When I remember bygone days
I think how evening follows morn;
So many I loved were not yet dead,
So many I love were not yet born.

Ogden Nash, *The Middle.*

In memory of the lives of Edward Ellman and Larry Spector,
in anticipation of the lives of Noah and Avi, and in awe of my
marvelous luck 36 years ago when I married Tara.
I.M.E.

To Dad, whom I miss every day, to Mom, who keeps us
together, to my loving sisters, and most especially
to my beloved Carol and Benji and to Claire
who now has completed our family
P.M.K.

To Bob, Christy and Adam, with all my love,
and in memory of Carol,
who taught us many lessons about the meaning of family.
E.S.

To Zachary and Cara (the lights of my life), and in memory of
my mother Corinne (a woman for all seasons).
L.A.W.

To Karen and David.
B.B.

PREFACE

This new edition of Family Law brings changes. The most important are two new authors. Ira Ellman, Paul Kurtz and Elizabeth Scott are delighted to welcome Lois Weithorn and Brian Bix to our partnership. The Fourth Edition reflects the steady efforts of all five of us, and it has benefitted enormously from this multiplicity of perspectives.

Family law continues to change rapidly, and this edition includes developments through the early summer of 2004. But it does not merely tack new authorities on an otherwise static presentation. Even while making many revisions and additions to incorporate new scholarship as well as new law, we have pruned nearly 200 pages. We achieved this reduction by applying a careful eye throughout the text, and every chapter has contributed to the result. About half these page savings, however, have been achieved in two places. Chapter Four, on alimony and property division, has been shortened substantially. Our coverage of this material still remains the most comprehensive available in a law school casebook, and the abridgment sacrifices nothing in the breadth or sophistication of the treatment. Our belief, however, is that it will allow instructors to make much better use of the chapter. We have also reluctantly chosen to drop much of the material that in the third edition had been covered in Chapter 10: primarily, coverage of the basic law of abortion and contraception. The deletion of this chapter reflects the reality that in every law school the basic constitutional law of procreative liberties is addressed in the Constitutional Law course. Most teachers therefore find they cannot justify repeating this material in Family Law, given the large number of other Family Law topics, not covered elsewhere in the curriculum, that they must address. Of course, we have retained material on the special problems involved in the invocation of procreative liberties by minors. Those subjects, including the foundational cases of *Bellotti and Carey*, are found in the revised chapter on State Regulation of the Parent-Child Relationship (now Chapter Ten).

Throughout this revision process we have been mindful to keep the Fourth Edition faithful to the pedagogical philosophy that has been this book's hallmark from the outset: a comprehensive and multidisciplinary treatment of legal and policy issues that includes extensive textual material. The text performs two important functions. Along with excerpts from relevant social science literature, some textual material acquaints law students with learning from other fields that bears on the important public policy issues presented by Family Law. Other textual material explains and clarifies legal doctrine more effectively and efficiently than the traditional use of case excerpts. We believe that casebook notes should not only call attention to difficult questions of legal doctrine and policy, they should illuminate them. We have worked hard to satisfy that ambitious goal and hope we have had at least some success in meeting it. Our purpose is to provide the foundation necessary to allow the instructor to spend class time both exploring the policy issues, and honing the students' ability to apply the relevant legal doctrine, obviously an essential part of legal education. The first edition of Family Law pioneered the use of

Problems as an excellent mechanism for developing this ability, and this edition continues that tradition. Many of the problems have been revised and many new problems have been added.

We have benefitted from the assistance of many people in preparing this and earlier editions. Many of the contributions that our good friend and cherished colleague, Katharine Bartlett, made to the Second Edition can still be discerned in this volume. Part way through our work on this edition, illness forced the retirement of Kay Winn, who from the first edition had managed many details of the manuscript preparation with unfailing competence. She was missed, but with the willing help of several members of the ASU staff we managed to get through. Ira Ellman would also like to take this opportunity to once again thank the professional staff of the Arizona State University law library, and especially Marianne Alcorn, for invaluable assistance and unfailing good cheer in tracking down nonlegal as well as legal sources, in this and other projects.

I.M.E.,
P.M.K.,
E.S.,
L.A.W.,
B.B.

ACKNOWLEDGMENTS

Excerpted material appearing in this book is reprinted by permission, as listed below.

American Law Institute, PRINCIPLES OF THE LAW OF FAMILY DISSOLUTION. Copyright © 2002 by The American Law Institute. Reprinted by permission of the American Law Institute. All Rights Reserved.

Anderson, Is Women's Labor a Commodity?, 19 PHILOSOPHY & PUBLIC AFFAIRS (1988). Copyright © 1988. Reprinted by permission of Blackwell Publishing. All Rights Reserved.

Andrews, *Surrogate Motherhood: The Challenge for Feminists*, 16 LAW MEDICINE & HEALTH CARE 72 (1988). Copyright © 1988. Reprinted by permission of the author.

Barrett, *Wendt Divorce Dissects Job of "Corporate Wife,"* Wall St. J. December 6, 1996, at B1. Copyright © 1996, The Wall Street Journal. Reprinted by permission of the Wall Street Journal.

Blumberg, *Cohabitation Without Marriage: A Different Perspective*, 28 UCLA L. REV. 1125, 1161-67 (1981). Copyright © 1981 by UCLA LAW REVIEW. Reprinted by permission of UCLA Law Review and Grace Blumberg. All Rights Reserved.

Blumberg, *The Regularization of Nonmarital Cohabitation: Rights and Responsibilities in the American Welfare-State*, 76 NOTRE DAME L. REV. 1265, 1275-83, 1287-88 (2001). Copyright © 2001 by Notre Dame L. Review and Grace Blumberg. Reprinted by permission of Notre Dame Law Review and Grace Blumberg. All Rights Reserved.

Casad, *Unmarried Couples and Unjust Enrichment: From Status to Contract and Back Again*, 77 MICH. L. REV. 47, 52-56 (1978). Copyright © (1978). Reprinted by permission of the author.

Cherlin, MARRIAGE, DIVORCE, REMARRIAGE 21-27. Reprinted by permission of the publisher from MARRIAGE, DIVORCE, REMARRIAGE by Andrew J. Cherlin, Cambridge, Mass.: Harvard University Press, Copyright © 1981 by the President and Fellows of Harvard College.

Commentary to MODEL PENAL CODE § 213.1. Copyright © 1985 by The American Law Institute; as Adopted at the 1962 Annual Meeting of The American Law Institute. Reprinted by permission of the American Law Institute.

Developments in the Law: The Law of Marriage and Family, 116 HARV. L. REV. 1997, 2201-12 (2003). Copyright © 2003 by Harvard Law Review. Reprinted by permission of Harvard Law Review. All Rights Reserved.

Ellman, *"Contract Thinking" Was Marvin's Fatal Flaw*, 76 NOTRE DAME L. REV. 1365, 1365-73 (2001). Copyright © 2001 by Notre Dame Law Review. Reprinted by permission of the author.

Ellman, *Fudging Failure: The Economic Analysis Used to Construct Child Support Guidelines*, 2004 UNIVERSITY OF CHICAGO LEGAL FORUM. Copyright © 2004. Reprinted by permission of the author.

Ellman, *The Misguided Movement to Revive Fault Divorce*, 11 INTERNATIONAL JOURNAL OF LAW, POLICY & FAMILY 216 (1997). Copyright © 1997, The Oxford University Press, Oxford, United Kingdom. Reprinted by permission of Oxford University Press and the author.

Ellman, *The Place of Fault in a Modern Divorce Law*, 28 ARIZONA STATE LAW JOURNAL 773 (1996). Copyright © 1996 by Arizona State Law Journal. Reprinted by permission of the author.

Ellman, *The Theory of Alimony*, 77 CALIFORNIA LAW REVIEW 1, 7-9, 25-28 (1989). Copyright © 1989 by California Law Review. Reprinted by permission of the author.

Ellman, *Thinking About Custody and Support in Ambiguous-Father Families*, 36 FAMILY LAW QUARTERLY 499, 50-55, 62, 63, 77-78 (2002). Copyright © 2002 by American Bar Association. Reprinted by permission of the author.

Ellman & Sugarman, *Spousal Emotional Abuse as a Tort?*, 55 MD. L. REV. 1268, 1291-92 (1996). Copyright © 1996 by Maryland Law Review. Reprinted by permission of the author. All Rights Reserved.

Fineman, THE AUTONOMY MYTH: A THEORY OF DEPENDENCY 60-64 (2004). Copyright © 2004. Reprinted by permission of the author.

Friedman, AMERICAN LAW IN THE TWENTIETH CENTURY 434-38 (2002). Copyright © 2002 by Lawrence Friedman. Reprinted by permission of the author, Lawrence M. Friedman, Professor of Law, Stanford University, Stanford, California.

Friedman, AMERICAN LAW: AN INTRODUCTION 254-276 (1984). Copyright © 1984 by Lawrence Friedman. Reprinted by permission of the author, Lawrence M. Friedman, Professor of Law, Stanford University, Stanford, California.

Friedman, A HISTORY OF AMERICAN LAW 204-207, 498-504 (2d ed. 1985). Copyright © 1985 by Lawrence Friedman. Reprinted by permission of the author, Lawrence M. Friedman, Professor of Law, Stanford University, Stanford, California.

Glendon, THE TRANSFORMATION OF FAMILY LAW 5-10 (1989). Copyright © 1989. Reprinted by permission of The University of Chicago Press, Chicago,

SUMMARY TABLE OF CONTENTS

TABLE OF CONTENTS

PART III NONTRADITIONAL FAMILIES

PART IV PARENT AND CHILD

CHAPTER 10 STATE REGULATION OF THE PARENT-CHILD RELATIONSHIP 1077

Part I

Introduction

Chapter 1

INTRODUCTION

§ A. THE THEMES OF FAMILY AND FAMILY LAW

MARY ANN GLENDON, ABORTION AND DIVORCE IN WESTERN LAW 10 (1987)

. . . Much of family law is no more — and no less — than the symbolic expression of certain cultural ideals. The older continental European civil codes told wives that they should obey their husbands, and children of all ages that they should honor and respect their parents. Today, modernized versions of the same codes tell husbands and wives that they are equal partners in running a household, and a recent Swedish law tells parents that they should not punish by spanking or otherwise humiliating their children. Probably no other area of law is so replete with legal norms that communicate ideas about proper behavior but that have no direct sanctions.

MARTHA MINOW, "FORMING UNDERNEATH EVERYTHING THAT GROWS": TOWARD A HISTORY OF FAMILY LAW, 1985 Wis. L. Rev. 819, 819

Family law is in two senses "underneath" other areas of the law. Its low status within the profession is well-known. But it is also "underneath" other legal fields in the sense that its rules about roles and duties between men and women, parents and children, families and strangers historically and conceptually underlie other rules about employment and commerce, education and welfare, and perhaps the governance of the state.

JOHN WITTE, JR., FROM SACRAMENT TO CONTRACT: MARRIAGE, RELIGION, AND LAW IN THE WESTERN TRADITION 2 (1997)

The Western Christian Church has, from its apostolic beginnings, offered four perspectives on marriage. A *religious perspective* regards marriage as a spiritual or sacramental association, subject to the creed, cult, and canons of the church community. A *social perspective* treats marriage as a social estate, subject to the expectations and exactions of the local community and to special state laws of contract, property, and inheritance. A *contractual perspective* describes marriage as a voluntary association, subject to the wills and preferences of the couple, their children, and their household. Hovering in the background is a *naturalist perspective* that treats marriage as a created institution, subject to the natural laws of reason, conscience, and the Bible. In Voltaire's quip: "Among Christians, the family is either a little church, a little state, or a little club" blessed by nature and nature's God.

These perspectives are, in an important sense, complementary, for they each emphasize one aspect of marriage — its religious sanction, communal legitimation, voluntary formation, and natural origin, respectively. These perspectives, however, have also come to stand in considerable tension, for they are linked to competing claims of ultimate authority over the form and function of marriage — claims by the church, by the state, by family members, and by God and nature. Some of the deepest fault lines in the historical formation and in the current transformation of Western marriage ultimately break out from this central tension of perspective.

LAWRENCE M. FRIEDMAN, A HISTORY OF AMERICAN LAW 206 (2ND ED., 1985)

. . . . Nor was the rising divorce rate [in the 19th century] so obviously a sign that the family was breaking down. The family was indeed changing. There were new strains on marital relationships. William O'Neill put it this way: "when families are large and loose, arouse few expectations, and make few demands, there is no need for divorce." That need arises when "families become the center for social organization." At this point, "their intimacy can become suffocating, their demands unbearable, and their expectations too high to be easily realizable. Divorce then becomes the safety value that makes the system workable." Moreover, a divorceless state is not a state without adultery, prostitution, fornication. It may be, rather, a place sharply divided between zones of official law and zones of unofficial behavior.

L. POGREBIN, FAMILY POLITICS: LAWS AND POWER ON AN INTIMATE FRONTIER 21–22, 24–26 (1983)

If not in crisis all these years, the family has been "in transition." Depending on which theorist you read it has been moving from an institutional to a companionship form, from an economic to an affectional unit, from a child-centered to a couple-centered entity, from one lifelong bond to serial connections, from asymmetrical to quasi-egalitarian roles, from kinship groups to extended families to nuclear to "reconstituted" families.

Here's the point: I believe one can acknowledge that the traditional patriarchal family oppresses women and creates distorted gender relations, but still choose not to jettison family as a way of life. Furthermore, I'm aware that for many women the family has been "a source of power" as often as a "tool of oppression." I think it insulting, not to mention irresponsible, to overlook the psychological satisfactions many women find in marriage, motherhood, homemaking and heterosexuality. What's more, in many black, white ethnic and poor communities, there is great pride in families' "adaptive resiliency and strength" and there is more confidence in the reliability of the family for support, succor and sheer survival than might be the case in more affluent, educated classes where the luxury of individualism can be indulged.

With all this in mind, I concluded it won't do to just trash the family; we must transform it. Thousands of my contemporaries have reached the same conclusion. Moreover, regardless of what we conclude, the plain fact is that family living, in one form or another, remains the condition or the goal of a vast majority of Americans.

What is it about the family that survives dissection, defamation, reports of its imminent demise, and the burdens of its own imperfection? Why do seven out of ten divorced people choose to remarry within five years despite bitter experience, and make new families despite the problems of stepparenthood? Why do so many people form "chosen families" to take the place of legal ones? (The latest census revealed that more than three million U.S. households are composed of unrelated people living together. According to *The New York Times,* what these unmarried couples, same-sex roommates, and elderly companions are seeking is not just cost-sharing but "the semblance of family," tribal attachments, and the sense of "coming home.") Can family be all bad if the urge to have a family and be a family is so strong?

MARTHA ALBERTSON FINEMAN, THE AUTONOMY MYTH: A THEORY OF DEPENDENCY 60–64 (2004)

While it is true that law initially defines the family, controlling entry into the privileged status, once it is formed and given content, the family is a powerful construct. Family has symbolic significance to many groups within society and can be manipulated by politicians and others with ideological objectives to mobilize a variety of constituencies. In addition, perceived family strengths (or weaknesses) can be utilized to place pressure on political institutions. The adjustments and accommodations that may result can alter the very nature of the state's relationship to the family and the individual.

The family is currently subsidized on both a material and a cultural level in its traditional, preferred (marital) form. Supporters argue the legitimacy of allocating public resources to the marital family. Such subsidy is facilitated and enhanced by the symbolic position the preferred family has in political rhetoric and American ideology. One implication of this preference for the marital family form is the demand for access to marital status by those who are in unions that do not conform to the ideal form. The more favored the preferred family is, the more pressure is generated from outsiders to the institution demanding entry into or expansion of the subsidized family category.

Because of the interactive relationship between the family and other institutions within society, it is much more accurate to view the family not as existing in or constituting a separate sphere, but rather, as being a constructed institution contained within the larger society. As such, the extent and functioning of other societal institutions profoundly affects the nature and shape of the family. By the same token, the nature and functioning of the family profoundly affects other social institutions, particularly the state. . . .

. . . .

. . . I am concerned with those institutions that are clearly contained within and defined by the state. It is those institutions that are correctly understood as "coercively constituted," in that they are creatures of the state. While law may affect voluntary entities, it is those institutions, such as the family and the market, that are actually created and constituted as coherent institutions through law. Their very existence as objects of state regulatory concern comes into being through law: it is law that gives them consequence and meaning even outside of the wishes and demands of their members.

Of course, these various state-constructed entities may spill over into the voluntary field. There is a well-developed sense of family in religion, for example. So, too, individuals and groups outside of the regulated space may clamor for entry into it, willing to trade the freedom of nonlegal status for the benefits of the legal and privileged institutional form. Such overlapping interest on the part of the coercive and voluntary realms in regard to an entity such as the family might provide an occasion for tension, even for transformation or adjustment in state rules. In this way these coercive institutions are potentially dynamic in nature. The state has the authority and power to monitor (or impede) their transformations.

If this model of the family/state relationship is accurate, it has important implications for public policy. In the first instance, it indicates that the family's relationship to the state is not fixed or static. State policies can profoundly affect the form and functioning of the family. Correspondingly, if the family is constructed through interaction with the state and society, the family cannot be posited as a "natural" entity with a form that is constant over time and culture. Nor can a preferred family form be assumed essential to family functioning, such as caring for children or providing emotional and psychological support for members. Instead, the state defines the nature of the preferred family as a *political* matter. Definitions of what constitutes a family can change, and perhaps will inevitably change, in response to political and social pressures.

Altered state regulation, support, and subsidy for the preferred family may affect that family; it may empower it or create tensions and pressures that lead to demands for accommodation or regulation of other institutions with which the family interacts. Changes in the family can spur changes in other societal institutions, such as the workplace. As a societal institution within the state, the family competes with other institutions for allocation of state resources, including political and ideological capital. Since other institutions are also inherently state constructs, existing in law and grounded in state regulatory authority, the state, acting through law, can mandate accommodation and change in those institutions.

BRUCE C. HAFEN, THE CONSTITUTIONAL STATUS OF MARRIAGE, KINSHIP, AND SEXUAL PRIVACY — BALANCING THE INDIVIDUAL AND SOCIAL INTERESTS, 81 Mich. L. Rev. 472, 476, 480–81 (1983)

. . . The objectives of a democratic society based on established patterns of marriage and kinship should not be terribly mysterious; . . . [f]or instance, a stable environment is crucial to the developmental needs of children. . . .

The unarticulated policy roots of family law are also related to the political ends of democracy, because it is primarily through family bonds that both children and parents learn the attitudes and skills that sustain an open society. . . .

The commitments of close kinship and marriage represent the last modern vestiges of Status as a source of duty. Much of what family members — especially marital partners — "owe" one another cannot be enforced in a court of law; yet the sense of family duty has an uncanny power to produce obedience to the unenforceable in ways that defy Adam Smith's assumption that self-interest is man's dominant value. In this way, the family tradition is a prerequisite to a successful individual tradition. Through the commitments of marriage and kinship both children and parents experience the need for and the value of authority, responsibility, and duty in their most pristine forms. . . .

There is, however, an even more political meaning to the formal family's place as a mediating structure in our system. Our system is committed to pluralism and diversity as political values, because those values maximize the opportunity for individual choice and control. . . .

. . . Monolithic control of the value transmission system is "a hallmark of totalitarianism"; thus, "for obvious reasons, the state nursery is the paradigm for a totalitarian society." An essential element in maintaining a system of limited government is to deny state control over childrearing, simply because childrearing has such power.

GARY S. BECKER, A TREATISE ON THE FAMILY 363 (Rev. Ed., 1991)

We believe that a surprising number of state interventions mimic the agreements that would occur if children were capable of arranging for their own care. Stated differently, our belief is that many regulations of the family improve the efficiency of family activities. To be sure, these regulations raise the welfare of children, but they also raise the welfare of parents, or at least they raise the combined welfare of parents and children.

NOTE ON FAMILY LAW AND CULTURAL NORMS

More than other legal fields, family law traditionally reflected core cultural norms, and has been more densely packed with rules that have no important function other than the affirmation of particular cultural values. This is the point made above by Mary Ann Glendon. In an extension of that idea, Martha Minow suggests that these norms and the rules that reflect them may influence our thinking in other fields as well.

Yet a field of law so closely tied to the most personal aspects of prevailing culture is placed under great stress when the culture is itself under pressure or in transition. Two important modern pressures today are the decline in the proportion of the population whose family lives conform to the traditional ideal of the nuclear family (see data in Chapter 9) and the changing cultural consensus concerning gender roles. The second movement is far too complex to be encapsulated here effectively, although the Pogrebin excerpt provides a small window into its possible impact on family law. Finally, the excerpt from Hafen offers two important traditional arguments concerning society's stake in family law — arguments which do not point in the same direction.

One is the importance of stable family values to stable societal values, which suggests a justification for legal regulation of the family; the other is the value placed on pluralism by modern liberal political theory (so influential in the formation of the American political system), which would seem to require great restraint in the regulation of the family.

This last question — the extent to which society ought to regulate the family — brings us full circle to where we began. For just as the law reflects cultural values, it may in turn influence them. One important theme of feminist reformers, for example, is that we should root out family law rules that assume gender roles even when they have no immediate enforceability, for they still stand as symbolic statements of how things ought to be, and such official endorsements are not only offensive, but are capable, by their apparent authority alone, of perpetuating the norms that originally created them.

Note the tension in the discussions of marriage and the family, between those, like Fineman and Friedman, who see the institutions as basically fluid, subject (or at least potentially subject) to radical changes over time; and those, like Hafen and Witte, who emphasize continuity and seem willing to think in terms of the family's "basic nature." Whether one sees marriage and the family as something we are given or something we construct will obviously color one's view of family law doctrine and policy.

The conflicting themes of pluralism and stability identified by Hafen are just two of the overarching tendencies that compete to influence family law, as the following excerpt from Schneider points out.

CARL E. SCHNEIDER, MORAL DISCOURSE AND THE TRANSFORMATION OF AMERICAN FAMILY LAW, 83 Mich. L. Rev. 1803, 1807–08, 1827–28, 1835–39, 1847–48 (1985)

. . . Four forces . . . have shaped modern family law. They are the legal tradition of noninterference in family affairs, the ideology of liberal individualism, American society's changing moral beliefs, and the rise of "psychologic man." These forces have occasioned a crucial change: a diminution of the law's discourse in moral terms about the relations between family members, and the transfer of many moral decisions from the law to the people the law once regulated. I do not mean that this change is complete or will ever be completed. I do not suppose that it is occurring in every aspect of family law, or everywhere in the country with equal speed. I emphasize that there are other trends, and that there is a considered and considerable reaction to the trend impelled by a revived conservatism and a politicized fundamentalism. But I do suggest that the change is widespread jurisdictionally, institutionally, and doctrinally; that it is deep-seated; and that it is transforming family law.

. . . [L]egal actors and those they govern distinguish between decisions made on moral grounds and decisions made on social, economic, psychological, or "legal" grounds. . . .

The differences between these kinds of decisions may be illustrated by the various rationales for prohibiting incest. A decision made on moral grounds turns on whether particular conduct is "right" or "wrong," whether it accords with the obligations owed other people or oneself. Incest might be prohibited on moral grounds because it is with coercion or because it violates natural or divine law which prescribes standards of right and wrong. A decision made on psychological grounds turns on whether particular conduct promotes psychological health. Incest might be prohibited on psychological grounds because the prohibition eases resolution of the Oedipal conflict. A decision made on social grounds turns on whether particular conduct promotes the effective functioning of society as a whole. Incest might be prohibited on social grounds because "the prohibition of incest establishes a mutual dependency between families, compelling them, in order to perpetuate themselves, to give rise to new families." A decision made on economic grounds turns on whether particular conduct promotes economic efficiency. Incest might be prohibited on economic grounds because such a prohibition, by discouraging endogamy, encourages capital formation. A decision made on "legal grounds" turns on whether particular conduct is required in order to comply with authoritatively promulgated principles. A court might enforce a prohibition against incest quite apart from its own beliefs about the wisdom of such a prohibition because it believed that the legislature intended that such a prohibition be enforced and that the decision to prohibit such conduct was constitutionally confided in the legislature.

In each of these different situations, the governmental actor will consult a different rationale and will speak a different language; and the people acted upon will understand what has happened in different ways. It is, of course, always possible to reach a given result through several rationales and with varying language. But in analyzing legal problems, we legitimately test the merits of the rationales offered for a result, and we properly remember that the way we talk about problems can change the way we think about them. In this paper I direct attention to changes in the way we talk about and justify modern family law because those changes change the way we think about it and act on it. . . .

Perhaps the oldest impediment to moral discourse in family law is the legal tradition of noninterference in the family. That tradition rests in large measure on the practical difficulties of enforcing family law and the practical consequences of trying to do so. Because of this tradition, the moral problems associated with many kinds of family disputes do not enter legal discourse. The tradition is an old one, has telling rationales, and may be growing in appeal.

The strength of the tradition of noninterference is attested to by its age,[120] by the extreme circumstances in which the law has heeded it, and by the multiplicity of reasons for it. Each of these testimonies may be illumined by examining the unusually direct, eloquent, and provocative opinion in *State v. Rhodes,* an 1868 criminal prosecution of a husband for the assault and battery of his wife. The court condemned the evil the husband had done and expressly denied he had any "right" to do it. Nevertheless, the court forbade

---

[120] As family law traditions go, this one, because it dates at least to the mid-nineteenth century, is quite old. But it is worth recalling that the view of the family as a haven and regard for family privacy and autonomy are primarily products of the nineteenth century. Earlier centuries did not perceive clear boundaries between the family and society, and were willing to intervene directly in families and to use families to carry out the policies of the state. See generally L. Stone, THE FAMILY, SEX AND MARRIAGE IN ENGLAND 1500-1800 (1977).

intervention in the absence of "permanent or malicious injury" or "intolerable" conditions, since each family has a "domestic government . . . formed for themselves, suited to their own peculiar conditions, and . . . supreme, and from [which] there is no appeal except in cases of great importance requiring the strong arm of the law. . . ."

Several fears underlay the court's holding. First, the court feared the burden of dealing with "every trifling family broil." Second, it feared the complexities of deciding "what would be the standard?"

> Suppose a case coming up to us from a hovel, where neither delicacy of sentiment nor refinement of manners is appreciated or known. The parties themselves would be amazed, if they were to be held responsible for rudeness or trifling violence. . . . Take a case from the middle class, where modesty and purity have their abode but nevertheless have not immunity from the frailties of nature, and are sometimes moved by the mysteries of passion. . . . Or take a case from the higher ranks, where education and culture have so refined nature, that a look cuts like a knife, and a word strikes like a hammer; where the most delicate attention gives pleasure, and the slightest neglect pain; where an indignity is disgrace and exposure is ruin. Bring all these cases into court side by side, with the same offense charged and the same proof made; and what conceivable charge of the court to the jury would be alike appropriate to all the cases. . . .

Third, the court feared that, once in court, each family member would endeavor "to justify himself or herself by criminating the other, [and] that which ought to be forgotten in a day, will be remembered for life." Finally, the court feared "the evils which would result from raising the curtain, and exposing to public curiosity and criticism, the nursery and the bed chamber."

Each of these rationales applies in substance, if not in language or in particulars, today. Indeed, although a modern court would be unlikely to use them to dismiss a criminal prosecution for assault, they are regularly used in discussions of how police and prosecutors should handle spousal-assault complaints. And, to take an example from the civil side, courts commonly use them in declining to intervene in family disputes even where a husband and wife have by prenuptial agreement solicited intervention.

The law not only suspects that intervention will do harm; it doubts that intervention will do good: in family law as in few other areas of the law, the enforcement problems are ubiquitous and severe. . . .

Enforcement difficulties arise first because much of what family law seeks to regulate — from child and spouse abuse to fornication — occurs in private. The distastefulness of investigating private life is sharp enough to have been used to justify the doctrine of constitutional privacy and to have contributed to the rise of no-fault divorce. Family privacy is often hard to breach because the parties all participated in the violation of law, because they wish to protect those who did participate, or because they are ashamed to have people know about the incident in which the state is interested. . . .

Family law's second enforcement problem is that the person enforced against is often specially able to injure the very person the law intervened to protect. The spouse who wishes to resist divorce, the abused child or spouse, the pregnant woman, and her fetus are all vulnerable in this way. Legal intervention in these situations thus may be fruitless, or, worse, might provoke the person enforced against to retaliate against the person the law wants to protect. Because the person to be protected often depends on the person enforced against, even legal punishment itself can injure the person to be protected by depriving him or her of the presence or affection of the other.

The third enforcement difficulty arises from the fact that, in many critical areas of family law, the people the law wishes to regulate live in emotional settings and under psychological pressures which make them little susceptible to the law's persuasion or even coercion. . . .

In short, the law has long avoided many of the moral issues facing families under the authority of the tradition of "nonintervention."

[The Rise of Psychologic Man]

For our purposes, a central feature of the psychologic view is that it replaces moral discourse with medical discourse and moral thought with therapeutic thought. That shift may usefully be understood in terms of the role attributed to human happiness in social life. The old view held that men and women were obligated to lead a good life as that was defined by religious or social convention. Happiness was not the purpose of these conventions, but was expected to be a by-product of performing one's duties. If it did not come, however, one would be consoled by knowing one had led the right kind of life. The psychologic view, at least in its ideal type, denies that there are religious or social conventions that are independently valid. It holds that life's goal is the search for personal well-being, adjustment, and contentment — in short, for "health." Adherence to a religious or social convention may serve that end, but if it does not, other paths to well-being should be tried and used. In short, says Rieff mordantly,

> [E]vil and immorality are disappearing, as Spencer assumed they would, mainly because our culture is changing its definition of human perfection. No longer the Saint, but the instinctual Everyman, twisting his neck uncomfortably inside the starched collar of culture, is the communal ideal, to whom men offer tacit prayers for deliverance from their inherited renu[n]ciations.[170]

On the old view, the right life was difficult: one's duties were numerous and onerous (though not necessarily unpleasant); distractions from duty were numerous and dangerous. Thus codes of family morality were aspirational and ascetic. As Professor Rieff observes:

> Heretofore, the saving arrangements of Western culture have appeared as symbol systems communicating demands by stoning the sensual with deprivations, and were thus operated in a dynamically ambivalent mode. Our culture developed, as its general technique of salvation, assents to moral demands that treated the sensual part of

---

[170] *Id.* at 8. Rieff continues, "Freud sought only to soften the collar; others, using bits and pieces of his genius, would like to take it off."

the self as an enemy. From mastery over this enemy-self there developed some triumphant moral feeling; a character ideal was born.

The psychologic view concedes that "stoning the sensual with deprivations" can work, but doubts it will. That view sees the drive of the instincts as crucial to understanding human motivation, believes that confining the drive of the instincts tends to be unhealthy, and, more specifically, sees sexual expression as central to human happiness.

BRUCE C. HAFEN, INDIVIDUALISM AND AUTONOMY IN FAMILY LAW: THE WANING OF BELONGING, 1991 B.Y.U. L. Rev. 1, 31–34

A friend shared this experience with me: his daughter came home from elementary school one day, crying and upset. "Is it true that I don't really belong to you, Mom?", she asked her mother. Knowing this was her natural child, the startled mother asked what her daughter meant. The girl explained that her teacher had told her class that everyone is free to control his or her own life, and no one belongs to anyone else. Children don't belong to parents; husbands don't belong to wives; nobody belongs to anybody. The girl looked up at her mother and asked, "I am yours, aren't I, Mom?" The mother took the child in her arms and said, "Of course you're mine — and I'm yours, too." As the two embraced, they both felt the love and the security of really belonging to each other.

A couple I know adopted a young child after having had other natural children. When the adoption was to be finalized, the child was old enough to speak a few sentences. As soon as the formal adoption proceedings ended, the family members reached out their arms to the child in a gesture of complete acceptance. The little boy smiled broadly as he looked into his parents' eyes and exclaimed, "Now we are ours!" Note the possessive form: ours.

A man and woman who love each other also feel joy and meaning in the thought that they could "belong" to each other. Many of our phrases in the language of romantic love are based on the idea of belonging. "Be mine," say the little candy hearts we see on Valentine's Day. "I'm yours," proclaimed a hit song of the 1950s. And the opening line of another once-popular song reads, "If I give my heart to you, will you handle it with care?"

. . . To offer our hearts is to offer our innermost selves. And if the offer is accepted, there may one day be a wedding — that ancient and sacred ritual in which a man and woman gladly give themselves to each other in the "bonds" of matrimony. [¶] We have always known that people who offer their hearts to others take the risk of getting those hearts banged up, and sometimes getting them broken. . . . [¶] These days, however, a fear more bewildering than the risk of a broken heart clouds our willingness to give ourselves to one another. The teacher's comment to her school class reminds us appropriately that family members should not treat each other as slaves or inanimate objects. But it also intimates that many people in today's society are increasingly unsure whether the bonds of kinship and marriage are valuable ties that bind, or are sheer bondage.

The sense of possession implicit in the concept of belonging can imply relationships as beautiful as romantic love (familistic relationships) or relationships as ugly as slavery (compulsory relationships). In earlier times, our common sense told us the obvious differences between these opposite ends of the spectrum of human interaction. But in these days of personal liberation, some say we are not really free until we break loose from all relationships and commitments that seem to tie us down. For these people, belonging is by definition enslaving rather than enriching. Yet those who break loose from the arms and bonds that hold them may replace their previous sense of belonging only with a sense of longing, as this age of liberation becomes more and more the age of isolation and loneliness. Ours is the age of the waning of belonging.

Of course . . . when I express concern about the waning of belonging, I am acutely aware of the harm inflicted by abusive parents and spouses, or by insensitive authority figures who take advantage of those who are dependent on them. Still, the fact that some have used the vulnerability of intimate relationships to harm others is no reason to suppose that sustained intimacy itself is the problem. Yet many voices in our culture have become deeply suspicious of the serious, long-range commitments on which marriage and family ties are based.

For example . . . some wish to "liberate" children from the "captivity" of their family ties. As one writer put it, "[t]he child's subjugated status [is] rooted in the same benevolent despotism that kings, husbands, and slave masters claimed as their moral right." Yet the deepest psychological and emotional needs of children require continuity and stability in their relationships with parents — relationships that can be the key factor in their eventual development of mature, personal freedom. Ironically, the most ardent advocates of children's liberation gloss over the reality that prematurely cutting children's family ties can have the effect of abandoning them.

. . .

In HABITS OF THE HEART, Robert Bellah and his colleagues drew on their empirical studies to describe how Americans have shifted their view of marriage from that of a relatively permanent social institution to a temporary source of personal fulfillment. As a result, when marriage commitments intrude on their preferences and their convenience, people feel entitled — even normatively obliged — to walk away. Yet, ironically, Bellah's group also found that despite Americans' preoccupation with self-interest, most of the people they interviewed still cling, perhaps in a hopelessly dreamy sense, to the nostalgic notion of marriage and family life based upon loving and permanent commitments as "the dominant American ideal."

Amid these paradoxical impressions of a desire for self-protection on one hand and a need for familial commitment on the other, many perceive the legal system as having become less judgmental of what people should expect of one another. This creates an impression that family law has lost its normative expectation that family members should feel a sense of personal responsibility to uphold their commitments. Thus, it is easy to assume that the law no longer seeks to restrain our almost unwilling self-indulgence. The very absence of demands by the law now seems to confirm our spreading fear that long-term, loving relationships are impossible to find anymore.

NOTE

Schneider helps us to see the different kinds of arguments that can be made in connection with any particular family law regulation. While he chose incest to illustrate his point, a similar argument could be made with respect to most other family law rules. The next chapter, for example, begins with a discussion of the rules for entering marriage. One might ask why we should have rules requiring any formalities, such as ceremonies or marriage licenses, or rules setting substantive requirements, such as that the potential spouses be of a different gender or above a certain age. Arguments based on moral, social, economic, psychological or "legal" grounds can and have been offered to support or attack any particular regulation.

Hafen picks up on another of Schneider's themes, that elements of modern culture portray marriage and family as merely one possible route to self-fulfillment and happiness, in contrast to the traditional view of family as life's primary source of commitment and responsibility. If this cultural characterization is correct, has the legal system been a cause of the change, or merely a reflection of it? Can the legal system be used to influence or resist it? Should it? Note the tension Hafen's analysis reveals between the metaphors of possession that traditional culture uses to describe family relationships, and modern liberal ideas of autonomy and human dignity. Are these merely word games, or does his discussion reveal a true conflict of a kind that is inevitably reflected in legal policy debates?

There is finally one more theme to consider: the historical. Even changing systems always carry with them a history, and in family law particularly, such histories may become traditions that assume a force of their own — whether or not the rationale that originally motivated them has any remaining relevance. This may be particularly important in family law because, as Mary Ann Glendon emphasizes, marriage and family preceded legal institutions. The relevant history is cultural history, not legal history. Do we need to consider anthropology to understand it properly? Consider the following excerpt from Glendon.

MARY ANN GLENDON, THE TRANSFORMATION OF FAMILY LAW 5–10 (1989)

[I]t will be useful to distinguish for analytical purposes between what a particular legal system may classify as "families" or "marriages" and the conduct which an anthropologist or sociologist is likely to describe as family or marriage behavior. . . .

The Tinker's Wedding

In John Synge's play, *The Tinker's Wedding,* the principal characters, Michael Byrne and Sarah Casey, are tinkers — traveling menders of metal household utensils. Their association began one day at Rathvanna, when Michael hit Sarah "a great clout in the lug," after which she came along with him "quiet and easy . . . from that hour to this present day." By the time we meet them, Sarah has been "going beside [him] a great while, and rearing a lot of them." The action of the play is set in motion by Sarah's sudden demand, backed up by a threat of leaving, that she and Michael be married. We can infer from their spirited and affectionate banter that Sarah's demand is not a symptom of any serious trouble that has arisen between Michael and herself. Except for this one point, she seems generally happy, "thriving, and getting [her] good health by the grace of the Almighty God." As the play opens, Michael has already agreed to go along with Sarah's desire for a wedding, although he does not understand it, and he is putting the finishing touches on her home-made wedding ring. All that remains to be done is to find a priest to do the job.

But things are not so easily arranged. The local priest comes walking along the road by the tinkers' camp, but he rejects as preposterous Sarah's request that he perform a wedding ceremony for them for no fee and give them a bit of silver into the bargain "to pay for the ring." After some discussion, he says he could see his way clear to offer the tinkers a special reduced price of one pound. But Michael and Sarah do not have a pound. Finally, after prolonged bargaining, the priest agrees to marry the couple for ten shillings and a gallon can which Michael has almost finished making — such a little sum "as wouldn't marry a child." The priest is not moved by Sarah's claim of poverty, unkindly pointing out that the tinkers are well known to steal "east and west in Wicklow and Wexford and the County Meath."

After the deal is struck, the wedding is set for the next day. But alas, during the night, Michael's old mother, Mary, is overcome by the temptation to take the newly made can and to sell it at the local pub in order to get a "pint for her sleep." To put off the moment of reckoning with Sarah, she sneaks a couple of empty bottles into the sack which had contained the can. Naturally, when the priest opens the sack the next day and finds only the bottles, he thinks that Michael and Sarah have tried to deceive him. He indignantly refuses to marry them for ten shillings without the can. After increasingly harsh words are exchanged, Sarah's disappointment turns to anger and the play ends with the priest trussed and thrown into a ditch. As the tinkers leave him, Sarah places her wedding ring on his finger to remind him of the promise he has made — under duress — not to tell the police he has been roughed up.

This little tale poses a number of interesting questions. It is Sarah's desire to get "married" that precipitates the action. But are not Michael and Sarah already married? A sociologist would probably consider that Michael and Sarah had been married for some time according to the long-standing customs of the subculture of the traveling people of Ireland. In the play, all indications are that Michael and Sarah intended that their union would be of some duration, and it is clear from the text that they held themselves out to the community of tinkers as belonging together. Furthermore, Michael's account of how he "got" Sarah at Rathvanna is reminiscent of descriptions by anthropologists of "marriage by capture," which is not really a kind of marriage, but rather a form of *wedding*. Thus, from a sociologist's or anthropologist's point of view, the "tinker's wedding" may well have taken place when Michael hit Sarah in the lug and carried her off.[10]

If the union of Michael and Sarah constituted behavior which a sociologist would call "marriage," is that the only sense in which they are married? In Ireland at the turn of the century, when Synge's play takes place, a couple validly married under the law of the Church was also married under the law of the state. Now, there is little doubt that Michael and Sarah would have been considered married under canon law as it stood until the Council of Trent made the presence of a priest at weddings mandatory in 1563. Prior to that time, Christians, like other people, could form marriages simply by exchanging consents and cohabiting. But [the rule] was expressly limited to marriages of baptized persons. The priest in Synge's play repeatedly alludes to the "heathen" state of the tinkers. This does not seem to be a mere epithet. At one point the priest speculates, "I'm thinking you were never christened, Sarah Casey," and remarks, "It would be a queer job to go dealing Christian sacraments unto the like of you."

If, in fact, Michael and Sarah were unbaptized persons, their marital status under canon law is unaffected by the marriage legislation of Trent. Under canon law, marriages between unbaptized persons are presumptively valid, provided the crucial element of consent exists. Furthermore, even if Michael and Sarah were baptized persons, and the Tridentine formalities were in principle required, the Church does not always insist on the priest's presence if compliance with this requirement would present "grave inconvenience." Grave inconvenience, it has been said, can arise from poverty.

Why then, if Michael and Sarah are already married in one or more senses of the word, should it be important to the state, to the Church, or to the parties, that a "wedding" should take place or that they should be "married" in another sense? If we ask this question from the point of view of the state and the Church, we fall upon a point of great significance for our inquiry into the changing relationship of family law to family life. In the case of Michael and Sarah, poor itinerants in Ireland at the turn of the century, it is fairly clear that neither the state nor the Church had much interest in their marital status. They belonged to what Max Rheinstein called the "neglected groups" of society and the law. By that he meant that, historically, family law paid little attention to the concerns of the poor, or of such ethnic minority groups as the Indians of North and South America or the Afro-Americans of the United States. Prior to the twentieth century, propertyless individuals came to the attention of the legal system chiefly as subjects of the criminal law. As Rheinstein observed, one of the great trends presently transforming the

---

[10] The formation of marriage, in simple societies, is often better understood as a process rather than an event, with the "wedding" of relatively minor importance. Customary marriages may be initiated by negotiation between families or by a ceremony of some sort, but often they merely involve living together, having a child, and gradually becoming accepted as a couple by relatives and neighbors. This is the case today, for example, for most New Guineans. See Owen Jessep and John Luluaki, PRINCIPLES OF FAMILY LAW IN PAPUA NEW GUINEA (Waigani: University of Papua New Guinea Press, 1985), 17–28. The marriages of as many as a fifth of the English population as late as the eighteenth century could also be characterized as having come into being in this way. See Stephen Parker, *The Marriage Act 1753: A Case Study in Family Law-Making*," 1 INTERNATIONAL JOURNAL OF LAW AND THE FAMILY 133, 139 (1987).

law of the family is precisely that of paying increasing attention to the needs and demands of hitherto neglected groups.

But we are running ahead of our story. Suffice it to say that Synge's priest repeatedly makes it plain that he considers tinkers to be outside the normal scope of his sphere of action and interest. He regards Michael and Sarah as different from "my own pairs living here in the place." He is, in fact, as puzzled about why Sarah wants to get married as are Michael and Michael's mother. When, during their haggling over the price of the wedding, Sarah begins to cry at the thought that she may never get married, the priest exclaims in surprise, "It's a queer woman you are to be crying at the like of that, and you your whole life walking the roads."

When we turn to the question of why Sarah, a member of a neglected group, with its own customary way of marrying, seeks nevertheless to be married in another way, we have a number of theories from which to choose. Yet those apt to come to mind first today can be ruled out. The playwright gives us no reason to believe that Sarah is motivated by any thought of improving her economic position or "legitimizing"[16] her children through bringing herself within the framework of legal rights and duties attaching to marriage. Nor does Synge give us the slightest hint that Sarah thought marriage by a priest was somehow related to the salvation of her immortal soul. Rather, it seems that she is concerned about the social approval of groups other than tinkers. After she is married, she thinks, "there will be no one have a right to call me a dirty name and I selling cans in Wicklow or Wexford or the city of Dublin itself."

But why should a hastily performed ritual make such a difference? For the purposes of our inquiry, this question opens up the subject of how imaginative representations in the law can sometimes affect the way people perceive and experience the reality of something as central to our lives as marriage. We are accustomed to viewing law as importantly shaped by beliefs and behavior, but we frequently overlook the reflexive and continuous nature of the interaction among laws, ideas, feelings, and conduct. Often mesmerized by the coercive power of law, we tend to minimize its persuasive and constitutive aspects.

In Synge's play, it is Mary Byrne who has the last word (inspired no doubt by the necessity of putting the best possible light on the situation which her own great thirst has brought about). To Michael, still fearful about Sarah's earlier threat to leave him if he doesn't marry her, she says: "And you're thinking it's paying gold to his reverence would make a woman stop when she's a mind to go?" With Sarah, whose hopes of marriage have been dashed, the rough, boozy old woman for the first time adopts a gentle tone: "It's as good a right you have surely, Sarah Casey, but what good will it do? Is it putting that ring on your finger will keep you from getting an aged woman

---

[16] Note that the legal classification of children born outside legal marriage as "illegitimate" may or may not correspond to social concepts of legitimacy. The legal definition of legitimacy is a function of the definition of legal marriage, whereas a sociologist's definition of legitimacy has to take into consideration other cultural norms besides legal ones. Note, too, that the legal category of "illegitimacy" may include children who are living in families with both of their parents, while the set of "legitimate" children includes many who are living with only one parent.

and losing the fine face you have, or be easing your pain?" Feeling a little guilty about what has happened — but not too guilty — Mary affirms the folkways of the traveling people: "[I]t's a long time we are going our own ways — father and son and his son after him, or mother and daughter and her own daughter again — and it's little need we ever had of going up into a church and swearing."

And so, in the end, Sarah's notion of getting married is left in the ditch with the priest and the wedding ring. Why would a poor tinker, married and wedded in custom and the eyes of God, want in addition to be married by an official? It may, suggests Mary, have been the "changing of the moon." But, at the turn of the century, Ireland was changing too. And as part of that change, people like Sarah all over the world were beginning to associate legitimacy with legality.

NOTES

1. ***The Nonlegal Environment of Family Law Rules.*** The legal topic most related to the Synge story that Glendon ponders is the rules for entering marriage, the topic that begins the next chapter. As with any legal topic, we will sometimes ask why the rules should be formulated as they are — what societal interests are served, what larger policies are vindicated. But as the Glendon excerpt reminds us, we should also ask why any of this matters to the parties themselves — why do they wish to transform their informal "marriage" into a formal one? Surely their motivations — or their ambivalence — are relevant to the way we formulate the rules, and perhaps also to understanding what constitutes the societal interest. We must remember that the urge of people to "marry" predates the existence of legal rules that could effectively generate any practical consequences to their decision. Perhaps psychological realities or cultural norms generated such consequences. Do they still? Are they as important as legally generated consequences? We typically assume people enter commercial contracts at least in part to generate legally enforceable obligations. Is this true in marriage as well, or are the motivations largely religious, cultural or social? These may be important questions to ponder as one considers the policy implications of the legal rules.

2. ***Contrasting Norms.*** Cultural norms change over time, but also at any one time they vary across nations and among subgroups within nations. For example, at one time "arranged" marriages were common in Western Europe, but today they are rare. This swing reflects a corresponding change in these cultures' understanding of the function of marriage. At one time, at least among wealthier classes, marriage was viewed as a social and economic tool, while today its purpose is almost exclusively personal and romantic. *See* MARY ANN GLENDON, THE NEW FAMILY AND THE NEW PROPERTY 12–32 (1981). Yet arranged marriages continue to be common in some non-European cultures, and even in some cultural subgroups within Western Europe and the United States. *See, e.g.,* Lehner, *For Better or Worse, Arranged Marriages Still Thrive in Japan*, WALL ST. J., July 2, 1983, at 1.

Similar traditions also persisted in India, even among the otherwise more westernized, affluent groups. "Not only is the traditional [arranged marriage] generally accepted, it is widely defended as working at least as well as what is seen here as the West's chancy, unreliable system of courtship." Stevens, *The Past Still Shadows Marriage in India*, N.Y. TIMES, May 14, 1984, at 14. The system is based on the assumption that companionship and affection are secondary considerations in making a match, and there is little expectation that love will develop between the spouses. The "girl" is expected to pass inspection by the groom's family, and "physical defects . . . must by honor be declared."

Indian legal prohibitions on dowries are widely disregarded, and marriages frequently involve financial settlements in which the bride's family makes a payment to the groom. The size of the dowry may depend on the occupational status of the "boy" — and Indians who hold American "green cards," allowing them to work here, may command especially high dowries. At the same time, middle class Indians more often give the prospective spouses some say in the match, sometimes even allowing them to date a few times before making up their minds. Some believe this hybrid system gives them the best of both worlds, because the couple has freedom to refuse but has "the security of knowing that [their] parents are looking out for [their] interests." *Id*. According to Ramdas Menon, a sociology professor at Texas A. & M. University, the rate of arranged marriages in the United States increased with increases in Indian and Pakistani immigration. He reported that issues of an Indian weekly published in the United States which in 1971 typically carried 30 matrimonial ads now carry 180. Asra Q. Nomani, *To Wed, Some Fans of Rock and Pizza Revert to Tradition*, WALL ST. J., Apr. 14, 1988, at 1.

3. *Transitions in Family Law.* The changes in family law over the past four decades have been dramatic. If the law is seen as the reflection of societal values, then these legal changes reveal dramatic shifts in American values beginning in the 1960s. Most of these transformations in American family law are addressed in succeeding chapters and concern matters such as on the law governing the termination of the marital status; the consequences of divorce on division of marital property, child custody and support obligations; the treatment of unmarried families; and the recognition of procreative liberties. Most recently, challenges to state laws restricting entry to marriage to opposite-sex couples have begun to chip away at the prohibition against same-sex marriages. More broadly, gay and lesbian couples, individuals, and their children have sought, and in some contexts been granted, rights and benefits equivalent to, or approaching, those enjoyed by heterosexuals.

Yet, despite the dramatic changes in family law that the second half of the 20th century has brought with it, we should not lose sight of the continuities. For example, in examining family law transitions and debates over the prior century, historian Michael Grossberg observes:

> What has struck me the most about a comparison of family law in the 1890s and 1990s is not so much the commonality or differences in particular issues or even the importance placed on family well-being, but rather the persistent way we talk about the complex relationship between families and law. . . . [W]e have inherited a way of talking about American family law that fundamentally frames our disputes over marriage, divorce, child custody, abortion, and other contested

family issues of our time. . . . [¶] The persistent discourse of domestic relations has two critical components. First, we tend to talk about family law problems in metaphorical terms of balancing. Teeter-totter-like, we speak of balancing individual and family rights and autonomy with state interests . . . . Examples fill every chapter of the domestic relations tests used in classes in 1894 and 1994; the right to wed and the state regulation of marital choices, the right to leave a troubled marriage and the state interests in family preservation, the right to a child and the public interest in child protection, and so forth. [¶] Second, . . . the sides shift in these rhetorical balancing acts because of critical timebound elements that spring from the constant reality of American family diversity. That is, now, as at any moment in the past, there is no single American family. Quite the contrary, there are, and always have been, a wide range of family forms and choices. Debate focuses on the legal standing of these various family forms, and it generally emerges in contests between what I would call functional families and ideological families. Functional families are those various ways women, men, and children actually live together; ideological families are the forms of family life recognized in the public narratives and the law. . . . The two do not always coincide [and c]lashes over them provoke debate and controversy because they raise the basic questions of family law: What is a legal family? What are the responsibilities of family members to each other and to the community? Who can marry and form a legal family? Who ought to be recognized as a parent? Answers to these questions repeatedly upset the legal balance and spill out into the public sphere. They did in 1894, and they do so now.

Michael Grossberg, *Balancing Acts: Crisis, Change, and Continuity in American Family Law, 1890–1990*, 28 IND. L. REV. 273, 273–74 (1995).

§ B. THE "FAMILY" AS A REGULATORY CLASSIFICATION

[1] ZONING RULES

MOORE v. CITY OF EAST CLEVELAND

431 U.S. 494 (1977)

MR. JUSTICE POWELL announced the judgment of the Court, and delivered an opinion in which MR. JUSTICE BRENNAN, MR. JUSTICE MARSHALL, and MR. JUSTICE BLACKMUN joined.

East Cleveland's housing ordinance, like many throughout the country, limits occupancy of a dwelling unit to members of a single family. § 1351.02. But the ordinance contains an unusual and complicated definitional section that recognizes as a "family" only a few categories of related individuals.

§ 1341.08. [2] Because her family, living together in her home, fits none of those categories, appellant stands convicted of a criminal offense. The question . . . is whether the ordinance violates the Due Process Clause of the Fourteenth Amendment.

Appellant, Mrs. Inez Moore, lives in her East Cleveland home together with her son, Dale Moore, Sr., and her two grandsons, Dale, Jr., and John Moore, Jr. The two boys are first cousins rather than brothers; . . . John came to live with his grandmother and with the elder and younger Dale Moores after his mother's death.

In early 1973, Mrs. Moore received a notice of violation from the city, stating that John was an "illegal occupant" and directing her to comply with the ordinance. When she failed to remove him from her home, the city filed a criminal charge. Mrs. Moore moved to dismiss, claiming that the ordinance was constitutionally invalid on its face. Her motion was overruled, and upon conviction she was sentenced to five days in jail and a $25 fine. The Ohio Court of Appeals affirmed after giving full consideration to her constitutional claims, and the Ohio Supreme Court denied review. We noted probable jurisdiction of her appeal, 425 U.S. 949 (1976).

The city argues that our decision in *Village of Belle Terre v. Boraas*, 416 U.S. 1 (1974), requires us to sustain the ordinance attacked here. *Belle Terre*, like *East Cleveland*, imposed limits on the types of groups that could occupy a single dwelling unit. Applying the constitutional standard announced in this Court's leading land-use case, *Euclid v. Ambler Realty Co.*, 272 U.S. 365 (1926), we sustained the *Belle Terre* ordinance on the ground that it bore a rational relationship to permissible state objectives.

But one overriding factor sets this case apart from *Belle Terre*. The ordinance there affected only unrelated individuals. It expressly allowed all who were related by "blood, adoption, or marriage" to live together, and in sustaining the ordinance we were careful to note that it promoted "family needs" and "family values." 416 U.S., at 9. *East Cleveland*, in contrast, has chosen to regulate the occupancy of its housing by slicing deeply into the

---

[2] Section 1341.08 provides:

    "'Family' means a number of individuals related to the nominal head of the household or to the spouse of the nominal head of the household living as a single housekeeping unit in a single dwelling unit, but limited to the following:

    "(a) Husband or wife of the nominal head of the household.

    "(b) Unmarried children of the nominal head of the household or of the spouse of the nominal head of the household, provided, however, that such unmarried children have no children residing with them.

    "(c) Father or mother of the nominal head of the household or of the spouse of the nominal head of the household.

    "(d) Notwithstanding the provisions of subsection (b) hereof, a family may include not more than one dependent married or unmarried child of the nominal head of the household or of the spouse of the nominal head of the household and the spouse and dependent children of such dependent child. For the purpose of this subsection, a dependent person is one who has more than fifty percent of his total support furnished for him by the nominal head of the household and the spouse of the nominal head of the household.

    "(e) A family may consist of one individual."

family itself. This is no mere incidental result of the ordinance. On its face it selects certain categories of relatives who may live together and declares that others may not. In particular, it makes a crime of a grandmother's choice to live with her grandson in circumstances like those presented here.

When a city undertakes such intrusive regulation of the family, neither *Belle Terre* nor *Euclid* governs; the usual judicial deference to the legislature is inappropriate. "This Court has long recognized that freedom of personal choice in matters of marriage and family life is one of the liberties protected by the Due Process Clause of the Fourteenth Amendment." *Cleveland Board of Education v. LaFleur*, 414 U.S. 632, 639–640 (1974). A host of cases, tracing their lineage to *Meyer v. Nebraska*, 262 U.S. 390, 399–401 (1923), and *Pierce v. Society of Sisters*, 268 U.S. 510, 534–535 (1925), have consistently acknowledged a "private realm of family life which the state cannot enter." *Prince v. Massachusetts*, 321 U.S. 158, 166 (1944). . . .

When thus examined, this ordinance cannot survive. The city seeks to justify it as a means of preventing overcrowding, minimizing traffic and parking congestion, and avoiding an undue financial burden on East Cleveland's school system. Although these are legitimate goals, the ordinance before us serves them marginally, at best. For example, the ordinance permits any family consisting only of husband, wife, and unmarried children to live together, even if the family contains a half dozen licensed drivers, each with his or her own car. At the same time it forbids an adult brother and sister to share a household, even if both faithfully use public transportation. The ordinance would permit a grandmother to live with a single dependent son and children, even if his school-age children number a dozen, yet it forces Mrs. Moore to find another dwelling for her grandson John, simply because of the presence of his uncle and cousin in the same household. We need not labor the point. Section 1341.08 has but a tenuous relation to alleviation of the conditions mentioned by the city.

The city would distinguish the cases based on *Meyer* and *Pierce*. It points out that none of them "gives grandmothers any fundamental rights with respect to grandsons," and suggests that any constitutional right to live together as a family extends only to the nuclear family — essentially a couple and their dependent children.

To be sure, these cases did not expressly consider the family relationship presented here. They were immediately concerned with freedom of choice with respect to childbearing, *e.g.*, *LaFleur*, *Roe v. Wade*, *Griswold*, *supra*, or with the rights of parents to the custody and companionship of their own children, *Stanley v. Illinois*, *supra*, or with traditional parental authority in matters of child rearing and education. *Yoder, Ginsberg, Pierce, Meyer, supra*. But unless we close our eyes to the basic reasons why certain rights associated with the family have been accorded shelter under the Fourteenth Amendment's Due Process Clause, we cannot avoid applying the force and rationale of these precedents to the family choice involved in this case. . . .

Substantive due process has at times been a treacherous field for this Court. . . . [¶] [But appropriate] limits on substantive due process come not from drawing arbitrary lines but rather from careful "respect for the teachings of history [and] solid recognition of the basic values that underlie our society."

Griswold v. Connecticut, 381 U.S., at 501 (Harlan, J., concurring). Our decisions establish that the Constitution protects the sanctity of the family precisely because the institution of the family is deeply rooted in this Nation's history and tradition. It is through the family that we inculcate and pass down many of our most cherished values, moral and cultural.

Ours is by no means a tradition limited to respect for the bonds uniting the members of the nuclear family. The tradition of uncles, aunts, cousins, and especially grandparents sharing a household along with parents and children has roots equally venerable and equally deserving of constitutional recognition. Over the years millions of our citizens have grown up in just such an environment, and most, surely, have profited from it. Even if conditions of modern society have brought about a decline in extended family households, they have not erased the accumulated wisdom of civilization, gained over the centuries and honored throughout our history, that supports a larger conception of the family. Out of choice, necessity, or a sense of family responsibility, it has been common for close relatives to draw together and participate in the duties and the satisfactions of a common home. Decisions concerning child rearing, which *Yoder, Meyer, Pierce* and other cases have recognized as entitled to constitutional protection, long have been shared with grandparents or other relatives who occupy the same household — indeed who may take on major responsibility for the rearing of the children. Especially in times of adversity, such as the death of a spouse or economic need, the broader family has tended to come together for mutual sustenance and to maintain or rebuild a secure home life. This is apparently what happened here.

Whether or not such a household is established because of personal tragedy, the choice of relatives in this degree of kinship to live together may not lightly be denied by the State. *Pierce* struck down an Oregon law requiring all children to attend the State's public schools, holding that the Constitution "excludes any general power of the State to standardize its children by forcing them to accept instruction from public teachers only." 268 U.S., at 535. By the same token the Constitution prevents East Cleveland from standardizing its children — and its adults — by forcing all to live in certain narrowly defined family patterns.

Reversed.

[JUSTICE STEVENS concurred in the judgment, finding the challenged zoning regulation an unconstitutional "taking" of appellant's property because the city "failed totally" to explain the need for a rule allowing a homeowner to have grandchildren live with her if they are brothers but not if they are cousins. The other four Justices dissented.]

DAVID D. HADDOCK & DANIEL D. POLSBY, FAMILY AS A RATIONAL CLASSIFICATION, 74 Wash. U. L.Q. 15, 16–32 (1996)

. . . Does a legislative preference for "family" amount to an irrational classification? [¶] The question was squarely raised in *Santa Barbara v. Adamson*. According to the California Supreme Court, the city violated the state's constitution by pegging its residential land use regulations to the subsistence of a "family" (as traditionally and legally constituted). [8] That sequitur follows from the major premise that privacy is an inalienable right, and the minor premise that it is essentially a private matter whether a person lives in a marital household, a hippie commune, or some variant that, according to the court, could be termed "an alternate family."

The court characterized the city's legislative purpose as preventing the moral hazards that communes pose to traditional families and their children. However, the court stated that to pursue such objectives by means of a flat ban amounts to erecting an "irrebuttable presumption" that communal life is immoral or socially corrosive. The city's legitimate goals — to head off the damage and misconduct that communards may (but do not always) do — and that traditional family members sometimes also do (if less frequently) — can be less-restrictively brought about by zeroing in on how the property is used rather than by whom it is used. Using family as an operational surrogate in a statutory plan aimed at assuring the stability of a neighborhood is overbroad because it thereby rules out many legitimate associations that would not introduce neighborhood instability. Additionally, family is underinclusive in that it allows many arrangements that would undermine neighborhood stability.

[W]hy should organized society care, one way or another, about the family? If most people want to live in families, fine; if others do not, so what? [¶] . . . From ancient times, it has been widely recognized that there exists an essential connection between families and the larger societies that contain them. It is not only that families are the schools of first instance, in which children learn to embrace their deepest and most primitive assumptions about life and other people. It is also, as Confucius, Plato, and probably a hundred of their forerunners recognized, that the family is a sort of molecule, the very stuff of which the larger society is composed, so that the welfare of the one and the other are indissolubly coherent. As we should say in the patois of modern policy wonk-speak, families generate positive externalities for society relative to other living arrangements. One might suppose that so rooted an intuition would attract little skepticism. But a good deal of modern family law appears to accept the subtly inconsistent premise that how a person chooses to live, and with whom, is essentially a private matter into which the community intrudes as a hostile and officious stranger. According to our argument, that premise is specious. A matter, even a sensitively intimate one like a person's domestic living arrangements, can hardly be "private" if seen as threatening to result in important external harm.

. . .

What is the basis for the fireside induction that "families" behave differently from a demographically matched group of non-family members? The answer is largely one of the stability of relationships, and the costs that members of any relational group will ordinarily encounter when they try to control the behavior of other group members. [¶] [T]he relative probabilities of exit,

---

[8] . . . "Family" is defined in the Santa Barbara city ordinance as, "1. An individual, or two (2) or more persons related by blood, marriage or legal adoption living together as a single housekeeping unit in a dwelling unit. 2. A group of not to exceed five (5) persons, excluding servants living together as a single housekeeping unit in a dwelling unit."

emotional as well as physical, from the household [is different for families]. The ease or difficulty of exit carries implications for the ability of the domestic unit to acquire and preserve reputational capital, which in turn affects the stake that household members have in investing in the household's "brand name."

. . .

Family members have incentives to constrain one another's behavior in order to maximize the family's equity in such reputational assets as honesty, virtue, trustworthiness, community-mindedness, and so on, because "having a good name" will translate into increased latitude for the members of the family as they function in the larger community. The full value of reputation emerges only over time. Short-term players have very different incentives, an insight that is reflected, among other ways, by the insinuation of malevolence that goes with the term *drifter*. Private markets display the same horse-sense when they ordain discernibly higher rental rates for transients than for a long-term tenant of the same abode. It often makes more sense to tax nuisances expectationally than to try to punish only that subset of actors that ultimately proves to be miscreant. When deterrence is unacceptably costly, a "misbehavior premium" is pooled across all the individuals in a risk category. The unavoidable downside of such a procedure is that certain unoffending people will end up bearing added costs to which their behavior will not at all have contributed.

"Reputation" is a familial public good, and like any public good it is subject to underinvestment, exploitation, and degradation by free riders. The larger society characteristically tries to prevent free riders on public goods by means of taxation or prosecution. Within families, free riders are usually dealt with more directly. There is typically a hierarchy of authority that can police collective goods problems at the source and at comparatively low cost. Costs are low, in turn, because the constabulary — parents usually — are already in possession of much arcane and useful information about the constituents. (Even though mom was not there, she knows that the lamp was broken because somebody was using the sofa as a trampoline, and she knows who generally tries to use the sofa as a trampoline.) Furthermore, the strict requirements of justice (in particular, due process) which are so costly in the public realm, are considerably relaxed within the family.

. . .

There [are] then, not only . . . anecdotes, but also a rather familiar theory which tells us that Santa Barbara was right: Communes, hippie or otherwise, can be expected to behave differently from families, even if one holds the demographic characteristics of their memberships constant, because communes and families expectationally have different time horizons, and thus different behavioral incentives. Like any other law, that "prediction" is overinclusive and underinclusive and contains a "conclusive presumption" (i.e., that deviation from the formal requirement of the law will tend to produce, though it may not always produce, the harm sought to be avoided). A highway speed limit is also over-and underinclusive, in addition to being a "conclusive presumption." So what? Nothing follows.

[Consider] the court's suggestion that the city attempt to enforce its interest behaviorally rather than structurally . . . . [This method of regulation would be costly to enforce, and] awkward for the state to scrutinize [in that it requires access to] the confidential dealings of families. Regulation, if it is required, must operate in domains that are accessible at reasonable cost. [Bright-line rules, such as those excluding certain family structures,] applies to easy-to-see conduct. . . . [¶] Santa Barbara can make [this] sort of case for its zoning law. The city's police resources are limited. Rather than sending a squad car to investigate every stereo that might disturb the neighbors at two o'clock in the morning — and fingering the actual perpetrator in a house full of suspects may quite strain officers' patience and competence — the city would just as soon restrict certain residential-only zones to entities — families — whom it believes are less likely to be blaring the stereo in the first place. Additionally, in a family, one person can usually be found to take responsibility for the doings of the household. Even if the individuals upon whom the regulation impinged were standing on a highly preferred personal right, the law's impact was marginal. Santa Barbara did legally tolerate Bohemian living arrangements; it simply did not do so everywhere. In seeking to segregate what might reasonably be considered mutually incompatible lifestyles, the city effectively increased the amount of neighborhood lifestyle diversity within its jurisdiction.

In *City of Belle Terre v. Boraas*, the United States Supreme Court acknowledged the validity of that sort of regulatory construction of the entropies of communal life. [The authors quote the *Belle Terre* definition of family, reprinted in Note 1, *supra*.] Uses meant to be excluded, according to the Court, were "lodging houses, boarding houses, fraternity houses, or multiple-dwelling houses." The excluded arrangements encompassed Mr. Boraas and his five fellow college-student roommates. But the court was noticeably woolly about the justification for such a land-use regulation. Living arrangements of the Boraas genre, said the court, "present urban problems. More people occupy a given space; more cars rather continuously pass by; more cars are parked; noise travels with crowds."

The explanation would be apropos if "more people" was what the village had attempted to regulate — but it was not. [For as JUSTICE MARSHALL said in dissent, the *Belle Terre* ordinance] "permits any number of persons related by blood or marriage, be it two or twenty, to live in a single household, but it limits to two the number of unrelated persons bound by profession, love, friendship, religious or political affiliation, or mere economics who can occupy a single home. *Belle Terre* imposes upon those who deviate from the community norm in their choice of living companions significantly greater restrictions than are applied to residential groups who are related by blood or marriage. . . ."

Justice Marshall's opinion [explains why] cases of this kind are not . . . about communes and ad hoc college dorms [but about] "lifestyle decisions" — people choosing . . . with whom to live. *Boraas* . . . challenged the Court to articulate a theory upon which the discriminatory fencing-out of such decisions could be defended. Instead of accepting the challenge, the Court ducked. But a few terms later . . . a plurality had the rudiments of the theory . . . in *Moore v. City of East Cleveland*.

Moore . . . struck down a law practically identical in effect to the one in *Boraas*, because "it makes a crime of a grandmother's choice to live with her grandson in circumstances like those presented here." Municipalities [can] limit the use of single dwellings to "families," but . . . have [no] blanket authority to dictate what "families" are. The state is obliged to recognize that . . . certain kinds of arrangements simply are families. What makes them so, although the Court did not explicitly recognize it, is this: Blood kinship and the legal constraints entailed by marriage or adoption amount to a bond against exit, an imperfect bond though it is. The existence of such a bond, and the accumulation of common assets that it facilitates, is key to the stability and welfare of the community. In that regard at least, from the standpoint of the community, families are not the same thing as fraternity houses or communes. They're better.

. . . .

. . .What you get when you have a household whose members intend to stay together for less than a year, and in which no one has legal or moral authority to speak up on behalf of group-enhancing norms of conduct, is Animal House. And what you get when you have a group of people who intend to live together indefinitely, and in which there are agents with legal and moral authority to speak for the interests of the group, is the Benedictine friars — or a family.

. . .

. . . Anyone who has ever seen the kitchen sink in a college dorm will readily grasp the point: Members of such households will stop working on common projects too soon for the common good unless the household has some means to control shirking. . . . [¶] When members of a household . . . injure the well-being of neighbors, they demean the reputation of the household to the detriment of all its members. But a transgressor who does not plan to stay around for long will have less reason to be daunted. He compares the entire personal benefit of the act with the loss of household reputation only as it trickles down to him in his role as a member of the household. And if he plans to exit presently, that comparison will tilt ever more strongly toward selfishness. Unless the household itself can prevent it, some of its members will have strong self-interested reasons for behaving in ways that inflict collective injury.

NOTES

1. *Other Cases on Regulatory Definitions of Family.* Prior to *East Cleveland*, the Supreme Court considered two other cases raising similar issues. In *Department of Agriculture v. Moreno*, 413 U.S. 528 (1973), the Court struck down a provision of the Food Stamp Act which denied assistance to households containing any unrelated individuals. The *Moreno* plaintiffs were an appealing group: most were traditional family units which had taken in unrelated individuals either as a charitable gesture, or to ease difficult financial problems by sharing expenses. Moreover, the household restriction had no apparent connection with the Act's stated purposes of stimulating the agricultural economy and assisting the poor with their nutritional needs. The actual motivation behind the provision was congressional hostility to some of the alternative lifestyle communes which had arisen in the 1960s, even though, as *Moreno* itself showed, the statutory language cast a broader net. The Court's opinion addressed the congressional motivation directly, observing that the legislative history revealed

> . . . that that amendment was intended to prevent so-called "hippies" and "hippie communes" from participating in the food stamp program. . . . The challenged classification clearly cannot be sustained by reference to this congressional purpose. For if the constitutional conception of "equal protection of the laws" means anything, it must at the very least mean that a bare congressional desire to harm a politically unpopular group cannot constitute a legitimate governmental interest. As a result, "[a] purpose to discriminate against hippies cannot, in and of itself and without reference to [some independent] considerations in the public interest, justify the 1971 amendment."

413 U.S. at 534. Such language would suggest that the "bare desire" to exclude communes or cohabitants could not sustain any classification. Such a broad reading of *Moreno* appears to be foreclosed, however, by the middle case in this trio, *Belle Terre v. Boraas*, 416 U.S. 1 (1973), to which the *Moore* opinion refers. *Belle Terre*'s zoning ordinance restricted occupancy to one-family units, with family defined as "one or more persons related by blood, adoption, or marriage, living or cooking together as single housekeeping unit, exclusive of household servants." The definition contained an exception permitting two unrelated persons to constitute a family, but no more than two such persons in any housekeeping unit. When the village enforced the ordinance against a property owner who had rented his house to six students at the nearby state university, the Second Circuit Court of Appeals held it unconstitutional. The Supreme Court reversed. The opinion emphasized that the zoning power extends to ensuring "quiet seclusion" and an area hospitable to "family values." Little effort was otherwise made to distinguish *Moreno*. A footnote in *Belle Terre* did point out, however, that the ordinance, unlike the statute in *Moreno*, did not operate against an unmarried couple, since it did include two "unrelated" individuals within the definition of family, suggesting the Court would strike down a zoning ordinance excluding unmarried couples entirely.

The definitional problem wrestled with in *Moore* — what is a "family" — arises in other regulatory schemes as well. *See, e.g., Hann v. Housing Authority of the City of Easton,* 709 F. Supp. 605 (E.D. Pa. 1989) (holding that categorical exclusion of unmarried couples from eligibility under low-income housing programs violates United States Housing Act); *In re Cummings,* 30 Cal. 3d 870, 640 P.2d 1101, 180 Cal. Rptr. 826 (1982) (rejecting inmate's constitutional challenge to prison regulations limiting the definition of "family" for the purpose of overnight visitation including the exercise of "conjugal rights" to a "legal spouse," explicitly excluding "persons with only a common-law relationship to the inmate").

2. *Distinguishing* Moore *and* Belle Terre. The Court reconciles *Moore* and *Belle Terre* by emphasizing that the purpose of the *Belle Terre* ordinance was to promote "family values," while the *Moore* rule actually required the separation of families. This analysis therefore assumes a definition of family broad enough to encompass the extended family of *Moore* and narrow enough to exclude communes or groups of roommates, as in *Belle Terre.* As such, in determining which collections of individuals constitute a family whose privacy falls within the protection of the Due Process Clause of the Fourteenth Amendment, the Court stays within the parameters of the familiar formal categories of relation (blood, marriage, or adoption), although extending the boundaries beyond the nuclear family. Some commentators view *Belle Terre* "as simply excluding unrelated college students from single-family neighborhoods and not reaching the question of whether an alternative [functional] family can be excluded from the same neighborhoods." *E.g.*, Barbara J. Cox, *Alternative Families: Obtaining Traditional Family Benefits Through Litigation, Legislation and Collective Bargaining*, 15 WIS. WOMEN'S L.J. 93, 106 (2000). Are there other ways to distinguish the households in *Moore* and *Belle Terre?* Consider, for example, the various "factors" set forth in *Braschi v. Stahl Associates Co,* 543 N.E.2d 49 (N.Y. 1989), *infra* at page 34, and apply them to the *Moore* and *Belle Terre* "families." Haddock and Polsby assert that one key distinction between "families" and groups of "non-family members" is the stability of their relationships. How should stability be measured? In *Braschi, infra*, the court refers to "longevity." Are the two synonymous in this context? If not, what distinguishes them? How do the *Moore* and *Belle Terre* households compare with respect to either the stability or longevity of the relationships? Stability is only one part of what Haddock and Polsby see as the critical distinction. They also say that it is more difficult for persons to exit a family unit, both emotionally and physically, and that the "ease or difficulty of exit carries implications for the ability of the domestic unit to acquire and preserve reputational capital, which in turn affects the stake that household members have in investing in the household's 'brand name'." They believe this is the key feature families that makes them more likely than other groups to conform to social norms, and thus the rationale for treating them more favorably in some regulatory schemes. Consider what implication this argument has for how such regulatory schemes should define families. For example, would Haddock and Polsby approve of the definition of family used by New Jersey in the *Glassboro* decision described below in Note 4?

3. Zoning Ordinances and Subtexts Relating to Race, Class, and Other Distinctions. In his concurring opinion in *Moore*, Justice Brennan notes that the family type excluded by the East Cleveland ordinance is one that is more prevalent in African-American families, an issue the plurality opinion by Justice Powell did not acknowledge.

> The "extended" form is especially familiar among black families. We may suppose that this reflects the truism that black citizens, like generations of white immigrants before them, have been victims of economic and other disadvantages that would worsen if they were compelled to abandon extended, for nuclear, living patterns. Even in husband and wife households, 13% of black families compared with 3% of white families include relatives under 18 years old, in addition to the couple's own children. In black households whose head is an elderly woman, as in this case, the contrast is even more striking: 48% of such black households, compared with 10% of counterpart white households, include related minor children not offspring of the head

of the household. I do not wish to be understood as implying that East Cleveland's enforcement of its ordinance is motivated by a racially discriminatory purpose: The record of this case would not support that implication. But the prominence of other than nuclear families among ethnic and racial minority groups, including our black citizens, surely demonstrates that the "extended family" pattern remains a vital tenet of our society.

Moore, 431 U.S. at 509 (Brennan, J., concurring). Justice Stewart pointed out, in a footnote to his dissenting opinion, that "East Cleveland is a predominantly Negro community, with a Negro City Manager and City Commission." Professor Robert Burt suggests the following interpretation, noting that while the *Moore*

> plurality viewed the ordinance as directed against "overcrowding, minimizing traffic and parking congestion, and avoiding an undue financial burden on [the] school system" and observed that these "legitimate goals" could be pursued by other means, [it] did not consider that the purpose of the ordinance was quite straightforward: to exclude from a middle-class, predominantly black community, that saw itself as socially and economically upwardly mobile, other black families most characteristic of lower-class ghetto life.

The Constitution of the Family, 1979 SUP. CT. REV. 329, 388–89. As such, Professor Burt suggests that the Court has been "exceedingly solicitous of white middle-class communities' attempts to preserve common social identity," as in *Belle Terre,* but seemed less willing to endorse the preferences of "the current [African-American] majority . . . in East Cleveland." However one views the motives of the East Cleveland city officials (and the Court's lack of deference to their judgment), Professor Burt's comments highlight the reality that zoning ordinances may exclude particular racial, ethnic, socioeconomic groups, whether or not that is the intent of the particular local government. For further discussion of some of the issues and subtexts relating to race and class in residential zoning and city planning policies, see, *e.g.,* David Dante Troutt, *Ghettoes Made Easy: The Metamarket/Antimarket Dichotomy and the Legal Challenges of Inner-City Economic Development,* 35 HARV. C.R.-C.L. L. REV. 427, 441–47 (2000); Richard Thompson Ford, *The Boundaries of Race: Political Geography in Legal Analysis,* 107 HARV. L. REV. 1841 (1994); James J. Harnett, *Affordable Housing, Exclusionary Zoning, and American Apartheid: Using Title VIII to Foster Statewide Racial Integration,* 68 N.Y.U. L. REV. 89 (1993).

For further commentary on *Moore* and *Belle Terre,* see, *e.g.,* Katia Brener, Note, *Belle Terre and Single-Family Home Ordinances: Judicial Perceptions of Local Government and the Presumption of Validity,* 74 N.Y.U. L. REV. 447 (1999); William Graham, *There Goes the Neighborhood: The Evolution of "Family" In Local Zoning Ordinances,* 9 TOURO L. REV. 699 (1993): Joel Kosman, *Toward an Inclusionary Jurisprudence: A Reconceptualization of Zoning,* 43 CATH. U. L. REV. 59 (1993); J. Gregory Richards, *Zoning for Direct Social Control,* 1982 DUKE L.J. 761.

4. ***State Court Scrutiny of Residential Zoning Ordinances.*** State courts have been split in their willingness to follow *Belle Terre.* Some adopt the Supreme Court's reasoning, applying a deferential standard to zoning ordinances excluding unrelated persons from single-family homes. *See, e.g., Dinan v. Bd. of Zoning Appeals*, 595 A.2d 864 (Conn. 1991); *State v. Champoux*, 555 N.W.3d 69 (Neb. App. 1996). Others rely on state constitutional provisions to reach a contrary result, as did the California Supreme Court in *Santa Barbara v. Adamson*, 27 Cal. 3d 123, 610 P.2d 436, 164 Cal. Rptr. 539 (1980), discussed in Haddock and Polsby's excerpt *supra. See also Charter Twp. of Delta v. Dinolfo*, 351 N.W.2d 831 (Mich. 1984). A series of New Jersey cases also illustrate the latter approach. In *State v. Baker*, 405 A.2d 368 (N.J. 1979), Baker appealed a conviction for violating a Plainfield zoning ordinance prohibiting more than four unrelated individuals from sharing a single housing unit. The unit in question housed Mr. and Mrs. Baker, their three daughters, Mrs. Conata, and her three children. The court stated: "The two groups view each other as part of one large family and have no desire to reside in separate homes. Defendant, an ordained minister of the Presbyterian Church, testified that the living arrangement arose out of the individuals' religious beliefs and resultant desire to go through life as 'brothers and sisters.' The Bakers and Conatas ate together, shared common areas and held communal prayer sessions." The court accepted as legitimate the city's stated purpose of preserving the neighborhood's "family" character, but found the ordinance's particular restrictions to be insufficiently related to this goal. In holding the ordinance unconstitutional, noting that "[r]egulations based upon biological traits or legal relationships necessarily reflect generalized assumptions about the stability and social desirability of households comprised of unrelated individuals . . . which in many cases do not reflect the real world." *Id.* at 107.

The same court held in 1990 that a group of ten college sophomores constituted a "family" under a zoning ordinance defining family as "one or more persons occupying a dwelling unit as a single nonprofit housekeeping unit, who are living together as a stable and permanent living unit, being a traditional family unit or the functional equivalency [sic] thereof." *Borough of Glassboro v. Vallorosi*, 568 A.2d 888 (N.J. 1990). (The ordinance was enacted after "a rowdy weekend celebration by Glassboro State College students." *Id.* at 889.) The court stated that "in order for a group of unrelated persons living together as a single housekeeping unit to constitute a single family for the purpose of a zoning regulation, it must exhibit a kind of stability, permanency and functional lifestyle which is equivalent to that of the traditional family unit." Even though the court conceded that "it is a matter of common experience that . . . student relationships do not readily lead to the formation of a household as stable and potentially durable as the one described in this record," *id.* at 894–95, it focused on the students' sharing of domestic activities (*e.g.*, preparing meals and eating together), payment of living expenses from a common fund, and intention to stay together throughout college as sufficiently indicative of a functional family to satisfy the ordinance's requirements.

5. Foster Families and Group Homes. Many of these zoning battles involve foster families or group homes. For example, in *Children's Home of Easton v. Easton*, 417 A.2d 830, 832 (Pa. Commw. Ct. 1980), the Pennsylvania court held that the definition of family in a city zoning ordinance was unconstitutional in its exclusion of a foster family headed by a married couple who had two of their own children and custody of three foster children. Distinguishing the proposed household from the "six unrelated college students" in *Belle Terre*, the court concluded that "the foster family proposed [is akin] in all respects . . . to a 'natural' family. There would be no professional counselors involved, nor any 'days off' for the foster parents. The 'hope' would be that the foster children would remain in the home until graduation from high school. The foster parents would be expected to provide all the services that would have been expected from natural parents. They would serve in a 'nurturing, supervisory and caring role.' In sum, the foster family in this instance would be the functional equivalent of a biologically related family." In a different context, the Supreme Court has implied that under certain circumstances, foster parent-child relationships might be entitled to more constitutional protection than other collections of individuals, because of their similarity to natural families, see *Smith v. Organization of Foster Families*, 431 U.S. 816 (1977) (see Chapter 10). *See also Saunders v. Clark County Zoning Dep't*, 421 N.E.2d 152 (Ohio 1981) (holding that a household consisting of a minister, his wife and five children, and up to nine foster children who had been adjudicated as juvenile delinquents, constituted a "family" for the purpose of the relevant zoning ordinance, asserting that "definitions of 'family,'[should not be] encrust[ed] with the barnacles of one's own notions and prejudices of what [constitutes a] 'family'"); *City of White Plains v. Ferraisli*, 313 N.E.2d 756, 357 N.Y.S.2d 449 (Sup. Ct. N.Y. 1974) (holding that a married couple living with their two children as well as ten foster children constituted a family entitled to live in a neighborhood zoned as "single family," emphasizing that the essential characteristic of "family" for zoning purposes was "a relatively permanent household" rather than "a framework for transients or transient living"). Not all courts have viewed foster homes as functional families. *See, e.g., Metropolitan Dev. Comm'n of Marion Cty. v. Villages Inc.*, 464 N.E.2d 367 (Ind. App. 1984) (holding that the undefined term "family" in the zoning ordinance did not encompass a single-family residence housing a married couple caring for up to ten foster children placed there by child protective services, noting that those states that have construed the term "family" to encompass such groups have "exceed[ed] the constitutional requirements set forth in *Belle Terre* [and] *Moore*).

Cases involving group homes housing children or adults with special needs, such as the mentally disabled or mentally ill, have been more complicated. The cases we have discussed thus far have been decided on the question of whether the household constitutes a "family" for the purposes of a zoning ordinance, and if not, whether the definition is unconstitutional in its exclusion of such household groups. Another group of cases has been decided on equal protection grounds. *See Cleburne v. Cleburne Living Center, Inc.*, 473 U.S. 432 (1985) (holding that the city's requirement of a special use permit for a group home for mentally-retarded residences, while not requiring such a permit for certain other uses, was irrational in light of the city's stated zoning goals). Assisted by 1988 Amendments to the Fair Housing Act, which prohibit discrimination in housing on the basis of an individual's "handicap," those who seek to establish group homes for a range of special populations have relied on various theories in challenging the ordinance's exclusion. For a discussion of these issues, including the U.S. Supreme Court's decision, *City of Edmonds v. Oxford House, Inc.*, 514 U.S. 725 (1995), interpreting the 1988 Fair Housing Act provisions, see Michael J. Davis & Karen L. Gaus, *Protecting Group Homes for the Non-Handicapped: Zoning in the Post-Edmonds Era*, 46 U. KAN. L. REV. 77 (1998); Daniel Lauber, *A Real Lulu: Zoning for Group Homes and Halfway Houses Under the Fair Housing Amendments Act of 1988*, 29 JOHN MARSHALL L. REV. 369 (1996).

PROBLEMS

Problem 1-1. Two married couples, the Rademans and the Beravers, are each unable to afford a home of their own. As they are good friends, they decide to pool their resources and jointly purchase a single home which they will share. The home is in an area zoned for single family residences. The city zoning administrator brings an action against them for violation of the zoning laws, contending that they do not constitute a single family. What result? What should be the result?

Problem 1-2. Opus Dei is an organization of Roman Catholic laymen, recognized by the Roman Catholic Church. The Opus Dei Center of St. Louis consists of seven laymen and a Roman Catholic priest. While continuing to work in their secular occupations, the seven men are fully committed to a single life so that they are completely available to carry out the spiritual and educational mission of Opus Dei. The Center acquires a home for the group to live in. The home is in an area zoned single-family, and the town denies Opus Dei an occupancy permit because they do not constitute a family. The zoning law defines family as "one or more persons living as a single housekeeping unit, all of whom or all but two of whom are related to each other by birth, adoption or marriage, as distinguished from a group occupying a boarding house or hotel." Opus Dei seeks judicial review of the zoning board's decision. What result? What should be the result?

Problem 1-3. Alice and Tom are both divorced. They begin living together but decide to postpone any marriage plans, preferring instead their oral understanding that they would share all income and expenses while together, but would have no obligations to each other if either decides to separate. They each have two children by their earlier marriage, and each has custody. Their housekeeping unit therefore includes six people. They rent a home in a single-family zone. The city zoning law defines a family as a single housekeeping unit that includes no more than two "unrelated" individuals. The city brings an action against them for violation of the zoning law. What result? What should be the result?

Problem 1-4. You are the city attorney of Familytown. The council has decided to do everything it can to suppress unconventional living arrangements, in order to preserve the family character of the town from the influences of the nearby city and its university. It wants to suppress communes, unmarried cohabitation and groups of roommates, but not "genuine" extended families.

The Council realizes that there may be constitutional restrictions, but wants to go as far as it can. It is willing to enact a law which might get challenged, so long as the chance of ultimately prevailing on appeal is reasonably good. It is not interested in enacting an ordinance that is likely to be struck down.

Draft a law for the council to consider. Assume that state law allows the city all authority you might need for criminal provisions, land-use regulations or other appropriate provisions.

[2] RENT CONTROL REGULATION

BRASCHI v. STAHL ASSOCIATES CO.

543 N.E.2d 49 (N.Y. 1989)

TITONE, J. . . . .

Appellant, Miguel Braschi, was living with Leslie Blanchard in a rent-controlled apartment located at 405 East 54th Street from the summer of 1975 until Blanchard's death in September of 1986. In November of 1986, respondent, Stahl Associates Company, the owner of the apartment building, served a notice to cure on appellant contending that he was a mere licensee with no right to occupy the apartment since only Blanchard was the tenant of record. In December of 1986 respondent served appellant with a notice to terminate informing appellant that he had one month to vacate the apartment and that, if the apartment was not vacated, respondent would commence summary proceedings to evict him.

[Braschi] initiated an action seeking a permanent injunction and a declaration of entitlement to occupy the apartment. [He] then moved for a preliminary injunction, pendente lite, enjoining respondent from evicting him until a court could determine whether he was a member of Blanchard's family within the meaning of 9 NYC [Rent and Eviction Regulations] R 2204.6(d). After examining the nature of the relationship between the two men, Supreme Court concluded that [Braschi] was a "family member" within the meaning of the regulation . . . and, accordingly, that a preliminary injunction should be issued. The court based this decision on its finding that the long-term interdependent nature of the 10-year relationship between [Braschi] and Blanchard "fulfills any definitional criteria of the term 'family.' "

The Appellate Division reversed, concluding that section 2204.6 (d) provides non-eviction protection only to "family members within traditional, legally recognized familial relationships." Since [Braschi's] and Blanchard's relationship was not one given formal recognition by the law, the court held that appellant could not seek the protection of the noneviction ordinance. . . . We now reverse.

. . . .

The present dispute arises because the term "family" is not defined in the rent-control code and the legislative history is devoid of any specific reference to the noneviction provision.

. . . .

. . . [S]ection 2204.6 of the New York City Rent and Eviction Regulations (9 NYCRR 2204.6), which authorizes the issuance of a certificate for the eviction of persons occupying a rent-controlled apartment after the death of the named tenant, provides, in subdivision (d), noneviction protection to those occupants who are either the "surviving spouse of the deceased tenant or some other member of the deceased tenant's family who has been living with the tenant [of record]." The manifest intent of this section is to restrict the landowners' ability to evict a narrow class of occupants other than the tenant of record. The question presented here concerns the scope of the protections provided. Juxtaposed against this intent favoring the protection of tenants, is the over-all objective of a gradual "transition from regulation to a normal market of free bargaining between landlord and tenant". . .

Emphasizing the latter objective, [landlord] argues that the term "family member" as used in 9 NYCRR 2204.6(d) should be construed, consistent with this State's intestacy laws, to mean relationships of blood, consanguinity and adoption in order to effectuate the over-all goal of orderly succession to real property. Under this interpretation, only those entitled to inherit under the laws of intestacy would be afforded noneviction protection. Further, [landlord argues] that since the relationship between [Braschi] and Blanchard has not been accorded legal status by the Legislature, it is not entitled to the protections of section 2204.6 (d). . . .

. . . . [W]e conclude that the term family, as used in 9 NYCRR 2204.6(d), should not be rigidly restricted to those people who have formalized their relationship by obtaining, for instance, a marriage certificate or an adoption order. The intended protection against sudden eviction should not rest on fictitious legal distinctions or genetic history, but instead should find its foundation in the reality of family life. In the context of eviction, a more realistic, and certainly equally valid, view of a family includes two adult lifetime partners whose relationship is long term and characterized by an emotional and financial commitment and interdependence. This view comports both with our society's traditional concept of "family" and with the expectations of individuals who live in such nuclear units. [See] BALLANTINE'S LAW DICTIONARY 456 [3d ed. 1969] ["family" defined as "(p)rimarily, the collective body of persons who live in one house and under one head or management"]. . . . Hence, it is reasonable to conclude that, in using the term "family," the Legislature intended to extend protection to those who reside in households having all of the normal familial characteristics. Appellant Braschi should therefore be afforded the opportunity to prove that he and Blanchard had such a household.

This definition of "family" is consistent with both of the competing purposes of the rent-control laws: the protection of individuals from sudden dislocation and the gradual transition to a free market system. Family members, whether or not related by blood or law, who have always treated the apartment as their family home will be protected against the hardship of eviction following the death of the named tenant, thereby furthering the Legislature's goals of preventing dislocation and preserving family units which might otherwise be broken apart upon eviction. This approach will foster the transition from rent control to rent stabilization by drawing a distinction between those individuals who are, in fact, genuine family members, and those who are mere roommates or newly discovered relatives hoping to inherit the rent-controlled apartment after the existing tenant's death.

The determination as to whether an individual is entitled to noneviction protection should be based upon an objective examination of the relationship of the parties. In making this assessment, the lower courts of this State have looked to a number of factors, including the exclusivity and longevity of the relationship, the level of emotional and financial commitment, the manner in which the parties have conducted their everyday lives and held themselves out to society, and the reliance placed upon one another for daily family services. These factors are most helpful, although it should be emphasized that the presence or absence of one or more of them is not dispositive since it is the totality of the relationship as evidenced by the dedication, caring and self-sacrifice of the parties which should, in the final analysis, control. [Braschi's] situation provides an example of how the rule should be applied.

[Braschi] and Blanchard lived together as permanent life partners for more than 10 years. They regarded one another, and were regarded by friends and family, as spouses. The two men's families were aware of the nature of the relationship, and they regularly visited each other's families and attended family functions together, as a couple. Even today, [Braschi] continues to maintain a relationship with Blanchard's niece, who considers him an uncle.

In addition to their interwoven social lives, [Braschi] clearly considered the apartment his home. He lists the apartment as his address on his driver's license and passport, and receives all his mail at the apartment address. Moreover, [his] tenancy was known to the building's superintendent and doormen, who viewed the two men as a couple.

Financially, the two men shared all obligations including a household budget. The two were authorized signatories of three safe-deposit boxes, they maintained joint checking and savings accounts, and joint credit cards. In fact, rent was often paid with a check from their joint checking account. Additionally, Blanchard executed a power of attorney in [Braschi's] favor so that [Braschi] could make necessary decisions — financial, medical and personal — for him during his illness. Finally, [Braschi] was the named beneficiary of Blanchard's life insurance policy, as well as the primary legatee and coexecutor of Blanchard's estate. Hence, a court examining these facts could reasonably conclude that these men were much more than mere roommates.

Accordingly, the order of the Appellate Division should be reversed and the case remitted to that court for a consideration of undetermined questions.

NOTES

1. Braschi *and a Functional Definition of Family.* The court in *Braschi* abandoned the traditional bases for defining family as a legal category — blood, marriage, and adoption — for a purely functional approach. The judicial inquiry is directed at distinguishing roommates and friends from family members. In *Braschi*, the couple had lived together in a relationship analogous to that of a married couple. They shared checking and savings accounts, went to family functions together, and were regarded by their associates as spouses.

Braschi held a power of attorney for Blanchard, and was the principal beneficiary of his life insurance policy and legatee of his will.

After *Braschi*, a lower appellate court held that the provision protecting family members under the Rent Stabilization Code also applied to a gay couple, using a functional definition of family. *E. Tenth St. Assoc. v. Goldstein*, 552 N.Y.S.2d 257 (App. Div. 1990). Unlike the rent control law at issue in *Braschi*, the rent stabilization statute defines "family members" quite specifically to include 24 enumerated relationships (husband, wife, son, daughter, stepson, stepdaughter, father, mother, . . . sister, . . . nephew, niece, . . . son-in-law, etc.), but the definition does not include gay partners. Nonetheless, the court held that *Braschi* was controlling because the two regulatory schemes have a similar underlying purpose.

In 1990, the Division of Housing and Community Renewal (DHCR) issued regulations defining "family members" entitled to succeed to a rent-regulated apartment on the death or departure of a tenant under both the rent control and rent stabilization laws. 9 N.Y.C.R.R. 2401.6; 2204.6. "Family member" under the regulations includes "any other person residing with the tenant . . . in the housing accommodation as a primary . . . residence, who can prove emotional and financial commitment and interdependence between such person and the tenant." The regulations list several factors to be considered, emphasizing that no single factor is determinative:

i)   the longevity of the relationship;

ii)   whether household expenses are shared;

iii)   intermingling of finances;

iv)   whether they engage in family-type activities;

v)   whether they have formalized legal obligations toward one another;

vi)   whether they hold themselves out as family members;

vii)   whether they regularly perform family functions;

viii)   any other pattern of behavior showing evidence of an intention to create a long term emotionally committed relationship.

The regulations were upheld against a constitutional challenge by a landlord group, who argued that the regulations effected an unconstitutional taking of property without just compensation. *See Rent Stabilization Ass'n v. Higgins*, 630 N.E.2d 627 (N.Y. 1993).

The DHCR regulations prohibit requiring or considering evidence of a sexual relationship in determining family status. It is not clear, however, whether the purpose is to exclude evidence which intrudes into privacy or to expand the definition of family members to include parties who are not in sexual relationships. In practice, although both same-sex and heterosexual couples in long-term committed relationships may qualify as family members, individuals in relationships without sexual intimacy may have a harder time. For example, a woman who claimed a sibling-like relationship to the tenant was found to be more like a "good friend and roommate." *Seminole Realty Co. v. Greenbaum*, 209 A.D.2d 345, 619 N.Y.S. 2d 5 (1994). The couple did not intermingle finances, execute documents formalizing the relationship, or jointly own property. Although the court implied that a real sibling-like relationship might qualify for functional family status, it would seem that a typical adult sibling relationship probably would fall short.

2. *Functional Definitions of Family in Other Contexts*. Courts in New York and elsewhere have been reluctant to apply functional definitions to family relationships in other legal contexts to extend legal benefits to non-traditional families. For example, same-sex couples have been unsuccessful in their efforts to claim spousal rights in a decedent's estate, on the basis of a spouselike relationship with the decedent. New York courts have refused to apply *Braschi's* functional definition of family in this context, on the ground that the statute regulating the distribution of estates specifies "husband and wife." *In the Matter of the Estate of Cooper*, 149 Misc. 2d 282, 564 N.Y.S. 2d 684 (Surr. Ct. N.Y. 1990). Courts have also rejected arguments based on *Braschi* that the husband-wife testimonial privilege in criminal cases should extend to a couple in a long term cohabitation relationship. *See State v. Suarez,* 148 Misc. 2d 95, 560 N.Y.S. 2d 68 (S. Ct. N.Y. 1990). A Colorado appellate court upheld a decision to deny family sick leave benefits to same-sex domestic partners. *Ross v. Denver Dept. of Health and Hospitals*, 883 P.2d. 516 (Colo. A.P. 1994). The court reasoned that the definition of "family" is a policy question for the legislature. It distinguished *Braschi* on the ground that, in contrast to New York's rent control law, the Colorado regulations included a definition of "family." For further discussion of legal treatment of same-sex partnerships, see Chapter 9, note 3 below.

One of the most important contexts in which parties have made claims based on functional family relationships is on issues of child custody, visitation, and adoption. In *Alison D. v. Virginia M.,* the Court of Appeals upheld a lower court decision rejecting the petition for visitation by a former lesbian partner of the child's biological mother, who claimed that she was the child's functional parent. 572 N.E.2d 27 (N.Y. 1991). The couple had decided together to have the child, who had been conceived through artificial insemination. Both partners were fully involved in rearing, until the couple separated when the child was three years old. The court held that the plaintiff was not a "parent" under the custody statute, and thus had no basis for claiming visitation rights. In the lower court opinion, 552 N.Y.S.2d 321 (App. Div. 1990), the majority and dissent argued about the relevance of *Braschi* analysis to the case. The majority asserted that the definition of family under rent control law was simply inapposite to the definition of parent under the custody statute. The dissent argued that the court's refusal to inquire "into the realities of the relationship" between the partner and the child by subjecting the definition of "parent" to functional analysis was at odds with the underlying spirit and policy of *Braschi*. For further discussion of custody and adoption in gay families, see Chapters 6 and 9.

3. *Evaluating Formal vs. Functional Definitions of Family*. Same-sex partners have a particularly compelling claim to recognition of their status as functional family members, because they are prohibited from marrying in almost all states (See Chapter 2), and the alternative formal statuses available to them approach marriage in few states as well. (See Chapter 9). Adopting a functional definition of family permits the extension of legal protection to non-traditional family relationships. Such extensions serve important social functions of family. By cutting the legal definition of family loose from its traditional moorings, however, the *Braschi* court has raised many questions.

For example, if the legal test for family, which heretofore was a bright line rule, is transformed into a broad, indeterminate standard, judges acquire broad discretion to determine which characteristics are important in defining family relationships. Furthermore, these determinations invite what may be intrusive inquiries into family life. For example, a landlord may be motivated to observe the activities of tenants and their visitors to acquire evidence that a couple is *not* in a family relationship. The risks of a functional standard, and the advantages of formal categories are suggested by a case involving an unsuccessful effort by a landlord to argue that a married couple was not a "family" under *Braschi*, based on evidence that the husband was gay and the couple had separate bank accounts. *John C. v. Martha A.*, 156 Misc. 2d. 222, 592 N.Y.S. 2d 229 (1992). The court declined to "peer behind the marriage, into the parties' sexual and economic relationship," an inquiry that may be necessary under a functional test.

Martha Minow has criticized the use of functional tests to define family on several grounds, including indeterminacy — although ultimately she endorses functional definitions of families where the individuals have freely chosen family-like relationships. Martha Minow, *Redefining Families: Who's In and Who's Out?* 62 Colo. L. Rev. 269 (1991). However, Minow opposes the use of functional definitions by the state to punish or impose obligations on individuals. Some commentators have argued that domestic partnership registries, through which individuals in nontraditional relationships can formalize their family status, offer a superior means for these individuals to receive legal benefits associated with family status. Describing an innovative proposal for identifying "family" relationships building upon the domestic part-nership and registration schema, see Note, *Looking for A Family Resemblance: The Limits of the Functional Approach to the Legal Definition of Family*, 104 Harv. L. Rev. 1640 (1991). For a thoughtful discussion of the context-specificity of definitions of family, and distinctions between those components of definitions that focus on "associations of choice," from "kinships of responsi-bility," see Barbara Bennett Woodhouse, *"It all Depends on What you Mean by Home": Toward a Communitarian Theory of the "Nontraditional" Family*, 1996 Utah. L. Rev. 569.

For further discussion of *Braschi* and its contribution to the functional models of family definition, see William C. Duncan, *"Don't Ever Take a Fence Down:" The "Functional" Definition of Family — Displacing Marriage in Family Law*, 3 J. L. & Fam. Stud. 57 (2001); Craig W. Christensen, *Legal Ordering of Family Values: The Case of Gay and Lesbian Families*, 18 Cardozo L. Rev. 1299 (1997); Joseph G. Arsenault, *"Family" But Not "Parent": The Same-Sex Coupling Jurisprudence of the New York Court of Appeals*, 58 Alb. L. Rev. 813 (1995) (comparing *Braschi* with *Alison D.*); Paris R. Baldacci, *Pushing the Law to Encompass the Reality of Our Families*, 21 Fordham Urb. L.J. 973 (1994); Jana B. Singer, *The Privatization of Family Law*, 1992 Wis. L. Rev. 1444 (1992).

§ C. FAMILY, WORK, AND GENDER

[1] PATTERNS OF EMPLOYMENT, FAMILY RESPONSIBILITIES, AND GENDER ROLES: THEN AND NOW

DAPHNE SPAIN AND SUZANNE M. BIANCHI, BALANCING ACT: MOTHERHOOD, MARRIAGE, AND EMPLOYMENT AMONG AMERICAN WOMEN 77–78, 85, 167–69, 171–76, 195–99 (1996)

In a single generation, the lives of American women have undergone a remarkable transformation. Women who started families in the 1950s generally stayed home to raise their children; their daughters most often choose to work as they raise families. That such an enormous change in family lifestyle could occur in the span of a few decades testifies not only to changing attitudes about women's participation in the workforce but also to a labor market that has been able to attract and absorb women's labor.

Baby boom women have attended to the demands of jobs and babies simultaneously rather than sequentially for a variety of reasons [such as] later age at marriage, rising educational attainment, the high divorce rate and women's ensuing realization that they must be able to support themselves (and their children) financially, the women's movement and changing attitudes about the desirability of working outside the home, the contraceptive revolution and the increased control these women had over the timing of their fertility, [and] the stagnating wages of males after 1974 necessitating two-income families. . . .

. . . .

Throughout the 1970s and 1980s, the group with the lowest rate of labor force participation historically — married women with young children — increased participation rapidly. In 1970, 44 percent of married women with young children worked during the year and only 10 percent worked full time, year round (see table 6.4). By 1990, 68 percent of married women with young children worked outside the home and 28 percent worked full time, year round. By 1990, most married mothers of young children had some involvement in market work, although they typically were employed part time.

. . . .

The majority of American women have always been mothers, and now a majority of mothers are also employees. The dual responsibilities of child care and paid employment are particularly problematic for the growing number of single mothers. The economic realities of women's lives — that they earn less than men and are more likely to live in poverty — mean that the balancing act between motherhood and employment is less often a choice than a necessity. . . .

. . . .

Although the physical demands of housework are less strenuous for each generation of women, the total amount of house-work to be done has remained fairly constant throughout this century. . . . In most households, women still bear the large brunt of housework. The persistence of employed wives' primary responsibility for child care and domestic tasks has been labeled the "stalled revolution" (Hochschild 1989) because of its seeming intransigence in the face of additional market work by women. . . .

. . . .

Given the increasing amount of time women spend in market work (men's traditional domain), it is reasonable to ask how much time men spend in housework and child care (women's traditional sphere). Over the past two decades, married mothers have experienced a sizable decline in their hours of housework (from about thirty hours to about twenty hours per week); married fathers, however, picked up only part of the slack, increasing their household work from about five hours a week to about ten hours. By 1985, married mothers performed about two-thirds of all housework compared with three-quarters in 1965. More recent data on time budgets corroborate the decline in hours that mothers spend on housework and the failure of fathers to compensate fully for mothers' increased market work. . . .[¶] Household tasks continue to differ by gender. . . .

. . . .

Employed women and men face different dilemmas when juggling home and work responsibilities. Women's family roles tend to intrude on their work roles, whereas men's work roles tend to intrude on their family time. For example, when a child in day care becomes sick, the wife is more likely than the husband to leave work; when an overnight business trip is required, the husband is more likely than the wife to have the job that demands it. Husbands can "take work home" in ways that advance their careers, while taking "home to work" limits women's career development. As long as men have fewer family responsibilities and women have many more, the potential exists for women to choose or accept lower occupational status and earnings, which in turn affects their bargaining position within the marriage.

Academic researchers seem more troubled by the division of household labor than the women they interview, many of whom think their household arrangement is equitable. The psychological theory of cognitive dissonance suggests that most people perceive their lives to be fair because they need to reconcile expectations with reality (for better or worse). Women are no exception. Most married women are satisfied with, the amount of housework they perform, even though most wives do far more housework than their husbands. The majority of husbands and wives believe that housework should be shared equally if both spouses work year round and full time, but these beliefs may not always translate into practice.

Social exchange theory proposes that power and dependency influence how people assess fairness, and that power depends on individual resources (such as income). Applying this framework to the family means that the spouse with fewer economic resources, and so fewer alternatives, has less influence on family decision-making . . . Under this model, wives would have a greater interest in maintaining the marriage than husbands because their earnings are lower, in contemporary society the probability of divorce is high, and wives' investments tend to be in intangible family relationships while husbands' investments tend to produce tangible benefits. A wife's dissatisfaction with the household division of labor, however, can lead to thoughts of divorce. [¶] . . . . Other explanations for women's perceptions of fairness include the importance of gender ideology. Some women believe they *should* do most of the housework regardless of their employment status. The more conventional an employed wife's view of a woman's role in the family, the more likely she is to perceive an unequal division of household work as fair. . . .

. . . .

Women juggling home and employment adopt various adaptive strategies[.] . . . . [¶] . . . . Women who work outside the home have fewer children than women who are not employed. In 1992, employed women aged eighteen to thirty-four had an average of 0.9 children compared with an average of 1.7 children for women not in the labor force. Employed women also are more likely to expect to remain childless: 11 percent in 1992 compared with 6 percent of women not in the labor force. . . . [¶][B]oth childbearing and employment create "hard choices" [for women] that must constantly be renegotiated throughout life. The ultimate reason for the negative correlation between fertility and employment — regardless of causation — is that the role of mother often contradicts that of a paid employee. Many women try to resolve this conflict by taking part-time jobs.

Part-time jobs may be compatible with child rearing, but the economic costs are great compared with working full time. A loss of income is not the only penalty: women who work part time also suffer an erosion of their wage rate, a loss of seniority, and often a loss of benefits and job security. . . . [¶] In addition to working part time, women may choose certain occupations that accommodate family responsibilities. Mothers therefore tend to self-select into jobs that make employment and parenthood easier to balance. [W]omen choose jobs that permit easy exit and reentry in order to minimize wage and skills loss. . . . [¶] Another adaptation that employed women make to family responsibilities is to work closer to home than men. Since a wife is typically the secondary wage earner, her job choices may be more limited than those of her husband. Convenience may therefore become a deciding factor in accepting a job . . . .

. . . .

. . . . Overall . . . men and women seem more receptive to the *addition* of roles for women than to the equal division of domestic responsibilities . . . . [¶] Each younger generation has questioned a bit more the "fairness" of an unequal division of labor in the home, but change is gradual. it originates more from the replacement of generations than from dramatic shifts in the behavior of adults during their lifetime.

. . . .

. . . . Women juggle a variety of roles out of preference *and* necessity. They will become more successful at it the closer society gets to defining the balancing act as a "family" rather than a "women's" issue. Until that time, women will continue to pay a higher price than men for negotiating the transitions necessary to combine family and employment. . . . [¶] [If] the past is any indication, change comes slowly, and permanent transformation results from a process of cohort replacement. Mothers see differences between their own experiences and those of their children: their daughters juggle home and work in ways that seem almost incomprehensible, and their sons and sons-in-law complete household chores their fathers never did. They see great shifts in gender roles, even as significant differences continue.

Meanwhile, their daughters, especially those now in school or who have recently entered the work force, are impatient with the pace of change. Their earnings remain unequal to men's and will likely continue that way throughout their labor force career. The division of labor in their homes is also unequal, and men's care and responsibility toward children and housework are responding only slowly. But failing to recognize that change is occurring is to miss the revolution that has already transformed the economic activity of women, one that will echo for years to come in the domestic roles of men *and* women.

IRA MARK ELLMAN, DIVORCE RATES, MARRIAGE RATES, AND THE PROBLEMATIC PERSISTENCE OF TRADITIONAL MARITAL ROLES, 34 Fam. L. Q. 1, 19-31 (2000)

. . . The disproportionate responsibility for domestic duties shouldered by working wives has been a familiar theme of feminist literature, and no one really contests the factual claim. Explaining it is another matter. It must in some sense result from the interaction of common preferences of men and women, whether or not one regards the preferences as unfairly or improperly constrained. One story assumes that few men will accept a financially dependent, domestic, marital role. So while successfully employed women may look for husbands more interested in child care than careers, they cannot find them. Some may then settle for a less ideal arrangement, even if it is not their first preference, because they regard remaining unmarried as even less desirable. Others may not marry. A second story is that women don't want domestically inclined men anyway, that even successfully employed women prefer husbands who can earn more than they do — who earn enough to pay for the especially high opportunity cost incurred when a highly skilled woman foregoes some of her earning potential to care for her children. In this story, women end up performing more of the domestic role because they wish to. (Of course, they may have a greater interest in some portions of it, such as child care, than in other portions, such as house care — but settle for the best available package.) [¶] [I]f this second story is true, then one reason why women usually earn less than their husbands is their choice of husband: they seek men with earning potentials greater than their own. Social scientists have certainly observed that this is the traditional preference pattern of men and women.

My own suspicion is that both stories describe the preferences of a large proportion of men and of women, although of course not everyone. . . . It is one thing to say that women are more likely to be attracted to men capable of comfortably supporting them and their children; it is another thing to say it is all they care about. . . .

B. Marital Roles and Labor Force Participation

Everyone knows that a dramatic increase in the proportion of women in labor force was a major demographic story of the second half of the twentieth century. Has that translated into a change in proportion of marriages in which the wife is the dominant breadwinner? One way to look at that question is to ask about the proportion of marriages that conform to the traditional model, in which the husband works and the wife does not work, and the proportion that conform to a complete role-reversal, in which the wife works and the husband does not. Figure 3 gives these proportions for the years 1978 to 1998, the most recent year for which we have data.

Figure 3

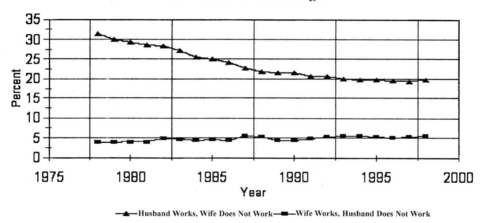

Traditional and Role-Reversal Marriage
As Percent of All Marriages

—▲—Husband Works, Wife Does Not Work—■—Wife Works, Husband Does Not Work

Figure 3 tells us several things. First, the traditional marriage of breadwinner-husband and homemaker-wife has indeed declined in frequency. On the other hand, its converse has not increased: marriages in which the wife is the sole breadwinner are just as uncommon as they were a decade ago, remaining fixed at about one in twenty. [Indeed, some of the marriages counted here as among the one-in-twenty involve a husband who has retired with a wife who has not, and it is probably mistaken to count these as role-reversal marriages, because this snapshot of the spouses' senior years is probably inconsistent with the pattern prevailing during most of their marriage. Others may involve husbands who became disabled.] True role-reversal marriages are thus probably fewer than one in twenty.

Figure 3 also shows [that] about 1988 . . . the rate of decline for traditional marriages eased. The proportion of marriages in which the husband was the sole breadwinner has held steady since 1990, even increasing slightly. [Other data show a similar pattern. We can, for example, avoid the complication of retired husbands by looking only at marriages in which the husband works (full time or part time) to see the proportion in which the wife earns more than her working husband. In 1981 that proportion was 10 %, but it rose to 16.5 % by 1992. Since then, however, there has been little change; it was 17.2 % in 1997. Data on the relative earnings of men and women generally tell a similar story of recent role stability. It is also useful to break [these] data down by age group:

Median earnings of Women Working Full Time, as % of Male Median, By Age

		1981	1992	1997
Persons who are:	16 and older	64.5%	75.8%	74.5%
	20 to 24 years old	82.5%	94.2%	90.6%
	25 to 34 years old	70.4%	82.0%	82.9%

[These data show that] the gap in the earnings of men and women closed considerably between 1981 and 1992, but hardly narrowed at all since that time. [They also show that] younger women have earnings much closer to their male peers than older women have to theirs. The youngest adult women employed full time have a wage and salary median income that is over 90 percent that of men's. This would not appear to be generational effect, given that the major share of progress toward gender equality in earnings took place in the 1980's rather than more recently. It would seem instead to be the result of diverging life choices as men and women age. As women become wives and mothers, and men become husbands and fathers, their earnings are affected. Wives are more likely than single women to work part time, which may affect their earnings not only during their period of part time work, but afterward as well, even if they return to full time labor. Only forty-six percent of married women worked full time in 1997, compared to 83 percent of married men.

Even among those working full time, the figures may be misleading. The Bureau of Labor Statistics, which is the source of such earnings data, considers everyone working more than 35 hours a week to be "full-time"; those working fifty hours a week are thus lumped together with those working thirty-five. But women working full time work fewer hours than men working full time, even when they have the same educational attainment and same profession. This difference almost surely rises from the impact, on the overall averages, of women with children [who, because they] bear a larger share than their husbands of the responsibility for the family's domestic chores, even when they work full time, ... may advance less rapidly in their earnings potential than do those who work more. . . . So sacrifices in earnings potential for the sake of the marriage will be common even among wives who work full time during marriage, and also make it more likely that husbands will outearn their wives. Those sacrifices will be more reasonable to make if the husband, whose earning potential is not sacrificed, has a higher earning potential than the wife to start with.

. . . . Victor Fuchs, writing in 1988, [observed that] between 1980 and 1986 . . . women's wages as a percentage of men's increased by seven percent — an unprecedented rate of change. Why was there progress just then. . .? Anti-discrimination laws apparently worked little change in the wage gap between their enactment in the 1960's and 1980, and it was implausible to suggest that the sudden progress after 1980 was the result of increased enforcement vigor by the Reagan administration, which had then come to office. [¶] Fuchs found that [these] gains were disproportionately [attributable to] very large gains by women then younger than 40. These women on average had significantly fewer children, and were significantly more likely to divorce than their older sisters. Fuchs . . . found that women's greater willingness than men to make career sacrifices for their children was by far the most important source of their lower average earnings, swamping other factors such as employer discrimination. [H]ourly earnings of women aged 30 to 39 . . . declined proportionately with the number of children [even after controlling for age and education level.] He observed that a survey of corporate officers found that more than half the women were childless, while over 95 percent of the men were fathers, a reflection of the disproportionate family sacrifice that women must make for career success — a sacrifice he doubted most men were prepared to make. In other words, Fuchs saw the gender differences in economic data as a function of marital roles, while I have been asking whether trends in marriage and divorce rates could be a function of the economic data.

Surely both perspectives can be correct. If women earn less because they sacrifice earnings opportunities to care for their children, they may also favor husbands with incomes high enough to soften the impact of the earnings sacrifice they expect to make. The problem may arise from the fact that as their earnings potential increases, so does their sacrifice. Thus, the earnings they will require in a husband will also increase, accordingly.

1. Preferences and Economic Pressures

The claim that women work less because they prefer to have more time to care for their children does run up against some apparently conflicting facts[, such as the] significant increase in the proportion of marriages in which the wife works [either full-or part-time]. The proportion of wives ages 25 to 54 who work full-time increased from 23 percent to 46 percent between 1969 and 1998. Surely this is also evidence of a preference — a preference for market work and, presumably, for a reduced domestic role. Survey data of ever-married women under 45 [support] this inference. In 1970 80% of them told interviewers they agreed with the statement that "It is much better for everyone involved if the man is the achiever outside the home and the woman takes care of the home and the family"; by 1989 less than 30% agreed with that statement. In 1970, about half agreed that "A working mother can achieve just as warm a relationship with her children as a mother who does not work"; in 1989 about 78% agreed. These figures evidence a remarkably large change in attitude over a relatively short time. Maybe, then, we are in a transition period of changing preferences. Perhaps increasing numbers of women will be content to focus more on career and less on family.

A change in attitude can of course be the product, as well as the cause, of a change in behavior. Women who worry about the impact of their working on their children or their marriage, but who felt constrained, by economic factors or otherwise, to work more hours, might be expected to resolve those doubts by changing their beliefs so that they were in less tension with their behavior. This follows from the classic psychological theory of cognitive dissonance. This observation does not suggest that the change in attitude is any less real, and indeed, it may then feed further changes in behavior. But it does suggest that both the work behavior and the reported attitudes of women constrained by economic realities to work more hours may be an unreliable guide to the preferences they might express, or act upon, if less constrained by economic pressures. What we thus might want to know is what proportion of the 46 % of wives now working full-time would in fact work part-time, if their economic circumstances permitted.

No one can offer a precise answer to the last question, but there is evidence to suggest that economic pressures played a large role in the trend toward wives' increased market hours. . . . The years during which wives increased their labor force participation were years during which many Americans experienced declining returns to each hour of market labor. The American expectation of economic progress, of advancing in the economic ladder over the level of one's parents, became increasingly difficult to achieve for families with only one breadwinner. A recent report of the Department of Labor . . . which looks at aggregate hours of market labor performed by husband and wife . . . . shows that all married couples, except for those in the lowest ten percent of the income distribution, together worked more hours in 1997 than in 1979. [Yet, the same report reveals that only] families in the upper thirty percent of the income distribution experienced a growth in income per hour of labor. . . . For a large swath of married couples, increased labor was apparently necessary for income maintenance, much less income growth. With the great majority of husbands already working full time, increased market labor by wives may have been the primary or perhaps exclusive potential source of additional hours of market labor that the couple had available to deploy. Other data from the Department of Labor [show] that over this same time period the real weekly earnings of men between 25 and 54 years of age actually declined, except for those in the upper 20% in weekly earnings. By contrast, women's weekly hours of labor not only increased during this same time period, but that their real weekly earnings increased disproportionately to their increase in hours. So during the 1980's and 1990's, additional hours of paid labor by wives was clearly the most economically rational choice for married couples seeking to maintain or improve upon their parents' living standards.

So there is good reason to believe that an important factor in wives' increased market hours is financial pressure. One way to pursue this question is to see how wives' work choices are affected by their husband's income: Presumably, the higher her husband's income, the less economic pressure there will be on the wife to work. From unpublished data collected in the 1997 Current Population Survey, provided me by the Bureau of Labor Statistics, it was possible to derive the results presented in Figure 6, which shows the percentage of wives between the ages of 18 and 64, with minor children, who work full time, grouped by both husband's income, and the wife's educational attainment. . . .

As one might expect, wives' full time labor force participation is higher, at most levels of husband's income, when they are better educated. The opportunity cost of the wife's withdrawal from full time work obviously increases, on average, with her level of education. But for most couples there is a level of husband's income which, once reached, induces them to incur this opportunity cost. Even wives with graduate and professional degrees do not usually work full time when their husband's income exceeds $75,000. For less well-educated wives, withdrawal from full-time work occurs at a lower levels of husband's income. It thus appears that as economic pressures on their choice lessen, American wives increasingly choose to work part time rather than full time, regardless of their educational level. If that is their preference, then one would also expect most women to prefer potential spouses with an income potential sufficient to permit them to exercise it, which means that the income potential they will require in their prospective husband will rise along with their own.

Figure 6

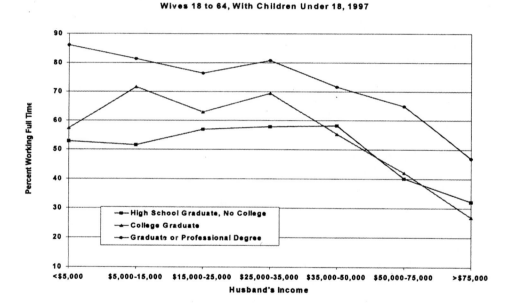

Wives 18 to 64, With Children Under 18, 1997

NOTES

1. *Changing Rates of Women's Labor Force Participation.* Economists and demographers have observed that the "increase in the proportion of women who are working . . . has been one of the most significant social and economic trends in modern U.S. history." Howard V. Hayghe, *Developments in Women's Labor Force Participation,* MONTHLY LABOR REV. 41 (Sept. 1997). In contrast to the steady increase in women's labor force participation, men's labor force participation declined in all age groups during the second half of the 20th century. The most significant decline occurred in the older age groups, primarily as a result of Social Security and the availability of employment benefits which enabled older men to retire. Howard N. Fullerton,

Jr., *Labor Force Participation: 75 Years of Change, 1950–1998 and 1998–2025*, MONTHLY LABOR REV. 3, 5 (Dec. 1999).

The best measure of the impact of women's work force participation on family life is the dramatic change in the percentage of *mothers* in the labor force over time. This percentage nearly tripled between 1955 and 2001, rising from 27% to 72%. Sixty-four percent of mothers with a child under six were in the labor force in 2001, compared with only 18.2% in 1955. Breaking down these data by the age of the women's youngest child, in the year 2001, 64% of women had children under age 6, and 79% of women had children between the ages of 6 and 17 years. Mothers' labor force participation increased most dramatically (over 350%) for women with children under age 6, whose labor force participation in 1955 was only 18.2%. Not only have more mothers of minor children participated in the labor force in recent decades, but more of them have worked full-time and year-round. Despite these increases in full-time employment of mothers, most married mothers still work primarily part-time. Donald R. Williams, *Women's Part-Time Employment: A Gross Flows Analysis,* MONTHLY LABOR REV. 36 (Apr. 1995). As Ellman shows, the proportion who work full-time declines with increasing husband income. As one might guess from that statistic, mothers without husbands are even more likely to work full time. *See, e.g.*, Phillip N. Cohen & Suzanne M. Bianchi, *Marriage, Children, and Women's Employment: What do We Know?* MONTHLY LABOR REV. 22 (Dec. 1999).

2. *The Second Shift*. Increasing participation of women in the labor force has not been accompanied by proportionate declines in their share of domestic labors. Attention was focused on this point in 1989 with the publication of a book by University of California sociologist Arlie Hochschild (with Anne Machung), who coined the now-common phrase "second shift" to refer to this phenomenon. THE SECOND SHIFT: WORKING PARENTS AND THE REVOLUTION AT HOME (1989). Hochschild studied fifty families over an eight-year period, examining the ways in which these families manage their work and family responsibilities. Although both spouses in her sample worked full-time, most men in her study did not contribute equally to domestic chores. The stories told by these mothers certainly helps show why women who can afford to forego full-time earnings might prefer part-time employment. Both before and after work, mothers, but not fathers, routinely put in a "second shift" at home. Hochschild estimated that the effect was, on average, an extra month's work each year, compared to their husbands. Hochschild eloquently described the *emotional* and *physical* toll that this allocation takes on mothers in the labor force, and on their marriages.

> The women I interviewed seemed to be far more deeply torn between the demands of work and family than were their husbands. . . . They felt the second shift was *their* issue and most of their husbands agreed. . . . [¶] [¶] One reason women take a deeper interest than men in the problems of juggling work with family life is that even when husbands happily shared the hours of work, their wives felt more *responsible* for home and children. More women kept track of doctors' appointments and arranged for playmates to come over. More mothers than fathers worried about the tail on a child's Halloween costume

or birthday present for a school friend. They were more likely to think about their children while at work and to check in by phone with the baby-sitter.

Partly because of this, more women felt torn between one sense of urgency and another, between the need to soothe a child's fear of being left at daycare, and the need to show the boss she's "serious" at work. More women than men questioned how good they were as parents . . . .

. . . . There is no more time in the day than there was when wives stayed home, but there is twice as much to get done. It is mainly women who absorb this "speed-up." Twenty percent of the men in my study shared housework equally. Seventy percent of men did a substantial amount (less than half but more than a third), and 10 percent did less than a third. Even when couples share more equitably in the work at home, women do two-thirds of the *daily* jobs at home, like cooking and cleaning up — jobs that fix them into a rigid routine. Most women cook dinner and most men change the oil in the family car. But, as one mother pointed out, dinner needs to be prepared every evening around six o'clock, whereas the car oil needs to be changed every six months, any day around that time, any time that day. Women do more childcare than men, and men repair more household appliances. A child needs to be tended daily while the repair of household appliances can often wait "until I have time." Men thus have more control over *when* they make their contributions than women do. They may be very busy with family chores but, like the executive who tells his secretary to "hold my calls," the man has more control over his time. The job of the working mother, like that of the secretary, is usually to "take the calls."

Another reason women may feel more strained than men is that women more often do two things at once — for example, write checks and return phone calls, vacuum and keep an eye on a three-year-old, fold laundry and think out the shopping list. Men more often cook dinner *or* take a child to the park. Indeed, women more often juggle three spheres — job, children, and housework — while most men juggle two — job and children. For women, two activities compete with their time with children, not just one.

Beyond doing more at home, women also devote proportionately more of their time at home to housework and proportionately less of it to childcare. Of all the time men spend working at home, more of it goes to childcare. That is, working wives spend relatively more time "mothering the house"; husbands spend more time "mothering" the children. Since most parents prefer to tend to their children than clean house, men do more of what they'd rather do. More men than women take their children on "fun" outings to the park, the zoo, the movies. Women spend more time on maintenance, feeding and bathing children, enjoyable activities to be sure, but often less leisurely or "special" than going to the zoo. Men also do fewer of the "undesirable" household chores: fewer men than women wash toilets and scrub the bathroom.

As a result, women tend to talk more intently about being overtired, sick, and "emotionally drained." Many women I could not tear away from the topic of sleep. They talked about how much they could "get by on" . . . six and a half, seven, seven and a half, less, more. They talked about who they knew who needed more or less. Some apologized for how much sleep they needed — "I'm afraid I need eight hours of sleep" — as if eight was "too much." They talked about the effect of a change in baby-sitter, the birth of a second child, or a business trip on their child's pattern of sleep. They talked about how to avoid fully waking up when a child called them at night, and how to get back to sleep. These women talked about sleep the way a hungry person talks about food.

All in all, if in this period of American history, the two-job family is suffering from a speed-up of work and family life, working mothers are its primary victims. . . .

Id. at 6–9. Research reveals very little change in the past decade with respect to the special impact that competing family and work demands have upon women's careers, marital satisfaction, and emotional and physical well-being. *See, e.g.,* Terry Arendell, *Conceiving and Investigating Motherhood: The Decade's Scholarship,* UNDERSTANDING FAMILIES INTO THE NEW MILLENNIUM: A DECADE IN REVIEW 411 (R.M. Milardo, ed. 2001); Maureen Perry-Jenkins, Rena L. Repetti & Ann C. Crouter, *Work and Family in the 1990s,* in UNDERSTANDING FAMILIES, *supra* at 200. The studies, however, point to the complexity of these phenomena. For example, we know that employment can be a very positive facet of women's lives, even when women are balancing careers and family obligations. This is particularly true when the women's employment status is consistent with her own and her husband's preferences, and when she experiences job satisfaction. Arendell, *supra* at 417; Glenna Spitze, *Women's Employment and Family Relations,* 50 J. MARR. & FAM. 595, 599 (1988). In fact, in some dual-income households, married mothers experience more positive emotion at work than at home, whereas it is the reverse for their husbands. The explanation for this phenomenon is that the return to home at the end of the work day usually signals relaxation and leisure for men, while it signals the onset of the "second shift" (that is, housework, cooking, and childcare) for women. *See* Arendell, *supra* at 416.

Thus, clearly, it is not women's employment per se that is problematic. It is the *conflict* between the demands of work and family that deserves the attention of scholars and policymakers. "Work-family conflict" has been defined as "a form of interrole conflict in which the role pressures from the work and family domains are mutually incompatible in some respect." Linda Elizabeth Duxbury & Christopher Alan Higgins, *Gender Differences in Work-Family Conflict,* 76 J. APPLIED PSYCHOL. 60, 61 (1991). Resolving this incompatibility has generally been viewed as the job of the mothers who experience it by society, by employers, by fathers, and by the mothers themselves.

Mothers actively and continuously strategize the handling of family life and employment[, relying] on their own resources and innovations in managing work and child raising. Their personal and individual solutions are due . . . to the dearth of formal programs and supports to which to turn for assistance. Mothers alter their strategies for coordinating work and family in accord with their perceptions of children's developmental trajectories and well-being. They cope with the two roles by emphasizing efficiency and organization, planning ahead . . . .

Arendell, *supra* at 418.

3. ***Women's Earnings and Future Trends***. " 'Fifty-nine cents on the dollar' — for decades the ratio of women's to men's earnings among full-time, year-round workers — was a rallying cry of the women's movement during the late 1960s and 1970s." SPAIN & BIANCHI, *supra* at 107. "[S]tatistics on wage equality by gender show that the gap [in earnings between men and women] has recently narrowed but has not been eliminated." *Id.* at 107–08. The ratio of women's to men's median annual earnings hovered around 59% throughout the 1960s and 1970s, rising slowly beginning around 1982 (to about 62%). By 1990, the ratio reached about 71%, and by 2000, 73.3%. The ratio of women's median weekly earnings for full-time, year-round workers is slightly higher, reaching 76% in 2000, suggesting that some proportion of these full-time female workers lose income because of absences from the job during the year, possibly due to family care responsibilities. Institute for Women's Policy Research, *The Gender Wage Ratio: Women's and Men's Earnings,* Fact Sheet (2001).

A breakdown of the ratio of women's to men's wages by the ages of the men and women provides some support to Spain and Bianchi's suggestion that greater equality for women in the work force and in the home may accompany "cohort replacement" (that is, the emergence into the work force and into parenthood of new generations with more progressive attitudes and different skills). Younger women, particularly those of the "Baby Boom" generation and "Generation X," who have had greater educational opportunities than their mothers and grandmothers, are partly responsible for the narrowing of this gap. SPAIN & BIANCHI, *supra* at 112–122; Marisa DiNatale & Stephanie Boraas, *The Labor Force Experience of Women from "Generation X,"* MONTHLY LABOR REV. 3 (2002). Yet men earn more even if one compares men and women matched for educational level. Fuchs and Ellman observe that differences between older and younger women's behavior may reflect, at least in part, not a changing ethic across generations so much as their different places in the life cycle and, for younger women, the fact that they have fewer children overall, and bear them at an older average age than did women in earlier generations. Perhaps, then, as these younger women grow older and have more children, their behavior may shift to look more like their older sisters'.

In an attempt to balance their jobs with their family obligations, women make choices that may affect their earnings. Women may opt for part-time positions and jobs with flexible hours or choose an employer closer to their children's school. They may exit and re-enter the job market in response to the needs of their families. They may decide not to apply for a promotion, or a job that entails significant travel. Studies cited in the excerpt from Ellman, *supra*, reveal that even among nominally full-time workers in the same occupational classification, men average longer work-weeks than women.

Although familiar forms of gender discrimination in the workplace may account for one source of women's lower earnings, various studies suggest that disproportionate domestic burdens are far more important than discrimination by employers in explaining the limited success women have had in the workplace. *See especially* V. FUCHS, WOMEN'S QUEST FOR ECONOMIC EQUALITY (1988). Joan Williams and Nancy Segal have recently argued that workplace conditions that disfavor workers who combine their work with caregiving roles constitute a form of employment discrimination. *Beyond the Maternal Wall: Relief for Family Caregivers who are Discriminated Against on the Job,* 26 HARV. WOMEN'S L.J. 77 (2003). They cite a growing number of cases in which women and men have succeeded in challenging practices by employers, such as penalizing employees who request or return from maternity or paternity leaves, by giving them negative performance evaluations, passing them over for promotions, or assigning them inappropriate work.

4. *Remedies at the Termination of Marital and Cohabiting Relationships.* Clearly, the allocation of gender roles during an intact family relationship bears on the circumstances in which the two parents find themselves if their relationship dissolves. Disproportionate contributions by one spouse or the other to market work versus domestic work may result in inequities at the dissolution of a marital or marriage-like cohabiting relationship, if not addressed in the financial remedies imposed at the termination of the relationship. For divorcing couples, the issues of fairness in the allocation of property, post-divorce income, and custodial responsibilities and opportunities become extremely important here, and are covered in Chapters 4, 5, and 6. Analogous questions relevant to unmarried parents are treated in Chapter 9.

[2] FUTURE DIRECTIONS FOR LEGAL POLICY

If a principle explanation for women's relative disadvantage in the workplace is that they bear a greater share of the family's domestic responsibilities, how can policymakers respond to reduce the work-family conflict described above, whether it is experienced by women or by men? The first question to ask is: Is there really a problem here, and if so, where does that problem lie? There are perhaps several different ways to conceptualize the *locus* as well as the *nature* of the problem. First, we can focus on the relative allocation of income-earning and home-based obligations between spouses. Second, we can focus on the way in which paid employment (and perhaps other institutions) are structured in our society. Third, we can focus on the availability (or not) of various governmental services, subsidies, or supports for working families, geared toward relieving the family's economic burdens or providing them with greater flexibility in choosing between various work and family commitments.

Looking first at the relative allocation of responsibilities between spouses, Spain and Bianchi, and Ellman have pointed out that, to the puzzlement of sociologists and other academics, surveyed women typically report that they do not find the allocation of work and home responsibilities between themselves and their husbands to be unfair. Professor Ellman suggests that one interpretation of these findings is that women want a different family-market balance than do men, and thus *want* to trade some market presence for a larger domestic role. Another explanation he considers is that women want a larger market role but cannot find husbands who would pick up the domestic labors they would forego if they chose differently. He suggests that the first story identifies the key preferences that women bring to marriage; the second emphasizes the preferences of men. If the first story is correct, the problem is arguably less severe; many women and men are in fact living the life they want. The main improvement we could achieve would be to reduce the deleterious impact on a woman's career when she reduces her market commitment. If the second story is correct, the problem is more severe, and carries with it an overtone of unfairness in the relative situations of men and women. Of course, either story is problematic for those who want a world less organized by gender roles, and who are not satisfied even if current roles reflect current preferences. If this is one's view then the key question is whether, and how, we can change these preference patterns so as to reduce gender roles. Are such preferences malleable? Perhaps. In truth we do not know for sure.

A second perspective is one that focuses not on the relative allocation of work and home responsibilities between spouses, but on the structure of paid employment and various societal institutions. This perspective asserts that changes in the preference patterns of men and women would be unlikely to solve the problem of work-family conflict: a role-reversal marriage would face the same difficulty today as a conventional marriage; it would simply place the difficulty of satisfying the multiple obligations of caregiver and wage-earner on the father rather than the mother. Redistribution of household and childrearing burdens between mothers and fathers, of course, does nothing to alter the work-family conflict experienced by the large number of single parents in our society, nor does it speak to the circumstances of same-sex couples. Thus, irrespective of the gender of the parent who is fulfilling the lion's share of the family-based needs, work-family conflicts will be faced by such caregivers because

> family responsibilities . . . take place in mutually-exclusive locations and times. Work, school, and medical care in America are still organized around the 1950s myth that every household has a full-time mother at home, available to chauffeur children to doctor and dentist appointments in the middle of the day, pick up elementary school children on early dismissal days, and stay home when a child has the flu. [¶] Consequently, many parents — especially mothers, who are still expected to take prime childrearing responsibility — are intensely ambivalent about the tradeoffs between work and parenting. Such ambivalence is fed by a stream of often-contradictory research and wild speculation about the effects of maternal employment on children.

STEPHANIE COONTZ, THE WAY WE NEVER WERE: AMERICAN FAMILIES AND THE NOSTALGIA TRAP 215–16 (1992). Obviously, that way of organizing the world is in tension with current reality in that *most* mothers today work, at least part-time, and many full-time. Some authors, such as Professor Williams in her excerpt below, suggest that market work must change so as not to disfavor working parents. She proposes a gender-neutral approach to restructuring the workplace to provide women and men with choices that allow them to engage in successful careers while attending to the needs of their families.

A third emphasis in the search for solutions to work-family conflict is one that focuses on the role that *government* should play in offering a variety of services, subsidies, and supports to working parents. Perhaps such policies might even include state subsidization of childcare services or parental leaves incentives to employers to provide workers with greater flexibility to meet family responsibilities. It might encompass financial incentives to employers (such as tax breaks) if employees actually *use* leave policies. Such incentives may be necessary to remedy the overt or subtle reprisals that exist in many workplaces, as discussed in Professor Malin's excerpt below, when employees take advantage of so-called "family-friendly" policies. Professor Malin discusses some of the constraints on the choices of men who seek a more active role in parenting without jeopardizing their professional success.

The final reading in this subsection of the chapter is one by Professor Ellman. He provides a comparative perspective, revealing attitudes of men and women in several nations as to their preferences for allocation within families of income-earning versus domestic responsibilities. In reviewing Swedish policy in some depth, his analysis underscores the potential inefficacy of social policies that seek to alter gender role *preferences* of men and women within families. He suggests that attempts to alter traditional gender roles may not work because the preference patterns of men and women may not be as malleable as those seeking to alter such roles might hope. This perspective is quite consistent with those of Professors Williams and Malin, who do not seek to orchestrate changes in gender *roles*, but rather to modify gender *expectations* in the workplace, and perhaps also in society-at-large. In other words, their view is that social reforms should offer *real* choices in a gender-neutral manner to those seeking to balance work and family obligations. If, in the face of such choices, those parents who raise a child together with an opposite-sex partner wish to divide the domestic responsibilities along traditional gender roles, such an allocation would not be problematic. But, to the extent that couples or single parents wish to stray from traditional gender roles, there should be viable options allowing them to do so without incurring disproportionate penalties in the workplace.

JOAN WILLIAMS, UNBENDING GENDER: WHY FAMILY AND WORK CONFLICT AND WHAT TO DO ABOUT IT, 1– 5 (2000)

. . . .Domesticity is a gender system comprised most centrally of the organization of market work and family work that arose around 1780, and the gender norms that justify, sustain, and reproduce that organization. Before then, market work and family work were not sharply separated in space or time. By the turn of the nineteenth century this way of life was changing, as domesticity set up the system of men working in factories and offices, while women (in theory) stayed behind to rear the children and tend the "home sweet home."

Domesticity remains the entrenched, almost unquestioned, American norm and practice. As a gender system it has two defining characteristics. The first is its organization of market work around the ideal of a worker who works full-time and overtime and takes little or no time off for childbearing or childrearing. Though this ideal-worker norm does not define all jobs today, it defines the good ones: full-time blue-collar jobs in the working-class context, and high level executive and professional jobs for the middle-class and above. When work is structured in this way, caregivers often cannot perform as ideal workers. Their inability to do so gives rise to domesticity's second defining characteristic: its system of providing for caregiving by marginalizing the caregivers, thereby cutting them off from most of the social roles that offer responsibility and authority.

. . . .

[M]arket work continues to be structured in ways that perpetuate the economic vulnerability of caregivers. Their vulnerability stems from the way we define the ideal worker, as someone who works at least forty hours a week year round. This ideal worker norm, framed around the traditional life patterns of men, excludes most mothers. . . .[¶] Moreover, full-time work is no guarantee of avoiding economic vulnerability: even mothers who work full-time often find themselves on the "mommy track." In addition, full-time workers who cannot work overtime often suffer economically because many of the best jobs now require substantial overtime. A rarely recognized, but extraordinarily important fact is that jobs requiring extensive overtime exclude virtually all mothers: (93 percent).[¶] Our economy is divided into mothers and others. Having children has a very strong negative effect on women's income, an effect that actually increased in the 1980s despite the fact that women have become better educated.

. . . .

Domesticity takes a toll in a second way: by minimizing fathers' involvement. . . .[¶] Domesticity also takes a toll on men by pressuring them to perform as ideal workers in an age when that often requires long hours of work: roughly one-third of fathers work forty-nine hours a week or more. The current fathers' rights and men's movements need to be seen not only as continued assertions of male privilege (which they are), but also as protests against the gender role domesticity assigns to men. That role includes both breadwinning and the narrow emotional range we associate with conventional masculinities . . . .

. . . .

. . . .My goal is not to advocate sameness or androgyny, but to deconstruct domesticity and encourage the development of new ways of organizing work as well as family, emotional, and political life. The guiding principles are that society needs not only market work but also family work, and that adults who do family work should not be marginalized.

. . . .

Eliminating the ideal-worker norm in market work requires restructuring work around the values people hold in family life, in particular around the norm of parental care . . . . Work/family activists have tried for twenty years to persuade companies to offer part-time jobs and other flexible policies by showing the productivity and other benefits to be gained by doing so. These attempts have had limited success. Their primary result is a pyrrhic victory:

a set of mommy-track policies that offer flexibility at the price of work success. What we need is not a mommy track, but market work restructured to reflect the legitimate claims of family life. This requires a new legal theory that defines the current structuring of market work as discrimination against women. . . .

[T]he current design of work discriminates against mothers. This analysis starts from the fact that the current work ideal is someone who works full-time (and often overtime) and who can move if the job "requires it." This way of defining the ideal worker is not ungendered. It links the ability to be an ideal worker with the flow of family work and other privileges typically available only to men. [Professor Williams proceeds to review empirical data suggesting that flexible, family-friendly and gender-neutral employment policies, such as job-sharing and caregiving leaves, would promote, rather than detract from, workplace efficiency and productivity. She reviews litigation strategies to challenge various aspects of the current system, ranging from salary inequities and promotion policies.]

MARTIN H. MALIN, FATHERS AND PARENTAL LEAVE, 72 Texas L. Rev. 1048–55, 1066–79 (1994)

The characterization of work-family conflicts as "women's issues" has also been necessary to a certain extent. The maternal role has had a substantial negative impact on the development of women's careers. Whereas the careers of single women without children tend to follow the male pattern, women with children often interrupt their careers, begin them later, or otherwise find that child-care responsibilities limit their career involvements. Recognition that the absence of adequate parental leave policies has inhibited women's roles in the workplace was a major reason for the enactment of the Family & Medical Leave Act (FMLA).

[Research on actual and anticipated use by fathers of paternal leave policies revealed that] only seven percent of male workers would take a twelve-week unpaid leave following the birth or adoption of a child whereas forty-three percent of working women would do so. Even liberal estimates place the participation rate of American fathers in parental leave programs at less than ten percent. [¶] Low paternal participation rates in parental leave programs are matched by low paternal participation rates in child-care tasks. . . .

. . . .

Largely missing from the debate over maternal work-family conflicts is any discussion of paternal work-family conflicts. The two, however, are linked to a significant extent. Just as the absence of adequate maternal leave policies has been a barrier to women's roles in the workplace, the absence of adequate paternal leave policies has been a barrier to men's roles in the home. Furthermore, as long as parental leave remains de facto maternal leave, work-family conflicts will remain a significant barrier to women's employment and a significant source of discrimination against women.

. . .

Current practices in the division of family labor reinforce the stereo-typed views concerning the relative competence of mothers and fathers in caring for young children. The threshold decision facing new parents is who will take leave from employment to care for the newborn baby. In the typical dual-worker family, the mother will take leave but the father will not. Consequently, the mother has much greater opportunity to participate and gains much more practice in child care than the father. This may lead to greater or more rapid development of the mother's parenting skills than the father's. [¶] . . . . Thus, when fathers do not take parental leave following the birth of their children, they rapidly fall behind their wives in gaining experience with the child and are perceived to be less competent. This results in marginalizing the father's role in child care and in placing the predominant burden on the mother.

If the absence of paternal leave fuels maternal domination of child-care responsibilities, one would expect that significant paternal use of parental leave would lead to a more equal division of child care between mothers and fathers. Evidence from Sweden suggests that it does.

   . . . .

Unfortunately for men, their role as breadwinners interferes with their involvement with their children. Childbirth means substantial increases in household expenses and is often accompanied by a decrease in maternal contribution to household income. Fathers caught in this economic squeeze often respond by working more hours to enable the family to make ends meet. Feminists have rightly observed that many women who appear to have chosen to subordinate their careers to child-care responsibilities in reality have no choice. They often assert that men, in contrast, have the freedom to choose to have children without sacrificing their careers. Men's choices, however, are also limited. The father's primary role in providing economic security functions as a barrier to increased paternal involvement in the family. Fathers are often torn between their desires to provide financial security for their families and their desires to establish close relationships with their children. Indeed, fathers commonly express their desires to have more time with their children and to play a larger role in nurturing them.

   . . . .

[M]ost men do take time off immediately following the births of their children. They do so by using accrued vacation and personal days. Fathers take this approach either because it is all they can get — that is, family leave as such is not available to them — or they believe it is all they can get away with — that is, taking a real family leave will jeopardize their careers because of employer hostility. These make-shift leaves are quite short . . . [Most employers do not offer parental leave. And, even when they do, p]aid paternal leave policies are extremely rare. . . . [T]he absence of pay poses a major barrier to the father's ability to take leave.

[Furthermore, although e]mployer sensitivity to the need to accommodate workers' family responsibilities is increasing steadily[, many] employers' willingness to make such accommodations is limited to women workers. Men's accommodation requests are often met by, "Your wife should handle it." [¶] . . . . It appears that many employers extend parental leave to fathers so that they can give the appearance of gender-neutral policies, but never intend for fathers to use it. [One research study revealed] glaring and pervasive employer hostility toward men taking parental leave. . . . [H]uman resource and other managers [have been] quite candid in their assessments that their companies would take a very negative view of fathers who might take leave to care for their children. Another study found executives more likely to accommodate the family needs of women employees than similarly situated men, including being more likely to grant a female accountant's request for a one-month child-care leave than a male's. Fathers who take parental leave justifiably fear for their jobs and their families' financial security.[¶] Employers are not the only source of workplace hostility. Co-worker hostility can generate powerful peer pressure. Such peer pressure can intimidate and deter fathers from taking leave. [¶] [T]here is anecdotal evidence in the United States that when an employer not only provides parental leave, but also sanctions its use, men actively participate in the program.

. . . .

IRA MARK ELLMAN, DIVORCE RATES, MARRIAGE RATES, AND THE PROBLEMATIC PERSISTENCE OF TRADITIONAL MARITAL ROLES, 34 Fam. L.Q. 1, 33-38 (2000)

One way to examine the likelihood that the preferences of American men and women will change and converge is to look at the preference patterns in other countries: this can perhaps tell us how malleable the preferences are, under the impact of cultural forces. A 1996 cross-national Gallup survey seems to suggest that Americans have persisted in a preference for traditional families more than the residents of some other developed countries. Two-thirds of Americans believe that one working parent is better for society than two, higher than in the UK (50%), France (56%), Spain (34%) or even Japan (52%). Gallup also asked whether the respondent favored men working with women taking care of the family. Interestingly, while the proportion answering "yes" varied considerably from country to country, within each country the responses given by men and women were remarkably similar. Women were, in other words, more likely to give the same answer as given by their male compatriots, than the answer given by women in other countries. On one hand, the results confirm the implications of the economic data that many American women prefer traditional marriage. On the other hand, they also suggest a broader cultural malleability in women's work/home preference than some might expect. Gallup's results are set out in Table Four.

Table 4

Percentage Who Favor Men Working and Women Caring for Family

Country	Men	Women
USA	47	49
UK	34	33
France	50	45
Hungary	67	64
Japan	50	43
Mexico	27	33
Panama	33	31

Country	Men	Women
Thailand	25	25
China	37	37
Iceland	35	28
Germany	30	26
Latvia	43	35
Lithuania	27	29

So Americans are much more likely to favor traditional marriage than the British, but only slightly more than the French or Japanese. None of the other surveyed countries, however, favor traditional marriage nearly so much as the Hungarians. Because the data suggest a high degree of cultural variation, it seems plausible to think the American view could shift. But on another scale, American and Hungarian women are far apart. Gallup also asked respondents whether they would want to be reborn as the opposite sex. In every country but Iceland, more women than men answered yes, suggesting that women generally find themselves less well-treated than men. But the size of the gender gap in the answers varied enormously among countries. The results are set out in Table Five. By this crude measure, American women are relatively happy with their situation, while Hungarian women appear to be miserable (but not nearly so miserable as Thai or Chinese women):

Table 5

Would You Want to Be Reborn as the Opposite Sex?
(Percentage Answering "Yes")

Country	Men	Women	Gap
US	4	8	4
UK	7	19	12
France	9	18	9
Hungary	6	21	15
Japan	10	27	17
Mexico	5	17	12
Panama	6	13	7
Thailand	3	41	38
China	11	41	30
Iceland	9	9	0
Latvia	4	16	12
Lithuania	3	25	22
Germany	7	19	12

The conclusion one might thus draw is that while Hungarian women prefer traditional marital roles, they don't much like being women. American women, by contrast, combine a relatively high preference for traditional marital roles with a very high level of contentment with being women — higher than in any country but Iceland. The American data do not appear to be the stuff that a revolution in marital roles is made of.

The distinctiveness of the American situation may be of a different character than these numbers first suggest, however, because differences in reported attitudes may not bear much relationship to differences in actual practice. For example, although the proportion of German men and women who tell

Gallup that they reject the traditional sexual division of labor is considerably greater than in the U.S., contemporaneous data [show] that American women in fact have a higher employment rate than German women. The same pattern appears to prevail when we compare ourselves to the British. So perhaps the real difference between Americans and others lies in our relative consistency between what we say we believe and how we act. One cannot tell, of course, whether the Germans and the British report less commitment to traditional gender models than they actually have, or whether they feel constrained to act more committed to traditional gender models than they actually believe appropriate. Either conclusion could explain why their expressed preferences differ from ours in one direction, while their actual behavior differs in the opposite direction. And either could perhaps also explain why they are, on average, less content than Americans with their gender. [¶] . . . Americans have in general a more individualistic culture than many others: we are perhaps less inclined than Europeans to think that our own preference ought to accord with prevailing ideology, less embarrassed to admit that it does not. . . .

The Swedish experience may offer a lesson in the difficulty of using public policy to alter the distribution of preferences between the genders. The sharing of family responsibilities between mothers and fathers is an explicit goal of Swedish law. Swedish law makes no distinction between maternity and paternity leave: it allows the father and the mother to share the statutory parental leave between them however they want, after the child's birth. The Swedes have apparently achieved much more market equality between the genders than have Americans: the gender wage differential is much less, and workplace child care facilities much more available. But when one looks at the choices actually made by mother and fathers, a familiar pattern emerges — but even more so. The proportion of women who work part time is much greater in Sweden than in America, both absolutely, and relative to the proportion of men who work part-time. While 85 percent of Swedish women between 25 and 64 are in the labor force, about 60 percent of employed women with children between 2 and 6 work only part-time. By comparison, 90 percent of Swedish men are in the labor force, and only about 5 % of those with children between 2 and 6 work part-time.

One survey picked a random week during the year and asked whether parents were absent from work that week to care for their children. Twenty-four percent of Swedish women with children below 7 were absent for the entire week, but only 2 percent of the men. Eighty-six percent of the women with children under a year of age were absent for a week, but only 6 percent of the men. While better educated Swedish women work more hours than the less-well educated, even those with a college education only work about 65% of the hours that men work, during the first ten years of their child's life — assuming that they have only one child. Those with more than one child work less, perhaps half the hours that men work. A Swedish researcher sympathetic to the announced Swedish policy, but frustrated by its apparent ineffectiveness in altering gender patterns in work and family behavior, concluded that it was inadequate to urge young women to choose "male" subjects in their education. "A second line of attack is to induce men to behave more like women in their career choices." But she had no ready strategy for achieving that goal either. Observing as well that local surveys indicated that most Swedish women are "quite content with their lot," she concluded with some apparent resignation that "[p]erhaps we should avoid equating gender equality with 'sameness' and give more allowance for gender-specific personal fulfillment."

NOTES

1. *What Would a "Restructured" Workplace Look Like?* What does Professor Williams mean when she says that "eliminating the ideal-worker norm in market work requires restructuring work around the values people hold in family life, in particular around the norm of parental care"? And how does her model compare with what has been labeled as the "Mommy Track"? The "Mommy Track" (labeled as such after a 1989 article by Felice Schwartz in the *Harvard Business Review*) is an approach that allows parents in some higher-echelon jobs (such as law firms) to elect a less demanding work schedule with the goal of balancing career and family obligations. The idea is that such employees could still progress in work although perhaps, in recognition of their less demanding schedule, at a slower pace. This approach has been applauded by many as an essential option allowing women to balance work and family, even though they may decry what some see as its pejorative label. *See, e.g.,* Judith Kaye, *"Mommy Track" in Practice,* NAT'L L.J., May 22, 1989, at 13. Kaye, Chief Judge of the New York Court of Appeals, portrays herself as a successful example of the Mommy Track.

Yet, Williams refers to the creation of a "Mommy Track" as a "pyrrhic victory." Why? She points out that these positions typically permit the worker flexibility, but "at the price of work success." For example, in law firms, part-time Mommy-Track workers have not typically progressed along a partnership track, but have been placed *outside of* the partnership track. As Williams suggests in her other writings, these workers are "marginalized." Furthermore, workers on this type of track in many professions are not paid in a manner commensurate with the proportion of a full-time schedule which they work, nor do they have access to benefits, progress toward seniority, and so on. Often they are passed over for preferable work assignments, even when such assignments could be successfully performed with their particular work schedule. Thus, the choice between being a full-time "ideal worker" versus a "Mommy Track" worker has often been a choice between achieving compensation, recognition, and progress appropriate to one's skills, actual efforts, and job performance *versus* forsaking all of the foregoing in order to obtain certain employer concessions to family obligations.

The following true anecdote provides an example of what a "restructured workplace" might look like. In the late 1990s, the principal of a public elementary school sought to address the needs of two of her classroom teachers, both of whom were about to become mothers. The teachers sought reduced hours, but wished to remain classroom teachers. The parties ultimately arrived at the idea of the two teachers sharing a classroom, an arrangement sometimes referred to as a "job-share." Each teacher would receive compensation appropriate to working a just-slightly-greater-than 50% share of hours, with benefits and measures of employer recognition commensurate with the proportion of a full-time schedule they worked. Each teacher would work 2

1/2 days weekly, with some additional overlapping time for coordination between the two of them. While some parents of school children initially viewed this type of arrangement with concern about "consistency" of the classroom experience for children, the concerns were not lasting. Parental evaluations ultimately refocused on the *quality* of the teaching, unrelated to the job-share. Some parents *preferred* the job-share arrangement, viewing their children's exposure to two complimentary teaching styles as a net gain for the children. Six years later, the school boasted a half-dozen job-shares of this type. While one may view this type of innovation as a form of "Mommy Track," it bears important distinctions from the prototypical "Mommy Track." In law firms and certain other settings, the Mommy Track is, in fact, a *different* career path from the one followed by regular workers. It can be a "dead-end," and workers may find it difficult to transition out of that track, or find they must begin all over again, like new workers, if they try to return to "ideal worker" status. By contrast, the restructured workplace envisioned by Williams would allow workers, male or female, to continue on their career path, but to do so in a manner and at a pace that allowed them to meet familial obligations. By contrast, a traditional Mommy Track in the elementary school context described above would have relegated the part-time workers to being "substitute teachers," or teaching aides, or perhaps administrative workers, and would have precluded their continued functioning in a manner consistent with their training, skills, and available hours.

Is Professor Williams' vision of a restructured workplace truly feasible in our capitalistic system? She asserts that flexible, family-friendly and gender-neutral employment policies, such as job-sharing and caregiving leaves promote, rather than detract from, workplace efficiency and productivity. If her economic analysis is correct, wouldn't we expect at least some private employers to adopt her proposals voluntarily? Private employers who themselves believe such a policy would improve workplace efficiency and productivity would also believe it in their self-interest to adopt it. And if that belief is correct and their productivity in fact improved, competitive forces would lead remaining employers to adopt it as well. Might market imperfections or regulatory barriers explain employer resistance, or are employers in fact assessing the efficiency and productivity issues correctly, if differently than Williams, and thus acting in an economically rational manner? We cannot devote the space here to exploring these questions, but doing so would seem important in assessing both the practicality and desirability of Williams' proposals. Note, though, that even if one concluded that her proposals would yield some loss in productivity, one might believe the price (assuming you could calculate it) was worth paying. Perhaps, for example, we believe overall human happiness would be enhanced in a society in which the accepted balance between market and home was different, even if it resulted in fewer material resources. Consider whether the dominant European view is not in fact different than the American in just this dimension. Surveys seem to show that Americans work longer hours than Europeans, and today even work longer than the Japanese. On one hand, the European economy functions in this climate. On the other hand, this difference in work ethic has been identified by economists as one important reason why the American economy has outperformed the European in recent decades. Responding to such an analysis, some European governments have in recent years on occasion sought reforms that would move their economy closer to the American model, in order to improve their global competitiveness, but such proposals have often met with fierce public opposition. This difference between Europe and the United States seems cultural as much as legal. Clearly, there is a choice to be made here, and the correct choice may not be as obvious as those on either side of this debate would claim.

2. *American Policy: The Family and Medical Leave Act.* The 1993 Family and Medical Leave Act ("FMLA"), 29 U.S.C. § 2601 et seq. (2004), signed by President Clinton, constitutes the only federally-mandated parental leave policy in the United States. The Act was designed "to balance the demands of the workplace with the needs of families[;] to promote the stability and economic security of families[;] to promote national interests in preserving family integrity [;] to entitle employees to take reasonable leave for medical reasons, for the birth or adoption of a child, and for the care of a child, spouse, or parent who has a serious health condition"; and to do so in a manner that "accommodates the legitimate interests of employers" and minimizes the potential for employment discrimination on the basis of sex." 29 U.S.C. § 2601(b) (2004). The legislation requires certain employers to provide eligible employees with a total of 12 weeks of leave during a 12-month period for any of several circumstances, including the birth or adoption of a child, or provision of care to a qualifying family member who suffers from a "serious health condition." 29 U.S.C. § 2612 (2004). Substantial litigation has ensued over the question of what constitutes a "serious health condition." Jessica Beckett-McWalter, Note, *The Definition of "Serious Health Condition" Under the Family Medical Leave Act*, 55 HAST. L.J. 451 (2003). The Act does not require or provide for employee compensation during the leave. The absence of replacement income contrasts with the policies in most European nations. *See* Barry D. Roseman, *Family and Medical Leave Act*, SJ012 ALI-ABA 281 (2003) (summarizing the income replacement policies of various European nations). The lack of an income during the leave renders the policy an impractical option for many employees in all but dire emergencies. Marc Mory & Lia Pistilli, Note, *The Failure of the Family and Medical Leave Act: Alternative Proposals for Contemporary American Families*, 18 HOFSTRA LAB. & EMP. L.J. 689 (2001). The primary benefit to employees under the FLMA is thus the right to reinstatement upon return to work. Some critics have argued that judicial interpretation of this provision has undercut the efficacy of the FLMA in achieving its goals. *See, e.g.,* Stacey A. Hickox, *The Elusive Right to Reinstatement Under the Family Medical Leave Act*, 91 KY. L. J. 477 (2002–03); Emily A. Hayes, *Bridging the Gap Between Work and Family: Accomplishing the Goals of the Family and Medical Leave Act of 1993*, 42 WM. & MARY L. REV. 1507 (2001). In a victory for proponents of a broader application of the FLMA, the United States Supreme Court recently held that state employees can sue to recover damages from noncompliant employers. *See Nevada Department of Human Resources v. Hibbs,* 123 S. Ct. 1972 (2003). Some state policies provide more generous benefits to employees than does the FLMA. For a summary of state law provisions regulating parental and medical care leaves, see Michael Faillace, *ADA/FMLA/Military Leaves,* 697 PLI/LIT 219, 405–18 (2003).

3. *American Policy: Childcare.* Affordable childcare is important to workers at all wage levels, but is of most pressing importance to lower-income earners, single-parents, and those returning to employment pursuant to reforms in federal and state welfare policies. Many commentators have criticized welfare reforms for failure to create and subsidize childcare resources, seen as an inextricable component to successful workforce reentry for parents with young children. *See, e.g.*, Martha Albertson Fineman, *The Inevitability of Dependency and the Politics of Subsidy*, 9 STAN. L. & POL'Y REV. 89 (1998); Kerri Harper, Note, *Stereotypes, Childcare, and Social Change: How the Failure to Provide Childcare Perpetuates the Public Perception of Welfare Mothers*, 4 N.Y.U. J. LEGIS. & SOC. POL'Y 387 (2000–2001); Peter Pitegoff, *Child Care Policy and the Welfare Reform Act,* 6 J. AFFORDABLE HOUSING & COMMUNITY DEV. L. 113 (1997). For further analysis and critique of American childcare policy, see Mildred Warner et al., *Addressing the Affordability Gap: Framing Child Care as Economic Development*, 12 J. AFFORDABLE HOUSING & COMMUNITY DEV. L. 294 (2003); Meghan Thompson, Comment, *The Role of Business and Government in the Provision of Child Care Assistance: A Comparative Analysis of the United States and Canada*, 17 U. PA. J. INT'L ECON. L. 1209 (1996).

4. *The Importance of Fathers.* Until relatively recently the role of fathers in childrearing was largely ignored by scholars as well as policymakers. That has changed. *See, e.g.*, MICHAEL E. LAMB (ED.), THE ROLE OF THE FATHER IN CHILD DEVELOPMENT (4th ed. 2003); William Marsiglio, Paul Amato et al., *Scholarship on Fatherhood in the 1990s and Beyond*, in UNDERSTANDING FAMILIES IN THE NEW MILLENNIUM: A DECADE IN REVIEW 392 (R.M. Milardo ed. 2001); ALAN BOOTH & ANN C. CROUTER (EDS.), MEN IN FAMILIES (1998). Scholars have increasingly concluded that an exclusive focus in developmental psychology and in the law on *mothers'* contributions to their children's well-being presents an inaccurate picture of developmental processes. *See, e.g.,* Catherine McBride-Chang et al., *Mother-Blaming, Psychology and the Law*, 1 S. CAL. REV. L. & WOMEN'S STUD. 69 (1992). Of course, studies showing the importance of a paternal role in child development typically rely on data collected from families in which the mothers are the primary caretaker of the children, since that arrangement continues to describe most families.

5. *The Swedish Model.* If Europeans generally have a more "family-friendly" work environment than Americans, the Swedes probably have policies as family-friendly as any in Europe. Even the Swedes have not gone as far as Williams would urge, but they come as close as anyone, and we can perhaps learn something from their experience. The Swedish researcher quoted in the last paragraph of the excerpt from Ellman is Bretta Höem, whose work is also the source of much of the information Ellman provides. *See* Bretta Höem, *The Way of the Gender-Segregated Swedish Labour Market*, in GENDER AND FAMILY CHANGE IN INDUSTRIALIZED COUNTRIES 279 (K. Mason & A. Jenson, eds. 1995). *See also* Marianne Sundström & Anne-Zofie E. Duvander, *Gender Division of Childcare and the Sharing of Parental Leave among New Parents in Sweden*, 18 EUR. SOC. REV. 433 (2002). Sundström and Duvander provide some additional details on how the current Swedish leave program works and updated reports on how Swedes use it.

They explain that in Sweden, employed mothers and fathers of newborns have a right to fifteen months leave of absence, which may be taken at any time up to the child's eighth birthday. During leave, the parent receives benefits based on their earnings record during the 240 days preceding the birth. These scaled benefits, paid from tax revenues without cost to the employer, are 90 percent of their normal earnings, up to a benefit ceiling that equaled $32,000 in 1999. Benefits during the thirteenth, fourteenth, and fifteenth month are paid at a lower flat rate. Parents who had no earnings before the birth also receive the lower flat rate payment. The authors observe that "[t]his difference in benefits has given young women strong incentives to establish themselves in the labour market before giving birth and even to postpone births until earnings are sufficiently high." Both parents cannot use benefits full time at the same time, but they may both use benefits half time. "For parents of children born in 1995 or later. . ., one of the 15 months is reserved for each parent — one mummy-month and one daddy-month — and cannot be transferred to the other parent. . . . Multiple births give a right to 180 days of extra benefits per child." The program began in 1974, with a guarantee of six months' leave; the leave duration was then increased in several steps till reaching the current fifteen-month duration in 1989.

What has been the result? In some ways, as Ellman reports, the Swedes have achieved success. For example, Swedish women have high rates of labor force participation, and the gender earnings gap in Sweden is certainly lower than in the United States. Yet it is also true that gender roles have not disappeared in Sweden. In 1999, fathers accounted for only 11.6% of all the benefit days claimed, a proportion that was roughly constant since the beginning of that decade. About half of all fathers never claim any leave at all. What accounts for this continued gender division?

Sundström and Duvander report that the "father's work situation" was the most frequent answer given by both mothers and fathers who were asked why the father did not take more leave. It thus appears that both parents are likely to see the father's market work as more important to protect than the mother's. Fathers were more likely than mothers to report employer obstacles to parental leave-taking, while mothers were more likely than fathers to report positive responses from their employer. This appears to suggest that the employers continued to view child care responsibilities through a gendered lens, despite official policy to the contrary. Perhaps then they are more likely to accept a woman's claim to domestic obligations at face value, and more likely to suspect that men who seek parental leave are really shirkers. Another possibility is that the employers do not actually respond so differently to men and women, but that male and female employees interpret the same employer response differently. For example, perhaps men react more negatively than women to employers who communicate that those who take parental leave are likely to advance more slowly in their career. Whatever the explanation, the phenomenon is certainly not confined to Sweden. Recall that Malin reported similar negative reactions to paternal leave requests by American employers. For more on this question in the United States, see Martin H. Malin, *Fathers and Parental Leave Revisited*, 19 N. ILL. U.L. REV. 125 (1998); Chuck Halverson, *From Here to Paternity: Why Men Are Not Taking Paternity Leave Under the Family and Medical Leave Act*, 18 WIS. WOMEN'S L.J. 257 (2003);

Keith Cunningham, *Father Time: Flexible Work Arrangements and the Law Firm's Failure of the Family,* 53 STAN. L. REV. 967 (2001).

But employers were hardly the only source of resistance for fathers. It turns out that one important reason why so many fathers took no leave at all is that half the mothers wanted it all for themselves. Fathers were more likely to take leave when the employed mother was highly educated; one might speculate that such mothers were more likely to have jobs they liked and thus to be among the half of mothers who did not seek all the leave-time for themselves. Fathers were more likely to take at least one month's leave for first-born children than for later-born children, a finding that Sundström and Duvander replicated in this study. The authors note other studies indicating that the division of parental labor becomes more gender-based with additional children. Sundström and Duvander also found that fathers took more leave when mothers earned more, but that, in general, the father's own earnings had much more impact of the likelihood of his taking leave than did the earnings level of the mother. But the impact of the father's own earning on his leave taking were complex. The likelihood of the father's taking leave actually increased with his earnings for one group of men — those with incomes above the mean, but below the benefit ceiling. The authors speculate that those above the mean were better able to forgo the ten percent of father's income that leave-taking entails. And of course, the earnings sacrifice from taking parental leave would be greater for men with earnings above the benefit ceiling.

For an interesting and very different view of the possible societal impact that policies like the Swedes' may have, see Neil Gilbert & Rebecca A. Van Voorhis, *The Paradox of Family Policy,* 40 SOC'Y No. 6, Sept./October 2003, at pp. 51–56. Gilbert and Van Voorhis note that, in addition to the parental leave policies already examined, the Swedes provide parents with free day care services, subsidized, in effect, by as much as $11,900 per child, paid from tax revenues. The "paradox" Gilbert and Van Voorhis examine is that the European countries with more generous parental leave policies and more heavily subsidized and available childcare also have lower birth rates. They note that in 2000 the American fertility rate was 2.06, close to the replacement rate of 2.11, while, *e.g.,* the Swedish rate was 1.54. They ask why women are having fewer children in the countries that make it easier for them to combine children with market work. They, like Sundström and Duvander, observe that the Swedes create an incentive structure that encourages young women to become attached to the labor force before they have children, and to rely on others to take care of their children after they have them. They speculate about whether the effect is not to devalue family over market in a way that affects women's preferences with respect to the number of their children. Such a connection is of course difficult to show, as the authors appreciate. They find it suggestive, however, that in 1998 Norway initiated a policy to pay cash benefits to families with children under three who did *not* enroll their children in state-subsidized child care, thus in effect removing the financial incentive to have others care for your children rather than caring for them yourself. Finland has a program similar to Norway's, and the authors note that both these countries have higher marriage and fertility rates than Sweden.

Not surprisingly, in light of its social programs, Sweden reveals the highest rate of women's participation in the labor force among all developed countries. SPAIN & BIANCHI, *supra* at 101. Next highest, according to 1990 data, are the United States, England, Canada, and Australia. France, Germany, and Italy have somewhat lower levels (with Italy at about 33%). There is substantial variability across nations in the comparative earnings of men and women. As in the United States, the gap in women's and men's earnings has narrowed since the 1950s, and in some nations, such as Australia, Sweden, Denmark, and France, women's wages have approached 80–90% of men's. *Id.* at 136. The gap in the United States is among the highest in industrialized nations, although the reasons are related at least in part to more fundamental differences between economies that are not particularly gender related. The income range in most western European countries is more compressed than in the United States, with smaller differences generally between upper and lower economic strata than we have.

6. *Considering Spouses' Perceptions of the Choices Between Home and Market.* Recall that Spain and Bianchi characterize mothers' part-time employment as a concession they make to allow them to meet their family's expectations of their domestic role. Yet social scientists have repeatedly found "that although dual-earner wives do two to three times the amount of domestic work their husbands do, less than one third of wives report the division of the daily family work as unfair." Alan J. Hawkins, Christina M. Marshall & Sarah M. Allen, *The Orientation Toward Domestic Labor Questionnaire: Exploring Dual-Earner Wives' Sense of Fairness About Family Work,* 12 J. FAM. PSYCHOL. 244 (1998). Indeed, there has been no change in this observation over decades. *See, e.g.*, Stacy J. Rogers & Paul R. Amato, *Have Changes in Gender Relations Affected Marital Quality?* 79 SOC. FORCES 731 (2000), who find no difference in this fairness assessment when one compares cohorts of married couples interviewed in the 1960s, 1970s and 1980s, with those interviewed more recently. (There is a difference, however, in the share of domestic work that wives say their husbands do. It increases from about 1/4 to about 1/3, between the earlier and later time periods.)

Spain and Bianchi suggest that these findings illustrate psychological theories like cognitive dissonance or social exchange, or perhaps a commitment to an outdated gender ideology. The common thread of these explanations is the assumption that the allocation of domestic tasks is in fact unfair, so that the contrary belief of the wives themselves must be explained as the product of a psychological process, conscious or not, that allows them to adapt to a reality that is in fact oppressive but which they cannot change. Spain and Bianchi's implication is that if wives *truly* had their choice, they would work more in the market, and their husbands would carry a larger share of the domestic burden. Certainly, for gender roles to change in response to workplace reforms like the Swedes', one has to assume that mothers and fathers *want* that change and will act accordingly, if only given the chance. But if married partners today find their current allocation of family responsibilities fair, such an assumption about their true desires is put in doubt. So it is perhaps relevant to consider further whether it is correct to doubt the fairness assessment made by most wives themselves. Is it correct to treat it as a psychological adaptation to a reality that is in fact objectively unfair? Consider the following:

> [C]ontractual obligations are well-defined in both time and nature, while the reciprocities expected in close social relationships are not; contractual obligations are discrete; social obligations are embedded in a larger relationship on which they depend for their existence and meaning. The strength of a friendship may be inversely proportional to the extent to which either party feels a need to keep careful tabs on favors extended or received. In all these regards marriages are like friendships, only more so. If lovers have bargains, they are complex emotional bargains, and they themselves may not easily identify the quids and quos. Sociologists have found that even though wives almost always do much more of the housework, most of these wives say they believe this division of labor is fair. Not equal — fair. How can wives believe this? Presumably because they see their relationship as a whole, not as a series of discrete transactions, and believe that in the relationship as a whole, both partners are contributing. They also see their relationship as existing over time, with a past and a future, in which the balance sheet need not tally day-by-day. [Citing Steven Nock, *Time and Gender in Marriage*, 86 VA. L. REV. 1971 (2000).] Husbands undoubtedly make similar kinds of assessments. How else could so many traditional husbands who work long hours providing most of the family's income nonetheless feel they gain so much from their marriage? It is the rare outsider who has a clear enough window into another person's marriage to see how or why it works — or does not. We can be surprised when a marriage we thought we knew fails, and we are sometimes surprised that other marriages survive.

Ira Mark Ellman, *Why Making Family Law Is Hard*, 35 ARIZ. ST. L.J. 699, 712–13 (2003).

If sociologists found that men in traditional marriages believed it was fair for them to support their wives financially, would we assume they were confused or misled? Marriages aren't just about housework, or housework plus income; they involve a host of reciprocities, some of which may be invisible to the partners themselves, but the fairness of which must be assessed as a package — and it is difficult for anyone other than the parties themselves to make that overall assessment. Of course, unfairness may result if the longer time horizon assumed by one party to the relationship is cut short by the other, even if the same arrangement is not unfair if the marriage endures. That point must be kept in mind when thinking about the remedies at divorce: we may believe that effective remedies at divorce must provide the reassurance necessary to allow marital partners to structure their ongoing relationship in ways compatible with their preferences. Note also that it is wives in current, intact marriages who are asked in these studies about the fairness of the domestic labor allocation. We might get very different responses from former wives asked for retrospective assessments of their now-dissolved marriage.

7. *Viewing the Swedish Data Through A Different Lens*. In his excerpt, Professor Ellman interprets the inefficacy of the Swedish policy reforms in achieving one of the asserted goals: altering the gender-based preferences of the marital partners regarding the distribution of market versus domestic work across. For example, despite the existence of greater gender equality in a range of aspects of the Swedish workforce, such as wages and availability of leaves, more Swedish than American women work part-time as contrasted with full-time. Yet, Professor Williams and others who share her perspectives might focus less on a goal of altering the gender-based preferences of workers, and more on whether workers who choose part-time options can do so with fewer sacrifices to their incomes, job satisfaction, and future career paths. Thus, it is possible that if the Swedish reforms and culture incorporate workers who choose part-time positions into the mainstream, with a proportionate wage and preservation of the employees' professional future, more workers will exercise the part-time options. Here, in the United States, the consequences of choosing a part-time position is more deleterious to the worker and her family than simply a proportionate dip in salary. Thus, workers would be expected to choose a part-time option in the United States primarily in those situations when they view themselves as having no other choice, or as Professor Ellman has discussed, when one spouse's salary is sufficiently high to permit the other spouse to reduce her income flows and wage-earning contributions in order to devote more time to domestic tasks.

8. *Further Reading*. For elaboration of the legal strategies suggested by Professor Williams, see Joan Williams and Nancy Segal, *Beyond the Maternal Wall: Relief for Family Caregivers who are Discriminated Against on the Job*, 26 HARV. WOMEN'S L.J. 77 (2003). For further discussion of workplace policies responsive to families, see Jane Waldfogel, *Family Friendly Policies for Families with Young Children*, 5 EMPLOYEE RIGHTS & EMPLOYMENT POL'Y J. 273 (2001); Nancy E. Dowd, *Work and Family: The Gender Paradox and the Limitations of Discrimination Analysis in Restructuring the Workplace*, 24 HARV. C.R.-C.L. L. REV. 79 (1989); Kathryn Abrams, *Gender Discrimination and the Transformation of Workplace Norms*, 42 VAND. L. REV. 1183 (1989). For particular attention to the work-family conflicts experienced by lawyers and some of the responses by their employers, see Joan Williams and Cynthia Thomas Calvert, *Balanced Hours: Effective Part-Time Policies for Washington Law Firms: The Project for Attorney Retention: Final Report*, 8 WM. & MARY J. WOMEN & L. 357 (2002); Jacqueline Slotkin, *Should I Have Learned to Cook? Interviews with Women Lawyers Juggling Multiple Roles*, 13 HASTINGS WOMEN'S L.J. 147 (2002); Deborah Rhode, *Balanced Lives for Lawyers*, 70 FORD. L. REV. 2207 (2002); Keith Cunningham, Note, *Father Time: Flexible Work Arrangements and the Law Firm's Failure of the Family*, 53 STAN. L. REV. 967 (2001); CYNTHIA FUCHS EPSTEIN ET AL., THE PART-TIME PARADOX: TIME NORMS, PROFESSIONAL LIVES, FAMILY, AND GENDER 5 (1999). For a comparison of maternity leave policies in different nations, see Dorothea Alewell and Kerstin Pull, *An International Comparison and Assessment of Maternity Leave Legislation,* 22 COMP. LABOR L & POL'Y J. 297 (2001).

Part II

Marriage and Divorce

Chapter 2

MARRIAGE

§ A. ENTERING MARRIAGE

[1] FORMAL REQUIREMENTS

[a] Licensure and Solemnization

MODEL MARRIAGE AND DIVORCE ACT § 206

§ 206. [*Solemnization and Registration*]

(a) A marriage may be solemnized by a judge of a court of record, by a public official whose powers include solemnization of marriages, or in accordance with any mode of solemnization recognized by any religious denomination, Indian Nation or Tribe, or Native Group. Either the person solemnizing the marriage, or, if no individual acting alone solemnized the marriage, a party to the marriage, shall complete the marriage certificate form and forward it to the [marriage license] clerk.

(b) If a party to a marriage is unable to be present at the solemnization, he may authorize in writing a third person to act as his proxy. If the person solemnizing the marriage is satisfied that the absent party is unable to be present and has consented to the marriage, he may solemnize the marriage by proxy. . . .

(c) Upon receipt of the marriage certificate, the [marriage license] clerk shall register the marriage.

(d) The solemnization of the marriage is not invalidated by the fact that the person solemnizing the marriage was not legally qualified to solemnize it, if either party to the marriage believed him to be so qualified.

NOTES

1. *Licensing Process.* All American states prescribe certain formalities for marriage entry. While details vary, regulations fall into two categories — licensure and solemnization. Contrary to popular belief, generally sexual intercourse is not required to solemnize a ceremonial marriage. *See In re Burnside,* 777 S.W.2d 660 (Mo. App. 1989).

All states have marriage license laws. Applicants provide certain information to a government official (usually a clerk) concerning age, existing relationship of the parties by blood or marriage, previous marriages, etc. This information helps in compiling vital statistics and could facilitate enforcement of substantive marriage regulations. For example, if the application revealed the bride and groom were siblings, the license would be denied under laws prohibiting incestuous marriages. In practice, the license law does little to restrain intentional violation of substantive regulations, because little effort is made to confirm the truth of the license application information.

Most states require a physical examination as a prerequisite for a marriage license.

> Most of the statutes require an examination for venereal disease alone. A few also require tests for tuberculosis, for mental incompetence, for rubella immunity and for sickle cell anemia. In all instances except the examination for rubella immunity and for sickle cell immunity, the physician's statement certifying freedom from the specified disease is required to be presented before the license may issue. There is usually provision in the statutes for waiver of the examination by a court upon proof of circumstances warranting such action.

H. CLARK, THE LAW OF DOMESTIC RELATIONS § 2.3 at 36–7 (2d ed. 1988).

Louisiana and Illinois experimented with requiring pre-marital AIDS testing requirements. Neither conditioned issuance of a license on "passing" the exam. Both statutes were quickly repealed. During the Illinois statute's first year, the issuance of marriage licenses dropped 25% from the prior year. Only 44 of the 221,000 people applying for a license tested positive for the HIV virus during the first 18 months. Health officials estimated about 12 were false positives and that the total cost of the testing was $5.4 million. Wilkerson, *Illinois Legislature Repeals Requirement for Prenuptial AIDS Tests,* N.Y. TIMES, June 25, 1989, at 12. It has been argued that mandatory pre-marital AIDS testing is unconstitutional. Closen et al., *Mandatory Premarital HIV Testing: Political Exploitation of the AIDS Epidemic,* 69 TUL. L. REV. 71 (1994). A Utah statute declaring void any marriage in which either party was infected with AIDS, UTAH CODE ANN. § 30-1-2 (1995), was held to violate the Americans with Disability Act and the Rehabilitation Act of 1973. *T.E.P. v. Leavitt,* 840 F. Supp. 110 (D. Utah 1993).

Do the state interests served by physical exam requirements require denial of permission to marry or would they be satisfied by requiring both parties to be made aware of the exam results?

2. *Waiting Period.* Many states impose a waiting period (of either 3 or 5 days), either between application and issuance of the license or between issuance and performance of the ceremony. Often the waiting period is waived under certain circumstances, *e.g.,* where the woman is pregnant, where the parties are already the parents of a child, where both parties are adults or where one party is about to leave for an overseas military assignment. The waiting period requirement, as well as the entire licensing procedure, is explained as impressing upon the parties the seriousness of the entry into marriage. For a discussion of biases that can affect the pre-marital decision-making process and of how a waiting period can improve that process, see Scott, *Rational Decisionmaking About Marriage and Divorce,* 76 VA. L. REV. 9 (1990).

3. *Ceremony and Registration.* All states have statutes governing solemnization of marriage. While there is no explicit format for the marriage ceremony, some statutes require the couple to declare in the presence of the presiding official and the required witnesses that "they take each other as husband and wife." N.Y. DOM. REL. LAW § 12 (McKinney 1999). Each state has a statutory list of officials authorized to perform marriages, normally focusing on judges, justices of the peace and clergy.

Noting that the Universal Life Church permits all its members to become "ministers," a New York case found ministers of the Church not "clergymen" under the relevant statute and, thus, not authorized to perform weddings. *Ranieri v. Ranieri*, 539 N.Y.S.2d 382 (App. Div. 1989); *but see In re Blackwell*, 531 So. 2d 1193 (Miss. 1988) (upholding marriage performed by ULC minister). A 1997 Tennessee court remanded for a determination of whether Islamic law requires that a person have an official position in a mosque to be competent to perform a marriage ceremony. *Aghili v. Saadatnejadi*, 958 S.W. 2d 784 (Tenn. App. 1997). Contrary to popular belief, there apparently are no statutes authorizing ship captains to perform ceremonies on the high seas.

Section 206(a) of the Model Act illustrates another common requirement — registration of a marriage certificate. This document, often printed on the reverse side of the license, is usually filed with a county or state official.

4. *Proxy Marriage.* Section 206(b) of the Model Act allows proxy marriages. While rare, marriage by proxy is necessary if one party cannot be present for the ceremony. While its most prominent use has been in wartime with one party on duty overseas, sometimes it is used by prisoners. *See Lyle Menendez Marries Girlfriend in Secret*, BUFFALO NEWS, Feb. 1, 1997, p. 5A (brother Erik served as best man during conference call ceremony held on the day the pair were sentenced to life in prison for killing their parents.) Statutes requiring both parties' presence would appear to forbid proxy marriage, but there is some case law to the contrary. *See, e.g., State v. Anderson,* 396 P.2d 558 (Or. 1964) (permitting invocation of marital privilege).

STATE v. DENTON

983 P.2d 693 (Wash. App. 1999)

BECKER, J. — Mark Denton invoked the spousal privilege to prevent his wife from testifying against him. The trial court allowed her to testify, after finding the marriage invalid. . . . The ruling was in error. In Washington, failure to procure a [marriage] license does not invalidate a ceremonial marriage. Denton's conviction for theft is reversed. In 1986, Denton was active in the Bellevue Jaycees, a non-profit community service organization whose members were involved in various charitable fundraising projects. Denton set up and operated a Fourth of July fireworks stand to raise money for the Washington State Sudden Infant Death Syndrome (SIDS) Foundation. With three other officers of the Jaycees, he opened a bank account in Redmond in the name of Eastside Parents for SIDS. In 1989, the Bellevue Jaycees disbanded. . . . Denton continued to receive monthly statements. Bank records show the account remained inactive for seven years with a balance of over $ 2,000. In 1996, Denton withdrew the funds and used them for his own purposes.

His transaction came to the attention of the police through Jill Bowersox, an acquaintance of Denton's who became suspicious in the course of helping him withdraw the funds. . . . Denton told [Bowersox] in January 1996 he needed to close out an old account that had less than $ 100 remaining in it. He explained that the money belonged to the Bellevue Jaycees and he was going to send it to the SIDS Foundation. Denton told Bowersox that he needed her help . . . because he could not locate the former officers whose names were on the bank's signature card for the account. . . . Bowersox . . . agreed to assist Denton by adding her signature to the new card. The new card already bore the signatures of Denton, his 15-year-old daughter, and his wife. . . . According to the bank's policy, two of four signers were needed to authorize banking transactions. . . . Bowersox went to the bank with Denton to authorize the closing of the account. . . . Bank records show that Denton deposited a check for $ 2,610.38 into his own bank account [after the closing of the account]. . . . The State's theory was that Denton knew the money was not his but decided to convert the account to his own use when he encountered personal financial difficulty.

Before trial, Denton attempted to invoke the spousal testimonial privilege to prevent his wife, Leona Rosser, from testifying. The State argued that the Denton-Rosser marriage, though solemnized in a church wedding ceremony, was invalid because the couple did not procure a marriage license. The trial court . . . allowed Rosser to testify. Rosser, separated from Denton at the time of trial, testified that during the early years of their marriage, bank statements arrived at their home addressed to the Bellevue Jaycees. She said Denton told her he was going to send the money from the account to the State Jaycee organization. She also testified that in January or February 1996, she herself loaned Denton $2,000 to help him out with business debts. The jury convicted Denton as charged, and he appeals. Denton maintains his marriage to Rosser was valid and that the court erred in refusing to honor his exercise of the spousal privilege.

Washington's spousal privilege is provided by statute, in part: "A husband shall not be examined for or against his wife, without the consent of the wife, nor a wife for or against her husband without the consent of the husband; nor can either during marriage or afterward, be without the consent of the other, examined as to any communication made by one to the other during marriage." *RCW 5.60.060(1)*. The statute affording the spousal privilege contemplates legal marital status. . . . Denton and Rosser not only lived together and held themselves out as husband and wife for years, they . . . began their marriage relationship with a religious ceremony in which they promised to take each other to be husband and wife. The question is whether their ceremonial marriage was valid notwithstanding the lack of a license. . . . [T]he Court [in the earlier case] relied on the common law principle that a marriage without a license is universally held to be valid in the absence of an express declaration by the Legislature that such a marriage is void. [That] remains the rule today. In the eyes of the common law, marriage is a civil contract. As Blackstone put it, the law treats marriage "as it does all other contracts: allowing it to be good and valid in all cases, where the parties at the time of making it were, in the first place, willing to contract; secondly, able to contract; and, lastly, actually did contract, in the proper forms and solemnities required by law." *Picarella v. Picarella, 316 A.2d 826, 832, n. 10 (Md. App. 1974),* quoting Blackstone, Commentaries, Book I, ch. 15, sec. 433 (Lewis's Ed.). The policy favoring valid marriages is strong. It justifies recognition of an unlicensed ceremony unless the licensing statute plainly makes an unlicensed marriage invalid. See e.g., *Carabetta v. Carabetta, 438 A.2d 109, 112–113 (Conn. 1980).* New Jersey's statute is an example of an express declaration making a marriage license necessary for a valid marriage; it provides that "no marriage . . . shall be valid unless the contracting parties shall have obtained a marriage license". Where such a statute exists, even a ceremonial marriage is invalid without a license. But where there is no such statute, a marriage license is not integral to the creation of a valid marriage. Washington has a statutory requirement for a marriage license. "Before any persons can be joined in marriage, they shall procure a license from a county auditor". *RCW 26.04.140.* But Washington does not have a statute plainly making an unlicensed marriage invalid. Therefore, the . . . license requirement is purely regulatory. The regulatory purpose cannot be enforced by "the radical process of rendering void and immoral a matrimonial union otherwise validly contracted and solemnized." *Feehley v. Feehley, 99 A. [663] at 665 [(Md. 1916)].* Intentional failure to procure a license is punishable as a misdemeanor, *RCW 26.04.200,* but it does not render a marriage void or even voidable. See *RCW 26.04.130* (marriage voidable when party is unable to consent, or where consent obtained by force or fraud). The spousal privilege, although strictly construed, does apply when there is a valid, existing marriage. Because Denton and Rosser were parties willing and able to contract for marriage, and did contract for it in the solemnities required by law, their marriage was valid. We are aware of no authority for declaring a marriage to be valid for some purposes but not for others. The court erred in allowing Rosser to testify without Denton's consent.

[The court further determined that admission of the wife's testimony was reversible error because it materially affected the trial's likely outcome by casting significant doubt on defendant's defense of a good faith claim of title.]

Reversed.

NOTES

1. *Violation of Formalities*. *Denton* reflects the general rule that violations of formality requirements do not void the marriage. In the court's language, such rules are normally found "purely regulatory." *See also Accounts Management v. Litchfield,* 576 N.W. 2d 233 (S.D. 1998) (failure to record a marriage license does not invalidate marriage); *Fryar v. Roberts,* 57 S.W.3d 727 (Ark. 2001) (intentional burning of marriage license before filing did not invalidate marriage); *Yun v. Yun,* 908 S.W.2d 787 (Mo. App. 1995) (presumption of validity of marriage not rebutted by uncorroborated statement by "husband" that he did not obtain a license before ceremony); *Johnson v. Johnson,* 851 P.2d 866 (Ariz. App. 1993) (marriage performed in Puerto Rico with Arizona license not invalid for that reason). Lack of legal authority in the presiding official has also often been held not to make a marriage void. *See* Annot., *Validity of Marriage as Affected by Lack of Legal Authority of Person Solemnizing It,* 13 A.L.R.4th 1323 (1982).

But in *Nelson v. Marshall*, 869 S.W.2d 132 (Mo. App. 1993), the court held the license requirement was designed to eliminate common law marriage and failure to obtain a license rendered the attempted marriage void even though there was a ceremony (on the day before decedent's death) following a 12-year relationship. *See also In re Khalil*, 2003 U.S. Dist. LEXIS 6229 (D.V.I.)(Virgin Islands statute on licensure is mandatory); *Estate of DePasse*, 97 Cal. App. 4th 92 (2002) (failure to obtain marriage license before deathbed ceremony fatal to claim of marriage); *Moran v. Moran*, 933 P.2d 1207 (Ariz. App. 1996) (finding license requirement mandatory and, therefore, the marriage non-existent).

Denton's facts illustrate the majority rule's rationale. According to the court, "Denton and Rosser not only lived together and held themselves out as husband and wife for years, they formally began their marriage relationship with a religious ceremony in which they promised to take each other to be husband and wife." Not only did they hold themselves out as a married couple, they obviously believed they were a married couple. This has led most courts to apply what Professor Clark calls the principle of "validation" to ratify the parties' intentions. *See* CLARK, LAW OF DOMESTIC RELATIONS § 2.7 (2d ed. 1988). While this principle appears to leave the formality requirement with no sanction to enforce it, in fact most people comply anyway. Their compliance is not surprising; most people do not want ambiguity in their marital status.

Note that even where failure to comply with formality requirements does not affect the marriage's validity, other sanctions may apply. Those who knowingly perform a wedding ceremony in violation of the requirements may violate the criminal law. For example, in Georgia it is a misdemeanor for an official or clergyman to officiate at any unlicensed wedding or at any ceremony where "any disability of either of the parties . . . would render a contract of marriage improper and illegal. . . ." GA. CODE ANN. § 19-3-48 (1999). Similarly, some statutes punish the government official who illegally issues a license. *See, e.g.*, GA. CODE ANN. § 19-3-32 (1999) (misdemeanor to wrongfully issue a license). Additionally, the parties may commit perjury by fraudulently obtaining a license or, as in Washington according to *Denton*, the failure to obtain a license might be a crime. *See* Annot., *Perjury as Predicated upon Statements upon Application for Marriage License*, 101 A.L.R. 1263 (1936). Nonetheless, prosecutions under such laws are rare.

2. ***Void Versus Voidable.*** *Denton,* in rejecting the state's argument that the marriage was invalid, held that the parties were indeed married. It should be noted, however, that lack of validity would not necessarily mean that the marriage was void. Under the influence of English ecclesiastical law (the origin of much of our marriage law), cases and statutes have created a halfway house for some marriages — the "voidable" marriage.

A voidable marriage is neither valid nor void. It is not valid because a marriage regulation, either formal or substantive, has been violated. On the other hand, it is valid until a court decrees invalidity in an annulment action. The annulment, declaring the parties never were married, differs from a divorce, which terminates a marriage that once existed. Historically, the distinction between annulment and divorce was important because children born of later-annulled marriages were illegitimate and alimony or marital property claims were unavailable in annulments. Neither distinction is common today.

However, there are still theoretical reasons to inquire whether violation of a particular regulation renders the marriage void or voidable. First, a void marriage should need no judicial declaration of invalidity and be attackable in any collateral proceeding. (By contrast, a voidable marriage exists until annulment.) Second, a truly void marriage can be attacked (or ignored) by anybody, while voidable marriages usually can be attacked only by the parties, and sometimes only by one of the them. For example, usually an underage marriage can be attacked only by the underage party. *See* CLARK, THE LAW OF DOMESTIC RELATIONS § 2.10 at 93 (2d ed. 1988); *Harris v. Harris*, 506 N.W.2d 3 (Mich. App. 1993)(knowing bigamist can assert bigamy as ground for annulment because such marriages are void). Third, a voidable marriage can be ratified, while a void marriage cannot. Fourth, there could be financial consequences. A New York case held division of marital property may validly take place in an annulment, but not when a marriage is declared void. *Rashkov v. Rashkov*, 522 N.Y.S.2d 782 (Sup. Ct. 1987).

The void/voidable distinction, however, often is ignored or confused. For example, some cases hold that while a particular marriage was statutorily "void," only a party can attack it. *See, e.g., Ragan v. Cox*, 194 S.W.2d 681 (Ark. 1946). Similarly, some statutes describe certain marriages as void, yet prescribe annulment as the means of terminating them. *See, e.g.,* GA. CODE ANN. § 19-3-5 (1999). Likewise, some cases permit ratification of statutorily "void" marriages. *See* CLARK, THE LAW OF DOMESTIC RELATIONS § 2.10 at 96 (2d ed. 1988).

3. *The Marital Communication Privilege.* The communication privilege whose applicability was at issue in *Denton* was designed to encourage marital communication and frankness. Tracing its roots far back in English legal history, the rule has survived largely intact. Under UNIFORM RULES OF EVIDENCE § 504 (1974), a criminal defendant "has a privilege to prevent his spouse from testifying as to any confidential communication between the accused and the spouse." Most states apply the privilege in civil cases also. *See, e.g.,* MAINE RULES OF EVID. § 504 (2003); WIS. STAT. § 905.05 (2000). There are several exceptions, such as criminal prosecutions for crimes committed on one spouse by the other, actions against third parties for injury to the marital relation and interspousal litigation such as divorce. J. STRONG, McCORMICK ON EVIDENCE 131 (5th ed. 1999).

A recent case, focusing on the privilege's rationale, found admissible a wife's testimony about her husband's "boastful" confession that he had raped his stepdaughter (her biological daughter) and his specific plans to have sexual intercourse with their two daughters. *Commonwealth v. Spetzer*, 813 A. 2d 707 (Pa. 2002). "It would be perverse, indeed," wrote the court, "to indulge a fiction of marital harmony to shield statements which prove the declarant spouse's utter contempt for, and abuse of, the marital union." The court found that, under these circumstances, the communications were not confidential.

[b]   Common Law Marriage: Exception to Formality Requirements

IN RE ESTATE OF HALL

67 Ohio App. 3d 715; 588 N.E.2d 203 (1990)

STEPHENSON, Judge: . . . .

The following facts . . ., many . . . undisputed, appear in . . . a transcript of proceedings two hundred pages in length embodying the testimony of twenty-two witnesses and forty-nine documentary exhibits for [Denise] and three for [Burnworth].

. . . . In 1986 both Denise and decedent [Alan] were separated from their respective spouses and began living together in June. . . . Divorce actions were then pending. In August 1986, Denise was divorced from her husband and on January 23, 1987, decedent was divorced from his wife. Thereafter, Denise and decedent continued to reside together and had a close relationship, not only working together but also spending the non-working hours together in social and other activities.

At a family outing on July 4, 1988, tragically, decedent accidentally drowned while swimming. On July 13, 1988, Randall G. Burnworth was appointed administrator of the estate, the application not setting forth the name of a surviving spouse. On August 2, 1988, [Denise] filed an application to remove [Burnworth] and appoint her since she was the common-law spouse . . . .

. . . [T]he court . . . denied the removal motion. The decision, *inter alia*, set forth findings as follows:

"Decedent and Denise started cohabiting in June 1986. . . . They cohabited continuously until decedent's untimely death.

"At no time after decedent's divorce did the parties enter into a civil marriage contract. However, according to Denise, they did plan to participate in a civil marriage ceremony after they finished remodeling decedent's house on the west side of Marietta.

"During the time they lived together they shared expenses. They each had separate checking accounts. Denise at times paid financial obligations which were solely those of the decedent from her own account. Although Denise named the decedent as beneficiary on her individual retirement account, on her private life insurance policy and on her employment life insurance policy, decedent did not reciprocate.

"They were employed at the same job site. They spent a great deal of their work time, as well as their leisure time together. They took vacations together; and while in Florida they purchased a time share interest in a condominium for one week per year. However, they signed the purchase contract in their individual names, making no reference to their marital status.

"They attempted to borrow money in November/December 1987 from the Marietta Savings and Loan Company for the purpose of remodeling decedent's house on the west side of Marietta. In this application, the parties held themselves out as being unmarried.

"On their 1987 federal income tax returns decedent and Denise listed their marital status as 'single' and not as 'married filing singly.'

"In September 1988, Denise filed an application for death benefits as beneficiary of decedent with the Plumbers & Pipefitters Union. On the application she listed herself as beneficiary but did not list herself as decedent's spouse.

"At no time after his divorce . . . did the decedent change or attempt to change the name of the beneficiary on any of his life insurance policies or pensions into Denise's name. The decedent in fact is reported to have made statements very near to the time of his death that he would never marry Denise and that he had aspirations of some day reconciling with his former wife.

"Decedent and Denise acted in some respects similarly to the way a married couple would act. Although some of their acquaintances thought they were married, others did not think they were married.

"The court finds that Denise A. Chancellor has failed to prove by clear and convincing evidence that she and the decedent entered a mutual agreement of marriage in the present; that they cohabited as husband and wife; and that they were treated and received as husband and wife in the community in which they lived."

The law of Ohio respecting establishment of common-law marriage is succinctly summarized in . . . *Nestor v. Nestor* (1984):

"A common law marriage is the marital joinder of a man and a woman without the benefit of formal papers or procedures. Such marriages are not favored in Ohio, but have long been recognized as lawful if certain elements or circumstances are found to be present.

    . . . .

" 'An agreement of marriage in praesenti when made by parties competent to contract, accompanied and followed by cohabitation as husband and wife, they being so treated and reputed in the community and circle in which they move, establishes a valid marriage at common law . . .'

"The fundamental requirement . . . is a meeting of the minds between the parties who enter into a mutual contract to presently take each other as man and wife. The agreement to marry in praesenti is the essential element of a common law marriage. Its absence precludes the establishment of such a relationship. . . .

"The contract of marriage in praesenti may be proven either by way of direct evidence which establishes the agreement, or by way of proof of cohabitation, acts, declarations, and the conduct of the parties and their recognized status in the community in which they reside.

However, all of the essential elements to a common law marriage must be established by clear and convincing evidence.

> ". . . [T]estimony regarding cohabitation and community reputation tends to raise an inference of the marriage. This inference is given more or less strength according to the circumstances of the particular case. The inference is generally strengthened with the lapse of time during which the parties are living together and cohabiting as man and wife."

No evidence was adduced by [Denise] of an express agreement . . . . [She] sought to establish her claim . . . based upon the nature and continuing relationship of the parties. There was evidence . . . tending to establish by inference a common-law marriage. While the lower court's factual findings are supported in the record, there was also evidence of open cohabitation, the intermingling of finances, the joint purchase of property and stock, recognition of at least part of decedent's family as to a common-law marriage, including placement of [Denise]'s name on the tombstone as wife, and on occasion the introduction of [Denise] by decedent as his wife.

The thrust of [Denise's] argument . . . is that the court below erred in evaluating the evidence by application of a burden of proof greater than that of clear and convincing evidence. . . .

. . . .

We are not . . . persuaded that the decision of the court below applied an incorrect standard. . . .

. . . [W]e also conclude that there is probative and substantial evidence to support the judgment below.

. . . .

Finally, this writer approves of the statement by Justice William B. Brown writing in dissent in *Nestor* . . .:

> "Moreover, I call upon the legislature, in this last quarter of the Twentieth Century, to act to abolish the antiquated institution of common law marriage in Ohio. The days of the walking preacher and of the bishop on horseback are long gone. As was stated in *In re Estate of Maynard* (1962):
>
> " 'Is it not an amazing fact, that, in a matter which so profoundly affects the dignity and stability of a family institution, society should be slow to take enlightened action? Surely, no legislative reform is more needed than clear and positive statutes declaring such loosely contracted unions null and void.' "

For the reasons above set forth, the assignment of error is overruled and the judgment affirmed.

GREY, Judge, concurring.

I concur . . . but . . . cannot agree with the suggestion that common-law marriages no longer be recognized. The ultimate philosophical question . . . is should we have laws which reflect the way we want people to behave, or should we have laws which reflect the way they actually behave? Some common-law marriages are of long duration, and have brought stability and happiness into the lives of the parties. Whatever the reason parties do not choose a ceremonial marriage, the unmistakable fact of life is that there are many long-term common-law marriages, which are real marriages in every sense of the word.

Common-law marriages occasionally cause a problem for the courts which have to decide whether or not a common-law marriage, in fact, exists. This is not a major problem . . ., particularly in light of the clear standards for deciding such a case . . . .

If we refuse to recognize these kinds of marriages, we will often work a terrible injustice. A woman may have lived with a man for forty years, held herself out as his wife, borne his children, helped him through the bad times, celebrated the good times, and done everything a good and faithful wife might have done. But when he dies, we will ignore the fact of their life together, deny her survivor benefits, her right to share in his estate, even her right to bury him, for in the eyes of the law, this helpmate of a lifetime is only a legal stranger. . . .

The issue is not whether common-law marriages are antiquated, because we still get them regularly. The question is whether we will continue to have the common decency to recognize them.

. . . .

NOTES

1. *Status as Marriage.* A common law marriage where recognized is not simply "living together." It is a real marriage which requires capacity to marry under the same regulations applicable to ceremonial marriage. For example, two persons of the same sex cannot contract a valid common law marriage. *DeSanto v. Barnsley*, 476 A.2d 952 (Pa. Super. 1984). Likewise, a common law marriage is not created when one party is under the age of consent for marriage, *Mueggenborg v. Walling*, 836 P.2d 112 (Okla. 1992), and an existing marriage by either party prevents creation of a valid common law marriage, *In re Fisher*, 176 N.W.2d 801 (Iowa 1970). There is no concept of "common law divorce" to parallel "common law marriage." If there has been a marriage (whether ceremonial or common law), death or divorce must dissolve it to free either party to marry again. *See, e.g., In re Estate of Stodola*, 519 N.W.2d 97 (Iowa App. 1994).

While common law marriage claims often are made to establish a share in a decedent's estate as in *Hall*, it is not the only occasion. The case may involve invocation of the evidentiary marital privilege, *Bowler v. United States*, 480 A.2d 678 (D.C. App. 1984), a claim for insurance (life or health) benefits as a member of the insured's family, *Whyte v. Blair*, 885 P.2d 791 (Utah 1994), death benefits under a scheme of government entitlements, a divorce action, *Crosson v. Crosson*, 668 So. 2d 868 (Ala. App. 1995), or claim for division of marital property.

2. *History of Common Law Marriage.* Traditionally, the sole requirement for a so-called common law marriage was an agreement to be married. *See*

Davis v. Stouffer, 112 S.W. 282 (Mo. App. 1908); STONE, UNCERTAIN UNIONS & BROKEN LIVES 10-35 (1995). Some argue this doctrine was developed in England before American colonization, II POLLACK & MAITLAND, HISTORY OF ENGLISH LAW 368 (1898); others believe the early American jurists who recognized the doctrine were misreading the English precedents. The doctrine was fairly widely utilized. Chief Justice Gibson, in *Rodebaugh v. Sanks,* 2 Watts 9, 11 (Pa. 1833), wrote: "a rigid execution of [the marriage laws requiring a ceremony] would bastardize a vast majority of the children which have been born within the state for half a century."

As American conditions changed, so did acceptance of common law marriage. Critics claim the doctrine encourages fraudulent assertion of marriage after a party's death (note *Hall*'s facts), condones vice, frustrates state interests behind formality requirements and debases ceremonial marriage. Common law marriage is also described as unnecessary. As one court put it, "Cost is certainly not prohibitory, and a plethora of public and quasi-public officials are available to solemnize such an important and socially significant occasion." *Johnson v. Young,* 372 A.2d 992, 996 (D.C. 1977); *see also People v. Lucero,* 747 P.2d 660 (Colo. 1987) (public acknowledgment required to "guard against fraudulent claims"). It is also argued that abolition of common law marriage facilitates administrative efficiency and reduces litigation. That is, limitation of marriage to the formal, ceremonial marriage is alleged to serve the same purposes as the Statute of Frauds does in requiring certain important agreements to be written.

Others defend the institution. In addition to justice-based arguments offered by the *Hall* concurrence, others assert fraud can be defeated by a heightened burden of proof and Dead Man's statutes limiting evidence about communications with people now dead. As for the promotion of vice, Clark argues that recognition of such relationships actually reduces vice by accepting its legitimacy. H. CLARK, THE LAW OF DOMESTIC RELATIONS § 2.4, at 60 (2d ed. 1988).

A recent commentator argues vigorously for a return of the doctrine

> because it protects the interests of women, especially poor women and women of color, more effectively than any of the theories suggested to address the problems created by its absence. Most of the original reasons for abolishing common law marriage — fears of fraud, protection of morality and the family, racism, eugenics, and health-related reasons — do not withstand scrutiny; and other arguments, based on administrative convenience, are outweighed by more important values. The impact of nonrecognition is clearly disparate: it hurts most those women who are most vulnerable, and its effect is greatest on issues with a significant impact on their welfare, such as the ability to leave [a] violent relationship or to obtain a variety of benefits upon the death of a family's breadwinner.

Bowman, *A Feminist Proposal to Bring Back Common Law Marriage*, 75 ORE. L. REV. 709, 779 (1996). *See also* Note, *Governing Through Contract: Common Law Marriage in the Nineteenth Century*, 107 YALE L.J. 1885 (1998)(asserting common law marriage "represents one private, common law antecedent of later public policies to handle the problem of female poverty").

Texas tries to avoid the marital status ambiguities which constitute one objection to common law marriage by allowing registration of the marriage by the parties. TEX. FAM. CODE ANN. §§ 2.402, 2.403, 2.404 (1998) (registering parties must swear that they agreed to be married, live together as husband and wife, and hold themselves out to others as married). Such registration is not required however; Texas also recognizes unregistered common law marriages. *See* TEX. FAM. CODE § 2.401(a)(2) (1998).

3. *Present Status.* Only 10 states and the District of Columbia currently clearly recognize common law marriages contracted within their borders (Alabama, Colorado, Iowa, Kansas, Montana, Oklahoma, Rhode Island, South Carolina, Texas and Utah). Pennsylvania's status is not clear. In *Staudenmayer v. Staudenmayer*, 714 A.2d 1016 (Pa. 1998), a plurality of the state supreme court wrote that the doctrine's "continued viability is seriously in question," but the full court did not address the merits of the claim for abolition because the parties had not raised the issue. In 2003, however, in a case in which the issue was preserved and fully argued, the Superior Court (a mid-level appellate court) prospectively abolished common law marriage, citing the usual complaints concerning the state interests vindicated by cere-monial marriage, judicial inefficiencies, uncertainties caused by the continu-ance of common law marriage and easy alternatives to the institution. *PNC v. Workers' Compensation Appeal Board*, 831 A.2d 1269 (Pa. 2003).

Ohio is among three states that have recently abolished it, following the *Denton* majority's suggestion. *See* GA. CODE § 19-3-1.1 (1999); IDAHO CODE § 32-201 (1996); OHIO REVISED CODE ANNOT. § 3105.12 (2000). In all three states, however, common law marriages created before repeal continue to be recognized.

By contrast, Utah's recognition of common law marriage is recent, in a 1987 statute. UTAH CODE ANN. § 30-1-4.5 (1995). The law requires official recogni-tion by a court or agency, which can occur in the context of a suit predicated on the marriage's existence, such as litigation against an insurer claiming coverage as a family member of the insured. *See Whyte v. Blair*, 885 P.2d 791 (Utah 1994). At least one commentator believes the statute was motivated by concerns over fraud rather than the interests of those who conducted them-selves as married without complying with the formalities. The alleged goal was elimination of welfare claims by mothers with *de facto* husbands they had never formally married. Note, *Tom Green, Common-Law Marriage, and the Illegality of Putative Polygamy*, 17 B.Y.U. J. PUB. L. 141, 148 (2002).

4. *Current Requirements.* *Hall* states the usual modern requirements in states that continue to allow common law marriage. While older cases required only an agreement to be married, *Hall* not only imposes a high evidentiary burden of proof on the proponent ("clear and convincing evidence"), but also adds to the substantive elements by requiring public declaration and continu-ous cohabitation. *See also Krier v. Krier*, 676 So. 2d 1335 (Ala. Civ. App. 1996); *Chandler v. Central Oil Corp.*, 853 P.2d 649 (Kan. 1993); *Winfield v. Renfro*, 821 S.W.2d 640 (Tex. App. 1991) (finding insufficient evidence of holding out to the community); *Copeland v. Richardson,* 551 So. 2d 353 (Ala. 1989). A few states are less stringent. *See Commonwealth v. Wilson*, 672 A.2d 293 (Pa. 1996) (requiring only agreement, with cohabitation and holding out raising presumption of agreement); *East v. East*, 536 A.2d 1103 (D.C. App. 1988) (rejecting requirement of clear and convincing evidence and adopting ordinary preponderance standard). Contrary to popular belief, however, no state prescribes a minimum cohabitation period.

The desire to thwart fraudulent claims causes courts to emphasize more "public" kind of evidence, such as cohabitation and representation to others that there is a marriage, rather than the more easily fabricated claim that the parties agreed to be married. At least one court has held proof of cohabitation and holding out eliminates the need for any evidence of agreement. *Owens v. Owens*, 466 S.E.2d 373, 375 (S.C. App. 1995). Indeed, the *Owens* court refused to characterize the wife's testimony that "his mother would die and he knew it if he ever married me, but he said if he ever married anybody it would be me" as an express disavowal of agreement.

5. *Impediment Removal.* In *Hall* plaintiff and decedent began their relationship when both were already married and, thus, ineligible to marry. Suppose they also had satisfied the objective requirements of a common law marriage (agreement, cohabitation and holding out to community) *before* they were both free to remarry on January 23, 1987 (when the second divorce was entered). Would a common law marriage have arisen between Denise and Alan immediately at the point of removal of the impediment to their marriage?

Treatment of such cases depends upon the parties' knowledge. If either party was ignorant of the impediment at the creation of the relationship, a marriage is created immediately upon the impediment's removal. *See, e.g., Bowlin v. Bowlin,* 285 S.E.2d 273 (N.C. App. 1981). On the other hand, if both knew of the impediment at the inception of their relationship, many courts require proof of a new agreement after the impediment's removal. *See, e.g., Johns v. Johns*, 420 S.E.2d 856 (S.C. App. 1992) ("A relationship illicit at its inception does not ripen into a common law marriage once the impediment . . . is removed. . . . [T]he parties must enter into a common law marriage after the impediment is removed."). Some courts, acknowledging the unlikelihood of a new post-removal agreement, do not require a new agreement, but find a marriage if the parties continue to cohabit and hold themselves out as married. *See, e.g., In re Estate of Alcorn*, 868 P.2d 629 (Mont. 1994).

6. *Conflict of Law and Common Law Marriage.* Common law marriage is more important than the short list of recognizing states in note 2 might suggest because of the general conflicts rule that a marriage valid where contracted is recognized elsewhere.

Three basic fact patterns appear in the case law. In the first (the "circle" situation), two people agree to be married, cohabit and hold themselves out as married in a non-recognizing jurisdiction. Then, after spending time in a recognizing jurisdiction, they return home. At some later point (often the death of one "spouse"), the home state must decide if the couple was married.

In this situation, many courts find a marriage, often despite merely ephemeral connection to the common law marriage state. *See, e.g., Katebi v. Hooshiari*, 288 A.D.2d 188 (2001) (family vacations to common law marriage state are sufficient); *Carpenter v. Carpenter*, 617 N.Y.S.2d 903 (App. Div. 1994) (two visits of no more than a week each occurring 20 years apart); *Blaw-Knox*

Construction Equip. Co. v. Morris, 596 A.2d 679 (Md. Spec. App. 1991) (two-day visit); *Renshaw v. Heckler,* 787 F.2d 50 (2d Cir. 1986) (eight two-day visits en route to vacations elsewhere); *Coney v. R.S.R. Corp.,* 563 N.Y.S.2d 211 (App. Div. 1990) (three-day visit). When a court in a non-common law marriage state finds a marriage, what is it saying about the forum's expressed policy against such relationships? Note that most cases recognizing marriage in these circumstances involve lengthy relationships and/or a particularly deep-pocketed defendant such as the government or an insurance company.

Some cases refusing to recognize marriage here frankly ground their analysis in what is described as a strong forum policy against common law marriage. *See, e.g., Lynch v. Bowen*, 681 F. Supp. 506 (N.D. Ill. 1988) (applying Illinois law); *Hesington v. Hesington,* 640 S.W.2d 824 (Mo. App. 1982). Other courts reject the marriage claim through application (and sometimes distortion) of the common law marriage state's law. *See Smith v. Anderson*, 821 So. 2d 323 (Fla. App. 2002) (finding insufficient connection to Georgia to support a finding of a common law marriage there); *In re Estate of Landolfi*, 283 App. Div. 2d 497 (2001) (rejecting alleged marriage created by brief visits to Pennsylvania for lack of agreement in that state); *Estate of Burroughs*, 486 N.W.2d 113 (Mich. App. 1992) (rejecting alleged Texas common law marriage for lack of cohabitation); *Goldin v. Goldin,* 426 A.2d 410 (Md. Spec. App. 1981) (lack of intent to marry in common law state bars recognition).

Two other fact patterns ought to be noted. In contrast to the circular situation above, these scenarios can be described as "chains." In the first, a couple, having contracted a common law marriage in a recognizing state, moves to a non-recognizing state where the marriage's validity is litigated. Almost all courts recognize the marriage here, particularly if there was a significant connection to the common law state. *See Johnson v. Lincoln Square Properties*, 571 So. 2d 541 (Fla. App. 1990); *Delaney v. Delaney,* 405 A.2d 91 (Conn. Super. 1979); *Mission Ins. Co. v. Industrial Comm'n,* 559 P.2d 1085 (Ariz. 1976). In contrast, a recent Virginia decision rejected a claim of marriage where the couple stayed one night each in two common law marriage states during a trip. *Kelderhaus v. Kelderhaus*, 467 S.E.2d 303 (Va. App. 1996) (recognition here would "distort and trivialize" the doctrine recognized by common law marriage states).

The final pattern reverses the second one. In *Travers v. Reinhardt,* 205 U.S. 423 (1907), the couple lived together in several non-common law marriage states, then moved to New Jersey, then a recognizing state. There was no proof of any new agreement in New Jersey, but the Supreme Court found a marriage, based on an inferred continuing agreement. While *Travers* might simply reflect an earlier era when common law marriage enjoyed wider acceptance, more recent cases also adopt the *Travers* result. *See, e.g., Marriage of Winegard,* 257 N.W.2d 609 (Iowa 1977); *but see Estate of Maynard,* 192 N.E.2d 281 (Ohio App. 1962) (because original state of residence did not recognize common law marriage, any claim of such a marriage in forum requires proof of an agreement in the forum).

[c] Putative Spouse Doctrine: Form over Substance or Substance over Form?

CALIFORNIA FAMILY CODE §§ 2251, 2254 (West 1994)

§ 2251. (A) If a determination is made that a marriage is void or voidable and the court finds that either party or both parties believed in good faith that the marriage was valid, the court shall:

(1) Declare the party or parties to have the status of a putative spouse.

(2) If the division of property is in issue, divide . . . that property acquired during the union that would have been community property or quasi-community property if the union had not been void or voidable. . . . This property is known as "quasi-marital property."

§ 2254. The court may, during the pendency of a proceeding for nullity of marriage, order a party to pay for the support of the other party . . . if the party for whose benefit the order is made is found to be a putative spouse.

IN RE ESTATE OF VARGAS

36 Cal. App. 3d 714, 111 Cal. Rptr. 779 (1974)

FLEMING, Associate Justice. For 24 years Juan Vargas lived a double life as husband and father to two separate families, neither of which knew of the other's existence. This terrestrial paradise came to an end in 1969 when Juan died intestate in an automobile accident. In subsequent heirship proceedings the probate court divided his estate equally between the two wives. Juan's first wife Mildred appeals, contending that the evidence did not establish Juan's second wife Josephine as a putative spouse, and that even if Josephine were considered a putative spouse an equal division of the estate was erroneous.

Mildred . . . and Juan married in 1929, raised three children, and lived together continuously in Los Angeles until Juan's death in 1969. From 1945 . . . Juan never spent more than a week or 10 days away from home. They acquired no substantial assets until after 1945.

Josephine . . . met Juan in 1942 while employed in his exporting business. They married in Las Vegas in February 1945. . . . Josephine knew Juan had been previously married, but Juan assured her he had acquired a divorce. In July 1945 they moved into a home in West Los Angeles and there raised a family of four children. After 1949 Juan no longer spent his nights at home, explaining to Josephine that he spent the nights in Long Beach in order to be close to his business, but he and Josephine continued to engage in sexual relations until his death in 1969. He visited Josephine and their children every weekday for dinner, spent time with them weekends, supported the family, and exercised control over its affairs as husband and father. Throughout the years Josephine continued to perform secretarial work for Juan's business at home without pay.

The foregoing evidence amply supports the court's finding that Josephine was a putative spouse. An innocent participant who has duly solemnized a matrimonial union which is void because of some legal infirmity acquires the status of putative spouse. Although Josephine's marriage was void because Juan was still married to Mildred, Josephine, according to her testimony, married Juan in the good-faith belief he was divorced from his first wife. Her testimony was not inherently improbable; her credibility was a question for determination by the trial court; and court acceptance of her testimony established her status as a putative spouse.

The more difficult question involves the equal division of Juan's estate between Mildred and Josephine.

California courts have relied on at least two legal theories to justify the award of an interest in a decedent's estate to a putative spouse. The theory of "quasi-marital property" equates property rights acquired during a putative marriage with community property rights acquired during a legal marriage. Subsequent to the time of Juan's death this theory was codified in Civil Code section 4452: [quoted earlier in its renumbered form].

A second legal theory treats the putative marriage as a partnership: "In effect, the innocent putative spouse was in partnership or a joint enterprise with her spouse, contributing her services — and in this case, her earnings — to the common enterprise. Thus, their accumulated property was held in effect in tenancy-in-common in equal shares. Upon death of the husband, only his half interest is considered as community property, to which the rights of the lawful spouse attach." (*Sousa v. Freitas*)

In practice, these sometimes-conflicting theories have proved no more than convenient explanations to justify reasonable results, for when the theories do not fit the facts, courts have customarily resorted to general principles of equity . . . . For example, in *Brown v. Brown,* the court found that a legal wife's acquiescence in a putative wife's 28-year marriage equitably estopped the legal wife from claiming any interest in the community property.

. . . [T]he laws regulating succession and the disposition of marital property are not designed to cope with the extraordinary circumstance of purposeful bigamy at the expense of two innocent parties.[2]

The laws of marital succession . . . do not provide for contingencies arising during the course of felonious activity. For this reason resort to equitable principles becomes particularly appropriate here. . . . Equity need not wait upon precedent "but will assert itself in those situations where right and justice would be defeated but for its intervention." (*Satterfield v. Garmire*). For example, in *Estate of Krone*, where the putative husband died intestate and there was no legal wife, the court awarded the entire quasi-marital estate to the putative wife, even though the putative wife had no legal claim to the husband's share of the quasi-marital estate.

In the present case, depending on which statute or legal theory is applied, both Mildred, as legal spouse, and Josephine, as putative spouse, have valid

---

[2] "[I]n most, if not all, of the reported decisions involving a putative spouse, the supposed husband did in fact separate from his lawful wife." (Luther and Luther, [24 HASTINGS L.J.] at p. 318.)

or plausible claims to at least half, perhaps three-quarters, possibly all, of Juan's estate. The court found that both wives contributed in indeterminable amounts and proportions to the accumulations of the community. Since statutes and judicial decisions provide no sure guidance for the resolution of the controversy, the probate court cut the Gordian knot of competing claims and divided the estate equally between the two wives, presumably on the theory that innocent wives of practicing bigamists are entitled to equal shares of property accumulated during the active phase of the bigamy. No injury has been visited upon third parties, and the wisdom of Solomon is not required to perceive the justice of the result.

The judgment is affirmed.

NOTES

1. ***Vargas "II" (or "III"?).*** While *Vargas* reads like a law professor's dream hypothetical, news reports of such situations surface with some frequency. For example, upon the 1991 death of Dr. Norman J. Lewiston, a prominent lung specialist at Stanford University, it was discovered that he had continuing relationships with three wives. His first spouse, who married him in 1960, lived in Palo Alto. He married a second spouse in 1985 and shared a house with her in the nearby town of Los Altos. A third spouse, who married him in 1989, had a home with him in San Diego. None of the spouses knew of the others before his death and each assumed that a very busy professional life, including travel, accounted for the doctor's failure to spend much time with her. His third wife, demonstrating some sense of perspective, commented, "The only thing I want to inherit is his frequent-flier miles." Dalton, *Bigamy: Professor Led Full Life; Multiple Wives Kept Stanford's Medical Pioneer on the Move*, SAN DIEGO UNION-TRIBUNE, Oct. 8, 1991, p. A-1. For those thinking this is purely a California phenomenon, see Donohue, *DA: Plumber with 2 Wives Wrenches Law*, N.Y. DAILY NEWS, Nov. 20, 1996 (defendant had one wife in Queens and another in Manhattan and allegedly "used the odd hours of a plumber on call to conceal a double life"); Muller, *"I Still Have Feelings for Him, That's Why I Feel Betrayed"; Bigamist's First Wife Tries Hard to Forgive*, ARIZ. REPUBLIC, Dec. 29, 1994, p. B1 (defendant "juggled" four wives in three states for several months; he "kept a log and took notes during conversations" to keep track of the stories he told each wife).

2. ***Putative Spouse Doctrine.*** The putative spouse doctrine exists primarily in states with a civil law tradition. It protects a party ignorant of an impediment which made the marriage either void or voidable. For other cases applying the doctrine, see *Alfonso v. Gravois*, 739 So. 2d 946 (La. App. 1999) (dealing with property division on divorce); *Xiong v. Xiong*, 255 N.W. 2d 900 (Wis. 2002) (wrongful death); *Estate of DePasse*, 97 Cal. App. 4d 92 (2002) (court rejects claim of putative spousehood in probate litigation where both parties were aware their "marriage" ceremony occurred without required license); *Gilvary v. Gilvary*, 648 So. 2d 317 (Fla. App. 1995) (attorney's fees in annulment litigation); *Kindle v. Kindle*, 629 So. 2d 176 (Fla. App. 1993) (permanent alimony); *Garduno v. Garduno,* 760 S.W.2d 735 (Tex. App. 1988) (property division). The Model Marriage and Divorce Act's optional putative spouse section (§ 209) creates property division and maintenance rights after

termination of the relationship. Some non-community property states have adopted this provision. *See, e.g.,* ILL. ANN. STAT., ch. 750, § 5/305 (Smith-Hurd 1999); MINN. STAT. ANN. § 518.055 (West 1994); Mont. Code Ann. § 40-1-404 (2001). The putative spouse is also protected under the Social Security statute. 42 U.S.C.S. § 416(h)(1)(B)(i) (2000).

Several states legislatively recognize putative spouse claims: in wrongful death actions, CAL. CIV. PROC. CODE § 377.60(b) (2003 Supp.); worker's compensation benefits, CAL. LABOR CODE § 3503 (1989); division of property in non-death termination of the relationship, LA. CIV. CODE art. 96 (1999); and alimony, COLO. REV. STAT. § 14-2-111 (1997). For a survey of the law, see Blakesley, *The Putative Marriage Doctrine,* 60 TUL. L. REV. 1 (1985).

3. *Good Faith Belief.* Putative spousehood terminates upon a party's loss of good faith belief that he or she is married. *Welch v. State,* 83 Cal. App. 4th 1374 (2000). What *is* good faith? In *Marriage of Flores,* 252 Cal. Rptr. 687 (App. 1988), the parties were first cousins who had gone through a wedding ceremony 21 years earlier after being told by court personnel that such a marriage was prohibited. The court held there could be no good faith belief in the validity of the marriage, but affirmed an alimony order on an estoppel theory. In *In re Vryonis,* 248 Cal. Rptr. 807 (App. 1988), the court held that a belief that the couple had been married according to Islamic law in a "Muta" ceremony was insufficient. Holding good faith requires a belief in a legally-recognized marriage, the court held "(w)here there has been no attempted compliance with the procedural requirements of a valid marriage, and where the usual indicia of marriage and conduct consistent with a valid marriage are absent, a belief in the existence of a valid marriage, although sincerely held, would be unreasonable and therefore lacking in good faith." *Id.* at 813. For recent cases exploring the good faith requirement, see *Thomason v. Thomason,* 776 So. 2d 553 (La. App. 2000) (upholding claim of putative spousehood where parties obtained license and "went to a man" though there was no ceremony); *Kelderhouse v. Kelderhouse,* 467 S.E.2d 303 (Va. App. 1996) (rejecting claim of putative spousehood under California law). Several cases applying Louisiana law impose a duty to investigate when informed of a partner's prior marriage. *See Schaefer v. Schaefer,* 379 So. 2d 864 (La. App. 1980).

There is authority to support recognition of a putative common law marriage in a state which generally recognizes common law marriage. *Garduno v. Garduno,* 760 S.W.2d 735 (Tex. App. 1988) (finding, however, no good faith in instant case); *but see Welch v. State,* 83 Cal. App. 4th 1374 (2000) (despite 30-year relationship, appellant's "subjective belief that she was married, even if honestly held, does not constitute good faith" in non-common law marriage state).

4. *Putative Spousehood vs. Common Law Marriage.* A common law marriage is a marriage, while a putative marriage is not. Thus, common law marriage is impossible where the parties are ineligible for marriage, as in *Vargas.* On the other hand, divorce is unnecessary to terminate a putative marriage; a marriage by Josephine after "marrying" Juan in 1945 would have been valid. A recent case contrasted the two doctrines by noting that a common law spouse can invoke the marital testimonial privilege, while a putative spouse cannot. *Weaver v. State*, 855 S.W.2d 116 (Tex. App. 1993). Note also that the putative spouse doctrine would offer an alternative remedy for violations of the formality requirements (*e.g.*, failure to obtain a marriage license).where the rule violation made the marriage void or voidable. An innocent "spouse" who believed in good faith that a valid marriage resulted from the ceremony would qualify as a putative spouse.

5. *Lawful Versus Putative Spouse.* Competing claims by a lawful and a putative spouse may arise in connection with an estate, as in *Vargas*, as well as in other circumstances. There may, for example, be competitive wrongful death actions, or life insurance claims. The equal division adopted in *Vargas*, while attractive on those facts, would not always be appropriate. Consider, *e.g.*, a case in which decedent's legal spouse split from decedent after 3 years, whereupon decedent moved in with the putative spouse and they lived together for 35 years until death. Section 209 of the MMDA, the model for most current statutes recognizing putative spousehood, provides:

> If there is a legal spouse or other putative spouses, rights acquired by a putative spouse do not supersede the rights of the legal spouse or those acquired by other putative spouses, but the court shall apportion property, maintenance, and support rights among the claimants as appropriate in the circumstances and in the interests of justice.

6. *The Presumption of the Validity of the Latest Marriage.* Although Josephine, Juan's second "wife" in *Vargas,* claimed putative spousehood, she might have argued her marriage was valid, utilizing a well-known evidentiary presumption — the presumption of the validity of the latest marriage. This presumption, along with such family law doctrines as the putative spouse concept and recognition of cohabitational contracts (see Chapter 9 at pp. 876-918), operate in tension with the broadly-stated monogamy principle, limiting people to one spouse at a time. *See* pp. 140-42, *infra*.

There are several recurring fact patterns in which this presumption is utilized. Common are situations where two individuals both seek: life insurance benefits, *Metropolitan Life Ins. Co. v. Jackson*, 896 F. Supp. 318 (S.D.N.Y. 1995); retirement benefits, *Croskey v. Ford Motor Co.*, 2002 U.S. Dist. LEXIS 8824 (S.D. N.Y.); Social Security death benefits, *McKnight v. Schweiker,* 516 F. Supp. 1102 (D. Md. 1981); intestate succession rights, *Estate of Loveless,* 64 S.W. 3d 564 (Tex. App. 2001); or rights under a will. *Estate of Bajurczak,* 742 N.E. 2d 1191 (Ohio App. 2000) (court rejects presumption's existence). Occasionally, the second spouse seeks annulment, or defends a divorce suit, claiming the "marriage" was bigamous. *See, e.g., Callaway v. Callaway*, 739 So. 2d 1134 (Ala. Civ. App. 1999); *Loera v. Loera*, 815 S.W.2d 910 (Tex. App. 1991) (refusal to annul second marriage because of failure to rebut the presumption of legitimacy). In *Carr v. Carr*, 724 So. 2d 937 (Miss. App. 1998), a father asserted the presumption to defend his second marriage's validity in a custody action in which his first wife sought to limit visitation based on the fact that the second marriage was invalid. The appellate court upheld a finding that the presumption had been rebutted, but also found that the father's non-marital status did not affect his visitation rights.

The presumption is said to be based on the principle that the "law presumes innocence, not criminality (bigamy); morality, not immorality; and marriage, not concubinage," *Rainer v. Snider,* 369 N.E.2d 666 (Ind. App. 1977); *Grey v. Heckler*, 721 F.2d 41 (2d Cir. 1983); and requires the party attacking the later marriage to bear the burden of proof. Thus, the party asserting bigamy faces the difficult task of proving a negative: nondissolution of the first marriage. Given our society's mobility and the ease of divorce, this can be time-consuming and expensive. It is often made more difficult by judicial imposition of a heightened standard of proof: "to a moral certainty," *McKnight v. Schweiker, supra;* "so cogent and conclusive as to fairly preclude any other result," *Smith v. Weir,* 387 So. 2d 761 (Miss. 1980); "strong, distinct, satisfactory, and conclusive," *Johnson v. Young,* 372 A.2d 992 (D.C. 1977). The presumption has been described as "one of the strongest, if not the strongest, known to law," *Estate of Loveless,* 64 S.W. 3d 564 (Tex. App. 2001), which increases as the length of the second marriage increases. *Lambertini v. Lambertini*, 655 So. 2d 142 (Fla. App. 1995); *Stokes v. Heckler*, 773 F.2d 990 (8th Cir. 1985).

For example, the presumption has been found unrebutted by testimony by Wife-1 that she had not filed for divorce and had received no notice of a divorce action. *In re Estate of Lucas*, 909 S.W.2d 365 (Mo. App. 1995). Likewise, failing to find a divorce record in the first marriage's domiciliary state has been found insufficient because there might have been a divorce in another state or country. *Croskey v. Ford Motor Co.*, 2002 U.S. Dist. LEXIS 8824 (S.D. N.Y.) (applying Michigan law): *Brown v. Brown*, 57 S.W. 3d 354 (Mo. App. 2001); *Miller v. AMF Harley-Davidson Motor Co.*, 328 N.W.2d 348 (Iowa 1982); *Medrano v. Medrano*, 701 S.W.2d 337 (Tex. App. 1985).

Some cases describe a weaker presumption. For example, in some states the introduction of any rebuttal evidence eliminates the presumption, making the question of which marriage is valid a simple fact question. *See, e.g., Hewitt v. Firestone Tire & Rubber Co.,* 490 F. Supp. 1358 (E.D. Va. 1980); *Claveria v. Claveria,* 615 S.W.2d 164 (Tex. 1981). In Georgia, the attacker need prove only that both parties to the first marriage were alive at the time of the second marriage; the defender of the second marriage must then prove dissolution. *See, e.g., Johnson v. Johnson,* 238 S.E.2d 437 (Ga. 1977); *Scott v. Jefferson*, 331 S.E.2d 1 (Ga. App. 1985). Courts sometimes acknowledge that appealing facts may weaken the presumption. Thus, in *In re O'Rourke*, 246 N.W.2d 461 (Minn. 1976), the court found the presumption inapplicable where the second marriage occurred only four months before the litigation and produced no children. At least one court has rejected the presumption altogether, writing "[w]here . . . both marriages have been lawfully solemnized and the record is silent as to whether there has been a divorce . . . there is a presumption that the status of the parties to the first marriage continues. . . ." *Estate of Bajurczak,* 742 N.E. 2d 1191 (Ohio App. 2000).

Theoretically, the presumption would be available in any case, such as *Vargas,* where a person had contracted more than one marriage. The fact that courts (and apparently litigants) routinely ignore the presumption in such cases (*Vargas* omits any reference) suggests many trial courts ignore the "rule" of a strong presumption and apply a weaker version. Nevertheless, several recent cases (cited earlier in this Note) restate the strong version of the presumption.

For an article canvassing the cases in the area and discussing issues such as the rationale for the presumption, its relationship to other family law presumptions, the burden of proof and how it is carried, etc., see Swisher & Jones, *The Last-in-Time Marriage Presumption*, 29 FAM. L.Q. 409 (1995).

PROBLEMS

Problem 2-1. In 1971, Harold Jones married Corinne Smith in a church wedding. They split up in 1981, but because both abhorred the notion of divorce, neither obtained one. After seven years on his own, Harold fell in love with his next-door neighbor, Wilma, a 21-year old single woman living with her parents. During their courtship, Harold told Wilma he had been married before. She asked him "Where is your former wife?" His reply was, "She's left town, I don't know where she's gone."

In early 1989, Harold and Wilma were married before a minister. They obtained a license as required by state law, but failed to wait the prescribed three days because they were in a hurry to get on with their honeymoon. On the way to the airport after the ceremony, Harold was killed in an accident. Wilma seeks advice as to the claims she might make against Harold's estate. He died without a will but with 1,000 acres of prime farmland and investments worth $500,000. In your investigation, you discover all the above facts, plus the fact that Corinne never left town after her separation from Harold. Your jurisdiction recognizes common law marriage and the putative spouse doctrine. What theories might you offer on Wilma's behalf? How do you think the court would respond to these theories?

Problem 2-2. Alice and Benton were married in a ceremonial marriage in 1989. In 1994, Alice filed for divorce. Benton signed a voluntary appearance in the law suit and signed a property settlement agreement. Notice of the hearing was mailed to Benton at his home address. Neither Benton nor anybody representing him appeared at the hearing where the divorce was granted. After the divorce, both parties lived together for another 9 years. They held themselves out as husband and wife and had three children. They split up in 2003.

Benton comes to you as a client in late 2003, seeking to represent him in a divorce action against Alice. Your research reveals that the divorce had been granted in 1994. When you ask Benton about it he tells you "I signed some papers back then when we were having trouble. Alice, who is an attorney, handled all the business stuff in our marriage. She told me she had filed the divorce, but then she told me that she had dismissed it." He denies ever having received any notice of a divorce hearing, noting that because he worked a strange shift, Alice always retrieved the mail. You also discover that a large amount of property was obtained between 1994 and 2003. Alice earned considerably more money than Benton and virtually all the property was titled in her name. Your jurisdiction has the following statute, which was enacted in 1991:

When the court finds that a party entered into the contract of marriage in good faith supposing the other to be capable of contracting, and the marriage is declared a nullity, such fact shall be entered in the decree and the court may order such innocent party compensated as in the case of dissolution of marriage, including an award for costs and attorney fees.

How will you argue on behalf of your client in seeking to claim a portion of the assets titled in Alice's name? What responses do you expect from the other side?

[2] SUBSTANTIVE REQUIREMENTS

[a] Constitutional Restraints Upon Substantive Requirements

ZABLOCKI v. REDHAIL

434 U.S. 374 (1978)

MR. JUSTICE MARSHALL delivered the opinion of the Court.

At issue . . . is the constitutionality of a Wisconsin statute . . . which *[Issue]* provides that members of a certain class of Wisconsin residents may not marry . . . without first obtaining a court order granting permission to marry. The class is . . . any "Wisconsin resident having minor issue not in his custody and which he is under obligation to support by any court order or judgment." . . . [C]ourt permission cannot be granted unless the marriage applicant submits proof of compliance with the support obligation and, in addition, demonstrates that the children covered by the support order "are not then and are not likely thereafter to become public charges." No marriage license may lawfully be issued in Wisconsin to a person covered by the statute, except upon court order; any marriage entered into [in violation of the statute] is declared void; and persons acquiring marriage licenses in violation of the section are subject to criminal penalties. . . .

[A 1972 judgment found Redhail father of a baby girl and ordered child support. In 1974, having failed to pay support for over two years, his marriage license application was denied for failure to satisfy the statute. It was stipulated that the child, who was on welfare, would have been "a public charge even if [Redhail] had been current in his support payments. . . ."] *[D was denied a marriage licence]*

[The trial court] analyzed the . . . statute under the Equal Protection Clause and concluded that "strict scrutiny" was required because the classification . . . infringed upon a fundamental right, the right to marry. The court then proceeded to evaluate the interests advanced by the State to justify the statute, and, finding that the classification was not necessary for the achievement of those interests, the court held the statute invalid. . . . *[lower ct finds it invalid]*

[The state] brought this direct appeal. . . . We agree . . . that the statute violates the Equal Protection Clause.

II

Ct gives critical examination of statute

In evaluating [the statute] under the Equal Protection Clause, "we must first determine what burden of justification the classification created thereby must meet, by looking to the nature of the classification and the individual interests affected." *Memorial Hospital v. Maricopa County.* Since our past decisions make clear that the right to marry is of fundamental importance, and since the classification at issue here significantly interferes with the exercise of that right, we believe that "critical examination" of the state interests advanced in support of the classification is required.

The leading decision . . . on the right to marry is *Loving v. Virginia,* 388 U.S. 1 (1967). In that case, an interracial couple who had been convicted of violating Virginia's miscegenation laws challenged the statutory scheme on both equal protection and due process grounds. The Court's opinion could have rested solely on the ground that the statutes discriminated on the basis of race in violation of the Equal Protection Clause. But the Court went on to hold that the laws arbitrarily deprived the couple of a fundamental liberty protected by the Due Process Clause, the freedom to marry. The Court's language on the latter point bears repeating:

Marriage is a personal right and long recognized

"The freedom to marry has long been recognized as one of the vital personal rights essential to the orderly pursuit of happiness by free men.

"Marriage is one of the 'basic civil rights of man,' fundamental to our very existence and survival." *Id.,* at 12, quoting *Skinner v. Oklahoma ex rel. Williamson,* 316 U.S. 535, 541 (1942).

[Justice Marshall here discussed prior Supreme Court authority dealing with privacy, procreative decisionmaking and family autonomy, discussed in Chapter 9, *infra.* No prior case squarely held there was a right to enter marriage, but there was some dicta to that effect.]

Marriage has significant importance and deserves protection

It is not surprising that the decision to marry has been placed on the same level of importance as decisions relating to procreation, childbirth, child rearing, and family relationships. As the facts of this case illustrate, it would make little sense to recognize a right of privacy with respect to other matters of family life and not with respect to the decision to enter the relationship that is the foundation of the family in our society. The woman [Redhail] desired to marry had a fundamental right to seek an abortion of their expected child, or to bring the child into life to suffer the myriad social, if not economic, disabilities that the status of illegitimacy brings. Surely, a decision to marry and raise the child in a traditional family setting must receive equivalent protection. And, [Redhail]'s right to procreate means anything at all, it must imply some right to enter the only relationship in which the State of Wisconsin allows sexual relations legally to take place.

legit regulations may be imposed
※

[W]e do not mean to suggest that every state regulation which relates in any way to the incidents of or prerequisites for marriage must be subjected to rigorous scrutiny. To the contrary, reasonable regulations that do not significantly interfere with decisions to enter into the marital relationship may legitimately be imposed. The statutory classification at issue here, however, clearly does interfere directly and substantially with the right to marry.

Under the challenged statute, no Wisconsin resident in the affected class may marry in Wisconsin or elsewhere without a court order, and marriages contracted in violation of the statute are both void and punishable as criminal offenses. Some of those in the affected class, like [Redhail], will never be able to obtain the necessary court order, because they either lack the financial means to meet their support obligations or cannot prove that their children will not become public charges. These persons are absolutely prevented from getting married. Many others, able in theory to satisfy the statute's requirements, will be sufficiently burdened by having to do so that they will in effect be coerced into forgoing their right to marry. And even those who can be persuaded to meet the statute's requirements suffer a serious intrusion into their freedom of choice in an area in which we have held such freedom to be fundamental.

Undue infringement on affected class

III

When a statutory classification significantly interferes with the exercise of a fundamental right, it cannot be upheld unless it is supported by sufficiently important state interests and is closely tailored to effectuate only those interests. [The state] asserts that two interests are served by the challenged statute: the permission-to-marry proceeding furnishes an opportunity to counsel the applicant as to the necessity of fulfilling his prior support obligations; and the welfare of the out-of-custody children is protected. We may accept for present purposes that these are legitimate and substantial interests, but, since the means selected by the State for achieving these interests unnecessarily impinge on the right to marry, the statute cannot be sustained.

State's interests in this statute (2)

Ct finds statute too broad

There is evidence that the challenged statute, as originally introduced in the Wisconsin Legislature, was intended merely to establish a mechanism whereby persons with support obligations to children from prior marriages could be counseled before they entered into new marital relationships and incurred further support obligations. Court permission to marry . . . was automatically to be granted after counseling was completed. The statute actually enacted, however, does not expressly require or provide for any counseling whatsoever, nor for any automatic granting of permission to marry by the court, and thus it can hardly be justified as a means for ensuring counseling. . . .

With regard to safeguarding the welfare of the out-of-custody children, . . . [the state]'s counsel suggested that, since permission to marry cannot be granted unless the applicant shows that he has satisfied his court-determined support obligations to the prior children and that those children will not become public charges, the statute provides incentive for the applicant to make support payments to his children. This "collection device" rationale cannot justify the statute's broad infringement on the right to marry.

First, with respect to individuals who are unable to meet the statutory requirements, the statute merely prevents the applicant from getting married, without delivering any money at all into the hands of the applicant's prior children. More importantly, regardless of the applicant's ability or willingness to meet the statutory requirements, the State already has numerous other means for exacting compliance with support obligations, means that are at least as effective as the instant statute's and yet do not impinge upon the right to marry. . . . [C]ourt-determined support obligations may be enforced directly via wage assignments, civil contempt proceedings, and criminal penalties. And, if the State believes that parents of children out of their custody should be responsible for ensuring that those children do not become public charges, this interest can be achieved by adjusting the criteria used for determining the amounts to be paid under their support orders.

There is also some suggestion that [the statute] protects the ability of marriage applicants to meet support obligations to prior children by preventing the applicants from incurring new support obligations. But the challenged provisions . . . are grossly underinclusive with respect to this purpose, since they do not limit in any way new financial commitments . . . other than those arising out of the contemplated marriage. The statutory classification is substantially overinclusive as well: Given the possibility that the new spouse will actually better the applicant's financial situation, by contributing income from a job or otherwise, the statute in many cases may prevent affected individuals from improving their ability to satisfy their prior support obligations. And, although it is true that the applicant will incur support obligations to any children born during the contemplated marriage, preventing the marriage may only result in the children being born out of wedlock, as in fact occurred in [Redhail]'s case. Since the support obligation is the same whether the child is born in or out of wedlock, the net result of preventing the marriage is simply more illegitimate children.

The statutory classification . . . thus cannot be justified by the interests advanced in support of it. The judgment of the District Court is, accordingly,

Affirmed.

MR. JUSTICE STEWART, concurring in the judgment.

[While agreeing the statute was unconstitutional, Justice Stewart concluded this was not an equal protection case, but rather, a substantive due process case.]

I

I do not agree . . . that there is a "right to marry" in the constitutional sense. That right, or more accurately that privilege, is under our federal system peculiarly one to be defined and limited by state law. A State may not only "significantly interfere with decisions to enter into the marital relationship," but may in many circumstances absolutely prohibit it. Surely, for example, a State may legitimately say that no one can marry his or her sibling, that no one can marry who is not at least 14 years old, that no one can marry without first passing an examination for venereal disease, or that no one can marry who has a living husband or wife. But, just as surely, in regulating the intimate human relationship of marriage, there is a limit beyond which a State may not constitutionally go.

. . . [I]t is settled that the "liberty" protected by the Due Process Clause of the Fourteenth Amendment embraces more than those freedoms expressly enumerated in the Bill of Rights. And the decisions of this Court have made clear that freedom of personal choice in matters of marriage and family life is one of the liberties so protected.

It is evident that the Wisconsin law now before us directly abridges that freedom. The question is whether the state interests that support the abridgment can overcome the substantive protections of the Constitution.

[Justice Stewart found state concerns on behalf of collection of support for existing obligees and the prospective family's economic well-being were legitimate, but the "State's legitimate concern with the financial soundness of prospective marriages must stop short of telling people they may not marry because they are too poor or because they might persist in their financial irresponsibility. The invasion of constitutionally protected liberty and the chance of erroneous prediction are simply too great."]

Mr. Justice Powell, concurring in the judgment.

. . . . I write separately because the majority's rationale sweeps too broadly in an area which traditionally has been subject to pervasive state regulation. The Court apparently would subject all state regulation which "directly and substantially" interferes with the decision to marry in a traditional family setting to "critical examination" or "compelling state interest" analysis. Presumably, "reasonable regulations that do not significantly interfere with decisions to enter into the marital relationship may legitimately be imposed." The Court does not present, however, any principled means for distinguishing between the two types of regulations. Since state regulation in this area typically takes the form of a prerequisite or barrier to marriage or divorce, the degree of "direct" interference with the decision to marry or to divorce is unlikely to provide either guidance for state legislatures or a basis for judicial oversight. [Justice Powell here repeated the discussion of prior privacy cases, concluding that "the Court has yet to hold that all regulation touching upon marriage implicates a 'fundamental right' triggering the most exacting judicial scrutiny.[1] "

. . . Although *Loving* speaks of the "freedom to marry" as "one of the vital personal rights essential to the orderly pursuit of happiness by free men," the Court focused on the miscegenation statute before it. . . . [which denied] a "fundamental freedom" on a wholly unsupportable basis — the use of classifications "directly subversive of the principle of equality at the heart of the Fourteenth Amendment. . . ." It does not speak to the level of judicial scrutiny of, or governmental justification for, "supportable" restrictions on the "fundamental freedom" of individuals to marry or divorce.

In my view, analysis must start from the recognition of domestic relations as "an area that has long been regarded as a virtually exclusive province of

---

[1] Although the cases [indicate] that there is a sphere of privacy or autonomy surrounding an existing marital relationship into which the State may not lightly intrude, they do not necessarily suggest that the same barrier of justification blocks regulation of the conditions of entry into or the dissolution of the marital bond. See generally Henkin, *Privacy and Autonomy,* 74 Colum. L. Rev. 1410, 1429–1432 (1974).

the States." *Sosna v. Iowa* . . . . The State, representing the collective expression of moral aspirations, has an undeniable interest in ensuring that its rules of domestic relations reflect the widely held values of its people. . . . State regulation has included bans on incest, bigamy, and homosexuality, as well as various preconditions to marriage, such as blood tests. Likewise, a showing of fault on the part of one of the partners traditionally has been a prerequisite to the dissolution of an unsuccessful union. A "compelling state purpose" inquiry would cast doubt on the network of restrictions that the States have fashioned to govern marriage and divorce.

II

State power over domestic relations is not without constitutional limits. The Due Process Clause requires a showing of justification "when the government intrudes on choices concerning family living arrangements" in a manner which is contrary to deeply rooted traditions. *Moore v. East Cleveland* (plurality opinion). Due process constraints also limit the extent to which the State may monopolize the process of ordering certain human relationships while excluding the truly indigent from that process. . . .

Th[is statute] does not pass muster under either due process or equal protection standards. . . . The . . . Court amply demonstrates that the asserted counseling objective bears no relation to this statute. . . .

The so-called "collection device" rationale presents a somewhat more difficult question. I do not agree with the suggestion in the Court's opinion that a State may never condition the right to marry on satisfaction of existing support obligations simply because the State has alternative methods of compelling such payments. To the extent this restriction applies to persons who are able to make the required support payments but simply wish to shirk their moral and legal obligation, the Constitution interposes no bar to this additional collection mechanism. The vice inheres, not in the collection concept, but in the failure to make provision for those without the means to comply with child-support obligations. [Justice Powell here cited *Boddie v. Connecticut* which struck down filing fees for divorce actions as applied to those unable to pay]. The monopolization [here] is total, for Wisconsin will not recognize foreign marriages that [violate the statute].

The third justification . . . is that the statute preserves the ability of marriage applicants to support their prior issue by preventing them from incurring new obligations. The challenged provisions . . . are so grossly underinclusive with respect to this objective, given the many ways that additional financial obligations may be incurred [aside] from a contemplated marriage, that the classification "does not bear a fair and substantial relation to the object of the legislation."

 . . . . This statute does more than simply "fail to alleviate the consequences of differences in economic circumstances that exist wholly apart from any state action." *Griffin v. Illinois* (Harlan, J., dissenting). It tells the truly indigent, whether they have met their support obligations or not, that they may not marry so long as their children are public charges or there is a danger that their children might go on public assistance in the future. Apparently, no other jurisdiction has embraced this approach. . . . Because the State has not established a justification for this [bar to marriage for many citizens based on poverty], I concur in the judgment. . . .

[Justice Stevens concurred, finding denial of permission to those whose children were public charges "either futile or perverse insofar as it applies to childless couples, couples who will have illegitimate children if they are forbidden to marry, couples whose economic status will be improved by marriage, and couples who are so poor that the marriage will have no impact on the welfare status of their children. . . ." Justice Rehnquist dissented. Applying rational relationship scrutiny, he found the statute within a state's "power to regulate family life and to assure the support of minor children, despite its possible imprecision in the extreme cases envisioned in the concurring opinions."]

NOTES

1. **Scope of Zablocki.** After establishing that marriage is "a right of fundamental importance," the majority rejects rigorous scrutiny for laws which "do not significantly interfere with decisions to enter into the marital relationship." Justice Marshall notes the *Zablocki* regulation "clearly does interfere directly and substantially with the right to marry" and, therefore, applies searching scrutiny. How are regulations which "significantly interfere" with marriage to be distinguished from those which do not? As you study the various marriage regulations, consider which level of scrutiny is appropriate under *Zablocki*.

2. **Importance of Poverty to Zablocki's Holding.** Consider the following statute: "All those who have been ordered to pay child support and are in arrears cannot enter into a marital relationship until those arrearages are eliminated; provided, those who can show they are financially unable to pay these arrearages can marry." Justice Marshall presumably would find this version of the statute equally objectionable, but it would appear to satisfy Justice Powell.

3. **What Is Zablocki Protecting?** One might ask what precisely is protected by a "right to marry." The Court states, *e.g.*, "marriage is the only relationship in which the state . . . allows sexual relations legally to take place." Would the statute be equally defective if extramarital sexual relations were permitted?

What constitutionally protected interest would the marriage restriction deny a couple who may cohabit legally? It could be access to alimony or property division claims on divorce. Yet many states today allow cohabitants to create binding contractual obligations to one another (*see* Chapter 9, Nontraditional Families, at pp. 876-918), which might eliminate this concern. Is *Zablocki* acting to protect any future children from the burden of non-marital status? Not likely. The couple may not have children and, anyway, non-marital status rarely is relevant, under modern law, in the child's claims for support, intestate succession, etc. (*See* Chapter 9 at pp. 1035-38). Then, is a right to marry designed to protect couples so they can file joint tax returns, inherit intestate, sue for wrongful death, or obtain the family rate at a local country club?

In sum, is *Zablocki* about the practical benefits of marriage or is it instead protecting access to the symbolic status of marriage? From the perspective of a potential spouse, do people choose to marry rather than cohabit because of practical consequences, or because of custom, psychic need, symbolic significance or religious belief? To suggest *Zablocki* protects access to a symbolic act is not to suggest it is wrong; rather it is to suggest this symbol is extraordinarily important.

While people can claim they are married even though the state refused them a license, the state has a practical "monopoly" over access to the marriage label. Most people probably believe state approval, obtained by adherence to state rules, is necessary to create a legitimate marriage. Access to legally recognized marriage is thus usually essential to social recognition of it and this is more important than the legal consequences which they likely never stopped to consider. The couple wants to be married not only in their own eyes, but also in the perception of others.

Thus, the significant state power over marriage which is the subject of *Zablocki* is a very strange power: it is a power over a symbol, enforced by social convention. This is good to keep in mind in considering substantive restrictions on entering marriage.

4. A Dissent on the Right to Marry. Not all commentators accept the Supreme Court's right to marry jurisprudence uncritically. Professor Earl Maltz argues "the case law dealing with the . . . right to marry is far more ambiguous than is often assumed." Maltz, *Right to Marry: A Dissenting View*, 60 Geo. Wash. L. Rev. 949, 954 (1992). He points out that

> government . . . plays a different role in *Loving* and *Redhail* than in many other cases involving claims of a fundamental right. Assertions of . . . free speech, for example, rest on the view that the government should not be allowed to interfere with certain practices that are independent of government itself. . . . [R]ather than a right to be free from state interference, [however],the right to marry can only be conceptualized as the right to place the power of the state behind previously agreed-to, consensual arrangements, and to forge a linkage between . . . different rights and obligations derived from those arrangements.

Id. at 955. The author identifies four aspects of the marital relationship which have been claimed to justify strict scrutiny of regulation (the "emotional support and public commitment provided by a marriage, the economic benefits derived from the marital relationship, the sexual relationship . . . and the relationship between the husband, wife, and offspring of the marriage") and finds each wanting as a basis upon which to conclude that the right to marry is fundamental. *Id.* at 956–67.

PROBLEMS

Problem 2-3. Ramona was employed by a company which assisted the police department in processing insurance claims of current and former police officers. In that capacity, she had access to files containing confidential information about the officers. She became romantically involved with an incarcerated felon and planned to marry him. When her supervisor learned of this plan, she told Ramona to either end the relationship or terminate her employment. Ramona resigned and now has come to you wanting to file a lawsuit seeking damages or to get her job back. Without regard to the appropriate remedy, how will you argue the case and what kind of response do you expect from the other side?

Problem 2-4. Your state has recently enacted the following statute:

> In a divorce action, the judge shall, as the evidence and the nature of the case may warrant, direct whether the party against whom the judgement of divorce is made be permitted to marry again. In situations where a person is denied permission to remarry, it shall be competent for a judge, upon motion and proper proof, to allow the moving party to marry again, as justice may seem to require.

As an Assistant Attorney General, draft an opinion on the constitutionality of this legislation.

Problem 2-5. Judith is a state prison inmate serving a life sentence. She has fallen in love with Brian, an old friend with whom she went to high school. They've known each other for 30 years, each having been divorced for over 10 years. Following state statutory rules, each wrote a letter to the prison administrator seeking permission to marry. The matter was referred to the prison's marriage committee which, after separately interviewing the parties, denied permission to marry. The committee's memorandum stated "this marriage would not be in the best interest of either party or the institution. Both parties are unrealistic about the length of Judith's sentence and both seem to believe it will be reduced. She will not be eligible for parole under current rules for 21 years. Brian spoke of building a log cabin for the couple to live in after her release. While both spoke of a lengthy relationship, they were very vague about its details and, except for the last six months when contact was re-established, the relationship could not be documented. Judith was very nervous during the interview and talked mostly about how she did not commit the crime for which she is incarcerated. Brian was very sarcastic. Each stated that the other was 'pushing' to get married." The administrator accepted the committee's recommendation and Judith has filed suit to overturn the refusal to grant her permission to marry. As law clerk to the judge hearing the suit, review the relevant Supreme Court authority and outline the arguments you expect from both sides.

[b]   Same-Sex Prohibitions

GOODRIDGE v. DEPARTMENT OF PUBLIC HEALTH

798 N.E.2d 941 (Mass. 2003)

MARSHALL, C.J.. Marriage is a vital social institution. The exclusive commitment of two individuals to each other nurtures love and mutual support; it brings stability to our society. For those who choose to marry, and for their children, marriage provides an abundance of legal, financial, and social benefits. In return it imposes weighty legal, financial, and social obligations. The question . . . is whether, consistent with the Massachusetts Constitution, the Commonwealth may deny the protections, benefits, and obligations conferred by civil marriage to two individuals of the same sex who wish to marry. We conclude that it may not. The Massachusetts Constitution . . . forbids the creation of second-class citizens. [The State] has failed to identify any constitutionally adequate reason for denying civil marriage to same-sex couples.

. . . [O]ur decision marks a change in the history of our marriage law. Many people hold deep-seated religious, moral, and ethical convictions that marriage should be limited to the union of one man and one woman, and that homosexual conduct is immoral. Many hold equally strong religious, moral, and ethical convictions that same-sex couples are entitled to be married. . . . Neither view answers the question before us. Our concern is with the Massachusetts Constitution. . . .

Whether the Commonwealth may use its formidable regulatory authority to bar same-sex couples from civil marriage is a question not previously addressed by a Massachusetts appellate court. It is a question the United States Supreme Court left open as a matter of Federal law in *Lawrence* [*v. Texas*, 123 S. Ct. 2472 (2003)] where it was not an issue. There, the Court affirmed that the core concept of common human dignity protected by the *Fourteenth Amendment to the United States Constitution* precludes government intrusion into the deeply personal realms of consensual adult expressions of intimacy and one's choice of an intimate partner. The Court also reaffirmed the central role that decisions whether to marry or have children bear in shaping one's identity. The Massachusetts Constitution is, if anything, more protective of individual liberty and equality than the Federal Constitution; it may demand broader protection for fundamental rights; and it is less tolerant of government intrusion into the protected spheres of private life.

Barred access to the protections, benefits, and obligations of civil marriage, a person who enters into an intimate, exclusive union with another of the same sex is arbitrarily deprived of membership in one of our community's most rewarding and cherished institutions. That exclusion is incompatible with the constitutional principles of respect for individual autonomy and equality under law.

[The court noted that the seven plaintiff couples had relationships of from 4 to 30 years and several lived with their children. Noting plaintiffs included "business executives, lawyers, an investment banker, educators, therapists, and a computer engineer," the court acknowledged they] have employed such legal means as are available to them — for example, joint adoption, powers of attorney, and joint ownership of real property — to secure aspects of their relationships. Each . . . attests a desire to marry his or her partner in order to affirm publicly their commitment to each other and to secure the legal protections and benefits afforded to married couples and their children.

The Department of Public Health (department) is charged . . . with safeguarding public health. Among its responsibilities, [it] oversees the registry of vital records and statistics (registry), which "enforces all laws" [regarding] issuance of marriage licenses and . . . keeping of marriage records. . . .

[Each of the plaintiff couples, which uncontestedly "met all of the facial qualifications to obtain marriage licenses," were denied licenses by the relevant government official. Specific instances of denial of the "full legal protections of civil marriage" suffered by plaintiffs and their families included one partner's "difficulty gaining access to [partner] and their newborn daughter at the hospital" and the necessity of gaining separate health insurance policy for one partner because his partner's family health policy rejected his inclusion as a dependent.]

. . .[P]laintiffs filed suit . . . against the department and the commissioner seeking a judgment that "the exclusion of the plaintiff couples and other qualified same-sex couples from access to marriage licenses, and the legal and social status of civil marriage, as well as the protections, benefits and obligations of marriage, violates Massachusetts law." The plaintiffs alleged violation of the laws of the Commonwealth, including but not limited to their rights under arts. 1, 6, 7, 10 . . . and Part II, c. 1, § 1, art. 4, of the Massachusetts Constitution.[7]

. . . .

[Ruling on cross motions for summary judgment, the trial court dismissed a claim that the marriage statutes "should be construed to permit marriage

---

[7] Article 1 . . . provides: "All people are born free and equal and have certain natural, essential and unalienable rights; among which may be reckoned the right of enjoying and defending their lives and liberties; that of acquiring, possessing and protecting property; in fine, that of seeking and obtaining their safety and happiness. Equality under the law shall not be denied or abridged because of sex, race, color, creed or national origin."

Article 6 provides: "No man . . . or association of men, have any other title to obtain advantages, or particular and exclusive privileges, distinct from those of the community, than what arises from the consideration of services rendered to the public . . . ."

Article 7 provides: "Government is instituted for the common good; for the protection, safety, prosperity, and happiness of the people; and not for the profit, honor, or private interest of any one man, family or class of men: Therefore the people alone have an . . . indefeasible right to institute government; and to reform, alter, or totally change the same, when their protection, safety, prosperity and happiness require it."

Article 10 provides . . .: "Each individual of the society has a right to be protected by it in the enjoyment of his life, liberty and property, according to standing laws . . . ."

. . . .

Part II, c. 1, § 1, art. 4 . . . provides . . . that "full power and authority are hereby given and granted to the said general court . . . to . . . establish all manner of wholesome and reasonable orders, laws . . . so as the same be not repugnant or contrary to this constitution, as they shall judge to be for the . . . welfare of this Commonwealth."

between persons of the same sex." The trial court judge then] held that the marriage exclusion does not offend the liberty, freedom, equality, or due process provisions of the Massachusetts Constitution, and that the Massachusetts Declaration of Rights does not guarantee "the fundamental right to marry a person of the same sex." He concluded that prohibiting same-sex marriage rationally furthers the Legislature's legitimate interest in safeguarding the "primary purpose" of marriage, "procreation." The Legislature may rationally limit marriage to opposite-sex couples, he concluded, because those couples are "theoretically . . . capable of procreation," they do not rely on "inherently more cumbersome" noncoital means of reproduction, and they are more likely . . . to have children, or more children.

. . . .

[Plaintiffs] focus, quite properly, on the marriage licensing statute, which controls entry into civil marriage. As a preliminary matter, we summarize the provisions of that law.

[The relevant statute serves "gatekeeping" functions (prohibiting polygamous and incestuous marriages, those with an underage party and those in which a party has communicable syphilis. It also identifies those authorized to solemnize a marriage. As for "record-keeping provisions," the statute requires the filing of information forms and medical certificates, payment of fees and outlines the process of issuance and filing of the marriage license and certificate.]

In short, for all the joy and solemnity that normally attend a marriage, [the statute] is a licensing law. The plaintiffs argue that because nothing in that licensing law specifically prohibits marriages between persons of the same sex, we may interpret the statute to permit "qualified same sex couples" to obtain marriage licenses, [to avoid the constitutional question]. This claim lacks merit.

We interpret statutes to carry out the Legislature's intent, determined by the words of a statute interpreted according to "the ordinary and approved usage of the language." The everyday meaning of "marriage" is "the legal union of a man and woman as husband and wife," BLACK'S LAW DICTIONARY 986 (7th ed. 1999), and the plaintiffs do not argue . . . "marriage" has ever had a different meaning under Massachusetts law. This definition of marriage . . . derives from the common law. Far from being ambiguous, the undefined word "marriage" confirms the General Court's intent to hew to the term's common-law and quotidian meaning concerning the genders of the marriage partners.

The [statute's] intended scope . . . is also evident in its consanguinity provisions. [It is] silent as to the consanguinity of male-male or female-female marriage applicants. The only reasonable explanation is that the Legislature did not intend that same-sex couples be licensed to marry. We conclude that [the statute] may not be construed to permit same-sex couples to marry.

The larger question is whether . . . government action that bars same-sex couples from civil marriage constitutes a legitimate exercise of the State's authority to regulate conduct, or whether . . . this categorical marriage exclusion violates the Massachusetts Constitution. We have recognized the long-standing statutory understanding. . . . But that history cannot and does not foreclose the constitutional question.

The plaintiffs' claim . . . can be analyzed in two ways. Does it offend the Constitution's guarantees of equality before the law? Or do the liberty and due process provisions of the Massachusetts Constitution secure the plaintiffs' right to marry their chosen partner? In matters implicating marriage, family life, and the upbringing of children, the two constitutional concepts frequently overlap, as they do here. *See, e.g.,* . . . *Lawrence* ("Equality of treatment and the due process right to demand respect for conduct protected by the substantive guarantee of liberty are linked in important respects, and a decision on the latter point advances both interests"). . . . Much of what we say concerning one standard applies to the other.

We begin by considering the nature of civil marriage itself. Simply put, the government creates civil marriage. . . . No religious ceremony has ever been required to validate a Massachusetts marriage. In a real sense, there are three partners to every civil marriage: two willing spouses and an approving State. While only the parties can mutually assent to marriage, the terms of the marriage — who may marry and what obligations, benefits, and liabilities attach to civil marriage — are set by the Commonwealth. Conversely, while only the parties can agree to end the marriage (absent [death or a void marriage]), the Commonwealth defines the exit terms.

Civil marriage is created by the state and monitored by police power

Civil marriage is created and regulated through exercise of the police power. "Police power" . . . is an old-fashioned term for the Commonwealth's lawmaking authority, as bounded by the liberty and equality guarantees of the Massachusetts Constitution and its express delegation of power from the people to their government. In broad terms, it is the Legislature's power to enact rules to regulate conduct, to the extent that such laws are "necessary to secure the health, safety, good order, comfort, or general welfare of the community." *Opinion of the Justices,* 168 N.E.2d 858 (Mass. 1960).

Without question, civil marriage enhances the "welfare of the community." It is a "social institution of the highest importance." Civil marriage anchors an ordered society by encouraging stable relationships over transient ones. It is central to the way the Commonwealth identifies individuals, provides for the orderly distribution of property, ensures that children and adults are cared for and supported whenever possible from private rather than public funds, and tracks important epidemiological and demographic data.

Civil marriage benefits the community

Marriage also bestows enormous private and social advantages on those who choose to marry. Civil marriage is at once a deeply personal commitment . . . and a highly public celebration of the ideals of mutuality, companionship, intimacy, fidelity, and family. . . . Because it fulfils yearnings for security, safe haven, and connection that express our common humanity, civil marriage is an esteemed institution, and the decision whether and whom to marry is among life's momentous acts of self-definition.

policy

Tangible as well as intangible benefits flow from marriage. The marriage license grants valuable property rights to those who meet the entry requirements, and who agree to what might otherwise be a burdensome degree of government regulation of their activities.[13] The Legislature has conferred

benefits

---

[13] For example, married persons face substantial restrictions, simply because they are married, on their ability freely to dispose of their assets.

on "each party [in a civil marriage] substantial rights concerning the assets of the other which unmarried cohabitants do not have." *Wilcox, 693 N.E.2d 141 (1998)*. [The court noted case law rejecting cohabitants' equitable distribution claims at the conclusion of their relationship, loss of consortium damages and alimony.].

Statutes and rights relating to marriage

The benefits accessible only by way of a marriage license are enormous, touching nearly every aspect of life and death. The department states that "hundreds of statutes" are related to marriage and to marital benefits. With no attempt to be comprehensive, we note that some of the statutory benefits conferred by the Legislature on those who enter into civil marriage include, as to property: joint Massachusetts income tax filing; tenancy by the entirety ([which] provides certain protections against creditors . . .); extension of the benefit of the homestead protection . . .; automatic rights to inherit the property of a deceased spouse who does not leave a will; the rights of elective share and of dower (which allow surviving spouses certain property rights where the decedent spouse has not made adequate provision for the survivor in a will); entitlement to wages owed to a deceased employee; eligibility to continue certain businesses of a deceased spouse; the right to share the medical policy of one's spouse; thirty-nine week continuation of health coverage for the spouse of a person who is laid off or dies; preferential options under the Commonwealth's pension system; preferential benefits in the Commonwealth's medical program . . .; access to veterans' spousal benefits and preferences; financial protections for spouses of certain Commonwealth employees (fire fighters, police officers, prosecutors, among others) killed in the performance of duty; the equitable division of marital property on divorce; . . . alimony rights; the right to . . . support on separation of the parties . . .; and the right to bring claims for wrongful death and loss of consortium, and for funeral and burial expenses and punitive damages resulting from tort actions.

Exclusive marital benefits that are not directly tied to property rights include the presumptions of legitimacy and parentage of children born to a married couple; and evidentiary rights, such as the prohibition against spouses testifying against one another about their private conversations, applicable in both civil and criminal cases. Other statutory benefits . . . include qualification for bereavement or medical leave to care for individuals related by blood or marriage; an automatic "family member" preference to make medical decisions for an incompetent or disabled spouse . . .; the application of predictable rules of child custody, visitation, support, and removal out-of-State when married parents divorce; priority rights to administer the estate of a[n intestate] spouse. . ., and requirement that surviving spouse must consent to the appointment of any other person as administrator; and the right to interment in the lot or tomb owned by one's deceased spouse.

Children's benefits

Where a married couple has children, their children are also directly or indirectly . . . the recipients of the special legal and economic protections obtained by civil marriage. Notwithstanding the Commonwealth's strong public policy to abolish legal distinctions between marital and nonmarital children . . ., the fact remains that marital children reap a measure of family stability and economic security based on their parents' legally privileged status that is largely inaccessible, or not as readily accessible, to nonmarital children. Some of these benefits are social, such as the enhanced approval that still attends the status of being a marital child. Others are material, such as the greater ease of access to family-based State and Federal benefits that attend the presumptions of one's parentage.

It is undoubtedly for these concrete reasons, as well as for its intimately personal significance, that civil marriage has long been termed a "civil right." *See, e.g., Loving.* The United States Supreme Court has described the right to marry as "of fundamental importance for all individuals" and as "part of the fundamental 'right of privacy' implicit in the Fourteenth Amendment's Due Process Clause." *Zablocki.*

[margin note: Civil marriage is a civil right]

Without the right to marry — or more properly, the right to choose to marry — one is excluded from the full range of human experience and denied full protection of the laws for one's "avowed commitment to an intimate and lasting human relationship." *Baker v. State* [a parallel Vermont Supreme Court case discussed in Note 1 following this opinion]. Because civil marriage is central to the lives of individuals and the welfare of the community, our laws assiduously protect the individual's right to marry against undue government incursion. Laws may not "interfere directly and substantially with the right to marry." *Zablocki* [15]

[margin note: w/o right to marry person is excluded from experience]

Unquestionably, the regulatory power . . . over civil marriage is broad, as is the Commonwealth's discretion to award public benefits. Individuals who have the choice to marry each other and nevertheless choose not to may properly be denied the legal benefits of marriage. But that same logic cannot hold for a qualified individual who would marry if she or he only could.

[margin note: ✳]

For decades, indeed centuries, in much of this country (including Massachusetts) no lawful marriage was possible between white and black Americans. That long history availed not when the Supreme Court of California held in 1948 that a legislative prohibition against interracial marriage violated the due process and equality guarantees of the Fourteenth Amendment, *Perez v. Sharp* or when, nineteen years later, the United States Supreme Court also held that a statutory bar to interracial marriage violated the Fourteenth Amendment, *Loving.* [16] As both *Perez* and *Loving* make clear, the right to marry means little if it does not include the right to marry the person of one's choice, subject to appropriate government restrictions in the interests of public health, safety, and welfare. In this case . . . a statute deprives individuals of access to an institution of fundamental legal, personal, and social significance — the institution of marriage — because of a single trait: skin color

[margin note: Right to marry includes choice of person]

---

[15] The department argues that this case concerns the rights of couples (same sex and opposite sex), not the rights of individuals. This is incorrect. The rights implicated in this case are at the core of individual privacy and autonomy. . . .

[16] The department argues that the *Loving* decision did not profoundly alter the by-then common conception of marriage because it was decided at a time when antimiscegenation statutes were in "full-scale retreat." But the relationship the department draws between popular consensus and the constitutionality of a statute oppressive to a minority group ignores the successful constitutional challenges to an antimiscegenation statute, initiated some twenty years earlier. When the Supreme Court of California decided *Perez* . . . racial inequality was rampant and normative, segregation in public and private institutions was commonplace, the civil rights movement had not yet been launched, and the "separate but equal" doctrine of *Plessy v. Ferguson* . . . was still good law . . . .

in *Perez* and *Loving*, sexual orientation here. As it did in *Perez* and *Loving*, history must yield to a more fully developed understanding of the invidious quality of the discrimination.

The Massachusetts Constitution protects matters of personal liberty against government incursion as zealously, and often more so, than does the Federal Constitution, even where both Constitutions employ essentially the same language. That [this is so] is not surprising. Fundamental to the vigor of our Federal system of government is that "state courts are absolutely free to interpret state constitutional provisions to accord greater protection to individual rights than do similar provisions of the United States Constitution." *Evans,* 514 U.S. 1 (1995).

. . . .

Statute can't be arbitrary & capricious

The Massachusetts Constitution requires, at a minimum, that the exercise of the State's regulatory authority not be "arbitrary or capricious." Under both the equality and liberty guarantees, regulatory authority must, at very least, serve "a legitimate purpose in a rational way"; a statute must "bear a reasonable relation to a permissible legislative objective.". . . .

P challenges on due process and equal protection grounds

The plaintiffs challenge the marriage statute on both equal protection and due process grounds. . . .[W]e must first determine the appropriate standard of review. Where a statute implicates a fundamental right or uses a suspect classification, we employ "strict judicial scrutiny." For all other statutes, we employ the " 'rational basis' test." For due process claims, rational basis analysis requires that statutes "bear[] a real and substantial relation to the public health, safety, morals, or some other phase of the general welfare." For equal protection challenges, the rational basis test requires that "an impartial lawmaker could logically believe that the classification would serve a legitimate public purpose that transcends the harm to the members of the disadvantaged class."

Ct uses Rational basis test

Statute fails rational basis test

The department argues that no fundamental right or "suspect" class is at issue here, and rational basis is the appropriate standard of review. For the reasons we explain below, we conclude that the marriage ban does not meet the rational basis test for either due process or equal protection [and, thus,] we do not consider the plaintiffs' arguments that this case merits strict judicial scrutiny.

D's argument (3)

The department posits three legislative rationales for prohibiting same-sex couples from marrying: (1) providing a "favorable setting for procreation"; (2) ensuring the optimal setting for child rearing, which the department defines as "a two-parent family with one parent of each sex"; and (3) preserving scarce State and private financial resources. We consider each in turn.

Civil marriage does not require procreation

The [trial] judge . . . endorsed the first rationale, holding that "the state's interest in regulating marriage is based on the traditional concept that marriage's primary purpose is procreation." This is incorrect. Our laws of civil marriage do not privilege procreative heterosexual intercourse between married people above every other form of adult intimacy and every other means of creating a family. [The statute] contains no requirement that the applicants for a marriage license attest to their ability or intention to conceive children by coitus. Fertility is not a condition of marriage, nor is it grounds for divorce. People who have never consummated their marriage, and never plan to, may be and stay married. People who cannot stir from their deathbed may marry. While it is certainly true that many, perhaps most, married couples have children together (assisted or unassisted), it is the exclusive and permanent commitment of the marriage partners to one another, not the begetting of children, that is the sine qua non of civil marriage.[23]

Moreover, the Commonwealth affirmatively facilitates bringing children into a family regardless of whether the intended parent is married or unmarried, whether the child is adopted or born into a family, whether assistive technology was used to conceive the child, and whether the parent or her partner is heterosexual, homosexual, or bisexual. If procreation were a necessary component of civil marriage, our statutes would draw a tighter circle around the permissible bounds of nonmarital child bearing and the creation of families by noncoital means. The attempt to isolate procreation as "the source of a fundamental right to marry," (Cordy, J., dissenting), overlooks the integrated way in which courts have examined the complex and overlapping realms of personal autonomy, marriage, family life, and child rearing. Our jurisprudence recognizes that, in these nuanced and fundamentally private areas of life, such a narrow focus is inappropriate.

The "marriage is procreation" argument singles out the one unbridgeable difference between same-sex and opposite-sex couples, and transforms that difference into the essence of legal marriage. Like "Amendment 2" to the Constitution of Colorado, which effectively denied homosexual persons equality under the law and full access to the political process, the marriage restriction impermissibly "identifies persons by a single trait and then denies them protection across the board." *Romer v. Evans,* 517 U.S. 620. In so doing, the State's action confers an official stamp of approval on the destructive stereotype that same-sex relationships are inherently unstable and inferior to opposite-sex relationships and are not worthy of respect.

The department's first stated rationale, equating marriage with unassisted heterosexual procreation, shades imperceptibly into its second: that confining marriage to opposite-sex couples ensures that children are raised in the "optimal" setting. Protecting the welfare of children is a paramount State policy. Restricting marriage to opposite-sex couples, however, cannot plausibly further this policy. "The demographic changes of the past century make it difficult to speak of an average American family. The composition of families varies greatly from household to household." *Troxel v. Granville,* 530 U.S. 57 (2000). Massachusetts has responded supportively to "the changing realities of the American family" and has moved vigorously to strengthen the modern family in its many variations. . . . Moreover, we have repudiated the common-law power of the State to provide varying levels of protection to children

[handwritten margin note: Protection of children is important, but not furthered by the statute]

---

[23] It is hardly surprising that civil marriage developed historically as a means to regulate heterosexual conduct and to promote child rearing, because until very recently unassisted heterosexual relations were the only means short of adoption by which children could come into the world, and the absence of widely available and effective contraceptives made the link between heterosexual sex and procreation very strong indeed. . . . But it is circular reasoning, not analysis, to maintain that marriage must remain a heterosexual institution because that is what it historically has been. . . .

best interest of the child does not restrict gay couples

based on the circumstances of birth. . . . The "best interests of the child" standard does not turn on a parent's sexual orientation or marital status.

same-sex couples may be good parents

The department has offered no evidence that forbidding marriage to people of the same sex will increase the number of couples choosing to enter into opposite-sex marriages in order to have and raise children. There is thus no rational relationship between the marriage statute and the . . . goal of protecting the "optimal" child rearing unit. Moreover, the department readily concedes that people in same-sex couples may be "excellent" parents. These couples (including four of the plaintiff couples) have children for the reasons others do — to love them, to care for them, to nurture them. But the task of child rearing for same-sex couples is made infinitely harder by their status as outliers to the marriage laws. While establishing the parentage of children as soon as possible is crucial to the safety and welfare of children, same-sex couples must undergo the sometimes lengthy and intrusive process of second-parent adoption to establish their joint parentage. While the enhanced income provided by marital benefits is an important source of security and stability for married couples and their children, those benefits are denied to families headed by same-sex couples. While the laws of divorce provide clear and reasonably predictable guidelines for child support, child custody, and property division on dissolution of a marriage, same-sex couples . . . find themselves and their children in the highly unpredictable terrain of equity jurisdiction. Given the wide range of public benefits reserved only for married couples, we do not credit the department's contention that the absence of access to civil marriage amounts to little more than an inconvenience to same-sex couples and their children. Excluding same-sex couples from civil marriage will not make children of opposite-sex marriages more secure, but it does prevent children of same-sex couples from enjoying the immeasurable advantages that flow from the assurance of "a stable family structure in which children will be reared, educated, and socialized." (Cordy, J., dissenting).

No one disputes that the plaintiff couples are families, that many are parents, and that the children they are raising, like all children, need and should have the fullest opportunity to grow up in a secure, protected family unit. Similarly, no one disputes that, under the rubric of marriage, the State provides a cornucopia of substantial benefits to married parents and their children. The preferential treatment of civil marriage reflects the Legislature's conclusion that marriage "is the foremost setting for the education and socialization of children" precisely because it "encourages parents to remain committed to each other and to their children as they grow." (Cordy, J., dissenting).

P denied b/c State objects to sexual orientation

In this case, we are confronted with an entire, sizeable class of parents raising children who have absolutely no access to civil marriage and its protections because they are forbidden from procuring a marriage license. It cannot be rational . . . to penalize children by depriving them of State benefits because the State disapproves of their parents' sexual orientation.

D's 3rd argument

The third rationale advanced . . . is that limiting marriage to opposite-sex couples furthers the Legislature's interest in conserving scarce State and private financial resources. The marriage restriction is rational, it argues, because the General Court logically could assume that same-sex couples are more financially independent than married couples and thus less needy of public marital benefits, such as tax advantages, or private marital benefits, such as employer-financed health plans that include spouses in their coverage.

An absolute statutory ban on same-sex marriage bears no rational relationship to the goal of economy. First, the department's conclusory generalization — that same-sex couples are less financially dependent on each other than opposite-sex couples — ignores that many same-sex couples, such as many of the plaintiffs . . ., have children and other dependents (here, aged parents) in their care. The department does not contend, nor could it, that these dependents are less needy or deserving than the dependents of married couples. Second, Massachusetts marriage laws do not condition receipt of public and private financial benefits to married individuals on a demonstration of financial dependence on each other . . . . *ct disagrees*

The department suggests additional rationales . . . . It argues that broadening civil marriage . . . will trivialize or destroy the institution of marriage as it has historically been fashioned. Certainly our decision today marks a significant change in the definition of marriage as it has been inherited from the common law, and understood by many societies for centuries. But it does not disturb the fundamental value of marriage in our society.

Here, the plaintiffs seek only to be married, not to undermine the institution of civil marriage. They do not want marriage abolished. They do not attack the binary nature of marriage, the consanguinity provisions, or any of the other gate-keeping provisions of the marriage licensing law. Recognizing the right of an individual to marry a person of the same sex will not diminish the validity or dignity of opposite-sex marriage, any more than recognizing the right of an individual to marry a person of a different race devalues the marriage of a person who marries someone of her own race.[28] If anything, extending civil marriage . . . reinforces the importance of marriage to individuals and communities. That same-sex couples are willing to embrace marriage's . . . obligations of exclusivity, mutual support, and commitment . . . is a testament to the enduring place of marriage in our laws and in the human spirit.

[At this point, the court rejected a separation of powers argument, concluding "[t]he . . . Constitution requires that legislation . . . not extend beyond certain limits. It is the function of courts to determine whether these criteria are met and whether these limits are exceeded. In most instances, these limits are defined by whether a rational basis exists to conclude that legislation will bring about a rational result. The Legislature in the first instance, and the courts in the last instance, must ascertain whether such a rational basis exists."]

. . . .

---

[28] Justice Cordy suggests that we have "transmuted the 'right' to marry into a right to change the institution of marriage itself," because marriage is intimately tied to the reproductive systems of the marriage partners and to the "optimal" mother and father setting for child rearing. That analysis hews perilously close to the argument . . ., that men and women are so innately and fundamentally different that their respective "proper spheres" can be rigidly and universally delineated. . . .

The department has had more than ample opportunity to articulate a constitutionally adequate justification for limiting civil marriage to opposite-sex unions. It has failed to do so. The [alleged state interests] are starkly at odds with the comprehensive network of vigorous, gender-neutral laws promoting stable families and the best interests of children. It has failed to identify any relevant characteristic that would justify shutting the door to civil marriage to a person who wishes to marry someone of the same sex.

D's arguments fail

The marriage ban works a deep and scarring hardship on a very real segment of the community for no rational reason. The absence of any reasonable relationship between . . . an absolute disqualification of same-sex couples . . . and . . . protection of public health, safety, or general welfare, suggests that the marriage restriction is rooted in persistent prejudices against persons who are (or who are believed to be) homosexual. "The Constitution cannot control such prejudices but neither can it tolerate them. Private biases may be outside the reach of the law, but the law cannot, directly or indirectly, give them effect." *Palmore,* 466 U.S. 429 (1984). Limiting the protections, benefits, and obligations of civil marriage to opposite-sex couples violates the basic premises of individual liberty and equality under law protected by the Massachusetts Constitution.

the ban is based on discrimination

. . . .

We consider next the plaintiffs' request for relief. We preserve as much of the statute as may be preserved in the face of the successful constitutional challenge. . . .

what type of relief is appropriate?

Here, no one argues that striking down the marriage laws is an appropriate form of relief. Eliminating civil marriage would be wholly inconsistent with the Legislature's deep commitment to fostering stable families and would dismantle a vital organizing principle of our society. We face a problem similar to one that recently confronted the Court of Appeal for Ontario, the highest court of that Canadian province, when it considered the constitutionality of the same-sex marriage ban under Canada's Federal Constitution, the Charter of Rights and Freedoms (Charter). See *Halpern v. Toronto (City),* 172 O.A.C. 276 (2003). Canada, like the United States, adopted the common law of England that civil marriage is "the voluntary union for life of one man and one woman, to the exclusion of all others." In holding that the limitation . . . to opposite-sex couples violated the Charter, the Court of Appeal refined the common-law meaning of marriage. We concur with this remedy. . . .

Ct likes Canada's approach redefine "marriage"

We construe civil marriage to mean the voluntary union of two persons as spouses, to the exclusion of all others. This reformulation redresses the plaintiffs' constitutional injury and furthers the aim of marriage to promote stable, exclusive relationships. It advances the two legitimate State interests the department has identified: providing a stable setting for child rearing and conserving State resources. It [accepts] the Legislature's broad discretion to regulate marriage.

New definition →

In their complaint the plaintiffs request only a declaration that their exclusion and the exclusion of other qualified same-sex couples from access to civil marriage violates Massachusetts law. We declare that barring an individual from the protections, benefits, and obligations of civil marriage solely because that person would marry a person of the same sex violates the Massachusetts Constitution. We vacate the summary judgment for the department. We remand this case . . . for entry of judgment consistent with this opinion. Entry of judgment shall be stayed for 180 days to permit the Legislature to take such action as it may deem appropriate in light of this opinion.

DISSENT

SPINA, J. (dissenting, with whom SOSMAN and CORDY, JJ., join). What is at stake in this case is not the unequal treatment of individuals or whether individual rights have been impermissibly burdened, but the power of the Legislature to effectuate social change without interference from the courts . . . . The power to regulate marriage lies with the Legislature. . . . Today, the court has transformed its role as protector of individual rights into the role of creator of rights. . . .

Issue

1. Equal protection. Although the court did not address the plaintiffs' gender discrimination claim, [the statute] does not unconstitutionally discriminate on the basis of gender. [It] enumerates certain qualifications for obtaining a marriage license. It creates no distinction between the sexes, but applies to men and women in precisely the same way. . . . [B]oth men and women are similarly limited to marrying a person of the opposite sex.

statute doesn't discriminate based on gender

Similarly, the marriage statutes do not discriminate on the basis of sexual orientation. . . . [C]onstitutional protections are extended to individuals, not couples. The marriage statutes do not disqualify individuals on the basis of sexual orientation from entering into marriage. . . . Whether an individual chooses not to marry because of sexual orientation or any other reason should be of no concern to the court.

statute doesn't discriminate based on sexual orientation

The court concludes, however, that [the statute] unconstitutionally discriminates against the individual plaintiffs because it denies them the "right to marry the person of one's choice" where that person is of the same sex. To reach this result the court relies on *Loving* . . . and transforms "choice" into the essential element of the institution of marriage. The *Loving* case did not use the word "choice" in this manner, and it did not point to the result that the court reaches today. In *Loving*, the Supreme Court . . . concluded that the [anti-miscegenation] statute was intended to preserve white supremacy and invidiously discriminated against non-Caucasians because of their race. The "choice" to which the Supreme Court referred was the "choice to marry," and it concluded that with respect to the institution of marriage, the State had no compelling interest in limiting the choice to marry along racial lines. The Supreme Court did not imply the existence of a right to marry a person of the same sex.

Loving case does not extend to same sex marriages

Unlike the [anti-miscegenation] cases, the Massachusetts Legislature has erected no barrier to marriage that intentionally discriminates against anyone. Within the institution of marriage, anyone is free to marry, with certain exceptions that are not challenged. In the absence of any discriminatory purpose, the State's marriage statutes do not violate principles of equal protection. This court should not have invoked even the most deferential standard of review within equal protection analysis because no individual was denied access to the institution of marriage.

2. Due process. The marriage statutes do not impermissibly burden a right protected by our constitutional guarantee of due process . . . . There is no

Marriage statutes do not violate due process

restriction on the right of any plaintiff to enter into marriage. Each is free to marry a willing person of the opposite sex.

. . . .

SOSMAN, J. (dissenting, with whom SPINA and CORDY, JJ., join). Based on our own philosophy of child rearing, and on our observations of the children being raised by same-sex couples to whom we are personally close, we may be of the view that what matters to children is not the gender, or sexual orientation, or even the number of the adults who raise them, but rather whether those adults provide the children with a nurturing, stable, safe, consistent, and supportive environment in which to mature. Same-sex couples can provide their children with the requisite nurturing, stable, safe, consistent, and supportive environment in which to mature, just as opposite-sex couples do. It is therefore understandable that the court might view the traditional definition of marriage as an unnecessary anachronism, rooted in historical prejudices that modern society has in large measure rejected and biological limitations that modern science has overcome.

It is not, however, our assessment that matters. Conspicuously absent from the court's opinion today is any acknowledgment that the attempts at scientific study of the ramifications of raising children in same-sex couple households are themselves in their infancy and have so far produced inconclusive and conflicting results. Notwithstanding our belief that gender and sexual orientation of parents should not matter to the success of the child rearing venture, studies to date reveal that there are still some observable differences between children raised by opposite-sex couples and children raised by same-sex couples. Interpretation of the data gathered by those studies then becomes clouded by the personal and political beliefs of the investigators . . . . Even in the absence of bias or political agenda behind the various studies of children raised by same-sex couples, the most neutral and strict application of scientific principles to this field would be constrained by the limited period of observation that has been available. Gay and lesbian couples living together openly, and official recognition of them as their children's sole parents, comprise a very recent phenomenon, and the recency of that phenomenon has not yet permitted any study of how those children fare as adults and at best minimal study of how they fare during their adolescent years. The Legislature can rationally view the state of the scientific evidence as unsettled on the critical question . . .: Are families headed by same-sex parents equally successful in rearing children . . . as families headed by parents of opposite sexes? Our belief that children raised by same-sex couples should fare the same as children raised in traditional families is just that: a passionately held but utterly untested belief. The Legislature is not required to share that belief but may . . . wish to see the proof before making a fundamental alteration to that institution.

. . . .

CORDY, J. (dissenting, with whom SPINA and SOSMAN, JJ., join).

. . . .

[T]he Legislature could conclude that redefining . . . marriage to permit same-sex couples to marry would impair the State's interest in promoting and supporting heterosexual marriage as the social institution that it has determined best normalizes, stabilizes, and links the acts of procreation and child rearing. While the plaintiffs argue that they only want to take part in the same stabilizing institution, the Legislature conceivably could conclude that permitting their participation would have the unintended effect of undermining to some degree marriage's ability to serve its social purpose.

As long as marriage is limited to opposite-sex couples who can at least theoretically procreate, society is able to communicate a consistent message to its citizens that marriage is a (normatively) necessary part of their procreative endeavor; that if they are to procreate, then society has endorsed the institution of marriage as the environment for it and for the subsequent rearing of their children; and that benefits are available explicitly to create a supportive and conducive atmosphere for those purposes. If society proceeds similarly to recognize marriages between same-sex couples who cannot procreate, it could be perceived as an abandonment of this claim, and might result in the mistaken view that civil marriage has little to do with procreation: just as the potential of procreation would not be necessary for a marriage to be valid, marriage would not be necessary for optimal procreation and child rearing to occur.[79] In essence, the Legislature could conclude that the consequence of such a policy shift would be a diminution in society's ability to steer the acts of procreation and child rearing into their most optimal setting.[80]

The court recognizes this concern, but brushes it aside with the assumption that permitting same-sex couples to marry "will not diminish the validity or dignity of opposite-sex marriage," and that "we have no doubt that marriage will continue to be a vibrant and revered institution." Whether the court is correct in its assumption is irrelevant. What is relevant is that such predicting is not the business of the courts. A rational Legislature, given the evidence, could conceivably come to a different conclusion, or could at least harbor rational concerns about possible unintended consequences of a dramatic redefinition of marriage.

There is no question that many same-sex couples are capable of being good parents, and should be (and are) permitted to be so. The policy question that

---

[79] The court contends that the exclusive and permanent commitment of the marriage partnership rather than the begetting of children is the sine qua non of civil marriage and that "the 'marriage is procreation' argument singles out the one unbridgeable difference between same-sex and opposite-sex couples, and transforms that difference into the essence of legal marriage." The court has it backward. Civil marriage is the product of society's critical need to manage procreation as the inevitable consequence of intercourse between members of the opposite sex. Procreation has always been at the root of marriage and the reasons for its existence as a social institution. Its structure . . . reflects society's judgment as how optimally to manage procreation and the resultant child rearing. The court . . . transforms the form of the structure into its purpose. In doing so, it turns history on its head.

[80] Although the marriage statute is overinclusive because it comprehends within its scope infertile or voluntarily nonreproductive opposite-sex couples, this overinclusiveness does not make the statute constitutionally infirm. The overinclusiveness . . . here is constitutionally permissible because the Commonwealth has chosen, reasonably, not to test every prospective married couple for fertility and not to demand of fertile prospective married couples whether or not they will procreate. It is satisfied, rather, to allow every couple whose biological opposition makes procreation theoretically possible to join the institution.

[handwritten margin note: Legislature should make the choice not the cts]

a legislator must resolve is a different one, and turns on an assessment of whether the marriage structure proposed by the plaintiffs will, over time . . . prove to be as stable and successful a model as the one that has formed a cornerstone of our society since colonial times, or prove to be less than optimal, and result in consequences . . . adverse to the State's legitimate interest in promoting and supporting the best possible social structure in which children should be born and raised. Given the critical importance of civil marriage as an organizing and stabilizing institution of society, it is eminently rational for the Legislature to postpone making fundamental changes to it until such time as there is unanimous scientific evidence, or popular consensus, or both, that such changes can safely be made.

. . . .

NOTES

1. *Constitutionality of Same-Sex Marriage Bans.* For over 20 years, litigants have asserted claims that exclusion of same-sex couples from marriage is unconstitutional. No attack based on the federal constitution has yet been successful. *See e.g.*, *Dean v. District of Columbia*, 653 A.2d 307 (D.C. App. 1995); *Adams v. Howerton*, 486 F. Supp. 1119 (C.D. Cal. 1980), *aff'd*, 673 F.2d 1036 (9th Cir. 1982); *cf. Shahar v. Bowers*, 836 F. Supp. 859 (N.D. Ga. 1993), *aff'd*, 114 F.3d 1097 (11th Cir. 1997) (termination of state employment after public marriage ceremony with same-sex partner did not violate employee's constitutional rights). Especially between 1986 (when the U.S. Supreme Court decided *Bowers v. Hardwick)* and 2003 (when it decided *Lawrence v. Texas*) (*Bowers* and *Lawrence* are discussed *infra* at pp. 120-22), a federal constitutional claim seemed futile. Litigants therefore focused their strategy on state constitutions.

Goodridge is the most successful such attack, though earlier state court decisions had provided at least partial victories for the claims of same-sex couples. In *Baehr v. Lewin*, 852 P. 2d 44 (Hawaii 1993), the court held that its state constitution required strict scrutiny of the same-sex marriage ban. On remand, the trial court found exclusion of same-sex couples failed strict scrutiny for lack of a compelling state interest. In response, the state constitution was amended to authorize legislative limitation of marriage to opposite-sex couples, while also establishing a new form of legally recognized relationship called "reciprocal beneficiaries." Hawaiian reciprocal beneficiaries are not provided all the tangible benefits of marriage — there are some differences. Indeed, there is no general statement in the statute that reciprocal beneficiaries are entitled to all the benefits of married couples. Instead, there is an explicit statement that "unless a particular statute explicitly states otherwise, they 'shall not have the same rights and obligations under the law that are conferred through marriage . . . .' " Note, *Developments in Law and Policy: Emerging Issues in Family Law*, 21 YALE L.& POL'Y REV. 169 (2003) (quoting statute). The Hawaiian system is discussed in Chapter 9. For an account of the Hawaii litigation, see *Symposium: Same-Sex Marriage: The Debate in Hawaii and the Nation*, 22 U. HAWAII L. REV. 1 (2000).

In 1999, the Vermont Supreme Court, in *Baker v. State*, 744 A. 2d 864 (Vt. 1999), found under the state constitution's Common Benefits Clause (similar to the federal constitution's Equal Protection Clause) that same-sex couples "may not be deprived of the statutory benefits and protections afforded persons of the opposite sex who choose to marry." Note, however, the relative narrowness of the *Baker* court's holding, which did not grant petitioners the right to get married. Later in the opinion, the court explicitly stated that the Legislature might "establish an alternative legal status to marriage for same-sex couples, impose similar formal requirements and limitations, create a parallel licensing or registration scheme, and extend all or most of the same rights and obligations provided by the law to married partners." Indeed, that was the legislature's response. While the details of the Vermont civil union statute are covered in Chapter 9, the Vermont system (mandated by *Baker*) confers on same-sex civil union partners essentially all the attributes of a married couple regarding state law issues, including, *e.g.*, a "marital" property system. (State law cannot compel federal agencies, such as the Internal Revenue Service or the Immigration and Naturalization Service, to treat civil union partners like spouses.)

The final sentence of the *Goodridge* majority opinion grants the Legislature 180 days to "take such action as it may deem appropriate in light of this opinion." While some speculated that this suggested that a civil union statute similar to Vermont's might be such "appropriate" action, the court, in a 4-3 Advisory Opinion in which the judges were arrayed identically to the original *Goodridge* decision, held that a proposed civil union statute in which same-sex partners would be granted "all the same benefits, protections, rights and responsibilities under law as are granted to spouses in a marriage" did not satisfy the state constitution. Noting that the bill would allow only same-sex couples to enter into a civil union and continue to prohibit them from marrying, the court majority wrote:

> For no rational reason the marriage laws . . . discriminate against a defined class; no amount of tinkering with language will eradicate that stain. The bill would have the effect of maintaining and fostering a stigma of exclusion that the Constitution prohibits. It would deny to same-sex "spouses" only a status that is specially recognized in society and has significant social and other advantages. The Massachusetts Constitution . . . does not permit such invidious discrimination, no matter how well intentioned.

Opinions of the Justices to the Senate, 802 N.E. 2d 565 (Mass. 2004). Plans to amend the state constitution, just as had been done in Hawaii in response to the *Baehr* opinion, were immediately announced, but the amendment process required approval by two consecutive sessions of the Legislature and approval by the voters, a process which could not be completed until 2006. Belluck, *Massachusetts Gives New Push to Gay Marriage*, N.Y. Times, Feb. 5, 2004, p. A1.

2. *Constitutional Overview of Same-Sex Marriage Prohibitions*.

a. *Sex Discrimination?* *Goodridge's* analysis under rational relationship scrutiny did not require consideration of whether same-sex marriage bans constitute sexual discrimination. While virtually all courts, including *Baker*, have rejected such a claim. *Baehr* found sex discrimination under a state constitutional provision. The argument for it depends upon what has been described as a wooden understanding of a classic racial discrimination case, *Loving v. Virginia*, 388 U.S. 1 (1967), in which the Court struck down a statute barring interracial marriage. In reaching that result, the Court rejected a state argument that its law did not discriminate racially because it treated blacks and whites alike: each could marry members of their own racial group and neither could marry members of the other group. The claim that a same-sex marriage ban is sex discrimination assumes that the only defense against such an assertion is one analogous to this rejected Virginia argument: that it is not gender discrimination because men and women suffer the same legal disability under this rule. If this defense is no good, the argument goes, then this is sex discrimination.

The Supreme Court clearly was correct in seeing the Virginia statute as motivated by racial animus and, thus, forbidden racial discrimination, despite Virginia's claim that the rule satisfied a literal test of equality. The very opposite is also clear, however, in the case of the sex-discrimination challenge to the same-sex marriage ban. While it was obvious that the purpose of the Virginia law was to maintain the social segregation of African-Americans, it is equally obvious that the purpose of the same-sex marriage ban is *not* to maintain the social segregation of men or women. It is rather to make clear that gay relationships — male or female — are different from, and less favored than, heterosexual relationships. After *Lawrence v. Texas*, discussed below, that may also be a constitutionally suspect goal. But it is not sex discrimination — discrimination based upon the fact that one is female or male. It is rather discrimination based upon one's sexual orientation.

For an article analogizing treatment of mixed-race and same-sex marriages, see Ross, *The Sexualization of Difference: A Comparison of Mixed-Race and Same-Gender Marriage,* 37 HARV. CIV. R.-CIV. LIB. L. REV. 255 (2002). Professor Ross argues that same-sex marriages have been "sexualized" by society just as mixed-race marriages were sexualized in the past. "Sexualization" means the relationships are "viewed as essentially sexual and . . . not about commitment, communication or love." Ross argues that "sexualization is a cause as well as a symptom of disempowerment" for both kinds of relationship. She also asserts defending a same-sex marriage ban on the ground that this encourages mixing of the sexes would imply that a state could also forbid individuals from marrying members of their own race in order to encourage racial mixing, a result she finds absurd.

b. *Fundamental Right to Marry?* *Zablocki* establishes that access to marriage is of fundamental federal constitutional importance. One can also argue, however, that the very definition of marriage inherent in this constitutional status assumes heterosexual unions only. The Hawaii Supreme Court in *Baehr, supra*, adopted this position, though the court accepted state constitutional arguments separate from the fundamental right approach. The *Goodridge* court, because it used rational relationship scrutiny, did not address the question of whether heightened scrutiny was appropriate because of interference with the fundamental right to marry. It did, however, as part of the remedy in the case reinterpret the concept of marriage "to mean the voluntary union of two persons as spouses, to the exclusion of all others."

c. *General Substantive Due Process.* The possibility of a substantive due process argument prevailing against the same-sex marriage ban became far more plausible after the Supreme Court's decision in *Lawrence v. Texas*, 539 U.S. 558 (2003) (reprinted and discussed more fully in Chapter 9). *Lawrence* overruled *Bowers v. Hardwick*, 478 U.S. 186 (1986), in which the Court had upheld the constitutionality of a criminal prosecution of two adult men for violation of Georgia's sodomy statute. *Bowers* defined the question before it as whether the Constitution conferred on homosexuals a fundamental right to engage in sodomy. *Lawrence* is important because it redefined the question.

> To say that the issue in *Bowers* was simply the right to engage in certain sexual conduct demeans the claim . . ., just as it would demean a married couple were it to be said marriage is simply about the right to have sexual intercourse. The laws involved in *Bowers* and here are, to be sure, statutes that purport to do no more than prohibit a particular sexual act. Their penalties and purposes, though, have more far-reaching consequences, touching upon the most private human conduct, sexual behavior, and in the most private of places, the home. The statutes . . . seek to control a personal relationship that, whether or not entitled to formal recognition in the law, is within the liberty of persons to choose without being punished as criminals.
>
> . . .
>
> When homosexual conduct is made criminal . . ., that declaration in and of itself is an invitation to subject homosexual persons to discrimination both in the public and in the private spheres. . . . *Bowers'* . . . continuance as precedent demeans the lives of homosexual persons. [¶] . . . . The [criminal defendants] are entitled to respect for their private lives. The State cannot demean their existence or control their destiny by making their private sexual conduct a crime. Their right to liberty under the Due Process Clause gives them the full right to engage in their conduct without intervention of the government. "It is a promise of the Constitution that there is a realm of personal liberty which the government may not enter." [Quoting *Casey*]. The Texas statute furthers no legitimate state interest which can justify its intrusion into the personal and private life of the individual.

Does the ban on same-sex marriage demean the existence of homosexuals and deprive them of respect for their private lives? If so, does it further a legitimate state interest sufficiently important to justify the ban? Analysis of these questions must surely be informed by *Zablocki* which teaches marriage is a core part of an individual's private life protected from unjustified state regulation. The combination of *Zablocki* and *Lawrence* could suggest that government may not justify a ban on same-sex marriage with the goal of demeaning, discouraging or controlling the private lives of homosexuals. It must offer some other purpose for excluding their relationships from the advantages sought by persons who marry.

What is the other purpose and is it adequate?

Despite the apparently powerful arguments available in any challenge to the same-sex marriage ban, most commentators would be surprised if the Court accepted them, at least in the near future. Justice O'Connor, concurring in *Lawrence*, made clear she would distinguish and reject a constitutional challenge to the gay marriage ban. Justice Kennedy, speaking for the other five Justices in the majority, was more circumspect. He wrote only that *Lawrence* "does not involve whether the government must give formal recognition to any relationship that homosexual persons seek to enter." The matter, in other words, was reserved, not decided (this is the conclusion drawn by the *Goodridge* majority about *Lawrence*'s treatment of the same-sex marriage question). The majority thus made clear it was not committed to finding homosexuals have a right to marry and, by going out of its way to announce this, might have been hinting that the decision, when made, will be against same-sex marriage. Alternatively, this language may simply express political prudence. Finally, perhaps the choice of language — "any relationship" — suggests future adoption of the *Baker* approach: rejecting a demand for state recognition of same-sex "marriage," but requiring the state to make available to gay couples an alternative form of legal status substantially equivalent to marriage in terms of benefits accorded those who choose it.

Writing for the *Lawrence* dissenters, Justice Scalia argued the majority's

> reasoning leaves on pretty shaky grounds state laws limiting marriage to opposite-sex couples. Justice O'Connor seeks to preserve them by the conclusory statement that "preserving the traditional institution of marriage" is a legitimate state interest. But "preserving the traditional institution of marriage" is just a kinder way of describing the State's *moral disapproval* of same-sex couples. Texas' interest in [eliminating homosexual sodomy] could be recast in similarly euphemistic terms: "preserving the traditional sexual mores of our society." (emphasis in original).

Is it possible there might be state interests insufficient to justify criminal punishment, but sufficient to validate refusal of a state to offer its symbol of legitimacy to a relationship it didn't approve of?

3. *More on the Interests of Gay Couples*. As discussed in the notes following *Zablocki*, marriage is surely a symbol. Persons enter marriage to symbolize love and commitment to one another and they usually want others, including the state, to accept and acknowledge their marriage. One might therefore argue that the couple's most important interest is the symbolic one of state recognition, especially because the alternative rule — a ban on same-sex marriage — is not merely neutral, but an affirmative denigration of the relationship, at least in comparison with heterosexual families. Symbolic interests may seem unimportant to some, yet in human relationships they are often crucial. As the *Zablocki* notes point out, they seem to be an important part of the fundamental right recognized in that case. To the extent the symbolic issue is key, the *Baker* solution — the marriage alternative — falls short by continuing to affirm that same-sex relationships are different from, and in some sense less than, heterosexual relationships. The *Goodridge* majority's Advisory Opinion makes it clear that the symbol of marriage has importance independent of the tangible benefits of the status.

Of course, symbolic interests are not the entire story. In *What If? The Legal Consequences of Marriage and the Legal Needs of Lesbian and Gay Male Couples*, 95 MICH. L. REV. 447 (1996), Professor David Chambers concludes the laws assigning consequences to marriage today have much more coherence than has been commonly recognized, largely falling within three sorts of regulation; that each of these three sorts of regulation would, as a whole, fit the needs of long-term gay male and lesbian couples; that while the law has changed in recent years to recognize nonmarital relationships in a variety of contexts, the number of significant distinctions resting on marital status remains large and durable; that in some significant respects the remaining distinctive laws of marriage are better suited to the life situations of same-sex couples than they are to those of the opposite-sex couples for whom they were devised; and, most broadly, that the package of rules relating to marriage, while problematic in some details and unduly exclusive in some regards, are a just response by the state to the circumstances of persons who live together in enduring, emotionally based attachments. Legal marriage, somewhat surprisingly to a person long dubious of the state's regulation of nonviolent private relationships, has much to be said for it.

Id. at pp. 447–48. Professor Chambers' three categories are: (1) "regulations that recognize emotional attachments" (including those giving spouses decisionmaking authority when a person is incompetent, intestacy laws, family leave laws); (2) "regulations dealing with parenting" (laws dealing with stepparent status, surrogacy and the new technology of reproduction and adoption and foster care); (3) "laws regulating the economic relationships of couples or between the couple and the state" (including tax laws, property division and maintenance laws, forced share statutes). These are of course precisely the kinds of regulations that Vermont makes available to same-sex couples who enter civil unions. The question is whether this is an adequate response to the constitutional claim.

4. *More on the State's Interests.* Lynn Wardle, who opposes recognizing same-sex relationships, has offered this summary of "important public interests in and social purposes" supporting that position:

. . . . These include (1) safe sexual relations; (2) responsible procreation; (3) optimal child rearing; (4) healthy human development; (5) protecting those who undertake the most vulnerable family roles for the benefit of society, especially wives and mothers; (6) securing the stability and integrity of the basic unit of society; (7) fostering civic virtue, democracy, and social order; and (8) facilitating interjurisdictional compatibility.

On the basis of history and common experience across cultures, advocates of preserving marriage exclusively for male-female couples may reasonably assert that committed heterosexual unions we call marriages make unique and important contributions to achieving the public and social purposes of marriage. [H]eterosexual . . . marriage seem[s] to provide the best setting for the safest and most beneficial expression of sexual intimacy. [It] also appears to provide the best environment into which children can be born. Heterosexual marriage reasonably may be assumed to provide the most advantageous environment in which children can be reared, providing profound benefits of dual gender parenting to model intergender relations and show children how to relate to persons of their own and the opposite gender. [It] has been believed to provide the most enriching and liberating relationship to facilitate human adults to personally develop and achieve their fullest potential. . . . [I]t has long been believed that heterosexual marriage provides the best security for those who take the greatest risks and invest the greatest personal effort in establishing and maintaining families, especially wives and mothers. [It] appears to provide the strongest and most stable companionate unit of society, and the most secure setting for intergenerational transmission of social knowledge and skills, and reflects the understanding of marriage that has been constant across cultures and throughout history.

Wardle, *"Multiply and Replenish": Considering Same-Sex Marriage in Light of State Interests in Marital Procreation,* 24 HARV. J. L. & PUB. POL'Y 771 (2001).

Review Wardle's list carefully. Many of the interests he identifies assume certain facts. Do you think there is in fact agreement on the facts he assumes? (*E.g.*, would a gay person agree that for him or her, a heterosexual union would "provide the most enriching and liberating relationship to facilitate human adults to personally develop and achieve their fullest potential"? Or, assuming it is true that heterosexual marriages are a more stable "companionate unit" than same-sex relationships, is it possible that this is a *consequence* of our refusal to recognize same-sex relationships, rather than a *reason* for refusing?). Perhaps even more importantly, a state interest is relevant to the constitutional analysis only if recognition of same-sex marriage would somehow place it in jeopardy. Opponents of same-sex marriage seem to assume that its recognition would necessarily burden heterosexual marriage. But does that necessarily follow? Could it possibly follow? It may not be possible to offer any arguments in response to these questions, on either side, that many on the other side would credit. The final question is how much deference should then be given to the legislature's answer.

5. *Conflict Within the Gay/Lesbian Community*. The gay and lesbian community is not united in its view of same-sex marriage. Professor William Eskridge has stated

same-sex marriage is good for gay people and good for America and for the same reason: it civilizes gays and it civilizes America. . . . For most of the twentieth century, lesbians, gay men, and bisexuals have been outlaws. The law relevant to us was the criminal code. . . . The law relevant to us today is found in the civil code. . . . Virtually no one in the gay and lesbian community would deny that this "civilizing" shift in the law reflects enormous progress and that such progress is incomplete until gay people enjoy the same rights and responsibilities as straight people. Marriage is the most important right the state has to offer. . . . As a formal matter, law's civilizing movement will not be complete until the same-sex married couple replaces the outlawed sodomite. . . . [Additionally], [t]his country would be edified — civilized, if you will — if it would end all vestiges of legal discrimination against its homosexual population. Essential to this project is the adoption of laws guaranteeing rights for lesbian and gay couples.

ESKRIDGE, THE CASE FOR SAME-SEX MARRIAGE 8, 10 (1996); *see also* Wolfson, *Crossing the Threshhold: Equal Marriage Rights for Lesbians and Gay Men and the Intra-Community Critique*, 21 NYU REV. L.& SOC. CHANGE 567 (1994) (supporting litigation attacking state marriage entry regulations).

Others prefer to oppose the institution of marriage altogether:

> For lesbians, the abolition of marriage would mean that our relationships would not be in a different legal category from other legal relationships. . . . [T]he state would not relate to its citizens on the basis of their intimate relations. . . . Abolishing marriage would also mean that a nation could not resort to formalistic legal relations to determine the rights of its citizens.

ROBSON, SAPPHO GOES TO LAW SCHOOL 146, 149–50 (1998); *see also* Warner, *Normal and Normaller: Beyond Gay Marriage*, 5 GLQ: A JOURNAL OF LESBIAN AND GAY STUDIES 119, 121 (1999) ("If reform of marriage was the goal [of those seeking legalization of same-sex marriage], the tactics of legal advocacy have not worked; in some way they have made the problem worse. . . . [N]ow that the ship has run aground, we might ask whether it was headed in the right direction.") Polikoff, *We Will Get What We Ask For: Why Legalizing Gay and Lesbian Marriage Will Not "Dismantle the Legal Structure of Gender in Every Marriage,"* 79 VA. L. REV. 1535, 1536 (1993) ("the desire to marry in the lesbian and gay community is an attempt to mimic the worst of mainstream society, an effort to fit into an inherently problematic institution that betrays the promise of both lesbian and gay liberation and radical feminism"); Note, *Against Marriage*, 29 HARV. CIV. R.-CIV. LIB. L. REV. 507, 530 (1994) ("[m]arriage is not the same thing as love. For their part, heterosexuals have shown us what marriage is worth and how long it lasts. . . .[W]e have learned from our outlaw status a great deal about love — what it is worth, and how long it lasts. Rather than accept the narrowness under which heterosexuals themselves chafe, why not invite them to share in what we know . . .? . . . . Let them come to us.).

6. *Changing Religious Views on Same-Sex Marriage?* Beginning in the mid-1980s a number of religious groups have endorsed the concept of same-sex relationships, either in marriage or quasi-marriage. For example, in 1984, the Unitarian Universalist Association General Assembly, the governing body of the Unitarian Church, affirmed "the growing practices of some of its ministers of conducting services of union of gay and lesbian couples and urges member societies to support their ministers in this important aspect of our movement's ministry to the gay and lesbian community." *Unitarians Make U.S. History, Acknowledge Gay Marriages*, SAN DIEGO UNION-TRIBUNE, June 29, 1984, p. A-4. Likewise, the Central Conference of American (Reform) Rabbis, in 1996 endorsed legally-recognized marriage for same-sex couples. *See* Wallach, *Who Among Us Fit to Judge Same-Sex Marriages?*, HOUSTON CHRONICLE, Apr. 22, 1996, p. 19. The group followed this in 2000 by affirming that "gay relationships [are] 'worthy of affirmation' through Jewish ritual and that Reform rabbis who decided to officiate at same-sex ceremonies would have the support" of the Conference. Niebuhr, *Reform Rabbis Back Blessing of Gay Unions*, N.Y. TIMES, March 30, 2000, p. A1.

The Reconstructionist Rabbinical Association (representing a movement with over 100 congregations in North America) has adopted a similar position. Alpert, *Religious Liberty, Same-Sex Marriage, and the Case of Reconstructionist Judaism* in GOD FORBID: RELIGION AND SEX IN AMERICAN PUBLIC LIFE (2000). The United Church of Christ permits its ministers to perform same-sex unions. Kloehn, *Protestants Face Schism on Homosexuality; Many Mainline Denominations Beset with Rifts on Gay Issues*, CHICAGO TRIB., May 3, 1999, p.1. Similarly, the Christian Church (Disciples of Christ) has "voted to allow same-sex unions." *Disciples D.C. Church Oks Same-Sex Unions*, CHRISTIAN CENTURY, December 18–31, 2002, p. 16. A major American Buddhist group, Soka Gakkai, which claims 300,000 followers in the United States also has decided to "support the [same-sex] couple in expressing their commitment" and the head monk at a California Buddhist Meditation Center reported having performed ten same-sex weddings even before the formal acceptance of the concept by the organization. Dart, *For Buddhists, Gay Marriage is as Holy as Any Other Kind*, L.A. TIMES, July 1, 1995, at p. B11. The Metropolitan Community Churches, whose membership is predominantly gay and lesbian, report performing approximately 6,000 same-sex marriages annually. Whitaker, *Gay Couples Pop Big Question, But the States' Reply is the Same*, N.Y. TIMES, Feb. 15, 2003, p. 15. An article in 2004 reports that clergy are "seeing a growing number of religiously observant gay couples who are sidestepping the debate over legal rights and seeking to consecrate their unions in churches and synagogues." Goodstein, *Gay Couples Seek Unions in God's Eyes*, N.Y. TIMES, January 30, 2004, p. A1. As one participant stated, "[w]e didn't want it to be like going to a justice of the peace or anything. We would be more concerned about breaking vows we'd promised to God than to some guy in a suit."

Support for same-sex marriage is not limited to the smaller religious groups in the country. "Interestingly, clerical sympathy for same-sex marriage exists in denominations that have most fervently opposed same-sex unions." ESKRIDGE, THE CASE FOR SAME-SEX MARRIAGE 102 (1996) (identifying fundamentalist and Roman Catholic clergy who officiate at same-sex weddings); *see also* Rotello, *To Have and to Hold: The Case for Gay Marriage*, THE NATION, June 24, 1996, p. 11 (reporting "religious groups have been faster on the draw [than liberal political groups]; also cited are "many Quaker and Buddhist denominations and many individual Protestant congregations, Episcopal bishops and high-ranking clerics of many faiths"); *Rebuked Pastor Plans More Same-Sex Rites*, CHRISTIAN CENTURY, May 17, 2003, p. 15 (reporting Presbyterian minister's insistence on performing weddings for same-sex couples despite Presbyterian Church (U.S.A.) position that such ceremonies should not be designated weddings).

7. *Public Opinion on Same-Sex Unions*. Public opinion on the question has undergone enormous change in recent decades. In 1977, The Gallup Organization first asked a national sample whether "homosexual relations between consenting adults should or should not be legal?" Americans were evenly split, with 43% on each side of the question and 14% undecided. In

May, 2003, 60% of the sample favored legalization with 35% opposed and 5% undecided. Newport, *Six in Ten Americans Agree That Gay Sex Should Be Legal*, THE GALLUP POLL NEWS RELEASES (June 27, 2003). Not only is acceptance broadening in the general population, but much of the support is concentrated on the younger generation. In the 2003 survey, 66% of 18-to 29-year-olds and 65% of those between 30 and 49 favored legalization. *Id.* Perhaps not surprisingly, support for legalization varied across different regions of the country. Only 49% of respondents in the South favored legalization, while support in the West was 73%. Howlett, *Attitudes on Gay Relations Tied to Demographics*, USA TODAY, June 27, 2003, p. 6A. Legalization was favored by college graduates (71%), those earning more than $75,000 (72%) and those reporting they seldom attend religious services (76%). *Id.*

In response to the question of whether "homosexuality should be considered an acceptable alternative lifestyle," the 2003 poll reported 54% found it acceptable with 43% opposed. This compares with 34% and 51%, respectively, in a 1982 survey posing the same question. Newport, *supra.* Interestingly, though, the 2003 survey reported a majority of Americans (52%–44%) continued to find homosexual behavior to be "morally wrong."

Attitudes toward same-sex marriage are less accepting. A 1994 poll reported almost 40% of the American public believe "homosexuals should have equal rights to marry one another." The same survey reported that 56% of respondents between the ages of 18 and 29 agreed with the statement as did 42% of those between 30 and 39. *Homosexual Unions*, THE AMERICAN ENTERPRISE, Vol. 6, July, 1995, at p. 106 (reporting results from ABC/Washington Post poll). A 1996 Gallup Poll, however, found only 27% of the national sample approved of legalization of same-sex marriages. Moore, *Public Opposes Gay Marriage*, THE GALLUP POLL MONTHLY, April 1996, at pp. 19, 21. The same poll showed greater acceptance for same-sex marriages among young people (41% among those between 18 and 29 and 30% in the group between 30 and 49). The poll also found women generally much more accepting of gay marriage than men (33% vs. 20%). *Id.* A 2003 poll conducted immediately after *Lawrence*, found 39% supporting same-sex marriage, with 61% of those between 18-29 supporting the concept, but only 37% of those between 30-49 favoring it. Jones, *Young Adults Back Gay Marriages*, USA TODAY, July 1, 2003, p. 8A.

There has been a dramatic shift in Americans' understanding of whether homosexuality is "something a person is born with or . . . due to factors such as upbringing or environment." "In 1977, when the question was first asked in a Gallup poll, 56% of the public said that homosexuality was environmental, while only 13% said it was genetic." Newport, *Some Change Over Time in American Attitudes Toward Homosexuality, But Negativity Remains*, THE GALLUP POLL MONTHLY, March 1999, at p. 28. In the May 2003 survey, only 44% of the respondents saw homosexuality as the product of upbringing and environment and 38% believed it was something one was "born with." Newport, *Six in Ten Americans Agree That Gay Sex Should Be Legal*, THE GALLUP POLL NEWS RELEASES (June 27, 2003). Perhaps as the public comes to believe homosexuality is genetically-determined, it may find it unfair to exclude same-sex couples from the institution of marriage.

8. Same-Sex Unions in Other Countries. In the spring of 2003, the Canadian Cabinet announced plans to seek federal legislation authorizing same-sex marriage. Krauss, *Canadian Leaders Agree to Propose Gay Marriage Law*, N.Y. TIMES, June 18, 2003, p. A1. This was in the wake of decisions in three Canadian provinces declaring the same-sex marriage ban unconstitutional under the federal Charter of Rights and Freedoms. The decisions were rendered by the Quebec Superior Court, the British Columbia Court of Appeal and the Ontario Court of Appeal. *See Halpern v. Canada (Attorney General)*, 2003 Ont. C.A. LEXIS 271 (June 10); *EGALE Canada Inc. v. Canada (Attorney General)*, 2003 BCCA 251 (May 1); *Quebec Gays Hail Court Ruling*, TORONTO STAR, September 7, 2002, p. A9. The Ontario decision said that by refusing to accept same-sex marriages, the law "offends the dignity of persons in same-sex relations." Because there is no residency requirement for a Canadian marriage license, a significant number of same-sex couples from the United States likely will travel north to marry. The legal efficacy of such marriages in the United States is considered below in the Notes on Conflict of Law and Marriage Regulation.

Two European nations permit same-sex couples to marry. The Belgian Parliament overwhelmingly passed a new law in early 2003. Simons, *Belgium: Parliament Approves Gay Marriage*, N.Y. TIMES, January 31, 2003, p. A6. Under the Belgian law, such marriages can be contracted by foreigners, but partners in such a marriage cannot adopt children. In 2001, the Netherlands became the first country to authorize same-sex marriage. Richburg, *Gay Partners Make It Official; Same-Sex Couples are First to Marry Under Dutch Law*, WASH. POST, April 1, 2001, p. A21. The Dutch law grants same-sex couples all rights possessed by opposite-sex couples. Only Dutch residents or those of other countries authorizing same-sex marriages, however, are eligible to enter such marriages.

Many other countries have adopted domestic partnership or civil union legislation under which same-sex couples may gain most of the legal rights of married couples. Such legislation has been enacted in Denmark, Norway, Sweden, Iceland, Finland, Hungary, France, Germany and Portugal. *See* MERIN, EQUALITY FOR SAME-SEX COUPLES: THE LEGAL RECOGNITION OF GAY PARTNERSHIPS IN EUROPE AND THE UNITED STATES (2002); LEGAL RECOGNITION OF SAME-SEX PARTNERSHIPS (Wintemute & Andenaes eds. 2001); Note, *Developments — The Law of Marriage and Family*, 116 HARV. L. REV. 1996, 2004–27 (2003).

9. *Literature on Same-Sex Marriage*. There is a rich literature dealing with same-sex marriage from many different perspectives. In a provocative application of economic analysis, Professor Jennifer Brown argued that New Mexico and Vermont both had strong incentives to become "first movers." Based on assumptions about the country's gay and lesbian population, expected wedding-related expenditures and the marriage rate among the gay population, in 1995 she estimated the "present value of the revenue to be generated by the first state than legalizes same-sex marriage is at least $3 billion to $4 billion." Brown, *Competitive Federalism and the Legislative Incentives to Recognize Same-Sex Marriage*, 68 S. CAL. L. REV. 745 (1995). For other recent articles, see Backer, *Religion as the Language of Discourse of Same Sex Marriage*, 30 CAP. U.L. REV. 221 (2002); Donovan, *Rock-Salting the Slippery Slope: Why Same-Sex Marriage is Not a Commitment to Polygamous Marriage*, 29 N. KY. L. REV. 521 (2002); Note, *Defending Marriage: A*

Litigation Strategy to Oppose Same-Sex "Marriage," 14 REGENT U.L. REV. 487 (2001-2); Ross, *Sex, Marriage and History: Analyzing the Continued Resistance to Same-Sex Marriage*, 55 SMU L. REV. 1657 (2002); Culhane, *A Tale of Two Concurrences: Same-Sex Marriage and Products Liability*, 7 WM. & MARY J. WOMEN & L. 447 (2001); Linton, *Same-Sex "Marriage" Under State Equal Rights Amendments*, 46 ST. LOUIS L.J. 909 (2002); Becker, *Family Law in the Secular State and Restriction on Same-Sex Marriage: Two are Better Than One*, 2001 U. ILL. L. REV. 1; Sparling, *All in the Family: Recognizing the Unifying Potential of Same-Sex Marriage*, 10 LAW & SEX. 187 (2001); Bradley, *Same-Sex Marriage: Our Final Answer?*, 13 NOTRE DAME J. L. ETHICS & PUB. POL'Y 729 (2000); Wriggins, *Marriage Law and Family Law: Anatomy, Interdependence, and Couples of the Same Gender*, 41 B.C. L. REV. 265 (2000).

10. *Marriage Involving a Transsexual.* In *M.T. v. J.T.,* 355 A.2d 204 (N.J. App. 1976), the court held valid a marriage in which the wife had been born with male sex organs, but had them surgically removed and replaced with a vagina and labia "adequate for sexual intercourse." The husband was aware of (and funded) the surgery, so fraud was not an issue. The court held the transsexual had "become physically and psychologically unified and fully capable of sexual activity consistent with her reconciled sexual attributes of gender and anatomy. Consequently, plaintiff should be considered a member of the female sex for marital purposes." Similarly, a Florida trial court in 2003 upheld a marriage between a woman and a female-to-male transsexual who had undergone sex reassignment surgery before the ceremony. *Kantaras v. Kantaras,* 29 FAM. L. REP. 1195 (Fla. Cir. Ct., Feb. 21, 2003). In an 809-page opinion, the trial judge granted the husband a divorce and custody of the two children (one was the product of artificial insemination of the wife and the other was her child by a prior relationship and adopted by husband). The judge held the gender designated on a person's birth certificate "may be relevant but is not . . . dispositive." *But see In re Application for a Marriage License*, 2003 Ohio App. Lexis 6513 (holding amended Massachusetts birth certificate of transsexual could be ignored under the public policy exception to the Full Faith and Credit clause; upholding refusal to permit post-surgery male to marry female); *In re Estate of Gardiner,* 42 P. 3d 120 (Kan. 2002) (rejecting petition to be administrator of estate; court held sex reassignment surgery four years prior to marriage to decedent was legally ineffective to change sex; petitioner did not "fit the common meaning of female"); *J. v. S-T*, THE INDEPENDENT, Nov. 26, 1996 (English Court of Appeal affirmed refusal to grant alimony-like claim in annulment action by party who deceived partner during 17-year relationship concerning status as female-to-male transsexual); *In re Ladrach,* 32 Ohio Misc. 2d 6 (Prob. 1987) (concluding "sex is determined at birth," court denied marriage license to male and post-operative transsexual female). *See* Comment, *Transsexualism as Metaphor: The Collision of Sex and Gender*, 43 BUFF. L. REV. 835 (1995).

NOTES ON CONFLICT OF LAW AND MARRIAGE REGULATION

1. *General Rule*. In a mobile society with 50 states, each able to enact marriage entry regulations, conflict of laws questions often arise regarding a marriage's validity. As noted above in the common law marriage materials, the general rule is that a "marriage is valid everywhere if valid under the law of the state where the marriage takes place." SCOLES & HAY, CONFLICT OF LAWS § 13.5 (2d ed. 1992); RESTATEMENT, SECOND, CONFLICT OF LAWS § 283(2) (1971). The strongest rationale for this *lex loci* rule is the validation principle. That is, because the parties getting married intend that status and often have traveled to a place where the marriage is permitted, the law should treat them as being married.

There are two exceptions to this general rule. One is a public policy exception under which the forum state where the marriage's validity is being litigated finds that the marriage offends a deeply-held public policy of the forum. *See* D'Amato, *Conflict of Laws Rules and the Interstate Recognition of Same-Sex Marriages*, 1995 U. ILL. L. REV. 911; RESTATEMENT (SECOND) CONFLICTS OF LAWS § 283(2) (state can ignore marriage if "it violates the strong public policy of [a state] which had the most significant relationship to the spouses and the marriage at the time of the marriage"); *New York v. Ezeonu*, 588 N.Y.S.2d 116 (Sup. Ct. 1992) (refusing to recognize polygamous marriage contracted in Nigeria); *but see Mason v. Mason*, 775 N.E. 2d 706 (Ind. App. 2002) (rejecting claim that Tennessee marriage between cousins violated Indiana public policy); *Leszinske v. Poole,* 798 P.2d 1049 (N.M. App. 1990) (recognizing woman's Costa Rican marriage to her uncle; local law voiding such a marriage as incestuous found not to express strong public policy).

2. *Evasion of Domicile Law*. The other exception to the *lex loci* rule applies when a domiciliary goes to another state for the purpose of avoiding the strictures of the home state's marriage law. R. WEINTRAUB, COMMENTARY ON THE CONFLICT OF LAWS § 5.1A (4th ed. 2001). Some states refuse to recognize marriages contracted out of state by their own domiciliaries which violate the home state's marriage law. *See* ARIZ. REV. STATS. § 25-112(C) (2000); GA CODE § 19-3-43 (1999); *In re Estate of Toutant*, 633 N.W. 2d 692 (Wis. App. 2001) (applying statute refusing to recognize any marriage contracted in state or out of state within 6 months of divorce regardless of where the divorce occurred).

In 1912, the National Conference of Commissioners on Uniform State Laws promulgated the Uniform Marriage Evasion Act. Under the Act a marriage which was void under home state law would also be void if contracted elsewhere. The statute, however, was never broadly adopted and was withdrawn in 1943. Hovermill, *A Conflict of Laws and Morals: The Choice of Law Implications of Hawaii's Recognition of Same-Sex Marriages*, 53 MD. L. REV. 450, 455–56 (1994). The Conference' subsequent Model Marriage and Divorce Act omits any such provision, instead adopting the general *lex loci* rule. M.M.D.A. § 210.

3. *Marriage Invalid Where Performed*. While most marriages are valid in the state where the wedding takes place, what if the marriage is invalid where performed but valid in the domiciliary state? Some cases hold such a marriage invalid under the *lex loci* rule. *See, e.g., Hudson Trail Outfitters v. Dep't of Employment Services*, 801 A.2d 987 (D.C. App. 2002)(ignoring Nicaragua wedding not registered according to law); *Police & Firemen's Disability and Pension Fund v. Redding,* 2002 Ohio 3891 (App.) (rejecting asserted common law marriage contracted in a non-recognizing state); *Farah v. Farah*, 429 S.E.2d 626 (Va. App. 1993) (refusing to recognize proxy marriage which would be void in England where performed). The RESTATEMENT (2D) OF CONFLICTS, § 283, Comment (*I*), however, suggests that the "fact that a marriage does not comply with the requirements of the state where it was contracted should not therefore inevitably lead to the conclusion that the marriage is invalid." It suggests instead that the marriage be recognized "unless the intensity of the interest of the state where the marriage was contracted in having its invalidating rule applied outweighs the policy of protecting the expectations of the parties . . . and the interest of the other state with the validating rule." In suggesting how to gauge the "intensity" of the state interests involved, the Restatement continues

> The state where the marriage was contracted has a substantial interest in having persons who marry within its territory comply with its local requirements as to formalities at least to the extent that these requirements are mandatory. . . .

> The state where the marriage was contracted will probably have no similar interest in the application to a marriage between non-residents of such of its marriage rules as do not relate to formalities. So . . . there would seem to be little reason to invalidate a marriage between first cousins by application of a rule of the state where the marriage was contracted if such a marriage would be valid under the local law of the state where the parties were domiciled both before and immediately following their marriage. . . .

See also Donlann v. Macgurn, 55 P. 3d 74 (Ariz. App. 2002) (recognizing Mexican marriage performed by unauthorized person on grounds that domestic law would recognize the marriage); *In re Estate of Banks*, 629 N.E.2d 1223 (Ill. App. 1994) (upholding bigamous marriage contracted in Arkansas because impediment was later removed, even though its removal would not validate the marriage in Arkansas).

4. ***Defense of Marriage Act.*** Article IV, § 1 of the United States Constitution provides:

> Full Faith and Credit shall be given in each State to the public Acts, Records, and judicial Proceedings of every other State. And the Congress may by general Laws prescribe the Manner in which such Acts, Records and Proceedings shall be proved, and the Effect thereof.

In 1996, responding to speculation that the Full Faith and Credit Clause's first sentence might require all states to recognize a same-sex marriage legally contracted in one state (at that time, Hawaii seemed about to legalize such marriages) the Congress passed the Defense of Marriage Act (DOMA), relying on its authority under the Clause's second sentence. The first of DOMA's two substantive provisions, codified at 28 U.S.C.S. § 1738C (2000), provides:

> No State . . . shall be required to give effect to any public act, record or judicial proceeding of any other State . . . respecting a relationship between persons of the same sex that is treated as a marriage under the laws of such other State . . . or a right or claim arising from such relationship.

This legislation retroactively authorized a wave of then-recent state legislation which refused recognition of any legal same-sex marriages. *See, e.g.*, ALASKA STAT. § 25.05.013 (2002) ("A marriage entered into by persons of the same sex . . . that is recognized by another state . . . is void in this state, and contractual rights granted by virtue of the marriage, including its termination, are unenforceable in this state"); IDAHO CODE § 32-209 (1996) ("[Marriages valid where performed are valid in this state] unless they violate the public policy of this state. Marriages that violate the public policy of this state include, but are not limited to, same-sex marriages. . . .").

As of 2003, a total of 38 states had passed such statutes or constitutional provisions (often referred to as "state DOMA's"), including at least one which extended non-recognition to same-sex couples in "a civil union, domestic partnership or other similar same-sex relationship. . . ." NEB. CONST. Art. 1, § 29 (2002): Elliott, *Same-Sex Measure Easily Clears House; Perry is Expected to Sign Bill into Law*, HOUSTON CHRONICLE, May 1, 2003, at p. A27.

It is not clear whether Congressional permission to ignore a legal same-sex marriage contracted in another state is, on the one hand, necessary in light of the Supreme Court's interpretation of the Full Faith and Credit clause or, on the other hand, whether the Clause empowers Congress to do so. As for its necessity, it is not clear that marriages are "public Acts, Records, [or] judicial Proceedings" in the language of the Full Faith and Credit Clause. Silberman, *Can the Island of Hawaii Bind the World? A Comment on Same-Sex Marriage and Federalism Values*, 16 QUINNIPIAC L. REV. 191, 192–96 (1996) (noting that the Supreme Court has long distinguished, under the Full Faith and Credit Clause, the respect due to other states' laws and other states' judicial judgments). Even if marriages conducted under another state's laws are covered by the Clause, there is Supreme Court authority for the existence of a public policy exception to the Clause, *see Nevada v. Hall*, 440 U.S. 410 (1979), which might permit a second state to ignore a valid same-sex marriage in another state. *But see Baker v. General Motors*, 522 U.S. 222 (1998) (casting doubt on the existence of such an exception); Kramer, *Same-Sex Marriage, Conflict of Laws, and the Unconstitutional Public Policy Exception*, 106 YALE L.J. 1965 (1997). On the other hand, one can argue that under *Lawrence v. Texas* (discussed *supra* at pp. 120-22) a state may not single out for condemnation otherwise valid marriages involving a same-sex couple legally married in another state. Indeed, the same argument can be used to support a claim that DOMA itself is unconstitutional.

To sample literature on the Act's constitutionality and related issues, see Note, *Developments —The Law of Marriage and Family*, 116 HARV. L. REV. 1996, 2028–51 (2003) (examining constitutional constraints on interstate same-sex marriage recognition); Note, *The Malleable Use of History in Substantive Due Process Jurisprudence: How the "Deeply Rooted" Test Should Not Be a Barrier to Finding the Defense of Marriage Act Unconstitutional Under the Fifth Amendment's Due Process Clause*, 44 B.C. L. REV. 177 (2002); Whitten, *Exporting and Importing Domestic Partnerships: Some Conflict-of-Laws Questions and Concerns*, 2001 B.Y.U. L. REV. 1235; Strasser, *Some Observations About DOMA, Marriages, Civil Unions, and Domestic Partnerships*, 30 CAP. U.L. REV. 363 (2001); Ryan, *Love and Let Love: Same-Sex*

Marriage, Past, Present, and Future, and the Constitutionality of DOMA, 22 U. HAWAII L. REV.185 (2000); Strasser, Loving *the* Romer *Out of* Baehr: *On Acts in Defense of Marriage and the Constitution*, 58 U. PITT. L. REV. 279 (1997); Estin, *When* Baehr *Meets* Romer: *Family Law Issues After Amendment 2*, 68 COLORADO L. REV. 349, 370 (1997); Eskridge, *Credit is Due*, THE NEW REPUBLIC, June 17, 1996, at p. 11 ("Unless the Defense of Marriage Act merely implements a valid public policy exception, it raises grave constitutional concerns"); Statement of Professor Cass R. Sunstein, *Hearing Before the Senate Judiciary Committee on S. 1740*, July 11, 1996, at pp. 42–48 (enabling clause may only give Congress "affirmative" power to insure inter-state recognition of other states' actions, but not "negative" power to authorize non-recognition by other states).

What about same-sex marriages validly contracted in a foreign country? (*See* Note 8 following *Goodridge, supra*). The Full Faith and Credit Clause does not cover foreign laws or judgments. Applicable instead is the principle of "comity," which the Supreme Court has defined as "the recognition which one nation allows within its territory to the legislative, executive or judicial acts of another nation, having due regard both to international duty and convenience, and to the rights of its own citizens or of other persons who are under the protection of its laws." *Hilton v. Guyot*, 159 U.S. 113, 164 (1895); *see also* Yntema, *The Comity Doctrine*, 65 MICH. L. REV. 9 (1966) (tracing comity back to the seventeenth century in the Netherlands). While there has been no litigation on this point, it would seem that a state without a DOMA provision would be more likely to extend comity to a valid foreign same-sex marriage than a state in which a public policy against such marriages had been expressed legislatively.

The federal DOMA's second provision, codified at 1 U.S.C. § 7 (2000), defines "marriage" and "spouse" for purposes of federal legislation, administrative rulings and regulations as follows:

the word "marriage" means only a legal union between one man and one woman as husband and wife, and the word "spouse" refers only to a person of the opposite sex who is a husband or a wife.

While Congress would seem to be able to define particular words as it chooses, this portion of the legislation might also be subject to attack on the ground that *Lawrence* prohibits a definition of marriage which excludes same-sex marriages. Assuming its constitutionality, this provision would be an obstacle to an American citizen, having contracted a legal same-sex marriage in another country, obtaining immediate relative treatment for his or her spouse. *See* Krauss, *Married Gay Canadian Couple Barred from U.S.*, N.Y. TIMES, Sept. 19, 2003, A4 (married gay couple denied permission to enter the U.S. as a single family, though they would be permitted to do so as two individuals). A commentator has urged the Immigration and Naturalization Service to "end its policy of discrimination by granting immigration benefits to lawful same-sex spouses." Reed, *When Love, Comity, and Justice Conquer Borders: INS Recognition of Same-Sex Marriage*, 28 COLUM. HUMAN RIGHTS L. REV. 97 (1996) (arguing DOMA's definition of marriage is unconstitutional); *see also* Comment, *Queer Reasoning: Immigration Policy,* Baker v. State of Vermont, *and the (Non)Recognition of Same-Gender Relationships*, 10 L. & SEX. 211 (2001).

In the wake of *Goodridge*, a number of federal constitutional amendments on the subject of same-sex marriage were introduced in Congress. One read as follows:

> Marriage in the United States shall consist only of the union of a man and a woman. Neither this Constitution or the Constitution of any state, nor state or federal law, shall be construed to require that marital status or the legal incidents thereof be conferred upon unmarried couples or groups.

Stevenson, *Bush Expected to Endorse Amendment on Marriage*, N.Y. TIMES, February 5, 2004, p. A27. Would this Amendment prohibit a state legislature from passing a same-sex marriage law? Would it make the Vermont civil union statute unconstitutional?

[c]   Other Restrictions on Available Marital Partners

[i]   Age

NOTES

1. *Age Regulations.* Four types of age restrictions in American marriage law exist: 1) the age of consent when a person may choose to marry without consultation or permission of anyone; 2) an age when marriage is permitted with approval of a parent or parent-substitute; 3) age below the age of parental permission at which, in exceptional circumstances, marriage is authorized; 4) age of marriage capacity establishing the minimum "age of marriageability." Wardle, *Rethinking Marital Age Restrictions,* 22 J. FAM. L. 1 (1983–84). As of that time, the age of consent was 18 in virtually all states and all states had a parental permission period before 18. Most commonly, parental consent is required for older minors and both parental and judicial permission is required for younger children or in "other exceptional circumstances" such as the bride's pregnancy. Very few states have a true minimum age of marriageability which would void a marriage in violation of it.

A parental permission requirement was upheld against a *Zablocki*-based constitutional attack. *Moe v. Dinkins,* 669 F.2d 67 (2d Cir. 1982). In *Phelps v. Bing,* 316 N.E.2d 775 (Ill. 1974), the court struck down a statute which created different age requirements for men and women. The state offered no justification for the gender restrictions and the court found none. *Cf. Stanton v. Stanton,* 421 U.S. 7 (1975) (rejecting assertion that woman's intended role of wife and mother justified state law providing different ages of majority for men and women).

The Supreme Court of Nevada sustained a statute permitting a 15-year-old to marry with permission of only one parent and trial court approval, *Kirkpatrick v. Eight Judicial District Court,* 64 P.3d 1056 (Nev. 2003), rejecting the non-consenting parent's claim that this deprived him of his fundamental right to the parent-child relationship. The court held that the "statute strikes a balance between an arbitrary rule of age for marriage and accommodation of individual differences and circumstances."

   2. Rationale. The standard justification for age restrictions has been the claim that "[m]arriages involving teenagers are more unstable than other marriages and are more likely to end in divorce than other marriages." Wardle, *supra*, at 26. A positive correlation between youthful marriage and subsequent marital instability has been established. *See, e.g.*, Lee, *Age at Marriage and Marital Satisfaction: A Multivariate Analysis with Implications for Marital Stability,* 39 J. MARRIAGE & FAM. 493 (1977). It is unclear, however, that the participants' youth is what causes their marital failure. Indeed one author suggested that the relationship between age at marriage and marital instability is caused by those marrying young: 1) being attracted to others who share a tendency toward rash decisionmaking or antisocial behavior or 2) having "been driven out of an abusive or combative family of origin whose values are inimical to marital stability." Thus, "both values [are] being determined by some common social or psychological antecedent." South, *Do You Need to Shop Around-Age at Marriage, Spousal Alternatives, and Marital Dissolution,* 16 J. FAM. ISSUES 432 (1995). Many studies point to non-age related factors as important predictors of marital failure. Ironically, premarital pregnancy, often a statutory exception to age requirements, is a significant predictor of divorce. *See, e.g.*, Bumpuss & Sweet, *Differentials in Marital Instability, 1970,* 37 AM. SOC. REV. 754, 759 (1972).

PROBLEM

   Problem 2-6. Tom Bennett is a 17-year-old high school senior who recently married his long-time girlfriend, Robin Smith, age 15. Soon after the wedding, Robin gave birth to their child. The relevant state statutes set the age of individual consent at 18, permit those between 16 and 18 to marry with parental permission and are silent regarding those under 16. Tom's parents gave their permission, but Robin falsely gave her age as 17 and forged her parents' signatures.

   Tom, who has competed for three years in football, basketball and baseball, learned after the wedding of the state high school athletic association rule providing: "Students who are or have ever been married are ineligible for interscholastic athletic competition." This has caused a great deal of anger and frustration within the Bennett home. Tom asks if you can find a way to "help me out of this mess. I want to play baseball this spring." What do you advise?

[ii]   Non-Relation

MODEL MARRIAGE AND DIVORCE ACT § 207

§ 207. [Prohibited Marriages.]

   (a) The following marriages are prohibited: . . .

(2) a marriage between an ancestor and a descendant, or between a brother and a sister, whether the relationship is by the half or the whole blood, or by adoption;

(3) a marriage between an uncle and a niece or between an aunt and a nephew, whether the relationship is by the half or the whole blood, except as to marriages permitted by the established customs of aboriginal cultures.

––––––––––

The American Law Institute's Model Penal Code (§ 230.2) criminalizes sexual intercourse and marriage within certain degrees of consanguinity. The Commentary identifies at least five different explanations for the "continuation of a criminal prohibition against incest." In addition to the religious rationale, the ALI asserted

> the laws against incest may . . . serve the civil and utilitarian function of preventing such inbreeding as would result in defective offspring. . . . [C]lose kinsmen are more likely to be genetically similar than are persons randomly selected from the population. Inbreeding therefore yields an increased . . . chance that the offspring will receive an identical genetic contribution from each parent. If the pedigree contains a recessive abnormality — a genetic defect that does not appear in an individual unless both parents transmit the appropriate determinant — the increased probability of homozygosity in the first generation of offspring may have tragic consequences.

The Institute acknowledged, however, that standard incest laws are typically overbroad in prohibiting more than child-bearing. Overbreadth is also reflected in those statutes barring marriages or sexual intercourse of those who are not blood relations. Moving on to consanguineous mating, the Commentary reports

> . . . [g]eneticists are not agreed in their assessments of the relative dangers posed by inbreeding, and the number of serious genetic disorders related to inbreeding is quite limited. More importantly, some have argued that any decrease in the number of first-generation defectives resulting from the prevention of consanguineous marriages will be balanced by an increase in later generations, as the dispersal of unfavorable genes among the general population through exogamous matings raises the frequency with which the marriage of unrelated persons produces the unfavorable characteristic. . . .

The ALI also noted "various social objectives that the incest prohibition might serve. Perhaps the most persuasive theory is that social strictures against incest promote the solidarity of the nuclear family. . . . A critical component of [socialization of children within the nuclear family] is the channeling of the individual's erotic impulses into socially acceptable patterns. The incest prohibition regulates erotic desire in two ways that contribute to preservation of the nuclear family. First, the prohibition controls sex rivalries and jealousies within the family unit. . . . Second, by ensuring suitable role models, the incest restriction prepares the individual for assumption of familial responsibility as an adult. . . ."

The final goals of such statutes identified by the Commentary are the reinforcement of community norms and prevention of "sexual imposition." In connection with the latter rationale, the Commentary states "[t]he actual incidence of prosecution for incest suggests that such laws have operated primarily against a kind of imposition on young and dependent females. A study of 30 appellate decisions on incest in the United States from 1846 to 1954 disclosed that all prosecutions were against males and that in 28 of the 30 cases the other party was the daughter or stepdaughter of the defendant. . . .

GRADY, FEW RISKS SEEN TO THE CHILDREN OF FIRST COUSINS, N.Y. Times, Apr. 4, 2002, Section A, p. 1, col. 3.

Contrary to widely held beliefs and longstanding taboos in America, first cousins can have children together without a great risk of birth defects or genetic disease, scientists are reporting today. They say there is no biological reason to discourage cousins from marrying.

First cousins are somewhat more likely than unrelated parents to have a child with a serious birth defect, mental retardation or genetic disease, but their increased risk is nowhere near as large as most people think, the scientists said.

In the general population, the risk that a child will be born with a serious problem like spina bifida or cystic fibrosis is 3 percent to 4 percent; to that background risk, first cousins must add another 1.7 to 2.8 percentage points, the report said.

Although the increase represents a near doubling of the risk, the result is still not considered large enough to discourage cousins from having children, said Dr. Arno Motulsky [of] the University of Washington. . . .

"In terms of general risks in life it's not very high," Dr. Motulsky said. Even at its worst, 7 percent, he said, "93 percent of the time, nothing is going to happen."

. . .

He and his colleagues said no one questioned the right of people with genetic disorders to have children, even though some have far higher levels of risk than first cousins. For example, people with Huntington's disease, a severe neurological disorder that comes on in adulthood, have a 50 percent chance of passing the disease to their children.

The researchers, a panel convened by the National Society of Genetic Counselors, based their conclusions on a review of six major studies conducted from 1965 to August 2000, involving many thousands of births.

. . .

 . . . . [N]o countries in Europe have such prohibitions, and in parts of the Middle East, Africa and Asia, marriages between cousins are considered preferable.

. . . .

Dr. Motulsky said . . . some of the revulsion [against cousin marriages] might have stemmed from the eugenics movement, which intended to improve the human race by deciding who should be allowed to breed. The movement flourished in this country early in the 20th century.

It is not known how many cousins marry or live together. Estimates of marriages between related people, which include first cousins and more distant ones, range from less than 0.1 percent of the general population to 1.5 percent. In the past, small studies have found much higher rates in some areas. A survey in 1942 found 18.7 percent in a small town in Kentucky and a 1980 study found 33 percent in a Mennonite community in Kansas.

The report made a point of saying that the term "incest" should not be applied to cousins but only to sexual relations between siblings or between parents and children. Babies who result from those unions are thought to be at significantly higher risk of genetic problems, the report said, but there is not enough data to be sure.

. . . .

The small increase in risk is thought to occur because related people may be carrying some of the same disease-causing genes, inherited from common ancestors. The problems arise from recessive genes, which have no effect on people who carry single copies, but can cause disease in a person who inherits two copies of the gene, one from each parent. When two carriers of a recessive gene have a child, the child has a one-in-four chance of inheriting two copies of that gene. When that happens, disease can result. Cystic fibrosis and the fatal Tay-Sachs disease, for example, are caused by recessive genes. Unrelated people share fewer genes and so their risk of illness caused by recessive genes is a bit lower.

Keith T., 30, said he married his cousin seven years ago and in 1998, frustrated by the lack of information for cousins who wanted to marry, he started a Web site, cousincouples.com. It is full of postings from people who say they have married their cousins or want to do so.

The site highlights famous people who married their first cousins, including Charles Darwin, who, with Emma Wedgwood, had 10 children, all healthy, some brilliant. Mr. T. asked that his full name not be used because he said he did business in a small town and feared that he would lose customers if they found out his wife was also his cousin.

. . . .

NOTES

1. *Consanguinity Prohibition.* A 1984 survey reported that virtually every state banned at least some consanguineous marriages (between parties who share at least one common ancestor). The only exception is Alabama, which does criminalize incestuous marriage. ALA. CODE § 13A-13-3 (1998). All states ban marriages between siblings, between parent and child, and between grandparents and grandchildren. The web site referred to toward the end of the *New York Times* excerpt above currently reports that approximately

one-half the states permit marriage between first cousins. For a current compilation of incest laws, see LEITER, NATIONAL SURVEY OF STATE LAW at pp. 301–312 (2d ed. 1997).

Most jurisdictions include within their consanguinity prohibitions those related either by the whole blood (two common parents) or the half blood (one common parent). Several recent cases find half-blood relationships covered by statutes silent on the question. *See Tapscott v. State*, 684 A.2d 439 (Md. App. 1996) (upholding incest conviction of a man who had intercourse with his niece by the half-blood); *see also Singh v. Singh*, 569 A.2d 1112 (Conn. 1990); Annot., *Sexual Intercourse Between Persons Related by Half Blood as Incest*, 34 A.L.R. 5th 723 (1995).

2. *Affinity Prohibition.* Those related by virtue of a marriage are said to be related by affinity. The classic affinity relationships are step-relationships and in-law relationships. According to Bratt, *supra*, 15 states forbid certain marriages between affinial relations. What state interests are furthered by prohibiting such marriages? For an article attacking the legitimacy of statutes banning affinial marriages, see Metteer, *Some "Incest" is Harmless Incest: Determining the Fundamental Right to Marry of Adults Related by Affinity Without Resorting to State Incest Statutes*, 10 KAN. J.L.& PUB. POL'Y 262 (2000).

Does an affinity relationship outlive the marriage upon which it is based? *E.g.*, in a state banning marriage between a woman and her son-in-law could the couple marry after the son-in-law's divorce? Some statutes make clear that affinity prohibitions "continue notwithstanding the dissolution, by death or divorce, of the marriage by which the affinity was created." MASS. ANN. LAWS ch. 207, § 3 (1998). By contrast, some cases hold such relationships cease with the end of the relationship-creating marriage. *See, e.g., Gish v. State*, 352 S.E.2d 800 (Ga. App. 1987); *Henderson v. State,* 157 So. 884 (Ala. App. 1934).

3. *Adoption and Incest.* While adoption statutes often require treatment of an adopted child as if she were the adoptive parents' natural child (*see* Chapter 11 at pp. 1294-97), several marriage cases raise doubts that these statutes mean what they say. For example, in *State ex rel. Miesner v. Geile,* 747 S.W.2d 757 (Mo. App. 1988), the court permitted an uncle and his niece-by-adoption to marry. The court relied on statutory silence regarding adoptive relationships. *See also Bagnardi v. Hartnett,* 366 N.Y.S.2d 89 (Sup. Ct. 1975) (approving marriage between adoptive father and daughter); *State v. Bale*, 512 N.W.2d 164 (S.D. 1994) (sexual intercourse with adopted child is not criminal incest; "adoption statute cannot erase lineal consanguinity and then create a new lineal consanguinity").

In *Israel v. Allen,* 577 P.2d 762 (Colo. 1978), the court struck down a statute prohibiting marriage between siblings related by adoption (groom's father had adopted bride). The court rejected the asserted state interest in family harmony, finding the law "illogical" and unconstitutional. The *Israel* couple never lived in the same household after adoption. Would the result have been different had they lived with their parents after the parental marriage? *See In re MEW & MLB,* 4 Pa. D. & C.3d 51 (C.P. Allegheny 1977) (parties lived in same household "for a short period" and marriage license was denied, at least partly because of fear of encouragement of sexual rivalry within the household). Relatedly, the Indiana Supreme Court has upheld an incest conviction of a father who impregnated his natural daughter who was another man's adoptive daughter. *Bohall v. State,* 546 N.E.2d 1214 (Ind. 1989).

4. *Effect of Incestuous Marriage.* "The great majority of states . . . pronounce those marriages void which violate the incest statute. The meaning of 'void' in this context seems to be that the purported marriage is an absolute nullity, which cannot be ratified by the parties, and which may be attacked at any time, either collaterally or directly, either before or after the death of a party." CLARK, THE LAW OF DOMESTIC RELATIONS § 2.9 at 85 (2d ed. 1988). Thus, in *Weeks v. Weeks,* 654 So. 2d 33 (Miss. 1995), the court held that, because it was void, an uncle-niece marriage could not support a suit for separate maintenance upon separation after nine years. The court rejected plaintiff's assertion of equitable estoppel, concluding both parties were in *pari delicto. See Adams v. Adams,* 604 P.2d 332 (Mont. 1979) (rejecting equitable estoppel claim in case of void first cousin marriage); *Catalano v. Catalano,* 170 A.2d 726 (Conn. 1961) (rejecting widow's allowance in void uncle-niece marriage); *but see May's Estate,* 114 N.E.2d 4 (N.Y. 1953).

[iii] Monogamy

All states prohibit marriages where either partner is already married. Any such attempted marriage is void and, in most states, a criminal act.

NOTES

1. *First Amendment and Polygamy.* The Supreme Court of the United States has consistently rejected assertions that religious freedom protects the practice of polygamy. *See Reynolds v. United States,* 98 U.S. 145 (1878); *Cleveland v. United States*, 329 U.S. 14 (1946) (upholding criminal conviction of polygamous Mormon fundamentalists travelling interstate). *Zablocki* has not changed the view of the lower federal courts. In *Potter v. Murray City,* 585 F. Supp. 1126 (D. Utah 1984), the court upheld the firing of a policeman for violating the criminal prohibition of polygamy. The court cited Justice Powell's *Zablocki* concurrence for its recognition of a state interest in "ensuring that its rules of domestic relations reflect the widely held values of its people" and rejected plaintiff's contention that this interest could be effectuated by a judicially-created exemption for those with plural marriages based upon "sincere religious belief." The court found *Zablocki* added nothing to the strength of plaintiff's case. *See also Barlow v. Blackburn,* 798 P.2d 1360 (Ariz. App. 1990) (permitting administrative proceedings against peace officer with three wives). For recent literature asserting polygamy should be recognized as protected under the First Amendment, see Sealing, *Polygamists Out of the Closet: Statutory and State Constitutional Prohibitions Against Polygamy are Unconstitutional Under the Free Exercise Clause,* 17 GA. ST. U. L. REV. 691 (2001); Note, *The Absolution of* Reynolds: *The Constitutionality of Religious Polygamy,* 8 WM. & MARY BILL RTS. J. 497 (2000).

2. *Polygamy in the United States.* Polygamy prohibitions have not been completely effective in eliminating the practice. A recent article estimated that between 30,000 and 60,000 currently practice polygamy. Note, *Tom Green,*

Common-Law Marriage, and the Illegality of Putative Polygamy, 17 B.Y.U. J. PUB. L. 141 (2002). The most well-publicized stronghold of the practice is in a community straddling the Arizona-Utah border (Hildale, Utah and Colorado City, Arizona) which is populated almost exclusively by members of the Fundamentalist Church of the Latter Day Saints. This group's separation from the mainline Church of the Latter Day Saints, commonly known as the Mormon Church, dates from the latter's acceptance of *Reynolds, supra*. For a brief history of the separatist movement, see Dougherty, *Polygamy's Odyssey*, PHOENIX NEW TIMES (News Section, March 13, 2003).

In 2001, Tom Green, a prominent polygamist, was successfully prosecuted for bigamy. While Green had been careful to never be married ceremonially to more than one person at a time, the prosecution convinced a jury that his continuing cohabitation with his initial wife after their legal divorce constituted a common law marriage under Utah law. Thus, his cohabitation with his other four "spiritual wives" constituted four counts of bigamy under the Utah statute punishing married individuals who "cohabit with another person." UTAH CODE ANN. § 76-7-101 (1999). For an account of the prosecution and a critique of the prosecutorial theory accepted by the court, see the Note, *supra*.

Recently, the then-Attorney General of Arizona (now-Governor Janet Napolitano) began an investigation of alleged criminal activity in the Colorado City area, including child abuse, misuse of state money and bigamy. *See* Sherwood & Wagner, *Polygamy Investigators Defend Work*, ARIZ. REPUB. p. B6 (Oct. 11, 2002). At the same time, a deputy marshal who serves both Hildale and Colorado City (a member of the Fundamentalist Church of the Latter Day Saints) was indicted in Utah on bigamy charges for his "spiritual marriage" to his wife's sister while still legally married. Wagner, *Bigamy Sex Charges Filed Vs. Lawman*, ARIZ. REPUB. p. A1 (Oct. 8, 2002) (defendant also charged with unlawful sex with a minor). The first wife was indicted for aiding and abetting her husband's bigamous relationship with her sister. It was reported that she recruited her sister to marry her husband in order to gain an ally in her constant battles with a third wife. Dougherty, *Bound by Fear: Polygamy in Arizona*, PHOENIX NEW TIMES (News Section, Mar. 13, 2003). The recent anti-polygamy campaign follows many prior efforts in the same vein. In 1953, Arizona state officials raided Short Creek (former name of Colorado City), arresting many residents for polygamy. After the raid, then-Governor Howard Pyle credited the officers with "quelling a rebellion that endangered 'the lives and futures of 263 children, the products and the victims of the foulest conspiracy you could imagine.'" No convictions were obtained. *See also* BRADLEY, KIDNAPPED FROM THAT LAND: THE GOVERNMENT RAIDS ON THE SHORT CREEK POLYGAMISTS (1993); Slivka, *Polygamous Sect Persists Despite "Persecutions" Past and Present*, ARIZ. REPUB. p A1 (Oct. 11, 2002).

In 1985, when the town officially incorporated as Colorado City, the first mayor was Daniel Barlow, who had five wives. One town elder had fathered more than 80 children. "The town's founder and spiritual leader, 98-year old Leroy Johnson, married wife No. 16 in 1984; 13 wives survive." Schlender, *Colorado City, Ariz., Has Five First Ladies But Just One Mayor*, WALL ST. J., Jan. 6, 1986, at A1. For a discussion of empirical research on family relationships in the contemporary Mormon fundamentalist community conducted by an academic psychologist, see Altman, *Polygamous Family Life: The Case of Contemporary Mormon Fundamentalists*, 1996 UTAH L. REV. 367.

3. *Polygamy in Other Countries.* Polygamy is practiced in many cultures. Even in those societies, however, the practice is not without controversy. The Koran allows a man to take as many as four wives simultaneously. In 1979, Egypt enacted a statute which required a man to officially inform his first wife that he was taking a second. The first could then obtain a divorce, receive alimony immediately, retain custody of any marital children and either retain the marital abode or obtain a new residence to be provided by the husband. This women's rights law was heavily criticized by Islamic fundamentalists.

A 1985 Egyptian Supreme Court decision struck down the statute, reinstating earlier provisions under which a woman need not be informed of a divorce or a taking of a second wife. "No longer is a second marriage automatically grounds for divorce; a woman must . . . prove in court that the second marriage has harmed her." Miller, *Egypt Divided by Court's Abolition of Law Guarding Rights of First Wives,* N.Y. TIMES, June 10, 1985, at A4, col. 1.

4. *Enoch Arden Situation.* A classic problem raising polygamy concerns arises when one spouse is absent without explanation for a lengthy period, during which the other spouse remarries. Does the absent spouse's return render the second marriage void and/or criminal? This has been called the Enoch Arden situation, after the Tennyson poem in which the seaman returns after a 10-year absence (due to shipwreck) to find his wife remarried.

Most criminal bigamy statutes do not punish the second marriage in this situation. *See, e.g.,* ILL. REV. STAT. ch. 720, § 5/11-12(b)(3)(2002) (creating "affirmative defense . . . that the prior spouse had been continually absent for a period of five years during which time the accused did not know the prior spouse to be alive"). Some statutes allow the deserted spouse to dissolve the first marriage based upon a presumption of death. *See, e.g.,* PA. STAT. tit. 23, § 1701(b) (2001) (seven years' absence sufficient for finding of death and "[t]he fact that an absentee was exposed to a specific peril of death may be a sufficient ground for finding that he died less than seven years after he was last heard from"). With no statute, the deserted spouse would be wise to file for a divorce before remarrying. While no case law has tested the proposition, absence for an extended period would seem to authorize a no-fault divorce on grounds of, *e.g.,* "irretrievable breakdown" or a fault divorce based on abandonment.

[d] Consent Requirements

GEORGIA CODE §§ 19-3-2, 19-3-4 (1999)

§ 19-3-2. To be able to contract marriage, a person must:

(1) Be of sound mind. . . .

§ 19-3-4. To constitute an actual contract of marriage, the parties must consent thereto voluntarily without any fraud practiced upon either. Drunkenness at the time of marriage, brought about by art or contrivance to induce consent, shall be held as fraud.

NOTES

1. ***Capacity to Consent.*** As GA. CODE ANN. § 19-3-4 indicates, a valid marriage requires both parties' consent. Such consent necessarily includes capacity to consent. GA. CODE ANN. § 19-3-2 defines this capacity in terms of each party being "of sound mind." *See also* PA. STAT. tit. 23, § 1304(c) (2001) (prohibiting license for the "weak minded, insane" or those "of unsound mind"). The cases interpreting such requirements define the mental competence standard fairly minimally. It is often defined as the ability to comprehend the nature of marriage and the duties and responsibilities attendant thereto. *See In re Hendrickson*, 805 P.2d 20 (Kan. 1991); *Pape v. Byrd*, 582 N.E.2d 164 (Ill. 1991). A recent case, however, annulled a marriage for lack of capacity where an 86-year old suffered from Alzheimer's Disease. *Moss v. Davis*, 794 A. 2d 1288 (Del. Fam. 2001). Little, if anything, is done to screen out those without capacity in the licensing process. If incompetence is ever raised, it is in a suit for annulment.

2. ***Fraudulently Induced Consent.*** Assuming both parties *could* consent, the next question is *did* they consent. There are two groups of cases in which lack of consent is alleged. In one, the claimant asserts fraudulent inducement. While fraudulently induced marriages generally are voidable, courts are very reluctant to find fraud. Rather than applying contracts doctrine, under which fraud requires only a material misrepresentation causing consent, annulment courts traditionally require a misrepresentation concerning the "essentials" of marriage.

The essentials test traces to an old Massachusetts case, *Reynolds v. Reynolds,* 3 Allen 605 (1862). While the definition of "essentials" is not consistent among courts, misrepresentations concerning wealth, temper or character ordinarily are not grounds for annulment. By contrast, misrepresentation about a party's fertility, or willingness or ability to engage in sexual relations, goes to the "essentials." Recent cases applying the essentials test in rejecting annulments include *Pavel v. Navitlal*, 627 A.2d 683 (N.J. Super. 1993) (Indian bride's failure to reveal her mother had lived with a person of a different caste during a marital separation); *Johnston v. Johnston*, 22 Cal. Rptr. 2d 253 (App. 1993) (concealed drinking problem and intention not to work); *Tobon v. Sanchez,* 517 A.2d 885 (N.J. Super. 1985) (failure to disclose existence of two non-marital children); *Woy v. Woy,* 737 S.W.2d 769 (Mo. App. 1987) (failure to reveal premarital lesbian behavior and drug use). Some decisions define marital "essentials" using a subjective approach. *See, e.g., Bilowit v. Dolitsky,* 304 A.2d 774 (N.J. Super. Ct. Ch. Div. 1973) (false self-description as Orthodox Jew sufficient); *Wolfe v. Wolfe,* 389 N.E.2d 1143 (Ill. 1979). In fact, some cases appear to go so far as to adopt a materiality test for fraud. *See, e.g., Charley v. Fant*, 892 S.W.2d 811 (Mo. App. 1995); *Kober v. Kober,* 211 N.E.2d 817 (N.Y. 1965).

Professor Clark asserted the "trend of the law since *Reynolds* has been to add to the kinds of fraud which entitle one to annulment." CLARK, THE LAW OF DOMESTIC RELATIONS 109 (2d ed. 1988). A more recent commentator reports that:

> there is great variation in the way courts delineate . . . the essentials standard. Some courts have specified that it covers only frauds

affecting sexual relations between the parties. Others take the view that the "essentials" cannot be definitively listed and will be determined on a case-by-case basis. . . . [T]he recurring themes are sex and procreation.

Note, *Sex, Procreation and the State Interest in Marriage*, 102 COLUM. L. REV. 1089, 1097 (2002). The widespread availability of no-fault divorce has removed the motivation of many for seeking annulment, leading to a decline in the number of cases addressing these questions and in judicial inclination to expand the grounds. For collections of cases on particular grounds for fraud annulments, see Annot., *Incapacity for Sexual Intercourse as Ground for Annulment*, 52 A.L.R.3d 589 (1973); Annot., *Religion: Concealment or Misrepresentation Relating to Religion as Ground for Annulment*, 44 A.L.R.3d 972 (1972); Annot., *Homosexuality, Transvestism, and Similar Sexual Practices as Grounds for Annulment of Marriage*, 68 A.L.R.4th 1069 (1989).

3. *Duress-Induced Consent.* The other type of case raising questions about apparent consent involves claims of duress. A marriage in which the consent of one party has been obtained by duress is voidable. There are relatively few such modern cases. But in *Marriage of Weintraub*, 213 Cal. Rptr. 159 (App. 1985), an annulment was awarded where a woman was abducted "by force, physical beatings, and threat of physical harm and taken [to another state] where . . . against her will and as the result of coercion, physical beatings, intimidation and threats upon the safety of her family, [she] went through a marriage ceremony." Many old cases find a threat of prosecution for criminal seduction or bastardy to be insufficient to prove duress. For a thorough criticism of these cases, see Wadlington, *Shotgun Marriage by Operation of Law*, 1 GA. L. REV. 183 (1967).

4. *Limited Purpose Marriage.* Fraud, duress and incapacity are theories alleging that the consent, though proper in form, lacks the required substance. Other cases do not challenge the *fact* of consent, but its *scope,* claiming that the consent was for a marriage of limited purpose — so limited that no genuine marriage was intended at all. Unlike claims of fraud, duress and incapacity, this attack ordinarily is brought by the government rather than a marriage party because the alleged limited purpose often is the obtaining of a government benefit available only upon marriage — most often, favorable immigration status for an alien married to a citizen. For a case dealing with a serviceman relying on a sham marriage to obtain a favorable housing allowance, see *United States v. Bolden*, 28 MIL. J. REP. 127 (Ct. Mil. App. 1989).

Typically the government denies the benefit, asserting a sham marriage. The facts usually suggest the parties married, at least in part, to obtain the benefit. Is that motivation sufficient to void the marriage, or is more needed?

While some cases suggest a motivation inquiry, *see Ryan v. Ryan*, 281 N.Y.S. 709 (Sup. Ct. 1935) (annulment where woman married solely for money), this cannot be the test because there is no societal consensus on appropriate motivations for marriage. Is love required or may one marry for money or status or lust? Instead, courts dealing with the question in the immigration area have looked at intent, not motivation. For example, in *Bark v. INS*, 511 F.2d 1200, 1202 (9th Cir. 1975), the court asked if the parties intended "to establish a life together." This changes the issue from *why* the marriage occurred to what *type* of marriage was intended.

But this reformed inquiry also has difficulties. First, it is subjective in nature: the question is what the parties meant, not what they did. *E.g.*, in *Bark,* the INS rejected the marriage because the couple separated shortly after the wedding. In reversing, the court wrote, "(c)onduct of the parties after marriage is relevant only to the extent that it bears upon their subjective state of mind at the time they were married." Because many couples who intend a "real" marriage nonetheless soon separate, their quick separation was not conclusive that they had not intended "a life together." *See also Dabaghian v. Civiletti,* 607 F.2d 868 (9th Cir. 1979) (divorce filed four months after marriage immediately after grant of favorable immigration status not dispositive on lack of proper intent).

Establishing subjective intent obviously is difficult. While the law sometimes (*e.g.*, in criminal mens rea) inquires into subjective intent, the limited purpose marriage inquiry is peculiar because of the intent required for a valid marriage. In determining whether the parties intended a "real" marriage, the court necessarily must have some concept of a "real marriage." At a time when many marriages fail despite "good" intentions and many others depart from traditional patterns, this is very difficult. As *Bark* pointed out, "[a]liens cannot be required to have more conventional or more successful marriages than citizens." 511 F.2d at 1201.

Not only is application of a rule requiring intent to create a "real marriage" difficult, there is also a certain irony in such a rule. As discussed earlier, most persons entering a "normal" marriage do not first study its legal consequences: their purpose usually has more to do with emotions and symbols. Their indifference (even opposition) to the legal consequences of marriage is irrelevant to its validity. By rejecting limited purpose marriage, the law would be punishing parties who often have studied at least some of the legal consequences and intend them. Because, however, they are indifferent to matrimony's emotional and symbolic aspects, their marriage is denied legal effect as being not real.

Although the intent inquiry is a relatively unusual one, it is consistent with the understanding of legal marriage suggested *supra,* in the post-*Zablocki* notes: it is not marriage's legal consequences that give it constitutional importance, but its social and symbolic significance. It is, thus, not surprising that courts look for the presence of these same factors in deciding if a marriage is real and quite possible that these non-legal aspects of marriage are what prompted Congress to give alien spouses of citizens special consideration. Most courts hold that state family law and federal immigration law can reach different conclusions as to a marriage's validity. *See, e.g.*, *Villanueva v. Brown,* 1997 U.S. Dist. LEXIS 23759 (S.D. Ohio); *Ponce-Gonzalez v. INS,* 775 F.2d 1342 (5th Cir. 1985); *Skelly v. INS,* 630 F.2d 1375 (10th Cir. 1980).

5. *More on "Immigration Marriages."* During the 1980s, though hard data was unavailable, it was claimed that many aliens were contracting marriages with American citizens "fraudulently" for the purpose of gaining permanent residence here. According to a 1985 article, 111,653 foreigners were granted permanent American residency via marriage in 1984, twice as many as in 1974. Brooks, *Marriage Fraud Aimed at Single Mothers,* N.Y. TIMES, June 13, 1985, at p. 19. The article reported an "epidemic" increase in "illegal" marriages. In a common pattern, a foreigner might pay a citizen a fee to marry, with final payment deferred until the grant of permanent residency status. *See* Wade, *Limited Purpose Marriages,* 45 MOD. L. REV. 159, 161 (1982) (claiming lax divorce laws and lessening stigma of divorce contributes to rise in such marriages).

Problems can arise, however. The *Times* article quoted an immigration official's estimate that 2/3 of the suspicious marriages investigated involved single mothers, who are often financially pressed. Some women are never paid as promised. More importantly, many are unaware that a marriage valid under state law may support valid claims on their assets by their husbands at divorce. Likewise, a valid marriage could terminate alimony payments from a prior husband. Of course, state law may reject the marriage's validity. *See, e.g., Faustin v. Lewis,* 427 A.2d 1105 (N.J. 1981) ("immigration marriage" annulled; no "meaningful" marital relationship intended). In 2003, four "career brides" who had applied for multiple marriage licenses were arrested by New York police and charged with selling their service as a bride for $1,000. One woman had applied for 27 licenses in 19 years. Saulny, *Here Comes the Bride, Again, and Again. . .,* N.Y. TIMES, July 10, 2003, p. A1.

At least partially in response to assertions of a wave of fraudulent marriages, the federal Immigration Marriage Fraud Amendments, 8 U.S.C. §§ 1154(h), 1255(e), were passed in 1986. A study presented to Congress by the Immigration and Naturalization Service purported to show that 30% of marriage-based visa petitions involved sham marriages. In later litigation attacking the Act's constitutionality, an INS official acknowledged "this figure had no statistical basis." Sheard, *Ethical Issues in Immigration Proceedings,* 9 GEO. IMMIGR. L.J. 719, 737 (1995); Gordon, *The Marriage Fraud Act of 1986,* 4 GEO. IMMIGR. L.J. 183 (1990). One analysis asserts the IMFA were produced by "misinformation and anti-alien sentiment fueled by groups lobbying to restrict, if not close altogether, our borders to aliens." Sfasciotti & Redmond, *Marriage, Divorce, and the Immigration Laws,* 81 ILL. B.J. 644, 645 (1993).

Under the amendments, an alien married to a citizen for less than two years is granted conditional status with reexamination of the marriage's bona fides and continuance after two years at which time permanent resident status may be granted upon petition of both spouses. If the marriage, however, takes place during deportation or exclusion proceedings, generally the alien must leave the United States for two years *before* obtaining the conditional resident status.

Citing the Supreme Court's traditional reluctance to disturb Congressional action on immigration, *Fiallo v. Bell,* 430 U.S. 787 (1977), several courts have rejected equal protection and due process attacks on the Amendments. *See Azizi v. Thornburg,* 908 F.2d 1130 (2d Cir. 1990); *Bright v. Parra,* 919 F.2d 31 (5th Cir. 1990); *Gomex-Arauz v. McNary,* 746 F. Supp. 1071 (W.D. Okla. 1990). *Anetekhai v. INS,* 876 F.2d 1218 (5th Cir. 1989); *Almario v. Attorney General,* 872 F.2d 147 (6th Cir. 1989). One court, however, found unconstitutional the two-year exclusion after marriage during deportation, finding a procedural due process violation. *Escobar v. INS,* 896 F.2d 564 (D.C. Cir. 1990) (distinguishing *Fiallo* as recognition of plenary Congressional power in *substantive,* not procedural, aspects of immigration policy), but the opinion was later withdrawn on a finding of mootness. *See* 925 F.2d 488 (D.C. Cir. 1991).

Further amendments in 1990 make it somewhat easier for an alien who marries a citizen during deportation or exclusion proceedings to remain here and expand the exceptions to the rule requiring a petition by both spouses to establish a marriage's bona fides after two years of conditional residency. For a discussion of the 1990 amendments, see Sfasciotti & Redmond, *supra,* at p. 648.

The legislative attention and judicial resources expended on the issue may not have made a major difference in the flow of immigrants married to American citizens. The number of spouses being admitted as an immediate relative of citizens continues to increase significantly. In 1984, 111,653 spouses of American citizens entered the country. By 2001, this number had more than doubled (270,545). Compare STATISTICAL YEARBOOK OF THE IMMIGRATION AND NATURALIZATION SERVICE, 1984 at p. 12 with STATISTICAL YEARBOOK OF THE IMMIGRATION AND NATURALIZATION SERVICE, 2001 at p. 25. The overwhelming number of petitions for permanent resident status after the two-year waiting period are approved. Motomura, *The Family and Immigration: A Roadmap for the Ruritanian Lawmaker*, 43 AM. J. COMP. L. 511, 531 (1995) (reporting over 80,000 applications were granted of the 90,000 cases eligible for such a grant in 1993). In 1994, the parallel totals were 90,243 of 96,033 cases (94%). STATISTICAL YEARBOOK OF THE IMMIGRATION AND NATURALIZATION SERVICE, 1994 at p. 70.

Some marriages of citizens and non-citizens result from the "mail-order bride" industry in which brokers, using catalogs describing and often picturing available mates, arrange marriages between women from foreign countries and American men. This business, largely unregulated, has grown exponentially in recent years. According to one commentator, the industry, which existed during the settlement of the North American continent, "resurfaced in the 1970's when men discontented with the Women's Movement in the United States began looking overseas for wives with 'old-fashioned' values." Note, *The Mail-Order Bride Industry: The Perpetuation of Transnational Economic Inequalities and Stereotypes*, 17 U. PA. J. INT'L ECON. L. 1155, 1160 (1996). A 1999 report to Congress on "international matchmaking organizations" estimated between 4,000 and 6,000 marriages arranged by the industry each year. Kelly, *Marriage for Sale: The Mail-Order Bride Industry and the Changing Value of Marriage*, 5 J. GENDER RACE & JUST. 175 (2001) (detailing allegations of rampant domestic abuse and fraud in mail-order marriages); *see also* Vergara, *Abusive Mail-Order Bride Marriage and the Thirteenth Amendment*, 94 NW. U.L. REV. 1547 (2000): Note, *Mail-Order Brides: Gilded Prostitutes and the Legal Response*, 28 U. MICH J. L. REF. 197, 201 (1994) (estimating over 200 American matchmaking businesses operating internationally).

PROBLEMS

Problem 2-7. (a) Molly and Stanley had a sexual relationship which had continued for several years. When Molly informed Stanley she was pregnant, he responded by proposing marriage, saying that while he really didn't want to get married, he didn't believe in abortions or non-marital children. He made no attempt to verify her pregnancy. The couple married and Stanley later discovered that Molly was not and never had been pregnant and never had really thought she was. He is outraged and comes to you anxious to "get rid of her." What is your advice?

(b) Assume Molly had actually been pregnant, but when she spoke to Stanley she knew the child's father was her old boyfriend, Harry. Would this change your advice?

Problem 2-8. Elizabeth and Charles are first cousins and were born in England. Charles emigrated to Arizona in 1980 and is now an American citizen. In 1988, he invited Elizabeth to move to Arizona to live with him. They soon fell in love and decided to marry. Arizona law bars marriage between first cousins, but California permits it. They went to California, got married and immediately returned to Tempe, where they both are Arizona State University law professors. Elizabeth seeks to stay in Arizona, claiming she is entitled to permanent resident status as an American citizen's spouse. The Immigration and Naturalization Service, however, rejects her application, asserting she is not married to Charles. You are the federal judge before whom this dispute has been brought. How do you decide the case? What difference, if any, would the presence or absence of a marriage evasion statute make?

[3]   BREACH OF PROMISE TO MARRY: "A CHANGE OF HEART"

NOTES

1. *"Pure" Breach of Promise Action*. The common law recognized an action for breach of the promise to marry. While formally a contract action, the damages recoverable are tort-like in that plaintiff "may recover for loss to reputation, mental anguish, injury to health . . . expenditures made in preparation for the marriage and loss of the pecuniary and social advantages which the promised marriage offered." *Stanard v. Bolin*, 565 P.2d 94 (Wash. 1977). *Stanard* summarized the widespread criticism of the action:

> (1) [it] is used as an instrument of . . . blackmail; (2) engaged persons should be allowed to correct their mistakes without fear of publicity and legal compulsion; (3) [it] is subject to great abuse [by] juries; (4) it is wrong to allow under the guise of contract an action that is essentially tortious and penal . . . (5) the measure of damages is unjust because damages are allowed for loss of social and economic position, whereas most persons marry for reasons of mutual love and affection.

Stanard is one of the relatively few recent cases continuing to recognize the action based solely on emotional injury, failed expectations and compensation for pre-wedding expenditures. Defendant had told plaintiff he was worth in excess of $2 million, would soon retire, and that plaintiff would not have to work again. After she quit her job, sold most of her furniture, put her house on the market, and arranged for the ceremony and reception, defendant cancelled the wedding with one month's notice. The appellate court overturned a dismissal of plaintiff's action, writing that it did "not feel these injuries should go unanswered merely because the breach-of-promise-to-marry action may be subject to abuses. . . ." The court refused, however, to permit recovery for damages of loss of expected financial and social position.

Is the court's distinction between damages for mental anguish (permissible) and loss of social position or financial advantage (impermissible) a sensible one? While the court's statement that most people do not marry for such material reasons is likely correct, what if that *was* an important motivation in a particular case? Should the law define the *proper* reason for marriage?

In *Hoffman v. Boyd*, 698 So. 2d 346 (Fla. App. 1997), a *written* contract provided for liquidated damages, requiring open-ended support of the plaintiff if defendant did not marry her within 12 months. Her suit for breach was rejected by both trial and appellate courts, both because of the state's Heart Balm statute (for details of such statutes, see Section C3 at p. 199) abolishing breach of promise actions and because both parties were married to others at the time of the contract which, thus, promoted divorce. The court rejected plaintiff's assertion of estoppel, finding the agreement void.

While retaining the action, some states have legislatively modified it. For example, Illinois imposes a one-year statute of limitations, restricting recovery to actual damages. ILL. ANN. STAT. ch. 740, §§ 15/6, 15/2 (2002); *see Wildey v. Springs*, 840 F. Supp. 1259 (N.D. Ill. 1994), *rev'd on other grounds*, 47 F.3d 1475 (7th Cir. 1995) (according to diversity court, pain and suffering included within "actual damages"). A Tennessee plaintiff must either have written proof of the contract or testimony by two disinterested witnesses. Plaintiffs over 60 may recover only actual damages. TENN. CODE ANN. §§ 36-3-401-05 (2001); *see Rivkin v. Postal*, 2001 Tenn. App. LEXIS 682 (rejecting plaintiff's parents as disinterested witnesses).

2. *The Engagement Ring and Other Conditional Gifts.* Akin to breach of promise is a suit brought (usually by a jilted groom) to get back property (usually the engagement ring) after cancellation of wedding plans. While it follows a broken engagement, this typically is not seen as a breach of promise action, but instead a quantum meruit action which survives enactment of a Heart Balm statute. *Aronow v. Silver,* 538 A.2d 851 (N.J. Super. 1987); *Brown v. Thomas,* 379 N.W.2d 868 (Wis. App. 1985). At least one court, however, refused to carve out a Heart Balm exception which it perceived as gender-biased in favor of men. In *Albinger v. Harris*, 48 P.3d 711 (Mont. 2002), the court held that an engagement ring is not a conditional gift and need not be returned upon the breakup. Finding the Heart Balm statute often deprives women, who "often still assume the bulk of pre-wedding costs," of a cause of action, *Albinger* held that "[i]f this court were to fashion a special exception for engagement ring actions. . ., we would perpetuate the gender bias attendant upon the Legislature's decision to [reject] all actions for breach of antenuptial promises." *See* Note, *Rules of Engagement*, 107 YALE L.J. 2583 (1998) (criticizes "particularly gendered effects of current doctrine, which requires the return of engagement gifts while allowing no redress for pre-wedding expenses borne mainly by women"); Blecher, *Broken Engagements: Who is Entitled to the Engagement Ring?*, 34 FAM. L.Q. 579 (2000).

Some Heart Balm statutes explicitly preserve such actions. *See, e.g.*, N.Y. CIVIL RIGHTS LAW § 80-b (2001); *Bruno v. Guerra*, 549 N.Y.S.2d 925 (Sup. Ct. 1990); *but see Estate of Lowe*, 379 N.W.2d 485 (Mich. App. 1985) (conditional gift of engagement ring became unconditional on death of fiancé); *Dastugue v. Fernan*, 662 So. 2d 538 (La. App. 1995) (no recovery where plaintiff gave engagement ring to wife before marriage and returned it to her after divorce).

Other gifts conditioned on marriage have been ordered returned. In *Fanning v. Iverson*, 535 N.W.2d 770 (S.D. 1995), plaintiff recovered the value of a half-interest in a real estate investment made in contemplation of marriage. The court held plaintiff was "not asking for damages for loss of marriage or humiliation. Rather, he seeks to assert his equitable common-law right to recover property for which he paid and solely owns because the condition precedent . . . was not fulfilled." *See also Volodarsky v. Malamud*, N.Y. L.J., Oct. 1, 1996 (Civ. Ct. Queens) (granting restitution of payment of defendant's pre-marital debts intended as gift conditioned on marriage).

The cases are divided on fault's role in such suits. Many courts limit recovery to "innocent" plaintiffs. *See Spinnell v. Quigley*, 785 P. 2d 1149 (Wash. App. 1990); RESTATEMENT OF RESTITUTION § 58, comment c (1937). In *Curtis v. Anderson*, 106 S.W. 3d 251 (Tex. App. 2003), the court relied on prior law requiring the ring's return by a defendant at fault to find that the plaintiff who had broken the engagement for "vague reasons" was not entitled to the ring's return. Most of the more recent cases, however, return property regardless of fault, likely influenced by the no-fault divorce regime. *Vigil v. Haber*, 888 P.2d 455 (N.M. 1995), applied what it viewed as a minority rule. Characterizing a ring as a gift either expressly or impliedly conditioned on marriage, it concluded that if the condition was not met for any reason, the gift or its equivalent value should be returned. *See also Benassi v. Back & Neck Pain Clinic*, 629 N.W.2d 475 (Minn. App. 2001); *Meyer v. Mitnick*, 625 N.W. 2d 136 (Mich. App. 2000); *Fierro v. Hoel*, 465 N.W.2d 669 (Iowa App. 1990). *See generally* Annot., *Rights in Respect of Engagement and Courtship Presents When Marriage Does Not Ensue*, 44 A.L.R.5th 1 (1996). Some cases turn on whether a particular ring was an engagement ring or, *e.g.*, a birthday present. *See Busse v. Lambert*, 773 So. 2d 182 (La. App. 2000).

After the wedding, who owns the engagement ring? In *Winer v. Winer*, 575 A.2d 518 (N.J. App. 1990), during the engagement the bride-to-be was given a 4-carat ring which throughout the seven-year marriage was kept in a safe-deposit box and worn only on special occasions. On divorce, husband argued that because the conditional gift became absolute at the wedding it then became marital property. The court rejected the argument, finding an engagement ring is intended to become wife's separate property. *See also Ward v. Ward*, 585 N.W.2d 551 (Neb. App. 1998); *Hanover v. Hanover*, 775 S.W.2d 612 (Tenn. App. 1989).

3. *Fraudulent Promises.* Breach of promise actions assume defendant broke a genuine promise. What should a court do, in a state with a Heart Balm statute, where plaintiff alleges defendant never intended to marry, making the promise fraudulent at the outset? Courts facing this question have split on whether to permit such a suit. *See, e.g., Waddell v. Briggs*, 381 A.2d 1132

(Me. 1978) (dicta barring such an action as inconsistent with rejection of heart balm actions); *Piccininni v. Hajus,* 429 A.2d 886 (Conn. 1980) (entertaining deceit action). *See* Note, *Heartbalm Statutes and Deceit Actions,* 83 MICH. L. REV. 1770 (1985) (arguing such actions, if "carefully construed and managed by courts, are outside the statutory bar of the heartbalm statutes and are not subject to the grave abuses once feared").

Some defendants conceal a matter other than an intention not to marry and the fraud is not discovered until long after marriage. For example, in *Askew v. Askew*, 22 Cal. App. 4th 942 (1994), the jury found against defendant who defrauded her prospective husband by claimed "lust," "passion" and "sexual desire" for him at the time of their wedding 13 years earlier. Plaintiff alleged these false statements led to his transfer of separate property to defendant. Terming this a breach of promise action "gussied up as a fraud action," the appellate court reversed the verdict, concluding "words of love, passion and sexual desire are simply unsuited to the cumbersome strictures of common law fraud and deceit." *See also Yang v. Lee,,* 163 F. Supp. 2d 554 (D. Md. 2001) (holding Maryland law prohibited suit by defrauded wife and her parents for defendant's misrepresentations concerning his sexual identity and history); *M.N. v. D.S.*, 616 N.W.2d 284 (Minn. App. 2000) ("if no cause of action can exist in tort for a fraudulent promise to marry, then . . . no cause of action can exist for a fraudulent promise by a married man to leave his wife and impregnate a woman who is not his wife"); *Charley v. Fant*, 892 S.W.2d 811 (Mo. App. 1995) (affirming dismissal of fraud action based on pre-marital concealment of prior marriage).

Despite the trend toward abolition of causes of action where questions of sexual behavior and misbehavior are central to the litigation, a commentator has argued forcefully for recognition of a "sexual fraud" action. Larson, *Women Understand So Little, They Call My Good Nature "Deceit": A Feminist Rethinking of Seduction*, 93 COLUM. L. REV. 374 (1993). The author urges liability for one "who fraudulently makes a misrepresentation . . . for the purpose of inducing another to consent to sexual relations in reliance upon it." Recovery would be awarded for "serious physical, pecuniary, and emotional loss. . . ."

PROBLEMS

Problem 2-9. Christine Bock was 18 when she married Marine Corps Major Frank Frist. After 15 years, while Frank was at sea, a married girlfriend invited her to dinner. Without Christine's knowledge, her friend had invited a dinner date for her, Captain David Shutt, a married naval officer. Christine and David began to date and commenced a sexual relationship. After four months, they decided to marry and divorced their spouses.

Preparing for their wedding, the couple ordered wedding bands and arranged for the church, organist, caterer, florist and baker. Christine purchased a wedding dress, a silk bouquet, shoes and a nightgown for the wedding night and bought David a desk set inscribed with the wedding date. The day before the ceremony, however, David confessed to some doubts. On the wedding day after the 150 guests had gathered, David arrived a half hour late and had a long talk with Christine and the minister, during which he confessed "there's somebody else and I can't marry you." The wedding was cancelled. David soon married a high school sweetheart.

Christine has sued for breach of promise. She has testified she was "humiliated, devastated, nauseated and, from time to time, suicidal." She has undergone $3,000 worth of psychiatric treatment. She has also testified as follows:

> I am very upset about the loss of my first husband. While life with Frank was not always great, I could have lived with him forever. He makes a good living and always treated me very well. The marriage could have been saved had it not been for David and the promise of a better life with him.

Christine is working, for the first time in her adult life, at a local bookstore. She makes little and survives on her divorce settlement. Frank wants nothing to do with her and, in fact, has remarried.

Christine obtains a jury verdict of $60,000. David seeks your representation on appeal. Your research reveals your state recognizes breach of promise, but has never discussed the elements of damages. There is no statutory authorization and the most recent appellate case was decided in 1951. What will you argue on appeal?

Problem 2-10. Assume the same facts as above, except that the minister talked David into proceeding with the wedding. Three weeks later, however, certain that it was a mistake, he filed for divorce. A no-fault divorce was quickly granted and, given the short marriage and absence of children, Christine got neither alimony nor property division. Her three-week marriage, however, ended her monthly alimony payments from Frank. They provided a supplement to her bookstore income that made the difference between subsistence and a comfortable life. Does she have a claim against David for breach of promise? For some other tort? Should she?

§ B.   LAW OF THE INTACT MARRIAGE

[1]   DUTY TO SUPPORT

MCGUIRE v. MCGUIRE

59 N.W.2d 336 (Neb. 1953)

MESSMORE, Justice. . . . [Plaintiff's suit for separate maintenance was successful at trial, in which a decree was entered to require defendant to "pay for certain items in the nature of improvements and repairs, furniture, and appliances . . .;. . . purchase a new automobile with an effective heater within 30 days;. . . pay travel expenses of the plaintiff for a visit to each of her daughters at least once a year; . . . [provide] a personal allowance . . . of $50 a month . . . . As an alternative to house improvements, defendant could "purchase a modern home elsewhere. . . ."]

. . . [P]laintiff and defendant were married . . . on August 11, 1919. . . . [D]efendant was a bachelor 46 or 47 years of age and had a reputation for more than ordinary frugality, of which the plaintiff was aware. She had . . . known him for about 3 years prior. . . . The plaintiff had been previously married. Her first husband died . . . leaving . . . plaintiff and two daughters [each a one-third interest in] 80 acres of land. . . . At the time . . . plaintiff's daughters were 9 and 11 years of age. . . .

At the time of trial plaintiff was 66 years of age and the defendant nearly 80 years of age. No children were born to these parties. The defendant had no dependents except the plaintiff.

The plaintiff . . . was a dutiful and obedient wife, worked and saved, and cohabited with the defendant until the last 2 or 3 years. She worked in the fields, did outside chores, cooked, and attended to her household duties such as cleaning the house and doing the washing. For a number of years she raised as high as 300 chickens, sold poultry and eggs, and used the money to buy clothing, things she wanted, and groceries. She . . . testified . . . defendant was the boss of the house and his word was law; that he would not tolerate any charge accounts and would not inform her as to his finances or business; and that he was a poor companion. The defendant did not complain of her work, but left the impression . . . that she had not done enough. On several occasions the plaintiff asked the defendant for money. He would give her very small amounts, and for the last 3 or 4 years he had not given her any money nor provided her with clothing, except a coat about 4 years previous. The defendant had purchased the groceries the last 3 or 4 years, and permitted her to buy groceries, but he paid for them by check. There is apparently no complaint about the groceries. . . . The defendant had not taken her to a motion picture show during the past 12 years. They did not belong to any organizations or charitable institutions, nor did he give her money to make contributions to any charitable institutions. The defendant belongs to the Pleasant Valley Church which occupies about 2 acres of his farm land. At the time of trial there was no minister for this church so there were no services. For the past 4 years or more, the defendant had not given the plaintiff money to purchase furniture. . . . Three years ago he did purchase an electric, wood-and-cob combination stove which was installed in the kitchen, also linoleum floor covering for the kitchen. [T]he house is not equipped with a bathroom, bathing facilities, or inside toilet. . . . She does not have a kitchen sink. Hard and soft water is obtained from a well and cistern. She has a mechanical . . . refrigerator, and the house is equipped with electricity. There is a pipeless furnace which she testified had not been in good working order for 5 or 6 years, and she testified she was tired of scooping coal and ashes. [Defendant refused to buy a new furnace.] She related that the furniture was old and she would like to replenish it, at least to be comparable with some of her neighbors; that her silverware and dishes were old and were primarily gifts, outside of what she purchased; that one of her daughters [gave her] at least a dress a year, or sometimes two; that the defendant owns a 1929 Ford coupe equipped with a heater which is not efficient, and on the average of every 2 weeks he drives the plaintiff to . . . visit her mother; and that he also owns a 1927 Chevrolet pickup. . . . The plaintiff was privileged to use . . . the rent money . . . from the 80-acre farm, and when she goes to see her daughters . . . she uses part of the rent money for that purpose, the defendant providing no funds for such use. . . . At the present time the plaintiff is not able to raise chickens and sell eggs. . . . The plaintiff has had three abdominal operations for which the defendant has paid. . . . The plaintiff further testified . . . use of the telephone was restricted, indicating that defendant did not desire that she make long distance calls, otherwise she had free access to the telephone.

. . . [D]efendant owns 398 acres of land with 2 acres deeded to a church, the land [valued at] $83,960; . . . he has bank deposits . . . of $12,786.81 and government bonds [worth] $104,500; and . . . his income . . . is $8,000 or $9,000 a year. . . .

. . . .

[The court noted prior state case law permitting maintenance actions where the parties had been separated and cases in other states allowing support actions where, while living in the same house, the parties had separate bedrooms, were not communicating and were generally leading separate lives.]

[T]here are no [Nebraska] cases cited by the plaintiff . . . that will sustain the action such as she has instituted in the instant case.

. . . .

[T]he marital relation has continued for more than 33 years, and the wife has been supported in the same manner during this time without complaint on her part. The parties have not been separated or living apart from each other at any time. In the light of the cited cases it is clear . . . that to maintain an action such as the one at bar, the parties must be separated or living apart from each other.

The living standards of a family are a matter of concern to the household, and not for the courts to determine, even though the husband's attitude toward his wife, according to his wealth and circumstances, leaves little to be said in his behalf. As long as the home is maintained and the parties are living as husband and wife it may be said that the husband is legally supporting his wife and the purpose of the marriage relation is being carried out. Public policy requires such a holding. It appears that the plaintiff is not devoid of money in her own right. She has a fair-sized bank account and is entitled to use the rent from the 80 acres of land. . . .

Reversed and remanded with directions to dismiss.

YEAGER, Justice (dissenting). . . .

. . . .[I]f this plaintiff were living apart from the defendant she could in equity and on the facts . . . be awarded appropriate relief. . . .

In the light of . . . the basis of the right to maintain an action for support, is there any less reason for extending the right to a wife who is denied the right to maintenance in a home occupied with her husband than to one who has chosen to occupy a separate abode?

If [separation is required] equity and effective justice would be denied where a wealthy husband refused proper support . . . to a wife physically or mentally incapable of putting herself in a position [to separate from her husband].

. . . .

In *Earle v. Earle,* it was said: "The question is, whether . . . plaintiff shall be compelled to resort to a proceeding for a divorce, which she does not desire to do, and which probably she is unwilling to do, from conscientious convictions, or, in failing to do so, shall be deprived of [appropriate] support. . . ."

NOTES

1. **Common Law Duty of Support.** As part of the legal fiction that the wife had no separate existence apart from the husband, the common law obligated him to provide for her in return for which she was obligated to render "services." *See Manby v. Scott,* 86 Eng. Rep. 781 (1659). Curiously, this gender-based reciprocal relationship survived the 19th century recognition of wives' independent status by enactment of Married Women's Property Acts in most American states. *See* Krauskopf & Thomas, *Partnership Marriage: The Solution to an Ineffective and Inequitable Law of Support,* 35 OHIO ST. L.J. 558, 560–62 (1974). Recent statutes codify spousal obligations in gender-neutral terms (*see, e.g.,* CAL. FAMILY CODE § 720 (1994)) (spouses "contract toward each other obligations of mutual respect, fidelity, and support").

2. **Refusal to Interfere.** What explains the courts' general refusal to provide a direct remedy for the neglected spouse where spouses live together? With no direct remedy to effectuate a "right" to support, it can be argued no right actually exists.

> A very technical explanation at common law was that the wife had no legal existence. . . . A more likely explanation was the judicial reflection that the husband's authority in the home was not to be questioned and the belief that if the wife could live with him surely she could influence him to provide adequately for her. . . . The thought was that by ordering [support], the court would render the wife capable of leaving the husband.

Krauskopf & Thomas, *supra,* at 566.

A separate rationale underlying the *McGuire* rule is judicial fear of a heavy caseload or a regime requiring courts to decide issues such as whether a new set of furniture was needed, etc. As one court put it, courts refused to become "a sounding board for domestic financial disagreements, nor a board of arbitration to determine the extent to which a husband is required to recognize the budget suggested by the wife. . . ." *Commonwealth v. George,* 56 A.2d 229, 231 (Pa. 1948).

A recent article sees *McGuire* as adopting an "entity" approach under which:

> the family is regarded as a freestanding thing, or phenomenon, or group . . . distinct from . . . the state, and must be given some decisional space. By marrying, Mr. and Mrs. McGuire formed a precinct that stands apart from and is ordinarily closed to state authority.

Teitelbaum, *The Family as a System: A Preliminary Sketch,* 1996 UTAH L. REV. 537, 542. Dean Teitelbaum contrasts the entity view with a view of the family as an aggregation of individuals "who define for themselves the relationship into which they enter." *Id.* at 544. As a third perspective, he describes a "systems" approach in which a system is

> understood as a network that 'integrate[s] parts into a whole.' This understanding incorporates both the sense of an identifiable, special relationship and the sense of membership by individuals that seem characteristic of families.

Id. at p. 549.

Divorce courts do inquire into the marriage's financial aspects and one might argue there is, thus, little reason to refuse involvement here. In divorce, of course, the courts have practically no choice — the marriage is effectively over and, in order to free the parties to remarry a final financial accounting must be made. The only practicable way for courts to minimize this kind of judicial "business," is to follow *McGuire* and refuse to hear disputes within the intact marriage. Is it not possible, however, that some marriages might be "saved" by providing a direct action *during* marriage to resolve some financial disagreements?

3. *Marital Autonomy.* Cases like *McGuire* can be characterized as establishing a common law family autonomy zone into which the state rarely intrudes. This same notion resurfaces in the constitutional law decisions dealt with in Chapters 9 and 10. This refusal to adjudicate spousal rights in the ongoing marriage is not universal. For example, Switzerland provides for "judicial adjustment of disputes about questions of family life in general." Rheinstein & Glendon, *Interspousal Relations,* IV INTERNATIONAL ENCYCLO-PEDIA OF COMPARATIVE LAW 12 (Chloros ed. 1980). In Spain, a spousal dis-agreement over location of the family's place of residence should be can be resolved in court, if the parties have children. *Id.* at 12–13. Consider also the following statutes:

> Art. 168. — The husband and the wife shall . . . resolve by common agreement all that is conducive to managing the home, to the upbring-ing and education of the children and to the administration of the property appertaining thereto. In case of disagreement, the judge . . . shall resolve what is proper.

> Art. 169. — The spouses may have whatever employment activity they wish except that which harms the morale of the family or its structure. Either of them can oppose the other's employment activity, and the judge . . . shall resolve the disagreement.

THE MEXICAN CIVIL CODE 42 (Gordon transl. 1980).

4. *Fault and Action for Support.* At one time, marital misconduct was "highly relevant" in separate maintenance suits. H. CLARK, LAW OF DOMESTIC RELATIONS 184 (1st ed. 1968). Thus, defendant could defeat the support claim by showing plaintiff's abandonment or adultery. Cases also generally exoner-ated the husband where the wife's "intolerable" behavior caused him to leave and sometimes required plaintiff to prove defendant's fault as an element of the suit for support.

In recent years, though, just as no-fault divorce has become the norm (*see* Chapter 3), fault has been eliminated in most support actions. *See* MMDA

§ 308. Some statutes retain fault as a relevant issue in support actions. *See, e.g.*, GEORGIA CODE ANN. §§ 19-6-1; 19-6-4 (1999); NEV. REV. STATS. § 123.100 (2001).

NORTH CAROLINA BAPTIST HOSPITALS v. HARRIS

354 S.E.2d 471 (N.C. 1987)

MEYER, Justice. [Defendant's husband received necessary treatment at the hospital.]

At the time of Mr. Harris' admission . . ., the hospital's business office submitted to his wife, defendant Vern Dell Harris, a form to sign authorizing treatment. Vern Dell signed this form in her husband's name, "by Vern Dell Harris." She declined to sign as guarantor. . . . [She] neither requested her husband's admission . . ., anticipated that he would be admitted, nor agreed to pay. . . .

The hospital charged $3,303.61 for the services provided to defendant Donnie Harris. Neither Donnie nor Vern Dell has paid this bill to date.

We [must] decide whether, in the absence of an express undertaking on her part, a wife may be held responsible for the necessary medical expenses incurred by her husband. We hold that she may be and that the "doctrine of necessaries," heretofore applicable only to medical services provided to the wife, applies to such services provided to either spouse.

At common law it was the duty of the husband to provide for the necessary expenses of his wife. . . . The doctrine of necessaries was a recognition of the traditional status of the husband . . . as the financial provider of the family's needs and has been enforced even where the husband was incompetent or where the wife was financially capable of providing for her own needs. . . .

    . . . .

The traditional allocation of marital rights and duties [by which husband was obligated to support in exchange for wife's services] was based at least in part on the legal disability of married women to manage their own financial affairs. . . .

[The North Carolina doctrine survived enactment of the Married Women's Property Act which gave "a married woman the right to dispose of her own property without the permission of her husband. . . ."]

We have consistently held that a wife is responsible for her own necessaries upon her express contract or on equitable principles when the husband was unable to pay, notwithstanding her husband's concurrent liability. [This case is one of first impression in this court.]

Most jurisdictions . . . have held that the doctrine of necessaries should be applied in a gender-neutral fashion. Some states have eliminated it from their common law altogether. See, *e.g.*, *Condore v. Prince George's County*, 425 A.2d 1011 (Md. 1981); *Schilling v. Bedford County Memorial Hospital, Inc.*, 303 S.E.2d 905 (Va. 1983). Other jurisdictions have expanded the doctrine to apply equally to either gender. See, *e.g.*, *Jersey Shore Medical Center-Fitkin Hospital v. Baum's Estate,* 417 A.2d 1003 (N.J. 1980); *Richland Memorial Hospital v. Burton,* 318 S.E.2d 12 (S.C. 1984). Still other jurisdictions have imposed liability on the wife where the husband is unable to pay for his own necessaries. See, *e.g., Borgess Medical Center v. Smith,* 386 N.W.2d 684 (Mich. App. 1986); *Marshfield Clinic v. Discher,* 314 N.W.2d 326 (Wisc. 1982). One jurisdiction reaching this issue recently has held that the common law doctrine, as historically applied, is still the law. See *Shands Teaching Hosp. and Clinics, Inc. v. Smith,* 497 So. 2d 644 (Fla. 1986). . . . Our concern here must be with the policy of North Carolina. . . .

. . . .[W]ife relies on *Presbyterian Hospitals v. McCartha,* 310 S.E.2d 409 (N.C. App. 1984). There the Court of Appeals . . . determined that a wife was not liable for the medical expenses of her husband. The court reasoned that since the hospital was looking to the husband for payment and not relying on the wife's credit, there was no basis in law or equity for her to be held liable.

A review of several historical developments in the law of our state indicates a trend toward "gender neutrality." Many of the statutory provisions that formerly applied only to males now apply to both genders. [Court cited gender-neutral provisions on non-support, alimony eligibility and child support.]

Perhaps the most convincing evidence that our legislature intends to bring gender neutrality into the law of domestic relations is the Equitable Distribution Act. This act [treats] parties to a marriage as equal partners in a joint enterprise and appears . . . to be a clear break from the archaic notions reflected in earlier statutes.

We followed the legislative trend toward gender neutrality in our recent case of *Mims v. Mims.* There, we considered the judge-made rule that where a wife buys property and puts it in her husband's name, a resulting trust . . . arises in her favor; yet where the husband buys property and puts it in his wife's name, the law presumes it to have been a gift to her. . . . In deciding that this gender-biased rule was no longer in keeping with the modern concept of the marriage and with recent legislative trends already alluded to, we said:

> These notions no longer accurately represent the society in which we live, and our laws have changed. . . . No longer must the husband be, nor is he in all instances the sole owner of the family wealth. No longer is the wife viewed as "little more than a chattel in the eyes of the law". . . .

We find that the reasoning in *Mims* is sound and applies equally well to the judge-made gender-biased rule requiring a husband to pay for the necessaries of his wife, but relieving her of a reciprocal duty. We . . . hold that a wife is liable for the necessary medical expenses provided for her husband. To the extent that the Court of Appeals opinion in *McCartha* conflicts with our ruling, that case is overruled.

Defendant contends that a gender-neutral application . . . would be better accomplished by abolishing the doctrine of necessaries altogether. We see no reason to take this course. The doctrine has historically served several beneficial functions. Among these are the encouragement of healthcare providers and facilities to provide needed medical attention to married persons and the recognition that the marriage involves shared wealth, expenses, rights, and duties. . . . [T]he benefits to the institution of marriage will be enhanced by expanding . . . the doctrine. . . . Our decision is a recognition of a . . . duty of each spouse to support the other, a duty arising from the . . . relationship itself and carrying with it the corollary right to support from the other spouse.

Because this obligation . . . arises from the marriage relationship, attempts by the wife, as here, to disavow this duty have no effect.

. . . [W]e turn to the question of whether the dismissal of plaintiff's action . . . was proper. In order to make out a prima facie case . . ., the following must be shown:

(1) medical services were provided to the spouse;

(2) the medical services were necessary for the health and well-being of the receiving spouse;

(3) [defendant] was married to the person to whom the medical services were provided at the time such services were provided; and

(4) the payment for the necessaries has not been made.

. . . . [I]t appears that all of the elements of a prima facie case have been proven or stipulated to by the parties and that no affirmative defenses have been shown. . . . We conclude, therefore, that plaintiff is entitled to recover of Vern Dell Harris $3,303.61, the cost of the medical services provided for her husband by plaintiff.

Reversed and Remanded

NOTES

1. *Necessaries Doctrine.* The common law necessaries doctrine provided an indirect remedy for husband's failure to fulfill his support obligations. Merchants could sue him for the cost of necessaries provided to wife. Thus, for example, Mrs. McGuire could have obtained the "new automobile with an effective heater" which she needed and the car dealer could seek payment from Mr. McGuire.

This doctrine was not tremendously effective in providing support for the needy spouse. First, merchants might not extend credit without husband's signature on a contract. Additionally, because the doctrine only covered "necessaries," merchant had the burden of proving necessity in the family's circumstances. For example, the *McGuire* issue would be whether the "new car with a heater" was necessary in the circumstances of that particular marriage. Also, husband generally would not be liable if he had already provided wife the necessaries or money to purchase them. *See Hubbard v. Suniland Furn. Co.,* 302 S.W.2d 688 (Tex. Civ. App. 1957). In some courts, husband's failure to provide was an element of plaintiff's case. *See* Annot., *Necessity, in Action Against Husband for Necessaries Furnished Wife, of Proving Husband's Failure to Provide Necessaries,* 19 A.L.R.4th 432 (1983).

Finally, the necessaries doctrine was tied to the fault-based divorce law. Thus, many courts held husband not liable if wife had wrongfully left him. *See Holiday Hosp. Ass'n v. Schwarz,* 166 So. 2d 493 (Fla. App. 1964). The merchant had to determine whether the parties were separated and, if so, who caused the split. (This latter doctrine explains newspaper legal column items announcing "I am no longer liable for the debts of. . . .") The fault-based nature of the necessaries doctrine has, in fact, survived the move to no-fault divorce in some states. *See, e.g., Bartrom v. Adjustment Bureau, Inc.,* 618 N.E.2d 1 (Ind. 1993). For recent applications of the necessaries doctrine, see *Francis v. Francis,* 2001 Tenn App. LEXIS 434 (doctrine covers funeral expenses); *North Shore Community Bank & Trust Co. v. Kollar,* 710 N.E.2d 106 (Ill. App. 1999) (refusing to apply Family Expense Statute, a codification of the necessaries doctrine, to decedent-spouse's promissory note).

2. *Current Status of the Necessaries Doctrine.* Despite the hazards to the creditor, the necessaries doctrine is utilized surprisingly often, particularly in cases like *Harris,* where necessary medical care is provided.

The major task facing modern courts is reconciling the traditional doctrine with current marketplace realities and the abandonment of gendered conceptions of family roles. A rule holding men, but not women, liable for a spouse's debts would appear to violate the Supreme Court's modern interpretation of the Equal Protection Clause. *See* Mahoney, *Economic Sharing During Marriage: Equal Protection, Spousal Support and the Doctrine of Necessaries,* 22 J. FAM. L. 221, 237 (1983). The only recent courts affirming the common law doctrine found the constitutional issue not before the court. *Davis v. Baxter Cty. Region. Hosp.,* 855 S.W.2d 303 (Ark. 1993); *Shands Teaching Hosp. v. Smith,* 497 So. 2d 644 (Fla. 1986).

Harris notes two obvious gender-neutral schemes: abolition of the doctrine altogether or a mirror-image expansion making wives liable in the same way husbands have been liable. For courts abolishing the doctrine, either for policy or constitutional reason, and remanding the creditor to ordinary contract relief, see *North Ottawa Comm. Hosp. v. Kieft,* 578 N.W.2d 267 (Mich. 1998); *Med. Ctr. Hosp. v. Lorrain,* 675 A.2d 326 (Vt. 1996); *Southwest Fla. Reg. Med. Center v. Connor,* 668 So. 2d 175 (Fla. 1995); *but see Queen's Med. Ctr. v. Kagawa,* 967 P.2d 686 (Hawaii App. 1998) (opting for mirror-image expansion).

A third alternative was adopted in New Jersey, in *Baum's Estate,* cited in *Harris.* Under *Baum,* the creditor can seek payment from the spouse only after failing to collect from the spouse who obtained the goods or services. This rule is easily administered from the creditor's perspective and satisfies constitutional mandates as gender-neutral. This alternative seems to represent the emerging trend. *See, e.g., Cheshire Med. Ctr. v. Holbrook,* 663 A.2d 1344 (N.H. 1995); *Landmark Med. Ctr. v. Gauthier,* 635 A.2d 1145 (R.I. 1994); *Bartrom v. Adjustment Bureau, Inc.* 618 N.E.2d 1 (Ind. 1993); *St. Francis Reg. Med. Ctr. v. Bowles,* 836 P.2d 1123 (Kan. 1992). However, Professor Mahoney argues that, under *Baum,* in a traditional family where wife "makes the purchases for the day to day operation of the household . . . the homemaker . . . is . . . prejudiced." Mahoney, *supra,* at 254.

In *Marshfield Clinic v. Discher,* 314 N.W.2d 326 (Wis. 1982), the court adopted a different approach, holding that, in a society where women generally earn less than men, husbands are always primarily liable for debts of either spouse. The court found this rule "lets a creditor know how to proceed in collecting for necessary expenses incurred by either spouse. The creditor does not have to delve into a family's financial background in order to ascertain from which spouse it can collect. . . . Such a fixed rule is essential in the commercial world." The court held its rule satisfied the intermediate Equal Protection scrutiny appropriate for analysis of gender discrimination. *See also Swidzinski v. Schultz,* 493 A.2d 93 (Pa. Super. 1985); *Borgess,* cited in *Harris* (wife liable where husband's estate is insolvent).

A final alternative would be a case-by-case approach with liability based on the parties' respective financial resources with each spouse's responsibility based on a pro rata share of total spousal resources. *Discher* held this would be constitutionally acceptable, but concluded such a rule would "destroy any certainty on the part of providers. . . . How is the seller of goods to know which spouse possesses the greatest financial resources in any individual situation?"

Professor Mahoney endorses this approach and would require suit against both parties, permitting the court to determine how much compensation was due from each party. She argues this would rarely be a significant burden for the creditor. "An exception could be made . . . where one spouse is outside the state or for some other compelling reason cannot be brought within the court's jurisdiction. . . . A discretionary power in the court to consider the respective circumstances of husband and wife in rendering judgment against one or both of them would provide a basis for equitable allocation of necessaries obligations and protection of dependent spouses." Mahoney, *supra,* at 259–60.

The case-by-case approach would also avoid any question of contribution which is raised under most other gender-neutral schemes. Under traditional law, the only person who could be sued was the husband who ultimately had sole financial responsibility. Where the duty of support is not gender-specific, a defendant-spouse successfully sued by a family creditor might seek contribution in a separate suit from the non-paying spouse.

3. *Criminal Non-Support.* Another indirect means of effectuating the support obligation is criminal prosecution for non-support. Virtually all states have statutes punishing willful non-support. This is generally held to require proof of financial ability to provide support. *See State v. Mehaffey,* 534 S.W.2d 563 (Mo. App. 1976). Interestingly, though, there is authority for the proposition that the state can place the burden of persuasion regarding ability to pay on the defendant. *See, e.g., Cooper v. State,* 760 N.E.2d 660 (Ind. App. 2001); *State v. Mays,* 1995 Ohio App. LEXIS 556. This state court authority is premised on a finding that ability to pay is *not* an element of the crime of non-support. If it were an element, the burden on the issue could not constitutionally be placed on the criminal defendant.

PROBLEM

Problem 2-11. Shirley and Melvin are married, but have not lived together in three years. They remain on a relatively friendly basis, but do not plan to divorce in the near future. One day Melvin felt faint and called Shirley to drive him to the hospital. He was admitted as a patient, describing himself as married to Shirley. He remained in the hospital for three months and eventually died, owing $45,000. His estate was closed without paying this bill. The hospital has now sued Shirley under the necessaries doctrine. You are the trial court judge hearing the case. Both sides have moved for summary judgment. What legal issues are presented by this case and how would you decide it?

[2] SPOUSAL CONTROL OVER EARNINGS AND PROPERTY

Traditionally, marriage under the common law gave overriding financial power to the husband. His usual role of breadwinner was important because marriage did not alter his sole authority over his earnings and all property held in his name. As the prior section illustrates, the wife had no claim upon the husband's assets except the limited right to purchase necessaries on his credit and to seek support directly if the parties were separated. Indeed, the older rules gave him control over her earnings and property as well. For a discussion of the married woman's limited rights at common law, see H. CLARK, THE LAW OF DOMESTIC RELATIONS 286–89 (2d ed. 1988).

In the middle and late 19th century, all states enacted what were known as Married Women's Property Acts, which were designed to ameliorate the married woman's position. Generally these statutes gave wives the right to acquire, own and transfer property without their husbands' participation, the right to make contracts and keep their own earnings, the right to make a will, the right to sue and be sued individually and the ability to testify in court. *See generally* HARTOG, MAN AND WIFE IN AMERICA: A HISTORY (2000) (providing interesting history of marital property reform). The reforms gave the wife no control or management rights over property titled in her husband's name and, thus, gave no assistance to the wife who lacked significant resources of her own.

Providing an apparent contrast to the status of wives under the common law was the community property system, which governed spousal property rights in the eight states whose marriage law has French or Spanish roots: Arizona, California, Idaho, Louisiana, New Mexico, Nevada, Texas and Washington. While details vary, community property typically includes all "property acquired by either husband or wife during the marriage. . .except for property that is . . . [a]cquired by gift, devise or descent." ARIZ. REV. STAT. § 25-211(1) (2003). This broad definition means every dollar acquired during marriage by *either* party, including all earnings, belongs to *both* husband and wife. There are, of course, further details in the community property law's classification rules; *e.g.*, acquisitions during marriage traceable to separate property typically retain their separate character, in contrast to earnings during marriage from either spouse's labor, which are community property, These details are explored further in Chapter 4's discussion of property division at divorce. Here we explore treatment of community property during marriage.

Under the original American community property system, the wife was hardly better off during marriage than in a common law state, because the husband had sole management authority over all community property. The wife could claim her share of the community upon divorce or her husband's death, but during marriage her interest in the community was described as a "mere expectancy." *Van Maren v. Johnson*, 15 Cal. 308, 311 (1860). *See* Prager, *The Persistence of Separate Property Concepts in California's Community Property System, 1849–1975*, 24 U.C.L.A. L. REV. 1, 35–39, 47–52 (1976). For example, in *Wilcox v. Wilcox*, 98 Cal. Rptr. 319 (App. 1971), the husband complained that his wife had "secreted" $30,000 of community funds and the appellate court recognized his claim:

> By statute a husband "has the management and control of the community personal property, with like absolute power of disposition, other than testamentary, as he has of his separate estate," subject to certain [irrelevant] exceptions. . . . The right of the husband . . . is invaded . . . when [wife] deprives him thereof by taking, secreting and exercising exclusive control over community funds.

The court recognized a cause of action without specific statutory authority.

Wilcox was a last hurrah for male management prerogatives. The 1970s saw a wave of reform in community property states which replaced "husband as manager" provisions with various forms of dual or coequal management. Louisiana was the last holdout. Its husband-dominated management system was struck down in *Kirchberg v. Feenstra*, 450 U.S. 55 (1981). Although again details vary, no community property state has male management provisions today. What does "equal management" of the community mean? Consider the relatively straightforward Arizona statute:

> A. Each spouse has the sole management, control and disposition rights of each spouse's separate property.
>
> B. The spouses have equal management, control and disposition rights over their community property and have equal power to bind the community.
>
> C. Either spouse separately may acquire, manage, control or dispose of community property or bind the community, except that joinder of both spouses is required in any of the following cases:
>
> > 1. Any transaction for the acquisition, disposition or encumbrance of an interest in real property other than an unpatented mining claim or a lease of less than one year.
> >
> > 2. Any transaction of guaranty, indemnity or suretyship. . . .

ARIZ. REV. STAT. § 25–214 (2003).

Note that the statute states both a default rule allowing either spouse to bind the community, and exceptions requiring agreement of both spouses. Federal law adds to this list of exceptions, with respect to plans covered under ERISA, the federal law that regulates tax-qualified pension plans. Pension plans typically offer retiring employees a choice between a pension that continues until the employee's death ("Life"), or one that continues until both the employee and the employee's spouse have died ("Joint Life"). Because the expected term of payments will be greater, the monthly payout is less with the joint-life plan. Because a pension is a community asset to the extent that it was earned by employment during marriage, the choice of plan is a community property management decision. Under general management rules such as those in the Arizona statute, either spouse could bind the community to a choice, although before ERISA pension plan administrators would ask only the employee. Employees choosing higher payouts that ended with their death left disappointed survivors who sometimes challenged the decision, but under applicable community property principles they usually lost. *Brown v. Boeing Co.,* 622 P.2d 1313 (Wash. App. 1980) (decedent-husband's choice of Life plan binding even though she objected to husband during his life). Under the Retirement Equity Act of 1984 (29 U.S.C. § 1055), ERISA now requires pension plans to obtain the non-employee spouse's written consent to selection of an annuity with no survivor benefits. This requirement applies to all covered pension plans (which is most plans); the spouse's consent is thus required in both common law and community property jurisdictions.

NOTES

1. ***Analogous Management Choices.*** Choice of pension plan is hardly the only management decision that may prove important to both spouses even though made only by one. It is common, *e.g.,* for one spouse alone to make decisions about investment accounts with community funds. For another everyday example, consider *Johnson v. Farmers Insurance Company*, 817 P.2d 841 (Wash. 1991), involving a choice of auto insurance coverage. After separation, a couple's daughter was injured in an accident in which the responsible third-party was uninsured. Her claim under their policy's Uninsured Motorist (UIM) coverage was limited by the father's unilateral pre-divorce decision waiving full coverage (in exchange for a reduced premium). The mother lost her challenge to the waiver. The court explained:

> As one spouse manages community affairs with the effect of binding or benefiting the community, then the other spouse enjoys the same benefits and incurs the same obligations. The . . . burden both [spouses] incurred under the insurance contract once they waived full UIM coverage was the burden of having to take affirmative steps with their insurer if they later desired to reacquire full UIM coverage.

> [E]ither spouse is authorized to act in management of community affairs. . . . Either [spouse] could have bound the other by individually executing a valid waiver, with that waiver surviving the termination of the marriage. Such a construction is consistent with the equal management authority principle.

2. ***Three Kinds of Gender-Neutral Management.*** *Brown v. Boeing* and *Johnson* illustrate the traps that exist when either spouse can bind the other. Particularly because third parties may rely upon the directions of either spouse, the first spouse to act often will prevail. The husband's purchase of a new car with community funds cannot be undone by wife; if the wife buys a certificate of deposit, the husband cannot avoid the early withdrawal penalty by asserting his lack of consent. At least for most day-to-day transactions, however, there does not seem to be any alternative. A rule requiring both spouses' consent to every management transaction would get very tedious. For

example, it would mean both spouses would have to sign every credit card transaction. No community property state employs this rule. Instead, the Washington rule applied in *Brown* and *Johnson* is the most common formulation.

There is also a pattern to the statutory exceptions under which particular kinds of transactions require the consent of both spouses. The sale or encumbrance of real estate, identified by the Arizona statute quoted above, is such a common exception. *Droeger v. Friedman, Sloan & Ross*, 812 P.2d 931 (Cal. 1991) (wife's unilateral encumbrance of community real estate, in violation of statute requiring both spouses' consent to such transactions, voidable by husband by timely objection).

On the other hand, for some transactions, state law may give one spouse, selected on a gender-neutral basis, exclusive management authority. For example, some states give the entrepreneur-spouse sole management authority over a community property business "to assure the smooth functioning of the concern, on the assumption that joint decision-making is potentially divisive in a way that would be destructive of the community's ultimate interest in the business' success." Bruch, *Management Powers and Duties Under California's Community Property Laws: Recommendations for Reform,* 34 Hastings L.J. 227, 274 (1982); *see, e.g.,* Cal. Fam. Code § 1100(d) (2003) ("a spouse who is operating or managing a business . . . that is . . . community . . . property has the primary management and control of the business or interest. Primary management and control means that the managing spouse may act alone in all transactions but shall give prior written notice to the other spouse of any sale, lease . . . or other disposition of . . . substantially all of the . . . property used in the operation of the business . . . whether or not title to that property is held in the name of only one spouse"); La. Civ. Code art. 2352 (2003) (spouse who is a partner has "exclusive right" to manage partnership interest); Nev. Rev. Stats. § 123.230(6) (2003) (where one spouse "participates in the management" of a business, that spouse may take actions "in the ordinary course of business" without consent "of the non-participating spouse"). In sum, gender-neutral management means: 1) often either spouse can act alone and bind the other, 2) sometimes both must consent, and 3) sometimes sole management authority is allocated to one spouse on a gender-neutral basis.

Finally, one cannot ignore the reality that factors unrelated to marital property law may give one spouse effective sole management authority over at least some community property. For example, commercial relations in a community property state lacking any "entrepreneur-spouse" exception as described in the preceding paragraph may effectively ensure the same result. In fact, sole management may be the effective rule for some assets outside the entrepreneur-spouse rule:

> As a practical matter, if stocks are registered in the name of one spouse, only that spouse can sell. True, the stock may be community property despite the paper title in the name of one spouse, and theoretically the non-titled spouse has "equal" power to manage; but the broker will transfer only on the signature of the registered owner. If one spouse manages an unincorporated business, the commercial

world [normally] will deal only with that spouse. . . . If one spouse is a partner with third persons, partnership law gives the other spouse no power to act for the partnership. In short, "equal" management is fine in theory but is unrealistic in practice. It is probably harmless, however, to leave equal management statutory provisions as they are.

Effland, *Arizona Community Property Law, Time for Review and Revision,* 1982 ARIZ. ST. L.J. 1, 15.

3. *Open Questions.* Does one spouse have an enforceable right to an accounting of community assets concealed by the other? Does one spouse have a claim against the other for negligent mismanagement of the assets? Where either can act alone for the community, can one spouse prevent the other from acting by informing the third party of his or her opposition? (For example, can husband prevent wife's sale of their boat by informing a prospective buyer that he has decided not to sell?)

Not all these questions have been answered in each community property state. California imposes on each spouse a fiduciary duty to the other when managing community assets. This duty includes "the obligation to make full disclosure to the other spouse of the existence of assets in which the community has an interest and debts for which the community may be liable, upon request. . . ." CAL. FAM. CODE § 1100(e) (2003). Either spouse may bring an action for an accounting to "determine the rights of ownership in, the beneficial enjoyment of, or access to, community property, and the classification of all property of the parties to a marriage," or an action for "any breach of the fiduciary duty that results in impairment to the claimant spouse's present undivided one-half interest in the community estate, including, but not limited to, a single transaction or a pattern or series of transactions, which. . .have caused or will cause a detrimental impact to the claimant spouse's undivided one-half interest. . . ." CAL. FAM. CODE § 1101 (2003). *See* Bruch, *Protecting the Rights of Spouses in Intact Marriages: The 1987 California Community Property Reform and Why It Was So Hard to Get,* 1990 WIS. L. REV. 731 (recounting history of these provisions).

Two community property states have somewhat different management systems which avoid or deal with some of these questions. Texas' unique system makes each spouse sole manager of community property "that he or she would have owned if single." TEX. FAM. CODE ANN. § 3.102 (2003). This gives each spouse sole control over his or her earnings, although the manager cannot "unfairly dispose of the other spouse's one-half interest in the community." *Mazique v. Mazique,* 742 S.W.2d 805 (Tex. App. 1987). New Mexico provides, in effect, that written title to personal community property determines whether management control is in both spouses or one spouse. Control is given to the party or parties "named in a document evidencing ownership." N.M. STAT. ANN. § 40-3-14 (2003). In a unique provision, New Mexico permits a spouse to claim sole management authority by entering into a written agreement with a third party which designates that spouse as having that authority. *Id.* The apparent purpose is to protect merchants who enter into agreements with one spouse. *See* Bingaman, *The Community Property Act of 1973: A Commentary and Quasi-Legislative History,* 5 N. MEX. L. REV. 1 (1974).

4. *Common Law Applications.* The Uniform Marital Property Act (UMPA), promulgated in 1983 by the National Conference of Commissioners on Uniform State Laws, largely follows community property principles while shunning community property labels, perhaps to make the proposal more palatable to traditionalists in common law states. Property obtained during marriage is "marital," not "community" property. Property brought into the marriage is "individual" not "separate." Wisconsin is the only state to have adopted UMPA to date. WIS. STAT. ANN. §§ 766.001 to .097 (2003). The state had considered adopting a community property system in earlier years, and, in opting for UMPA, the legislature understood it was moving toward a community property system. Reppy, *The Uniform Marital Property Act: Some Suggested Revisions for a Basically Sound Act,* 21 HOUS. L. REV. 679, 686–87 (1984).

In many ways UMPA's management provisions follow New Mexico's title principle. Section 5 gives each spouse management authority over most untitled marital property (real and personal) with certain exceptions, including property held in one spouse's name, which may be managed by that spouse only. Both spouses must concur in management of property if their names appear on the title joined by an "and"; either can act alone if their names are joined by an "or." Section 15 establishes remedies for one spouse against another arising from the spouse's interest in marital property. The complete text of UMPA, as well as extensive commentary, may be found in *Uniform Marital Property Act Symposium,* 21 HOUS. L. REV. 595 (1984).

[3] VARYING THE MARRIAGE "CONTRACT"

NOTES

1. *Traditional Rule on Enforcement of Marital Contracts.* As reflected in cases such as *Graham v. Graham,* 33 F. Supp. 936 (E.D. Mich. 1940), traditionally marriage was conceived as a tri-lateral contract between husband, wife and state. While individuals had virtually free choice of whether to marry, when to marry and whom to marry, once the marriage occurred the state mandated its own "standard-form" contract which defined the husband as head of household (and entitled to determine marital domicile) and supporter of his wife. Thus, *Graham* refused to enforce an agreement under which a man gave up his job and his right to determine marital domicile in exchange for his wife's support. In explanation, the court wrote:

> The [traditional rule forbidding private alteration of the marital contract] is based on sound foundations of public policy. If they were permitted to . . . contract [about] where the parties are to live and whether the husband is to work or be supported by his wife, there would . . . be no reason why married persons could not contract as to the allowance the husband or wife may receive, the number of dresses she may have, the places where they will spend their evenings and vacations, and innumerable other aspects of their personal relationships. Such right would open an endless field for controversy and bickering and would destroy the element of flexibility needed in

making adjustments to new conditions. . . . [Voluntary behavior along these lines is acceptable.] The objection is to putting such conduct into a binding contract. . . . It would be unfortunate if in making . . . adjustments [to unforeseen developments] the parties should find their hands tied. . . .

Thus, at the same time the state is quite reluctant to intervene to require marital partners to conform to *state*-created expectations (see *McGuire*), it also refuses to enforce any *private* agreements which vary those expectations.

A recent court reiterated the traditional approach. In *Diosdado v. Diosdado*, 97 Cal. App. 4th 470 (2002), a marital contract was signed after the husband's extra-marital affair had caused a separation. One clause obligated both parties to "emotional and sexual fidelity" and defined as a breach "any [voluntary] kissing on the mouth or touching in any sexual manner of any person outside of said marital relationship, as determined by a trier of fact." A liquidated damages clause provided for payment of $50,000. The trial court dismissed the wife's suit claiming husband had breached by kissing another woman. The appellate court affirmed, holding enforcement of the agreement would be inconsistent with a no-fault divorce regime under which the court will not assess blame for a marriage's dissolution.

2. *Modern Developments.* Resistance to allowing marital partners contractual autonomy recently has softened in other areas of family law. Both antenuptial and separation agreements defining the financial consequences of a divorce are likely to be enforced by modern courts. In both areas, the once-perceived significant state interest in the details of the arrangements has diminished. See Chapter 8. Likewise, unmarried cohabitants are increasingly permitted to contract with each other. (See Chapter 9 at pp. 876-918). Though the contracts in most of the cohabitation cases deal with financial issues like those addressed by antenuptial or separation agreements, the contract principles applied in them would seem to reach other matters as well, particularly because the issue would arise outside the context of the traditional rules confining marital arrangements.

Marriage contract advocates argue that if contractual freedom is not extended to marriage contracts, the law will be encouraging those who want flexibility in their relationships to stay outside of marriage. A number of recent commentators have urged enforcement of agreements between marital partners creating specific obligations and rights in various aspects of the marriage. For example, Professor Lenore Weitzman suggests parties might want provisions defining: the duration of the marriage, the decision-making process to be used concerning jobs and education, the nature of property obtained by either partner during marriage (marital v. non-marital), living arrangements, responsibility for household tasks, surname(s) to be used, the nature of sexual relations, religious commitments, relationships with friends and family, intent to bear children and childrearing philosophies. WEITZMAN, THE MARRIAGE CONTRACT (1981).

Professor Weitzman's book includes five actual contracts. One involved David, a first-year medical student, and Nancy, an aspiring dancer who was turning down a two-year fellowship in Paris to marry. Madly in love, she agrees to trade her fellowship and career for life as a doctor's wife. After making explicit this overarching exchange whereby Nancy would gain the "usual benefits of being a doctor's wife (*i.e.*, a beautiful home and summer home, expensive clothing, vacations in Europe, child care and private schools for her children, and a full-time housekeeper)," the contract includes, among others, the following provisions:

Statement of Interest

1. The parties consider this a contract for a lifetime partnership.

2. The parties consider themselves equal partners. . . .

3. The parties recognize that although Nancy's contribution to the partnership will be less tangible financially, her financial support during school, her home and child care afterwards, and her continuing emotional and psychological nurturance are of equal worth to the partnership.

4. The parties agree to share equally all income, property, and other gains that may accrue to either. . . . They consider any gains that accrue to the income-earning partner to be the result of . . . joint efforts — and thereby to belong to both parties equally.

. . . .

Domicile

The location of the family domicile will be decided by David; the main consideration in making such a decision will be the best interest of David's career.

Name

Both parties will use David's surname.

Housekeeping Responsibilities

Nancy will be responsible for the administration of the household, eventually with the assistance of a full-time housekeeper.

Other Responsibilities

1. Nancy agrees to further David's career by maintaining appropriate social relationships with other doctors and their wives.

2. Nancy agrees to participate actively in church and country club activities, to serve on medical auxiliary and hospital benefit committees, and to socialize with David's colleagues and other physicians.

3. Nancy promises to give a dinner party or to otherwise aid David's professional advancement by entertaining at least twice a week.

4. David agrees to accompany Nancy to the ballet at least once a month.

5. David also agrees to schedule at least two two-week vacations with her each year, at least one of them in Europe.

Id. at pp. 295–98.

3. *Enforcement of Non-financial Matters in Marriage Contracts.*
Should courts enforce provisions of marital contracts that go beyond financial
matters, such as Nancy's obligation to maintain "appropriate relationships
with other doctors and their wives" or David's agreement on scheduling
vacations? There are obvious enforcement difficulties with such provisions.
One may question whether there is any point to a marriage which requires
such an agreement.

Would creation of a new court that would issue decrees of rebuke or condemnation to those who violate marital contract terms help facilitate recognition
of marital contracting? Would such decrees be effective? Would such a process
be more acceptable than traditional legal remedies? Perhaps a court would
not be required to provide such remedies — a private agency might suffice.
Enforcement might thus not require injunctive relief or even judicial appraisal
of damages for such a breach. Is that enough to make enforcement likely or
desirable?

Perhaps resistance to enforcement is related to resistance to recognizing
a limited purpose marriage as "real" (discussed earlier). That is, while we are
increasingly willing to allow couples to modify the financial consequences of
marriage, we reject enforcement (and resulting legal legitimacy) of their
contracts about the personal and symbolic aspects of marriage — the same
aspects which courts, in other contexts, have treated as indicators of whether
a marriage is real. Perhaps these personal matters, rather than marriage's
financial aspects, are now the "essentials" which cannot be modified.

One commentator contrasted judicial willingness to enforce interspousal
agreements dealing with property division and alimony with the refusal to
enforce "nonmonetary" contractual provisions such as those in Note 2. Silbaugh, *Marriage Contracts and the Family Economy*, 93 Nw. U. L. Rev. 65
(1998). Asserting that the "rule of selective enforcement disproportionately
benefits those who bring more money to a marriage, who are more likely to
be men than women," Professor Silbaugh urges that, because the "nonmonetary aspects of marriage" cannot be meaningfully enforced, "equity dictates
that we should at least have a presumption against the enforcement of
monetary contracts."

4. *Ramifications of Marriage Contracting.* Some defend the legitimacy
and efficacy of enforcement of marital contracts. One commentator argues that
"[s]ince the new function of marriage is happiness and fulfillment of the individuals, it also follows that personal preferences as to the substance of the
marriage should be honored. Our society is based on . . . tolerance of . . .
diversity. If marriage has truly become a personal rather than a social institution, we would defer to personal private ordering of the relationship." Temple,
Freedom of Contract and Intimate Relationships, 8 Harv. J. L. & Pub. Pol'y
121 (1985); *see also* Shultz, *Contractual Ordering of Marriage: A New Model
for State Policy*, 70 Calif. L. Rev. 204 (1982). Temple asserts bargaining is
not inimical to intimate relationships, nor is it inherently hostile or adversary.
Problems such as overreaching by one party and change of circumstances can
be dealt with by ordinary contract principles. While conceding judicial dispute
resolution concerning such contracts might be problematic, Temple urges

creation of alternative methods for resolution of marital contract disputes, such as mediation, arbitration or conciliation courts. As for remedies, Temple argues money damages sometimes would be appropriate, but also suggests the possibility of specific performance in some situations and urges use of liquidated damages clauses in the contracts themselves.

A critic argues enforcement of marital contracts might produce "unintended consequences" such as increasingly intrusive notions of unconscionability and overreaching, a shift in general contract law damages from money damage to specific performance or restrictions on divorce resulting from the use of standard form church-drafted marriage contracts. Helmholz, *Comment: Recurrent Patterns of Family Law,* 8 HARV. J.L. & PUB. POL. 175, 181–83 (1985).

§ C. CONSEQUENCES OF MARITAL STATUS

[1] NAMES

IN RE NATALE

527 S.W.2d 402 (Mo. App. 1975)

DOWD, Judge. [Judith appealed denial of her name change petition. She wanted to change her name because, as an attorney, she wanted to list her home phone number in telephone directories. Her husband (who joined her petition), a school administrator, did not want to receive phone calls from parents or students during off-work hours. She asserted a name change would not defraud creditors. She sought to use the name "Montage" which was not her pre-marriage name. During her pre-marriage life, she had been known by three different surnames due to her mother's remarriage and her adoption.]

. . . [T]he court [denied] the Petition . . . on the ground that "[Judith] is lawfully married and resides with her legal spouse" and "that under such circumstances the granting of said petition could be detrimental to others in the future.". . . [A]t the hearing, the court had commented, "Where a married couple who do have and in the future are likely to have many obligations for which they are liable, I can see circumstances that would be detrimental. . . ." It appears, therefore, that the trial court found that the fact of a woman's ongoing marriage is prima facie evidence of detriment to creditors sufficient to deny her petition for change of name.

. . .[P]etitioner's first argument is that she has the right at common law to change her name, regardless of her marital status. . . .

Surnames arose as descriptive terms applied to individuals to differentiate between parties with the same baptismal name, eventually becoming a required part of a person's legal name. Even so, names could be adopted and abandoned at will, and all members of a family, including the husband and wife, were not necessarily known by the same surname. Gradually, the custom that all members of the family bear the same, fixed surname developed as surnames lost their character as descriptions of particular individuals. Since the husband and wife customarily adopted the name of the spouse with the most property and since men typically held more property than women, most women took the husband's name. However, the custom never became law. The English common law view was that a woman's surname was not bound to her marital status and arose only through her use of a name.

The law of England . . . recognized the right to change names by the nonfraudulent use of another. The right was never limited to males; indeed, it was through this common law method that a woman changed her surname to that of her husband after marriage. . . . [M]arried women in Missouri are free to adopt another name by the common law method if this right has not been invalidated by constitutional or statutory mandate.

This court is unaware of any constitutional or statutory provision which abrogates the English common law right to change names through usage. . . .

Policy argues in favor of acknowledging that a woman may exercise the common law right to change names. The custom of restricting a married woman's right to use a surname other than her husband's is an outgrowth of societal compulsion and economic coercion[3] inconsistent with developments granting women equal legal rights. The concept that the husband and wife are one, the "one" being the husband, has been abandoned. Insistence that a married couple use one name, the husband's, is equally outmoded.

[We have found] no appellate decision in any state which affirmed . . . denial of a married woman's name change petition on the ground of an ongoing marriage.

We are persuaded that the trial court abused its discretion in denying [Judith] her requested name change. . . .

In view of Judith's common law right to change her name, the requested name change is proper. . . . The law will not keep a wife under her husband's thumb by compelling her to keep his name once she has chosen another. The record . . . is devoid of evidence of harm to third parties. Since Judith's husband joined in her petition, no harm to her husband can be presumed, and possible harm to children born to the marriage in the future is too speculative. No harm to the state is shown . . . since Judith did not request a name which is bizarre, obscene, offensive, or of a governmental body.

. . . The damage to the couple's creditors is no greater than that to the creditor of any person whose name has been changed, yet creditors have not complained of undue harm when women have assumed their husband's name upon marriage or changed their names following divorce. . . . Given the notice provided creditors by [the name change statutes], it is at least as possible to defraud a creditor by nondisclosure of the existence of a spouse with

---

[3] It is not difficult to understand a married woman's assumption of her husband's name given the disabilities and privileges afforded a married woman under the common law. . . .

[Judith] chose to petition for a court ordered change of name . . . rather than use the common law method to change her name. . . . [The name change statutes] do not abrogate . . . the common law method of name change.

Under the common law, the change of name is accomplished by usage or habit. . . . The primary difference between the two methods is, therefore, the speed and certainty of the change of name under the statutory procedure. . . .

the same name as the existence of a spouse with a different name. In addition, it does not seem difficult or uncommon to include the spouse's name, whether it be the same or different, whenever marital status is requested by creditors.

. . . [A] wife's property is not automatically subject to the debts of her husband and . . . a wife is deemed a feme sole for most purposes. It is difficult to imagine prima facie harm to creditors under these circumstances. Both spouses will be known when they seek credit together. The husband's creditors have no automatic right to proceed against the wife's property. The wife's creditors gain an unexpected advantage if they have extended credit to a woman believed to be single who is married and whose husband is found to be obligated for the particular debt involved. In times past, the management of a woman was "given" to the woman's husband by her father in the marriage ceremony. The woman was symbolically, if not literally, traded from father to husband like a chattel. Today, a woman is under new management, her own. . . .

The judgment is reversed. . . .

NOTES

1. ***Marriage as a Name Change.*** The *Natale* petitioner came to be known by her husband's surname in the same way as most women who change their name upon marriage . . . . by using what can best be described as self-help through consistent, non-fraudulent use of her husband's surname. But *Natale* makes clear, as almost all modern courts have, that marriage itself does not change the wife's surname. Most such litigation involves a wife seeking to use a name other than husband's for purposes of: voting, see *Keltch v. Alfalfa County Election Bd.,* 737 P.2d 908 (Okla. 1987); *State v. Taylor,* 415 So. 2d 1043 (Ala. 1982); car registration, *Davis v. Roos,* 326 So. 2d 226 (Fla. App. 1976); a driver's license, *Traugott v. Petit,* 404 A.2d 77 (R.I. 1979); filing a dissolution action, *Malone v. Sullivan,* 605 P.2d 447 (Ariz. 1980); registration of vital statistics, *Secretary v. City Clerk of Lowell,* 366 N.E.2d 717 (Mass. 1977). Other married women, like the *Natale* petitioner, seek a court order changing her name. In all these cases, the bureaucrat's or trial judge's non-cooperation was rejected by an appellate court reaching the same conclusion as the *Natale* appellate court.

In 13th and 14th century England, a researcher asserts, it was "not unusual for a married heiress to retain her father's family name." Daum, *The Right of Married Women to Assert Their Own Surnames,* 8 J.L. REFORM 64, 67 (1974). One commentator concluded it was more common, in fact, for both spouses to be known by the wife's, not the husband's, surname. L.G. PINE, THE STORY OF SURNAMES 23 (1966). A recent commentator reports a trend in this country of men adopting their wives' surnames upon marriage. Rosenaft, *Comment: The Right of Men to Change Their Names Upon Marriage,* 5 U. PA. J. CONST. L. 186 (2002) (asserting many states act unconstitutionally by making it easier for women to change their name on marriage than men).

Only two courts in the past 60 years have held marriage automatically changes a woman's surname. *Forbush v. Wallace,* 341 F. Supp. 217 (M.D. Ala.

1971), *aff'd without opinion,* 405 U.S. 970 (1972), held Alabama common law changed a woman's name upon marriage. Note, however, that the Alabama Supreme Court (in *Taylor, supra*) later held *Forbush* had misinterpreted Alabama law. An Illinois appellate court, *People ex rel. Rago v. Lipsky,* 63 N.E.2d 642 (Ill. App. 1945), also held the common law worked a change of name at marriage. In *Whitlow v. Hodges,* 539 F.2d 582 (6th Cir. 1976), a divided court held Kentucky could require married women to apply for driver's licenses in their husbands' surnames regardless of whether marriage automatically changed their name.

While legislation mandating a name change of a married woman to that of her husband is difficult if not impossible to find, it has been reported that as recently as 1971 the State Department wrote to a married woman who had requested a passport that "the legal name of a married woman is her husband's surname [and] the wife at marriage loses her maiden name. . . ." STANNARD, MRS. MAN 256 (Germainbooks 1977) (quoting this letter without further attribution); *see also* Augustine-Adams, *The Beginning of Wisdom is to Call Things by Their Right Names,* 7 S. CAL. REV. L.& WOMEN'S STUD. 1 (1997) (surveying history of naming practices in the U.S. and "naming practices and concomitant social meanings across . . . cultures" and other countries).

2. *Can More Than One Name Be Used?* May a married woman continue using her birth name professionally, but be known as Mrs. _____ socially? The cases do not address this issue explicitly, but a judge complained when a court apparently foreclosed the two-name option. In *Kruzel v. Podell,* 226 N.W.2d 458 (Wis. 1975), the dissent argued that the majority, by finding the only way a married woman acquires her husband's surname is to "habitually use" it, had forced her to elect one or the other. In the dissent's words, "[i]f she doesn't use it, she doesn't get it. If she blurs the situation by using both her maiden name and her married name, she will be hard put to qualify as an 'habitual user' under the [majority's] test." A recent Ohio court wrote "[a] person may change his name at any time or *even use several different names,* so long as he does not do so for a fraudulent purpose." *State v. Hayes,* 774 N.E.2d 807 (Ohio Mun. Ct. 2002) (reversing a conviction for displaying a fictitious identification designating driver as Santa Claus; court noted defendant had used this name, along with his given name, for approximately 20 years and no fraud was involved).

Should the law accommodate the wishes of women who want to use different names for different purposes? Would *Natale's* assurance of minimal risk to creditors apply in this context?

3. *Election of Remedies.* As noted in *Natale,* in addition to self-help as a method of changing one's name, most states have a judicial name change procedure. The existence of this procedure, however, does not usually displace the self-help method. *But see In re Bobrowich,* 2003 N.Y. Misc. LEXIS 52 (Civ. Ct) (suggesting self-help's availability implies judicial discretion to refuse to authorize name change); *Traugott v. Petit,* 404 A.2d 77 (R.I. 1979). At least one state, however, requires use of the statutory mechanism. *See* OKLA. STAT. tit. 12, § 1637 (1993) (exceptions for those who change their names after marriage, divorce or adoption). Eliminating self-help may be a concession that it often is ineffective. One commentator describes the common law method as "practically meaningless. The realities of contemporary society require a state-sponsored corroboration to establish our identity. . . . It is doubtful whether a credit card company will issue new cards to someone calling up and declaring a common law name change." Rosenaft, *Comment: The Right of Men to Change Their Names Upon Marriage*, 5 U. Pa. J. Const. L. 186, 206 (2002). *See also* 83 Op. Att'y Gen. Cal. No. 00-205 (2000) ("the inability to establish one's name for purposes of life's daily transactions, although perhaps only occasionally resulting when sole reliance is placed on the common law method, can be a substantial inconvenience when it occurs"). The availability of self-help was cited by a court who rejected a man's attempt to force a woman to stop using his surname after the annulment of their marriage. *Smithers v. Smithers*, 804 So. 2d 489 (Fla. App. 2001) (no fraud involved and plaintiff lacked standing to seek to change another person's name).

A third method of changing names is available in some states, which grant divorce court judges power to restore wife's maiden name upon divorce. Some statutes make grant of the request mandatory, if requested. *See, e.g.*, Ga. Code Ann. § 19-5-16 (1999). ("If a divorce is granted, the judgment . . . shall . . . restore to the party the name [sought] in the pleadings."). Indeed, the Georgia statute speaks in terms of "restoration of a maiden or prior name," thus making clear that a husband who had adopted his wife's name upon marriage could return to his pre-marital surname. While divorce courts routinely grant such requests even without such mandatory language, some trial courts have expressed reluctance to grant the ex-wife/mother's name change request. *See Miller v. Miller,* 670 S.W.2d 591 (Mo. App. 1984) (reversing trial court's requirement that applicant prove no detriment to children).

What factors would affect the choice of method for changing one's name?

4. *Limits on Freedom to Change Names.* There apparently are some limits on the ability to change one's name. Thus, it has been written that a person may be known by any name "in the absence of fraud, misrepresentation or interference with the rights of others." *In re Linda Ann A.,* 480 N.Y.S.2d 996 (Sup. Ct. 1984). Note the additional restraints suggested by *Natale* ("bizarre, obscene, offensive, or of a governmental body"). Another court wrote:

> [denial of a name change is warranted] when there is factual proof of an "unworthy motive, the possibility of fraud on the public, or the choice of a name that is bizarre, unduly lengthy, ridiculous or offensive to common decency and good taste."

In re Porter, 31 P. 3d 519 (Utah 2001*); see also In re Bobrowich,* 2003 N.Y. Misc. LEXIS 52 (Civ. Ct) (denial appropriate for "obscene, pornographic, or offensive" names or those which "violate . . . public policy or morals"). Some statutes require sworn testimony concerning petitioner's criminal record. *See State v. Barkwell,* 600 S.W.2d 497 (Mo. App. 1979).

Thus, most courts will grant the petition of the married woman (or anybody else) so long as there is no evidence of fraud or misrepresentation, but some cases and statutes seem to require a justification. In *In re Mohlman,* 216 S.E.2d 147 (N.C. App. 1975), the court affirmed refusal of name changes for several married women who asserted only "personal and professional reasons" for the change. The court held that a statute permitting a change "for good cause shown and for good and sufficient reasons" (N.C. GEN. STAT. § 101-2 (2001)) required something more. Perhaps understandably, the court did not detail what such good reasons might be. More recently, appellate courts have suggested a change from a male to a female name was inappropriate for a male with a history of "significant periods of gender confusion" without sex-change surgery, *In re DeWeese*, 772 N.E.2d 692 (Ohio App. 2002), and inappropriate where a person wanted to change his name to "Steffi Owned Slave." *In re Bobrowich*, 2003 N.Y. Misc. LEXIS 52 (Civ. Ct).

Natale rejects the claim that children suffer sufficient harm when the parent(s) they live with don't share their name to justify rejection of a proposed name change. For further discussion of this claim, see Chapter 6 at pp. 634-35.

5. *What Names are Being Used?* A 1993 survey conducted for AMERICAN DEMOGRAPHICS concluded only 10 percent of married women in this country use something other than their husband's last name. Brightman, *Why Hillary Chooses Rodham Clinton*, AMERICAN DEMOGRAPHICS, March, 1994 at p. 9. The survey reported half those using non-traditional names use hyphenated surnames which include their birth name and their husband's. Twenty percent use their own birth name exclusively, while 30% "use other alternatives," including use of their birth name as a middle name.

Education, income and age are important variables correlated to women's use of non-traditional names. For example, 21% of women with a post-graduate education do not use their husband's name as compared to 5% of women whose education stopped after high school. Fourteen percent of those under 30 use non-traditional names and only 5% of those over 60. Household income, however, does not present as neat a picture. Thirteen percent of women in households with $60,000 or more are in the non-traditional category, as compared to 7% of those whose income is between $12,500 and $39,999. One tenth of those below $12,500, however, use non-traditional names. A more recent article describes a national survey of 2,000 married women reporting that 95% took their husband's names. A Danish academic at Radcliffe College reported that in her native country women went from taking their husbands' names to retaining their names "within one generation in the 1970s." By way of explanation, she speculated that "the United States may have a more romantic notion of marriage, which keeps the name issue associated with emotional love, rather than a reminder of an old system in which a woman was the property of her husband." Wen, *Tradition in Name Only*, BOSTON GLOBE, Mar. 17, 2001, at p. A1.

[2] LIABILITY FOR SPOUSAL VIOLENCE

SIEGEL, "THE RULE OF LOVE": WIFE BEATING AS PREROGATIVE AND PRIVACY, 105 Yale L.J. 2117, 2118 (1996)

The . . . common law originally provided that a husband, as master of his household, could subject his wife to corporal punishment or "chastisement" so long as he did not inflict permanent injury. . . . During the nineteenth century, an era of feminist agitation for reform. . ., authorities in England and the United States declared that a husband no longer had the right to chastise his wife. Yet, for a century after . . ., the American legal system continued to treat wife beating differently from other cases of assault and battery. . . .[A]uthorities . . . intervened only intermittently in cases of marital violence: Men who assaulted their wives were often granted formal and informal immunities from prosecution, in order to protect the privacy of the family and to promote "domestic harmony." In the late 1970s, the feminist movement began to challenge the concept of family privacy that shielded wife abuse, and since then, it has secured many reforms designed to protect women from marital violence. Yet violence in the household persists. The U.S. Surgeon General recently found that "battering of women by husbands, ex-husbands or lovers '[is] the single largest cause of injury to women in the United States.' "[5] "[T]hirty-one percent of all women murdered in America are killed by their husbands, ex-husbands, or lovers."

[The author asserts "repudiation of chastisement precipitated a shift in the rules and rhetoric of laws regulating interspousal violence — giving rise to a new doctrinal regime couched in discourses of affective privacy that preserved, to a significant degree, the marital prerogative that chastisement rules once protected." This was reflected in both criminal and tort law through the early 20th century. In the criminal law, while courts explicitly rejected chastisement, they often refused to entertain prosecutions of husbands for wife-beating on grounds of family privacy. "If no permanent injury has been inflicted, nor malice, cruelty nor dangerous violence shown . . ., it is better to draw the curtain, shut out the public gaze, and leave the parties to forget and forgive." *State v. Oliver*, 70 N.C. 60 (1874). The tort interspousal immunity doctrine, based on marital privacy, kept assault and battery claims by wives against husbands out of court.]

By the beginning of the twentieth century, [marital privacy] . . . found institutional expression in the criminal justice system. . . . [C]ities began to establish special domestic relations courts staffed by social workers to handle complaints of marital violence. . . . The family court system sought to decriminalize marital violence. [A] New York City judge explained . . . "domestic trouble cases are not criminal in a legal sense."

Rather than punish those who assaulted their partners, the judges and social workers urged couples to reconcile, providing informal or formal counseling designed to preserve the relationship whenever possible. Battered wives were discouraged from filing criminal charges against their husbands, urged to accept responsibility for their role in provoking the violence, and encouraged to remain in the relationship and rebuild it rather than attempt to separate or divorce. The police adjusted their arrest procedures to accord with the new philosophy. . . .

The criminal justice system regulated marital violence in this "therapeutic" framework for much of the twentieth century. . . . [T]he criminal justice

---

[5] Zorza, *The Criminal Law of Misdemeanor Domestic Violence, 1970-1990*, 83 J. Crim. L. & Criminology 46, 46 (1992) (quoting Hightower & McManus, *Limits of State Constitutional Guarantees: Lesson from Efforts to Implement Domestic Violence Policies*, 49 Pub. Admin. Rev. 269 (1989)).

system developed a set of formal procedures for handling marital violence . . . that provided informal immunity . . . in many circumstances. In the 1960s, for example, the training bulletin of the international association of chiefs of police offered the following instructions for handling "family disturbances":

> For the most part these disputes are personal matters requiring no direct police action. . . . Once inside the home, the officer's sole purpose is to preserve the peace . . . attempt to soothe feelings, pacify parties . . . [and] suggest parties refer their problem to a church or a community agency. . . . In dealing with family disputes . . . arrest should be [used] as a last resort. The officer should never create a police problem when there is only a family problem existing.

Until the last decade, this set of instructions was quite typical. . . .

. . . . Today, after numerous protest activities and law suits, there are shelters for battered women and their children, new arrest procedures for police departments across the country, and even federal legislation making gender-motivated assaults a civil rights violation. . . .

Because statistics on domestic violence document chastisement's continuing legacy in a different narrative mode, it is worth considering the recent figures in a bit more detail. As of 1995, justice department statistics show that:

- About three-quarters of all lone-offender violence against women was perpetrated by an offender whom the victim knew.

- In 29% of all violence against women by a lone offender, the perpetrator was a husband, ex-husband, boyfriend, or ex-boyfriend — an intimate.

- Female victims of violent incidents were more likely to be injured when the perpetrator was an intimate than when the assailant was a stranger.

The gender asymmetry of violence between intimates remains dramatic. The Justice Department has estimated that 90% to 95% of domestic violence victims are women. Compared to men, women were about six times more likely to experience violence committed by an intimate. Female homicide victims were more than nine times more likely to have been killed by a husband, ex-husband, or boyfriend than male homicide victims were to have been killed by their wife, ex-wife, or girlfriend. In 1992 approximately 28% of female victims of homicide were known to have been killed by their husband, ex-husband, or boyfriend; in contrast, just over 3% of male homicide victims were known to have been killed by their wife, ex-wife, or girlfriend. In considering these statistics, it should be kept in mind that they include assaults by women undertaken in self-defense.

As the statistics on homicide of women by intimates suggest, assaults between intimates can involve significant amounts of violence. The Justice Department estimates that one-third of domestic violence attacks, if reported, would be classified as felony rapes, robberies, or aggravated assaults. The rest would be classified as simple assaults, though many of them involved " 'bodily injury at least as serious as the injury inflicted in 90 percent of all robberies and aggravated assaults.' " And the American Medical Association's Council on Scientific Affairs reports that "over 80% of all assaults against spouses and ex-spouses result in injuries, compared with 54% of the victims of stranger violence; victims of marital violence also have the highest rates of internal injuries and unconsciousness." (In a 1985 survey of intact couples, nearly one of every eight husbands had carried out an act of physical aggression against his female partner. "Over one-third of these assaults involved severe aggression such as punching, kicking, choking, beating up, or using a knife or a gun.")

Finally, domestic violence remains widespread. The Journal of the American Medical Association reports that approximately four million women are believed to be battered every year by their partners, and estimates that at least one-fifth of all women will be physically assaulted by a partner or ex-partner during their lifetime. The 1985 National Family Violence Survey found that "154 out of every 1000 pregnant women were assaulted by their mates during the first four months of pregnancy, and 170 per 1000 women were assaulted during the fifth through the ninth months" of pregnancy. Women who are assaulted by their male partners are more likely to be repeatedly attacked, raped, injured, or killed than are women assaulted by other types of assailants.

As these statistics suggest, marital violence persists, notwithstanding profound changes in the laws and mores of marriage since [1900]. And, despite the contemporary feminist movement's efforts to pierce the veil of privacy talk surrounding the practice, Americans still reason about marital violence in the discourse of affective privacy. O.J. Simpson invoked this tradition in 1989 when he shouted at police who had responded to his wife's call for help: " 'The police have been out here eight times before, and now you're going to arrest me for this? This is a family matter. Why do you want to make a big deal out of it when we can handle it?' " . . . .

More recently, the Chief Justice of the United States invoked this discourse of the private when he objected to provisions in the new Violence Against Women Act that create a federal cause of action for gender-motivated violence. The bill's "broad definition of criminal conduct is so open-ended, and the new private right of action so sweeping," Chief Justice Rehnquist complained, "that the legislation could involve the federal courts in a whole host of domestic relations disputes."

NOTES

1. *Estimates of Family Violence.* In 1988, two leading researchers summarized the various estimates of family violence (including their own) in the United States. Professors Straus and Gelles defined violent acts as: throwing an object at another person, pushing, grabbing, shoving, slapping, spanking, kicking, biting, punching, choking, threatening with a knife or gun or using a knife or gun. Under this definition, they estimated 8.7 million people were victims of spousal violence in 1985 (16.1% of couples). Victims of "severe violence" (kicking, biting, punching, beating up, choking, use or threatened use of a weapon) totaled, according to their estimate, 3.4 million (6.3% of all couples). In summarizing other studies, they reported estimates of spousal violence ranging from 12.1% to 51%. Straus & Gelles, *How Violent*

Are American Families? Estimates from the National Family Violence Resurvey and Other Studies, in FAMILY ABUSE AND ITS CONSEQUENCES: NEW DIRECTIONS IN RESEARCH (Hotaling, et al., eds. 1988). According to Straus and Gelles, the rate of spousal violence reported in the National Crime Survey (NCS) is less than 3%, as compared to their estimate of 16.1% from the National Family Violence Survey.

> The most likely reason for the tremendous discrepancy lies in differences between the context of the NCS versus the other studies. The NCS is presented to respondents as a study of crime, whereas the others are presented as studies of family problems. The difficulty with a "crime survey" as the context for determining incidence rates of intrafamily violence is that most people think of being kicked by their spouses as wrong, but not a "crime". . . . Thus only a minute proportion of assaults by spouses are reported in the National Crime Survey.

> *Id.* at 20.

A 1997 New York City Department of Health study reported "more women in New York City are killed by their husbands or boyfriends than in robberies, disputes, sexual assaults, drug violence, random attacks or any other crime in cases where the motive for murder is known." Belluck, *A Woman's Killer is Likely to be Her Partner, a Study Finds*, N.Y. TIMES, Mar. 31, 1997, at p. A12. The researchers noted the cause of death of every woman killed in the city between 1990 and 1994. Nearly half the women for whom a cause of death could be identified "were killed by current or former husbands or boyfriends. . . ." *Id.* The study also noted that "in nearly one-third of the cases where husbands and boyfriends killed women, the men also tried to kill themselves." *Id.*

Research also suggests a link between family violence and violence outside the family. A 1989 article, using two national household surveys and a student survey as a basis for its claims, asserts that domestic violence victims and perpetrators are more likely than others to perpetrate aggression outside the family. Hotaling et al, *Intrafamily Violence, and Crime and Violence Outside the Family*, 11 CRIME AND JUSTICE 315 (1989). The authors note that these links remain when controlling for socioeconomic status, gender and severity of family violence and is inconsistent with the notion that family violence is fundamentally different from "ordinary" violence or "crime in the streets." The breadth of family violence across a broad spectrum of socioeconomic strata is reflected by a recent spate of disciplinary actions against attorneys based on domestic abuse convictions. *See, e.g., In re Grella*, 777 N.E.2d 167 (Mass. 2002) (suspending attorney for two months based on misdemeanor assault and battery committed against wife while their four children were in the home); *In re Melvin*, 807 A.2d 550 (Del. 2002) (suspending attorney for 18 months for two misdemeanor convictions for violating family court order protecting spouse).

Domestic violence often has a direct impact on victims outside the family. It has been reported that "more police die in connection with domestic violence encounters than during any other aspect of their work." Fain, *Conjugal Violence: Legal and Psychosociological Remedies*, 32 SYR. L. REV. 497, 504 (1981) (reporting 22.2% of all police homicides occur during domestic violence calls). This sometimes results from feuding spouses joining against the officer as a common enemy and at least partly explains the police manual language quoted by Professor Siegel.

2. *Men as Victims of Spousal Abuse.* Professor Siegel asserts women are more often the victims of spousal abuse than men. In fact, data derived from The National Crime Victimization Survey suggests husbands commit spousal violence more than 10 times more often than wives do. National Family Violence Survey data, however, paints a very different picture. According to the 1985 Survey (utilizing a nationally representative sample of 6,002 married and cohabiting couples), women commit slightly more minor assaults than men on their mates and men are slightly more often guilty of severe assaults on their mates than women. Straus, *Physical Assaults by Women Partners: A Major Social Problem* in WOMEN, MEN AND GENDER: ONGOING DEBATES at p. 210 (M. R. Walsh, ed. 1997) [hereinafter WOMEN, MEN AND GENDER]. Professor Straus suggests the difference between the Justice Department and Family Violence Survey data is caused by the fact that:

> in the context of a crime survey, people tend to report attacks only when they have been experienced as "real crimes" — because they resulted in injury or were perpetrated by former partners.

Id. at p. 212. Professor Straus asserts that every study that is not "self-selective . . . has found a rate of assault by women on male partners that is about the same as the rate of assault by men on female partners." *Id.* at p. 211.

Even if Straus' claim that women commit severe attacks almost as often as men do are true, female domestic violence victims clearly sustain greater injuries than males. For example, 3% of female victims in the Violence Survey needed medical treatment for their injuries, while only 0.4% of male victims required such attention. Stets & Straus, *Gender Differences in Reporting Marital Violence and Its Medical and Psychological Consequences* in PHYSICAL VIOLENCE IN AMERICAN FAMILIES: RISK FACTORS AND ADAPTATIONS TO VIOLENCE IN 8,145 FAMILIES at p. 157 (Straus & Gelles eds. 1990) [hereinafter PHYSICAL VIOLENCE IN AMERICAN FAMILIES]. Also, it is generally assumed that a significant portion of female-to-male violence is in self-defense, though Professor Straus finds the evidence ambiguous. He cites studies claiming at least "25–30 percent of violent relationships are violent solely because of attacks by the woman." WOMEN, MEN AND GENDER at p. 214.

He argues further that even if female violence can be explained as self-defense, it nevertheless must be dealt with by society because the "moral justification of assault implicit when she slaps or throws something at him for something outrageous strengthens implicit norms which justify assaults *by men.*" (emphasis in original). PHYSICAL VIOLENCE IN AMERICAN FAMILIES. For other work on men as victims of spouse abuse, see Detschelt, *Recognizing Domestic Violence Directed Towards Men: Overcoming Societal Perceptions, Conducting Accurate Studies, and Enacting Responsible Legislation*, 12 KAN. J. L.& PUB. POL'Y 249 (2003) (asserting "domestic violence against men is . . . a serious social issue that must be fully addressed" and suggesting, among other reforms, gender-neutralization of domestic violence statutes); Migliaccio,

Abused Husbands: A Narrative Analysis, 23 J. FAM. ISSUES 26 (2002) (reporting on interviews with male victims of domestic violence); COOK, ABUSED MEN: THE HIDDEN SIDE OF DOMESTIC VIOLENCE (1997); Saunders, *When Battered Women Use Violence: Husband Abuse or Self-Defense?*, 1 VIOLENCE AND VICTIMS 47 (1986).

3. ***Criminally Prosecuting Family Violence.*** The crimes of assault and battery are available for prosecution of spousal violence. "Not a single jurisdiction has chosen to exempt domestic assaults from the ambit of the criminal law." Marcus, *Conjugal Violence: The Law of Force and the Force of Law,* 69 CALIF. L. REV. 1657, 1662 (1981). As indicated in Professor Siegel's article, though, police and prosecutors traditionally have treated domestic violence differently from other similar incidents.

> Discriminatory enforcement policies . . . can be found in official statements as well as individual cases. . . . Victims are told that courts are not in session and that no judge is available. These directions . . . are remarkable for their failure to predicate arrest on relevant criteria such as seriousness of the injury, use of weapons, acts of violence committed in the officer's presence or outstanding orders of protection indicating repeated prior attacks.
>
> Prosecutors have required extra elements before proceeding . . ., including witnesses other than the victim and children, a record of prior attacks, a police report already on file and serious visible injuries. Even when the victim is ready to testify and the additional criteria are met, such cases may be rejected automatically on the theory that securing a conviction is more difficult than in nonfamilial cases. . . .

Id. at 1688–91. Empirical studies demonstrate relatively few arrests are made in domestic violence incidents. *See* Buzawa, *Responding to Crimes of Violence Against Women: Gender Differences Versus Organizational Imperatives*, 41 CRIME & DELINQ. 443 (1995); Note, *Mandatory Arrest for Domestic Violence,* 11 HARV. WOMEN'S L.J. 213, 217 (1988) (citing surveys showing arrest rates from 3% to 10% and a Philadelphia study finding arrests in only 13% of the cases in which police observed injuries to victim*).*

4. ***Civil Rights Actions Claiming Failure to Enforce Laws Against Domestic Violence***. A series of cases in the 1980s recognized a federal § 1983 civil rights cause of action on behalf of abused spouses against municipalities which failed to respond to domestic violence reports or applied special arrest policies in such cases. *See, e.g., Hynson v. City of Chester,* 864 F.2d 1026 (3d Cir. 1988); *Watson v. Kansas City,* 857 F.2d 690 (10th Cir. 1988); *Balistreri v. Pacifica Police Dep't,* 855 F.2d 1421 (9th Cir. 1988); *Thurman v. City of Torrington,* 595 F. Supp. 1521 (D. Conn. 1984); *Bartalone v. Berrian Cty.,* 643 F. Supp. 574 (E.D. Mich. 1986). The *Thurman* plaintiff was awarded $2.3 million by a jury. Eppler, *Battered Women and the Equal Protection Clause: Will the Constitution Help Them When the Police Won't?*, 95 YALE L.J. 788, 795 at n. 31 (1986).

The efficacy of § 1983 in such cases, however, was limited by *DeShaney v. Winnebago Cty. Dep't of Social Servs.,* 489 U.S. 189 (1989) (generally "State's failure to protect an individual against private violence simply does not constitute a violation of the Due Process Clause"). Claims of a § 1983 violation based on gender discrimination may remain a viable theory in seeking damages against a police department. *See Fajardo v. Los Angeles County*, 179 F.3d 698 (9th Cir. 1999) (remanding for determination whether domestic 911 calls were given lower priority than others and, if so, whether such a policy survived rational relationship Equal Protection review). Additionally, a recent case held that violation of a mandatory arrest statute gave rise to a procedural Due Process claim cognizable under § 1983. *Gonzales v. Castle Rock*, 307 F.3d 1258 (10th Cir. 2002). *See also* Note, *Due Process and Equal Protection Challenges to the Inadequate Response of the Police in Domestic Violence Situations*, 68 S. CAL. L. REV. 1295 (1995) (detailing avenues available to civil rights plaintiffs); Note, *Battered Women Suing Police for Failure to Intervene: Viable Legal Avenues After* DeShaney v. Winnebago Department of Social Services, 75 CORNELL L. REV. 1393 (1990).

5. *Mandatory Criminal Arrest and Prosecution*. A 2002 survey reported 16 state statutes requiring arrest when the law enforcement official discovers domestic violence. Epstein, *Procedural Justice: Tempering the State's Response to Domestic Violence,* 43 WM. & MARY L. REV. 1843 (2002)(also noting 24 states with statutes mandating arrest on probable cause that a protective order has been violated); *see, e.g.*, CONN. GEN. STAT. ANN. § 46b-38b (2003 Supp.) (requiring arrest where officer "determines on speedy information that a family violence crime has been committed within his jurisdiction"); OR.. REV. STAT. § 133.055 (1998 Supp.) (family violence exception to general policy permitting citation in lieu of arrest); *Campbell v. Campbell*, 682 A.2d 272 (N.J. Super. 1996) (approving action against police officer for negligent failure to abide by mandatory arrest statute). It is not at all clear, however, that mandatory arrest statutes actually reduce domestic violence. A leading researcher concludes such policies "may be doing more harm than good." SHERMAN, POLICING DOMESTIC VIOLENCE at 1 (1993). In the early 1980's, Professor Sherman conducted the "Minnesota experiment" testing arrest's effectiveness in reducing domestic violence. The experiment concluded "arrest and a night in jail for the suspect cut in half the risk of repeat violence against the same victim over a six-month follow-up period, from about 20% to 10%" *Id.* at 2. This study was used by many to justify mandatory arrest policies.

But Professor Sherman later tried to replicate the Minnesota experiment in five cities and reported evidence in three cities (Milwaukee, Charlotte and Omaha) that arrest *increases* the frequency of future domestic violence. On the other hand, in addition to Minneapolis (the original test site), Colorado Springs and Miami data suggest arrest works. The dividing line between "arrest deters" and "arrest doesn't deter" cities is in the "racial composition of the samples. On average, the proportion of black victims and suspects is substantially lower in the 'arrest deters' cities, and higher in the 'arrest backfires' cities." *Id.* at 3. The methodology of the follow-up studies has been criticized, see Niemi-Kiesilainen, *The Deterrent Effect of Arrest in Domestic Violence: Differerentiating Between Victim and Perpetrator Response*, 12 HAST. WOMEN'S L.J. 283 (2001) (urging focus on impact of arrest on victim's future behavior, including willingness to report; theorizes that "arrest deters violence *and* encourages victims to call the police"); Note, *Mandatory Arrest: A Step*

Toward Eradicating Domestic Violence, But is It Enough?, 1996 ILL. L. REV. 533, 555–57 (asserting mandatory arrest is important part of a comprehensive criminal justice policy); Zorza, *Must We Stop Arresting Batterers? Analysis and Policy Implications of New Police Domestic Violence Studies*, 28 NEW ENG. L. REV. 929 (1994), while others have used the follow-up to argue for a flexible policy of arrest preserving discretion for law enforcement personnel. Comment, *Mandatory Arrest of Domestic Abusers: Panacea or Perpetuation of the Problem of Abuse?*, 43 DEPAUL L. REV. 1133 (1994). There is some evidence, in fact, that even in jurisdictions with such policies, law enforcement personnel do not actually make arrests in domestic violence cases. Mignon & Holmes, *Police Response to Mandatory Arrest Laws*, 41 CRIME & DELINQ. 430 (1995).

A recent commentator, reviewing several experiments on the effects of arrest on domestic violence, concluded:

> The lesson of these studies is that formal (legal) sanctions are effective when reinforced by informal social controls. . . . [T]he deterrent effects of arrest will be greater for batterers who perceive higher social costs associated with the act of violence and with arrest. These costs include loss of job, relationship and children, social status in the neighborhood, and whatever substantive punishment they receive.

FAGAN, THE CRIMINALIZATION OF DOMESTIC VIOLENCE: PROMISES AND LIMITS at p. 22 (National Institute of Justice 1996). For an annotated bibliography on police response to spouse abuse, see Egan, *The Police Response to Spouse Abuse: A Selective, Annotated Bibliography*, 91 L. LIB. J. 499 (1999); *see also* Fedders, *Lobbying for Mandatory-Arrest Policies: Race, Class, and the Politics of the Battered Women's Movement*, 23 N.Y.U. REV. L. & SOC. CHANGE 281 (1997) (asserting "mandatory-arrest advocates are from a limited demographic base, ascribe to a narrow theoretical framework, and have an advocacy agenda that reflects this homogeneity").

Similar issues are raised by "no-drop" policies under which "the state pursues cases regardless of the victim's wishes. Thus, attempts to intimidate or dissuade the victim from proceeding would be ineffective. The community would understand that the state takes domestic violence cases seriously and that prosecution is consistent, not arbitrary." Hanna, *No Right to Choose: Mandated Victim Participation in Domestic Violence Prosecutions*, 109 HARV. L. REV. 1849, 1852 (1996). Professor Epstein's article, *supra*, cites a survey indicating 2/3 of "prosecutor's offices in major urban centers . . . had adopted such policies." Under such a policy, victims may be subpoenaed to testify and face the possibility of jail for contempt for refusal to testify. Professor Hanna recognizes the risks posed by such a policy for victims, but asserts more "aggressive domestic violence policies" by prosecutors can "reduce the likelihood that the victim will ever have to take the stand." *Id.* at 1857. Such policies include putting more effort into gathering physical and medical evidence by creating "specific evidence-gathering and arrest protocols to ensure that the arrest of the batterer leads to prosecution and not to case dismissal." *Id.* at 1901. Professor Hanna, a former prosecutor of such cases, argues "prosecutors have both a responsibility and a duty to present evidence that communicates that the harm of domestic violence extends beyond the victim's home and produces consequences for the whole community." *Id.* at 1908. *See also* Note,

No-Drop Policies in the Prosecution of Domestic Violence Cases: Guarantee to Action or Dangerous Solution?, 63 FORD. L. REV. 853 (1994); Kirsch, *Problems in Domestic Violence: Should Victims Be Forced to Participate in the Prosecution of Their Abusers?*, 7 WM. & MARY J. WOMEN & L. 383(2001) (reporting empirical study of one prosecutor's office in Indiana; assesses costs and benefits of no-drop policies); Robbins, *No-Drop Prosecution of Domestic Violence: Just Good Policy, or Equal Protection Mandate*, 52 STAN. L. REV. 205 (1999) (advocating adoption of no-drop policy along with "careful *ad hoc* consideration of victim safety" as best way to insure compliance with the Constitution).

For a critique of a range of mandatory policies, including those requiring arrest, prosecution and reporting by medical personnel, see Mills, *Killing Her Softly: Intimate Abuse and the Violence of State Intervention*, 113 HARV. L. REV. 550 (1999) (social work professor argues "state interventions designed to eradicate the intimate abuse in battered women's lives all too often reproduce the emotional abuse of the battering relationship"); *see also* Coker, *Crime Control and Feminist Law Reform in Domestic Violence Law: A Critical Review*, 4 BUFF. CRIM. L. REV. 801 (2001) (asserting mandatory policies "may further state control of women"). Professor Mills presents "survivor-centered model" of intervention as an alternative. *See also* Han, *Mandatory Arrest and No-Drop Policies: Victim Empowerment in Domestic Violence Cases*, 23 B.C. THIRD WORLD L.J. 159 (2003) (urging arrest and prosecution policies be considered separately and arguing an "important component of a victim-centered approach to justice is the recognition that mandatory policies are problematic in their lack of flexibility").

Even if an arrest is made in such an incident and the case is prosecuted, judges and juries may treat it differently from other types of violence. *See* Note, *The Battered Woman Syndrome and Self-Defense,* 72 VA. L. REV. 619 (1986); Blair, *Making the Legal System Work for Battered Women,* in BATTERED WOMEN 114–15 (1979); Comment, *The Case for Legal Remedies for Abused Women,* 6 N.Y.U. REV. L.& SOC. CHANGE 135, 151 (1976); Comment, *Wife Beating: Law and Society Confront the Castle Door,* 15 GONZAGA L. REV. 171, 197 (1979). Also, the jury may acquit despite overwhelming evidence of guilt. Jury nullification has been defended, in another context, as introducing into law enforcement the "mollifying influence of current ethical [standards]." *United States ex rel. McCann v. Adams,* 126 F.2d 774, 775 (2d Cir. 1942) (Hand, J.).

6. *Is Spousal Violence on the Decline?* It has been suggested that efforts by the legal system to condemn and punish domestic violence, to provide shelters for victims and provide alternative such as restraining orders (*see* Note 7) may be having some effect on the rates of domestic violence. Straus & Kaufman Kantor, *Paper Presented at the 13th World Congress of Sociology, Bielefeld, Germany*, July 19, 1994 (on file with Professor Kurtz). Using the National Family Violence Surveys of 1975 and 1985 and the 1992 National Alcohol and Family Violence Survey (all focused on couples who were either married or cohabiting), the authors find a constant decrease in the rate of severe assaultive behavior by men in the domestic context. It should be noted, however, that during this time there also has been a general decline in crime rates. While acknowledging the decline in male domestic violence may be based merely on increasing reluctance by men to report having assaulted their partner, rather than an actual decline in wife-beating, the authors argue that

> even if the entire decrease (in male violence) reflects differences in willingness to report, that would still be an important achievement because it indicates a heightened sensitivity . . . and . . . awareness that hitting one's wife is condemned by society. That heightened awareness is probably a necessary part of the process of changing the rate of actual assaults.

By contrast, the authors found both the 1985 and 1992 surveys reflect no change in the rate of assaults by wives, as compared to the 1975 baseline. They conclude "part of the reason may be that there has been no effort to condemn assault by wives parallel to the effort to condemn assaults by husbands." *Id.*

As for cultural norms concerning domestic violence, Straus and Kaufman Kantor report four national surveys between 1968 and 1994 reflect a constantly declining percentage of approval of the statement, "Are there any situations that you can imagine in which you would approve of a husband slapping his wife's face?" Approval of slapping by husbands went from 20% in 1968 to 10% in 1994. Approval by both men and women of slapping by wives, however, "has not changed significantly." Straus & Kaufman Kantor, *Change in Cultural Norms Approving Marital Violence,* in OUT OF THE DARKNESS: CONTEMPORARY RESEARCH PERSPECTIVES ON FAMILY VIOLENCE (Kaufman Kantor & Jasinski, eds., 1997) (reporting 21% approval of slapping by wives in 1968 and 22% in 1994).

7. *Non-Criminal Response to Spousal Abuse.* Virtually every state has legislation providing for "civil orders of protection" for domestic violence victims. Such statutes often broadly define family, so as to protect victims unrelated by blood or marriage to their attackers. For example, the Minnesota Domestic Abuse Act provides for protection orders for violence between "family or household members" and defines the latter as

> spouses and former spouses; parents and children; persons related by blood; persons who are presently residing together or who have resided together in the past; persons who have a child in common regardless of whether they have been married or have lived together at any time; a man and a woman if the woman is pregnant and the man is alleged to be the father. . .; and persons involved in a significant romantic or sexual relationship.

MINN. STATS. ANN. § 518B.01, subd. 2(b) (2003 Supp.). The statute's breadth would seem to include, for example, a cohabiting or formerly cohabiting same-sex couple. A recent commentator identified 48 state statutes protecting cohabitors from domestic violence, while 6 such statutes explicitly exclude same-sex couples. Note, *Queer Justice: Equal Protection for Victims of Same-Sex Domestic Violence*, 30 VAL. L. REV. 335, 345 (1995); *see also Ohio v. Yaden,* 692 N.E.2d 1097 (Ohio App. 1997) (applying similar criminal domestic violence statute in same-sex context); *Ireland v. Davis,* 957 S.W.2d 310 (Ky. App. 1997) (finding the word "couple" in a domestic violence statute includes homosexual relationship); *see also* Note, *Same-Sex Domestic Violence: Addressing the Issues for the Proper Protection of Victims*, 4 J.L. IN SOC'Y 99 (2002); Knauer, *Same-Sex Domestic Violence: Claiming a Domestic Sphere While Risking Negative Stereotypes*, 8 TEMP. POL. & CIV. RTS. L. REV. 325 (1999); Comment, *Trouble in Paradise: Barriers to Addressing Domestic Violence in Lesbian Relationships*, 9 LAW & SEX. 311 (1999).

Does coverage of violence between those "who have resided together in the past," in the language of the Minnesota statute, last indefinitely? New Jersey's statute, which applies to "former household members," has been the source of much litigation. Recent cases rejected jurisdiction where the litigants were middle-aged brothers who had not lived together for over 20 years, *Jutchenko v. Jutchenko*, 660 A.2d 1267 (N.J. App. Div. 1995), and where the parties had ended a cohabitational relationship over four years before with only one intervening telephone call. *Sperling v. Teplitsky*, 683 A.2d 244 (N.J. Super. Ct., Chanc. Div. 1996). On the other hand, a more recent case granted standing to seek a protective order where the parties had not lived under the same roof for 19 years, *Storch v. Sauerhoff,* 757 A. 2d 836 (N.J. Ch. Div. 2000) (noting defendant was petitioner's stepmother and parties had lived in separate residences on same street for 11 years), and a former dating partner had standing where the relationship had ended four years earlier. *Tribuzio v. Roder*, 813 A.2d 1210 (N.J. Super. Ct. App. Div. 2003) (noting frequent attempted contact by defendant during intervening time period). For a New Jersey case holding college dormitory suitemates were members of the same household under the domestic violence statute, see *Hamilton v. Ali*, 795 A.2d 929 (N.J. Ch. Div. 2002). For another case dealing with coverage under a civil domestic violence statute, see *Embry v. Balfanz*, 817 A.2d 6 (Vt. 2002) (finding brothers-in-law outside statute protecting "family members" and "household members").

Generally short-term protective orders are obtained in an *ex parte* proceeding and may order the abuser's eviction, temporary child support and custody arrangements and, in some situations, mandatory counseling. After a hearing where both parties can be present, such orders may be made "permanent," usually for up to a year. Some statutes criminalize violation of protection orders. Because they are non-criminal, protection proceedings use a civil standard of proof (preponderance of the evidence) and focus on prevention of future anti-social conduct, rather than punishing prior behavior. Addressing the protective order's advantages and disadvantages, one commentator has written:

> Civil protection orders provide the only remedy for abuse that is not yet criminal. . . . Civil protection orders alone can provide victims with relief when the victim does not want the batterer charged criminally. . . . Due to fear of retaliation, many women do not want their partner arrested. In addition, if he were given a criminal record or jailed, he might lose his job and be unable to support the woman and their children. Moreover, the children might turn against their mother for "throwing dad in jail." Furthermore, most women are interested in stopping the battering, not punishing their partner. . . .

Many people have questioned whether civil protection orders against domestic abuse are effective. [They] have been criticized for failing to prevent further violence, for reinforcing a "soft" approach to a serious criminal problem, for being susceptible to fraud, and for being difficult to enforce.

. . . .

Finn, *Statutory Authority in the Use and Enforcement of Civil Protection Orders Against Domestic Abuse,* 23 FAM. L.Q. 43, 44–45 (1989); *see also* Ko, *Civil Restraining Orders for Domestic Violence: The Unresolved Question of Efficacy,* 11 S. CAL. INTERDISC. L.J. 361 (2002) (reviewing empirical studies of effectiveness of orders, both from victim's perspective and an objective approach assessing post-order abuse; finds impact much more positive from former perspective); Balos & Trotzky, *Enforcement of the Domestic Abuse Act in Minnesota: A Preliminary Study,* 6 LAW & INEQUALITY 83 (1988) (concluding orders usually eliminate violence).

For a fairly current 50-state survey of protective order statutes, see Note, *Victims of Abuse and Discrimination: Protecting Battered Homosexuals Under Domestic Violence Legislation,* 28 HOFSTRA L. REV. 1095, 1114–5 & nn. 171–76 (2000).

Is personal jurisdiction over a defendant required for issuance of a protective order? A recent Iowa decision analogized domestic violence litigation to divorce litigation in which courts have power over the marital status even without personal jurisdiction over one of the parties. *Bartsch v. Bartsch,* 636 N.W.2d 3 (Iowa 2001). Thus, the court approved issuance of a protective order against a Colorado resident sought by his former wife who had returned to her home state after their divorce in Utah. For decisions requiring and finding personal jurisdiction, see *A.R. v. M.R.,* 799 A.2d 27 (N.J. Super. Ct. App. Div. 2002) (phone calls from out of state to ascertain petitioner's residence after her flight from defendant's home in Mississippi); *Beckers v. Seck,* 14 S.W. 3d 139 (Mo. App. 2000) (harassing phone calls from out of state).

8. ***Federal Response to Domestic Violence.*** While not limited to domestic violence, the Violence Against Women Act of 1994 (VAWA) was a major entry into the field by the federal government. The Act, Pub. L. 103-322, authorized creation of a national, toll-free hotline for domestic violence victims, and authorized grants for battered women's shelters, for implementation of mandatory domestic violence arrest policies and for judicial and youth education about domestic violence. The Act created a federal crime for interstate travel resulting in bodily injury to the actor's "spouse or intimate partner." *See United States v. Bailey,* 112 F.3d 758 (4th Cir. 1997) (rejecting constitutional attack).

The Act's most controversial provision guaranteed "all persons within the United States. . . the right to be free from crimes of violence motivated by gender. . ." and created a federal cause of action (including compensatory and punitive damages) for victims of such crimes. *See* 42 U.S.C.S. § 13981 (Supp. 1996). The legislation asserted Congressional authority both under the Commerce Clause and § 5 of the Fourteenth Amendment.

In 2000, however, the Supreme Court held, in a 5-4 decision in *United States v. Morrison,* 529 U.S. 598 (2000), that Congress exceeded its Constitutional power in creating the private cause of action. In affirming the *en banc* decision of the Fourth Circuit, the Court majority rejected both Commerce Clause and Fourteenth Amendment assertions of power. Applying *United States v. Lopez*, 514 U.S. 549 (1995), the Court found "[g]ender-motivated crimes of violence are not, in any sense of the phrase, economic activity." It also noted there was no "jurisdictional element" tying the cause of action to interstate commerce and found insufficient the Congressional findings of an impact on interstate commerce by domestic violence. Section 5 of the Fourteenth Amendment was rejected as a source of Congressional authority for lack of state action. Two dissenting opinions were filed. For critical commentary on the Court's decision, see Resnik, *The Programmatic Judiciary: Lobbying, Judging, and Invalidating the Violence Against Women Act*, 74 S. Cal. L. Rev. 269 (2000); Anderson, *Women Do Not Report the Violence They Suffer: Violence Against Women and the State Action Doctrine*, 46 Vill. L. Rev. 907 (2001).

Other VAWA provisions have withstood constitutional attack in the lower courts. *See, e.g.,United States v. Al-Zubaidy*, 283 F.3d 804 (6th Cir. 2002) (upholding Act's interstate stalking provision against Commerce Clause attack); *United States v. Gluzman*, 154 F.3d 49 (2d Cir. 1998) (upholding criminalization of committing or attempting a crime of violence after traveling in interstate commerce with that purpose); *United States v. Von Foelkel*, 136 F.3d 339 (2d Cir. 1998) (rejecting constitutional attack on provision criminalizing crossing of state lines with intent to violate a protective order).

In 1996, the Lautenberg Amendment made it a federal crime for anyone "who has been convicted . . . of a misdemeanor crime of domestic violence" to ship, possess or receive "any firearm or ammunition" in interstate or foreign commerce. 18 U.S.C. § 922(g)(9). For commentary on this legislation, see Saylor , *Federalism and the Family After Morrison: An Examination of the Child Support Recovery Act, the Freedom of Access to Clinic Entrances Act, and a Federal Law Outlawing Gun Possession by Domestic Violence Abusers*, 25 Harv. Women's L.J. 57 (2002); Note, *Examining the Lautenberg Amendment in the Civilian and Military Contexts: Congressional Overreaching, Statutory Vagueness, Ex Post Facto Violations, and Implementational Flaws*, 29 Fordham Urb. L.J. 427 (2001); Note, *The Lautenberg Amendment: An Essential Tool for Combating Domestic Violence*, 75 N.D. L. Rev. 365 (1999); Note, *At the Intersection of Domestic Violence and Guns: The Public Interest Exception and the Lautenberg Amendment*, 85 Cornell L. Rev. 822 (2000); *see also United States v. Emerson*, 270 F.3d 203 (5th Cir. 2001) (rejecting Second Amendment claim by defendant prosecuted under related statute penalizing possession of a handgun by one subject to a temporary restraining order).

9. *Insurance Discrimination Against Domestic Violence Victims*. A recent commentator reports:

> . . . [T]he increased documentation of abuse-related injuries . . . has . . . resulted in a discrete and extremely counterproductive form of discrimination. Some insurance companies use . . . evidence of spousal abuse to discriminate against the victim by denying her access to all forms of insurance.

Note, *Insurance Discrimination Against Battered Women: Proposed Legislative Protections*, 72 Ind. L.J. 259, 260 (1996). The author predicts "victims may stop seeking help or reporting incidents of abuse in order to preserve necessary insurance coverage." *Id..* A 1998 Note identified 16 states which prohibit insurance discrimination against abuse victims. Note, *Review of Selected 1997 California Legislation: Ensuring the Victims of Domestic Abuse are Not Discriminated Against in the Insurance Industry,* 29 McGeorge L. Rev. 677, 682 (1998).

10. *Domestic Violence in the Workplace.* Domestic violence presents increasing problems in the workplace. It has been estimated that annually domestic violence causes 175,000 days of missed employment. Comment, *Employer Liability for Domestic Violence in the Workplace: Are Employers Walking a Tightrope Without a Safety Net?,* 31 Tex. Tech. L. Rev. 139, 143 (2000). In addition to its impact on the safety and productivity of the workplace, domestic violence may create liability on an employer who fails to provide protection to domestic abuse victims from their abusers. *See id.; see also* Robertson, *Addressing Domestic Violence in the Workplace: An Employer's Responsibility,* 16 Law & Ineq. J. 633 (1998). While workers' compensation coverage normally provides the exclusive remedy for employees injured on the job, exceptions to this exclusivity have been established in a number of jurisdictions. One such exception is recovery for damages caused by "injuries connected to inherently private relationships." Comment, *supra,* at p. 146 (detailing unreported Louisiana case permitting suit against employer where plaintiff was shot during work hours by spouse). *See also* Beaver, *Beyond the Exclusivity Rule: Employer's Liability for Workplace Violence,* 81 Marq. L. Rev. 103 (1997).

A different type of workplace victimization of domestic abuse targets has been reported. In *Green v. Bryant,* 887 F. Supp. 798 (E.D. Pa. 1995), the court rejected plaintiff's wrongful discharge claim based on her firing after being beaten and raped by her ex-husband. The court, however, suggested a claim would be recognized if "plaintiff alleged that she was discharged because she had applied for victim compensation or had sought a protective order." *See* Note, *Working Towards Freedom From Abuse: Recognizing a "Public Policy" Exception to Employment-at-Will for Domestic Violence Victims,* 59 N.Y.U. Ann. Surv. Am. L. 121 (2003) (urging recognition of cause of action for victims dismissed because of any "reason directly stemming from intimate partner abuse").

11. *Marital Rape Exemption.* A particularly egregious form of domestic violence is the rape of a woman by her husband. The common law, however, did not criminally punish such behavior. In 1984, the New York Court of Appeals summarized the history and rationale for the common law position:

> The assumption . . . is traceable to a statement made by the 17th century English jurist Lord Hale, who wrote: "[T]he husband cannot be guilty of a rape committed by himself upon his lawful wife, for by their mutual matrimonial consent and contract the wife hath given up herself in this kind unto her husband, which she cannot retract" (1 Hale, History of Pleas of The Crown, p. 629). Although Hale cited no authority for his statement it was relied on by State Legislatures . . . and by courts which established a common law exemption for husbands.

[An 1857 Massachussetts opinion] stated in dictum that it would always be a defense to rape to show marriage to the victim. . . . Decisions to the same effect by other courts followed, usually with no rationale or authority cited other than Hale's implied consent view. . . .

. . . .

. . . . Any argument based on a supposed consent, however, is untenable. Rape is not simply a sexual act to which one party does not consent. Rather, it is a degrading, violent act which violates the bodily integrity of the victim and frequently causes severe, long-lasting physical and psychic harm. To ever imply consent to such an act is irrational and absurd. Other than in the context of rape statutes, marriage has never been viewed as giving a husband the right to coerced intercourse on demand. Certainly, then, a marriage license should not be viewed as a license for a husband to forcibly rape his wife with impunity. A married woman has the same right to control her own body as does an unmarried woman. If a husband feels "aggrieved" by his wife's refusal to engage in sexual intercourse, he should seek [a divorce, but should not engage] in "violent or forceful self-help" (*State v. Smith*, 85 N.J. 193, 206).

The other traditional justifications . . . were the common law doctrines that a woman was the property of her husband and that the legal existence of the woman was "incorporated and consolidated into that of the husband" Both these doctrines, of course, have long been rejected in this State. . . .

People v. Liberta, 474 N.E.2d 567, 572–73 (N.Y. 1984). *See also* Hasday, *Contest and Consent: A Legal History of Marital Rape,* 88 CALIF. L. REV. 1373 (2000).

In finding the marital exemption unconstitutional, the *Liberta* court rejected the assertion that it protected marital privacy. The court found that only consensual acts were protected by privacy doctrine. Likewise, it dismissed arguments that marital rape would be a difficult crime to prove and that "vindictive" wives would likely fabricate rape charges. The court noted rape is always a difficult crime to prove and found wives to be no more likely than unmarried women to falsify rape charges, pointing out the criminal justice system's ability to weed out false complaints. *Liberta* was later applied to New York's marital exemption for third degree sexual abuse. *People v. Naylor*, 609 N.Y.S.2d 954, 956 (App. Div. 1994); *see also People v. M.D.*, 595 N.E.2d 702 (Ill. App. 1992) (citing *Liberta*, while striking down scheme providing marital exemption for lesser crimes of sexual abuse, but no exemption for aggravated sexual assault).

12. *Model Penal Code Position.* The Model Penal Code includes a marital exemption, applying it to "persons living as man and wife, regardless of the legal status of their relationship" until entry of a judicial separation decree. *See* §§ 213.1, 213.6(2). The 1980 commentary explains:

[Certainly a woman] may marry without surrendering to sex on demand. If on occasion she refuses, the husband has no right to compel her to submit. If he does so by force or physical menace, he may be guilty of assault. . . . Liability for rape is another matter. Rape may consist of wholly non-violent conduct, but where force is used, rape carries sanctions more severe than . . . assault. . . . [A] prior and continuing relation of intimacy . . . is not irrelevant. . . .

First, marriage . . . does imply a kind of generalized consent that distinguishes some versions of . . . rape from parallel behavior by a husband. The relationship itself creates a presumption of consent, valid until revoked. At a minimum, therefore, husbands must be exempt from those categories of liability based . . . on a presumed incapacity . . . to consent [such as sexual intercourse with a person who is unconscious] at least unless there are aggravating circumstances. . . . Plainly there must also be some form of spousal exclusion applicable to . . . statutory rape. . . .

[As for rape committed by force or threat,] in many such situations . . . the law of rape . . . would thrust the prospect of criminal sanctions into the ongoing process of adjustment in the marital relationship. Section 213.1, for example, defines as gross sexual imposition intercourse coerced "by any threat that would prevent resistance by a woman of ordinary resolution." [Perhaps] a woman of ordinary resolution would be prevented from resisting by her husband's threat to expose a secret to her mother, for example. Behavior of this sort within [a marriage] is no doubt unattractive, but it is a risky business for the law to intervene by threatening criminal sanctions. . . .

[As for sex] coerced by force or threat of physical harm, . . . the law already authorizes a penalty for assault. If the actor causes serious bodily injury, the punishment is quite severe. The issue is whether the still more drastic sanctions of rape should apply. The answer depends on whether the injury caused by forcible intercourse by a husband is equivalent to that inflicted by someone else. The gravity of the crime . . . derives not merely from its violent character but also from its achievement of a particularly degrading kind of unwanted intimacy. Where the attacker stands in an ongoing relation of sexual intimacy, that evil, as distinct from the force used to compel submission, may well be thought qualitatively different. The character of the voluntary association of husband and wife . . . may be thought to affect the nature of the harm involved . . . . That, in any event, is the conclusion long endorsed by the law of rape and carried forward in the Model Code provision.

Part II, Vol. 1, MODEL PENAL CODE & COMMENTARIES 344–46 (1980).

The Commentary posits a "generalized consent" to justify exonerating a husband who has sex with his unconscious wife. While echoing Lord Hale's view that marriage deprives women of the power to say no to sex, this provision seems sensible. While a husband who has sex with his unconscious wife has done something wrong, he certainly hasn't raped her.

But the Code exempts many more cases from its rape statute. For example, the cohabiting husband whose threats force his wife into sex is not a rapist under the statute. Why not? Is it clear that "the voluntary association of husband and wife" changes the nature of the harm imposed by unwanted intercourse? One study reports that more victims of marital rape suffer severe long-term effects than victims of stranger rape. RUSSELL, RAPE IN MARRIAGE 192–93 (1982). On the other hand, consider a situation where a married couple regularly has sex twice weekly (Monday and Wednesday). If the husband forces his wife to have sex on a Saturday morning, is she harmed in the same way as if a stranger had broken into the house and done the same acts?

Why is it "risky business for the law to intervene" where a wife is threatened by her husband with exposure of a secret? Is it any riskier, *e.g.*, than when a co-worker threatens to "tell the boss"? Even if one accepts the Commentary's rationale, it does not support an exemption until legal separation. The "ongoing relation of sexual intimacy," asserted by the Commentary to justify the spousal exemption, often is over long before a legal separation is obtained.

13. *Current Status of the Marital Rape Exemption.* According to one commentator:

> By 1990, no state retained an absolute marital rape exemption, although thirty-five states placed limits on the prosecution of marital rapists. Such prosecutorial limitations include non-cohabitation or aggravated force requirements, ceilings on punishment, specifications on when — and to whom — marital rape must be reported, and the creation of alternative, frequently misdemeanor, sexual assault statutes that applied [to felony rape behavior when committed by a spouse]. Within one year, ten of those thirty-five states revoked or revised these provisions. By 1994, twenty-four states had abolished any form of marital rape exemption — either through legislative reform or judicial interpretation of existing statutes. Nevertheless, at least thirteen states still offer preferential or disparate treatment to perpetrators of spousal sexual assault.

Note, *Ultimate Weapon?: Demythologizing Spousal Rape and Reconceptualizing Its Prosecution*, 48 STAN. L. REV. 677, 681–82 (1996).

A Note in the mid-1980s reported a counter-trend which actually expands the marital rape exemption. "[N]early one-quarter of the states have recently expanded the marital rape exemption to cover unmarried cohabitators and 'voluntary social companions.'" Note, *To Have and to Hold: The Marital Rape Exemption and the Fourteenth Amendment*, 99 HARV. L. REV. 1255 (1986) (criticizing trend as "modern version of Hale's theory that women who enter into relationships with men give an implied consent to sexual intercourse or that those who consent to intercourse once are forever bound"). While many of the statutes collected by the Note have been repealed since 1986, at least some remain. *E.g.*, Connecticut grants an affirmative defense in a number of sexual offenses where "defendant and the alleged victim were, at the time of the alleged defense, living together by mutual consent in a relationship of cohabitation, regardless of the legal status of their relationship." CONN. GEN. STAT. ANN. § 53a-67(b) (West 1994).

PROBLEMS

Problem 2-12. Paul and Mary's 10-year marriage was a stormy one. After four years they separated, but reconciled after four months. The tenth year of marriage was particularly difficult, however, and despite their many common interests, they agreed to a trial separation to "see if we want to divorce or not."

They continued to see each other occasionally but had no intimacies. Five months into the separation they impulsively decided to have dinner together, after leaving a joint appointment with their lawyer. It was a good dinner and they both had some wine. Paul escorted Mary back to her apartment, which they had formerly shared, but rather than leaving he made some affectionate approaches. Mary's feelings were ambivalent. She knew she did not wish to engage in sexual intercourse, but she also felt somewhat kindly and affectionate toward Paul, because of the warmth of the evening's conversation which revived memories of many of the good times in their marriage. She tried to be firm but kind in rejecting his advances, but her signals were apparently too subtle for Paul.

As she got more definite he got more aggressive. He finally got angry when he realized she really meant to reject him. He pushed her onto the bed, pulled off her clothes while holding her and achieved sexual penetration. She yelled at him and clearly resisted, but was unable to rouse neighbors. Paul never actually hit or bruised her during the attack, but her clothes were ripped and she had numerous scratches. This was the first violent incident in their relationship.

Two days later Mary files a rape complaint. Their state has recently abolished the marital rape exemption entirely. Forcible rape is a felony under state law punishable by a minimum term of imprisonment of 20 years. Aggravated assault (an assault using a deadly weapon) is a lesser felony with maximum punishment set at 15 years' imprisonment. Simple assault is a class-one misdemeanor, punishable by up to 2 years' imprisonment. You are the district attorney. What, if anything, would you charge Paul with? What penalty would you ask for?

Problem 2-13. Betty and Joseph had a violent marriage which eventually ended after 10 years in divorce. Soon after the divorce was finalized, Betty obtained a protective order against Joseph because of repeated abusive and threatening episodes. According to the terms of the protective order, "Joseph shall not have any contact with Betty and will remain at least 100 yards away from her at all times." The order was to be in effect for 1 year. Six months after entry of the order, Betty invited Joseph to her home for the birthday celebration of their three-year-old daughter. During the party, Betty and Joseph consumed a considerable amount of alcohol and this led to a physical altercation in which Joseph seriously injured Betty. Joseph was charged with the crime of violation of the protective order. Betty is also charged with being an accomplice to Joseph's crime. The state code makes it a crime "to intentionally or recklessly violate the terms of a protective order." The code also includes a criminal complicity provision which states "no person, acting with the kind of culpability required for the commission of an offense shall aid, abet, assist, encourage or facilitate another in committing the offense." Betty's lawyer has filed a motion to dismiss the charges. As clerk to the presiding judge, prepare a memo outlining both sides' likely arguments.

Problem 2-14. Harry and Sally have been married 15 years and have an active and mutually satisfactory sexual relationship. One evening they return home from a party both having had too much to drink. By the time they get to bed, Sally is nearly passed out. Harry had been looking forward to sexual intercourse with his wife and proceeds despite Sally's semi-conscious state. During a breakfast discussion the next morning, Sally reports no recollection of the sexual episode. Moreover, she expresses her irritation when she learns what he did, particularly because he proceeded without contraceptive protection, which she would have objected to had she been able to. Sally, fortunately, does not become pregnant.

Eight months later, the couple is having marital difficulties. When he discovers that she has had an affair with a co-worker, he announces he wants a divorce. Sally learns, by a consultation with an attorney, that her state's divorce courts are permitted to consider marital misconduct in allocating marital property and awarding alimony. She files a rape charge against Harry with the police. State law provides that first degree rape includes intercourse with a woman who is incapacitated from consenting. There is no marital rape exemption of any kind.

Should the district attorney prosecute? Assume she does proceed, the facts as stated above are established, and the jury convicts under appropriate instructions. Should the appellate court affirm? Should the legislature change the law? If so, to what? Do your answers to any of the questions change if the incident recited above had happened more than once, despite Sally's objection, and her rape charge was filed immediately after the most recent such incident?

[3] EVIDENCE, TORTS AND CRIMINAL RESPONSIBILITY

EVIDENTIARY CONSEQUENCES OF MARRIAGE

The common law's vision of spousal unity fostered several special evidentiary rules applicable solely to married couples. In addition to the marital communication privilege discussed in Note 3 after *Denton* at p. 79, the common law created the rule of spousal disqualification, under which one could not testify for or against a spouse in civil or criminal proceedings. Wigmore identified several rationales for this rule in addition to the legal unity fiction: 1) identity of interest — both spouses had the same interest in the outcome of any suit. Just as a party could not testify, likewise a party's spouse was ineligible; 2) as for pro-spouse testimony, a spouse could likely be biased; 3) adverse spousal testimony would interfere with the marital relationship. *See* WIGMORE, EVIDENCE § 2227 (McNaughton rev. 1961).

As for the current state of the rule, a "spouse is now everywhere a competent witness for his or her spouse in criminal and civil cases." CARLSON, IMWINKEL-RIED, KIONKA & STRACHAN, EVIDENCE: TEACHING MATERIALS FOR AN AGE OF

SCIENCE & STATUTES 173 (5th ed. 2002). The states are split, however, concerning adverse testimony. In civil cases, spouses generally are competent to testify against a spouse and in only a few jurisdictions are they privileged to refuse to so testify. *Id.* At least one statute permits a spouse to exclude adverse testimony by his spouse. *See* COLO. REV. STAT. § 13-90-107(1) (1997) (requiring consent — with some exceptions — of both spouses when either testifies); *In re Bozarth,* 779 P.2d 1346 (Colo. 1989) (statute permits custodial mother to exclude second husband's testimony in custody modification action filed by first husband).

The situation in criminal cases is more complicated. In 1980, the Supreme Court identified four positions with regard to the spousal disqualification rule in criminal cases: 1) the common law rule of ineligibility (8 states); 2) privilege against adverse spousal testimony vested either in defendant, or in witness and defendant (16 states); 3) privilege against adverse testimony vested solely in witness (9 states); 4) total abolition of the common law rule, thus rendering adverse spousal testimony competent and compellable (17 states). *See Trammel v. United States,* 445 U.S. 40, 48–49 n. 9 (1980). Where it exists, the privilege applies to any adverse testimony, not only to communications. Thus, it can bar adverse eyewitness testimony by a spouse. In a recent case where the privilege was vested in defendant, the Minnesota Supreme Court refused to find a marriage was a sham designed to take advantage of the privilege. The court also declined to adopt a joint participant exception under which the privilege would be unavailable when the spouses were participating together in a crime. *State v. Gianakos,* 644 N.W.2d 409 (Minn. 2002).

In interpreting FED. R. EVID. § 501 which governs federal court litigation, *Trammel* chose the third position, granting the witness the right to refuse to testify. It held this rule "furthers the important public interest in marital harmony without unduly burdening legitimate law enforcement needs." *Id.* at 53. Does the state interest in preserving marital harmony justify exempting a witness-spouse from the citizen's ordinary obligation to assist law enforcement? A recent commentator criticized the privilege's continued existence, particularly noting the problem posed in domestic violence cases:

> Courts and commentators may declare loudly that domestic violence is no longer tolerated in this society, and that married women have the right to feel secure in their homes, but such rights, with little way to prove entitlement to the rights, echo emptily. [States in which the prosecutor cannot compel testimony in domestic violence cases as in other criminal cases] send an obvious message: When a man beats his wife it is not a crime that offends the state — it is simply a private matter. . . . Even those jurisdictions with a spousal violence exception leave married women unprotected by the legal system because of very narrow and uninformed views of what constitutes spousal violence.

Seymore, *Isn't It a Crime: Feminist Perspectives on Spousal Immunity and Spousal Violence,* 90 Nw. L. REV. 1032, 1035–36 (1996); *see Commonwealth v. Kirkner,* 805 A. 2d 514 (Pa. 2002) (spousal testimony compellable in cases where defendant is charged with domestic violence against witness).

By contrast, others urge a broadening of the *Trammel* privilege:

[*Trammel*] sanctioned attempts by the government to induce, if not coerce, the defendant's spouse to testify against her or him. This change rewrote an ancient social contract, striking a new balance between the social importance of law enforcement and the family. . . . Fifteen years ago the *Trammel* Court decided that the societal interest in assisting law enforcement was more important than preserving marriage from further erosion. Today, there are voices suggesting a different conclusion.

Mullane, Trammell v. United States: *Bad History, Bad Policy and Bad Law*, 47 ME. L. REV. 105, 109,162 (1995); *see also* Regan, *Spousal Privilege and the Meanings of Marriage*, 81 VA. L. REV. 2045, 2050 (1995) (explaining privilege as part of an "internal stance" toward marriage "which highlights the way in which spouses' lives become intertwined, which makes them acutely dependent on each other"); Note, *"Honey, the Judge Says We're History": Abrogating the Marital Privileges Via Modern Doctrines of Marital Worthiness*, 77 CORN. L. REV. 843 (1992) (arguing *Trammel* is one of several judicial doctrines showing "disrespect for both the purposes of the privileges and for state prerogatives in domestic relations law"). Another common law evidentiary rule linked to the marital relationship was Lord Mansfield's Rule, under which the spouses "shall not be permitted to say after marriage that they have had no connection and therefore that the offspring is spurious." *Goodright v. Moss,* 98 Eng. Rep. 1257 (1777). Some states still apply this rule, *see, e.g., Markov v. Markov,* 758 A.2d 75 (Md. App. 2000), despite severe criticism of it. *See* Strong, *supra,* at 108 (endorsing Wigmore's description of the rule as "inconsistent and obstructive"); Annot., *Rule as Regards Competency of Husband or Wife to Testify as to Nonaccess,* 49 A.L.R.3d 212 (1973).

PROBLEM

Problem 2-15. Sally and Sam were partners in a stormy marriage. After many fights and separations, Sally began an adulterous relationship with Kenny. One night while Kenny waited outside Sally and Sam's house he witnessed a particularly violent and nasty argument between them. During the altercation, Sally shot Sam, who died from his injuries. Although she was charged with murder in the first degree, she asserted self-defense. The morning of trial, with Kenny under subpoena as a witness in the murder trial and Sally out on bond, Kenny and Sally got married. At trial, Sally sought to invoke the spousal testimonial privilege. At the hearing on the motion to quash Kenny's testimony, the next-door neighbor testifies Sally told him "Yeah, I really put one over on that damned prosecutor. I married Kenny and that means that he cannot testify against me. That's why we got married."

As judge in the case, your research indicates your jurisdiction recognizes the privilege and vests it in both witness and defendant. Will you require Kenny to testify to what he saw on the night of the killing?

NOTES ON TORTS AND THE MARRIED COUPLE

1. Interspousal Immunity. Like the law of evidence, tort law has grown beyond special treatment for married people. Interspousal immunity long insulated spouses from tort claims, but during the past 100 years there has been a significant trend toward its abolition. A leading hornbook announced in 2000 that a majority of states now permit litigation between spouses, at least in some circumstances. DOBBS, LAW OF TORTS 752 (2000). The demise of interspousal immunity, along with the simultaneous rise of no-fault divorce, has provided a context in which some litigants have sought to file tort actions, alleging intentional infliction of emotional distress or assault, along with their divorce actions. These actions are discussed in Chapter 4.

For recent cases abolishing interspousal immunity, see *Waite v. Waite*, 618 So. 2d 1360 (Fla. 1993); *Beattie v. Beattie*, 630 A.2d 1096 (Del. Super. Ct. 1993); *Burns v. Burns,* 518 So. 2d 1205 (Miss. 1988); *Heino v. Harper,* 759 P.2d 253 (Or. 1988); *Flagg v. Loy,* 734 P.2d 1183 (Kan. 1987); *Moran v. Beyer,* 734 F.2d 1245 (7th Cir. 1984) (finding immunity unconstitutional); *Jones v. Jones,* 376 S.E.2d 674 (Ga. 1989) (immunity unconstitutional in wrongful death actions) *but see Bozman v. Bozman*, 806 A.2d 740 (Md. App. 2002) ("[d]espite its antiquity, the doctrine remains a part of Maryland's common law"). *Burns* and *Harper* include state-by-state analysis of the doctrine's status, listing 39 states which have abolished it and 8 others which have significantly restricted it. For a comprehensive treatment of the current status of interspousal tort immunity, see Wanamaker, Waite v. Waite: *The Florida Supreme Court Abrogates the Doctrine of Interspousal Immunity*, 45 MERCER L. REV. 903-906-07 (1994) (footnotes comprehensively list cases and citation); Tobias, *Interspousal Tort Immunity in America,* 23 GA. L. REV. 359 (1989) (doctrine is "one of the truly 'sick men' of American tort jurisprudence for whom the requiem may soon play").

Interspousal immunity's poor reputation in modern courts was underscored in *Boone v. Boone*, 546 S.E.2d 191 (S.C. 2001). Plaintiff sued her husband for injuries suffered in a car accident as a passenger while he drove. The accident occurred in Georgia, which recognizes interspousal immunity. The South Carolina court, conceding conflict of laws principles ordinarily would apply the Georgia rule, refused to do so, applying the public policy exception to traditional choice of law doctrine. The immunity rule is contrary to "natural justice," according to the court, and the rationales behind it are "simply not justified in the twenty-first century."

2. *Marriage-Related Torts.* The common law simultaneously created several marriage-related torts. First, a husband could recover from third-party tortfeasors who deprived him of his wife's services due to injuries. Wives had no parallel action for loss of a husband's consortium because he did not owe her any services. DOBBS, *supra,* at 842. Most states now permit either spouse to bring such actions.

Two related torts, criminal conversation and alienation of affections, helped compensate the cuckolded husband. Criminal conversation required proof of defendant's adulterous (consensual or nonconsensual) sexual intercourse with plaintiff's wife. DOBBS, *supra,* at 1246. Rather than address the obvious constitutional issue concerning gender-based discrimination, many states have abolished this tort. *See Saunders v. Alford*, 607 So. 2d 1214 (Miss. 1992); *Thomas v. Siddiqui,* 869 S.W.2d 740 (Mo. 1994); *Norton v. Macfarlane,* 818 P.2d 8 (Utah 1991) (noting plaintiff's spouse might be just as much at fault as defendant); *but see Nunn v. Allen*, 574 S.E.2d 35 (N.C. App. 2002) (outlining elements of criminal conversation, rejecting proposal to abolish it and affirming a jury verdict which included punitive damages); *Oddo v. Presser*, 581 S.E.2d 123 (N.C. App. 2003) (upholding verdicts for criminal conversation and alienation of affections and delineating appropriate elements of damages, including punitives); *Neal v. Neal*, 873 P.2d 871 (Idaho 1994). In jurisdictions maintaining the action, it appears to be assumed that it is no longer gender-specific and either spouse may be a plaintiff.

Many jurisdictions also have abolished the tort of alienation of affections. "The gist of the tort is not sexual intimacy but an interference with the marital relation that changes one spouse's mental attitude toward the other." Keeton, *supra,* at 918. While judicial abolition is relatively rare, several courts have done so. *See Russo v. Sutton*, 422 S.E.2d 750 (S.C. 1992); *Hoye v. Hoye*, 824 S.W.2d 422 (Ky. 1992) (abolishing tort of intentional interference with the marital relation, a combination of criminal conversation and alienation of affections); *O'Neil v. Schuckardt,* 733 P.2d 693 (Idaho 1986) (asserting 28 jurisdictions have either abolished or severely restricted the action). Even states retaining the action have severely modified it by, *e.g.,* eliminating money damages, apparently permitting only an action for injunction. *See, e.g.,* ALA. CODE § 6-5-331 (1993); VT. STAT. ANN. tit. 15, § 1001 (2002).

Some courts, however, continue to accept the tort. In *Nelson v. Jacobsen,* 669 P.2d 1207 (Utah 1983), the court said the tort protected each spouse's "valuable interest in the marriage *relationship,* including its intimacy, companionship, support, duties and affection" (emphasis in original). The court acknowledged recovery does not restore the marriage, but held it can compensate plaintiff's loss. As for claims that the tort can be used for extortion, the court noted other types of actions can be used similarly. Conceding that in some such cases the marriage is already shaky when a partner seeks an outsider's companionship, the court required proof of a happy marriage and that defendant's relationship with plaintiff's spouse was the "controlling or effective" cause of the "loss and alienation of such love and affection." *See also Bland v. Hill,* 735 So. 2d 14 (Miss. 1999) (abolition would, "in essence, send the message that we are devaluing the marital relationship. We decline this invitation"); *Cooper v. Shealy,* 537 S.E.2d 854 (N.C. App. 2000) (accepting long-arm jurisdiction in an alienation of affections action where foreign defendant's phone calls to the state were the basis of the claim); *Hutelmyer v. Cox*, 514 S.E.2d 554 (N.C. App. 1999) (upholding $1 million jury verdict); *Pankratz v. Miller,* 401 N.W.2d 543 (S.D. 1987) (reaffirming alienation of affections, after having abolished criminal conversation).

Many states have Heart Balm statutes which, in addition to abolishing the marital torts discussed above, eliminate the breach of promise action discussed at pp. 148-49. Such statutes are consistent with a modern view of sexual autonomy. The same distaste for public airing of "dirty linen" which helped foster the divorce reform movement (see Chapter 3 at pp. 212-17) motivated the trend toward abolition of Heart Balm actions. For a commentary seeking a reversal of the trend toward abolition aimed at "punishing intentional interference with the husband-wife relationship and the violation of accepted canons of social conduct," see Corbett, *A Somewhat Modest Proposal to Prevent Adultery and Save Families: Two Old Torts Looking for a New Career*, 33 ARIZ. ST. L.J. 985 (2001).

In recent years, imaginative litigants have used the intentional infliction of emotional distress label for claims formerly made in the abolished marriage-related torts. These efforts have met with mixed success. In *Quinn v. Walsh*, 732 N.E.2d 330 (Mass. App. 2000), the court affirmed the dismissal of a suit by a man and his son against the wife/mother's alleged lover. It rejected assertions that the injury's intentional infliction and the plaintiffs' emotional harm differentiated this action from traditional alienation of affection and criminal conversation actions.

By contrast, in *Bailey v. Searles-Bailey*, 746 N.E.2d 1159 (Ohio App. 2000), the court held an intentional infliction of emotional distress claim by a husband whose wife and lover concealed the parentage of her child born during marriage survived an assertion that it was merely a disguised alienation of affections/criminal conversation action. The court held the suit was based on plaintiff's emotional trauma upon discovery that his wife's child was not his. Judgment for the plaintiff, however, was reversed for lack of the required level of outrageousness. *See also Williams v. Jeffs*, 57 P.3d 232 (Utah App. 2002) (requisite outrageousness not demonstrated); *Rosenthal v. Erven*, 17 P.3d 558 (Ore. App. 2001) (affair with wife not "so far beyond the bounds of social toleration that it should be actionable. . ."); Weiner, *Domestic Violence and the Per Se Standard of Outrage*, 54 MD. L. REV. 183 (1995) (analyzing use of intentional infliction as remedy by domestic violence victims, urging per se standard of outrage which would be met by proof of violation of protective order).

A number of emotional distress claims have been brought against clergy for sexual relationships with plaintiff's spouse. In *Osborne v. Payne*, 31 S.W.3d 911 (Ky. 2000), the court reversed summary judgment against plaintiff who alleged defendant priest's adulterous relationship with plaintiff's wife during a counseling relationship. The court held abolition of the amatory torts did not eliminate recovery and that the allegations, if proven, would constitute outrageous conduct sufficient for recovery for intentional infliction of emotional distress. *See also Jacqueline R. v. Household of Faith Family Church*, 97 Cal. App. 4th 198 (Cal. App. 2002) (church pastor should not be held to same standard of care as licensed marriage counselor); *Odenthal v. Minnesota Conference of Seventh-Day Adventists*, 649 N.W.2d 426 (Minn. 2002) (rejecting claim that First Amendment bars negligent counseling claim based on relationship between pastor and plaintiff's wife during counseling). *Osborne*, however, affirmed dismissal of the church as a defendant under vicarious liability, concluding that while the priest's counseling was well within his job, his employment responsibilities did not include commission of adultery. *See also Mercier v. Daniels*, 533 S.E.2d 877 (N.C. App. 2000) (rejecting vicarious liability of defendant's employer for alienation of affections); *Thornburg v. Federal Express Corporation*, 62 S.W.3d 421 (Mo. App. 2001) (same).

For analysis and criticism of the marital torts, see Spector, *All in the Family — Tort Litigation Comes of Age*, 28 FAM. L.Q. 363–67 (1994); Karp & Karp, *Beyond the Normal Ebb and Flow . . . Infliction of Emotional Distress in Domestic Violence Cases*, 28 FAM. L.Q. 389 (1994).

NOTE ON MARRIAGE AND CRIMINAL RESPONSIBILITY

The unity of husband and wife led the common law to hold that spouses could not be convicted as the sole parties to a conspiracy. LaFave, Criminal Law 607–8 (3rd ed. 2000). While virtually all modern courts have rejected the rule, in 1960, four justices of the Supreme Court stated:

> It is not necessary to be wedded to fictions to approve the [common law rule], for one of the dangers which that doctrine averts is the prosecution and conviction of persons for "conspiracies" which Congress never meant to be [prosecuted]. A wife, simply by virtue of the intimate life she shares with her husband, might easily perform acts . . . sufficient to involve her in a criminal conspiracy with him, but which might be far removed from the arms-length agreement typical of that crime.

United States v. Dege, 364 U.S. 51, 57–58 (1960) (Warren, C.J., dissenting).

> Additionally, the common law exempted wives from criminal liability for acts committed under duress of husbands. While duress was a generally recognized defense, wives were treated differently from others claiming it. If the wife
>
>> committed the criminal act in her husband's presence, there was a rebuttable presumption that he had coerced her. Something less in the way of pressure was required for a wife to be coerced than for an ordinary person to meet the requirements of the defense of duress; one early English case held that the husband's mere command would do.
>
> LaFave, *supra,* at 475. Virtually all modern statutes and courts reject any special rule of coercion for wives. Some states, however, continue the presumption, while terming it a slight one. *See, e.g., Barnhart v. State,* 559 P.2d 451 (Okla. Crim. App. 1977).

Chapter 3

DISSOLVING THE MARITAL STATUS

INTRODUCTION

This chapter deals with one aspect of the law of divorce: the rules governing the termination of the marital status itself, as distinct from the financial and child custody issues which arise from the termination. California was the first state to eliminate *all* fault-based divorce provisions in 1970. Prior to the passage of California's divorce reform law, a handful of states allowed spouses to end their marriage on the basis of "incompatibility," a ground that focused less on the "fault" of one or both parties, and more on the breakdown of the marital relationship. Yet, these incompatibility grounds existed beside fault-based provisions in the statutes of these states. California's reform, by contrast, represented an unambiguous departure from prior law, in that the legislature repealed all fault provisions. The variations among the states in their implementation of no-fault divorce laws were substantial, and will be discussed in some detail below. For now, however, we note that the idea that parties should be able to end their marriage without proof of fault "spread like prairie fire. By 1974, . . . forty-five states already possessed a no-fault procedure." HERBERT JACOB, SILENT REVOLUTION: THE TRANSFORMATION OF DIVORCE LAW IN THE UNITED STATES 80 (1988). In the subsequent decade, the final five states joined the rest, with South Dakota as the last in 1985. *Id.* Most states added their new no-fault provisions while leaving fault-based divorce grounds intact. Many states retained fault as a consideration in marital property distributions or awards of spousal support. While the transition to no-fault divorce appears to be one of the most dramatic changes in 20th century American family law, the foundation for these developments was laid gradually throughout the century. Furthermore, although all states now have no-fault statutes, there remains substantial variability among the states, including retention of fault-based standards in most jurisdictions (i.e., approximately two-thirds of the states). It appeared that the battle over the rules governing the termination of marital status was largely over, but in the past decade, opponents of no-fault have sought to repeal, or at least reform, modern divorce statutes.

In this Chapter, we examine the history of divorce law in the United States and analyze the various transitions that characterized the law on the books and the law in action throughout the last century and into the present one. What policies drove the no-fault reforms? How do no-fault and fault-based grounds function, side-by-side? Are the results of the no-fault "revolution" what the reformers expected? How will attempts to "reform the reforms" change modern divorce law?

§ A. THE ORIGINS AND HISTORY OF AMERICAN DIVORCE LAW

A culture's beliefs about marriage are reflected in its rules for divorce. From the 16th to the 18th century, there was a gradual change in Europe from a conception of marriage as an economic alliance between families to a conception of it as a romantic bond between individuals — what has been called "companionate" marriage. MARY ANN GLENDON, THE NEW FAMILY AND THE NEW PROPERTY 13-17, 23 (1981). The French Civil Code of 1804 reflected the older conception, providing for the continued connection of any title in land to the blood family of each spouse. The relevant provisions, valid until 1965, existed to protect both families' financial interests. Alterations in this rule were permissible only by premarital agreement. Once marriage was contracted, the spouses could not alter the arrangements. Depending upon the role marriage plays in a particular society, the personal preferences of the marital partners may have more or less importance in determining whether the marriage will continue. The shift to a companionate marriage model ultimately was accompanied by the increasing centrality of the marital partners in determining whether or when the marriage dissolves. The American history of divorce law is of course somewhat different from the European, but the basic trends in the law are essentially the same, as the following selection indicates.

[1]   EARLY AMERICAN DIVORCE

LAWRENCE M. FRIEDMAN, A HISTORY OF AMERICAN LAW 204-07, 498-504 (2ND ED., 1985)

England [was] a "divorceless society,". . . until 1857. There was no . . . judicial divorce. The very wealthy might squeeze a rare private bill of divorce out of Parliament. Between 1800 and 1836 there were, on the average, three of these a year. For the rest, unhappy husbands and wives had to be satisfied with annulment (no easy matter), or divorce from bed and board *(a mensa et thoro),* a form of legal separation which did not entitle either spouse to marry again. . . .

In the [United States, during the] colonial period, the South was generally faithful to English tradition. Absolute divorce was unknown, divorce from bed and board very rare. In New England, however, courts and legislatures occasionally granted divorce. In Pennsylvania, Penn's laws of 1682 gave spouses the right to a "Bill of Divorcement" if their marriage partner was convicted of adultery. Later, the governor or lieutenant governor was empowered to dissolve marriages on grounds of incest, adultery, bigamy, or homosexuality. There is no evidence that the governor ever used this power. . . .

After Independence, . . . regional differences remained quite strong. In the South, divorce continued to be unusual. The extreme case was South Carolina. Henry William Desaussure, writing in 1817, stated flatly that South Carolina had never granted a single divorce. He was right. There was no such thing as absolute divorce in South Carolina, throughout the 19th century. In other

Southern states, legislatures dissolved marriages by passing private divorce laws. The Georgia constitution of 1798 allowed legislative divorce, on a two-thirds vote of each branch of the legislature. . . . Between 1798 and 1835, there were 291 legislative divorces in Georgia. The frequency curve rose toward the end of the period. . . .

North of the Mason-Dixon line, courtroom divorce became the normal mode, rather than legislative divorce. Pennsylvania passed a general divorce law in 1785, Massachusetts one year later. Every New England state had a divorce law before 1800, along with New York, New Jersey, and Tennessee. Grounds for divorce varied somewhat from state to state. New York's law of 1787 permitted absolute divorce only for adultery. Vermont, on the other hand, allowed divorce for impotence, adultery, intolerable severity, three years' willful desertion, and long absence with presumption of death (1798). Rhode Island allowed divorce for "gross misbehaviour and wickedness in either of the parties, repugnant to and in violation of the marriage covenant." In New Hampshire, it was grounds for divorce if a spouse joined the Shaker sect — not an unreasonable rule, since the Shakers did not believe in sexual intercourse.

. . . . The size of the demand doomed the practice of divorce by statute. Like corporate charters, private divorce bills became a nuisance, a pointless drain on the legislature's time. [By the end of the 19th century], private divorce laws became extinct.

. . . . What was the source of this sudden desire for a simpler way to divorce? The divorce rate in the 19th century, of course, was the merest trickle in comparison to the rate in more recent times. Still, it was noticeable, and it was growing; to some self-appointed guardians of national morals, it was an alarming fire bell in the night, a symptom of moral dry rot, and a cause in itself of still further moral decay. President Timothy Dwight of Yale, in 1816, called the rise in divorces "dreadful beyond conception." Connecticut faced "stalking, barefaced pollution"; if things went on, the state would become "one vast Brothel; one great province of the World of Perdition." The "whole community," he warned, could be thrown "into a general prostitution". . . .

Easy divorce laws grew out of the needs of the middle-class mass. The smallholder had to have some way to stabilize and legitimize relationships, to settle doubts about ownership of family property. It was the same general impulse that lay behind the common-law marriage. Divorce was simplest to obtain and divorce laws most advanced in those parts of the country — the West especially — least stratified by class.

Divorce was, then, genuinely popular. . . .[¶] . . . . Divorce laws were a kind of compromise. In general, the law never recognized full, free consensual divorce. It became simpler to get a divorce than in the past; but divorce was not routine or automatic. In form, divorce was an adversary proceeding. . . . Eventually, of course, the collusive or friendly divorce became the normal case.

The collusive divorce did not dominate the dockets until later in the century. But it was not unknown, say, in 1840.

. . . .

. . . . The divorce statutes were somewhat variable. From about 1850 to 1870, some states adopted rather loose divorce laws. In Connecticut, any "misconduct" was grounds for divorce, if it "permanently destroys the happiness of the petitioner and defeats the purposes of the marriage relation." In Maine, a supreme court justice could grant a divorce if he deemed it "reasonable and proper, conducive to peace and harmony, and consistent with the peace and morality of society." Divorce laws in states as different as North Carolina, Indiana and Rhode Island were also quite permissive. Some states which did not go as far as Maine or Connecticut broadened their statutes considerably; they added to the traditional list of grounds for divorce (adultery, desertion, and impotence, for example) new and vaguer ones such as "cruelty." In the Tennessee Code of 1858, for example, divorce was available on grounds of impotence, bigamy, adultery, desertion, felony conviction, plus the following: attempting to take a spouse's life by poison; concealing a pregnancy by another man at the time of marriage; nonsupport. In addition, the court might, in its "discretion," free a woman from the bonds of matrimony if her husband had "abandoned her, or turned her out of doors," if he was guilty of cruel and inhuman treatment, or if he had "offered such indignities to her person as to render her condition intolerable and force her to withdraw."

After 1870, the tide began to turn. Influential moral leaders had never stopped attacking loose divorce laws. Horace Greeley thought that "easy divorce" had made the Roman Empire rot. A similar fate lay in store for America, "blasted by the mildew of unchaste mothers and dissolute homes." Theodore D. Woolsey, president of Yale University, wrote a book in 1869 denouncing the divorce laws of his state as immoral and unscriptural. . . . In his view, "petitions for divorce become more numerous with the ease of obtaining them"; lax laws caused the disintegration of the family, the backbone of American life. . . . [¶] Naturally, there were two sides to the question. Militant feminists took up the cudgels for permissive divorce. A furious debate raged in New York. Robert Dale Owen, son of the Utopian reformer, went into battle against Horace Greeley. Owen . . . felt that strict divorce laws, not lax ones, led to adultery. . . .

One thing was certain: the divorce rate was rising. The number of divorces rose from 9,937 in 1867, to 25,535 in 1886, far more than population increase can explain, and despite tightened divorce laws; by 1900, more than 55,000 divorces were granted each year.

How is this fact to be accounted for? There are two possibilities. Either dry rot had affected family life; or more people wanted formal acceptance of the fact that their marriages were dead. . . . [T]he second [explanation] seems far more likely. Just as more of the middle class wanted, and needed, their deeds recorded, their wills made out, their marriages solemnized, so they wanted the honesty and convenience of divorce, the right to remarry in bourgeois style, to have legitimate children with their second wife (or husband), and the right to decent, honest disposition of their worldly goods. Only divorce could provide this. . . .

. . . .

The migratory divorce, for people with money and the urge to travel, was [a] detour around strict enforcement of divorce law. To attract the "tourist trade," a state needed easy laws and a short residence period. Indiana was one of these states, before the 1870s. . . . [I]n 1873, the legislature passed a stricter law that shut the divorce mill down. South and North Dakota, too, had their day. Finally, Nevada became the place. . . . [I]ts career as national divorce mill lasted longer than any other state's.

[2] AMERICAN DIVORCE IN THE TWENTIETH CENTURY

The late 19th century law of divorce, described by Professor Friedman as a "hodgepodge," remained largely unchanged until the 1970s. The divorce laws of every state assumed an adversary proceeding in which the plaintiff had to prove the defendant's "fault." Just what sort of "fault" was necessary depended upon the state's particular statutory language. All states recognized adultery as a ground for divorce (until 1967, adultery was the *only* permissible ground for divorce in New York) and most states recognized desertion or abandonment. Plaintiffs claiming desertion were required to show that the defendant had abandoned all marital duties and that, for a minimum period of time often specified by statute, the parties had not cohabited. A few jurisdictions granted divorce on desertion grounds even though cohabitation continued if the defendant had refused performance of marital duties, most commonly sexual relations, for the minimum statutory period. Because of the fault premise underlying the statutory scheme, the defendant could defeat a desertion-based divorce action by showing that the plaintiff had consented to the defendant's absence, or that the defendant's departure was justified by the plaintiff's conduct. Precisely what conduct could be offered in justification varied from state to state. A third common ground permitted under the traditional divorce laws was "cruelty." The law of many states required the plaintiff alleging cruelty to show bodily harm as a result of the defendant's actions, although some states accepted proof of mental suffering as well.

The fault-based logic permeating the system was further exemplified by the defenses recognized under the traditional divorce law. The most notorious defense was "recrimination," that is, showing that the plaintiff was also guilty of conduct which the law recognized as a ground for divorce. If both plaintiff and defendant proved the other's fault, neither party was granted a divorce. Within the fault-based system, divorce was a remedy available only to an innocent spouse. As one court bound by the recrimination doctrine observed: "[D]ivorce would perhaps be the better solution for the difficulties facing the parties." *Kucera v. Kucera*, 117 N.W.2d 810, 817 (N.D. 1962).

Most divorces were uncontested and thus undefended. An uncontested divorce case, however, was a rather peculiar legal animal. Divorce by mutual consent was not formally available. Thus, the court could not issue the decree simply because the spouses agreed that it should. Some statutory ground for divorce still had to be proven in court. In form, an adversary proceeding was required, even if the parties were not, in fact, adversaries. Particularly where the jurisdiction had relatively restrictive rules on grounds for divorce, the official divorce law of the books often bore no relation to the law in action Several practices arose in response to the disconnect between formal legal notions of marital breakup and the circumstances that, in reality, led couples to seek a dissolution of their marriage. In some jurisdictions, the courts granted divorces on facts far short of the standards articulated in the case law. For example, in the 1968 edition of his family law treatise, Homer Clark observed that his discussion of the ground of cruelty was confined to "the law of the statutes and reported cases," which he underscored was "by no means the same as the law in action." He stated further:

> [I]n uncontested cases divorces will often be granted upon evidence of cruelty which would not qualify [under] the reported cases. Cruelty in those circumstances has proven to be capable of nearly limitless expansion, in the face of pronouncements by appellate courts which would lead one to think that the definition of cruelty had not changed much for one hundred and fifty years. In many states, especially in the West, a divorce for cruelty may be had for the asking, providing it is uncontested. Whether this condition be labeled hypocritical or sophisticated, it . . . ought to be made known to laymen. It is the means by which divorce has become easy in most of the United States without the necessity for enlarging the statutory grounds.

HOMER CLARK, LAW OF DOMESTIC RELATIONS 341 (1968).

In states with more restrictive divorce grounds, the challenges for a couple seeking a consensual divorce were greater. Wealthier residents of states with restrictive divorce laws often established an allegedly-permanent domicile in a state with more relaxed grounds for divorce, such as Nevada, in order to avail themselves of the more lenient divorce statutes. Chapter 7 examines the special jurisdictional rules governing domestic relations matters, many of which arose out of this tradition of "migratory" divorce. More commonly, domiciliaries of states with restrictive divorce statutes had to prove specific behavior demonstrating the defendant's faults. As the following excerpts reveal, these requirements invited collusion between the parties in manufacturing the "evidence" necessary to prove the required statutory ground.

NOTE, COLLUSIVE AND CONSENSUAL DIVORCE AND THE NEW YORK ANOMALY, 36 Colum. L. Rev. 1121-33 (1936)

. . .[C]ollusion has been held to comprehend an agreement between husband and wife for (1) the commission of an offense for the purpose of obtaining a divorce, or (2) the introduction of false evidence of an offense not actually committed, or (3) the suppression of a valid defense. . . .

. . . [P]rocedural, as well as substantive rules have been evolved to prevent the practice. Thus, five states require the complainant to take a special oath that his petition is not founded on collusion. And generally a divorce will not be granted on default; the facts must thereafter be proved to the satisfaction of the court. Corroboration will be required to bolster the confessions or admissions of the parties, and the mutual corroboration of the spouses will not suffice. A higher standard of proof than that ordinarily required in civil cases may even be demanded. Direct sanctions against attorneys in the form of disbarment or contempt of court, and the inability of an attorney to represent both sides with their consent in a divorce suit, as well as a variety of other procedural regulations, have also sought the same objective. But "hotel evidence,"[33] which has lost some of its probative force in England, is still sufficient to create a *prima facie* case in most American jurisdictions.

. . . .

But in spite of the vast array of substantive and procedural weapons that have been utilized, no satisfactory method of eliminating collusion has been devised. [The author cites judges and lawyers who assert that collusive divorce is rampant, ranging from 75% to 100% of all cases, according to some.]

Factual Evidence of Collusion in New York. . . . Prominent . . . is the huge number of cases which are uncontested on the merits . . .[60] Similarly persuasive are the large percentage of co-respondents who remain unnamed, the surprising state of undress in which the defendant and co-respondent are generally found,[65] and the close relationships generally existing between the defendant and witnesses for the complainant. And the unusually short period commonly intervening between the alleged adultery and the service of process would constitute at least a suspicious circumstance. . . .

Conclusion. That the law relating to collusion is not serving its purpose is abundantly clear. Moreover, positive evils have grown up in its wake. Perjury arises to aid in the creation of legal farces, attorneys resort to degrading tactics, [and] the profession of co-respondents makes an appearance. . .][70]

LAWRENCE M. FRIEDMAN, AMERICAN LAW IN THE TWENTIETH CENTURY 434-38 (2002)

. . . . Marriage (in legal theory) was a contract between man and wife; but unlike most contracts, once the two were in it, it was devilishly hard to get out. A contract to buy a horse can be called off if both buyer and seller want

---

[33] In England this normally consisted of a hotel bill being sent home by the husband, and witnesses testifying that he stayed at the hotel and occupied a bedroom with a woman not his wife. . . .

[60] In the Special Term for Trials in New York County, matrimonial actions disposed of were:

	1931	1932	1933	1934
Defended Matrimonials	188	239	188	196
Undefended Matrimonials Referred to Official Referees	1341	1186	1250	1417

The figures include matrimonials of all types. The Judicial Statistics of the Work of the Supreme Court of New York in the First Judicial Department (1931–1934) 23. The U.S. Bureau of Census, Marriage and Divorce (1931) gives approximately 5% for New York "contested" divorces.

[65] [P]eople do not ordinarily open a door, even partially, to permit someone to enter unless they are more suitably clothed than the cases indicate. The information was available in 483 cases as to the clothing of the male and 488 as to that of the female. As tabulated by Jackson, the cases show:

For the male, absolutely nude, 21; wrapped in towel, 2; wrapper, 1; nightgown, 8; B.V.D. or underwear, 119; bathrobe or dressing gown, 101; pajamas, 227; kimono, 4.

For the female: absolutely nude, 55; brassiere, 2; bloomers, 2; negligee, 67; slip, 5; wrapper, 1; chemise, 24; underwear, 26; lingerie, 5; nightgown, 126; pajamas, 73; bathrobe or dressing gown, 32; combination, 2; kimono, 68.

[70] See, *e.g.,* Jarvis, *I Was the Unknown Blonde in 100 New York Divorces,* SUNDAY MIRROR MAGAZINE, March 11, 1934. After performing their services at the "chosen hotel room . . . these divorce aiders receive their $50 (now often reduced to $25) and go home."

to call it off; but a marriage contract is not like buying a horse. Only a court could dissolve a marriage, and only when one party, herself quite innocent, could prove the other guilty of an offense against the marriage — the so-called grounds for divorce.

Admissible grounds varied from state to state. In South Carolina absolute divorce was not available at all, for any reason; divorce arrived in South Carolina only in 1948. In the other states, the common grounds were adultery, desertion, and cruelty; but there were all sorts of state idiosyncrasies. Drunkenness, failure to provide, imprisonment, and impotence were grounds in some states. Leprosy was grounds for divorce in Hawaii; in Virginia a husband could divorce his wife if he discovered she had been a prostitute. Cruelty became the grounds of choice in the twentieth century; it overtook adultery in 1922, and in 1950 accounted for almost three-fifths of all divorces. Most states recognized cruelty as a valid reason for divorce — New York was a prominent exception.

What accounts for this outbreak of marital cruelty? Nothing. It was, in fact, an outbreak of collusion. Most "cruelty" cases were uncontested. The plaintiff (usually the wife) filed for divorce. The husband made no defense. Divorce was granted, by default. Collusive divorce had become common in the late nineteenth century; in the twentieth century, it was absolutely pervasive. In legal theory, a collusive divorce was void. Husband and wife had no right to agree to split. In practice, collusion was the rule, not the exception; and the judges all knew it. . . .

The precise form of collusion did vary from state to state. It mirrored the state statute; it was, in a sense, "cheating in the shadow of the law." In California, as in most states, cruelty was the courtroom favorite. In case after case after case, the wife complained that her husband cursed her and hit her, and made her life miserable. . . .

In New York divorce was available, practically speaking, only for adultery. This was an extreme situation; but any and all attempts to amend the law ended in shipwreck in the legislature. The demand for divorce, however, was as strong in New York as it was elsewhere. . . .

New York also developed a weird form of collusive adultery — one might even call it soft-core adultery. A man would check into a hotel, a woman (usually a blonde) would appear, together with a photographer; the photographer would take pictures of the couple, in pajamas or underwear or even naked; the woman would get her fifty-dollar fee; and lo and behold! here was evidence of adultery. . . .

Collusion was by far the most popular, and practical, detour around tough divorce laws. But the federal system opened another door: the migratory divorce. There had been a number of divorce "mills" in the nineteenth century: states that attracted birds of passage with easy divorce laws. The clergy and respectable people usually objected to this rather tawdry business; and most divorce mills — South Dakota was one — were soon closed down. . . .

. . . . Divorce had become a classic example of what one might call a dual system — a system with a radical disjuncture, or gap, between the official system and the living law. Of course, official law and living law are never perfectly congruent; but in a true dual system, the two systems are entirely separate, operating almost in two different worlds. [¶] . . .Dual systems arise from a number of causes. Divorce was kind of a stalemate. The forces that opposed it were powerful. Divorce was absolutely forbidden to Roman Catholics; other religions tolerated it, but barely. It carried a stigma. Yet, the demand for divorce continued to rise; and it proved impossible to confine it within the narrow channels of the official law. An irresistible force (the popular desire for divorce) had met an immovable object (the opposition to easy divorce).

. . . .

There were, of course, costs to the dual system. It was tawdry and unpopular; it was expensive; it degraded everybody who took part in it. Yet there was no easy way for the system to change. It was rotting from within; but the constant calls for reform made little headway. . . .

NOTES

1. *Evading Divorce Restrictions with Annulments.* In the face of restrictive divorce laws, parties desiring to end their marriage sought annulments. Grounds for annulment are discussed in Chapter 2, on page 78 *et seq.* In 1963, for example, 36% of all New York decrees terminating marriages were annulments rather than divorces. National Center for Health Statistics, *Divorce Statistics Analysis 1963,* at 10. New York annulments were available on a showing that one of the parties was fraudulently persuaded to enter the marriage. It is estimated that more than 150 types of fraud were recognized by New York courts, including one party's assertion that the other had fraudulently misrepresented his or her desire to have a family. Richard H. Wels, *New York: The Poor Man's Reno,* 35 CORNELL L.Q. 303, 319-20 (1950). With the advent of no-fault divorce, the importance of annulment declined. In fact, the California Governor's Commission (discussed *infra* at page 213) recommended abolishing annulments entirely, although its recommendation was not adopted.

Professor Mary Ann Glendon observed a parallel phenomenon within the Roman Catholic Church, which recognizes annulment but not divorce. THE NEW FAMILY AND THE NEW PROPERTY, 35, 122 (1981). In the United States,

> where Roman Catholics divorce in roughly the same proportion as the rest of the population, annulment law has been developing in a pattern reminiscent of the [the liberalized practice prevalent under the] old-fashioned fault-based secular divorce laws.

> . . . The Church's version of migratory divorce has its basis in the fact that many couples seek to find a ground for jurisdiction in a diocese where the tribunals are known to be more lenient in granting annulments. (In 1977, a mere 14 of 147 dioceses handed down 43 per cent of the annulment decisions.) [¶ How] can a tribunal declare that the marriage of a couple who had children and who lived together for many years, at least some of the time harmoniously, never existed? The answer is, quite easily. Lack of consent, capacity, or consummation, the tried and true grounds for annulment, have all undergone sea-changes in the case law of the marital tribunals.

Thus, consent may have been rendered defective not only by fraud and duress, but by emotional immaturity. A person may be incapable if she is the sort who cannot live up to her marital obligations. The long marriage may not really have been consummated (despite the two children) if the spouses have not attained a spiritual and emotional, as well as physical, union. Here we see the same legal mind that was at work adapting the old cruelty grounds to the rising demand for secular divorce in the late 1950s and the 1960s.

Id. at 122-24. Despite revisions of canon law that were expected to restrain the trend toward increased availability of annulments, *Pope Set to Issue New Church Laws,* N.Y. TIMES, Jan. 23, 1983, at A1, church annulments continue and are criticized by some. *See, e.g.,* Steinfels, *Beliefs,* N.Y. TIMES, March 17, 1997 (citing 1996 book, *Shattered Faith,* by Sheila Rauch Kennedy, former wife of Representative Joseph Kennedy II of Massachusetts, critique the church policy that authorized the annulment of her marriage). It observed that "the church in the United States has . . . broadened the grounds for annulments to embrace the insights of modern psychology about states or mind or personality disorders that may prevent an individual from truly entering into a sacramental marriage," and has granted over 60,000 annulments annually, "a vast increase since the 1950's." *Id.*

2. *Additional Reading.* For further discussion of the 20th century divorce law and the mechanisms and customs employed to avoid the laws' harsh effects, see Lawrence M. Friedman, *A Dead Language: Divorce Law and Practice Before No-Fault,* 86 VA. L. REV. 1497 (2000) [hereinafter "Friedman, *A Dead Language*"]. For an analysis of these issues with particular attention to changing status of women during the 20th century, see Herma Hill Kay, *From Second Sex to the Joint Venture: An Overview of Women's Rights and Family Law in the United States During the Twentieth Century,* 88 CAL. L. REV. 2019 (2000) [hereinafter "Kay, *From Second Sex to Joint Venture*"].

[3] THE DEVELOPMENT OF THE NO-FAULT APPROACH

Prior to California's elimination of its fault-based grounds for divorce in 1970, a handful of states had a no-fault ground on the books. For example, in 1933, New Mexico added the statutory ground of "incompatibility." Friedman, *A Dead Language, supra* at 1527. In 1968, Professor Clark identified four jurisdictions that accepted "incompatibility" as a ground for divorce. CLARK, *supra,* at 350. He observed that "the courts seem to be so strongly conditioned to the idea that divorce may only be granted upon a showing of fault by the defendant that they have had great difficulty in dealing with the fact that incompatibility statutes contain no mention of fault." For a detailed account of the difficulties of dealing with an apparently no-fault ground like incompatibility in the context of a fault-based law, see Walter Wadlington, *Divorce Without Fault Without Perjury,* 52 VA. L. REV. 32 (1966). Yet, by the 1970s, most states were ready to embrace some version of no-fault divorce provisions.

MAX RHEINSTEIN, MARRIAGE STABILITY, DIVORCE AND THE LAW 373-81 (1972)

In 1963, the movement to modify the divorce law of California started as an effort not to turn the tide of conservative resistance to divorce but to stem the rising tide of divorce, to lessen the very high divorce rate of the state as a whole and of some counties in particular.

. . . [T]he governor, on 11 May 1966, established the Governor's Commission on the Family. . . .

[T]he California commission recommended the abandonment of the principle of matrimonial offense. The reasons were: commission of a matrimonial offense constitutes guilt in a formalistic sense only; guilt in the true sense almost always lies with both parties; the commission of a matrimonial offense does not by itself indicate that the marriage is no longer viable; the necessity of alleging a matrimonial offense creates an atmosphere of hostility in which it is difficult to settle the issues of child custody and support, of property settlement and alimony; the commission of an offense can be feigned so that insincerity and perjury may be induced to the detriment of the respect for the law and the courts. The commission added another ground, the incompatibility of the principle of offense with the function of a family court as envisaged by the commission. While it would thus no longer be necessary or sufficient to prove adultery, desertion, cruelty, or any other of the matrimonial offenses enumerated in the existing law of California, it should be possible to obtain a divorce upon the initiative of either party. The proceedings could be assumed normally to last about eight months. . . .

The commission's extreme liberality in stating the grounds for divorce was counterbalanced by the proposal of an elaborate system of family courts. It is hard to say whether this proposal was meant as a serious check or as window dressing. . . .[¶] A family court was to be a division of the superior court of each county. . . . [T]he new court was to have comprehensive jurisdiction in all matters of family law. . . . The judges, it was hoped, would be interested and experienced in family matters. They were to be aided by a staff of professionals trained in counseling. This staff was to go to work when a petition of inquiry had been filed. . . . It was . . . to proceed . . . to explore whether and in what ways a reconciliation might be possible, to help the parties, through efforts of its own or through recommendation of an outside counselor or agency, and, if it appeared that the parties would not decide to be reconciled, consult with them "for the purpose of working out a settlement of the circumstances attendant upon the dissolution of the marriage including the problems of child custody and visitation." The counselor would then submit a report to the judge. [Additional steps were then provided.]

The plan of the California governor's commission was a compromise. [T]he commission sought to bring together the essentially conservative family court plan and a divorce law of the books that in effect was to be more liberal than even the existing California law in action. While the former tendency was emphasized, the latter required some scrutiny to be discovered.

[T]he report did not meet with a friendly reception by the bar. . . .

The bar may have been primarily responsible for the elimination from California divorce reform of the family court plan. Helped by taxpayers' desire for economy and the difficulty of finding sufficient numbers of trained personnel, tendencies to broaden the existing scheme of conciliation courts were also stopped. . . .

Elimination from the proceedings of allegation of misconduct and wrangling about guilt is one of the principal aims of the new California law. This desire has found expression not only in the substitution of the objective ground of breakdown for the former misconduct grounds, but also in what constitutes the most far-reaching innovation of the new scheme, the elimination of guilt as a determinant in the decision about property settlement, alimony, and child custody.

———————

In 1970, the Commissioners on Uniform State Laws approved a Model Marriage and Divorce Act, heavily influenced by the California developments. Section 302, as originally approved by the Commissioners, provided for entry of a dissolution decree if the court "finds that the marriage is irretrievably broken." Because this proposal sparked intense opposition in the Family Law Section of the American Bar Association, the ABA originally declined to approve it. The chairman of the Family Law Section later explained:

> [The Family Law Section] has opposed the draft . . . because that Act provides for no-fault divorce even against the wishes of one of the spouses, without regard to the fact that the marriage may have been of long duration and without an adequate cooling-off period or other delay. The FLS further opposes the Uniform Act as it contains no adequate provisions available for reconciliation and conciliation inquiries, during which period it could be ascertained whether the marriage is in fact dead or whether the break-up is merely a whim of one of the parties. The FLS therefore proposed amendments . . . which will provide for an adequate delay before a divorce, together with necessary reconciliation inquiry and conciliation processes, where advisable.
>
> This writer answers those who seek to achieve a system of divorce on demand, without delay, that such a step will lead to the destruction of marriage and the family unit as social institutions and ultimately of society in general. A dead marriage . . . should be buried, but not so long as there is the slightest breath of life still left in it. The best test of whether the marriage is dead is a suitable period of living apart for at least one year prior to commencement of a divorce action; this separation should be coupled with an attempt at reconciliation. This then, should be the basis for establishing that the marriage is irretrievably broken and constitutes the ground for a no-fault divorce, not just a speedy and easy divorce. . . .
>
> The FLS revision . . . clearly defines irretrievable breakdown to be "(a) that the parties have lived separate and apart for a period of more than one year next preceding the commencement of this proceeding

or, (b) that such serious marital misconduct has occurred which has so adversely affected the physical or mental health of the petitioning party as to make it impossible for the parties to continue the marital relation, and that reconciliation is improbable." This definition of irretrievable breakdown removes what the FLS understands to be the practice in many courts, where breakdown is the ground, of accepting a mere statement by the petitioning party that the marriage is irretrievably broken as sufficient to warrant dissolution. . . .

Hon. Ralph J. Podell, *The Case for Revision of the Uniform Marriage and Divorce Act,* 18 S.D. L. REV. 601, 603 (1973). For a sample of the debate as it was then waged, *see also* Robert J. Levy, *Introduction to a Symposium on the Uniform Marriage and Divorce Act,* 18 S.D. L. REV. 531 (1973); Henry H. Foster, Jr., *Divorce Reform and the Uniform Act,* 18 S.D. L. REV. 572 (1973). The prospect of two competing Uniform Acts was averted when the ABA accepted an amended version of the Commissioners' draft. That version, still current, is reprinted below, at pages 217-218. (For the story of how this version was developed, see Harvey L. Zuckman, *The A.B.A. Family Law Section v. NCCUSL,* 24 CATH. U.L. REV. 61 (1974)).

Divorce reform percolated rapidly through the various state legislatures. In *Silent Revolution: The Transformation of Divorce Law in the United States,* Herbert Jacob explores how such an immense change could take place with so little public debate. By 1985, every state in the union had adopted some form of no-fault provision. There remained, and still remains, substantial variability in the wording of the statutes and whether the no-fault provisions coexist with fault-based provisions. Section B *infra,* examines the nature and variability in current divorce statutes, and how these provisions work in practice.

NOTES ON COMPARATIVE LAW OF DIVORCE

1. *English Marriage and Divorce Law.* LAWRENCE STONE, ROAD TO DIVORCE: ENGLAND 1530-1987 (1990), provides a comprehensive history of English marriage and divorce law. Two companion volumes offer collections of case studies, many quite colorful. *See, e.g.,* LAWRENCE STONE, UNCERTAIN UNIONS: MARRIAGE IN ENGLAND 1660-1753 (1992) (discussing marriage laws sufficiently ambiguous "that very large numbers of perfectly respectable people . . . could never be sure whether they were married or not," N.Y. REV. BOOKS, Nov. 4, 1993); LAWRENCE STONE BROKEN LIVES: SEPARATION AND DIVORCE IN ENGLAND 1660-1857 (1993) (dealing with the difficulties of ending unsatisfactory marriages).

Divorce reform was taking place in Europe during the same time that it occurred here. The Archbishop of Canterbury appointed a committee whose 1966 report, *Putting Asunder: A Divorce Law for Contemporary Society,* influenced American as well as British developments in its support of marital breakdown as the exclusive ground for divorce. In Britain, as in so many American states, compromise was necessary to achieve enactment and reforms were hedged. An uncontested no-fault divorce became available only after a two-year separation, while a unilateral no-fault divorce required a five-year separation. Because of these lengthy separation requirements, approximately 70% of divorces in England proceed under fault-based provisions which allow for a speedier dissolution of the marriage. D. MARIANNE BLAIR & MERLE H. WEINER, FAMILY LAW IN THE WORLD COMMUNITY 264 (2003). In response to proposals to eliminate fault-based grounds completely from the statutes and to reduce the waiting period to one year, Parliament passed the Family Law Act of 1996, which incorporated such provisions. Yet, controversy surrounding the Act led to delays of implementation, the addition of various amendments requiring petitioning couples to participate in interventions geared toward saving marriages, and several years of "pilot" projects to examine the effects of the law and the amendments. *Id.* at 265-66. Ultimately, the law was repealed in 2001, never having gone into effect nationwide. For further discussion of the struggles over divorce law in 20ᵗʰ century England see Carol Smart, *Divorce in England 1950-2000: A Moral Tale?* In CROSS CURRENTS: FAMILY LAW AND POLICY IN THE US AND ENGLAND 363 (eds. S.N. Katz, J. Eekelaar & M. MacLean 2000).

2. *Divorce Reform in Europe*. Mary Ann Glendon noted that "[b]etween 1969 and 1985 divorce law in nearly every Western country was profoundly altered. Among the most dramatic changes was the introduction of civil divorce in the predominantly Catholic countries of Italy and Spain, and its extension to Catholic marriages in Portugal." ABORTION AND DIVORCE IN WESTERN LAW 66 (1987). The particulars of the new laws varied, with some jurisdictions following a path similar to that of California in eliminating fault-based grounds completely, others retaining fault grounds while adding no-fault grounds, and still others regulating divorces fairly restrictively (*e.g.*, by requiring lengthy waiting periods or providing courts with discretion to deny unilateral divorces). *Id.* at 67-69. *See* MARY ANN GLENDON, THE TRANSFORMATION OF FAMILY LAW 159-82 (1989), for an in-depth discussion of the divorce reforms in France and West Germany, which occurred at the same time as the transition to no-fault in the United States.

The Scandinavian countries followed a different path, introducing some form of no-fault divorce early in the 1900s. For example, although Sweden further liberalized its divorce law in 1973, it had permitted divorce on the basis of marital breakdown since 1915. Denmark, Finland, and Iceland followed Sweden's lead within a few years thereafter. Glendon, *supra*, THE TRANSFORMATION OF FAMILY LAW 182-88.

Marching to a different drummer than every other state in Western Europe, Ireland barred divorce altogether until 1995. For accounts of the debate and varying reform proposals, see MICHELLE DILLON, DEBATING DIVORCE: MORAL CONFLICT IN IRELAND (1993); BLAIR & WEINER, *supra,* at 268-75. In a referendum on November 24, 1995, Ireland voted by a narrow margin (0.6%) to lift its constitutional ban on divorce. *Id.* at 270. The new Irish law allows divorce if the couple has lived apart for at least four of the preceding five years, there is no reasonable prospect of reconciliation, and proper provision has been made for the spouses and children. Ireland thus went directly from a complete bar on divorce to allowing unilateral no-fault divorce, but with a very long waiting period. *See* Christine P. James, *Cead Mile Failte? Ireland Welcomes Divorce: The 1995 Irish Divorce Referendum and the Family (Divorce) Act of*

1996, 8 DUKE J. COMP. & INT'L L. 175 (1997) (discussing the historical and cultural context of the referendum); Jennifer A. Carter, Note, *Breaking the Bonds and Splitting the Assets: Women and Divorce in Ireland*, 15 B.U. INT'L L.J. 511 (1997) (analyzing the operation of the new divorce laws and their economic consequences for women).

3. *Divorce in Non-Western Nations*. For a discussion of divorce laws and reform movements in Asian, African, and Middle Eastern countries, see BLAIR & WEINER, *supra*, at 281-87, 298-306. Reportedly, Chile is the only nation in the world in which divorce remains completely unavailable, despite attempts at legal reform in the 1990s. Patrick Thurston, *The Development of Religious Liberty in Chile 1973-2000*, 2000 BYU.L. REV. 1185, 1257. Yet, the restrictive divorce laws in Chile seem not to have prevented many couples who wish to separate from doing so. There are high numbers of annulments in Chile, primarily available to those who can afford the fees. *Id.* Furthermore, observers report that a substantial proportion of legally-married couples effect *de facto* marital separations. Robert M. Gordon, *The Limits of Limits on Divorce*, 1007 YALE L.J. 1435 (1998) (citing estimates that "nearly half of all married adults [in Chile] have separated unofficially").

§ B.   THE MODERN LAW IN ACTION

[1]   PURE NO-FAULT SYSTEMS

MODEL MARRIAGE AND DIVORCE ACT §§ 302, 305

§ 302. [DISSOLUTION OF MARRIAGE; LEGAL SEPARATION]

(a) The [_____] court shall enter a decree of dissolution of marriage if:

    . . . .

(2) the court finds that the marriage is irretrievably broken, if the finding is supported by evidence that (i) the parties have lived separate and apart for a period of more than 180 days next preceding the commencement of the proceeding, or (ii) there is serious marital discord adversely affecting the attitude of one or both of the parties toward the marriage;

(3) the court finds that the conciliation provisions of Section 305 either do not apply or have been met;

(4) to the extent it has jurisdiction to do so, the court has considered, approved, or provided for child custody, the support of any child entitled to support, the maintenance of either spouse, and the disposition of property; or has provided for a separate later hearing to complete these matters.

(b) If a party requests a decree of legal separation rather than a decree of dissolution of marriage, the court shall grant the decree in that form unless the other party objects.

§ 305. [Irretrievable Breakdown]

(a) If both of the parties by petition or otherwise have stated under oath or affirmation that the marriage is irretrievably broken, or one of the parties has so stated and the other has not denied it, the court, after hearing, shall make a finding whether the marriage is irretrievably broken.

(b) If one of the parties has denied under oath or affirmation that the marriage is irretrievably broken, the court shall consider all relevant factors, including the circumstances that gave rise to filing the petition and the prospect of reconciliation, and shall:

(1) make a finding whether the marriage is irretrievably broken; or

(2) continue the matter for further hearing not fewer than 30 nor more than 60 days later, or as soon thereafter as the matter may be reached on the court's calendar, and may suggest to the parties that they seek counseling. The court, at the request of either party shall, or on its own motion may, order a conciliation conference. At the adjourned hearing the court shall make a finding whether the marriage is irretrievably broken.

(c) A finding of irretrievable breakdown is a determination that there is no reasonable prospect of reconciliation.

NOTES

1. *No-Fault Statutes in the U.S.* The MMDA, a product of the compromise described above, allows the court to find that the marriage is "irretrievably broken" if the parties have lived apart for 180 days. But even this half-year waiting period may be avoided if the court finds, in the alternative, that "there is serious marital discord adversely affecting the attitude of one or both of the parties toward the marriage." A party thus need not wait at all if he or she can show that the marriage is no longer viable, without regard to *why* it isn't, or whether the marital failure is the petitioner's fault. The Model Act is thus a "pure" no-fault statute, because it makes dissolution available to either party by a "no-fault" showing of marital failure. The parallel provision of the pioneering California law which inspired the MMDA requires a court finding of "irreconcilable differences," a formulation which some other states have also chosen.

As the introduction to this chapter indicates, by 1985 every state in the nation had added a no-fault provision to its divorce statutes. Some states, like California, repealed the fault-based grounds and thus, like the MMDA, may be characterized as pure no-fault systems, while other jurisdictions added no-fault grounds to the existing statutes. In these latter jurisdictions with "limited" no-fault systems, one or more no-fault grounds exist together with fault grounds. Section B2 examines some of the issues involved in resolution of cases in limited no-fault jurisdictions.

A 1987 survey found that sixteen states had pure no-fault laws: Arizona, California, Colorado, Delaware, Florida, Hawaii, Iowa, Kentucky, Michigan, Minnesota, Montana, Nebraska, Oregon, Washington, Wisconsin and Wyoming. Herma Hill Kay, *Equality and Difference: A Perspective on No-Fault Divorce and Its Aftermath,* 56 U. CIN. L. REV. 1, 5-6 (1987) [hereinafter "Hill,

Equality and Difference"]. Only slight changes occurred with respect to this category in the next fifteen years. Most notably, the District of Columbia's fault-based grounds were repealed, moving the District from the limited no-fault to pure no-fault group. D.C. CODE § 16-904 (2003). One pure no-fault state, Arizona, adopted "covenant marriage" as an optional alternative to standard marriage, which reintroduces fault-based divorce provisions. (*See* discussion of covenant marriage *infra* at page 260.) ARIZ. REV. ST. § 25-901 *et seq.* (2003). The remaining thirty-five states simply added a modern no-fault ground to their traditional fault grounds.

The no-fault provisions in both pure and limited no-fault jurisdictions fall into one of two categories: "marital breakdown" standards, and those rules granting divorce upon evidence that the parties have "lived separate and apart" for a statutorily-required period of time. Marital breakdown standards, adopted by over two-thirds of the states, require a finding that the marriage is "irretrievably" or "irremediably" broken (*e.g.*, GA. CODE ANN. § 19-5-3(13) (2003)); or that the spouses' relationship is characterized by "incompatibility" (*e.g.*, 43 OKLA. ST. § 101 (7) (2003), "insupportability" (*e.g.*, TEX. FAM. CODE § 6.001 (2003), or by "irreconcilable differences" (*e.g.*, S.D. § 25-4-2(7) (2003)). The influence of the MMDA is apparent; most of those states taking this approach adopt the terminology of irretrievable or irremediable breakdown. Unlike the MMDA, however, most states do not provide, in the alternative, that irretrievable breakdown can be demonstrated either by proof of marital discord or that the parties lived separate and apart for 180 days. Thus, even though a separation period of six months may constitute probative evidence that the marriage is over, determinations of such are technically left in the hands of the trial court judges (but see note 4, *infra* at p. 221, for a discussion of how such provisions are applied in practice).

Those states granting no-fault divorces upon a finding that the couple has lived "separate and apart" for a specified period of time reveal substantial variability in the length of the required separation periods. The periods range from six months in Vermont, 15 VT. ST. § 551 (2003), and Montana, MT. ST. § 40-4-104(1) (2003), to three years in Rhode Island, R.I. ST. 15-5-3(a) (2003), and Utah, UTAH ST. § 30-3-1-(3)(j) (2003). The remaining states in this group require, respectively, periods of one year, eighteen months, or two years. A handful of states, such as Hawaii and Texas, offer alternative no-fault grounds of marital breakdown and a period of separation. *See, e.g.*, HI. ST. § 580.41 (2003) (permitting a decree of divorce upon a finding of either irretrievable breakdown or a two-year period of separation); TEX. FAM. CODE §§ 6.001, 6.006 (2003) (permitting the court to grant a divorce upon a finding that the marriage is insupportable or a three-year period of separation without cohabitation). Many laws in this last group actually predated the California no-fault reform, although some of these states shortened their required periods of separation after the reform movement took hold. Despite the apparent no-fault divorce "revolution," much of the old divorce law remains remarkably intact in some states. This is especially true in states which have added a lengthy separation period as the only no-fault ground. Depending upon the parties' situations, proceeding on fault grounds may be preferable to waiting several years.

2. *Can a No-Fault Petition Be Resisted Successfully?* An early California no-fault case suggested that the courts might take seriously the requirement that there be a meaningful showing that there were, indeed, irreconcilable differences between the parties. In *McKim v. McKim,* 6 Cal. 3d 673, 677, n.3, 493 P.2d 868, 890, 100 Cal. Rptr. 140, 142 (1972), the wife, who was the petitioner, did not personally appear. The husband filed no responsive pleading to the wife's petition, but appeared at the hearing as her witness:

Q. Mr. McKim, you are the respondent in this case; is that correct? A. Right.

Q. At the time the petition in this matter was filed, was it your belief that there were irreconcilable differences between you and your wife? A. Right.

Q. Since that time, have you and your wife attempted to resolve these differences? A. Yes.

Q. In fact, you reconciled for a period of time; is that correct? A. Yes.

Q. That reconciliation did not work out? A. No.

Q. Is it your opinion that at the present time there are irreconcilable differences? A. Right.

Q. Is it your opinion that any further waiting period or conciliation would assist in saving this marriage? A. No.

Q. As far as you are concerned, there is no longer a marriage? A. No.

Although this *pro forma* showing of "breakdown" has since become typical, in 1972 the California Supreme Court did not accept it. It affirmed the trial court's refusal to grant the divorce:

> [T]he wife urges that collusion precluding the granting of a judgment of dissolution cannot exist under the Family Law Act because any agreement by the spouses that their marriage should be dissolved establishes their irreconcilable differences and the breakdown of their marriage.
>
> . . .[A] traditional justification of the collusion doctrine with its implementing procedural rules is the state's interest in preserving the institution of marriage. . . . Under the Family Law Act the court, not the parties, must decide whether the evidence adduced supports findings that irreconcilable differences do exist and that the marriage has broken down irremediably and should be dissolved.

But it soon became clear that courts would not probe into the facts of the parties' relationship. *McKim* is probably the last case in California denying an unopposed dissolution petition. *See* Elayne Carol Berg, Note, *Irreconcilable Differences: California Courts Respond to No Fault Dissolutions,* 7 Loy. L.A. L. Rev. 453 (1974). "No fault" divorce thus quickly became the vehicle for acceptance of divorce by mutual consent. Iowa adopted a no-fault law soon after California, and a 1973 study found that dissolution hearings in uncontested cases averaged fifteen to twenty minutes. Stephen L. Sass, *The Iowa No Fault Dissolution of Marriage Law in Action,* 18 S.D. L. Rev. 629, 650 *et seq.* (1973). Similar results were reported by a 1978 study of Nebraska's no-fault law. Alan H. Frank, John J. Berman & Stanley F. Mazur-Hart, *No Fault*

Divorce and the Divorce Rate: The Nebraska Experience — An Interrupted Time Series Analysis and Commentary, 58 NEB. L. REV. 1, 61-65 (1978). A 1972 Iowa Supreme Court decision proved a better signal than *McKim* of how no-fault laws would be implemented, even in California:

> The requirement for corroboration is almost repugnant to the concept of "no-fault" dissolution of marriage. . . . Corroborative evidence is required mainly to prevent collusion between the parties. . . . In truth, if it were demonstrated that the parties were in collusion to bring about a termination of the marriage relationship, it would further evidence the fact of the marriage breakdown. *In re Marriage of Collins,* 200 N.W.2d 886, 890 (Iowa 1972).

3. *Summary Proceedings.* In fact, California and other states soon adopted summary dissolution procedures designed to achieve a convenient divorce by mutual consent — precisely the goal thwarted by the *McKim* court. Summary dispositions typically dispense with a hearing altogether. They are usually available only for childless marriages, or those with no minor children, and require as well that the parties submit affidavits or other sworn statements indicating that they have agreed upon the disposition of any marital property and waive any claim for support. California also sets a ceiling on the marital assets which a couple seeking a summary dissolution may have. CAL. FAM. CODE § 2400 *et seq.* (2003). Washington and Colorado allow summary dissolutions even when there are minor children. WASH. REV. CODE ANN. § 26.09.030 (2003); COLO. REV. STAT. ANN. § 14-10-120.3 (2003). For other summary dissolution procedures, see CONN. GEN. STAT. ANN. § 46b-51(a) (2003) (divorce on grounds of irretrievable breakdown available upon written stipulation of the parties); HAW. REV. STAT. § 580-42 (2003) (court may forgo hearing if fact of irretrievable breakdown uncontested); 750 ILL. COMP. STAT. ANN. § 5/451 *et seq.* (2003) ("Joint Simplified Dissolution Procedure" available to parties married eight years or less who waive support claims, have no minor children, have no real property and limited personal property, have combined income less than $35,000, have been separated for at least 6 months, who agree that marriage is irretrievably broken, and who have a written agreement dividing assets and liabilities); FLA. FAM. L.R. PROC. 12.105 (2003) ("Simplified Dissolution Procedure" available to parties without minor children who file financial statement and petition stating they have settled all issues; parties must appear at expedited hearing but will not have to give testimony unless court specifically requires it); OR. REV. STAT. § 107.485 (2003) (for marriages less than ten years with no minor children, no real property, limited other property, and no spousal support claims).

4. *Unilateral Divorce.* Studies in California, Iowa, and Nebraska revealed that the opponents of no-fault were correct in forecasting that these reforms would ultimately permit unilateral divorce. Berg, *supra* (California); Sass, *supra* (Iowa); Frank, Berman & Mazur-Hart, *supra* (Nebraska). In Iowa, petitions were granted in all of 211 contested divorce cases. In the Nebraska study a "survey of 10,000 dissolution cases failed to reveal a single instance in which it could be said with certainty that a divorce which was desired by even one of the spouses was ultimately refused." Frank, Berman & Mazur-Hart, *supra,* at 66-67. As the Nebraska investigators observed:

it is difficult to imagine what evidence a respondent spouse could introduce to counter the impressive demonstration of marital breakdown which is exhibited when one of the parties to a marriage steadfastly insists that the relationship has come to an end. The strained and hostile atmosphere and the ugly courtroom confrontation that would attend a contest over whether marital breakdown has occurred would only further evidence the fact that it had.

Very few state laws recognize this reality officially. Washington is an exception. In the absence of a denial on the part of either party that the marriage is irretrievably broken, the court must enter a decree of dissolution. If one party denies that the marriage is irretrievably broken, "the court shall consider all relevant factors, including the circumstances that gave rise to the filing of the petition and the prospects for reconciliation and shall" either "make a finding that the marriage is irretrievably broken and enter a decree of dissolution" or order counseling in the hopes of inspiring reconciliation. If such a request is granted, the court must still order the dissolution within 60 days if the parties are not reconciled and "either party continues to allege that the marriage is irretrievably broken." WASH. REV. CODE ANN. § 26.09.030 (2003). But while Washington's official recognition of unilateral divorce may be unique, few disagree that unilateral divorce is, in practice, granted in most jurisdictions. Thus, there remains a dual law of divorce, but the nature of the duality has changed. Today, while the law in the books does not recognize unilateral divorce, in most states the law in action does.

5. *Requiring Counseling as Part of the Divorce Process.* California never adopted the elaborate proposal for "family courts" that the Governor's Commission originally recommended, but more modest versions of the same idea were enacted in many states, often under the label of "conciliation courts." The Commission's recommendation reflects the hope that some divorces could be avoided by equipping domestic relations courts with marriage counselors and empowering domestic relations judges to order counseling. Yet, data were discouraging with respect to the effectiveness of conciliations courts. Frank, Berman & Mazur-Hart, *supra,* at 82-90. The recent trend has been to shift from marriage counseling to divorce counseling. The goal is not to preserve the marriage, but rather to assist the divorcing couple in reaching a divorce settlement, and (for those with minor children) working out a post-decree relationship supportive of the child's needs.

6. *Constitutional Right of Access to Divorce and to Block the Effect of No-Fault Reforms.* The U.S. Supreme Court has not directly held that the right to divorce is fundamental. In *Boddie v. Connecticut,* 401 U.S. 371 (1971), the Court struck down the application of filing fee requirements to indigent divorce petitioners. It held the state could not constitutionally deny indigents access to the only legally available means for terminating their marriage. In *United States v. Kras,* 409 U.S. 434 (1973), the Court distinguished *Boddie* in holding that filing fees could be imposed on indigents seeking bankruptcy. The only way to reconcile the cases is by attaching a special constitutional significance to divorce, although the Court in *Kras* conceded only that *Boddie* relied in part on "the marital relationship and the associated interests that surround it." 409 U.S. at 444. Yet, in *Sosna v. Iowa,* 419 U.S.

393 (1975), the Court applied only a rational basis test in rejecting a challenge to a durational residency requirement imposed on divorce petitioners. Several years later, in 1978, the Court, in *Zablocki v. Redhail* (reprinted in Chapter 2, p. 95), held that there is a fundamental right to marry. Does this right to marry necessarily implicate a right to divorce, since impediments to divorce burden the right to remarry? It is possible that had the Court decided *Zablocki* first, the *Sosna* Court might have arrived at a different result.

Some no-fault opponents have claimed unsuccessfully that certain no-fault divorce policies are unconstitutional. *See, e.g., Waite v. Waite*, 64 S.W.3d 217 (Tex. App. (2001) (no-fault does not violate Federal Establishment or Free Exercise Clauses or various state constitutional provisions); *Richter v. Richter*, 625 N.W.2d 490 (Minn. App. 2001) (marriage is not a "contract" within meaning of state and federal constitutions prohibiting restrictions on contracts).

[2] LIMITED NO-FAULT SYSTEMS

MISSOURI ANNOTATED STATUTES § 452.320 (2003)

1. If both of the parties by petition or otherwise have stated under oath or affirmation that the marriage is irretrievably broken, or one of the parties has so stated and the other has not denied it, the court, after considering the aforesaid petition or statement, and after a hearing thereon shall make a finding whether or not the marriage is irretrievably broken and shall enter an order of dissolution or dismissal accordingly.

2. If one of the parties has denied under oath or affirmation that the marriage is irretrievably broken, the court shall consider all relevant factors, including the circumstances that gave rise to the filing of the petition and the prospect of reconciliation, and after hearing the evidence shall

(1) Make a finding whether or not the marriage is irretrievably broken, and in order for the court to find that the marriage is irretrievably broken, the petitioner shall satisfy the court of one or more of the following facts:

(a) That the respondent has committed adultery and the petitioner finds it intolerable to live with the respondent;

(b) That the respondent has behaved in such a way that the petitioner cannot reasonably be expected to live with the respondent;

(c) That the respondent has abandoned the petitioner for a continuous period of at least six months preceding the presentation of the petition;

(d) That the parties to the marriage have lived separate and apart by mutual consent for a continuous period of twelve months immediately preceding the filing of the petition;

(e) That the parties to the marriage have lived separate and apart for a continuous period of at least twenty-four months preceding the filing of the petition; or

(2) Continue the matter for further hearing not less than thirty days or more than six months later, or as soon thereafter as the matter may be

reached on the court's calendar, and may suggest to the parties that they seek counseling. No court shall require counseling as a condition precedent to a decree, nor shall any employee of any court, or of the state or any political subdivision of the state, be utilized as a marriage counselor. At the adjourned hearing, the court shall make a finding whether the marriage is irretrievably broken as set forth in subdivision (1) above and shall enter an order of dissolution or dismissal accordingly.

MARRIAGE OF MITCHELL

545 S.W.2d 313 (Mo. App. 1976)

KELLY, Judge. Sharon Kay Mitchell, respondent in the trial court, takes this appeal from an order . . . granting a decree of dissolution of her marriage with Glenn Gary Mitchell, the petitioner. The sole issue on appeal is whether there is sufficient evidence to support the order of the trial court finding that the marriage is irretrievably broken and granting the decree of dissolution. We reverse. . . .

[Glenn's petition alleged that the parties separated on October 20, 1973, had two minor children, and that] there is no reasonable likelihood that the marriage . . . can be preserved, and is therefore irretrievably broken. He prayed that the marriage be dissolved.

[Sharon's] Answer . . . alleged that although she and petitioner have not lived together on a continuing basis since about October 20, 1973, he left without her consent and she at all times has desired, and at the time of the separation did desire to continue cohabiting with him. She denied the allegation . . . that there was no reasonable likelihood that the marriage could be preserved and was irretrievably broken.

. . . . At the time of the marriage [Glenn] was 21 years of age and [Sharon], 22.

. . . . The basis for [Glenn's] conclusion that the marriage was irretrievably broken was that for three years he has felt that he no longer loves his wife. They have been separated on two occasions; the first time, between October of 1972 to May of 1973, and again from October 1973 to the date of trial. It was he who left home on each occasion. They had undergone counseling prior to the first separation with the family physician, a psychiatrist, a priest, a minister, friends and family. He cannot continue married life with the respondent.

[Glenn] admitted on cross-examination that during his periods of separation he had associated with women other than his wife and on one occasion had intercourse with one of the women. He admitted that when he returned home in May, 1973, he resumed marital relationships with [Sharon], and maintained the "husband-wife father-children" relationship until he left the marital home the last time in October, 1973.

[Sharon] testified that between 1973 and 1974 she and petitioner had "quarrels"[1] about normal husband and wife things — "No big thing." She was dissatisfied with [Glenn's] role as a husband around the home because he said he would do things and then he would not do them. She had guests at the home when they could afford it, but they could not afford to have guests often. They had guests at home more frequently than once every three months. She never refused to have friends over to the house and was happy entertaining when they had the money, but they had financial troubles throughout their married life. [Glenn] managed the money throughout the marriage and was still managing it. . . Prior to their first separation [Glenn] had to be at work by 7:30 a.m. As a consequence they would retire between 10 and 12 p.m. On occasion, when she was sewing for the children and had a deadline to meet, he would retire before she did. They had some late night discussions over problems with the children, on normal husband and wife problems, and normal every day happenings. She did not feel that she had enough help with the children's disciplining because [Glenn] was at work so much of the time. He said that it was necessary that he be at work so much, and she accepted this.

About five years ago, for the first time, she realized something was wrong with the marriage but she did not know what it was. She concluded that the children and she were not as important to [Glenn] as they had been. He did not want to be home. He had to attend dinner meetings and "things" with General Motors, his employer, and she was not included in these activities. He told her she was not welcome at these dinners. She became ill and lost 25 pounds. She went to her family physician who gave her all of the help he could. [Glenn] . . . told her that some of the girls at work went to a psychiatrist for their problems, and suggested that she consult him. She did. After [Sharon] saw the psychiatrist, he wanted to see [Glenn]. [Glenn] went to see the psychiatrist and [Sharon] returned to his care also. After a time the psychiatrist told her he wanted to see [Glenn] again, but [Glenn] would not go see him this time. The psychiatrist referred [Sharon] to . . . a marriage counselor and both she and [Glenn] went to see the marriage counselor a number of times between May, 1972, and October, 1972. She talked with one priest initially when she began to suspect a problem with the marriage and then again . . . with another priest. . . . She also talked with a minister.

After [Glenn] returned to his familial role in May of 1973 he continued to remain away from home. He always had a dinner meeting, or a golf game, or another job. When he did come home it was late at night, or he only came home when it involved the children. He said, "he was going to try."

She believed the marriage could be preserved because [Glenn] had left before, returned and resumed marital relations with her and took up his place in the home. With respect to his sexual relations with the other woman, although she had heard about it, when she questioned [Glenn], he told her that it was a rumor and untrue. She believed him until she heard him testify at the hearing; however, she believed he was just sowing some wild oats in that relationship.

---

[1] "Quarrels" was the word used by petitioner's counsel in his question and adopted by respondent initially; however, throughout the greater part of her testimony she insisted the word "discussions" was more appropriate to these husband and wife conversations.

. . . . [¶] [Glenn] . . . was employed for the year prior to the hearing . . . with a contracting company "in the sales aspect of selling home improvements and obtaining leads to do the same" on a commission basis. Prior to that he had been employed by the General Motors Parts Division for seven years. . . .

[Sharon], after graduating from high school, was employed by Sears-Roebuck in the credit office doing sales and billing. She terminated this employment in 1963 when she became pregnant with her daughter and has not been employed out of the home since then. [¶] . . . She is a voluntary physical education teacher at the school the children attend and she does share in the activities of the Campfire Girls in which her daughter participates. She makes most of her own clothing as well as that of the daughter. . . . [¶] [Sharon] has no special training other than that which she obtained in high school.

At the conclusion of the evidence, [Sharon's] counsel moved for a judgment in her behalf for the reason that the evidence failed to establish the basis for a dissolution of marriage under the provisions of § 452.320.2. . . . [T]he trial court advised counsel that . . . it thought that the marriage was irretrievably broken and there is no reasonable likelihood that it may be preserved. The trial court felt that the parties had made every effort to try to reconcile by going to counselors, a psychiatrist, and [Sharon] to priests and ministers; that it was the clear intent of the Legislature in the enactment of the present Divorce and Marriage Act, which no longer contained the word "divorce," that where a situation has arisen, without trying to place fault on "A" or "B," the law recognizes that they cannot be forced to cohabit and live together. It was the trial court's opinion that if the parties demonstrate in their testimony that they are really irreconcilably situated at the time, the Legislature recognizes that fact. The inability of the trial court to make people happy in matrimony was decried and although the court could send them to marriage counselors and make them go through what they have already gone through, it saw no reason for doing so. . . . Shortly thereafter the decree of dissolution was entered.

Both parties are in agreement that one basis for the trial court's finding that the marriage was irretrievably broken in this contested case is subparagraph 2(1)(b) of § 452.320, "[t]hat *respondent* has behaved in such a way that petitioner cannot reasonably be expected to live with respondent." (Emphasis supplied). However, they do not agree on the requisite scope of the inquiry by the trial court in ascertaining whether the parties' marriage is irretrievably broken. [Glenn] takes the position that the sole issue in this case is whether this marriage is irretrievably broken and if it is then the trial court did not err in granting the dissolution decree. [Sharon] argues that in order for the trial court to make a finding that the marriage is irretrievably broken, where the respondent denies that it is, there must be substantial evidence of wrongdoing on the respondent's part so that the petitioner cannot reasonably be expected to live with her. She contends that there is no evidence in this record of any wrongdoing on her part and that the only evidence in the case for the petitioner's conclusion that the parties' marriage is irretrievably broken is his testimony that he no longer loves her.

The evidence [Glenn] contends supports the trial court's finding that the marriage is irretrievably broken is the following:

1) [Sharon] recognized five years prior to the filing of his petition for dissolution of the marriage that there was something wrong with the marriage,

2) while [Glenn] was attending dinner meetings with General Motors, his employer, [Sharon] was not included,

3) [Sharon] did not read newspapers or books or attempt personal growth by belonging to a church, civic or women's group,

4) when [Glenn] returned home after a long day's work, [Sharon] would bring up problems late at night,

5) the marriage relationship continued to deteriorate,

6) [Glenn] maintained a steady course of employment and supported the family while [Sharon] was confused and needed help,

7) to assist [Sharon], [Glenn] suggested psychiatric help and on advice of the psychiatrist undertook professional marriage counseling with [Sharon],

8) [Sharon] sought other help, but despite all this the marriage did not improve and it continued to weaken and break apart until a separation followed between October, 1972, and May, 1973,

9) during the separation [Glenn] occasionally dated and had one affair, and

10) after [Glenn] returned nothing changed and after six months [Glenn] realized that he could not continue to live with [Sharon].

There is today in Missouri one ground for the granting of a decree dissolving a marriage, and that is where the trial court finds that there remains no likelihood that the marriage can be preserved and therefore the marriage is irretrievably broken. § 452.305.1(2). . . .

Unlike other states which have adopted the "no fault" concept of divorce reform laws . . . of Missouri clearly did not enact a total "no fault" dissolution law. Rather, our General Assembly adopted a "modified no fault" dissolution law. In those jurisdictions where the true "no fault" dissolution law is in effect all that needs to be shown to authorize the entry of a decree of dissolution is that the marriage is "irretrievably broken." In most "no fault" laws the term "irretrievably broken" is left undefined and no definitive standards or guidelines are given to control the dissolution process and consideration is given to each case individually. . . . All that the trial court must find from the evidence presented at the hearing on the petition is that the parties can no longer live together because of difficulties so substantial that no reasonable efforts could reconcile them. . . .

However, we conclude that . . . the Missouri General Assembly . . . unlike those jurisdictions where the legislatures have enacted true "no fault" dissolution laws, intended that a spouse, who by his or her actions makes the life of the other spouse intolerable or whose behavior makes it unreasonable for the marriage to be expected to continue, should not profit by his or her own wrongdoing and thereby obtain a dissolution of the marriage over the objection of the other perhaps innocent spouse. This intention is evidenced, we think, by the establishment of guidelines within the Law itself for trial courts . . . [Where the respondent denies] under oath or affirmation that the marriage is irretrievably broken, . . . § 452.320.2 is applicable. It is this . . . circumstance that we have here. . . .

. . .[This section provides that] *"in order for the court to find that the marriage is irretrievably broken,* the petitioner shall satisfy the court of one or more of" five facts. (Emphasis supplied). Of these five facts . . ., three are couched in terms which involve wrongdoing by the respondent. . . . The first wrongdoing . . . is adultery committed by the respondent; the second, that the respondent has behaved in such a way that the petitioner cannot reasonably be expected to live with the respondent; and the third, abandonment of the petitioner by the respondent for a continuous period of at least six months preceding the presentation of the petition.

Alternatively, in the absence of any "wrongdoing" on the part of the respondent, the trial court may then find the marriage is irretrievably broken if it is satisfied by petitioner's evidence (1) that the parties to the marriage have lived separate and apart by *mutual consent* for a continuous period of at least twelve months preceding the filing of the petition or (2) that they have lived separate and apart for a continuous period of at least twenty-four months preceding the filing of the petition.

The last time these parties separated was October 20, 1973. This petition for dissolution of marriage was filed on July 24, 1974. A period of nine months had intervened and there is no evidence that [Sharon] consented to the separation. Therefore, there is no evidence upon which the trial court could have based its finding of fact under § 452.320.2(1)(d) or (e) that the marriage is irretrievably broken.

Likewise, there is no evidence that [Sharon] has committed adultery, nor that she has abandoned [Glenn] for a continuous period of at least six months preceding the presentation of the petition.

The only remaining "fact" . . . [that could support a finding] that the marriage was irretrievably broken is that [Sharon] has behaved in such a way that he cannot reasonably be expected to live with her. His sole reason for his inability to live with [Sharon] was that he no longer loved her. He specified no behavior on her part which caused him to arrive at this conclusion. . . . From this evidence we conclude that it was the wife, rather than the husband, who undertook to preserve the marriage. . . . All of the evidence is that here was a mother who was burdened alone with the child-rearing of the minor children of the family, whose discussions concerning the children were categorized by [Glenn's] counsel as "quarrels" when never once during [Glenn's] testimony did he complain that it was these "quarrels" or "discussions" which made it unreasonable to expect [Glenn] to live with [Sharon]. We find in the record no complaint from [Glenn] that his wife's failure to read the newspapers or books was a behavior trait which contributed to the downfall of the marriage. Nor, are we impressed with [his] argument . . . that . . . [Sharon, after his return], failed to recognize that the manner in which the parties functioned would have to change in order for there to be a likelihood for the marriage to be preserved. We note that the evidence is clear that after [Glenn] returned he did not change; he continued attending his company dinners at which [Sharon] was unwelcome. The behavior in this record which would make it unreasonable to expect one of the parties to live with the other is essentially [Glenn]'s not [Sharon]'s.

This marriage may well be beyond saving, and in holding as we do we are but delaying the inevitable; nevertheless, we as an appellate court construe and apply the law, we do not make it. It is commonly recognized that the Divorce Reform Act of this State is not, and was not meant to be, a true "no fault" dissolution law.

We hold that under the evidence in the record before us the trial court erred in finding that the marriage of these parties was irretrievably broken . . . and reverse the decree of dissolution entered thereon.

NOTES

1. Mitchell *Sequel.* Five months after *Mitchell* was decided, the husband again filed for dissolution, this time on the no-fault ground that the parties had been separated for two years. When the trial court granted the husband's decree, the wife again appealed, contending that in reckoning the period of separation, the trial court should not have counted the portion of their separation which had occurred before the previous appellate decision. The court rejected this claim and ordered the dissolution. *Mitchell v. Mitchell,* 581 S.W.2d 871 (Mo. App. 1979).

2. *Other Interpretations of Missouri Statute.* Contrast *Mitchell* with the contemporaneous opinion of another Missouri court in *Gummels v. Gummels,* 561 S.W.2d 442 (Mo. App. 1978). In rejecting the husband's arguments that the marriage was not "irretrievably broken," as the wife claimed, the court said:

> Defendant-husband appeals, contending only that . . . the evidence did not warrant a finding . . . that he had behaved in such a way that his wife cannot reasonably be expected to live with him. . . .
>
> Defendant's only cited case on the merits is *In re Marriage of Mitchell.* There, . . . the plaintiff-husband's sole reason for his inability to live with his wife — without explanation — was his bald statement he no longer loved her. That case is distinguishable.
>
> Here, there was evidence of the parties' deteriorating relationship and the waning of their affections for several years. . . . She testified that only she disciplined their two children; that defendant usually consoled them and would not "back her up." Plaintiff also testified she and defendant were "unable to communicate"; that they could not "iron out our differences"; they couldn't live together, and she "needed some peace of mind." Plaintiff testified . . . she no longer loved him and believed there was no likelihood the marriage could be preserved.
>
> Defendant-husband testified his wife's complaints were "built out of all proportion" and concluded he did not believe their marriage was irretrievably broken.
>
> . . . [W]e find no reversible error in the court's conclusion that there remains no reasonable likelihood the marriage can be preserved and is irretrievably broken.

A perusal of Missouri cases suggests that *Gummels* presents a more accurate picture than *Mitchell* of how Missouri's law usually works in practice. But the picture is not uniform, and the spirit of *Mitchell* can still be seen in subsequent cases. *Compare Nieters v. Nieters*, 815 S.W.2d 124 (Mo. App. 1991) (adulterous husband denied divorce over opposition of wife where only eight months of the parties' multi-year separation were before filing of the divorce petition; and husband's testimony that parties were sometimes "unable to get along," disagreed on some financial and child-raising matters, and were sometimes mutually violent did not establish that he could not reasonably be expected to live with wife; court concedes that it is "but delaying the inevitable" but is bound by the statute) *with Welsh v. Welsh*, 869 S.W.2d 802 (Mo. App. 1994) (deferring to trial court's judgment that wife could not reasonably be expected to live with husband where she believed he was "not compassionate or considerate" and testified to several specific incidents, contested by him, to support that conclusion).

3. *What Is "Living Apart"?* For states which rely on lengthy periods of *de facto* separation to establish eligibility for a no-fault divorce, questions can arise as to what constitutes "living apart." Missouri and Illinois courts have held, for example, that parties have "lived apart" for the purpose of these statutes even though they lived in the same home, where they did not share a bedroom, did not communicate with each other and in general led "separate lives." *In re Marriage of Kenik,* 536 N.E.2d 982 (Ill. App. 1989); *In re Marriage of Uhls,* 549 S.W.2d 107 (Mo. App. 1977). A North Carolina court held that a couple had not begun living apart when the husband had taken a job in Boston, so long as he flew home to North Carolina for the holidays and the couple maintained a public posture of an intact marriage. *Hall v. Hall,* 363 S.E.2d 189 (N.C. App. 1987).

4. *Requiring Mutual Consent.* A few states go beyond requiring long waiting periods for unilateral divorce: they bar it altogether. New York, among the most reluctant converts to no-fault, recognizes only one ground for a no-fault divorce: living apart for the requisite period of time. But in New York (unlike Missouri and most other limited no-fault states), "living apart" qualifies only if it is pursuant to either a written separation agreement (and thus mutual consent) or to a judgment of legal separation, N.Y. DOM. REL. LAW § 170 (2003). Legal separation in turn can be obtained only on fault grounds, N.Y. DOM. REL. L. § 200 (2003). Thus, in New York, a spouse who cannot be shown "at fault" can effectively block a divorce indefinitely by refusing to enter into a voluntary written separation agreement. A task force appointed by the New York State Bar to review the state's family law statutes issued its report in 1996. It recommended that New York repeal the restrictive rules and adopt unilateral no-fault divorce. Ira M. Ellman & Sharon Lohr, *Marriage as Contract, Opportunist Violence, and Other Bad Arguments for Fault Divorce*, 1997 U. ILL. L. REV. 719, 723 n.8. No such revision succeeded. Mississippi and Tennessee follow a similar approach, although in those states the no-fault ground requiring agreement by the parties is "irreconcilable differences." MISS. CODE ANN. §§ 93-5-1, 93-5-2 (2003); TENN. STAT. ANN. §§ 36-4-101 (14), 36-4-103(b) (2003). Rules that effectively require mutual consent as the only alternative to proof of fault are subject to the same concerns raised with respect to long waiting periods for unilateral divorce. For discussion of these problems, see excerpt by Professor Ellman, at page 246 *infra*.

5. *Continued Use of Fault Grounds*. There are several reasons why a spouse might claim fault grounds in a state that provides both fault and no-fault divorce: (1) Spouses who have settled their divorce may agree on a fault ground in order to dissolve their marriage more quickly than is allowed under the no-fault rule prevailing in states that impose a waiting period on no-fault divorce; (2) Where there is no settlement, a fault divorce may provide one party an advantage in settling the financial aspects of the divorce. About half the states allow their courts to consider marital misconduct in deciding upon alimony awards, and a smaller group allow its consideration even in the allocation of marital property. *See* Chapter 4. In some of these states, only a spouse who obtains a fault divorce can take advantage of such provisions. The result is that even today, some cases read like classic fault-based litigation in some states. *See, e.g., Bacon v. Bacon*, 351 S.E.2d 37 (Va. App. 1986) (decree based on one year's separation reversed because trial court must consider wife's claim for divorce based on husband's desertion, since such grounds may be relevant in determining alimony); *Hughes v. Hughes*, 531 S.E.2d 645 (Va. App. 2000) (trial judge erred in granting divorce on adultery grounds because wife's cohabitation in same home with the man she intended to marry was insufficient proof of adultery, given their separate bedrooms; even "highly suspicious circumstances" are insufficient as proof of adultery; remand to consider granting of a divorce on grounds of one year's separation).

Parties are even more likely to seek a fault-based divorce in the small number of states that bar unilateral no-fault divorce, such as Tennessee and Mississippi. *See, e.g., Simpson v. Simpson,* 716 S.W.2d 27 (Tenn. 1986) (considering whether insanity may be offered as a defense to a claim for fault divorce based on cruel and inhumane treatment); *Earls v. Earls*, 42 S.W.2d 877 (Tenn. App. 2000) (reversing trial court's refusal to grant a divorce to husband on the fault ground of "inappropriate marital conduct"— the ground which replaced the former fault ground of "cruel and inhumane treatment"). In Mississippi, in *Lewis v. Lewis*, 602 So. 2d 881, 883 (1992), the state supreme court reversed the trial court's grant of divorce on fault grounds. In this case, husband claimed wife treated him cruelly and inhumanely, and wife claimed that husband regularly committed adultery. The trial court judge granted divorce, stating: "I don't think either one of you has proven a ground for divorce. But, I feel like this is one of those occasions where you people are not going to be able to live together." On appeal, the supreme court held that no divorce can be granted on fault grounds without the specific findings of fault required by statute. (In this case, the wife's appeal was grounded in her hope that a finding of fault against her husband might enhance her claim for alimony, as in *Bacon, supra*.) *See also Bowen v. Bowen*, 688 So. 2d 1374 (Miss. 1997) (divorce denied to both parties, the court finding that neither had made a sufficient showing of "habitual cruel and inhuman treatment," even though testimony was provided by the couple's children concerning the couple's physical altercations); *Harmon v. Harmon*, 757 So.2d 305 (Miss. App. 2000) (neither the condonation or recrimination defenses barred wife's divorce action grounded on husband's adultery).

6. *The Perceptions of Parties in Limited No-Fault Jurisdictions.* English law is quite similar to Missouri's in its combination of fault and no-fault grounds for divorce. A study of English law concluded that no-fault reform failed in its purpose of shifting the parties' perception of the divorce process from one based on a "fault" principle to one based on a no-fault "break-down" principle.

> The law tells the parties, on one hand, that the sole ground for divorce is irretrievable breakdown, and on the other hand, that unless they are able to wait for at least two years after separation, a divorce can only be obtained by proving fault. Not surprisingly, the subtlety that the facts are not ground for divorce, but merely evidence of breakdown, is seldom grasped.

British Law Commission, *Facing the Future: A Discussion Paper on the Ground for Divorce* 17, Law Com. No. 170 (1988). Another British study concluded that the presentation of evidence to demonstrate the fault "facts" generates the same kind of hostility that prior fault-based regimes produced, and which the no-fault reforms were supposed to lessen. G. Davis & M. Murch, Grounds for Divorce (1988).

§ C. REPRISE: RE-EVALUATING NO-FAULT, FAULT, AND THE LAW'S ROLE IN PROMOTING MARITAL STABILITY

Did the no-fault reforms go too far, making divorce too easy to obtain? Some argue yes and assert that the consequences of these reforms have been deleterious for the parties, their children, and society. Some propose revising no-fault divorce laws in one way or another. The arguments for "reforming the reforms" are of several kinds. One view posits that in removing legal obstacles to divorce, the no-fault "revolution" opened the floodgates, causing skyrocketing divorce rates by virtue of the ease with which marital dissolution could now be achieved. A second argument suggests that the impact of no-fault reforms have been more subtle — that the accessibility of divorce has altered social norms. According to this view, no-fault divorce laws weaken the institution of marriage by undercutting the social norm that marriage is a life-long commitment. *See, e.g.,* Linda J. Waite & Maggie Gallagher, The Case for Marriage: Why Married People are Happier, Healthier and Better Off Financially 195-99 (2000); Elizabeth Scott, *Social Norms and the Legal Regulation of Marriage*, 86 Va. L. Rev. 1901 (2000). Some allege that no-fault divorce encourages a moral decline. It ostensibly promotes a retreat from the traditional ideal of an intact family unit comprised of a married couple and their children, which is asserted to be the core building block of our society. Some conservative politicians have called for a return to "family values," such as reversal of the "trend toward automatic divorce." Kay, *From Second Sex to Joint Venture, supra,* at 2068-69 (citing White House Working Group on the Family, The Family: Preserving America's Future 6 (1986)). Because many of these calls to turn back the clock assume that modern divorce statutes *caused* the high divorce rates, their proponents suggest that making divorce more difficult to obtain is likely to *reduce* the divorce rate. In Section C1, *infra,* we consider the data and alternative interpretive arguments.

A second theme is concerned with working justice between divorcing spouses. To this end, some commentators argue either: (a) because marriage is a contract the law should not allow one party to end it unilaterally; or (b) restrictions on unilateral divorce are necessary to protect the innocent spouse. Below, we consider the arguments and counter-arguments relevant to these contentions. More generally, some commentators blame no-fault policies for the disproportionate impoverishment of women and children following divorce. There is little dispute that divorce has far-ranging financial consequences for many families, and that women and children experience these economic consequences more severely than do men. Yet, the precise nature and extent of the gender discrepancies is the subject of significant debate. For an analysis of the competing claims, see Note on the Debate Over Differences in the Financial Impact of Divorce on Men and Women, *infra* at p. 367. Most scholars have concluded that no-fault divorce laws are not the cause of these consequences, but that the problems lie with legal policies governing the characterization and distribution of marital property and of post-dissolution spousal and child support. *See, e.g.,* AMERICAN LAW INSTITUTE, PRINCIPLES OF THE LAW OF FAMILY DISSOLUTION: ANALYSIS AND RECOMMENDATIONS (2000) (proposing reforms of property distribution and support provisions in divorce law); STEPHEN D. SUGARMAN & HERMA HILL KAY (EDS.), DIVORCE REFORM AT THE CROSSROADS (1990) (reviewing, with several essays, alternative approaches to improving economic well-being of women and children following divorce). Chapter 4 examines this subject in greater depth, and thus we will not address it further here.

Third, critics of no-fault divorce also claim that divorce reform is responsible for increasing the numbers of children who suffer emotionally because of parental divorce. Apart from the implicit but contested assumption that no-fault laws have caused an increase in the divorce rate, the impact of divorce on children is also in dispute. While few disagree that a parental divorce is an emotionally-challenging transition for children to endure, the "soundbites" as to the allegedly universal and devastating consequences of divorce for children typically oversimplify the issues. Section 2c, *infra,* summarizes the relevant social science evidence and examines some of the conclusions suggested by recent studies. This discussion of the effects of divorce on children continues in Chapter 6.

Fourth, in response to the concerns raised above, the legislatures of many states considered proposals to return to fault-based standards during the 1990s. Across the board, these bills were defeated. In 1997, however, Louisiana became the first state to offer those who marry a choice between a standard marriage (governed by the state's existing no-fault divorce provisions) and "covenant marriage" (governed by more traditional fault-based standards). In Section 2d, *infra*, we discuss the phenomenon and its implications. Finally, an additional set of reforms has emerged from the discussions noted above, focusing on encouraging forethought before marriage and on enhancing the stability of existing marriages, and these proposals are discussed as well.

[1] THE DATA ON MARRIAGE AND DIVORCE RATES

[a] What Are the Trends?

There is more than one way to calculate divorce rates. One good measure is the number of divorces per 1,000 existing marriages. Figure 1-5 reports annual measures of these statistics, and reflects "the particular social and economic conditions of each year." ANDREW CHERLIN, MARRIAGE, DIVORCE, REMARRIAGE 20-21 (Revised and Enlarged Edition, 1992).

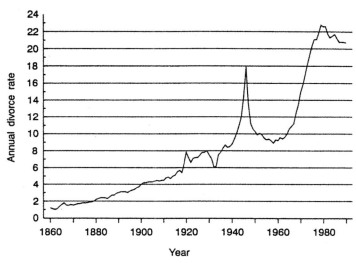

Figure 1-5 Annual divorce rates, United States. For 1920-1988: divorces per 1,000 married women aged 15 and over; for 1860-1920: divorces per 1,000 existing marriages.

Professor Cherlin notes the rise of divorce rates after major wars (*e.g.*, Civil War, World Wars I and II) and the lowering of these rates during the Depression. The rates in the period from 1950 to 1960 depart from the pattern of long-term rise. *Id.* at 21-22. Following this sharp drop is a correspondingly sharp rise, with a peak around 1979, and a subsequent decline. Many of those who posit a causal relationship between changes in divorce laws in the 1970s and subsequent rates of marriage view a truncated version of these figures, comparing the annual rates from 1960s with those following the divorce law reforms in the 1970s and 1980s. These observers therefore, miss the big picture of rising divorce rates throughout the 20th century and the latter portion of the 19th century.

Professor Cherlin provides another, more revealing, picture of the pattern in divorce rates throughout this same period of time. Figure 1-6 charts the "proportion of all marriages begun in every year between 1867 and 1985 which will have ended, or will end, in divorce before one of the spouses dies." *Id.*

at 22-23. The dots in the chart indicate actual data; the smooth line is the curve that most closely fits the pattern revealed by these dots and which therefore suggests the long-term trend. One value of the second chart, Cherlin explains, is that it gives us a better picture of the general trends. "We can see from the dotted line that the proportion of all marriages in a given year that eventually end in divorce has increased at a faster and faster rate since the mid-nineteenth century. Moreover, the increase has been relatively steady, without the large fluctuations which the annual rates show in times of war or depression." *Id.* at 23.

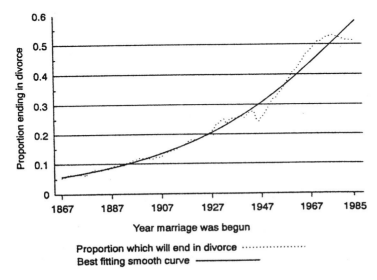

Figure 1-6 Proportion of marriages begun in each year that will end in divorce, 1867 to 1985.

Divorce rates are most commonly calculated as divorces per 1,000 people, and these are the only data available presently for the 1990s and early 2000s. The American divorce rate peaked, at 5.3 divorces per 1,000 people in 1979 and 1981 (it was 5.2 in 1980). The rate then declined to 5.0 in 1982, and remained there until the decline resumed in 1986. The rate has dropped steadily since. It was 4.7 in 1990, 4.3 in 1995, 4.2 in 2000, and 4.0 in 2001. U.S. Census Bureau, STATISTICAL ABSTRACT OF THE UNITED STATES: 2002, Table No. 66, p. 59. This latter figure reflects an almost 25% decrease from the 1979/1981 peaks. Presently the rate of divorce per 1,000 in the population is at the lowest level in the United States since 1972.

One study, using 1988 data, estimated that 43% — a figure somewhat lower than the frequently-cited one-half — of all marriages in the United States fail. Robert Schoen & Robin M. Weinick, *The Slowing Metabolism of Marriage: Figures from 1988 U.S. Marital Status Life Tables*, 30 DEMOGRAPHY 737, 742 (1993). More recently, researchers report disruption of approximately 20% of first-time marriages by separation or divorce within the first five years, one-third within ten years, and 43% by the fifteen-year mark. Matthew D.

Bramlett & William D. Mosher, *First Marriage Dissolution, Divorce, and Remarriage: United States,* ADVANCE DATA # 323, May 31, 2001. The percentage of marriages that end in formal divorce is, of course, somewhat lower than those ending in divorce or separation, although about 75% of the separations lead to divorce within about two years, and 90% within five years. The researchers examined some of the variables that relate to the likelihood a marriage will terminate early. In particular, if the wife was a teenager (or even 18-19), her marriage was significantly more likely to dissolve early than were marriages of women age 20 and older. The relationship between marriages of persons under age 20 and higher rates of divorce is a frequently-cited finding. *See, e.g.,* The National Marriage Project, THE STATE OF OUR UNIONS 2002, at 21 (available at: marriage.rutgers.edu/Publications/SOOU/SOOU2002.pdf). Furthermore, racial factors were also relevant to the likelihood that a marriage would terminate within the first fifteen years. Bramlett and Mosher examined the marital patterns from the perspective of the women partners, and found that Asian-American women had the lowest rate of marital dissolution, African-American women had the highest, and Caucasian and Hispanic women fell between the two extremes.[1]

Rates of marriage have also dropped in the second half of the 20th century, although not following a linear course. The rate of marriage, measured as the number per 1,000 in the population, was 11.1 in 1950, 8.5 in 1960, and 10.6 in 1970. It spiked briefly to 10.9 in 1972, dropped to 10.6 in 1980, to 9.8 in 1990, to 8.9 in 1995, and to 8.5 in 2000, matching the 1960 rate. U.S. Census Bureau, STATISTICAL ABSTRACT OF THE UNITED STATES: 2002, Table No. 66, p. 59. In 2001, the rate dropped to 8.4. Does the decline in marriage rates arise from a declining interest in marriage? A 1996 Roper survey found that 86% of Americans between the ages of 18 and 29 say a happy marriage is "part of the good life" — a 14% *increase* over the percentage who so answered that question in 1991. The opinions of older Americans changed much less over that same time period. Half of all adult Americans (including those who were single) said they had a happy marriage in 1996, about the same as in 1991, but less than the 60% who so reported in 1975. *The Big Picture,* AMERICAN DEMOGRAPHICS, August 1997, at 35.

Average marital duration is affected by death as well as divorce, and mortality rates declined this century while divorce rates were rising. As a result, the aggregate dissolution rate — the number of marriages ending by either divorce or death, per 1,000 existing marriages — actually remained quite stable between 1860 and 1970. At the beginning of that period, the

---

[1] Note that no national divorce statistics have been systematically collected since January 1996. *Notice: Changes in Marriage and Divorce Data Available from the Center for Health Statistics,* 60 FED. REG. 64437-64438 (1995) (summary available at: www.cdc.gov/nchs/datawh/datasite/frnotice.htm). Since that time, only "provisional" data only have been collected. These data differ from the "final" data collected prior to this change, in that they are incomplete and do not include data from counties or perhaps even states that have not reported at the time the data are compiled. While the editors are not aware of any studies that have made systematic comparisons between such provisional data and the final data that were previously collected, casual inspection of provisional and final data collected before 1996 suggests that provisional data systematically overestimated divorce rates. One must therefore exercise caution in comparing divorce statistics from before 1996 with the provisional statistics available for later years, as this more recent data may also overestimate post-1995 divorce rates.

combined rate was 33.2 dissolutions per 1,000 marriages, while in 1970 the combined rate was 34.5. At least one scholar has therefore speculated that divorce may merely be a functional substitute for death, made necessary by increasing longevity. L. STONE, THE FAMILY, SEX AND MARRIAGE IN ENGLAND, 1500-1800, 56 (1977). Stone observed that as a result of the mortality rates "one very firm conclusion about the pre-modern family . . . was [that it was], statistically speaking, a transient and temporary association both of husband and wife and of parents and children." *Id.* at 55. The steep rise in divorce rates in the 1970s far exceeded mortality reductions, however, pushing the aggregate dissolution rates to 40.5 dissolutions per 1,000 marriages in 1978. Indeed, by the mid-1970s, for the first time in American history, more marriages ended every year in divorce than in death.

Estimates of remarriage rates vary, although it is clear that the remarriage rate declines with age, particularly for women. Bramlett and Mosher, *supra* at 9-10, found that 75% of divorced women remarry within ten years of their divorce, and that remarriage rates are significantly higher for women who are younger at divorce. *See also* Peter Uhlenberg, Teresa Cooney & Robert Boyd, *Divorce for Women After Midlife,* 45 J. GERONTOLOGY S3, S5 (1990) (measuring remarriages per 1,000 divorced women and reporting 1985 rates of 264 per 1,000 for women under 25, 184 per 1,000 for women 25 to 29, 80 per 1,000 for women 35 to 44, and 29 per 1,000 for women 45-64). Men are more likely to remarry than are women. THE STATE OF OUR UNIONS, *supra* at 20-21. Consistent with the gender differences in remarriage rates across the lifespan, older men remarry more often than older women. For example, ten percent of divorced men aged 45 to 54 married in 1988, compared to five percent of divorced women of that age. Dewitt, *supra.* Is it true that remarriages are more likely to end in divorce than first marriages? Yes, but the difference is not very great. U.S. Census Bureau, NUMBER, TIMING, AND DURATION OF MARRIAGES AND DIVORCES: 1996, p. 9 (2002) (noting that the median number of years from first marriage to divorce was about 8 years for men and women, and the median number of years from remarriage to divorce was about 7 years for men and women). Overall, between 80 to 90% of men and women in the United States are projected to marry at some point in their lives. *Id.* at 16.

[b]   Did the Move to No-Fault Divorce Laws Cause the Rise in Divorce Rates, and If Not, What Did?

Social scientists frequently remind us that "correlation does not imply causation." In other words, the fact that two variables or trends appear to be associated, such as a change in divorce laws and a rise in the divorce rates, does not demonstrate that one *caused* the other. *See e.g.,* Maire Ni Bhrolchain, *"Divorce Effects" and Causality in the Social Sciences,* 17 EUROPEAN SOCIOL. REV. 33, 44-53 (2001); V.R. McKim & S.P. Turner, CAUSALITY IN CRISIS? (eds. 1997). Two sets of changes may be unrelated, both sets might be caused by a third variable, or the direction of causality may be the reverse of that postulated by observers. Frequently, with complex social phenomena like divorce rates, a combination of multiple-interacting factors may explain observed changes. We examine the patterns of change in divorce rates in relation to the passage of no-fault statutes below, together with other social and cultural shifts, analyzing what factors may have contributed to the observed increases in divorce rates.

Look again at Figure 1-5, *supra*. Putting aside the one-time spike associated with the return of soldiers from World War II, the picture divides into three clear segments: a long-term gradual upward trend in divorce rates from the year when data first became available, 1860, through the early 1960s; a dramatically accelerated upward trend between the early 1960s and 1979; then a leveling off and decline. Most of the shift to no-fault laws occurred between the early 1970s and 1980 — *after* the largest increases in divorce rates had already occurred.

This aggregate picture is replicated when one looks at the relative timing of rises in divorce rates and transition to no-fault laws in the individual states. In fact, state-by-state analyses bring the chronology of the trends into even starker relief than do aggregate national data, because each state adopted no-fault reforms at different times during the fifteen year period between 1970 and 1985. In Arizona, for example, the divorce rate rose from 5.0 per thousand population in 1961 to 7.9 in 1971 under a regime of fault divorce. No-fault divorce was adopted in 1973. Only once between 1973 and 1979 — in 1976 — did the divorce rate exceed the 1971 fault-divorce level. The Arizona divorce rate peaked in 1979 at 8.2, but by 1994 had declined nearly 30 %, to 5.8. This decline occurred entirely under the state's new no-fault divorce law. Similar patterns are observed in most states, where divorce rate increases preceded no-fault reforms. For a detailed analysis of the state-by-state data, see Ira Mark Ellman & Sharon L. Lohr, *Dissolving the Relationship Between Divorce Rates and Divorce Laws*, 18 INT'L REV. L. & ECON. 341 (1998) [hereinafter Ellman & Lohr, *Dissolving the Relationship*].

This chronological sequence indicates that the no-fault statutes *followed*, rather than preceded, the rise in divorce rates. To the extent one ventures hypotheses as whether the legal changes and rising divorce rates are causally related to each other, no-fault laws were more likely a *result* of the increasing divorce rate, rather than its cause. Recall the discussion in Section A of the costs of the fault-based regime on the participants and on the legal system. "When divorce rates began a steep rise in the late 1960s, an increasing proportion of the population began experiencing this charade [of colluding to manufacture and testify to "evidence" sufficient to allow for a fault-based divorce adjudication]. More lawyer time was spent producing it, and more judge time was spent listening to it. In that way the rising divorce rate itself enlarged the constituency for divorce law reform." Ira Mark Ellman, *Divorce Rates, Marriage Rates, and the Problematic Persistence of Traditional Marital Roles*, 34 FAM. L.Q. 1, 5 (2000) [hereinafter Ellman, *Divorce Rates*].

Furthermore, there are rich bodies of historical and sociological evidence indicating that the increase in divorce rates and the transition to no-fault statutes were *both* caused by a plethora of sociocultural changes which dramatically affected American family life in the latter decades of the 20th century. Without question, the most commonly-cited factor affecting the divorce rate is the entrance of women into the labor market. *See, e.g.,* Cherlin, *supra* at 51 ("[A]lmost every well-known scholar who has addressed [the rise in divorce and separation] in the twentieth century has cited the importance of the increase in the employment of women."); HERBERT JACOB, SILENT REVOLUTION: THE TRANSFORMATION OF DIVORCE LAW IN THE UNITED STATES 17-18 (1988) (after 1940, married women's participation in workforce "exploded" with a rise of 10% per decade; by 1985, 54.3% of all married women were in the labor force, including a majority of married mothers with children under age three). The relationships between women's employment and divorce are complex, but many researchers agree that the decreasing economic dependence of employed women on their husbands made it easier for a couple to end an unhappy marriage. Cherlin, *supra* at 53; Jacob, *supra* at 18-19. *See* Ellman, *Divorce Rates, supra* at 13-14 & n.33, for a discussion of the role that wives' employment played in the rise of divorce rates and a summary and analysis of empirical research on the subject.

Furthermore, as discussed in Chapter 1, women's increasing participation in the labor market was not accompanied by commensurate reductions in their responsibilities in the home. Children and households still needed as much care as before, and husbands did not take over a significant portion of the load. *See, e.g.,* Jacob, *supra* at 19; SUZANNE M. BIANCHI & DAPHNE SPAIN, AMERICAN WOMEN IN TRANSITION 160 (1986). In addition, few workplaces responded flexibly to familial demands on their female employees. JOAN WILLIAMS, UNBENDING GENDER: WHY FAMILY AND WORK CONFLICT AND WHAT TO DO ABOUT IT (2000). Women struggled, and continue to struggle, with balancing their obligations to the workplace and home, a fact that often contributes to marital stress and dissatisfaction. ARLIE HOCHSCHILD & ANNE MACHUNG, THE SECOND SHIFT (1989).

Concurrent with these changes were the ideological shifts triggered by the women's movement. "Although only a small minority of American women ever openly declared themselves to be feminists, . . . the arguments of the women's movement dramatically altered women's attitudes toward family roles, marital relationships, femininity, and housework." STEVEN MINTZ & SUSAN KELLOGG, DOMESTIC REVOLUTIONS: A SOCIAL HISTORY OF AMERICAN FAMILY LIFE 208 (1988). The women's movement in the United States followed on the heels of the struggle for racial equality, focusing initially on gender discrimination in the workplace. As the movement progressed, the agenda expanded and came to embrace the goal of women's equality more broadly. Ultimately, feminism advanced a new way of thinking of marital relationships. "Talk of marriage as a contract between equals became more common and undermined the traditional view of marriage as a . . . relationship in which the husband dominated by natural right." Jacob, *supra* at 23. Although coverture of married women had, in theory, ended a century earlier, most American families did not internalize the view of women as equal partners of husbands until the latter decades of the 20th century.

Thus, a range of factors relating to women's entry into the labor market, their attempts to juggle family and workplace obligations, and shifting perceptions of women's place in the family led to transitions in marital roles and relationships. In many cases, partners had married with expectations that each would play more traditional marital roles, and these sociocultural changes crept up on them unexpectedly, altering the expectations of at least one of the partners. Some marriages adapted, others did not.

Expectations for marriage as a source of personal satisfaction also soared during the 1960s and 1970s: "[I]n addition to its traditional functions of caring for children, providing economic security, and meeting is members' emotional needs, the family has become the focus of the new expectations for sexual fulfillment, intimacy, and companionship." Mintz & Kellogg, *supra,* at 205. *See also* PAUL R. AMATO & ALAN BOOTH, A GENERATION AT RISK: GROWING UP IN AN ERA OF FAMILY UPHEAVAL 12 (1997) [hereinafter Amato & Booth, 1997]. Reflecting the continuation of this trend, a recent study of young adults reports that an overwhelming majority (94%) are searching for a marital partner who will be a "soul mate," that is, someone with whom they can share a "deep emotional and spiritual connection, and with whom they can communicate about their deepest feelings." Barbara Dafoe Whitehead & David Popenoe, *Who Wants to Marry a Soul Mate? New Survey Findings on Young Adults' Attitudes about Love and Marriage,* THE STATE OF OUR UNIONS: 2001 at 6, 8 (available at: marriage.rutgers.edu/Publications/SOOU/ NMPAR2001.pdf). Whereas higher expectations of personal satisfaction from one's marriage may, in some instances, propel a couple to a more rewarding relationship, in other cases it can lead to disappointment in the marriage. In fact, survey data reveal that the percentage of people who reported their marriages as "very happy," gradually declined between 1973 and 1988. Norval D. Glenn, *The Recent Trend in Marital Success in the United States,* 53 J. MARR & FAM. 261 (1991). *See* Amato & Booth, 1997*, supra* at 11 (summarizing studies). Furthermore, while research in prior decades revealed that married people reported being happier with their lives than did single people, the gap between the groups has narrowed; never-married men and women in the 1980s reported higher levels of personal happiness than they did in the 1970s, and young married women's reports of personal happiness declined between these two decades. *Id.* The lengthening of Americans' lifespans and the attendant lengthening of the lifespans of marriages created circumstances in which "marriages which are not companionate [could be experienced as] intolerable. Intolerable marriages more frequently lead to divorce. . . ." Jacob, *supra* at 26.

Scholars also cite other critical attitudinal changes that occurred in the latter half of the 20th century as contributing both to the rise in divorce rates and the move to no-fault divorce. The trend toward enhanced "commitment to individual choice and private ordering" was one such change. Michael Grossberg, *Balancing Acts: Crisis, Change, and Continuity in American Family Law,* 28 IND. L. REV. 273, 295 (1995). "Before no-fault divorce, the law retained for itself much of the responsibility for the moral choice whether to divorce; after no-fault, most of that responsibility was transferred to the husband and wife." Carl E. Schneider, *Moral Discourse and the Transformation of American Family Law,* 83 MICH. L. REV. 1803, 1809-10 (1985). Other beliefs about marriage and divorce had changed as well. The notion that marriages fail primarily because one spouse was wronged by the other no longer meshed with popular beliefs. Divorce and those who obtained it became less stigmatized because people had stopped believing the message fault-based divorce laws were sending. People also rejected the premise that the state should be in the business of enforcing the aspiration that marriages should last a lifetime. Schneider, *supra* at 1809.

The language used by a majority of the U.S. Supreme Court in *Boddie v. Connecticut*, a 1971 case holding unconstitutional a Connecticut statute that required those petitioning for divorce to pay a filing fee (*see* Note 6 *supra*, at p. 222) further reveals how dramatically public attitudes toward divorce had changed. In *Boddie*, the Court referred to divorce as an "adjustment of a fundamental human relationship," and divorce procedures as the method by which "two consenting adults may divorce and mutually liberate themselves from the constraints of legal obligations that go with marriage, and more fundamentally the prohibition against remarriage." *Id.* at 383, 376; *see* discussion at Grossberg, *supra* at 296. To the extent that the views articulated by the Court serve as a barometer of public attitudes, it is noteworthy that in 1971, eight of the nine justices concurred that the state must not put onerous obstacles in the path of couples who seek a divorce. *Boddie* preceded no-fault divorce reforms in most states by several years. Although the issue in *Boddie* concerned exclusion of economically-disadvantaged parties from access to the divorce process, the language used reveals a morally-neutral acceptance that divorce and remarriage are facts of life in America.

The list of explanations for the rise in divorce rates and transition to no-fault statutes set forth above is not exhaustive. *See, e.g.,* Ellman, *Divorce Rates, supra* at 7-13 (discussing the relationship of mobility and divorce). In the final analysis, the relationship between high divorce rates and changes in divorce laws may be characterized as one of reciprocal influence, much like the relationship between law and social change more generally:

> [M]ajor social change begins outside the legal system, that is, in society. . . . When we look at [the complete transformations in Western legal systems since the Middle Ages,] it is clear that the legal system has been carried along by great waves of social force. . . . Social forces in the larger society create [law], shape it, twist it and turn it, pull it and push on it. But these forces produce a system that becomes itself part of social life; once in place, the system works its own influence on society, on how we live, how we think, how we feel.

LAWRENCE M. FRIEDMAN, AMERICAN LAW: AN INTRODUCTION 254-276 (1984). Thus, once no-fault divorce became a fixture in America's legal landscape, it no doubt had an effect on social attitudes. "Law is a . . . thing that is shaped by culture, and in turn shapes the culture." Carol Weisbrod, *On the Expressive Functions of Family Law*, 22 U.C. DAVIS L. REV. 991-93 (1989). The empirical data, however, simply do not support the conclusion that the passage of no-fault divorce statutes is responsible for the *long-term* increase in divorce rates reported above. Although there appear to have been short-term increases in divorce rates in some jurisdictions immediately after the enactment of no-fault statutes, no long-term effect has been demonstrated. *See, e.g.,* Justin Wolfers, *Did Unilateral Divorce Laws Raise Divorce Rates? A Reconciliation and New Results* (2003) (available at: papers.ssrn.com/paper.taf?abstract_id=444620).

For articles concluding that no-fault statutes played a causative role in the rise in divorce rates, *see, e.g.,* Margaret F. Brinig & F.H. Buckley, *No-Fault Laws and At-Fault People*, 18 INT'L J. L. POL'Y & FAM. 225 (1997); Leora

Friedberg, *Did Unilateral Divorce Raise Divorce Rates?*, 88 AM. ECON. REV. 608 (1998). For analyses disputing a causal role of no-fault reforms in stimulating a long-term rise in divorce rates, see Cherlin, *supra* at 48; Ira Mark Ellman, *The Misguided Movement to Revive Fault Divorce*, 11 INT'L J. L. POL'Y & FAM. 216 (1997); Ellman, *Divorce Rates, supra* at n.7; Ellman & Lohr, *Dissolving the Relationship, supra*; Norval D. Glenn, *A Reconsideration of the Effect of No-Fault Divorce on Divorce Rates,* 59 J. MARR. & FAM. 1023 (1997); Norval D. Glenn, *Further Discussion of the Effects of No-Fault Divorce on Divorce Rates,* 361 J. MARR. & FAM. 800 (1999); Wolfers, *supra. See also* Ian Smith, *European Divorce Laws, Divorce Rates, and their Consequences,* In THE LAW AND ECONOMICS OF MARRIAGE 212, 226-27 (A.W. Dnes & R. Rowthorn, eds. 2002) (concluding that the move to no-fault divorce laws in European nations was not responsible for the rise in divorce rates, and that both trends were likely "jointly determined" by social, cultural, and economic forces). It is noteworthy, however, that even those authors who attribute some of the rise in divorce rates to the passage of no-fault statutes assert only a relatively small causative effect to these legal reforms. For summaries and critiques of the various studies, and in-depth discussion of their methodologies, see Wolfers, *supra*; Ellman, *Divorce Rates, supra* at n.7; Ellman & Lohr, *Dissolving the Relationship, supra.*

Given that the enactment of no-fault statutes does not explain the long-term rise in divorce rates, it is unlikely that a repeal of no-fault statutes would lead to substantial reductions in the divorce rate. As before the transition to no-fault, parties seeking divorces would likely resort to whatever path to divorce provides the least resistance, whether it be proceeding on fault grounds or obtaining a marital dissolution in a more divorce-friendly jurisdiction. In conclusion, it is worthwhile to recall that divorce rates have declined steadily since they peaked in 1979 and 1981, and are now lower than at the point when no-fault reforms were enacted in most states. Thus, with no-fault statutes in force in every state, the United States has experienced the only period in its history during which divorce rates have declined consistently for a quarter century.

[2] THEMES IN THE REVIVED POLICY DEBATES ON NO-FAULT

[a] Legal Strategies, New and Old: Commitment and Delay

ELIZABETH SCOTT, MARRIAGE AS PRECOMMITMENT, IN MARRIAGE IN AMERICA: A COMMUNITARIAN PERSPECTIVE 161-171 (M.K. WHYTE, ED. 2000)

A different approach to promoting marital stability is one in which the law's role is to assist couples to achieve their goal of lasting marriage. Most people enter marriage aspiring to a lifelong relationship, and view the success of their marriage as important to a good life. . . . [¶] As divorce statistics reveal, for many people the commitment and optimism with which they enter marriage does not last. Life presents stresses and temptations, and decisions are made that weaken or destroy the bond between spouses. Gradually (or suddenly), the marriage succumbs. The original commitment is "nonbinding" under the current no-fault divorce regime and can be readily set aside. Not only are there few legal restraints to provide disincentive to divorce, but under current law, the couple may not be permitted to voluntarily undertake a more binding commitment through restrictions on divorce.

I . . . argue . . . that divorce law should build on the aspirations with which many people enter marriage, by providing couples with the means to reinforce their commitment to the marital and family relationships that they are undertaking. From an ex ante perspective, the voluntary reinforcement of the marital commitment through restriction on divorce serves two important functions. First, the restrictions can serve as precommitment mechanisms, which discourage each spouse from pursuing transitory preferences that are inconsistent with the couple's self-defined long term interest in lasting marriage. Second, each spouse, knowing that the other's commitment is enforceable, receives assurance that his or her investment in the relationship will be protected. If marriage is a relationship that can be easily terminated at any time by either party, trust will be impaired and investment will be tentative. Allowing couples entering marriage to undertake a greater commitment to the relationship than the law currently encourages or allows would have a direct effect on the decision to divorce and indirect effects on attitude toward and behavior in marriage. [¶] . . . . [C]urrent divorce law undermines commitment, by assuming that commitment is antithetical to personal freedom. To the contrary, basic contract principles demonstrate that freedom to commit extends our ability to fulfill our ends. . . .

        . . . .

[Sometimes marriages fail because t]he long-term rewards of the relationship . . . seem remote and incompatible with immediate desires and preferences. In most marriages, even successful ones, both spouses will be tempted to engage in selfish or uncooperative behavior, which reflects current preferences that may be transitory but which undermine the stability of the relationship. There are obvious examples: immersion in career at the expense of family, pursuit of other relationships, disputes over family finances and children, withdrawal, boredom; etc. A pattern of uncooperative behavior can cause retaliation, estrangement, erosion of the marital commitment and ultimately can lead to the breakdown of the relationship.

        . . . . Described in this way, the failure of marriage is analogous to other situations in life in which individuals make choices based on transitory preferences that temporarily dominate and undermine the fulfillment of their long term goals. A commitment to a healthy diet to lose weight, moderate use of alcohol, completion of a project, or saving money for a new home can involve sacrificing pleasures that, at a particular moment may represent the more compelling choice than adherence to the long term goal. . . . A familiar corrective . . . involves the use of precommitment mechanisms. Precommitments are self-management strategies designed to penalize the short term choice that the decisionmaker wants to avoid (eating the cake) or to reward adherence to her long term goal (losing 10 pounds). Through the use of enforceable penalties or rewards, she reinforces her initial commitment to her goal and reduces the likelihood that she will be diverted by temporarily attractive temptations. . . .

. . . Suppose, for example, that the couple agrees before marriage to a three year mandatory waiting period before divorce. This barrier imposes a substantial cost on the decision to exit the marriage, and thus reduces the likelihood that divorce will take place unless the costs of remaining in the marriage are substantial (or the benefits minimal). In other words, as the unhappy spouse makes a choice between continued marriage and divorce, the precommitment shifts the calculus in favor of remaining in the marriage. Predictably, decisions to divorce will be less common and more carefully made.

More subtly but perhaps more importantly, precommitments that impose restrictions on divorce can promote stability in marriage by influencing the couple's attitude about the kind of relationship that they have undertaken, which in turn may affect their behavior in marriage. The decision by the couple to undertake a binding commitment signals the seriousness with which each enters the marriage. Moreover, at least indirectly, knowledge that exit will not be easy can encourage cooperation and assist each spouse to resist the temptation to pursue her short term self interest. In a marriage bounded by precommitment, the original cooperative intentions may be less likely to be forgotten because the relationship cannot be readily abandoned if it becomes unsatisfactory. This may influence the parties to protect the marriage by avoiding behavior that could lead them to confront the costly decision to divorce. Such a conception of marriage might be expressed as follows: "We have made a commitment to this marriage and we're not getting out of it easily. Since we're in for the duration, we might as well make the best of it."

. . . .

. . . . By restricting her or his own freedom, each spouse gains greater assurance of the commitment of the other, and confidence that the relationship will endure through good and bad times. This sense of security promotes a level of trust in the partner that fosters substantial investment in the marriage, in terms of time, energy, emotions and resources. Indeed the kind of interdependence that is often associated with a successful marriage may only be possible with the level of trust that is conditioned on a binding commitment. . . .

. . . .

Courts have been lukewarm toward premarital contracts in which the couple seeks to reinforce their commitment to one another by restricting divorce, a response that is curiously inconsistent with the liberal premises of modern regulation of marriage. . . .[¶] Individuals who are about to marry may tend to be influenced by emotional and cognitive biases that could distort decision-making. . . . [¶] The effect of these cognitive biases on decision-making about marital precommitment is not easy to predict. Optimism could lead some couples to see no need for precommitment [i.e., "undercommitment"]. Other couples may . . . reject the possibility that their own marriage will fail. [¶] The upshot of this latter response may be "overcommitment," a more onerous restriction on divorce than most observers would conclude was rational under the circumstances. Thus, the couple might agree never to divorce or create a prohibitive fine to be imposed on the spouse who ends the marriage. . . . Thus, legal regulation is necessary to ensure that precommitments impose only moderate obstacles to divorce.

Sometimes, precommitments that are moderate in most cases may be unacceptable because of the conduct of one spouse and the resulting vulnerability of the other. In cases of spousal abuse, for example, obstacles to divorce may increase the harm to the victims, and exemption should be readily available. In general, any precommitment that insists on continued cohabitation or even direct association is risky and should be unenforceable. Procedures should be readily available to expedite spousal and child support upon separation in cases involving dependent spouses and minor children. That is not to say that mandatory delay before final divorce or remarriage cannot be prescribed, under conditions in which financial support for a dependent is provided.

Caution is required on other grounds as well. A precommitment that is likely to have a differential impact on the spouses because of different marital roles is undesirable. Thus, monetary penalties — includ[ing] those affecting spousal support — are problematic unless the spouses have equal assets and earning capacity, which in most marriages will not be the case. The homemaker spouse, for example, would be systematically disadvantaged by this type of precommitment, because it presents her with a greater barrier than it poses for her husband. Furthermore, since the ultimate policy goal of promoting marital stability is to enhance the welfare of children, only precommitments that serve that objective are acceptable. Thus, precommitments withholding access to visitation or child support, or otherwise undermining children's security, should not be enforced.

. . . .

A mandatory waiting period of some substantial duration before divorce (perhaps two or three years) is the optimal precommitment . . . because it serves several functions. First, a mandatory period of delay serves well the standard precommitment purposes. It creates a barrier to divorce that makes leaving the marriage more costly, and at the same time it defines the relationship as one that is not easily set aside, subtly influencing the spouses' attitudes and behavior. Beyond this, an extended waiting period promotes better decisionmaking. The spouse who is unhappy in the marriage can more accurately assess whether her decision reflects her long term interest or transitory intense preferences. In general, time is a good tool for making better decisions and avoiding cognitive errors. Finally, a waiting period undermines the ability of a spouse quickly to establish a new family, a step that dilutes interest in children of an earlier marriage.

Fault-based divorce laws served a little noticed precommitment function that was sacrificed in the movement toward no-fault divorce. . . . Should fault be reintroduced as a precommitment? [¶] In some regards, fault would seem to serve quite well as a precommitment. . . . It may . . . influence marital behavior in a direction that stabilizes the relationship. Fault grounds certainly create barriers and restrict divorce. [¶] In many regards, however, fault grounds do not function well as precommitments. . . . The proving of fault [before no-fault reforms] undermined the integrity of the judicial process and surely undermined the parties' future relationship, an important concern if the objective is to promote the welfare of the children whose lives currently are disrupted by instability. In general, I would hesitate to reintroduce fault as a precommitment.

IRA MARK ELLMAN, THE MISGUIDED MOVEMENT TO REVIVE FAULT DIVORCE, 11 Int'l J. of Law, Policy, and the Family 216, 221-37 (1997)

. . . [Consider the imposition of waiting periods on mutual consent divorces.] Proponents . . . apparently believe that couples made to wait might change their minds and reunite, and live happily — or at least functionally — ever after. They apparently think that many couples with children divorce casually, without thinking much about what they are doing, and that they therefore will stay together if we just make them think about it some more. [This seems unlikely. Consider too that] a waiting period for divorce is really a waiting period for remarriage, for remarriage is the only thing that is truly delayed [since the parties will still separate physically, and a court may still grant a legal separation with custody and support provisions]. Do we want [to delay remarriage]? For what purpose? Do waiting period proponents want the [divorced] to avoid establishing new relationships, or to cohabit without marrying?

. . .

. . .[J]urisdictions with lengthy waiting periods typically apply them only to no-fault divorces. . . . The result, of course, is that couples who agree on divorce also quickly agree on some fault ground that they can present to the court so as to avoid the waiting period. [¶]Consider, for example, some recent data from England, which requires two years' separation before a mutual consent no-fault divorce can be granted (and five years' separation before a unilateral no-fault divorce is ordered). The result: there are very few no-fault mutual consent divorces. Where wives are the petitioner, 76% of divorces were granted on grounds of adultery or "unreasonable behavior"; only 19% on two years' mutual separation and 5 percent on five years' unilateral separation. Among the 30 percent of divorces in which the husband was the petitioner, fault grounds were less dominant, but still accounted for a clear majority of all decrees. Similar patterns are found in the American statistics as well as in other British data. . . . What this means is that the primary consequence of imposing waiting periods for no-fault divorces is the revival of the sham "fault" proceedings that were common under the old fault regimes, in which the spouses collude in presenting the fault grounds necessary to obtain the quicker decree.

There is a further detail in this recent British data that is even more interesting: both husbands and wives were even less likely to wait the two (or five) year period if they had children under 16: the percentage who instead relied upon fault grounds increased 6% among petitioning wives, and 11% among petitioning husbands (46% of whom charged their wives with adultery). Indeed, the younger that the youngest child was, at the time of divorce, the more likely were the parents to avoid the waiting periods and petition instead on fault grounds. The parents apparently knew something that the law's draftsmen did not: that once a marriage fails, prolonging the divorce process is unlikely to be good for the children, particularly if the divorce is likely to exacerbate parental conflict.

. . .

. . . [W]hat then of a common companion proposal, an even longer waiting period — five years has been suggested — before a unilateral no-fault divorce is allowed. . . . [¶] Imagine [*Marriage of Mitchell*, page 224, *supra*] decided under [that] regime. . . . Mr. Mitchell, after moving out for the last time, must wait five more years for divorce — while Mrs. Mitchell presumably waits for him to return. Will denying Mr. Mitchell the right to remarry during this time drive him back to Mrs. Mitchell? No one reading the court's opinion could think that likely, nor would they believe it necessarily the best result for Mrs. Mitchell or her children. And surely a five year wait followed by divorce would not help them. Mrs. Mitchell needs to rebuild her life, and sooner is better than later, especially for her children.

. . .[And] while the law can keep Mr. Mitchell from remarrying, it is unlikely to keep him celibate. What then happens when he develops a close relationship with Mrs. Smith? The enforced wait means he cannot legally commit himself to her and her child. Perhaps they will cohabit in any event — and perhaps produce a nonmarital child during that time. While that is surely not the result that waiting period proponents intend, it may be the result they achieve. Their effort to protect Mrs. Mitchell will thus burden Mrs. Smith.

And [c]onsider Mrs. Mitchell's sister, Mrs. Jones. She is unhappy in her marriage because Mr. Jones is an insensitive, domineering bully who psychologically mistreats both her and their child. Mr. Smith would be a far better husband for her and they would like to marry. But Mr. Jones, who has no immediate interest in remarrying, gets in his last licks at Mrs. Jones by refusing to cooperate with her in obtaining a consensual divorce. So now the only way Mrs. Jones can avoid waiting five years before marrying Mr. Smith is to assume the burden of proving Mr. Jones' fault. But his nasty, demeaning conduct, though real enough, is not so simple to prove in a contested proceeding — and perhaps Mrs. Jones also worries that he might defend with proof of an adulterous act between her and Mr. Smith. Surely adultery is also misconduct under the fault law, and would be an effective defense under classic fault regimes.

So Mrs. Jones has a dilemma. Should she incur the cost of a contest over his fault, in the hope she can prevail — and prevail soon enough to make the effort worthwhile? Or should she perhaps try to induce Mr. Jones' agreement to a quicker consensual no-fault divorce, by offering to accept a reduced share of their marital property? This is probably not the scenario that waiting period proponents have in mind, but it is surely one that their proposals are likely to produce. Fans of fault often make the mistake of thinking that fault laws protect the innocent. They do not. They protect the person who does not care about delaying the divorce, at the expense of the person who does — and who may have very good reasons for wanting out. That is why the "bargaining chip" rationale for these rules doesn't work: no matter how we design them, it is inevitable that in many cases they will give bargaining leverage to the wrong spouse. We can achieve the goal of protecting the financially vulnerable spouse far more effectively by the direct strategy of reforming the law of alimony than by the indirect one of hoping that the imposition of a waiting period will allow the financially vulnerable spouse to negotiate a better deal.

NOTES

1. *Existing Laws on Mandatory Waiting Periods.* As *Mitchell* illustrates, some states never permitted unilateral no-fault divorce without long waiting periods. *Mitchell* required 2 years. The original MMDA "compromise" draft required that "marital breakdown" be "shown" by evidence of 180 days' separation. Missouri effectively imposes delay on unilateral divorces only, since parties who agree may present the court with fault grounds that require no wait. That is in fact what many do, as the English data cited by Ellman on page 246 illustrate. One can instead impose delay on all divorces, in one of two ways: by requiring that the initial divorce decree be interlocutory, with a "final" divorce decree issued only after an additional delay, or by imposing a statutory delay following service of process in a divorce suit. Prior to 1989, Nebraska employed both techniques, requiring a sixty-day wait following service of process, and another six months once the judge enters the decree of divorce. A 1978 study found that about 25% of Nebraska divorce actions are in fact dropped during these waiting periods. Frank, Berman & Mazur-Hart, *No Fault Divorce and the Divorce Rate: The Nebraska Experience — An Interrupted Time Series Analysis and Commentary,* 58 Neb. L. Rev. 1, 78, 80 n.329. But, whether any lasting reconciliation has occurred in these cases is not known, and if so, whether these reconciliations were the result of delay imposed by the process, or would have occurred without it. For example, about 10% of currently-married American couples have experienced a separation and reconciliation in their marriage, and about one-third of women who attempted a reconciliation were still married to their husband more than one year afterward. See the sources cited in Wineberg, *The Resolutions of Separation: Are Marital Reconciliations Attempted?,* 15 Population Res. & Pol'y Rev. 297 (1996).

2. *Premarital and Separation Agreements Limiting or Expanding Available Grounds for Termination Beyond Those Set Forth by Statute.* Professor Scott observes that the courts have been "lukewarm" toward premarital agreements restricting divorce. There are not many cases on point. In *Penhallow v. Penhallow,* 649 A.2d 1016 (R.I. 1994), a court enforced a premarital agreement that penalized the spouse who initiated a divorce action in the allocation of marital property. In *Massar v. Massar,* 652 A.2d 219 (N.J. App. Div. 1995), a court enforced a separation agreement in which the husband promised to vacate the marital home in exchange for the wife's agreement not to petition for divorce on a fault-based ground. Given that New Jersey's statutes authorized unilateral no-fault divorce only on the basis of "living separate and apart for a period of 18 months or more," the agreement required the wife to incur this waiting period rather than seek a quicker divorce with a petition alleging fault grounds. When the wife petitioned six months later on grounds of extreme cruelty, the court enforced the agreement,

rejecting the wife's claim that the agreement was unenforceable as violating public policy. Yet, the court's language suggested that it might not be willing to enforce a premarital agreement limiting a parties' access to a fault-based divorce. It noted that in the instant case, the parties contracted "with full knowledge of the conduct of each during the marriage which could form the basis for a cause of action for divorce. We do not suggest that the parties could enter an agreement which would preclude seeking a judgment of divorce on [fault grounds arising from] conduct which occurred after the execution of the agreement." *Id.* at 223.

A court's willingness to enforce a premarital agreement stipulating the grounds on which a divorce can proceed, or how evidence of "fault" will affect property distribution and support, may depend, in part, on whether the substantive provisions in the agreement conflict with the state's public policy. California, for example, has thoroughly rejected fault-based divorce and its vestiges, in both the enumeration of grounds for divorce and the principles set forth for property division and support orders. Thus, it is not surprising that in 2002, an appellate court refused to enforce a provision in a premarital contract that required one spouse to pay "liquidated damages" as part of a divorce action if that spouse had committed adultery, asserting that it was contrary to the public policy of California, adopted with the no-fault divorce laws in 1969, to "look to fault in dissolving the marriage, dividing property, or ordering support." *Diosdado v. Diosdado*, 97 Cal. App. 4th 470, 473, 118 Cal. Rptr. 2d 494, 496 (2002).

See Section D for a discussion of "covenant marriage," which allows marital partners to choose a fault-based divorce regime at the time of entry into marriage. For discussion of the enforcement of obligations set forth in contracts entered into as part of religious traditions, see *Avitzur v. Avitzur,* 58 N.Y.2d 572, 459 N.Y.S.2d 572 (App. Div. 1983) (enforcing a provision in a Jewish marriage contract, *i.e.*, a "Ketubah," permitting a religious court to summon the parties for marital counseling). *See also Akileh v. Elchahal*, 666 So. 2d 246 (Fla. App. 1996), described below in Chapter 8, page 781 (addressing an Islamic marriage contract).

[b] Working Justice Between Divorcing Spouses

Have no-fault divorce laws transformed marriage into a contract with no remedy for breach by one party? Whereas Professor Scott relies on a contract analogy to argue for a precommitment strategy for strengthening marital bonds, thus focusing on the notion of parties' agreeing in advance to the terms governing *termination* of their marriage, a different version of the contract argument focuses on the parties' terms for *conducting* the marriage. Professors Brinig and Crafton and Professor Ellman have debated the applicability of the contract analogy in this context.

> While marriage has many of the characteristics of relational con-
> tracting, it has become in many places a kind of unenforceable, illusory
> contract; it is splendid as long as both spouses are committed to the
> relationship but ethereal once one spouse decides to take advantage
> of the other. [T]he terms of the marriage contract are, to a great extent,
> the expectations of the parties as to the allowable parameters of

marital behavior. . . . [Legal] changes . . . that make marital promises unenforceable . . . allow opportunistic behavior [and that is what
is done by] the enactment in many states of no-fault divorce with the
simultaneous removal of fault (breach) as a consideration in grants
of spousal support and property division. A marriage is, as are many
business relationships, now terminable at will, *but* without penalties
for breach of other conditions.

Margaret F. Brinig & Steven M. Crafton, *Marriage and Opportunism*, 23 J.
LEGAL STUDIES 869, 871-72 (1994). Professor Ellman rejects this model,
arguing that unlike commercial contracts, the ordinary marital "contract" is
insufficiently specific enough to allow a court to determine when there has
been a breach.

The most fundamental requirement of contract is the ability to
identify when there is a breach: a contract's terms must be sufficiently
clear to permit this. What are the terms of the marriage contract . . .?
[Brinig and Crafton suggest that] the words of the typical wedding
ceremony — that the parties take each other "for richer or poorer, in
sickness and in health . . . as long as life shall last" and will "love
and cherish" one another — are intended to create contractual obligations, rather than to express by well-known ritual the parties' feelings
of mutual love and commitment. . . . But neither contract theory nor
existing law would treat such statements of intent as unconditional
commitments to "care for," "live with," or "cherish" the other spouse,
no matter what. Everyone understands that this is not what the
parties really mean. [T]he wife who later ceases to love or cherish her
husband is [not] always in breach. Even the most fault-regarding of
divorce regimes would want to know the reason for her change of
heart. Did she cease to love him because he turned out to be a poor
provider or a bad father, or because she later decided she did not want
to be the housewife that both of them initially expected her to be, or
because she found she felt more passion for the neighbor across the
street, or because as she matured and changed she concluded he was
not worth her affection?

The "contract" terms derivable from the wedding ceremony itself are
. . .inadequate to tell us whether the answers to such questions
matter. [Brinig and Crafton] suggest . . . that . . . the "terms of the
marriage contract are the expectations of the parties as to the allowable parameters of marital behavior." But [they themselves] concede
. . . that "the parties [are] incapable of reducing important terms of
the arrangement to well-defined obligations." How then can this be
contract?. . . [Because of the absence of such terms] judgments
purportedly based on the parties' . . . values will in reality be based
on the judge's, which means that thinking of such an alimony remedy
in contract terms obscures rather than reveals what is actually
happening.

Ira Mark Ellman & Sharon Lohr, *Marriage as Contract, Opportunistic
Violence, and Other Bad Arguments for Fault Divorce*, 1997 ILL. L. REV. 719,
746. Some critics of no-fault reform express concern that fault-based divorce

policies are needed to protect an innocent spouse. Such protection could take any of several forms. If the "guilty" spouse cannot easily obtain a divorce over the objections of the "innocent" spouse, the "innocent" spouse has a bargaining chip in the negotiations regarding the financial aspects of the dissolution not available under no-fault. Furthermore, about half of the states still permit the consideration of marital misconduct in alimony awards, and a smaller group in the allocation of property. Professor Ellman argues that a rule awarding money at divorce on the premise that one spouse has caused the other harm has more in common with tort than with contract. Ira Mark Ellman, *The Place of Fault in a Modern Divorce Law*, 28 ARIZ. ST. L.J. 773 (1996). He states that such a rule is based on the defendant's violation of a duty to the person harmed, rather than on breach of promise. For a discussion of the special difficulties involved in using tort ideas to compensate individuals for marital misconduct, see Ira Mark Ellman & Stephen Sugarman, *Spousal Emotional Abuse As a Tort?*, 55 MD. L. REV. 1268 (1996). For a discussion on the idea of using fault rules to protect the innocent spouse from a feminist perspective, see Barbara Bennett Woodhouse & Katherine Bartlett, *Sex, Lies, and Dissipation: The Discourse of Fault in a No-Fault Era*, 82 GEORGETOWN L.J. 2525 (1994). The question of tort claims between divorcing spouses is treated more fully in Chapter 4.

What if the dissolution will cause one spouse far more harm than the other, in ways that cannot be remedied by the divorce court? The British no-fault reforms gave judges discretion to deny a divorce, regardless of whether adequate grounds exist, where one of the parties has shown that dissolution "will result in grave financial or other hardship to him and that it would in all circumstances be wrong to dissolve the marriage." Divorce Reform Act, 1969, C. 55, § 4(2)(6). An Indiana case, *Abney v. Abney*, 374 N.E.2d 264 (Ind. App. 1978), *cert. denied*, 439 U.S. 1069 (1979), provides an example of what the English drafters may have had in mind. James Abney had been denied a divorce in Tennessee, where Dorothy Abney lived after their separation. He was paying support to her under a Tennessee separation decree, and the Tennessee courts had ordered Abney not to seek dissolution in Indiana. Indiana declined to honor this Tennessee order.

> Dorothy Abney argues that the trial court should have exercised equitable discretion to deny the dissolution, notwithstanding its finding that the marriage was irretrievably broken. . . . [¶] . . . When . . . the marriage is . . . irretrievably broken . . . the Act directs the trial court to grant dissolution. . . . [¶] The . . . trial court [has] no alternative.

> We are not insensitive to Dorothy Abney's ultimate concern. . . . She suffers from severe rheumatoid arthritis which requires costly medical treatment. [T]he assistance she has been receiving through James Abney's military benefits terminates upon dissolution. . . . Dorothy Abney claims these benefits are her "life blood" and respectfully asserts that the equities compel us to reverse the dissolution decree.

> . . . Admittedly, the trial court found that James Abney . . . is economically unable to. . . offset the loss of the medical benefits. Yet

we are without authority to reverse a dissolution decree . . . solely because the . . . dissolution will . . .terminate benefits . . . advantageous to one of the parties.

Abney, 374 N.E. 2d at 269-70. For other installments of the *Abney* saga, see *Abney v. Abney,* 360 N.E.2d 1044 (Ind. App. 1977); 456 S.W.2d 364 (Tenn. App. 1970), and 433 S.W.2d 847 (Tenn. 1968). *See also Bartz v. Bartz,* 452 N.W.2d 160 (Wis. App. 1989) (trial court may not refuse divorce even though loss of husband's health insurance would impose financial hardship for wife).

The British considered repeal of their "hardship" provision, *Facing the Future: A Discussion Paper on the Ground for Divorce, (supra),* but decided against it, British Law Comm., *The Ground for Divorce* (Law Com. No. 192, 1990). It only applies to divorces sought on the basis of five years' separation, less than 6 % of all British divorces, and has been successfully invoked in only two reported cases, both involving lost pensions. Ingman, *Reform of the Ground for Divorce,* FAMILY LAW 94 (1989). French law has a similar provision, allowing a judge to dismiss a petition for a no-fault divorce (available only after six years' separation) if the divorce would entail "material or moral consequences of exceptional hardship" for the unwilling spouse or their children. French courts have applied this provision in cases to deny divorce where the court concludes that the nonconsenting spouse's physical or mental health would be deleteriously affected, as where the wife "who suffers already from having been abandoned by her husband, would be subject to reproach" in her Catholic community. MARY ANN GLENDON, ABORTION AND DIVORCE IN WESTERN LAW 72-74 (1987).

[c] The Effects of Divorce on Children

Few subjects relating either to family law or to the psychological well-being of children have garnered as much attention from the media and the general public as has the topic of the effects of divorce on children. It is therefore not surprising that discourse about these effects would be dominated by overly-simplified "soundbites" highlighted by exaggerated claims. These soundbites mask the complexities in the data and obscure the important messages that the data could transmit to policymakers, lawyers, mental health professionals, and parents.

The release of Judith Wallerstein and Joan Kelly's 1980 book, SURVIVING THE BREAKUP: HOW CHILDREN ACTUALLY COPE WITH DIVORCE, stimulated concerns about the psychological consequences of divorce for children. Painting a bleak picture, and widely quoted in the popular press, Wallerstein and Kelly's report garnered the attention of policymakers and others, and etched into the American consciousness the notion that parental divorce is uniformly and irreversibly damaging to children. *See also* the 2000 sequel, Judith S. Wallerstein, Julia M. Lewis, & Sandra Blakeslee, THE UNEXPECTED LEGACY OF DIVORCE. Social scientists from a range of disciplines, however, severely criticized Wallerstein's work because of methodological shortcomings, such as the absence of control groups, and the use of a sample drawn from families seeking psychological services (*i.e.,* families that were already encountering emotional difficulties). Wallerstein's work has been so discredited by researchers and scholars that it does not even appear in the reference list of the important summaries and analyses of empirical studies (unless the author's purpose is to criticize the study). *See, e.g.,* Paul R. Amato & Bruce Keith, *Parental Divorce and the Well-Being of Children: A Meta-Analysis,* 110 PSYCHOL. BULL. 26 (1991); ROBERT E. EMERY, MARRIAGE, DIVORCE, AND CHILDREN'S ADJUSTMENT (2d ed. 1999) (hereinafter "EMERY, MARRIAGE, DIVORCE & CHILDREN'S ADJUSTMENT"); E. Mavis Hetherington, Margaret Bridges, & Glendessa M. Insabella, *What Matters? What Does Not? Five Perspectives on the Association Between Marital Transitions and Children's Adjustment,* 53 AM. PSYCHOLOGIST 167 (1998).

Contrary to various assertions, parental divorce is neither a destructive force that renders most children who encounter it maladjusted, nor is it a life event that is irrelevant to children's well-being. Parental divorce is an experience that might best be thought of as introducing certain stressors into a child's life. Robert E. Emery, *Postdivorce Family Life for Children: An Overview of Research and Some Implications for Policy,* in THE POSTDIVORCE FAMILY: CHILDREN, PARENTING, AND SOCIETY 3 (R.A. Thompson & P.R. Amato eds. 1999) (hereinafter "Emery, *Postdivorce Family Life*"). For example, divorce changes living arrangements, leads to periods of separation from one or both parents, and brings economic hardships to many families. These factors and others accompanying divorces place psychological challenges in the path of children. Yet, researchers repeatedly emphasize that "despite the increase in risk, *resilience* is the normative outcome of divorce for children, that is, most children from divorced families function as well as children from married families on various commonly used indices of their adjustment." *Id.* at 4. In other words, most children who experience their parents' divorce will negotiate those stressors quite well, and emerge from parental divorce without notable long-term difficulties. *Id.* Many exhibit short-term adjustment difficulties, and most report experiencing sadness, anxiety, or other unpleasant emotions during the transitions associated with marital dissolution. Yet most children cope with the challenges successfully, and end up as relatively well-adjusted adults, enjoying "satisfying social and intimate relationships." *See, e.g.,* E. MAVIS HETHERINGTON & JOHN KELLY, FOR BETTER OR FOR WORSE: DIVORCE RECONSIDERED 252 (2002).

Despite these general findings, however, some children who experience parental divorce encounter greater difficulties coping and reveal longer-term adjustment difficulties. One recent meta-analysis revealed "that children of divorced parents, as a group, continue to fare more poorly than children with continuously married parents," demonstrating less adaptive academic, behavioral, emotional, and interpersonal functioning. Paul R. Amato, *Children and Divorce in the 1990s: An Update of the Amato and Keith (1991) Meta-Analysis,* 15 J. FAM. PSYCHOL. 355, 366 (2001). *See also* Hetherington, Bridges & Insabella, *supra* at 169-70. These differences remain, even into early adulthood. *See, e.g,* Paul R. Amato & Bruce Keith, *Parental Divorce and Adult Well-Being: A Meta-Analysis,* 53 J. MARR. & FAM. 43 (1991); Hetherington, Bridges & Insabella, *supra* at 169-70. And, although the *magnitude* of the differences between the divorced-parent and married-parent groups is generally reported to be small, *see, e.g.,* Emery, *Postdivorce Family Life, supra* at 13, researchers sensibly are turning their attention to identifying which variables predict adaptive versus maladaptive postdivorce outcomes for children. The findings that emerge from this latter endeavor offer the promise of promoting development of strategies to minimize the likelihood that children will experience such difficulties.

A handful of research teams have prospectively studied large samples of children and families over several-decade time periods, using sophisticated methodologies and increasingly sensitive analyses of a wide range of variables and their interactions. *See, e.g,* Andrew Cherlin, P. Lindsay Chase-Lansdale & Christine McRae, *Effects of Parental Divorce on Mental Health Throughout the Life Course*, 63 AM. SOCIOL. REV. 239 (1998); Hetherington & Kelly, *supra;* Paul R. Amato & Alan Booth, A GENERATION AT RISK: GROWING UP IN AN ERA OF FAMILY UPHEAVAL (1997). Although there are many questions yet unanswered, several important themes emerge from the current literature. First, we are reminded that caution should govern conclusions about causal connections between two associated variables, such as divorce and children's adjustment. Many writers have incorrectly assumed that a direct causal relationship exists between parental divorce and any problems in children's postdivorce adjustment. Such conclusions are not warranted by the available data. For a discussion of these issues, see Maire Ni Bhrolchain, *"Divorce Effects" and Causality in the Social Sciences,* 17 EUROPEAN SOCIOL. REV. 33, 44-53 (2001); Maire Ni Bhrolchain, Roma Chappell et al., *Parental Divorce and Outcomes for Children: Evidence and Interpretation*, 16 SOCIOL. REV. 67 (2002). To the contrary, recent studies have demonstrated that children whose parents divorce reveal adjustment difficulties in social, emotional, and academic realms *well before* (sometimes as far ahead as five to ten years) a divorce occurs. Andrew J. Cherlin, *Going to Extremes: Family Structure, Children's Well-Being, and Social Science*, 36 DEMOGRAPHY 421 (1999). Given the convergent findings of several studies published in the 1990s, Cherlin concludes that "the evidence that precursors of the difficulties associated with divorce are visible to some extent in children years before the break-up . . . . is now a well-established finding." *Id.* at 435. Thus, it is important to keep in mind that any differences in psychological, social, academic, or occupational functioning observed between individuals who experienced parental divorce as children and those who did not is subject to these interpretive limitations regarding causality.

In addition to these insights about the impact of predivorce factors on children's well-being after divorce, recent scholarship has also addressed the role that postdivorce factors play as well:

> The postdivorce family has its origins before the parents have divorced, even before they have begun to contemplate marital separation. It begins with the quality of marriage that shapes how children experience family life and subsequently cope with divorce. Considerable research shows that postdivorce adjustment is significantly influenced by the conditions of predivorce family life, such as the frequency and intensity of marital conflict . . . and the psychological resources that accompany children through the process of divorce. Many of the problems that children exhibit in the years following marital dissolution may arise, in fact, from family problems preceding divorce — *and these problems often continue after divorce.*

Ross A. Thompson & Paul A. Amato, *The Postdivorce Family: An Introduction to the Issues*, in THE POSTDIVORCE FAMILY: CHILDREN, PARENTING, AND SOCIETY xi, xiv-xv (R.A. Thompson & P.R. Amato, eds. 1999) (emphasis added). The focus on predivorce and postdivorce factors and their impact on children's well-being has led to a reformulation of divorce as an occurrence that is not "a discrete event" marked by the occurrence of the formal legal marital dissolution,

> But . . . part of a series of family transitions and changes in family relationships. The response to any family transition will depend both on what precedes and follows it. The response to divorce and life in a single-parent household will be influenced by individual adjustment and the quality of family relationships before the divorce as well as circumstances surrounding and following the divorce.

E. Mavis Hetherington, Tracey C. Law & Thomas G. O'Connor, *Divorce: Challenges, Changes, and New Chances*, in FAMILY IN TRANSITION 176, 177 (A.S. Skolnick & J.H. Skolnick eds., 9th ed. 1997). "[M]arital disruption [is] a multistage process that may begin long before families dissolve and extend many years after divorce or separation." Yongmin Sun, *Family Environment and Adolescents' Well-Being Before and After Parents' Marital Disruption: A Longitudinal Analysis*, 63 J. MARR. & FAM. 697, 699 (2001).

The understanding of the role of postdivorce factors creates a positive opportunity to interrupt potentially negative effects of divorce on children. In some families, postdivorce family relationships and patterns perpetuate predivorce problems and do not promote children's positive adjustment to the changes brought by the divorce. Yet, in other families, divorce creates the opportunity for positive change in any of several domains. Professor Robert Emery explains:

> Many differences [in the psychological adjustment of children following parental divorce] are attributable to postdivorce family relationships, especially: (a) the quality of the children's relationship with their residential parent, (b) the degree and manner in which conflict is expressed between the parents, (c) the family's economic standing, and (d) the children's contact and relationship with the nonresidential parent.

Emery, *Postdivorce Family Life*, *supra* at 4. Thus, perhaps the most important conclusion that can be drawn from current research is that *the effects of divorce on children are not irrevocably predetermined*. In other words, children's fates are not sealed by virtue of their parents' decisions to dissolve the marriage. Adjustment to life stressors is a dynamic process that does not occur in one moment in time. The growing body of knowledge about children's resilience in response to life stressors informs us that environmental factors, particularly healthy supportive relationships with caring adults, can do much to mitigate the ill effects of challenging life circumstances. Such positive factors can promote healthy adaptation to stressful life events of all types, including parental divorce. *See generally* E. MAVIS HETHERINGTON (ED.), COPING WITH DIVORCE, SINGLE PARENTING, AND REMARRIAGE: A RISK AND RESILIENCY PERSPECTIVE (1999); ROBERT J. HAGGERTY, LONNIE R. SHERROD ET AL.,

STRESS, RISK, AND RESILIENCE IN CHILDREN AND ADOLESCENTS: PROCESSES, MECHANISMS, AND INTERVENTIONS (1996).

How should policymakers respond to these findings? Some have advocated a return to fault grounds, arguing that divorce is deleterious to children's well-being, and that exit from marriage should be limited to those situations in which a spouse has violated one of certain limited statutory grounds. The argument here is that keeping all of the non-qualifying marriages together will be in the best interest of children in those families.

A second set of proposals argue that policymakers should focus on keeping marriages *with minor children* together, and should do so by making marital exit more difficult when marriages involve children. These authors suggest creation of a dual standard of sorts, treating marriages with children differently than other marriages with respect to divorce standards. Thus, for example, some recommend longer waiting periods for divorce by couples with minor children. *See, e.g.,* Waite & Gallagher, *supra* at 195-96 (citing with approval pre-no-fault waiting periods of two to three years in the United States and five-to-seven years in Europe); Elizabeth S. Scott, *Divorce, Children's Welfare, and the Culture Wars,* 9 VA. J. SOC. POL'Y & L. 95, 105 (2001) (suggesting that couples entering marriage, particularly couples with children, be permitted to commit voluntarily to a legally-enforceable period, such as two years, to serve as a waiting period prior to marital termination). The authors assert that such a waiting period would serve as a barrier to divorce, requiring parties to deliberate and reconsider the choice to end their marriage, and perhaps to work harder toward the success of the marriage. Waite & Gallagher, *supra* at 195; *see also* Scott, *supra* at 105-06. Furthermore, these authors suggest that such policies would send the proper messages to the populace about the marriage as a life-long commitment.

There is, of course, another side to the debate about whether making marital exit more difficult will promote children's well-being. Opponents of policies to restrict access to divorce would first reject the premise that making divorce harder to obtain will result in fewer divorces or reductions in the deleterious effects associated with growing up in a family disrupted by divorce. Ellman, *The Misguided Movement to Revive Fault Divorce, supra.* Second, given evidence that much of children's postdivorce adjustment problems can be tied to *predivorce* factors, critics of this set of proposals would assert that restrictive divorce laws merely maintain the *de jure* marital status of dysfunctional families, while forcing them to remain together. Some of the proposals would force them to live separately during a several-year waiting period. Some proposals require a long period of separation before couples access divorce. Yet, long waiting periods risk "freezing" family processes at the height of crisis, placing children in an extended period of "limbo"— living with parental separation and the knowledge of an impending divorce. Particularly problematic for these children is the uncertainty as to whether, when, and how a divorce will change their lives. Living quarters may be temporary, other facets of everyday life make-shift and unsettled, and family relationship issues unresolved. Such circumstances are highly unlikely to promote children's well-being.

Furthermore, as the first half of this chapter emphasizes, couples still find ways to divorce under a fault-based system or a system with long waiting periods. Couples manufacture fault grounds where none exist, avoid long wait-ing periods, seek annulments, or take advantage of friendlier policies in other jurisdictions. Thus, fault-based standards and long waiting periods are unlikely to prevent divorce. And, of even greater concern, the obstacles placed in the paths of unhappy couples may be more likely to exacerbate interparen-tal conflict (by requiring an adversarial determination of fault) and to tax the families' financial resources (by requiring hefty outlays of funds for legal fees). As such, proposals imposing substantial barriers to divorce may even *enhance* the likelihood that children will be exposed to risk factors known to have deleterious effects on children such as parental conflict and economic hardship.

In recent years, there has been a new "twist" to the proposals in singling out marriages involving minors children for special treatment. The new approach distinguishes between those couples with minor children appropri-ate for a "fast track" (i.e., easy access to divorce), and those couples with minor children appropriate for a "slow track" (*i.e.*, more difficult access to divorce). The "fast track" would be reserved for those parents whose divorces involving fault on the part of one spouse, mutual consent between spouses, or a high degree of interparental conflict. *See, e.g.,* William A. Galston, *The Law of Marriage and Divorce: Options for Reform*, in MARRIAGE IN AMERICA: A COMMUNITARIAN PERSPECTIVE 179, 185 (M.K. Whyte, ed. 2000). Those couples not triaged into the "fast track" would be required to wait for "years rather than months" to obtain a divorce. Judges would retain discretion to determine which track is most appropriate for any particular couple. The inclusion of high-conflict divorces in the "fast-track" grouping invokes the findings of one study which noted that while divorce seemed to *improve* the prospects for adjustment for children whose parents' marriages were characterized by *high* levels of conflict, divorce seemed to lead to a net "loss" in such prospects for children whose parents' marriages were characterized by *low* levels of conflict. *See* Alan Booth & Paul R. Amato, *Parental Predivorce Relations and Offspring Postdivorce Well-Being*, 63 J. MARR. & FAM. 197 (2001). This finding surprised the researchers, who interpret it as relating, in part, to the following:

> Children in households where parents engage in a long-term process of overt, unresolved conflict are at risk for a variety of developmental and emotional problems. . . . When a divorce occurs, these children are freed from a dysfunctional home environment and may genuinely welcome the shift to a calmer single-parent household. Under these circumstances, children's conflict-related symptoms are likely to improve over time. By contrast, children in households in which par-ents engage in relatively little overt conflict are at low risk for developmental and emotional problems. [These children] are likely to view divorce under these circumstances as an unexpected, unwelcome, and uncontrollable event, an event that sets into motion a series of stressful circumstances (a decline in standard of living, loss of contact with one parent, and moving) with no compensating advantages. Under these circumstances, children may exhibit a variety of stress-related symptoms. . . .

Id. at 199. Further research is needed to replicate and better understand this particular finding. For the moment, however, advocates who wish to make divorce more difficult for parents with minor children now argue that this study supports placement of barriers to marital exit in the paths of those parents whose relationships fall into the "low conflict" group.

The retort to this proposal emphasizes that conditioning access to a "fast track," or quicker, divorce upon these factors may create perverse incentives. Given what we know about the lengths to which unhappy marital partners will go to obtain a divorce, some may be motivated to create a higher level of spousal conflict so that the couple will "qualify" for the fast track. Such policies may therefore promote precisely the types of family interaction patterns we know are most damaging to children's well-being.

While it seems sensible to provide parents whose unhappy marriages are not characterized by the high levels of conflict with various support services, *forcing* such couples to stay together is a very different proposition. Sociologist Paul Amato, the study's author and the chief proponent of providing assistance to parents in "good enough marriages," flatly rejects the notion that legal policies should be crafted to make divorce less accessible for these couples. Paul R. Amato, *Good Enough Marriages: Parental Discord, Divorce, and Children's Long-Term Well-Being*, 9 VA. J. SOC. POL'Y & L. 71, 92-94 (2001). Professor Amato's point echoes assertions made by other scholars as well. They argue that it would make more sense to focus on interventions that could preserve marriages *in fact* as well as *in form*, and might promote healthier relationships within marital families. Professor Andrew Cherlin and colleagues argue that society could better improve the welfare of children by working to prevent the increasingly-predictable downward spiral from family dysfunction to divorce, paying "[a]t least as much attention . . . to the processes that occur in troubled, intact families" as is now paid to children's postdivorce functioning. Cherlin, Furstenberg et al., *supra* at 1388.

If the law of divorce, by itself, cannot reduce the incidence of family breakup, perhaps it can reduce the negative impact of divorce by focusing on the known risk factors summarized above by Emery. The last several decades have seen some attempts along those lines. Most notably, child custody law reforms beginning in California and ultimately adopted in many jurisdictions mandate child custody mediation as an alternative to litigation. Mediation proponents hoped that this type of alternate dispute resolution could circumvent exacerbation of the discord between divorcing parents frequently associated with adversarial child custody litigation. Proponents hypothesized that custody mediation might have salutary benefits for children by reducing their exposure to the conflict surrounding custody disputes.

Evaluation studies reveal that child custody mediation failed to realize the hoped-for benefits for children's well-being. It has, however, increased participant satisfaction with the legal process, reduced relitigation of custody orders, increased compliance with these orders, and has been an economically-efficient alternative to courtroom adjudication. Joan B. Kelly, *Psychological and Legal Interventions for Parents and Children in Custody and Access Disputes: Current Research and Practice*, 10 VA. J. SOC. POL'Y & L. 129, (2002). *See also* Connie J.A. Beck & Bruce D. Sales, *A Critical Reappraisal of Divorce Mediation Research and Policy*, 6 PSYCHOL. PUB. POL'Y & L. 898 (2000). In light of recent findings that predivorce factors play an important role in children's adjustment after divorce, it makes sense that a brief intervention during the family's active involvement with the legal system might be ineffective in altering adjustment patterns. That said, given the benefits identified above, child custody mediation certainly appears to play a useful role in the armamentarium of a legal system in response to child custody disputes.

California also invented legally-sanctioned joint custody in order to promote children's continuing relationships with both parents after divorce. Such policies sought to prevent or reduce the phenomenon referred to as "father drift," that is, the gradual disengagement of noncustodial parents from their relationships with their children. Sadly, research findings revealed that many children in divorced families had little or no contact with their noncustodial fathers as the years passed, and that the loss of this relationship was a risk factor portending poor postdivorce adjustment for many children. *See, e.g.,* Michael E. Lamb, *Noncustodial Fathers and Their Impact on the Children of Divorce*, in THE POSTDIVORCE FAMILY, *supra* at 105.

While mandatory mediation has not had significant impact on children's postdivorce adjustment, joint custody *has* had such an impact. In general, joint custody placements appear to be associated with more positive postdivorce outcomes for children. Robert Bauserman, *Child Adjustment in Joint-Custody Versus Sole-Custody Arrangements: A Meta-Analytic Review*, 16 J. FAM. PSYCH. 91, 97-99 (2002) (concluding that: "children in joint [physical or legal] custody are better adjusted, across multiple types of measures, than children in sole" custody; children in joint custody did not differ in adjustment from children whose parents remained married; causal conclusions about the findings are limited by the reality that "those parents who have better relationships prior to, or during, the divorce process may self-select into joint custody"). Researchers caution, however, that some joint-custody arrangements, such as those that require ongoing parental cooperation and interaction, are typically inappropriate for high-conflict divorces, particularly those in which there is domestic violence. Janet R. Johnston, *High-Conflict Divorce*, 4 THE FUTURE OF CHILDREN: CHILDREN AND DIVORCE 165 (1994).

For a discussion of the history of the California policy reforms geared toward improving the outcomes of children following divorce, see Senate Task Force on Family Equity, California Senate Judiciary Committee, FINAL REPORT (1987); ELEANOR E. MACCOBY & ROBERT H. MNOOKIN, DIVIDING THE CHILD: SOCIAL AND LEGAL DILEMMAS OF CUSTODY 9-10 (1992).

Many jurisdictions have adopted policies or funded pilot projects requiring divorcing parents to attend "divorce education" classes, the main purpose of which is to instruct the parents on how to minimize the negative effects of their divorce on their children. While these studies have not yet reported long-term results in reducing postdivorce difficulties in children, the preliminary indications are that such efforts may have some benefits. *See, e.g.,* Brenda L. Bacon & Brad McKenzie, *Parent Education After Separation/Divorce*, 42 FAM. CT. REV. 85 (2004). *See also* Kelly, *supra* at 133-37 (summarizing types of programs and initial research findings); Sanford L. Braver, Melanie C. Smith & Stephanie R. DeLuse, *Methodological Considerations in Evaluating Family Court Programs*, 35 FAM. & CONCILIATION CTS. REV. 9 (1997) (critiquing the absence of formal evaluations of court-based intervention programs and discussing methodological problems in such evaluations). Furthermore, divorce education programs for *children,* "designed to help children develop a better understanding of their parents' divorces and skills for coping with them" have developed nationwide, and are currently undergoing empirical evaluation. Kelly, *supra* at 136-37.

Given research findings demonstrating that the quality of parent-child relationships is highly predictive of children's postdivorce adjustment, availability of low-cost psychological intervention programs geared toward improving postdivorce parenting and parent-child relationships might be particularly helpful to children's welfare. In light of the role that reduced standards of living and economic opportunities play in hindering children's adaptive postdivorce adjustment, legal policies that promote adequate support for the child and custodial parent are essential. For example, Professor Glendon proposes a "children first" policy in divorce cases. MARY ANN GLENDON, ABORTION AND DIVORCE IN WESTERN LAW 94-99 (1987). In other words, "the judge's main task would be to piece together, from property and income and inkind personal care, the best possible package to meet the needs of the children and their physical custodian"; property distribution and spousal support awards would be governed by this principle, relegating other rationales and formulas for distribution as secondary. Further creative policymaking geared toward improving family and children's adjustment before, during, and after divorce holds the promise of yielding positive benefits to children. It is critical, however, that evaluation components be part of any such initiatives, in order to learn if the hoped-for benefits have been achieved.

[d] Covenant Marriage and Other Proposals for Strengthening Marriage and Reducing the Divorce Rate

In 1997, Louisiana provided for a statutory innovation called "covenant marriage." Leaving intact its "standard" no-fault divorce provisions, which allow divorce after a six-month period of separation, LA. CIV. CODE ART. 102 (2003), the legislature created different rules for exit from covenant marriage. LA. REV. ST. §§ 9:272 to 9:275, 9:307 to 9:309 (2003). Since August 15, 1997, those marrying in Louisiana have had the option of choosing between standard marriage or covenant marriage, and already-married couples have been permitted to "convert" their existing marriages into covenant marriages. Parties entering covenant marriage must recite words expressing the following:

> We do solemnly declare that marriage is a covenant between a man and a woman who agree to live together as husband and wife for so long as they both may live. We have chosen each other carefully and disclosed to one another everything which could adversely affect the decision to enter into this marriage. We have received premarital counseling on the nature, purposes, and responsibilities of marriage. We have read the Covenant Marriage Act, and we understand that a Covenant Marriage is for life. If we experience marital difficulties, we commit ourselves to take all reasonable efforts to preserve our marriage, including marital counseling.

LA. ST. REV. § 9:273 (2003). Prior to the ceremony, the parties must submit evidence that they have received premarital counseling and that they understand the terms and provisions of the covenant marriage statutes. Section 9:307 governs dissolutions of covenant marriages, and lists several fault grounds (*i.e.,* proof of adultery, sentence of death or imprisonment at hard labor for conviction of a felony, abandonment of the marital domicile for at least one year and refusing to return, physical or sexual abuse of the petitioner or a child of one of them), and also permits divorce upon a period of two years living separate and apart without reconciliation. The statute also provides for dissolution if there are no minor children of the marriage and the parties have lived separate and apart for one year without reconciliation after a judgment of separation was obtained. By contrast, if the parties have a minor child or children, they must live separate and apart for 18 months after a judgment of separation. The 18-month period is reduced to one year in cases where domestic violence or child abuse has occurred. LA. ST. REV. § 9:307A(6)(a)&(b) (2003). Judgments of separation are available on the same grounds as dissolution, including one additional ground of "habitual intemperance of the other spouse, or . . . cruel treatment or outrages of the other spouse . . . that render their living together insupportable." LA. ST. REV. § 307B(6) (2003).

The provisions governing dissolution of covenant marriage in Louisiana are not, in substance, highly unusual. After all, several states require a period of separation of two years or more before granting divorce (*e.g.*, Maryland, New Hampshire, Pennsylvania, Rhode Island), and in these states, the no-fault separation period exists as an alternative to traditional fault grounds. Thus, what makes Louisiana's adoption of covenant marriage unique is that Louisiana is the first state to adopt a statute that makes divorce *harder* to obtain since no-fault swept the country between 1970 and 1985. It is noteworthy that covenant marriage appeared after several years of completely unsuccessful attempts by no-fault opponents in a handful of states to repeal no-fault reforms. *See, e.g.,* Laura Bradford, Note, *The Counterrevolution: A Critique of Recent Proposals to Reform No-Fault Divorce Laws*, 49 STAN. L. REV. 607, 617-620 (1996). No-fault opponents were forced to reconcile themselves to the reality that state legislatures were simply unwilling to roll back no-fault reforms. Covenant marriage was, to some extent, an alternative method by which no-fault opponents could reintroduce fault, while leaving existing no-fault statutes intact. Its advocates argue that it is a form of private ordering, allowing couples to choose the marital regime that is most congruent with their values and goals. From this vantage point, one can analogize covenant marriage to a premarital contract with predetermined nonwaivable terms. Unlike premarital contracts, which can be modified by mutual agreement of the parties at any time, covenant marriage statutes make no provision for mutually-consensual modification. Along similar lines, the statutes do not permit conversion *from* covenant marriage to standard marriage, even when both parties agree.

Professor Elizabeth Scott characterizes covenant marriage as introducing a type of precommitment mechanism. *Marriage as Precommitment, supra* at 172. Although she views the fault-based provisions of covenant marriage regimes as detracting from their virtues, she believes such statutes are a "first step toward an approach to reform of no-fault divorce law that [treats] restriction on divorce as precommitment undertaken by the couple entering marriage, to assist them to achieve their goals for a lasting relationship." Obviously, within this framework, allowing spouses to modify or rescind the terms of the exit provisions would undercut the purposes covenant marriage was designed to serve. Covenant marriage proponents assert that this institution will strengthen marriage by means of mechanisms such as premarital counseling requirements, provisions for resolving marital problems through "reasonable efforts to preserve the marriage," and creation of barriers to marital exit. Furthermore, proponents assert that covenant marriage conveys to marrying partners the message that marriage is a life-long commitment. Other advantages include the invitation to religious and other community organizations to help support marriages, and the asserted restoration of "some power and some protection to the 'innocent' spouse who desires to continue the marriage." Katherine Shaw Spaht, *Louisiana's Covenant Marriage: Social Analysis and Legal Implications*, 59 LA. L. REV. 63, 74-78 (1998).

Are there any negative implications to the existence and availability of covenant marriage? The first criticism of the concept of covenant marriage is that the evidence does not exist that making divorce harder to obtain reduces the divorce rate or makes marriage stronger or more stable. A corollary criticism asserts that the same objections lodged against fault-based divorce can be lodged against covenant marriage. *See, e.g.,* Amy L. Stewart, Note, *Covenant Marriage: Legislating Family Values*, 32 IND. L. REV. 509, 522-23, 535 (1999) (referring to covenant marriage as "the ghost of a system that was declared dead three decades ago"). *See also* Heather K. McShain, *For Better or Worse: A Closer Look at Two Implications of Covenant Marriage*, 32 FAM. L.Q. 629 (1998). For example, unhappy spouses may replicate the patterns of their predecessors who engaged in collusion and evasion to avoid restrictive divorce laws. As noted in Section C2c *supra,* long waiting periods before divorce may be particularly difficult for children to weather. Furthermore, victims of psychologically-abusive relationships, who do not have a fault-based remedy under Louisiana's covenant marriage divorce statute, may be prevented from escaping such marriages in timely manner, subjecting them, and possibly also their children, to sustained emotional harm.

Given the voluntary nature of covenant marriage, however, proponents view its selection by couples as a positive manifestation of pluralism in marital choice. From this perspective, the existence of covenant marriage invokes some of the same considerations raised by enforcement of premarital contracts more generally. That is, to what extent should people entering marriage be permitted to bind themselves before marriage to terms governing marital exit? And, what factors should be considered in deciding whether or not such agreements should be enforced? These questions are the subject of debate with respect to premarital contracts generally, and are discussed in Chapter 8. There is a twist, however, in the case of covenant marriage, not present with ordinary premarital contracts: the state will enforce the terms of a covenant marriage even if both parties wish to modify the terms or rescind the covenant. One author has argued that this feature constitutes a critical distinction between covenant marriage and ordinary premarital contracts, in that it is the state that ultimately binds couples to the terms, even if, upon reflection or after the passage of time, both parties agree that the "choice . . . was ill-conceived or ill-advised." Chauncey E. Brummer, *The Shackles of Covenant Marriage: Who Holds the Keys to Wedlock?* 25 U. ARK. LITTLE ROCK L. REV. 261, 289 (2003). For a thoughtful analysis of the potential impact of covenant marriage, examining arguments by both its proponents and critics, see Jean Louise Carriere, *"It's Déjà vu All Over Again": The Covenant Marriage Act in Popular Cultural Perception and Legal Reality*, 72 TUL. L. REV. 1701 (1998).

How have other states responded to Louisiana's innovation? While approximately twenty state legislatures have considered covenant marriage statutes, Lynne Marie Kohm, *A Comparative Survey of Covenant Marriage Proposals in the United States*, 12 REGENT U.L. REV. 31 (1999-2000) (reviewing state proposals), only two states (Arizona and Arkansas) have joined Louisiana in enacting them. ARIZ. REV. ST. § 25-901 et seq. (2003) (adopted in 1998); ARK. CODE §§ 9-11-802 et seq. (2003) (adopted in 2001). While similar in principle, these statutes differ slightly. For example, Arizona permits covenant marriage spouses to avoid the fault grounds and the two-year waiting period by mutual consent. ARIZ. REV. ST. § 25-903.8 (2003).

Florida, the site of the first covenant marriage proposal (in 1990), failed repeatedly to pass the bill and appears to have stopped trying. The number of state legislatures considering covenant marriage proposals has dropped annually. In 2003, proposals were introduced in the legislatures of Indiana, Iowa, Mississippi, Missouri, Oklahoma, Texas, Utah, and Virginia. The bills never emerged from committees in some states. In other states, the proposals failed to pass one or both legislative houses. In South Carolina in 2002, after a covenant marriage bill failed to progress in the state senate, the legislature established a State Covenant Marriage Study Committee to evaluate the bill and report back to the legislature. At the time of this writing, the Committee had not yet issued its report. In an interesting follow-up to Louisiana's enactment of its covenant marriage statutes, in 1998 the state legislature asked the Louisiana State Law Institute to make recommendations as to the merits of reinstating fault as a prerequisite to *all* Louisiana divorces. In 2002, the Institute published its report, and strongly recommended against such a move. Kenneth Rigby, *Report and Recommendations of the Louisiana State Law Institute to the House Civil Law Committee of the Louisiana Legislature Relative to the Reinstatement of Fault as a Prerequisite of Divorce*, 62 LA. L. REV. 561 (2002) (concluding a return to fault would not improve the quality of marriage and would promote animosity between spouses, even if it prolonged marriage).

Not only have state legislatures failed to embrace the covenant marriage concept, but very few marrying couples in the covenant marriage states have chosen to avail themselves of the option. For example, data obtained from the Louisiana State Center for Health Statistics reveal that in 1998, 1999, and 2000 respectively, covenant marriages constituted 1.54%, 1.21%, and 1.16% of the annual number of new marriages. State Center for Health Statistics, Office of Public Health, State of Louisiana, Vital Statistics Data Tables (available through links beginning at: oph.dhh.state.law.us/recordsstatistics/statistics;page0cda.html?page=117). The number of covenant marriages in this three-year period totaled 1,577. (Unfortunately, Louisiana's published statistics do not indicate how many existing marriages converted to covenant marriages, and what proportion of divorces, if any, were covenant marriage divorces.) Arizona statistics likewise demonstrate only minimal interest in the institution by the public. During the period from enactment (1998) through January of 2000, the Maricopa County (Phoenix) Recorder issued 316 licenses for covenant marriages as compared with 16,168 ordinary marriage licenses (thus, covenant marriages constituted 1.95% of the new marriages). *Covenant Marriages Haven't Exactly Caught On In State*, THE ARIZONA REPUBLIC, February 18, 2001, at page A12.

Some of the more interesting questions about the effects of covenant marriage, such as whether, in the long run, it reduces divorce, will be difficult to study because those who enter covenant marriage comprise a self-selected group. Comparisons with those who do not elect covenant marriage will tell us less about the effects of covenant marriage and more about the characteristics of those who opt in and those who do not. Such information will be interesting, even if only descriptive. The first comparison of couples choosing covenant versus standard marriage in Louisiana reveals that the two groups differ on a range of demographic and attitudinal variables, such as their levels of religious involvement, whether they cohabited prior to marriage, and whether they favor more egalitarian or more traditional gender roles in marriage. Steven L. Nock, Laura Sanchez, et al., *Covenant Marriage Turns Five Years Old,* 10 MICH. J. GENDER & L. 169 (2003). These findings are consistent with earlier attitudinal surveys revealing that persons who hold more conservative gender-role ideologies and are more active in their religious institutions are more likely to endorse the concept of covenant marriage. *See, e.g.,* Alan J. Hawkins, Steven L. Nock et al., *Attitudes About Covenant Marriage and Divorce: Policy Implications from a Three-State Comparison,* 51 FAM. RELATIONS 166 (2002); Laura Sanchez, Steven L. Nock et al., *Setting the Clock Forward or Back? Covenant Marriage and the "Divorce Revolution,"* 23 J. FAM. ISSUES 91 (2002).

The institution of covenant marriage raises, of course, interesting legal issues, such as those relating to what happens when spouses of covenant marriage seek divorces in other states. *See, e.g.,* Brian H. Bix, *Choice of Law and Marriage: A Proposal,* 36 FAM. L.Q. 255, 260 (2002); Brian H. Bix, *State of the Union: The States' Interest in the Marital Status of their Citizens,* 55 U. MIAMI L. REV. 1, 21 (2000); Katherine Shaw Spaht & Symeon C. Symeonides, *Covenant Marriage and the Law of Conflicts of Laws,* 32 CREIGHTON L. REV. 1085 (1999); Mark Strasser, *Baker and Some Recipes for Disaster: On DOMA, Covenant Marriages, and Full Faith and Credit Jurisprudence,* 64 BROOK. L. REV. 307 (1998).

Other initiatives seeking to reduce divorce by strengthening marriage have gained support in various jurisdictions. These approaches might best be characterized as falling into two groups: those seeking to encourage forethought regarding decisions to enter marriage, and those seeking to strengthen existing marriages by providing support, education, and counseling. These approaches differ from legal policies regulating divorce in that they seek to prevent dysfunctional marriages from coming into being, and to ameliorate marital problems, rather than simply restricting unhappy couples' access to divorce. For example, approaches that seek to improve the quality of couples' decisions to marry include statutes providing minor incentives (such as reductions in the marital license fee) for couples' participation in a premarital counseling program. *See e.g.,* 43 OKLA. ST. § 5.A.2 (2003). Florida, Maryland, and Minnesota also have similar initiatives. National Conference of State Legislatures, *State Trends in Marriage and Divorce Legislation* (available at: www.ncsl.org/programs/cyf/marriagefact.htm). Some states encourage applicants for marriage licenses to attend a premarital education course. *See, e.g.,* TEX. FAM. CODE § 2.013 (2003). Under Florida's Marriage Preparation and Preservation Act, those seeking marriage licenses are given a marriage preparation handbook. Furthermore, graduation from high school in Florida now requires a course relating to relationship skills.

Approaches geared toward improving the quality of marriage include those in Oklahoma (Oklahoma Marriage Initiative, www.okmarriage.org/survey.htm, bringing together policymakers, social scientists, community and religious leaders to develop strategies to strengthen marriage;); New Hampshire (creating a committee to develop a marriage education and enhancement program); and Arizona (creating an advisory Marriage and Communication Skills Commission in 2000). For a summary and description of marital promotion and support policies and proposals across the states, see Karen N. Gardiner, Michael E. Fishman, et al., *State Policies to Promote Marriage* (2002) (available at: aspe.hhs.gov/hsp/marriage02f/). At the time of this writing, state legislatures consider a wide range of proposals of these types, aimed at improving premarital decisionmaking and enhancing marital quality.

In a parallel movement, private community efforts to promote and support marriages have become increasingly popular. Most such efforts have been organized by religious institutions, with explicit goals of encouraging better decisions regarding marital entry and providing support and counseling to those couples who marry. For example, as of 2002, clergy in approximately 130 cities nationwide had adopted the Community Marriage Covenant, founded in Modesto, California in 1986. Rigby, *supra* at 599. One version of the program was adopted by fourteen congregations in Shreveport, Louisiana. It encourages a four-month delay between engagement and marriage, provides for premarital counseling, as well as mentoring of newlyweds and couples considering divorce, and offers counseling and support to divorced or separated couples, and to newly-formed stepfamilies. *Id. See also, e.g., Across our Nation,* INDIANAPOLIS NEWS/INDIANAPOLIS STAR, Dec. 6, 2003 (describing signing of the Covenant by 50 clergy leaders in Indianapolis); Deidre Erin Murphy, *To Have and To Hold,* PORTLAND PRESS HERALD, June 7, 2003 (describing similar movement in Portland, Maine).

[e] Epilog: The Role of Family Law in Producing Social Change

In recommending reform of no-fault divorce laws, Linda Waite and Maggie Gallagher state:

> The legal story of marriage is now directly at odds with social purposes and cultural meaning of the marriage vow. Thanks to pure no-fault

statutes, the law now sends the message to couples that marriage is a temporary commitment that can be abrogated unilaterally by either partner at any time and for any reason. . . *The law is a power tool.* A recent study found that the move to no-fault divorce by itself caused a 6 percent increase in divorce. . . .

THE CASE FOR MARRIAGE, *supra* at 195 (emphasis added). Waite and Gallagher assert that the law is a potent weapon in producing social change, whether that social change is manifested in public attitudes and values, or in measurements of the public's use of social institutions. Compare this view to the following:

> In principle, law can buttress the social forces that support the institution of marriage. The law should certainly try to do so. But I believe that familial institutions must rest primarily on culture rather than on law. . . . [F]amily law is feeble. . . . [¶] . . . . Family law, as much as any area of law, persistently encounters . . . "enforcement problems." Law has enough trouble regulating public conduct, as I am reminded every time I drive to work [and people pass by me at 95 miles per hour.] Regulating private conduct is much harder, especially conduct that concerns life's most volatile interests and emotions. . . . [¶] . . . .[A]ny real strengthening of marriage would have to come not from law but from social and cultural reform. [I doubt] that family law, in and of itself, can do much to help re-institutionalize marriage."

Carl E. Schneider, *Fixing the Family: Legal Acts and Cultural Admonitions*, in REVITALIZING THE INSTITUTION OF MARRIAGE FOR THE TWENTY-FIRST CENTURY 177, 178-79 (A.J. Hawkins, L.D. Wardle & D.O. Coolidge eds. 2002). These opposing views can be used not only to construct different interpretations of the relationship between no-fault reforms and rising divorce rates in the 20th century, but also to understand the relationship between divorce rates in the 1990s and 2000s, and the advent of policies such as covenant marriage. Consider how the views of these authors, and then Professor Friedman, *supra* pages 204 and 209, might explain the more recent attempts, failures, and successes in promoting legal policies designed to discourage divorce and encourage stability in marriage.

PROBLEMS

Consider the statutory proposals set forth in the following problems and explain (a) how they would change the law of your state, or why they would not change the law of your state; (b) why they would or would not be good policy; and (c) what changes or amendments you would suggest.

Problem 3-1. Upon the joint verified petition of any husband and wife, filed with the clerk of the superior court, the clerk shall issue a decree of divorce terminating their marital status. If the petition provides for the custody of any minor children, the support obligations of either of the spouses, or the division of the spouses' property, the decree shall incorporate the provisions. If the petition does not provide for these matters, the spouses may later submit a joint sworn petition which does, and the clerk shall cause the original decree to be amended to incorporate the provisions of the second petition. Either spouse may separately petition the court to seek an order covering matters not dealt with in a decree issued pursuant to a joint sworn petition, or to modify an order for support or custody incorporated in such a decree. Such a separate petition shall be dealt with according to the ordinary rules for handling post-decree matters in domestic relations cases.

Problem 3-2. The clerk of the superior court shall issue a decree terminating a marriage on the 91st day following the filing of a sworn request for such a decree by either spouse. Notice of the request shall be given to the non-moving spouse within 10 days of its filing, by first class, certified, or registered mail. If before the issuance of the order the clerk receives a sworn statement of both spouses providing for the division of their property, their support obligations, or the custody of their children, the decree terminating the marriage shall incorporate these provisions. Either spouse may separately petition the court for an order covering such matters, if not dealt with by a joint sworn statement, or to modify an order for support or custody based upon such a statement. Such a separate petition shall be dealt with according to the ordinary rules for handling post-decree matters in domestic relations cases.

Problem 3-3. No decree of divorce shall be issued in any marriage in which there are minor children, except when the following conditions have been met:

(a) at least one year has passed since a petition for divorce has been filed, and

(b) for a period of at least one year, both spouses have regularly met with a licensed marriage counselor in an effort to effect a reconciliation, and

(c) the court finds that there are no realistic prospects for reconciliation, and

(d) there is clear and convincing evidence that termination of the marriage is consistent with the best interests of the minor children.

Problem 3-4. When applying for a marriage license, each couple shall file with the county clerk a notarized statement, signed by each, setting forth the grounds upon which their marriage may be terminated. In particular, the statement may indicate:

(a) that either spouse shall have the right to terminate the marriage without cause, and, if so, any required notice period before such termination is effective;

(b) that cause shall be required for termination on the petition of either spouse, and, if so, what cause shall be sufficient;

(c) that the marriage may not be terminated for any reason, including the mutual consent of the spouses, either for a specified period after its solemnization, or at all;

(d) that the marriage be terminated solely upon the mutual consent of the spouses; or

(e) that the marriage may be terminated only in accordance with the religious principles of a specified faith, provided that the statement specifies a religious authority which shall rule on any divorce petition that may be filed.

Any marriage for which such a statement has been filed may not be terminated except in accordance with its terms. If no such statement has been filed, a marriage may be terminated by either spouse, without cause and upon 90 days' notice.

Chapter 4
PROPERTY DIVISION AND ALIMONY UPON DIVORCE

INTRODUCTION

In most divorce cases, a large portion of the lawyer's efforts focus on the financial issues: property division, alimony (or as it is increasingly called, spousal support or maintenance) and child support. In this chapter, we deal with the first two. The introductory materials that follow place the doctrinal discussions of property division and alimony in a larger practical context. Of course, most divorces are settled, so that litigated alimony and property disputes, like litigated child support and custody disputes, are uncommon. But in this field as in all others, the terms that parties agree upon in reaching their settlements are affected by the legal rules a judge would apply if they litigated it. They are also affected by the tax laws, which treat alimony but not property allocations as income to the recipient with a corresponding deduction for the obligor. (Child support is also not income to the recipient and not deductible for the obligor; dispositions of property may or may not trigger capital gains taxes depending on how they are arranged.) Tax laws as well as family law rules are thus important considerations to attorneys fashioning an agreement.

THE RELATION OF PROPERTY DIVISION TO ALIMONY

Although we defer consideration of alimony until after exploring property division, their relationship to each other is so great that it must be acknowledged at the outset. Because they are both simply awards of resources, in judging the fairness of the divorce's financial result it is necessary to look at both the property division and the alimony award, which constitute a single economic package. Both property awards and alimony can be structured either as lump sum payments or as periodic payments (though it is more usual for alimony to be periodic); and periodic payments for a specified period of time are financially equivalent to a lump-sum payment. In the course of negotiating the terms of dissolution, there are a variety of reasons for preferring a property award over an alimony obligation, or vice versa. Some of these reasons have to do with current ability to pay, a preference for the certainty of current payment over a future obligation, or the desire to prevent modification of the obligation. For many couples, the most important reasons for choosing one over the other are the different treatments of property division and alimony under tax law and bankruptcy.

RULES OF MARITAL PROPERTY

AMERICAN LAW INSTITUTE, PRINCIPLES OF THE LAW OF FAMILY DISSOLUTION 21–23 (2002)

The common-law treated property owned by the spouses during their marriage as the individual property of one of them unless, as to a particular piece of property, they had acted to create joint ownership. The title in which property was held was critical. The usual effect was to vest ownership in the spouse who earned the money with which the property was purchased, although that owner could make a gift to the other spouse by shifting property to joint title, or sole title in the other spouse's name. At divorce each spouse was allocated his or her property. The result in most cases was to allocate the bulk of the property to the husband. Alimony was therefore often the only financial remedy available to meet claims the divorced wife might have on her own behalf, as contrasted with claims of child support she might make on behalf of her children.

Community-property law begins with the contrary presumption: all earnings from spousal labor during the marriage are the property of the marital "community" in which each spouse has an undivided one-half interest. Property acquired with spousal earnings is therefore ["community property" which is] owned equally by the spouses, regardless of whether purchased with funds earned by the husband, the wife, or both, unless the parties change the character of the property by agreement or gift. In three community-property states [California, Louisiana, and New Mexico], all community property is divided at divorce into spousal shares equal in value, although not necessarily identical in kind. Alimony (renamed as "spousal support" or "maintenance" in most jurisdictions) may also be allowed, as determined on a case-by-case basis.

This sharp dichotomy between common-law and community-property traditions no longer prevails in the United States. All the common-law states now allow the divorce court to distribute ["marital property," which includes all property derived from earnings during marriage] between [the divorcing spouses,] on a basis other than common-law principles of ownership, under a doctrine known generally as "equitable distribution." Five of the eight community property states also instruct their divorce courts to divide the community-property between the spouses "equitably" (rather than "equally"). Equitable distribution is the dominant rule today, followed everywhere but in the three "equal division" community-property states.

The consensus, however, is not so great as first appears. In community property states, the concept of joint ownership is pervasive, applicable not only at dissolution but also at death and during the intact marriage. The common-law states, in contrast, generally retain their traditional separate-ownership principles in all matters other than the system of equitable distribution they apply at divorce. These different starting points in the basic underlying concepts of ownership may yield differences in the application of equitable-distribution rules that are similar in form. The two most critical features of any law of equitable distribution are its rules for identifying the pool available for allocation on equitable grounds, and its default or presumptive allocation rule. The trend in equitable division states has favored a presumption, whether formal or in practice, that an equitable division of property is an equal division, but not all states follow this pattern, and its strength varies among those that do. Such differences in the default allocation rule are sometimes related to differences in the definition of property available for allocation. Strong presumptions of equal division are more common among states that limit the pool of allocable property by excluding inherited property, or property owned by the spouses individually before their marriage. States that put all property owned by either spouse into the allocable pool tend to employ more discretionary rules of allocation. California is a leading example of the first kind; it requires equal division in all cases, but has detailed and comprehensive rules distinguishing the equally divided community property from each spouse's "separate property," which the court cannot reallocate to the other spouse.

Looking behind these differences nonetheless reveals some common substantive themes. For example, even in those states that do not require or strongly presume equal division, property acquired with marital labor (that is, labor by a spouse during marriage) is often divided equally at dissolution. At the same time, courts in states that in principle allow the court to allocate all property owned by the spouses, in fact tend nonetheless to treat property inherited by one spouse during the marriage differently than property acquired through marital labor. Important distinctions among the states thus emerge primarily at the next level of detail: when is a case not "ordinary," so that an equal-division presumption should not apply? When, if ever, should the court be allowed to divide property that one of the spouses inherited or owned before the marriage?

(footnotes omitted)

One helpful overview of property division issues was given by Robert J. Levy, Reporter for the Model Marriage and Divorce Act. Levy states that a family lawyer facing a property division question should ask four questions regarding any item potentially subject to division:

(1)   is an item property?

(2)   is it marital or separate property?

(3)   how much is it worth (valuation)?

(4)   what is the basis/standard for division/distribution?

Robert J. Levy, *An Introduction to Divorce-Property Issues*, 23 FAM. L.Q. 147, 147 (1989).

All of these questions and distinctions will be revisited in the coming sections.

§ A. PROPERTY DIVISION: GENERAL PRINCIPLES

[1] THE CLASSIC COMMON LAW TITLE RULE

As already mentioned, prior to their adoption of equitable division as the principle of property division at divorce, common law states divided property at divorce according to who owned title. This usually produced a one-sided division in the husband's favor, as (1) many women did not work outside the home; (2) those who did work outside the home usually made far less than their husbands did; and (3) in those times and jurisdictions where the traditional rule of "coverture" applied, whatever property the wife brought to the marriage automatically became the property of the husband.

The harshness of the classic common law title approach is exemplified by *Saff v. Saff*, 61 A.D.2d 452, 402 N.Y.S.2d 690 (1978), *appeal dismissed*, 46 N.Y.2d 969, 389 N.E.2d 142, 415 N.Y.S.2d 829 (1979). Mr. and Mrs. Saff were married in 1936. Both worked at various jobs and held the accumulated funds jointly. In 1946, Mr. Saff and a partner founded Jamestown Fabricated Steel; each invested $2000. Mr. Saff's contribution came from the Saffs' joint funds; however, Mrs. Saff never had an express legal interest in the business. At the time of divorce, the company was estimated to have a net worth exceeding $500,000. The court stated:

> A minority of the court would grant [Mrs. Saff] relief by imposing a constructive trust. . . .

> Before the court may declare that [Mr. Saff] holds his separately owned property as a trustee for [Mrs. Saff]'s benefit, [Mrs. Saff] must prove that there was (1) a promise by him — express or implied, (2) which caused her to transfer property to him relying on the promise, (3) that a confidential relationship existed between the parties and (4) that [Mr. Saff] has been unjustly enriched at her expense by his conduct.

> Marriage is a confidential relationship, of course, and there was a transfer of funds and labor by [Mrs. Saff] to [Mr. Saff]. The remedy of constructive trust, however, requires more. There must be proof that the transfer was made in reliance on a promise that the property transferred would be held for the benefit of [Mrs. Saff], and that [Mr. Saff] was enriched unjustly by retaining the fruits of the transfer.

> We find no express promise by [Mr. Saff]. [Mrs. Saff] testified that from 1946 to 1960, apparently after the purchase of the business, [Mr. Saff] told her on various occasions, "Baby girl, what is mine is yours; you're my wife. It's always all half yours, you're my wife." Such representations undoubtedly reflected the emotions of a happier time but they most assuredly did not constitute a promise by [Mr. Saff] that he held one-half of his corporate stock as trustee for [Mrs. Saff]. The statements meant precisely what most people would interpret them to mean — not that [Mrs. Saff] had a proprietary interest in every personal belonging of [Mr. Saff], be it clothing or corporate stock, but

rather that the parties would share their successes equally in raising their family and enjoying their life together.

The court went on to reject the conclusion that there has been an implied promise, adding: "The remedy of constructive trust may not be applied randomly to adjust general equities between spouses or as a punitive measure to divvy up a husband's separately owned property because of his past indiscretion."

After noting that Mrs. Saff had been compensated, by salary, for some of her work for the company, the court commented:

> There was no unjust enrichment of [Mr. Saff]. [Mrs. Saff] has been more than adequately compensated for her efforts and in ways fully to be expected in a marriage. [Mr. Saff] has kept the couple happily circumstanced for 30 years. All of his earnings from the company were deposited in the couple's joint accounts and were used to support [Mrs. Saff]. Generous purchases of property and investments were made from these funds for her. The income has been sufficient to enable her to travel, to enjoy the satisfying social and athletic life which she described in her testimony as the routine of "the most beautiful marriage in the world." [Mrs. Saff] will continue to enjoy the support available through [Mr. Saff]'s efforts, by the separately owned property accumulated for her or, if her needs require it, by [Mr. Saff]'s income for as long as he is able to do so. There is no need for a division of [Mr. Saff]'s capital. . . .

> [Mrs. Saff] is not penniless. She came to this marriage with few material assets but she has lived a financially secure life for over 30 years since then. The Trial Court granted her exclusive, tax free use of the marital residence and the extensive furnishings in it. She has joint ownership in $100,000 in stocks, several thousand dollars of various stocks in her own name, $15,200 in savings and ownership of a sizeable insurance policy on her husband's life. In addition to this, she receives $12,500 a year income from her part-time employment at Jamestown Steel and she has dividend income of $3,600 per year. Neither the Trial Court nor the majority of this court find alimony justified on these facts.

> This case is a vivid illustration of the dangers of creating a judicial version of a community property law. A businessman or busineswoman ought to be able to determine whether his or her spouse is a partner in business, a partner in marriage, or both, without obtaining a judicial decree, after the fact, based upon nebulous and subjective concepts of what is equitable. The result sought by [Mrs. Saff] here would foist an unwanted business partner on [Mr. Saff and his partner], a business partner who may be motivated by considerations unrelated to the best interests of Jamestown Steel, those who own it and those who are employed by it. It is one thing to make an equitable adjustment of real and personal property of divorced spouses. It is quite another thing for a court of equity to trifle with corporate enterprises involving the vital interests of innocent third parties.

The common law title system effectively employed a narrow "contribution" principle: property is allocated between the spouses in proportion to their direct financial contribution to the marriage. The traditional homemaker earned nothing and was therefore entitled to nothing: to obtain a portion of the accumulated property, she had to show that she earned part of it herself by "direct business services of the type which an employee or partner" would contribute. *Patterson v. Patterson,* 277 S.E.2d 708, 712 (W. Va. 1981). The "constructive trust" doctrine was the only escape from the title system under the traditional common law, and it had limited utility. Constructive trust is an equitable remedy available to the party who can show that he or she is the true owner of property held by another, which most wives could not do under traditional common law principles (the dissenters in *Saff* supported the application of "constructive trust" in that case, but, as seen, the majority rejected that approach).

Some common-law courts avoided the harsher results of the traditional title system by applying the constructive trust doctrine more flexibly to aid wives who had participated directly in their husbands' businesses. Some courts also divided property under the guise of "alimony" awards giving the wife, for example, the family car and a life estate in the family residence. *Patterson v. Patterson, supra,* at 709. Such tactics often achieved a more equitable result, but did not approach either the generosity of the community property system or the flexibility of an equitable distribution system.

[2] EQUAL DIVISION

The historic American alternative to the common law title system was the community property system. Essential to that system is the distinction between community property and separate property briefly explained in the introductory section's excerpt from the *ALI Principles*. Each spouse took his or her separate property at the marriage's conclusion, but community property is divided at divorce between the spouses. Today, the common law states use a largely analogous set of rules that distinguish what they call "marital property" from separate property. Income earned during the marriage is community or marital property, while property received during the marriage by gift or inheritance is separate. Property acquired by either spouse before the marriage is also separate. As a general matter, property acquired in exchange for other property assumes the character of the property traded for it. Thus, if a spouse buys shares of stock with funds earned during the marriage, the shares are community or marital. If the same spouse owned stock before the marriage, sells it during the marriage, and buys new stock with the proceeds, the new stock is separate property (as were the predecessor shares). This rule can require tracing assets the spouses hold at divorce back to their source. A spouse cannot change community property into separate property by unilateral action. For example, a car purchased with earnings during marriage is community property even though the spouse who bought it had title placed in his or her name alone. Common law states usually follow the same rule with respect to marital property. The foregoing sets forth the basics; complications can and do arise, and Section B below examines the classification rules in more detail. In this section, we begin our examination of the allocation rule itself: how is marital (or community) property divided at divorce?

Most states employ a rule of "equitable" distribution, detailed in the next section, which allows the trial court some discretion in deciding upon the fair division of the marital or community property between the spouses. A smaller group, however, employs a rule of equal division. Most of these are community property states. Three require strict equal division in all cases, including, most importantly, California, CAL. FAM. CODE § 2550 (West 1994 & Supp. 2003). Louisiana has a similar provision, LA. REV. STAT. ANN. § 9:2801(4)(b) (West 1997 & Supp. 2003) ("court shall divide the community assets and liabilities so that each spouse receives property of an equal net value"); and New Mexico has reached the same result by judicial decision. *Ruggles v. Ruggles*, 860 P.2d 182, 188, (N.M. 1993) ("property attributable to community earnings must be divided equally when the community is dissolved"). These three are all community property states; the other community property states (Arizona, Idaho, Nevada, Texas and Washington), follow a rule of "equitable distribution." A 1990 survey found, however, that Arizona, Texas, and Idaho apply a *presumption* of equal division, Herma Hill Kay, *Beyond No-Fault: New Directions in Divorce Reform*, in DIVORCE REFORM AT THE CROSSROADS 6 (Stephen D. Sugarman & Herma Hill Kay eds., 1990). *See, e.g.*, IDAHO CODE, § 32-712(1)(A) (Michie 1996 & Supp. 2003) ("Unless there are compelling reasons otherwise, there shall be a substantially equal division in value, considering debts, between the spouses."). In 1993, Nevada adopted a similar provision, requiring "an equal disposition of the community property of the parties" unless "the court finds a compelling reason" to make an unequal distribution and "sets forth in writing the reasons for making the unequal disposition." NEV. REV. STAT. § 125.150(1)(b) (Lexis 1998 & Supp. 2003). No common law property state has a rule *mandating* equal division, but some have presumptions similar to the Nevada rule, that marital property should be divided equally in the absence of identified countervailing considerations, *e.g.*, *Brown v. Brown*, 914 P.2d 206 (Alaska 1996), or find equal division to be an appropriate place from which to start the analysis, *e.g.*, *Cherry v. Cherry*, 421 N.E.2d 1293 (Ohio 1981).

The distinction between community and separate property is obviously more critical when the allocation rules governing each are more disparate. They are most disparate in the three community property states with strict equal division rules. As one might therefore expect, California has a rich trove of statutory and caselaw plumbing the distinction between community and separate property. Common law equitable distribution states, on the other hand, have no reason to distinguish marital and separate property apart from divorce, and even then precise accuracy in characterizing property may seem less essential, particularly among states with a tendency to treat all difficult-to-characterize items as marital property on the assumption that one can then rely on the court's discretion to allocate them in some reasonable fashion. This substitution of judicial discretion for clear rules has drawbacks as well as advantages, as we shall see further below.

Compliance with an equal division rule requires accurate valuations of every item that is not itself divided in half, and it is the rare divorce that does not include at least some such items. Careful valuations (like careful characterization of property as community or separate) may be more easily foregone under an equitable distribution system. Even though one would think that accurate valuation of the marital property is necessary to know whether any particular allocation of property is fair or equitable, some equitable distribution jurisdictions simply rely on the trial court's instincts and discretion. The need to obtain accurate valuations can be viewed as either an advantage or a disadvantage of the equal division rule. On one hand, valuations may be time consuming or expensive. On the other hand, because they are necessary only when the parties cannot agree on the division of their property the need for careful valuation may impose a useful discipline on the court, avoiding a kind of "rough justice" approach which may be unfair to one party. Of course, equitable distributions states can also require careful valuations if they choose to do so.

When careful valuation is required in a contested proceeding, one spouse may need to compel discovery of information held by the other, especially in the case of business assets. *E.g., In re Petition of B & F Towing & Salvage,* 551 A.2d 45 (Del. 1989) (wife entitled to discovery of financial records of three corporations in which the husband held an interest). In a community property state a spouse can claim access not only under normal discovery rules, but also as a co-owner of the property. *Schnabel v. Superior Ct.,* 5 Cal. 4th 704, 854 P.2d 1117, 21 Cal. Rptr. 2d 200 (1993) (close corporation that employed husband, who owned 30% of shares, must comply with the wife's subpoena for production of financial records, including corporate tax returns; shares were community property even though record title was in husband's name, entitling her to the same access as any other shareholder).

Spouses may agree upon one of several methods to divide their assets, of which the most familiar is the "piece of cake" approach, in which one spouse divides the property into two lists of items and the other chooses which list he or she wants. Devising a truly equitable method, however, is not without its difficulties, particularly where the assets are not fungible and the parties attach different values to them. A mathematician and political scientist jointly developed a version of the "one values, the other chooses" method said to ensure an equitable and "envy-free" division (in the sense that neither party would be willing to exchange his/her share for the other's share). *See* Peterson, *Formulas for Fairness,* 149 SCIENCE NEWS 284 (May 4, 1996).

PROBLEM

Problem 4-1. Joan and Fred have been married ten years. During that time, Fred has been a full-time homemaker and Joan has operated a business. Upon divorce their assets include:

a. the business (a closely-held corporation in which all stock is held by Joan);

b. Joan's vested interest in a pension;

c. a home titled in both their names;

d. two cars, one titled in each of their names;

e. a large interest in a mutual fund, purchased with Fred's inheritance from his father and held solely in his name;

f. two joint bank accounts.

Except for the mutual fund, which is only a small part of the entire value of the property, all assets were acquired with funds earned by Joan during the marriage. How would each asset be divided on divorce in California (a community property state following an equal division property rule) and how would it likely be divided in a common law equitable division state?

[3]　EQUITABLE DIVISION

"Equitable Distribution" is today the dominant form of property distribution on divorce. But many different practices are packaged under that label. Two samples follow: the first from a common law state, the second from a community property state.

MICHAEL v. MICHAEL

791 S.W.2d 772 (Mo. App. 1990)

PUDLOWSKI, Presiding Judge.

This is an appeal from a judgment and decree of dissolution which awarded respondent [Deborah Michael] the majority of marital property and awarded appellant [Dennis Michael] . . . no maintenance.

[Dennis] and [Deborah] . . . married in August 1972 and separated in April 1987. There were no children. . . . Both [Dennis] and [Deborah] are well educated. [Dennis] holds a baccalaureate degree in political science and a master's degree in journalism. [Deborah] holds a baccalaureate degree in journalism and a master's degree in public administration.

[T]he day following the parties' marriage, the couple moved to Little Rock, Arkansas where [Deborah] was going to work for Southwestern Bell Corporation. While . . . in Little Rock, [Dennis] was employed as a reporter for a local newspaper.

In June 1974, [Deborah] received a promotion and was transferred back to St. Louis. In St. Louis, [Dennis] worked for APC Skills Company and then for Maritz, Inc. In 1978, [Dennis] was fired from Maritz, Inc. [T]he couple [then] agreed that [Dennis] would not seek outside employment but instead would devote time to writing fiction. In that same year [Deborah] received another transfer and the couple moved to Oklahoma City.

While living in Oklahoma, [Dennis] . . . abandoned [his writing career] without ever having written a chapter. . . .[He then] worked briefly in a food store and spent 8–9 months working free-lance public relations. When [Dennis] was not employed outside of the home, the couple agreed that [he] would be responsible for the general upkeep of the house and . . . the preparation of the evening meal. [He] spent several hours a day preparing the couple's dinner. [Deborah] claimed that [Dennis]'s other domestic chores were very lax. For two years while the couple was living in Oklahoma [Dennis] drove [Deborah] to and from work. However, for the rest of the mornings, [Dennis] slept until 10 or 11:00 a.m. [¶] In 1984 [Deborah] was again transferred to St. Louis. [Dennis] continued to cook the couple's dinner [and] periodically took [Deborah] to work but did not seek outside employment.

Throughout the marriage, the couple's lifestyle improved and they had a significant amount of disposable income. They were able to purchase homes whenever [Deborah] accepted a job transfer and the couple took many trips including visits to Europe. In addition, [Deborah] . . . provided her mother annually with support . . . of $5,000.

At the time of trial, [Deborah] had been working for Southwestern Bell for more than 15 years and was earning over $70,000 per year. [Deborah also had] vested pension benefits through the Southwestern Bell Corporation Management Pension Plan equal to $1,169.58 monthly payable at age sixty-five (65), as of March 1, 1988. [Dennis has] no income from employment, however he receives $75 per month in interest, and his share of the gross income on the previous year's Federal Income Tax Return was $1200.

[C]ertainly the sex of the parties should have no bearing on the division of marital property or on the allowance or prohibition of maintenance.

The trial court allocated $51,347 or 75.5% of the parties' marital property to [Deborah] and $14,128 or 21.5% to [Dennis]. The court granted [Dennis] no maintenance. . . .[¶] [Dennis] claims that the trial court abused its discretion by its distribution of the parties' marital property [and] by awarding [him] no maintenance. . . .

    . . .

Section 452.330 RSMo 1988 directs the trial court to divide the marital property in a just manner, after considering all relevant factors including . . .

(1) The economic circumstances of each spouse at the time the division of property is to become effective. . . .

(2) The contribution of each spouse to the acquisition of the marital property, including the contribution of a spouse as a homemaker;

(3) The value of the non-marital property set apart to each spouse;

(4) The conduct of the parties during the marriage; and

(5) Custodial arrangements for minor children.

There are two guiding principles inherent in § 452.330: "[F]irst property division should reflect the concept of marriage as a shared enterprise similar to a partnership; and, second property division should be utilized as a means of providing future support for an economically dependent spouse." Krauskopf, *A Theory for "Just" Division of Marital Property in Missouri*, 41 Mo. L. Rev. 165 (1976).

[A]pplying these guiding principles . . . we find that the trial court abused its discretion. . . . Throughout the course of the marriage, [Dennis] has become economically dependent on [Deborah]. At . . . dissolution . . . [Dennis] was unemployed, had not been employed in his chosen field of journalism for fifteen years, and had not been employed full-time since 1978. Conversely, at . . . dissolution . . . [Deborah] had elevated herself within the Southwestern Bell organization to a position directing press relations.

With regard to the second statutory factor, the trial court found that . . . the funds used to acquire the marital property had been earned almost solely by [Deborah]. Also, the court found that [Dennis] made no substantial contribution to the marriage as a homemaker because he showed a marked disinclination to undertake the normal domestic duties of a homemaker, engaging only in those duties, such as cooking the evening meal, which he found fulfilling, stimulating and interesting.

. . . While [Dennis]'s performance of traditional domestic chores was often times lax, he did prepare dinner. We are not finding that [Dennis]'s contributions entitled him to an equal division of the marital property, however, we do hold that the trial court's division of property is against the weight of the evidence and therefore an abuse of discretion.

[Dennis] claims . . . the trial court . . . abused its discretion in awarding no maintenance to [him]. [Dennis] argues that although he is educated and possesses a degree in journalism and public administration, the fact that he is 40 years old and has not held employment in either of these fields for the past fifteen (15) years will have a negative effect on his ability to . . . support himself. [He] does not claim that he is completely unable to support himself. However . . . he requires a period of rehabilitative maintenance. [Dennis] argues that he would require an additional two and one half or three years of education to take course work that would enable him to be self-supporting as a journalist.

We have said that maintenance is awarded when one spouse has detrimentally relied on the other spouse to provide the monetary support during the marriage. If the relying spouse's withdrawal from the marketplace so injures his/her marketable skills that he/she is unable to provide for his/her reasonable needs maintenance may be awarded. "Rehabilitative maintenance" should be awarded for a term reasonably sufficient to receive job training. Rehabilitative maintenance is appropriate where there is substantial evidence that the party seeking maintenance will or should become self-supporting. [¶] We . . . find that the trial court did . . . abuse its discretion. . . .

. . .

. . . Our disposition of the issues of marital property and maintenance is consistent with the generally accepted principles . . ., that marriage is a shared enterprise and that maintenance should be utilized as a means of providing support for an economically dependent spouse until said spouse is self-reliant. [¶] . . . This matter is remanded for further proceedings consistent with this opinion.

Crandall, Judge, dissenting. I believe the trial court acted within its discretion. [¶] If we accept the concept of marriage as a shared enterprise similar to a partnership, husband had a negative impact on that partnership. Husband did not sacrifice his career for wife, rather he was a hindrance to her progress. On the issue of maintenance, husband has simply shown that he is unwilling, rather than unable, to support himself through appropriate employment. [¶] . . . I would affirm. . . .

PROVINZANO v. PROVINZANO

570 P.2d 513 (Ariz. App. 1977)

HAIRE, Judge. On this appeal the contentions raised by the appellant-wife concern . . . the disposition of the community property . . . and spousal maintenance. . . . When the decree of dissolution was entered the parties had been married for approximately 32 ½ years.

[A]t the time of the hearing . . . appellee-husband was 53 years of age, and immediately prior to the hearing, had voluntarily retired for physical disability reasons after over 30 years . . . with the United States Post Office Department. [T]he Post Office Retirement plan . . . was community property [and provided] [¶] $807.95 per month. [T]he husband also received a military service disability payment . . . of $233.00 per month [resulting] from disabilities [he] incurred . . . in World War II, at a time when the parties were married.

[T]he wife was 52 years of age and worked as a sales clerk, with a gross income averaging approximately $400.00 per month. [T]he trial court awarded to the husband the entire community interest in the . . . retirement and disability benefits yielding a total monthly payment of $1,041; a life insurance policy having a cash surrender value of between $3,500 and $3,600; funds remaining from a savings account in the sum of $968; and miscellaneous unvalued personal property including a 1968 Chrysler, a stamp and coin collection, and the husband's guns, tools, art supplies and books.

The appellant-wife was awarded her community interest in the residence . . . having an approximate net value of $5,250 (value of the wife's one-half interest); miscellaneous household furniture; and a 1962 Nova automobile. In addition, the wife was awarded the husband's interest in the community residence "as a lump sum maintenance payment."

A.R.S. § 25-318 directs that . . . the trial judge shall "divide the community, joint tenancy, and other property held in common equitably, though not necessarily in kind." As we stated in *Lindsay v. Lindsay,* 565 P.2d 199 (Ariz. App. 1977):

> While the trial court . . . has wide discretion, it cannot without reason create a gross disparity, or make its award arbitrarily. [I]n the absence of sound reasons appearing in the record which justify a contrary result, the apportionment of the community estate upon dissolution must be substantially equal.

The trial judge did not make a substantially equal disposition of the community property . . ., but rather awarded the entire community interest in the retirement and disability benefits to the husband. [W]e find no evidence which would justify such an extreme departure from the equality of disposition principles. . . . It is true . . . the husband's disabilities probably precluded future employment on his part, while . . . the wife was physically able and was employed and earning a gross amount of approximately $400 per month at the time. Certainly the trial court was entitled to consider this discrepancy in earning ability in making an equitable disposition . . . since neither party possessed other income-producing property. But, the disposition . . . would take away the wife's entire interest in this community property and give it to the husband, thereby giving him a monthly income of $1,041 per month, while leaving the wife without any income except that which she could earn as a sales clerk, approximating $400 per month. While the trial judge did award to the wife the husband's interest in the community residence "as a lump sum maintenance payment", this small maintenance award could not reasonably be considered as off-setting the substantial discrepancy created by the above disposition. . . .

The wife should be awarded a 29% interest in the monthly retirement and disability payments. Such a distribution would give her approximately $302 per month for a total income potential of $702 per month. Subtracting the $302 from the $1,041 presently allocated to the husband would leave him with a monthly income from community property alone of $739. Considering the husband's disabilities and the wife's employment income potential, . . . such a modification would constitute a more equitable disposition. . . .

NOTES AND QUESTIONS

1. *What Does "Equitable" Distribution Mean?* Consider the summary contained in § 4.09, Comment *a* of the *ALI Principles:*

> [In the] dominant . . . "equitable distribution [model]," . . . the governing statute provides a list of "factors" that the trial judge is authorized or directed to consider in deciding the fairest allocation of the property. These statutes typically provide the judge no guidance in weighing the relative importance of the various factors. Although these lists often include eight or 10 factors, most of the factors are specific examples of two basic but conflicting principles: Property should be allocated in proportion to the spousal contributions to its acquisition, and property should be allocated according to relative spousal need.

For an example of a state law's list of eleven factors, based on the Model Marriage and Divorce Act, see the excerpt from the Pennsylvania law on pp. 284-85. One survey of state equitable distribution statutes found that in the aggregate they list 38 purportedly different factors, but the two most common were "the economic circumstances of the parties at the time of the division," and "the contributions of each party to the acquisition of marital property." The third most commonly listed factor is the length of the marriage. Howard I. Lipsey and William I. Weston, *Determining Factors in Equitable Distribution of Marital Property* § 19.03[1] (1991) in 1 VALUATION AND DISTRIBUTION OF MARITAL PROPERTY, Ch. 19 (Matthew Bender 1996).

It is difficult to see how marital duration can operate as an independent factor, as it is generally the same for both parties. It is perhaps intended to affect the application of the primary factors of contribution (which perhaps lessens in importance with increasing duration) and need (which perhaps increases in importance with increasing duration). It has been noted, however, that an equal division rule will in most cases automatically adjust the impact of need and contribution by duration in just this way: the longer the parties have been married, the more marital or community property they will usually accumulate — so that more property is shifted from the spouse whose market labor earned it to the other spouse. Mary Ann Glendon, *Family Law Reform in the 1980's*, 44 LA. L. REV. 1553, 1561–62 (1984).

"Equitable" is merely a four-syllable word for "fair." As any group of schoolchildren dividing a bag of candy know, the default meaning of fair is "equal." Anyone proposing an unequal allocation must provide persuasive arguments for that position. In the case of "equitable distribution," what might those arguments be? Any effort to answer that question must begin by analyzing how the parties' relative need, or their relative contribution to the acquisition of property, are relevant to the allocation of the property.

2. Need as a Factor in Equitable Distribution and the Award's Relationship With Alimony. While financial need is one of the two most commonly cited factors to consider in allocating property under equitable distribution, it is also the most dominant factor offered to justify awards of alimony. Because income flows and capital assets can be substituted for one another and valued on a common scale, an enhanced share of marital property may in principle always substitute for a fixed-term alimony award. This was in fact the premise sometimes relied upon early in the no-fault reform era by those who hoped equitable distribution reforms, by recognizing the wife's property claims, would replace alimony. Those hopes were frustrated in practice. Few divorcing couples have capital assets sufficiently large to provide an adequate substitute for any but the most modest of alimony awards. Nonetheless, need remains a critical factor in most equitable distribution statutes, often in language that duplicates the language of the state's alimony provisions. The overlap arises because the policy basis for awarding alimony is largely indistinguishable from the basis for allowing one spouse an enhanced share of the marital property. "Need" is the most common rationale for both under existing law. Whatever "need" might mean, there is no reason it should mean different things in these two contexts.

The question of how to handle need-based claims will be largely postponed until we examine alimony. There are, nonetheless, some points that should be previewed now.

a. *The appropriateness of a property allocation to meet need.* How would a court in California (a mandatory equal division state) have dealt with the *Provinzano* facts? Of necessity, it would allocate the property equally — probably by allocating the pension equally — and would then in addition make an award of alimony to the husband. What would be the advantages of this solution, as compared with Arizona's use of the property award to respond to the husband's need? The disadvantages?

b. *Do courts now allocate property on the basis of need?* The language of most equitable distribution statutes makes possible need-based claims to an enhanced share of the property. *E.g., Schwartz v. Linders,* 426 N.W.2d 97 (Wis. App. 1988) (noting that four of its state's typical list of "factors" relate to spousal needs). One commentator concludes, however, that allocations under equitable distribution laws in common law states have focused more heavily on spousal contributions than on relative spousal needs. Reynolds, *The Relationship of Property Division and Alimony: The Division of Property to*

Address Need, 56 FORDHAM L. REV. 827 (1988). If need were the *preeminent* consideration (and if "need" were understood, as it frequently is, to mean something like a right to a standard of living close to that experienced during the marriage), the spouse with less earning capacity would receive a more than equal (often much more than equal) share of the accumulated property, even if his or her contribution to its acquisition was less. Many courts, however, have rejected such distributions as inequitable. *E.g.,* in both *Sattari v. Sattari,* 503 A.2d 125 (R.I. 1986) and *Schnarr v. Schnarr,* 491 N.E.2d 561 (Ind. App. 1986), awards of virtually all of the assets to the wife, premised on the husband's greater earning capacity, were overturned on appeal. Courts have split on whether less extremely disparate allocations are defensible on grounds of the favored spouse's lower earning capacity. *Compare, e.g., In re Marriage of Agazim,* 530 N.E.2d 1110 (Ill. App. 1988) (wife, with limited earning potential, entitled to 76% of property, after 11-year marriage in which husband was principal wage-earner) and *Goller v. Goller,* 758 S.W.2d 505 (Mo. App. 1988) (trial court award to homemaker wife of 36% of $2.3 million estate too low because she needed the property as means of providing future support), *with Longo v. Longo,* 533 So. 2d 791 (Fla. App. 1988) (wife's lower earning capacity and more modest separate assets did not justify giving her nearly two-thirds of the marital property). Community property equitable distribution states may be more willing than their common law counterparts to favor a needy spouse in allocating the property, as did *Provinzano. See, e.g., McNabney v. McNabney,* 782 P.2d 1291 (Nev. 1989) ("preeminent example" of case in which unequal allocation is equitable "is that of the wife and mother in a long-term marriage who has given up career opportunities to devote herself to her family" because in such cases equity might require giving the wife more than half).

c. *Need and the marital home.* Where there are minor children of the marriage, it may seem sensible to award the marital home to the custodial parent. In many cases, however, the marital home is so large a portion of the community assets that it is impossible to offset it with an equal award to the noncustodial spouse. Under a rule of equitable division the court may conclude it is not necessary to do so, at least if the needs of the custodial spouse and children are thought proper considerations in applying the rule of equity. *See, e.g.,* N.C. GEN. STAT. § 50-20(c)(4) (Lexis 2003). One common order defers sale of the home while giving the custodial spouse exclusive use of it during this deferral period. An equitable division state may conclude this is appropriate even where the noncustodial spouse receives no offsetting benefit in exchange for deferring realization of his or her share of the equity. *E.g., Cenci v. Cenci,* 16 Fam. L. Rep. 1069 (N.Y. Sup. Ct. 1989) (rent-controlled apartment leased in husband's name awarded to wife/custodial parent).

Because its purpose is to serve the children's interests, the cost of a deferred sale can be thought of as a form of child support, *In re Marriage of Herrmann,* 84 Cal. App. 3d 361, 148 Cal. Rptr. 550 (1978), thereby providing a rationale for departing from equal division in states which require it. At sale, the former spouses divide the proceeds equally, perhaps with adjustments for expenditures on the home in the interim. Bruch, *The Definition and Division of Marital Property in California: Towards Parity and Simplicity*, 33 HASTINGS L.J. 769, 848–50 (1982); *Marriage of Duke,* 101 Cal. App. 3d 152, 161 Cal. Rptr.

444, 446 (1980) ("immediate loss of a long established family home" would result in "adverse economic, emotional and social impacts on minor children" with roots in the "school and social milieu of their neighborhood"). Deferral may be problematic, however, if the effect is to deny the non-custodial spouse access to his principal asset for many years. *In re Marriage of Horowitz,* 159 Cal. App. 3d 368, 205 Cal. Rptr. 874, 879 n.6 (1984) (*Duke* should apply only where children are old enough that sale will occur in two or three years); *In re Marriage of Stallworth,* 192 Cal. App. 3d 742, 237 Cal. Rptr. 829 (1987) (where home equity is major community asset, deferring sale until son reached 18 improper where no evidence showing sale of home would yield an adverse impact on the minor child; very young child's emotional attachment to home is minimal, and in any event a sale could occur at natural transition point, as when child changes schools, rather than await child's majority). California has now codified its rules for dealing with the marital home at CAL. FAM. CODE §§ 3800–3810 (West 1994 & Supp. 2003).

3. *The Contribution Rationale and the Residual Effects of Title*. While no common law state still divides property strictly according to title, the effects of the old title-based approach can still be seen. For example, the Pennsylvania law, 23 PA. CONS. STAT. ANN. § 3502 (West 2001 & Supp. 2004), adopts most of the language of § 307 of the Model Marriage and Divorce Act. It uses typical language in empowering the court to

"equitably divide, distribute or assign, in kind or otherwise, the marital property . . . without regard to marital misconduct in such proportions and in such manner as the court deems just after considering all relevant factors including:

(1) The length of the marriage.

(2) Any prior marriage of either party.

(3) The age, health, station, amount and sources of income, vocational skills, employability, estate, liabilities and needs of each of the parties.

(4) The contribution by one party to the education, training, or increased earning power of the other party.

(5) The opportunity of each party for future acquisitions of capital assets and income.

(6) The sources of income of both parties, including but not limited to medical, retirement, insurance or other benefits.

(7) The contribution or dissipation of each party in the acquisition, preservation, depreciation or appreciation of the marital property, including the contribution of a party as homemaker.

(8) The value of the property set apart to each party.

(9) The standard of living of the parties established during the marriage.

(10) The economic circumstances of each party, including Federal, State and local tax ramifications, at the time the division of property is to become effective.

(11) Whether the party will be serving as the custodian of any dependent minor children."

Some Pennsylvania courts held that property should be divided equally under this authority unless the listed factors or some other important equitable consideration required otherwise. *E.g., Paul W. v. Margaret W.,* 130 Pittsburgh L.J. 6 (Ct. C.P. Allegheny County 1981) ("property division based on the concept of marriage as a shared enterprise [must initially assume] that the contributions of both parties were sufficiently significant that the parties shall be deemed equal partners of the marital assets"). But to other judges the idea of "marriage as a shared enterprise" sounded more like a community property concept than they believed the Pennsylvania legislature intended. *E.g., Fratangelo v. Fratangelo,* 520 A.2d 1195 (Pa. App. 1987):

> . . . . *Paul W.*['s adoption of] a starting point of fifty-fifty distribution . . . simply ignores the legislative mandate and adopts the easiest solution which, in keeping with human nature, will be the only solution. Once the fifty-fifty starting point is universal, lip service will be paid to equitable distribution and we will, in fact, if not in word, be distributing property in the manner of community property regimes. . . . [the] automatic bestowal of the separate property of one spouse upon the other, as is the law in community property states, . . . is unconstitutional as a deprivation of property in violation of due process. . . . In Perlberger, *Pennsylvania Divorce Code,* 1980, § 5.2 The Concept of Equitable Distribution, it is stated: "[W]hile many factors go into the formula for post-divorce division, it is important to note that record ownership of assets remains significant and the court must find that equity requires a transfer of ownership from one party to the other. . . ." Marital property is not property that is thrown into the pot to be divided equally as in community property states, but property impressed with equitable consideration which must be evaluated before apportionment is considered. We cannot, therefore, approve a starting point of fifty-fifty without consideration of section 401(d) factors.

The continuing influence of the title approach is obvious in *Fratangelo.* The idea that the property really "belongs" to the spouse who earned it is reinforced by the schizophrenic character of the common law marital property system: during the intact marriage the spouses in fact have no ownership interest in one another's earnings. The concept of marital property thus appears only at divorce, making it seem more natural for the divorce court to assign property to the spouse who earned it unless "equitable" factors make it fair to *transfer* ownership of some portion to the other spouse. In a community property state, of course, notions of "transferring" ownership could arise only when one did *not* divide the property equally. Common law and community property judges may thus approach equitable division with very different attitudes.

The lingering impact of the common law title system can also be seen in the limits some states place on the authority of divorce courts to allocate property under their "equitable division" regime. For example, one common law state does not allow courts to transfer ownership of real or personal property from one spouse to the other, even though it can grant a monetary award in accordance with the "equities and rights of the parties." MD. ANN. CODE FAM. LAW §§ 8-202; 8-205 (Lexis 1999 & Supp. 2003). Others get around the strictures of the title system by defining alimony to include the transfer of property from one spouse to another, *e.g.*, N.C. GEN. STAT. § 50-16.7(a) (Lexis 2003). Another halfway measure which was engrafted upon the title system in some states was a doctrine allowing transfer of property only to wives who have shown "special equity." *See*, *e.g.*, *Wilson v. Wilson*, 241 S.E.2d 566, 569 (S.C. 1978); *Morris v. Morris*, 232 S.E.2d 326, 327 (S.C. 1977); *Canakaris v. Canakaris*, 382 So. 2d 1197, 1200 (Fla. 1980). These partial fixes have gradually been replaced with full-fledged equitable distribution systems, *e.g.*, FLA. STAT. ANN. § 61.075 (West 1997 & Supp. 2003).

Some common law states have left the title system far behind, and have established a presumption that property acquired during the marriage should be divided equally in the absence of countervailing equitable considerations. *E.g.*, *Hayes v. Hayes*, 756 P.2d 298 (Alaska 1988), and *Cherry v. Cherry*, 421 N.E.2d 1293 (Ohio 1981). However, even where the doctrine favors equal division as the norm, it may not in practice be the result. For example, five years after New York's adoption of equitable distribution its high court said marriage is an economic partnership in which the "contributions [of the spouses] should ordinarily be regarded as equal." *O'Brien v. O'Brien*, 66 N.Y.2d 576, 489 N.E.2d 712, 498 N.Y.S.2d 743 (1985), quoting from a Memorandum of the Governor in signing the reform legislation. Yet a study conducted in that same year found that in 70 sampled cases women received, on the average, only 30% of the marital assets. *Divorce Law Is Called Unfair by Bar and Women's Groups*, N.Y. TIMES, Aug. 5, 1985, at 1, col. 3. More recent New York data suggests that the average division of assets is now half and half (but with considerable dispersion about this average, especially for settled cases). Marsha Garrison, *How Do Judges Decide Divorce Cases: An Empirical Analysis of Discretionary Decision Making*, 74 N.C. L. REV. 403 (1996).

Note that contribution is not relevant under the community property system. Spousal labor is pooled, and it does not matter which spouse's labor accounts for the asset's acquisition — it is community property. What of property acquired through no labor at all, but sheer luck, such as a winning lottery ticket? In community property states, if the ticket was purchased from community property, such as current earnings, as it almost always is, then the winnings are also community property. *See*, *e.g.*, *In re Marriage of Rossi*, 90 Cal. App. 4th 34, 108 Cal. Rptr. 2d 270 (2001) (wife's lottery winnings were community property, and her efforts to hide them during the divorce proceedings constituted fraud, justifying the award of those winnings entirely to the husband); *Lynch v. Lynch*, 791 P.2d 653 (Ariz. App. 1990) (husband's $2 million lottery winnings treated as community property, even though received during the course of the divorce action and two years after the couple physically separated). Common law states have largely reached the same result, generally justifying the result, as they should, on the basis that the lottery tickets were bought with "marital property." *Ullah v. Ullah*, 555 N.Y.S.2d 834 (App. Div. 1990) ($8 million lottery winnings); *In re Mahaffey*, 564 N.E.2d 1300 (Ill. App. 1990) ($3.6 million lottery ticket); *Swartz v. Swartz*, 512 N.W.2d 825 (Iowa 1993) (trial court's equal division of wife's winning $7.2 million lottery ticket "equitable").

4. *Broadening the Contribution Principle with Homemaker Provisions*. Concerned that the common law contribution principle might be particularly burdensome to the traditional homemaker, many common law states added "homemaker" provisions to their equitable distribution states. Homemaker provisions would be superfluous in community property equitable distribution states, as the homemaker spouse owned half of all the property attributable to the other spouse's earnings during marriage. The typical provision adds a spouse's contributions as a homemaker to the list of factors the court may or should consider in allocating marital property. Yet some of these provisions allow consideration of homemaker services only to the extent they contributed to "the acquisition, preservation and maintenance, or increase in value of marital property." W. VA. CODE § 48-7-103(2)(A) (Michie 2001 & Supp. 2003).

If that requirement were applied as written, the homemaker would not often do well. While it may be easy to show that the homemaker wife contributed greatly to her husband's comfort or happiness, it is less easy to show that her services yielded a significant contribution to "the acquisition, preservation and maintenance, or increase in value of marital property." Married men do earn more, on average, than do bachelors, but that is not necessarily because having a wife increases a man's earning potential. One can just as plausibly hypothesize that men with better earnings prospects have more success in attracting a wife, or that certain traits help a man both in courting women and in earning money. *See, e.g.,* Cohen and Haberfeld, *Why Do Married Men Earn More than Unmarried Men?,* 20 SOC. SCI. RES. 29 (1991).

It thus matters greatly whether a "homemaker" statute is read to create an irrebuttable presumption that the homemaker's economic contribution is equal, or merely to create an opportunity for the homemaker to try to show how her services contributed to the parties' assets. *Compare Axtell v. Axtell,* 482 A.2d 1261, 1264 (Me. 1984) (husband's financial contributions to 23-year marriage held "responsible for by far the greater portion of the value of the increase in the marital assets" as compared to contribution of homemaker wife) *with Ferguson v. Ferguson,* 357 N.W.2d 104 (Minn. App. 1984) (statutory presumption that homemaker's contributions are equal to earner's conclusive in allocating property of ten-year marriage). Note also that the homemaker spouse might not be much aided by shifting strategies and demonstrating the market value of her services, rather than the financial contribution made to creation of the parties' property, because housecleaning and child care are invariably low-paid occupations. At the typical hourly wage for this work, the homemaker spouse married to a physician, attorney or successful corporate executive could not come close to showing an equal market value for their labor, even if, as is usually the case, the homemaker worked very long hours.

The foregoing may suggest only that it is misleading to rest the claim for equal division of property accumulated during a marriage on a homemaker's *financial* contributions. Indeed, one might even argue that insisting on such a narrow vision of that spouse's contribution trivializes rather than recognizes her role. In thinking about the appropriate way to treat the contribution of the spouse who is not the primary breadwinner, consider *Michael.* Should Dennis Michael share equally in the parties' accumulated assets? If you believe so, is it because of his contribution as a homemaker? If you believe not, is it because he did not do such a great job as a homemaker?

5. *Different Rule for High Asset Divorces?* Where the community or marital property estate is very large, common law states are far more likely than community property states to order an unequal division favoring the primary breadwinner. In these cases the differing property heritage of the two groups of states has a very clear impact. The estate's size has no effect on the foundational premise of equal ownership from which community property courts reason. The common law states, by contrast, have great difficulty justifying the transfer of so much property, for they cannot conclude that the homemaker's contribution was worth that much no matter how fine the homemaking job. *See* Barrett, *Wendt Divorce Dissects Job of "Corporate Wife,"* Wall St. J., December 6, 1996, at B1:

> Gary Wendt has had a stellar 20-year career at General Electric Co. and now, at the age of 54, is one of its top executives. His wife, Lorna, 53, has been behind him every step of the way — giving advice on job applicants, making small talk with foreign dignitaries, even minding the offspring of colleagues. [¶] . . . Mr. Wendt, chief executive of GE's giant and hugely profitable GE Capital unit, says the [marital] estate is . . . $52 million. . . . He is offering [Mrs. Wendt] $8 million, plus $250,000 a year in alimony indefinitely, Mrs. Wendt's lawyers say.

> . . .

> [In cases with such large marital estates, few divorce courts in common law states give the wife half.] Knowing [that], lawyers for women often persuade them to settle for less than half. . . .[¶] [But] Mrs. Wendt has decided to take her chances in court. In testimony . . ., she said that the question wasn't what she "needed" but what she deserved after decades of organizing GE dinner parties and trips abroad, giving other "GE wives" tips on shopping and entertaining and generally being "the ultimate hostess." "I took my job very seriously," she testified . . .

> . . .

> By the time Mr. Wendt had taken over the GE subsidiary that generates 36% of the parent's profits, Mrs. Wendt testified, she was orchestrating black-tie dinners for 90 at their luxurious Stamford home. . . .

> Testifying in the drab, tiny Fairfield County courtroom, a stylishly dressed Mrs. Wendt spoke alternately with affection and resentment in her voice. "He loved to entertain," she said of her husband. "He just didn't see that it was a lot of work." Mrs. Wendt wasn't compensated by GE. Her husband earns roughly $2 million a year in salary and bonus. . . .

> . . .

> Mr. Wendt, a famously tough corporate negotiator, asserted in his deposition that it was he who had worked hard and sacrificed and

therefore deserved to keep a much larger share of the couple's assets. "There is no attempt at meanness, but there is an understanding of how hard I've worked and what I've accomplished and the stress I put myself under and what the rest of my life might in fact be like because of that." . . . [¶] "My rewards were financial, and I think her rewards were perhaps emotional," specifically, "the satisfaction of being with the children". . . .

Should Mrs. Wendt have received half the $52 million marital estate? *See* JUNE CARBONE, FROM PARTNERS TO PARENTS 147–51 (2000) (discussing the *Wendt* case and mentioning that the trial court in that case awarded Mrs. Wendt $20 million).

Wendt is hardly alone. From reported cases and other anecdotal evidence, many of the cases involving a large disparity in income or assets (*e.g.*, where one of the spouses is a corporate executive, successful athlete, celebrity actor, or the like) result in a division of property that deviates significantly from an equal split. *See* CARBONE, at 147–53. It is not easy either to explain or to justify why the division in high-asset, high-differential divorces should be so much more one-sided than the division in marriages with a more modest or more equal level of assets.

In these cases, the reasoning of the court often offers little guidance as to its thinking, as the division is simply offered as what is "equitable" in the context of all the factors that the court has been directed to consider. One possible explanation of the courts' approach in these cases is that the high-income spouse simply "contributed" more than the other spouse, even when the lower-income spouse's housework and other non-financial contributions to the marriage are considered. If that is the basis for these unequal divisions in high-asset cases, then it is far from persuasive (and is, in some ways, self-refuting — why would Mrs. Wendt's homemaker services be worth $20 million, while spouses who gave comparable homemaking services in other marriages were awarded a small fraction of that?). If the basic idea of marriage is that the spouses are "in it together," for better and for worse, then a presumption of equal division is the logical starting point, and an exceptional ability to earn money is no more a justification for deviation than a particular facility at raising children. Any deviation from rough equality would seem to require justification, though, as the next Note discusses, the criteria the legislatures require courts to consider often end up increasing discretion (and lack of accountability) rather than offering any sort of structure for decision.

6. A Discretionary System? Appellate courts in equitable distribution states that do not follow a clear presumption of equal division typically emphasize the trial judge's discretion whenever the property allocation is challenged on appeal. "While the trial court must consider the delineated statutory criteria, no single criterion is preferred over the others, and the court is accorded wide latitude in varying the weight placed upon each item under the peculiar circumstances of each case." *Sunbury v. Sunbury*, 553 A.2d 612 (Conn. 1989). Can there be meaningful appellate review under such a system? One Indiana judge observed that the trial court's range of choice in equitable distribution "is virtually limitless and [appellate] review little more than pretense." *Baker v. Baker*, 488 N.E.2d 361, 366 (Ind. App. 1986) (Young, J., concurring). *See also* Mary Ann Glendon, *Family Law Reform in the 1980's*, 44 LA. L. REV. 1553, 1556 (1984) (the movement to equitable distribution is more aptly described as a movement to "discretionary distribution, since what consistently distinguishes [it] from [its] predecessors is not that [it is] more equitable, but that [it is] more unpredictable"). A classic article points out that unpredictability in judicial decision puts a negotiating burden on the risk-averse spouse. While it makes that point in the context of child custody disputes, much of its analysis applies equally to property division. Robert H. Mnookin & Lewis Kornhauser, *Bargaining in the Shadow of the Law: The Case of Divorce*, 88 YALE L.J. 950 (1979). But despite all the criticisms of a discretionary allocation system, many jurisdictions continue to resist the move towards an equal division presumption. In 1992, the Hawaii Supreme Court disapproved property allocation guidelines developed by its intermediate appellate courts because they improperly deprived trial judges of discretion. *Gussin v. Gussin*, 836 P.2d 484 (Haw. 1992).

The *ALI Principles* recommends a strong presumption of equal division, § 4.09, and English law seems also to have moved towards that conclusion. *See* Stephen Cretney, *Community of Property Imposed by Judicial Decree*, 119 L.Q. REV. 349 (2003).

7. Rebutting an Equal Division Presumption. Common law states using a rebuttable presumption of equal division struggle with the question of what it takes to rebut it. For example, Oregon law directs the court to make a "just and proper" division of the property, and to consider homemaker contributions, and then concludes that "[t]here is a rebuttable presumption that both spouses have contributed equally to the acquisition of property during the marriage, whether such property is jointly or separately held." O.R.S. § 107.105(1)(f) (2003). In *Marriage of Stice,* 779 P.2d 1020 (Or. 1989), husband and wife both worked for Teledyne during their 25-year marriage, had nearly equal incomes, and had separate bank accounts. They had agreed to an equal division of their property, with the exception of certain stock.

> The disputed stock [was] acquired by wife in her sole name . . . through monthly payroll deductions to Teledyne's employee stock plan. In all, she paid $10,296 for the stock, which . . . is now valued at over $400,000. Husband holds in his name about $72,000 in Teledyne and related stock he received . . . as bonuses. Husband also purchased other stocks, which, in the words of the trial court, "didn't pan out.". . .

> The trial court found that the "wife has always been the saver and purchaser throughout the marriage. She saved from her earnings and purchased the furniture the parties have from those savings. When they originally bought a beach house in Waldport, it was purchased from her savings. [Husband] has generally been a spender, and he has used most of his income above that needed for the monthly expenses for his enjoyment and hobbies. The Court is satisfied that the [disputed] Teledyne and related stocks were accumulated through [wife's] industry and frugality. It was her interest and perseverance that allowed the parties to obtain the . . . property that is being awarded to [husband]. I am satisfied, however, that [wife] was able to do this

with her income, because of the financial support she received from [husband] in paying the monthly bills."

On the basis of these findings the trial court awarded most of the stock to the wife. The Oregon Supreme Court reversed:

> In a long-term marriage in which the parties' properties were acquired during the marriage, the parties should separate on as equal a basis as possible. In *Jenks, . . .* we explained:

> "When couples enter marriage, they ordinarily commit themselves to an indefinite shared future of which shared finances are a part. Acquisitions are made, foregone or replaced for the good of the family unit rather than for the financial interests of either spouse. Property is bought, sold, enhanced, diminished, intermixed and used without regard to ease of division upon termination of the marriage. . . . [B]y the nature of the marital relationship, couples ordinarily pledge their troth for better or worse until death parts them and their financial affairs are conducted accordingly.

> "If the marriage is terminated before the parties' financial affairs become commingled or committed to the needs of children to the point that the parties cannot readily be restored to their premarital situations, then property division is a relatively simple task in the nature of a rescission. With each common financial act or decision, however, extrication upon dissolution becomes increasingly difficult. The origin of each item becomes less significant in making a property division which is 'just and proper in all the circumstances.' "

As to the wife's claim that she had performed the major share of the homemaking services, as well as contributing equally if not more to the marriage's finances, the court said:

> We do not find the ORS 107.105(1)(f) "homemaker" provision relevant to the facts of this case. The provision primarily was intended to recognize that "non-earning spouses who maintain the home, do the cooking and cleaning and raise the children, also contribute to the acquisition of property in a tangible way." The provision effectively places the homemaker-spouse's non-economic contributions on a par with the breadwinner-spouse's direct economic contribution to the acquisition of property.

> We find no legislative intent, however, that a spouse [who] works outside the home and, additionally, performs "homemaker" duties, should be able to rely upon the homemaker provision to establish that she or he contributed more than 50 percent to the acquisition of property.

8. *Are Homemaker Provisions Obsolete?* Although much of the discussion of marital property regimes assumes a homemaker wife, she is becoming uncommon. In 1940, only one of seven married women (with their husband present) was working outside the home or looking for work. By 1979, it was one of two. Hayghe, *Two-Income Families*, AMERICAN DEMOGRAPHICS 35–36 (Sept. 1981). Government data shows that in recent years the number of "traditional households" (in which the husband was the sole breadwinner) has hovered at slightly under 20%. *See* Ira Mark Ellman, *Divorce Rates, Marriage Rates, and the Problematic Persistence of Traditional Marital Roles*, 34 FAM. L.Q. 1, 21–22 (2000) (summarizing and discussing the data). It may therefore seem that modern marital property law should not assume a traditional family organization.

One writer, anticipating these developments, suggested that as women come to participate fully and equally in the workplace, separate property regimes would protect their interests more than community property, or reformed common law equitable distribution systems. Glendon, *Is There a Future for Separate Property?*, 8 FAM. L.Q. 315 (1974). But a closer look at the data reveals some important realities: many wives do not work full-time, and even most of those who do earn less than their husband. *E.g.*, Hayghe and Bianchi found that in 1992 only 43 percent of married mothers with children between ages 6 and 17 worked *full-time* for the whole year, and only 31 percent of married mothers with children under six did so. In short, about half the working mothers worked less than full time. This contrasts with the experience of married men, who are *more* likely to work, and to work full time, if they have children. The emergence of the "working wife" is thus not the same as the demise of the homemaker wife. As a factual matter, most working wives still base their employment decisions on the assumption that they bear the primary responsibility for household tasks and child rearing, and this constraint has been estimated to account for 70% of the difference in earnings between married men and women. Riche, *All About Working Women,* AM. DEMOGRAPHICS 6 (Oct. 1981). Even where both spouses work, they are unlikely to make career decisions on the same basis as if they were not married. Most couples are likely to pool their resources on the assumption, perhaps unspoken, that they are partners in a sharing relationship. Prager, *Sharing Principles and the Future of Marital Property Law,* 25 U.C.L.A. L. REV. 1, 7–11, 13 (1977). This reality argues strongly for "sharing principles" as a foundation of marital property regimes, on the simple premise that it would be unfair to allocate to one spouse all of the financial benefits of the preferred career. And as a matter of social policy, Prager said, we may wish to encourage "sharing principles" by our marital property law:

> A separate property system encourages each person to function as an earner by refusing to compensate a spouse who remains in the home for some significant period. [¶] But if many couples in fact make decisions with the special exigencies of the marital relationship in mind, a system of property law which assumes decisions ought to be made on an individual basis may produce two quite different ill effects. First, one spouse may ultimately be treated unfairly if the couple does not alter its behavior to conform to the individualistic orientation of the separate property model. Second, if behavior is indeed responsive to a legal structure which dictates putting oneself first, other social values will suffer. By dictating that a married person behave as if unmarried with respect to certain choices or suffer the consequences of subsequent property disadvantage for not doing so, the individually oriented model works to reward self-interested choices which can be detrimental to the continuation of the marriage. At the same time it

punishes conduct of accommodation and compromise so important to furthering and preserving the relationship. From a social engineering standpoint, an individualistic property system will begin to produce behavior that is at cross-purposes with other values, such as stability and cooperation in marital relationships.

Id. at 12.

9. *Marital Misconduct as a Factor in Equitable Distribution*. A full examination of whether marital misconduct should influence the financial terms of a divorce is deferred until Section G of this chapter. But note that even states that permit its consideration in alimony awards often allocate property on a no-fault basis. The Model Marriage and Divorce Act, provides in § 307 that property is allocated by the court "without regard to marital misconduct." Under the old common law there was little opportunity to consider marital misconduct in allocating property because property allocation involved no equitable judgment. Property was simply allocated to the spouse who held title to it. Before the no-fault revolution, some community property states did consider marital fault in allocating community property upon divorce. Equitable distribution came to the common law states at about the same time as no-fault divorce, and most followed the MMDA's lead. But fifteen states permit their courts broad authority to consider marital misconduct when allocating property at divorce: Alabama, Connecticut, Georgia, Maryland, Massachusetts, Michigan, Mississippi, Missouri, New Hampshire, North Dakota, Rhode Island, South Carolina, Texas, Vermont, and Wyoming. *ALI Principles*, at 43–49, 68, 77–82.

In these fifteen states misconduct claims are a wild card with unpredictable results that vary with the trial judge. As the *ALI Principles* explain:.

> The problem of creating standards by which to determine the dollar consequences of a fault finding is particularly intractable. Appellate decisions in fault states sometimes caution that fault is only one factor relevant to the allocation of property or granting of alimony, and should not be given disproportionate weight. *E.g., Sparks v. Sparks*, 485 N.W.2d 893 (Mich. 1992). But the meaning of such cautionary language is at best obscure. For example, in *Sparks* itself, the trial court had awarded the husband 75 percent of the marital property after finding that the wife's adultery was the principal cause of the marital failure. The Michigan Supreme Court held that the trial court had given the wife's fault disproportionate weight in this disposition, but was unable to state any rule [to] determine the proportionate weight to accord such misconduct. . . .

> In a number of fault states, appellate courts have attempted to establish rules that explain when findings of fault may appropriately affect the award, but such guidelines do not seem to create effective bounds on trial-court discretion. For example, Missouri opinions specify that "the conduct factor becomes important . . . when the conduct of one party to the marriage is such that it throws upon the other party marital burdens beyond the norms to be expected in the marital relationship." *Burtscher v. Burtscher*, 563 S.W.2d 526, 527 (Mo. App. 1978). Even in laying down this rule, the court observed that "it is

unnecessary and probably impossible to lay down any precise guidelines for the weight to be given to the conduct factor." So in *Burtscher* itself the appeals court declined to reverse the trial court's conclusion that husband's adultery was counterbalanced by his wife's insistence on playing bingo four nights a week over the husband's objection.

ALI Principles at 83. The *ALI Principles* themselves endorse a no-fault approach to property allocation. Early in the no-fault divorce era, the New Jersey Supreme Court explained its adoption of a no-fault rule with two salient observations:

> First of all, marriage is such an intricate relationship that often it is difficult, if not impossible, to ascertain upon whom the real responsibility for the marital breakup rests.[¶]. . .
>
>   . . .
>
> Second, equitable distribution is merely the recognition that each spouse contributes something to the marital estate. The concept of fault is not relevant to such distribution since all that is being effected is the allocation to each party of what really belongs to him or her.

Chalmers v. Chalmers, 320 A.2d 478 (N.J. 1974). Note *Chalmers'* emphasis on equitable distribution as simply allocating each spouse "what really belongs to him or her." Misconduct then seems less relevant in dividing property than it would if the process is instead framed as deciding whether equitable considerations require awarding one spouse property that belongs to the other. It is therefore not surprising that there is only one community property state among the fifteen that permit consideration of marital misconduct. It may also be true that the common law states most inclined to divide property equally upon divorce are also those least likely to consider marital misconduct.

New York occupies something of a middle ground between the fifteen states that consider fault and the majority that do not. Marital fault is excluded from consideration in equitable distribution except for "egregious cases that shock the conscience." *O'Brien v. O'Brien*, 66 N.Y.S.2d 576, 489 N.E.2d 712, 498 N.Y.S.2d 743, 750 (1985) (except for such extreme cases, misconduct is not a "just and proper" consideration as it is inconsistent with the premise of economic partnership). It appears that only serious felonies meet this standard. "[V]erbal harassment, threats and several acts of minor domestic violence" is not egregious misconduct, *Kellerman v. Kellerman*, 187 A.D.2d 906, 590 N.Y.S.2d 570, 571 (1992), nor is the husband's refusal to have children in violation of an explicit promise, *McCann v. McCann*, 156 Misc. 2d 540, 593 N.Y.S.2d 917 (Sup. 1993) (discussing the rule at length), nor the combination of the wife's open adultery, physical abuse (scratching, biting, and pulling hair of husband), verbal abuse (repeatedly berating him in front of coworkers and friends), and wounding of her husband with a knife while breaking into his locked briefcase, *Stevens v. Stevens*, 107 A.D.2d 987, 484 N.Y.S.2d 708 (1985), nor necessarily the husband's verbal and physical abuse of wife, which may not be sufficiently extreme or outrageous to allow reduction in his share of marital property, *Orofino v. Orofino*, 215 A.D.2d 997, 627 N.Y.S.2d 460 (1995). Attempted murder is egregious misconduct, *Brancoveanu v. Brancoveanu*, 145 A.D.2d 395, 535 N.Y.S.2d 86 (1988) and *Wenzel v. Wenzel*,

122 Misc. 2d 1001, 472 N.Y.S.2d 830 (Sup. Ct. 1984); as is rape, *Thompson v. Thompson*, N.Y. L.J., Jan. 5, 1990, at 28 (rape of wife's daughter by husband-stepfather); and repeated physical abuse in which, over a 20-year period, the husband: slapped defendant's face weekly; broke her foot by stamping on it; broke her finger, leaving it permanently deformed; pushed her, causing a broken arm with a permanent 40 percent loss of use, and punched her so that she sustained dental damage requiring caps and root canal work. *Debeny v. Debeny*, N.Y. L.J., Jan. 24, 1991, at 29.

10. *Financial Misconduct*. All states permit the dissolution court to consider, in allocating marital property, misconduct directly affecting the amount or value of the property available for allocation. Even a pure no-fault system committed to equal division of community property must take account of misconduct by one spouse that would deprive the other of a true half-share. In many states the rule often is statutory, though the statutes are of varying formulation. *E.g.*, ARIZ. REV. STAT. ANN. § 25-318(A) (West 2000 & Supp. 2002) (court may consider, in allocating property, a spouse's "abnormal expenditures, destruction, concealment or fraudulent disposition" of assets); CAL. FAM. CODE § 2602 (West 1994 & Supp. 2003) (court may deduct from a spouse's share of the community property an "amount the court determines to have been deliberately misappropriated by the party to the exclusion of the interest of the other party in the community estate"); KAN. STAT. ANN. § 60-1610(b)(1) (Supp. 2002) (court may consider a spouse's "dissipation" of assets).

Excluding claims of marital misconduct is not inconsistent with allowing claims of financial misconduct, as analogy to a business partnership's dissolution makes clear. A court allocating a dissolving partnership's assets among the business partners may consider a claim that one partner fraudulently conveyed partnership assets to a confederate and has therefore already realized much or all of his share. But it would be inappropriate for the court to consider one partner's claim that another's nasty conduct caused the complainant great emotional distress or that another partner had committed a battery. Resolution of a fraudulent conveyance claim is necessarily part of any complete accounting of the dissolving partnership's assets, while the battery or emotional distress claim is a collateral matter to be decided under tort law. Note too that the intractable problem of establishing standards by which to gauge the financial value of a marital misconduct claim does not arise in most cases of financial misconduct.

But the term "financial misconduct" is sufficiently broad and vague to raise some difficult questions. Consider the rule of Kansas and others allowing the court dividing marital property to consider a spouse's "dissipation" of marital assets. As the *ALI Principles* observe, "[w]hile the term ['dissipation'] communicates the conclusion that a particular use of the assets was improper, it provides no criteria for distinguishing improper uses from the many unfortunate but lawful ways in which funds may be lost, including poor judgment." § 4.10, Comment *a*.

Gambling losses are frequently held to constitute dissipation, but not investment losses, even where the investment was of high risk — at least if it was not inconsistent with the general investment pattern within the marriage. *Compare Harrison v. Harrison*, 787 S.W.2d 738 (Mo. App. 1989) (dissipation found where wife surreptitiously took funds from joint account and lost them in 12-hour gambling spree) *and Booth v. Booth*, 371 S.E.2d 569 (Va. App. 1988) (wife "wasted" $60,000 lost in a speculative stock market investment) *with Hauge v. Hauge*, 427 N.W.2d 154 (Wis. App. 1988) (investment in Arabian horses not dissipation) *and Marriage of Drummond*, 509 N.E.2d 707 (Ill. App. 1987) (commodities trading not dissipation where husband had experience with it).

What if a spouse's gambling losses are part of the long-term marital pattern? Can a spouse who has apparently tolerated them — perhaps even participating at times in the gambling activities — suddenly disavow the losses at dissolution? In *Marriage of Williams*, 927 P.2d 679 (Wash. App. 1996), the court concluded that the wife's $12,000 gambling losses were not dissipation because her gambling activities were legal under state law and were essentially entertainment costs indistinguishable from other expenditures on entertainment that either spouse might make. The court noted that her husband was aware of the wife's gambling activities. The court presumably felt that his failure to object, or at least the willingness to continue the marriage despite the objectionable behavior, suggests that he accepted this behavior as part of an overall marital arrangement. Having done so, the spouse cannot later disfavor just those parts of the marital relationship he or she did not like. Note that this principle would not apply to alleged acts of dissipation that occurred once the marital relationship had effectively ended. In apparent reliance on such reasoning, some courts limit dissipation claims to losses that occurred in the "waning days" of the marriage, or after its "breakdown." *Siegel v. Siegel*, 574 A.2d 54 (N.J. Super. Ct. Ch. Div. 1990) (husband's gambling losses of $227,000 treated as dissipation where incurred after marriage was "irreparably fractured"). This restriction has been held crucial to prevent spouses from using the dissolution action to question every spending decision made during the marriage and thereby requiring courts to "become auditing agencies for every marriage that falters." *In re Marriage of Getautas*, 544 N.E.2d 1284, 1288 (Ill. App. 1989). *See also Panhorst v. Panhorst*, 390 S.E.2d 376, 379 (S.C. App. 1990) ("One spouse . . . may have spent marital funds foolishly or selfishly or may have invested them unprofitably. The statute wisely prevents the other spouse from resurrecting these transactions at the end of the marriage to gain an advantage in the equitable distribution.")

While there is a certain logic to this approach, the experience of Illinois, a principal proponent of it, suggests that the uncertainty of a test framed in terms of whether the dissipation occurred after the marital breakdown may invite litigation. *See, e.g., Marriage of Harding*, 545 N.E.2d 459, 467 (Ill. App. 1989) (appellate court reverses finding that breakdown occurred, for purpose of judging validity of dissipation claim, when wife stopped cooking for husband; "no evidence of an irreconcilable breakdown of the marriage until the point at which petitioner filed for dissolution. . . ."). An alternative to the breakdown standard that still attempts to vindicate the logic of the approach is to employ a more objective indicator of the marital termination, such as the parties' separation. *See, e.g.*, N.C. GEN. STAT. § 50-20(b)(1) (Lexis 2003), allowing the court to consider, in making an equitable distribution, "[a]cts of either party to . . . waste, neglect, devalue or convert such marital property, during the period after separation of the parties and before the time of distribution." But fixing the time of separation may also be subject to dispute. Thus, *ALI Principles* § 4.10 takes this approach a step further, limiting most dissipation claims to a fixed period of time prior to service of the dissolution petition.

Note too that while the line between financial misconduct and marital misconduct is real, it is also permeable. Gifts to paramours are a frequent fact pattern in dissipation claims, *e.g.*, *Marriage of Charles*, 672 N.E.2d 57 (Ill. App. 1996) (trial court reversed for failing to consider whether husband's purchase of house and furniture for his mistress after parties' separation was dissipation); *Zeigler v. Zeigler*, 530 A.2d 445 (Pa. Super. 1987) (reimbursement ordered where husband used marital funds toward down-payment on home titled in girlfriend's name), as are expenditures on adulterous relationships, *e.g.*, *Noll v. Noll*, 375 S.E.2d 338 (S.C. App. 1988) (reimbursement required where wife spent $2,000 of joint funds on cruise with boyfriend). Judicial willingness to treat such expenditures as dissipation is undoubtedly influenced by disapproval of the financed conduct. But note as well that a dissipation claim is necessarily limited to recovering the lost marital funds, so that its contours are far more well-defined than a general claim in a true fault system for an enlarged property award as compensation for the other spouse's adultery.

PROBLEMS

Problem 4-2. Alice and Jerry marry in 1992. During the marriage, Alice attends schools, pursues hobbies and keeps house, while Jerry works for a computer software company. In the evenings, Jerry works at home designing computer programs, and in 1994 he comes up with a new program which he markets himself through Softsell, a company he creates for this purpose. Jerry is the sole proprietor of Softsell, which he started with savings accumulated since 1992. The program is an immense success, and by 1995, Softsell is worth $2 million. In 1996, it is worth $10 million. Also in 1996, Alice files for divorce, complaining Jerry is spending too much time with the computer and not enough with her. Alice has never been interested in computers and has never participated in Softsell in any way. How would the Softsell Company be treated on divorce, in community property and common law equitable distribution states?

a) Would it matter if during the pending divorce proceedings, Alice inherited $1 million when her father passed away? Should it?

b) Suppose Alice, miffed that Jerry is spending many evenings working on the computer rather than spending time with her, begins seeing other men. Unbeknownst to Jerry, by the end of 1994, she has a regular boyfriend named Vincent. Unfortunately, Vincent is an aspiring painter of questionable talent who cannot provide Alice with many material goods. By 1996, however, Alice decides she can no longer put up with Jerry's nerdish ways and commences divorce proceedings. She assures Vincent that with her share of Softsell (which she has found out is now worth $10 million), they will both be able to live comfortably while Vincent paints. Is she right? Should she be?

c) Would it matter whether the capital Jerry put into Softsell came from a gift from his mother, rather than savings accumulated during the marriage? Should it?

Problem 4-3. During their 12-year marriage, H and W attended jai-alai matches every Saturday, at which H placed regular bets. At the dissolution of the marriage, W seeks to have her share of the marital property augmented to reflect the losses from those bets. W alleges that she did not participate in the betting and objected to H's gambling. H alleges that W enjoyed the gambling and shared eagerly in the winnings. Is it necessary to resolve their factual dispute to decide this case? What is the appropriate resolution?

§ B.   PROPERTY DIVISION: PROBLEMS IN CLASSIFYING PROPERTY AS MARITAL OR SEPARATE

[1]   THE BASICS

ALI PRINCIPLES § 4.03 DEFINITION OF MARITAL AND SEPARATE PROPERTY (2002)

(1) Property acquired during marriage is marital property, except as otherwise expressly provided in this Chapter.

(2) Inheritances, including bequests and devises, and gifts from third parties, are the separate property of the acquiring spouse even if acquired during marriage.

(3) Property received in exchange for separate property is separate property even if acquired during marriage.

(4) Property acquired during marriage but after the parties have commenced living apart pursuant to either a written separation agreement or a judicial decree, is the separate property of the acquiring spouse unless the agreement or decree specifies otherwise.

(5) For the purpose of this section "during marriage" means after the commencement of marriage and before the filing and service of a petition for dissolution (if that petition ultimately results in a decree dissolving the marriage), unless there are facts, set forth in written findings of the trial court . . ., establishing that use of another date is necessary to avoid a substantial injustice.

The old Model Marriage and Divorce Act (MMDA) recommended that common law states adopt a version of equitable distribution that authorized courts to allocate all the spouses' property, rather than limiting the allocation to marital property. MMDA § 307. This has been called the "hotchpot" system. Most common law states did not follow the MMDA, however. They instead adopted a system in which the divorce court has equitable authority to distribute only marital property. One recent tabulation found 16 common law property states and one community property state (Washington) which allow the distribution of both marital and separate property. JOHN DEWITT GREGORY, JANET LEACH RICHARDS & SHERYL WOLF, PROPERTY DIVISION IN DIVORCE PROCEEDINGS: A FIFTY STATE GUIDE § 2.02 n.3 (2003). This count may be controversially high; at the least, one must consider nuances in the application of the rules that could make the "hotchpot" designation at least partly misleading. *See ALI Principles*, § 4.03, Reporters Notes, Comment *a*. Many cases in the purported hotchpot states show the court in fact *not* ignoring the distinction between marital and separate property, finding "the fact that property subject to distribution was acquired by one of the parties prior to the marriage is a consideration weighing in favor of that party," *Fraase v. Fraase*, 315 N.W.2d 271, 274 (N.D. 1982), and that inherited property should ordinarily go to the spouse who inherited it, *Bonelli v. Bonelli*, 576 A.2d 587 (Conn. App. 1990); *see also* J. Thomas Oldham, *Tracing, Commingling, and Transmutation*, 23 FAM. L.Q. 219, 220 n.5 (1989); Robert J. Levy, *An Introduction to Divorce Property Issues*, 23 FAM. L.Q. 147, 151–56 (1989); Mary Ann Glendon, *Family Law Reform in the 1980's*, 44 LA. L. REV. 1553, 1556 (1984) (no consensus supports "a view of marriage in itself as engaging all one's property no matter when or how acquired.").

In short, there are few true hotchpot systems, in which no distinction is made between marital and separate property. The real question is whether the distinction is to be drawn by the application of property classification rules or through the exercise of trial court discretion in allocating property from the hotchpot. Examination of appellate cases in hotchpot states suggests that they are most likely to give one spouse a share of the other's "separate" property (as other states would call it) when the dissolved marriage was long-term and the spouses' financial capacity would otherwise be very disparate. *See, e.g., Zeh v. Zeh*, 618 N.E.2d 1376 (Mass. App. 1993) (at dissolution of 24-year marriage, trial court required to include within the hotchpot the husband's $420,000 inheritance, which dwarfed the parties' other assets); *Steele v. Steele*, 759 P.2d 304 (Or. App. 1988) (wife's inherited property should be divided equally with husband at dissolution of 57-year marriage); *Taylor v. Taylor*, 856 P.2d 325 (Or. App. 1993) (wife allocated one-third of H's inheritance at dissolution of 18-year marriage); *Becker and Becker*, 858 P.2d 480 (Or. App. 1993) (wife must pay out to husband $2 million of her trust assets at the dissolution of their 27-year marriage, where parties had used the trust income to supplement the husband's income during marriage, and had not saved for retirement upon the assumption that his pension and her trust assets would be adequate to ensure their financial security); *In re Debord*, 770 P.2d 81 (Or. App. 1989) (usual equal division presumption does not apply in short-term marriages, largely to avoid recognizing a claim in such marriages on the other spouse's "separate" property). Much the same approach, working from the other end, is achieved by some states that usually distinguish between marital and separate property. *See, e.g.*, MINN. STAT. 518.58 (2002) (if the court finds that the division of marital property alone would "work an unfair hardship," up to one half of the separate property may be apportioned). The *ALI Principles* reflect these authorities, albeit in less discretionary form, by adopting the distinction between marital and separate property, but also providing that a very gradually increasing share of each spouse's separate property is recharacterized as marital property as their marriage lengthens, if the parties have not taken steps to provide otherwise. *ALI Principles*, § 4.18.

NOTES

1. *When Does the Marital Community Begin and End?* While the marriage ceremony provides a convenient bright line for the beginning of the marriage, difficulties arise where the parties acquire some significant asset during a period of nonmarital cohabitation preceding marriage. While the acquisition is clearly not "during the marriage" in the literal sense, some courts permit the inclusion of such assets in the marital estate. *E.g., Marriage of Dubnicay*, 830 P.2d 608 (Or. App. 1992) (relying in part on the fact that parties commingled their assets during this period); *Northrop v. Northrop*, 622 N.W.2d 219 (N.D. 2001) (in the context of a case involving the division of a pension earned partly during the seven-year cohabitation that preceded a marriage of less than two years, the court reaffirms that courts may consider premarital cohabitation). Other courts allow separate actions to enforce claims based on premarital cohabitation, following *Marvin v. Marvin*, 18 Cal. 3d 660, 557 P.2d 106, 134 Cal. Rptr. 815 (1976) (*see* Chapter 9), but reject claims that such cohabitation should affect the division of marital property. *Rolle v. Rolle*, 530 A.2d 847 (N.J. Super. Ch. Div. 1987); *Marriage of Leversee*, 156 Cal. App. 3d 891, 203 Cal. Rptr. 481 (1984). A third group not only hold the premarital cohabitation period irrelevant to the division of marital property but also reject any *Marvin* claims based upon it, either because the court rejects *Marvin* in general, *Marriage of Crouch*, 410 N.E.2d 580 (Ill. App. 1980), or rejects its application in this context, *Mangone v. Mangone*, 495 A.2d 469, 471 (N.J. Super. Ch. Div. 1985) (property acquired during premarital cohabitation not subject to equitable distribution, and any contract rights that wife may once have had arising from the cohabitation "merged into the greater contract of marriage"); *see also Stoner v. Stoner*, 2001 Tenn. App. Lexis 30 (Jan. 18, 2001) (refusing to treat as marital property husband's stock accounts accumulated during cohabitation of nearly 20 years that preceded the short-lived marriage).

Several possibilities exist for the termination of (the creation of) marital or community property. Some jurisdictions choose the date upon which the divorce petition is filed, which might be called the "petition rule." *See, e.g., Painter v. Painter*, 320 A.2d 484 (N.J. 1974). The *ALI Principles*, § 4.03(5), endorses the petition rule as the presumptive termination date, but allows the court to substitute a different date in order to avoid a substantial injustice. Such a case might arise, for example, if the parties move to separate cities and commence leading entirely separate lives years before either seeks a legal termination of their marriage.

Another group of states choose the date of the final divorce decree, holding that all earnings and acquisitions prior to that moment to be "during the marriage." *Friedman v. Friedman*, 384 S.E.2d 641 (Ga. 1989); *Alston v. Alston*, 629 A.2d 70 (Md. 1993); *Giha v. Giha*, 609 A.2d 945 (R.I. 1992) ($2.4 million lottery prize is marital property when won six months after entry of the interlocutory divorce decree but before entry of final decree). This "decree rule" often gives bargaining leverage to the lower-earning spouse, who may gain by imposing strategic delays in settlement of the divorce action, because these delays permit her to continue sharing in the other spouse's accumulations of property, including, for example, pension benefits. Ohio follows the decree rule, but like the *ALI Principles* allows the court to depart from it in exceptional cases to avoid injustice. OHIO REV. CODE ANN. § 3105.171(A)(2)(b) (Anderson 2003).

California uses a third rule, under which spousal earnings acquired while the spouses live "separate and apart" are separate property, CAL. FAM. CODE § 771(a) (West 1994 & Supp. 2003). The case by case determinations that this rule requires — asking in each case just when the parties separated — would seem a likely source of difficulty, particularly as couples often go through one or more physical separations over several years before deciding definitely to end their marriage. California, however, has applied the rule so strictly, requiring a "complete and final break," *Marriage of Von Der Nuell*, 23 Cal. App. 4th 730, 28 Cal. Rptr. 2d 447 (1994), that the time of separation would not often be much before the time of the petition. *See also Marriage of Hardin*, 38 Cal. App. 4th 448, 45 Cal. Rptr. 2d 308 (1995). For discussion of the inherent problems in applying the California rule, see Carol S. Bruch, *The Legal Import of Informal Separations: A Survey of California Law and a Call for Change*, 65 CAL. L. REV. 1015, 1021–24 (1977). Washington is the only other community property state following the California rule, WASH. REV. CODE § 26.16.140 (West 1997 & Supp. 2003). Under a fourth approach, there is no rule at all, but instead the matter is within trial court discretion. This is the Alaska approach. *Schanck v. Schanck*, 717 P.2d 1, 3 (Alaska 1986) (each "case must be judged on its facts to determine when the marriage has terminated as a joint enterprise").

2. As of What Date Is Marital Property Valued? Note 1 discusses the alternative rules for determining the "closing date" of the marital community. The "valuation date" is a separate question. Assume marital acquisitions cease as of January 1, when the divorce petition is filed, and that the court actually divides the property on the following July 1, when it formulates its decree. At that later time it must assess the value of the various assets in order to make an equitable or equal distribution. But the value as of which date: January 1, July 1, or something in between? *See ALI Principles*, § 4.03, Comment *f*:

> As a general matter a court should always use the most recent valuation date practical, even though marital property acquisitions cease on an earlier date. Use of the most recent date helps ensure that the parties are affected equally by market fluctuations, during the pendency of a divorce proceeding, in the value of their marital property. A different rule is appropriate, however, where the value of marital property is altered by the labor of either spouse after the cut-off date for marital acquisitions.

See Quinn v. Quinn, 575 A.2d 764 (Md. App. 1990) (trial court erroneously failed to consider whether husband's post-separation labor increased the value of marital property).

[2] SOME SPECIAL PROBLEMS

While state statutes or judicial decisions may set bright lines for determining when a marriage has begun and ended for the purpose of determining which property is subject to division at divorce, there are recurrent complicating issues that arise in situations when efforts during the period of the marriage lead to property acquired after — sometimes, long after — the end of the marriage. While this section explores general principles for such property, one important sub-category, pensions, will be covered separately in the next section.

NIROO v. NIROO

545 A.2d 35 (Md. 1988)

MURPHY, Chief Judge. The question . . . is whether anticipated renewal commissions on insurance policies sold by a spouse during marriage but accruing after dissolution of the marriage are "marital property" [under state law which] defines "marital property" as

> "property, however titled, acquired by 1 or both parties during the marriage.
>
> (2) 'Marital property' does not include property:
>
> (i) acquired before the marriage;
>
> (ii) acquired by inheritance or gift from a third party;
>
> (iii) excluded by valid agreement; or
>
> (iv) directly traceable to any of these sources."

I

The appellant, David Niroo (the husband) . . . challenges the determination of the trial judge that future renewal commissions accruing on insurance policies sold by him or his agents during the marriage were marital property.

The couple was married in 1977. In 1978, the husband began work as an insurance salesman for Pennsylvania Life Insurance Company (Penn Life) [and] received commissions on individual policies sold. In 1980, he became a branch manager and entered into agency manager agreements with Penn Life. . . . Under these agreements, the husband shared in the profits (and the losses) of the company as determined by specific "office codes," or blocks of insurance, assigned to agents under him and for whom he was responsible. The husband was entitled under the agreements to receive income derived from net profits generated if and when insurance policies coming under his office codes were renewed, provided that certain conditions . . . were satisfied [including,] inter alia, a covenant not to compete, an exclusivity clause, and a required renewal volume. . . .

At trial, both parties presented expert testimony as to the present day [sic] value of these renewal commissions after expenses were deducted, i.e., what the husband could expect to receive from the renewal policies. This valuation was based on industry "persistency rates," explained by the husband's expert witness as "the portion of the premiums that are in force in one year that renew and hence are paid and are still in force in the following year." This expert included only those renewal commission profits on policies sold during the marriage.

The trial judge determined that the husband's interest in the renewal income constituted marital property. He . . . found the present discounted profit value of the renewal commissions to be $410,000. The court also took into account various "advances" made to the husband by the insurance companies which were chargeable against renewal commissions. Under the agreements, these advances were considered as loans, repayable on demand. At the time of trial, the husband was indebted to the companies in the amount of $267,000. . . . [T]he trial judge determined that although the renewal income was marital property, the husband's $267,000 debt was not marital debt, but instead was to be taken into account as an "economic circumstance." The court arrived at a final monetary award of $200,000; in doing so, it considered various statutory factors, including the economic circumstances of the parties.

The husband appealed. We granted certiorari . . . .

II

In 1978 . . . the General Assembly enacted the Property Disposition in Divorce and Annulment Act, which significantly changed traditional notions as to property rights between spouses upon dissolution. . . . Enacted to remedy the inequities inherent under the previous system of allowing the property to remain with whichever spouse held title to it during the marriage, the Act . . . does not authorize the court to transfer title, nor require that all property be evenly divided, [but] does allow . . . a monetary adjustment to more fairly and equitably allocate the various property interests between the divorcing spouses. . . .

[T]he statute imposes a three-step process whereby the trial judge first determines what property is marital property . . .; then assigns a value to it . . .; and thereafter may grant a monetary award to whichever spouse would not otherwise receive his or her fair share of the marital assets. . . . In determining the proper amount and method of payment of this award, the court must consider the following factors provided under [the statute]:

"(1) the contributions, monetary and nonmonetary, of each party to the well-being of the family;

(2) the value of all property interests of each party;

(3) the economic circumstances of each party at the time the award is to be made;

(4) the circumstances that contributed to the estrangement of the parties;

(5) the duration of the marriage;

(6) the age of each party;

(7) the physical and mental condition of each party;

(8) how and when specific marital property was acquired, including the effort expended by each party in accumulating the marital property;

(9) any award of alimony and any award or other provision that the court has made with respect to family use personal property or the family home; and

(10) any other factor that the court considers necessary or appropriate to consider in order to arrive at a fair and equitable monetary award."

III

The husband. . . . asserts that due to the speculative and contingent nature of [the renewal] commissions, they are not within the definition of marital property [under] § 8-201(e). Furthermore, he argues that as it is necessary for him to "work" and nurture these accounts through activities performed after the marriage was dissolved, the income thereby derived is not "acquired" during the marriage. Thus, he contends, classification of renewal commissions as marital property would improperly give his former wife the fruits of his future efforts and would penalize him if the renewal commissions were not actually realized.

. . . [W]e have repeatedly noted that the meaning of property within the statutory definition of "marital property" . . . " 'embraces everything which has exchangeable value or goes to make up a man's wealth — every interest or estate which the law regards of sufficient value for judicial recognition.' " [¶] Under this broad concept . . . we have found that marital property includes: that portion of a husband's workers' compensation award for permanent partial disability which compensated for wages lost during the marriage; pension rights accumulated during the marriage; and a work-related contributory disability pension plan. On the other hand, we have found the following interests not includable as marital property: an inchoate personal injury claim arising from an accident occurring during the marriage, and a medical degree or license.

[We have] found that the right to pension benefits accumulated during marriage was a contractual right and therefore enforceable as a property right rather than as a mere conditional expectation. [W]e said that the proper analysis . . . was, first, to decide whether the property right was acquired during the marriage and secondly, whether it is equitable to include it as marital property, without regard to whether the right is vested or not. Moreover, we noted that the fact that the right to the pension benefit may be contingent upon continued employment did not matter, as such contingent future interests constituted property. Finally, it was clear that both spouses were relying on the pension benefits to provide for their future, so that an equitable distribution of the benefits was indeed proper. [¶] [We have also found the portion of any worker's compensation award] which compensated for the loss of earning capacity during the marriage was marital property, while his loss of future earning capacity arising after dissolution of the marriage was not marital property, [and that] a personal injury claim arising from an injury which occurred while the injured spouse was married was so uniquely personal that it could not be considered marital property "acquired" during the marriage, as required by the statute. . . .[¶]

When analyzed under the principles set forth in our cases, we think it clear that contractually vested rights in renewal commissions are . . . marital property. . . . [A]n insurance agent has a vested right in commissions on renewal premiums when provided for by contract. . . . This contractual right was clearly established in the husband's agency contract [and] cannot be terminated unilaterally by the company, but instead would require an affirmative surrender by the agent to forfeit the future commissions due. [T]he agency contract provided that should the husband die or become disabled, his right to receive the renewal commissions, as well as his heirs' right thereto, would not be affected. [The agency contract also made] the husband's right to the renewal commission . . . assignable with the prior written consent of the company . . . [T]he husband's right amounts to more than a "mere expectancy," or a "mere historical possibility of gain" as he alternatively characterizes it.

The husband claims that after the dissolution . . ., he must continue to "service" his accounts after their initial procurement if he is to realize the renewal commissions. He thereby seeks to distinguish his situation from that involving pension benefits. We are not persuaded by his argument. The husband's primary effort was expended in acquiring the original policies. Evidence at trial showed that on a national average, 72% of the existing policies will be automatically renewed after the first year; 82% will be renewed after the second year; and 88% will be renewed thereafter. The husband nevertheless maintains that he must satisfy certain conditions not present with pension benefits, thus rendering his right to the commissions only a tenuous property interest. Specifically, he refers to the covenant in the agency agreements not to compete and to certain requirements as to renewal volume, the violation or nonattainment of which could result in forfeiture or diminishment of his commissions. He also asserts that uncertainties inherent in renewals, such as customer preferences, economic conditions, and agency turnover, render the renewal commissions too speculative for valuation. While we recognize these concerns, we do not find these conditions so onerous, and the contingencies so uncertain, as to make the contractual right to renewal commissions beyond valuation, particularly when the insurance industry itself assigns a value to them based on statistical persistency rates.

Courts in other jurisdictions have reached like conclusions. . . .

These cases support the view that the claim to renewal commissions is not the type of right that is uniquely personal to the holder, as in a personal injury claim or a professional degree. Instead, it is . . . part of the compensation package developed during the marriage by one of the spouses that each could have justifiably relied upon to provide for their economic future. [I]t is a . . . valuable asset not separable from the original policies sold during the marriage, and thus properly a part of the couple's shared assets during marriage. This determination, we think, is consistent with the declared policy of the Marital Property Act, . . ., "that marriage is a union between a man and a woman having equal rights under the law." Plainly, this policy recognizes the nonmonetary contributions made by the wife in this case in accumulating the assets. . . .

IV.

The husband next argues that the advances received by him as a loan from Penn Life should have reduced the present value of the future commissions in valuing marital property. [T]he husband asserts that he borrowed the money against the profits from the anticipated renewal commissions to finance his agency operation; and that the debt therefore was an encumbrance upon the renewal income to be paid to him in the future. The wife . . . argues that the husband did not use the advances for the purpose of acquiring renewal commissions but rather for family expenses, including high personal expenditures of his own to support a lavish life style. The wife suggests that the husband's annual income, particularly in the later years of his agency business, was sufficiently high that no need existed to borrow money from Penn Life to meet the expenses of his branch manager operation.

The trial judge [found] that the loans . . . were used for family living expenses and that a sufficient nexus had not been established between the debt and the renewal income for it to be considered marital debt. . . . The trial judge considered the debt . . . a nonmarital "economic circumstance" of the husband under § 8-205(a)(3), to be taken into account in determining the amount and the method of payment of the monetary award to the wife. In doing so, the court recognized that no renewal commissions may have been available had the advances not been taken by the husband; nevertheless, it found that "the real use of those monies was not to purchase renewal commissions" but was for family living expenses.

On the record before us, we think the trial judge was wrong. In *Schweizer v. Schweizer*, 301 Md. 626, 484 A.2d 627 (1984), we said:

> "[A] 'marital debt' is a debt which is directly traceable to the acquisition of marital property. Conversely, 'nonmarital debt' is a debt which is not directly traceable to the acquisition of marital property. That part of marital property which is represented by an outstanding marital debt has not been 'acquired' for the purpose of an equitable distribution by way of a monetary award. Therefore, the value of that marital property is adjusted downward by the amount of the marital debt."

In considering the legal effect . . . of the advances drawn by the husband against future commissions, the trial judge seemingly applied the second sentence quoted above without regard to the context in which that sentence was written.

Schweizer presented the question . . . of whether debt incurred by the husband during the marriage which was not secured by marital property could be used to reduce the value of unencumbered marital property. Because none of the husband's debt was secured by marital property, the wife submitted that the husband's total debt was . . . only . . . an economic circumstance [the court could consider] . . . when [it set] the amount of any monetary award. The husband in *Schweizer*, on the other hand, contended that all of his liabilities should be deducted from marital property, . . . which under the facts in *Schweizer* would have resulted in a negative valuation of marital property.

We rejected both contentions. The wife's contention was too narrow and the husband's contention was too broad. [W]e said that a debt which could be traced to the acquisition of marital property reduced the value of the marital property and that a debt which could not be so traced did not reduce the value of marital property. We remanded for the trial court to determine what portion, if any, of the husband's indebtedness was "marital debt."

Nothing . . . in *Schweizer* contradicted that part of the wife's contention which recognized that encumbrances on marital property reduce its value. In effect, the value of encumbered marital property is ordinarily the value of its equity. . . .

In the instant matter the advances drawn by Mr. Niroo against future insurance commissions are repayable on demand. If called, the debt can be set off by Penn Life against future commissions. The debt, in economic effect, is an encumbrance on the future commissions which reduces their present value. The trial judge therefore erred in not subtracting the debt of $267,000 from the value of the renewal income.

. . .

JUDGMENT AFFIRMED IN PART AND REVERSED IN PART; CASE REMANDED . . . FOR FURTHER PROCEEDINGS CONSISTENT WITH THIS OPINION.

NOTES

1. Niroo *as Exemplifying the Maturing Marital Property System.*
Common law courts asked to resolve the more difficult questions of marital property law find a plentiful selection of relevant precedent in the community property states, and many seem more willing than they were years ago to take guidance from the community property states' greater experience with what are now essentially identical property classification issues. That is not to say that no differences remain between the two systems. Note, for example, that the Maryland law applied in *Niroo* does not permit the court to transfer title to property, but only to make a monetary judgment. Title thus retains a significance in Maryland, and in some other common law states, that it does not have under community property regimes.

Niroo touches on many different issues in its discussion, including the treatment of pensions, personal injury claims, degrees, and debts, and the husband's claim that some portion of the property in question derives its value from post-dissolution labor. We return to the question of degrees, and of the treatment of spousal labor as property, in Section C of this chapter, which addresses a number of issues that intersect both property and alimony concepts. We explore the other issues now in the following notes.

2. *The Case of Deferred Compensation: In General.* The applicable principle is simple to state: income earned during the marriage is classified as marital property even though its receipt is deferred until after divorce. The renewal commissions at issue in *Niroo* are treated as marital property because they were earned during the marriage. This is the usual result. *See Marriage of Skaden*, 19 Cal. 3d 679, 139 Cal. Rptr. 615, 566 P.2d 249 (1977); *Marriage of Wade*, 923 S.W.2d 735 (Tex. App. 1996); *Bigbie v. Bigbie*, 898 P.2d 1271 (Okla. 1995) (relying on *Niroo*); *but see Lawyer v. Lawyer*, 702 S.W.2d 790 (Ark. 1986) (possible future termination payments, used to compensate for lost commissions, too speculative to be marital property). Pensions are the most prominent example of this principle's application, involved in a high percentage of divorces, and the special complications they raise are treated in a separate section beginning at p. 316, *infra*. Royalties paid out after divorce on work completed during marriage is another example. *E.g.*, *Heinze v. Heinze*, 631 N.E.2d 728 (Ill. App. 1994) (books); *Marriage of Worth*, 195 Cal. App. 3d 768, 241 Cal. Rptr. 135 (1987) (books as one type of artistic work); *Dunn v. Dunn*, 802 P.2d 1314 (Utah App. 1990) (royalties from invention of surgical instrument). Accounts receivable — as-yet-unpaid invoices owed to either spouse at divorce, for work that spouse performed during the marriage — are another common example. But while the principle is clear, its application to particular cases can raise knotty problems.

a. *Allocation issues*. Questions sometimes arise as to whether a particular post-dissolution income stream is the product of marital labor or of post-divorce labor. Mr. Niroo claimed, for example, that the renewal commissions were the result, at least in part, of his labors in servicing the renewing accounts — labors that would continue after divorce, along with the commissions. The claim is at least plausible. Clients of Mr. Niroo's whose business was sought by competing agents might be tempted to switch — and thus cancel their policies with him — if they believed he was not responding adequately to their requests. The commission penalty he would incur if his renewals fell below specified percentages would seem aimed at providing him with additional incentives to maintain good relationships with his clients so as to encourage their renewals, suggesting that the insurance company itself agrees that renewals depend, at least to some extent, on the agent's continuing efforts.

The court nonetheless rejects Mr. Niroo's claim with two observations. It first says that over 70 percent of policies are renewed. This observation is a non-sequitur. The fact that most people renew does not suggest that agents are not working to make sure of that result. More important is the court's second point, that "the husband's primary effort was expended in acquiring the original policies." The question is what to do with that plausible factual conclusion. One could theoretically allocate the income between marital and separate property components in proportion to one's estimate of the relative contributions that the pre-and post-divorce labor provide towards acquiring it. That estimate might be difficult to devise, both in principle (how does one measure the relative contribution? are hours an adequate measure, or are some hours more crucial than others?) and in fact (how accurately can one forecast the future labor required to maintain the accounts?). Perhaps because of these practical difficulties, many courts do not attempt such allocations, remaining content to treat as marital property any income attributable primarily to marital labor. *See, e.g.*, *Skaden*, *supra* (rejecting husband's claim that a portion of his agent's "termination payments," based primarily on renewal commissions, should be treated as separate property because attributable to his post-dissolution labor). This practice can work in both directions. Consider, for example, a major league baseball player who performs superbly during the 2003 season, and then goes on the free agent market in which he obtains a very lucrative contract for the next three seasons. He is divorced after signing the contract but before the 2004 season commences. Is any portion of the post-dissolution pay he will earn under this contract marital property? The conventional answer in such cases is no, yet surely much of the 2004 pay could be attributed to his labor during 2003. *See Chambers v. Chambers*, 840 P.2d 841 (Utah App. 1992) (wife's marital property claim on husband's post-divorce income under remaining three years of his five-year basketball contract with the Phoenix Suns rejected, because the income would derive from his post-marital labor, "rather than from some past effort or a product produced during the marriage").

Other courts do make such allocations, however. For example, one large and important group of cases in which courts routinely unravel the relative contributions of marital and nonmarital labor to post-marital payments are pension allocations, where the stakes are relatively high for a relatively large proportion of divorcing couples. It is also the case with pensions that extensive experience with the matter in many states has given rise to well-accepted methods for approximating, if not calculating, an appropriate allocation. (*See* Section B3, p. 316.) *See also Heinze, supra* (husband awarded only 25% of royalties received after marriage on books wife wrote during marriage because future book sales were attributable in part to wife's post-marital promotional labors); *Dunn, supra* (value of time spent by husband after dissolution in generating royalty income deducted from wife's otherwise equal share in royalties).

b. *Estimating future income flows*. How could *Niroo* award the wife a share in the renewal commissions the husband would receive in the future when he had not received them? This problem will arise, of course, in any award of marital income to be realized in the future. Where the future compensation, or its amount, is uncertain, a court, generally, has three options: it can set now the shares each spouse will obtain if and when there are such payments; it can reserve jurisdiction to make an appropriate order when the payments are actually received or their amount established with relative certainty; and it can make an immediate lump sum payment, as occurred in *Niroo*.

In order to make an immediate lump sum distribution to the wife, the *Niroo* court had to fix a value for the future income. It relied upon expert witnesses who estimated the future income, based upon industry data on the average renewal rate, and then calculated a present value for this estimated future income flow. *See also Quinn v. Quinn*, 575 A.2d 764 (Md. App. 1990) (urging division at divorce, despite the valuation difficulties). On the other hand, where the amount of future income is uncertain, courts sometimes refuse to allocate it at all, because its receipt is too "speculative." *Marriage of Teitz*, 605 N.E.2d 670 (Ill. App. 1992) (speculative nature of attorney's contingent fees, where case has not yet reached final conclusion, distinguishes them from accounts receivable); *Beasley v. Beasley*, 518 A.2d 545, 554 (Pa. Super. 1986) (contingent fees excluded where assigning value at time of dissolution would be "tenuous and risky"). This approach denies the other spouse any share in the contingent fees even though most of the labor performed to earn them occurred during marriage. Other courts (and the *ALI Principles*, § 4.08) conclude that in such situations jurisdiction should be reserved. *E.g., Garrett v. Garrett*, 683 P.2d 1166 (Ariz. App. 1984) (jurisdiction reserved for the purpose of dividing contingent fees when they are in fact received by the law firm); *Marriage of Weiss*, 365 N.W.2d 608 (Wis. App. 1985) (same).

3. *Personal Injury and Worker's Compensation Awards*. Generally, personal injury recoveries and workers' compensation claims are marital property to the extent that they provide compensation for the loss of a marital asset, of which the most important example is the loss of income that the injured spouse would otherwise have earned during the marriage. Because post-divorce income is separate property, compensation for its loss is separate as well. *Niroo* quotes a prior case that follows this rule with respect to workers' compensation benefits. Most courts classify compensation for pain and suffering, typically available in tort awards but not in workers' compensation claims, as separate property, leaving the portion of the tort award intended to replace marital earnings as the main marital property component. Because tort awards are typically undifferentiated, the divorce court often must examine the circumstances to make the allocation itself. *See, e.g., Ramsey v. Ramsey*, 682 So. 2d 797 (La. App. 1996) (affirming trial court allocation of undifferentiated award between community property portion compensating for lost wages, and separate property portion compensating for pain and suffering); *Bandow v. Bandow*, 794 P.2d 1346 (Alaska 1990) (similar); *Landwehr v. Landwehr*, 545 A.2d 738 (N.J. 1988) (similar). Some courts avoid the allocation issue by following a mechanical approach under which tort recoveries are classified entirely according to the timing of their receipt rather than according to the losses for which they provide compensation. The *ALI Principles*, § 4.08(2)(b), suggest characterizing disability pay and worker's compensation payments according to the nature of the wages they replace, and this approach has been adopted by at least one jurisdiction. *Holman v. Holman*, 84 S.W.3d 903 (Ky. 2002) (citing the *Principles* in an application to disability retirement benefits).

4. *Dividing Debts*. Courts have struggled with devising a sensible rule on the allocation of debts and *Niroo*'s treatment is characteristically incomplete. State statutes typically contain no definition of a marital debt. *See Marriage of Welch*, 795 S.W.2d 640 (Mo. App. 1990). There is nonetheless little difficulty in dealing with an encumbered asset such as the mortgaged marital home; as *Niroo* suggests, one simply takes the debt into account in valuing the asset. That is effectively how the court dealt with Mr. Niroo's renewal commissions, which apparently served as security for his debt to the company. So long as the debt and the asset are both marital rather than separate, this is clearly correct. Because Mr. Niroo is alone legally responsible for marital debt, then an equal division requires that he be allocated an offsetting amount of marital property. The court therefore netted the debt against the asset, giving Mrs. Niroo a share of the excess only. Note that the parties differed over the characterization of the debt: was it separate or marital? The importance of that dispute should be clear: if the debt was Mr. Niroo's separate obligation rather than the spouses' joint obligation, then his liability for it would not justify allocating him an offsetting share of the marital property. The characterization of debts as separate or marital, while therefore important, is an issue which many courts have found difficult.

Generally, debts incurred during the marriage, like assets obtained during the marriage, are presumed to be marital debts. While courts sometimes say that the characterization test is whether the debt was incurred for "the joint benefit of the parties," this is probably not a good description of the test the courts are actually applying or should apply. Inevitably, many expenditures within a marriage will inure primarily to the benefit to one spouse or the other. It is only when debts support activities that will have ongoing benefits to one spouse only — the paradigmatic case being educational loans — that the courts tend to characterize such debts as "separate" rather than "marital." *See ALI Principles*, § 4.09, Comment h.

Some jurisdictions also expressly allow an unequal division of marital debts where there is sharply disparate income or wealth (and thus ability to repay the debts), or where other factors might make an unequal division "equitable." CAL. FAM. CODE § 2622 (West 1994 & Supp. 2003) (where parties' debts exceed their assets, the general equal division rule does not apply; court shall instead divide debts equitably after giving due consideration to relative incomes and other unspecified factors); *see also ALI Principles*, § 4.09(2)(c).

5. *Appreciation of Separate Property During Marriage.* As for appreciation of separate property during marriage, community property states distinguish appreciation attributable to either spouse's labors from the property's "natural increase" in value. In every community property state, the "natural increase" is also separate. So if the wife enters marriage owning 100 shares of Acme Corporation, which double in value during marriage, the increase as well as the original 100 shares remain her separate property. On the other hand, any increase in value of separate property attributable to either spouse's labor during marriage is community property, following the general rule that the community owns the fruits of marital labors. Many common law states today apply the same rule. *Merriken v. Merriken*, 590 A.2d 566, 575 (Md. Spec. App. 1991) (wife had claim on appreciation of husband's separate real property because its appreciation was largely traceable to his marital labor); *Knowles v. Knowles*, 588 A.2d 315, 317 (Me. 1991) (wife had interest in appreciation of husband's separate property business resulting from his labor); KY. REV. STAT. ANN. § 403.190(2) (Lexis 1999 & Supp. 2002) (separate property appreciation resulting from spousal labor is marital); MO. ANN. STAT. § 452.330(2)(5) (West 2003) (same); ILL. ANN. STAT. ch. 750, para. 5/503 (West 1999 & Supp. 2003); VA. CODE. ANN. § 20-107.3(A)(3) (Lexis 2000 & Supp. 2002); OHIO REV. CODE ANN. § 3105.171(A)(6)(a) (Anderson 2002) ("passive" appreciation is separate, implying appreciation resulting from spousal labor is marital). It is difficult, however, to characterize comprehensively current law in the common law states on this question because in many cases the governing authority is sparse or unclear. Some statutes provide only that the appreciation of separate property remains separate, without more. *E.g.*, ARK. CODE ANN. § 9-12-315(b) (Lexis 2002) (though Arkansas is also a state that allows recourse to separate property if necessary for an equitable division of property, *id.* at § 9-12-315(a)(2)). A few states treat all appreciation as marital property. *See* COLO. REV. STAT. § 14-10-113(4) (2002); 23 PA. CONS. STAT. ANN. DOM. REL. § 3501 (West 2001 & Supp. 2003). Other states will treat the appreciation as marital property (entirely or partially) if the appreciation was due in large part to marital funds or the efforts of the spouse who was not the property's owner. *See, e.g., Innerblicher v. Innerblicher*, 752 A.2d 291 (Md. 2000); *Godley v. Godley*, 429 S.E.2d 382 (N.C. Ct. App. 1993).

Under the community property rule, apportionment will be necessary in many cases because the property has increased in value due both to "natural" reasons and spousal labor. One common example arises when one spouse begins a business before marriage, with separate property capital, but continues to operate it during marriage. If the business is worth more at divorce than at the time of marriage, the increase must be allocated between the original capital and its natural increase (separate property) and the fruits of the spousal labor (community or marital property). No neutral, established accounting principles exist by which to make such an apportionment and courts have developed different, and conflicting, rules. One line of cases finds no community property component in the incremental value where the entrepreneur spouse took compensation from the business during marriage which was reasonable in light of market standards for that kind of work. This approach (called *Van Camp* after the case that first announced it) seems mistaken in excluding the possibility that this spouse's labor was more valuable than the norm: the marital community owns all the returns to his labor, including unusually lucrative ones. The consequence of *Van Camp* is sometimes to attribute, by implication, implausibly high returns to the initial separate-property capital stake. The competing *Pereira* line of authority attributes an ordinary rate of return to the separate property capital, and allocates all the return above this amount to spousal labor. A California case that reviews both lines of authority is *Marriage of Dekker*, 17 Cal. App. 4th 842, 21 Cal. Rptr. 2d 642 (1993). *Dekker* rejects *Van Camp*'s application to the facts before it. Section 4.05 of the *ALI Principles*, which adopts the basic community property rule, generally favors the *Pereira* rule. *See also* Oldham, *Separate Property Businesses That Increase in Value During Marriage,* 1990 WIS. L. REV. 585; Perkins, *Appreciation of the Separately Owned, Closely Held Business,* 14(3) COMM. PROP. J. 62 (1987); Messinger, *Unification of the Pereira and Van Camp Rules: The Economics Underlying the Division of a Business Between Separate and Community Property in California Divorce Proceedings,* 9 COMM. PROP. J. 286 (1982).

Common-law states addressing the apportionment problem have divided. Some follow *Van Camp. Meservey v. Meservey*, 841 S.W.2d 240 (Mo. App. 1992) (increase in value of H's family farm entirely separate because W did not prove H had received inadequate compensation from the farm); *Marriage of Werries*, 616 N.E.2d 1379 (Ill. App. 1993); *Huger v. Huger*, 433 S.E.2d 255 (Va. App. 1993) (evidence failed to show increased value of stock in spousal business was due to uncompensated spousal efforts, and was therefore separate). Two decisions in common law states are more consistent with *Dekker* and *Pereira. Schorer v. Schorer*, 501 N.W.2d 916 (Wis. App. 1993) (appreciation of company stock marital property where husband's labor largely responsible for business's increased value; irrelevant whether owning spouse "fairly" compensated); *Knowles v. Knowles*, 588 A.2d 315 (Me. 1991) (described *supra*). Other common law states do not apportion the appreciation of separate property between marital and separate property components, but instead treat the characterization as requiring an all or nothing resolution. TENN. CODE ANN. § 36-4-121 (Lexis 2001 & Supp. 2002) (all appreciation is marital if nontitled spouse contributed to it); *Zelnick v. Zelnick*, 169 A.D.2d 317, 573 N.Y.S.2d 261 (1991) ("wife is entitled to an award based upon the appreciation of the property unless the appreciation was completely unrelated to any effort expended by her and due solely to the fluctuations of the real estate market"); *Bowen v. Bowen*, 543 So. 2d 1284 (Fla. App. 1989) (orange grove worked by husband is entirely marital property even though premarital assets were used to acquire option to purchase it and to make down payment).

In many common law states, of course, placing all of the appreciation in the marital property pot merely permits the court to exercise discretion in its allocation. The other spouse's claim to share it thus becomes an appeal to equity, in contrast with the community property view that the spousal interest is a property right with precise contours that the court is required to identify.

6. *Income Realized During Marriage from Separate Property.* Most of the eight traditional community property states, including California, follow the "American rule," which treats income from separate property as separate. The only complete exception is Texas, whose state supreme court in 1925 held that the Spanish rule, treating the income as marital property, was required by the state constitution. The California Supreme Court had earlier reached a contrary result in applying an identical state constitutional provision. See the history as recounted in Thomas R. Andrews, *Income from Separate Property: Towards a Theoretical Foundation*, 56 LAW & CONTEMP. PROBS. 171, 182–85 (Spring 1993). While Louisiana is usually listed as a Spanish rule jurisdiction, it allows the separate owner unilaterally to declare the income separate by filing a statement of this intention in the "conveyance records" of the appropriate parish. LA. CIV. CODE ANN. art. 2339 (1985 & Supp. 2003). Wisconsin adopted the Louisiana approach when it enacted the Uniform Marital Property Act. WIS. STAT. ANN. § 766.59 (West 2001 & Supp. 2002) ("spouse may unilaterally execute a written statement which classifies . . . income [from separate] property as [separate] property"). Idaho, the only other purported Spanish rule state, achieves much the same result as Louisiana and Wisconsin with a rule that the income from separate property remains separate if the conveyance by which the property is acquired so declares, IDAHO CODE § 32-906 (Michie 1996 & Supp. 2002); *see* Andrews, *supra*, at 189. Characterization of the common law states is more difficult because authority is sparse. Andrews concluded, however, that of the common law states that have addressed the question, 11 treat the income from separate property as separate and 7 treat it as marital, but that only a handful of the states have actually given the matter careful consideration. Andrews, *supra*, at 192–99. Income from separate property is less likely than its appreciation to give rise to significant disputes at divorce. There are few marriages with significant separate property income, and any income that the parties do realize is often consumed during marriage, leaving no opportunity to dispute its allocation at divorce.

7. *Assets Acquired With a Blend of Separate and Marital Capital.* This problem arises most frequently in connection with the marital home. If one party owns a home before the marriage, it is that party's separate property, but mortgage payments may be made from marital earnings. Or the marital home may be purchased with a down payment made from the separate property of one spouse, such as a gift to that spouse from his or her parents, but the mortgage paid from marital earnings. Or the mortgage may be paid off with a separate property inheritance, while all payments before that were from marital property. At divorce the court must allocate the property's value between marital and separate property components.

The allocation may be made in one of two ways. The choice between them becomes significant principally when the property has appreciated so that its value at divorce is higher than the value of the two contributions (marital and separate) combined. One approach allocates the value according to the relative proportions of the marital and separate contributions. *E.g., Thomas v. Thomas,* 377 S.E.2d 666 (Ga. 1989) (proceeds from house sale divided between separate and marital property in proportion to the contributions of the spouses, both jointly and separately, to its purchase). The other approach characterizes the property as entirely marital or entirely separate, often by applying an "inception" rule under which the house retains the characterization it had at the moment of its acquisition. Under this approach, for example, a house purchased with a separate property down payment would remain entirely separate even though subsequent mortgage payments and improvements were financed from marital property sources. Courts applying such a rule often also find, however, that in such cases the marital estate must be reimbursed for the marital property contributions. One can see that the marital community does less well under the reimbursement approach, than under the shared equity approach, if the property has appreciated in value, but it may do better in a declining market. Note finally that some common law states reject both allocation methods but instead, as in other areas, choose to rely on the trial court to do "equity" by taking these facts into account in making the allocation. *E.g., Yeldell v. Yeldell,* 551 A.2d 832 (D.C. 1988) (Husband's payment of mortgage on home owned by the wife before the marriage establishes an equitable interest in it).

There are additional complications as well, including the handling generally of assets acquired on credit. For much more on this topic, and more generally on the treatment of assets acquired with a blend of marital and separate funds, see § 4.06 of the *ALI Principles.* See also Comment, *The Division of the Family Residence Acquired with a Mixture of Separate and Community Funds,* 70 CAL. L. REV. 1263 (1982).

8. *Bankruptcy.* The traditional rule was that child or spousal support orders were not dischargeable in bankruptcy, but that inter-spousal obligations arising from the divorce court's settlement of marital property claims were. For example, an order under which one spouse must buy out the other's share in a large item of marital property might require installment payments for some years after the divorce. What happens if the obligor-spouse subsequently goes bankrupt? The debt would be dischargeable in bankruptcy under traditional rules, although of course it might receive some priority if, for example, it was secured by the assets of the business. In October of 1994, however, Congress passed the Bankruptcy Reform Act, Pub. L. No. 94-393. This act adds property transfers at divorce to the list of debts that are not dischargeable in bankruptcy. The new language, codified as 11 U.S.C. § 523(a)(15), provides that debts other than those classified as alimony, maintenance or child support are also not dischargeable if the debt is incurred by the debtor in the course of a divorce or separation or in connection with a separation agreement, divorce decree or other order of a court of record, a determination made in accordance with State or territorial law by a governmental unit unless—

(A) the debtor does not have the ability to pay such debt from income or property of the debtor not reasonably necessary to be expended for the maintenance or support of the debtor or a dependent of the debtor and, if the debtor is engaged in a business, for the payment of expenditures necessary for the continuation, preservation, and operation of such business; or

(B) discharging such debt would result in a benefit to the debtor that outweighs the detrimental consequences to a spouse, former spouse, or child of the debtor.

The provision is somewhat odd, one author stating that it is the first time the bankruptcy law has used the nondischargeability provisions to, in effect, condition a debtor's right to discharge on his or her prospective inability to pay the obligation. The same author argues that the legislative history demonstrates that Congress only intended to make property awards nondischargeable when they were made "in lieu of alimony" or pursuant to hold-harmless agreements, even though the language of the act does not so state. Bowles, *Matrimonial Implications of the Bankruptcy Reform Act of 1994*, FAIRSHARE, Vol. 15, No. 3, at 4 (March 1995). Both Bowles and the writer for the *Equitable Distribution Journal* conclude that the limitations to the nondischargeability provisions contained in subsections A and B make the amendment's effect difficult to predict. *Bankruptcy Reform*, 11 EQUITABLE DISTRIBUTION JOURNAL 133 (December, 1994). For a review of the problems that bankruptcy courts have had with implementing the new rules, and suggestions for changes in the bankruptcy law, see Meredith Johnson, Note, *At the Intersection of Bankruptcy and Divorce: Property Division Debts Under the Bankruptcy Reform Act of 1994*, 97 COLUM. L. REV. 91 (1997). For an overview of all the intricate interactions of bankruptcy law and family law, see JUDITH K. FITZGERALD & RAMONA M. ARENA, BANKRUPTCY AND DIVORCE: SUPPORT AND PROPERTY DIVISION (2d ed., 1994 & Supp. 2003).

PROBLEMS

Problem 4-4. Sam, a movie producer, is the CEO and sole shareholder of a closely owned corporation, Sam's Productions Inc (or SP), through which he produces his movies. He marries Sophie, and during the marriage SP agrees to produce a new movie, *The British Patient*. SP employs Sam in this endeavor. *British Patient* is a smash hit, and the various contractual rights owned by SP become enormously valuable. Sam and Sophie divorce. Sophie claims a share in the increased value of SP. Sam says SP, having been created before the marriage, is his separate property. He concedes, of course, that the salary SP paid him during the marriage is marital property. Does Sophie also have a marital property interest in SP's enhanced value?

Problem 4-5. After filing her petition to dissolve her 15-year marriage with Ronald, Rhonda learns that she is among a group of employees to be released in a corporate downsizing. The company provides released employees severance pay equal to one month's salary for each year of employment at the company. Rhonda therefore receives ten months' salary, or $40,000. Rhonda, a hard worker, had also accumulated a month's worth of unused vacation time during her years of employment, worth another $4,000. Ronald claims all $44,000 is marital property, Rhonda claims it is all separate property. What is the correct result?

Problem 4-6. Joan, a trial attorney, wins a $500,000 verdict for her client in a contingent fee case in which she is entitled to 35% of any recovery. The defendant has filed an appeal which is scheduled to be heard in six months. Joan will handle the appeal for the plaintiff. Her husband has now filed a divorce petition. He claims that Joan's contingent fee is marital property. Is he right?

Problem 4-7. Tom's prized Alfa Romeo, bought with his own funds before his marriage to Tonya, is his separate property. In January of 1996, Tom, testing the Alfa's limits on a back country road, has a serious accident. In consequence his Alfa is totaled, and he suffers chronic injuries leaving him too disabled to continue his prior employment. In June of 1996, Tom and Tonya file for divorce. Among their assets are: a) a check for $45,000 from the Acme Insurance Company, for the total loss of the Alfa; b) monthly payments of $5,000 from the Acyou Insurance Co., on a disability insurance policy the company had previously issued on Tom, and which will continue until Tom ceases to be disabled; and c) a term life insurance policy issued by the Acwe Insurance Co, expiring in October of each year, which is automatically renewable. Because of Tom's current medical condition, he would not otherwise be able to purchase life insurance. The premiums on all three policies were made from Tom's earnings during marriage. Which of these are marital assets? Which separate? Are any not property at all?

[3] APPLYING MARITAL PROPERTY RULES TO PENSIONS

In many marriages, the pension or other retirement benefits earned by one or both spouses during the marriage may be the only significant asset available for division. Therefore, the rules and procedures regarding the division of this asset are central to much divorce practice.

[a] State Law Issues

NOTES

All states treat pensions as marital property divisible on divorce. There are a number of issues that arise in working out the details, however:

1. *Should the Court Divide Unvested Pension Rights?* Pension benefits are typically funded, at least in part, by the employer's contributions. While these contributions are made in each pay period, the employee typically does not acquire a right to receive them upon retirement until she has worked for the employer a specified period of time. At that moment, the employee's pension rights are said to "vest." An early California case found no community interest in unvested pension rights, but this rule was later reversed, *In re Marriage of Brown,* 15 Cal. 3d 838, 544 P.2d 561, 126 Cal. Rptr. 633 (1976), *overruling French v. French,* 17 Cal. 2d 775, 112 P.2d 235 (1941). Nearly all states now treat unvested pensions as marital property. Grace G. Blumberg, *Marital Property Treatment of Pensions, Disability Pay, Workers' Compensation, and Other Wage Substitutes: An Insurance, Or Replacement, Analysis,* 33 U.C.L.A. L. REV. 1250, 1263 (1986). Recent cases so holding include *Stoller v. Wood,* 687 A.2d 636 (Me. 1996); *Cohen v. Cohen,* 937 S.W.2d 823 (Tenn. 1996); *Burns v. Burns,* 84 N.Y.2d 369, 643 N.E.2d 80, 618 N.Y.S.2d 761 (1994). Two apparently still valid authorities, however, excluding unvested pension plans from the marital property pot are *Charles v. Charles,* 713 P.2d 1048 (Okla. App. 1986) and *Skirvin v. Skirvin,* 560 N.E.2d 1263 (Ind. App. 1990) (pension vesting 32 days after divorce decree not marital property).

There are basically two options when treating unvested pensions. First, a court could defer the pension's distribution until vesting, when its value becomes more certain. *See Laing v. Laing,* 741 P.2d 649 (Alaska 1987) (concluding immediate distribution of unvested pension benefit would unfairly place full risk of forfeiture on employee-spouse); *see also ALI Principles* § 4.08(3) & Comment d. Alternatively, the value of the pension can be discounted to reflect the risk of nonvesting and distributed immediately. Especially where the amounts are small and the time of vesting is some time off, this may be more convenient for the parties. *See Lowry v. Lowry,* 544 A.2d 972, 983 (Pa. Super. 1988) (finding that unvested pension can be distributed immediately to the nonemployee spouse by discounting its value).

2. *Deferred vs. Immediate Distribution of Pension Benefits.* A court can fix each spouse's share of future annuity payments when the employee spouse retires. If there are sufficient assets, the court can allocate the entire pension to the employee-spouse, with the non-employee spouse allocated an enhanced share of the remaining property as an offset. Such an immediate distribution requires establishing the current value of the pension so that the amount of the required offset can be determined. One can see that immediate and deferred distributions each have advantages and difficulties whose importance varies with the facts of each case. When the parties are relatively young, their accumulated pension entitlements are usually small, and their retirement is far in the future — a combination of facts that suggests that immediate distribution makes the most sense. When the parties are older and on the verge of retirement, pension values are usually high, and it usually makes more sense to fix the spouses' respective shares of the annuity payments as they are made, typically monthly.

Decisions favoring an immediate lump-sum distribution of the pension rights emphasize that it completes the property arrangements, thus reducing the need for the former spouses to remain in contact with each other ("clean break"), and also eliminates potential enforcement problems in ensuring that the nonemployee spouse receives his share of each pension payment when made. *Koelsch v. Koelsch,* 713 P.2d 1234 (Ariz. 1986); *Dewan v. Dewan,* 506 N.E.2d 879 (Mass. 1987); *Moore v. Moore,* 553 A.2d 20 (N.J. 1989); *Cross v. Cross,* 363 S.E.2d 449 (W. Va. 1987). Where it is not feasible for one spouse to buy out the other with one lump-sum payment, these courts sometimes permit a schedule of payments over a relatively short period of time. *E.g.*, *Moore*, *supra*, at 29 (trial court decision giving husband two years to buy out wife's pension rights "defensible" where resources lacking for immediate, full payment); *Cross*, *supra*, at 445 (where lump-sum buy-out is not feasible the next-best solution is to require monthly payments for a term of years by which the employee spouse pays out the present value of pension rights, with interest).

Decisions favoring the deferred distribution method emphasize the hardship of a buyout on the employee-spouse when the value of currently available assets is small relative to the pension entitlement, as well as the difficulties in calculating at divorce the value of an unvested pension or the present value for the annuity provided by a defined benefit plan. *Marriage of Nelson*, 746 P.2d 1346 (Colo. 1987); *Marriage of Hobbs*, 442 N.E.2d 629 (Ill. App. 1982); *Rask v. Rask*, 445 N.W.2d 849 (Minn. App. 1989); *Hodgins v. Hodgins*, 497 A.2d 1187 (N.H. 1985); *Bailey v. Bailey*, 745 P.2d 830 (Utah App. 1987). Deferred distributions pose a problem if the employee-spouse chose to work beyond the date on which she was eligible to retire, thus delaying receipt of the pension. While the delay would provide compensating benefit to the employee whose pension account was thereby enlarged, it provided no benefit to the other spouse, who has no claim on the increment in the pension benefit earned by post-marital labor, and who therefore can only lose by the additional delay in receipt of the pension benefits. Some courts once held that the employee could not postpone the former spouse's realization of her share of the pension by delaying retirement. Where the employee cannot afford to buy out the former spouse or to fund equivalent substitute payments himself, such decisions effectively require the employee to retire early and forego potentially important benefits. *Gillmore v. Gillmore*, 29 Cal. 3d 418, 174 Cal. Rptr. 493, 629 P.2d 1 (1981); *Koelsch v. Koelsch*, 713 P.2d 1234, 1243 (Ariz. 1986).

Today, however, the conflict of interest between the spouses as to the employee's choice of when to retire is not an important consideration in most cases. Governing law usually allows the dissolution court to "bifurcate" the pension and require the pension plan administrator to make monthly payments directly to each spouse of his or her share of the pension. The timing of the employee spouse's retirement becomes irrelevant under such a bifurcation, because the court can require the pension plan to begin payments to the nonemployee spouse at the employee's earliest retirement eligibility date, even if the employee does not choose to then retire. The plan administrator will make payments to the nonemployee spouse that are equal to her share of the payments that *would* have been due the employee *if* the employee-spouse had then retired. The pension plan funds these payments to the nonemployee-spouse with compensating reductions in the payments eventually made to the employee-spouse at his actual retirement.

The most important source of law allowing the dissolution court to order such bifurcations is the federal Employee Retirement Income Security Act (ERISA), 29 U.S.C. § 1001 *et seq* (West 1998 & Supp. 2003). The Act defines a Qualified Domestic Relations Order (QDRO) as including a state court judgment pursuant to state domestic relations or community property law that meets certain formal requirements and assigns to an "alternate payee" (that is, a payee other than the pension beneficiary) the right to "receive all or a portion of the benefits payable" to a participant in a covered pension plan. *Id.* at § 1056(d)(3). Covered pension plans are required to "establish reasonable procedures . . . to administer distributions under such qualified orders," *Id.* At § 1056(d)(3)(G)(ii). The Act specifies that a QDRO may "require[] the payment of benefits . . . to the alternate payee" prior to the employee's actual retirement, so long as the order, among other things, provides that benefits are payable to the alternative payee "as if the participant had retired on the date on which such payment is to begin under such order (but taking into account only the present value of benefits actually accrued and not taking into account the present value of any employer subsidy for early retirement)," *id.* at § 1056(d)(3)(E); *see* Howard A. Massler, *Qualified Domestic Relations Orders*, in 3 Valuation and Distribution of Marital Property 47-1 (Matthew Bender 1996). Not every pension plan is covered by ERISA, however. Most importantly, the Act excludes public pension plans from coverage. Some states have enacted analogous provisions, however, to cover various state and local employees. *See, e.g.*, Grace G. Blumberg, Community Property in California 341 (2d ed. 1993) (describing Cal. Gov't Code § 21215 *et seq.* and Cal. Educ. Code § 22650, et seq.); *Grieve v. Mankey,* 679 A.2d 814 (Pa. Super. 1996) (discussing Pennsylvania statute that authorizes QDROs for public school employee pensions). But many gaps remain. *See, e.g., Bryant v. Employees Retirement System of Georgia*, 455 S.E.2d 839 (Ga. App. 1995) (while husband's retirement benefits are marital property subject to division, trial court had no authority under state or federal law to order state retirement system to make payments directly to wife).

3. *Valuation of Pensions.* As explained in Note 2, fashioning an appropriate order at dissolution often requires establishing a value for the pension that has been earned during the marriage. The approach taken to this valuation usually depends upon whether the pension plan is a "defined benefit" or "defined contribution" plan. While attorneys commonly hire experts to make such valuations, it is important for the attorney to understand what the expert is doing. See the *ALI Principles*, § 4.08, Comment *e*:

> In a defined-contribution plan, contributions to a pension fund are made on the employee's behalf during employment. The accumulated contributions and the investment income derived from them are then available to fund the employee's retirement, often by the purchase of an annuity. At any point up to that time, the amount accumulated on the employee's behalf can in principle be determined. On this basis a determination can be made of the marital-property share, which equals the accumulations during the marriage plus the investment return attributable to them. Difficulties can sometimes arise when accurate values are, as a practical matter, unavailable for the particular assets allocable to the employee.

> "Defined-benefit" plans create a contractual obligation of the employer to provide an annuity fixed by a formula that has no necessary connection to any amounts nominally set aside to fund it. It is thus inappropriate to value it by reference to such nominal contributions.

An alternative method used to value some defined-benefit pensions calculates a present value for the annuity entitlement earned as of the time the valuation is made. Defined-benefit plans, for example, may set the annuity payment by multiplying the employee's average salary during his final working years by a particular percentage and by the total years of service. One could apply the formula to the employee spouse at divorce, whether or not the spouse is then eligible to retire, and then calculate a present value for that flow of payments . . . by assuming a retirement date and a life expectancy. In a variation of this approach, one could calculate the present value of the annuity to which the employee would be entitled at retirement, assuming the additional years of post-marriage service remaining to that time, and then reduce the resulting value in proportion to the nonmarital years of service assumed in its calculation. Other possibilities emerge from the particular characteristics of the pension plan in question.

Any such calculation of course requires an assumption about the employee-spouse's life expectancy, to project the number of years over which payments will be made, but in most cases a projection based upon standard actuarial tables will permit an adequate valuation of the payment flow. The uncertainties of projecting the employee's life span are alone usually surmountable.

An individual may begin employment before marriage, continue it during his marriage, and remain at it after the marriage ends. That individual's spouse is entitled to share in only the portion of the pension entitlement earned during the marriage. How is this apportionment between marital and non-marital portions made? *See ALI Principles*, § 4.08, Comment *f*:

The apportionment formulas used are generally variants of either of two basic methods, which can be called the relative-value rule and the relative-time rule. The relative-value rule in principle provides an accurate apportionment method for defined contribution plans. It takes the total contributions that were made during the marriage, combined with the investment gains (or losses) derived from those contributions, and classifies this total as marital property for the purpose of calculating a lump-sum distribution. If a deferred distribution is made one can then determine, at the time of retirement, the ratio of this marital-property share to the total of all accumulated contributions and investment returns. This same proportion of each annuity payment, when made, is considered marital property. Accuracy requires identifying the actual investment results on the marital- and separate-property contributions, rather than assuming they are proportional to the relative value of the contributions themselves. This adjustment is necessary because returns on contributions made in the early years of employment will ordinarily be proportionately greater than the returns from more recent years, which will have been invested for less time. While in principle the relative-value rule provides the most accurate method for apportioning a defined-contribution pension, it may be difficult in some cases to obtain the information necessary to apply it.

. . .

. . . The relative-time rule apportions the pension between its marital-and separate-property components by assuming that all years of labor contribute equally to the pension entitlement. It thus classifies as marital property the same proportion of the pension as the marital years of labor bear to the total years of labor. It may be implemented by establishing a fraction (sometimes called the "coverture factor") in which the numerator is the period of employment during the marriage and the denominator is the total period of employment (considering, of course, only employment giving rise to the pension entitlement at issue).

For a recent case upholding the use of the relative-time rule in a community property state, see *Hunt v. Hunt*, 43 P.3d 777 (Idaho 2002).

[b]   Federal Preemption of State Law

A series of Supreme Court decisions affects the inclusion of pension rights within the community and marital property pot. *Hisquierdo v. Hisquierdo,* 439 U.S. 572 (1979), involved a husband's Railroad Retirement Act pension. The California court had held the wife entitled to share in the pension, but the Supreme Court reversed. The Court found Railroad Retirement pensions resembled social welfare benefits more than private contractual rights, because Congress can alter or eliminate them at any time. Moreover, the social welfare scheme contained a number of provisions which arguably evidenced a considered decision to exclude Mrs. Hisquierdo's claim. One section barred assignment, garnishment or attachment of the benefits, except to satisfy a child support or alimony obligation, while another section defined "alimony" for this purpose as "excluding any payment . . . in compliance with any community property settlement, equitable distribution of property, or other division of property between spouses or former spouses." *Id.* at 577. Relying upon these provisions, the Court found that Congress had intended to exclude community property claims to these pension rights. Under the Supremacy Clause, California community property law was therefore preempted by the federal pension law. The Court held further that California was barred from frustrating this "federal policy" by giving the wife an offsetting award from presently available community assets, to compensate her for the denial of pension rights.

Hisquierdo was noteworthy because of the Court's willingness to find a federal preemption in an area traditionally reserved for state law. The Court itself quoted earlier decisions holding that a preemption of state family law requires a finding that the state law would impose "major damage" on "clear and substantial federal interests" and that "Congress has positively required by direct enactment" that the state law be preempted. 439 U.S. at 581.

The Court's approach was similar in its next case in the area, *McCarty v. McCarty,* 453 U.S. 210 (1981). *McCarty* involved military retired pay. Such pay was arguably compensation for current services rather than deferred compensation, and in fact lower courts had divided on that question. Only if it were deferred compensation for services rendered during the marriage would it be community property in which the former wife had an interest. The Supreme Court declined to decide, however, "whether federal law prohibits a State from characterizing retired pay as deferred compensation," 543 U.S. at 233, because the Court concluded that here, as in *Hisquierdo,* federal law preempted state marital property rules.

Implicit in the Court's reasoning was an assumption that a congressional failure to acknowledge a spouse's interest in the other's pay was equivalent to a considered decision to override that interest. A much more plausible conclusion from the evidence was that Congress, in designing military retired pay as well as the compensation schemes for other federal employees, never thought much at all about the impact of state marital property law. That conclusion would not support preemption under established rules, as the dissent vigorously pointed out. Nonetheless, the Court made no attempt to show why active duty pay would not come within its holding, and even "reserved" the question, suggesting the possibility of a much broader net, in fact reaching all earnings of most federal employees. 453 U.S. at 225, n.17.

McCarty itself was overruled by Congress in September 1982, by the Uniformed Services Former Spouses Protection Act, 966 Stat. 730, codified in part at 10 U.S.C. § 1408, which provides, subject to certain limitations, that a court "may treat disposable retired pay . . . either as property solely of the member or as property of the member and his spouse in accordance with the law of the jurisdiction of such court." The statute is prospective only, and does not permit reopening of pension rights settled before it became effective. It contains certain procedural devices to assist the claimant. A former spouse in a marriage of at least 10 years entitled to share in the monthly payments under a state court order may receive the payments directly from the government. 10 U.S.C. § 1408(d) (West 1998 & Supp. 2003). State courts may also divide pension rights arising in shorter marriages, although in such cases direct payments from the government will not be available. *E.g., Konzen v. Konzen,* 693 P.2d 97 (Wash. 1985).

While the Former Spouses' Protection Act applies only to the military, and does not deal generally with deferred (or present) compensation of federal employees, it was hoped that its enactment would limit judicial extension of *McCarty* to other federal workers or compensation programs. But in *Mansell v. Mansell,* 490 U.S. 581 (1989), the Court refused to accept that Congress really meant to overrule *McCarty* in the Uniformed Services Former Spouses' Protection Act. *Mansell* dealt with a federal rule allowing a military pensioner also eligible for disability pay, to collect it only to the extent he waives an equivalent amount of pension rights; the rule is intended to prevent double-dipping. Waiving the retirement pay in favor of the disability pay is nonetheless advantageous to the veteran because disability benefits are exempt from federal and local income taxes. After *Mansell,* it has the additional advantage of shielding the payments from a former wife's claims, since the Court found that the federal law barred a state from treating as divisible marital property the disability pay taken in lieu of the divisible retirement pay.

The Court dealt with the intersection of ERISA and community property law (in this case, from Louisiana) again in *Boggs v. Boggs,* 520 U.S. 833 (1997). *Boggs* dealt with a conflict between the decedent's second wife and his sons by his first wife, who had predeceased him. The first wife had bequeathed the sons her community property share of their father's retirement benefits, which included a monthly annuity, an individual retirement account, and shares in an employee stock ownership plan. At the time of her death he had not yet retired. The Court held that her bequest of the IRA and ESOP (Employee Stock Ownership Plan) shares was an "assignment" or "alienation" barred by the Act, both in the transfer of the interest from her husband to her, and in her testamentary transfer of it to her sons. Note that this reasoning does not apply to QDRO's issued by divorce courts, which Congress, in the Retirement Equity Act of 1984, specifically excepted from these anti-alienation provisions. One might hope that attention will at some point be paid to Justice Breyer's dissent in which, in a portion joined by O'Connor, Rehnquist, and Ginsberg, he argued against the Court's application of the anti-alienation and assignment provisions to the first wife's possession of the retirement benefits:

> [The first wife's] interest arose not through assignment or alienation, but through the operation of Louisiana's community property law itself. Thus, [the second wife's] claim must be that community property law's grant of an undivided one-half interest in retirement benefits to a nonparticipant wife or husband itself violates some congressional purpose. But what purpose could that be? Congress has recognized that community property law, like any other kind of property law, can create various property interests for nonparticipant spouses. See 29 U.S.C. § 1056(d)(3)(B)(ii)(II). Community property law, like other property law, can provide an appropriate legal framework for resolving disputes about who owns what. § 1056(d)(3). The anti-alienation provision is designed to prevent plan beneficiaries from prematurely divesting themselves of the funds they will need for retirement, not to prevent application of the property laws that define the legal interest in those funds. One cannot find frustration of an "anti-alienation" purpose simply in the state law's definition of property.

In *Egelhoff v. Egelhoff*, 532 U.S. 141 (2001), the Court dealt with the interaction of a Washington statute and ERISA. While Washington is a community property state, the issue presented in *Egelhoff* is relevant in all states. ERISA specifies that it "shall supersede any and all State laws insofar as they may now or hereafter relate to any employee benefit plan" covered by it. The husband had designated his wife as the beneficiary of his employer-provided pension and life insurance plans, both of which were covered by ERISA. He was then divorced, and died unexpectedly two months later, intestate and unmarried, and without having removed his wife as the beneficiary. Under Washington law, as that of many other states, her beneficiary status was revoked automatically by the divorce. If the Washington law prevailed, the husband's children from a prior marriage would succeed to the assets. ERISA directs the plan administrator to make payments to a beneficiary "in accordance with the documents and instruments governing the plan." 29 U.S.C. § 1104(a)(1)(D). The majority held that this language effectively required that payment be made to the wife despite the Washington law, thus preempting it. This result makes little sense. The wife had already been allocated her fair share of the community property, including the pension, in the divorce proceeding itself (in which she received certain stock and business assets as a setoff against her share of the pension, which was allocated entirely to the husband). Under this decision she now receives the pension as an add-on to her divorce settlement. It is difficult to believe that Congress intended by its general language to override state laws designed to avoid just this sort of result. These points were made by Justice Breyer, in a dissent joined by Justice Stevens (the dissent also urged that there was in fact no direct conflict or contradiction between the Washington statute and the plan documents at issue when the two are read carefully).

PROBLEMS

Problem 4-8. You handled Gloria's divorce action, which was completed in 1996 with a separation agreement. The parties had been married since 1973, and during that entire time, her husband George worked for a small private corporation owned entirely by Edward. George had been Edward's right-hand man, but retired in 2000. Shortly afterward, Gloria comes to you to say that she has heard that Edward recently gave George a large interest in a ranch, worth something like $300,000. She wants to know if she can get a share of it.

Problem 4-9. W has worked for 20 years for the police force. She is eligible to retire and receive her now-vested pension benefits. She wants to continue working, however, in order to reach the rank of a sergeant and to make herself eligible for the greater pension available after 30 years of service. The couple has few other assets and H has no pension of his own. You represent the husband. What is your problem and how might you solve it?

Problem 4-10. Robert began working for Acme in 1965. In 1990, when he was 55, he married Roberta. In 1997 they divorce. Under his defined benefit retirement plan Robert, who has risen high in the company, is eligible, in 1997, to retire with an annual annuity payments totaling $70,000. Had he retired in 1990, he would have received only $30,000 under the benefit plan formula. Roberta argues that the marital share of Robert's pension is an annuity of $40,000 — the difference between what he would receive if he retired now, at the time of divorce, and what he would have received had he retired at the time of marriage. She wants an award of her share now, even if Robert wishes to continue working until his late 60's. What is she entitled to?

§ C. SHOULD EARNING CAPACITY, PROFESSIONAL CREDENTIALS, OR GOODWILL BE TREATED AS MARITAL PROPERTY?

[1] EARNING CAPACITY AND PROFESSIONAL CREDENTIALS

The traditional and still dominant rule is that earning capacity is not property. That rule is no longer always followed, however. A handful of jurisdictions have departed from it overtly; more do so covertly, or perhaps even inadvertently. The following decision by the New York Court of Appeals is by far the most important one overtly treating earning capacity as property, although it does so only in the limited context of professional licenses. No other state high court has followed its lead, and many have rejected it. Why?

O'BRIEN v. O'BRIEN

66 N.Y.2d 576, 498 N.Y.S.2d 743, 489 N.E.2d 712 (1985)

SIMONS, Judge. In this divorce action, the parties' only asset of any consequence is the husband's newly acquired license to practice medicine. . . .[¶] We . . . hold that [husband]'s medical license constitutes "marital property" within the meaning of Domestic Relations Law § 236(B)(1)(c) and . . . is . . . subject to equitable distribution. . . .

Ct holds medical license is marital property

I

[Husband] and [wife] married on April 3, 1971. At the time both were employed as teachers at the same private school. [Wife] had a bachelor's degree but required 18 months of postgraduate classes at an approximate cost of $3,000, excluding living expenses, to obtain permanent certification in New York. The trial court found she had relinquished the opportunity to obtain permanent certification while [husband] pursued his education. At the time of the marriage, [husband] had completed only three and one-half years of college but shortly afterward he returned to school at night to earn his bachelor's degree. In September 1973 the parties moved to Guadalajara, Mexico, where [husband] became a full-time medical student. While he pursued his studies [wife] held several teaching and tutorial positions and contributed her earnings to their joint expenses. The parties returned to New York in December 1976 so that [husband] could complete the last two semesters of medical school and internship training here. [Wife] resumed her former teaching position and remained in it at the time this action was commenced. [Husband] was licensed to practice medicine in October 1980. He commenced this action for divorce two months later. At the time of trial, he was a resident in general surgery.

both were teachers when H went to med school

W continued teaching while H went to school

After H got his license he filed for divorce

During the marriage both parties contributed to the living and educational expenses and they received additional help from both . . . families. [I]n addition to performing household work and managing the family finances [wife] was gainfully employed throughout the marriage. . . . The trial court found that she had contributed 76% of the parties' income exclusive of a $10,000 student loan obtained by [wife]. Finding that [husband]'s medical degree and license are marital property, the court received evidence of its value and ordered a distributive award to [wife]. [Wife] presented expert testimony that the present value of [husband]'s medical license was $472,000. Her expert . . . arrived at this figure by comparing the average income of a college graduate and that of a general surgeon between 1985, when [husband]'s residency would end, and 2012, when he would reach age 65. After considering Federal income taxes, an inflation rate of 10% and a real interest

lower ct found W contributed 76% of money and was entitled to share of license

Expert values license

rate of 3% he capitalized the difference in average earnings and reduced the amount to present value. . . .

The court, after considering the life-style that [husband] would enjoy from the enhanced earning potential his medical license would bring and [wife]'s contributions and efforts toward attainment of it, made a distributive award to her of $188,800, representing 40% of the value of the license, and ordered it paid in 11 annual installments of various amounts. . . . The court also directed [husband] to maintain a life insurance policy on his life for [wife]'s benefit for the unpaid balance of the award. . . . It did not award [wife] maintenance. [¶] A divided Appellate Division . . . concluded that a professional license acquired during marriage is not marital property subject to distribution. . . .

II

The Equitable Distribution Law contemplates only two classes of property: marital . . . and separate property. . . . The former, which is subject to equitable distribution, is defined broadly as "all property acquired by either or both spouses during the marriage and before the execution of a separation agreement or the commencement of a matrimonial action, *regardless of the form in which title is held*" (Domestic Relations Law § 236[B][1][c] [emphasis added]). [Husband] does not contend that his license is excluded from distribution because it is separate property; rather, he claims that it is not property at all but represents a personal attainment in acquiring knowledge. He rests his argument on decisions in similar cases from other jurisdictions and on his view that a license does not satisfy common law concepts of property. Neither contention is controlling because decisions in other States rely principally on their own statutes, and the legislative history underlying them, and because the New York Legislature deliberately went beyond traditional property concepts. Instead, our statute recognizes that spouses have an equitable claim to things of value arising out of the marital relationship and classifies them [according to] the marital status of the parties at the time of acquisition. Those things acquired during marriage and subject to distribution have been classified as "marital property" although . . . they hardly fall within the traditional property concepts because there is no common law property interest remotely resembling marital property. Having classified the "property" subject to distribution, the Legislature did not attempt to go further and define it but left it to the courts to determine what interests come within the terms of section 236(B)(1)(c).

. . . .

Section 236 provides that in making an equitable distribution of marital property, "the court shall consider: . . . (6) any equitable claim to, interest in, or direct or indirect contribution made to the acquisition of such marital property by the party not having title, including joint efforts or expenditures and contributions and services as a spouse, parent, wage earner and homemaker, and *to the career or career potential* of the other party [and] . . . (9) the impossibility or difficulty of evaluating any component asset or any interest in a business, corporation or *profession*" [emphasis added]. . . .

Where equitable distribution of marital property is appropriate but "the distribution of an interest in a business, corporation or profession would be contrary to law" the court shall make a distributive award in lieu of an actual distribution of the property. . . . The words mean exactly what they say: that an interest in a profession or professional career potential is marital property which may be represented by direct or indirect contributions of the non-title-holding spouse, including financial contributions and nonfinancial contributions made by caring for the home and family.

Ct can award a distribution in lieu of equitable distribution

The history which preceded enactment of the statute confirms this interpretation. . . . [E]xperience had proven that application of the traditional common law title theory of property had caused inequities. . . . The Legislature replaced the existing system with equitable distribution of marital property, an entirely new theory which considered all the circumstances of the case and of the respective parties to the marriage. . . . Equitable distribution was based on the premise that a marriage is, among other things, an economic partnership to which both parties contribute as spouse, parent, wage earner or homemaker. . . .

Policy – avoid inequity

The determination that a professional license is marital property is also consistent with the conceptual base upon which the statute rests. As this case demonstrates, few undertakings during a marriage better qualify as the type of joint effort that the statute's economic partnership theory is intended to address than contributions toward one spouse's acquisition of a professional license. Working spouses are often required to contribute substantial income as wage earners, sacrifice their own educational or career goals and opportunities for child rearing, perform the bulk of household duties and responsibilities and forego the acquisition of marital assets that could have been accumulated if the professional spouse had been employed rather than occupied with the study and training necessary to acquire a professional license. In this case, nearly all of the parties' nine-year marriage was devoted to the acquisition of [husband]'s medical license and [wife] played a major role in that project. She worked continuously during the marriage and contributed all of her earnings to their joint effort, she sacrificed her own educational and career opportunities, and she traveled with [husband] to Mexico for three and one-half years while he attended medical school there. The Legislature has decided, by its explicit reference in the statute to the contributions of one spouse to the other's profession or career, . . . that these contributions represent investments in the economic partnership of the marriage and that the product of the parties' joint efforts, the professional license, should be considered marital property.

Wife helped H get his license. W made economic contributions to acquire the property

. . . .

[Husband]'s principal argument . . . is that a professional license does not fit within the traditional view of property as something which has an exchange value on the open market and is capable of sale, assignment or transfer. The position does not withstand analysis. . . . First, . . . it ignores the fact that whether a professional license constitutes marital property is to be judged by the language of the statute which created this new species of property. . . . Thus, whether the license fits within traditional property concepts is of no consequence. Second, it is an overstatement to assert that a professional license could not be considered property even outside the context of section

A license is a valuable property right B/c it has no market is irrelevant

236(B). A professional license is a valuable property right, reflected in the money, effort and lost opportunity for employment expended in its acquisition, and also in the enhanced earning capacity it affords its holder, which may not be revoked without due process of law. That a professional license has no market value is irrelevant. Obviously, a license may not be alienated as may other property and for that reason the working spouse's interest in it is limited. The Legislature has recognized that limitation, however, and has provided for an award in lieu of its actual distribution.

H's second argument

Ct rejects #2 argument

[I]t has been suggested that even if a professional license is considered marital property, the working spouse is entitled only to reimbursement of his or her direct financial contributions. By parity of reasoning, a spouse's down payment on real estate or contribution to the purchase of securities would be limited to the money contributed, without any remuneration for any incremental value in the asset because of price appreciation. Such a result is completely at odds with the statute's requirement that the court give full consideration to both direct and indirect contributions "made to the acquisition of such marital property by the party not having title, including joint *efforts* or expenditures and *contributions and services as a spouse, parent, wage earner and homemaker*" . . . [emphasis added]. If the license is marital property, then the working spouse is entitled to an equitable portion of it, not a return of funds advanced. Its value is the enhanced earning capacity . . . and although fixing the present value of that enhanced earning capacity may present problems, the problems are not insurmountable. Certainly they are no more difficult than computing tort damages for wrongful death or diminished earning capacity resulting from injury and they differ only in degree from the problems presented when valuing a professional practice for purposes of a distributive award, something the courts have not hesitated to do. The trial court retains the flexibility and discretion to structure the distributive award equitably, taking into consideration factors such as the working spouse's need for immediate payment, the licensed spouse's current ability to pay and the income tax consequences of prolonging the period of payment. . . .

Concurrence

MEYER, Judge (concurring). I . . . write separately to point up for consideration by the Legislature the potential for unfairness involved in distributive awards based upon a license of a professional still in training. An equity court normally has power to "change its decrees where there has been a change of circumstances". . . . [H]owever . . . a distributive award . . . is not subject to change. Yet a professional in training who is not finally committed to a career choice when the distributive award is made may be locked into a particular kind of practice simply because the monetary obligations imposed by the distributive award made on the basis of the trial judge's conclusion (prophecy may be a better word) as to what the career choice will be leaves him or her no alternative.

What if it never becomes a doctor?

The present case points up the problem. . . . Here it is undisputed that [husband] was in a residency for general surgery at the time of the trial, but had the previous year done a residency in internal medicine. [Wife]'s expert based his opinion on the difference between the average income of a general surgeon and that of a college graduate of [husband]'s age and life expectancy, which the trial judge utilized, impliedly finding that [husband] would engage in a surgical practice despite [husband]'s testimony that he was dissatisfied with the general surgery program he was in and was attempting to return to the internal medicine training. . . . The trial judge had the right, of course, to discredit that testimony, but the point is that equitable distribution was not intended to permit a judge to make a career decision for a licensed spouse still in training. Yet the degree of speculation involved in the award made is emphasized by the testimony of the expert on which it was based. Asked whether his assumptions and calculations were in any way speculative, he replied: "Yes. They're speculative to the extent of, will Dr. O'Brien practice medicine? Will Dr. O'Brien earn more or less than the average surgeon earns? Will Dr. O'Brien live to age sixty-five? Will Dr. O'Brien have a heart attack or will he be injured in an automobile accident? Will he be disabled? I mean, there is a degree of speculation. That speculative aspect is no more to be taken into account, cannot be taken into account, and it's a question, again, Mr. Emanuelli, not for the expert but for the courts to decide. It's not my function nor could it be."

The equitable distribution provisions of the Domestic Relations Law were intended to provide flexibility. . . . But if the assumption as to career choice on which a distributive award payable over a number of years is based turns out not to be the fact (as, for example, should a general surgery trainee accidentally lose the use of his hand), it should be possible for the court to revise the distributive award to conform to the fact. . . .

POSTEMA v. POSTEMA

471 N.W.2d 912 (Mich. 1991)

MAHER, J.:

[Both parties challenge] the property distribution provisions of a . . . judgment of divorce. The primary issue concerns the valuation of defendant's law degree and whether the trial court erred in finding the law degree to be a marital asset. We affirm in part and remand.

Plaintiff and defendant were married on August 11, 1984. At the time of their marriage, defendant was employed as a cost accountant and plaintiff was working as a licensed practical nurse and attending school in pursuit of an associate's degree in nursing so that she could become a registered nurse. It was the plan of the parties when they married that defendant would enroll in law school and that plaintiff would postpone her schooling and work full-time to support them while defendant attended school. Accordingly, shortly after the marriage, the parties moved from Grand Rapids to the Detroit area, where they stayed from September 1984 until May 1987 while defendant attended Wayne State University Law School. In furtherance of the parties' plan, plaintiff obtained a full-time job at an area hospital, earning approximately $ 53,000 during the period defendant was in law school. Plaintiff also assumed the primary responsibility of maintaining the household, doing all cooking and cleaning, and running all errands. Though defendant did not work at all during his first year in law school, he later worked as a law clerk, full-time during the summers following his first and second years in law school and then part-time during his second and part of his third years. In all, defendant earned approximately $ 12,000 from clerking. The parties' earnings were used primarily for their support, while defendant's education was financed mostly through student loans totaling $ 15,000.

Defendant proved to be a successful law student and wrote for the school's law review. After defendant graduated in May 1987, the parties moved back to the Grand Rapids area, where defendant accepted a position as an associate attorney with a local law firm at a starting annual salary of $ 41,000. The following September, plaintiff resumed classes in pursuit of her associate's degree in nursing. In November 1987, however, the parties separated. Despite the separation, plaintiff continued her classes and eventually received her associate's degree in May 1988, although she had to support herself during that period by working full-time at a local hospital.

Plaintiff testified that marital problems developed early in the marriage. She said defendant would often complain that she was overweight, saying it embarrassed him, and that he would start many verbal fights, usually over things that were insignificant. She claimed the situation got to the point where her whole life revolved around trying not to agitate defendant. Defendant testified that he often asked plaintiff to leave, complained that she was a "fanatic" about cleaning, and admitted that he once presented her with a list of things for her to remember to do so that she wouldn't "irritate" him. Although defendant agreed that he was sometimes difficult to live with and that he treated plaintiff badly from time to time, he blamed it on the stress of law school. According to plaintiff, defendant would often apologize the day after a fight, sometimes verbally and sometimes in a letter. The parties finally separated . . . after defendant informed plaintiff that he had met another woman and had gone out with her a couple of times while plaintiff was working.

The trial court found that the breakdown of the marriage was primarily the fault of defendant, and announced it had considered this fact in its property distribution. After awarding each of the parties their respective automobiles, the trial court awarded plaintiff specific household goods and bank funds totaling $5,000, while awarding defendant specific goods and funds totaling $3,000. Defendant was also held solely responsible for repayment of $14,000 in student loans. Finally, the trial court determined that defendant's law degree was a marital asset subject to distribution. The court valued the degree at $80,000, and awarded plaintiff, as her share of the degree, $32,000 on the basis that this amount would equalize the parties' respective distributive shares. The court ordered this obligation to be paid off in monthly installments of $ 371.55 or more, at seven percent interest, until fully paid. The court did not award either party alimony.

[D]efendant challenges various aspects of the . . . property distribution, with his primary objection being the court's inclusion of his law degree in the marital estate and the resultant valuation of that degree. On cross appeal, plaintiff also challenges the trial court's valuation of the law degree. . . .

The goal . . . with respect to the division of the marital estate is a fair and equitable distribution under all of the circumstances. The division is not governed by any rigid rules or mathematical formula and need not be equal. . . . The primary question is what is fair. ✻

Panels of this Court have expressed different views concerning the treatment, characterization, and valuation of an advanced degree. . . . Nevertheless, most panels have agreed that fairness dictates that a spouse who did not earn an advanced degree be compensated whenever the advanced degree is the end product of a concerted family effort involving mutual sacrifice and effort by both spouses. [W]e will begin by first discussing the rationale behind the recognition that a nonstudent spouse must be compensated whenever a concerted family effort is involved in obtaining an advanced degree, which discussion will include an application of the concept "concerted family effort" to the facts of the instant case. Secondly, we will discuss what we believe to be the appropriate and preferable means of characterizing a claim for compensation involving an advanced degree. Finally, we will address the factors and methods that we believe are relevant in valuing such a claim upon divorce.

Nonstudent spouse should be compensated

. . . The relevancy of fairness is that, in Michigan, equitable considerations form the underlying basis for recognizing a claim for compensation involving an advanced degree, and that the ultimate goal in every divorce case is to do what is necessary to accord complete equity under the facts and circumstances of the case. Second, the concept "concerted family effort" stresses the fact that it is not the . . . degree itself that gives rise to an equitable claim for compensation, but rather the fact of the degree being the end product of the mutual sacrifice, effort, and contribution of both parties as part of a larger, long-range plan intended to benefit the family as a whole. The concept is premised, in part, on the fact that the attainment of an advanced degree is a prolonged undertaking involving considerable expenditure of time, effort, and money, as well as other sacrifices. Where such an undertaking is pursued as part of a concerted family effort, both spouses expect to be compensated for their respective sacrifices, efforts, and contributions by eventually sharing in the fruits of the degree. Where, however, the parties' relationship ends in divorce, such a sharing is impossible. Although the degree holder will always have the degree to show for the efforts, the nonstudent spouse is left with nothing. Therefore, a remedy consistent with fairness and equity requires that an attempt be made to at least return financially to the nonstudent spouse the value of what that spouse contributed toward attainment of the degree.

Policy behind "concerted family effort"

Fairness dictates financial compensation

Generally, the existence of a concerted family effort will be reflected in many ways[, such as] through a spouse's tangible efforts and financial contributions associated with working and supporting the mate while the mate pursues the advanced degree, [and] through other intangible, nonpecuniary efforts and contributions, such as where a spouse increases the share of the daily tasks, child-rearing responsibilities, or other details of household and family management undertaken in order to provide the mate with the necessary time and energy to study and attend classes. A concerted family effort is also exemplified by the fact that both spouses typically share in the emotional and psychological burdens of the educational experience. For the nonstudent spouse, these burdens may be experienced either directly, such as through the presence of increased tension within the household, or indirectly, such as where the spouse shares vicariously in the stress of the educational experience. Finally, the attainment of an advanced degree during marriage is

Nonstudent spouse's contribution is varied.

usually accompanied by considerable sacrifice on the part of both spouses. For the nonstudent spouse, such sacrifice may be reflected by a change in life style during the educational process, the availability of less time to pursue personal interests, or even a decision to either give up or temporarily postpone one's own educational or career pursuits as part of the larger, long-range plan designed to benefit the family as a whole.

[P]laintiff temporarily postponed her pursuit of an associate's degree in nursing, moved with defendant to the Detroit area so that he could attend law school, and then worked full-time to support [them while he] attended classes. This was all done as part of a larger plan to benefit both parties as a whole. Plaintiff, in addition to being the primary financial provider while defendant attended school, wherein she accounted for approximately eighty percent of the parties' total financial support, also bore primary responsibility for the daily household tasks. Moreover, the stress of the law school experience was certainly experienced by both parties, as reflected by the fact that defendant repeatedly blamed his inappropriate behavior toward plaintiff on the stress of law school, and by plaintiff's testimony explaining that her whole life revolved around her trying not to agitate defendant.

We conclude, therefore, that defendant's law degree was clearly the end product of a concerted family effort giving rise to an equitable claim for compensation in favor of plaintiff. . . .

. . . [Our] panels are in disagreement over the appropriate manner in which a claim for compensation should be considered. While some panels have characterized an advanced degree as a marital asset subject to property division, other panels have held that an advanced degree is more properly considered as a factor in awarding alimony.

After reviewing the various decisions addressing the issue and taking into consideration the underlying principles upon which an award of compensation for an advanced degree is premised, we reject the view holding that an advanced degree is more properly considered as a factor in awarding alimony.

The cases adhering to the alimony view, have stated that a degree is simply not "property" for the reasons expressed in *Graham v Graham*, 194 Colo 429, 432; 574 P.2d 75 (1978):

> An educational degree . . ., is simply not encompassed even by the broad views of the concept of "property." It does not have an exchange value or any objective transferable value on an open market. It is personal to the holder. It terminates on death of the holder and is not inheritable. It cannot be assigned, sold, transferred, conveyed or pledged. An advanced degree is a cumulative product of many years of previous education, combined with diligence and hard work. It may not be acquired by the mere expenditure of money. It is simply an intellectual achievement that may potentially assist in the future acquisition of property. In our view, it has none of the attributes of property in the usual sense of that term.

In rejecting the alimony approach, we first recognize that the basic purpose of paying alimony is to assist in the other spouse's support. Unlike alimony, however, the principles underlying an award of compensation based on the attainment of an advanced degree are neither rooted in nor based on notions of support. . . . [W]here a concerted family effort is involved, a spouse's entitlement to compensation constitutes a recognized right; it is not dependent upon factors related to the need for support. . . .

Moreover . . . an award in terms of alimony may unfairly jeopardize a spouse's recognized right to compensation because a trial court has broad discretion in deciding whether to grant alimony, because an award of alimony is dependent on factors different from those related to the division of marital property, and because . . . alimony may be terminated if the spouse receiving it remarries. Regarding this latter observation, we agree with the panel in [*Lewis v Lewis*, 181 Mich. App. 1, 6; 448 N.W.2d 735 (1989)], which stated: "Because the value of an advanced degree does not 'evaporate' upon the nondegree-earning spouse's remarriage, we do not find an award of alimony a satisfactory method of recognizing that spouse's efforts toward earning the degree." Furthermore, we note that it is often the case that a nonstudent spouse will already have demonstrated the ability of self-support by virtue of having supported the degree-earning spouse through graduate school. While such fact would ordinarily militate against an award of alimony, we do not believe it should operate to deprive the nonstudent spouse of a recognized right to be compensated for unrewarded sacrifices, efforts, and contributions toward attainment of the degree.

Finally, . . . we do not believe that the consideration of an advanced degree when making the property distribution would be improper merely because a degree cannot be characterized as "property" in the classic sense. Rather, we agree with [*Woodworth v. Woodworth*, 126 Mich. App. 258, 263; 337 N.W.2d 332 (1983)], that "whether or not an advanced degree can physically or metaphysically be defined as 'property' is beside the point[;] [c]ourts must instead focus on the most equitable solution to dissolving the marriage and dividing among the respective parties what they have." Furthermore, as I stated in my concurring opinion in Olah, [*Olah v. Olah*, 135 Mich. App. 404, 412; 354 N.W.2d 359 (1984)]: "This is an equitable distribution jurisdiction, in which classification of an item as either property or non-property is not decisive in determining the best division of the parties' holdings on divorce." Finally, in *Lewis, supra*, p. 6, this Court added: "[T]he fundamental question in cases involving advanced degrees is not whether a degree is property, but rather 'whether the facts in the case give rise to an equitable claim regarding the degree so that a property division can be considered fair and equitable between the parties.'"

We conclude, therefore, that [in a case like this], there arises a "marital asset" subject to distribution, wherein the interest of the nonstudent spouse consists of an "equitable claim" regarding the degree.

Having found that a marital asset giving rise to an "equitable claim" subject to distribution exists . . ., we will now discuss the appropriate factors and considerations relative to an evaluation of such a claim for purposes of distributing property. *Woodworth, supra*, pp. 268–269, discussed two methods of compensating a nonstudent spouse . . .: (1) awarding a percentage share of the present value of the future earnings attributable to the degree, or (2) restitution. The first method focuses on the degree's present value by attempting to estimate what the person holding the degree is likely to make in a particular job market and subtracting therefrom what that person would probably have earned without the degree. *Id.*

[The court here recounts the steps taken by the trial court to value the wife's share of the degree. Dissatisfied, the court said:]

Accordingly, we conclude that the appropriate remedy . . . is to remand . . . for revaluation of plaintiff's "equitable claim" in light of this opinion. On remand, we do not believe that the present value method . . ., purportedly used by plaintiff's expert, is an appropriate means by which to evaluate plaintiff's equitable claim involving the degree. Such a method emphasizes the notion that a nonstudent spouse possesses some sort of pecuniary interest in the degree itself. We believe such a notion misconstrues the underlying premise upon which an award of compensation involving an advanced degree is based. As we have attempted to explain throughout this opinion, an award of compensation is premised upon equitable considerations, wherein the goal is to attempt to financially return to the nonstudent spouse what that spouse contributed toward attainment of the degree. Because such an award is not premised upon the notion that a nonstudent spouse possesses an interest in the degree itself, we do not believe the actual value of the degree is a relevant consideration.

Among the arguments advanced by defendant in support of his contention that an advanced degree should not be considered when dividing the marital estate are: (1) that marriage is not a commercial venture, (2) that the value of an advanced degree cannot be ascertained with reasonable certainty, and (3) that consideration of a degree as part of the property division would be akin to involuntary servitude. Inherent in each of these arguments, however, is the notion that a nonstudent spouse possesses some type of pecuniary interest in a degree or is entitled to be compensated for a portion of the so-called "value" of the degree, views we specifically reject. Again, we emphasize that the focus of an award involving an advanced degree is not to reimburse the nonstudent spouse for "loss of expectations" over what the degree might potentially have produced, but to reimburse that spouse for unrewarded sacrifices, efforts, and contributions toward attainment of the degree on the ground that it would be equitable to do so in view of the fact that that spouse will not be sharing in the fruits of the degree.

[The] Appellate Division of the Superior Court of New Jersey in *Mahoney v Mahoney*, 182 N.J. Super. 598; 442 A.2d 1062 (1982) [stated]:

> The termination of the marriage represents, if nothing else, the disappointment of expectations, financial and nonfinancial, which were hoped to be achieved by and during the continuation of the relationship. It does not, however, in our view, represent a commercial investment loss. Recompense for the disappointed expectations resulting from the failure of the marital entity to survive cannot, therefore, be made to the spouses on a strictly commercial basis. . . .
>
>   * * *
>
> If the plan fails by reason of the termination of the marriage, we do not regard the supporting spouse's consequent loss of expectations by itself as any more compensable or demanding of solicitude than the

loss of expectations of any other spouse who, in the hope and anticipation of the endurance of the relationship and its commitments, has invested a portion of his or her life, youth, energy and labor in a failed marriage.

In our view, any valuation of a nonstudent spouse's equitable claim involving an advanced degree involves a two-step analysis. First, an examination of the sacrifices, efforts, and contributions of the nonstudent spouse toward attainment of the degree. Second, given such sacrifices, efforts, and contributions, a determination of what remedy or means of compensation would most equitably compensate the nonstudent spouse under the facts of the case. In this regard, . . . the length of the marriage after the degree was obtained, the sources and extent of financial support given to the degree holder during the years in school, and the overall division of the parties' marital property are all relevant considerations. . . .

[handwritten: Ct's 2 step valuation process]

. . .

[A]n equitable remedy may be exemplified in different ways. For example, as this Court recognized in [*Krause v Krause*, 177 Mich. App. 184, 197–198; 441 N.W.2d 66 (1989)]: "[I]f [the nonstudent spouse] wishes to pursue [an] education or take other similar steps to improve . . . employability or income earning potential, it is reasonable and equitable to require the [degree-holding spouse] to assist . . . in those endeavors." Thus, in this type of situation, an award consistent with fairness and equity would be one which requires the degree-earning spouse to provide assistance, in the form of financial support, equivalent to that provided by the nonstudent spouse during the marriage.

Where, however, a nonstudent spouse does not wish to further pursue an education, then perhaps equity would best be served by an award reimbursing the spouse for the amount of financial assistance provided toward attainment of the degree, while also recognizing the other intangible, nonpecuniary sacrifices made and efforts expended.

. . .

We note . . . the parties separated shortly after defendant attained his law degree. Thus, plaintiff received little reward, if any, for her sacrifices, efforts, and contributions toward defendant's degree. Further, while defendant did contribute some financial support during the degree-earning period, it was plaintiff who accounted for the vast majority of it, approximately eighty percent. Moreover, while defendant certainly worked hard in obtaining his degree, it is abundantly clear from the record that plaintiff's nonpecuniary efforts and contributions toward the degree were indeed significant also, and that she certainly endured many hardships and sacrifices as a result of her participation in the law school experience. We also note that while plaintiff did ultimately further her own career objectives in the manner she chose, she was required to do so on her own and did not have nearly the same benefits, financial or otherwise, that defendant had while he attended school. Defendant was, however, primarily responsible for the actual cost of his education, which was financed mostly through student loans for which he remains solely responsible. These are just some of the factors which were not discussed by the trial court, but yet are relevant to the valuation of plaintiff's equitable

[handwritten: Trial ct failed to look at some factors]

claim involving the degree. Therefore, these factors shall be considered by the trial court on remand.

After valuing plaintiff's equitable claim, the trial court may order that the amount determined to be due be payable in monthly installments over a fixed period of time. . . .

. . .

Affirmed in part and remanded for proceedings consistent with this opinion regarding the valuation of plaintiff's equitable claim involving defendant's law degree. We do not retain jurisdiction.

ALI PRINCIPLES OF THE LAW OF FAMILY DISSOLUTION, § 4.07 EARNING CAPACITY AND GOODWILL

(1) Spousal earning capacity, spousal skills, and earnings from post-dissolution spousal labor are not marital property.

(2) Occupational licenses and educational degrees are not marital property.

(3) Business and professional goodwill earned during marriage are marital property to the extent they have value apart from the value of spousal earning capacity, spousal skills, or post-dissolution spousal labor.

(a) Evidence of an increment during marriage in the market value of business or professional goodwill establishes the existence of divisible marital property in that amount except to the extent that market value includes the value of post-dissolution spousal labor.

(b) Business or professional goodwill that is not marketable is nevertheless marital property to the extent a value can be established for it that does not include the value of spousal earning capacity, spousal skills, or post-dissolution spousal labor.

Comment:

a. Earning capacity and the relation between property and compensatory payments. . . .[¶] "Earning capacity" has no meaning or existence independent of the method used to measure it. It is generally measured by finding a present value for . . . the individual's future earnings, and is thus no more than a shorthand term for that present value. A rule characterizing earning capacity as marital property is a rule treating future earnings as marital property, which in operation requires that those earnings be estimated at divorce so that their present value can then be fixed and allocated between the spouses.

Traditionally, however, spousal claims on post-divorce earnings were made under the rubric of alimony. . . . A major purpose of Chapter 5 is to reconceive alimony in a form that provides a more reliable and consistent remedy, in cases of disparate earning capacity, than is offered by the existing law. It is likely that the historical unreliability of the alimony remedy is an important reason why some potential alimony claimants recast their claim on post-marital earnings into property terms. The ease with which any income flow can be described as a property interest of equivalent value facilitates this strategy. . . .[¶] While property and alimony remedies are financially fungible, they have different procedural and substantive traditions that bear on the kind of claims best treated under each. These traditions explain why courts that confront the question directly usually decline to treat earning capacity as property. . . .

Procedurally, alimony awards are exercises of continuing equitable authority and typically remain modifiable, while a division of marital property is an ordinary civil judgment and therefore final and nonmodifiable. The finality and nonmodifiability that are critical to adjudications of property ownership make these judgments poor instruments by which to allocate future spousal earnings. Not only may the earnings of the former spouses vary in unpredictable ways, but also spousal claims on one another's post-dissolution income are properly affected by some post-dissolution events, such as the obligee's remarriage. . . .

The traditional procedural differences between alimony and property are related to their divergent substantive heritage. An alimony obligee's improved living standard after divorce can provide substantive grounds for terminating the alimony award, while it would violate substantive norms to require a newly fortunate spouse to return some of the marital property he or she was allocated at dissolution. Increased prosperity does not compromise previously established property rights. . . . [A] regime that treats earning capacity acquired during marriage as marital property approaches the cases according to property rules designed to serve other policies, rather than according to the equitable considerations with which the law of alimony has traditionally been concerned. The treatment of earning capacity as property would therefore deny relief to many deserving spouses while allowing it to others with no equitable claim.

. . .

The preceding observations relate to a broader theme from which the differences between property and alimony in part emerge. The law has treated alimony as appropriate in only a subset of divorces in which there are circumstances, sometimes temporary, that justify equitable adjustments in post-marriage income between former spouses. In contrast, marital-property claims are normally viewed as property entitlements created by the marriage alone, even if subject to equitable adjustment. The principle underlying this difference is that marriage creates property entitlements to certain *things* acquired during it, but does not create property entitlements against the *person* of the other spouse. Marriage does not create a lifetime claim by one spouse on the other's talents and labor, even though a long-term or even permanent claim on a former spouse's post-marriage earnings does result from the combination of marriage with other factors of the kind traditionally considered under the rubric of alimony and addressed in Chapter 5 of these *Principles*. Section 4.07(1) therefore reflects the law's longstanding distinction between claims on things and claims on another's personal attributes.

. . .

c. *Educational degrees and occupational licenses.* Paragraph (2) [of § 4.07] bars marital property claims on educational degrees and occupational licenses.

This bar is an application of the more fundamental principle stated in Paragraph (1). Any value assigned to degrees or licenses is necessarily a valuation of spousal earning capacity. Degrees and licenses are not marketable nor is there any market data on which their valuation can be based. The few decisions that recognize a marital property interest in a degree or license value them by projecting the probable difference, over the holder's lifetime, between the earnings of an individual with the license or degree and the earnings of one without it. Under this formulation, the credential's value is simply the average increment in income earned by its holders. Other skills or entitlements that increase average earnings cannot be distinguished, even if their acquisition is not recognized in a formal document such as a degree. The principle that treats degrees or licenses as marital property would necessarily extend, for example, to job seniority and promotions.

Some cases rejecting property claims on degrees rely entirely on the fact that degrees are not marketable. That explanation sweeps too broadly, however, for nonmarketable assets are routinely and properly treated as marital property. Pension rights, which are typically nontransferable, perhaps provide the most common example. The principle on which this section relies is not marketability and it therefore does not exclude property claims on spousal pensions. Pensions differ from degrees because, even though pensions are not saleable, market data can establish a value for them that does not include the value of "spousal earning capacity, spousal skills, and post-marital spousal labor". . . .

Marital-property claims to degrees and licenses are often made by persons who supported their spouse in school or in training. The decisions rejecting such property claims often allow instead an alimony claim based upon these facts.

NOTES

1. O'Brien's *Logic, and Other Cases on Licenses and Degrees.* ***Marriage of Graham**, 574 P.2d 75 (Colo. 1978), quoted in *Postema*, preceded the New York decision in *O'Brien*. The *Graham* court read the Colorado law, based upon the Model Marriage and Divorce Act, quite differently than *O'Brien* read the New York law.

Graham has proven far more influential than *O'Brien*. *O'Brien* itself conceded that other states have reached the opposite result. A 1987 National Law Journal survey, found New York was then the only state with surviving authority for classifying a professional degree as property. State high court cases decided since then uniformly favor *Graham*. These include *Guy v. Guy*, 736 So.2d 1042 (Miss. 1999); *Simmons v. Simmons*, 708 A.2d 949 (Conn. 1998); *Becker v. Perkins-Becker*, 669 A.2d 524 (R.I. 1996); *Downs v. Downs,* 574 A.2d 156 (Vt. 1990); *Hodge v. Hodge,* 520 A.2d 15 (Pa. 1986); *Marriage of Francis,* 442 N.W.2d 59 (Iowa 1989); *Drapek v. Drapek,* 503 N.E.2d 946 (Mass. 1987); *Sweeney v. Sweeney,* 534 A.2d 1290 (Me. 1987); *Stevens v. Stevens,* 492 N.E.2d 131 (Ohio 1986); *Nelson v. Nelson,* 736 P.2d 1145 (Alaska 1987); *Hoak v. Hoak,* 370 S.E.2d 473 (W. Va. 1988); and *Archer v. Archer*, 493 A.2d 1074 (Md. 1985); *see generally Simmons, supra,* at 955 n.7 (listing cases from each state). Most cases rejecting degree-as-property claims conclude that other remedies can be found to reimburse one spouse for the support provided the other for schooling, sometimes by way of alimony and sometimes by creating restitutionary remedies designed just for this purpose. For more on these alternative remedies, see Notes 3 & 4. The *ALI Principles* similarly reject *O'Brien* in favor of the majority rule.

O'Brien emphasizes a phrase in the New York statute defining marital property as all property acquired after the marriage "regardless of the form in which title is held," as if that phrase were unusually dramatic. In fact, variants of this phrase can be found in nearly all modern equitable distribution statutes, including § 307 of the Model Marriage and Divorce Act (permitting division of property "whether title thereto is in the name of the husband or wife or both") upon which the Colorado statute construed in *Graham* is based. The intent of such language likely was to make clear the reformers' purpose of overruling the common law's traditional emphasis on title in allocating property on divorce, and thereby ensure that the title's form would not bar the court from allocating it under the new law. In making the title to property irrelevant it did not alter common understandings of what was property. One can make similar observations about the New York statute's list of factors relevant to the allocation of marital property, also mentioned in *O'Brien*. New York's inclusion, as one factor on this list, of one spouse's contributions to the other's career is entirely typical, as we saw above in Section A1, and offers no basis for suggesting that New York's law is unusual. And of course the list of factors is meant to guide the courts in *dividing* property, not in *defining* it.

O'Brien was reaffirmed and actually expanded by *McSparron v. McSparron*, 87 N.Y.2d 275, 639 N.Y.S.2d 265, 662 N.E.2d 745 (1995). *McSparron* reviewed a series of decisions by lower New York courts that had declined to apply *O'Brien* to a degree held by a spouse who had subsequently established a successful professional practice that was also subject to division. These lower courts had found that in such cases the degree or license had "merged" into the practice and need not be divided separately from it. Many expected the court to overrule *O'Brien*, but the contrary occurred. *McSparron* disapproved these lower court decisions and suggested that ensuring the separate treatment of the license as marital property is necessary in order to *avoid* introducing "nettlesome legal fictions" in the law. Its discussion of *O'Brien* does not acknowledge its unanimous rejection by other state high courts. After *McSparron*, the New York State Bar Association urged the legislature to overrule *O'Brien*. New York State Bar Association, *Report of the Task Force on Family Law* 15 (August 19, 1996); Spencer, *No-Fault Divorce Endorsed By State Bar, Uphill Battle Predicted for State Legislature*, N.Y. L.J., January 27, 1997, at 1.

2. Applying O'Brien. One New York lower court concluded early on that advances during marriage in the wife's acting career were marital property. *Golub v. Golub*, 139 Misc. 2d 440, 527 N.Y.S.2d 946 (Sup. 1988):

> Plaintiff . . . contends that her celebrity status is neither "professional" nor a "license" and hence not an "investment in human capital subject to equitable distribution." Moreover, plaintiff argues that

because a career in show business is subject to substantial fluctuation, it should not be considered. In *O'Brien,* the fact that the professional license itself had no market value was irrelevant. It is the enhanced earning capacity that the license affords the holder that is of value. In this respect, all sources of enhanced earning capacity become indistinguishable.

. . . *O'Brien* is the law. If it is to remain as good law, the rule should be uniformly applied. There seems to be no rational basis upon which to distinguish between a degree, a license, or any other special skill that generates substantial income.

See also Elkus v. Elkus, 169 A.D.2d 134, 572 N.Y.S.2d 901 (1991) (husband's claim to wife's successful career as an opera singer); *Allocco v. Allocco,* 152 Misc.2d 529, 578 N.Y.S.2d 995 (Sup. 1991) (husband's successful completion of civil service examinations for police lieutenant is divisible property which his wife should share because she contributed to his success); *but see McAlpine v. McAlpine,* 176 A.D.2d 285, 574 N.Y.S.2d 385 (1991) (even if husband's successful completion of last five actuary examinations during marriage had added to his earning capacity, wife had no claim because husband performed most household duties during marriage and wife did not contribute to his examination success or sacrifice her own career prospects to further it). While this effort to limit *O'Brien*'s reach is understandable, any serious requirement that the claimant show a direct causal link between his or her contributions and the spouse's career success would probably doom most claims.

For other applications of *O'Brien*, see *Morrongiello v. Paulsen,* 195 A.D.2d 594, 601 N.Y.S.2d 121 (1993) (where marriage occurred after husband finished one year of law school, two-thirds of his degree, equal to $189,474, is marital property); *Finocchio v. Finocchio,* 162 A.D.2d 1044, 556 N.Y.S.2d 1007 (1990) (license to practice law); *Di Caprio v. Di Caprio,* 162 A.D.2d 944, 556 N.Y.S.2d 1011 (1990) (master's degree and permanent certification in school administration); *Shoenfeld v. Shoenfeld,* 168 A.D.2d 674, 563 N.Y.S.2d 500 (1990) (medical license); *Holihan v. Holihan,* 159 A.D.2d 685, 553 N.Y.S.2d 434 (1990) (guidance counselor license); *Morimando v. Morimando,* 145 A.D.2d 609, 536 N.Y.S.2d 701 (1988) (physician's assistant certification); *McGowan v. McGowan,* 142 A.D.2d 355, 535 N.Y.S.2d 990 (1988) (master's degree); *Marcus v. Marcus,* 135 A.D.2d 216, 525 N.Y.S.2d 238 (1988) (medical license, merged with practice itself); *Anderson v. Anderson,* 153 A.D.2d 823, 545 N.Y.S.2d 335 (1989) (master's degrees in health care administration and labor and industrial relations, nursing home administrator license).

Some lower courts have developed rules of equity under which the degree, while treated as marital property, should not be divided between the spouses, or at least not in anything approaching an equal division. In *Gandhi v. Gandhi,* 283 A.D.2d 782, 724 N.Y.S.2d 541 (2001), the court said that neither the husband's accounting degree, earned partially before marriage, nor the wife's paralegal degree, earned partially after the marriage, should be allocated. In justification, the court observed (among other things) that the husband's CPA license was attributable in part to his intelligence and hard work. In *Brough v. Brough,* 285 A.D.2d 913, 727 N.Y.S.2d 555 (2001), the court granted the husband only 10% of the wife's enhanced earnings arising from the B.A., M.A., and teacher's certificate she earned during their 20 year marriage, reasoning that even though the husband fully supported the wife during her education, and gave her personal assistance with her studies, the degrees and licenses were primarily the result of her own abilities and efforts. *Conasanti v. Conasanti*, 296 A.D.2d 831, 744 N.Y.S.2d 614 (2002), similarly granted the wife only 30% of the husband's medical degree, because "while [the wife's] efforts certainly contributed to the ability of [the husband] to obtain his medical license and advanced degrees, those achievements were accomplished primarily through [his] own ability and Herculean effort as well as his own capacity for hard work" (citing *Brough*). Of course, similar claims could have been made for the license-holding spouse in *O'Brien* and in most of the cases that have followed. While requiring the court to decide on the relative importance of the contributions of the degree-holding spouse and the supporting spouse to the holder's achievement may avoid some of the absurd results *O'Brien* seems to entail, wildly inconsistent results appear inevitable. Their one "reliable" common feature is that as property rather than alimony awards, their allocations of post-divorce income will not be modifiable to correct the erroneous projections of the degree-holder's future economic circumstances that courts will inevitably make in some cases.

3. *Alternative Remedies I:* Postema, *etc.* As *Postema* indicates, there are alternatives to *O'Brien*'s treatment of licenses as marital property. First, one could find the license or degree obtained during the course of the marriage irrelevant to the financial terms of divorce, but consider the greater earning power the license or degree may have brought relevant, particularly in alimony decisions (treated in Note 4 and Section D, *infra*). The advantage of alimony over *O'Brien*'s property treatment is that it does not require the court to hazard a guess of the value of the license or degree — which, if wrong, could create a windfall for the non-degree-holding spouse at the degree-holding spouse's expense. At the least, a high evaluation of the value of the license or degree could unjustly constrain the degree-holding spouse's career options (*e.g.*, forcing a lawyer to choose corporate law firm work over public interest or public sector work). An alimony award can be modified over time, as it becomes clearer whether and to what extent obtaining a license or degree has increased its holder's earning capacity.

An additional advantage of alimony becomes clear when one notes that the same degree or license may be acquired in a marriage of three years' duration or during the first three years of a thirty-year marriage. The *O'Brien* rule does not distinguish these cases: in both, the degree's entire value is marital property. Within a long-term marriage, (1) as *Postema* points out, the non-degree-owning spouse will likely have benefited significantly, if indirectly, from the license and the increased earning power it brought; and (2) if the marriage ends with a significant difference in earning potential between the two spouses, most courts allow the lower earner (usually the non-degree-holder) a share in the other spouse's earnings through an alimony award.

The disadvantages of a traditional alimony award are: (1) as *Postema* points out, that it implies that the payments are at the discretion of the court, and perhaps based on "need" or "status," rather than any sort of entitlement; and (2) in many jurisdictions, alimony is subject to modification based on the obligor's ability to pay, and it is terminated on the death of either former spouse or the remarriage of the recipient (all three factors reflecting the view of alimony as discretionary rather than an entitlement). *Postema* sought a middle ground that would avoid the problems of both property treatments of degrees and alimony awards. However, *Postema*'s compromise does not seem successful; its decision proclaims a quasi-property entitlement which articulated, leaves trial courts with little guidance and a great deal of discretion. The solution may be not much better than (and not much different from) the problems it was seeking to remedy.

One obvious alternative response to a situation where property is inappropriate and alimony inadequate, is to fix the alimony option — to make it more of an entitlement, and less discretionary and unpredictable. As is discussed in the following Note, a number of jurisdictions, and the *ALI Principles*, have taken that path.

4. *Alternative Remedies II: Reimbursement Alimony.* While the discussion of alimony is left to Section D, brief mention should be made here of the way alimony is commonly used to respond to marriages where one spouse has supported the other in obtaining a degree (with the marriage ending during the degree program or shortly after the degree is attained). Many states have statutes which expressly authorize the award of alimony to the spouse who "[c]ontributed to the educational opportunities of the other spouse," without regard to need, or to whether the claimant intended to return to school herself. A.R.S. 25-319(a)(3) (West 2000 & Supp. 2002). Such provisions are now common. In other states, courts have relied upon more flexible statutory language to create a remedy called "reimbursement alimony," available to the supporting spouse without regard to that spouse's educational plans. *See, e.g., DeLa Rosa v. DeLa Rosa*, 309 N.W.2d 755 (Minn. 1981). In that case, Pedro DeLa Rosa and Elena DeLa Rosa married in 1972, when Pedro was beginning his undergraduate education. By agreement, Elena supported him through his undergraduate education and in his medical school training. Pedro filed for divorce during his second year of medical education.

> Prior to their separation, [Elena] was the primary source of financial income, thus permitting her husband to focus his energies upon obtaining an undergraduate degree, entering and attending medical school. The trial court found that [she] earned approximately $41,000 during coverture which was used for the parties' joint living expenses. [Pedro's] contributions were nominal; he earned $2,300 and received Veterans' educational benefits . . . of $9,031. He also received a grant to attend medical school . . . of $5,680. [Pedro] had incurred student loans of approximately $10,000 at the time of separation. The record reveals that tuition for [Pedro's] undergraduate and medical educations during the parties' marriage was roughly $8,811.

The trial court concluded (and the Minnesota Supreme Court agreed) that Elena was not entitled to alimony under the Minnesota statute, due to her ability to support herself through appropriate employment. However, the trial court awarded Elena $29,669 for contributions she made to [Pedro's] education. The Minnesota Supreme Court commented:

The trial court's award was grounded in equity and represented restitution of the financial support [she] provided to [him] during the time he was attending college and medical school.

[Elena] had a reasonable expectation that she would be rewarded for her efforts by a higher standard of living when [Pedro] began practicing medicine. We find that the trial court did not abuse its discretion in making an equitable award to [Elena] for the financial support she provided . . . during his schooling in light of the facts and circumstances of this case.

However, the court modified the original award (reducing it to $11,400) based on the following reasoning:

It is this Court's view that the award should have been limited to the monies expended by [Elena] for [Pedro]'s living expenses and any contributions made toward [his] direct educational costs. To achieve this result, we subtract from [her] earnings her own living expenses. This has the effect of imputing one-half of the living expenses and all the educational expenses to the student spouse. The formula subtracts from [her] contributions one-half of the couple's living expenses, that amount being the contributions of the two parties which were not used for direct educational costs: Working spouse's financial contributions to joint living expenses and educational costs of student spouse *less* 1/2 (working spouse's financial contributions *plus* student spouse's financial contributions less cost of education) *equals* equitable award to working spouse.

DeLa Rosa's approach to measuring reimbursement alimony is consistent with the bulk of existing authority — *e.g.*, *Mahoney v. Mahoney*, 453 A.2d 527 (N.J. 1982); *Hubbard v. Hubbard*, 603 P.2d 747, 750–53 (Okla. 1979); *Hoak v. Hoak*, 370 S.E.2d 473 (W.Va. 1988); *Geer v. Geer*, 353 S.E.2d 427 (N.C. App. 1987); *Donahue v. Donahue*, 384 S.E.2d 741 (S.C. 1989) — and also with *ALI Principles* § 5.12.

California requires "reimbursement" upon divorce to the marital community "for community contributions to education or training of a party that substantially enhances the earning capacity of the party." CAL. FAM. CODE § 2641 (West 1994 & Supp. 2003). The statute distinguishes between long-and short-term marriages in a portion that allows for departures from the required reimbursement when the education or training had occurred so long ago that "the community has substantially benefited" from it already. The statute creates a rebuttable presumption that such benefit has accrued where the education occurred more than ten years before divorce. The long-term spouse is thus excluded from reimbursement, but may benefit, of course, from an alimony award based on the degree holder's larger earnings.

Some authorities that authorize reimbursement alimony do not allow recovery for living expenses, as compared with the direct costs of the other spouse's education. *Bold v. Bold*, 574 A.2d 552 (Pa. 1990); CAL. FAM. CODE § 2641 (West 1994 & Supp. 2003); IND. CODE ANN. § 31-15-7-6 (Michie 1997 & Supp. 2002). Some statutes and cases make support for the other spouse's education a relevant factor in considering an alimony claim without providing any specific guidance for calculating the entitlement. *E.g.*, N.H. Rev. Stat. Ann. § 458:16-a(II)(h) (Lexis 1992 & Supp. 2000) (one factor in determining an equitable division of the property is "direct or indirect contribution made by one party to help educate or develop the career . . . of the other"); Ariz. Rev. Stat. § 25-319(A)(3) (2000 & Supp. 2002) (a basis for alimony); N.C. Gen. Stat. §§ 50-20(b)(2), (c)(7) (Lexis 2003) (to be considered in alimony; degrees not considered marital property); Tenn. Code Ann. § 36-4-121 (Lexis 2001 & Supp. 2002) (a factor in allocating marital property, but degrees are not themselves property); *Schmitz v. Schmitz*, 801 S.W.2d 333, 336 (Ky. App. 1991) (there is no "set formula" for reimbursement alimony); *Downs v. Downs*, 574 A.2d 156 (Vt. 1990). California statutes allow both property and alimony remedies, although presumably not in the same case. See *Watt v. Watt*, 214 Cal. App. 3d 340, 262 Cal. Rptr. 783 (1989) (finding the wife ineligible for property award but entitled to alimony).

Comment *a* of *ALI Principles* § 5.12 explains the reimbursement award for educational expenses as a limited exception to the usual rule rejecting claims based on inequities in the allocation of financial resources during the marriage — an exception justified by two factors:

> First, arrangements under which one spouse supports the other through school are often seen as separable from other spousal arrangements. . . . Second, the equities favoring a remedy are thought particularly strong when the educated spouse leaves the marriage with an advantage in earning capacity achieved with the other's uncompensated assistance.

However, matters change with a longer marriage:

> [C]ompensation is available only when the divorce occurs reasonably soon after completion of the education or training. With the passage of time the spousal arrangements for support of the education can no longer be treated as a distinct transaction to be evaluated independently from the rest of the marital give and take. Spouses still married 10 years after one of them has completed an education with the other's support will normally have both enjoyed benefits . . . from the earning capacity enhancement it brought, and will share as well in marital property purchased with those incremental earnings. (*Id.*)

See also, Pyeatte v. Pyeatte, 661 P.2d 196, 203–04 (Ariz. App. 1983) (in the ordinary case the value of each spouse's labor during marriage "is consumed by the community in the on-going relationship and forms no basis for a claim); *Mahoney v. Mahoney*, 453 A.2d 527, 533 (N.J. 1982) (marriage cannot be treated as "a business arrangement in which the parties keep track of debits and credits, their accounts to be settled upon divorce").

Does a claim for reimbursement alimony require that the claimant spent money directly on his spouse's *education*? In *Bold* the wife provided much of her husband's living expenses through school, but made no direct contribution to his educational expenses, which he paid from loans and grants. The lower court held she therefore had no reimbursement claim, because she had merely satisfied her ordinary duty of support in the marriage. In reversing and sustaining an award, the Pennsylvania Supreme Court allowed her a claim for all support she paid in excess of the "bare minimum" she was legally obliged to provide. *Bold v. Bold,* 574 A.2d 552 (Pa. 1990). Does a reimbursement claim require that the claimant herself suffered a loss from having supported her spouse, as by foregoing one's own education in order to support one's spouse? Minnesota seemed to require this element in the *DeLa Rosa* sequel of *Ellesmere v. Ellesmere,* 359 N.W.2d 48 (Minn. App. 1984). The wife earned three advanced degrees during the marriage while the husband, a physician, supported her. Relying on *DeLa Rosa,* he sought on divorce to recover his expenditures on her education, but was rebuffed in part because he incurred no "sacrifice and foregoing of the enjoyment of earned income significant enough to fit within the *DeLa Rosa* principle." What then of a schoolteacher who continues her teaching career unhampered after a divorce from her physician husband? A later Minnesota case, citing *DeLa Rosa* without further explanation, allowed restitution under just such facts for the teacher's support of her periodontist husband's education, despite a dissent citing *Ellesmere. In re Marriage of Williams,* 388 N.W.2d 432 (Minn. App. 1986).

5. Equity, Entitlement, and Sympathy. One might wonder whether the courts' evaluations of the equities in *O'Brien, Postema,* and *DeLa Rosa,* were affected by unarticulated assumptions concerning marital fault. The stereotypic facts that many assume in these sorts of claims involves a husband who leaves his wife for another woman after she has supported him through school. Would we be as sympathetic to Mrs. O'Brien's claim for half of her former husband's lifetime earnings as a physician if after his graduation she instead had left him for their impecunious next-door neighbor, the two of them planning to live comfortably ever after on half of Mr. O'Brien's future earnings? Would we think differently about the reimbursement of expenses for Mrs. Postema and Mrs. DeLa Rosa if the reason for their marriage's ending was their cruel treatment or adultery? If we do not wish to introduce fault into marital property allocations, then we need rules which are equitable without regard to whose actions caused the breakup. That is one argument that might be offered for allowing short-term spouses only reimbursement of their outlays, while allowing longer-term spouses a share in the other's post-dissolution income, when it is much greater than the claimant's.

[2] GOODWILL

Definitions of goodwill found in the cases often quote Justice Story's classic description in COMMENTARIES ON THE LAW OF PARTNERSHIPS, § 99, at 170 (6th ed. 1868), which has even found its way into statute, CAL. BUS. & PROF. CODE § 14100 (West 1964 & Supp. 2004) ("The 'good will' of a business is the expectation of continued public patronage."). But if we really want to know what goodwill means, these statements are of little help. It is better to ask: how is goodwill measured? And, indeed, if we put aside their testimony in lawsuits, and look instead at how accountants measure goodwill in their actual practice, there are some well-established conventions. Those conventions assume a sale, which is ordinarily the only occasion, apart from lawsuits, on which goodwill is measured. When a business is sold, values may be assigned to its various components to establish their basis for subsequent tax treatment. Standard accounting principles applicable to publicly traded corporations specify that the value of goodwill is the excess of a business's market value — what it sells for — over its asset value — the sum of the value of each of the firm's identifiable assets. B. HARTMAN, R. HARPER, J. KNOBLETT & P. RECKERS, INTERMEDIATE ACCOUNTING Chapter 13 (1994). The value of the goodwill thus depends upon the firm's market value, as the *ALI Principles* observe in § 4.07, Comment *d*:

> Standard accounting practice . . . give[s] goodwill a purely operational definition: it is no more (and no less) than the amount by which the market value of a going concern exceeds the total value of its tangible assets. . . . [¶] . . . One may speculate that this additional value arises from factors such as the business's reputation or location but such speculations have no relevance in accounting for the sale: the difference between sale price and asset value is entered as goodwill on the buyer's balance sheet, without regard to the explanation for it. . . . [B]uyers are willing to pay more than simple asset value for an operating business when they believe the business will generate an income, in their hands, that justifies the enhanced price. The greater the income expectation, the greater a premium over asset value buyers will be willing to pay, and the greater will be the goodwill component that accountants will assign to the purchase price. But this relationship between income expectations and goodwill is essentially circular, with no meaning apart from the definitional conventions employed by accountants. . . . Goodwill is not some "thing" which is the source of the income flow, and which is therefore marital property if acquired during marriage. Goodwill is simply the label placed on the price that a buyer is willing to pay for the income flow. . . .

Thus, once the market sets a value for the business as a whole, the definitional conventions employed by accountants yield a value for its goodwill. Before the market value for the business is established, the accountant cannot tell whether the business has any goodwill value at all; after it is established, the accountant cannot tell why the goodwill value is X rather than Y.

Why do domestic relations lawyers care how much of the market value of a business is accounted for by goodwill? Ordinarily, they don't. If Sally creates a business during her marriage to John, using marital capital, then the entire value of the business is marital property. And if we know what the business would sell for, we ordinarily know its value, for in the ordinary case the market value of a business is its value for marital property purposes as well. It matters not whether a buyer's accountant, after the sale, would conclude that goodwill accounted for fifty percent, ten percent, or zero percent of the purchase price; the entire purchase price, and no more, is marital property in all three cases. For the ordinary saleable business, for which a market price can be established, there is thus no occasion for disputes over the value of goodwill.

The occasion for such disputes arises instead when the business is not saleable, or when the claim is made that the market price does not reflect the full value of the business for marital property purposes. The most common example is the professional practice. Regulatory rules may bar or restrict the sale of a professional practice, so that it has no market price, or a depressed market price that the professional's spouse believes is less than its marital property value. The question then is this: What benchmark other than the market price can be used to fix the practice's value? One common approach seeks a market value for each component of the business (books, furniture, office equipment, and the like), as well as the goodwill. In such a case then, the usual accountant's convention is turned on its head: a value is offered for the goodwill (as well as the other components) in order to establish the full value of the business or practice. The consequence is then that one cannot employ the accountant's traditional definition of good will as the difference between the market value of a business and the sum of the value of each of its identifiable assets. If goodwill is simply what is left over after deducting the value of other assets from the total market value, then goodwill cannot be employed to calculate that market value. But then in this case it is not the market value that the evaluator seeks to establish. The whole point in this first place was to have a valuation that reflected the belief that, for marital property purposes, the business has a value that is something more than the market value. This observation identifies the problem but not the solution, which necessarily requires developing a method for valuing the goodwill, and thus the business, that differs from and does not depend upon knowing its market value.

Once one accepts the proposition that the value of an asset for marital property purposes is something other than its market value, the opportunities for contention over the valuation method become considerably enriched. There are no substitutes for market value that experts or courts agree upon. Ordinary appraisal methods seek to estimate the market price of an object, and that market value serves as a benchmark against which to judge the accuracy of an appraiser or his methods. What is the benchmark if market value is rejected? And what then is goodwill? These are the questions that many goodwill cases wrestle with, and all necessarily resolve, knowingly or not. The problem is particularly difficult because the purported experts in valuation relied upon in such cases do not always understand that their choice for the meaning of value, or of goodwill, must be driven by marital property rules and the policies that underlie them. In the midst of such confusion the opportunities for creative lawyering multiply. Indeed, if nonmarket meanings of value or goodwill are acceptable, why should they be limited to the case in which regulatory rules restrict or eliminate the market? Perhaps the true meaning of an asset for marital property purposes is different than its market value even where there is a market value.

While the conflicting authorities over the treatment of goodwill therefore spill over into a number of areas, the cases of professional practices remain the dominant arena. In contrast to professional licenses, and earning capacity itself, most courts agree that professional goodwill is divisible property. They differ, however, on the rules they adopt with respect to evidence of value. As one might expect from the preceding discussion, these measurement differences are more than technicalities. Not only can they yield dramatically different dollar amounts; they reflect fundamentally different conceptions of what constitutes divisible property. In some cases the measurement method used or adopted effectively includes earning capacity. It is therefore not possible to understand the policy at issue in the goodwill cases without mastering the valuation basics. Such mastery is also necessary for competent representation of a client in a case in which the marital property includes potentially valuable business or professional assets. The valuation evidence typically is offered by an expert witness who is an accountant or a business appraiser, but a lawyer who wants to persuade the court to accept one expert's valuation rather than another's must understand what the experts have in fact done. The following case, *Hanson v. Hanson*, involves two divorces in which two different valuation methods were used. One method relies upon establishment of a market value; the other is more mysterious.

HANSON v. HANSON

738 S.W.2d 429 (Mo. 1987)

ROBERTSON, Judge. These are consolidated appeals arising out of decrees of dissolution of marriage. . . . The husbands . . . are the sole partners in an oral surgery partnership. *In Hanson*, . . . the Circuit Court of Boone County valued the partnership at $324,862, including $233,727, an amount characterized as "goodwill" by the parties. In *Graham,* [another] Circuit Court . . . hearing virtually identical evidence, valued the same partnership at $90,280. . . .

We granted transfer to determine whether our dissolution of marriage laws recognize the existence of goodwill in a professional practice as a marital asset and to determine the extent to which those laws permit the division of such goodwill upon dissolution of marriage. . . .

I.

The Oral Surgery Partnership

Drs. Graham and Hanson formed their partnership for the practice of oral surgery in Jefferson City . . . in July, 1973. At trial, both Mrs. Hanson and Mrs. Graham employed Stephen Smith, a C.P.A., as an expert witness. Smith valued the oral surgery partnership as follows:

$ 39,750.00	equipment
$ 51,385.00	accounts receivable
$351,077.00	going concern value
$442,212.00	Total Value

Smith defined "going concern value" as the "opportunity to walk into a successful situation and to start work and earn money without having to build the practice." Smith further testified that going concern value represented the ability of the buyer to trade on the past reputation of the seller. [The court later concludes that "going concern value," as defined here, is equivalent to goodwill.]

Smith applied an 85 percent capitalization rate to the previous year's gross receipts to determine the value of the partnership. This capitalization rate was the product of Smith's assessment of the partnership's "monopolistic" position in the Jefferson City market, its expenses, the degree of risk attendant to the practice, and the reputation of the practice and the practitioners in the community. From these factors, Smith fashioned a tentative going concern value for the partnership. He compared his tentative conclusions to the national average sales price for oral surgery practices, for gross production per oral surgeon, and for average revenues and expenses for oral surgery partnerships containing five or fewer oral surgeons. From these considerations Smith reached his conclusion as to the appropriate capitalization factor to apply to the Graham and Hanson partnership. . . .

Both Dr. Hanson and Dr. Graham produced Elmer Evers, C.P.A. as an expert for purposes of valuing their partnership interests. Evers valued the partnership at $91,000, the approximate value of equipment, cash on hand and accounts receivable. Evers compared sales of professional practices in the area served by the partnership, the nature of the partnership's patronage, and the reputation of the partners to determine that neither goodwill nor going concern value existed in the partnership.

Dr. Thomas Coyle, an oral surgeon practicing in Columbia, . . . testified on behalf of Dr. Hanson. Dr. Coyle bought into a partnership . . . in Columbia in 1975. He testified that his purchase price included neither an amount for goodwill nor for the going concern value. . . . Upon the retirement of Dr. Coyle's partner, Dr. Coyle bought his partner's interest in the partnership; again, Dr. Coyle paid nothing for goodwill or going concern value.

Drs. Graham and Hanson introduced their partnership agreement in their respective cases. Paragraph eight of that agreement provided:

> The value of the interest of a withdrawing partner shall be the sum of: (a) One-half of the reasonable market value of the fixtures, equipment and contents of the office partnership; (b) His proportionate share of the accrued net profits; (c) One-half of all accounts receivable as of the date of dissolution which can be reasonably expected to be collected in the first six months following the date of dissolution; (d) No value for goodwill or firm name shall be included in any computations of a partner's interest; (e) If a net loss has been incurred to the date of dissolution, his share of such loss shall be deducted.

Dr. Hanson testified that profits were drawn from the partnership account twice monthly; there were no accrued net profits.

The Hanson Marriage

Dr. and Mrs. Hanson married on March 20, 1974. By the time of the marriage, Dr. Hanson had already completed his oral surgery training, had retired all but $1,000 of the debt he incurred to finance his education and had opened the oral surgery practice with Dr. Graham. Mrs. Hanson [had] a nursing degree. Following the marriage, Mrs. Hanson continued to pursue her nursing career. She earned a Master's Degree in nursing in December, 1981. At the time of the trial, Dr. Hanson earned approximately $120,000 per year in his oral surgery practice; Mrs. Hanson earned approximately $7,000 per year. There were no children.

The Boone County Circuit Court valued the partnership at $324,862.00, an amount which included the fair market value of the partnership's equipment

($39,750), the accounts receivable ($51,385) and the partnership's ordinary income for 1984 ($233,727). . . .

Dr. Hanson appeals the valuation of his partnership interest. . . .

The Graham Marriage

Dr. and Mrs. Graham married on May 24, 1969. The marriage produced two children. By the time of the marriage, Dr. Graham had completed his dental studies; he finished his oral surgery training during the marriage. Mrs. Graham completed registered nurse training prior to the marriage. In 1978, the Grahams began investing in real estate. The couple accumulated several parcels of improved real estate[.] Mrs. Graham managed the couple's properties. In 1980, she obtained a real estate license and began selling real estate on a full-time basis. In 1983, Mrs. Graham grossed approximately $27,000 as a real estate salesperson. After the couple's separation in 1983, her income declined to $5,000 in 1984. Dr. Graham earned approximately $120,000 per year at the time of the trial.

The Circuit Court of Cole County dissolved the marriage, valued Dr. Graham's interest in the partnership at $45,140, divided the marital property equally between the parties, awarded Mrs. Graham permanent maintenance of $500 per month to continue until remarriage, death or modification by court order. . . .

Both parties appealed the trial court's order. Mrs. Graham assigns error to the court's valuation of Dr. Graham's interest in the oral surgery partnership. . . .

II.

Section 452.330.1, RSMo 1986, authorizes the court to "set apart to each spouse his property and . . . divide the marital property in such proportions as the court deems just. . . ."

A.

Is goodwill property? Our courts have long recognized that "the goodwill of a business is property. . . ." Goodwill produced in a professional setting is no less property than that arising from a commercial setting.

[G]oodwill which can be sold, and is therefore property, attaches not to an individual but to a business entity. Goodwill has no separate existence; it has value only as an incident of a continuing business.

B.

In addressing the question of the existence and value of goodwill in a professional context as marital property, the courts have not spoken with a uniform voice.

1.

In *Dugan v. Dugan,* 92 N.J. 423, 457 A.2d 1 (1983), the New Jersey Supreme Court found that goodwill in the law practice of a sole practitioner is property subject to distribution in a dissolution action. The court recognized that reputation is "at the core" of any consideration of professional goodwill. 457 A.2d at 6. While acknowledging that future earning capacity is not *per se* goodwill, the New Jersey justices noted that when "future earning capacity has been enhanced because reputation leads to probable future patronage from existing and potential clients, goodwill may exist and have value." *Id. Dugan* has been criticized, and properly so in our view, for its failure to distinguish between the reputation of the professional as an individual and the reputation of the professional practice as a business entity. Parkman, *The Treatment of Professional Goodwill in Divorce Proceedings,* 18 Fam. L.Q., 213, 219 (Summer 1984).

In *In the Matter of the Marriage of Fleege,* 91 Wash. 2d 324, 588 P.2d 1136 (banc 1979), the Washington Supreme Court defined the critical question as "not whether the goodwill of the practice could be sold . . . but whether it [the goodwill] has value to [the practitioner]." 588 P.2d at 1138–9. In determining the value of the such [*sic*] goodwill, *Fleege* outlined several factors for consideration: "[T]he practitioner's age, health, past earning power, reputation in the community for judgment, skill and knowledge, and his comparative professional success." 588 P.2d at 1138. Each of these factors is, in our view, directly attributable to the professional as a person. For this reason, we find that the *Fleege* analysis is mired in the same mixture of personal reputation and entity reputation as is found in *Dugan.*

2.

Several courts have refused to acknowledge professional goodwill as property. A leading case is *Holbrook v. Holbrook,* 103 Wis. 2d 327, 309 N.W.2d 343 (App. 1981). There the court refused to follow "the twisted and illogical path that other jurisdictions have made in dealing with the concept [of professional goodwill] in the context of divorce." The court continued, "[t]he concept of professional goodwill evanesces when one attempts to distinguish it from future earning capacity. . . . The goodwill or reputation of such a business accrues to the benefit of the owners only through increased salary." 309 N.W.2d at 354. . . .

3.

Between the opposing results reached in *Dugan* and *Holbrook,* several courts have attempted to chart a course which recognizes that goodwill is marital property, but only insofar as it exists independently of the individual professional's reputation. Characteristic of these cases is *Taylor v. Taylor,* 222 Neb. 721, 386 N.W.2d 851 (1986). There the Nebraska Supreme Court concluded that "goodwill must be a business asset with value independent of the presence or reputation of a particular individual, an asset which may be sold, transferred, conveyed, or pledged. . . ." *Taylor,* 386 N.W.2d at 858–9. . . .

C.

As we have said, goodwill is recognized as property in this state. . . . Goodwill may exist in both commercial and professional entities. Irrespective of the setting . . ., the meaning of goodwill does not change. It is property which attaches to and is dependent upon an existing business entity; the reputation and skill of an individual entrepreneur — be he a professional or a traditional businessman — is not a component of the intangible asset we identify generally as goodwill.

Holding and definition of goodwill

With the caveats which follow, we hold that goodwill in a professional practice acquired during a marriage is marital property subject to division. . . . We define goodwill within a professional setting to mean the value of the practice which exceeds its tangible assets and which is the result of the tendency of clients/patients to return to and recommend the practice irrespective of the reputation of the individual practitioner. Our understanding of goodwill is thus consistent with and no broader than the economic, accounting and legal definition which existed prior to the advent of *Dugan, Fleege* and cases reaching similar results.

Goodwill is not dependent, however, on the manner in which the professional practice is organized nor the size of the practice itself. We recognize . . . that goodwill will more likely exist in larger professional practices than in the offices of sole practitioners. This is so because reliance by patients/clients on the reputation and skill of the individual practitioner is, in most cases, inversely related to the number of practitioners in the practice. However, to the extent that, for instance, competent evidence exists that clients/patients will return to the place of the practice — or recommend it to acquaintances who have not yet patronized it — irrespective of the presence of the individual professional, goodwill exists in the solo practice.

Professional goodwill may not be confused with future earning capacity. We have not declared future earning capacity to be marital property. We do not now do so. Instead, we leave to the trial court broad discretion in striking an appropriate balance between husband and wife in the division of property and any award of maintenance. . . .

D.

1.

Proof of the existence of goodwill is particularly troublesome in a professional context [because] the reputation of the individual practitioner and the goodwill of his enterprise are often inextricably interwoven. Because of the difficulties inherent in separating the reputation of the professional from that of his enterprise, evidence that other professionals are willing to pay for goodwill when acquiring a practice is, in our view, the only acceptable evidence of the existence of goodwill. Thus, as a matter of proof, the existence of goodwill is shown only when there is evidence of a recent actual sale of a similarly situated professional practice, an offer to purchase such a practice, or expert testimony and testimony of members of the subject profession as to the existence of goodwill in a similar practice in the relevant geographic and

Proof

professional market. Absent such evidence, one can only speculate as to the existence of goodwill.[1]

Divisions of marital property may not be based on speculation as to the very existence of the property being divided.

2.

As to the issue of valuation, *In re the Marriage of Hall,* 103 Wash. 2d 236, 692 P.2d 175, 179–80 (1984), outlines five major formulae for establishing goodwill value. Of these, three are accounting formulae. The first utilizes a straight capitalization method. The average net profits of the professional are capitalized. The result is the total value of the business including tangible and intangible assets. Book value of the assets is subtracted to determine goodwill value.

5 methods for valuation
1

The second formula is the capitalization of excess earnings method. The annual salary of the average employee practitioner is subtracted from the average net income of the practice. The remaining amount is multiplied by a capitalization rate to determine goodwill value.

2

The third method is the Internal Revenue Service variation of capitalized excess earnings. Under this formula, a reasonable rate of return based on the business' average net tangible assets is subtracted from the average net income of the business for the last five years. From this amount a comparable net salary is subtracted. A capitalization rate is applied to determine goodwill value.

3

The fourth *Hall* formula focuses on fair market value. The value of goodwill, if any, is determined by the price the practice would bring were it sold on the open, relevant market to a qualified professional.

4

The fifth valuation method is based on a buy-sell agreement. The value established in a partnership agreement, for example, determines the value of any goodwill in the practice.

5

Of the suggested formulae, we state our strong preference for the fair market value approach. First, the fair market value approach "does not take explicitly into consideration the future earning capacity of the professional goodwill or the post-dissolution efforts of the professional spouse." Comment, *Professional Goodwill in Louisiana: An Analysis of Its Classification, Valuation and Partition,* 43 LA. L. REV. 139, 142 (1982). As we have previously said, in Missouri, the future earning capacity of one of the marital partners is not *per se* property. . . .

Ct adopts #4

Second, fair market value evidence appears to us to be the most equitable and accurate measure of both the existence and true value of the goodwill of an enterprise. Evidence of a recent actual sale of a similarly situated practice, an offer to purchase the subject or a similar practice, or expert testimony and

---

[1] Courts which have employed capitalization formulae, see discussion, *infra,* often appear to mix concepts of value with concepts of proof. See, *e.g., In re Marriage of Hall,* 692 P.2d at 175. Expert testimony concerning the value of goodwill based on capitalization formulae is not tantamount to proof of the existence of goodwill. An expert can simply assume the existence of goodwill and, using a capitalization formula, produce a value.

testimony of members of the subject profession as to the present value of goodwill of a similar practice in the open, relevant, geographical and professional market is the best evidence of value.

Third, the fair market value method is most likely to avoid the "disturbing inequity in compelling a professional practitioner to pay a spouse a share of intangible assets at a judicially determined value that could not be realized by a sale or another method of liquidating value." *Holbrook,* 309 N.W.2d at 355. We therefore reject the notion advanced by some courts that goodwill may exist and be subject to division in a dissolution proceeding even though it may not be sold. See, *e.g., In re Marriage of Freedman,* 23 Wash. App. 27, 592 P.2d 1124 (1979); *Hall,* 692 P.2d at 175.

Under certain circumstances, the buy-sell agreement method for determining goodwill value may be appropriate. We believe the trial court is best suited to determine when a buy-sell agreement constitutes competent evidence of goodwill value, *In re Marriage of Morris,* 588 S.W.2d 39, 43–4 (Mo. App. 1979), recognizing that "the professional spouse may be influenced by many factors other than fair market value in negotiating the terms of the agreement. . . ." *Hall,* 692 P.2d at 180.

We reject the use of capitalization formulae as a substitute for fair market value evidence of the value of goodwill in a professional practice.[2] The very purpose of capitalization formulae is to place a present value on the future earnings of the business entity being valued. *Beasley [v. Beasley,* 518 A.2d 545] at 552 [(Pa. Super. 1986)]. The formulae draw no distinction between the future earning capacity of the individual and that of the entity in which he or she practices. And as we have said previously, the future earning capacity of the individual professional is not, *per se,* an item of marital property subject to division in a dissolution proceeding. . . .

Hanson v. Hanson

Dr. Thomas Coyle stated that he paid nothing for either goodwill or going concern value when he joined an established oral surgeon in a partnership in Columbia or when he purchased his partner's interest in the practice upon the partner's retirement. The husbands' [Graham and Hanson's] expert, Mr. Evers, testified that in his experience similar practices were sold in the geographic area of the partnership without payment for goodwill or going concern value. He concluded that there was no going concern value or goodwill in the partnership. Mr. Smith, the wives' expert, provided no fair market value evidence for goodwill or going concern value in the relevant geographical market, relying instead on a capitalization formula we have rejected. . . .

The Circuit Court of Boone County valued the partnership at $324,862. This included $233,727, the partnership's ordinary income for 1984. Ostensibly, the trial court based its valuation on paragraph eight of the partnership agreement. We find no support for the trial court's conclusion in either that document or in the evidence. . . . The fair market value evidence in the record

---

[2] We recognize that evidence of the fair market value of the goodwill of an entity may reveal that such value is the product of the application of a capitalization rate to the gross receipts or net income of the entity. To the extent that fair market value as shown by the evidence includes such a product, we obviously do not reject it.

indicates no goodwill value in the partnership. . . . [W]e therefore remand the case to the Circuit Court . . . with directions to assign a value to Dr. Hanson's share in the oral surgery partnership which does not reflect either goodwill or accrued net profits. . . .

Graham v. Graham

The only evidence of fair market value before the trial court in the *Graham* case consisted of the testimony of Elmer Evers, Dr. Graham's expert. As he did in the *Hanson* case, Mr. Evers stated that in his experience in the relevant market, practices similar to that of the Graham and Hanson oral surgery partnership are sold without payment for goodwill or going concern value. The court heard no contrary fair market value evidence. We must, therefore, affirm the trial court's valuation of the oral surgery partnership. . . .

BILLINGS, C.J., BLACKMAR, DONNELLY, RENDLEN, HIGGINS, J.J., and PREWITT, Special Judge, concur.

WELLIVER, J., not sitting.

NOTES

1. *Capitalization of Income Flows: the Basics.* Although the opinion does not make clear precisely what calculations Expert Smith performed, one can in general describe the "capitalization" method he employed. While that method is rejected by *Hanson,* it has been accepted by more than a few other courts. Perhaps the leading authority favoring a capitalization approach is *Dugan,* which endorses the method described by *Hanson* as "capitalization of excess earnings." This method is employed by most experts asked to do such a valuation of nonmarketable goodwill. *Dugan* explains it this way:

> Goodwill is to be differentiated from earning capacity. It reflects not simply a possibility of future earnings, but a probability based on existing circumstances. Enhanced earnings reflected in goodwill are to be distinguished from a license to practice a profession and an educational degree. In that situation the enhanced future earnings are so remote and speculative that the license and degree have not been deemed to be property.
>
> . . . An individual practitioner's inability to sell a law practice does not eliminate existence of goodwill. . . . [D]ifficulty in fixing its value does not justify ignoring its existence. Goodwill should be valued with great care, for the individual practitioner will be forced to pay the ex-spouse "tangible" dollars for an intangible asset at a value concededly arrived at on the basis of some uncertain elements. For purposes of valuing the goodwill of a law practice, the true enhancement to be evaluated is the likelihood of repeat patronage and a certain degree of immunity from competition. Identification of goodwill in this fashion differs from that utilized in evaluating goodwill in businesses where an identification of a return on tangible assets is made.
>
> . . . "[A] lawyer's practice and good will may not be offered for sale."
> H. Drinker, LEGAL ETHICS 161 (1953) (footnote omitted); accord R.

Wise, LEGAL ETHICS 204 (2d ed. 1970) ("Goodwill cannot be sold as clients are not chattels or merchandise and a lawyer is not a tradesman") (footnote omitted). This principle has been accepted and announced by our Advisory Committee on Professional Ethics, Op. 48, 87 N.J. L.J. 459 (1964). . . . [¶] However . . . goodwill may be of significant value irrespective of these limitations.

One appropriate [measure] of goodwill of a law practice [is] the amount by which the attorney's earnings exceed that which would have been earned as an employee by a person with similar qualifications of education, experience and capability. . . . An attorney who earns $35,000 per year as an employee would, as any employee, not have goodwill properly ascribable to his employment. The same attorney earning a net income of the same amount from his individual practice should likewise not be considered to have property consisting of goodwill in ascertaining the value of his practice.

The court should first ascertain what an attorney of comparable experience, expertise, education and age would be earning as an employee in the same general locale. The effort that the practitioner expends on his law practice should not be overlooked when comparing his income to that of the hypothetical employee. A sole practitioner who, for example, works a regular sixty-hour week may have a significantly greater income than an employee who regularly works a forty-hour week, and the income may be due to greater productivity rather than the realization of income on the sole practitioner's goodwill. Next, the attorney's net income before federal and state income taxes for a period of years, preferably five, should be determined and averaged. The actual average should then be compared with the employee norm. If the attorney's actual average realistically exceeds the total of (1) the employee norm and (2) a return on the investment in the physical assets, the excess would be the basis for evaluating goodwill.

This excess is subject to a capitalization factor. The capitalization factor is generally perceived as the number of years of excess earnings a purchaser would be willing to pay for in advance in order to acquire the goodwill. 2 J. Bonbright, VALUATION OF PROPERTY 731 (1937). The minimum capitalization factor is zero. The precise capitalization factor would depend on other evidence. Such evidence could consist of a comparison of capitalization factors used to measure goodwill in other professions, such as medicine or dentistry, adjusted, however, for ingredients peculiar to law, such as the inability to sell the practice and nonavailability of a restrictive covenant. The age of a lawyer may be particularly important because a sole practitioner's goodwill would probably terminate upon death, contrary to that of a doctor.

. . . .

[The expert who testified at trial on the value of the attorney's goodwill] used a [capitalization] factor of five. . . . No evidence supported capitalization at that figure. Our New Jersey inheritance practice indicates a frequent use of three in evaluating goodwill in close corporations or partnerships and Bonbright points out that in New York three is the factor regarded as least in need of justification. See 2 J. Bonbright, *supra,* at 731. When calculating the value of an attorney's goodwill, the court should also consider the risks and competitiveness of the practice. A string of recent successes in contingent fee cases, for example, may lead to overestimating expected income, although averaging over a number of years will correct for many . . . such distortions. Even a properly adjusted estimate may reflect a portion of income attributable to return on risk-taking by the attorney, rather than on his reputation. Similarly, a practice in a highly competitive field might reduce the estimated value of an attorney's goodwill. If consideration is given to plaintiff's work life expectancy, to his inability to sell the practice, to his inability to grant a restrictive covenant, and to the competitiveness and risks of the practice, a factor of five is inordinately high. . . .

Note that the method endorsed by *Dugan* has two steps, each of which depends upon certain assumptions. The first step involves identifying that portion of the lawyer's income attributable to "goodwill." The apportionment is necessary because, as even *Dugan* and *Hanson* agree, the lawyer's entire potential income is not divisible property. Rather, *Dugan* treats as divisible property only that portion of the income attributable to the practice's (not the lawyer's) "goodwill." Under *Hanson*, if there is no market for the goodwill then it doesn't exist; if there is a market, then it is worth what it would sell for, as with any other marital asset. By contrast, *Dugan* holds goodwill often exists even if it is nonsaleable, and so *Dugan* must offer a method for identifying and valuing it. To establish the existence of such nonsaleable goodwill, *Dugan's* first step asks whether the lawyer has "excess earnings" — earnings that derive from this nonmarketable professional goodwill. We return in Note 2 to examining the criteria *Dugan* employs for determining what portion of the lawyer's future expected income is "excess." For now we proceed to the second step, which is placing a value on those excess earnings.

Mathematically, this second step is rather straightforward. There is a standard formula for establishing the current value of a future income flow. This is sometimes called "capitalizing" the income flow, and is sometimes called figuring its "present value." The process is mathematically equivalent to calculating a mortgage, but from the bank's perspective rather than the borrower's. One can think of a bank as buying an income flow — the mortgage payments it will receive over the loan's life, which might last 30 years into the future — with a lump sum it has to pay out right now: the amount of money it lends to the borrower. The equation that solves the calculation has four key values: the principal amount of the mortgage, the interest rate, the term of the mortgage in years, and the monthly payments. Once you know three of these values, the fourth is determined.

The same calculation exactly applies to capitalizing, or figuring the present value of, an income flow. To calculate what a future income flow is worth in current dollars, one must have two other facts: the number of years over which this income will flow, and the prevailing interest rate, sometimes also called the "discount rate." The interest rate is presumably taken from prevailing market rates at the time the calculation is made. Finding a benchmark for the term of years is a bit trickier (called the "capitalization factor" by *Dugan*). For the ordinary income producing asset — a bond, a patent, a franchise, a business — this number would be fixed by the market: how many years of income is a buyer willing to pay for? Some income is so far in the future that it has little or no current value. Income not so far in the future may also have little value; if potential buyers believe there is a substantial risk it will not be realized. This perception of risk will vary with the asset. The market will employ shorter capitalization factors for assets viewed as riskier, longer ones for less risky assets. But of course in the case of attorney income addressed by *Dugan*, there is no market. Establishment of the "capitalization factor" is thus rather arbitrary. Perhaps for this reason, *Dugan* takes a fairly conservative approach, finding a factor of five "inordinately high" and suggesting three as more appropriate.

Once one has all the terms — the amount of excess income per year, the interest rate, and the number of years — the calculation is done by employing the same formula used to calculate a mortgage. The income flow is the equivalent of the mortgage payments, the period of years over which the income is capitalized is equivalent to the term of the mortgage, and of course, the interest rate serves the same function in both cases. The "capitalized" amount of the income flow which the expert offers as the present value of the goodwill is equivalent to the principal amount of the mortgage loan. Looking at a mortgage from the bank's perspective, one can see that the process is the same, since for the bank the question is: how much money will we lend the borrower for this secured promise to provide us with an income flow over the next X years?

(Some of the above discussion, and the discussion that follows, is grounded on the assumption that law practices cannot be sold. The ethical rule forbidding the sale of practices is being modified in some jurisdictions, *see, e.g.*, Charles M. Kidd, *Survey of 1997 Developments in the Law of Professional Responsibility*, 31 IND. L. REV. 723, 730–33 (1998), and such developments will obviously affect the manner of measuring professional goodwill in those jurisdictions where sales of practices are allowed.)

2. Identifying Excess Earnings in the Nonmarket Valuation Method. Now we return to the more fundamental question. Anyone with a business calculator can perform a present value calculation for an income flow which provided the numbers described in Note 1. But how does one determine the amount of income, monthly or annual, to be plugged into the formula? This is the key question of the entire valuation enterprise. In the case of a lawyer's practice, *Dugan* uses "the amount by which the attorney's earnings exceed that which would have been earned as an employee by a person with similar qualifications of education, experience and capability" — otherwise known as the attorney's "excess earnings." Yet the key question is *why* the attorney has such "excess earnings." Most jurisdictions do not recognize the attorney's personal attributes or skills as marital property, an important basis for their rejection of *O'Brien*. Also, the returns on post-dissolution labor are not marital property anywhere. These "excess earnings" therefore cannot be properly treated as marital property unless one identifies them as arising from some source other than the professional's personal skills or post-dissolution labor (for example, if the cause is the business' location, which the owner acquired with marital assets, this "goodwill" should clearly be considered a marital asset). *ALI Principles*, § 4.07, Comment d, adds:

> Some authorities, apparently concerned that the division of professional goodwill is necessarily a mechanism for treating earning capacity as property, suggest that it is never divisible property. However, in many professions, a practice is saleable, and its market value will exceed the value of its tangible assets. The price paid for a medical practice, for example, may reflect income expectations resulting from receipt of the seller's medical records, a list of the patients, office location, and a letter from the seller to his patients recommending the buyer's services. A market value that reflects these components is properly treated as marital property. As with businesses, however, care must be taken to exclude value attributable to the seller's post-divorce labors or personal skills. For example, the sale of a medical practice might include the seller's agreement to remain at the office for a transitional period in which patient loyalties were gradually transferred to the buyer. This is a payment for the seller's labor, and if the labor is post-divorce then it is not marital property.

3. Current State of the Law. The question of whether a professional practice has goodwill is a mixed question of fact and doctrine. Under any plausible doctrinal treatment, some law practices will have goodwill, and others will not. A successful major big city law firm almost certainly has goodwill: it has a brand name that brings business to its partners that they would not get if they left to practice on their own. Other law firms, especially small ones, may get very little business on the basis of institutional reputation, even though the individual attorneys may attract clients on the basis of their personal skills and reputation. Indeed, even within any one law firm, the appropriate result may differ from attorney to attorney. The institutional goodwill may provide no additional income to the firm's major rainmaker, even though it does for his or her partners.

There has been a gradual increase in the sophistication with which courts have handled goodwill questions. Cases from the early and mid-1980's tended to treat the question of professional goodwill as exclusively one of doctrine, and one commentator writing at that time observed, with respect to valuation of nonmarketable goodwill, that "there appear to be almost as many formulas as there are accountants." Bruch, *The Definition and Division of Marital Property in California: Towards Parity and Simplicity,* 33 HASTINGS L.J. 769, 811 (1982). Especially in an equal distribution state like California, some may have found advantage in having a marital asset with no objectively determinable value, because it gave courts the freedom to use it as a fudge term allowing them to reach an overall result they think equitable. The same commentator observed that many attorneys have remarked "we know how much the goodwill is worth; it's worth the equity in the house." Bruch, *supra,* at 812. More recent cases generally sort themselves according to whether, like *Hanson,* they will accept only market evidence of goodwill, or whether, like *Dugan,* they will accept evidence based on capitalization of some portion of the professional's earnings. Cases that follow *Hanson* typically do not consider the possibility that there may be nonmarketable goodwill that nonetheless reflects something other than the professional's personal attributes, while cases that follow *Dugan* typically do not acknowledge that the methods for valuing goodwill which they allow are likely to treat post-dissolution income arising from the professional's personal attributes or post-dissolution labor as part of goodwill.

Cases adopting *Dugan's* valuation approach include *Marriage of Hull*, 712 P.2d 1317 (Mont. 1986) (uses same method to determine goodwill of anesthesiology practice); *Marriage of Watts*, 171 Cal. App. 3d 366, 217 Cal. Rptr. 301, 305 (1985) ("the mere fact that a professional practice cannot be sold . . . will not justify a finding that the practice has no goodwill nor that the . . . goodwill has no value"; its value is found by capitalizing the "excess earnings"); *Marriage of Brooks*, 756 P.2d 161, 166 n.10 (Wash. App. 1988) (goodwill of husband's law practice found by capitalizing difference between "reasonable average income" and his income without regard to partnership agreement fixing lower price at which partner can be bought out); *Clark v. Clark*, 782 S.W.2d 56 (Ky. App. 1990) (following *Dugan*); *Porter v. Porter*, 526 N.E.2d 219 (Ind. App. 1988) (medical practice had goodwill despite lack of marketability and partnership agreement excluding goodwill from purchase price); *Molloy v. Molloy*, 761 P.2d 138 (Ariz. App. 1988) (same, with regard to lawyer's practice); *Ford v. Ford*, 782 P.2d 1304 (Nev. 1989) (explicitly rejects *Hanson* and endorses *Dugan*).

Cases which, like *Hanson*, are skeptical of goodwill claims in the absence of saleability include *Thompson v. Thompson*, 576 So. 2d 267, 270 (Fla. 1991) (goodwill is marital property only if it is "separate and distinct from the presence and reputation of the individual attorney"; fair market value is the preferred valuation method); *McCabe v. McCabe*, 575 A.2d 87, 89 (Pa. 1990) ("future income is not marital property because it has not been acquired during the marriage"); *Mocnik v. Mocnik*, 838 P.2d 500, 504 (Okla. 1992) (same); *Sorenson v. Sorenson*, 769 P.2d 820 (Utah 1989) (goodwill of dental practice divided where expert testified as to practice's market value, but court cautions that goodwill valuations may not be based on projections of future earnings); *Depner v. Depner*, 478 So. 2d 532 (La. App. 1985); *Smith v. Smith*, 709 S.W.2d 588 (Tenn. App. 1985); *Taylor v. Taylor*, 386 N.W.2d 851 (Neb. 1986); *Prahinski v. Prahinski*, 540 A.2d 833 (Md. App. 1988); *Antolik v. Harvey*, 761 P.2d 305 (Haw. App. 1988); *Richmond v. Richmond*, 779 P.2d 1211 (Alaska 1989); *Theilen v. Theilen*, 847 S.W.2d 116 (Mo. App. 1992) (husband's dental practice had no goodwill value where the only evidence of value was the capitalization method).

Even courts following *Hanson*, and considering only market data, are sometimes offered wildly varying valuations, presumably because available market data is sparse. *E.g.*, in *Makowski v. Makowski*, 613 So. 2d 924 (Fla. Dist. Ct. App. 1993), the wife's and husband's experts estimates of the market value of the husband's surveying practice were, respectively, $190,000 and $24,197. (The trial court's judgment valuing the practice at $60,000 was affirmed.) The scarcity of real data may blur the line between honest efforts at a difficult evaluation, and entirely dishonest ones. *Cf. Carden v. Getzoff*, 190 Cal. App.

3d 907, 235 Cal. Rptr. 698 (1987) (tort claim alleging expert fabricated "comparable" medical practices used to establish value of plaintiff's practice). Perhaps concerned with the scarcity of good data, some courts go further than *Hanson* and hold that professional goodwill is always indistinguishable from earning capacity and is therefore never marital property, in the absence of a sale. *Marriage of Zells*, 572 N.E.2d 944, 945–56 (Ill. 1991) (treating goodwill as divisible marital asset "results in gross inequity"; goodwill is merely "income potential" which is already reflected in support award, rendering further consideration of it "duplicative and improper"); *Powell v. Powell*, 648 P.2d 218, 223 (Kan. 1982) ("[t]he practice is personal to the practitioner"); *Nail v. Nail*, 486 S.W.2d 761, 764 (Tex. 1972) (practice of ophthalmologist is "no more than an expectancy wholly dependent upon the continuation of existing circumstances" and not a marital asset). Even these states recognize, of course, that saleable business goodwill is property. Illinois, for example, has distinguished between "personal goodwill," which is not marital property, and "enterprise goodwill," which is. *Marriage of Talty*, 652 N.E.2d 330, 333 (Ill. 1995) (car dealership may have "enterprise goodwill," but valuation must distinguish that from "personal goodwill" which is not divisible under *Zells*); *Yoon v. Yoon*, 711 N.E.2d 1265 (Ind. 1999); *Solomon v. Solomon*, 611 A.2d 686 (Pa. 1992); *Howell v. Howell*, 523 S.E.2d 514 (Va. Ct. App. 2000); *Moretti v. Moretti*, 766 A.2d 925 (R.I. 2001).

Zells emphasizes, in explaining why it does not treat personal goodwill as property, that double counting would result: because a spouse's future earnings are a primary consideration in fashioning an alimony award, they should not also be treated as property under the rubric of a goodwill measure that reduces future earnings to a present value. *See also Peerenboom v. Peerenboom*, 433 N.W.2d 282, 284 (Wis. App. 1988) (only marketable goodwill may be divided to ensure its distinction from earning capacity). But another court following the *Dugan* approach rejected this argument against dividing nonmarketable goodwill because "the capitalization of excess earnings method used to value goodwill examines appellant's past earnings, not his future earnings. Thus, there was no double recovery. . . ." *Clark v. Clark,* 782 S.W.2d 56 (Ky. App. 1990). Is this response persuasive? What if one is dealing with a jurisdiction where alimony is rarely awarded (or usually only awarded at modest levels and for a short duration)?

For a general survey, see Annot., *Valuation of Goodwill in Accounting Practice for Purpose of Divorce Court's Property Distribution,* 77 A.L.R.4th 609 (1990); Annot., *Valuation of Goodwill in Law Practice for Purpose of Divorce Court's Property Distribution,* 77 A.L.R.4th 683 (1990); Helga White, *Professional Goodwill: Is it a Settled Question or is there "Value" in Discussing It?,* 15 J. AM. ACAD. MATRIMONIAL L. 495 (1998).

4. *Implications of Allowing Recovery for Professional Goodwill.* If an attorney has "goodwill" value in a practice even though he cannot sell it, what of an author or an artist? Would Agatha Christie have goodwill in her bookwriting business, or Pablo Picasso in his painting business, that is distinct from earning capacity and thus divisible? While the suggestion may seem amusing, it was not to comedian Joe Piscopo, who was told by a New Jersey appellate court that his talents had created divisible goodwill:

The trial judge in this case analogized the celebrity goodwill of plaintiff to the professional goodwill of *Dugan*. Plaintiff's record of past earning was undisputed. It was also undisputed that whatever plaintiff had achieved as a celebrity had taken place during the marriage. While the trial judge recognized that it would be difficult to value plaintiff's celebrity goodwill, that difficulty would not affect its includability in the marital estate.

Piscopo v. Piscopo, 557 A.2d 1040 (N.J. App. Div. 1989). Is there a principled distinction between *Dugan* and *Piscopo*? If not, are they both right or both wrong? For some criticisms of *Piscopo*, see Donahue & Skoloff, *Court Views Celebrity Good Will as Part of Assets in Divorce Case*, NAT'L L.J., Aug. 14, 1989, at 18.

PROBLEMS

Problem 4-11. *W* has a successful business manufacturing a specialty product for the electronics industry. *W* invented the product and his personal reputation makes the product saleable. The business was started with capital that came in part from *H*'s parents; the remainder came from funds which *W* had saved out of her salary as an engineer, earned during the first years of the marriage. *H* worked in the business during its early years, as a bookkeeper. He did much of the work at home while also tending the couple's children and keeping house. He never received compensation from the business for this work. For the last several years, a professional bookkeeper has worked for the business.

The couple has been married 20 years. Their children are now 16, 17 and 19. *H* has never held regular employment since their marriage, but he is a high school graduate. *W* reported $65,000 in income last year, but they appear to live at a higher level than that, with frequent traveling, four cars, and a nicely furnished, expensive home. The children have always had summer jobs in the business. You represent *H*. What is your approach?

Problem 4-12. Harry owns and operates a car dealership, which is entirely marital property. At his divorce his wife's expert testifies that the value of the dealership is $1.4 million. Harry's expert testifies to a value of $800,000. The difference between them is due entirely to the inclusion by the wife's expert of a value for goodwill of $600,000. Harry's annual income from the car dealership varies between $400,000 and $600,000. You are representing one of the parties to the divorce. What additional facts do you wish to develop and what arguments can you make concerning valuation of the dealership?

Problem 4-13. Shortly after marrying Joan, John is hired as an Administrative Assistant to the Governor, specializing in legislative liaison. Five years later, he files for divorce and resigns his post. At the time of his resignation, his annual salary is $75,000. After his resignation, he opens a law practice and solicits business as a lobbyist. In his first year as a self-employed lobbyist, he earns $150,000. His new success is known before the divorce decree is entered, and Joan seeks to share in his new wealth. She claims a portion of the goodwill value of John's practice. What is her best argument? What is his best argument? Assume they are in a state in which the accumulation of "marital" or "community" property ends when the divorce petition is filed.

Problem 4-14. Dentist Bridge signs a contract to sell his dental practice. The sales contract specifies a payment to Bridge of $60,000 for the practice itself, and $225,000 for Bridge's "covenant not to compete," under which he promised to never open a competing dental practice in the same metropolitan area. At the time of the sale Bridge also files for divorce. His wife claims the dental practice as a marital asset, since it was begun during the marriage using only marital funds. What is the value of the practice for marital property purposes?

Problem 4-15. Lawyer Loretta has had a very successful solo practice in the small suburban town where she lives with her husband, earning $250,000 annually, on average. But she's now had enough, and wishes to work less. She hires Associate Alice, an ambitious young lawyer whose work for opposing firms has impressed Loretta. Their understanding is that Loretta will gradually reduce her workload to part-time, as Alice assumes the major share of the lawyering work. A year later Loretta is working half time, and Alice is working long weeks, and both are earning about $150,000 annually. Loretta suggests to Alice that if she continues, Loretta will eventually retire and leave the entire practice to her. With her new found free time, Loretta acquires a boyfriend and files for divorce. Loretta's law practice is marital property. Her husband claims that its value includes an important component of goodwill. What is the appropriate valuation method?

§ D. ALIMONY

[1] HISTORY AND HISTORICAL JUSTIFICATIONS

AMERICAN LAW INSTITUTE, PRINCIPLES OF THE LAW OF FAMILY DISSOLUTION 23–25 (2002)

Alimony was originally a remedy of the English ecclesiastical courts developed at a time when complete divorce was available only by special legislative action, and gender roles in marriage were rigid and unquestioned. The husband had a legal and customary duty to support his wife. This duty continued after divorce because there was no divorce in the modern sense, but only legal separation. When judicial divorce became available in the 18th and 19th centuries, alimony remained a remedy even though its initial justification — the duty of the husband to support his wife – no longer applied. One explanation was that the duty to support his wife could not be extinguished by the husband's own misconduct. Following that rationale, some jurisdictions allowed alimony claims only by "innocent" wives divorcing "guilty" husbands. Other jurisdictions, focusing on women's financial dependency, in theory allowed claims by guilty wives as well. This view was eventually adopted by the English ecclesiastical courts from their concern that the wife might otherwise "be turned out destitute on the streets or led into temptation," the assumption being that women were limited to domestic skills and could not support themselves by employment. The traditional explanation for alimony was weakened considerably once absolute divorce was allowed, and was undermined completely by modern reforms removing fault from divorce and rejecting gender roles. Yet the financial dependency of wives continued in most marriages. On a practical level a doctrine such as alimony was thus necessary even though the law had no theory to explain it.

Unease over the continuing validity of the traditional rationale for alimony affected decisions early in the modern regime of no-fault divorce. These decisions granted only limited-duration alimony to women who had been homemakers in long-term marriages, and expressed the view that alimony's principal purpose was to provide short-term transitional assistance to such women. The inability to articulate any basis for an indefinite continuation of the husband's support obligation, and the conviction that where possible divorce should effect a "clean break" between the marital partners, combined to push the courts in this direction. The result was buttressed by the expectation that the homemaker would develop marketable skills sufficient to afford her an acceptable living standard, at least when combined with her share in the equitable distribution of their accumulated property, an entitlement which was then relatively new in many common-law states.

But these expectations were often frustrated, and this vision of alimony does not describe the law that one finds today in most appellate opinions. At least in long-term marriages one instead finds a widespread view that marital dissolution should not dissolve all financial ties between the former spouses if the result would be a significant disparity in the spouses' post-dissolution financial standing. However this apparent consensus exists only in very general terms, and has produced no dominant theory to explain the alimony award. The prevailing statutory formulation allows the court to grant alimony (now usually called "spousal support" or "maintenance") to the spouse who is in need. Neither the statutes nor the cases, however, explain why a needy person's former spouse should be liable for his or her support rather than the needy person's parents, children, or society as a whole. The result is that the meaning of "need" — the most fundamental issue created by such statutes — is hopelessly confused. Some opinions find an alimony claimant in "need" only if unable to provide for her basic necessities; others find need if the claimant is unable to support himself at a moderate middle-class level; and still others find need when the claimant is unable to sustain the living standard enjoyed during the marriage even if it was lavish. There can be no principled basis for choosing among these definitions of need without an explanation for imposing the obligation to meet it. In fact, "need" is often used in the law as a conclusory term whose only meaning is that a court has found the spouse entitled to an award of alimony.

It is therefore not surprising that research studies find that trial court decisions on alimony vary widely, even within the same jurisdiction. Some decisional variation would be expected in even a perfect system, because trial courts must have discretion in these matters to deal appropriately with factual variations that no statute can comprehensively anticipate. But it seems clear that the variation arises at least in part because trial courts apply different principles as often as they face different facts. As a consequence, decisions are very difficult to predict. This unpredictability affects the negotiations that settle the great majority of cases.

NOTES

1. *Stereotype Reinforcement.* In *Orr v. Orr*, 440 U.S. 268 (1979), the United States Supreme Court held that Alabama's divorce law, which allowed alimony awards for divorced wives, but not divorced husbands, violated the Equal Protection Clause. Because the alimony applicant had to show "need" in any event (not all divorced wives qualified), Alabama's claim that gender served as a proxy for need could not explain the law. More importantly, the Court rejected Alabama's argument that its public policy of encouraging the traditional family could justify the gender classification. The Court agreed that some permissible purposes could justify gender classifications "substantially related" to them, but held that encouraging traditional family forms was not among them. *Orr* makes clear that that the law cannot fashion rules with the purpose of disfavoring couples who choose non-traditional marital roles. The "tender years" doctrine, an older and once common rule for deciding child custody disputes, raises some of the same issues. *See* Chapter 6.

2. *Traditional Statutes.* The Alabama statute invalidated in *Orr* was a typical traditional enactment: it allowed an alimony award to the wife who obtained a divorce based on "the misconduct of the husband" and specified that such an award "must be as liberal as the estate of the husband will permit." On the other hand, it also allowed the court to make no award, and gave the court discretion to make an award to the wife divorced for her own misconduct in an amount "regulated by the ability of the husband and the nature of the misconduct of the wife." The combination of the fault provisions and the general language gave the court wide discretion to make an award of almost any amount or no amount at all.

One traditional consideration, the standard of living during the marriage, remains a common statutory criterion for setting the amount of the award, sometimes as one factor among others, *e.g.*, Model Marriage and Divorce Act § 308, 9A (Part I) U.L.A. 159, 446 (1998), other times as a more fundamental but not invariable benchmark, *e.g.*, CAL. FAM. CODE § 4320 (West 1994 & Supp. 2003) (in determining amount of award, court must consider "[t]he extent to which the earning capacity of each party is sufficient to maintain the standard of living established during the marriage"). There are many examples of modern cases that employ this traditional standard in long-term marriages. *Heim v. Heim,* 763 P.2d 678, 683 (Nev. 1988) (35-year marriage; wife allowed more alimony than the $1,500 monthly she asked for, since she is "entitled . . . to live as nearly as fairly possible to the station in life that she enjoyed before the divorce"); *Simmons v. Simmons*, 409 N.E.2d 321, 326-29 (Ill. App. 1980) (court applying statutory language identical to Model Marriage and Divorce Act orders maintenance to childless wife earning $1,750 monthly to allow her to approach marital living standard); *Rosenberg v. Rosenberg*, 595 N.E.2d 792, 793 (Mass. App. 1992) (29-year marriage; in affirming alimony award of $2,000 weekly to wife allocated $5.38 million in property division, court notes "the central objective of alimony is, subject to the availability of resources, maintenance of the more dependent spouse in an economic style close to which the spouse had become accustomed during the marriage"). Clearly, unless the parties have more income after their divorce than they had during their marriage, it will not be possible for both to enjoy the marital living standard once their single household becomes two. In *Marriage of LaRocque*, 406 N.W.2d 736 (Wis. 1987), the court held that the marital living standard is the "goal" of maintenance, and even where beyond reach is a relevant benchmark justifying reversal of smaller awards to the extent the obligor's income allows. Nonetheless, the historic reality is that most alimony awards fall well short of permitting the obligee to maintain the marital living standard. Does that reality reflect an intuition that a different standard is in fact more appropriate? We pursue that question further below.

3. Frequency. One thing to keep in mind in considering the issues relating to alimony is that alimony is awarded in this country infrequently, relative to the number of divorces. It appears that this was equally true during the fault divorce era and since the advent of no-fault. *See, e.g.*, BUREAU OF THE CENSUS, CHILD SUPPORT AND ALIMONY: 1985 14 (1987) (nation-wide figure of 14.6%); LENORE J. WEITZMAN, THE DIVORCE REVOLUTION 169 (1985) (in a study of California divorces, the percentage of wives receiving alimony was 18.8% during the fault regime of 1968, 12.9% during the no-fault year of 1972, and 16.5% in 1977).[1] As indicated by later discussions, the rate of alimony is inevitably higher for longer marriages and marriages with children. (It is also important to note that where the financial provisions are determined by party agreement, as occurs in the vast majority of divorces, a spouse might "trade off" alimony for a larger share of the property or higher child support payments.)

[2] THE STRUGGLE FOR A MODERN RATIONALE

MODEL MARRIAGE AND DIVORCE ACT

§ 308. [Maintenance.]

(a) In a proceeding for dissolution of marriage, legal separation, or maintenance following a decree of dissolution of the marriage by a court which lacked personal jurisdiction over the absent spouse, the court may grant a maintenance order for either spouse only if it finds that the spouse seeking maintenance:

(1) lacks sufficient property to provide for his reasonable needs; and

(2) is unable to support himself through appropriate employment or is the custodian of a child whose condition or circumstances make it appropriate that the custodian not be required to seek employment outside the home.

---

[1] Data from the March 2002 Data Supplement to the Annual Demographic Survey, a joint project between the Bureau of Labor Statistics and the Bureau of the Census, gives a rough basis for approximating more recent divorce figures. According to the Survey, in 2001, there were 12.24 million divorced women over the age of 18, and 8.67 million divorced men. However, only 453,000 people (of either gender) over the age of 15 receive alimony. *See* ferret.bls.census.gov/macro/032002/perinc/toc.htm (Tables PINC-02, PINC-08) (last accessed, June 2004). Beyond the slight problem of the different age definitions (over 18 as against over 15), the numbers are also low in part because the figures do not reflect those who had been awarded temporary alimony that has terminated.

(b) The maintenance order shall be in amounts and for periods of time the court deems just, without regard to marital misconduct, and after considering all relevant factors including:

(1) the financial resources of the party seeking maintenance, including marital property apportioned to him, his ability to meet his needs independently, and the extent to which a provision for support of a child living with the party includes a sum for that party as custodian;

(2) the time necessary to acquire sufficient education or training to enable the party seeking maintenance to find appropriate employment;

(3) the standard of living established during the marriage;

(4) the duration of the marriage;

(5) the age and the physical and emotional condition of the spouse seeking maintenance; and

(6) the ability of the spouse from whom maintenance is sought to meet his needs while meeting those of the spouse seeking maintenance.

NOTE: GENDER PATTERNS IN ALIMONY CLAIMS

Although all modern alimony statutes are gender-neutral, alimony awards go disproportionately to women, at least in part because wives make alimony claims far more often than husbands. That is hardly surprising in light of the fact that women remain far more likely to be economically dependent on their spouse. ("According to the U.S. Census Bureau's March 2002 Current Population Survey, among two-parent households, there were 189,000 children with stay-at-home dads [compared with] 11 million children with stay-at-home moms. . . ." Kemba J. Dunham, *Stay-at-Home Dads Fight Stigma*, WALL ST. J., AUG. 26, 2003.) Nonetheless, the picture is gradually changing. The extent of the change is summarized in the articles and notes given in Chapter 1, Section C.

The gendered factual background of alimony claims undoubtedly affects the way men and women think about the appropriate rules. Men are much more likely to think of themselves as potential obligors; women as potential obligees. It may also suggest that the formal gender neutrality of the governing law may mask possibly relevant facts. Consider: if we react differently to claims by men than by women, is that because we are making different assumptions about the stories that lie behind their claims? If so, those assumptions need be made more overt, and their relevance assessed.

One thing that is clear is that, on average, divorce affects men and women differently. What are the differences in financial impact? The next note explores that question.

NOTE: THE DEBATE OVER DIFFERENCES IN THE FINANCIAL IMPACT OF DIVORCE ON MEN AND WOMEN

Do modern divorce laws leave women worse off financially than men? The perception that they do is largely traceable to the extraordinary impact of a book, Lenore Weitzman's 1985 publication, THE DIVORCE REVOLUTION. Her thesis was that the shift to no-fault divorce robbed financially dependent women of bargaining leverage with husbands who abandoned them. In making this case, she captured attention largely through data showing dramatic differences between the post-divorce standard of living of men and women. We defer until Section E the specific question of whether *no-fault rules* are the source of any inequity, as that section addresses more generally the question of whether courts should consider marital misconduct in alimony and property adjudications. Here we look at two more fundamental questions: a) what do we know about the post-divorce finances of men and women, and b) are the disparities that surely exist a consequence of inequitable *divorce laws* (as compared to other possible sources of inequity). Men and women historically entered marriage with different earnings histories and different earnings prospects. They usually leave marriage the same way. Divorce laws may or may not enlarge or contribute to that result, and to observe a difference is not necessarily to establish that it is inequitable. Just what financial arrangements the law should require at divorce is of course the central question of this entire chapter. So while this note raises some important questions of equity, it does not conclude them. We continue to address them throughout this chapter and into others, such as Chapter Five's discussion of the appropriate levels of child support. But we turn first to the facts, and to the controversy over Weitzman's data.

[a] The Weitzman Data on the Gender Impact of Divorce

Weitzman's dramatic claims were first made in her 1981 article, *The Economics of Divorce: Social and Economic Consequences of Property, Alimony and Child Support Awards*, 28 U.C.L.A. L. REV. 1181, 1249–53 (1981) (reprinted in THE DIVORCE REVOLUTION, at 337–43). She claimed that data from a sample of divorced California families showed that one year after divorce men experienced a 42% improvement in their post-divorce standard of living, while women experienced a 73% loss. This bleak picture was widely reported. Weitzman's percentages on the spouses' relative standard of living was quoted often in publications ranging from serious academic articles to Dear Abby, often with erroneous attribution to official government studies which had themselves merely quoted Weitzman. However, after years of challenge by other researchers, Weitzman ultimately conceded that her published data were wrong, as explained below.

In fact, there were many other studies of this question both before and after Weitzman's, and all found a significant gender gap in the financial consequences of divorce. However, those studies all found that wives' post-divorce decline in living standard was about 30%, rather than the 73% Weitzman claimed. Duncan & Hoffman, *A Reconsideration of the Economic Consequences of Divorce*, 22 DEMOGRAPHY 485 (1985); Weiss, *The Impact of Marital Dissolution on Income and Consumption in Single-Parent Households*, 46 J. MARRIAGE & FAMILY 115 (1984). These other studies received much less attention than Weitzman's, undoubtedly because their numbers and conclusions were less dramatic, but are today regarded as more accurate. The debate that led to this conclusion is worth review here, both because the truth of the matter is important to family law policy, and because it provides an important lesson in why those interested in family law policy must be sophisticated consumers of the social science data often offered in these policy debates.

The first step in understanding this debate is to be clear that the effect that all researchers sought to measure was the change after divorce in the spouses' standard of living, not in their income. The two are not the same. Weitzman never claimed, for example, that the average husband's income increased by 42% in the year after divorce, nor would such a figure be plausible. His standard of living would increase, however, if his income remained relatively constant while his needs declined. Why might needs decline? The most obvious reason would be a decline in family size. In fact, the needs of both husbands' and wives' *households* typically decline after divorce, if they do not remarry, because their household size declines. If, for example, we assume that the pre-divorce family consisted of husband, wife and two minor children, then the post-divorce family size of a noncustodial husband is one, a reduction of three, and the post-divorce family size of a custodial wife is three, a reduction of one. Either post-divorce family can maintain the same standard of living that it enjoyed pre-divorce with a lower income than the pre-divorce family had, although of course the family of three will need more to maintain that standard than would a family of one. If the incomes of custodial mothers and their former husbands are, say, equal after taking account of alimony and child support payments, their standards of living will not be. It is this reality which Weitzman and other researchers seek to capture by comparing standards of living rather than income. There are a variety of methods for comparing the living standards of households of different size, and opinions vary among economists about their relative virtues; all have flaws. We will look at some of the problems below. But this was not the reason why Weitzman's figures were different than that of others, because her choice of method was not different than theirs. The problem with her published results appeared to be logistical rather than conceptual: as ultimately demonstrated by Richard Peterson, one simply could not derive her published results from her raw data. Peterson, *A Revolution of the Economic Consequences of Divorce,* 61 AM. SOC. REV. 528 (1996). The explanation for this discrepancy is still not known for certain, but in response to Peterson, Weitzman conceded the problem, and blamed errors by her computer staff. Weitzman, *The Economic Consequences of Divorce Are Still Unequal: Comment On Peterson,* 61 AM. SOC. REV. 537 (1996). Peterson's own analysis of Weitzman's raw data showed a 27% drop in wives' post-divorce living standards, very close to the figure obtained by the other researchers, and a ten percent average increase in their husband's living standards, also consistent with other sources.

There are some general lessons to be learned from this small bit of social science history. Perhaps the most important is that the attention social scientists receive for their work is often more proportional to the dramatic impact of its social claims than to the soundness of its methodology. The fame of a piece of research cannot be taken as a proxy for its quality. Any serious effort to look to social science sources for policy guidance requires a reasonably comprehensive and methodologically informed review of the relevant literature.

[b] Beyond Weitzman: Assessing the Gender Impact of Divorce

As Peterson says, nearly all researchers in the field find an average post-divorce decline of about 30 % in wives' living standards. He also suggests that the ten percent average increase in husbands' living standard shown by a correct analysis of Weitzman's data is consistent with other sources. Let us assume these figures are correct. Are not these results sufficiently disparate to suggest an important inequity?

Perhaps. Whatever the raw figures, their policy implications require some interpretation: Do the figures capture the full financial picture of the spouses? Is the financial picture they paint long-term or merely transitional? Are there nonfinancial factors that also must be taken into account in assessing the relative fairness of the outcome? To what extent is the divorce law a cause of the disparate financial picture? These are important questions to ask if one wants to move from the data to the making of legal policy. In fact, much of the literature attacked Weitzman's conclusions on these grounds, rather than attacking the figures themselves. *See, e.g.,* Jacob, *Faulting No-Fault*, 1986 A.B.F. Res. J. 773; Jacob, *Another Look at No-Fault Divorce and the Post Divorce Finances of Women*, 23 Law & Soc. Rev. 95 (1989); Abraham, *"The Divorce Revolution" Revisited: A Counter-Revolutionary Critique*, 9 N. Ill. U.L. Rev. 251 (1989). Some of the most interesting criticisms, from a policy standpoint, are made in Sugarman, *Dividing Financial Interests at Divorce*, in S. Sugarman & H. Kay, eds., Divorce Reform at the Crossroads 130-259 (1990). While Weitzman's own numbers are no longer on the table, the points made in this literature are still important to consider.

1. *Do the Cost of Living Figures Reflect the Parties' Complete Financial Situation?* A problem could arise if the calculations were based upon assessments of what is required to maintain a particular standard of living that left out or undercounted expenses that did not affect men and women equally. There is at least one possible example of importance: taxes. Researchers in this area generally base their assessments of comparative living standards on the parties' gross income (before taxes). If the parties are paying roughly equivalent portions of their income in taxes, then the choice between gross and net income does not matter. But several tax rules combine to suggest that noncustodial fathers pay a higher proportion of their income in taxes than do custodial mothers. The child support obligor must typically pay taxes on the portion of his income that is paid out in child support, while the obligee does not count child support received as part of taxable income. (This point does not matter, of course, to the obligee who in fact receives no child support. But to the extent one wishes to use this data in choosing a policy for deciding upon the appropriate size of child support or other required spousal income transfers, the point is quite relevant.) The custodial parent may also benefit from child care credits, the lower tax rate accorded heads of households, and the tax credit for low earners. One researcher has tentatively concluded that these and other tax factors compress the standard of living differences between the typical custodial mother and non-custodial father sufficiently to eliminate most of them. Sanford L. Braver, *The Gender Gap in Standard of*

Living After Divorce: Vanishingly Small?, 33 FAM. L.Q. 111 (1999). Difficult methodological issues, however, ensure that this study is not the final word.

2. *What is the Long-Term Financial Situation of Divorced Men and Women After Divorce?* At what point should the comparison be made? Weitzman took a single snapshot at one year after divorce. Compare a study by Duncan and Hoffman that looked at the economic situation five years after divorce. By then divorced wives who were still single had a living standard that was on average about 94% of the standard they enjoyed in the year before divorce — a 6% decline in living standard, rather than the 30% decline that nearly all researchers find after one year. Duncan & Hoffman, *Economic Consequences of Marital Instability*, in M. David & T. Smeeding, HORIZONTAL EQUITY, UNCERTAINTY, AND ECONOMIC WELL-BEING 427, 437 (1985). Similar conclusions are suggested by the 1992-93 National Survey of Families and Households, which asked women who had split from their husband since the prior survey, taken in 1987-88, how their finances compared to their situation during the marriage. Forty-three percent said their finances were better than during their marriage, while only 40% said they were worse. Furstenberg, *The Future of Marriage*, AMERICAN DEMOGRAPHICS, June 1996, at 36–37. Perhaps, then, the problem uncovered by the one-year data is more a problem of transition, requiring different remedies than would be required to correct a long-term difficulty.

3. *Should We Consider Remarriage?* The parties' post-divorce economic status will be affected by whether they remarry; remarriage may be the most important change that is captured by extending the comparison past the first year after divorce. Only four to six percent of the women in Weitzman's sample had remarried in the year after divorce, Weitzman, *supra*, at 328, 333. Andrew Cherlin's important study concludes that about two-thirds of divorced women eventually remarry, and that a significant portion of the remainder enter a nonmarital union. A. CHERLIN, MARRIAGE, DIVORCE, REMARRIAGE 28 (revised ed., 1992). Duncan and Hoffman's five year followup study, noted above, found that divorced women who had remarried on average enjoyed a living standard five years after divorce that was 25% *greater* than in the last year of their prior marriage. Duncan & Hoffman, *supra*, at 437.

4. *Should the Gender Comparison Include Non-Financial Factors?* Some argue that if non-financial factors are weighed in the balance, a different impression is given of the comparative outcomes for men and women. Weitzman herself found that women as well as men report a rise in "competence and self esteem" in the first year after divorce. Weitzman, *supra*, at 345. Indeed, in most of the non-financial post-divorce measures she took, women fare better than men; a larger percentage "feel better about themselves," consider themselves "more competent in their work," feel "more physically attractive" and "possessed of better parenting skills" than during the marriage. *Id.* at 345–46. Data from the 1992-93 National Survey of Families and Households suggest the same result. The survey asked women who had split from their husband since the 1987-88 survey to compare their situation in several non-financial respects: Seventy-seven percent said they were happier than during their marriage, 65% said their home life had improved, 57% said their social life had improved, and 55% said their parenting had improved.

Furstenberg, *The Future of Marriage*, AMERICAN DEMOGRAPHICS, June 1996, at 36–37. Sugarman argues that custodial arrangements are the most important omitted consideration: "[W]here women have physical custody of the children and men feel that they have, as a result, lost something terribly important to them, it is deeply troubling to compare the former spouses' living standards in terms that treat the children solely as a liability." Sugarman, *supra*, at 151. (Children are a "liability" in standard of living comparisons because their presence in the household increases "need," and thus results in a lower percentage of "need" being met at a given level of income.)

These points perhaps explain why, despite women's relatively worse financial situation, a 1985 poll found that 85% of divorced or separated women say that they are happier since the dissolution of their marriage, while only 58% of men so report. Harper's Index, HARPER'S MAGAZINE, Nov. 1985 at 15 (reporting on poll conducted for USA TODAY). It may also explain why, roughly two thirds of the time, it is the wife who instigates the separation or divorce. Braver, Whitley, & Ng, *Who Divorced Whom? Methodological and Theoretical Issues*, 20 J. DIVORCE & REMARRIAGE 1 (1993); *cf.* Margarat F. Brinig & Douglas W. Allen, *"These Boots are Made for Walking": Why Most Divorce Filers are Women*, 2 AM. J. L. & ECON. 126 (2000) (arguing higher filing rates for wives is due to desire to obtain child custody). Of course, the fact that women are happier after divorce does not of itself demonstrate that the divorce process treated them fairly. If their marriage was oppressive enough, then even an unfair divorce settlement could be an improvement in their lives. Another approach to getting at the question is to ask divorcing parties whether they believe they were treated fairly in the divorce process. Such inquiries give mixed results. A study of couples divorcing in Maricopa County (Phoenix) in 1986, with at least one child fifteen or less, found that one year after divorce wives reported themselves significantly more satisfied than did husbands with the custody, visitation, property division, and "other financial provisions" of their divorce decree (defined as everything other than child support and property division). But interviewed again three years after divorce, the wives now were significantly less satisfied than their former husbands with the financial terms of the divorce, while their greater satisfaction than men with the custody and visitation terms remained — and indeed, the satisfaction gap between them on this measure had increased. V. L. Sheets & S. L. Braver, *Gender Differences in Satisfaction with Divorce Settlements*, 45 FAMILY RELATIONS 336–342 (1996). While such data certainly suggest that a different picture is painted if one looks at the entire situation rather than at the financial issues alone, it does not resolve the more difficult policy question of deciding upon the significance of this comparison.

This discussion can hardly resolve the question of whether existing divorce law or practice contains a systematic gender bias. It does provide a background against which to consider the principal question addressed in the remainder of this chapter: what constitutes a fair law of alimony?

NOTE: THE ALIMONY PUZZLE

The Model Marriage and Divorce Act sought to establish the convention, as the no-fault era began, that alimony would be a short-term remedy, based on "need," and awarded without regard to fault. There is currently a fairly wide consensus that it is appropriate to impose an alimony obligation of some length at the dissolution of a long-term marriage when the parties would otherwise have very disparate living standards. The basis of that obligation remains unclear, however, with the consequence that the consensus rapidly disappears as the facts vary or more detailed questions are put. (How much of the disparity should be eliminated? For how long should the award continue?) In fact, if alimony cannot be based on gender roles, nor limited to cases in which it can be justified by the obligor's fault for ending the marriage, it is not so easy to explain its basis. That is the modern alimony puzzle to which we now turn.

People often develop a view on alimony with some particular fact pattern in mind. That is not necessarily a bad way to start, but any set of principles must deal with many fact patterns. To test your own intuitions on this difficult problem, you might want to keep in mind the following hypotheticals, and ask yourself: should there be an alimony award in this case? Why or why not? What principle am I following, and is it consistent with my treatment of the other hypotheticals? And you might do the mind experiment of posing these same questions to the authors of materials excerpted below, as you read them.

a. *The classic case.* Alice and Barry (both 48) divorce after 23 years of marriage. Alice has been a homemaker and also worked part time. Their children are now grown and Alice is available for full time work although she has not done it since she was much younger and would not have planned on returning to full time work but for the divorce. Barry, who always worked full time during the marriage, earns $60,000 annually. Alice's current earning potential as a retail clerk, her best prospect for full time work, is about $25,000 annually. The parties' net assets at divorce, about $50,000 in home equity and savings, have been divided equally.

b. *The classic case, professional version.* Lionel and Anne met in law school, and married in their third year. They both obtained desirable law firm jobs after graduation. After their first child was born in the fourth year of their marriage, Anne took a year's maternity leave. She returned to the firm on a part time "mommy track." When their second child was born two years later, she left the firm altogether. After their younger child turned four, Anne began regular volunteer work with a local public interest firm. By the time the children were both in school, her volunteer work turned into a half time position. After fifteen years of marriage, the parties seek divorce. The children are eleven and eight. Anne earns $25,000 annually in her half-time position, which the public interest firm has offered to convert to full time at twice the pay. She likes the work and has no desire to seek more lucrative employment at private firms, although she probably could obtain such work because of her litigation experience. Lionel remained at his original firm, made partner, and at divorce is earning $200,000 annually.

c. *The role reversal case.* Carl and Denise are in the same situation as Alice and Barry, except that Carl was the homemaker and Denise earns $60,000 annually. This was not the couple's original plan when they married. Carl had dreams of becoming a novelist, and wrote while also doing odd jobs to generate some income. Denise, who had no similar aspirations, began work as an administrative assistant in a business office, thinking that this would be a suitable temporary post until Carl's career developed. Over time, however, Denise's quiet competence and reliability won her promotions to her current executive position. Over the same period, Carl's writing ambitions, repeatedly frustrated by publisher's rejections, faded. So the parties slid into a pattern in which Denise was the primary breadwinner while Carl was the homemaker, who stayed home with the couple's two children, who are now grown.

d. *The classic case with further facts, No. 1.* Alice and Barry grew apart over the last ten years of their marriage. Barry developed a friendship with a coworker which eventually developed into a romantic relationship. Once the children were grown, he decided it was time to end the marriage so that he could begin a new life with a new spouse. Alice was not surprised at this development, as she was fully aware that the mutual affection she and Barry once had for one another had left their marriage. But while she is not emotionally crushed by this development, neither is she happy about it, as she has no potential new mate.

e. *The classic case with further facts, No. 2.* Same as Version D, except that it is Alice rather than Barry who develops a new relationship, with an attorney for whom she did some part time office work. She therefore initiates divorce proceedings. During those proceedings, however, Alice and the attorney end their relationship. With no plans to remarry after the divorce, Alice requests alimony.

f. *The role reversal case with further facts, No. 1.* Over the last ten years of their marriage, Denise has become increasingly impatient with Carl, whom she realizes is a loser. She contrasts her own ability to develop job skills and ambition, as the circumstances required, with Carl's inability to reorient and develop another useful and remunerative skill once it became clear his writing career would not work out. She feels Carl, a college graduate, could have done more to develop his life once the children were older and more independent. When she begins to develop an enjoyable social relationship with an executive at another firm with whom she deals, she concludes her marriage is empty and should be ended. She therefore files for divorce.

g. *The role reversal case with further facts, No. 2.* Carl, feeling unappreciated by Denise and insecure in his own self-image, takes refuge in a relationship he develops with a woman neighbor who is usually home during the day. With her encouragement, he starts writing again. Feeling he can begin his life over with her, he files for divorce. Knowing that the neighbor's earning capacity is limited and that his own earning prospects from writing are speculative at best, Carl seeks an alimony award.

[3] WHY DO WE HAVE ALIMONY?

CLAPP v. CLAPP

653 A.2d 72 (Vt. 1994)

DOOLEY, Justice. Michael Clapp appeals a decision . . . in the divorce action between him and his former wife, Elizabeth Clapp, challenging both property and maintenance orders contained therein. . . .

The parties were married in 1967 following [Michael]'s first year of law school. When [Michael] graduated in 1969, the parties returned to Vermont and he began his legal practice that continues. . . . The parties' son was born in 1970 and their daughter in 1972. [Elizabeth] remained home to care for the children full time until 1975, at which time she began pursuing her master's degree in education. In 1977, having received her degree, [Elizabeth] began work as a junior high school guidance counselor. In 1981, she became a high school guidance counselor and has continued in that job. . . . In 1987, after twenty years of marriage, the parties separated. [Elizabeth] filed for divorce in 1989. In 1991, her annual income before taxes was $45,237; [Michael]'s annual income before taxes was $137,600.

The parties were divorced by final order . . . entered in February 1993. At that time, both parties were forty-eight years old. The court found that the parties' assets totaled $1,257,577, and their liabilities $498,773. Finding that the merits of the situation favored [Elizabeth] wife slightly, the court ordered the parties' assets to be split 60% to wife and 40% to husband. In so decreeing, the court awarded each spouse the respective homes, but required that both homes be sold and the equity divided 60/40.

The court ordered [Michael] to pay maintenance and set the amount temporarily at $2,000 per month. Thereafter, it required a calculation of maintenance based on an equalization of the parties' after-tax income from June 1987 to the date of the divorce. This maintenance amount had not been calculated at the time of the appeal, and the parties had widely divergent claims about the result of the calculation. [Elizabeth claimed the correct amount was $4,333.33 per month; Michael claimed it was either $2,460 or $2,720 per month.] Once calculated, the base maintenance amount would be adjusted annually based on . . . the Consumer Price Index.

. . . .

[Michael] argues any maintenance award cannot exceed the amount necessary to enable the obligee to meet her reasonable needs. [He argues that the family court improperly exceeded this amount] in order to compensate [Elizabeth] for past contributions as a homemaker [but that] the statute does not allow for restitutionary or compensatory awards.

Much of [Michael]'s argument is based on the statutory language, which provides:

§ 752. Maintenance

(a) In an action under this chapter, the court may order either spouse to make maintenance payments, either rehabilitative or permanent in nature, to the other spouse if it finds that the spouse seeking maintenance:

> (1) lacks sufficient income, property, or both, including property apportioned . . ., to provide for his or her reasonable needs, and

> (2) is unable to support himself or herself through appropriate employment at the standard of living established during the marriage or is the custodian of a child of the parties.

The argument specifically emphasizes § 752(a)(1) which requires a threshold finding that the prospective obligee lacks income or property to meet "reasonable needs." In [Michael]'s view, the court must first determine reasonable need without regard to the income available during the marriage, or the obligor's current income, and award maintenance only if this need is not met by the obligee's nonmaintenance income and property. [¶] [Michael]'s argument involves an overly narrow reading of § 752(a)(1). The statute is based on a concept of relative, not absolute, need. [The] court can award maintenance even though the wife is meeting her needs through employment where [a] vast inequality in [the] parties' financial position remains. [R]easonable need is not to be judged in relation to subsistence [but] "in light of the standard of living established during the marriage." [T]he term "reasonable needs" allow[s] the court "to balance equities whenever the financial contributions of one spouse enable the other spouse to enhance his or her future earning capacity." [O]ne purpose of maintenance under § 752(a) is to compensate a homemaker for contributions to family well-being not otherwise recognized in the property distribution.

We do not have to plunge deeply into the detail of [Elizabeth]'s post-separation needs to affirm the award of maintenance in this case. According to the findings, the parties were living on an after-tax income of approximately $130,000 per year and spending most of it. Of this, about $33,000 is attributable to [Elizabeth]. Both parties had attained maximum vocational skills and employability. [Michael]'s earning capacity should, however, grow at a faster rate as he approaches retirement. [¶] [Elizabeth] would not maintain the standard of living realized during the marriage on her share of the marital income. . . . In light of the standard of living of the parties, the court acted within its discretion in awarding maintenance in this case.

[Michael] attacks the amount of maintenance awarded. [T]he court found that the deficit in [Elizabeth]'s income to pay expenses amounted to about $1,000 per month. It also recognized that [Elizabeth] had made a significant nonmonetary contribution to the marriage as a homemaker, and had reduced her earnings over the years because of this contribution. For the dual purpose of avoiding "an adverse economic impact upon [Elizabeth]" and compensating her for her nonmonetary contributions during the marriage, the court ordered such permanent maintenance as would equalize after-tax income, as calculated over the period from the date of separation to the date of divorce. . . .

The amount is not adjusted on a regular basis because of changes in either party's income, although it is adjusted for inflation.

[T]he family court has broad discretion in determining the amount of maintenance, and we will reverse only if there is no reasonable basis to support the award. In determining the amount of maintenance to award, the court must consider all relevant factors, including seven statutory factors. [Similar to Section 308(b) of the Model Act, excerpted above.] Most of the statutory factors figured into the family court's decision, including the ability of the obligee to meet her needs without maintenance, the standard of living established during the marriage, the duration of the marriage, the age and physical and emotional condition of each spouse, and the ability of the obligor to meet reasonable needs while paying maintenance. The award was tailored to maintain for [Elizabeth] the standard of living during the marriage. This objective was supported by the length of the marriage, twenty-five years. It is also supported in this lengthy marriage by the need to compensate [Elizabeth] for homemaker contributions to family well-being not otherwise recognized in the financial awards.

It is important to recognize the difference between the income equalization approach of this award and the approach we rejected in *Delozier*. In *Delozier*, the income equalization award was prospective and permanent so each spouse was to receive half of their joint income for the remainder of their lives. On facts somewhat similar to those here, . . . we held that permanent income equalization may "wind up being punitive rather than compensatory." *Delozier*, 640 A.2d at 60.

Here, income equalization was used as a method to calculate an appropriate monthly maintenance award, but the amount of the award will not change in the future because of changes in the income of either of the parties. In light of the court's conclusion that the gap between the income of the parties would grow over time, this award equalized income for only a year, with [Michael] keeping an increasing share of the combined income in the future. We believe the award equalized income for "an appropriate period of time". . . .

Need here should also be viewed in relation to the standard of living established during the marriage, another statutory factor. The main objective of the award was to maintain that standard of living for [Elizabeth].

[Also] restitution for past homemaker contributions is a basis [for alimony we] explicitly recognized in *Klein*, 555 A.2d at 387. We see no reason to abandon that recognition here. [Michael] claims that consideration of this factor was not warranted because there was no evidence of the extent of the contribution. The court found that [Elizabeth] delayed her education and entry into the job market in order to raise the parties' children while they were infants. Thereafter, the parties jointly decided that [Elizabeth] should work in a school system, rather than in other employment with higher remuneration, in order to care for the children and manage the home. This also enabled her to stay in the home during the summer. In comparison, [Michael] consistently put in night and weekend hours at his law office.

Homemaker contributions are, by their nature, nonmonetary so they cannot be quantified or put into a monetary formula to specify their impact on the ultimate maintenance award. The court's characterization of these contributions as "significant . . . over many years" is probably as specific as is possible. . . .[¶] [T]he family court acted within its discretion in awarding permanent maintenance to [Elizabeth], and the amount is also within its discretion.

[The trial court had also ordered Michael to sell a lakefront home he had purchased as his separate property for $415,000, because his mortgage payments made it impossible for him to meet his maintenance payments. Michael argued that the court could not order sale of property in which there was no marital equity.] In our view, this is a distinction without a controlling difference. Just as the house in which [Elizabeth] resides is being sold to give [Michael] his interest in it, [Michael]'s house is being sold to give [Elizabeth] her interest in his income, an interest that cannot realistically exist as long as so much of the income is diverted to a house payment.[4]

. . . .

MARRIAGE OF WILSON

201 Cal. App. 3d 913, 247 Cal. Rptr. 522 (1988)

HADEN, J. Elma Wilson appeals an order terminating her spousal support after 58 months following a 70 month marriage. Having found her permanently disabled and her former husband able to pay continued support, the trial court weighed the length and nature of the marriage, and the duration of spousal support payments and ruled husband no longer had the legal obligation to support his former spouse. We affirm.

Factual and Procedural Background

Thomas and Elma Wilson (Tom and Elma) were married in May 1976 and separated in March 1982, after 70 months. Elma was injured in a fall two years before separation. As a result of her injuries or subsequent infection following dental work, she could no longer work as a bartender. In 1983 her doctor believed her neurologic deficit would remain permanent but recommended some rehabilitation to enable her to pursue work which would not require verbalization. A clinical psychologist opined Elma suffered brain damage which left her "lacking in social judgment, common sense, and social intelligence." The psychologist felt Elma would probably not succeed where she had to make decisions using common sense.

In the November 1983 stipulated interlocutory judgment, Tom received, inter alia, his Navy pension and a Volkswagen while Elma took the house, a Jaguar automobile, and spousal support of $500 per month for two years plus medical insurance coverage for the same period.

---

[4] After the divorce, [Michael] can, of course, purchase any property he desires, and the new property will not fall within the jurisdiction of the family court under 15 V.S.A. § 751(a). Any new mortgage lender will, however, be aware of [Michael]'s outstanding obligation to pay maintenance in determining whether [Michael]'s income is adequate to meet his mortgage payments.

In September 1985 Elma sought continued spousal support. She anticipated further brain surgery in one to two years. The same clinical psychologist reexamined her and concluded "[i]t appears unlikely that Mrs. Wilson could succeed in today's competitive job market. . . . [S]he would have difficulty with any job that required an intellectual component that was above the mildly mentally retarded level." The psychologist further stated, "[I]t appears doubtful that Mrs. Wilson is able to profit from training that could lead to employment." In December 1985 the trial court extended the $500 per month spousal support for one year. After considering Elma's serious physical problems, the court went on to explain this was not a lengthy marriage, there were no children born of the marriage, and the ages of the parties at the time of the marriage indicated they had established their lives before they married. In April 1986 the court temporarily reduced support to $350 per month when Tom was unemployed.

In September 1986 Elma once again sought continuing spousal support, claiming she was still unemployed and neither rehabilitated nor capable of rehabilitation. She continued to receive $436 per month in social security benefits. She noted her daughter and son-in-law had been living with her since May 1986 and he began earning $5.00 per hour in September 1986 but was unemployed by the December 1986 hearing. Her daughter was in rehabilitation for injuries suffered in an automobile accident. In October 1986 Tom declared he earned over $2,200 per month in salary plus over $1,000 in Navy retirement.

At a hearing on the support issue in December 1986 Tom argued Elma should not be entitled to lifetime support from him based on a 70-month marriage. The court found Tom, age 46, had the earning capacity to continue to make support payments and Elma, age 48, had a need for such payments because she was both disabled and could not regain her previous income earning status. The court considered the length of the marriage (70 months) and the length of the spousal support period (58 months). The court then stated, "My question . . . that I'm faced with is at what point in time does the obligation to assist Mrs. Wilson become one of society's as distinguished from an obligation that is Mr. Wilson's, and I find that it is society's at this point in time." The court continued support for four months and then terminated it.

Discussion

I

A promise to "love, honor and cherish as long as we both shall live" is in fact easily and frequently revocable today. It is lamentable that many decide to live together without benefit of such vows and many who take them soon forget them. However, we are concerned here with legal, not moral, obligations. We are asked to decide whether following a childless marriage of short duration it was an abuse of discretion to terminate spousal support even though the supported spouse was permanently disabled.

II

Civil Code section 4801 provides for spousal support in any amount and for any period just and reasonable, provided the trial court in making the award considers all of the [eight factors specified]. . . . The record reflects the trial court weighed each of these eight factors before exercising discretion to terminate support. Tom had the earning capacity to continue to make support payments. Elma had virtually no marketable skills and could not regain her previous income. This was not a marriage in which Elma's earning capacity was impaired by unemployment incurred to permit her to attend to domestic duties. The parties were in their forties when they married and, the court noted, had already established their lives. There were no children of this marriage. There was no evidence Elma had contributed to the attainment of Tom's career. His military career must have been completed or substantially completed when the couple married. Elma had a need for support because she was disabled, the court balanced the equities and decided under these circumstances the obligation to assist Elma should shift from Tom to society.

. . . .

Elma contends it was an abuse of discretion to terminate spousal support where there was no present evidence of her ability to be self-supporting. . . . Specifically, Elma argues the trial court failed to comply with *In re Marriage of Morrison* (1978) 20 Cal. 3d 437 [143 Cal. Rptr. 139, 573 P.2d 41]. . . . *Morrison,* however, concerned a lengthy marriage of 28 years during which wife at husband's insistence devoted her time principally to maintaining the home and raising two children. In this context a trial court should . . . retain jurisdiction over support unless the record indicates the supported spouse will be able adequately to meet his or her financial needs at the time of termination. [But] *Morrison* need not apply here.

. . . .

The order is affirmed.

Todd, Acting P. J., and Benke, J., concurred.

NOTES

1. *Problematic Rationales For Alimony: Need.* The wife in *Clapp* leaves the marriage at the age of 48 with no dependents (the parties' children being grown), a share of the marital property worth about $455,000 (60% of the total marital equity), and an apparently secure job paying $45,000 annually. The court concludes that she also qualifies for a substantial and permanent alimony award, with automatic adjustments for inflation. The wife in *Wilson* leaves her marriage substantially disabled and dependent for her basic needs upon charity or public assistance. The court concludes that her modest alimony award must expire after a fixed-term of around five years. *Clapp* was decided under a statute whose basic terms closely track the Model Marriage and Divorce Act — an Act that established "need" as the announced basis for alimony in the no-fault era. But the *Clapp* court is quite straightforward in rejecting need as the principal touchstone for alimony awards, treating it as just one of several relevant factors. Need is thus not a necessary condition for an alimony award. *Wilson* teaches that it is also insufficient — that need alone, without more, is inadequate. *Clapp* and *Wilson* are not atypical in their rejection of need as the dispositive consideration in alimony awards, although they may be somewhat atypical in the overtness with which they reach this result. Because many statutes still follow the M.M.D.A.'s lead in appearing to establish need as the primary consideration, some courts are more reluctant than *Clapp* to state otherwise. Nor is obfuscation in this matter difficult. Need can easily be thought of as varying with the obligee — some "need" to enjoy a higher standard of living more than others. In the end, need becomes, as the *ALI Principles* observe, a conclusion rather than an explanation. The difficulties with need as an underlying concept for alimony have been understood for some time. *See* Ellman, *The Theory of Alimony,* 77 CAL. L. REV. 1, 5 (1989).

Divorced spouses even more comfortable than Elizabeth Clapp have been awarded alimony. *See, e.g., Johnston v. Johnston,* 649 N.E.2d 799 (Mass. App. 1995) (weekly alimony of $1250 for wife who also received $3 million distribution of marital property, "not excessive"); *Wrobleski v. Wrobleski,* 653 A.2d 732 (R.I. 1995) (sustaining five-year alimony award of $5000 monthly, and $2000 monthly thereafter, to wife awarded $1.3 million in marital assets). In *Marriage of McNaughton,* 145 Cal. App. 3d 845, 194 Cal. Rptr. 176, 179 (1983), the court sustained a maintenance award of $3,500 monthly to wife with $3 million in property, at the conclusion of a 32-year childless marriage, saying "[a]rguments that a spouse could live with less are properly addressed to the trial court. The award may seem excessive, but given the lavish lifestyle of the parties, the financial needs of Wife, and the Husband's ability to pay, another judge could reasonably make the same order under the same circumstances." Those who try to force such results into the rubric of need sometimes appeal to notions of "social need," that women accustomed to the life of "the highest and most prosperous socioeconomic group" by virtue of their husband's income require such awards because otherwise "the moorings of their identification with a certain social class, and with it the core of their self-esteem — formerly exclusively determined by the husband's education, occupation, and income — [would otherwise be] shaken loose." J. WALLERSTEIN & J. KELLY, SURVIVING THE BREAKUP 23 (1980).

Cases like *Wilson* are perhaps less common. In *Marriage of Heistermann,* 234 Cal. App. 3d 1195, 286 Cal. Rptr. 127 (1991), where the facts were otherwise similar, the initial decree, unlike *Wilson,* provided permanent alimony, and the court declined to modify it because there were no new circumstances. In *Marriage of Biderman,* 5 Cal. App. 4th 409, 6 Cal. Rptr. 2d 791 (1992), the parties had separated in 1984 after 20 years of marriage, and each was awarded about $350,000 in property. The husband was also awarded $650 monthly in spousal support for one year. Seeking an extension, he claimed he was still disabled by depression and unable to support himself. The trial court granted the extension but the appeals court reversed, concluding that even if he was disabled, his assets could provide sufficient support to make alimony unnecessary.

Does "need" in high-income divorces include savings? In *Drapeau v. Drapeau,* 93 Cal. App. 4th 1086, 114 Cal. Rptr. 2d 6 (2001), review denied

(Feb. 13, 2002), the husband earned $1 million annually. The wife argued that the trial court's $12,206 monthly alimony award was too low because it would not allow her to save at the same rate as the parties saved during the marriage ($15,000 monthly). The appeals court remanded with directions to the trial court to consider this savings history, although it did not require an award that would allow the wife to duplicate it. The Florida Supreme Court took precisely the opposite view in *Mallard v. Mallard*, 771 So.2d 1138 (Fla. 2000). The *Mallard* parties lived modestly despite their high income, allowing them to save at least 25% of their income and amassing considerable assets. Lower courts had allowed the wife an alimony award based upon that income rather than their life style, intentionally allowing her to continue the savings pattern. The Florida Supreme Court held, however, that amassing savings was not part of the purpose of an alimony award and therefore could not be considered in setting its amount.

2. *Problematic Rationales for Alimony: Contract.* Can one simply infer a contract between the parties whose terms explain the alimony obligation? The *ALI Principles* conclude not. Comment b of § 5.05 explains:

> Contract analogies are sometimes relied upon to explain alimony awards to the long-time homemaker. . . . [A] conventional contract rationale would require describing the spousal relation in exchange terms that seem inapt because the parties define their relation by its nonfinancial aspects even though financial sharing is an important part of it. Spouses pool their financial affairs as part of a more general expectation of a shared life in which they have emotional and personal obligations as well as financial ones. At dissolution, no compensation is provided either spouse for loss of these nonfinancial aspects of their marriage. Nor is compensation provided for the loss of the nonfinancial services, such as homemaking, or home maintenance, which spouses typically provide each other during their marriage. Even if marriage as a whole were susceptible to being understood strictly in contract terms, a contract rationale could not explain why the financial obligations of marriage should alone survive dissolution when the larger relationship upon which those obligations depended does not.

Note as well that if alimony is viewed as roughly analogous to damages for breach of contract, then it would be available only to claimant who could show that it was their spouse, and not them, who breached the agreement — which is close to making alimony turn on marital "fault." Few commentators or courts would find such a rule desirable, *and* it is not the law anywhere today. For more on the contract rationale for alimony and the difficulties with it, see Ira Mark Ellman, *Why Family Law is Hard*, 35 ARIZ. ST. L.J. 699, 709-14 (2003), and Ira Mark Ellman and Sharon Lohr, *Opportunistic Violence, Marriage as Contract, and Other Bad Arguments for Fault Divorce*, 1997 U. ILL. L. REV. 719. For commentators more favorably inclined toward the contract approach, see Carbone, *Economics, Feminism, and the Reinvention of Alimony: A Reply to Ira Ellman*, 43 VAND. L. REV. 1463 (1990); Allen M. Parkman, *Reform of the Divorce Provisions of the Marriage Contract*, 8 B.Y.U. J. PUB. L. 91 (1994); Cynthia Starnes, *Application of a Contemporary Partnership Model for Divorce*, 8 B.Y.U. J. PUB. L. 107 (1993). Some commentators employ contract concepts more metaphorically, and their conclusions are not necessarily inconsistent with the ALI's approach. *E.g.*, Elizabeth Scott, *Rehabilitating Liberalism in Modern Divorce Law,* 1994 UTAH L. REV. 687 and Carol Weisbrod, *The Way We Live: A New Discussion of Contracts and Domestic Arrangements,* 1994 UTAH L. REV. 777.

3. *Problematic Rationales for Alimony: Restitution.* If no contract can be inferred, perhaps relief can be premised upon a quasi-contract doctrine like unjust enrichment, or restitution — an approach sometimes used in other contexts to work justice when the formal requirements of contract cannot be met. The husband in *Clapp* argued that the trial court improperly based its award "on a theory of restitution for past homemaker services," but the Vermont Supreme Court held that alimony can be granted on this basis even though not mentioned in the governing statute. But *Clapp* makes no formal inquiry into whether that doctrine's requirements were in fact met. What if it had? *See Pyeatte v. Pyeatte,* 661 P.2d 196 (Ariz. App. 1983), an unusual case because both parties conceded the existence of an agreement under which the spouses would take turns attending school and rely upon the support of the other. They divorced after the husband completed his schooling but before the wife began hers, and she sued. The court rejected her contract claim because the husband's reciprocal obligations under the agreement could not be established with sufficient specificity to enforce. But it did allow her restitution of the support she had provided. Yet the very success of the *Pyeatte* restitution claim points out the doctrine's limits as a broadly applicable rationale for alimony. *See* Ellman, *The Theory of Alimony,* 77 CAL. L. REV. 1, 25-28 (1989):

> There are three elements to a restitution claim in modern law: First, the defendant must have received a cognizable benefit; second, the benefit must have been conferred at the plaintiff's expense; and third, the defendant's retention of the benefit must be unjust. There is ordinarily no difficulty in cases like *Pyeatte* in establishing the first two elements of restitution, that the defendant benefitted at the plaintiff's expense. The only real question becomes whether the defendant's gratuitous retention of the benefit is "unjust." The general rule is that there is no unjustness where the benefit was originally conferred with "donative intent." Conversely, retention of a benefit is unjust where there was "an expectation of payment or compensation for services at the time they were rendered." The existence of a contract, even one that fails for indefiniteness, suggests that both parties understood that some compensation would be due – that the benefit was not conferred as a gift. Precisely this reasoning led the court in *Pyeatte* to conclude that the requirement of unjustness was met. Thus *Pyeatte's* precedential force is limited: Even though it provides a remedy without requiring a breach of contract, it necessarily relies heavily on the incomplete agreement whose existence was conceded by both parties.
>
> Because other claimants are unlikely to have an agreement to rely upon, they will have considerably more difficulty showing that the other spouse's retention of the benefit is unjust. In *Pyeatte* the

agreement dealt with a specific and rather limited aspect of the marriage, the immediate educational plans of each party. While all of the terms were not spelled out in detail, there was no difficulty establishing what benefit had been conferred on the husband (support during school), and the nature of the compensation both parties agreed upon in return. We know both that the wife's intent was not donative and that she did not receive the expected compensation. We could therefore conclude that the husband's retention of his benefit without some payment to the wife was unjust.

It is harder to find nonpayment in the case of the long-term homemaker. The benefit she conferred is presumably her many years of companionship and homemaking service. Perhaps the parties expected the wife to receive lifetime support in return, even if the marriage dissolved. In that case, the wife remains without full compensation, so that the husband has been unjustly enriched. Yet just as plausibly, the quid pro quo might have been the companionship and financial support that she has *already* received over the years in which they lived together. Or perhaps the parties had no defined expectations, but simply gave to each other out of love — that is, with a donative intent rather than with an expectation of repayment. If a court can determine which set of motivations accurately describes the particular case before it, then it can determine whether one spouse "unjustly" retains a benefit conferred by the other. In many cases, however, the court will find no unjustness using traditional criteria, and in many others the facts simply will not be clear enough to allow any conclusion. In the end, . . . the court attempting a restitution analysis will inevitably be drawn to its own understanding of the marital relation to test whether there was "unjust" enrichment. The parties' own expectations or understandings, having been expressed unclearly (or else they would have a valid contract) will be less important.

This can be seen from the *Pyeatte* case itself. The court took pains to distinguish the facts before it from the kind of homemaker case we have just been discussing: "Where both spouses perform the usual and incidental activities of the marital relationship, upon dissolution there can be no restitution for performance of these activities." Restitution, the court felt, is appropriate only where "the facts demonstrate an agreement between the spouses and an extraordinary or unilateral effort by one spouse which inures solely to the benefit of the other by the time of dissolution." Traditional marital roles cannot constitute such "extraordinary or unilateral effort."

Some will agree with the *Pyeatte* court's description of the marital relation; others will undoubtedly find it too narrow or unrealistic. But it is precisely this debate that ultimately dooms restitution as a workable solution to the problem of alimony, for it demonstrates that a court can resolve a restitution claim only by referring to its own unguided conception of marriage. In the end, restitution principles do no more than direct the court to order repayment where it feels that to do otherwise would be "unjust." Since directives from the parties themselves are absent, the court can only employ its own sense of the marital obligations and claims necessarily flowing from marriage in deciding what justice requires.

The doctrine of restitution thus offers no conceptual framework that explains generally why post-marriage payments are appropriate in some cases but not in others. Before the doctrine can be applied coherently, one must first have an established understanding of the social and economic conventions that ordinarily govern the relationship between the parties, against which to test claims that there has been an "unjust" enrichment. In the business and employment relations in which the doctrine is ordinarily applied, such conventions exist. In marriage they once did, but do not any longer. The doctrine of unjust enrichment cannot replace these conventions, because its application requires their prior existence. . . .

What conception of marriage must one have to ground the *Clapp* award on the idea of restitution? It is perhaps suggested by the court's observation that the wife took employment that "enabled her to stay at home during the summer" while in contrast, the husband "consistently put in night and weekend hours at his law office." But is this necessarily an argument for the wife, as the court seems to think, or could it also be offered as an argument for the husband? Could he have a restitution claim for the excess support he provided during the marriage? Which spouse, if either, made contributions that exceeded "the usual and incidental activities of the marital relationship"? If neither made such contributions, how can a restitution claim succeed?

4. Problematic Rationales for Alimony: Contribution. Courts like *Clapp,* as well as some governing statutes, often refer to a spouse's contributions to the marriage as a basis for alimony without tying the contributions to some doctrinal explanation for an award, such as contract or restitution. This contribution argument is often connected with the observation that the contributing spouse gave up other opportunities. *Marriage of LaRocque,* 406 N.W.2d 736 (Wis. 1987) (because parties did not accumulate a great deal of property during marriage, alimony rather than property distribution must be relied upon to "compensate" the homemaker wife for her contribution and her loss of a stream of income); *McNamara v. McNamara,* 443 N.W.2d 511, 516 (Mich. App. 1989) (24-year marriage in which homemaker wife said to "contribute significantly" to lawyer-husband's success "by not pursuing her own career opportunities and by providing the comfort and support, financial and otherwise, needed for defendant's well-being while he was climbing a professional and financial ladder."); *Rosenberg v. Rosenberg,* 155 A.D.2d 428, 547 N.Y.S.2d 90, 92 (1989) ("wife had contributed to the economic partnership as a parent and homemaker"). In that sense the claim may be just a less explicit version of unjust enrichment. But putting aside the problems we have already seen with unjust enrichment, we might ask how such contributions could be taken into account.

In offering the contribution argument itself, *Clapp* says that "homemaker contributions are, by their nature, nonmonetary so that they cannot be quantified or put into a monetary formula to specify their impact on the ultimate maintenance award." Of course, housekeeping and child care services can be purchased, and their monetary value thus established. The court's point makes sense, however, if one assumes a broader view of homemaking functions that includes intangible factors like emotional support, or spousal and parental love. These items are not available in market transactions and are therefore not easily valued in dollar amounts. But if Mrs. Clapp's intangible contributions to the marriage are considered, surely Mr. Clapp's also made contributions. Perhaps the alimony claimant should be required to present evidence of the spouses' respective intangible contributions, to establish that she contributed more than her share. If courts should neither make assumptions about the spouses' relative contributions, nor require evidence on the question, then how can such contributions be made relevant to the alimony decision?

There is another version of the contribution argument: the claim is that compensation is due for the homemaker's contributions to the breadwinner's career success, whether on an unjust enrichment rationale or on some more general claim of equity. If that is the rationale, should obligors be able to defend the claim by showing, if they can, that they would have done as well financially without their spouses? (Recall *Michael v. Michael,* p. 277, *supra.)* Or do we mean instead to explain alimony by reference to a more general proposition that homemakers typically "contribute" to their spouse's success, and thereby justify a general remedy for homemakers that is available without regard to the particular facts of their case. The problem with that view is that it is actually quite uncertain whether, as a general matter, husbands earn more than bachelors *because* of their wives' homemaking contributions. It is at least equally plausible that married men earn more because women are more likely to choose financially successful men for husbands, or because many of the attributes that make a man more likely to enjoy financial success also make him more able to attract a wife. *See* Yinon Cohen & Yitchak Haberfeld, *Why Do Married Men Earn More Than Unmarried Men?,* 20 SOC. SCI. RES. 29 (1991).

Yet another version of the contribution argument is that a homemaker spouse's support makes the breadwinner spouse more comfortable or more happy. Clearly true in many marriages, it may be less often true in precisely those marriages that end in divorce. In any event, the converse is equally plausible, that the homemaker is more comfortable or more happy during marriage by virtue of sharing in the financial rewards of the other spouse's market efforts. The point, of course, is that at dissolution each spouse loses the benefits conferred by the other spouse in an intact marriage, and therefore a claim of compensation requires more explanation than the simple recognition of that loss (or we would end up allowing remedies to both spouses).

5. *The Importance of Marital Duration.* One obvious difference between *Clapp* and *Wilson* is the length of the respective marriages. Marital duration appears to be a critical factor for nearly every court asked to make an award of "support alimony" — alimony with no definite termination date that is intended to provide the obligee with a more comfortable living standard. For example, see Rosalyn B. Bell, *Alimony and the Financially Dependent Spouse in Montgomery County, Maryland,* 22 FAM. L.Q. 225, 253 (1988) (survey of appellate decisions concludes that, excluding cases involving minor children, permanent alimony rarely awarded in marriages of less than 30 years duration). Studies of trial court decisions suggest the same result, *id.* at 288 (median marital duration in contested cases in which fixed-term alimony awards were granted was 14 years; median marital duration for contested cases in which awards of indefinite term were granted was 27 years).

Why should the length of the marriage matter? One might distinguish between two kinds of cases. The first group are those for which we believe the spouse's "need" in some sense arises from the marriage. *Clapp* seems to make this point when it argues that the wife delayed her education and entry into the job market in order to take primary responsibility for raising the marital children. The longer the marriage, the more plausible is the claim that the homemaker has lost significant earning capacity, and the more plausible is the intuition that the potential obligor in fact benefitted from the homemaking labors that now give rise to the need asserted by the obligee. For this group of claims, then, we may look to the length of marriage as a rough indication of the extent to which the former spouse should be liable for current needs, because the length of marriage will be correlated with the factors that justify imposing the obligation in the first place.

Wilson, however, is an example of a second kind of case, in which the need does not arise from the marriage, even though it arises *during the* marriage. (*Wilson*'s factual premise is that the husband bore no responsibility for the wife's disability.) *Wilson* concludes that where one has an inadvertent accident or illness, one's spouse does not necessarily incur a lifetime obligation to provide the financial assistance which is thereby made necessary, but it suggests it would be more receptive to such a claim if the marriage had been of longer duration. But why? If the marital commitment is "revocable," as *Wilson* suggests, then we might think it is just as revocable after 20 years as after two years.

There is no accepted answer to this question, but the *Wilson* court's instinct that the length of the marriage matters in both kinds of cases is widely shared. Some might argue there is rough justice in the claim that "I've given you the best x years of my life and if you want to leave me now, when things aren't going so well, for somebody else, you ought to pay for it in spades." That argument cannot carry the day, however, because it assumes the obligor is at fault for leaving: what if the potential obligee ends the marriage? Or what if things have never gone well, and one spouse finally decides to call it off? Should a long-term award be allowed in that case? *See, e.g., Andersen v. Andersen,* 16 FAM. L. REP. 1345 (N.Y. Sup. Ct. 1990) (wife who supported her alcoholic husband during their 27-year marriage ordered to pay $3,000 per month in rehabilitative alimony for set term of three years). If we want to answer "yes" without relying upon assumptions of fault, the rationale needs to be set out more clearly than it is in most cases. Perhaps we believe that as the spouses age, their reliance on the marital commitment increases because one's life course becomes harder to change and the prospects of finding a new spouse decline. Note too that some of *Wilson*'s language suggests the length of the husband's obligation should be proportional to the length of the marriage. Under that approach, we would not classify marriages as "long term" or "short term," but would instead employ a sliding scale of obligation.

6. *The ALI Approach.* For many of the reasons just surveyed, the *ALI Principles* conclude that neither need nor contribution provides a satisfactory explanation of alimony. The *Principles* observe that alimony has historically been a residual category encompassing any financial claim at divorce that was not a property or child support claim, and that several different kinds of claims have in fact been allowed, each with its own rationale. The *Principles* separates these threads more clearly into separate claims, with set criteria for each, which when met create a presumption of entitlement to an award of a specified amount. An individual may qualify for more than one kind of claim. Another significant change is the *Principles'* reconceptualization of alimony as compensation for losses, rather than the meeting of needs. Thus, each of the claims recognized under the *Principles* is a claim for a different kind of loss. Comment *a* to Section 5.02 of the *Principles* lays out the basic approach:

> The principal conceptual innovation of this Chapter is . . . to recharacterize The remedy it provides as compensation for loss rather than relief for need. A spouse frequently seems in need at the conclusion of a marriage because its dissolution imposes a particularly severe loss on him or her. The intuition that the former spouse has an obligation to meet that need arises from the perception that the need results from the unfair allocation of the financial losses arising from the marital failure. This perception explains why . . . all alimony claims cannot be adjudicated by reference to a single standard of need. If the payment's justification is not relief of need but the equitable reallocation of the losses arising from the marital failure, then need is not an appropriate eligibility requirement for the award. While many persons who have suffered an inequitable financial loss will be in need, others will not, and the remainder will vary in their degree of need. At the same time, some formerly married individuals may find themselves in need for reasons unrelated to the marriage and its subsequent dissolution. In that case, there may be no basis for imposing a special obligation to meet that need on their former spouses.
>
> . . . [F]ocusing on loss permits more coherent definition of the cases qualifying for compensatory payments [the term used instead of "alimony" or "maintenance"] than is possible in a system judging all claims on the single but ill-defined goal of relieving need. The shift in analysis from need to loss thus facilitates more precise rules of adjudication, with a correspondingly reduced disparity of result. . . .
>
> Equally important, recharacterizing the award's purpose from the relief of need to the equitable allocation of loss transforms the claimant's petition from a plea for help to a claim of entitlement. Although conceptual confusion over the grounds of alimony has undoubtedly contributed to mistaken judgments in both directions, inadequate or missing awards have been the more frequent problem. This failure of alimony has created pressure to expand the relief available through the division of property so as to reach claims for which that remedy is ill-suited. Reconceptualizing alimony as compensatory payments for

losses arising from the marriage and its failure established it as an entitlement providing a more reliable remedy for the divorce-related financial claims.

Section 5.03 lists the "compensable losses" — the losses for which claims arise. As explained in § 5.02, these are limited to financial losses; there are no claims, for example, for emotional damage (although the *Principles* do not preclude tort claims). Claims are also limited to financial losses arising from the marriage's dissolution, as compared to claims for financial inequities during the marriage. Some of the claims (such as reimbursement for support during school – discussed above, in Section C, p. 342) arise only at the dissolution of short-term marriages. By far the most important of the claims recognized by the *Principles* are the two that would replace, in existing law, the traditional claim of "support alimony" – potentially long-term awards meant to assist the obligee in maintaining a level of support. Section 5.03 describes those two losses this way:

(a) In a marriage of significant duration, the loss in living standard experienced at dissolution by the spouse who has less wealth or earning capacity. . . .

(b) An earning-capacity loss incurred during marriage but continuing after dissolution and arising from one spouse's disproportionate share, during marriage, of the care of the marital children or of the children of either spouse. . . .

Homemakers in long-term marriages with children will typically qualify for both awards. As for the second award, its basic rationale is that because care for marital children is a joint obligation of both spouses, financial losses arising from marital child care that endure after the marriage ends ought also to be shared (as they are when the marriage is intact). The *Principles* provides that the size of the award increases with the duration of the child care period. The *Principles* offers the following rationale for the first award, compensation for the loss of living standard:

Section 5.04, Comment *c*:

[T]he cases reflect an enduring intuition that the homemaker in a long-term marriage has some claim on her spouse's post-divorce income. That intuition does not depend on any assumption that the parties made explicit promises to one another, but on the belief that the relationship itself gives rise to obligations. Anglo-American legal traditions, individualistic as they are, recognize duties between relative strangers that arise from even fleeting interactions in which one person's behavior affects another. Further duties may be owed those with whom one has a more established relationship. The relationship of employer and employee, landlord and tenant, and shareholder and corporate officer, all give rise to legal duties. Some may be waivable by contract and some not, but few are dependent upon contract to establish their existence. They emerge from entry into the relationship itself, whether or not the parties expressly adopt them. The relationship of husband and wife is of this kind, but more so. Its effects may accrete slowly, but with great impact as the spouses' lives become entwined over time.

In understanding the nature of the obligation that arises in the long-term marriage, it is useful to think first about the traditional home-maker wife, as perhaps the clearest case. . . . That wife has more at risk, financially, from the dissolution of a long-term marriage than does her breadwinner spouse. The observation is not limited to full-time homemakers but applies equally to anyone economically depen-dent on his or her spouse, which typically includes part-time home-makers who are also employed but earn much less than their spouse[s]. The marital dissolution may leave both spouses financially less well off, but whenever the spouses have significantly different earning capacities, the loss for the lower-earning spouse will be much greater than for the other. Under this section, when there is such an income differential, and the marriage exceeds some minimum dura-tion, there will usually be a remedy in favor of the lower-earning spouse in an amount that is proportional to both the income differen-tial and the marital duration.

The remedy is proportional to the marital duration because the obligations recognized under this section do not arise from the mar-riage ceremony alone, but develop over time as the parties' lives become entwined. . . . To leave the financially dependent spouse in a long marriage without a remedy would facilitate exploitation of the trusting spouse and discourage investment by the nervous one.

The *Principles*, in Sections 5.04 and 5.05, provide in effect guidelines that set a presumptive award amount, once the entitlement criteria have been shown. The awards equal a percentage of the difference between the two spouse's incomes, with that percentage gradually increasing with either marital duration or the duration of the child care. The combined value of the two awards is capped (the suggested cap is 40% of the income difference). The emphasis on duration can be understood on two grounds. First, duration pro-vides a rough measure of the size of the claimant's loss: a longer child care period will usually entail a greater loss of earning capacity; also the longer the marriage, the greater is the dependent spouse's sense of the marriage's more affluent living standard as the benchmark against which to compare her post-divorce situation. Second, duration provides a rough measure of the obligor-spouse's duty to share the other spouse's loss, as the parties' obliga-tions to one another increase the longer they are married. (The commentary to § 5.05 recognizes that the loss of earning capacity may not be related to the difference in the spouses' incomes at dissolution, but concludes that insurmountable measurement difficulties preclude a more direct measure of that loss, and offers theoretical reasons why the earnings difference may in any event be an appropriate benchmark.)

7. *Alimony Guidelines.* As will be discussed in Chapter Five, child support guidelines, creating (for better or for worse) relatively predictable results for child support cases within a jurisdiction, now rule that area of post-divorce financial obligations. In most such cases, the presumptive amount of support to be ordered is determined by a formula that uses the income of the obligor parent or the income of both parents. While there has been significant debate about the merits of such guidelines, there is little doubt that they have made child support determinations more consistent and more predictable. As discussed in the previous note, the *ALI Principles'* treatment of alimony seeks a similar predictability in the results for alimony. Additionally, according to one review, at least 12 states have experimented, either at a state-wide level, or at the county level, with guidelines for setting alimony, or alimony *pendente lite. See* Virginia R. Dugan & Jon A. Feder, *Alimony Guidelines: Do They Work?*, 25 FAMILY ADVOCATE 20 (2003). However, these guidelines tend to give only rough or "rule of thumb" guidance as to whether to order alimony, or at what level. They tend to set a minimum duration of the marriage before alimony can be awarded, a preference for rehabilitative or permanent alimony, and, occasionally, some formula for determining the level of support. One barrier for alimony guidelines is that the varied purposes for alimony affects perceptions of the appropriate amount. For this reason, any suggested set of guidelines is unlikely to seem appropriate across the full range of cases. It remains to be seen whether the ALI's recommendations have any impact on the process of establishing alimony guidelines. The Family Court of Maricopa County, Arizona (Phoenix) has adopted guidelines that are in some respects similar to the ALI recommendations, although considerably less comprehensive. *See* Ira Mark Ellman, *The Maturing Law of Divorce Finances: Toward Rules and Guidelines*, 33 FAM. L.Q. 801 (1999).

8. *Ex Ante vs. Ex Post Considerations.* A standard tension in the analysis, and in lawmaking in general, is rules which do justice between the parties (looking back on the facts of their case ("ex post")) may not create the best incentives for other people's behavior in the future ("ex ante"). Sometimes this distinction is put in terms of considerations of fairness versus considerations of (economic) efficiency. In any event, such tensions potentially arise in connection with the rules of alimony. Some feminist theorists have argued against rules that compensate spouses who sacrifice for the sake of the marital household, on the basis that such rules, though perhaps offering just compensation for those sacrifices, improperly encourage women to (continue to) make economically disabling choices, perpetuating their financial dependence on men and their inequality in society. June Carbone, *Economics, Feminism, and the Reinvention of Alimony*, 43 VAND. L. REV. 1463 (1990). Of course, whether incentives created by the laws of divorce in fact have any effect on people's choices in their domestic lives is itself a matter of dispute. For those who believe that there are such effects, a choice may be necessary between doing justice between the parties and encouraging changes in the way marriages are conducted in the future.

PROBLEM

Problem 4-16. Suppose the disability in *Wilson* developed just after the spouses separated, rather than just before. Should the husband have any obligation in that case, for even a short period of assistance? What if the marriage were of 16 years' duration, rather than 6?

[4] SIZE AND DURATION OF AWARDS FOLLOWING A LONG-TERM MARRIAGE

RAINWATER v. RAINWATER

869 P.2d 176 (Ariz. App. 1993)

FIDEL, Chief Judge. Sam Rainwater ("husband") appeals from the trial court's award of spousal maintenance to Barbara Rainwater ("wife") until her death or remarriage. He argues that unless the receiving spouse, through age, disability, or lack of earning capacity, is permanently unable to become self-sustaining, Arizona law permits spousal maintenance only for a finite, transitional, rehabilitative term. We find that husband's argument gives inadequate weight to marital standard of living as a factor in maintenance awards, and to the receiving spouse's contribution to the earning ability of the paying spouse. We conclude that the trial court did not exceed its discretion in awarding indefinite maintenance in this case.

I.

In June of 1988, wife petitioned . . . to dissolve the parties' twenty-two-year marriage. Resolving all other issues by stipulation, the parties went to trial on the . . . appropriate spousal maintenance for wife.

Wife through much of the parties' marriage worked full time outside the home. In the early years, she helped support husband while he worked toward an engineering degree. In later years, . . . she contributed socially and emotionally to husband's career. Additionally, wife maintained the home and was primary caretaker for the parties' two children, who now are grown. After husband received his degree, his income rose substantially. In the year of the divorce and for two years prior, husband's earnings exceeded $100,000.

At the time of dissolution, wife, a forty-one-year-old secretary, was working toward a Bachelor of Arts degree, but neither party showed the extent to which her earning capacity would be enhanced by that degree. Weighing wife's needs in the context of her marital standard of living, the trial court found that wife "would not be able to meet her reasonable needs . . . nor enjoy the standard of living established during the marriage based on reasonably anticipated income from her investments and her employment." Specifically, the trial court estimated wife's after-tax income from labor and pre-tax income from investments as $20,000 per year and her reasonable needs as $41,000 per year. Finding that husband's earnings exceeded his needs, the trial court awarded wife $1900 per month for three years or until one year after completion of her B.A. degree, whichever should first occur, and $1200 per month thereafter till her death or remarriage.

Although husband argued in the trial court that wife should receive no spousal maintenance, on appeal he challenges only the duration and amount of the award. Husband argues that the trial court erred by entering an award that would allow his able-bodied former wife "to live off his labors forever."

He argues that, in the absence of evidence that wife is permanently unable to become self-sustaining, Arizona public policy permits only a fixed-term award to assist her in transition to an independent life. Wife responds that our maintenance law requires a case-by-case determination, that it is flexible enough to permit an indefinite award when justified by statutorily enumerated considerations, and that those considerations support indefinite maintenance in this case.

II.

Arizona law extends the trial court substantial discretion to set the amount and duration of spousal maintenance. The framework for that discretion is largely provided by Ariz. Rev. Stat. Ann. ("A.R.S.") section 25-319 (1991). First, to justify any award, the evidence must support a finding . . . that the receiving spouse lacks sufficient property and ability to meet reasonable living expenses. That finding is not contested in this case. Second, in deciding the duration and amount of maintenance, the trial court must balance the factors listed in section 25-319(B). [2]

To strike the proper balance, the trial court need not apply every factor listed. . . . In what is necessarily a case-by-case inquiry, some factors will not apply. The trial court may abuse its discretion, however, by neglecting an applicable factor.

We turn to husband's claim that the 25-319(B) balance is weighted by public policy in favor of maintenance that is transitional, rehabilitative, and limited in term. We agree up to a point. Citing *Schroeder v. Schroeder*, 778 P.2d 1212 (Ariz. 1989), husband emphasizes the supreme court's statement that

> the current aim [of spousal maintenance] is to achieve independence for both parties and to require an effort toward independence by the party requesting maintenance. The temporary award of maintenance in its present form reflects both of these values. In most cases of temporary maintenance, the key issue for the parties and the court will be whether that independence will be achieved by a good faith effort.

This general statement is best examined in the context of the facts.

In *Schroeder*, the trial court had initially awarded wife four years of spousal maintenance, but later extended maintenance until her death or remarriage

---

[2] The factors listed in section 25-319(B) are:

1. The standard of living established during the marriage.

2. The duration of the marriage.

3. The age, employment history, earning ability and the physical and emotional condition of the spouse seeking maintenance.

4. The ability of the spouse from whom maintenance is sought to meet his or her needs while meeting those of the spouse seeking maintenance.

5. The comparative financial resources of the spouses, including their comparative earning abilities in the labor market.

6. The contribution of the spouse seeking maintenance to the earning ability of the other spouse.

7. The extent to which the spouse seeking maintenance has reduced his or her income or career opportunities for the benefit of the other spouse.

or the further order of the court. The supreme court upheld the modified award. The court explained that maintenance awards are modifiable both in amount and in duration, unless the parties have expressly agreed to the contrary and the trial court has so ordered. The wife in *Schroeder* was fifty and had worked primarily as a homemaker before her twenty-eight-year marriage ended. Although the initial award of four years' duration was "intended to support [wife's] transitional growth of earning capacity," by the time of the petition for modification, wife had only found relatively unlucrative work as a filing clerk, and her expenses had increased to include chemotherapy treatment for cancer. Because time had disproved the trial court's apparent initial expectation that four years of transitional support would enable wife to become self-supporting, the supreme court concluded that the evidence now justified an indefinite maintenance award.

Schroeder indeed recognizes the transition toward independence as a principal objective of maintenance. . . . But *Schroeder* also reaffirms the trial court's discretion to award indefinite maintenance when it appears . . . that independence is unlikely. . . . Additionally, *Schroeder* shows that assessing the likelihood of a successful transition to independence requires a prediction that may vary not only from case to case, but from time to time within a case.

III.

It does not resolve this case to recognize that maintenance orders, whenever possible, should promote a transition toward financial independence. The crux of husband's argument is that indefinite maintenance can be awarded only to a spouse who is "permanently unable to be self-sustaining."

The principal flaw in this argument is husband's failure to define "self-sustaining" by reference to any standard of living. The evidence certainly suggests that wife can be self-sustaining beyond the minimal subsistence level. Yet the trial court expressly found that wife's "reasonably anticipated income" would not meet her "reasonable needs," when those needs were determined by reference to "the standard of living established during the marriage."

Marital standard of living has long been listed by our legislature among the factors pertinent to the duration and amount of spousal maintenance. And though Arizona courts have stated that public policy favors fixed-term maintenance as a means to promote a diligent effort to become self-sustaining, we have repeatedly cautioned that this goal "must be balanced with some realistic appraisal of the probabilities that the receiving spouse will in fact subsequently be able to support herself in some reasonable approximation of the standard of living established during the marriage." [¶] In 1987, when the legislature enacted the most recent amendments to section 25-319, it expanded subsection (B) by adding [factors 6, 7, and 8, as reprinted in footnote 2]. It is apparent from these changes that the legislature does not regard a 25-319(B) decision as exclusively an inquiry into the speed with which the receiving spouse might become self-supporting without maintenance. See *Elliott v. Elliott*, 796 P.2d at 938 (Factors 6 and 7 "differ from most of the other section 25-319(B) factors in that they are not based upon the parties' needs.").

We do not suggest that at the end of every marriage, the party of lesser earning capacity is entitled to enough support to maintain the standard of living achieved during the marriage. First of all, divorce often requires a lesser standard of living for both parties. The statute requires consideration of "[t]he ability of the spouse from whom maintenance is sought to meet his or her needs while meeting those of the spouse seeking maintenance." A.R.S. § 25-319(B)(4). Second, there will be case-to-case variance in the degree to which the marital standard of living may be seen as a product of the marriage. For this reason, such factors as length of the marriage, the receiving spouse's contributions to the education and earning capacity of the paying spouse, and the receiving spouse's reduction in income or career opportunities for the benefit of the family home and children bear heavily on the trial court's effort to establish an equitable award. . . .

In this case, the parties had a marriage of long duration, to which wife contributed financially and by assuming the role of primary caretaker for the family home and children. She contributed to husband's support as he worked toward an engineering degree, and she contributed socially and emotionally to his professional advancement once his formal education was complete. The parties had achieved a relatively high standard of living by the last years of their marriage, which the trial court properly regarded as a product of their sustained common efforts for 23 years. The trial court built an incentive toward independence into its maintenance award by reducing wife's monthly payment from $1900 to $1200 after the expiration of a reasonable period for getting her B.A. degree. But the trial court also concluded — and the evidence permits the conclusion — that wife could not foreseeably expect to maintain her standard of living without ongoing support from husband at a level reasonably within his ability to provide. Under all of these circumstances, we find that the trial court properly balanced the many relevant factors of 25-319(B), and we find no abuse of discretion in the trial court's award.

We add that our decision is strongly affected by the presumptive modifiability of spousal maintenance awards. Because maintenance awards are modifiable, an award of maintenance until death or remarriage does not lock long-term maintenance irrefutably into place. Rather, it places the burden on the paying spouse to prove a later change in circumstances sufficiently substantial to warrant shortening the duration of the award. A fixed-term award, by contrast, places the burden on the receiving spouse to prove a change in circumstances sufficiently substantial to warrant extending the award.

The allocation of the burden of seeking modification order represents a prediction of when independence will occur, and that the effects of changing circumstances should not be borne solely by the receiving spouse. [¶] An award until death or remarriage is a prediction that one spouse will never be able to independently approximate the standard of living established during marriage, and that the other spouse will remain financially able to contribute to the first spouse's support. When, as in this case, that finding is supported by the evidence, we find no inequity in placing the burden on the paying spouse to later prove that a substantial and continuing change of circumstances has occurred.

. . .

We affirm the trial court's order of spousal maintenance.

[The Arizona Supreme Court denied the husband's Petition for Review, but Justice Martone dissented: "[T]his case decides an important issue of law. . . . There is no existing authority for the proposition that a spouse 'needs' to live forever in the style to which he or she has become accustomed. It can be argued that the allowance of lifetime maintenance at the standard of living established during marriage turns the institution of marriage into a lifetime annuity. This important issue warrants our consideration." *Rainwater v. Rainwater*, 869 P.2d 175 (Ariz. 1994). Ed.]

HECKER v. HECKER

568 N.W.2d 705 (Minn. 1997)

KEITH, CHIEF JUSTICE. . . .[¶] Dennis and Sandra Hecker were married on February 23, 1973. . . . Dennis enjoyed considerable success in the auto sales business while Sandra engaged in traditional homemaking responsibilities, including caring for the parties' two children. . . . In August 1982, Dennis petitioned the district court to dissolve the marriage. [A] marital termination agreement . . . award[ed] Sandra sole physical custody of the parties' 5-and 8-year-old daughters, child support in the amount of $800 per month per child, certain real and personal property, and temporary spousal maintenance of $800 per month for 121 months until June 1, 1993. The [May 1983] judgment . . . incorporated the terms of this agreement.

[Sandra obtained modifications of the judgment in 1985 and again in 1986, which together gave her an additional $155,000 in a lump sum settlement of property claims, increased her child support to $900 per month per child, and increased spousal maintenance to $1,000 per month for a five-year period, after which it returned to the original $800 per month until its scheduled termination on June 1, 1993.]

On February 2, 1993, four months before her temporary spousal maintenance award was to expire, Sandra again moved the district court to modify the judgment and decree by increasing her monthly maintenance to $2,000 and designating it as a permanent award. In support of her claim that changed circumstances rendered the original award unreasonable or unfair, Sandra stated that she was then 45 years old and, because of her responsibilities with regard to the children, she never completed vocational training as she had intended at the time of the marriage dissolution entered ten years earlier. She claimed that her monthly income from child support and maintenance was $3,196.92 and that her monthly expenses for herself and the youngest child were $3,107, but because the oldest child was to graduate from high school in June 1993, the loss of support for that child and that the expiration of the temporary maintenance period would leave her without sufficient means to provide for her own support. While Dennis acknowledged that he had sufficient income to support a modification, he opposed it based upon the parties' earlier agreements.

Sandra, who was 35 at the time of the marriage dissolution, apparently initially appreciated that, because of her stipulation for durational, not permanent maintenance, it was necessary for her to retrain or otherwise enter the labor market. Within a year of that dissolution in 1984, she obtained a part-time position at the YMCA, performing various tasks during her eight-year employment. She earned approximately $6 per hour during that employment period. She left the YMCA in October 1992 and, from December 1992 to February 1993, was employed as an interviewer for a temporary job service earning $7 to $7.50 per hour. During this time, she applied for several full-time positions, stating that she had initially preferred part-time employment so that she could retain flexibility and meet her children's needs.

The referee granted Sandra's motion for an increased and permanent award in its entirety, finding that she had failed to rehabilitate and that this failure constituted the requisite substantial change in circumstances that rendered the original award unreasonable and unfair. The referee's award of $2,000 per month was affirmed by the district court [but reversed by a divided appeals panel and remanded to the district court for further proceedings to address, *inter alia*, the reasons for her failure to rehabilitate]. [T]he appellate court appears to have suggested . . . that the reasons for Sandra's failure to rehabilitate must be ascertained because, at the time of the dissolution, the parties contemplated that she would be the primary custodian of the children and, as far as the record was developed, there existed no *changed* circumstances — that is, the fact that Sandra would devote considerable time to the care of the children was expected when the parties agreed to her sole physical custody.

On remand. . . . Dennis' . . . vocational expert [testified] that Sandra could expect entry-level earnings of $16,000 per year in retail management and, with three years' experience, could increase those earnings to $25,000 per year. The expert commented that during the time since the marriage was dissolved, Sandra was "minimally involved" in preparing for or pursuing a career and that she could have improved her earning capacity had she made a greater effort. The report was not rebutted.

The referee found that Sandra "chose not to make any serious effort at obtaining vocational training or work experience, but rather decided to rely upon the possibility that she would continue to receive spousal maintenance, despite the terms of the decree." The referee found no evidence to support Sandra's claim that her health problems, the health or needs of the children, the stress of divorce or the need to appear in court for periodic litigation restricted her achievement of better employment with greater income. Based upon Sandra's failure to make any reasonable effort toward rehabilitation, the referee [attributed] to her an annual income of $25,000 which, when coupled with annual investment income of $5,400 [based on the earlier $155,000 property settlement], would result in an approximate net monthly income of $1,825. Finding also that Sandra's reasonable monthly expenses are $3,200, the referee awarded her permanent monthly spousal maintenance of $1,375 — the difference between the monthly expenses and the total of investment and attributed income — to allow Sandra to meet her needs. The district court affirmed [the referee]. [¶] On Dennis' second appeal. . . . the court of appeals [affirmed,] holding that Sandra's willful failure to rehabilitate did not preclude her from receiving further maintenance if, after attributing to her the maximum earning capacity attainable by diligent efforts, she failed to become self-supporting.

. . . . Minn. Stat. § 518.64, subd. 2 (1996) . . . provides. . . .

> The terms of an order respecting maintenance or support may be modified upon a showing of one or more of the following: (1) substantially increased or decreased earnings of a party; (2) substantially increased or decreased need of a party * * *; (3) receipt of assistance * * *; (4) a change in the cost of living for either party * * *, any of which makes the terms unreasonable and unfair * * *.

That statute places a dual burden on the party seeking modification — first, to demonstrate that there has occurred a substantial change in one or more of the circumstances identified in the statute and second, to show that the substantial change has the effect of rendering the original award unreasonable and unfair.

Here, the parties originally stipulated to their respective rights and obligations, including that Sandra would receive temporary or durational spousal maintenance in presumed anticipation of her efforts to achieve some level of self-sufficiency. [It has] relevance in a modification context [as an] identification of the baseline circumstances against which claims of substantial change are evaluated. . . .

The referee implicitly concluded that the requisite substantial change in circumstances was . . . the frustration of the parties' expectations of [Sandra's] self-sufficiency. . . . [The trial court did not abuse its discretion accepting this finding and] recasting Dennis' obligation for spousal maintenance as permanent.

[T]he referee . . . fashioned an award which attributed to her the income that the unrefuted expert testimony demonstrated could have been produced by reasonable effort. . . . The result is . . . consistent with . . . the principle embodied in the statutory maintenance provision, which calls for a "just" award.

Affirmed.

[Justice Page's short concurring opinion not included]

NOTES

1. *The Size of Alimony Awards.* Recall that *Clapp* approved an alimony award intended to equalize the parties' incomes, with annual inflation adjustments. The *Rainwater* award is considerably less generous, although it is difficult to make a precise calculation. We are told that the husband's earnings "exceed" $100,000 annually, presumably a pre-tax income figure, and that the wife's after-tax annual income is $20,000. The wife is allowed a transitional award of $1900 monthly, and a long-term award of $1,200 monthly, equivalent to annual amounts of $22,800 and $14,400, respectively. If we assume the husband's after-tax income is $80,000, then the parties respective after-tax annual incomes, after the alimony payments, would be $57,200 and $44,800, during the transitional period, and $65,600 and $34,400, once that period had ended. Of course, the alimony reduction after the transitional period is premised on the assumption that the wife will achieve greater earnings once she acquires her B.A. degree. If one assumes an after-tax income for her of $40,000 annually rather than $20,000, her post-transition income is $55,000, not so far below the husband's net of $65,600. But it is probably unrealistic to assume that her after-tax income will double while his stays constant. In any event it seems likely that some gap between their incomes will continue long into their future. Is that gap appropriate? What standard should the court adopt for setting the size of the alimony award?

Income equalization is an easily understood benchmark, but is rarely adopted by the courts. *Rainwater*, like many other courts, refers to the marital standard of living as an appropriate goal. It is obvious, however, that if the spouses' incomes are the same after divorce as during the marriage, they cannot both retain the marital living standard. For example, if the aggregate income of both Rainwater spouses was $120,000 during the marriage and also after it, then an income equalization rule would give each $60,000 after post-divorce alimony payments. However, it surely would require more than $60,000 for one person to have the same living standard as a two-person household can achieve at $120,000. To provide Mrs. Rainwater with the marital living standard would thus require an award that *exceeded* income equalization, transferring more than half of Mr. Rainwater's income to his former wife, and driving his living standard considerably below hers. Not surprisingly, no court endorses that result. The marital living standard is thus an aspiration, not a rule, as *Rainwater* appreciates when it notes that "divorce often requires a lesser standard of living for both parties." When could divorce *not* require a reduction from the marital living standard, for at least one party? Only when the spouses' aggregate income after divorce is higher than during marriage. This does sometimes happen, either because a former homemaker devotes more hours to market labor after divorce, or because spousal incomes rise with the passage of time. If the obligor's income were to rise enough after divorce, he could make an alimony payment sufficient to provide his former spouse with the marital living standard while still retaining an even better standard for himself. (Imagine, for example, that Mr. Rainwater achieved an annual income of $200,000 after divorce.) In such atypical cases, an alimony award that falls *short* of income equalization could nonetheless provide the obligee with funds sufficient to maintain the marital living standard.

Rainwater's struggle with this problem reflects both the concerns and the confusion inherent in existing law. On one hand, cases often suggest that maintenance at the marital living standard is the appropriate goal of an alimony award, and is therefore required whenever the obligor can afford to provide it to a former spouse unable to achieve that standard on his own. *E.g.*, see *Marriage of LaRocque*, 406 N.W.2d 736 (Wis. 1987). Courts sometimes go even a bit further. The same court that decided *LaRocque*, for example, later held that the maintenance claim arising at the end of a 20-year marriage with two children could consider the standard of living the parties "anticipated" as well as that which they actually experienced during their marriage, where the husband's income had increased from $88,000 at the time of filing to over $400,000 at the time of the decree. *Hefty v. Hefty*, 493 N.W.2d 33 (Wis. 1992). On the other hand, at least one state provides by statute that an indefinite alimony award is permitted only when the recipient cannot be "self-supporting" or the "respective standards of living of the parties will be unconscionably disparate." MD. CODE ANN., FAM. LAW, § 11-106(c) (Lexis 1999 & Supp. 2002), which also suggests that an award reducing the disparity to a level that is not "unconscionable" satisfies the statute.

Vermont, as *Clapp* suggests, has in at least some cases held it appropriate to allow an alimony award that equalizes the parties' post-divorce incomes, see *Guiel v. Guiel*, 682 A.2d 957 (Vt. 1996) (23-year marriage). Other courts reject the goal of income equalization, *Stone v. Stone*, 488 S.E.2d 15 (W. Va. 1997) (alimony award cannot be based on goal of equalizing parties' incomes); *Marriage of Bancroft*, 773 P.2d 21, 22 (Or. App. 1989) (spousal support need not equalize parties' earning capacity, so long as their standards of living are "not overly disproportionate to . . . [that] enjoyed during the marriage"). A commentator who supports post-divorce income-equalization concluded, after surveying the cases, that "none of [the reported cases] have divided all income equally. . . . Even judges who have expressed concern with the disparity of income capacity have typically kept women at income levels half that of their former husbands. Although spousal support statutes typically list a range of factors to be considered in setting support, not a single state suggests that equality should be the goal of post-divorce support." Jane Rutherford, *Duty in Divorce: Shared Income as a Path to Equality*, 58 FORDHAM L. REV. 539, 578–79 (1990).

2. *Rehabilitation and An Alimony Award's Duration.* Why should an alimony award ever have a fixed termination date? The *ALI Principles* offer two possible rationales for a fixed term, depending upon the facts of a particular case. They are a) expectation of rehabilitation, and b) limitations on the obligor's responsibility.

a. Expectation of rehabilitation. Possibly the obligee will not "need" the award after an adequate period for rehabilitation. This presents a choice in framing the initial decree — a choice between alternatives exemplified by the lower courts in *Rainwater* and *Hecker*. The *Rainwater* trial court ordered alimony for an indefinite period, observing that the award could always be modified if the obligee later acquired additional resources or earning capacity, while in *Hecker* an initial award for a fixed term was later modified into a permanent award. Because alimony awards are modifiable, one might think that it matters little whether the initial decree is for an indefinite or fixed term: in either case the trial court's initial projection about the parties' future circumstances can be corrected if it turns out wrong. But as *Rainwater* aptly points out, the award's initial characterization determines which party will have the burden of persuasion in any modification proceeding. In addition, as the *ALI Principles* point out, the initial award also communicates the law's expectations. "A fixed-term award communicates the law's expectation that after its expiration the former spouses will no longer have financial obligations to or claims upon one another. This expectation encourages both spouses to plan their future accordingly." § 5.06, Comment *a*. That expectation is, in effect, given bite by the burden allocation that *Rainwater* notes.

The problem is that under some traditional procedural rules, the bite associated with the fixed term award may be too deep. Those rules often constrain the court's ability to extend a fixed-term alimony award past its initial termination date. In some states the court cannot extend it at all; in some it cannot do so unless its initial order expressly reserved jurisdiction for that purpose; in many it cannot in any event revive an alimony award that has expired. These rules may encourage courts to rely more on indefinite awards than they otherwise would, for fear that mistaken projections of obligee rehabilitation will be more difficult to correct than mistakes in the other direction. The more recent trend is to abandon these procedural restrictions. *See, e.g., Milner v. Milner,* 672 A.2d 206 (N.J. App. 1996) (reversing trial court holding that "rehabilitative alimony may be modified but cannot be changed into permanent alimony"). California had such procedural constraints until it amended its law in 1987 to provide that in the absence of either a court order terminating spousal support, or of the parties' agreement to the contrary, the court retains jurisdiction over spousal maintenance awards "indefinitely" in marriages of long duration. CAL. FAM. CODE § 4336 (West 1994 & Supp. 2004); *see Beck v. Beck,* 57 Cal. App. 4th 341, 67 Cal. Rptr. 2d 79 (1997) (finding no jurisdiction to reinstate support 16 years after it had expired under the original decree because marriage predated the amendment and was not governed by it).

The trend toward relaxation of these procedural rules has its origins in cases decided soon after the original no-fault reforms, in which long-term homemakers were given fixed-term awards on the basis of idealistic assumptions about their capacity to re-enter the job market at the age of 40 or 50. Lack of modifiability often resulted in injustice. In an important decision, the California Supreme Court held that "[a] trial court should not terminate jurisdiction to extend a future support order after a lengthy marriage, unless the record clearly indicates that the supported spouse will be able to adequately meet his or her financial needs. . . . In making its decision . . . the court must rely only on the evidence in the record. . . . It must not engage in speculation." *In re Marriage of Morrison,* 20 Cal. 3d 437, 143 Cal. Rptr. 139, 573 P.2d 41, 52 (1978). While the short term "rehabilitative award" was still the ideal, the court was to retain jurisdiction to extend the term, indefinitely if necessary, if the former homemaker turned out to be unable to secure employment that would allow her to be self-supporting at the middle class level reasonably similar to that to which she was accustomed.

b. The limits of obligor responsibility. Even if the obligee's loss or need is indefinite in duration, the obligor's responsibility to share it may not be. This is essentially the basis of *Wilson,* reprinted above, and is probably an important if silent rationale in other cases as well. *See, e.g., Marriage of Bevers,* 326 N.W.2d 896 (Iowa 1982) (college-educated homemaker wife allowed alimony for two years after termination of 11-year marriage). One is most likely to reach this conclusion in comparatively short marriages such as *Wilson.*

There are important implications to justifying a fixed term by limitations on the obligor's responsibility, rather than by optimistic projections of the obligee's future earning capacity. Equity requires that fixed terms based upon such projections of the obligee's future income remain modifiable in case they prove inaccurate. In contrast, the extent of the obligor's responsibility to share any financial shortfall of the obligee's, whatever it is, can be fully assessed at the time of the initial decree. While the size of the obligee's loss (to use the *ALI* terminology) may be affected by post-divorce developments, the extent of the obligor's responsibility for it cannot be.

3. Policing Obligee's Rehabilitation Attempts. *Hecker* confronts a recurring issue: Does the obligee's continuing income shortfall arise from the impact of the marriage on earning capacity or from a failure to make reasonable efforts to maximize earnings? *Hecker* is typical of many courts that apply some version of a "diligence" test. For example, the court may issue an order setting an alimony award with a termination date based upon the expectation that with reasonable diligence the obligee will by then have become self-supporting. *See, e.g., Marriage of Richmond*, 105 Cal. App. 3d 352, 164 Cal. Rptr. 381 (1980). The court can later extend the award beyond the cutoff date for the obligee who has not become self-supporting despite reasonable diligence. As in *Hecker*, the court must evaluate the particular facts to determine if adequate rehabilitation efforts have been made. *See, e.g., Berland v. Berland,* 215 Cal. App. 3d 1257, 264 Cal. Rptr. 210 (1989) (wife's unrealistic efforts to find employment as a paid fundraiser delayed her rehabilitation, justifying reduction of her alimony award); *see also* OR. REV. STAT. § 107.412(2) (2003) ("if the . . . party receiving support has not made a reasonable effort during the previous ten years to become financially self-supporting and independent of the support provided under the decree, the court shall order that support terminated.").

PROBLEM

Problem 4-17 Husband and wife married for 10 years. No children are born to the marriage, and at the time of divorce, wife is 47 years old. She is a college graduate, but her employment experience was limited to two years before the marriage as a social worker. During the marriage, the wife did not work, but accompanied her husband in business-related travel and helped to entertain business clients. Wife is a diabetic, suffers from a thyroid condition, and often does not feel well, but she does not claim that the illness is entirely disabling or that she is prevented from working at least part time. The parties agree to split the interest in the husband's business. Additionally, wife seeks permanent alimony, arguing that the property does not allow her to meet her reasonable living expenses. Husband argues that any alimony should be restricted to a fixed term, in order to give the wife an incentive to gain the employment she requires to meet her own needs. Is permanent or temporary alimony appropriate? What criteria should the trial court use to answer this question?

NOTE: EARNING CAPACITY LOSSES AND THEIR RECOVERY

While establishing the exact dollar value of the earning capacity loss incurred by any particular person who, during a long marriage, foregoes the labor market (because accurate calculation would require knowing, and projecting the consequences of, the different decisions that particular individual would have made if living a different life), some studies attempt to gauge the average effects, usually by comparing groups of women with varying work histories but similar in other relevant respects. These studies consistently find that a traditional domestic role has a significant negative impact on a women's earning capacity, although they differ on the precise size of the impact, whether the earning capacity can be restored, and on the length of time required to restore it. Many studies focus on the residual loss in earning capacity produced by a parent's temporary withdrawal from market labor. For an early example see Mary E. Corcoran, *Work Experience, Labor Force Withdrawals, and Women's Wages: Empirical Results Using the 1976 Panel of Income Dynamics*, in WOMEN IN THE LABOR MARKET 216 (Cynthia B. Lloyd, Emily S. Andrews & Curtis L. Gilroy eds., 1979).

What of the duration of the earning capacity decline caused by leaving the workforce? Joyce P. Jacobsen and Laurence M. Levin, *The Effects of Intermittent Labor Force Attachment on Female Earnings*, 118 MONTHLY LABOR REV. 14 (Sept. 1995), looked at data from the mid-1980s. They defined "gappers" as women taking a break from work of six months or longer after attainment of their final educational degree. The average length of the most recent "gap" for such women in their study was 7.5 years. The gappers were on average less well-educated, older, and less productive than "non-gapper" women. In order to determine the effects of the gap itself, they compared two groups of women after correcting for these differences. They found that gappers reentering the workforce on average earned 14 percent less than the "non-gappers," but that 32 months after reentry the wage difference had declined to 10 percent. They conclude that the income effects of gaps clearly decline over time, but that some difference may persist after even 20 years.

A more optimistic view of the speed of wage recovery for gappers is found in Mincer & Ofek, *Interrupted Work Careers: Depreciation and Restoration of Human Capital*, 17 J. HUM. RESOURCES 3 (1982), although they also find a small permanent loss. They found that in the short run the average cost of a year's interruption was a wage reduction of between 3.3 and 7.6 percent, but that in the long run, this average cost declined to between 1.5 and 1.8 percent for each year away. Their data, however, includes women who withdrew from the labor force because of layoffs, ill health, or migration, and these groups experienced greater depreciation of their earning capacity per year away than did other women. They also found that the duration of the work interruption is inversely related to the worker's level of education.

Employment gaps are not the full story, however. The birth of children usually affects the earning capacity of women who continue to work full time as well as those who do not. See Joni Hersch, *The Impact of Nonmarket Work on Market Wages*, 81(2) AM. ECON. REV. 157 (1991), who found that, while the time spent on housework is positively correlated with the number of children for both men and women, the wages of married women, but not married men, are reduced by time spent on housework. (This difference probably results from the fact that married men consistently spend less than half the time of married women in housework. *Id.* at 158. With the range of time on housework so restricted for married men, variations within that range may have little effect on wages.) Hersch suggests that the effect of housework on women's wages results from either a reduction in the effort they put in their market labor, or their demand that employers accommodate their working conditions to their household role, which results in their lower wages. *Id.* at 160. In either case, a residual loss in earning capacity is likely.

A comprehensive study by a distinguished economist concludes that disproportionate responsibility for child care is by far the most important single factor explaining the difference in the earnings of men and women, swamping all other possible factors including discrimination by employers. VICTOR FUCHS, WOMEN'S QUEST FOR ECONOMIC EQUALITY (1988). For example, by looking at women aged 30 to 39 who worked at least 1,000 paid hours during the year, and controlling for both age and education, Fuchs found that women's relative wage declines in a nearly straight line with the number of children in the household, so that women in households with four or more children earn 70 percent of the hourly wage earned by women with no children. The identical result is obtained whether one looks at data from 1960 or 1986, despite the passage of anti-discrimination legislation during this period. *Id.* at 62. On the other hand, while women's wages as a percentage of men's was virtually unchanged between 1960 and 1980, they increased by an unprecedented seven percent between 1980 and 1986. There is no reason to believe that this increase resulted from increased vigor in enforcement of employment discrimination laws. Fuchs concludes that it was instead due largely to the increased proportion of women workers who were born after 1946 and had fewer children than their older sisters. *Id.* at 65–66. *See also* Gary S. Becker, *Human Capital, Effort, and the Sexual Division of Labor*, 3(1) J. LAB. ECON. 533 (Supp. 1985).

Average data will not accurately describe individual cases. Any general rule is thus necessarily a compromise. However, the difficulty of determining the correct length on a case-by-case basis requires use of a general rule if compensation is to be provided at all.

Should alimony awards seek to compensate homemakers in long-term marriages for the full value of their lost earning capacity? Only some portion of the value, so that their loss is shared by both spouses? Should such compensation be paid even to the obligee who can achieve a reasonably satisfactory income without it? Does it matter whether the obligor derived any *financial* benefit from the homemaker's efforts, or whether the obligor's earning capacity as the marriage's end is significantly higher than the obligee's? These are the kinds of questions any systematic approach to alimony must address.

PROBLEMS

Problem 4-18 Jim and Alice, two school teachers, divorce after 23 years of marriage. They have two grown children. Jim's income at divorce is $40,000, Alice's is $28,000. The income differential arises almost entirely from the ten-year leave from teaching that Alice took to care for the children when they were younger. Alice can live comfortably on $28,000, but not as well as Jim can live on $40,000. Alice seeks a permanent alimony award that would equalize the parties' post-dissolution incomes. Will she get it? Should she get it?

Problem 4-19. Fred and Mildred divorce after 18 years. They have no children. Mildred is a family practice physician and Fred a registered nurse. Two years before their divorce, however, Mildred commenced a specialty in hair transplants. This work is phenomenally successful, and Mildred's income has increased from $80,000 to $350,000 annually. Fred's fortunes are less favorable. He developed an immune system disorder which is debilitating. During the marriage, Fred introduced Mildred at a party to a social acquaintance who, in their ensuing conversation, gave her the idea for the hair transplant business. Fred made no other contributions to the business's success. The spouses' marital assets at dissolution, worth $500,000, were mostly acquired through Mildred's new business venture. The court divides them equally. Fred also seeks permanent maintenance at a level based upon Mildred's newly enhanced income. Mildred objects. What will be the result? What should be the result?

Problem 4-20. During his marriage Bill, an actuary, regularly earned in excess of $120,000 annually by averaging 60-hour work weeks. Pat, his wife, was the primary caretaker of the couple's children and did not work outside the home. Subsequent to the parties' separation, Bill reduced his regular work week to 45 hours, with a corresponding reduction in his income. At divorce, Pat seeks an alimony award based upon the marital living standard. Bill seeks an award based upon his lower, post-separation income. What result? What should be the result?

Problem 4-21. Joan and Michael have one child. Joan is a schoolteacher. When the child was two years old, Michael lost his job in a corporate downsizing. After unsuccessfully seeking comparable work, he opened a consulting business. The business never did well, however, and Joan's income provided the majority of the family's support. Joan was also the primary caretaker of their child, performing the majority of domestic chores. When their child was 8, the parties filed for divorce. At this time Joan's income is $38,000 annually, while Michael income's is sporadic but averages between $10,000 and $20,000. Joan seeks spousal maintenance, arguing that her role as homemaker and primary caretaker has burdened her earning capacity, and she is entitled to payments from him to compensate her for that loss. She offers evidence that she had good prospects for advancement to a principal's post but could not apply because she could not commit herself to the job's additional hours away from home. What result? What should be the result? Why?

Problem 4-22. Jack and Jill married 20 years ago after Jack finished his medical training. After marriage, Jill went back to school and earned a credential as a special education teacher. She worked in this field throughout their marriage, and eventually became a district-wide administrator for special education. Last year, however, the district consolidated its program with an adjoining school district, as a result of which Jill's job was eliminated. She could go back to being a classroom teacher, at lower pay, but has no interest in doing that. Jack and Jill have two children at home, ages 9 and 11, and Jill has been thinking that for now she would prefer to spend more time with them. She has been doing that for the past few months, but now she and Jack have agreed to divorce. Even with child support, she will need a substantial alimony award to maintain something close to the standard of living she has been accustomed to, unless she can find new employment that pays as well as her former job. Even then, she would need an alimony award to come close to the living standard that Jack will enjoy. The parties have agreed that Jill will have primary custody of their children.

a) Would Jill be able to get a long-term, substantial alimony award to allow her to be a full-time homemaker until her children are grown? Should she? Assume her best employment prospect is the classroom teaching job she very much does not want.

b) Assume Jill takes the classroom teaching job. Will she be able to get a permanent alimony award sufficient to bring her standard of living up to the same level as Jack's? Should she? Assume that Jack's annual income as a physician is $150,000, that her teaching job, with her seniority, would pay her $35,000, and that the alimony award necessary to achieve financial equivalence with Jack would be $2,000 per month (in addition to the $3,000 per month Jack will pay in child support).

c) Assume Jill decides she would like to go to law school. Because she also wants to spend time with her children, she feels it is feasible for her to return to school only if she does not have to work. She seeks an alimony award from Jack that will pay her educational costs and allow her to live at her accustomed living standard while she is in school. Will she get such an award? Should she?

§ E. RESCISSION AFTER THE SHORT-TERM MARRIAGE

ROSE v. ROSE

755 P.2d 1121 (Alaska 1988)

BURKE, J. Debra E. Rose and Duane A. Rose were married in Anchorage, Alaska, on November 17, 1984. They [separated] in May 1986. The marriage produced no children, but each partner had children from a previous marriage. Debra's two children, Victoria and Jonathan, lived with the couple throughout the marriage, as did Duane's daughter, Brandy.

The parties each brought assets into the marriage. Debra owned a condominium and Duane owned a house. The family used Duane's home as a residence during their marriage. Each party had an automobile. During their marriage, both parties were employed, Duane as a police officer, earning approximately $63,000 per year, and Debra as a service order clerk, earning approximately $27,000 per year. Both Duane and Debra have retirement plans through their employers. Likewise, each party has a vacation plan which allows them to accumulate leave time which may be converted to cash. During the marriage Duane accumulated 216 hours of leave time; Debra accumulated seventeen hours.

Shortly after the parties were married, Duane, who had substantial premarital savings, made a down payment on property in Kenai and took title in his own name. Thereafter, the family began using the Kenai property for recreational purposes. While there, the family stayed in a camper/trailer which Duane had purchased approximately two months prior to the parties' marriage. The family also enjoyed the use of a boat and motor purchased by Duane after the couple's marriage.

During the marriage, the parties maintained the separate checking and savings accounts they had established prior to the marriage. Their paychecks were directly deposited into their respective accounts. Debra made payments on her condominium and her automobile from her account, and Duane made his own house payments and the monthly payments on the Kenai lot from his account. The trailer, the boat and the motor were purchased by Duane using his separate funds. Both parties bought groceries and clothing for the family. The parties agree that Duane contributed approximately $47,500 to the mutual household expenditures during the course of the marriage, while Debra contributed approximately $20,000.

At trial, the parties stipulated to a number of facts, including the values and dispositions of some of the properties involved in this marriage. They agreed, for example, that the condominium that Debra brought into the marriage and the house that Duane brought into the marriage would be retained by the respective parties. They also agreed that each would retain the automobile in his or her possession at the time of separation. Consequently, the only items in dispute at the time of trial were the Kenai property, the boat and motor, the trailer, and Duane's accumulated leave time and pension assets.

. . . . Debra contended . . . that the Kenai property, though purchased with savings accumulated by Duane prior to the marriage, was marital property subject to division. She also contended that the trailer, . . . was a precoverture asset subject to division under *AS 25.24.160(a)(4)*.[8] Debra requested that the court award her one-half the value of the foregoing assets, as well as one-half the value of Duane's accumulated leave time and pension, and one-half the value of the boat and motor. Duane argued that the couple had never "come together" as an "economic marriage" and, hence, he should be entitled to keep 100% of the disputed items, since they were acquired in his name and with his funds.

[The trial court] agreed with Duane, awarding him 100% of all of the disputed items of property. Debra appeals. . . .

We have long recognized the trial court's broad discretion in determining a just disposition of property . . ., and . . . we will reverse the trial court's

---

[8] *AS 25.24.160(a)(4)* provides:

In a judgment in an action for divorce or action declaring a marriage void or at any time after judgment, the court may provide

(4) for the division between the parties of their property, whether joint or separate, acquired only during coverture, in the manner as may be just, and without regard to which of the parties is in fault; however, the court, in making the division, may invade the property of either spouse acquired before marriage when the balancing of the equities between the parties requires it. . . .

determination only where it is clearly unjust. Nonetheless, we have established . . . an accepted method of legal analysis to be followed in determining property dispositions under *AS 25.24.160(a)(4)*. The first step . . . is to determine the specific property available for distribution. Such property includes all assets acquired by the parties during marriage, plus any premarital property which the "balancing of equities" suggests should be divided. Second, the court must determine the value of all property available for distribution. Finally, the court must determine the most equitable allocation of the property between the parties, beginning "with the presumption that the most equitable division of the property is an equal division." [*Wanberg v. Wanberg,* 664 P.2d 568, 570, 574–75 (Alaska 1983)]. The principal factors the trial court must consider . . . are

> the respective ages of the parties; their earning ability; the duration and conduct of each during the marriage; their station in life; the circumstances and necessities of each; their health and physical condition; their financial circumstances, including the time and manner of acquisition of the property in question, its value at the time and its income producing capacity if any.

Merrill v. Merrill, 368 P.2d 546, 547–48 n.4 (Alaska 1962).

It is apparent, from an examination of the record in this case, that the court below did not strictly adhere to the *Wanberg / Merrill* analysis. . . . The court made no determination in its findings as to whether the Kenai property and the trailer were items subject to distribution under *AS 25.24.160(a)(4)*. . . . Moreover, the record makes no mention of the *Merrill* factors and gives no indication that the court began with the "equal division" presumption. Although it might be divined from the record that the court considered some of the *Merrill* factors, *e.g.,* the duration of the marriage, the conduct of parties during marriage, and the time and manner in which the property at issue was acquired, the court gave no discernible consideration to the ages of the parties, their earning capacity, their station in life, their circumstances and necessities, their health, or their financial condition.

Instead, the court took an alternative approach [reasoning] as follows:

> Concerning the division of property, *this is a marriage of an extremely short duration. It's possible to untangle these parties' financial activities and to trace their respective contributions.* I also take into account their expectations, and what reasonable people expect under this type of circumstance, and what the community expects. When people have been together a number of years, there's an expectation that essentially what they have is theirs, but *when people are together a very short time, as these two people were, there's not that expectation,* nobody expects that, even though, of course, one's dreams and hopes are burst, *it's still economically not a unit and if tracing can be done, tracing should be done.*

(Emphasis added). [The court] further noted that both parties had contributed monetarily to the marital estate, in the form of food, clothing and other household expenses, and that neither party had been forced to "scrimp and save to make sure that the marital unit survived while the other party was building his own assets." In light of the short duration of this marriage and the fact that these parties, by their conduct, had indicated that they were "economically not a unit," the court concluded that the best course was to "leave the parties as [it found] them. Mr. Rose tak[ing] his property [and] Mrs. Rose tak[ing] hers." We must decide whether such an alternative analysis was justified . . .

[The court here cited two Oregon cases using the same reasoning as the trial court.]

We are persuaded by the reasoning of these decisions. . . . [T]he parties were married only eighteen months. During that period, they maintained completely separate economic identities, carrying on their individual fiscal affairs in the same manner as they had prior to their marriage. Neither party was forced to forego employment opportunities, and neither party withheld family contributions to the detriment of the other. Finally, none of the items in dispute here appreciated in value during the course of the marriage. We see no compelling reason why, under these circumstances, the trial court should have been bound to begin with an "equal division" presumption, or to engage in a painstaking analysis under the *Merrill* factors before concluding that assets Duane accrued or purchased with his separate, uncommingled funds were his to retain. We believe that the disposition arrived at by the trial court put the parties in, as nearly as possible, the financial position they would have occupied had no marriage taken place. Accordingly, we cannot say that the result reached was clearly unjust.

We conclude that, in marriages of short duration, where there has been no significant commingling of assets between the parties, the trial court may, without abusing its discretion, treat the property division as an action in the nature of rescission, aimed at placing the parties in, as closely as possible, the financial position they would have occupied had no marriage taken place. Our reading of the record . . . convinces us that the trial court recognized this principle and applied it appropriately. The judgment is therefore AFFIRMED.

[The dissenting opinion by Justice Compton is omitted.]

NOTES

1. *Rescission*. The idea of rescission comes primarily from the area of contract law, and its application to family law is not entirely comfortable. Even the few jurisdictions which have expressly endorsed the option of rescission have emphasized that this conclusion should be reached only in cases where the marriage has been short *and* there has been no significant commingling of funds *and* there are no other equitable factors pointing to a different sort of division. *See, e.g., Marriage of Massee*, 970 P.2d 1203 (Or. 1999) (all criteria must be met); *Bell v. Bell*, 794 P.2d 97 (Alaska 1990) (though marriage only 16 months long, rescission inappropriate because of significant commingling of funds).

2. *ALI Principles*. In dissolving short-term marriages, the *ALI Principles*, § 5.13, adopt the guiding principle that the divorce court should return the parties to the position they were in before they were married. The *Principles* also recognize, however, that there are facts other than commingling which could render rescission inappropriate even in a very short marriage such as the kind of situation faced in *Lill v. Lill*, 520 N.W.2d 855 (N.D. 1994) (alimony award appropriate at termination of short marriage where claimant left employment because of marriage and at divorce could only find employment at "a significantly lower wage"; award's purpose is to "place the disadvantaged spouse in the position she could have been in if it were not for the marriage").

§ F. MODIFICATION OF AWARDS: SOME SPECIAL PROBLEMS

[1] BASIC RULES

MODEL MARRIAGE AND DIVORCE ACT, § 316

(a) Except as otherwise provided in subsection (f) of Section 306 [pertaining to separation agreements] the provisions of any decree respecting maintenance or support may be modified only as to installments accruing subsequent to the motion for modification and only upon a showing of changed circumstances so substantial and continuing as to make the terms unconscionable. The provisions as to property disposition may not be revoked or modified, unless the court finds the existence of conditions that justify the reopening of a judgment under the laws of this state.

(b) Unless otherwise agreed in writing or expressly provided in the decree, the obligation to pay future maintenance is terminated upon the death of either party or the remarriage of the party receiving maintenance.

(c) Unless otherwise agreed in writing or expressly provided in the decree, provisions for the support of a child are terminated by emancipation of the child but not by the death of a parent obligated to support the child. When a parent obligated to pay support dies, the amount of support may be modified, revoked, or commuted to a lump sum payment, to the extent just and appropriate in the circumstances.

———

The MMDA provision is fairly straightforward, as well as typical in most of its results: property division is not modifiable, while maintenance and child support are; maintenance is presumed to terminate at the remarriage of the receiving spouse, while neither child support nor property settlement is so affected. Death of either party terminates maintenance obligations, but not claims based upon the allocation of marital property. These results have a certain logic which should make them relatively easy to keep in mind. If a property division award is based upon property rights, then a judgment regarding those property rights should be as final, and nonmodifiable, as any other civil judgment, and should survive the parties as assets or liabilities of their respective estates. Support judgments, on the other hand, were historically based upon current facts concerning the needs and resources of the parties, which may change. They are continuing obligations, and as with analogous forms of equitable relief, can be reevaluated if a change in circumstances warrants. Because of the historical basis of spousal support, it is not surprising that it would normally be presumed to terminate upon the receiving spouse's remarriage, but there is no similar basis for presuming that the custodial spouse's right to child support payments would also end, unless a new spouse undertakes legal responsibility for the children by adopting them.

Not all jurisdictions follow the MMDA rules. For example, contrary to subsection (c), most states provide that child support obligations die with the obligor, and many states require the modification petitioner to prove only that there has been a change in circumstances justifying the modification, and not that there has been a change "so substantial" as to make the existing order "unconscionable." Second, the MMDA rules do not always apply comfortably to some modern categories of award developed after these rules were written. For example, courts usually hold reimbursement awards are not modifiable and are unaffected by the obligee's remarriage, even if made under the rubric of "alimony." *See Marriage of Francis*, 442 N.W.2d 59 (Iowa 1989); *Reiss v. Reiss*, 490 A.2d 378 (N.J. Super. Ch. Div. 1984); *Petersen v. Petersen*, 737 P.2d 237 (Utah App. 1987). Likewise, conceiving of alimony as a form of compensation suggests a different treatment of obligee's remarriage than traditional law. We will examine that question further below.

Finally, although the modification rules differentiate among child support, alimony and property division, judicial decrees and separation agreements do not always distinguish explicitly the financial elements of an award. Poor drafting is not the only reason. The parties may have a tax incentive to treat periodic payments as alimony rather than child support (because the higher earning obligor can typically make more effective use of the tax deduction) and for similar reasons may wish to manipulate alimony/property settlement characterization for tax purposes. An ambiguous agreement may result from the desire to have a particular element characterized one way for divorce law purposes and another for tax purposes. The form of the award is not necessarily dispositive. A division of property might be satisfied in periodic payments, either to make it look like an alimony award in order to achieve a certain tax result, or simply because the amount is too great for the obligor to pay in one lump sum. Whether such manipulations are effective under the tax law turns on the changing tax rules. Here our point is to make clear that for divorce law purposes it is the actual function and justification of the award, rather than the label attached to it, that normally determines how it is treated in divorce law for modification purposes.

Some examples will make the point. In *Zullo v. Zullo*, 613 A.2d 544 (Pa. 1992), the husband had been ordered to make payments to the wife for 48 months following divorce, as his contribution toward retiring the marital debt — a debt the wife had settled by mortgaging her house. Because the trial court labeled the payments alimony, another trial court terminated them upon her remarriage. Were they really alimony? Not if one considers the allocation of debts an aspect of property division, and the original order merely a tool by which this debt was equitably allocated. That is essentially what the Pennsylvania Supreme Court concluded in finding no termination upon remarriage.

See also Andrews v. Whitaker, 453 S.E.2d 735 (Ga. 1995) (suggesting functional criteria for distinguishing alimony from property); *Wagoner v. Wagoner*, 648 A.2d 299 (Pa. 1994) (payments intended to approximate wife's share of husband's pension are property even though parties labeled them alimony); *Amos v. Amos*, 879 S.W.2d 856 (Tenn. App. 1994) (payments terminating on death or obligee's remarriage are not property but alimony); *Erickson v. Erickson,* 449 N.W.2d 173 (Minn. 1989) (payments labeled alimony for tax purposes are really child support, and should now be relabeled so that they can continue past recipient's remarriage); *Lieberman v. Lieberman,* 568 A.2d 1157 (Md. Sp. App. 1990) (payments unallocated for tax reasons are modifiable because they are in fact child support); *Schaffer v. Schaffer,* 643 P.2d 1300 (Or. App. 1982) (payment labeled "alimony" by agreement, for tax purposes, is really non-modifiable property settlement). In at least one case, the wife's property interest in her husband's federal pension was labeled "alimony" in order to preserve a garnishment remedy because of federal rules barring garnishment to enforce property division (but not alimony) obligations. When the wife remarried, the former husband sought termination of the payments, but the court held that these alimony payments could continue past remarriage since they substituted for property division. *McGhee v. McGhee,* 131 Cal. App. 3d 408, 182 Cal. Rptr. 456 (1982). The wife thus reaped the benefit of having the payment considered as alimony for purposes of federal law, while treated as property division under state law.

[2] REMARRIAGE OF THE OBLIGEE

When alimony reflected the law's acceptance of a gender-based support duty, it followed naturally that any claim would terminate upon the woman's remarriage:

> [I]t is against public policy that a woman should have support or its equivalent during the same period from each of two men. . . . Aside from positive unseemliness, it is illogical and unreasonable that she should have the equivalent of an obligation for support by way of alimony from a former husband and an obligation from a present husband for an adequate support at the same time.

Wolter v. Wolter, 158 N.W.2d 616, 619 (Neb. 1968), quoting *Bowman v. Bowman*, 79 N.W.2d 554 (Neb. 1956). But this rationale is undercut by the modern rule making alimony available to a needy spouse of either sex. If the alimony obligee's need continues after the remarriage, why should alimony terminate? The cases do not much address this question, even though they continue to enforce the rule ending alimony at remarriage. *E.g.*, in *Dunaway v. Dunaway*, 560 N.E.2d 171 (Ohio 1990), obligee remarried 10 years after divorce, but new husband's only income was his disability payments. Claiming continued need, she resisted a motion to terminate her alimony. In rejecting her claim, the Ohio Supreme Court said:

> It is clear to us that when parties marry they assume mutual obligations of maintenance and support. It is a conscious election to share life together, and this necessarily includes financial circumstances. To hold a first spouse responsible for continued support of

a former spouse who has remarried is tantamount to imposing a legal obligation to support another couple's marriage. We therefore hold that where a dependent divorced spouse remarries, the obligation of the first spouse to pay sustenance alimony terminates as a matter of law, unless. . .the parties have executed a separation agreement in contemplation of divorce that expressly provides for the continuation of sustenance alimony after the dependent party remarries. . . .

Consequently, the fact that defendant chose to marry Barnard when his sources of income consisted of approximately $830 per month in Social Security benefits and $553 per month in retirement benefits in no way diminishes the choice she voluntarily made to share her living expenses with him. While Barnard may not be wholly able to support defendant, Ohio law recognizes defendant's obligation to assist in supporting her new husband.

In an opinion that provides a comprehensive review of authorities nation-wide, the Massachusetts Supreme Court concluded that most states' statutes specify automatic termination of alimony upon the obligee's remarriage, and that most of the rest apply a judicially-created rule that remarriage termi-nates alimony in the absence of extraordinary circumstances. *Keller v. O'Brien*, 652 N.E.2d 589 (Mass. 1995); *see also* Annotation, *Alimony as Affected by Recipient Spouse's Remarriage in Absence of Controlling Specific Statute*, 47 A.L.R.5th 129 (1997). In adopting the extraordinary circumstance rule itself, *Keller* echoed the sentiments of *Dunaway* and observed that such extraordinary circumstances are "rare." The court provided but one example of such a circumstance: where the obligee would otherwise become a public charge.

A small number of states take a contrary approach — treating marriage (as most states treat cohabitation — see the next section) as an event that *might* affect the recipient's level of need, but which will not cause an *automatic* termination. *See, e.g., Taylor v. Taylor*, 819 A.2d 684 (Vt. 2002); *Marriage of Jones and Jones*, 17 P.3d 491 (Ore. App. 2001).

Does the *Dunaway* analysis also apply if alimony is based not on need, but on a compensation rationale such as that adopted by the ALI? Perhaps. If an alimony obligee who remains in "need" despite her remarriage nonetheless loses her award under current law, then perhaps the obligee whose financial loss continues after remarriage may be denied further compensation.

One's rationale for ending alimony at the obligee's remarriage may have implications for how the law should treat nonmarital cohabitation by the obligee. It is often said that nonmarital cohabitation is relevant only insofar as it has an impact on the obligee's financial circumstances. That does not appear to be the principle applied to remarriage, which ends alimony nearly everywhere without regard to financial consequences for the obligee. Are any of the foregoing efforts successful at explaining that result? If so, one should perhaps reconsider them when we address cohabitation in the next section.

NOTES

1. *Agreements to Continue Alimony Past Remarriage.* Most states will enforce the parties' agreement to continue alimony beyond the obligee's remarriage. What if an agreement-based decree specifies events that will terminate maintenance, such as the obligee's death, but does not mention the obligee's remarriage? Some courts conclude such an omission is intentional and continue the alimony. *E.g., In re Marriage of Sherman,* 162 Cal. App. 3d 1132, 208 Cal. Rptr. 832 (1984); *Raymond v. Raymond,* 447 A.2d 70 (Me. 1982); *Sprentall v. Sprentall,* 75 Misc. 2d 405, 347 N.Y.S.2d 659 (Sup. Ct. 1973). Other courts will require explicit language for continuance of the alimony. *Gunderson v. Gunderson,* 408 N.W.2d 852 (Minn. 1987); *In re Williams,* 796 P.2d 421 (Wash. 1990); *In re Thornton,* 95 Cal. App. 4th 251, 115 Cal. Rptr. 2d 380 (2002); *Moore v. Jacobsen,* 817 A.2d 212 (Md. 2003). A California court held an agreement specifying that alimony "shall be nonmodifiable for any reason whatsoever" was insufficiently explicit to override the statutory presumption that alimony ends on the recipient's remarriage, since "nonmodifiable" is not the same as "nonterminable." *In re Marriage of Glasser,* 181 Cal. App. 3d 149, 226 Cal. Rptr. 229 (1986).

2. *Agreement to Revive Alimony If Second Marriage Fails.* The general rule is that alimony obligations terminated upon remarriage do not revive if the remarriage ends in divorce: the former obligee must seek relief from the second spouse. But of course alimony claims against the second spouse may fail if the second marriage is short. The remedy for the foresighted is an agreement that provides for the revival of the first spouse's alimony obligation in such a case. *See, for example, Diedrich v. Diedrich,* 424 N.W.2d 580 (Minn. App. 1988) (court enforces first husband's promise to reinstate his maintenance payments if the wife's second marriage ended in divorce within five years). The first husband might make such an agreement to encourage his former wife to remarry, in the hope that the remarriage will last and thus end his obligation.

3. *The Annulled Second Marriage.* Because an annulment theoretically declares that a marriage never existed in the first place, arguably the obligee's annulled remarriage should not affect the obligor's alimony obligations. Although conceptually neat, this reasoning often leads to unreasonable results. Under the old fault-oriented divorce laws, spouses might have sought an annulment rather than divorce only because divorce was difficult to obtain. Under some modern statutes, the conceptual distinction may no longer be so clear, because there is no difference in the grounds for divorce and the grounds for annulment.

Although the annulment issue does not arise often, especially under modern divorce laws which have reduced the use of annulments, the general rule today is that alimony obligations terminated on account of the recipient's remarriage are not revived if the remarriage is held void. *In re Harris,* 560 N.E.2d 1138 (Ill. App. 1990); *Falk v. Falk,* 462 N.W.2d 547 (Wis. App. 1990). Some courts reaching this result qualify it by saying that the annulled remarriage must be valid on its face in order to terminate the first spouse's alimony obligations. *Hodges v. Hodges,* 578 P.2d 1001 (Ariz. App. 1978); *Joye v. Yon,* 547 S.E.2d 888 (S.C. App. 2001) (wife's remarriage annulled because of her would-be new husband's previous undissolved marriage; court reinstates alimony on the basis that the wife's second marriage was "void" rather than "voidable"). *See* Note, *Annulment: Effect on Prior Spousal Support and Maintenance Obligations,* 20 ARIZ. L. REV. 1053 (1978). The real point may be that some flexibility is necessary to avoid unreasonable results. *See, e.g., Marriage of Weintraub,* 167 Cal. App. 3d 420, 213 Cal. Rptr. 159 (1985) (wife could reclaim lost alimony payments after annulment upon proof that she had consented to annulled second marriage only because she had been abducted, beaten and threatened with harm to her family).

PROBLEMS

Problem 4-23. Sam and Alice were married for 20 years when they were divorced. Alice, who was a homemaker throughout their marriage, was awarded permanent alimony of $1,500 monthly. Six months later, Sam and Alice reconciled and remarried. Sadly, however, their new marriage lasted only three months, when they concluded that they indeed could no longer live together. They filed for divorce. It is virtually unheard of in this jurisdiction to obtain an alimony award in connection with the dissolution of a marriage of only three months' duration. Could Alice get her original alimony award reinstated? Should she be able to? Are there other arguments to be made on her behalf?

Problem 4-24. Alice was awarded $2,500 monthly alimony from George, who divorced her after a 20-year marriage. Their children are grown, so Alice has no custodial responsibilities and receives no child support. The alimony award was based on the fact that Alice had never worked during the marriage and could not now realistically expect to obtain employment that would maintain her at the economic level that she was accustomed to in her marriage with George. George is a successful businessman earning $160,000 annually.

Alice falls in love with Pablo and they marry. Pablo is a painter. He earns nothing now, although some say he shows promise. He might be able to obtain some kind of unskilled employment while still painting, but it would produce little income and interfere with his painting. He has no ability to earn much more than minimum wage in any event (unless his paintings start selling).

(a) George seeks to eliminate alimony payments based upon Alice's remarriage. What result? What should be the result? Assume that by the time the hearing on George's motion is held, Alice's marriage to Pablo had already failed, and divorce proceedings concluded. Does this alter the result? Should it?

(b) Suppose before remarriage, Alice had come to you for legal advice on the impact of her plans. What would you have advised her to do?

[3] COHABITATION OF THE OBLIGEE

MELLETZ v. MELLETZ

638 A.2d 898 (N.J. App. Div. 1994)

DREIER, J.A.D. [Husband] appeals from [denial of] his motion to suspend alimony payments because of [wife]'s alleged cohabitation with a male friend. [the court] determined that the cohabitation clause in the parties' settlement agreement was unfair, inequitable and unenforceable, and thus refused to suspend [husband]'s alimony obligation. However, as the clause was a material aspect of the settlement agreement, the judge decided that the agreement could now be renegotiated if [husband] so desired.

The parties were divorced on November 13, 1991, and negotiated a settlement agreement which was incorporated into the final judgment of divorce. Under the agreement, [wife] was to receive alimony in the amount of $400 a week, but the alimony payments would terminate upon the death of either party or upon [wife]'s remarriage, and would be suspended for any period during which [wife] cohabited with an unrelated male. The cohabitation provisions read as follows:

> Husband's alimony obligation shall be suspended during the period of cohabitation if the wife cohabits with a male unrelated to her by blood or marriage. Cohabitation for the purposes of this agreement, shall be defined as the wife and the unrelated male (hereinafter "male") generally residing together in a common residence, or residences where they generally engage in some, but not necessarily all, of the following:
>
> (a) Meals taken together at the residence(s);
>
> (b) Departing from and returning to the residence of the other for employment and/or social purposes;
>
> (c) Maintaining clothing at the other's residence;
>
> (d) Sleeping together at the residence or the residence of the other;
>
> (e) Receiving telephone calls at the residence or the residence of the other.
>
> The occurrence of any of the following shall not defeat cohabitation as the parties have defined that term herein:
>
> (a) Temporary interruptions of the relationship . . .;
>
> (b) Alternating of residences;
>
> (c) Maintenance of a separate residence by the male.

The parties have expressly agreed that the purpose of this provision was specifically negotiated for, and represents the end product of, a bargained for agreement. Specifically, the parties intend that the economic contribution component of *Gayet* shall not be applicable and the mere cohabitation, as defined herein, shall be the basis for suspension of the husband's alimony obligation.

Wife represents that she is not currently cohabiting and if that representation is false, the husband shall have the right to reimbursement of alimony paid during cohabitation. In the future, if it is determined that wife is cohabiting, any relief would be retroactive to the date cohabitation commenced.

Since the judge found the provisions unenforceable, he made no factual determination whether the parties were cohabiting under the standards of the agreement. [¶] At the November 13, 1991 hearing [wife] testified that she had gone through each of the terms of the agreement with her attorney, that she understood the terms, that she was entering into the agreement voluntarily and that she accepted the terms of the agreement as fair and equitable. The [divorce] judge subsequently determined that the agreement had been entered into voluntarily and that it was "believed to be fair and equitable under all the circumstances of this case with both parties being represented by counsel." The judge, however, made no finding as to the reasonableness of the agreement.

On October 11, 1991, over a month prior to the divorce, [husband], his then-fiancée (now his wife) and one of her friends began surveilling [wife]'s condominium unit. Eventually, [husband] also hired two private investigation firms to watch [wife]. [Husband] was thus aware of [wife]'s relationship with a male friend, Mr. "C," prior to the November 13, 1991 negotiation. In fact, at the plenary hearing, [husband] testified that the cohabitation clause was designed "to stop what [was] going on." [Wife] testified that she was aware of the allegations of her cohabitation at the time of the agreement, but did not contemplate that her relationship constituted cohabitation under the agreement. We note parenthetically that [husband] has lived with his present wife since shortly after separating from [wife] in March of 1989.

It is undisputed that [wife] and her friend had a relationship. The trial judge found the following:

> During this period [August 30, 1991 through November 1991], the wife maintained a social or dating relationship with an individual identified as [Mr. C.]. At all times material, the wife and [the friend] maintained separate residences but socialized and dated by engaging in such activities as shopping, going out to restaurants, eating meals at the residence of the other and remaining over night with each other. The wife, during her testimony recalled at least ten overnight stays by [the friend] at [wife's] new condominium in Mount Laurel, New Jersey. Both the wife and [the friend], during their testimony, described their relationship as "just dating" and as a warm friendship.

[Husband] maintains that [wife] and her friend were "cohabiting" as that term is defined in the settlement agreement.

. . . .

In New Jersey, the test for determining whether cohabitation by the dependent spouse should reduce an alimony award has always been based on a theory of economic contribution. In *Gayet v. Gayet*, 456 A.2d 102 (N.J.

1983), the Supreme Court. . . .ruled that the test. . . .was "whether the relationship has reduced the financial needs of the dependent former spouse." The Court found that a supporting spouse is entitled to a modification "only if one cohabitant supports or subsidizes the other under circumstances sufficient to entitle the supporting spouse to relief."

More recently we were confronted with a property settlement agreement [that required] the wife to sell the marital home [if] she lived there with an unrelated male. [Husband] subsequently tried to [enforce this clause]. [Wife] admitted that "a non-related adult male" spent three weekends a month and at least one day a week at the home. We held, however, that this did not constitute cohabitation. We focused on the economic impact of the relationship:

> [T]he agreement should be regarded as having principally an economic purpose, that is, to assure that [husband]'s interest in the former marital home is not used to subsidize [wife]'s relationship with a male cohabitant.

Pugh v. Pugh, 524 A.2d 410 (N.J. App. Div. 1987).

Thus we were able to rely upon contractual interpretation, and were not faced with the question of whether parties could vary the parameters of the economic contribution rule by contract.

. . . .

In the case before us the parties recognized the rule in *Gayet*, and, specifically citing it, stated in so many words that they wished to reject it. . . . Under the agreement, [husband] is entitled to suspend his payment of alimony if [wife] cohabits, regardless of the economic impact of such cohabitation.[1]

The one-sided agreement attempts to control the wife's behavior in terms of suspension of her total alimony, even though the prohibited behavior may have no economic impact on her life. This is basically an *in terrorem* clause seeking to regulate the ex-wife's otherwise legal activities. We could even consider a hypothetical mirror image of this case. If the wife agreed to one-half of the alimony justified by the parties' circumstances on condition that the husband refrain from similar behavior, would such a clause have a different legal consequence from the one before us? We think not.

. . . . Should the law be concerned with enforcement of agreements by which a payor divorced spouse attempts to control the payee's behavior that has no economic impact on the payor or other effect in an area of recognized mutual concern? For example, can a payor require that alimony payments to which the payee spouse is statutorily entitled will be made only so long as the payee dyed his or her hair a particular color, or lived in a particular neighborhood, or engaged in a particular occupation? Matters of personal preference, residence, or occupation, insofar as they do not reflect changes in income or expenses or other matter of recognized mutual concern, simply are

---

[1] [Husband] is currently paying alimony in the amount of $400 a week. There was no evidence of the alimony that would have been due [wife] in the absence of the cohabitation clause. Therefore neither we nor the trial judge could determine whether [wife] received additional consideration by way of increased alimony for agreeing to the cohabitation clause.

not the business of a former spouse. They do not relate to the payee's right to adequate support. Nor in the usual case are the courts inclined to apply precious resources to the enforcement of or adjudicating the breach of such agreements. So too with matters of cohabitation. It is enough that we must monitor the economic impact of cohabitation. . . .

We therefore hold that, apart from the economic impact upon either need or the ability to pay recognized in *Gayet*. . . . the payor spouse may not through loss or suspension of statutory alimony control the social activities of the payee.[3] If the issue involves conduct, legal for the participants, but detrimental to children in the household, the parties may, of course, agree on generally-recognized standards of social behavior. But these issues are non-economic and cannot be used for economic coercion. The divorce cuts the ties that permit one spouse to control the other's behavior where their respective economic rights and responsibilities or other matters of recognized continuing mutual concern are not implicated. [¶] [A]llowing [husband] to attach conditions to [wife]'s receipt of her statutorily mandated alimony which are unrelated to her financial status would contravene the very purpose of alimony.

[Husband]'s motivation was made clear when he admitted that the clause was "to stop what [was] going on." [Wife] testified that she wouldn't "dare go out with anybody anymore because I would never ever put any other man in the circumstances that [Mr. C.] was put into." In fact, both [wife] and her friend testified that their relationship was over, presumably because of the strain of this litigation. [The court] properly found that "the [wife] is rendered social and economic hostage of the property settlement agreement. The agreement leaves very little latitude for the [wife] to engage in even a casual or social relationship without fear of losing her economic support. . . ."

. . . .

The order appealed from is affirmed. . . .

[The concurring opinion of Judge Brochin is omitted.]

O'CONNOR BROTHERS ABALONE CO. v. BRANDO

40 Cal. App. 3d 90, 114 Cal. Rptr. 773 (1974)

COMPTON, Associate Justice. In July of 1968, in connection with the annulment of their marriage, Marlon and Movita Brando executed a written agreement purporting to settle certain financial matters and child custody rights.

As a part of that agreement Marlon undertook to make monthly payments of $600 for the support of the minor children and monthly payments of $1400

---

[3] It might be thought that [the obligee willing to reduce her standard of living could employ alimony payments] to support a paramour. *Gayet* [does] not stand for such a proposition. Also the rule has been established. . . that where the payee and a paramour share a residence, the support of or by the paramour is presumed, thus implicating an economic impact. While the parties here may have intended to bring [wife] within the rule of these cases, the indicia of a common residence were expanded here beyond reason.

for the support of Movita. Only the latter payments to Movita are at issue here. . . .

The resolution of this dispute turns on whether, under the terms of the agreement . . ., her conduct was such as to terminate Marlon's obligation to make further payments. The crucial provision . . . is as follows:

> "(a) Defendant agrees to pay . . . Plaintiff, the amount of $1,400.00 per month . . . for a period of one-hundred fifty-six (156) months, *or until she remarries or dies, whichever occurs sooner. For the purposes of this Agreement, 'remarriage' shall include, without limitation, Plaintiff's appearing to maintain a marital relationship with any person, or any ceremonial marriage entered into by Plaintiff even though the same may later be annulled or otherwise terminated or rendered invalid."* (Emphasis added.)

In reliance on this "remarriage" clause, Marlon ceased to make the payments in April 1971. He contends that in 1968, Movita entered into a relationship with one James Ford which . . . was within the provisions of the term "remarriage". . . .

The evidence . . . left little doubt that Movita and Ford enjoyed a relationship of substantial duration, which . . . bore the objective indicia of marriage. By their own admission they engaged in frequent sexual intercourse. Ford kept his clothes at [Movita's] residence in Coldwater Canyon, he ate meals there, many of which he prepared. Ford frequently purchased groceries for their meals by charging them to Movita's account at the market, he drove her cars and was authorized to use her charge account at one of the major department stores.

Additionally, Ford on significant occasions gave the Coldwater Canyon address as his own. He used that address in applying for a driver's license and in reporting to his probation officer. The two were often in company together and in company with Movita's children in public.

The trial court's finding that they "lived" together is well supported. The further finding that such relationship could not be reasonably interpreted as indicating that Ford and Movita were in fact married apparently flowed from the absence of any evidence that they told anyone they were married.

The parties' real dispute centers on whether the above described relationship is one contemplated by the Agreement . . .

O'Connor contends, and the trial court concluded, that the phrase "appearing to maintain a marital relationship" means a holding out by Movita that she was in fact married or conduct on her part that would imply a marriage in fact. According to this version, a meretricious relationship, no matter how intimate and enduring, would not terminate the obligation for support payments so long as it was made clear to the world that Movita and her paramour were *not* married. This interpretation would place a premium on the persistence with which Movita publicized the illicit nature of the relationship.

On the other hand, Marlon contends that the Agreement was designed to prevent Movita from maintaining a relationship with a male companion as a result of which the latter appeared to enjoy the usual rewards of marriage without assuming the obligations which flow from a ceremony of marriage. According to Marlon the Agreement means a "marital type" relationship and such interpretation is necessary to avoid what he sought to avoid, i.e., the possibility that Movita's male companion, in sharing Movita's shelter, bed and board, would also benefit from the support payments which Marlon was providing. . . .

Marlon testified his intent was ". . . that I was not to pay for any man that she might be living with through the support payments; that if she were going to live with somebody, then they would have to support her, and it would not fall to me, outside of the support for the children, it would not fall to me to pay for her continuing support." Movita testified that she understood that if she "lived" with another man the support payments would stop.

Mr. Garey, the attorney, testified that his client Marlon's and his intent were to provide for terminating the payments if Movita lived with another man who would benefit from the support payments and if the relationship would be demeaning to Marlon in the eyes of the public.

The final Agreement evolved from two previously written drafts. The first draft simply used the phrase "until she remarries" without further definition. To this Marlon objected. The second draft defined remarriage as "cohabitation by plaintiff with any person." To this Movita objected.

Mr. Garey testified that Movita's attorney indicated that the objection to "cohabitation" was based on a fear that the word might apply to so-called "one night stands." . . .

Clearly the purpose of the Agreement was not to circumscribe Movita's sexual activity per se as she was free to engage in sexual intercourse with other men. The Agreement sought to embrace actual ceremonial marriages on the one hand and on the other, relationships which were not marriages but which had the attributes of marriage such as companionship of substantial duration, the sharing of habitation, eating together and sexual intimacy. The characterization of such a relationship as "marital" does not depend on whether third persons are led to believe the existence of a ceremonial marriage. In fact, public belief that Movita and Ford were actually married would be less demeaning to Marlon than their conduct of "living" together while disavowing an actual marriage.

What is important here from the standpoint of the objectives of the Agreement is that such a relationship creates the strong probability that the male partner will derive benefit from the support payments. And that, in fact, is what occurred here. O'Connor contends in its brief that there was no common financial or economic relationship between Ford and Movita and that this detracts from the "marital" character of the relationship. Interestingly enough, however, in respondent's support of this argument it is admitted that Movita paid for the upkeep of her cars which Ford drove. She paid for the groceries which Ford charged, and she paid for the department store purchases which Ford charged. It appears without contradiction that Movita paid for the maintenance of the house in which they lived.

We interpret the phrase "appearing to maintain a marital relationship" as including the appearance of "living together" under circumstances such as existed here, whether or not there is the appearance of marriage in fact. This appears to us to be the only possible reasonable interpretation of the Agreement.

[Thus, O'Connor lost.]. . . .

NOTES

1. *The Effect of Obligee's Cohabitation When Parties Have No Agreement.* Both the cases deal with the application of the parties' separation agreement. What is the rule if there is no agreement concerning cohabitation? States vary.

a. *The traditional rule.* The traditional rule, surviving in many states, recognizes that the obligee's cohabitation can be a basis for terminating alimony, apart from its financial impact. *E.g.*, GA. CODE. ANN. § 19-6-19(b) (Lexis 1999 & Supp. 2002) (in addition to change in income or financial status, "the voluntary cohabitation of [the obligee] with a third party in a meretricious relationship shall also be grounds to modify. . .alimony"); NEW YORK DOM. REL. L. § 248 (West 1999 & Supp. 2003) ("annulling" alimony orders for an ex-wife "habitually living with another man" if she "hold[s] herself out" as his wife); UTAH CODE ANN. § 30-3-5(9) (Lexis 1998 & Supp. 2002) ("Any [alimony] order . . . terminates upon establishment by the [obligor] that the former spouse is cohabitating with another person."); ILL. ST. CH. 750 § 5/510(c) (West 1999 & Supp. 2003) ("Unless otherwise agreed by the parties in a written agreement set forth in the judgment or otherwise approved by the court, the obligation to pay future maintenance is terminated. . .if the party receiving maintenance cohabits with another person on a resident, continuing conjugal basis"); *see Marriage of Herrin*, 643 N.E.2d 1168 (Ill. App. 1994) (effect of cohabitation on obligee's need not be "controlling"; cohabitation rule based on "the inequity created when the ex-spouse receiving maintenance becomes involved in a husband-wife relationship but does not legally formalize it").

If financial need is not the test, particular care is necessary in defining the "cohabitation" that can trigger the provision. The principal difficulty, as illustrated by the Brando negotiations, is distinguishing between couples who share a household and those who do not even though they may see one another regularly. Courts are in fairly wide agreement that cohabitation means more than an intimate relationship, and even where the parties do live together, a minimum duration may be thought necessary to trigger a statutory rule. *See, e.g., Leming v. Leming*, 590 N.E.2d 1027 (Ill. App. 1992) (obligee's four-month cohabitation does not meet statutory test). At the same time, a longer cohabitation may be inadequate lacking other indicia of "cohabitation." *Marriage of Nolen*, 558 N.E.2d 781 (Ill. App. 1990) (alimony should not be terminated even though obligee's room and board were provided by the man in whose house she lived, in exchange for nursing and housekeeping services, where there was no de facto marriage between them). Consider *Melletz* again. Is the real problem in this case the language of the agreement, or the fact pattern to which the husband sought to apply it? For a comprehensive review of the many different ways that cohabitation clauses have been phrased in agreements, see *Gordon v. Gordon,* 675 A.2d 540 (Md. 1996) (holding such agreements enforceable but concluding wife was not "cohabiting" within contractual meaning of that term). The Illinois Supreme Court held one alimony obligee to be cohabiting within the meaning of its statute even though her partner was impotent. *Marriage of Sappington,* 478 N.E.2d 376, 379 (Ill. 1985) ("[I]f to avoid the application of this section all that a person had to do was to claim impotency or deny any sexual relations, then the purpose of this statute could easily be defeated.")

b. *The recent trend.* The recent trend appears to favor the financial impact rule: the obligee's cohabitation is relevant only insofar as it affects her need and thus her financial eligibility for the award. Recent cases favoring this approach include *Lyon v. Lyon,* 728 A.2d 127 (Me. 1999) (cohabiting obligee's alimony should not have been reduced because the cohabitation did not change her financial circumstances sufficiently to justify the modification); *Ozolins v. Ozolins,* 705 A.2d 1230 (N.J. Super. 1998) (fact of cohabitation alone insufficient to justify termination of alimony, evidence of financial consequence of cohabitation in this case justified only reduction of alimony amount); *Marriage of Chew,* 888 P.2d 428 (Mont. 1995) (trial court wrong to provide alimony would terminate if recipient cohabited, since test is financial need); *Hollowell v. Hollowell,* 369 S.E.2d 451 (Va. App. 1988) (cohabitation provides a basis for modification only when it results in a change in financial circumstances); *McVay v. McVay,* 429 S.E.2d 239 (W. Va. 1993) (same); *Ramsbottom v. Ramsbottom,* 542 A.2d 1098 (R.I. 1988) (same); *Gottsegen v. Gottsegen,* 492 N.E.2d 1133 (Mass. 1986) (same); *Bisig v. Bisig,* 469 A.2d 1348 (N.H. 1983) (same); *Myhre v. Myhre,* 296 N.W.2d 905 (S.D. 1980) (same); *Combs v. Combs,* 787 S.W.2d 260 (Ky. 1990) (same). Courts sometimes say they follow a financial test when it appears they do not. For example, in *Marriage of Toole,* 653 N.E.2d 456 (Ill. App. 1995), the court said the purpose of the Illinois cohabitation rule is not to control or comment upon the obligee's morals, but denied the wife a rehabilitative alimony award after a 22-year marriage on the basis of her cohabitation.

For the British law on this subject, see Hayes, *Cohabitation Clauses in Financial Provision and Property Adjustment Orders — Law, Policy and Justice,* 110 LAW Q. REV. 124 (1994).

2. *The Validity of Contractual Terms on the Effect of Cohabitation.* *Melletz* disallows an agreement that makes cohabitation relevant. *Melletz is* supported by *Ramsbottom v. Ramsbottom,* 542 A.2d 1098 (R.I. 1988). For precisely the contrary result, see *Bramson v. Bramson,* 404 N.E.2d 469 (Ill. App. 1980), in which the court holds that the Illinois law described in Note 1 (making continuous cohabitation a ground for terminating alimony) is "mandatory" and cannot be "avoided" by the parties' agreement. Neither approach is common, nor does either seem to make much sense. Separation agreements are ordinarily submitted to the court for approval, and could in any event be set aside for procedural unconscionability (*see* Chapter 8). The question here is whether an agreement that passes these process tests should be rejected because of public policy objections to its substantive content. Given the split among the states as to the appropriate rule on cohabitation, it seems remarkable for courts to decide that *either* choice is so far from reasonable that parties may not voluntarily adopt it. On the other hand, one might also take the position that while the parties may agree to make the obligee's cohabitation relevant, they may not condition the obligee's alimony on remaining celibate. Can *Melletz* be explained on that basis?

3. *Conceptual Difficulties with the Financial-Impact Rule.* Cases limiting consideration of cohabitation to its financial impact sometimes say that reduced need is the only financial impact that matters. That is, they purport to make cohabitation relevant only to the extent that the obligee is being supported by his or her cohabitant. However, when pushed, many courts concede (as does *Melletz,* in footnote 3) that one may also consider whether the obligee is using alimony payments to pay the cohabitant's living expenses — the precise concern said to have motivated Brando. This concession poses two difficult problems for courts that adopt the financial-impact rule.

There is first the problem that it is nearly always true that when two people pool their resources to conduct a joint household, they both benefit financially — as is known by every unmarried person who has ever taken a roommate. (People may see personal costs in taking a roommate — but they often do so despite those personal costs just because of the economic advantages.) So it would seem that the financial-impact requirement will be met in nearly every case of true cohabitation, if the court concedes that support of the obligee's cohabitant satisfies the requirement.

Second, there is a more fundamental conceptual problem, for the concession comes back to bite the very argument that is offered for the financial-impact rule by courts like *Melletz:* their argument that the financial impact of cohabitation is the only aspect of it that is the obligor's business. However, why is it the obligor's business whether the obligee spends her income to support a paramour? The only answer is that this is a special kind of expenditure. For surely any court would agree that the obligor cannot normally complain about how the obligee chooses to spend her funds — nice clothes or vacation, or whatever (unless her choices demonstrate that she has more resources than the court was led to believe when the amount of obligation was established, an entirely different matter). In short, it is difficult to see how courts like *Melletz* can have it both ways; if they really believe the obligee's living arrangements are of no legitimate interest to the obligor, then they cannot concede that the obligors have any legitimate complaint when the obligee uses her alimony to support her paramour as well as herself. In this sense, the usual financial impact rule seems too broad when it reaches the case in which the obligee provides financial benefit to her cohabiting partner.

Yet in another way, the usual rule is also too narrow. Consider, for example, CAL. FAM. CODE § 4323 (West 1994 & Supp. 2003), which offers one typical statement of the test:

> (a)(1) Except as otherwise agreed to by the parties in writing, there is a rebuttable presumption, affecting the burden of proof, of decreased need for spousal support if the supported party is cohabiting with a person of the opposite sex. Upon a determination that circumstances have changed, the court may modify or terminate the spousal support. . .

(2) Holding oneself out to be the husband or wife of the person with whom one is cohabiting is not necessary to constitute cohabitation as the term is used in this subdivision.

The presumption of decreased need only applies under this rule when the "supported party" cohabits "with a person of the opposite sex." Why so limit the presumption? Doesn't *any* pooling of resources permit the supported party a higher living standard, thus reducing her "need"? One explanation for the "opposite sex" requirement is, of course, that the obligee's decision to economize on her housing arrangements by taking a roommate (perhaps so that she may have more funds for other purposes) does not ordinarily give rise to a presumption of decreased need because *ordinarily* an obligee's particular preference in allocating her resources remains her choice alone — unless a new intimate relationship is involved. (Notice that footnote 3 of *Melletz,* describing its very similar rule, says the presumption arises when the obligee shares a residence with her "paramour.") The presumption thus requires not only the economy of a joint household, but the existence of an intimate relationship. *See, e.g., Marriage of Thweatt,* 96 Cal. App. 3d 530, 157 Cal. Rptr. 826 (1979) (wife is not "cohabiting" within the meaning of this section where there was no evidence of a sexual relationship, a romantic involvement, or even a homemaker-companion relationship between her and either of her two male boarders). Of course, an intimate relationship between same-sex partners is also possible. In *Van Dyck v. Van Dyck,* 425 S.E.2d 853 (Ga. 1993), the court held Georgia's cohabitation statute (see Note 1, above) applied only to heterosexual relationships. *Van Dyck* was subsequently overruled by the legislature, which made clear that its concern was with intimate relationships with partners of either gender. *See* GA. CODE ANN. § 19-6-19(b) (Lexis 1999 & Supp. 2002) ("cohabitation means dwelling together continuously and openly in a meretricious relationship with another person regardless of the sex of the other person"). A Pennsylvania court, in *Kripp v. Kripp,* 784 A.2d 158 (Pa. App. 2001), held that the former wife's live-in relationship with another woman was not "cohabition" for the purpose of an agreement terminating alimony payments were the wife to "co-habitate." But whether the requirement of an intimate relationship is met by a homosexual relationship or not, the main point is unaffected: A true financial impact rule cannot exclude non-intimate cohabitees, it would seem.

So why not replace the prevalent approach to cohabitation with a true, pure financial impact rule to avoid these conceptual problems? Consider a case that did so, *Van Dyke v. Van Dyke,* 902 P.2d 1372 (Ariz. App. 1995). The wife was awarded alimony of $13,000 monthly. Her fiancée moved into her home six months after the divorce decree, and they planned a large wedding a year later. But the wife cancelled the wedding ceremony a month before its scheduled date, when she realized her remarriage would terminate her alimony. The "newlyweds" nonetheless went forward with the wedding party and honeymoon, and continued an apparently permanent cohabitation in her home (the sale of which would have also terminated her alimony under the decree, apparently because of her substantial equity in it). Because the fiancée paid her no rent, and provided her with no other financial support that her former husband could establish as altering her economic circumstances, the court — applying a pure financial-impact rule — denied him any modification of his alimony obligation.

The problem is obvious: Given that we terminate alimony upon remarriage without regard to its financial impact on the obligee, it is difficult to explain why we do not do so when the obligee enters a *de facto* marriage. In an earlier era in which social mores sharply distinguished between marital and nonmarital cohabitation, this point would be less important. But if the law makes such a distinction at a time when social mores do not, strategic behavior is invited. There is, to be sure, one difference that often exists between the marital and non-marital relationships: the law may recognize no alimony or marital property claim at the termination of the nonmarital relationship. Is that difference sufficient to justify the distinction? Some courts think so. *See Marriage of Sasson,* 129 Cal. App. 3d 140, 180 Cal. Rptr. 815, 819-20 (1982). But even this distinction may be evaporating. Just as few financial claims typically arise at the dissolution of the short marriage, courts today increasingly recognize financial claims at the termination of a long-term cohabiting relationship (*see* Chapter 9). Nonetheless, where the cohabiting parties make no explicit agreement to share property, or for the payment of support at the termination of their relationship, many courts will deny such relief. One could fashion a test terminating alimony on the obligee's cohabitation if, and only if, that cohabitation also satisfies whatever requirements the court would apply before granting remedies when *that* relationship ends. Is this a satisfactory resolution?

4. *Administrative Difficulties With Pure Financial Impact Rule.* What if the wife's new partner in *Van Dyke* (see Note 3) had substantial resources, but made no apparent contribution to the joint household? Should a court applying a pure financial impact test look at the partner's capacity to assist the alimony obligee and thus reduce her need, or is it only concerned with whether he or she in fact does so? Most courts assume the latter, a plausible position given that the cohabitants have no legal obligation of mutual support. But what then of "under the table" transfers. In a case decided under the California statute, the wife attempted to rebut the presumption of decreased need with evidence that she collected no rent from her cohabiting partner. But he did make repairs and improvements to the house and had given her a $4,200 diamond ring. The court held the cohabiting wife cannot "evade [the new statute's] strictures by accepting 'gifts' in lieu of monetary reimbursement for joint household expenses, and thereby create a situation of apparent continuing need." *In re Marriage of Schroeder,* 192 Cal. App. 3d 1154, 238 Cal. Rptr. 12, 17 (1987). Wisconsin faced a similar issue in *VanGorder v. VanGorder,* 327 N.W.2d 674 (Wis. 1983). The former wife sought to retain her alimony award of $700 monthly, which by its own terms continued only so long as her income did not exceed $8,000 per year. She worked as a typist and earned about $600 a month, but then began cohabiting with a man whose net monthly income was $2,250. Yet she claimed he made no contribution to the rent, utilities or any of her personal expenses, but paid only for his share of the meals and for the couple's entertainment. She thus argued that her financial needs had not changed, entitling her to keep the alimony. The trial court had terminated the alimony, but the Wisconsin Supreme Court held that before termination the trial court must find that he was in fact supporting her. Appreciating the strategic possibilities made available by such a rule, however, the court also held the parties were not free to "fashion their relationship and finances in a manner that is intended solely to prevent the modification of maintenance payments." The meaning of these instructions is difficult to fathom. Suppose the trial court believes the wife's testimony that she receives no rent, utilities or personal support from her companion, but finds that in the absence of her alimony income he would offer such support, and she would accept it. Is this sufficient evidence that they have "fashioned their relationship" with an eye toward the maintenance payments? How important is the word "solely" in the court's instructions? The *VanGorder* opinion itself is not especially helpful on these points.

PROBLEM

Problem 4-25. Mabel and Ernest divorce after 20 years of marriage and two children. Mabel, who is 39, receives an alimony award of indefinite duration that reflects the fact that, as the primary caretaker of the couple's children, she gave up educational and career opportunities that now make it unlikely she will ever come close to matching Ernest's substantial income as an attorney. A year after the divorce she begins a serious relationship with Fernando. Fernando, 30 years old, is an aspiring novelist. He has supported himself as a waiter, but works fewer hours after moving in with Mabel so that he can devote more time to his writing. He tells Mabel he does not want to marry until he feels he can make a more substantial financial contribution to their relationship. A year later Ernest moves to terminate the alimony award of $3000 a month. Mabel earns $1500 a month taking telephone orders for a mail-order retailer. Fernando once earned $2000 a month as a waiter, but with his reduced hours brings in only $500. Fernando and Mabel plan to continue to live together. The parties' separation agreement does not address the effect of Mabel's nonmarital cohabitation. State law ends alimony automatically upon the obligee's remarriage. Should Ernest's motion be granted? Will it?

[4] ECONOMIC CHANGES

[a] Increase in Obligor's Income

An increase in alimony can generally not be grounded solely on an increase in the obligor's income, given that the measure of the alimony recipient's needs is ordinarily based on the marital standard of living. *See, e.g., Cole v. Cole*, 409 A.2d 734 (Md. App. 1979). The exception is where the original award was set too low (because of the obligor's temporary inability to pay more), and the obligor's increased income allows a modification that merely raises the award to where it should have been originally. *See Marriage of Hopwood*, 214 Cal. App. 3d 1604, 263 Cal. Rptr. 401 (1989); *Marriage of Smith*, 225 Cal. App. 3d 469, 274 Cal. Rptr. 911, 926 (1990). Yet, where the obligor's income increases dramatically after the marriage has ended, it seems inevitable that the court will hear the recipient's claims more sympathetically.

It should be noted that some states, by case-law, statute, or some combination of the two, expressly allow modification of alimony grounded solely on the obligor's increased income. *Bedell v. Bedell*, 583 So.2d 1005, 1007 (Fla. 1991) (holding that "a substantial increase in the financial ability of the paying spouse, standing alone, may justify but does not require an order of increased alimony"); *cf.* Minn. Stat. § 518.64 (2002) ("an order respecting maintenance or support may be modified upon a showing of one or more of the following: (1) substantially increased or decreased earnings of a party;. . . .").

Note that there is a better argument for increasing child support on account of post-marriage increases in the obligor's income. The children, unlike the former spouse are ordinarily thought entitled to share in the post-marital prosperity of their parents. "Parental relationships and obligations continue after the parents divorce each other. The children are not thereby divorced from either parent. They have a right to expect the same support and care they would have reasonably expected if their parents had remained married." *Colizoli v. Colizoli*, 474 N.E.2d 280, 283 (Ohio 1984) (allowing increase in child support award but not in alimony award).

[b] The Obligor's Retirement or Change in Employment

Any spousal support or child support proceeding contains the potential issue of whether the actual earnings of either party are a fair indicator of what they could or should earn. We consider here the case in which a party's income *declines* after the initial award is set, perhaps because of a later retirement or loss of employment. In deciding whether the income change justifies a modification of the award, the court frequently must decide whether the party whose earning capacity is at issue has acted reasonably.

The obligor's voluntary retirement may be complete, or may involve a change to less lucrative employment. Should an alimony award be reduced to reflect the obligor's reduced earnings? Where the retirement occurs at a typical retirement age, the answer almost always is "yes." *See Sylvan v. Sylvan*, 632 A.2d 528 (N.J. App. Div. 1993) (while retirement at 65 does not justify an automatic reduction in alimony, obligor is entitled to hearing on whether changed circumstances justify reduction). When it occurs early, the case is more difficult. *Ellis v. Ellis*, 262 N.W.2d 265 (Iowa 1978) is a classic example. The obligor, a veterinarian, had a high-level Department of Agriculture position in Iowa at the time of divorce. But a few years later, at age 62, he sought to retire from this position and move to Florida with his new wife, their small child, and his mother-in-law. He testified that work had become "too much for him" and a warmer climate would "be a lot better for my upper respiratory tract." He provided no medical evidence to support a need to move away from winter, and did not claim to be unable to work in his field. He bought a house in Florida for cash and owned a sailboat, and his new wife intended to attend school there. The court denied his modification petition:

> We do not dispute the sincerity of his wish to leave his employment
> and move to a warmer climate. We do not doubt his desire to see his
> present wife continue her education. Nor do we question his devotion

to their child and his mother-in-law. Although . . . his health problems are not as serious as he makes them out to be, we do not think they are imaginary. However, he is not free to plan his future without regard to his obligation to his first wife. He cannot arbitrarily freeze her out of his future. Similar obligations in and apart from family life compel many persons to maintain employment which may be difficult, undesirable and even physically or mentally painful.

See also Marriage of Sinks, 204 Cal. App. 3d 586, 251 Cal. Rptr. 379 (1988) (refusing to reduce alimony obligation of 62-year-old husband so that he could take advantage of chance to retire with full pension benefits); *Barbarine v. Barbarine,* 925 S.W.2d 831 (Ky. App. 1996) (modification denied to husband seeking to retire at 62 because advantages to him did not substantially outweigh disadvantage to former spouse); *Marriage of Shaughnessy,* 793 P.2d 1116 (Az. App. 1990). For a more sympathetic treatment of a retiring obligor, see *Burns v. Burns,* 331 A.2d 768 (Pa. Super. 1975) (husband retiring in response to his son's death and his own failing health; court added, "even if he and his wife were living together there could be no complaint [by] the wife that her income would be reduced."); *Reeves v. Reeves,* 803 S.W.2d 52 (Mo. App. 1990) (59-year-old husband allowed to reduce alimony upon retirement where wife had increased her income); *Bogan v. Bogan,* 60 S.W.2d 721 (Tenn. 2001) (establishing principle that "when an obligor's retirement is objectively reasonable, it does constitute a substantial and material change in circumstances — irrespective of whether the retirement was foreseeable and voluntary — so as to permit modification of the support obligation").

Many reasons other than retirement may motivate an obligor to reduce his income. In one group of cases the obligor seeks to return to school. In *Stiltz v. Stiltz,* 223 S.E.2d 689 (Ga. 1976), the husband sought relief from his $150 per month alimony obligation when he quit work to attend a seminary. The court held it had "no authority to relieve appellant of his obligations even for the worthy purpose of entering the ministry." Similarly, in *Goldberger v. Goldberger,* 624 A.2d 1328 (Md. App. 1993), both parents were Orthodox Jews, and they had six children. The father had never worked, having always intended, in the Orthodox tradition, to be a permanent Torah and Talmud student. The court held that the father's study plans amounted to voluntary impoverishment justifying a support award set according to his earning capacity. Left for the trial court to figure out was the earning capacity of an unemployed Talmud student who had never had a job. But in *Meegan v. Meegan,* 11 Cal. App. 4th 156, 13 Cal. Rptr. 2d 799 (1992), the court reduced the former husband's spousal support obligations to zero when he quit his employment to enter a monastery with the goal of entering the priesthood. The change was permanent because the husband's plans included taking a vow of poverty.

Courts are sometimes more favorably inclined when the obligor's educational plans seem likely to enhance his earning capacity, to the eventual economic benefit of his dependents. *E.g., Arce v. Arce,* 566 So. 2d 1308 (Fla. App. 1990) (physician allowed to reduce alimony and child support obligations while completing 3-year cardiology fellowship); *but see Ilas v. Ilas,* 12 Cal. App. 4th 1630, 16 Cal. Rptr. 2d 345 (1993) (pharmacist who quit to attend medical school was told that his spousal and child support obligations would be measured by earning capacity rather than earnings).

When an obligor caught up in a corporate downsizing accepts his company's severance offer, how should the courts respond to requests for alimony modification? The cases tend to be highly fact-sensitive, and may turn on how sympathetic the parties are, or the general inclinations of the judges. In one case, the obligor, a 59-year old supervisor at Otis Elevator in San Diego, accepted the company's offer of 8.5 months salary as a severance pay bonus for accepting early retirement. The court found his decision reasonable because the only alternative was to risk involuntary layoff with no similar accompanying severance pay. But it also required that alimony continue at pre-layoff levels during the 8.5 month severance pay period. The decision of whether to reduce it then was deferred to permit the court to assess his earning capacity under the economic circumstances prevailing when the severance pay period ran out. *Marriage of Stephenson*, 39 Cal. App. 4th 71, 46 Cal. Rptr. 2d 8 (1995). In another case, an obligor, reassigned from his supervisory position at Johnson Wax and told that further advancement was unlikely, accepted the company's buyout package to purchase a video rental franchise. Upon his separation he prepaid a year's worth of child support, signed over to his former wife her interest in his separation benefits, and later sought an order suspending further child support and maintenance payments until he had his new business sufficiently well-established to draw an income from it. The court found that while the father's income reduction was well intended it fell within the state's "shirking" rule because it was unreasonable in light of the father's child support obligations. Because the court felt the father should have kept his Johnson Wax job, it continued his support obligations as if he had. *Van Offeren v. Van Offeren*, 496 N.W.2d 660 (Wis. App. 1992).

Courts have held that the obligor's reduction in earnings were not voluntary and therefore did justify reducing the alimony award, where the income loss arose from alcoholism, *Haas v. Haas,* 552 So. 2d 252 (Fla. App. 1989), and participation in a strike, *Reep v. Reep,* 565 So. 2d 814 (Fla. App. 1990). For a comprehensive overview of the area, and a proposal for reform, see Becker, *Spousal and Child Support and the "Voluntary Reduction of Income "Doctrine,"* 29 CONN. L. REV. 647 (1997).

[c] Voluntary Employment Changes by the Obligee

Most litigation on the obligee's earning capacity involve competing claims regarding the obligee who is returning to the labor market, or whose rehabilitative award is about to end. These cases are treated above, at pp. 396 – 402. The same issue could arise if an obligee leaves lucrative employment for a less well-paying position. Such cases are unusual because alimony obligees ordinarily are not well-employed, since the very fact of their lucrative employment would typically defeat their alimony claim. The issue does arise in the context of child support, however.

[d] Inflation

In the 1970's modifications based upon inflation were an important consideration in alimony awards. The issue has subsided in importance with changing economic conditions, but of course economic cycles come and go. It is sometimes said in passing that inflation does not justify a modification of a support award, since it equally affects both parties. *Baker v. Baker,* 332 S.E.2d 550, 552 (S.C. App. 1985); *Fakouri v. Perkins,* 322 So. 2d 401 (La. 1975); *Binder v. Binder,* 390 N.E.2d 260 (Mass. App. 1979). Such a statement oversimplifies the problem considerably. To the extent the obligee relies upon a fixed award, inflation surely reduces her standard of living, while the obligor's income typically rises over time. The problem with a claim based only on general indicators of inflation is that modifications are supposed to be based on changes in the circumstances of the particular party subject to the original order, not on general societal indicators. In any particular case, the obligor may not have a rising income or the obligee may benefit from increases in her own resources. Other courts acknowledge this. *Goldberg v. Goldberg,* 332 N.E.2d 710 (Ill. App. 1975); *Edelstein v. Edelstein,* 28 A.D.2d 979, 283 N.Y.S.2d 658 (1967). An increase in the obligor's earnings combined with inflation-created erosion in the obligee's standard of living should be enough to justify an increase in the award. *See, e.g., Pope v. Pope,* 342 So. 2d 1000 (Fla. App. 1977); *Alexander v. Alexander,* 540 P.2d 457 (Wash. App. 1975); *but see Nichols v. Nichols,* 236 S.E.2d 36 (W. Va. 1977) (court reversed increase in support despite such a showing, after concluding increase in obligor's earnings was contemplated at outset). Some jurisdictions respond to the problem by ordering that orders for alimony or child support include automatic adjustments for changes in cost of living. *See, e.g.,* MINN. STAT. § 518.641 (2002) ("biennial adjustment in the amount to be paid based on a change in the cost of living" as determined by an index such as the consumer price index).

PROBLEMS

Problem 4-26. Joan and Larry were married for 20 years at divorce. Larry operated a service station and earned about $20,000 annually. Joan had worked at a meat packing plant for ten years, by the end of which she was earning $8.95 per hour. She quit two years before their divorce, when her pension partially vested, to help Larry with the service station business. When they were later divorced, she went to work at a popcorn packing plant, earning $3.65 an hour. She could have resumed her old job in the meat packing plant, although it would pay only $5.50 because she had now lost her seniority. Joan contends that she is entitled to an award of alimony based upon her current earnings at the popcorn plant; Larry contends that the court should give her a lower award, based on her earning capacity at the meat packing plant. Joan does not want to return to the meat packing plant because the job there is grueling and she is concerned about its effects on her health. What is the appropriate result?

Problem 4-27. The divorce decree requires Richard to pay Sally $400 monthly in spousal maintenance and $600 monthly in child support. It also provides that the payments should be increased annually in proportion to any increases in Richard's income. Richard has a bachelor's degree and is employed as a bookkeeper by a large corporation. He decides to go to law school, with the thought that he will become a tax lawyer, increasing his earnings substantially. When school begins he shifts to part time work for his former employer, reducing his income from $30,000 annually to $18,000. He adjusts his payments to Sally accordingly. Sally seeks enforcement of the original amount. What result? What should be the result?

§ G. SHOULD COURTS CONSIDER CLAIMS OF MARITAL MISCONDUCT?

[1] AS A FACTOR IN ALIMONY OR MARITAL PROPERTY ADJUDICATIONS?

Until the no-fault divorce revolution, claims of marital misconduct were central to divorce litigation, as the usual (sometimes exclusive) grounds for divorce. They were also central to divorce's financial issues. Many states would not allow the award of alimony to a wife who had committed adultery (a rule still in force in a few states, as we will see). This was at a time when an award of alimony was likely to be the only money a wife could take out of a dissolved marriage. Alimony, like the dissolution itself, was to be a reward to "an innocent and victimized" wife and unavailable to a "guilty" wife.

The grounds for divorce have changed significantly in recent decades, as have the rules of property ownership during marriage, property division after marriage, and the principles governing the grant of alimony. While fault plays a far smaller role than it once did as a grounds of divorce, some jurisdictions continue to give it a role in the financial terms of divorce.

ELLMAN, THE PLACE OF FAULT IN A MODERN DIVORCE LAW, 28 Ariz. St. L.J. 773 (1996)

Prior to 1968, consideration of marital misconduct, or "fault," was almost universally allowed. The two decades that followed saw considerable change in the law. The Uniform Marriage and Divorce Act (UMDA), initially approved in 1970, provides unambiguously that both allocation of marital property and determinations of spousal support or maintenance (the new terms for "alimony") be made "without regard to marital misconduct". [¶] . . . Published surveys typically report that approximately half the states now share the Uniform Act's position. Yet two categories — fault and no-fault — are inadequate to describe the major variations in state policy. The tables that follow place states in one of five categories. Some preliminary comments are necessary to explain these classifications.

There are two senses in which marital misconduct affects property disposition and alimony orders in even the most thoroughly no-fault jurisdictions. One might call them the "financial cost" exceptions to the no-fault principle. First, it appears that all states recognize the power of dissolution courts to consider, in allocating marital property, misconduct that has affected directly the amount of property available for allocation. Second . . . misconduct affects both alimony and property allocations to the extent it enlarges either spouse's need. . . . [as] when domestic violence leaves one spouse with increased medical costs or a reduced earning capacity. Because existing law in no-fault states emphasizes that disparities in post-dissolution living standards are the primary basis for alimony awards, it can respond to such facts without explicit consideration of the misconduct that has altered the disparity. . . .

Categorization of fault states is complicated by the variation among them in the definition of both the relevant misconduct and the financial issues to which it applies. Some allow consideration of only specified forms of misconduct; some leave the matter to trial court discretion; and some leave the matter to trial court discretion but attempt to contain its exercise through rules that in general terms limit the kind of conduct that may be considered.

. . .

The classifications of state law employed here adopt the following conventions.

1. Pure no-fault (20 states). These states exclude consideration of marital misconduct entirely, subject to the two universal "financial cost" exceptions. Many employ the language of the Uniform Marriage and Divorce Act in their statutes, stating clearly that both property allocations and spousal maintenance adjudications are made "without regard to marital misconduct."

2. Pure no-fault property, almost pure no-fault alimony (5 states). The states in this category all adopt a pure no-fault position with regard to property, but may allow some very limited consideration of misconduct with respect to alimony. In one state in this group, it appears that the state supreme court is gradually retreating from a 1973 decision allowing consideration of fault with respect to alimony, and in 1995 came within one vote of excluding it altogether. In the second there is caselaw that allows consideration of misconduct in alimony adjudications but few reported decisions that actually do so. In the third a 1990 amendment deleted the requirement that alimony claimants be free from fault, establishing instead need and ability to pay as the primary basis for the awards; it is not yet clear whether any consideration of fault survives this amendment. In the fourth there are a handful of twenty-year-old cases from intermediate appellate courts considering fault in fixing alimony awards. While these have never been formally overruled, more recent practice seems identical to states in Category 1. In the fifth very recent legislation allows but does not require courts to consider fault in alimony adjudications. While established case law in that state strongly suggests that its courts will not embrace this invitation, there is not yet an authoritative interpretation of the new provision.

3. Almost pure no-fault (3 states). These states seem very much like those in Category 1, but the slight possibility of considering fault that exists under their law applies to both alimony and property allocation. Two of the three could easily be placed in Category 1: In one the governing state supreme court decision establishes a no-fault rule with language that is nearly absolute, and in fact there have been no reported decisions in that state allowing consideration of misconduct since that case was decided. In the second there is a single decision of the state supreme court that allowed an exception (to the state's otherwise complete no-fault approach) in a case of murder. The third state in this group has an apparently unique rule that in practice excludes fault from consideration except in cases of serious violent assault.

4. No-fault property, fault in alimony (7 states). These states have a pure no-fault position with regard to marital property allocations, but give their trial courts considerable discretion to consider fault in alimony awards.

5. Full-fault (15 states). These are true fault states. They give their courts discretion to consider the parties' marital misconduct in both alimony adjudications and property allocations. In some, authoritative appellate opinions have on occasion attempted to describe the range of misconduct that trial courts should consider, or suggest restraint in the weight to be accorded misconduct. These states are nonetheless classified as "full-fault" because their appellate opinions also embrace the importance of trial judge discretion, and the pattern of reported cases suggests that the hortatory language in the more cautious fault opinions has little impact on the decisions in others.

. . .

The *[ALI] Principles* . . . reconceptualize alimony claims as compensation for the disproportionate share of the financial losses that the obligee spouse incurs at the dissolution of the marriage. . . .[¶] [This] understanding of alimony's function helps define the question presented by the fault debate. . . . Assessments of misconduct have no logical connection to the factual foundation upon which [the *Principles'*] presumptions of entitlement are based. Such misconduct would not itself cast doubt on the existence and size of the loss recognized by the presumptions, or on their basis for asserting joint responsibility for losses: the duration of the parties' relationship and of the period of foregone employment opportunity.

In that case fault can be relevant only to vindicate interests not addressed by the basic alimony award — interests that in a given case require a concurrent financial award which can be added to, or offset against, the award based upon the compensatory payment rationale. An examination of the policy question must therefore begin by identifying these other interests to determine whether they should in fact be considered in the dissolution action.

III. The Possible Functions of Fault

. . .

A. A Fault Rule as An Agent of Morality: Rewarding Virtue and Punishing Sin.

Punishing the wrongdoer has been a persistent but troubled theme in the law of fault states. Punishment is more usually the function of the criminal law. [E]ven in fault states, punitive [alimony] awards are ordinarily condemned — when they are recognized as such. On the other hand, many fault states apply rules that cannot be explained as anything but punitive. The clearest example is the rule that inflexibly bars alimony awards to every adulterous spouse, without regard to any other facts of the case.[29] The caselaw's oft-stated rejection of punitive awards[30] seems preferable to these silent impositions of them.

. . .

Some courts appeal to a rationale that seems at first to avoid the punitive nature of a fault award by casting it as compensation for the financial costs of splitting one household in two, costs that necessarily arise in most dissolutions. These courts argue that a fault-based award is justified because it allocates more of those costs to the spouse whose conduct caused them, by causing the dissolution. Framing the rule this way thus casts it as compensation rather than punishment even though no losses are identified beyond the financial consequences present in nearly every dissolution.

Closer examination suggests, however, that this principle . . . necessarily relies on sleight of hand in application. The problem is the principle's reliance on being able to establish which spouse "caused" the dissolution. Inquiring into the cause of marital dissolution is different from inquiring into the cause of chicken pox, or of a plumbing failure. The fundamental problem is that the inquiry is ultimately one of morality, not science. Some individuals tolerate their spouse's drunkenness or adultery and remain in their marriage. Others may seek divorce if their spouse grows fat, or spends long hours at the office. Is the divorce caused by one spouse's offensive conduct or the other's unreasonable intolerance? In deciding that question the court is assessing the parties' relative moral failings, not the relationship between independent and dependent variables. And the complexity of marital relations of course confounds the inquiry. The fading of affective ties makes spouses less tolerant of one another. So of course the decisionmaker inquiring into "cause" should ask about the reason for the loss of affection in order, for example, to determine whether it is the complainant's apparently unreasonable intolerance that is the cause of the marital failure, rather than conduct of the other spouse that

---

[29] The potential recipient's adultery is a complete bar to alimony, without regard to any other facts of the case, in Georgia, North Carolina, South Carolina, and West Virginia. In Virginia it is a complete bar unless the court finds that its denial "would constitute a manifest injustice based upon the respective degrees of fault during the marriage and the relative economic circumstances of the parties." In Mississippi it is generally a bar, but not after a long marriage if the adulterous spouse would otherwise be "destitute," in which case a reduced award may be allowed. The Mississippi rule was applied to limit the alimony that would otherwise have been allowed the wife in the dissolution of a 25-year marriage, even though the husband in that case also committed adultery. Adultery is an "appropriate consideration" in many other fault states; decisions sustaining its consideration without any apparent important limitation on the trial court's discretion include Alabama (trial court reversed for failing to consider H's adultery in allocating marital property); Connecticut; Kentucky (W's adultery may reduce alimony award, but H's adultery cannot be the basis for increasing it); Louisiana; South Dakota (H's adultery may also be considered); Maryland (trial court reversed for refusing to hear testimony of W's adultery); New Hampshire; North Dakota (trial court properly allocated 83 percent of property to H after 19-year marriage, where W guilty of adultery); Tennessee; Texas; and Vermont. See Appendix A.

[30] This sentiment is expressed even in full-fault states, Young v. Young, 609 S.W.2d 758 (Texas 1980) (court should use fault to make "a just and right division" of the community property, not to "punish" the guilty spouse); *Paul v. Paul*, 616 P.2d 707, 712 (Wy. 1980) (court should not use its discretion to reward one party and punish the other).

prompted the complainant's loss of affection (and which in turn encouraged the intolerance). Perhaps courts in fault states sometimes engage in such tracing, although surely many do not. But in either case the inquiry is not really about cause in the true sense of that term. It is not about the conduct that caused the dissolution, but about the misconduct that can be assigned the blame for it. Was the marital breakdown in Marriage One caused by one spouse's adultery or the other's emotional insensitivity? In Marriage Two, by the first's adultery or the second's failure to keep fit? The court's answer tells us which conduct it finds more blameworthy, not which [caused] the other.

This analysis does not suggest, of course, that it is wrong to assign the costs of dissolution to the spouse whose conduct was more blameworthy. It only reveals that this is what the court is in fact doing. Once that is revealed, however, a problem is uncovered: by dressing up its conclusion in the neutral language of causation, the court can assign such blame without identifying the standards under which it does so. Much mischief can result from allowing courts to assign liability to non-tortious conduct by application of unarticulated — and effectively unreviewable — standards of blameworthiness. Nor is such a rule necessary to reach serious misconduct. Offensive conduct in marriage that does violate norms of tort or criminal law will normally be actionable whether or not it is the "cause" of the actor's marital dissolution.

In sum, courts that purport to allocate the unavoidable costs of dissolution by assessing the cause of the marital failure are in fact rewarding virtue and punishing sin. They are not compensating one spouse for a harm "caused" by the other. If the behavior they punish could properly be held tortious, it ought to give rise to damages on those grounds. If not, the language of "cause" serves only to conceal, perhaps from the court itself, that the judgment's true function is to assign liability to behavior that may not be blameworthy under the better established standards of tort law.

B. Fault Law as a Source of Compensation for Harms Caused by Wrongful Conduct.

Compensation is a more palatable rationale than punishment for fault-based adjustments in alimony awards. . . . But just what kind of loss would the fault-based rule provide compensation for? No-fault principles already recognize financial losses traceable to spousal misconduct, under the two [financial cost exceptions to no-fault identified above]. . . . What additional losses would a fault system recognize, beyond these losses of property and earning capacity? The answer is non-financial losses.

That is, a compensation-based rationale for considering marital misconduct is, in its essence, an argument to provide compensation at dissolution for non-financial losses. This seems true even though existing law in fault states probably does not now provide such compensation. . .reliably, simply because existing fault law includes no standard for setting the dollar consequences that should flow from a finding of fault.[35] It is hardly an exaggeration to

---

[35] Courts in full-fault states do sometimes describe their consideration of fault as serving this compensation function. *E.g., Robinson v. Robinson*, 444 A.2d 234, 234–35 (Conn. 1982) (in considering the "gravity" of the wife's adultery as it applies to the allocation of property, the court

say that the existing law in fault states leaves the dollar consequence of a fault finding largely to the whim of the trial court judge. But the argument for considering fault must rest on this rationale of compensating for non-financial losses, even if current practice does not implement it. Could a reformed law implement this principle more effectively? This question seems central to examining any proposal to consider marital misconduct at dissolution. The first step is to identify more precisely just what these additional non-financial losses are. There are in principle two possibilities, each of which has a tort analog:

1. Compensation for emotional losses arising from the other spouse's misconduct. (Intentional or negligent infliction of emotional distress.)

2. Compensation for the pain and suffering arising from the other's misconduct. (General damages in battery or assault actions.)

In short, a fault rule would serve compensation functions that may already be served by the tort law. Such duplication is inadvisable. There is no reason to reinvent compensation principles under the rubric of fault adjudications, nor to incorporate tort principles into divorce adjudications. A jurisdiction that wants concurrent consideration of tort claims and dissolution remedies may permit their joinder. . . .

In comparing the virtues of recognizing certain interspousal claims in tort or in dissolution, it might seem natural to assume that their incorporation into dissolution law would have the advantage of facilitating such claims by lowering the procedural or transactional hurdles that confront them. But whether a fault-regarding dissolution law would actually have this effect, as compared to a rule allowing the joinder of the dissolution and tort actions, is hardly clear. Even more importantly, however, one cannot in fact assume that sound policy favors such encouragement of tort claims. Most acts that meet the formal elements of battery, or of intentional infliction of emotional distress, do not lead to tort claims. Both inside and outside the family, people do not sue over every shove, punch, or outrageously mean and hurtful act. Their reticence is usually regarded as a good thing, not as a problem to be solved. There is no general enthusiasm abroad for encouraging more tort suits by finding ways that people can conveniently add their claims to the end of forms they must file anyway for other reasons. Interspousal tort claims present no reason for a different view. To the contrary, an effective strategy to encourage spousal tort claims could easily, if unintentionally, tap the anger and bitterness often present at divorce, yielding additional tort suits that are disproportionately of the sort that should not be brought. Some tort claims might be made for tactical advantage in the divorce settlement negotiations.

---

may consider the "humiliation and mental anguish" that it imposed on the husband). And it seems clear that in exercising the wide discretion typically allowed them in full-fault jurisdictions, trial judges often think of themselves as awarding damages in the guise of alimony or property allocations. Whether those damages are compensatory or punitive in nature is typically difficult to ascertain, however, because of the fault law's disinclination to acknowledge either purpose overtly. For a telling illustration, see *Martone v. Martone*, 611 A.2d 896, 901 (Conn. App. 1992) (trial judge initially refers to award of $15,000 to W as "damages" for H's conduct in "brutally causing the breakup of this marriage," *id.* at 899, but subsequently recharacterizes it as alimony; award affirmed on appeal since fault is valid factor in alimony and court's "later characterization" of its award should control).

A conclusion that more claims would be brought, were it possible to easily add them to the dissolution petition, would be cause for caution. The question is not whether incorporating the tort law into dissolution action would yield more claims. It is rather whether the tort law provides an adequate opportunity to obtain a remedy for worthy claims that should be brought. If it does, then inviting additional claims in the dissolution action is a problem, not a solution.

NOTES

1. *State Law Variations.* The Ellman article contains appendices that describing the law of every state, with supporting authorities; a similar breakdown is given in JOHN DEWITT GREGORY, JANET LEACH RICHARDS & SHERYL WOLF, PROPERTY DIVISION IN DIVORCE PROCEEDINGS: A FIFTY STATE GUIDE § 12.04 (2003). As a logical matter, there are three possible ways for considering fault: it may be an eligibility requirement (the claimant must prove his spouse at fault in order to receive alimony); it may be a bar (the claimant otherwise eligible for alimony is disqualified if at fault); or it may be a factor affecting the amount of alimony, rather than entitlement to it. Until recently, North Carolina treated fault as an eligibility requirement, but it no longer does so, and it appears that no other state now does. Footnote 29 in Ellman, *supra*, identifies states that treat the obligee's adultery as a bar. Note that these possibilities may be combined. For example, before its recent amendment North Carolina treated fault as a bar as well as an eligibility requirement. It can also be both a bar and a factor, so that the claimant free from fault may point to the obligor's fault to enhance the amount of the award. In fact, all the states that consider fault treat it as a factor, whether or not they also consider it a bar.

2. *Do Wives Do Better Under Fault Laws?* One of Professor Lenore Weitzman's most important claims (*supra*, pp. 368-69) was that no-fault divorce contributed to the relative poverty of divorced women — that women were better off under the predecessor fault system. The argument that the change of available grounds for divorce made divorced women financially worse off than before the reform focused on the bargaining process:

> The fault rules gave great bargaining leverage to the spouse who felt no urgency to end the marriage, especially if it would be difficult to prove that spouse guilty of "fault." Knowing the difficulty of obtaining a divorce in a truly contested proceeding in which her fault would have to be shown, such an innocent spouse might offer to cooperate with a "consent" decree only if certain financial demands were met. So, for example, the older married man who abandoned his long-term wife for a younger woman could not obtain his "freedom" to remarry her without buying it from his first wife. In such a system the laws governing property division and alimony often didn't matter, since in many cases the wife had great [bargaining] leverage regardless of their content. This is not to say that the system necessarily produced equitable results. While it protected the marital investment of an "innocent" spouse, or one whose "fault" would be tricky to prove,

it failed entirely to protect the "guilty" spouse who had invested a great deal in her marriage, while giving bargaining leverage to the innocent spouse who had invested very little.

No-fault reform created a sea-change in this legal environment. Although motivated in large part by a desire to end the charade of perjured testimony and falsified residency that permeated consent divorces under the fault system, its effects went considerably further. The no-fault reform effectively recognized unilateral divorce. The man who wants to end his marriage now simply files a petition alleging that it is irretrievably broken; there is no defense against such an allegation. The wife seeking alimony, property division, or child support has no leverage to demand such compensation as the price of her husband's "freedom," but must rely instead on the substantive law governing these issues. Thus, the law of alimony and property division now count in a way neither did before.

Ellman, *The Theory of Alimony*, 77 Cal. L. Rev. 1, 7–8 (1989).

It thus seemed plausible to think that the no-fault reforms adversely affected the financial outcome of divorce for women. And perhaps as well, the typically concomitant change in many states from fault-regarding alimony rules to no-fault alimony rules, somehow also had the unintended effect of burdening women. These are ultimately empirical propositions, not theoretical ones, and it turns out the evidence is at best uncertain whether women fare worse under no-fault divorce. One might note that if women want out of their marriage as often as men, then no-fault reforms that remove the bargaining lever previously held by the party resisting divorce would burden women as often as men. In fact, available evidence suggests that, at least today, women are *more* likely than men to be the instigators of their divorce. Braver, Whitley & Ng, *Who Divorced Whom? Methodological and Theoretical Issues*, 20 J. Divorce & Remarriage 1 (1993); Margaret F. Brinig & Douglas W. Allen, *"These Boots Are Made for Walking": Why Most Divorce Filers Are Women*, 2 Am L. & Econ. Rev. 126 (2000). Finally, if one believes women do less well than justice requires in the financial remedies at divorce, one must consider whether one is better off reforming the substantive law of alimony and property division, or restoring fault in the hope it will give bargaining leverage to the right party.

On the basic empirical question — did women in fact do less well in California after its adoption of no-fault divorce? — Weitzman's conclusions drew some criticism even before the fundamental flaws in her data analysis were exposed. The critics were of two kinds. Some, looking at other data, concluded that no-fault had little impact, *e.g.*, Jacob, *Another Look at No-Fault Divorce and the Post-Divorce Finances of Women*, 23 Law & Soc. Rev. 95, 112–13 (1989). Others, examining Weitzman's own published data, concluded that she had misinterpreted it. *See especially* Sugarman, *Dividing Financial Interests at Divorce*, in S. Sugarman & H. Kay, Divorce Reform at the Crossroads 130, 132–34 (1990). More recently, it has been pointed out that while Weitzman focused on California divorces, in the common law states the ascendancy of no-fault divorce occurred during much the same period as the transition to equitable distribution, making it likely that women's situations might well have improved over this period. Ellman, *The Misguided Movement to Revive Fault Divorce*, 11 INT'L J. LAW, POLICY, & THE FAMILY 216, 242 n.45 (1997). For an examination of the interaction of different marital property rules and fault divorce, see Gray, *The Economic Impact of Divorce Law Reform*, 15 POP. RES. & POLICY REV. 275 (1996). Despite its theoretical plausibility, the claim that no-fault divorce adversely affected divorced women is, at best, unproven.

[2] AS THE BASIS OF AN INTERSPOUSAL TORT CLAIM?

The prospect of tort suits for marital misconduct is made possible by the gradual abandonment, in most states, of the doctrine of interspousal tort immunity, for both personal injury and intentional torts. Ironically enough, this movement took place at the same time as the movement to eliminate fault adjudications in divorce actions. By 1994, 39 jurisdictions had totally abrogated interspousal immunity and 10 states had partially nullified it. Laura H. Wanamaker, Waite v. Waite: *The Florida Supreme Court Abrogates the Doctrine of Interspousal Immunity*, 45 MERCER L. REV. 903, 906–07 (1994) (footnotes give a comprehensive list of case and statutory citations). Only Hawaii, *Peters v. Peters*, 634 P.2d 586 (Haw. 1981), and Louisiana, LA. REV. STAT. ANN. § 9:291 (West 2000 & Supp. 2003), appear to retain full interspousal tort immunity. The trend to abrogate the immunity has been endorsed by commentators, F. HARPER, F. JAMES & O. GRAY, THE LAW OF TORTS 569 (2d ed. 1986) ("the total abolition of the immunity [seems] eminently desirable") as well as by the American Law Institute, RESTATEMENT (SECOND) OF TORTS § 895F and Comment *f* (1979). These authorities agree that allowing such suits seems particularly plausible after divorce, where "there [is] no home to disrupt and no domestic harmony to disturb." Harper et al., *supra*, at 565–66, criticizing, *inter alia, Aldrich v. Tracy*, 269 N.W. 30 (Iowa 1936) (applying immunity in case where wife had been murdered by husband), and *Counts v. Counts*, 266 S.E.2d 895 (Va. 1980) (applying immunity in suit brought after divorce, seeking damages against former husband for the injuries inflicted by a would-be assassin he hired to murder wife during coverture). Courts that have abandoned absolute interspousal tort immunity may still employ special rules restricting recovery to a specified class of interspousal torts. *See* W.P. KEETON, PROSSER AND KEETON ON TORTS 903–04 (5th ed. 1984).

The movement to abolish interspousal tort immunity was motivated largely by the perception that the principal consequence of the immunity doctrine was to deny someone injured by his spouse's negligence the ability to recover compensation from the spouse's insurance carrier, and by the conclusion that any concern that the spouses might collude with one another on fraudulent insurance claims could be met by a response less drastic than complete immunity. But, of course, insurance coverage is not a factor in intentional torts, so that concerns over fraudulent claims could never provide an adequate explanation for immunity as to them. Is there some other rationale for caution in recognizing claims of intentional torts between spouses? With the general abolition of interspousal tort immunity, that question has now been put. Consider the following:

[a] Ordinary Battery Claims

It is difficult to think of plausible policy arguments that could be offered to justify a rule disallowing battery claims between separated, divorcing or divorced spouses. The arguments for no-fault divorce have no application to such a battery suit. Without revisiting all the arguments here, recall one in particular: that making the outcome of a divorce action turn on assessments of blame for the breakup of the marriage will not work because allocating such blame is often beyond the court's ken. (Is the wife who leaves her husband "at fault"? Surely that must depend upon why she left. If she left because he treated her cruelly, then he must be at fault. If because she went to live with her lover, then she is at fault. But what if he treated her cruelly and she went to live with her lover? Is it then critical which occurred first? But what occurred before that?) Reformers found this kind of inquiry pointless and unproductive. But no such inquiry is necessary to resolve a battery suit between former spouses. Because physical violence is an actionable wrong without regard to whether we think the perpetrator had good reason to be angry with the victim, the court need not attempt to determine whether it believes he did.

If battery claims are generally allowed, and if spousal violence is not rare, why aren't battery claims common among divorcing spouses? Consider the speculations in Ellman and Sugarman, *Spousal Emotional Abuse As a Tort?*, 55 Mᴅ. L. Rᴇᴠ. 1268, 1291–92 (1996):

It is not entirely clear to us why spousal battering victims so rarely seek special financial redress. Because we do not know the actual explanation, we can only consider the various possibilities. . . .

One explanation that seems likely is that neither the battery victim nor her lawyer even considers the tort suit possibility. A common pattern, we imagine, involves battery incidents that leave the victim with no permanent physical loss, even though they are painful and humiliating when they occur. Perhaps the victim initially responds to these experiences by trying to avoid events or situations that might provoke the batterer, or by staying out of his way at those times. When these strategies fail, the victim eventually leaves the marital home, and at some point then consults a divorce lawyer. Especially if the victim has no permanent physical injury, it might not occur to a divorce lawyer — who may have never handled a personal injury case, and who does not think of himself as a personal injury lawyer — that a tort claim is a possibility, even though the lawyer would understand, if the matter were raised, that it is doctrinally clear that a battery has been committed. But the victim may never raise the question because the goal foremost in her mind when she consults the lawyer is ending her relationship with the batterer. She is also likely to be concerned about the custody and support of her children, and perhaps about leaving with a fair share of accumulated property. Again, however, these concerns translate much more easily into traditional divorce rather than tort claims.

Even if the tort possibility is raised, we can imagine more than a few reasons why the battery victim and her lawyer would decide not to pursue it, especially in the case in which there is no remaining physical injury. In the basic pattern we imagined, the victim's avoidance efforts may have been successful in reducing the frequency of incidents considerably — and claims resting on some, or even all, of the physical strikings may now be barred by the statute of limitations. The price of having acted in ways designed to forestall further battering may, of course, have been great stress for the victim, but that stress does not itself present a battery claim. With only few recent incidents of physical attack, the victim and her lawyer might believe there is little prospect for obtaining an award large enough to warrant the additional lawyer time. Indeed, they may foresee that a battery claim will provoke some retaliatory legal strategy that will further increase the cost and hassle of the divorce process.

Other spousal battering victims may pursue no legal remedy against their abusers because they may fear further and more serious postseparation physical abuse. Others may find the psychological price of such a claim too high. They may feel personal shame in having been abused, leaving them either unwilling to reveal it in a public process, or believing it too painful to relive the abuse by testifying to it in a legal proceeding. Finally, whether warranted or not, many may doubt that their claims will be sympathetically received. They may worry that the court will dismiss their charges as manufactured, especially if they suffered abuse for some time and have no witnesses or physical evidence to offer. Some battering victims may assume that because of their own conduct judges and juries will not be sympathetic. Suppose the victim is a drug addict, or a drinker, or an adulterer, or a whiner and complainer. While. . . none of this remotely entitles the other spouse to engage in physical abuse, the victim may nonetheless fear that if she takes the matter to court she will be thought to have earned the beating.

Ellman and Sugarman note that battery claims brought at the marriage's end might be time-barred under the ordinary statute of limitations. Courts have developed doctrines under which the statute of limitations may be waived in some such cases, however. *See, e.g., Giovine v. Giovine*, 663 A.2d 109 (N.J. App. Div. 1995) (allowing wife to include claims for battering incidents that would ordinarily be time-barred, if she was victim of "battered woman's syndrome" and rendered incapable of bringing earlier action); *but see Mustilli v. Mustilli*, 671 A.2d 650, 651 (N.J. Super. Ct., Ch. Div., 1995) ("psychological paralysis" argument accepted in *Giovine* may only be made by a woman).

[b] Emotional Distress Claims Based Upon Adultery

In *Ruprecht v. Ruprecht*, 599 A.2d 604 (N.J. Super. Ct. Ch. Div. 1991), the parties' marriage appeared stable from its commencement in 1960 to about

1980, when the wife returned to work after the children had grown. Over the next decade there were several separations and during these years the husband repeatedly asked his wife whether she was having an affair with her boss, which she consistently denied. But soon after filing for divorce in 1990 the husband learned that she had maintained an adulterous relationship with her employer during her entire period of employment. He then added a claim for intentional infliction of emotional distress (IIED) to his divorce action. The New Jersey court decided that while interspousal IIED claims would be allowed in principle, these facts did not meet the "outrageousness" requirement which is part of such causes of action.

Ruprecht seems typical of the general pattern: IIED claims based upon adultery fail, the court holding either that there are general policy reasons for rejecting interspousal IIED claims altogether, or that in any event claims of unfaithfulness are insufficient to satisfy the tort's outrageousness requirement. *See, e.g., Whittington v. Whittington*, 766 S.W.2d 73, 74 (Ky. Ct. App. 1989) (holding conduct not outrageous); *Browning v. Browning*, 584 S.W.2d 406, 408 (Ky. Ct. App. 1979) (public policy bars emotional distress claim against wife for "openly consorting" with another man); *Alexander v. Inman*, 825 S.W.2d 102, 105 (Tenn. App. 1991) (holding extramarital affair is not sufficiently extreme or outrageous to support claim); *Perkins v. Dean*, 570 So. 2d 1217, 1219 (Ala. 1990) (extramarital affair may be morally or socially repugnant, but does not normally constitute outrageous conduct); *Weicker v. Weicker*, 22 N.Y.2d 8, 290 N.Y.S.2d 732, 237 N.E.2d 876 (1968) (rejecting IIED claims in marital context for policy reasons); *Pickering v. Pickering*, 434 N.W.2d 758, 761 (S.D. 1989) (holding IIED unavailable in divorce action for public policy reasons). Similar results have followed in claims for IIED or fraud arising from husband's discovery that wife had misled him over the paternity of a child born during the marriage. *See Steve H. v. Wendy S.*, 57 Cal. App. 4th 379, 67 Cal. Rptr. 2d 90 (1997) (based partly upon protecting child's interests, but also expressing skepticism about permitting IIED claims between divorcing spouses).

[c] Other Interspousal Claims for Outrageous Infliction of Emotional Distress

Emotional distress claims have often been allowed when the distress is said to arise from the defendant's battery and the IIED and battery claims are joined, *Noble v. Noble*, 761 P.2d 1369 (Utah 1988); *Stuart v. Stuart*, 421 N.W.2d 505 (Wis. 1988); *McCoy v. Cooke*, 419 N.W.2d 44 (Mich. App. 1988).

If one allows battery actions between divorcing or former spouses, there seems little reason to exclude companion emotional distress claims based upon the battering conduct. But the IIED claim adds little, because the damages available to the successful battery plaintiff in any event include compensation for severe emotional distress resulting from the battery. The more difficult question is how to treat the IIED claim that is for the most part based upon conduct that does *not* constitute assault or battery. Many courts have held that for such claims to be recognized in the marital setting, the threshold of "outrageousness" to be proven must be set very high. *See, e.g., Hakkila v. Hakkila*, 812 P.2d 1320 (N.M. App. 1991) (husband's insults, outbursts, minor assaults, and refraining from sexual intercourse insufficient to ground claim). The *Hakkila* court expressed concern that such claims become a basis for a public investigation into all aspects of a marriage. One might similarly worry that if allowed, tort claims for emotional distress might be routinely added to divorce petitions filed by bitter or spiteful spouses, perhaps as a strategy to increase their bargaining leverage in the property and spousal maintenance negotiations. Yet no similar phenomenon seems to have happened with battery claims. Is there reason to think the experience might be different?

Another possible concern is that there is no satisfactory standard of liability to apply to spousal claims for emotional distress. One scholar has observed that successful emotional distress claims arise almost entirely where there is some established relationship between the parties, such as landlord and tenant or debtor and creditor, that gives the court sufficient context for establishing limits of decency by which to judge whether the defendant's conduct was adequately outrageous. Givelber, *The Right to Minimum Social Decency and the Limits Of Evanhandedness: Intentional Infliction of Emotional Distress by Outrageous Conduct,* 82 COLUM. L. REV. 42, 46–50 (1982). Can we articulate analogous "limits of decency" for conduct within marriage? Surely there are some things that can quickly be identified as beyond the bounds — physical violence being the most obvious. But are there objective standards when one gets beyond physical mistreatment covered by the criminal law, to accusations of unacceptable emotional mistreatment? For claims of that sort, an objective standard may be hard to discern, and it may be equally difficult to extract one from the couple's own relationship. *See* Ellman & Sugarman, *supra*, 1318, *et seq.* Ellman and Sugarman suggest later in their article that interspousal tort claims should be permitted when the tortious conduct is also a criminal violation, but not otherwise. So, for example, battery and false imprisonment would be actionable, but outrage as well as many forms of invasion of privacy would not be. Does this solution make sense?

[d]   Criminal Conversation and Related Tort Actions

Among the traditional common law causes of action that once potentially applied to the break-up of a marriage were *criminal conversation* (an action by one spouse against someone who had committed adultery with his or her spouse) and *alienation of affection* (intentional interference with a marriage by a third party — usually involving an outside lover, but actual adultery need not be proven; and cases could also, in principle, be brought against friends and relatives who tried to break up a marriage). Most states, by statute or case-law, have abolished these "heart balm" actions (along with other related actions, including "breach of promise to marry" and "seduction" (brought by a parent against a man who had enticed a daughter of chaste character to have sex)). *See, e.g.*, Helsel v. Noellsch, 107 S.W.3d 231 (Mo. 2003) (abolishing the tort of alienation of affection); MINN. STAT. § 553.01 (2002) (abolishing the causes of action of breach of promise to marry, seduction, alienation of affection, and criminal conversation). While only a handful of states still recognize causes of action for alienation of affection or criminal conversation, one can still find a few large verdicts being returned on such actions. *E.g.*,

Veeder v. Kennedy, 589 N.W.2d 610 (S.D. 1999) (upholding a $265,000 judgment for alienation of affection); *Hutelmyer v. Cox*, 514 S.E.2d 554 (N.C. App. 1999) (upholding a judgment of one million dollars for criminal conversation and alienation of affection); *Jones v. Swanson*, 341 F.3d 723 (8th Cir. 2003) (affirming a large alienation of affection judgment subject to acceptance of a remittitur, which would reduce a judgment of $450,000 in compensatory damages and $500,000 in punitive damages to $150,000 compensatory and $250,000 punitive). (The history and current law relating to the causes of actions discussed in this Note are discussed at greater length in Chapter 2.)

PROBLEMS

Problem 4-28. At marriage, Faith and Hubert are devout members of an orthodox religious congregation which understands its sacred texts to treat both homosexuality and adultery as an outrage. Ten years after their marriage Faith realizes, when she finds herself in love with another woman, that she is a lesbian — a truth that she had denied to herself during her years of religious training. When she tells Hubert of her new self-understanding and of her new relationship, he not only seeks divorce but sues for intentional infliction of emotional distress. He claims that in the context of their marriage, her adulterous lesbian affair is outrageous conduct. What result? What should be the result?

Problem 4-29. Joan repeatedly tells her husband John that she prefers privacy while dressing. After he nonetheless enters their bedroom without knocking on several occasions, she files a tort claim for invasion of privacy. Assume that the claim would clearly be good if the parties were strangers. What result here? What should be the result?

Problem 4-30. Henrietta and Horace have a stormy relationship, caused in part by Henrietta's temper and impulsive behavior. After a bout of yelling and screaming when Horace refused to apologize for making plans with his family for Thanksgiving, rather than hers, Henrietta called the local police and filed a formal complaint accusing Horace of beating her. The report was entirely false, as Horace had never attacked her physically nor had he ever threatened to do so. Horace nonetheless spent 24 hours in jail until his lawyer obtained his release, and he was not exonerated for another two months. During that two-month period Henrietta made repeated phone calls not only to Horace but also to other members of his accounting firm, accusing him of domestic violence. As a result of her behavior, Horace had to resign from the firm. In his subsequent divorce action against Henrietta, he joins tort claims for damages for false imprisonment and intentional infliction of emotional distress, as well as compensation for his lost employment. What result? What should be the result?

Problem 4-31. Unbeknownst to Chastity, her husband Clyde sets up a digital camera in their bedroom which takes pictures of their lovemaking. He posts those pictures on the Internet. She discovers this when a coworker tells her he enjoyed viewing them and asks her out to lunch. She files for divorce and adds a tort claim for invasion of privacy. What result? What should be the result? Does it matter whether the pictures are legally obscene? Would it matter if Clyde was provoked by anger at learning that Chastity has performed a striptease at the office Christmas party?

Chapter 5

CHILD SUPPORT

INTRODUCTION

All American jurisdictions recognize a parental duty to support minor children. In the intact family, the state intervenes only in the rare case where support is so inadequate as to constitute child neglect. At divorce, however, the state must be willing to set and enforce child support owed by the non-custodial parent to the custodial household. These orders are the subject of this chapter. Most support rules apply equally to non-marital children, but the special problems in enforcing such support obligations are covered in Chapter 9.

At one time, the support duty was paternal rather than parental. The mother's lack of financial responsibility was explained by the wife's common law disabilities and the natural differences between the sexes. Any duty imposed on the mother was secondary to the father's obligation. Today the law imposes an equal duty of support on mothers and fathers, a regime generally believed mandated by the Fourteenth Amendment or by state equal rights amendments. *Cotton v. Municipal Court,* 130 Cal. Rptr. 876 (App. 1976); Annot., *Constitutionality of Gender-Based Classifications in Criminal Laws Proscribing Nonsupport of Spouse or Child,* 14 A.L.R.4th 717 (1982); *but see In re Marriage of Bruske,* 656 S.W.2d 288 (Mo. App. 1983).

The support duty is not based upon the obligor's consent to sexual relations, much less intent to conceive a child. For example, in *State ex rel. Hermesmann v. Seyer,* 847 P.2d 1273 (Kan. 1993), the defendant (a 12-year old) had a sexual relationship with his 16-year-old babysitter. After a child was born, the defendant argued in a support action that, because he was protected by the statutory rape law, he was legally incapable of giving consent to the intercourse which produced the child. The court found his age irrelevant, concluding that "as a father he has a common-law duty, as well as a statutory duty, to support his child." *See also County of San Luis Obispo v. Nathaniel J.,* 50 Cal. App. 4th 842 (1996) (rejects same defense where mother was convicted of statutory rape of father); *Jevning v. Cichos,* 499 N.W.2d 515 (Minn. App. 1993) (20-year-old woman successful in support suit against 15-year-old male). Indeed, the precise rationale for imposing the duty to support children on their parents is rarely discussed or articulated. *See* Altman, *A Theory of Child Support,* 17 INT. J. L., POL'Y & FAM. 173 (2003) (arguing private child support duties should be viewed "primarily as remedies for parental wrongs" a theory which "has specific consequences for issues of support allocation, including who should be declared a parent, and how much child support parents owe"); Sheldon, *Unwilling Fathers and Abortion: Terminating Men's Child Support Obligations?,* 66 MODERN L. REV. 175 (2003) (arguing there is no explanation for compelling support from the father given the mother's exclusive control over the procreation decision and arguing that therefore support should be a public, not a private, obligation).

Section A of this chapter outlines the contours of the duty of support. Section B covers reduction of the legal obligation to a specific amount of support. Section C discusses enforcement of support orders. Section D focuses on interstate support issues.

§ A. DUTY OF SUPPORT

[1] DURATION

[a] General Rule

At the very least, parents must support their children during the child's minority or, in some states, until graduation from high school. *See, e.g.,* KAN. STAT. ANN. § 60-1610(a) (2001) (duty lasts through high school); *Carr v. Carr,* 834 P.2d 970 (Okla. 1992) (statute extends duty to 19th birthday for high school students); *Walworth v. Klauder,* 615 So. 2d 219 (Fla. App. 1993) (same); *Freyer v. Freyer,* 427 N.W.2d 348 (N. D. 1988) (duty lasts through high school); *Paaso v. Paaso,* 428 N.W.2d 724 (Mich. App. 1988) (reduction of age of majority to 18 not intended to cut off support of high school students).

Some states once ended the obligation to support daughters earlier than the obligation to support sons, on the assumption that women were ready for their life's work — housewifery — sooner than men, who need more education for their tasks. This distinction was held to violate the Equal Protection Clause. *Stanton v. Stanton,* 421 U.S. 7 (1975); *Stanton v. Stanton,* 429 U.S. 501 (1977).

Despite the general rule, some circumstances may extend the support obligation into the child's majority and other circumstances may extinguish the obligation before the child reaches majority.

[b] Post-Majority Support for Disabled Children

The disabled child incapable of self-support is a widely recognized exception to the general rule terminating the support obligation at the child's majority. *See, e.g.,* ARIZ. REV. STAT. ANN. § 25-320 B (Supp. 2003); HAWAII REV. STAT. § 580-47(a) (2001 Cum. Supp.); TEX. FAM. CODE ANN. § 154.001(a)(4) (2002); *Cohn v. Cohn,* 934 P.2d 279 (N.M. App. 1997) (common law duty to support handicapped adult whose disability dates from minority); *Streb v. Streb,* 774 P.2d 798 (Alaska 1989); *Nelson v. Nelson,* 548 A.2d 109 (D.C. App. 1988) (surveying authority in other states); *but see Pierce v. Pierce,* 770 A.2d 867 (R.I. 2001) (discussing statute which overruled judicial precedent authorizing extended support for disabled children); *In re Thurmond,* 715 N.E. 2d 814 (Ill. App. 1999) (overturning extended support order for "slow learner" who had graduated from high school, had a job and been accepted to college).

States recognizing a duty to support disabled children split on whether the disability must exist before the child reaches majority. *Compare Towery v. Towery,* 685 S.W.2d 155 (Ark. 1985) (no duty when crippling injury occurred after majority) with *Racherbaumer v. Racherbaumer,* 844 S.W.2d 502 (Mo. App. 1992) (duty exists where disabled child is adult at time of divorce) and *Riggs v. Riggs,* 578 S.E.2d 3 (S.C. 2003) (support can be ordered where genetic degenerative disease did not reveal itself until adulthood, 8 years after divorce).

[c] Post-Majority Support for Higher Education

NOTES

1. ***Authority to Award Post-Majority Educational Support.*** Even when the age of majority in most states was 21, a college education was often held outside the parental child support obligation. *See* Note, *Educational Support Obligations of Noncustodial Parents,* 36 RUTG. L. REV. 588, 593–603 (1984). By contrast, many current statutes specifically authorize the award of post-majority parental support for higher education. *See, e.g.,* COLO. REV. STAT. ANN. § 14-10-115 (1.5)(b)(I) (2002 Supp.) ("if the court finds it appropriate for the parents to contribute to the costs of a program of postsecondary education"); HAW. REV. STAT. § 580-47(a) (2001 Cum. Supp.); ILL. REV. STAT. ch. 750, § 5/513 (2003 Supp.); IND. CODE ANN. § 31-16-6-2 (1997); MO. ANN. STAT. § 452.340(5) (2003); N.H. REV. STAT. ANN. § 458:20 (1997); N.J. REV. STAT. ANN. § 2A:34-23(a)(5) (2000); N.Y. DOM. REL. LAW § 240(1-b) (b)(2) (2003 Supp.) (support may include amounts for the "education of any unemancipated child under the age of twenty-one years"); OR. REV. STAT. § 107.108 (1998 Supp.); WASH. REV. CODE Ch. 26.19, Child Support Schedule Appendix, *Postsecondary Education Standards* (2003 Supp.); W. VA. CODE § 48-13-702(2001).

Awards for post-majority educational support are not necessarily limited to undergraduate school. *See, e.g., Ross v. Ross,* 400 A.2d 1233 (N.J. Super. 1979) (law school); *Kopp v. Turley,* 518 A.2d 588 (Pa. Super. 1986) (commercial art school); *but see In re Holderrieth,* 536 N.E.2d 946 (Ill. App. 1989) (no support for trade school); *cf. delCastillo v. delCastillo,* 617 A.2d 26 (Pa. Super. 1992) (agreement to fund education "beyond high school" excludes graduate school expenses). However, some courts have been very careful to separate educational costs from general support. *See, e.g., In re: Gilmore,* 803 A.2d 601 (N.H. 2002) (transportation, clothing, medical and dental coverage not properly included in "educational expenses"); *Meek v. Warren,* 726 So. 2d 1292 (Miss. App. 1998). College expense statutes often require the child to inform the non-custodial parent of academic progress and to enroll and complete a minimum amount of credits to continue eligibility. *See Mandel v. Eagleton,* 90 S.W.3d 527 (Mo. App. 2002) (failure to enroll in statutory minimum of college credits is an emancipation, rendering child ineligible for future support); *but see Rogers v. Rogers,* 87 S.W.3d 368 (Mo. App. 2002) (failure to provide transcripts to non-custodial parent does not authorize reimbursement of college expenses already paid).

By contrast, some courts refuse to authorize post-majority support for educational purposes, relying "on the argument that if the marriage had continued, the parents would have been free to decide not to send their child to college, and that divorce should not deprive them of that discretion." CLARK,

THE LAW OF DOMESTIC RELATIONS, § 17.1 at 718 (2d ed. 1988). *See, e.g., Dowling v. Dowling,* 679 P.2d 480 (Alaska 1984); *In re Plummer,* 735 P.2d 165 (Colo. 1987); *Grapin v. Grapin,* 450 So. 2d 853 (Fla. 1984); *Cariseo v. Cariseo,* 459 A.2d 523 (Conn. 1983); *Jones v. Jones,* 257 S.E.2d 537 (Ga. 1979); *Peterson v. Peterson,* 319 N.W.2d 414 (Minn. 1982). That argument, however, seems weak because parents in intact families are generally free to choose any level of support above the minimal threshold needed to avoid liability for neglect while child support awards always exceed this minimum if parental resources permit.

Divorced parents have argued that requiring support for a college education is unconstitutional, claiming an equal protection violation because married parents are not similarly obligated. Most courts reject such arguments, usually citing state interests in educating its youth and in ameliorating the particular hardships for children of divorce. *See, e.g. In re Crocker,* 22 P.3d 759 (Or. 2001); *Kohring v. Snodgrass,* 999 S.W.2d 229 Mo. 1999); *LeClair v. LeClair,* 624 A.2d 1350 (N.H. 1993) (rational to conclude that "absent judicial involvement, children of divorce may be less likely than children of intact families to receive college financial support from both . . . parents"); *Kujawinski v. Kujawinski,* 376 N.E.2d 1382 (Ill. 1978); *but see Curtis v. Kline,* 666 A.2d 265 (Pa. 1995) (holding legislation authorizing post-majority educational support violates federal Equal Protection Clause). At least one state allows courts to order post-majority support for children of divorce but not for non-marital children. This law was sustained over an Equal Protection challenge in *Johnson v. Louis,* 654 N.W.2d 886 (Iowa 2002).

Discussion of post-majority educational support by non-custodial parents can be found in Horan, *Postminority Support for College Education — A Legally Enforceable Obligation in Divorce Proceedings?,* 20 FAM. L.Q. 589 (1987); Annot., *Responsibility of Noncustodial Divorced Parent to Pay for, or Contribute to, Costs of Child's College Education,* 99 A.L.R.3d 322 (1980).

2. *Indirect Educational Support.* Courts that cannot directly order post-majority college support sometimes employ indirect approaches to achieve this goal. Some require maintenance of a trust or insurance policy during minority, with proceeds paid for college education after the child reaches majority. *Nash v. Mulle,* 846 S.W.2d 803 (Tenn. 1993) (while *payments* cannot be ordered after child is adult, no reason why *benefits* of payments cannot continue into child's majority); *In re Paternity of Tukker M.O.,* 544 N.W.2d 417 (Wis. 1996). Another method has been to include tuition money for child in mother's alimony. *Nicolay v. Nicolay,* 387 So. 2d 500 (Fla. App. 1980); *but see Grapin, supra,* Note 1 (rejecting this as a subterfuge).

In most states, even though a divorce court cannot order post-majority support, a decree can incorporate a parental agreement to that effect, thus establishing an enforceable obligation. *See, e.g.,* CAL. FAM. CODE § 3587 (1994) (". . .the court has the authority to approve a stipulated agreement . . . for the support of an adult child or for the continuation of child support after [age 18] and to make a support order to effectuate the agreement"); VT. STAT. ANN. tit. 15, § 659(b) (2002) ("If the parties agree, the court may include . . . an additional amount designated for the purpose of providing for postsecondary education"); *Hayward v. Lawrence,* 312 S.E.2d 609 (Ga. 1984) (father in contempt for failing to comply with incorporated agreement); *Acrey v. Acrey*, 356 S.E.2d 437 (S.C. App. 1987). Alternatively, the court may decline to incorporate a parental agreement into the divorce decree, but enforce it as a contract. *Solomon v. Findley*, 808 P.2d 294 (Ariz. 1991); *Madson v. Madson*, 636 So. 2d 759 (Fla. App. 1994) (separation agreement announcing father's "moral obligation" and "intention" to support children through college is unenforceable).

3. Can An Obligor Condition Support on Student's Behavior? In *Mayes v. Fisher*, 854 S.W.2d 430 (Mo. App. 1993), the court rejected the obligor's claim that his daughter's enrollment in a single community college course was a "sham" created solely to extend his support obligation. The court found the daughter's financial circumstances did not permit her to enroll in more courses and the limited nature of her course load did not justify termination of the support obligation. In *In re Sandlin*, 831 P.2d 64 (Ore. App. 1992), the obligor sought to eliminate support payments to his college-student daughter who was living with her boyfriend. Finding the statutory eligibility requirements had been met, the court found the daughter's lifestyle irrelevant to the support issue.

Other obligors have been treated more sympathetically. In *Moss v. Nedas*, 674 A.2d 174 (N.J. Super. App. Div. 1996), the court found daughter had treated obligor solely as a "wallet" when, in violation of prior court orders, the father was denied input into her selection of a college and information on her performance at school. The appellate court found the "obstructive behavior" justified terminating the support obligation. *See also McKay v. McKay*, 644 N.E.2d 164 (Ind. App. 1994) (college student's refusal to have any relationship with father relieves obligor of duty of support).

4. The ALI Approach. Section 3.12 of the *ALI Principles* makes support for college, along with other important "life opportunities," dependent upon an inquiry into both the parental resources and the likelihood that such support would have been forthcoming had there been no divorce. See page 477 of this chapter.

PROBLEMS

Problem 5-1. Karen Miller relates the following: After 22 years of marriage, she and David separated in December of their son Caleb's final year in high school. Caleb (then 18) remained in the marital home with Karen. Soon after, however, she and Caleb began having problems. He violated his curfew, refused to study and neglected household chores. Several violent arguments ensued, during which Caleb shoved her and spat in her face. In March, he moved in with his father and ceased communication with her.

After graduating from high school, Caleb entered the University of Richmond, earning a 3.0 grade point average as a freshman. His father paid all educational expenses and Caleb returned to his father's home during vacations. After his freshman year, he transferred to Occidental College in California. Before enrolling there, Caleb (through his father) filed a support action seeking $5,000 toward his college expenses. Karen and David are both fairly well-off financially. Karen tells you, "I can afford it, but I don't think

I need to pay." Caleb wants no communication with his mother. The parents are not divorced.

In David and Karen's jurisdiction a divorce court has power to order post-majority support for educational purposes. The leading appellate case directs trial courts to consider two factors in deciding whether to order support: "the child's desire and ability to successfully pursue post-secondary education and the parents' ability to contribute to that effort without undue hardship." Lower court cases have additionally considered the child's independent financial resources, whether private school is appropriate for the child and parental educational background. The jurisdiction has a no-fault divorce statute.

How would you argue on behalf of Karen and what arguments would you expect to hear from opposing counsel?

Problem 5-2. Jerry and Mary's divorce decree incorporated the following provision from their separation agreement: "Mary will pay all of the children's college expenses, including room, board, tuition, reasonable transportation expenses, school supplies and similar costs. She will have a say in the choice of college for each child and will have the right to approve or disapprove a particular college but will exercise that right in a reasonable fashion." Three years after the divorce, Mary filed a motion to terminate her support obligation for the couple's second child, Oren. The motion alleged that Oren had turned 18, graduated from high school and was not attending college. The relevant age of majority was 18. At a pre-trial conference, Mary learned for the first time that Oren had indeed been enrolled in community college for a semester and was in the middle of his second semester. She was unaware of these developments because she had not exercised any visitation with Oren or communicated with him in the three years since the divorce. She now insists that she need not provide college support because the divorce provision has been violated. How should the court rule on her claim?

Problem 5-3. Fred and Ethel were divorced in Georgia in 1991, when their daughter, Michelle, was 12. The decree ordered weekly support payments by Fred. The decree was silent about support beyond the age of 18, Georgia's age of majority, at which time all support obligations stop. Ethel and Michelle moved to Columbia, South Carolina, while Fred remains in Georgia in a border town from which he commutes daily to his job as a physician in South Carolina. He has paid his support regularly and exercises his visitation rights. Michelle has done fairly well academically in high school. South Carolina law is clear that an order for post-majority support for educational purposes is within judicial discretion, upon consideration of factors such as parental ability to so provide, the child's ability to succeed and the advantages which might be obtained by such an education. Michelle has been accepted at a private college and her mother has retained you to represent them. What are the issues and how would you argue on behalf of your client?

Problem 5-4. Sam and Janet were divorced when their daughter Ilene was 15. Ilene had been diagnosed with an autism-related chronic condition (Asperger's syndrome) for which she had begun receiving treatment when she was 9. Janet obtained custody of Ilene and Sam was ordered to pay support until Ilene turned 21. Now, 35 years later, Ilene is 50, having lived with her mother since the divorce. Janet has just died and Ilene comes to your office wondering if she might be able to obtain support from Sam, who is now very wealthy. Ilene has never worked and is unable to do so. She had been supported by Janet alone since the support order terminated on her 21st birthday. What do you advise her?

[d] Pre-Majority Termination of Support

Many states adhere to the common law rule terminating the support obligation with the obligor's death. *See, e.g., Benson v. Patterson*, 830 A.2d 966 (Pa. 2003) (reviewing case law, declaring common law rule to be the majority rule); *Hirst v. Dugan*, 611 A.2d 616 (N.H. 1992) (duty to marital and non-marital children terminated); TEX. FAM. CODE ANN. § 154.006 (2002). This is said to be consistent with the "generally accepted view in American law that a parent may disinherit his minor children if he wishes. . . ." CLARK, THE LAW OF DOMESTIC RELATIONS § 17.2 at p. 733 (2d ed. 1988). Even in states following this rule, the parties may agree that support shall survive the obligor's death. *See, e.g., In re North Carolina Inheritance Taxes*, 277 S.E.2d 403 (N.C. 1981). This is often accomplished by requiring the obligor to maintain life insurance naming the child as beneficiary.

In contrast, the Model Marriage and Divorce Act § 316(c) provides that on the obligor's death "the amount of support may be modified, revoked, or commuted to a lump sum payment, to the extent just and appropriate. . . ." In rejecting an automatic cutoff, states adopting this view may recognize that "disinherited children are in fact protected where the marriage does not end in divorce, since in most states the surviving spouse is given a statutory forced share of the decedent's estate which can then be subjected to the child's claim for support." CLARK, *supra. See Kujawinski v. Kujawinski*, 376 N.E.2d 1382 (Ill. 1978). Some courts find power to order post-death support where the statute is silent. *See, e.g., Knowles v. Thompson*, 697 A.2d 335 (Vt. 1997) (court can order obligor to purchase life insurance with children as beneficiaries because "it is reasonable to assume that [obligor] would have provided for his children in his will"); *Scott v. Wagoner*, 400 S.E.2d 556 (W. Va. 1990) (post-death support can be ordered if "compelling equitable considerations" exist); *Koidl v. Schreiber*, 520 A.2d 759 (N.J. Super. 1986); Annot., *Death of Parent as Affecting Decree for Support of Child*, 14 A.L.R.5th 557 (1993); Annot., *Divorce: Provision in Decree That One Party Obtain or Maintain Life Insurance for Benefit of Other Party or Child*, 59 A.L.R.3d 9 (1974).

Another event terminating the support obligation before majority is emancipation. At common law, the minor child's marriage or entry into the military service terminated or suspended the parental support obligation. *See Bishop v. Bishop*, 671 A.2d 644 (N.J. Super. Ch. Div. 1995) (child enrolled at United States Military Academy is, by definition, emancipated); *Porath v. McVey*, 884 S.W.2d 692 (Mo. App. 1994) (same); Katz, Schroeder & Sidman, *Emancipating Our Children — Coming of Legal Age in America*, 7 FAM. L.Q. 211 (1973). Many current statutes establish procedures for judicial emancipation at the behest of the child or, sometimes, the parent. They vary widely on the standard for and the scope of an emancipation. Several commentators have urged a uniform emancipation statute. *See, e.g.*, Cady, *Emancipation of Minors*, 12 CONN. L. REV. 62 (1979); Comment, *The Uncertain Status of the Emancipated*

Minor: Why We Need a Uniform Statutory Emancipation of Minors Act (USEMA), 15 U. SAN FRAN. L. REV. 473 (1981); *see also* Note, *The Status of Emancipated Minors in Iowa: The Case for a Clearly Drafted Statute*, 44 DRAKE L. REV. 39 (1995).

Many cases find a child emancipated because of his or her behavior. *See, e.g.*, *Caldwell v. Caldwell*, 823 So. 2d 1216 (Miss. App. 2002) (emancipation where daughter had non-marital child, quit school, chose not to seek employment and accepted child support from child's father); *P.K. v. M.K.*, 19 FAM. L. REP. 1362 (N.Y. Fam. Ct. 1993) (child's unreasonable refusal to permit visitation justifies suspension of support); *Hunter v. Hulgan*, 609 So. 2d 5 (Ala. Civ. App. 1992) (support termination justified by 16-year-old's marriage and fatherhood of child). A child's gainful employment has been held to constitute emancipation. In *Ware v. Ware*, 391 S.E.2d 887 (Va. App. 1990), the divorce decree obligated the father to support the children until majority or until they "married, died, or become otherwise emancipated." The court held a 17-year-old daughter earning over $15,000 annually in a full-time job while living with her mother was emancipated. The court held the parties contemplated an emancipation when the child "earned sufficient funds to fully provide for herself."

While some cases declare an emancipation on extreme facts, generally courts are reluctant to terminate support obligations based on the child's behavior. *See, e.g.*, *In re Schoby*, 4 P.3d 604 (Kan. 2000) (16-year-old boy's marriage did not automatically terminate support obligation; divorce decree incorporating agreement that support would be terminated by marriage not dispositive); *Dunson v. Dunson*, 769 N.E.2d 1120 (Ind. 2002) (child living outside home not emancipated because he was not self-supporting); *Carroll v. Carroll*, 593 So. 2d 1131 (Fla. App. 1992) (support continued where child had successfully petitioned to terminate obligor's visitation rights); *Allison C. v. Susan C.*, 598 N.Y.S.2d 970 (App. Div. 1993) (lack of parent-child contact was obligor's fault); *Wulff v. Wulff*, 500 N.W.2d 845 (Neb. 1993) (emancipation rescinded where child who had left home and given birth returned to the parental home); *In re Brown*, 597 N.E.2d 1297 (Ind. App. 1992) (17-year-old's refusal to visit non-custodial parent does not justify finding of emancipation); *Trosky v. Mann*, 581 A.2d 177 (Pa. Super. 1990) (imposing obligation where 16-year-old said he "wanted absolutely nothing" from his parents after leaving home; court found child incapable of self-support and unwelcome in his parents' home).

PROBLEM

Problem 5-5. You are a Legal Aid attorney who works with prisoners. Fred Felon reports he was divorced from Sally three years ago and ordered to pay $50 per week support for their child. Last month, he was convicted of theft and incarcerated for a term of six-to-ten years. The earliest he will be eligible for release is in three years. He earns approximately $24 a week while in prison. He wants relief from his support obligation. If you seek to modify or suspend his obligations during his imprisonment, what counter-arguments do you expect from Sally? How should the court decide such a suit? Is it relevant that Fred was current on his obligations upon entering prison? Is it relevant that he had been awarded one-half the equity in the parties' marital home (the only marital asset) at the time of divorce?

[2] SUPPORT OF STEP-CHILDREN

Step-relationships are established by the remarriage of a widowed or divorced parent. Census Bureau statistics indicate 7.25 million children (15.9% of all children in the U.S.) were living with a step-parent in 1990. *See* U.S. Dep't of Commerce, Bureau of the Census, *Marriage, Divorce, and Remarriage in the 1990s*, P-23, no. 180 at 10, 12 (Oct. 1992). In the late 1980s, it was estimated that 25% of children then alive would live with a step-parent by the age of 16. Zill, *Behavior, Achievement, and Health Problems Among Children in Stepfamilies: Findings from a National Survey of Child Health* in THE IMPACT OF DIVORCE, SINGLE PARENTING AND STEPPARENTING ON CHILDREN 325–68 (Hetherington & Arasteh eds. 1988). Another study, based on data from the same general period, estimated between 33% and 40% of all U.S. children then alive eventually would live at some point with a step-parent. HUNTLEY, UNDERSTANDING STEPFAMILIES: IMPLICATIONS FOR ASSESSMENT AND TREATMENT at ix (1995) (citing 1988–89 study). More recent data, based on survey questions in the 2000 Census different from those used in the earlier data collection, found approximately 5.2% of all children who lived with a householder were the step-child of the householder. U.S. Dep't of Commerce, Bureau of the Census, *Adopted Children and Stepchildren: 2000*, Census 2000 Special Reports, CENSR-6RV, p. 2 (Oct. 2003). This figure does not include a householder's biological children who live with a step-parent married to the householder.

[a]   General Rule of Non-Liability

At common law, the step-relationship itself imposed no legally enforceable support obligation. Some courts held that accepting a step-child into one's home established an obligation to support because the step-parent was acting *in loco parentis*, but this "obligation" was terminable at will by the step-parent. Today, similar rules are usually provided by statute, see, *e.g.*, DEL. CODE ANN. tit. 13, § 501(b) (1999) (expanding duty to include cohabitors if natural parent is not supporting); MONT. CODE ANN. § 40-6-217 (2003); N.D. CENT. CODE § 14-09-09 (1997), or by judicial decision. *See In re Farrell*, 835 P.2d 267 (Wash. App. 1992) (holding state family expense statute which included stepchildren did not change common law rule); *but see Harmon v. Dep't of Soc. & Health Servs.*, 922 P.2d 201 (Wash. App. 1996) (rejecting *Farrell*'s interpretation of the statute). This traditional rule creates step-parent obligations that are illusory at best. No support can be ordered at divorce or separation and, during the marriage between parent and step-parent, the obligation — like all support obligations in the intact family — is satisfied by minimal support. Practically, of course, a step-parent in fact does support the child by virtue of sharing the same household. This reality presumably was the basis of older federal law requiring states to include stepparent income in determining the eligibility of a child's family for public assistance. 42 U.S.C. § 602(a)(31) (Supp. 1996). Ramsey & Masson, *Stepparent Support of Stepchildren: A Comparative Analysis of Policies and Problems in the American and English*

Experience, 36 SYRACUSE L. REV. 659 (1985). Under the 1996 welfare reform act (the Personal Responsibility and Work Opportunity Reconciliation Act), states can determine for themselves how to treat step-parental income.

[b] Imposing Liability on Step-Parents

One exception to the limited support liability of step-parents are family expense statutes which protect creditors who provide goods and services to family members including step-children. WASH. REV. CODE ANN. § 26.16.205 (1997). Of potentially greater significance is the occasional imposition of step-parent support obligations through equitable estoppel. *Miller v. Miller,* 478 A.2d 351 (N.J. 1984), estopped a divorcing step-parent from denying a post-divorce obligation to support his step-children. During the marriage, defendant tore up support checks from the natural father, who was serving a prison term for narcotics offenses, not wanting to be connected to narcotics activities. *See also W v. W.,* 779 A.2d 716 (Conn. 2001) (defendant had represented himself as father for 12 years, interfered with relationship with natural father and caused detrimental reliance by child).

Step-parents have been held liable for post-divorce support via contract. *See Dewey v. Dewey,* 886 P.2d 623 (Alaska 1994); *Duffey v. Duffey,* 438 S.E.2d 445 (N.C. App. 1994) (enforcing separation agreement, but finding step-parent secondarily liable to biological parents); *In re Marriage of Dawley,* 551 P.2d 323 (Cal. 1976) (enforcing antenuptial agreement to support wife's child for 14 months, a period longer than the marriage lasted); *L. v. L.,* 497 S.W.2d 840 (Mo. App. 1973) (enforcing pre-marital promise to "treat the child as his" during and after marriage). In a related fact pattern, courts have acknowledged that grandparents might have a support obligation, either through contract, *Mooney v. Mooney,* 538 S.E.2d 864 (Ga. App. 2000), or the doctrine of equitable adoption. *Johnson v. Johnson,* 617 N.W.2d 97 (N.D. 2000). Guardianship status alone, without a support agreement, has been held not to create a support obligation. *Favrow v. Vargas,* 647 A.2d 731 (Conn. 1994); *Tilley v. Tilley,* 489 N.W.2d 185 (Mich. App. 1992). *See generally,* Annot., *Stepparent's Postdivorce Duty to Support Stepchild,* 44 A.L.R.4th 520 (1986).

For discussions of the obligations of step-parents, see Fisher, *Stepparent Responsibility for Child Support in California's Community Property System,* 22 LOYOLA L. REV. 73 (1988); Mahoney, *Stepfamilies in the Federal Law,* 48 PITT. L. REV. 491 (1987) (focusing on Social Security programs and immigration); Bartlett, *Rethinking Parenthood as an Exclusive Status: The Need for Legal Alternatives When the Premise of the Nuclear Family Has Failed,* 70 VA. L. REV. 879, 912 *et seq.* (1984) (discussing support, custody and visitation). For a recent article urging expansion of the duty to support beyond biological parenthood, see Nolan, *Legal Strangers and the Duty of Support: Beyond the Biological Tie — But How Far Beyond the Marital Tie?,* 41 SANTA CLARA L. REV. 1 (2000) (argues duty should extend to legal strangers "to the extent that their own actions and conduct would bind them under the principles of *in loco parentis,* contract law, or equitable estoppel").

[c] Same-Sex Partners as Step-Parents?

The status of a same-sex partner of a biological parent, which could be analogized to a stepparent, is treated in Chapter 9 at pp. 1043-73.

[3] RELATIONSHIP BETWEEN VISITATION AND SUPPORT OBLIGATIONS

Visitation and support are often intertwined in the minds of divorced parents. A support obligor may feel he need not pay child support when the custodial parent has interfered with his access to the child, and a custodial parent may feel justified in limiting or denying access to a non-custodial parent who is in arrears.

Most states treat child support and visitation as independent obligations. This means one parent cannot defend a failure to pay support or allow visitation with evidence of the other parent's failure to comply with the court order. This ban on "self-help" does not necessarily bar a *court* from linking the obligations, however, as a tool of enforcement — an approach on which the states are split. Under Model Marriage and Divorce Act (MMDA) § 315, a party's failure to comply with the decree does not affect "the obligation of the other party to make payments for support or maintenance or to permit visitation . . .; but he may move the court to grant an appropriate order." The MMDA thus allows a wronged parent to seek a judicial order conditioning support on visitation, or visitation on support. *See also* MINN. STAT. ANN. § 518.612 (2002). By contrast, under the Uniform Interstate Family Support Act § 305(d) the court "may not condition the payment of a support order . . . upon compliance . . . with provisions for visitation."

Some state statutes specifically authorize decrees linking visitation and support obligations. *See, e.g.,* OR. REV. STAT. § 107.431 (1998 Supp.). A New York statute permitting suspension of alimony or cancellation of arrears for the withholding of visitation rights was applied to child support, *Vigo v. Vigo,* 467 N.Y.S.2d 436 (App. 1983); *but see* N.Y. DOM. REL. LAW § 241 (1999) (making clear that any suspension must be prospective and not retroactive); *Smith v. Bombard,* 741 N.Y.S.2d 336 (App. Div. 2002). For more on this topic, see Ellman, *Should Visitation Denial Affect the Obligation to Pay Support?,* in COMANOR, ed., THE LAW AND ECONOMICS OF CHILD SUPPORT PAYMENTS (2004), reprinted in _____ ARIZ. ST. L.J. _____ (2004).

A support obligor who engages in self-help and ceases payments when the other parent refuses to permit visitation may also find that the rule against retroactive modification of support arrearages bars consideration of his claim on the merits. See pp. 505-507 of this chapter.

PROBLEMS

Problem 5-6. Ward and June's marriage produced two sons, Wallace and Theodore. The couple divorced after ten years and June was ordered to pay Ward, the custodial parent, $250 monthly in support. Two years later, Ward married a wealthy nightclub entertainer, Margaret Anderson. Euphoria, where all relevant events occurred, has a law requiring step-parents who "accept children of their spouse into their home" to support them while they are in the home.

Ward and Margaret moved with the boys to an expensive home. June, who was earning $25,000 annually when she and Ward divorced, now earns

$30,000 annually. She asks you whether, in light of the boys' new living situation, she can seek a reduction in her child support payments. What is your response?

Problem 5-7. Your client Bill is involved in a bitter divorce with Camilla. The couple has two children, a 13-year-old girl and a 16-year-old boy. In the divorce decree, the judge has ordered maintenance, property division, and $500 monthly support for the two children. Additionally, because the parents are well-educated and Bill's financial resources are ample, he's been ordered to buy $150,000 of life insurance with the two children as beneficiaries.

The order provides that if Bill dies while either child is in college or under the age of 19, the insurance proceeds shall be put in a trust fund to be used for costs at their chosen undergraduate school and "graduate education if appropriate." They are to split any funds remaining when the younger turns 30. Bill wants to appeal the insurance portion of the order. What will you need to know about your state's law and how will you argue the case?

Problem 5-8. Soon after Anne married John, he adopted her four children from her marriage to Bill. Ten years later John was ordered, in his divorce from Anne, to pay $320 monthly support. After the divorce, Anne got back together with Bill, who moved into the house where she lived with the children.

Anne and Bill remarried and relocated (with the children) from Ohio, where all parties had always lived, to California. Bill now wanted to be their legal father again. Anne asked John for his consent. "After all," she said, "he's their real father, he'll be living with them in California and you've had difficulties with them anyway." John agreed and signed a "Waiver of Notice and Consent to Adoption" which permitted an adoption without notice to him.

Bill filed for adoption as soon as the family arrived in California in the fall of 2003. The children enrolled in school using his last name. Later in the fall, however, because of serious marital troubles and the children's sudden reluctance, Bill and Anne postponed the adoption hearing. In February, Anne wrote John, relating the problems and asking him to resume his support which he had halted when he signed the consent to adoption. In April 2004, Bill and Anne were divorced and no support was ordered. Immediately thereafter, Anne and the children returned to Ohio.

Anne has filed an action in an appropriate Ohio court seeking child support arrearages since John stopped paying and a declaration that his obligations continue into the future. What advice can you give John?

Problem 5-9. Father and Mother's divorce agreement provided for shared child care responsibilities and costs and gave Father custody on alternate weekends during the year and a month during the summer. Two years later, Mother comes to you complaining that Father has never exercised his summer custody rights and often cancels his weekend visitation, sometimes on short notice. What do you advise?

§ B. ESTABLISHING THE AMOUNT OF SUPPORT: FROM DISCRETION TO GUIDELINES TO A SUPPORT ORDER

[1] EXISTING GUIDELINE MODELS, AND HOW WE GOT HERE

Traditionally, courts had wide discretion in applying the general duty of support to specific cases. Consider, *e.g.*, Model Marriage and Divorce Act § 309:

> In a proceeding for . . . child support, the court may order either or both parents owing a duty of support . . . to pay an amount reasonable or necessary . . ., without regard to marital misconduct, after considering all relevant factors including:
>
> (1) the financial resources of the child;
>
> (2) the financial resources of the custodial parent;
>
> (3) the standard of living the child would have enjoyed had the marriage not been dissolved;
>
> (4) the physical and emotional condition of the child and his educational needs; and
>
> (5) the financial resources and needs of the noncustodial parent.

The exercise of judicial discretion resulted in wide variation in the amount of child support ordered in like cases. *See* Yee, *What Really Happens in Child Support Award Cases: An Empirical Study of Establishment and Enforcement of Child Support Orders in the Denver District Court*, 57 DEN. L.J. 21, 38–42 (1979); White & Stone, *A Study of Alimony and Child Support Rulings with Some Recommendations*, 10 FAM. L.Q. 75, 83 (1976). Because of the breadth of the trial court's discretion, such variation largely went uncorrected in the appellate courts. While some courts tried to regularize child support through the use of guidelines, others rejected any limitation on judicial discretion. In *Powell v. Powell*, 433 So. 2d 1374 (Fla. App. 1983), e.g., the court found bar association support guidelines violated the state law granting judicial discretion to award "such [child] support as from the circumstances of the parties and the nature of the case is equitable." *Id.* at 1375.

Although the law of child support was often said to be based on the standard of living maintained during the marriage, the greater expense of maintaining two households necessarily leads to a lower standard of living. Many commentators complained that orders under the discretionary system often did not meet a child's minimum needs, much less maintain the prior standard of living. Weitzman & Dixon, *Child Custody Awards: Legal Standards and Empirical Patterns for Child Custody, Support and Visitation After Divorce*, 12 U.C.D. L. REV. 473, 494–501 (1979); Hunter, *Child Support Law and Policy: The Systematic Imposition of Costs on Women*, 6 HARV. WOMEN'S L.J. 1 (1983). Consequently, a disproportionate share of the financial burden of divorce was placed on the custodial parent, usually the mother.

As part of a major federal child support initiative (discussed more fully in Section C at pp. 512-15), in the 1980s Congress required, as a condition of federal funding of state welfare programs, that each state create specific child support guidelines. The Family Support Act of 1988 requires guidelines which create a rebuttable presumption in all support proceedings. Pub. L. 100-485, 42 U.S.C. § 667(b) (2001). (The term "guideline," although widely used, does not accurately portray current child support law in most jurisdictions. "Formulas" and "tables," along with many presumptive rules, is a more accurate description.)

The states, thus, had to develop generally applicable rules designed to produce uniform results in like cases. While Federal law does not prescribe the support levels set by the guidelines, the guideline amount is presumptively correct and courts must justify any award which departs from it. Before examining what the states have done in response to this mandate, it is worth considering the policy question. How would you give concrete content to the duty to support a child? How would you approach the task of creating child support guidelines? Early on, states, encouraged by studies funded by HHS, looked toward data on how much people spend on their children. In particular, an early study by Espenshade, originally done for other purposes and before the law required support guidelines, was very influential in channeling thinking about how to approach the construction of guidelines.

THOMAS J. ESPENSHADE, INVESTING IN CHILDREN: NEW ESTIMATES OF PARENTAL EXPENDITURES 1–6 (1984)

Rearing children requires expenditures of both time and money. Money expenditures consist of out-of-pocket direct maintenance expenses for items such as food, clothing, shelter, medical care, education, and other categories. Time or opportunity expenditures refer to the opportunities forgone by the time spent with children. These opportunity expenditures are . . . often measured by the income the mother gives up by reducing her labor force participation below what it would be without children.

[The rest of this excerpt discusses out-of-pocket expenditures only.]

Persons wanting to know how much couples spend on their children often ask, "How much does it cost to raise a child?" In our opinion, however, asking about the *cost* of raising a child is unsatisfactory, not only because it invites answers that focus on some minimum level required for biological subsistence but also because the question implies a single answer. . . . The following example clarifies the latter point. Suppose one asked, "What does it cost to own a car today?" Obviously, the answer depends on what kind of car one owns — old model versus new model, the cost of car insurance, the car's repair record, gas mileage, and the like. Thus, in this study, we distinguish between the concepts of cost and expenditure. . . . [W]e are estimating parental expenditures on children. . . .

. . . .

Examining dollar expenditures on children does not by itself paint the whole picture of the economic responsibilities of parenthood because parents' ability to pay . . . varies. *Perhaps a more complete view emerges when the percentage of total family consumption that represents expenditure on the children is analyzed. Our results show that this fraction varies remarkably little with a family's socioeconomic status but depends significantly on the number of children. Families with one child can expect to commit about 30 percent of total family expenditures to their child; in families with two children the proportion rises to between 40 and 45 percent; and in families with three children nearly 50 percent of total family spending is for the children. . . .[emphasis added]*

As children age they tend to become more expensive. . . . [A]pproximately 26 percent of total child-related expenditures to age 18 arise at ages 0–5, and roughly equal amounts occur at ages 6–11 (36 percent) and 12–17 (38 percent). . . .

We have disaggregated expenditures on children to age 18 into seven major categories of consumption including food, clothing, housing, transportation, recreation, medical care, and miscellaneous. Transportation (25.1 percent of the total), housing (24.1 percent), and food (22.5 percent) are typically the three most important budget items for children. . .

. . . .

[Our estimates] are cast in 1981 prices. What can a family anticipate in future expenditures if their first child is born in 1981 and if we factor future inflation into the estimates? Under the low-inflation scenario, which assumes an annual rate of inflation of 5.2 percent, expenditures to age 18 in our two-child middle-American family rise from $82,400 per child . . . to $149,000 per child in projected future dollars. At the medium-inflation level (8.0 percent . . .), our estimate . . . reaches $200,000 per child; and with the high-inflation scenario (9.3 percent . . .) the total climbs to $228,000 per child. Moreover, accounting for anticipated college costs could boost the expense of rearing a child from birth through four years of college to between $196,000 and $310,000, depending on the type of four-year institution and the assumption regarding future inflation.

NOTES

1. *Parents Underestimate Expenditure on Children.* In a later article, Professor Espenshade reported that:

> People tend to underestimate substantially their expenditure on children. For example, in response to a survey . . . in the early 1970s, Caucasian parents in Hawaii estimated the child-related proportion of their family spending at 15% — while our data would show the actual proportion to be two or three times that.

Espenshade & Calhoun, *The Dollars and Cents of Parenthood*, 5 J. POLICY ANALYSIS & MGMT. 813, 815 (1986).

2. *Expenditures as the Basis of Child Support Guidelines: the Continuity of Expenditure Principle.* See Ellman, *Fudging Failure: The Economic Analysis Used to Construct Child Support Guidelines*, _____University of Chicago Legal Forum _____(2004):

> The federal Department of Health and Human Services has since 1989 required all states to have child support guidelines "based on specific descriptive and numeric criteria" that lead to the computation

of a specific child support award in each case. State law must also provide that the amount yielded by application of the required guidelines is presumed to be the correct amount of the . . . award, although the presumption can be rebutted if the court explains why it is "inappropriate or unjust" in the particular case. Each state must review its guidelines every four years to ensure that they continue to provide for an appropriate child support award. But the federal rules are oblique at best in suggesting the criteria by which to determine whether an award is "appropriate." The only hint is contained in 45 C.F.R. 302.56(h), which specifies that in the required quadrennial review of the support guidelines, "a State must consider economic data on the cost of raising children." This provision is misleading. It appears to assume that objective data on the cost of raising children exists and ought to be important, and perhaps even primary, in setting the level of . . . awards. Yet that was not the accepted understanding at the time the federal government adopted these regulations. In the standard work on the topic then available, Thomas Espenshade explained that "asking about the cost of raising a child is unsatisfactory" for two reasons: "it invites answers that focus on some minimum level required for biological subsistence," and "implies a single answer when in fact a range of answers is possible." Indeed, a range of answers is inevitable once one goes beyond subsistence measures, because the cost of a child, like the cost of an adult, depends upon the living standard one means to reference: the cost of living, in other words depends upon the standard of living. An upper-class life style costs more than middle-class which costs more than lower-class which costs more than the poverty threshold. Espenshade thus emphasized that he was "estimating parental expenditures on children, not the cost of raising them. . . .," and parental expenditures varied with parental income. This view was echoed in all three of the reports later commissioned under H.H.S. auspices. The prevalent understanding, therefore, is while the regulation refers to costs, the relevant data is really about expenditures, and because parental expenditures on children vary with parental income, so does the "cost" of children and thus also the level of the appropriate . . . award. . . .

   . . .

   . . .Given the . . . focus on parental child expenditures, what parents in intact families in fact spend on their children became the norm by which guidelines are constructed. This norm can be called the continuity-of-expenditure rule, and can best be formulated in percentage rather than dollar terms: parents ought to contribute the same percentage of their income to child support after a divorce that they would have contributed if their relationship had not dissolved. Under this approach, one calculates the average amount spent on children by parents in an intact family, at any given income level. Divorced parents with the same aggregate income are then required to pay the same percentage of that income in child support. Each parent's respective share of the obligation is proportional to that parent's share of the total parental income. The support order requires the noncustodial parent to pay an amount equal to that parent's share; the rule assumes the custodial parent necessarily contributes her share in the course of maintaining the custodial household. Because of both constitutional and policy imperatives requiring that marital and nonmarital children be treated equally, the same guideline number is applied to support awards for children whose parents were never married and never lived with one another in an intact family relationship."

3. *Alternative Implementations of the Continuity-of-Expenditure Rule: Income Shares, POOI, and the Melson Formula.* While nearly all American states have guidelines based upon the continuity-of-expenditure principle, there is considerable variation in their implementation of it. Most fundamentally, most American states have adopted an "income shares" guideline, but a substantial minority have adopted a "percentage of obligor income" (POOI) guideline. (One recent compilation found 33 income shares states and 13 POOI states. Venohr & Williams, *The Implementation and Periodic Review of State Child Support Guidelines*, 33 FAM. L.Q. 7, 19 (1999).) Under the income shares approach, the incomes of both parents are used to calculate the total expected parental expenditure on the child. Each parent is then expected to contribute a pro rata share of that total expenditure; each parent's share is equal to that parent's share of the total parental income. For example, assume the parents have one child and net incomes of $50,000 for the noncustodial father and $25,000 for the custodial mother. For the moment, let's assume further that their expenditures equal their net income. Recall that Espenshade concluded that in one-child families 30% of parental expenditures are attributable to the child. If we were to construct an income shares guideline based on Espenshade's estimate, we would assume the average two-parent family at this income level spends 30% of $75,000 on their child, or $22,500. The noncustodial parent should contribute two-thirds of this amount, because he earns two-thirds of net parental income. Our guideline would thus require him to pay $15,000 in child support to the mother. The custodial mother is assumed to contribute her share in the course of meeting her custodial responsibilities.

Note that one could simplify the guideline calculation considerably by simply requiring the noncustodial parent in a one-child family to pay 30% of his net income in child support, as one would get the same result: 30% of $50,000 is also $15,000. This is the premise of the POOI states, whose simpler guidelines apply a standard percentage to the obligor's income, varying the percentage only according to the number of children. In that case, why should anyone ever use a more complex income shares formula? Part of the reason is public relations: the income shares approach makes explicit what the POOI formula only assumes, that the custodial parent, as well as the noncustodial parent, is contributing to the child's support. The more substantive explanation arises from the way income shares guidelines are in fact constructed. While nearly all studies suggest parents with different net incomes devote the same percentage of their *expenditures* on children, that does not necessarily mean that they spend the same percentage of their net (after-tax) *income* on their children. This brings us back to the assumption we made in our example, that our hypothetical parents' expenditures equaled their net income. We could have instead assumed they spent only 95% of their net income. In that case the Espenshade estimate of child expenditures would also decline by 5%, as would the ultimate calculation of the father's support obligation. If we assume that people spend the same percentage of their net income across the entire income range addressed by the guidelines, this simple reduction would address the question.

But what if people spend a lower percentage of their income as their income goes up? That is in fact the assumption generally made in income shares states, and that is why their guidelines typically produce different results than the POOI model. While POOI states typically apply a constant percentage to obligor income across income ranges, incomes shares states generally do not. The numbers in their guidelines are instead usually computed on the premise that family expenditures decline, as a percent of family income, as income rises. So, for example, an income shares guideline that assumes that 95% of income is expended in our hypothetical where the total parental income was $75,000, might assume that only 80% of income was expended when the total parental income was $120,000. The result is that while total child expenditures in the first case would be calculated as 30% of *95%* of $75,000, or $21,375, in the second case they would be calculated as 30% of *80%* of $125,000, or 30,000, to be allocated between the parents in proportion to their incomes. Considered then as a percentage of income, the obligor in our hypothetical pays 28.5%, while the obligor in the higher income family pays 24%. Indeed, as we shall see below, the economic data on which income shares states based their guidelines may actually assume that upper income parents spend as little as 60 percent of their income.

The Melson formula is a third variant of the continuity-of-expenditure model, adopted by the Delaware Family Court in 1979. It is an Income Shares formula with a self-support reserve. A self-support reserve is a set-aside from parent income, intended to allow the parent to devote that amount entirely to himself or herself *before* he or she is tapped for child support. A reserve may be given to either the custodial or the non-custodial parent, or to both. The effects of parental self-support reserves depend on how they are constructed.

The most current version of the Melson formula (promulgated in 2002) incorporates a monthly self-support reserve of $850 for each parent and then requires the parents to contribute 100% of net income until the children have been provided a minimal "primary support allowance." Each adult self-support reserve is intended to meet the parent's minimum needs living alone, but the child's reserve will suffice only if the custodial parent actually has the $850 base. For one child, that amount is $350. If the custodial parent lacks the full $850 for self-support, the $350 child support allowance will not save the child from poverty. Once all self-support requirements are satisfied, the formula applies a rate of 16% to the non-custodial parent's additional net income. The total primary support allowance increases with the number of children ($650 for two children, $920 for 3 children, $1170 for 4 children, and each additional child is allocated $220) and the child support percentage of the parent's additional net income also increases (26% for two children, 33% for three, 39% for four and 4% for each additional child). For recent cases applying the Melson

Formula, see T.E.N. v. T.J.O., 2003 Del. Fam. Ct. LEXIS 117; In re: D.J.D., Jr. v. K.L.D., 2003 Del. Fam. Ct. LEXIS 151; In re Marriage of Eugene J.R. & Gail M.R., 1996 Del. Fam. Ct. LEXIS 99 (including detailed worksheet demonstrating Melson Formula in operation).

The Melson reserves have little effect when the incomes of both parents are relatively equal and exceed the amounts of the self-support reserves. If, for example, each parent of an only child has monthly income of $1025 ($850 + ($350 ÷ 2)), all self-support reserves will be satisfied. The child's primary support allowance, $350, is 17% of $2,050, the combined amount of parent income. Sixteen percent is the percentage that the formula applies to net earnings beyond the amount necessary to satisfy the self support reserves. Thus, so long as each parent has net income of at least $1025 monthly, it makes little difference whether one applies the self-support reserves or a simple 17% of net income. Yet the self-support reserve does have real bite when the custodial parent has little or no income. Then the support obligor, who may also have low income, must provide most or all of the child's self-support reserve.

4. _Data Problems in Expenditure Estimates._ As explained in Note 3, the premise underlying the typical incomes shares guideline is that people spend a lower percentage of their net income as their income rises. It is plausible that people with more income are able to save a higher percentage of their income. The question is whether that relationship is true within the income range addressed by the typical guideline grid. For example, one could imagine that expenditures decline significantly, as a percentage of income, for families in the upper five percent of the income distribution, but not for the vast majority below this elite group. Nonetheless, the question is an empirical one, and in discerning the facts the economic consultants are dependent upon data collected by the Bureau of Labor Statistics in the Consumer Expenditure Survey. The CES is the only source of national data on household expenditures by income group. It turns out, however, that this data set has serious flaws which are likely to distort these estimates. In particular, the CES shows expenditures in excess of income for about half the population — those in the lower half of the income distribution — and expenditures at an implausibly low percentage of income (around 60%) for those in the upper fifth of the income distribution. The Ellman study, excerpted in Note 2, _supra,_ reviews the available information on this data and concludes that the likely problem is disproportionate underreporting of income in the bottom half and disproportionate underreporting of expenditures in the upper twenty percent. The result is that the economic studies upon which income-shares guidelines are typically based probably yield estimates of child expenditures that are too high at the lower income levels and too low at the higher income levels. Ellman's analysis notes other potential problem areas as well, including the exclusion of certain outlays from the expenditure total, and the corrections for taxes, that cast further doubt on the estimates.

5. _Continuity of Expenditure, As Implemented, Is Continuity of_ Marginal _Expenditure._ The data difficulties aside, we have seen that both the income shares and POOI systems share the premise that child support awards ought to be based upon an estimate of what parents in intact families spend on their children (the continuity of expenditure principle), even if they differ as to whether upper income parents spend the same percentage of income on their children as lower income parents. Determining what parents in intact families in fact spend on their children thus becomes the fundamental inquiry every time a POOI or Incomes Shares state (which is nearly every state) reviews its guidelines. This task is difficult both conceptually and practically. As a conceptual matter, many household expenditures are devoted to items such as heat, the cost of which is unaffected by the number of persons in the household. There is not even in principle any unique correct method for allocating the cost of such "household public goods" among household members. And as a practical matter, even for household private goods, such as food, which in principle *are* individually allocable, there is no data. The only available data (the CES) does not break down household consumption by individual. The result is that we actually have no direct data on how much people spend on their children. Economists asked to assist guideline writers therefore face a difficult methodological problem.

To solve this difficulty, economic consultants employed to provide expenditure estimates to guideline committees generate those estimates with a tool called an "equivalence scale." There are several equivalence scales identified in the economic literature, based upon different ways of estimating when two households of different composition have equal living standards. The two most commonly used such estimators are the Engel and the Rothbarth. The Engel estimator assumes that two households have the same standard of living if they devote the same *percentage* of their total household expenditures to groceries. The Rothbarth estimator assumes that two households have the same living standard if they spend the same *dollar amount* on items that are exclusively used for adults. (Given limitations in the available data, the "adult goods" typically employed in implementing the Rothbarth estimator is adult clothing.) Whichever estimator is used, the method is the same. The researcher relies upon the equivalence scale to determine how much more money a family with children must spend in order to have a standard of living that is equivalent to a childless couple. For example, the researcher may conclude that a family with two parents and two children that spends $80,000 achieves the same living standard as a childless couple who spend $50,000 (because these two households either devote the same percentage of total expenditures on groceries (Engel) or the same dollar amount on adult clothing (Rothbarth)). The researcher then treats the *additional* amount spent by the family with children (here, $30,000) as the child expenditure for families that spend, in total, $80,000. The final step is to decide what *income* level is associated with expenditures of $80,000. Suppose, for example, the researcher concludes that families with incomes of $100,000 have expenditures of $80,000 (the remaining $20,000 going to taxes, savings, or other non-expenditure items). The consultant would then conclude that families with two children earning $100,000 spend $30,000, or 30% of their income, on their children. To understand this process in more detail, see the Ellman paper excerpted in Note 2 above.

For our purposes, however, it is important primarily to understand that this method calculates only the additional expenditures made when children are added to the household — what an economist would call the *marginal* expenditure. For that reason the fundamental rule underlying most modern support guidelines is more accurately the "continuity of *marginal* expenditure" principle. A simplified example explains that point. Assume that a childless couple lives in a one-bedroom apartment that rents for $1000. They now have a child, and to maintain the equivalent housing standard, they could rent a two-bedroom apartment in the same complex for $1300. The logic that underlies the equivalence scale methodology would conclude that the housing expenditure on the child is $300. Similarly, if the childless couple already own two cars, and continue to own only two cars after they have a child, there may be no marginal transportation expenditures on children (unless perhaps more miles are driven). While the equivalence scale method actually proceeds globally, rather than item by item in this manner, these examples communicate its fundamental logic. Yet any household has many joint consumption items; all its members benefit from the living room, the kitchen, the heating system, and the cars. A child's welfare obviously depends upon sharing in the expenditures that provide the family with these joint consumption items, but the equivalence table method systematically excludes them, in their entirety, from the accounting of child expenditures. Ellman concludes:

> There is no inherent reason why a continuity of expenditure rule need be a continuity of *marginal* expenditure, as the economic consultants who implement the expenditure approach seem to assume. Marginal cost analysis is central to economic theory, of course. A factory owner deciding upon whether to enlarge his output would rationally consider only the marginal cost of the additional output, not the average cost; so long as he can sell the additional output for more than its marginal cost he is better off. But someone considering going into the widget supply business who wanted to know what it cost to make widgets would be wrong to look only at the marginal cost of the last widget made by an existing manufacturer. For this new entry the marginal cost of the first widget would include all the capital costs of building the factory, which he would of course have to incur to go into the business. Indeed, the prospective new entrant really needs to know his likely average cost, at various projected outputs, and his likely sales volume, because he doesn't want to enter the market at all unless his average selling price will be more than his average cost.

> So whether one is interested in average costs or marginal costs depends upon the reason for asking the question. If the question is how much additional income a childless couple will need to maintain their living standard, if they have a child, then the child's marginal cost is indeed the answer. If the question is whether the custodial household has sufficient resources to provide the child with an appropriate environment, the marginal costs of providing for that child if he or she were added to some other theoretical but factually nonexistent household — the intact family — is quite irrelevant. We could calculate the marginal costs of all the members of the custodial household in this manner, and if we allowed that household a total budget equal to the sum of their individual marginal costs, thus calculated, they likely all would starve. Reconstituted post-dissolution households are . . . start-ups. They can no more survive on a budget

based on their theoretical marginal costs of adding children to an existing household, then could our prospective industrialist profit by selling his first ten widgets at a price equal to the marginal costs incurred for the last ten made by the current market leader.

The equivalence scale methodology suffers from other flaws as well. Most importantly, different equivalence estimators, such as Engel and Rothbardt, yield different estimates of the marginal expenditures on children. Yet, as Ellman explains, no empirical test is possible to determine which method yields more accurate results, and there probably also is no theoretical basis upon which to prefer one to the other. A competing method for estimating expenditures on children is adopted by the Agricultural Department, which issues its estimates annually. *See, e.g.,* Mark Lino, *Expenditures on Children by Families: 2001 Annual Report,* U.S. Department of Agriculture, Center for Nutrition Policy and Promotion, Miscellaneous Publication No. 1528-2001 (2002). This approach allocates some expenditures, such as housing, on a per capita basis, while allocating others on marginal expenditure basis. The Agriculture Department's estimates of expenditures on children are typically higher than the estimates of guideline consultants, and the author of its reports argues its estimates would provide a better basis for guidelines than estimates based upon the Engel or Rothbardt estimators.

6. *What Are Current Equivalence Scale Estimates?* As explained above, most guidelines are based upon estimates of child expenditures as a percentage of all household expenditures, and this figure does not change appreciably with family income. It does change, however, with the choice of Rothbarth or Engel equivalence estimator. It also changes over time with changes in the data on which the estimates are based, the ongoing interviews conducted for the Consumer Expenditure Survey. It may also change, of course, with the identity of the economist who makes the estimates based on the data, as there are necessarily many judgment calls which must be made in that enterprise. Professor David Betson of Notre Dame is the person whose estimates are by far the most frequently used. A 2003 report to the Arizona guideline committee by PSI, a consulting company that employs the Betson estimates, provided four sets of estimates prepared by Professor Betson: his original estimates employing data from the early 1980's, and more recent estimates using data from the late 1990's. There are four estimates because for each set of data one estimate uses the Engel equivalence estimator, and one uses the Rothbarth estimator:

Average Child-rearing Expenditures as a Percent of Total Family Expenditures

Estimate and Data Source	One Child	Two Children	Three Children
Betson-Engel (1980–86 data)	33%	49%	59%
Betson-Engel (1996–99 data)	30%	44%	52%
Betson-Rothbarth (1980–86 data)	25%	37%	44%
Betson-Rothbarth (1996–99 data)	25%	35%	41%

Note that in general, estimates based upon newer data are lower than estimates based upon older data, and that estimates using the Rothbarth estimator are lower than those using the Engel estimator. PSI will prepare estimates for its client states using either estimator, but recommends Rothbarth, and states have generally been moving in that direction according to PSI's report to the Michigan child support committee. (*See generally* the Ellman paper in Note 2.) In consequence of this trend toward the Rothbarth estimator, as well as the impact of more recent data, one would expect to find a trend toward declining child support guidelines. One might wonder why estimates of what parents spend on their children would decline over time. It seems unlikely that parental values are so fickle on this matter. One possible explanation is that the sort of items purchased in larger quantity by families with children are cheaper today, relative to other consumer purchases, than they were in the early 1980s. Alternatively, the data simply may be flawed, suggesting changes in the real world that are not in fact there, or that the declining estimates are an artifact of an equivalence scale methodology that is sensitive to changes in the data that actually are irrelevant. There is, at the moment, no way to tell what the actual explanation is.

Note that all the preceding estimates are based upon expenditure patterns in two-parent families. These are the estimates upon which current guidelines are based. Clearly, adding children to a single parent household will require a larger percentage increase in expenditures, to maintain the same living standard, than adding children to a household that already has two adults. In 1990 Professor Betson offered estimates for one-parent families, based upon the Rothbarth estimator, that were 40%, 55%, and 60%, respectively, for one, two, and three-child households. Betson, ALTERNATIVE ESTIMATES OF THE COST OF CHILDREN FROM THE 1980–86 CONSUMER EXPENDITURE SURVEY 57 (1990), Final Report to the U.S. Department of Health and Human Services.

[2] ALTERNATIVE WAYS TO THINK ABOUT GUIDELINE CONSTRUCTION

The material in the preceding section explained that modern guidelines are based largely upon estimates of the marginal expenditures on children in two-parent families. But are such estimates in fact the right benchmark for support guidelines to use? *Consider* Ellman, *Fudging Failure: The Economic Analysis Used to Construct Child Support Guidelines*, _____University of Chicago Legal Forum _____(2004):

> As a principle of fairness, and of social policy, the continuity-of-expenditure norm is plausible. What people on average spend on their children in intact families, when the parents are not in conflict, can be seen as a convenient and reasonable benchmark of society's view as to the fair and appropriate amount to require of divorced parents. Yet, it is not the inevitable benchmark. For one thing, the usual analysis only attempts to determine the *average* expenditure level on children in families at given income levels, but there is reason to think that expenditures of actual families vary quite considerably around that mean. In that case, one could move some distance above or below

the mean figure and still claim nearly as substantial an endorsement from the expenditure data — which means that policy considerations arising from other sources can reasonably be given proportionately more weight. More fundamentally, if one considers the question (how much income should the noncustodial parent share with the custodial household?) from scratch, without first being channeled into thinking in expenditure terms, one might take a very different approach. One would first decide whether the primary reason for requiring support is to serve the child's interests, to achieve fairness as between the parents, or to serve a balanced blend of the two. If one believes the child's interests are paramount, for example, one might believe the support level should be set high enough to ensure that the child, who is presumably the innocent victim of the marital failure, suffers no financial harm at all from the divorce, even if that principle requires an award which gives the child a higher post-divorce living standard than the support obligor. Yet an exclusive focus on the child might also lead one to conclude that a custodial parent with sufficient resources to provide the child a comfortable environment should receive no compelled support from the other parent, because the child welfare value of any award could not be shown. In other words, if child welfare concerns were paramount, we would presumably require the highest support levels from which the child would derive benefit, but no higher — and so in writing the guidelines we would mainly want to know all we could about the benefits that flow to children from various levels of support payments.

In contrast, if fairness as between the parents is thought paramount, one would require support even if it added little or no child benefit to the comfortable environment that a financially secure custodial parent might alone be able to provide, because one would still want to ensure that the noncustodial parent contributes his fair share (freeing some of the custodial parent's resources for non-child expenditures). We might also decline to make some awards that were appropriate on child welfare grounds because they would be regarded as unfairly burdensome to the obligor.

So child welfare and fair treatment of the child's parents can yield conflicting outcomes. A rational child support system must reflect an appropriate compromise between them.

How should one determine the content of a rational compromise? Do guidelines based upon marginal child support expenditures in intact families reflect an appropriate compromise, or is a different approach arguably superior? The American Law Institute considered this question in formulating the child support recommendations contained in the Family Dissolution Principles. It concluded that the best way to consider the matter was to ask how the two households, custodial and noncustodial, fared. In other words, the ALI would measure the fairness of a child support guideline according to the economic circumstances that resulted from its application in each of the post-dissolution households.

While the interests of both parents, the child, and state were all noted, the core of the analysis is reconciling the claims of the noncustodial parent and of the child. The analysis proceeds by imagining what the strongest plausible claim of each party might be. From the perspective of the noncustodial parent, the fact of divorce should not free the obligor from his duty to his child, but neither should it enlarge that duty by requiring him to pay *more* than he would have spent on the child if no divorce had occurred. This sounds very much like the continuity of expenditure principle. And indeed, in its strongest form, this claim argues the support obligation should be calculated using the marginal expenditure in the intact household as the benchmark. From the perspective of the support obligor, a support obligation based on this benchmark is fair because it leaves him the same amount of money to spend on himself that he would have had for non-child expenditures had no divorce occurred — no more, and no less.

What is the strongest plausible claim that can be made on the child's behalf? One might argue that the child can claim he should not suffer financially at all from the divorce, for surely the child is the innocent victim of the marital failure. In application, however, such a claim would mean that the obligor would have to pay an amount of child support sufficient to maintain all of the members of the custodial household (including the custodial parent) at the marital living standard. This would, in almost all cases, place the obligor considerably below the marital living standard. A rule that would require the obligor to maintain the child and the custodial parent at a higher living standard than himself does not in fact appear plausible to most policymakers. The child's next strongest claim is for an amount of support sufficient to ensure that the child suffer no more financially from the divorce than does any other member of the family. In other words, both post-divorce households may be less well off than the prior, intact marital household, but their loss would be equal. The child would suffer financially from the divorce, but no more than either parent. This is, of course, an equal living standards (ELS) principle, and equality always has plausibility as a principle of justice. While no state has adopted ELS as a principle of child support, it has been urged by feminists and supported in some of the public policy literature. *See, e.g.,* Cassetty, Sprinkle, White & Douglass, *The ELS (Equal Living Standards) Model for Child Support Awards*, in ESSENTIALS OF CHILD SUPPORT GUIDE-LINES DEVELOPMENT: ECONOMIC ISSUES AND POLICY CONSIDERATIONS 329, 336 (1986) and Betson, et al., *Trade-Offs Implicit in Child-Support Guidelines*, 11 J. POLICY ANAL. & MGT. 1 (1992).

As seen below, in most cases the support payment required to satisfy an ELS principle is greater than the support payment required under the continuity-of-marginal-expenditure principle that our hypothetical obligor would favor. But that only partially explains the obligor's likely opposition to this principle. Perhaps even more problematic, from the obligor's perspective, is that payments based upon an ELS principle would necessarily require him to pay enough to bring *all* members of the custodial household to this level, not only the children to whom he has a duty. The other parent, as well as that parent's new children or spouse, if any, will also benefit. This is inevitable because all members of the custodial household necessarily share a living standard. But the fact that this consequence of satisfying the child's claim for equality is unavoidable, does not make it unobjectionable, to the obligor. Another concern with an ELS model is the possibility that it would substantially discourage the custodial parent's labor force participation. Guidelines based upon ELS effectively require the custodial parent to share every dollar she earns with the non-custodial parent, because as she raises her income on her own the support award will decline proportionately. Even its supporters acknowledge that guidelines based upon ELS could reduce labor force participation of custodial parents by as much as a third. *Id.* Although reduced labor force participation may serve the short-term interests of custodial parents, it conflicts with their long-term interests because children grow up and the child support entitlement eventually ends. At this point, custodial parents have an interest in having maximized prior labor force participation to the extent consistent with the needs of the children. This point was also emphasized by the ALI in its rejection of ELS. Notice, however, that the reasonableness of any objections to the ELS model is affected by the incomes of the parents. That is, if the parents have equal incomes before any child support transfer, the objections are much weaker. First, if the custodial parent has the same income as the noncustodial parent, it would seem only fair that she also enjoy the same living standard, rather than have her living standard compromised by the fact of her custodial responsibilities. Thus, the noncustodial parent's objections to an ELS principle lose plausibility in this case . Nor do objections based on discouraging labor market participation have much bite here, for the custodial parent is already earning enough to maintain the same living standard when the child leaves home and child support ends.

The ALI's compromise of these competing claims takes account of all these factors. The basic rule appears in § 3.04 of the Family Dissolution Principles, which directs construction of guidelines so that the child enjoys "a standard of living not grossly inferior to that of either parent." The obligor's interest is recognized in that the child's claim to equal treatment is not fully met, but the child's interest is also recognized in that the obligor must pay enough to ensure that the child's living standard — and unavoidably, the custodial parent's as well — is not "grossly inferior" to the obligor's. The ALI would implement this principle by requiring guidelines that provide a sliding supplement to the marginal expenditure support calculation. But that supplement is zero when the parents are equal earners. No supplement is required in that case because it turns out that a marginal expenditure award alone will ensure the custodial household at least an equal living standard. Similarly where the custodial parent earns more than the noncustodial parent, no supplement is needed. The supplement is triggered when the noncustodial parent earns more than the custodial parent, and gradually increases with the size of that earnings gap, calibrated to meet the "not grossly inferior" standard. Thus, while the ALI rejects the ELS principle, unlike the continuity-of-marginal-expenditure model it acknowledges the likelihood of a living standards gap and manages it explicitly.

The ALI's recommended approach still requires, for its implementation, the use of equivalence scales, because that is the only method for comparing the living standards of households of different size. (The dominant "continuity of marginal expenditure" model relies on equivalence scales as a tool with which to estimate the marginal expenditures on children.) To the extent the equivalence scale methodology has flaws, both approaches are thus affected. Nonetheless, because equivalence scales are commonly employed in child support debates, and no ready substitute for them has been developed, it is useful and appropriate to consider how any particular guideline fares when scrutinized under this lens.

To take an example of how this methodology might be employed in assessing child support guidelines, consider the Bureau of Labor Standards (BLS) Household Equivalence Scale, a widely-used formulation for comparing the standards of living in households of different size and composition. BLS used the Engel estimator, which we have already noted tends to attribute relatively higher marginal costs to children than does the Rothbarth estimator. We can use the BLS scale to tell us how much income each of the two post-divorce households would require to maintain the same living standard of the pre-divorce marital household. The required income is expressed as a percentage of the pre-divorce income. *See* Bureau of Labor Statistics, U.S. Department of Labor, *Revised Equivalence Scale For Estimating Equivalent Incomes or Budget Costs by Family Type* 14 (Table A-1), Bulletin No. 1570-2 (1968). In the BLS table, NCP stands for the non-custodial parent. CP&C stands for the custodial parent and child(ren). Here are its figures:

	1 child	2 children	3 children	4 children
NCP	46%	38%	33%	29%
CP&C	71%	77%	84%	90%
Total	117%	115%	117%	119%

The BLS table, for example, demonstrates that when a household composed of two adults and one child breaks down, the non-custodial parent (if living alone), requires 46% of the pre-separation family income to maintain the pre-separation living standard, while the custodial parent and child require 71%. Thus, the two households together require 117% of the pre-separation income in order for both to maintain their standard of living. (In this example, the head of household is assumed to be between 35-54 and the child between 6-15.) That is, the unsurprising conclusion is that family members cannot maintain their living standard after divorce without additional sources of income. We might assume that most families will not immediately have such extra resources. The BLS figures can also be used to calculate the relative incomes required in each of the post-divorce households to ensure that they have equal living standards. This calculation is provided in the following table, which shows the percentages of total family income that each post-dissolution household must have for their living standards to be equal.[1] Of course, this calculation of the percentages required for equal living standards applies no matter whether this equal standard is lower, equal to, or higher than the marital living standard. For families which do not increase their income after

---

[1] These figures are derived by simple cross multiplication:

one child family:	$46/117 = x/100; x = 39\%$
	$71/117 = x/100; x = 61\%$
two child family:	$38/115 = x/100; x = 33\%$
	$77/115 = x/100; x = 67\%$
three child family:	$33/117 = x/100; x = 28\%$
	$84/117 = x/100; x = 72\%$
four child family:	$29/119 = x/100; x = 24\%$
	$90/119 = x/100; x = 76\%$

divorce sufficiently to allow them to maintain the pre-separation living standard, this allocation would distribute equally the divorce's economic impact.

	1 child	2 children	3 children	4 children
NCP	39%	33%	28%	24%
CP&C	61%	67%	72%	76%
Total	100%	100%	100%	100%

This second table is particularly useful in assessing the results that flow from any particular child support guideline. For example, consider the following:

Illustration:

1. Assume Jurisdiction A requires payment of 22% of net income for the support of one child, 34% for two children, and 44% for three children. Tom and Mary are divorcing and Mary will have custody of their only child, Sandy. Tom and Mary have equal incomes of $2,000 net monthly. Tom must pay Mary $440 monthly ($2,000 times .22), and Mary is presumed to devote another $440 ($2,000 times .22) to Sandy in the custodial household. After the child support transfer, Mary's custodial household will have $2,440 monthly and Tom will have income of $1,560 monthly. That is, the custodial household will have 61% of the total family income of $4000, and the noncustodial household will have 39%. The BLS table thus suggests the households will have equal living standards. Given that the parents in this example have equal incomes, it seems appropriate that they enjoy equal living standards after the child support transfer.

But the outcomes under this guideline seem less satisfactory when the incomes of the parents are substantially unequal.

Illustrations:

2. Change Illustration 1's facts so that Tom has net income of $2,000 monthly and Mary has net income of $1,000 monthly (a typical earnings ratio for (male) non-custodial and (female) custodial parents). After Tom pays child support of $440, Mary's custodial household has income of $1,440 to support Mary and Sandy, and Tom has income of $1,560 ($2,000 minus $440) to support himself. Applying the BLS household equivalence table, at $1,440 of income, the members of the custodial household will experience a 32% decline from the marital standard of living, while Tom, with $1,560 of income, will experience a 13% increase.

3. James, the non-custodial parent earns $1,600 net monthly and Martha, the custodial parent, earns $800 net monthly at full-time minimum wage employment. They have one child, Bobby. James pays child support of $352 ($1,500 times .22). After payment of child support, the custodial household has income of $1,152 to maintain two people and the non-custodial parent has income of $1,248 to maintain himself. Applying the BLS table, the members of the custodial household experience a 32% decline in standard of living and the non-custodial parent experiences a 13% increase.

This kind of examination, which is the basis of the ALI recommendations, can be useful in evaluating any set of guidelines. One must be cautious, however. The BLS calculations depend upon the same problematic method — the equivalence scale — as does the methodology now used to generate the dominant continuity of marginal expenditure guidelines. In addition, there are further adjustments one needs to consider to produce an accurate estimate of the actual impact of any set of guidelines. One issue is the treatment of taxes — in some cases the income tax system will have substantial effect on the relative financial welfare of the two post-divorce households. For some concrete recommendations on how a support guideline committee might proceed in the face of these methodological difficulties, see Ellman, *Fudging Failure: The Economic Analysis Used to Construct Child Support Guidelines*, _____University of Chicago Legal Forum _____(2004), which also explores the methodological issues in considerably more depth.

PROBLEM

Problem 5-10. The official web page of the New York City Administrator of Children Services, Office of Child Support Enforcement, explains that the goal of New York's guidelines "is to give children the same standard of living they would have if their parents were together." A pamphlet issued by the New York State Division of Child Support Enforcement, entitled "What Non-Custodial Parents Need to Know About Child Support" (Pub. 4721) explains: "The guideline was put in the law to make sure that people pay an amount for support that is actually close to what it costs to care for a child." The June, 2001 New York State Child Support Standards Act Quadrennial Evaluation explains that: "The guidelines, as written, produce awards roughly in line with the accepted standard of requiring the noncustodial parent to pay in support what he or she would have contributed to the children in an intact family." Are these three contemporary descriptions of the same state guidelines consistent with one another? Assuming the New York guidelines are an example of the dominant continuity-of-expenditure approach, are any of these descriptions accurate?

[3] ASPECTS OF SUPPORT NOT INCLUDED WITHIN THE ORDINARY GUIDELINE

[a] Expenditure for Child Care Required by the Custodial Parent's Gainful Employment

For the gainfully employed custodial parent, treatment of child care required for employment may be a matter of great significance. Child care expenditure should not be understood to be part of the basic marginal expenditure child support obligation because (i) consumer expenditure data for two-parent families shows little expenditure for child care and (ii) the amount of child care required by a one-parent family is highly variable and hence unsuitable for treatment by a generalized formula. The ordinary marginal expenditure measure of child support necessarily assumes full employment, or some effective equivalent, by both parents, because a *marginal* measure of child support is conceptually meaningless without a base to which the marginal amount is added.

Marginal expenditure Income Shares jurisdictions, which nominally consider the incomes of both parents, usually provide that the cost of child care required by a parent's gainful employment should be shared by the child's parents, either equally or in proportion to their relative incomes. *See, e.g.*, CAL. FAM. CODE §§ 4061 and 4062 (West 1994). Yet the minority POOI (obligor income only) jurisdictions usually make no provision for child care required by the custodial parent's employment, effectively imposing all such costs on the custodial parent.

The ALI model initially apportions child care expenses between parents according to their relative incomes. The non-custodial parent's share is effectively capped, however, as part of a tradeoff against the benefits that the ALI's formula generally offers the custodial parent.

[b]   Expenditure for Health Insurance and for Uninsured Health Care Costs

Federal law requires that state guidelines take account of health care costs. Like child care required by the custodial parent's employment, health care expenditure is highly variable, as is parent access to reasonable or inexpensive health insurance. Consequently, Income Shares guidelines typically add the costs of health insurance and uninsured medical expenditure to the amount of support required by the guideline (formula) and apportion such costs to the parties either equally or according to their relative incomes. *See, e.g.*, CAL. FAM. CODE §§ 3753, 4061, 4062 (West 1994); ALI, PRINCIPLES § 3.05 (7) (2002) (requiring child's medical and dental insurance costs and expenditures for child's uninsured medical and dental care be "shared by the parents according to their relative incomes"). Often, one parent will have an employment benefit package that allows that parent to provide the child with health insurance at a lower cost than the other parent. In such cases, the best result is obtained by requiring that parent to include the child in his or her health insurance and then adjusting the support order to ensure that the actual cost is allocated appropriately.

[c]   Rethinking Postsecondary Education and Other Issues in Light of the Marginal Expenditure Principle

The law concerning a parent's obligation to assist a child with postsecondary education was largely developed before the now almost-universal adoption of the concept of marginal expenditure as a principle of child support. What are the implications of the principle that, at a minimum, a parent should ordinarily spend on a child with whom he does not reside what would be spent on the child if he were residing with the child?

The *ALI Principles* § 3.12 subsume postsecondary education in the category of "life opportunities." The commentary explains that in deciding whether to order support for post-secondary education under this standard, the trier of fact must first decide whether the parent would provide the opportunity if the child were residing with the parent. If there are no objective indicia of what the parent would do (such as the fact that the parent has paid for the education of another child), then "the parent should be assumed to do what residential parents of similar wealth and background ordinarily do." The second question (reached only if one concludes that post-secondary education would have been provided in the intact family) is whether the parents can now contribute to it without undue hardship to themselves or their other dependents.

[4]   DETERMINING THE OBLIGOR'S RESOURCES

IN RE MARRIAGE OF DENNIS

344 N.W.2d 128 (Wis. 1984)

STEINMETZ, Justice. The issue . . . is whether the circuit court may in enforcing a child support order require this divorced father to make a search for other employment to increase or to add to his limited income. *[handwritten: Issue]*

. . . .

[In a divorce action, defendant was ordered to pay $35 weekly for temporary "family maintenance."]

On February 25, 1980, Dennis appeared [at a contempt hearing where] the court reduced his support obligation to $15 per month, which was $5 per child per month, and ordered payment of $5 monthly toward arrearages of $560. *[handwritten: Trial ct reduced child support award]*

[At the final hearing on March 24, 1981], the court ordered:

> . . . that the respondent should pay $300.00 per month for child support. It appears that respondent does not have the present ability to do so. . . . That he should look for additional or alternative work because it appears that he has never made over $3,500.00 per year in his past endeavors. That respondent . . . use his good faith efforts to apply for other work at least in ten places per month. . . . that he is to . . . report . . . any additional or alternative employment obtained. . . .

. . . Dennis filed a motion for reconsideration . . . asking the court to reconsider the "seek-work" order [because] such an order constituted an abuse of discretion.

At the hearing . . . the court again took notice of the fact that Dennis had never earned over $3,500 per year and then stated that this income was insufficient to permit reimbursement of the AFDC payments for his family. The court reasoned that Dennis's earning history strongly suggested that in the future he would not earn enough to meet the AFDC payments. . . .

On July 20, 1981 . . . Dennis introduced into evidence a list of 30 separate employers he had contacted regarding employment. He testified that he had called each . . ., inquiring as to whether they were accepting employment applications. He stated that in many cases, the employers were not taking applications and so he did not drive to those places. . . .

Ct ordered Dennis to apply to 10 places for work each month

The court renewed its order at the . . . hearing. . . . This renewed order again required Dennis to apply for work with ten separate employers per month, and the judge [additionally required] Dennis to apply to both Polk County and Barron County Job Services, and to follow all leads suggested by such Job Services. The court ordered Dennis to appear again . . . on September 14, 1981 . . . to demonstrate compliance. . . .

. . . [T]he court ordered Dennis to appear on October 22, 1981 [at which time he] testified that he had not kept a list of employers to whom he had submitted applications. However, he stated he had talked to several people in an effort to seek work and named three specific persons and that he had talked to "quite a few people" with no success. He stated he had not been to either county Job Service, but had watched the "help wanted" section of the newspaper.

. . . Dennis . . . had been in the car repair business off and on for 20 years, although steadily for ten years, but had operated his present automobile garage business at its present location for only about a year. His business gross receipts averaged $500 to $700 monthly with his take-home pay at about $300 monthly. His personal monthly expenses included $200 for food, part of which went to feed his three children who spent some weekends with him. As part of the property division . . ., Dennis mortgaged his trailerhouse for half its value, and thereby paid his wife $2,000. His monthly payment toward that mortgage was $105. His monthly gasoline expenses . . . were $160 which included driving to and from work and driving to auto parts suppliers to obtain parts for his work. He deducted his gasoline expenses from his gross receipts. His other monthly business expenses were telephone charges of $15 to $20, gas and oxygen charges for welding purposes of $40 to $50, electricity charges of $20 to $25, and rental of the building for which he did mechanical work for the landlord as payment.

Dennis complained he could not meet ct's order

Dennis testified that because of his limited income and monthly expenses, he could not afford to comply with the court's order that he apply for ten different jobs per month. Nor could he afford to drive weekly to both Polk and Barron County Job Services and to follow up leads those services might suggest. At the time of the hearing, he had nothing in his checking account and did not have any savings [and] still owed nearly the entire $2,000 [mortgage].

Dennis indicated he worked six days per week and worked between 8:00 a.m. and 6:00 p.m. He testified he never passed up nor avoided any work unless it was unlikely that he would be paid for his services. There was no direct evidence at any hearing that Dennis intentionally shirked or avoided work. Mrs. Dennis testified that he had always been a hard and steady worker. . . .

Ct finds him in contempt

. . . [T]he court found Dennis in willful contempt of court. Dennis was sentenced to 60 days in the Barron county jail under the work release program and was allowed to purge the contempt by payment of $800. . . . The court found him in contempt on two bases:

(1) For failing to make application for work as ordered, and

(2) For failing to make child support payments of $15 per month or $5 per month on the arrears as ordered.

The court of appeals affirmed the . . . holding that the court had the inherent power to order Dennis to look for other work. The court held Dennis's testimony incredible which led . . . to the "inescapable conclusion" that Dennis had undisclosed income. The trial court had not made such a finding. The court of appeals found the holding of contempt sustained by the evidence and that the purge . . . was within Dennis's ability to meet by borrowing on his remaining equity in the lot and mobile home.

. . . What is before this court is the order which required the defendant to "seek work" other than or in addition to his present business. . . . The defendant also contests the trial court's authority to retain jurisdiction over him . . . after the final divorce hearing for the purpose of enforcing the "seek-work" order.

The trial court did not order the defendant to take another or different job, but only to seek other work. The rule of *Balaam v. Balaam,* therefore is not controlling. In *Balaam,* we held:

> A divorced husband should be allowed a fair choice of a means of livelihood and to pursue what he honestly feels are his best opportunities even though he might for the present, at least, be working for a lesser financial return. This rule is, of course, subject to reasonableness commensurate with his obligations to his children and his former wife.

Id. at 867.

The *Balaam* rule is not an absolute prohibition against . . . requiring a divorced supporting spouse to consider a change in livelihood, especially where as here Dennis's income as a mechanic has never exceeded $3,500 per year . . . and it has not increased since he has become a garage operator. Not present in *Balaam* was the supporting father's claimed inability to pay $5 per month per child and $5 per month toward arrearage pursuant to the trial court's order as in this case. If ever there was a minuscule support order recognizing the party's lack of present earnings, this is it. It shows great respect and restraint by the trial judge . . . and in no way reflects that the trial court was insisting that the defendant repay the AFDC payments his family was receiving.

Edwards v. Edwards, dealt with the issue of consideration of . . . father's potential earning capacity rather than . . . actual earnings at . . . divorce. . . .

. . . .

However, until the trial court requires the defendant to "seek work" . . ., there can be no accurate and informed finding as to [his] ability to earn. . . . Until that is known, the court has no way of testing the person's economic worth,. . . . It is to the defendant's benefit to learn his own value, and . . . perhaps to be better able to meet his financial responsibilities. . . . [D]efendant should be interested in supporting his children the best he can and not be satisfied with society supporting them minimally on AFDC. He was not ordered to earn enough to repay AFDC but rather to seek work to investigate whether he is complacent by continuing in . . . non-productive work just so he can feed, house and clothe himself.

[handwritten margin notes: "Ct of Appeals affirmed"; "Trial ct did not order Dennis to another job, just to look for work"; "Balaam rule"; "seeking work is the only way to test the person's economic worth"]

Until the defendant and the judge know what other work and income is available, there is no way the judge can determine . . . that the defendant can do no better and there is no way, except by way of inference, to determine that the defendant is satisfied with his own lot in life and is willing to allow society to support his children. To obtain definite and meaningful information, the order of the trial court is reasonable. . . . Telephone calls at random to possible employers do not appear to be a sincere nor effective means of seeking work information. The defendant . . . has not been ordered to abandon his occupation. . . . He was ordered to seek work and report to the court. The trial court read *Edwards* correctly, since in *Edwards* we held: "While a $3,200 a year income is obviously low, no attempt was made to ascertain whether better barbering jobs were available . . . and, if so, how much he could be expected to earn in such a job." The *Edwards* court thereby informed trial courts to have the supportive parent seek other work to learn whether his lot was improvable. . . .

Affirmed

The "seek-work" order was not an abuse of discretion.

. . . .

Concurring

ABRAHAMSON, Justice (concurring). . . .

This case presents issues somewhat different from other child support cases, since both the husband and the wife are subsisting below the poverty line. In this case the supporting parent . . . earned very little per month, both before and after the divorce. Before the divorce proceedings, [his] income apparently was sufficient to support the family without government assistance; after the divorce proceedings began, the same income was insufficient to support two family units without government assistance for one unit. . . . While I concur in the court's decision, I have . . . reservations about the court's analysis of the issues. . . .

I am uneasy with the majority's characterization of the circuit court's order as a "seek-work order" issued for the purpose of enabling the trial court "to make an accurate and informed finding as to the defendant's ability to earn and what his worth is economically." . . . I agree that under the *Edwards* dictum the trial court may issue a reasonable seek-work order to gather information about the income of the supporting parent. . . . But I am concerned that this . . . order does not comport with . . . *Edwards* . . . in several respects.

Seek work order should have been more narrowly drawn

Edwards speaks about examining job opportunities in the same profession in which the parent is trained. Yet the order in this case requires the father to seek employment generally. An order designed to help the trial court ascertain whether the father was fulfilling his earning capacity through diligent work in his chosen trade should have been more narrowly drawn. . . .

Edwards speaks in terms of giving a parent a fair choice of a means of livelihood subject to reasonableness commensurate with obligations. The order in this case was not specifically designed to determine "fair choice" or "reasonableness." Prior to issuing the order, it appears that the trial court may have concluded that the father had had enough time to make a "go" of work in the car repair field and that his fair choice had been used up. . . .

If the trial court's order were interpreted as not merely information gathering but as requiring the father to get another job, the order may not be within the trial court's discretion under the rules set forth [in our prior cases].

Under these rules, the support order must be based on the actual earnings of $300 per month, unless the trial court finds that the father was not fairly or diligently working at an occupation for which he is best suited or that he has wilfully accepted employment and lowered compensation in order to reduce the ability to pay child support. There is no evidence in this record to support such a finding. . . . [T]he record indicates that the father was diligent, that he was working at the job for which he was trained, and that his income in his chosen trade has remained stable over many years. Under these circumstances the . . . court appropriately based its support order on the father's actual income. For the trial court . . . to order the father to change his trade so as to increase his income so that the . . . court can increase the support order may be a clear abuse of discretion. . . .

As a matter of constitutional law, strict standards must be met before the highly protected freedom from compulsory work can be infringed. Without a finding of wilfulness or lack of diligence an order directing the supporting parent to take alternative employment raises questions of due process, equal protection, and involuntary servitude. . . .

As to the reasonableness of such an order, I wonder whether a man in this father's situation is likely to find a much better-paying job. . . . He is 43 years old; he does not have a high school diploma; he has had 20 years' experience in the car repair business and has had no other job experience; he is accustomed to operating his own business; his compensation has been at the same level for a number of years; and he is earning $3,600 a year, the most he has ever earned. And even if he is successful in finding a job, I wonder what the prospects for job stability are, considering his employment history and his being forced to work at a job he does not want. With these reservations, I concur in the holding.

CECI, Justice (dissenting). I dissent . . . because a clear reading of the entire record indicates to me a defendant who clearly does not wish to exert himself in any respect for purposes of supporting his children.

. . . .

The record indicates that during this period of nearly zero effort by this defendant, he was able to trade off repair work for a membership in the golf country club, which was valued at $100. Had the defendant truly been making any effort to support his . . . children, he could have used the $100 [to] pay . . . the support the court had ordered for a period of five months and all of the amounts ordered to be paid on the arrearages for a period of five months. Instead, this defendant chose to trade off his labor and efforts so that he could go golfing.

[T]he entire record indicates . . . this defendant was totally satisfied that the taxpayers were supporting his . . . children. My reading . . . indicates an individual who just did not care to comply with the court's orders. I would affirm.

[Margin annotations: *Dissent* — *Dennis just doesn't want to support his children* — *He trades work for golf – not exactly good for making money*]

NOTES

1. *Establishing Obligor's Ability to Pay.* Ordinarily a court or guideline looks to the obligor's income in setting the amount of the child support obligation. What should be done when the actual earnings are much less than earning capacity? A court might use earning capacity rather than the actual earnings to set the award, thus leaving the obligor to deal with the problem, presumably by finding new work. This is often described as imputing income to the obligor. When the court is not certain that the obligor has an earning capacity greater than his current income, a "seek-work" order might be an apt solution. By requiring a search for more lucrative work, the court will presumably find out if, in fact, obligor can obtain it. That is the problem addressed by the *Dennis* trial court and the solution it adopted.

While the seek-work order may seem attractive, the *Dennis* opinions suggest the conflicting policies at work here. On the one hand, obligees (and the state which is paying welfare benefits) argue obligors ought to support their children to the extent permitted by their earning capacity. On the other hand, the obligor argues for the same right other people have to choose employment free from state coercion, particularly where his income, which was relatively constant, was sufficient to support the family during the marriage. Certainly, both support of children and freedom to work at one's chosen profession are policies worthy of recognition and support. In dealing with these conflicting policies, most appellate courts direct trial courts to follow some version of the rules set out in Justice Abrahamson's concurrence. That is, the trial courts have discretion to resolve conflicts between obligee and obligor interests on a case-by-case basis.

A seek-work order is no help in the case of the incarcerated obligor. The California courts have held that no income should be imputed to a prisoner-obligor unless there is an opportunity to work for pay while in prison. *Oregon v. Vargas*, 70 Cal. App. 4th 1123 (5th Dist. 1999). A later court, in dealing with a modification case raising the same issue, refused to create a "public policy exception" to *Vargas* where the incarcerated obligors had been convicted of offenses such as child molestation and child pornography. *Smith v. Smith*, 90 Cal. App. 4th 74 (5th Dist. 2001). Some other jurisdictions have refused to exempt prisoners from the imputation of income or have simply included incarceration as one factor to be considered. *See, e.g., Richardson v. Ballard*, 681 N.E.2d 507 (Ohio App. 1996)(incarceration is a voluntary lowering of income as foreseeable result of criminal behavior); *Mooney v. Brennan*, 848 P.2d 1020 (Mont. 1993) (same); *In re Marriage of Burbridge*, 738 N.E.2d 979 (Ill. App. 2000) (incarceration is one factor to be considered); *Thomasson v. Johnson*, 903 P.2d 254 (New. Mex. 1995) (same). For an article asserting incarcerated parents are often overlooked as a source of child support, see Cavanaugh & Pollack, *Child Support Obligations of Incarcerated Parents*, 7 CORNELL J. L. & PUB. POL'Y 531 (1998); *see also* Comment, *Imputing Parental Income in Child Support Determinations: What Price for a Child's Best Interests?*, 49 CATH. U. L. REV. 167 (1999) (discussing imputation of income in general); *Petitto v. Petitto*, 808 A.2d 809 (Md. App. 2001)(imputation of income to *obligee* should also be done in appropriate circumstances).

2. *Seek-Work Orders*. The *Dennis* trial court, rather than litigating the question of ability to pay in a vacuum, ordered the defendant to explore other employment possibilities. While this order was approved by the appellate court, such orders are rarely issued. But in a post-*Dennis* case, the trial court was criticized for *failure* to issue a seek-work order. In *In re Marriage of Wallen*, 407 N.W.2d 293 (Wis. App. 1987), the father was laid off from his factory job, which paid almost $30,000 annually and immediately took a minimum wage job at a theme park. The court ordered substantial child support (his entire salary plus $25 weekly) because it believed obligor "has taken a very low paying job . . . when he could have sought and obtained employment that was higher paying. . . ." The appellate court found no evidence of shirking. Citing *Dennis,* the court held "use of a seek-work order here would have put the trial court in a much better position to determine . . . whether [the father] was shirking his obligations by refusing, or failing to seek, suitable employment."

[5]   CUSTOMIZING A CHILD SUPPORT ORDER

As indicated above, the Family Support Act of 1988 requires all support guidelines to identify a presumptive amount of child support. After this baseline is calculated, either obligor or obligee can attempt to convince the court that the particular circumstances render an award at this level inappropriate. Of course, the number of variations in this situation are almost infinite. Consider the following cases.

DONOHUE v. GETMAN

432 N.W.2d 281 (S.D. 1988)

MILLER, Justice. Virginia Getman Donohue appeals from an order which set Richard Getman's child support payments at $120 per month. We reverse.

Richard and Virginia were divorced in 1982 [and] Richard received physical custody of their three children. Both parties subsequently remarried, and their new spouses either have custody of or pay child support for children from prior marriages.

In 1986 the trial court . . . awarded sole . . . custody of the parties' three children to Virginia. The court denied Virginia's request for child support, finding that Richard did not have the means or ability to make support payments.

Shortly thereafter, Virginia petitioned the trial court for child support based on the guidelines set forth in SDCL 25-7-7, since Richard was receiving worker's compensation and social security disability benefits totaling $1,405.33 per month. The trial court found that Richard is totally disabled within the meaning of worker's compensation and social security law. Richard has a severe degenerative condition of the spine and a herniated disc; as a result, he suffers pain, has occasional blackouts, and is experiencing atrophy of his arms. Richard has undergone surgery at least four times due to these problems, and his present wife cannot work because she must stay at home

[margin note: Trial ct found D's new family had medical expenses and thus lowered P's award]

to take care of him. The trial court also found that the children of Richard's new spouse are experiencing medical problems which will require surgery, and Richard will be obligated to pay those medical bills. The trial court concluded that even though the statutory guidelines would require Richard to pay between $539 and $578 per month . . ., he should pay only $120 per month. The trial court gave the following reasons for its deviation . . .: Richard's medical condition and total disability; his monthly expenses and large indebtedness; his future medical expenses; his inability to hold any kind of gainful employment; and the medical condition of his step-children, which will require further expenditures of money.

Did the trial court abuse its discretion by deviating from the child support guidelines . . .?

[margin note: Standard of review = abuse of discretion]

This court will not disturb an award . . . unless it clearly appears that the trial court abused its discretion. Virginia argues that the trial court abused its discretion when it failed to enter findings with regard to all five factors listed in SDCL 25-7-7 before deviating from the guidelines. Virginia also contends that it was an abuse of discretion to allow expenses from Richard's second family to [justify] deviation from the guidelines. We agree.

SDCL 25-7-7 states in part:

[margin note: Factors determining child support award]

> These guidelines shall be used in setting child support. *Deviation from the guidelines may be made only upon the entry of specific findings based upon the following factors:*
>
> (1) Financial condition of the parents, including . . . income of a new spouse or contribution of a third party to the income or expenses of that parent;
>
> (2) The standard of living of the child;
>
> (3) The age and special needs of the child;
>
> (4) The effect of provisions relating to custody and visitation; or
>
> (5) Child care. (emphasis added)

Very recently, in *Bruning v. Jeffries,* we addressed the guidelines set forth in SDCL 25-7-7 and stated:

[margin note: Cannot deviate from guidelines w/o specific findings]

> As the above quoted portion of SDCL 25-7-7 indicates, *there may be no deviation from the guidelines unless there is an entry of specific findings regarding the five listed factors.* The question becomes whether Secretary (and hearing examiner) must consider these factors in every case he hears. We conclude . . . that *the legislature intended that these factors be considered in each proceeding* (emphasis added).

422 N.W.2d at 580.

[margin note: Trial ct failed to follow all factors]

Here, the trial court entered findings regarding the financial condition of Richard and his second family, but none on the financial condition of Virginia or the other four [statutory] factors. . . . [T]he failure of the trial court to address these factors constitutes an abuse of discretion. The trial courts of this state must consider the totality of both parents' financial condition and the needs of the children, . . . before deviating from the statutory guidelines.

Furthermore, it is well settled that a parent's responsibility to support his children is paramount; other debts are secondary. This includes obligations resulting from remarriage. *Brunick v. Brunick.* In this case the trial court failed to address the financial needs of Richard's natural children, while focusing on the needs of Richard's step-children by his second marriage and his other debts. The trial court then used the step-children's needs as a basis for reducing Richard's support for his natural children. This is contrary to our holdings . . . and constitutes a further abuse of the trial court's discretion.

[handwritten margin note: D has responsibility to children regardless of remarriage]

We therefore reverse . . . and remand for reconsideration. . . .

[handwritten margin note: Reversed]

NOTES

1. *Variation from Guideline Amount.* South Dakota's statute is like many in defining the information relevant to deciding whether to order less or more than the guideline amount. Some statutes provide less guidance to the court. Other statutes are very detailed, mentioning parental financial resources, relative standards of living, child's resources, tax consequences, disparity between parental incomes, step-children of the obligor and in-kind contributions by each parent. *See, e.g.,* GA. CODE ANN. § 19-6-15(c) (1999) (17 specific factors); N.Y. DOM. REL. L. § 240, 1-b, (f) (2003) (nine factors). Listed factors often are described as illustrative and not exhaustive.

A constitutional attack on child support guidelines by a group of support obligors, asserting they constituted an improper "irrebutable presumption" because courts would not consider arguments that a particular child's needs were below the guideline amount, was rejected in *Parents Opposed to Punitive Support (POPS) v. Gardner,* 998 F.2d 764 (9th Cir. 1993). The court held that even if the statutory amount was irrebutable, it was constitutionally acceptable as a substantive legislative judgment that "divorcing parents will be required to sustain their children at a certain standard of living determined by the parents' income." A state constitutional attack based on an alleged violation of separation of powers doctrine was rejected in *Gallaher v. Elam,* 104 S.W.3d 455 (Tenn. 2003) (legislative delegation to executive agency of power to promulgate guidelines was acceptable because appropriate standards for guidelines were provided).

Federal law specifies that the guideline amount may be rebutted only by a "written finding or specific finding on the record that the application of the guidelines would be unjust or inappropriate in a particular case, as determined under criteria established by the state. . . ." 42 U.S.C. § 667(b) (2001) and this requirement is reflected in the typical state statute. Some cases, however, accept fairly flimsy "specific findings." *See, e.g., Manzanares v. Manzanares,* 769 P.2d 156 (Okla. 1989) (trial court varied amount "based on the equities of the case"). Why require express or written findings?

What if the parties reach an agreement on child support which specifies an amount different from that which the guidelines would provide? Is the agreement itself a reason to award a non-guideline amount? Blackletter law has always provided that "an agreement of the parties cannot usurp the authority of the court to ultimately determine the child support award." MORGAN, CHILD SUPPORT GUIDELINES: INTERPRETATION AND APPLICATION p. 4-70

(2003 Supp.).Many states, however, either via statute or case law, identify an agreement as a circumstance which is appropriate to consider in determining whether to vary from the guideline level of support. *Id.* at pp. 4–71 and 4–72; *see, e.g., In re Marriage of Rosenthal*, 903 P.2d 1174 (Col. App. 1995).

2. *Obligor's Second Family as Justifying Variance.* Courts often must deal with the financial demands of the obligor's new family when the obligor seeks to *reduce* existing child support obligations. *Donohue,* however, faced the issue in establishing a support order. The same establishment issue might arise where a married obligor was asked to support a non-marital child or an obligor was separated from the child's parent and cohabiting with a new family.

While *Donohue* (and the South Dakota statute) recognize the relevance of such financial demands, note the court's signal as to the appropriate weight of this factor. The court notes "a parent's responsibility to support his children is paramount; other debts are secondary. This includes obligations from remarriage." A trial judge on remand might have difficulty operationalizing this mandate. Must the second family subsidize the obligor's marital child? If the marital child doesn't get all the support otherwise due is he subsidizing the second family? Recall the Wisconsin statute found unconstitutional in *Zablocki v. Redhail* in Chapter 2. Would your answer depend on whether the children of the second marriage were the obligor's step-children (and whether state law required stepparental support) or were the obligor's "natural" children? The South Dakota court later rejected an Equal Protection clause attack on the preference for the first family. *Feltman v. Feltman,* 434 N.W.2d 590 (S.D. 1989). Similarly, the Tennessee Supreme Court upheld the constitutionality of support guidelines under which other dependents of the obligor can be considered only where such dependents are beneficiaries of a court order. *See Gallaher, supra* (rejecting Equal Protection and Due Process attacks, noting statute permits consideration of other dependents without a decree in "extreme circumstances").

In *Betty v. Betty*, 552 S.E.2d 846 (Ga. 2001), the Georgia Supreme Court noted that obligations to prior children justified variance under the state statute only where an existing order requires support of those children. While obligor had legal custody of his older child, the child was living with obligor's mother, he was not under any order to support that child and no evidence suggested he was doing so. In this context, the court found no reason to consider the fact that obligor had legal custody of his prior child in setting support in the current divorce case. *See also State ex rel. Crippen v. Johnson,* 2001 Tenn. App. LEXIS 72 (in setting support for non-marital child, it is irrelevant that three other children are living with obligor).

3. *Guidelines Versus Discretion.* What effect has the introduction of guidelines had on the level of awards? An early (1989) study in three states with different models (Hawaii — Melson Formula; Colorado — Income Shares; Illinois — Percentage of Obligor's Income) reported a modest closing of the asserted adequacy gap between the amount needed and the amount ordered in the pre-guideline discretion era, with support ordered in the three states (as a group) increasing by 15%. The study offered reasons for the relatively modest increase in awards. "The picture we have generated may be only temporary, with full impact requiring a longer implementation phase. The most dramatic effects of guidelines may only be realized when they are applied to the modification of previously established orders." Pearson, Thoennes & Tjaden, *Legislating Adequacy: The Impact of Child Support Guidelines*, 23 LAW & SOC. REV. 569, 586–87 (1989). *See also* New Jersey Administrative Office of the Court, *New Jersey Child Support Guidelines, First Year Evaluation* (1987) (finding increase of 30% in the award level in the first year of Income Shares model guidelines). Perhaps the most important point, however, is that only with the adoption of guidelines can any systematic discussion of the appropriate level of child support even take place. The ALI's thoughtful consideration of how to set appropriate support levels, reviewed in some detail above at pp. 470-75, may eventually yield higher support awards.

The other major impetus behind the guideline movement has been a sense that guidelines will make support awards more consistent. The sparse empirical research on actual awards suggests the pre-guideline system resulted in wide disparity in the amount of support ordered in similar circumstances. For example, a Denver study in the 1970s reported non-custodial parents were ordered to make payments ranging from 6% to 33.3% of their incomes to support one child and 5.6% to 40% of their incomes to support two children. Yee, *What Really Happens in Child Support Award Cases: An Empirical Study of Establishment and Enforcement of Child Support Orders in the Denver District Court*, 57 DEN. L.J. 21, 38–42 (1979); *see also* White & Stone, *A Study of Alimony and Child Support Rulings With Some Recommendations*, 10 FAM. L.Q. 75, 83 (1976). The Pearson, Thoennes & Tjaden study cited above reports a reduction in variability of the level of support awards in the three states studied. 23 LAW & SOC. REV. at 577. On the other hand, a commentator in 1998 found existing empirical data suggest that the goals of increased award levels and decreased award variability have not been met by the enactment of guidelines. Garrison, *An Evaluation of Two Models of Parental Obligation*, 86 CALIF. L. REV. 41 (1998) (urging adoption of ELS guidelines as exemplifying author's "Community Model" of support); *see also* Graves, *Comparing Child Support Guidelines*, 34 FAM. L.Q. 149 (2000); *Child Support Symposium*, 33 FAM. L.Q. 1 (1999).

STATE v. HALL

418 N.W.2d 187 (Minn. App. 1988)

CRIPPEN, Judge. [A parentage action was instituted by Zabloski and welfare authorities against entertainer Daryl Hall. After paternity was acknowledged, Zabloski was granted custody and support was ordered. This appeal followed.]

Zabloski and Hall['s] . . . relationship consisted of a single sexual encounter early in 1983. Their son was born on January 8, 1984.

Zabloski is currently 24 years old and lives in Duluth. She also has a minor daughter. . . . She and her two children live in a small one-bedroom apartment.

Zabloski was on public assistance from October 1983 until October 1986, when she began receiving temporary child support from Hall. Her monthly

[handwritten: Z rec's child support from Hall]

income during that time consisted of approximately $437 in A.F.D.C. benefits and an average of $120 in food stamps. Since the birth of her daughter, she has also received $95 per month in child support . . . which she expects will soon increase to $250 per month.

At trial, Zabloski . . . submitted a proposed monthly budget of $3,143, based on the purchase of an $80,000 three-bedroom home, a new car, monthly food expenditures of $400, and monthly spending of $800 for her son (including $175 for clothing, $200 for toys/books, $125 for school needs, $53 for musical training/supplies, and $300 monthly toward the purchase of a $9,000 piano).

Experts . . . testified that the amount of money a parent spends on a child is largely a matter of personal choice. Zabloski's expert testified that on a net monthly income of $43,000, approximately 13 percent or $5,590 per month would be spent on a 3-year-old child, with an increase to 25 percent at age 6. . . . Hall is 40 years old and resides in . . . a three-bedroom home . . . on 160 acres of land. He is unmarried and has no other children. He . . . has achieved commercial success, and his current net income approximates . . . $116,000 per month. He testified . . . most of his personal monthly expenses of $8,250 are for travel and business-related needs. [He] described his personal lifestyle as "frugal" and "simple" [and argued] he would want his son . . . to grow up as he did, without expensive music lessons or tutoring.

. . . Hall was ordered to pay . . . support of $1,000 per month, to provide health and dental coverage . . . and to pay for any uninsured medical or dental expenses. Absent an upward deviation, no higher award is provided under statutory child support guidelines. . . . On appeal, Zabloski [asserts] the ongoing child support award is unsatisfactory.

Did the trial court abuse its discretion in declining to deviate from the child support guidelines?

[The court noted appellate courts reverse support awards only if "clearly erroneous."]

The statutory . . . guidelines are a starting point. . . . Where an obligor's net monthly income is $4,000 or above, the guidelines set child support for one child at $1,000. The statute further provides:

(a) [Absent an agreement of the parties] the court shall order child support in accordance with the guidelines and the other factors set forth in paragraph (b) and any departure therefrom.

(b) In addition to the child support guidelines, the court shall take into consideration the following factors in setting or modifying child support:

(1) all earnings, income, and resources of the parents. . .;

(2) the financial needs and resources, physical and emotional condition, and educational needs of the child. . .;

(3) the standards of living the child would have enjoyed had the marriage not been dissolved.

. . . .

(e) The above guidelines are binding in each case unless the court makes express findings of fact as to the reason for departure below or above the guidelines.

MINN. STAT. 518.551, subd. 5.

Thus, while the statute provides for departure above or below the guidelines amount, . . . a court . . . must make express findings on the reasons for deviation . . . Zabloski [asserts] that the trial court abused its discretion by failing to fully consider Hall's standard of living, the factor listed in subdivision 5(b)(1).

z claims ct failed to acct for Hall's lifestyle in making award

In *Thompson v. Newman,* this court held that the intent of the standard of living factor "is that a child is entitled to enjoy the benefits of the incomes of both parents." We further held that ". . . [subd. 5(b)(1)] must be considered to determine what standard of living the child would have enjoyed if she or he had the benefit of both parents' incomes."

. . . In *Pitkin [v. Gross],* the obligor had net monthly income of $12,000. Although application of guidelines . . . would have resulted in [$1500 monthly] . . . support . . . the trial court . . . awarded $900 per month. In so doing, the court suggested that it was inappropriate to consider the financial needs of a custodial parent . . . and that such consideration would lead to an award which would be "grossly excessive when viewed solely from the standpoint of the needs of [the child]." In rejecting this reasoning, we noted that the needs of the child and of the custodial parent are relevant factors. . . . Thus, a downward deviation such as in *Pitkin* based on a child's limited needs could not occur without consideration of the custodial parent's needs. Because the trial court in *Pitkin* made no findings on the particular needs of either the child or the mother, its decision could not be upheld.

The need of the custodial parent is a relevant factor

In this case, the trial court's findings address not only the father's income, assets, and expenses, but also the mother's earning ability, living circumstances, and the child's personal needs. It found that if Zabloski were to complete her high school education, she would still be able to "generate only minimum or slightly above minimum wage income." It found . . . the child "appears to be a child of above-average intelligence who suffers from no . . . disabilities, and does not require any special attention or special care or training."

Trial ct's findings

. . . .

In support of its decision not to deviate, the . . . court identified several reasons which are persuasive. First, after reciting Zabloski's claimed needs, the court found that she "has not prepared or presented to this Court an estimate of how much of this proposed budget would represent the actual monthly expenses of the minor child." Based on the [expert evidence] regarding the amount of income which would normally be spent on a normal child, the court determined that the personal needs of the child are much less than the total sum claimed necessary by the mother. . . . Thus, the court determined that the child's personal needs did not exceed $1,000 per month.

z failed to show how much the child needs

The court [also distinguished] between the support which is legally required to be provided under the guidelines and the freedom of a parent to choose whether additional contributions are to be given. . . . [T]he legislature has effectively declared that a child's needs are normally not higher than $1,000 per month. *See . . . Moylan* (Yetka, J., concurring specially) (Touching on concept that legislature cannot require parents to provide a minimum dollar amount for the support of their children beyond adequate food, clothing, and medical care: "This is because some families, even with great financial resources, might want to raise their children in a spartan atmosphere in order to impress upon their children the value of money and the sacrifice and effort required to raise it. Other parents might be extremely generous, granting their children material privileges few other children will ever see or experience in their lifetimes. Such is life.")

[margin note: Cannot use child support to upgrade parent's standard of living]

The court finally implied that while the mother's needs may be considered, it would be inappropriate to use a child support obligation to upgrade her standard of living. In this sense, a distinction was made between the mother's needs and the standard of living to be enjoyed by a family. The maximum appropriate award under the guidelines effectively suggests a normal "cap" on the use of support to upgrade a child's standard of living.

Similar reasoning has been adopted by courts in other jurisdictions. In *Jane Doe VI v. Richard Roe VI*, 736 P.2d 448 (Haw. App. 1987), a paternity proceeding, the non-custodial father appealed the award. . . . Hawaii statutes required that the court consider the standard of living and circumstances of the parents. . . . Based on the father's average annual income of $110,000, the appellate court ordered "basic child support" to be set at $1,600. . . . Of particular importance to this case are the following statements of the appellate court:

[margin note: Raising the parent's standard of living is an impermissible obligation]

> We do not agree with [the father] that the need of the child is controlling. Nor do we believe, however, that the child's support should be determined mainly on the non-custodial father's standard of living. The court must be cognizant of the fact that "to raise [the mother's] standard of living through the vehicle of child support would constitute the imposition of an unauthorized obligation on part of the father toward the mother." *Kathy G. J. v. Arnold D.*, (App. Div. 1986). Also, an award for child support is for the child's current needs based on the child's appropriate standard of living and not for the purpose of saving portions thereof for future needs.

Jane Doe VI, 736 P.2d at 456–57.

Examination of the trial court's findings and memorandum in this case satisfy us that Hall's standard of living was properly considered. We conclude that the court exercised its discretion within appropriate limits when it declined to deviate from the guidelines.

[It is also urged] that the trial court failed to properly and fully assess the child's special needs. . . . The guardian's demands, however, go beyond the ability of the trial court or of this court to predict what unusual or special needs this 3-year-old child might have at some point. . . . Any identifiable special needs may be an appropriate topic for modification as those needs are encountered.

. . . .

[margin note: Affrm]

The trial court's child support award is affirmed.

NOTES

1. *High Income Obligors.* Different methods of dealing with high-income obligors have been developed. Within the percentage-of-obligor-income model, some guidelines, like Minnesota's, establish a relatively low maximum guideline amount and make the obligor's high income a factor upon which an upward deviation may be based. When *Hall* was decided, the limit on net obligor income considered by the guideline was $4,000 monthly. The percentage payable by an obligor for one child was 25%. Thus, the *Hall* "guideline amount" was $1,000, even though defendant earned $116,000 monthly. While *Hall* ultimately approved the guideline amount, it recognized that subdivision (b)(1) allowed consideration of the obligor's income as a basis for departing from the guideline.

In contrast, Georgia (another POOI state) sets no maximum guideline amount, though the court can consider an obligor's "unusually high income" as a factor justifying an award different from the otherwise applicable percentage. GA. CODE § 19-6-15(c)(11)(B) (1997) (defining unusually high income as annual gross income of more than $75,000). While both states thus allow consideration of an obligor's high income, they frame the issue quite differently.

In *Hall,* the *obligee* must prove that $1,000 monthly support is inadequate because "a child's needs are normally not higher than $1,000 per month." In Georgia, the *defendant* in a case with facts identical to *Hall* would have to show that $19,720 to $26,680 (guideline amounts based on the 17% to 23% of income payable for a single child) were inordinately high. One can therefore imagine a different result in *Hall* under Georgia law. *See also Ford v. Ford,* 600 A.2d 25 (Del. 1993) (under Melson Formula, defendant obligor must rebut presumption that the Formula calculation is appropriate).

The *ALI Principles* point in a different direction from the Minnesota and Georgia approaches to the high income obligor. Like Georgia, they reject the Minnesota approach of setting a cap on the amount of obligor income subject to the formula and agree that unusually high income enter the analysis only as a rebuttal factor offered by the obligor. Yet, the *Principles* argue, the ultimate issue in high income cases is not the amount of obligor income, but achievement of child well-being. The *Principles* thus provide:

§ 3.07 Presumptive Effect of the Child-Support Formula

(1) The child support rules should provide that the obligation established by the child-support formula is presumptively just and appropriate. Unless the presumption is rebutted . . ., the amount determined by the child-support formula should be incorporated in the child support award.

(2) The presumption established by paragraph (1) is a presumption affecting the burden of proof. It should be rebuttable only by proof that, taking into account the interests of the child, the amount determined by the child-support formula would be unjust or inappropriate, under the particular circumstances of the case, for one or more of the following reasons:

(a) the support obligor has extraordinarily high income and the amount determined under the formula exceeds an amount necessary to insure that (i) the child enjoys a standard of living that is both adequate and not grossly inferior to that of either parent and (ii) the child's . . . life opportunities are adequately secured . . .

Comment:

. . .

b. *Presumptive effect of formula.* Giving the formula presumptive effect is required by federal law as well as by sound practice. Efficient mass administration of child-support obligations requires uniform rules subject only to narrow and clearly defined exceptions. The burden of proof encompasses both the burden of going forward with the evidence and the burden of persuasion.

c. *When the support obligor has extraordinarily high income.* The principle that a parent should share income with a child seeks to ensure that the child enjoys economic adequacy and a standard of living not grossly inferior to that of either parent, and that the child is not deprived of important life opportunities that would have been available had the child resided with that parent. . . . When the amount of child support generated by application of the formula is sufficient to accomplish all these objectives, the rationale for continued sharing of income loses much of its force, although the court may still require that some percentage of additional income be shared with the child on the unqualified principle that a parent should share income with a child.

The exception for support obligors with extraordinarily high income should be treated as a rebuttal factor, rather than as a general limitation on the amount of income subject to the formula. Some states have unwisely taken the latter path, often cutting off application of the formula at inappropriately low limits of obligor or total parent income. That a nonresidential parent enjoys a high income does not imply that a child support obligation expressed as a *percentage* of this income will provide similarly or even adequately for the child. It is only when the income of an obligor is extraordinarily high that this result is certain to occur. With the illustrative ALI formula, such cases are likely to involve only support obligors whose annual net income exceeds $200,000 and such cases are in any event likely to require individualized treatment by the trier of fact.

ALI, Principles, pp. 477–79 (2002).

Some Income Shares states provide that if the combined parental income exceeds the highest amount listed on the chart, the court should exercise discretion in determining the basic support obligation (which is then divided proportionately between the parents). *See* N.Y. Dom. Rel. L. § 240(1-b)(c)(3) (2003 Supp.) (for combined annual net income above $80,000, court shall consider list of factors and/or standard percentage establishing basic child support obligation); Colo. Rev. Stats. § 14-10-115(10)(a)(II)(E) (2002 Supp.) (court may exercise "discretion where combined monthly gross income exceeds

$15,000" but support must be at least the amount appropriate where combined monthly income was $15,000); MD. FAM. LAW CODE § 12-204(d) (1999) (discretion where income exceeds guideline maximum of $10,000 joint monthly adjusted). *See also Downing v. Downing*, 45 S.W.3d 449 (Ky. App. 2001) (above-chart income should be considered on case-by-case basis; rejecting mechanical extrapolation from chart requiring 4% of all beyond-chart income as support).

The New York statute was interpreted in *Cassano v. Cassano*, 651 N.E.2d 878 (N.Y. 1995), where the combined parental income was approximately $100,000. After a hearing on the circumstances of both parents, the court had applied the 17% figure applicable where the combined income is under $80,000. On appeal, the father complained that the trial court was obligated to explain, on the basis of the child's needs, why any support was being ordered from the "excess" $20,000. The court rejected this argument, noting that the statute directs the trial court to use *either* the statutory list of factors or the standard percentage. The court did, however, require some explanation by the trial court as to why it chose the formula and not the statutory list of factors. "The stated basis for an exercise of discretion to apply the formula to income over $80,000 should reflect both that the court has carefully considered the parties' circumstances and that it has found no reason why there should be a departure from the prescribed percentage."

Must a high-income obligor reveal the exact height of his income? In *Hubner v. Hubner*, 94 Cal. App. 4th 175 (2d Dist. 2001), the father asserted that so long as he stipulated that he could afford to pay whatever support was ordered he had a right to keep the amount of his income private. The appellate court held that the need to have sufficient information to "properly assess the child's needs" outweighed any privacy interest. Noting that both obligor and obligee had complained about the support order, the fact that it was based on "fictional gross income assumptions" left the court "unable to assess whether either party is correct." A remand to develop accurate information was ordered. An issue arising with some frequency in cases involving high income obligors is the appropriate treatment of stock options. *See In re Cheriton*, 111 Cal. Rptr. 2d 755 (App. 2001); *Murray v. Murray*, 716 N.E.2d 288 (Ohio App. 1999); Isard, *Stock Options and Child Support: The Price of Accuracy*, 14 HAST. WOMEN'S L.J. 215 (2003).

2. *Disparity Between Parental Incomes in Nonmarital Support Cases.* *Hall* involved not only a high-income obligor, but also a custodial parent with very little income to whom the obligor had never been married. Such a situation forces the court to confront head-on the tension between the idea that the obligor should share income with his child and the reality that the custodial parent — to whom the obligor has no legal duty — will also benefit from the award of child support. The *Hall* trial court noted the mother's proposed budget did not indicate "the actual monthly expenses of the minor child." It was concerned she would use the child support for her own needs, concluding "it would be inappropriate to use a child support obligation to upgrade (mother's) standard of living." Note the proposed purchase of an $80,000 home by the mother, who apparently was living on welfare, food stamps and child support for her other child. *Hall*'s reasoning suggests that if the mother were better off, the support order would be higher. Some statutes identify disparity of parental income as a factor in deciding whether to vary the guideline amount. *See, e.g.,* NEV. REV. STATS. § 125B.080(9)(l) (2001) ("relative income of both parents"); N.Y. DOM. REL. L. § 240(1-b)(f)(7) (2003 Supp.).

Can this dilemma be resolved without penalizing either the child or the non-custodial obligor? One appellate court, reversing an award it found too low in a case involving great disparity, suggested the court could order the support paid directly to the provider of specific services for the child. *In re Marriage of Hubner,* 252 Cal. Rptr. 428 (App. 1988). Other courts simply accept the fact that in the disparate income situation, part of the appropriate child support award may enhance the life of the custodial parent. *See In re Marriage of Catalano,* 251 Cal. Rptr. 370 (App. 1988) ("where the supporting parent enjoys a lifestyle that far exceeds that of the custodial parent, child support must to some degree reflect the more opulent lifestyle even though this may . . . produce a benefit for the custodial parent"). But this latter attitude is more difficult to accept where a non-marital partner has no legal or moral claim to alimony or a share in the other parent's property.

In a case strikingly similar to *Hall,* the defendant was a "world-famous entertainer" who had fathered a non-marital child with a woman on welfare. *Kathy G.J. v. Arnold D.,* 501 N.Y.S.2d 58 (App. Div. 1986). While New York (like many states) has separate statutes concerning support statutes for marital and non-marital children, the court found the only "potentially significant difference" between the statutes was the former's reference to the "marital standard of living" as a relevant factor in determining support. "The reason for this distinction is an important, valid and constitutional one. Using the marital standard of living as a guidepost in determining a marital child's support decreases the possibility that such a child will have to face the additional trauma of adjusting to a new standard of living, while adjusting to all of the other changes engendered by the breakup of a marriage." The court noted that if a non-marital child had lived with his parents and established a "non-marital family," that standard of living would be relevant in setting support.

In affirming the support order and rejecting the mother's claim that her child had been treated unfairly because of her non-marital status, the court held "a fair balance must be struck, taking into consideration all relevant circumstances. [Both statutes] seek . . . to achieve the same end, that is, to provide for the needs of the particular child . . . according to the circumstances of the parents and the child. Simply because another [marital] child of the same father, in different circumstances, receives more support, does not mean that equal protection has been denied . . .; it only means that the relevant circumstances differ." *Cf. Illinois ex rel. Graham v. Adams,* 608 N.E.2d 614 (Ill. App. 1993) (while marital and non-marital children are entitled to equal treatment, child's actual needs are relevant, for both marital and non-marital children, where custodial parent has custody of other children who the obligor is not obligated to support). New York now seems to have abandoned this distinction, however, because the state's guidelines do not recognize it. *See Jones v. Reese,* 642 N.Y.S.2d 378, 379 (App. Div. 1996) (rejecting *Kathy G.J.*'s reasoning and holding marital and non-marital children should be treated identically); *see also Shuba v. Division of Child Support Enforcement ex rel. Reese,* 564 A.2d 1084 (Del. 1989) (rejecting father's claim that Melson Formula's Standard of Living Adjustment was inapplicable because parents had never cohabited). For further discussion of constitutional limits on any distinction in support rules between marital and non-marital children, see pp. 973-78 in Chapter 9.

3. *Low Income Support Obligor Cases.* As of 2001, sixteen states provided for a mandatory minimum monthly award, usually between $20 and $50. MORGAN, CHILD SUPPORT GUIDELINES: INTERPRETATION AND APPLICATION pp. 4–59 through 4-60 (2001 Supp.); *see, e.g.,* COLO. REV. STATS. § 14-10-115(10)(b) (2002 Supp.) ($20 to $50 minimum). In *Rose ex rel. Clancy v. Moody,* 629 N.E.2d 378 (N.Y. 1993), however, the court struck down a $25 monthly minimum for all obligors. The court found this pre-empted by the federal requirement of "rebuttable" guidelines. *See also Hunt v. Hunt,* 648 A.2d 843 (Vt. 1994) (Dooley, dissenting) (no federal requirement of at least nominal support in all cases). The *Moody* dissenter argued that the federal statute did not prohibit imposition of a minimum support obligation and that such a minimum, rather than conflicting with federal interests, actually furthered the interest in strengthening the support enforcement program. The dissent also noted state law protection of the obligor, a mother with custody of two of her three children whose sole income was welfare benefits, from actual enforcement of the $25 monthly obligation. Some courts have discretion to award a lesser amount than the "minimum" on a finding of inability to pay. *See, e.g.,* NEV. REV. STATS. § 125B.080(4) (2001).

4. *Other Factors Justifying Variance.* A myriad of factors are listed in various statutes as relevant to the question of variance from guideline amounts. These factors include joint custody arrangements, extraordinary medical or educational expenses for the child, unusual expenses of the obligor or obligee, transportation for visitation, age of the child, in-kind contributions of either parent and custodial parent's income (in states which adopt the percentage of obligor's income model). Georgia also specifies "historical spending in the family for children which varies significantly from the percentage table." GA. CODE ANN. § 19-6-15(c)(12) (1999).

Should the child's income be considered? In *In re Emerson,* 850 P.2d 942 (Kan. App. 1993), the court refused to consider the fact that the child received Social Security benefits based on the child's disability. Describing the benefits as a "gratuity from a governmental agency," the court noted such benefits are available only for the disabled who have inadequate income from other sources. Thus, these payments are designed to *supplement,* not *replace* child support payments. In fact, the Social Security payments might be reduced or eliminated after the award and receipt of child support. *See also Paton v. Paton,* 742 N.E.2d 619 (Ohio 2001) (adopting same rule in context of modification motion); *Nelson v. Nelson,* 454 N.W.2d 533 (S.D. 1990); *but see Velez v. Velez,* 552 So. 2d 1271 (La. App. 1989).

Emerson distinguished the situation where the child received Social Security benefits as a dependent of a disabled obligor. In that situation, the benefits are designed to replace the obligor's income and are based on contributions made by the obligor. Courts regularly credit such payments to the disabled obligor's support obligation. *See Ford v. Ford*, 816 So. 2d 1193 (Fla. App. 2002); *Brooks v. Brooks*, 881 P.2d 955 (Utah App. 1994); *In re Henry*, 622 N.E.2d 803 (Ill. 1993). Similar treatment is accorded Social Security payments to the child based on the obligor's retirement. *In re: Marriage of Belger*, 654 N.W.2d 902 (Iowa 2002); *In re Allsup*, 926 S.W.2d 323 (Tex. App. 1996).

[6] NON-JUDICIAL PROCESSES FOR ESTABLISHING SUPPORT

Support orders have traditionally been entered by courts, but recently, under pressure from Congress, many states have adopted administrative and quasi-judicial processes. The Child Support Enforcement Amendments of 1984 required creation of "expedited processes" to establish support orders in cases handled by the state's child support enforcement agency. 42 U.S.C. § 666(a)(2) (2001); 45 C.F.R. § 303.101 (2002). (These agencies, more fully described in Section C, *infra,* were established to collect support due obligees receiving welfare assistance. They are known as IV-D agencies after the title of the Social Security Act mandating their creation, 42 U.S.C. § 654(3) (2001), and now are used also by non-welfare obligees.). The expedited process must assure that, in most categories of establishment cases, an order is entered within a year of the time of filing by the agency. 45 C.F.R. § 303.101(b)(2) (2002). A waiver of the expedited process requirement is available to a state whose judicial system is equally efficacious. 42 U.S.C. § 666(d) (2001).

In response to this federal mandate, some states have chosen to offer these expedited processes to all support obligees, not simply those served by the child support enforcement agency. In about half the states, these processes involve quasi-judicial officials such as masters, referees or commissioners who either enter an order subject to review by a judge or recommend an order to the judge.

Other states use an administrative process to establish support obligations. In such a system, an executive agency (*e.g.*, department of social services) has the power to determine support duties and to enter orders. Administrative adjudication is similar to judicial process. A parent may be represented by a lawyer. There is notice, a right to a hearing, and judicial review. In practice, this administrative process has had minimal participation by attorneys. Proponents argue the administrative approach is cheaper and quicker because it avoids court calendar problems. Judges have higher salaries and larger staffs and decide fewer cases per day.

The federally-mandated guidelines apply in both judicial and non-judicial proceedings. Appeals are available from administrative proceedings, though the states are split on whether this review is de novo or on the record. In Maine, an administrative process state, only one percent of agency decisions were appealed to the judicial system in 1987. Ball, *Administrative Process,* in INTERSTATE CHILD SUPPORT REMEDIES, at 125 (Haynes ed. 1989). Some states authorize agencies to modify support decrees as well as establish them initially. A recent Montana Supreme Court decision found such a scheme violated the state constitution's separation of powers provisions. *Seubert v.*

Seubert, 13 P. 3d 365 (Mont. 2000). The court noted that, unlike statutory provisions in other states, in Montana there was no automatic judicial review of the agency determination. *See also Hilburn v. Staeden*, 91 S.W.3d 607 (Mo. 2002) (rejecting constitutional attack on administrative proceeding requiring payment of support); *State ex rel. Allee v. Gocha*, 555 N.W.2d 683 (Iowa 1996) (rejecting state constitutional attack on administrative modification).

For an overview of the use of the administrative process to establish child support, see Ball, *supra* (especially Appendix V-2, indicating range of treatment of recurring issues); Cooper, et al., A Guide for Designing and Implementing an Administrative Process for Child Support Enforcement (1985); Roberts, *Expedited Processes and Child Support Enforcement: A Delicate Balance, Parts I and II*, 19 Clearing. Rev. 483, 620 (1985); Silvester & Cooper, The Administrative Adjudication of Child Support Obligations (1981).

[7] MODIFICATION OF CHILD SUPPORT AWARDS

Like alimony awards, child support judgments are based upon current facts concerning the parties' needs and resources, which may change. As continuous obligations, they can be reevaluated if warranted by a change in circumstances. Either obligor or obligee can seek modification. The traditional rule permitted modification upon a "material change in circumstances," sometimes with the additional requirement that the change be "substantial and continuing." Some statutes imposed a more stringent burden on the movant. The Model Marriage and Divorce Act § 316(a) requires that the change of circumstances be "so substantial and continuing as to make the terms [of the original award] unconscionable." The drafters designed this provision to "discourage repeated or insubstantial motions for modification." *Commentary*, MMDA § 316. Some courts explicitly require proof that the change of circumstances was unforeseen and unforeseeable at the time of the original order. *See, e.g., In re Marriage of Feustel*, 467 N.W.2d 261 (Iowa 1990); *Miller v. Miller*, 384 S.E.2d 715 (S.C. 1989).

At one time, a party seeking an increase in child support had to show increased needs of the child as well as an increase in available obligor resources. *See* Morgan, Child Support: Guidelines: Interpretation and Application at p. 5-4 (2000 Supp.) [hereinafter Morgan]; *Kerby v. Kerby*, 60 P.3d 1038 (Okla. 2002) (four-fold increase in obligor income is cause to review support award, but "trial court . . . must consider all the relevant factors including the needs of the children . . . and the parents' income"); *Yeatman v. Gortney*, 562 So. 2d 258 (Ala. Civ. App. 1990); *Wexelman v. Donnelly*, 782 S.W.2d 72 (Mo. App. 1989). Such a requirement, though, is inconsistent with the modern approach to setting the initial award, which abandons the unhelpful "needs" formulation and instead focuses upon parental income. Under a principle that the child is entitled to share in post-divorce increases in the parent's prosperity, just as the child typically would in an intact family, higher obligor income is sufficient by itself to justify an increase in the child support award. *Miller v. Schou*, 616 So. 2d 436 (Fla. 1993) ("child is . . . entitled to share in the good fortune of his parent consistent with an appropriate life-style"); *Graham v. Graham*, 597 A.2d 355 (D.C. 1991) (doubling of obligor's income justifies increase).

Federal regulations permit a state to provide that an "inconsistency" between the original award and the guideline amount under the current facts is sufficient to justify modification without inquiry into the child's "needs." 45 C.F.R. § 303.8(c) (2002). While the regulations apply only to Title IV-D cases, most states apply the federal rule to all cases. MORGAN, at p. 5–10 (2002 Supp.). Under the rule, states are permitted to establish a "reasonable, quantitative" standard by which to determine whether the necessary "inconsistency" is shown. 45 C.F.R. § 303.8(c)(2002). Most states have identified a certain percentage of variance as their quantified standard (ranging from 10% to 30%). MORGAN, at pp. 5–12 and 5–13. It would seem that if the inconsistency between the guidelines and the current guideline amount stems from a variance or rebuttal of the guideline amount in the original action, the moving party should be obligated to prove that changed circumstances nullify the original variance. *See Smith v. Collins*, 667 N.E.2d 1236 (Ohio App. 1995).

The traditional modification process left awards unchanged unless a party initiated legal action to change them. The transaction costs involved deterred modifications and likely resulted in many support awards becoming inadequate over time. *See generally* Oldham, *Abating the Feminization of Poverty: Changing the Rules Governing Post-Decree Modification of Child Support Obligations*, 1994 BYU L. REV. 841; Note, *Preserving the Purchasing Power of Child Support Awards: Can the Use of Escalator Clauses Be Justified After the Family Support Act?*, 69 IND. L.J. 921 (1994). Since 1988, federal law has required routinized periodic review and modification of certain support orders without demonstration of a substantial change of circumstances. The current version of this periodic review is mandated by § 351 of the Personal Responsibility and Work Opportunity Reconciliation Act. 42 U.S.C. § 666(a)(10) (2001). Under this provision, the state must select one of three options for periodic review of IV-D orders:

   1) periodic review in which the court seeks current economic data from the parties and recalculates the support award according to the guidelines;

   2) application of a cost-of-living adjustment; or

   3) an automated method in which the state can use earnings information already in its possession, including wage or State income tax data, to identify those orders which should be adjusted and to adjust them.

This periodic review and adjustment must be available at least once every three years. If a state chooses either the second or third option, both parties must be given an opportunity to contest any resulting modification. States have increasingly adopted some form of automatic periodic review for all cases, rather than limiting it to those within the IV-D system. For example, in New Hampshire, while a change in circumstance modification is always available, either party can move for modification three years after its issuance. N.H. REV. STATS. ANN. § 458-C:7 (2002 Supp.). While the statute is silent, the adjustment apparently brings the order into compliance with the existing guidelines using the parties' current economic data. Nevada requires, upon request of the state or either parent, a review "at least every 3 years . . . to determine whether the order should be modified or adjusted." NEV. REV. STATS. § 125B.145(1)(2001). The order can be reviewed "at any time on the basis of changed circumstances." NEV. REV. STATS. § 125B.145(4)(2001).

Another approach requires all support decrees to include a cost of living adjustment. *See, e.g.,* MINN. STAT. ANN. § 518.641(1)(a) (2002) (unless court accepts contrary agreement, every support award "shall provide for a biennial adjustment in the amount to be paid based on a change in the cost of living"). The court must specify the cost of living index to be applied. The obligee must notify the obligor of an intention to claim the adjustment, giving the latter an opportunity to seek judicial elimination or reduction of the COLA on the ground that any increase in the obligor's income has not matched inflation. MINN. STAT. ANN. § 518.641(2) (2002). Courts in other states have endorsed similar decrees. *See, e.g., Cochran v. Rodenbarger,* 736 N.E.2d 1279 (Ind. App. 2000) (approving agreement-based self-modifying order, even though court could not enter similar order outside of parental agreement); *Roya v. Roya,* 494 A.2d 132 (Vt. 1985); *H.P.A. v. S.C.A.,* 704 P.2d 205 (Alaska 1985).

In addition to self-modifying orders and traditional modification triggered by one party, the *ALI Principles* require periodic review of all awards at least every three years, to be carried out by a state agency designated either by the court or legislature. *ALI, Principles* § 3.19 (2002). The designated agency would be empowered to gather, either from the parties or from others, such as employers, any information necessary for the calculation of the appropriate award. The parties could avoid such a review by reaching an agreement, either rejecting review or agreeing on a new level of support. The *Principles* also recommend that "whenever practicable," child support awards be self-modifying by their own terms, "automatically and continuously . . . as all relevant income changes." *Id.* at § 3.18(1). The *Principles* suggest that compliance with this requirement could be achieved by expressing support orders as a percentage of obligor's income, which would account for post-divorce decreases in income as well as increases. The Commentary acknowledges, however, that such an automatic modification system may be inconsistent with current federal regulations.

NOTES

1. *Change of Guidelines or Post-Award Developments Changing Applicable Guideline Amount.* Does promulgation of a (new) set of child support guidelines itself constitute a substantial change of circumstances justifying support modification? One group of states, either by statute or case law, has answered in the affirmative. *See, e.g.,* CAL. FAM. CODE § 4069 (1994) ("establishment of the statewide uniform guideline constitutes a change of circumstances"); S.D. COD. LAWS ANN. § 25-7-6.13 (2003 Supp.) (support orders entered before promulgation of new guidelines may be modified in accordance with guidelines without showing of change of circumstances); *Schmitt v. Schmitt,* 477 N.W.2d 563 (Neb. 1991) (enactment of new guidelines entitles obligee to recalculation of support); *Parkinson v. Parkinson,* 796 P.2d 229 (Nev. 1990). The opposite answer has been reached in another group of

states. *See, e.g.*, D.C. CODE ANN. § 16-916.01(o)(3) (2003 Supp.); N.Y. DOM. REL. LAW § 240(1-b)(l) (2003 Supp.); *Willingham v. Willingham*, 410 S.E.2d 98 (Ga. 1991); *In re Marriage of Kukes*, 852 P.2d 655 (Mont. 1993).

One commentator reports that "in most of the cases where the court determined that enactment of the guidelines constituted a change in circumstances, the petitioning party was the custodial parent seeking an upward modification; in most of the cases where the court determined enactment of the guidelines did not constitute a change in circumstances, the petitioning party was the noncustodial parent seeking a downward modification." MORGAN, at p. 5–9 (2002 Supp.). The same commentator reports that most states have taken an intermediate position and found that when there is a "material or substantial" variance between the extant award and the new guidelines a modification will be permitted. *Id.* This ensures "similar amounts of support for similarly situated children, as well as the public policy goal of administrative efficiency."

2. *Serial Families and Modification.* The custodial parent's remarriage ordinarily is not a basis for modifying the obligor's support obligation. Under the traditional rule, the legal parents retain the primary support obligation, which does not shift to a step-parent. Nonetheless, the reality that the custodial parent's new spouse has resources which are available to the child may lead courts to consider that income in allowing a reduction, particularly where the claim for reduction has additional grounds which make it plausible. *See, e.g., Snyder v. Snyder*, 499 N.E.2d 320 (Ohio App. 1985). The obligor's remarriage may, at least in some states, increase his obligations. Courts in several community property states have held that the obligor's claim to income earned by the new spouse expands the resources available to him to support his children. *See, e.g., Rodgers v. Rodgers*, 887 P.2d 269 (Nev. 1994); *Fleishmann v. Fleishmann*, 562 So. 2d 464 (La. App. 1990); *DeTevis v. Aragon*, 717 P.2d 558 (N.M. App. 1986). In other community property states, the income of new spouses is expressly excluded from child support calculations. *See, e.g.*, ARIZ. REV. STATS. § 25-320 (Appendix), § 4(f) ("income of a parent's new spouse is not treated as income of that parent") (2003 Supp.).

A particularly difficult issue arises when a second marriage (or relationship) results in new children. In one situation, a support obligor seeks a reduction in support to enable him to meet the needs of his new children. A different situation arises if that second marriage also ends, and a court must now set a child support order for the second set of children. Here the question is typically whether the existing support order for the first children should be deducted from the obligor's income in fixing the award to the second set of children.

There is no consensus on how to handle the first situation. Some states provide a fairly firm rule of "first in time, first in right" and reject downward modification motions based on the demands of a second family. *See, e.g., In re Marriage of Vucic*, 576 N.E.2d 406 (1991) (new family obligation does not lessen duty to support children from prior marriage); *Bock v. Bock*, 506 N.W.2d 321 (Minn. App. 1993) (subsequent children provide no reason to deviate from presumptive obligation to prior children); *Feltman v. Feltman*, 434 N.W.2d 590 (S.D. 1989) (obligor who becomes responsible for supporting new children does so knowing of continuing responsibility to existing children). *Feltman*, in fact, rejected a constitutional attack on the statutory preference for the first family, finding the classification rational.

By contrast, other states, either by statute or case law, provide that consideration of obligations to subsequent children is appropriate or required. *See, e.g., Martinez v. Martinez*, 660 A.2d 13 (N.J. Ch. Div. 1995) (subsequent child's right to adequate support not dependent on timing of birth); *Rohr v. Rohr*, 911 P.2d 133 (Idaho 1996) (remarriage and new child states claim for downward modification); *In re Marriage of Paulin*, 54 Cal. Rptr. 2d 314 (App. 1996) ("hardship deduction" available for obligor seeking downward modification who has twins with new wife). Many states take an intermediate position. Some admit facts about the new family as part of the exercise of the trial court's discretion. Another way to handle the issue is to "provide that the consideration of subsequent children may only be used 'defensively' and not 'offensively.' This means that an obligor may not . . . seek a modification on the support obligation on the grounds that he or she has new children. . . . The obligor may, however, defend a motion for an upward modification . . . on the grounds that he or she has new children. . . ." MORGAN, at p. 3–48 (2001 Supp.). *See also Taylor v. McGlothin*, 919 P.2d 1349 (Alaska 1996) (trial court did not abuse discretion in setting support for prior children less than guideline level after considering obligor's subsequent children); *Molstad v. Molstad*, 535 N.W.2d 63 (Wis. App. 1995) (trial court properly considered needs of subsequent children in addressing modification petition brought by mother of children of first marriage).

In the second situation, the guidelines of a "vast majority of states . . . provide that an existing child support obligation, arising out of a court order or separation agreement and actually paid, is deducted from that parent's gross income" for calculation of resources available to support the subsequent children. MORGAN, at pp. 3–42 (2003 Supp.) (collecting citations to relevant state guidelines). Other states provide that such obligations provide a reason for variation from the otherwise applicable guideline amount and Texas has a separate formula for such cases. *Id.* at pp. 3–43. This approach favoring the prior children is, perhaps, inevitable because modification of an existing order is not feasible in the second litigation. The prior children are not parties to the litigation and may not even be within the jurisdiction of the court establishing the new order. This approach, though universal, has not gone uncriticized. A student commentator urged that the later children should not be burdened by their parent's procreative decisions and that a systematic preference for existing children presents an Equal Protection problem. Note, *Second Children Second Best? Equal Protection for Successive Families Under State Child Support Guidelines*, 18 HASTINGS CON. L.Q. 881 (1991).

3. *Downward Modifications: Some Special Cases.* Many obligors seek a downward modification based on a return to school or a new job or career. In *Kelly v. Hougham*, 504 N.W.2d 440 (Wis. App. 1994), the court reduced father's obligation when he returned to graduate school and quit his full-time job. The court was influenced by the fact that the custodial mother, a law student with only part-time employment at the time of the original decree, was at this point earning a full-time annual salary of $45,000. Also, the father intended to continue to work part-time during graduate school and, during marriage, had intended to return to school after his wife finished law school. *See also Marriage of Meegan*, 13 Cal. Rptr. 2d 799 (App. 1992) (reducing support to zero when obligor entered priesthood); *but see Marriage of Ilas*, 16 Cal. Rptr. 2d 345 (App. 1993) (rejecting downward modification proposed by pharmacist who had quit his job to attend medical school; obligations would be measured against earning capacity, not earnings, regardless of good faith); *Goldberger v. Goldberger*, 624 A.2d 1328 (Md. Sp. App. 1993) (father's plans to be permanent Torah and Talmud student amount to voluntary impoverishment, even though he had done this throughout the marriage and had never had a paying job).

Should obligor be permitted to reduce a support obligation because of a decision to leave the workplace and return home to care for a new-born baby? The Mississippi Supreme Court said no in *Bailey v. Bailey*, 724 So. 2d 335 (Miss. 1998). Acknowledging the obligor likely had no intent to jeopardize the interests of her older children, the court concluded she was compromising their interests in favor of her new baby, which amounted to a "neglect or refusal to fulfill some duty . . . by some interested . . . motive" and, thus, satisfied a standard definition of bad faith.

A former major league baseball player was unsuccessful in seeking a downward modification after loss of his minor league general manager's job. In *Phelps v. LaPoint*, 284 App. Div. 2d 605 (3d Dept. 2001), the support obligation was set in 1996 at $100 weekly. After losing his baseball job, LaPoint was working as manager of a bar owned by his new wife, earning $24,000, rather than his prior annual salary of $40,000. The appellate court found this a "quintessential fact pattern" demonstrating a purposeful attempt to avoid family obligations. The court noted obligor's assignment of a $1 million receivable to his current wife, his country club membership, numerous golf vacations and "tens of thousands of dollars in annual credit card charges." The court found obligor's post-baseball efforts to obtain employment consistent with his earning capacity "woefully inadequate." *See also In re Malloy*, 2001 Iowa App. LEXIS 464 (permitting downward modification based on obligor's retirement from the National Guard, noting retirement was caused, in part, by obligor's exercise of visitation with his children).

Many modification cases involve incarcerated obligors seeking to reduce or terminate their obligation. The cases are badly split. Some courts grant such petitions, concluding the obligor's income is drastically reduced and he has no capacity for greater earnings while in prison. *See, e.g., In re Marriage of Willis*, 840 P.2d 697 (Ore. 1992); *Voecks v. Voecks*, 491 N.W.2d 107 (Wisc. App. 1992). By contrast, other courts reject such petitions, often theorizing that the criminal activity which resulted in incarceration was voluntary and, thus, the reduced income can be seen as voluntary. *See Glenn v. Glenn*, 848 P.2d 819 (Wyo. 1993) (obliging father, however, to pay support on basis of his prison income); *In re Marriage of Phillips*, 493 N.W.2d 872 (Iowa App. 1992). Understandably, courts are particularly reluctant to permit an incarcerated obligor to reduce or eliminate a support obligation where the incarceration results from conviction for failure to support the child. *See, e.g., Commissioner of Human Resources v. Bridgeforth*, 604 A.2d 836 (Conn. 1992).

PRICE v. PRICE

912 S.W.2d 44 (Ky. 1995)

STEPHENS, C.J. This appeal arises from an order of the . . . Circuit Court relieving [David's] obligation to pay child support arrearages which accrued from October 31, 1990, until February 14, 1992. The Court of Appeals affirmed this decision. We do not agree. *[Issue]*

David . . . (hereinafter Father) and Janet Price (hereinafter Mother) were divorced in 1987. [T]he couple had one minor son (hereinafter Child). . . . Mother was awarded custody . . . Father was ordered to pay $1400 per month in . . . support. . . . *[child support award]*

In an attempt to correct some behavioral problems, the parents agreed to change Child's residence, from Mother to Father. The change occurred on October 31, 1990. The Child remains in Father's home. Father stopped all payment . . . as of [that date]. Mother filed a motion to compel Father to pay . . . arrearages on February 14, 1992. Father [then] filed for modification of the child support decree and a legal change of custody. Thereafter . . . Mother and Father entered into an agreed order changing custody from Mother to Father. *[Child then lives with Father and Father obtains custody]*

. . . Father maintains that because he was in physical custody of Child and providing for all necessities of Child that he was not obligated to pay Mother child support between October 31, 1990 and [the date of the order changing custody in 1992]. [¶] It is undisputed that . . . legal custody of Child was not changed from Mother until the agreed order of April 27, 1992.

The trial court found that. . ."it would be unfair to require that child support be paid" by Father after October 31, 1990. The Court of Appeals . . . found no abuse of discretion. . . . This Court finds that the trial judge had no power to relieve Father of his . . . obligations which became due between the time Child changed residences and the filing of the motion for a modification of that order. *[Trial ct found Father to not owe child support. Appeals affirmed]*

. . . KRS § 403.213 . . . explicitly states that "the provisions of any decree respecting child support may be modified only as to installments accruing subsequent to the filing of a motion for modification. . ." [No] motion for modification was made to the court prior to Father's motion [in] 1992. . . . There is no ambiguity in the wording of this statute. *[Statute obligates Father to pay]*

This statute is in place to avoid litigation when one parent decides what is best for the child, much like the case before us now. Once a court has issued an order for . . . child support, neither parent can unilaterally decide upon a different course of action. In issuing this order, the court, along with the legislature, has made a determination as to what is best for the child. It is unfortunate that divorcing parents are often unable to make these decisions, but divorce by its nature is a time of conflict. We have recognized that many parents do agree, without the aid of the courts, as to modifications of custody and child support. In those instances, a court has the power to recognize the modification of the child support obligation and reduce the arrearages accordingly.

A court will enforce a private agreement . . . if it meets certain requirements. If the agreement is oral it must be proven with reasonable certainty and the court must find "that the agreement is fair and equitable under the circumstances." *Whicker v. Whicker.* Moreover, the agreement, once proven, will only be enforced if the "modification might reasonably have been granted, had a proper motion to modify been brought." *Id.*

Furthermore, . . . *Whicker* reinforces the fundamental concept that child support can only be modified prospectively. This Court has long understood "that unpaid periodical payments for maintenance of children, . . . become vested when due." *Dalton v. Dalton.* As a result and "as a matter of fact, each installment of child support becomes a lump sum judgment, unchangeable by the trial court when it becomes due and is unpaid." *Stewart v. Raikes.* Accordingly, "the courts are without authority to 'forgive' vested rights in accrued maintenance." *Mauk.* In the case before us, . . . there was no agreement . . . as to a modification. . . . We will not reach into this dispute and find an implicit agreement.

Appellee urges that equitable principles require the courts to relieve him of the court ordered child support because he, in fact, supported his child while Child lived in Father's home. We understand that "equity provides relief where the law does not furnish a remedy." *Heisley v. Heisley.* Here, appellee's recourse was at law, by the filing of a motion for modification or at least coming to an agreement with the custodial parent when circumstances warranted. Moreover, appellee took his child into his home in an attempt to correct some problems Child was having. The support given, while admirable, is the support of a parent. That does not impact the court ordered child support. As we stated long ago:

> . . . . If a party wishes to contribute to the support of his children in some manner other than that in which a court has directed, the court is always open to a timely application for modification. If he does it without such permission it is not incumbent on the court to give him any credit for it.

Tucker v. Tucker, Ky., 398 S.W.2d 238, 239 (1965)

. . . [T]he trial court abused its discretion in relieving appellee's child support arrearages. Under the circumstances, the trial court did not . . . have the power to do so. Accordingly, the Court of Appeals is reversed and this case is remanded for proceedings in conformity with this opinion.

WINTERSHEIMER, Justice, Dissenting. . . . [T]he oral agreement between the parties satisfied any . . . obligation. The change in actual custody and the ending of child support payments constituted a complete acquiescence by the wife to the oral modification of the custody agreement. Equity prevents the wife from receiving . . . payments for the period that the husband provided all the support for the son.

The parties may modify child support by oral agreement. Such agreements are enforceable prospectively if they can be proven with reasonable certainty and they are fair and equitable and if the modification is on the same terms as might reasonably been granted [by the court]. This Court has recognized that many parents can agree without the aid of the legal system to a modification of custody and child support. Clearly, a court [can] recognize the modification . . . and . . . reduce the arrearage accordingly.

The situation presented here is highly inequitable. The mother waived her right to child support by surrendering physical custody of the child for almost two years. . . . There is no equitable reason to provide a windfall. . . . The trial judge was acting with proper discretion. . . . The Court of Appeals . . . properly found no abuse of discretion. . . . Now a majority of this Court "finds" that the trial judge had no power to relieve the father of his . . . obligations. This is clearly an invasion of the factfinding authority of the trial judge. Neither the law nor equity supports such a substitution of findings.

This case teaches a very harsh lesson to . . . litigants in a domestic relations matter. . . . [I]t is always necessary to obtain such modification in writing and with the specific approval of the circuit court. It is a primary but hard lesson that voluntary payments and even beneficial conduct are simply that, only voluntary, and clearly have no legal support.

NOTE

Rule Against Retroactive Modification. *Price* is a particularly harsh application of the rule, required by federal law, 42 U.S.C.A. § 666(a)(9)(C) (1997 Supp.), barring retroactive modification of child support payments. The act, familiarly known as the Bradley Amendment, mandates that every "payment or installment of support under any child support order . . . is (on and after the date it is due) . . . not subject to retroactive modification" in any state. There are no exceptions, although a court may modify a support obligation as of the date on which the modification petition itself was filed, *see* 45 C.F.R. §§ 302.70(a), 303.106 (2002).

The federal law was well-motivated. At one time, support obligors who believed themselves entitled to a reduction in their obligation commonly would simply pay less, forcing the obligee to seek enforcement of the full award. If such enforcement was sought, the obligor would counterclaim for retroactive modification. The obligor thus had little to lose by the self-help tactic of reducing his payments, and he might benefit inappropriately if the obligee left his reduction unchallenged for any period of time — as she might if she were financially unable to incur the cost of an enforcement action, especially one that was made more complex by a counterclaim for modification.

There is now an emerging consensus, however, that the wooden and inflexible federal rule has itself led to serious injustices. *Price* offers a good example: One parent recovers substantial child support for a lengthy period of time during which the child, by parental agreement, was in the other parent's custody. This fact pattern is not rare. *See also Houser v. Houser*, 535 N.W.2d 882 (S.D. 1995) (father ordered to pay $32,000 in arrearages accrued during a ten-year period when two of the couple's three children were living with him.)

The retroactive modification ban also can combine with the rule refusing credit for nonconforming payments to produce inequitable results. In *Niemi v. Fisher*, 547 N.W.2d 801 (Wisc. App. 1996), obligor paid the custodial parent directly, rather than through the court clerk; the obligee then obtained a judgment for "unpaid" arrearages, plus interest. The appeals court, affirming, wrote:

> We confess that the results . . . are troublesome because . . . [obligor] made direct payments. Because [the relevant statutes] preclude recognition of these payments, [obligee] is unfairly enriched by double payments. This is a public policy decision made by the legislature, apparently on the belief that the public interest in addressing the problem of nonpayment of child support is best served by limiting payments to those made in accordance with the divorce judgment. This policy fixes arrearages with certainty and facilitates the determination as to who owes arrearages and what amount.

Id. at p. 815. *See also In re: Marriage of Lehr*, 740 N.E.2d 417 (Ill. App. 2000) (rejecting reimbursement for voluntary overpayment of support because it would constitute retroactive modification).

Despite the rule against modification, some courts rely on doctrines of equity to estop obligees from seeking arrearages in some situations. *See, e.g., Nill v. Martin*, 666 N.E.2d 936 (Ind. App. 1996) (no arrearage recovery where parents agreed to reduce support when one of three children died, even though award itself specified a gross amount rather than an amount per child); *Bowens v. Bowens*, 668 A.2d 90 (N.J. App. 1995) (permitting retroactive modification to date of child's attainment of majority or emancipation); *Brakke v. Brakke*, 525 N.W.2d 687 (N.D. 1994) (permitting retroactive modification where child changed residence and lived with obligor); *Ours v. Glock*, 514 N.W.2d 724 (Wisc. App. 1993) (obligee estopped from seeking arrearages for six-year period during which children lived with obligor); *Johnston v. Johnston*, 552 N.E.2d 93 (Ill. App. 1990) (mother estopped from collecting arrearages accruing while child lived with father, when she had told him he need not pay). In one kind of case, the support obligor cannot make current support payments that will reach the child because the custodial parent has concealed herself and the child. When the custodial parent reappears, can she now collect arrearages covering the concealment period? Courts have divided. *See, e.g., In re Shorten*, 967 P.2d 797 (Mont. 1998) (concealment of child for 8 years by custodial parent leads to an estoppel); *In re Marriage of Damico*, 872 P.2d 126 (Cal. 1994) (mother estopped from seeking arrearages where she actively concealed child from obligor); *but see In re Vroenen*, 94 Cal. App. 4th 1176 (Cal. App. 2001) (rejecting concealment as basis for estoppel where concealment ended before child reached majority). For more on these cases, see Ellman, *Should Visitation Denial Affect the Obligation to Pay Support?*, in COMANOR, ed., THE LAW AND ECONOMICS OF CHILD SUPPORT PAYMENTS (2004), reprinted in ——————— ARIZ. ST. L.J. ——————— (2004).

A Massachusetts court rejected a former prisoner's suit for rescission of his child support debts which accrued during his imprisonment. *D'Avella v. McGonigle*, 711 N.E. 2d 882 (Mass. 1999). The court noted the lack of explicit exceptions to the statutory ban on retroactive modification of child support debts. A similar situation with an egregious twist was reported more recently. Clarence Brandley, a Texas school janitor, was released from prison in 1992 on a finding by a state appeals court that he had been wrongfully convicted of murder. In 1993, however, his wages were garnished for about $35 weekly for support arrearages which accrued during his nine years of wrongful imprisonment. Brandley described the situation as a "double insult," and asserted the state ought to forgive or pay his arrears because it had wrongfully placed him on death row for nine years. A spokesman for the Attorney General's office, acknowledging "special circumstances," said the "obligation for child support does not go away." An attorney who represented Brandley in a support arrearage action in 1993 noted the action was begun "shortly after Brandley filed a $120 million civil rights lawsuit against an array of state agencies" which was later dismissed on the basis of sovereign immunity. Rice, *"It's Like a Double Insult"; Free From Prison, Brandley Baffled by Order to Pay Back Child Support,* HOUST. CHRON., Apr. 27, 2002, p. 1.

PROBLEMS

Problem 5-11. You serve on the staff of the legislative committee with jurisdiction over child support matters. Your chair wants a draft of a statutory provision dealing with claims by custodial parents that the obligor's support obligation should include payment of private school tuition for minor children. What factors do you think should be relevant? Should religiously-supported private schools be treated the same as secular schools? Should the obligor's objections to the "elitist" nature of a particular private school be considered?

Problem 5-12. Tammy and Jim are divorcing after a 15-year marriage with three children, now aged 11, 5 and 3. For most of the marriage, Jim was a trial lawyer in a major firm. After seven years, he was made a partner and earned approximately $150,000 annually for the next seven years. About a year ago, when the marriage began to crumble, Jim quit and entered a seminary to train to be a clergyman. During the last year, the family has lived on savings and Jim's part-time job at a local supermarket where he grossed about $275 per week. Tammy, who has a high school education, is a secretary and grosses about $17,000 per year. Tammy seeks your advice on what child support she can expect to receive. All events take place in Georgia.

Problem 5-13. Patricia and Joseph are divorcing. Your client, Joseph, owns real estate appraised at approximately $1.5 million. The property is not income-producing and consists of a vineyard, two dilapidated commercial buildings (currently being renovated) and two pieces of undeveloped land. During the marriage, Joseph was not gainfully employed and used his investment income from stocks and bonds to support the family. The trial court has awarded support to Patricia for the couple's two children, basing his calculation of Joseph's income, in part, on an imputation of a 6% return on the value of his real estate. What is your response on appeal?

§ C. ENFORCEMENT OF SUPPORT ORDERS

[1] TRADITIONAL DIFFICULTIES IN COLLECTING SUPPORT

According to reports from custodial parents, in surveys conducted by the Census Bureau, a significant proportion of children do not receive support from an absent parent. Non-marital fathers are disproportionately represented in the group of non-supporters. It seems the usual problem is not that a support order is ignored but that no order has been obtained. In the 2002 survey, only 59% of the 13.4 million parents living with children under 21 whose other parent was not living in the household reported having either a decree or an agreement for child support. U.S. Department of Commerce, Bureau of the Census, *Custodial Mothers and Fathers and Their Child Support: 2001, Current Population Reports, Consumer Income,* Series P60-225 (October 2003) [hereinafter *2001 Data*].

Several types of explanations were offered by parents without an award or agreement. Perhaps surprisingly, of the 5.9 million such parents, only about one in six (16.9%) claimed to be unable to locate the absent parent. *Id.* at Fig. 4. More than 32% reported they "did not feel the need to make (support arrangements) legal." A total of almost 37% reported either that they "did not want the other parent to pay" (19.3%) or that they did "not want to have contact with the other parent" (17.4%). *Id.* While 63% of female custodial parents had obtained an award or agreement for child support, only 39% of male custodial parents reported agreements or awards imposing a support obligation on non-custodial mothers. *Id.* at Table 8.

What would explain a refusal to seek support? Some custodial parents, because of their partner's attitude or meager resources, conclude a support suit would be futile. Others want to minimize or eliminate further interaction with the absent parent. The phenomenon of custodial parents entitled to, yet not seeking, support may be a particular example of the common situation in which a right-holder fails to enforce his or her rights either in court or elsewhere. But, of course, here the custodial parent is failing to enforce his or her child's or children's support rights.

In those same surveys, custodial parents who do have awards or support agreements often report that they did not receive payments that were due. Of custodial parents to whom child support was owed in 2001, only 44.8% reported receiving the full amount due, 29.2% reported partial payment, and 26% received none of the expected support. *Id.* at Fig. 5. From other studies, it seems certain that comparable surveys of noncustodial parents would produce reports of greater compliance. Unfortunately it is not possible to be certain of the actual facts. A study in the late 1980's of 378 divorcing families in Maricopa County, Arizona (Phoenix) found a higher compliance rate regarding child support obligations than that found by the Census Bureau surveys, with only 16% of divorced custodial mothers reporting no child support payments as opposed to approximately 25% in the Census Bureau data. Custodial mothers reported 71% of all court-awarded support paid, compared to the Census data which, during that time period using a different methodology than currently used, reported full receipt in the 60–65% range. The difference can be traced in part to the fact that the Arizona study was limited to divorcing families, while the Census data includes never-married custodial mothers. Such a finding is consistent with the popular perception of non-marital fathers being less involved with their children than the fathers of in-wedlock children.

The Arizona study also tested the Census Bureau's methodology by asking support *obligors* how much support had been paid. Not surprisingly, the reports were not identical. Obligors reported having paid 93% of their obligations. Fully 2/3 of obligors reported having paid at least 100% of their support obligations during the preceding 12 months (11% reported having paid more than the required amount). By contrast, only 45% of custodial parents reported their ex-spouse was current in support payments. *See* Braver, Fitzpatrick & Bay, *Noncustodial Parent's Report of Child Support Payments,* 40 FAMILY RELATIONS 180 (1991). The authors did not speculate on whether the custodial or noncustodial parents are being more truthful.

The increased efforts at enforcement detailed in the rest of this Chapter seem to be having a positive impact on the effectiveness of child support collection. Between 1993 (when the Census Bureau changed its methodology and thus rendered earlier data non-comparable) and 2001, the percentage of custodial parents reporting full payment of owed support rose from 36.9% of those who were owed support to 44.8% in 2001, an increase of over 20%. *2001 Data* at Figure 5. Interestingly, however, in the latter year 45.4% of custodial mothers reported received full payment, while only 39% of custodial fathers received full payment. *Id.* at Table A. Comparison of the Census data in 1993 and 2001 also makes clear that while more custodial parents reported receiving all support due in 2001, the percentage reporting partial receipt declined from 38.9% in the earlier year to 29.2% in the latter year. *Id.* at Figure 5. Thus, the percentage of parents receiving at least some money did not increase but, in fact, slightly declined from 75.8% to 74%. *Id.* This suggests that the new enforcement techniques were most effective in getting more money from those already paying something.

It has long been asserted that there is a linkage between contact with the child and the payment of child support. The 2001 data supports the existence of such a link. At least some child support was reported paid in approximately 77% of the cases in which the obligor had either joint custody or visitation privileges, as compared to only 55.8% of the cases lacking any legally-mandated access to the child. *2001 Data* at p. 8.

The average child support payments reported received in 1991 was $2,961, U.S. Department of Commerce, Bureau of the Census, *Child Support for Custodial Mothers and Fathers: 1991, Current Population Reports, Consumer Income,* Series P60-187 at p. 18, an increase of approximately 1/3 over 1985, probably reflecting the impact of the adoption of child support guidelines. Custodial parents reported $17.7 billion in payments due in 1991 and $11.9 billion actually received. *Id.* at p. 2. Custodial mothers received about 68% of support due during 1991, while custodial fathers reported collecting only 53% of the aggregate support due to them. *Id.* at p. 10. While approximately 76% of all custodial parents who were due money actually received some during 1991, 88% of those who were relying on agreements received some payments, while only 71% of those relying on court orders received any of the support due. *Id..* The 2001 figures reflected further improvement for those actually receiving child support. The average support received was $3,200 per custodial parent family, approximately 12% higher, in real terms, than in 1993. *2001 Data* at p. 8. Non-custodial mothers seemed to be more reliable than non-custodial fathers with approximately 68% of the support owed by the former being reported received, while only 62.1% of the money owed by fathers was reported received. *Id.*

What explains non-collection of support orders? The most important impediment is the fact that such orders usually require multiple periodic payments. Obviously there is a greater risk of non-compliance when compliance requires performance of a series of acts over a long period of time. Enforcing support judgments, therefore, requires enforcement mechanisms such as the threat of jail or garnishment of wages. Some courts, however, are reluctant to jail non-paying obligors. Another factor contributing to under-enforcement is difficulty in identifying and locating obligors (particularly those living far from the child) or the obligor's assets. Another difficulty is that the obligor may have inadequate financial resources. There is no easy solution where parents of limited financial means incur more obligations than they can fulfill. (Recall Wisconsin's unsuccessful attempt to deny marriage licenses to obligors delinquent in existing support obligations in *Zablocki,* reprinted in Chapter 2.) Traditionally, enforcement was left to the custodial parent, who had to initiate the necessary legal proceedings. The need to pursue the non-paying parent often presented a financial or emotional obstacle for a custodial parent not anxious for contact with the absent parent. Incomplete records concerning payments often make such litigation difficult. Such problems have contributed to increasing government involvement in the enforcement of support.

[2] GOVERNMENTAL INVOLVEMENT IN SUPPORT ENFORCEMENT

LEGLER, THE COMING REVOLUTION IN CHILD SUPPORT POLICY: IMPLICATIONS OF THE 1996 WELFARE ACT, 30 Fam. L.Q. 519, 520–24 (1996)

We have seen the American family undergo dramatic structural changes in the last thirty years. The skyrocketing increase in . . . out-of-wedlock births coupled with the high rate of divorce means that more and more families are single parent families. The custodial parent . . . is often the sole source of financial support, and since that parent is often a mother with low income, millions . . . are subject to a childhood of poverty. Efforts to reduce poverty for children in single parent families will require a broad, comprehensive strategy. One part of that comprehensive strategy . . . is the need for increased child support collections through better child support enforcement.

Efforts to increase child support enforcement are not new. Congress first passed an amendment to the Social Security Act in 1975 which required each state to develop its own child support enforcement program, commonly known as the "IV-D" program.[11] It established the child support system as a joint federal and state effort with the federal government providing partial funding for IV-D programs and providing oversight and technical assistance. The federal government also operates the Federal Parent Locator Service (FPLS). States operate their own IV-D programs with substantial discretion but with certain program requirements imposed by federal law.

The original legislation creating the IV-D program has been . . . expanded several times.[15] State IV-D programs must currently provide child support services to all cases where the custodial parent receives AFDC or Medicaid. These individuals must assign their right to receive child support to the state. State agencies must also serve any other individual custodial parent who requests services. . . . It is estimated that 60 percent or more of all child support cases are now in this public IV-D collection system. Non-IV-D cases . . . are handled through private arrangements.

. . . .

Yet, despite some successes, . . . we still have a long way to go. A . . . report issued in 1994 by the Urban Institute showed just how far the current child support system falls short.[24] The report showed an immense gap between what is currently collected in child support and what could theoretically be collected. According to the findings, if child support orders, reflecting current ability to pay, were to be established for all children with a living noncustodial father, and these orders were fully enforced, aggregate child support payments would have been as high as $48.2 billion dollars in 1990. Only $14.4 billion was actually received. Thus, there is a gap between what is currently received and what could theoretically be collected of $33.8 billion dollars per year.[25]

. . . .

Three facts that emerge . . . are striking. First, the total picture the reports show is bleak — millions of children are not receiving the support they deserve. Second, the gap from the inadequacy of awards ($7.0 billion) is as large as from the failure to collect what is owed ($7.2 billion). Third, and perhaps most importantly, the largest part of the gap ($19.6 billion) is due to the failure to obtain child support awards. Because the lack of paternity

---

[11] . . . . [S]tates that wish to participate in AFDC are also required to take part in Title IV-D. [The new welfare act, the Personal Responsibility and Work Opportunity Reconciliation Act of 1996 (PRWORA)] §101 continues this cooperative federalism arrangement.

[15] The Child Support Amendments of 1984 . . . mandated the adoption of a number of state laws and procedures. . . . The Family Support Act of 1988 added additional requirements for state programs, including standards for paternity establishment, income withholding from noncustodial parent's wages, presumptive support guidelines . . ., periodic review and adjustment of some orders, and the development of statewide automated systems. . . .

[24] Elaine Sorenson, Urban Institute, NONCUSTODIAL FATHERS: CAN THEY AFFORD TO PAY MORE CHILD SUPPORT? (1994) [hereinafter Urban Institute].

[25] According to the study, 21% of the $33.8 billion, or $7.2 billion, is due to a failure to collect what is ordered; another 21%, or $7.0 billion, is due to inadequate awards; and 58%, $19.6 billion, is due to the fact that many potentially eligible custodial parents do not have a legal child support award or order. Some caution must be taken in using the numbers from this study. The collection gap of $34 billion dollars represents what could "theoretically" be collected, not court ordered child support that was not paid. . . .

establishment is the chief reason for a lack of awards, improving paternity establishment is crucial to closing the collection gap.[28]

NOTE ON FEDERAL INVOLVEMENT IN SUPPORT ENFORCEMENT

As noted by Legler, Congress in the past three decades has mandated many improvements and expansion of state techniques of enforcing child support. "Quietly — almost without notice — Congress has spent the last 15 years altering the nature of America's family law system." ROBERTS, TURNING PROMISES INTO REALITIES: A GUIDE TO IMPLEMENTING THE CHILD SUPPORT PROVISIONS OF THE FAMILY SUPPORT ACT OF 1988, at 1 (Center for Law and Social Policy 1989). The IV-D child support enforcement agency described in the excerpt was designed to "help locate absent parents, establish paternity, obtain support orders and enforce those orders." Roberts, *supra,* at 1.

In some states, the IV-D agency is located within the human services or welfare department. In other states, the local contact is affiliated with the county attorney's office or as an administrative branch of the courts. The trend is toward incorporating the IV-D agency responsibilities within a state government agency with other significant law enforcement responsibilities, such as the Attorney General's Office or the State Department of Revenue.

Most IV-D "clients" have been welfare recipients. Services to welfare families were pursued more vigorously by the states because of their taxpayers' pocketbook interest in seeking reimbursement and elimination of AFDC awards. Federal law makes clear, however, that non-welfare families must have equal access to IV-D services. *In re Marriage of Lappe*, 680 N.E.2d 380 (Ill. 1997) (state provision of such services is mandated by Federal statutes and not violative of state constitutional provision limiting expenditure of public funds to "public purposes"); *Cabinet for Human Resources v. Houck*, 908 S.W.2d 673 (Ky. 1995) (same). While ordinarily obligees are served by the support agency, obligors may also use the agency in various matters such as the establishment of parenthood, petition for a downward modification, etc.

In fact, a substantial number of IV-D cases do not involve "welfare" clients. According to data quoted in *Lappe, supra*, virtually half of the litigants assisted by the state IV-D agency in fiscal year 1995 were non-AFDC clients (243,551 of 495,833). Between 1991 and 1998, the non-AFDC caseload of IV-D agencies nationally increased over 100% (from 5.4 million to 10.9 million), while the AFDC portion increased only from 8 million cases to 8.5 million. Thus, by the latter year, the IV-D agencies were handling more non-welfare cases than welfare cases. U.S. Department of Health and Human Resources, Office of Child Support Enforcement, *Twentieth Annual Report to Congress* 41 (1997); U.S. Department of Health and Human Resources, Office of Child Support Enforcement, *Twenty-Third Annual Report to Congress* 21 (2000). Indeed, by 2002 because of the late 1990's welfare reform limiting access to TANF, the vast majority of IV-D child support collection cases involved obligees who were not currently receiving government assistance. According

---

[28] Paternity, a prerequisite to establishing a support award, has not been established in about half of these cases. . . .

to the federal Office of Child Support Enforcement only 2.8 million of the 16 million IV-D cases were welfare cases in 2002 (because of changes in methodology the 2002 data is not directly comparable to earlier data). www.acf.hhs.gov/programs/cse/pubs/2003/reports/prelim_datareport/ Table 1.

Non-welfare custodial parents may be required to pay for IV-D services. Retained counsel may use IV-D services such as the parent locator service. Once the absent parent is located, legal procedures to obtain or enforce an order can be instituted, either by the agency or by private counsel.

The 1984 Child Support Amendments (Pub. L. 98-378) used the conditional spending power to encourage states to enact a number of specific remedies and procedures designed to improve support enforcement and to equalize treatment of welfare and non-welfare families. States, for example, were required to create expedited processes for establishment of support orders in IV-D cases. Additional requirements applicable to all child support cases (not just IV-D cases) included automatic wage withholding for obligors in arrears and allowing establishment of paternity at any time until the child's 18th birthday. The 1988 Family Support Act (Pub. L. 100-485) and the Personal Responsibility and Work Opportunity Reconciliation Act of 1996 (Pub. L. 104-193) [hereinafter PRWORA] imposed additional requirements concerning enforcement, some of which are noted below.

The latter statute transformed the AFDC entitlement program to a block grant program known as Temporary Assistance for Needy Families (TANF). It required each state and the federal government to create a Directory of New Hires which will provide a new database for use in establishing and enforcing support obligations. PRWORA §§ 313, 316. All employers, regardless of size, must report information (including Social Security Number) on new hires within 20 days to the State Directory, which shares the data with the Federal Directory. The Act also requires use of Social Security numbers in a range of contexts, such as applications for many licenses, including marriage and occupational, death certificates, support orders and divorce decrees. PRWORA § 317. The Act imposes a generally-applicable five-year limit on the receipt of federal welfare cash assistance, thus making the effectiveness of child support enforcement especially important for poor parents whose further receipt of welfare funds is time-barred. *See* Brustin, *The Intersection Between Welfare Reform and Child Support Enforcement*, 52 Cath. U.L. Rev. 621 (2003).

The Tenth Circuit rejected an attack on PRWORA's restrictions in *Kansas v. United States*, 214 F. 3d 1196 (10th Cir. 2000). Kansas had objected to federal requirements mandating information sharing, mass case processing, and uniformity in exchange for federal welfare funding, the establishment of a Case Registry containing all support orders, the required Directory of New Hires, the required adoption of the Uniform Interstate Family Support Act and laws facilitating genetic testing and paternity establishment. The argument was that the federal government could not constitutionally impose such requirements on the states as a condition of federal funding of welfare programs. The court, however, held that the limits on the Congressional Spending Power outlined in *South Dakota v. Dole*, 483 U.S. 203 (1987), had not been breached, noting that the new law actually offered individual states more options than the previous Aid to Families with Dependent Children. *See*

Elrod, *Child Support Reassessed: Federalization of Enforcement Nears Completion,* 1997 U. ILL. L. REV. 695 (predicts improvement of support enforcement alone will not solve problem of child poverty and argues current law reduces public support for families by focusing on support enforcement rather than assistance to needy families); Estin, *Federalism and Child Support,* 5 VA. J. OF SOC. POL'Y & L. 541 (1998) (discusses use of Commerce and Spending Power to promulgate federal support legislation; argues "boundaries between national and state power are worth preserving in family law and . . . Congress and the courts have important roles to play in helping to preserve the balance").

While responsibility for support enforcement remains with the states, considerable federal resources are available to initiate and finance state programs. States meeting the minimum standards established by OCSE receive substantial federal funding for the administrative costs of collection programs.

How successful has the effort to increase support collection been? Collections by the state IV-D agencies continue to increase every year. Support collection of current year's support went from $6.0 billion in FY 1990 to $9.5 billion in FY 1998 to $15 billion in FY 2002. U.S. Department of Health and Human Services, Office of Child Support Enforcement, *Thirteenth Annual Report to Congress,* at 6–7 (1990); U.S. Department of Health and Human Services, Office of Child Support Enforcement, *Twenty-Third Annual Report to Congress,* at p. 32 (2000); www.acf.hhs.gov/programs/cse/pubs/2003/reports/ prelim_datareport/ Table 9.

Understood as a percentage of the support owed, collection also has become more successful in the past two decades. For FY 1986, the states collected 45.8% of the amount of current support owed. For FY 1994, they collected 53% of the current support owed. By FY 2002, the comparable percentage was 57%.

While the IV-D program has become progressively more effective in collecting support, a significant part of the improvement stems from the movement of non-welfare cases into the IV-D collection machinery. Thus, while total IV-D collections increased from $1.8 billion to $3.9 billion from 1978 to 1987 (an increase of 117%), total collections reported in the Census Bureau surveys of obligees increased only from $8.2 billion to $10 billion (an increase of only 22%) over the same period. (In fact, total reported collections by obligors decreased from 1978 to 1983 and from 1983 to 1985.) Put another way, in 1978, IV-D collections represented 23% of the total collections reported, while in 1987 they represented 39% of total collections. U.S. House Committee on Ways & Means, *Background Material and Data on Programs Within the Jurisdiction of the Committee on Ways and Means,* at 633 (1990 ed.). In FY 2002, less than $1 billion of the $15 billion in current support collected was on behalf of welfare recipients.

Some insist that improvement in support collection has not been significant enough and have proposed use of the Internal Revenue Service for child support collection and disbursement. Clymer, *Child-Support Collection Net Usually Fails,* N.Y. TIMES, July 15, 1997 at p. 8. Representative Henry Hyde, a co-sponsor, argued "child support collection efforts must be consolidated at the Federal level and support must be collected with the same efficiency and resolve with which . . . taxes are collected." The proposal, which has languished because of Congressional hostility to the IRS, would require informing the employer of the amount of any court-ordered obligation. Failure to report would be punishable by up to a year in prison. *See* Note, *Collecting and Enforcing Child Support Orders with the Internal Revenue Service: An Analysis of a Novel Idea*, 20 WOMEN'S RTS. L. REP. 137 (1999).

Another alternative to current enforcement mechanisms is suggested by the recent establishment of a number of private child support collection agencies to track down absent obligors. Lewin, *Private Firms Help Single Parents Get What's Due*, N.Y. TIMES, May 21, 1994, p. 1. Working on a contingency fee, the firms identify the location of non-paying obligors and property which can be attached. The article reports the creation of many such firms in the early 1990's. The industry appears to be relatively unregulated, though a 2003 article details some legislative enactments and proposals, along with litigation concerning complaints by aggrieved obligors and obligees. Swank, *The National Child Non-Support Epidemic*, 2003 DET. C.L.L. REV. 357.

[3]   ENFORCEMENT REMEDIES

[a]   Income Withholding

Traditionally, wage garnishment was rarely employed to enforce child support awards. State and federal law often barred garnishment for certain categories of workers. Even where available, garnishment could be obtained only where an obligor was in arrears and required a new action by the obligee ordering payment of a specific amount of money. Because future payments were not yet debts (because they had not become due), no garnishment order could be obtained to secure their payment. Thus, a garnishment order would expire upon satisfaction of the arrearage. Meanwhile, the obligor might have missed current payments, creating a new arrearage which required reduction to judgment for a new garnishment order. Another difficulty under traditional rules was the inability to gain jurisdiction over an obligor's out-of-state employer. *Champion Int'l Corp. v. Ayars*, 587 F. Supp. 1274 (D. Conn. 1984). Thus, at one time that main successful enforcement technique was imprisonment for contempt rather than garnishment as shown in a famous study by Professor David Chambers detailed in Subsection b.

Today this has all changed. Largely because of new federal requirements imposed during the 1980s, wage garnishment (now known as income withholding) has become the most important and effective tool for enforcement of support awards. Income withholding orders require the obligor's employer to deduct the employee's obligation from the paycheck, much like income tax withholding. While distribution formerly could be made either directly to the obligee or to a governmental collection and disbursement agency, the PRWOA (§ 312) generally requires all withholding be collected in a centralized governmental agency and disbursed to the obligee within two business days. Income withholding orders today are not limited to arrearages.

In fact, the success of this technique led Congress — in the Family Support Act — to require all child support orders entered on or after Jan. 1, 1994, to include an income withholding order unless the court finds "good cause" for not ordering it or the parties agree in writing to an alternative payment plan. The Child Support Enforcement Amendments of 1984 separately require such income withholding provisions where the obligor is one month in arrears and the "good cause" exception is unavailable in cases of arrearage. The most recent data from the federal Office of Child Support Enforcement reports that approximately 65% ($15.5 billion) of the state IV-D agencies' support collections in Fiscal Year 2002 was accomplished via income withholding. U.S. Department of Health and Human Services, *Child Support Enforcement Preliminary Report for FY 2002*. www.acf.hhs.gov/programs/cse/pubs/2003/reports/prelim_datareport, Figure 4. This reflects a quantum leap from the data reported merely four years earlier, when the parallel percentage was 56% of the collections or $6.1 billion. U.S. Department of Health and Human Services, Office of Child Support Enforcement, *Twenty-Third Annual Report to Congress*, at p. 31 (2000). As recently as FY 1988, this technique collected only $1.7 billion.

States also must make their income withholding procedures available for interstate collection of support. 42 U.S.C. § 666(b)(9) (2001); *see* 45 C.F.R. § 303.100(f) (2002). The Child Support Project of the American Bar Association and the National Conference of State Legislatures proposed a Model Interstate Income Withholding Act. Office of Child Support Enforcement, U.S. Dep't of Health and Human Services, *Model Interstate Income Withholding Act with Commentary* (1984); *see* DEL. CODE ANN. tit. 13, §§ 401-412 (1999). At least partly because the Act was not widely adopted, PRWORA (§ 321) requires states to adopt the Uniform Interstate Family Support Act which requires employers to comply with income withholding orders of another state (§ 501). While enormously helpful, income withholding is not a panacea. Until enactment of the PRWORA (§ 314) in 1996, federal law required only wage withholding and not all obligors earn wages. There are many forms of income other than wages, such as, *e.g.*, a partnership draw in a law firm, patent or book royalties or periodic payments under a mortgage. The Welfare Reform Act required states to enact an expanded definition of accessible resources. Under 42 U.S.C. § 666(b)(8) (2001), "income" means "any periodic form of payment due to an individual, regardless of source, including wages, salaries, commissions, bonuses, workers' compensation, disability, payments pursuant to a pension of retirement program, and interest." *See also* ARIZ. REV. STATS. § 25-320 (Appendix) § 4a (2003 Supp.) ("income from any source [including, but not limited to] salaries, wages, commissions, bonuses, dividends, severance pay, pensions, interest, trust income, annuities, capital gains, social security benefits. . ., worker's compensation benefits, . . . recurring gifts, prizes, and spousal maintenance"); OHIO REV. CODE § 3121.01(D)(2003 Supp.); TEX. FAM. CODE § 101.011 (2002) ("a payment to or due . . . regardless of source and how denominated. [Earnings include] a periodic or lump-sum payment. . .").

While an expanded definition of income certainly helps obligees, there may be practical difficulties in identifying the obligor's non-wage sources of income. Even if the obligor earns income under the state definition, a change of jobs requires transfer of the withholding order to the new employer. Additionally, while federal law now requires states to accommodate interstate withholding, a move by the obligor to a new state may create difficulties in locating the obligor and his or her sources of income. Also, it should be noted that the federal Consumer Credit Protection Act, 15 U.S.C. § 1673(b) (2001), limits the amount which can be withheld from an employee's pay check and states may enact lower ceilings. *See, e.g., Wilcox v. Wilcox,* 575 A.2d 127 (Pa. Super. 1990) (applying state limit of 50% instead of federal ceiling of 65%); Wyo. Stats. § 20-6-210 (1989) (limiting withholding to 35% of obligor's disposable income rather than the CCPA's 50%-65% ceiling). Due process requirements, most importantly allowing the obligor to correct mistakes of fact, must be satisfied by the withholding statute and by the procedures utilized in the individual case. For litigation addressing the adequacy of state withholding procedures, see *State ex rel. Sheppard v. Money,* 529 N.E.2d 542 (Ill. 1988) (applying *Matthews v. Eldridge,* 424 U.S. 319 (1976)); *State ex rel. Keasling v. Keasling,* 442 N.W.2d 118 (Iowa 1989) (upholding statute permitting child support agency to order wage attachment).

Finally, while federal law prohibits dismissal of an employee because his wages are subject to withholding, 15 U.S.C. § 1674 (2001), there "is a good deal of evidence that this provision is of limited value." Roberts, Turning Promises into Realities: A Guide to Implementing the Child Support Provisions of the Family Support Act of 1988, at 50 (1989). The risk of retaliatory dismissal, however, may decline as a greater proportion of the work force becomes subject to support withholding. For the federally-mandated wage withholding procedures, see 45 C.F.R. § 303.100 (2002).

[b] Contempt

Prior to the routine use of income withholding, imprisonment for contempt of court was perhaps the most commonly used remedy for recalcitrant support obligors. While perhaps relatively less common today, it is still available in difficult cases.

NOTES

1. *Civil Versus Criminal Contempt.* One traditional enforcement tool is an action alleging defendant is in contempt of the court's order that he pay child support. A contempt action may be civil or criminal in nature. While a jail sentence or fine is usually authorized under state law for either type of contempt, the sanctions have different purposes. *Hicks v. Feiock*, 485 U.S. 624 (1985). Criminal contempt results in a fine or jail sentence of definite amount or duration imposed as punishment for violation of a court order. A criminal contempt action must comply with constitutional rules protecting criminal defendants.

By contrast, the purpose of civil contempt is to coerce compliance with the court order, and it normally results in placing the defendant in jail until he complies by paying. Some contempt proceedings result in a finding of both civil and criminal contempt. Thus, the obligor may be sentenced to a precise term, with the further condition that he will not be released until he "purges" himself of the contempt by paying his debts. While *Hicks* holds federal constitutional rights afforded criminal defendants inapplicable in civil contempt, state constitutional or statutory law often grant such rights. Thus, *e.g.*, some states provide a jury trial in civil contempt. See, *e.g.*, *Mead v. Batchlor,* 460 N.W.2d 493 (Mich. 1990); *Johansen v. State,* 491 P.2d 759 (Alaska 1971). Likewise, several cases hold that the possibility of any jail sentence (whether civil or criminal contempt) guarantees an indigent defendant appointed counsel. *See, e.g., Black v. Div. of Child Supp. Enforcement,* 686 A.2d 164 (Del. 1996)(jail time impermissible without right to counsel); *Santa Clara Cty. v. Superior Court (Rodriguez),* 2 Cal. App. 4th 1686 (1992) (appointment of counsel mandated by legislative authorization for governmental payment for indigents' counsel); *Cox v. Slama,* 355 N.W.2d 401 (Minn. 1984); *In re Stahira,* 509 N.E.2d 1117 (Ind. App. 1987). *See also* Comment, U. CHI. L. REV. 326 (1983); Annot., *Right to Counsel in Contempt Proceedings,* 52 A.L.R.3d 1002 (1973). *Hicks* also makes clear that the classification of a particular proceeding as civil or criminal contempt is itself a question of federal constitutional law.

For a study examining the effect of the presence of counsel on time spent in jail by civil contemnors, see Hermann & Donahue, *Fathers Behind Bars: The Right to Counsel in Civil Contempt Proceedings,* 14 N. MEX. L. REV. 275 (1984). The authors found unrepresented (72%) defendants spent an average of 14 days in jail, while represented defendants spent an average of three days in jail.

2. *Incarceration and Compliance.* An extensive study in Michigan by Professor David Chambers makes clear that jail for contempt is effective in improving support collections. CHAMBERS, MAKING FATHERS PAY (1979); Chambers, *Men Who Know They Are Watched: Some Benefits and Costs of Jailing for Nonpayment of Support,* 75 MICH. L. REV. 900 (1977).

Created in 1917, the Michigan Friend of Court is a support enforcement agency in each county. Support payments are made to the agency, which forwards them to the obligee. The agency can investigate nonpayment, issue warnings and initiate actions to secure payment, such as contempt proceedings. In his study of 28 counties, Chambers found jail sentences served both as a specific and general deterrent. Not only did those jailed pay more often after their imprisonment, but compliance among those never jailed was higher in areas of well-organized enforcement. The most important factors in explaining the level of support collection were: a) whether the Friend of Court acted on its own in seeking contempt or awaited a complaint by the obligee; b) the frequency of jail sentences (not their length); and c) county size (smaller counties consistently collected a higher percentage of support owed).

Chambers also found that a "credible threat of jail improves the payment record of every identifiable group of men — whether classified by age, type of employment, race, income or events following divorces." The study also refutes claims that aggressive collection techniques are "not worth the expenditures, because you spend more than you collect." For example, it concludes that a "generous" estimate of costs of the enforcement program in one county was $400,000 as compared to almost $3.5 million in support collected. MAKING FATHERS PAY, at 101.

Though his data shows jail is effective, Chambers is philosophically opposed to jailing people for nonpayment, in part because he believes the sanction is applied unequally. *Id.* at 253. He suggests many who are incarcerated are less blameworthy than those who are not. He found unskilled blue collar workers and men with employment difficulties or alcohol problems overrepresented in jail and managers and professionals underrepresented. *Id.* at 201–16.

He also discredits the notion that attorneys are unnecessary in civil contempt because defendant has "the jailhouse keys in his pocket." He reports courts did not inquire whether defendant had money available to pay the portion of arrearages required as the price of release. MAKING FATHERS PAY, at 187. Although more than half the jailed men in the study paid enough to be released from jail, Chambers cautions against concluding that this proves that a man is capable of making regular support payments, because the source of the "release" money may be someone other than the jailed man himself. *Id.* at 218–20.

In 1983, Michigan revised its civil contempt procedures to designate jail as the last resort for support violations. Commitment is limited to 45 days for the first contempt order and 90 days for any subsequent order. While incarcerated for contempt, a person may have the privilege of released time to seek or continue work. *See* MICH. COMP. L. §§ 552.633, 552.637 (2003 Supp.).

In an attempt to handle nonsupport cases efficiently and to deter nonpayment, several states have conducted roundups of delinquent obligors. For example, approximately 480 civil contempt actions were initiated simultaneously in Florida against obligors. The cases were assembled before a single judge who disposed of them during a four-day period. Respondents found in contempt who failed to pay immediately were jailed. Over 100 respondents were committed to jail and over $140,000 was collected. Thirty-eight fathers who were held in contempt obtained reversals on appeal, alleging due process violations in the cursory hearings and the lack of record support for the finding of guilt. While willing to tolerate a degree of informality, the court deplored the total absence of oaths, court reporters, witnesses, and rules of evidence. *Robbins v. Robbins,* 429 So. 2d 424 (Fla. App. 1983).

3. *Imprisonment for Debt?* Jail terms for contempt in support cases do not violate state constitutional prohibitions on imprisonment for debt because child support is generally held not a debt within the meaning of the prohibition. *In re Pettit,* 626 N.E.2d 444 (Ind. 1993); *Gould v. Gould,* 823 S.W.2d 890 (Ark. 1992); *Ex parte Wilbanks,* 722 S.W.2d 221 (Tex. App. 1986); *Marriage of Lenger,* 336 N.W.2d 191 (Iowa 1983). In fact, some state constitutional provisions prohibiting imprisonment for debt explicitly exempt support debts. *See* MD. CONST. ART. III, § 38.

PROBLEM

Problem 5-14. David has fathered nine children by four different women over the past 15 years. He has been ordered to pay child support for each child, but has not been regular in his payments. He has been convicted of criminal non-support of one child and the trial judge has sentenced him to three years in prison followed by five years of probation. One of the probation conditions is that "David cannot have any more children unless he demonstrates the ability to support new children and that he is supporting his existing children."

In the non-jury trial, the judge found that David had the ability to support his existing children, but refused to work. You are law clerk to a judge on the appellate court which will hear David's appeal. What are the issues and how should they be resolved?

[c] Other Enforcement Techniques

[i] Criminal Prosecution

All states criminally punish nonsupport (or abandonment or desertion) of children. About half of these statutes are patterned after the Uniform Desertion and Nonsupport Act. Promulgated in 1910, it read:

> Any . . . parent who shall without lawful excuse, desert or wilfully neglect or refuse to provide for the support and maintenance of his or her child or children under the age of sixteen . . . in destitute or necessitous circumstances, shall be guilty of a crime.

10 UNIFORM LAWS ANN. § 1 (1922). *See* VA. CODE § 20-61 (2000); WYO. CODE § 20-3-101 (2003). A more modern model act adopted in several states is Model Penal Code § 230.5 (MPC) which provides:

> A person commits a misdemeanor if he persistently fails to provide support which he can provide and which he knows he is legally obliged to provide to a spouse, child or other dependent.

See ALA. CODE § 13A-13-4(a) (1994); NEB. REV. STATS. § 28-706 (1995) (excluding failure to pay for abortion if parent wasn't consulted or abortion was not therapeutic); KY. REV. STATS. § 530.050(1) (1995).

Nonsupport is criminal under the Uniform Act only if the child is left without basic necessities, while the MPC punishes any failure to meet the defendant's "legal" obligation. By incorporating the general standards of child support, the MPC requires more than mere subsistence support. *See, e.g., State v. Davis,* 469 S.W.2d 1 (Mo. 1971) (interpreting MPC-type provision to require support "reasonably suitable to the condition in life and commensurate with the defendant's ability").

While statutes rarely include specific language dealing with mens rea, most courts, because of a reluctance to impose criminal strict liability unless such is clearly provided for in the statute, require proof of at least recklessness. *See State v. Collins*, 733 N.E.2d 1118 (Ohio 2000)(lacking evidence of mistake or misdirected payments, failure to pay over a number of years provides sufficient evidence from which recklessness or even intent can be found beyond a reasonable doubt).

Most states treat nonsupport as a misdemeanor, and the remainder usually set the maximum incarceration at three years. CLARK, LAW OF DOMESTIC RELATIONS 269-70 (2d ed. 1988). At least one state varies the punishment based on the amount of arrearages. *See* NEV. REV. STATS. § 201.020(1)(a) (2001). Some states punish defendants more severely if they have left the state. *See* GA. CODE § 19-10-1(b) (1999); OKLA. CODE 2001 tit. 21, § 852. The United States Supreme Court has upheld such a statute against a constitutional attack based on the right to interstate migration. *Jones v. Helms,* 452

U.S. 412 (1981). Many statutes explicitly authorize intermittent or suspended sentences to allow defendants to maintain jobs. *See, e.g.*, GA. CODE § 19-10-1(j) (1999 Supp.).

Does prior conviction for criminal contempt provide a double jeopardy defense in a criminal non-support prosecution? No, according to *Iowa v. Rater*, 568 N.W.2d 655 (Iowa 1997). Defendant had been convicted of criminal contempt for failure to support between December, 1992 and September, 1993. In a prosecution alleging non-support in a later period, he asserted non-support was a single continuous offense and, therefore, any criminal prosecution would constitute double jeopardy. The court rejected this claim, finding each failure to make a monthly payment a separate offense.

Criminal prosecutions for non-support are relatively rare, because similar penalties are obtained more easily through contempt proceedings. The crime may be charged in egregious circumstances where there is no existing support order, however, because most criminal statutes do not require a prior support order. The states are split on whether the state or the defense has the burden of proof on defendant's ability to pay. *See* Melli, *Remedies in Child Support Enforcement,* in 2 ALIMONY, CHILD SUPPORT & COUNSEL FEES — AWARD MODIFICATION & ENFORCEMENT, at 15–31 and 15–32 (Melli & Stanton eds. 1989); *see also State v. Burg*, 648 N.W.2d 673 (Minn. 2002)(Due Process requires state to prove absence of lawful excuse for non-payment, an element of criminal non-support under the statute).

The Federal Child Support Recovery Act of 1992 criminalized failure to pay support for a child in another state. *See* 18 U.S.C. § 228. Subsection (a) punishes the defendant who "willfully fails to pay a past due support obligation with respect to a child who resides in another State. . . ." A past due support obligation is defined as one which has been unpaid for at least a year or is more than $5,000. The statute authorizes imprisonment for 6 months for a first offense and up to 2 years for subsequent offenses. Restitution in the amount of the unpaid support is required. The Act (since renamed the Deadbeat Parents Punishment Act as part of a 1998 stiffening of punishment levels) has, in the lower courts, survived a number of constitutional attacks based on *United States v. Morrison*, 529 U.S. 598 (2000) (striking down a portion of the Violence Against Women Act), claiming it exceeded Congressional Commerce Clause authority. *See United States v. Klinzing*, 315 F.3d 803 (7th Cir. 2003); *United States v. Monts,*311 F.3d 993 (10th Cir. 2002); *United States v. King*, 276 F.3d 109 (2d Cir. 2002); *United States v. Lewko*, 269 F.3d 64 (1st Cir. 2001); *United States v. Faasse,* 265 F.3d 475 (6th Cir. 2001); *cf. United States v. Ballek*, 170 F.3d 871 (9th Cir. 1999) (rejecting 13th Amendment attack in a case where defendant had refused to work in order to avoid support obligations).

In addition to the consideration of constitutional attacks, the federal courts have been busy interpreting the Act. For example, the definition of the word "child" in the phrase "child support" was at issue in *United States v. Molak*, 276 F.3d 45 (10th Cir. 2002). The *Molak* defendant argued the trial court had ordered restitution of too much money because a portion of the child support order which he had failed to pay was attributable to post-majority support for such items as college tuition and interest. He contended child support was limited to money due before the beneficiary reached his or her 18th birthday. The Tenth Circuit rejected this argument. Acknowledging that the Act itself does not define "child," the court noted that the definition of "support obligation" ties the meaning of child to the specific order alleged to have been violated. State courts are in a better position than federal courts to determine who the appropriate beneficiaries of a support order are, held the court, and federal courts "should accept state-court support orders as they are written and avoid relitigating matters already decided in the family courts." *See also United States v. Gill*, 264 F.3d 929 (9th Cir. 2001) (restitution award appropriately included both principal and interest); *United States v. Craig*, 181 F.3d 1124 (9th Cir. 1999) (arrearage award can appropriately include all arrearages, not simply amount accruing during period specified in the indictment). For venue purposes the crime defined by the CSRA occurs in both the place where the obligor is and the place where the children live. *See United States v. Muench*, 153 F.3d 1298 (11th Cir. 1998). In *United States v. Mattice*, 186 F.3d 219 (2d Cir. 1999), the court found the statutory mens rea is intent to violate the support obligation, not intent to violate the Act. It has been held that a defendant may defend by collaterally attacking (for lack of personal jurisdiction) the support order alleged to have been violated. *United States v. Kramer*, 225 F.3d 847 (7th Cir. 2000). It has also been held that the civil statute of limitations governing the original decree is irrelevant in the criminal prosecution. *Monts, supra.*

Prosecutions under the Act have been relatively rare. A 1995 Student Note reported "[s]lightly more than fifty cases have been prosecuted nationwide, with fewer than half resulting in convictions." Note, *The Constitutionality of Punishing Deadbeat Parents: The Child Support Recovery Act of 1992 After United States v. Lopez*, 64 Ford. L. Rev. 1089, 1098 (1995). The author speculated that the paucity of prosecution may be due to the wilfulness requirement and a lack of resources for prosecution. *Id.* at p. 1099. U.S. Justice Department guidelines for prosecution, quoted in the Note, limit prosecution to egregious cases where "all reasonably available civil and state remedies have been exhausted or where state remedies have proven ineffective." *Id. See* Note, *Deadbeat Dads, Welfare Moms, and Uncle Sam: How the Child Support Recovery Act Punishes Single-Mother Families*, 53 Stan. L. Rev. 729 (2000) (arguing for state or local prosecution of obligors, with federal funds devoted instead to training single mothers and subsidizing day care facilities).

[ii] Civil Remedies

The 1984 Child Support Enforcement Amendments require states to provide several additional enforcement devices including: 1) income tax refund offsets, 2) security and 3) liens. The appropriateness of these procedures depends upon such factors as obligor's payment record and availability of other remedies. Federal income tax refund intercepts (under which the obligor's refund is sent, in full or in part, to the obligee) are available through IV-D agencies for collection of support arrearages (but not current child support or any spousal support). 42 U.S.C. § 664(a) (2001); 45 C.F.R. § 303.72 (2002). States with income taxes must allow intercepts of refunds in IV-D cases. 42 U.S.C. § 666(a)(3) (2001). Such intercepts are not subject to the limits of the

Consumer Credit Protection Act. *Kokoszka v. Belford,* 417 U.S. 642 (1974); *Usery v. First Nat'l Bank of Arizona,* 586 F.2d 107 (9th Cir. 1978).

Due process guarantees entitle obligors to advance notice of and a chance to contest an intercept. Defenses are limited to challenging: 1) jurisdiction of the court entering the support order, 2) the determination that arrearages exist and 3) the amount owed. For federal litigation concerning the precise requirements of due process in the Tax Refund Intercept Program, see *Anderson v. White,* 888 F.2d 985 (3d Cir. 1989); *McClelland v. Massinga,* 786 F.2d 1205 (4th Cir. 1986); *Nelson v. Regan,* 731 F.2d 105 (2d Cir. 1984); *see* Motz & Baida, *The Due Process Rights of Postjudgment Debtors and Child Support Obligors,* 45 MD. L. REV. 61 (1986).

Federal law requires states to provide in all support cases a procedure by which the court can require obligor to give security, post a bond, or otherwise guarantee payment of overdue support. 42 U.S.C. § 666(a)(6) (2001). A guarantee need not be required in every case. The use of a security, bond or other guarantee is most appropriate where obligor is self-employed or has income not easily reached by other means or is likely to leave the state. If required payments are not forthcoming, the court may (after notice and hearing) declare the security forfeited.

Each state must provide a procedure, available in all support cases, for the creation of a lien on obligor's real or personal property for support arrearages. 42 U.S.C. § 666(a)(4) (2001). As a practical matter, an existing lien prevents sale or transfer of the property until it has been satisfied. Some statutes permit a support decree itself (with recordation in the appropriate office) to operate as a lien. *See, e.g.,* NEB. REV. STAT. § 42-371 (2002 Supp.) (liens "upon real property and any personal property registered with any county office. . . ."); IND. CODE ANN. § 12-17-2-33 (2003 Supp.) (automatic lien on motor vehicle titles). Some states had required arrearages to be reduced to judgment before creation of a lien, but the PRWORA, requires (§ 368) that all states create liens on real and personal property which will exist by operation of law, without reduction to a specific money judgment of an arrearage. The statute also mandates interstate recognition of such liens. Recordation may still be required. While ordinarily there are statutory exemptions from liens, either in terms of a type of asset or a particular value of obligor's assets, some states permit support obligees to overcome such exemptions. *See, e.g.,* 42 PA. STATS. § 8123(b) (1998); IDAHO CODE § 11-607(1) (1998); *Redick v. O'Brien,* 468 A.2d 735 (N.J. Super. 1983). *See generally* Ball & Sablan, EFFECTIVE USE OF LIENS IN CHILD SUPPORT CASES (1990).

Finally, while the prior collection devices derive from state law (albeit with the federal government's "encouragement"), a purely federal enforcement technique also is available. The Internal Revenue Service can collect a support arrearage "as it would attempt to collect federal taxes." Dodson, *IRS Full Collection Procedure and Use of Federal Courts* in INTERSTATE CHILD SUPPORT REMEDIES at 159 (Haynes & Dodson eds. 1989); *see* 26 U.S.C. § 6305 (1996). The state IV-D agency must certify the amount of arrearages to the Office of Child Support Enforcement, which requests IRS help. *See* 42 U.S.C. § 652(b) (2001); 45 C.F.R. § 303.71 (2002). There must be at least $750 in arrearages and reasonable attempts to use other collection techniques must have been made. *Id.*

[iii] Revocation or Denial of State-Created Privileges

A 1996 survey reported over 30 states with license revocation programs under which obligors with outstanding support debts may lose their driver's or professional licenses. Fondacaro & Stolle, *Revoking Motor Vehicle and Professional Licenses for Purposes of Child Support Enforcement: Constitutional Challenges and Policy Implications*, 5 CORN. J.L. & PUB. POL'Y 355, 358 at fn. 10 (1996). The authors note the exclusion of attorneys from many license revocation statutes. They explain that this

> is because in many states attorney discipline is under the exclusive jurisdiction of the state supreme court, whereas the discipline of all other professional groups is subject to regulation by the state legislature. . . .

Id. at 389. The authors note a Florida Supreme Court rule extending to attorneys the same license revocation rules applicable to other professionals. *Id.* at 390. The PRWORA (§ 369) requires license suspension laws for obligors who are delinquent or fail to respond to a warrant. The licenses covered include driver's, occupational and recreational licenses. Passports also can be denied or revoked for obligors owing more than $5,000 in support. *Id.* at § 370. A newspaper report announced that Maine had collected $26 million from over 13,000 obligors in a two-year period after threatening license suspension. "In that period, only 100 licenses were actually suspended." Dao, *New York Plans to Take Driver's Licenses of Some Parents Who Owe Child Support*, N.Y. TIMES, Aug. 7, 1995, at B12. In a related enforcement mechanism, a 1996 Presidential Executive Order makes it more difficult for support obligors in arrears to obtain federal loans. Exec. Order No. 13019, 61 Fed. Reg. 51763 (Sept. 28, 1996).

In *Berntson v. Indiana Div. Of Fam. & Child.*, 737 N.E.2d 1208 (Ind. App. 2000), the court rejected obligor's assertion that an earlier finding of contempt of a support order precluded revocation of his license as a certified public accountant. While conceding that inability to pay would be a valid defense in a license revocation action, the court found that the claim had been raised and rejected on factual grounds at trial. *See also Dep't of Revenue v. Beans*, 965 P.2d 725 (Alaska 1998) (obligor has constitutional right to assert and prove inability to pay defense in driver's license revocation proceeding).

The above-quoted law review article on license revocation schemes analyzes possible constitutional attacks, particularly those based on Due Process (both substantive and procedural) and Equal Protection. The authors are confident that such statutes are constitutional. 5 CORN. J.L. & PUB. POL'Y at 398–99. Under either substantive due process or equal protection analysis, a rational relationship between the statute's goal and its provisions would be required. What is the goal of such a license revocation statute? Is there an acceptable means/end relationship between such a statute and that goal? In a related area, recent cases have rejected constitutional attacks on provisions of federal law authorizing revocation of the passports of obligors who are more than $5,000 in arrears. In *Eunique v. Powell*, 281 F.3d 940 (9th Cir. 2002), the court rejected an attack based on the right to travel. Citing Supreme Court precedent, the court noted the right to travel internationally is merely part of the liberty protected by the Due Process Clause and, as such, is significantly narrower than the separately-guaranteed right to interstate travel. Applying rational relationship scrutiny, the majority found the scheme related to special concerns about the problems of enforcement where obligor has left the jurisdiction. The dissent applied intermediate scrutiny and found the statute wanting. *See also Weinstein v. Albright*, 261 F.3d 127 (2d Cir. 2001) (rejecting Procedural Due Process and Equal Protection attacks on same provision). *See* Annot., *Validity and Application of Statute or Regulation Authorizing Revocation or Suspension of Driver's License for Reasons Unrelated to Use of, or Ability to Operate, Motor Vehicle*, 18 A.L.R. 5th 542 (1994).

[iv] Termination of Parental Rights

The ultimate sanction for failure to support is termination of parental rights. Failure to support one's children can be used to justify a finding of abandonment, which in turn is a commonly available statutory ground for parental rights termination. Bell, *Termination of Parental Rights: Recent Judicial and Legislative Trends*, 30 EMORY L.J. 1065, 1075 n.50 (1981). Most states, however, find failure to pay simply one factor in determining abandonment. In *In re Schoffstall*, 369 S.E.2d 459 (W. Va. 1988), the court found father's refusal to pay in an attempt to force compliance with a visitation order was insufficient to show abandonment.

At any rate, termination of parental rights and obligations, including the support obligation, is of dubious value to the child in need of financial support. Termination actually relieves the chronically delinquent obligor of the legal duty to support and could leave a child with no parent obligated to provide support. Therefore, termination of parental rights for nonsupport is rarely pursued unless adoption seems likely.

[4] DEFENSES TO ACTIONS TO COLLECT ARREARAGES

When the obligee seeks to collect unpaid arrearages on an outstanding support order, res judicata generally precludes any attempt to raise substantive objections to the order's existence or amount. While historically some states allowed such defenses under the rubric of "retroactive modifications," federal law, described above, now severely limits the availability of such modification. However, other defenses are sometimes raised. Some are obvious, if unusual, as where defendant claims mistaken identity or asserts the order was for less than the obligee claims. Other defenses are more common and include:

[a] Prior Payment

The obligor may claim to have already made the payments in question. This happens most often where the payments were made in a different manner than that prescribed in the order. The discrepancy can be "technical," as where the obligor made direct payments to the obligee rather than through the court as provided by the order. Obligors sometimes argue that "in kind" payments of toys, clothing, entertainment or allowance should be credited on his obligation. The usual rule is that support must be rendered according to the order's provisions and nonconforming payments do not count. *Olson v.Palagi,* 627 N.W.2d 765 (Neb. App. 2001) (voluntary payment of college expenses not recoverable); *Stringer v. Sheffield,* 451 So. 2d 109 (Ala. App. 1984) (no credit for purchases of clothing and sports and automotive equipment); *Glover v. Glover,* 598 S.W.2d 736 (Ark. 1980); Annot., *Right to Credit on Accrued Support Payments for Time Child is in Father's Custody or for Other Voluntary Expenditures,* 47 A.L.R.3d 1031 (1973). Crediting non-conforming payments would erode the custodial parent's authority to determine the details of the child's upbringing. *Williams v. Budke,* 606 P.2d 515 (Mont. 1980).

However, equitable considerations may require crediting such payments, as where the custodial parent consented to the substituted payment method. For example, in *Payson v. Payson,* 442 N.E.2d 1123 (Ind. App. 1982), support was payable to the court clerk, but obligor had paid directly to obligee's landlord with obligee's consent. The court granted credit in an action for contempt and declaration of arrearages. *See also Kinsey v. Kinsey,* 425 So. 2d 483 (Ala. App. 1983) (direct payments to child which were used for tuition).

[b] Custodial Changes

Unless the decree provides otherwise, the noncustodial parent generally is not entitled to a support payment deduction for visitation periods. *See, e.g., Peak v. Peak,* 772 P.2d 775 (Kan. 1989); *Marriage of Eagen,* 640 P.2d 1019 (Or. 1982). Visitation periods are ordinarily contemplated in the decree and, in any event, most expenses for children do not decline during a temporary absence from home. *Escott v. Escott,* 325 N.E.2d 395 (Ill. App. 1975). Sometimes the parents informally change the child's primary residence without modifying the decree. In such cases, obligors often find the de facto custodial change is no defense to non-payment of support, even though it may provide grounds for prospective changes in the support award.

[c] Delay

Some support defendants assert the equitable defense of laches, arguing obligee's failure to pursue support for a lengthy period excuses non-payment. Courts are relatively hostile to such defense claims, often summarily dismissing the defense for lack of demonstrated prejudice. *See, e.g., State ex rel. Bennett v. Peterson,* 657 N.W.2d 698 (S.D. 2003) (12-year delay in bringing suit on behalf of non-marital child did not prejudice defendant or any other parties, such as new family); *Myers v. Myers,* 768 N.E.2d 1201 (Ohio App. 2002) ("length of delay [28 years] alone is insufficient to constitute material prejudice. The mere inconvenience of having to meet an existing obligation imposed by an earlier order . . . cannot be called material prejudice"); *In re Marriage of Capetillo and Kivett,* 932 P.2d 691 (Wash. App. 1997) (10-year delay insufficient; "defendant cannot prove damage simply by showing he is having to do now what he has been legally obligated to do for years"); *LeMaster v. LeMaster,* 596 So. 2d 1117 (Fla. App. 1992) (10-year period of concealment of child does not justify imposition of laches); *Connin v. Bailey,* 472 N.E.2d 328 (Ohio 1984) (no prejudice where obligee waited 35 years and obligor was now dead); *but see In re: Hilborn,* 58 P.3d 905 (Wash. App. 2002) (18-year delay in bringing paternity action deprived defendant of chance for relationship and court-ordered visitation); *Davis v. Davis,* 689 So. 2d 433 (Fla. App. 1997) (15-year delay which "denied [obligor] the opportunity to share in the upbringing of his child" sufficient, especially where obligor has no property and more expenses than income); *Pyne v .Black,* 650 So. 2d 1073 (Fla. App. 1995) (12-year lapse and loss of opportunity to maintain parent-child relationship because of denial of visitation sufficient to show legal prejudice); *Kerrigan v. Kerrigan,* 642 A. 2d 1324 (D.C. App. 1994) (8-year delay and obligor's change of position in reliance on obligee's failure to seek enforcement, along with his expenditure of large amounts on child, including wedding expenses, sufficient to present prima facie case of laches). Rather than examining prejudice to the defendant in applying laches, some courts categorically reject laches in support enforcement cases, usually concluding the custodial parent cannot, as a trustee for the child, forfeit her rights through mere inaction. *See, e.g., Hammond v. Hammond,* 14 P. 3d 199 (Wyo. 2000) (finding arrearages to be an action at law, while laches is an equitable defense); *Lamon v. Hamm,* 702 So. 2d 449 (Ala. 1997); *Rogers v. Woodlin,* 672 A.2d 814 (Pa. Super. 1996). *See generally* Annot., *Laches or Acquiescence as Defense, So As to Bar Recovery of Arrearages of Permanent Alimony or Child Support,* 5 A.L.R. 4th 1015 (1981).

Closely related is a statute of limitations defense. While there may be a relevant statute, it may begin to run only when the child reaches majority. *See Marriage of Wight,* 264 Cal. Rptr. 508 (App. 1989) (five-year statute begins at majority); *Harvey v. McGuire,* 635 S.W.2d 8 (Ky. 1982). The length of statutes of limitations to enforce child support varies considerably. *Valley v. Selfridge,* 639 P.2d 225 (Wash. App. 1982) (six years); *Huff v. Huff,* 634 S.W.2d 5 (Tex. Civ. App. 1982) (ten years); *Kroeger v. Kroeger,* 353 N.W.2d 60 (Wis. 1984) (20 years).

The same fact pattern that may suggest a laches or statute of limitations defense has also given rise to an argument that arrearages should not be collectible because the child is now an adult, but that argument is generally rejected. *See Cramer v. Petrie,* 637 N.E.2d 882 (Ohio 1994).

[d] Estoppel

In a variety of situations, defendant may claim the custodial parent is estopped from seeking to enforce a support order. While a major element of most such cases will be the delay involved, often there are other factors, such as a parental agreement or the custodial parent's wrongful hiding of the child. In *Hendrickson v. State,* 72 S.W. 3d 124 (Ark. App. 2002), the trial court was told to consider whether equitable estoppel was a defense in an arrearage action. The obligor had asserted an oral agreement with obligee to split custody 50/50 and eliminate all support obligations. The trial court should not have relied on a "mistaken understanding that unless the agreement of the parties was incorporated in a modification to the divorce decree, the agreement was not enforceable." *See also* Chapter 8's discussion of separation agreement provisions waiving support.

[e] Nature of Obligor's Resources

Defendants sometimes argue that their only resources are privileged against the particular enforcement device. For example, in *Rose v. Rose,* 481 U.S. 619 (1987), the obligor's contempt defense was that his main source of income, VA disability benefits, were paid under a federal statute providing that such benefits "shall not be liable to attachment, levy, or seizure by or under any legal or equitable process whatever, either before or after receipt by the beneficiary." Interpreting the federal statute as creating the benefits for the assistance of both obligor and his family, *Rose* rejected defendant's claim, finding no preemption. *But see Ridgway v. Ridgway,* 454 U.S. 46 (1981) (finding preemption in allocation of military insurance proceeds). The *Rose* statute would in most circumstances prohibit entry of an order of garnishment or wage withholding against VA disability benefits.

Several cases have held Social Security disability benefits subject to garnishment. *See, e.g., Mariche v. Mariche,* 758 P.2d 745 (Kan. 1988); *Marriage of Schonts,* 345 N.W.2d 145 (Iowa App. 1983); *Barbour v. Barbour,* 642 S.W.2d 904 (Ky. App. 1982); *but see Department of Human Servs. ex rel. Young v. Young,* 802 S.W.2d 594 (Tenn. 1990) (distinguishing Social Security SSI payments, finding them protected). State entitlements also may be protected from particular types of enforcement. *See, e.g., Lapeer Cty. v. Harris,* 453 N.W.2d 272 (Mich. App. 1990) (state general assistance benefits immune from wage withholding); Epps, *To Pay or Not to Pay, That is the Question: Should SSI Recipients Be Exempt From Child Support Obligations,* 34 RUTG. L. REV. 63 (2002) (arguing disabled obligors should be exempt from making support payments and urging creation of an alternative "monthly benefit to the children involved, to ensure that they have a minimum level of income").

[f] Bankruptcy

The federal Bankruptcy Code precludes a debtor from discharging debts "to a spouse, former spouse, or child of the debtor, for alimony to, maintenance for, or support of such spouse or child, in connection with a separation agreement, divorce decree or other order of a court." 11 U.S.C. § 523(a)(5) (1997). While child support debts assigned to the state were once dischargeable in bankruptcy, federal law has been amended to reverse this rule. 42 U.S.C. § 656(b) (1997 Supp.).

[5] SPECIAL PROCEDURES IN ENFORCEMENT OF SUPPORT FOR INDIGENT FAMILIES

The child support collections process for indigent families typically begins when the custodial parent applies for benefits from the state Temporary Assistance to Needy Families agency, which entitles parent to support enforcement services without charge. As a condition of eligibility for TANF, a parent must cooperate with the support enforcement agency in identifying and seeking support from the absent parent and assign the right to support to the agency, making the debt due directly to the state. 42 U.S.C. § 608(a)(2) and (3) (2001). Generally the obligor will be liable to the state only up to the amount he is obligated to pay under a support order. *See, e.g.,* ALASKA STATS.

§ 25.27.120 (2002). Because of the state's right to reimbursement, it is entitled to notice of any proceeding to modify the support obligation. *See Marriage of Mena,* 260 Cal. Rptr. 314 (App. 1989) (agency indispensable party to modification proceeding).

An applicant refusing to cooperate with the agency may be denied benefits of at least 25% and perhaps as much as 100% of the grant. 42 U.S.C. § 608(a)(2)(2001). There is a "good cause" exception to the duty to cooperate in securing support payments, applicable if there is reasonable likelihood of physical or emotional harm to applicant or child. 42 U.S.C. § 654(29) (2001)); 45 C.F.R. §§ 260.52, 264.30 (2002); *See* Notar & Turetsky, *Models for Safe Child Support Enforcement,* 8 Am. U. J. Gender, Soc. Pol'y & L. 657 (2000) (analyzing appropriate balance between protecting against abuse and collecting support). There is no exception to the assignment requirement.

The TANF agency must make all relevant records available to the IV-D enforcement agency. An attempt to recover support is begun regardless of whether there was ever a marriage, a support judgment, or paternity action or acknowledgment. All support is paid to and disbursed by the enforcement agency. Former law provided that the first $50 of any support payment went directly to the family and the rest was devoted to reimbursing the state and federal governments for past payments to the family. 42 U.S.C. § 602(a)(8)(A)(vi) (1990 Supp.). This is no longer mandated, or subsidized, by the federal government. PRWORA § 302.

PROBLEMS

Problem 5-15. Dick and Jane had two children. Their divorce decree ordered Dick to "pay support for the two minor children at the rate of $400 monthly." Six years later, the couple's older child, Sam, has entered the Navy, at age 17. That was six months ago. The younger child, Sally, is now 14. When Dick heard Sam had enlisted, he immediately reduced his monthly check to $200. Jane thinks this entirely inadequate and seeks your advice. The age of majority in your jurisdiction is 18. What options do you have?

Problem 5-16. Jeffrey and Polly were divorced three years ago. She has custody of the couple's two children and he was ordered to pay $350 per month support. Six months ago, without notice, he stopped paying. Representing Polly, you have learned that Jeffrey has joined a religious organization called the "Bride of Christ," which forbids members from having separate earnings or supporting non-members. The members are supported by a church business. How do you advise Polly? How would Jeffrey respond to your actions?

Problem 5-17. Raymond and Christi were divorced two years ago. Christi got custody of their three children and Raymond was ordered to pay $50 monthly support for each child. Soon afterward, Raymond was declared totally disabled and awarded Social Security disability benefits of $700 monthly. Each child was awarded $89 monthly in "child's insurance benefits" under the Social Security Act. Christi was named representative payee for the children. Raymond now seeks to end his support obligations. As judge, how will you decide the case?

Problem 5-18. Rodney was ordered to pay child support in his divorce from Patricia. He ceased payments about three years ago. The support agency has been unable to obtain wage assignments because he works as a carpenter on many different jobs. Each time the agency tracks him down he has gone to a different job. Rodney's union refuses to inform the agency of his jobs.

In response to these problems, the agency has asked the court to join the union (whose hiring hall refers its members to various jobs) as a party to the continuing divorce action. An order requiring the union to inform the agency when it sends Rodney out on a job (along with the employer's name, address and telephone number) also has been sought. What arguments do you expect from the union and how would you decide the case?

Problem 5-19. Edward was ordered to pay $300 monthly support for his daughter, Michelle. He has complied fully. He complains, however, that often when Michelle, now 15, visits she is so ill-clothed he must purchase clothes for her. He also reports she is usually hungry when he sees her. Edward suspects his ex-wife is spending the support money on herself rather than on Michelle. He does not mind spending money for the child's well-being, but is generally upset about his daughter's condition. What options does he have?

Problem 5-20. Lois and Clark were divorced after a 15-year marriage which produced three children. Clark was awarded custody and Lois was ordered to pay support, but never complied. Three years later, the couple remarried. Support arrearages of over $12,000 had accrued at the time. In discussions at the time of the remarriage, they laughed about the arrearages and Clark said, "That's okay, I got along well enough as it was." Unfortunately, the second marriage didn't last very long. After eight months, Clark walked out on Lois. Clark seeks your advice concerning the arrearages and future support payments. How do you respond? Would the analysis differ if the order was for their non-marital child?

Problem 5-21. (a) Jennifer, wanting nothing to do with her soon-to-be ex-husband Michael, agrees to forego maintenance and support in return for his promise to leave her and their children alone. She expects to rely on her family's help to get by on her income of $28,000. Michael earns $45,000 annually at a local factory. Should the court accept such an agreement?

(b) The court accepted the agreement in (a), dividing the marital property but awarding no maintenance or support. Two years later, Jennifer has lost her job and is on welfare. As required by law, she assigned her rights to the welfare agency which has now sought reimbursement from Michael for benefits provided his children. State law provides: "An obligor is liable to the state in the amount of assistance granted to a child whom the obligor owes a duty of support except that if a support order has been entered, the obligor's liability may not exceed the amount of support provided for in the support order." You are the judge. What will the arguments of the parties be and how will you decide the case?

§ D. INTERSTATE SUPPORT LITIGATION

Even before the statutory developments outlined below that were designed to make interstate litigation more accessible, at least one-fourth of all child support litigation involved obligors and obligees residing in different states. U.S. GENERAL ACCOUNTING OFFICE, INTERSTATE CHILD SUPPORT: MOTHERS REPORT RECEIVING LESS SUPPORT FROM OUT-OF-STATE FATHERS 3 (Jan. 1992). Interstate support disputes may involve either initial support awards or petitions to modify or enforce them. The issues are the same whether or not the parties were ever married. A different kind of interstate dispute occurs when the interstate movement of one or both parties occurs *after* a support order is issued in a divorce or paternity action and one party seeks to enforce or modify the decree. In many interstate cases, the moving party (obligor or obligee) could obtain long-arm jurisdiction over the respondent in petitioner's state of residence, under the jurisdictional rules discussed in Chapter 7. Alternatively, the petitioner can file in the respondent's state. There are difficulties, however, with both choices. Sometimes the petitioner cannot obtain jurisdiction in her own state, while litigating in the courts of the respondent's state may be difficult and expensive.

This section considers a third alternative. Its basic structure was established in 1950 by the Uniform Reciprocal Enforcement of Support Act (URESA) promulgated by the National Conference of Commissioners on Uniform State Laws (NCCUSL) and eventually adopted, in some form, by all states. In this "two-state" litigation, the petitioner remains in his or her state and the respondent need not leave his or her state. URESA was eventually replaced by the Uniform Interstate Family Support Act (UIFSA), now the law in all states.

JOHN J. SAMPSON AND PAUL M. KURTZ, UIFSA: AN INTERSTATE SUPPORT ACT FOR THE 21ST CENTURY, 27 Fam. L. Q. 85–89 (1993)

. . . .

. . . . The National Conference of Commissioners on Uniform State Laws [hereinafter NCCUSL or the Conference] has been dealing with the subject of interstate support for most of this century. Its major effort, however, began in 1950 with the promulgation of the Uniform Reciprocal Enforcement of Support Act [hereinafter URESA]. That act was amended in 1952 and again in 1958. By 1968, enough experience had been gathered to lead to an even more extensive revision; in fact, the amendments were so sweeping that the new act was retitled the Revised Uniform Reciprocal Enforcement of Support Act [hereinafter RURESA]. [By 1992, all states and the District of Columbia had enacted some version of URESA or RURESA.]

By 1988 it had become apparent . . . that the time had come for another version of URESA. During the ensuing process . . ., the focus shifted from revision . . . to a complete overhaul of the URESA system and the establishment of a new approach. Four years of effort culminated [in 1992], when the . . . Conference voted unanimously to replace RURESA with the Uniform Interstate Family Support Act [hereinafter UIFSA].

. . . .

[F]or its time URESA was a . . . breakthrough in legal thought by providing a means to establish and enforce . . . support obligations . . . across state lines

. . . without requiring the custodial parent to travel to any distant forum in which the obligor might reside. Rather, the obligee was represented on both ends of the lawsuit by a governmental attorney. The process of filing a petition in State A . . . forwarding it to State B, . . . where the noncustodial parent resides or owns property, and establishing or enforcing a support order in that distant forum is a complex task. . . . Part of the difficulty is caused by the inevitable problems of "lost paper" endemic to bureaucratic structures. When time and distance are added to the equation, along with certain structural defects in URESA itself, the difficulty . . . is readily apparent.

The Family Support Act of 1988 established the U.S. Commission on Interstate Child Support, . . . charged with the task of identifying ways to improve interstate child support enforcement and report its findings and recommendations to Congress. The Commission was specifically directed to work with NCCUSL in an effort to improve URESA. . . . UIFSA provides a new beginning.

How does the new Act differ from URESA?. . . . Probably the most significant improvement offered by UIFSA is the elimination of the multiple-order system. . . . Orders entered under URESA have been defined as additional to, and not replacements of, prior support orders. Thus, at any particular time, two or more orders covering the same child might exist with different levels of support set by each one. When combined with the general family law rule permitting modifications of existing child support orders on the basis of changed circumstances, the resultant chaos and confusion is certainly understandable.

By contrast, UIFSA adopts the concept of continuing, exclusive jurisdiction to establish and modify the levels of child support due to a particular child. Thus, once a court or administrative agency enters a support decree with jurisdiction, it is the only body entitled to modify it so long as it retains continuing, exclusive jurisdiction under the Act. Another state, while required by UIFSA to enforce the existing decree, has no power . . . to modify the original decree or enter a support order at a different level.

UIFSA also recognizes, for the first time in a uniform act, the role of each state's support enforcement agency. . . . Likewise, the Act recognizes that some states have elected to have support orders entered by administrative agencies, rather than courts, and extends recognition to such awards in the interstate context.

Efficiency in the interstate support context is an explicit goal. . . . The Act recognizes certain situations in which interstate . . . enforcement can be sought directly by an obligee without utilization of courts or agencies in his or her own state. Thus, an obligee with an existing order may have it sent directly to the obligor's employer or to a support enforcement agency in the obligor's state. Alternatively, the obligee can file the case in . . . the obligor's state without the intervention of any support enforcement agency.

. . . .

The Act includes several rules designed to speed up the processing of interstate cases. Federal forms presently in use in only certain cases are mandated for all cases in order to ensure complete information; authority is given for transmission of information and documents through modern technology; interstate telephone conferencing is authorized; and tribunals and state enforcement agencies are required to keep parties informed of the progress of their interstate cases. Visitation issues are explicitly severed from support issues to eliminate delay in the establishment and enforcement of support obligations.

. . . .

[1] ESTABLISHING A SUPPORT DECREE THROUGH UIFSA

§ 102. Definitions

. . . .

(4) "Home State" means the State in which a child lived with a parent or person acting as parent for at least six consecutive months immediately preceding the time of filing of a [petition]. . . and, if a child is less than six months old, the State in which the child lived from birth with any of them. A period of temporary absence of any of them is counted as part of the six-month . . . period.

. . . .

§ 203. Initiating and Responding Tribunal of this State.

Under this [Act], a tribunal of this State may serve as an initiating tribunal to forward proceedings to another state and as a responding tribunal for proceedings initiated in another state.

§ 204. Simultaneous Proceedings.

(a) A tribunal of this State may exercise jurisdiction to establish a support order if the [petition] . . . is filed after a [petition] . . . is filed in another state only if:

(1) the [petition] . . . in this State is filed before the expiration of the time allowed in the other state for filing a responsive pleading challenging the exercise of jurisdiction by the other state;

(2) the contesting party timely challenges the exercise of jurisdiction in the other state; and

(3) . . . this State is the home state of the child.

(b) A tribunal of this State may not exercise jurisdiction to establish a support order if the [petition] . . . is filed before a [petition] . . . is filed in another state if:

(1) the [petition] . . . in the other state is filed before the expiration of the time allowed in this State for filing a responsive pleading challenging the exercise of jurisdiction by this State;

(2) the contesting party timely challenges the exercise of jurisdiction in this State; and

(3) . . . the other state is the home state of the child.

§ 301. Proceedings Under This [Act].

. . . .

(b) An individual . . . or a support enforcement agency may initiate a proceeding authorized under this [Act] by filing a [petition] in an initiating tribunal for forwarding to a responding tribunal or by filing a [petition] . . . directly in a tribunal of another state which has or can obtain personal jurisdiction over the [respondent].

§ 303. Application of Law of this State.

Except as otherwise provided in this [Act], a responding tribunal of this State shall:

(1) apply the procedural and substantive law generally applicable to similar proceedings originating in this State and may exercise all powers and provide all remedies available in those proceedings; and

(2) determine the duty of support and the amount payable in accordance with the law and support guidelines of this State.

§ 304. Duties of Initiating Tribunal.

(a) Upon the filing of a [petition] . . ., an initiating tribunal of this State shall forward the [petition] and its accompanying documents:

(1) to the responding tribunal or appropriate support enforcement agency in the responding state; or

(2) . . . to the state information agency of the responding state with a request that they be forwarded to the appropriate tribunal. . . .

. . . .

§ 305. Duties and Powers of Responding Tribunal.

(a) When a responding tribunal of this State receives a [petition] . . . from an initiating tribunal or directly pursuant to Section 301(b), it shall cause the [petition] . . . to be filed and notify the [petitioner]. . . .

(b) A responding tribunal of this State, to the extent not prohibited by other law, may . . .:

(1) issue . . . a support order . . . or determine parentage;

(2) order an obligor to comply with a support order, specifying the amount and the manner of compliance;

(3) order income withholding;

(4) determine the amount of any arrearages . . .;

. . . .

(8) order an obligor to keep the tribunal informed of the obligor's current residential address, telephone number, employer, address of employment, and telephone number at the place of employment;

(9) issue a [bench warrant; capias] for an obligor who has failed after proper notice to appear at a hearing . . .;

(10) order the obligor to seek appropriate employment by specified methods;

(11) award reasonable attorney's fees and other fees and costs; and

(12) grant any other available remedy.

(c) A responding tribunal of this State shall include in a support order . . . the calculations on which the support order is based.

(d) A responding tribunal of this State may not condition the payment of a support order issued under this [Act] upon compliance by a party with provisions for visitation.

. . . .

§ 316. Special Rules of Evidence and Procedure.

(a) The physical presence of a nonresident party . . . in a tribunal of this State is not required for the establishment . . . of a support order or the rendition of a judgment determining parentage.

. . . .

(e) Documentary evidence transmitted from another state . . . by telephone, telecopier, or other means that do not provide an original record may not be excluded from evidence on an objection based on the means of transmission.

(f) In a proceeding under this [Act], a tribunal of this State shall permit a party or witness residing in another state to be deposed or to testify by telephone, audiovisual means, or other electronic means. . . .

(g) If a party called to testify at a civil hearing refuses to answer on the ground that the testimony may be self-incriminating, the trier of fact may draw an adverse inference from the refusal.

(h) A privilege against disclosure of communications between spouses does not apply in a proceeding under this [Act].

(i) The defense of immunity based on the relationship of husband and wife or parent and child does not apply in a proceeding under this [Act].

(j) A voluntary acknowledgment of paternity, certified as a true copy, is admissible to establish parentage of the child.

§ 317. Communications Between Tribunals.

A tribunal of this State may communicate with a tribunal of another state or foreign country . . . in a record, or by telephone or other means, to obtain information concerning the laws, the legal effect of a judgment, decree, or order of that tribunal, and the status of a proceeding in the other state or foreign country. . . . A tribunal of this State may furnish similar information by similar means. . . .

§ 401. [Petition] to Establish Support Order.

(a) If a support order entitled to recognition under this [Act] has not been issued, a responding tribunal of this State may issue a support order if:

(1) the individual seeking the order resides in another state; or

(2) the support enforcement agency seeking the order is located in another state.

(b) The tribunal may issue a temporary child support order if the tribunal determines that such an order is appropriate and the individual ordered to pay is:

(1) a presumed father of the child;

(2) petitioning to have his paternity adjudicated;

(3) identified as the father of the child through genetic testing;

(4) an alleged father who has declined to submit to genetic testing;

(5) shown by clear and convincing evidence to be the father of the child;

(6) an acknowledged father as provided by [applicable state law];

(7) the mother of the child; or

(8) an individual who has been ordered to pay child support in a previous proceeding and the order has not been reversed or vacated.

(c) Upon finding, after notice and opportunity to be heard, that an obligor owes a duty of support, the tribunal shall issue a[n] order directed to the obligor and may issue other orders [under] Section 305.

§ 701. Proceeding to Determine Parentage.

A court of this State authorized to determine parentage of a child may serve as a responding tribunal in a proceeding to determine parentage brought under this [Act] or a law substantially similar to this [Act].

NOTES

1. *Establishing a Support Order Under the Uniform Interstate Family Support Act.* Since its promulgation by NCCUSL in1992, UIFSA has been enacted in all states and the District of Columbia. The 1996 Welfare Reform Act required every state, as a condition for the receipt of welfare block grants, to have UIFSA in effect on January 1, 1998. 42 U.S.C. § 666(f) (2001). Since its original promulgation, UIFSA twice has been amended by NCCUSL, in 1996 and in 2001. The statutory provisions reprinted above are from the current version of the Uniform Act. Individual states, of course, may have slightly different versions. *See* Sampson & Brooks, *Uniform Interstate Family Support Act (2001) with Prefatory Note and Comments*, 36 FAM. L.Q. 329 (2002).

As suggested in the Sampson & Kurtz excerpt above, UIFSA makes several dramatic changes in the area of interstate child support litigation but maintains the basic structure of URESA's two-state suit. That is, under § 401, a petitioner-obligee (or the support enforcement agency-the IV-D agency mentioned in the Enforcement materials above) may file a petition to establish an obligation if "a support order entitled to recognition . . . has not been issued." The latter language is designed to establish one of the main differences between the old and new Uniform Acts. Under URESA, courts would routinely enter new orders involving children for whom orders had already been entered in other states. At the heart of the "one-order" world of UIFSA is the proposition that once an order covering a particular child has been issued no other court ("tribunal" in the Act's language to account for the fact that some states empower administrative agencies to order support) can issue an order for the support of the same child unless the Act's restrictive rules concerning modification (discussed below) are satisfied.

The mechanics of filing a suit to establish support are summarized in § 301, which authorizes either the petitioner or a IV-D agency acting on his or her behalf to file a petition in an initiating tribunal for forwarding to the responding tribunal where the respondent resides. While URESA permitted only this method of initiating an interstate action, UIFSA also permits petitioner to contact the IV-D agency in his or her home state who can forward the information to the IV-D agency in the respondent's state. Other alternatives include the use of private attorneys (specifically authorized under § 309) or direct contact by the petitioner with the IV-D agency in the respondent's state. Section 307 empowers the support enforcement agency in the responding state to "take all steps necessary to enable an appropriate tribunal . . . to obtain jurisdiction over the respondent." Most petitioners using UIFSA use the services of a IV-D agency.

Once personal jurisdiction over the respondent is obtained, the responding tribunal is directed by § 303(1) to treat the case as it would any other support case that was not interstate in nature. Thus, e.g., the parties would be notified of any hearing, responsive pleadings would be permitted, etc. The special nature of two-state litigation with the parties in different states is dealt with by § 316 which makes clear, e.g., that the presence of the non-resident party is not required in the responding state and that any restrictions imposed by the hearsay rule are trumped by use of federally-mandated forms. The determination of a support obligation in a responding tribunal without the personal appearance of the petitioner there was a standard occurrence under URESA and raises no problem with the Confrontation Clause, which is concerned solely with criminal proceedings. Section 401 authorizes issuance of a temporary support order in certain circumstances, while § 305 authorizes the responding tribunal to issue a permanent order.

As detailed in Chapter 7, UIFSA contains a long-arm provision which can be used by petitioner where the parties live in different states to force respondent to litigate, not in a two-state format, but instead in "one-state litigation" in the petitioner's state. URESA had no similar provision and, thus, during the URESA era there was a wide range of provisions, with many states having no specific family law long-arm statute. For material generally comparing the two Acts and their provisions, see Oliphant, *Is Sweeping Change Possible? Minnesota Adopts the Uniform Interstate Family Support Act*, 21 WM. MITCHELL L. REV. 989 (1996); Note, *Interstate Child Support Enforcement System:*

Juggernaut of Bureaucracy, 46 MERCER L. REV. 921 (1995); Note, *The Uniform Interstate Family Support Act: The New URESA*, 20 DAYT. L. REV. 425 (1994); *see also* Kemper, *Annot., Construction and Application of the Uniform Interstate Family Support Act,* 90 A.L.R.5th 1 (2001).

2. *Choice of Law under UIFSA.* The fact that in the two-state litigation the petitioner (and usually the child) are in one jurisdiction and the respondent (usually the obligor) is elsewhere raises the question of which state's law should be applied. Under UIFSA § 303, the responding tribunal generally applies its own law (substantive, procedural, and choice of law), with specific direction in subsection (b) to apply its own state's support guidelines. While other plausible policy choices existed (*e.g.*, apply the law of the jurisdiction where the child is or apply whichever law best promotes the child's interest), the section's Official Comment explains § 303 as an attempt to insure efficiency in interstate litigation. As the drafters put it, "it is vital that decision-makers apply familiar rules of substantive and procedural law. . . ."

Thus, in *Department of Human Services v. Frye*, 754 A.2d 1000 (Me. 2000), respondent argued for application of Florida law (where his son was living) which would restrict any retroactive award to 24 months' worth of support and mandate imputation of income to the child's mother who had chosen not to work. The court held that even if Maine choice of law rules would provide for application of Florida law, § 301(b) mandated application of the Maine rules concerning these issues. The court concluded that "[t]here is good reason for this position, to [among other reasons] assure ease of calculation. . . ." *See also State v. Frisard*, 694 So. 2d 1032 (La. App. 1997); Sampson, *Uniform Interstate Family Support Act (1996) (with More Unofficial Annotations by John J. Sampson)*, 32 FAM. L.Q. 390, 451 (1998).

Several of the Act's provisions create rules for the conduct of interstate litigation which are exceptions to the general local law rule. Section 316 includes various evidentiary rules, § 312 permits the sealing of identifying information where a party's or child's health or safety might be threatened if disclosed to another party, authority is granted by § 313 to award fees and costs, including attorney's fees, and immunity from service or the exercise of personal jurisdiction in other actions is provided by § 314. Notice, also, that the preface to § 305(b)'s laundry list of powers of a responding tribunal specifically grants such power "to the extent not prohibited by other law." This provision grants power to the responding court in interstate cases that it might not have in domestic cases.

3. *Simultaneous Proceedings*. As part of UIFSA's commitment to a system with only one order for each child rather than the multiple orders permissible under URESA, it imposes self-restraint on a state in exercising jurisdiction where more than one action concerning support of a particular child has been filed. Section § 204(a) is directed to a State-2 tribunal considering a petition to establish a support order when such a petition already is pending in State-1. State-2 can entertain an action only if: a) the second action is filed before the expiration of the time for challenging State 1's exercise of jurisdiction; b) a timely challenge to State-1's exercise of jurisdiction is filed; and c) State-2 is the child's "home state" under 102(4). The latter concept was borrowed from the Uniform Child Custody Jurisdiction

Enforcement Act and the Federal Parental Kidnaping Prevention Act. Subsection (b) of § 204 speaks to the State-1 court in the above scenario.

The Act's preference for application of forum law could, without § 204, encourage forum shopping and competition between states in the exercise of support jurisdiction. For example, consider a situation where a married couple (X and Y) lives with their young child in Jurisdiction A, near its border with Jurisdiction B. Y moves alone to Jurisdiction B, whose support laws are less congenial to the obligor than A (*e.g.*, higher levels of support and a longer duration of support). Given the choice of law rule of § 303, X would prefer to litigate the support issues in Jurisdiction B, while Y would rather litigate in Jurisdiction A. If each filed a lawsuit to establish the support obligation in their preferred jurisdiction, § 204's rules would be used to decide which suit could proceed. Under the facts as outlined, so long as Y challenged B's exercise of jurisdiction in a timely fashion, the litigation would occur in Jurisdiction A, the child's home state.

4. *Establishment of Parentage Under UIFSA*. Because of ambiguous language in the URESA, pre-UIFSA courts were split on whether to permit interstate litigation to establish parentage of a child. A federal commission charged in the late 1980s with proposing improvements to the interstate support system reported that under the old Uniform Act, "[s]ome responding courts will not resolve parentage in a contested case unless the out-of-state petitioner physically appears and participates in the hearing. If the petitioner . . . lacks the resources to make the trip, the URESA case remains in limbo until parentage is determined elsewhere." U.S. COMMISSION ON INTERSTATE CHILD SUPPORT, SUPPORTING OUR CHILDREN: A BLUEPRINT FOR REFORM 232 (1992); *see, e.g., Packard v. Cargile*, 546 N.E.2d 301, 302 (Ind. 1989) ("[o]ne does not have a duty to support because of allegations of one's paternity"). Likely, this interpretation of URESA was bolstered by a sense that a respondent-alleged father would be prejudiced by his inability to subject the testimony against him to cross-examination. *Cf. State ex rel. T.L.R. v. R.W.T.*, 7373 So. 2d 688 (La. 1999) (rejecting respondent's claim that finding of paternity in such a context was unconstitutional).

Section 701 of UIFSA makes clear that a determination of parentage can be made in the interstate litigation itself. While the Drafters did not explicitly respond to the kind of complaint made by the respondent in *R.W.T.*, above, presumably such a response would stress the importance of resolving parentage and the availability, under § 316, of testimony and deposition evidence via electronic means. Traditionally, paternity litigation is filed by a mother seeking a declaration that the defendant is the child's father, but under the Act a petitioner can obtain a declaration that he is the father. According to the Commentary, the Act also permits a "'pure' parentage action . . ., *i.e.,* an action not joined with a claim for support." While § 701 adheres to the Act's general approach in applying local law to the parentage determination, the draft of UIFSA originally presented to the NCCUSL would have imposed a series of substantive rules governing UIFSA parentage litigation. For a recounting of the Conference's debate and rejection of the draft, see Sampson & Kurtz, *UIFSA: An Interstate Support Act for the 21st Century*, 27 FAM. L.Q. 85, 167, fn. 165 (1993).

[2] UIFSA LITIGATION WHEN AN ORDER EXISTS

§ 205. Continuing, Exclusive Jurisdiction.

(a) A tribunal . . . that has issued a child-support order consistent with the law of this State has and shall exercise continuing, exclusive jurisdiction to modify its child-support order if the order is the controlling order and:

(1) at the time of the filing of a request for modification this State is the residence of the obligor, the individual obligee, or the child. . .; or

(2) . . . the parties consent . . . that the tribunal of this State may continue to exercise jurisdiction to modify its order.

(b) A tribunal . . . may not exercise continuing, exclusive jurisdiction to modify the order if:

(1) all of the parties who are individuals file consent . . . with the tribunal of this State that a tribunal of another State . . . may modify the order and assume continuing, exclusive jurisdiction. . . .

(c) If a tribunal of another State has issued a child-support order pursuant to the [Uniform Interstate Family Support Act] . . . which modifies a child-support order of a tribunal of this State, tribunals of this State shall recognize the continuing, exclusive jurisdiction of the tribunal of the other State.

(d) A tribunal of this State [lacking modification jurisdiction] may serve as an initiating tribunal to request a tribunal of another State to modify a support order issued in that State.

(e) A temporary support order issued ex parte or pending resolution of a jurisdictional conflict does not create continuing, exclusive jurisdiction. . . .

§ 206. Continuing Jurisdiction to Enforce Child-Support Order.

(a) A tribunal . . . that has issued a child-support order consistent with the law of this State may serve as an initiating tribunal to request a tribunal of another state to enforce:

(1) the order if the order is the controlling order and has not been modified [pursuant to UIFSA]; or

(2) a money judgment for arrears . . . on the order accrued before a determination that an order of another State is the controlling order.

. . . .

§ 207. Determination of Controlling Child-Support Order.

(a) If a proceeding is brought under this [Act] and only one tribunal has issued a child-support order, the order of that tribunal controls and must be so recognized.

(b) If a proceeding is brought under this [Act], and two or more child-support orders have been issued . . . with regard to the same obligor and same child, a tribunal of this State . . . shall apply the following rules and by order shall determine which order controls:

(1) If only one of the tribunals would have continuing, exclusive jurisdiction under this [Act], the order of that tribunal controls. . . .

(2) If more than one of the tribunals would have continuing, exclusive jurisdiction under this [Act]:

(A) an order issued by a tribunal in the current home State of the child controls; but

(B) if an order has not been issued in the current home State of the child, the order most recently issued controls.

(3) If none of the tribunals would have continuing, exclusive jurisdiction under this [Act], the tribunal of this State shall issue a child-support order, which controls.

(c) If two or more child-support orders have been issued for the same obligor and same child, upon request of a party . . ., a tribunal of this State having personal jurisdiction over both the obligor and the obligee. . . . shall determine which order controls. . .

. . . .

(e) The tribunal that issued the controlling order under subsection (a), (b), or (c) has continuing jurisdiction to the extent provided in Section 205 or 206.

. . . .

(g) Within [30] days after issuance of an order determining the controlling order, the party obtaining the order shall file a certified copy of it in each tribunal that issued or registered an earlier order. . . . The failure to file does not affect the validity or enforceability of the controlling order.

. . . .

§ 315. Nonparentage as a Defense.

A party whose parentage of a child has been previously determined by or pursuant to law may not plead nonparentage as a defense to a proceeding under this [Act].

§ 501. Employer's Receipt of Income-Withholding Order of Another State.

An income-withholding order issued in another State may be sent . . . to the . . . obligor's employer . . . without first filing a [petition] . . . or registering the order with a tribunal. . . .

§ 502. Employer's Compliance with Income-Withholding Order of Another State.

(a) Upon receipt of an income-withholding order, the obligor's employer shall immediately provide a copy of the order to the obligor.

(b) The employer shall treat an income-withholding order issued in another State which appears regular on its face as if it had been issued by a tribunal of this State.

(c) Except as otherwise provided in subsection (d) and § 503, the employer shall withhold and distribute the funds as directed in the withholding order by complying with terms of the order which specify:

(1) the duration and amount of periodic payments of current child-support. . .;

(2) the person designated to receive payments . . .;

(3) medical support, whether in the form of periodic cash payment, stated as a sum certain, or ordering the obligor to provide health insurance coverage for the child under a policy available through the obligor's employment;

(4) . . . fees and costs for a support enforcement agency, the issuing tribunal, and the obligee's attorney, stated as sums certain; and

(5) . . . arrearages and interest on arrearages, stated as sums certain.

(d) An employer shall comply with the law of the State of the obligor's principal place of employment for withholding from income with respect to:

(1) the employer's fee for processing an income-withholding order;

(2) the maximum amount permitted to be withheld . . .; and

(3) the times within which the employer must implement the withholding order and forward the child-support payment.

§ 504. Immunity From Civil Liability.

An employer who complies with an income-withholding order [in compliance] with this article is not subject to civil liability . . . with regard to the employer's withholding of child support from the obligor's income.

§ 506. Contest by Obligor.

(a) An obligor may contest the validity or enforcement of an income-withholding order issued in another State and received directly by an employer in this State by registering the order in a tribunal of this State and filing a contest to that order as provided in Article 6, or otherwise contesting the order . . . as if [it] had been issued by a tribunal of this State.

. . . .

§ 507. Administrative Enforcement of Orders.

(a) A party or support enforcement agency seeking to enforce a support order or an income-withholding order, or both, issued by a tribunal of another State may send the documents required for registering the order to a support enforcement agency of this State.

(b) . . .[T]he support enforcement agency . . . shall consider and, if appropriate, use any administrative procedure authorized by the law of this State to enforce a support order or an income-withholding order, or both. If the obligor does not contest administrative enforcement, the order need not be registered. If the obligor contests the validity or administrative enforcement of the order, the support enforcement agency shall register the order pursuant to this [Act].

§ 601. Registration of Order for Enforcement.

A support order or income-withholding order issued by a tribunal of another State may be registered in this State for enforcement.

§ 602. Procedure to Register Order for Enforcement.

(a) A support order or income-withholding order of another State may be registered in this State by sending the following . . . to the [appropriate tribunal] in this State:

(1) a letter of transmittal . . . requesting registration and enforcement;

(2) two copies, including one certified copy, of the order to be registered, including any modification of the order;

(3) a sworn statement by [petitioner] or a certified statement by the custodian of the records showing the amount of any arrearage;

(4) [identifying information about the obligor an any of the obligor's property in the state not exempt from execution]

(5) except as otherwise provided in § 312, the name and address of the obligee and, if applicable, the person to whom support payments are to be remitted.

(b) On receipt . . ., the registering tribunal shall cause the order to be filed as a foreign judgment. . . .

. . . .

(d) If two or more orders are in effect, the [petitioner] shall:

(1) furnish . . . a copy of every support order asserted to be in effect in addition to the documents specified in this section;

(2) specify the order alleged to be the controlling order, if any; and

(3) specify the amount of consolidated arrears, if any.

(e) A request for a determination of which is the controlling order may be filed separately or with a request for registration and enforcement or for registration and modification. . . .

§ 603. Effect of Registration for Enforcement.

(a) A support order or income-withholding order issued in another State is registered when the order is filed in the registering tribunal of this State.

(b) A registered order issued in another State is enforceable in the same manner and is subject to the same procedures as an order issued by a tribunal of this State.

(c) Except as otherwise provided in this article, a tribunal of this State shall recognize and enforce, but may not modify, a registered order if the issuing tribunal had jurisdiction.

§ 604. Choice of Law.

(a) . . . [T]he law of the issuing State governs:

(1) the nature, extent, amount, and duration of current payments under a registered support order;

(2) the computation and payment of arrearages and accrual of interest on the arrearages under the support order; and

(3) the existence and satisfaction of other obligations under the support order.

(b) In a proceeding for arrears under a registered support order, the statute of limitation of this State or of the issuing State, whichever is longer, applies.

(c) A responding tribunal of this State shall apply the procedures and remedies of this State to enforce current support and collect arrears and interest due on a support order of another State registered in this State.

. . . .

§ 605. Notice of Registration of Order.

(a) When a[n] order . . . issued in another State is registered, the registering tribunal shall notify the nonregistering party. . . .

(b) A notice must inform the nonregistering party:

(1) that a registered order is enforceable as of the date of registration in the same manner as an order issued by a tribunal of this State;

(2) that a hearing to contest the validity or enforcement of the registered order must be requested within [20] days after notice;

(3) that failure to contest the validity or enforcement of the registered order in a timely manner will result in confirmation of the order and enforcement of the order and the alleged arrearages; and

(4) of the amount of any alleged arrearages.

(c) If the registering party asserts that two or more orders are in effect, a notice must also:

(1) identify the two or more orders and the order alleged by the registering person to be the controlling order and the consolidated arrears, if any;

(2) notify the nonregistering party of the right to a determination of which is the controlling order;

(3) state that the procedures provided in subsection (b) apply to the determination of which is the controlling order; and

(4) state that failure to contest the validity or enforcement of the order alleged to be the controlling order in a timely manner may result in confirmation that the order is the controlling order.

(d) Upon registration of an income-withholding order for enforcement, the registering tribunal shall notify the obligor's employer pursuant to [the income-withholding law of this State].

§ 606. Procedure to Contest Validity or Enforcement of Registered Order.

(a) A nonregistering party seeking to contest the validity or enforcement of a registered order in this State shall request a hearing within [20] days after notice of the registration. The nonregistering party may seek to vacate the registration, to assert any defense to an allegation of noncompliance . . ., or to contest the remedies being sought or the amount of any alleged arrearages pursuant to § 607.

(b) If the nonregistering party fails to contest the validity or enforcement of the registered order in a timely manner, the order is confirmed by operation of law.

(c) If a nonregistering party requests a hearing . . ., the registering tribunal shall [set a] hearing and give notice to the parties. . . .

§ 607. Contest of Registration or Enforcement.

(a) A party contesting the validity or enforcement of a registered order or seeking to vacate the registration [must prove] . . . :

(1) the issuing tribunal lacked personal jurisdiction over the contesting party;

(2) the order was obtained by fraud;

(3) the order has been vacated, suspended, or modified by a later order;

(4) the issuing tribunal has stayed the order pending appeal;

(5) there is a defense under the law of this State to the remedy sought;

(6) full or partial payment has been made;

(7) the statute of limitation under § 604 precludes enforcement . . .; or

(8) the alleged controlling order is not the controlling order.

(b) If a party presents evidence establishing a full or partial defense . . ., a tribunal may stay enforcement of the registered order, continue the proceeding to permit production of additional relevant evidence, and issue other appropriate orders. . . .

(c) If the contesting party does not establish a defense under subsection (a) . . ., the registering tribunal shall issue an order confirming the order.

§ 608. Confirmed Order.

Confirmation of a registered order, whether by operation of law or after notice and hearing, precludes further contest of the order with respect to any matter that could have been asserted at the time of registration.

§ 609. Procedure to Register Child-Support Order of Another State for Modification.

A party . . . seeking to modify . . . a child-support order issued in another State shall register that order in this State in the same manner provided in [the earlier registration provisions] if the order has not been registered. A [petition] for modification may be filed at the same time as a request for registration, or later [and] must specify the grounds for modification.

§ 610. Effect of Registration for Modification.

A tribunal of this State may enforce a child-support order of another State registered for purposes of modification, in the same manner as if the order had been issued by a tribunal of this State, but the registered order may be modified only if the requirements of § 611, § 613, or § 615 have been met.

§ 611. Modification of Child-Support Order of Another State.

(a) If § 613 does not apply,. . ., upon [petition] a tribunal of this State may modify a child-support order issued in another State which is registered in this State if, after notice and hearing, the tribunal finds that:

(1) the following requirements are met:

(A) [no party] resides in the issuing State;

(B) a [petitioner] who is a nonresident of this State seeks modification; and

(C) the [respondent] is subject to the personal jurisdiction of the tribunal of this State; or

(2) this State is the State of residence of the child, or a party who is an individual is subject to the personal jurisdiction of the tribunal of this State, and all of the parties who are individuals have filed consents . . . in the issuing tribunal for a tribunal of this State to modify . . . and assume continuing, exclusive jurisdiction [over the order].

(b) Modification of a registered child-support order is subject to the same requirements, procedures, and defenses that apply to the modification of an order issued by a tribunal of this State and the order may be enforced and satisfied in the same manner.

(c) . . . [A] tribunal of this State may not modify any aspect of a child-support order that may not be modified under the law of the issuing State, including the duration of the obligation of support. If two or more tribunals have issued child-support orders for the same obligor and same child, the order that controls and must be so recognized under § 207 establishes the aspects of the support order which are nonmodifiable.

(d) In a proceeding to modify . . ., the law of the State that is determined to have issued the initial controlling order governs the duration of the obligation of support. The obligor's fulfillment of the duty of support established by that order precludes imposition of a further obligation of support by a tribunal of this State.

(e) On the issuance of an order [of modification] by a tribunal of this State . . ., the tribunal of this State [obtains] continuing, exclusive jurisdiction.

§ 612. Recognition of Order Modified in Another State.

If a child-support order issued by a tribunal of this State is modified by a tribunal of another State [under UIFSA], a tribunal of this State:

(1) may enforce its order that was modified only as to arrears and interest accruing before the modification;

(2) may provide appropriate relief for violations of its order which occurred before the effective date of the modification; and

(3) shall recognize the modifying order of the other State, upon registration, for the purpose of enforcement.

§ 613. Jurisdiction to Modify Child-Support Order of Another State When Individual Parties Reside in This State.

(a) If all of the parties who are individuals reside in this State and the child does not reside in the issuing State, a tribunal of this State has jurisdiction to enforce and to modify the issuing State's child-support order in a proceeding to register that order.

. . . .

HARBISON v. JOHNSTON

28 P.3d 1136 (N.M. App. 2001)

SUTIN, Judge.

. . . . (Mother) appeals the district court's order dismissing . . . her motion to modify and enforce the child support provisions of a Texas support and visitation judgment. Mother raises two issues: (1) whether . . . (Father) submitted to personal jurisdiction in the New Mexico district court when he initiated proceedings to enforce the visitation provisions of the Texas judgment, and (2) whether the district court had subject matter jurisdiction to modify or enforce the child support provisions of the same judgment. . . .

. . . . Mother and Father are parents of a child . . . born in El Paso, Texas, in May 1995. When Child was one year old, Father filed an action in Texas . . . to establish paternity. [In]1996, the . . . court entered a judgment . . . adjudicating Father as parent, granting Mother permanent custody, awarding Father visitation rights, and ordering Father to pay child support.

For about two years, Father exercised his visitation rights. . . . In July 1998 Mother and Child moved from El Paso to Las Cruces, New Mexico, so Mother could finish her studies at New Mexico State University. In August 1998 Father moved to California to perform temporary work on a reservoir construction project, whereupon his visitation with Child ceased, except for one week . . . when Child visited him in California. After . . . approximately nine months, Father returned to El Paso and tried, unsuccessfully, to resume visitation with Child, who continued to live with Mother in Las Cruces.

In November 1999 Father filed a petition in New Mexico . . ., requesting that it recognize and enforce the visitation provisions . . . in the Texas judgment and hold Mother in contempt for violating its requirements. Mother responded . . . and also filed a countermotion to modify and enforce the child support provisions . . . in the Texas judgment. . . . Father [moved] to dismiss the child support action. Father argued that the New Mexico court had neither personal jurisdiction nor subject matter jurisdiction to modify and enforce the Texas support order and that Texas had continuing, exclusive jurisdiction over the support order.

Following an evidentiary hearing . . ., the district court entered an order giving full faith and credit to the Texas judgment, modifying its visitation provisions. . . . Following a later hearing, the district court dismissed Mother's motion . . . regarding child support. The district court determined New Mexico lacked both subject matter jurisdiction and personal jurisdiction over Father, and concluded Texas retained exclusive jurisdiction over the support order. Mother appeals from the dismissal.

. . . .

[The court determined the trial court had personal jurisdiction over Father for purposes of the support action, holding that under the state long-arm statute, patterned after UIFSA § 201 (*see* Chapter 7), Father had submitted to jurisdiction by entering a general appearance in New Mexico seeking enforcement of the Texas visitation order. "Once Father invoked and submitted himself to the jurisdiction of New Mexico, he could not then attempt to limit his appearance solely to attacking the personal jurisdiction of the court in the support portion of the proceedings." The court acknowledged that the *Texas* child custody jurisdiction statute [based on § 109 of the Uniform Child Custody Jurisdiction Enforcement Act] would provide a petitioner immunity from personal service in another action when pursuing a custody action under it, but there was no parallel immunity under New Mexico law.]

Mother contends the district court erred in determining that it did not have [subject matter] jurisdiction to consider her motion to modify and enforce the Texas support order. The crux of her argument appears to be that because Father [sought] enforcement of the Texas visitation order, the district court also acquired jurisdiction to hear her motion to modify and enforce the Texas support order.

Two statutory acts govern: the Child Custody Jurisdiction Act (CCJA) and the UIFSA. Jurisdiction over the issue of visitation is governed by the CCJA. Jurisdiction over the modification and enforcement of another state's child support order is governed by UIFSA. The standards under each act are different and assign jurisdiction independently. A court's jurisdiction to hear a custody or visitation dispute under the CCJA does not confer jurisdiction . . . to determine issues of child support under the UIFSA. Similarly child support jurisdiction under UIFSA does not confer jurisdiction [over]custody or visitation. We hold the district court's jurisdiction over the visitation proceeding did not confer subject matter jurisdiction to modify and enforce the Texas support order.

Under the UIFSA, a New Mexico court "shall recognize the continuing, exclusive jurisdiction of a tribunal of another state which has issued a child-support order pursuant to a law substantially similar to the Uniform Interstate Family Support Act." [Ed.'s Note: this is the language of UIFSA § 205(d) as it was promulgated in 1992. While this precise language no longer exists in the current version of the Uniform Act, it still accurately describes the position taken by UIFSA] Texas . . . has adopted the UIFSA. Therefore, the two acts are "substantially similar." Under its continuing jurisdiction provision, identical to [New Mexico's], Texas, as the state that issued the child support order, still has continuing, exclusive jurisdiction to modify the order because Father continues to reside in Texas, and the parties have not mutually agreed to confer jurisdiction to New Mexico.

A New Mexico court's power to modify another state's child support order is specifically governed by [UIFSA § 611(a). Ed.'s Note: again, this is the 1992 version, the substance of which remains the law under the 2001 version]. That provision states in pertinent part:

> After a child support order issued in another state has been registered in this state, the responding tribunal of this state may modify the order only . . . after notice and hearing the tribunal finds that:
>
> (1) the following requirements are met:
>
>> (A) the child, the individual obligee, and the obligor do not reside in the issuing state;
>>
>> (B) a petitioner who is a nonresident of this state seeks modification; and
>>
>> (C) the respondent is subject to the personal jurisdiction of the tribunal of this state; or
>
> (2) the child, or a party who is an individual, is subject to the personal jurisdiction of the tribunal of this state and all of the parties who are individuals have filed . . . written consents for a tribunal of this state to modify the support order and assume continuing, exclusive jurisdiction over the order[.]

As a threshold matter, we determine that the Texas judgment . . . was "registered" in New Mexico when Father filed it in the district court for purposes of enforcing its visitation provision.

We conclude, however, that the other statutory prerequisites for New Mexico district court modification of the support order were not met in this case. First, Father still resided in the issuing state of Texas. Second, Mother and Father did not consent in writing for New Mexico to assume continuing, exclusive jurisdiction over the support order. Finally, Mother was a New Mexico resident and thus did not meet the requirement that the party seeking modification be a non-resident of the forum state. Therefore, the district court did not have jurisdiction to modify the Texas support order.

Mother nevertheless argues that the district court had jurisdiction to modify the support order under the federal Full Faith and Credit for Child Support Orders Act (FFCCSOA), 28 U.S.C. § 1738B (1997). Although Mother did not raise [this] below, we address her argument . . . because the FFCCSOA governs subject matter jurisdiction and full faith and credit for support orders and, thus, may be considered for the first time on appeal.

The FFCCSOA . . . is intended to work in tandem with the UIFSA and essentially mirrors its jurisdictional concepts. *See Gentzel v. Williams*, 965 P.2d 855, 860 (Kan. App. 1998) ("FFCCSOA is similar to UIFSA both in . . . structure and intent."); *see generally* Patricia Wick Hatamyar, *Critical Applications and Proposals for Improvement of the Uniform Interstate Family Support Act and the Full Faith and Credit for Child Support Orders Act*, 71 ST. JOHN'S L. REV. 1 (1997).

According to subsections (a) and (c) of § 1738B, if a child support order is made by a court that had jurisdiction and gave the parties notice and an opportunity to be heard, a court of another state cannot modify the order except as provided. That is, the FFCCSOA allows modification of a valid order only if (1) neither the child nor any of the parties remain in the issuing state, and the forum state has jurisdiction over the parties; or (2) all parties have consented to the jurisdiction of the forum state to modify the order. 28 U.S.C. § 1738B(e). Because Father remains a resident of Texas and the parties have not consented to a change in jurisdiction, Texas retains continuing, exclusive jurisdiction over modification of the support order under the FFCCSOA. We do not find Section 205(d) of the UIFSA to be in direct conflict with the FFCCSOA and the full faith and credit clause of the United States Constitution, as Mother suggests.

Mother also asked the district court to enforce certain provisions of the Texas support order. In particular, Mother sought employment and financial information as required by the order and a determination of the amount of past child support owed by Father. . . .

We conclude the district court incorrectly concluded it did not have jurisdiction to enforce the support order. Under the UIFSA, if a child support order of another state is properly registered, the registering state is obligated to enforce the order in the same manner as if it had issued the order, even though it remains an order of the issuing state for purposes of modification. [See UIFSA § 603(c) ("Except as otherwise provided in this article, a tribunal of this state shall recognize and enforce, but may not modify, a registered order if the issuing tribunal had jurisdiction.")]

The FFCCSOA similarly obligates states to give full faith and credit to child support orders properly issued by other states and to refrain from modifying such orders unless the limited conditions of the act are met. 28 U.S.C. § 1738B(a), (e). The intended purpose and effect of the enforcement provisions in the UIFSA and the FFCCSOA are to facilitate the enforcement of child support orders among the states. *See generally* Patricia Wick Hatamyar, *Interstate Establishment, Enforcement, and Modification of Child Support Orders*, 25 OKLA. CITY U. L. REV. 511, 541–43 (2000).

We hold the district court had personal jurisdiction over Father regarding the Texas judgment he registered in New Mexico and subject matter jurisdiction to enforce, but not modify, the child support order in that judgment. We reverse and remand for further proceedings consistent with this opinion.

NOTES

1. *Restriction of Modification of Child Support Orders Under UIFSA.*
As noted in the Sampson & Kurtz excerpt above, under URESA courts would
often, in an interstate action, enter a support order for a particular child with
terms that differed from the terms of a previously-existing support order.
Usually the second, or URESA, order would be for a lesser amount. Generally
this second order was not conceived of as a modification of the existing order.
See, e.g., Jefferson County Child Support Enforcement Unit v. Hollands, 938
S.W.2d 302 (Ark. 1997); *Alaska v. Valdez*, 941 P.2d 144 (Alas. 1997); *In re
Kramer*, 625 N.E.2d 808 (Ill. App. 1993) (URESA decree which set lower
payments than divorce decree did not stop accumulation of arrearages under
the latter); *Dep't of Health & Rehab. Servs. v. Franklin*, 630 So. 2d 661 (Fla.
App. 1994); Annot., *Construction and Effect of Provision of Uniform Reciprocal
Enforcement of Support Act That No Support Order Shall Supersede or Nullify
Any Other Order*, 31 A.L.R.4th 347 (1984). Indeed URESA § 31, the so-called
anti-supersession clause, stated that a URESA order did not "nullify" any prior
order "unless otherwise specifically provided by the [URESA] court. . . ." Courts
would rarely even attempt to take advantage of the final proviso, likely
because of the awkwardness of a court purporting to change the terms of an
order of another state. Instead, most URESA courts likely imagined themselves as merely "enforcing" the prior order, even if only partially, by entering
an order for the same or a lesser amount of support than had previously been
ordered.

Why was URESA constructed in such a way as to permit or even encourage
multiple orders concerning support of the same child? Apparently, the drafters
found protection of state sovereignty (of the original issuing state) to be an
important value, particularly considering that in interstate actions at most
only one of the parties physically appeared in the responding court. The fine-
tuning of support obligations with only one party able to testify and respond
to cross-examination was seen as risky at best. However, a world in which
multiple orders from several states each requiring different amounts of
support for the same child was a very confusing one, both for obligors and
obligees.

Thus, UIFSA's drafters set out to establish a system under which, rather
than multiple orders possibly setting different levels of support for the same
child, at any one time there would be only one support order for any child.
Section 205 of UIFSA is designed to carry out this intent by providing that
the court which issued the original order shall have "continuing, *exclusive*
jurisdiction" [CEJ] to modify it unless certain conditions are met. While
UIFSA does not explicitly define "modify," the federal Full Faith and Credit
for Child Support Orders Act (FFCCSOA), 28 U.S.C. § 1738B (1997) (referred
to in *Harbison* and discussed at Note 7, *infra*) provides a very broad definition
of the concept which, when combined with UIFSA § 205, means a UIFSA court
lacking modification jurisdiction can do very little where a support order
already exists. Under FFCCSOA (which, as federal law, controls in determining when and in what ways full faith and credit must be given to existing
support orders), modification is defined as "a change in a child support order
that affects the amount, scope, or duration of the order and modifies, replaces,

supersedes or *otherwise is made subsequent to the child support order."* § 1738B(b) (emphasis added).

Under UIFSA § 205, no other court can gain jurisdiction to modify an existing order if one party currently lives in the jurisdiction which issued the original decree. Thus, because Father in *Harbison* was living in Texas, which had issued the original decree, New Mexico had no subject matter jurisdiction to modify that order. Originally, UIFSA provided that the issuing state would retain continuing, exclusive jurisdiction to modify *"as long as [it] remains"* the residence of one of the parties. In 2001, the language was changed to make explicit that the issuing state would regain CEJ if a party (such as the *Harbison* Father) left the issuing state, but returned before any modification had been issued. *Harbison* (and the statute) distinguish between personal and subject matter jurisdiction, making clear that both are required and that the presence of the former does not guarantee the existence of the latter.

Now that New Mexico has told Mother in *Harbison* that it has no jurisdiction to modify the original support order, what would you advise her to do?

2. *Jurisdiction to Modify Under UIFSA.* While the UIFSA rules for modification are much more restrictive than the URESA regime, there are some narrow situations in which a second state can modify another state's support order and assume CEJ to make any future modifications. Two sections deal with modification of an order issued by another state. Under § 611, there must be a finding that either: 1) all the parties have left the issuing state, and the petitioner is a non-resident of the forum and the respondent is subject to the forum's personal jurisdiction **or** 2) all parties have agreed to a modification determination in the forum, so long as the forum is either child's residence or has personal jurisdiction over a party. Thus, *e.g.*, if an Idaho decree was entered when all parties lived there, but now the obligor lives in Iowa and the obligee lives with the child in Maine, Iowa could be a forum under UIFSA for a modification action brought by the obligee. Similarly, Maine would be able to issue a modification order in an action brought by the obligor. Once a court in either state issued such a modification, it would become the CEJ court with power to deal with any future modifications. Alternatively under § 611, the parties can agree to give a new state the power to modify an existing order so long as it has connection to the litigation by either having personal jurisdiction over a party or being the child's residence. Under § 613, if all parties reside in the forum state and the child has left the issuing state, there is modification jurisdiction.

3. *Enforcing an Existing Support Order Under UIFSA.* The UIFSA approach to enforcement of existing orders is very different from its approach to modification. The statute [§ 603] makes clear that any state can and, indeed, must recognize and enforce the support decrees of other states. Thus, the *Harbison* appellate court held that the trial court had UIFSA jurisdiction to order Father to turn over employment and financial information required under the Texas order and the ability to determine arrearages owed under the Texas decree. Note the breadth of the court's enforcement powers under § 305 reprinted above. It could, *e.g.*, "specify a method of payment" of any arrearages it had determined to exist, it could "enforce orders by civil or criminal contempt," it could "order income withholding," etc.

Of course, not only could the appropriate New Mexico court enforce the order against Father, but Texas, as the issuing state, could also enforce its order so long as Father remained subject to its jurisdiction. In fact, even if another state eventually modified the Texas order under modification jurisdiction obtained under § 611 or § 613, the issuing tribunal in Texas, under § 612(1), could enforce its order to the extent that "arrears and interest" had accrued before the modification.

4. ***The Mechanics of Modifying or Enforcing an Existing Order.*** Article Six of UIFSA (selected provisions of which appear above) outlines the details of the process of modifying or enforcing an existing order. While registration is required as a pre-requisite to modification in the new state, there are situations (*see* Note 6, *infra*) in which enforcement in a non-issuing state can be accomplished without registration. The UIFSA rules for registering an existing order are set out in § 602 which, although titled as a procedure "for enforcement" is made applicable to the modification proceeding by § 609. Note that *Harbison* held that the Texas decree had been properly registered for purposes of UIFSA.

The filing of the foreign order under § 602 constitutes registration under § 603 and the order thereby becomes enforceable in the registering state. The Commentary to §§ 602 and 603 makes clear that the registering of a foreign order in State-2 does not convert a State-1 order into an order of the new state. Instead, as stated in the Commentary to § 603, "the registering tribunal must bear in mind that the enforcement procedures taken, whether to enforce current support or to assist collecting . . . arrears are made on behalf of the issuing State, and are not to be viewed as modifications of the . . . order."

Sections 605 through 608 explain registration contests by the non-registering party. Under § 605, the latter is informed that he or she has 20 days in which to contest the registered order. The respondent may, according to § 606(a), "seek to vacate the registration, to assert any defense to an allegation of noncompliance. . .or to contest the remedies being sought or the amount of any alleged arrearages. . ." The grounds for contesting the validity or enforcement of a registered order are detailed in § 607(a). If no contest is filed or if no defense is proven under § 607(a), the order is confirmed which, under § 608, precludes the respondent from raising any claim that "could have been asserted at the time of registration."

5. ***Choice of Law in Enforcement of Existing Orders.*** As noted earlier, UIFSA's general choice of law rule (§ 303) directs the forum tribunal to apply the law of its own state. Section 303, based on a policy of allowing a forum court to apply familiar rules, acknowledges that other UIFSA provisions make exceptions to the general rule. The most important such provision is § 604, which deals with the enforcement of an existing decree in another state. It states that the law of the issuing state will control "the nature, extent, amount, and duration of current payments" in a situation where it is being enforced in a second state. Thus, *e.g.*, if State A's order provides for support "until adulthood" which is defined in State A as the age of 21 and it is registered in State B, which has an 18-year-old age of majority, the latter state will be obligated to enforce the order until the age of 21. *See, e.g., Robdau v. Va. Dept. Soc. Servs.*, 543 S.E.2d 602 (Va. App. 2001); *State ex rel. Harnes* *v. Lawrence*, 538 S.E.2d 223 N.C. App. 2000). The rationale for this rule is explained by the Drafters as deriving from the Act's insistence that the second state is not creating a new order, but simply assisting in the enforcement of the first state's order. Thus, the law of the issuing state is the logical one to look to for the determination of the meaning of its terms.

A different choice of law rule is provided in subsection (b) for the statute of limitations for collection of arrearages. This provision directs the court to the law of either the forum or the issuing state, whichever is longer. *See Attorney General v. Litten*, 999 S.W.2d 74 (Tex. App. 1999). According to the Commentary, this rule was designed to insure that "the obligor should not gain an undue benefit from the choice of residence if the forum State has a shorter statute of limitations. . . ." The Drafters assert that if the forum state's statute provides for a longer period of recoverability than the issuing state's the obligor cannot justly complain about being treated the same as all other obligors in the forum state. While not mentioned by the Commentary, this rule might be even more persuasively justified by its child-centered nature. Local law governs, under § 604(c), in determining the procedures available for enforcement. Thus, the enforcement court could, *e.g.*, rely on its license revocation statute even if the issuing state did not have a similar law.

6. *Direct Enforcement of Child Support Orders and Wage Withholding Orders.* One of UIFSA's major innovations is direct enforcement of existing orders in a second state without involvement by any tribunal in the second state. Under § 501, a wage withholding order issued by State X can be sent to the obligor's employer in State Y "without first filing a [petition] . . . or registering the order with a tribunal. . . ." Under § 502(b), upon receipt of such an order, the employer is to treat it "as if it had been issued by a tribunal" of State Y and, under subsection (c), comply with the order's terms concerning the duration and amount of periodic payments, medical support, fees and costs of attorneys and child support agencies and arrearages. Subsection (d) provides, however, that the law of the obligor's state shall govern limits on the amount the employer can charge for processing, the maximum amount which can be withheld from the obligor's income and time limits on employer compliance. Failure to comply with a foreign income withholding order will subject the employer, under § 505, to whatever penalties exist for failure to withhold under an in-state order. Under § 506, an obligor seeking to contest the validity of enforcement of an out-of-state order received by his or her employer must register the order and then file a contest under §§ 605-608 (Note 4, *supra*).

A separate provision of the statute, § 507, deals with administrative enforcement of a support order by the support enforcement agency of the obligor's state, again without involvement of a tribunal. Under subsection (a) a party or agency in the obligee's state can send a copy of the order to the agency in obligor's state. That agency is authorized, under subsection (b), to use any administrative procedures available for domestic orders to enforce the out-of-state order. As the Commentary to § 507 states, "[f]or example, if the administrative hearing procedure must be exhausted for an intrastate order before a contesting party may seek relief in a tribunal, the same rule applies to an interstate order received for administrative enforcement."

7. *The Federal Full Faith and Credit for Child Support Orders Act of 1994.* Between the initial promulgation of UIFSA in 1992 and the passage of the federal mandate to the states to enact UIFSA (in the 1996 Welfare Reform Act), Congress passed the Full Faith and Credit for Child Support Orders Act of 1994 (FFCCSOA, codified at 28 U.S.C. § 1738B) which, like UIFSA, was designed to replace the multiple orders of URESA with a "one-order" regime. The rationale for enacting the Federal law merely two years after the Uniform Act had been proposed has been described as "somewhat elusive." Hatamyar, *Critical Applications and Proposals for Improvement of the Uniform Interstate Family Support Act and the Full Faith and Credit for Child Support Orders Act*, 71 St. John's L. Rev. 1 (1997). Professor Hatamyar reports, however, that

> [s]ome child support advocates . . . worried that piecemeal, state-by-state adoption of UIFSA would delay receipt of the intended benefits by interstate obligees. In addition, given the states' patchwork adoption of variants of URESA . . . UIFSA supporters believed that the "uniform law" would become anything but uniform.

Id. at p. 6. *See also* Hatamyar, *Interstate Establishment, Enforcement, and Modification of Child Support*, 25 Okla. City U.L. Rev. 511 (2000).

Under the statute, states must enforce support orders of other states so long as the original order was entered consistently with the provisions of § 1738B(c). The latter subsection in turn requires that the original order be entered with jurisdiction (both personal and subject matter) and consistent with due process requirements of notice.

The federal statute, like UIFSA, restricts a second state's ability to modify an existing support order. According to § 1738B(e), modification is allowed only when there is no longer a court with continuing, exclusive jurisdiction or all parties have agreed to transfer continuing, exclusive jurisdiction to a new state. Critically, the federal law does not permit a second state to use the URESA-era charade that it was not modifying a prior support order but merely issuing an independent order. As mentioned in Note 1, *supra*, the Act defines modification as "a change in a child support order that affects the amount, scope, or duration of the order and modifies, replaces, supersedes or *otherwise is made subsequent to the child support order.*" § 1738B(b) (emphasis added). *See Isabel M. v. Thomas M.*, 624 N.Y.S.2d 356 (Fam. Ct. 1995) (finding italicized phrase prohibits action filed under New York's version of URESA, the Uniform Support of Dependents Law, where another state has continuing, exclusive jurisdiction over existing order).

The federal act has been upheld against constitutional attack. *Kilroy v. Superior Court*, 63 Cal. Rptr. 2d 390 (App. 1997). Noting continuing, exclusive modification jurisdiction remained in the Georgia courts where petitioner and child remained and there was no agreement for the California courts to consider the modification, *Kilroy* found FFCCSOA clearly prohibited a California modification. In addressing petitioner's argument that the Act exceeded Congressional power under the Commerce Clause, the court distinguished *United States v. Lopez*, 514 U.S. 549 (1995), in which the Gun-Free School Zone Act of 1990 was found unconstitutional. The court found "payments between parents in different states substantially affects interstate commerce,"

63 Cal. Rptr. 2d at 400, noting extensive Congressional findings identifying the particular problems faced by children and custodial parents in interstate litigation. *Kilroy* also rejected petitioner's Tenth Amendment attack, noting express Congressional authority under the Full Faith and Credit Clause, Art. IV, § 1, to provide for the proof of the acts of other states and "prescribe . . . the effect thereof."

For other cases interpreting FFCCSOA, see *Peddar v. Peddar*, 683 N.E.2d 1045 (Mass App. 1997) (personal jurisdiction over defendant-obligor insufficient to override Act's jurisdictional rules); *Lewis v. Lewis*, 1997 Ohio App. LEXIS 1130 (finding Act supports subject matter modification jurisdiction in Ohio, but refusing to apply choice of law rules retroactively where petition pre-dated Act); *V.G. v. Bates*, 1997 Minn. App. LEXIS 430 (rejecting constitutional attacks and applying Act to Texas judgment obtained before Act's effective date).

8. *Sorting Through Multiple Orders.* Despite UIFSA's determination to move from a world of multiple orders to one in which there is only one effective order at any time, the possibility of more than one existing support order for a particular child remains. For example, a prior order under URESA might exist, or a court in a UIFSA case might have erroneously entered an order without jurisdiction or a modification order might have been entered without jurisdiction in a default proceeding. In *P.A.N. v. R.N.*, 1996 Del. Fam. Ct. LEXIS 139, the court found a pre-UIFSA Delaware decree to be a nullity. The decree, entered under URESA, ordered payment of the same amount of support ordered by a prior New York divorce. The declaration of nullity was based upon UIFSA § 207(a)(2) [now § 207(b)(1)], which provides that where multiple support orders for the same child exist and only one of the issuing courts would have continuing exclusive jurisdiction under the Act that the latter was the order entitled to recognition. In *P.A.N.*, the obligee and the child remained in New York which, thus, retained continuing exclusive modification jurisdiction.

Section 207's rules designed to guide a court in determining what order is the UIFSA "one-order" will be especially important in the transition period as the country moves from the URESA multiple order regime to the UIFSA world with only one binding order at any time. As the Official Comment to the section states,

> [E]ven assuming universal enactment of UIFSA, many years will pass before its one-order system will be completely in place. . . . [This provision] is designed to span the gulf between the one-order system and the multiple order system in place under RURESA. . . . [M]ultiple orders issued under RURESA number in the tens of thousands; it can be reasonably anticipated that those orders . . . will continue in effect far into the future.

In a recent case, a URESA order had been entered in New Jersey and then an administrative order was issued in Maryland. While both were valid, the court found that under UIFSA's rules, the original order controlled because New Jersey remained the child's home state. Because it provided for continued support throughout the child's enrollment in college, it overrode the Maryland administrative decree terminating support on the child's 18th birthday. *Teare v. Bromley*, 753 A.2d 764 (N.J. Super. 2000); *see also Cohen v. Powers*, 43 P.3d 1150 (Ore. App. 2002) (applying transition rules to determine controlling order where three prior orders existed).

PROBLEMS

Problem 5-22. Morris and Kitty are married with two children, living in Nevada. Morris leaves one morning "for work" and does not communicate with Kitty any further. She discovers that he now lives in Maine. She would like to be rid of Morris and get support for their children, one of whom is 6 and the other of whom is 4. Assume both states have enacted UIFSA. What do you advise? Which state's law will govern the duration of any child support order she might obtain? Which state's guidelines govern?

Problem 5-23. George and Martha divorce and he is awarded custody of their only child, Denzel. Martha is ordered to pay $250 monthly child support. She moves to another state. After three years, George reports Martha hasn't paid support in two years and also has obtained a new job which pays a lot more money. George would like to collect the arrearages and seek an upward modification. Both states have enacted UIFSA. What are his options?

Problem 5-24. Rebecca and Dan's New Jersey divorce decree ordered Dan to pay $300 monthly in support for their children. Three years later, with all parties having moved to Florida, a court there ordered Dan to pay off his $8,000 in arrearages at a rate of $150 per month in addition to the $300 monthly support. Two years after that, when Dan moved back to New Jersey, Rebecca sought an order from the original divorce court, ordering him to pay arrearages at a rate of $300 monthly. Neither Rebecca in her petition nor Dan in his response mentioned the Florida decree. The judge granted Rebecca's petition changing the arrearage payment schedule. Now Dan has sought a rehearing claiming a violation of UIFSA and FFCCSOA. As clerk to the judge who will decide the case, outline your analysis of the issues, the best arguments on both sides and your recommended resolution.

Problem 5-25. John and Betsy are divorced in State A. Though they have three children, their divorce decree omits mention of support, but does provide for alimony, property division and custody. John subsequently moves to State B. The duty to support in State A extends to age 18, while State B requires support until age 21. Betsy has filed a UIFSA action in State A which is forwarded to State B. In this action, she seeks support for the children until age 21. Personal jurisdiction over John has been obtained. What are the issues and the parties' likely arguments? Would your answer change if the State A divorce decree, instead of ignoring child support had said that it "reserves the question of support until John is released from his current jail sentence"?

Problem 5-26. Eduardo and Helga are married, have two children and live in Tennessee. On a business trip to Illinois, Eduardo meets Natasha, with whom he falls madly in love. When Helga finds out, she divorces Eduardo in Tennessee. The decree orders Eduardo to pay $250 monthly child support. Subsequently, Eduardo loses his job in Tennessee and moves to Illinois to live with Natasha. Because he has not been paying his support, Helga files a UIFSA petition in Tennessee which is forwarded to Illinois. After obtaining personal jurisdiction over Eduardo, the Illinois court enters an order for $300 monthly in support, failing to address arrearages, which were not mentioned in the pleadings. After futile attempts to find gainful employment in Illinois, Eduardo is kicked out of their home by Natasha and moves to Wyoming. Helga moves to Illinois with the children to live with her parents and files an action in Wyoming seeking to register the Illinois decree providing for prospective payment of $300 monthly and seeks arrearages in Wyoming under the Tennessee divorce decree. Is she entitled to such relief?

Chapter 6

CHILD CUSTODY

§ A. INTRODUCTION

Custody of a minor child ordinarily encompasses a broad set of rights, including the right to live with the child in a shared residence and decision-making authority with respect to such matters as discipline, the child's name, where the child lives, who visits the child, and the child's education, earnings, medical treatment, and religious training. With these rights comes the duty to provide the child protection and support. But when a divorce court allocates custody between the parents, one or the other parent may lose some of these rights. Nonetheless, even when one parent is awarded primary custody, the other usually retains visitation rights, support duties, and the right to make certain decisions, particularly when the child is temporarily with that parent. In joint custody awards, courts often divide the broad concept of "custody" into legal custody, which refers to authority to make important decisions for the child such as those relating to education and medical care, and physical custody, which refers to rights to physical care and control.

Custody disputes between separating parents should be distinguished from child abuse proceedings, in which the state may deprive either or both parents of some or all parental rights, including physical custody, temporarily or permanently. These proceedings are addressed in Chapter 10. While in abuse proceedings the state must justify the limitation of parental rights as necessary to protect the child from harm, showings of harm are not required in private custody proceedings. Custody disputes can arise between two loving and entirely adequate parents: although in such a case neither parent could show that the other's custody risked harm to the child, the court must still resolve the parents' custody dispute. Harm can be at issue in custody proceedings, of course, and a showing of harm is normally necessary before one of the separating parents can be deprived of all contact with the child. This chapter deals with custody disputes between divorcing parents, as well as disputes between parents and third parties, typically relatives of the child. Chapter 9 deals with the special problems that arise in custody disputes between parents who have never been married to each other.

[1] BRIEF HISTORY OF INTER-PARENTAL CUSTODY DISPUTES

Roman law vested absolute power in custodial matters in the father. In fact, in ancient Rome a father could sell his children or even put them to death. FORSYTH, CUSTODY OF INFANTS 8 (1850). By contrast, a mother was not considered the child's natural guardian, even where the father died intestate. Thus, no custody disputes between parents were adjudicated in Roman courts, because the father's "will was practically absolute, and no amount of cruelty, neglect of duty or immorality on his part, affected in the slightest degree his claim to the custody of his children." *Id.*

English law adopted the Roman view of absolute paternal power and right to custody. The father had no right under English law to kill or sell a child, however. "The power of a parent by our English laws is much more moderate [than the laws of ancient Rome]; but still sufficient to keep the child in order and obedience." 1 BLACKSTONE, COMMENTARIES at 452. Blackstone wrote that "a mother, as such, is entitled to no power, but only to reverence and respect." 1 BLACKSTONE, COMMENTARIES 453. In the oft-cited case of *Rex v. DeManneville,* 102 Eng. Rep. 1054 (K.B. 1804), the court ordered an eight-month-old nursing infant removed from the mother and returned to the father, despite the mother's uncontested allegations that the parental separation was due to the father's extreme cruelty. The broadly-stated paternal preference rule of English and Roman law never gained a significant foothold in the United States. While some early 19th century American courts approvingly cited the English rule, *see, e.g., Commonwealth v. Briggs,* 16 Pick. 203 (Mass. 1834), the American rule quickly became the "best-interests-of-the-child." Many rules of thumb have been used to apply this standard. One mid-19th century commentator suggested that in divorce disputes, most courts followed the general rule that "children will be best taken care of and instructed by the innocent party." BISHOP, COMMENTARIES ON THE LAWS OF MARRIAGE AND DIVORCE 520 (1852). Although this principle today is outdated, remnants of the fault notion persist.

The "tender years" doctrine, under which the mother was deemed to be the more suitable custodian for young children, was developed in the 19th century. In 1813, the Pennsylvania Supreme Court reasoned: "[C]onsidering [the children's] tender age, they stand in need of that kind of assistance, which can be afforded by none so well as a mother." *Commonwealth v. Addicks,* 5 Binn. 520 (Pa. 1813). The presumption favoring mothers was justified both by the assumed biological superiority of mothers as parents and by social custom, which assigned responsibility for parenting to mothers. Early defenses of this doctrine glorified maternal love. *See, e.g. Krieger v. Krieger,* 81 P.2d 1081, 1083 (Idaho 1938) (the maternal preference "needs no argument to support it because it arises out of the very nature and instincts of motherhood; nature has ordained it"); *Tuter v. Tuter,* 120 S.W.2d 203, 205 (Mo. App. 1938) ("[t]here is but a twilight zone between a mother's love and the atmosphere of heaven.")

The tender years presumption was the dominant rule for resolving custody disputes through much of the twentieth century. It eroded in the 1970s and has been formally abolished in virtually all states. The decline of the presumption can be attributed in part to a rejection by courts of the sharply differentiated gender roles. Although in actual practice roles are changing slowly, courts and legislatures are reluctant to assume that maternal custody is in the child's best interest. Courts in the 1980s described the tender years presumption as based on "outdated stereotypes." *Pusey v. Pusey,* 728 P.2d 117 (Utah 1986). The decline of the legal preference for mothers in custody disputes was hastened by a series of constitutional challenges. The United States Supreme Court has never addressed the constitutionality of a gender preference rule in divorce custody cases, but many lower courts have struck down such a rule, either on constitutional grounds or under the best-interests principle. *See, e.g., Ex parte Devine,* 398 So. 2d 686 (Ala. 1981) (unconstitutional); *Bazemore v. Davis,* 394 A.2d 1377 (D.C. 1977) (violates best-interests principle); *State ex rel. Watts,* 350 N.Y.S.2d 285 (1973) (both); *see also Commonwealth ex rel. Spriggs v. Carson,* 368 A.2d 635 (Pa. 1977) (doctrine of questionable constitutionality). At least one court has found it violative of a state Equal Rights Amendment. *People ex rel. Irby v. Dubois,* 354 N.E.2d 562 (Ill. App. 1976).

[2] CHILDREN AND DIVORCE: PERSPECTIVES FROM SOCIAL SCIENCE

The impact of family dissolution on children has been a subject of considerable interest to social scientists. While experts tend to agree on the importance of the child's need for continuity, there is variation of opinion about what type of continuity is most important. Three well-known psychoanalysts, Joseph Goldstein, Anna Freud, and Albert Solnit emphasize the child's need for an undisturbed bond with a psychological parent, who has unconditional parental authority. This focus, which derives from psychological attachment theory, holds that the child's healthy psychological development is only possible if this critical parent-child bond is protected. This emphasis, in the divorce context, leads these authors to favor giving the primary caregiver sole authority and to permit only so much visitation with others as that parent deems appropriate. J. GOLDSTEIN, A. FREUD & A. SOLNIT, BEYOND THE BEST INTERESTS OF THE CHILD 38 (1973).

Other experts have emphasized that continued, meaningful contact with both parents after divorce is important to a child's well-being. In the 1970s and 1980s, research on children's relationships with their fathers confirmed that fathers play an important role in children's development. *See generally* M. LAMB (ED.), THE ROLE OF FATHERS IN CHILD DEVELOPMENT (1976). This evidence provided support for those who argued that continued paternal involvement after divorce is important to children's well being. Thompson, *The Father's Case in Child Custody Disputes: The Contributions of Psychological Research,* FATHERHOOD AND FAMILY POLICY 53 (M. LAMB & A. SAGI, EDS. 1983). Although social scientists agree that exposure to intense conflict between their parents is harmful to children, in most families, maintaining parent-child relationships with both parents is now viewed by many psychologists as important for children's adjustment. The post-divorce family must be restructured, but family relationships should be maintained. R. EMERY, RENEGOTIATING FAMILY RELATIONSHIPS: DIVORCE, CHILD CUSTODY, AND MEDIATION 184-93 (1994).

Another issue on which expert opinion varies is on the impact of divorce on children. Most psychologists emphasize the harmful impact to children of divorce, but some researchers have stressed the diversity of children's responses, noting that some children even gain maturity during their parents' divorce. In general, long-term predictions about the impact of divorce or what arrangement is best for children may be problematic.

HETHERINGTON, STANLEY-HAGAN & ANDERSON, MARITAL TRANSITIONS: A CHILD'S PERSPECTIVE, 1989
Am. Psych. 303, 303-10

There is great diversity in children's responses to their parents' marital transitions. . . .

Following the initial responses to the crisis period in their parents' divorce and remarriage, some children exhibit remarkable resiliency and in the long term may actually be enhanced by coping with these transitions; others suffer sustained developmental delays or disruptions; still others appear to adapt well in the early stages of family reorganization but show delayed effects that emerge at a later time, especially adolescence. . . . The most commonly reported problem behaviors found in children from divorced and remarried families are aggressive, noncompliant, and acting-out behaviors; decrements in prosocial behavior; problems in academic achievement and school adjustment; and disruptions in peer and heterosexual relations. . . . Although there are some reports of greater depression or internalizing disorders in these children when they reach adolescence . . . these findings are less well substantiated and less consistently found than those citing externalizing problems. . . . Researchers consistently find that children adapt better in a well-functioning single-parent or step-parent family than in a conflict-ridden family of origin. . . .

    . . . .

Temperamentally difficult children have been found to be less adaptable to change and more vulnerable to adversity than are temperamentally easy children. . . . Other individual attributes such as intelligence, independence, internal locus of control, and self-esteem also are related to children's adaptability in the face of stressful life experiences. . . .

The adaptation of children to family transitions also varies with their developmental status. . . . [T]he type of behavior problems and coping mechanisms differ for children of different ages. Although nothing is known about the effects of divorce on infants, young children's responses are mediated by their limited cognitive and social competencies, their dependency on their parents, and their restriction to the home. During the interval immediately following divorce, preschool children are less able to appraise accurately the divorce situation, the motives and feelings of their parents, their own role in the divorce, and possible outcomes. Thus young children may blame themselves for the divorce, may fear abandonment by both parents, may misperceive parents' emotions, needs, and behaviors, and may harbor fantasies of reconciliation. . . .

The cognitive immaturity that creates profound anxieties for the child who is young at the time of [the] parents' divorce may prove beneficial over time. Ten years after divorce these children have fewer memories of either parental conflict [or] their own earlier fears and suffering . . . and they typically have developed a close relationship with the custodial parent. . . . In contrast, those who had been adolescents and who retain memories of the conflict and stress associated with the divorce may be more consciously troubled. . . .

. . . [Older children] are better able to accurately assign responsibility for the divorce, to resolve loyalty conflicts, and to assess and cope with additional stresses such as economic changes and new family role definitions. The older child also is able to take advantage of extra-familial support systems. Adolescents may show remarkable maturity as they assume greater responsibilities . . . but many experience premature detachment from their families. It is estimated that one-third of older children and adolescents become disengaged from their families. If this disengagement leads to greater involvement in a prosocial peer group, school attainment, or nurturant, constructive relationships outside of the family this can be an adaptive, positive coping mechanism. If, however, it is associated with involvement in antisocial groups and activities with little adult concern [or] monitoring, the outcomes can be disastrous. . . .

. . . .

. . . The deleterious effects of marital discord, divorce and life in a single-parent family in which the mother has custody are more pervasive for boys than for girls. . . . [B]oys . . . show a higher rate of behavior disorders and problems in interpersonal relations both in the home and in the school with teachers and peers. Boys also are more likely to show more sustained noncompliant, aggressive behavior even two to three years after divorce. . . . Disturbances in social and emotional adjustment in girls living with their mothers have largely disappeared by two years after divorce; however, problems may reemerge at adolescence in the form of precocious sexual behavior and disruptions in heterosexual relations. . . . There is some evidence that school-aged children adapt better in the custody of a parent of the same sex. . . .

The balance between conflict and cooperation and the conflict resolution strategies used by divorced parents seem to play an especially important role in the adjustment of children. . . . Although parents may feel angry or resentful, if they are able to control their anger, cooperate in parenting, negotiate differences, and not directly expose their children to quarrels or violence, children show fewer emotional and social problems. Most children wish to maintain relations with both parents, and continued positive relations with both parents has been shown to be an important factor in children's successful adjustment to family transitions. . . .

In single-parent families, the well-being of the custodial parent and the quality of the parent-child relationship become central to the adjustment of the child. Yet the stress of separation and divorce places both men and women at risk for psychological and physical dysfunction. . . . Alcoholism, drug abuse, depression, psychosomatic problems, and accidents are more common among divorced than non-divorced adults. . . .

. . . The significance of these . . . changes is that children are encountering an altered parent at a time when they need stability. . . . Furthermore, parents and children may exacerbate each other's problems. A physically ill, emotionally disturbed, or preoccupied parent and a distressed, demanding, noncompliant child may have difficulty giving each other support or solace.

. . . .

———

In 2002, Mavis Hetherington and John Kelly published a comprehensive reflection on the impact of divorce on children, drawing on Hetherington's 30 years of research. E. M. HETHERINGTON & J. KELLY, FOR BETTER OR FOR WORSE: DIVORCE RECONSIDERED (2002). *See also* R. EMERY, MARRIAGE, DIVORCE, AND CHILDREN'S ADJUSTMENT (2d ed. 1999) (summarizing current research evidence on children and divorce); R. EMERY, RENEGOTIATING FAMILY RELATIONSHIPS: DIVORCE, CHILD CUSTODY, AND MEDIATION 184-93 (1994). In an important longitudinal study, Paul Amato and Alan Booth compared the adjustment and well being of young adults whose parents divorced during the 20 years of the study with those whose families remained intact. P. AMATO & A. BOOTH, A GENERATION AT RISK: GROWING UP IN AN ERA OF FAMILY UPHEAVAL (1997). These researchers found that children who were exposed to serious conflict in their parents' marriages were better off when the conflict was reduced by divorce. Children whose parents' marriages involved low to moderate conflict (perhaps a majority of divorces), however, experienced negative consequences when their parents divorced, as compared to a similar group whose parents remained married.

§ B.   THE BEST INTEREST OF THE CHILD STANDARD

[1]   INTRODUCTION

In most states today, the best interest of the child standard is the legal rule applied to child custody decisions. In considering this rule, it is important to recognize that custody determinations under the best interest standard differ in significant ways from most other forms of adjudication.

1. *Child custody determinations are "person-oriented" disputes.* Most legal rules require a determination of the facts relating to some event and are thus "act-oriented." Child custody determinations under the best interest standard, in contrast, are "person-oriented," making relevant "the attitudes, dispositions, capacities, and shortcomings of each parent." Mnookin, *Child-Custody Adjudication: Judicial Functions in the Face of Indeterminacy,* 39 LAW & CONTEMP. PROBS. 226, 250-51 (Summer 1975). Indeed, because each parent's goal is to persuade the judge that the child's welfare will be promoted by giving that parent custody, each is motivated to present evidence about his or her strengths and about the other parent's deficiencies. It is not surprising that pursuit of this goal generates a great deal of acrimony between parents, an unfortunate outcome since they will continue to have a relationship, the quality of which may affect their child's welfare.

2. *Custody determinations involve predictions about the future.* Most adjudication "requires determination of *past* acts and facts. Child custody determinations under the best-interests standard, on the other hand, require individualized predictions: with whom will this child be better off in the years to come?

Proof of what happened in the past is relevant only insofar as it enables the court to decide what is likely to happen in the future." *Id.* at 251-52.

3. *Future behaviors of many persons, including the loser's, may be relevant.* The predictions about the future necessary in child custody determinations under a best-interest standard depend in part on the future behavior of the parties. Even the "loser's" future behavior – how cooperative a parent will he be in a particular visitation arrangement, for example – may be an important factor in determining what result will be best for the child. How the best-interests-of-the-child rule is applied may create incentives for certain kinds of behavior and disincentives for others. *Id.* at 252-53.

4. *Trial courts have wide discretion and appellate review is difficult.* Statutory versions of the best interest standard are either simply a reiteration of the policy objective (to make the decision that reflects the child's best interest) or a list of factors to be considered by the court, with no direction about rank ordering or about the weight that should be attached to any particular factor. (The Minnesota statute below is a good example). Thus, a court resolving a custody dispute is free to consider anything that seems relevant under the circumstances to the child's interest, and to weigh the evidence as the judge sees fit — unless it is excluded under the statute or on constitutional grounds. (*See Palmore v. Sidoti, infra*). As a broad discretionary standard, the best interest test does little to constrain judges who might be inclined to base the custody decision on their personal moral and social values. One effect is that the outcome of adjudication is less predictable than it would be under a bright line rule. In the face of this uncertainty, a risk-averse parent for whom having custody is important may be inclined to make concessions to the other spouse in negotiations in order to secure custody by agreement, rather than leave the decision to a court. Moreover, because the standard allows so much discretion, "[p]rior reported cases . . . provide little basis for controlling or predicting the outcome of a particular case." This fact makes appellate review very difficult, and results in wide discretion for trial courts. Mnookin, *supra* at 253-54. *See also* Scott, *Pluralism, Parental Preference and Child Custody,* 80 CAL. L. REV. 615 (1992), for a discussion of the shortcomings of the best interest standard.

5. *Adjudication is rare.* The final point is that actual adjudication is relatively rare, in part, as suggested above, because risk-averse parents, faced with an uncertain outcome, favor agreement. Parties often agree about who should have custody. *See* Mnookin & Maccoby, *Private Ordering Revisited: What Custodial Arrangements Are Parents Negotiating?,* in DIVORCE REFORM AT THE CROSSROADS 52 (S. Sugarman & H. Kay eds. 1990) (parents agree from the beginning in 78.1% of divorce cases). Even when they initially disagree, parents often settle their disagreements before going to court. In some states, mandatory mediation and court-ordered custody evaluations reduce further the necessity of adjudication. These topics are considered in Chapter 8 Section B (mediation) and Section D of this chapter.

Statutory Frameworks

MINN. STAT. ANN. § 518.17 (West Supp. 2003)

Subdivision 1. The best interests of the child.

(a) "The best interests of the child" means all relevant factors to be considered and evaluated by the court including:

(1) the wishes of the child's parent or parents as to custody;

(2) the reasonable preference of the child, if the court deems the child to be of sufficient age to express preference;

(3) the child's primary caretaker;

(4) the intimacy of the relationship between each parent and the child;

(5) the interaction and interrelationship of the child with a parent or parents, siblings, and any other person who may significantly affect the child's best interests;

(6) the child's adjustment to his home, school, and community;

(7) the length of time the child has lived in a stable, satisfactory environment and the desirability of maintaining continuity;

(8) the permanence, as a family unit, of the existing or proposed custodial home;

(9) the mental and physical health of all individuals involved;

(10) the capacity and disposition of the parties to give the child love, affection, and guidance, and to continue educating and raising the child in the child's culture and religion or creed, if any; and

(11) the child's cultural background;

(12) the effect on the child of the actions of an abuser, if related to domestic abuse. . . .

The court may not use one factor to the exclusion of all others. The primary caretaker may not be used as a presumption in determining the best interests of the child. The courts must make detailed findings on each of the factors and explain how the factors led to its conclusions and to the determination of the best interests of the child.

(b) The court shall not consider conduct of a proposed custodian that does not affect the custodian's relationship to the child.

MODEL MARRIAGE AND DIVORCE ACT (as amended 1973)

§ 402. [Best Interest of Child].

The court shall determine custody in accordance with the best interest of the child. The court shall consider all relevant factors including:

(1) the wishes of the child's parent or parents as to his custody;

(2) the wishes of the child as to his custodian;

(3) the interaction and interrelationship of the child with his parent or parents, his siblings, and any other person who may significantly affect the child's best interest;

(4) the child's adjustment to his home, school, and community; and

(5) the mental and physical health of all individuals involved.

The court shall not consider conduct of a proposed custodian that does not affect his relationship to the child.

[2] DETERMINING THE CHILD'S BEST INTERESTS

[a] Gender and Caretaking Roles

BURCHARD v. GARAY

42 Cal. 3d 531, 724 P.2d 486, 229 Cal. Rptr. 800 (1986)

BROUSSARD, J. This case concerns the custody of William Garay, Jr., age two and one-half at the date of trial. Ana Burchard, his mother, appeals from an order . . . awarding custody to the father, William Garay.

As a result of a brief liaison between Ana and William, Ana became pregnant. Early in her term she told William that she was pregnant with his child, but he refused to believe that he was the father. . . .

. . . Ana undertook the difficult task of caring for her child, with the help of her father and others, while working at two jobs and continuing her training to become a registered nurse. William continued to deny paternity, and did not visit the child or provide any support.

. . . Ana [subsequently] brought a paternity and support action. After court-ordered blood tests established that William was the father, he stipulated to paternity and to support in the amount of $200 a month. Judgment entered accordingly on November 24, 1980. In December . . . William visited his son for the first time. In the next month he moved in with Ana and the child in an attempt to live together as a family; the attempt failed and six weeks later he moved out.

William asked for visitation rights; Ana refused and [sought] exclusive custody. William responded, seeking exclusive custody himself. . . .

. . . .

. . . Applying the "best interests" test, [the court] awarded custody to William. Its decision appears to be based upon three considerations. The first is that William is financially better off — he has greater job stability, owns his own home, and is "better equipped economically . . . to give constant care to the minor child and cope with his continuing needs." The second is that William has remarried, and he "and the stepmother can provide constant care for the minor child and keep him on a regular schedule without resorting to other caretakers"; Ana, on the other hand, must rely upon babysitters and day care centers while she works and studies. Finally, the court referred to

William providing the mother with visitation, an indirect reference to Ana's unwillingness to permit William visitation.

Pursuant to the court order William took custody of the child on August 15, 1982. Ana appealed from the order . . . and William, Jr., remained in his father's custody pending this appeal.

. . . .

[W]e conclude that the trial court erred in applying [the best-interests] standard. . . .

The trial court's decision referred to William's better economic position, and to matters such as homeownership and ability to provide a more "wholesome environment" which reflect economic advantage. But comparative income or economic advantage is not a permissible basis for a custody award. . . . If in fact the custodial parent's income is insufficient to provide a proper care for the child, the remedy is to award child support, not to take away custody.

The court also referred to the fact that Ana worked and had to place the child in day care, while William's new wife could care for the child in their home. But in an era when over 50 percent of mothers and almost 80 percent of divorced mothers work, the courts must not presume that a working mother is a less satisfactory parent or less fully committed to the care of her child. A custody determination must be based upon a true assessment of the emotional bonds between parent and child. . . . It must reflect also a factual determination of how best to provide continuity of attention, nurturing, and care. It cannot be based on an assumption, unsupported by scientific evidence, that a working mother cannot provide such care — an assumption particularly unfair when, as here, the mother has in fact been the primary caregiver. . . .

All of [the grounds relied on by the trial court] . . . are insignificant compared to the fact that Ana has been the primary caretaker for the child from birth to the date of the trial court hearing, that no serious deficiency in her care has been proven, and that William, Jr., under her care, has become a happy, healthy, well-adjusted child. We have frequently stressed . . . the importance of stability and continuity in the life of a child, and the harm that may result from disruption of established patterns of care and emotional bonds. The showing made in this case is, we believe, wholly insufficient to justify taking the custody of a child from the mother who has raised him from birth, successfully coping with the many difficulties encountered by single working mothers. . . .

. . . .

The order is reversed.

BIRD, C. J., Concurring. I write separately to underscore that the trial court's ruling was an abuse of discretion not only in its failure to give due weight to the importance of continuity and stability in custody arrangements but in its assumption that there is a negative relation between a woman's lack of wealth or her need or desire to work and the quality of her parenting. As this case so aptly demonstrates, outmoded notions such as these result in harsh judgments which unfairly penalize working mothers.

. . . .

When the record contains no evidence as to which parent does provide [the greatest] care, clearly the "working mother" factor operates as a negative presumption. Even more clearly, this factor operates unfairly when the record indicates that the mother has in fact been the primary caregiver. The use of such a presumption as a basis for a custody award is of dubious constitutionality.

Furthermore, the presumption is inappropriate because the relationship between maternal employment and the "presumed facts" about the child's best interests is not supported by reason or experience. Typically, it is the mother who provides most day-to-day care, whether or not she works outside the home. . . . A presumption which ignores this fact is likely to lead to erroneous and unfair decisions.

Moreover, there is no accepted body of expert opinion that maternal employment per se has a detrimental effect on a child. . . .

The burden of the trial court's reasoning would certainly fall most heavily on women. In those cases where the father contests custody, he is the parent likely to have superior economic resources. . . . This alone would give him an advantage under the trial court's reasoning. Further, such resources may well include the ability to support a nonworking spouse. Conversely, the mother is likely to have no choice about working, particularly if she does not remarry. . . . In the 25 to 44 age range, the remarriage rate of divorced men is almost double that of divorced women. . . .

Yet, under the trial court's rationale, it is the mother — and not the father — who would be penalized for working out of the home. She and she alone would be placed in this Catch-22 situation. If she did not work, she could not possibly hope to compete with the father in providing material advantages for the child. She would risk losing custody to a father who could provide a larger home, a better neighborhood, or other material goods and benefits.[5]

. . . .

If she did work, she would face the prejudicial view that a working mother is by definition inadequate, dissatisfied with her role, or more concerned with her own needs than with those of her child. This view rests on outmoded notions of a woman's role in our society. Again, this presumption is seldom, if ever, applied even-handedly to fathers. The result — no one would take an unbiased look at the amount and quality of parental attention which the child was receiving from each parent. . . .

The double standard appears again when, as here, the father is permitted to rely on the care which someone else will give to the child. It is not uncommon for courts to award custody to a father when care will actually be provided by a relative, second wife, or even a babysitter. . . . However, the implicit assumption that such care is the equivalent of that which a nonworking mother

---

[5] For example, in *Porter v. Porter* (N.D. 1979) 274 N.W.2d 235, the reviewing court affirmed a custody award to a working father because "he is in a position to lend more stability and guidance to nurturing the development of the children during those periods of time in which he would not be actually pursuing his employment. . . ." As the wife had forsaken a career during marriage to care for the children, the husband's earning capacity was substantially greater than hers. It was this greater earning capacity which apparently was the source of his "stability and guidance."

would provide "comes dangerously close to implying that mothers are fungible — that one woman will do just as well as another in rearing any particular children." (Polikoff, *Why Are Mothers Losing?* 7 WOMEN'S RIGHTS L. REP. 235, 241 (1982)). This is scarcely consistent with any enlightened ideas of childrearing. . . .

NOTES

1. *Past Caretaking as a Consideration in Custody Decisions.* The *Burchard* court, in ordering maternal custody, emphasized the mother's experience as the child's primary caretaker. In general, this is a key consideration in custody determinations. Under the tender years presumption, maternal custody was presumed to be in the child's best interest because mothers were primarily responsible for their children's care. Although that presumption has been abandoned, the parents' past caretaking roles continue to be an important consideration in custody determinations. Under the best interest standard, of course, courts can consider many other factors — the focus of our inquiry in this section. This should not be taken to mean that parents' childrearing roles in the intact family no longer are central to custody determinations. Indeed, it is fair to say that a fundamental debate in custody law and policy focuses on how much weight should be given to past caretaking in deciding future custodial arrangements.

Some courts and legislatures have concluded that custody should be decided primarily on the basis of past caretaking roles. In the past generation, a few states have adopted a primary caretaker preference. *See Garska v. McCoy,* 278 S.E.2d 357 (W. Va. 1981). Recently, the American Law Institute has modernized the primary caretaker preference, adopting a standard that allocates custody in proportion to each parents' fulfillment of caretaking responsibilities during marriage. AMERICAN LAW INSTITUTE, PRINCIPLES OF THE LAW OF FAMILY DISSOLUTION SECT. 2.08-2.09 (2002). Reforms of the best interest standard that base the custody determination on parents' past caretaking will be explored at length in Section C2, below. *See* Scott, *Pluralism, Parental Preference and Child Custody,* 80 CAL. L. REV. 615 (1992).

As *Burchard* suggests, under the best interest standard, each parent's past role in caring for the child has an uncertain status. For this reason, feminists and others have argued that mothers are seriously disadvantaged under the best interest standard in ways that are fundamentally unfair.

2. *Gender Roles and Fairness to Parents.* Chief Justice Bird's concurrence emphasizes the disadvantages divorced women would face in custody cases if a parent's economic advantage and/or remarriage to a stay-at-home spouse were factors a court could take into account. The statutes require that custody be decided according to the child's best interests, not those of the parents. Are the interests of the child and the mother in conflict in *Burchard?* Remarriage of a parent, of course, offers the child a two-parent home, which may have some advantages for that child. Similarly, economic stability is, generally speaking, good for children. Granting that these factors should not outweigh other, more important, factors, is it consistent with the child's best interest to disregard them altogether? In a case like *Burchard,* should the

outcome be different if research demonstrated that home care by a relative or stepparent was better for children than paid day care? [In reality, no such research findings exist.]

Recently, a number of courts have concluded that favoring the parent who can provide home care for the child disadvantages women since most mothers work after divorce and divorced men are more likely to remarry spouses who are not employed outside the home. *See e.g., West v. West*, 21 P.3d 838 (Alaska 2001) (reversing trial court's custody award to father, whose fiancé nurse (with whom the child had little relationship) would care for child; the father was in Coast Guard and was subject to deployment, while the working mother lived near her parents who could help with child care); *Ireland v. Ireland,* 547 N.W.2d 686 (Mich. 1996) (reversing trial court's transfer of custody to father on the ground that mother was a college student and child was in day care); *Linda R. v. Richard E.*, 561 N.Y.S. 2d 29 (App. Div. 1990) (reversing custody award to father where trial court expected mother, but not father, to give priority to child over career). However, some courts may continue to apply different "baselines" to mothers and fathers, giving a lot of credit to fathers who are more involved than traditional fathers (perhaps coaching a team or performing some child care functions), because he is being measured against the role of traditional father, while deeming the working or student mother deficient because she is measured against the performance of a traditional mother.

For a feminist critique of courts for treating mothers like "draftees" (taking for granted their responsibility for children), and fathers like "volunteers," whose efforts are encouraged and appreciated, *see* Czapanskiy, *Volunteers and Draftees: The Struggle for Parental Equality,* 38 U.C.L.A. L. Rev. 1415 (1991).

3. *Who Wins Custody Contests?* Despite the elimination of explicit gender preferences in most jurisdictions, most divorces still conclude with the mother as the primary custodial parent. Although the research is a little dated, many studies have put the figure at about 90%. Robert Mnookin and Eleanor Maccoby, in a study of divorce custody cases in two California counties in the mid-1980s, found that only 10% of families had an arrangement in which fathers had custody and mothers visitation. In 70%, mothers had sole custody and in 20% custody was shared. E. Maccoby & R. Mnookin, Dividing the Child: Social and Legal Dilemmas of Custody (1992).

Many fathers who express a desire for sole or joint custody do not actually petition for custody. Maccoby and Mnookin found that only 30% of fathers expressed a preference for maternal custody. The authors suggest that fathers may voice desires for custody but that their preferences are weaker than those of mothers. Also, some fathers may realize that they might desire custody, but are not prepared to assume the responsibilities of child rearing, a role with which they have little experience. *Id.* at 100-03.

As for the results of contested custody hearings, research results have varied considerably. Maccoby and Mnookin found that in cases in which parents contested custody, mothers were granted the arrangements they requested twice to four times as often as fathers. The most typical conflict was when mothers requested sole physical custody and fathers requested joint physical custody. *Id* at 103-4. Where each parent sought sole custody, mothers won

46% of the time, fathers 11% and joint custody was ordered in the rest. *See* Pearson & Ring, *Judicial Decisionmaking in Contested Custody Cases,* 21 J. FAM. L. 713, 719 (1982-83) (in three Colorado counties, fathers won custody in 32.3%, 15.5% and 21.2% of cases). Other studies have shown fathers to be more successful. *See, e.g.,* Polikoff, *Why Are Mothers Losing?,* 7 WOMEN'S RIGHTS L. REP. 235, 236 (1982) (citing various studies, giving father success rates ranging from 38% to 63%); Atkinson, *Criteria for Deciding Child Custody in the Trial and Appellate Courts,* 18 FAM. L.Q. 1, 10-11 (1984) (fathers win custody in 51% of cases).

Feminist authors continue to challenge the gender-neutral best interest standard. *See, e.g.,* Byran, *Reasking the Woman Question at Divorce,* 75 CHI.-KENT L. REV. 713 (2000) (discussing how gender stereotypes disadvantage women in custody proceedings, and examining feminism's relevance to these problems); Fineman, *Fatherhood, Feminism and Family Law,* 32 MCGEORGE L. REV. 1031 (2001) (arguing that the movement for gender-neutrality in custody proceedings focuses too much on achieving egalitarian results, ignoring important differences between the sexes and ultimately doing mothers a disservice); Bartlett, *Comparing Race and Sex Discrimination in Custody Cases,* 28 HOFSTRA L. REV. 877 (2000) (arguing that the similarities between race and sex discrimination support a categorical ban on all types of discrimination in the *ALI Principles*).

4. *Same-Sex Preference.* Another gender-based rule is the preference in custody disputes involving older children for the parent of the same sex. The psychological data demonstrating the importance to adolescent and pre-adolescent children of close relationships with the same-sex parent — both boys and girls — is collected in Hetherington, Stanley-Hagan & Anderson, *Marital Transitions: A Child's Perspective,* 1989 AM. PSYCH. 303, 306, and Wallerstein, *Child of Divorce: An Overview,* 4 BEHAVIORAL SCIENCE & THE LAW 105, 113 (1986). As with the tender years rule, there is no explicit statutory authority for a same-sex parent preference. Still, courts, citing psychological evidence, sometimes conclude that a child's best interest requires custody with the same-sex parent, at least at certain ages. *See, e.g., Warner v. Warner,* 534 N.E.2d 752 (Ind. App. 1989) (upholding custody award to father based in part on psychologist's testimony that as child gets older, identification with same-sex parent is important); *Matter of Marriage of Clement,* 627 P.2d 1263 (Or. App. 1981) (stressing importance of mother as role model for five-year-old girl). *But see Giffen v. Crane,* 716 A.2d 1029 (Md. 1998) (citing Maryland's Equal Rights Amendment, court rejects trial court's custody award to mother on ground that teen-age daughter "needs a female hand"); *Tresnak v. Tresnak,* 297 N.W.2d 109 (Iowa 1980) (rejecting "a *priori* notion of parental fitness . . . based on the sex of parent or child").

PROBLEM

Problem 6-1 Emma was born to Jane and Eric, who were both nineteen years old and were unmarried. They separated before Emma was born. Eric got a job in a neighboring town and lived with his mother, while Jane stayed in Somerville and cared for Emma. Eric visited his daughter every two weeks or so and contributed sporadically to her support. When Emma was a year old, Jane became a full-time student at Somerville College, working part-time and getting some financial help from her parents. About a year later, Eric petitioned for custody, on the ground that Emma would be better cared for by his mother, Emma's grandmother, than by "strangers" in the day care center where Emma spent several hours a day while Jane worked, studied and went to classes. Also he presented evidence that Jane had lived in two different student family housing units since she started school and argued that Emma would be better off in the stable quiet neighborhood where his mother lived. He claimed, and Jane did not dispute, that Jane would be involved in her studies for many years because she planned to go on to law school after graduating from college. Who should be awarded custody if this case is decided under the Minnesota statute on page 617?

NOTE ON DOMESTIC VIOLENCE AS A FACTOR IN CUSTODY DECISIONS

A parent's abusive conduct toward a child will be central (probably dispositive) in a custody decision. What about abusive conduct toward the other parent? In an earlier era, domestic violence by one parent against the other may have been considered tangential to consideration of the child's interest. However, in the past decade or so, this has changed; almost every state today considers whether a parent has engaged in domestic violence in the custody analysis. Recently, many states have taken a tougher stance, creating a presumption against awarding custody to perpetrators of domestic violence.

This trend is a response to heightened concern generally about domestic violence and to the growing recognition that children may experience harm from violence directed at another family member. First, the parent who is violent toward his spouse may also abuse his children. Studies show a correlation between spousal or partner abuse and child abuse. Strauss, *Supervised Visitation and Family Violence*, 29 FAM. L.Q. 229, 237-8 (1995). The parent who is violent to his partner has revealed a capacity for violence that may create a risk for the child, even if he has not yet engaged in child abuse. Moreover, even if the child has not suffered physical injury, the likelihood that he has experienced psychological harm is substantial. Children exposed to domestic violence experience anxiety and other adjustment problems. Hughs, *Impact of Spousal Abuse on Children of Battered Women* 2(12) VIOLENCE UPDATE (1992). Further, these children are more likely than others to engage in domestic abuse themselves when they become adults.

The clear statutory trend is toward a rebuttable presumption against awarding custody to a parent who has engaged in domestic violence, although there is considerable variation among jurisdictions. *See* MICH. COMP. LAWS ANN. §§ 722.25 (West 2002). Some statutes take a narrow approach, applying the presumption only in cases where there has been a substantial history of domestic violence. *See, e.g.,* MASS. GEN. LAWS ch. 209A, § 3 (2001) (requiring a pattern or serious incident); ARIZ. REV. STAT. § 25-403(N) (2001) (serious incident of violence or a pattern of abusive behavior; presumption not applicable if both parents engaged in domestic violence); TEX. FAM. CODE ANN. § 153.004 (Vernon Supp. 2002) ("history or pattern"). Sometimes conviction of a felony is required for the presumption to operate. FLA. STAT. ANN.

§ 61.13(2)(b)(2) (West Supp. 2003). Courts sometimes also have narrowed the construction of statutes. A grandmother who alleged that the mother had assaulted her was found to lack standing as a non-parent to petition for custody under the domestic violence statute. *J.M.R. v. S.T.R.*, 15 P.3d 253 (Alaska 2001). Other states, in contrast, have been willing to apply the presumption without limiting it to recurring or egregious incidents of abuse. OR. REV. STAT. § 107.137(2) (2001). California does not require a pattern or serious incident, but does require that the incident of domestic violence have occurred within five years of the custody dispute before the presumption will be applied. CAL. FAM. CODE § 3044 (West Supp. 2002). *See also Tulintseff v. Jacobsen*, 615 N.W.2d 129 (N.D. 2000) (statutory presumption does not apply where abuse occurred long before custody proceeding). In other states, this factor must be considered, although there is no presumption. Does a broad presumption against awarding custody to a parent who has engaged in domestic violence become unworkable in the situation in which both parents are violent?

Many courts emphasize the potential link between domestic violence and parenting capacity, and assume that custody in a parent who has abused his spouse will likely have harmful effects on the child. *See, e.g., Acevedo v. Acevedo*, 606 N.Y.S.2d 307 (App. Div. 1994) (father's physical abuse of mother "reveals that [he] possesses a character that is manifestly ill-suited to the difficult task of providing young children with moral and intellectual guidance"); *Rohan v. Rohan*, 623 N.Y.S. 390 (App. Div. 1995) (reversing custody award to father who committed "egregious acts of spousal abuse," which the trial court weighed insufficiently; the appellate court suggested that "it [was] possible that [the child] at some future point might become the victim of petitioner's explosive emotions and may also develop a pattern of abuse, thereby becoming an abuser himself when he matures"). In the notorious dispute between O.J. Simpson and the parents of his murdered wife, Nicole, the appellate court reversed the trial court rulings excluding evidence of domestic violence and evidence that Simpson had killed his wife. *Guardianship of Simpson*, 79 Cal. Rptr. 2d 389 (Cal. App. 1999).

Courts are not likely to order joint custody in families with a history of domestic violence. Joint custody requires more contact and cooperation between the parents than sole custody, and even non-violent conflict can be harmful to the children. Moreover, the parent who was a victim of marital violence may be subject to intimidation. A number of custody statutes include a prohibition or a rebuttable presumption against joint custody in this situation. *See e.g.*, ARIZ. REV. STAT. ANN. § 25-403 (E) (Supp. 2002) ("joint custody shall not be awarded if the court makes a finding of the existence of significant domestic violence"); IOWA CODE ANN. § 598.41 (1)(b) (West 2001) (rebuttable presumption). *See also Caven v. Caven*, 966 P.2d 1247 (Wash. 1998) (joint legal custody (mutual decision-making power under parenting plan) prohibited where there is history of domestic violence).

A parent who is the victim of domestic violence may leave the home to escape. This may put her in a vulnerable position in a custody dispute, even when she takes the children with her, and particularly if she does not. If the woman goes to a shelter or moves in with family or friends, her living arrangements are likely to be temporary and the home that she offers the child may seem less "stable" than that of the father who remains in the family home. Uncertainty about the effect of her circumstances on the custody decision may lead the victim to return to the abuser. Statutory provisions that require courts to consider one parent's acts of domestic violence against the other can partially offset the disadvantage created by the victim's circumstances. Further, some custody statutes address this concern directly by providing that abandonment of the home by a victim of abuse can not be considered in determining the best interest of the child. COLO. REV. STAT. § 14-10-124(1.5)(b)(V)(4) (2002); IOWA CODE ANN. § 598.41 (1)(d) (West 2001).

Some observers have challenged the wisdom of a broad categorical presumption that a parent who engages in domestic violence should not get custody. The argument is that the empirical assumptions (about harm to the child and parenting capacity of the parent) on which the presumption is based have not been demonstrated by research. The research suggests that various patterns of domestic violence exist, and that the batterer who terrorizes his partner and traumatizes his children is only one type. Other patterns involve mutual and occasional violence that is not usually injurious (sometimes called "common couple violence"). Children may be differentially affected depending on the type of violence to which they are exposed. Some courts decline to consider domestic violence where both parties have initiated violence, even if one initiated more often. *See King v. King*, 50 P.3d 453 (2002). To date, research shedding light on how less severe violence may affect children is sparse. *See* Johnson & Ferraro, *Research on Domestic Violence in the 1990s: Making Distinctions*, 62 J. MARRIAGE & THE FAMILY 948 (2000); Johnston & Campbell, *Parent-child Relationships in Domestic Violence Families Disputing Custody*, 31(3) FAM. & CONCILIATION CTS. REV. 282 (1993).

For comprehensive overviews of the law in this area, see Lemon, *Statutes Creating Rebuttable Presumptions Against Custody to Batterers: How Effective Are They?*, 28 WM. MITCHELL L. REV. 601 (2001); Family Violence Project of the National Council of Juvenile and Family Court Judges, *Family Violence in Child Custody Statutes: An Analysis of State Codes*, 29 FAM. L.Q. 197 (1995).

[b]　Sexual Conduct and Moral Unfitness

VAN DRIEL v. VAN DRIEL

525 N.W.2d 37 (S.D. 1994)

MILLER, Chief Justice.

Appellant James Mark Van Driel (James) appeals the trial court's award of primary physical custody of his minor children to their mother, appellee Lori Ann Van Driel (Lori), citing their mother's lesbian relationship and the parties' status as joint legal custodians as grounds for reversal . . . We affirm. . . .

James and Lori were married on May 23, 1981. In 1989 or 1990, the couple separated. During this period of separation, Lori became involved in a lesbian relationship and began sharing a residence with her lesbian partner.

James and Lori divorced on January 3, 1991. Pursuant to a settlement agreement, James and Lori shared joint legal and physical custody of their two children, an eight-year-old daughter and a five-year-old son. Under this arrangement, the children lived with each parent on an alternating weekly basis.

Approximately three weeks after the finalization of her divorce, Lori "exchanged vows" with her lesbian partner, with the intent to enter into a permanent and monogamous relationship. Considering Lori's lesbian relationship, James objected to Lori having custody, fearing the children would be ridiculed by their peers and would react negatively in the future to their mother's sexual orientation. Therefore, in August 1991, James petitioned the court for a modification of custody. . . . In a memorandum opinion, the trial court awarded primary physical custody to Lori, subject to reasonable and liberal visitation with James. . . .

James argues that Lori's cohabitation with a woman in a lesbian relationship was *per se* not in the best interests of the children, and the trial court's designation of Lori as the primary custodial parent constituted an abuse of discretion for this reason. We disagree. . . .

The trial court found that both James and Lori were loving and caring parents who had the best interests of their children at heart. Although James suggests that Lori's relationship with another woman is immoral *per se,* "immoral conduct by one parent does not automatically render that parent unfit to have custody of the children and require an award of custody to the other parent." *Shoop v. Shoop,* 460 N.W.2d 721, 724 (S.D.1990) (citing *Williams,* 425 N.W.2d 390). The parent's conduct must be shown to have had some harmful effect on the children. *Id.* at 724-25. . . . Furthermore, the issue properly before us is whether the trial court abused its discretion in awarding primary custody of these children to their mother. We are called upon to make a judicial review of the trial court's decision rather than a moral evaluation of the parties' conduct. . . .

James mistakenly relies on *Chicoine,* 479 N.W.2d 891, to bolster his argument that Lori's lesbian relationship automatically disqualifies her as a custodial parent. The facts in this case and those in *Chicoine* are so wholly dissimilar as to render *Chicoine* irrelevant. In *Chicoine,* this Court held that the trial court abused its discretion in awarding unsupervised overnight visitation to a lesbian mother without first ordering a home study and enforcement measures to ensure compliance with restrictions on visitation. This Court's ruling was triggered by evidence that the mother had experienced a myriad of psychological problems, had taken the children to gay bars, had allowed the children to sleep with her and her partner while the mother was unclothed, had kissed and caressed her partner in front of the children despite protests by her oldest son, and had continued a sexual encounter rather than comfort her child after the child had discovered her engaged in sexual activity. *Id.* at 893-94.

In contrast, there is no evidence of this type of behavior in this case. The record indicates that both Lori and her partner are affectionate and attentive toward the children, while being discreet about the sexual aspects of their own relationship. Contrary to James' fears, there was no evidence that the children were ridiculed by classmates or the larger community because of their mother's sexual orientation or that the children were repulsed or embarrassed by, or otherwise showed adverse reactions to, their mother's living arrangement. Indeed, the children's own statements, as reported by the clinical psychologist, indicated that they would prefer living with their mother. Finally, a custody evaluation issued by a clinical psychologist who was retained by both parties recommended that the court award physical custody of the children to Lori. This recommendation was based on a wealth of information, including interviews, psychological tests, and clinical observations of the parties and the children, collateral contacts with the parties' friends and family, and psychological literature concerning the effect of gay or lesbian parents on child development. In light of all of this evidence, this Court cannot conclude that the trial court's custody decision was an abuse of discretion.

NOTES

1. *Rationales for Considering a Parent's Sexual Behavior.* Both heterosexual and homosexual behavior by parents may be brought into evidence in litigated custody disputes. Courts are sometimes asked to take into account conduct that some believe to be "immoral" or, in the case of homosexual behavior, actually illegal in some states. One rationale for considering the behavior is that the parent's conduct will influence a child's and that it is detrimental to a child for his parent to set a "bad example." This rationale, however, raises many difficulties. Children will not necessarily be aware of their parent's sexual conduct, and even if they are, little is known about the circumstances under which they will emulate that conduct. As to the influence of gay parents on their children's sexuality, in particular, the little evidence there is indicates that children in the sole custody of lesbian mothers do not have identifiably different development of sexual identity than those residing with heterosexual parents. *See* C. Patterson & R. Redding, *Lesbian and Gay Parents and Their Children: Legal and Public Policy Implications of Social Science Research*, 52 J. Soc. Issues 29 (1996); N. Gartrell et al., *The National Lesbian Family Study*, 66 Am. J. Orthopsychiatry 272 (1996); C. Patterson, *Children of Lesbian and Gay Parents*, 63 Child Dev. 1025 (1992).

Another reason that courts and some commentators offer for considering a parent's sexual (particularly homosexual) behavior is that the child will experience psychological harm from being reared by parents who do not conform to conventional sexual norms. Here the assumption is that children living with gay and lesbian parents will experience social stigma and rejection, which will contribute to low self esteem, poor social adjustment and psychiatric problems. Again, the evidence does not support the allegations. Children raised by lesbian parents do not evidence greater social adjustment problems, poorer self esteem or more emotional problems than those raised in heterosexual households. *See* C. Patterson & R. Redding, *supra*.

2. *The Legal Standards.* Some custody statutes specifically address the issue of morality. The Alabama custody statute, for example, directs courts to consider "the moral character and prudence of the parents," ALA. CODE § 30-3-1 (West 1998). *See also* MICH. COMP. LAWS ANN. § 722.23(f) (West 2002) ("moral fitness of the parties involved" is factor to be considered by court deciding custody); UTAH CODE ANN. § 30-3-10(1)(a) (Supp. 2002) ("the court shall consider . . . the past conduct and demonstrated moral standards of each of the parties"). The Minnesota statute, *supra*, in contrast, precludes consideration of "conduct of a proposed custodian that does not affect his relationship to the child." MINN. STAT. ANN. § 518.17(13)(b) (West Supp. 2003). This general language could encompass a whole range of parental conduct, of which sexual behavior is just one example. The District of Columbia appears to be the only jurisdiction which directly speaks to the question of sexual orientation. D.C. CODE ANN. § 16-914(a) (2001) ("with respect to matters of custody and visitation . . . sexual orientation, in and of itself, of a party shall not be a conclusive consideration").

The majority rule with respect to non-marital, heterosexual behavior is that such conduct alone cannot justify denial of custody to a parent, unless adverse effects on the child are shown. In *Fletcher v. Fletcher*, 504 N.W.2d 684 (Mich. App. 1993), an appellate court reversed a trial court decision awarding custody of the children to father because of the "poor moral example" set by mother in having two extramarital affairs. There was no evidence, held the court, that the children were even aware of the affairs. Beyond that, even if they had been aware, the court reiterated that adultery alone is insufficient for a finding of immorality. *See also Lackey v. Fuller*, 755 So. 2d. 1087 (Miss. 2000) (holding that mother's pre-divorce extra-marital affair could not be the basis of custody award to father); *Judith R. v. Hey*, 405 S.E.2d 447 (W.Va. 1991) (reversing trial court order requiring a custodial mother who was cohabiting with a man to either marry him within 30 days or lose custody to former husband). *But see V.A.E. v. D.A.E.*, 873 S.W.2d 262 (Mo. App. 1994) (mother's post-separation heterosexual affair which produced a child was one factor to be considered in the custody decision). Few recent appellate court opinions have reviewed custody decisions in which a parents' heterosexual conduct was an issue, suggesting the declining importance of this issue.

Courts traditionally have tended to be harder on parents involved in same sex relationships, perhaps because of a view that the child will experience stigma and that her sexual identity will be affected. Many courts assume that exposure to a parent's same sex relationship is likely to be harmful to children, and therefore it can be the basis of a custody award to the other parent without a showing of adverse effects of the behavior on the child. *See Pulliam v. Smith*, 501 S.E.2d 898 (N.C. 1998) (order upheld changing custody to mother after father's partner moved in, despite no showing of an adverse impact on the children); *Tucker v. Tucker*, 910 P.2d 1209 (Utah 1996) (custody award to father reinstated, because mother's lesbian cohabitational relationship before and after divorce demonstrated "lack of moral example"). Some courts continue to express moralistic condemnation of homosexuality in custody disputes, and to emphasize the likelihood of social stigma and negative role modeling). *See, e.g. In re H.H.,* 830 S.2d 21 (Ala. 2002)(concurring opinion) ("Homosexual conduct by it's very nature is immoral").

The traditional response is exemplified by *Roe v. Roe,* 324 S.E.2d 691 (Va. 1985), a case in which the mother sought modification of custody, based on the custodial father's conduct of living and sleeping with his gay partner, and kissing and hugging in front of the child.

> . . . The father's continuous exposure of the child to his immoral and illicit relationship renders him an unfit and improper custodian as a matter of law. Indeed . . . adultery is a class four misdemeanor in Virginia (Code § 18.2-365) which is seldom prosecuted, while the conduct inherent in the father's relationship is punishable as a class six felony (Code § 18.2-361) which is prosecuted with considerable frequency and vigor. . . . [W]e have no hesitancy in saying that the conditions under which this child must live daily are not only unlawful but also impose an intolerable burden upon her by reason of the social condemnation attached to them, which will inevitably afflict her relationships with her peers and with the community at large. . . . The father's unfitness is manifested by his willingness to impose this burden upon her in exchange for his own gratification.

> The trial court was, as stated above, seriously concerned as to the impact of the father's conduct upon the child, but took the position that its worst features could be allayed by ordering him out of his lover's bedroom. We are not so persuaded. The child's awareness of the nature of the father's illicit relationship is fixed and cannot be dispelled. The open behavior of the father and his friends in the home can only be expected to continue. The impact of such behavior upon the child, and upon any of her peers who may visit the home, is inevitable. We conclude that the best interests of the child will only be served by protecting her from the burdens imposed by such behavior, insofar as practicable. In the circumstances of this case, this necessitates not only a change of custody to the mother, but also a cessation of any visitations in the father's home, or in the presence of his homosexual lover, while his present living arrangements continue. . . .

In light of the 2003 Supreme Court opinion in *Lawrence v. Texas* 123 S. Ct. 2472 (2003), page 847 above, the *Roe* court's stance that homosexual parents are *per se* unfit because they are engaging in criminal conduct is no longer viable. In *Lawrence,* the Court struck down a Texas sodomy law that criminalized consensual sexual relations between same sex partners and denounced in strong language the stigma and intrusiveness of such laws. *See* Chapter 9. Can courts continue to consider a parents' sexual orientation after *Lawrence*? It would seem that courts will need to find some actual harm to the child in living with a gay or lesbian parent. Whether social stigma or concerns about role modeling will suffice remains to be seen.

Even before *Lawrence,* as *Van Driel* suggests, the response of courts to a parent's homosexual behavior had begun to change. The judicial trend is to require that homosexual behavior, like heterosexual conduct, be shown to be harmful before a court may take it into account. For example, the Mississippi

Supreme Court reversed a custody award to a father, emphasizing that adultery *per se* was not a ground for denial of custody, and that it was irrelevant whether the affair was heterosexual or homosexual. *Hollan v. Hollan,* 784 So. 2d 943 (Miss. 2001). The mother had provided most of the child care, and since the separation, the father often paid child support only through wage garnishment. Moreover, the mother's work schedule was more conducive to caring for the child. Finding that the clear weight of the evidence favored the mother as the child's custodian, the appellate court determined that the chancellor abused his discretion in giving too much weight to one factor ("moral fitness") and ignoring evidence favoring the mother. *See also Fox v. Fox,* 904 P.2d 66 (Okla. 1995) (reversing modification based on mother's lesbian behavior; no evidence of change in children's school performance, behavior or relationships); *Stroman v. Williams,* 353 S.E.2d 704 (S.C. 1987); *Guinan v. Guinan,* 477 N.Y.S.2d 830 (App. Div. 1984); *Doe v. Doe,* 452 N.E.2d 293 (Mass. App. 1983). *See also In re Marriage of D.F.D.,* 862 P.2d 368 (Mont. 1993) (husband's cross-dressing behavior held not grounds for denial of joint custody, absent finding of significant risk of harm to the couple's two-year old boy); Annot., *Initial Award or Denial of Child Custody to Homosexual or Lesbian Parent,* 62 A.L.R. 5th 591 (1998).

The *ALI Principles* prohibits consideration of both sexual orientation and of extramarital sexual conduct unless shown to have an adverse impact on the child. § 2.12 (1) (d) & (e).

3. Legal Commentary. There is a substantial amount of recent legal commentary on the relevance of homosexuality in child custody determinations. *See, e.g.,* Gill, *Best Interest of the Child? A Critique of Judicially Sanctioned Arguments Denying Child Custody to Gays and Lesbians,* 68 TENN L. REV. 361 (2001); Chambers & Polikoff, *Family Law and Gay and Lesbian Family Issues in the Twentieth Century,* 33 FAM. L.Q. 523 (1999); Shapiro, *Custody and Conduct: How the Law Fails Lesbian and Gay Parents and their Children,* 71 IND. L.J. 623 (1996).

PROBLEM

Problem 6-2. Theresa has custody of her three daughters, ages 12, 10 and 7. Because of her unsatisfying marriage, Theresa has sworn off men altogether, and has remained celibate since her divorce. She has told her daughters that men are not worth the trouble. She has also told them that if a woman decides to get involved with a man, she should live with him for a long time before marriage, in order to be sure that they are sexually compatible. The girls' father, Donald, strongly objects to this advice, which he considers both immoral and a violation of the criminal statute against contributing to the delinquency of a minor. Does Donald have adequate grounds for a modification of custody in his favor? Advise him.

[c]   Race

PALMORE v. SIDOTI

466 U.S. 429 (1984)

CHIEF JUSTICE BURGER delivered the opinion of the Court.

We granted certiorari to review a judgment of a state court divesting a natural mother of the custody of her infant child because of her remarriage to a person of a different race.

When petitioner Linda Sidoti Palmore and respondent Anthony J. Sidoti, both Caucasians, were divorced in May 1980 in Florida, the mother was awarded custody of their three-year-old daughter.

In September 1981 the father sought custody of the child by filing a petition to modify the prior judgment because of changed conditions. The change was that the child's mother was then cohabiting with a Negro, Clarence Palmore, Jr., whom she married two months later. . . .

After hearing testimony from both parties and considering a court counselor's investigative report, the court . . . . made a finding that "there is no issue as to either party's devotion to the child, adequacy of housing facilities, or respect[a]bility of the new spouse of either parent." . . .

The court then addressed the recommendations of the court counselor . . . for a change in custody because "[t]he wife [petitioner] has chosen for herself and for her child, a life-style unacceptable to her father and to society . . . The child . . . is, or at school age will be, subject to environmental pressures not of choice."

The court then concluded that the best interests of the child would be served by awarding custody to the father. The court's rationale is contained in the following:

> The father's evident resentment of the mother's choice of a black partner is not sufficient to wrest custody from the mother. It is of some significance, however, that the mother did see fit to bring a man into her home and carry on a sexual relationship with him without being married to him. Such action tended to place gratification of her own desires ahead of her concern for the child's future welfare. This Court feels that despite the strides that have been made in bettering relations between the races in this country, it is inevitable that Melanie will, if allowed to remain in her present situation and attains school age and thus more vulnerable to peer pressures, suffer from the social stigmatization that is sure to come. . . .

The judgment of a state court determining or reviewing a child custody decision is not ordinarily a likely candidate for review by this Court. However, the court's opinion, after stating that the "father's evident resentment of the mother's choice of a black partner is not sufficient" to deprive her of custody, then turns to what it regarded as the damaging impact on the child from remaining in a racially-mixed household. . . . This raises important federal concerns arising from the Constitution's commitment to eradicating discrimination based on race.

The Florida court did not focus directly on the parental qualifications of the natural mother or her present husband, or indeed on the father's qualifications to have custody of the child. The court found that "there is no issue as to either party's devotion to the child, adequacy of housing facilities, or respect[a]bility of the new spouse of either parent." . . . This, taken with the absence of any negative finding as to the quality of the care provided by the mother, constitutes a rejection of any claim of petitioner's unfitness to continue the custody of her child.

The court correctly stated that the child's welfare was the controlling factor. But that court was entirely candid and made no effort to place its holding on any ground other than race. Taking the court's findings and rationale at face value, it is clear that the outcome would have been different had petitioner married a Caucasian male of similar respectability.

A core purpose of the Fourteenth Amendment was to do away with all governmentally-imposed discrimination based on race. . . . Such classifications are subject to the most exacting scrutiny; to pass constitutional muster, they must be justified by a compelling governmental interest and must be "necessary . . . to the accomplishment" of its legitimate purpose, *McLaughlin v. Florida,* 379 U.S. 184 (1964).

The State, of course, has a duty of the highest order to protect the interests of minor children, particularly those of tender years. In common with most states, Florida law mandates that custody determinations be made in the best interests of the children involved. The goal of granting custody based on the best interests of the child is indisputably a substantial governmental interest for purposes of the Equal Protection Clause.

It would ignore reality to suggest that racial and ethnic prejudices do not exist or that all manifestations of those prejudices have been eliminated. There is a risk that a child living with a step-parent of a different race may be subject to a variety of pressures and stresses not present if the child were living with parents of the same racial or ethnic origin.

The question, however, is whether the reality of private biases and the possible injury they might inflict are permissible considerations for removal of an infant child from the custody of its natural mother. We have little difficulty concluding that they are not. The Constitution cannot control such prejudices but neither can it tolerate them. Private biases may be outside the reach of the law, but the law cannot, directly or indirectly, give them effect. "Public officials sworn to uphold the Constitution may not avoid a constitutional duty by bowing to the hypothetical effects of private racial prejudice that they assume to be both widely and deeply held. *Palmer v. Thompson,* 403 U.S. 217, 260-261 (1971). (WHITE, J., dissenting).

This is by no means the first time that acknowledged racial prejudice has been invoked to justify racial classifications. In *Buchanan v. Warley,* 245 U.S. 60 (1917), for example, this Court invalidated a Kentucky law forbidding Negroes from buying homes in white neighborhoods.

It is urged that this proposed segregation will promote the public peace by preventing race conflicts. Desirable as this is, and important as is the preservation of the public peace, this aim cannot be accomplished by laws or ordinances which deny rights created or protected by the Federal Constitution.

Id., at 81.

Whatever problems racially-mixed households may pose for children in 1984 can no more support a denial of constitutional rights than could the stresses that residential integration was thought to entail in 1917. The effects of racial prejudice, however real, cannot justify a racial classification removing an infant child from the custody of its natural mother found to be an appropriate person to have such custody.

The judgment . . . is reversed.

NOTES

1. ***The Limits of*** **Sidoti?** The Court in *Sidoti* concedes that "a child living with a stepparent of a different race may be subject to a variety of pressures and stresses not present if the child were living with parents of the same racial or ethnic origin," but concludes that these pressures and stresses are not "permissible considerations" in a custody dispute. Is there a limit to the amount or severity of "pressures" and "stresses" a child should have to sustain in order that the law not give effect to private biases? One student notewriter suggests that where a child has actually sustained harm from a difficult racial situation, *Sidoti* does not preclude consideration of that harm in custody determinations. *See* Note, *Race as a Factor in Custody and Adoption Proceedings,* 71 CORNELL L. REV. 209 (1985). At least one court has hinted in dictum that it agreed. *Holt v. Chenault,* 722 S.W.2d 897 (Ky. 1987) (child's reaction might be taken into account if it is significant and severe). For a comprehensive and critical analysis of the use of race in custody decisions, see Perry, *Race and Child Placement: The Best Interests Test and the Cost of Discretion,* 29 J. FAM. L. 51 (1990-91). *See also* Bartlett, *Comparing Race and Sex Discrimination in Custody Cases,* 28 HOFSTRA L. REV. 877 (2000) (arguing that the similarities between race and sex discrimination support a categorical ban on all types of discrimination in the *ALI Principles*).

2. ***Custody of Bi-racial Children.*** Can race be taken into account as a positive factor if one parent is more likely to contribute to the child's minority racial identity? Would this be allowed under the Minnesota custody statute, *supra,* which provides for considering the "child's cultural background" and the capacity of the parent to "continue educating the child in the child's culture?" Some courts have found such consideration to be precluded by *Palmore. See In re Marriage of Brown*, 480 N.E.2d 246, 248 (Ind. Ct. App. 1985). Other courts have found that the special needs of bi-racial children justify taking race into account. In *Ebirim v. Ebirim,* a Nebraska court concluded that race was one factor among many to be considered in the custody decision, but upheld an award to the white mother. 620 N.W.2d 117 (Neb. App. 2000). The Nigerian-born father argued that he was better able to raise the child to appreciate his biracial heritage, pointing out that there were no other black

children in the town where the mother lived, and that some members of the mother's family had made racist comments in the past. The court posited that when individuals of different races have a child, neither gains priority on grounds of race alone. *But see Jones v. Jones* (542 S.W.2d. 119 (S.D. 1996)(awarding custody of a bi-racial child to a Native American father, as more likely than mother to expose the child to his racial heritage).

The *ALI Principles* prohibit consideration of race or ethnicity as a factor in the custody decision. Sect. 2.12 (1)(a). The Reporter's comments acknowledge the importance of children having a positive racial identity, but reject the notion that a bi-racial child shares his race with only one parent, and that, on that basis, custody should be awarded to the parent of the stigmatized race. The *Principles* allow consideration of the parents' capacity to nurture self esteem, including positive racial identity. Professor Randall Kennedy argues that race should be excluded as a consideration in both custody and adoption cases. RANDALL KENNEDY, INTERRACIAL INTIMACIES: SEX, MARRIAGE, IDENTITY AND ADOPTION (2003). In Kennedy's view, racial identity should not be socially ascribed, but instead, chosen by individuals.

For a comparison of judicial treatment of race and religious practice as considerations in the custody decision, see notes following *Leppert, infra.*

PROBLEM

Problem 6-3. Billy, aged 11, is the son of Mary, who is white and John, who is African American. During their marriage, Mary and John adopted traditional roles. Mary was a homemaker and Billy's primary caretaker, and John was a busy history professor. Most of Billy's friends were African American and he identified himself as African American, although he was very close to his mother and there is no evidence that his racial identity has interfered with his relationship with her. Mary and John separate and both parents seek custody of Billy. The judge appoints you as Billy's guardian *ad litem* to investigate the family situation and to advise in making the custody decision. Do you have an opinion about which parent should get custody? What information should you seek to assist the judge?

NOTE ON CUSTODY AND PARENTAL HEALTH

Difficult questions arise when a parent's ability to function is affected by physical or mental disability, conditions that are beyond the parent's control. The Model Marriage and Divorce Act, p. 566 *supra*, and many statutes permit consideration of factors such as "the mental and physical health of all individuals involved." *See, e.g.*, COLO. REV. STAT. § 14-10-124(1.5)(a)(V) (2002); MINN. STAT. ANN. § 518.17(a)(9) (West Supp. 2003). Although a physical condition might sometimes be relevant to the custody determination, courts try to weigh carefully how much the condition actually impairs important parenting functions, and to avoid decisions based on prejudiced assumptions about the incapacities of disabled persons. *See, e.g., Bednarski v. Bednarski*, 366 N.W.2d 69 (Mich. App. 1985) (reversing trial court award of custody of child to grandparents because, although mother was deaf, the children had adequate alternatives for learning verbal and oral communication skills). In recent years, both federal and state governments have pursued policies of full integration into society of disabled persons through laws that prohibit discrimination in employment, education, housing, transportation and public access. *See, e.g.* Americans with Disabilities Act, 42 U.S.C. §§ 12101 *et seq.* (2000). Although these laws have not focused on child custody decisions, courts have recognized that full integration encompasses fulfillment of family roles to the extent possible. *In re Carney*, 598 P2d 36 (Cal. 1979). Where the disability seriously affects the parent's ability to care for the child, however, it will be considered. In a recent South Dakota case, the Court reiterated that a physical disability was not *per se* an impediment to custody, but then upheld a custody award of a three-year-old to her mother, where the father suffered from cerebral palsy and had an attendant. *Arneson v. Arneson,* 670 N.W.2d 904 (S.D. 2003). The trial court based its decision largely on the opinion of an evaluator, who concluded that, although the father could care for the child, he might have difficulty responding to emergencies until she was older.

PROBLEM

Probem 6-4 Tom Card lived in California with his two sons and his partner, Marie, who acted as a stepmother. Tom had custody of the boys under a separation agreement with his wife, who had moved to New York after the divorce. Five years later, Tom was injured in a car accident that left him quadriplegic. Tom's former wife sued for a change in custody. Should she prevail?

[d]   Religion

LEPPERT v. LEPPERT

519 N.W.2d 287 (N.D. 1994)

NEUMANN, Justice. Joel Leppert appeals from a divorce judgment awarding physical custody of his three youngest children to their mother, Quinta Leppert. We reverse and remand to the district court.

Joel and Quinta were married June 18, 1984. Five children were born of this marriage . . . On January 14, 1992, Judge Mikal Simonson issued an . . . order granting temporary physical custody of the three youngest children to Quinta, with the physical custody of the two older children alternating between the parents on a bimonthly basis. . . .

The guardian recommended custody of all five of the children should be with Joel, allowing for limited periods of visitation with Quinta. Concluding his report, the guardian stated "Quinta, despite her many admirable traits, is likely to provide parenting that is in several crucial respects, extremely dangerous to the children's psychological and emotional health, personality and characterological development, their physical well being and even their life."

One of the guardian's primary concerns was the harmful impact of Quinta's beliefs and resulting actions. Specifically, Quinta is a devout follower of the teachings of her father, Gordon Winrod (Winrod). Her father is the supreme leader of his own religious sect known as Our Savior's Church. . . . His church is not affiliated with any religious denomination, but purports to follow the teachings of the Bible.

Winrod and his followers believe there are only two types of people in the world: God's enemies, and those who are obedient to God. Those who do not follow Winrod's teachings are not obedient to God, and they are consequently evil, and are to be hated as God's enemies.[1] Testimony at trial stated Winrod teaches lying to God's enemies, stealing from God's enemies, and violent behavior toward God's enemies. He also rejects the authority of governments, and his followers therefore refuse to pay taxes, refuse to register with selective service, ignore hunting and fishing regulations, and refuse to buy liability insurance on their vehicles as required by law. Quinta believes she has a duty to raise her children to follow Winrod. She insists that her children adopt all of his teachings and beliefs.

Joel was at one time a follower of Winrod, but has since stopped following his teachings. Since the marital separation, Quinta has moved to live with her father and several of his followers in a commune-like residence in Gainsville, Missouri. Joel has continued to live and work on the Leppert family farm in Dickey, North Dakota.

Prior to the separation, Quinta home-schooled the two oldest children. Since the separation, Joel enrolled the two oldest children in public school in Jud, North Dakota. When the children enrolled in classes, evaluation assessments showed James' reading and writing skills were significantly below the norm for his age.[2] The children's social skills lagged far behind those of their classmates.[3]

Testimony was introduced at trial that supported Joel's contention that Quinta was attempting to poison the children's relationship with Joel and his family. Tape recorded telephone conversations between Quinta and the two oldest children, James and Stephanie, include statements by Quinta, such as:

> ". . . [Y]our daddy's such a pin head . . ., birds of a feather flock together so do pigs and swine, that's the way your father is, he's a pig and he's a swine. . . .

> ". . . You know I thought some day maybe he [Joel]would grow up so I waited for seven years but all he did was grow hideous . . . his heart rotted out till he's an evil man now, just evil. . . .

---

[1] A major theme in Winrod's teaching is to hate "Jews," and supporters of "Jews." Persons who do not agree with Winrod's interpretation of the Bible are considered supporters of "Jews" and therefore are to be hated. . . .

[2] Testimony of teacher Kristi Kumpf included: ". . . I'm not sure that he ever opened a reading book before because he had no idea how sentences were put together, which is way below first grade level. He had reading-wise maybe three words, four words that he could write for me."

[3] Kristi Kumpf further testified: "When [Stephanie and James] first came to school, they didn't interact at all with other children. They were shy, withdrawn. When I questioned them, they wouldn't answer. . . ."

". . . [Delores Leppert is] wicked and evil, and I'm gonna talk like that and your daddy can hear it whether he likes it or not. She's evil and she's made him evil, and your Uncle Tim is evil and Danny's evil and they're evil there."

Joel also testified that the younger children started to exhibit behavior that suggests Quinta is poisoning them against Joel as well.

Home studies were conducted both in Quinta's home in Missouri, and Joel's home in North Dakota. The results of the studies were that both households would be adequate for raising the five children.

. . . .

Child custody determinations are findings of fact. N.D.R.Civ.P. Rule 52(a); *e.g.*, *Weber v. Weber*, 512 N.W.2d 723, 726 (N.D.1994). On appeal, findings of fact are not disturbed unless clearly erroneous.

Joel argues that the trial court clearly made a mistake when it awarded custody of the three youngest children to Quinta. Specifically, he argues the court erred when it refused to consider the harmful impact of Quinta's beliefs when determining the best interests of the children. We agree.

In its memorandum opinion, the trial court clearly addressed each of the enumerated factors of our best interests statute. NDCC § 14-09-06.2. Subsection (f) of the best interests statute is entitled "moral fitness of the parents." Addressing this subsection, quoting *Hanson v. Hanson*, 404 N.W.2d 460 (N.D.1987), the district court stated "that physical and [sic] emotional harm must be clearly shown, before religious beliefs may become a determining factor" in the best interests of the child analysis, but went on to find that there was not a clear showing of physical and emotional harm to the children from Quinta's practices and beliefs. We cannot agree. The guardian's report unequivocally stated that Quinta's parenting, because of her beliefs, constituted an extreme danger to the children, both physically and emotionally. Based upon such a record, the district court's finding is clearly erroneous.

Although we agree with the district court that Quinta must not be discounted from consideration as a custodial parent simply because of her religious beliefs, this does not mean her religiously motivated actions, which are emotionally and physically harmful to the children, should be ignored when determining the children's best interests. Such a holding would immunize from consideration all religiously motivated acts, no matter what their impact on the children. Carl E. Schneider, *Religion and Child Custody*, 25 U. MICH. J.L. REF. 879, 888 (1992). Almost all of the behavior of members of "other-worldly" sects would be excluded from consideration. *Id.* Not only would we be ignoring the best interests of the child, but the "worldly" parent would be comparatively disadvantaged. Schneider, *supra*, at 888.

Consideration of the harmful impact of a parent's beliefs when determining the best interests of the child is in no way intended to punish parents. . . . Schneider, *supra*, at 883. To the contrary, the goal in custody determinations is to foster the health and well-being of the child, not to punish either of the parents.

The only reason for any consideration of religious beliefs when determining the best interests of the child is to take into account any harmful impact the belief system may have on the child. The best interests factors enumerated in § 14-09-06.2 are secular in nature, and the courts' functions do not include determining the road to salvation. Although secular courts have no place deciding one religion is better than another, they do have the duty of objectively determining whether a belief system's secular effects are likely to cause physical or emotional harm to children. We acknowledge that, ultimately, secular courts may not fully accommodate the desires of those who wholly reject secular standards. Remedying a conflict such as that, however, is beyond the scope of this appeal.

There are factors the trial court appeared to ignore in the best interests analysis because they were religiously motivated. Applying the correct standard for considering the adverse impact that Quinta's beliefs are likely to have on the children, it is in the best interests of all five children that their physical custody be with Joel. . . .

NOTES

1. **When Can Religious Practice be Considered in the Custody Decision?** Although parents' religious beliefs *per se* are not considered in custody cases, religious practices may be taken into account under some circumstances. Courts have used various tests to determine whether parents' religious practices are relevant to the decision. Some courts apply a general best interest test, allowing courts to consider such evidence "to the extent that such views or practices are demonstrated to bear upon the physical or emotional welfare of the child." *Bienenfeld v. Bennett-White,* 605 A.2d 172, 182 (Md. Spec. App. 1992). *See also Burnham v. Burnham,* 304 N.W.2d 58 (Neb. 1981) (early and much-cited case awarding custody to father where mother's church taught anti-semitism and advocated cessation of communication with non-believers, beliefs that could have a "deleterious effect upon the well being of the child herself"). Other courts allow consideration of religious beliefs and practices if there is a reasonable likelihood that the practice will jeopardize the child's physical safety or mental health. The Colorado Supreme Court requires a showing of substantial or reasonable likelihood of present or future harm. *In re Short,* 698 P.2d 1310 (Colo. 1985). *See also Hadeen v. Hadeen,* 619 P.2d 374 (Wash. App. 1980) (religious practices can be considered to the extent that they create likelihood of "immediate or future impairment"). A stricter test requires a showing that the religious practice poses an imminent danger to the child. The Maine Supreme Court applied a variation of the strict test, in rejecting the claim of a father that the Jehovah's Witness mother should be denied custody because she could not authorize a blood transfusion for her child under any circumstances. *Osier v. Osier,* 410 A.2d 1027 (Me. 1980). Because the child was normal and healthy and did not need a blood transfusion, the court found that custody in the mother did not constitute endangerment.

The strictest standard requires that actual harm from the religious practice be demonstrated. *Quiner v. Quiner,* 59 Cal. Rptr. 503 (Cal. Ct. App. 1967). Under the *Quiner* test, impairment of physical, emotional and mental well-being is necessary and evidence offered by psychologists and psychiatrists of the projected effect of a parent's religious practices on the child is excluded.

ALI Principles adopt a test that strictly limits the admissibility of evidence of religious practice to situations where the practice threatens severe and almost certain harm. Sect. 2.12 (1)(c). *Leppert* stresses the need to show that the mother's religious practices have a "harmful impact" on the child, which sounds like the strict *Quiner* test, but it then concludes that the mother's beliefs and practices are in fact causing harm to her children, without offering any clear evidence that this is the case.

In some sense, *Osier* presents an "easy" case; the religious practice of refusing blood transfusions is discrete, and the potential impact simple to evaluate — and, in the case itself, not likely to affect the child's life. Much harder are cases like *Leppert*, in which the parent's religious practice defines her life on a day-to-day basis — and will shape the children's lives if she has custody. When the parent's religious belief and practice have a range of important secular effects on how the parent rears her children, can those effects be excluded from consideration by the court choosing between the parents in a custody dispute? Will the Leppert children be affected by the mother's isolation from society and hostility toward outsiders, including the father, and by her attitude toward education? In *Johnson v. Johnson*, 564 P.2d 71 (Alaska 1977), the mother was a Jehovah's Witness who did not believe that secular education was important, did not teach the children to count money or wash themselves, opposed celebration of holidays and birthdays, and believed that her former husband (who had been "disfellowshipped" by the church) was subject to satanic control. The father proposed to offer the children "exposure to the usual experiences of children their age," *id.* at 74, and planned to send them to college. In a case like this, if evidence of the mother's religious practice is excluded from consideration, how can the parents be compared to determine which parents' custody promotes the children's welfare?

As courts recognize, however, consideration of evidence of parents' religious practice raises serious concerns. Not only are the parents' Free Exercise rights implicated, but a court's preference for one religious view over another would raise Establishment Clause concerns. It is not surprising that courts have struggled to limit consideration of this kind of evidence, while still focusing on the welfare of the children who are the subject of the dispute.

Carl Schneider offers a thoughtful treatment of these issues, in an article heavily relied upon by the *Leppert* court. *See* Schneider, *Religion and Child Custody,* 25 U. MICH. J.L. REF. 879 (1992). Schneider argues that focusing on whether parents' religious practices have secular effects that are harmful to the child is legitimate and, indeed, that any other policy would immunize all religiously motivated behavior. James Dwyer challenges the position that parents have a right to inculcate their children in their religious beliefs and argues that religious practices that are contrary to children's temporal interest are not protected. *See* Dwyer, *Parents' Religion and Children's Welfare: Debunking the Doctrine of Parents' Rights*, 82 CAL. L. REV. 1371 (1994). In a similar vein, see Bergman, *Dealing with Jehovah's Witness Custody Cases,* 29 CREIGHT. L. REV. 1483 (1996). This author contends the child-rearing practices of Jehovah's Witnesses are "not conducive to achieving the goals that most deem important for their children. These goals include being socially involved in school, attending college, pursuing a career, utilizing appropriate medical treatment, and developing tolerance toward persons of a variety of religious faiths and orientation."

2. Custody and the Child's Prior Religious Upbringing. Ordinarily the custodial parent will determine the child's religious training. This may result in a child being raised after the divorce in a different religion than the one in which he or she was earlier raised. Some courts have allowed consideration of the child's prior religious training and practice to be weighed in the custody decision, often in response to statutory guidelines directing that courts making custody determinations consider the child's "religious needs." *See Bonjour v. Bonjour*, 592 P.2d 1233 (Alaska 1979) (under statute requiring consideration of child's religious needs, court can consider which parent is better situated to meet those needs). *See also Boylan v. Boylan,* 577 A.2d. 218 (Pa. Super. Ct. 1990) (children's religious faith favors same faith parent, but is not determinative). The ALI standard allows consideration of the parents' and child's religious practice where necessary to protect the child's ability to practice a religion that has been a significant part of her life. *See* § 212 (1)(c) *supra*.

Religious practice can be an issue in disputes about the freedom of non-custodial parents to take children to religious services during visitation. *See* Section B2, *infra*.

PROBLEMS

Problem 6-5. George seeks your advice about whether he can protect his children from the bizarre religious practices of his former wife, Karen, who has custody. Karen is a devoted and loving mother, but she has become increasingly committed to a religious sect that teaches near-total separation from non-church members, who are deemed "unclean." Karen instructs the children to associate only with church members at school, and prohibits them from participating in any school or after-school activities, including sports, Boy or Girl Scouts, drama, and clubs. She also prohibits them from listening to the radio, watching T.V., playing with video games or reading books unless she first approves them. The children have also been taught that adults in their sect do not vote or participate in any civic, political or governmental activities. George travels a great deal in his job and does not want to seek custody himself. Should he be able to obtain a court order placing conditions on Karen's continued custody, such as that she permit the children to socialize with other children? That she refrain from teaching her children that non-church-members (including their father) are "unclean"?

Problem 6-6. What if Karen's teachings and rules, described above, are based not upon religious convictions, but upon her personal views that present-day society is corrupt and immoral, and that the less her children have to do with it, the better? To what extent does this improve George's position?

[e] Alienation of the Child's Affections

RENAUD v. RENAUD

721 A.2d 463 (Vt. 1998)

The parties had one child, a son, born in January 1994. In May 1996, the parties separated following father's disclosure that he was having an affair with a co-worker and wanted a divorce. At the time of trial in April and May of 1997, mother was living with the three-year-old child in the marital home, and father was living with the co-worker and her children. . . .

Almost immediately [after the separation], mother began to impede father's contact with the child, forcing father to file a number of motions to establish an emergency visitation schedule. Following a hearing in July 1996, the court established a temporary visitation schedule. Thereafter, mother filed a succession of relief-from-abuse petitions, alleging that father had physically and sexually abused the minor. The allegations ranged from evidence of diaper rash, to sunburn, cuts and bruises, and inappropriate touching. . . .

None of the abuse allegations was substantiated, and all . . . were ulti-mately dismissed. Indeed, the court found that father had never abused the minor, that the factual support for the "excessive number of motions and petitions" was "weak at best". . . . The court further found that mother's actions were the result of a heightened distrust of father because of his marital unfaithfulness, and that her "baseless suspicions ha[d] adversely affected [the minor] in that he is no longer as loving towards [father] as he once was." A team of psychiatric experts appointed by the court observed that the child interacted well with each parent, but noted that mother's repeated accusations had damaged the child's relationship with father, and warned that if such accusations continued they could seriously compromise the father-child relationship. . . .

In light of the court's express findings that mother had undermined the child's relationship with father by filing excessive and baseless abuse allega-tions, father contends that the court's decision to award mother sole parental rights and responsibilities was a patent abuse of discretion. Like the trial court here, we are reluctant to condone any conduct by a parent that tends to diminish the child's relationship with the other parent. Indeed, in awarding parental rights and responsibilities, the court is statutorily required to consider "the ability and disposition of each parent to foster a positive relationship and frequent and continuing contact with the other parent, including physical contact, except where contact will result in harm to the child or to a parent." 15 V.S.A. § 665(b)(5). Across the country, the great weight of authority holds that conduct by one parent that tends to alienate the child's affections from the other is so inimical to the child's welfare as to be grounds for a denial of custody to, or a change of custody from, the parent guilty of such conduct.

The paramount consideration in any custody decision, however, is the best interests of the child. Children are not responsible for the misconduct of their parents toward each other, and will not be uprooted from their home merely to punish a wayward parent. Nevertheless, a child's best interests are plainly furthered by nurturing the child's relationship with both parents, and a sustained course of conduct by one parent designed to interfere in the child's relationship with the other casts serious doubt upon the fitness of the offending party to be the custodial parent. See *Young v. Young,* 628 N.Y.S.2d 957, 958 (1995) (interference with relationship between child and non-custodial parent raises " 'a strong probability that the offending party is unfit to act as a custodial parent' ") (quoting *Maloney v. Maloney,* 617 N.Y.S.2d 190, 191 (1994)).

This is not to say that evidence of alienation of affection automatically precludes the offending parent from obtaining custody. . . . Courts should be wary, however, of over-reliance on such otherwise significant considerations as the child's emotional attachment to, or expressed preference for, the offending parent, or on such factors as stability and continuity. For as one court has observed, "The desires of young children, capable of distortive manipulation by a bitter, or perhaps even well-meaning, parent, do not always reflect the long-term best interest of the children." *Nehra v. Uhlar,* 372 N.E.2d 4, 7 (N.Y.1977). And although stability is undoubtedly important, the short-term disruption occasioned by a change of custody may be more than compensated by the long-term benefits of a healthy relationship with both parents.

Thus, where the evidence discloses a continual and unmitigated course of conduct by a parent designed to poison a child's relationship with the other parent, a change of custody from the offending parent may well be in the child's long-term best interests. . . .

A more subtle, but no less invidious, form of interference in parent-child relations may take the form of persistent allegations of physical or sexual abuse. In *Young,* for example, the court reversed an award of custody to the mother where the trial court had inexplicably ignored uncontradicted evidence that the mother had filed numerous false accusations of sexual abuse by the father. As the court observed, "[t]hese repeated uncorroborated and unfounded allegations of sexual abuse brought by the mother against the father cast serious doubt upon her fitness to be the custodial parent." 628 N.Y.S.2d at 962.

 . . . . The situation is more difficult where the allegations of abuse, although ultimately found to be baseless, may initially be in doubt. Society has a strong interest in encouraging parents to take action if they suspect that their child is being abused. Accordingly, courts should infer an ulterior motive in the filing of such charges only where a parent knew, or reasonably should have known, that they were groundless. . . .

The record mitigates in favor of mother in this regard. The evidence showed that she did not act precipitously in filing the petitions, but consulted with the child's pediatrician and therapist, as well as her own therapist, about her suspicions. The child's pediatrician . . . informed her that the child's physical condition did not necessarily suggest abuse or neglect, [but]he also told her that if the child's sunburns continued he would "be quite alarmed," and would feel that the "caregiver [father] is not able to protect [the child] from an obvious source of harm". . . .

Mother also expressed her concerns to the child's therapist. She was particularly anxious about statements by the child suggesting that father had manipulated the child's penis. The therapist recalled . . . that mother "chiefly wanted guidance." Although he ultimately concluded that it was unlikely the child had been abused, he was sufficiently concerned to contact Social and Rehabilitation Services. . . . Although the court again found the allegations of abuse to be groundless, it stressed that it was "not at all suggesting that the mother's reaction wasn't appropriate. She was obviously concerned. . . ."

Thus, the record evidence does not support a finding that mother's purpose was to alienate the child from his father, or that her concerns were wholly unreasonable. It is particularly significant in this regard that mother repeatedly sought expert guidance before acting and received ambiguous messages, suggesting on the one hand that the physical evidence of abuse was weak, but on the other hand that her concerns were not entirely unfounded and certainly warranted investigation.

. . . . Although there was conflicting evidence on this point, substantial credible expert evidence supported the conclusion that mother's actions were a transient reaction to a highly volatile emotional situation, and that she had progressed to the point where she could within a reasonable period of time cooperate with father and foster a healthy relationship with the child. We note that the child's tender years may facilitate the healing process envisioned by the court, whereas an older child might not be so amenable to change.

NOTE

In recent years, courts deciding custody have focused increasingly on the extent to which each parent is supportive of the other's relationship with the child. An important goal of modern custody law is to promote continued contact between the child and both parents, and some statutes direct courts to consider which parent is more likely to support the child's relationship with the other parent. Many statutes include provisions directing the court deciding between the parents to consider "[t]he ability of the parties to encourage the sharing of love, affection, and contact between the child and the other party." See COLO. REV. STAT. § 14-10-124 (1.5)(a)(VI) (2002). Such "friendly parent" provisions are designed to discourage the parents from letting their hostility toward one another affect their children. See ILL. STAT. ANN. Sect. 750 para. 5/602(a)(8) (Smith-Hurd 1993). See Morehouse v. Morehouse, 452 S.E.2d 632 (S.C. App. 1995) (father awarded custody because he encouraged good relationship between child and mother, though mother claimed he had engaged in "almost every kind of misconduct"); Garrett v. Garrett, 527 N.W.2d 213 (Neb. 1995) (Jehovah's Witness mother awarded custody despite depression, because father tried to alienate children); In re Marriage of Quirk-Edwards, 509 N.W.2d 476 (Iowa 1993) (refusal of one parent to provide opportunity for other parent to have meaningful contact with child without just cause shall be considered harmful to the child's interest).

Courts and commentators have focused recently on a variation of this theme where one parent claims that the other has purposely alienated the child's affections. See Begins v. Begins, 721 A.2d at 473 (Vt. 1998) (custody transferred to mother where father poisoned the sons' relationship with the mother, who had been the primary caretaker). In a dispute described as the "worst case of parental alienation syndrome. . .in the history of the United States," a North Dakota trial court not only ordered that custody be changed from the mother to the father, but also denied the mother visitation for a year. *Hendrikson v. Hendrikson*, 603 N.W.2d 896 (2000). The Appellate court ordered supervised visitation, but upheld the change in custody due to the mother's frustration of visitation and poisoning of the relationship between the children and their father. However, the trial court later returned custody to the mother because of the children's unruly behavior in their father's custody. 622 N.W.2d 720 (2001). The claim of alienation has become more common (and has gained some notoriety) due to its designation as a pathology — parental alienation syndrome. Child psychiatrist Richard Gardner described this syndrome in which one parent "brainwashes" the child to hate and fear the other parent, and parent and child become enmeshed in a *folie a deux*. RICHARD GARDNER, THE PARENTAL ALIENATION SYNDROME (2nd ed. 1998). Gardner argues that the syndrome is implicated in many (false) allegations of child sexual abuse in custody disputes, as well as in other situations. Separation of the child and the offending parent is often indicated, in Gardner's view, a conclusion that, if accepted, would have important implications for custody decisions. Other researchers studying parental alienation reject Gardner's syndrome as having little scientific foundation, but still advocate remedial intervention. *See* Kelly & Johnston, *The Alienated Child: A Reformulation of Parental Alienation Syndrome*, 39 FAM. CT. REV. 249 (2001).

This emphasis on alienation of the child's affections as a factor in custody cases has been the subject of sharp criticism. Carol Bruch challenges Gardner's theory as having little scientific basis, and argues that focusing on parental alienation places an unjustified burden on the complaining parent and child, and may divert attention from actual abuse. Bruch, *Parental Alienation Syndrome and Parental Alienation: Getting It Wrong in Child Custody Cases*, 35 FAM. L.Q. 527 (2001). Bruch strongly objects to alienation being a factor in the custody decision. She points out that the child's alienation is usually a transitory response, which the child regrets as she matures.

[f] Child's Preference: The Role of Child Preferences in Custody Decisions

Statutes in most jurisdictions identify the child's preference as a factor to be considered in determining custody. Some statutes make the preferences of older children virtually dispositive. For example, the Georgia law provides that a child of 14 "shall have the right to select the parent with whom he desires to live. The child's selection shall be controlling, unless the parent so selected is determined not to be a fit and proper person to have the custody of the child." GA. CODE § 19-9-1(3)(A) (Supp. 2002). Under such a standard, the parent not selected must prove the selected parent's unfitness. *See also* W.Va Code § 44-10-4 (2001) (minor over 14 years can nominate parent to serve as custodian who shall be approved by the court unless unfit).

Most states give courts more discretion, providing that the child's preference be considered and given weight if it reflects a level of mature judgment. For example, the Florida statute provides that the best interests determination includes the "reasonable preference of the child, if the court deems the child to be of sufficient intelligence, understanding, and experience to express a preference." FLA. STAT. ANN. § 61.13(3)(i) (West Supp. 2003). What is a "reasonable preference"? Many courts will evaluate the reasons given for the preference and discount it if convinced there is an illegitimate basis for the child's choice, or if one parent has put undue pressure on the child. *See, e.g., Marriage of Black*, 837 P2d 407 (Mont. 1992) (upholding trial court's denial of father's petition for custody modification, where court concluded that children's preference for father was based in part on fact that he took them more places, bought them more things and did not make them work around the house); *Leo v. Leo,* 213 N.W.2d 495 (Iowa 1973) (child preferred father because he permitted him to drink alcoholic beverages and play pool in father's nightclub where boy could regularly view "go-go girls who at times engaged in lewd acts with customers"). Sometimes courts reject the importance of reasons given by the child that seem legitimate. For example a North Dakota court chided children for trying to "hold on to the past" where their preference for their father was based on a desire to stay in the same town and school. *Gould v. Miller*, 488 N.W. 2d 42, 44 (N.D. 1992). Of course, the determination of the maturity of a preference provides another opportunity for the judge to inject value-laden opinions into the decision.

There is conflicting evidence about how much weight judges actually give to the child's preferences, although it seems likely that older children's preferences are considered carefully. In a 1995 survey which did not focus on the child's age, Indiana judges ranked the child's preference near the bottom in order of importance in a list of criteria to be considered in custody decisions. Hodges, *Judges Agree on the Issues in Divorces, Study Says,* Det. News, June 17, 1996, at B1. A survey of California judges, on the other hand, reported the desires of children and the custody investigation report are the most important single factors in child custody determinations. Reidy, Silver & Carlson, *Child Custody Decisions: A Survey of Judges,* 23 FAM. L.Q. 75 (1989). A Virginia study established a clear correlation between the child's age and the degree to which the child's preference is considered. *See* Scott, Reppucci & Aber, *Children's Preference in Adjudicated Custody Decisions,* 22 GA. L. REV. 1035 (1988). Although the Virginia custody statute does not make the child's preference a factor, nearly 90% of judges surveyed reported that the preferences of children age 14 and older were either "dispositive . . . or extremely important"; the preferences of children age 10-13 were given somewhat less weight; the preferences of younger children were "discounted significantly."

Is it clear a child's preference should be solicited and considered in a custody proceeding? Consider the following:

> Having the child choose has much to commend it. The child, after all, is the focus [of] social concern. Moreover, in the face of indeterminacy, why not have the child's values inform the choice? The child, better than the judge, may have an intuitive sense of the parent's love, devotion, and capacity. But particularly for infants, this standard is little more than a random process, and for the younger child, what would

this standard mean? Would the child be able to express a preference? If so, would the child's choice be pressured or corrupted by the prelitigation behavior of one parent? Is it desirable or fair to ask the child to choose? This rule might make the child, in the parents' eyes, responsible for the choice. This might often be a very great burden for the child. Furthermore, if the child were made responsible, the child's relationship with the nonchosen parent might be substantially injured.

Mnookin, *Child-Custody Adjudication: Judicial Functions in the Face of Indeterminacy,* 39 LAW & CONTEMP. PROBS. (No. 3) 226, 285 (1975).

How should the child's preference be obtained? Children rarely testify in court in divorce custody proceedings, although the Virginia study found that many judges felt obligated to allow such testimony if one parent insisted. More common are *in camera* interviews of the child by the judge. What rules apply to such interviews? Some courts allow no one else to be present, raising the concern that parties may be disabled from responding to important evidence offered by the child. Scott, *et. al., Children's Preference in Adjudicated Custody Decisions, supra.* Some statutory procedures deal with this concern. Consider a Minnesota statute:

> The court may interview the child in chambers to ascertain the child's reasonable preference as to custodian, if the court deems the child to be of sufficient age to express preference. The court shall permit counsel to be present at the interview and shall permit counsel to propound reasonable questions to the child either directly or through the court. The court shall cause a record of the interview to be made and to be made part of the record in the case unless waived by the parties.

MINN. STAT. § 518.166 (West 1990).

This statute is intended to provide a way for the child to give useful information to the judge, while giving parents the ability to question child witnesses. A record of the interview makes meaningful review of trial court decisionmaking possible. Such statutory protections in favor of parents have been strictly enforced. *See, e.g., Smith v. Smith,* 425 N.W.2d 854 (Minn. 1988); *Williams v. Cole,* 590 S.W.2d 908 (Mo. 1979). A few states even require that evidence of the child's preference be given in open court. *See, e.g., Stevens v. Stevens,* 215 S.E.2d 991 (N.C. App. 1975); *Jethrow v. Jethrow,* 571 So. 2d 270 (Miss. 1990) (parent has right to call child as witness in divorce action).

Ohio takes quite a different approach. While providing that a court, in its discretion, may conduct an interview of the child in chambers, the Ohio statute also contemplates special circumstances in which the court might determine that "it would not be in the best interests of the child to determine the child's wishes and concerns. . . ." OHIO REV. CODE ANN. § 3109.04(B)(2)(b) (Anderson 1996). If an interview is held, "no persons other than the child, the child's attorney, the judge, any necessary court personnel, and, in the judge's discretion, the attorney of each parent shall be permitted to be present in the chambers during the interview." *Id.* Not only is there no provision for a record to be taken of the interview, but the statute provides specifically, that "no court, in determining the child's best interest . . . shall accept or consider a written or recorded statement or affidavit that purports to set forth the child's wishes and concerns. . . ." The Michigan Supreme Court held that a trial court can interview the child who is the subject of a custody contest *in camera*, but only for the limited purpose of eliciting the child's preference about custody. *Molloy v. Molloy,* 637 N.W.2d 803 (Mich. Ct. App. 2001).

The child's preference seems to have increased in importance in recent years. Some courts have found the failure to consider the preferences of quite young children to be reversible error. *See, e.g., Hensgens v. Hensgens,* 653 So. 2d 48 (La. Ct. App. 1995) (court should have considered the preferences of mature, intelligent children aged eight and ten); *Ellison v. Ellison,* 628 So. 2d. 855 (Ala. Civ. App. 1995) (reversible error for court to refuse to allow testimony of mentally retarded ten-year-old); *Bowers v. Bowers,* 475 N.W.2d 394 (Mich. Ct. App. 1991) (reversible error not to interview 6- and 9-year-old children).

NOTE ON THE ROLE OF THE CHILD'S ATTORNEY

If the child's preference is an important consideration in the custody dispute, should children have a right to representation by an attorney who will advocate for the outcome favored by her client? Guardians *ad litem* are often appointed by courts in litigated custody disputes to represent the child's interests, but views vary widely about their appropriate role. Should a guardian ad litem treat the child like any other client? Many observers support this position, but it may not be feasible (or advisable) with younger children.

In a famous Note, Kim Landsman and Martha Minow reported their study in which they interviewed attorneys and found two competing models of legal representation of children in custody disputes — advocates and fact finders. Landsman & Minow, *Lawyering for the Child: Principles of Representation in Custody and Visitation Disputes arising from Divorce,* 87 YALE L.J. 1126 (1978). Advocates generally urged conferral of party status on the child and argue that the attorney's role is to advocate for the child's preference. Under the fact-finder model, the principal role of the attorney is that of impartial investigator; to "insure that all considerations regarding the best interests of the child will have been brought to the Court's attention." Landsman and Minow argue that both of these models offers a limited conception of legal representation, because neither addresses the needs of a child during the period of litigation. They urge a more flexible approach and propose guidelines for attorneys representing children.

> (1) The attorney should invite the child to participate and should provide explanation to the extent of the child's desire and capacity. He should also respect a child's desire not to participate. . . .

> (2) The attorney should be wary of opposing the child's preference; there may be good reasons for the preference that are not readily observable.

> (3) The attorney should act to enhance existing parent-child relationships; this requires a duty to the parents greater than avoiding the infliction of needless harm.

(4) The attorney should take advantage of his unique opportunity to act as mediator and arbitrator in a manner consistent with the child's interests.

The authors also discourage attorneys from relying on investigative agencies or experts, and from seeking psychological evaluations, which are deemed intrusive.

Courts have had a mixed response to requests by children for independent representation in custody disputes. An Arizona court held that the trial court abused its discretion in rejecting the request of a 7-year-old boy for independent counsel in his parents' divorce proceedings. The court noted that state statutes provided discretion to the trial court, but found that where the divorce involved allegations of mistreatment by each parent and the child was able to articulate his feelings well, counsel should have been appointed. *J.A.R. v. Superior Ct.*, 877 P.2d 1323 (Ariz. 1994). *See also G.S. v. T.S.*, 582 A.2d 467 (Conn. App. 1990) (same, in case involving allegation of sexual abuse). A Maryland court, however, followed what is probably the majority rule, in denying the request of the children, ages 12 and 14, to intervene in their parents' custody proceeding through their own attorney. *Auclair v. Auclair*, 730 A.2d 1260 (Md. Spec. App. 1999). The children argued that their guardian *ad litem* failed to communicate their preferences forcefully to the court. The trial court replaced the first guardian *ad litem* with a second (with whom the children refused to meet), but rejected the petition to intervene through their chosen attorney, and further ordered the attorney not to speak with them. The appellate court held that the children were not entitled to independent representation because they were not parties to the proceeding. Moreover, the court noted that, where attorneys have been allowed, they are appointed by the court and not chosen by the children, to assure competence and independence from either parent. [Here, the mother had chosen the attorney.] In rejecting the children's right to independent representation, the court pointed to the added burden of time and expense that would be incurred. However, the lower court was found to have erred in prohibiting the children from consulting with counsel of their choice. Since the primary task of the guardian *ad litem* is to investigate and obtain information from the children, private counsel could play an important role in providing the children with information and legal advice on effective formulation of their preferences.

For further commentary on the role of attorney for the child and other questions relating to the representation of children in custody proceedings, see Guggenheim, *A Paradigm for Determining the Role of Counsel for Children*, 64 FORDHAM L. REV. 1399 (1996). Guggenheim argues that the appropriate role of lawyers for younger children is not to advocate for a particular outcome, but to assure that judges are in the best position to make a considered judgment based on accurate information. This is also the position of the standard adopted by the American Academy of Matrimonial Lawyers. REPRESENTING CHILDREN: STANDARDS FOR ATTORNEYS AND GUARDIANS AD LITEM IN CUSTODY OR VISITATION PROCEEDINGS (1995). The A.B.A. has undertaken a pro bono project that focuses on expanding access to justice for children in custody cases. www.abachildcustodyproject.org

PROBLEM

Problem 6-7. You have been appointed to represent a twelve-year-old child, Sarah, in a bitterly contested custody fight. In your discussion with Sarah, she states firmly and consistently that she wants to live with her mother, Hannah, because "Mommy has always taken care of me, and I take care of her too." After conducting a full investigation of the case, you learn that the mother has a history of rather serious emotional problems and was hospitalized for depression last year. You also learn that Hannah has had a secret problem with alcohol abuse over the past decade; she admits that in the past she has been intoxicated around Sarah occasionally. Although Hannah insists that her drinking problem is under control, you are concerned that under stress, she may start drinking again. Sarah's father, Mike, is a stable and affectionate parent, although he is a busy lawyer and has always left Sarah's care to Hannah. Although Sarah is not as close to him as she is to her mother, you are convinced that in the long run, she will receive better care and greater stability with her father. From your discussions with the father and with his attorney, it is clear that neither knows of the mother's drinking problem.

In the custody proceedings, do you advocate the position that corresponds to Sarah's preferences, or the position that you believe is in her long-term best interests? What alternative courses of action do you have? Do you tell the father's attorney or the court about the mother's alcohol problems?

§ C.   ALTERNATIVE CUSTODY DECISION RULES

The best interest of the child standard has been criticized over the years on the ground that it provides little guidance to courts about what factors should be given priority in the custody decision. *See* discussion in Section B1, *supra*. Indeed, it might be said that the best interest standard hardly qualifies as a legal rule at all; more accurately, it simply describes the court's goal in determining custody — to decide the child's custodial arrangements according to her best interests. As the preceding section demonstrates, most doctrinal developments have focused on whether certain controversial factors (race, religion, gender, sexual behavior) should be *excluded* from consideration under the best interest standard. The best interest standard gives courts vast discretion, allowing judges' subjective values and biases to influence the custodial choice. Moreover, adjudication of custody disputes under this standard, which effectively invites each parent to marshal evidence about the other's deficiencies, is likely to have a particularly damaging impact on the parties' future relationship. To the extent that parents' cooperation in the post-dissolution period serves their children's interests, the best interest standard paradoxically may undermine children's interests.

Many observers have argued that the best interest of the child standard should be replaced with a more determinate decision rule that narrows the discretion of courts. We will consider the two most important alternatives to emerge in the past generation. The first approach is for parents to share responsibility and authority for their children under an order for joint physical or legal custody. The rationale for joint custody is that it promotes the child's welfare by preserving her relationships with both parents after separation.

Although joint physical custody has not gained the popularity that advocates predicted in the 1980s, joint legal custody is routinely ordered in many states. The second approach focuses on the parents' caretaking role in the child's life before the family broke down. Until recently, the dominant version of this approach was the primary caretaker preference, under which custody was awarded to the parent who assumed primary responsibility for the child's care before dissolution. *See Garska v. McCoy*, 278 S.E.2d 357 (W. Va. 1981). This rule was essentially a gender-neutral version of the tender years presumption; it assumed that the child had only one primary caretaker, but that either parent might fill the role. Recently, this approach has been adapted to recognize both parents' caretaking roles. Under the A.L.I. standard, custodial responsibility is allocated between the parents so as to approximate each parent's caretaking role before separation. Sect. 2.08-2.09.

[1] JOINT CUSTODY

Courts have an option today that was not available in most states until the 1980s of awarding legal or physical custody to both parents. This approach to custody, mostly accomplished through statutory reform, reflects an underlying policy of encouraging both parents to maintain post-divorce relationships with the child. Although the overriding policy goal of joint custody is clear, the term is used in a confusing way because it includes two types of legal arrangements. Joint physical custody involves a relatively equal sharing by the parents of physical care of the child; the term refers to the child's residential placement. Joint legal custody involves sharing by the parents of the authority to make important decisions affecting the child's welfare — decisions relating to education, medical care and religious training and practice. Although advocates of joint custody generally seek to promote joint physical custody, commentators, courts and even legislatures formulating statutes tend to be unclear about which form is intended. The following case addresses the distinctions between joint physical and joint legal custody.

McCARTY v. McCARTY

807 A.2d 1211 (Md. Spec. App. 2002)

MOYLAN, Judge. This case concerns the award of joint legal custody to the estranged parents of three-year-old Jessica McCarty. The appellant, Carol Marie McCarty (the Mother), and the appellee, Douglas Neal McCarty (the Father), were married on January 31, 1998. Jessica was born on August 8, 1999. The parties separated on November 17, 2000. The Father filed a motion in the Circuit Court for Montgomery County, asking for both joint legal custody and joint physical custody of his daughter. The Mother filed a counter-complaint in the same court, asking for a limited divorce and for sole custody, both legal and physical, of her daughter. [The trial court] awarded sole physical custody to the Mother but joint legal custody to the Mother and Father. The Mother has taken this appeal from that award of joint legal custody.

Initially, it will be helpful to contrast joint legal custody and joint physical custody. Although the landmark case of *Taylor v. Taylor*, 508 A.2d 964 (Md. 1986), discusses both forms of joint custody, it is careful to distinguish the two from each other. . . .

[A] distinction must be made between sharing parental responsibility in major decision-making matters and sharing responsibility for providing a home for the child. Embraced within the meaning of "custody" are the concepts of "legal" and "physical" custody. Legal custody carries with it the right and obligation to make long range decisions involving education, religious training, discipline, medical care, and other matters of major significance concerning the child's life and welfare. Joint legal custody means that both parents have an equal voice in making those decisions, and neither parent's rights are superior to the other. . . .

Physical custody, on the other hand, means the right and obligation to provide a home for the child and to make the day-to-day decisions required during the time the child is actually with the parent having such custody. Joint physical custody is in reality "shared" or "divided" custody. Shared physical custody may, but need not, be on a 50/50 basis, and in fact most commonly will involve custody by one parent during the school year and by the other during summer vacation months, or division between weekdays and weekends, or between days and nights. . . .

Proper practice in any case involving joint custody dictates that the parties and the trial judge separately consider the issues involved in both joint legal custody and joint physical custody, and that the trial judge state specifically the decision made as to each.

The only issue before us in this case is joint legal custody, and not joint physical custody. . . .

The Mother points to two factors to support her claim that Judge Sundt was guilty of a clear abuse of discretion in awarding joint legal custody. One is her own reluctance to share legal custody. . . . This is a factor that self-evidently applies to joint legal custody and joint physical custody alike. "Generally, the parents should be willing to undertake joint custody or it should not be ordered." 508 A.2d 964.

. . . . [T]he Court of Appeals rejected the proposition "that a trial judge may never order joint legal custody over the objection of one parent." *Id*. It was unwilling to grant either parent "veto power" over such a possibility.

A caring parent, believing that sole custody is in the best interest of the child, may forcefully advance that position throughout the litigation but be willing and able to fully participate in a joint custody arrangement if that is the considered decision of the court. 508 A.2d 964.

The Mother's reluctance to share legal custody, moreover, does not come across to us as an adamantine or Shermanesque refusal to participate in the event that such an arrangement were to be ordered by the court. She had moved, after all, for sole legal custody in herself and her position on joint custody, expressed in her brief, simply supports that position.

A mere reluctance to participate in an arrangement is not tantamount to a refusal to participate and should not be given the same weight as the judge assesses the prospects for a successful resolution.

The other factor cited by the Mother as a contraindication of joint legal custody is the inability of the Mother and Father to communicate effectively with each other. This is a . . . factor that is particularly pertinent to joint legal custody.

This is clearly the most important factor in the determination of whether an award of joint legal custody is appropriate, and is relevant as well to a consideration of shared physical custody. Rarely, if ever, should joint legal custody be awarded in the absence of a record of mature conduct on the part of the parents evidencing an ability to effectively communicate with each other concerning the best interest of the child, and then only when it is possible to make a finding of a strong potential for such conduct in the future.

508 A.2d 964.

It is that "rarely, if ever, . . ." dictum . . . on which the appellant essentially hinges this appeal. The trial judge would obviously need a substantial basis for looking beyond the surface appearance of poor communication.

In this case, the actual "track record" of the Mother and Father for effective communication had been, to be sure, abysmal. Indeed, on September 7, 2001, Judge Sundt deferred making a final decision on joint legal custody for six months and ordered both the Mother and the Father to "work with a parent coordinator, Dr. Linda Gordon," whose "primary purpose shall be to facilitate communication between the parties, to reduce the conflict between the parties."

It was the relative optimism of Dr. Gordon, six months later, based on improvements in the attitude of both parties, that persuaded Judge Sundt to award joint legal custody. Ordinarily the best evidence of compatibility with this criterion will be the past conduct or "track record" of the parties. We recognize, however, that the tensions of separation and litigation will sometimes produce bitterness and lack of ability to cooperate or agree. The trial judge will have to evaluate whether this is a temporary condition, very likely to abate upon resolution of the issues, or whether it is more permanent in nature. . . .

Admittedly, tensions and disagreements between the parties have escalated. Nevertheless, after hearing the testimony, and judging the credibility and demeanor of the witnesses, the trial court concluded that the parties could resolve their differences and act together in [the child's] best interest.

. . . . Judge Sundt found that, after six months of the parties' working with Dr. Gordon, there had been "enormous improvement" in their ability and willingness to communicate with each other. Linda Gordon talked about the successes first, the fact that there had been sharing of information, and the way the she had institutionalized that was through faxes on a weekly basis, so that the parties could communicate as to what was going on with Jessica.

She talked about the reduction of conflict and strategies that she had been working with the parties on, even small language strategies, so that Mrs. McCarty, who has demonstrated, by both experts' testimony, real learning skills in handing off Jessica — even there, in small nuances of language, could turn a phrase so that it might appear more positive than pejorative as she is getting Jessica ready to go on visits — and certainly with Mr. McCarty, who had a longer road to travel, doing whatever he could to, if not mask his hostility toward his wife, at least put on a civil face and address her and in a tone of voice that would not be threatening or would not be perceived as frightening.

In a case in which there is not an established "track record" of good communication, . . . the trial court must articulate the bases for any optimistic expectation on its part that the situation will improve.

In this case, Judge Sundt did just that. She pointed to 1) the fact that the tensions of litigation were subsiding and 2) the continuing help of a third party. . . .

In terms of that third-party help, part of Judge Sundt's final order, moreover, was her firm directive that both parties must continue, at their own mutual expense, to work with Dr. Gordon for an additional six months in the effort to improve their communicative skills. Judge Sundt was emphatic:

Neither one of you is to make a major decision without consulting the other, and, as I said, if you run into an impasse, that is the time you meet with Dr. Gordon. I want you to meet with her no fewer than 10 times over these six months. So, that is roughly every other week.

I think you can do legal custody. . . . [T]he primary factor in joint legal custody has to do with valuing and respecting each other so that you can actually confer and consult.

But I am relying on Linda Gordon in this respect. Her sense was that to the extent that . . . the conflict is situational, and to the extent that you have been able to move past that and that there are ways of communicating without having to do it face-to-face and certainly not in Jessica's presence, it will come.

And I tend to adopt her view that the alternative is worse — that a period of time right now for one of you to be making the decisions without the other's input will be perceived as such disrespect and such disregard that the conflict will not abate — that the only way that conflict is going to abate is with your having to be civil, courteous, and respectful.

We cannot say that Judge Sundt's decision constituted a clear abuse of discretion.

NOTES

1. *The Dual Meaning of Joint Custody.* The *McCarty* court describes the difference between joint physical custody and joint legal custody and emphasizes that only joint legal custody is at issue in this case in which the mother is awarded primary physical custody. Other courts are far less clear, and even statutes can be ambiguous. For example, the Iowa statute creates a preference favoring joint custody. IOWA CODE SECT. 598.41 (2002). Iowa judicial opinions clarify, however, that the preference applies only to joint *legal* custody, and even conclude that joint physical custody is to be awarded only in exceptional circumstances — a conclusion that the statute itself certainly does not indicate. *See In re Marriage of Will*, 489 N.W.2d 394 (Iowa 1992). The Maryland court in *McCarty* suggests that the factors to be considered in deciding whether joint physical custody is appropriate differ from those that would be considered in a decision about joint legal custody. Other than logistical factors such as the proximity to one another of the parties' homes, how would the inquiry be different? The ability of the parties to communicate with one another would be important both in joint legal and physical custody — probably more important when physical custody is shared. Would a court considering joint physical custody have found these parents' communication to be adequate?

One effect of the confusion about the meaning of "joint custody" is that it is hard to evaluate the prevalence of joint custody and the impact of the trend. The most comprehensive study of joint custody to date is the California study conducted by Eleanor Maccaby and Robert Mnookin, described earlier. E. MACCOBY & R. MNOOKIN, DIVIDING THE CHILD: SOCIAL AND LEGAL DILEMMAS OF CUSTODY (1992). These researchers found that joint legal custody (awarded in 79% of cases) is much more common than joint physical custody (19.6% of cases). Moreover, in about 45% of the families with joint physical custody, a "drift" took place over the next three years, and the arrangements became *de facto* sole custody arrangements, with children living with their mother. Complicating the issue further is the fact that what distinguishes joint and sole physical custody is the amount of time the child spends with each parent, and it may not be clear where the line between sole and joint physical custody lies. The *McCarty* court emphasizes that a 50\50 division of time is not necessary. Do parents have joint custody when the child spends two days a week with one parent (and five with the other)? Three days with one and four with the other?

2. *The Legal Trend.* While precedential authority for joint custody awards dates from early in the last century (*see, e.g., Baer v. Baer,* 51 S.W.2d 873 (Mo. App. 1932)), the modern availability of joint custody as an alternative to traditional sole custody has been described as a "small revolution . . . in child custody law." Scott & Derdeyn, *Rethinking Joint Custody,* 45 OHIO ST. L.J. 455, 455 (1984). Beginning in the late 1970's, many courts have authorized joint custody without express statutory support. *See, e.g., Taylor v Taylor,* 508 A.2d 964 (Md. 1986)(discussed in *McCarty*); *Beck v. Beck,* 432 A.2d 63 (N.J. 1981); *Daniel v. Daniel,* 238 S.E.2d 108 (Ga. 1977). The 1980s saw a flood of legislation, such that a 1989 article found 34 states with joint custody statutes of one sort or another. Freed & Foster, *Family Law in the 50 States,* 22 FAM. L.Q. 367, 467 (1989). A few were enacted in the 1990s. *See* D.C. CODE ANN. § 16-911, 16-914 (2001).

The momentum behind joint custody legislation has come in part from the political efforts of fathers' groups. Fathers who are involved with their children have been frustrated by traditional sole custody arrangements, under which their access to their child and parental status generally is quite limited. M. ROMAN & W. HADDAD, THE DISPOSABLE PARENT (1978). The receptiveness to joint custody and the legal reforms that have resulted may be attributed, in part, to a belief that fathers with joint custody will maintain their relationship with their children, and thus will be more likely to continue to provide financial support. The continued involvement of both parents in their children's lives after divorce is expressed as a policy goal under many custody laws.

3. *State Law Variations.* State statutes reveal a wide range of policies with respect to joint custody. Consider the following state statutes:

CAL. FAM. CODE § 3040 (West Supp. 2003).

(a) Custody should be awarded in the following order of preference according to the best interests of the child. . . .:

(1) To both parents jointly . . . or to either parent. In making an order for custody to either parent, the court shall consider, among other factors, which parent is more likely to allow the child or children frequent and continuing contact with the noncustodial parent, . . .

(b) This section establishes neither a preference nor a presumption for or against joint legal custody, joint physical custody, or sole custody. . . .

§ 3080 (West 1994).

There is a presumption, affecting the burden of proof, that joint custody is in the best interests of a minor child where the parents have agreed to an award of joint custody or so agree in open court. . . .

§ 3081 (West 1994).

On the application of either parent, joint custody may be ordered in the discretion of the court. . . .

FLA. STAT. ANN. § 61.13 (West Supp. 2003).

(2)(b)2. The court shall order that the parental responsibility for a minor child be shared by both parents unless the court finds that shared parental responsibility would be detrimental to the child. . . .

a. In ordering shared parental responsibility, the court may consider the expressed desires of the parents and may grant to one party the ultimate responsibility over specific aspects of the child's welfare or may divide those responsibilities between the parties based on the best interests of the child. Areas of responsibility may include primary residence, education, medical and dental care, and any other responsibilities which the court finds unique to a particular family.

b. The court shall order "sole parental responsibility, with or without visitation rights, to the other parent when it is in the best interests of" the minor child.

The statutes show considerable variation. Some create a preference for joint (legal) custody and direct courts to consider several factors to determine whether this arrangement is appropriate. These factors include whether each parent would be a suitable custodian; whether the parents can communicate with each other regarding the child's needs; whether both parents have actively cared for the child before and since the separation; and whether each parent can support the other parent's relationship with the child. Some states require joint custody to be considered if one parent petitions, while others simply authorize joint custody. A few states, like California, *supra* create a preference in favor of joint custody that only applies if both parents agree. *See* CONN. GEN. STAT. ANN.§ 46b-56b (2001). In others, the preference is overcome by a showing that another award is in the child's best interests. *See* MICH. COMP. LAWS ANN. § 722.26a(1) (2001). A few statutes prohibit an award of joint custody unless the parents agree. *See* OR. REV. STAT. § 107.169(3) (1999); VT. STAT. ANN tit. 15 § 665(a) (2001).

Some courts have tended to interpret joint custody statutes restrictively. In Nebraska, a judicially-created rule requires a hearing to determine whether joint physical custody is in the best interest of the child, even when the parents agree to it. *Hildebrand v. Hildebrand,* 477 N.W.2d 1, 4 (1991). *See* note 1 *supra.*

4. ***Joint Custody Over Parental Objection.*** Most joint custody statutes at least implicitly allow courts to order joint custody over the objection of one parent, and many permit a joint custody order even if neither parent seeks this arrangement. (Some statutes require parental agreement, and others have been interpreted in this way.) As the *McCarty* court suggests, a parent's opposition to joint custody is usually treated as simply one of the several factors weighed by the court when the other parent has requested joint custody. *See, e.g., Squires v. Squires,* 854 S.W.2d 765 (Ky. 1993) (a requirement of agreement would give one parent a veto that could be exercised in bad faith). As *McCarty* suggests, this view assumes (and some social scientists agree) that some parents who have been hostile to one another can set aside their disagreements and cooperate in a joint custody arrangement, if ordered to do so by a court. *See, e.g.,* McKinnon & Wallerstein, *Joint Custody and the Preschool Child,* 4 BEHAV. SCI. & L. 169, 177 (1986); Greif, *Fathers, Children, and Joint Custody,* 49 AM. J. ORTHOPSYCHIATRY 311, 318 (1979). *See* Note, *Whose Child Is It Anyway? Awarding Joint Custody Over the Objection of One Parent,* 15 FORDHAM URBAN L.J. 625 (1987).

Recently, a few courts have ordered joint custody *because* one (or both) parent is hostile and seeks to alienate the child from the other parent. In *Barton v. Hirshberg,* a Maryland court upheld an award of joint legal custody, based on a diagnosis of Parental Alienation Syndrome, caused by the mother's hostility toward the father. 767 A2d 874 (Md. App. 2000). The court justified the order (along with increased visitation) on the ground that the mother's alienating behavior could result in the child being "distanced from his father. . .and. . .impede his emotional maturation." The court concluded (optimistically) that the parents would be able to communicate adequately after the tensions surrounding the legal proceedings abated. *See also Scott v. Scott,* 579 S.E.2d 620 (S.C. 2003) (joint physical custody ordered where both parents seek to alienate the child from the other; either parent with sole custody would compromise the child's relationship with the other). Are these courts elevating the importance of maintaining the child's relationship with both parents over every other consideration? Is this a consideration in *McCarty?*

By contrast, some courts are unwilling to coerce parents into a joint custody arrangement, reasoning that there is no reasonable hope of post-divorce cooperation in such an arrangement unless the parents are committed to it. *See, e.g., Emerick v. Emerick,* 502 A.2d 933 (Conn. App. 1985); *Frey v. Wagner,* 433 So. 2d 60 (Fla. App. 1983). This view is also supported by some research indicating that court-ordered joint custody does not promote cooperative parenting. *See* Steinman, *Joint Custody: What We Know, What We Have Yet to Learn, and the Judicial and Legislative Implications,* 16 U.C.D. L. REV. 739, 759 (1983). A great deal of psychological research supports the proposition that exposure to conflict between their parents has a destructive impact on children after divorce (or in an intact family, for that matter), an impact that may be more harmful than reduced contact with a parent. *See* research summarized in Scott and Derdeyn, *Rethinking Joint Custody, supra* note 1. Thus, coercing a continued relationship (through a joint custody arrangement) between parents who are extremely hostile toward one another may be more disruptive to the child than a sole custody arrangement.

5. *Logistical Complications of Physical Joint Custody Arrangements.* As the Mnookin and Maccoby study suggests, even in California, only a small proportion of divorced couples share physical custody. One constraint on joint physical custody is mobility. Many people relocate after divorce and sharing in the child's care becomes impractical. Relocation is discussed in Section E2, *infra.* Moreover, courts are resistant to complicated, or constantly shifting residential arrangements. *See, e.g., Lukens v. Lukens,* 587 N.W. 2d 141 (N.D. 1998) (court rejects award rotating custody on a monthly basis); *Evans v. Lungrin,* 708 So. 2d 731 (La. 1998) (trial court abused discretion in ordering custody to alternate in four month blocks between Louisiana father and Washington mother).

6. *Resolving Disputes Between Parents with Joint Custody.* In joint physical custody arrangements, the potential for conflict over everyday matters of scheduling, discipline, etc. is great. Substantial parental conflict which detrimentally affects the child can result in modification to a sole custody arrangement. Parents with joint legal custody may disagree about the decisions that are the subject of shared authority. Many courts will resolve the dispute by deciding the matter itself, while some will designate the parent with decisionmaking authority. An example of the latter approach is *Hight v. McKinney,* 627 N.Y.S.2d 271 (Fam. Ct. 1995), in which the court gave the mother the authority to decide whether the child should attend sex education classes to which the father objected. In *In re Debenham,* 896 P.2d 1098 (Kans. App. 1995), joint custodial parents had deadlocked over where to send their child to school. The appellate court affirmed the order directing the child's continued attendance at the private school chosen by the primary physical custodian, but emphasized it was not adopting a *per se* rule in favoring the primary physical custodian's decision and stressed that the other parent could return to court to renew his request for a different educational plan for the child. The court acknowledged that this solution, with its built-in invitation for continued litigation, was not very satisfactory. However, it blamed the legislature for "declar[ing] joint custody and equal decisional rights as the public policy of this state." *Id.* at 1101. *See also Sotnick v. Sotnick,* 650 So. 2d 157 (Fla. App. 1995) (court resolves issue of where child should attend school when parents with shared responsibility deadlock).

7. *"Friendly Parent" Provisions and Joint Custody.* The California statute, *supra,* includes a "friendly parent" provision directing the court to consider "which parent is more likely to allow the child. . .frequent. . . contact with the non-custodial parent" if it decides to award sole, rather than joint, custody. Such provisions can present a formidable obstacle to the parent who opposes a joint custody petition by the other. Consider one court's statement: "[A] court may properly consider that a parent's unreasonable or obdurate resistance to joint custody is a factor which can weigh in favor of awarding sole custody to the other parent." *In re Marriage of Weidner,* 338 N.W.2d 351(Iowa 1983). Critics of "friendly parent" provisions argue these provisions discourage well-intentioned parents from opposing joint custody, for fear that this might be used to label the complainer as a non-friendly parent and, therefore, an inappropriate candidate for a sole custody award. *See* Schulman & Pitt, *Second Thoughts on Joint Child Custody: Analysis of Legislation and Its Implications for Women and Children,* 12 GOLDEN GATE U.L. REV. 538, 554-55 (1982). *Weidner* and other cases have emphasized, however, that a parent's good faith opposition to joint custody should not penalize her request for sole custody. *See, e.g., Rolde v. Rolde,* 425 N.E.2d 388 (Mass. App. 1981); *In re Marriage of Heinel and Kessel,* 637 P.2d 1313 (Or. 1981). Nonetheless, seeking to prove good faith opposition carries some risk.

8. *The Feminist Critique of Joint Custody.* Some feminists point out that the joint custody movement has been dominated by fathers' rights groups, and argue that the reforms are detrimental to women. They claim that laws favoring joint custody give fathers additional leverage, which is used to exact concessions from mothers during divorce negotiations, or to manipulate or harass women after the divorce. Moreover, awarding custody rights to fathers who have had minimal involvement with their children is unfair to primary caretaking mothers.

As Martha Fineman has argued:

> In most marriages, one parent, normally the mother, assumes day-to-day primary care. Shared parenting in these situations seldom means equally divided responsibility and control: typically one parent sacrifices more than the other in order to care for the child. The sense of sharing in this context is not based on the actual assumption of divided responsibilities by the parents. . . . Yet an unrealistic and idealized vision of shared parenting *independent* of the relationship is now imposed on couples after divorce. . . . [T]his amounts to furthering the interests of non-caretaking fathers over the objections and against the interests of caretaking mothers.

Fineman, *Dominant Discourse, Professional Language and Legal Change in Child Custody Decisionmaking,* 101 HARV. L. REV. 727, 768 (1988).

See also Scott & Derdeyn, *Rethinking Joint Custody, supra;* Schulman & Pitt, *supra;* Singer & Reynolds, *A Dissent on Joint Custody,* 47 MD. L. REV. 497 (1988); Post, *Arguments Against Joint Custody,* 4 BERKELEY WOMEN'S L.J. 316 (1989-90) ("joint custody is more often an arrangement designed to protect the divorcing father's rights rather than the best interests of the children").

A response to this critique is that a party in a legal dispute always has more leverage in negotiations when the legal rule favors that party. So just as a joint custody presumption gives fathers leverage, a primary caretaker presumption gives mothers leverage. The question, of course is not whether one party or the other benefits from a legal rule, but rather whether the rule allocates those benefits appropriately as a matter of public policy. Fineman and others argue that a joint custody rule does not, because it favors the parent who has not exercised responsibility for the child comparable to the other parent when the family was intact. Certainly a presumption favoring joint custody might have this effect. Supporters, however, argue that by promoting the involvement of both parents, joint custody benefits children. Schepard, *Taking Children Seriously: Promoting Cooperative Custody After Divorce*, 64 TEX. L. REV. 687 (1985).

Another criticism of joint custody is that women may be required to "cooperate" with their physically abusive former spouses. Some statutes create a presumption against joint custody where one parent has engaged in acts of domestic violence against the child or other parent. WIS. STAT. ANN. § 767.24 (West Supp. 2002); CAL. FAM. CODE § 3011 (West Supp. 2003). *See also* ALASKA STAT. § 25.20.090(8) (Michie 2002); ARIZ. REV. STAT. ANN. § 25-403 (E) (West Supp. 2002). Courts also have addressed this issue. *See, e.g., In re Marriage of Brainard* 523 N.W.2d 611 (Iowa App. 1994); *Bishop v. Bishop*, 457 So. 2d 264 (La. App. 1984) (rejecting joint custody because of impact of physical abuse and extreme antagonism between parents on child); *In re Marriage of Hickey*, 689 P.2d 1222 (Mont. 1984) (reversing joint custody decree because of father's history of violent temper and threats against wife).

Some feminists acknowledge the deficiencies of joint custody, but defend this arrangement, arguing that it expresses egalitarian parenting roles, which ultimately serve women's interests as well as those of men. *See* Bartlett & Stack, *Joint Custody, Feminism and the Dependency Dilemma*, 2 BERKELEY WOMEN'S L.J. 9 (1985).

PROBLEM

Problem 6-8. Your client, Jane, is divorcing her husband Fred, who has left her for a young associate in his law firm. Jane tells you that Fred is a decent parent who loves his children, Mary and Liza, ages 5 and 7. However, because of his busy professional life, he has played a small role in their upbringing. Fred is seeking joint physical custody of the children. Jane tells you that she is adamantly opposed to joint custody and wants sole custody. She does not believe that Fred is capable of caring for the children and she does not believe that they can cooperate — in part, because she is so angry with him about his treatment of her. Assume that your jurisdiction has adopted a statute similar to Florida's, and a friendly parent provision. What do you advise Jane?

[2] PAST PARENTAL CARETAKING ROLES

The role of each parent in caring for the child before separation has long been an important consideration in deciding custody under the best interest of the child standard. *See* Section B2(a). Feminists and others who are dissatisfied with the best interest standard have argued that awarding custody to the primary caretaker is the best means to promote the child's best interests. *See, e.g.,* Fineman, *Dominant Discourse, Professional Language, and Legal Change in Child Custody Decisionmaking,* 101 HARV. L. REV. 727 (1988). In the 1980s a few states adopted this approach and, in others, custody statutes gave priority to this factor. Recently, a new custody standard based on past parenting roles has been proposed. Rather than awarding sole custody to the primary caretaker, the *ALI Principles'* approximation standard allocates custodial responsibility *between* the parents in proportion to their caretaking roles in the intact family. This standard, which has been adopted by West Virginia (a former primary caretaker state), is responsive to many of the criticisms that have been directed toward other custody standards. Below we consider each of these approaches.

[a]   Primary Caretaker Preference

The primary caretaker presumption takes one factor under the best interest standard and designates it as the most important in choosing the custodial parent. In *Garska v. McCoy,* the West Virginia Supreme Court adopted what might be called a strong version of the presumption; the primary caretaker is awarded custody unless she is unfit. 278 S.E.2d 357 (W. Va. 1981). A weaker form would give the other parent the burden of proving that the child's interest is not served by custody in the primary caregiver. The presumption could also serve as a tie-breaker rule under the best interest standard. Indeed, it seems quite likely that courts applying the best interest standard informally utilize the weaker variations of the presumption, because of the widespread acceptance of the importance to the child of the relationship with her primary caretaker.

Garska offered the following guidelines for determining the primary caretaker:

> In establishing which . . . parent is the primary caretaker, the trial court shall determine which parent has taken primary responsibility for, *inter alia,* the performance of the following caring and nurturing duties of a parent: (1) preparing and planning of meals; (2) bathing, grooming and dressing; 3) purchasing, cleaning, and care of clothes; (4) medical care, including nursing and trips to physicians; (5) arranging for social interaction among peers after school, i.e. transporting to friends' houses or, for example, to girl or boy scout meetings; (6) arranging alternative care, i.e. babysitting, day-care, etc.; (7) putting child to bed at night, attending to child in the middle of the night, waking child in the morning; (8) disciplining, i.e. teaching general manners and toilet training; (9) educating, i.e. religious, cultural, social, etc.; and, (10) teaching elementary skills, i.e., reading, writing and arithmetic. *Id* at 363.

As compared with the best interest standard, the primary caretaker presumption substantially narrows the judicial inquiry. It shifts the court's task from predicting the future (with whom will the child be better off?) to deciding historical facts (who was the child's primary caretaker?). This rule also discourages qualitative inquiry about which parent will function more effectively to meet the child's needs. Neither parent's deficiencies (either past or future) are relevant to the decision — unless they are of such severity as to render the parent unfit to have custody. Because qualitative evidence is excluded, a parent has less incentive to focus on the failings of the spouse, an effect that may reduce acrimony in the litigation. It is clear that, in theory at least, a primary caretaker presumption is more determinate than the best interest standard and can be more easily applied by courts. Moreover, because the parties can better predict the outcome of adjudication, the presumption may also discourage strategic bargaining and generally reduce the costs of negotiation. For a discussion of the impact of different custody decision rules on divorce bargaining, see Scott, *Pluralism, Parental Preference and Child Custody*, 80 CAL. L. REV. 615, 635 (1992).

Whether the presumption results in custody decisions that promote the child's best interest depends on whether the underlying premise is correct: that nothing is more important to the child's future welfare after family dissolution than undisturbed continuity of her relationship with her primary caregiver. Many child development experts agree with this premise, at least as to younger children. It derives from attachment theory, which posits that the child forms a critical attachment to the adult who cares for his needs from infancy, and that healthy psychological development (emotional security, self esteem and the ability to form relationships later in life) is based on the stability and continuity of the child's relationship with that person. When attachment theory was developed, that relationship was presumed to be the mother-child bond, but today it is described in gender-neutral terms. *See, e.g.,* GOLDSTEIN, FREUD AND SOLNIT, BEFORE THE BEST INTERESTS OF THE CHILD (1974).

A primary caretaker rule can also be justified on fairness grounds. *See* Chambers, *Rethinking the Substantive Rules for Custody Disputes in Divorce*, 83 MICH. L. REV. 477, 499-503 (1984); Elster, *Solomonic Judgments: Against the Best Interests of the Child,* 54 U. CHI. L. REV. 1, 16-21 (1987). On this view, if the spouses implicitly divided roles in marriage, the primary caretaker has invested most of her efforts in her parenting role. Continuing to fulfill that role after divorce is likely to be extremely important to her, and the loss of custody may be devastating. Presumably, she has made sacrifices, having foregone the opportunity to have a career (and the earning capacity that goes with it). The breadwinner, on the other hand, has invested in his career and his role in rearing his children has been a more limited one. He will leave the marriage with a valuable asset — his earning capacity developed over years of work. If he also gets custody when the couple divorces, the primary caretaker leaves the marriage with little to show for her efforts. On the other hand, what if the secondary parent wanted to be the primary caretaker, but sacrificed his or her preferences in order to be the family breadwinner?

Although the primary caretaker preference has generated support among feminist and other academics, few states have formally adopted this legal standard in place of the best interest standard. The Minnesota Supreme Court adopted the presumption only to have it abolished by the legislature several years later. *Pikula v. Pikula,* 374 N.W.2d 705 (Minn. 1985) (*See* Minnesota statute, *supra*). For an analysis of the Minnesota experience, see Crippen, *Stumbling Beyond Best Interest of the Child: Reexamining Child Custody Standard Setting in the Wake of Minnesota's Four Year Experiment with the*

Primary Caretaker Preference, 75 MINN. L. REV. 427 (1990) (attributing failure of preference to broad exceptions allowed and to introduction of fault). The West Virginia legislature recently abolished the statutory presumption, replacing it with the ALI standard, outlined below. A few states rank past parental care as the most important consideration in the custody decision without creating a formal presumption. The Washington statute directs courts making "residential provisions" to give "greatest weight" to "[t]he relative strength, nature and stability of the child's relationship with each parent, including whether a parent has taken greater responsibility for performing parenting functions relating to the daily needs of the child." WASH. REV. CODE ANN. § 26.09.187(3)(a)(i) (West 1997). This statute also provides that the best interest of the child is ordinarily served when the existing pattern of interaction between a parent and child is altered only to the extent necessitated by the changed relationship of the parents or as required to protect the child from physical, mental, or emotional harm. The Washington Supreme Court, however, rejected a lower court holding that this provision creates a primary caretaker presumption. *Kovacs v. Kovacs*, 854 P.2d 629, 632 (Wash. 1993). The court recounted the legislative history of the statute — and the explicit rejection by the legislature of such a presumption — in reaching this conclusion. Other states such as South Carolina, through judicial opinion, have recognized the importance of this factor, without creating a presumption. *See, e.g., Parris v. Parris,* 460 S.E.2d 571 (1996) (father wins as primary caregiver). *See also Lamb v. Wenning*, 600 N.E. 2d 96 (Ind. 1992); *Harris v. Harris*, 546 A.2d. 208 (Vt. 1988) (rejecting primary caretaker rule, but concluding that relationship should be given great weight).

Why have courts and legislatures not embraced the primary caretaker preference as a custody rule with many advantages over the best interest standard? Some critics may reject this presumption as simply a re-creation of the tender years presumption. Although the primary caretaker test is ostensibly gender neutral, the vast majority of primary caretakers of young children are women, and most advocates are motivated to protect mothers, who, they believe, are disadvantaged under the best interest standard. In a world of changing gender roles, one might question whether the primary caretaker presumption is a very useful aid in child custody determinations. As women enter the work force and men become more involved in rearing their children, fewer parents may have traditional roles of primary caretaker and breadwinner. At present, the vast majority of married mothers who work continue to perform the bulk of child rearing responsibilities. If this pattern were to change so that many parents substantially shared child care responsibilities in the future, the primary caretaker preference may become obsolete.

If these criticisms have some merit, but maintaining the stability of the child's relationships is critical to her welfare, then perhaps what is needed is a custody rule that bases custody on past parental roles, but does not presume that one parent is the primary caretaker. This is the approach of the ALI custody standard, below.

[b] The ALI Standard — Approximation of Past Parental Roles

W. Va. Code Ann. § 48-9-206 (Michie 2001)

(a) Unless otherwise resolved by agreement of the parents . . . or unless manifestly harmful to the child, the court shall allocate custodial responsibility so that the proportion of custodial time the child spends with each parent approximates the proportion of time each parent spent performing caretaking functions for the child prior to the parents' separation or, if the parents never lived together, before the filing of the action, except to the extent . . . necessary to achieve any of the following objectives:

(1) To permit the child to have a relationship with each parent who has performed a reasonable share of parenting functions;

(2) To accommodate the firm and reasonable preferences of a child who is fourteen years of age or older, and with regard to a child under fourteen years of age, but sufficiently matured that he or she can intelligently express a voluntary preference for one parent, to give that preference such weight as circumstances warrant;

(3) To keep siblings together when the court finds that doing so is necessary to their welfare;

(4) To protect the child's welfare when, under an otherwise appropriate allocation, the child would be harmed because of a gross disparity in the quality of the emotional attachments between each parent and the child or in each parent's demonstrated ability or availability to meet a child's needs;. . . .

(6) To avoid an allocation of custodial responsibility that would be extremely impractical or that would interfere substantially with the child's need for stability in light of economic, physical or other circumstances, including the distance between the parents' residences, the cost and difficulty of transporting the child, the parents' and child's daily schedules, and the ability of the parents to cooperate in the arrangement. . . .

(b) In determining the proportion of caretaking functions each parent previously performed for the child under subsection (a) of this section, the court shall not consider the divisions of functions arising from temporary arrangements after separation, whether those arrangements are consensual or by court order. The court may take into account information relating to the temporary arrangements in determining other issues under this section.

(c) If the court is unable to allocate custodial responsibility under subsection (a) of this section because the allocation under that subsection would be manifestly harmful to the child, or because there is no history of past performance of caretaking functions, as in the case of a newborn, or because the history does not establish a pattern of caretaking sufficiently dispositive of the issues of the case, the court shall allocate custodial responsibility based on the child's best interest . . . preserving to the extent possible this section's priority on the share of past caretaking functions each parent performed. . . .

§ 48-9-207. Allocation of significant decision-making responsibility

(a) Unless otherwise resolved by agreement of the parents . . ., the court shall allocate responsibility for making significant life decisions on behalf of the child, including the child's education and health care, to one parent or to two parents jointly, in accordance with the child's best interest, in light of:

(1) The allocation of custodial responsibility under section 9-206 of this article;

(2) The level of each parent's participation in past decision-making on behalf of the child;

(3) The wishes of the parents;

(4) The level of ability and cooperation the parents have demonstrated in decision-making on behalf of the child;

. . . .

(b) If each of the child's legal parents has been exercising a reasonable share of parenting functions for the child, the court shall presume that an allocation of decision-making responsibility to both parents jointly is in the child's best interests. The presumption is overcome if there is a history of domestic abuse, or by a showing that joint allocation of decision-making responsibility is not in the child's best interest.

(c) Unless otherwise provided or agreed by the parents, each parent who is exercising custodial responsibility shall be given sole responsibility for day-to-day decisions for the child, while the child is in that parent's care and control, including emergency decisions affecting the health and safety of the child.

The West Virginia legislature adopted this statute, based on the ALI custody standard, in 1999, and repealed the state's primary caretaker preference. The adoption of the ALI standard appears to have been a legislative compromise of sorts, in response to intense pressure both from groups advocating the adoption of a joint physical custody presumption and from supporters of retaining the primary caretaker preference. A key supporter of the ALI standard argued that both of these alternative rules encouraged parents to raise allegations of unfitness against one another. Karin Fischer, *Changes in Custody Law Concern Some; Predictability of Primary Caregiver Positive, Negative,* Charleston Daily Mail, May 5, 1999, 1A.

Like the primary caretaker preference, the ALI standard directs courts to allocate custodial responsibility after divorce on the basis of parents' roles in caring for the child in the intact family. Relevant evidence would include the same tasks and duties described by the West Virginia court in *Garska*. This standard differs from the primary caretaker preference, however, in recognizing that many parents divide childrearing responsibilities in ways that do not follow the primary caretaker model. For each family, the ALI standard allocates custody after divorce to quantitatively approximate the parents' predivorce division of responsibility. Thus, a court applying this standard might order a custodial arrangement that is similar to joint physical custody, but only if the parents shared child care equally when the family was intact. On the other hand, if one parent was the primary caretaker, that parent will be awarded a greater proportion of custodial time after divorce. Moreover, under the ALI formulation, "parenting functions" are defined somewhat more broadly than caretaking, such that a traditional father who supports his children, but does little caretaking, will qualify for a minimum custody allocation. The standard also creates a rebuttable presumption that decision-making responsibility should be shared jointly, on the assumption that this is the understanding in most intact families. For a feminist defense of this standard, see Brinig, *Feminism and Child Custody Under Chapter Two of the American Law Institute's Principles of the Law of Family Dissolution,* 8 DUKE J. GENDER & L. POL. 301 (2001).

Professor Elizabeth Scott, who first proposed the approximation standard adopted by the ALI, argues that this rule effectively promotes the child's best interests. Her analysis also supports the intuition of the West Virginia legislator, *supra,* that allegations of parental unfitness may be less common under the new standard.

SCOTT, PLURALISM, PARENTAL PREFERENCE AND CHILD CUSTODY, 80 Cal. L. Rev. 615 (1992)

[T]he inquiry regarding future custody arrangements should focus on the past relationship of each parent to the child and do so in a more precise and individualized way than either the best interests standard or the reform alternatives require. The custody decision is an announcement and prescription of the future part each parent will play in the child's life over the years of her minority. There is . . . no sounder basis for this prescription than past relationships. Therefore, in most cases the law's goal should be to approximate, to the extent possible, the predivorce role of each parent in the child's life. . . .

Divorce, which by any measure is a period of upheaval in a child's life, should not be treated as an opportunity for restructuring parent-child relationships. Child development experts emphasize the harmful impact of the disruption associated with divorce, and the link between continuity of the parent-child relationship and healthy child development. Custody law can minimize disruption of the child's habitual routines and relationships after divorce by perpetuating patterns of parental care established in the intact family. A rule that preserves the continuity of family relationships would seem to reflect the best interests of the child as accurately as this elusive concept permits.

The approximation approach . . . accommodates two strands of child development research and theory that have been drawn into the policy debate over custody and are currently treated as irreconcilable. The first strand, . . . [a]ttachment theory would support the assertion that the gravest deficiency of the best interests standard is the risk of disrupting the relationship between the child and her primary caretaker. More recently, however, other researchers have suggested that the role of fathers in their children's lives has been undervalued and that attachment theory exaggerates the uniqueness and exclusiveness of the primary caretaker-child bond. Some observers argue that this research supports a stronger claim for father custody or, at least, weakens the viability of a primary caretaker preference. Taken together, these two psychological perspectives point to a legal response that does not choose between parents or split custody of the child but rather seeks to gauge the strength of existing bonds and to perpetuate them through the custody arrangement. Thus, for example, if both parents have been active caretakers, the child should not have to suffer from the disruptive effects of relegating one parent's status to that of visitor. On the other hand, if one parent's involvement and care for the child has been dominant, that strong bond should not be disturbed. The secondary role of the other parent, however, should also be recognized.

Structuring future custody [in this way] could also mitigate the observed tension between two goals of custody law: encouraging the participation of both parents after divorce and avoiding exposure of the child to excessive interparental conflict. The joint custody debate demonstrates this tension, with advocates stressing the harm of lost parental contact while opponents emphasize the detriment to the child from exposure to interparental conflict. It is plausible to assume that basing custody roles on past patterns of caretaking would provide optimal parental involvement with minimal conflict. Joint physical custody, which provides the greatest opportunity for conflict, will be ordered under this approach only if it replicates the pattern of childrearing that occurred during the marriage. In such a situation, the couple's prior experience of shared responsibility increases the likelihood of mutual commitment, competency, and respect. Thus, the prospect of a cooperative adjustment is better than it would be were new roles thrust upon parents. The resentment of joint custody by primary caretaker mothers and the potential conflict that it could generate might be reduced if custody is formulated on the basis of past roles. . . .

[The] contention that parents are generally inclined to track predivorce roles is consistent with the growing body of empirical research on custody. Children of divorce in single-parent homes are overwhelmingly in the custody of their mothers, an arrangement that is closer to patterns of parent-child relationships in most intact families than is the alternative of exclusive paternal custody. When the menu of custody arrangements expands to include joint custody, the importance of predivorce roles seems even clearer. Joint legal custody, which . . . reflects typical role allocation more accurately than does sole custody, has been accepted by both mothers and fathers and is now the prevailing norm in some jurisdictions. In comparison, parents have been less receptive to joint physical custody, suggesting that parents resist radically altering patterns of care and authority established in the intact family. Moreover, researchers in California have found that, even in custody arrangements that began as joint physical custody, children of divorce tended over time to live primarily with their mothers. This trend suggests that parents might be revealing their true preferences through their conduct, "drifting" toward arrangements that may reflect predivorce patterns of care. Parental resistance to the transformation of established roles might also contribute to the poor adjustment and high relitigation rates associated with court-ordered joint custody in which one party, usually the mother, resists the arrangement. In general, the experience with joint custody is consistent with [the] hypothesis that parents tend to accept and adapt to this innovation to the extent that it comports with past roles.

Implicit in this analysis is the conclusion that a rule that reflects parents' preferences for custody is also in the best interests of the child. . . . Parents adopt roles and functions in the family according to complex sets of values and preferences and with little legal supervision. The law can look to these family patterns as the best reflection of the parents' true preferences and the best predictor of the future stability of custody arrangements. . . .

NOTES

1. *The ALI Standard as a Decision Rule.* As a legal decision rule, the ALI standard shares many advantages with the primary caretaker preference. It is far more determinate than the best interest standard and thus should yield more predictable results. Adjudication should be easier because the inquiry is narrower and focuses on concrete facts about each parent's care of the child. As the Comment for § 208 explains:

> . . .[The standard] requires factfinding that is less likely than the traditional best-interests test to require expert testimony about such matters as the child's emotional state or developmental needs, the parents' relative abilities and the strength of their emotional relationships to the child. Avoiding expert testimony is desirable because such testimony, within an adversarial context, tends to focus on the weaknesses of each parent and thus undermines the spirit of cooperation and compromise necessary to successful post-divorce custodial arrangements. . . .

> Some parents will disagree over how caretaking roles were previously divided, making the past division of caretaking functions itself a litigation issue The difficulties in applying the standard, however, must be evaluated in light of the available alternatives. While each parent's share of past caretaking will in some cases be disputed, these functions encompass specific tasks and responsibilities about which concrete evidence is available and thus offer greater determinacy than more qualitative standards, such as parental competence, the strength of the parent-child emotional bond or . . . the child's best interests. These qualitative criteria are future oriented and highly subjective, whereas how the parents divided caretaking responsibilities in the past is a concrete question of historical fact, like other questions courts are accustomed to resolving.

A.L.I. PRINCIPLES, COMMENT, § 2.08.

Although focusing on past parenting roles will simplify fact finding in custody adjudication, it is unlikely to be error-proof. In a recent Vermont case, the court accepted the trial court conclusion that the father has "a slightly more active engagement in the children's lives," while the dissent argued persuasively that uncontested evidence suggested that the mother spent twice as many waking hours with the children as did the father. *Hoover (Letourneau) v. Hoover*, 764 A.2d 1192 (Vt. 2000).

2. *Rejection of the "Custody/Visitation" Distinction.* The second major innovative feature of the ALI Standard (besides narrowing the custody inquiry to parents' past caretaking roles) is that it abolishes the categories of custody and visitation, and instead simply directs the allocation of custodial responsibility between the parents. In part, this is a matter of terminology. A parent who played little role in childrearing when the family was together may receive an allocation of custodial time that is similar to a standard visitation award. However, the abolition of the hierarchical categories of custody and visitation has important symbolic meaning. Neither parent is relegated to the inferior status of "visitor" and the custody award is less likely to be characterized as the prize in a zero sum game. Further, as Professor Scott puts it, by rejecting traditional categories and "recognizing the role allocation that each couple has adopted, this framework removes barriers to the evolution of parental roles erected by legal rules that give exclusive custody to one parent." Scott, *supra* at 672.

3. *The Presumption of Shared Decisionmaking Authority.* The ALI Custody Principles (§ 2.09) create a rebuttable presumption that the parents will share decisionmaking authority legal custody if both have been reasonably involved in rearing the child. The presumption shifts the burden of proof on this issue to the parent opposed to joint decisionmaking to show that it is not in the child's best interests or that it is inappropriate because of a history of domestic violence. Factors relevant to this best interest determination include the past involvement of each parent in decisionmaking, and the parents' ability to cooperate. Each parent, under § 209, also has authority over day-to-day decisions while the child is in that parent's custodial care. Thus, even if the vegetarian mother has been awarded sole decisionmaking, the meat-eating father can feed the children hamburgers when they are with him. *See* Comment Sect. 2.09.

This approach reflects a modest move toward shared decisionmaking. *See* discussion of joint legal custody, Section C1 *supra*. Some commentators have argued that parents who are denied decisionmaking authority may feel disenfranchised as parents and that this may undermine their commitment to their parental role. *See* Scott, *Parental Autonomy and Children's Welfare*, Wm. & Mary Bill of Rights J. (2003). A study by Professor Judith Selzer found that joint legal custody had a positive correlation with increased visits by parents, but not with better compliance with child support orders. Selzer, *Father By Law: Effects of Joint Legal Custody on Non-Resident Fathers Involvement with Children*, 35 Demography 135 (May 1998).

PROBLEM

Problem 6-9. Elaine and Vic were married in 1990. In 1995, their son Jay was born and Elaine quit her job as a web page designer. From 1995 to 1999, Elaine remained at home caring for Jay, while Vic supported the family with his job as a college professor. In 1999, Elaine got a part-time job in a graphic design firm. Vic arranged his schedule so that he could be home in the afternoons three days a week while Elaine worked. When Jay started school in 2000, Vic met the school bus in the afternoons and stayed with Jay until Elaine arrived home at 6:00. During this time, Elaine continued to get Jay up and ready for school; she also prepared his meals, arranged play dates and doctors' appointments, bought his clothes and bathed him and put him to bed. In October 2002, Vic moved out, but he continued to meet the bus and stay with Jay until Elaine got home from work. In 2003, Elaine filed for divorce. Both parties sought custody. You are a trial judge in a jurisdiction that has adopted the ALI custody standard. How should custodial responsibility be allocated? Which parent should get custody in a jurisdiction that has adopted the primary caretaker presumption?

§ D.   RIGHTS OF THE NONCUSTODIAL PARENT

[1]   VISITATION RIGHTS

Although joint legal custody is becoming the norm in some states, most child custody decrees today give sole physical custody to one parent and "visitation rights" to the other. Access by both parents is strongly favored in the law and visitation will be granted unless the custodial parent shows that visitation is likely to lead to some serious harm or detriment to the child. *See, e.g.*, ILL. COMP. STAT. ANN. ch. 750, para. 5/607(a) (Smith-Hurd Supp. 2003) (parent not granted custody "is entitled to reasonable visitation rights unless the court finds . . . that visitation would endanger seriously the child's physical, mental, moral or emotional health"); CAL. FAM. CODE § 3100 (a) (West Supp. 2003) (visitation refused only if shown to be "detrimental to the best interests of the child"). Courts take this admonition seriously. In *Smith v. Smith*, 869 S.W.2d 55 (Ky. 1994), for example, the Kentucky Supreme Court reversed a trial court that denied visitation to a father incarcerated for murder, robbery and kidnapping, because there had been no hearing, and thus no finding that visitation would endanger the child. While courts rarely address constitutional considerations, the noncustodial parent's right to have access to his or her child is generally considered to be constitutionally grounded. *See also Damiani v. Damiani*, 2002 Fla. App. LEXIS 17138 (Fla. App. 11\20\02) (court order conditioning mother's visitation on $100,000 bond was abuse of discretion, despite her non-compliance with previous court orders to produce the child, as it would effectively eliminate visitation). *See Zummo v. Zummo, infra; see also* Chapter 9 (discussing constitutional protection of unmarried father's access to his children); Chapter 10 (discussing parental authority generally).

The strong presumption favoring visitation can be overcome, of course, in dire situations. For example, a Rhode Island court upheld a denial of visitation where the father, a convicted murderer serving a life sentence without parole, made accusations against the mother and child and evidenced "distorted thinking." *Laurence v. Nelson*, 785 A.2d 519 (R.I. 2001). Standard fact patterns for denial of visitation include violence or the threat of violence, *In re D.M.*, 771 A.2d 360 (D.C. App. 2001); drug addiction, *Soltis v. Soltis*, 470 So. 2d 1250

(Ala. App. 1985); sexual abuse, *Nelson v. Jones,* 781 P.2d 964 (Alaska 1989); severe conflict between parents, *In re Jones,* 462 P.2d 680 (Or. App. 1978); and absolute refusal by the child to cooperate, *In re Two Minor Children,* 249 A.2d 743 (Del. 1969).

Views about visitation rights are not uniform. In general, these rights are accepted as minimally fair recognition of parents who have lost full parental status. Moreover, in general, it is assumed that visitation benefits the child and is not simply a right of the non-custodial parent. This view has support in recent social science research which indicates the children benefit from meaningful contact with their noncustodial fathers. *See, e.g.* Lamb, *Noncustodial Fathers and Their Impact on the Children of Divorce,* in R. THOMPSON AND P. AMATO, EDS., THE POSTDIVORCE FAMILY 105 (1999). One tangible benefit is that non-custodial parents who are afforded the opportunity to maintain a relationship with their children may be more likely to fulfill their parental responsibilities. However, visitation rights have also been criticized, most famously in J. GOLDSTEIN, A. FREUD & A. SOLNIT, BEYOND THE BEST INTERESTS OF THE CHILD (1973). These psychoanalysts argue that in order to protect the security of the relationship between the child and the custodial parent, "the noncustodial parent should have no legally enforceable right to visit the child, and the custodial parent should have the right to decide whether it is desirable for the child to have such visits." Feminist scholar Martha Fineman makes a similar argument. M. FINEMAN, THE NEUTERED MOTHER, THE SEXUAL FAMILY, AND OTHER TWENTIETH CENTURY TRAGEDIES (1995). This view has not been adopted by courts or legislatures. One trial court was reversed on appeal when it gave a custodial mother discretion to decide about visitation by a father who had been convicted of shooting her. *Lewis v. Lewis*, 637 A.2d 70 (D.C. 1994). The appellate court made clear that the court might curtail visitation, but could not delegate this power to the mother.

ZUMMO v. ZUMMO

574 A.2d 1130 (Pa. Super. 1990)

KELLY, J. . . .

The facts and procedural history of this case were set forth by the trial court in its opinion as follows:

Pamela S. Zummo (mother) and David S. Zummo (father) were married [in 1978], separated [in 1987], and divorced [in 1988]. Three children were born of this marriage, namely Adam, age eight; Rachael, age four; and Daniel, age three. Mother was raised a Jew and has actively practiced her faith since childhood. Father was raised Roman Catholic but . . . attended Catholic services only sporadically. Prior to their marriage, mother and father discussed their religious differences and agreed that any children would be raised in the Jewish faith.

During the marriage, the Zummo family participated fully in the life of the Jewish faith and community. They became members of the

Norristown Community Jewish Center in 1983, celebrated Sabbath every Friday night and attended all of the high holiday services as well. In addition, mother and father participated in a social couples' group at their Synagogue and joined B'nai B'rith. All three of the children were formally given Hebrew names.

Before the parties separated, the children attended no religious services outside of the Jewish faith. Adam will begin preparing for his Bar Mitzvah this fall. Customary instruction would require attendance at two classes each week after school, participation in Saturday services and attendance at Sunday School. . . .

Since separation, father has refused to arrange for Adam's attendance to Sunday School while exercising visitation rights on alternate weekends. Father also wishes to take the children to occasional Roman Catholic services as he sees fit. Father suggests the children would benefit from a bi-cultural upbringing and should therefore be exposed to the religion of each parent. Mother opposes visitation by father to the extent it disrupts the formal Jewish training to the children. She further opposes exposing the children to a second religion which would confuse and disorient them.

. . . The parties agreed to share legal custody [and that] Mother should have primary physical custody subject to Father's partial physical custody on alternating weekends, as well as certain holidays and vacation periods.

[The trial court then resolved the remaining issues under the following order:]

5. Father shall be obligated during his weekend visitations to arrange for the children's attendance at their Synagogue's Sunday School. . . .

6. Father shall not be permitted to take the children to religious services contrary to the Jewish faith, however, this provision shall not be construed so as to prevent father from taking the children to weddings, funerals, or family gatherings and shall not be construed so as to prevent father from arranging for the presence of the children [at] events involving family traditions at Christmas and Easter.

Father has appealed this Order to the Superior Court, asserting that his Constitutional rights and those of his children were violated by the Order.

The trial court. . .concluded that restrictions upon the father's right to expose his children to his religious beliefs were permissible and appropriate. The trial court noted several factors in support of the challenged restrictions: the Zummo's had orally agreed prior to their marriage that any children to their marriage would be raised as Jews; during the marriage the children were raised as Jews; it was in the children's best interests to preserve the stability of their religious beliefs; the father's practice of Catholicism was only sporadic while the mother's practice of Judaism had been active; Judaism and Catholicism are irreconcilable; and, exposure to both religions might "unfairly confuse and disorient the children, and perhaps vitiate all benefits flowing from either religion.". . .

IV. *Pre-Divorce Religious Training Agreements*

In this case the parents orally agreed prior to their marriage that any children they might have would be raised as Jews. The parents, not surprisingly, had a different understanding of this vague agreement. The mother understood the agreement to envision intense and exclusive Jewish religious indoctrination with exposure to only the most secular aspects of the father's Italian/Catholic heritage. The father on the other hand explained that while he understood that their informal agreement envisioned that his children would receive formal Jewish education, he did not understand it to preclude him from exposing the children to Catholic mass and other aspects of his cultural and religious heritage on a periodic basis. The indefiniteness of the instant oral agreement precludes enforcement on ordinary contract principles as it demonstrates no meeting of minds on the critical issues. . . .

The excessive entanglement difficulties are also manifest in the instant case. The father is prohibited from taking his children to "religious services contrary to the Jewish" faith. . . . An exemption is provided for weddings, funerals, and "family gatherings and event[s] involving family traditions at Christmas and Easter." How does one determine which events are "family gatherings or events?" How broadly are "Christmas" and "Easter" defined? Do they include Advent? Epiphany? Lent? The Ascension? Pentecost? Both the subject matter and the ambiguities of the order make excessive entanglement in religious matters inevitable if the order is to be enforced.

Finally, there is a broader and more fundamental entanglement problem with enforcement of such agreements. Enforcement plainly encroaches upon the fundamental right of individuals to question, to doubt, and to change their religious convictions, and to expose their children to their changed beliefs.

The constitutional freedom to question, to doubt, and to change one's convictions, protected by the Free Exercise and Establishment Clause, is important for very pragmatic reasons. . . . [I]t would be difficult, if not impossible, for an interreligious couple engaged to be married to project themselves into the future so as to enable them to know how they will feel about religion, in order to accurately anticipate the circumstances under which religious upbringing agreements would be enforced if such agreements were given legal effect. . . . Consequently, a hopeful and perhaps naive prenuptial assurance of a future commitment to an agreed (usually vague) course of religious instruction for then as yet unborn children in the event of divorce (an often unconsidered possibility), must remain as legally unenforceable in civil courts as the wedding vows the parties even more solemnly exchanged. . . .

The decision to grant [significant] weight [to the oral pre-nuptial agreement] was constitutionally impermissible and an abuse of discretion. . . .

V. *The Children's Pre-Divorce Religious Training*

[Analyzing the mother's claim that the children were "assiduously" grounded in the Jewish faith, the court concluded that the children were] too young to assert a religious identity for themselves. . . .

Moreover, even if the children had expressed a personal religious identity it is not clear that the children would have had any constitutional right to resist, or to be protected from, attempts by either parent to exercise their constitutional rights to inculcate religious beliefs in them contrary to their declared preferences prior to their legal emancipation. . . .

VI. *Stability of Children's Religious Beliefs*

The trial court also opined that "stability and consistency in a child's religious inculcation has been recognized as an important factor in determining the best interests of a child.". . .

This Court has noted in several cases that stability with regard to with whom the children live, and where the children live, is an important consideration in custody/visitation cases. . . .

. . . We are compelled, however, to expressly disavow the suggestion . . . that governmental interests in maintaining stability in spiritual inculcation exist which could provide a justification to encroach upon constitutionally recognized parental authority and First Amendment Free Exercise rights of a parent to attempt to inculcate religious beliefs in their children. Notwithstanding the genuine comfort and reassurance a child may derive from any religion in a time of turmoil like divorce, the government simply cannot constitutionally prefer stability in religious beliefs to instability.

. . . Because government cannot presume to have any knowledge as to which if any religions offer . . . eternal rewards or repressive delusions, a child's "best interests" with regard to the spiritual aspect of religion cannot be determined by any governmental authority.

Moreover, the prohibition on preferring some religion to none, may not be avoided by suggesting that religion or religious stability is only being considered because of the secular rather than spiritual benefits expected to arise from protecting the stability of a child's religious beliefs. We are aware of the wide body of research which suggests that religiosity may be linked to various physical, intellectual, emotional, and moral benefits. While different benefits may vary between and among religions and sects, we find that even assuming that some religion may lead to more secular benefits than no religion generally, the First Amendment as construed by the United States Supreme Court nonetheless precludes a preference for some religion over none, regardless of the secular benefits presumed to be at stake. . . . The exclusion of the benefits of stability in religious inculcation and of religiosity in general are apparently part of the price which must be paid for religious freedom and constitutional recognition of parental rights.

Thus, we conclude that while the desire to provide or maintain stability in the already tumultuous context of a divorce is generally a significant factor in custody determinations, courts constitutionally cannot have any interest in the stability of a child's religious beliefs. The consideration [of the children's] presumed interests in spiritual stability was constitutionally impermissible and an abuse of discretion.

VII. *Relative Parental Devoutness*

. . . . It is clear . . . that neither determination of, nor consideration of, parents' relative devoutness or activeness in religious activities has any place in custody determinations. . . .

VIII. *Relevance of Perceived Difference in Religions*

The trial court took "judicial notice" that "the practice of Judaism and that of Roman Catholicism cannot be squared. . . . [and] that exposure of children being raised as Jews to Catholicism would harm the children. *Id.* This was improper. . . . [T]he extent to which Judaism may be "reconcilable" with Christianity involves theological and philosophical issues far beyond our ken or cognizance. . . . Consideration of the presumed irreconcilability of Judaism and Christianity in this case was constitutionally impermissible and an abuse of discretion.

IX. *Perceived Probability of Harmful Effects From Exposure to "Inconsistent" Religions*

The trial court's [principal] justification, to which each of the preceding factors were deemed to relate, was the perceived risk of harm to the children arising from their exposure to Catholicism. The trial court concluded that, "to expose the children to a competing religion after so assiduously grounding them in the tenets of Judaism would unfairly confuse and disorient them and quite possibly vitiate the benefits flowing from either religion.". . .

For children of divorce in general, and children of intermarriage and divorce especially, exposure to parents' conflicting values, lifestyles, and religious beliefs may indeed cause doubts and stress. However, stress is not always harmful, nor is it always to be avoided and protected against. The key . . . is not whether the child experiences stress, but whether the stress experienced is unproductively severe. . . .

. . . Assuming that the father's religion is or becomes a source of conflict between him and his children, it is nonetheless important that, absent unproductively severe conflict and distress, the father and the children be permitted to work through the conflict in developing their post-divorce parent-child relationships. Restrictions on this process may themselves generate stress from the artificial or incomplete nature of the exchange. For this reason too, restrictions must be imposed sparingly.

It is also important to note the problem of causation. In order for the presence of unproductive stress to provide a basis for governmental intervention in a religious upbringing dispute, the unproductively severe stress must result from the religious upbringing dispute. If the child is distressed because the parents have divorced or because of other factors unrelated to the religious upbringing dispute, imposing an orthodoxy in the child's religious training will not remove that distress. . . .

. . . [F]ar from being established "beyond dispute," our research reveals there is no objective basis to support either parental or expert predictions of future harm to a particular child based upon an assumption that such exposure is generally harmful. The caselaw, commentaries, and empirical studies all suggest, if not compel, an opposite conclusion — that while some may suffer emotional distress from exposure to contradictory religions, most do not. . . .

We hold that in order to justify restrictions upon parent's rights to [inculcate] religious beliefs in their children, the party seeking the restriction must demonstrate by competent evidence that the belief or practice of the party to be restricted actually presents a substantial threat of present or future physical or [emotional] harm to the particular child or children involved in absence of the proposed restriction, and that the restriction is the least intrusive means adequate to prevent the specified harm. Because the evidence presented in this case was wholly insufficient to meet this standard . . . [the order] forbidding the father to take his children to religious services "contrary to the Jewish faith," must be vacated.

X. *Obligations to Take Children to Religious Services*

The trial court found "little if any distinction between prohibiting the father's affirmative act of taking his children to Catholic services and its direction that the father present the children at the Synagogue for Sunday School." We, on the other hand, find a material and controlling distinction; and consequently, affirm that part of the order requiring the father to present his children at the Synagogue for Sunday School.

Both parents have rights to inculcate religious beliefs in their children. Accordingly, the trial court may constitutionally accommodate the mother's rights with a directive of the type imposed here, which essentially carves out a time period each Sunday during which the mother has the right to custody and control of the children. . . .

Here, despite the father's argument to the contrary, we find that adequate accommodation of the father's visitation right was made. The Saturday religion classes desired by the mother will be made up on weeknights. Moreover, the mother has indicated willingness to allow the father reasonable weeknight visitation to compensate for the portion of Sunday taken up by the mother's chosen religious indoctrination for her children. The mother's cooperation on this point is noteworthy and commendable. . . .

NOTES

1. *Religion and Visitation.* What exactly is the basis of the court's opinion in *Zummo*? There are various possibilities: the constraint on the court of the Establishment Clause; the father's First Amendment Free Exercise right, including his right not to be compelled to practice, or support, a particular religion; his constitutional parental right to visit his child, free from burdensome restrictions (religious or otherwise); and the child's best interests. Likewise, the mother's arguments may be seen from alternative perspectives: her own First Amendment rights; her right to control her child's upbringing, including religious training; and the child's best interests.

Is the outcome in *Zummo* determined by the fact that the parents have joint legal custody, which gives both the legal authority to make important decisions for the child? The court does not emphasize this point, although it would seem to be important. Under the court's analysis, would a court order giving one parent the authority to control the child's religious upbringing constitute an impermissible preference by the state for a particular religion (presumably in violation of the Establishment Clause of the First Amendment)? A neutral rule might be that the children's religious training and upbringing should continue in whatever tradition they followed before the divorce, absent evidence that the religious practice was harmful. Under the *ALI Principles*, decisionmaking authority can be allocated "to protect the child's ability to practice a religion that has been a significant part of the child's life." § 2.12(1)(c) (2002).

Moreover, is restriction of the noncustodial parent's right to inculcate his or her child in the parent's religious belief as problematic as the court suggests? Parents have a right to inculcate children on the basis of their parental rights, and noncustodial parents generally have more limited rights to make decisions for their children than do parents in intact families. For example, the Supreme Court has held that the right of parents to guide the child's educational upbringing is constitutionally protected under the Fourteenth Amendment. *See Meyer v. Nebraska* and *Pierce v. Society of Sisters*, Chapter 10, *infra*. Yet, noncustodial parents generally lose this right upon divorce. How is the parent's right to make decisions about religious observance different? Perhaps the restriction is based on the parent's own Free Exercise rights.

Courts have generally followed the approach of *Zummo,* restricting noncustodial parent's activities during visitation only when the custodial parent can demonstrate harm to the child. For example, a Florida court found that the custodial father's claim that he felt "uncomfortable" with mother's "charismatic" church was insufficient to justify the trial court order prohibiting the mother from taking the children to services or educating them in her religious faith. *Mesa v. Mesa*, 652 So. 2d 456 (Fla. App. 1995). *See also In re Jensen-Branch*, 899 P.2d 803 (Wash. App. 1995) (reversing an order barring noncustodial father from teaching his children the precepts of his church, the Worldwide Church of God); *Brown v. Szakal,* 514 A.2d 81 (N.J. Super. Ct. Ch. Div. 1986) (denying restriction sought by custodial mother against father's violation of Jewish Sabbath and dietary laws). In a highly publicized case dealing with non-custodial parents' inculcation rights, the Supreme Court recently held that a noncustodial father of an elementary school student lacked prudential standing to challenge in federal court the reciting of the Pledge of Allegiance in his daughter's public school. *Oak Grove Unified School Dist. v. Newdow*, 124 S. Ct. 2301 (2004). The atheist father's objection was based on the "under God" language in the pledge which the father argued was unconstitutional on Establishment Clause grounds. After the 9th Circuit Court of Appeals had ruled in favor of Newdow, the mother, who had sole legal custody, intervened in the case, arguing that it was not in her child's interest to be a party in the law suit because she and her mother were Christians. A California court enjoined the father from suing as Lisa's next friend. The Supreme Court avoided deciding the issue on the merits. Instead, emphasizing the deference of federal courts to state law in the area of domestic relations, the Court concluded that because Newdow could not sue as his daughter's next friend under California law, he lacked prudential standing to sue on her behalf in federal court. The Court noted that although Newdow had the right to instruct his daughter in his religious beliefs, he did not have the right "to forestall [her] exposure to religious ideas that her mother, who wields a form of veto power, endorses," or to "dictate to others what they may and may not say to his child respecting religion."

Restrictions on religious practice have been upheld where the custodial parent shows some actual harm to the children. The Vermont Supreme Court upheld a trial court order prohibiting a non-custodial father from taking his children to Jehovah's Witness religious meetings or inculcating them as Jehovah's Witnesses, where conflict between the religious beliefs of the mother and father was causing extreme confusion and anxiety in the children. *Meyer v. Meyer*, 789 A.2d 921 (Vt. 2001). The court found no First Amendment Establishment Clause violation, noting that it was not interfering with the father's ability to practice his religious faith or favoring one parent's religion over the other, but merely giving effect to the mother's decision as the custodial parent charged with the legal responsibility for the children. *See also Kendall v. Kendall*, 687 N.E.2d 1228 (Mass. 1997) (restriction upheld based on clear evidence that exposure to the father's Christian fundamentalist religion caused substantial harm to the children; father's beliefs included conviction that those not of his religion were damned to go to hell; beliefs distressed the children by interfering with their Jewish identities, alienating them from their mother, and forcing them to choose between their parents); *Sagar v. Sagar*, 781 N.E.2d 54 (Mass. App. 2003) (father prohibited from initiating child in Hindu religious ceremony, absent agreement of both parents); *Baker v. Baker*, 1997 Tenn. App. Lexis 837 (father's inculcation efforts in his Jehovah's Witness faith caused children's confusion and withdrawal, which the court found to be clear and affirmative harm as a result of exposure to their parents' conflicting religious beliefs).

Can you reconcile courts' refusal to restrict noncustodial parents' religious inculcation efforts with requirements that they accommodate the custodial parent's religious training of the child? Other courts have also agreed with *Zummo* on this issue. In *Nelson v. Nelson*, 736 N.Y.S.2d 532 (App. Div. 2002), an appellate court upheld an order requiring the father to return the children to their mother on weekends when he has visitation, so that she could take them to church. The court emphasized that this restriction did not impermissibly interfere with the father's own religious practices or with his visitation time. *See also Colley v. Colley*, 606 N.Y.S.2d 796 (App. Div. 1994) (Presbyterian father must take his children to Catholic mass during his visitation weekends, although the children were not baptized as Catholics until after the marital breakup).

2. *Parental Agreements About Religious Upbringing.* Note the *Zummo* court's position on the significance of premarital parental agreements about their children's religious upbringing: parents cannot be expected to anticipate the direction their religious views might take, and courts should not be "entangled" in the enforcement of any agreements parents have previously made on this subject. Do First Amendment concerns justify the refusal to enforce agreements about religious upbringing? In cases in which the parties were complying with the terms of the agreement before divorce, the contract may well represent the best evidence that exists both about what is in a child's best interests and about what is fair to the parents. New York courts have upheld agreements that the custodial parent continue the family's religious practices and traditions. *See, e.g., Smith v. Smith*, 17 FAM. L. REP.1024 (N.Y. Fam., Monroe Cty. 1990) (enforcing parental agreement that custodial mother continue to raise children as Roman Catholics, even after mother changed her religion); *Gruber v. Gruber,* 451 N.Y.S.2d 117 (1982) (enforcing parental agreement that child should attend full-time yeshiva); *Perlstein v. Perlstein,* 429 N.Y.S.2d 896 (N.Y. App. 1980) (failure of custodial mother to comply with agreement to observe orthodox Jewish practices will trigger change of custody provision, unless court determines that change of custody is detrimental to the child).

3. *Visitation and Parents' Sexual Activities*. Another issue that is often litigated involves efforts by custodial parents to restrict non-custodial parents' sexual activities during overnight visitation. A typical case involves the custodial mother's objection when the father's girlfriend spends the night while the children are visiting. Today, courts generally are reluctant to intervene, where heterosexual non-marital sexual activities are involved, unless it is shown that the parent's sexual activities are detrimental to the child. *See Kelly v. Kelly,* 524 A.2d 1330 (N.J. Super. Ct. Ch. Div. 1986). In *Kelly,* the court rejected the mother's petition to prohibit visitation "in the presence of an unrelated person of the opposite sex." She argued that, in light of the family's Catholic faith, the father's activities violated their agreement not to do anything that would have an adverse effect on the children's moral welfare. Based on the testimony of a psychologist, the court concluded that denial of visitation would be harmful to the children's development. Where the parent, as in *Kelly,* is "managing" his or her visitation activities under circumstances that appear to be sensitive to the emotional needs of the children, and where the children do not appear to be harmed, overnight visits usually will not be limited. *See, e.g., Jones v. Haraway,* 537 So. 2d 946 (Ala. Civ. App. 1988); *Nowicki v. Nowicki,* 393 N.W.2d 797 (Wis. App. 1986).

Courts have been more willing to intervene in cases involving parents in same-sex relationships. *See, e.g., J.P. v. P.W.,* 772 S.W.2d 786 (Mo. App. 1989) (trial court order banning lover from house during visitation remanded for further visitation restrictions, including supervision and no overnight visits). Some courts have gone even further, directing that the children should not be around the mother's partner during the visitation period or be exposed to a "gay lifestyle." In *Ex Parte D.W.W.,* 717 So. 2d 793 (Ala. 1998), the court concluded that any exposure could greatly traumatize the children, because the mother's conduct was immoral and criminal. *See also Marlow v. Marlow,* 702 N.E.2d 733 (Ind. Ct. App. 1998) (upholding order prohibiting gay non-custodial father from involving the children in social, religious or educational activities that were "sponsored by or otherwise promote the homosexual lifestyle"). In *Marlow,* the court justified the restrictions on the ground that the children's mother continued to raise them as fundamentalist Christians, and they were too young to understand or resolve the conflicts between their mother's and father's lifestyles. The court rejected the father's constitutional challenge, based on *Palmore v. Sidotti, supra,* that the restriction was based on private bias against homosexuality, and thus was a violation of his Equal Protection rights. Instead, the court concluded, it was based on concern for the welfare of the children.

Increasingly, courts take a different view, finding these restrictions impermissible absent a finding that the child was physically or emotionally harmed by the experiences. Thus, for example, in *Dorworth v. Dorworth,* 33 P.3d 1260

(Colo. App. 2001), a trial court order prohibiting the father from having overnight visitors during visitation (and from taking his daughter to his gay church) was reversed on appeal. The court pointed out that under Colorado's statutory provision, parenting time could not be restricted on the basis of sexual orientation, and observed that no evidence was presented that the child was physically or emotionally harmed. One court, accepting the analogy to *Palmore v. Sidotti*, rejected the argument that the child's embarrassment about others' reactions to his mother's lesbian relationship was a sufficient reason to bar visitation in the presence of the mother's lover. *Blew v. Verta*, 617 A.2d 31 (Pa. Super. 1992). *See also Eldridge v. Eldridge*, 42 S.W.3d 82 (Tenn. 2001) (upholding trial court order authorizing unrestricted overnight visitation for a lesbian mother who lived with her partner where no evidence showed that the child had been, or would be, subject to physical or emotional harm).

Many courts seem inclined to ignore or tolerate parental behavior in the visitation context that might get more attention in a custody decision. A showing of real risk of harm, of course, may result in restriction or prohibition. *See, e.g., Bacon v. Goff*, 20 Fam. L. Rep. 1012 (Rich. Cty. Fam. Ct., S.C., Oct., 8, 1993) (non-custodial mother ordered not to smoke around her asthmatic son). However, sexual conduct by parents (particularly same-sex conduct) that might be deemed important in choosing between parents in a custody dispute may not be restricted in visitation. Perhaps this is because the noncustodial parent has such a limited protected interest in his relationship with his child that courts are reluctant to burden it further. There also may be a concern that the parent might choose his sexual partner over his children if he is not permitted to continue to associate with them together. In *Kelly*, above, for example, the court did not consider ordering the father not to have his girlfriend present during visitation. It considered only the options of permitting her presence or sacrificing the children's relationship with their father. Encouraging noncustodial parents to continue to stay involved with their children is an important goal of legal regulation in this area.

4. *Child's Wishes in Visitation.* How important should the child's wishes be in resolving conflicts between parents over visitation? Note *Zummo*'s conclusion that the children's wishes as to their religious upbringing would not be considered. On the other hand, we saw that courts often give considerable weight to the preferences of children, especially older children, in deciding which parent will get custody. Generally, courts give less weight to the child's preference in visitation matters than in custodial determinations. For example, in *Roberts v. Roberts*, 371 A.2d 689 (Md. App. 1977), the court held the opposition of a 14-year-old to visitation by her mother should be given only slight consideration, if any. By comparison, a teenager's preference normally would be accorded great weight in choosing a custodian.

NOTE ON THE ENFORCEMENT OF VISITATION ORDERS

The Child's Opposition. Many circumstances can frustrate the rights of the noncustodial parent under a visitation order. First, the child may refuse to cooperate in visitation. What relief is available for the parent? Some courts will go far indeed to encourage cooperation. In *In re Marriage of Marshall*,

663 N.E.2d 1113 (Ill. App. 1996), the trial judge found two children in direct contempt for refusing to visit their father in North Carolina, and put the older (12-year-old) child in a juvenile detention facility until she agreed to go. The appellate court upheld the finding of contempt, but reversed the sanctions as inappropriate, because the trial court did not consider whether they were the least restrictive alternatives which would lead to visitation — although the appellate court did not rule out incarceration as a last resort.

A few older cases have found such refusals by children sufficient grounds for termination of child support, *e.g.*, *Tyrrell v. Tyrrell,* 359 So. 2d 62 (Fla. App. 1978), particularly if the child's uncooperative attitude is the product of the custodial parent's influence and the custodial parent has sufficient resources to care for the child without child support. *Cooper v. Cooper,* 375 N.E.2d 925 (Ill. App. 1978). In general, however, courts are reluctant to harm children by denying them support and most courts insist support and visitation are independent obligations. *See Farmer v. Farmer,* 735 N.E. 2d 285 (Ind. Ct. App. 2000). This topic is treated more extensively in Chapter 5, which deals with child support.

Breach by the Custodial Parent. The custodial parent may also frustrate visitation rights. That parent may (1) remove the child from the custodial home at visitation time; (2) report (truthfully or otherwise) that the child does not want visitation; or (3) simply refuse to permit entry into the custodial home to pick up the child.

Courts can act quite coercively to encourage the custodial parent to cooperate and to support the noncustodial parent's relationship with the child. In *Hendrikson v. Hendrikson*, 603 N.W.2d 896 (N.D. 2000), for example, the court considered (for the third time) a long and bitter dispute in which the mother seemed to work relentlessly to frustrate the father's visitation efforts and to alienate the children from him. The appellate court upheld the trial court's order transferring custody to the father, agreeing that the mother's interference with visitation in this case was a changed circumstance. The lower court's order denying the mother all visitation for a year was reversed, however; instead, the appellate court ordered supervised visitation in the mother. *Hendrikson* illustrates how difficult it is to fashion effective remedies for interference with visitation in extreme cases. In this case, custody was later returned to the mother due to the children's extreme hostility to the father. Other remedies such as an action for contempt or termination or reduction of alimony or child support payments; also may not be totally effective. In *Hendrikson,* the trial court found the mother to be in contempt, but was reluctant to put her in jail, because it thought the children would be harmed. As noted above, most courts find the duties of support independent of the right to visitation, although this may be changing. Where all else fails, as in *Hendrikson,* should this remedy be used? This is the conclusion of one commentator. Ellman, *Should Visitation Denial Affect The Obligation to Pay Support?*, in THE LAW AND ECONOMICS OF CHILD SUPPORT PAYMENTS (W. COMANOR, ED., 2003). *See* discussion of child support and visitation in Chapter 5.

An innovative remedy for parents wrongfully denied visitation rights is authorized by MICH. COMP. LAWS ANN. § 552.642 (West Supp. 2003). Under this statute, the "friend of the court" (a court official who has the responsibility for investigating custody disputes and supervising compliance with custody decrees) is authorized to formulate a makeup visitation policy. Under such a policy, a wrongfully denied visitation day can be made up at a time chosen by the noncustodial parent within one year after the wrongful denial. The makeup day shall be "the same type and duration of parenting time as the parenting time that was denied. . . ." § 552.642(1)(a). The statute provides for a referee or trial judge to determine whether there has been a wrongful denial of visitation. What kind of conduct on the part of the custodial parent should qualify?

The Non-Visiting Parent. What of the situation, not infrequent, where the noncustodial parent fails to exercise visitation rights? Instead of defining the noncustodial parent's access to the child as a right, should there be an enforceable duty to maintain the relationship with the child? An unusual Arizona statute authorizes courts to sanction defaulting parents by holding them in contempt, ordering compliance with visitation orders, requiring education or counseling or imposing fines (up to $100 per violation). ARIZ. REV. STAT. ANN. § 25-414 (West. Supp. 2002). Courts have generally declined to find such a duty (or to find that the child has a right to visitation). *See In re Mitchell,* 745 N.E.2d 167 (Ill. App. 2001). One scholar has argued that courts ought to order noncustodial parents to visit their children on a regular basis. Bruch, *Making Visitation Work: Dual Parenting Orders,* 1 FAM. ADVOCATE 22, 26 (Summer 1978). Given the recognized goal of maintaining post-divorce relationships between both parents and the child, why do you think this has not happened? Perhaps enforcement costs would be too high. What sanction would be appropriate? Professor Bruch suggests that recalcitrant noncustodial parents be required to pay the custodial parent an increased amount of child support to cover "the costs of increased child care requirements" imposed by the failure to visit. *Id.* at 42. In *Mitchell,* the court acknowledged that the purpose of the custody statute was to promote a close relationship between the child and the non-custodial parent, but questioned whether forcing visitation between the child and a reluctant parent would truly be in the child's best interest.

PROBLEMS

Problem 6-10. Lou, the custodial father, is very health conscious, and is very concerned about recent news reports of the dangers of "passive" smoking. Lily, the non-custodial mother, and Lily's parents, with whom she lives, all are smokers. Can Lou obtain a modification of Lily's visitation privileges to prevent Lily from smoking while visiting with their 6-year-old daughter, Jill? Can he get a court order requiring that all visitations occur in a smoke-free environment, even if that means overnight visitations can occur only in a hotel (which Lily cannot afford)?

Problem 6-11. Bill's favorite activity during his biweekly weekend visitations with his 8-year-old son, Eddy, is to ride mini-trail bikes around the hills and woods in a nearby state park. It is an activity which Eddy also enjoys immensely, and which gives him a great sense of accomplishment and camaraderie with his dad. Eddy's custodial mother, June, has researched the safety of the mini-bikes and found the accident rate for children Eddy's age is 20 times greater than the accident rate on normal bicycles. June has spoken with Bill about her concern for Eddy's safety, but Bill insists that it is a safe sport, that he and Eddy are careful, and that he should decide the visitation activities. June wants a court order forbidding mini-bike riding during Bill's visitation periods. Should she be successful? What should June have to prove?

Problem 6-12. Stan and Dianne are the divorced parents of a 4-year-old daughter, Nicole. Under the terms of the divorce decree, Stan has custody of Nicole and Dianne has visitation rights each summer for two weeks and every other weekend throughout the year. Nicole is enrolled in nursery school during the week. The formal program ends at 3 p.m., but Stan has made arrangements with the school to provide day care from 3 p.m. until 5 p.m. when he picks up Nicole on his way home from the office. Dianne has come to school and asked Nicole's teacher to permit her access to the child from 3 to 5 every afternoon. She has not told Stan about this. The teacher's impression is that the divorce was bitter and hard-fought. The teacher asks your advice. What is your response?

NOTE ON CUSTODY AGREEMENTS AND PARENTING PLANS

As divorce has become commonplace in the past generation or so, many commentators have advocated that children's welfare is promoted if parents assume responsibility for making decisions about their children's future custody. *See* Scott, *Parental Autonomy and Children's Welfare*, 11 Wm. & M. Bill of Rights J. 1071 (2003). The past generation has seen a trend toward private ordering of custody disputes and encouragement of parents to plan for their children's future. This trend, perhaps most evident in the enthusiasm for mediation (see Chapter 8), reflects the view that when parents can reach agreement about custody arrangements, the resulting plan may be more likely to prove satisfactory over time than one imposed by a court over the objection of one or both parents. Parents know more about their children's needs and their own preferences than a court is likely to learn in an adversary proceeding. In general, enforcement costs over the post divorce period are likely to be lower when parents participate in and agree to the custody plan. *See* E. Maccoby and R. Mnookin, Dividing the Child: Social and Legal Dilemmas of Custody, 41-42; Scott & Scott, *Parents as Fiduciaries*, 81 Va. L. Rev. 2401 (1995).

Traditionally, courts had considerable formal authority to review parents' custody agreements (although it seems unlikely that courts ever made a practice of routinely overriding parents' agreements). Even today, statutes direct courts to review agreements concerning custody and child support to determine whether the child's best interest is promoted. *See, e.g.* Alaska Stat § 25.24.220 (h), (I) (2001) (court shall review agreement to determine whether it furthers child's best interests). Such review is deemed justified on the ground that parents in the midst of divorce can not be relied on to act to promote their children's welfare. Children's rights advocates, who are generally skeptical of parental authority, see a fundamental conflict of interest between parent and child in this context that justifies active judicial oversight of parents' agreements. *See* Richards, *Redefining Parenthood: Parental Rights Verses Children's Rights,*40 WAYNE L. REV. 1227 (1994). Moreover, judicial oversight of agreements may be justified because mothers may sacrifice property and support to secure custody.

Although most states continue to recognize the *parens patriae* authority of courts to review custody agreements, the evidence suggests that parents' custody agreements rarely are set aside, suggesting that courts view arrangements agreed upon by the parents to be more likely to be successful than those imposed by a court. *See* E. MACCOBY & R. MNOOKIN, *supra*, at 41. Beyond this, some modern statutes limit judicial freedom in this area. In many states today, courts are directed by statute to approve parents' agreements unless they are found to be contrary to the child's best interest. N.J. STAT. ANN. § 9:2-4(d) (2002). Under some statutes, the court must explain why it has declined to enter a custody order based on the parents' agreement. *See* PA. CONS. STAT. ANN. § 5307 (2001) (court must state on the record the reasons for declining to base its order on the parents' agreement). A higher standard of proof is required to override parental agreements in some states. *See* MICH. COMP. LAWS ANN.§ 722.27a(2)(2001) (court must determine by clear and convincing evidence that agreement is not in child's best interest to override). Joint custody agreements are given special deference under some statutes, probably because legislatures assume courts may be more likely to set them aside. California, for example, creates a rebuttable presumption that such agreements are in the best interests of the child. CAL. FAM. CODE § 3080 (2001). *See also* CONN. GEN. STAT. § 46b-56a(b)(2001)(same).

The *ALI Principles* are strongly deferential toward parental custody agreements, directing courts to order custody on the basis of a knowing, voluntary custody agreement unless it is harmful to the child. Sect. 2.06. The Comments justify this approach on the ground that courts have neither the time nor resources to review agreements meaningfully. Moreover, an arrangement based on parental agreement is more likely to be successful than one imposed on unwilling and objecting parents. Sect. 2.06 Comment a.

A more recent development is the promotion of parenting plans. Statutory provisions in many states direct or authorize courts to order parents to plan for their children's future with some specificity. Parenting plans form the basis of custody orders that are more detailed and specific than the traditional formulations which, in the extreme, simply awarded primary custody to one parent and "reasonable visitation" to the other. Typical parenting plans include provisions for each parent's rights and responsibilities for the care of the child and for educational and health care decisions, a schedule for the child's living arrangements, including holidays and vacations, and procedures for communication and dispute resolution between parents. WASH. REV. CODE ANN. § 26.09.181 (West 1997); VT. STAT. ANN. tit. 15, § 666 (2002) (plan to include (1) physical living arrangements, (2) parent-child contact, (3) education (4) medical, dental and health care, (5) travel arrangements, (6) procedures for communicating about the child's welfare, and (7) procedures for resolving disputes).

Psychologists advocate comprehensive planning at the time of divorce as a means to promote future cooperation between parents by reducing the potential for uncertainty and misunderstandings that can lead to later conflict. R. EMERY, RENEGOTIATING FAMILY RELATIONSHIPS: DIVORCE, CHILD CUSTODY AND MEDIATION (1994). Ideally, the process of creating a parenting plan involves both parents in working together to make decisions about the child's future, and commits both to the agreements they reach. Legislative drafters of the Washington law, the first statute mandating parenting plans, described its goals along these lines — to encourage parents to take responsibility for creating a plan that reflects their individualized needs, rather than having families subject to court-devised formulas; to encourage continued participation of both parents in their children's lives through shared parenting; to focus parents on their future parental responsibilities; and to reduce conflict. *See* Ellis, *Plans, Protections and Professional Interventions: Innovations in Divorce Custody Reform and the Role of Legal Professionals*, 24 U. MICH. J.L. REFORM 65, 80-94 (1990).

States vary in the extent to which parenting plans are required in custody cases. The Washington Parenting Act requires a parenting plan in every custody case. WASH. REV. CODE ANN. § 26.09.181 et seq. (1999). More typically, plans are required when parents plan to share physical custody. ILL. ANN. STAT. ch. 750, para. 5\602.1(b)(2001); OHIO REV. CODE ANN. § 3109.04(G); MASS. GEN. LAWS ch. 208, § 31 (2001). In some states, courts have discretion to order parents to submit a parenting plan. CAL. FAM. CODE § 3040 (a)(1); MICH. COMP. LAWS § 722.27a(8).

The *ALI Principles* require all parents seeking custody to submit parenting plans to the court, and, indeed, describes the parenting plan as "the core concept" of its custody regulation. Sect. 2.05, Comment a. The requirement encourages parents to cooperate because plans to which parents agree generally must be adopted by the court. Moreover, the parenting plan concept recognizes the diversity of parenting arrangements and encourages parents to tailor their plans to accommodate their family needs. *Id.* Like many statutory provisions, the *Principles* require parents to include provisions for dispute resolution and to establish remedies in order to discourage relitigation. Sect. 2.05 (5)(c).

[2] NAMING THE CHILD

The issue of children's surnames arises typically when a custodial mother wants to change the child's surname to her own "maiden" or remarried name after divorce or when an unmarried father seeks to have the child adopt his surname. There is some traditional authority for the view that a father has a protectable interest in having his children bear his surname. *See, e.g., In re Harris*, 236 S.E.2d 426, 429 (W. Va. App. 1977), but the modern trend is to resolve disputes over the child's name under a best interest standard. In *In re Willhite*, 706 N.E.2d 778 (Ohio 1999), the court adopted the best interests standard and directed the trial court to consider several factors: the effect of the change on the child's relationship with each parent, the identification of the child as part of a family unit, the length of time the child has had the surname, the preference of a child with sufficient maturity, and whether the child's surname is different from the residential parent's and any embarrassment that might cause.

Courts increasingly have allowed name changes where the mother offers a plausible justification, despite the father's objections. *See, e.g., In re Douglass*, 205 Cal. App. 3d 1046 (1988) (granting mother's petition for name change based upon desire to avoid embarrassment to the children of having last name different from other family members). Modern courts tend to respond less positively to claims that the father's future relationship with the child will be undermined if the child does not bear his name. *See, e.g., In re Marriage of McManamy*, 18 Cal. Rptr. 2d 216 (1993) ("Kate's understanding of her father's role in her life will not be based solely on her surname, but will develop in light of his conduct and attitudes, particularly his active involvement in her life").

Courts have also responded to name change disputes arising between parents who were never married by favoring the custodial mother. The New Jersey Supreme Court has announced a "strong presumption" that the custodial parent has the right to choose the child's surname. In *Gubernat v. Deremer*, 657 A.2d 856 (N.J. 1995), the court concluded that the traditional presumption favoring the father's surname was grounded in a patriarchal legal regime and that it should not be applied today. The presumption favoring the custodial parent is rebuttable upon a demonstration by the noncustodial parent that another surname served the child's interests (for example, when the child had carried the noncustodial parent's surname for some period of time and would be confused or embarrassed by a change). *See also Workman v. Olszewski*, 993 P.2d 667 (Mont. 1999) (upholding a lower court's decision that the child should retain his mother's surname — and acknowledging preference for the father's surname in its earlier decisions); *Huffman v. Fisher*, 987 S.W.2d 269 (Ark. 1999) (rejecting decision to change surname of a child of unmarried parents to the father's name, and directing a best interest inquiry).

PROBLEM

Problem 6-13. Mary Dolan and Bill Williams were not married and separated shortly after Sarah was born. Sarah, who is now 5 years old, has used her father's surname since she was born. Mary recently married Brad Grady, who has two children living with him. Mary (now Mary Grady) would like to change Sarah's name to Grady. Bill objects to the name change. Although he only sees Sarah 2 or 3 times a year, he provides modest financial support on a regular basis. Bill objects to changing Sarah's name. Should the court order a name change?

§ E.　MODIFICATION OF CUSTODY

[1]　GENERAL PRINCIPLES

BURCHARD v. GARAY

724 P.2d 486 (Cal. 1986)

[The facts and the court's analysis of the merits of the modification petition are set forth in section B2a, *supra*. The court reversed the trial court award of custody to the father.]

. . . [W]e first consider the function of the changed-circumstance rule in child custody proceedings. In deciding between competing parental claims to custody, the court must make an award "according to the best interests of the child.". . . This test, established by statute, governs all custody proceedings. . . . The changed-circumstance rule is not a different test, devised to supplant the statutory test, but an adjunct to the best-interest test. It provides, in essence, that once it has been established that a particular custodial arrangement is in the best interests of the child, the court need not reexamine that question. Instead, it should preserve the established mode of custody unless some significant change in circumstances indicates that a different arrangement would be in the child's best interest. The rule thus fosters the dual goals of judicial economy and protecting stable custody arrangements. . . .

"The change of circumstances standard is based on principles of *res judicata*." (Sharp, *Modification of Agreement-Based Custody Decrees: Unitary or Dual Standard?* (1982) 68 Va. L. Rev. 1263, 1264, fn. 9.) The rule established in a majority of jurisdictions, which we here endorse, applies [the changed circumstances] standard whenever custody has been established by judicial decree. A minority of states . . . [apply] it only when custody was determined through an adversarial hearing. No state, so far as we have ascertained, applies the changed-circumstance standard when there has been no prior judicial determination of custody.

Ana [the child's mother] argues that the trial court erred in failing to apply the changed circumstance rule [on the grounds that, although there was no prior custody determination, she has had custody for a significant period. Thus, she argues, the father] should have the burden of persuading the court that a change in custody is essential or expedient for the welfare of the child. We agree in substance with this argument: in view of the child's interest in stable custodial and emotional ties, custody lawfully acquired and maintained for a significant period will have the effect of compelling the noncustodial parent to assume the burden of persuading the trier of fact that a change is in the child's best interest. That effect, however, is different from the changed-circumstance rule, which not only changes the burden of persuasion but also limits the evidence cognizable by the court.

. . . .

The contrary [rule that the changed-circumstance standard protects a "de facto" custody arrangement[3] is in our opinion unsound, unworkable, and potentially harmful. It is unsound because, absent some prior determination of the child's best interests as of some past date, the courts have no warrant to disregard facts bearing upon that issue merely because such facts do not constitute changed circumstances. It is unworkable because . . . absent such a prior determination the courts have no established basis on which they can assess the significance of any change. And it is potentially harmful because it could compel the court to make an award inconsistent with the child's best interest.[5]

. . . .

In most cases, of course, the changed-circumstance rule and the best interest test produce the same result. When custody continues over a significant period, the child's need for continuity and stability assumes an increasingly important role. That need will often dictate the conclusion that maintenance of the current arrangement would be in the best interests of that child. But there will be occasional cases where it makes a difference. Consider, for example, a case in which a couple separate, and in the emotional turmoil of the separation the less suitable spouse takes custody of the child. In a later custody proceeding, the noncustodial parent may be able to prove that the custodial parent is unable to provide proper care, but not that his or her ability to do so has deteriorated since the separation. In such a case the changed-circumstance rule might require the court to confirm a custody not in the best interest of the child. Or, to take another example, a child may be born out of wedlock to a woman who for some reason is not able to give it suitable care. The changed-circumstance rule would require the father, when he seeks custody, to prove not only that the mother is unsuitable, but that she has become more so since the baby's birth. In this example, the changed-circumstance rule again might require the court to endorse a custodial arrangement harmful to the child.[7]

. . . .

We conclude that custody in the present case should be decided on the basis of the best interests of the child without requiring William to prove in addition that changed circumstances render it essential that he receive custody. . . .

---

[3] The parties use the term "de facto custody" to refer to custody established without a court order. Strictly speaking, Ana's custody of William, Jr., was "de jure," since under Civil Code section 197 as a matter of law an unmarried woman acquires sole custody of her child at birth when there is no presumed father.

[5] The risk of harm to the child would be reduced, but not eliminated, by requiring a rather long period of custody before it becomes "significant" enough to invoke the changed-circumstances rule. . .

[7] To avoid the danger that the changed circumstances rule might dictate a result harmful to the child's best interests, Justice Mosk's concurring opinion suggests two possible ways to modify that rule. The first is that "when the noncustodial parent shows that custody has remained unchanged but inadequate since its inception, he need prove only that a change is essential or at least expedient for the welfare of the child in order to obtain custody." We assume that "welfare of the child" is equivalent to "best interests of the child." If so, this proposal would permit the noncustodial parent to prevail by showing that a change in custody would promote the best interests of the child as demonstrated by either changed or unchanged circumstances. So modified, the changed-circumstances test is identical to the statutory best-interests test.

[The trial court abused its discretion.]

MOSK, J., concurring. I concur in the reversal . . . but strongly disagree with the manner in which the majority reach that result. . . .

. . . .

. . . [T]he limited application of the changed-circumstances rule that the majority adopt is in conflict with the primary purpose of the rule. The child whose custody was established by means other than judicial decree has the same need for and right to stability and continuity — and accordingly the same entitlement to the protection the rule is intended to provide — as the child whose custody was established by judicial decree. Because it is not unreasonable to assume that the children of two-parent and relatively more affluent families are disproportionately represented in the class of children whose custody was originally established by judicial decree, the majority's holding, I fear, will effectively deny needed protection disproportionately to children of single-parent and less affluent families.

. . . .

The [majority states that absent a prior determination of the child's best interests], "courts have no established basis on which they can assess the significance of any change." But "[i]dentification of a base line against which to measure a subsequent change of conditions is not as difficult as the [majority] suggest. The simple fact is that a demonstration of changed conditions does not normally require a preexisting record of all the facts that prevailed at the time [custody was originally established]. . . .

NOTES

1. *The Changed-Circumstances Rule.* "The traditional custody modification standard allows modification of an initial custody decree if the court determines that a subsequent, substantial change of circumstances warrants a change of custody in order to promote the best interests of the child." Wexler, *Rethinking the Modification of Child Custody Decrees,* 94 YALE L.J. 757, 761 (1985). As it is usually described, the rule requires that the changed circumstances must have occurred since the degree was entered and have been unanticipated by the parties. *Lizzio v. Jackson,* 640 N.Y.S.2d 330 (N.Y.App. Div. 1996) (asthmatic child's allergic reaction to custodial mother's smoking is not a changed circumstance, since mother smoked at time of divorce). While this rule is well-grounded in the principle of *res judicata* and also comports with the widely held view that a child's interest is best served by stable custody orders, courts vary a great deal in their conclusions about what constitutes a sufficient change of circumstance to warrant a change of custody. For some, the threshold is quite low. *See, e.g., Marriage of Richardson,* 622 N.E.2d 178 (Ind. 1993) (age change from 8 to 12 and increased interest in athletics was sufficient change of circumstance to modify custody); *Butland v. Butland,* 1996 WL 362038 (Ohio Ct. App.) (children's preference together with their desire to participate in extracurricular activities were changed circumstances). Others apply a stricter test. *See, e.g., Pierce v. Pierce,* 620 N.E.2d 726 (Ind. App. 1993) (significant improvement in mother's depression is not a change of circumstances). Remarriage (or marriage, in the case of

unmarried parents) of either the custodial and noncustodial parent is some-times viewed as a changed circumstance, but generally remarriage alone will not warrant a change of custody. *Porter v. Porter*, 298 S.E.2d 130 (W.Va. 1982) (custodial mother's remarriage is changed circumstance warranting custody reconsideration, but alone creates no presumption that change of custody is warranted); *Seeley v. Jaramillo*, 727 P.2d 91 (N.M. App. 1986). The modifica-tion rules in the *ALI Principles* follow this approach. Sect. 2.15 (3)(b) (2002).

2. The Exceptions. Some jurisdictions apply a relaxed standard when the original custody award was based upon a settlement agreement or a default judgment, allowing facts that occurred before the custody order to be consid-ered, because they were never formally adjudicated. *See, e.g., Wetch v. Wetch,* 539 N.W.2d 309 (N.D. 1995) (when original custody is based on settlement agreement or default judgment, it was error not to consider pre-divorce conduct); *Hill v. Hill,* 620 P.2d 1114 (Kan. 1980) (default judgment). *See also* DEL. CODE ANN. TIT. 13, § 729 (2001) (order based on parties' consent may be modified under best interest standard; order entered after full hearing on the merits may not be modified within two years, absent endangerment or emotional impairment). Given that more than 90% of custody arrangements are based on parental agreement, (*see* E. MACCOBY & R. MNOOKIN, DIVIDING THE CHILD: SOCIAL AND LEGAL DILEMMAS OF CUSTODY 137 (1992)), this exception has the effect of severely undercutting the rule. Justice Mosk, in his *Burchard* concurrence, rejects this approach:

> . . . [T]he fact remains that even when custody is not adjudi-cated. . . ., we may nevertheless presume that such custody is in the child's best interest and as a result require the noncustodial parent to show that a material change of circumstances has subsequently occurred.
>
> Such a presumption is justified when custody is established by agreement. "First, most parents genuinely love their children, and it is reasonable to assume that the children's welfare is a vital consider-ation in the parents' decision to resolve their dispute by agree-ment. . . . Second, parents have a better informational base upon which to make a decision about custody. The adversarial process is an inadequate means to assemble sufficient 'facts' to resolve custodial disputes satisfactorily. Third, it is difficult to protect a child from the painful pull of divided loyalties when his parents fail to agree. Parental agreements help to preserve an atmosphere of at least superficial peace between parents and thereby facilitate a much easier and more meaningful future relationship between the child and the non-custodial parent." (Sharp, *Modification of Agreement-Based Cus-tody Decrees: Unitary or Dual Standard?* (1982), 68 VA. L. REV. 1263, 1280.)

The California Supreme Court has revisited and somewhat qualified the *Burchard* approach recently, holding that the modification of an initial custody order is subject to the changed circumstances rule only if the parties clearly intended that the stipulated order was a final judgment. *Montenegro v. Diaz,* 27 P.3d 289 (Cal. 2001). The court upheld the trial court's application of the best interest standard to a father's request that the earlier stipulated order be modified to provide for joint physical custody, because it was not clear that the parties had intended that the stipulated order be final. In the court's view, stipulated orders are often meant to be temporary, and parties would be wary of entering such orders if they were treated as final judgments.

Some courts simply abandon any rule of *res judicata* when the facts of the individual case seem compelling enough. The usual justification is that, in the end, the best interests of the child must always be the predominant consideration. *See, e.g., Elmer v. Elmer,* 776 P.2d 599 (Utah 1989) ("the *res judicata* aspect of the rule must always be subservient to the best interests of the child").

3. *De Facto Custody Arrangements. Burchard* holds that the changed-circumstances rule should apply only to court-ordered, not to de facto, custody arrangements. Other courts treat both situations alike, as Justice Mosk urges in his concurrence, requiring proof of changed circumstances in both situations.

> First, as between the parent who undertakes to provide care and the parent who fails or refuses to do so, custody with the former must be deemed to serve the child's best interests. Thus, it is altogether reasonable to require the latter to demonstrate changed circumstances should he subsequently attempt to obtain custody. Second, as Dr. Andrew Watson, psychiatrist and professor of law, has observed, stability is "practically the principal element in raising children" and "a child can handle almost anything better than he can handle instability."

For consistency, should a jurisdiction use the same approach for *de facto* arrangements as for settlement agreements? Montana, for example, which applies the changed-circumstances rule to orders based upon a settlement agreement or a default judgement (*In re Marriage of Hay,* 786 P.2d 1195 (Mont. 1990)), also applied the rule to a *de facto* custody arrangement, on the theory that stability in such an arrangement was as important as stability of court-ordered arrangements. *See Andre v. Bobson (McAllister),* 761 P.2d 809 (Mont. 1988).

4. *Future-Oriented Provisions in Custody Orders and Agreements.* Custody orders and agreements sometimes include provisions directing that custody arrangements be changed in the future. The question sometimes arises whether such provisions should be enforced or are subject to the modification rule. Particularly in jurisdictions that require parenting plans, this issue may arise, because parenting plans frequently include provisions for future modifications of the plans. *See Ellis, Plans, Protections, and Professional Interventions: Innovations in Divorce Custody Reform and the Role of Legal Professionals* 24 U. MICH. J. L. REF. 65, 144 (finding 23 % of plans in King Co., Wash. include future modification provision provisions). The *ALI Principles* note this development and takes the position that provisions in a parenting plan that deal with future changes in custodial arrangements under certain conditions should be treated as implementations and not modifications of the plan. § 2.15, Comment b. For example, provisions in the plan directing a change of custody when the child reaches a certain age or when a custodial parent relocates should not be subject to the changed circumstances rule. This stance is compatible with the general deference to parental agreements. *See Principles,* § 2.06 (directing courts to adopt parents' agreements, unless harmful to the child).

Some courts reject *in futuro* provisions in agreements and court orders. The North Dakota Supreme Court refused to enforce a provision in the custody agreement of two Air Force personnel (and included in the divorce judgment) that custody would be transferred to the father if the custodial mother accepted an assignment to be transferred out of state. *Zeller v. Zeller,* 640 N.W.2d 53 (N.D. 2002). When the mother was assigned to Fort Leonard Wood, Mo., she petitioned to relocate and the father sought to enforce the custody-change provision. The appellate court rejected the trial court's order changing custody to the father, finding the stipulation to change custody to be unenforceable as against public policy. The trial court, instead, should have applied the standard for considering a petition by the custodial parent to relocate. *See also Frauenshuh v. Geise,* 599 N.W.2d 153 (Minn. 1999) (rejecting stipulation in divorce agreement that best interest standard be applied to modification; holding parties must apply state standard based on endangerment). Court orders directing future custody changes have also been rejected. A Maryland court reversed a Solomonic custody order awarding custody of the two-year-old child to his mother until 30 days following the completion of the fifth grade, at which time custody was to go to the father, who would have custody until the child was eighteen years old. *Schaefer v. Cusack,* 722 A.2d 73 (Md. Ct. App. 1998). The appellate court held that modification of custody must be based on a contemporaneous assessment of whether substantial changed circumstances exist that warrant the change. "We have not the faintest idea of what the situation of the parents may be at the time when this child finishes the fifth grade . . . [or] what effect a change of custody might have on the child." 722 A.2d at 78. Would such a provision in an agreement between the parents be enforceable under the *Principles*?

5. *Time Limitations on Modification Actions.* Many statutes prohibit modification petitions made within a short time after the initial custody decree. A typical period is two years after the most recent court order, although some statutes have shorter periods. *See* COLO. REV. STAT. § 14-10-131(1) (2000) (two years after most recent decree); WIS. STAT. ANN. § 767.325 (1) (2001) (two years after initial order). These provisions seek to promote stability in the custodial arrangements and to deter petitions by disgruntled non-custodial parents. Exceptions to these rules are often allowed where the child's health or emotional well-being is endangered, or where the custodial parent can no longer care for the child. *See e.g.,* the Arizona provision ARIZ. REV. STAT. ANN. § 25-403(T) (modification allowed if court believes current environment may endanger child's "physical, mental, moral or emotional health"); *Naylor v. Kindred,* 620 N.E.2d 520 (Ill. App. 1993) (custodial mother incarcerated).

6. *Modification Actions Affecting Joint Custody.* Should the rule for modification of joint custody awards be different from other awards? Some states have abandoned the changed circumstances rule in this context, based on an implicit (and sometimes explicit) concern that joint custody arrangements may be undesirable if cooperation between the parents breaks down, but that this may not be seen as a basis for modification. A few courts have resolved the problem by explicitly holding that the parents' inability to cooperate is a material changed circumstance, warranting modification. *See, e.g., Word v. Remmick*, 58 S.W.3d 422 (Ark. App. 2001). Other courts have held that the changed circumstance rule does not apply to joint custody arrangements, and that petitions to modify joint custody should be considered under the best interest standard. *In re Pasquale*, 777 A.2d 877 (N.H. 2001). In this case, both parents agreed that the joint custody arrangement was not working, but the mother, after losing custody, challenged the use of the best interest standard. *See Lewis v. Lewis*, 557 S.E.2d 40 (Ga. App. 2001); *Weigle v. Weigle*, 43 P.3d 740 (Colo. Ct. App. 2002). *See* Utah Code Ann. § 30-3-10.4(1) (a) (2001) (joint legal custody order can be modified if unworkable or inappropriate under the circumstances).

Jurisdictions that favor joint custody, on the other hand, have made modification of sole custody to joint custody easier than other modifications. *See, e.g. In re Marriage of Wall*, 868 P.2d 387 (Colo. 1994) (joint custody statute requires best interests standard, rather than a change of circumstance standard for modification from sole custody to joint custody); *Karis v. Karis*, 544 A.2d 1328 (Pa. 1988). A few courts have held that to modify a joint custody award, a higher standard is appropriate. *See, e.g., In re Burke*, 541 N.E.2d 245 (Ill. App. 1989) (change from joint custody requires "clear and convincing evidence" of changed circumstances, even where parents have agreed to change).

PROBLEM

Problem 6-14. Elwyn consults you about obtaining a modification of a court order issued two years ago giving custody of his children to his former wife Mary. Two weeks after the decree, Elwyn remarried. He and his wife have had a child, and Elwyn's wife stays at home to care for the child. Also since the decree, Mary has gone back to work and sought psychotherapy for periodic depression. The children are now ages 9 and 14.

Would any of these factors be relevant to Elwyn's attempt to obtain a modification order? Should they be sufficient to justify modification if the court concluded that it was in the best interests of the children? What if Elwyn simply wants a modification to give him joint legal custody and increase his visitation time?

[2] THE PROBLEM OF RELOCATION

MARRIAGE OF LAMUSGA

88 P.3d 81 (Cal. 2004)

MORENO, J.

. . . .

Susan LaMusga . . . filed [a] petition for dissolution of marriage on May 10, 1996, and requested sole physical custody of the children [Garrett, age 4 and Devlen, age 2], who were living with her in the family residence. The father objected and requested joint legal and physical custody. . . .

[T]he superior court awarded the parties joint legal custody of the children, with the mother having "primary physical custody". . . .

The mother subsequently married Todd Navarro and, on September 16, 1999, gave birth to a daughter. The father also remarried. His wife, Karin, has a daughter from her prior marriage.

On February 13, 2001, the mother filed an order to show cause to modify the visitation order to permit her to relocate with the children to Cleveland, Ohio. She alleged that she had family in the Cleveland area and her husband had received an offer for a more lucrative job there. . . .

The father objected to the mother's plan to move the children to Ohio and asked that primary custody of the children be transferred to him if the mother moved to Ohio. The father declared that the mother had attempted to alienate him from their sons since their separation and feared that moving the boys to Ohio would result in his "being lost as their father."

. . . . The court . . . [appointed] Dr. Stahl "to [evaluate] whether the relocation of the parties' two minor children is in the best interest of said children."

Dr. Stahl's . . . report notes that the mother has wanted to move ever since the divorce. . . . The move would improve her family's "economic standard of living, and . . . inherent quality of life. . . ." The mother "believes that she will have no difficulty supporting the boys in their relationship with their dad," asserting ". . . . that she is not a contributor to any alienation that the boys might feel. . . ."

Dr. Stahl was concerned "that the boys might not maintain any positive relationship with their dad if they move," noting that such a loss "would be significant." But he added that this "must be balanced with the potential losses that the boys might experience if their mother moves, and they stay," observing: "They have been in the primary care of their mother since the parents' divorce and they will likely have a significant loss [if] she moves without them. They also have a very close relationship with their sister Aisley, as well as Todd, and they will feel those losses as well. Third, they have their own desire to move. . . . If they don't move, they're likely to feel that their wishes aren't being heard." Dr. Stahl also observed that forcing the children to remain in California could cause them to further reject their father. . . .

Although the mother stated that she wanted to move to Ohio because that "is where she is originally from and where she has family support," Dr. Stahl suggested an additional motive: "Underneath, however, it has always appeared that [the mother] has wanted to move so that she can remove herself and the boys from the day-to-day interactions with [the father]. She has difficulty dealing with him and prefers to have as little communication with him as possible.". . .

Dr. Stahl [recommended that . . . the mother should not be permitted to move the children to Ohio, stating: "[T]here is no evidence that. . .[the mother] will really do what she said she will do. . . [i]n terms of being supportive of the boys' relationship with their father. . . . [I]t is still a tenuous relationship. . .[that could] get worse if the move is allowed."

Dr. Stahl acknowledged that the father also bore some of the responsibility for his strained relationship with his sons. . . . [H]e contributes to the children's alienation to the extent he perpetuates his conflict with the mother.

The [superior] court acknowledged that the mother is not purposely trying to alienate the children from their father, but noted that the mother's inability to "let go" of her anger toward the father caused her to project those feelings onto their children and to reinforce the children when they expressed negative feelings toward their father. . . . The court also acknowledged that this was not "a bad faith move away. I don't think this is an instance where [the mother is] attempting to relocate with the children for the specific purpose of limiting their contact or relationship with their father". . . .

"The primary importance, it seems to me at this point, is to be able to reinforce what is now a tenuous and somewhat detached relationship with the boys and their father. . .[A] relocation of the children out of. . .California . . . would inevitably under these circumstances be detrimental to their welfare. . . . If [the mother] wishes to relocate to the state of Ohio, certainly she is entitled to do that. Should she choose to do so, then I [order] primary physical custody of the children, at least during the school year, to Mr. Lamusga. . . . [I]f [the mother] decides not to relocate, then the existing custodial arrangement will remain."

The mother appealed and the Court of Appeal reversed the judgment. . . . We granted review. . . .

[In *In re Marriage of Burgess,* 13 Cal. 4th 25 (1996),][w]e observed that "[i]n an initial custody determination, the trial court has 'the widest discretion to choose a parenting plan that is in the best interest of the child.' (Fam.Code, § 3040, subd. (b).)." . . . Citing Family Code section 7501, which states that "[a] parent entitled to custody of a child has a right to change the residence of the child, subject to the power of the court to restrain a removal that would prejudice the rights or welfare of the child," we noted that the court must also consider "the presumptive right of a custodial parent to change the residence of the minor children, so long as the removal would not be prejudicial to their rights or welfare." . . .

We rejected the Court of Appeal's holding that the mother was required to show that it was "necessary" for her to move. . . .

Although *Burgess* involved an initial determination of custody, we held that "the same conclusion applies when a parent who has sole physical custody under an *existing* judicial custody order seeks to relocate:" . . . . But we recognized that, as with any allegation that "changed circumstances" warrant a modification of an existing custody order, the noncustodial parent has a substantial burden to show that "'some significant change in circumstances indicates that a different arrangement would be in the child's best interest.' . . . ." In a 'move-away' case, a change of custody is not justified simply because the custodial parent has chosen, for any sound good faith reason, to reside in a different location, but only if, as a result of relocation with that parent, the child will suffer detriment rendering it "essential or expedient for the welfare of the child that there be a change."

We were quick to emphasize, however, that "bright line rules in this area are inappropriate: each case must be evaluated on its own unique facts. Although the interests of a minor child in the continuity and permanency of custodial placement with the primary caretaker will most often prevail, the trial court, in assessing 'prejudice' to the child's welfare as a result of relocating even a distance of 40 or 50 miles, may take into consideration the nature of the child's existing contact with both parents . . . and the child's age, community ties, and health and educational needs. Where appropriate, it must also take into account the preferences of the child. . . .

Recently, the Legislature codified our decision in *Burgess* by amending Family Code section 7501 to add subdivision (b), which reads: "It is the intent of the Legislature to declare[*Burgess*] to be the public policy and law of this state."

[The Court then reviewed several cases applying *Burgess*, most of which upheld decisions by lower courts permitting relocation, including two cases permitting relocation to Australia and Isreal, the custodial mothers' homes. The Court emphasized the broad discretion allowed lower courts. In one of the few cases in which an appellate court reversed the superior court's granting permission to relocate, the trial court considered only whether the custodial parent was acting in bad faith and failed to consider whether 'as a result of relocation with [the custodial] parent, the child will suffer detriment rendering it " 'essential or expedient for the welfare of the child that there be a change.]

The Court of Appeal in the present case held that the superior court abused its discretion [because it] "neither proceeded from the presumption that Mother had a right to change the residence of the children, nor took into account this paramount need for stability and continuity in the existing custodial arrangement. Instead, it placed undue emphasis on the detriment that would be caused to the children's relationship with Father if they moved." We disagree.

We reaffirm our statement in *Burgess* that "the paramount need for continuity and stability in custody arrangements — and the harm that may result from disruption of established patterns of care and emotional bonds with the primary caretaker — weigh heavily in favor of maintaining ongoing custody arrangements. But there is nothing in the record before us that indicates that the superior court failed to consider the children's "interest in stable custodial and emotional ties" with their mother. . . . The court placed "primary importance" on the effect the proposed move would have on "what is now a tenuous and somewhat detached relationship with the boys and their father," concluding that the proposed move would be "extremely detrimental" to the children's welfare because it would disrupt the progress being made by the children's therapist in promoting this relationship. . . . In future cases, courts would do well to state on the record that they have considered this interest in stability, but the lack of such a statement does not constitute error and does not indicate that the court failed to properly discharge its duties. . . .

. . . . [T]he superior court's function in determining custody is not to reward or punish the parents for their past conduct. . . . But this does not mean that the court may not consider the past conduct of the parents in determining what future arrangement will be best for the children. . . .

. . . . The court was correct that the situation might have been far different had the parents shown a history of cooperative parenting. If that had been the case, it might have appeared more likely that the detrimental effects of the proposed move on the children's relationship with their father could have been ameliorated by the mother's efforts to foster and encourage frequent, positive contact between the children and their father. . . . [T]he court concluded that the mother's past conduct made it unlikely that she would facilitate the difficult task of maintaining the father's long-distance relationship with the boys.

The Court of Appeal was concerned about the superior court's reliance upon the detriment to the children's relationship with their father that would be caused by the proposed move, because "[t]here is inevitably a significant detriment to the relationship between the child and the noncustodial parent" whenever the custodial parent relocates with the children. . . . We do not suggest that a showing that a proposed move will cause detriment to the relationship between the children and the noncustodial parent *mandates* a change in custody. But it is within the wide discretion of the superior court to order a change of custody based upon such detriment, if such a change is in the best interests of the children in light of all the relevant factors. . . .

. . . . [T]he Court of Appeal in [*In re Marriage of Edlund & Hales*] may have inadvertently generated some confusion when it stated as a general conclusion: "The showing of 'changed circumstances' required of the noncustodial parent must consist of more than the fact of the proposed move". . . .

. . . . [S]ome courts have mistakenly interpreted [this] statement. . . to mean that the likely consequences of a proposed move can never constitute changed circumstances that justify a reevaluation of an existing custody order. . . This is incorrect. The likely consequences of a proposed change in the residence of a child, when considered in the light of all the relevant factors, may constitute a change of circumstances that warrants a change in custody, and the detriment to the child's relationship with the noncustodial parent that will be caused by the proposed move, when considered in light of all the relevant factors, may warrant denying a request to change the child's residence or changing custody. . . .

The Court of Appeal in the present case held that the father bore the burden of showing "that modification of custody is essential for the child's welfare". . . . In doing so, the Court of Appeal placed too great a burden on the noncustodial parent in a move-away case.

. . . . A change in custody is "essential or expedient" within the meaning of *Burgess,* therefore, if it is in the best interests of the child.

The Court of Appeal in the present case further concluded that the superior court improperly used its conditional order transferring primary physical custody to the father as a device to restrain the mother from relocating. We agree that a court must not issue such a conditional order for the purpose of coercing the custodial parent into abandoning plans to relocate. . . . There is nothing to indicate that the order transferring primary physical custody of the children to the father if the mother relocated was issued to coerce the mother into abandoning her plans to move.

The mother places great emphasis on the superior court's finding that she was not acting in "bad faith." . . . .

. . . . In . . . [*Burgess*], we observed that ". . . . Once the trial court determined that the mother did not relocate in order to frustrate the father's contact with the minor children, but did so for sound 'good faith' reasons, it was not required to inquire further into the wisdom of her inherently subjective decisionmaking." . . . .

In *In re Marriage of Bryant,* 91 Cal. App. 4th 789, . . . the Court of Appeal . . . overstate[d] the importance of the superior court's finding that the mother was not acting in bad faith, holding that once the superior court found that the mother was not acting in bad faith, "[n]o further inquiry [into the reasons for the proposed move] was necessary or appropriate." . . . .

This is not what we said in *Burgess.* . . . [W]e did not say that the reasons for a proposed move are irrelevant if the custodial parent is acting in good faith. . . .

Even if the custodial parent has legitimate reasons for the proposed change in the child's residence and is not acting simply to frustrate the noncustodial parent's contact with the child, the court still may consider whether one reason for the move is to lessen the child's contact with the noncustodial parent and whether that indicates, when considered in light of all the relevant factors, that a change in custody would be in the child's best interests.

. . . . [T]his area of law is not amenable to inflexible rules. Rather, we must permit our superior court judges — guided by statute and the principles we announced in *Burgess* and affirm in the present case — to exercise their discretion to fashion orders that best serve the interests of the children in the cases before them. Among the factors that the court ordinarily should consider when deciding whether to modify a custody order in light of the custodial parent's proposal to change the residence of the child are the following: the children's interest in stability and continuity in the custodial arrangement; the distance of the move; the age of the children; the children's relationship with both parents; the relationship between the parents including, but not limited to, their ability to communicate and cooperate effectively and their willingness to put the interests of the children above their individual interests; the wishes of the children if they are mature enough for such an inquiry to be appropriate; the reasons for the proposed move; and the extent to which the parents currently are sharing custody. . . .

The judgment of the Court of Appeal is reversed and the matter is remanded to that court with directions to affirm the superior court's postjudgment order transferring custody of the children to the father if the mother moves to Ohio. . . .

Dissenting Opinion by KENNARD, J.

A parent with custody of minor children has a "presumptive right" to change the children's residence. (*In re Marriage of Burgess* (1996) 13 Cal. 4th 25, 32, 38; see also Fam.Code, § 7501.) A noncustodial parent opposing such a change of residence bears the initial burden of showing that the move will cause some detriment to the children. Once this showing of detriment has been made, the trial court must then weigh the likely effects on the child's welfare from moving with the custodial parent, against the likely effects from a change in custody. Only if the child's interests are better served by changing custody than by relocating with the custodial parent may a court order custody transferred to the other parent.

Here, the trial court's explanation for its ruling shows that it properly considered how relocation to Ohio might detrimentally affect the children — including the impact on their tenuous relationship with their father. But the trial court was also required to weigh this detriment against the detriment that would result from removing the boys from the mother's custody. This the court did not do. In its statement of reasons, the court said: ". . . . *The issue is the effect on these children of relocating, and the effect of the relationship with their father if they are permitted to relocate.*" (Italics added.) But the effect of the relocation on the children's relationship with the father . . . just one of the potential detriments shown by the evidence that the trial court was required to consider. Equally important was the potential detriment from disrupting the existing custodial arrangement by transferring custody from the mother to the father.

This court has stressed that the "paramount need for continuity and stability in custody arrangements — and the harm that may result from disruption of established patterns of care and emotional bonds with the primary caretaker — weigh heavily in favor of maintaining ongoing custody arrangements." (*In re Marriage of Burgess, supra,* 13 Cal. 4th at pp. 32-33.) Here, the trial court's explanation for its ruling provides no assurance that the trial court gave any weight to the importance of continuity and stability in custody arrangements.

. . . . [A] trial court abuses its discretion whenever it applies the wrong legal standard to the issue at hand. . . .

. . . . [N]othing in the record indicates that the court [considered the children's 'interest in stable custodial and emotional ties' with their mother]. . . . In the absence of such a statement, or some other evidence in the record showing that the trial court affirmatively considered and weighed the required factors, I cannot conclude that the trial court properly exercised its discretion.

NOTES

1. *The Dilemma of Relocation*. Almost one half of Americans move in a five year period, according to the U.S. Bureau of the Census statistics. Thus the legal response to a custodial parent's desire to relocate is a very important issue. These cases "present some of the knottiest and most disturbing problems" that courts face *Tropea v. Tropea*, 642 N.Y.S.2d 575 (1996), pitting the custodial parent's wish to better her circumstances by moving to a place where presumably she can have a better life against the noncustodial parent's desire to continue to have a relationship with his child that involves frequent contact.

The custodial parent's claim may be compelling. If she was the homemaker in the marriage, she may have moved to the location where the family has lived only because of her husband's employment, and she may have strong ties to another locale. Sometimes, the custodial parent may seek to move because of a job or a new marriage, or to return to home and family, reasons that courts usually find to be legitimate. In *LaMusga*, the custodial mother had family in Ohio and her new husband had a better job there. Why did the court reject her petition? If relocation is strongly deterred by the legal response, the custodial parent may be "forced" to continue to reside in a particular community where she has few opportunities or ties, only because it suits the interest of her former spouse to live there. Thus, a restrictive relocation policy may be extremely burdensome to the primary caregiver. Moreover, some courts have suggested that the primary custodian and children make up a new family unit after divorce, all of whose members may benefit from the move. *Ireland v. Ireland*, 717 A.2d 676 (Conn. 1998). Courts cite social science evidence suggesting that "in general, what is good for the custodial parent, is good for the child." J. Wallerstein & T. Tanke, *"To Move or Not to Move: Psychological and Legal Considerations in the Relocation of Children Following Divorce,"* 30 FAM. L.Q. 305, 315 (1996). *See Baures v. Lewis*, 770 A.2d 220 (N.J. 2001) (citing this claim).

On the other hand, relocation of the custodial parent and child to a distant locale can inflict considerable costs on both the noncustodial parent and the child if they have had a close relationship. In *LaMusga*, the court weighed heavily the harm to even a tenuous relationship between the father and children, should the children move to Ohio. Moreover, a rule that creates no barriers to relocation by the custodial parent may encourage her to move for frivolous or spiteful reasons; at a minimum, it makes it less likely that she will weigh the cost to the relationship between the noncustodial parent and child in her decision. Such a rule gives her a weapon to use against the noncustodial parent in the not uncommon situation in which she finds proximity to him distasteful. Was this a consideration in *LaMusga*? Finally, many social scientists disagree with the views of Wallerstein and Tanke, above. *See* Kelly and Lamb, *Developmental Issues in Relocation Cases Involving Young Children: When, Whether, and How?,* 17 J. FAM. PSYCHOLOGY _ (2003); Warshak, *Social Science and Children's Interest in Relocation Cases: Burgess Revisited,* 34 FAM L. Q. 83 (2000) (criticizing the research support for the benefits of relocation). One recent study indicates that college students who experienced a parent's relocation showed negative effects as compared to those whose parents did not move. Braver, Ellman, & Fabricus, *Relocation*

After Divorce and Children's Best Interests: New Evidence and Legal Considerations, 17 J. FAM. PSYCHOLOGY 206 (2003).

Some courts and commentators find that a restrictive relocation rule that effectively ties the custodial parent to a particular geographic area interferes with that parent's constitutional right to travel. The Wyoming Supreme Court found that the right to travel "carries with it the right of a custodial parent to have the children move with that parent," and that it could only be impaired upon a clear showing that another change of circumstances exists and that the move would have a detrimental effect on the child. *Watt v. Watt,* 971 P.2d 608, 616 (Wyo. 1999). *See also In re D.M.G.,* 951 P.2d 1377 (Mont. 1998) (rejecting a trial court directive that the mother return to Montana from Oregon or relinquish custody, and holding that interference with the right to travel justified only where the party seeking the restriction demonstrates it is in the child's best interest); *Jaramillo v. Jaramillo,* 823 P.2d 299, 305 (N.M. 1991) (placing the burden of proof on the custodial parent is an unconstitutional impairment of the parent's right to travel); *Holder v. Polanski,* 544 A.2d 852, 856 (N.J. 1988) (allowing relocation unless adverse to child's best interests avoids the unconstitutional burden on parent's right to travel). There is no question that this interest is burdened if continued custody is contingent on remaining in the jurisdiction. *See* WIS. STAT. ANN. § 767.327 (West Supp. 2002). However, the noncustodial parent also has a constitutionally protected interest in his relationship with his child, which is impaired if the custodial parent is free to move to a distant location. Although courts do not tend to focus on this interest (perhaps because parental rights are inherently restricted for noncustodial parents), either outcome will burden a constitutional interest of one parent. *See* LaFrance, *Child Custody and Relocation: A Constitutional Perspective,* 34 U. LOUISVILLE J. FAM. L. 1 (1996).

A threshold consideration in many relocation cases is the good faith of either the relocating custodial parent or of the noncustodial parent who is seeking to block the child's relocation. Courts want to discourage spiteful and strategic behavior by either parent. Thus, for example, it is not surprising that courts have paid attention to the actual extent of involvement of the noncustodial parent with the child (and not just the contact allowed under the custody/ visitation order). *Taylor v. Taylor,* 849 S.W.2d 319 (Tenn. 1993) (court reversed order prohibiting mother's move, emphasizing that father failed to visit under schedule on 20 or more occasions). The underlying premise is that a parent who has not been significantly involved with the child has little legitimate basis for objecting to the move. Of course, the good faith of the relocating parent is also important. Even under liberal relocation laws, the custodial parent must offer a reasonable good faith basis for the relocation. In some states this fulfills her obligation to justify the move. In New Jersey, for example, "any sincere, good-faith reason will suffice," even though the relocating parent can not show a "real advantage" to the move. *Holder v. Polanski,* 544 A2d 852, 56 (N.J. 1988). In others, the burden then shifts to the noncustodial parent to demonstrate that relocation is not in the child's interest. *Ireland v. Ireland, supra. LaMusga* suggests that some California courts misinterpreted *Burgess* to require only good faith on the part of the relocating parent. Instead, the Court says *Burgess* treats the relocating parent's good faith as simply a threshold requirement.

Most cases, however, do not involve bad faith on the part of either parent, but rather a conflict between two parents each with legitimate interests. This may explain why courts have struggled with this issue, such that the legal response has been varied and unstable (see note 3 below).

2. *Relocation and the Modification Standard.* The fact that one parent wants to relocate is sometimes considered in the initial custody decision. More often the issue arises later, perhaps because the parent who wants to move is reluctant to have this factor weighed in the initial decision. Thus, often an important question is whether the planned move by the custodial parent constitutes a "changed circumstance" so as to trigger a reconsideration of custody under the modification standard. Some courts hold the custodial parent's move does not justify reexamination of the basic custody decision. *See, e.g., Taylor v. Taylor, supra; Pitt v. Olds,* 511 S.E.2d 60 (S.C. 1999). Other courts treat the relocation itself as a changed circumstance, justifying a new inquiry and decision about custody. *See Rowland v. Kingman,* 629 A.2d 613 (Me. 1993) (relocation constitutes a substantial change of circumstances); *Rice v. Shephard,* 877 S.W.2d 229 (Mo. App. 1994) ("residential change of the custodial parent to a distant location away from the non-custodial parent is a change of circumstances"); *Dominigues v. Johnson,* 593 A.2d 1133 (Md. 1991) (same). *LaMusga* suggests that under recent California law, while the move is not *per se* a changed circumstance, under some circumstances, it may be treated as such.

A related issue involves orders that condition the custodial parent's continued right to custody on remaining in the jurisdiction, (and automatically transfer custody to the other parent if she moves), with no separate determination that a change of custody is warranted. Some courts have upheld conditional orders with automatic transfer provisions. *See Lozinak v. Lozinak,* 569 A.2d 353 (Pa. Super. 1990) (upholding order transferring custody to the father if mother left Pennsylvania); *Maeda v. Maeda,* 794 P.2d 268 (Haw. App. 1990) (upholding conditional order). These conditional orders are often transparently designed to discourage the custodial parent from relocating. Courts may conclude that they lead to the best outcome; *i.e.,* the custodial parent stays in the jurisdiction and retains custody. This is suggested by a New York opinion in which the court conditioned the mother's custody on her not moving, after concluding that the child's best interest would not be served by a transfer of custody to the father. *Sullivan v. Sullivan,* 594 N.Y.S.2d 276 (N.Y. App. 1993). *LaMusga* somewhat disingenuously rejects the argument that the conditional order was designed to deter the mother.

Other courts reject an automatic transfer of custody upon relocation, and require instead that the change of custody must be justified under legal modification standards. In *Korn v. Korn,* 2003 Ala. Civ. App. LEXIS 42, the appellate court concluded that the trial court abused its discretion in holding that custody would automatically switch to the father if the mother, who was from Israel, left the United States. The court emphasized that custody could not be changed on the basis of a parent's relocation unless the non-custodial parent met the standard for modification of custody which required him to demonstrate that the relocation amounts to a material change of circumstances, that the change of custody will promote the child's best interests, and that the benefits of changing custody outweigh the disruption. *See also Moeller-Prokosch v. Prokosch*, 53 P.3d 152 (Alaska 2002) (order giving mother custody as long as she stayed within reasonable distance of father's school choice for child was reversed; trial court instructed to determine whether mother's reasons for moving were legitimate and whether mother's or father's custody was in child's interest).

Whether relocation results in a change of primary custody, it usually will result in some modification of the custody arrangements. Thus, it is useful to think of most relocation cases as belonging to a unique category of modification cases, which in most states are subject to special rules. For example, the *ALI Principles* treat relocation as a substantial changed circumstance when it impairs either parent's ability to continue to exercise custodial responsibilities. Sect 2.17 (1). The court is then directed to modify the parenting plan in accordance with the child's best interests. However, where one parent has had primary custodial responsibility, she will be allowed to relocate if she demonstrates a valid purpose and good faith, and the location is reasonable in light of the purpose. *See Hayes v. Gallacher*, 972 P.2d 1138 (Nev. 1999) (adopting ALI relocation standard). *See also* Note 3.

3. The Contemporary Legal Trend. Generalizations about the legal response to moves by custodial parents are dangerous, although the current trend appears to be toward a rule that allows greater freedom to relocate by a parent with primary custody. Relatively restrictive rules that placed the burden of justifying the move on the custodial parent seeking to relocate with the child have been supplanted in many states by rules that direct a more neutral multi-factored inquiry, or that place the burden of demonstrating harm to the child on the parent seeking to block the move. The trend has certainly not been linear, however.

California law, and particularly *LaMusga*, demonstrate the unpredictability of doctrine in this area. Before *In re Marriage of Burgess*, 913 P.2d 473 (1996), discussed at length in *LaMusga*, lower appellate courts in California responded inconsistently to relocation cases. Some courts favored the relocating parent while others placed the burden on that parent to prove that the move was in the child's best interest. In *Burgess*, the state supreme court interpreted the statute, which had not changed in a century, to require that the non-custodial parent challenging relocation must meet the modification test; he must prove that a change of custody is "essential or expedient for the welfare of the child." Until *LaMusga*, most courts and commentators interpreted *Burgess* to afford the custodial parent substantial freedom to relocate. In 2003, with *LaMusga* pending, the legislature adopted a statute that provided that "a parent entitled to custody of a child has a right to change residence of the child [unless the removal would] prejudice the rights or welfare of the child." Cal. Fam. Code Sect. 7501. The statute also expressly affirmed *Burgess* as "the public policy and law of the state." *LaMusga* upholds the trial court's rejection of the mother's petition to relocate, despite the fact that the trial court seems to have based its decision mostly on the cost of relocation to the noncustodial father's relationship with his children. Although *LaMusga* seeks to align its conclusion with *Burgess* by noting repeatedly that *Burgess* emphasized the importance of deference to trial court discretion, without question, *LaMusga* has seriously undermined *Burgess*. After *LaMusga*, no clear legal standard would seem to govern relocation cases in California. For the time being, trial courts are left to decide these cases, virtually without restraint.

Until recently, New York may have had the most restrictive relocation standard of any state, putting the burden on the relocating parent to demonstrate "exceptional" or "compelling" circumstances relating to the child's best interests. *See Daghir v. Daghir,* 439 N.E.2d 324 (N.Y. 1982) (test not met where mother moved with her husband when he was transferred to France). More recently, however, the New York "exceptional circumstances" test has been interpreted to allow a custodial parent to move with the child even in very unexceptional circumstances. *See, e.g., Aldrich v. Aldrich,* 516 N.Y.S.2d 328 (N.Y. App. Div. 1987) (mother allowed to move from New York to California where her husband resided). In *Tropea v. Tropea, supra* note 1, the Court of Appeals officially abandoned the "exceptional circumstances" test in favor of a balancing test that requires that all relevant facts and circumstances be evaluated. Under the new test, important considerations include the impact of the move on the relationship between the child and the non-custodial parent, the reasons for the move, the feasibility and desirability of a change of custody, the quality of the lifestyle the child will experience in the new location, each parent's good faith, and the possibility of developing a visitation schedule that will enable the child and non-custodial parent to maintain their relationship. This test, although it gives courts discretion to weigh the non-custodial parent's interest in preventing the move, is far more favorable to relocation than the former "exceptional circumstances" test. *See Ireland v. Ireland,* 717 A.2d 676 (Conn. 1998) (adopting *Tropea* factors under test in which non-custodial parent must demonstrate that move is not in child's best interest).

Several other states have established burdens of proof or presumptions that require the noncustodial parent to demonstrate that the proposed relocation is not in the best interests of the child. *See Ireland, supra; Sefkow v. Sefkow,* 427 N.W.2d 203, 214 (Minn.1988) (removal allowed absent showing by noncustodial parent that such action would endanger child's well-being); *Lane v. Schenck,* 614 A.2d 786 (1992) (relocation must be allowed unless noncustodial parent proves that best interests of child would be "so undermined by a relocation . . . that a transfer of custody is necessary");

Some courts continue to disfavor relocation. *See, e.g., Rowland v. Kingman,* 629 A.2d 613 (Me. 1993) (relocation constitutes a substantial change of circumstances). Others put the burden of proof on the relocating parent to demonstrate that relocation is in the child's best interest. *Brown v. Brown,* 621 N.W.2d 70 (Neb. 2000) (same); *Stout v. Stout,* 560 N.W.2d 903, 913 (N.D.1997) (same). Illinois puts the burden of proof on the relocating parent by statute. ILL. STAT. ANN. ch. 750 para. 5/609 (Smith-Hurd 1993). In *In re Marriage of Collingbourne* 791 N.E.2d 532 (Ill. 2003), the Illinois Supreme Court upheld the trial court's grant of the mother's petition to relocate, emphasizing that the court should weigh benefits of the relocation to the custodial parents that indirectly benefited the child.

The *ALI Principles* allows parents with primary custody freedom to relocate if they act in good faith and for a valid purpose; this stance is described as consistent with the "modern view" that a "primary purpose" of divorce is "to allow each party to go his or her way." *Principles* § 2.17. Comment. The *Principles* direct that courts should recognize the following as valid purposes: To be closer to family; to address health problems; to protect the child or other family members from harm; to pursue an employment or educational opportunity; to be with a spouse or domestic partner; or to significantly improve the family's quality of life. The relocating parent must prove that other purposes are valid.

4. *Joint Custody and Relocation.* Not surprisingly, parents with joint physical custody are generally subject to a restrictive relocation rule. Thus, under the *ALI Principles*, where neither parent has been exercising a clear majority of custodial responsibility, the court simply resolves the relocation dispute under the best interest standard, considering all relevant factors including the benefits and disruptive effects of the relocation. § 2.17 (4)(c). Similarly, a de novo determination of custody is required for California couples with joint physical custody where one parent plans to relocate. Other states also distinguish sole and joint custody cases. In allocating the burden of proof, for example, the Wisconsin statute distinguishes circumstances in which the relocating parent has custody "for the greater period of time" (burden on party resisting move) from circumstances in which the parents have "substantially equal periods of physical" custody (burden of proof on party seeking move). *See* Wis. Stat. Ann. § 767.327(3) (West Supp. 2002). In Nevada, however, the supreme court clarified that a joint custody order should not be considered a bar to relocation, and that courts should consider the established relocation factors (the extent to which relocation improved the quality of life for parent and child, the motives of each parent, opportunities for reasonable visitation, etc.). *McGuiness v. McGuiness*, 970 P.2d 1074 (Nev. 1998). The court chided trial courts for "chain[ing] custodial parents, most often women, to the state of Nevada." 970 P.2d at 1079. The dissenting justice pointed out that the court's holding was in tension with its previously announced preference for joint custody.

In jurisdictions that apply a different rule to joint custody vs. sole custody arrangements, it may be important whether the protesting parent actually took responsibility for the child under a joint custody order. *In re Marriage of Francis*, 919 P.2d 776 (Colo. 1996); *Rogero v. Pitt*, 759 S.W.2d 109 (Tenn. 1988) (court reverses order denying mother's petition to relocate, noting that, despite joint custody order, children spent most of their time with mother). The Maccoby -Mnookin study of divorced California families found that in about half of those families with joint physical custody orders, one parent (usually the mother) had primary *de facto* custody. *See* Section A2, *supra*.

5. *Critiques and Alternatives.* A large literature has examined relocation issues, much of it sympathetic to relocating parents. *See, e.g.*, Bruch and Bowermaster, *The Relocation of Children and Custodial Parents: Public Policy Past and Present*, 30 Fam L. Q. 245 (1996). These authors provide a comprehensive description of the legal trend toward liberalized relocation rules and argue that this trend is justified because the relationship between the child and the custodial parent is central to the child's well-being. They view restrictive rules as providing "inappropriate opportunities for abuses of power by former partners" and "doing a great disservice to children and their primary caretakers." *Id* at 246. Because custodial parents are most often women, some critics have been concerned about how restrictive relocation rules have a disparate impact upon women. *See, e.g.*, Note, *Post-Divorce Child Custody and Family Relocation,* 9 HARV. WOMEN'S L.J. 135 (1989). Still other commentators opposed to restrictive relocation rules have focused on the right-to-travel issue. *See, e.g.*, Raines, *Joint Custody and the Right to Travel: Legal and Psychological Implications,* 24 J. FAM. L. 625 (1985-86). Some observers argue for more a restrictive relocation policy, or at least one that allows consideration of the child's interest.. *See, e.g.*, Warshak; Braver, Ellman, & Fabricus, both Note 1 above; Adams, *Child Custody and Parent Relocations: Loving Your Children From a Distance,* 33 DUQ. L. REV. 143 (1994) (arguing greater weight should be given to the importance of the noncustodial parent-child relationship).

§ F.   PARENT – NON-PARENT DISPUTES

[1]   CUSTODY DISPUTES BETWEEN LEGAL AND DE FACTO PARENTS

V.C. v. M.J.B.

748 A.2d 539 (N.J. 2000)

LONG, J.

In this case, we are called on to determine what legal standard applies to a third party's claim to joint custody and visitation of her former domestic partner's biological children, with whom she lived in a familial setting and in respect of whom she claims to have functioned as a psychological parent. Although the case arises in the context of a lesbian couple, the standard we enunciate is applicable to all persons who have willingly, and with the approval of the legal parent, undertaken the duties of a parent to a child not related by blood or adoption.

V.C. and M.J.B., who are lesbians, met in 1992 and began dating on July 4, 1993. On July 9, 1993, M.J.B. went to see a fertility specialist to begin artificial insemination procedures. . . .

According to V.C., early in their relationship, the two discussed having children. However, V.C. did not become aware of M.J.B.'s visits with the specialist and her decision to have a baby by artificial insemination until September 1993. . . .

During M.J.B.'s pregnancy, both M.J.B. and V.C. prepared for the birth of the twins by attending pre-natal and Lamaze classes. . . .

The children were born on September 29, 1994. V.C. took M.J.B. to the hospital and she was present in the delivery room at the birth of the children. . . . After the children were born, M.J.B. took a three-month maternity leave and V.C. took a three-week vacation.

The parties opened joint bank accounts for their household expenses, and prepared wills, powers of attorney, and named each other as the beneficiary for their respective life insurance policies. At some point, [they] also opened savings accounts for the children, and named V.C. as custodian for one account and M.J.B. as custodian for the other.

The parties also decided to have the children call M.J.B. "Mommy" and V.C. "Meema." M.J.B. conceded that she referred to V.C. as a "mother" of the children. . . . M.J.B. encouraged a relationship between V.C. and the children and sought to create a "happy, cohesive environment for the children." M.J.B. admitted that, when the parties' relationship was intact, she sometimes thought of the four of them as a family. However, although M.J.B. sometimes considered the children "theirs," other times she considered them "hers".

M.J.B. agreed that both parties cared for the children but insisted that she made substantive decisions regarding their lives. . . . V.C. countered that she was equally involved in all decision-making regarding the children. Specifically, V.C. claimed that she participated in choosing a day care center for the children, and it is clear that M.J.B. brought V.C. to visit the center she selected prior to making a final decision.

M.J.B. acknowledged that V.C. assumed substantial responsibility for the children, but maintained that V.C. was a mere helper and not a co-parent. However, according to V.C., she acted as a co-parent to the children and had equal parenting responsibility. Indeed, M.J.B. listed V.C. as the "other mother" on the children's pediatrician and day care registration forms. M.J.B. also gave V.C. medical power of attorney over the children.

Together the parties purchased a home in February 1995. Later that year, . . .[they] held a commitment ceremony where they were "married."

. . . . V.C., M.J.B. and the twins attended family functions, holidays, and birthdays. . . . V.C. claimed that the children were very close to V.C.'s family. Apparently, the children referred to S.D. [V.C.'s mother] as "Grandma," and to V.C.'s grandmother, as "great-grandma."

. . . . M.J.B. testified that the parties considered adoption and in June 1996 consulted an attorney on the subject. M.J.B. paid a two thousand dollar retainer, and the attorney advised the parties to get letters from family and friends indicating that the parties and the twins functioned as a family. The parties never actually attempted to get the letters or proceed with the adoption. . . .

Just two months later, in August 1996, M.J.B. ended the relationship. The parties then took turns living in the house with the children until November 1996. In December 1996, V.C. moved out. M.J.B. permitted V.C. to visit with the children until May 1997. During that time, V.C. spent approximately every other weekend with the children, and contributed money toward the household expenses.

In May 1997, M.J.B. went away on business and left the children with V.C. for two weeks. However, later that month, M.J.B. refused to continue V.C.'s visitation with the children, and at some point, M.J.B. stopped accepting V.C.'s money. . . . Eventually, V.C. filed this complaint for joint legal custody. . . .

The trial court denied V.C.'s applications for joint legal custody and visitation. . . .

M.J.B. contends that there is no legal precedent for this action by V.C. She asserts, correctly, that a legal parent has a fundamental right to the care, custody and nurturance of his or her child. . . . According to M.J.B., that right entitles her to absolute preference over V.C. in connection with custody and visitation of the twins. She argues that V.C., a stranger, has no standing to bring this action. We disagree. . . .

According to M.J.B., because there is no allegation by V.C. of unfitness, abandonment or gross misconduct, there is no reason advanced to interfere with any of her constitutional prerogatives. What she elides from consideration, however, is the "exceptional circumstances" category. . . that has been recognized as an alternative basis for a third party to seek custody and visitation of another person's child. . . .

Subsumed within that category is the subset known as the psychological parent cases in which a third party has stepped in to assume the role of the legal parent who has been unable or unwilling to undertake the obligations of parenthood.

At the heart of the psychological parent cases is a recognition that children have a strong interest in maintaining the ties that connect them to adults who love and provide for them. That interest, for constitutional as well as social purposes, lies in the emotional bonds that develop between family members as a result of shared daily life. That point was emphasized in *Lehr v. Robertson,* 463 *U.S.* 248, 261, (1983), where the Supreme Court held that a stepfather's *actual* relationship with a child was the determining factor when considering the degree of protection that the parent-child link must be afforded. . . .

To be sure, prior cases in New Jersey have arisen in the context of a third party taking over the role of an unwilling, absent or incapacitated parent. The question presented here is different; V.C. did not step into M.J.B.'s shoes, but labored alongside her in their family. However, because we view this issue as falling broadly within the contours we have previously described, and because V.C. invokes the "exceptional circumstances" doctrine based on her claim to be a psychological parent to the twins, she has standing to maintain this action separate and apart from the statute. . . .

The next issue we confront is how a party may establish that he or she has, in fact, become a psychological parent to the child of a fit and involved legal parent. . . . The most thoughtful and inclusive definition of *de facto* parenthood is the test enunciated in *Custody of H.S.H.-K.,* 533 *N.W.*2d 419, 421 (Wis.1995). . . . Under that test,

> [t]o demonstrate the existence of the petitioner's parent-like relationship with the child, the petitioner must prove four elements: (1) that the biological or adoptive parent consented to, and fostered, the petitioner's formation and establishment of a parent-like relationship with the child; (2) that the petitioner and the child lived together in the same household; (3) that the petitioner assumed the obligations of parenthood by taking significant responsibility for the child's care,

education and development, including contributing towards the child's support, without expectation of financial compensation [a petitioner's contribution to a child's support need not be monetary]; and (4) that the petitioner has been in a parental role for a length of time sufficient to have established with the child a bonded, dependent relationship parental in nature.

[*Custody of H.S.H.-K., supra,* 533 *N.W.*2d at 421. . . .]

. . . . We are satisfied that that test provides a good framework for determining psychological parenthood in cases where the third party has lived for a substantial period with the legal parent and her child.

Prong one is critical because it makes the biological or adoptive parent a participant in the creation of the psychological parent's relationship with the child. Without such a requirement, a paid nanny or babysitter could theoretically qualify for parental status. To avoid that result, in order for a third party to be deemed a psychological parent, the legal parent must have fostered the formation of the parental relationship between the third party and the child. By fostered is meant that the legal parent ceded over to the third party a measure of parental authority and autonomy and granted to that third party rights and duties vis-a-vis the child that the third party's status would not otherwise warrant. . . .

The requirement of cooperation by the legal parent is critical because it places control within his or her hands. That parent has the absolute ability to maintain a zone of autonomous privacy for herself and her child. However, if she wishes to maintain that zone of privacy she cannot invite a third party to function as a parent to her child and cannot cede over to that third party parental authority the exercise of which may create a profound bond with the child.

Two further points concerning the consent requirement need to be clarified. First, a psychological parent-child relationship that is voluntarily created by the legally recognized parent may not be unilaterally terminated after the relationship between the adults ends. Although the intent of the legally recognized parent is critical to the psychological parent analysis, the focus is on that party's intent during the formation and pendency of the parent-child relationship. The reason is that the ending of the relationship between the legal parent and the third party does not end the bond that the legal parent fostered and that actually developed between the child and the psychological parent. . . .

In practice, that may mean protecting those relationships despite the later, contrary wishes of the legal parent in order to advance the interests of the child. As long as the legal parent consents to the continuation of the relationship between another adult who is a psychological parent and the child after the termination of the adult parties' relationship, the courts need not be involved. Only when that consent is withdrawn are courts called on to protect the child's relationship with the psychological parent.

The second issue that needs to be clarified is that participation in the decision to have a child is not a prerequisite to a finding that one has become a psychological parent to the child. . . .

The third prong, a finding that a third party assumed the obligations of parenthood, is not contingent on financial contributions made by the third party. . . . Obviously, as we have indicated, the assumption of a parental role is much more complex than mere financial support. It is determined by the nature, quality, and extent of the functions undertaken by the third party and the response of the child to that nurturance.

Indeed, we can conceive of a case in which the third party is the stay-at-home mother or father who undertakes all of the daily domestic and child care activities in a household with preschool children while the legal parent is the breadwinner engaged in her occupation or profession. . . .

It bears repeating that the fourth prong is most important because it requires the existence of a parent-child bond. A necessary corollary is that the third party must have functioned as a parent for a long enough time that such a bond has developed. What is crucial here is not the amount of time but the nature of the relationship. How much time is necessary will turn on the facts of each case including an assessment of exactly what functions the putative parent performed, as well as at what period and stage of the child's life and development such actions were taken. Most importantly, a determination will have to be made about the actuality and strength of the parent-child bond. Generally, that will require expert testimony. . .

This opinion should not be viewed as an incursion on the general right of a fit legal parent to raise his or her child without outside interference. What we have addressed here is a specific set of circumstances involving the volitional choice of a legal parent to cede a measure of parental authority to a third party; to allow that party to function as a parent in the day-to-day life of the child; and to foster the forging of a parental bond between the third party and the child. In such circumstances, the legal parent has created a family with the third party and the child, and has invited the third party into the otherwise inviolable realm of family privacy. By virtue of her own actions, the legal parent's expectation of autonomous privacy in her relationship with her child is necessarily reduced from that which would have been the case had she never invited the third party into their lives. Most important, where that invitation and its consequences have altered her child's life by essentially giving him or her another parent, the legal parent's options are constrained. It is the child's best interest that is preeminent as it would be if two legal parents were in a conflict over custody and visitation. . . .

Once a third party has been determined to be a psychological parent to a child, under the previously described standards, he or she stands in parity with the legal parent. Custody and visitation issues between them are to be determined on a best interests standard giving weight to the factors set forth in [the New Jersey custody statute]. . . .

That is not to suggest that a person's status as a legal parent does not play a part in custody or visitation proceedings in those circumstances. . . . The legal parent's status is a significant weight in the best interests balance because eventually, in the search for self-knowledge, the child's interest in his or her roots will emerge. Thus, under ordinary circumstances when the evidence concerning the child's best interests (as between a legal parent and psychological parent) is in equipoise, custody will be awarded to the legal parent.

Visitation, however, will be the presumptive rule,. . . as would be the case if two natural parents were in conflict. . . . [V]isitation rights are almost "invariably" granted to the non-custodial parent. [T]he denial of visitation rights . . . should be invoked only. . . where. . . the granting of visitation will cause physical or emotional harm to the children or where it is demonstrated that the parent is unfit. . . .

[The court concluded that remand was unnecessary, because V.C. was clearly a psychological parent to the twins. It ordered visitation but declined to order joint legal custody because V.C. had not been involved in making decisions for the children for nearly four years due to the pendency of the proceedings.].

NOTES

1. *Parent — Non-Parent Custody Disputes.* Custody disputes between parents and non-parents can arise in many contexts. The parent may seek the return of a child from a non-parent who has been living with and caring for the child, or the non-parent may seek to take custody from a parent on the ground that the parent is not providing adequate care. Another type of dispute pits a step-parent who has been living with the child and the custodial parent against the noncustodial parent, when custodial parent dies or becomes unable to care for the child. Finally, in cases like *V. C. v. M.J.B.*, a same sex partner or step-parent living with the custodial parent and the child may seek custody or visitation on dissolution of the relationship. The legal treatment of *de facto* parents who have shared childrearing responsibilities with parents has been the focus of a great deal of attention in recent years. We address this issue in Note 3, below.

Many states continue to apply the traditional rule, which does not distinguish among various kinds of cases, but holds that a parent prevails against a non-parent in a dispute over custody, unless the parent is shown to be unfit or to have abandoned his or her rights. *See, e.g.,* WIS. STAT. ANN. § 767.24(3)(a) (West Supp. 2002) (custody may be awarded to a relative if "neither parent is able to care for the child adequately or. . .is fit or proper to have custody."). In a case raising perhaps the most troubling variation of the parent-non-parent dispute, the North Dakota Supreme Court relied on the parental preference in affirming award of custody of a 9-year-old to her non-custodial mother instead of custodial father's widow. *Simons v. Gisvold*, 519 N.W.2d 585 (N.D. 1994). Although the daughter had lived with father and his second wife for eight years, the court noted the strong bond between mother and child and lack of evidence that maternal custody would be detrimental to the child. The Supreme Court of Missouri went one step further in reversing a custody award to the older half-sister of the children on the death of the mother, in a case in which the father had little previous involvement and failed to pay child support. *Cotton v. Wise*, 977 S.W.2d 263 (Mo. 1998). The court concluded that under the Missouri statute, the father was entitled to custody unless he was unfit, unwilling, or unable to assume responsibility for the children, even if their welfare would be detrimentally affected. *See also Ex Parte S.T.S.*, 806 So. 2d 336 (Ala. 2001) (father wins custody over grandmother, absent unfitness or voluntary relinquishment).

In most jurisdictions, the parental preference is somewhat weaker, and can be set aside not only where the parent is unfit, but also on a showing that parental custody will cause substantial harm to the child. This is a difficult standard for the challenger to meet, and courts make clear that it is not sufficient for the non-parents to demonstrate that their custody is in the child's best interest. Thus in *In re the Custody of Anderson*, 890 P.2d 525, 526 (Wash. App. 1995), the court awarded custody to the child's mother, while acknowledging that her aunt and uncle, who cared for the child for two years, "could offer her a superior home environment and a greater opportunity for optimum growth and development." *See also Lewis v. Donoho*, 993 S.W.2d 1 (Tenn. 1999) (mother awarded custody over non-parent, with whom eight-year-old child had lived almost since birth, absent showing of "substantial harm"); *Kinnard v. Kinnard,* 43 P3d 150 (Alaska 2002) (upholding shared custody based on stepmother's demonstration that she was psychological parent to child and that severing bond would be detrimental); *Froelich v. Clark,* 745 N.E.2d 222 (Ind. App. 2001) (*de facto* custodian with whom child lived for 8 years must overcome presumption favoring parental custody to retain custody).

California, by statute applies a similar rule. *See* CAL. FAM. CODE § 3041 (West Supp. 2003) (non-parent may be awarded custody if "granting custody to a parent would be detrimental to the child and granting custody to the nonparent is required to serve the best interest of the child.") In the highly publicized custody dispute between O.J. Simpson, the former football star, and his deceased wife's parents, Louis and Juditha Brown, the trial court applying this statute granted Simpson custody, but the appellate court reversed, finding that evidence of Simpson's involvement in his wife's murder (based on the verdict against him in the civil action) must be admitted in the custody determination. *Simpson v. Brown*, 79 Cal. Rptr. 2d 389 (Ct. App. 1998). However, the Browns subsequently agreed to relinquish physical custody to Simpson. *O.J. Getting the Kids / In-laws Will Let Them Go to Fla.*, L.A. Times, Aug. 7, 2000, at A08.

New York permits a non-parent to win custody against a fit parent only if "extraordinary circumstances" can be proved. *Bennett v. Jeffreys*, 356 N.E.2d 277 (N.Y.1976) (non-parent had cared for child for long period of time). This creates a substantial hurdle for non-parents, as the Court of Appeals demonstrated in *In re Michael B.*, 590 N.Y.S.2d 60 (N.Y. 1992). The court reversed a grant of custody to foster parents who had been custodians of the child for five years (characterized by the court as "temporary foster care"). The father sought custody of the child, who had been voluntarily placed in state-sponsored foster care by his mother. The court emphasized that there had been no finding of parental unfitness, and distinguished *Bennett v. Jeffreys*, which involved a private unsupervised placement with the non-parent, rather than a state placement. As the court in *V.C.* explains, *de facto* parents in New Jersey can also invoke "extraordinary circumstances" doctrine. However, for other nonparent claimants, New Jersey courts have narrowly construed this basis of rebutting the parental presumption. *See, e.g., Watkins v. Nelson*, 748 A.2d 558 (N.J. 2000) (affirming strong parental presumption emphasizing narrowness of exceptions).

In some jurisdictions the parental preference rule is applied when the child lives with the parent, but it is set aside, and a best interest standard applied, in cases in which the non-parent has lived with the child and functioned in a parental role for some significant length of time, and the parent has not had custody. *See, e.g., Price v. Howard*, 484 S.E.2d 528 (N.C. 1998) (where parent voluntarily relinquished child to non-parent, with whom child has lived for substantial period, best interest test applies). Some courts have gone a step further, applying the changed circumstances modification rule to parents' efforts to gain custody from custodial non-parents. In *C.R.B. v. C.C.*, 959 P.2d 375 (Alaska 1998), the grandparents obtained custody after their daughter, who had been awarded custody upon divorce, became unable to care for the children due to her cocaine addiction. After almost three years without contact, the father sought modification of the custody order when he established himself with a new wife and business in Seattle. The court rejected the father's argument that the changed circumstance standard should be relaxed when a parent seeks modification of custody in a non-parent. Although parents are preferred in the initial custody proceeding, once a non-parent is granted custody in spite of this preference, the goal of preserving stability in the child's life outweighs the parental preference at modification. *See also Blair v. Badenhope*, 77 S.W.3d 137 (Tenn. 2002). For an argument that a standard be applied in cases of "removal" (from the parents) should be different from that which is applied when the parent seeks "reunification" with a child who has been cared for by a third party who seeks to continue care, *see* Kaas, *Breaking Up a Family or Putting It Back Together Again: Redefining the Preference in Favor of the Parent in Third Party Custody Cases*, 37 WM. & MARY L. REV. 1045 (1996).

The Model Marriage and Divorce Act § 401 (1987), gives non-parents standing to contest custody but only where the child "is not in the physical custody of one of his parents." This approach has been adopted in a number of states. *See, e.g.*, ILL. ANN. STAT. ch. 750, para. 5/601(b)(2) (Smith-Hurd Supp. 1999); WASH. REV. CODE ANN. § 26.10.030 (West Supp. 2003).

The Supreme Court opinion in *Troxel v Granville*, 530 U.S. 57 (2000), Section F2, *infra*, has cast a shadow on custody disputes between parents and non-parents, although it focuses on a narrower related issue of the constitutional limits on the authority of courts to order grandparent visitation over the objection of fit custodial parents. Some courts view *Troxel* as limiting their freedom to award custody to non-parents. In a recent Michigan case, an appellate court rejected a ruling based on precedent, under which parents carried the burden of persuasion in challenging a non-parent with custody in an "established parental environment." *Heltzel v. Heltzel*, 638 N.W.2d 123 (Mich. App. 2001). In light of *Troxel*, the court held, courts must give "special weight" to the mother's fundamental liberty interest in raising her children, under a presumption that can be rebutted only by clear and convincing evidence. Several courts have recently focused on the constitutional importance of the presumption favoring parents in custody disputes with third parties. The Florida Supreme Court struck down a statute that applied the best interest standard to custody disputes between a parent and grandparent with whom the child resided in a stable relationship. *Richardson v. Richardson,* 766 So. 2d 1036 (Fla. 2000). The statute was facially unconstitutional, in the court's view, because it equated grandparents with parents, and did not require a finding that parental custody would be detrimental as a predicate to awarding custody to a non-parent. *See also State v. Wooden,* 57 P.3d 583 (Ore. App. 2002) (best interest standard no longer applies post *Troxel* to parent-grandparent custody dispute; father awarded custody despite sporadic contact with child, where child lived with mother and grandparents). In *Clark v. Wade,* 544 S.E.2d 99 (Ga. 2001), in which the grandparents succeeded in their custody claim, the court distinguished *Troxel,* pointing out that the grandparents were not intruding in the parent-child relationship; rather, the parents were intruding in an established family relationship. The Georgia statute, as construed by the court, requires non-parents to demonstrate by clear and convincing evidence that custody in the parents would result in physical or emotional harm to the child, and that the non-parent's custody is in the child's best interest.

A few states seem to give the parental preference relatively little weight, applying a fairly straightforward best-interests standard in any custody dispute between a non-parent and parent. The Hawaii statute provides that "custody may be awarded to persons other than the father or mother whenever the award serves the best interest of the child." Haw. Rev. Stat. Ann. § 571-46(2) (Michie Supp. 2002). Hawaii even favors the "person who has had de facto custody of the child in a stable and wholesome home" over the parent who has not had custody. Other courts maintain the preference, but do not treat it as presenting much of a hurdle to nonparent's claims. The Pennsylvania Supreme Court concluded that the presumption favoring the father was overcome by a clear showing that the stepfather's custody was in the child's best interest. *Charles v. Stehlik,* 744 A.2d 1255 (Pa. 2000). *See also McDonel v. Sohn,* 762 A.2d 1101 (Pa. Super. Ct. 2000).

2. The Concept of Psychological Parenthood. The concept of "psychological parenthood" has been influential in the weakening of the parental rights approach in parent-third party disputes. Under one well-known proposal, the legally favored parent would be the adult who has actually functioned as the child's primary caregiver, and whom the child identifies, psychologically, as the parent. *See* J. Goldstein, A. Freud & A. Solnit, Beyond the Best Interests of the Child (1973). These authors approach the custody decision from a psychoanalytic perspective. Their argument that the psychological parent should be favored in custody disputes rests on attachment theory, which holds that the child's healthy psychological development depends on the security of the bond with her attachment figure, the adult who cares for her basic needs from infancy. Thus, in the custody determination, little weight would be given to one party's status as biological parent.

Although few courts weigh psychological parenthood as heavily as the authors advocate, the concept has had an important influence in disputes between parents and non-parents and is at the heart of the rationale for recognizing claims by *de facto* parents. *See* Note 3, *supra*. In another context, the Colorado Supreme Court, in *C.R.S. v. T.A.M.*, 892 P2d 246 (Colo. 1995), awarded custody to prospective adoptive parents in a failed adoption case, on the ground that they were psychological parents. Emphasizing that the foster parents had raised the child since birth and fulfilled his psychological needs, the court concluded that disrupting the emotional bond that had formed between them (by awarding custody to the mother) "would likely prove devastating to the child." Continuation of that relationship was "presumed to be in the child's best interests." Oregon has recognized the psychological parenthood concept statutorily, by allowing anyone who has "established emotional ties creating a child-parent relationship . . . with a child" to petition for custody or visitation. OR. REV. STAT. § 109.119 (Supp. 1999). The statute defines child-parent relationship as:

> . . . a relationship that exists or did exist . . . and in which relationship a person having physical custody of a child or residing in the same household as the child supplied, or otherwise made available to the child, food, clothing, shelter and incidental necessaries and provided the child with necessary care, education and discipline, and which relationship continued on a day-to-day basis, through interaction, companionship, interplay and mutuality, that fulfilled the child's psychological needs for a parent as well as the child's physical needs.

Id. at 109.119(6)(a).

3. *Custody and Visitation Claims by De Facto Parents.* Custody disputes between former domestic partners often present compelling nonparent claims. Many of these contests involve lesbian couples who created families through the artificial insemination of one partner, after which both partners function fully as parents and share childrearing responsibilities. In some jurisdictions, the partner who is not the biological parent can legally adopt the child. *See* Chapter 11. In many states, however, this route to recognized parental status is foreclosed. When the lesbian partners' relationship ends, the *de facto* parent may contest custody or seek visitation. In doing so, these *de facto* parents assert their interest in a continued parental relationship with children with whom they have lived in a family unit — often since the child's birth.

This is an area in which legal doctrine is evolving as courts respond to social change. Traditionally, courts have been hostile to custody or visitation claims by same-sex *de facto* parents. In *Alison D. v. Virginia M.*, 572 N.E.2d 27 (NY 1991), for example, the court rejected the *de facto* parent's visitation petition, declining to recognize her parental status under the doctrine of *in loco parentis*, even though she had shared fully with the biological parent in planning and caring for the child. *See also Titchenal v. Dexter*, 693 A.2d 682 (Vt. 1997) (lesbian partner of adoptive mother could have adopted child, but court has no statutory or equitable authority to adjudicate visitation petition). In recent years, as *V. C.* suggests, courts have begun to respond positively to these claims and to develop legal standards for determining when claimants have parental status.

The test announced by the New Jersey Supreme Court is very similar to that adopted by the *ALI Principles*, which provide that courts can allocate residential responsibility to an individual who has resided with the child for a significant period and has performed many parenting functions without financial compensation. *Id.* § 2.03(1)(c), § 2.18. Like the New Jersey test, the ALI standard emphasizes the acquiescence of the legal parent to the development of the parent-child relationship between the *de facto* parent and the child (or the complete default of any legal parent). Unlike the New Jersey test, under which the amount of time that the claimant has functioned in a parental role is not crucial, the *ALI Principles* sets a minimum two-year time period. The latter approach seems likely to considerably reduce litigation.

Other courts have recognized the visitation claims of *de facto* parents, often citing with approval the *ALI Principles* or New Jersey test. *See Rubano v. DiCenzo,* 759 A.2d 959 (R.I. 2000) (enforcing a written visitation agreement, after determining that the domestic partner was the child's *de facto* parent); *E.L.O. v. L.M.M,* 711 N.E.2d 886 (Mass. 1999) (upholding recognition of lesbian domestic partner as *de facto* parent, citing the ALI standard, and awarding visitation). Both the ALI and the New Jersey Supreme Court acknowledge the influence of an earlier Wisconsin test offered in *In re Custody of H.S.H.-K.,* 533 N.W. 2d 419 (Wis. 1995).

Although *V.C.* holds that *de facto* parents stand in parity with legal parents (and thus the best interest standard applies to their disputes), it recognizes that usually these claimants will be awarded visitation rights and not custody. How does the court reach this conclusion? Many courts have held explicitly, under the general parental preference rule, that if the legal parent is both a fit parent and has had custody of the child, *de facto* parents can only seek visitation. *In re Custody of H.S.H.-K.,supra.* (*de facto* parent has no standing to sue under custody statute absent showing of unfitness);. *Kazmierazak v. Query,* 736 So. 2d 106 (Fla. Dist. Ct. App. 1999)(same). The ALI approach provides that the *de facto* parent should not get the majority of custodial responsibility. Sect. 2.18.

Courts have also recognized *de facto* parents other than domestic partners. Stepparents often get visitation after divorce as *de facto* parents, of course. *See* Gregory, *Defining the Family in the Millennium: The Troxel Follies,* 32 U. MEM. L. REV. 687, 690-91(2002) (describing statutes that expressly or implicitly authorize step-parent visitation). A Massachusetts court awarded visitation to an aunt who had cared for the child for 11 years, in a contest with the father, who was taking the child to his home in Georgia. Citing the *Principles,* the court held that the aunt was the child's *de facto* parent. *Youmans v. Ramos,* 711 N.E.2d 165 (Mass. 1998).

Some courts use other doctrinal paths to protect the relationships of children and *de facto* parents. The Pennsylvania Supreme Court, for example, invoked the common law doctrine of *in loco parentis* in awarding visitation to the mother's domestic partner, who lived with the child until she was almost three years old. *T.B. v. L.R.M.,* 786 A.2d 913 (Pa. 2001). Equitable estoppel has also been applied to these disputes, where parents held the non-parent out as the child's parent. For example, a mother who married the petitioner when she was pregnant and held him out to the world (and the child) as the child's father was estopped from denying his standing to seek custody or visitation. *Jean Maby H. v. Joseph H.,* 676 N.Y.S.2d 677 (App. Div. 1998). The *Principles* recognize custody claims by parents by estoppel, defined as an individual who fulfilled full parental responsibilities either because he thought he was the child's biological father or on the basis of agreement with the legal parent. Sect. 2.03(1)(b).

The *de facto* parent test is not expansive. For example, a post-*V.C.* New Jersey court denied *de facto* parent status to the mother's romantic partner, who lived with the mother and was very involved with the child, but was not held out to the child or to others as the child's parent by the mother. *A.F. v. D.L.P.*, 771 A.2d 692 (N.J. Super. Ct. App. Div. 2001). The court reasoned that this requirement was essential to afford constitutional protection to the parent-child relationship. *See also Swiss v. Cabinet for Families and Children*, 43 S.W.3d 796 (Ky. App. 2001) (foster parents were not *de facto* parents because agency provided financial support).

For further discussion of the issue of the legal response to same-sex families, see Chapter 9. For further discussion of the response to a parent's homosexuality in custody and visitation matters, see Sections B and D.

Much commentary has focused on the legal treatment of de facto parents and on the ALI approach to this issue. *See* Buss, Parental Rights, 88 Va. L. Rev. 635 (2002) (critiquing the ALI *de facto* parent status as interfering with legal parent's rights); Loken, *The New Extended Family: "De Facto" Parenthood and Standing Under Chapter 2*, 2001 B.Y.U. L. Rev. 1045 (arguing that the costs to biological parents of the ALI standard exceed any possible gains); Woodhouse, *Horton Looks at the ALI Principles*, 4 J.L. & Fam. Stud. 151 (2002) (criticizing Principles' treatment of *de facto* parenthood for ignoring children's developmental needs). *See also* Polikoff, *This Child Does Have Two Mothers: Redefining Parenthood to Meet the Needs of Children in Lesbian-Mother and Other Nontraditional Families*, 78 Geo. L.J. 459 (1990) (arguing that all functional parental relationships formed with the cooperation and consent of the biological parent should be legally recognized, in both custody and visitation cases).

PROBLEMS

Problem 6-15. In 1998, Jessica moved in with Marie and her five-year-old daughter, Sarah. Jessica was an English professor, whose schedule is flexible, while Marie often worked evenings and weekends as a manager of a local department store. Jessica took care of Sarah on weekends when Marie worked and usually picked her up after school and gave her dinner. As Sarah got older, Jessica often helped her with homework, took her to soccer practice, and to play dates and birthday parties. The couple pooled their financial resources; they had joint checking and savings accounts. Marie made all important decisions affecting Sarah, including medical and educational decisions, and important disciplinary decisions. Usually she went to teachers' conferences, although occasionally Jessica performed this function. After five years, when Sarah was 10 years old, the couple split up. You represent Jessica in her effort to get custody or visitation. Is she likely to be recognized as a *de facto* parent? What other information might be important? The court has ordered a psychological evaluation of all parties. What should be the focus of the psychologist's evaluation?

Problem 6-16. Julie and Mark hired Dasha as a live-in nanny for their children when their first child was three months old. They now have three children, ages 6, 8, and 10, and have decided to terminate Dasha to save money and retrieve some of their privacy. Dasha is extremely attached to the children, and wants to continue to see them on a regular basis. Julie and Mark believe it would be better for the children to make a clean break with Dasha.

As a matter of policy, should Dasha have standing to petition a court for visitation? Is she a *de facto* parent under the New Jersey test? Under the American Law Institute approach?

Problem 6-17 Jane and Jim of Tacoma, Washington, are the aunt and uncle of Sam, age 23, a young man with serious emotional problems. In 1998, Sam and his girl friend, Ellie, had a child, Michael. Jane and Jim became involved with the young family, spending time with them, giving advice, and buying clothes, books, and toys for Michael. They had raised three children, loved kids, and wanted to bring stability and support to Michael's life. Ellie was a loving mother, but she was immature and somewhat erratic and she managed to care for Michael only with much difficulty. In 2000, Sam and Ellie split up and Ellie took off for Alaska with Michael. She moved from place to place, getting jobs that allowed Michael to be with her and living in whatever accommodations she could find. Jane and Jim traveled to Alaska and persuaded Ellie to let them take Michael home to Washington. A few months later, having earned enough money to travel, Ellie returned to Washington and asked that Michael be returned to her. Jane and Jim refuse and petition for custody of Michael. Will they be successful?

[2] GRANDPARENT VISITATION

TROXEL v. GRANVILLE

530 U.S. 57 (2000)

Justice O'CONNOR announced the judgment of the Court and delivered an opinion, in which THE CHIEF JUSTICE, Justice GINSBURG, and Justice BREYER join. . . .

Tommie Granville and Brad Troxel shared a relationship that ended in June 1991. The two never married, but they had two daughters, Isabelle and Natalie. Jenifer and Gary Troxel are Brad's parents, and thus the paternal grandparents of Isabelle and Natalie. After Tommie and Brad separated in 1991, Brad lived with his parents and regularly brought his daughters to his parents' home for weekend visitation. Brad committed suicide in May 1993. Although the Troxels at first continued to see Isabelle and Natalie on a regular basis after their son's death, Tommie Granville informed the Troxels in October 1993 that she wished to limit their visitation with her daughters to one short visit per month.

In December 1993, the Troxels commenced the present action by filing . . . a petition to obtain visitation rights with Isabelle and Natalie. The Troxels filed their petition under . . . Wash. Rev. Code 26.10.160(3) (1994) . . . Section

26.10.160(3) provides: "Any person may petition the court for visitation rights at any time including, but not limited to, custody proceedings. The court may order visitation rights for any person when visitation may serve the best interest of the child whether or not there has been any change of circumstances." At trial, the Troxels requested two weekends of overnight visitation per month and two weeks of visitation each summer. Granville did not oppose visitation altogether, but instead asked the court to order one day of visitation per month with no overnight stay. In 1995, the Superior Court issued an oral ruling and entered a visitation decree ordering visitation one weekend per month, one week during the summer, and four hours on both of the petitioning grandparents' birthdays. . . .

[The Washington Court of Appeals reversed the visitation order and dismissed the Troxels' petition on statutory grounds. 940 P.2d 698 (Wash. Ct. App. 1997). The Washington Supreme Court affirmed, 969 P.2d 21 (Wash. 1998), rejecting the statutory ground, but agreeing with the lower court that the Troxels could not obtain visitation. During the appeal process, Granville married and her husband adopted the chidren.]

The [Washington Supreme] [C]ourt rested its decision on the Federal Constitution, holding that § 26.10.160(3) unconstitutionally infringes on the fundamental right of parents to rear their children. . . .

We granted certiorari, and now affirm the judgment. . . .

The demographic changes of the past century make it difficult to speak of an average American family. . . . While many children may have two married parents and grandparents who visit regularly, many other children are raised in single-parent households. In 1996, children living with only one parent accounted for 28 percent of all children under age 18 in the United States. . . . Understandably, in these single-parent households, persons outside the nuclear family are called upon with increasing frequency to assist in the everyday tasks of child rearing. In many cases, grandparents play an important role. . . .

The nationwide enactment of nonparental visitation statutes is assuredly due, in some part, to the States' recognition of these changing realities of the American family. Because grandparents and other relatives undertake duties of a parental nature in many households, States have sought to ensure the welfare of the children therein by protecting the relationships those children form with such third parties. The States' nonparental visitation statutes are further supported by a recognition . . . that children should have the opportunity to benefit from relationships with . . . their grandparents. The extension of statutory rights in this area to persons other than a child's parents, however, comes with an obvious cost. For example, the State's recognition of an independent third-party interest in a child can place a substantial burden on the traditional parent-child relationship. . . .

The Fourteenth Amendment provides that no State shall "deprive any person of life, liberty, or property, without due process of law." . . . The Clause . . . includes a substantive component that "provides heightened protection against government interference with certain fundamental rights and liberty interests."

The liberty interest at issue in this case — the interest of parents in the care, custody, and control of their children — is perhaps the oldest of the fundamental liberty interests recognized by this Court. . . . *Meyer v. Nebraska*, 262 U.S. 390 (1923) . . . *Pierce v. Society of Sisters*, . . . *Stanley v. Illinois*, . . . *Wisconsin v. Yoder*, . . . *Quilloin v. Walcott*, . . . *Parham v. J. R.*, . . . *Santosky v. Kramer.* . . .

Section 26.10.160(3), as applied to Granville and her family in this case, unconstitutionally infringes on that fundamental parental right. The Washington nonparental visitation statute is breathtakingly broad. According to the statute's text, "*[a]ny person* may petition the court for visitation rights *at any time*," and the court may grant such visitation rights whenever "visitation may serve *the best interest of the child.*" § 26.10.160(3) (emphases added). That language effectively permits any third party seeking visitation to subject any decision by a parent concerning visitation of the parent's children to state-court review . . . [in which] a parent's decision that visitation would not be in the child's best interest is accorded no deference. Section 26.10.160(3) contains no requirement that a court accord the parent's decision any presumption of validity or any weight whatsoever. . . . Should the judge disagree with the parent's estimation of the child's best interests, the judge's view necessarily prevails. Thus, in practical effect, in the State of Washington a court can disregard and overturn any decision by a fit custodial parent concerning visitation whenever a third party affected by the decision files a visitation petition, based solely on the judge's determination of the child's best interests. The Washington Supreme Court had the opportunity to give § 26.10.160(3) a narrower reading, but it declined to do so. . . .

Turning to the facts of this case, the record reveals that the Superior Court's order was based on precisely the type of mere disagreement we have just described and nothing more. The Superior Court's order was not founded on any special factors that might justify the State's interference with Granville's fundamental right to make decisions concerning the rearing of her two daughters. . . . [T]he combination of several factors here compels our conclusion that Sect. 26.10160(3), as applied, exceeded the demands of the Due Process Clause. . . .

First, the Troxels did not allege, and no court has found, that Granville was an unfit parent. That aspect of the case is important, for there is a presumption that fit parents act in the best interests of their children. As this Court explained in Parham:

> "[O]ur constitutional system long ago rejected any notion that a child is the mere creature of the State and, on the contrary, asserted that parents generally have the right, coupled with the high duty, to recognize and prepare [their children] for additional obligations. . . . [I]t has recognized that natural bonds of affection lead parents to act in the best interests of their children." 442 U.S., at 602.

Accordingly, so long as a parent adequately cares for his or her children (*i.e.*, is fit), there will normally be no reason for the State to inject itself into the private realm of the family to further question the ability of that parent to make the best decisions concerning the rearing of that parent's children. . . .

The problem here is not that the Washington Superior Court intervened, but that when it did so, it gave no special weight at all to Granville's determination of her daughters' best interests. More importantly, it appears that the Superior Court applied exactly the opposite presumption. . . .

The judge's comments suggest that he presumed the grandparents' request should be granted unless the children would be "impact[ed] adversely." In effect, the judge placed on Granville, the fit custodial parent, the burden of *disproving* that visitation would be in the best interest of her daughters. . . .

The decisional framework employed by the Superior Court directly contravened the traditional presumption that a fit parent will act in the best interest of his or her child. In that respect, the court's presumption failed to provide any protection for Granville's fundamental constitutional right to make decisions concerning the rearing of her own daughters. . . . In an ideal world, parents might always seek to cultivate the bonds between grandparents and their grandchildren. Needless to say, however, our world is far from perfect, and in it the decision whether such an intergenerational relationship would be beneficial in any specific case is for the parent to make in the first instance. And, if a fit parent's decision of the kind at issue here becomes subject to judicial review, the court must accord at least some special weight to the parent's own determination.

Finally, we note that there is no allegation that Granville ever sought to cut off visitation entirely. . . . Granville did not oppose visitation but instead asked that the duration of any visitation order be shorter than that requested by the Troxels. . . . The Superior Court gave no weight to Granville's having assented to visitation even before the filing of any visitation petition or subsequent court intervention. . . . Significantly, many other States expressly provide by statute that courts may not award visitation unless a parent has denied (or unreasonably denied) visitation to the concerned third party. *See, e.g.* . . . Ore. Rev. Stat. § 109.121(1)(a)(B) (1997) (court may award visitation if the "custodian of the child has denied the grandparent reasonable opportunity to visit the child"). . . .

Considered together with the Superior Court's reasons for awarding visitation to the Troxels, the combination of these factors demonstrates that the visitation order in this case was an unconstitutional infringement on Granville's fundamental right to make decisions concerning the care, custody, and control of her two daughters. The Washington Superior Court failed to accord the determination of Granville, a fit custodial parent, any material weight. In fact, the Superior Court made only two formal findings in support of its visitation order. First, the Troxels "are part of a large, central, loving family, all located in this area, and the [Troxels] can provide opportunities for the children in the areas of cousins and music." App. 70a. Second, "[t]he children would be benefitted from spending quality time with the [Troxels], provided that that time is balanced with time with the childrens' [sic] nuclear family." *Ibid.* These slender findings . . . show that this case involves nothing more than a simple disagreement between the Washington Superior Court and Granville concerning her children's best interests. . . . As we have explained, the Due Process Clause does not permit a State to infringe on the fundamental right of parents to make childrearing decisions simply because a state judge believes a "better" decision could be made. . . . Accordingly, we hold that § 26.10.160(3), as applied in this case, is unconstitutional.

Because we rest our decision on the sweeping breadth of § 26.10.160(3) and the application of that broad, unlimited power in this case, we do not consider the primary constitutional question passed on by the Washington Supreme Court — whether the Due Process Clause requires all nonparental visitation statutes to include a showing of harm or potential harm to the child as a condition precedent to granting visitation. We do not, and need not, define today the precise scope of the parental due process right in the visitation context. . . . Because much state-court adjudication in this context occurs on a case-by-case basis, we would be hesitant to hold that specific nonparental visitation statutes violate the Due Process Clause as a *per se* matter. . . .

There is . . . no reason to remand the case for further proceedings in the Washington Supreme Court. . . . [I]t is apparent that the entry of the visitation order in this case violated the Constitution. We should say so now, without forcing the parties into additional litigation that would further burden Granville's parental right. We therefore hold that the application of § 26.10.160(3) to Granville and her family violated her due process right to make decisions concerning the care, custody, and control of her daughters.

Accordingly, the judgment of the Washington Supreme Court is affirmed.

Justice SOUTER, concurring in the judgment.

I concur in the judgment affirming the decision of the Supreme Court of Washington, whose facial invalidation of its own state statute is consistent with this Court's prior cases addressing the substantive interests at stake. I would say no more. . . .

[T]he state court authoritatively read [the statutory] provision as placing hardly any limit on a court's discretion to award visitation rights. As the court understood it, the specific best-interests provision in the statute would allow a court to award visitation whenever it thought it could make a better decision than a child's parent had done. . . .

Justice THOMAS, concurring in the judgment.

. . . . [I] agree with the plurality that this Court's recognition of a fundamental right of parents to direct the upbringing of their children resolves this case. . . . The opinions of the plurality, Justice KENNEDY, and Justice SOUTER recognize such a right, but curiously none of them articulates the appropriate standard of review. I would apply strict scrutiny to infringements of fundamental rights. Here, the State of Washington lacks even a legitimate governmental interest — to say nothing of a compelling one — in second-guessing a fit parent's decision regarding visitation with third parties. On this basis, I would affirm the judgment below.

Justice STEVENS, dissenting.

. . . . The second key aspect of the Washington Supreme Court's holding — that the Federal Constitution requires a showing of actual or potential "harm" to the child before a court may order visitation continued over a parent's objections — finds no support in this Court's case law. While, as the Court recognizes, the Federal Constitution certainly protects the parent-child relationship from arbitrary impairment by the State, we have never held that the parent's liberty interest in this relationship is so inflexible as to establish a rigid constitutional shield, protecting every arbitrary parental decision from any challenge absent a threshold finding of harm. The presumption that parental decisions generally serve the best interests of their children is sound, and clearly in the normal case the parent's interest is paramount. But even a fit parent is capable of treating a child like a mere possession.

Cases like this do not present a bipolar struggle between the parents and the State over who has final authority to determine what is in a child's best interests. There is at a minimum a third individual, whose interests are implicated in every case to which the statute applies — the child.

   . . . .

A parent's rights with respect to her child have thus never been regarded as absolute, but rather are limited by the existence of an actual, developed relationship with a child, and are tied to the presence or absence of some embodiment of family. These limitations have arisen, not simply out of the definition of parenthood itself, but because of this Court's assumption that a parent's interests in a child must be balanced against the State's long-recognized interests as *parens patriae*, see, *e.g.*, . . . *Prince v. Massachusetts*, 321 U.S. 158, 166 (1944), and, critically, the child's own complementary interest in preserving relationships that serve her welfare and protection, *Santosky*, 455 U.S., at 760.

While this Court has not yet had occasion to elucidate the nature of a child's liberty interests in preserving established familial or family-like bonds, it seems to me extremely likely that, to the extent parents and families have fundamental liberty interests in preserving such intimate relationships, so, too, do children have these interests, and so, too, must their interests be balanced in the equation. At a minimum, our prior cases recognizing that children are, generally speaking, constitutionally protected actors require that this Court reject any suggestion that when it comes to parental rights, children are so much chattel. The constitutional protection against arbitrary state interference with parental rights should not be extended to prevent the States from protecting children against the arbitrary exercise of parental authority that is not in fact motivated by an interest in the welfare of the child.

This is not, of course, to suggest that a child's liberty interest in maintaining contact with a particular individual is to be treated invariably as on a par with that child's parents' contrary interests. Because our substantive due process case law includes a strong presumption that a parent will act in the best interest of her child, it would be necessary, were the state appellate courts actually to confront a challenge to the statute as applied, to consider whether the trial court's assessment of the "best interest of the child" incorporated that presumption. Neither would I decide whether the trial court applied Washington's statute in a constitutional way in this case. . . . For the purpose of a facial challenge like this, I think it safe to assume that trial judges usually give great deference to parents' wishes, and I am not persuaded otherwise here.

But presumptions notwithstanding, we should recognize that there may be circumstances in which a child has a stronger interest at stake than mere protection from serious harm caused by the termination of visitation by a "person" other than a parent. The almost infinite variety of family relationships that pervade our ever-changing society strongly counsel against the creation by this Court of a constitutional rule that treats a biological parent's liberty interest in the care and supervision of her child as an isolated right that may be exercised arbitrarily. It is indisputably the business of the States, rather than a federal court employing a national standard, to assess in the first instance the relative importance of the conflicting interests that give rise to disputes such as this. Far from guaranteeing that parents' interests will be trammeled in the sweep of cases arising under the statute, the Washington law merely gives an individual — with whom a child may have an established relationship — the procedural right to ask the State to act as arbiter, through the entirely well-known best-interests standard, between the parent's protected interests and the child's. It seems clear to me that the Due Process Clause of the Fourteenth Amendment leaves room for States to consider the impact on a child of possibly arbitrary parental decisions that neither serve nor are motivated by the best interests of the child. . . .

Justice SCALIA, dissenting.

. . . . Only three holdings of this Court rest in whole or in part upon a substantive constitutional right of parents to direct the upbringing of their children — two of them from an era rich in substantive due process holdings that have since been repudiated. *See Meyer v. Nebraska.* . . .; *Pierce v. Society of Sisters*; *Wisconsin v. Yoder*, ... The sheer diversity of today's opinions persuades me that the theory of unenumerated parental rights underlying these three cases has small claim to *stare decisis* protection. . . . While I would not now overrule those earlier cases (that has not been urged), neither would I extend the theory upon which they rested to this new context. . . .

[Dissenting opinion by Justice KENNEDY omitted.]

NOTES

1. *Grandparents Visitation Rights — The Background.* In the years before the Supreme Court decided *Troxel*, most states enacted statutes giving grandparents and, to a lesser extent, other non-parents, standing to petition for visitation, over the objection of custodial parents. The traditional common-law rule gave grandparents no legal right to continue their relationship with their grandchildren when their own child (the grandchild's parent) died, divorced, or had her parental rights terminated. This position was compatible with the general stance that the custodial parent is entitled to exclusive custody against the entire world, a right which includes the authority to decide who (including relatives) can associate with the child. *See, e.g., Thomas v. Pickard,* 195 S.E.2d 339 (N.C. App. 1973); *Odell v. Lutz,* 78 Cal. App. 2d 104, 177 P.2d 628 (1947). Largely through lobbying efforts by grandparent groups, state legislatures across the country enacted statutes authorizing courts to order grandparent visitation under some circumstances. In part, this sweeping legal reform was likely driven by a view that both children and grandparents have a special interest in this unique relationship that justifies trumping parental authority. Moreover, legislatures, to some extent, were responding to particularly compelling claims by grandparents who had cared for their grandchildren as *de facto* parents, or those whose relationships with grandchildren were severed when their own children died (as happened in *Troxel*) or lost parental rights. Some statutes were limited to these compelling cases. *See e.g.* MINN. STAT. ANN. § 257C.08 (subd. 3) (West Supp. 2003) (only grandparent who lived with child for more than 12 months had standing). The sweeping Washington statute at issue in *Troxel*, of course, contained none of these limits, allowing the trial judge to order visitation in favor any third party. *See also* N.H. REV. STAT. ANN. § 458:17(VI) (Supp. 2002). Subsequent to *Troxel*, courts generally upheld narrower statutes and some legislatures revised and limited standing along these lines. For a survey of the judicial and legislative response to *Troxel,* see Notes 2 and 3 *infra*.

Grandparent visitation has always had its critics, despite its popularity in the period before *Troxel*. Many observers have challenged the wisdom of courts' overriding the decisions of responsible custodial parents who may have good reasons not to allow the contact. The issue, of course, is not whether it is generally beneficial to children to have contact with their grandparents, but whether courts or parents should make that decision. Moreover, this kind of intervention can also be challenged on fairness grounds. Unlike noncustodial parents, most grandparents (like the Troxels) have never lived with the children or taken responsibility for their upbringing — and they have no support obligation. *See* Scott, *Parental Autonomy and Children's Welfare*, 11 WM & M. BILL OF RIGHTS J. 1071 (2003). For an early critique by a child psychiatrist, see Derdeyn, *Grandparent Visitation Rights: Rendering Family Dissension More Pronounced*, 55(2) AM. J. ORTHOPSYCHIATRY 277 (1985).

Even before *Troxel*, some lower courts either limited or overturned broadly written grandparent visitation statutes, and some even found narrower formulations to violate parental autonomy. Particularly, courts found statutory provisions authorizing visitation over the objection of parents in an intact family (including the grandparent's own child) to be unconstitutional, or they simply refused to apply general statutory authorization of grandparent visitation to this kind of case. *See, e.g., Brooks v. Parkerson*, 454 S.E.2d 769 (Ga. 1995) (holding statute permitting visitation in intact families to be unconstitutional state interference in family autonomy, unless harm to child is shown). In 1996, the Georgia legislature amended the statute to require that visitation be ordered only where denial resulted in harm to the child. *See* 1996 GA. LAWS, Act 954. *See also Herbst v. Sayre*, 971 P.2d 395 (Okla. 1998) (statute unconstitutional as applied to parents in an intact family, absent demonstrable harm to the child or parental unfitness; *Williams v. Williams*, 501 S.E.2d 417 (Va. 1998) (same).

2. Troxel *and its Aftermath — The Judicial Response.* The broadly written Washington statute gave trial court authority to grant visitation to any third party whenever doing so was in the child's best interests. Yet Justice O'Connor's plurality opinion did not find the statute to be unconstitutional *on its face*, but only as applied in the *Troxel* case itself. Given the extraordinary breadth of the Washington statute, it would seem that every contemporary statute would pass facial constitutional muster. It is therefore surprising perhaps that, after *Troxel* a number of lower courts have ruled various state provisions facially unconstitutional. Michigan highest court did so by announcing that the Supreme Court in fact had found the Washington statute to be unconstitutional despite the failure of the O'Connor plurality to acknowledge this directly. *DeRose v. DeRose*, 666 N.W.2d 636 (Mich. 2003). Because the Michigan statute also failed to require deference to a fit parent's objection to visitation, the state court found it facially unconstitutional. The Illinois Supreme Court recently struck down that state's statute because it put non-parent and parent on equal footing, and contravened the presumption that parents are fit and act in the best interest of their children. In language far broader than *Troxel*, the court stated, "A fit parent's constitutionally protected liberty interest to direct the care, custody and control of his or her children mandates that parents — not judges — should be the ones to decide with whom their children will and will not associate". *Wickham v. Byrne*, 769 N.E.2d 1 (Ill. 2002). *See also In re Marriage of Howard*, 661 N.W.3d. 183 (Iowa 2003) (provision permitting visitation petition when parents are divorced is unconstitutional on face); *Cf. Linder v. Linder*, 72 S.W.3d 841 (Ark. 2002) (statute authorizing visitation over parents' objection categorically unconstitutional as applied to fit parents; but not as applied to an entity (such as state agency) without fundamental interest). *Linder* applied strict scrutiny, a position advocated only by Justice Thomas in his *Troxel* concurrence, and found grandparent visitation to be a major intrusion on the fundamental right of parents to rear their children.

The O'Connor plurality expressly left undecided the question of whether the Constitution required a showing that the parent's denial of visitation was harmful to the child before the court could justify ordering visitation. The Connecticut Supreme Court prescribed such a harm requirement. *Roth v. Weston*, 789 A.2d 431 (Conn. 2002) (party seeking visitation must have a parent-like relationship with the child and demonstrate by clear and convincing evidence that denial of visitation would cause significant harm to the child, of a kind that is contemplated by the neglect/dependency statute). *See also Neal v. Lee* 14 P.3d 347 (Okla. 2000) (unless parent is unfit, court should order grandparent visitation only on the basis of clear and convincing evidence that children would suffer harm without visitation); *Scott v. Scott*, 80 S.W.3d 447 (Ky. Ct. App. 2002).

Other courts have explicitly rejected the claim that a showing of harm to the child was constitutionally required before visitation can be ordered over a parent's objections. *Kan. Dep't of Soc. and Rehab. Serv. v. Paillet*, 16 P.3d 962 (Kan. 2001) (petitioner must rebut presumption that a fit parent acts in child's best interest, by showing that visitation is in child's best interest); *Zeman v. Stanford*, 789 So. 2d 798 (Miss. 2001) (best interest of child is paramount); *State ex. rel. Brandon L. v. Moats*, 551 S.E.2d 674 (W. Va. 2001) (court must find visitation is in child's best interest and that it represents no substantial interference with parental authority); *Rideout v. Riendeau*, 761 A.2d 291 (Me. 2000) (showing of parentlike relationship with child or harm of denial of visitation are alternative means of showing compelling state interest).

Would the actual custody decision in *Troxel* have been sustained if made pursuant to a more narrow statute? For example, a statute that allows the court to grant visitation only to grandparents, and only those whose own child had died, would be much narrower than the Washington statute. However, unless such a statute required the judge to give some special deference to the parental decision, it would seem, based on O'Connor's analysis, that the constitutional flaw would remain. The plurality opinion, however, offers little guidance about acceptable statutory formulations. Justice O'Connor recognizes that allowing the parent's decision to be overruled only if harm to the child is shown would be satisfactory, but does not tell us whether some less demanding formulation would also be adequate.

In the face of this these ambiguities, state courts have wrestled, post-*Troxel*, with custody decisions rendered under narrower statutes. These statutes are interpreted to give special weight to the parents' decision and/or restrict visitation that substantially interferes with the parent-child relationship. Thus, in a case involving a grandmother who had been a *de facto* parent to the child, the Supreme Court of Maine upheld a visitation order under a statute that includes a threshold standing requirement that the grandparent must have a sufficient existing relationship with the child; the statute then directs the court to consider the parent's objection and order visitation only if it does not significantly interfere with the parent-child relationship. *Rideout v. Riendeau, supra.* Some grandparent visitation statutes have been upheld on the basis of narrowing interpretations, although trial courts are left with considerable discretion. The Mississippi Supreme Court approved a statute that restricts petitioners seeking visitation to grandparents (unlike *Troxel*), but gives courts rather broad authority to order visitation. *Zeman v. Stanford,* 789 So. 2d. 798 (Miss. 2001). The court emphasized that the statute had been interpreted earlier to require courts to analyze numerous factors in deciding whether visitation is in the child's best interest, including that the grandparent would not interfere with the parents' child rearing. The court deemphasized the burden to parents' interests imposed by court-ordered grandparent visitation, and stressed that the child's best interest is paramount. *See also Galjour v. Harris,* 795 So. 2d 350 (La. 2001) (statute applying best interest standard upheld because it was limited to a narrow category of petitioners (parents of deceased, absent or noncustodial parents)); *Kan. Dep't of Soc. and Rehab. Serv. v. Paillet, supra* (statute upheld, although unconstitutionally applied, that requires "substantial relationship" and places burden on petitioner to demonstrate that visitation is in the child's best interest); *State ex. rel. Brandon L. v. Moats, supra* (statute upheld; requires finding that visitation does not substantially interfere with the parent-child relationship; best interest standard identifies twelve factors to guide court); *Blixt v. Blixt,* 774 N.E. 2d 1052 (Mass. 2002) (statute limiting grandparent visitation to families in which parents do not reside together upheld against facial equal protection challenge).

3. *Post-Troxel Statutory Reform.* In response to *Troxel*, many state legislatures reexamined their grandparent visitation statutes, and narrowed judicial authority to order visitation over parents' objections. *See, e.g.,* N.D. CENT. CODE § 14-09-05.1 (2002) (permitting grandparent visitation only where a finding is made that it would be in the best interests of the minor and would not interfere with the parent-child relationship, and removing the presumption that grandparent visitation is in the best interests of the child);

2001 MAINE. LAWS 696 (providing that a grandparent who has been designated as an interested person or participant, or who has been granted intervenor status, may petition for reasonable visitation); ORE. REV. STAT. § 109.119 (2001) (permitting any person having a parent-child relationship with a child to be awarded custody, guardianship, or rights of visitation if it is in the child's best interests, but requiring the petitioning party to overcome by clear and convincing evidence the presumption that the legal parent acts in the best interest of the child); S.D. CODIFIED LAWS § 25-4-52 (2001) (permitting grandparent visitation if it would be in the best interests of the child, and either the visitation would not significantly interfere with the parent-child relationship, or the parent or custodian of the child has unreasonably denied the grandparent reasonable opportunity to visit the child; also providing for a presumption that grandparent visitation is in the best interests of a grandchild if a parent of that grandchild, who is also the child of that grandparent, has died); TENN. CODE ANN. § 36-6-306 (2001) (identifying conditions which necessitate a hearing when a grandparent petitions for visitation, and providing that grandparent visitation may be ordered upon a finding of danger of substantial harm to the child of denial, and a finding that such visitation would be in the child's best interests); UTAH CODE ANN. § 30-5-2 (2000) (creating a rebuttable presumption that the parent's decision as to grandparent visitation is in the best interests of the child, and permitting courts to consider the child's wishes in regard to visitation).

Under the *ALI Principles*, grandparents would have standing to seek a portion of custodial responsibility only if they qualify as *de facto* parents or parents by estoppel — *i.e.*, they must have resided with the child and performed many parenting functions with the parent's acquiescence. § 2.03(1). Because the *Principles* abolish the conventional "visitation" category, and limit custodial access to adults who have lived with and cared for the child, most grandparents would lack standing.

4. *Other Non-Parent Visitation.* Note that under the Washington statute, "any person" could petition for visitation. Aside from grandparents, most non-parent visitation petitions involve step-parents or *de facto* parents who resided with the child. *See* Gregory, *Defining the Family in the Millennium: The Troxel Follies*, 32 U. MEM. L. REV. 687 (2002) (discussing statutes authorizing step-parent visitation after *Troxel*. In some states, however, the statutory language allows others to seek visitation. *See, e.g.,* OR. REV. STAT. § 109.119(8) (1999) (any person who "has maintained an ongoing personal relationship with substantial continuity for at least one year, through interaction, companionship, interplay and mutuality" may petition for visitation). Some statutes specifically authorize sibling visitation, see, *e.g.,* N.J. STAT. ANN. § 9:2-7.1 (West Supp. 1997), and some courts have ordered sibling visitation without express statutory authority. In *State v. Ken W.*, 529 N.W.2d 548 (Neb. App. 1995), the court upheld a sibling visitation order sought by a boy who was in state custody because he was uncontrollable. The court, in granting the boy visitation with his two-year-old sister over their parents' objection, concluded that siblings (unlike grandparents) have a direct right of access. On the facts of the case, the court found that visitation would benefit the brother while there was "no evidence that the supervised sibling visitation would have a negative impact" on his sister.

5. *Literature on Troxel.* Much has been written about *Troxel* and its implications. For two excellent analyses and critiques of the opinion, see Buss, *Adrift in the Middle: Parental Rights After* Troxel v. Granville, 2000 SUP. CT. REV. 279 (2000) and Gilles, *Parental (and Grandparental) Rights after* Troxel, 9 SUP. CT. ECON. REV. 69 (2001). *See also* Buss, *"Parental" Rights*, 88 VA. L. REV. 635 (2002) (criticizing grandparent visitation, arguing that the Constitution grants strong protection to parental child rearing rights, but weaker protection to any individual's claim to parental identity); Dolgin, *The Constitution as Family Arbiter: A Moral in the Mess?*, 102 COLUM. L. REV. 337 (2002) (arguing that constitutional jurisprudence is inadequate to the task of determining the proper scope of familial relationships, because constitutional law presumes individual autonomy). An excellent symposium on *Troxel* appears in 32 RUTGERS LAW JOURNAL 695 *et. seq.* and includes articles by Earl M. Maltz, David Meyer, Margaret Brinig, Sally Goldfarb, and Nancy Polikoff.

PROBLEM

Problem 6-18. Sam and Ilsa Jameson, who lived in San Francisco, were very fond of their grandchildren, Ann and Lois, who lived in Canton, Ohio, with the Jameson's daughter Ariel, and her husband Mark. The Jamesons saw the family twice a year at Christmas and in the summer. The visits were memorable experiences for both grandparents and grandchildren. The children loved being with their grandparents; Sam and Ilsa took them to museums, theater performances and did other special things with them. As the children got older, they developed a close bond with their grandparents. However, the visits were always a little stressful because Sam and Ilsa were quite critical of Ariel and Mark's parenting. They felt that Mark particularly let the children do whatever they wanted to do, never disciplined them, and allowed them to live on junk food. Although Sam and Ilsa tried to keep their views to themselves, they sometimes could not restrain themselves from expressing their concern. In 2000, when Ann was 10 years old and Lois was 8, Ariel died in a car accident. After her death, Mark was less than eager for the Jamesons to visit with their grandchildren. During one tense visit in 2001, the Jamesons had an argument with Mark over how much unmonitored TV the children were watching. Mark said he thought it would be better for the children if they didn't see their grandparents. The next time the Jamesons suggested a visit, Mark refused. Sam and Ilsa petition for visitation with the children. How should the court respond?

§ G. THE ROLE OF THE ATTORNEY IN CUSTODY CASES

Lawyers representing parents in custody disputes may be constrained in their role because, although the attorney is responsible primarily to her client, the purpose of the proceeding is to promote the best interest of the child. For example, although attorneys are prohibited under the attorney-client privilege from disclosing confidential communications from their clients, an attorney may be required to disclose her client's whereabouts where the client has taken the child out of the jurisdiction in violation of a court order. *See Bersani v. Bersani*, 565 A.2d 1368 (Conn. Super. 1989). Attorneys advising their clients must explain the limits of the privilege.

Attorneys for the parents in custody disputes have been subject to substantial criticism because they have traditionally understood their role to be that of zealous advocate for their client's interest, even if the child's interest is sacrificed. As part of a larger effort to define the ethical obligations of divorce attorneys under a model that deemphasizes the "zealous advocate" role, the American Academy of Matrimonial Lawyers, a reform group, has promulgated standards that encourage attorneys to consider the interest of the child in representing the parent. *The Bounds of Advocacy, Standards of Conduct*, 9 J. AMER. ACAD. MATRIMONIAL LAWYERS 1 (Fall 1992). The introduction to this section of the standards describes the basis of the obligation of parent's attorney to consider the welfare of the children:

> One of the most troubling issues in family law is determining a lawyer's obligation to children. The lawyer must represent the client zealously, but not at the expense of children. The parents' fiduciary obligations for the well-being of a child provide a basis for the attorney's consideration of the child's best interests consistent with traditional adversary and client loyalty principles. It is accepted doctrine that the attorney for a trustee or other fiduciary has an ethical obligation to the beneficiaries to whom the fiduciaries obligations run. To the extent that statutory or decisional law imposes a duty on the parent to act in the child's best interest, the attorney for the parent might be considered to have an obligation to the child that would, in some instances, justify subordinating the wishes of the parent.

The standards direct the parent's attorney to consider the welfare of the children (Standard 2.23). The attorney is also prohibited from contesting custody for financial leverage or vindictiveness, and is directed to seek to withdraw if the client persists in such strategic pursuits (Standard 2.25 and Comment). *See also* Becker, *Ethical Concerns in Negotiating Family Law Agreements*, 30 FAM. L.Q 587 (1996). Becker suggests that, under the ABA Model Rules of Professional Conduct, the attorney should counsel a parent against pursuing a course that is detrimental to the child. (Rule 2.1).

PROBLEM

Problem 6-19. (a) A is attorney for F in his divorce action against M. F seeks custody of the three children. A's investigation of the case reveals that F is not a very good father. He often leaves the family for days at a time, has a poor relationship with his children, and often refuses, for no apparent reason, to allow his children to play with their neighborhood friends. M, on the other hand, is an excellent parent and A therefore believes she ought to be awarded custody of the children. What can A do, consistent with his ethical obligations as an attorney?

(b) Suppose A has learned, from a discussion with the children, that F has in fact molested his daughter. M appears to be ignorant of this fact; in any event, it is clear that she has not told her attorney. What are A's obligations?

Chapter 7

DIVORCE JURISDICTION

§ A. TERMINATION OF MARITAL STATUS

SOSNA v. IOWA

419 U.S. 393 (1974)

MR. JUSTICE REHNQUIST delivered the opinion of the Court.

[Carol Sosna filed a divorce petition in Iowa within a month of her arrival in the state with her three children. Her husband, Michael, who had remained in New York after the couple's separation, was served during a trip to Iowa to visit his children. The trial court dismissed for lack of jurisdiction because Carol had not been, as required by statute, "for the last year a resident of the state." A three-judge Federal District Court rejected Carol's constitutional challenge to the statute.]

[We] . . . hold that the Iowa durational residency requirement for divorce does not offend the United States Constitution.

I

[The Court rejected a mootness claim.]

II

The durational residency requirement . . . is a part of Iowa's comprehensive statutory regulation of domestic relations, an area that has long been regarded as a virtually exclusive province of the States. Cases decided by this Court over a period of more than a century bear witness to this historical fact. In *Barber v. Barber* (1859), the Court said: "We disclaim altogether any jurisdiction in the courts of the United States upon the subject of divorce. . . ." In *Pennoyer v. Neff* (1878), the Court said: "The State . . . has absolute right to prescribe the conditions upon which the marriage relation between its own citizens shall be created, and the causes for which it may be dissolved."

The statutory scheme in Iowa, like those in other States, sets forth . . . the grounds upon which a marriage may be dissolved and the circumstances in which a divorce may be obtained. Jurisdiction . . . is . . . in "the county where either party resides" and the Iowa courts have construed the term "resident" to have much the same meaning as is ordinarily associated with the concept of domicile. . . .

The imposition of a durational residency requirement for divorce is scarcely unique to Iowa, since 48 States impose such a requirement. . . . [T]he periods

681

. . . range from six weeks to two years. The one-year period selected by Iowa is the most common length of time prescribed.

[Carol] contends that the Iowa requirement of one year's residence is unconstitutional for two separate reasons: *first,* because it establishes two classes of persons and discriminates against those who have recently exercised their right to travel to Iowa, thereby contravening the Court's holdings in *Shapiro v. Thompson*; *Dunn v. Blumstein*; and *Memorial Hospital v. Maricopa County*; and, *second,* because it denies a litigant the opportunity to make an individualized showing of bona fide residence and therefore denies such residents access to the only method of legally dissolving their marriage. *Vlandis v. Kline*; *Boddie v. Connecticut.*

P claims Iowa's residency requirement unconstitutional for 2 reasons

State statutes imposing durational residency requirements were, of course, invalidated when imposed by States as a qualification for welfare payments, *Shapiro;* for voting, *Dunn;* and for medical care, *Maricopa County.* But none of those cases intimated that the States might never impose durational residency requirements, and such a proposition was in fact expressly disclaimed. . . . [T]he durational residency requirements they struck down were justified [by] budgetary or recordkeeping considerations which were held insufficient to outweigh the constitutional claims of the individuals. But Iowa's divorce residency requirement is of a different stripe. [Carol] was not irretrievably foreclosed from obtaining some part of what she sought, as was the case with the welfare recipients in *Shapiro,* the voters in *Dunn,* or the indigent patient in *Maricopa County.* She would eventually qualify for the same sort of adjudication which she demanded virtually upon her arrival in the State. Iowa's requirement [only] delayed her access to the courts. . . .

Iowa's residency requirement may reasonably be justified on grounds other than purely budgetary considerations or administrative convenience. A decree of divorce is not a matter in which the only interested parties are the State as a sort of "grantor," and a divorce petitioner such as [Carol] in the role of "grantee." Both spouses are obviously interested in the proceedings, since it will affect their marital status and very likely their property rights. Where a married couple has minor children, a decree of divorce would usually include provisions for their custody and support. With consequences of such moment riding on a divorce decree issued by its courts, Iowa may insist that one seeking to initiate such a proceeding have the modicum of attachment to the State required here.

Such a requirement additionally furthers the State's parallel interests both in avoiding officious intermeddling in matters in which another State has a paramount interest, and in minimizing the susceptibility of its own divorce decrees to collateral attack. A State . . . may quite reasonably decide that it does not wish to become a divorce mill. . . . Until . . . Iowa is convinced that [Carol] intends to remain in the State, it lacks the "nexus between person and place of such permanence as to control the creation of legal relations and responsibilities of the utmost significance." *Williams v. North Carolina,* (1945). Perhaps even more important, Iowa's interests extend beyond its borders and include the recognition of its divorce decrees by other States under the Full Faith and Credit Clause of the Constitution, Art. IV, § 1. For that purpose, this Court has often stated that "judicial power to grant a divorce — jurisdiction, strictly speaking — is founded on domicile." *Williams, supra.* Where a divorce decree is entered after a finding of domicile in *ex parte* proceedings, this Court has held that the finding of domicile is not binding upon another State and may be disregarded in the face of "cogent evidence" to the contrary. . . . The State's decision to exact a one-year residency requirement . . . is therefore buttressed by a quite permissible inference that this requirement not only effectuates state substantive policy but likewise provides a greater safeguard against successful collateral attack than would a requirement of bona fide residence alone. This is precisely the sort of determination that a State in the exercise of its domestic relations jurisdiction is entitled to make.

We therefore hold that the state interest in requiring that those who seek a divorce from its courts be genuinely attached to the State, as well as a desire to insulate divorce decrees from the likelihood of collateral attack, requires a different resolution of the constitutional issue presented than . . . in *Shapiro, Dunn* and *Maricopa County.*

. . .

In *Boddie, supra,* this Court held that Connecticut might not deny access to divorce courts to those persons who could not afford to pay the required fee. Because of the exclusive role played by the State in the termination of marriages, it was held that indigents could not be denied an opportunity to be heard "absent a countervailing state interest of overriding significance." But the gravamen of [Carol's] claim is not total deprivation, as in *Boddie,* but only delay. The operation of the filing fee . . . served to exclude forever a certain segment of the population from obtaining a divorce. . . . No similar total deprivation is present in appellant's case. . . .

Affirmed.

NOTES ON DIVORCE JURISDICTION

1. *Domicile as Basis of Jurisdiction to Terminate.* The notion that termination of marital status may have special jurisdictional rules has a long history. *Pennoyer*, which established federal constitutional boundaries for state court jurisdiction, lumped "cases affecting the personal status of the plaintiff" with "*in rem*" cases for purposes of jurisdictional rules. Because being married or divorced is such a personal status, jurisdiction to terminate marriage is determined by *in rem* rather than *in personam* rules. Under the usual *in rem* analysis, the presence of the affected res "before the court" is both necessary and sufficient for jurisdiction. The analogous requirement for jurisdiction over a status is that the person whose status is being adjudicated is a forum domiciliary. While this is a generally-recognized principle, it has been argued that personal jurisdiction over the respondent should be required for divorce.

The special jurisdictional rule for divorce was addressed in *Williams v. North Carolina,* 317 U.S. 287 (1942) (*Williams I*) and *Williams v. North Carolina,* 325 U.S. 226 (1945) (*Williams II*), both of which arose during the fault divorce era. The question of jurisdiction then was of immense practical importance, in part because of an established choice of law rule under which the forum applied its own divorce law. For example, it was critically important for New York residents to know the circumstances under which one could escape their state's restrictive divorce rules (limiting divorce to cases of adultery) by seeking divorce elsewhere, such as Nevada.

The *Williams I* issue was whether North Carolina had to honor Nevada divorces granted to two North Carolinians who had traveled to Las Vegas to obtain divorces. Both stayed for the six weeks required under Nevada law, served their spouses by mail or delivery, obtained the decree, and then remarried (each other). They were welcomed on their return to North Carolina with a bigamy prosecution. Their convictions were reversed in *Williams I*. Because the divorce proceedings contained no contrary evidence, the Supreme Court felt bound by the Nevada court's finding that the couple were Nevada domiciliaries and held the Full Faith and Credit Clause required North Carolina to honor the divorces. *Williams I* thus established the principle relied upon in *Sosna:* one party's domicile supports a state's jurisdiction to terminate a marriage.

2. Is There an Acceptable Jurisdictional Substitute for Domicile? While *Williams I* held domicile *sufficient* for jurisdiction, it did not decide whether it was *necessary*. That is, could a state end a marriage on a jurisdictional basis other than domicile? Suppose, *e.g.*, a court had personal jurisdiction over both spouses, but neither was a forum domiciliary. Because the Supreme Court has never been presented with this question, it has not answered it.

Nonetheless, states have fashioned their laws on the assumption that divorce jurisdiction requires domicile and state courts routinely interpret statutes as if domicile of at least one party is a constitutional necessity. For example, in *Fletcher v. Fletcher*, 619 A.2d 561 (Md. Spec. App. 1993), no statute explicitly required domicile and, in fact, a procedural rule appeared to permit divorce if one party merely did business in the state. Nevertheless, describing domicile as the basis for divorce jurisdiction as one which "has a Constitutional underpinning and remains firmly intact," the appellate court, citing *Sosna* and several state court decisions, required domicile of at least one party. *See also Carr v. Carr*, 724 So. 2d 937 (Miss. 1998) (citing *Williams II* for proposition that domicile is cornerstone of divorce jurisdiction).

3. Divorces Involving Military Personnel. There is no direct Supreme Court authority upholding any non-domiciliary assertion of jurisdiction. Nonetheless, one standard exception to the domicile requirement seems defensible only if personal jurisdiction under traditional presence standards can substitute for domicile. Military personnel often present special jurisdictional problems in divorce cases. They typically are not domiciled where they are stationed because they are there involuntarily and do not wish to establish a new domicile. They thus remain domiciled in a state where they may have not actually lived for some years, where their spouse may have no contact, and where a divorce action may be inconvenient. To solve these practical problems, the typical statute claims divorce jurisdiction where one spouse is a resident who is a member of the armed services. *See*, *e.g.*, M.M.D.A. § 302(a)(1) (asserting jurisdiction if, at commencement of the action, either party "was stationed in this State while a member of the armed forces" and such "military presence" was maintained for 90 days).

While most divorce jurisdictional issues involving military respondents are raised in the state of respondent's residence, suit may also be filed in respondent's domicile. In *Wamsley v. Wamsley*, 635 A.2d 1322 (Md. 1994), a divorce petitioner sued in a jurisdiction where respondent had not lived during his 11 years of naval service. Citing cases from other courts as authority, the court upheld jurisdiction, noting respondent had a Maryland driver's license, was registered to vote there and paid state income taxes. Thus, respondent was domiciled there and could be sued for divorce.

4. *When Does a Finding of Domicile Bind Other Courts?* *Williams I and II,* and particularly the dicta suggesting domicile was necessary for jurisdiction as well as sufficient, created issues which were addressed in a series of cases.

a. *Can State-2 re-examine a divorce court's finding of domicile?* This issue was reserved in *Williams I,* because the record did not raise the bona fides of the spouses' Nevada domicile. That is, *Williams I* held only that domicile conferred jurisdiction; it did not address the proof of domicile or the circumstances under which it can be challenged. The Court left North Carolina free to examine these questions, and the state court on remand rejected Nevada's finding that the parties were Nevada domiciliaries. In *Williams II,* the Supreme Court found North Carolina was not bound by Nevada's decision on domiciliary status.

Williams II held that while North Carolina was bound to "respect" the Nevada finding, it could reach its own judgment on whether this jurisdictional prerequisite was met because it was not party to the Nevada litigation. Thus, the Court permitted North Carolina's challenge, apparently because as the original domiciliary state it has an adequate interest in the divorce decision. The result is that for *ex parte* divorces such as the Nevada decree in *Williams,* the finding of domicile had to be persuasive enough to withstand scrutiny by another court. This rule underlies *Sosna's* observation that by requiring a year's residence, Iowa was furthering a valid state interest in ensuring its divorce decrees would be honored elsewhere. Of course, a state is not *compelled* to impose a durational residency requirement. For example, Alaska has no durational residency requirement, though residence is required. *Perito v. Perito,* 756 P.2d 895 (Alaska 1988) (upholding finding of residence when suit was filed the day after petitioner's arrival).

b. *Can State-1's jurisdiction be collaterally attacked where both spouses participated in the divorce proceedings, acknowledging domicile and jurisdiction?* The Supreme Court held that it could not, *Sherrer v. Sherrer,* 334 U.S. 343 (1948), not even by some third parties. *Johnson v. Muelberger,* 340 U.S. 581 (1951). Although no direct authority exists, the prevailing view is that the original domiciliary state is also bound, thus limiting it to "the protection of the stay-at-home spouse against unilateral (*ex parte*) actions by the other [spouse] in a distant forum." SCOLES, HAY, BORCHERS & SYMEONIDES, CONFLICT OF LAWS § 15.11 at p. 619 (3d ed. 2000). In combination with *Williams II,* this meant: first, one spouse could not unilaterally evade his state's restrictive divorce laws by obtaining a Nevada decree based upon sham residence there, because another state could redetermine the validity of Nevada domicile; but second, if the spouses cooperated they *could* evade their state law through a joint appearance in Nevada, which would insulate their divorce decree from collateral attack.

   5. *"Sham" Domicile and Lack of Contact By Respondent.* Because domicile of one party is sufficient for divorce jurisdiction, essentially a party can unilaterally grant a state jurisdiction over termination by establishing domicile there. What if this move is made for a "bad" reason or to a state with which the other party has no contact? The cases are clear that the reason for changing domicile is irrelevant. In *Fletcher* (Note 2, *supra*), the court observed:

> The [trial] court . . . seemed concerned that Louis had moved here solely to take advantage of . . . more favorable divorce law. That may well be so, and if it is so, it is unfortunate. But jurisdiction does not hinge on why he moved here, only whether he moved here . . . and whether, at present, he intends to remain here for the foreseeable future, which it appears he does. . . .

619 A.2d at 566. Note, however, that the petitioner's domicile does not alone establish jurisdiction over the respondent for any purpose other than terminating the marital status. *See* Sections B & C, *infra*. Domicile does not require citizenship. *Cho v. Jeong*, 1997 Tenn. App. LEXIS 407 (petitioner with student spouse visa); *Kimura v. Kimura*, 471 N.W.2d 869 (Iowa 1991) (permanent resident alien).

   6. *Foreign Divorces.* Recognition of a foreign divorce is not governed by the Full Faith and Credit Clause. As a matter of comity, American states generally recognize divorces granted by foreign countries if one party was domiciled in that country. *Mori v. Mori*, 931 P.2d 854 (Utah 1997); *Atassi v. Atassi*, 451 S.E.2d 371 (N.C. App. 1995). During the fault divorce era, Americans sometimes sought foreign divorces to avoid restrictive local rules, but such divorces were usually held invalid when neither spouse actually lived abroad. For cases reviewing this law, see *Carr v. Carr*, 724 So. 2d 937 (Miss. 1998); Annot., *Domestic Recognition of Divorce Decree Obtained in Foreign Country and Attacked for Lack of Domicil or Jurisdiction of Parties*, 13 A.L.R.3d 1419 (1965). In a rule adopted during the era of very limited divorce grounds, New York recognizes foreign divorces even without a domiciliary attachment to the foreign country if both parties were before the foreign court. *Rosenstiel v. Rosenstiel*, 16 N.Y.2d 64, 209 N.E.2d 709 (1965) (recognizing Mexican divorce, noting that even though parties were only there very briefly, "Nevada gets no closer to the real public concern with the marriage than Chihuahua").

   7. *Modern Relevance of Domicile Rule.* The problem of divorce jurisdiction is quite different today than when the above-discussed cases were decided. The dominance of no-fault divorce has reduced the incentives for seeking a traditional divorce haven like Nevada and a home state's incentives to restrict its residents' ability to seek divorce elsewhere. At the same time, people are increasingly mobile, so that while a move to Nevada to establish a sham domicile is less likely, an individual may in fact move to Nevada or Iowa or Maine, before or after the termination of the marital status. In that case, which state court should divide their property, decide the custody of their children and determine the level of child or spousal support? As one commentator has observed, the problem today is not so much migratory divorce as migratory people. Garfield, *The Transitory Divorce Action: Jurisdiction in the No-Fault Era,* 58 TEX. L. REV. 501, 504 (1980). We now turn to these jurisdictional problems.

§ B.   JURISDICTION TO ISSUE SUPPORT ORDERS AND DIVIDE PROPERTY

In addition to terminating the marital status, a divorce decree usually fixes rights to support, custody, and property. The rules in the preceding section do not establish jurisdiction over these issues, which today form the most important part of any divorce action. This difference in jurisdictional rules creates the possibility of "divisible divorce"; while the marital status can always be terminated by a spouse's domiciliary state, it cannot bind an absent spouse to determinations of property and alimony without personal jurisdiction over him. *Estin v. Estin,* 334 U.S. 541 (1948); *Vanderbilt v. Vanderbilt,* 354 U.S. 416 (1957). The termination of the marital status by the domiciliary state thus "divides" the divorce issues with the financial and custody issues left for determination elsewhere. *See, e.g., Ellithorp v. Ellithorp,* 575 S.E.2d 94 (W. Va. 2002) (Texas had jurisdiction to terminate the marriage, but only West Virginia had jurisdiction over financial and custody issues); *Muckle v. Muckle,* 102 Cal. App. 4th 218 (2002) (jurisdiction to terminate marriage found present in California, but property issues must be litigated in Georgia); *Snider v. Snider,* 551 S.E.2d 693 (W. Va. 2001) (Illinois decree terminating marriage does not deprive West Virginia court of jurisdiction over property division or alimony issues); *Poston v. Poston,* 624 A.2d 853 (Vt. 1993) (rejecting Texas decree purporting to extinguish party's right to maintenance without personal jurisdiction).

In requiring personal jurisdiction over respondent to adjudicate the financial issues, *Estin* did not focus so much upon the absent spouse's Due Process rights as upon permitting each state to decide the matters of its "dominant" concern. In *Estin,* Nevada could adjudicate the marital status of its domiciliary, the husband; New York could adjudicate the support rights of its domiciliary, the wife. While the Court would reach the same result today, it would be based more explicitly upon the non-resident's Due Process rights; as in any other civil action, the Constitution requires personal jurisdiction over an individual in order to fix his or her rights or obligations regarding property or support. The following case applies this rule.

KULKO v. SUPERIOR COURT OF CALIFORNIA

436 U.S. 84 (1978)

MR. JUSTICE MARSHALL delivered the opinion of the Court. The issue before us is whether, in this action for child support, the California state courts may exercise *in personam* jurisdiction over a nonresident, nondomiciliary parent of minor children domiciled within the State. . . . [W]e hold that the exercise of such jurisdiction would violate the Due Process Clause of the Fourteenth Amendment.

I

. . . Ezra Kulko married . . . Sharon Kulko Horn in 1959, during [Ezra's] three-day stopover in California en route . . . to a tour of duty in Korea. At the time of this marriage, both parties were domiciled in . . . New York State. Immediately following the marriage, Sharon . . . returned to New York, as did [Ezra] after his tour of duty. [The couple's two children were born in New York. The [family] resided together . . . in New York City continuously until March 1972, when the Kulkos separated.

Following the separation, Sharon . . . moved to San Francisco. . . . A written separation agreement was drawn up in New York; in September 1972, Sharon . . . flew to New York City in order to sign this agreement. The agreement provided, *inter alia,* that the children would remain with their father during the school year but would spend their Christmas, Easter, and summer vacations with their mother. . . . Ezra . . . agreed to pay his wife $3,000 per year in child support for the periods when the children were in her care, custody, and control. Immediately after execution of the separation agreement, Sharon . . . flew to Haiti and procured a divorce there; the divorce decree incorporated the terms of the agreement. She then returned to California. . . .

[Both parties complied with the agreement] until December 1973. At this time, just before Ilsa was to leave New York to spend Christmas vacation with her mother, she told her father that she wanted to remain in California after her vacation. Ezra bought his daughter a one-way plane ticket, and Ilsa [began] living in California with her mother during the school year and spending vacations with her father. In January 1976, appellant's other child, Darwin, called Sharon from New York and advised her that he wanted to live with her in California. Unbeknownst to Ezra, Sharon sent a plane ticket to her son, which he used to fly to California where he took up residence with his mother and sister.

Less than one month after Darwin's arrival. . ., [Sharon] commenced this action . . . in the California Superior Court. She sought to establish the Haitian divorce decree as a California judgment; to modify the judgment so as to award her full custody of the children; and to increase [Ezra's] child-support obligations. [Ezra attacked personal jurisdiction for lack of "minimum contacts" under *International Shoe*.]

The trial court summarily denied the motion to quash, and [Ezra] sought review in the California Court of Appeal. . . . The appellate court affirmed the denial of [Ezra's] motion to quash, reasoning that, by consenting to his children's living in California, appellant had "caused an effect in th[e] state". . . .

The California Supreme Court . . . sustained the rulings of the lower state courts. It noted first that the California Code of Civil Procedure demonstrated an intent that the courts of California utilize all bases of *in personam* jurisdiction "not inconsistent with the Constitution.". . . [T]he Supreme Court stated that, where a nonresident defendant has caused an effect in the State . . ., personal jurisdiction . . . in causes arising from that effect may be exercised whenever "reasonable." It went on to hold that such an exercise was "reasonable" in this case because [Ezra] had "purposely availed himself of the benefits and protections of the laws of California" by sending Ilsa to live with her mother. . . . — [T]he court concluded that it was "fair and reasonable for [Ezra] to be subject to personal jurisdiction for the support of both children, where he has committed acts with respect to one child which confers [sic] personal jurisdiction and has consented to the permanent residence of the other child in California."

II

The Due Process Clause . . . operates as a limitation on the jurisdiction of state courts to enter judgments affecting rights or interests of nonresident defendants. See *Shaffer v. Heitner,* 433 U.S. 186 (1977). . . . [A] valid judgment imposing a personal obligation or duty . . . may be entered only by a court having jurisdiction over the person of the defendant. . . . The existence of personal jurisdiction, in turn, depends upon the presence of reasonable notice . . ., and a sufficient connection between the defendant and the forum State to make it fair to require defense of the action in the forum. . . . In this case, [Ezra] does not dispute the adequacy of the notice . . ., but contends that his connection with . . . California is too attenuated. . . .

. . .[T]he constitutional standard for determining whether the State may enter a binding judgment against [Ezra] here is that set forth in this Court's opinion in *International Shoe Co.:* that a defendant "have certain minimum contacts with [the forum State] such that the maintenance of the suit does not offend 'traditional notions of fair play and substantial justice.' " While the interests of the forum State and of the plaintiff in proceeding with the cause in the plaintiff's forum of choice are, of course, to be considered, . . ., an essential criterion in all cases is whether the "quality and nature" of the defendant's activity is such that it is "reasonable" and "fair" to require him to conduct his defense in that State. . . .

. . .[T]he "minimum contacts" test of *International Shoe* is not susceptible of mechanical application; rather, the facts of each case must be weighed to determine whether the requisite "affiliating circumstances" are present. . . .

A

. . .[T]he California Supreme Court did not rely on [Ezra's] glancing presence in the State some 13 years before the events that led to this controversy, nor could it have. [Ezra] has been in California on only two occasions [on stopovers to and from service in Korea.]. To hold such temporary visits to a State a basis for the assertion of *in personam* jurisdiction over unrelated actions arising in the future would make a mockery of the limitations on state jurisdiction. . . . Nor did the California court rely on the fact that [Ezra] was actually married in California on one of his two brief visits. We agree that where two New York domiciliaries, for reasons of convenience, marry in the State of California and thereafter spend their entire married life in New York, the fact of their California marriage by itself cannot support a California court's exercise of jurisdiction over a spouse who remains a New York resident in an action relating to child support.

Finally, . . .the court below carefully disclaimed reliance on the fact that [Ezra] had agreed at the time of separation to allow his children to live with their mother three months a year and that he had sent them to California each year pursuant to this agreement. . . . [T]o find personal jurisdiction in a State on this basis, merely because the mother was residing there, would discourage parents from entering into reasonable visitation agreements. Moreover, it could arbitrarily subject one parent to suit in any State of the Union where the other parent chose to spend time while having custody of their offspring pursuant to a separation agreement. As we have emphasized:

> "The unilateral activity of those who claim some relationship with a nonresident defendant cannot satisfy the requirement of contact with the forum State. . . ."

Hanson v. Denckla, supra, at 253.

The "purposeful act" that the California Supreme Court believed did warrant the exercise of personal jurisdiction over [Ezra] . . . was his "actively and fully consent[ing] to Ilsa living in California for the school year . . . and . . . sen[ding] her to California for that purpose." We cannot accept the proposition that [Ezra's] acquiescence in Ilsa's desire to live with her mother conferred jurisdiction. . . . A father who agrees, in the interests of family harmony and his children's preferences, to allow them to spend more time in California than was required under a separation agreement can hardly be said to have "purposefully availed himself" of the "benefits and protections" of California's laws. . . .

Nor can we agree with the assertion of the court below that the exercise of *in personam* jurisdiction here was warranted by the financial benefit [Ezra] derived from his daughter's presence in California for nine months of the year. This argument rests on the premise that, while [Ezra's] liability for support payments remained unchanged, his yearly expenses for supporting the child in New York decreased. But this circumstance, even if true, does not support California's assertion of jurisdiction here. Any diminution in [Ezra's] household costs resulted, not from the child's presence in California, but rather from her absence from [Ezra's] home. Moreover, an action by [Sharon] to increase support payments could now be brought, and could have been brought when Ilsa first moved to California, in the State of New York; a New York court would clearly have personal jurisdiction over [Ezra] and, if a judgment were entered by a New York court increasing [Ezra's] child-support obligations, it could properly be enforced against him in both New York and California. Any ultimate financial advantage to [Ezra] thus results not from the child's presence in California, but from [Sharon's] failure earlier to seek an increase. . . .

B

In light of our conclusion that [Ezra] did not purposefully derive benefit from any activities relating to the State of California, it is apparent that the California Supreme Court's reliance on [Ezra's] having caused an "effect" in California was misplaced.

The circumstances [here] clearly render "unreasonable" California's assertion of personal jurisdiction. There is no claim that [Ezra] has visited physical injury on either property or persons within the State of California. The cause of action herein asserted arises, not from the defendant's commercial transactions in interstate commerce, but rather from his personal, domestic relations. . . . [Ezra's] activities cannot fairly be analogized to an insurer's sending an insurance contract and premium notices into the State to an insured resident of the State. Furthermore, the controversy . . . arises from a separation that occurred in the State of New York; [Sharon] seeks modification of a contract that was negotiated in New York and that she flew to New York to sign. As in *Hanson,* the instant action involves an agreement . . . with virtually no connection with the forum State.

Finally, basic considerations of fairness point decisively in favor of [Ezra's] State of domicile as the proper forum for adjudication. . . . It is [Ezra] who has remained in the State of the marital domicile, whereas it is [Sharon] who has moved across the continent. . . . As noted above, [Ezra] did no more than acquiesce in the stated preference of one of his children to live with her mother in California. This single act is surely not one that a reasonable parent would expect to result in the substantial financial burden and personal strain of litigating a child-support suit in a forum 3,000 miles away, and we therefore see no basis on which it can be said that [Ezra] could reasonably have anticipated being "haled before a [California] court," *Shaffer.* To make jurisdiction . . . turn on whether [Ezra] bought his daughter her ticket or instead unsuccessfully sought to prevent her departure would impose an unreasonable burden on family relations, and one wholly unjustified by the "quality and nature" of appellant's activities in or relating to the State of California. . . .

III

. . .[Sharon] argues that California has substantial interests in protecting the welfare of its minor residents and in . . . a healthy and supportive family environment. . . . These interests are unquestionably important. But . . . the fact that California may be the "center of gravity" for choice-of-law purposes does not mean that California has personal jurisdiction over the defendant. And California has not attempted to assert any particularized interest in trying such cases in its courts by, *e.g.,* enacting a special jurisdictional statute.

California's legitimate interest in ensuring the support of children resident in California without unduly disrupting the children's lives, moreover, is already being served by the State's participation in the Revised Uniform Reciprocal Enforcement of Support Act of 1968. . . .

Accordingly, we conclude that [Ezra's] motion to quash service . . . was erroneously denied. . . . The judgment . . . is, therefore,

Reversed.

NOTES

1. *Variations.* *Kulko* applies, in the divorce context, the general rule requiring personal jurisdiction over respondent (along with the constitutional minimum contacts analysis) as a pre-requisite to an order determining financial rights and obligations. While directly covering only modification of child support, the principle also covers establishment of child support, establishment or modification of spousal maintenance and property division. The case's central point is made in part II's last paragraph: fairness principles require the traveling party, not the one who has remained in the state of the marital home, to bear the burden of litigating in another state. This principle will decide many (if not most) disputes over the application of long-arm jurisdiction in domestic relations cases. For a recent case applying *Kulko*, see *In re Crew*, 549 N.W.2d 527 (Iowa 1996) (payment of child support in state, communication via letter and telephone and sending children back to state to custodial parent insufficient for personal jurisdiction for support modification);

In many marriages, of course, the parties have lived in more than one state, so that more than one state could assert jurisdiction. Consider, *e.g.*, the couple who spends ten years of married life in State *A*, and then relocates to State *B*. After a year, they divorce and custodial mother returns to *A* with the couple's children. Both State *A* and State *B* could obtain personal jurisdiction over the father in the mother's child support action, under ordinary jurisdiction rules, for the father has strong contacts with State *A* related to the dispute and lives in State *B*.

Nonetheless, the passage of time alone may cause a state to lose sufficient contact to sustain jurisdiction. *E.g.*, in *Garrett v. Garrett*, 668 So. 2d 991 (Fla. 1996), the court found no jurisdiction over a non-resident who had fathered a child in the state, lived there with his family for 12 years and periodically returned to visit. Noting the state had been abandoned (by both parties) as the marital domicile eight years before the suit and that they had lived for five of the intervening years in Texas, the court found that an exercise of jurisdiction facts here "would empower the Florida courts to exercise jurisdiction over any party to a dissolution proceeding if the couple had ever lived in the state, for however brief a time. This would clearly violate the Due Process Clause of the United States Constitution." *See also Morris v. Morris*, 672 So. 2d 622 (Fla. App. 1996) (applying *Garrett*); *but see Panganiban v. Panganiban*, 736 A.2d 190 (Conn. App. 1999) (extending jurisdiction over defendant absent from state for 11 years after living there with wife for 6 years).

Of course, as *Kulko* suggests, availability to the obligee of an interstate enforcement mechanism, such as the Revised Uniform Reciprocal Enforcement of Support Act of 1968 (since replaced by the Uniform Interstate Family Support Act) removes some pressure to stretch jurisdictional rules to allow such actions, at least to the extent one believes the interstate statute effective. (UIFSA is discussed in Chapter 5). No such action was available to the wife in *Khan v. Superior Ct.*, 251 Cal. Rptr. 815 (App. 1988), whose husband had divorced her in a Saudi Arabian court by repeating "I divorce you" three times. The couple had lived in California an aggregate of nine years during their thirty-year marriage, most of the remaining 21 years having been spent in various Middle Eastern locales. But they maintained California contacts even during foreign stays, including ownership of two California homes. Despite the husband's presence in Saudi Arabia since 1974, the court found sufficient

contact with California to distinguish *Kulko* and find jurisdiction over maintenance and marital property claims. The court may have been relying on
plaintiff's lack of other forums, a factor considered in long-arm jurisdiction
cases in ordinary civil suits.

As in other civil actions, personal jurisdiction over the divorce respondent
can be established by serving respondent with process while in the forum
state, even if there is no other contact with the state. *Burnham v. Superior
Court,* 495 U.S. 604 (1990) (in personam jurisdiction over father in mother's
divorce action established by service on him while he was in state visiting
his children); *see also In re Peterson,* 843 P.2d 1107 (Wash. App. 1993) (finding
Burnham precludes respondent's minimum contacts argument against in-state
personal service).

2. *Long-arm Statutes.* California's broad long-arm statute provided simply
jurisdiction "on any basis not inconsistent with the Constitution. . . .",
making it easier for the *Kulko* petitioner to argue that the state intended to
exercise jurisdiction over her former husband. States with less-sweeping
language in their long-arm statutes require the petitioner to fit the support
or property division claim within a particular provision and this can be
difficult. Courts have held, *e.g.,* that support claims normally cannot be
brought under the "transacts any business" portion of the typical long-arm
statute, while the negotiation and execution of a separation agreement within
the state may qualify as the conduct of "business" within the statute. *Warren
v. Warren,* 287 S.E.2d 524 (Ga. 1982); *but see Poindexter v. Poindexter,* 594
N.W.2d 76 (Mich. App. 1999)(asserting jurisdiction for support order against
defendant who had been out of state for 22 years; fathering child creates quasi-
contractual obligation under long-arm provision covering those who contract
with state citizens).

To avoid such problems, many states have enacted special domestic relations provisions in their long-arm statutes. In fact, as of January 1, 1998,
states are required as a condition of their receipt of Federal welfare funding
(see 42 U.S.C. § 666(f)(1997)), to have enacted the Uniform Interstate Family
Support Act, which includes a long-arm provision for child and spousal support
claims. The Uniform Act provides:

> SECTION 201. BASES FOR JURISDICTION. . . . In a proceeding
> to establish, enforce, or modify a support order or to determine
> parentage, a [court] may exercise personal jurisdiction over a nonresi-
> dent . . . if:
>
> (1) the individual is personally served . . . within this State;
>
> (2) the individual submits to the jurisdiction of this State by
> consent. . .;
>
> (3) the individual resided with the child in this State;
>
> (4) the individual resided in this State and provided prenatal
> expenses or support for the child;
>
> (5) the child resides in this State as a result of the acts or direc-
> tives of the individual;
>
> (6) the individual engaged in sexual intercourse in this State and
> the child may have been conceived by that act of intercourse;

. . . or

(8) there is any other basis consistent with the constitutions of this State and the United States for the exercise of personal jurisdiction.

Given the inclusion of the California-style subsection (8), the earlier subsections might seem superfluous. The drafters may have included the specific provisions in hopes that reliance on a narrowly-drafted provision might satisfy any notice requirements implicit in the Due Process clause. Alternatively, the inclusion of such specific language might express the drafters' opinion that any of the facts in the subsections would satisfy minimum contacts requirements. If so, are they right? What if, *e.g.*, the respondent's only connection with the forum state was residence there with the child which had ended ten years earlier? *See Levy v. Levy*, 592 N.Y.S.2d 480 (App. Div. 1993) (Constitution not violated by application of long-arm where forum marital domicile had ended ten years earlier). Similarly, would brief marital residency in the forum confer jurisdiction on a defendant who had been absent for 20 years? *See Strickland v. Strickland*, 534 S.E.2d 74 (Ga. 2000) (finding exercise of jurisdiction in such a situation unconstitutional).

Another explanation for the appearance of subsection 8 is reflected in a recent North Carolina case which noted that most of UIFSA's provisions define jurisdiction in child support litigation. Other than personal service or consent (in subsections 1 and 2, respectively), the only ground for exercise of jurisdiction over alimony or property division issues is subsection 8. *Butler v. Butler*, 566 S.E.2d 707 (N.C. App. 2002). It upheld subsection (8) jurisdiction where defendant had jointly purchased a home in the forum, decided to move his wife and children to the state because of the good schools and visited them (from his home in the Bahamas) several days each month over a two-year period.

3. *Continuing Jurisdiction.* The usual rule is that personal jurisdiction, once established in a case, is not lost through subsequent events. Courts of equity claim continuing jurisdiction to enforce or modify their orders even if the parties move. This principle applies in support actions. *See, e.g., Bailey v. Bailey*, 867 P.2d 1267 (Okla. 1994) (constitutional attack based on lack of minimum contacts rejected in support modification where neither parent nor children remained in forum); *see also Hall v. Hall*, 524 So. 2d 370 (Ala. Civ. App. 1988); Annot., *Necessity of Personal Service within State Upon Nonresident Spouse as Prerequisite of Court's Power to Modify Its Decree as to Alimony or Child Support in Matrimonial Action*, 62 A.L.R.2d 544 (1958). In light of *Kulko*'s emphasis on fairness to an absent defendant, is it possible that at some point the exercise of continuing jurisdiction might violate the minimum contacts doctrine? For example, imagine a case where both parties had left the forum state immediately after the decree 10 years before, neither was domiciled in the forum state when modification was sought and the respondent had not set foot in the forum since the decree was rendered. Could modification jurisdiction be exercised constitutionally?

4. *Modification by Another State.* In general, of course, a final judgment made by a court with jurisdiction is entitled to full faith and credit in sister states. While this principle applies to judgments for alimony, maintenance, and child custody, the result is a bit different than with ordinary civil judgments because the Supreme Court has held the Constitution requires recognition only of final decrees and, to the extent family law decrees are modifiable, there is no mandate for recognition. *Aldrich v. Aldrich,* 378 U.S. 540 (1964); *Barber v. Barber,* 323 U.S. 77 (1944); *Sistare v. Sistare,* 218 U.S. 1 (1910). Thus, a second state need not enter its own decree ordering future (and thus modifiable) payments of child support or maintenance. While a state is not bound to honor modifiable decrees, it may choose to do so by adopting (often known as domesticating) the existing decree and rendering a new judgment of its own. *Griffin v. Griffin,* 327 U.S. 220 (1946). After adopting the decree, the second state may modify it. *Norwood v. Craig,* 658 So. 2d 212 (La. App. 1995); *Watson v. Blakely,* 748 P.2d 984 (N.M. App. 1987); *Walzer v. Walzer,* 376 A.2d 414 (Conn. 1977). Of course, to modify the new order the second state will need personal jurisdiction over the respondent. *Laney v. Nigro,* 905 S.W.2d 902 (Mo. App. 1995); *Scott (Anderson) v. Scott,* 492 N.W.2d 831 (Minn. App. 1992). Two different Uniform Acts each provide mechanisms for the domestication of one state's judgment in another state. *See* UNIFORM ENFORCEMENT OF FOREIGN JUDGMENTS ACT, 13 U.L.A. 149 (1986); UNIFORM INTERSTATE FAMILY SUPPORT ACT, Vol. 9, Part IB U.L.A. 42 (2003 Supp.). To reduce multiple relitigation in multiple jurisdictions over the appropriate level of child support, Congress has restricted the ability of states to exercise modification jurisdiction. *See* Full Faith and Credit for Child Support Orders Act, 28 U.S.C. 1738B (2000) (discussed in Chapter 5).

5. *Real Property Outside the Forum State.* A complicating factor in divorce jurisdiction arises where the couple owns divisible real property outside the forum. Traditionally, only the state where real property is located has power to affect title to it. SCOLES, HAY, BORCHERS & SYMEONIDES, CONFLICT OF LAWS § 24.10 (3d ed. 2000). This would bar a change in title by a non-situs state, even one with personal jurisdiction over the owner. Almost 100 years ago the Supreme Court applied this rule in the divorce context, affirming Nebraska's refusal to recognize a Washington decree awarding wife title to Nebraska realty. *Fall v. Eastin,* 215 U.S. 1 (1909). Despite the fact that some applications of this rule would appear inconsistent with modern jurisdictional standards, it survives, though not without serious questioning. *See* Weintraub, *An Inquiry into the Utility of "Situs" as a Concept in Conflict Analysis,* 52 CORN. L.Q. 1 (1966); Hancock, *Full Faith and Credit to Foreign Laws and Judgments in Real Property Litigation: The Supreme Court and the Land Taboo,* 18 STAN. L. REV. 1299, 1310–14 (1963).

As a practical matter, the rule is unworkable for a divorce court making an equitable division of property. Only the court settling the parties' entire financial arrangement can determine the proper disposition of their real property, and in any event that court's law will govern the division of property upon divorce, not the law of the situs. Thus, despite the absence of constitutional compulsion, situs states typically recognize decrees of non-situs divorce courts fixing spousal property rights. Usually, the divorce court avoids any attempt to affect directly the title and instead orders the spouses to make whatever conveyance is necessary to effect the property disposition. *In re Marriage of Day,* 904 P.2d 171 (Ore. App. 1995) (directing distribution of equity of California property); *Eckard v. Eckard,* 636 A.2d 455 (Md. 1994) (upholding order to ex-wife to authorize ex-husband to sell Florida land). If the order was issued with personal jurisdiction over the defendant, the situs state will recognize and enforce it. Some states do this as a matter of comity, while others assert Full Faith and Credit compulsion, distinguishing such orders from those directly affecting title to land. *In re Marriage of Hanley*, 245 Cal. Rptr. 441 (App. 1988) (recognizing efficacy of Washington decree requiring conveyance of California property). A court with personal jurisdiction over owner-spouse can hold him in contempt for refusing to comply with its order to convey non-situs real property. *Collins v. Collins*, 898 P.2d 1316 (Okla. App. 1995).

6. *Jurisdiction Based on Marital Property?* In *Abernathy v. Abernathy*, 482 S.E.2d 265 (Ga. 1997), the divorcing couple had never lived in Georgia and apparently the wife had never been within the state. After their separation in Louisiana, however, the husband moved to Georgia and established domicile. He brought some marital property with him and also earned marital property in Georgia before filing for divorce. He sought division of the marital property, both real and personal, located in Georgia.

The Georgia Supreme Court affirmed the trial court's exercise of jurisdiction to divide the property, finding exercise of jurisdiction not inconsistent with the analysis of *Shaffer v. Heitner*. The majority relied on the following language in *Shaffer* which suggested that in some cases the mere presence of property in the forum necessarily would satisfy the required *International Shoe* minimum contacts analysis:

> [W]hen claims to the property itself are the source of the underlying controversy between the plaintiff and the defendant, it would be unusual for the State where the property is located not to have jurisdiction. In such cases, the defendant's claim to property located in the State would normally indicate that he expected to benefit from the State's protection of his interest. The State's strong interests in assuring the marketability of property within its borders and in providing a procedure for peaceful resolution of disputes about the . . . property would also support jurisdiction, as would the likelihood that important records and witnesses will be found in the State.

Id. at 207–8. This is not the *quasi in rem* jurisdiction disallowed in *Shaffer* because the courts' jurisdiction was limited to adjudicating interests in the property before it. However, whether it is consistent with the constitutional requirements for limited jurisdiction may be disputed. *E.g.*, an *Abernathy* dissenter noted the wife "has never lived here and she did not participate in the decision of her husband to acquire property in this state. . . . Forcing the wife to litigate her interests in marital assets wherever her husband happens to relocate violates 'traditional notions of fair play and substantial justice.'" *See Hoffman v. Hoffman*, 821 S.W.2d 3 (Tex. App. 1992) (citing *Shaffer* for proposition that court may sometimes "lack jurisdiction to divide property within the [forum] state").

7. *Military Pensions.* The federal Uniformed Services Former Spouses Protection Act (summarized in Chapter 4's discussion of pension division), bars a divorce court from exercising jurisdiction over a spouse's military pension using the ordinary minimum-contacts analysis usually used in property claims. Under the federal law, jurisdiction requires that the pensioned spouse is resident or domiciled in the forum state, or has consented to jurisdiction. *In re Tucker,* 277 Cal. Rptr. 403 (App. 1991); *Mortenson v. Mortenson,* 409 N.W.2d 20 (Minn. App. 1987).

PROBLEMS

Problem 7-1. Husband *H* and Wife *W* marry in California, where they live together for ten years. They then separate, and *H* moves to Oregon with his new girlfriend. *W,* who remains behind in California, files an action for divorce there. What may the California court adjudicate?

Problem 7-2. Assume the same facts as in Problem 7-1, except that instead of remaining in California, *W* moves to New York where her family lives. *W* now seeks to bring a divorce action which will include claims for property division, alimony and child support. Can a unitary action addressing all matters be brought by her in New York? In Oregon? In California?

Problem 7-3. Suppose, in Problem 7-2, *W* could not bring a unitary action in Oregon because state law required a divorce petitioner to be a domiciliary. In a constitutional challenge to this requirement, would *Sosna* control?

Problem 7-4. Harry and Sally were married in the State of Bliss which was where her parents had moved when she left the original family home in Oregon. Immediately after the wedding, they left Bliss and spent the next 16 years traveling around the world where each had assignments as journalists. The only time during this period in which they were in the United States for more than a week was when they spent 6 months in Georgia in the mid-90's. During the marriage, all federal income tax forms and returns were sent to Harry and Sally at her parents' home in Bliss. From 1991 to 1997 Harry had his salary direct deposited into a Bliss bank account. From 1989 to 2000, Harry had a Bliss driver's license. Harry's will named his parents-in-law co-executors of his estate. Harry and Sally had an investment account in Bliss for the last 7 years of their marriage. After their separation in 2003, Sally returned to Bliss to live with her parents. She has filed for divorce there, seeking alimony. State law provides for personal jurisdiction over the parties in any case "that arises out of the marital relationship within this State, notwithstanding subsequent departure from the State, if the other party to the marital relationship continues to reside in this state." Is the statute satisfied and is the Constitution satisfied?

Problem 7-5. Beverly and James were married in Massachusetts. After living there for 7 years, the childless couple moved to Florida. Eleven years later, pregnant with their first child, Beverly left her husband to move back to Massachusetts, where the child was born. Several years later, she filed for divorce in Massachusetts, claiming cruel and abusive treatment by James throughout their marriage and seeking child support. Her affidavit asserts the only way she could support herself and her child after her separation was to live in her parents' home in Massachusetts. James has never owned any real estate in the state, has transacted no business there in over 15 years and has visited the state only once since Beverly moved there to see his daughter perform in her third grade play. The state statute authorizes the exercise of personal jurisdiction over any person:

> 1) "who acts directly or by an agent, as to a cause of action arising from the person's maintaining a domicile in this commonwealth while a party to a personal or marital relationship out of which arises a claim for divorce, alimony, property settlement, parentage of a child, child support or child custody; or the commission of any act giving rise to such a claim;. . . .6) where the claim is for child support and the child resides in this Commonwealth as a result of the acts of the defendant. . . ."

Is the statute satisfied? Is the Constitution satisfied?

§ C. JURISDICTION TO ADJUDICATE CUSTODY DISPUTES

[1] CONSTITUTIONAL FRAMEWORK

Section B applied ordinary personal jurisdiction rules to cases adjudicating the financial incidents of divorce, noting that generally the minimum contacts principle determines whether judicial power over the respondent exists. Does this rule also apply to child custody adjudications? Surprisingly, the Supreme Court's most recent opinion on this point, now over 50 years old, leaves this question unanswered. In *May v. Anderson,* 345 U.S. 528 (1953), the wife left her husband in Wisconsin and moved to Ohio with their children. Soon after, the husband commenced a Wisconsin divorce action. The wife failed to appear, though she was served in Ohio. Wisconsin's grant of custody to father was unchallenged for four years, until mother refused to surrender the children after her summer visitation period.

In the father's *habeas corpus* action, the Ohio courts held full faith and credit required recognition of the Wisconsin custody order, accepting father's claim that the children remained Wisconsin domiciliaries despite their physical presence in Ohio and Wisconsin retained jurisdiction over them. The Supreme Court, however, held Ohio was not bound by the Wisconsin decree, finding the children's domicile irrelevant, because "that does not give Wisconsin . . . the personal jurisdiction that it must have in order to deprive their mother of . . . their immediate possession." *Id.* at 534.

The case reads oddly today because of its restrictive notions of personal jurisdiction. The modern Court likely would uphold Wisconsin's exercise of personal jurisdiction over wife where (a) it had long been the marital home, (b) the father remained there, and (c) the wife had been personally served soon after departing.

In any event, *May* is less important than one might expect. While it frees states from any obligation to honor custody decrees rendered without personal jurisdiction over the respondent spouse, in practice there always had been little application of full faith and credit to custody decrees anyway. The Clause has been held to require only that a second state give a judgment the same effect as it has in the rendering state. Because all states permit modification of custody awards upon changed circumstances, almost all custody decrees have been considered reviewable by a second state, at least for changed circumstances. *See Ford v. Ford,* 371 U.S. 187 (1962); *Kovacs v. Brewer,* 356 U.S. 604 (1958).

May would have mattered more had it found that due process requires personal jurisdiction over respondent spouse for a binding custody decision, but the Court never quite said that. To the modern ear, any distinction between the dictates of due process, and of full faith and credit, may sound strange. The current assumption is that full faith and credit is required for all decrees obtained with jurisdiction, thus making due process and full faith and credit coextensive. But in a concurring opinion, Justice Frankfurter, the fifth member of the five-justice *May* majority, found that while personal jurisdiction over the respondent spouse was required for full faith and credit, a decree in the absence of such jurisdiction would not offend the Due Process Clause. That is, "one-state jurisdiction" which did not require interstate respect was possible; a state constitutionally could render a custody decree enforceable within its borders but without effect elsewhere.

The remaining members of the majority never spoke to this question, however, and it remains uncertain whether personal jurisdiction over respondent spouse is required under due process as well as under the Full Faith and Credit Clause. One explanation for the Frankfurter view is that custody, like termination of the marriage, is an adjudication of "status," to which the personal jurisdiction requirements of due process do not apply. Even many years after *May,* after the Court extended the personal-jurisdiction principles of *International Shoe* to *quasi-in-rem* actions, the Court reiterated the status rules. *Shaffer v. Heitner,* 433 U.S. 186, 208 n.30 (1977).

States and Congress consistently have acted to authorize custody jurisdiction without personal jurisdiction over the respondent parent. This approach is exemplified by the traditional state law rule basing custody jurisdiction solely on the presence of the subject child. This was analogized to the power of the state to adjudicate marital status based solely on one spouse's presence even without personal jurisdiction over the respondent. Such traditional rules would be valid only if Frankfurter's understanding of *May* were adopted.

Today traditional state law rules governing custody jurisdiction have been supplanted by new statutes — the Uniform Child Custody Jurisdiction and Enforcement Act (UCCJEA) and the Parental Kidnapping Prevention Act (PKPA) — considered at length below. The *May* issue survives, however, because these statutes sometimes assert jurisdiction without personal jurisdiction over an absent parent. Some lower courts have ignored Frankfurter's concurrence, reading *May* as holding due process forbids enforcement of custody decrees in such cases. *Pasqualone v. Pasqualone,* 406 N.E.2d 1121 (Ohio 1980); *In re Dean,* 447 So. 2d 733 (Ala. 1984). However, most courts and commentators conclude that a custody decree complying with the UCC-JEA (or its predecessor, the UCCJA) is constitutionally acceptable, even without satisfaction of the minimum contacts test. *See, e.g., In re Thomas J.R.,* 663 N.W.2d 734 (Wisc. 2003) (termination of parental rights under UCCJA despite lack of minimum contacts); *Balestrieri v. Miliska,* 622 So. 2d 561 (Fla. App. 1993) (finding custody within *Shaffer v. Heitner*'s "status exception");

Coombs, *Interstate Child Custody: Jurisdiction, Recognition, Enforcement,* 66 MINN. L. REV. 711 (1982). Professor Atwood agrees that personal jurisdiction over the absent parent is not and ought not be required. Instead, she proposes requiring "territorial jurisdiction" to be determined through analysis of "child-centered contacts with the forum state." Atwood, *Child Custody Jurisdiction and Territoriality,* 52 OHIO ST. L.J. 369, 372–73 (1991).

[2] THE MODERN STATUTORY FRAMEWORK

Frankfurter's approach left each state free to devise its own custody jurisdiction rules, because due process imposed no threshold for permissible assertions. When most custody disputes remained within one state, interstate divisions over appropriate jurisdictional rules did not matter much, but custody disputes became increasingly multi-state. A parent dissatisfied with a custody decision often would seek a new one elsewhere. The second state usually was able and often willing to render a new decree, which as a practical matter would be enforceable if the child was physically within the jurisdiction. Child snatching, thus, was encouraged. This unfortunate situation became a target of reform, resulting in successive uniform state laws and a federal statute. In 1968, the Commissioners on Uniform Laws proposed the Uniform Child Custody Jurisdiction Act (UCCJA). While it was eventually adopted in each state, before its universal adoption (and likely in an effort to encourage the remaining states to adopt it), Congress in 1980 passed the Parental Kidnapping Prevention Act (PKPA), which defines the jurisdictional bases for custody decrees which are entitled to respect by other states. While the two acts were similar, there were critical differences between them concerning the appropriate bases for jurisdiction. Because of those differences and also because of widely varying interpretations of the UCCJA over the prior 29 years, in 1997 the National Conference of Commissioners on Uniform State Laws, with the endorsement of the American Bar Association, proposed a replacement, the Uniform Child Custody Jurisdiction and Enforcement Act (UCC-JEA). By spring, 2004, this Act had been passed in 35 states. The remaining jurisdictions retain their version of the UCCJA. For the history of the Uniform and federal legislation, see Hoff, *The ABC's of the UCCJEA,* 32 FAM. L.Q. 267 (1998); Coombs, *Child Custody and Visitation by Non-Parents Under the New Uniform Child Custody Jurisdiction and Enforcement Act: A Rerun of Seize-and-Run,* 16 J. AM. ACAD. MATRIMONIAL LAW. 1 (1999); Stoner, *The Uniform Child Custody Jurisdiction and Enforcement Act (UCCJEA) — A Metamorphosis of the Uniform Child Custody Jurisdiction Act (UCCJA),* 75 N. DAK. L. REV. 301 (1999); *see also* Minneman, Annotation, *Construction and Operation of Uniform Child Custody Jurisdiction and Enforcement Act,* 100 A.L.R.5th 1 (2003).

UNIFORM CHILD CUSTODY JURISDICTION AND ENFORCEMENT ACT

§ 102. DEFINITIONS. In this [Act]:

. . . .

(3) "Child-custody determination" means a judgment, decree, or other order of a court providing for the legal custody, physical custody, or visitation with respect to a child. The term includes a permanent, temporary, initial, and modification order. . . .

(4) "Child-custody proceeding" means a proceeding in which legal custody, physical custody, or visitation with respect to a child is an issue. The term includes a proceeding for divorce, separation, neglect, abuse, dependency, guardianship, paternity, termination of parental rights, and protection from domestic violence, in which the issue may appear. The term does not include a proceeding involving juvenile delinquency, contractual emancipation, or enforcement. . . .

. . . .

(7) "Home State" means the State in which a child lived with a parent or a person acting as a parent for at least six consecutive months immediately before the commencement of a child-custody proceeding. In the case of a child less than six months of age, the term means the State in which the child lived from birth with any of the persons mentioned. A period of temporary absence of any of the mentioned persons is part of the period.

(8) "Initial determination" means the first child-custody determination concerning a particular child.

. . . .

(11) "Modification" means a child-custody determination that changes, replaces, supersedes, or is otherwise made after a previous determination concerning the same child, whether or not it is made by the court that made the previous determination.

. . . .

(13) "Person acting as a parent" means a person, other than a parent, who:

(A) has physical custody of the child or has had physical custody for a period of six consecutive months, including any temporary absence, within one year immediately before the commencement of a child-custody proceeding; and

(B) has been awarded legal custody by a court or claims a right to legal custody under the law of this State.

. . . .

§ 103. PROCEEDINGS GOVERNED BY OTHER LAW. This [Act] does not govern an adoption proceeding. . . .

. . . .

§ 105. INTERNATIONAL APPLICATION OF [ACT].

(a) A court of this State shall treat a foreign country as if it were a State. . . .

. . . .

(c) A court of this State need not apply this [Act] if the child custody law of a foreign country violates fundamental principles of human rights.

§ 106. EFFECT OF CHILD-CUSTODY DETERMINATION.

A child-custody determination made by a court of this State that had jurisdiction under this [Act] binds all persons who have been served in accordance with the laws of this State or notified in accordance with [the laws of this state or of the state in which service is made] or who have submitted to the jurisdiction of the court, and who have been given an opportunity to be heard. As to those persons, the determination is conclusive as to all decided issues of law and fact except to the extent the determination is modified.

. . . .

§ 110. COMMUNICATION BETWEEN COURTS.

(a) A court of this State may communicate with a court in another State concerning a proceeding arising under this [Act].

(b) The court may allow the parties to participate in the communication. If the parties are not able to participate . . ., they must be given the opportunity to present facts and legal arguments before a decision on jurisdiction is made.

. . . .

§ 201. INITIAL CHILD-CUSTODY JURISDICTION.

(a) Except as otherwise provided in § 204, a court of this State has jurisdiction to make an initial child-custody determination only if:

(1) this State is the home State of the child [at] the commencement of the proceeding, or was the home State . . . within six months before the commencement of the proceeding and the child is absent from this State but a parent or person acting as a parent continues to live in this State;

(2) a court of another State does not have jurisdiction under paragraph (1), or . . . the home State of the child has declined to exercise jurisdiction on the ground that this State is the more appropriate forum under § 207 or § 208, and:

(A) the child and the child's parents, or the child and at least one parent or a person acting as a parent, have a significant connection with this State other than mere physical presence; and

(B) substantial evidence is available in this State concerning the child's care, protection, training, and personal relationships;

(3) all courts having jurisdiction under paragraph (1) or (2) have declined to exercise jurisdiction on the ground that a court of this State is the more appropriate forum. . . .; or

(4) no court of any other State would have jurisdiction under the criteria specified in paragraph (1), (2), or (3).

(b) Subsection (a) is the exclusive jurisdictional basis for making a child-custody determination by a court of this State.

(c) Physical presence of, or personal jurisdiction over, a party or a child is not necessary or sufficient to make a child-custody determination.

§ 202. EXCLUSIVE, CONTINUING JURISDICTION.

(a) Except as otherwise provided in § 204, a court of this State which has made a child-custody determination consistent with § 201 or § 203 has exclusive, continuing jurisdiction over the determination until:

(1) a court of this State determines that neither the child, nor the child and one parent, nor the child and a person acting as a parent have a significant connection with this State and that substantial evidence is no longer available in this State concerning the child's care, protection, training, and personal relationships; or

(2) a court of this State or a court of another State determines that the child, the child's parents, and any person acting as a parent do not presently reside in this State.

. . . .

§ 203. JURISDICTION TO MODIFY DETERMINATION.

Except as otherwise provided in § 204, a court of this State may not modify a child-custody determination made by . . . another State unless a court of this State has jurisdiction to make an initial determination under § 201(a)(1) or (2) and:

(1) the court of the other State determines it no longer has exclusive, continuing jurisdiction under § 202 or that a court of this State would be a more convenient forum under § 207; or

(2) a court of this State or a court of the other State determines that the child, the child's parents, and any person acting as a parent do not presently reside in the other State.

. . . .

SECTION 204. TEMPORARY EMERGENCY JURISDICTION.

(a) A court of this State has temporary emergency jurisdiction if the child is present in this State and the child has been abandoned or it is necessary . . . to protect the child because the child, or a sibling or parent of the child, is subjected to or threatened with mistreatment or abuse.

(b) [If there is no existing order or ongoing litigation elsewhere], a child-custody determination made under this section remains in effect until an order is obtained from a court of a State having jurisdiction under [the Act]. If a child-custody proceeding has not been or is not commenced in a court of a State having jurisdiction under [the Act], a child-custody determination made under this section becomes a final determination, if it so provides and this State becomes the home State of the child.

(c) If there is a previous child-custody determination that is entitled to be enforced under this [Act], or a child-custody proceeding has been commenced in a court of a State having jurisdiction under [the Act, the emergency jurisdiction shall] specify in the order a period [during which petitioner must obtain an order from the court which issued the prior order]. The order issued in this State remains in effect until [such]an order is obtained . . . within the period specified or the period expires.

. . . .

§ 206. SIMULTANEOUS PROCEEDINGS.

(a) Except as otherwise provided in § 204, a court of this State may not exercise its jurisdiction under this [article] if, at the time of the commencement of the proceeding, a proceeding concerning the custody of the child has been commenced in a court of another State having jurisdiction substantially in conformity with this [Act], unless the proceeding has been terminated or is stayed by the court of the other State because a court of this State is a more convenient forum under § 207.

(b). . . . If the court determines that a child-custody proceeding has been commenced in a court in another State having jurisdiction substantially in accordance with this [Act], the court of this State shall stay its proceeding and communicate with the court of the other State. If the court of the State having jurisdiction substantially in accordance with this [Act] does not determine that the court of this State is a more appropriate forum, the court of this State shall dismiss the proceeding.

. . . .

§ 207. INCONVENIENT FORUM.

(a) A court of this State which has jurisdiction under this [Act] to make a child-custody determination may decline to exercise its jurisdiction at any time if it determines that it is an inconvenient forum under the circumstances and that a court of another State is a more appropriate forum. The issue of inconvenient forum may be raised upon motion of a party, the court's own motion, or request of another court.

(b) Before determining whether it is an inconvenient forum, a court . . . shall consider whether it is appropriate for a court of another State to exercise jurisdiction. . . . [T]he court shall allow the parties to submit information and shall consider all relevant factors, including:

(1) whether domestic violence has occurred and is likely to continue in the future and which State could best protect the parties and the child;

(2) the length of time the child has resided outside this State;

(3) the distance between the court in this State and the court in the State that would assume jurisdiction;

(4) the relative financial circumstances of the parties;

(5) any agreement of the parties as to which State should assume jurisdiction;

(6) the nature and location of the evidence required to resolve the pending litigation, including testimony of the child;

(7) the ability of the court of each State to decide the issue expeditiously and the procedures necessary to present the evidence; and

(8) the familiarity of the court of each State with the facts and issues in the pending litigation.

(c) If a court of this State determines that it is an inconvenient forum and that a court of another State is a more appropriate forum, it shall stay the proceedings upon condition that a child-custody proceeding be promptly commenced in another designated State and may impose any other condition the court considers just and proper.

(d) A court of this State may decline to exercise its jurisdiction under this [Act] if a child-custody determination is incidental to an action for divorce or another proceeding while still retaining jurisdiction over the divorce or other proceeding.

§ 208. JURISDICTION DECLINED BY REASON OF CONDUCT.

(a) Except as otherwise provided in § 204 [or by other law of this State], if a court of this State has jurisdiction under this [Act] because a person seeking to invoke its jurisdiction has engaged in unjustifiable conduct, the court shall decline to exercise its jurisdiction unless:

(1) the parents and all persons acting as parents have acquiesced in the exercise of jurisdiction;

(2) a court of the State otherwise having jurisdiction under §§ 201 through 203 determines that this State is a more appropriate forum under § 207; or

(3) no court of any other State would have jurisdiction under the criteria specified in §§ 201 through 203.

(b) If a court of this State declines to exercise its jurisdiction pursuant to subsection (a), it may fashion an appropriate remedy to ensure the safety of the child and prevent a repetition of the unjustifiable conduct, including staying the proceeding until a child-custody proceeding is commenced in a court having jurisdiction under §§ 201 through 203.

(c) If a court dismisses a petition or stays a proceeding because it declines to exercise its jurisdiction pursuant to subsection (a), it shall assess against the party seeking to invoke its jurisdiction necessary and reasonable expenses. . . .

PARENTAL KIDNAPPING PREVENTION ACT, 28 U.S.C. § 1738A

(a) The appropriate authorities of every State shall enforce according to its terms, and shall not modify except as provided in subsections (f), (g), and (h) of this section, any custody . . .or visitation determination made consistently with the provisions of this section by a court of another State.

(b) As used in this section, the term—

(1) "child" means a person under the age of eighteen;

(2) "contestant" means a person, including a parent or grandparent, who claims a right to custody or visitation of a child;

(3) "custody determination" means a judgment, decree, or other order of a court providing for the custody of a child, and includes permanent and temporary orders, and initial orders and modifications;

(4) "home State" means the State in which, immediately preceding the time involved, the child lived with his parents, a parent, or a person acting as parent, for at least six consecutive months, and in the case of a child less than six months old, the State in which the child lived from birth with any of such persons. Periods of temporary absence of any of such persons are counted as part of the six-month or other period;

(5) "modification" and "modify" refer to a custody or visitation determination which modifies, replaces, supersedes, or otherwise is made subsequent to, a prior custody or visitation determination concerning the same child, whether made by the same court or not;

(6) "person acting as a parent" means a person, other than a parent, who has physical custody of a child and who has either been awarded custody by a court or claims a right to custody;

(7) "physical custody" means actual possession and control of a child;

(8) "State" means a State of the United States, the District of Columbia, the Commonwealth of Puerto Rico, or a territory or possession of the United States; and

(9) "visitation determination" means a judgment, decree, or other order of a court providing for the visitation of a child and includes permanent and temporary orders and initial orders and modifications.

(c) A child custody or visitation determination made by a court of a State is consistent with the provisions of this section only if—

(1) such court has jurisdiction under the law of such State; and

(2) one of the following conditions is met:

(A) such State (i) is the home State of the child on the date of the commencement of the proceeding, or (ii) had been the child's home State within six months before the date of the commencement of the proceeding and the child is absent from such State because of his removal or retention by a contestant or for other reasons, and a contestant continues to live in such State;

(B) (i) it appears that no other State would have jurisdiction under subparagraph (A), and (ii) it is in the best interest of the child that a court of such State assume jurisdiction because (I) the child and his parents, or the child and at least one contestant, have a significant connection with such State other than mere physical presence in such State, and (II) there is available in such State substantial evidence concerning the child's present or future care, protection, training, and personal relationships;

(C) the child is physically present in such State and (i) the child has been abandoned, or (ii) it is necessary in an emergency to protect the child because the child, a sibling, or parent of the child has been subjected to or threatened with mistreatment or abuse;

(D) (i) it appears that no other State would have jurisdiction under subparagraph (A), (B), (C), or (E), or another State has declined to exercise jurisdiction on the ground that the State whose jurisdiction is in issue is the more appropriate forum to determine the custody or visitation of the child, and (ii) it is in the best interest of the child that such court assume jurisdiction; or

(E) the court has continuing jurisdiction pursuant to subsection (d) of this section.

(d) The jurisdiction of a court of a State which has made a . . . . determination consistently with the provisions of this section continues as long as the requirement of subsection (c)(1) of this section continues to be met and such State remains the residence of the child or of any contestant.

(e) Before a . . . determination is made, reasonable notice and opportunity to be heard shall be given to the contestants, any parent whose parental rights have not been previously terminated and any person who has physical custody of a child.

(f) A court of a State may modify a determination of the custody of the same child made by a court of another State, if—

(1) it has jurisdiction to make such a child custody determination; and

(2) the court of the other State no longer has jurisdiction, or it has declined to exercise such jurisdiction to modify such determination.

(g) A court of a State shall not exercise jurisdiction in any proceeding . . . commenced during the pendency of a proceeding in a court of another State where such court of that other State is exercising jurisdiction consistently with the provisions of this section to make a custody determination.

(h) A court of a State may not modify a visitation determination made by a court of another State unless the court of the other State no longer has jurisdiction to modify such determination or has declined to exercise jurisdiction to modify such determination.

[a] Jurisdiction to Render Initial Custody Decree

WELCH-DODEN v. ROBERTS

42 P.3d 1166 (Ariz. App. 2002)

BARKER, Judge

This opinion resolves a statutory conflict in the meaning of "home state" as that phrase is used to determine initial jurisdiction between competing states in child custody disputes under Arizona's newly adopted Uniform Child Custody Jurisdiction and Enforcement Act ("UCCJEA"). . . .

[Mother and Father married in Arizona in 1996. After moving to Oklahoma, their child was born there in April, 1999. Subsequently, mother and child moved several times between the two states to permit mother to research job opportunities in Arizona. The child was in Oklahoma for the first 7 ½ months of life. Mother and child then were in Arizona for 3 months, Oklahoma for 6 months and then Arizona for four months when Mother filed for divorce, seeking custody. Immediately thereafter father, still in Oklahoma, filed there. He contested jurisdiction in the Arizona action and the Arizona trial court, finding Oklahoma the child's home state, dismissed the action for lack of jurisdiction. Mother appealed this dismissal.]

. . . .

. . . . The question of "home state" jurisdiction under the UCCJEA is of first impression, has statewide importance, and is likely to recur. . . .

. . . .

We consider several issues: First, does the UCCJEA provide that home state jurisdiction is based on a child residing in a state (a) for a six-month period *immediately prior* to the filing of a custody petition, or (b) for a six-month period that is completed *at any time within* six months of the filing?

Second, if a state has home state jurisdiction, does home state jurisdiction then become pre-eminent, thereby precluding a court without home state jurisdiction from considering the child's best interests for jurisdictional purposes?

And finally, does a state with home state jurisdiction have jurisdictional priority when a petition in another state was filed first-in-time?

. . . .

[UCCJEA § 201] is the statutory starting place for determining initial jurisdiction. In summary, subsection (b) makes it clear that Arizona *only* has jurisdiction pursuant to subsection (a). Subsection (a), paragraph (1) provides for Arizona to have jurisdiction when Arizona qualifies as a home state. If a state is the "home state" under this paragraph, it has jurisdiction. There is no further factual inquiry on the *jurisdictional* issue. Paragraphs (2)-(4) . . . provide the circumstances whereby Arizona may have jurisdiction when it does *not* qualify as the home state. Paragraph 2, in particular, requires the court to consider whether the child has a significant connection to the state (as well as other factors) before jurisdiction may be found. Subsection (c) clarifies that the presence of the child is neither necessary nor sufficient to establish jurisdiction.

In considering [§ 201] . . ., we must . . . take into account [that] [Section 102(7)] defines "home state" as follows:

> . . .The state in which a child lived with a parent or a person acting as a parent for *at least six consecutive months immediately before the commencement of a child custody proceeding*, including any period during which that person is temporarily absent from that state.

. . . [T]his definition of "home state" to [§ 201] [confcts with § 201 which provides that] a state has jurisdiction if [it]

> is the [1] home state of the child *on the date of the commencement of the proceeding*, or [2] was the home state of the child *within six months before the commencement* of the proceeding and the child is absent from this state but a parent or person acting as a parent continues to live in this state.

The definition of "home state" . . . provides, however, that a state is a "home state" *only* when "a child lived with a parent . . . for at least six consecutive months *immediately before* the commencement of a child custody proceeding." (Emphasis added.)

Thus, applying literally the definition of "home state" from [§ 102] to element one of [§ 201(a)(1)] renders superfluous the language . . . that says jurisdiction lies when a state is the home state "on the date of the commencement of the proceeding." That latter phrase merely restates what is already required by the definition of "home state". . . .

Element two of [§ 201(a)(1)] poses a more significant problem in statutory construction when the home state definition . . . is applied: the two statutes directly conflict. Element two . . . provides that a state has jurisdiction if it is the "home state . . . *within six months before*" the commencement of the child custody proceeding. Section [102(7)] requires that in order to be a "home state" . . ., a child must have lived in a state for six consecutive months "immediately before" the child custody proceeding. Thus, if a child's home state two months before a proceeding was commenced is different from the state to which a child has permanently moved (and in which the proceeding was commenced), [§ 102] would indicate there is no home state at all. Initial jurisdiction would then be determined based on substantial connections to the state and other factors under [§ 201]. On the other hand, under the same facts, element two of [§ 201(a)(1)] would declare the *prior state* the home state because it was the home state *within* six months of the filing. Initial jurisdiction would then be in the prior state regardless of any significant connections to the state in which the filing was made.

The statutory conflict . . . is directly at issue here. The child lived in Oklahoma for six consecutive months ending in September 2000. The child then resided in Arizona for the next four months, immediately before the petition was filed in January 2001. Thus, under father's (and the trial judge's) reading of the statute, Oklahoma is the home state . . . under element two of [§ 201(a)(1)]. Oklahoma, under this view, was the home state (from March to September 2000) *within* six months of the filing of the petition in January 2001 and thus has initial jurisdiction.

Under mother's reading of the statute, however, neither Oklahoma nor Arizona is the home state as neither state meets the requirement of [§ 102(7)]. . . . Under that scenario, Oklahoma does not have initial jurisdiction. The trial court would be required to . . . determine whether there were significant connections with Arizona and other factors per [§ 201(a)(2)], to determine whether Arizona should have initial jurisdiction. . . .

. . . .

To appropriately resolve the conflict here, it is critical to examine the stated purposes behind the changes in home state jurisdiction brought about by the UCCJEA.

. . . .

The precursor to the UCCJEA was the . . . [UCCJA]. The stated purposes of the UCCJA were to avoid jurisdictional competition and conflict, promote cooperation between states, discourage the use of the interstate system to continue custody controversies, deter abductions, avoid relitigation in different states, and facilitate enforcement of custody decrees between states.

All fifty states, the District of Columbia and the Virgin Islands adopted the UCCJA. 9 U.L.A. 261–62. However, many states departed from its original text, and subsequent litigation produced substantial inconsistencies in interpretation among state courts — defeating the goals of a uniform interstate jurisdictional act.

. . . .

In particular, prior to the adoption of the UCCJEA, the UCCJA provided four separate bases to take initial jurisdiction in child custody disputes. Those bases included (1) domicile or home state, (2) significant connections to the state and a consideration of the child's relationships, training, care and protection, (3) the child's best interests, and (4) emergency.

The . . . drafters of the UCCJA had assumed that home state jurisdiction was the most appropriate factor in demonstrating the best interests of the child. They also thought that a state should be able to proceed without delay and, therefore, should find jurisdiction on any acceptable basis. Thus, the drafters included the four separate bases for jurisdiction. However, state courts were split as to whether the four bases were equal or whether home state was preferred. These conflicts created an unworkable and non-uniform interstate act.

Additionally, . . . a significant federal statute was passed by the United States Congress. That statute, the [PKPA] was aimed at interstate custody problems that continued to exist after the adoption of the UCCJA. It mandated states to apply full faith and credit to interstate custody decisions. Importantly, it did not allow for full faith and credit on the four bases as set forth in the UCCJA. Instead, enforceability under the PKPA was based on the priority of home-state jurisdiction:

> [The court here cited (c)(2) of the PKPA.]

In 1997, [the UCCJEA was promulgated]. As the drafters . . . noted, lack of uniformity between jurisdictions "increases the costs of the enforcement action; it decreases the lack of certainty of outcome; and it often turns enforcement of a child custody or visitation order into a long and drawn out process." The National Conference of Commissioners on Uniform State Laws, *Uniform Child Custody Jurisdiction and Enforcement Act* (2001). Arizona adopted the UCCJEA effective January 1, 2001.

The UCCJEA drafters dealt specifically with the conflict created by differing jurisdictions taking contrary views of the four bases of jurisdiction. They reconciled the jurisdictional provisions of the UCCJA with the PKPA:

> The UCCJA, however, specifically authorizes four independent bases of jurisdiction without prioritization. Under the UCCJA, a significant connection custody determination may have to be enforced even if it would be denied enforcement under the PKPA [which prioritizes home state jurisdiction]. *The UCCJEA prioritizes home state jurisdiction*[.]

9 U.L.A. 650-51 (emphasis added). The drafters made it clear that the new act was to give priority to a finding of home state jurisdiction over any other jurisdictional provisions.

Furthermore, the UCCJEA completely eliminates a determination of "best interests" of a child from the jurisdictional inquiry. These changes advance a more efficient and "bright line" jurisdictional rule consistent with the UCCJEA's purpose. The UCCJEA specifically seeks to avoid a judicial analysis of substantive issues in the determination of jurisdiction. . . . [A]s noted above, the statutory text of [§ 201] allows consideration of other substantive factors *only* if no state qualifies as a "home state."

It is clear from the drafters' intent that the UCCJEA should be construed to promote one of its primary purposes: avoiding the jurisdictional competition and conflict that flows from hearings in competing states when each state substantively reviews subjective factors (such as "best interests") for purposes of determining initial jurisdiction. With this fundamental purpose in mind, when there is a statutory conflict in the application of home state jurisdiction, the conflict should be resolved to strengthen (rather than dilute) the certainty of home state jurisdiction. This course is consistent with the UCCJEA's statutory purpose.

. . . .

Given the fundamental purpose of the UCCJEA to establish the certainty of home state jurisdiction, it is clear to us that [§ 201(a)(1)] acts to enlarge and modify the definition of home state. . . . We hold that "home state" for purposes of determining initial jurisdiction under [§ 201(a)(1)] is not limited to the time period of "six consecutive months immediately before the commencement of a child custody proceeding[.]" Instead, the applicable time period to determine "home state" in such circumstances is "within six months before the commencement of the [child custody] proceeding." [§ 201]. This interpretation promotes the priority of home state jurisdiction that the drafters specifically intended. [Mother's theory] would increase the number of potentially conflicting jurisdictional disputes in competing jurisdictions. This is contrary to the UCCJEA's purpose.

Even though the UCCJEA is a uniform act, which has been adopted by twenty-seven states and introduced in nine states, we have found no cases that construe the statutory conflict at issue. While not discussing the conflict, other states have ruled in a manner that is consistent with the interpretation we adopt here. *E.g., In re McCoy*, 52 S.W.3d 297, 303–304 (Tex. App. 2001) (finding that Texas was not the children's home state at any time during the six months prior to the filing of the suit); *Nesa v. Baten*, 290 A.D.2d 663, 736 N.Y.S.2d 173, 174 (N.Y.A.D. 2002) ("New York had not been the children's home state at the time of commencement of the custody proceeding or within the preceding six months.").

. . . .

Thus, we conclude that the trial court did not err in rejecting mother's position and concluding that Oklahoma had home state jurisdiction.

. . . .

Mother also contends that even if Oklahoma is the home state according to the foregoing analysis, the trial judge still erred in not conducting a hearing to determine if jurisdiction was in the child's best interests. Mother puts forth two reasons: (1) Arizona's version of UCCJEA requires it, and (2) it would be inequitable and unfair not to consider the child's best interests in a determination of initial jurisdiction. We address each argument in turn.

First, in contending that Arizona's version of the UCCJEA requires a "best interests" hearing even though home state jurisdiction is found elsewhere, mother relies on the prefatory phrase in [§ 201(a)]: "[A] court of this State has jurisdiction to make an initial child custody determination only if *any of the following is true.*" Mother argues the phrase "if any of the following is true" allows courts to choose between the four bases of jurisdiction . . . much as courts chose between the four bases of jurisdiction provided under the UCCJA. This argument is directly contrary to the express language of the statute.

. . . .

Second, mother argues that the equitable issues presented in a case such as this one (child having always been with mother; mother and child having significant connections in Arizona; mother and child having lived in Arizona for the four months prior to filing) or in a hypothetical case (child lives five months and 29 days in one state, but the prior six months in another resulting in home state jurisdiction in the prior case) require a hearing to consider the child's best interests. Mother's argument does not consider that the UCCJEA expressly provides for a factual hearing *in the home state* in which that state may decline to exercise its jurisdiction and allow another jurisdiction to proceed. [§ 207]. This hearing may include a "best interests" determination.

The drafters . . . expressly recognized — and sought to eliminate — the jurisdictional disputes that resulted when "best interests" was used to determine initial jurisdiction. That language and inquiry, present in the previously enacted UCCJA, was intentionally omitted from the newly-drafted UCCJEA. The drafters stated:

The *"best interest" language* in the jurisdictional sections of the UCCJA was *not intended to be an invitation to address the merits of the custody dispute in the jurisdictional determination* or to otherwise provide that "best interests" considerations should override jurisdictional determinations or provide an additional jurisdictional basis.

[This draft] eliminates the term "best interests" in order to clearly distinguish between the jurisdictional standards and the substantive standards relating to custody and visitation of children.

9 U.L.A. at 651–652 (emphasis added).

Thus, the "best interests" analysis does not take place in determining jurisdiction. "Best interests" may be fully explored and considered in the context of a request under [§ 207]. . . .

The issue of an inconvenient forum "may be raised on motion of a party, the court's own motion or request of another court." Any such request, however, must be pursued in Oklahoma rather than Arizona, as Oklahoma has home state jurisdiction. . . . This is critical: To allow the state without home state jurisdiction to conduct the hearing would lead to the jurisdictional competition the drafters sought to avoid. Thus the equitable arguments that mother wishes to pursue are not eliminated, but are merely re-directed to the home state. . . . [M]other can ask the Oklahoma court to relinquish jurisdiction.

Accordingly, mother's argument that the trial judge erred in not considering the "best interests" of the child . . . is wrong. The trial judge correctly determined that this was an issue for the Oklahoma court.

. . . .

Mother also argues, relying on [§ 206(a)], that Arizona should have jurisdiction as her filing was first-in-time. This argument fails as well. . . .

Mother's argument is that this provision mandates jurisdiction in Arizona as the filing was first-in-time. What mother ignores is that the first-in-time filing must be in a state "having jurisdiction substantially in conformity with this chapter." [§ 206(a)]. Because Oklahoma had home state jurisdiction, Arizona did not have jurisdiction "substantially in conformity with this chapter." *Id.* Thus, the first-in-time filing granted mother no rights. The trial court did not err by rejecting mother's request that a first-in-time filing conferred initial jurisdiction upon the Arizona Court.

. . . .

NOTES

1. Priority of Home State Jurisdiction. The UCCJA § 3 identified four different bases for jurisdiction to issue a custody decree, the most important of which were home state and significant connection. Because they were listed as alternatives, the natural reading of the statutory language gave no jurisdictional priority to the home state as compared with a state with significant connection to the child and a parent. *See, e.g., Weinstein v. Weinstein,* 408 N.E.2d 952 (Ill. App. 1980); Foster, *Child Custody Jurisdiction: UCCJA and PKPA,* 28 N.Y.L. Sch. L. Rev. 297 (1981). Such priority for the home state was favored, however, by Professor Bodenheimer. As Reporter for the UCCJA, she had been unable to get approval for statutory language explicitly giving priority to the home state, but she argued this result was the necessary implication of the organization of § 3, which placed home state jurisdiction first on the list of alternative grounds for jurisdiction. Bodenheimer, *Interstate Custody: Initial Jurisdiction and Continuing Jurisdiction Under the UCCJA,* 14 Fam. L.Q. 203 (1981). Some states, before the promulgation of the UCCJEA, modified their versions of the UCCJA to give priority to home state jurisdiction. *See, e.g.,* Tenn. Fam. Code Ann. §§ 36-6-203(a)(1) & (2) (1996); Tex. Fam. Code §§ 11.53 (1) & (2) (1996). Of course, piecemeal amendment of the Uniform Act by a few states had relatively little impact. For example, any state which had enacted the UCCJA as promulgated could exercise significant interest jurisdiction even though Texas was the home state, although Texas might not have been required under its own law to recognize that other state's decree (because it had not been rendered under jurisdictional rules substantially the same as Texas).

At the same time, subsection (c)(2)(B) of the federal Parental Kidnapping Prevention Act (PKPA) required full faith and credit for home state decrees, but not for a decree based upon significant connection jurisdiction if a home state existed at the time it was issued. Of course, nothing in the PKPA *barred* the exercise of significant connection jurisdiction when another state was the home state, although some courts mistakenly so held. *See, e.g., Rogers v.*

Rogers, 907 P.2d 469 (Alaska 1995); *Michael P.* v. *Diana G.*, 553 N.Y.S.2d 689 (App. Div. 1995).

As noted in *Welch-Doden*, the major difference between the UCCJEA and its predecessor is the clear statement of priority for home state jurisdiction announced in subsections (a)(2), (a)(3) and (a)(4) of § 201. The "significant connection" jurisdiction of (a)(2) can be exercised only if there is no home state or the home state has declined to exercise jurisdiction under § 207 (forum non conveniens) or § 208 (unclean hands). Likewise, (a)(3) jurisdiction cannot be exercised unless all courts with home state or significant connection jurisdiction have deferred to the forum and, finally, (a)(4) jurisdiction can be exercised only if no courts have jurisdiction under any of the other three grounds.

2. *Conflict Between Definition of Home State and Description of Home State Jurisdiction?* The *Welch-Doden* court resolved what it characterized as a conflict between the definition of home state in § 102 and the description of § 201(a)(1) home state jurisdiction. It is not clear that there is actually a conflict between the two sections. While Oklahoma was clearly not the home state at the time of the beginning of the Arizona litigation, it is equally clear that, under § 201(a)(1), home state *jurisdiction* is a broader concept than that of home state and it can be exercised for six months after a jurisdiction's status as home state has been lost, so long as a parent or a person acting as a parent remains in the state. The purpose of this provision, which has its roots in UCCJA § 3(a)(1) and the PKPA, is to discourage the use of self-help by a parent to deprive a home state of custody jurisdiction. The new provision is slightly different from both the prior Uniform Act and the PKPA. As explained in the UCCJEA commentary,

> The UCCJA provided that home state jurisdiction continued for six months when the child had been removed by a person seeking the child's custody or for other reasons and a parent or a person acting as a parent continues to reside in the home State. Under this Act, it is no longer necessary to determine why the child has been removed. . . . This change provides a slightly more refined home state standard than the UCCJA or the PKPA [(c)(2)(A)], which also requires a determination that the child has been removed "by a contestant or for other reasons." The scope of the PKPA's provision is theoretically narrower than this Act. However, the phrase "or for other reasons" covers most fact situations where the child is not in the home State and, therefore, the difference has no substantive effect.

9 U.L.A. Part IA p. 672 (1997).

The PKPA home state jurisdiction provision extends jurisdiction for six months so long as a "contestant" remains in the home state. Under subsection (b), the federal statute defines "contestant" as any person "including a parent or grandparent, who claims a right to custody or visitation." The UCCJEA, by contrast, extends jurisdiction only if a parent or a person acting as a parent remains in the former home state. As the UCCJEA commentary states,

> This eliminates the undesirable jurisdictional determinations which would occur as a result of differing state substantive laws on visitation involving grandparents and others. For example, if State A's law

provided that grandparents could obtain visitation with a child after the death of one of the parents, then the grandparents, who would be considered "contestants" under the PKPA, could file a proceeding within six months after the remaining parent moved and have the case heard in State A.

Id. While the UCCJEA commentary finds the result under the PKPA definition "undesirable,"according to Professor Russell Coombs, a drafter of the PKPA, the UCCJEA result where only a grandparent (and not the child or any parent) remains in the home state is the inappropriate one. He argues the UCCJEA provisions are "cause for grave concern among grandparents and numerous other non-parents who visit minor children or sometimes have their custody." Coombs, *Child Custody and Visitation by Non-Parents Under the New Uniform Child Custody Jurisdiction and Enforcement Act: A Rerun of Seize-and-Run*, 16 J. Am. Acad. Matrimonial Law. 1, 3 (1999). He notes, however, that a UCCJA state that issued the initial decree would retain jurisdiction under its own law so long as a grandparent with visitation rights under that decree remained in that state — even if the parents and children moved to a UCCJEA state. He further asserts that the PKPA would require full faith and credit for that initial decree in the parents' new state. While Professor Combs views this as illustrating a problem with the UCCJEA, others would argue the problem is with statutes that make parents and children subject to jurisdiction in a distant state to which only grandparents retain a connection. Professor Coombs criticizes other aspects of the UCCJEA as well, including its provisions on notice and joinder, modification and its interaction with other federal statutes. He speculates that, at least in some situations, it may be unconstitutional. *Id.* at pp. 78–91.

In a case similar to *Welch-Doden* in which the litigation was brought in the child's original home state, the Alaska Supreme Court held, in *Atkins v. Vigil*, 59 P.3d 255 (Alaska 2002), that "extended home state jurisdiction" was satisfied even though the action was filed six months and a week after the child had left the state for California to be with his maternal grandparents. The court held that, under the PKPA and UCCJEA definitions of home state, a period of temporary absence constitutes presence in the determination of home state. Because the child's original departure to California was intended to be temporary, Alaska had been the home state within six months and could exercise extended home state jurisdiction at the time of the father's filing. *See also In re Oliver v. Oliver*, 61 Va. Cir. 88 (Fairfax Cty. 2003) (home state jurisdiction found on basis of six months' presence followed by four-year series of temporary absences in various countries because of father's State Department work assignments); *but see In re Calderon-Garza*, 81 S.W.3d 899 (Tex. App. 2002) (even if mother, a Mexican domiciliary, was in Texas "temporarily" when child was born, Texas is still child's home state; child cannot be temporarily away from a place she had never been).

3. *Significant Connection Jurisdiction.* While the UCCJEA and the PKPA both require states to defer to the child's home state in making an initial custody award, sometimes there is no home state. For example, in *In re Amberley D.*, 775 A.2d 1158 (Me. 2001), the 14-year-old child had lived with her mother in New Hampshire for several months, but then ran away from home to Maine to live with her stepfather's parents who soon thereafter filed a petition seeking a guardianship over the girl. The child's mother asserted New Hampshire was the home state, but the Maine court held there was no home state under the UCCJEA and PKPA (because the child had not been in New Hampshire for six months when the petition was filed in Maine) and that Maine could claim jurisdiction as a state with a "significant connection" to the child in which a person acting as a parent lived. Also required under both statutes is substantial evidence, in the words of the UCCJEA, "concerning the child's care, protection, training and personal relationships," within the forum state. The court found this present because the child had visited the petition-ers often in the past and had attended school in Maine for six years earlier in her childhood. *See also In re Brilliant*, 86 S.W. 2d 680 (Tex. App. 2002) (finding jurisdiction where grandfather had lived in state for over 25 years and assisted in raising of child, child had much interaction with extended family and child's medical records were in state).

4. *Forum Non Conveniens under UCCJEA § 207.* Under the Act, there are several situations in which a court with § 201 jurisdiction might decline (or in some situations be barred from exercising) that jurisdiction. Section 207 (reprinted above) outlines the Act's "inconvenient forum" doctrine under which the forum court would defer to the jurisdiction of another state. According to the Commentary, this section is based on UCCJA § 7 and "authorizes courts to decide that another state is in a better position to make the custody determination, taking into consideration the relative circumstances of the parties." 9 U.L.A. Part IA at p. 683. For example, in *Welch-Doden*, the Okla-homa court might later on decide to defer to Arizona after all, in light of the mother and child's presence there. While not intended to be exhaustive of the possibly relevant factors, subsection (b) suggests considering any history of domestic violence and the ability of both courts to protect the victim from further violence. A recent Montana Supreme Court offers an example. *Stone-man v. Drollinger*, 64 P.3d 997 (Mt. 2003). The court noted the UCCJEA's rejection of the UCCJA's explicit focus on the child's best interests in the inconvenient forum determination. The court held that, trial courts should "give priority to the safety of victims of domestic violence when considering jurisdictional issues under the UCCJEA." It found the victim-mother felt safer in Washington "where she is surrounded by extended family and where [abuser-father] does not know her address or daily pattern of activities," and, after analyzing the relevance of the other factors in § 207(b), reversed the lower court's refusal to defer to Washington. *See also McNabb v. McNabb*, 65 P.3d 1068 (Kan. App. 2003) (abuse allegations appropriately considered by Virginia court in deciding to withdraw its deference to Kansas and, thus, Kansas custody proceeding was inappropriate); *Shanoski v. Miller*, 780 A.2d 275 (Maine 2001) (facts that child had lived 80% of her life in North Carolina, her care providers and teachers were there and more evidence was to be found there, supported Maine finding of inconvenient forum); *VanWechel v. Mueller*, 662 N.W.2d 371 (Iowa App. 2003) (refusal to find inconvenient forum affirmed where recent evidence concerning child was in Iowa and all parties lived in Iowa at time of filing of modification suit).

A determination that another forum would be more convenient results in a stay of the forum proceedings upon condition that a proceeding be instituted "promptly" in the other jurisdiction. Other conditions might be imposed and temporary orders issued to govern until the other state issues a decree. The order can also specify that jurisdiction would be resumed if the other state declines to hear the case.

Section 207 expressly applies to all situations in which the forum court has UCCJEA jurisdiction. This has been held to include a situation where the court has continuing, exclusive modification jurisdiction under § 202 (discussed more fully in the following subsection on modification jurisdiction). *Lord v. Lord*, 2001 Conn. Super. LEXIS 2646 (while Connecticut had § 202 modification jurisdiction, child had lived in New York for four years after living in forum for only 9 months and most relevant evidence concerning her was located in New York). The *Lord* court stayed the Connecticut action on the condition that a modification action was filed in New York within 45 days.

5. *Unclean Hands under UCCJEA § 208.* Even in a UCCJEA world in which ordinarily there will be only one jurisdiction with custody at any point, the clean hands doctrine recognized in UCCJA § 8 will sometimes still be relevant. For example, a parent may abduct a child and establish a new home state which, after the 6 months of "extended home state jurisdiction" in § 201(a)(1), theoretically will have priority over any other state attempting to exercise jurisdiction. Under § 208, however, if the court in the new home state concludes that its jurisdiction exists "because a person seeking to invoke" it "has engaged in unjustifiable conduct" the court must reject the exercise of such jurisdiction. In attempting to define the concept of "unjustifiability," the UCCJEA's Reporter has written that the "focus on unjustifiable conduct represents a continuation of the balancing process [of the UCCJA]. The court should balance the wrongfulness of the conduct of the parent that establishes jurisdiction against the reasons for the parent's conduct." Spector, *Uniform Child-Custody Jurisdiction and Enforcement Act (with Prefatory Note and Comments by Robert G. Spector)*, 32 Fam. L.Q. 303, 359 at fn. 124.(1998).

Focusing on the behavior of domestic violence victims in fleeing such violence with the child, the Commentary to § 208 warns courts not to characterize "technically illegal" conduct as "unjustifiable." ". . . [I]f a parent flees with a child to escape domestic violence and in the process violates a joint custody decree, the case should not be automatically dismissed. . . . An inquiry must be made into whether the flight was justified under the circumstances. . . . However, an abusive parent who seizes the child and flees to another State to establish jurisdiction has engaged in unjustifiable conduct and the new State must decline to exercise jurisdiction under this section." *Id.* at p. 685.

6. *Simultaneous Proceedings under UCCJEA § 206.* Simultaneous custody proceedings in more than one state can arise under the UCCJEA if there is no home state, there is no existing decree and more than one state is able to assert significant connection jurisdiction. Under the UCCJEA, however, the priority of home state jurisdiction expressed in § 201 should handle the vast majority of disputes. The effectiveness of the home state prioritization in solving the problem of simultaneous proceedings is reflected in *Welch-Doden*. While the Arizona litigation had been filed first, the appellate court ordered deference to the later-filed Oklahoma suit. The court recognized Arizona was not the home state and that Oklahoma, though also not the home state when the suit was filed, could still exercise "extended home state" jurisdiction, preferred under § 201 to Arizona's significant connection jurisdiction. UCCJEA § 206 deals with the remaining problem of "dueling proceedings" by adopting a first in time rule, though subsection (b) orders communication with the court of another state where prior litigation was filed, and deference on inconvenient forum grounds is authorized.

7. Tribal Jurisdiction. The Indian Child Welfare Act of 1978, 92 Stat. 3069, largely codified at 25 U.S.C. § 1901 *et seq.*, provides for exclusive tribal court jurisdiction over adoptive or foster care placement of Indian children in certain classes of cases, but specifically excludes from its jurisdictional provisions "an award, in a divorce proceeding, of custody to one of the parents." 25 U.S.C. § 1903. Much litigation and commentary has addressed the appropriate factors in determining the ICWA's applicability in a particular case. *See, e.g., In re Suzanna L.*, 104 Cal. App. 4th 223 (2002) (ICWA's notice provisions applicable even if child might not belong to a tribe or existing family doctrine might exclude tribal jurisdiction); *In re J.L.*, 654 N.W.2d 786 (S.D. 2002) (forum non conveniens analysis appropriate in determining whether to transfer case to tribal court); Davis, *The Existing Indian Family Exception to the Indian Child Welfare Act*, 69 N. DAK. L. REV. 465 (1993); Atwood, *Fighting Over Indian Children: The Uses and Abuses of Jurisdictional Ambiguity,* 36 U.C.L.A. L. REV. 1051 (1989). Substantively, the Act's provisions favor the child's extended family, other members of the child's tribe and other Indians. *See generally* Annot., *Construction and Application of Indian Child Welfare Act of 1978 Upon Child Custody Determinations*, 89 A.L.R.5d 195 (2001).

PROBLEMS

Problem 7-6. Mary is a resident of Florida who was pregnant with her sixth child when she left the state to go to Arkansas after learning that termination proceedings were about to be filed with regard to her new child as soon as she was born. Child neglect proceedings were pending on each of her five older children (who remained in Florida with relatives) at the time she left Florida. Three months after the birth of Mary's daughter, Cheyenne, the Arkansas child welfare agency received a "pick up order" issued by a Florida trial court directing that Cheyenne be taken to Florida. The Florida court based its order on its understanding of state law that the filing of termination of parental rights regarding the five older children would automatically include the new child at birth. As soon as Cheyenne was picked up in Arkansas by the child welfare authorities, the child's maternal grandmother (who had been housing Mary and Cheyenne) filed a guardianship proceeding and sought an order halting the child's removal. Arkansas has adopted the UCCJEA. What arguments do you foresee being made by both sides and what result?

Problem 7-7. Wilton and Marsha are the grandparents of Johnny, whose parents are Sybil and Tyrone. All the parties are residents of Confusion. After Sybil's death, however, Tyrone moves with Johnny to Nirvana. Under the law of Confusion, while grandparents cannot seek visitation during an intact marriage, they can seek court-ordered visitation within six months of the death of a parent. Wilton and Marsha come to your office three weeks after Tyrone and Johnny have left for Nirvana, seeking to file a Confusion visitation action. Both Confusion and Nirvana have adopted the UCCJEA. What will be your advice and why?

Problem 7-8. Mary Jo and Frank are the parents of a child. They have separated, however, and Frank has moved with their child to a different state. After eight months in his new state, he files for divorce and seeks a determination that he is entitled to be the primary custodian of the child. Mary Jo has remained in the original marital home and has never been to Frank's state. Does Frank's state have jurisdiction under the UCCJEA to determine custody? Does Frank's state have jurisdiction to determine child support?

Problem 7-9. Steve and Beth are husband and wife, but their marriage is a stormy one. One night after an especially traumatic episode of spousal abuse in which she received physical injuries, Beth takes the couple's 6-year old child and flies to a distant state, where her parents live. The morning after she arrives, her mother suggests that a protective order ought to be obtained from the court in the new state. No protective orders were ever sought or issued in the original marital home state. Assuming the UCCJEA has been enacted in the new state, what jurisdictional issue(s) are raised by Beth's action?

Problem 7-10. Sandra and Larry met when Larry was on temporary assignment in Sandra's home state of New Mexico. During his three months' sojourn there, a close personal relationship arose and Sandra became pregnant, though she did not tell Larry of her pregnancy until the birth of their child, Benjamin. By that time Larry was back in his home state of Connecticut. When he learned of Benjamin's birth, Larry began to urge Sandra to bring the child and live as a family with him in his home. After four months of his entreaties, Sandra assented and moved to Connecticut. She did not, however, want to move in with Larry, saying she was not sure about their relationship or about living so far away from her parents in New Mexico. Instead, she signed a one-year lease at a condominium in the next town from Larry, who paid 50% of the rent. The entire rent was prepaid (Sandra used an inheritance she had been left by her Aunt Viola). She enrolled Benjamin in day care and began work for a company which places secretaries as temporary employees. After about five and a half months of this, she left Connecticut with Benjamin without notifying Larry or her landlord. Three days later, Larry comes to your office anxious to file a law suit seeking custody of Benjamin or at least visitation rights. Connecticut is a UCCJEA state. What are the issues and what is your advice?

[b]   Jurisdiction to Modify an Existing Decree

SNOW v. SNOW

74 P.3d 1137 (Ore. App. 2003)

HASELTON, P. J.

. . . . Respondents . . . (father) and . . . (mother) are the parents of "S" who is now nine years old. Petitioner is . . . S's paternal grandmother. [Grandmother] acted as S's primary caregiver from mid-1995 until June 2001.

[Father was granted custody of S in a 1995 North Dakota divorce which gave Mother "reasonable visitation rights." Father soon moved to Oregon, leaving S with Grandmother in North Dakota. In 1997, Grandmother and S rejoined Father in Oregon. Mother has remained in North Dakota. In June 2001, Grandmother, suspecting S had been abused by Father, had an altercation with Father, whereupon he removed S to California and then to England, where she lives with father's half-sister.]

In July 2001, [Grandmother] filed a petition . . . seeking custody of S. That petition, which named only father as a respondent, asserted . . . that (1) mother "has had no contact with [S] for over six years and her whereabouts are unknown"; (2) "Oregon is [S's] home state * * * and it appears that no other state would have jurisdiction"; and (3) [Grandmother] should be awarded sole custody of S [with supervised visitation by Father].

. . . [Grandmother] amended her petition to name mother as an additional respondent [acknowledging that Mother was a North Dakota resident] and that the . . . dissolution . . . decree [granted Father custody and Mother visitation. [Grandmother] also acknowledged both parents should be permitted visitation.] Both respondents appeared and opposed the amended petition.

. . . [Grandmother] argued . . . that Oregon had jurisdiction under the UCCJEA because it was "the home state of [S], father, and grandmother for the past four years" and because it was "the most convenient forum" in that "most evidence concerning the child's formative years and relationships is in Oregon."

Father responded that Oregon lacked jurisdiction . . . because mother continued to live in North Dakota, "which is the state which made the initial determination regarding custody." Father asserted . . . that North Dakota had neither . . . determined that "it does not have exclusive, continuing jurisdiction" nor that Oregon was "the most convenient forum."

The trial court dismissed the petition, concluding that Oregon "does not have subject matter jurisdiction" under the UCCJEA and that "continuing jurisdiction" resides in North Dakota. . . . [Grandmother appeals.]

On appeal, the parties dispute the applicability and operation of various UCCJEA provisions, including [§§ 202, 203, 206] . . . [W]e conclude that [§ 203] is dispositive and, consequently, we do not address the potential applicability of other UCCJEA provisions that might also preclude subject matter jurisdiction.

. . . .

The application of [§ 203] . . . depends on the resolution of two questions. First, did the . . . petition here seek to "modify a child custody determination made by a court of another state"? Second, if so, were the requisites of modification jurisdiction . . . satisfied in this case?

[Section 102] of the UCCJEA defines both "modification" and "child custody determination." [The court here recited the Oregon definitions which are virtually identical to the UCCJEA language in § 102.]

Applying those definitions [here], the petition . . . seeks to "modify" the "child custody determination" rendered in the . . . North Dakota . . . decree of dissolution. [Grandmother] seeks sole custody of S. A judgment granting such relief would, necessarily, "change," "replace," or "supersede" the North Dakota court's prior award of sole custody to father. The plain language of [§ 203] read in conjunction with [§ 102] is conclusive. . . .

[Grandmother] argues, nevertheless, that subjecting her petition to the jurisdictional strictures of [§ 203] cannot be reconciled with our analysis and holding in *Fenimore v. Smith*, 930 P.2d 892 (1996). We disagree.

In *Fenimore*, the petitioner was the stepfather of a 12-year-old child. [A California divorce decree had granted the parents joint legal custody of their then-three year old child and gave mother physical custody.] After the divorce, the mother married the stepfather, and the child grew up in their home in California. When the child was 11, she moved with her mother and stepfather to Oregon. A few months later, her mother died. The father and the stepfather disputed custody, and the stepfather filed a petition [here] seeking custody. . . . The trial court dismissed . . . for lack of jurisdiction under . . . the [UCCJA].

On appeal, we reversed that dismissal. In so holding, we observed:

> "*It is important to keep in mind that this is an initial action seeking custody.* . . .
>
> "However, under the UCCJA even if there is a jurisdictional basis . . . for this child custody proceeding, Oregon would be barred from exercising that jurisdiction . . . if a modification of another state's custody decree was sought and that state retained and had not declined jurisdiction. . . . *The modification bar of the UCCJA is . . . inapplicable as this is an initial custody proceeding between stepfather and father, not the modification of the divorce decree between mother and father.*"

145 Ore. App. at 506 (emphasis added; footnote omitted). Petitioner invokes the emphasized language as compelling the conclusion that her . . . petition cannot be deemed to seek "modification". . . .

Fenimore is substantively distinguishable, and noncontrolling, because it was decided under a different statute, the UCCJA, not the UCCJEA, and the pertinent statutory provisions are materially different. The UCCJA's "modification jurisdiction" provision read as follows:

> "If a court of another state has made a custody decree, a court of this state shall not modify that decree unless it appears . . . that the

court which rendered the decree does not now have jurisdiction under jurisdictional prerequisites substantially in accordance with [the UCCJA] or has declined to assume jurisdiction to modify the decree and the court of this state has jurisdiction."

The UCCJA included no definition of "modify" or "modification" but did define "modification decree" as:

> "[A] custody decree which modifies or replaces a prior decree, whether made by the court which rendered the prior decree or by another court."

ORS 109.710(7) (1995).

Thus, under the UCCJA, "modification" connoted alteration or replacement of the prior decree. Conversely, under the UCCJEA, "modification" seems much more broadly to encompass any child custody determination that "changes, replaces, [or] supersedes" any "previous determination concerning the same child." Given that distinction, while [the UCCJA provision] could be narrowly construed (as in *Fenimore*) to apply only to literal modification of the same judgment or decree, [the UCCJEA provision] is not plausibly susceptible to such a construction.[1] Under [§ 203], it is irrelevant whether modification is sought in a continuation of the original proceeding or in a new proceeding, or even whether the party seeking custody was a party to the original proceeding — so long as the petition seeks to change, replace, or supersede the prior award of custody, it seeks "modification" and must satisfy the statute's jurisdictional requisites.

We thus conclude that the petition here is subject to [§ 203]. Under the statute, the court can exercise modification jurisdiction only if two cumulative conditions are satisfied. First, the Oregon court must have jurisdiction to make an initial determination under [§ 201]. And, second, *either* (1) the court of the other state must determine that it no longer has "exclusive, continuing jurisdiction," as described in [§ 202] or that the Oregon court would be a "more convenient forum," [§ 207]; *or* (2) either the Oregon court or the court of the other state must determine that "the child's parents and any person acting as a parent do not presently reside in the other state." [§ 203].

We need not address, and decide, whether the first of those two cumulative conditions is satisfied, because the second is not. In particular, the North Dakota court has not determined that it no longer has "exclusive, continuing jurisdiction" or that Oregon would be a "more convenient forum." Further, because mother continues to live in North Dakota, no court could render the necessary determination [that none of the parents or persons acting as parents still live in North Dakota.] In sum, [§ 203] precludes subject matter jurisdiction. . . .

     . . . .

Affirmed.

---

[1] We note one final consideration that may have underlay our analysis in Fenimore: There, the mother, who had been awarded physical custody, had died; consequently, the stepfather's petition did not seek to divest the custodial parent of custody, effectively nullifying the prior judgment. Here, however, that is precisely the relief that petitioner seeks. . . .

NOTES

1. *Continuing Exclusive Jurisdiction.* *Snow* illustrates a major change made by the UCCJEA. Sections 202 and 203 were added to remedy what the drafters described as a "failure of the UCCJA to clearly enunciate that the decree-granting State retains exclusive continuing jurisdiction to modify a decree. . . ." UCCJEA Prefatory Note, 9 U.L.A. Part IA, at p. 651 (1997). While the idea that a court, having issued a custody decree, continued to have jurisdiction to modify it was certainly recognized in many, if not all, states, the UCCJA's failure to articulate a uniform set of rules setting the duration of such jurisdiction created a chaotic situation with many conflicting custody decrees. As the UCCJEA drafters described the situation under the UCCJA,

> "States . . . have different interpretations as to how long continuing jurisdiction lasts. Some courts have held that modification jurisdiction continues until the last contestant leaves the State, regardless of how many years the child has lived outside the State or how tenuous the child's connections to the State have become. Other courts have held that continuing modification jurisdiction ends as soon as the child has established a new home State, regardless of how significant the child's connections to the decree State remain. Still other States distinguish between custody orders and visitation orders. . . .

Id. This murky situation was further complicated by the PKPA provision requiring states to give full faith and credit to decree modifications made under continuing jurisdiction so long as the issuing state had jurisdiction under its own law and the child or any contestant still lived there. § 1738A(d).

UCCJEA §§ 202 and 203 aim to create clarity and uniformity to reduce the number of conflicting custody decrees. Under § 202, a state which has issued a custody decree is the only state (with one exception described in Note 2 below) which can modify that determination until one of two events occurs. The first is when the child, the parents, and anyone "acting as a parent" have all moved away from the issuing state. The second is described in § 202(a)(1), which itself is not a model of drafting clarity. This provision is designed to cover a situation where a parent or person acting as a parent remains in the issuing state. Here, the Commentary explains, continuing jurisdiction is ended when the decree state no longer has "the general requisites of the 'substantial connection' jurisdiction provisions of § 201. . . . If the relationship between the child and the person remaining in the [original] State. . . . becomes so attenuated that the court could no longer find significant connections and substantial evidence, jurisdiction would no longer exist." *Id.* at p. 674. Thus, the decree state might well retain exclusive jurisdiction to modify the original decree long after another state had become the child's home state. For example, in *In re Bellamy*, 67 S.W.3d 482 (Tex. App. 2002), the child had lived with her mother in Louisiana for well more than six months. Her father remained in Texas, however, and she still attended school in Texas (using her grandparents' home address as her residence for attendance purposes) and stayed with her father for six weeks each year, plus some holidays and weekends. the court held that it retained exclusive modification jurisdiction. *See also In re McCormick*, 87 S.W.3d 746 (Tex. App. 2002) (where both issuing state and another state have significant connection jurisdiction, exclusive modification jurisdiction is retained in the issuing state); *but see In re M.B. II,* 756 N.Y.S.2d 710 (Nassau Fam. Ct. 2002) (decree state renounces continuing jurisdiction because of lack of significant connection and lack of substantial evidence within state).

At this point, a review of the requirements of "significant connection" jurisdiction under § 201(a)(2) might be helpful. Have the goals of clarity and uniformity been met by extending exclusive modification jurisdiction until a court concludes the parties no longer have "significant connection with [a] state other than mere physical presence" and that "substantial evidence is available in [the forum] state concerning the child's care, protection, training, and personal relationships"? While reasonable minds might disagree on whether the jurisdiction-terminating facts exist, under UCCJEA § 202(a)(1) ("a court of this state"), only the issuing state can make the decision. Thus, *e.g.,* in the *Bellamy* case, *supra,* only Texas (not Louisiana) could decide that Texas had lost continuing exclusive modification jurisdiction under § 202(a)(1) for lack of significant connection jurisdiction. By contrast, Louisiana would be authorized, under § 202(a)(2), to determine that all of the relevant parties had left Texas. This determination seems to be a more objective one. Section 203 defines modification jurisdiction from the perspective of the potential modification state and, as such, was the one which *Snow* had to apply. This companion to § 202 states that, with the exception of emergency jurisdiction described in Note 2, a court lacks the power to modify another state's custody determination unless one of three events have occurred: 1) the issuing court has decided it no longer has continuing jurisdiction; 2) the issuing court has deferred under forum non conveniens under § 207; or 3) all the relevant parties have abandoned the issuing state. If one of those conditions exists, the court can modify if it has jurisdiction under § 201.

The UCCJEA's continuing exclusive jurisdiction provisions are narrower than the PKPA's parallel provisions. Subsection (d) of the federal statute mandates full faith and credit to modification decrees issued by a state in which any "contestant" continues to reside and the latter word encompasses anybody, including grandparents or other third parties, who claims a right to custody or visitation. § 1738A(b)(2). While the "contestants" category obviously is broader than the parties referred to in § 202(a)(2), there is no conflict between the federal and the uniform statute because subsection (d) also requires that the issuing state have continuing jurisdiction under its own law. If it has enacted the UCCJEA, the state simply would be claiming, under § 202, less continuing jurisdiction than the PKPA would recognize. The UCCJEA drafters decided that the continued presence of a third party, such as a grandparent, who might be claiming only a right to visitation, was an inadequate basis for continuing modification jurisdiction. During the transition to nationwide adoption of the new Uniform Act, however, "some states may continue to base continuing jurisdiction on the continued presence of a contestant. . . . The PKPA will require that such decisions be enforced. The problem will disappear as states adopt [the UCCJEA] to replace the UCCJA." *Id.* at p. 675.

2. Emergency Jurisdiction. Section 204 provides an exceptional type of jurisdiction separate from § 201's initial jurisdiction and § 203's modification jurisdiction. Based on the child's presence in the state, jurisdiction is premised on the child being abandoned or in need of protection "because the child, or a sibling or parent of the child, is subjected to or threatened with mistreatment or abuse." § 204(a). Subsection (a)'s use of "mistreatment or abuse" as triggering conditions was designed to harmonize it with the parallel PKPA provision. Protective order proceedings to deal with family violence (discussed in Chapter 2) often deal with custody and visitation questions. So long as the child is present in the state, jurisdiction to handle custody and visitation matters would exist under § 204.

In one of the few cases under § 204, in *P.E.K.v. J.M. and C.Y.M.*, 52 S.W.3d 653 (Tenn. App. 2001), the trial court issued a custody decree concerning a child not within the state who was in need because of threatened or actual abuse. The court apparently viewed the statute as providing two alternative jurisdictional predicates (abandoned in the state OR in need of protection because of abuse, actual or threatened). After examining the prior UCCJA provision, the appellate court rejected this interpretation of § 204, finding "no indication that the legislature intended to involve the courts of this state in emergencies existing in other states."

Unlike its predecessor, the new statute's emergency jurisdiction is explicitly temporary, though it may become a final order if the conditions of subsection (b) are satisfied. Emergency jurisdiction may be exercised whether or not there is an existing order and even if there is ongoing custody litigation elsewhere. If there is an existing order or ongoing litigation, the statute requires that the emergency order provide a specific amount of time in which petitioner is to obtain an order from the appropriate other court. § 204(c). Subsection (d) of the statute requires "emergency jurisdiction" courts and "regular jurisdiction" courts to communicate with each other "to resolve the emergency, protect the safety of the parties and the child, and determine a period for the duration of the temporary order."

3. *Other UCCJEA Innovations.* The new act makes many other changes to the UCCJA regime. It provides an explicit definition of the types of proceedings qualifying as custody proceedings (§ 102(4) which notably excludes adoption proceedings, jurisdiction of which is covered by the Uniform Adoption Act). As *Welch-Doden* acknowledged, the Act eliminates any reference to the child's best interests to emphasize that the substantive decision concerning disposition of custody is an issue to be decided only *after* the decision on the existence of jurisdiction. The Act also has a section dealing with the enforcement of custody and visitation orders of other states. As the drafters noted in the Prefatory Note to the UCCJEA,

> . . . [S]tate borders have become one of the biggest obstacles to enforcement of custody and visitation orders. If either parent leaves the State where the custody determination was made, the other parent faces considerable difficulty in enforcing the visitation and custody provisions of the decree. Locating the child, making service of process, and preventing adverse modification in a new forum all present problems.
>
> There is currently no uniform method of enforcing custody and visitation orders validly entered in another State. . . . [D]espite the

fact that both the UCCJA and the PKPA direct the enforcement of visitation and custody orders entered in accordance with mandated jurisdictional prerequisites and due process, neither act provides enforcement procedures or remedies.

. . . [T]he lack of specificity in enforcement procedures has resulted in the law of enforcement evolving differently in different jurisdictions. In one State, it might be common practice to file a Motion to Enforce or a Motion to Grant Full Faith and Credit to initiate an enforcement proceeding. In another State, a Writ of Habeas Corpus or a Citation for Contempt might be commonly used. In some States, Mandamus and Prohibition also may be utilized. . . . While many States tend to limit considerations in enforcement proceedings to whether the court which issued the decree had jurisdiction to make the custody determination, others broaden the considerations to scrutiny of whether enforcement would be in the best interests of the child.

Lack of uniformity complicates the enforcement process in several ways: (1) It increases the costs of the enforcement action. . . .; (2) It decreases the certainty of outcome; (3) It can turn enforcement into a long and drawn out procedure. . . .

UCCJEA Prefatory Comment, 9 U.L.A. Part IA, p. 652 (1997).

4. *International Custody Disputes.* In 1988, the United States became a contracting party to the 1980 Hague Convention on Child Abduction. The International Child Abduction Remedies Act, 42 U.S.C. § 11601 *et seq.*, is the implementing legislation. As of fall, 2002, there were 74 contracting states. *See Hague Convention Web Site* (www.hcch.net).

The Convention applies to children under 16 who were "habitually resident" in a contracting state "immediately before any breach of custody or access rights." An existing custody decree is not a pre-requisite and pre-decree removal of the child by a parent can violate the other parent's access rights. Moreover, the wrongdoer's obtaining of a favorable custody decree in the asylum State does not affect rights under the Act, although a court may consider the reasons underlying such a decree when asked to apply the Convention. Lacking criminal sanctions or extradition provisions, the Convention's sole purpose is to create a civil remedy under which the aggrieved party can regain access to or custody of the child. The abduction is wrongful if it violates custody rights, as determined by the law of the child's habitual residence. Every contracting state must establish a Central Authority to receive claims under the Convention by citizens of that state or from any other contracting state. The United States' Central Authority is the Department of State's Office of Citizen's Consular Services. Norko, *Mandatory Implementation of the Hague Convention on International Child Abduction: An Open Letter to President William Clinton*, 8 CONN. J. INT. L. 575, 577 (1993).

Under Article 13, there are three exceptions to the general obligation to defer to the "habitual residence" of the child: 1) the objecting party was not actually exercising custody or consented to such removal or retention; 2) the child would be exposed to "physical or emotional harm" or other "intolerable situation" upon return; and 3) a mature child objects to the return. The second exception's scope was at issue in *Tahan v. Duquette*, 613 A.2d 486 (N.J. App. Div. 1992). The father opposing his child's return to Canada was not allowed to present evidence about alleged possible psychological harm caused by returning the child to live with mother. The appellate court affirmed the trial court's refusal to admit the evidence, holding

> the Article 13b inquiry was not intended to deal with issues or factual questions . . . appropriate for consideration in a plenary custody proceeding. Psychological profiles, detailed evaluations of parental fitness, evidence concerning lifestyle and the nature and quality of relationships all bear upon the ultimate issue.

The court did note that trial courts must be permitted to "evaluate the surroundings to which the child is to be sent and the basic personal qualities of those located there." In another Article 13 case, the appellate court affirmed a trial court finding that respondent-grandparents had wrongfully taken two children from their father in Mexico and should be returned. *March v. Levine*, 249 F.3d 462 (6th Cir. 2001). Believing their daughter to have been murdered by their son-in-law, the grandparents had obtained an Illinois visitation order which a Mexican court enforced. They refused to return the children at the end of the visit, triggering father's petition. The court rejected the claim that petitioner should be "disentitled" from bringing the action because of unclean hands. Noting that the Convention mandates proof by clear and convincing evidence of an Article 13 exception, the court upheld summary judgment in favor of petitioner. *See also Miller v. Miller*, 240 F.3d 392 (4th Cir. 2001) (affirming order requiring father to return two daughters to ex-wife in Canada; children had been forcibly removed from mother's possession and no Convention exception was proven); *Escaf v. Rodriquez,* 200 F. Supp. 2d 603 (E.D. Va. 2002) (return of child to Colombia required); *Vaile v. District Court*, 44 P.3d 506 (Nev. 2002) (finding Norway the children's habitual residence as matter of law and ordering their return); *Brennan v. Cibault*, 643 N.Y.S.2d 780 (App. Div. 1996) (finding child "habitual resident" of France and ordering return); *Friedrich v. Friedrich*, 78 F.3d 1060 (6th Cir. 1996) (finding child's removal from Germany by mother wrongful and mother's alleged defenses unproven); *Walton v. Walton*, 925 F. Supp. 453 (S.D. Miss. 1996) (child "habitual resident" of Australia and return ordered); *Zajaczkowska v. Zajaczkowska*, 932 F. Supp. 128 (D. Md. 1996) (no hearing on merits is contemplated by Convention; proper procedural rules are those of habeas corpus).

The remedies by the Convention are not exclusive. Thus, a litigant claiming wrongful taking or retention of a child might sue under state custody law or, alternatively, seek a return order under the Convention. It has been held, however, that utilization of state law may waive rights under the Convention. *See, e.g., Holder v. Holder*, 2002 Cal. App. Unpub. LEXIS 2898 (2002); *see also Journe v. Journe*, 911 F. Supp. 43 (Dist. P.R. 1995) (failure to win custody in French courts prevents later use of Convention to relitigate same issues).

For relevant secondary authority, see Weiner, *Navigating the Road Between Uniformity and Progress: The Need for Purposive Analysis of The Hague Convention on the Civil Aspects of International Child Abductions*, 33 COLUM. HUM. RTS. L. REV. 275 (2002) (analyzing federal court activism in interpreting Convention, especially in cases involving domestic violence victims who flee transnationally with children); Symposium, *The Past and Promise of the 1980 Hague Convention on the Civil Aspects of International Child Abduction*, 33 N.Y.U. J. INTL. L. & POL'Y 1 (2000); Johnson, *The Foul Rag-and-Bone Shop of the Heart: Enforcing the Hague Convention Through the Tort of Intentional Interference with Parental Rights*, 10 TRANSNAT'L L. & CONTEMP. PROBS. 665 (2000); Lopez, *U.S./Mexico Cross-Border Child Abduction — the Need for Cooperation*, 29 N.M. L. REV. 289 (2000); Note, Blondin v. DuBois: *A Closer Step to Safeguarding the Welfare of Abducted Children?*, 26 BROOK. J. INT'L L. 721 (2000); Comment, *The Hague Convention on the Civil Aspects of International Child Abduction: When Domestic Violence and Child Abuse Impact the Goal of Comity*, 13 TRANSNAT'L LAW. 391 (2000); Kreston, *Prosecuting International Parental Kidnaping,* 15 NOTRE DAME J. L. ETHICS & PUB. POL'Y 533 (2001); Note, *The Views of a Child: Emerging Interpretation and Significance of the Child's Objection Defense Under the Hague Child Abduction Convention*, 22 BROOK. J. INT. L. 434, 436 (1996); Note, *Due Process Rights of Parents and Children in International Child Abductions: An Examination of the Hague Convention and Its Exceptions*, 26 VAND. J. TRANSNAT. L. 865 (1993) (arguing while U.S. courts must be faithful to Convention purpose of "allowing custody decisions to be made by the state of the child's habitual residence, court must be willing to invoke the Convention's exceptions [where] abducting parent will not be given . . . a custody hearing . . . consistent with United States notions of due process").

The most famous recent international custody case centered on Elian Gonzalez. Because there was no allegation that the child was wrongfully taken from Cuba by his custodial mother, the Hague Convention was not implicated. Instead the case revolved around the law of asylum, separation of powers, judicial review and related matters. *See Gonzalez v. Reno*, 212 F.3d 1338 (11th Cir. 2000); *see also* Comment, *Where to Decide the "Best Interests" of Elian Gonzalez: The Law of Abduction and International Custody Disputes*, 31 U. MIAMI INTER-AM. L. REV. 323 (2000).

The most recent Hague Convention dealing with international custody disputes is the 1996 Convention on Jurisdiction, Applicable Law, Recognition, Enforcement and Cooperation in Respect of Parental Responsibility and Measures for the Protection of Children. An American law professor who was one of three U.S. delegates negotiating the Convention described its main purpose as the "establish[ment of] international standards of jurisdiction and enforcement of judgments for custody cases." Silberman, *The 1996 Hague Convention on the Protection of Children: Should the United States Join?*, 34 FAM. L.Q. 239 (2000). As of the fall of 2003, six states have ratified the Convention and two have acceded to it. *See Hague Convention Web Site* (www.hcch.net)

PROBLEMS

Problem 7-11. Janet and Sammy were Texas residents whose marriage produced one child, Melissa. The couple separated in June, 2001 and Sammy filed for divorce the next month in Texas. Temporary orders were entered naming the couple joint legal custodians and granting Sammy primary physical custody. Janet immediately moved to New York City. In January

2002, Sammy died, while the divorce suit was still pending. Rather than uproot Melissa immediately, Janet allowed her to stay in Texas with her maternal grandparents. After four months of this arrangement, Janet brought Melissa to New York. In September, 2002, Sammy's parents filed suit under a Texas statute which allows a court to order visitation of a grandchild within one year of the death of a child's parent. Texas is a UCCJEA state. State law also provides that the death of a parent with legal custody terminates the custody order. You are law clerk to the judge in whose court the lawsuit has been filed. Write a memorandum outlining the issues and your proposed resolution of Janet's motion to dismiss for lack of jurisdiction.

Problem 7-12. Timothy was born to Sara and John (who were never married to each other) in California. Sara is a drug addict, has a lengthy criminal record and has been investigated numerous times on charges of abusing her other five children. When Timothy was four months old, he was removed from Sara's care and placed with his paternal grandmother (Laura) who was appointed his guardian in a court proceeding. The guardianship order directed John and Sara to stay away from the child. Five years later, with her health failing, Laura sent Timothy to Alaska to live with Lynne, John's former wife who was the mother of Timothy's two half-siblings. After writing a notarized letter purporting to transfer guardianship of Timothy to Lynne, Laura died. For the past five years Timothy has lived with Lynne and his half-siblings in Alaska. The Alaska child welfare agency has filed suit to terminate Sara's parental rights on the grounds that she has not seen the child in five years. Alaska is a UCCJEA state. You are a law clerk to the judge hearing the case. What jurisdictional issues do you see in this case and what do you think you need to know about California law to resolve them?

Problem 7-13. Weldon and Mary Ann have a troubled marriage. After years of physical and emotional abuse, she obtains a domestic violence protective order in Minnesota (their home state) which prohibits him from seeing her and requires him to undertake anger management counseling for 8 months. Weldon completes his required counseling and seems to have turned over a new leaf. In the intervening period, however, Mary Ann has left for Hawaii with the couple's child, Joshua. She and the child have been in Hawaii for seven months and she has told Weldon by phone "I have no intention of ever living anywhere within 100 miles of you and I don't have any intention of having Joshua being exposed to your evil ways and miserable temper." Weldon comes to you in your Minnesota law office wanting to file a suit to obtain joint custody of Joshua with visitation rights. You know Minnesota is a UCCJEA state. What else will you need to know before you know whether you will be able to obtain jurisdiction?

Problem 7-14. Dennis and Sheila were divorced in New York in 1999. The decree provided for joint legal custody of their child, Jacob, with primary physical custody in the father. Sheila was given reasonable visitation. Since 2002, however, Jacob has lived with Sheila in her new residence in the Virgin Islands with the permission of Dennis. You are clerking in the New York court which entered the original decree and in which Sheila has moved for a modification (in 2004) to grant her sole legal custody and child support. You know that New York enacted the UCCJEA in 2001 and enacted the UIFSA in 1998. What issues do you foresee and how would you expect them to be resolved?

DOMESTIC RELATIONS JURISDICTION AND FEDERALISM

Federal courts consistently have refused to hear domestic relations cases that would otherwise qualify for diversity jurisdiction. This domestic relations "exception" to federal jurisdiction excludes, *e.g.*, a petition to modify an existing custody decree, even though the contestants live in different states. The exception traces from United States Supreme Court dicta in *Barber v. Barber*, 21 How. 582 (1859). In its most recent analysis of the issue, the Court found the exception statutory rather than constitutional. *Ankenbrandt v. Richards*, 504 U.S. 689 (1992). *Ankenbrandt* held that the Judiciary Act of 1789, in providing for federal diversity jurisdiction of "all suits of a civil nature at common law or in equity," did not reach most domestic relations issues, which traditionally were within the jurisdiction of the English Chancery Court. Finding Congressional failure to overrule *Barber*'s dicta constituted approval of it, the Court held that actions for divorce or alimony, as custody determinations, fell within the exception. At the same time, however, the Court stated that "*Barber* . . . did not intend to strip the federal courts of authority to hear cases arising from the domestic relations of persons unless they seek the granting or modification of a divorce or alimony decree," before adding custody to the list of excluded topics. On the *Ankenbrandt* facts, the Court permitted litigation of a mother's tort claim based upon assertions of physical and sexual abuse by a father and his new wife.

A number of recent lower courts have approved the exercise of jurisdiction, despite claims of violation of the domestic relations exception. In *Dunn v. Cometa*, 238 F.3d 38 (1st Cir. 2001), a diversity plaintiff sued on behalf of his disabled son and himself, alleging financial misfeasance by his former daughter-in-law during the waning days of the marriage. Discovery into these matters in the divorce action had been abandoned. The divorce judge found "not a shred of evidence to support a finding of economic misconduct or fraud." Soon after the divorce, the federal action was filed. While conceding the alleged economic misconduct could have had an impact on the level of alimony, the appellate court found federal jurisdiction, noting that sometimes events can simultaneously have relevance to different types of relationships. *See also Rash v. Rash*, 173 F.3d 1376 (11th Cir. 1999)(entertaining suit seeking declaratory judgment as to which of two divorce decrees was valid); *Shelar v. Shelar*, 910 F. Supp. 1307 (N.D. Ohio 1995) (suit against former spouse for intentional infliction of emotional distress for concealing or misapplying marital property during divorce proceeding); *Strasen v. Strasen*, 897 F. Supp. 1179 (E.D. Wisc. 1995) (conspiracy, fraudulent misrepresentation by divorcing spouse); *Lannan v. Maul*, 979 F.2d 627 (8th Cir. 1992) (contract action against parent's estate alleging breach of parental agreement incorporated in divorce decree); *Rubin v. Smith*, 817 F. Supp. 987 (D.N.H. 1993) (domestic relations exception inapplicable in federal question litigation based on childnapping by father and policemen); *but see McLaughlin v. Cotner*, 193 F.3d 410 (6th Cir. 1999) (upholding dismissal of diversity suit alleging breach of separation agreement); *Bidwell v. Baker*, 2001 U.S. Dist. LEXIS 12503 (D. Ore.) (dismissing suit alleging violation of a post-judgment oral agreement to modify result of a divorce action); *Johnson v. Rodrigues*, 226 F.3d 1103 (10th Cir. 2000) (dismissing action seeking return of child to biological father because of alleged constitutional invalidity of adoption notification procedure); *Mazur v. Woodson*, 932 F. Supp. 144 (E.D. Va. 1996) (dismissing action challenging appointment of guardian of allegedly incompetent person); *Johnson v. Thomas*, 808 F. Supp. 1316 (W.D. Mich. 1992) (dismissing palimony action). *See* Stein, *The Domestic Relations Exception to Federal Jurisdiction: Rethinking an Unsettled Federal Courts Doctrine*, 36 BOST. COLL. L. REV. 669 (1995).

Some lower federal courts had held the PKPA created an implied federal cause of action to resolve custody jurisdictional conflicts between state courts, but the Supreme Court found to the contrary, noting state courts can themselves implement the statute's purpose of applying full faith and credit principles to custody decisions. *Thompson v. Thompson,* 484 U.S. 174 (1988).

The same emphasis on state primacy over domestic relations cases which keeps most family law cases out of federal court animates a body of law holding that domestic relations litigation involving foreign diplomats based in the United States can be litigated in state courts. Thus, in *Ohio ex rel. Popovici v. Agler*, 280 U.S. 379 (1930), the Supreme Court upheld Ohio jurisdiction in a diplomat-defendant's divorce action despite Constitutional and federal legislative provisions establishing diplomatic immunity in state courts. *See also Salvatierra v. Calderon*, 836 So. 2d 149 (La. App. 2002) (diplomatic status did not prevent establishment of state domicile by diplomat's spouse or exercise of personal jurisdiction over diplomat-defendant); *Duran-Ballen v. Duran-Ballen*, 40 N.Y.S.2d 617 (Sup. Ct. 1943) (state could obtain jurisdiction over diplomat in declaratory judgment action dealing with validity of his foreign divorce).

Chapter 8

FIXING THE CONSEQUENCES OF DIVORCE BY AGREEMENT OF THE PARTIES

INTRODUCTION

This chapter deals with premarital agreements and separation agreements. A separation agreement fixes the terms of the couple's separation and, usually, their divorce; it is also often called a settlement agreement. A premarital (or "antenuptial") agreement may also fix the consequences of the marriage's dissolution, but is made before the parties enter the marriage rather than after they have decided to end it. The traditional premarital agreement applied only when the marriage ended by the death of a spouse, because the traditional law did not allow enforcement of agreements "contemplating" divorce. That limitation has now been widely abandoned, leaving timing as the major difference between premarital and separation agreements. The difference in timing leads to other process differences, however. For example, premarital agreements, like other contracts, are extrajudicial when made; courts see them for the first time when their enforcement is sought, which may be years after their execution. In contrast, divorce settlement agreements ordinarily are presented to the divorce court for approval soon after they are made, because the parties usually want their terms incorporated in the divorce decree. Perhaps because of this difference, it is unusual for settlement agreements to be upset later, while successful attacks on the validity of premarital agreements were historically common. This chapter's treatment of premarital agreements therefore focuses on the rules that govern their enforceability, while its treatment of settlement agreements gives more attention to the negotiating process and the role of lawyers in that process. Sometimes spouses who are not planning a separation make an agreement during their marriage. Such "during-marriage" agreements, sometimes called marital agreements, function much like premarital agreements and are covered in the premarital agreement section of this chapter. While largely similar, they may present special procedural problems, and are sometimes subject to different requirements.

Throughout this chapter, reference will be made from time to time to the provisions on premarital and separation agreements contained in Chapter 7 of the PRINCIPLES OF THE LAW OF FAMILY DISSOLUTION, adopted in May of 2000 by the American Law Institute and published in May of 2002. This chapter will be referred to by the short reference, *ALI Principles*.

§ A. PREMARITAL AGREEMENTS

[1] INTRODUCTION

Why do parties seek premarital agreements? The usual explanation is to protect children from a prior marriage from competing financial claims by the new spouse. This explanation is consistent with old data showing that the overwhelming majority of parties in reported cases on premarital agreements had been married before and were older than 40 at the time of the agreement. Gamble, *The Antenuptial Contract,* 26 MIAMI L. REV. 732 (1972). The increasing number of second marriages may therefore make premarital agreements more important. In 46% of 1988 marriages, at least one of the newlyweds had been married before, DeWitt, *The Second Time Around,* AMERICAN DEMOGRAPHICS, November, 1992, at 60, 63. Cautious but wealthy individuals marrying for the first time and without children may also seek a premarital agreement to limit any financial claims their new spouse might have if the marriage fails. One can also imagine premarital agreements that deal with nonfinancial issues, such as custody arrangements in the event of divorce, or with the conduct of the marriage rather than the consequences of its dissolution. Terms concerning such nonfinancial issues are typically not binding however, see pages 776-782 below.

The possible impact of a premarital agreement on property arrangements will vary with local law. In a "hotchpot" system in which all property is normally before the court, the agreement could exclude premarital acquisitions from the divorce court's reach. In the majority of states in which divorce courts divide only community or marital property, the agreement could opt out of the community property or marital property regime entirely, reserving to each spouse all property earned by that spouse during the marriage. The parties might agree to exclude from divisible property the appreciation, during the marriage, of any separate assets, which some states otherwise would reach. This could be important where one spouse enters the marriage with an operating business he expects will prosper. The agreement might also avoid rules transforming separate property into marital property when assets are commingled. Finally, the agreement could affect the availability or size of an alimony award although, as we shall see, there are occasional restrictions on provisions limiting alimony that do not apply to property provisions.

NOTES

1. *Echoes of the Traditional Rule.* The traditional rule barring agreements that "contemplated divorce" was consistent with the prevailing law of the fault-divorce era: given that the law barred divorce by mutual consent, one would expect it to also look skeptically on premarital agreements setting forth divorce terms. As no-fault divorce was widely adopted during the 1970s and 1980s, this limitation on premarital agreements gradually disappeared as well. *Scherer v. Scherer,* 292 S.E.2d 662 (Ga. 1982) was typical of this transition. The Scherer agreement, executed in 1976, required the husband to maintain life insurance policies that would pay the wife death benefits of

about half a million dollars, if the parties were married at the time of his death, but provided that the wife would otherwise have no claims on his sizeable stock holdings in a family business. A second provision stated simply that "in the event of the termination of marriage other than by death, the intent and provisions hereof shall be considered and applied to the extent permitted by law." The agreement's language thus carefully avoided even mentioning the word "divorce," for fear of putting the entire agreement in legal jeopardy. When husband sought a divorce in 1980, the question was whether the agreement applied. In holding that it did, Scherer quoted approvingly language from *Volid v. Volid*, 286 N.E.2d 42, 46–47 (Ill. App. 1972), that "Public policy is not violated by permitting these persons . . . to anticipate the possibility of divorce and to establish their rights by contract in such an event as long as the contract is entered with full knowledge and without fraud, duress or coercion."

Scherer and *Volid* reflect the current prevailing view; *see also Gentry v. Gentry,* 798 S.W.2d 928 (Ky. 1990). This trend was strengthened by the Uniform Premarital Agreement Act (UPAA), § 3 of which authorizes spouses to contract about their rights with respect to the "property of either or both of them whenever and wherever acquired or located." That Act was adopted in about 25 states, although, as explained below in Note 1 following *Bonds* and *Simeone*, other provisions of it have proven controversial and adoption has slowed.

2. *Requirement of a Writing.* As a general matter, premarital agreements fall within the provision of the Statute of Frauds applying to promises made in consideration of marriage, and the cases require a writing whenever marriage is even part of the contract's consideration. Clark, *Antenuptial Contracts,* 50 Colo. L. Rev. 141, 143 (1979). Section 2 of the Uniform Premarital Agreement Act requires a writing, as does the American Law Institute's *Principles of the Law of Family Dissolution*, § 7.04(1). The usual rule is that an oral agreement otherwise barred by the Statute of Frauds may be enforceable if one of the parties has performed in reliance upon it. That rule has been applied in the context of marital or premarital agreements. *See, e.g., Marriage of Benson*, 7 Cal. Rptr. 3d 905 (App. 2003) (enforcing parties' oral agreement that husband's retirement account would remain his separate property in exchange for husband abandoning any community property interest in the marital residence, where deed transferring the residence to a trust of which wife was sole beneficiary had already been executed).

3. *Agreements "Encouraging" Divorce*. Modern courts still occasionally say they will not enforce agreements "encouraging" divorce, but no one appears to know precisely what this means. *Marriage of Noghrey*, 215 Cal. Rptr. 153 (App. 1985), relied on this principle in refusing to enforce a provision in a *ketuba*, the traditional Jewish marriage contract. The *ketubah* typically requires a payment from the husband to the wife in the event of divorce. In modern Jewish weddings the specified payment is usually small and symbolic, but the disputed provision in *Noghrey* required the husband to pay the wife $500,000. The court held the provision void because it was not meant to adjust property rights arising from the marriage, and created an incentive for the wife to seek divorce. The parties were Iranians, and the wife had claimed the payment was meant to compensate her for the difficulty she would have in finding a new Iranian husband when she was no longer a virgin. An analogous provision in a Jordanian marriage contract was involved in *Marriage of Dajani*, 251 Cal. Rptr. 871 (App. 1988), and the court relied on *Noghrey* in refusing to enforce it, even though here the required payment was only 5,000 Jordanian dinars, about $1,600 at the time. More recently, in *Bellio v. Bellio*, 129 Cal. Rptr. 2d 556 (App. 2003), the court considered a provision allowing the wife a lump sum payment of $100,000 if the marriage ended by either divorce or the husband's death; the agreement otherwise provided that the spouse's respective earnings would remain separate. The wife was 48 and the husband 71 at the time of the marriage; the husband, a multimillionaire, had asked wife to agree that all accumulations during the marriage would remain separate, and the wife had insisted on the lump-sum provision in exchange. Her earnings were modest and she depended upon alimony payments from her first husband, which would terminate with this second marriage, and she was therefore concerned that at the end of the second marriage she would be left in precarious financial circumstances. The trial court had nonetheless held the provision invalid under *Noghrey* and *Dajani*, but the appeals court reversed and enforced it. It distinguished *Noghrey* as involving a bonus payment so large as to induce the divorce, and said that *Dajani* was wrongly decided because the payment there was too small to have that effect. Is $100,000 large enough to induce divorce? It might seem so. But the court sensibly explained its enforcement of the provision by reference to a different principle: the payment involved no more than reasonable financial planning that would assure the wife that the marriage could not make her worse off than before. Although the court did not note it, the provision was also surely a reasonable —indeed, modest — *quid* for the *quo* of her waiving any community property claims that would otherwise have arisen during the marriage — putting the provision in a very different light than those involved in the earlier cases.

Consider whether such decisions cast doubt upon the premarital agreement entered into by Donald Trump and Marla Maples, who announced in May of 1997 that they would divorce "as friends" after "a long relationship and a three-and-a-half year marriage." According to reports from "a person familiar with Mr. Trump's portfolio and marital situation," the separation was his idea and "was happening now for reasons of economy." This source reported that the parties premarital agreement "which would pay Ms. Maples $1 million to $5 million in the event of divorce, is to expire within 11 months, after which she would be entitled to a settlement based on a percentage of Mr. Trump's net worth. [¶] If he's really worth $2.5 billion, 'even . . . a small percentage is a lot of money,' the person said." According to this person there was no third party involved in the divorce, which occurred because Mr. Trump "has been forced economically to act. . . . Unless you're married to someone you have 1000 percent surety in, you just can't do [otherwise]." *Donald and Marla Headed for Divestiture*, N.Y. Times, May 3, 1997, at 20.

Note that the cases just described all involve provisions in which the payments in question did *not* depend upon who sought the divorce. Provisions that create penalties for the party seeking divorce raise different issues. See the *Penhallow* case discussed in the notes on pages 780-781, below.

[2] SHOULD COURTS ENSURE THE PROCEDURAL OR SUBSTANTIVE FAIRNESS OF PREMARITAL AGREEMENTS?

Should courts scrutinize premarital agreements more carefully than commercial contracts, before enforcing them? The traditional law contemplated such heightened scrutiny. But then the Uniform Premarital Agreement Act, adopted by the Commissioners in 1983, treated premarital agreements more like commercial contracts, with very limited judicial review for substantive or procedural fairness, and in the fifteen years that followed this seemed to be the trend in the law. But adoptions of the UPAA have slowed, and the more recent recommendations of the American Law Institute seek instead to clarify and systemize the traditional approach of heightened scrutiny. Which policy is best? We examine examples of both.

[a] The Traditional Rule of Heightened Scrutiny

WISCONSIN STATUTES § 767.255(3) (2003)

The court shall presume that all [marital] property. . .is to be divided equally between the parties, but may alter this distribution without regard to marital misconduct after considering all of the following:

. . .

> (L) Any written agreement made by the parties before or during the marriage concerning any arrangement for property distribution; such agreements shall be binding upon the court except that no such agreement shall be binding where the terms of the agreement are inequitable as to either party. The court shall presume any such agreement to be equitable as to both parties.

BUTTON v. BUTTON

388 N.W.2d 546 (Wis. 1986)

SHIRLEY S. ABRAHAMSON, JUSTICE. This is an appeal from a judgment . . . dividing property upon divorce in accordance with the terms of a written property agreement which the circuit court found binding under § 767.255. . . .

[1. The Facts]

. . . The parties married on September 12, 1969, having known each other for approximately five years. . . . Both . . . had been married previously; Mrs. Button had one adult child . . . and Mr. Button had three adult children. When they were married, Mrs. Button was 50 years old, and Mr. Button 61 years old. Mrs. Button began the divorce action in 1983.

Prior to the marriage, Mrs. Button had acquired some personal property and other assets with a total worth of no more than $3,000 and a life insurance policy on the life of her former husband in the amount of $12,000. Mr. Button had an upholstery business, a stock portfolio, personal property and real estate upon which a duplex residence and the business were located. He had inherited a substantial part of this property and, under sec. 767.255, inherited property is considered separate property not generally subject to division upon divorce.

The parties entered into a written prenuptial agreement on August 15, 1969. While this prenuptial agreement is not the agreement in issue here, the facts relating to the execution of the 1969 agreement may bear on the determination of whether the 1974 agreement is inequitable.

Mrs. Button testified that there was no discussion of Mr. Button's finances prior to their marriage, although she was aware that he owned a duplex house, an upholstery business, a car, and a snowmobile. Mrs. Button also testified that Mr. Button's attorney told her that "if [you] wanted to take it to another attorney [you] could, but if [you] did that then you would say that you didn't trust Charles and Charlie said that's right. . . ." Mrs. Button also stated that she did not read the agreement before signing it. Mr. Button's attorney testified that he believed that both parties understood the agreement, although he has no record of any financial disclosures being made between the parties. Mr. Button testified that he did not make any financial disclosures to Mrs. Button. Neither Mrs. Button nor Mr. Button's attorney had any recollection of Mrs. Button's being advised of the rights she was surrendering by signing the agreement.

. . .

In June 1974, after Mr. Button sold his upholstery business to his son for $85,000, the parties signed a postnuptial agreement which expressly rescinded and terminated the 1969 prenuptial agreement. Mr. Button's assets had appreciated in value during the marriage to approximately $110,000. Mrs. Button's assets were essentially the same as before marriage. . . .

The 1974 agreement was drafted by Mr. Button's attorney. Mrs. Button did not have independent counsel. She testified that the agreement was never explained to her and that no financial disclosures were made. Mrs. Button also testified, however, that she was generally aware of Mr. Button's property, that they filed joint tax returns and that she had access to copies of the returns. She also testified that she was unfamiliar with tax returns, having never prepared one herself. Furthermore, Mr. Button acknowledged that the full extent of his financial holdings could not be discerned from his tax returns.

The 1974 postnuptial agreement provided that in the event of a divorce all property owned by either party prior to marriage would remain the separate property of that party and that all property acquired after the marriage would be deemed the separate property of the party acquiring the property. In the event of divorce, Mrs. Button was to accept as full property settlement her own articles of personal property, her own separate property and one-half of all properties acquired jointly by the parties.

At the time of divorce Mrs. Button was in ill health, confined to a skilled care nursing home receiving public assistance. In addition to receiving $255,103 in property, Mr. Button was working part-time after the divorce.

[At the dissolution of this 14-year marriage . . . the circuit court awarded Mrs. Button assets valued at $7,882.10 and awarded Mr. Button assets valued at $255,103.99. Florence S. Button appeals only from that part of the judgment directing a division of property pursuant to the 1974 written agreement. The circuit court's entire finding relating to the division of property . . . is as follows:

> ". . . Mrs. Button was 54 years of age when she signed the June 19, 1974 agreement, some five years after the initial agreement and the marriage of the parties. . . . [S]he had already given her daughter $12,000 from funds brought to the marriage by her from funds she received at the time of the death of her first husband. She clearly wanted to be able to dispose of her own property as she saw fit and it is reasonable to assume she understood that Mr. Button would be able to do the same thing as a result of this agreement. In light of the entire record, the Court is convinced that Mrs. Button was well aware of the consequences of the June 19, 1974 agreement and it is enforceable as written with regard to the distribution of the property."]

[2. The Court's Analysis]

[2a. In general]

We now turn to the question of what is an inequitable agreement for purposes of § 767.255. The statute does not define inequitable. . . . [¶] The legislature has recognized that prenuptial and postnuptial agreements dividing property. . . allow parties to structure their financial affairs to suit their needs and values and to achieve certainty. This certainty may encourage marriage and may be conducive to marital tranquility by protecting the financial expectations of the parties. The right to enter into an agreement regulating financial affairs in a marriage is important to a large number of citizens.

Section 767.255 however, sets forth a competing public policy when it empowers a divorce court to override the parties' agreement if the agreement is inequitable. This latter policy reflects the unique role of the marriage contract in society. Marriage is not simply a contract between two parties. Marriage is a legal status in which the state has a special interest. Certain rights and obligations dictated by the state flow from marriage, and the legislature requires a divorce court to scrutinize an agreement between the spouses carefully. The parties are free to contract, but they contract in the shadow of the court's obligation to review the agreement on divorce to protect the spouses' financial interests on divorce.

[We conclude that an agreement is inequitable under § 767.255 if it fails to satisfy any one of the following requirements: each spouse has made fair and reasonable disclosure to the other of his or her financial status; each spouse has entered into the agreement voluntarily and freely; and the substantive provisions of the agreement dividing the property upon divorce are fair to each spouse. The first two requirements must be assessed as of the time of the execution of the agreement. As we shall explain, the third requirement is assessed as of the time of the execution of the agreement and, if circumstances significantly changed since the agreement, then also at the divorce.]

[3b. Procedural Fairness]

Fairness in procurement depends on two factors: whether each spouse makes fair and reasonable disclosure . . . of his or her financial status, and whether each spouse enters into the agreement voluntarily and freely. Obviously these two factors are determined as of the date of the execution of the contract. If the parties fail to satisfy either of these factors, the agreement is inequitable. . . .

An agreement is inequitable if either spouse has not made fair and reasonable disclosure to the other of his or her assets, liabilities and debts. A party might not have entered into the agreement had she or he known the facts. Where it can be shown that a spouse had independent knowledge of the opposing spouse's financial status, this independent knowledge serves as a substitute for disclosure. This case does not raise the question of whether a spouse may waive disclosure and we do not decide that issue. . . . Married persons and persons about to marry stand in a confidential relationship and must deal fairly with each other. Fair and reasonable disclosure of financial status is a significant aspect of the duty of fair dealing.

An agreement is also inequitable if it is not entered into voluntarily and freely. In determining [this], the relevant inquiry is whether each spouse had a meaningful choice. Some factors a circuit court should consider are whether each party was represented by independent counsel, whether each party had adequate time to review the agreement, whether the parties understood the terms of the agreement and their effect, and whether the parties understood their financial rights in the absence of an agreement. If the agreement was not entered into voluntarily and freely, the agreement is inequitable. . . .

[3c. Substantive Fairness]

. . . The third requirement is an issue of "substantive fairness." Substantive fairness is an amorphous concept. We can set forth general principles, but the courts must determine substantive fairness on a case by case basis.

An agreement need not approximate a division a circuit court might make under § 767.255 to meet the requirement of substantive fairness. If the parties are permitted to do only that which a circuit court would do under § 767.255, the parties would not have a meaningful right to contract or to divide their property as they wish. [To meet the requirement of substantive fairness, an agreement should, in some manner appropriate to the circumstances of the parties, take into account that each spouse contributes to the prosperity of the marriage by his or her efforts.]

In framing the agreement the parties should consider the circumstances existing at the execution of the agreement and those reasonably foreseeable. The parties should consider that the duration of the marriage is unknown and that they wish the agreement to govern their financial arrangements whether the marriage lasts a short time or for many years. The parties should consider such factors as the objectives of the parties in executing an agreement, the economic circumstances of the parties, the property brought to the marriage by each party, each spouse's family relationships and obligations to persons other than to the spouse, the earning capacity of each person, the anticipated contribution by one party to the education, training or increased earning power of the other, the future needs of the respective spouses, the age and physical and emotional health of the parties, and the expected contribution of each party to the marriage, giving appropriate economic value to each party's contribution in homemaking and child care services.

In assessing the fairness of the substantive terms of the agreement, a circuit court considers these factors and evaluates the terms of the agreement from the perspective of the parties at the execution of the agreement. We conclude that the court should look at the substantive fairness of the agreement as of the time it was made if the court is to give effect to the parties' freedom to contract. At execution the parties know their property and other relevant circumstances and are able to make reasonable predictions about the future; they should then be able to draft a fair agreement considering these factors.

Clearly an agreement fair at execution is not unfair at divorce just because the application of the agreement at divorce results in a property division which is not equal between the parties or which a court might not order under § 767.255. If, however, there are significantly changed circumstances after the execution of an agreement and the agreement as applied at divorce no longer comports with the reasonable expectations of the parties, an agreement which is fair at execution may be unfair to the parties at divorce. [¶] . . . This approach protects the parties' freedom to contract and the parties' financial interests at divorce.

[Conclusion]

. . .[¶] Because the circuit court has not considered this agreement in this case under the three-part test we have set forth, we remand the cause to the circuit court to exercise its discretion under the test set forth herein. . . .

GANT v. GANT, 329 S.E.2d 106 (W. Va. 1985). The middle-aged parties, both previously married, entered into a premarital agreement the day before their 1979 wedding, under which the wife waived all her rights to post-divorce alimony. They separated in 1981 and, after an apparent reconciliation failed, the wife brought a divorce action in 1982. The husband, a physician, though impaired by mental problems, apparently had more earning capacity than the wife, a licensed realtor and vocational nurse. In upholding the agreement, the court said:

> Many courts supervise prenuptial agreements by inquiring into their "fairness," either at the time they were entered into, or at the time of divorce, or at both times. We have no problem accepting . . . that prenuptial agreements must be voluntarily and knowledgeably entered and validly procured, but we are loath to apply a vague and entirely subjective standard of "fairness." Throughout all of contract law there is the recurring problem of disparity of bargaining power; thus if mere disparate bargaining power alone is grounds for invalidating contracts, contracts between rich and poor or between strong and weak will always be of questionable validity. Such, however, is not the rule elsewhere in contract law, and we see no policy reasons to make it so in the law of prenuptial agreements.

The term "fair," without some further elaboration, gives no guidance whatsoever concerning which agreements will be binding and which agreements will be struck down. Furthermore, candor compels us to raise to a conscious level the fact that, as in this case, prenuptial agreements will almost always be entered into between people with property or an income potential to protect on one side and people who are impecunious on the other. Measuring an agreement by an undefined judicial standard of fairness is an invitation to the very wealth redistribution that these agreements are designed to prevent.

[W]hen courts talk about "fairness" in the setting of a prenuptial agreement, they are usually not talking about an entirely subjective, open-ended concept that allows judges to renegotiate contracts and substitute their own judgment for the agreement of the parties. Rather, what other courts are really concerned about is "foreseeability." [¶] In the case of Larry and Elana Gant there is no reason not to honor the parties' prenuptial agreement because circumstances have transpired exactly as the parties foresaw that they might transpire at the time the prenuptial agreement was made. Basically, things did not work out romantically between two middle-aged adults, and that was the exact eventuality about which they had bargained and contracted.

But what . . . if Elana and Larry had had an idyllic relationship for five years and had decided to have three children? Certainly that was not a foreseen event, and if ten years after entering into this prenuptial agreement, with three hypothetical children aged four, three, and one, Larry had decided to divorce, these hypothetical, unforeseen, intervening events would compel us to think very hard about whether to honor the prenuptial agreement's waiver of alimony. Elana would need support for herself so that she could care for the children, but neither party had contemplated having children at the time they entered into the agreement. . . .

Accordingly, we hold today that. . . .the burden of demonstrating the invalidity of a prenuptial agreement is upon the person who would have it held invalid. Although advice of independent counsel at the time parties enter into a prenuptial agreement helps demonstrate that there has not been fraud, duress, or misrepresentation, and that the agreement was entered into knowledgeably and voluntarily, such independent advice is not a prerequisite to enforceability when the terms of the agreement are understandable to a reasonably intelligent adult, as long as both parties had the opportunity to consult with independent counsel.

Unless a prenuptial agreement is so outrageous as to come within unconscionability principles as developed in commercial contract law, West Virginia courts will not evaluate the substantive fairness of prenuptial agreements. . . . Nonetheless, prenuptial agreements will be enforced in their explicit terms only to the extent that circumstances at the time the marriage ends are roughly what the parties foresaw at the time they entered into the prenuptial agreement. In this regard the passage of time, a change of position based upon reasonable reliance on the permanence of the marriage, and the birth of children are relevant factors, among others, for a court to consider.

In [this] case we find nothing unreasonable about Elana's waiver of alimony. . . . Both parties were middle-aged, both had been married before, and the divorce occurred sufficiently close in time (5 years) to the signing of the prenuptial agreement that this divorce was an event that was contemplated and foreseen at the time the agreement was entered into.

[b] The Contractual Model

UNIFORM PREMARITAL AGREEMENT ACT

§ 1. *Definitions*

As used in this Act:

(1) "Premarital agreement" means an agreement between prospective spouses made in contemplation of marriage and to be effective upon marriage.

(2) "Property" means an interest, present or future, legal or equitable, vested or contingent, in real or personal property, including income and earnings.

§ 2. *Formalities*

A premarital agreement must be in writing and signed by both parties. It is enforceable without consideration.

§ 3. *Content*

(a) Parties to a premarital agreement may contract with respect to:

(1) the rights and obligations of each of the parties in any of the property of either or both of them whenever and wherever acquired or located;

(2) the right to buy, sell, use, transfer, exchange, abandon, lease, consume, expend, assign, create a security interest in, mortgage, encumber, dispose of, or otherwise manage and control property;

(3) the disposition of property upon separation, marital dissolution, death, or the occurrence or nonoccurrence of any other event;

(4) the modification or elimination of spousal support;

(5) the making of a will, trust, or other arrangement to carry out the provisions of the agreement;

(6) the ownership rights in and disposition of the death benefit from a life insurance policy;

(7) the choice of law governing the construction of the agreement; and

(8) any other matter, including their personal rights and obligations, not in violation of public policy or a statute imposing a criminal penalty.

(b) The right of a child to support may not be adversely affected by a premarital agreement.

§ 4. Effect of Marriage

A premarital agreement becomes effective upon marriage.

§ 5. Amendment, Revocation

After marriage, a premarital agreement may be amended or revoked only by a written agreement signed by the parties. The amended agreement or the revocation is enforceable without consideration.

§ 6. Enforcement

(a) A premarital agreement is not enforceable if the party against whom enforcement is sought proves that:

(1) that party did not execute the agreement voluntarily; or

(2) the agreement was unconscionable when it was executed and, before execution of the agreement, that party:

(i) was not provided a fair and reasonable disclosure of the property or financial obligations of the other party;

(ii) did not voluntarily and expressly waive, in writing, any right to disclosure of the property or financial obligations of the other party beyond the disclosure provided; and

(iii) did not have, or reasonably could not have had, an adequate knowledge of the property or financial obligations of the other party.

(b) If a provision of a premarital agreement modifies or eliminates spousal support and that modification or elimination causes one party to the agreement to be eligible for support under a program of public assistance at the time of separation or marital dissolution, a court, notwithstanding the terms of the agreement, may require the other party to provide support to the extent necessary to avoid that eligibility.

(c) An issue of unconscionability of a premarital agreement shall be decided by the court as a matter of law.

§ 7. Enforcement: Void Marriage

If a marriage is determined to be void, an agreement that would otherwise have been a premarital agreement is enforceable only to the extent necessary to avoid an inequitable result.

§ 8. Limitation of Actions

Any statute of limitations applicable to an action asserting a claim for relief under a premarital agreement is tolled during the marriage of the parties to the agreement. However, equitable defenses limiting the time for enforcement, including laches and estoppel, are available to either party.

§ 9. *Application and Construction*

This [Act] shall be applied and construed to effectuate its general purpose to make uniform the law with respect to the subject of this [Act] among states enacting it.

MARRIAGE OF BONDS

24 Cal. 4th 1, 5 P.3d 815, 99 Cal. Rptr. 2d 252 (Cal. 2000)

GEORGE, CHIEF JUSTICE . In this case we consider whether appellant Susann (known as Sun) Margreth Bonds voluntarily entered into a premarital agreement with respondent Barry Lamar Bonds. We conclude that the Court of Appeal erred [when it concluded] that because Sun, unlike Barry, was not represented by independent counsel when she entered into the agreement, the voluntariness of the agreement must be subjected to strict scrutiny. Instead, we determine that the circumstance that one of the parties was not represented by independent counsel is only one of several factors that must be considered in determining whether a premarital agreement was entered into voluntarily. Further, as we shall explain, we conclude that substantial evidence supports the determination of the trial court that the agreement in the present case was entered into voluntarily.

I

Sun and Barry met in Montreal in the summer of 1987. . . . In November 1987, Sun moved to Phoenix to take up residence with Barry and, one week later, the two became engaged. . . . [T]hey decided to marry before the commencement of professional baseball's spring training. On February 5, 1988, in Phoenix, the parties entered into a written premarital agreement in which each party waived any interest in the earnings and acquisitions of the other party during marriage. That same day, they flew to Las Vegas, and were married the following day.

Each of the parties then was 23 years of age. Barry, who had attended college for three years and who had begun his career in professional baseball in 1985, had a contract to play for the Pittsburgh Pirates. His annual salary at the time of the marriage ceremony was approximately $ 106,000. Sun had emigrated to Canada from Sweden in 1985, had worked as a waitress and bartender, and had undertaken some training as a cosmetologist, having expressed an interest in embarking upon a career as a makeup artist for celebrity clients. Although her native language was Swedish, she had used both French and English in her employment, education, and personal relationships when she lived in Canada. She was unemployed at the time she entered into the premarital agreement.

Barry petitioned for legal separation [later amended to divorce] on May 27, 1994, in California, the parties then being California residents. Sun requested custody of the parties' two children, then three and four years of age. In addition, she sought child and spousal support, attorney fees, and a determination of property rights. . . . Child support was awarded in the amount of

$ 10,000 per month per child. Spousal support was awarded in the amount of $ 10,000 per month, to terminate December 30, 1998. Only the. . .validity of the premarital agreement is before this court.

Barry testified that he was aware of teammates and other persons who had undergone bitter marital dissolution proceedings involving the division of property, and recalled that from the beginning of his relationship with Sun he told her that he believed his earnings and acquisitions during marriage should be his own. He informed her he would not marry without a premarital agreement, and she had no objection. He also recalled that from the beginning of the relationship, Sun agreed that their earnings and acquisitions should be separate, saying "what's mine is mine, what's yours is yours." Indeed, she informed him that this was the practice with respect to marital property in Sweden. She stated that she planned to pursue a career and wished to be financially independent. Sun knew that Barry did not anticipate that she would shoulder her living expenses while she was not employed. She was not, in fact, employed during the marriage. Barry testified that he and Sun had no difficulty communicating.

Although Barry testified that he had previous experience working with lawyers in the course of baseball contract negotiations and the purchase of real property, his testimony at trial did not demonstrate an understanding of the legal fine points of the agreement.

Sun's testimony at trial differed from Barry's in material respects. She testified that her English language skills in 1987 and 1988 were limited. Out of pride, she did not disclose to Barry that she often did not understand him. She testified that she and Barry never discussed money or property during the relationship that preceded their marriage. She agreed that she had expressed interest in a career as a cosmetologist and had said she wished to be financially independent. She had very few assets when she took up residence with Barry, and he paid for all their needs. Their wedding arrangements were very informal, with no written invitations or caterer, and only Barry's parents and a couple of friends, including Barry's godfather Willie Mays, were invited to attend. No marriage license or venue had been arranged in advance of their arrival in Las Vegas. . . .

Sun testified that on the evening before the premarital agreement was signed, Barry first informed her that they needed to go the following day to the offices of his lawyers. . . . She was uncertain, however, whether Barry made any reference to a premarital agreement. She testified that only at the parking lot of the law office where the agreement was to be entered into did she learn, from Barry's financial adviser, Mel Wilcox, that Barry would not marry her unless she signed a premarital agreement. She was not upset. She was surprised, however, because Barry never had said that signing the agreement was a precondition to marriage. She did not question Barry or anyone else on this point. She was under the impression that Barry wished to retain separate ownership of property he owned before the marriage, and that this was the sole object of the premarital agreement. She was unaware the agreement would affect her future and was not concerned about the matter, because she was nervous and excited about getting married and trusted Barry. Wilcox's statement had little effect on her, because she had no question but that she and Barry were to be married the following day.

Sun recalled having to hurry to arrive at the lawyers' office in time both to accomplish their business there and make the scheduled departure of the airplane to Las Vegas so that she and Barry could marry the next day. Sun recalled that once they arrived at the lawyers' office on February 5, 1988, she, her friend Margareta Forsberg, Barry, and. . .Mel Wilcox were present in a conference room. She did not recall asking questions or her friend asking questions, nor did she recall that any changes were made to the agreement. She declared that her English language skills were limited at the time and she did not understand the agreement, but she did not ask questions of anyone other than Margareta Forsberg or ask for more time, because she did not want to miss her flight and she was focussed on the forthcoming marriage ceremony. She did not believe that Barry understood the agreement either. Forsberg was unable to assist her. Sun did not recall the lawyers telling her that she should retain her own lawyer, that they were representing Barry and not her, that the applicable community property law provided that a spouse has an interest in the earnings and in acquisitions of the other spouse during marriage, or that she would be waiving this right if she signed the agreement. The lawyers may have mentioned the possibility of her being represented by her own lawyer, but she did not believe she needed one. She did not inform anyone at the meeting that she was concerned about the agreement; the meeting and discussion were not cut short, and no one forced her to sign the agreement.

Forsberg, a native of Sweden and 51 years of age at the time the agreement was signed, confirmed that she was present when [Barry's attorneys] Brown and Megwa explained the agreement, that Wilcox also was present, that no changes to the agreement were made at Sun's or Forsberg's request, and that she had been unable to answer Sun's questions or explain to Sun the terminology used in the agreement. She confirmed that Sun's English was limited, that the lawyers had explained the agreement, and that Sun never stated that she was considering not signing the agreement, that she did not understand it, or that she was not signing of her own free will. Sun never said that Barry threatened her or forced her to sign, that she wanted to consult independent counsel concerning the agreement, or that she felt pressured. Forsberg understood that Brown and Megwa were Barry's attorneys, not Sun's. She testified that when the attorneys explained the agreement, she did not recall any discussion of Sun's community property rights.

Barry and other witnesses offered a different picture. . . . Barry and his attorney, Brown, recalled that approximately two weeks before the parties signed the formal agreement, they discussed with Sun the drafting of an agreement to keep earnings and acquisitions separate. Brown testified that he told Sun at this meeting that he represented Barry and that it might be in her best interest to obtain independent counsel.

Barry, Brown, and Megwa testified that. . .the attorneys informed Sun of her right to independent counsel. All three recalled that Sun stated she did not want her own counsel, and Megwa recalled explaining that he and Brown did not represent her. Additionally, all three recalled that the attorneys read the agreement to her paragraph by paragraph and explained it as they went through it, also informing her of a spouse's basic community property rights in earnings and acquisitions and that Sun would be waiving these rights.

Megwa recalled it was clearly explained that Barry's income and acquisitions during the marriage would remain Barry's separate property, and he recalled that Sun stated that such arrangements were the practice in Sweden. Furthermore, Barry and the two attorneys each confirmed that Sun and Forsberg asked questions during the meeting and were left alone on several occasions to discuss its terms, that Sun did not exhibit any confusion, and that Sun indicated she understood the agreement. They also testified that changes were made to the agreement at Sun's behest. Brown and Megwa experienced no difficulty in communicating with Sun, found her confident and happy, and had no indication that she was nervous or confused, intimidated, or pressured. No threat was uttered that unless she signed the agreement, the wedding would be cancelled, nor did they hear her express any reservations about signing the agreement. Additionally, legal secretary Illa Washington recalled that Wilcox waited in another room while the agreement was discussed, that Sun asked questions and that changes were made to the agreement at her behest, that Sun was informed she could secure independent counsel, that Sun said she understood the contract and did not want to consult another attorney, and that she appeared to understand the discussions and to feel comfortable and confident.

The trial court observed that the case turned upon the credibility of the witnesses [and determined] that Sun entered into the agreement voluntarily, "free from the taint of fraud, coercion and undue influence . . . with full knowledge of the property involved and her rights therein". . . .[¶] The court also determined that Barry and Sun were not in a confidential relationship at the time the agreement was executed. The trial court also declared that pursuant to a pretrial stipulation the burden of proof rested upon Sun, but that even if the court were to place the burden of proof upon Barry, Barry had demonstrated by clear and convincing evidence "that the agreement and its execution [were] free from the taint of fraud, coercion or undue influence" and that Sun "entered the agreement with full knowledge of the property involved and her rights therein,". . . .

The Court of Appeal in a split decision reversed the judgment rendered by the trial court and directed a retrial on the issue of voluntariness. The majority stressed that Sun lacked independent counsel, determined that she had not waived counsel effectively, and concluded that under such circumstances the evidence must be subjected to strict judicial scrutiny to determine whether the agreement was voluntary. The majority asserted that Attorneys Brown and Megwa failed to explain that Sun's interests conflicted with Barry's, failed to urge her to retain separate counsel, and may have led Sun to believe they actually represented her interests as they explained the agreement paragraph by paragraph. . . .[¶] We granted Barry's petition for review.

II

. . .We [first] conclude [the court of appeals] erred in holding that a premarital agreement in which one party is not represented by independent counsel should be subjected to strict scrutiny for voluntariness. Such a holding is inconsistent with Family Code § 1615, which governs the enforceability of premarital agreements.

A

From the inception of its statehood, California has retained the community property law that predated its admission to the Union and consistently has provided as a general rule that property acquired by spouses during marriage, including earnings, is community property. [¶] At the same time, applicable statutes recognized the power of parties contemplating a marriage to reach an agreement containing terms at variance with community property law. Thus in 1850, the Legislature provided that community property principles shall govern the rights of the parties "unless there is a marriage contract, containing stipulations contrary thereto." [¶] . . .In order to encourage enforcement of [premarital] agreements on a more certain and uniform basis, while, according to the drafters of the act, retaining some "flexibility," the Uniform Premarital Agreement Act (hereafter sometimes referred to as the Uniform Act) was promulgated in 1983. [¶] In 1985, the California Legislature adopted most of the provisions of the Uniform Act. . . .

B

The California enactment, like the Uniform Act, . . . provides in pertinent part:

(a) A premarital agreement is not enforceable if the party against whom enforcement is sought proves either of the following:

(1) That party did not execute the agreement voluntarily.

(2) The agreement was unconscionable when it was executed and, before execution of the agreement, all of the following applied to that party:

(A) That party was not provided a fair and reasonable disclosure of the property or financial obligations of the other party.

(B) That party did not voluntarily and expressly waive, in writing, any right to disclosure of the property or financial obligations of the other party beyond the disclosure provided.

(C) That party did not have, or reasonably could not have had, an adequate knowledge of the property or financial obligations of the other party.

Pursuant to [this excerpt from] Family Code § 1615, a premarital agreement will be enforced unless the party resisting enforcement of the agreement can demonstrate either (1) that he or she did not enter into the contract voluntarily, or (2) that the contract was unconscionable when entered into *and* that he or she did not have actual or constructive knowledge of the assets and obligations of the other party and did not voluntarily waive knowledge of such assets and obligations. In the present case, the trial court found no lack of knowledge regarding the nature of the parties' assets, a necessary predicate to considering the issue of unconscionability, and the Court of Appeal accepted the trial court's determination on this point. We do not reconsider this factual determination, and thus the question of unconscionability is not before us. . . . Thus, the only issue we face concerns the trial court's determination that Sun entered into the agreement voluntarily.

Neither the article of the Family Code in which section 1615 is located, nor the Uniform Act, defines the term "voluntarily.". . .[¶] To the extent it is unclear on the face of the statute what was intended by the Legislature in employing the term "voluntarily," we consult the history of the statute and consider its general intent in order to determine the sense in which the Legislature used the term.

The debate that preceded the adoption of the Uniform Act indicated a basic disagreement between those commissioners at the National Conference of Commissioners on Uniform State Laws who placed the highest value on certainty in enforcement of premarital agreements and the vocal minority of commissioners who urged that such contracts routinely should be evaluated for substantive fairness at the time of enforcement. Indeed, over sharp and repeated objection from commissioners of the minority view, eventually it was settled that the party against whom enforcement of a premarital agreement was sought only could raise the issue of unconscionability, that is, the substantive unfairness of an agreement, if he or she also could demonstrate lack of disclosure of assets, lack of waiver of disclosure, *and* lack of imputed knowledge of assets. The language adopted was intended to *enhance* the enforceability of premarital agreements and to convey the sense that an agreement voluntarily entered into would be enforced without regard to the apparent unfairness of its terms, as long as the objecting party knew or should have known of the other party's assets, or voluntarily had waived disclosure. The commissioners, however, did not supply a definition of the term "voluntarily," nor was there much discussion of the term.

We find an indication of the commissioners' understanding of the term in their official comment to the enforcement provision of the Uniform Act, stating that the conditions to enforcement "are comparable to concepts which are expressed in the statutory and decisional law of many jurisdictions." (9B West's U. Laws Ann., *supra*, Uniform Act, com. to § 6, p. 376.) In support of this statement, the comment cites cases from various jurisdictions examining the voluntariness of premarital agreements. . . . In the majority of these cases. . .the question is viewed as one involving such ordinary contract defenses as fraud, undue influence, or duress, along with some examination of the parties' knowledge of the rights being waived, or at least knowledge of the intent of the agreement.

These cases demonstrate the commissioners' belief that a number of factors are relevant to the issue of voluntariness. In considering defenses proffered against enforcement of a premarital agreement, the court should consider whether the evidence indicates coercion or lack of knowledge. . . . Specifically, the cases . . . direct consideration of the impact upon the parties of . . . the coercion that may arise from the proximity of execution of the agreement to the wedding, or from surprise in the presentation of the agreement; the presence or absence of independent counsel or of an opportunity to consult independent counsel; inequality of bargaining power — in some cases indicated by the relative age and sophistication of the parties; whether there was full disclosure of assets; and the parties' understanding of the rights being waived under the agreement or at least their awareness of the intent of the agreement.

The cases cited in the comment to the enforcement provision of the Uniform Act indicate that the commissioners considered that . . . voluntariness . . . may turn in part upon whether the agreement was entered into knowingly, in the sense that the parties understood the terms or basic effect of the agreement. . . . [These cases also] indicate that the parties' general understanding of the effect of the agreement constitutes a factor for the court to consider in determining whether the parties entered into the agreement voluntarily.

The commissioners' debate over the problem of unconscionability throws further light on their view of the voluntariness requirement, which, as noted, did not receive much explicit discussion. Those taking the minority view noted with concern that the proposed Uniform Act would enforce agreements that might be declared void as unconscionable under the Uniform Commercial Code, because the Uniform Act precluded consideration of the substantive fairness of the agreement unless the party challenging the agreement also could prove lack of notice of the other party's assets and obligations. Commissioners who valued substantive fairness over certainty of enforcement urged, for example, that if a premarital agreement waiving property rights is entered into between a pregnant teenager — who wishes to ensure the legitimacy of her child — and an older man, the agreement should be subject to searching scrutiny for unconscionability; those taking the majority position countered that the requirement that the contract be entered into voluntarily provided adequate protection to the weaker party. In addition, it was clear from their discussion that the commissioners anticipated that such defenses as lack of capacity, fraud, duress, and undue influence would apply in determining the voluntariness of the agreement.

In sum, it is clear from the cases cited in the comment to the enforcement section of the Uniform Act and from the record of the proceedings of the National Conference of Commissioners on Uniform State Laws that the commissioners intended that the party seeking to avoid a premarital agreement may prevail by establishing that the agreement was involuntary, and that evidence of lack of capacity, duress, fraud, and undue influence, as demonstrated by a number of factors uniquely probative of coercion in the premarital context, would be relevant in establishing the involuntariness of the agreement.

Not only did the commissioners intend that the above factors be considered in determining whether a premarital agreement was entered into voluntarily, but the same intention safely may be attributed to the California Legislature, because an examination of the history of the enactment of Family Code § 1615 in California indicates that the Legislature adopted the views of the commissioners in all respects relevant to the present discussion.

. . . .

We have considered the range of factors that may be relevant to establish the involuntariness of a premarital agreement in order to consider whether the Court of Appeal erred in according such great weight to one factor — the presence or absence of independent counsel for each party. . . .

It is clear. . .that the commissioners rejected the view that independent counsel was essential. . . . Although the proposed Uniform Act initially contained a proviso stating that premarital agreements were presumptively valid unless the party against whom enforcement was sought was not represented by independent legal counsel or there was not full disclosure, the commissioners eventually removed any reference to independent counsel. A commissioner explained the action of the executive committee in removing the proviso: "We feel that, certainly, that representation would be a *factor* in determining whether the party acted voluntarily and knowingly. We do not believe, however, that legal representation alone would be a desirable basis for enforcement." An amendment was proposed to restore the omitted provision, but it was rejected . . . (Proceedings, Uniform Act, *supra*, pp. 61–62.)

. . .

Finally, and perhaps most significantly, the rule created by the Court of Appeal would have the effect of shifting the burden of proof on the question of voluntariness to the party seeking enforcement of the premarital agreement, even though the statute expressly places the burden upon the party challenging the voluntariness of the agreement. . . .[¶] We conclude that although the ability of the party challenging the agreement to obtain independent counsel is an important factor in determining whether that party entered into the agreement voluntarily, the Court of Appeal majority erred in directing trial courts to subject premarital agreements to strict scrutiny where the less sophisticated party does not have independent counsel and has not waived counsel according to exacting waiver requirements.

C

[Despite our conclusions concerning] independent counsel . . . we . . . agree with the Court of Appeal majority that considerations applicable in commercial contexts do not necessarily govern the determination whether a premarital agreement was entered into voluntarily.

. . .Even apart from the circumstance that there is no statutory requirement that commercial contracts be entered into voluntarily as that term is used in Family Code § 1615, we observe some significant distinctions between the two types of contracts. A commercial contract most frequently constitutes a private regulatory agreement intended to ensure the successful outcome of the business between the contracting parties — in essence, to guide their relationship so that the object of the contract may be achieved. Normally, the execution of the contract ushers in the applicability of the regulatory scheme contemplated by the contract and the endeavor that is the object of the contract. As for a premarital agreement (or clause of such an agreement) providing solely for the division of property upon marital dissolution, the parties generally enter into the agreement anticipating that it never will be invoked, and the agreement, far from regulating the relationship of the contracting parties and providing the method for attaining their joint objectives, exists to provide for eventualities that will arise only if the relationship founders, possibly in the distant future under greatly changed and unforeseeable circumstances.

Furthermore, marriage itself is a highly regulated institution of undisputed social value, and there are many limitations on the ability of persons to contract with respect to it, or to vary its statutory terms, that have nothing to do with maximizing the satisfaction of the parties or carrying out their intent. Such limitations are inconsistent with the freedom-of-contract analysis espoused, for example, by the Pennsylvania Supreme Court. (See *Simeone v. Simeone,* 581 A.2d 162, 165–166.) We refer to rules establishing a duty of mutual financial support during the marriage and prohibiting agreements in derogation of the duty to support a child of the marriage; the unenforceability of a promise to marry; the circumstance that a party may abandon the marriage unilaterally under this state's no-fault laws; and the pervasive state involvement in the dissolution of marital status, the marriage contract, and the arrangements to be made for the children of the marriage — even without consideration of the circumstance that marriage normally lacks a predominantly commercial object. We also observe that a premarital agreement to raise children in a particular religion is not enforceable. We note, too, that there is authority — as conceded by the commissioners who considered the Uniform Act — to the effect that a contract to pay a spouse for personal services such as nursing cannot be enforced, despite the undoubted economic value of the services. These limitations demonstrate further that freedom of contract with respect to marital arrangements is tempered with statutory requirements and case law expressing social policy with respect to marriage.

There also are obvious differences between the remedies that realistically may be awarded with respect to commercial contracts and premarital agreements. Although a party seeking rescission of a commercial contract, for example, may be required to restore the status quo ante by restoring the consideration received, and a party in breach may be required to pay damages, the status quo ante for spouses cannot be restored to either party, nor are damages contemplated for breach of the marital contract. In any event, the suggestion that commercial contracts are strictly enforced without regard to the fairness or oppressiveness of the terms or the inequality of the bargaining power of the parties is anachronistic and inaccurate, in that claims such as duress, unconscionability, and undue influence turn upon the specific context in which the contract is formed. (See Bix, *Bargaining in the Shadow of Love: The Enforcement of Premarital Agreements and How We Think About Marriage (1998) 40 Wm. & Mary L. Rev. 145, 163, 182, 188, 205;* see also Atwood, *Ten Years Later: Lingering Concerns About the Uniform Premarital Agreement Act (1993) 19 J. Legis. 127, 146.)*

We also have explained generally that we believe the reference to voluntariness in the Uniform Act was intended to convey an element of knowing waiver that is not a consistent feature of commercial contract enforcement. Further, although the Uniform Act contemplated that contract defenses should apply, in the sense that an agreement should be free from fraud (including constructive fraud), duress, or undue influence, it is clear from the debate of the commissioners who adopted the Uniform Act and the cases cited in support of the enforcement provision of the Uniform Act that subtle coercion that would not be considered in challenges to ordinary commercial contracts may be considered in the context of the premarital agreement. The obvious distinctions between premarital agreements and ordinary commercial contracts lead us to conclude that factual circumstances relating to contract defenses that would not necessarily support the rescission of a commercial contract may suffice to render a premarital agreement unenforceable. The question of voluntariness must be examined in the unique context of the marital relationship.

On the other hand, we do not agree with Sun and the Court of Appeal majority that a *premarital* agreement should be interpreted and enforced under the same standards applicable to *marital* settlement agreements. First, although persons, once they are married, are in a fiduciary relationship to one another (*Fam. Code, § 721*, subd. (b)), so that whenever the parties enter into an agreement in which one party gains an advantage, the advantaged party bears the burden of demonstrating that the agreement was not obtained through undue influence, a different burden applies under the Uniform Act in the premarital setting. Even when the premarital agreement clearly advantages one of the parties, the party challenging the agreement bears the burden of demonstrating that the agreement was not entered into voluntarily. Further, under the Uniform Act, even when there has been a failure of disclosure, the statute still places the burden upon the party challenging the agreement to prove that the terms of the agreement were unconscionable when executed, rather than placing the burden on the advantaged party to demonstrate that the agreement was not unconscionable. Thus the terms of the act itself do not support the Court of Appeal's conclusion that the Legislature intended that premarital agreements should be interpreted in the same manner as agreements entered into during marriage.

In particular, we believe that both the Court of Appeal majority and Sun err to the extent they suggest that the Uniform Act or its California analog established that persons who enter into premarital agreements must be presumed to be in a confidential relationship, a status that would give rise to the fiduciary duties between spouses expressly established by § 721 of the Family Code. California law prior to the enactment of the Uniform Act was to the contrary, and we discern nothing in the Uniform Act suggesting that its adoption in California was intended to overrule our earlier decision.

The primary consequences of designating a relationship as fiduciary in nature are that the parties owe a duty of full disclosure, and that a presumption arises that a party who owes a fiduciary duty, and who secures a benefit through an agreement, has done so through undue influence. For example, a transaction in which an attorney gains an advantage over his or her client "is presumptively invalid, and the attorney must show not only that it was fair, but that the client was fully informed of all facts necessary to enable him to deal at arm's length." (1 Witkin, Summary of Cal. Law, *supra*, Contracts, § 425, pp. 381–382, italics omitted.) It long has been the rule that "[w]hen an interspousal transaction advantages one spouse, '[t]he law, from considerations of public policy, presumes such transactions to have been induced by undue influence.' " (*In re Marriage of Haines, supra*, 33 Cal. App. 4th at p. 293, quoting *Brison v. Brison (1888) 75 Cal. 525, 529 [17 P. 689].)*

. . .

Because the Uniform Act was intended to enhance the enforceability of premarital agreements, because it expressly places the burden of proof upon the person challenging the agreement, and finally because the California statute imposing fiduciary duties in the family law setting applies only to spouses, we do not believe that the commissioners or our Legislature contemplated that the voluntariness of a premarital agreement would be examined in light of the strict fiduciary duties imposed on persons such as lawyers, or imposed expressly by statute upon persons who are married. Although we certainly agree that persons contemplating marriage morally owe each other a duty of fair dealing and obviously are not embarking upon a purely commercial contract, we do not believe that these circumstances permit us to interpret our statute as imposing a *presumption* of undue influence or as requiring the kind of strict scrutiny that is conducted when a lawyer or other fiduciary engages in self-dealing. On the contrary, it is evident that the Uniform Act was intended to *enhance* the enforceability of premarital agreements, a goal that would be undermined by presuming the existence of a confidential or fiduciary relationship.

. . .

D

The Court of Appeal majority, suggesting that counsel for the party who proposed the premarital agreement has a duty to provide a warning to the other party if he or she is unrepresented, stated: "Counsel, at a minimum, must explain to the unrepresented party (1) that the attorney's responsibility is to pursue and protect only the interests of his or her client; (2) that spousal interests are probably not identical and are likely to conflict; (3) that the spouses' interests will change over time and the attorney will not be concerned with providing for all the changed circumstances that could possibly impact the unrepresented spouse; and (4) that signing this agreement will eliminate or modify his or her statutory rights."

Both Sun and Barry contend that counsel for the represented party cannot effectively or ethically explain to the unrepresented party what rights are being waived under the agreement. Barry claims that such a warning would be unethical, because it would be inconsistent with the attorney's duty to serve only his or her own client's interest. Sun adds that such a rule would be improper because it would violate a rule of professional conduct prohibiting counsel for one party from giving legal advice to an opposing party who is unrepresented, in that such advice might cause the unrepresented party to believe counsel is serving both parties.

We do not believe that the case before us presents an appropriate occasion to delineate the duties that must guide an attorney in drafting a premarital agreement. The issue before us is the enforceability of a premarital agreement, not the extent, if any, of counsel's duty to an unrepresented party to the agreement, or the imposition of discipline upon an attorney who does not comply with that duty. We do observe, however, that it is consistent with an attorney's duty to further the interest of his or her client for the attorney to take steps to ensure that the premarital agreement will be enforceable. After discussing the matter with his or her client, an attorney may convey such information to the other party as will assist in having the agreement upheld, as long as he or she does not violate the duty of loyalty to the client or undertake to represent both parties without an appropriate waiver of the conflict of interest. We also observe that, obviously, the best assurance of enforceability is independent representation for both parties.

III

Finally, we conclude that the trial court's determination that Sun voluntarily entered into the premarital agreement in the present case is supported by substantial evidence. . . .[¶] The trial court made specific findings of fact regarding the factors we have identified as relevant to the determination of voluntariness. These findings. . .should have been accepted by the Court of Appeal majority. . . .

. . .

[A]lthough Sun lacked legal counsel, the trial court determined that she had a reasonable opportunity to obtain counsel. The trial court stated: ". . . . Respondent was advised at a meeting with Attorney Brown at least one week prior to execution of the Agreement that she had the right to have an attorney represent her and that Attorneys Brown and Megwa represented Petitioner, not Respondent. On at least two occasions during the February 5, 1988, meeting, Respondent was told that she could have separate counsel if she chose. Respondent declined. Respondent was capable of understanding this admonition."

. . . .[¶] The Court of Appeal majority surmised that Sun did not have a reasonable opportunity to consult counsel because a copy of the agreement was not provided in advance of the February 5, 1988, meeting, and because Sun had insufficient funds to retain counsel and was not informed that Barry would pay for independent counsel's services. Again, this determination is contradicted by the conclusion of the trial court that Sun had "an adequate and reasonable opportunity to obtain independent counsel prior to execution of the Agreement." . . . Additionally, there was evidence supporting the inference that she declined counsel because she understood and agreed with the terms of the agreement, and not because she had insufficient funds to employ counsel. [T]he Court of Appeal . . . majority's opinion departed from the appropriate standard of review in this respect. . . .

IV

The judgment of the Court of Appeal is reversed to the extent that it reversed the judgment of the trial court on the issue of the voluntariness of the premarital agreement. The matter is remanded to the Court of Appeal to determine whether, consistent with this opinion, its remand to the trial court for reevaluation of the termination of spousal support remains necessary, and to consider other issues it declared moot in light of its determination that the agreement was not enforceable: namely, (1) whether the trial court denied Sun due process by excluding evidence supporting her claim that Barry should be estopped from enforcing the agreement, and (2) whether the trial court erred in various respects in interpreting and enforcing the agreement.

Mosk, J., Kennard, J., Baxter, J., Werdegar, J., Chin, J., and Brown, J., concurred.

SIMEONE v. SIMEONE, 581 A.2d 162 (Pa. 1990): "At issue in this appeal is the validity of a prenuptial agreement executed between the appellant, Catherine E. Walsh Simeone, and the appellee, Frederick A. Simeone. At the time of their marriage, in 1975, [Catherine] was a twenty-three year old nurse and [Frederick] was a thirty-nine year old neurosurgeon. [Frederick] had an income of approximately $90,000 per year, and [Catherine] was unemployed. [Frederick] also had assets worth approximately $300,000. On the eve of the parties' wedding, [Frederick]'s attorney presented [Catherine] with a prenuptial agreement to be signed. [Catherine], without the benefit of counsel, signed the agreement. [Frederick]'s attorney had not advised [Catherine] regarding any legal rights that the agreement surrendered. The parties are in disagreement as to whether [Catherine] knew in advance of that date that such an agreement would be presented for signature. [Catherine] denies having had such knowledge and claims to have signed under adverse circumstances, which, she contends, provide a basis for declaring it void.

"The agreement limited [Catherine] to support payments of $200 per week in the event of separation or divorce, subject to a maximum total payment of $25,000. . . . The Superior Court [upheld the agreement and enforced this limit].

". . . .There is no longer validity in [the] implicit presumption [of earlier cases]that . . . spouses are of unequal status and that women are not knowledgeable enough to understand the nature of contracts that they enter. Society has advanced, however, to the point where women are no longer regarded as the "weaker" party in marriage, or in society generally. Indeed, the stereotype that women serve as homemakers while men work as breadwinners is no longer viable. . . . Nor is there viability in the presumption that women are uninformed, uneducated, and readily subjected to unfair advantage in marital agreements. . . . [¶] . . . [T]he standards governing prenuptial agreements [in earlier cases] reflected a paternalistic approach that is now insupportable.

". . .Prenuptial agreements are contracts, and, as such, should be evaluated under the same criteria as are applicable to other types of contracts. . . . Absent fraud, misrepresentation, or duress, spouses should be bound by the terms of their agreements. [¶] Contracting parties are normally bound by their agreements, without regard to whether the terms thereof were read and fully understood and irrespective of whether the agreements embodied reasonable or good bargains. [T]he present prenuptial agreement must be . . . binding, without regard to whether the terms were fully understood by [Catherine]. *Ignorantia non excusat.*

"Accordingly, we find no merit in a contention raised by [Catherine] that the agreement should be declared void on the ground that she did not consult with independent legal counsel. . . . [¶] Further, the reasonableness of a prenuptial bargain is not a proper subject for judicial review. . . . [¶] [E]veryone who enters a long-term agreement knows that circumstances can change during its term, so that what initially appeared desirable might prove to be an unfavorable bargain. Such are the risks that contracting parties routinely assume. Certainly, the possibilities of illness, birth of children, reliance upon a spouse, numerous other events that can occur in the course of a marriage cannot be regarded as unforeseeable. If parties choose not to address such matters in their prenuptial agreements, they must be regarded as having contracted to bear the risk of events that alter the value of their bargains."

[c]   Current Trends and the ALI's Proposals

1. *The Overview.* One may police premarital agreements by imposing special procedural requirements, or by imposing special tests of substantive fairness. *Button* does both. It allows enforcement only if: 1) the parties had knowledge of each other's assets, either independently or through disclosure; *and* 2) the agreement was "voluntary," meaning that the parties had a "meaningful choice"; *and* 3) its terms were fair at the time of execution; *and* 4) it is fair to apply it at the time of divorce. The third and fourth are obviously requirements of substantive fairness, and the first is a procedural fairness requirement. As we shall see below in Note 2, the "voluntariness" requirement becomes procedural as well, once one tries to give it meaning. All four of these requirements go well beyond what courts ordinarily demand before enforcing a commercial contract. At the other end of the spectrum is *Simeone,* which largely adopts normal contractual rules.

In between the endpoints of *Button* and *Simeone* lie *Gant, Bonds*, and the UPAA, in approximately that order. As explained further below, the recommendations of the American Law Institute's *Principles* adopt *Gant's* foreseeability test for substantive fairness, while also imposing some procedural fairness requirements that are more carefully defined than the test of voluntariness found in both *Button* and the UPAA. Following the decision in *Bonds*, the California legislature amended that state's version of the UPAA in several respects, overruling *Bonds* and adopting some provisions that follow the ALI's recommendations. *See* Notes 4 and 5, *infra.*

The UPAA has come under increasing criticism for its relative willingness to enforce premarital agreements in circumstances that the commentators believe inappropriate. *See* Barbara Atwood, *Ten Years Later: Lingering Concerns about the Uniform Premarital Agreement Act,* 19 J. Legis. 127, 128 (1993) ("Despite the representations of N.C.C.U.S.L., the U.P.A.A. departs, sometimes dramatically, from the common law of many states"); Katharine Silbaugh, *Marriage Contracts and the Family Economy*, 93 Nw. U. L. Rev. 65 (1998) (critical of the trend toward enforcement of agreements, noting that accepted arguments against enforcement of some nonmonetary terms may apply to monetary terms as well); Gail F. Brod, *Premarital Agreements and Gender Justice*, 6 Yale J.L. & Feminism 229, 295 (1994) (arguing that the UPAA fails to give adequate weight to policies other than freedom of contract and personal autonomy, such as the "attainment of economic justice for the economically vulnerable spouse at the end of marriage"). Whether for this reason or otherwise, the Act's initial acceptance has waned, and the pace of adoption has declined. In the first seven years from its promulgation in 1983, the UPAA was adopted by 15 states. In the next 10 years, through 2000, it was adopted by 10 more states and the District of Columbia. But only three of those 10 new adoptions came after 1995. Uniform Laws Annotated (Westlaw, May 12, 2000). Nearly one-third of the adopting states (8 states) have varied from the official text in some important respect; some of these departures are noted below.

2. *The Voluntariness Requirement: A Form of Procedural Fairness*. The UPAA, as well as all the preceding cases but *Simeone*, make special note that agreements must be "voluntary" to be enforceable. Much of the *Bonds* opinion is an exploration of the meaning of this requirement, which the UPAA itself leaves undefined. As *Bonds* notes, the narrow majority of Uniform Act commissioners who favored the UPAA's severe limits on the unconscionability doctrine (more on this below in Note 4) defended their position in the Uniform Act debates with assurances that the requirement of voluntariness would prevent the enforcement of questionable contracts. *E.g.*, the drafting committee was asked why it deleted language making an agreement's enforcement dependent upon the parties having "understood [its] effect" ("[W]as it that the 'voluntary' carries the freight . . . or you don't care whether they understood it or not?"). The committee's spokesman responded "We think the 'voluntary' covers it." National Conference of Commissioners on Uniform State Laws, Proceedings in the Committee of the Whole, Uniform Premarital Agreements Act, at p. 63 (July 23, 25, and 26, 1983). And as *Bonds* notes, when concern was raised over the case of a young pregnant girl, asked to sign a one-sided agreement as a condition of marriage to the father, the draft's defenders said that agreement would be unenforceable as involuntary because that doctrine would reach cases of "oppression," *id*. at 72–73. But these hints are all we have of the intended meaning of "voluntary," and the act itself does not define the term. Courts thus have wide latitude in its construction. But the legislative history at the Uniform Commissioner deliberations, as well as earlier case law using the term, strongly suggests that it is meant to add *something* to the usual requirements for enforcing a contract. This seems to be agreed upon by all the other authorities other than *Simeone*.

Those usual contract principles deny enforcement of agreements entered into under "duress," a seeming close cousin of "involuntary." But in fact contract law's traditional duress requirement has a very limited reach, leaving plenty of room for the additional requirement of voluntariness to add real meaning. *E.g.*, the duress rule offers no basis for voiding an agreement just because the disfavored party did not understand its effect. Consider as well that in the commercial contract context, courts have held that a defense of economic duress usually requires a showing that the promisor's dire circumstances were the result of the promisee's acts. E. ALLAN FARNSWORTH, I FARNSWORTH ON CONTRACTS 486, n.26 (2d ed. 1998). Could an analogous showing be made in the debated case of the pregnant teenage bride, thus sustaining a duress defense to such an agreement? Not necessarily. In *Hamilton v. Hamilton*, 591 A.2d 720, 722 (Pa. Super. 1991), the wife was 18, unemployed, and three months pregnant (by the husband) when the parties married. The husband had conditioned marriage on the wife's agreement to waive all alimony claims; the wife's counsel had advised her against signing but she signed anyway. The court enforced the waiver, concluding that "[w]here a party has been free to consult counsel before signing an agreement, the courts have uniformly rejected duress as a defense to the agreement." *See also Lebeck v. Lebeck*, 881 P.2d 727 (N.M. App. 1994) (duress not shown by wife with independent counsel, who signed agreement demanded by her attorney-husband because she wished to legitimate their daughter; "a threat to do that which the demanding party has the right to demand is not sufficient to support a claim of duress.") By contrast, compare *Williams v. Williams*, 617 So. 2d 1032 (Ala. 1992), which evaluates such claims by reference to ideas of voluntariness rather than duress. It found that under a rule requiring "that the agreement was entered into freely and voluntarily," the lower court must decide whether, as a question of fact, "the father's conditioning the marriage on the pregnant mother's signing the antenuptial agreement, joined with the mother's moral objection to abortion and the importance of legitimacy in a small town, created a coercive atmosphere in which the mother had no viable alternative to accepting the father's condition for marriage. . . .").

So the concept of "voluntariness" must go beyond conventional ideas of "duress" in order to deny enforcement of contracts that the enforcement-oriented commissioners conceded were problematic. But how far beyond, and to where? *Button*'s definition of voluntary — did the actor have a "meaningful choice" — does not help very much to answer this question. Any choice in which one has a lot at stake may seem meaningful. *Bonds* tries to discern the UPAA's understanding of "voluntary" by looking at the fact patterns that recur in the cases cited by the UPAA, and concludes "that the voluntariness of a premarital agreement may turn in part upon whether the agreement was entered into knowingly, in the sense that the parties understood the terms or basic effect of the agreement." Yet it is of course difficult to know what someone really understood. This requirement therefore tends to get redefined into procedural safeguards to make sure the party had every chance to understand it: *e.g.*, was the party advised by independent counsel, were assets disclosed, and was an adequate explanation of the agreement's significance provided? A second thread *Bonds* finds in the voluntariness cases reflects the view of some drafting Commissioners that the voluntariness requirement deals with cases of "oppression." What does voluntary mean in this context? A rule of voluntariness cannot require looking at the soul of each party to the contract to determine whether his or her free will is intact. The victim of the armed robber makes a choice when told "your money or your life," and he probably would rather have that choice, than not. We nonetheless call the choice "involuntary" because threatening to kill people is an improper bargaining tactic, and we do not bind people to choices made in response to such threats. So we say that one party's improper — "oppressive" — bargaining tactics denies the other party a "voluntary" choice. But it is our condemnation of the bargaining tactic, not the psyche of its victim, that is key.

Of course the usual premarital agreement dispute does not involve death threats. To assess whether bargaining tactics are improper in the more typical case, courts must make some subtle distinctions. On one hand, for example, an agreement is not involuntary merely because one party insisted upon it as a condition of marriage, because the "threat of a refusal to marry is not wrongful in the eyes of the law." *Liebelt v. Liebelt*, 801 P.2d 52, 55 (Idaho App. 1990); *accord, Gardner v. Gardner*, 527 N.W.2d 701, 706 (Wis. App. 1994); *Howell v. Landry*, 386 S.E.2d 610, 617–18 (N.C. App. 1989); *Taylor v. Taylor*, 832 P.2d 429, 431 (Okla. App. 1992). But on the other hand, one party's insistence on conditioning the marriage to the other's consent to an agreement may be regarded as improper if the demand is made, for the first time, on the eve of the wedding. "The presentation of an agreement a very short time before the wedding ceremony will create a presumption of overreaching or coercion if . . . the postponement of the wedding would cause significant hardship, embarrassment or emotional stress. . . [¶] The meaningfulness of the opportunity of the nonproponent party to seek counsel before executing an antenuptial agreement is . . . [significant in determining] whether coercion or overreaching occurred." *Fletcher v. Fletcher*, 628 N.E.2d 1343 (Ohio 1994) (but upholding the particular agreement before it because in this particular case the wedding's postponement would not have caused hardship or embarrassment). Similarly, conditioning marriage on an agreement may be thought improper in pregnant-bride cases like *Williams*, *supra*, if the groom is seen as exploiting the bride's vulnerability, to gain an unfair advantage. To the extent that the idea of voluntariness captures this exploitation concern, it protects the vulnerable party in situations in which courts might otherwise rely upon the unconscionability doctrine to reach the same result. *See* Note 6, *infra*.

3. *The ALI Principles' Approach to the Voluntariness Requirement.* The *ALI Principles* follow the analysis of the prior note and avoid any use at all of the term "voluntary." "The best understanding of the frequently stated voluntariness requirement is that it expresses the law's heightened sensitivity to duress and coercion concerns in the context of premarital agreements. . . . Consent is involuntary when it is elicited by . . . problematic bargaining tactics." *ALI Principles* § 7.04, Comment *b*. The ALI recommends special procedural requirements as a more effective and more certain alternative to reliance upon the vague requirement of "voluntariness." It requires the party seeking to enforce the agreement to show that the other party's consent was informed and not obtained under duress. Section 7.04(3) then gives the agreement's proponent the benefit of a presumption (rebuttable) that this burden has been met, if the proponent shows that:

(a) [the agreement] was executed at least 30 days before the parties' marriage;

(b) both parties were advised to obtain independent legal counsel, and had reasonable opportunity to do so, before the agreement's execution; and,

(c) in the case of agreements concluded without the assistance of independent legal counsel for each party, the agreement states, in language easily understandable by an adult of ordinary intelligence with no legal training,

(i) the nature of any rights or claims otherwise arising at dissolution that are altered by the contract, and the nature of that alteration, and

(ii) that the interests of the spouses with respect to the agreement may be adverse.

Section 7.05 thus deals directly with the principal issues that recur under the rubric of voluntariness: the parties' understanding of the agreement's terms and its significance, reasonable opportunity to consult independent counsel, and last minute demands for an agreement. The agreement's proponent may prevail even if these requirements are not met, but only by carrying the burden of proving that "the other party's consent was informed and not obtained under duress."

The requirement of execution at least 30 days prior to the wedding is not generally found in prevailing American law. The *Principles* explain

> [T]he late insistence on an agreement places the offeree in a dilemma. [It] may give the offeree doubts about the marriage. Yet, by this time, the parties have already agreed to marry, and perhaps publicly announced their commitment. The newly created doubts, even if worrisome, may come too late to reverse the momentum of the existing marital plans, or to overcome the offeree's preexisting emotional commitment to the marriage, as well as the offeree's naturally optimistic expectations of married life with the offeror. So the agreement is signed.

> Because no one is ever obliged to marry, people are generally free to insist on an agreement as a condition for entering marriage. The difficulty in these cases is the late hour at which this insistence is expressed — often some time after the parties had decided to marry, and after they have acted on that decision in both their public and private behavior. In this context, the proffered premarital agreement resembles new terms that one party insists upon adding to an agreement to marry that had already been reached and partially executed. . . .[¶] Premarital agreements are rarely proposed on impulse. They are usually planned. The party who wants the agreement typically hires a lawyer to draft it. There is usually no reason why this process cannot begin early enough to be completed a month before the wedding.

In § 7.04(5), the *Principles* also require the disclosure of a party's assets and income for the enforcement of any provision limiting the other party's financial claims at divorce, or proof that the other party knew the first party's assets and income, at least approximately.

4. *Disclosure of Assets and Unconscionability in Premarital Agreements.* Disclosure is probably the most universal of the heightened procedural requirements applied to premarital agreements, required under pre-UPAA law as well as the *ALI Principles*. Even *Simeone*, in a passage not included in the excerpt above, holds that absent a "full and fair disclosure of the financial positions of the parties. . . material misrepresentation in the inducement for entering a prenuptial agreement may be asserted." Mandatory disclosure is of course one way to vindicate a concern that consent to an agreement is "knowledgeable," an important part of the "voluntariness" rubric. One might also argue that concealment of one's assets is precisely the kind of bargaining tactic barred under the rubric of voluntariness. The Uniform Premarital Agreement Act's treatment of the disclosure requirement is therefore puzzling. Under § 6(a)(2), disclosure is important only if the agreement is also unconscionable, as the failure to disclose does not alone affect the agreement's validity. The UPAA would therefore enforce an unfair agreement the disadvantaged party would not have signed if disclosure had been made, unless it is so unfair as to be unconscionable.

Note that the reverse problem is also possible under the UPAA; an agreement is immune from attack as unconscionable, if either disclosure was made, or the disadvantaged party had knowledge of the other party's assets. *Bonds* relies on this very point in concluding that the issue of unconscionability cannot be before the court because the parties had agreed that Sun had knowledge of Barry's assets. Moreover, § 6(a)(2)(ii) of the UPAA allows a party to waive disclosure, creating the stunning possibility that an unconscionably unfair agreement could be enforced against an uninformed party who waived disclosure. Three states that have otherwise adopted the UPAA changed its language to avoid the implication that disclosure can be waived. *See* Conn. Gen. Stat. Ann. § 46b-36g(a)(3); Iowa Code Ann. § 596.7(2)(c); N.J. Stat. Ann. § 37:2-38(c)(1). There may be reason to wonder whether the Commissioners really intended the result apparently called for under this UPAA language. Perhaps the drafters expected the Act's vague requirement of voluntariness to protect parties who would have unconscionability claims but for the Act's unique provisions. But in the end it is difficult to be confident of what the UPAA drafters had in mind. The official UPAA commentary to § 6 cites with approval the case of *Del Vecchio v. Del Vecchio*, 143 So. 2d 17 (Fla. 1962), but that case is inconsistent with these UPAA provisions. It requires disclosure and disallows its waiver, and does not treat disclosure as "cleansing" an otherwise unconscionable agreement so as to allow its enforcement. For more on this point, see the Reporter's Notes to Comment *g* of § 7.04 of the *ALI Principles.*

5. *More on Independent Counsel.* Recall that under the *ALI Principles* the agreement's proponent will benefit from a presumption that the other party's consent was informed, and free from duress, only if, among other requirements, "both parties were advised to obtain independent legal counsel, and had reasonable opportunity to do so, before the agreement's execution." In the event there in fact was no independent counsel, there is the additional requirement set forth in § 7.04(3)(c), reprinted above in Note 3, that the agreement contain a plain language explanation of both its significance, and that the parties' interests may be adverse. In this respect (as others, see Note 7 below) the *ALI Principles* follow *Gant*, which also requires either independent counsel or an agreement reasonably understandable to the layman. Most authorities are not as explicit on the counsel requirement, however. As *Bonds* point out, for example, there is no mention of independent counsel in the UPAA, an omission that was apparently intentional. On the other hand, as *Bonds* also points out, the presence or absence of independent counsel, and the availability of an understandable explanation of the agreement's terms and significance, are factors that can be weighed in assessing whether consent was "voluntary," even though their absence does not shift the burden of proof, as it effectively does under the *ALI Principles.* In fact, after *Bonds* was decided, the California legislature amended its statute to adopt provisions very similar to the *ALI Principles'* recommendations. Newly-enacted CALIF. FAM. CODE § 1615(c) provides that an agreement is not voluntary unless two conditions are both met:

(1) The party against whom enforcement is sought was represented by independent legal counsel at the time of signing the agreement or, after

being advised to seek independent legal counsel, expressly waived, in a separate writing, representation by independent legal counsel.

(2) The party against whom enforcement is sought had not less than seven calendar days between the time that party was first presented with the agreement and advised to seek independent legal counsel and the time the agreement was signed.

It is thus apparent that the *Bonds* agreement itself would not be enforceable under current provisions of California law.

Did Sun Bonds have a "reasonable opportunity" to obtain counsel, as specified in § 7.04(3) of the *ALI Principles*? One question is whether Sun Bonds could *afford* independent counsel. In commentary, the *ALI Principles* conclude that a party does *not* have "reasonable opportunity" to consult independent counsel if that party cannot afford to pay counsel. *See* § 7.04, Comment *e*. Thus, to obtain the benefit of the presumption of validity under the *ALI Principles*, Barry would have had to have offered to pay for independent counsel for Sun, if Sun did not have adequate funds of her own. The court of appeals believed she did not, an important factor contributing to its conclusion that her agreement was not voluntary. In reversing, the California Supreme Court relied on the trial court's finding that Sun had reasonable opportunity to obtain counsel, but there is no indication that the trial court considered Sun's ability to pay counsel as bearing on its conclusion. Nor do the general provisions ultimately adopted by the legislature in § 1615(c) address this question (is the waiver allowed under § 1615(c)(1) valid, when executed by a party who could not pay for counsel?). Note that California now applies a special requirement for counsel applicable to provisions waiving spousal support. *See* Note 6, *infra*.

6. *Special Rules With Respect to Provisions Limiting Alimony.* Note that Sun in fact received a large alimony award, and there was apparently no provision in their agreement — or at least none that Barry sought to enforce — which limited her spousal support claim. Historically, some courts and legislatures have been more resistant to enforcing waivers of alimony than waivers of marital property rights, and this resistance can still be seen. Indiana added language to its version of the UPAA allowing its courts to require spousal maintenance, despite contract terms to the contrary, when a spouse would otherwise suffer "extreme hardship under circumstances not reasonably foreseeable at the time of the execution of the agreement." *See Rider v. Rider*, 669 N.E.2d 160, 163–64 (Ind. 1996). Illinois has adopted the same language, ILL. COMP. STAT. 10/7-§ 7(b). Four other states that adopted the UPAA (California, Iowa, New Mexico, and South Dakota) changed its text to delete spousal maintenance from the list of subjects that a valid agreement may address. In a decision handed down with *Bonds*, the California Supreme Court held that this omission was not intended to bar agreements on maintenance, *Pendleton v. Fireman*, 5 P.3d 839 (Cal. 2000). In response, the California legislature then barred enforcement of agreements waiving spousal support if they are "unconscionable at the time of enforcement" or if the waiving party was not represented by independent counsel at the time of the waiver. CAL. FAM. CODE § 1612(c).

7. *Substantive Fairness, the Doctrine of Unconscionability, and the ALI's Proposals.* Section 208 of RESTATEMENT SECOND, CONTRACTS states the classic rule:

> If a contract or term thereof is unconscionable at the time the contract is made a court may refuse to enforce the contract, or may enforce the remainder of the contract without the unconscionable term, or may so limit the application of any unconscionable term as to avoid any unconscionable result.

The Restatement does not attempt to define unconscionability with any further precision. It is not inadvertent, however, that § 208 specifies that the question is whether an agreement is unconscionable "at the time the contract is made," not at some later time when its enforcement is sought. This feature of the unconscionability principle is inherent in its rationale. As explained in Comment *d* of § 7.01 of the *ALI Principles,*

> The doctrine goes primarily to defects in the bargaining process, including unfairness in the negotiating tactics used to obtain agreement. Along with procedural defects, however, the law has also recognized substantive unconscionability, or a gross one-sidedness in terms. The two often go hand in hand, for one may tend to prove the other. A grossly one-sided agreement may corroborate unconscionable bargaining tactics, while unfair bargaining tactics may most often be employed to obtain a one-sided agreement.

In other words, one would not usually expect a competent adult to agree to contract terms that are oppressive — substantively unconscionable — at the time of the agreement, unless there was a defect in the bargaining process. That process defect might be of the sort contemplated by other contract doctrines, such as misrepresentation or duress. But it might not, and then the unconscionability doctrine is important. An example is the unfair exploitation, by one party, of the other's special vulnerability. *See* Eisenberg, *The Bargain Principle and Its Limits,* 95 HARV. L. REV. 741 (1982) (explaining how the unconscionability doctrine is necessary to deny enforcement of the stranded desert traveler's promise to pay a million dollars for a jug of water). Substantive unconscionability thus suggests the likelihood of procedural unconscionability, and can be said to depend upon that likelihood as part of its rationale for denying enforcement of an unconscionable agreement. But procedural unconscionability is not suggested by terms that seemed fair at the time of execution, even if they may be very unfair under the facts prevailing at some later time when enforcement is sought. We still may wish, of course, to deny enforcement of terms that, as things turn out, are enormously one-sided. But doing so requires the development of a different doctrine, for while substantive unconscionability exists as a legal concept, it is not entirely independent from concerns with procedural unconscionability.

That need for a different doctrine is obscured by courts and statutes which deny enforcement of an agreement if it is unconscionable at the time of enforcement. Some states that adopted the UPAA have modified it to add such language. *E.g.*, CONN. GEN. STAT. ANN. § 46b-36g(a)(2) (agreement is not enforceable if "unconscionable when it was executed or when enforcement is sought"; N.D. CENT. CODE § 14-03.1-06(1) (*similarly, see Lutz v. Schneider,* 563 N.W.2d 90 (N.D. 1997)); N.J. STAT. ANN. 37:2-38(b) (defining as unconscionable any agreement that "would provide a standard of living far below that which was enjoyed before the marriage"); CALIF. FAM. CODE § 1612(c) (with respect to spousal support terms only). It may seem that asking whether an agreement is "unconscionable" at the time of enforcement merely applies an established doctrine to a new situation, but the temporal shift robs the doctrine of much of its rationale. *Button* avoids the word "unconscionable," simply holding that an agreement can be reviewed for "fairness" as of the time of enforcement. This may not be entirely satisfactory either, for it seems inconsistent with basic ideas of contract law to allow courts to reject any agreement they find "unfair." Indeed, concern with just such freewheeling judicial scrutiny is what appears to have motivated the Uniform Commissioners to circumscribe the unconscionability doctrine in the UPAA. The challenge, then, is to develop a doctrine dealing with agreements that seem wrong to enforce because of circumstances prevailing at the time of enforcement, while doing so in a way that is more limited than just allowing courts to refuse enforcement of any contract they believe very unfair.

Gant takes up this challenge. It is probably correct in concluding that when courts talk about unfairness at the time of *enforcement*, they are really talking about the unforeseeability, at the time of *execution*, of the circumstances under which enforcement is sought. This is not a problem of unconscionability in the classic sense, because it is not a case in which one party has necessarily imposed unfairly on the other. It may even be a case in which *neither* party really foresaw, at the time of execution, the impact of enforcing its terms later. In adopting *Gant*'s general approach, the *ALI Principles* necessarily must fill in some details. These are found in § 7.05:

AMERCAN LAW INSTITUTE, *Principles of the Law of Family Dissolution*, § 7.05

§ 7.05 When Enforcement Would Work a Substantial Injustice

(1) A court should not enforce a term in an agreement if, pursuant to Paragraphs (2) and (3) of this section,

(a) the circumstances require it to consider if enforcement would work a substantial injustice; and

(b) the court finds that enforcement would work a substantial injustice.

(2) A court should consider whether enforcement of an agreement would work a substantial injustice if, and only if, the party resisting its enforcement shows that one or more of the following have occurred since the time of the agreement's execution:

(a) more than a fixed number of years have passed, that number being set in a rule of statewide application;

(b) a child was born to, or adopted by, the parties, who at the time of execution had no children in common;

(c) there has been a change in circumstances that has a substantial impact on the parties or their children, but when they executed the agreement the parties probably did not anticipate either the change, or its impact.

Comment: . . . .

b. . . . . [N]early all premarital agreements involve special difficulties arising from unrealistic optimism about marital success, the human tendency to treat low probabilities as zero probabilities, the excessive discounting of future benefits, and the inclination to overweigh the importance of the immediate and certain consequences of agreement — the marriage — as against its contingent and future consequences. Paragraph (2), however, does not call for the court's examination at divorce of all premarital agreements, but only a subset in which these difficulties are particularly likely. Paragraph (2)(a) identifies contracts made more than a fixed period of years before enforcement is sought, that period having been set in a uniform rule of statewide application. A period of about 10 years would ensure scrutiny of agreements whose enforcement is particularly likely to be problematic, while leaving a clear majority of divorces unaffected (because most divorces occur after fewer years of marriage). Paragraph (2)(b) identifies for scrutiny those cases in which the parties had no children in common at the time of the agreement, but do so at the time that its enforcement is sought. Even childless parties who anticipate having children are often unable to anticipate the impact that children will have on their values and life plans. Once they are parents, the effect of the terms they earlier agreed upon are therefore likely to seem quite different than they expected when childless. Note that, when the parties have children, there are policy issues as well. See Comment *c.*

Most of the fact patterns justifying a substantial-injustice inquiry when enforcement is sought will be captured by Paragraphs (2)(a) and (2)(b), but not all. There are additional cases in which the cognitive difficulties are particularly severe, but which are not easily identified by the simple objective indicators employed in Paragraphs (2)(a) and (2)(b). Paragraph (2)(c) states a more general standard under which at least some of these problem cases may be reached. It requires the party resisting enforcement to show a change in life circumstances that was probably unanticipated by the parties but that has a substantial impact on them or their children. To meet this burden, the party resisting enforcement need not show the nature of the parties' deliberations and their cognitive capacities at the time of execution, which may have been many years earlier. As an initial matter, the resisting party may satisfy this burden by showing that normal, competent individuals would not usually anticipate either the circumstances at the time of divorce, or the change in the impact of the agreement's terms under those new circumstances. The party seeking to enforce the agreement may rebut such a showing, however, with evidence that the particular parties were in fact likely to have anticipated the new circumstances and to have considered the impact that enforcement of the agreement would have on them if those circumstances arose.

Illustrations:

1. Prior to their marriage, Susan and George enter into an agreement that keeps most of their property separate rather than marital, and that limits claims for compensatory payments. At the time of the contract, they are childless, have no plans to have children, and work at jobs yielding similar, comfortable incomes. Two years after their marriage, Susan's sister dies unexpectedly, and Susan becomes the legal guardian of her two nieces, then four and seven. Susan changes to part-time work so that she can spend more time with the children. She eventually reduces her employment even further, with George's acquiescence, to devote more time to her nieces.

In the eighth year of their marriage, George and Susan divorce. Susan will remain the children's primary caretaker. Their state has set 10 years as the applicable period under Paragraph (2)(a). Paragraph (2)(a) therefore does not apply because 10 years have not passed since the agreement was executed. Paragraph (2)(b) does not apply, because Susan and George have no children in common. (The conclusion would be different had they adopted Susan's nieces.) However, under Paragraph (2)(c), the court should consider whether the enforcement of this agreement would work a substantial injustice. There has been a change in the parties' circumstances since the agreement was executed that significantly alters the impact of the agreement's enforcement on the parties. Susan has not worked full time for some years. It is unlikely that contracting parties would anticipate the events that brought about this change. Moreover, the changes in the marriage are similar to those that might have occurred if the parties had their own children, in which case Paragraph (2)(b) would have applied. Paragraph (2)(c) requires the same result here, and therefore the court should consider whether enforcement would work a substantial injustice.

―――――――

The ALI thus offers an approach to fairness that is more limited than *Button* because it permits the inquiry in only a subset of premarital agreement cases. Another subsection not reprinted above lists the considerations that bear upon whether an agreement works a substantial injustice. This subsection, informed by the discussion of it in the accompanying commentary, guides the substantial injustice inquiry. The limitation in the circumstances under which the inquiry can be made at all remains, however, the most important reason why the *ALI Principles* do not in fact allow the kind of open ended review of an agreement's fairness that the Uniform Commissioners also wished to avoid.

8. *More on the Rationale for Heightened Scrutiny.* Why impose special process requirements on premarital agreements, and why allow courts ever to inquire into the fairness of enforcing them? The *ALI Principles* summarizes the arguments it relies upon, in Comment *c* of § 7.02::

> While there are good reasons to respect contracts relating to the consequences of family dissolution, the family context requires some departure from the rules that govern the commercial arena. First, the relationship between contracting parties who are married, or about to marry, is different than the usual commercial relationship in ways that matter to the law's treatment of their agreements. Persons planning to marry usually assume that they share with their intended spouse a mutual and deep concern for one another's welfare. Business people negotiating a commercial agreement do not usually have that expectation of one another. . . . These distinctive expectations that persons planning to marry usually have about one another can disarm their capacity for self-protective judgment, or their inclination to exercise it, as compared to parties negotiating commercial agreements. This difference justifies legal rules designed to strengthen the parties' ability and inclination to consider how a proposed agreement affects their own interest, such as rules that require transparency in the agreement's language and that encourage parties to seek independent legal counsel.

> Second, even though the terms of agreements made before, or during, an ongoing family relationship address the consequences of its dissolution, the parties ordinarily do not expect the family unit to dissolve. Even if the possibility of dissolution is considered, it is necessarily imagined as arising at some indefinite time in the future. The remoteness of dissolution in both likelihood and timing, as well as the difficulty of anticipating other life changes that might occur during the course of the marriage, further impedes the ability of persons to evaluate the impact that the contract terms will have on them in the future when its enforcement is sought. . . .

> The two concerns just identified describe distinctive limits on the cognitive capacity with which persons may enter family contracts, as contrasted with commercial agreements. There is, in addition, the point that the rights and obligations that parties might seek to waive through private agreements are designed to protect the interests of persons who enter into family relationships, and the interests of their children. Enforcement of agreements about the consequences of family dissolution therefore present a different policy question than enforcement of commercial agreements between persons who otherwise have no claims on one another's property or income. Family contracts set aside otherwise applicable public policies while commercial agreements do not. Two implications of this difference are noted here. First, when a contract departs from otherwise applicable public policies that are designed to protect parties, the law can reasonably require greater assurance that the parties understand and appreciate what they are doing, than when the contract does not. Second, vindication of the public policies may require rules that limit the enforcement of private agreements that significantly infringe upon them. These policy concerns thus suggest a rationale for special rules for family contracts

that is additional to the rationale based upon the cognitive limitations that are likely to impinge upon persons entering into family contracts. . . .[¶] Indeed, the cases in which the parties are most likely to make errors of cognition overlap considerably with those in which significant public policies are most likely implicated: long marriages and marriages producing children. . . .

The Institute thus offers two complementary explanations for treating premarital agreements differently than ordinary commercial contracts: a cognitive rationale, and a policy rationale. The cognitive rationale, as the Institute later explains, arises from the fact that "[c]ontract law is. . .based not only upon a philosophical commitment to individual autonomy, but also upon a factual assumption about the abilities of contracting parties." In this respect, the Institute relies on modern studies from behavioral economics which suggest that the cognitive capacities necessary for the kind of assessment of self-interest assumed by contract doctrine are more likely to be deficient in the premarital agreement context than in the commercial context, and particularly so in the case of long marriages and marriages with after-born children. The policy rationale notes that the obligations arising from family relationships are not based upon contract in the first place, and thus not necessarily waivable by contract either. This point seems obvious with respect to the obligations of parents to their children, but applies as well, the Institute argues, to duties arising between spouses in a long-term relationship. While obligations imposed by law cannot always be waived by contract, the law may allow their partial waiver, or their waiver under specified conditions — which is the approach taken by the *ALI Principles*. A more complete explanation for the Institute's recommendation for a limited time-of-enforcement fairness review can be found in Comments *b* and *c* of § 7.05 of the *ALI Principles*. For further development of the argument that obligations between spouses in a long-term relationship are not based upon contract ideas, see Ellman, *Contract Thinking Was Marvin's Fatal Flaw*, 76 NOTRE DAME L. REV. 1365 (2001), which is excerpted at pages 898-900 of Chapter 9.

Some passages toward the beginning of Section C of *Bonds* not only adopt the same view as the *Principles* with respect to differences between commercial agreements and premarital agreements, but also agree that these differences call for a different legal treatment of these two kinds of contract. But *Bonds*, believing itself constrained by governing statutes based upon the UPAA, does not endorse as demanding a review of premarital agreements as recommended by the ALI. Closer to the approach of *Gant* and the ALI is *McKee-Johnson v. Johnson,* 444 N.W.2d 259 (Minn. 1989) (enforcement may be denied to a premarital agreement fair at its inception "if the premises upon which [the contract was] originally based have so drastically changed that enforcement would not comport with the [original] reasonable expectations of the parties . . . to such an extent that . . . enforcement would be unconscionable.").

Compare these sources with the final paragraph of the excerpt from *Simeone,* reprinted above: "the possibilities of illness, birth of children, reliance upon a spouse, numerous other events that can occur in the course of a marriage cannot be regarded as unforeseeable. If parties choose not to address such matters in their prenuptial agreements, they must be regarded as having contracted to bear the risk of events that alter the value of their bargains." Is the issue whether parties anticipate having children, or anticipate all the changes in their life that the presence of children may bring? *See* Eisenberg, *The Limits of Cognition and the Limits of Contract*, 47 STAN. L. REV. 211, 254–58 (1995) ("It is almost impossible to predict the impact that a prenuptial agreement will have if it does come into play. Personal income may increase or decrease; job skills may be acquired or lost; family obligations may vary in regard to both the other spouse and children; personal expectations may change. Change in the course of marriage is foreseeable, but the specifics of the change are not. The limits of cognition therefore provide a strong justification for a second-look approach to prenuptial agreements.")

9. *"Fiduciary Relationships" and the Difference Between Marital and Premarital Agreements.* *Bonds* says that while *spouses* are in a fiduciary or "confidential" relationship with one another, those just planning their marriage to one another are not. A "fiduciary relationship" most typically arises when one person has power over another's property, and is in consequence bound to heightened duties when dealing with it. Such is clearly not the case at the time prospective spouses enter into an agreement. But fiduciary responsibilities are also imposed on someone in a "position of trust"— a "confidential relationship" — such that the other party has come to rely upon the fiduciary. For example, a lawyer might be in a fiduciary relation with his or her client, and therefore bound to heightened obligations in other dealings with him or her. As *Bonds* suggests, one common consequence of a fiduciary relationship is that the fiduciary will have the burden of justifying any contract between the parties which confers any benefit or advantage upon the fiduciary, and that burden might include a showing that no "undue influence" was applied. If prospective spouses are in a confidential relationship with one another, then whichever spouse seeks to enforce a premarital agreement that advantages that spouse, would have this burden. *Bonds* reads the UPAA as rejecting this position, and therefore declines to put such a burden on the agreement's proponent, although its reasoning suggests that it would impose such a burden on the proponent of a *marital* agreement, executed after the spouses had married. (Such agreements are not governed by the UPAA.)

By contrast, note that *Button* itself involves both a premarital agreement, and a later marital agreement which replaced it, and neither the Wisconsin Supreme Court, nor the Wisconsin statute it applies, suggest that the two kinds of agreement should be tested against different standards. The implication is that fiduciary obligations arise in premarital as well as marital agreements. Other courts have been explicit on this point. *E.g.*, the court in *Friedlander v. Friedlander,* 494 P.2d 208 (Wash. 1972), said: "[A]n engagement to marry creates a confidential relationship. Parties to a pre-nuptial agreement do not deal with each other at arm's length. Their relationship is one of mutual confidence and trust which calls for the exercise of good faith, candor and sincerity in all matters bearing upon the proposed agreement." The *ALI Principles* clearly adopt the *Friedlander* position with respect to the underlying factual assumption about the conduct and attitudes that persons planning their marriage are likely to have toward one another. Perhaps the *Bonds* court would have as well, had it not considered itself constrained from doing so by provisions of the UPAA.

More generally, the authorities are divided on whether marital and premarital agreements should be governed by the same rules. In addition to Wisconsin Statutes § 767.255(3), other statutes applying the same rules to both premarital and marital agreements include: N.Y. DOM. REL. LAW § 236(B)(1) ("An agreement by the parties, made before or during the marriage, shall be valid and enforceable in a matrimonial action if such agreement is in writing, subscribed by the parties, and acknowledged"); N.C. G.S. § 52-10(a) ("Contracts between husband and wife not inconsistent with public policy are valid, and any persons about to be married and married persons may release rights which they might respectively acquire or may have acquired"). One recent case takes the same position. *Reese v. Reese*, 984 P.2d 987 (Utah 1999) ("spouses or prospective spouses may make binding contracts with each other and arrange their affairs as they see fit, insofar as the negotiations are conducted in good faith and do not unreasonably constrain the court's equitable and statutory duties"). On the other hand, a 1994 Minnesota enactment requires marital agreements to meet certain requirements not imposed on premarital agreements: Each party must be represented by separate legal counsel, MINN. STAT. ANN. § 519.11(1a)(2)(c); each spouse must have property worth more than $1,200,000, § 519.11(1a)(2)(d); and neither spouse can commence an action for legal separation or divorce within two years of its execution, § 519.11(1a)(2)(e). Louisiana, in an apparently unique provision, requires marital agreements, but not premarital agreements, to be judicially approved, the judge being required to find that the agreement serves both parties' "best interests" and that both understood "the governing rules and principles." LA. ARTICLE 2329.

One modern case concludes that marital and premarital agreements should be treated differently. *Pacelli v. Pacelli*, 725 A.2d 56 (N.J. App. Div. 1999) (inappropriate to treat a "mid-marriage" agreement similarly to a premarital agreement because "the dynamics and pressures" are different). The *ALI Principles* embrace the result in *Pacelli*, which declined to enforce the marital agreement before it, but not its doctrinal position. The *Principles* adopt the same legal principles for both marital and premarital agreements, but conclude they are likely to apply differently in the two kinds of cases. The *Principles* suggest that the unconscionability doctrine is more likely to have application in the context of marital agreements, while if premarital agreements are problematic it is more likely to be because of circumstances at the time of enforcement that the parties could not anticipate at the time of execution. *See ALI Principles*, § 7.01, Comment *e*. For a thoughtful piece that discusses some of the difficulties with contracts between persons already married, see Michael Trebilcock & Steven Elliott, *The Scope and Limits of Legal Paternalism: Altruism and Coercion in Family Financial Arrangements*, in THE THEORY OF CONTRACT LAW (Peter Benson ed., Cambridge University Press, 2001).

10. *Amendment by Conduct.* While the law is generally clear that a writing is required to establish a premarital agreement, courts have occasionally held that the parties' conduct during their marriage negated an earlier written agreement. *E.g.*, in *Baxter v. Baxter*, 911 P.2d 343 (Ore. App. 1996), the parties had kept their finances separate during the first half of their 13-year marriage, but during the second half the wife left her own employment and worked without pay as manager of the husband's golf course, and applied some of her separate assets to the business's debts. The court found that this conduct "demonstrated mutual intent to rescind" their agreement to retain separate ownership of their assets. See the compilation of such cases in Annotation, *Antenuptial Contracts: Parties' Behavior During Marriage as Abandonment, Estoppel, or Waiver Regarding Contractual Rights*, 56 A.L.R.4th 999 (1987). The UPAA has been criticized for appearing to bar such modifications of agreements by later conduct. Barbara Atwood, *Ten Years Later: Lingering Concerns about the Uniform Premarital Agreement Act*, 19 J. LEGIS. 127, 147 (1993). It is important that *Baxter* and like cases involve more than a claim of an oral agreement to modify the earlier writing: They claim as well (or instead) that the parties have in fact conducted their lives differently than they had contemplated at the time of the agreement. One can perhaps understand these cases as an application of the rule that partial performance takes a contract out of the Statute of Frauds (the contract being one to modify to the original agreement), or instead as an instance of an equitable doctrine (most plausibly, estoppel) serving its traditional purpose of providing relief from an injustice that would otherwise result from the application of technical legal rules. The latter approach is of course most easily adopted in jurisdictions that permit their courts broad equitable authority to decline to enforce premarital agreements. *E.g.*, *Krejci v. Krejci*, 667 N.W.2d 780 (Wisc.App. 2003) (concluding it would be inequitable to enforce an agreement that excluded the appreciated value of resort hotel from marital property division where during their 18-year marriage the parties combined their resources, including inheritances, savings, and incomes, operated the resort as a partnership, and generally ignored the agreement, which no longer comported with their expectation). One must distinguish these cases, which conclude the parties mutually agreed to amend or rescind their agreement, from claims that one party's marital misconduct should allow the other to avoid it. This latter claim is not ordinarily allowed. *E.g.*, *Perkinson v. Perkinson*, 802 S.W.2d 600 (Tenn. 1990) (wealthy widow had signed agreement providing husband with $150,000 in full satisfaction of any claim he might have on her separate property; provision cannot be avoided by wife's allegation, in divorce action, of cruel and inhumane treatment).

11. *General Sources.* For surveys of the extent to which the law polices premarital agreements for procedural or substantive fairness, see Annot., *Enforceability of Premarital Agreements Governing Support or Property Rights Upon Divorce or Separation as Affected by Fairness or Adequacy of Those Terms — Modern Status*, 53 A.L.R.4th 161 (1987), and Annot., *Enforceability of Premarital Agreements Governing Support or Property Rights Upon Divorce or Separation as Affected by Circumstances Surrounding Execution — Modern Status*, 53 A.L.R.4th 85 (1987).

PROBLEMS

Problem 8-1. Carol and Doug have been married for six years, and have two children, ages four and two. Doug is a physician earning a substantial income. Carol is an R.N.. She works occasionally in order to maintain her job skills and her license, but has been the children's primary caretaker since the first child's birth. Doug is a doting father, and does all he can to make sure he has time with the children on weekday evenings, and on weekends when he is not out on call. Carol and Doug live in Sweet Lake, a small city near the Rocky Mountains, where Doug completed his medical training. He is affiliated with the University's medical school.

Carol has never liked Sweet Lake, and has long wanted to return to New York, where she grew up and where her family still lives. Her discontent has affected her marriage. Assured of support from her family, optimistic about her job prospects in New York when she is ready to return to work, and interested in renewing her relationship with an old boyfriend there, she tells Doug she intends to divorce him and return there with the children. Doug is devastated, not only about the demise of his marriage, but also about the loss of daily contact with his young children if Carol returns to New York. He consults a lawyer who advises him that, under applicable law, Carol, as the children's primary caretaker, is nearly certain to be awarded primary custody, and is likely to prevail if he were to oppose her relocation to New York with the children. He begs Carol to reconsider.

Carol agrees to remain in Sweet Lake with Doug for at least two more years, if Doug will agree that, if they later divorce, she will receive sixty percent of their marital property, and spousal support for a nonmodifiable term of at least 10 years, calculated on the assumption that she is unavailable for work, and to continue even if she remarries. Desperate to maintain daily contact with his children, and hopeful that in two years' time he can persuade Carol to remain in the marriage, Doug agrees. After two years, Carol files for divorce and seeks primary custody of the children, and their relocation, with her, to New York. Due to a current shortage of R.N.s, well-paying jobs with flexible hours are in fact available to Carol in N.Y., and under applicable law she would therefore receive a relatively small support award for a short term, which would end if she remarried. Carol, however, seeks enforcement of the parties' agreement: a) a guaranteed 10-year term of compensatory payments, even if she remarries, and calculated on the basis that she has no income, even if she chooses to work; and b) 75 percent of the parties' marital property, rather than the half she would receive under otherwise applicable law.

Should their agreement be enforced? Would it be enforced in California? In a jurisdiction following the *ALI Principles*? Does it matter that it is a marital rather than premarital agreement? How?

Problem 8-2. Jean and Julius meet at a class reunion when they are both 60. Both have grown children from an earlier marriage that ended with the death of their respective spouses. Jean and Julius begin dating, and eventually acquire a common primary residence. After living together four years, they decide to marry so that Jean will be covered under Julius' health insurance policy. Julius has been employed for 30 years by the same bank, where he is now a regional manager. He has his secretary type up a premarital agreement for them to sign, based upon a form provided him by a friend who is an attorney. The agreement specifies that each party gives up any claims he or she might have to marital property, in the event of their divorce, as well as any claims to the surviving spouse's share to which they would otherwise be entitled under their state's probate law, in the event of the other's death. The agreement specifies that the parties disclosed their assets to one another in attached schedules, which in fact they do. The parties sign the agreement before a notary, and marry the next day. Six months later, they both consult an attorney Jean knows, to prepare their wills. Jean's will leaves all of her property to her son, and Julius's will leaves all of his property to his two children. Julius assets' total about $750,000; Jean's, about $250,000.

The parties divorce after three years of marriage. Under otherwise applicable law, property acquired during the four years they lived together, as well as that acquired during their marriage, is marital property that is ordinarily divided equally. The effect of the agreement is to exclude these acquisitions from such a division. Julius seeks to enforce it. Should it be enforced?

Problem 8-3. After Paul and Helen decide to marry, Paul asks his attorney, Delores, to draft a premarital agreement. Delores arranges for Helen to meet separately with another attorney, Frank, whose office was down the hall from hers. Delores supplies Frank and Helen with a copy of the proposed agreement just as Frank and Helen meet for the first time. But the copy lacks the attachments referred to in the agreement, detailing Paul's financial situation. Helen's meeting with Frank was interrupted after a half-hour by Paul, who arrived unannounced to inquire "what was taking so long." The wedding was then canceled, but the parties reconciled a few weeks later and married hurriedly so that they could take the honeymoon arranged in connection with their original wedding plans. The agreement was signed the day before the wedding at Delores's office, with no further meetings between Helen and Frank. The attachments were included in the signed copies. The parties divorce ten years later. The agreement denies Helen any share in property acquired by Paul during the marriage and limits her alimony claims to a two-year rehabilitative award. It allows her a lump sum of $50,000 in lieu of any further alimony or property claim. The couple has no children. Paul has substantial assets that would be marital property but for the agreement, and a healthy annual income. Helen is an R.N. and can obtain reasonable employment. She has few assets. Should this agreement be enforced?

Problem 8-4. Eugene and Delores enter into an agreement before they marry under which all their property will remain separate and neither will have a claim for spousal support. At the time they enter this agreement, they are both employed full time, have comparable incomes, and have no children. They have lived together for four years, and feel they know each other well. Both of them enjoy their work as well as their time together. They sign the agreement after jointly consulting an attorney they both know. He suggested that they may wish to have separate attorneys, but they assure him it is unnecessary because the agreement is their mutual idea. They both believe this kind of arrangement is fair and "eliminates problems." They each have a very good idea of the other's income and assets, given their four years of living together. They feel they are equals, and wish a marital arrangement that reflects that. They do not plan to have children, but when questioned by their attorney they say that if they do, they will share child care duties equally and make equal adjustments in their work schedules.

They file for divorce 15 years later. They now have two children, seven and 11. Delores has been the children's primary caretaker since their birth, and her income potential, at the time of divorce, is considerably less than Eugene's. When their first child was born they planned alternate leaves from work, but Delores was much more comfortable with taking a leave than was Eugene. Eugene would have hired a live-in nanny to allow both of them to keep working, but Delores was uneasy with that arrangement, preferring less hired child care and more care by her. This is therefore the arrangement they came to. Both agree that Delores will continue to be the primary residential parent after their divorce. Under the law applicable but for their agreement, she would have a substantial claim for spousal support, and an equal share in the property accumulated with Eugene's much greater earnings. Under the agreement she has neither. Eugene seeks to enforce the agreement, while Delores seeks the support and property awards allowed under otherwise applicable law.

Should the agreement be enforced? Would it be enforced under the UPAA, the *ALI Principles*, *Bonds*, and *Button*?

[3] LIMITATIONS ON SUBJECTS GOVERNED BY PREMARITAL AGREEMENTS

DIOSDADO V. DIOSDADO

118 Cal. Rptr. 2d 494 (App. 2002)

EPSTEIN, ACTING P. J. In this case we conclude that a contract entered into between a husband and wife, providing for payment of liquidated damages in the event one of them is sexually unfaithful to the other, is unenforceable. [¶] For the purpose of reviewing this grant of judgment on the pleadings, we take as true the allegations of the complaint and the facts presented to the trial court in an offer of proof.

Donna and Manuel Diosdado were married in November 1988. In 1993, Manuel had an affair with another woman. When Donna learned of this, the parties separated but did not divorce. Instead, they entered into a written "Marital Settlement Agreement" (hereafter the agreement) intended to "preserve, protect and assure the longevity and integrity of an amicable and beneficial marital relationship between them."

Section 1 of the agreement provides that if either party expresses concern that the goals of the marriage are not being met, they agree to seek counseling and make a good faith effort to resolve their problems to preserve the relationship.

Section 2 is labeled "Obligation of Fidelity," and provides: "It is further acknowledged that the parties' marriage is intended to be an exclusive relationship between Husband and Wife that is premised upon the values of emotional and sexual fidelity, and mutual trust. The parties hereto are subject to a legal obligation of emotional and sexual fidelity to the other. It shall be considered a breach of such obligation of fidelity to volitionally engage in any act of kissing on the mouth or touching in any sexual manner of any person outside of said marital relationship, as determined by a trier of fact. The parties acknowledge their mutual understanding that any such breach of fidelity by one party hereto may cause serious emotional, physical and financial injury to the other."

Section 3 is labeled "Liquidated Damages." It provides:

In the event it is shown by a preponderance of the evidence in a court of competent jurisdiction that either party has engaged in any breach of the obligation of sexual fidelity as defined hereinabove . . . and, additionally, that election is made by one or both parties to commence an action to terminate the marriage by divorce because of said breach, the following terms and conditions shall become effective:

(a) The party shown to have committed the breach shall vacate the family residence immediately upon the completion of a showing of breach as defined above;

(b) The party shown to have committed the breach will be solely responsible for all attorney fees and court costs incurred as a result of or in connection with the litigation of any issue surrounding or relating to said breach;

(c) The party shown to have committed the breach will pay the other party (hereinafter, the 'recipient') liquidated damages for said breach in the sum of $ 50,000, said sum to be paid over and above, and irrespective of, any property settlement and/or support obligation imposed by law as a result of said divorce proceeding. Said damages shall be due and payable on a date that is no later than six (6) months following entry of judgment of dissolution of marriage by a court of competent jurisdiction. Said damages shall become the sole and separate property of the recipient, except that, should said recipient remarry at any time following such payment, said damages shall be fully and completely refunded to the party shown to have committed the breach. Said refund shall be due and payable on a date no later than six (6) months following the date of the recipient's remarriage.

(d) Both parties shall cooperate in the negotiation and execution of a reasonable property settlement and support agreement for the resolution of said divorce proceeding so as to minimize the emotional and financial expense of said litigation.

The agreement was drafted by Manuel's attorney, and both Donna and Manuel signed it voluntarily in December 1993. They resumed living together. [¶] In 1998, Manuel again had an affair with another woman. When Donna learned of it, she confronted Manuel, who denied it. Donna obtained independent verification from a witness who saw Manuel kissing this other woman. The parties separated in August 1998, and thereafter divorced. [¶] Donna then brought this action for breach of contract in February 2000, seeking to enforce the liquidated damages clause of the agreement. On the first day of trial, the trial court, on its own motion, granted a judgment on the pleadings in favor of Manuel. Donna appeals from the judgment.

The only question before this court is whether the agreement is enforceable. The trial court found that it was not because it was contrary to the public policy underlying California's no-fault divorce laws. That reasoning is sound.

In 1969, California enacted Civil Code section 4506 (now Fam. Code, § 2310), providing for dissolution of marriage based on irreconcilable differences which have caused the irremediable breakdown of the marriage. This change was explained in *Marriage of Walton* (1972) 28 Cal. App. 3d 108, 119 [104 Cal. Rptr. 472]: "After thorough study, the Legislature, for reasons of social policy deemed compelling, has seen fit to change the grounds for termination of marriage from a fault basis to a marriage breakdown basis."

With certain exceptions (such as child custody matters or restraining orders), "evidence of specific acts of misconduct is improper and inadmissible" in a pleading or proceeding for dissolution of marriage. (Fam. Code, § 2335.) Fault is simply not a relevant consideration in the legal process by which a marriage is dissolved. Recovery in no-fault dissolution proceedings "is basically limited to half the community property and appropriate support and attorney fee orders — no hefty premiums for emotional angst." (*Askew v. Askew*, 28 Cal. Rptr. 2d 284 (1994).)

Contrary to the public policy underlying California's no-fault divorce laws, the agreement between Donna and Manuel attempts to impose just such a premium for the "emotional angst" caused by Manuel's breach of his promise of sexual fidelity. . . .[¶] The family law court may not look to fault in dissolving the marriage, dividing property, or ordering support. Yet this agreement attempts to penalize the party who is at fault for having breached the obligation of sexual fidelity, and whose breach provided the basis for terminating the marriage. This penalty is in direct contravention of the public policy underlying no-fault divorce.

To be enforceable, a contract must have a "lawful object." (Civ. Code, § 1550, subd. 3.) A contract is unlawful if it is contrary to an express provision of law, contrary to the policy of express law, or otherwise contrary to good morals. (Civ. Code, § 1667.) Here, where the agreement attempts to impose a penalty on one of the parties as a result of that party's "fault" during the marriage, it is contrary to the public policy underlying the no-fault provisions for dissolution of marriage. For that reason, the agreement is unenforceable.

Donna claims a different result is required, by [*Marriage of Bonds.*] [¶] In *Bonds*, the court addressed the enforceability of a premarital agreement. . . .[¶] What is informative in *Bonds* is the distinction the court drew between the freedom of contract found in ordinary commercial contracts and the existence of limitations in marital agreements. The court recognized that "marriage itself is a highly regulated institution of undisputed social value, and there are many limitations on the ability of persons to contract with respect to it, or to vary its statutory terms, that have nothing to do with maximizing the satisfaction of the parties or carrying out their intent. . . . These limitations demonstrate further that freedom of contract with respect to marital arrangements is tempered with statutory requirements and case law expressing social policy with respect to marriage." *Bonds* does not support Donna's position.

Judgment on the pleadings was properly granted in this case. [¶] The judgment is affirmed.

HASTINGS, J., and CURRY, J., concurred.

NOTES AND QUESTIONS

1. *Can a Premarital Agreement Establish Fault Standards for Alimony and Property?* *Diosdado* was followed in *Marriage of Dargan*, 13 Cal. Rptr. 3d 522 (App. 2004), which held unenforceable the husband's agreement to grant the wife his interest in specified items of community property if he used drugs. The position taken in *Diosdado* is also consistent with *Atkinson v. Evans*, 787 A.2d 1033 (Pa. Super. 2001), in which the parties separated after 21 years of marriage when the husband discovered the wife's affair with Evans. They then reconciled, pursuant to an agreement under which the wife promised to terminate her relationship with Evans and to not engage "in any other adulterous relationship." When her affair with Evans apparently later resumed, the husband brought this action against him for interference with a contractual relationship — claiming Evans had induced the wife to break her agreement. The court sustained a general demurrer, viewing the claim as an attempted end-run around the state's abolition of the tort of alienation of affections. These cases are also consistent with § 7.08 of the *ALI Principles*, which states:

A term in an agreement is not enforceable if

(1) it limits or enlarges the grounds for divorce otherwise available under state law;

(2) it would require or forbid a court to evaluate marital conduct in allocating marital property or awarding compensatory payments, except as the term incorporates principles of state law that so provide; or

(3) by its terms, it penalizes a party for initiating the legal action leading to a decree of divorce or legal separation.

The *Principles* go on to explain:

. . .While there have been significant changes during the second half of the 20th century in the state law governing the grounds for divorce, there has been little change in the principle that this law reflects a fundamental policy choice not subject to alteration by the parties. The rationale for this principle may be somewhat different under modern no-fault statutes than it was under the older fault-oriented divorce laws. Classic fault-based divorce laws did not accept mutual consent as a ground for divorce, and it is nearly tautological to observe that it would be inconsistent with this policy to permit parties to avoid it by agreement. Modern no-fault divorce laws reflect, among other things, a policy of limiting the role of legal institutions in monitoring and policing the details of intimate relationships, and it would defeat that purpose if parties were permitted, by their own agreement, to require courts to decide if either of them was at fault for their relationship's decline.

In principle, a state could adopt laws that allowed parties to choose, at the time of their marriage, the rules that would govern its potential dissolution. This section neither endorses nor opposes this possibility. Parties may agree to any set of rules permitted by state law. Historically, however, state law has offered no such choice, and even recent legislative proposals contemplate a choice between only two alternatives. This section reflects the view that such state-law rules articulate public-policy choices binding upon individual parties. In the United States, the state has always been the exclusive source of the legal rules by which the status of marriage is created and dissolved.

By contrast, consider the case of *Penhallow v. Penhallow*, 649 A.2d 1016 (R.I. 1994), in which the parties' agreement made the financial consequence of divorce turn upon which party first filed: Susan would keep half John's property if he divorced her, but not if she divorced him. He was 78, and she 50, at the time of their marriage. About four years after their marriage, the parties had a conflict, the details of which were not resolved by the court, but which led to the wife's having the husband served with a "protection from abuse" order requiring him to leave the marital home. The following month he petitioned for divorce. He claimed that their dispute arose from the wife's refusal to return his bankbooks, which she had taken without his consent; the wife claimed it arose from the husband's spending "excessive" amounts of time with a younger woman who was a tenant on his farm. The court held the agreement enforceable under Rhode Island's recently adopted version of the UPAA, but remanded to the lower court for a determination of whether the wife's having filed for the order of protection was in effect an initiation of a divorce under the agreement. On remand, the trial court held it was, and this interpretation was affirmed on appeal, *Penhallow v. Penhallow*, 725 A.2d 896 (1998), thus denying the wife any share of the property. The court's willingness to enforce the agreement under these facts seems surprising, but the court apparently felt compelled to reach this result under the governing statute. The Rhode Island legislature had altered the UPAA in several respects before adopting it, and all of its changes had the effect of making it more difficult to deny enforcement of a premarital agreement.

The court's interpretation of the agreement is more difficult to explain. The wife argued that since she was not the one to file the divorce complaint, she did not "initiate" the divorce within the meaning of the agreement, but the court gave a different meaning to the term "initiate," apparently treating it as a synonym for "precipitate." The issue, then, as the court read the agreement, was which spouse's conduct was the cause of the divorce. Or at least that would appear to be the court's construction, although it never addressed this point explicitly. It relied instead on the trial court's resolution of the question on remand, which in turn emphasized the wife's poor impression as witness. The case may perhaps be best offered as a fine example of why most states abolished fault divorce law in the first place. *Penhallow* is explicitly rejected by the *ALI Principles*, which observe in Comment *c* of § 7.08: "A provision that by its terms disfavors a party because that party initiates the divorce action. . .effectively imposes a penalty upon a party's invocation of the state's rules governing the availability of divorce. The imposition of such a burden restricts the legally available grounds for divorce and violates the policy underlying § 7.08(1). It is therefore barred by [§ 7.08(3)]."

See also *Akileh v. Elchahal*, 666 So. 2d 246 (Fla. App. 1996), in which the parties' *sadaq*, traditional in Islamic culture, provided a "postponed dowry" to the wife from the husband of $50,000, in case of divorce. The question was whether the *sadaq* provided that the wife forfeited the payment if she sought the divorce (as the husband believed) or only if she had been sexually unfaithful (as the wife believed). Both parties thus believed that the agreement incorporated some form of fault standard for determining whether the wife would collect the *sadaq*; they simply differed on what that standard was. Florida is a no-fault state that does not normally consider marital misconduct in the allocation of property or the awarding of alimony, *Heilman v. Heilman*, 610 So. 2d 60 (Fla. App. 1992), but it enforced the *sadaq* (sustaining the wife's interpretation of it). While Rhode Island law allows the court to consider the parties' conduct, its state supreme court has not encouraged placing much weight on fault considerations, see *Rochefort v. Rochefort*, 494 A.2d 92 (R.I. 1985) and *Fisk v. Fisk*, 477 A.2d 956 (R.I. 1984). Thus, both Florida and Rhode Island seem to accept agreements that are likely to alter the way in which fault considerations would otherwise affect the outcome under their state law.

At least one author has urged judicial recognition of this kind of agreement. *See* Haas, *The Rationality and Enforceability of Contractual Restrictions on Divorce*, 66 N. Car. L. Rev. 879 (1988). *See also* Stake, *Mandatory Planning for Divorce*, 45 Vand. L. Rev. 397, 431–32 (1992), who would require parties to enter premarital agreement and recognizing that some might choose to include fault terms, and Scott, *Rational Decisionmaking About Marriage and Divorce*, 76 Va. L. Rev. 9 (1990), who offers a precommitment approach she believes will aid marital stability. Stake develops his views further in Rasmussen and Stake, *Lifting the Veil of Ignorance: Personalizing the Marriage Contract*, 73 Indiana L.J. 453 (1998).

Would you urge an agreement of the form that the *Akileh* wife thought she had? How would that agreement apply to the case in which both spouses had committed adultery? In short, are fault terms imposed by contract any less problematic than those imposed by law? Another court enforced the parties' agreement that neither could file an action for divorce on any grounds other than 18 months' continuous separation. *Masser v. Masser*, 652 A.2d 219 (N.J. App. Div., 1994). While New Jersey is a no-fault state, its statute also allows parties to seek divorce on fault grounds, but in this case the wife's petition for divorce on grounds of extreme cruelty was dismissed as violative of the agreement.

2. *Terms Affecting Children*. The traditional rule is that a contract between prospective spouses cannot bind a court in deciding child support or child custody matters, Comment, *Enforceability of Antenuptial Agreements Concerning the Education of Children*, 43 Calif. L. Rev. 132 (1955). Section 3(b) of the UPAA seems to continue this restriction with respect to child support. Arguably, however, the UPAA restriction operates in one direction only, and would not bar enforcement of a provision enlarging support, as, *e.g.*, by obliging a parent to support a child in college where the governing state law would not otherwise impose that duty. As to custody, the UPAA is silent.

Custody is omitted from § 3's list of specific items that the agreement may address, but neither is it specifically barred by any other provision analogous to § 3(b)'s bar of any provision adversely affecting the right to child support. The question for a court in a UPAA state would therefore be whether a custody provision violated "public policy" under § 3(a)(8). Long tradition in the domestic relations area would seem to ensure, however, that courts would not consider themselves bound by custody provisions they believed injurious to the child's interest. The law of separation agreements in every state is explicit on that point, and there is no reason why premarital agreements would be treated differently. *See Combs v. Combs*, 865 P.2d 50 (Wyo. 1993) (provision in agreement executed one month after parties' marriage, providing that "any progeny resulting from this union, should this contract be terminated, shall remain in the custody of the parent of that progeny's sex," is not enforceable because state law forbids basing custody determinations solely on the gender of the parent).

Arbitration of support or custody disputes is arguably a different matter, and comes up more often in the context of separation agreements than with premarital agreements. *See* pp. 830-832 *infra*. On one hand, the recent trend, exemplified by *Kelm v. Kelm*, 623 N.E.2d 39 (Ohio 1993*)*, favors such agreements. *See* Annot., *Validity and Construction of Provisions for Arbitration of Disputes As to Alimony or Support Payments or Child Visitation or Custody Matters*, 38 A.L.R.5th 69 (1993). On the other hand, courts typically indicate some reservation of power to override the arbitrator's award where the interest of the child so requires, as *Kelm* also appears to do. Such a rule is inconsistent, however, with the usual understanding of arbitration, under which courts have no authority at all to reexamine the merits of the arbitrator's decision. Judicial review of arbitration is ordinarily limited to fundamental challenges to the arbitrator's authority, rather than to the substance of the decision — to matters such as whether the issue in question was in fact within the scope of the arbitration agreement, or whether the arbitrator's decision was based upon a bribe. This tension between recognition of the merits of arbitration, and the desire to preserve in the court some residual authority to protect the child's interest, remains largely unresolved. For recent commentary on this topic, see E. Gary Spitko, *Reclaiming the "Creatures of the State": Contracting for Child Custody Decisionmaking in the Best Interests of the Family*, 57 WASH. & LEE L.REV. 1139 (2000).

PROBLEMS

Problem 8-5. Susan Rose consults you for advice on a premarital agreement. She is an Orthodox Jew planning to marry. Her intended husband, David, is also Jewish but has not heretofore been completely faithful to traditional practices. He has agreed, however, to conduct himself according to Jewish law from now on. While satisfied of his sincerity, she seeks some assurance in a premarital agreement. Two points are especially important to her. The first is that their children be raised according to traditional Orthodox practice. She has no concern about their training during the marriage, since she will be the primary caretaker of the children, but wants to guarantee that if the marriage should end by divorce, or her death, that any children be raised in an Orthodox Jewish home. The second point concerns the authority of the Beth Din, or Jewish religious tribunal, over their marriage. In particular, she wants to be certain that if she and David did obtain a civil divorce, he would cooperate in also appearing before the Beth Din, so that she would be eligible to remarry under Jewish law as well.

What do you advise? How would you prepare an appropriate agreement?

Problem 8-6. Richard comes to consult you about a premarital agreement. He is 38-years-old, and a successful businessman. This is his second marriage. His first ended in divorce after seven years, when his wife left him for another man. He is still bitter, especially because the divorce court gave his first wife a major share of his business, allowing her and her new husband to live well as a result of his efforts. It rankles him that, as he sees it, she was allowed to profit by her adultery, even though he was faithful. He is determined to avoid a repetition of that experience.

He has heard that it is possible to agree in advance that his wife would not share in his property. While such an agreement is acceptable to him, it goes further than he would demand. If the marriage is successful, as he expects it to be, he would be happy for her to share in his financial successes. What he wants to be certain of, however, is that if his wife commits adultery, he can divorce her without paying her either alimony or a share in the property he is able to accumulate during their marriage. He is quite willing for the agreement to be reciprocal, although it is not clear to him how that would work, since she has relatively little prospect to earn significant sums herself. He suggests he might agree to pay her a liquidated sum, such as $100,000, in the event that he commits adultery.

He has mentioned the possibility of a premarital agreement to his fiancée once, in a general way. While they discussed it only briefly then, he had the feeling that she was not happy about it. He did not discuss particular terms with her. He has no children by his first marriage, and is not expecting any to result from this one.

What do you advise?

§ B. SEPARATION AGREEMENTS

The sense that courts and lawyers ought to promote settlement certainly transcends the field of divorce. One set of reasons typically given for preferring settlement focuses on the parties: settlement is said to give them more satisfaction than litigated outcomes, is more responsive to their needs, saves them time and money, and spares them from unwanted risk and emotional stress. Settlement is also said to yield outcomes that are superior because they are based upon superior knowledge of the parties' preferences, involve compromise (which is assumed to be superior), can be based upon a wider range of norms than permitted in litigation, can be more flexible and inventive in the solutions adopted, and are more likely to be complied with by the parties. Settlement is said to promote judicial efficiency, and even to change the parties for the better. Whether settlement in fact achieves all or any of these objectives may not be as certain as one might think, nor is the available evidence entirely favorable to settlement. *See* Galanter and Cahill, *"Most Cases*

Settle": Judicial Promotion and Regulation of Settlements, 46 STAN. L. REV. 1339 (1994). But a full exploration of the settlement literature is beyond our charge. Most divorces, like most other lawsuits, are in fact resolved by a settlement agreement negotiated by the parties and their lawyers. In this section we examine that process as it operates in divorce, and consider as well alternative methods of achieving settlement — primarily, mediation.

[1] ACHIEVING AN AGREEMENT

[a] The Traditional Bargaining Process

[i] Factors Influencing Whether a Case is Settled

Divorcing spouses generally expect to settle. Parties in one study of Wisconsin divorces "spent very little time weighing the costs of litigation against settlement because most — even those who were most reluctant — viewed settlement as the better solution." Melli, Erlanger & Chambliss, *The Process of Negotiation: An Exploratory Investigation in the Context of No-Fault Divorce*, 40 RUTGERS L. REV. 1133, 1143 (1988). This expectation of settlement is shared by the lawyers as much as by the divorcing spouses themselves. Contrary to the claims one sometimes hears, lawyers usually push their clients toward settlement, not toward litigation. A study of 115 divorce cases in California and Massachusetts concluded: "Although some of our lawyers occasionally advised clients to ask for more than the client had originally contemplated or to refuse to concede on a major issue when the client was inclined to do so, most seemed to believe that it is generally better to settle than contest divorce disputes." Sarat & Felstiner, *Law and Strategy in the Divorce Lawyer's Office,* 20 LAW & SOC'Y REV. 93, 109 (1986). Studies of British and Dutch lawyers reached the same conclusion. Ingleby, *The Solicitor as Intermediary,* in R. DINGWALL & J. EEKALAAR, DIVORCE MEDIATION AND THE LEGAL PROCESS 43, 44–45 (1988); Griffiths, *What Do Dutch Lawyers Actually Do in Divorce Cases?,* 20 LAW & SOC'Y REV. 135, 154 (1986).

Sarat and Felstiner describe in detail the lawyer-client discussions in one "typical" case. The client-wife felt keenly that an injustice had been done by the judge who granted her husband's *ex parte* request for an order restraining her from entering the marital home, and for that reason wanted to fight. Her lawyer agreed that the order was wrong, but urged her to focus on negotiating a favorable property settlement. He believed that contesting the restraining order would be unduly costly, and would interfere with the negotiations, and thus would not be in her interest, especially as she had already agreed to allow her husband to buy out her share in the home. Much of the discussion between the wife and her lawyer involved his efforts gently to bring her around to this view, while agreeing with her that the restraining order was indeed unjust. The lawyer, focusing on the practical and the long-term, pushed negotiation on a client who was reluctant because she was focusing on gaining vindication in a symbolic matter of short-term interest. The lawyer pushed settlement, even though he liked trial work, and went into a divorce practice in part because of the trial opportunities it offered. At one point in the discussions, he invoked the advice of the client's therapist in support of his advice to settle.

Id. at 111–13. Sarat and Felstiner conclude that "it is clear that this lawyer, and most of those we observed, construct an image of the appropriate mode of disposition . . . that is at odds with the conventional view in which lawyers are alleged to induce competition and hostility, transform noncontentious clients into combatants, and promulgate a 'fight theory of justice.' " *Id.* at 113.

Why do lawyers prefer to settle divorce cases? Ingleby suggests that lawyers appreciate the fact that in divorce cases, goodwill and cooperation are necessary to perform the agreement, creating an advantage for non-adversarial bargaining over confrontational strategies. Ingleby, *supra,* at 47. He reports that a main thread in the reasoning of solicitors is the belief that the parties are more likely to observe an agreement they made themselves than a court-ordered one. Ingleby also notes that less contentious cases are less demanding on the lawyer, and that the additional burdens of litigation are not always accompanied by proportionately increased fees. Melli *et al.* note that in divorce, as in other areas, there is pressure from the court to settle, which often becomes explicit in judicial comments made at pretrial conferences. They also found many spouses anxious to settle to avoid the emotional costs associated with prolonging the divorce process, including the burdens they perceived this would impose upon their children. *Id.* at 1156. And of course, one cannot exclude the possibility that lawyers urge settlement at least in part because in most cases they see it as furthering their client's interests, as did the lawyer described above in the Sarat and Felstiner study.

It may be that matrimonial lawyers are more likely to encourage settlement than lawyers in some other fields. Gilson and Mnookin developed a game theory model of litigation that takes account of the fact that it is carried out by lawyer-agents on behalf of their clients, and distinguishes between the client, typically a one-time player in the litigation game, and the lawyer, a repeat player who has the opportunity to establish a reputation for either a cooperative or adversarial style. They show that the ordinary game theory model suggests that disputants in many legal conflicts find themselves in a classic "prisoner's dilemma" in which they have strong incentives to be contentious, but that the introduction of lawyer-agents makes it possible for disputants to overcome this dilemma by "selecting cooperative lawyers whose reputations credibly commit each party to a cooperative strategy." They hypothesize that matrimonial practice, as compared to commercial litigation, might have two structural characteristics that would make such a reputational market for cooperativeness more possible. First, divorce practice may be a non-zero sum game in which gains from cooperation may be more easily achieved. If both spouses care about their children, then arrangements that benefit the children produce gains to both. Because of differences in the parties' preferences, and in the relative values they attach to different assets or activities, value can be created through trades — an opportunity that cannot arise in a commercial dispute in which dollars are the only thing at issue. Second, because family law practice tends to be both localized and specialized, it is more possible than in some other fields for lawyers to develop and sustain reputations for cooperativeness. They also observe that while "the strong emotions attending divorce may pose a formidable barrier to collaborative rational problem solving," that barrier can be overcome by negotiation through lawyer-agents committed to cooperative strategies. Interviews conducted by the authors with California family law specialists seemed to confirm their analysis by suggesting that many lawyers did develop a reputation as cooperative problem solvers, that clients often sought attorneys with such reputations, and that such attorneys often turned away clients who sought a more adversarial approach. Gilson and Mnookin, *Disputing Through Agents: Cooperation and Conflict Between Lawyers in Litigation*, 94 COLUM. L. REV. 509 (1994).

Of course, lawyers cannot decide whether a case is settled, or alone decide upon a bargaining strategy. Clients matter too. For an examination of how lawyers and clients manage their relationship in divorce cases, see Felstiner & Sarat, *Enactments of Power: Negotiating Reality and Responsibility in Lawyer-Client Interactions*, 77 CORNELL L. REV. 1447 (1992). One study using Mnookin and Maccoby's data set of California divorces involving minor children found three factors that reduced the likelihood a divorce would require adjudication: when the wife had more education, the time between separation and divorce was longer, or the parties owned a home. Settlement was less likely the higher the husband's income and when lawyers were present. Amy Farmer and Jill Tiefenthaler, *The Determinants of Pretrial Settlement*, 21 INT'L REV. L. AND ECON. 157 (2001). Note that these correlations do not of course demonstrate cause. *E.g.*, parties who have more assets may be more likely to have lawyers and also more likely to litigate, or parties who are more likely to litigate in any event may for that reason also be more likely to have an attorney.

Just what percentage of divorces settle? Of 349 cases examined by Melli *et al., supra,* only 32 (about 9 percent) went to trial because the parties themselves could not reach agreement on the substantive issues. (Some others went to trial due to third-party objections by state agencies seeking reimbursement for welfare costs, or for other unrelated reasons.) Melli's data cannot tell us precisely why these particular cases did not settle, but she concluded from her interviews that the parties' attitude toward divorce is an important factor. Wisconsin, where she conducted this research, has a pure no-fault law in which irretrievable breakdown is the only ground for divorce, so that one spouse cannot block the other's decision to end the marriage. Apparently, such unilateral breakups are disproportionately represented among the unsettled cases, and the lawyers in her sample felt that this resulted from the inclination of the party who did not want the divorce to fight about whatever there was that could be fought over.

The fact that settlement is the norm does not mean that the legal rules governing divorce are irrelevant, for they obviously influence the negotiating process. Recall from Chapter 6 that encouragement of settlement is one argument made in support of deciding custody disputes by the more predictable primary-caretaker doctrine rather than by the vague best-interests test. This argument reflects the conventional wisdom that parties are more likely to settle when the outcome of litigation is easy to predict, because there is then little point to litigating. Griffiths confirmed this prediction in the Netherlands, where the alimony and child support rules are framed in a way that makes judicial decision highly predictable. Griffiths, *supra*, at 161 n.24.

Surely lawyers who see defeat as certain are unlikely to urge their clients to litigate, and confident predictions of defeat are more likely when the decision rules are clear. Yet the American law of support, property division, and custody has historically ceded much to trial judge discretion, which makes outcomes difficult to predict. While the conventional wisdom concludes that this uncertainty reduces the probability of settlement, some argue that extreme unpredictability also creates pressure to settle, at least for risk-averse clients who then view the courtroom as a high-risk enterprise. Griffiths, *id.,* quoting Felstiner & Sarat. The same studies in which Felstiner and Sarat found that lawyers typically urge settlement also found that divorce lawyers frequently emphasize to clients that trial court decisions in divorce are arbitrary and depend more on the particular personnel involved than on any general rules of justice. Sarat & Felstiner, *supra,* and Sarat & Felstiner, *Lawyers and Legal Consciousness: Law Talk in the Divorce Lawyer's Office,* 98 YALE L.J. 1663 (1989).

For an excellent and more recent study, see LYNN MATHER, CRAIG MCEWEN, AND RICHARD MAIMAN, DIVORCE LAWYERS AT WORK : VARIETIES OF PROFESSIONALISM IN PRACTICE (2001).

[ii]   Factors Influencing the Terms of a Settlement

If the parties are more likely to settle when the legal rules are clear, it is because they have those rules in mind during the negotiations. The classic study of the effect of legal rules on negotiations is Mnookin & Kornhauser, *Bargaining in the Shadow of the Law: The Case of Divorce,* 88 YALE L.J. 950 (1979), on which portions of this note are based. They point out (among other things) that rules that would favor a party at trial also give that party leverage during negotiations. But the relevant legal doctrine consists of more than the rules establishing each party's entitlements. On one hand, while the rules of property division, child support, and alimony are doctrinally separate, in many cases they will be at least partly fungible. Financially all can be reduced to a present value, and if there are not items of property that have important noneconomic value to one or the other spouse, then the labels property, child support, and alimony are merely names for essentially one thing: money. Of course, the parties' relative preference between money now (lump sum) and money later (as in payments over time) may differ, creating the possibility for trade-offs. Moreover, legal doctrine may be important in calculating how much money a particular award is really worth. For example, alimony is less valuable to the recipient than child support because it is taxable. If it is labeled alimony, it will probably terminate when the recipient remarries or becomes employable, while child support will last until the children reach majority. In part, negotiating a separation agreement will involve manipulating these labels to obtain an overall package that appeals to both parties, and some arrangements may produce more total value for the spouses (and less for the government). But to the extent the negotiations focus on maximizing each party's financial outcome, they are in principle no different than the negotiation of commercial disputes. The lawyer's skills can help to enlarge the pot, and to advise clients on how much of it they are likely to obtain in a contested proceeding.

As observed in the preceding section of this note, however, parties to a divorce are more likely than parties to a commercial dispute to have negotiating goals other than the maximization of financial gain. The sample case from Sarat and Felstiner illustrates one way in which symbolic or emotional issues peculiar to divorce may compete with purely financial motivations. Melli provides another example. One client told her "50 lawyers could tell me to go after more money and I wouldn't have. I just didn't want to buck [my husband]. . . . I just wanted it over." Melli *et al.,* at 1156.

A variety of emotional attitudes can affect the negotiated terms substantially. Some spouses are driven to settle for less than they might otherwise have gotten because they feel guilty about ending the marriage, because they are genuinely concerned about their former spouse's welfare, because they simply want to "put this behind" them, or because they hope that amiability in the bargaining process may trigger a desired settlement. Others are driven to hard bargaining because they want to punish the other spouse for walking out on the marriage, because they want to protect the financial standing of the children, or because they believe that hard bargaining may force the other spouse to give up and return to the marriage. And of course, some have multiple emotions that push them in opposite directions.

Data that Melli gathered in a small sample of cases also suggest the importance of spousal attitudes toward the divorce. Examining cases involving minor children, she and her co-investigators looked at the amount of child support called for in the agreement, calculated as a percentage of the obligor's total income. From their interviews with clients and their lawyers, they also classified the parties' attitude as "impatient" to end the marriage, "reluctant" to end the marriage, or "accepting" of the marital termination. They found that "reluctant" obligors agreed to pay an average of 19% of their income in support, "accepting" obligors 24%, and "impatient" obligors 29%. The differences were even more striking when payments were classified according to the attitude of the obligee. Reluctant obligees received an average of 30% of the obligor's income in child support, accepting obligees 24%, and impatient obligees 19%. These data do not mean that legally relevant financial factors have no importance in the negotiation of support awards. To the contrary, Melli also found that 50 percent of the variation among cases in the amount of child support was accounted for by three clearly relevant factors: the number of children, the income of the obligor, and the couple's estimated net worth. Attitude toward divorce was an important additional factor that influenced the settlement amount when the parties negotiated, but it did not supplant these other factors.[1]

We have thus far focused exclusively on financial issues, but of course there is also often the question of child custody, which complicates the analysis considerably. The parts of the financial package are all fungible, but potential tradeoffs between money and custody are more difficult to evaluate. For many,

---

[1] The small size of Melli's sample also counsels caution in interpreting her results. A temporary support order had been issued in one-third of the cases Melli examined, and in those cases it was a very important additional factor. In four of five such cases, the parties settled on exactly the same amount as that contained in the temporary order. Of course, the temporary order itself might have been the result of stipulation — of an agreement between the parties.

obtaining primary custody will have overriding importance, so that the financial terms will be minor in comparison. Others, however, do not even want primary custody, and a few may even be indifferent to their visitation rights. A party indifferent to his custody rights may still use it as a bargaining lever; if the other parent has a strong preference for custody, the indifferent parent can threaten to contest it unless the other parent agrees to unfavorable financial terms. This kind of strategy has no ready analog in a commercial dispute in which money is the only issue, for the parties are not going to value money differently from one another, in the way that divorcing spouses may attach different values to custody.

This potential interaction between custody and the financial issues is, of course, affected by the jurisdiction's rule for deciding custody disputes. Consider that a party less willing than the other to risk litigation is at a bargaining disadvantage in settlement negotiations. This bargaining handicap is appropriately imposed upon a party who resists litigation because she is likely to lose under prevailing legal rules: that party settles for a "bad deal" in the negotiations because it is all she is entitled to under the law. But rules of divorce may lead a party to avoid litigation for other reasons that yield less defensible results. The outcome of custody disputes decided under a best-interests standard that invests the trial court with considerable discretion may be difficult to predict for even competent, experienced attorneys. In that case lawyers will advise their clients that custody litigation is chancy (as well as unpleasant or worse). Mnookin and Kornhauser point out that this advice gives the bargaining advantage to the parent more willing than the other to risk the litigation "lottery" as well as emotional stress and harm to the child. This is not necessarily the parent that a sensibly designed policy would favor. And as Solomon knew, the parent more anxious to spare his children the trauma of custody litigation is then put at a bargaining disadvantage — and may therefore agree to unfavorable financial terms in return for an agreement on custody. There are thus a variety of reasons why parties may settle on terms that appear unfair, and that is one reason why § 306 of the M.M.D.A., as the law of most states, requires some form of judicial review of separation agreements before they become incorporated in the divorce decree.

Is another solution to bar settlement agreement involving custody tradeoffs? Should a party be able to avoid an unfavorable financial settlement by showing that she agreed to it only to avoid such a custody contest? We address this question below at pages 811-815 of this chapter. We first complete this section, however, by examining a method for reaching an agreement that is an alternative to the traditional process of negotiations between lawyers: mediation.

[b] Mediation as a Means of Achieving Agreement

Within the last generation, much attention has been paid to mediation as a route to agreement. "Mediation is a process in which an impartial third party — a mediator — facilitates the resolution of a dispute by promoting voluntary agreement (or 'self-determination') by the parties to the dispute." AMERICAN ARBITRATION ASSOCIATION, SOCIETY OF PROFESSIONALS IN DISPUTE RESOLUTION, AND THE AMERICAN BAR ASSOCIATION, THE STANDARDS OF CONDUCT FOR

MEDIATORS I (1996). In contrast to an arbitrator, who decides for the parties, the mediator facilitates dispute settlement by the parties. It has been described as a "solution to overcrowded dockets and a way to rid judges of unsavory divorce cases. Moreover, . . . proponents tell divorce lawyers that mediation offers a 'better way' of resolving divorce disputes. In contrast with traditional lawyer representation, the informality of mediation, they explain, honors client autonomy and family privacy, preserves post-divorce family relationships, fosters greater compliance with final decrees, and permits idiosyncratic agreements unconstrained by the insensitive dictates of formal law." Bryan, *Reclaiming Professionalism: The Lawyer's Role in Divorce Mediation*, 28 FAM. L.Q. 177 (1994). For more on why some believe that meditation has important advantages over traditional negotiation, see Loeb, *New Forms of Resolving Disputes — ADR*, 33 FAM. L.Q. 581 (1999); Bush, *"What Do We Need a Mediator For?": Mediation's "Value-Added" for Negotiators*, 12 OHIO ST. J. ON DISP. RES. 1 (1996).

In recent years, many mediation programs have been created through court-affiliated conciliation courts, which originally sought to reunite couples (see Chapter 3). Additionally, many private mediation centers have been created and a number of mediators have established practices on their own. A 1989 survey reported "divorce mediation has been implemented in one form or another in 36 states and the District of Columbia, with more than 120 programs operating in the states." Myers et al., *Court-sponsored Mediation of Divorce, Custody, Visitation, and Support: Resolving Policy Issues*, 13 STATE CT. J. 24 (Winter 1989); *but see* King, *Burdening Access to Justice: The Cost of Divorce Mediation on the Cheap*, 73 ST. JOHN'S L. REV. 375 (1999) (arguing mandatory "party-paid. . .mediation presents jurisprudential as well as policy problems concerning fair access to justice which outweigh the benefit").

What does mediation look like?

> . . . there are tremendous variations in the ways that the mediation process takes place. . . There may be one mediator, or a pair of co-mediators, or even a group of mediators who work together as a panel. . . . The makeup of the mediation team may also neutralize potential power imbalances by providing specific gender, ethnicity, or other diverse representation. The mediators may meet alone with the disputants one at a time, or may never speak separately with any disputant. The process may be highly structured, or completely fluid. The mediators may truly leave the outcome in the parties' hands, or may take a strong role in encouraging, influencing, or even coercing settlement. The mediators may, or may not, suggest to the parties what they ought to do. The mediators may encourage, permit, or forbid attorneys to be present.

BENNETT & HERMANN, THE ART OF MEDIATION 15 (NITA 1996). Mediation of family law disputes has its own distinctive features:

> Because of the emotional issues involved and the nature of the disputes between the parties, many of the original divorce mediation practitioners felt that the mediation sessions should be broken down over a period of weeks. The parties need time to adjust to their

renegotiated relationship and to think through major life changes. Consequently, divorce mediation sessions are often limited to approximately an hour, and take place once a week until all matters are settled.

KOVACH, MEDIATION: PRINCIPLES AND PRACTICES 35 (West 2000). *See also* Coogler, STRUCTURED MEDIATION IN DIVORCE SETTLEMENT: A HANDBOOK FOR MARITAL MEDIATORS (1978).

NOTES

1. *Who Are the Mediators?* At least four basic patterns have emerged: (1) the mediator is a lawyer; (2) the mediator is a marriage counselor, child psychologist or social worker; (3) team mediation with lawyers and non-lawyers working together; (4) the mediator is a "pure" dispute resolution specialist who is neither an attorney nor a mental health or social welfare professional. Any of these kinds of mediators may also bring into the process specialists or consultants to help parties to assess particular aspects of their dispute (*e.g.* a financial planner to help parties assess the short and long-term costs of particular settlements.)

Those mediators with a legal background tend to emphasize divorce's legal consequences and the need to protect the parties' rights, while non-lawyers often emphasize divorce's trauma and the need to protect the parties' emotional interests. *Compare* Callner, *Boundaries of the Divorce Lawyer's Role*, 10 FAM. L.Q. 389 (1977) *with* Haynes, DIVORCE MEDIATION: A PRACTICAL GUIDE FOR THERAPISTS AND COUNSELORS (1981). For an explanation of the advantages and disadvantages of the various patterns, see Note, *Turf Battles and Professional Biases: An Analysis of Mediator Qualifications in Child Custody Disputes*, 11 OHIO ST. J. DISP. RES. 469 (1996). The Note concludes that "empirical studies suggest no differences in user satisfaction rates" among them. *Id.* at p. 486. The most important variable linked to party satisfaction is the mediator's experience level rather than professional background. *Id.* In fact, the Note finds little difference in satisfaction rates when comparing professional to volunteer mediators. *Id.* at p. 487.

2. *Mediation Ordered by Law*. Some statutes impose mandatory mediation, at least in certain circumstances. The following statutory provisions, are taken from the CALIFORNIA FAMILY CODE (1994):

§ 3164. Qualifications of mediator

(a) The mediator may be a member of the professional staff of a family conciliation court, probation department, or mental health services agency, or may be any other person or agency designated by the court.

(b) The mediator shall meet the minimum qualifications required of a counselor of conciliation as provided in Section 1815 [which requires a master's degree in "psychology, social work, marriage, family and child counseling" or other relevant behavioral science, and, among other things, knowledge of the court system and knowledge of "child development, child abuse, clinical issues relating to children, the effects of divorce on children, the effects of domestic violence on children, and child custody research. . . ."].

§ 3170. Setting contested issues for mediation

(a) If it appears on the face of a petition . . . to obtain or modify a temporary or permanent custody or visitation order that custody, visitation, or both are contested, the court shall set the contested issues for mediation.

. . . .

§ 3177. Confidentiality of proceedings

Mediation proceedings . . . shall be held in private and shall be confidential. . . .

. . . .

§ 3181. Separate mediation following history of domestic violence

(a) . . .[W]here there has been a history of domestic violence between the parties or where a protective order . . . is in effect, at the request of the party alleging domestic violence in a written declaration under penalty of perjury or protected by the order, the mediator . . . shall meet with the parties separately and at separate times.

. . . .

§ 3182. Exclusion of counsel from participation

(a) The mediator has authority to exclude counsel from participation in the mediation proceedings . . . if [it] is appropriate or necessary.

. . . .

§ 3183. Recommendations to court

(a) The mediator may . . . submit a recommendation to the court as to the custody of or visitation with the child.

(b) Where the parties have not reached agreement . . ., the mediator may recommend to the court that an investigation be conducted . . . or that other services be offered to assist the parties to effect a resolution of the controversy. . . .

(c) In appropriate cases, the mediator may recommend that restraining orders be issued . . . to protect the well-being of the child involved in the controversy.

Most statutes do not themselves mandate mediation but instead grant trial court judges the power to do so in appropriate situations. The Kansas statute, e.g., grants the court the power to appoint a mediator to help resolve any child custody or visitation issue. KAN. STAT. ANN. § 23-602(a) (2003 Supp.). For a collection of statutes dealing with divorce mediation, see Tondo, Coronel & Drucker, *Mediation Trends: A Survey of the States*, 39 FAM. CT. REV. 431 (2001). This survey finds: 10 states that have statutes mandating mediation in divorce cases; 24 in which mediation is "discretionary"; 5 states that mandate mediation in particular circumstances (commonly in cases involving children); and 12 states with no statutes on point. The authors caution:

"Findings to date show that mediation of family relations is not used in the precise [same] manner in any two states. . . . This finding in and of itself suggests the need for uniformity." *Id* at 433.

Where a party is ordered to mediate, what constitutes compliance with the order? Clearly, neither the court nor a statute can require an agreement. The test must instead be whether the party participated. An objective participation standard (did the party attend a mediation session?) seems the only practical test of compliance. *See* Lande, *Using Dispute System Design Methods to Promote Good-faith Participation in Court-Connected Mediation Programs* 50 UCLA L. REV. 69 (2002) (concluding good faith requirements are unworkable and proposing pre-mediation information, limited attendance requirements, and protections against misrepresentation as more effective methods to assure participation); Note, *Participation Standards in Mandatory Mediation Statutes: "You Can Lead a Horse to Water. . . .",* 11 OHIO ST. J. DISP. RES. 187 (1996).

3. ***Should Lawyers Participate in Mediation?*** One set of authors argues for a "lawyer-participant" model, their description of the pattern they say is used in Maine and other states. McEwen, Rogers & Maiman, *Bring in the Lawyers: Challenging the Dominant Approaches to Ensuring Fairness in Divorce Mediation,* 79 MINN. L. REV. 1317 (1995). Under this model, lawyers attend mediation sessions and, in Maine, "believe that their primary role in mediation is to provide a check on unfairness." *Id.* at p. 1360. On the basis of a Maine empirical study, the authors conclude lawyer participation does not reduce the number of settlements, does not create an adversarial atmosphere and does not result in the lawyers "taking over the process."

At the same time, lawyers increasingly are being advised on how to advocate effectively for their clients in mediation. For example, the National Institute for Trial Advocacy has published a manual for "Mediation Advocacy," including advice on "delineating the extent of the client's verbal participation," which includes: "the client should face the mediator when speaking . . . the client should state only facts . . . the client should never argue . . . the client should never ask difficult questions." COOLEY, MEDIATION ADVOCACY 85 -104 (NITA 1996). Advice for the attorney includes how to make opening statements, how to gain tactical advantages through private caucuses with the mediator, and how to select conflict behaviors that maximizes a client's gains. *Id* at 103 – 123. *Compare* Kovach, *New Wine Requires New Wineskins: Transforming Lawyer Ethics for Effective Representation in a Non-adversarial Approach to Problem Solving: Mediation,* 28 FORDHAM URB. L.J. 935 (2001).

A distinctive form of lawyer participation in family disputes is called "collaborative lawyering." Under this practice, clients contract with their lawyers solely to negotiate settlement of a divorce; by contract, the lawyers will not represent these clients in a later divorce, if needed. "Collaborative law arose as a response to the harms of family law litigation and the limitations of family mediation. It consists of lawyers and clients working exclusively toward settlement. The lawyers and neutral experts are disqualified if the parties should litigate." Tesler, *Collaborative Law: A New Paradigm for Divorce Lawyers,* 5 PSYCHOL. PUB. POL'Y & L. 967 (1999). *See also* Lawrence, *Collaborative Lawyering: A New Development in Conflict Resolution,* 17 OHIO ST. J. ON DISP. RESOL. 431 (2002).

4. *Confidentiality of Mediation.* Note that § 3183 of the California Family Code, quoted in Note 2, permits local courts to hear a mediator's recommendations concerning custody disposition, presumably if the parties fail to reach agreement. After unsuccessful mediation, could a party or the court subpoena the mediator at trial? While mediation contracts often assure the parties of confidentiality, it is not at all clear that such provisions would survive a court order to produce the evidence. It has been held, for example, that contracts providing for suppression of evidence are contrary to public policy. *Simrin v. Simrin*, 43 Cal. Rptr. 376 (App. 1965). One commentator has stated flatly,

> [M]ediation programs habitually assert that the confidentiality of the process will be protected, even from court intrusion. This is inaccurate and, in New Jersey and elsewhere, the mediator may be called to court and questioned as to admissions made by either party. This would be true even though the "rules" governing the mediation provide to the contrary, in the absence of some statute or court rule which would assure such confidentiality.

Cornblatt, *Matrimonial Mediation*, 23 J. FAM. L. 99, 102 (1984–85).

The ABA Standards of Practice for Lawyer Mediators in Family Disputes state:

> II. (A) At the outset of mediation, the parties should agree in writing not to require the mediator to disclose to any party any statements made in the course of mediation. The mediator shall inform the participants that the mediator will not voluntarily disclose . . . any of the information obtained through the mediation process, unless such disclosure is required by law, without the prior consent of the participants. The mediator also shall inform the parties of the limitations of confidentiality such as statutory or judicially mandated reporting.
>
> (B) If subpoenaed or otherwise noticed to testify, the mediator shall inform the participants immediately so as to afford them an opportunity to quash the process.
>
> (C) The mediator shall inform the participants of the mediator's inability to bind third parties to an agreement not to disclose information furnished during the mediation in the absence of any absolute privilege.

See also Standard V, MODEL STANDARDS OF CONDUCT FOR MEDIATORS (1996), which states, "The mediator shall not disclose any matter that a party expects to be confidential unless given permission by all parties or unless required by law or other public policy."

In 2001, the National Conference of Commissioners on Uniform State Laws promulgated a Uniform Mediation Act (UMA). The Act, which has been adopted in several states, creates a broad-based privilege for any "mediation communication," UMA §§ 4 -8, which is defined as "a statement, whether oral or in a record or verbal or nonverbal, that occurs during a mediation or is made for purposes of considering, conducting, participating in, initiating, continuing, or reconvening a mediation or retaining a mediator." *Id* § 2(2). The privilege permits parties to prevent disclosures of any mediation communication. The mediator may prevent disclosure of any mediation communication "of the mediator." *Id* § 4(b)(1) & (2). The Act provides for waiver of the privilege and delineates a series of exceptions; it also limits the reports that a mediator may make to any tribunal which must later rule on the dispute. *Id* § 7. For debate on the Act's approach, *see* Hughes, *The Uniform Mediation Act: to the Spoiled Go The Privileges*, 85 MARQ. L. REV. 9 (2001); *and* Deason, *The Quest for Uniformity in Mediation Confidentiality: Foolish Consistency or Crucial Predictability?* 85 MARQ. L. REV. 79 (2001).

The UMA emerged from what one commentator reported as a "profusion of mediation privilege statutes and rules." Kirtley, *The Mediation Privilege's Transition from Theory to Implementation: Designing a Mediation Privilege Standard to Protect Mediation Participants, The Process and the Public Interest*, 1995 J. DISP. RES. 1. This survey reports the typical statute provides that all the mediator's work product, as well as any communication made in the course of mediation is "confidential" and "not subject to disclosure in any judicial or administrative proceeding." *See* MASS. GEN. LAWS Ann., Ch. 233, § 23C (2000); FLA. STAT. ANN. § 44.102 (3) (2003); OKLA. STAT. ANN., tit. 12, § 1805 (1993). What interests favor confidentiality of mediation? Professor Kirtley observes that: "A principal purpose of the mediation privilege is to provide mediation parties protection against these downside risks of a failed mediation. Participation will diminish if perceptions of confidentiality are not matched by reality." 1995 J. DISP. RES. at pp. 9–10.

Not all commentators support a broadly-defined privilege, suggesting countervailing interests such as protection of individual rights and enforcement of the criminal law. *See* Kirtley, *supra* (citing need for consideration of exceptions dealing with "fraud, unconscionability, 'manifest injustice,' public health and safety issues, or violations of law"); Note, *Confidentiality in Mediation: The Best Protection Has Exceptions*, 19 AM. J. TR. ADV. 411 (1995); Note, *Keeping the Lid on Confidentiality: Mediation Privilege and Conflict of Laws*, 10 OHIO ST. J. DISP. RES. 157 (1994).

5. *Criticism and Limits of Mediation.* Mediation has not met with universal approval and even its advocates acknowledge it is not appropriate in every case. Many argue that the process requires trust between the parties and a willingness to reach a fair settlement. Those who would rather fight to "win" the divorce battle at any cost and those who are bitter or highly emotional are not likely to reach a mediated agreement. "Divorcing couples come to mediation with their personal and economic lives on the line. They come at a time when feelings of anger, guilt and failure run high. And they come with established patterns of reacting to each other." BROWN, THE EMOTIONAL CONTEXT OF DIVORCE: IMPLICATIONS FOR MEDIATION 43 (1982). While some may be able to simultaneously handle their emotions and the mediation process, the capacity of others may be temporarily diminished by the emotional upheaval of divorce. To guard against emotional incapacity to bargain, a cooling-off period before an agreement would become enforceable, has been suggested. Mnookin, *Divorce Bargaining: The Limits on Private Ordering*, in THE RESOLUTION OF FAMILY CONFLICT 364 (J. Eekelaar & S. Katz eds. 1984).

Perhaps the broadest criticism leveled at mediation is the feminist critique. Some fear that a system that requires parties to negotiate with each other directly, rather than through lawyer-agents, may advantage the more aggressive or dominant spouse. Fineman, *The Illusion of Equality: The Rhetoric and Reality of Divorce Reform* at pp. 144–46 (1991) (contending women are hurt by mediation's bias toward joint custody); Grillo, *The Mediation Alternative*, 100 YALE L.J. 1545 (1991); Bryan, *Killing Us Softly: Divorce Mediation and the Politics of Power*, 40 BUFF. L. REV. 441 (1992); Shaffer, *Divorce Mediation: A Feminist Perspective*, 46 U. TORONTO FAC. L. REV. 163 (1988); *but see* Marcus, et al., *To Mediate or Not to Mediate: Financial Outcomes in Mediated Versus Adversarial Divorces*, 17 MEDIATION Q. 143 (1999) (reporting on Connecticut empirical study showing that the mediated cases resulted in women receiving more of the marital assets, longer periods of alimony and more child support than the litigated cases); Pearson, *Ten Myths About Family Law*, 27 FAM. L.Q. 279 (1993); Rosenberg, *In Defense of Mediation*, 33 ARIZ. L. REV. 467 (1991).

A separate non-gender-based critique asserts that mediation is inappropriate where there has been domestic violence or neglect, or where one party has serious psychological problems. Note, *The Dangers of Mediation in Domestic Violence Cases*, 8 CARDOZO WOMEN'S L.J. 235 (2002). Critics sometimes draw a distinction between court-mandated mediation and voluntary mediation. *See* Grillo, *supra*, (criticizing mandatory mediation); Wheeler, *Mandatory Family Mediation and Domestic Violence,* 26 S. ILL. U. L.J. 559 (2002). Within court-mandated mediation, the primary issues include whether to exempt domestic violence cases, how to screen for domestic violence, and how to respond when the fact of violence emerges in mediation. Note, *Mediating Family Disputes in a World with Domestic Violence: How to Devise a Safe and Effective Court-Connected Mediation Program*, 17 OHIO ST. J. DISP. RESOL. 95 (2001); Zylstram, *Mediation and Domestic Violence: a Practical Screening Method for Mediators and Mediation Program Administrators*, 2001 J. DISP. RESOL. 253; Gerenscer, *Family Mediation: Screening for Domestic Abuse*, 23 FLA. ST. U. L. REV. 43 (1995); Utzig, *Entering the Debate on Spousal Abuse Divorce Mediation: Safely Managing Divorce Mediation When Domestic Violence Is Discovered*, 7 BUFF. WOMEN'S L. J. 51 (2001). As for voluntary mediation, while some critics argue against any mediation of these cases, others advocate for the victim's right to choose mediation. Ver Steegh, *Yes, No, and Maybe: Informed Decision Making about Divorce Mediation in the Presence of Domestic Violence* 9 WM. & MARY J. WOMEN & L. 145 (2003).

Others question some of the claims made by mediation enthusiasts about both mediation and the adversarial system. Consider the following:

> That mediation enthusiasts continually oversimplify the problem suggests . . . commitment to the institution and desire to enhance its image by distinguishing its process and values . . . from the "adversarial system."
>
> . . . [M]ediation literature usually implies (and often . . . contends) that mediators share a number of values as to process and outcomes which distinguish . . . their enterprise from . . . the "traditional adversarial approach." For example, such notions as shared post-divorce parenting responsibilities. . .; more rapid processing; lower legal costs; maximized self-determination for the divorcing spouses;

minimized interpersonal and legal conflict during and after the divorce.

. . .[B]ut a great many nonmediator lawyers would like to lessen the legal costs of divorce. Many lawyers, whose clients have returned time and again to relitigate their divorces endlessly in one form or another, share mediators' concerns as to post-divorce "recidivism." Many lawyers and judges . . . believe that children are better off if their parents are satisfied with only one trial. Yet all such perspectives and policy choices are the products of values and hunches — anecdotal experiences sprinkled liberally with personal background factors and emotion. There is . . . very little known as to the relative utility of various possible treatments, and no consensus as to the values about the adjustment of divorced persons and their children which should inform choices.

Consider our ignorance about the couples who endlessly relitigate. Some of them must be so full of interpersonal venom that: (a) they would never permit a professional to "mediate" their differences; (b) their relitigations are symbolic spousal batterings which [replace] physical assaults; or, (c) their children do "better" when the parents are litigating, because so long as they are fighting . . . in court they do not fight with the children at home. Continuing litigation may be, at least for some . . . , a "healthy adaptation."

Levy, *Comment on the Pearson-Thoennes Study on Mediation*, 17 FAM. L.Q. 525, 531–33 (1984). *See also* Gangel-Jacob, *Some Words of Caution About Divorce Mediation*, 23 HOFSTRA L. REV. 825 (1995). Justice Gangel-Jacob, a New York trial court judge, concluded:

A civilized divorce may be an oxymoron, but it is less likely to be when there is economic justice. . . . [B]uzz words that connote fairness are "joint custody," "shared decision making power," "no fault divorce," and "mediation." what could be more civilized than a nice, mediated settlement which results in joint custody, few economic burdens on the monied spouse, and a quick divorce? I propose that far more civilized is a fair economic package that takes into consideration the children's economic and emotional needs and makes adequate provision for the non-monied spouse.

. . . I appeal to . . . legislators, those who influence legislators, those who are academics . . . those who are judges and administrators . . . those who are lawyers . . . and those who are law students . . . not to cast matrimonial attorneys as the "villains" and mediators as the "saviors". . . .

Id. at pp. 835–36.

6. Empirical Evidence. A study reported in 1994 "found no differences in children's problems when children whose parents had used mediation were compared with those whose parents had used litigation to settle their child custody dispute one year earlier." Kitzmann & Emery, *Child and Family Coping One Year After Mediated and Litigated Child Custody Disputes*, 8 J. OF FAM. PSYCHOLOGY 150 (1994). The study, however, was relatively small (involving fewer than 60 families) and the mediating couples each experienced 4 to 8 hours of mediation. The same study did document a dramatic reduction in post-divorce court hearings and an increase in party satisfaction and compliance with child support orders. Emery, Matthews & Kitzmann, *Child Custody Mediation and Litigation: Parents' Satisfaction and Functioning One Year After Settlement*, 62 J. OF CONSULT. & CLIN. PSYCHOLOGY 124 (1994). A long-term study found that nine years after resolution of a custody dispute those who had mediated their case reported greater current contact with their children and greater involvement in current decisions. The mediating parents also reported more frequent communication with each other about the children during the post-resolution period. Dillon & Emery*, Divorce Mediation and Resolution of Child Custody Disputes: Long-Term Effects*, 66 AM. J. OF ORTHOPSYCHIATRY 131 (1996). In addition to the report of the specific study involved, the latter article surveys the empirical literature.

For other studies, see Emery, *Easing the Pain of Divorce for Children: Children's Voices, Causes of Conflict and Mediation. Comments on Kelly's "Resolving Child Custody Disputes,"* 10 VA. J. SO. POL'Y & L. 164, 167 (2002); BECK & SALES, FAMILY MEDIATION: FACTS MYTHS AND FUTURE PROSPECTS (2001); Caprez & Armstrong, *A Study of Domestic Mediation Outcomes with Indigent Parents*, 9 FAM. CT. REV. 415 (2001); Emery, RENEGOTIATING FAMILY RELATIONSHIPS: DIVORCE, CHILD CUSTODY, AND MEDIATION (1994).

[2] THE REQUIREMENT THAT DIVORCE SETTLEMENTS BE JUDICIALLY APPROVED

[a] In General

Divorcing spouses are not done when they reach agreement on the terms of their marital dissolution, for they must still obtain a decree from the divorce court. Ordinarily, the divorce decree will reflect the terms of the parties' agreement. Nonetheless, a variety of issues may arise. A party may have a change of heart after reaching an agreement but prior to the decree's issuance, and may thus challenge the agreement's terms before the court asked to issue the decree based upon it. Or, a party may challenge the terms *after* the issuance of the decree, seeking a change in the judicial order on the grounds that there were defects in the agreement upon which it was based. Finally, a party may seek what would ordinarily be a permissible modification of a divorce decree, upon the grounds of changed circumstances, but be met with the claim that he or she is contractually bound by the agreement's provisions so that the decree also is not modifiable. In this section we examine each of these issues in turn.

MODEL MARRIAGE AND DIVORCE ACT § 306

§ 306. Separation Agreement

(a) To promote amicable settlement of disputes between parties to a marriage attendant upon their separation or the dissolution of their marriage, the parties may enter into a written separation agreement containing provisions for disposition of any property owned by either of them, maintenance of either of them, and support, custody, and visitation of their children.

(b) In a proceeding for dissolution of marriage or for legal separation, the terms of the separation agreement, except those providing for the support, custody, and visitation of children, are binding upon the court unless it finds, after considering the economic circumstances of the parties and any other relevant evidence produced by the parties, on their own motion or on request of the court, that the separation agreement is unconscionable.

(c) If the court finds the separation agreement unconscionable, it may request the parties to submit a revised separation agreement or may make orders for the distribution of property, maintenance, and support.

(d) If the court finds that the separation agreement is not unconscionable as to disposition of property or maintenance, and not unsatisfactory as to support:

(1) unless the separation agreement provides to the contrary, its terms shall be set forth in the decree of dissolution or legal separation and the parties shall be ordered to perform them, or

(2) if the separation agreement provides that its terms shall not be set forth in the decree, the decree shall identify the separation agreement and state that the court has found the terms not unconscionable.

(e) Terms of the agreement set forth in the decree are enforceable by all remedies available for enforcement of a judgment, including contempt, and are enforceable as contract terms.

(f) Except for terms concerning the support, custody, or visitation of children, the decree may expressly preclude or limit modification of terms set forth in the decree if the separation agreement so provides. Otherwise, terms of a separation agreement set forth in the decree are automatically modified by modification of the decree.

WEBER v. WEBER

589 N.W.2d 358 (N.D. 1999)

SANDSTROM, Justice. Ruby Moos appealed from the judgment of the district court vacating the property settlement agreement between her and Herbert Weber. The district court found the agreement unconscionable and set it aside in its entirety. We affirm, concluding the district court did not err in finding the agreement unconscionable.

I

Moos and Weber were married on September 13, 1995. Twenty-seven days later, Moos retained an attorney to begin a divorce action. Moos signed a property settlement agreement at a meeting with Weber on October 12, 1995. Weber was not represented by counsel. Moos was represented by attorney Thomas Bair, who advised Weber he represented only Moos and Weber should retain his own attorney. Weber declined to retain his own attorney and signed the document after reviewing it. The property settlement agreement was accompanied by a quitclaim deed giving Moos ownership of a condominium worth about $ 70,000 and owned by Weber prior to the marriage. [¶] The property settlement agreement was filed in . . . court on October 16, 1995. [On the same day,] Weber retained an attorney and moved the . . . court to set aside the . . . agreement, including the quitclaim deed executed in conjunction with it. On October 20, 1995, Weber filed a motion to repossess the condominium, and on October 24, 1995, Weber filed a motion of lis pendens with the . . . court.

In denying Weber's motions, the district court found Weber was able to act independently of the plaintiff and freely to protect his own interests. The district court also found no mistake, fraud, or undue duress. Weber appealed from the district court's judgment. [¶] In *Weber v. Weber*, 548 N.W.2d 781 (N.D. 1996), we remanded to the district court, saying its analysis and ruling were too narrow. In reviewing the property settlement agreement giving substantial property to Moos, the district court limited its review to the contractual capacity of the parties and to whether the contract was entered freely and knowingly, without fraud, duress, menace or undue influence, or genuine mistake of fact or law. We concluded the district court should have considered whether the property settlement agreement was unconscionable.

On remand, the district court addressed three issues for unconscionability. First, was the property settlement agreement "one-sided"? Second, did the agreement create a hardship on either party? And third, given the station in life of each of the parties, and considering the Ruff-Fischer guidelines for property division, was the agreement fair, just, and proper? Applying these, the district court found the October 12, 1995, property settlement agreement . . . unconscionable, and set it aside in its entirety. Moos appealed.

II

. . .

B

When a divorce is granted, N.D.C.C. § 14-05-24 requires a trial court to "make such equitable distribution of the real and personal property of the parties as may seem just and proper." In doing so, however, we have encouraged district courts to recognize valid agreements between divorcing parties. The public policy on divorce favors a "prompt and peaceful resolution of disputes." *Wolfe v. Wolfe*, 391 N.W.2d 617, 619 (N.D. 1986)). "To the extent that competent parties have voluntarily stipulated to a particular disposition of their marital property, a court ordinarily should not decree a distribution of property that is inconsistent with the parties' contract." *Wolfe*, 391 N.W.2d at 619.

District courts should not, however, blindly accept property settlement agreements. See Principles of the Law of Family Dissolution: Analysis and Recommendations, Tentative Draft No. 2, A.L.I. § 4.01 comment (1996) (stating "agreements between spouses have traditionally been subject to various procedural and substantive rules beyond those which apply to contracts generally"). We have noted the district court's duty to make a just and proper distribution of property under N.D.C.C. § 14-05-24 includes the authority to rewrite a property settlement agreement for mistake, duress, menace, fraud, or undue influence under N.D.C.C. § 9-09-02(1). See *Wolfe*, 391 N.W.2d at 619.

We have also held a district court should not enforce an agreement if it is unconscionable. See also Uniform Marriage and Divorce Act, 9A U.L.A. 306(b) (1998) (stating "the terms of a separation agreement . . . are binding upon the court unless it finds, after considering the economic circumstances of the parties and any other relevant evidence produced by the parties, on their own motion or on request of the court, that the separation agreement is unconscionable"). Unconscionability is a doctrine by which courts may deny enforcement of a contract "because of procedural abuses arising out of the contract formation, or because of substantive abuses relating to terms of the contract." Black's Law Dictionary, 6th Ed., 1524.

Therefore, district courts should make two findings when considering whether a settlement agreement between divorcing parties should be enforced. The first inquiry is whether the agreement is free from mistake, duress, menace, fraud, or undue influence under N.D.C.C. § 9-09-02(1). On remand, the district court stated:

> The Court has determined in its previous judgment that the parties and their resulting agreement did not occur as the result of fraud, deceit, misrepresentation, or mistake of law or fact. Further, that the Supreme Court decision herein did not reverse the Court's findings thereon. Accordingly, the trial court is left to determine whether or not the result of the property settlement agreement of the parties is unconscionable.

The district court did not err in finding the agreement free from mistake, duress, menace, fraud, or undue influence. The inquiry does not, however, end there.[¶]. . .The district court [also] found the result of the property settlement agreement . . . unconscionable. The court first found the agreement to be "one-sided," based on the brevity of the marriage, the additional assets of $ 75,000 Moos received during the brief marriage, the gifts given to Moos by Weber in this very short marriage, and Weber giving up his only residence.

Moos argues the district court was clearly erroneous in this finding. . . . [Moos] argues the agreement between her and Weber must be perceived as more than unfair or "one-sided," it must be "blatantly one-sided" and "rankly unfair," citing language from *Crawford*, 524 N.W.2d 833. [¶] Although the district court does not call the agreement between Moos and Weber "rankly unfair" or "blatantly one-sided," that does not mean it could not have been described as such. The agreement left Weber with far less than he brought into the one-month marriage. This appears to be the kind of agreement no rational, undeluded person would make, and no honest and fair person would accept. The district court did not err in finding the agreement one-sided. Whether it was characterized as "rankly" or "blatantly" one-sided is not important.

The district court's second finding on unconscionability was that the agreement created a greater hardship on Weber. Weber gave up his condominium and lost his household furnishings, and he would have had to expend a substantial portion of his retirement assets to replace the condominium. Moos, on the other hand, could resume renting an apartment comparable to her previous accommodations without reducing her assets. Moos argues the agreement allowed Weber to retain 73% of the marital estate. This argument fails, however, to consider Weber brought nearly 100% of the estate into the one-month marriage. The district court did not err in finding the agreement placed a greater hardship on Weber.

Finally, the district court applied the Ruff-Fischer guidelines and found the agreement "unfair and unjust under the circumstances with respect to [Weber]."[2] Traditionally, the Ruff-Fischer guidelines are applied in divorce cases to distribute property of divorcing spouses, absent an agreement. While Ruff-Fischer is not the standard in a domestic relations case to determine unconscionability of a settlement agreement of divorcing parties, it is appropriate for a district court to consider. The Ruff-Fischer guidelines are proper because a domestic relations agreement should not be scrutinized in the same way as a business contract. Thus, the district court did not err in applying Ruff-Fischer to determine unconscionability.

The haste with which the agreement was entered and the involvement of only one attorney is also troubling. The action by Weber to rescind immediately after having signed the agreement is also persuasive. As we said in *Peterson v. Peterson*, 555 N.W.2d 359, 362 (N.D. 1996), "a stipulation in a divorce proceeding which occurs this rapidly with the use of one attorney and under serious threats of harm to one of the parties should be viewed with great skepticism." Although there were no serious threats of physical harm, Weber was under strain from the threat of losing considerably more of his life's earnings if he did not sign the agreement. The skepticism we noted in *Peterson* was correctly applied to this agreement.

The district court did not err in finding the agreement unconscionable. The decision of the district court is affirmed.

---

[2] The Fuff-Fischer guidelines are applied to distribute property in a divorce in the absence of an ante-or postnuptial agreement. Considered under the Ruff-Fischer guidelines are: "'the respective ages of the parties, their earning ability, the duration of the marriage and conduct of the parties during the marriage, their station in life, the circumstances and necessities of each, their health and physical condition, their financial circumstances as shown by the property owned at the time, its value at the time, its income-producing capacity, if any, whether accumulated before or after the marriage, and such other matters as may be material." Weir v. Weir, 374 N.W.2d 858, 862 (N.D. 1985).

———————

ALI Principles, Chapter One, Introduction, at Pp. 40–41: "Separation agreements resolving the [divorcing parties' alimony and property division arrangements] are favored, both under existing law and these Principles. . . . In negotiating a separation agreement in the shadow of state default rules that set the standard for fairness, the parties can often settle their affairs more efficiently and more to their satisfaction than a court can. The greater favor shown to separation agreements than to premarital agreements may also reflect the different negotiating context. The parties to a premarital agreement are contracting about a speculative future event, dissolution, in a setting dominated by a quite different and immediate event, marriage. In contrast, at dissolution the parties are contracting for events that are already upon them. They are better able to comprehend the circumstances in which the agreement will be enforced and thus to grasp the significance of the terms of the agreement. Given the demise of their relationship, the parties may generally be expected to bargain at arm's length. Although parties making agreements before or during marriage may assume that the other party is acting for their common good, parties bargaining about the terms of an impending dissolution are more likely to appreciate that each party has individual interests to advance and safeguard.

"Thus, the law should enforce separation agreements unless the rules of contract, viewed in the context of family dissolution, have been violated, or the terms of the agreement would frustrate some important policy of the law of family dissolution. . . .[¶] These Principles impose few formal requirements for the enforceability of separation agreements. Recognizing that parties may not settle until the hour of trial, separation agreements may either be in writing or stipulated by the parties before the court. The party seeking enforcement need only show the prima facie existence of an agreement, that is, a signed writing or a stipulation. The party resisting enforcement bears the burden of showing that the agreement should not be enforced.

". . . . Judicial economy is better served by limiting court oversight to those relatively few cases in which a term of an agreement is ultimately contested than by requiring courts to examine all separation agreements, including those that are unproblematic or may never be contested. In any event, these Principles acknowledge the reality that most courts do not have the resources to exercise meaningful oversight of all separation agreements. Therefore the Principles do not require judicial approval of agreements regulating property disposition or compensatory payments, and instead require judicial inquiry only when one party objects to the terms of an agreement."

NOTES AND QUESTIONS

1. *In general.* While modern divorce law encourages negotiated settlement, it usually requires the parties to present their agreement to the court, which may in theory reject it. The MMDA instructs the court to approve the provisions concerning alimony and property division unless it finds them "unconscionable," but provides more vigorous review of terms on custody and child support. The purpose is to assure, through judicial supervision of the parties, that the interests of the children are not submerged in an effort to accommodate the spouses, while giving the spouses broad authority to set terms affecting only themselves. Most states have similar provisions for judicial review of separation agreements. The *ALI Principles* also require approval of custody and child support terms, which directly affect children, but conclude that routine review of the property or alimony portions of a separation agreement are usually unnecessary, and are unlikely to provide meaningful oversight in any event. While it therefore dispenses with the pretense of routine review, it does allow post-agreement challenges to the settlement's terms at the instance of a party, under standards described below.

2. Can Routine Judicial Review of All Agreements Really Work? Note that in *Weber* itself a careful review of the agreement occurred because one of the parties had a change of heart and objected to it by the time judicial approval was sought. But how can a requirement of routine review work in the usual case, where the parties remain in agreement so that the court cannot depend upon the adversarial process to bring out the critical facts? If the requirement were to be meaningful it would appear that the court would have to probe for the facts *sua sponte,* yet existing law generally does not put courts under any obligation to make such an unprompted investigation, *Dow v. Dow,* 732 S.W.2d 906 (Mo. 1987), and they rarely will. It is thus not surprising that there are few reported decisions rejecting an agreement endorsed by both husband and wife. Melli's study revealed the same pattern in the trial courts. The court rejected the parties' agreement in only one case of 349 she examined, and that case arose from an objection by the state child support agency, which pointed out that the custodial parent had agreed to the support terms only because additional funds were being provided through AFDC. Where judges made inquiries about the agreement, they asked only whether the parties understood and supported it. Like the trial court in *Weber*, they never inquired into the agreement's substantive fairness; they limited themselves to verifying that it was voluntarily entered. Indeed, in three-fourths of Melli's cases, the file before the judge did not contain the financial information that would be necessary to make a substantive evaluation, and even financial disclosure forms required by state law were often missing or incomplete. Melli, Erlanger & Chambliss, *The Process of Negotiation: An Exploratory Investigation in the Context of No-Fault Divorce,* 40 RUTGERS L. REV. 1133, 1145–47 (1988).[2]

The court's failure to give an agreement meaningful review will not normally provide a basis for later upsetting the decree which incorporates it. For example, in *Monroe v. Monroe,* 413 A.2d 819 (Conn.), *appeal dismissed,* 444 U.S. 801 (1979), the former wife sought to vacate a divorce decree based upon

---

[2] Other studies support the impression left by Melli's data. See the authorities cited in Mnookin & Kornhauser, *Bargaining in the Shadow of the Law,* 88 YALE L.J. 950, 954 (1979). A survey of Nebraska judges suggests that some scrutiny of provisions concerning children may take place, but even when such cases were counted the judges reported alteration of less than five percent of the agreements. Frank, Berman & Mazur-Hart, *No Fault Divorce and the Divorce Rate: The Nebraska Experience — An Interrupted Time Series Analysis and Commentary,* 58 NEB. L. REV. 1, 77 n. 311 (1978). See also Sharp, *Modification of Agreement Based Custody Decrees: Unitary or Dual Standard?,* 68 VA. L. REV. 1263, 1279 n. 69.

a negotiated agreement. Among other grounds, she argued that she had not actually consented to the agreement, or to its submission to a court-appointed referee, who handled uncontested divorces. The referee's review of the agreement was so cursory that he made no effort even to verify that the wife consented to it. The Connecticut Supreme Court observed:

> The plaintiff claims that she was coerced by her attorney into agreeing to the order of reference and into appearing before the referee, but there are no findings of fact to support those allegations. The plaintiff's argument would have us impose upon the defendant, the burden of establishing that the plaintiff's relationship with her counsel was one of informed consent. This we are not prepared to do.
>
> Although the plaintiff . . . has not sustained her burden, the questions indirectly raised by her appeal are not trivial. Lawyers who represent clients in matrimonial dissolutions have a special responsibility for full and fair disclosure, for a searching dialogue, about all of the facts that materially affect the client's rights and interests. . . . It is . . . noteworthy that the referee who accepted the stipulated divorce settlement and incorporated it into his decree did so completely upon the representations of counsel. Although both parties — were present, the referee made no inquiry whatsoever to ascertain the parties' actual consent to the proposal before him. Because of the emotionally-laden circumstances under which negotiations about marital dissolutions necessarily take place, reasonable [inquiries] should be made to ensure, as far as possible, that reasonable settlements have been knowingly agreed upon. Nonetheless, even judicial failure to conduct a searching inquiry into the acceptability of a divorce settlement does not make the subsequent judgment of divorce vulnerable to collateral attack as a miscarriage of justice.

Monroe suggests both judges and attorneys may have a special obligation to protect the divorcing parties from settlements which are unfair or which do not in fact reflect the parties' desires. But the court still denies the wife's claim, saying that the husband need not prove her informed consent to the agreement. This combination of strong words with little action is typical. *See also Marriage of Manzo,* 659 P.2d 669, 674 (Colo. 1983).

How would a trial court proceed if it actually wanted to do the policing that most statutes seem in principle to require? In *Linnenburger v. Linnenburger,* 741 S.W.2d 872 (Mo. App. 1987), the court found the trial court had erred in setting its own amounts for child support and maintenance, even though it did not disagree with the trial court that the provisions in the parties' agreement were unconscionable. The agreement had waived maintenance and set support at only $35 per week; the trial judge had ordered support payments of $50 weekly and maintenance of $100 per month. The appeals court held that the trial judge should have either ordered the parties to submit a revised separation agreement, or held a separate evidentiary hearing. It also held that the trial court could not set aside the maintenance and support provisions while honoring the agreement's property terms; the agreement must stand or fall in its entirety.

3. What Standards Should Govern Challenges to Agreements? What standards should a court apply in cases like *Weber*, when a party asks a court to reject the agreement he had previously accepted but which has not yet been incorporated into the decree? *Weber* suggests that courts should subject these agreements to standards more demanding than would be imposed on a commercial agreements, but the opinion does not make entirely clear what the more demanding standards consist of. "Mistake, duress, menace, fraud, or undue influence" are all terms identifying doctrines that apply to contracts generally, as does the unconscionability doctrine. The first group are all defects in process, while unconscionability may arise from substantive as well as process failures. In suggesting that it is appropriate for a court to compare the result under the agreement with the property allocation that a court might order under North Dakota law absent any agreement, however, the court implies that in this realm, as compared to commercial agreements, there are legally established substantive standards setting forth benchmarks of fairness and that agreements may be substantively unconscionable if they depart too dramatically from those standards. Other courts have also suggested a fuller substantive review of challenged divorce agreements than contract law alone would usually accept, sometimes relying upon statutory language. For example, in *Sharp v. Sharp*, 877 P.2d 304 (Ariz. App. 1994), the parties negotiated with each other directly and over the course of several weeks reached agreement on a divorce settlement. But the wife's attorney rejected the agreement after he was asked by both spouses to prepare the necessary papers to finalize the divorce, and the wife therefore opposed it when the husband filed. She offered several arguments based upon defects in the bargaining process that were rejected but the trial court was reversed nevertheless for failure to determine whether the agreement was "fair" — the standard adopted (rather than unconscionability) in the state's version of MMDA § 306(b). The court held, in effect, that the wife's objections to the agreement created a factual dispute about its fairness that could not be resolved without an examination of the parties' financial particulars. As in *Weber*, the appellate court held that the trial court could not bypass the task by relying upon the parties' having agreed on the terms.

Process and substantive concerns are of course inevitably related; concerns about the negotiating process can motivate or justify a fuller substantive review. The process claims of the wife in *Sharp* were hardly implausible, even though rejected by the court. She was imprisoned in Hawaii on criminal charges while negotiating with her husband in Arizona. While conceding she may have been in distress due to "external circumstances," the court found that this distress did not transform her husband's "entreaties to sign the agreement" into "duress, coercion or undue influence," noting that he was not responsible for the charges against her. In *Weber* the objecting spouse was uncounseled and the process hurried; one might wonder whether the husband's initial willingness to proceed that way might have arisen from an overriding desire to bring a stressful episode to conclusion. Yet divorce is typically a stressful experience, and thus many settlements would become vulnerable to challenge if emotional turmoil alone were grounds for upsetting a divorce agreement. *See, e.g., Beattie v. Beattie*, 368 N.E.2d 178 (Ill. App. 1977) (wife's claim of "anxiety neurosis" at the time of settlement insufficient to permit her to disavow the agreement). This seems to be the position taken by most courts, although there are exceptions. *E.g.*, in *Jenks v. Jenks*, 657 A.2d 1107 (Conn. 1995) (affirming trial court findings of duress arising from husband's threatening and intimidating behavior in divorce negotiations).

Nor is it uncommon for parties to settle on the eve of trial under what in retrospect might seem precipitous circumstances. For example, in *Marriage of Steadman*, 670 N.E.2d 1146 (Ill. App. 1996), the parties and their attorneys reached a comprehensive agreement during hallway negotiations conducted just before their scheduled hearing on the husband's motion to enjoin the wife from taking their children out of state, and their agreement was then presented to the court, which accepted it. But the wife challenged the agreement a month later, before the court actually entered a judgment based upon it. In rejecting her claim the appeals court conceded that "the oral settlement agreement was contrived during two hours of negotiations" but emphasized that the parties "negotiated for two hours at arms length with the aid of counsel." While the court agreed "that the record demonstrates wife may have been unhappy with the settlement terms," as she claimed, she could still be held to her stipulation in open court that accepted them: "this unhappiness does not negate the fact that she stated under oath to counsel and the trial court that this was her agreement." For a similar result on similar facts, see *Richardson v. Richardson,* 392 S.E.2d 688 (Va. App. 1990).

Stookey v. Stookey, 554 S.E.2d 472 (Ga. 2001), would seem to go a step further. The wife's attorney negotiated a deal on her behalf in a telephone conversation with the husband's attorney, in which the wife also participated. Her attorney then informed the court that a scheduled hearing could be cancelled because settlement had been reached. But the wife refused to sign the agreement later prepared by the husband's attorney, denying she had authorized a settlement on those terms. Finding the wife bound by her attorney's representations because she had authorized him to settle on her behalf, the Georgia Supreme Court held that a binding agreement had in fact been entered. Note that the *ALI Principles* would distinguish between these cases: it accepts oral stipulations before a court as creating a binding agreement, but requires nonjudicial agreements to be in writing. *See* § 7.09. In contrast to both the *ALI Principles* and *Stookey* is the decision of the Virginia Supreme Court in *Flanary v. Milton*, 556 S.E.2d 777 (Va. 2002), which held unenforceable the wife's oral agreement, entered into before the court, to accept a lump-sum payment in settlement of her marital property claims. Virginia law includes a general statutory provision applying the state's version of the Uniform Premarital Agreement to agreements between spouses; the court held that the UPA's requirement of a writing therefore applied to this agreement as well.

For more on this general topic, see Mnookin, *Divorce Bargaining, The Limits of Private Ordering,* in J. EEKELAAR & S. KATZ, RESOLUTION OF FAMILY CONFLICTS: CONTEMPORARY LEGAL PERSPECTIVES 364 (1984), on which portions of the preceding note are based.

4. *Possible Reforms: Replacing Pro Forma Routine Review with Demanding But Focused Review*. On one hand, it appears that many courts are disinclined to allow parties to avoid agreements whenever they were made under emotional stress or pursuant to fast, high-pressure negotiations, because such rules would make too many agreements vulnerable. On the other hand, one commentator has argued that it is just because such circumstances are in fact common that appropriate rules would require fairness in the results of the agreement, going beyond ordinary contract doctrines that focus on the bargaining process and generally accept a wide range of results as conscionable. Sally Sharp, *Fairness Standards and Separation Agreements: A Word of Caution on Contractual Freedom,* 132 U. PA. L. REV. 1399 (1984). This may be the implied message of cases like *Weber* and *Sharp,* described above. It is also the approach taken by the American Law Institute. When an agreement is challenged by a party before it has been incorporated into the decree, the ALI would subject it to more searching substantive scrutiny than commercial contracts receive. The Institute's key recommendations are contained in the following excerpt from § 7.09 of the *ALI Principles*:

§ 7.09 The Enforceability of a Separation Agreement

(1) The terms of a separation agreement providing for the disposition of property or for compensatory payments are enforceable and, under § 7.10, are binding on the court if

(a) the agreement is in writing and signed by the parties, or is stipulated by the parties before the court;

(b) the agreement otherwise satisfies the requirements of an enforceable contract;

(c) prior to accepting the agreement, each party had full and fair opportunity to be informed of the existence and value of the parties' marital and separate assets, each party's current earnings and prospects for future earnings, and the significance of the terms of the agreement;

(d) the agreement satisfies any other requirements of state law specially applicable to separation agreements; and

(e) the terms of the agreement have not been found unenforceable under Paragraph (2).

(2) Except as provided in the last sentence of this Paragraph, the terms of a separation agreement providing for the disposition of property or for compensatory payments are unenforceable if they substantially limit or augment property rights or compensatory payments otherwise due under law, and enforcement of those terms would substantially impair the economic well-being of a party who has or will have

(a) primary or dual residential responsibility for a child or

(b) substantially fewer economic resources than the other party.

Nevertheless, the court may enforce such terms if it finds, under the particular circumstances of the case, that enforcement of the terms would not work an injustice.

(3) The party seeking enforcement of a separation agreement must demonstrate that it satisfies Paragraph (1)(a). The party opposing enforcement must show that the separation agreement is unenforceable under another provision of Paragraph (1) or Paragraph (2).

These provisions set modest process requirements: disclosure, analogous to the typical requirements for an enforceable premarital agreement, is the only significant process requirement added to the usual prerequisites for any enforceable contract. But the court's authority to reject a substantively unfair agreement is also made clear in certain specified cases: where the disadvantaged party is a custodial parent, or has "substantially fewer economic resources" than the other party. In those cases, the agreement is unenforceable if it substantially limits the financial claims that party would otherwise have under applicable law, and such that it yields results that "substantially impair the economic well-being" of that party, unless the court also finds that its unfavorable terms do not "work an injustice." Thus, the goal is to specify a subset of cases in which the judicial scrutiny will take place, but to ensure that in those cases the scrutiny is real rather than *pro forma*. The special focus is on children, and those who are financially much worse off than their former partner.

5. *Fiduciary Duties Between Spouses.* If one wished to impose heightened process requirements to separation agreements, one might argue that spouses have special duties to one another beyond those imposed on parties to a commercial agreement. And indeed, in separation agreements as in premarital agreements, courts sometimes say that. *Marriage of Smith,* 115 S.W.3d 126 (Tex. App. 2003) ("because of the confidential relationship between husband and wife, courts closely scrutinize property agreements made by spouses during marriage and have imposed the same duties of good faith and fair dealing on spouses as required of partners and other fiduciaries"); *Manes v. Manes,* 717 N.Y.S.2d 185, (App. Div. 2000) ("In view of the fiduciary relationship existing between spouses, separation agreements are more closely scrutinized by courts than ordinary contracts and may be set aside upon the demonstration of good cause, such as mistake, fraud, duress or overreaching or when found to be unconscionable."). These duties are said to require disclosure of assets, and in general to bar one marital partner from using his superior knowledge, or his influence over the other, to obtain some advantage to the other's detriment. But in many states, any confidential relation between spouses may cease to exist when a divorce petition is filed, separation occurs, or attorneys are hired, depending upon the law of the particular state. *E.g.,* *Webb v. Webb*, 431 S.E.2d 55 (Va. App. 1993) ("if parties have separated, have employed independent counsel and are then negotiating agreement, it is arms length transaction and their former fiduciary relationship is deemed to have ended"); *Sidden v. Mailman,* 529 S.E.2d 266 (N.C. App. 2000) (a fiduciary relationship exists between husband and wife unless they have become adversaries negotiating over the terms of a separation or property settlement agreement). In these states, the protective rules applying to confidential relations have no application to the typical separation agreement problem. *See* Sharp, *Fairness Standards and Separation Agreements,* 132 U. Pa. L. Rev. 1399, 1414–23 (1984). In community property states, the spouses' fiduciary duty to one another in their handling of community assets continues while the community is intact. *See* Sharp at 1415; *Miller v. Bechtel Corp.,* 663 P.2d 177 (Cal. 1983) (fiduciary relationship between spouses continues to exist, even during separation, when one spouse controls community property).; *Compton v. Compton,* 612 P.2d 1175, 1182 (Idaho 1980). Community property states divide on whether the community ends when the spouses commence living apart, or only at divorce. Where the rule is "living apart," there can obviously be some difficulties in construction.

6. *The Attorney's Obligations in Settlement.* An attorney may be held liable for negligently advising a client to settle. *Grayson v. Wofsey et al.,* 646 A.2d 195 (Conn. 1994); *McWhirt v. Heavey,* 550 N.W.2d 327 (Neb. 1996). In these jurisdictions the attorney can be liable in malpractice for negligence in the settlement process even though the agreement was approved by the court as fair and equitable. *E.g.,* in *Grayson* a $1.5 million judgment was upheld against an attorney charged with failing to adequately investigate and value the husband's estate and business interests, in consequence of which the wife accepted an agreement that gave her too little property and less alimony than she should have received. In *Heavey* the husband obtained a judgment of $91,000 against an attorney where he accepted a settlement offer after the attorney inaccurately advised him that his inherited property would be considered marital property under local law, and that his wife was likely to receive a long-term alimony award. In both cases there were also more general allegations, including inadequate trial preparation. No malpractice liability should arise from the attorney's exercise of judgment in advising the client with respect to the amount to accept or pay, as contrasted with mistaken advice about the law or about the impact of the agreement on the client's rights and obligations. *McMahon v. Shea,* 657 A.2d 938 (Pa. Super.1995).

7. *Where There Are No Lawyers*. One way for the indigent or thrifty to obtain divorce is to act as their own lawyers. With the advent of no-fault divorces — and especially summary divorce procedures — such pro se divorces have increased. One study found that 47 percent of the divorces obtained in the Superior Court in Phoenix, Ariz., during 1985 did not involve lawyers. Those most likely to obtain a divorce pro se were under 30, in a low-income job, married less than ten years, and without children. *Self Helpers on the Increase,* A.B.A. JOURNAL 40 (1988). By 1990 neither spouse had an attorney in 52 percent of the divorces filed in Phoenix, Sales, Beck, and Haan, *Is Self-Representation a Reasonable Alternative to Attorney Representation in Divorce Cases?,* 37 St. LOUIS U. L. REV. 553, 571 n.81 (1992), and more recent data from the court indicate even higher rates. The domestic relations court in Phoenix has now created a "self-help" center that includes automated access to forms and other legal assistance, a library of self-help materials, and limited access to consultations with volunteer lawyers. Similar efforts have been undertaken in other jurisdictions. *See* Yegge, *Divorce Litigants Without Lawyers,* 28 FAM. L.Q. 407 (1994). Sales, et al., *supra,* includes an empirical study that confirms the earlier findings on the demographic characteristics of Phoenix pro se divorce litigants and some comparative data on pro se and attorney-represented litigants.

What happens if the party to a no-lawyer divorce later claims that the spousal agreement is tainted by a bargaining process that was inadequate or coercive? Probably because no-lawyer divorces usually involve parties with few assets, such claims seem uncommon. Consider, however, *Carsey v. Carsey,* 508 A.2d 533 (Md. App. 1986), in which an extraordinarily informal agreement was enforced. The husband, then president of a local community college, suddenly "chucked it all," leaving both his job and his wife of 14 years. He took all their liquid assets but left her two notes and a tape, all composed without counsel. One note "relinquished all claims" to their joint estate and disclaimed all responsibilities for their debts, the second told her of the physical and emotional mess he found himself in, and referred her to a tape with more information about the family finances. When she later filed for divorce, the court found that there was no marital property to divide because the husband's notes constituted an offer of all their joint property in exchange for assuming liability for their obligations, an offer which the wife accepted by her subsequent actions.

[b] Special Rules To Govern Bargaining Over Children

Consider *Marriage of Lawrence,* 642 P.2d 1043 (Mont. 1982), in which the parties' agreement allocated the wife property and support payments worth about $60,800, while estimates of the husband's share ranged from $227,000 to $422,500. The wife had been advised by her attorney that the agreement was unwise, and that she could probably do better if she went to trial, but, according to the attorney, she rejected this advice and gave no indication she felt coerced. Yet she later sought to set the agreement aside as unconscionable, saying she signed it because her husband had threatened he would otherwise contest custody with evidence of her adultery.

The court rejected her claim, concluding that "custody is frequently a bargaining chip in negotiations whether we like it or not," and declining to adopt a rule that would "encourage a challenge of negotiated property settlement agreements where custody rights have been settled on an arm's length basis as here." The court relied heavily upon her separate representation by competent counsel and her apparently knowing rejection of counsel's advice. The agreement involved no fraud, nor coercion as that term would be understood in policing commercial contracts: the husband's threat, after all, amounted to no more than a statement that if his wife did not agree to a provision with respect to one term in the agreement, he would press his legal rights with respect to another term. Or, to cast it in even more palatable terms, he offered to forgo a tenable legal claim he had to one item on the negotiating table, if the wife would forgo a claim she had to another. This is, of course, the ordinary stuff of negotiated agreements. Why, then, does this agreement leave us uneasy? There is at least one apparent explanation.

In commercial settlement negotiations, the threat to litigate a particular item has leverage primarily to the extent the party making the threat has a good claim on the merits, or at least, a claim that would be difficult to defeat. While parties also desire to avoid litigation, this mutual preference gives neither side a negotiating advantage unless litigation would impose greater costs on one party than the other. Custody contests, however, have the unusual feature that heavy costs — perhaps the highest costs — are imposed on third parties (the children). A negotiating advantage thus lies with the party less concerned about the burden of litigation on the children. We may find a special kind of unfairness in allowing one spouse to achieve a negotiating advantage by exploiting the other's more responsible concern for the children's welfare. Good advice from independent counsel will not ameliorate this concern. Whether this is the reason or not, some courts, unlike *Lawrence,* have held that under appropriate facts a one-sided property agreement may be later upset on grounds of duress where a disfavored party shows that she agreed to it only in response to her spouse's threat to otherwise contest custody. *Brockman v. Brockman,* 240 Cal. Rptr. 96 (App. 1987) (wife gave up all claims to couple's substantial community property in exchange for husband's agreement to forfeit a $100,000 bond if he should ever contest the custody or support order; trial court must give wife opportunity to show that she was thereby coerced).

Yet there are of course also cases in which both parents are sincere in wanting a larger share of the custodial responsibilities than the other parent wishes to accept. If settlement of such conflicts is to be encouraged — and surely we do not wish to push them all to litigation — then musn't we allow agreements in which the parent who concedes more on custody obtains more on something else? The problem, in other words, may lie in distinguishing this kind of case from one in which a divorcing spouse threatens a custody claim for strategic advantage only, rather than from a genuine desire to undertake more residential responsibility for his or her children. Or is this the right distinction? One author tried to capture the difference between acceptable and problematic tradeoffs by comparing three hypotheticals:

> 1. Allan explicitly threatens to litigate custody if not given most of the marital property. He does not want custodial time. He is motivated by spite and self-interest. He settles for twenty percent custodial time and seventy-five percent of the marital property.

> 2. Bob makes no explicit threat. He simply proposes a settlement in which he has sixty percent custodial time and fifty percent of the marital property. He makes the proposal with the hope and belief that it will induce his wife to make a counter-proposal in which she gets eighty percent custody and twenty-five percent of the marital property. When she does, he accepts it.

> [3. Charlie proposes a settlement identical to Bob's. He wants sixty percent custodial time because he thinks the children are best off spending time with him. After difficult negotiations he accepts twenty percent custody, and seventy-five percent of the marital property. His wife refused to compromise about time. So he accepted her terms to avoid litigation for the children's sake. He demanded the property because he felt taken advantage of if he did not get something in exchange for giving up time.]

I see no reason to judge Bob less harshly than Allan. If he would have given his wife eighty percent custody without extracting marital property had he not seen the chance to use custody as leverage, he has coerced his wife by depriving her of an important option. The use of this leverage was exploitative if he benefits financially because she cares for the children and perhaps because she cannot afford to fight for them.

Whether trades are less problematic if initiated by the person seeking more custodial time rather than by the person seeking more money is not obvious. Consider for example a mother who suggests receiving lower child support payments if the father does not seek primary custody. Perhaps her initiation indicates that she has reason to believe the father would actually have litigated had she not agreed to less child support. If so, the transaction was not coercive because it provides a benefit to both parents. However, payor initiation might indicate only that the mother fears litigation, which need not reflect actual likelihood of litigation.

Of course, not all trades of custodial terms for financial benefits coerce or exploit. . . . Because Charlie did not enter the negotiations demanding payment for something he would otherwise give for free, he has not coerced his wife. Nothing in the example suggests that he used his wife's desperation or attachment to the children to gain marital property.

Altman, *Lurking in the Shadow*, 68 So. CALIF. L. REV. 493, 515–16 (1995). Do you find Altman's distinctions persuasive? Would it matter if Charlie, in Hypothetical 3, agreed to the tradeoff not because he felt the need to spare his children the custody fight, but because he thought his chance of winning the fight wasn't good enough to make persistence worthwhile?

Even if one agrees upon a principle that distinguishes proper from improper bargaining, it may still be difficult to develop a practical legal rule that reliably implements it. For example, would it be a practical rule that allowed subsequent attacks on settlement agreements only when they resulted from negotiations in which one party threatened to seek custody he did not really want? There is an obvious difficulty in making such assessments of a party's motivations at some time in the past. One state attempted to address this problem by experimenting with bifurcated proceedings in contested divorces, in which adjudication of custody disputes did not take place until all other matters in the divorce had been decided. ARIZ. REV. STAT. ANN. § 25-328 (1976). (Alternative child support orders are formulated, and the appropriate one selected after the custody determination.) The goal was to eliminate custody contests that were actually the product of one party's hard bargaining for economic advantage. With the economic issues settled, there is no point to contesting custody unless one actually wants it. Perhaps the threat to contest custody is also less effective under such a rule, at least where the other spouse believes the threatener does not truly want custody, since the threat cannot be carried out until such time as it can achieve no purpose other than obtaining custody. In its current form the statute still requires that custody be decided last when a party so requests, but in the absence of a request that sequence is not required. ARIZ. REV. STAT. ANN. § 25-328 (2004).

The *ALI Principles* conclude that "a distinction between good-faith and bad-faith threats of litigation is unworkable" even while also expressing concern that "the potential for oppressive bargaining is substantial." *ALI Principles* § 3.13, Comment *d*. In the context of considering when to approve agreements that call for "substantially less child support" than the court would otherwise award, perhaps as a trade-off to forestall a threatened custody claim, the *Principles* call for the court to reject the child support terms unless it determines that the agreement "as a whole" is "consistent with the interests of the child." *ALI Principles* § 3.13. When would lower child support amount satisfy this test? One relatively easy case suggested by Illustration 1 of § 3.13 involves an agreement under which the obligor provides other financial assistance to the custodial household that he might not otherwise be required to provide, and which confers benefits upon the child equivalent to the foregone support. More generally, the *Principles* observe that clear and appropriate custody allocation rules are perhaps the most effective way to suppress improper bargaining tactics over custody. Referring to the custody allocation rules that the *Principles* themselves adopt in its Chapter Two, Comment *d* to § 3.13 explains:

> The frequency of cases in which a custody challenge is threatened and then relinquished in exchange for a reduction of that parent's child-support obligation is a function of the bargaining positions of the parties, which derive in part from the rules regulating the allocation of custodial responsibility. The stronger a parent's claim to custodial responsibility, the less vulnerable the parent is to pressure to compromise child support in order to preserve that connection. In Chapter 2, these Principles base the allocation of custodial responsibility on past exercise of caretaking functions. Thus, the parent likely to have the stronger connection to the child should experience less pressure to compromise child support in order to preserve that connection. Similarly, the other parent's interest in access is guarded by a guarantee of access sufficient to maintain a strong relationship with the child even though that may be more contact than otherwise justified by that parent's preseparation caretaking role. Thus, Chapter 2 minimizes the extent to which either parent may be pressured to compromise child support in order [to] maintain an appropriate relationship with the child.

Does the problem of strategic threats to contest custody arise often enough to require a solution? Data on that point is hard to obtain, because of course one cannot easily establish the motivation for a threatened or actual custody contest. Altman surveyed members of the Family Law Section of the California Bar, and asked in what percentage of their prior year's family law cases involving minor children had "opposing counsel or their clients ever stated or clearly implied that they might litigate over custodial time if your client did not agree to a favorable financial settlement, [including proposals reported to you by your clients]." Forty percent said this had not happened in any of their cases; the mean response of all attorneys was 13 percent of the cases. Altman also reports data from several surveys in other states, but they use widely varying methods and obtain widely varying results.

It does not appear that standards of professional conduct would bar an attorney from tactical assertions of custody claim intended to obtain some other benefit for the client. *See* Becker, *Ethical Concerns in Negotiating Family Law Agreements*, 30 Fam. L.Q. 587, 628–29 (1996).

Note that the law generally imposes substantive limitations on custody and child support terms in separation agreements that do not arise from concerns over improper bargaining tactics. Most important is the general rule that such provisions always remain modifiable as necessary to protect the child's interest (the precise standard for modification varying among the states). Trade-offs of custody and support may also be vulnerable under such provisions. In that sense, the parties do not possess complete contractual freedom to specify by agreement the support and custody terms of their divorce. More consideration to these substantive limitations is given at pages 827-830 *infra*.

[3] WHERE THERE IS ONLY ONE ATTORNEY

[a] Joint Representation

It is common for separation agreements to be negotiated and executed by parties who are jointly assisted by a single attorney. The ethical obligations applicable to attorneys in these situations are addressed below in Notes 1 and 2. But the question of whether the resulting agreement is itself vulnerable to attack by an aggrieved party is in principle separate from the question of whether the lawyer complied with all applicable rules of professional conduct. In general, enforcement of the agreement cannot be resisted on this basis. In *Levine v. Levine*, 56 N.Y.2d 42, 436 N.E.2d 476, 451 N.Y.S.2d 26 (1982),

> The separation agreement was prepared by an attorney, related to the husband by marriage, who had previously represented the husband in connection with his business and who had known both parties for a number of years. The husband initially contacted the attorney and informed him that he had discussed the possibility of a separation agreement with his wife and that the couple had agreed on the essential terms. The attorney then arranged to meet with the wife at his office.
>
> At this meeting, the attorney told the wife that he was involved in the matter only because the basic terms of the agreement had already been settled by the parties and that the wife was free to seek the advice of another attorney. Based on conversations with both parties, the attorney prepared a draft agreement. Further negotiations and consultations followed, after which a final agreement was drawn up, thoroughly reviewed by plaintiff, and then signed by her. . . .

The court held that the fact that the same attorney represented both parties in the preparation of the agreement did not require its "automatic nullification."

> While the absence of independent representation is a significant factor to be taken into consideration when determining whether a separation agreement was freely and fairly entered into, the fact that each party retained the same attorney does not, in and of itself, provide a basis for rescission. . . . [W]here one attorney has represented both parties to the agreement, a question of overreaching on the part of the party who is the prime beneficiary of the attorney's assistance may arise. Nevertheless, as long as the attorney fairly advises the parties of both the salient issues and the consequences of joint representation, and the separation agreement arrived at was fair, rescission will not be granted. While the potential conflict of interests inherent in such joint representation suggests that the

husband and wife should retain separate counsel, the parties have an absolute right to be represented by the same attorney provided "there has been full disclosure between the parties, not only of all relevant facts but also of their contextual significance, and there has been an absence of inequitable conduct or other infirmity which might vitiate the execution of the agreement."

In *Marriage of Egedi*, 105 Cal. Rptr. 2d 518 (App. 2001), the husband seeking to avoid enforcement of the settlement agreement claimed the attorney's disclosures were insufficient to permit his informed consent to the dual representation. While the trial court agreed with him, he lost on appeal. It may in fact be difficult to imagine what more the attorney could have done. He initially resisted the parties' request that he represent them both (he had previously represented each of them individually in unrelated matters), forcefully asserted his concern over a conflict of interest, and insisted on their signed acknowledgment that he advised them to seek independent counsel. After the parties reached an understanding and reduced it to writing without any participation by the attorney, he explained that his only role would be to type up their agreement after adding some "standard provisions." He thus obtained their consent to excluding any "advisory capacity" from his role, and he consistently refused to discuss the substance of the agreement's terms with either spouse. All this was applauded by the appeals court, which even observed that a "single attorney acting as a scrivener should not advise the parties of the pros and cons of their agreement so that they might 'unagree.' This would defeat the very purpose for which they sought assistance." *Id.* at 523.

What if the *Egedi* agreement contained terms that the attorney believed grossly one-sided? Is he supposed to remain silent in the face of such facts? Might not the parties, despite their understanding, assume from his silence that their agreement contained no unreasonable, unconscionable, or obviously unenforceable provisions, or provisions that, for example, subject them to avoidable tax liabilities? Recognizing this possibility the court observes in footnote that in such a case the attorney might "decline to act as a scrivener," but the court believed this case itself presented no such facts.

On one hand, the *Egedi* court seems right that the attorney was clear as could be about the limited nature of his role. On the other hand, is it appropriate for an attorney to agree to such a limited role? If the parties only want a scrivener, why do they need an attorney at all, one might ask. This court didn't, and that is surprising in light of an earlier California Case, *Ishmael v. Millington,* 241 Cal. App. 2d 520, 50 Cal. Rptr. 592 (1966). After discovering that in the divorce agreement she signed away most of her community property rights, the wife brought a malpractice action against the attorney who handled their divorce. His defense was that she had "sought no advice from the attorney and was given none," and that even in her deposition the wife conceded that "in signing the complaint and property settlement agreement she relied solely on her husband and did not rely on the attorney." The court observed:

> Divorces are frequently uncontested; the parties may make their financial arrangements peaceably and honestly; vestigial chivalry may

impel them to display the wife as the injured plaintiff; the husband may then seek out and pay an attorney to escort the wife through the formalities of adjudication. We describe these facts of life without necessarily approving them. Even in that situation the attorney's professional obligations do not permit his descent to the level of a scrivener. . . . A husband and wife at the brink of division of their marital assets have an obvious divergence of interests. Representing the wife in an arm's length divorce, an attorney of ordinary professional skill would demand some verification of the husband's financial statement; or, at the minimum, inform the wife that the husband's statement was unconfirmed, that wives may be cheated, that prudence called for investigation and verification. Deprived of such disclosure, the wife cannot make a free and intelligent choice. Representing both spouses in an uncontested divorce situation (whatever the ethical implications), the attorney's professional obligations demand no less. He may not set a shallow limit on the depth to which he will represent the wife.

The trial court's summary judgment in the attorney's favor was reversed, although the ultimate outcome of the malpractice action is not reported. *Egedi* and *Ishmael* could be reconciled by observing that a rule denying the cheated spouse the right to avoid the agreement need not also deny that spouse recovery for the loss against the attorney who failed to advise of the danger. Yet *Egedi* hardly invites that reading; to the contrary, it suggests that the attorney has a duty to avoid pointing out possibly unfair terms to the disadvantaged spouse, for fear of upsetting the agreement. If that is indeed the rule, then surely the attorney finding herself in that position ought to withdraw, as the *Egedi* court suggests she may. Consider, however, whether such a withdrawal might not inevitably suggest to the parties that the attorney believes the agreement problematic.

Intimately connected with the question of whether an attorney's conduct in joint representation constitutes malpractice is the question of whether it violates rules of professional conduct. The old A.B.A. Code of Professional Responsibility took a very skeptical approach toward joint representation. It provided in Disciplinary Rule 5-105(c) that

> a lawyer may represent multiple clients if it is obvious that he can adequately represent the interest of each and if each consents to the representation after full disclosure of the possible effect of such representation on the exercise of his independent professional judgment on behalf of each.

Under this language, even the consent of both clients may be insufficient to permit joint representation, since it may not be "obvious that [the lawyer] can adequately represent the interest of each" client if there is in fact a potential conflict between them.

Most states today follow the A.B.A.'s newer Model Rules of Professional Conduct, first promulgated in 1983. In its original form it had two provisions potentially applicable to the question of joint representation at divorce. Model Rule 1.7 stated the general rule dealing with conflicts of interest that can arise when a lawyer represents two persons whose interests may be adverse, while

Rule 2.2 dealt with "intermediation," and was intended to apply to the case where the lawyer acted to facilitate such parties' reaching an agreement. The American Bar Association adopted major changes to the Model Rules in 2002; included among them was deletion of Rule 2.2 and the revision of Rule 1.7. Many states had not yet adopted these changes at the time of this book's preparation.

The language of new Rule 1.7 seems both more clear and less tolerant of multiple representation. Subdivision (a) states the basic rule ordinarily barring an attorney from representing two clients whenever "the representation of one client will be directly adverse to another client." Subsection (b) nonetheless creates a limited exception permitting such representation if

(1) the lawyer reasonably believes that the lawyer will be able to provide competent and diligent representation to each affected client;

(2) the representation is not prohibited by law;

(3) the representation does not involve the assertion of a claim by one client against another client represented by the lawyer in the same litigation or other proceeding before a tribunal; and

(4) each affected client gives informed consent, confirmed in writing.

Divorcing spouses must eventually become opposing parties in a lawsuit, at which point the Rule clearly bars joint representation under subsection (b)(3), even if both spouses consented. Nonetheless, lawyers often consult with both spouses up to the point of concluding their separation agreement, even though the lawyer can be counsel of record for only one of them in the divorce papers then filed before the court. Is that practice consistent with Rule 1.7? Paragraph 4's requirement of written informed consent means that it cannot be if the lawyer does not first obtain consent in writing from both spouses, after having explained to them the risks and dangers of such joint representation, including its effects on the attorney obligations of loyalty and confidentiality. Official Comment 19 to the Code suggests that clients may wish to weigh the added cost of securing a second attorney against such risks. Such added costs are of course a common concern in divorce proceedings. What seems clear from the Rule, however, is that it is for the client, and not the attorney, to make the judgment of whether the monetary savings justify the risks of joint representation. The client cannot weigh those risks properly if the attorney does not adequately describe them. An adequate description ought to include, one might think, more than abstractions. Specific illustrations of potential conflicts between the parties about the identification, classification, and valuation of property could, for example, bring home the nature of the risk to the naiive client who might not otherwise appreciate it. On the other hand, such illustrations might have little meaning to some clients who have no significant property. The trick lies in assessing the kind of warnings most appropriate to particular clients in advance of undertaking their joint representation.

It is also important to keep in mind that consent is not sufficient in every case. Subsection (b)(1) bars joint representation if the lawyer does not "reasonably believe" that it is possible to provide "competent and diligent representation" to both of the spouses. This independent requirement is not avoided by client consent, even fully informed client consent. The trick here is to determine when a lawyer can "reasonably believe" these facts. This question is addressed through example in G. HAZARD & W. HODES, THE LAW OF LAWYERING §§ 11.4, 11.11, and 11.15, at pages 11–12, 11–28, and 11–47 (3d. Edition, 2004 Supp.)

The illustration involves a case in which both husband and wife come to the lawyer claiming to have worked out the details of their separation agreement, and ask him to "look over the figures" and then "represent them both in their 'amicable' divorce." The authors conclude that while the relationship between the parties is not antagonistic, it is "surely . . . directly adverse," so that Rule 1.7(a) applies. Thus the dispositive question is whether the clients can give effective consent. The authors point out that there is an unavoidable risk of as yet unknown magnitude that the lawyer cannot offer his best efforts on behalf of one client without materially limiting his representation of the other. Effective representation would be "extremely difficult," the authors conclude, if the attorney senses that the parties are not equally committed to the figures that they present, or would not equally welcome suggested revisions to their draft agreement. If the lawyer views the agreement as one-sided, as compared to agreements in comparable situations, the lawyer must feel free to express that view or he is not properly serving the interests of the disadvantaged client. Yet his duty to the advantaged client is to remain silent.

Is representation in this context "consentable," or must the reasonable lawyer conclude that competent and diligent representation cannot be provided simultaneously to both parties? The answer may require a deeper understanding of the clients' goals. Perhaps, for example, one is confident that both clients appreciate the possibility of such potential conflicts but consent anyway because both believe it best to settle on terms seen as fair by objective third parties. They thus affirmatively desire the attorney's assessment, even if the consequence would be a refashioning of the terms that altered the relative outcome. Persons who see themselves in a long-term relationship may well think in such terms, believing that any short-term advantage realized from a one-sided agreement would be offset by its longer-term costs to a relationship they wish to maintain. Divorcing parties could feel this way even though they are obviously ending their marital relationship, for any of a variety of reasons, such as their joint interest in maintaining a cooperative approach in their post-divorce parental roles. Assisting the parties to reach this kind of fair agreement is the kind of situation contemplated by the now abandoned Rule 2.2. At least some informed commentators, such as Hazard and Hodes, believe it may still be permissible under the revised Rule 1.7. But even they also caution that the lawyer must be alert to the possibility that the parties are not equally committed to such a vision of their task. If the lawyer does not have confidence that they are, then the common representation is not consentable because the lawyer cannot reasonably believe it possible to provide both clients with adequate representation. Making this judgment may be extremely difficult. The attitude of divorcing spouses may be more volatile than at first appears. Comment 29 to Rule 1.7 in the newly revised Model Rules cautions that the clients should be advised that common representation requires each client to assume greater responsibility for decisions than is necessary when they are separately represented with each lawyer free to pursue his own client's interest more vigorously.

It should not necessarily be assumed that separate representation is more likely to lead to a relationship of animosity. An attorney with clearly undivided loyalty to one spouse may be more effective in persuading that spouse that a less aggressive stance on short-term goals will be more effective in furthering his or her long-term interests, than would an attorney attempting to represent both parties. Common representation would seem unlikely to offer much advantage to the parties apart from the potential savings on attorney fees when it is successful. Yet those savings will be important to many divorcing spouses. For those with limited resources especially, the risk that common representation will leave one or both inadequately counseled may seem low enough to accept, given that less may be at stake in their allocation of property or the size of any support award. Ultimately, the ethical rules appear to reflect the uneasy tension between the ideal of separate representation and the reality for many divorcing couples of limited resources.

It must also be noted that the risk of common representation is greater where the attorney has a preexisting relationship with one of the spouses. The attorney may not be able to maintain his obligation of confidentiality with respect to information gained in that prior representation without compromising his obligations to the other spouse. If the spouse with the prior relationship is unwilling to waive the attorney's duty of confidentiality, common representation in the divorce would not be possible. *See* Comment 31 to Rule 1.7. Finally, the position of the American Academy of Matrimonial Lawyers is considerably less nuanced than the Model Rules on the question of joint representation. "An attorney should not represent both husband and wife even if they do not wish to obtain independent representation." American Academy of Matrimonial Lawyers, THE BOUNDS OF ADVOCACY § 2.20, at p. 25 (1991). While acknowledging that such common representation was permitted within the limitations of Model Rule 2.2, (which was still part of the Model Rules when the Academy's standards were adopted), the comment to this section concludes that "it is impossible for the attorney to provide impartial advice" to both husband and wife and that "even a seemingly amicable separation or divorce may result in bitter litigation over financial matters or custody." The Academy's standards do not have legal force but they do represent the collective judgment of this voluntary association.

[b]   Where Only One Party is Represented

The material in the preceding section considered the problems confronted by the attorney who attempts to service both husband and wife. One way to deal with the conflict, of course, is to define only one of the spouses as your client. The other is then unrepresented. While this approach eliminates the problem of conflict, it can raise its own difficulties. *Tenneboe v. Tenneboe*, 558 So. 2d 470 (Fla. App. 1990), provides a good example. The husband sought to set aside an agreement that obligated him to pay $700 monthly in alimony and child support against a net income of only $800 monthly, earned in a seven-day work week. The agreement also called for the husband to quit claim to the wife all his interest in the marital home, leaving her with the parties' full equity of $30,000. He assumed all their debts, and kept only a pension plan and credit union account worth approximately $10,500.

> The husband . . . was not represented by an attorney at the time of either the preparation or execution of the agreement, which was drafted in its entirety by the attorney representing the wife. He testified that when he signed the agreement at the wife's attorney's office, he protested that the payments were more than he "could handle," and inquired of the wife's attorney whether, by virtue of the agreement, the permanent alimony payments were set for the rest of his life. In response, the wife's attorney told him that he could return to court at a future time to have the payments modified, but according to the husband, the wife's attorney did not tell him that he would have to show a substantial change in circumstances or financial ability in order to obtain such reduction. . . . The husband testified that he signed the agreement at that time in reliance on the attorney's representation, and that he would not have signed the agreement had he known that in order to prevail on a later request for modification, he would have to establish a change in circumstances or financial ability.

While the wife and her attorney disputed the precise content of the conversation, it was undisputed that her attorney had a conversation with the husband concerning his ability to pay the amounts called for in the agreement. The trial court nonetheless denied his motion to set aside the agreement, but the appeals court reversed.

> If the wife's attorney told the husband that he could return to court later to have the payments reduced, without also explaining that he would have to establish a substantial change in circumstances or financial ability, he misinformed him. Indeed, the husband's efforts to obtain relief in the trial court met with resounding defeat, both at the hearing on the motion to set aside the agreement as well as at the final hearing of dissolution, which only served to confirm the intricacies inherent in successfully obtaining such relief. In any event, the advice given by the wife's attorney was, at best, an oversimplification. [¶] . . . [W]e conclude that the trial court abused its discretion in refusing to set aside the property settlement agreement. The husband's evidence on the matters of misrepresentation and overreaching was persuasive enough to steer the exercise of discretion in the direction of affording the husband relief from the rigorous provisions of the agreement.

Rule 4.3 of the Model Rules of Professional Conduct applies to a lawyer dealing with an unrepresented opposing person. It requires the lawyer to refrain from saying or implying that he is "disinterested," and requires the lawyer to correct any misunderstandings the unrepresented party may have as to the lawyer's role. *Tenneboe* quotes the comment to Rule 4.3 that the unrepresented party might think the lawyer is "a disinterested authority on the law even when the lawyer represents a client" and cautions that the "lawyer should not give advice to an unrepresented person other than the advice to obtain counsel." Revisions to the Rules after *Tenneboe* strengthen these points by moving them from the Comment to the Rule itself. The Comment now explains that the lawyer can negotiate with an unrepresented person on behalf of the client, by explaining the terms on which the client will settle a dispute and preparing the necessary papers for signature by the other person as well as the client. But it cautions that the lawyer can undertake such a role only after explaining that he or she represents the client only. The conduct of the *Tenneboe* attorney probably violated these guidelines, for both husband and wife agreed — and the attorney did not deny — that he discussed the alimony provision with the husband. Even if his explanation of it was accurate — a matter in dispute — he still appeared to give the husband legal advice on the substance of the agreement he had prepared as the wife's attorney. *See also* Note, *Professional Responsibility: Duties Owed to An Unrepresented Party*, 44 Fla. L. Rev. 489 (1992).

[4] THE IMPACT OF THE DECREE ON THE AGREEMENT: OF MERGER AND MODIFICATION

ALI Principles § 7.10

§ 7.10 Incorporation of the Terms of a Separation Agreement in a Decree

(1) Except as provided by Paragraph (3), if the court has not found the terms of a separation agreement unenforceable under § 7.09 and if the agreement does not provide otherwise, the court should incorporate the terms of the separation agreement in the decree of dissolution. . . .

(2) Unless otherwise agreed by the parties, terms of a separation agreement that are incorporated in a decree are merged in the decree.

(3) In those jurisdictions that do not allow a court to enforce decree terms that the court does not have the power to order on its own, terms of a separation agreement that a court does not have the power to enforce as decree terms, but that are otherwise enforceable as contract terms, are not incorporated in the decree and survive the decree as enforceable contract terms.

(4) Terms of a separation agreement incorporated in a decree are enforceable by all remedies available for the enforcement of judgments generally.

(5) Incorporated terms of a separation agreement that survive the decree as contract terms are automatically modified by modification of the decree.

NOTES

1. *Merger of the Agreement Into the Decree.* Generalization on the subject of merger is difficult because of subtle variations among the states in the applicable procedural rules. Do the parties' intentions as expressed in their agreement determine whether merger occurs? Is there a particular form in which those intentions must be expressed to be effective? In the absence of any expression by the parties, does the agreement merge or not? In answering these sorts of questions, state law may vary enormously. Compare,

for example, *Binder v. Binder,* 390 N.E.2d 260 (Mass. App. 1979), holding that merger is precluded if the agreement provides that it survives the decree, even if the decree incorporates the agreement by reference, with *Appels-Meehan v. Appels,* 805 P.2d 415 (Ariz. App. 1991), holding that there is merger unless the agreement contains language "unequivocally precluding merger," and *Walters v. Walters,* 298 S.E.2d 338 (N.C. 1983), holding that any separation agreement brought to the court for its approval merges into the decree, no matter what it says. *See* Sharp, *Semantics as Jurisprudence: The Elevation of Form Over Substance in the Treatment of Separation Agreements in North Carolina,* 69 N.C. L. Rev. 319 (1991).

Nonetheless, § 7.10 of the *ALI Principles* sets forth the basic framework as generally understood. The parties' agreement is normally but a prelude to the divorce decree that incorporates its terms. Whatever the necessary local procedure, the usual result is that the agreement is merged into the decree once it has been issued. One effect of merger is that the agreement no longer has independent status as a contract, and contract actions to enforce it therefore become unavailable. The contract terms are instead enforceable as terms of the decree. As a general matter, this is an enforcement advantage, because there are remedies available for enforcement of a decree that are not available in a contract action and which are usually more effective. For example, the spousal maintenance and child support portions of a decree (but not a contract) can be enforced by contempt, as well as periodic wage withholding or the diversion of tax refunds. *E.g., Ex Parte Hall*, 854 S.W.2d 656 (Tex. 1993) (contempt not available as remedy to enforce support and maintenance payments based upon premarital agreement rather than judicial decree). On the other hand, state law typically allows courts to modify the child support and alimony provisions of a decree, including decrees based upon agreements, while contract terms of course cannot normally be modified except by the agreement of both parties. Nonetheless, the modification of agreement-based decrees is itself a matter on which state law varies, and is addressed in more detail in Notes 3 and 4, and with respect to alimony, at pages 832-834 below.

State law also varies as to the consequences of nonmerger. For example, in *Binder,* the court held that without merger, the separation agreement survives as a contract creating obligations independent of the decree, that the contract is enforceable by an ordinary contract action, and that the decree is enforceable like an ordinary decree. Needless to say, having two potential remedies for any nonpayment can be confusing, especially since the contract cannot ordinarily be modified but the decree can, and modification of the obligation established in the decree would not affect the parties' contractual obligations. Other cases hold that where the agreement specifies it shall be incorporated into the decree but not merged, the result is not only survival of the agreement as a contract, but also preclusion of any judicial modification of the decree or enforcement of it by contempt. *Riffenburg v. Riffenburg,* 585 A.2d 627 (R.I. 1991) (alimony); *Mendelson v. Mendelson,* 541 A.2d 1331 (Md. Sp. App. 1988) (alimony provision); *Sonder v. Sonder,* 549 A.2d 155 (Pa. Super. 1988) (child support provision). Especially as to child support, this last result is not without difficulty; if the parties may not initially bind the court to an agreement to waive child support entirely, it would seem they should also be unable to prevent the enforcement of child support obligations through contempt.

One reason the parties may wish to avoid merger is that they have agreed on a contract that includes terms that the divorce court could not order on its own. The most common example is an agreement to pay child support past the age of majority while the child attends college. Many states do not allow support orders for college students over age 18, even if the parties agree. In these states the only way such a term can be enforced is to ensure that it does not merge into the decree, but survives as a contract term enforceable in an action for breach. *Solomon v. Findley,* 808 P.2d 294 (Ariz. 1991). In other states, however, a provision in the agreement that the court could not order on its own can nonetheless be incorporated into the decree and enforced as any other provision; in these states merger is probably preferable. *See, e.g., Foltz v. Foltz,* 232 S.E.2d 66 (Ga. 1977) (provision obligating husband to support wife's child); *Peterson v. Leonard,* 622 A.2d 87 (Me. 1993) (same).

For a general treatment of the problem of merger, see Brogan, *Divorce Settlement Agreements: The Problem of Merger or Incorporation and the Status of the Agreement in Relation to the Decree,* 67 NEB. L. REV. 235 (1988).

2. *Challenges to An Agreement After Merger.* In *Weber* and *Tennenboe* objections to the agreement were raised before the decree had been issued or the terms approved under the jurisdiction's procedures for routine review of all agreements. But what if objection is first raised later, after the court presumably approved the agreement and merged it into the resulting decree? One basis for upsetting a decree already entered is fraud, and it is possible, for example, for an attorney's conduct with an unrepresented opposing party to cross that line. *See, e.g., Adkins v. Adkins,* 186 Cal. Rptr. 818 (App. 1982) (agreement held void as having been secured by fraud where wife's attorney secured the uneducated husband's consent by misleading him concerning his rights). Yet, the traditional fraud rule may not be adequate to deal with all cases of abuse. Part of the problem is the distinction between intrinsic and extrinsic fraud. The traditional rule requires "extrinsic" fraud to set aside a judgment. Some courts have abandoned this distinction, in part because it is so difficult to apply, *e.g., St. Pierre v. Edmonds,* 645 P.2d 615 (Utah 1982). Other courts continue to struggle with explaining the difference. *Stevenot v. Stevenot,* 202 Cal. Rptr. 116 (App. 1984), explains it this way:

> Fraud is extrinsic where the defrauded party was deprived of the opportunity to present his or her claim or defense to the court, that is, where he or she was kept in ignorance or in some manner, other than from his or her own conduct, fraudulently prevented from fully participating in the proceeding. . . .
>
> Any fraud is intrinsic if a party has been given notice of the action and has not been prevented from participating therein, that is, if he or she had the opportunity to present his or her case and to protect himself or herself from any mistake or fraud of his or her adversary, but unreasonably neglected to do so.

Under this approach, intrinsic fraud permits reopening the matter addressed by the decree, but extrinsic fraud does not. For example, in *Marriage of Alexander,* 261 Cal. Rptr. 9 (App. 1989), neither party had counsel; the husband prepared their *pro se* divorce papers based on his wife's waiver of any interest in his pension, their joint bank accounts or spousal support. But there was no extrinsic fraud because the wife "was not deliberately kept in ignorance of the proceeding or fraudulently prevented . . . from presenting her claims. Any failure was due to her own failure to act diligently." She was thus denied the chance to reopen the settlement agreed to 15 months earlier. Compare *Grissom v. Grissom,* 35 Cal. Rptr. 2d 530 (App. 1994), in which the husband told the wife that the papers he presented to her were needed to dismiss their pending divorce action. The papers in fact divided their property and allowed him to proceed with a divorce without notifying her. He filed the papers while continuing to live with the wife for ten years as if they were married — at which time the wife discovered they were not. Her motion to set aside both the dissolution and the marital settlement was allowed, the court finding extrinsic fraud.

One common claim is that one party intentionally misled the other as to the value of certain marital property assets; the defense will often be that the statement of value was an opinion rather than a fact, and cannot therefore constitute fraud. The cases divide. *E.g., Greger v. Greger,* 578 A.2d 162 (Conn. App. 1990) (constitutes fraud); *contra, Billington v. Billington,* 578 A.2d 674 (Conn. App. 1990) (*Greger* does not apply where fraud perpetrated only on party and not on the court, and where the party had not exercised diligence in protecting herself from the fraud). See also the cases collected in *Hresko v. Hresko,* 574 A.2d 24 (Md. Sp. App. 1990) and *Fraud and Duress — Relief from Judgment,* 12 EQUITABLE DIST. J. 73 (1995). Provisions in the separation agreement in which the parties each warrant that they have made full disclosure can provide a basis for later claims. *E.g., Hess v. Hess,* 580 A.2d 357 (Pa. Super. 1990) (wife allowed compensatory and punitive damages for fraud and breach of contract where husband concealed assets and agreement warranted that each party had made full disclosure). One court found extrinsic fraud where the husband and the wife's attorney were having an affair during the divorce proceedings. *Nobles v. Earhart,* 769 S.W.2d 869 (Tenn. App. 1988).

Some courts stretch traditional fraud doctrine to permit a post-judgment attack on egregious separation agreements. Professor Sharp suggests the law would be better served by a general rule requiring disclosure. Sharp, *Fairness Standards and Separation Agreements,* 132 U. PA. L. REV. 1399, 1410, 1426–27. See *Miranda v. Miranda,* 449 N.W.2d 158 (Minn. 1989) and the cases collected at 3 EQUITABLE DIST. J. 73–76, 154–55 (1986). Note that even with claims of fraud, statutes of limitation may bar later attack on the judgment.

The American Law Institute recommends abandoning reliance on the fraud doctrine in favor of a simpler approach, set out in § 7.11 of the *ALI Principles.* This provision generally allows the court to set aside any decree based upon an agreement that it would have rejected under § 7.09 (described above), had objection then been raised, if the "incorporated terms of the decree were substantially less favorable to the moving party than they would have been without the agreement." This power is subject to two limitations only: time limitations imposed by state law, and the rights of third parties. A typical source of time limitations under state law are provisions of state procedural rules modeled upon Rule 60 of the Federal Rules of Civil Procedure, which allows the court, on such terms as are just, to grant relief from judgment on diverse grounds, including: (1) mistake, inadvertence, surprise, or excusable neglect; (2) newly discovered evidence; (3) fraud (whether extrinsic or intrinsic), misrepresentation, or other misconduct of an adverse party; or (6) "any other reason justifying relief from the operation of the judgment." Rule 60 provides that the motion shall be made within a reasonable time and, for reasons (1), (2), and (3), not more than one year after entry of judgment. As for the rights of third parties, ordinary equity principles would usually bar compromising the claims of innocent third parties to property they purchased for value subsequent to its allocation under the challenged decree.

3. *Should Agreement-Based Custody and Support Terms Be More Modifiable Than Adjudication-Based Ones?* Some courts treat agreement-based decrees as *more easily* modifiable than custody decrees ordered by the court after litigation. Courts that apply such a "dual standard" to modification petitions may believe that judges can make better custody decisions than parents, perhaps because they are objective, or have the assistance of professionals such as social workers or psychologists, so that an initial custody decision made by a judge is entitled to more deference than one made by the parents. For a critical review of these cases, see Sharp, *Modification of Agreement Based Custody Decrees: Unitary or Dual Standard?*, 68 VA. L. REV. 1263, 1278–79 (1982).

If the custody terms of an agreement are more modifiable than those imposed by a judge, what of the agreement's child support terms? *Consider Thomas v. Thomas,* 120 Cal. App. 3d 33, 173 Cal. Rptr. 844 (1981). The husband sought a reduction in child support from $125 to $100 monthly. The original order had been entered in 1976 pursuant to the parties' agreement, and the record supporting the 1976 order contained no evidence of the circumstances at that time. (Such an empty record will be common in settled cases, as has been noted in other contexts as well, Fiss, *Comment, Against Settlement,* 93 YALE L.J. 1073 (1984)). Over the wife's objection, the court concluded that the trial judge had discretion to revise the child support award on the basis of current circumstances alone, without considering whether the circumstances had changed:

> Our decision should not be construed as discouraging parties from entering into stipulated dispositions because of the concern they will later be upset without a showing of changed circumstances. Parties may either include in their stipulation the relevant circumstances on which it is based or, at either interlocutory time or on motion to modify, file a financial declaration or otherwise show his or her version of the circumstances. On motion to modify the resisting party may assert and show the lack of change as a bar to the motion. The record does not show any of these things was done in this case.

For a similar result, see *Essex v. Ayres,* 503 So. 2d 1365 (Fla. App. 1987). Does the problem of an empty record explain the lack of deference to the agreement's custody terms as well?

4. *Should Agreement Based Decrees Be Less Modifiable?* One might conclude they should, on the reasoning that the contract would not be modifiable without approval of both parties, and therefore the decree based upon it should be subject to the same rule. Because the court's obligations to protect the interests of children are regarded as paramount, this claim is not usually accepted with respect to child support or child custody — indeed, the opposite inclination is sometimes seen, as explained in Note 3. But alimony may be a different matter. Even though they are normally modifiable, one might regard it inappropriate to alter alimony terms based on a decree, given the likelihood that they are part of an overall financial package that includes nonmodifiable provisions on property allocation. This conclusion might be strengthened if the agreement itself provided for such non-modifiability These possibilities are all considered below in Section B5c, on the enforceability of no-modification clauses. The next section also gives fuller consideration to the enforceability of provisions concerning children.

[5] LIMITATIONS ON THE SUBJECT OR TERMS OF SEPARATION AGREEMENTS

[a] Children

Almost any separation agreement ending a marriage with children will contain custody arrangements and child support terms. But in these areas courts assert a special role. Section 3.06 of the MMDA excludes terms "providing for the support, custody, and visitation of children" from the rule that otherwise makes provisions of a separation agreement binding on the court unless it finds them unconscionable. The same section also provides that these terms remain modifiable even if the agreement attempts to limit their modifiability. These rules are typical, and have the purpose of ensuring that the court can always revise the agreement, initially or through modification, as needed to protect the interests of the child.

Should courts retain such power to overrule parental decisions? The *ALI Principles* retain but limit that judicial authority, providing in § 206 that the court should order the custody terms agreed upon by the parents unless "the agreement is not knowing or voluntary, or would be harmful to the child." Thus, apart from defects in the bargaining process considered in the prior section, the court's power to overrule the parental arrangements may be exercised only when it finds such harm.

In *Ayo v. Ayo*, 235 Cal. Rptr. 458 (App. 1987), Patricia had a four year old son by a prior relationship at the time of her marriage to Larry. Larry adopted him within a year. The parties were divorced when the boy was 8 and support and visitation orders were entered. But almost immediately the parties had disputes over both the visitation and support arrangements. When the boy's biological father began to visit him a year after the divorce, the parties agreed to terminate visitation, and Patricia agreed to "hold Larry harmless from any claims" involving the boy. Their agreement was incorporated into the court's decree in 1979 when the boy was 9. But in 1985 Patricia sought current child support from Larry, who argued that even if he had to pay currently, he should have a right to eventual reimbursement from Patricia under their agreement. The court rejected this claim.

[T]o uphold Larry's contention would mean that the broad powers of the courts regarding the support of minor children could be thwarted by the subterfuge of an indemnity provision in a contract between the parties. [U]nder such a provision a parent could find himself or herself allocating resources for indemnification that would otherwise be used to support the child, thereby harming the child's welfare. In sum, the 1979 agreement fails on public policy grounds. . . . [¶] [T]he rights of the contracting parties under agreements such as this one affecting children must yield to the welfare of the children. [¶] [T]he 1979 agreement was an attempt to completely obviate the clear and strong policy of this state that a parent must support his children. . . .

Saying it was "not without sympathy" for Larry, given the earlier judicial approval of the agreement and his reliance upon that, the court noted that Patricia had not sought support arrearages for the period between the 1979 agreement and her 1985 claim to renew Larry's support obligation, and observed that were she to seek such arrearages, "issues of waiver and estoppel would undoubtedly have to be addressed." In effect then, the *Ayo* court suggested that it would accept the agreement subject to the court's power to modify it as the children's needs required. But the case can also be read to suggest that the initial judicial approval of the agreement was mistaken, so that Larry should never have been allowed to avoid support obligations pursuant to it, even if the court was not prepared to penalize him now for the earlier court's mistake.

Was the original decision in *Ayo* wrong to have approved this agreement? The *Ayo* fact pattern is not uncommon: an estranged father agrees to forego visitation in exchange for the custodial mother's agreement to forego child support. The deal may be struck, as in *Ayo,* after the divorce, when the father-child estrangement has occurred. Or it may be the parental arrangement from the outset. Such understandings seem particularly common between nonmarital parents. What is unusual about *Ayo* is that the parties formalized this arrangement in an agreement incorporated in a judicial decree. Because most courts would find such agreements not in the child's interests, they are rarely offered to courts and more rarely accepted. *Ayo* demonstrates they may not be enforceable even if approved, at least as to future support. Recall as well that most states hold that a spousal agreement does not alone justify a child support award that departs from prevailing guidelines. Such a rule clearly casts doubt on any no-visitation/no-support agreement, which by definition does not comply with support guidelines. *See DePalmo v. DePalmo*, 679 N.E.2d 266 (Ohio 1997) (holding husband's waiver of all support invalid, as the court has the obligation to test any proposal put forth by the parents against the support guidelines).

Sometimes the parties attempt to settle the child support obligation in a lump sum; the entire agreement may or may not include a visitation tradeoff as well. For example, in *Kelley v. Kelley*, 449 S.E.2d 55 (Va. 1994), the divorce decree incorporated the parties' agreement under which the husband relinquished to the wife his share of the equity in the marital home, valued at $40,000, in exchange for which "the husband shall never be responsible for payment of child support." The agreement also required the wife to indemnify the husband were he ever ordered to pay support. Six years later the husband petitioned "for definite periods of visitation" with the children, the wife counterclaimed for child support, and the husband replied with a motion asking the court to order the wife to reimburse him for any support he was required to pay. The court held the support provisions of the agreement, and the decree that incorporated them, void as a violation of the rule that "parents cannot contract away their children's right to support nor can a court be precluded by agreement from exercising its power to decree child support." It therefore affirmed the trial court order requiring support and barring the indemnification. For a similar result on similar facts, but with the genders reversed, see *Reimer v. Reimer*, 502 N.W.2d 231 (N.D. 1993).

The *ALI Principles* may be somewhat more willing to accept parental arrangements in these cases. *See* Illustration 3 of § 3.13 of the *Principles*:

> Sandra and Richard are the parents of eight-year-old Charlene, who was born while Sandra was still in high school and living in her parents' home. Sandra and Richard have never lived together and Sandra has always been Charlene's residential parent. Richard, a low-wage earner who has been able to pay only small amounts of child support, has visited Charlene sporadically, generally arriving unannounced on major holidays, sometimes in a state of inebriation. Sandra married Bob three years ago. Bob, a pharmacist, earns good wages and he and Sandra have had a child together. Charlene is deeply attached to her little brother Billy and to Bob, who are equally attached to her. The entire family is disturbed by Richard's holiday visits. Charlene has become increasingly distressed during holiday periods and becomes visibly depressed and withdrawn during and after Richard's visits. Sandra proposed to Richard that she waive child support in return for his agreement not to visit Charlene until she feels differently about his visits. Richard agreed. The court should approve this agreement.

Some may be disturbed by this result because it seems to allow Richard to use his own irresponsible behavior as a bargaining chip allowing him to obtain an agreement that frees him from his financial responsibilities to his child. On the other hand, it seems clear that the relatively modest payments Richard would otherwise be required to make would probably provide little real financial benefit for the child, who is adequately provided for in any event. In light of that, it is plausible to think that on balance the child is better off with this agreement than without it. Under such circumstances, the *Principles* take the position that the court should defer to the parental judgment expressed in the agreement. Note that this example from the *Principles* does not address whether Richard should remain immune from any claim for future child support were Charlene's circumstances to change. Suppose, for example, Charlene and Bob were to divorce, placing Charlene in a financially less comfortable situation. Should Richard then be liable for current support if he were financially capable of providing it? Most courts would probably say yes, although depending upon the facts a plausible case could be made that the support obligation should then fall to Bob rather than Richard.

For a case that might seem consistent with the approach of the *Principles*, see *Albins v. Elovitz*, 791 P.2d 366 (Ariz. App. 1990). Although stating that such agreements were not "binding" where the child's interests were adversely affected, the court held that "a custodial parent can waive child support" and that the noncustodial parent, "in consideration of the waiver," can surrender visitation rights. The court nonetheless allowed the father to resume visitation, despite his agreement waiving it, although it also declined to enforce the contract's liquidated damage provision, which would have required the father to pay an amount equal to the past due support that would have been ordered but for the agreement. In short, *Albins* seems to endorse both the view that such agreements may be accepted and the caution that the court may still modify their application at a later time if the child's interests so require.

NOTE

Agreements concerning relocation. The relocation of a custodial parent to a distant location is one of the most contentious issues that can arise after divorce. *See* Chapter 6, pp. 643-655. Some parties may anticipate the issue at the time of the initial decree and provide for it in their agreement. Should such an agreement be enforced? Consider *Bell v. Bell*, 572 So. 2d 841 (Miss. 1990), in which the parties provided that the children would live near Tupelo (the marital home) and that "neither husband nor the wife shall remove the children . . . without the express written consent of the other." These terms were incorporated in the 1986 divorce decree, but in 1988 the wife sought to move with the children from Tupelo to Jackson, over the husband's objection. The court conceded that the agreement barred the move, but held it unenforceable and evaluated the parties' conflict with the same kind of best interest analysis it would apply had there been no agreement (with the result that the mother was allowed to take one child with her, but not the other, a teenager who wished to remain with his father).

The decision in *Bell* appears typical; see the Reporter's Notes to Comment *h* of § 2.17 of the *ALI Principles* for a review of the cases. The *Principles* nonetheless recommend honoring such agreements unless the parent who seeks to relocate can make out a case for modifying the custody decree, which under the *Principles* requires a showing of an unanticipated and substantial change in circumstances. *See ALI Principles* § 2.17, Comment *h*. The comment points out that parties may find it easier to reach agreement on custodial arrangements initially if they can include provisions concerning such relocation. Suppose in *Bell* the husband had obtained his wife's agreement to the "no-move" provision in exchange for a financial settlement more generous to the wife than the court would ordinarily be expected to order: should that matter?

[b] Arbitration Clauses

Parties may provide in their settlement agreement for arbitration of disputes that may arise under it, or of petitions for its modification. At one time courts may have been more skeptical of such arbitration clauses, but today they are more likely to be accepted. *Hampton v. Hampton*, 689 N.Y.S.2d 186 (App. Div. 1999) (holding that arbitration of child support, pursuant to clause in separation agreement, is not incompatible with the Child Support

Standards Act). Some courts, however, still refuse to enforce arbitration awards concerning child custody. *Lipsius v. Lipsius*, 673 N.Y.S.2d 458 (App. Div. 1998) (holding that disputes over custody and visitation are not subject to arbitration). In *Miller v. Miller*, 620 A.2d 1161 (Pa. Super. 1992), the mother sought to enforce a custody award by the arbitrator under the arbitration process created by the parties' separation agreement. Although holding that such an arbitration clause was not void as against public policy, and offering many kind words about the virtue of parental agreement and of arbitration, the court concluded:

> We cannot ignore our duty to protect the rights and interests of children once called upon to do so. Therefore, while arbitration proceedings in custody disputes are not void as against public policy, the question of the enforceability of arbitration awards in this context is a very different matter. [W]hile agreements entered into between parties are binding as between the parties, they may not bind the court once its jurisdiction is invoked. It follows necessarily that an award rendered by an arbitration panel would be subject to the supervisory power of the court in its parens patriae capacity in a proceeding to determine the best interests of the child. It has long been recognized by the courts that it is the Commonwealth who is charged with the duty of protecting the rights and interests of children.

This seems a common response. For example, in *Sheets v. Sheets,* 22 A.D.2d 176, 254 N.Y.S.2d 320 (1964), the court declared that "there seems to be no clear and valid reason why the arbitration process should not be made available in the area of custody." But the court also said (in a passage cited by *Miller* with approval):

> Upon any showing that a provision of an award might be adverse to the best interest of a child, the Court could take such action that was necessary for the best interest of the child. Once the court's paternal jurisdiction is invoked, it would examine into the matter, de novo, and in doing so could utilize the proof adduced before the arbitration tribunal, could call for new proof, or could employ a combination of both. The Court could then determine what was necessary for the best interest of the child.

> However, the award could not be effectively attacked by a dissatisfied parent merely because it affected the child. Obviously every such award will have that effect. What must be shown to evoke judicial intervention is that the award adversely affects the welfare and best interest of the child — clearly a much narrower issue.

These courts seem to be looking for a way to encourage arbitration agreements, and to move some dispute resolution to the arbitration process, without ceding the ultimate judicial authority with respect to custody matters. Whether any have found a formula to achieve that result is uncertain.

Courts may be reluctant to enforce child custody arbitration provisions because the arbitrator is limited to deciding the dispute on the basis of the agreement of the parties, while courts consider the child's best interests in deciding custody disputes. Two commentators have offered the following illustrative example: In deciding whether a noncustodial father ought to be required to pay for a child's psychiatric care under a clause obligating him to pay medical expenses, an arbitrator would properly focus on what parties usually mean when they use this kind of language and whether that accepted meaning includes psychiatric care. By contrast, a judge might properly consider the child's interests and whether the father was in a position to pay for the care. Spencer & Zammit, *Mediation and Arbitration: A Proposal for Private Resolution of Disputes Between Divorced or Separated Parents,* 1976 DUKE L.J. 911, 921–22. It has been suggested that to assuage any such fears by the courts, properly drafted arbitration clauses could require the arbitrator to consider the child's best interests in making arbitration awards. Additionally, independent representation could be provided for the children in the arbitration. Note, *Agreements to Arbitrate Post-Divorce Custody Disputes,* 18 COLUM. J.L. & SOC. PROBS. 419, 452–59 (1985); Spencer & Zammit, *Reflections on Arbitration Under the Family Dispute Services,* 32 ARB. J. 111 (1977). For recent commentary on this topic, see E. Gary Spitko, *Reclaiming the "Creatures of the State": Contracting for Child Custody Decisionmaking in the Best Interests of the Family,* 57 WASH. & LEE L.REV. 1139 (2000).

An arbitration clause must be explicit. For example, in *Parrinelli v. Parrinelli,* 138 Misc. 2d 49, 524 N.Y.S.2d 159 (N.Y. Sup. 1988), the parties had agreed "to consult with each other with respect to [their] child's education," but had failed to provide any mechanism such as arbitration to settle their differences if they could not agree. The father sought to enforce this provision when the custodial mother unilaterally changed the child's school without even notifying him, but the court concluded that the clause at issue was no more than "an agreement to agree" and unenforceable under basic contract principles.

[c] No-Modification Clauses

As explained above at pages 822-824, once an agreement is merged into the divorce decree it is no longer enforceable as a contract but is instead enforceable as a decree. Alimony provisions in a decree are ordinarily modifiable. Is their modifiability for changed circumstances affected by the fact that they are based on the parties agreement? On one hand, alimony, unlike child support, is not subject to the rule that the court must retain the power to modify the obligation as necessary to protect the child's interest. On the other, the alimony provisions may be part of an overall financial settlement that includes non-modifiable terms on property allocation, so that modifications of the alimony provisions alone may seem unfair to one party.

State laws vary considerably on this question. Some courts take a contract approach and provide that the terms of a separation agreement, even though merged in the decree, are not modifiable unless the parties' agreement expressly permits modification. *Husband B. v. Wife H.,* 451 A.2d 1165 (Del. Super. 1982) (but court retains power to modify child support provision). Such a policy may even be extended, in part, to child support awards, *McInturff v. McInturff,* 644 S.W.2d 618 (Ark. App. 1983) (court retains power to modify child support awards only where the portion intended as child support can be determined; aggregate award which is partially child support is not modifiable). Other courts make agreement-based decrees subject to the same modification rules as judge-made decrees. *E.g.*, *Lepis v. Lepis,* 416 A.2d 45 (N.J. 1980). One state with restrictive alimony rules manages to take both positions depending upon whether the alimony obligation in question could have been ordered by the court. *Voigt v. Voigt,* 670 N.E.2d 1271 (Ind. 1996) (state law allows only rehabilitative alimony limited to three years, unless the obligee is either physically or mentally incapacitated and therefore unable to support himself, or is unable to work because he must care for a child with a physical or mental incapacity; agreement-based alimony not modifiable by the court unless the facts were such that the court could have imposed the alimony award in question).

In a jurisdiction which ordinarily allows modification of agreement-based alimony orders, what happens if the agreement expressly bars or limits such modifications of the alimony terms? Again, the states vary. One approach allows enforcement of "no-modification" clauses, but only if they meet strict requirements. California seems to take this approach. *Hufford v. Hufford,* 199 Cal. Rptr. 726 (App. 1984) (spousal support modifiable despite general language in agreement precluding alteration; effective no-modification clause must be in "specific, unequivocal language"); *In re Marriage of Benson,* 171 Cal. App. 3d 907, 217 Cal. Rptr. 589 (1985) (relies on *Hufford* in allowing extension of spousal support despite an agreement-based decree specifying support would terminate after eight years); *Marriage of Jones,* 222 Cal. App. 3d 505, 271 Cal. Rptr. 761 (1990) (similar). *Compare In re Marriage of Zlatnik,* 197 Cal. App. 3d 1284, 243 Cal. Rptr. 454 (1988) (agreement stating "in no event shall husband be obligated to pay spousal support after April 30, 1986" (seven years from the decree) sufficiently explicit to satisfy *Hufford* and effectively precludes an extension). Limits on no-modification clauses may still be imposed where required by children's welfare, *In re Marriage of Stevens,* 221 Cal. Rptr. 78 (App. 1985) (provision prohibiting wife from seeking modification explicit enough to make family support award nonmodifiable, but court retains power to modify where necessary to provide for children).

Other courts are less grudging in permitting enforcement of no-modification clauses, at least for alimony. In *Karon v. Karon,* 435 N.W.2d 501 (Minn. 1989), the parties' agreement called for spousal maintenance for ten years and contained a provision waiving "any right to maintenance except as provided therein" and divesting the court "of jurisdiction to alter the agreement or maintenance." Five years later, the wife sought an increase in maintenance because she had lost her job and her former husband was doing well. In a split decision, the court turned her down in language strongly suggesting this was largely a matter of contract. ("[I]ntelligent adult women, especially when represented by counsel, must be expected to honor their contracts the same as anybody else." *Id.* at 504.) The Wisconsin Supreme Court held that a father whose income had declined could not obtain a child support reduction because the agreement contained a no-modification provision which explicitly bound him "notwithstanding a reduction in his income." The court avoided the question of whether it would enforce an agreement limiting increases in child support. *Honore v. Honore,* 439 N.W.2d 827 (Wis. 1989).

No-modification clauses may render seemingly unreasonable results when events turn out in ways the parties did not anticipate. For example, in *Josic v. Josic*, 397 N.E.2d 204 (Ill. App. 1979), the parties' 1975 agreement provided that the husband's alimony obligations to the wife would be non-modifiable. He later had a stroke which he "alleged. . .rendered him permanently disabled and thus permanently unemployed and unable to make the payments." The court nonetheless enforced the agreement as permitted under state law. *In Toni v. Toni*, 636 N.W.2d 396 (N.D. 2001), the court enforced a provision in the parties' separation agreement barring modification of the alimony terms. At the1999 dissolution of the parties' 28-year marriage the husband earned $14,000 monthly as a urologist while the wife earned only $1,000 as a bookstore clerk. Their agreement allowed her $5,000 monthly in alimony but terminated all payments at her remarriage or in April 2001, whichever occurred first. She agreed to this limited term because she expected soon to remarry. When her marital plans fell through she sought the extension which the court here denied. Note that under § 7.12 (3) of the *ALI Principles*, an agreement to limit the modifiability of "compensatory payments" (the ALI's replacement for alimony) is not enforceable if "the court finds that modification is required to avoid a substantial injustice." Recall that the *Principles* allow courts to examine the substantive fairness of premarital agreements in specified categories of cases in which it seems particularly likely that the circumstances under which enforcement is sought were not anticipated by the parties; the concern is that enforcement should not be available where it would yield very unfair results under such unanticipated circumstances. The principle that the *ALI* applies here to separation agreements seems similar.

As a planning matter, the attorney drafting a separation agreement intended to govern the parties' relationship over a long period may well want to build some flexibility into it. Permitting petitions for judicial modification is the traditional answer, but may provide too much flexibility. Another approach is to establish by agreement both standards for modification and for the arbitration of disputes between the parties on the application of these standards.

PROBLEMS

Problem 8-7. *H* asks you to prepare a separation agreement for him and his wife. They have mutually agreed upon divorce and want to proceed with it amicably and simply. They have already produced their own rough draft without legal assistance and need you only to take care of the legal technicalities. You do not know *H* well, although a few years ago you reviewed a limited-partnership agreement for him in connection with an investment he was considering. The couple have been married for 15 years, and have two children. For the last ten years, *W* has not worked outside the home; *H* has been a plant manager for the American Can Company. *H* tells you he's agreed to give *W* custody of the children, reasonable child support (around $250 a month for the two of them), possession of the marital home, including the household furnishings, until the younger child (now 11) reaches 18, and one of their cars. *H* will make the mortgage and insurance payments on the home, and has already given *W* a lump-sum of $5,000, since she was interested in buying an ice-cream business. He also mentioned that he was putting aside $25,000 for each of the children, to be given them upon their graduation from high school, and that he had promised *W* that each child would receive at least one-fourth of his estate.

How do you proceed?

Problem 8-8. Attorney *A* calls to arrange your being counsel for *W*. He has prepared a separation agreement for the couple but feels that *W* should have her own counsel. When *W* arrives for an appointment the next day, she is accompanied by *H*. How do you proceed?

Problem 8-9. The Johnsons come to consult about a separation agreement. They present you with a rough draft working out most of the terms. You have represented *H* on some prior business dealings, from which you have a general idea of his financial standing. It seems to you the agreement gives *W* relatively little. Nonetheless, they do not seem interested in having you review the substance of their agreement, except for tax considerations or other "legal technicalities." When you suggest that *W* probably ought to have separate counsel, *H* makes it clear that he thinks that would be an unnecessary expense "since we've already worked everything out." *W* says nothing, but agrees with *H* when you ask her opinion. In explaining the agreement to you, *H*, who generally seems to dominate the discussion, emphasizes that it gives *W* sole custody of their two children, ages 8 and 6.

How do you proceed?

Problem 8-10. An agreement between *H* and *W* provided that *W* would sell their house, receiving the first $60,000 of net proceeds, while *H* would receive the rest. When the agreement was negotiated and signed, *H* was unrepresented. But he assumed that the agreement would result in net proceeds to him of about $50,000. In fact, the house did not sell at the original listing price, as a result of which *W* lowered it. She now expects to net a total of about $70,000 from a sale, leaving $10,000 for *H*. *H* seeks your advice, since he now wants to challenge the agreement, which has not yet been approved by the court. What do you advise?

Problem 8-11. *H* and *W*'s 1983 separation agreement required *H* to provide 36% of his gross income in support, assist in the two children's medical expenses as well as the cost of the college education, and to share in the purchase of a home for *W* and the children. At the time the agreement was made, the children, then of preschool age, suffered severely from cystic fibrosis, and the parties assumed *W* would be needed in the home full-time to tend the children's medical needs. Eight years later, *H* seeks relief from the agreement. The children's condition has improved well beyond prior expectations so that they now lead essentially normal lives. *W* has received an inheritance of $140,000, and is employed at a salary of $18,500. H's annual salary of $36,000 produces a monthly net of $1,837, of which about $1,100 must be paid per month under the agreement.

Can he obtain an order modifying the agreement's provisions for child support?

Part III

Nontraditional Families

Chapter 9

NONTRADITIONAL FAMILIES

INTRODUCTION

United States Supreme Court Justice O'Connor recently noted that the "demographic changes of the past century make it difficult to speak of an average American family. The composition of families varies greatly from household to household." *Troxel v. Granville,* 530 U.S. 57, 63 (2000). These changes include increases in numbers of unmarried heterosexual couples living together and of children born and raised outside of marriage. Same-sex partners are more visible in American society, and many are raising children together. This Chapter examines the legal system's responses to these changing demographics. Courts and legislatures have varied greatly in the pace and manner with which they have recognized nontraditional family forms. The resulting mosaic of policies offers a fascinating study of how the law responds to social change. Section A examines federal constitutional doctrines of particular relevance to nontraditional families. Section B addresses legal treatment of nonmarital cohabitant relationships. Finally, Section C considers the legal status of nonmarital children and their relationships with their parents, with special attention to the obstacles that have faced gays and lesbians who seek to adopt children.

§ A. CONSTITUTIONAL PROTECTION OF NONTRADITIONAL FAMILIES

"[D]omestic relations, [is] an area that has long been regarded as a virtually exclusive province of the States. Cases decided by the Court over a period of more than a century bear witness to this historical fact." *Sosna v. Iowa,* 419 U.S. 393, 404 (1975). And yet, "[s]tate power over domestic relations is not without constitutional limits." *Zablocki v. Redhail,* 434 U.S. 374, 398 (1978). In the past several decades, federal constitutional doctrines have been particularly important in delineating the contours of permissible state regulation of families. For example, the Supreme Court struck down various state laws affecting families as violating the Equal Protection Clause. *See, e.g., Loving v. Virginia,* 388 U.S. 1 (1967) (holding unconstitutional Virginia's criminal prohibition of interracial marriage); *Orr v. Orr,* 440 U.S. 268 (1979) (holding unconstitutional Alabama's spousal support statute, which imposed alimony obligations on husbands but not on wives); *Clark v. Jeter,* 486 U.S. 456 (1988) (striking down Pennsylvania's six-year statute of limitations for child support actions by nonmarital children against their fathers, where no such limitation existed for marital children). The Court has relied on the guarantee of liberty found in the Due Process Clause of the Fourteenth Amendment to invalidate specific statutes regulating family and intimate relationships, and personal decisionmaking about certain matters. Section 1 reviews the development of the constitutional right of privacy as it relates to family life and personal relationships. Section 2 explores the application of constitutional principles to same-sex relationships.

[1] EVOLUTION OF THE RIGHT OF PRIVACY

In 1923, the U.S. Supreme Court first suggested that liberty, as guaranteed by the Constitution, includes "not merely freedom from bodily restraint but also the right of the individual to . . . marry, establish a home and bring up children. *Meyer v. Nebraska,* 262 U.S. 390, 399. Two years later, in *Pierce v. Society of Sisters*, 268 U.S. 510, 534 (1925), the Court struck down an Oregon statute requiring children between the ages of 8 and 16 to attend public (rather than private) school: "The Act . . . unreasonably interferes with the liberty of parents . . . to direct the upbringing and education of their children. . . ." In language that appeared to celebrate the Constitution as the protector of pluralism and diversity, *Pierce* concluded that: "The fundamental theory of liberty . . . excludes any general power of the state to standardize its children. . . . The child is not the mere creature of the state. . . ." *Id.* at 535. Two decades later, addressing the limits of parental autonomy in childrearing in *Prince v. Massachusetts*, the Court nonetheless underscored that its decisions recognize "the private realm of family life which the state cannot enter." 321 U.S. 158, 166 (1944).

In 1965, in *Griswold v. Connecticut*, 381 U.S. 479, the Court returned to these early building blocks of what has come to be known as the constitutional right of privacy. In *Griswold,* the Court struck down a Connecticut criminal statute that punished any person using contraception with a fine or up to a year in prison. The appellants in question were Planned Parenthood personnel charged as accessories for prescribing contraceptives to "married persons." In the Opinion for the Court, Justice Douglas stated that the challenged law operated "directly on an intimate relation of husband and wife." *Id.* at 482.

> [S]pecific guarantees in the Bill of Rights have penumbras, formed by emanations from those guarantees that help give them life and substance. Various guarantees create zones of privacy. The right of association contained in the penumbra of the First Amendment is one . . . The Third Amendment in its prohibition against the quartering of soldiers "in any house" in time of peace without the consent of the owner is another facet of that privacy. The Fourth Amendment explicitly affirms the "right of the people to be secure in their persons, houses, papers, and effects, against unreasonable searches and seizures." The Fifth Amendment in its Self-Incrimination Clause enables the citizen to create a zone of privacy which government may not force him to surrender to his detriment. The Ninth Amendment provides: "The enumeration in the Constitution, of certain rights, shall not be construed to deny or disparage others retained by the people."

>   . . . .

> The present case, then, concerns a relationship lying within the zone of privacy created by several fundamental constitutional guarantees. And it concerns a law which, in forbidding the *use* of contraceptives

rather than regulating their manufacture or sale, seeks to achieve its goals by . . . having a maximum destructive impact upon that relationship. . . . Would we allow the police to search the sacred precincts of marital bedrooms for telltale signs of the use of contraceptives? The very idea is repulsive to the notions of privacy surrounding the marriage relationship. [¶] We deal with a right of privacy older than the Bill of Rights — older than our political parties, older than our school system. Marriage is a coming together for better or for worse, hopefully enduring, and intimate to the degree of being sacred. It is an association that promotes a way of life, not causes; a harmony in living, not political faiths; a bilateral loyalty, not commercial or social projects. Yet it is an association for as noble a purpose as any involved in our prior decisions.

Id. at 484–86. In a concurrence, Justice Goldberg identified the Ninth Amendment as the constitutional source of the right. Citing with approval Justice Brandeis' dissent in the 1928 case of *Olmstead v. United States*, 277 U.S. 438, Justice Goldberg "summarized the principles underlying the Constitution's guarantees of privacy":

The [Framers] undertook to secure conditions favorable to the pursuit of happiness. They recognized the significance of man's spiritual nature, of his feelings and of his intellect. They knew that only a part of the pain, pleasure and satisfactions of life are to be found in material things. They sought to protect Americans in their beliefs, their thoughts, their emotions and their sensations. They conferred, as against the government, the right to be let alone — the most comprehensive of rights and the right most valued by civilized men.

Griswold, 381 U.S. at 494 (Goldberg, J., concurring) (citing *Olmstead*, 277 U.S. at 478 (Brandeis, J., dissenting)). Justice Goldberg also relied on Justice Harlan's dissenting opinion in *Poe v. Ullman*, 367 U.S. 497 (1961):

[T]he State is asserting the right to enforce its moral judgment by intruding upon the most intimate details of the marital relation with the full power of the criminal law. Potentially, this could allow the deployment of all the incidental machinery of the criminal law, arrests, searches and seizures; [and requiring courtroom] testimony as to the mode and manner of the married couples' sexual relations. . . . In sum, the statute allows the State to enquire into, prove and punish married people for the private use of their marital intimacy. [¶]. . . . This enactment involves what . . . must be granted to be a most fundamental aspect of "liberty," the privacy of the home in its most basic sense, and it is this which requires that the statute be subjected to "strict scrutiny." [¶] [H]ere we have not an intrusion into the home so much as [the] privacies of the life within. . . . The home derives its pre-eminence as the seat of family life. And the integrity of that life is something so fundamental that it has been found to draw to its protection the principles of more than one explicitly granted Constitutional right. . . .

Griswold, 381 U.S. at 496 (Goldberg, J., concurring) (citing *Poe v. Ullman*, 367 U.S. at 548, 551–52 (Harlan, J., dissenting)).

Justice Harlan's *Griswold* concurrence characterized the right to use contraceptives as a liberty right, consistent with the language used in *Meyer* and *Pierce*:

> In my view, the proper constitutional inquiry in this case is whether this Connecticut statute infringes the Due Process Clause of the Fourteenth Amendment because the enactment violates basic values "implicit in the concept of ordered liberty," *Palko v. State of Connecticut*, 302 U.S. 319, 325 [(1937)]. For reasons stated at length in my dissenting opinion in *Poe v. Ullman,* . . . I believe that it does. While the relevant inquiry may be aided by resort to one or more of the provisions of the Bill of Rights, it is not dependent on them or any of their radiations. The Due Process Clause of the Fourteenth Amendment stands, in my opinion, on its own bottom.

Griswold, 381 U.S. at 500 (Harlan, J., concurring).

Six years after *Griswold*, the Court was confronted with the question of whether unmarried individuals were also protected by this right of privacy. *Eisenstadt v. Baird*, 405 U.S. 438 (1971). The Court did not formally address this question, but instead focused on the challenged statute's distinction between married and unmarried persons. The statute permitted married persons to obtain contraceptives to prevent pregnancy, but not unmarried persons. Finding this classification irrational, the Court held that the law violated the Equal Protection Clause. Yet, the Court's language declared that privacy rights belong to *individuals*, as well as to married couples:

> [May the Massachusetts statute] be sustained simply as a prohibition on contraception? . . . We need not and do not . . . decide that important question in this case because, whatever the rights of the individual to access to contraceptives may be, the rights must be the same for the unmarried and the married alike.
>
> . . . . It is true that in *Griswold* the right of privacy in question inhered in the marital relationship. Yet the marital couple is not an independent entity with a mind and heart of its own, but an association of two individuals each with a separate intellectual and emotional makeup. If the right of privacy means anything, it is the right of the *individual,* married or single, to be free from unwarranted governmental intrusion into matters so fundamentally affecting a person as the decision whether to bear or beget a child. *See Stanley v. Georgia* (1969); *see also Skinner v. Oklahoma ex rel. Williamson* (1942); *Jacobson v. Massachusetts* (1905).

Eisenstadt, 405 U.S. at 453–54. The language referring to the right of privacy as an *individual* right led many to speculate that the Court had expanded the *Griswold* doctrine from one protecting *marital* intimacy to a general right of intimate association. Yet, absent more explicit language, observers had to await future decisions for greater clarity. Also unclear were the contours of the right the Court had recognized. Did this emerging doctrine of privacy establish a narrow right of access to contraceptives, a broader right to decide when and whether to procreate, an even broader right of decisional autonomy in personal or family matters, or a right of intimate association? While leaving many questions about the parameters of the right of privacy unanswered, the Court again invoked this right in *Roe v. Wade*, a constitutional challenge to the Texas criminal abortion statutes. 410 U.S. 113 (1973).

> The Constitution does not explicitly mention any right of privacy. [T]he Court has recognized that a right of personal privacy, or a guarantee of certain areas or zones of privacy, does exist under the Constitution. In varying contexts, the Court or individual Justices have, indeed, found at least the roots of that right in the First Amendment, . . . in the Fourth and Fifth Amendments,. . . in the penumbras of the Bill of Rights, . . . in the Ninth Amendment; or in the concept of liberty guaranteed by the first section of the Fourteenth Amendment. . . . These decisions make it clear that only personal rights that can be deemed "fundamental" or "implicit in the concept of ordered liberty," are included in this guarantee of personal privacy. They also make it clear that the right has some extension to activities relating to marriage [*Loving v. Virginia*]; procreation [*Skinner v. Oklahoma*]; contraception [*Eisenstadt v. Baird*]; family relationships [*Prince v. Massachusetts*]; and child rearing and education [*Pierce v. Society of Sisters, Meyer v. Nebraska*]. [¶] This right of privacy, whether it be founded in the Fourteenth Amendment's concept of personal liberty and restrictions upon state action, as we feel it is, or, as the District Court determined, in the Ninth Amendment's reservation of rights to the people, is broad enough to encompass a woman's decision whether or not to terminate her pregnancy.

Id. at 152–53. Four years later, in *Carey v. Population Servs. Int'l*, 431 U.S. 678 (1977), the Court extended *Griswold's* and *Eisenstadt's* protection of the right of access to contraceptives to minors. These decisions, together with others, clarified that the right of privacy encompassed protection of certain *individual* liberties as well as certain *family* relationships. In *Planned Parenthood of Central Missouri v. Danforth,* the Court resolved a conflict between these two clusters of core values, holding that a state cannot require a pregnant woman to obtain her husband's consent for an abortion. 428 U.S. 52 (1976).

The Court has also been confronted with the question of *which* family relationships fall within the protected zone, and in particular, whether the definition of "family" in family privacy extends to relationships established outside of the nuclear marital family. In 1972, in *Stanley v. Illinois*, 405 U.S. 981, the Court established that unmarried fathers have certain constitutionally-protected rights regarding their biological children. (See excerpts and discussion of *Stanley* on page 981.) In *Moore v. City of East Cleveland*, 431 U.S 494 (1977), the Court held unconstitutional an East Cleveland ordinance that precluded a grandmother from living in a single family home with her son and two grandchildren. The ordinance's definition of "family" excluded certain three-generational groupings. Referring to the challenged ordinance as "slicing deeply into the family itself," the Court stated that "freedom of personal choice in matters of marriage and family life is one of the liberties protected by the Due Process Clause of the Fourteenth Amendment." *Id.* at 498–99. (*Moore* is reprinted and discussed in Chapter 1, *supra*, at page 18.) *See also United States Dep't of Agriculture v. Moreno*, 413 U.S. 528 (1973) (holding unconstitutional a statute treating parties living in a household with unrelated persons as ineligible for food stamps). Delineation of precisely which nontraditional family or family-like relationships are protected by the Constitution remains an important avenue of inquiry in the field of family law, and will be addressed throughout the remainder of this chapter.

[2] CONSTITUTIONAL PROTECTION OF PRIVATE CONSENSUAL SEXUAL CONDUCT AND SAME-SEX RELATIONSHIPS

Family privacy jurisprudence flourished in the 1970s with cases like *Roe v. Wade, Carey v. Population Services International, Zablocki v. Redhail, Wisconsin v. Yoder, Stanley v. Illinois, Moore v. City of East Cleveland* and others. Citations in each new case cross-referenced the others, emphasizing that the right of privacy encompassed the right to make procreative decisions, the right to marry, and the right to exercise discretion in raising one's children. Yet, scholarship revealed certain fundamental disagreements as to the essential elements of the right of privacy. Whereas some classic scholarly analyses articulated an expansive reading of the doctrine, *see, e.g.,* Kenneth L. Karst, *The Freedom of Intimate Association*, 89 YALE L.J. 624 (1980); Lawrence H. Tribe, AMERICAN CONSTITUTIONAL LAW (1978); J. Harvie Wilkinson III & G. Edward White, *Constitutional Protection for Personal Lifestyles*, 52 CORNELL L. REV. 563 (1977), others offered more restrained and critical analyses, *see, e.g.,* Bruce C. Hafen, *The Constitutional Status of Marriage, Kinship and Sexual Privacy — Balancing the Individual and Social Interests*, 81 MICH. L. REV. 463 (1983); Robert A. Burt, *The Constitution of the Family*, 1979 SUP. CT. REV. 329. For an overview, see *Developments in the Law, The Constitution and The Family*, 93 HARV. L. REV. 1156 (1980). Commentators and jurists disagreed as to whether there was a unitary conceptual thread linking all of the rights identified as falling within the protected ambit of privacy. One scholar suggested that the Court had substituted a "lengthy and undifferentiated string" of citations for a conceptual analysis of what constitutes the right of privacy. John Hart Ely, *Foreword: On Discovering Fundamental Values*, 92 HARV. L. REV. 5, 11 n.40 (1978).

These debates anticipated the 1986 challenge by Michael Hardwick to the constitutionality of a Georgia statute criminalizing sodomy. *Bowers v. Hardwick*, 478 U.S. 186. In 1986, approximately half of the states still proscribed sodomy, even between consenting adults in the privacy of their homes. Many of these statutes applied to heterosexual as well as homosexual conduct. Prosecutions were rare. Yet, the continued existence and validity of these statutes signaled the government's formal disapproval of homosexuality.

Michael Hardwick had been charged with violating the Georgia law by engaging in sodomy with another adult male in the bedroom of his home. Although the charges against him were dropped, Hardwick brought suit challenging the constitutionality of the statute's criminalization of consensual sodomy. He "asserted that he was a practicing homosexual, that the Georgia sodomy statute, as administered by the defendants, placed him in imminent danger of arrest, and that the statute for several reasons violates the Federal

Constitution." The Court framed the issue as "whether the Federal Constitution confers a fundamental right upon homosexuals to engage in sodomy and hence invalidates the laws of the many States that still make such conduct illegal and have done so for a very long time." *Id.* at 190. In a 5-4 decision, a majority of the Court rejected Hardwick's position that the right of privacy extended to homosexual sodomy. It characterized the relevant precedents as dealing with childrearing and education, with family relationships, with marriage, with procreation, with contraception, and with abortion. As such, the Court concluded that

> none of the rights announced in [our] cases bears any resemblance to the claimed constitutional right of homosexuals to engage in acts of sodomy. . . . No connection between family, marriage, or procreation on the one hand and homosexual activity on the other has been demonstrated. . . . Moreover, any claim that these cases nevertheless stand for the proposition that any kind of private sexual conduct between consenting adults is constitutionally insulated from state proscription is insupportable. . . . [¶] Precedent aside, however, respondent would have us announce . . . a fundamental right to engage in homosexual sodomy. This we are quite unwilling to do. . .

Id. at 190–91. Justice Blackmun, in dissent (joined by Justices Brennan, Marshall and Stevens) roundly criticized the Court's narrow and highly specific characterization of the right in question, asserting that: "This case is [not] about 'a fundamental right to engage in homosexual sodomy,' as the Court purports to declare. . . . Rather, this case is about 'the most comprehensive of rights and the right most valued by civilized men,' namely, 'the right to be let alone.' " *Id.* at 199. Justice Blackmun argued that the Court's privacy precedents protected the "freedom an individual has to *choose* the form and nature of . . . personal bonds," stating that the majority's decision had "refused to recognize . . . the fundamental interest all individuals have in controlling the nature of their intimate associations with others." *Id.* at 206.

Bowers v. Hardwick generated much commentary, most of it critical. *See, e.g.,* Thomas B. Stoddard, Bowers v. Hardwick: *Precedent by Personal Predilection*, 54 U. CHI. L. REV. 649 (1987); Jed Rubenfeld, *The Right of Privacy*, 102 HARV. L. REV. 737 (1989); Brenda Sue Thornton, *The New International Jurisprudence on the Right to Privacy: A Head-On Collision with* Bowers v. Hardwick, 58 ALBANY L. REV. 725 (1995); William N. Eskridge, Jr., Hardwick *and Historiography*, 1999 U. ILL. L. REV. 631 (1999). *But see* Norman Viera, Hardwick *and the Right of Privacy*, 55 U. CHI. L. REV. 1181 (1988) (arguing that "underlying doctrinal deficiencies . . . not merely . . . the shortcomings of the *Hardwick* opinion" are to blame for the result); Richard F. Duncan, *"They Call Me 'Eight Eyes' ":* Hardwick's *Respectability,* Romer's *Narrowness, and Same-Sex Marriage*, 32 CREIGHTON L. REV. 241 (1998) (arguing that *Bowers v. Hardwick* should not be overruled).

Justice Powell, who cast the decisive fifth vote upholding the Georgia statute in *Hardwick*, acknowledged four years later that he thought he had "made a mistake" in joining Justice White's opinion. In a conversation with law students at New York University, the then-retired justice said that he had initially voted in conference to strike down the Georgia statute, but changed his mind and joined Justice White's opinion. Linda Greenhouse, *When Second Thoughts in Case Come Too Late,* N.Y. TIMES, Nov. 5, 1990, at A14. The New York Times reported: "In his conversation with the law students, Justice Powell did not explain his current view. According to an account . . . in The National Law Journal, the retired Justice, who is 83 years old, said that when he reread the decision a few months after it was issued, 'I thought the dissent had the better of the arguments.' " *Id*. For a detailed discussion of Justice Powell's viewpoints on this case, see John C. Jeffries, Jr., JUSTICE LEWIS F. POWELL, JR.: A BIOGRAPHY 515-30 (1994). *See also* E. Nathaniel Gates, *Justice Stillborn: Lies, Lacunae, Incommensurability, and the Judicial Role,* 19 CARDOZO L. REV. 971, 1026–31 (1997). Twelve years after *Hardwick*, the Georgia Supreme Court unanimously invalidated the state's sodomy statute, grounding the decision in the state constitutional right of privacy. *Powell v. State,* 510 S.E.2d 18 (1998).

A decade later, in *Romer v. Evans*, 517 U.S. 620, 624 (1996), the Court struck down an amendment to the Colorado Constitution that barred local governments and state agencies from adopting "any statute, regulation, ordinance or policy whereby homosexual, lesbian or bisexual orientation, conduct, practices or relationships shall constitute or otherwise be the basis of or entitle any person or class of persons to have or claim any minority status, quota preferences, protected status or claim of discrimination." In a 6-3 decision authored by Justice Kennedy, the Court held that the Colorado amendment violated the Equal Protection Clause of the U.S. Constitution. The Court applied rational basis analysis, and concluded that Colorado's passage of the amendment was "inexplicable by anything but animus toward the class that it affects" and that as such, "it lacks a rational relationship to legitimate state interests." *Id*. at 632. The majority further noted that the challenged amendment "classifies homosexuals not to further a proper legislative end but to make them unequal to everyone else. This Colorado cannot do. A State cannot so deem a class of persons a stranger to its laws. Amendment 2 violates the Equal Protection Clause. . . ." *Id*. at 635.

Justice Scalia, in a vociferous dissent joined by Chief Justice Rehnquist and Justice Thomas, noted that the majority had not mentioned *Bowers v. Hardwick*. Justice Scalia claimed that *Romer's* holding "that homosexuality cannot be singled out for disfavorable treatment. . . . contradicts a decision, unchallenged here, pronounced only 10 years ago. . ." *Id*. at 636. He asserted: "If it is constitutionally permissible for a State to make homosexual conduct criminal, surely it is constitutionally permissible for a State to enact other laws merely disfavoring homosexual conduct. . . . And *a fortiori* it is constitutionally permissible for a State to adopt a provision *not even* disfavoring homosexual conduct, but merely prohibiting all levels of state government from bestowing special *protections* upon homosexual conduct." *Id*. at 641. For the next several years, scholars debated the fundamental question of whether *Romer* impliedly overruled *Hardwick*. *Compare* Cass Sunstein, *Foreword: Leaving Things Undecided*, 110 HARV. L. REV. 4, 67–68 (1996) (arguing that the two cases can be distinguished) *with* Thomas Grey, Bowers v. Hardwick *Diminished*, 68 U. COLO. L. REV. 373, 373–74 (1997) (arguing that the cases cannot be reconciled). For other commentary on the relationship between *Bowers* and *Romer*, *see, e.g.,* Lynn A. Baker, *The Missing Pages of the Majority*

Opinion in Romer v. Evans, 68 U. COLO. L. REV. 387 (1997); Andrew M. Jacobs, Romer *Wasn't Built in a Day: The Subtle Transformation in Judicial Argument Over Gay Rights*, 1996 WIS. L. REV. 893 (1996). For a relevant pre-*Romer* piece, see Janet E. Halley, *Reasoning about Sodomy: Act and Identity in and after* Bowers v. Hardwick, 79 VA. L. REV. 1721 (1993). Until 2003, however, such commentary could only speculate as to the Court's treatment of a post-*Romer* challenge to statutes such as the one reviewed below in *Lawrence v. Texas*.

LAWRENCE v. TEXAS

123 S. Ct. 2472 (2003)

JUSTICE KENNEDY delivered the opinion of the Court.

Liberty protects the person from unwarranted government intrusions into a dwelling or other private places. In our tradition the State is not omnipresent in the home. And there are other spheres of our lives and existence, outside the home, where the State should not be a dominant presence. Freedom extends beyond spatial bounds. Liberty presumes an autonomy of self that includes freedom of thought, belief, expression, and certain intimate conduct. The instant case involves liberty of the person both in its spatial and more transcendent dimensions.

I

The question before the Court is the validity of a Texas statute making it a crime for two persons of the same sex to engage in certain intimate sexual conduct.

In Houston, Texas, officers of the Harris County Police Department were dispatched to a private residence in response to a reported weapons disturbance. They entered an apartment where one of the petitioners, John Geddes Lawrence, resided . . . The officers observed Lawrence and another man, Tyron Garner, engaging in a sexual act. The two petitioners were arrested, held in custody over night, and charged and convicted. . . .

The complaints described their crime as "deviate sexual intercourse, namely anal sex, with a member of the same sex (man)." [Texas] Penal Code Ann. § 21.06(a) . . . provides: "A person commits an offense if he engages in deviate sexual intercourse with another individual of the same sex." The statute defines "[d]eviate sexual intercourse" as follows: "(A) any contact between any part of the genitals of one person and the mouth or anus of another person; or (B) the penetration of the genitals or the anus of another person with an object." § 21.01(1).

[In further proceedings, the petitioners unsuccessfully] challenged the statute as a violation of the Equal Protection Clause of the Fourteenth Amendment and of a like provision of the Texas Constitution. [They] were each fined $200 and assessed court costs of $141.25.

The Court of Appeals for the Texas Fourteenth District considered the petitioners' federal constitutional arguments under both the Equal Protection and

Due Process Clauses of the Fourteenth Amendment [and concluded that] our decision in *Bowers v. Hardwick,* 478 U.S. 186 (1986), [was] controlling on the federal due process aspect of the case. . . . We granted certiorari to consider three questions:

"1. Whether Petitioners' criminal convictions under the Texas 'Homosexual Conduct' law — which criminalizes sexual intimacy by same-sex couples, but not identical behavior by different-sex couples — violate the Fourteenth Amendment guarantee of equal protection of laws?

"2. Whether Petitioners' criminal convictions for adult consensual sexual intimacy in the home violate their vital interests in liberty and privacy protected by the Due Process Clause of the Fourteenth Amendment?

"3. Whether *Bowers v. Hardwick,* should be overruled?"

The petitioners were adults at the time of the alleged offense. Their conduct was in private and consensual.

II

We conclude the case should be resolved by determining whether the petitioners were free as adults to engage in the private conduct in the exercise of their liberty under the Due Process Clause of the Fourteenth Amendment to the Constitution. For this inquiry we deem it necessary to reconsider the Court's holding in *Bowers.*

There are broad statements of the substantive reach of liberty under the Due Process Clause in earlier cases, including *Pierce v. Society of Sisters,* 268 U.S. 510 (1925), and *Meyer v. Nebraska,* 262 U.S. 390 (1923); but the most pertinent beginning point is our decision in *Griswold v. Connecticut,* 381 U.S. 479 (1965).

[The Court reviews *Griswold* and *Eisenstadt* and their holdings, citing with approval the oft-quoted language from *Eisenstadt:* "If the right of privacy means anything, it is the right of the *individual,* married or single, to be free from unwarranted governmental intrusion into matters so fundamentally affecting a person as the decision whether to bear or beget a child."] [¶] The opinions in *Griswold* and *Eisenstadt* were part of the background for the decision in *Roe v. Wade,* 410 U.S. 113 (1973). . . . *Roe* recognized the right of a woman to make certain fundamental decisions affecting her destiny and confirmed once more that the protection of liberty under the Due Process Clause has a substantive dimension of fundamental significance in defining the rights of the person. [¶] In *Carey v. Population Services Int'l,* 431 U.S. 678 (1977), the Court [invalidated] a New York law forbidding sale or distribution of contraceptive devices to persons under 16 years of age. . . . Both *Eisenstadt* and *Carey,* as well as the holding and rationale in *Roe,* confirmed that the reasoning of *Griswold* could not be confined to the protection of rights of married adults. This was the state of the law with respect to some of the most relevant cases when the Court considered *Bowers v. Hardwick.*

The facts in *Bowers* had some similarities to the instant case. A police officer . . . observed Hardwick, in his own bedroom, engaging in intimate sexual conduct with another adult male. . . . in violation of a Georgia statute making it a criminal offense to engage in sodomy. One difference between the two cases is that the Georgia statute prohibited the conduct whether or not the participants were of the same sex, while the Texas statute, as we have seen, applies only to participants of the same sex. Hardwick was not prosecuted, but he brought an action in federal court to declare the state statute invalid. He alleged he was a practicing homosexual and that the criminal prohibition violated rights guaranteed to him by the Constitution. The Court, in an opinion authored by Justice White, sustained the Georgia law. Chief Justice Burger and Justice Powell joined the opinion of the Court and filed separate, concurring opinions. Four Justices dissented [Justices Blackmun, Brennan, Marshall, and Stevens].

The Court began its substantive discussion in *Bowers* as follows: "The issue presented is whether the Federal Constitution confers a fundamental right upon homosexuals to engage in sodomy and hence invalidates the laws of the many States that still make such conduct illegal and have done so for a very long time." That statement, we now conclude, discloses the Court's own failure to appreciate the extent of the liberty at stake. To say that the issue in *Bowers* was simply the right to engage in certain sexual conduct demeans the claim the individual put forward, just as it would demean a married couple were it to be said marriage is simply about the right to have sexual intercourse. The laws involved in *Bowers* and here are, to be sure, statutes that purport to do no more than prohibit a particular sexual act. Their penalties and purposes, though, have more far-reaching consequences, touching upon the most private human conduct, sexual behavior, and in the most private of places, the home. The statutes . . . seek to control a personal relationship that, whether or not entitled to formal recognition in the law, is within the liberty of persons to choose without being punished as criminals.

. . . . It suffices for us to acknowledge that adults may choose to enter upon this relationship in the confines of their homes and their own private lives and still retain their dignity as free persons. When sexuality finds overt expression in intimate conduct with another person, the conduct can be but one element in a personal bond that is more enduring. The liberty protected by the Constitution allows homosexual persons the right to make this choice.

Having misapprehended the claim of liberty there presented to it, and thus stating the claim to be whether there is a fundamental right to engage in consensual sodomy, the *Bowers* Court said: "Proscriptions against that conduct have ancient roots." [The Court reviews various historical sources to reach the following conclusions:] [T]here is no longstanding history in this country of laws directed at homosexual conduct as a distinct matter. . . . [E]arly American sodomy laws were not directed at homosexuals as such but instead sought to prohibit nonprocreative sexual activity more generally. . . .[¶] Laws prohibiting sodomy do not seem to have been enforced against consenting adults acting in private. A substantial number of sodomy prosecutions and convictions for which there are surviving records were for predatory acts against those who could not or did not consent, as in the case of a minor or the victim of an assault. . . .[¶] [Historical records reveal that prosecutions for these crimes were relatively infrequent. T]hat infrequency makes it difficult to say that society approved of a rigorous and systematic punishment of the consensual acts committed in private and by adults. . . . [¶] . . . [F]ar from possessing "ancient roots," American laws targeting same-sex couples did not develop until the last third of the 20th century. . . .

It was not until the 1970's that any State singled out same-sex relations for criminal prosecution, and only nine States [did so.] Over the course of the last decades, States with same-sex prohibitions have moved toward abolishing them. . . . [¶]. . . . In summary, the historical grounds relied upon in *Bowers*. . . . at the very least, are overstated.

It must be acknowledged, of course, that the Court in *Bowers* was making the broader point that for centuries there have been powerful voices to condemn homosexual conduct as immoral. The condemnation has been shaped by religious beliefs, conceptions of right and acceptable behavior, and respect for the traditional family. For many persons these are not trivial concerns but profound and deep convictions accepted as ethical and moral principles to which they aspire and which thus determine the course of their lives. These considerations do not answer the question before us, however. The issue is whether the majority may use the power of the State to enforce these views on the whole society through operation of the criminal law. "Our obligation is to define the liberty of all, not to mandate our own moral code." *Planned Parenthood of Southeastern Pa. v. Casey,* 505 U.S. 833, 850 (1992).

Chief Justice Burger joined the opinion for the Court in *Bowers* and further explained his views as follows: "Decisions of individuals relating to homosexual conduct have been subject to state intervention throughout the history of Western civilization. Condemnation of those practices is firmly rooted in Judeo-Christian moral and ethical standards.". . . . [Yet,] "history and tradition are the starting point but not in all cases the ending point of the substantive due process inquiry."

This emerging recognition should have been apparent when *Bowers* was decided. In 1955 the American Law Institute promulgated the Model Penal Code and made clear that it did not recommend or provide for "criminal penalties for consensual sexual relations conducted in private." ALI, Model Penal Code § 213.2, Comment 2, p. 372 (1980). It justified its decision on three grounds: (1) The prohibitions undermined respect for the law by penalizing conduct many people engaged in; (2) the statutes regulated private conduct not harmful to others; and (3) the laws were arbitrarily enforced and thus invited the danger of blackmail. . . .

The sweeping references by Chief Justice Burger to the history of Western civilization and to Judeo-Christian moral and ethical standards did not take account of other authorities pointing in an opposite direction. A committee advising the British Parliament recommended in 1957 repeal of laws punishing homosexual conduct. . . . Parliament enacted the substance of those recommendations 10 years later.

Of even more importance, almost five years before *Bowers* was decided the European Court of Human Rights considered a case with parallels to *Bowers* and to today's case. . . . The court held that the laws proscribing [private consensual homosexual] conduct were invalid under the European Convention on Human Rights. . . . Authoritative in all countries that are members of the Council of Europe (21 nations then, 45 nations now), the decision is at odds with the premise in *Bowers* that the claim put forward was insubstantial in our Western civilization.

In our own constitutional system the deficiencies in *Bowers* became even more apparent in the years following its announcement. The 25 States with laws prohibiting the relevant conduct referenced in the *Bowers* decision are reduced now to 13, of which 4 enforce their laws only against homosexual conduct. In those States where sodomy is still proscribed, whether for same-sex or heterosexual conduct, there is a pattern of nonenforcement with respect to consenting adults acting in private. . . .

Two principal cases decided after *Bowers* cast its holding into even more doubt. In *Casey,* the Court reaffirmed the substantive force of the liberty protected by the Due Process Clause. The *Casey* decision again confirmed that our laws and tradition afford constitutional protection to personal decisions relating to marriage, procreation, contraception, family relationships, child rearing, and education. . . .:

> These matters, involving the most intimate and personal choices a person may make in a lifetime, choices central to personal dignity and autonomy, are central to the liberty protected by the Fourteenth Amendment. At the heart of liberty is the right to define one's own concept of existence, of meaning, of the universe, and of the mystery of human life. Beliefs about these matters could not define the attributes of personhood were they formed under compulsion of the State.

Persons in a homosexual relationship may seek autonomy for these purposes, just as heterosexual persons do. The decision in *Bowers* would deny them this right.

The second post-*Bowers* case of principal relevance is *Romer v. Evans,* 517 U.S. 620 (1996). There the Court struck down class-based legislation directed at homosexuals as a violation of the Equal Protection Clause. *Romer* invalidated an amendment to Colorado's constitution which named as a solitary class persons who were homosexuals, lesbians, or bisexual either by "orientation, conduct, practices or relationships," and deprived them of protection under state antidiscrimination laws. We concluded that the provision was "born of animosity toward the class of persons affected" and further that it had no rational relation to a legitimate governmental purpose.

As an alternative argument in this case, counsel for the petitioners and some *amici* contend that *Romer* provides the basis for declaring the Texas statute invalid under the Equal Protection Clause. That is a tenable argument, but we conclude the instant case requires us to address whether *Bowers* itself has continuing validity. Were we to hold the statute invalid under the Equal Protection Clause some might question whether a prohibition would be valid if drawn differently, say, to prohibit the conduct both between same-sex and different-sex participants.

Equality of treatment and the due process right to demand respect for conduct protected by the substantive guarantee of liberty are linked in important respects, and a decision on the latter point advances both interests. If protected conduct is made criminal and the law which does so remains unexamined for its substantive validity, its stigma might remain even if it were not enforceable as drawn for equal protection reasons. When homosexual conduct is made criminal by the law of the State, that declaration in and of itself is an invitation to subject homosexual persons to discrimination both in the public and in the private spheres. [The] continuance [of *Bowers*] as precedent demeans the lives of homosexual persons.

The stigma this criminal statute imposes, moreover, is not trivial. The offense, to be sure, is but a class C misdemeanor, a minor offense. . . . Still, it remains a criminal offense with all that imports for the dignity of the persons charged. The petitioners will bear on their record the history of their criminal convictions. . . . We are advised that if Texas convicted an adult for private, consensual homosexual conduct under the statute here in question the convicted person would come within the registration laws of at least four States. . . . This underscores the consequential nature of the punishment and the state-sponsored condemnation attendant to the criminal prohibition. Furthermore, the Texas criminal conviction carries with it the other collateral consequences always following a conviction, such as notations on job application forms. . . .

. . . . In the United States criticism of *Bowers* has been substantial and continuing, disapproving of its reasoning in all respects, not just as to its historical assumptions. . . . [¶] To the extent *Bowers* relied on values we share with a wider civilization, it should be noted that the reasoning and holding in *Bowers* have been rejected [in other nations]. There has been no showing that in this country the governmental interest in circumscribing personal choice is somehow more legitimate or urgent.

The doctrine of *stare decisis* is essential to the respect accorded to the judgments of the Court and to the stability of the law. It is not, however, an inexorable command. . . . *Bowers* itself causes uncertainty, for the precedents before and after its issuance contradict its central holding.

The rationale of *Bowers* does not withstand careful analysis. In his dissenting opinion in *Bowers* Justice STEVENS came to these conclusions:

> Our prior cases make two propositions abundantly clear. First, the fact that the governing majority in a State has traditionally viewed a particular practice as immoral is not a sufficient reason for upholding a law prohibiting the practice; neither history nor tradition could save a law prohibiting miscegenation from constitutional attack. Second, individual decisions by married persons, concerning the intimacies of their physical relationship, even when not intended to produce offspring, are a form of "liberty" protected by the Due Process Clause of the Fourteenth Amendment. Moreover, this protection extends to intimate choices by unmarried as well as married persons. 478 U.S., at 216.

Justice STEVENS' analysis, in our view, should have been controlling in *Bowers* and should control here.

Bowers was not correct when it was decided, and it is not correct today. It ought not to remain binding precedent. *Bowers v. Hardwick* should be and now is overruled.

The present case does not involve minors. It does not involve persons who might be injured or coerced or who are situated in relationships where consent might not easily be refused. It does not involve public conduct or prostitution. It does not involve whether the government must give formal recognition to any relationship that homosexual persons seek to enter. The case does involve two adults who, with full and mutual consent from each other, engaged in sexual practices common to a homosexual lifestyle. The petitioners are entitled to respect for their private lives. The State cannot demean their existence or control their destiny by making their private sexual conduct a crime. Their right to liberty under the Due Process Clause gives them the full right to engage in their conduct without intervention of the government. "It is a promise of the Constitution that there is a realm of personal liberty which the government may not enter." The Texas statute furthers no legitimate state interest which can justify its intrusion into the personal and private life of the individual.

Had those who drew and ratified the Due Process Clauses of the Fifth Amendment or the Fourteenth Amendment known the components of liberty in its manifold possibilities, they might have been more specific. They did not presume to have this insight. They knew times can blind us to certain truths and later generations can see that laws once thought necessary and proper in fact serve only to oppress. As the Constitution endures, persons in every generation can invoke its principles in their own search for greater freedom.

. . . .

Justice O'Connor, concurring in the judgment.

The Court today overrules *Bowers v. Hardwick*. I joined *Bowers,* and do not join the Court in overruling it. Nevertheless, I agree with the Court that Texas' statute banning same-sex sodomy is unconstitutional. Rather than relying on the substantive component of the Fourteenth Amendment's Due Process Clause, as the Court does, I base my conclusion on the Fourteenth Amendment's Equal Protection Clause.

The Equal Protection Clause of the Fourteenth Amendment "is essentially a direction that all persons similarly situated should be treated alike." *Cleburne v. Cleburne Living Center, Inc.,* 473 U.S. 432 (1985). . . . Under our rational basis standard of review, "legislation is presumed to be valid and will be sustained if the classification drawn by the statute is rationally related to a legitimate state interest." *Cleburne, supra* at 440; see also *Department of Agriculture v. Moreno,* 413 U.S. 528 (1973); *Romer v. Evans,* 517 U.S. 620 (1996). . . .

Laws such as economic or tax legislation that are scrutinized under rational basis review normally pass constitutional muster. . . . We have consistently held, however, that some objectives, such as "a bare . . . desire to harm a politically unpopular group," are not legitimate state interests. When a law exhibits such a desire to harm a politically unpopular group, we have applied a more searching form of rational basis review to strike down such laws under the Equal Protection Clause.

We have been most likely to apply rational basis review to hold a law unconstitutional under the Equal Protection Clause where, as here, the challenged legislation inhibits personal relationships. . . . [In] *Romer,* we disallowed a state statute that "impos[ed] a broad and undifferentiated disability on a single named group"— specifically, homosexuals. . . .

The statute at issue here makes sodomy a crime only if a person "engages in deviate sexual intercourse with another individual of the same sex." Sodomy between opposite-sex partners, however, is not a crime in Texas. That is, Texas treats the same conduct differently based solely on the participants. . . . [¶] The Texas statute makes homosexuals unequal in the eyes of the law by making particular conduct — and only that conduct — subject to criminal sanction. It appears that prosecutions under Texas' sodomy law are rare. This case shows, however, that prosecutions under § 21.06 *do* occur. And while the penalty imposed on petitioners in this case was relatively minor, the consequences of conviction are not. As the Court notes, petitioners' convictions, if upheld, would disqualify them from or restrict their ability to engage in a variety of professions, including medicine, athletic training, and interior design.

And the effect of Texas' sodomy law is not just limited to the threat of prosecution or consequence of conviction. Texas' sodomy law brands all homosexuals as criminals, thereby making it more difficult for homosexuals to be treated in the same manner as everyone else. Indeed, Texas itself has previously acknowledged the collateral effects of the law, stipulating in a prior challenge to this action that the law "legally sanctions discrimination against [homosexuals] in a variety of ways unrelated to the criminal law," including in the areas of "employment, family issues, and housing."

. . . .

. . . . This case raises a different issue than *Bowers:* whether, under the Equal Protection Clause, moral disapproval is a legitimate state interest to justify by itself a statute that bans homosexual sodomy, but not heterosexual sodomy. It is not. Moral disapproval of this group, like a bare desire to harm the group, is an interest that is insufficient to satisfy rational basis review under the Equal Protection Clause. Indeed, we have never held that moral disapproval, without any other asserted state interest, is a sufficient rationale under the Equal Protection Clause to justify a law that discriminates among groups of persons. . . . The Texas sodomy law "raise[s] the inevitable inference that the disadvantage imposed is born of animosity toward the class of persons affected."

Texas argues, however, that the sodomy law does not discriminate against homosexual persons. Instead, the State maintains that the law discriminates only against homosexual conduct. While it is true that the law applies only to conduct, the conduct targeted by this law is conduct that is closely correlated with being homosexual. Under such circumstances, Texas' sodomy law is targeted at more than conduct. It is instead directed toward gay persons as a class. "After all, there can hardly be more palpable discrimination against a class than making the conduct that defines the class criminal." *Id.,* at 641 (SCALIA, J., dissenting). When a State makes homosexual conduct criminal, and not "deviate sexual intercourse" committed by persons of different sexes, "that declaration in and of itself is an invitation to subject homosexual persons to discrimination both in the public and in the private spheres.

. . . .

. . . .The Texas sodomy statute subjects homosexuals to "a lifelong penalty and stigma. . . ." [¶] Whether a sodomy law that is neutral both in effect and application . . . would violate the substantive component of the Due Process Clause is an issue that need not be decided today. I am confident, however, that so long as the Equal Protection Clause requires a sodomy law to apply equally to the private consensual conduct of homosexuals and heterosexuals alike, such a law would not long stand in our democratic society. In the words of Justice Jackson:

> The framers of the Constitution knew, and we should not forget today, that there is no more effective practical guaranty against arbitrary and unreasonable government than to require that the principles of law which officials would impose upon a minority be imposed generally. Conversely, nothing opens the door to arbitrary action so effectively as to allow those officials to pick and choose only a few to whom they will apply legislation and thus to escape the political retribution that might be visited upon them if larger numbers were affected."

. . . .

A law branding one class of persons as criminal solely based on the State's moral disapproval of that class and the conduct associated with that class runs contrary to the values of the Constitution and the Equal Protection Clause, under any standard of review. I therefore concur in the Court's judgment that Texas' sodomy law banning "deviate sexual intercourse" between consenting adults of the same sex, but not between consenting adults of different sexes, is unconstitutional.

JUSTICE SCALIA, with whom THE CHIEF JUSTICE and JUSTICE THOMAS join, dissenting.

"Liberty finds no refuge in a jurisprudence of doubt." *Casey,* 505 U.S. at 844. That was the Court's sententious response, barely more than a decade ago, to those seeking to overrule *Roe v. Wade.* The Court's response today, to those who have engaged in a 17-year crusade to overrule *Bowers v. Hardwick* (1986), is very different. The need for stability and certainty presents no barrier.

Most of the rest of today's opinion has no relevance to its actual holding — that the Texas statute "furthers no legitimate state interest which can justify" its application to petitioners under rational-basis review. Though there is discussion of "fundamental proposition[s]," and "fundamental decisions," nowhere does the Court's opinion declare that homosexual sodomy is a "fundamental right" under the Due Process Clause; nor does it subject the Texas law to the standard of review that would be appropriate (strict scrutiny) if homosexual sodomy *were* a "fundamental right." Thus, while overruling the *outcome* of *Bowers,* the Court leaves strangely untouched its central legal conclusion: "[R]espondent would have us announce . . . a fundamental right to engage in homosexual sodomy. This we are quite unwilling to do." Instead the Court simply describes petitioners' conduct as "an exercise of their liberty"—which it undoubtedly is—and proceeds to apply an unheard-of form of rational-basis review that will have far-reaching implications beyond this case.

I

I begin with the Court's surprising readiness to reconsider a decision rendered a mere 17 years ago in *Bowers v. Hardwick.* I do not myself believe in rigid adherence to *stare decisis* in constitutional cases; but I do believe that we should be consistent rather than manipulative in invoking the doctrine. . . . [¶] [¶] Today, however, the widespread opposition to *Bowers,* a decision resolving an issue as "intensely divisive" as the issue in *Roe,* is offered as a reason in favor of *overruling* it. . . .

. . . .

To tell the truth, it does not surprise me, and should surprise no one, that the Court has chosen today to revise the standards of *stare decisis* set forth in *Casey.* It has thereby exposed *Casey*'s extraordinary deference to precedent for the result-oriented expedient that it is.

II

Having decided that it need not adhere to *stare decisis,* the Court still must establish that *Bowers* was wrongly decided and that the Texas statute, as applied to petitioners, is unconstitutional.

Texas Penal Code Ann. § 21.06(a) (2003) undoubtedly imposes constraints on liberty. So do laws prohibiting prostitution, recreational use of heroin, and, for that matter, working more than 60 hours per week in a bakery. . . . The Fourteenth Amendment *expressly allows* States to deprive their citizens of "liberty," *so long as "due process of law" is provided:*

> "No state shall . . . deprive any person of life, liberty, or property, *without due process of law.*" Amdt. 14 (emphasis added).

Our opinions applying the doctrine known as "substantive due process" hold that the Due Process Clause prohibits States from infringing *fundamental* liberty interests, unless the infringement is narrowly tailored to serve a compelling state interest. *Washington v. Glucksberg,* 521 U.S., at 721. We have held repeatedly, in cases the Court today does not overrule, that *only* fundamental rights qualify for this so-called "heightened scrutiny" protection — that is, rights which are " 'deeply rooted in this Nation's history and tradition,' ". . . . All other liberty interests may be abridged or abrogated pursuant to a validly enacted state law if that law is rationally related to a legitimate state interest.

Bowers held, first, that criminal prohibitions of homosexual sodomy are not subject to heightened scrutiny because they do not implicate a "fundamental right" under the Due Process Clause. . . [¶] The Court today does not overrule this holding. Not once does it describe homosexual sodomy as a "fundamental right" or a "fundamental liberty interest," nor does it subject the Texas statute to strict scrutiny. Instead, . . . the Court concludes that the application of

Texas's statute to petitioners' conduct fails the rational-basis test, and overrules *Bowers'* holding to the contrary [:]"The Texas statute furthers no legitimate state interest which can justify its intrusion into the personal and private life of the individual."

. . . .

III

I turn now to the ground on which the Court squarely rests its holding: the contention that there is no rational basis for the law here under attack. . . . [¶] The Texas statute undeniably seeks to further the belief of its citizens that certain forms of sexual behavior are "immoral and unacceptable" — the same interest furthered by criminal laws against fornication, bigamy, adultery, adult incest, bestiality, and obscenity. *Bowers* held that this *was* a legitimate state interest. The Court today reaches the opposite conclusion. . . . The Court embraces instead Justice STEVENS' declaration in his *Bowers* dissent, that "the fact that the governing majority in a State has traditionally viewed a particular practice as immoral is not a sufficient reason for upholding a law prohibiting the practice." This effectively decrees the end of all morals legislation. If, as the Court asserts, the promotion of majoritarian sexual morality is not even a *legitimate* state interest, none of the above-mentioned laws can survive rational-basis review.

. . . .

V

Finally, I turn to petitioners' equal-protection challenge, which [only] JUSTICE O'CONNOR . . . embraces. . . . [¶] [¶] JUSTICE O'CONNOR argues that the discrimination in this law which must be justified is not its discrimination with regard to the sex of the partner but its discrimination with regard to the sexual proclivity of the principal actor. . . . Of course the same could be said of any law. A law against public nudity targets "the conduct that is closely correlated with being a nudist," and hence "is targeted at more than conduct"; it is "directed toward nudists as a class." But be that as it may. Even if the Texas law *does* deny equal protection to "homosexuals as a class," that denial *still* does not need to be justified by anything more than a rational basis, which our cases show is satisfied by the enforcement of traditional notions of sexual morality.

JUSTICE O'CONNOR simply decrees application of "a more searching form of rational basis review" to the Texas statute. The cases she cites [*i.e.*, *Romer v. Evans, Cleburne v. Cleburne Living Center, Inc, Department of Agriculture v. Moreno*] do not recognize such a standard, and reach their conclusions only after finding, as required by conventional rational-basis analysis, that no conceivable legitimate state interest supports the classification at issue. Nor does JUSTICE O'CONNOR explain precisely what her "more searching form" of rational-basis review consists of. It must at least mean, however, that laws exhibiting " 'a . . . desire to harm a politically unpopular group,' " are invalid *even though* there may be a conceivable rational basis to support

This reasoning leaves on pretty shaky grounds state laws limiting marriage to opposite-sex couples. JUSTICE O'CONNOR seeks to preserve them by the conclusory statement that "preserving the traditional institution of marriage" is a legitimate state interest. But "preserving the traditional institution of marriage" is just a kinder way of describing the State's *moral disapproval* of same-sex couples. Texas's interest in § 21.06 could be recast in similarly euphemistic terms: "preserving the traditional sexual mores of our society." In the jurisprudence JUSTICE O'CONNOR has seemingly created, judges can validate laws by characterizing them as "preserving the traditions of society" (good); or invalidate them by characterizing them as "expressing moral disapproval" (bad).

*   *   *   *   *   *

Today's opinion is the product of a Court, which is the product of a law-profession culture, that has largely signed on to the so-called homosexual agenda, by which I mean the agenda promoted by some homosexual activists directed at eliminating the moral opprobrium that has traditionally attached to homosexual conduct. I noted in an earlier opinion the fact that the American Association of Law Schools (to which any reputable law school *must* seek to belong) excludes from membership any school that refuses to ban from its job-interview facilities a law firm (no matter how small) that does not wish to hire as a prospective partner a person who openly engages in homosexual conduct.

One of the most revealing statements in today's opinion is the Court's grim warning that the criminalization of homosexual conduct is "an invitation to subject homosexual persons to discrimination both in the public and in the private spheres." It is clear from this that the Court has taken sides in the culture war, departing from its role of assuring, as neutral observer, that the democratic rules of engagement are observed. Many Americans do not want persons who openly engage in homosexual conduct as partners in their business, as scoutmasters for their children, as teachers in their children's schools, or as boarders in their home. They view this as protecting themselves and their families from a lifestyle that they believe to be immoral and destructive. . . .

Let me be clear that I have nothing against homosexuals, or any other group, promoting their agenda through normal democratic means. Social perceptions of sexual and other morality change over time, and every group has the right to persuade its fellow citizens that its view of such matters is the best. That homosexuals have achieved some success in that enterprise is attested to by the fact that Texas is one of the few remaining States that criminalize private, consensual homosexual acts. But persuading one's fellow citizens is one thing, and imposing one's views in absence of democratic majority will is something else. I would no more *require* a State to criminalize homosexual acts — or, for that matter, display *any* moral disapprobation of them — than I would *forbid* it to do so. What Texas has chosen to do is well within the range of traditional democratic action, and its hand should not be stayed through the invention of a brand-new "constitutional right" by a Court that is impatient of democratic change. It is indeed true that "later generations can see that laws once thought necessary and proper in fact serve only to oppress," and when that happens, later generations can repeal those laws. But it is the premise of our system that those judgments are to be made by the people, and not imposed by a governing caste that knows best.

One of the benefits of leaving regulation of this matter to the people rather than to the courts is that the people, unlike judges, need not carry things to their logical conclusion. The people may feel that their disapproval of homosexual conduct is strong enough to disallow homosexual marriage, but not strong enough to criminalize private homosexual acts — and may legislate accordingly. The Court today pretends that it possesses a similar freedom of action, so that that we need not fear judicial imposition of homosexual marriage, as has recently occurred in Canada (in a decision that the Canadian Government has chosen not to appeal). At the end of its opinion — after having laid waste the foundations of our rational-basis jurisprudence — the Court says that the present case "does not involve whether the government must give formal recognition to any relationship that homosexual persons seek to enter." Do not believe it. More illuminating than this bald, unreasoned disclaimer is the progression of thought displayed by an earlier passage in the Court's opinion, which notes the constitutional protections afforded to "personal decisions relating to *marriage,* procreation, contraception, family relationships, child rearing, and education," and then declares that "[p]ersons in a homosexual relationship may seek autonomy for these purposes, just as heterosexual persons do." Today's opinion dismantles the structure of constitutional law that has permitted a distinction to be made between heterosexual and homosexual unions, insofar as formal recognition in marriage is concerned. If moral disapprobation of homosexual conduct is "no legitimate state interest" for purposes of proscribing that conduct, and if, as the Court coos (casting aside all pretense of neutrality), "[w]hen sexuality finds overt expression in intimate conduct with another person, the conduct can be but one element in a personal bond that is more enduring," what justification could there possibly be for denying the benefits of marriage to homosexual couples exercising "[t]he liberty protected by the Constitution,"? Surely not the encouragement of procreation, since the sterile and the elderly are allowed to marry. This case "does not involve" the issue of homosexual marriage only if one entertains the belief that principle and logic have nothing to do with the decisions of this Court. . . .

JUSTICE THOMAS, dissenting.

I join JUSTICE SCALIA's dissenting opinion. I write separately to note that the law before the Court today "is . . . uncommonly silly." *Griswold v. Connecticut,* 381 U.S. 479, 527 (1965) (Stewart, J., dissenting). If I were a member of the Texas Legislature, I would vote to repeal it. Punishing someone for expressing his sexual preference through noncommercial consensual conduct with another adult does not appear to be a worthy way to expend valuable law enforcement resources. [¶] Notwithstanding this, I recognize that as a member of this Court I am not empowered to help petitioners and others similarly situated. My duty, rather, is to "decide cases 'agreeably to the Constitution and laws of the United States.'" And, just like Justice Stewart, I "can find [neither in the Bill of Rights nor any other part of the Constitution a] general right of privacy," or as the Court terms it today, the "liberty of the person both in its spatial and more transcendent dimensions."

NOTES

1. *What is the Essential Holding of* Lawrence? Most observers expected that the Texas statute would fail to survive the Court's review in *Lawrence*. Unlike the Georgia statute upheld in *Bowers v. Hardwick*, Texas' anti-sodomy law applied only to same-sex partners. Thus, the Court's striking of that law seemed a logical extension of the principles announced in *Romer*. Such an approach, laid out in Justice O'Connor's *Lawrence* concurrence, would have allowed the Court to invalidate the statute without directly overruling *Hardwick*. Given this Court's tendency toward moderation, few anticipated that a 5-4 majority of the Court would ground its ruling in the Due Process Clause, explicitly rejecting *Hardwick*.

Yet, it is not completely clear what aspects of *Hardwick* the *Lawrence* Court did overrule and how broad is its holding. While the majority clearly reversed *Hardwick's* holding that a state could constitutionally prohibit private, consensual, noncommercial sodomy between adult partners, Justice Kennedy's decision stopped short of declaring that there exists a fundamental right to engage in such conduct. Was such a conclusion implicit in the Court's language? Justice Kennedy's reliance on precedents such as *Griswold, Eisenstadt,* and *Roe* certainly suggests that the interest at stake is a privacy right. Yet the majority opinion refers to the underlying interest in *Lawrence* as a form of "liberty" and avoids the terms "privacy" and "fundamental" in defining this interest. Is this just a matter of semantics, or does this aspect of the Court's language portend limitations in *Lawrence's* reach as precedent? This question is already puzzling scholars. *See, e.g.,* Randy E. Barnett, *Justice Kennedy's Libertarian Revolution:* Lawrence v. Texas (2003) (available at: www.bu.edu/law/faculty/papers); Brett H. McDonnell, *Is Incest Next?* 10 CARDOZO WOMEN'S L.J. (forthcoming); Cass R. Sunstein, *What Did* Lawrence *Hold? Of Autonomy, Desuetude, Sexuality, and Marriage* (2003) (available at: www.law.uchicago.edu/Lawecon/index.html) (noting four possible viewpoints as to the mode of analysis employed in *Lawrence*). To the extent that the characterization of the underlying right in *Lawrence* mandates a particular standard of review, the characterization of that right is likely to have important implications for the extension of *Lawrence* to other contexts.

In his dissent, Justice Scalia blasted the majority for failing to articulate its standard of review. He is correct that nowhere does the *Lawrence* majority enunciate or apply the familiar language of strict scrutiny, the heightened level of review used by the Court when evaluating the constitutionality of statutes that infringe on fundamental rights such as privacy. In fact, the only language reminiscent of one of the tiers of constitutional review is Justice Kennedy's statement in *Lawrence* that "[t]he Texas statute furthers no legitimate state interest which can justify its intrusion into the personal and private life of the individual." Justice Scalia cites this passage as indicating that the Court applied a version of the rational basis test in *Lawrence*. If this is the case, and the Court's review parallels the rational basis review in *Romer*, statutes challenged after *Lawrence* may stand if a reviewing court can identify some legitimate or permissible state purpose that the statute might reasonably achieve. Conceivably, however, *Lawrence* rejected the two-tiered framework completely, rendering its impact in other contexts even more unpredictable.

The *Lawrence* opinion is not the first characterizing privacy-like interests as a form of liberty requiring a review less searching than strict scrutiny. In *Cruzan v. Director, Missouri Health Dep't.*, 497 U.S. 261 (1990), the Court noted: "Although many state courts have held that a right to refuse treatment is encompassed by a generalized constitutional right to privacy, we have never so held. We believe this issue is more properly analyzed in terms of a Fourteenth Amendment liberty interest." *Id.* at 279, n.7. The Court did not articulate its standard of review in *Cruzan,* but appears to balance the patient's liberty interests against the relevant state interests. *See* David L. Faigman, *Madisonian Balancing: A Theory of Constitutional Adjudication,* 88 Nw. U.L. Rev. 641 (1994) (discussing the relationship between balancing tests and tiered constitutional review). In *Casey,* 505 U.S. at 850, the Court departed from *Roe's* characterization of the underlying right as a fundamental right to privacy, referring to it instead as a liberty interest. In *Casey,* the Court replaced the strict scrutiny review of *Roe* with the "undue burden" standard. Thus, to the extent that these precedents bear on *Lawrence,* various privacy-like liberty interests do not necessarily trigger strict scrutiny, and may be analyzed outside of the familiar two-tiered due process analysis. Precisely what is the proper mode of analysis for those cases using *Lawrence* as precedent is not clear, and is likely to be the source of substantial commentary until the Court provides further guidance. *See, e.g.,* Barnett, *supra* (viewing *Lawrence* as "revolutionary" in its rejection of the traditional two-tiered analysis, while requiring government to justify its restriction on liberty); Sunstein, *supra.*

2. *Shifts in Approach Evident in the Majority Opinion in* Lawrence. The *Lawrence* opinion rejects many of the analytic tools that *Hardwick,,* as well as certain other cases, *e.g.*, *Michael H. v. Gerald D.* (reprinted in Section C *infra*), employed to limit the scope of the underlying constitutional interest. First, *Lawrence* flatly rejected *Hardwick's* highly-specific definition of the underlying right. Instead, it searched for the general principle of which the right in question might be but one example. In *Lawrence,* Justice Kennedy referred to the liberty interests involved as including "autonomy of self," "freedom of . . . intimate conduct," the right of adults to "choose to enter" relationships that encompass intimate sexual conduct, and the "right to engage in [private sexual conduct] without intervention from the government." Second, in *Lawrence,* the Court deemphasized the importance of our nation's historical or traditional protection of the right in the determination of whether the right deserves constitutional protection. Third, *Lawrence* rejected a strict constructionist approach to interpreting the Constitution in this context, suggesting that the Framers' use of general, rather than specific, language in the text of the Constitution was meant to accommodate the needs of each generation to apply its principles to issues arising in their unique moments in history. Finally, the Court rejected the *Hardwick* Court's use of "morality" as a primary yardstick for what is or is not constitutionally protected. These shifts, taken together, open the door for constitutional considerations to reflect changing social values, and to vindicate the rights of those engaging in harmless conduct that departs from social norms.

The Court, in addition, revealed a newly-found interest in evaluating American law by comparing it with policies and precedents of other nations and of international tribunals. *Lawrence* was one among several opinions written by various justices in recent years revealing a nascent concern with how our law compares with those of others in the world community. For a critique of this phenomenon, see Robert H. Bork, *Whose Constitution Is It, Anyway?* 55 NATIONAL REVIEW, Dec. 8, 2003.

3. *The Ramifications of* Lawrence *for the Rights of Gays and Lesbians in the Context of Family Law and Intimate Relations*. How will *Lawrence* affect other areas of family law in which gays and lesbians are disfavored? Will it open the door to same-sex marriage, facilitate gay and lesbian adoptions of children, or restrict consideration of a party's sexual orientation in child custody determinations? Justice Kennedy asserted that the *Lawrence* ruling "does not involve whether the government must give formal recognition to any relationship that homosexual persons seek to enter." *Id*. at 2484. However, courts are, of course, free to apply the principles announced in *Lawrence* to the particular questions before them. At first blush, the equal protection analysis set forth in Justice O'Connor's *Lawrence* concurrence appears to lend itself more readily to such extensions than does the majority opinion. Justice O'Connor concluded that classifications based solely on "the State's moral disapproval of a class and the conduct associated with that class" are unconstitutional, particularly where "the challenged legislation inhibits personal relationships." *Id*. at 2484, 2488 (O'Connor, J., concurring). Thus, to the extent that a state restricts the equal opportunities of gays and lesbians to engage in family relationships or to obtain legal recognition for those relationships, and those restrictions appear grounded *solely* in animus toward or moral disapproval of homosexuals, such distinctions would not be constitutionally sustainable under Justice O'Connor's analysis. However, policymakers often ground legal distinctions between heterosexuals and homosexuals in the family context on assertions that children's best interests are better served in a home with heterosexual, rather than homosexual, parents. (See the discussion of these claims in Chapter 6, and in Section C4 of this chapter.) Thus, to the extent that such views are persuasive, the reach of Justice O'Connor's equal protection analysis would be limited, because a rational basis for the distinction could be offered even if the evidence supporting such a distinction was weak, anecdotal, or contested.

More complicated, and somewhat less intuitive, are arguments for extending the *Lawrence* Court's due process analysis to those areas of family law in which gays and lesbians are disfavored. To the extent that policymakers rely on the existence of criminal proscriptions against homosexual conduct to legitimize *civil* distinctions between homosexuals and heterosexuals, *Lawrence* will disable such arguments. In his recent commentary on the *Lawrence* decision, Professor Laurence Tribe underscores the power that resides in criminal sanctions, even when unenforced, in affecting a societal subgroup's status in society:

Given that the criminal laws [prohibiting sodomy] . . . almost from the start, have languished without enforcement, Lawrence quickly becomes a story about how the very fact of criminalization, even unaccompanied by any appreciable number of prosecutions, can cast already misunderstood or despised individuals into grossly stereotyped roles, which become the source and justification for treating those individuals less well than others. The outlawed acts — visualized in ways that obscure their similarity to what most sexually active adults themselves routinely do — come to represent human identities, and this reductionist conflation of ostracized identity with outlawed act in turn reinforces the vicious cycle of distancing and stigma that preserves the equilibrium of oppression in one of the several distinct dynamics at play in the legal construction of social hierarchy.

Laurence H. Tribe, Lawrence v. Texas: *The "Fundamental Right" That Dare Not Speak Its Name*, 117 HARV. L. REV. 1893, 1895 (2004).

Lawrence also rejected, in no uncertain terms, the use of "morality" as the sole justification for policies that disfavor gays and lesbians, eliminating another device often used to support such distinctions. For a discussion of the implications of *Lawrence* for policy justifications relying on claims of morality, see Suzanne B. Goldberg, *Morals-Based Justifications for Lawmaking Before and After* Lawrence v. Texas, 88 MICH. L. REV. 1233 (2004). Taking the possible impact of *Lawrence* a step further, Justices Kennedy and Scalia both imply, albeit from different vantage points, that the Court's invocation of liberty as the basis for its ruling both encompasses and expands upon the protections inherent in an equal protection analysis. "Equality of treatment and the due process right to demand respect for conduct protected by the substantive guarantee of liberty are linked in important respects, and a decision on the latter point advances both interests. . . . When homosexual conduct is made criminal by the law of the State, that declaration in and of itself is an invitation to subject homosexual persons to discrimination in the public and in the private spheres [which] demeans the lives of homosexual persons." *Lawrence*, 123 S. Ct. at 2482. One might argue that if the only factor that distinguishes homosexuals from heterosexuals is the nature of the intimate sexual conduct engaged in by each, and that conduct has been held to fall within our cherished right of liberty, it is difficult to justify legal disabilities based solely on that distinction. Justice Scalia concedes as much when he dismisses the majority's claim that the "present case 'does not involve whether the government must give formal recognition to any relationship that homosexual persons seek to enter.' " *Id.* at 2497–98 (Scalia, J., dissenting). For further discussion of the relationship between equal protection and due process analyses in *Lawrence*, see Tribe, *supra* at 1897-98, and Pamela S. Karlan, *Loving* Lawrence (2004) (available at http://ssrn.com/abstract=512662).

Is Justice Scalia correct that the majority opinion in *Lawrence* opens the door to challenges against same-sex marriage prohibitions? He links the Court's discussion of "the constitutional protections afforded to 'personal decisions relating to *marriage*, procreation, contraception, family relationships, child rearing and education' " to its declaration that " '[p]ersons in a homosexual relationship may seek autonomy for these purposes, just as heterosexuals do.'" *Id.* at 2498 (emphasis in original). In other words, concludes Justice Scalia, "[t]oday's opinion dismantles the structure of constitutional law that has permitted a distinction to be made between heterosexual and homosexual unions, insofar as formal recognition of marriage is concerned. If moral disapprobation of homosexual conduct is [not a] legitimate state interest for purposes of proscribing that conduct,. . . . what justification could there possibly be for denying the benefits of marriage to homosexual couples exercising '[t]he liberty protected by the Constitution'?" *Id.* Whereas it is not necessarily as clear as Justice Scalia suggests that *Lawrence* leads directly to the conclusion that states *must* make marriage available to same-sex couples, courts will clearly be required to examine differential legal distinctions of heterosexuals and homosexuals more carefully than they have been required to do in the past.

Since *Lawrence* was decided, certain closely-watched decisions affecting the rights of gays and lesbians have been issued. The most dramatic post-*Lawrence* development is the Massachusetts' Supreme Judicial Court's 4-3 holding that "barring an individual from the protections, benefits, and obligations of civil marriage solely because that person would marry a person of the same sex violates the Massachusetts Constitution." *Goodridge v. Dept. of Public Health*, 798 N.E.2d 941, 969 (2003) (reprinted in Chapter 2). The Massachusetts court avoided the question of whether the denial of marriage licenses to same-sex couples implicated a fundamental right or created a suspect classification. Because the Massachusetts court held that the statute did not survive rational basis review, it determined that the more searching inquiries were unnecessary. Rejecting each of the state's asserted rationales for the exclusion of same-sex couples, the court gave the legislature six months to take action appropriate with the opinion. Although the decision interpreted provisions of the Massachusetts Constitution and relied heavily on Massachusetts precedent, *Lawrence* clearly had an impact. In particular, the court cited *Lawrence* most directly when eschewing government imposition of lawmakers' own moral codes at the expense of liberty, and when referring to decisions "[w]hether and whom to marry [and] how to express sexual intimacy [as] among the most basic of every individual's liberty and due process rights." *Id.* at 959.

The dissenters argued for a more limited reading of *Lawrence,* suggesting that *Lawrence* articulated a right to be free from government intrusion into private intimate relations that occur behind bedroom doors. *Goodridge*, 798 N.E.2d at 974, 978 (Spina, J., dissenting). Quoting Justice Kennedy's assertion that *Lawrence* "does not involve whether the government must give formal recognition to any relationship that homosexual persons seek to enter," the *Goodridge* dissenters suggested that "by extending the marriage laws to same-sex couples the [*Goodridge* majority] has turned substantive due process on its head and used it to interject government into the plaintiffs' lives." *Id.* at 978.

In February 2004, in response to an inquiry from the Massachusetts State Senate, the Supreme Judicial Court of Massachusetts clarified its November 2003 decision. *Opinion of the Justices to the Senate*, 802 N.E.2d 565 (Mass. 2004). The justices held that if the state legislature created a special status for same-sex couples rather than permitting these couples to marry, the new law would violate the equal protection clause of the Massachusetts Constitution, even if the new status provided for the same rights, benefits, and obligations as marriage. "The dissimilitude between the terms 'civil marriage' and 'civil union' is not innocuous; it is a considered choice of language that reflects a demonstrable assigning of same-sex, largely homosexual, couples to second-class status." *Id.* at 570. Several days later, Massachusetts assembled a constitutional convention to consider whether to amend the state constitution in a manner that would limit or avoid the effect of this court decision. In March 2004, the assembly approved a compromise amendment precluding same-sex marriage but establishing civil unions as a status with legal incidents identical to marriage. The Massachusetts constitutional amendment process requires a second convention two years later to reenact the same amendment, followed by the endorsement of two-thirds of the voters, before it becomes effective. Pam Belluck, *Effort to Undo Gay Marriage Ruling Fails, For Moment*, NEW YORK TIMES, Feb. 12, 2004.

A month before the Massachusetts court rendered its *Goodridge* decision, the Arizona Court of Appeals cited the same passage in Justice Kennedy's *Lawrence* opinion, and decided that Arizona's preclusion of gay marriage is constitutional, applying a rational basis analysis. *Standhardt v. Superior Court,* 77 P.3d 451 (Ariz. App. 2003) *rev. denied* (2004). Also in 2003, unpublished decisions in New Jersey and Indiana agreed with the conclusions reached by the *Standhardt* court. *See, e.g., Lewis v. Harris*, No. MER-L-15-03, 2003 WL 23191114 (N.J. Super. Ct. Law Div. 2003) (holding that New Jersey's restriction of marriage to opposite-sex couples does not violate the federal or New Jersey constitutions); *Morrison v. Sadler,* No. 49D13-0211-PL-001946, 2003 WL 23119998 (Ind. Super. Ct. 2003) (holding that Indiana's statute defining marriage as a union between a man and woman does not violate the Indiana Constitution). See Chapter 2 for further discussion of the current status of same-sex marriage restrictions.

In another post-*Lawrence* development, a three-judge panel of the Eleventh Circuit unanimously affirmed a lower court ruling sustaining Florida's ban against homosexual individuals or couples adopting a child in that state. *Lofton v. Sec'y of Dep't of Children and Family Serv., 358 F.3d 804 (2004).* The court distinguished between the criminal proscription at issue in *Lawrence* and the adoption of children. It rejected the plaintiff's contention that *Lawrence* established a fundamental right to "private sexual intimacy." It observed the inconsistency between the language in *Lawrence* and the standard fundamental rights analysis. Thus, it applied rational basis review, and concluded that Florida's interest in placing adoptive children in a home with an "optimal family structure" (that is, a married mother and father) justified the prohibition of adoptions by gays or lesbians. The American Civil Liberties Union, which represents the plaintiffs, indicated an intention to appeal.

For further discussion of the implications of *Lawrence* for the legal status of gays and lesbians, see *Symposium: Gay Rights after* Lawrence v. Texas, 88 MINN. L. REV. 1017 (2004). For a general survey of the legal status of gays and lesbians in areas such as employment, family, civil, immigration, and criminal law matters, prior to the *Lawrence* decision, see Rhonda R. Rivera,

Our Straight-Laced Judges: The Legal Position of Homosexual Persons in the United States, 50 HASTINGS L.J. 1015 (1999). For a discussion of the history of litigation for the rights of gays and lesbians in the United States prior to the 1990s, see Patricia A. Cain, *Litigating for Lesbian and Gay Rights: A Legal History,* 79 VA. L. REV. 1551 (1993); Mary Anne Case, *Couples and Coupling in the Public Sphere: A Comment on the Legal History of Litigating for Lesbian and Gay Rights*, 79 VA. L. REV. 1643 (1993).

4. *The Implications of* Lawrence *for State Statutes Proscribing Sodomy, Fornication, Cohabitation, and Adultery.* After *Lawrence,* it is clear that state sodomy laws cannot be enforced against private consensual acts between adults, although public or commercial sexual acts can still be criminalized, as can sexual acts involving minors. *See, e.g., Doe v. Pryor*, 344 F.3d 1282 (11th Cir. 2003) (referring to a "supplemental briefing" submitted to the court by the state's Attorney General concluding *Lawrence* rendered Alabama's sodomy statute unconstitutional). Consistent with this conclusion, it is not surprising that prosecutors in several states where sodomy remains a crime dropped pending cases, or changed their policies of enforcement, of sodomy laws post-*Lawrence. See, e.g.,* Meredith Oakley, *Sex Ought to be Private,* ARKANSAS DEMOCRAT GAZETTE, June 29, 2003, 2003 WL 57084398 (noting that Missouri prosecutors dropped cases of "deviate sexual intercourse" against six men following *Lawrence*); Christina C. Breen, *Sodomy Arrest Guideline Revised,* CHARLOTTE OBSERVER, July 6, 2003, *available at* www.charlotte.com/mld/observer/news/local/6242528.htm (last visited July 21, 2003) (describing revised guidelines for North Carolina police officers requiring that for arrests on suspicion of soliciting sodomy, the solicitation must be for a meeting in a public, rather than private, place). It is noteworthy, however, that a Kansas Court of Appeal rejected a defendant's challenge to a Kansas statute that provides substantially harsher penalties for the crime of sodomy of a minor when the perpetrator and victim are of the same sex, as contrasted with when the two individuals are of the opposite sex. *State v. Limon*, 83 P.3d 229 (Kan. 2004). The Kansas court reconsidered the statute's constitutionality after the U.S. Supreme Court remanded in light of *Lawrence. Limon v. Kansas*, 123 S. Ct. 2638 (2003). In this case, the defendant received a 206-month sentence; if the victim had been female, the sentence would likely have been approximately 15 months. Linda Greenhouse, *High Court Applies New Ruling to Teen's Sodomy Conviction*, SAN DIEGO UNION-TRIBUNE, June 28, 2003. In upholding the statute and the sentence, the Kansas court distinguished *Lawrence* on the basis that the Kansas statute under review sought to protect minors from sexual offenses, while *Lawrence* involved consenting adults.

a. *Anti-Fornication Statutes*. Fornication, usually defined as sexual intercourse between unmarried adults, is still a crime in about two dozen states. Traci Shallbetter Stratton, Note, *No More Messing Around: Substantive Due Process Challenges to State Laws Proscribing Fornication*, 73 WASH L. REV. 767 (1998); *In re J.M.*, 575 S.E.2d 441 (2003) (holding that Georgia's anti-fornication statute violated state constitutional privacy guarantees). To the extent that fornication laws focus on private, consensual conduct between adults, such laws may be repealed or judicially invalidated following *Lawrence*. Within days of the *Lawrence* decision, the Virginia State Crime

Commission subcommittee voted to limit the reach of the state's fornication, cohabitation, and adultery laws to "public" conduct. Tyler Whitley, *Panel: Strike Sodomy Statutes; Assembly May Not Listen to Suggestion,* THE RICHMOND TIMES-DISPATCH, July 17, 2003. This restriction often appeared in statutes even prior to *Lawrence. See, e.g.,* IL. ST. Ch. 720 § 5/11-8 (2003) (fornication prohibition limited to behavior that is "open and notorious"); *Adultery and Fornication,* AM. JUR. 2D (2003 update) (observing fornication prosecutions are rare in modern times, and some statutes have been interpreted not to apply to private conduct).

b. Anti-Cohabitation Statutes. While a single sexual act could, in principle, violate an anti-fornication statute, laws criminalizing cohabitation typically require more. At a minimum, "cohabitation" would appear to involve some form of living arrangement, and sharing a residence, with at least some regularity. Some states require that the cohabitation be "open and notorious" or "lewd and lascivious." *See, e.g.,* MICH. PEN. CODE § 335 (2003). Anti-cohabitation statutes, in one form or another, remain in several states, among them Idaho, Massachusetts, Michigan, Minnesota, Mississippi, North Carolina, North Dakota, South Carolina, Utah, Virginia, and West Virginia. Prosecutions under these statutes is rare. *See Doe v. Duling*, 782 F.2d 1202 (4th Cir. 1986) (holding that a couple could not challenge Virginia's anti-cohabitation statute because there was no threat of prosecution, given that the last recorded conviction for private, consensual cohabitation occurred in 1883). In April 2003, the North Dakota state Senate rejected a bill to repeal the state's 113-year-old criminal anti-cohabitation statute. This action garnered the attention of various observers, including a television talk-show host, *N.D. Legislature: More Comedy than Content*, GRAND FORKS HERALD, Apr. 29, 2003, and a New York Post writer commented: "Those who break the law . . . face up to 30 days in jail. No doubt, in separate cells." Marsha Kranes, *Weird But True*, NEW YORK POST, Apr. 5, 2003.

c. Anti-Adultery Statutes. A 1996 compilation found that 23 states and the District of Columbia still criminalized adultery. Richard Posner and Katharine Silbaugh, A GUIDE TO AMERICAN'S SEX LAWS 103-110. Although that number has dropped slightly in the past several years, anti-adultery statutes remain in many states. *See* Stratton, *supra*, at n.2. While adultery prosecutions are rare, they do occur, generally in circumstances suggesting another offense such as prostitution. *See, e.g., Commonwealth v. Stowell*, 449 N.E.2d 357 (Mass. 1983) (sustaining statute against privacy-based constitutional claim). Criminal prohibitions against adultery have also been used to justify disciplinary actions against married employees who have extramarital affairs. In at least two cases such use of the statutes to discipline police officers have been sustained over constitutional objections. *Sherman v. Henry*, 928 S.W.2d 464 (Tex. 1996) (police officer denied promotion); *Oliverson v. West Valley City*, 875 F. Supp. 1465 (D. Utah 1995) (police officer sanctioned).

After *Lawrence,* are adultery statutes likely to be sustained as constitutional? One might argue that adultery directly undercuts marriage and family because, by definition, it involves an extramarital relationship. Thus, whereas private consensual conduct between married partners or unmarried partners is clearly within the scope of *Lawrence's* holding, extension to adultery may require one more step that some courts might be reluctant to take. For thoughtful analysis of these issues, see Mark Strasser, *Sodomy, Adultery, and Same-Sex Marriage: On Legal Analysis and Fundamental Interests,* 8 UCLA WOMEN'S L.J. 313 (1998); Martin J. Siegel, *For Better or For Worse: Adultery, Crime, and the Constitution,* 30 J. FAM. L. 45 (1991/1992).

5. *Lawrence and the Future of State Restrictions on Polygamy and Incest*. Justice Scalia predicts that the *Lawrence* decision will pave the way for the striking of proscriptions against bigamy and adult incest. All states prohibit bigamous (and therefore also polygamous) marriages, as well as marriages between two persons who stand in particular family relations to one another. All states criminalize sexual relations between such family members, and most criminalize bigamy. *See* Ryan D. Tenney, Note, *Tom Green, Common-Law Marriage, and the Illegality of Putative Polygamy,* 17 BYU J. PUB. L. 141, 155 (2002) (reporting that forty-four states explicitly criminalize bigamy). Is *Lawrence* likely to affect these proscriptions? In *Lawrence,* Justice Kennedy limited the decision to situations where there is no "injury to a person or abuse of an institution the law protects." 123 S. Ct. at 2478. It is likely that defenders of criminal prohibitions of incest and bigamy will argue that these two practices are harmful either to the parties involved, or to the stability and welfare of the family as an institution. Historically, courts have been satisfied merely to refer to such harms, and have required little or no evidence that these practices are, in fact, harmful. One court recently considered a challenge to that state's incest statute which the defendant grounded in *Lawrence. State v. Freeman,* 801 N.E.2d 906 (Ohio App. 2003). The court rejected the defendant's arguments, distinguishing the incest proscription from the sodomy statute struck down in *Lawrence,* referring generally to the notion that harms accompany incestuous relations. An adjudication of the precedential value of *Lawrence* for polygamy proscriptions may be forthcoming from the Utah Supreme Court. Tom Green and Rodney Holm, two men living polygamous lifestyles, and convicted of violating Utah's bigamy statutes, have cited *Lawrence* as authority in their appeal. *See* Tony Mauro, *Double-Edged Ruling, "Lawrence v. Texas" a Boon for Gay Rights — Or Is It?* THE RECORDER, Feb. 9, 2004; Pamela Manson, *Appeals Seek Polygamy Right,* SALT LAKE TRIBUNE, Dec. 15, 2003. For the unpublished court of appeals decision, see *State v. Green,* No. 20010076-CA, 2001 WL 422825 (2001).

In considering how far *Lawrence* will reach, it is useful to consider the social context of the decision. In the latter decades of the 20th century, gay and lesbian individuals and couples became more visible in society. As such, people have learned that family members, friends, co-workers, and favorite television personalities are gay or lesbian. The media has increasingly portrayed gays and lesbians as people we can respect and admire and with whom we can identify. Social attitudes are shifting, and Americans have increasingly accepted gays and lesbians as "normal" in a variety of contexts. The process perpetuates itself, as greater social acceptance of gays and lesbians encourages such persons to be more open about their sexual orientation, further widening the circle of those who learn that people they like and respect are gay or lesbian. With such knowledge, the biases of many give way to acceptance. In dramatic contrast, no such change in social attitudes has occurred with respect to those who engage in polygamy or incest. One might even speculate that most forms of these practices remain as disdained by the populace today as they were when the criminal proscriptions were first enacted. In his analysis of the implications of *Lawrence,* Professor Cass Sunstein argues that public opinion was critical to the Court's decision in *Lawrence*:

> [T]he Court's decision [in *Lawrence*] was less about sexual autonomy, as a freestanding idea, and closer to a kind of due process variation on the old common law idea of desuetude. According to that concept, laws that are hardly ever enforced are said, by courts, to have lapsed, simply because they lack public support. The rationale here is that unenforced laws lack support in public convictions, and may not be brought to bear, in an unpredictable and essentially arbitrary way, against private citizens. . . . [¶]. . . . The decision should not be read to say that each and every criminal statute becomes unenforceable if it is rarely enforced. . . . At a minimum, it is also necessary to say that the rarity of enforcement is a product of the anachronistic nature of the moral judgment that underlies it. Building on this idea, the notion of desuetude might be applied whenever a criminal statute is rarely invoked because the public no longer supports the moral argument behind it.

Sunstein, *supra,* at 19. *See also* McDonnell, *supra* Note 1, at 26–28 (distinguishing sodomy and incest bans, in part, by the absence of a political movement advocating repeal of incest bans, and by social norms relating to both practices). Sunstein's perspective has much in common with the emphasis on social norms discussed in Chapter 3 in the discussion of the no-fault divorce reforms. *See* page 217 *supra*. To a great extent, law follows, rather than leads, social change. From this vantage point, the primary difference between the *Hardwick* and *Lawrence* decisions is the 17 years that separated them, and the critical shift in the social acceptance of gays and lesbians that occurred in that interval. For a discussion of changing societal attitudes as they relate to *Lawrence* and to constitutional decisionmaking more generally, see William N. Eskridge, Jr., Lawrence's *Jurisprudence of Tolerance: Stakes of Identity Poiltics*, 88 MINN. L. REV. 1021 (2004).

PROBLEM

Problem 9-1. After *Lawrence* was decided, Joe, a former Army officer, filed a federal lawsuit challenging the military policy commonly referred to as: "Don't Ask, Don't Tell." This policy permits any branch of the armed forces to discharge its members for homosexual conduct or for "stat[ing] that he or she is a homosexual or bisexual, or words to that effect." 10 U.S.C. § 654(b) (2003). Joe's briefs state that "he was discharged in 1997, eight days shy of his 20-year retirement date [and is] seeking to recoup $1.1 million in lost pension benefits." His suit also challenges the military's criminal prohibition against "unnatural carnal copulation," set forth in Article 125 of the Uniform Code of Military Justice, even though he was not prosecuted under that provision. He argues that the military's criminal *investigation* of his case under Article 125 was a factor in his discharge. Several federal circuit courts decided challenges against Section 654(b) before *Lawrence,* and rejected equal protection and first amendment claims by service men and women. *See, e.g,* *Able v. U.S.,* 155 F.3d 628 (2nd Cir. 1998); *Holmes v. California Army Nat'l Guard,* 124 F.3d 1126 (9th Cir. 1997); *Steffan v. Perry,* 41 F.3d 677 (D.C. Cir. 1994). As attorney for Joe, how might you argue Joe's case after *Lawrence*? To what extent do you think that the traditional deference to military policies will affect the result?

Problem 9-2. Alice and Harry had been married for six years and had one child, Cathy. The two divorced when Alice indicated that she is a lesbian and planned to move in with another woman. Prior to *Lawrence*, Alice and Harry engaged in a bitter custody fight, and Harry succeeded in obtaining primary custody of Cathy on the basis that Alice's homosexuality rendered her an unfit mother. Alice now challenges the trial court's decision in light of *Lawrence*, and argues that the state's statute permitting consideration of the "morality" of parental conduct in the determination of a child's custody is unconstitutional after *Lawrence* if it is applied to exclude a parent based on her sexual orientation. What are the strongest arguments for and against Alice's claims? How, if at all, would your arguments differ if Justice O'Connor's concurrence in *Lawrence* had been adopted by the Court's majority?

§ B. NONMARITAL COHABITATION

[1] THE DEMOGRAPHICS OF UNMARRIED COHABITATING COUPLES IN THE UNITED STATES

Between 1960 and 2002, the number of unmarried heterosexual couples living together increased more than ten-fold. *See* Table 9-1. During the same time period, the number of married couples did not even double. The ratio of unmarried heterosexual couples to married couples in the United States increased from 1.1 in 1960 to 8.6 in 2002. Furthermore, increasing proportions of the population have lived in at least one cohabiting relationship at some time in their lives. Larry Bumpass & Hsien-Hen Lu, *Trends in Cohabitation and Implications for Children's Family Contexts in the United States,* 54 POPULATION STUDIES 29, 31–32 (2000). In 1995, almost half of surveyed women between the ages of 25 and 40 reported having cohabited at some time during their lives. These numbers reflect substantial increases over comparable data collected in 1987-1988.

Research also reveals that heterosexual cohabiting relationships are less stable than are marriages. Approximately half of such relationships last one year or less, one-sixth last about three years, and only one-tenth last five years or longer. *Id.* at 33. In addition, couples who cohabit before marriage are more likely to divorce than are couples who did not cohabit before marriage. *Id.* at 33. Although this phenomenon is not well understood, most sociologists suggest that couples who choose to cohabit before marriage differ from other married couples in ways that ultimately affect the durability of their marriages. *See, e.g.,* Judith A. Seltzer, *Families Formed Outside of Marriage,* 62 J. MARR. & FAM. 1247 (2000); Lee A. Lillard, Michael J. Brien & Linda J. Waite, *Premarital Cohabitation and Subsequent Marital Dissolution: A Matter of Self-Selection?* 32 DEMOGRAPHY 437 (1995); Elizabeth Thomson & Ugo Colella, *Cohabitation and Marital Stability: Quality or Commitment?*, 54 J. MARR. & FAM. 259 (1992).

Table 9-1
Unmarried Heterosexual Couple Households in the United States, by Presence of Children: 1960 to 2002[1]

Year	Total Married Couples	UNMARRIED HETEROSEXUAL COUPLE HOUSEHOLDS		Ratio of Unmarried Couples Per 100 Married Couples
		Total	Without Children Under 15	With Children Under 15	

Year	Total Married Couples	Total	Without Children Under 15	With Children Under 15	Ratio of Unmarried Couples Per 100 Married Couples
2002	56,747,000	4,898,000	3,245,000	1,654,000	8.6
2001	56,592,000	4,893,000	3,178,000	1,716,000	8.6
2000	55,311,000	4,736,000	3,061,000	1,675,000	8.6
1999	54,770,000	4,486,000	2,981.,000	1,505,000	8.2
1998	54,317,000	4,236,000	2,716,000	1,520,000	7.8
1997	53,604,000	4,130,000	2,660,000	1,470,000	7.7
1996	53,567,000	3,958,000	2,516,000	1,442,000	7.4
1995	53,858,000	3,668,000	2,349,000	1,319,000	6.8
1990	52,317,000	2,856,000	1,966,000	891,000	5.5
1985	50,350,000	1,983,000	1,380,000	603,000	3.9
1980	49,112,000	1,589,000	1,159,000	431,000	3.2
1970	44,728,000	523,000	327,000	196,000	1.2
1960	39,254,000	439,000	242,000	197,000	1.1

Although most nonmarital cohabitants are in their 20s, 30s and 40s,[2] there has been a rise in such cohabitation among older Americans. One study reported an increase from 9,600 cohabitors age 60 and older in 1960 to 407,000 senior cohabitors in 1990. Most observers attribute this rise largely to the economic disincentives of marriage for elder couples, combined with the growing social acceptance of nonmarital cohabitation. Elders who marry risk loss of or reduction in public assistance, Supplemental Security Income, or pension survivor benefits, and their Social Security benefits may be subject to higher taxes following marriage. Albert Chevan, *As Cheaply as One:*

---

[1] Table 9-1 was compiled and adapted from the following sources: U.S. Census Bureau, Table HH-1. Households, by Type: 1940 to Present, June 12, 2003 (available at: www.census.gov/population/www/socdemo/hh-fam/tabHH-1.csv); U.S. Census Bureau, Table UC-1. Unmarried-Couple Households, by Presence of Children: 1960 to Present, June 12, 2003 (available at: www.census.gov/population/www/socdemo/hh-fam/tabUC-1.csv). For additional information regarding data collection methods, see the Statistical Note on page 874.

[2] Data from the year 2000 reveal that 47.4% of male and 42.2% of female unmarried cohabiting adults were ages 35 and older, that 37% of the men and 33.2% of the women were ages 25 to 34 years old, and that the remaining 15.6% and 24.5%, respectively, were ages 24 and younger. U.S. Census Bureau, *America's Families and Living Arrangements* (2000).

Cohabitation in the Older Population, 58 J. MARR. & FAM. 656, 660 (1996). As today's cohabiting couples age, we are likely to see continuing increases in rates of nonmarital cohabitation in older age groups. *Id.*; *see generally* T.P. Gallanis, *Aging and the Nontraditional Family*, 32 U. MEM. L. REV. 607 (2002).

Demographic data on same-sex cohabitating couples has been somewhat more difficult to obtain. Prior to 1990, the only data on nonmarital cohabitation available from the United States Census Bureau was collected by a survey of telephone interviews of a random representative sample of American households. The results of these surveys, called Current Population Surveys ("CPS"), were then extrapolated to the larger U.S. population, resulting in data such as those presented in Table 9-1. Beginning in 1990, however, the decennial census, which tracks population data by sending questionnaires to every household in the country at the beginning of each decade, added a new category. This category, which appeared again on the 2000 census, allows a respondent to check a box labeled "unmarried partner" in the section of the survey inquiring about the nature of the relationship between the respondent and others with whom she or he lives.[3] Table 9-2 examines data obtained in the 1990 and 2000 decennial census surveys and breaks down households in the United States by composition, with particular emphasis on whether "coupled households" are headed by married couples or by unmarried opposite-sex or same-sex couples. The data reveal that in 2000, of the almost 60 million households headed by an adult couple, about 5.5 million, or 9.13% of those couples were unmarried. Of the 5.5 million cohabiting *unmarried* couples, about 594,391 couples or 10.91% are same-sex couples. Same-sex couples comprised approximately one percent of the total adult-couple households in the year 2000.

Comparing the decennial census data obtained in 2000 with those obtained in 1990,[4] the percentage of adult couples living together who identify themselves as unmarried partners appears to have risen substantially, from 5.81% in 1990 to 9.13% in 2000. In addition, the percentage of adult couples living together who identify themselves as same-sex partners has risen from.026% in 1990 to approximately 1% in 2000. Table 9-3 offers another way to look at these data. It examines the ratio of unmarried-partner couples to married couples in 1990 and 2000, and presents the ratios of opposite-sex couples and same-sex couples to married couples. These data suggest fairly dramatic increases in all of the categories of unmarried cohabiting partners between 1990 and 2000.

---

[3] For more information on the relationship between the decennial census data and the data reported in Table 9-1, see the Statistical Note on page 874.

[4] See Statistical Note, page 874 of this chapter, for additional information about the comparability of the 1990 and 2000 decennial census data on same-sex couples reported here.

Table 9-2
Same-Sex Partner Households in the United States, Compared with Married and Unmarried Heterosexual Partner Households: 2000 and 1990[5]

Census Year	Total Households	Total Coupled Households	Married-Couple Households	Unmarried Opposite-Sex Partners	Same-Sex Partners: Male	Same-Sex Partners : Female
2000	105,480,101	59,969,000	54,493,232	4,881,377	301,026	293,365
1990	91,993,582	54,905,986	51,718,214	3,042,642	81,343	63,787

It is important to note, however, that the data presented thus far examine *household composition only*. That is, they do not tell us how many people identify themselves as gay or lesbian, or how many people are in gay or lesbian relationships, but *not* sharing a household. Many same-sex and opposite-sex unmarried couples may consider themselves to be in a committed relationship, perhaps even spending extended periods of time living together in one partner's home, while still maintaining separate legal residences. When confronted with a formal document such as a Census questionnaire, many such persons will not classify themselves as sharing a household. Furthermore, it is likely that in some cases, a survey respondent living with a same-sex partner may choose not to identify the unrelated person with whom she or he is lives as an "unmarried partner." Rather, some respondents may check the box for "housemate" or "roommate," as the Census form permits, because of reluctance to reveal the nature of their intimate relationships on a governmental questionnaire.

---

[5] Adapted from: U.S. Census Bureau, *Married-Couple and Unmarried-Partner Households: 2000*, Feb. 2003 (available at: www.census.gov/prod/2003pubs/censr-5.pdf); U.S. Census Bureau, *1990 Census of Population: Social and Economic Characteristics, United States* (available at: www.census.gov/prod/cen1990/cp2/cp-2-1.pdf). For a discussion of the limitations of comparing the 2000 and 1990 data on same-sex cohabiting couples, see *Technical Note on Same-Sex Unmarried Partner Data From the 1990 and 2000 Censuses*. (Available at: www.census.gov/population/www/cen2000/samesex.html.)

Table 9-3
Ratio of Unmarried-Partner Couples Living Together to Married Couples Living Together: 2000 and 1990

Year	Unmarried-Partner Couples Per 100 Married Couples	Opposite-Sex Partner Couples Per 100 Married Couples	Same-Sex Couples Per 100 Married Couples
2000	10.0	8.9	1.1
1990	6.2	5.9	.2

What do we know about the frequency with which Americans identify themselves as gay or lesbian? Recent studies suggest that approximately 2.8% of men identify themselves as gay, and 1.4% of women identify themselves as lesbian. *See* Dan Black, Gary Gates, et al., *Demographics of the Gay and Lesbian Population in the United States: Evidence from Available Systematic Data Sources*, 37 DEMOGRAPHY 139, 140 (2000). This figure should be distinguished from the percentage of persons who report having had "homosexual desire," which has been reported to be 7.7% for men and 7.5% for women. *Id.* Black, Gates and colleagues underscore that attempts to obtain population estimates of gay and lesbian individuals must confront the "complicated question of what it means to be gay or lesbian." *Id.* at 141. For example, how frequent or exclusive must one's sexual contacts with same-sex persons be before one is classified as gay or lesbian? These are issues that researchers are beginning to address, but certainly have not fully resolved, and thus, data sets differ depending upon the definitions employed. *Id.*

What proportion of persons identifying themselves as gay or lesbian report involvement in a current relationship? One study suggested that approximately 34% of persons reported involvement in current same-sex partnerships. *Id.* at 143. *See also* sources cited in David Chambers, *What If? The Legal Consequences of Marriage and the Legal Needs of Lesbian and Gay Male Couples*, 95 MICH. L. REV. 447, 449 (1996) (indicating that, at any given time, nearly half of persons identifying themselves as gay, and more than half of those identifying themselves as lesbians, report themselves "in a relationship with a primary partner," and many of these have exchanged rings or otherwise engaged in a commitment ceremony).

STATISTICAL NOTE

A brief history of the Census Bureau's measurement of nonmarital cohabitation rates can assist in the interpretation of the statistics reported in Chapter 9, relating to nonmarital cohabitation by opposite and same-sex couples. Prior to 1990, the United States Census Bureau did not have any category to measure nonmarital cohabitation in the decennial census. The decennial census tracks population data by sending questionnaires to every household in the country at the beginning of each decade. In 1990, the decennial census added a category called "unmarried partner" in the section of the survey that asks the nature of the relationship between the respondent and others with whom she or he lives.

The data reported in Table 9-1, on page 871, which date back to 1960, do not derive from the decennial census. Rather, they derive from the Census Bureau's Current Population Surveys ("CPS"), obtained via telephone interviews of a random sample of American households, and extrapolate from those data to obtain estimates for the national population. For several decades, the CPS has included a category of Person of Opposite Sex Sharing Living Quarters ("POSSLQ"), which is the category referred to in Table 9-1 as "unmarried heterosexual couple households." This category counts those households containing an unrelated adult man and woman sharing a housing unit with each other, and with no other adults. In some unknown percentage of the cases, assumed to be relatively small, the man and woman do not have an intimate relationship, but are merely roommates. Furthermore, this category does not include the small percentage of nonmarital cohabiting heterosexual couples who are intimate partners, but happen to share a residence with other adults. The reason that these distinctions are important is that there are some discrepancies between the data collected by the CPS and reported in Table 9-1, and the more accurate data collected in 1990 and 2000 through the decennial census. Compare the 1990 and 2000 figures from Table 9-1, of 2.86 million and 4.74 million couples respectively with the 1990 and 2000 figures from the decennial census of 3.04 and 4.88 million couples respectively. In both instances, the decennial census indicates slightly higher figures. Despite these discrepancies, the Census Bureau represents the CPS data reported in Table 9-1 to provide a fairly good estimate of historical trends.[6]

By contrast, the Census Bureau firmly rejects the utility of the CPS, as collected for any year thus far, as a source for data on cohabitation of same-sex couples.[7] Although such data exist, and are an "extension" of the POSSLQ data, allowing for designation that the other adult with whom one is living is of the same sex as the respondent, the figures estimate the numbers of household units in the United States comprised of two unrelated adults of the same sex. Because many, perhaps even most, of these units house persons who are merely roommates and/or perhaps also friends, rather than a couple involved in a gay or lesbian relationship, the CPS data should *not* be represented as reflecting the numbers of cohabiting same-sex couples in the United States.

Rather, the Census Bureau represents that the most accurate data are those collected as part of the 2000 decennial census, which permitted not only designation of whether one was living with an unmarried partner, but whether that partner was of the same or opposite sex as the respondent.[8] Complicating the situation further, however, the Census Bureau has taken the formal position

---

[6] Telephone conversation with Jason Fields, Family Demographer, Fertility and Family Statistics Branch, Population Division, U.S. Census Bureau (August 5, 2003).

[7] *Id.* (stating the position of the Census Bureau).

[8] *Id.* Telephone conversation with Tavia Simmons, Family Demographer, U.S. Census Bureau, (August 5, 2003).

that the *1990* decennial census data on same-sex partner households are not comparable to the 2000 decennial data, because of discrepancies in the scoring of these data, which it describes in detail in a Technical Note it has disseminated.[9] Despite this caveat, however, the Census Bureau has, in fact, compared the data from these two time periods in a 2003 report it has published on *Married Partner and Unmarried-Partner Households.*[10] Some of the data found in this 2003 report are presented in Table 9-2, on page 873 of this chapter.

[2] ENFORCING OBLIGATIONS BETWEEN COHABITANTS

[a] Contract-Based Remedies

MARVIN v. MARVIN

18 Cal. 3d 660, 557 P.2d 106, 134 Cal. Rptr. 815 (1976)

TOBRINER, Justice. During the past 15 years, there has been a substantial increase in the number of couples living together without marrying. Such nonmarital relationships lead to legal controversy when one partner dies or the couple separates. Courts of Appeal, faced with the task of determining property rights in such cases, have arrived at conflicting positions: two cases have held that the Family Law Act requires division of the property according to community property principles, and one decision has rejected that holding. We take this opportunity to resolve that controversy and to declare the principles which should govern distribution of property acquired in a nonmarital relationship.

We conclude: (1) The provisions of the Family Law Act do not govern the distribution of property acquired during a nonmarital relationship; such a relationship remains subject solely to judicial decision. (2) The courts should enforce express contracts between nonmarital partners except to the extent that the contract is explicitly founded on the consideration of meretricious sexual services. (3) In the absence of an express contract, the courts should inquire into the conduct of the parties to determine whether that conduct demonstrates an implied contract, agreement of partnership or joint venture, or some other tacit understanding between the parties. The courts may also employ the doctrine of *quantum meruit,* or equitable remedies such as constructive or resulting trusts, when warranted by the facts of the case.

[P]laintiff and defendant lived together for seven years without marrying; all property acquired during this period was taken in defendant's name. When

---

[9] *See Technical Note on Same-Sex Unmarried Partner Data From the 1990 and 20000 Censuses.* (Available at: www.census.gov/population/www/cen2000/samesex.html.)

[10] U.S. Census Bureau, *Married-Couple and Unmarried-Partner Households: 2000*, Feb. 2003 (available at: www.census.gov/prod/2003pubs/censr-5.pdf); U.S. Bureau of the Census, *1990 Census of Population: Social and Economic Characteristics, United States* (available at: www.census.gov/prod/cen1990/cp2/cp-2-1.pdf).

plaintiff sued to enforce a contract under which she was entitled to half the property and to support payments, the trial court granted judgment on the pleadings for defendant, thus leaving him with all property accumulated by the couple during their relationship. Since the trial court denied plaintiff a trial on the merits of her claim, its decision conflicts with the principles stated above, and must be reversed.

1. The factual setting of this appeal

Since the trial court rendered judgment for defendant on the pleadings, we must [determine] whether such allegations state, or can be amended to state, a cause of action. . . .

Plaintiff avers that in October of 1964 she and defendant "entered into an oral agreement" that while "the parties lived together they would combine their efforts and earnings and would share equally any and all property accumulated as a result of their efforts whether individual or combined." Furthermore, they agreed to "hold themselves out to the general public as husband and wife" and that "plaintiff would further render her services as a companion, homemaker, housekeeper and cook to . . . defendant."

Shortly thereafter plaintiff agreed to "give up her lucrative career as an entertainer [and] singer" in order to "devote her full time to defendant . . . as a companion, homemaker, housekeeper and cook;" in return defendant agreed to "provide for all of plaintiff's financial support and needs for the rest of her life."

Plaintiff alleges that she lived with defendant from October of 1964 through May of 1970 and fulfilled her obligations under the agreement. During this period the parties as a result of their efforts and earnings acquired in defendant's name substantial real and personal property, including motion picture rights worth over $1 million. In May of 1970, however, defendant compelled plaintiff to leave his household. He continued to support plaintiff until November of 1971, but thereafter refused to provide further support.

On the basis of these allegations plaintiff asserts two causes of action. The first, for declaratory relief, asks the court to determine her contract and property rights; the second seeks to impose a constructive trust upon one half of the property acquired during the course of the relationship. . . .

2. Plaintiff's complaint states a cause of action for breach of an express contract

. . . . Although [the trial] court did not specify the ground for its conclusion that plaintiff's contractual allegations stated no cause of action, defendant offers [several] theories to sustain the ruling; we proceed to examine them.

Defendant . . . relies on the contention that the alleged contract is so closely related to the supposed "immoral" character of the relationship between plaintiff and himself that the enforcement of the contract would violate public policy. He points to cases asserting that a contract between nonmarital partners is unenforceable if it is "involved in" an illicit relationship, or made in "contemplation" of such a relationship. A review of the numerous California decisions concerning contracts between nonmarital partners, however, reveals that the courts have not employed such broad and uncertain standards to strike down contracts. The decisions instead disclose a narrower and more precise standard: a contract between nonmarital partners is unenforceable only *to the extent* that it *explicitly* rests upon the immoral and illicit consideration of meretricious sexual services.

. . . . Numerous other cases have upheld enforcement of agreements between nonmarital partners in factual settings essentially indistinguishable from the present case.[5] [¶] Although the past decisions hover over the issue in the somewhat wispy form of the figures of a Chagall painting, we can abstract from those decisions a clear and simple rule. The fact that a man and woman live together without marriage, and engage in a sexual relationship, does not in itself invalidate agreements between them relating to their earnings, property, or expenses. Neither is such an agreement invalid merely because the parties may have contemplated the creation or continuation of a nonmarital relationship when they entered into it. Agreements between nonmarital partners fail only to the extent that they rest upon a consideration of meretricious sexual services. Thus the rule asserted by defendant, that a contract fails if it is "involved in" or made "in contemplation" of a nonmarital relationship, cannot be reconciled with the decisions.

The . . . cases cited by defendant which have declined to enforce contracts between nonmarital partners involved consideration that *was* expressly founded upon . . . illicit sexual services. In *Hill v. Estate of Westbrook,* 95 Cal. App. 2d 599, 213 P.2d 727 (1952), the woman promised to keep house for the man, to live with him as man and wife, and to bear his children; the man promised to provide for her in his will, but died without doing so. Reversing a judgment for the woman based on the reasonable value of her services, the Court of Appeal stated that "the action is predicated upon a claim which seeks, among other things, the reasonable value of living with decedent in meretricious relationship and bearing him two children. . . . The law does not award compensation for living with a man as a concubine and bearing him children. . . . As the judgment is, at least in part, for the value of the claimed services for which recovery cannot be had, it must be reversed." (95 Cal. App. 2d at 603, 213 P.2d at 730.) Upon retrial, the trial court found that it could not sever the contract and place an independent value upon the legitimate services performed by claimant. We therefore affirmed a judgment for the estate. [¶] In . . . *Updeck v. Samuel,* 123 Cal. App. 2d 264, 266 P.2d 822 (1964), the contract "was based on the consideration that the parties lived together as husband and wife." (123 Cal. App. 2d at 267, 266 P.2d at 824.) Viewing the contract as calling for adultery, the court held it illegal.

. . . *Hill* and *Updeck* . . . demonstrate that a contract . . . expressly made in contemplation of a common living arrangement is invalid only if sexual acts form an inseparable part of the consideration . . . even if sexual services are

---

[5] Defendant urges that all [but perhaps two of the cases cited by the court to support this proposition] can be distinguished on the ground that the partner seeking to enforce the contract contributed either property or services additional to ordinary homemaking services. No case, however, suggests that a pooling agreement in which one partner contributes only homemaking services is invalid. . . . A promise to perform homemaking services is, of course, a lawful and adequate consideration for a contract. . . .

part of the contractual consideration, any *severable* portion of the contract supported by independent consideration will still be enforced.

The principle that a contract between nonmarital partners will be enforced unless expressly and inseparably based upon an illicit consideration of sexual services not only represents the distillation of the decisional law, but also offers a far more precise and workable standard than that advocated by defendant. . . .[¶] [A] standard which inquires whether an agreement is "involved" in or "contemplates" a nonmarital relationship is vague and unworkable. Virtually all agreements between nonmarital partners can be said to be "involved" in some sense in the fact of their mutual sexual relationship, or to "contemplate" the existence of that relationship. Thus defendant's proposed standards, if taken literally, might invalidate all agreements between nonmarital partners, a result no one favors. Moreover, those standards offer no basis to distinguish between valid and invalid agreements. By looking . . . only to the consideration underlying the agreement, we provide the parties and the courts with a practical guide to determine when an agreement between nonmarital partners should be enforced.

. . . . [Defendant also] contends that enforcement of the oral agreement between plaintiff and himself is barred by Civil Code section 5134, which provides that "All contracts for marriage settlements must be in writing. . . ." A marriage settlement, however, is an agreement [relating to] marriage. . . . The contract at issue here does not conceivably fall within that definition, and thus is beyond the compass of section 5134.

Defendant finally argues that enforcement of the contract is barred by Civil Code section 43.5, subdivision (d), which provides that "No cause of action arises for . . . [b]reach of a promise of marriage." This rather strained contention proceeds from the premise that a promise of marriage impliedly includes a promise to support and to pool property acquired after marriage, to the conclusion that pooling and support agreements not part of or accompanied by promise of marriage are barred by the section. We conclude that section 43.5 is not reasonably susceptible to the interpretation advanced by defendant. . . .

In summary, we base our opinion on the principle that adults who voluntarily live together and engage in sexual relations are nonetheless as competent as any other persons to contract respecting their earning and property rights. Of course, [cohabiting adults] cannot lawfully contract to pay for the performance of sexual services, for such a contract is, in essence, an agreement for prostitution and unlawful for that reason. But they may agree to pool their earnings and to hold all property acquired during the relationship in accord with the law governing community property; conversely they may agree that each partner's earnings and the property acquired from those earnings remains the separate property of the earning partner. So long as the agreement does not rest upon illicit meretricious consideration, the parties may order their economic affairs as they choose, and no policy precludes the courts from enforcing such agreements.

In the present instance, plaintiff alleges that the parties agreed to pool their earnings, that they contracted to share equally in all property acquired, and that defendant agreed to support plaintiff. The terms of the contract as alleged do not rest upon any unlawful consideration. . . . The trial court consequently erred in granting defendant's motion for judgment on the pleadings.

3. Plaintiff's complaint can be amended to state a cause of action founded upon theories of implied contract or equitable relief

. . . [B]oth causes of action in plaintiff's complaint allege an express contract; neither assert any basis for relief independent from the contract. In *Marriage of Cary,* 34 Cal. App. 3d 345, 109 Cal. Rptr. 862 (1973), however, the Court of Appeal held that, in view of the policy of the Family Law Act, [which requires equal division of community property when married partners divorce,] property accumulated by nonmarital partners in an actual family relationship should be divided equally. . . . Although our conclusion that plaintiff's complaint states a cause of action based on an express contract alone compels us to reverse the judgment for defendant, resolution of the *Cary* issue will . . . resolve a conflict . . . in published Court of Appeal decisions. . . .[11]

. . . .

[T]he cases prior to *Cary* exhibited a schizophrenic inconsistency. By enforcing an express contract between nonmarital partners unless it rested upon an unlawful consideration, the courts applied a common law principle as to contracts. Yet the courts disregarded the common law principle that holds that implied contracts can arise from the conduct of the parties. Refusing to enforce such contracts, the courts spoke of leaving the parties "in the position in which they had placed themselves" (*Oakley v. Oakley,* 82 Cal. App. 2d 188, 192, 185 P.2d 848, 850 (1947)), just as if they were guilty parties "*in pari delicto.*"

Justice Curtis noted this inconsistency in his dissenting opinion in *Vallera,* pointing out that "if an express agreement will be enforced, there is no legal or just reason why an implied agreement to share the property cannot be enforced." [*Vallera v. Vallera* 21 Cal. 2d 681, 686, 34 P.2d 761, 764 (Cal. 1943) [¶] Still another inconsistency in the prior cases arises from their treatment of property accumulated through joint effort. To the extent that a partner had contributed *funds* or *property,* the cases held that the partner obtains a proportionate share in the acquisition, despite the lack of legal standing of the relationship. Yet courts have refused to recognize just such an interest based upon the contribution of *services.* As Justice Curtis points out "Unless it can be argued that a woman's services as cook, housekeeper, and home-maker are valueless, it would seem logical that if, when she contributes money

---

[11] We note that a deliberate decision to avoid the strictures of the community property system is not the only reason that couples live together without marriage. Some couples may wish to avoid the permanent commitment that marriage implies, yet be willing to share equally any property acquired during the relationship; others may fear the loss of pension, welfare, or tax benefits resulting from marriage. Others may engage in the relationship as a possible prelude to marriage. In lower socio-economic groups the difficulty and expense of dissolving a former marriage often leads couples to choose a nonmarital relationship; many unmarried couples may also incorrectly believe that the doctrine of common law marriage prevails in California, and thus that they are in fact married. Consequently we conclude that the mere fact that a couple have not participated in a valid marriage ceremony cannot serve as a basis for a court's inference that the couple intend to keep their earnings and property separate and independent; the parties' intention can only be ascertained by a more searching inquiry into the nature of their relationship.

to the purchase of property, her interest will be protected, then when she contributes her services in the home, her interest in property accumulated should be protected" [*Vallera, supra,* 21 Cal. 2d at 686–687, 134 P.2d at 764 (Curtis, J., dissenting opinion)].

Thus as of 1973, the time of the filing of *In re Marriage of Cary,* the cases apparently held that a nonmarital partner who rendered services in the absence of express contract could assert no right to property acquired during the relationship. . . .

　　　. . . .

[A]lthough we reject the reasoning of *Cary* . . . we share the perception of the [*Cary* court] that the application of former precedent in [similar factual settings] would work an unfair distribution of the property accumulated. . . . [¶] The principal reason why the pre-*Cary* decisions result in an unfair distribution of property inheres in the court's refusal to permit a nonmarital partner to assert rights based upon accepted principles of implied contract and equity. We have examined the reasons advanced to justify this denial of relief, and find that none have merit.

First, we note that the cases denying relief do not rest their refusal upon any theory of "punishing" a "guilty" partner. Indeed, to the extent that denial of relief "punishes" one partner, it necessarily rewards the other by permitting him to retain a disproportionate amount of the property. Concepts of "guilt" thus cannot justify an unequal division of property between two equally "guilty" persons.

Other reasons advanced in the decisions fare no better. The principal argument seems to be that "[e]quitable considerations arising from the reasonable expectation of . . . benefits attending the status of marriage . . . are not present [in a nonmarital relationship]." (*Vallera v. Vallera, supra,* 21 Cal. 2d at 685, 134 P.2d at 763.) But, although parties to a nonmarital relationship obviously cannot have based any expectations upon the belief that they were married, other expectations and equitable considerations remain. The parties may well expect that property will be divided in accord with the parties' own tacit understanding and that in the absence of such understanding the courts will fairly apportion property accumulated through mutual effort. We need not treat nonmarital partners as putatively married persons in order to apply principles of implied contract, or extend equitable remedies; we need to treat them only as we do any other unmarried persons.[22]

The remaining arguments advanced from time to time to deny remedies to the nonmarital partners are of less moment. There is no more reason to presume that services are contributed as a gift than to presume that funds are contributed as a gift; in any event the better approach is to presume, as Justice Peters suggested, "that the parties intend to deal fairly with each other." (*Keene v. Keene, supra,* 57 Cal. 2d 657, 674, 371 P.2d 329, 339 (dissenting opn.))

---

[22] In some instances a confidential relationship may arise between nonmarital partners, and economic transactions between them should be governed by the principles applicable to such relationships.

The argument that granting remedies to the nonmarital partners would discourage marriage must fail; as *Cary* pointed out, "with equal or greater force the point might be made that the pre-1970 rule was calculated to cause the income-producing partner to avoid marriage and thus retain the benefit of all of his or her accumulated earnings." (34 Cal. App. 3d at p. 353, 109 Cal. Rptr. at p. 866.) Although we recognize the well-established public policy to foster and promote the institution of marriage . . ., perpetuation of judicial rules which result in an inequitable distribution of property accumulated during a nonmarital relationship is neither a just nor an effective way of carrying out that policy.

In summary, we believe that the prevalence of nonmarital relationships in modern society and the social acceptance of them, marks this as a time when our courts should by no means apply the doctrine of the unlawfulness of the so-called meretricious relationship to the instant case. [T]he nonenforceability of agreements expressly providing for meretricious conduct rested upon the fact that such conduct . . . pertained to . . . prostitution. To equate the nonmarital relationship of today to such a subject matter is to do violence to an accepted and wholly different practice. [¶] We are aware that many young couples live together without the solemnization of marriage, in order to make sure that they can successfully later undertake marriage. This trial period, preliminary to marriage, serves as some assurance that the marriage will not subsequently end in dissolution to the harm of both parties. . . .

The mores of the society have . . . changed so radically in regard to cohabitation that we cannot impose a standard based on alleged moral considerations that have apparently been so widely abandoned by so many. Lest we be misunderstood, however, we take this occasion to point out that the structure of society itself largely depends upon the institution of marriage, and nothing we have said in this opinion should be taken to derogate from that institution. The joining of the man and woman in marriage is at once the most socially productive and individually fulfilling relationship that one can enjoy in the course of a lifetime.

We conclude that the judicial barriers that may stand in the way of a policy based upon the fulfillment of the reasonable expectations of the parties to a nonmarital relationship should be removed. . . . We add that in the absence of an express agreement, the courts may look to a variety of other remedies in order to protect the parties' lawful expectations.[24] [¶] The courts may inquire into the conduct of the parties to determine whether that conduct demonstrates an implied contract or implied agreement of partnership or joint venture or some other tacit understanding between the parties. The courts may, when appropriate, employ principles of constructive trust or resulting trust. Finally, a nonmarital partner may recover in *quantum meruit* for the reasonable value of household services rendered less the reasonable value of

---

[24] We do not seek to resurrect the doctrine of common law marriage, which was abolished in California by statute in 1895. Thus we do not hold that plaintiff and defendant were "married," . . . or putative spouses; we hold only that she has the same rights to enforce contracts and to assert her equitable interest in property acquired through her effort as does any other unmarried person.

support received if he can show that he rendered services with the expectation of monetary reward.[25]

Since we have determined that plaintiff's complaint states a cause of action for breach of an express contract, and, as we have explained, can be amended to state a cause of action independent of allegations of express contract[,][26] we must conclude that the trial court erred in granting defendant a judgment on the pleadings. [¶] The judgment is reversed and the cause remanded for further proceedings consistent with the views expressed herein.

HEWITT v. HEWITT

394 N.E.2d 1204 (Ill. 1979)

UNDERWOOD, Justice. The issue in this case is whether plaintiff Victoria Hewitt, whose complaint alleges she lived with defendant Robert Hewitt from 1960 to 1975 in an unmarried, family-like relationship to which three children have been born, may recover from him "an equal share of the profits and properties accumulated by the parties" during that period.

[The plaintiff's divorce action was dismissed because the parties had never married.] Plaintiff thereafter filed an amended complaint alleging . . . (1) that because defendant promised he would "share his life, his future, his earnings and his property" with her and all of defendant's property resulted from the parties' joint endeavors, plaintiff is entitled in equity to a one-half share; (2) that the conduct of the parties evinced an implied contract entitling plaintiff to one-half the property accumulated during their "family relationship"; (3) that because defendant fraudulently assured plaintiff she was his wife in order to secure her services, although he knew they were not legally married, defendant's property should be impressed with a trust for plaintiff's benefit; (4) that because plaintiff has relied to her detriment on defendant's promises and devoted her entire life to him, defendant has been unjustly enriched.

[She further alleged] that in June 1960, when she and defendant were students at Grinnell College in Iowa, [she] became pregnant; that defendant thereafter told her that they were husband and wife and would live as such, no formal ceremony being necessary, and that he would "share his life, his future, his earnings and his property" with her; that the parties immediately announced to their respective parents that they were married and thereafter held themselves out as husband and wife; that in reliance on defendant's promises she devoted her efforts to his professional education and his establishment in the practice of pedodontia, obtaining financial assistance from her parents for this purpose; that she assisted defendant in his career with her own special skills and although she was given payroll checks for these services

[25] Our opinion does not preclude the evolution of additional equitable remedies to protect the expectations of the parties to a nonmarital relationship in cases in which existing remedies prove inadequate; the suitability of such remedies may be determined in later cases in light of the factual setting in which they arise.

[26] We do not pass upon the question whether, in the absence of an express or implied contractual obligation, a party to a nonmarital relationship is entitled to support payments from the other party after the relationship terminates.

she placed them in a common fund; that defendant, who was without funds at the time of the marriage, as a result of her efforts now earns over $80,000 a year and has accumulated large amounts of property, owned either jointly with her or separately; that she has given him every assistance a wife and mother could give, including social activities designed to enhance his social and professional reputation.

The amended complaint was also dismissed, the trial court finding that Illinois law and public policy require such claims to be based on a valid marriage. The appellate court reversed, stating that because the parties had outwardly lived a conventional married life, plaintiff's conduct had not "so affronted public policy that she should be denied any and all relief," and that plaintiff's complaint stated a cause of action on an express oral contract. . . .

The appellate court, in reversing, gave considerable weight to the fact that the parties had held themselves out as husband and wife for over 15 years. The court noted that they lived "a most conventional, respectable and ordinary family life" that did not openly flout accepted standards, the "single flaw" being the lack of a valid marriage. Indeed the appellate court went so far as to say that the parties had "lived within the legitimate boundaries of a marriage and family relationship of a most conventional sort," an assertion which that court cannot have intended to be taken literally. Noting that the Illinois Marriage and Dissolution of Marriage Act does not prohibit nonmarital cohabitation and that the Criminal Code of 1961 makes fornication an offense only if the behavior is open and notorious, the appellate court concluded that plaintiff should not be denied relief on public policy grounds.

In finding that plaintiff's complaint stated a cause of action on an express oral contract, the appellate court adopted the reasoning of the California Supreme Court in the widely publicized case of *Marvin v. Marvin.* . . .

It is apparent that the *Marvin* court adopted a pure contract theory, under which, if the intent of the parties and the terms of their agreement are proved, the pseudo-conventional family relationship which impressed the appellate court here is irrelevant; recovery may be had unless the implicit sexual relationship is made the explicit consideration for the agreement. In contrast, the appellate court here, as we understand its opinion, would apply contract principles only in a setting where the relationship of the parties outwardly resembled that of a traditional family. It seems apparent that the plaintiff in *Marvin* would not have been entitled to recover in our appellate court because of the absence of that outwardly appearing conventional family relationship.

The issue of whether property rights accrue to unmarried cohabitants cannot, however, be regarded realistically as merely a problem in the law of express contracts. Plaintiff argues that because her action is founded on an express contract, her recovery would in no way imply that unmarried cohabitants acquire property rights merely by cohabitation and subsequent separation. However, the *Marvin* court expressly recognized and the appellate court here seems to agree that if common law principles of express contract govern express agreements between unmarried cohabitants, common law principles of implied contract, equitable relief and constructive trust must govern the parties' relations in the absence of such an agreement. In all probability the latter case will be much the more common, since it is unlikely that most couples who live together will enter into express agreements regulating their property rights. The increasing incidence of nonmarital cohabitation referred to in *Marvin* and the variety of legal remedies therein sanctioned seem certain to result in substantial amounts of litigation, in which, whatever the allegations regarding an oral contract, the proof will necessarily involve details of the parties' living arrangements.

Apart, however, from the appellate court's reliance upon *Marvin* to reach what appears to us to be a significantly different result, we believe there is a more fundamental problem. We are aware, of course, of the increasing judicial attention given to claims of unmarried cohabitants to jointly accumulated property, and the fact that the majority of courts considering the question have recognized an equitable or contractual basis for implementing the reasonable expectations of the parties unless the sexual services were the explicit consideration. The issue of unmarried cohabitants' mutual property rights, however, as we earlier noted, cannot appropriately be characterized in terms of contract law, nor is it limited to considerations of equity or fairness as between the parties to such relationships. There are major public policy questions involved. . . . Of substantially greater importance than the rights of the immediate parties is the impact of such recognition upon our society and the institution of marriage. Will the fact that legal rights closely resembling those arising from conventional marriages can be acquired by those who deliberately choose to enter into what have heretofore been commonly referred to as "illicit" or "meretricious" relationships encourage formation of such relationships and weaken marriage as the foundation of our family-based society? In the event of death shall the survivor have the status of a surviving spouse for purposes of inheritance, wrongful death actions, workmen's compensation, etc.? And still more importantly: what of the children born of such relationships? What are their support and inheritance rights and by what standards are custody questions resolved? What of the sociological and psychological effects upon them of that type of environment? Does not the recognition of legally enforceable property and custody rights emanating from nonmarital cohabitation in practical effect equate with the legalization of common law marriage — at least in the circumstances of this case? And, in summary, have the increasing numbers of unmarried cohabitants and changing mores of our society reached the point at which the general welfare of the citizens of this State is best served by a return to something resembling the judicially created common law marriage our legislature outlawed in 1905?

. . . .

It is true, of course, that cohabitation by the parties may not prevent them from forming valid contracts about . . . matters [independent of sexual services], for which it is said the sexual relations do not form part of the consideration. . . . [S]everal courts have reasoned that the rendition of housekeeping and homemaking services such as plaintiff alleges here could be regarded as the consideration for a separate contract between the parties, severable from the illegal contract founded on sexual relations. . . .

The real thrust of plaintiff's argument here is that we should abandon the rule of illegality because of certain changes in societal norms and attitudes.

It is urged that social mores have changed radically in recent years, rendering this principle of law archaic. It is said that because there are so many unmarried cohabitants today the courts must confer a legal status on such relationships. . . . If this is to be the result, however, it would seem more candid to acknowledge the return of varying forms of common law marriage than to continue displaying the naiveté we believe involved in the assertion that there are involved in these relationships contracts separate and independent from the sexual activity, and the assumption that those contracts would have been entered into or would continue without that activity.

Even if we were to assume some modification of the rule of illegality is appropriate, we return to the fundamental question earlier alluded to: If resolution of this issue rests ultimately on grounds of public policy, by what body should that policy be determined? *Marvin*, viewing the issue as governed solely by contract law, found judicial policy-making appropriate. Its decision was facilitated by California precedent and that State's no-fault divorce law. In our view, however, the situation alleged here was not the kind of arm's length bargain envisioned by traditional contract principles, but an intimate arrangement of a fundamentally different kind. The issue, realistically, is whether it is appropriate for this court to grant a legal status to a private arrangement substituting for the institution of marriage sanctioned by the State. The question whether change is needed in the law governing the rights of parties in this delicate area of marriage-like relationships involves evaluations of sociological data and alternatives we believe best suited to the superior investigative and fact-finding facilities of the legislative branch in the exercise of its traditional authority to declare public policy in the domestic relations field. That belief is reinforced by the fact that judicial recognition of mutual property rights between unmarried cohabitants would, in our opinion, clearly violate the policy of our recently enacted Illinois Marriage and Dissolution of Marriage Act. Although the Act does not specifically address the subject of nonmarital cohabitation, we think the legislative policy quite evident from the statutory scheme.

[The court quotes from the introductory section of the Marriage and Divorce Act which says that its purpose, *inter alia*, is to "strengthen and preserve the integrity of marriage and safeguard family relationships."] We cannot confidently say that judicial recognition of property rights between unmarried cohabitants will not make that alternative to marriage more attractive by allowing the parties to engage in such relationships with greater security. . . . In thus rotationally enhancing the attractiveness of a private arrangement over marriage, we believe that the appellate court decision in this case contravenes the Act's policy of strengthening and preserving marriage.

. . .

While the appellate court denied that its decision here served to rehabilitate the doctrine of common law marriage, we are not persuaded. Plaintiff's allegations disclose a relationship that clearly would have constituted a valid common law marriage in this State prior to 1905. The parties expressly manifested their present intent to be husband and wife; immediately thereafter they assumed the marital status; and for many years they consistently held themselves out to their relatives and the public at large as husband and wife. Revealingly, the appellate court relied on the fact that the parties were, to the public, husband and wife in determining that the parties living arrangement did not flout Illinois public policy. It is of course true, as plaintiff argues, that unlike a common law spouse she would not have full marital rights in that she could not, for example, claim her statutory one-third share of defendant's property on his death. The distinction appears unimpressive, however, if she can claim one-half of his property on a theory of express or implied contract.

. . . .

[T]he fault in the appellate court holding in this case is that its practical effect is the reinstatement of common law marriage. . . .

We accordingly hold that plaintiff's claims are unenforceable [because] they contravene the public policy, implicit in the statutory scheme of the Illinois Marriage and Dissolution of Marriage Act, disfavoring the grant of mutually enforceable property rights to knowingly unmarried cohabitants. The judgment of the appellate court is reversed. . . .

NOTES

1. ***Michelle Triola Marvin's Recovery on Remand***. On remand the trial court found no contract between Lee and Michelle. Relying upon footnote 25 of the California Supreme Court's opinion ("Our opinion does not preclude the evolution of additional equitable remedies to protect the expectations of the parties. . . ."), it awarded her $104,000 for economic rehabilitation, so that she could become self-supporting. The court of appeals reversed:

> [T]he trial court expressly found that plaintiff benefited economically and socially from her relationship with defendant and suffered no damage therefrom, even with respect to its termination. Furthermore, the trial court also expressly found that defendant never had any obligation to pay plaintiff a reasonable sum as and for her maintenance and that defendant had not been unjustly enriched by reason of the relationship or its termination and that defendant had never acquired anything of value from plaintiff by any wrongful act.

> Furthermore, the special findings in support of the challenged rehabilitative award merely established plaintiff's need therefor and defendant's ability to respond to that need. This is not enough. The award, being nonconsensual in nature, must be supported by some recognized underlying obligation in law or in equity. A court of equity admittedly has broad powers, but it may not create totally new substantive rights under the guise of doing equity.

> The trial court in its special conclusions of law addressed to this point attempted to state an underlying obligation by saying that plaintiff had a right to assistance from defendant until she became self-supporting. But this special conclusion obviously conflicts with the earlier, more general, finding of the court that defendant has never had and did not then have any obligation to provide plaintiff with a reasonable sum for her support and maintenance and, in view of the

already-mentioned findings of no damage (but benefit instead), no unjust enrichment and no wrongful act on the part of defendant with respect to either the relationship or its termination, it is clear that no basis whatsoever, either in equity or in law, exists for the challenged rehabilitative award. It therefore must be deleted from the judgment.

Marvin v. Marvin, 122 Cal. App. 3d 871, 876, 176 Cal.Rptr. 555, 558–59 (App. 1981). Compare this approach to that traditionally taken upon the dissolution of marriage where "need" has been considered a very appropriate, perhaps even central, consideration in making spousal support awards. The sharp contrast between such applications of *Marvin* and the remedies available after marriage has led some to propose that long-term cohabiting relationships be treated like marriages upon dissolution. See discussion of status-based remedies below.

2. *Comparing Marvin and Hewitt.*

(a) Household services versus market labor and economic contributions. In footnote 5, *Marvin* rejects the defendant's proffered distinctions between cases in which the plaintiff contributed directly to the acquisition of property (with material, labor or money) and those in which the plaintiff's claim is grounded in performance of household services. Indeed, many pre-*Marvin* cases sustained a party's equitable interests in a joint *economic* venture independent of the partners' cohabitation. *Compare, e.g., Garza v. Fernandez,* 248 P.2d 869 (Ariz. 1952) (woman claimed business partnership with decedent; action for accounting allowed without regard to their cohabitation) *with Stevens v. Anderson,* 256 P.2d 712 (Ariz. 1953) (woman denied relief against decedent's estate after 30 years' cohabitation; *Garza* distinguished as not involving a contract for a meretricious relationship). Even *Hewitt* concedes: "cohabitation by the parties will not prevent them from forming contracts about independent matters." Indeed, recovery has been allowed in Illinois, following *Hewitt,* under other facts: "Unlike the plaintiff's claims in *Hewitt,* the claims of Donna Spafford are based on evidence that she furnished substantially all of the consideration for the purchase of several vehicles and . . . permitting the defendant to retain all of the vehicles would constitute an unjust enrichment which equity should not permit. [Her] claims . . . are substantially independent of the nonmarital relationship of the parties and are not based on rights arising from their cohabitation." *Spafford v. Coats,* 455 N.E.2d 241 (Ill. App. 1983). Claims like Spafford's are based on conventional rules regarding property rights (that is, if she paid for it, it is hers). By contrast, homemaker services provided within the context of an intimate relationship have not traditionally been viewed in terms of their economic productivity. Professor Katharine Silbaugh asserts that such services are typically characterized as expressions of affection and caregiving, not as labor that contributes to the economic well-being of the couple. *Turning Labor into Love: Housework and the Law*, 91 Nw. U.L. Rev. 1 (1996). Although various approaches to property distribution and spousal support at divorce explicitly or implicitly incorporate notions of the economic value of non-wage services provided by spouses (see Chapter 4), contract-based approaches in the nonmarital cohabitation context must contend with the characterization of homemaker services described by Professor Silbaugh. For a discussion of the concept of homemaker services expressed in *Marvin* and their relevance for cohabitation and marriage, see Margaret F. Brinig, *The Influence of Marvin v. Marvin on Housework During Marriage,* 76 NOTRE DAME L. REV. 1311 (2001).

(b) The severability of the sexual relationship. Where the plaintiff made no *financial* contribution to the home, and thus there is no joint economic venture, the cohabiting relationship and the household and other services provided within that relationship form the basis of the claim. What criteria distinguish such a contract from an illegal agreement for prostitution? *Marvin* required that the sexual relationship between the cohabiting parties be *severable* from the rest of their agreement. Thus, the valid portion of the contract can be enforced, and recognition denied to any portion that rests explicitly on sexual services. Can this distinction be made? The *Hewitt* majority observes that typically, cohabitation contracts would not be made in the absence of a sexual relationship between the parties. According to this view, the sexual component of the relationship is integral and cannot be severed from the rest of the contract. Compare the formulation set forth in *Latham v. Latham*, 547 P.2d 144, 147 (Or. 1976), where the Oregon Supreme Court did not require that the sexual relationship be *severable*, but rather that "the agreement contemplated all the burdens and amenities of married life" and was not *primarily* a contract for sexual services.

(c) What constitutes cohabitation? Which living arrangements between nonmarital couples should be construed as "cohabitation"? Sociologists and demographers note that there is a continuum of living arrangements which may or may not fit within various concepts of cohabitation. *See, e.g.,* Judith Teitler & Nancy E. Reichman, *Cohabitation: An Elusive Concept*. Center for Research on Child Wellbeing Working Paper #01-07-FF (2001) (available at: crcw.princeton.edu/fragilefamilies/ffpapers.html). Romantically-involved couples often do not spend every night together, and their relationship may not be sexually exclusive. *Id.* What indices of cohabitation are essential in order to trigger *Marvin's* remedies? A California appellate court has provided a partial response. In *Cochran v. Cochran*, 89 Cal. App. 4th 283, 106 Cal. Rtpr. 899 (App. 2001), Patricia Cochran claimed that her unmarried companion of 25 years, attorney Johnnie Cochran, had breached his agreement to provide her with lifetime support. The couple had lived together two to four days a week, in the home which Johnnie had purchased in their names as joint tenants. The couple also had a child together. During a portion of this relationship, they held themselves out to the world as husband and wife. (Johnnie was married to another woman during the first decade of their relationship.) Johnnie argued that he had never "cohabited" with Patricia in a manner consistent with the meaning of that term under *Marvin*. The court rejected Johnnie's position: "We save for another day the issue of whether consenting adults need cohabit at all in order to enter an enforceable agreement regarding their earnings and property. Assuming . . . that cohabitation is required, . . . the rationale of *Marvin* is satisfied . . . by a cohabitation arrangement that is less than full-time." *Cochran*, 89 Cal. App. 4th at 291, 106 Cal. Rptr. at 905. "Here, the parties shared a long-term, stable and significant relationship. In this context, evidence that they lived together two to four days a week . . .

is sufficient to raise a triable issue of fact that they cohabited under *Marvin.*" 89 Cal. App. 4th at 293, 106 Cal. Rptr. at 906.

Yet, it does appear that some threshold level of cohabitation may be required in order to trigger remedies under *Marvin. See, e.g., Bergen v. Wood,* 14 Cal. App. 4th 854, 18 Cal. Rptr. 2d 75 (App. 1993). Although the relationship in *Bergen* lasted seven years, the couple never cohabited. The court noted that "in addition to rendering sexual services, Bergen acted as Wood's 'social companion' and 'hostess.' Because services as a social companion and hostess are not normally compensated and are inextricably intertwined with the sexual relationship, Bergen failed to show any consideration independent of the sexual aspect of the relationship. Therefore, the agreement was unenforceable. . . ." 14 Cal. App.4d at 859–860. Consider what principles should guide line-drawing between those couples the law considers cohabitants and those it does not.

(d) Distinguishing recognition of cohabitation remedies from revival of common law marriage. *Hewitt* characterized recognition of legally-enforceable rights emanating from nonmarital cohabitation as tantamount to legalization of common law marriage. *See also Carnes v. Sheldon,* 311 N.W.2d 747, 753 (Mich. App. 1981) ("recovery based on principles of contracts implied at law essentially would resurrect the old common-law marriage doctrine which was specifically abolished by the Legislature"); *Glidewell v. Glidewell,* 790 S.W.2d 925, 927 (Ky. App. 1990) (to imply that the "performance of domestic and household work produce[s] any rights analogous to those of a spouse . . . 'would be reinstituting by judicial fiat common law marriage' "). Yet, *Marvin,* in footnote 24, disclaims that its decision resurrects common law marriage. Which characterization is correct? Common law marriage, although effectuated by an informal agreement between the parties, is a legally-binding marriage in those states recognizing it, and it is accompanied by all of the legal rights and obligations of marriage. (See Chapter 2.) Not only does the status of marriage create a wide range of legal rights and obligations between the parties, but also between the couple and third parties, including the state. *Marvin* does not create a marriage-like status between nonmarital cohabitants, nor does it enable the parties to create such a status for themselves. It does, however, allow nonmarital cohabitants to agree on certain financial implications arising out of their relationship. In many instances, the asserted financial arrangements, such as a particular distribution of property acquired during the life of the relationship, or promises of post-relationship support, are similar to the state-supplied terms that accompany marital dissolution. Yet, to the extent that the contracts enforced are express or implied-in-fact, the state's role is limited to private dispute settlement. By contrast, the state's role in the regulation of marriage extends well beyond this function, seeking to promote an institution to serve as the cornerstone or foundation of its society. *See, e.g., Maynard v. Hill,* 125 U.S. 190 (1887).

3. *State Recognition of Contract-Based Remedies.* Most states will, in principle, recognize express or implied-in-fact contracts, and claims grounded in equity. *See, e.g., Doe v. Burkland,* 808 A2d 1090 (R.I. 2002) (holding that unmarried cohabitants may enter into enforceable contracts and that in the absence of such, equitable doctrines may be applied); *Salzman v. Bachrach,*

996 P.2d 1263, 1267, 1269 (Colo. 2000) (en banc) ("we now join the majority of courts in other states in holding that nonmarried cohabiting couples may legally contract with each other" and courts may apply "general contract laws and equitable rules" in adjudicating disputes); *Goode v. Goode,* 396 S.E.2d 430 (W. Va. 1990) (same); *Boland v. Catalano,* 521 A.2d 142, 146 (Conn. 1987) (same); *Watts v. Watts,* 405 N.W.2d 303 (Wis. 1987) (same).

Only three states, Illinois, Georgia, and Louisiana, have refused to enforce such agreements on public policy grounds. Georgia courts have concluded that "immoral" sexual services are an inseparable component of cohabitation agreements, and that to enforce such agreements would sanction meretricious contracts. *See, e.g., Rehak v. Mathis,* 238 S.E.2d 81, 82 (Ga. 1977); *Liles v. Still,* 335 S.E.2d 168, 169 (Ga. App. 1985). In *Schwegman v. Schwegman,* a Louisiana court drew similar conclusions, asserting that nonmarital cohabitation must be discouraged in order to protect "the moral fabric of society and its preservation against those who flaunt its standards and values." 441 So. 2d 316, 326 (La. App. 1983). For a discussion of some of the policy considerations raised with respect to enforcement of nonmarital cohabitation contracts, see Harry G. Prince, *Public Policy Limitations of Cohabitation Agreements: Unruly Horse or Circus Pony?* 70 MINN. L. REV. 163 (1985).

Yet, even in these jurisdictions, claims by cohabitants are allowed when viewed as incidental to the parties' cohabitant relationship. *See, e.g., Crooke v. Gliden,* 414 S.E.2d 645, (Ga. 1992) (upholding written contract regarding real estate specifying sharing of expenses and assets, relying on parol evidence rule to exclude evidence of "immoral [cohabiting] relationship" as irrelevant); *Spafford v. Coats,* 455 N.E.2d 241 (Ill. App. 1983) (imposing constructive trust with regard to vehicles jointly purchased because claims were independent of relationship). Yet, the distinctions between claims permitted versus not can be exceedingly fine. Thus, while one Illinois court permitted a former cohabitant's claim for return of $47,188 that she had given him to pay off the mortgage on *his* home, *Kaiser v. Strong,* 735 N.E.2d 144, 148–149 (Ill. App. 2000), another denied relief to a woman who made monetary contributions to the home in which she and cohabitant lived together for ten years. *Ayala v. Fox,* 564 N.E.2d 920, 922 (Ill. App. 1990). In distinguishing these cases, the *Kaiser* court construed the plaintiff's "lump sum" payoff of the mortgage on her boyfriend's home as a financial investment which he convinced her to make. By contrast, the monthly mortgage payments in *Ayala* seem to have been viewed as regular living expenses, and the relief sought as "akin to a marital relationship." For criticism of *Ayala,* arguing it as an extension of *Hewitt,* see Jan Skelton, *Hewitt to Ayala: A Wrong Turn for Cohabitants' Rights,* 82 ILL. B.J. 364 (1994).

(a) States requiring a writing. The Statute of Frauds typically applies to agreements made "upon consideration of marriage." Although the California Supreme Court explicitly declined to extend the statute of frauds to cohabitation, the legislatures of two states, Minnesota and Texas, have determined that cohabitation agreements must be in writing to be enforceable. In 1980, the Minnesota legislature adopted such a rule after its supreme court followed *Marvin* in *Carlson v. Olson,* 256 N.W.2d 249 (Minn. 1977). *See* MINN. STAT. § 513.075 (2003). The pertinent statutory sections read: "a contract between a man and a woman who are living together . . . out of wedlock . . . is enforceable . . . concerning the property and financial relations of the parties only if . . . the contract is written and signed by the parties." Texas amended its statute of frauds in 1987 to add a provision that incorporated "agreement[s] made on consideration of . . . nonmarital conjugal cohabitation." TEX. BUS. & COM. CODE § 26.01(b)(3) (2003). *See also* TEX. FAM. CODE § 1.108 (2003) ("A promise or agreement made on consideration of . . . nonmarital conjugal cohabitation is not enforceable unless [it is] in writing and signed by the person obligated by the promise or agreement.") In addition, courts in Florida and North Dakota have held that cohabitation agreements fall within the statute of frauds. *See Posik v. Layton*, 695 So. 2d 759, 761 (Fla. App. 1997); *Kohler v. Flynn*, 493 N.W.2d 647 (N.D. 1992).

In practice, few cohabitants have written agreements today. *See, e.g.,* Jennifer Robbennolt & Monica Kirkpatrick Johnson, *Legal Planning for Unmarried Committed Partners: Empirical Lessons for a Therapeutic and Preventative Approach*, 41 ARIZ. L. REV. 417 (1999). Thus, the requirement of a writing is likely to result in denial of relief in many cases. *See, e.g., Roatch v. Puera*, 534 N.W.2d 560 (Minn. App. 1995). Minnesota law provides for a limited exception to this requirement. It permits enforcement of oral agreements between cohabitants where, for example, the agreements concern "a claim by an individual to recover, preserve, or protect his or her own property, which he or she acquired 'independent of any service contract related to cohabitation. . . .'" *Estate of Palmen*, 588 N.W.2d 493, 495 (Minn. 1999) (quoting *Estate of Eriksen*, 337 N.W.2d 671 (Minn. 1983)) (enforcing oral promise by a decedent that he could reimburse plaintiff cohabitant for the labor and funds she had contributed to construction of a log cabin). In general, courts have applied this category of exception very narrowly, denying enforcement of unwritten contracts whenever the claim is not based *exclusively* upon the claimant's contribution of financial assets or market labors. *See, e.g., Mechura v. McQuillan,* 419 N.W.2d 855 (Minn. App. 1988). *See also* William A. Reppy, Jr., *Choice of Law Problems Arising When Unmarried Cohabitants Change Domicile*, 55 SMU L. REV. 273, 283–285 (2002) (reviewing existing state law on enforcement of agreements between nonmarital cohabitants); Kim Kantorowicz, *Contracts — Cohabitation in Minnesota: From Love to Contract — Public Policy Gone Awry:* In Re *Estate of Palmen*, 558 N.W.2d 493 (Minn. 1999), 26 WM. MITCHELL L. REV. 213 (2000); Buddy Brixley, Comment, *Texas Legislation on the Statute of Frauds in Palimony Suits: Is an Oral Contract Worth the Paper It's Written On?*, 25 HOUS. L. REV. 979, 993–1000 (1988).

(b) States requiring that oral contracts be express. The high courts of New York, *Morone v. Morone*, 50 N.Y.2d 481, 413 N.E.2d 1154, (N.Y. 1980), New Hampshire, *Tapley v. Tapley,* 449 A.2d 1218 (N.H. 1982), and New Mexico, *Merrill v. Davis*, 673 P.2d 1285 (N. Mex. 1983), have held that they will enforce *express* agreements only, although no writing is required. In *Morone*, a couple lived together for over 20 years, had two children, and held themselves out to the community as husband and wife. After their separation, plaintiff claimed that "she has performed domestic duties and business services at the request of defendant with the expectation that she would receive full compensation for them, and that defendant has always accepted her services knowing that she expected compensation for them." 50 N.Y.2d at 484–85, 413 N.E.2d at 1155. The New York court decisively refused to consider this claim. It reasoned that the task of finding an implied contract, as permitted in *Marvin*, is "conceptually so amorphous as practically to defy equitable enforcement." It continued:

> The major difficulty with implying a contract from the rendition of services for one another by persons living together is that it is not reasonable to infer an agreement to pay for the services rendered when the relationship of the parties makes it natural that the services were rendered gratuitously. As a matter of human experience personal services will frequently be rendered by two people living together because they value each other's company or because they find it a convenient or rewarding thing to do. . . . For courts to attempt through hindsight to sort out the intentions of the parties and affix jural significance to conduct carried out within an essentially private and generally noncontractual relationship runs too great a risk of error. Absent an express agreement, there is no frame of reference against which to compare the testimony presented and the character of the evidence that can be presented becomes more evanescent. There is, therefore, substantially greater risk of emotion-laden afterthought, not to mention fraud, in attempting to ascertain by implication what services, if any, were rendered gratuitously and what compensation, if any, the parties intended to be paid.

50 N.Y.2d 481, 484, 488, 413 N.E.2d 1154, 1154–55, 1158. *See also Wilcox v. Trautz*, 693 N.E.2d 141, 146 (Mass. 1998) (holding express contracts enforceable, rejecting "those portions of *Marvin* . . . which grant property rights to a nonmarital partner in the absence of an express contract").

Whereas most states are willing to recognize oral express contracts between cohabitants, the plaintiff must prove the existence of such a contract. Michele Marvin, for example, was ultimately unable to convince the court that an oral contract existed. *Marvin II,* 122 Cal. App. 3d 871, 176 Cal. Rptr. 555 (App. 1981). *See, e.g., Wood v. Collins*, 812 P.2d 951, 954 (Alaska 1991) (holding alleged promise by cohabitant "that everything would be taken care of if they separated" not sufficiently credible or clear to demonstrate existence of express contract); *Aehegma v. Aehegma*, 797 P.2d 74, 79 (Haw. App. 1990) (rejecting evidence of joint checking account as insufficient to prove existence of express contract). Where the courts find oral express contracts, often the plaintiff's testimony is not the sole evidence. *See, e.g., Kozlowski v. Kozlowski*, 403 A.2d 902, 906 (N.J. 1979) (plaintiff's daughter, son-in-law, and niece also testified to knowledge of the agreement).

(c) Recognition of implied-in-fact contracts and equitable claims. In the absence of an express contract, courts willing to enforce implied-in-fact contracts must first identify the nature and terms of the underlying contract. This requirement becomes even more challenging when courts determine whether or not to imply a contract at law.

> The decisions in cases granting or withholding these remedies may be couched in terms of contract or trust: a contract may be "implied-in-law" or a constructive trust may "arise." But in modern analysis, such

terms really mean that the court has found a remediable unjust enrichment. In short, if a court allows restitution, it does so because the defendant has received a cognizable benefit; the benefit was at the plaintiff's expense; and the defendant's retention of it was unjustified. The modern law of restitution is, in the main, the elaboration of these three fundamental elements.

. . . . Household services . . . are economically valuable, and despite the difficulty of precisely assessing that value, its transfer can certainly supply the benefit. [¶]. . . . If the value of those beneficial services exceeds the value of the benefits received from the defendant — in goods or services — a court may appropriately allow the plaintiff to recover for the defendant's net benefit.

The most troublesome problem . . . lies in the . . . "unjustness" element. Not all uncompensated benefits are unjust enrichment. If one confers a benefit with donative intent, the recipient's retention of it cannot, of course, be called unjustified. . . . [¶] [W]e are considering couples who . . . cohabit fully aware of the relevant facts. . . . Even if the parties did not actually agree about the transfer of benefits from one to the other, they probably contemplated that the benefits they would receive — material and non-material — would offset the burdens they undertook. Neither party anticipated paying for the material benefits received from the other except by contributing to the relationship. Each party understood that the material benefit received would depend upon what the other chose to contribute. Under those assumptions, neither party's contributions could unjustly enrich the other. . . . If one party becomes dissatisfied with the arrangement or feels that he is giving more than receiving, the remedy is to give less, or simply to stop giving — to end the relationship.

That solution is not always easy. . . . When one party works in the marketplace and the other in the home, they may not be . . . equally free to end their association. [The fact that] [b]reaking off the relationship . . . could lose [the homemaker partner] all economic support . . . might well deter him from ending . . . the association. . . . But without a contract or unconscionable conduct by the other party, how could he, when the relationship ends, call the other's enrichment unjust?

Robert Casad, *Unmarried Couples And Unjust Enrichment: From Status To Contract And Back Again*, 77 MICH. L. REV. 47, 52–56 (1978). Applying Casad's understanding of the law, it is not surprising that, despite widespread adoption of the *Marvin* principles and the breadth of potential remedies, claims grounded in implied contract or equitable principles infrequently succeed. Ann Laquer Estin, *Ordinary Cohabitation*, 76 NOTRE DAME L. REV. 1381, 1395 (2001). Courts are generally willing to provide relief to a cohabitant who loaned money to her former partner or invested in the former partner's property, or who contributed market-type services to her former partner's business ventures or assets. *Id.* at 1398–1400. By contrast, equitable claims grounded in a cohabitant's provision of homemaker services, or in the relationship itself, are rare. *Compare, e.g., Slocum v. Hammond,* 346 N.W.2d 485 (1984) (rejecting unjust enrichment claim for equitable division of assets acquired during cohabitation) *with Shold v. Goro,* 449 N.W.2d 372 (1989) (permitting recovery by a woman for repayment of funds advanced to cohabitant during their six-year relationship, despite absence of formal loan agreement). In short, most jurisdictions adopting *Marvin* agree that "an unmarried cohabitant does not have the type of claim to a share of the other partner's earnings that a spouse could make in a divorce proceeding[, nor does it] give rise to a presumption of shared property rights." Estin, *supra* at 1400.

For analyses of trends in state enforcement of contract-based claims between nonmarital cohabitants, see *Symposium: Unmarried Partners and the Legacy of Marvin v. Marvin,* 76 NOTRE DAME L. REV. 1261 (2001), which contains articles by Grace Ganz Blumberg, Margaret F. Brinig, David L. Chambers, Ira Mark Ellman, Ann Laquer Estin, J. Thomas Oldham, Milton C. Regan, Jr., and David Westfall. For further discussion and analysis of trends in state laws, see also George L. Blum, Annot., *Property Rights Arising from Relationship of Couple Cohabiting Without Marriage,* 69 A.L.R.5th 219 (1999); William A. Reppy, Jr., *Choice of Law Problems Arising When Unmarried Cohabitants Change Domicile,* 55 SMU L. REV. 273, 275–288 (2002); Mark Strasser, *A Small Step Forward: The ALI Domestic Partners Recommendation,* 2001 B.Y.U. L. REV. 1125, 1146–1157. For an influential pre-*Marvin* discussion of these issues, see Carol Bruch, *Property Rights of De Facto Spouses Including Thoughts on the Value of Homemaker Services,* 10 FAM. L.Q. 101 (1976). *See also* Herma Hill Kay & Carol Amy, Marvin v. Marvin: *Preserving the Options,* 65 CALIF. L. REV. 937 (1977) (exploring *Marvin's* implications shortly after the decision).

4. *Applying Marvin to Same-Sex Couples.* Most courts have held that cohabitation agreements between gay partners are enforceable on the same basis as those between heterosexual partners. *See Posik v. Layton,* 695 So. 2d 759 (Fla. App. 1997) and the cases cited therein. *See also Crooke v. Gliden,* 414 S.E.2d 645 (Ga. 1992); *Marimba v. Clyburn,* 949 S.W.2d 822 (App. Tex. 1997); *Wharton v. Dillingham,* 248 Cal. Rptr. 405, 202 Cal. App. 3d 447 (App. 1988). For further discussion of legal treatment of same-sex cohabitants, see Amy D. Romer, *Homophobia: In the Closet and In the Coffin,* 21 LAW & INEQ. 65 (2003); Angie, Note, *That's the Ticket: A New Way of Defining Family,* 10 CORNELL J. L. PUB. POL'Y 629 (2001).

5. *Separation Agreements for Cohabitants.* Even if state law is unsettled on a particular cohabitation claim, the cohabitation version of a separation agreement should still be enforceable as a contract, on the grounds that a contract to settle claims is valid without reference to the validity of the underlying claims. *See, e.g., Kinnison v. Kinnison,* 627 P.2d 594 (Wyo. 1981). Courts may be particularly inclined to honor such agreements as a device for avoiding potentially difficult claims of unjust enrichment or implied contract. *See, e.g., Silver v. Starrett,* 176 Misc. 2d 511, 674 N.Y.S. 2d 915 (N.Y. Sup. Ct. 1998).

6. *Effect of Cohabitation on Subsequent Marriage and Divorce.* If a couple lives together before marriage, should their cohabitation and the showing of *Marvin*-type agreements affect the division of their property upon divorce? In *Meyer v. Meyer,* 620 N.W.2d 382, 386 (Wis. 2000), the Wisconsin Supreme Court held that premarital contributions made by one spouse to the other's "education, training, or increased earning power" could be considered in setting spousal support awards allowed at marital dissolution. Courts permitting marital property divisions reflecting prior periods of cohabitation include: *Kerekes v. Kerekes,* 446 N.W.2d 356 (Mich. App. 1989); *Nelson v. Nelson,* 384 N.W.2d 468 (Minn. App. 1986); *Malek v. Malek,* 768 P.2d 243 (Haw. App. 1989); *Chestnut v. Chestnut,* 499 N.E.2d 783 (Ind. App. 1986); *Burton v. Burton,* 758 P.2d 394 (Or. App. 1988). Some courts divide property acquired during a preceding period of cohabitation only if the property was acquired "in contemplation of marriage," see, *e.g., In re Marriage of Malter,* 133 Ill. App. 3d 168, 478 N.E.2d 1068 (1985); *Weiss v. Weiss,* 543 A.2d 1062 (N.J. App. Div. 1988). *But see Wilen v. Wilen,* 486 A.2d 775 (Md. App. 1985). By contrast, California requires that property claims arising from premarital cohabitation be brought in a separate *Marvin* action, see *Watkins v. Watkins,* 192 Cal. Rptr. 54 (App. 1983), although it may consolidate that action with the divorce proceedings. *See In re Marriage of Leversee,* 203 Cal. Rptr. 481 (App. 1984). California applied a similar rule to a spousal support claim in *Bukaty v. Bukaty,* 180 Cal. App. 3d 143, 225 Cal. Rptr. 492 (App. 1986), where the parties lived together for more than 25 years before marrying, but the marriage lasted less than two years, and the wife sought to have the premarital cohabitation period considered by the court. Finally, Illinois courts have read *Hewitt* to bar cohabitation-based enhancement of marriage-based property awards. *In re Goldstein,* 423 N.E.2d 1201 (Ill. App. 1981); *In re Marriage of Crouch,* 410 N.E.2d 580 (Ill. App. 1980). For commentary on these issues, see Jennifer K. Neth, Note, *The Effect of Premarital Contributions on Maintenance in Wisconsin: Meyer v. Meyer,* 2003 WIS. L. REV. 225 (2003); Barbara Freedman Wand, *The Relevance of Premarital Cohabitation to Property Division Awards in Divorce Proceedings,* 63 B.U.L. REV. 105 (1983).

[b] The Status Alternative to Contract Remedies

In recognizing cohabitation agreements, *Marvin* responded to real and important changes in social mores. Yet, "*Marvin* has been much criticized as unworkable, inapt, artificial, and inadequately responsive to a range of worthy claims." Grace Ganz Blumberg, *The Regularization of Nonmarital Cohabitation: Rights and Responsibilities in the American Welfare State,* 76 NOTRE DAME L. REV. 1265, 1292 (2001). This section explores such criticisms, and examines the status alternative proposed by the American Law Institute in the *Principles of the Law of Family Dissolution (ALI Principles),* which built upon the work of Professors Blumberg, Ellman, and others.

[i] Critiques of the Contract Approach

GRACE GANZ BLUMBERG, COHABITATION WITHOUT MARRIAGE: A DIFFERENT PERSPECTIVE, 28 U.C.L.A. L. Rev. 1125, 1161–67 (1981)

For most cohabitants, the last resort claim under contract theory is the quasi-contractual remedy of quantum meruit. In this context, quantum meruit operates as a variation on the now discredited theme that marriage is the exchange of (male) support for (female) services. If the value of support is less than the value of the services, the difference is owed to the service-providing cohabitant. Unlike the wife in the traditional formulation, the female cohabitant does not owe her cohabitant any sexual services. Indeed, to provide them for compensation would be unlawful or at least "against public policy." In computing this measure of recovery, the value of the cohabitant's nonsexual companionate services is ignored as well. Her services are thus reduced to their domestic component; she is valued at a maid's salary. Surely, the last fifty years have produced no more degrading or useless formulation of the role and value of a homemaker. In addition, quantum meruit has a distressing tendency to commodify and hence to degrade what is probably the most important and certainly the most intimate human relationship.

Objection to the artificiality of implied contract and quantum meruit theories is more than aesthetic. Ostensibly based on the "intent" of the parties, these theories are often used by sympathetic judges to work economic justice between the separating cohabitants. Since the judicial frame of reference is state matrimonial property and maintenance law, the results bear great similarity to those in divorce cases. In *Marvin,* for example, on remand the trial court awarded Michelle Triola rehabilitative alimony. Indeed, results that do not resemble divorce remedies may be inappropriate. For example, the quantum meruit measure of value of services less value of support bears no relationship to the likely rehabilitative needs of the homemaker at the termination of a cohabitation relationship. Dawn Oliver, an English scholar, argues that the *Marvin* theory of express and implied contract is artificial in that the parties never have any sort of agreement, and that this artificiality will generate a sense of unfairness in men. There would be much less "unfairness" if the courts imposed divorce remedies directly without pretending concern for cohabitants' "intent."

. . . .We have had our romance with freedom of contract, epitomized in the notorious *Lochner* case. The inequality between the baker and his employer was greater in scale but was not significantly different in kind from the inequality between the sexes. In general, the essence of a cohabitation or marriage contract between heterosexual cohabitants is that the man gives up wealth that would otherwise accrue to him in order to insure the woman some semblance of economic dignity. Self-interest would lead the man to give up as little as possible. The woman has scant leverage with which to persuade him otherwise. She lacks economic power. . . Thus, the cohabitants' unequal bargaining power leads to unjust results under contract theory. . . .

Furthermore, it may not be desirable for couples to contract on the eve of cohabitation about future circumstances that can be only dimly foreseen. . . . Domesticity and maternity surprise and alarm even the most astute women. The life of economic achievement and independence which a woman may anticipate is often severely disrupted. Additionally, the economic and social integration that will take place during the relationship has not yet begun on the eve of cohabitation or marriage. The fixing of individualistic rights and duties at this point is premature and may well impede the process of economic and social integration. The interest of the parties in the success of their relationship may best be served by postponing their recognition of their conflicting interests until they are firmly established as a couple. Recognition of unequal contribution to material wealth, for example, is likely to pass with little effect after the birth of a child, but might pose a serious stumbling block to negotiation of a cohabitation contract. The provisions that fix rights for married cohabitants — equitable distribution and elective share laws — are written, as they should be, from the vantage point of an ongoing mature marriage. This is the perspective of a majority of the public and the legislators.

IRA MARK ELLMAN, "CONTRACT THINKING" WAS MARVIN'S FATAL FLAW, 76 Notre Dame L. Rev. 1365, 1365–1373 (2001)

Marvin v. Marvin held that claims that unmarried partners might have against one another at the conclusion of their relationship would be governed primarily by principles of contract law. [¶] [¶] The main defect with contract as the conceptual underpinning for claims between intimate partners is that couples do not in fact think of their relationship in contract terms. [D]ecades of urging by contract enthusiasts have led few couples (married or unmarried) to make express contracts. . . . [C]ourts have no sensible rule to apply in dealing with end-of-relationship disputes between the typical unmarried partners who have no express agreement. Some courts hold that in the absence of an express agreement there can be no claim at all, but more seem to follow *Marvin* and ask whether an agreement between parties can be implied from their conduct. The difference between these two approaches may be more apparent than real, however. If couples do not in fact think of their relationship in contract terms, then a doctrine that directs courts to decide their disputes by looking for a contract is unlikely to find one. . . . Do we want courts to think broadly about the rules that yield a fair dissolution of an unmarried couple's relationship, or do we want to limit courts to searching the parties' conduct for evidence that at some point in the past they agreed upon terms that should now govern their mutual obligations?

The contract inquiry is obviously the more narrow one, for contract focuses on one particular aspect of fairness, keeping one's promises. The very idea of contract is to bind parties now to terms that they agreed upon earlier, to require the later self to remain true to the earlier self's commitments . . . Yet, there is considerable social science evidence that perfectly competent adults lack the capacity to evaluate rationally the contractual commitments involved in an agreement about the consequences that should flow from the dissolution of their intimate relationships — a dissolution which they do not expect to occur and which may well occur, if it does occur, many years in the future when their lives are dramatically different. [See in particular Melvin A. Eisenberg, *The Limits of Cognition and the Limits of Contract,* 47 STAN. L. REV. 211, 254–58 (1995).] Relationships develop over time in ways that competent adults will often fail to anticipate and that may change their lives fundamentally. . . .

If such concerns over the ability of spouses to foresee the long-term consequences of premarital agreement require limits on their enforceability, then surely those same concerns also cast doubt on any rule that would decide claims between unmarried partners by reference to express contracts they made years earlier. Even more doubtful would be a rule directing the court, if there is no express contract, to decide the claim by attempting to plumb the intentions that the parties may have brought to the relationship years before their current dispute arose. Contracts bind parties forever to the terms they agreed upon at execution, and this static conception of obligation is unsuited to the realities of intimate relationships.

One need only look at some of the cases to see how far a contract rubric takes one from results that sensibly and fairly coordinate with actual human behavior. *Friedman v. Friedman*, [24 Cal. Rptr. 2d 892 (App. 1993)], a California case, was decided nearly twenty years after *Marvin*, but involved a couple (Terri and Elliott) who began living together in 1967, before *Marvin* had been decided. Children of the 1960s, they did not believe official marriage necessary for the lifetime commitment they intended and so vowed to be "partners in all respects 'without any sanction by the State.' " They purchased property in Alaska as "Husband and Wife," had two children together, and in the late 1970s moved to Berkeley where Elliott attended law school and prospered economically.

By 1982, their attitude about relationships had perhaps changed, because they made plans to marry. Yet when bad weather kept Elliott from returning from a business trip in time for the wedding, it was never rescheduled, suggesting perhaps that the interest in marriage was not entirely mutual. By the mid-1980s, Terri, who had performed the classic homemaking role throughout their relationship, became disabled with serious back problems. Their relationship apparently deteriorated with her back, and in 1992, Terri filed a legal complaint seeking equitable relief, including support. The trial court found the parties had an "implied contract" providing that if they separated Elliott would support Terri in the same manner as if they had married and, accordingly, ordered temporary support pending final determination of Terri's claim. The couple had no express agreement defining the obligations they would have to one another at their relationship's end, and the appeals court, plausibly enough, held the evidence of implied agreement also insufficient to sustain the trial court's order. Indeed, the parties' decision to live together "without any sanction by the State" was inconsistent, the court concluded, with Terri's claim that they agreed to be bound by the support rules applicable to marriage. As Elliot said of Terri's claim for post-relationship support: "That was not part of our life. It was not part of what we were doing. . . . [W]hen we split up, we split up."

Even those most sympathetic to Terri's claims must concede that Elliot's understanding of the couple's arrangement, at the time they decided to live together, was entirely plausible. Young persons in their twenties, with no children, few responsibilities, and many prospects in front of them, may see little reason to bind themselves to lifetime obligations that could outlast their mutual affection. But for Terri, 1967 is then; 1992 is now. Much of a lifetime has passed. Should the law really say that after twenty-five years together raising two children, Elliott can leave their relationship lucratively employed and with no obligations at all to Terri, who has become disabled, because she cannot show that at some earlier time he had entered into a contract agreeing to them?. . . .

. . . .The *Marvin* doctrine does not [work justice at the dissolution of cohabiting relationships]. There are other cases like Elliott's and Terri's with similar results.[39] There are also cases in which the court responds to similar facts by stretching contract doctrine beyond recognition in order to justify a remedy,[40] as the dissenting judge urged in *Friedman* itself.[41] Either response would seem to indicate a mismatch between the problem (what do people owe one another when it is over?) and the doctrine these courts employ to deal with it.

[ii]   The Status Alternative

Under Chapter 6 of the American Law Institute's ("ALI") *Principles of the Law of Family Dissolution* ("the *Principles*"), couples who are "domestic partners" are treated almost identically to married couples with respect to property claims at dissolution, and claims for post-dissolution income transfers (called "compensatory payments" rather than alimony in the ALI formulation). The ALI permits domestic partners, like married couples, to enter into agreements before or during their relationship to alter the usual property or support rules that would otherwise apply at termination of their relationship. (See Chapter 8 for further discussion of approaches to enforcement of premarital agreements.) Note that the ALI's use of the term "domestic partners" must be distinguished from the use of that term to identify a *formal* status alternative available to nonmarital cohabitants requiring registration. The latter type of domestic partnership is discussed later in this Chapter, beginning on page 929, and is distinct from the ALI proposal. The ALI's recommendations apply equally to opposite-sex and same-sex couples. One commentator supportive of the ALI's approach puts particular emphasis on this aspect of its proposal. Nancy Polikoff, *Making Marriage Matter Less: The ALI Domestic Partner Principles Are One Step In The Right Direction*, 2004 Univ. Chi. Legal Forum ____. *See also* Dee Ann Habegger, *Living in Sin and the Law: Benefits for Unmarried Couples Dependent Upon Sexual Orientation?*, 33 IND. L. REV. 991 (2000).

---

[39] Other cases involving long-term relationships for which the contract rubric provided little basis for relief, despite compelling equitable claims, include Rissberger v. Gorton, 597 P.2d 366, 370 (Or. Ct. App. 1979) (reversing a trial court finding of intent to share equally a duplex and other personal property), and Featherston v. Steinhoff, 575 N.W.2d 6, 10–11 (Mich. Ct. App. 1997) (involving an eight year relationship that produced a child; reversing a trial court finding of implied contract of support).

[40] See, e.g., Kozlowski v. Kozlowski, 403 A.2d 902, 906–07 (N.J. 1979) (finding the man bound by an express agreement to provide support for the woman when, in the course of their relationship, he said he would provide for her for the rest of her life, if she would return and live with him).

[41] "The result reached by the majority may be, in the eyes of some, good law; it is lousy justice." Friedman, 24 Cal. Rptr. 2d at 896 (Poche, J., dissenting).

**AMERICAN LAW INSTITUTE, PRINCIPLES OF THE LAW
OF FAMILY DISSOLUTION: ANALYSIS AND
RECOMMENDATIONS (2002)**

§ 6.03 Determination That Persons Are Domestic Partners

(1)　For the purposes of defining relationships to which this Chapter applies, domestic partners are two persons of the same or opposite sex, not married to one another, who for a significant period of time share a primary residence and a life together as a couple.

(2)　Persons are domestic partners when they have maintained a common household, as defined in Paragraph (4), with their common child, as defined in Paragraph (5), for a continuous period that equals or exceeds a duration, called the *cohabitation parenting period,* set in a rule of statewide application.

(3)　Persons not related by blood or adoption are presumed to be domestic partners when they have maintained a common household . . . for a continuous period that equals or exceeds a duration, called the *cohabitation period*, set in a uniform rule of statewide application. The presumption is rebuttable by evidence that the parties did not share life together as a couple, as defined by Paragraph (7).

. . . .

(6)　When the requirements of Paragraphs (2) or (3) are not satisfied, a person asserting a claim under this Chapter bears the burden of proving that for a significant period of time the parties shared a primary residence and a life together as a couple, as defined in Paragraph (7). Whether a period of time is significant is determined in light of all the Paragraph (7) circumstances of the parties' relationship and, particularly, the extent to which the circumstances wrought change in the life of one or both parties.

(7)　Whether persons share a life together as a couple is determined by reference to all the circumstances including:

(a)　the oral or written statements or promises made to one another, or representations jointly made to third parties, regarding their relationship;

(b)　the extent to which the parties intermingled their finances;

(c)　the extent to which their relationship fostered the parties' economic interdependence, or the economic dependence of one party upon the other;

(d)　the extent to which the parties engaged in conduct and assumed specialized or collaborative roles in furtherance of their life together;

(e)　the extent to which the relationship wrought change in the life of either or both parties;

(f)　the extent to which the parties acknowledged responsibilities to one another, as by naming one another the beneficiary of life insurance or of a testamentary instrument, or as eligible to receive benefits under an employee benefit plan;

(g)   the extent to which the parties' relationship was treated by the parties as qualitatively distinct from the relationship either party had with any other person;

(h)   the emotional or physical intimacy of the parties' relationship;

(i)   the parties' community reputation as a couple;

(j)   the parties' participation in some form of commitment ceremony or registration as a domestic partnership;

(k)   the parties' participation in a void or voidable marriage that, under applicable law, does not give rise to the economic incidents of marriage;

(l)   the parties' procreation of, adoption of, or joint assumption of parental functions toward a child;

(m)   the parties' maintenance of a common household. . . .

Comment:

a. . . .

b. . . . In the United States, courts . . . split on whether to recognize implied contracts. Those that do . . . differ in their inclination to infer contractual undertakings. . . . Some courts reach much further than others. In doing so, they appear to vindicate an equitable rather than a contractual principle. That is, having concluded that a particular set of facts demands a remedy, they may stretch ordinary contract principles to fit the remedy within a contractual rubric. This result is not surprising. Parties may share their lives for many years without having any clear agreement, express or implied, that sets out the financial consequences of terminating their relationship. To find such an agreement may therefore require filling many gaps with terms that flow more from the court's sense of fairness than from any mutual intentions inferable from the parties' conduct.

This section approaches the matter in a more straightforward manner. It identifies the circumstances that would typically lead such a court to find a contract, and defines those circumstances as giving rise to a domestic partnership. Remedies then follow unless the parties have made an enforceable contract to the contrary. In formulating a rubric combining expansive notions of contract with equitable remedies, one court observed that it is appropriate in these cases to presume "that the parties intend to deal fairly with each other." This suggests that, as in marriage, in the ordinary case the law should provide remedies at the dissolution of a domestic relationship that will ensure an equitable allocation of accumulated property and of the financial losses arising from the termination of the relationship. The result, in comparison with a narrow contractual approach, is a system that places the burden of showing a contract on the party wishing to avoid such fairness-based remedies, rather than imposing it on the party seeking to claim them.

This section thus does not require as a predicate to finding the existence of a domestic partnership, that the parties had an implied or express agreement, or even that the facts meet the standard requirements of a quantum meruit claim. It instead relies, as do the marriage laws, on a status classification: property claims and support obligations presumptively arise between persons who qualify as domestic partners, as they do between legal spouses, without inquiry into each couple's particular arrangement, except as the presumption is itself overcome by contract. This approach reflects a judgment that it is usually just to apply to both groups the property and support rules applicable to divorcing spouses, that individualized inquiries are usually impractical or unduly burdensome, and that it therefore makes more sense to require parties to contract out of these property and support rules than to contract into them. . . .

d. . . . Persons treated as domestic partners under this section must also meet the requirements of Chapter 5 . . . . See § 6.06. Chapter 5 imposes its own durational thresholds for award eligibility [and the] value of any award . . . is ordinarily proportional to the duration of the parties' cohabitation. The amount of the parties' property subject to division under § 6.05 will also, in the ordinary case, be proportional to the duration of the parties' cohabitation. *See* § 6.04. Thus, this section does not require long cohabitation periods to screen out inappropriate compensatory-payment or property-distribution awards.

The required durations do need to be long enough to make it likely that the parties have established a life together as a couple and that [this life together] has had some significant impact on the circumstances of one or both parties. . . . Cohabitation periods of two or three years have been used by Canadian provinces that have adopted an approach similar to Paragraph (3). The parties' procreation or adoption of a child with whom they share a household is itself sufficiently indicative of this likelihood that the duration required under Paragraph (2) need not be as long as that required under Paragraph (3). If a jurisdiction sets the Paragraph (3) cohabitation period at three years, a reasonable choice, a Paragraph (2) cohabitation parenting period of two years would be appropriate.

[iii]   The Blending of Contract and Status Frameworks

ELIZABETH S. SCOTT, MARRIAGE, COHABITATION AND COLLECTIVE RESPONSIBILITY FOR DEPENDENCY, 2004 U. Chi. Legal Forum 219

[Despite the] legitimate preference that lawmakers have for formal marriage with its set of clear obligations. . . . courts should enforce agreements between cohabiting parties' about property distribution and support under ordinary contract principles.

Many courts have adopted this view in recent years and have been ready to enforce these contracts. . . . Often, however, no express agreement can be proved and the claimant must seek to demonstrate that the parties had a contract implied in fact based on conduct. [¶] Courts' responses to financial claims by cohabitating parties based on conduct rather than express promise have been mixed. . . [¶] In general, although claimants have sometimes prevailed, enforcement of implied contracts by cohabitants is an uncertain and costly business. [T]he extent and nature of understandings about financial sharing and support varies in informal unions, and the ability of third parties (i.e. courts) to discern accurately the parties' expectations on the basis of their conduct in this context is limited. . . . . The unpredictability of outcomes discourages settlements. The upshot is that courts have struggled to achieve fair outcomes in response to these claims, but the results have been unsatisfactory from the perspective of protecting financially vulnerable parties.

Some commentators have responded to these difficulties by concluding that the contractual framework is unsuitable for this context because the parties' understandings are too ambiguous. The approach of the A.L.I. Domestic Partnership Principles is representative of this response. Ira Ellman. . . . argues that unmarried couples do not think in contractual terms, and seldom have understandings about financial obligations upon dissolution that are sufficiently clear to be subject to legal enforcement as contract terms. Ellman's (and the A.L.I.) response is to substitute a non-consensual status as the mechanism to enforce financial obligations between intimate partners.

[T]he A.L.I.'s abandonment of contract is undesirable. It is also unnecessary, in that contract law can provide efficient default rules to clarify the implied understandings about property and support obligations between parties in long-term intimate unions. The application of properly structured default rules can facilitate legal enforcement and simplify the judicial evaluation of these claims.

[W]here a couple provide[s] clear evidence through . . . conduct that [the] relationship is marriage-like, [an] agreement to assume marital obligations can be inferred — and legally enforced. Where a couple lives together for many years, sharing a life and financial resources, and holding themselves out as husband and wife, it is a sound presumption that they intend to share the property acquired during the relationship. Further, [partners] who assume traditional marital roles of wage earner and homemaker can be presumed to intend to provide the financially dependent partner with "insurance" in the form of support should the relationship dissolve. The default terms of the marriage contract represent mutual obligations that spouses incur whether or not they expressly agree; these obligations should also be incurred in marriage-like informal unions.

The challenge is to design clear criteria that separate marriage-like unions from those in which the parties are not married because they do not want marital commitment or obligations. The framework should be as simple as possible, in order to clarify obligations and promote certainty for both courts and parties. [A] cohabitation period of substantial duration is the best available proxy for commitment, and the only practical means to avoid intrusive and error-prone inquiry in the effort to distinguish marriage-like relationships from more typical informal unions that involve less financial interdependency. A period of five years or more, for example, supports a presumption that the relationship was marriage-like and discourages opportunistic and marginal claims. At that point, the party challenging the contractual obligation can fairly be required to demonstrate that the parties' intent was not to undertake marital obligations and that the union was of a different kind. A five year period will significantly limit the category of claimants, because most informal unions do not last this long.[97] This means that some deserving parties will not get the benefit of the default rule. However, dependent partners in unions of extended duration present the most compelling claims, and these parties will be protected.

The default rule framework represents a significant improvement over current law; today, many claims fail, although it seems likely either that the parties had some agreement (but what, exactly?) or that one partner misled or exploited the other. Default rules clarify that the conduct of parties in long term unions will be deemed promissory unless clear evidence is offered that it is not. The framework functions effectively whether or not the parties have similar understandings of the terms of their commitment to one another. For most parties in relationships of long duration, the presumption that the union is marriage-like probably represents accurately the parties' explicit or implicit understanding about property sharing and support, and thus the framework simply functions as a standard majoritarian default. Where the default rule does not reflect both parties' expectations, it has a useful information-forcing function, putting the burden on the dissatisfied party to identify himself explicitly as a "non-committer." [¶] [¶] The proposed framework presents the primary wage earner with two options: he can . . . accept the legal obligations that follow from the application of the default rule as the cost of being in a long term intimate union, or he can disclose to his partner his intentions not to engage in financial sharing. At this point, she can make an informed choice about whether to end the union or to remain in a role that leaves her financially vulnerable. A jurisdiction that wants to offer additional legal protection to the dependent partner can do so by requiring a written agreement to opt out of the default rule. In any event, the default rule allows the parties to act upon more complete information about the financial terms of their relationship, reducing both misunderstanding and exploitation.

As compared with current doctrine, the default rule approach simplifies the judicial determination of financial obligations between cohabitants; it avoids an open-ended inquiry into the parties' expectations in every case. . . . [T]he framework provides a means to enforce the sometimes opaque financial understandings between cohabiting partners and does so by using familiar legal tools. The default framework offers far greater financial security than current law to vulnerable partners who may otherwise be exploited or misled — or who may simply have a different understanding of the relationship than the primary wage earning partner.

. . . .

Outcomes under my proposed framework will often be quite similar to those obtained under the A.L.I.'s Domestic Partnership status, which also imposes marriage-like obligations on cohabitants. The contract-based default framework has some advantages, however over the A.L.I. approach. . . .

---

[97] Only a small percentage of informal unions last for 5 years. . . . Thus, a presumption based on this duration promises to be a relatively accurate sorting mechanism for separating marriage-like from casual unions. If the cohabiting couple have children together, it makes sense for the birth of the child to triggers the presumption. This is the A.L.I. approach, which I would endorse in this regard.

[A] contractual framework is compatible with liberal values and thus has a normative appeal that the status-based approach adopted by the A.L.I. lacks. The proposed default rule framework rests on realistic empirical assumptions about the intentions and expectations of many couples in informal unions, while at the same time offering protection to naive parties whose expectations may not be shared by their partners. It recognizes, however, that sometimes one party will reject financial sharing as a condition of continuing the relationship and his partner will choose to remain in the union. Parties are free to contract out of default rules, and *imposing* a marriage-like status on cohabiting parties, as the A.L.I. Principles do, excludes an option for intimate affiliation that some parties might choose. The A.L.I. approach assumes that financially vulnerable partners would always choose no relationship over a relationship without financial security; in fact, some may prefer a shared life without financial sharing. Adults with full information should be free to make these choices. To be sure, sometimes the outcome under the default framework may result in inequity. However, the alternative of paternalistically imposing financial obligations on unchoosing (and even unwilling) parties after a certain period of cohabitation is even less satisfactory. Although an imposed status may sometimes beneficially deter exploitation of dependent partners, it sacrifices the freedom of individuals to order their intimate lives.

Not so long ago, both law and morality narrowly circumscribed the freedom of individuals to make choices about intimate affiliation; today, some are nostalgic about a society in which marriage was the only acceptable intimate union. Most moderns, however, endorse the core liberal principle that government should not interfere with the freedom of individuals to pursue their goals for personal happiness, absent some evidence that their choices will cause harm to others. Some couples may want to live together without commitment or obligation in long term relationships. As long as each partner voluntarily chooses this arrangement and is free to leave, paternalistic government restrictions that inhibit freedom in this private realm are hard to justify.

NOTES

1. *Critiques of the ALI Proposals*. Tentative drafts of the ALI proposals circulated for several years prior to the promulgation of the final version. During these years, the proposals generated substantial scholarly debate. *See, e.g., Symposium on the ALI Principles of the Law of Family Dissolution,* 2001 BYU L. REV. 857; *Symposium: Unmarried Partners and the Legacy of* Marvin v. Marvin, 76 NOTRE DAME L. REV. 1261 (2001). While some have greeted the unmarried cohabitant provisions with enthusiasm, *see, e.g.,* Mary Coombs, *Insiders and Outsiders: What the American Law Institute has Done for Gay and Lesbian Families,* 8 DUKE J. GENDER L. & POL'Y 87 (2001), others have been more critical. The critics have two principal contentions:

(a) *The ALI proposals and the traditional family*. In voicing one of the more vehement objections to Chapter 6, Professor Lynn D. Wardle claims that the creation of an "official, alternative, concubinage-like status of domestic partnership," could "seriously weaken and undermine the institution of marriage." *Deconstructing Family: A Critique of the American Law Institute's "Domestic Partners" Proposal,* 2001 BYU L. REV. 1189, 1193, 1206. On this question, the ALI drafters assert that the domestic partner provisions are likely to have the reverse effect. "[T]o the extent that some individuals avoid marriage in order to avoid responsibilities to a partner, this Chapter reduces the incentive to avoid marriage because it diminishes the effectiveness of this strategy . . . . Nor are domestic partnerships likely to provide a satisfactory alternative to marriage for those otherwise inclined to marry, because informal domestic relationships are not generally recognized by third parties, including governments, which often make marriage advantageous under various regulatory and benefit schemes." Comment b, § 6.02, American Law Institute, *Principles of the Law of Family Dissolution: Analysis and Recommendations* (2002). For a view contrasting with that of Professor Wardle, see Lynne Marie Kohm, *How Will the Proliferation and Recognition of Domestic Partnerships Affect Marriage,* 4 J. L. & FAM. STUD. 105 (2002).

(b) ***The ALI proposals and private ordering****.* Professor David Westfall argues that the provisions of Chapter 6 would "impos[e] marital obligations on parties in an informal relationship," which he views as "wholly at odds with some of the potentially liberating implications of the *Marvin* court's decision." *Forcing Incidents of Marriage on Unmarried Cohabitants: The American Law Institute's* Principles of Family Dissolution, 76 NOTRE DAME L. REV. 1467, 1470 (2001). Professor Westfall argues that the *"Principles'* recognition of domestic partners would substitute an emphasis on status, very similar to common-law marriage, for the powerful contemporary movement to recognize parties' freedom to contract about the terms of their relationship. And it would inject a troubling degree of uncertainty into the determination of when domestic partnership status exists." *Id.* at 1479. Chapter 6 does permit couples to contract out of some or all of the legal consequences of the domestic partner status, just as married partners can contract out of a range of state-supplied terms governing a dissolution of their marriage. Professor Westfall expresses dissatisfaction with this option, however, arguing that the procedural and substantive requirements for an enforceable contract under the *Principles* (which are the same as the *Principles* recommend for premarital contracts) are quite strict, potentially invalidating many agreements and making Chapter 6's provisions difficult to escape. For other discussions of the implications for private ordering of Chapter 6 of the *ALI Principles*, see Milton C. Regan, Jr., *Calibrated Commitment: The Legal Treatment of Marriage and Cohabitation,* 76 NOTRE DAME L. REV. 1435, 1446–1449 (2001); Margaret Brinig, *Domestic Partnership: Missing the Target?* 4 J. L. FAM. STUD. 19 (2002).

(c) ***Alternatives.*** Professor Scott, as evidenced above, argues that the contract framework is still a useful one for conceptualizing the obligations of nonmarital partners. As she notes, the remedies imposed by courts under her "default framework" may be quite similar to those required by adherence to the *ALI Principles*. Beyond the recommendation of a cohabitation period of five years in order to trigger the application of the default rules, Professor Scott asserts that her proposal differs from the ALI approach in that a primary function of her "default framework" is to signal to parties the rights and obligations that will attach to their relationship at the five-year point if they do not contract out of it. With such information and attendant freedom to opt out, she argues that enforcement of marriage-like post-dissolution remedies fits well within an implied contract model. In contrast to the ALI approach, under which she argues domestic partnership status is coercively imposed by a paternalistic state on unknowing and even unwilling parties, the contractual approach is based on implied consent. The problem is exaggerated, she argues, because, although a couple can contract out of domestic partnership status under the ALI Principles, courts have relatively broad discretion not to enforce such contracts. The ALI, however, would not agree with this description of its approach to the enforcement of agreements. For a comparison of the ALI's approach to premarital agreements (which is also applied to agreements to avoid domestic partner obligations) with existing law, see Chapter 8, pages 765-771.

Some commentators have proposed "compromises" between the ALI domestic partners proposal and the now-dominant contract-based regime. Concluding that the ALI proposals go too far in creating parity between married and unmarried couples, Professor Milton Regan would limit legal recognition of nonmarital cohabitant relationships in order to retain the "legally privileged" legal status of marriage. *Id.* at 1464. Yet, inter se claims between nonmarital cohabitants should be recognized, he argues, even in the absence of a contract, "when an individual is rendered vulnerable by virtue of her reliance on a nonmarital relationship" and where a partner can demonstrate that "failure to honor the claim would impose undue hardship." *Id.* at 1465, 1452. Professor Regan asserts that where "a claimant can establish that the relationship involved financial and emotional interdependence," the law should recognize that "individuals may have responsibilities of care toward one another that arise not simply from consent but by virtue of a shared life, whatever legal form it takes." *Id.* at 1450–51. Professor Thomas Oldham also asserts that the law should provide remedies where interdependence between nonmarital cohabitants results in "career damage" for one, particularly where there is a common child. J. Thomas Oldham, *Lessons From Jerry Hall v. Mick Jagger Regarding U.S. Regulation Of Heterosexual Cohabitants Or, Can't Get No Satisfaction*, 76 NOTRE DAME L. REV. 1409, 1427 (2001). He suggests that the law should protect parties in longer-term cohabiting relationships who have been disadvantaged by roles assumed during cohabitation, even where the parties had not formally agreed to enter the status, and that appropriate remedies could encompass either "transitional" post-relationship support or treatment of property acquired during the relationship as jointly owned. *Id.* at 1428–29.

2. *Understanding the ALI's Proposal.* Section 6.01(3) of the ALI Principles, not reprinted above, makes clear that its domestic partners rules do not displace other law that would enforce obligations between cohabitors that arise from contracts between them. While the ALI thus accepts contract as one source of obligation between cohabitors, it emphasizes an alternative non-contractual basis for obligation. It is thus the converse of *Marvin*, which suggests the possibility of an equitable basis for recovery but emphasizes contract. In part because the equitable branch of *Marvin* has never been developed, this difference can prove significant in the decision of actual cases, as Ellman's discussion of *Friedman v. Friedman* illustrates.

What is the non-contractual basis of cohabitor obligation upon which the ALI relies? As Ellman observes later in that same article:

Relationships are themselves the source of legal duties, without the need for any assistance from contract. This is not a new idea. Landlords and tenants, employers and employees, neighbors, lawyers and clients, and doctors and patients all incur legally enforceable duties to one another arising from their relationships. They may have a contract which itself creates obligations, and we may think of their mutual decision to enter into the relationship as a kind of contract. But in all these cases, the law may impose duties upon them which are based upon the relationship itself, not upon any agreement between them. [¶] . . . [F]amily law provides perhaps the oldest examples of legal duties arising from relationships, whether as husband and wife, or parent and child. [¶] . . . A sensible legal rule for deciding when legal duties arise between unmarried cohabitants will not ask whether they had a contract, but whether their nonmarital relationship shares with marriage those qualities which lead us to impose legal duties as between husbands and wives.

76 NOTRE DAME L. REV. at 1375-76. In the ALI's view, then, such relational duties arise between intimate partners who in fact "share a life together as a couple," whether or not they choose to formalize their relationship with a marriage ceremony. One can surely debate the precise nature of, and rationale for, relational duties, but their existence is widely acknowledged in the law as well as in popular understandings of moral obligation. For a sophisticated effort at exploring the basis of relational duties, see Samuel Sheffler, *Relationships and Responsibilities*, 26 Philosophy and Public Affairs 189 (1997).

While the law often enforces contracts between parties that alter their relational duties, their contractual freedom is often limited. We may deny or limit the right of parties to contract out of some obligations (such as the obligation to support a child, to use due care in performing surgery, or to provide a tenant with a habitable dwelling), or we may impose special procedural requirements upon such contracts. This same approach is also taken by the ALI Principles with respect to the obligations that arise between intimate partners who share a life together, whether they are married or not. The special procedural and substantive requirements applicable to premarital agreements, treated in Chapter 7 of the ALI Principles, are thus also applied to agreements that avoid obligations that would otherwise arise between domestic partners. However, § 7.04(6) of the ALI Principles does waive (for domestic partners only) most of the procedural requirements otherwise applied to such contracts, if the parties "have no children in common and enforcement is sought within five years of the agreement's execution." (The only exception to this waiver is the retention of the requirement that the agreement be in writing.) Thus, unmarried partners in a short-term, childless relationship can contract out of the domestic partner rules fairly easily, although such agreements would still be reviewable for unconscionability, or, under certain circumstances, for unanticipated changes in the parties' circumstances that make enforcement of their agreement, as written, a "substantial injustice." (For further explanation of this rule, see the discussion of the ALI's approach to premarital agreements at pages 766-769 in Chapter 8.)

Of course, to determine on a case by case basis whether two individuals have "shared a life together as a couple" could require the same kind of time-consuming inquiry that is necessary in a typical *Marvin* case like *Friedman*, in which the court must decide, in the face of the parties' conflicting stories, whether there was an oral or implied contract between them. A theme of the entire ALI project, running through its provisions on custody, compensatory payments, and property, as well as here, is to employ presumptions that reduce the need for or likelihood of such customized fact-finding. This is why the Principles call for the adoption of presumptions under which couples who share a primary residence together for more than the specified number of years may be treated as domestic partners without the need for such an inquiry. It is also typical of the *Principles* to leave the particular number of years unspecified; the *Principles* employ that same approach in the chapters on custody, compensatory payments, and property division, and for the same reason: On one hand, the *Principles* urge adoption of uniform presumption rules so as to achieve efficiency and consistency in adjudication. On the other hand, the Institute concluded that whether those rules should treat couples as domestic partners after living together three years or five years is not a question of fundamental principle, but rather one of practical judgment on which the Institute need not take a position.

This is not to say that the *Principles* offer no guidance on the appropriate time period. They do explain, as set out in Comment *d* quoted above, that the chosen period must be "long enough to make it likely that the parties have established a life together as a couple and that [this life together] has had some significant impact on the circumstances of one or both parties." The *Principles* are also clear in distinguishing between childless couples and couples with a child in common. For the latter, the presumption should not only arise after a shorter period of time than for couples without children, but it is made irrebuttable. So, for example, the ALI Principles would treat Terry and Elliott Friedman as domestic partners upon Terry's showing that they had a child together while sharing a primary residence for more than twenty years. Under the *Principles*, then, Elliott could avoid the obligations that flow from that status only by showing that he and Terry had a formal agreement so providing, and only if that agreement met the same procedural and substantive standards that the jurisdiction would apply to a premarital agreement waiving alimony or property claims.

A claimant like Michelle Marvin might also benefit from the ALI's approach, although the matter is less certain. Because Michelle and Lee shared a primary residence for six and a half years, a presumption would likely arise (unless the jurisdiction adopted an even longer durational requirement). But Lee, unlike Elliott, could rebut it if he could show that they had not "shared a life together as a couple," thus defeating Michelle's domestic partner claim entirely. Whether Lee would bother to attempt such a showing, however, might depend upon the jurisdiction's approach to financial claims at the dissolution of relatively short, childless marriages (because those same rules would apply to Lee and Marvin as domestic partners). Most states allow only modest claims in such cases — perhaps no more than the kind of transitional assistance that Lee provided Michelle voluntarily. (The *Marvin* opinion reports that he supported Michelle for a year and a half after she moved out.) It thus seems likely someone in Lee's place would have no reason to fight Michelle's domestic partner claim to avoid an alimony obligation, because he is prepared to pay more or less the modest amount that would be ordered in any event. The property claim, however, is another matter, and was undoubtedly the reason why both sides in *Marvin* itself believed their dispute worth fighting through two appellate levels and a retrial. California is a community property state with a strict equal division rule, under which Michelle would own half of all the property Lee accumulated during their relationship — property that she claimed included motion picture rights worth more than $1 million. Such a substantial property pot is obviously unusual, and many states would reject her claim to share equally in it even if they had married. Be that as it may, the ALI's position is that whatever rules the state finds appropriate to apply at the dissolution of a short-term childless marriage should apply as well to couples who live together in a true *de facto* marriage for the same time period. Of course, a high income person like Lee Marvin is just the kind of individual most likely and most able to obtain legal assistance in preparing a premarital, or pre-domestic-partner, agreement. An agreement limiting Michelle's claims if their childless relationship were to end after six years would be enforceable under the ALI's rules, as it is not "unconscionable" and would not even qualify for scrutiny of whether its enforcement would constitute a "substantial injustice." See pages 766-768 of Chapter 8.

It is useful to compare the ALI's likely resolution of these two cases with the result under competing formulations. The California courts tell us that a pure contract approach yields no claim for either Terry Friedman or Michelle Marvin, because neither woman could meet her burden of showing the existence of a contract between her and her partner. By contrast, the ALI puts the burden of proving a contract on Elliott or Lee if an unrebutted presumption of domestic partnership arises. Under the ALI one must contract *out* of relational duties, once they arise; under *Marvin* one must contract *into* them. Scott's proposed "contract default" rules offer what might be seen as an intermediate position. Like the ALI, she attaches importance to the duration of the parties' relationship. In both Terry's and Michelle's case the relationship's duration is long enough to trigger her default rules. For Scott, however, the default rules are not based upon relational duties imposed by the law, but instead express an assumption about the agreement the parties must have in fact intended — in effect, the contract we will assume they made in the absence of contrary evidence. That assumption would be rebutted, thus denying any recovery to Terry or Michelle, if Elliott or Lee persuaded the court that he had clearly expressed to his partner his rejection of the assumed default contract, because there would then be no basis for a contract-based remedy. How that rule would have played out in the actual *Marvin* and *Friedman* cases is uncertain. Those courts thought the evidence insufficient to show that Lee or Elliott had agreed to a contract creating post-relationship obligations, but that is not the same as concluding they had clearly expressed their rejection of such obligations. Certainly, however, that was Elliott's claim — he argued that he and Terry did have an understanding that when their relationship "was over, it was over." But of course the *Friedman* opinion does not itself test Elliot's factual claim under Scott's standard. Alternatively, Scott suggests her proposal might be implemented by requiring a written agreement to opt out of the obligations imposed by the default rule. Under that version of her proposal, Terry and Michele would succeed in establishing their claims.

Consider, however, the extent to which this version of Scott's proposal differs from the ALI's, which also imposes obligations on intimate partners who live together long enough, and also allows agreements to avoid the obligation. The main difference might be that Scott would accept some agreements to avoid intimate partner obligations that the ALI would decline to enforce. For more on the ALI's approach to premarital agreements (which it would also apply to agreements to avoid domestic partner obligations), see Chapter 8.

3. Washington's Status-Based Remedies. In 1984, the Washington Supreme Court held that property accumulated during a nonmarital cohabitant relationship is subject to the same equitable division principles that guide disposition of property after divorce if the parties had "stable, marital-like relationship where both parties cohabit with knowledge that a lawful marriage between them does not exist." *Marriage of Lindsey*, 678 P.2d 328, 330–331 (Wash. 1984), Following *Lindsey,* a Washington appellate court applied Washington's community property law to assets acquired over a ten-year period of cohabitation "during which the parties conducted themselves like a married couple and pooled their resources and services for joint projects." *Foster v. Thilges*, 812 P.2d 523, 525 (1991). The parties disagreed as to whether they had *intended* equal ownership of the property in question, but the court held that resolution of the factual dispute was unnecessary "[w]here the relationship was long-term, stable, pseudomarital and the undertakings were joint projects as in the instant case." *Id.* at 526. It concluded that "the couple's property [should] be divided justly and equitably, applying community property principles. . ." *Id.* The equitable distribution statute is not applied directly in cases such as these, but may be looked to "for guidance." *Connell v. Francisco*, 898 P.2d 831, 835 (Wash. 1995). Whereas Washington's community property laws permit the court to allocate both community and separate property at divorce, in cohabitation cases the court can distribute *only* that property which would have been community if the couple was married. *Id.*

More recently, in *Marriage of Pennington*, 14 P.3d 764 (2000) (en banc), the Washington Supreme Court reaffirmed the doctrine in principle, and noted five factors relevant to determining whether the required relationship exists in a particular case: "continuous cohabitation, duration of the relationship, purpose of the relationship, pooling of resources and services for joint projects, and the intent of the parties." *Id.* at 770. It concluded that the two sets of relationships before it did not satisfy the requirements, related in part to factors such as the sporadic nature of the cohabitation, inconsistencies in the sharing of expenses, and equivocal evidence of "the mutual intent of the parties to be in a [stable and committed] relationship." *Id.* at 772.

In 2004, a court of appeals applied the doctrine to a case involving a same-sex couple. *Gormley v. Robertson*, 83 P.3d 1042 (2004). The court emphasized that, while the question of whether same-sex couples can marry is a matter for the legislature, the extension of certain marriage-like property rights and obligations to intimate unmarried couples lies within the court's equitable powers, and that there was no basis for distinguishing between unmarried opposite-sex and same-sex couples in applying this doctrine. This decision was consistent with *Vasquez v. Hawthorne*, 33 P.3d 735, 737 (Wash. 2001), in which the Washington Supreme Court suggested that the application of this doctrine would not be "limited by the gender or sexual orientation of the parties."

Washington is not entirely alone in adopting a status approach. Many state courts have held that in considering cohabitation cases, they are not limited to contract ideas, and may also grant relief on general equitable grounds regardless of the parties' intent. *E.g.*, *Wilbur v. DeLapp*, 850 P.2d 1151, 1153 (Or. App. 1993) (in a nonmarital domestic relationship, primary consideration in distributing parties' property is their intent, but court is "not precluded from exercising [its] equitable powers to reach a fair result based on the circumstances of each case"); *Pickens v. Pickens*, 490 So. 2d 872 (Miss. 1986) (homemaker has equitable claim to property accumulated during long-term cohabiting relationship, without regard to contract inquiry); *Sullivan v. Rooney*, 533 N.E.2d 1372 (Mass. 1989) (relying upon constructive trust doctrine to award woman one-half interest in the home in which partners lived during the cohabitation, but which was titled solely in man's name); *Evans v. Wall*, 542 So. 2d 1055 (Fla. App. 1989) (same).

4. *Comparative Perspectives on Nonmarital Cohabitation.* Nonmarital cohabitation has become increasingly common in many developed nations. Some countries, like England and Ireland, offer limited remedies to cohabitants who have contributed to property acquired during cohabitation. JOHN MEE, THE PROPERTY RIGHTS OF COHABITEES: AN ANALYSIS OF EQUITY'S RESPONSE IN FIVE COMMON LAW JURISDICTIONS 34–92 (1999). Although grounded in notions of contract ("common intention") or equity (constructive trust), these remedies focus primarily on direct *financial* contributions to acquisition of property. *Id. See also* Gillian Douglas, *Marriage, Cohabitation, and Parenthood — from Contract to Status?* IN CROSS CURRENTS: FAMILY LAW AND POLICY IN THE US AND ENGLAND 211, 219–221 (S.N. Katz, J. Eekelaar & M. Maclean eds. 2000).

By contrast, several other jurisdictions have accorded more status-like legal recognition to nonmarital cohabitants. For example, in 2001, the New Zealand parliament passed the Property (Relationships) Act, which created parity between married persons and nonmarital cohabitants (referred to as "de facto partners") who have lived together as a couple for at least three years, Bill Akin, *The Challenge of Unmarried Cohabitation — The New Zealand Response*, 37 FAM. L.Q. 303 (2003). Prior to the 2002 effective date of this legislation, property rights upon dissolution of nonmarital relationships were governed by the equitable doctrine of "reasonable expectations," allowing the court to distribute property "fairly," irrespective of evidence of an actual agreement. Mee, *supra* at 266–93. The equitable doctrines that evolved in New Zealand, Canada, and Australia, unlike those in England and Ireland, permit consideration of one partner's provision of domestic services as relevant to property claims. *Id.* at 191, 235–38, 275.

By statute, certain Canadian provinces, such as Ontario and British Columbia, have addressed support obligations of nonmarital cohabitants following relationship dissolution. Grace Ganz Blumberg, *The Regularization of Nonmarital Cohabitation: Rights and Responsibilities in the American Welfare State*, 76 NOTRE DAME L. REV. 1265, 1300 (2001). Ontario treats nonmarital partners as "spouses" for such purposes if the couple has cohabited consecutively for at least three years or "lived together in a relationship of some permanence, if they are the natural or adoptive parents of a child." British Columbia focuses on the existence of a " 'marriage-like relationship for a period of at least 2 years.' " *Id.* at 1300–01 (quoting Ontario Family Reform Act and Family Relations Act of British Columbia). A national Canadian statute adopted in 2000 provides for parity in receipt of certain federal benefits among married couples and cohabiting couples (both opposite-sex and same-sex). Nicholas Bala, *Alternatives for Extending Spousal Status in Canada,* 17 CAN. J. FAM. L. 169 (2000).

One province of Australia, New South Wales, accords legislative recognition to nonmarital cohabiting relationships (referred to as "de facto relationships") through provisions that address property rights upon dissolution and death, and support rights upon dissolution. Blumberg, *supra* at 1301. Other Australian provinces have also extended some form of recognition to nonmarital cohabitants. Reg Graycar & Jenni Millbank, *The Bride Wore Pink . . . To the Property (Relationships) Legislation Amendment Act of 1999: Relationships Law Reform in New South Wales,* 17 CAN. J. FAM. L. 227, 244–48 (2000).

Several European nations have recognized rights to support and property upon dissolution of nonmarital relationships. In France, if a plaintiff can show that there was a *de facto* partnership between the cohabitants (an agreement to pool assets and to share profits and losses), she may be treated much like a spouse in the division of property, and perhaps even post-dissolution support. MARY ANN GLENDON, THE TRANSFORMATION OF FAMILY LAW 256–63 (1989). In general, "the more a particular free union [*i.e.*, de facto partnership] resembles a marriage in stability and in the way the partners conduct themselves toward each other and the community at large, the more likely it is to be given effects resembling those of legal marriage." *Id.* at 261. In other words, "French cohabitation law, new as well as old, often seems to imitate the law of marriage . . ." *Id.* at 262. Most recently, the French government enacted legislation (*Du Pacte Civil de Solidarite et du Concubinage* or "PACS") permitting nonmarital couples (opposite-and same-sex) to register as partners, thus creating a formal avenue for recognition. Eva Steiner, *The Sprit of the New French Registered Partnership Law — Promoting Autonomy and Pluralism or Weakening Marriage?* 12 CHILD & FAM. L. Q. 1 (2000). Commentators have noted that the provisions of this legislation continue the French tradition of providing for nonmarital cohabitants a "regime similar to the matrimonial regime of separation of assets," as well as access to various governmental benefits and other rights. *Id.* at 7; Claude Martin & Irene Thery, *The PACS and Marriage and Cohabitation in France,* 15 INT'L J. L., POL'Y & FAM. 135 (2001). In contrast to marriage, French PACS do not require a formal divorce and do not give rise to the adoption and parentage rights accompanying French marriage. Martin & Thery, *supra* at 14. Furthermore, the terms of PACS, but *not* marriages, can be contractually modified by the parties. David Bradley, *Regulation of Unmarried Cohabitation in West-European Jurisdictions — Determinants of Legal Policy,* 15 INT'L J. L., POL'Y & FAM. 22, 33 (2001)

Professor Mary Ann Glendon highlights the developments in Sweden and, to a lesser extent other Nordic countries, as characterized by "the convergence and consummation of three distinct trends [:] the emergence of informal marriage as a substantial social institution, its development as a legal institution, and the elimination from legal marriage of many of the features that previously distinguished it from informal marriage." Glendon, *supra* at 273. Specifically, she notes that legal differences between married couples and nonmarital cohabitants gradually eroded regarding a myriad of legal benefits and protections, including tax status. pension rights, capacity to sue for wrongful death of one's partner, and property division at dissolution. *Id.* at 274–77. Greater legal recognition of nonmarital relationships has occurred in other European nations as well, although at different paces and manners. *See, e.g.,* Dijana Jakovac-Lozic, *Croatia's New Family Act and its Implications on Marriage and Other Forms of Family Life*, 31 CAL. W. INT'L L.J. 83, 92–94 (2000) (discussing Croatia's legislation extending to nonmarital partners certain rights to property and post-relationship support); Bradley, *supra* (contrasting the nature of and path to legal recognition of nonmarital partnerships in Denmark, England, France, Germany, The Netherlands, Norway, Spain, and Sweden). For classic surveys and analyses of the comparative law of nonmarital cohabitation, see *Marriage and Cohabitation in Contemporary Societies* (J. Eekelaar & S. Katz eds. 1980); Mary Ann Glendon STATE, LAW AND FAMILY (1977); Carol S. Bruch, *Cohabitation in the Common Law Countries a Decade After* Marvin: *Settled In or Moving Ahead?,* 22 U.C. DAVIS L. REV. 717 (1989).

5. *Interstate Recognition of Nonmarital Cohabitant Relationships.* For a thoughtful analysis of the special issues raised when nonmarital couples begin their relationship in one jurisdiction and one or both of them change domiciles, see William A. Reppy, Jr., *Choice of Law Problems Arising When Unmarried Cohabitants Change Domicile*, 55 SMU L. REV. 273 (2002).

PROBLEMS

Consider how the following cases might be decided in a state following *Marvin, Hewitt,* or *Morone,* or under a status-based approach.

Problem 9-3. Cliff and Nancy lived together as a couple on and off during college. From 1992 to 1997, they lived together continuously in one half of a duplex which Cliff had purchased in his own name, using his separate funds for a down payment. The other half of the duplex was rented out, and Nancy helped to maintain it by cleaning between tenants, painting, showing it to prospective tenants, and so forth. Nancy and Cliff had joint savings and checking accounts, into which the rental payments and their separate earnings were always deposited. Mortgage payments as well as household purchases were also made from these funds. The parties kept no careful record of their respective earnings during this period of cohabitation, but it appears that Cliff earned significantly more than Nancy. In 1993, Nancy gave birth to a child, which Cliff admits is his. The parties owned a number of automobiles during the period, all of which were registered solely in Cliff's name. Some of their household items were gifts from their parents. Nancy had purchased a car in 1991, before they had begun living together, but when she stopped working after giving birth, she transferred title to Cliff, who took over the payments. Cliff later sold that car and used the proceeds to purchase a truck, in his own name.

At various times during their cohabitation, Nancy asked Cliff to put her name on the title to the duplex or the cars, but he always refused. She asked him to marry her on several occasions but he would not. She was hospitalized under his name on one occasion, and his health insurer paid her bills. Nancy claims that Cliff assured her that if he died, all his property would go to her and the child.

(A) After their relationship terminates, Nancy brings an action for a declaration of her rights in the duplex, automobiles, household furnishings and other personal property. What result?

(B) Suppose Nancy had come to you for advice before the relationship terminated. Would you suggest preparing a *Marvin* agreement for the parties to sign?

(C) Suppose Cliff had come to you for advice, seeking an agreement to present to Nancy, which will ensure that she has no claims upon him if their relationship ends. He confides that a few years ago, he came into a significant inheritance, which he invested in his brother's software company, and things have gone very well. Nancy doesn't know about any of these developments; he is reluctant to tell her for fear that she will pester him to spend money on things like a nicer home or better car, which he doesn't want to do. What do you advise?

Problem 9-4. Assume the facts of Problem 9-3, except that when Nancy became pregnant she came to seek your advice on whether it was important that she and Cliff marry. She knows that Cliff wants the child, and probably would marry her if she insisted upon it as a condition of her completing the pregnancy to term. She wants to know how important it is that she do that, and exactly how it would matter if they were married. What do you tell her?

(A) What if Cliff insists upon a premarital agreement that upon divorce, neither party will have any obligation to the other? Is there any reason for Nancy to prefer marriage with such a premarital agreement to cohabitation with a *Marvin* agreement?

(B) Suppose Cliff says that while he is willing to sign a cohabitation agreement stating that he will be financially responsible for the child, he will insist on also including provisions which deny any financial obligations to Nancy?

Problem 9-5. Irma was a 48-year-old Polish immigrant, married with two children, with little knowledge of English, when she met Thaddeus. Thaddeus, a sophisticated and well-to-do Polish businessman, was 42, married and the father of two children. He urged Irma to live with him and she consented. She raised both of their children and otherwise performed normal housewifely duties while he supported her and the children. He originally promised to divorce his wife and marry her, and he sought out her husband to arrange for a divorce for her. Irma was divorced, but Thaddeus never was. For some time he was evasive when questioned about marriage. In 1988, she left him after a serious argument. At this point, however, he made it clear that he would not marry her, but promised that he would "take care of her and provide for her for the rest of her life if she would only come back." She relented and returned. They continued living together until 1997, when Thaddeus became interested in another woman, 30 years younger. Irma left him, crushed and hurt, when she discovered that he had finally begun divorce proceedings against his wife so he could marry this new love.

Irma now brings an action to enforce Thaddeus' promise to provide for her for the rest of her life. What result?

Problem 9-6. Mario Bruno hired Angela into his business in 1969, and began an affair with her in 1970. Mario was married and had one adopted child, but frequently expressed to Angela his desire to have a child "of his own." He promised Angela that if she had his child he would support them and provide for the child in his will. He also promised to divorce his wife and marry Angela. Angela finally consented, but despite their efforts, Angela did not become pregnant until 1983. Their son was named Mario Bruno, Junior. Mario paid for all hospital expenses, visited Angela daily, both in the hospital and afterward, paid Angela's rent, and provided her with $60 per week support. As the years progressed, he spent more time with his son and Angela, and frequently bought gifts for them in addition to his regular support payments.

Bruno died suddenly in 1995. His will made no provision for either Angela or Mario Junior. Angela brings this action to obtain specific performance of Mario's agreement to provide for them in his will. Assume that as a general matter, contracts to make a will are enforceable. Is this one?

Problem 9-7. Contrast Problem 9-6 with the case of Joseph and Celeste. The couple began dating regularly in 1988. During that year, Celeste gradually increased the time she spent "staying over" at Joseph's home. Later that year, Joseph asked Celeste to move in with him permanently. She initially resisted, asserting that she "did not want to move in unless we were going to have a long range permanent husband and wife type of relationship." She reports that the next year, she did move into Joseph's home and that two "started living together by mutual agreement as Husband and Wife," including spending most of their time with one another and planning for their future together. She states: "We agreed that we were thereafter building our future together — personal, family, social contacts, community activities, our joint assets, debts and everything else was thereafter being done as husband and wife — not for Joe, not for Celeste, but for our joint benefit." Celeste prepared meals and managed the home. Celeste alleged that, in consideration of her moving in and "living together . . . as Husband and Wife," the two agreed that "all property acquired [with either party's skills, efforts, labor or earnings] were to be treated as their joint property." An integral part of the basic agreement, Celeste acknowledged in the trial court, was a commitment to try to "have a family." "Joe wanted me to get pregnant and have his children, to stop using birth control." And, indeed, they did: Celeste became pregnant in, apparently, late 1990; their first child, Joseph, Jr., was born in August 1991. The parties married in April 1992 and two more children, twin girls, were born to them in November 1996. Celeste filed a dissolution action in January 1998. How is she likely to fare in a claim for a half of the property accumulated by either one of them during the several-year period of premarital cohabitation?

Problems 9-8. Ann and Mary lived together for 12 years in a marriage-like relationship. During that period they both worked outside of the home: Mary as a preschool teacher, and Ann as a vice president of a clothing company. Ann's income was over four times as high as Mary's. In their domestic relationship, Mary performed most of the housekeeping chores while Ann managed their finances, which included stock investments as well as real estate. They each contributed similar proportions of their income to the investments, which were generally held solely in Ann's name. When their relationship ended, Mary brought this action seeking an equitable share in their accumulated property. She alleged an oral agreement "to commingle their resources and assets, to invest in real estate and other property, and to share the profits between themselves." Does she have a cause of action?

Problem 9-9. Phyllis and Robert begin an intimate relationship in 1991, around the time Phyllis decided to file for divorce from her husband. Phyllis completed the divorce in 1994, and the relationship continued until 1996. During much of this time, their affair was conducted clandestinely, and at no point did the parties actually cohabit. Beginning in 1994, Robert gave Phyllis the first of a series of payments intended to allow her to acquire and furnish a house, since Robert believed they would marry and the house would be their home. In fact, Phyllis later broke off the relationship. She refused to return the money, since "it was a gift for sexual services," and she "was prostituting herself for this home." Robert had purchased engagement and wedding rings in 1996; Phyllis wore the engagement ring for some time but then returned it. Robert wants to recover the monies he advanced for the home, totaling $21,000. What arguments does he have? Will he prevail?

[3] LEGAL STATUS OF UNMARRIED PARTNERS VIS A VIS THIRD PARTIES

Although most states are willing to enforce agreements between nonmarital cohabitants regarding property and sometimes also support, most have been reluctant to extend to unmarried partners rights as against third parties. Thus, with the notable exception of states that have created a formal status alternative to marriage, discussed in Subsection 3 below, the rights of nonmarital cohabitants vis a vis third parties are not well established, and vary substantially with the legal interests involved and across jurisdictions.

NOTES

1. *Torts Claims.* Unmarried partners have encountered substantial obstacles to recovery in tort for claims that require the court to recognize their relationship as analogous to a marriage. While the relatively recent statutory developments in Vermont and California extend all or most of the marital rights to sue in tort to registered partners, it is unusual for such rights to extend beyond marriage in the remaining states. The primary categories of tort claims that are grounded in the marital relationship include negligent infliction of emotional distress, loss of consortium, and wrongful death. Courts are wary of expanding the categories of potential plaintiffs who can bring an action based on any given negligent act. Thus, they have typically restricted the field of potential plaintiffs to persons standing in certain immediate family relationships to the victim. Generally, spouses are within that field, but nonmarital cohabitants are not.

In *Elden v. Sheldon,* 46 Cal. App. 3d 267, 758 P.2d 582 (Cal. 1988), the California Supreme Court denied a man's claim for negligent infliction of emotional distress experienced upon witnessing the accidental death of his alleged "de facto spouse." It expressed concern that courts would be over-burdened if required to determine which relationships are equivalent to a marriage. Hesitant to expand the numbers of persons to whom defendants owe a duty of due care, the court also cited the state's interests in promoting marriage. *Id.* Most state courts concur with *Elden's* approach. *See, e.g., Chiesa v. Rowe,* 486 F. Supp. 236 (W.D. Mich. 1980); *Sawyer v. Bailey,* 413 A.2d 165 (Me. 1980); *Tremblay v. Carter,* 390 So. 2d 816 (Fla. App. 1980); *Sostock v. Reiss,* 415 N.E.2d 1094 (Ill. App. 1980). In contrast, however, the New Jersey Supreme Court declined to follow *Elden* and allowed the decedent's fiancé-cohabitant to bring a claim for negligent infliction of emotional distress. *Dunphy v. Gregor,* 642 A.2d 372 (N.J. 1994). The Court rejected *Elden's* reasoning that a "bright line" definition of the bystander-victim relationship, as provided by a legally valid marriage, was necessary to an actionable claim. Instead, the court asserted that courts could determine whether the relationship between the victim and bystander was sufficiently intimate and "familial" to permit an action to be brought and proposed the following factors as pertinent to the inquiry: "the duration of the relationship, the degree of mutual dependence, the extent of common contributions to a life together, the extent and quality of shared experience, and . . . whether the plaintiff and the injured person were members of the same household, their emotional reliance on each other, the particulars of their day to day relationship, and the manner in which they related to each other in attending to life's mundane requirements." *Id.* at 378–380. The court also concluded that the state's interest in marriage would not be harmed by extension of the eligible category of plaintiffs to include certain unmarried cohabitants. The dissent, however, asserted that once the court opens the door to claims by persons other than spouses, there is no principled way to distinguish among the many persons with close emotional relationships to the victim, and that the standard set forth . . . would require the courts "to delve [intrusively] into the intimate details of claimants' lives." *Id.* at 380–81, 383 (Garibaldi, J., dissenting). In 2003, the New Hampshire Supreme Court adopted *Dunphy's* reasoning, permitting the deceased's nonmarital cohabitant/fiancée to bring a claim for negligent infliction of emotional distress. *Graves v. Easterbrook*, 818 A.2d 1255. It quoted *Dunphy's* conclusion that "courts are capable of dealing with the realities, not simply the legalities, of relationships. . ." *Id.* at 1260.

It is worth noting that the only two state supreme courts permitting non-marital cohabitants to bring bystander actions did so in cases where the cohabitants were engaged to be married at the time of the accident. Is it possible that these courts are relying not only on *functional* indicia of an intimate, familial relationship, but also the *quasi-formal* factor that the parties are engaged? For a survey of cases addressing claims for negligent infliction of emotional distress by persons who stand in nontraditional family relationships to the victim, see Dale Joseph Gilsinger, Annot., *Relationship Between Victim and Plaintiff-Witness as Affecting Right to Recover Under*

State Law for Negligent Infliction of Emotional Distress Due to Witnessing Injury to Another Where Bystander Plaintiff Is Not Member of Victim's Immediate Family, 98 A.L.R.5th 609 (2002).

Only rarely have courts permitted nonmarital cohabitants to bring loss of consortium actions. California's court of appeals decision permitting such actions, *Butcher v. Superior Court*, 139 Cal. App. 3d 58, 188 Cal. Rptr. 503 (App. 1983), was overruled in *Elden*, where the court invoked the same reasoning mentioned above to bar plaintiff from bringing a loss of consortium action. In 2003, the New Mexico Supreme Court became the first and only state supreme court to recognize a loss of consortium claim by an unmarried cohabitant. *Lozoya v. Sanchez*, 66 P.3d 948. In this case, the couple had been together for over 30 years, and had three children together. Citing *Dunphy's* emphasis on the "realities, not simply of legalities of relationships," the *Lozoya* court concluded that courts could make reliable assessments of which plaintiffs should be permitted to sue, and rejected the assertion that to allow recovery would be to recognize common law marriage. *Id.* at 954–56.

Wrongful death actions generally are authorized by statute rather than judge-made law, and plaintiffs are therefore limited to those classes of persons enumerated in the statutory provisions, typically including persons with formal legal relationships with the decedent, such as spouse or child. Courts have generally been reluctant to extend such legislative designations to nonmarital cohabitants. *See, e.g., Raum v. Restaurant Associates, Inc.*, 252 A.D.2d 369, 675 N.Y.S.2d 343 (App. Div. 1998); *Garcia v. Douglas Aircraft Co.*, 133 Cal. App. 3d 890, 184 Cal. Rptr. 390 (1982). In *Raum*, which involved a same-sex couple, the dissent argued that "precedent exists for preferring a functional over a literal interpretation of a statute whose purpose is to promote the public welfare, so that homosexual couples will not be disadvantaged by their inability to give their relationship a legal status." *Id.* at 345. To date, no *published* cases have interpreted the statutory designation of "spouse" to encompass nonmarital partners. Yet, in a departure from precedent, a California trial court determined that Sharon Smith could bring a wrongful death action against Marjorie Knoller and Robert Noel, the owners of a vicious dog who attacked and killed Smith's domestic partner Diane Whipple. *Smith v. Knoller*, Civ. No. 319532 (Cal. Super. Ct. Aug. 9, 2001). The court held that principles of equal protection under the California constitution required it to interpret the term "spouse" in the state's wrongful death statute to include a same-sex partner whose relationship with the deceased is analogous to that of a spouse. In addition, the court specified that the determination of whether the relationship in question was sufficiently similar to a marital relationship to permit the suit to go forward should be factual in nature, examining, *e.g.*, "whether the plaintiff and decedent are registered domestic partners. . . ., whether a common residence exists, the degree of economic cooperation, fidelity, and stability and duration. . . ." *Id.* at 4. For further discussion of tort-related claims by nonmarital cohabitants, see Shannon Minter, *Expanding Wrongful Death Statutes and other Death Benefits to Same-Sex Partners*, 30-Sum. HUM. RIGHTS 6 (2003); Michael Jay Gorback, Note, *Negligent Infliction of Emotional Distress: Has the Legislative Response to Diane Whipple's Death Rendered the Hard-Line Stance of* Elden *and* Thing *Obsolete?*, 54 HASTINGS L. J. 273, 276 (2002); Angie Smolka, Note,

That's the Ticket: A New Way of Defining Family, 10 CORNELL J. L. & PUB. POL'Y 629 (2001); John G. Culhane, *"Clanging Silence": Same-Sex Couples and Tort Law*, 89 KY. L. J. 911 (2000-2001); Laura M. Raisty, Note, *Bystander Distress and Loss of Consortium: An Examination of the Relationship Requirements in Light of* Romer v. Evans, 65 FORDHAM L. REV. 2647 (1997); Anne E. Simerman, *The Right of a Cohabitant to Recover in Tort: Wrongful Death, Negligent Infliction of Emotional Distress and Loss of Consortium*, 32 U. LOUISVILLE J. FAM. L. 531 (1993-1994).

2. *Unemployment compensation*. While unemployment compensation is ordinarily denied to persons who leave their employment voluntarily, California is among those states that compensates individuals if they leave their jobs for "good cause." CAL. UNEMP. INSUR. CODE § 1256 (2003). The governing statute sets forth certain rebuttable presumptions regarding the "good cause" requirement: "An individual may be deemed to have left his or her most recent work with good cause if he or she leaves employment to accompany his or her spouse or domestic partner to a place from which it is impractical to commute to the employment. For purposes of this section 'spouse' includes a person to whom marriage is imminent." *Id.* This language reflects a 2001 amendment which inserted the words "or domestic partner," creating parity between married couples and those who have registered as domestic partners in California. In addition, in 1988, the legislature added the definition of spouse, expanding the terms' reach to include persons for whom "marriage is imminent."

This latter language codified factors set forth in the pertinent regulations, which permitted courts to consider whether actions taken by the employee were related to a "legal or moral obligation" arising from a marriage or a prospective marriage. In *MacGregor v. Unemployment Ins. Appeals Bd.*, 37 Cal. 3d 205, 689 P.2d 453 (1984), the California Supreme Court unanimously sustained the unemployment benefits' claims of Patricia MacGregor, who had became engaged to her nonmarital partner, Dick Bailey, upon becoming pregnant with their child. The couple lived together as a family unit after the baby's birth, with Bailey acknowledging paternity, but they had not yet married. A month after the baby was born, while MacGregor was still on maternity leave, they moved to New York to care for Bailey's sick father, and MacGregor resigned from her job. The court held that she "established that her quitting was motivated by the need to preserve the family she had established with her nonmarital partner and their child, and that this need constituted good cause for her voluntary departure from work." 37 Cal. 3d at 207, 689 P.2d at 454.

This decision contrasted with the court's holding one year earlier in *Norman v. Unemployment Ins. Appeals Bd.*, 34 Cal. 3d 1, 663 P.2d 904 (1983). In *Norman*, the court rejected the claims of a woman who had left her job to accompany her nonmarital partner to Washington, D.C. The court noted that: "Plaintiff's decision to move to Washington came 10 months before her marriage was anticipated. [A]t oral argument more than 2 years later, we were informed that no marriage had as yet occurred. More significantly, nothing in her notification of termination to her employer or in her request for unemployment compensation benefits indicated that her presence in Washington was necessary. . . . [and plaintiff] did not, as a matter of law, establish 'good cause' for her voluntary departure from her employment. . ." 34 Cal. 3d at 9, 663 P.2d at 909. In distinguishing *Norman*, the MacGregor court focused on the "fundamental familial relationship [that] is created when two parents establish a home with their natural child," and California's policy of recognizing that relationship legally, even when parents are unmarried. 37 Cal. 3d at 212–13, 689 P.2d at 458–59. The court also emphasized the illness of Bailey's father, and concluded that the "intimate nature of the family bond among [mother, father, and child] would have been forever altered had MacGregor decided that she, or she and Leanna, should not accompany Bailey to New York." *Id.* Was the California Supreme Court's action one that was grounded in preserving the father-child relationship, as well as MacGregor's relationship with Bailey? Does this limit *MacGregor* to cases involving children, or is the child's existence merely evidence that the parties intend a serious, permanent relationship similar to marriage? If so, what other factors might provide evidence of these factors? *See, e.g., Reep v. Comm'n of Dep't of Employment & Training*, 593 N.E.2d 1297, 1300 (1992) (presumption of good cause when a married person leaves employment to move with spouse does not preclude "a nonmarital partner the right to prove, without benefit of that presumption, that his or her reasons for leaving employment are also 'urgent, compelling and necessitous' ").

3. *Employee Benefits.* Social Security and worker's compensation benefits generally flow to surviving spouses, but not to surviving cohabitants. The Social Security rule was sustained against constitutional challenge in *Califano v. Boles,* 443 U.S. 282 (1979). Some states provide worker's compensation benefits to surviving cohabitants if they can show economic dependency on the deceased employee, *see, e.g., West v. Barton-Malow Co.*, 230 N.W.2d 545 (Mich. 1975) (decedent's unmarried cohabitant of thirteen years eligible as dependent even though not married, given that they lived as, and regarded each other as, husband and wife). Other states exclude cohabitants altogether. *See, e.g., Banegas v. State Indus. Ins. System*, 19 P.3d 245 (Nev. 2001) (legislature did not intend to provide death benefits to dependents such as unmarried cohabitants lacking legally cognizable relationship with deceased worker). Oregon statutes require that those unmarried cohabitants who have lived together for over a year be treated as married for the purpose of the worker's compensation law. OR. REV. ST. § 656.226 (2003). The Oregon Supreme Court held, however, that a fatally injured worker's surviving cohabitant had no claim under Section 656.226 because the couple had separated a month before his death, analogizing such separation for unmarried couples to divorce for married partners. *Cottrell v. EBI Companies,* 743 P.2d 716 (Or. 1987) (en banc).

4. *Housing Discrimination.* Some landlords have refused to rent to unmarried couples, alleging that state nondiscrimination policies infringe upon their first amendment rights of free exercise of religion and free speech. These landlords argue that the policies force them to promote nonmarital cohabitation and fornication in violation of their religious beliefs. Some also claim that a state prohibition against inquiries as to the marital status of prospective tenants contravenes their freedom of speech. *See, e.g., Thomas v. Anchorage Equal Rights Comm'n,* 220 F.3d 1134 (9th Cir. 2000) (en banc). State courts have been mixed in their analyses of these cases. In those states upholding the landlords' claims, the courts have gleaned support from the formal disapproval of nonmarital cohabitation and fornication reflected in the state's criminal statutes. As such, the validity of those holdings may be in question if, as some predict, the United States Supreme Court's 2003 decision in *Lawrence* leads to the demise or repeal of state anti-cohabitation and anti-fornication statutes.

The North Dakota Supreme Court recently ruled on the question of whether a landlord refusing to rent to an unmarried couple violates that state's Human Rights Act. *North Dakota Fair Housing Council, Inc. v. Peterson*, 625 N.W.2d 551 (N.D. 2001). The Act prohibits discrimination on the basis of marital status, race, religion, age, and other factors. The landlord argued that the couple was seeking to cohabit unlawfully, in violation of North Dakota's criminal statutes. The court analyzed what it framed as a possible conflict between the two statutes, and held that the landlord did not violate the Human Rights Act. It grounded its result on a narrow interpretation of the meaning of marital status discrimination, concluding that the landlord's refusal was based on the couple's criminal *conduct* rather than their status as unmarried persons. The Minnesota Supreme Court arrived at a similar result in *Cooper v. French*, 460 N.W.2d 2 (1990), upholding a landlord's refusal to rent to an unmarried woman after learning who intended to live in the property with her fiancé. The landlord claimed that the state's nondiscrimination statute did not reach him because his religious convictions precluded him from renting to a couple who intended to violate the state's fornication statute. *See also Mister v. A.R.K. Partnership,* 553 N.E.2d 1152, 1157 (Ill. App. 1990); *Prince George's County v. Greenbelt Homes,* 431 A.2d 745 (Md. Spec. App. 1981) (cooperative association bylaws excluding unmarried couples do not violate local law prohibiting marital status discrimination).

Alaska, Massachusetts, and California courts have held that state nondiscrimination policies do protect nonmarital couples. The Alaska Supreme Court rejected a landlord's claim that the state's housing discrimination statute violated his religious freedom. *Swanner v. Anchorage Equal Rights Comm'n,* 874 P.2d 274 (Alaska 1994). First, the Alaska Supreme Court determined that a landlord's refusal to rent to an unmarried couple *is* discrimination based on marital *status*. Next, it determined that the legal restriction against landlords' refusals to rent to unmarried couples does not violate the state constitution's free exercise clause. The court indicated that its precedents limit constitutionally-protected "free exercise rights . . . to actions rooted in religious rituals, ceremonies, or practices." *Id.* at 280-82. Because renting a property does not fall within those categories, the nondiscrimination statute did not infringe the landlord's rights. *See also Smith v. Fair Employment and Housing Comm'n,* 913 P.2d 909 (1996); *Attorney General v. Desilets,* 636 N.E.2d 233 (Mass. 1994) (summary judgment for landlord reversed because state may have compelling interest sufficient to override landlord's religious objections to renting to unmarried couple).

In several New York cases, the courts have determined whether unmarried cohabitants fall within various definitions of "family" set forth in certain housing policies. Most recently, the state's highest court rejected the claims of lesbian medical students who sued Yeshiva University. *Levin v. Yeshiva*

University, 96 N.Y.2d 484, 754 N.E.2d 1099 (2001). The women challenged the university's policy of giving priority to married couples in school-owned housing, arguing that this preference constituted discrimination on the basis of marital status that had a disparate impact on gay and lesbian students in violation of the City Human Rights Act. The court held that the provision limiting housing "to only those in a legal, family relationship with the tenant" did not amount to marital discrimination. The court conceded that the plaintiffs might have a cause of action for disparate impact discrimination if they could demonstrate in further proceedings that the statute "disproportionately burdens lesbians and gay men." 96 N.Y.2d at 490, 496, 754 N.E.2d at 1102, 1106. Chief Judge Kaye's separate opinion cited the court's prior opinion in *Braschi v. Stahl Associates,* 74 N.Y.2d 201, 543 N.E.2d 49, 544 N.Y.S.2d 784 (1989), calling for recognition of tenants' same-sex partners as "members of their immediate family." *Id.* at 96 N.Y.S.2d at 501, 754 N.E.2d at 1110 (Kaye, J., concurring and dissenting). In *Braschi,* the court held that New York City's rent control laws, which protect members of a leaseholder's *de jure* family from eviction after his death, protected the homosexual partner of a recently deceased AIDS victim against eviction from the apartment in which they had lived together. (*Braschi* is reprinted in Chapter 1, *supra.*)

For further discussion on the relationship between nonmarital cohabitation, state antidiscrimination laws, and landlords' "rights," see, *e.g.,* Erin P.B. Zasada, *Civil Rights — Rights Protected and Discrimination Prohibited: Living in Sin in North Dakota? Not Under my Lease,* 78 N.D.L. REV. 539 (2002); Scott A. Johnson, Note, *The Conflict Between Religious Exercise and Efforts to Eradicate Housing Discrimination Against Nontraditional Couples: Should Free Exercise Protect Landlord Bias?* 53 WASH & LEE L. REV. 351 (1996); Kelly D. Eckel, Comment, *Legitimate Limitation Of A Landlord's Rights — A New Dawn For Unmarried Cohabitants,* 68 TEMP. L. REV. 811 (1995).

5. *Employment Discrimination*. In a few cases, litigants have successfully used state anti-discrimination laws to challenge employer refusals to hire them or continue their employment because of a nonmarital relationship. *See, e.g., McClure v. Sports and Health Club,* 370 N.W.2d 884 (Minn. 1985). Government employees disciplined or dismissed for engaging in unmarried cohabitation have occasionally sought relief in the courts, with mixed results. In a case that resulted in *six* different opinions from a panel of federal judges, Robin Shahar lost her claim against the state of Georgia after a job offer from the Georgia Attorney General's office was withdrawn. *Shahar v. Bowers,* 114 F.3d 1097 (11th Cir. 1997). Ms. Shahar claimed that the state had violated her rights of intimate and expressive association, freedom of religion, equal protection, and substantive due process by retracting its job offer upon learning of her lesbian commitment ceremony. All of her claims were rejected. For a survey of relevant cases, see Annot., *Refusal to Hire, or Dismissal from Employment, on Account of Plaintiff's Sexual Lifestyle or Sexual Preference as Violation of Federal Constitution or Federal Civil Rights Statutes,* 42 A.L.R. FED. 189 (1990).

Employees have had more success challenging disciplinary actions based on unmarried procreation because of the well-established constitutional interest in procreative decisions. *See, e.g., Lewis v. Delaware State College,*

455 F. Supp. 239 (D. Del. 1978) (employer college enjoined to reinstate unmarried mother to her position as Director of Residence Halls for Women because employee had a constitutionally protected right to bear a nonmarital child). *See also* Annot., *Discrimination Against Unwed Mothers or Unwed Pregnant Women as Prescribed Under Pregnancy Discrimination Act,* 91 A.L.R. FED. 178 (1990). Some employers have rules restricting the employment of spouses within the same employment setting. In *Espinoza v. Thoma,* 580 F.2d 346 (8th Cir. 1978), such a no-spouse rule was applied by analogy to deny employment to a woman cohabiting with another employee. The court sustained this application, finding that it followed logically from the purpose of the no-spouse rule.

6. *Probate.* In general, statutory rules which set forth intestate succession rights do not recognize cohabitants. *See* Mary Louise Fellows, Monica Kirkpatrick Johnson et al., *Committed Partners and Inheritance: An Empirical Study,* 16 LAW AND INEQ. 1, 15 (1998). An implied contract claim against an estate by a decedent's cohabitant may be allowed, *Byrne v. Laura,* 60 Cal. Rptr. 2d 908 (App. 1997); *In Matter of Estate of Steffen,* 290 N.W.2d 697 (Wis. 1980), as may a claim in *quantum meruit, Green v. Richmond,* 337 N.E.2d 691 (Mass. 1975) (services performed in reliance upon unenforceable oral agreement). Constitutional challenges to a state's inheritance and elective share statutes on the basis that they violate the equal protection clause have failed. *See In re Estate of Cooper,* 592 N.Y.S.2d 797, 187 A.D.2d 128 (N.Y. App. Div. 1993) (holding that "spousal-like" relationships do not give rise to spousal rights). Inheritance taxes typically treat surviving spouses more favorably than strangers, and a cohabitant taking under a will is a stranger under the tax law. *See, e.g., Cory v. Edgett,* 111 Cal. App. 3d 230, 168 Cal. Rptr. 686 (App. 1980) (rejecting claim by decedent's former wife that she should be treated as a surviving spouse for inheritance tax purposes where the couple had divorced after 33 years of marriage, subsequently resumed cohabitation, and the decedent left all of his assets to her). For a proposal urging reform of Uniform Probate Code to recognize unmarried cohabitants, see Marissa J. Holob, Note, *Respecting Commitment: A Proposal To Prevent Legal Barriers From Obstructing the Effectuation of Intestate Goals,* 85 CORNELL L. REV. 1492 (2000).

7. *Spousal Violence.* Do statutory provisions criminalizing spousal violence apply as well to unmarried cohabitants? In recent years, as awareness of the prevalence and dynamics of domestic violence has grown, nonmarital cohabitants have, increasingly, been recognized as falling within the purview of spousal abuse statutes. This is particularly important in light of empirical research revealing that unmarried women may be at greater risk for assaults by intimate partners than are married women. *See* Patricia Tjaden & Nancy Thoennes, EXTENT, NATURE, AND CONSEQUENCES OF INTIMATE PARTNER VIOLENCE, FINDINGS FROM THE NATIONAL VIOLENCE AGAINST WOMEN SURVEY iii (July 2000). Presently, most state statutes specifically refer to "partners" or "cohabitants" as well as spouses when delineating those categories of relationships that fall within the statutes' reach. *See, e.g.,* CAL. PENAL CODE § 273.5 (2003) (listing cohabitants and former cohabitants as two of the several categories of relationships falling within the statute's jurisdiction). Congress provided significant leadership in this regard, defining family violence to include acts "committed by a person against another individual . . . to whom such person is or was related by blood or marriage or otherwise legally related or with whom such person is or was lawfully residing." 42 U.S.C.A. § 10421 (2003). *See also* 18 U.S.C.A. § 921 (2003) (defining "intimate partner" to include "an individual who cohabits or has cohabited with the person" for purpose of special firearms provisions of federal criminal code). It is unclear whether same-sex cohabitants and intimate partners are included within this protection although the trend has been toward such inclusion. For further discussion of the reach of domestic violence statutes to same-sex relationships, see Marnie J. Franklin, *The Closet Becomes Darker for the Abused: A Perspective on Lesbian Partner Abuse*, 9 CARDOZO WOMEN'S L.J. 299 (2003); Krisana M. Hodges, *Trouble in Paradise: Barriers to Addressing Domestic Violence in Lesbian Relationships*, 9 L. & SEXUALITY 311 (1999-2000).

8. *Testimonial Privileges.* The testimonial privileges for marital communications and adverse testimony are generally statutory, and as such have not generally been judicially extended to a cohabitant. *See, e.g., People v. Delph*, 94 Cal. App. 3d 411, 156 Cal.Rptr. 422 (App. 1979) (the common law and statutory marital communication privileges do not extend to cohabitants in marriage-like relationships without formality of a ceremony); Annot., *Communication Between Unmarried Couple Living Together as Privileged*, 4 A.L.R.4th 422 (1981). For a proposal to extend the testimonial privileges to same-sex couples, see Jennifer R. Brannen, *Unmarried with Privileges: Extending the Evidentiary Privileges to Same-Sex Couples*, 17 REV. LIT. 311 (1998).

9. *Guardianship and Health Care.* In most jurisdictions, adults can execute an "advanced directive" or a "health care power of attorney" in order to nominate specific others to serve as proxy decisionmakers if they become incompetent to make their own health care decisions. *See* NANCY M.P. KING, MAKING SENSE OF ADVANCED DIRECTIVES (Rev. ed. 1996). As such, an individual can nominate any adult of her choosing, whether or not that person stands in a formal legal family relationship. Yet, most adults do not execute such documents, and in their absence, health care professionals must rely on the individuals identified by statute as default decisionmakers. Few states recognize nonmarital partners as "default" decision-makers. *But see* Health Care Surrogate Act, 755 ILL. COMP. STAT. 40/25(a) (1998) (recognizing "close friend" as default decision-maker). *Id.*

The best-known case addressing a dispute between a patient's family and her nonmarital cohabitant is *Guardianship of Kowalski*, 478 N.W.2d 790 (Minn. App. 1991). Sharon Kowalski's same-sex partner, Karen Thompson, petitioned the court to become Sharon's guardian after Sharon suffered severe brain damage in an accident. Opposed by Sharon's family, Karen litigated for eight years until a Minnesota appellate court ultimately granted her petition. For a discussion of this case, see Angie Smolka, Note, *That's the Ticket: A New Way of Defining Family*, 10 CORNELL J. L. & PUB. POL'Y 629, 636–37 (2001). For surveys of state laws and proposals for including nonmarital partners as decisionmakers, see Amy L. Brown, Note, *Broadening Anachronistic Notions of "Family" in Proxy Decisionmaking for Unmarried Adults*, 41 HASTINGS L.

J. 1029 (1990); Jonathan Andrew Hein, *Caring for the Evolving Family: Cohabiting Partners and Employee Sponsored Health Care*, 30 N.M. L. REV. 19 (2000). Finally, for a discussion of the issues relating to post-mortem decisions by proxy decisionmakers, see Jennifer E. Horan, Note, *"When Sleep at Last Has Come": Controlling the Disposition of Dead Bodies for Same-Sex Couples*, 2 J. GEN. RACE JUST. 423, 449–451 (1999).

10. *The Aftermath of 9/11*. As reviewed in the preceding notes, nonmarital partners generally are not treated in a manner equivalent to spouses with respect to a range of legal rights and benefits. The emotional and financial losses experienced by nonmarital cohabitants upon the death of their partners do not typically come to public attention. Sharon Smith's wrongful death suit following the death of her domestic partner Diane Whipple, discussed in note 1 *supra*, is exceptional in its notoriety and the degree to which it evoked public sympathy. In a similar manner, the losses experienced by nonmarital partners of victims of the September 11, 2001 terrorist attacks also captured the public's attention. Private relief agencies and the state and federal government faced the challenge of deciding whether spouse-*like* relationships would qualify survivors for benefits from the various victim compensation funds. The policies ultimately put in place reflect increasing recognition of the importance of nontraditional family relationships. For example, after some initial uncertainty, the American Red Cross determined that gay and lesbian partners of September 11th victims were eligible to receive survivor benefits. Cynthia Billhartz, *What is the Legal Status of Gay Unions?* ST. LOUIS POST-DISPATCH, June 16, 2003. The New York State World Trade Center Relief Fund, which provides financial relief to surviving spouses, children, and parents, extended eligibility for this benefit to domestic partners satisfying certain criteria. In applying for the surviving spouse benefits, the domestic partner must complete a "Domestic Partner Affidavit" declaring, in part: "We were each other's sole domestic partner, had been so for at least six months prior to the date of his/her death, and intended to remain so indefinitely. We were in a relationship of mutual support, caring, and commitment, and had assumed responsibility for each other's welfare." New York State World Trade Center Relief Fund, Surviving Spouse Application at 3 (available at: www.nysegov.com/news/wtcrf1_802.pdf). Applicants are further required to submit proof of cohabitation and financial interdependence. The requirements do not distinguish between opposite-sex and same-sex nonmarital relationships. Pennsylvania's fund also permits recovery by nonmarital partners. *See* Susan J. Becker, *Tumbling Towers as Turning Points: Will 9/11 Usher in a New Civil Rights Era for Gay Men and Lesbians in the United States?*, 9 WM. & MARY J. WOMEN & L. 207, 231–32 (2003). In contrast, the state of Virginia has denied compensation to surviving nonmarital partners of September 11th victims. *Id.* at 232.

Congress established the Federal September 11th Victim Compensation Fund of 2001 with its passage of the Air Transportation Safety and System Stabilization Act of 2001, Pub. L. No. 107-42, 115 Stat. 230 (2001) (codified at 49 U.S.C. §§ 40101, 44302-44306). *See generally* Erin G. Holt, Note, *The September 11th Victim Compensation Fund: Legislative Justice Sui Generis,* 59 N.Y.U. ANN. SURVEY AM. L. 513 (2004). While specifying some eligibility criteria, the legislation authorized the Justice Department to promulgate regulations and the Attorney General to designate a Special Master. The final regulations left unclear whether nonmarital partners of deceased victims would be eligible for compensation, prompting protests from a range of organizations, members of Congress, and state officials. *See, e.g.,* Lambda Legal, *Comments on the Interim Final Rule Implementing the September 11 Victims Compensation Fund,* Jan. 24, 2002 (available at: lambdalegal.org/cgi-bin/iowa/documents/record?record=980); *Gov, AG Object to 9/11 Compensation Fund Rules,* Press Release, Office of New York State Attorney General Eliot Spitzer, Jan. 23, 2002 (available at: www.oag.state.ny.us/press/2002/jan/jan23c_02.html). In the final analysis, however, the Fund's benefits have not been categorically denied to nonmarital partners. Rather, it appears that some nonmarital partners may succeed in their claims for benefits, particularly where the deceased's formal family (*e.g.,* parents or siblings) supports the partner's claim and where there is documentary evidence of the deceased's intent to make the partner a beneficiary in the event of her death (*e.g.,* on a life insurance policy) Becker, *supra* at 235.

In passing the Mychal Judge Police and Fire Chaplains Public Safety Officers' Benefit Act of 2002, Congress amended the Omnibus Crime Control and Safe Streets Act of 1968 to allow an "individual designated by [a public safety] officer as beneficiary under such officer's most recently executed life insurance policy" to receive the $250,000 federal death benefit available to survivors of fallen public safety officers in cases where there is no surviving spouse or child. PL 107-06, 116 Stat. 719 (2002) (codified at 42 U.S. C. § 3796(a) (2004)). This legislation implicitly recognizes nonmarital partners as potential recipients of these federal death benefits. *See, e.g., Developments — The Law of Marriage and Family,* 116 HARV. L. REV. 1997, 1999 (2003). For further discussion of the implications of the September 11th disaster for family law, see Nancy J. Knauer, *The September 11 Attack and Surviving Same-Sex Partners: Defining Family Through Tragedy,* 75 TEMP. L. REV. 31 (2002).

PROBLEMS

Problem 9-10. An employee group suggests that the employer extend benefits such as dependent health insurance to an employee's informal family. The employer asks for your advice on whether or how to make such changes. What do you advise?

Problem 9-11. The same-sex partner of a woman who was killed in a ferry accident seeks to be treated as a spouse in order to avail herself of tort remedies and to inherit from her deceased partner under the laws of intestate succession. What is her likelihood of success in various jurisdictions discussed *supra*?

[4] FORMAL STATUS ALTERNATIVES TO MARRIAGE IN THE INTERNATIONAL COMMUNITY AND IN THE UNITED STATES

In the past few decades, many nations, scores of local jurisdictions within the United States, and a handful of U.S. states have extended formal legal recognition to family-like relationships between same-sex partners. The nature and type of recognition has varied substantially. Some status alternatives grant partners the right to designate the other as qualifying family members for access to employee benefits, but no more. Under other schemes, same-sex partners are treated as "close family members" for the purposes of hospital visitation, of providing proxy consent for their partners' treatment, of making post-mortem decisions such as donation of their partners' organs, and/or other rights. Still other systems allow partners access to some or all of a range of governmental entitlements and rights typically reserved for married couples. Vermont's civil unions differ from marriage in name only, extending to registering partners all of the same rights, benefits, and obligations that accompany marriage. There are many variations and permutations of these status alternatives, which reflect the political and legal efforts that led to their creation and the values and culture of the regions in which they exist. While an exhaustive treatment of the nature, diversity, and prevalence of the various forms of nonmarital partnerships is beyond the scope of this book, it is clear that the trend toward extending legal recognition to nonmarital partnerships is proceeding with substantial momentum.

[a] Formal Registration Schemes Outside of the United States

"In many . . . West-European jurisdictions, introduction of a legal status for heterosexual cohabitation has operated to facilitate recognition of same-sex partnerships." David Bradley, *Regulation of Unmarried Cohabitation in West-European Jurisdictions — Determinants of Legal Policy*, 15 INT'L J. L., POL'Y & FAM. 22, 42 (2001). This pattern contrasts dramatically with that observed in the United States (discussed *infra*). In the U.S., the extension of legal protections to nonmarital partners has been fueled almost exclusively by the movement to extend to same-sex partners some of the rights, benefits, and obligations that have been unavailable to them because they are not permitted to marry. These efforts have resulted in the creation of various alternatives to marriage for same-sex couples, which may also be available to opposite-sex couples in very limited circumstances. This section will focus primarily on the process by which legal recognition of *same-sex* partnerships has occurred in the world community.

Commentators observe that an "incremental" approach has yielded continuing expansion of rights for same-sex couples in most of those nations in which expansion has occurred. *See, e.g.,* Kees Waaldijk, *Toward the Recognition of Same-Sex Partners in European Union Law: Expectations Based on Trends in National Law*, in LEGAL RECOGNITION OF SAME-SEX PARTNERSHIPS: A STUDY OF NATIONAL, EUROPEAN AND INTERNATIONAL LAW 635 & 649–50 (Appendix) (R. Wintemute & M. Andenaes eds. 2001); WILLIAM N. ESKRIDGE, JR., EQUALITY PRACTICE: CIVIL UNIONS AND THE FUTURE OF GAY RIGHTS 115–21 & Table 3.2 (2002). Examining policy reform in over two dozen countries, Waaldijk and Eskridge observe that legal recognition of the rights of same-sex couples has generally followed a step-wise and sequential pattern, and that each individual policy shift is relatively small. The progression typically begins with repeal of criminal sodomy statutes, followed by equalization of the ages of consent for same-sex, as contrasted with opposite-sex, sexual offenses. Prohibition of discrimination on the basis of sexual orientation and extension of certain legal benefits for same-sex cohabitants typically occur several years thereafter. The nations that have advanced to the next stage have created formal domestic partner registration systems. In Europe, one of the *last* developments is extension of legal rights to adopt children. Finally, according to Waaldijk and Eskridge, the progression culminates in the availability of marriage to same-sex couples. While Waaldijk focused on fifteen Western European nations, Eskridge has expanded the analysis to include Canada, Israel, Australia, South Africa, Hungary, and Russia, and also individual states or provinces within some nations. As the following summary suggests, the culmination of the progression may not always be marriage.

DEVELOPMENTS IN THE LAW: THE LAW OF MARRIAGE AND FAMILY, 116 Harv. L. Rev. 1997, 2207-12 (2003)

Progress toward the legalization of same-sex marriage has occurred most rapidly in Northern and Western Europe, where there is a relatively long history of extending civil rights to gays and lesbians. The Netherlands legalized same-sex marriage in 2001, when the country "opened up" the official definition of marriage to include "two persons of different sex or of the same sex.";B26;B26This change established complete parity between same-sex and opposite-sex couples, extending to same-sex couples identical rights to sanctify their relationships publicly, to label those relationships "marriages," and thereby to assume all the benefits and burdens associated with marriage, including the right to adopt children. The Belgian Parliament approved similar legislation permitting same-sex marriages in early 2003, though without accompanying rights of adoption. "Registered partnerships" — involving most, but not all, of the same rights and responsibilities as those associated with opposite-sex marriage — were legalized for same-sex couples in Denmark in 1989, in Norway in 1993, in Sweden in 1995, in Iceland in 1996, and in Finland in 2002. Less expansive forms of same-sex unions were legalized in Hungary in 1998, in France in 1999, in Germany in 2000, and in Portugal in 2001. . . .

. . . . The experience of some Western European nations demonstrates that the acceptance of same-sex marriage can occur relatively quickly. . . . [¶]. . . . Nevertheless, rapid change is far from the rule in Europe. To the contrary, the European experience provides considerable evidence that progress may stall, perpetuating the second-class status of same-sex couples. It is noteworthy that outside the Netherlands and Belgium, European recognition of same-sex unions has thus far ended with registered partnerships — and only in the Netherlands does same-sex marriage include full rights of adoption.

One explanation for this failure to carry reform to completion may be that, having obtained many of the rights associated with marriage, same-sex couples are not as motivated to advocate for marriage rights as they were when the rights gap was greater. Within the gay rights movement, some factions argue that gay men and lesbians should not seek formal marriage rights at all, because claiming such rights legitimizes state paternalism and the "hegemonic" history of marriage. Among opposite-sex couples, too, there is considerable evidence that the attractiveness of formalized marriage has waned as more limited forms of recognition, ranging from legalized cohabitation to registered partnerships, have become available.

A second explanation may be the pragmatic fear that too rapid a march toward marriage equality will engender a popular backlash — as occurred in Alaska and Hawaii. Professor William Eskridge, for example, has advocated "equality practice," arguing that "[a] process that forces minority rights onto an unwilling populace will often not 'stick' in a democracy," and concluding that "immediate full equality is not always possible, not practical, not even desirable."

Still a third explanation may be that popular acceptance of economic rights for same-sex couples does not necessarily imply a willingness to infringe on more established religious and cultural traditions of marriage and family. This notion finds some support in the adoption rights inequity that persists across Europe. Only the Netherlands, Denmark, and Iceland allow same-sex registered partners to adopt each other's children — and only in the Netherlands can such partners adopt unrelated children. In Norway, Sweden, France, and Germany, adoptions by same-sex couples are prohibited outright. . . . [R]eligious and cultural traditions [may] cause Europeans to distinguish between offering limited official recognition to same-sex couples and allowing such couples to marry and form families of their own. This explanation, in turn, suggests that incrementalism has its limits, such that the process of "small change" will not automatically culminate in full marriage equality, as it has in the Netherlands.

———

As the excerpt above reveals, there is variability in the specific benefits, rights, and obligations that accompany the legal partnerships available to same-sex couples in different nations. Furthermore, the list of jurisdictions cited by the *Harvard Law Review* is not exhaustive. In some instances, municipalities, states, or provinces extend certain protections to same-sex couples. For example, Catalonia, a state-like jurisdiction within Spain, has a partnership statute which creates "a legal status between partners, together with a bundle of personal and financial rights and duties." Miguel Martin Casals, *Same-Sex Partnership in the Legislation of the Spanish Autonomous Communities,* in LEGAL RECOGNITION OF SAME-SEX COUPLES IN EUROPE 54, 61 (K. Boele-Woelki & A. Fuchs eds. 2003). Other jurisdictions within Spain have followed Catalonia's lead. Most Canadian provinces have extended some form of recognition of same-sex couples, most typically in a manner similar to their recognition of opposite-sex nonmarital cohabitants, as has New Zealand and jurisdictions within Australia. In response to a 1999 Canadian Supreme Court decision, *M. v. H.,* 62 C.R.R. (2d) (Supreme Court of Canada), the Canadian legislature passed the Modernization of Benefits and Obligations Act, which amended sixty-eight "federal laws so that same-sex partners would enjoy the same rights and benefits as common law heterosexual couples. Included were the right to file joint tax returns, immigration rights, and other governmental benefits." YUVAL MERIN, EQUALITY FOR SAME-SEX COUPLES:

THE LEGAL RECOGNITION OF GAY PARTNERSHIPS IN EUROPE AND THE UNITED STATES, 160, 161 (2002). This pattern of provincial and federal recognition of same-sex cohabiting relationships has been overshadowed somewhat by more recent developments in Canada. In 2003, two Canadian provinces, British Columbia and Ontario, opened the status of marriage to same-sex couples, following appellate decisions holding restrictions against same-sex marriage unconstitutional. A lower court decision in Quebec reaching the same result has been appealed. The city of Buenos Aires passed an ordinance, effective July 2003, permitting same-sex couples to register for a status conferring some of the same rights available to married couples in Argentina, Jon Jeter, *Using New Law, Buenos Aires Men Celebrate Civil Union,* WASHINGTON POST, July 19, 2003, at P. A22, while several major cities in Brazil extended benefits to the same-sex partners of their employees. In response to a range of lawsuits and legislative initiatives, South Africa has made headway in securing some rights for same-sex couples, but a comprehensive civil union statute, while under consideration, has not been enacted as yet. Wendy Isaack, *Equal in the World of Law: The Rights of Lesbian and Gay People in South Africa,* 30 HUM. RIGHTS 19 (2003). Within the United Kingdom, the government is considering a proposal for a "civil partnership registration" system available to same-sex couples, extending many of the benefits, rights, and obligations of marriage. *See* Women & Equality Unit, Government of United Kingdom, CIVIL PARTNERSHIP: A FRAMEWORK FOR THE LEGAL RECOGNITION OF SAME-SEX COUPLES, June 2003 (available through links at: www.womenandequalityunit.gov.uk/lgbt/partnership.htm). For further discussion of legal recognition for same-sex partnerships from an international and comparative perspective, see LEGAL RECOGNITION OF SAME-SEX COUPLES IN EUROPE (K. Boele-Woelki & A. Fuchs eds. 2003); YUVAL MERIN, *supra*; LEGAL RECOGNITION OF SAME-SEX PARTNERSHIPS: A STUDY OF NATIONAL, EUROPEAN AND INTERNATIONAL LAW (R. Wintemute & M. Andenaes eds. 2001).

[b] Formal Registration Schemes Within the United States: Domestic Partnerships, Civil Unions, and Reciprocal Beneficiary Relationships

In the United States, formal status alternatives to marriage began to emerge in the late 1980s. These alternatives, referred to in various jurisdictions as domestic partnerships, civil unions, and reciprocal beneficiary relationships, developed in response to efforts by gay and lesbian couples to obtain legal recognition for their committed intimate relationships. The creation and evolution of these partnerships followed one of two distinct (but often intersecting) paths. Grace Ganz Blumberg, *The Regularization of Nonmarital Cohabitation: Rights and Responsibilities in the American Welfare State,* 76 NOTRE DAME L. REV. 1265 (2001). In some jurisdictions, recognition of same-sex partnerships followed the gradual, incremental approach described above as characterizing the advancement of rights for gay and lesbian couples in Europe. In others, however, the creation of a new status resulted from legislative compromise in the wake of state supreme court judgments holding unconstitutional the state's exclusion of same-sex couples from marriage or its legal incidents. In Hawaii and Vermont, for example, lawmakers scrambled to respond to judicial pronouncements that exclusion of same-sex couples from marriage or its benefits violated their state constitutions. (*See* Chapter 2, page 118 *infra*, for further discussion of the legal challenges to those states' marriage restrictions and of the legal developments that followed.) Hawaii ultimately amended its state constitution so as to nullify its supreme court's decision. At the same time, however, the legislature created the status of "reciprocal beneficiaries," providing registering couples with some of the rights and benefits enjoyed by marital partners. The Vermont legislature created "civil unions," a status intended to be the legal equivalent of marriage, when it was ordered by its supreme court to extend the benefits, rights, and obligations of marriage to same-sex couples. Both of these innovations will be discussed in more detail below.

While litigators challenged same-sex marriage restrictions in Hawaii, Alaska, Vermont, and Massachusetts, advocates adopting a step-by-step or "incremental" approach petitioned local governments to enact domestic partner ordinances. Eskridge, *supra* at 13; William N. Eskridge, Jr., *Comparative Law and the Same-Sex Marriage Debate: A Step-by-Step Approach Toward State Recognition*, 31 McGeorge L. Rev. 641 (2000). Although there is substantial variability in domestic partnership laws across jurisdictions, most such laws offer registration, and extension of employment benefits such as health insurance to same-sex partners of the city's or county's employees. Most early domestic partner ordinances provided few tangible benefits for registrants beyond the opportunity to designate one's partner as a beneficiary on health insurance and related benefit plans. For many, entering a domestic partnership had symbolic and psychological benefit. It permitted same-sex couples a mechanism to announce, formally and publicly, the partners' mutual commitment to the relationship. Furthermore, by creating the status, the sponsoring government implicitly conferred some measure of legitimacy on same-sex relationships. Such recognition was in marked contrast to its more traditional disapproval of gays and lesbians and the intimate relationships they formed.

The path to securing employee benefits for same-sex partners was not without roadblocks. In a series of lawsuits, most of which were brought by taxpayers, state courts across the country adjudicated the authority of various local governments to offer benefits to its employees' same-sex partners. While some ordinances were struck down, most survived review relatively intact. *Compare Heinsma v. City of Vancouver*, 29 P.3d 709 (Wa. 2001) (*en banc*) (city's definition of "dependents" for its employees' benefit plans as including domestic partners did not violate its authority under the state constitution); *City of Atlanta v. Morgan*, 492 S.E.2d 193 (Ga. 1997) (same); *Tyma v. Montgomery County*, 801 A.2d 148 (Md. App. 2002) (county ordinance did not infringe upon state's authority to regulate marriage and was within authority delegated to county); *Lowe v. Broward County*, 766 So. 2d 1199 (Fla. App. 2000) (same, but severable provisions authorizing domestic partners to make health care decisions for one another were unconstitutional); *Slattery v. City of New York*, 697 N.Y.S.2d 603 (App. Div. 1999) (domestic partner ordinance did not impermissibly legislate in area of marriage); *Crawford v. City of Chicago*, 710 N.E.2d 91 (Ill. App. 1999) (same); *Schaefer v. City and County of Denver*, 973 P.2d 717 (Colo. App. 1998) (city and county extension of health care benefits to "spousal equivalents" was not preempted by state statute) *with Devlin v. City of Philadelphia*, 809 A.2d 980 (Pa. App. 2002) (city impermissibly legislated in state-preempted field of domestic relations), *appeal granted* 833 A.2d 1115 (Pa. 2003); *Arlington County v. White*, 528 S.E.2d 706 (Va. 2000) (county exceeded its authority in interpreting the term "dependents" in its health insurance plan to include domestic partners); *Connors v. City of Boston*, 714 N.E.2d 335 (Mass. 1999) (same with respect to mayor's executive order); *Lilly v. City of Minneapolis*, 527 N.W.3d 107 (Minn. App. 1995) (same with respect to city council resolutions).

In a bold move, San Francisco distinguished itself from the other cities and counties with domestic partnership laws by adopting the Equal Benefits Ordinance, effective 1997. This enactment prohibits the city from contracting with any businesses that do not provide parity in benefits to their employees with domestic partners rather than spouses. *See* SAN FRANCISCO ADMIN. CODE §§ 12B.1(b), 12B.2(b) (2004). In that all companies doing business at San Francisco's International Airport fell within the reach of the nondiscrimination provision, it is not surprising that San Francisco was promptly sued by the trade association representing the airlines and by other affected employers. Although some components of the San Francisco scheme were struck down, most survived. *See Air Transport Ass'n of America v. San Francisco*, 992 F. Supp. 1149 (N.D. Cal. 1998); *aff'd* 266 F.3d 1064 (9th Cir. 2001); *see also S.D. Myers v. San Francisco*, 336 F.3d 1174 (2003). For further discussion of the San Francisco ordinance, see Emily V. Griffen, Comment, *"Relations Stop Nowhere": ERISA Preemption of San Francisco's Domestic Partner Ordinance*, 89 CAL. L. REV. 459 (2001) (discussing preemption of certain provisions by federal legislation governing employee benefits); Kathleen M. Meagher, *San Francisco's Equal Benefits Ordinance Litigation: Federal Preemption and Market Participation*, 188 PLI/CRIM 169 (2001) (analyzing district court's holding on the ordinance's violation of dormant Commerce Clause). Subsequent to San Francisco's enactment of its Equal Benefits Ordinance, a handful of other jurisdictions adopted similar provisions. *See* Yuval Merin, EQUALITY FOR SAME-SEX COUPLES 202 (2002) (listing as examples Berkeley, Los Angeles, and Seattle, among others). For further discussion of the legal challenges to domestic partner ordinances, see Mark A. Tumeo, *Civil Rights for Gays and Lesbians and Domestic Partner Benefits: How Far Could an Ohio Municipality Go?* 50 CLEV. ST. L. REV. 165 (2002-03); Heidi Eischen, *For Better or Worse: An Analysis of Recent Challenges to Domestic Partner Benefits Legislation*, 31 U. TOL. L. REV. 527 (2000).

The number of jurisdictions enacting domestic partner laws has expanded so rapidly within the last decade that observers seem to have stopped counting additions. In what it refers to as a "partial summary of domestic partner listings" one advocacy organization cites at least 75 cities and counties, and 11 states, as having adopted some form of domestic partner law. *See, e.g.*, Lambda Legal, *Partial Summary of Domestic Partner Listings* (Updated 8/01/01) (available at: www.lambdalegal.org/cgi-bin/iowa/documents/record?record=21).

In a parallel trend, hundreds of private employers have voluntarily extended benefits to domestic partners of their employees. One list is labeled "a sampling of the over 2,000 private companies that offer some form of domestic partner benefits." *See* Lambda Legal, *Partial Summary of Domestic Partner Listings* (Updated 8/01/01) (available at: www.lambdalegal.org/cgi-bin/iowa/documents/record?record=21). One author cites a document dated 2000 for the assertion that "3,572 private companies, colleges, universities, and governments offer domestic partnership benefits to their employees." William C. Duncan, *Domestic Partnership Laws in the United States: A Review and Critique,* 2001 B.Y.U. L. Rev. 961. Reportedly, in 1999, approximately 10% of all U.S. employers, and 25% of employers with more than 5,000 employees, offered such benefits. Merin, *supra* at 200. In most instances, no formal partnership registration with a government entity is required by private employers. Employees are permitted to designate a cohabiting nonmarital partner as a beneficiary in the absence of a spousal beneficiary. Most of these employers extend this option to opposite-sex nonmarital partners as well. *Id.* at 200-01.

Some domestic partner ordinances permit unmarried opposite-sex couples to register. *See, e.g.,* SAN FRANCISCO ADMIN. CODE § 62.2 (2004) (defining eligible parties as "two adults," without reference to gender); CAL. FAM. CODE § 297(b)(6) (B) (2003) (providing that "persons of opposite sexes may not constitute a domestic partnership unless both persons are over the age of 62" and satisfy specified Social Security eligibility requirements). Typically, though, domestic partner laws that extend *beyond* eligibility of partners for employee benefits are not available to couples legally capable of marrying in the jurisdiction. California's inclusion of opposite-sex senior citizen couples in its domestic partner scheme represents an exception, in recognition of the financial losses often incurred by Social Security recipients upon marrying. Given the strong concern among lawmakers in the United States that government *encourage* marriage, it is not surprising that policymakers have been reluctant to extend a status alternative to marriage to opposite-sex couples. Access to employee benefits, however, particularly health insurance, constitutes a logical exception to such exclusion, in light of the high proportion of individuals in this country who are without medical insurance, and the governments' interest in promoting individuals' access to such insurance. The constitutionality of domestic partner policies that exclude opposite-sex non-marital partners has been upheld by a federal appellate court. See *Irizarry v. Board of Education*, 251 F.3d 604 (7th Cir. 2001) (upholding Chicago Board of Education policy of providing health benefits to partners of employees in same-sex, but not opposite-sex, relationships). For an analysis of the issues concerning differential treatment of same-sex versus opposite-sex nonmarital partnerships in the United States, see Terry S. Kogan, *Competing Approaches to Same-Sex Versus Opposite-Sex, Unmarried Couples in Domestic Partnership Laws and Ordinances*, 2001 B.Y.U. L. Rev. 1023.

Unquestionably, employment benefits have played a much more important role in the growing recognition of same-sex partnerships in the United States than in other nations. In the absence of a national health system, Americans rely primarily on their employers to provide them with access to affordable health care. Blumberg, *supra* at 1282–92. It has been estimated that employment benefits may constitute as much as 40% of a worker's compensation. Merin, *supra* at 198. Thus, governmental endorsement of parity between spouses of married employees, and domestic partners of gay or lesbian employees, carries with it significant economic consequences for couples. Furthermore, such endorsement makes a statement about equal compensation for employees whose choice of partner precludes them from marrying. For further discussion of the history and evolution of domestic partner ordinances and statutes, see Nancy J. Knauer, *Domestic Partnership and Same-Sex Relationships: A Marketplace Innovation and A Less than Perfect Institutional Choice,* 7 TEMP. POL. & CIV. RTS. L. REV. 337 (1998); Raymond C. O'Brien, *Domestic Partnership: Recognition and Responsibility,* 32 SAN DIEGO L. REV. 163 (1995); Craig A. Bowman & Blake M. Cornish, *A More Perfect Union: A Legal and Social Analysis of Domestic Partnership Ordinances,* Note, 92 COLUM. L. REV. 1164 (1992).

[i] Civil Unions and Civil-Union-Like Domestic Partnerships

Following the Vermont Supreme Court's decision in *Baker v. State,* 744 A.2d 864 (Vt. 1999) (see Chapter 2, p. 118 *supra),* the state legislature created the status of civil unions, intended to provide to registering same-sex couples all of the rights, benefits, and obligations attendant to marriage in Vermont. 15 VT. STAT. § 1201 et seq. (2004). The status is available only to same-sex couples, and individuals are precluded from entering a civil union if they are already married or in a civil union with another person. 15 VT. STAT. § 1202 (2004). The legislation provides that

> (a) Parties to a civil union shall have all the same benefits, protections and responsibilities under law, whether they derive from statute, administrative or court rule, policy, common law or any other source of civil law, as are granted to spouses in a marriage. (b) A party to a civil union shall be included in any definition or use of the terms "spouse," "family," "immediate family," "dependent," "next of kin," and other terms that denote the spousal relationship, as those terms are used throughout the law. (c) Parties to a civil union shall be responsible for the support of one another to the same degree and in the same manner as prescribed under law for married persons. (d) The law of domestic relations, including annulment, separation and divorce, child custody and support, and property division and maintenance shall apply to parties to a civil union. . . . (f) The rights of parties to a civil union, with respect to a child of whom either becomes the natural parent during the term of the civil union, shall be the same as those of a married couple, with respect to a child of whom either spouse becomes the natural parent during the marriage.

15 VT. STAT. § 1204 (2004). Furthermore, the statutes set forth a "nonexclusive list of legal benefits, protections and responsibilities of spouses, which shall apply in like manner to parties to a civil union." 15 VT. STAT. § 1204(e) (2004). That list includes:

> (1) laws relating to title, tenure, descent and distribution, intestate succession, waiver of will, survivorship, or other incidents of the acquisition, ownership, or transfer, inter vivos or at death, of real or

personal property, including eligibility to hold real and personal property as tenants by the entirety (parties to a civil union meet the common law unity of person qualification for purposes of a tenancy by the entirety);

(2) causes of action related to or dependent upon spousal status, including an action for wrongful death, emotional distress, loss of consortium, dramshop, or other torts or actions under contracts reciting, related to, or dependent upon spousal status;

(3) probate law and procedure, including nonprobate transfer;

(4) adoption law and procedure;

15. VT. STAT. § 1204(e) (2004). Also included among the enumerated rights are a host of benefits relating to insurance, family leave, and public assistance, prohibitions of discrimination based upon marital status, testimonial privileges, hospital visitation privileges, and end-of-life proxy decisionmaking. *Id.* The legislation also provides that: "Parties to a civil union may modify the terms, conditions, or effects of their civil union in the same manner and to the same extent as married persons who execute an antenuptial agreement or other agreement recognized and enforceable under the law, setting forth particular understandings with respect to their union." 15 VT. STAT. § 1204 (2004). In addition, dissolutions of civil unions are subject to the same substantive and procedural rules as are marital dissolutions, and are handled by the family court. 15 VT. STAT. § 1206 (2004).

Although California's domestic partner legislation developed in a piecemeal fashion over a decade, the result is strikingly similar to Vermont's civil union status. While domestic partner benefits were available to state employees in California as early as 1994, the legislation creating the state registry was enacted in 1999, yet provided little more than the opportunity to register and access certain state benefits. CAL. FAM. CODE § 297 (2000). However, the state legislature expanded its provisions in subsequent years. In 2001, the legislature extended to domestic partners several sets of rights, including rights parallel to those of spouses to bring certain tort actions such as negligent infliction of emotional distress, CAL. CIV. CODE § 1701.14 (2004), and wrongful death, CAL. CODE CIV. PROC. § 377.6 (2004). Domestic partners also obtained the right to adopt their partner's children in a second-parent adoption analogous to step-parent adoption, CAL. FAM. CODE § 9000, as well as spouse-like hospital visitation privileges. CAL. HEALTH & SAFETY CODE § 1261 (2004). Effective July 2003, the legislature extended to domestic partners the same intestate succession rights to each others' separate property accorded spouses. CAL. PROB. CODE § 6402 (2004). These extensions culminated with the passage of the California Domestic Partner Rights and Responsibilities Act of 2003. 2003 CAL. LEGIS. SERV. Ch. 421 (A.B. 205). Effective January 1, 2005, the new package creates a status substantially similar to marriage. The key legislative provisions create parity between registered domestic partners and spouses with respect to the "rights, protections, and benefits" and "responsibilities, obligations, and duties under law, whether they derive from statutes, administrative regulations, court rules, government policies, common law, or any other provisions or sources of law, as are granted to and imposed upon spouses." CAL. FAM. CODE 297.5(a) (effective Jan. 1, 2005). One of the most dramatic effects of this new law is the extension of California's community property system to assets acquired by domestic partners during the partnership. The statute also sets forth that *former* registered domestic partners are treated in a legally-identical way as former spouses, CAL. FAM. CODE 297.5(b) (effective Jan. 1, 2005), and that *surviving* domestic partners likewise shall have the same legal status as spouses following the death of the other partner. CAL. FAM. CODE 297.5(c) (effective Jan. 1, 2005). The legislation also states that treatment of domestic partners "with respect to a child of either of them shall be the same as those of spouses." CAL. FAM. CODE 297.5(d) (effective Jan. 1, 2005). In California, domestic partnerships still differ from marriage in terms of the formalities required to enter them, and with respect to a requirement that the parties have a common residence. And, because most federal laws, such as tax laws, do not recognize domestic partnerships, the statutes make provisions to address potential inconsistencies in federal and state legal treatment. Thus, to the extent that the appellation "domestic partnership" signaled nothing more than registration and employee benefits when used in the United States, California has broken the mold, creating a status almost as similar to marriage as is Vermont's civil union.

[ii] Reciprocal Beneficiary Relationships

In response to the successful courtroom challenge of Hawaii's restriction of marriage to opposite-sex couples,

> the voters of Hawaii subsequently authorized their legislature to amend the state constitution to overrule *Baehr* insofar as it required Hawaii to recognize same-sex marriage. As an apparent quid pro quo, the Hawaii legislature provided "reciprocal beneficiary" legislation for persons legally unable to marry. [T]he Hawaii legislature side-stepped the issue of same-sex relationships by extending relief to any two unmarried individuals legally prohibited from marrying each other under state law. The legislative findings refer to brothers and sisters, a widowed mother and her unmarried son, and, finally, "two individuals who are of the same gender." The effect of the Hawaii legislation is to extend to same-sex couples some of the third-party benefits available to married couples, such as eligibility for derivative health insurance coverage for family members, hospital visitation privileges, wrongful death and loss of consortium claims, family and funeral leave from employment, and state employee pension rights and death benefits. The legislation includes reciprocal beneficiaries as spouses for state heirship and elective share legislation and the pretermitted spouse statute. Despite recognizing claims of one reciprocal beneficiary against another when their relationship ends at death, the Hawaii legislation creates no claims at inter vivos termination of the relationship. This gap is understandable in view of the broad scope of the legislation. One would not want to impose continuing obligations, for example, upon an unmarried son who, in order to marry, terminates a reciprocal beneficiary relationship with his mother. However, the nature of the relationship between persons who cannot marry because of consanguinity and the relationship of persons who cannot marry

because they are of the same sex is, or at least should be, distinctly different. An unmarried person who has access to benefits may commendably wish to share them with a less fortunate blood relative. That unmarried person should be able to terminate the relationship to the less fortunate relative without continuing obligation. On the other hand, same-sex partners who register as reciprocal beneficiaries are much more likely to be indistinguishable from opposite-sex couples who marry. Their relationship may include children as well as a much greater degree of financial interdependence than is likely in the case of reciprocal beneficiaries who are blood relatives. Thus, Hawaii's oblique treatment is one that is not fully satisfactory to persons other jurisdictions would characterize as "domestic partners."

Grace Ganz Blumberg, *The Regularization of Nonmarital Cohabitation: Rights and Responsibilities in the American Welfare State*, 76 NOTRE DAME L. REV. 1265, 1277–78 (2001). In an interesting postscript to its passage of civil union legislation, the Vermont legislature also enacted a reciprocal beneficiary statute. 15 VT. STAT. § 1301 et seq. (2004). This latter statute extends limited rights to "two persons who are blood-relatives or related by adoption the opportunity to establish a consensual reciprocal beneficiaries relationship," providing for particular spouse-like rights such as hospital visitation, surrogate medical decisionmaking, and decisionmaking regarding anatomical gifts and disposition of remains. 15 VT. STAT. § 1301 (2004). Because the provisions exclude parties who are either married or partners in a civil union, it is clear that the legislative purpose is to encourage connections and commitments among those family members who do not have a primary life partner, and to increase the likelihood that decisions regarding these individuals' health care and end-of-life choices will be made efficiently and by someone designated by the individual in question. Thus, an unintended and potentially positive consequence of the movement for legal recognition of same-sex relationships is a more generalized openness toward recognizing and encouraging mutually-caring and caregiving relationships among non-spousal family and family-like dyads.

NOTES

1. *The Demographics of Those Who Enter Vermont's Civil Unions.* In the first year, 2,479 couples entered civil unions in Vermont. Greg Johnson, *In Praise of Civil Unions*, 39 CAP. U. L. REV. 315, 334 (2002). Most of the couples (approximately three-quarters) were from out-of-state (hailing from 46 different states) or other nations. *Id.* Approximately three and one-half years after the legislation went into effect, 6,613 couples had entered the unions. Fred Bayles, *Vermont's Gay Civil Unions Mostly Affairs of the Heart; Law Didn't Spur Legal Battles or an "Invasion,"* USA TODAY, Jan. 7, 2004. About two-thirds of the couples are female, and most partners are college graduates with above-average incomes. Patricia Wen, *A Civil Tradition: Data Show Same-Sex Unions in Vt. Draw a Privileged Group*, BOSTON GLOBE, June 29, 2003, at B.1. A University of Vermont psychology professor, Esther Rothblum, is studying 400 couples who entered civil unions in Vermont in 2000 and 2001. She reports that, on average, the couples had been together for about 11 to 12 years prior to entering the formal union. Rona Marech, *Gay Couples Can be as Stable as Straights, Evidence Suggests,* SAN FRANCISCO CHRONICLE, Feb. 27, 2004, 2004 WL 58590405. For further information about the demographic and relationship characteristics of couples entering civil unions, see Sondra E. Solomon, Esther D. Rothblum & Kimberly F. Balsam, *Pioneers in Partnership: Lesbian and Gay Male Couples in Civil Unions Compared with Those Not in Civil Unions, and Married Heterosexual Siblings,* J. FAM. PSYCHOL. (forthcoming). Reportedly, slightly fewer than one-half of those Vermonters who identified themselves as cohabiting same-sex partners on the 2000 Census had entered civil unions in the first three years the law was in effect. Bayles, *supra.* By early 2004, of the 954 Vermont couples that had entered civil unions, 29 had obtained a formal dissolution of the union in the Vermont family courts. Betsy Rubiner and Wendy Cole, *Why Breaking Up is So Hard to Do,* NATION, Mar. 8, 2004.

   2. *Challenges to the Civil Union Statutes*. On April 26, 2000, Vermont's governor signed "An Act Relating to Civil Unions," which was scheduled to go into effect on July 1, 2000. Shortly before that date, "a group comprised of Vermont taxpayers, members of the Vermont House of Representatives, and three Vermont town clerks" filed various suits to enjoin the law's implementation. *Brady v. Dean,* 790 A.2d 428, 429 (Vt. 2000). In one action, taxpayers and legislators joined to challenge the validity of the legislation on the basis that "fourteen members of the House . . . participated in a 'dollar-a-guess' betting pool in connection with a preliminary vote on the civil unions bill." *Id.* Citing the independence of the legislature from judicial scrutiny of certain actions, the Vermont Supreme Court dismissed the action as a nonjusticiable political question. *Id.* at 545–46. The court also rejected the claims of several town clerks that their obligation to issue civil union licenses violated their free exercise of religion. *Id.* at 433–35. In contrast to the events in Hawaii, a state constitutional amendment that would have nullified the Vermont Supreme Court's decision in *Baker* was easily defeated in the state senate, 21 to 9. Adam Lisberg, *Vermont Senate Backs Civil Unions Bill,* GANNETT NEWS SERV., Apr. 19, 2000. Furthermore, polls revealed enough public support for the court's mandate to have caused such an amendment to fail if presented to the voters.

   While most legal scholarship views civil unions as a positive or neutral development, a small minority of writers is critical. *See, e.g.,* Lynn D. Wardle, *Counting the Costs of Civil Unions: Some Potential Detrimental Effects on Family Law,* 11 WIDENER J. PUB. L. 401, 442 (2002) (for an argument that civil unions will endanger the institution of marriage, will lead to confused and inconsistent family doctrines and to "suffering [and] costs disproportionately burden[ing] the most vulnerable" in society, such as children, because, for example, it will promote acceptance of gays and lesbians as parents). Other observers are critical of civil unions because Vermont created an alternate status for same-sex couples, and that such distinctions between marriages and same-sex committed relationships relegates the latter to an inferior status. *See, e.g., Baker v. State,* 744 A.2d 864, 897 (1999) (Johnson, J., concurring in part and dissenting in part); *Opinion of the Justices to the Senate,* 802 N.E.2d 565 (Mass. 2004).

3. *Interstate Recognition of Civil Unions.* Substantial scholarly commentary has considered the question of whether states will be required to recognize same-sex marriages performed elsewhere either under the Full Faith and Credit Clause of the U.S. Constitution or under common law principles. *See* Chapter 2 at page 129. The choice of law issues set forth in Chapter 2 are further complicated when parties seek recognition of a status such as a civil union. Although civil unions are legally identical to marriage within the state, they are not, technically-speaking, *marriages*. It is possible that states will view constitutional and common law requirements for recognition of an out-of-state marriage as inapplicable where the status in question is not technically a marriage, irrespective of the practical similarities between the status and marriage. Alternatively, a court may reason by analogy that it is required to accord the status with the same recognition as it does an out-of-state marriage, at least to the extent that the two statuses are similar with respect to the issue before the court. Matters become even more complicated when a status such as a domestic partnership or a reciprocal beneficiary relationship shares some but not all features in common with marriage.

Also uncertain is how the federal Defense of Marriage Act ("DOMA") and state statutes precluding recognition of same-sex marriages (*i.e.*, so-called "mini-DOMAs") will treat civil unions, domestic partnerships, reciprocal beneficiary relationships, and any other alternative-to-marriage statuses states create. These alternative statuses may escape application of these Defense of Marriage statutes because they are not, technically, marriages. Or, judges may focus on the similarities between the status and marriage with respect to the provisions at issue in the case. On the other hand, even in unfriendly jurisdictions, plaintiffs seeking to enforce particular provisions of a same-sex status might argue that *inter se* claims should be enforced on contract grounds. Earlier, this chapter discussed states' recognition of agreements between nonmarital cohabitants. *See* Section B2 *supra*. Given most states' willingness to enforce express contracts between nonmarital cohabitants, contract theory might allow recognition of claims concerning partners' rights and obligations to each other, eliminating the need for the court to recognize the underlying status. For a discussion of the special issues relating to interstate recognition of civil unions, domestic partnerships, and reciprocal beneficiary relationships, see Ralph U. Whitten, *Exporting and Importing Domestic Partnerships: Some Conflict-of-Laws Questions and Concerns*, 2001 B.Y.U. L. Rev. 1235. *See also* Elaine M. De Franco, *Choice of Law: Will a Wisconsin Court Recognize a Vermont Civil Union?* 85 Marq. L. Rev. 251 (2001); Lewis A. Silverman, *Vermont Civil Unions, Full Faith and Credit, and Marital Status*, 89 Ky. L.J. 1075 (2000-01); Barbara Cox, *Interstate Recognition of Marriages and Civil Unions*, 30 Hum. Rts. 5 (2003).

A handful of state courts have been asked to recognize a civil union outside of Vermont, with mixed results. For example, an appellate court in New York held that a deceased man's partner, with whom he had entered a Vermont civil union, was a "spouse" under New York's wrongful death statute. *Langan v. St. Vincent's Hospital,* 765 N.Y.S. 2d 411 (N.Y. App. Div. 2003). The court provided a nuanced analysis which examined the functional parallels between the partners' relationship and a marriage (including affidavits from family members alleging that the 16-year relationship between the partners was like that of a spouse). The court cited other New York precedents, such as *Braschi v. Stahl Associates* (see Chapter 1, p. 34), and the extension of family benefits by the New York State fund compensating victims of the September 11th tragedies. The New York court concluded that it was required under the Full Faith and Credit Clause to recognize this civil union as it would a marriage, given the absence of a public policy rationale for not doing so. Noting that New York had not passed a "mini-DOMA," *i.e.*, a statute precluding the state from recognizing same-sex relationships as marriages, the court held that recognition of Mr. Langan as a spouse furthered the underlying purposes of the wrongful death statutes.

In Massachusetts, a probate court judge dissolved a couple's civil union, relying on the state's high court's decision in *Goodridge*, reasoning that if the state constitution requires extension of marriage rights to same-sex couples, extension of the state's mechanisms for terminating relationships should be likewise available. Kathleen Burge, *Mass. Judge Grants "Divorce" to Gay Couple*, BOSTON GLOBE, Mar. 28, 2004. A Connecticut court of appeals, the highest state court adjudicating out-of-state dissolution of a civil union, held that a Vermont civil union is not a "marriage" for the purpose of giving the family court subject matter jurisdiction in order to dissolve the parties' union. *Rosengarten v. Downes*, 802 A.2d 170 (App. 2002). While a Texas family court granted a dissolution of a Vermont civil union to two men who petitioned jointly to terminate their union, the judge reversed his order following an opinion issued by the state attorney general that Texas law makes no provision for such dissolutions. *Lawyers' Delight — Gay Divorce*, THE ECONOMIST, Apr. 3, 2004, 2004 WL 62017472. An Iowa family court judge who granted a "divorce" to partners of a civil union (ostensibly without realizing that the partners were both women) subsequently altered his order to refer to the dissolution as a termination of a civil union rather than a marriage. *Id.*; Kathleen Burge, *supra*.

In *Burns v. Burns*, 560 S.E.2d 47 (Ga. App. 2002), a Georgia court determined that a civil union is not a civil marriage for the purpose of construing a consent order by a family court. The disputing parties were former marital partners, divorced in 1995. The father retained full custody of the couple's minor children. The mother had challenged her former husband's refusal to allow her to visit the children, which led to the issuance of a consent order by the family court. The order stated that the parties agreed that there would not be any "visitation or residence by the children with either party during any time where such party cohabits with or has overnight stays with any adult to which such party is not legally married . . ." *Id.* at 47. In the present action, Mr. Burns claimed that Ms. Burns violated this order. The court rejected Ms. Burns' claims that her relationship with her partner, with whom she had entered into a civil union, was analogous to that of spouses. Thus, it held she had violated the consent agreement when permitting her partner to cohabit.

Some state statutes address the question of recognition of civil unions and other similar statuses by statute. For example, in California's 2003 enactment of its expanded domestic partner statute, it explicitly provided for recognition of similar statuses entered into in other states. *See* CAL. FAM. CODE § 292.2 (2004). *See also* N.J. ST. § 26:8A-6 (2004) (extending recognition to civil unions, domestic partnerships, and reciprocal beneficiary relationships entered into in other states). By contrast, the Texas and Ohio legislatures passed bills indicating that the state will not recognize civil unions, 2003 Tex. S.B. 7 (enacted May 28, 2003), or any status that provides for the specific statutory benefits of legal marriage to same-sex couples. 2003 Ohio House Bill 272 (Enacted Feb. 6, 2004). Similar bills have been introduced in several other states. In 2004, both houses of the Wisconsin legislature passed a proposed state constitutional amendment that would prohibit recognition of either same-sex marriage or status alternatives extending the legal incidents of marriage to same-sex couples. The proposal must be passed again by the legislature in 2005, at which time the proposal can be placed on the ballot. *Action in State Laws on Gay Marriage,* Associated Press Newswires, Mar. 17, 2004.

4. *State Legislative Activity Regarding the Creation of Civil Unions, Domestic Partnerships, and Reciprocal Beneficiary Relationships.* During 2003, eight states considered bills that would have extended all or most of the legal rights, benefits, and obligations of marriage to same-sex couples. In six of those states (*i.e.*, Colorado, Connecticut, Hawaii, Massachusetts, Rhode Island, Washington), no proposal was adopted by the end of the year. One of those states, California, passed the comprehensive domestic partners bill discussed above. In late 2003, the eighth state, New Jersey, did not enact the civil union legislation, but enacted the "Domestic Partnership Act," Assembly Bill 3743, which extended to same-sex partners and opposite partners over age 62 certain limited rights available to married couples. Pub. L. 2003, c. 246, N.J. St. § 26:8A-1 et seq. (2004). Specifically, while the legislation provides for employee benefits for domestic partners of state employees, joint filing status for state tax purposes, and recognition of the domestic partner relationships with respect to hospital visitation and certain types of health care decisionmaking, it does not require private employers to recognize domestic partnerships for the purpose of insurance coverage. Furthermore, the statute does not extend to domestic partners a range of other benefits, such as mutual obligations and property division at dissolution, rights or obligations with respect to each others' children, various inheritance rights, or rights to be treated as a spouse for the purpose of certain tort actions. In 2004, in response to the Massachusetts Supreme Judicial Court's judgment in *Opinion of the Justices to the Senate,* 802 N.E.2d 565 (Mass. 2004) (holding that exclusion of same-sex couples from marriage in Massachusetts violates the state's constitution), the state legislature passed a constitutional amendment which would preclude same-sex marriages but permit civil unions. Ian Urbina, *Effort to Bar Gay Marriage Gains in Massachusetts Debate,* N.Y. Times, Mar. 29, 2004. In order to become effective, however, the proposed amendment must pass the state legislature twice more in 2006, and then must be endorsed by Massachusetts voters.

5. *Fiscal Implications of Civil Unions, Domestic Partnerships, and Reciprocal Beneficiary Relationships.* Some policymakers have expressed concern that extension of marriage-like benefits to same-sex couples will place a financial strain on state budgets as increasing numbers of couples become eligible for various state benefits. Yet, the economic analyses performed to date have found or predicted the fiscal effects of legal recognition of same-sex relationships for state budgets to be positive or nonsignificant. The 2002 Report of the Civil Union Commission in the Office of the Legislative Council in Vermont (available at: www1.law.ucla.edu/~williamsproj/vermontcommission.htm) concluded that civil unions had a positive financial impact on the couples entering them and no significant impact on the functioning of governmental agencies. A prospective analysis of the implications for California of passage of its expanded domestic partnership act predicted annual savings of between $8.1 to $10.6 million. M.V. Lee Badgett & R. Bradley Sears, *Equal Rights, Fiscal Responsibility: The Impact of AB 205 on California's Budget* (2003) (available at www1.law.ucla.edu/~williamsproj/AB205/). The authors of this policy study noted that Californians will make *less* use of public benefit programs as private employers cover same-sex partners of insured employees. And, they underscored, reduced reliance on public benefits will also follow the pooling of economic resources between partners, and the legal enforcement of financial obligations between partners and toward the partners' joint children upon relationship dissolution. Furthermore, the study predicted that increases in tourism would also help offset any additional state financial burdens that recognition of same-sex unions may have. A study by the same research team predicted that the New Jersey Domestic Partnership Act would save the state over $61 million annually. M.V. Lee Badgett, R. Bradley Sears & Suzanne Goldberg, *Supporting Families, Saving Funds: A Fiscal Analysis of New Jersey's Domestic Partnership Act* (2003) (available at: www.iglss.org).

§ C. UNMARRIED PARENTS AND THEIR CHILDREN

Children born to married mothers are usually also the biological, social, and legal child of her husband. But what of children born to unmarried mothers? This is the central topic of this chapter. Children born to unmarried mothers may live with her in a household that includes their biological father, or may not. If not, the household may include the mother's current partner, to whom she may or may not be married, and who may be a woman. Some children of unmarried mothers live in households with their father and not their mother, or with other adults altogether. Finally, consider that some children born to married mothers have biological fathers who are not the mother's husband. The child's mother and perhaps also the child's father are married, but not to one another. Such children may live with their mother and her husband, with their mother alone, or with their mother and her current partner who may or may not be the children's biological father. These situations are also addressed in this chapter.

The legal questions that arise do not ordinarily involve the child's relationship with the biological mother, who is also the child's legal mother in the absence of abuse and neglect proceedings terminating or suspending her parental rights. The child's relationship with other adults — the biological father and the mother's husband or partners — is more likely to present complications and their legal treatment is this section's primary focus. The law's characterization of these relationships — as parental, stranger, or something in-between — turns on its assessment of the relative importance of biological and social links. It also forces attention to gender differences.

Maternity is rarely uncertain, even temporarily, and most of these children live with their biological mothers. The social realities of maternity and paternity are thus different, and these differences led to differences in the rules the law historically applied to the recognition of legal maternity and paternity. But modern sensitivities to gender distinctions requires reexamination of these differences.

Part 1 of this section reviews the law governing the establishment of parentage — primarily, paternity. This law has been affected enormously by scientific advances that allow the confident identification of a child's biological father, and by the increased proportion of cases, as compared to decades ago, in which an unmarried father seeks rather than avoids responsibility for his child. Part 2 focuses on constitutional and state law responses to the paternal claims of unwed fathers, and to the special issues affecting the paternity of a child born to a married woman. Part 3 summarizes other constitutional rules protecting nonmarital children from discriminatory treatment by government. Finally, Part 4 reviews the legal treatment of gay and lesbian couples or individuals who are parents or seek to become parents. It makes sense, however, to first review the relevant demographic changes over recent decades.

In the year 2000, 1.35 million children were born to unmarried females in the United States. This number is up 15.6% from the 1.16 million children born to unmarried mothers in 1990. Even more dramatic, however, is the comparison of the number of nonmarital to marital births. Table 9-6 expresses these data as a percentage, revealing particularly steep increases between 1970 and 1990. The percentage of nonmarital births to Caucasian women has more than tripled between 1970 and 2000, while the percentage of nonmarital births to African-American women has not quite doubled during this same period. There are dramatic variations among other American subgroups as well. In 2000, nonmarital children comprised 7.6% of all births to Chinese mothers, 9.5% of children born to Japanese mothers, and 42.7% of births to women of Hispanic ancestry. *Statistical Abstract of the United States: 2000,* Table 74. These data reveal that nonmarital births, once stereotypically viewed as occurring primarily within certain minority groups, are increasingly common within the majority. Discussions about the possible consequences for children of growing up in a single-parent family cannot focus exclusively on divorce. Never-married mothers (as compared to divorced or separated mothers) grew from 17% of all single mothers in 1976, to 46% in 1997. Elaine Sorenson & Ariel Halpern, *Child Support Enforcement Is Working Better Than We Think,* Urban Institute Report No. A-31 (March, 1999), available at <http://newfederalism.urban.org/html/anf_31.html>.

Table 9-6
Nonmarital Births as Percent of All Births In the United States: 1970 to 2000[13]

Year	Total	White	Black
2000	33.2	27.1	68.5
1990	28.0	20.1	65.2
1980	28.4	11.0	55.2
1970	10.7	5.7	37.6

What accounts for the increase in nonmarital births? There is surely no simple answer to that question, which necessarily implicates many social trends. Some observations can be made, however. Any of the following, alone or in combination, would yield an increase in the proportion of births that are nonmarital: an increase in the proportion of pregnancies that are nonmarital; an increase in the proportion of nonmarital pregnancies that continue to term; and a decrease in the proportion of nonmarital pregnancies in which the mother marries before birth — what were once called "shotgun" marriages. One study, which defined a "shotgun marriage" as a marriage occurring within seven months prior to birth, calculated the shotgun marriage ratio, defined as the proportion of births conceived out of wedlock in which the mother marries before birth. It found that for whites, the shotgun marriage ratio declined from.61 in 1969 to.35 in 1988. The analogous decline for blacks was from.25 to.085. The authors then compared the nonmarital birth ratio during the four year period from 1965 to 1969 with the period from 1985 to 1989 and found that among whites, about three-fourths of the increase in nonmarital births between these two periods is accounted for by a decline in shotgun marriages, and about three-fifths of the increase among blacks. (They reach this conclusion by comparing the actual increase in nonmarital births to the increase that would have occurred if the same proportion of single pregnant women had married before their child's birth, in the late 1980s, as had done so in the late 1960s.) George A. Akerlof, et al., *An Analysis of Out-Of-Wedlock Childbearing in the United States*, 111 Quart. J. Econ. 277 (1996). It thus seems that the increase in non-marital births has been due less to an increase in non-marital pregnancy and more to a decrease in shotgun marriages. Why are fewer unmarried parents marrying after the pregnancy is known? The authors speculate that the availability of legal abortion may reduce the social pressure on the fathers to marry the mothers, even mothers who do not themselves wish to abort. Another possibility, of course, is that the mothers are not interested in marrying the fathers. A large proportion of unmarried mothers live in a social and economic milieu in which men with good jobs, or any jobs, are scarce. These women may not marry because they cannot find appealing candidates. If this is the explanation, then the most effective strategy for reducing the rate of nonmarital birth is to reduce poverty levels. *See* Ira Mark Ellman, *Why Making Family Law is Hard*, 35 Ariz. St. L.J. 699 (2004).

One must also remember, however, that an unmarried mother could nonetheless be cohabiting with the father at the time of the child's birth. Data

---

[13] Sources: Table 98, *Statistical Abstract of the United States: 1996*; Tables 74 & 75, *Statistical Abstract of the United States: 2002.*

reveal that an increasing proportion of nonmarital children are born into opposite-sex cohabiting relationships. One team of researchers commented that the United States "is rapidly moving towards the position of several European countries where an 'unmarried birth' is more likely to occur in a two-parent family than it is to create a mother-only family." Larry Bumpass & Hsien-Hen Lu, *Trends in Cohabitation and Implications for Children's Family Contexts in the United States*, 54 POPULATION STUDIES 29, 34–35 (2000). For example, between 1990 and 1994, approximately 40% of births to unmarried women occurred to cohabiting parents, up from 29% a decade earlier. *Id.* at 35. The most recent increases in nonmarital births appear to be "almost completely associated with cohabiting two-parent families." *Id.*

Referring back to Table 9-1, on page 871, the numbers of unmarried heterosexual couples living with children under the age of 15 has increased by over 700% between 1960 and 2002. Although the data reveal a drop in unmarried heterosexual couples living with children *under the age of 15* between the years 2000 and 2002, the numbers of these families with children *under the age of 18* continued to increase during these years, rising from 1,236,000 in 1996 to 1,295,000 in 1998, to 1,563,000 in 2000, and to 1,718,000 in 2002. These data indicate that an increasing proportion of the children living with a nonmarital heterosexual couple entered the age range of 15-and 18-years-old between 2000 and 2002.[14] Forty-one percent, or about two-fifths, of heterosexual unmarried-partner households included children under the age of 18 in 2000. This figure is only slightly less than the 46% of married-couple households with minor children. U.S. Census Bureau, *America's Families and Living Arrangements* (2000). Whereas some children born to unmarried mothers will be raised, at least for part of their minority, by two unmarried parents or by their mothers alone, some will be raised in other family constellations. Statistics on single-parent families can be misleading, in that many children counted as living in single-parent families actually live with a parent and nonmarital "stepparent." *See* Larry Bumpass, et al., *The Changing Character of Stepfamilies: Implications of Cohabitation and Nonmarital Childbearing*, 32 DEMOGRAPHY 425 (1995); Pamela J. Smock, *Cohabitation in the United States: An Appraisal of Research Themes, Findings, and Implications*, 26 ANN. REV. SOCIOL. 1, 2 (2000) (noting that in approximately 70% of the families in which cohabiting couples live with children, the children are the offspring of only one of the partners). And, of course, many children of unmarried mothers reside with their mothers and extended-family members. Children of unmarried mothers may experience a variety of household types, and their life histories may also include parental marriages, divorces, and separations.

What are the implications of birth into a nonmarital family? Children born to unmarried mothers, including those born to cohabiting parents, are more likely to experience certain disadvantages than are children born to married parents. Bumpass et al. *supra*; Smock, *supra*. Parental education and income levels are lower in nonmarital families, and as a result, children born outside

---

[14] U.S. Census Bureau data for unmarried heterosexual partner households with children *under the age of 18* are not available for years prior to 1996. Because data are available as far back as 1960 for households with children *under the age of 15*, Table 9-1 reflects only the latter numbers.

of marriage are more likely to experience poverty. Furthermore, the average duration of cohabitating relationships is significantly shorter than the average marital duration, which means that children living with cohabiting adults are more likely to experience the dissolution of their parents' relationship and separation from their fathers. But these studies cannot tell us whether their parent's unmarried status is the cause of these disabilities, or whether the nonmarital birth and the disabilities are both the product of other factors. Daniel T. Lichter & Deborah Roempke Graefe, *Finding a Mate? The Marital and Cohabitation Histories of Unwed Mothers*, in OUT OF WEDLOCK: CAUSES AND CONSEQUENCES OF NONMARITAL FERTILITY 317, 319 (L.L. Wu & B. Wolfe eds. 2001).

Some researchers interpret these data as suggesting that men and women with lower educational and income levels, or with a less stable commitment to each other, are simply less likely to marry, even once a child is conceived or born. Shelley Lundberg, *Nonmarital Fertility: Lessons for Family Economics*, in Wu & Wolfe, *supra*, at 383, 386. One creative study, using data from twins, concludes that unplanned births do appear to have large short-term effects on the economic well-being of single mothers, as compared to married mothers, and for black mothers these effects appear to continue. Bronars & Grogger, *The Economic Consequences of Unwed Motherhood: Using Twin Births As a Natural Experiment*, 84 AMER. ECON. REV. 1141 (1994). A massive project just recently underway will follow a birth cohort of approximately 5,000 children born to unmarried parents, and is likely to increase our understanding of these family considerably. Sara McLanahan, Irwin Garfinkel et al., *The Fragile Families and Child Wellbeing Study Baseline Report* (2001) (available at: crcw.princeton.edu/fragilefamilies/nationalreport.pdf). For more information on it, see crcw.princeton.edu/fragilefamilies/index.asp.

What about children living with same-sex couples? One team of researchers commented that although "adoption and parental rights policy for gay and lesbian couples is an intensely debated topic, we have virtually no empirical evidence regarding the current presence of children among gay and lesbian couples." Dan Black, Gary Gates et al., *Demographics of the Gay and Lesbian Population in the United States: Evidence from Available Systematic Data Sources*, 37 DEMOGRAPHY 139, 150 (2000). The existing evidence, however, suggests that approximately 21.7% of cohabiting lesbian couples and 5.2% of cohabiting male gay couples have children living with them. *Id.* Approximately three-quarters of these children are under the age of 18. Many were born into subsequently-dissolved heterosexual marriages. *Id.* Given the increasing visibility of gay and lesbian couples and individuals raising children in the past decade, it is likely that better estimates of the prevalence of such family arrangements will be forthcoming.

For further discussion of demographic, social, and economic factors associated with nonmarital cohabitation, childbearing, and childrearing, see also R. Kelly Raley, *Increasing Fertility in Coresident Union: Evidence for the Second Demographic Transition in the United States?*, 38 DEMOGRAPHY 59 (2001); Zheng Wu & Michael S. Pollard, *Economic Circumstances and the Stability of Nonmarital Cohabitation,* 21 J. FAM. ISSUES 303 (2000); Jay D. Teachman, *The Changing Demography of America's Families*, 62 J. MARR. &

FAM. 1234 (2000); Judith A. Seltzer, *Families Formed Outside of Marriage,* 62 J. MARR. & FAM. 1247 (2000); Wendy D. Manning & Daniel T. Lichter, *Parental Cohabitation and Children's Economic Well-Being*, 58 J. MARR. & FAM. 998 (1996); Steven L. Nock, *A Comparison of Marriages and Cohabiting Relationships,* 16 J. FAM. ISSUES 53 (1995); Zheng Wu, *The Stability of Cohabitation Relationships: The Role of Children,* 57 J. MARR. & FAM. 231 (1995); Deborah Roempke Graefe & Daniel T. Lichter, *Life Course Transitions of American Children: Parental Cohabitation, Marriage, and Single Mother-hood,* 36 DEMOGRAPHY 205 (1999).

[1] ESTABLISHING PATERNITY

Until quite recently, the old saw was still largely true: maternity is a question of fact, while paternity is a matter of opinion. No more. Maternity remains clear in almost all cases, although baby-switching cases occasionally arise (e.g., *Mays v. Twigg*, 543 So. 2d 241 (Fla. Dist. Ct. App. 1989), on remand *Twigg v. Mays*, 1993 WL330624 (Fla. Cir. Ct. 1993) (adjudicating request for parentage testing where two girls were allegedly switched in the hospital after birth)) and modern reproductive medicine offers new opportunities for such mistakes (e.g., *Perry-Rogers v. Fasano*, 715 N.Y.S.2d 19 (App. Div. 2000) (adjudicating parentage of twins whose embryos had mistakenly been implanted in the wrong woman at Fertility Clinic)). *See generally*, Tara R. Crane, *Mistaken Baby Switches: An Analysis of Hospital Liability and Resulting Custody Issues,* 21 J. LEG. MED. 109 (2000). Proof of maternity could also be needed if the biological mother abandons her newborn, if their biological relationship becomes relevant in a later proceeding.

Paternal ambiguity was historically more common. It can arise from paternal abandonment, of both mother and child, as well as from maternal concealment of the child from the biological father. Not only have disputes over paternity always been more common than disputes over maternity, but the increased proportion of children born to unmarried mothers in recent years only increases that gap. Yet the truly important change of the last several decades was the development of reliable scientific tests. Biological paternity has now also become, for the most part, a question of fact and not opinion.

[a] Methods of Proof

[i] Historical Difficulties

The classic paternity case was a maternal claim for support brought against a man alleged to be the child's father; proof of paternity was a prerequisite to a support order. But historically such proof was hard to make out. If the defendant denied sexual relations with the mother during the probable period of conception, one was left simply to choose between two stories. Direct corroboration of the plaintiff's testimony was rare, the relevant acts ordinarily having occurred in private. Perhaps in desperation, judges were sometimes known to permit exhibition of the child to the jurors, to resolve the conflict by assessing the child's resemblance to the putative father. Nor was the conduct of the case aided by a defense known as *exceptio plurium concubentium*, allowed in most jurisdictions, by which the defendant could escape liability, even if he had sexual relations with the mother during the period of conception, by showing that another man had also done so. Of course, were the other man then charged, he could use the same defense, relying upon the testimony of the initial defendant. The temptation to perjure oneself to help out a friend was too great for many to resist. In an often-cited Chicago study, an attempt was made to measure the incidence of perjury in paternity cases through the use of polygraph tests, but the tests (the accuracy of which are debatable) were not needed to make the point. Merely confronting witnesses with the machine elicited a startlingly high percentage of confessions. Fifty-seven percent of the witnesses who had testified to intercourse with the complainant (for the purpose of establishing an *exceptio plurium* defense), admitted they had lied. On the other hand, 48% of the mothers were shown to have lied in denying intercourse with another man during the period of conception, and 88% of the defendants admitted having lied in court about the number of times they had had intercourse with the mother. Arthur and Reid, *Using the Lie Detector to Determine the Truth In Disputed Paternity Cases*, 45 J. CRIM. L. C. & P. S. 213 (1954). Some courts attempted to deal with these difficulties by imposing, in paternity cases, a higher standard of proof, such as "clear and convincing," or by requiring corroborating evidence of sexual acts despite the implausibility of obtaining it. But a higher standard of proof hardly solves the problem of reaching accurate results; it merely reduces the risk of one kind of error, mistaken verdicts for the plaintiff, at the price of increasing the risk of another kind of error, mistaken verdicts for the defendant. A requirement of corroborating evidence may just encourage more perjury.

At one time, Sweden recognized a standard of proof in paternity cases quite different from that in American jurisdictions. Any man identified by the mother as having had sexual relations with her at the relevant time was considered the father, unless there was evidence, such as a blood test, making that conclusion obviously wrong. The defense of *exceptio plurium* was not allowed, and indeed was considered against "Swedish public order." But when the law was changed to give the nonmarital child full inheritance rights from his father and his father's family, requirements for proof of paternity were also tightened, becoming more similar to American rules. *See* Lodgberg, *The Reform of Family Law in the Scandinavian Countries,* in THE REFORM OF FAMILY LAW IN EUROPE 201, 213 (A. Chloros, ed. 1978). Denmark adopted another solution, imposing an obligation of support upon all men who had intercourse with the woman during the relevant time, rendering an *exceptio plurium* defense irrelevant. Such offspring were called "company children." *Id.* at 217.

Given the difficulties in establishing the biological father using traditional evidence, a reliable scientific test for paternity would obviously provide welcome relief. For many years, blood tests had been available to exclude putative fathers, but as explained below, their value was limited by the small proportion of exclusions they yielded. During the 1970s, however, new biological tests became available that were much more powerful, promising welcome relief from these problems of proof.

[ii] Development of Modern Parentage Testing

Why were traditional blood tests admitted only to exclude a man as the child's father, but not to prove his paternity? The logic underlying that rule also explains why modern paternity tests are not so limited. *See* Ira M. Ellman & David H. Kaye, *Probabilities and Proof: Can Hla and Blood Group Testing Prove Paternity?*, 54 N.Y.U. L. REV. 1131, 1135–52 (1979):

> The use of blood test evidence in paternity actions did not begin until the 1930's. Most frequently offered was a test based on the ABO blood typing system, but all such tests operate on the same basic principles. Human genes direct the expression of many easily identifiable characteristics. In particular, certain genes direct the synthesis of the chemicals, called antigens, which establish blood types. Since different versions, or alleles, as they are called, of these genes express distinct antigens, the presence of a specific antigen indicates a particular genetic composition, or genotype. Thus, the blood type antigens may be thought of as genetic markers.
>
> If one knows the father's genotype for a trait, such as blood type, then one also knows something about the child's. This is because humans. . . . possess genes in pairs, inherited one from each parent. If the putative father's pair of alleles for that characteristic are absent in the child — if neither of the child's pair is the same as either of the putative father's — then that man cannot be the father unless there has been a mutation. Mutations are sufficiently rare that they may be disregarded for the purpose of determining paternity. On the other hand, if the child and the putative father do share one allele of the gene pair in common, then it is possible the accused is indeed the father. And if that shared allele were unique to them — if no other person had a genotype which includes it — paternity would be established. However, most alleles are hardly unique. Indeed, under the traditional ABO testing system, the failure to exclude the accused meant, on the average, that he was one of the 86.6% of the male population that might have the possible genotype. Such evidence is obviously not very probative, and courts therefore have declined to admit it, since it is also deemed prejudicial.

Modern paternity tests are different than the traditional ABO tests precisely because they identify "infrequent" traits. If we know the actual father must have a particular genetic trait (because the child has the trait, and the mother does not), and if that trait is relatively rare (unlike most blood types, which are shared by large segments of the population) then the fact that paternity defendant has the required trait seems probative. But how probative? The "probability of exclusion" is one standard way to express how rare the trait in question is. It tells one the likelihood that a man chosen at random from the population would not have the trait. For example, a probability of exclusion of 95% means that 95 of 100 men, chosen at random, would, on average, be excluded as the child's father, because they do not possess the required trait. The greater the probability of exclusion, the more probative is a test that fails to exclude the paternity defendant. But the probability of exclusion is *not* the same as the probability of paternity.

An example helps to illustrate the difference between the probability of exclusion and the probability of paternity. Suppose it is known only that the mother lived in Los Angeles at the time of the child's conception, and that mother and child are Caucasian. One might assume that the actual father must also have lived in Los Angeles, but of course that is far from certain. He might have been visiting from elsewhere, or the mother might have become impregnated on a weekend trip to San Diego. But if we ignore those possibilities and limit our universe of possible fathers to Caucasian males past the age of puberty who resided in the Los Angeles area at the time of conception, we might have a suspect list of about two million. A test which eliminates even 95% of the suspects would still leave 100,000 possible fathers. The fact that the defendant was one of the remaining 100,000 is hardly overwhelming evidence. Although the test has a probability of exclusion of 95%, the probability of paternity in this example is only one in 100,000.

Of course this example has some unlikely features. Perhaps the most questionable aspect of our hypothetical is the assumption that our knowledge is strictly limited to the test results. Few defendants are chosen randomly from the population. We ordinarily know more, sometimes much more. In a typical case, the mother may testify that she had intercourse with the defendant, and only the defendant, during the period of conception, while the defendant might produce evidence that she had other lovers, and that he was out of town in the critical period. The problem is to determine how to combine our statistical information based on genetic frequency with the other evidence available. Only then can a number be produced which can sensibly be called the probability of paternity in that particular case.

Ellman and Kaye, supra.

The statistical problem that concerned Ellman and Kaye, who wrote in 1979, has largely ceased to exist. The reason is that modern parentage testing relies on traits that are so rare that even if one assumes the other evidence in the case lends little support for the conclusion that the paternity defendant is the father (a low "prior probability," in the parlance of Baysian probability analysis), the likelihood that a man who possesses the required trait is indeed the child's biological father is still quite high. As noted in a leading treatise on scientific evidence:

> . . . Increasingly, the full panoply of conventional genetic tests and DNA tests can produce posterior probabilities well in excess of 0.99 for virtually any plausible prior probability in the ordinary case. As a result, it has been suggested that

>> [W]e are approaching the point where explicit statistical analysis can be relegated to the background. Today, exclusions rarely are interpreted in terms of a paternity index or a probability of paternity, presumably because these numbers are so close to zero as to give no more guidance to a judge or jury than a simple statement that if the test results are correct, then it is practically impossible for the tested man to be the father. Likewise, an inclusion for which

the paternity index is clearly astronomical perhaps may be more profitably described as demonstrating that it is practically impossible for the putative father to be anything but the biological father.

MODERN SCIENTIFIC EVIDENCE: THE LAW AND SCIENCE OF EXPERT TESTIMONY § 26-1.5 (David L. Faigman, David H. Kaye, Michael J. Saks, Joseph Sanders, editors, 2d ed., 2002), quoting D.H. Kaye, *DNA Paternity Probabilities*, 24 FAM. L.Q. 279, 303–04 (1990).

But the establishment of reliable means to determine *biological* paternity does not necessarily settle the question of establishing *legal* paternity, as we consider in the next section.

[b]   Biological or Social Paternity? Of Procedures and Presumptions

IRA MARK ELLMAN, THINKING ABOUT CUSTODY AND SUPPORT IN AMBIGUOUS-FATHER FAMILIES, 36 Fam. L. Q. 49, 50–55 (2002)

Typical family composition has changed greatly [since 1970,] when most children were born to traditional families. Our image of that traditional family includes a husband who also fulfills the role of father. He provides a major portion of the child's financial support, lives with the child, spends at least some time in direct care of the child, and shares with the mother at least the major decisions of parenthood. Both he and the child view him as father, and third parties do as well. We can call this man the child's social father. . . . [T]he focus of this essay is on two . . . kinds [of paternal ambiguity]. Both of them . . . are much more common now than they once were. In the first, there is no dispute about the child's social father, but there is ambiguity about the legal father because the social father is not the biological father, and no formal adoption has taken place to align the two. In the second, the child has no social father, and one may therefore question whether the biological father should be considered the legal father. The resolution of these ambiguities tells us something, I believe, about the relationship between support obligations and custody claims.

When a married woman bears a child, both social conventions and legal presumptions have long treated her husband as the father. That was once how the rights and responsibilities of legal fatherhood were established for nearly all children, with little cost, contention or complication. During the final quarter of the twentieth century, however, things became more complex. The complexity arose from three developments, two social and one scientific. The two social developments were the increasing proportion of children born out of wedlock, and the increasing determination of policymakers to collect child support from absent fathers. Because of the first, there were more children whose father was not identified by the social conventions and legal presumptions applicable to marital children. Because of the second, identifying the legal father (and thus, the man responsible to provide support) became more important. The scientific development was the ability to establish biological paternity through genetic tests. This scientific development seemed to provide an answer to the problem created by the social developments. Legal paternity could be established by biology. But a new set of problems have been created by the possibility of establishing legal paternity in the absence of, or even in opposition to, social indicators of paternity.

Prior to the development of modern tissue tests, it was usually impossible to determine biological paternity. In consequence the law usually relied upon presumptions that typically attributed legal paternity to the child's social father — most importantly, to the mother's husband. States had varying rules concerning the admissibility of evidence to rebut the presumption of the husband's paternity. Some restricted such evidence very severely, while others might allow it. But even when courts accepted such rebuttal evidence, it was not often persuasive. The primitive blood tests then available were unlikely to exclude a man as the child's biological father even when he in fact was not. [That is, even most husbands who in fact were not the biological father of their wife's child would not be excluded by the test then available.] Under these conditions, husbands were almost always identified as the legal father of their wife's children. Because as recently as 1970 about ninety percent of all children were born to married mothers, the "marital presumption," as it is called, settled the question of legal paternity in the vast majority of cases. The presumption also identified as the legal father a man who was nearly always their social father. He was probably their biological father as well, but if he was not, few knew, at least not for certain. In short, the law did not then often face a forced choice between social and biological paternity.

For the relatively small proportion of children then born to unmarried women, the absence of the marital presumption usually left the child with no legally established father. A paternity action could be brought, of course. But prior to the advent of modern genetic testing, the typical paternity case consisted of conflicting testimony over the alleged father's sexual "access" to the mother during the probable period of conception, and over whether the mother had sexual relations during the same time period with other men. . . . In these muddied waters, the mother seeking to establish paternity was unlikely to meet her burden of proof, and her claim would fail. Doubtless many unmarried mothers never brought a paternity claim in the first place, anticipating this result. It would seem that this state of affairs ill served nonmarital children, who were deprived of the financial support that a finding of paternity would promise. On the other hand, it might not have much mattered, because child support orders, and especially those obtained against unmarried fathers, rarely fulfilled that promise anyway. This was the era before child support enforcement became a national policy priority.

While the outcomes for children born to married and unmarried mothers were thus very different, they were also consistent in one important respect: in both cases the attribution of legal paternity paralleled the reality of social paternity. The husband was the legal and social father of the marital child. And while no one was the legal father of the nonmarital child, typically no one was the child's social father either. Indeed, a nonmarital biological father who was the social father of his children was thought sufficiently rare that the law did not need to consider the possibility of his existence. For example, single mothers could alone consent to the adoption of their child, a core parental right. It was 1972 before American constitutional law recognized that the nonmarital father had any parental rights at all. In that case, the Supreme Court came to the assistance of Mr. Stanley, a nonmarital father who, rather atypically, had lived with his children and their mother for years. . . . [See discussion of *Stanley v. Illinois*, pages 975-977.] [¶] The Court ultimately decided four more cases on this general topic of nonmarital fathers' rights. Between the first and the last of these five cases (from 1972 to 1989), a sea change occurred in the science of paternity testing (and it has advanced even further since). In later cases the Court therefore had to confront a question that *Stanley* never raised: whether the Constitutional rights it had recognized arose from social paternity, biological paternity, or both. Its later decisions suggest that the Constitution guarantees the biological father some opportunity to establish a social connection with his offspring, but does not guarantee full paternal rights to the man who declines that opportunity. And the Court's decisions also suggest that state policymakers may treat a child's social father as the legal father, in preference to the biological father, although the Constitution does not require them to make this choice. So answers to the important questions were left largely to state policymakers.

Choosing the appropriate rule for assigning legal paternity becomes more difficult when social and biological paternity diverge. The newly-developed reliability in assessing biological paternity forces attention to this issue because it makes our knowledge of such divergence more likely. At the same time, the recent legislative determination to collect child support from absent fathers gives assignment of legal paternity enhanced importance in public policy. Moreover, a parent is not only obliged to provide support, but can also seek custody and is usually guaranteed at least some time with the child. Support duties and custody rights are in this way legally connected. Parents intuit the connection, and both custodial parents considering claims for support, and noncustodial parents considering claims for custody, sometimes forego their claim to avoid triggering the corresponding claim back from the other parent. The two also have a social connection: The biological father who has enjoyed a parental relationship with a child is more likely to pay support, and to want assured access, than the biological father who has not. So, in allowing the law to identify genetic fathers who have never known their child, modern science has given the law a challenge as well as a tool.

[i]   The Uniform Parentage Acts of 1973 and 2002

The Uniform Parentage Act, first drafted in 1973, was revised in 2000, and then amended again in 2002. The 2000 version of the act was adopted by Texas in 2001, Tex. Fam. Code §§ 160.001 et seq. (2003), and Washington in 2002, Wa. St. §§ 26.26.011 et seq. (2003). In 2003 Texas adopted many of the 2002 amendments. Delaware and Wyoming have recently enacted the 2002 version of the Act. Presently, the legislatures of three additional states (i.e., Minnesota, New Jersey, and New Mexico) are considering the Act as amended in 2002. Because the 1973 UPA was adopted by 19 states (Alabama, California, Colorado, Delaware, Hawaii, Illinois, Kansas, Minnesota, Missouri, Montana, Nevada, New Jersey, New Mexico, North Dakota, Ohio, Rhode Island, Texas, Washington, and Wyoming), most of which continue to operate under its provisions, the 1973 Act is still important today.

Below, we reprint portions of UPA (2002), including excerpts from the Preface, as well as Sections 4, 6, and 7 of the 1973 Act. (A catalogue of older state paternity statutes may be found in Jean E. Goldstein, Note, *"Children Born of the Marriage" — Res Judicata Effect on Later Support Proceedings,* 45 Mo. L. Rev. 307, 308 n.5 (1980).)

NATIONAL CONFERENCE OF COMMISSIONERS ON UNIFORM STATE LAWS, PREFATORY NOTE, UNIFORM PARENTAGE ACT (AS AMENDED 2002)

The National Conference of Commissioners on Uniform State Laws has addressed the subject of parentage throughout the 20th Century. In 1922, the Conference promulgated the "Uniform Illegitimacy Act," followed by the "Uniform Blood Tests To Determine Paternity Act" in 1952, the "Uniform Paternity Act" in 1960, and certain provisions in the "Uniform Probate Code" in 1969. The "Uniform Illegitimacy Act" was withdrawn by the Conference and none of the other Acts were widely adopted. As of June 1973, the Blood Tests to Determine Paternity Act had been enacted in nine states, the "Uniform Paternity Act" in four, and the "Uniform Probate Code" in five. The most important uniform act addressing the status of the nonmarital child was the Uniform Parentage Act approved in 1973 [hereinafter referred to as UPA (1973)]. . . .[¶] Case law has not always reached consistent results in construing UPA (1973). Moreover, widely differing treatment on subjects not dealt with by the Act has been common. . . . Finally, the incredible scientific advances in parentage testing since 1973 warrant a thoroughgoing revision of the Act. . . .

The promulgation of the UNIFORM PARENTAGE ACT in 2000, as amended in 2002, is now the official recommendation of the Conference on the subject of parentage. This Act relegates to history all of the earlier uniform acts dealing with parentage, to wit, UPA (1973), UPUFA (1988), and USCACA (1988). The amendments of 2002 are the end-result of objections lodged by the American Bar Association Section of Individual Rights and Responsibilities and the ABA Committee on the Unmet Legal Needs of Children, based on the view that in certain respects the 2000 version did not adequately treat a child of unmarried parents equally with a child of married parents. Because equal treatment of nonmarital children was a hallmark of the 1973 Act, the objections caused the drafters of the 2000 version to reconsider certain sections of the Act. Through extended discussion and a meeting of representatives of all the entities involved, a determination was made that the objections had merit. As a result of this process, the amendments shown in this Act were presented by mail ballot to the Commissioners and unanimously approved in November 2002.

[Comments to individual sections of UPA 2002 are reproduced below selectively, as are the sections of both UPA 1973 and UPA 2002. Omissions of sections or comments are not indicated individually.]

UNIFORM PARENTAGE ACT (1973)

SECTION 4. [*Presumption of Paternity.*]

(a) A man is presumed to be the natural father of a child if:

(1) he and the child's natural mother are or have been married to each other and the child is born during the marriage, or within 300 days after the marriage is terminated by death, annulment, declaration of invalidity, or divorce, or after a decree of separation is entered by a court;

(2) before the child's birth, he and the child's natural mother have attempted to marry each other by a marriage solemnized in apparent compliance with law, although the attempted marriage is or could be declared invalid, and

(i) if the attempted marriage could be declared invalid only by a court, the child is born during the attempted marriage, or within 300 days after its termination by death, annulment, declaration of invalidity, or divorce; or

(ii) if the attempted marriage is invalid without a court order, the child is born within 300 days after the termination of cohabitation;

(3) after the child's birth, he and the child's natural mother have married, or attempted to marry, each other by a marriage solemnized in apparent compliance with law, although the attempted marriage is or could be declared invalid, and

(i) he has acknowledged his paternity of the child in writing filed with the [appropriate court or Vital Statistics Bureau],

(ii) with his consent, he is named as the child's father on the child's birth certificate, or

(iii) he is obligated to support the child under a written voluntary promise or by court order;

(4) while the child is under the age of majority, he receives the child into his home and openly holds out the child as his natural child; or

(5) he acknowledges his paternity of the child in a writing filed with the [appropriate court or Vital Statistics Bureau], which shall promptly inform the mother of the filing of the acknowledgment, and she does not dispute the acknowledgment within a reasonable time after being informed thereof, in a writing filed with the [appropriate court or Vital Statistics Bureau]. If another man is presumed under this section to be the child's father, acknowledgment may be effected only with the written consent of the presumed father or after the presumption has been rebutted.

(b) A presumption under this section may be rebutted in an appropriate action only by clear and convincing evidence. If two or more presumptions arise which conflict with each other, the presumption which on the facts is founded on the weightier considerations of policy and logic controls. The presumption is rebutted by a court decree establishing paternity of the child by another man.

SECTION 6. [*Determination of Father and Child Relationship; Who May Bring Action; When Action May Be Brought.*]

(a) A child, his natural mother, or a man presumed to be his father under Paragraph (1), (2), or (3) of Section 4(a), may bring an action

(1) at any time for the purpose of declaring the existence of the father and child relationship presumed under Paragraph (1), (2), or (3) of Section 4(a); or

(2) for the purpose of declaring the non-existence of the father and child relationship presumed under Paragraph (1), (2), or (3) of Section 4(a) only if the action is brought within a reasonable time after obtaining knowledge of relevant facts, but in no event later than [5] years after the child's birth. After the presumption has been rebutted, paternity of the child by another man may be determined in the same action, if he has been made a party.

(b) Any interested party may bring an action at any time for the purpose of determining the existence or non-existence of the father and child relationship presumed under Paragraph (4) or (5) of Section 4(a).

(c) An action to determine the existence of the father and child relationship with respect to a child who has no presumed father under Section 4 may be brought by the child, the mother or personal representative of the child, the [appropriate state agency], the personal representative or a parent of the mother if the mother has died, a man alleged or alleging himself to be the father, or the personal representative or a parent of the alleged father if the alleged father has died or is a minor.

(d) Regardless of its terms, an agreement, other than an agreement approved by the court in accordance with Section 13(b), between an alleged or presumed father and the mother or child, does not bar an action under this section.

(e) If an action under this section is brought before the birth of the child, all proceedings shall be stayed until after the birth, except services of process and the taking of depositions to perpetuate testimony.

SECTION 7. [*Statute of Limitations.*]

An action to determine the existence of the father and child relationship as to a child who has no presumed father under Section 4 may not be brought later than [3] years after the birth of the child, or later than [3] years after the effective date of this Act, whichever is later. However, an action brought by or on behalf of a child whose paternity has not been determined is not barred until [3] years after the child reaches the age of majority. Sections 6 and 7 do not extend the time within which a right of inheritance or a right to a succession may be asserted beyond the time provided by law relating to distribution and closing of decedents' estates or to the determination of heirship, or otherwise.

———

UNIFORM PARENTAGE ACT (2002)

ARTICLE TWO: PARENT-CHILD RELATIONSHIP

Section 201. Establishment of Parent-Child Relationship.

. . . .

(b) The father-child relationship is established between a man and a child by:

(1) an unrebutted presumption of the man's paternity of the child under Section 204;

(2) an effective acknowledgment of paternity by the man under [Article] 3, unless the acknowledgment has been rescinded or successfully challenged;

(3) an adjudication of the man's paternity;

(4) adoption of the child by the man; [or]

(5) the man's having consented to assisted reproduction by a woman under [Article] 7 which resulted in the birth of the child [; or

(6) an adjudication confirming the man as a parent of a child born to a gestational mother if the agreement was validated under [Article] 8 or is enforceable under other law].

Section 202. No Discrimination Based on Marital Status.

A child born to parents who are not married to each other has the same rights under the law as a child born to parents who are married to each other.

Section 203. Consequences of Establishment of Parentage.

Unless parental rights are terminated, a parent-child relationship established under this [Act] applies for all purposes, except as otherwise specifically provided by other law of this State.

Section 204. Presumption of Paternity.

(a) A man is presumed to be the father of a child if:

(1) he and the mother of the child are married to each other and the child is born during the marriage;

(2) he and the mother of the child were married to each other and the child is born within 300 days after the marriage is terminated by death, annulment, declaration of invalidity, or divorce [, or after a decree of separation];

(3) before the birth of the child, he and the mother of the child married each other in apparent compliance with law, even if the attempted marriage is or could be declared invalid, and the child is born during the invalid marriage or within 300 days after its termination by death, annulment, declaration of invalidity, or divorce [, or after a decree of separation];

(4) after the birth of the child, he and the mother of the child married each other in apparent compliance with law, whether or not the marriage is or could be declared invalid, and he voluntarily asserted his paternity of the child, and:

(A) the assertion is in a record filed with [state agency maintaining birth records];

(B) he agreed to be and is named as the child's father on the child's birth certificate; or

(C) he promised in a record to support the child as his own; or

(5) for the first two years of the child's life, he resided in the same household with the child and openly held out the child as his own.

(b) A presumption of paternity established under this section may be rebutted only by an adjudication under [Article] 6.

ARTICLE 3 VOLUNTARY ACKNOWLEDGMENT OF PATERNITY

Comment

Voluntary acknowledgment of paternity has long been an alternative to a contested paternity suit. Under UPA (1973) § 4, the inclusion of a man's name on the child's birth certificate created a presumption of paternity, which could be rebutted. In order to improve the collection of child support, especially from unwed fathers, the U.S. Congress mandated a fundamental change in the acknowledgment procedure. The Personal Responsibility and Work Opportunity Reconciliation Act of 1996 (PRWORA, also known as the Welfare Reform Act) conditions receipt of federal child support enforcement funds on state enactment of laws that greatly strengthen the effect of a man's voluntary acknowledgment of paternity, 42 U.S.C. § 666(a)(5)(C). This statute. . . . provides that a valid, unrescinded, unchallenged acknowledgment of paternity is to be treated as equivalent to a judicial determination of paternity.

Because in many respects the federal act is nonspecific, the new UPA contains clear and comprehensive procedures to comply with the federal mandate. Primary among the factual circumstances that Congress did not take into account was that a married woman may consent to an acknowledgement of paternity by a man who may indeed be her child's genetic father, but is not her husband. Under the new UPA, the mother's husband is the presumed father of the child, see § 204, supra. By ignoring the real possibility that the child will have both an acknowledged father and a presumed father, Congress left it to the states to sort out which of the men should be recognized as the legal father.

Further, PRWORA does not require that a man acknowledging paternity must assert genetic paternity of the child. Section 301 is designed to prevent circumvention of adoption laws by requiring a sworn assertion of genetic parentage of the child.

Sections 302-305 clarify that, if a child has a presumed father, that man must file a denial of paternity in conjunction with another man's acknowledgment of paternity in order for the acknowledgement to be valid. If the presumed father is unwilling to cooperate, or his whereabouts are unknown, a court proceeding is necessary to resolve the issue of parentage.

Congress also directed that the acknowledgment can be "rescinded" within a particular time frame, and subsequently can be "challenged" without stating a time frame. Those procedures are dealt with in §§ 307–309.

Finally, the related issue of issuance or revision of birth certificates is left to other state law.

Section 301. Acknowledgment of Paternity.

The mother of a child and a man claiming to be the genetic father of the child may sign an acknowledgment of paternity with intent to establish the man's paternity.

Comment

. . .

PRWORA does not explicitly require that a man acknowledging parentage necessarily is asserting his genetic parentage of the child. In order to prevent circumvention of adoption laws, § 301 corrects this omission by requiring a sworn assertion of genetic parentage of the child. A 2002 amendment provides that a man who signs an acknowledgment of paternity declares that he is the genetic father of the child. Thus both the man and the mother acknowledge his paternity, under penalty of perjury, without requiring the parents to spell out the details of their sexual relations. Further, the amended language also takes into account a situation in which a man, who is unable to have sexual intercourse with his partner, may still have contributed to the conception of the child through the use of his own sperm. Henceforth, a man in that situation will be able to recognize legally his paternity through the voluntary acknowledgment procedure.

Section 302. Execution of Acknowledgment of Paternity.

(a) An acknowledgment of paternity must:

(1) be in a record;

(2) be signed, or otherwise authenticated, under penalty of perjury by the mother and by the man seeking to establish his paternity;

(3) state that the child whose paternity is being acknowledged:

(A) does not have a presumed father, or has a presumed father whose full name is stated; and

(B) does not have another acknowledged or adjudicated father;

(4) state whether there has been genetic testing and, if so, that the acknowledging man's claim of paternity is consistent with the results of the testing; and

(5) state that the signatories understand that the acknowledgment is the equivalent of a judicial adjudication of paternity of the child and that a challenge to the acknowledgment is permitted only under limited circumstances and is barred after two years.

(b) An acknowledgment of paternity is void if it:

(1) states that another man is a presumed father, unless a denial of paternity signed or otherwise authenticated by the presumed father is filed with the [agency maintaining birth records];

(2) states that another man is an acknowledged or adjudicated father; or

(3) falsely denies the existence of a presumed, acknowledged, or adjudicated father of the child.

(c) A presumed father may sign or otherwise authenticate an acknowledgment of paternity.

Comment

[Federal law requires states to establish] specific procedures for voluntary acknowledgment of paternity. This deceptively simple principle proved difficult to implement.

Problems most notably include . . . situations in which the mother is . . . married to someone other than the man who intends to acknowledge his paternity. With an acknowledgment the child would then have both an acknowledged father and a presumed father. To deal with this circumstance, many states have passed laws allowing the presumed father to sign a denial of paternity, which must be filed as part of the acknowledgment. This Act adopts this common sense solution; otherwise the acknowledgment would have no legal consequence because it cannot affect the legal rights of the presumed father.

At least two other provisions of this section warrant special emphasis. Subsection (a)(2) requires that the acknowledgment be "signed, or otherwise authenticated, under penalty of perjury," just as income tax returns and many other government documents require. Clearly, the potential punishment for false swearing is substantial, and the benefits from avoiding the complication of requiring witnesses and a notary are significant in this context. Mandating greater formality would greatly discourage the in-hospital signatures so earnestly desired in 42 U.S.C. § 666(a)(5)(C)(ii), see Appendix: Federal IV-D Statute Relating to Parentage, *infra*.

Similarly, in an attempt to ensure full disclosure and avoid false swearing, subsection (a)(4) requires that the results of genetic testing, if any, be reported along with confirmation that the acknowledgment is consistent with the results of that testing. This provision is also designed to avoid a possible subversion of the requirements for an adoption. A would-be "father" whose parentage of a child has been excluded by genetic testing may not validly sign an acknowledgment once that fact has been established.

Section 307. Proceeding for Rescission.

A signatory may rescind an acknowledgment of paternity or denial of paternity by commencing a proceeding to rescind before the earlier of:

(1) 60 days after the effective date of the acknowledgment or denial, as provided in Section 304; or

(2) the date of the first hearing, in a proceeding to which the signatory is a party, before a court to adjudicate an issue relating to the child, including a proceeding that establishes support.

Section 308. Challenge after Expiration of Period for Rescission.

(a) After the period for rescission under Section 307 has expired, a signatory of an acknowledgment of paternity or denial of paternity may commence a proceeding to challenge the acknowledgment or denial only:

(1) on the basis of fraud, duress, or material mistake of fact; and

(2) within two years after the acknowledgment or denial is filed with the [agency maintaining birth records].

(b) A party challenging an acknowledgment of paternity or denial of paternity has the burden of proof.

Comment

The federal statute also includes a provision for a "challenge" of an acknowledgment of paternity after the period for rescission of a voluntary acknowledgment of paternity has elapsed. Such a collateral attack is to be limited to a challenge based on alleged "fraud, duress, or material mistake of fact," and according to 42 U.S.C. § 666(a)(5)(c)(D)(iii), must be made "in court". . . .

ARTICLE 5: GENETIC TESTING

Section 505. Genetic Testing Results; Rebuttal.

(a) Under this [Act], a man is rebuttably identified as the father of a child if the genetic testing complies with this [article] and the results disclose that:

(1) the man has at least a 99 percent probability of paternity, using a prior probability of 0.50, as calculated by using the combined paternity index obtained in the testing; and

(2) a combined paternity index of at least 100 to 1.

(b) A man identified under subsection (a) as the father of the child may rebut the genetic testing results only by other genetic testing satisfying the requirements of this [article] which:

(1) excludes the man as a genetic father of the child; or

(2) identifies another man as the possible father of the child.

(c) Except as otherwise provided in Section 510, if more than one man is identified by genetic testing as the possible father of the child, the court shall order them to submit to further genetic testing to identify the genetic father.

ARTICLE SIX: PROCEEDINGS TO ADJUDICATE PARENTAGE

Section 602. Standing to Maintain Proceeding.

Subject to [Article] 3 and Sections 607 and 609, a proceeding to adjudicate parentage may be maintained by:

(1) the child;

(2) the mother of the child;

(3) a man whose paternity of the child is to be adjudicated;

(4) the support-enforcement agency [or other governmental agency authorized by other law];

(5) an authorized adoption agency or licensed child-placing agency; [or]

(6) a representative authorized by law to act for an individual who would otherwise be entitled to maintain a proceeding but who is deceased, incapacitated, or a minor [; or

(7) an intended parent under [Article] 8].

Section 606. No Limitation: Child Having No Presumed, Acknowledged, or Adjudicated Father.

A proceeding to adjudicate the parentage of a child having no presumed, acknowledged, or adjudicated father may be commenced at any time, even after:

(1) the child becomes an adult, but only if the child initiates the proceeding; or

(2) an earlier proceeding to adjudicate paternity has been dismissed based on the application of a statute of limitation then in effect.

Comment

[Federal law requires states] to "permit the establishment of the paternity of a child at any time before the child attains 18 years of age." States have chosen a wide range of age options: age 18 (20 states), age 19 (6 states), age 20 (2 states), age 21 (10 states), age 22 (2 states), age 23 (2 states), and no limitation (9 states). Several states limit the establishment of parental rights to a shorter period. [¶] The new UPA directs that an individual whose parentage has not been determined has a civil right to determine his or her own parentage, which should not be subject to limitation except when an estate has been closed. . . .

Section 607. Limitation: Child Having Presumed Father.

(a) Except as otherwise provided in subsection (b), a proceeding brought by a presumed father, the mother, or another individual to adjudicate the parentage of a child having a presumed father must be commenced not later than two years after the birth of the child.

(b) A proceeding seeking to disprove the father-child relationship between a child and the child's presumed father may be maintained at any time if the court determines that:

   (1) the presumed father and the mother of the child neither cohabited nor engaged in sexual intercourse with each other during the probable time of conception; and

   (2) the presumed father never openly held out the child as his own.

Section 608. Authority to Deny Motion for Genetic Testing.

(a) In a proceeding to adjudicate the parentage of a child having a presumed father or to challenge the paternity of a child having an acknowledged father, the court may deny a motion seeking an order for genetic testing of the mother, the child, and the presumed or acknowledged father if the court determines that:

   (1) the conduct of the mother or the presumed or acknowledged father estops that party from denying parentage; and

   (2) it would be inequitable to disprove the father-child relationship between the child and the presumed or acknowledged father.

(b) In determining whether to deny a motion seeking an order for genetic testing under this section, the court shall consider the best interest of the child, including the following factors:

   (1) the length of time between the proceeding to adjudicate parentage and the time that the presumed or acknowledged father was placed on notice that he might not be the genetic father;

   (2) the length of time during which the presumed or acknowledged father has assumed the role of father of the child;

   (3) the facts surrounding the presumed or acknowledged father's discovery of his possible nonpaternity;

   (4) the nature of the relationship between the child and the presumed or acknowledged father;

   (5) the age of the child;

   (6) the harm that may result to the child if presumed or acknowledged paternity is successfully disproved;

   (7) the nature of the relationship between the child and any alleged father;

   (8) the extent to which the passage of time reduces the chances of establishing the paternity of another man and a child-support obligation in favor of the child; and

   (9) other factors that may affect the equities arising from the disruption of the father-child relationship between the child and the presumed or acknowledged father or the chance of other harm to the child.

(c) In a proceeding involving the application of this section, a minor or incapacitated child must be represented by a guardian ad litem.

(d) Denial of a motion seeking an order for genetic testing must be based on clear and convincing evidence.

(e) If the court denies a motion seeking an order for genetic testing, it shall issue an order adjudicating the presumed or acknowledged father to be the father of the child.

Comment

This section incorporates the doctrine of paternity by estoppel, which extends equally to a child with a presumed father or an acknowledged father. In appropriate circumstances, the court may deny genetic testing and find the presumed or acknowledged father to be the father of the child. The most common situation in which estoppel should be applied arises when a man knows that a child is not, or may not be, his genetic child, but the man has affirmatively accepted his role as child's father and both the mother and the child have relied on that acceptance. Similarly, the man may have relied on the mother's acceptance of him as the child's father and the mother is then estopped to deny the man's presumed parentage. . . .

Section 609. Limitation: Child Having Acknowledged or Adjudicated Father.

(a) If a child has an acknowledged father, a signatory to the acknowledgment of paternity or denial of paternity may commence a proceeding seeking to rescind the acknowledgement or denial or challenge the paternity of the child only within the time allowed under Section 307 or 308.

(b) If a child has an acknowledged father or an adjudicated father, an individual, other than the child, who is neither a signatory to the acknowledgment of paternity nor a party to the adjudication and who seeks an adjudication of paternity of the child must commence a proceeding not later than two years after the effective date of the acknowledgment or adjudication.

(c) A proceeding under this section is subject to the application of the principles of estoppel established in Section 608.

Section 631. Rules for Adjudication of Paternity.

The court shall apply the following rules to adjudicate the paternity of a child:

(1) The paternity of a child having a presumed, acknowledged, or adjudicated father may be disproved only by admissible results of genetic testing excluding that man as the father of the child or identifying another man as the father of the child.

(2) Unless the results of genetic testing are admitted to rebut other results of genetic testing, a man identified as the father of a child under Section 505 must be adjudicated the father of the child.

(3) If the court finds that genetic testing under Section 505 neither identifies nor excludes a man as the father of a child, the court may not dismiss the

proceeding. In that event, the results of genetic testing, and other evidence, are admissible to adjudicate the issue of paternity.

(4) Unless the results of genetic testing are admitted to rebut other results of genetic testing, a man excluded as the father of a child by genetic testing must be adjudicated not to be the father of the child.

NOTES

1. *Comparing the Statutory Rules.* Section 4 of UPA 1973 sets out the classic paternity rules applied in most jurisdictions. Much of the section is devoted to specifying the boundaries of the marital presumption, while subsection (a)(4) states the equivalent of the marital presumption for the man who was not married to the child's mother but is the child's social father. Subsection (b) requires clear and convincing evidence to overcome any of these statutory presumptions, a standard that would often have been difficult to meet prior to the development of modern paternity tests. Under Section (a)(5) acknowledgment can also establish a presumption of paternity, but only if the mother does not object after being informed, and only if no other man is presumed to be the child's father. Section 6 strengthens the marital presumption further by setting clear time limits on any challenges to it; these limits do not apply to any of the nonmarital presumptions.

The need to accommodate modern scientific testing and new federal requirements leads to a more complex set of rules under UPA 2002. Most of the time paternity will be established by a presumption arising under § 204, or an acknowledgment arising under § 301; in their absence it will be established, typically, by genetic evidence under § 505 (as provided under § 631). A key question is the extent to which paternity established by acknowledgment or presumption can be challenged. An acknowledgment under § 301 can be rescinded under § 307, but only within 60 days of the acknowledgment. After that the acknowledgment can only be challenged under § 308, which has more demanding requirements as well as its own time limit of two years. Presumptions may be rebutted only as allowed under § 607 and § 608. As a general matter, challenges to presumed paternity are also barred more than two years after the child's birth; the only exception is the case in which the challenger can persuade the court that the mother and presumed father neither cohabited, nor had sexual relations during the probable time of conception, nor did the presumed father hold himself out as the father. Moreover, challenges to acknowledged as well as presumed paternity must be based on genetic evidence (§ 631), and under § 608 a court may refuse to order genetic testing even where the child is not yet two years old, if it believes that the challenger's conduct estops him from denying the presumed or acknowledged paternity, and that it would be inequitable to allow the challenge. One can thus see that while genetic evidence is very important under the Act, presumptions will still often prevail over any actual or potential genetic evidence to the contrary, either under this estoppel doctrine or because the child is more than 2 years old. The act thus makes clear that even though biological paternity and legal paternity are ordinarily the same, they need not be. In particular, the Act disallows genetic challenges to a child's social paternity — as reflected by the presumption and acknowledgment provisions — if brought too late. The Act establishes that more than two years after the child's birth is always too late, and provides that even earlier challenges may be too late if equity so requires.

The marital presumption initially established by UPA 1973 and strengthened by UPA 2002 thus reflects a public policy that the child's interests in maintaining settled social understandings about the child's parentage are more important then biological paternity. UPA 2002 thus resolves the possible conflict between social paternity and biological paternity, made so salient by modern scientific advances, in favor of social paternity. Where neither the biological father nor any other man is the social father, biological paternity will equal legal paternity. But where there is one social father who is not the biological father, UPA 2002 will usually identify that social father as the legal father. Sometimes, of course, there can be more than one man plausibly identified as the child's social father. These difficult cases are considered further below in connection with our review of *Michael H.* at page 1013.

2. The Traditional Marital Presumption and Its Allied Equitable Rules. The marital presumption codified by both versions of the UPA has long been part of the law. Some states, like California, had their own statutory provisions that effectively anticipated UPA 2002: California law has long barred all challenges to a husband's paternity more than two years after the child's birth, and excluded even timely challenges by anyone other than the husband, the wife, or (in consequence of recent amendments) men who qualify as presumed fathers under § 4 of UPA 1973. We examine third-party challenges of a husband's paternity below, at pages 1013-1035, in connection with the unsuccessful federal constitutional attack in *Michael H.* on California's exclusion of them. In this note we review how the rule operates to deny claims by the spouses themselves. Such challenges typically arise when either the husband challenges his paternity to avoid liability to support his wife's child, or the wife challenges his paternity in order to defeat his claims for custody of or visitation with the child.

Most states have had marital presumptions that are not as strong as California's or UPA 2002. The typical statutory law allows its rebuttal, and does not even impose the absolute five-year time limit on challenges contained in § 6(a)(2) of UPA 1973, much less a two-year limit. This is not to say that the presumption was, historically, easily overcome. It could be protected by high evidentiary standards, once nearly impossible to meet. Consider, for example, the traditional Massachusetts formulation: "The 'presumption of legitimacy may not be rebutted, even in a civil case, except on facts which prove, beyond all reasonable doubt, that the husband could not have been the father.' [citing 1861 case] . . . [A] child conceived by a married woman is presumed to be the child of the man to whom the mother was then married even if the mother and the husband are divorced at the time of the child's birth. This holding fosters the important social policy of affording legitimacy to children whenever possible." *P.B.C. v. D.H.,* 482 N.E.2d 1094 (Mass. 1985). Moreover, the usual marital presumption was often buttressed by judicially created equitable doctrines that pre-existed the availability of genetic evidence, and which in light of scientific advances are now even more important. For example, in the pre-genetic-test case of *Watts v. Watts,* 337 A.2d 350 (N.H. 1975), the wife sought a divorce after 21 years of marriage. Four children were born during the marriage, but the husband sought to show the two youngest were not his. The court denied his request for blood tests, even though the usual rule allowed their use to rebut the marital presumption, because "those rules do not apply in a situation such as this one where the defendant has acknowledged the children as his own without challenge for over fifteen years. To allow defendant to escape liability for support by using blood tests would be to ignore his lengthy, voluntary acceptance of parental responsibilities."

Note that *Watts* does not override blood test evidence; it rather denies a motion to obtain it. A possible difficulty with this approach is the implication that *if* scientific evidence of biological nonpaternity were available, the court would be obliged to follow it. By contrast, many other courts historically applied equitable rules that barred the claim itself, not just the gathering of evidence to support it. Some involved efforts by married mothers to defeat custody or visitation claims at divorce by husbands who had acted as the child's father during marriage. *E.g.*, *Atkinson v. Atkinson*, 408 N.W.2d 516, (Mich. App. 1987) (where husband had always treated the child as his during the marriage, was the only father the child had known, and now sought both the responsibilities and rights of fatherhood, he is treated as the child's "equitable parent" even though he is not the biological parent); *Pettinato v. Pettinato*, 582 A.2d 909 (R.I. 1990) (couple married 11 months after child's birth; mother who told husband he was father is estopped from challenging his paternity on divorce, six months later, in order to defeat his custody claim); *Seger v. Seger*, 547 A.2d 424 (Pa. Super. 1988) (husband could not be denied visitation for lack of biological parenthood where he had assumed parental duties during the marriage). There were similar results in cases involving married fathers who sought to deny support obligations for their wife's child. *E.g.*, *Johns v. Johns*, 443 N.W.2d 446 (Mich. App. 1989) ("Where, as in this case, a father rears a child as his own, he is estopped to deny the child is his"), and, more recently, *Miscovich v. Miscovich*, 688 A.2d 726 (Pa. App. 1997), *aff'd by an equally divided court*, 720 A.2d 764 (Pa. 1998) (husband could not disclaim legal paternity, despite DNA tests excluding biological fatherhood, in face of father-child relationship that had existed from the time of the child's birth); *W. v. W.*, 779 A.2d 716 (Conn. 2001), husband estopped from denying his paternity of wife's child he had treated as his for 12 years, even after he located purported biological father, from whom support might instead be sought; court relies in part on husband's discouraging wife from seeking support from the biological father at the time of birth or otherwise involving him in the child's life) *C.C.A. v. J.M.A.*, 744 So. 2d 515 (Fla. App. 1999) (husband estopped from disavowing at divorce a child of his wife's by a man she had intentionally chosen as a "surrogate" biological father, in light of the husband's vasectomy and his earlier agreement to such an arrangement with a different man; husband had treated the child as his long enough to support esopptel, "court declin[ing] to draw a bright line concerning" the required length of time but holding two years sufficient).

While these estoppel doctrines may serve an important purpose, they are ultimately less satisfactory than a rule like California's, or UPA 2002, in serving the child's interests.

The estoppel doctrine, unlike a simple two-year rule, necessarily requires a case-by-case examination of the facts, with far more variable results. Some courts apply the doctrine flexibly to bar either spouse from denying the husband's paternity whenever they have both treated the children as the husband's over a significant time period, if the disavowal has the potential for causing the children harm. But other courts adhere to the doctrine's technical requirements and therefore focus on facts that are irrelevant to the child's interests, such as whether the husband knew he was not the children's biological father when he treated them as his own. A narrow technical analysis leads other courts to reject a claim that the husband is estopped from denying his paternity, no matter how long he treated the children as his, unless he is directly responsible for the biological father's unavailability as a source of support. For example, these courts treat the mother's husband as the children's father if she sought severance of the biological father's parental status in reliance upon her husband's promise to support them, but will allow the husband to deny paternity, despite having treated the children as his throughout their life, if the biological father is unavailable because he is dead or cannot be found. Overall, then, the estoppel doctrine is poorly equipped as a general approach to these cases, although it can serve as a useful stopgap when better statutory provisions are not available.

Ira Mark Ellman, *Thinking About Custody and Support in Ambiguous-Father Families*, 36 FAM. L.Q. 49, 61-62 (2002).

We do not yet know whether UPA 2002 will be successful in moving the statutory law of most states toward the social paternity model. There certainly are good and weighty reasons in support of its approach, reflected in much (but not all) of this traditional estoppel caselaw.

3. Res Judicata Effect of Divorce Decree. Where a child support order is entered as part of a marital dissolution, ordinary res judicata principles would bar the former husband (as well as the former wife) from subsequently contesting his paternity of the marital children, even if the marital presumption did not. As the rules governing modification of custody decrees illustrate (see Chapter 6), courts sometimes relax ordinary res judicata principles to permit reconsideration of prior orders where the child's interests appear to require it. Nonetheless, reconsideration of divorce decree provisions premised on the husband's paternity is not ordinarily possible, even in states that do not impose normal res judicata principles. "Whatever the interests of the presumed father in ascertaining the genetic 'truth' of a child's origins, they remain subsidiary to the interests of the state, the family, and the child in maintaining the continuity, financial support, and psychological security of an established parent-child relationship. Therefore, absent a clear and convincing showing that it would serve the best interests of the child, a prior adjudication of paternity is conclusive." *Godin v. Godin*, 725 A.2d 904, 910 (Vt. 1998). The *Godin* father had sought to set aside the support order for the girl he raised as his daughter for eight years during his marriage and six more years after his divorce.

See also Marriage/Children of Betty L.W. v. William E.W., 569 S.E.2d 77 (W.Va. 2002) (former husband barred); *In the Interest of T.S.S.*, 61 S.W.3d

481 (Tex. App. 2001) (same); *Anderson v. Anderson,* 552 N.E.2d 546 (Mass. 1990) (same); *Gilbraith v. Hixon,* 512 N.E.2d 956 (Ohio 1987) (former husband barred; fact that divorce decree resulted from separation agreement irrelevant); *Sanders v. Sanders,* 558 A.2d 556 (Pa. Super. 1989) (former wife barred from seeking to establish another man's paternity in order to obtain support from him); *Van Nostrand v. Olivieri,* 427 So. 2d 374 (Fla. App. 1983) (former wife barred); *Mancini v. Mancini,* 440 N.E.2d 1232 (Ohio App. 1982) (former wife barred). Because prior judgments do not bind persons who were not parties to them, the divorce decree cannot bind the child, *Simcox v. Simcox,* 546 N.E.2d 609 (Ill. 1989) (child not represented in divorce action); *Gipson v. Enright,* 753 S.W.2d 122 (Mo. App. 1988) (same, allowing child to seek to establish paternity and thereby her right of inheritance).

There has been little retreat from this general rule despite the recent passage in some states of statutes permitting or requiring courts to reconsider paternity in the face of genetic test results contrary to the initial disposition. States apply these statutes directly to adjudicated *nonmarital* fathers but not usually to marital fathers' who seek to revisit their paternity as adjudicated in the divorce decrees. *See, e.g., Office of Child Support Enforcement v. Williams,* 995 S.W.2d 338 (1999) (holding that ARK. CODE ANN. § 9-10-115 does not limit the res judicata effect of paternity as adjudicated by a divorce decree); *Gann v. Gann,* 705 So. 2d 509 (ALA. CT. APP.1997) (same, interpreting ALA. CODE § 26-17A-1(a)).

4. *The "Nonmarital Presumption."* An important change in UPA 2002, as compared with the short-lived UPA 2000, is the later act's preservation of what might be called a "nonmarital presumption" — a presumption of paternity arising from a *de facto* family relationship that establishes a presumed father of a child born to an unmarried mother. That presumption, arising under UPA 2002 § 204(a)(5), is the successor to § 4(a)(4) of UPA 1973. The new provision applies only to the nonmarital father who lived with the child during the first two years of the child's life, while under the 1973 provision presumed paternity could be established later as well. On the other hand, the 2002 version, like all the presumptions arising under that law, has much greater force, because it can only be challenged within two years of the child's birth. Here again, this statutory reform may be necessary to protect the interests of nonmarital children, given especially that many courts will not apply the estoppel doctrine in connection with them. Consider, for example, *Van v. Zahorik,* 597 N.W.2d 15, 23 (Mich. 1999).

> The mother cohabited with Van for five years, and continued to see him after that. She led him to believe he was the father of the two children born to her during their relationship, and Van treated them as his children. When the children were 7 and 3 the couple's relationship ended. The mother now denied Van all access to them. When he sought legal relief she alleged, for the first time, that he was not their biological father. Tests confirmed her claim. The court refused to apply estoppel to protect Van because he was not married to the mother. The court conceded that the case presented "tragic circumstances":
>
> > [T]he children were suddenly separated from Mr. Van, the only father they had known; Mr. Van lost contact with the children whom

he helped raise and support; and Ms. Zahorik only belatedly introduced the biological fathers into the picture. However, the current
state of child custody law simply provides no means for Mr. Van, who
is not related to the children . . . either biologically or by marriage,
to pursue parental rights under. . .equitable estoppel. In short, he has
no legal right to continue a relationship with the children.

See also Price v. Howard, 484 S.E.2d 528 (N.C. 1997) (although man lived
together with child's mother from the time of her birth, held himself out as
the father, and was her primary caretaker at the time of the action, and
mother had represented to the man and to others that he was the child's
father, and the child believed that he was her father, parental rights doctrine
requires award of sole custody to child's biological mother, absent a finding
of her unfitness or that she engaged in conduct "inconsistent with the
constitutionally protected status of a natural parent") and *Petition of Bruce*,
522 N.W.2d 67 (Iowa 1994) (similar). Is the *Price* court correct in believing
that the mother's constitutionally protected parental rights bar the recognition
of her partner, the child's social father, as the child's legal father? The
difficulty with the court's position is that it assumes an answer to the question
being put — it assumes that the child's social father is *not* the child's legal
father. If that assumption is correct, than cases like *Troxel v. Granville*, 530
U.S. 57 (2000), reprinted *supra* in Chapter 6, indeed suggest that constitutional principles would limit a court's authority to require the mother to share
her custodial rights with this "legal stranger" to the child. But of course the
real question in this case is *whether* this man is a legal stranger to the child.
Constitutional principles do *not* enshrine biological paternity as the ultimate
or dispositive criterion of legal paternity, as will become more clear in the next
section of this chapter. For a persuasive discussion of the importance of
distinguishing constitutional rules protecting parental rights from rules for
identifying the parents, see Emily Buss, *Parental Rights*, 88 Va. L. Rev. 635
(2002).

PROBLEMS

Problem 9-12. Betty, unmarried, gives birth to daughter Joy. Just after
the birth she is visited in the hospital by her boyfriend Ben. During the visit
a hospital social worker approaches them and asks for both their signatures
on a form stating that Ben is Joy's father. They sign. The form states the
parties' belief that Ben is Joy's father, and asserts that no other man is her
presumed father or has acknowledged her paternity. Betty and Ben have in
fact never lived together, although they have known one another for several
years and have often been physically intimate during that time. They try
living together after Betty leaves the hospital, but it does not go well and by
the time Joy is 6 months old they are no longer seeing one another. When
Betty seeks public assistance, the social welfare agency files a claim against
Ben for child support. You are a legal services attorney advising Ben. He tells
you that one of the reasons he broke up with Betty was her continuing
relationship with Alan, an old boyfriend. At the time he signed the acknowledgment he thought it was possible that Alan was really Joy's father, but he
had believed Betty when she told him that she had hardly seen Alan for over

a year and wanted nothing to do with him anymore. Friends now tell him that Betty had been lying to him, and that she has told others she thought Alan was Joy's father. In fact, Ben just learned that Alan has moved in with Betty and Joy. Ben is angry with Betty, has no interest in Joy who he now thinks is not his daughter anyway, and certainly does not want to pay support to Betty while she is living with Alan. What defenses can be raised on Ben's behalf under UPA 2002? Under the law of your state, if it is different?

Problem 9-13. Assume the facts are the same as in Problem 9-12, except that Ben also tells you he has learned that Alan has just married Betty. Does this matter?

Problem 9-14. Assume the facts of Problem 9-12 except that Ben and Betty have an off and on relationship until they finally end their relationship permanently when Joy is two and a half years old, and shortly after that the welfare agency seeks support from Ben. Alan moves in with Betty when Joy is three.

Problem 9-15. Arzina and David are married with seven children. The sixth is Trudy. When Trudy is 15, her mother tells her that her real father is not David, but Cornelius. Thereafter, Trudy visits Cornelius often, and he acknowledges her as his daughter in front of others. Trudy remains part of the Arzina-David household, however. When Trudy is 27, Cornelius dies with no marital children. Cornelius is survived by two sisters, who nominate an executor for his estate. Trudy opposes their nomination and seeks appointment herself, as Cornelius' daughter. Her offer of proof includes not only the testimony of Arzina, but also genetic evidence that she cannot be David's daughter. David has never been told of Arzina's claim, nor of this proceeding brought by Trudy. Should Trudy be permitted to prove she is not David's daughter, but Cornelius'? Would she be allowed to under UPA 2002?

Problem 9-16. Edward asked Robin to marry him. Robin told him that she was then pregnant by another man. Edward assured her that it was all right: "We will have this child and he will have a father and a name." He promised her that he would not deny the child was his, and they were married in June. In September the child was born. The couple named him Edward Jr., and Edward was named as the father on the birth certificate. He acted as the child's father for the early part of their marriage, but before the marriage was two years old, it fell apart. In the divorce action which followed, Edward denied that the child was his and sought to be relieved of any obligation of support. What result under UPA 2002? Suppose the marriage had broken up two months after the child was born? A month before?

NOTE

Enforcing Paternal Support Obligations for Nonmarital Children: Some Special Considerations

The purpose of the traditional paternity action is to establish the defendant as the child's father so as to secure his support obligation. While Chapter 5's treatment of child support generally applies to both marital and nonmarital children, the establishment and collection of support for nonmarital children does raise additional problems. We survey them in this note. Collecting support from nonmarital fathers is an increasingly important social issue because nonmarital children account for an increasing share of the children on whose behalf support orders are issued. Never-married mothers (as compared to divorced or separated mothers) grew from 17% of all single mothers in 1976, to 46% in 1997. Elaine Sorenson and Ariel Halpern, *Child Support Enforcement Is Working Better Than We Think*, Urban Institute Report A-31, March, 1999, <newfederalism.urban.org/html/anf_31.html>.

> **a. Establishing paternity and collecting support.** Child support collections have always been much lower for nonmarital children than for children whose parents divorce. Historically, the obvious difficulty in proving paternity provided the most obvious explanation. Today, however, that explanation will not do. Yet it remains the case that the most important reason fathers of nonmarital children do not pay support is that there is no support order. While child support orders are routinely made in divorce cases involving minor children, for nonmarital children the support obligation must be enforced on its own.

> The Census Bureau tells us that 6.6 million custodial parents in 1997 had no formal, legal agreement for support payments. When asked why, 32% said they "did not feel need to make legal" (as characterized by the Bureau's truncated descriptions of the parents' responses.) Perhaps the father was contributing informally to the child's support in amounts the mother believed appropriate. . . . Another group said the other parent "provides what they can" (23%) or "could not afford to pay" (25%), and in fact researchers have estimated that thirty percent of the nonpaying fathers of nonmarital children are "poor" or "near-poor." Irwin Garfinkel, Sara Mc-Clanahan and Thomas Hanson, *A Patchwork Portrait of Nonresident Fathers,* in Irwin Garfinkel, Sara McLanahan, Daniel Meyer, and Judith Seltzer, eds. FATHERS UNDER FIRE: THE REVOLUTION IN CHILD SUPPORT ENFORCEMENT 31, 51 (1998). . . .[¶] Of greatest relevance, however, are the 19% who responded that they "did not want other parent to pay," and the 16% who said they "did not want to have contact with other parent." One imagines that this too is a diverse group. It must include some women who do not want contact with the father because they are afraid of him, including some who have been threatened explicitly with retaliation if a support order is sought. But it must also include others who simply prefer to live their lives free of the father's presence, and believe that they can get by well-enough without his financial assistance. Mothers receiving welfare benefits may be denied this choice by the relevant public agency, which will require their cooperation in locating the father unless persuaded the mother has "good cause" to refuse. But those not receiving welfare benefits will have more freedom of choice. They may be employed, have assistance from family members, or have established a relationship with another man who provides support.

Ellman, *Ambiguous-Father Families*, *supra*, at pages 69-70.

An important part of the most recent child support enforcement reforms have aimed directly at increasing the proportion of nonmarital children for whom a support order has been made. The proportion of never-married mothers reporting receipt of any child support payments increased from four percent in 1976 to 18 percent in 1997 — much greater than the gains reported by divorced mothers. Sorenson and Halpern, *Child Support Enforcement Is Working Better Than We Think, supra.* The 1996 federal welfare reform Act (PRWORA, for Personal Responsibility and Work Opportunity Reconciliation Act) is focused especially on this group. It requires states, with narrow exceptions, to treat an acknowledgment of paternity signed by the mother and putative father as establishing legal paternity — as UPA 2002 does. Massachusetts pioneered this technique before 1996, obtaining such acknowledgments, before the mother and child left the hospital, in an astonishing 70 % of all nonmarital births. Marilyn Rae Smith, *Child Support Reform in Action: New Strategies and New Frontiers in Massachusetts*, in MARRIAGE IN AMERICA: A COMMUNITARIAN PERSPECTIVE 269, 275 (Martin Whyte, editor 2000). Its success has apparently now been replicated elsewhere under the press of the new federal law. (Paul Legler, President Clinton's Assistant Commissioner in the Office of Child Support Enforcement, reported "astounding success" in the initial results from the new federal laws. Paul Legler, *The Impact of Welfare Reform on the Child Support Enforcement System*, in CHILD SUPPORT: THE NEXT FRONTIER, 46, 48 (Thomas Oldham and Marygold Melli, eds., 2000). But this program is of course dependent upon the father's knowledge that resistance is futile because genetic tests are available to establish paternity if needed. The 1996 welfare reform act requires states, with narrow exceptions, to authorize their child support enforcement agency to compel tests administratively if the agency receives a sworn statement of facts establishing "a reasonable possibility" of the requisite sexual contact. 42 U.S.C. § 666(a)(1)(B). While earlier reforms substantially improved the collection of child support for nonmarital children, the 1996 reforms promise much greater success.

Putative fathers may not appreciate the potentially dispositive and irreversible impact of a paternity acknowledgment, and most are probably unlikely to have legal counsel to caution them. Perhaps some will seek counsel once support enforcement has begun. As previously observed, under UPA 2002 § 308 they may usually rescind the acknowledgment if they act within 60 days, but after that the acknowledgment can only be challenged under § 307, which has more demanding requirements as well as its own time limit of two years.

b. The amount of support. Can a state apply different rules for calculating the amount of support owed by a noncustodial parent who was never married to the custodial parent, from the rules it applies to divorced parents? The answer is not entirely clear. In *Gomez v. Perez*, 409 U.S. 535 (1973), the Court held that Texas violated the Equal Protection Clause by denying nonmarital children any claim for paternal support, given that it recognized such claims on behalf of marital children. It would obviously be a further step to conclude that no distinction may be drawn in the *amount* of support for each. Nonetheless, the Court's evident concern about discriminatory treatment in the support law governing nonmarital children, not only in *Gomez* but also in other cases that are described in the next note on statutes of limitation for paternity claims, has led most state courts to be skeptical of any such distinctions. For example, a Massachusetts appellate court held that a nonmarital child between 18 and 21 years of age was entitled to support while living at home and dependent upon a parent, because a marital child would be entitled to such support under state law. *Doe v. Roe*, 504 N.E.2d 659 (Mass. App. 1987). The court held that differential treatment of the nonmarital child would violate the Equal Protection Clause.

The most important contrary authority arose in New York. In *Kathy G.J. v. Arnold D.*, 501 N.Y.S.2d 58 (App. Div. 1986), the court considered a support claim against a "world-famous entertainer" who had fathered a non-marital child with a woman on welfare. New York (like many states) at that time had separate statutes governing child support for marital and nonmarital children, but the court found the only "potentially significant difference" between them was the former's reference to the "marital standard of living" as a relevant factor in fixing the support level. "The reason for this distinction is an important, valid and constitutional one. Using the marital standard of living as a guidepost in determining a marital child's support decreases the possibility that such a child will have to face the additional trauma of adjusting to a new standard of living, while adjusting to all of the other changes engendered by the breakup of a marriage." The court agreed that if a nonmarital child had lived with his parents and established a "nonmarital family," their standard of living would be relevant in setting support.

This New York court thus found that a permissible line could be drawn that placed both marital and "nonmarital" families in one group, while placing in the other nonmarital children who had never lived with both parents in a family setting. In focusing on the de facto rather than the de jure family status of the unit, the court takes an approach that is quite similar to that adopted by the U.S. Supreme Court in determining which nonmarital fathers have their relationship with their children protected by the constitution. See pages [notes discussing *Quilloin*], *infra*. *Kathy G.J.* may also reflect the fact that a generous child support award unavoidably confers benefit on all members of the custodial household, including the custodial parent to whom no legal duty may be owed by the *nonmarital* noncustodial parent. *See Edgar v. Johnson*, 731 P.2d 131 (Ariz. App. 1986), which suggests this argument.

Whatever the merits of the arguments capsuled in *Kathy G.J.* or *Edgar*, the continuing validity of either case is in doubt. As the determination of child support obligations moved from a rule of judicial discretion to the application of guidelines, courts have increasingly concluded that no distinction ought to be made between marital and nonmarital children in the application of those guidelines. Whether or not the result is constitutionally compelled, courts typically find it is required under their state law establishing child support guidelines. *Ortiz v. Rappeport*, 820 P.2d 313, 314 (Ariz. App. 1991) ("The [child support] guidelines apply to all children whether they are born in or out of wedlock [and] . . . supersede any statements made in *Edgar*"); *Jones v. Reese*, 642 N.Y.S.2d 378 (App. Div. 1996) (rejecting *Kathy G.J.* on the basis that the child support guidelines are equally applicable to children born out of wedlock). *See also Shuba v. Reese*, 564 A.2d 1084 (Del. 1989) (rejecting nonmarital father's claim that Melson Formula's Standard of Living Adjustment should not be applied because parents had never cohabited). New York may nonetheless continue to follow *Kathy G.J.* in making child support determinations not governed by the guidelines. *Merithew v. Tuper*, 601 N.Y.S.2d 671 (Fam. Ct., 1993) (relies on *Kathy G.J.* in rejecting argument that nonmarital child cannot be denied an order directing father to name child as life insurance beneficiary, where such an order might be issued for marital child); *Orna S. v. Leonard G.*, 599 N.Y.S.2d 285 (App. Div., 1993) (similar).

c. Time limits on bringing a support action. Are there time limits within which a paternity action against a putative father must be brought? At one time many states had such limitations but they have been overriden by constitutional and statutory developments. First, *Gomez v. Perez,* 409 U.S. 535 (1979), held that Texas violated the Equal Protection Clause when it allowed marital but not nonmarital children to enforce a right to support. Then, *Mills v. Habluetzel,* 456 U.S. 91 (1982), and *Pickett v. Brown,* 462 U.S. 1 (1983), held respectively that both one-and four-year periods were too short to meet the state's constitutional obligation to allow "a reasonable opportunity" for a claim to be brought on the child's behalf. Finally, Justice O'Connor, writing for a unanimous Court, found unconstitutional a Pennsylvania rule barring most suits to establish the paternity of a nonmarital child brought more than six years after the child's birth. The Court relied on Equal Protection grounds, as the state allowed later actions on behalf of the children in certain situations, and allowed fathers to bring suits to establish their paternity without any statute of limitation. *Clark v. Jeter,* 486 U.S. 456 (1988).

Taken together, these opinions suggest that the Constitution requires allowing a paternity action to be brought at any time during child's minority. The constitutional question seems unlikely to present itself again, however, because after *Pickett,* Congress enacted the Child Support Enforcement Amendments of 1984, which effectively eliminate all statutes of limitation in paternity actions by requiring every state "to have procedures which permit the establishment of the paternity of any child at any time prior to such child's eighteenth birthday." 42 U.S.C.A. § 666(a)(5). The Family Support Act of 1988 further strengthened this provision by extending it to children whose earlier paternity action was dismissed because of a statute of limitations then in effect of less than 18 years. Using a carrot and stick, the Act also requires states to meet higher standards as to the percentage of out-of-wedlock children for whom paternity has been established (capping out at 50 percent). The Act also encourages states to set up a simple civil process for voluntary acknowledgment of paternity.

Long statutes of limitation are not without their complications, however. Especially troubling may be their interaction with the laws of some states that permit claims for support arrearages retroactive to the child's birth. Consider, for example, *Brad Mitchell v. Lee D.*, 564 N.W.2d 354 (Wisc.App. 1997). Brad was born to Catherine in 1977; she was unmarried and never sought to establish Brad's paternity. She changed her mind in 1992. Brad was now fifteen, and she became concerned about paying for his college education. She wrote Lee, asking for help. When he didn't reply she sought help from the county child support enforcement office, which obtained blood tests confirming Lee's paternity. All agreed that Lee never knew of Brad's existence before receiving Catherine's 1992 letter. But Lee, the court explained, was always liable for Brad's support; he just didn't know that he was. He was therefore ordered to pay retroactive support — arrearages — for the past fifteen years, as well as current support during the next three. During his fifteen years of ignorance, Lee had married, fathered two children, and ran a farm and logging business with his wife. Perhaps he had been setting aside college money for the two marital children he knew about; perhaps he would have made some life decisions differently during the past fifteen years if he had known he was responsible for a third child. But while expressing some sympathy for these concerns, the court concluded that Brad was nonetheless entitled to the money, for "the child cannot be held responsible . . . simply because the father was not aware of his child's birth."

The UPA does not itself speak to child support issues such as the collection of arrearages. Consider, however, that UPA 2002 § 606 allows the *adult* child to bring a parentage action. Why would someone do that? The reason could be entirely nonfinancial, such as the desire to establish family lineage for emotional, social, or symbolic reasons. (Recall, for example, news accounts during 2003 concerning the belated public recognition of then-deceased Senator Strom Thurmond's nonmarital bi-racial daughter, by that time a middle-aged woman.) There could possibly be a claim in probate. But there could also be a claim for support arrearages akin to *Brad*. *Tedford v. Gregory*, 959 P.2d 540 (N.M.App. 1998), provides a perhaps bizarre example. After their 1975 divorce, Tedford paid Nina support for all four children born during their marriage, including Jeanne, the youngest, who was 14 months when the marriage ended. When Jeanne was 16, Nina told her that Gregory, not Tedford, was her biological father, a fact that neither Jeanne nor Tedford had known. When she was 20, Jeanne sought child support arrearages from Gregory. After genetic tests confirmed his biological paternity, he was ordered to pay 18 years' support. Left unresolved was whether Tedford could claim reimbursement from Jeanne for funds collected from Gregory.

Cases like *Tedford* and *Brad* are not unique; see Annotation, *Liability of Father for Retroactive Child Support on Judicial Determination of Paternity*, 87 A.L.R.5th 361 (2001). There are good arguments that the collection of arrearages in such circumstances is unlikely to serve any of the policy purposes that normally explain enforcement of the support obligation. See the discussion of these cases in Ira Mark Ellman, *Should Visitation Denial Affect the Obligation to Pay Support?*, in THE LAW AND ECONOMICS OF CHILD SUPPORT PAYMENTS (WILLIAM COMANOR, ed. 2004), reprinted in 36 ARIZ. ST. L.J. 661 (2004). In fact, many states limit or disallow claims for arrearages arising before establishment of paternity. Ohio bars courts from ordering pre-decree arrearages when paternity is first established after the child's third birthday and the father "had no knowledge and had no reason to have knowledge of his alleged paternity of the child" before that initial paternity filing. OHIO REV. CODE ANN. § 3111.13(F)(3)(a)(ii) (West Supp. 2003). Maine limits arrearages to no more than six years prior to the decree, *Department of Human Services v. Bell*, 711 A.2d 1292 (Me. 1998) (applying statute). California bars pre-decree arrearages in their entirety in nearly all paternity cases. CAL. FAM. CODE § 4009 (West 1994 & Supp. 2004). *See Marriage of Goosmann*, 31 Cal. Rptr. 2d 613, 616 (Cal. App. 1994).

d. Res Judicata Effect of Paternity Adjudications. When factual disputes over actual paternity were common, before the availability of modern scientific evidence, paternity actions might be settled for a lump sum amount. The mother might agree to compromise the potential dollar amount of the father's support obligation, in exchange for his concession of his liability. Does that judgment bind the child in a later action? In *Gerhardt v. Estate of Moore,* 441 N.W.2d 734 (Wisc. 1989) the mother had settled her paternity claim for a lump sum of $3,600 in 1971, a year after the child was born. In 1984, the child brought an action against her father's estate for past and present support. The Wisconsin Supreme Court held that since such lump sum settlements of child support claims are not allowed to bar future support actions for marital children, no such bar could apply to nonmarital children under the Equal Protection Clause. The child was therefore free to bring an action. For a similar result see *Dones v. Thomas,* 534 N.W.2d 221 (Mich. App. 1995); *Willerton v. Basham,* 889 P.2d 823 (Nev. 1995); and *Caruthers v. Caruthers,* 37 Cal. Rptr. 2d 23 (App. 1995). Yet notice that while these cases allow reopening of the amount of support — the child can seek more than the lump sum the mother originally settled for — the fact of paternity cannot be reconsidered in light of the modern scientific evidence. The *Gerhardt* dissenters complained that it "is patently unfair and a violation of contract law principles to reopen, nineteen years later, one part of the bargain, the amount of child support, without reopening the other, the admission of paternity itself. But this is what the majority has done." *See Robert J. v. Leslie M.,* 59 Cal. Rptr. 2d 905 (App. 1997) (res judicata bars man who stipulated to judgment that he was the child's father from later challenging that judgment with blood test evidence excluding him); *Tandra S. v. Tyrone W.,* 648 A.2d 439 (Md. 1994) (similar, but reviewing authorities that allow reopening the judgment in such cases). The Michigan Supreme Court declined to follow *Gerhardt* in *Crego v. Coleman,* 615 N.W.2d 218 (Mich. 2000), sustaining the constitutionality of nonmodifiable support agreements.

Some state legislatures have responded to the application of *res judicata* principles in such cases with statutes expressly permitting the reopening of paternity adjudications. After the decision in *Tandra S, supra,* the legislature amended Maryland Code § 5-1038(a)(2)(i)2 to permit adjudicated fathers to present genetic evidence excluding their paternity, and in *Langston v. Riffe,* 754 A.2d 389 (Md. App. 2000), the court decided that the revisions statute should be applied retroactively, in light of the legislature's intent to "remedy the effect *Tandra S.* had on paternity decisions." 754 A.2d at 394. For similar statutory amendments, see ALA. CODE § 26-17A-1(a) (mandating reconsideration); ARK. CODE ANN. § 9-10-115 (2003) (same). Note that these provisions conflict with UPA 2002. Consider whether courts could still apply estoppel doctrines to bar at least some men from relying upon such statutory provisions to upset established paternity rulings.

e. Defense of Nonconsensual Paternity. Some paternity defendants concede biological paternity but argue that they should not incur child support obligations because their fatherhood was not consensual. Some claim the mother falsely said she was taking birth control pills at the time of intercourse, or that she had been sterilized. Such defenses have been consistently rejected, courts finding the father's failed expectations not relevant to his liability. *E.g., Wallis v. Smith,* 22 P.3d 682 (N. Mex. Ct. App. 2001) (birth control pills);

Murphy v. Myers, 560 N.W.2d 752 (Minn. App. 1997) (false claim of sterilization). *See also Straub v. B.M.T.*, 645 N.E.2d 597 (Ind. 1994) (refusing to enforce, as against public policy, the mother's agreement relieving defendant of prospective child support obligations, which he claimed she had signed to induce him to engage in unprotected intercourse with her) and *Budnick v. Ct. of Appeal*, 805 So. 2d 1112 (Fla.App. 2002) (similar). One group of cases involves support claims brought against boys by older women convicted of their statutory rape; even here, the courts have consistently refused the defense. *E.g., County of San Luis Obispo v. Nathaniel J.*, 57 Cal. Rptr. 2d 843 (App. 1996) (34-year-old woman, convicted of unlawful sexual intercourse with 15-year-old, entitled to child support judgment against him). These statutory rape cases were relied upon by the court in *S.F. v. T.M.*, 695 So. 2d 1186 (Ala. App. 1996) which found irrelevant the putative father's evidence that the mother had raped him while he was heavily intoxicated, including witnesses who testified the mother had bragged about having had intercourse with the defendant while he was passed out. It seems likely the evidence would have supported a conviction for rape of a woman analogously treated, but that did not matter given the court's conclusion that the child support claim would not be affected anyway. For an interesting and provocative feminist argument that permitting support claims in cases of nonconsensual paternity is inconsistent with feminist arguments justifying laws that give women exclusive control in deciding upon whether to abort, see Sally Sheldon, *"Sperm Bandits," Birth Control Fraud and the Battle of the Sexes*, 21 LEGAL STUDIES 460 (2001).

PROBLEMS

Problem 9-17. JoAnn and Bubba were a couple during high school, but they split up when JoAnn's family moved to another state after their graduation. Neither JoAnn nor Bubba knew that JoAnn was pregnant at the time of her family's move. By the time she learned she was, she had a new home and a new boyfriend, Ben. JoAnn and Ben planned to marry, and JoAnn let him think that the child was his. But in the end that relationship did not work out either. With some help from her parents, JoAnn got by on her own after her son Butch was born, never seeking support from either Bubba or Ben. But after her father died things became tough. JoAnn sought public assistance, and the local welfare agency asked her to name the child's father. She named Bubba. The agency brought a support enforcement action against him. By this time, Butch was 12 years old. JoAnn, who wanted to go back to school at her local community college, asked for arrearages as well, from the time of Butch's birth, believing that this lump sum would enable her to do that.

Bubba is surprised when served in this action, since he never saw JoAnn after she moved away and had no idea she had a child, much less his child. Bubba had since married and works in his father's auto repair business. He has two children with his wife, and had been trying to save money to pay for their college education. He cannot maintain his family at their current living standard and also pay the support sought without dipping into those savings. If he has to pay the arrearage claim also, his savings would be wiped out and he might have to borrow money. He concedes that he was still seeing JoAnn in June of 1992, just before she moved away, nine months prior to Butch's birth. However, even as a high school student Bubba was concerned about birth control. He had always used a condom in his relations with JoAnn. But during their last two weeks together JoAnn told him that she had begun taking birth control pills. She explained that she wanted their time together during this last month before she moved to be special, and wanted Bubba to experience sex with her without a condom. In fact JoAnn was not taking birth control pills, but she didn't think she would get pregnant because of the time in her menstrual cycle. She didn't tell that to Bubba, however, because she knew he would not be willing to skip the condom on that basis.

Assume UPA 2002 is in effect in your state. Does Bubba have any defense to the claim for current support, or to the support-arrearage claim? Should he?

Problem 9-18. A) Suppose JoAnn in Problem 9-17 had married the new boyfriend, Ben, that she acquired after the move, and Butch was born three months after the wedding. But Ben died when Butch was three. Would that affect the claim against Bubba? B) What if the marriage had instead ended in divorce when Butch was three, and Ben had been ordered to pay support for Butch. He did pay until he died when Butch was five.

[2]   ESTABLISHING PATERNAL RIGHTS

[a]   Constitutional Protection of the Unwed Father's Claim

Not so long ago, the law hardly considered the possibility that an unmarried father might seek to assert paternity rather than escape it, and procedures for such actions were often not available. This began to change with the decision in *Stanley v. Illinois,* 405 U.S. 645 (1972), the first of five Supreme Court cases over two decades that constitutionalized the law of paternal rights. Justice White, writing for the Court, explained:

> Joan Stanley lived with Peter Stanley intermittently for 18 years, during which time they had three children. When Joan Stanley died, Peter Stanley lost not only her but also his children. Under Illinois law, the children of unwed fathers become wards of the State upon the death of the mother. Accordingly, upon Joan Stanley's death, in a dependency proceeding instituted by the State of Illinois, Stanley's children were . . . placed with court-appointed guardians. Stanley appealed, claiming that he had never been shown to be an unfit parent and that since married fathers and unwed mothers could not be deprived of their children without such a showing, he had been deprived of the equal protection of the laws guaranteed him by the Fourteenth Amendment. The Illinois Supreme Court accepted the fact that Stanley's own unfitness had not been established but rejected the equal protection claim, holding that Stanley could properly be separated from his children upon proof of the single fact that he and the dead mother had not been married. Stanley's actual fitness as a father was irrelevant.

. . . .

The State's right — indeed, duty — to protect minor children through a judicial determination of their interests in a neglect proceeding is not challenged here. Rather, we are faced with a dependency statute that empowers state officials to circumvent neglect proceedings on the theory that an unwed father is not a "parent" whose existing relationship with his children must be considered. "Parents," says the State, "means the father and mother of a legitimate child, or the survivor of them, or the natural mother of an illegitimate child, and includes any adoptive parent," . . . but the term does not include unwed fathers.

Under Illinois law, therefore, while the children of all parents can be taken from them in neglect proceedings, that is only after notice, hearing, and proof of such unfitness as a parent as amounts to neglect, an unwed father is uniquely subject to the more simplistic dependency proceeding. By use of this proceeding, the State, on showing that the father was not married to the mother, need not prove unfitness in fact, because it is presumed at law. Thus, the unwed father's claim of parental qualification is avoided as "irrelevant."

The Court had granted certiorari "to determine whether this method of procedure by presumption could be allowed to stand in light of the fact that Illinois allows married fathers — whether divorced, widowed, or separated — and mothers — even if unwed — the benefit of the presumption that they are fit to raise their children." There was of course no difficulty in the Court's acknowledging the legitimacy and importance of the state interest furthered by its dependency law — protection of "'the moral, emotional, mental, and physical welfare of the minor." But as the Court noted, "the State registers no gain towards its declared goals when it separates children from the custody of fit parents. Indeed, if Stanley is a fit father, the State spites its own articulated goals when it needlessly separates him from his family."

It may be, as the State insists, that most unmarried fathers are unsuitable and neglectful parents It may also be that Stanley is such a parent and that his children should be placed in other hands. But all unmarried fathers are not in this category; some are wholly suited to have custody of their children. This much the State readily concedes, and nothing in this record indicates that Stanley is or has been a neglectful father who has not cared for his children. Given the opportunity to make his case, Stanley may have been seen to be deserving of custody of his offspring. Had this been so, the State's statutory policy would have been furthered by leaving custody in him.

Procedure by presumption is always cheaper and easier than individualized determination. But when, as here, the procedure forecloses the determinative issues of competence and care, when it explicitly disdains present realities in deference to past formalities, it needlessly risks running roughshod over the important interests of both parent and child. It therefore cannot stand. . . . [¶]. . . . Stanley's claim . . . is that failure to afford him a hearing on his parental qualifications while extending it to other parents denied him equal protection of the laws. We have concluded that all Illinois parents are constitutionally entitled to a hearing on their fitness before their children are removed from their custody. It follows that denying such a hearing to Stanley and those like him while granting it to other Illinois parents is inescapably contrary to the Equal Protection Clause.

When *Stanely* was decided, many worried that requiring states to give all unwed fathers notice and hearing might put unreasonable burdens upon state adoption procedures. They were concerned that the rationale of *Stanley* would seem to require paternal consent, or a finding of paternal unfitness, before the unwed mother could give her child up for adoption. They feared that required involvement of the father could frustrate favorable placement for such children for no good reason, because most unwed fathers, unlike Stanley himself, were in fact uninterested in their children and were often difficult to locate. This tension between protecting the paternal rights of unwed fathers and facilitating favorable placement for their children might seem central to the analysis of these cases. In fact, however, none of the Supreme Court decisions has involved a case in which the mother sought simply to relinquish the child for adoption over the actual or potential objection of a recalcitrant or absent father. There have always been other complications.

In *Stanley* itself, the Court addressed the adoption problem only briefly, in footnote 9:

> We note in passing that the incremental cost of offering unwed fathers an opportunity for individualized hearings on fitness appears to be minimal. If unwed fathers, in the main, do not care about the disposition of their children, they will not appear to demand hearings. If they do care, under the scheme here held invalid, Illinois would admittedly at some later time have to afford them a properly focused hearing in a custody or adoption proceeding.

> Extending opportunity for hearing to unwed fathers who desire and claim competence to care for their children creates no constitutional or procedural obstacle to foreclosing those unwed fathers who are not so inclined. The Illinois law governing procedure in juvenile cases . . . provides for . . . notice by publication when personal or certified mail service cannot be had or when notice is directed to unknown respondents under the style of "All whom it may Concern." Unwed fathers who do not promptly respond cannot complain if their children are declared wards of the State. Those who do respond retain the burden of proving their fatherhood.

This footnote served as the guidepost for many states which amended their adoption procedures in light of *Stanley.*

Six years later the Court decided *Quilloin v. Walcott,* 434 U.S. 246 (1978). The mother in *Quilloin* married after giving birth — but her husband was not the child's father. She later sought to have the child adopted by her husband. By the time of the dispute, the child was 11. The father had never lived with the mother and child, and had never wanted custody. He had never been under a court order of support, and the mother did not encourage him to visit the child. He had in fact visited and supported the child, but only irregularly. He now wanted to veto the husband's adoption (because it would necessarily terminate his paternal rights), and he also sought a visitation order. He believed the mother intended to bar his visits after her husband's adoption.

State law gave unwed fathers like Quilloin no claims to their children unless they had legitimated the child by marriage and acknowledgement, or by court order. Quilloin had done neither. Quilloin was permitted to appear at the adoption hearing, but the only issue at the hearing was whether the adoption was in the child's "best interests." The court concluded that it was, and effectively terminated Quilloin's rights by granting the adoption.

Quilloin argued that the Due Process Clause barred the termination of his parental rights without a finding of abandonment or unfitness. The state did require such a finding before terminating the rights of married fathers, as when a man's former wife, with custody, remarries, and wants her new husband to adopt her children. Quilloin also argued that this distinction between married and unmarried fathers violated the Equal Protection Clause.

The Supreme Court unanimously rejected both of Quilloin's claims. In doing so, the Court conceded that the Due Process Clause would probably require the state to show parental unfitness, before involuntarily separating a "natural family." But the Court found this principle inapplicable to Quilloin because he never "had, or sought, actual or legal custody of his child." In other words, the non-custodial relationship between Quilloin and his child did not qualify as a constitutionally-protected "family" relationship. The Court buttressed this result by arguing that the disputed adoption merely recognized "a family unit already in existence" — the unit of mother, child and stepfather-husband. It rejected the Equal Protection claim on similar reasoning, saying that Quilloin's interests were distinguishable from those of a married father, because "legal custody of children is . . . a central aspect of the marital relationship, and even a father whose marriage has broken apart will have borne full responsibility for the rearing of his children during the period of the marriage."

What stands out in *Quilloin* is the Court's emphasis on the substance of the parent-child relation, rather than on the legal formalities surrounding it. The state law at issue in *Quilloin* did give the father paternal rights if he obtained a court order legitimating the child, which Quilloin had not done. The Court might have disposed of the case by holding that the state may constitutionally require the unwed father to go through such a formality to protect his paternal interest, but it did not. Nor did the Court, in explaining why a married father may be treated differently, rely solely upon the fact of marriage itself. The Court instead argued that the substance of the married father-child relationship is typically custodial and therefore adequate to justify the additional protections guaranteed by state law. In sum, Quilloin lost his case not just because he failed to legitimate his child or marry the mother, but because he also failed to act sufficiently like a concerned father (as the Court saw the facts). The implication that the extent of paternal rights turns on the nature of biological father's relationship with his child has reappeared in ensuing cases. Indeed, in *Caban v. Mohammed*, 441 U.S. 380 (1978), which followed *Quilloin* by less than a year, the court pointed to the father's much greater paternal role in distinguishing him from Mr. Quilloin.

Doctrinally, however, *Caban* dealt with an issue that *Quilloin* had left undecided. The New York law at issue in *Caban* was similar to the Georgia law under which Quilloin lost his child. While the unwed father was afforded notice of any hearing concerning the adoption of his child, the adoption could be allowed over his objection if the court found it was in the child's best interests. The unwed mother's objection to any adoption was dispositive, however, unless her parental rights were terminated, which would require findings of unfitness. For procedural reasons, the Court had declined to consider Quilloin's separate claim that this rule constituted an unconstitutional gender classification, but in *Caban,* it decided this "gender-based distinction" was not "required by any universal difference between maternal and paternal relations" and that by "discriminate[ing] against unwed fathers even when their identity is known and they have manifested a significant paternal interest in the child," the rule exemplified an "overbroad generalization" barred by the Equal Protection Clause.

This last phrase's allusion to Mr. Caban's "significant paternal interest" was stressed by the Court in footnote seven, in which it characterized *Quilloin* as emphasizing "the importance of the appellant's failure to act as a father toward his children, noting that he 'has never exercised actual or legal custody over his child, and thus has never shouldered any significant responsibility with respect to the daily supervision, education, protection, or care of the child. . . . [I]ndeed, he does not even now seek custody of his child.' " Mr. Caban certainly presented a far different picture. He had lived together with the mother and their two children for seven years in a de facto marital relationship, and consistently sought to maintain his relationship with the children after he and the mother separated. He apparently sought custody of them with his new wife, but lost in the New York proceeding at issue in the Supreme Court, which terminated his paternal rights in order to allow adoption of the children by the mother's new husband. Thus, while the Court decided in Caban's favor the issue it had reserved in *Quilloin,* it did so in a way which suggested that Mr. Quilloin himself might still have lost, or at least that the state could permissibly treat him differently than Mr. Caban because of the differences in their respective relationships with their children.

Finally, the Court also seemed undecided as to whether the state's interests in facilitating adoption might be more persuasive in justifying disparate treatment of unwed fathers in a statute limited to newborns, given the possibility of "special difficulties attendant upon locating and identifying unwed fathers at birth." Presumably, the unwed father of the older child who has an established paternal relationship with the children, like Caban, can easily be found, while footnote 9 of *Stanley* made clear that no further account need be taken of the father with no relationship who cannot be found, if reasonable efforts were taken to give him notice. The unwed father of the newborn presents a possibly different problem, however, because there may have been no opportunity for him to develop a paternal relationship, and thus no basis for relying on his failure to do so to justify dispensing with his consent to adoption. In such a case, do we accord him the constitutional rights of the de facto father, even though he is not yet one, or do we treat him like the man who didn't care, even though he has had no chance to care? This puzzle, not really addressed by *Caban* or its predecessors, also arises in the case of the older child, if the father has no relationship with the child because the mother has denied him access to it. Such a fact pattern was presented to the Court five years after *Caban,* in *Lehr v. Robertson.*

Justice Stevens' opinion for the Court in *Lehr,* which is reprinted below, was foreshadowed by his dissent in *Caban.* In *Caban,* he argued that the Court resolved the gender discrimination claim improperly:

> Men and women are different, and the difference is relevant to the question whether the mother may be given the exclusive right to consent to the adoption of a child born out of wedlock. Because most adoptions involve newborn infants or very young children, it is appropriate at the outset to focus on the significance of the difference in such cases.

> Both parents are equally responsible for the conception of the child out of wedlock. But from that point on through pregnancy and infancy, the differences between the male and the female have an important impact on the child's destiny. Only the mother carries the child; it is she who has the constitutional right to decide whether to bear it or not. In many cases, only the mother knows who sired the child, and it will often be within her power to withhold that fact, and even the fact of her pregnancy, from that person. If during pregnancy the mother should marry a different partner, the child will be legitimate when born, and the natural father may never even know that his "rights" have been affected. On the other hand, only if the natural mother agrees to marry the natural father during that period can the latter's actions have a positive impact on the status of the child; if he instead should marry a different partner during that time, the only effect on the child is negative, for the likelihood of legitimacy will be lessened.

> These differences continue at birth and immediately thereafter. During that period, the mother and child are together. . . . The father, on the other hand, may or may not be present; his identity may be unknown to the world and may even be uncertain to the mother. These natural differences between unmarried fathers and mothers make it probable that the mother, and not the father or both parents, will have custody of the newborn infant.

> In short, it is virtually inevitable that from conception through infancy the mother will constantly be faced with decisions about how best to care for the child, whereas it is much less certain that the father will be confronted with comparable problems. . . . [A]s a matter of equal protection analysis, it is perfectly obvious that at the time and immediately after a child is born out of wedlock, differences between men and women justify some differential treatment of the mother and father in the adoption process.

> Most particularly, these differences justify a rule that gives the mother of the newborn infant the exclusive right to consent to its adoption. Such a rule gives the mother, in whose sole charge the infant is often placed anyway, the maximum flexibility in deciding how best

to care for the child. It also gives the loving father an incentive to marry the mother, and has no adverse impact on the disinterested father. Finally, it facilitates the interests of the adoptive parents, the child, and the public at large by streamlining the often traumatic adoption process and allowing the prompt, complete, and reliable integration of the child into a satisfactory new home at as young an age as is feasible. Put most simply, it permits the maximum participation of interested natural parents without so burdening the adoption process that its attractiveness to potential adoptive parents is destroyed.

Later in his opinion, Stevens emphasized the distinction the *Caban* majority suggests it might draw between cases involving newborns and those involving older children, saying that the "procedure . . . in cases involving infants . . . in the custody of their mothers . . . is entirely unaffected by the Court's holding or by its reasoning." He urged this narrow reading of the Court's opinion in part to avoid difficulties in the adoption process, which involves newborns disproportionately. Having concluded that the Court could not intend to apply the *Caban* rule to newborns, he argued the rule was also inappropriate for older children unless a challenger can show "that its unjust applications are sufficiently numerous and serious to render it invalid."

But Caban had "made no such showing," and Stevens doubted that cases like his were sufficiently numerous to warrant throwing out the general rule. For Stevens, the unwed father involved enough with his child to justify constitutional protection of their relationship is too unusual to provide the rationale for a constitutional principle that applies to all unwed fathers.

In sum, Justice Stevens' *Caban* dissent combines a number of arguments for a restrained view of the rights of unwed fathers: 1) according them rights will in most cases burden their children and their children's mothers, because it will frustrate the adoption process and the mother's freedom to deal with the adoption process, 2) the natural differences between men and women justify state rules which in general give unwed mothers more parental rights than unwed fathers, 3) only fathers with established relationships with their children (which necessarily means older children to whom they have had access) present a plausible case for constitutional protection, but they constitute too small a group to warrant imposing general rules protecting the interests of unwed fathers. Five years later, Justice Stevens had the opportunity to implement some of these views when he spoke for the Court in *Lehr*.

LEHR v. ROBERTSON

463 U.S. 248 (1983)

STEVENS, Justice. The question presented is whether New York has sufficiently protected an unmarried father's inchoate relationship with a child whom he has never supported and rarely seen in the two years since her birth. The appellant, Jonathan Lehr, claims that the Due Process and Equal Protection Clauses . . . give him an absolute right to notice and an opportunity to be heard before the child may be adopted. We disagree.

Jessica M. was born out of wedlock on November 9, 1976. Her mother, Lorraine Robertson, married Richard Robertson eight months after Jessica's birth. On December 21, 1978, when Jessica was over two years old, the Robertsons filed an adoption petition in the Family Court of Ulster County, New York. The court heard their testimony and received a favorable report from the Ulster County Department of Social Services. On March 7, 1979, the court entered an order of adoption. In this proceeding, appellant contends that the adoption order is invalid because he, Jessica's putative father, was not given advance notice of the adoption proceeding.

The State of New York maintains a "putative father registry." A man who files with that registry demonstrates his intent to claim paternity of a child born out of wedlock and is therefore entitled to receive notice of any proceeding to adopt that child. Before entering Jessica's adoption order, the Ulster County Family Court had the putative father registry examined. Although appellant claims to be Jessica's natural father, he had not entered his name in the registry.

In addition to the persons whose names are listed on the putative father registry, New York law requires that notice of an adoption proceeding be given to several other classes of possible fathers of children born out of wedlock — those who have been adjudicated to be the father, those who have been identified as the father on the child's birth certificate, those who live openly with the child and the child's mother and who hold themselves out to be the father, those who have been identified as the father by the mother in a sworn written statement, and those who were married to the child's mother before the child was six months old. Appellant admittedly was not a member of any of those classes. He had lived with appellee prior to Jessica's birth and visited her in the hospital when Jessica was born, but his name does not appear on Jessica's birth certificate. He did not live with appellee or Jessica after Jessica's birth, he has never provided them with any financial support, and he has never offered to marry appellee. Nevertheless, he contends that the following special circumstances gave him a constitutional right to notice and a hearing before Jessica was adopted.

On January 30, 1979, one month after the adoption proceeding was commenced in Ulster County, appellant filed a "visitation and paternity petition" in the Westchester County Family Court. In that petition, he asked for a determination of paternity, an order of support, and reasonable visitation privileges with Jessica. Notice of that proceeding was served on appellee on February 22, 1979. Four days later appellee's attorney informed the Ulster County Court that appellant had commenced a paternity proceeding in Westchester County; the Ulster County judge then entered an order staying appellant's paternity proceeding until he could rule on a motion to change the venue of that proceeding to Ulster County. On March 3, 1979, appellant received notice of the change of venue motion and, for the first time, learned that an adoption proceeding was pending in Ulster County.

On March 7, 1979, appellant's attorney telephoned the Ulster County judge to inform him that he planned to seek a stay of the adoption proceeding pending the determination of the paternity petition. In that telephone conversation, the judge advised the lawyer that he had already signed the adoption order earlier that day. According to appellant's attorney, the judge stated that he was aware of the pending paternity petition but did not believe he was required to give notice to appellant prior to the entry of the order of adoption.

Thereafter, the Family Court in Westchester County granted appellee's motion to dismiss the paternity petition, holding that the putative father's right to seek paternity ". . . must be deemed severed so long as an order of adoption exists." Appellant did not appeal from that dismissal.[6] On June 22, 1979, appellant filed a petition to vacate the order of adoption on the ground that it was obtained by fraud and in violation of his constitutional rights. The Ulster County Family Court received written and oral argument on the question whether it had "dropped the ball" by approving the adoption without giving appellant advance notice. [I]t denied the petition, explaining its decision in a thorough written opinion.

The Appellate Division of the Supreme Court affirmed. The majority held that appellant's commencement of a paternity action did not give him any right to receive notice of the adoption proceeding, that the notice provisions of the statute were constitutional, and that *Caban v. Mohammed* was not retroactive.[7] . . . . [¶] The New York Court of Appeals also affirmed by a divided vote. . . .

Appellant . . . offers two alternative grounds for holding the New York statutory scheme unconstitutional. First, he contends that a putative father's actual or potential relationship with a child born out of wedlock is an interest in liberty which may not be destroyed without due process of law; he argues therefore that he had a constitutional right to prior notice and an opportunity to be heard before he was deprived of that interest. Second, he contends that the gender-based classification in the statute, which both denied him the right to consent to Jessica's adoption and accorded him fewer procedural rights than her mother, violated the Equal Protection Clause.

The Due Process Claim. . . .

[The Court here reviews *Stanley, Quilloin,* and *Caban,* emphasizing "the clear distinction between a mere biological relationship and an actual relationship of parental responsibility."]

The difference between the developed parent-child relationship that was implicated in *Stanley* and *Caban,* and the potential relationship involved in *Quilloin* and this case, is both clear and significant. When an unwed father demonstrates a full commitment to the responsibilities of parenthood by "com[ing] forward to participate in the rearing of his child," *Caban,* 441 U.S., at 392, his interest in personal contact with his child acquires substantial protection under the due process clause. At that point it may be said that he "act[s] as a father toward his children." *Id.,* at 389, n.7. But the mere existence of a biological link does not merit equivalent constitutional protection. The actions of judges neither create nor sever genetic bonds. "[T]he importance

---

[6] Without trying to intervene in the adoption proceeding, appellant had attempted to file an appeal from the adoption order. That appeal was dismissed.

[7] *Caban* was decided on April 24, 1979, about two months after the entry of the order of adoption.

of the familial relationship, to the individuals involved and to the society, stems from the emotional attachments that derive from the intimacy of daily association, and from the role it plays in 'promot[ing] a way of life' through the instruction of children as well as from the fact of blood relationship." *Smith v. Organization of Foster Families for Equality and Reform,* 431 U.S. 816, 844 (1977) (quoting *Wisconsin v. Yoder,* 406 U.S. 205, 231–233 (1972)).

The significance of the biological connection is that it offers the natural father an opportunity that no other male possesses to develop a relationship with his offspring. If he grasps that opportunity and accepts some measure of responsibility for the child's future, he may enjoy the blessings of the parent-child relationship and make uniquely valuable contributions to the child's development.[18] If he fails to do so, the Federal Constitution will not automatically compel a state to listen to his opinion of where the child's best interests lie.

In this case, we are not assessing the constitutional adequacy of New York's procedures for terminating a developed relationship. Appellant has never had any significant custodial, personal, or financial relationship with Jessica, and he did not seek to establish a legal tie until after she was two years old.[19] We are concerned only with whether New York has adequately protected his opportunity to form such a relationship.

The most effective protection of the putative father's opportunity to develop a relationship with his child is provided by the laws that authorize formal marriage and govern its consequences. But the availability of that protection is, of course, dependent on the will of both parents of the child. Thus, New York has adopted a special statutory scheme to protect the unmarried father's interest in assuming a responsible role in the future of his child.

After . . . *Stanley,* the New York Legislature . . . enacted a statutory adoption scheme that automatically provides notice to seven categories of putative fathers who are likely to have assumed some responsibility for the care of their natural children. If . . . qualification for notice were beyond the control of an interested putative father, it might be thought procedurally inadequate. Yet, . . . the right to receive notice was completely within appellant's control. By mailing a postcard to the putative father registry, he

---

[18] Of course, we need not take sides in the ongoing debate among family psychologists over the relative weight to be accorded biological ties and psychological ties, in order to recognize that a natural father who has played a substantial role in rearing his child has a greater claim to constitutional protection than a mere biological parent. New York's statutory scheme reflects these differences, guaranteeing notice to any putative father who is living openly with the child, and providing putative fathers who have never developed a relationship with the child the opportunity to receive notice simply by mailing a postcard to the putative father registry.

[19] This case happens to involve an adoption by the husband of the natural mother, but we do not believe the natural father has any greater right to object to such an adoption than to an adoption by two total strangers. If anything, the balance of equities tips the opposite way in a case such as this. In denying the putative father relief in *Quilloin,* we made an observation equally applicable here:

> "Nor is this a case in which the proposed adoption would place the child with a new set of parents with whom the child had never before lived. Rather, the result of the adoption in this case is to give full recognition to a family unit already in existence, a result desired by all concerned, except appellant. . . ." 434 U.S., at 255.

could have guaranteed that he would receive notice of any proceedings to adopt Jessica. The possibility that he may have failed to do so because of his ignorance of the law cannot be a sufficient reason for criticizing the law itself. The New York legislature concluded that a more open-ended notice requirement would merely complicate the adoption process, threaten the privacy interests of unwed mothers, create the risk of unnecessary controversy, and impair the desired finality of adoption decrees. Regardless of whether we would have done likewise if we were legislators instead of judges, we surely cannot characterize the state's conclusion as arbitrary.

Appellant argues, however, that . . . he was nevertheless entitled to special notice because the court and the mother knew that he had filed an affiliation proceeding in another court. . . . The Constitution does not require either a trial judge or a litigant to give special notice to nonparties who are presumptively capable of asserting and protecting their own rights. Since the New York statutes adequately protected appellant's inchoate interest in establishing a relationship with Jessica, we find no merit in the claim that his constitutional rights were offended because the family court strictly complied with the notice provisions of the statute.

The Equal Protection Claim. . . .

. . . [The New York law] guarantees to certain people the right to veto an adoption and the right to prior notice of any adoption proceeding. The mother of an illegitimate child is always within that favored class, but only certain putative fathers are included. Appellant contends that the gender-based distinction is invidious. . . .

We have held that these statutes may not constitutionally be applied in that class of cases where the mother and father are in fact similarly situated with regard to their relationship with the child. In *Caban v. Mohammed,* the Court held that it violated the Equal Protection Clause to grant the mother a veto over the adoption of a four-year-old girl and a six-year-old boy, but not to grant a veto to their father, who had admitted paternity and had participated in the rearing of the children. The Court made it clear, however, that if the father had not "come forward to participate in the rearing of his child, nothing in the Equal Protection Clause [would] preclude[] the State from withholding from him the privilege of vetoing the adoption of that child." 441 U.S., at 392.

Jessica's parents are not like the parents involved in *Caban.* Whereas appellee had a continuous custodial responsibility for Jessica, appellant never established any custodial, personal, or financial relationship with her. If one parent has an established custodial relationship with the child and the other parent has either abandoned or never established a relationship, the Equal Protection Clause does not prevent a state from according the two parents different legal rights.

The judgment of the New York Court of Appeals is

Affirmed.

Justice White, with whom Justice Marshall and Justice Blackmun join, dissenting.

The question in this case is whether the State may, consistent with the Due Process Clause, deny notice and an opportunity to be heard in an adoption proceeding to a putative father when the State has actual notice of his existence, whereabouts, and interest in the child.

I

It is axiomatic that "[t]he fundamental requirement of due process is the opportunity to be heard 'at a meaningful time and in a meaningful manner.'" *Mathews v. Eldridge,* 424 U.S. 319, 333 (1976), quoting *Armstrong v. Manzo,* 380 U.S. 545, 552, (1965). As Jessica's biological father, Lehr either had an interest protected by the Constitution or he did not. If the entry of the adoption order in this case deprived Lehr of a constitutionally protected interest, he is entitled to notice and an opportunity to be heard before the order can be accorded finality.

According to Lehr, he and Jessica's mother met in 1971 and began living together in 1974. The couple cohabited for approximately 2 years, until Jessica's birth in 1976. Throughout the pregnancy and after the birth, Lorraine acknowledged to friends and relatives that Lehr was Jessica's father; Lorraine told Lehr that she had reported to the New York State Department of Social Services that he was the father.[2] Lehr visited Lorraine and Jessica in the hospital every day during Lorraine's confinement. According to Lehr, from the time Lorraine was discharged from the hospital until August, 1978, she concealed her whereabouts from him. During this time Lehr never ceased his efforts to locate Lorraine and Jessica and achieved sporadic success until August, 1977, after which time he was unable to locate them at all. On those occasions when he did determine Lorraine's location, he visited with her and her children to the extent she was willing to permit it. When Lehr, with the aid of a detective agency, located Lorraine and Jessica in August, 1978, Lorraine was already married to Mr. Robertson. Lehr asserts that at this time he offered to provide financial assistance and to set up a trust fund for Jessica, but that Lorraine refused. Lorraine threatened Lehr with arrest unless he stayed away and refused to permit him to see Jessica. Thereafter Lehr retained counsel who wrote to Lorraine in early December, 1978, requesting that she permit Lehr to visit Jessica and threatening legal action on Lehr's behalf. On December 21, 1978, perhaps as a response to Lehr's threatened legal action, appellees commenced the adoption action at issue here.

The majority posits that "[t]he intangible fibers that connect parent and child . . . are sufficiently vital to merit constitutional protection *in appropriate cases.*" . . . (emphasis added). It then purports to analyze the particular facts of this case to determine whether appellant has a constitutionally protected liberty interest. We have expressly rejected that approach. In *Board of Regents v. Roth,* 408 U.S. 564, 570–571 (1972), we stated that although "a weighing process has long been a part of any determination of the *form* of hearing required in particular situations, . . . to determine whether due process

---

[2] Under 18 NYCRR § 369.2(b), recipients of public assistance in the Aid to Families with Dependent Children program are required as a condition of eligibility to provide the name and address of the child's father. Lorraine apparently received public assistance after Jessica's birth; it is unclear whether she received public assistance after that regulation went into effect in 1977.

requirements apply in the first place, we must look not to the 'weight' but to the *nature* of the interest at stake . . . to see if the interest is within the Fourteenth Amendment's protection. . . ."

The "nature of the interest" at stake here is the interest that a natural parent has in his or her child, one that has long been recognized and accorded constitutional protection. We have frequently "stressed the importance of familial bonds, whether or not legitimized by marriage, and accorded them constitutional protection." *Little v. Streater*, 452 U.S. 1, 13 (1981). . . . It is beyond dispute that a formal order of adoption, no less than a formal termination proceeding, operates to permanently terminate parental rights.

Lehr's version of the "facts" paints a far different picture than that portrayed by the majority. . . . Appellant has never been afforded an opportunity to present his case. The legitimation proceeding he instituted was first stayed, and then dismissed, on appellees' motions. Nor could appellant establish his interest during the adoption proceedings, for it is the failure to provide Lehr notice and an opportunity to be heard there that is at issue here. We cannot fairly make a judgment based on the quality or substance of a relationship without a complete and developed factual record. This case requires us to assume that Lehr's allegations are true — that but for the actions of the child's mother there would have been the kind of significant relationship that the majority concedes is entitled to the full panoply of procedural due process protections.[3]

I reject the peculiar notion that the only significance of the biological connection between father and child is that "it offers the natural father an opportunity that no other male possesses to develop a relationship with his offspring." A "mere biological relationship" is not as unimportant in determining the nature of liberty interests as the majority suggests.

"[T]he usual understanding of 'family' implies biological relationships, and most decisions treating the relation between parent and child have stressed this element." *Smith v. Organization of Foster Families, supra*, 431 U.S., at 843. The "biological connection" is itself a relationship that creates a protected interest. Thus the "nature" of the interest is the parent-child relationship; how well-developed that relationship has become goes to its "weight," not its "nature."[4]

Whether Lehr's interest is entitled to constitutional protection does not entail a searching inquiry into the quality of the relationship but a simple

---

[3] In response to our decision in *Caban v. Mohammed*, the statute governing the persons whose consent is necessary to an adoption has been amended to include certain unwed fathers. The State has recognized that an unwed father's failure to maintain an actual relationship or to communicate with a child will not deprive him of his right to consent if he was "prevented from doing so by the person or authorized agency having lawful custody of the child." N.Y. DOM. REL. LAW § 111 (1) (d) (as amended by Chap. 575, L. 1980). Thus, even the State recognizes that before a lesser standard can be applied consistent with due process requirements, there must be a determination that there was no significant relationship and that the father was not prevented from forming such a relationship.

[4] The majority's citation of *Quilloin* and *Caban* as examples that the Constitution does not require the same procedural protections for the interests of all unwed fathers is disingenuous. Neither case involved notice and opportunity to be heard. In both, the unwed fathers were notified and participated as parties in the adoption proceedings.

determination of the fact that the relationship exists — a fact that even the majority agrees must be assumed to be established.

. . . Any analysis of the adequacy of the notice in this case must be conducted on the assumption that the interest involved here is as strong as that of *any* putative father. That is not to say that due process requires actual notice to every putative father or that adoptive parents or the State must conduct an exhaustive search of records or an intensive investigation before a final adoption order may be entered. The procedures adopted by the State, however, must at least represent a reasonable effort to determine the identity of the putative father and to give him adequate notice.

II

In this case, of course, there was no question about either the identity or the location of the putative father. . . . Lehr was entitled to due process, and the right to be heard is one of the fundamentals of that right. . . . [¶] The State concedes this much but insists that Lehr has had all the process that is due to him. It relies on § 111-a, which designates seven categories of unwed fathers to whom notice of adoption proceedings must be given, including any unwed father who has filed with the State a notice of his intent to claim paternity. The State submits that it need not give notice to anyone who has not filed his name, as he is permitted to do, and who is not otherwise within the designated categories, even if his identity and interest are known or are reasonably ascertainable by the State.

. . . .

The State asserts that any problem [with the inclusiveness of the categories] is overcome by the seventh category of putative fathers to whom notice must be given, namely those fathers who have identified themselves in the putative father register maintained by the State. Since Lehr did not [identify himself in this manner] he was not entitled to notice and a hearing even though his identity, location and interest were known to the adoption court prior to entry of the adoption order. I have difficulty with this position. First, it represents a grudging and crabbed approach to due process. . . . It makes little sense to me to deny notice and hearing to a father who has not placed his name in the register but who has unmistakably identified himself by filing suit to establish his paternity and has notified the adoption court of his action and his interest. [It] is the sheerest formalism to deny him a hearing because he informed the State in the wrong manner.

Because in my view the failure to provide Lehr with notice and an opportunity to be heard violated rights guaranteed him by the Due Process Clause, I need not address the question whether § 111-a violates the Equal Protection Clause by discriminating between categories of unwed fathers or by discriminating on the basis of gender.

Respectfully, I dissent.

NOTES

1. *The Due Process Claims in* **Lehr**. Lehr asserted two grounds on which he asked the Court to declare New York's statutory scheme unconstitutional:

due process and equal protection. The due process claim itself, however, has both procedural and substantive components. Lehr claimed that he had been deprived of "prior notice and an opportunity to be heard" on the matter of Jessica's adoption by Robertson. Thus, he argued that New York's statute violated his *procedural* due process rights. He necessarily grounded this argument, however, in the contention that the statute's operation infringed his *substantive* due process right to, or liberty interest in, a relationship with his biological daughter. Procedural due process rights are triggered by the deprivation of something in which one has a substantive liberty or property interest. *Mathews v. Eldridge*, 424 U.S. 319, 332 (1976) ("Procedural due process imposes constraints on governmental decisions which deprive individuals of 'liberty' or 'property' interests within the meaning of the Due Process Clause of the Fifth or Fourteenth Amendment.").

Does the court reject the proposition that Lehr has a constitutionally protected liberty interest at stake under these facts? On one hand, it seems not. The Court says "the New York statutes adequately protected appellant's inchoate interest in establishing a relationship with Jessica" by allowing him, through the registry, to ensure himself notice and an opportunity to be heard in any adoption proceeding. "If . . . qualification for notice were beyond the control of an interested putative father, it might be thought procedurally inadequate. Yet, . . . the right to receive notice was completely within appellant's control. By mailing a postcard to the putative father registry, he could have guaranteed that he would receive notice of any proceedings to adopt Jessica." The registry portion of New York's law is therefore important because the other methods it offers the unwed father to secure his procedural rights require the mother's cooperation; the registration alternative alone allows the unwed father to establish his claim by a *unilateral* act. Courts have read *Lehr* as requiring the state to afford the father at least one such unilateral method as the bare constitutional minimum. *See, e.g., B.G. v. H.S.,* 509 N.E.2d 214 (Ind. Ct. App. 1988) ("If Indiana law is to pass constitutional muster under *Lehr,* it must . . . provide some means by which fathers may unilaterally identify themselves as putative fathers and entitle themselves to notice of adoption proceedings."). This contruction is an application of a more general understanding that the biological connection alone does in fact trigger some level of procedural due process protection. *See, e.g., In re Baby Boy,* 988 P.2d 1270, 1274 (Okla. 1999) (biological father had right to notice and opportunity to be heard prior to termination of his parental rights where biological mother had concealed her pregnancy from him, depriving him "of the chance to grasp his parental opportunity interest"); *Adoption of B.G.S.,* 556 So. 2d 545 (La. 1990) ("We reject appellants' interpretation of the Supreme Court cases as holding that only an unwed father with a developed relationship with his child may have a constitutionally protected interest in his parenthood.").

So why then did Mr. Lehr himself lose? One might think of *Lehr* as applying a principle that while the state cannot deprive someone of a constitutionally protected liberty interest without procedural due process, it can require an individual to meet reasonable procedural requirements to avoid loss of these procedural rights. To take another example from the law of parent and child, a child support system may operate, as some now do, by imposing an automatic increase in the child support obligation on an individual who does not respond within a reasonable time to notice that such an increase is proposed. That failure to respond effectively waives that individual's right to a hearing on the factual assumptions offered to justify the increase. Registration is, by this way of thinking, an analogous and reasonable procedural requirement to impose on men like Lehr.

Yet at the same time, the Court makes clear that Lehr's constitutional claim is weaker than Stanley's or Caban's because he, unlike either of them, did not have an established relationship with his biological child. If he had, then the procedural claim he makes here might not have failed. Suppose, for example, the case were exactly the same except that Lehr had visited Jessica regularly, developed a warm relationship with her, and provided regular support to her during the first few years of her life, and only then lost contact with her because at this point (rather than earlier) Lorraine hid herself and the child from him. Even under these revised facts Lehr would not qualify for notice under the New York law at issue in the case, but its application to these circumstances would seem, given the Court's language, to call for a different result. In this portion of its opinion the Court deemphasizes the biological link between Lehr and Jessica, saying that biological paternity is important only because

> it offers the natural father an opportunity that no other male possesses to develop a relationship with his offspring. If he grasps that opportunity and accepts some measure of responsibility for the child's future, he may enjoy the blessings of the parent-child relationship and make uniquely valuable contributions to the child's development. If he fails to do so, the Federal Constitution will not automatically compel a state to listen to his opinion of where the child's best interests lie.

It is this weakened protection of Lehr's *procedural* rights to which Justice White objects in dissent. In one sense the majority's position seems almost circular because one cannot make the right to be heard depend upon factual conclusions concerning the *nature* of the relationship that can themselves be established only at a hearing. Justice White thus argues that whether "Lehr's interest is entitled to constitutional protection does not entail a searching inquiry into the quality of the relationship but a simple determination of the fact that the relationship exists — a fact that even the majority agrees must be assumed to be established." At least for the purpose of deciding procedural rights, the dissenters would not have a hierarchy of biological fathers arrayed according to the strength and nature of their parental relationship with the child. Of course, even Justice White's view depends upon the factual distinction between the likely biological father — the "putative father" — and the rest of the male population. Justice White would not impose on the state an unlimited obligation to find every plausible putative father and give him notice. But he concludes that the state's procedures "must at least represent a reasonable effort to determine the identity of the putative father and to give him adequate notice" — a standard which he believes New York's statute did not meet.

What if Lehr did appear at the adoption hearing — under what substantive standard could the trial court terminate his parental rights? This is a different substantive due process question, one the Court addressed in *Quilloin*. Recall the Court conceded in that case that the Due Process Clause would probably require the state to show parental unfitness, before involuntarily separating a "natural family." But the Court found this principle inapplicable to Mr. Quilloin because he never "had, or sought, actual or legal custody of his child." Mr. Lehr certainly never had custody of his child, and it is not clear he sought primary custody in any event. But his claims, which he never got to present in court, were that he sought regular access to the child so that he could maintain a parental relationship, and was prepared to provide financial support, and was prevented from doing either only because of the mother's having concealed herself from him. By his account, then, Mr. Lehr is what has been called a "thwarted" father — one who seeks to establish the relationship required by *Quilloin* but is prevented from doing so by the mother's resistance. The Court has never clearly established whether thwarted fathers are entitled to the same substantive constitutional protection that is accorded those who have succeeded in establishing a relationship. The language in *Quilloin* suggests they would be (since it notes that Mr. Quilloin never had "or sought" custody), but the Court has not had occasion to face that question squarely. Of course, in *Lehr* itself the Court seems unconcerned that it may have allowed the state to deny a hearing to a thwarted father, much less a favorable substantive rule. But that is not dispositive either, given the Court's view that Lehr was offered a reasonable procedure under which he would have been granted a hearing, and lost only because he failed to take advantage of it.

For more on the problem of thwarted fathers, which has occupied the attention of a number of state supreme courts, see Note 5 below. For more on the substantive rule applied in such hearings, when the child is a newborn, see Note 7 below, on page 1009.

2. The Equal Protection Claim in Lehr. Relying upon *Caban*, Lehr claimed that New York's failure to accord unwed fathers the same rights as unwed mothers to block their children's adoptions constituted a gender-based classification violating the Equal Protection Clause. There is no question the law distinguished parents on the basis of gender. The New York statute at issue in *Lehr* would require notice even to the mother who abandoned the child at birth to the father. Of course, such a mother would presumably lose on the merits of her objection, on the very ground of her abandonment. But the point is that the mother's rights to notice and hearing, and to have any petition to terminate her parental rights tested against the demanding standard of unfitness, do not depend on her having put her name on a registry or on having "participated in the rearing of the children," while the father's do. The Court nonetheless rejected the Equal Protection claim. It distinguished this case from *Caban* by pointing to the presence of a paternal relationship in that case and the absence of one in this case. "If one parent has an established custodial relationship with the child and the other parent has either abandoned or never established a relationship, the Equal Protection Clause does not prevent a state from according the two parents different legal rights." It is presumably necessary to the Court's treatment of this point that there was indeed no factual dispute about the absence of any relationship between Mr. Lehr and his daughter. If there were — if Lehr had claimed to have lived with the child for some time and to have provided support — it would then seem necessary to offer him the chance to prove his story. He would not be denied a hearing on the *assumption* that the facts are otherwise. In this sense, it must also be the case that the Court decided, *sub silentio*, that Lehr's claim he was a thwarted father was not relevant — that even if true, it would not entitle him to notice and a hearing.

To see the meaning of this last point, imagine two cases: the first is like *Lehr*, while in the second a father seeks to have his child adopted by his new wife, and claims no need to notify the child's mother of this potential termination of her rights because, he says, the mother never had any post-birth relationship with the child. Perhaps the mother concedes this fact, but claims that the reason is that father took the child shortly after birth and concealed himself and the child from her, thus denying her all contact with the child despite her considerable effort to find them. Or perhaps she has no such kidnapping claim, always knew where the father and child were, and never came by anyway. Either way, New York law would guarantee this mother notice and hearing before the adoption, even though this mother is at best in precisely the same situation as was Mr. Lehr. It is this differential treatment of mothers and fathers which the Court here necessarily says is permissible under the Equal Protection Clause. If one goes back to Justice Stevens' dissent in *Caban*, one can see how he would reach this result, because he believes that the biological differences in the roles of men and women in the procreative process lead to inevitable behavioral differences that the law of parent and child may constitutionally take into account. In *Lehr* Justice Stevens speaks for the entire Court, which appears to have adopted his view.

That appearance was further confirmed in *Nguyen v. Immigration and Naturalization Service*, 533 U.S.53 (2001), in which the issue came before the Court in the context of immigration law. Justice Kennedy wrote the opinion for the Court in *Nguyen*, joined not only by Stevens but also Rehnquist, Scalia and Thomas. The non-marital son of a U.S. serviceman and a Vietnamese woman was denied citizenship because his American father had not complied with the law's requirement that the child be legitimated, or his citizen father's paternity adjudicated or acknowledged, before he was 18. (His father did cooperate in establishing his paternity after the son's 18th birthday, and joined in this action.) Nonmarital children of citizen mothers and noncitizen fathers could be recognized as citizens without their mother's meeting any analogous requirement to establish parentage prior to the child's 18th birthday. The Court held 5-4 that this distinction was constitutional because it reflected natural differences between mothers and fathers, differences with consequences the Court believed important to the statute's valid policy objectives. That policy objective is to ensure that there is an actual parental relationship between a child born overseas and the citizen parent.

> Fathers and mothers are not similarly situated with regard to the proof of biological parenthood. The imposition of a different set of rules for making that legal determination with respect to fathers and mothers is neither surprising nor troublesome from a constitutional perspective. Section 1409(a)(4)'s provision of three options for a father seeking to establish paternity — legitimation, paternity oath, and court order of paternity — is designed to ensure an acceptable documentation of paternity.

Of course, this observation did not explain why the parentage of fathers, but not mothers, must be established before the child's 18th birthday to confer American citizenship. As the petitioners pointed out, modern DNA tests could establish biological paternity with confidence at any time. But biological parentage was not the government's sole interest, the Court explained:

> The second important governmental interest . . . is . . . to ensure that the child and the citizen parent have some demonstrated opportunity or potential to develop not just a relationship that is recognized, as a formal matter, by the law, but one that consists of the real, everyday ties that provide a connection between child and citizen parent and, in turn, the United States. In the case of a citizen mother and a child born overseas, the opportunity for a meaningful relationship between citizen parent and child inheres in the very event of birth, an event so often critical to our constitutional and statutory understandings of citizenship. The mother knows that the child is in being and is hers and has an initial point of contact with him. There is at least an opportunity for mother and child to develop a real, meaningful relationship.

> The same opportunity does not result from the event of birth, as a matter of biological inevitability, in the case of the unwed father. Given the 9-month interval between conception and birth, it is not always certain that a father will know that a child was conceived, nor is it always clear that even the mother will be sure of the father's identity. This fact takes on particular significance in the case of a child born overseas and out of wedlock. One concern in this context has always been with young people, men for the most part, who are on duty with the Armed Forces in foreign countries. Even if a father knows of the fact of conception, moreover, it does not follow that he will be present at the birth of the child. Thus, unlike the case of the mother, there is no assurance that the father and his biological child will ever meet. . . . [The law] takes the unremarkable step of ensuring that an opportunity [to develop a relationship], inherent in the event of birth as to the mother-child relationship, exists between father and child before citizenship is conferred upon the latter.

> The importance of the governmental interest at issue here is too profound to be satisfied merely by conducting a DNA test. The fact of paternity can be established even without the father's knowledge, not to say his presence. Paternity can be established by taking DNA samples even from a few strands of hair, years after the birth. Yet scientific proof of biological paternity does nothing, by itself, to ensure contact between father and child during the child's minority. . . .

>   . . .

>   . . . There is nothing irrational or improper in the recognition that at the moment of birth. . .the mother's knowledge of the child and the fact of parenthood have been established in a way not guaranteed in the case of the unwed father. This is not a stereotype. See *Virginia* ("The heightened review standard our precedent establishes does not make sex a proscribed classification. . . . Physical differences between

men and women . . . are enduring"). [¶] To fail to acknowledge even our most basic biological differences — such as the fact that a mother must be present at birth but the father need not be — risks making the guarantee of equal protection superficial, and so disserving it. . . . The distinction embodied in the statutory scheme here at issue is not marked by misconception and prejudice, nor does it show disrespect for either class. The difference between men and women in relation to the birth process is a real one, and the principle of equal protection does not forbid Congress to address the problem at hand in a manner specific to each gender.

Justice O'Connor's dissent, joined by Souter, Ginsberg, and Breyer, argues that the Congressional purpose could be served without relying upon gender as a proxy for the presence of a parental relationship. She argued that the challenged law's reliance upon gender

finds support not in biological differences but instead in a stereotype — *i.e.,* "the generalization that mothers are significantly more likely than fathers . . . to develop caring relationships with their children." Such a claim relies on "the very stereotype the law condemns," "lends credibility" to the generalization, and helps to convert that "assumption" into "a self-fulfilling prophecy." . . . Indeed, contrary to this stereotype, Boulais has reared Nguyen, while Nguyen apparently has lacked a relationship with his mother.

This statute, Justice O'Connor thunders, is "paradigmatic of a historic regime that left women with responsibility, and freed men from responsibility, for nonmarital children."

3. *More on Permitted Gender Distinctions in Parentage.* There are other examples of gender distinctions in legal rules about parents. Consider that the law makes important gender distinctions in the significance it attaches to the pre-birth behavior of the father as compared to the mother. No state accepts a mother's pre-birth relinquishment of her child to adoption (see page 1252 in Chapter 11), and efforts to terminate maternal rights on the basis of a mothers' pre-birth behavior, such as drug abuse that harms her unborn child, are highly controversial (see pages 1159-1165 in Chapter 10). Yet the father's uncaring or irresponsible pre-birth behavior can be relied upon in terminating his rights to his child. *See, e.g, Adoption of Michael H.,* 898 P.2d 891 (Cal. 1995), discussed below in Note 4. For an article concerned with devising an approach to paternal rights that properly walks the "fine line between adopting false gender-neutrality by treating men and women identically on the one hand, and reinforcing gender stereotypes on the other," see Mary Shanley, *Unwed Fathers' Rights, Adoption, and Sex Equality: Gender-Neutrality and the Perpetuation of Patriarchy,* 95 Colum. L. Rev. 60 (1995). For commentaries on the U.S. Supreme Court's decision in *Nguyen,* see Lica Tomizuka, *The Supreme Court's Blind Pursuit of Outdated Definitions of Familial Relationships in Upholding the Constitutionality of 8 U.S.C. 21 1409 in* Nguyen v. INS, 20 Law & Ineq. 275 (2002); Erin Chlopak, Comment, *Mandatory Motherhood and Frustrated Fatherhood: The Supreme Court's Preservation of Gender Discrimination in American Citizenship Law,* 51 Am. U. L. Rev. 967 (2002).

Well-established differences in the law governing paternal rights, as compared with paternal obligations, provide another example. Imagine the *Lehr* facts but the other way around. Suppose, that is, that Jessica's mother had filed a paternity action seeking Lehr's support of Jessica, rather than the adoption petition that cut off his rights. The absence of any developed father-child relationship between Lehr and Jessica would not matter. Yet if the state is not constitutionally required to provide Lehr notice of the adoption petition, how can it require him to pay child support? The Supreme Court has not ventured a view on this question. Of course, for many of these cases, there is a ready response: one can waive one's rights, but one cannot waive one's obligations. A biological father may therefore lose some or even all of his custodial and access rights to his children by failing to act responsibly with respect to them, but he cannot use his own irresponsible behavior as a defense in an action to enforce paternal obligations. Yet that response is not really satisfactory with respect to thwarted fathers, as Mr. Lehr appears to be. Indeed, even if the law did not necessarily allow the mother to defeat the *legal* claims of the biological father by concealing a child from him, a long-enough concealment period could obviously defeat his effort to establish an actual paternal relationship. In that case should the law reduce or repeal his legal obligations as well? For a suggestion that in some of these cases it should, see Ira Mark Ellman, *Should Visitation Denial Affect the Obligation to Pay Support?*, in The Law and Economics of Child Support Payments (William Comanor, Ed. 2004), reprinted in 36 Ariz. St. L.J. 661 (2004).

4. *Newborns.* The rules considered by the Court in *Lehr* did not apply to nonmarital children under six months of age. For them, the applicable New York statute required the consent of the *mother only*, unless the father had: (1) lived with the mother for six consecutive months immediately preceding the child's placement; (2) openly acknowledged his paternity during this period; and (3) paid reasonable pregnancy and birth expenses in accordance with his means. These rules were challenged in *Raquel Marie X*, 76 N.Y.2d 387, 559 N.E.2d 418, 559 N.Y.S.2d 855, *cert. denied, sub nom. Robert C. v. Miguel T.*, 498 U.S. 984 (1990), *on remand*, 570 N.Y.S.2d 604 (App. Div. 1991), New York's highest court held the requirement that the father live with the mother unconstitutional, because it "cuts off [a father's] interest by imposing as an absolute condition an obligation only tangentially related to the . . . relationship [between the father and the child] [¶] The 'living together' requirement. . . . permits adoption despite the father's prompt objection, even when he wishes to form or actually has attempted to form a relationship with the infant that would satisfy the State as substantial, continuous and meaningful by any other standard." 599 N.E.2d at 405.

Raquel Marie is consistent with the principle that the father is entitled to a *unilateral* method for establishing his procedural rights in any proceeding concerning the placement of his child (*see* Note 1, *supra*). The court in *Raquel Marie* held that, in determining whether an unwed father of a newborn has a right to be heard regarding the child's adoption, he must have demonstrated "a willingness himself to assume full custody of the child — not merely to block adoption by others, [and his] manifestation of parental responsibility must be prompt." *Id.* at 408. Further, the court held that during the critical six-month period preceding adoptive placement, the father must demonstrate indicia of responsibility such as "public acknowledgement of paternity, payment of pregnancy and birth expenses, steps taken to establish his legal responsibility for the child, and other factors evincing a commitment to the child." *Id.* at 408. On remand, New York's mid-level appellate court concluded that the conduct of Raquel Marie's father fell below this standard, rendering his consent to the adoption unnecessary. *See also Adoption of Michael H.,* 10 Cal. 4th 1043, 1060, 898 P.2d 891 (1995) (holding that unwed biological father who had failed to "promptly [come] forward and demonstrate[full] commitment to his parental responsibilities" could not block his child's adoption). Some states, however, require less of the father, accepting his willingness to share *financial* responsibility for the pregnancy, birth, and the child's subsequent needs as alone sufficient to trigger his rights; readiness to take on childrearing and custodial responsibilities are not also necessary. *See, e.g., Adoption of B.V.,* 33 P.3d 1083, 1087–88 (Utah App. 2001) (allowing unwed father of newborn to block adoption where he had agreed to be "legally responsible for" and made "reasonable efforts to contribute to medical and pregnancy related expenses"). Recall Justice Stevens' dissenting opinion in *Caban,* excerpted above on pages 986-987 in which he argued that the majority's holding should not apply to newborns. While the matter is not free from doubt, it seems likely that nonmarital fathers of newborns have the same *procedural* due process rights to notice and hearing as do fathers of older children. Less clear is whether Justice Stevens has prevailed or would prevail in his view that the substantive standard applied to terminating the parental rights of a newborn's nonmarital father can be less demanding than the standard applied to the fathers of older children.

5. *Unaware, Deceived, and Thwarted Fathers*. *Lehr* tells us that a state may impose the registry requirement to the detriment of the father who failed to register through his own ignorance of the registration requirement, even if he took other steps that showed his interest in the child. But does that principle also apply to a father who does not register because he is ignorant of the fact that he has a child?

The father who does not know he has a child because he left the mother may not seem a particularly sympathetic figure. One court concluded that such a father is "on notice," given his sexual relationship with the mother, "that a pregnancy and an adoption proceeding regarding that child may occur" and therefore responsible "to protect his own rights of notice and consent." *Adoption of B.B.D.,* 894 P.2d 967 (Utah, 1999) (citing Utah Code § 78-30-4.13(1)). *See also, Paternity of Baby Doe,* 734 N.E.2d 281, 287 (Ind. App. 2000) (refusing to invalidate an adoption where mother had not notified father of her pregnancy, concluding "that a child should . . . not be made to suffer when a putative father makes no inquiry regarding the possibility of a pregnancy after a sexual relationship with the mother"); *Matter of Adoption of S.J.B.,* 745 S.W.2d 606 (Ark. 1988) (same); *Baby Boy K.,* 546 N.W.2d 86 (S.D. 1996) (mother's failure to tell alleged father of pregnancy, and her misrepresentations to trial court concerning his identity, did not toll the statutory time period within which father required to assert his paternity); *In re Karen A.B.,* 513 A.2d 770 (Del. 1986) (where mother refuses to disclose identity of unwed father, and states he was unaware of her pregnancy, would be unsuitable as a custodian, and might harass her if he learned of the child's existence, court may terminate his rights and permit adoption without notice to him). The mother's simple failure to tell the father of the pregnancy, or identify him to the court, is not, under this understanding, enough to allow his claim when he finds out about the child later.

This view was well-articulated by New York in *Robert O. v. Russell*, 604 N.E.2d 99, 590 N.Y.S.2d 37 (1992). The father had been engaged to the mother, and lived with her for two months, but they then separated, and the mother never told him she had become pregnant. She consented to their child's adoption by friends and certified to the court that no other person's consent was required under New York law. The certification was correct because the father did not qualify under any of the New York rules for newborns. The father received no notice of the adoption. Thirteen months after the child's birth the parents reconciled, and five months later — after they had married — the mother told the father of the child's existence. He immediately filed with New York's putative father registry and, with the mother's support, sought to vacate the adoption. The court, however, held that this father must lose because he failed to meet the test of *Raquel Marie*, described *supra* in Note 4. In reaching this result the court found the record supported the trial court's conclusion that there was no "deception or concealment" by the mother.

> Petitioner analogizes his situation to that of the father in *Baby Girl S.* [a companion case to *Raquel* in which the court found that the father preserved his paternal rights because he sought "full custodial responsibility virtually from the time he learned of [the mother's] pregnancy [and] did everything possible to manifest and establish his parental responsibility."] Petitioner correctly reads *Lehr* and *Raquel Marie* to stand for the proposition that an unwed father who has promptly done all that he could to protect his parental interest is entitled to constitutional protection. His argument falters, however, in its conclusion that he has met that standard.

> [W]e stressed in *Raquel Marie* that the period in which the biological father must manifest his parental interest is limited in duration: if the father's actions are untimely, the State can deny a right of consent. In *Raquel Marie* we limited the period in which the father must act to the six continuing months immediately preceding the child's placement for adoption.

> To conclude that petitioner acted promptly once he became aware of the child is to fundamentally misconstrue whose timetable is relevant. Promptness is measured in terms of the baby's life not by the onset of the father's awareness. The demand for prompt action by the father at the child's birth is neither arbitrary nor punitive, but instead a logical and necessary outgrowth of the State's legitimate interest in the child's need for early permanence and stability. The competing interests at stake in an adoption — and the complications presented by petitioner's position — are clearly illustrated here: nearly a year and a half after the baby went to live with the adoptive parents, and more than 10 months after they were told by the court that the baby was legally theirs, petitioner sought to rearrange those lives by initiating his present legal action.

. . . .

> . . . No one, . . . let alone any State actor, prevented petitioner from finding out about Carol's pregnancy. His inaction . . . was solely attributable to him. Nothing in *Raquel Marie* or the Supreme Court decisions on which it rests suggests that the protections of constitutional due process must or should be extended to him under these circumstances.

What then of cases in which the mother has affirmatively "deceived" or "concealed"? Would New York or other states protect these men if they act promptly upon learning the truth, even if it is not soon after the child's birth? Such facts require a court to decide whether the state's "legitimate interest in the child's need for early permanence and stability" outweigh the father's paternal rights even when he is entirely blameless for his delay in asserting them.

Two well-publicized cases seem to suggest the Constitution requires protecting such fathers' paternal claims. In *Petition of Doe*, 638 N.E.2d 181 (Ill. 1994), the mother consented to adoption four days after birth but refused to reveal the father's name. In fact, she told the father the child had died. Suspicious, he investigated, learned the truth when the child was 57 days old, and immediately contested the adoption. The trial court found him unfit because he had failed to show "a reasonable degree of interest in the child in the first 30 days of life" as required by the Illinois Adoption Act. The Illinois Supreme Court eventually reversed, noting that there was no evidence to support the finding that the father had no early *interest* in the child. By the time of its decision the child was more than three years old, and had been with the adoptive parents throughout the appeals. But the court nonetheless ordered the child returned to the father, vindicating his paternal rights despite the disruption in the child's placement. In *B.G.C.*, 496 N.W.2d 239 (Iowa 1992), known popularly as the "Baby Jessica" case, the mother knowingly misrepresented her daughter's actual father in the adoption consent she gave two days after her birth. Ten days later she recanted and named the true father, who shortly thereafter intervened in the adoption case and filed his own paternity action seeking custody, and prevailed. Thus this case is in one sense not entirely on point because the father acted promptly, whether measured from the child's birth or from the time he learned of it. There was, however, considerable delay before he actually gained custody of the child, because the adoptive parents (the DeBoers) appealed, and retained custody of the child during those appeals. The appeals did not end until the little girl was two and a half, when the U.S. Supreme Court denied review of a decision of the Michigan Supreme Court, which had refused their plea to ignore the Iowa authorities and decide the matter anew. *In re Baby Girl Clausen*, 502 N.W. 2d 649 (Mich. 1993), *cert. denied sub nom, DeBoer v. Schmidt*, 509 U.S. 1301 (1993) (requiring the DeBoers' return of the child to the biological father (who by this time had married the biological mother) because the father's paternal rights "had not been terminated in accordance with Iowa law and therefore applicants were not entitled to adopt the child").

In both *Doe* and *Clausen* the considerable delay in effecting the child's final placement seemed disruptive to the child and prompted considerable, and unfavorable, attention in the popular media. Clearly, however, the father bore no responsibility for the delay in this case: it resulted instead from mistaken judicial decisions combined with the adopltive parents' recalcitrance. Perhaps significantly, however, given his views about the limited rights of nonmarital fathers with respect to newborns, Justice Stevens joined the denial of certiorari in *Clausen* with an opinion clearly rejecting the adoptive parents' claim. "Neither Iowa law, nor Michigan law, nor federal law authorizes unrelated persons to retain custody of a child whose natural parents have not been found to be unfit simply because they may be better able to provide for her future. [The DeBoers' claim that the child's interests require leaving her with them are grounded in part] on the relationship they have been able to develop with the child *after* it became clear that they were not entitled to adopt her." Both *Clausen* and *Doe* are also described in Chapter 11.

These cases present difficult conflicts between the child's interest in stability and the father's paternal rights. In *Clausen* and *Doe* the courts hold that the blameless father's paternal rights must prevail. But will they prevail no matter how long the delay before they are asserted? Consider what would happen if the mother in *Doe* had covered her tracks more effectively so that the father, despite his best efforts, did not learn the truth until the child was five years old? Ten years old? Perhaps at some point the result would shift. For further discussion of these issues, see Jeanette Mills, Comment, *Unwed Birthfathers and Infant Adoptions: Balancing a Father's Rights with the State's Need for a Timely Surrender Process*, 62 LA. L. REV. 615 (2002); Carol A. Gorenberg, *Fathers' Rights v. Children's Best Interests*, 31 FAM. L. Q. 169 (1997).

In an attempt to prevent unwed mothers from hiding their pregnancies from the biological fathers, and going forward with an adoption by third parties without the fathers' knowledge, Florida required mothers who place their children for adoption to publish certain information. FLA. ST. §§ 63.087-63.088 (2002). The required information included details as to the persons with whom the mother had sexual relations that may have resulted in the child's conception. A Florida court struck down the statute as unconstitutional, in an action by four women who argued that the statute infringed on their right of privacy as defined by the Florida Constitution. *G.P., C.M., C.H. and L.H. v. Florida*, 842 So. 3d 1059 (Fla. App. 2003). Most recently, some biological fathers have brought tort claims against the mothers or their attorneys whom they allege have intentionally concealed the child's birth or her plans to place the child for adoption. *See Kessel v. Leavitt*, 511 S.E.3d 720 (W. Va. 1998); *Smith v. Malouf*, 722 So. 2d 490 (Miss. 1998).

6. *More On Putative Father Registries*. Undoubtedly influenced by the Court's decision in *Lehr*, the putative father registry has proven a popular method for states to ensure that their statutes will meet constitutional standards. UPA 2002 adopts a registry in Article 4, the Prefatory Note to which observes that as of May, 2000, "at least 28 states had enacted legislation creating paternity registries." However, some of the state registry laws seem designed more to defeat paternal claims than to protect them. *See, e.g., Friehe v. Schaad*, 545 N.W.2d 740 (Neb. 1996) (sustaining a requirement that the putative father register within five days of the child's birth). Alabama created what appeared to be an absolute bar to adoption challenges by putative unwed fathers who do not file with its state registry within thirty days of the child's birth. *See* ALA. ST. § 26-10C-1 (2003). A divided Alabama Supreme Court held nonetheless that a man who had not filed with the registry, but had filed a legitimation and paternity action within fifteen days of child's birth, could pursue his paternity action. *S.C.W. v. C.B.,* 826 So. 2d 844, (2001). The legislature then amended the law to remove the ambiguity that the court had relied upon to avoid the registry requirement. ALA. ST. §§ 26-10C-1, 26-10A-7, 26-10C-9 (2003). For further discussion of these developments in Alabama, see Shirley D. Howell, *The Putative Father Registry; Behold Now the Behemoth (A Cautionary Tale),* 64 ALABAMA LAWYER 237 (2003). Some states that do not have registries have concluded that they don't need one because the provisions they do have satisfy *Lehr*'s constitutional requirements. *See, e.g., B.G. v. H.S.,* 509 N.E.2d 214 (Ind. Ct. App. 1988) (holding that statutes entitling a man to notice if he has filed a paternity action are sufficient).

After *Lehr* the Commisioners on Uniform State Laws initially rejected a registry in the Uniform Putative and Unknown Fathers Act. But UPA 2002, which supplants that Act, adopts the registry approach. The core registry provisions of UPA 2002 are §§ 402, 404, and 405. Some of the UPA definitional sections are also important.

UNIFORM PARENTAGE ACT (2002)

Section 102. Definitions. In this [Act]:

(1) "Acknowledged father" means a man who has established a father-child relationship under [Article] 3.

(2) "Adjudicated father" means a man who has been adjudicated by a court of competent jurisdiction to be the father of a child.

(3) "Alleged father" means a man who alleges himself to be, or is alleged to be, the genetic father or a possible genetic father of a child, but whose paternity has not been determined. The term does not include:

(A) a presumed father;

(B) a man whose parental rights have been terminated or declared not to exist; or

(C) a male donor.

. . .

(16) "Presumed father" means a man who, by operation of law under Section 204, is recognized as the father of a child until that status is rebutted or confirmed in a judicial proceeding.

Section 402. Registration for Notification.

(a) Except as otherwise provided in subsection (b) or Section 405, a man who desires to be notified of a proceeding for adoption of, or termination of parental rights regarding, a child that he may have fathered must register in the registry of paternity before the birth of the child or within 30 days after the birth.

(b) A man is not required to register if [:

(1)] a father-child relationship between the man and the child has been established under this [Act] or other law [; or

(2) the man commences a proceeding to adjudicate his paternity before the court has terminated his parental rights].

(c) A registrant shall promptly notify the registry in a record of any change in the information registered. The [agency maintaining the registry] shall incorporate all new information received into its records but need not affirmatively seek to obtain current information for incorporation in the registry.

Section 404. Termination of Parental Rights: Child under One Year of Age.

The parental rights of a man who may be the father of a child may be terminated without notice if:

(1) the child has not attained one year of age at the time of the termination of parental rights;

(2) the man did not register timely with the [agency maintaining the registry]; and

(3) the man is not exempt from registration under Section 402.

Section 405. Termination of Parental Rights: Child at Least One Year of Age.

(a) If a child has attained one year of age, notice of a proceeding for adoption of, or termination of parental rights regarding, the child must be given to every alleged father of the child, whether or not he has registered with the [agency maintaining the registry].

(b) Notice must be given in a manner prescribed for service of process in a civil action.

———

The way to understand a set of provisions like these is to ask which men are entitled under them to notice of an adoption or termination proceeding. The answer, where the child is under one year of age, is: a) those who have registered within 30 days of the child's birth; b) those who have already established their paternity of the child under the UPA or some other state law; and c) those who have initiated their own paternity action before the adoption or termination proceedings have become final. Where the child is at least one year old, notice must also be given to every alleged father, whether or not he has registered. One can immediately see that Mr. Lehr himself would have been entitled to notice under the UPA 2002 provisions because he had commenced his own paternity action prior to the entry of the adoption order.

What is added by Section 405? If one understands "alleged father" to mean only a man who has been alleged to be the father in an legal proceeding of some kind, not very much, for the man who has brought a paternity action is entitled to notice even if the child is less than one. The intended meaning, however, is broader: any man whom the mother identifies as the likely or perhaps even possible father, either in response to an adoption agency's inquiries or in her adoption petition, is also an "alleged father" entitled to notice when the child is more than one year old, even if he has not put himself in the adoption registry.

Also key under these provisions is understanding when "a father-child relationship between the man and the child has been established" under the UPA, because such men are entitled to notice even if unregistered. First, a man who has signed an acknowledgment of paternity under § 302 has an established father-child relationship because, as § 305 provides, "a valid acknowledgment of paternity filed with the [agency maintaining birth records] is equivalent to an adjudication of paternity of a child and confers upon the acknowledged father all of the rights and duties of a parent." Recall that under current child support enforcement programs such acknowledgment is routinely sought from putative fathers at the time of birth, and is increasingly obtained. Second, consider a man (call him Joe) who has lived with the mother and her child since the child's birth, holding himself out as the child's father. Perhaps he did not register because he saw no need to. Joe and the mother have a falling out and they part. The mother marries another man, and seeks to have him adopt the child. Must notice be given to Joe? Joe may be in touch with the mother, and know of her new relationship, but that alone does not guarantee that he would know of the adoption petition the mother has filed. If he had lived with the mother and child for at least two years from the child's birth, he is a presumed father under § 204(a)(5). Moreover, under § 607, the paternity of such a presumed cannot be challenged, even with genetic evidence, unless the challenger can show the presumed father never lived with the mother, never had sexual relations with her during the probable period of conception, and never held the child out as his own. Given that § 201 says that the "father-child relationship is established . . . by . . . an unrebutted presumption of the man's paternity . . . under Section 204," presumed fathers are established fathers entitled to notice. (This group includes husbands of the mother as well as men like Joe.)

By contrast, if Joe's falling out with the mother occurred when they had lived together only 20 months, he would not qualify as a presumed father. Nor would he if their period of cohabitation did not begin at the child's birth, even if it lasted more than two years. These "Joe-lights," so to speak, are not presumed fathers and are therefore not entitled to notice under §§ 402 or 405. To protect themselves, they must bring their own paternity action promptly after the falling out with the mother. If they do so prior to the entry of an adoption or termination order, they are guaranteed notice of any such action; otherwise they are not. What if the child is more than one year old at the time of the adoption proceeding, so that § 405 applies? This man will be entitled to notice even without filing such an action if the mother names him in the adoption petition as the likely father, as she should, because he is then an "alleged father" under that section. But what if she doesn't? Or more generally, what if an adoption order is entered without notice having been given to a man entitled to notice under the UPA? Adoption laws may allow the father to petition to annul the adoption. Adoption laws typically provide a time limit within which such an action must be brought. If the father acts within this limit he should be successful if he shows that he was indeed entitled to notice. Would our "Joe-light" succeed? If § 405 were read as written it would seem not, for even though the mother *should* have named him at the time of adoption she did not, and so he was not *then* an alleged father even though he should have been, and is now. Nonetheless, it seems likely that this provision will be read to vindicate such men on the ground that they would have been an alleged father at the time of adoption but for the mother's false statements to the adoption agency or in her adoption petition.

What happens under UPA 2002 with the deceived father (see Note 5 *supra*)? Consider, for example, the facts of *Petition of Doe*, described above in Note 5. Recall the mother told the father the child had died in childbirth. Suppose the father understandably does not register, and does not learn the truth until after the 30 day registration period has passed. Once again, his only recourse is to file his own paternity action, and hope he does so before entry of any adoption or termination order.

7. *The Substantive Criteria Applied in the Adoption Hearing*. If the unwed father receives notice of an adoption hearing and objects in a timely manner, what standard should be used to resolve the dispute between the father and those parties who wish the adoption to go forward? In *Quilloin,* the Supreme Court held that the state could approve an adoption over the father's objection on a best-interests standard. This standard, of course, gives strangers equal claims to the child as the nonmarital father, according him no deference. In reaching this result the Court emphasized that Mr. Quilloin did not have constitutionally-protected interests in a relationship with his child because he never "had, or sought, actual or legal custody of his child." *Quilloin* involved an older child whose whereabouts the father had known, and so he had had years of opportunity in which to assert his paternal rights. In *Caban,* by contrast, the Court found that the same rule, if applied to unwed fathers "even when their identity is known and they have manifested a significant paternal interest in the child," was a gender classification that violated the Equal Protection Clause (given that adoption could not be approved over the objection of the mother unless she was found unfit). Left unresolved was whether the unwed father of the newborn, whose interest in the child could not yet have been acted upon, was to be treated like Mr. Quilloin or Mr. Caban. There have been a fair number of state supreme court decisions addressing this question, however.

In *Adoption of Kelsey S.*, 1 Cal.4th 816, 823 P.2d 1216 (Cal. 1992), the California Supreme Court rejected the best interests standard. The biological father, Rickie M., brought an action to establish his paternity two days after the birth of his biological son, Kelsey. The mother, Kari S. had placed Kelsey with a prospective adoptive couple immediately after Kelsey's birth, and prevented Rickie from taking custody of the child, despite his statements to her that he wished to raise Kelsey. Rickie's action was consolidated with the adoption petition filed by that couple. The trial court terminated Rickie's rights on best interests grounds. Applying the UPA (1973), which California had adopted, the trial court had construed the plain language of the statute to exclude him as a "presumed father" because he did not qualify under any of the provisions relating to marriage or attempted marriage to the mother, and he had not received the child into his home, holding the child out as his own. If he had been determined to be a presumed father, California law would have precluded the adoption unless he was found to be unfit. Thus, although Rickie was permitted to appear in the adoption action to object, the trial court allowed the adoption after applying a the best interests standard.

The California Supreme Court agreed that Rickie was not a presumed father under the statute but held that federal constitutional principles required California to recognize his "reasonable and meaningful attempt to establish a relationship." 1 Cal.4th at 837, 823 P.2d at 1228. Overriding his objection to the adoption on a best interests standard was therefore unconstitutional:

> [The California] statutory scheme violates the federal constitutional guarantees of equal protection and due process for unwed fathers *to the extent that* the statutes allow a mother unilaterally to preclude her child's biological father from becoming a presumed father and thereby allowing the state to terminate his parental rights on nothing more than a showing of the child's best interest. If an unwed father promptly comes forward and demonstrates a full commitment to his parental responsibilities — emotional, financial, and otherwise — his federal constitutional right to due process prohibits the termination of his parental relationship absent a showing of his unfitness as a parent. Similarly, when the father has come forward to grasp his parental responsibilities, his parental rights are entitled to equal protection as those of the mother.

> . . . . The father's conduct both *before and after* the child's birth must be considered. Once the father knows or reasonably should know of the pregnancy, he must promptly attempt to assume his parental responsibilities as fully as the mother will allow and his circumstances permit. In particular, the father must demonstrate "a willingness himself to assume full custody of the child — not merely to block adoption by others." [citing *Raquel Marie*]. A court should also consider the father's public acknowledgment of paternity, payment of pregnancy and birth expenses commensurate with his ability to do so, and prompt legal action to seek custody of the child.

1 Cal. 4th at 849, 823 P.2d at 1236-37 (emphasis in original). The court emphasized further that "any finding of petitioner's unfitness must be supported by clear and convincing evidence. Absent such evidence, he shall be permitted to withhold his consent to the adoption." 1 Cal. 4th at 851, 823 P.2d at 1238. Finally, the court qualified that this standard applied solely to the question of whether the father can block the adoption. "Even if petitioner has a right to withhold his consent (and chooses to prevent the adoption), there will remain the question of the child's custody. That question is not before us, and we express no view on it." 1 Cal. 4th at 851, 823 P.2d at 1238. For a similar analysis, see *Baby Girl Eason,* 358 S.E.2d 459, 462–63 (Ga. 1987).

For more on this topic, see Katherine T. Bartlett, *Re-Expressing Parenthood*, 98 YALE L.J. 293 (1988), and Elizabeth Buchanan, *The Constitutional Rights of Unwed Fathers Before and After* Lehr v. Robertson, 45 OHIO ST. L.J. 313 (1984), on which *Eason* heavily relies.

PROBLEMS

Problem 9-19. (a) John and Mary have lived together for five years in a marriage-like relationship. They have a two-year-old child. They are now breaking up, and both want custody. State law provides that the unmarried mother should be given custody unless the father shows that maternal custody would be detrimental to the child. John loses the custody contest and challenges this standard. What result?

(b) John and Mary lived together for five years, but broke up when their child was six months old. In the year since then, John has visited the child irregularly and contributed occasionally to his support. Mary sought a formal order giving her custody and allowing her new husband to adopt the child. John opposed both. State law permits an adoption over the unmarried father's objection where it is in the best interests of the child. The law also prefers the mother for custody unless the father shows that maternal custody would be detrimental to the child. The mother prevails on both the custody and adoption petitions. John challenges the state law on appeal. What result?

(c) Suppose John and Mary had broken up during Mary's pregnancy. John has continually made efforts to see the child, but has been effectively stymied by Mary. His offers of support have been refused. Mary now seeks to have her new husband adopt the year-old child, who has never seen John. She knows that John will object, and therefore prefers to go forward with the adoption without notifying him. State law allows unwed fathers to register their interest in the child, but John, who has never consulted counsel, is unaware of the law and has never registered. Under state law, only married fathers and registered putative fathers must be notified of adoption proceedings. The adoption is completed without notification to John. Will he prevail on a subsequent constitutional challenge to the procedure?

(d) Assume the same facts as in (c), but John learns of the hearing and appears to object. Do constitutional rules permit the adoption petition to be granted on a best-interests standard?

(e) Assume the same facts as (c), but Mary has not remarried. She seeks to place the child for adoption in the home of a couple known to her doctor. She knows that John would oppose the adoption and would seek custody himself, and therefore wants to proceed without notifying him. Is notice constitutionally compelled? Assume that John learns of the adoption hearing and appears to object and seek custody. May the court grant the adoption on a best-interest standard?

Problem 9-20. Sally becomes pregnant by Sam while unmarried. After giving birth, she marries Sam, but remains firm that their child should be given up for adoption. Sam never sees the child, although he wanted to. Sally arranges for adoption of the child, although Sam had made clear to her that he objects. He is not notified of the hearing and does not appear. Does the adoption satisfy relevant constitutional requirements?

Problem 9-21. Jonathan and Jessica have a child together while unmarried but cohabiting. They raise the child together for a year and half, but then their relationship ends. Their separation is relatively amicable. Jessica retains primary custody of the child but Jonathan see the child several times a week and often has the child overnight. When the child is four Jessica moves in with a new boyfriend, and she becomes a bit less cooperative with Jonathan. Jessica then marries the new boyfriend. Jonathan is nervous that Jessica may try to cut off his access, but he has heard that there is a putative father registry in his state. He places his name and his claim to paternity of Jessica's child on the registry. Jessica and her husband begin proceedings shortly after to have him adopt the child. No notice of the adoption petition is given to Jonathan, in reliance upon a state law which requires such notice only to men who register within 30 days of the child's birth. State law also requires notice to presumed fathers, and includes a definition of presumed paternity taken from UPA 2002. Jonathan is not a presumed father under this definition because he did not live with mother and child for at least two years from the child's birth. The adoption petition is granted in conformity with state law. Jonathan learns of this for the first time when Jessica denies him access to the child shortly after the adoption is finalized. Jonathan promptly files an action to annual the adoption alleging that it is void because he was denied constitutionally required notice of the proceedings. Evaluate his constitutional claim.

Problem 9-22. Assume the facts of Problem 9-21 except that Jonathan and Jessica never live together because Jessica does not wish to live with Jonathan. Indeed, Jessica is uncooperative from the outset with Jonathan's attempts to see the child, and Jonathan begins to worry that she will give the child up for adoption. A friend tells him about the putative father registry and he files with it 45 days after the child's birth. Unbeknownst to him, an adoption proceedings have already been filed. The child is adopted by a couple Jessica has picked from the files of a local adoption lawyer. Jonathan challenges the adoption promptly claiming that he should have been given notice of the adoption proceeding. The failure to give him notice complied with state law because Jonathan had not registered within 30 days of the child's birth, had not filed a paternity action, and was not a presumed father under the state's UPA-inspired definition.

Problem 9-23. Assume in Problem 9-22 Jonathan heard about the adoption proceeding even though he was not provided notice, and files an objection to the adoption. Jessica does not contest Jonathan's standing to object but argues that adoption is in the child's best interest. The court grants the adoption under that standard. State law is clear that an adoption over the objection of the mother can be allowed only if the court finds the mother has abandoned the child or is unfit. Jonathan appeals the adoption order on both substantive due process and equal protection grounds. Jonathan does not wish primary custody of the child himself, but objects to the adoption because it would cut off his access to the child completely. What result? Suppose Jonathan does seek primary custody of the child?

[b]   The Unwed Father v. the Mother's Husband

Historically, cases in which unwed fathers claimed paternal rights with respect to a child born to a married women were rare. Does such an unwed father have a constitutional right to assert paternity that overrides state marital presumptions of paternity? Must states give such men the opportunity to rebut that presumption, or are there policies that justify, in such cases, ignoring biological paternity when assigning legal paternity? In 1989, the Supreme Court considered such a case.

MICHAEL H. v. GERALD D.

491 U.S. 110 (1989)

JUSTICE SCALIA announced the judgment of the Court and delivered an opinion, in which THE CHIEF JUSTICE joins, and in all but note 6 of which JUSTICE O'CONNOR and JUSTICE KENNEDY join.

Under California law, a child born to a married woman living with her husband is presumed to be a child of the marriage. The presumption of legitimacy may be rebutted only by the husband or wife, and then only in limited circumstances. The instant appeal presents the claim that this presumption infringes upon the due process rights of a man who wishes to establish his paternity of a child born to the wife of another man, and the claim that it infringes upon the constitutional right of the child to maintain a relationship with her natural father.

The facts of this case are, we must hope, extraordinary. On May 9, 1976, in Las Vegas, Nevada, Carole D., an international model, and Gerald D., a top executive in a French oil company, were married. The couple established a home in Playa del Rey, California in which they resided as husband and wife when one or the other was not out of the country on business. In the summer of 1978, Carole became involved in an adulterous affair with a neighbor, Michael H. In September 1980, she conceived a child, Victoria D., who was born on May 11, 1981. Gerald was listed as father on the birth certificate and has always held Victoria out to the world as his daughter. Soon after delivery of the child, however, Carole informed Michael that she believed he might be the father.

In the first three years of her life, Victoria remained always with Carole, but found herself within a variety of quasi-family units. In October 1981, Gerald moved to New York City to pursue his business interests, but Carole chose to remain in California. The end of that month, Carole and Michael had blood tests of themselves and Victoria, which showed a 98.07% probability that Michael was Victoria's father. In January 1982, Carole visited Michael in St. Thomas, where his primary business interests were based. There Michael held Victoria out as his child. In March, however, Carole left Michael and returned to California, where she took up residence with yet another man, Scott K. Later that spring, and again in the summer, Carole and Victoria spent time with Gerald in New York City, as well as on vacation in Europe. In the fall, they returned to Scott in California.

In November 1982, rebuffed in his attempts to visit Victoria, Michael filed a filiation action in California Superior Court to establish his paternity and right to visitation. In March 1983, the court appointed an attorney and guardian ad litem to represent Victoria's interests. Victoria then filed a cross-complaint asserting that if she had more than one psychological or de facto father, she was entitled to maintain her filial relationship, with all of the attendant rights, duties, and obligations, with both. In May 1983, Carole filed a motion for summary judgment. During this period, from March through July of 1983, Carole was again living with Gerald in New York. In August, however, she returned to California, became involved once again with Michael, and instructed her attorneys to remove the summary judgment motion from the calendar.

For the ensuing eight months, when Michael was not in St. Thomas he lived with Carole and Victoria in Carole's apartment in Los Angeles, and held Victoria out as his daughter. In April 1984, Carole and Michael signed a stipulation that Michael was Victoria's natural father. Carole left Michael the next month, however, and instructed her attorneys not to file the stipulation. In June 1984, Carole reconciled with Gerald and joined him in New York, where they now live with Victoria and two other children since born into the marriage.

In May 1984, Michael and Victoria, through her guardian ad litem, sought visitation rights for Michael pendente lite. To assist in determining whether visitation would be in Victoria's best interests, the Superior Court appointed a psychologist to evaluate Victoria, Gerald, Michael, and Carole. The psychologist recommended that Carole retain sole custody, but that Michael be allowed continued contact with Victoria pursuant to a restricted visitation schedule. The court concurred and ordered that Michael be provided with limited visitation privileges pendente lite.

On October 19, 1984, Gerald, who had intervened in the action, moved for summary judgment on the ground that under Cal. Evid. Code § 621 there were no triable issues of fact as to Victoria's paternity. This law provides that "the issue of a wife cohabiting with her husband, who is not impotent or sterile, is conclusively presumed to be a child of the marriage." Cal. Evid. Code Ann. § 621(a) (Supp. 1989). The presumption may be rebutted by blood tests, but only if a motion for such tests is made, within two years from the date of the child's birth, either by the husband or, if the natural father has filed an affidavit acknowledging paternity, by the wife. §§ 621(c) and (d).

On January 28, 1985, having found that affidavits submitted by Carole and Gerald sufficed to demonstrate that the two were cohabiting at conception and birth and that . . . Gerald was neither sterile nor impotent, the Superior Court granted Gerald's motion for summary judgment, rejecting Michael's and Victoria's challenges to the constitutionality of § 621. The court also denied their motions for continued visitation pending the appeal. . . . [because] such visitation would "violat[e] the intention of the Legislature by impugning the integrity of the family unit."

On appeal, Michael asserted, inter alia, that the Superior Court's application of § 621 had violated his procedural and substantive due process rights. Victoria also raised a due process challenge to the statute, seeking to preserve her de facto relationship with Michael as well as with Gerald. She contended, in addition, that as § 621 allows the husband and, at least to a limited extent, the mother, but not the child, to rebut the presumption of legitimacy, it violates the child's right to equal protection. Finally, she asserted a right to continued visitation with Michael. . . . [T]he California Court of Appeal affirmed the judgment . . . and upheld the constitutionality of the statute. . ., 236 Cal. Rptr. 810 (1987). It interpreted that judgment, moreover, as having denied permanent visitation rights . . . regarding that as the implication of the Superior Court's reliance upon § 621 and [other California authorities]. . . .

The . . . California Supreme Court denied discretionary review. . . . Before us, Michael and Victoria both raise equal protection and due process challenges. We do not reach Michael's equal protection claim, however, as it was neither raised nor passed upon below.

II

The California statute that is the subject of this litigation is, in substance, more than a century old. . . . In their present form, the substantive provisions of the statute are as follows:

"§ 621. Child of the marriage; notice of motion for blood tests

"(a) Except as provided in subdivision (b), the issue of wife cohabiting with her husband, who is not impotent or sterile, is conclusively presumed to be a child of the marriage.

"(b) Notwithstanding the provisions of subdivision (a), if the court finds that the conclusions of all the experts, as disclosed by the evidence based upon blood tests performed pursuant to Chapter 2 (commencing with Section 890) of Division 7 are that the husband is not the father of the child, the question of paternity of the husband shall be resolved accordingly.

"(c) The notice of motion for blood tests under subdivision (b) may be raised by the husband not later than two years from the child's date of birth.

"(d) The notice of motion for blood tests under subdivision (b) may be raised by the mother of the child not later than two years from the child's date of birth if the child's biological father has filed an affidavit with the court acknowledging paternity of the child.

"(e) The provisions of subdivision (b) shall not apply to any case coming within the provisions of Section 7005 of the Civil Code [dealing with artificial insemination] or to any case in which the wife, with the consent of the husband, conceived by means of a surgical procedure."

III

We address first the claims of Michael. . . . California law, like nature itself, makes no provision for dual fatherhood. Michael was seeking to be declared the father of Victoria. The immediate benefit he evidently sought to obtain from the status was visitation rights. See Cal. Civ. Code Ann. § 4601

(West 1983) (parent has statutory right to visitation "unless it is shown that such visitation would be detrimental to the best interests of the child"). But if Michael were successful in being declared the father, other rights would follow — most importantly, the right to be considered as the parent who should have custody. . . . All parental rights, including visitation, were automatically denied by denying Michael status as the father. . . . [since] California law denies visitation, against the wishes of the mother, to a putative father who has been prevented by § 621 from establishing his paternity.

Michael . . . [f]irst . . . asserts that requirements of procedural due process prevent the State from terminating his liberty interest in his relationship with his child without affording him an opportunity to demonstrate his paternity in an evidentiary hearing. We believe this claim derives from a fundamental misconception of the nature of the California statute. While § 621 is phrased in terms of a presumption, that rule of evidence is the implementation of a substantive rule of law. California declares it to be, except in limited circumstances, irrelevant for paternity purposes whether a child conceived during and born into an existing marriage was begotten by someone other than the husband and had a prior relationship with him. As the Court of Appeal phrased it:

> "The conclusive presumption is actually a substantive rule of law based upon a determination by the Legislature as a matter of overriding social policy, that given a certain relationship between the husband and wife, the husband is to be held responsible for the child, and that the integrity of the family unit should not be impugned." 191 Cal. App. 3d, at 1005, 236 Cal. Rptr., at 816, quoting *Vincent B. v. Joan R.,* 126 Cal. App. 3d, at 623, 179 Cal. Rptr. at 10.

Of course the conclusive presumption not only expresses the State's substantive policy but also furthers it, excluding inquiries into the child's paternity that would be destructive of family integrity and privacy.

This Court has struck down . . . certain "irrebuttable presumptions." Those holdings did not, however, rest upon procedural due process. . . . We therefore reject Michael's procedural due process challenge and proceed to his substantive claim.

Michael contends as a matter of substantive due process that because he has established a parental relationship with Victoria, protection of Gerald's and Carole's marital union is an insufficient state interest to support termination of that relationship. This argument is, of course, predicated on the assertion that Michael has a constitutionally protected liberty interest in his relationship with Victoria.

[T]he term "liberty" in the Due Process Clause extends beyond freedom from physical restraint. . . . [T]o limit and guide interpretation of the Clause, we have insisted not merely that the interest denominated as a "liberty" be "fundamental" (a concept that, in isolation, is hard to objectify), but also that it be an interest traditionally protected by our society.

. . . . Michael reads the landmark case of *Stanley* and the subsequent cases of *Quilloin, Caban,* and *Lehr,* as establishing that a liberty interest is created by biological fatherhood plus an established parental relationship — factors that exist in the present case as well. We think that distorts the rationale of those cases. As we view them, they rest not upon such isolated factors but upon the historic respect — indeed, sanctity would not be too strong a term — traditionally accorded to the relationships that develop within the unitary family. In *Stanley,* for example, we forbade the destruction of such a family when, upon the death of the mother, the state had sought to remove children from the custody of a father who had lived with and supported them and their mother for 18 years. As Justice Powell stated for the plurality in *Moore v. East Cleveland:* "Our decisions establish that the Constitution protects the sanctity of the family precisely because the institution of the family is deeply rooted in this Nation's history and tradition."

Thus, the legal issue in the present case reduces to whether the relationship between persons in the situation of Michael and Victoria has been treated as a protected family unit under the historic practices of our society, or [otherwise] has been accorded special protection. We think, . . . quite to the contrary, our traditions have protected the marital family (Gerald, Carole, and the child they acknowledge to be theirs) against the sort of claim Michael asserts.

The presumption of legitimacy was a fundamental principle of the common law. Traditionally, that presumption could be rebutted only by proof that a husband was incapable of procreation or had had no access to his wife during the relevant period. . . . BLACKSTONE'S COMMENTARIES 456 (Chitty ed. 1826). . . . The primary policy rationale underlying . . . common law's severe restrictions on rebuttal of the presumption appears to have been an aversion to declaring children illegitimate, thereby depriving them of rights of inheritance and succession, and likely making them wards of the state. A secondary policy concern was the interest in promoting the "peace and tranquility of States and families," . . . a goal that is obviously impaired by facilitating suits against husband and wife asserting that their children are illegitimate. . . . [¶] [E]ven in modern times — when, as we have noted, the rigid protection of the marital family has in other respects been relaxed — the ability of a person in Michael's position to claim paternity has not been generally acknowledged. . . .

. . . .What Michael asserts here is a right to have himself declared the natural father and thereby to obtain parental prerogatives. What he must establish, therefore, is not that our society has traditionally allowed a natural father in his circumstances to establish paternity, but that it has traditionally accorded such a father parental rights, or at least has not traditionally denied them. . . . What counts is whether the States . . . award substantive parental rights to the natural father of a child conceived within and born into an extant marital union that wishes to embrace the child. We are not aware of a single case, old or new, that has done so. This is not the stuff of which fundamental rights qualifying as liberty interests are made.

In *Lehr* . . . we observed that "[t]he significance of the biological connection is that it offers the natural father an opportunity that no other male possesses to develop a relationship with his offspring," and we assumed that the Constitution might require some protection of that opportunity. Where, however, the child is born into an extant marital family, the natural father's unique opportunity conflicts with the similarly unique opportunity of the husband of the marriage; and it is not unconstitutional for the State to give categorical preference to the latter. . . . In accord with our traditions, a limit is . . . imposed by the circumstance that the mother is, at the time of the child's conception and birth, married to and cohabiting with another man, both of whom wish to raise the child as the offspring of their union. It is a question of legislative policy and not constitutional law whether California will allow the presumed parenthood of a couple desiring to retain a child conceived within and born into their marriage to be rebutted.

We do not accept JUSTICE BRENNAN's criticism that this result "squashes" the liberty that consists of "the freedom not to conform." [T]hat reflects the erroneous view that there is only one side to this controversy. . . . [B]ut to provide protection to an adulterous natural father is to deny protection to a marital father, and vice versa. If Michael has a "freedom not to conform" (whatever that means), Gerald must equivalently have a "freedom to conform.". . . Our disposition does not choose between these two "freedoms," but leaves that to the people of California. JUSTICE BRENNAN's approach chooses one of them as the constitutional imperative, on no apparent basis except that the unconventional is to be preferred.

IV

We have never had occasion to decide whether a child has a liberty interest symmetrical with that of her parent, in maintaining her filial relationship. We need not do so here because, even assuming that such a right exists, Victoria's claim must fail. Victoria's due process challenge is, if anything, weaker than Michael's. Her basic claim is not that California has erred in preventing her from establishing that Michael, not Gerald, should stand as her legal father. Rather, she claims a due process right to maintain filial relationships with both Michael and Gerald. This assertion merits little discussion, for, whatever the merits of the guardian ad litem's belief that such an arrangement can be of great psychological benefit to a child, the claim that a State must recognize multiple fatherhood has no support in the history or traditions of this country. Moreover, even if we were to construe Victoria's argument as forwarding the lesser proposition that, whatever her status vis-à-vis Gerald, she has a liberty interest in maintaining a filial relationship with her natural father, Michael, we find that, at best, her claim is the obverse of Michael's and fails for the same reasons.

Victoria claims in addition that her equal protection rights have been violated because, unlike her mother and presumed father, she had no opportunity to rebut the presumption of her legitimacy. We find this argument wholly without merit. We reject, at the outset, Victoria's suggestion that her equal protection challenge must be assessed under a standard of strict scrutiny because, in denying her the right to maintain a filial relationship with Michael, the State is discriminating against her on the basis of her illegitimacy. Illegitimacy is a legal construct, not a natural trait. Under California law, Victoria is not illegitimate, and she is treated in the same manner as all other legitimate children: she is entitled to maintain a filial relationship with her legal parents.

We apply, therefore, the ordinary "rational relationship" test to Victoria's equal protection challenge. The primary rationale underlying § 621's limitation on those who may rebut the presumption of legitimacy is a concern that allowing persons other than the husband or wife to do so may undermine the integrity of the marital union. When the husband or wife contests the legitimacy of their child, the stability of the marriage has already been shaken. In contrast, allowing a claim of illegitimacy to be pressed by the child — or, more accurately, by a court-appointed guardian ad litem — may well disrupt an otherwise peaceful union. Since it pursues a legitimate end by rational means, California's decision to treat Victoria differently from her parents is not a denial of equal protection.

The judgment of the California Court of Appeal is

Affirmed.

JUSTICE O'CONNOR, with whom JUSTICE KENNEDY joins, concurring in part.

I concur in all but footnote 6 of JUSTICE SCALIA's opinion. This footnote sketches a mode of historical analysis to be used when identifying liberty interests protected by the Due Process Clause of the Fourteenth Amendment that may be somewhat inconsistent with our past decisions in this area. See *Griswold* and *Eisenstadt.* On occasion the Court has characterized relevant traditions protecting asserted rights at levels of generality that might not be "the most specific level" available. See *Loving v. Virginia,* 388 U.S. 1, 12 (1967); *Turner v. Safley,* 482 U.S. 78, 94 (1987). I would not foreclose the unanticipated by the prior imposition of a single mode of historical analysis.

JUSTICE STEVENS, concurring in the judgment.

[D]oes the California statute deny appellants a fair opportunity to prove that Victoria's best interests would be served by granting Michael visitation rights? [¶] [On this question] I do not agree with JUSTICE SCALIA's analysis. He seems to reject the possibility that a natural father might ever have a constitutionally protected interest in his relationship with a child whose mother was married to and cohabiting with another man at the time of the child's conception and birth. I think cases like *Stanley* and *Caban* demonstrate that enduring "family" relationships may develop in unconventional settings. I therefore would not foreclose the possibility that a constitutionally protected relationship between a natural father and his child might exist in a case like this. Indeed, I am willing to assume . . . that Michael's relationship with Victoria is strong enough to give him a constitutional right to try to convince a trial judge that Victoria's best interest would be served by granting him visitation rights. I am satisfied, however, that the California statute, as applied in this case, gave him that opportunity.

Section 4601 of the California Civil Code Annotated (West Supp. 1989) provides:

> "[R]easonable visitation rights [shall be awarded] to a parent unless it is shown that the visitation would be detrimental to the best interests of the child. In the discretion of the court, reasonable visitation rights may be granted *to any other person having an interest in the welfare of the child.*" (Emphasis added.)

The presumption established by § 621 denied Michael the benefit of the first sentence of § 4601 because, as a matter of law, he is not a "parent." It does not, however, prevent him from proving that he is an "other person having an interest in the welfare of the child." On its face, therefore, the statute plainly gave the trial judge the authority to grant Michael "reasonable visitation rights."

I recognize that my colleagues have interpreted § 621 as creating an absolute bar that would prevent a California trial judge from regarding the natural father as either a "parent" within the meaning of the first sentence of § 4601 or as "any other person" within the meaning of the second sentence. That is not only an unnatural reading of the statute's plain language, but it is also not consistent with the California courts' reading of the statute. . . .

[I]n this case, the trial judge not only found the conclusive presumption applicable, but also separately considered the effect of § 4601 and expressly found "that, at the present time, it is not in the best interests of the child that the Plaintiff have visitation. The Court believes that the existence of two (2) 'fathers' as male authority figures will confuse the child and be counter-productive to her best interests."

. . . Michael was given a fair opportunity to show that he is Victoria's natural father, that he had developed a relationship with her, and that her interests would be served by granting him visitation rights. On the other hand, the record also shows that after its rather shaky start, the marriage between Carole and Gerald developed a stability that now provides Victoria with a loving and harmonious family home. In the circumstances of this case, I find nothing fundamentally unfair about the exercise of a judge's discretion that, in the end, allows the mother to decide whether her child's best interest would be served by allowing the natural father visitation privileges. Because I am convinced that the trial judge had the authority under state law both to hear Michael's plea for visitation rights and to grant him such rights if Victoria's best interests so warranted, I am satisfied that the California statutory scheme is consistent with the Due Process Clause of the Fourteenth Amendment.

I therefore concur in the Court's judgment of affirmance.

JUSTICE BRENNAN, with whom JUSTICE MARSHALL and JUSTICE BLACKMUN join, dissenting.

In a case that has yielded so many opinions as has this one, it is fruitful to begin by emphasizing the common ground shared by a majority of this Court. Five Members of the Court refuse to foreclose "the possibility that a natural father might ever have a constitutionally protected interest in his relationship with a child whose mother was married to and cohabiting with another man at the time of the child's conception and birth." (STEVENS, J., concurring in judgment.) Five Justices agree that the flaw inhering in a conclusive presumption that terminates a constitutionally protected interest without any hearing whatsoever is a procedural one. See *infra,* (WHITE, J., dissenting); *ante,* (STEVENS, J., concurring in judgment). Four Members of the Court agree that Michael H. has a liberty interest in his relationship with Victoria, see *infra,* (WHITE, J., dissenting), and one assumes for purposes of this case that he does, see *ante,* (STEVENS, J., concurring in judgment).

In contrast, only two Members of the Court fully endorse JUSTICE SCALIA'S view of the proper method of analyzing questions arising under the Due Process Clause. See *ante,* (O'CONNOR, J., concurring in part). Nevertheless, because the plurality opinion's exclusively historical analysis portends a significant and unfortunate departure from our prior cases and from sound constitutional decisionmaking, I devote a substantial portion of my discussion to it. [Most of this discussion is omitted. —Ed.]

. . .

Today's plurality . . . does not ask whether parenthood is an interest that historically has received our attention and protection; the answer to that question is too clear for dispute. Instead, the plurality asks whether the specific variety of parenthood under consideration — a natural father's relationship with a child whose mother is married to another man — has enjoyed such protection.

If we had looked to tradition with such specificity in past cases, many a decision would have reached a different result. Surely the use of contraceptives by unmarried couples, *Eisenstadt,* or even by married couples, *Griswold;* the freedom from corporal punishment in schools, *Ingraham v. Wright,* 430 U.S. 651 (1977); the freedom from an arbitrary transfer from a prison to a psychiatric institution, *Vitek v. Jones,* 445 U.S. 480 (1980); and even the right to raise one's natural but illegitimate children, *Stanley,* were not "interest[s] traditionally protected by our society," at the time of their consideration by this Court. If we had asked, therefore, in *Eisenstadt, Griswold, Ingraham, Vitek,* or *Stanley* itself whether the specific interest under consideration had been traditionally protected, the answer would have been a resounding "no." That we did not ask this question in those cases highlights the novelty of the interpretive method that the plurality opinion employs today.

. . . We are not an assimilative, homogeneous society, but a facilitative, pluralistic one, in which we must be willing to abide someone else's unfamiliar or even repellant practice because the same tolerant impulse protects our own idiosyncrasies. Even if we can agree, therefore, that "family" and "parenthood" are part of the good life, it is absurd to assume that we can agree on the content of those terms and destructive to pretend that we do. In a community such as ours, "liberty" must include the freedom not to conform. The plurality today squashes this freedom by requiring specific approval from history before protecting anything in the name of liberty.

II

. . . Where the interest under consideration is a parent-child relationship, we need not ask, over and over again, whether that interest is one that society traditionally protects. . . . The better approach . . . is to ask whether the specific parent-child relationship under consideration is close enough to the interests that we already have protected to be deemed an aspect of "liberty" as well. [T]herefore, the question is not what "level of generality" should be used to describe the relationship between Michael and Victoria, see *ante,* at n.6, but whether the relationship under consideration is sufficiently substantial to qualify as a liberty interest under our prior cases.

On four prior occasions, we have considered whether unwed fathers have a constitutionally protected interest in their relationships with their children. [Citing *Stanley, Quilloin, Caban,* and *Lehr.*] . . . [T]hese cases have produced a unifying theme: although an unwed father's biological link to his child does not, in and of itself, guarantee him a constitutional stake in his relationship with that child, such a link combined with a substantial parent-child relationship will do so . . . This commitment is why Mr. Stanley and Mr. Caban won; why Mr. Quilloin and Mr. Lehr lost; and why Michael H. should prevail today. Michael H. is almost certainly Victoria D.'s natural father, has lived with her as her father, has contributed to her support, and has from the beginning sought to strengthen and maintain his relationship with her.

Claiming that the intent of these cases was to protect the "unitary family," the plurality waves *Stanley, Quilloin, Caban,* and *Lehr* aside. In evaluating the plurality's dismissal of these precedents, it is essential to identify its conception of the "unitary family.". . . Though it pays lip service to the idea that marriage is not the crucial fact in denying constitutional protection to the relationship between Michael and Victoria, *ante,* at n.3, the plurality cannot mean what it says.

The evidence is undisputed that Michael, Victoria, and Carole did live together as a family; that is, they shared the same household, Victoria called Michael "Daddy," Michael contributed to Victoria's support, and he is eager to continue his relationship with her. Yet they are not, in the plurality's view, a "unitary family," whereas Gerald, Carole, and Victoria [are]. The only difference between these two sets of relationships, however, is the fact of marriage. . . . However, the very premise of *Stanley* and the cases following it is that the marriage is not decisive in answering the question whether the Constitution protects the parental relationship under consideration. . . . It is important to remember, moreover, that in *Quilloin, Caban,* and *Lehr,* the putative father's demands would have disrupted a "unitary family" as the plurality defines it; in each case, the husband of the child's mother sought to adopt the child over the objections of the natural father. Significantly, our decisions in those cases in no way relied on the need to protect the marital family. Hence the plurality's claim that *Stanley, Quilloin, Caban,* and *Lehr* were about the "unitary family," as that family is defined by today's plurality, is surprising indeed.

The plurality's focus on the "unitary family" . . . conflates the question whether a liberty interest exists with the question what procedures may be used to terminate or curtail it. It is no coincidence that we never before have looked at the relationship that the unwed father seeks to disrupt, rather than the one he seeks to preserve, in determining whether he has a liberty interest in his relationship with his child. To do otherwise is to allow the State's interest in terminating the relationship to play a role in defining the "liberty" that is protected by the Constitution. According to our established framework under the Due Process Clause, however, we first ask whether the person claiming constitutional protection has an interest that the Constitution recognizes; if we find that she does, we next consider the State's interest in limiting the extent of the procedures that will attend the deprivation of that interest. By stressing the need to preserve the "unitary family" and by focusing not just on the relationship between Michael and Victoria but on their "situation" as well, *ante,* at 12, today's plurality opinion takes both of these steps at once.

The plurality's premature consideration of California's interest is evident from its careful limitation of its holding to those cases in which "the mother is, at the time of the child's conception and birth, married to and cohabiting with another man, *both of whom wish to raise the child as the offspring of their union.*" (emphasis added). . . . The highlighted language suggests that if Carole or Gerald alone wished to raise Victoria, or if both were dead and the State wished to raise her, Michael and Victoria might be found to have a liberty interest in their relationship with each other. But that would be to say that whether Michael and Victoria have a liberty interest varies with the State's interest in recognizing that interest, for it is the State's interest in protecting the marital family — and not Michael and Victoria's interest in their relationship with each other — that varies with the status of Carole and Gerald's relationship. . . .

III

[T]he effect of § 621 is to terminate the relationship between Michael and Victoria before affording any hearing whatsoever on the issue whether Michael is Victoria's father. This refusal to hold a hearing is properly analyzed under our procedural due process cases. . . . California's interest, minute in comparison with a father's interest in his relationship with his child, cannot justify its refusal to hear Michael out on his claim that he is Victoria's father.

A

We must first understand the nature of the challenged statute: it is a law that stubbornly insists that Gerald is Victoria's father, in the face of evidence showing a 98 percent probability that her father is Michael. What Michael wants is a chance to show that he is Victoria's father. By depriving him of this opportunity, California prevents Michael from taking advantage of the best-interest standard embodied in § 4601 of California's Civil Code, which directs that parents be given visitation rights unless "the visitation would be detrimental to the best interests of the child."

As interpreted by the California courts, however, § 621 not only deprives Michael of the benefits of the best-interest standard; it also deprives him of any chance of maintaining his relationship with the child he claims to be his own. When, as a result of § 621, a putative father may not establish his paternity, neither may he obtain discretionary visitation rights as a "nonparent" under § 4601. See *Vincent B.* JUSTICE STEVENS' assertion to the contrary, *ante,* is mere wishful thinking. . . . The California appellate court's decision will not support JUSTICE STEVENS' reading, as the court's reasoning applies to all putative fathers whom § 621 has denied the opportunity to show paternity. . . . Likewise, in the case before us, the court's finding that "the existence of two 'fathers' as male authority figures will confuse the child and be counterproductive to her best interests," is not an evaluation of the relationship between Michael and Victoria, but a restatement of the policies underlying § 621 itself. . . .

Section 621 as construed by the California courts thus cuts off the relationship between Michael and Victoria — a liberty interest protected by the Due Process Clause — without affording the least bit of process. This case, in other words, involves a conclusive presumption that is used to terminate a constitutionally protected interest — the kind of rule that our preoccupation with procedural fairness has caused us to condemn. . . .

. . . .

. . . Today's plurality [is] disturbing [in] its failure to recognize that the defect from which conclusive presumptions suffer is a procedural one: the State has declared a certain fact relevant, indeed controlling, yet has denied a particular class of litigants a hearing to establish that fact. This is precisely the kind of flaw that procedural due process is designed to correct.

. . . .

B

The question before us, therefore, is whether California has an interest so powerful that it justifies granting Michael no hearing before terminating his parental rights. . . .

. . . .

The purported state interests here . . . stem primarily from the State's antagonism to Michael and Victoria's constitutionally protected interest in their relationship with each other and not from any desire to streamline procedures. Gerald D. explains that § 621 promotes marriage, maintains the relationship between the child and presumed father, and protects the integrity and privacy of the matrimonial family. It is not, however, § 621, but the best-interest principle, that protects a stable marital relationship and maintains the relationship between the child and presumed father. . . .

. . . .

[T]o say that the State must provide Michael with a hearing to prove his paternity is not to express any opinion of the ultimate state of affairs between Michael and Victoria and Carole and Gerald. In order to change the current situation among these people, Michael first must convince a court that he is Victoria's father, and even if he is able to do this, he will be denied visitation rights if that would be in Victoria's best interests. See § 4601. . . .

The plurality's misunderstanding of Michael's claim leads to its assertion that "to provide protection to an adulterous natural father is to deny protection to a marital father." To allow Michael a chance to prove his paternity, however, in no way guarantees that Gerald's relationship with Victoria will be changed.

IV

The atmosphere surrounding today's decision is one of make-believe. Beginning with the suggestion that the situation confronting us here does not repeat itself every day in every corner of the country, moving on to the claim that it is tradition alone that supplies the details of the liberty that the Constitution protects, and passing finally to the notion that the Court always has recognized a cramped vision of "the family," today's decision lets stand California's pronouncement that Michael — whom blood tests show to a 98 percent probability to be Victoria's father — is not Victoria's father. When and if the Court awakes to reality, it will find a world very different from the one it expects.

JUSTICE WHITE, with whom JUSTICE BRENNAN joins, dissenting.

California law, as the plurality describes it, tells us that, except in limited circumstances, California declares it to be *"irrelevant* for paternity purposes whether a child conceived during and born into a lawful marriage was begotten by someone other than the husband," (emphasis in original). This I do not accept, for the fact that Michael H. is the biological father of Victoria is to me highly relevant to whether he has rights, as a father or otherwise, with respect to the child. Because I believe that Michael H. has a liberty interest that cannot be denied without due process of the law, I must dissent.

I

Like JUSTICES BRENNAN, MARSHALL, BLACKMUN and STEVENS, I do not agree with the plurality opinion's conclusion that a natural father can never "have a constitutionally protected interest in his relationship with a child whose mother was married to and cohabiting with another man at the time of the child's conception and birth." (STEVENS, J., concurring in judgment). Prior cases here have recognized the liberty interest of a father in his relationship with his child. In none of these cases did we indicate that the fathers' rights were dependent on the marital status of the mother or biological father. The basic principle enunciated in the Court's unwed father cases is that an unwed father who has demonstrated a sufficient commitment to his paternity by way of personal, financial, or custodial responsibilities has a protected liberty interest in a relationship with his child.

We have not before faced the question of a biological father's relationship with his child when the child was born while the mother was married to another man. . . .

. . . .

In the case now before us, Michael H. is not a father unwilling to assume his responsibilities as a parent. To the contrary, he is a father who has asserted his interests in raising and providing for his child since the very time of the child's birth. [Justice White here repeats the facts establishing the paternal relationship.] *Lehr* was predicated on the absence of a substantial relationship between the man and the child. . . . "When an unwed father demonstrates a full commitment to the responsibilities of parenthood . . . his interest in personal contact with his child acquires substantial protection under the Due Process Clause." *Lehr,* at 261. The facts in this case satisfy the *Lehr* criteria, which focused on the relationship between father and child, not on the relationship between father and mother. Under *Lehr* a "mere biological relationship" is not enough, but in light of Carole's vicissitudes, what more could Michael H. have done? . . . Michael H . . . has a liberty interest entitled to protection under the Due Process Clause. . . .

II

California plainly denies Michael this protection, by refusing him the opportunity to rebut the State's presumption that the mother's husband is the father of the child. . . . The grant of summary judgment against Michael H. was based on the conclusive presumption of § 621. The Court gives its blessing to § 621 by relying on the State's asserted interests in the integrity of the family (defined as Carole and Gerald) and in protecting Victoria from the stigma of illegitimacy and by balancing away Michael's interest in establishing that he is the father of the child.

The interest in protecting a child from the social stigma of illegitimacy lacks any real connection to the facts of a case where a father is seeking to establish, rather than repudiate, paternity. The "stigma of illegitimacy" argument harks back to ancient common law. . . . It may be true that a child conceived in an extra-marital relationship would be considered a "bastard" in the literal sense of the word, but whatever stigma remains in today's society is far less compelling in the context of a child of a married mother, especially when there is a father asserting paternity and seeking a relationship with his child. It is hardly rare in this world of divorce and remarriage for a child to live with the "father" to whom her mother is married, and still have a relationship with her biological father.

The State's professed interest in the preservation of the existing marital unit is a more significant concern. To be sure, the intrusion of an outsider asserting that he is the father of a child whom the husband believes to be his own would be disruptive to say the least. On the facts of this case, however, Gerald was well aware of the liaison between Carole and Michael. The conclusive presumption of evidentiary rule § 621 virtually eliminates the putative father's chances of succeeding in his effort to establish paternity, but it by no means prevents him from asserting the claim. It may serve as a deterrent to such claims but does not eliminate the threat. Further, the argument that the conclusive presumption preserved the sanctity of the marital unit had more sway in a time when the husband was similarly prevented from challenging paternity.

. . . .

As the Court has said: "The significance of the biological connection is that it offers the natural father an opportunity that no other male possesses to develop a relationship with his offspring. . . ." *Lehr,* 463 U.S., at 262. It is as if this passage was addressed to Michael H. Yet the plurality today recants. Michael H. eagerly grasped the opportunity to have a relationship with his daughter (he lived with her; he declared her to be his child; he provided financial support for her) and still, with today's opinion, his opportunity has vanished. He has been rendered a stranger to his child.

. . . I respectfully dissent.

NOTES

1. ***Framing the Issue.*** Justice Scalia asks whether "the relationship between persons in the situation of Michael and Victoria has been treated as a protected family unit under the historic practices of our society." This question arises, of course, from Justice Scalia's distinctive methodological approach to fundamental rights. He would fix the boundaries of the liberty protected by the Due Process Clause by asking whether the asserted interest is one that has historically or traditionally been protected by our society. This historical approach is not only rejected by the dissent but also by concurring Justices O'Connor and Kennedy. Justice Brennan's dissent also criticizes the *level of specificity* at which the plurality characterizes the right in question. That is, Justice Scalia describes the issue as whether a man who had an adulterous affair with a married woman has a constitutionally-protected relationship with the resulting child. Compare that to Justice Brennan's and Justice White's broader characterization of the right at issue.

Justice Scalia concludes that Michael H. has no liberty interest in his relationship with Victoria in part because Victoria's mother and her mother's husband, who were married at her conception and birth, jointly wish to raise the child as their own. Justice Brennan argues that this way of framing the issue is inconsistent with preexisting case law because the Court has never made the father's liberty interest turn on an examination of "the relationship the unwed father seeks to disrupt, rather than . . . the one he seeks to preserve." And as Justice White argues, even if *Lehr* is read to recognize a liberty interest in the biological father only when he has a demonstrated paternal relationship with the child, Michael H. surely qualifies.

On the other hand, recognizing that Michael H. has a liberty interest in maintaining a relationship with his daughter does not end the inquiry, for California explains its rule as necessary to its interest in protecting the integrity of the marital family. The question, then, is whether the latter interest justifies the burden on Michael H.'s paternal claim. Justice Brennan points out that California permits the rebuttal of the "unrebuttable" presumption by biological evidence of the husband's nonpaternity, and suggests that these exceptions undercut California's stated policy rationale. Consider whether his opinion is persuasive on this point. The statutory exceptions only allowed paternity claims brought by the husband or wife, and only if brought within two years of the child's birth. Perhaps it is plausible for California to assume that the integrity of the family will not be much aided by denying standing to the *spouse* who seeks to challenge the child's status: the integrity of that family has already been undone, if that is a spouse's inclination, whether or not the law chooses to recognize it. And by limiting even spouses to acting within two years after birth, California evinces a policy of protecting the settled expectations of the other family members as to the husband's paternal rights and obligations, even if one spouse seeks to upset them. The spousal exception thus concedes nothing about the validity of the basic policy of California law: a husband and wife united in their desire to treat a child born *during* their marriage as a child *of* their marriage cannot be challenged by a third party. On this policy California has been steadfast, denying standing even to the child who sought to prove that her father was someone other than her mother's husband. *Estate of Cornelius,* 35 Cal. 3d 461, 674 P.2d 245, 198 Cal. Rptr. 543 (1984).

Justice White, who would recognize a liberty interest in any biological father, also recognizes that the state's interest in the preservation of the existing marital unit "is a . . . significant concern," but would set it aside, at least on the facts of this case, since "Gerald was well aware of the liaison between Carole and Michael." Is this view persuasive? Or does it seem likely that allowing Michael to assert paternal claims of visitation, or perhaps even custody, would be "disruptive," to use Justice White's term, to this family unit as well? If so, then the real question presented by the case is whether California may constitutionally protect the marital unit from such disruption by denying Michael an opportunity to assert his paternity of Victoria. Or, to put it another way, may California declare that the biological paternity of the child born to a woman living with her husband is not relevant to the question of the child's *legal* paternity, when the mother and her husband decide to treat the child as their joint offspring? If so, then Michael H. can be denied a hearing in which to introduce his blood test evidence, because that evidence will not be relevant.

Justice Brennan frames the question as whether California can employ an irrebutable presumption, suggesting the defect in its law is procedural rather than substantive. After that doctrine was first employed by the court in *Vlandis v. Kline,* 412 U.S. 441 (1973), it was heavily attacked by most commentators as a "confusion" of equal protection and procedural due process, Note, *The Irrebuttable Presumption Doctrine in the Supreme Court,* 87 HARV. L. REV. 1534 (1974), and as a "fundamentally misconceived" analysis, "logically equivalent to an equal protection argument" but "standardless" and "illusory" in application, Note, *Irrebuttable Presumptions: An Illusory Analysis,* 27 STAN. L. REV. 449 (1975). It was thought to have been killed by the Court just two years after its birth, *Weinberger v. Salfi,* 422 U.S. 749 (1975) (the doctrine is "a virtual engine of destruction for countless legislative judgments which have heretofore been thought wholly consistent with [the Constitution].") Nonetheless, it "may survive for use where there are independent reasons for heightened scrutiny, as when 'fundamental interests' are protected," Gerald Gunther, *The Brief and Troubled Life of Irrebuttable Presumption Analysis,* in GUNTHER, INDIVIDUAL RIGHTS IN CONSTITUTIONAL LAW 519, 520 n.4 (1985).

California did not adopt the irrebuttable presumption as an administrative convenience. For example, it did *not* argue that the presumption is justified because most third parties asserting paternity of a married woman's child are not, in fact, the biological father, and that therefore it will save time and effort to assume their nonpaternity. It instead offered a policy of protecting the integrity of the marital family. The question then is the substantive one of whether this policy is a constitutionally adequate counterweight to the father's interest. The real issue, in other words, is not procedural but substantive: whether California has identified an interest that entitles it to treat a particular fact — biological paternity — as irrelevant to the question of legal paternity

2. *The Husband's Versus the Putative Father's Interests.* How important to the result in *Michael H.* was the paternity claim of the mother's husband? In evaluating the California policies at issue in this case, consider that he, like Michael H., also had a paternal relationship with Victoria. His paternal relationship with Victoria is surely also entitled to constitutional protection? Although the dissenters chastise the majority for their "pinched" and traditional view of family, perhaps the dissenters have a pinched view as well, if they believe that biological paternity should swamp all other factors that one might consider in identifying the legal father. One can view this case as a contest is between two men with equally plausible claims to being treated as the legal father, one on the basis of biological paternity, the other on the basis of his marital relationship with the mother, both of whom assumed responsibility for the child in the past and seek it now. Nothing in *Michael H.* bars a state from choosing to honor the biological father's claim. Or, like California, it could choose instead to protect the integrity of the traditional family unit — wife, husband, child — from all third parties who seek to disrupt it, even at the cost of denying the biological father any familial claims on his child. Or perhaps it could adopt a third approach, recognizing both father-child relationships. Plausible policy arguments might be offered for any of these approaches. Our experience with changing social conditions and our understanding of children's interests might all bear on the choice. But the question before the Court was of course not which policy is correct, but whether the Constitutions compels the choice among them. Yet if the dissent prevailed, we would have a rigid constitutional rule foreclosing California's particular answer to this difficult question. For discussion of these issues, see Katharine Bartlett, *Rethinking Parenthood as an Exclusive Status: The Need for Legal Alternatives When the Premise of the Nuclear Family Has Failed,* 70 VA. L. REV. 879 (1984).

3. *Justice Stevens' Concurrence.* Although Justice Stevens joins the Court's judgment, he notes that he does not necessarily agree with the plurality that someone in Michael's situation has no liberty interest in his relationship with his daughter. However, Justice Stevens concludes that Michael had his day in court because the family court had heard his petition for visitation under California's visitation statute (as contrasted with the statute's governing paternity). Justice Stevens concludes that the existence of that statute provides sufficient protection of whatever liberty interests Michael might have as a putative biological father of a married woman's child. As Justice Stevens reads that statute, Michael could obtain visitation by proving that such visitation would be in the child's interest. Justice Stevens concluded that the family court rejected Michael's visitation claim on the basis of a particularized judgment about Victoria's best interests, and not on the basis of the marital presumption. The statute to which Justice Stevens refers appears to permit judges to grant visitation to any person with an interest in the child. Consider, however, whether Justice Stevens view survives the Court's decision in *Troxel v. Granville,* reprinted and discussed in Chapter 6, beginning at page 667.

4. *Victoria's Due Process Claim*. In the plurality opinion, the Court notes that it "never had occasion to decide whether a child has a liberty interest symmetrical with that of her parent, in maintaining her filial relationship." But it deals with the issue by effectively reasoning back from its conclusion that California may constitutionally treat Gerald as the father to the further conclusion that therefore, even if Victoria had such reciprocal rights, they would protect her relationship with Gerald, not with Michael, and certainly not both men simultaneously because the law has not traditionally recognized "multiple fatherhood." For further discussion of this issue, see Justice Stevens' dissent in *Troxel v. Granville*, reprinted in Chapter 6, on pages 671-673, and also Emily Buss, *Children's Associational Rights? Why Less is More*, Public Law and Legal Theory Working Paper No. 41, U. of Chicago School of Law (2003) (Available at: www.law.uchicago.edu/academics/publiclaw/index.html) (arguing that because children rely on adults to exercise rights on their behalf, affording children associational rights such as preservation of relationships with non-parents will not necessarily foster the children's independent interests).

5. *Michael H. Epilog.* Born in 1980, Victoria was nine years old when the Supreme Court decided the case of *Michael H. v. Gerald D.* Our inquiry revealed that after the litigation, Michael H. was not permitted further contact with Victoria. They did have a meeting, on Father's Day of 2001. Michael H. reported that it had been fifteen years since he had seen her last. According to Michael, the intervening years made it difficult for the two to re-establish a parent-child relationship, and he has not seen his daughter since that date. He said, however, that Victoria did develop a strong father-daughter bond with Gerald, which has endured. (Telephone conversation with Michael H., March 6, 2003.)

6. *Revised California Law on Marital Presumption.* California recodified its family law statutes after *Michael H.* Former Evidence Code § 641, the conclusive presumption at issue in *Michael H.*, is now California Family Code § 7540. It remains largely intact, but there are two changes. Recall that the statute as described in *Michael H.* allowed husbands or wives to challenge the husband's paternity with a blood test sought before the child is two years old. In the new codification this exception to the conclusive presumption is set out in § 7541. After *Michael H.* was decided, § 7541 was amended to also allow such a blood-test challenge to the husband's paternity by a "presumed father" who seeks to establish his own paternity of the married woman's child. The amendment thus gives the "presumed father" the same time-limited opportunity as the mother's husband to challenge the marital presumption. California also adopted a definition of "presumed father" taken from § 4 of UPA 1973. Because Michael H. is a "presumed father" under § 4(a)(4) of UPA 1973, he would have fallen within the class of persons who could have challenged Gerald's paternity within two years of birth. It is perhaps unclear whether this revised California law would have allowed his particular challenge, however, given the two-year rule. His paternity claim was not lodged until Victoria's third year of life, and it would therefore have been too late then for him to seek the required blood test order. Could the challenge nonetheless be mounted with the blood test results that Gerald and the mother had apparently obtained previously on their own? Perhaps not, because § 7540(a) requires blood tests performed "pursuant to Chapter 2" of the Family Code, and it is not clear these would qualify. *See Rodney F. v. Karen M.*, 61 Cal. App. 4th 233, 71 Cal. Rptr. 2d 399 (1998) (blood tests erroneously ordered by court which indicated that husband was not the biological father of wife's child cannot be used to overcome the conclusive presumption of husband's paternity). For case in which a presumed father was allowed to challenge a husband's paternity because he did act within the two-year time limit, see *Brian C. v. Ginger K*, 77 Cal. App. 4th 1198, 92 Cal. Rptr. 2d 294 (2000). What about a man who wants to be a presumed father within the meaning of UPA 1973 but is not because the mother does not choose to live with him? He loses because he is not a man who can challenge her husband's paternity under the statute. *See Dawn D. v. Superior Court*, 17 Cal. 4th 932, 72 Cal. Rptr. 2d 871, 952 P.2d 1139 (1998) (putative father of child whose mother moved back with her husband during the pregnancy does not have standing to obtain blood tests to challenge husband's paternity, even though the action is brought four months before the child's birth, because he is not a presumed father).

7. *Extending California's Conclusive Presumption to Nonmarital Fathers.* Should the paternal status of an unmarried "father" who has taken the child into his home, and who is thus a presumed father under UPA 1973 (which still applies in California), be subject to rebuttal by biological evidence? The California Supreme Court, in a significant decision, held not, at least in some circumstances, in *Nicholas H.*, 120 Cal. Rptr. 2d 146 (Cal. 2002). Nicholas was born to Kimberly in 1995, who was then living with Thomas, with whom she continued to live till the end of 1997, and for a nine month period in 1999. The pregnancy had begun before Kimberly and Thomas has begun to live together, and the biological father could not be found. Kimberly and Thomas agreed to raise Nicholas as their child despite these facts. Kimberly herself was often homeless, usually unemployed, and used drugs. Thomas had some troubles of his own but did much better, and was "the constant" in Nicholas' life. After Thomas and Kimberly split up, Nicholas lived with Thomas pursuant to a January 2000 custody order, obtained after Kimberly had denied him access. The child preferred living with Thomas, according to the family services counselor's report to the court, because Kimberly "is mean to him, she hits and slaps him, and she smokes weed." Nonetheless, the intermediate appellate court held that while Nicholas was a presumed father under California's UPA, (as having taken the child into his own and held himself out as such), that the presumption had been rebutted by his admission that he was not the child's biological father. The California Supreme Court reversed, relying on statutory language allowing for the rebuttal of a presumption of paternity in an "appropriate case." This was not an appropriate case, the court decided, emphasizing both the child's interests and the fact that "no other man claims parental rights." Nicholas should not be left fatherless, nor should biological evidence be sought to make him so.

What then if the biological father had appeared, or reappeared, in a case like this, and sought himself to rebut the presumption? In *Kiana A.*, 113 Cal. Rptr. 2d 669 (App. 2001) the child had a paternal relationship with Kevin, who was living with the mother when the child was born, although another man, Mario, appeared as the father on her birth certificate. Mario married the mother two years after the child's birth. Both men were presumed fathers under the UPA 1973 provisions that govern in California, Mario because of the birth certificate and marriage, Kevin because he had treated the child as his, lived with her, and taken responsibility for her (not perfectly, but much more clearly so than Mario). The child herself thought of Kevin, not Mario, as her father. The appeals court held Kevin the father, denied Mario's request for genetic testing as untimely and in any event inappropriate as it could disrupt an established parental relationship. To similar effect under similar but not identical facts, is *Steven W. v. Matthew S.*, 39 Cal. Rptr. 2d 535 (App. 1995). Note that *Kiana* actually applies the social paternity policy underlying California's strong marital presumption to *defeat* the paternity claim of the mother's husband in favor of the child's social father. It could do this because California's conclusive marital presumption did not arise under the *Kiana* facts, as at the time of the child's birth the mother was not yet married to, or cohabiting with, the husband, even though he was named on the child's birth certificate and was, apparently, the child's biological father.

In its *Nicholas* opinion, the California Supreme Court expressly reserved the question of whether biological paternity should have been made to decide cases like *Kiana*, 120 Cal. Rptr. 2d at 157. Similarly, the court reserved judgement on the question presented by *Jerry P.*, 116 Cal. Rptr. 2d 123 (App. 2002), in which a man was held the father even though he was neither the biological father nor had ever lived with the child. He did live with the mother for a year, and also during her pregnancy, and while they broke up before birth he provided support to her and attended the child in the hospital after birth, presenting himself as the child's father. He sought to establish a paternal relationship but was thwarted by the failure of anyone to tell him that the social services agency had placed the child, who was born with cocaine in his blood, in a foster home. He finally found the child after four months and gained the right to see the child at the foster home. But he was ultimately denied reunification services as having no paternal relationship with the child since he was neither a presumed father nor the biological father. The appeals court held, however, that this man fell within the protection accorded biological fathers in *Kelsey S.* (see text *supra* at pages 1009-1010), essentially protecting him as a thwarted father (Note 5 at page 1002) who would have established a paternal relationship with the child had he not been kept by others from doing so.

The California Supreme Court initially granted a hearing in *Jerry P.*, but after deciding *Nicholas* it changed its mind and instead ordered publication of the appeals court decision. In sum, while formally reserving the question presented in *Jerry P.* and *Kiana,* the court has clearly indicated its receptiveness to rules protecting as parental the relationship between children and their social (but not biological) fathers, sometimes even over the objecting biological father, and in circumstances in which UPA 2002 would not recognize the man as a presumed father. This sense is further strengthened by the court's favorable references to the appeals court statutory analysis in *Raphael P.*, 118 Cal. Rptr. 2d 610 (App. 2002), which held that biological proof of nonpaternity did not necessarily preclude a man from presumed father status under UPA 1973, and indeed, decided that courts should not order genetic tests of presumed fathers. As the court explained, "where there is a man claiming presumed father status and no indication of another man asserting paternity, we question whether paternity can rightly be considered 'a relevant fact' [as required under the provision authorizing a court to order genetic testing]". *Raphel P.*, as quoted in *Nicholas H.* at 120 Cal. Rptr. 2d 156.

8. *State Constitutional Claims.* A handful of state supreme courts have accepted state constitutional claims analogous to the federal one that *Michael*

H. rejected. The Texas Supreme Court struck down Texas' irrebuttable marital presumption in *J.W.T.*, 872 S.W.2d 189 (Tex. 1994), as violating the due process clause of its state constitution. However, the decision is limited, for it applies only where the biological father "assert[s] his interest near the time of the child's birth" and "both (1) acknowledges responsibility for child support or other care and maintenance, and (2) makes serious and continuous efforts to establish a relationship with the child." Thus, for example, the irrebuttable presumption contained in the new UPA (2002) would appear to be constitutional under Texas law.) A sharply divided Iowa court rendered a more sweeping decision in *Callender v. Skiles*, 591 N.W. 182 (Iowa 1999), in which the mother became pregnant by another man during a brief period of separation from her husband. It struck down on state constitutional grounds an Iowa law barring the biological father from asserting his paternity of the child, with whom he had never lived and did not know. The court denied that the state could constitutionally protect the child's interests in maintaining the integrity of his existing family, responding that the family's integrity "suffered at the time of the extramarital affair" — even though the husband and wife were reconciled and united in their opposition to the biological father's claims. Subsequent cases may suggest some second thoughts; in reaffirmng after visitation was ordered on remand, 623 N.W.2d 852, 855 (Iowa 2001), the court conceded that the arrangement had caused the parties "anguish," and a year later, it affirmed a judgment in a different case in which the trial court dismissed the putative father's paternity action because it was not bought until seven years after the child's birth, during which time the mother and her husband (to whom she was married at the time of conception) raised the child as their own. *Huisman v. Miedema*, 644 N.W.2d 321 (Iowa 2002). For an older case, pre-*Michael H.*, see *R. McG. v. J.W.*, 615 P.2d 666 (Colo. 1980).

9. *Alternative State Rules on Third Party Challenges to the Marital Presumption.* California's bar on challenges to the marital presumption by third parties is distinctive only because of its mechanical nature — the automatic exclusion of all third-party challenges other than from men who qualify as presumed fathers, and the automatic exclusion of all challenges after the child's second birthday. Many other states have rules that are more fact sensitive. In many, for example, the court's evaluation of the child's best interests plays an important role, although it emerges in various doctrinal forms. Some permit third-party paternity claims to children born of a married woman only where the challenger can show that the action will serve the child's interest. *See, e.g., R.N. v. J.M.*, 61 S.W. 3d 149 (Ark. 2001) (putative father has standing to bring paternity action, but trial court has discretion to determine whether DNA testing is in the child's best interests); *Weidenbacher v. Duclos*, 661 A.2d 988 (Conn. 1995) (in determining whether putative father has standing to challenge marital presumption, court must show that his interests and the best interests of the child outweigh those of the marital family unit); *Ross v. Ross,* 783 P.2d 331 (Kan. 1990) (trial court abused its discretion in ordering paternity tests prior to determining whether doing so was in the best interest of children); *McDaniels v. Carlson,* 738 P.2d 254 (Wash. 1987) (trial court must make individualized determination as to whether paternity action is in child's best interests).

Massachusetts allows challenges to the husband's paternity only by men who have an established parental relationship with the child, in a judicially created version of the California rule allowing challenges only by "presumed fathers." The Massachusetts rule does not limit challenges to two years after the child's birth, however. *See, e.g., Paternity of Cheryl*, 746 N.E.2d 488 (2001); *C.C. v. A.B.*, 550 N.E.2d 365, 372 (1990) ("the existence of a substantial parent-child relationship" is the "controlling factor in determining whether" an unwed father can challenge the marital presumption). *See also Allen v. Stone*, 474 S.E.2d 554, 566 (W.Va. 1996) (the impact of putative father's paternity action on existing parent-child relationships "may be considered in both the standing and paternity determinations"). Some of these courts relied, in part, on the analysis urged in Note, *Rebutting the Marital Presumption: A Developed Relationship Test*, 88 COLUM. L. REV. 369 (1988). In an interesting twist on the typical constitutional argument, an Ohio court held in 1993 that the statute permitting an alleged biological father to challenge the mother's husband's paternity was unconstitutional in that it violated the marital family's fundamental rights to privacy. *Merkel v. Doe*, 635 N.E.2d 70 (Common Pleas). The court held that the statute was not narrowly tailored, in that it granted *any* man standing to allege biological fatherhood of a married woman's child. Ultimately, however, the court's reasoning emphasized preservation of the father-child bond, indicating that the mother's husband is "the only father [the child] has ever known. [The mother's husband] is, at the very least, John Jr.'s psychological father. . . ." *Id.* at 75.

Increasingly, in response to the virtual certainty of biological paternity determinations, and a growing sense that legal paternity should reflect the biological "truth," some courts and legislatures have been "relaxing" the marital presumption, are at times less apt to apply the equitable doctrines discussed at pages 968-970 *infra*, and do not require that the child's interests be considered as a prerequisite to, or element of, paternity actions. For example, Tennessee repealed its conclusive marital presumption, and now allows any man to file suit to prove paternity, without reference to the mother's marital status. See TENN. CODE ANN. § 36-2-304 (2003); *Cihlar v. Crawford*, 39 S.W.2d 172, 184 (Tenn. App. 2000). The statute does require paternity actions concerning a child born into a marriage to be brought within two years of the child's birth, however. TENN. CODE ANN. § 36-2-305 (2003). *See also Witso v. Overby*, 627 N.W.2d 63 (Minn. 2001) (interpreting Minnesota's statutes as permitting putative father seeking custody and visitation to litigate paternity of a child born into an intact marriage, despite unified objections from the mother and her husband); *K.S. v. R.S.*, 669 N.E.2d 399 (Ind. 1996) (permitting married woman's neighbor with whom she had had sexual relationship to bring paternity action based on statute, which makes no reference to marital status of mother, allowing "a man alleging that he is the child's biological father" to file a paternity action); *Doran v. Doran*, 820 A.2d 1279 (Pa. Super. 2003) (holding that former husband was not estopped from denying paternity of child that he held out as his own for ten years because he relied on his former wife's "fraudulent" assertions that the child was his).

Of course, if UPA 2002 becomes widely adopted, this variability will be reduced. UPA 2002 effectively adopts California's two-year limit on challenges to the husband's paternity, combined with recognition of equitable grounds for refusing even timely genetic challenges to the marital presumption.

10. *Dual Paternity.* One state, Louisiana, applies a concept of dual paternity. While any child born to a married woman is considered the "legitimate" child of the mother's husband, the mother can still establish the paternity and support obligation of the child's biological father. "Recognition of actual paternity, through filiation actions brought by the . . . child, the biological father, or the state, does not affect the child's . . . status as the legitimate offspring of [the mother's] husband." *Smith v. Cole,* 553 So. 2d 847 (La. 1989). Professor Mary Louise Fellows endorses this concept, indicating that it is the arrangement that "more clearly reflect[s] the realities of a child's complex life." *A Feminist Determination of the Law and Legitimacy,* 7 Tex. J. Women & L. 195, 207 (1998). *See also* Theresa Glennon, *Erosion of the Marital Presumption,* at 602–03.

PROBLEMS

Problem 9-24. Harry and Sally are married when Sally starts seeing Tom. When she becomes pregnant, she tells Tom the child is his, while also allowing Harry to think it is his. She divorces Harry two years later, receives custody, and then moves in with Tom. After five months, things don't work out and she moves out. Harry and Sally then remarry and deny Tom access to the child. A year later, Tom brings a paternity action to establish his parental rights. It is opposed by both Harry and Sally, although by this time they have filed for divorce again. The child calls the men "Daddy Harry" and "Daddy Tom," and both have a good paternal relationship with the child. Should the court allow Tom to proceed with his paternity action? Is its decision on this question constitutionally compelled?

Problem 9-25. Catherine became pregnant by Leslie during her short marriage to Gregory. She separated from Gregory in June of 1986, petitioned for dissolution of her marriage in October, gave birth in March of 1987, and obtained her final divorce decree in May. Neither Leslie nor Gregory knew of the child's existence until 1998, and in 1999 the district attorney sought child support from both. Blood tests excluded Gregory but showed Leslie the likely father. Who is the father under California's conclusive marital presumption? Under UPA 2002? Who should be the legal father? What should be his child support obligations?

[3] THE CONSTITUTIONAL PROTECTION OF NONMARITAL CHILDREN FROM DISCRIMINATORY TREATMENT BY GOVERNMENT

Traditionally, state and federal policies recognize a range of financial rights for marital or "legitimate" children that flow from the children's legal relationships with their parents. Many of these same rights were not available to nonmarital or "illegitimate" children, or were available only under certain limited circumstances or with particular restrictions or burdens that did not apply to children born into a legal marriage. In particular, children born out-of-wedlock did not have the same legally-enforceable rights as did marital children to parental support, to intestate succession, or to bring suits to recover for the wrongful death of a parent. Beginning in 1968, the United States Supreme Court decided a series of cases addressing the extent to which the Equal Protection Clause precludes the government from employing classifications that distinguish between marital and nonmarital children. In the final analysis, the Court elevated the scrutiny it used to review such classifications to an "intermediate" level, requiring a more searching examination of such classifications. GERALD GUNTHER AND KATHLEEN M. SULLIVAN, CONSTITUTIONAL LAW 725 (13th ed. 1997). Until the 1980s, however, the Court's decisions displayed marked ambivalence regarding the constitutionality of policies distinguishing between marital and nonmarital children.

In *Levy v. Louisiana,* 391 U.S. 68 (1968), five nonmarital children sought to recover for their mother's wrongful death. The Court held that the application of the Louisiana statute to permit only legitimate children to bring such actions constituted "invidious" discrimination against illegitimate children, and violated the Equal Protection Clause. In the same year, in *Glona v. American Guar. & Liab. Ins. Co.,* 391 U.S. 73, the Supreme Court reversed the denial of a mother's claim for her nonmarital son's wrongful death. The Court's opinions, written by Justice Douglas, held that the state's interest in promoting traditional married family life was not rationally related to the policies in question.

Yet, Justice Harlan, joined by Black and Stewart, dissented, arguing that every wrongful death statute necessarily employs arbitrary criteria to establish who may bring such an action. "Rather than hear offers of proof of love and affection and economic dependence from every person who might think or claim that the bell had tolled for him, . . . [l]egislatures . . . generally defined classes of proper plaintiffs by highly arbitrary lines based on family relationships, excluding issues concerning the actual effect of the death on the plaintiff." *Id.* at 76–77. He argued that extending a claim to legitimate, but not illegitimate children was no more arbitrary than any of the other lines drawn by the typical wrongful death statute.

In *Weber v. Aetna Cas. & Sur. Co.,* 406 U.S. 164 (1972), the Court rejected Louisiana's disfavor of unacknowledged nonmarital children in its worker's compensation law. Louisiana justified the statutory scheme by arguing that it furthered the state's interests in encouraging "legitimate family relations." In a passionate opinion authored by Justice White, the Court struck down the scheme as violating the Equal Protection Clause:

> The status of illegitimacy has expressed through the ages society's condemnation of irresponsible liaisons beyond the bonds of marriage. But visiting this condemnation on the head of an infant is illogical and unjust [and] is contrary to the basic concept . . . that legal burdens should bear some relationship to individual responsibility or wrongdoing. Obviously, no child is responsible for his birth and penalizing the illegitimate child is an ineffectual — as well as an unjust — way of deterring the parent.

406 U.S. at 175.

At common law, fathers were legally obligated to support their marital children, even after divorce, and this obligation was enforceable via civil proceedings and criminal sanctions. By contrast, no analogous principle mandated that a biological father support his nonmarital child. In 1973, in *Gomez v. Perez,* 409 U.S. 535, the U.S. Supreme Court held that Texas violated the Equal Protection Clause when it granted marital, but not nonmarital, children the right of paternal support.

In *Trimble v. Gordon,* 430 U.S. 762 (1977), the Court considered a challenge to an Illinois law that permitted illegitimate children to inherit by intestate succession from their mothers, but not their fathers, while legitimate children in Illinois could inherit from either parent. In *Trimble,* despite the existence of a prior adjudication of the decedent's paternity, the nonmarital child received no share of his estate. Although refusing to adopt a strict scrutiny standard of review for classifications based on illegitimacy, the Court noted that "illegitimacy is analogous in many respects to the personal characteristics that have been held to be suspect when used as the basis of statutory differentiations." 430 U.S. at 767. It noted that the appropriate standard of review "is not a toothless one," as the rational basis standard so often was. The Court went on to reject both of the state's justifications for its classification. The state's interest in promoting the marital family could not constitutionally be achieved by attempting "to influence the actions of men and women by imposing sanctions on the children born of their illegitimate relationships." 430 U.S. at 769. Furthermore, although the state did have a valid interest, the Court concluded, in establishing an accurate and efficient method of property disposition in probate, the Court held that the Illinois law was not "carefully tuned to alternative considerations" and failed "to consider the possibility of a middle ground between the extremes of complete exclusion and case by case determination of paternity." *Id.* at 770–72. Four members of the Court dissented.

The split among members of the Court on these issues was evident the next year, when the Court sustained a New York statute in *Lalli v. Lalli,* 439 U.S. 259 (1978). *Lalli* presented the Court with a statute only slightly more "tuned" than the one struck down in *Trimble.* New York's intestacy law allowed nonmarital children to inherit only if a court of competent jurisdiction had found during the decedent's lifetime that he was the father of the child. The *Trimble* child would have inherited under the New York law. In dissent, four justices (Justices Brennan, White, Marshall and Stevens) pointed out that the New York statute excluded the children with the most appealing claims. That is, those whose mother and father had lived together, and whose fathers supported them and openly acknowledged paternity (consistent with the facts in *Lalli),* would have been unlikely to seek a formal adjudication of paternity.

Lalli, however, was the first case in which the emerging "intermediate" standard of review was made explicit: in order to be sustained, a statute that distinguishes between legitimate and illegitimate children must be "substantially related to the important state interests the statute is intended to promote." *Id.* at 275–76. Furthermore, *Lalli* underscored that there may be special issues raised in cases involving inheritance and probate in which courts may find distinctions between marital and nonmarital children permissible. Specifically, the Court in *Lalli* noted that the state's interest in "just and orderly disposition of property at death [is] of considerable magnitude." *Id.* at 268. Underscoring that there are "peculiar problems of proof" in determining paternity, as contrasted with maternity, the Court concluded that these problems are particularly troublesome when the alleged father is deceased. *Id.* at 268.

Recall the description on pages 977-978 *supra*, of a series of cases in which the Court struck down state laws setting short statutes of limitation for child support claims. This line of cases culminated with *Clark v. Jeter,* 486 U.S. 456 (1988), in which a unanimous Court clearly embraced the heightened level of scrutiny it had applied with increasing conviction in recent years: "Between . . . extremes of rational basis review and strict scrutiny lies a level of intermediate scrutiny, which generally has been applied to discriminatory classifications based on sex or illegitimacy." *Id.* at 461. One might wonder whether the Court would have been as receptive to a claim of discrimination brought by nonmarital children in a case unrelated to child support, the collection of which has achieved bipartisan endorsement and a level of public approval that is relatively rare.

[4] GAY AND LESBIAN PARENTHOOD

The "unitary family" described by Justice Scalia in *Michael H.*, page 1013 *supra*, is comprised of one mother and one father and makes "no provision for dual fatherhood" and presumably, no provision for dual motherhood. Thus, to the extent that states endorse this model of family, parenting dyads of two men or two women and the children they raise do not enjoy legal recognition. Despite this, households with children parented by a same-sex couples are increasingly visible in American society. Making use of assisted reproductive technologies, some same-sex couples have planned and effected the conception of children biologically related to one of the partners. Others have jointly parented a child born to one of them in a previous heterosexual relationship. Others have adopted or sought to adopt children not related to either partner. These scenarios have set in motion a range of challenges to traditional family law doctrines.

Historically, American law has relied on biology, marriage, and adoption to establish legal parentage. With joint genetic procreation and marriage traditionally unavailable to same-sex couples, adoption law has become an increasingly important vehicle for legal recognition of the parent-like relationship that frequently exists between a child and her biological parent's same-sex partner. Such "second-parent" adoptions have broken new legal ground in some states, while other states have refused to grant them. In the absence of a second-parent adoption, the relationship between a biological parent's same-sex partner and her child is on uncertain legal ground. Most states regard the child and partner as legal strangers, even if the partner has coparented the child and participated fully in providing caregiving and support.

Public disapproval of homosexuality and homosexual conduct has also affected the legal rights of gay and lesbian parents as would-be parents. The opinions written by Justices Kennedy, O'Connor, and Scalia, in the case of *Lawrence v. Texas*, reprinted *supra*, review and set forth a range of attitudes toward homosexual conduct that may have characterized American viewpoints during the last century. Until fairly recently, gays and lesbians were disfavored in child custody determinations following divorce, even in the absence of any adverse effects on the child's well-being. More recently, courts in most jurisdictions have rejected the traditional approach of viewing homosexual conduct as evidence of *per se* parental unfitness, and have focused instead on the question of whether the parent's sexual conduct affects the child deleteriously. Social disapproval of homosexual conduct has also prevented gays and lesbians from adopting children in some jurisdictions. By statute, some states categorically bar adoptions by homosexuals or by unmarried individuals or couples. These statutes and challenges to them are discussed below, as are the legal issues relating to second-parent adoption and "de facto parent" claims by same-sex partners of a child's parents. See Chapter 6 for a discussion of the law affecting custody claims by gay or lesbian parents following marital dissolution.

One team of researchers commented that although "adoption and parental rights policy for gay and lesbian couples is an intensely debated topic, we have virtually no empirical evidence regarding the current presence of children among gay and lesbian couples." Dan Black, Gary Gates *et al.*, *Demographics of the Gay and Lesbian Population in the United States: Evidence from Available Systematic Data Sources*, 37 DEMOGRAPHY 139, 150 (2000). The existing evidence, however, suggests that approximately 21.7% of cohabiting lesbian couples and 5.2% of cohabiting male gay couples have children living with them. *Id.* Approximately three-quarters of these children are under the age of 18. Many were born into subsequently-dissolved heterosexual marriages. *Id.* Given the increasing visibility of gay and lesbian couples and individuals raising children in the past decade, it is likely that better estimates of the prevalence of such family arrangements will be forthcoming.

CHARLOTTE J. PATTERSON, FAMILY RELATIONSHIPS OF LESBIANS AND GAY MEN, 62 J. Marr. & Fam. 1052–1069 (2000)

The family lives of lesbian and gay people have been a subject of controversy during the past decade. Because of the stigma attached to nonheterosexual identities, those who declare lesbian or gay identities often do so at the risk of relationships in families of origin [as well as other risks]. Despite such obstacles, however, lesbian and gay people have often succeeded in creating and sustaining meaningful family relationships. . . .

. . . .

Many if not most lesbians and gay men express the desire for an enduring love relationship with a partner of the same gender. Indeed, research findings suggest that many are successful in creating such relationships. Survey data suggest that 40 to 60% of gay men and 45 to 80% of lesbians are currently involved in steady romantic relationships. [¶] When asked about their current relationship, lesbians and gay men report as much satisfaction with their relationships as do heterosexual couples; the great majority describe themselves as happy. [Studies reveal] no differences as a function of sexual orientation on any of the measures of relationship quality.

      . . .

When lesbian and gay couples experience problems in their relationships, some of these stem from the same roots from which difficulties in heterosexual relationships also arise. As in heterosexual relationships, problems can arise because of different religious, racial, ethnic, or socioeconomic backgrounds and because of the different values that these backgrounds may have inculcated. Relationship difficulties can also arise as a result of problems at either partner's job, financial pressures on the couple, friction with members of extended family networks, and so forth, just as they do in heterosexual relationships. Kurdek . . . reported that the top five areas of conflict for lesbian and gay couples were finances, driving style, affection/sex, being overly critical, and division of household tasks. [¶] There are some conflicts that are probably unique to lesbian and gay couples and prominent among these are issues created by negative social attitudes toward homosexuality. When a couple disagrees about the extent to which they should disclose the lesbian or gay nature of their relationship, problems in their relationship can ensue.

[Research examining the] longevity of lesbian and gay relationships [as contrasted with cohabiting opposite-sex or married-couple relationships reveals that for] couples who had been together 10 years, breakup rates over the 18 months of their study were low; only 6% of lesbian couples, 4% of gay couples, and 4% of married couples separated during this period. For couples who had been together less than 2 years, 22% of lesbian couples, 16% of gay couples, 17% of cohabiting (but unmarried) heterosexual couples, and only 4% of heterosexual married couples had separated; thus, being married was associated with low break-up rates, but otherwise there were no differences. A more recent study (see Kurdek, 1995) also found low rates of separation and no differences in break-up rates between lesbian and gay couples.

      . . . .

When considering lesbian and gay parents and their children, it is helpful to recognize the diversity of family constellations. One important distinction is between families in which children were born or adopted in the context of heterosexual marriages that later dissolved when one or both parents came out as gay or lesbian on the one hand, and those in which children were born or adopted after parents had affirmed lesbian or gay identities on the other. . . . [¶] Within each of these two types of families, there are of course many additional forms of diversity [e.g., ethnic, religious, economic.]

One important impetus for research in the area of lesbian and gay parents has come from extrinsic sources, such as judicial concerns about the psychological health and well-being of divorced lesbian mothers and their children compared with that of divorced heterosexual mothers and their children. . . . [¶]. . . . Thus, many studies have been conducted to evaluate the accuracy of negative expectations about lesbian and gay parents or about their children.

[A] number of studies have assessed the overall mental health of lesbian compared with heterosexual mothers [and have] found no differences between lesbian and heterosexual mothers on self-concept, happiness, overall adjustment, or psychiatric status. [¶]

. . . .

Although considerable research has focused on the overall psychological adjustment of [divorced] lesbian mothers compared with that of heterosexual mothers, no published studies of gay fathers make such comparisons with heterosexual fathers. [The author suggests that this dearth may be due, in part, to the disparity between post-divorce custody awards to mothers and fathers.] [¶] Research on the parenting attitudes of gay versus heterosexual divorced fathers has been reported, [however, and no meaningful statistically] significant differences [distinguished] gay and heterosexual fathers in their motives for parenthood. . . . [¶] [One study] asked gay and heterosexual fathers . . . to report on their behavior when interacting with their children. Although no differences emerged in the fathers' reports of involvement or intimacy, gay fathers reported that their behavior was characterized by greater responsiveness, more reasoning, and more limit setting than was that of heterosexual fathers. . . .

. . . .

Although for many years lesbian mothers and gay fathers were generally assumed to have become parents in the context of previous heterosexual relationships, both men and women are believed increasingly to be undertaking parenthood in the context of preexisting lesbian and gay identities. . . . [¶] [In one study,] more than half of the gay men who were not fathers indicated that they would like to rear a child. . . .

. . . .

Research on gender identity has failed to reveal any differences in the development of children as a function of their parents' sexual orientation. . . . [¶] A number of investigators have also studied sexual orientation, [and did not find any differences between children of gays and lesbians versus those of heterosexual parents in the likelihood that a child would identify as gay or lesbian.]

. . . .

Studies of other aspects of personal development among children of gay and lesbian parents have [revealed] no significant differences between children of lesbian or gay parents and children of heterosexual parents [on assessments of behavior problems, personality, self-concept, . . . moral judgment, and intelligence.] Concerns about possible difficulties in personal development among children of lesbian and gay parents have not been sustained by the results of research [and are thus] without empirical foundation. [¶]. . . . Research has consistently found that children of lesbian mothers report normal peer relations. . . .

. . . .

[The author focuses on recent studies of children born into lesbian relationships via donor insemination or in vitro fertilization. The results of these studies demonstrate no differences in psychological adjustment and development of children raised in lesbian versus heterosexual-parent families, with the following exceptions.] On two subscales of the self-concept measure . . . Patterson found that children of lesbian mothers reported feeling more reactions to stress (*e.g.*, feeling angry, scared, or upset), but a greater sense of well-being (*e.g.*, feeling joyful, content, and comfortable with themselves) than did the same-aged children of heterosexual mothers. . . . One possible interpretation of this result is that children of lesbian mothers reported greater reactivity to stress because, in fact, they experienced greater stress in their daily lives than did other children. Another possibility is that, regardless of actual stress levels, children of lesbian mothers were better able to acknowledge both positive and negative aspects of their emotional experience.

Contrary to stereotypes of these families as isolated from families of origin, most reported that children had regular (i.e., at least monthly) contact with one or more grandparents, as well as with other adult friends and relatives of both genders. In families headed by lesbian couples, the parents were likely to maintain egalitarian divisions of labor, but when differences occurred, biological lesbian mothers were likely to do somewhat more child care and nonbiological lesbian mothers were likely to spend somewhat more time engaged in paid employment. Even within the relatively small range represented in this sample, families in which child care was divided more evenly were also those in which children exhibited the most favorable adjustment. These results suggest the importance of family process variables as predictors of child adjustment in lesbian as well as in heterosexual families.

. . . .

Despite limitations, . . . central results of existing research on lesbian and gay couples and families with children are exceptionally clear. Beyond their witness to the sheer existence of lesbian and gay family lives, the results of existing studies, taken together, also yield a picture of families thriving, even in the midst of discrimination and oppression. Certainly, they provide no evidence that psychological adjustment among lesbians, gay men, their children, or other family members is impaired in any significant way. Indeed, the evidence suggests that relationships of lesbian and gay couples are just as supportive and that home environments provided by lesbian and gay parents are just as likely as those provided by heterosexual parents to enable psychosocial growth among family members.

* * * * *

For additional discussion of psychological research on gay and lesbian parenting, see SUZANNE M. JOHNSON & ELIZABETH O'CONNOR, THE GAY BABY BOOM: THE PSYCHOLOGY OF GAY PARENTHOOD (2002); Charlotte J. Patterson & Raymond W. Chan, *Families Headed by Lesbian and Gay Parents,* in "NONTRADITIONAL" FAMILIES 191 (M.E. Lamb ed. 1999); Patricia J. Falk, *The Gap Between Psychological Assumptions and Empirical Research in Lesbian-Mother Child Custody Cases,* in REDEFINING FAMILIES 131 (A.E. Gottfried &

A.W. Gottfried eds. 1994); Robert L. Barret & Bryan E. Robinson, *Gay Dads*, in REDEFINING FAMILIES, *supra,* at 157; FREDERICK W. BOZETT (ED.), GAY AND LESBIAN PARENTS (1987). For discussion of the mental health of gays and lesbians, and of gay or lesbian relationships, see generally RITCH C. SAVIN-WILLIAMS & KENNETH M. COHEN (EDS.), THE LIVES OF LESBIANS, GAYS, AND BISEXUALS: CHILDREN TO ADULTS (1996); ROBERT P. CABAJ & TERRY S. STEIN (EDS.), TEXTBOOK OF HOMOSEXUALITY AND MENTAL HEALTH (1996); JOHN C. GONSIOREK & JAMES D. WEINRICH (EDS.), HOMOSEXUALITY: RESEARCH IMPLICA-TIONS FOR PUBLIC POLICY (1991).

For application of these scientific findings to legal policy questions see Michael Wald, *Same-Sex Couple Marriage: A Family Policy Perspective*, 9 VA. J. SOC. POL'Y & L. 291 (2001) (concluding that the existing data base, while imperfect, does not provide a basis for limiting the rights of gays and lesbians to become parents); Lynn D. Wardle, *The Potential Impact of Homosexual Parenting on Children*, 1997 UNIV. ILL. L. REV. 833 (arguing that it is not in the best interests of children to be parented by gays or lesbians); Carlos A. Ball & Janice Farrell Pea, *Warring with Wardle: Morality, Social Science, and Gay and Lesbian Parents,* 1998 U. ILL. L. REV. 253 (providing a "point-by-point" rebuttal of Wardle's assessment of the social science literature).

[a] Adoptions by Same-Sex Couples and Gay or Lesbian Individuals

[i] Second-Parent Adoption

SHARON S. v. SUPERIOR COURT

31 Cal. 4th 417, 73 P.3d 554, 2 Cal. Rptr. 3d 699 (2003)

WERDEGAR, J.

This dispute arises in independent adoption proceedings commenced by a birth mother, Sharon S. . . . and her former domestic partner Annette F. . . . to effect Annette's adoption of Joshua (now three and a half years old) who, like his older brother Zachary (now six years old and previously adopted by Annette), was conceived by artificial insemination of Sharon and born during the partnership.[1] The question presented is whether an independent adop-tion in which the birth parent does not agree to termination of her parental rights is legislatively authorized and, if so, whether the statutes are constitutional. . . .

Sharon and Annette attended Harvard Business School together and were in a committed relationship from 1989 through mid 2000. In 1996, after being artificially inseminated with sperm from an anonymous donor, Sharon gave birth to Zachary. With Sharon's consent and approval, Annette petitioned to

---

[1] Independent adoptions are those in which no agency, state or private, joins in the adoption petition, although the state does have a role in investigating, evaluating and commenting upon the petition.

adopt Zachary in a "second parent" adoption, using official forms and proce-dures that expressly provided that Sharon consented to Zachary's adoption by Annette, but intended to retain her own parental rights.[2] The trial court approved Annette's adoption petition, and Annette has since been one of Zachary's two parents.

Three years later, in 1999, Sharon was inseminated again with sperm from the same anonymous donor and gave birth to Joshua. On August 30 of that year, Sharon signed an Independent Adoption Placement Agreement (Agree-ment), which begins: "Note to birth parent: This form will become a permanent and irrevocable consent to adoption. Do not sign this form unless you want the adopting parents named below to adopt your child." The Agreement goes on to recite Sharon's "permanent and irrevocable consent to the adoption on the 91st day after I sign" the Agreement.

The Agreement also recites that, upon the court's approval of the Agree-ment, Sharon will "give up all rights of custody, services, and earnings" with respect to Joshua. However, a written Addendum to Independent Adoption Placement Agreement (Addendum), a form developed by the California Department of Social Services (CDSS), was signed by Sharon and Annette on the same date as they signed the Agreement. The Addendum stated Sharon's intent, as Joshua's birth parent, to retain parental rights and control of Joshua while placing him with Annette for the purpose of independent adoption. These were essentially the same procedures and forms Sharon and Annette had used for Zachary's adoption.[3]

Subsequently, Annette filed a petition to adopt Joshua as a second parent with Sharon. The petition stated that Sharon, as "birth mother of the children [Zachary and Joshua,] consents to this adoption and will execute a limited written consent to the child's [Joshua's] adoption in the manner required by law." The petition also stated that Sharon "intends to retain all her rights to custody and control as to said child." In April 2000, the San Diego County Department of Health and Human Services (HHS), acting in its capacity as an agency licensed by CDSS under the Family Code to investigate and report upon proposed independent adoptions, recommended that the court grant An-nette's adoption petition.

Annette and Sharon's relationship has been somewhat volatile. . . . In mediation, the parties agreed on a temporary visitation schedule affording Annette time with both boys, but they could not reach an agreement respecting permanent custody or visitation. [¶] On October 23, 2000, Annette filed a motion for an order of adoption respecting Joshua, contending . . . that Sharon's consent had become irrevocable pursuant to section 8814.5 and that the adoption was in Joshua's best interest. [¶] After a family court mediator

---

[2] "The phrase 'second-parent adoption' refers to an independent adoption whereby a child born to [or legally adopted by] one partner is adopted by his or her non-biological or non-legal second parent, with the consent of the legal parent, and without changing the latter's rights and responsibilities". . . . As a result of the adoption, the child has two legal parents who have equal legal status in terms of their relationship with the child.

[3] CDSS forms and procedures for second parent adoptions have been developed over the past decade and presently are maintained in accordance with a policy announced by CDSS on November 15, 1999. . . .

recommended that Sharon and Annette share custody and that Annette have specified visitation, Sharon moved for court approval to withdraw her consent to the adoption. She contended there was no legal basis for the adoption. . . . HHS subsequently filed a supplemental report with the court, noting that Sharon had moved to withdraw her consent but had not done so within the statutorily specified period for revocation. HHS further reported that Annette had shared in Joshua's medical expenses and in the planning and handling of his daily care since birth, that Annette had a close and loving relationship with Joshua as his second parent, and that Annette's relationship with Joshua was similar to her relationship with Zachary. Finding that adoption continued to be in Joshua's best interest, HHS again recommended that Annette's petition to adopt Joshua be granted.

. . . .

"The right to adopt a child, and the right of a person to be adopted as the child of another, are wholly statutory.". . . . [¶] . . . Pursuant to the current statutory scheme, birth parents can consent to an independent adoption by entering into an adoption placement agreement with a prospective adoptive parent. The birth parent(s) have 30 days in which to revoke this consent. If they fail to do so, their consent becomes permanent and irrevocable. [¶] Once the adoption placement agreement has been signed, the prospective adoptive parent may petition for adoption. The court clerk must give CDSS notice of the petition and the petitioner must file a copy of the petition with CDSS.

Subsequently, it is incumbent on CDSS to "investigate the proposed independent adoption" and "ascertain whether the child is a proper subject for adoption and whether the proposed home is suitable for the child" [and submit a report to the court with a recommendation regarding the granting of the petition.] Assuming other statutory prerequisites are met, if the court is "satisfied that the interest of the child will be promoted by the adoption, the court may make and enter an order of adoption of the child by the prospective adoptive parent or parents."

Annette argues that these statutes authorize the superior court to finalize her adoption of Joshua, because she has complied with the substantive and procedural prerequisites for an independent adoption. Sharon contends that the adoption is not authorized, because section 8617 mandates full termination of birth parental rights in every independent adoption.

Section 8617 provides: "The birth parents of an adopted child are, from the time of the adoption, relieved of all parental duties towards, and all responsibility for, the adopted child, and have no right over the child." The section does not appear in the chapter devoted to independent adoptions, but is, rather, one of the general provisions. . . .

"The rule is that the adoption statutes are to be liberally construed with a view to effect their objects and to promote justice. Such a construction should be given as will sustain, rather than defeat, the object they have in view." *Dept. Soc. Welf. v. Super. Ct.*, 459 P.2d 897 (Cal. 1969) (en banc). Consistently with these principles, we previously have concluded that the Legislature did not intend section 8617's nearly identical precursor to bar an adoption when the parties clearly intended to waive the operation of that statute and agreed to preserve the birth parent's rights and responsibilities. *Marshall v. Marshall* 239 P. 36 (1925). Nothing in section 8617's text, context, history, or function justifies departure in this case from "the established rule that rights conferred by statute may be waived unless specific statutory provisions prohibit waiver." *Bickel v. City of Piedmont* 946 P.2d 427 (Cal. 1997).

. . . . The principles underlying *Bickel* are well established. As we have recognized for over a century, the law "will not compel a man to insist upon any benefit or advantage secured to him individually." Accordingly, a party may waive compliance with statutory conditions intended for his or her benefit, so long as the Legislature has not made those conditions mandatory. [¶] Applying these established principles "to determine whether in this case [section 8617] bars application of the waiver doctrine, we must ascertain (1) whether [the statute's provisions] are for the benefit of [the parties to an adoption petition] or are instead for a public purpose, and (2) whether there is any language in [the statute] prohibiting a waiver." *Bickel, supra.*

Addressing the latter point first, we immediately observe that section 8617 contains no language prohibiting the parties to an independent adoption from agreeing to waive its provisions. . . . [N]othing therein, or in any other statutory provision, prohibits the parties to an independent adoption from waiving the benefits of section 8617 when a birth parent intends and desires to coparent with another adult who has agreed to adopt the child and share parental responsibilities. [¶] Since section 8617's provisions are for the benefit of the parties to an adoption petition and the section contains no language prohibiting a waiver, we conclude that section 8617 declares a legal consequence of the usual adoption, waivable by the parties thereto, rather than a mandatory prerequisite to every valid adoption.[6]

. . . .

While California's adoption statutes nowhere concisely define "adoption," they do state the essential elements of a valid adoption. . . . 'The proceeding is essentially one of contract between the parties whose consent is required. . . . [¶] [T]he essential elements of every valid adoption are: a voluntary and informed parental consent to the adoption except where the parent has surrendered or has been judicially deprived of parental control, CAL. FAM. CODE §§ 8604-8606; a suitable adoptive parent at least 10 years older than, or in a specified preexisting family relationship with, the child, CAL. FAM. CODE §§ 8601, 8717, 8801, 8811–8811.5; and a judicial determination that "the interest of the child will be promoted by the adoption," CAL. FAM. CODE § 8612. When these essential elements are present, "the objective of the adoption statutes to protect the interests of both the natural or legal

---

[6] In so holding, we do not decide, contrary to what our concurring and dissenting colleagues suggest [see concurring and dissenting opinions of Justices Brown and Baxter, respectively], whether there exists an overriding legislative policy limiting a child to two parents. This case involves only a second parent adoption, so we have no occasion to address that point. Justice Baxter errs, therefore, in asserting that our decision today frees a family court to assign at will "as many legal parents as the lone judge deems in the child's best interest." While the Family Code contains in several sections language suggesting the Legislature may harbor a two-parent policy, those statutes are not in issue. Section 8617, which is in issue, does not speak to parental numerosity, except incidentally to recognize in its use of the plural, "birth parents," that a child ordinarily has two of these.

parent(s) and the child through the consent and best interests requirements" is not frustrated when statutory provisions like section 8617 are treated as nonmandatory. Patt, *Second Parent Adoption: When Crossing the Marital Barrier Is in a Child's Best Interests*, 3 BERKELEY WOMEN'S L.J. 96, 117 (1987-88) (discussing Civ. Code former § 229).

. . . .

" 'Independent Adoption' " means the adoption of a child in which neither the department nor an agency licensed by the department is a party to, or joins in, the adoption petition." CAL. FAM. CODE § 8524. In addition to the essential elements of all adoptions set out above, the independent adoption statutes require parental consent after notice and advisement, CAL. FAM. CODE §§ 8800, 8801.3, 8814, 8821, opportunities under specified conditions timely to revoke consent, CAL. FAM. CODE § 8814.5, or with court approval to withdraw it, CAL. FAM. CODE § 8815, selection of the adoptive parent or parents by the birth parent or parents personally, Cal. Fam. Code § 8801, advice to the birth parent of his or her rights by an adoption service provider or licensed out-of-state agency, CAL. FAM. CODE § 8801.5, execution of an adoption placement agreement satisfying specified requirements on a form prescribed by CDSS, CAL. FAM. CODE § 8801.3, administrative investigation by CDSS or its delegate, CAL. FAM. CODE § 8806-8811, 8817, an appropriate petition filed with the superior court, usually in the county in which the petitioner resides, CAL. FAM. CODE § 8802, and an appearance before the court by the prospective adoptive parents and the child, CAL. FAM. CODE § 8612, 8613, 8823. Nowhere does any mandate or requirement of relinquishment of a birth parent's rights and responsibilities appear. [¶] [S]ection 8617 neither prohibits a birth parent and another qualified adult from jointly waiving application of the statute in order to coparent an adoptable child, nor prohibits a court under such circumstances from ordering an otherwise valid adoption.

Decades ago, we held [the predecessor statute to] section 8617, was no bar to second parent adoption of a type — stepparent adoption — that was then not expressly provided for by statute. . . . [¶] In *Marshall,* the second husband of a widowed mother adopted her two minor children. . . . [¶] [W]e held in *Marshall* that "although no express authority therefor is to be found in the code, nevertheless a husband and wife may jointly adopt a child pursuant to the procedure therein prescribed, the result of which is to make the child, in law, the child of both spouses.". . . . [¶] In *Marshall,* we thus effectively read second parent adoption into the statutory scheme . . . In so doing, we necessarily determined that relinquishment of the birth parent's rights was not essential to adoption and that section 8617's predecessor was not mandatory.

. . . .

California's adoption statutes have always permitted adoption without regard to the marital status of prospective adoptive parents. . . . [N]o justification appears for treating section 8617 differently in this case than we did its predecessor in *Marshall.*

. . . .

Several important considerations of public policy also buttress our conclusion. Precisely how many second parent adoptions have been granted in

California over the years is difficult to know, partly because adoption proceedings are generally confidential, but published materials suggest they number 10,000 to 20,000. That the second parent adoption procedures promulgated by CDSS under the independent adoption statutes have received such widespread acceptance and have been so extensively used speaks not only to their utility in the modern context, but to their effectiveness in promoting the fundamental purposes that adoption has always served.

The basic purpose of an adoption is the "welfare, protection and betterment of the child," and adoption courts ultimately must rule on that basis. *Reeves v. Bailey,* 53 Cal. App.3d 1019, 1022–23 (1975). While the child's "best interest" is "an elusive guideline that belies rigid definition," obviously overall "[i]ts purpose is to maximize a child's opportunity to develop into a stable, well-adjusted adult." *Adoption of Michelle T.,* 44 Cal. App. 3d 699, 704 (1975). That there are a variety of "costs . . . if a legal relationship with a second parent is not established — costs that can be both financial and emotional" is well recognized. Doskow, *The Second Parent Trap,* 20 J. Juv. L. 1, 9 (1999). Second parent adoption can secure the salutary incidents of legally recognized parentage for a child of a nonbiological parent who otherwise must remain a legal stranger.

Second parent adoptions also benefit children by providing a clear legal framework for resolving any disputes that may arise over custody and visitation. Our explicitly recognizing their validity will prevent uncertainty, conflict, and protracted litigation in this area, all of which plainly are harmful to children caught in the middle. Unmarried couples who have brought a child into the world with the expectation that they will raise it together, and who have jointly petitioned for adoption, should be on notice that if they separate the same rules concerning custody and visitation as apply to all other parents will apply to them.

In addition, second parent adoptions offer the possibility of obtaining the security and advantages of two parents for some of California's neediest children, including many with "special needs" for whom a second parent adoption may constitute the "closest conceivable counterpart of the relationship of parent and child" available. The same is true as regards thousands of others in foster care for whom it is state policy to seek permanent adoptive placement.

    . . . .

Sharon argues that reversal of the Court of Appeal's decision will permit CDSS to authorize unusual adoptions, e.g., involving multiple parties, far removed from those contemplated by the Legislature. Justice Baxter also expresses concern that our decision will lead to "new and even bizarre family structures", while Justice Brown inexplicably refers to our supposed "irretrievabl[e] commit[ment] to . . . the-more-parents-the-merrier view of parenthood." Nonsense. While CDSS has for some time treated section 8617 as waivable, such scenarios have not materialized. Our explicit recognition in this case of the legal ground for second parent adoptions — a nonmandatory construction of section 8617 that comports with judicial precedent and ratifies administrative interpretation and practice in which the Legislature has acquiesced — obviously cannot be taken as authority for multiple parent or other novel adoption scenarios. Nothing we say in this case can validate an adoption that is not in the child's interest, omits any essential statutory element, or is in violation of a public policy the Legislature may express. . . .

In sum, adherence to the Court of Appeal's construction of section 8617 as precluding second parent adoption would unnecessarily eliminate access to a duly promulgated, well-tested adoption process that has become "routine in California" and that is fully consistent with the main purpose of the adoption statutes to promote "the welfare of children 'by the legal recognition and regulation of the consummation of the closest conceivable counterpart of the relationship of parent and child' " *Dept. Soc. Welf. v. Super. Ct., supra.*

The Court of Appeal's implication that California courts lack jurisdiction to grant second parent adoptions potentially called into question the legitimacy of existing families heretofore created in this state through established administrative and judicial procedures. Such families are of many types. [¶] Although second parent adoptions may involve children conceived, as in this case, by artificial insemination, others involve children placed directly by their birth parents or private agencies with two unmarried adoptive parents. Others involve dependent children, often with special needs because of prior abuse or neglect, who were placed by public agencies with an unmarried "fost-adopt" parent whose partner later became a second adoptive parent. Still others are "kinship" adoptions, in which a grandparent or other relative became a second legal parent of a child whose very young mother was unable to raise the child on her own. Such adoptions also have involved children born in other countries and adopted either in their country of origin or in California by an unmarried adult whose partner later became a second adoptive parent. Established practice in California thus has created settled expectations among many different types of adoptive families. Affirmance would unnecessarily risk disturbing these.

Affirmance not only would cast a shadow of uncertainty over the legal relationships between thousands of children and their adoptive parents (contrary to the clearly stated intention of all interested parties), but potentially could prompt some adoptive parents to disclaim their established responsibilities [and] "would invite attempts to nullify completed second party adoptions in myriad species of litigation including support/custody/visitation disputes, inheritance contests and withdrawals of entitlements to previously available health and pension benefits, both governmental and private. The ultimate financial and emotional losers will be children who are the intended beneficiaries of the adoption laws."

. . . .

For the foregoing reasons, we reverse the judgment of the Court of Appeal and remand the cause for further proceedings consistent with this opinion.

Concurring and Dissenting Opinion by BAXTER, J. [Joined by CHIN, J.]

The majority's principal holding — which recognizes second parent adoptions as valid in California — is unremarkable. At least 20 other jurisdictions have already done so, including the highest courts of three sister states. [Massachusetts, New York, and Vermont.] I join fully in that holding.

I part company with the majority, however, over its interpretation of Family Code section 8617, which states that from the time of adoption, the birth parent shall "have no right over the child." I would hold that the parties to an adoption may waive section 8617 in the limited circumstance of a second parent adoption. This is sufficient to resolve the case. Unfortunately, the majority does not stop there but makes the additional holding that section 8617 is a nonmandatory consequence of an adoption and can be waived *whenever* the parties agree to do so. Under the majority's approach, section 8617's termination of the birth parents' rights in *any* type of adoption — not merely those that seek to add a second parent — can be waived by mutual agreement, thus permitting a child to have three or more parents.

This makes new law, not only here but nationwide. Other states — even those states that have already validated second parent adoptions — have not taken this step. Unlike the majority, but in accordance with our sister states, I would hold that our termination-of-rights statute can be waived in the limited circumstance of a second parent adoption. [I]t is not necessary to make new law to uphold second parent adoptions in California.

I cannot fathom why the majority has deliberately chosen a rationale that is unnecessary to the disposition of this case *and* that has been avoided by other jurisdictions, but I do understand and fear the effect of the majority's additional holding: to put at risk fundamental understandings of family and parentage. Tomorrow, the question may be: *How many legal parents may a child have in California?* And the answer, according to the majority opinion, will be: *As many parents as a single family court judge, in the exercise of the broadest discretion in our law, deems to be in the child's best interest.*

. . . .

. . . . Commentators have recognized that a child may end up with any number of parents when family structure becomes a matter of private ordering. The available empirical evidence supports this prediction. An Alaska superior court's finding that a similar termination-of-rights statute was directory was followed quickly by an adoption in which neither natural parent severed ties with the child. "Accordingly, *the child now has three legal parents.*" (Patt, *Second Parent Adoption: When Crossing the Marital Barrier Is in a Child's Best Interests* (1987-1988) 3 Berkeley Women's L.J. 96, 132. . .) Moreover, at oral argument, Annette's counsel informed us that superior courts in this state have already allowed a child to have more than two legal parents, apparently based on counsel's theory that section 8617 is merely directory.

Since I am not a legislator, my own views as to whether children should be allowed to have three or more legal parents are not relevant here, although it does appear that such arrangements are highly problematic. The existence of multiple parents would also make more difficult the resolution of disputes that may arise over custody and visitation, as well as conflicts over other parental rights and responsibilities. In any event, the important point — and the one the majority deliberately ignores — is that "[e]xisting law recognizes a maximum of two parents per child." King, *Solomon Revisited: Assigning Parenthood in the Context of Collaborative Reproduction*, 5 UCLA WOMEN'S L.J. 329 (1995). Indeed, no commentator of whom I am aware shares the majority's agnosticism as to "whether there exists an overriding legislative policy limiting a child to two parents." Moreover, numerous provisions of the Family Code — including the sections cited by the majority — demonstrate the Legislature intended to limit a child to no more than two legal parents. . . . The majority's unique unwillingness to acknowledge section 8617's role in limiting a child to no more than two parents defies common sense.

. . . .

In sum, nothing in law or policy justifies the majority's evisceration of the important public purpose underlying section 8617 — namely, the legislative declaration and case authority that a child needs no more than two legal parents. [¶] Second parent adoptions by unmarried persons are consistent with California law. I would apply that settled law to decide this case. . . .

Concurring and Dissenting Opinion by BROWN, J.

This case raises questions concerning the past, present and future of California adoption law. Regarding the past, I agree that we should not disturb settled familial relationships. Regarding the present, Annette may deserve partial custody based on estoppel. The most important question, however, is whether the California Department of Social Services ought to continue authorizing these second parent adoptions in the thousands of cases that will arise in the future. The Legislature has heretofore required a legal relationship [of domestic partner] between the birth and second parent, and I would defer to this rule and bar second parent adoptions that violate the statutory scheme. [Justice Brown argues that by enacting statutes that permitted stepparent adoptions, and more recently, second-parent adoptions for domestic partners of the prospective adoptee's legal parent, the Legislature intended to limit the circumstances in which the natural parents need not sever parental rights in the adoption context to those two situations only. Like Justice Baxter, Justice Brown cites a concern that the majority's construction of Family Code § 8617 could lead to more than two parents for any given child (referring to the majority's position as its "the-more-parents-the-merrier view of parenthood"), and can lead to ambiguity as to which is a child's "real" parent. Justice Brown states that the majority trivializes family bonds by reducing parenthood to a contract.]

NOTES

1. *Case Law and Second-Parent Adoptions.* While most states agree with the result in *Sharon S.*, the dissenting justices are correct that no other appellate court has grounded its decision in the same legal theory. Courts construing adoption statutes broadly to authorize second-parent adoptions have concluded that doing so furthers the underlying purposes of the state's adoption statutes in promoting the child's best interests. For example, in *Adoptions of B.L.V.B. and E.L.V.B.*, 628 A.2d 1271, 1273–74 (Vt. 1993), the Vermont Supreme Court stated:

> In interpreting [our] statutes, we are mindful that the state's primary concern is to promote the welfare of children, and that application of the statutes should implement that purpose. In doing

so, we must avoid results that are irrational, unreasonable or absurd. We must look "not only at the letter of a statute but also its reason and spirit." [¶] [¶]. . . . [In enacting the step-parent adoption provision, the] legislature recognized that it would be against common sense to terminate the biological parent's rights when that parent will continue to raise and be responsible for the child, albeit in a family unit with a partner who is biologically unrelated to the child.

. . .Despite the narrow wording of the step-parent exception, we cannot conclude that the legislature ever meant to terminate the parental rights of a biological parent who intended to continue raising a child with the help of a partner. Such a narrow construction would produce the unreasonable and irrational result of defeating adoptions that are otherwise indisputably in the best interests of children. . . .

Courts have also focused on the particular benefits to children of an adoption by their legal parent's same-sex partner:

[The child's interests are] advanced . . . by allowing the two adults who actually function as a child's parents to become the child's legal parents. The advantages which would result from such an adoption include Social Security and life insurance benefits in the event of a parent's death or disability, the right to sue for the wrongful death of a parent, the right to inherit under rules of intestacy, and eligibility for coverage under both parents' health insurance policies. In addition, granting a second parent adoption further ensures that two adults are legally entitled to make medical decisions for the child in case of emergency and are under a legal obligation for the child's economic support.

Even more important, however, is the emotional security of knowing that in the event of the biological parent's death or disability, the other parent will have presumptive custody, and the children's relationship with their parents, siblings and other relatives will continue should the coparents separate. Indeed, viewed from the children's perspective, permitting the adoptions allows the children to achieve a measure of permanency with both parent figures. . . .

In re Jacob, 660 N.E.2d 398, 399, 636 N.Y.S.2d 716, 718 (N.Y. 1995). The number of state courts interpreting adoption statutes to permit second-parent adoption has increased annually. High court decisions authorizing second-parent adoptions include California, New York, *In re Jacob, supra,* and Vermont, *Adoptions of B.L.V.B. and E.L.V.B., supra,* Massachusetts, *In re Adoption of Tammy,* 619 N.E.2d 315 (Mass. 1993), and Pennsylvania, *In re Adoption of R.B.F.,* 803 A.3d 1195 (Pa. 2002). *See also In re M.M.D. & B.H.M.,* 662 A.2d 837 (D.C. App. 1995). State courts of appeal have approved second parent adoptions in several other jurisdictions. *See, e.g., In re Adoption of M.M.G.C., H.H.C, & K.E.A.C.,* 785 N.E.2d 267 (Ind. App. 2003); *Petition of K.M. and D.M.,* 653 N.E.2d 888 (Ill. App. 1995); *Adoption of Two Children by H.N.R.,* 666 A.2d 535 (N.J. App. Div. 1995). Although some sources state that approximately twenty states permit second-parent adoptions, only about half of those states have published decisions or statutes that tackle the question head-on. In others, trial courts have approved second-parent adoptions in individual cases, sometimes pursuant to a state department of family services policy of recommending such adoptions as in the best interests of the children, absent extenuating circumstances. A recent survey indicates that the following states fall within this category, based in part on "anecdotal evidence": Alabama, Alaska, Delaware, Hawaii, Iowa, Louisiana, Maryland, Minnesota, Nevada, New Mexico, Oregon, Rhode Island, Texas, and Washington. Human Rights Council, *Second-Parent Adoption*. Available at: www.hrc.org/familynet/printpage.asp?table = articles&ID = 209 (last visited August 6, 2003).

Some courts have rejected second-parent adoption petitions, awaiting explicit statutory authorization. Six of seven justices of the Connecticut Supreme Court took this position in *In re Adoption of Baby Z.,* 724 A.2d 1035 (1999). *See also In re Adoption of Luke,* 640 N.W.2d 365 (Neb. 2002) (same-sex companion of mother ineligible to adopt child under adoption statute absent termination of mother's parental rights); *In Matter of Adoption of T.K.J. and K.A.K,* 931 P.2d 488 (Colo. App. 1996) (liberal construction of adoption statute does not permit court to "rewrite" statute in granting second-parent adoption without explicit legislative authorization); *Interest of Angel Lace M.,* 516 N.W.2d 678 (Wis. 1994) (statutory provision requiring termination of mother's rights is mandatory and applies to adoption by her lesbian partner); *In re Adoption of Jane Doe,* 719 N.E.2d 1071 (Ohio App. 1998). For a general compilation of state policies, see Sonja Larsen, Annotation, *Adoption of Child by Same-Sex Partners,* 27 A.L.R.5th 54 (1995, updated 2000).

2. *Statutory Second-Parent Adoption Provisions*. Several states statutes explicitly authorize second-parent adoptions. As discussed in *Sharon S.,* California enacted Family Code § 9000(b), effective 2001, providing that a "domestic partner . . . desiring to adopt a child of his or her domestic partner may for that purpose file a petition in the county in which the petitioner resides." CAL. FAM. CODE § 9000(b) (2003). Immediately following the Connecticut Supreme Court's decision in *In re Baby Z., supra* note 1, the Connecticut legislature enacted a statute permitting a person who shares parental responsibility with the child's parent to adopt, or join in an adoption, even if the two adults are not married. CONN. ST. 45a-724(a)(3) (2003). Vermont enacted a similar provision as part of its civil union legislation, making second-parent adoptions by partners to a civil union analogous to step-parent adoptions by spouses. VT. ST. § 1204(e)(4) (2003). A bill permitting second-parent adoptions was introduced in the Wisconsin legislature following *Angel Lace M., supra* note 1, but was not enacted.

3. *The Concurring/Dissenting Justices Concerns in Sharon S.* All members of the California Supreme Court concurred that second-parent adoptions by same-sex partners were authorized by the independent adoption statutes that predated passage of Family Code Section 9000(b). Yet, three justices expressed concern that the majority's construction of the independent adoption statute was too broad, in allowing the parties to an adoption to waive the statutory requirement that natural parents' rights be terminated in situations beyond step-parent and second-parent adoptions. These justices argue that this construction could lead to adoption of a child who already has two legal parents. These concerns echo Justice Scalia's warning, in *Michael H.,* of the dangers that lie in recognizing two parents of the same gender. Whether or not one views three-or four-parent families as problematic, or agrees with Justices Baxter and Brown's characterizations of the majority opinion, their separate opinions remind us that new ground has been forged by expansions of legal doctrines in response to nontraditional family members' claims. We do not yet know all of the implications of the recent developments. For an argument in support of the proposition that more than two legal parents may serve children's best interests in some situations, see Pamela Gatos, Note, *Third-Parent Adoption in Lesbian and Gay Families*, 26 Vt. L. Rev. 195 (2001).

4. *Policy Positions of National Professional Associations.* In the past several years, several national professional groups have formally encouraged legal ratification of second-parent adoptions or have commented favorably on the adequacy of gays and lesbians as parents. *See, e.g.,* American Academy of Pediatrics, *Policy Statement on Coparent or Second-Parent Adoption by Same-Sex Parents*, 109 Pediatrics 339 (2002) (available at www.app.org/policy/020008.html) and Ellen C. Perrin and the Committee on Psychosocial Aspects of Child and Family Health, American Academy of Pediatrics, *Technical Report: Coparent or Second-Parent Adoption by Same-Sex Parents,* 109 Pediatrics 341 (2002) (concluding relevant developmental research supports legal extension of second-parent adoption policies); American Psychological Association, *Policy Statement: Legal Benefits for Same-Sex Couples*, adopted August 16, 1998, available at: www.apa.org/pi/lgbc/policy/statements.html#11); American Psychiatric Association, *Controversies in Child Custody; Gay and Lesbian Parenting; Transracial Adoptions; Joint versus Sole Custody; and Custody Gender Issues*, Adopted December 1997 (available at: www.psych.org/archives/970008.pdf); American Psychoanalytic Society, *Position Statement on Gay and Lesbian Parenting*, adopted May 16, 2002 (available at: www.apsa-co.org/ctf/cgli/parenting.htm).

5. *Scholarly Commentary.* Most scholarly commentary on the subject of second-parent adoption has recommended expansion of favorable policies, arguing that such policies protect children's best interests for the reasons articulated by the state supreme courts above. *See, e.g.,* Patricia J. Falk, *Second-Parent Adoption*, 48 Cleveland St. L. Rev. 93 (2000); Mark Strasser, *Courts, Legislatures, and Second-Parent Adoptions: On Judicial Deference, Specious Reasoning, and the Best Interests of the Child,* 66 Tenn. L. Rev. 1019 (1999); Theresa Glennon, *Binding the Family Ties: A Child Advocacy Perspective on Second-Parent Adoption*, 7 Temp. Pol. & Civ. Rts. L. Rev. 255 (1998); Maxwell S. Pelts, *Second-Parent Adoption: Overcoming Barriers to Lesbian Family Rights*, 3 Mich. J. Gender & L. 175 (1995). *But see* Lynn D. Wardle, *The Potential Impact of Homosexual Parenting on Children*, 1997 Univ. Ill. L. Rev. 833 (arguing adoption by homosexuals is not in children's best interests).

6. *Second-Parent Adoption Outside of the United States.* Certain Scandinavian and European countries which preceded American states in recognizing same-sex partnerships generally (see page 928 in this chapter), have been slower than many American states to permit same-sex couples to adopt. *See, e.g., Developments in the Law — The Law of Marriage and Family,* 116 HARV. L. REV. 1999, 2010–12 (2003) (hereinafter *"Developments"*). *See also* WILLIAM N. ESKRIDGE, JR., EQUALITY PRACTICE: CIVIL UNIONS AND THE PRACTICE OF GAY RIGHTS 89–117 & Table 3.2 at p. 116 (2001); YUVAL MERIN, EQUALITY FOR SAME-SEX COUPLES 253–262 (2002). The Scandinavian and European resistance to extending parental rights to same-sex couples demonstrates that "popular acceptance of economic rights for same-sex couples does not necessarily imply a willingness to infringe on more established religious and cultural traditions." *Developments,* supra., at 1011. According to one commentator, the traditional belief that a child is best off with two parents of different genders has been more tenaciously held in these countries than in the United States. Merin*, supra* at 254. Yet, the resistance is eroding. The Netherlands, Denmark, and Iceland now permit second-parent adoptions. *Developments,* at 1011. Furthermore, as part of a more comprehensive proposal to approve gay marriage set forth in its 2003 annual report on human rights to the European Union, the European Parliament recommended that gay men and lesbians be allowed to adopt children. *See European Parliament Backs Gay Marriage*, ADVOCATE.COM. Available at: www.advocate.com/new_news.asp?ID = 9774&sd = 9/06/03-09/08/03.

7. *An Alternative to Adoption?* On March 20, 1999, the birth of Maximillian Ehlert McAllister made headlines in California. Leslee Subak gave birth to Maximillian. Her same-sex partner, Linda McAllister, had provided the egg which was fertilized by an anonymous sperm donor and implanted in Leslee's uterus. Carol Ness, *Lesbian Moms Gain Rights,* SAN FRANCISCO EXAMINER, May 2, 1999. Judge Donna Hitchens issued a pre-birth decree recognizing both women as the child's legal mothers. *Id.* The legal conclusion that both women are Maximillian's mothers follows from the California Supreme Court's decision in *Johnson v. Calvert,* 19 Cal. Rptr. 494, 851 P.2d 776 (1993). In *Johnson,* two women, a gestational surrogate and the woman who hired her, claimed to be the resulting child's legal mother. The woman who had hired the surrogate (referred to by the court as the "intended mother") was also the child's genetic mother. Her ovum had been fertilized by her husband's sperm and implanted in the gestational surrogate's womb. The court concluded that California's statutes allow legal maternity to be established *either* by genetics or by giving birth. The court ultimately determined that the "intended mother" was the legal mother, "breaking the tie" between the two biological mothers with colorable claims by giving weight to intent. The decision opened an alternative avenue through which lesbian partners may be able to establish the legal maternity of both of them concurrently. If one woman contributes the genetic material and the other gives birth to the child, and they had jointly conceived the child for the purpose of coparenting the child together, both might be judged to be "intended parents," and thus legal parents as well.

[ii] Statutory Bars to Adoptions by Gay and Lesbian Couples and Individuals

LOFTON v. DEPARTMENT OF CHILDREN AND FAMILY SERVICES

358 F.3d 804 (11th Cir. 2004)

BIRCH, Circuit Judge. In this appeal, we decide . . . whether Florida Statute § 63.042(3), which prevents adoption by practicing homosexuals, is constitutional as enacted by the Florida legislature and as subsequently enforced. The district court granted summary judgment to Florida over an equal protection and due process challenge by homosexual persons desiring to adopt. We affirm.

I.

Since 1977, Florida's adoption law has contained a codified prohibition on adoption by any "homosexual" person.[1] For purposes of this statute, Florida courts have defined the term "homosexual" as being "limited to applicants who are known to engage in current, voluntary homosexual activity," thus drawing "a distinction between homosexual orientation and homosexual activity." During the past twelve years, several legislative bills have attempted to repeal the statute, and three separate legal challenges to it have been filed in the Florida courts. To date, no attempt to overturn the provision has succeeded. . . .

Six plaintiffs-appellants bring this case. The first, Steven Lofton, is a registered pediatric nurse who has raised from infancy three Florida foster children, each of whom tested positive for HIV at birth. By all accounts, Lofton's efforts in caring for these children have been exemplary, and his story has been chronicled in dozens of news stories and editorials as well as on national television. We confine our discussion of that story to those facts relevant to the legal issues before us and properly before us in the record. John Doe, also named as a plaintiff-appellant in this litigation, was born on 29 April 1991. Testing positive at birth for HIV and cocaine, Doe immediately entered the Florida foster care system. Shortly thereafter, Children's Home Society, a private agency, placed Doe in foster care with Lofton, who has extensive experience treating HIV patients. At eighteen months, Doe seroreverted and has since tested HIV negative. In September of 1994, Lofton filed an application to adopt Doe but refused to answer the application's inquiry about his sexual preference and also failed to disclose Roger Croteau, his cohabitating partner, as a member of his household. After Lofton refused requests from the Department of Children and Families ("DCF") to supply the missing information, his application was rejected pursuant to the homosexual adoption provision. . . .

---

[1] Fla. Stat. § 63.042(3) provides: "No person eligible to adopt under this statute may adopt if that person is a homosexual."

Plaintiff-appellant Douglas E. Houghton, Jr., is a clinical nurse specialist and legal guardian of plaintiff-appellant John Roe, who is eleven years old. Houghton has been Roe's caretaker since 1996 when Roe's biological father, suffering from alcohol abuse and frequent unemployment, voluntarily left Roe, then four years old, with Houghton. That same year, Houghton was appointed co-guardian of Roe along with one Robert Obeso (who otherwise has no involvement in this case). After Roe's biological father consented to termination of his parental rights, Houghton attempted to adopt Roe. Because of Houghton's homosexuality, however, he did not receive a favorable preliminary home study evaluation, which precluded him from filing the necessary adoption petition in state circuit court.

Plaintiff-appellants Wayne Larue Smith and Daniel Skahen, an attorney and real estate broker residing together in Key West, became licensed DCF foster parents after completing a requisite ten-week course in January of 2000. Since then, they have cared for three foster children, none of whom has been available for adoption. On 1 May 2000, Smith and Skahen submitted applications with DCF to serve as adoptive parents. On their adoption applications, both Smith and Skahen indicated that they are homosexuals. On 15 May 2000, they received notices from DCF stating that their applications had been denied because of their homosexuality.

Appellants. . . . alleged that the statute violates [their] fundamental rights and the principles of equal protection. Jointly, [they] asked the district court to declare Fla. Stat. § 63.042(3) unconstitutional and to enjoin its enforcement. . . . The district court . . . granted summary judgment in favor of the state on all counts. . . .

Appellants assert three constitutional arguments on appeal. First, appellants argue that the statute violates [their] rights to familial privacy, intimate association, and family integrity under the Due Process Clause of the Fourteenth Amendment. Second, appellants argue that the Supreme Court's recent decision in *Lawrence v. Texas*, 539 U.S. _____, 123 S. Ct. 2472 (2003) recognized a fundamental right to private sexual intimacy and that the Florida statute, by disallowing adoption by individuals who engage in homosexual activity, impermissibly burdens the exercise of this right. Third, appellants allege that, by categorically prohibiting only homosexual persons from adopting children, the statute violates the Equal Protection Clause of the Fourteenth Amendment. Each of these challenges raises questions of first impression in this circuit.

II.

. . . .

. . . . Under Florida law, "adoption is not a right; it is a statutory privilege." *Dept. Health & Rehab. Svcs. v. Cox,* 627 So.2d 1210 (Fla. Ct. App. 1993). Unlike biological parentage, which precedes and transcends formal recognition by the state, adoption is wholly a creature of the state. . . In formulating its adoption policies and procedures, the State of Florida acts in the protective and provisional role of *in loco parentis* for those children who, because of various circumstances, have become wards of the state. Thus, adoption law is unlike criminal law, for example, where the paramount substantive concern is not intruding on individuals' liberty interests, *see, e.g., Lawrence,* _____ U.S. _____ (2003); Roe v. Wade, 410 U.S. 113 (1973), and the paramount procedural imperative is ensuring due process and fairness. Adoption is also distinct from such contexts as government-benefit eligibility schemes or access to a public forum, where equality of treatment is the primary concern. By contrast, in the adoption context, the state's overriding interest is the best interests of the children whom it is seeking to place with adoptive families. . . . Florida, acting *parens patriae* for children who have lost their natural parents, bears the high duty of determining what adoptive home environments will best serve all aspects of the child's growth and development.

Because of the primacy of the welfare of the child, the state can make classifications for adoption purposes that would be constitutionally suspect in many other arenas. . . . In screening adoption applicants, Florida considers such factors as physical and mental health, income and financial status, duration of marriage, housing, and neighborhood, among others. Similarly, Florida gives preference to candidates who demonstrate a commitment to "value, respect, appreciate, and educate the child regarding his or her racial and ethnic heritage." FLA. ADMIN. CODE ANN. r. 65C-16.005(3) (2003). Moreover, prospective adoptive parents are required to sign an affidavit of good moral character. Many of these preferences and requirements, if employed outside the adoption arena, would be unlikely to withstand constitutional scrutiny. . . .

The decision to adopt a child is not a private one, but a public act. At a minimum, would-be adoptive parents are asking the state to confer official recognition — and, consequently, the highest level of constitutional insulation from subsequent state interference, on a relationship where there exists no natural filial bond. In many cases, they also are asking the state to entrust into their permanent care a child for whom the state is currently serving as *in loco parentis*. In doing so, these prospective adoptive parents are electing to open their homes and their private lives to close scrutiny by the state. . . .

In short, a person who seeks to adopt is asking the state to conduct an examination into his or her background and to make a determination as to the best interests of a child in need of adoption. In doing so, the state's overriding interest is not providing individuals the opportunity to become parents, but rather identifying those individuals whom it deems most capable of parenting adoptive children and providing them with a secure family environment. Indicative of the strength of the state's interest — indeed duty — in this context is the fact that appellants have not cited to us, nor have we found, a single precedent in which the Supreme Court or one of our sister circuits has sustained a constitutional challenge to an adoption scheme or practice by any individual other than a natural parent. . . .

Neither party disputes that there is no fundamental right to adopt, nor any fundamental right to be adopted. . . . Because there is no fundamental right to adopt or to be adopted, it follows that there can be no fundamental right to apply for adoption. [¶] Nevertheless, appellants argue that, by prohibiting homosexual adoption, the state is refusing to recognize and protect constitutionally protected parent-child relationships between Lofton and Doe and between Houghton and Roe. . . . Only by being given the opportunity to adopt, appellants assert, will they be able to protect their alleged right to "family integrity." [¶] [¶]. . . . Here, we find that under Florida law neither a foster parent nor a legal guardian could have a justifiable expectation of a permanent relationship with his or her child free from state oversight or intervention. Under Florida law, foster care is designed to be a short-term arrangement while the state attempts to find a permanent adoptive home. . . . Lofton and Houghton entered into relationships to be a foster parent and legal guardian, respectively, with an implicit understanding that these relationships would not be immune from state oversight and would be permitted to continue only upon state approval. The emotional connections between Lofton and his foster child and between Houghton and his ward originate in arrangements that have been subject to state oversight from the outset. We conclude that Lofton, Doe, Houghton, and Roe could have no justifiable expectation of permanency in their relationships. Nor could Lofton and Houghton have developed expectations that they would be allowed to adopt, in light of the adoption provision itself.

. . . .

We conclude that appellants' right-to-family-integrity argument fails to state a claim. There is no precedent for appellants' novel proposition that long-term foster care arrangements and guardianships are entitled to constitutional protection akin to that accorded to natural and adoptive families. Moreover, we decline appellants' invitation to recognize a new fundamental right to family integrity for groups of individuals who have formed deeply loving and interdependent relationships. Under appellants' theory, any collection of individuals living together and enjoying strong emotional bonds could claim a right to legal recognition of their family unit, and every removal of a child from a long-term foster care placement — or simply the state's failure to give long-term foster parents the opportunity to adopt — would give rise to a constitutional claim. Such an expansion of the venerable right of parental control would well exceed our judicial mandate as a lower federal court.

Laws that burden the exercise of a fundamental right require strict scrutiny and are sustained only if narrowly tailored to further a compelling government interest. *See, e.g., Zablocki v. Redhail*, 434 U.S. 374, 388 (1978); *Shapiro v. Thompson*, 394 U.S. 618, 634 (1969). Appellants argue that the Supreme Court's recent decision in *Lawrence v. Texas*, which struck down Texas's sodomy statute, identified a hitherto unarticulated fundamental right to private sexual intimacy. They contend that the Florida statute, by disallowing adoption to any individual who chooses to engage in homosexual conduct, impermissibly burdens the exercise of this right.

We begin with the threshold question of whether *Lawrence* identified a new fundamental right to private sexual intimacy. *Lawrence's* holding was that substantive due process does not permit a state to impose a criminal prohibition on private consensual homosexual conduct. The effect of this holding was to establish a greater respect than previously existed in the law for the right of consenting adults to engage in private sexual conduct. Nowhere, however, did the Court characterize this right as "fundamental." (Scalia, J., dissenting) (observing that "nowhere does the Court's opinion declare that homosexual sodomy is a 'fundamental right' under the Due Process Clause"). . . . We are particularly hesitant to infer a new fundamental liberty interest from an opinion whose language and reasoning are inconsistent with standard fundamental-rights analysis. . . . [¶] We conclude that it is a strained and ultimately incorrect reading of *Lawrence* to interpret it to announce a new fundamental right. . . . [¶] Moreover, the holding of *Lawrence* does not control the present case. Apart from the shared homosexuality component, there are marked differences in the facts of the two cases. The Court itself stressed the limited factual situation it was addressing in *Lawrence:*

> The present case does not involve minors. It does not involve persons who might be injured or coerced or who are situated in relationships where consent might not easily be refused. It does not involve public conduct or prostitution. It does not involve whether the government must give formal recognition to any relationship that homosexual persons seek to enter. The case does involve two adults who, with full and mutual consent from each other, engaged in sexual practices common to a homosexual lifestyle.

Lawrence, 123 S. Ct. at 2484. Here, the involved actors are not only consenting adults, but minors as well. The relevant state action is not criminal prohibition, but grant of a statutory privilege. And the asserted liberty interest is not the negative right to engage in private conduct without facing criminal sanctions, but the affirmative right to receive official and public recognition. Hence, we conclude that the *Lawrence* decision cannot be extrapolated to create a right to adopt for homosexual persons.

The Equal Protection Clause of the Fourteenth Amendment proclaims that "[n]o State shall . . . deny to any person within its jurisdiction the equal protection of laws." The central mandate of the equal protection guarantee is that "[t]he sovereign may not draw distinctions between individuals based solely on differences that are irrelevant to a legitimate governmental objective." *Lehr v. Robertson,* 463 U.S. 248 (1983). Equal protection, however, does not forbid legislative classifications. . . . Unless the challenged classification burdens a fundamental right or targets a suspect class, the Equal Protection Clause requires only that the classification be rationally related to a legitimate state interest. *Romer v. Evans,* 517 U.S. 620, 621 (1996). As we have explained, Florida's statute burdens no fundamental rights. Moreover, all of our sister circuits that have considered the question have declined to treat homosexuals as a suspect class. Because the present case involves neither a fundamental right nor a suspect class, we review the Florida statute under the rational-basis standard.

Rational-basis review, "a paradigm of judicial restraint," does not provide "a license for courts to judge the wisdom, fairness, or logic of legislative choices." *F.C.C. v. Beach Communications, Inc.* 508 U.S. 307, 313–14 (1993). The question is simply whether the challenged legislation is rationally related to a legitimate state interest. *Heller v. Doe,* 509 U.S. 312, 320 (1993). Under this deferential standard, a legislative classification "is accorded a strong presumption of validity," *id.* at 319, and "must be upheld against equal protection challenge if there is any reasonably conceivable state of facts that could provide a rational basis for the classification." *Id* at 320. This holds true "even if the law seems unwise or works to the disadvantage of a particular group, or if the rationale for it seems tenuous." *Romer v. Evans*, 517 U.S. at 632. . . . "[T]he burden is on the one attacking the legislative arrangement to negative every conceivable basis which might support it, whether or not the basis has a foundation in the record." *Heller, supra*, at 320–21.

. . . . Florida argues that the statute is rationally related to Florida's interest in furthering the best interests of adopted children by placing them in families with married mothers and fathers. Such homes, Florida asserts, provide the stability that marriage affords and the presence of both male and female authority figures, which it considers critical to optimal childhood development and socialization. In particular, Florida emphasizes a vital role that dual-gender parenting plays in shaping sexual and gender identity and in providing heterosexual role modeling. Florida argues that disallowing adoption into homosexual households, which are necessarily motherless or fatherless and lack the stability that comes with marriage, is a rational means of furthering Florida's interest in promoting adoption by marital families.

Florida clearly has a legitimate interest in encouraging a stable and nurturing environment for the education and socialization of its adopted children. . . . It is hard to conceive an interest more legitimate and more paramount for the state than promoting an optimal social structure for educating, socializing, and preparing its future citizens to become productive participants in civil society — particularly when those future citizens are displaced children for whom the state is standing *in loco parentis*.

More importantly for present purposes, the state has a legitimate interest in encouraging this optimal family structure by seeking to place adoptive children in homes that have both a mother and father. Florida argues that its preference for adoptive marital families is based on the premise that the marital family structure is more stable than other household arrangements and that children benefit from the presence of both a father and mother in the home. Given that appellants have offered no competent evidence to the contrary, we find this premise to be one of those "unprovable assumptions" that nevertheless can provide a legitimate basis for legislative action. Although social theorists from Plato to Simone de Beauvoir have proposed alternative child-rearing arrangements, none has proven as enduring as the marital family structure, nor has the accumulated wisdom of several millennia of human experience discovered a superior model. *See, e.g.,* Plato, *The Republic,* Bk. V, 459d-461e; Simone de Beauvoir, *The Second Sex* (H.M. Parshley trans., Vintage Books 1989) (1949). Against this "sum of experience," it is rational for Florida to conclude that it is in the best interests of adoptive children, many of whom come from troubled and unstable backgrounds, to be placed in a home anchored by both a father and a mother.

Appellants. . . . maintain that the statute is not rationally related to this interest[, that the statute] is both overinclusive and underinclusive, [and] that the real motivation behind the statute cannot be the best interest of adoptive children. . . . [¶] Appellants note that Florida law permits adoption by unmarried individuals and that, among children coming out [sic] the Florida foster care system, 25% of adoptions are to parents who are currently single.

Their argument is that homosexual persons are similarly situated to unmarried persons with regard to Florida's asserted interest in promoting married-couple adoption. According to appellants, this disparate treatment lacks a rational basis and, therefore, disproves any rational connection between the statute and Florida's asserted interest in promoting adoption into married homes. . . . [¶] [¶] The Florida legislature could rationally conclude that homosexuals and heterosexual singles are not "similarly situated in relevant respects." It is not irrational to think that heterosexual singles have a markedly greater probability of eventually establishing a married household and, thus, providing their adopted children with a stable, dual-gender parenting environment. Moreover, as the state noted, the legislature could rationally act on the theory that heterosexual singles, even if they never marry, are better positioned than homosexual individuals to provide adopted children with education and guidance relative to their sexual development throughout pubescence and adolescence.

. . . .

The possibility, raised by appellants, that some homosexual households, including those of appellants, would provide a better environment than would some heterosexual single-parent households does not alter our analysis. The Supreme Court repeatedly has instructed that neither the fact that a classification may be overinclusive or underinclusive nor the fact that a generalization underlying a classification is subject to exceptions renders the classification irrational. . . . We conclude that there are plausible rational reasons for the disparate treatment of homosexuals and heterosexual singles under Florida adoption law and that, to the extent that the classification may be imperfect, that imperfection does not rise to the level of a constitutional infraction.

Appellants make much of the fact that Florida has over three thousand children who are currently in foster care and, consequently, have not been placed with permanent adoptive families. According to appellants, because excluding homosexuals from the pool of prospective adoptive parents will not create more eligible married couples to reduce the backlog, it is impossible for the legislature to believe that the statute advances the state's interest in placing children with married couples.

We do not agree that the statute does not further the state's interest in promoting nuclear-family adoption because it may delay the adoption of some children. Appellants misconstrue Florida's interest, which is not simply to place children in a permanent home as quickly as possible, but, when placing them, to do so in an optimal home, i.e., one in which there is a heterosexual couple or the potential for one. According to appellants' logic, every restriction on adoptive-parent candidates, such as income, in-state residency, and criminal record — none of which creates more available married couples — are likewise constitutionally suspect as long as Florida has a backlog of unadopted foster children. The best interests of children, however, are not automatically served by adoption into *any* available home merely because it is permanent. Moreover, the legislature could rationally act on the theory that not placing adoptees in homosexual households increases the probability that these children eventually will be placed with married-couple families, thus furthering the state's goal of optimal placement. Therefore, we conclude that Florida's current foster care backlog does not render the statute irrational.

Noting that Florida law permits homosexuals to become foster parents and permanent guardians, appellants contend that this fact demonstrates that Florida must not truly believe that placement in a homosexual household is not in a child's best interests. . . . We have not located and appellants have not cited any precedent indicating that a disparity between a law and its enforcement is a relevant consideration on rational-basis review, which only asks whether the legislature could have reasonably thought that the challenged law would further a legitimate state interest. Thus, to the extent that foster care and guardianship placements with homosexuals are the handiwork of Florida's executive branch, they are irrelevant to the question of the *legislative* rationale for Florida's adoption scheme. To the extent that these placements are the product of an intentional legislative choice to treat foster care and guardianships differently than adoption, the distinction is not an irrational one. Indeed, it bears a rational relationship to Florida's interest in promoting the nuclear-family model of adoption since foster care and guardianship have neither the permanence nor the societal, cultural, and legal significance as does adoptive parenthood, which is the legal equivalent of natural parenthood. [¶]. . . . We conclude that the rationality of the statute is not defeated by the fact that Florida permits homosexual persons to serve as foster parents and legal guardians.

Appellants cite recent social science research and the opinion of mental health professionals and child welfare organizations as evidence that there is no child welfare basis for excluding homosexuals from adopting. They argue that the cited studies show that the parenting skills of homosexual parents are at least equivalent to those of heterosexual parents and that children raised by homosexual parents suffer no adverse outcomes. Appellants also point to the policies and practices of numerous adoption agencies that permit homosexual persons to adopt.

In considering appellants' argument, we must ask not whether the latest in social science research and professional opinion *support* the decision of the Florida legislature, but whether that evidence is so well established and so far beyond dispute that it would be irrational for the Florida legislature to believe that the interests of its children are best served by not permitting homosexual adoption. Also, we must credit any conceivable rational reason that the legislature might have for choosing not to alter its statutory scheme in response to this recent social science research. We must assume, for example, that the legislature might be aware of the critiques of the studies cited by appellants — critiques that have highlighted significant flaws in the studies' methodologies and conclusions, such as the use of small, self-selected samples; reliance on self-report instruments; politically driven hypotheses; and the use of unrepresentative study populations consisting of disproportionately affluent, educated parents. Alternatively, the legislature might consider and credit other studies that have found that children raised in homosexual households fare differently on a number of measures, doing worse on some of them, than children raised in similarly situated heterosexual households. Or the legislature might consider, and even credit, the research cited by appellants, but find it premature to rely on a very recent and still developing body of research, particularly in light of the absence of longitudinal studies following child subjects into adulthood and of studies of adopted, rather than natural, children of homosexual parents.

We do not find any of these possible legislative responses to be irrational. . . . Nor is it irrational for the legislature to proceed with deliberate caution before placing adoptive children in an alternative, but unproven, family structure that has not yet been conclusively demonstrated to be equivalent to the marital family structure that has established a proven track record spanning centuries. Accordingly, we conclude that appellants' proffered social science evidence does not disprove the rational basis of the Florida statute.

Finally, we disagree with appellants' contention that *Romer* requires us to strike down the Florida statute. In *Romer,* the Supreme Court invalidated Amendment 2 to the Colorado state constitution, which prohibited all legislative, executive, or judicial action designed to protect homosexual persons from discrimination. The constitutional defect in Amendment 2 was the disjunction between the "[s]weeping and comprehensive" classification it imposed on homosexuals and the state's asserted bases for the classification — respect for freedom of association and conservation of resources to fight race and gender discrimination. The Court concluded that the Amendment's "sheer breadth is so discontinuous with the reasons offered for it that the amendment seems inexplicable by anything but animus toward the class it affects."

Unlike Colorado's Amendment 2, Florida's statute is not so "[s]weeping and comprehensive" as to render Florida's rationales for the statute "inexplicable by anything but animus" toward its homosexual residents. . . . Thus, we conclude that *Romer's* unique factual situation and narrow holding are inapposite to this case.

NOTES

1. *State Prohibitions on Adoptions by Gay and Lesbian Individuals and Couples.* Most state statutes are silent on the eligibility of gay or lesbian couples or individuals to adopt children. A small minority of states have statutes that create categorical bars to adoptions by gay and lesbian or unmarried individuals or couples. In 1999, the New Hampshire legislature repealed a statute precluding "homosexuals" from adopting. N.H. Rev. Stat. Ann. § 170-B:4 (2003). Mississippi's ban was passed in 2000, and focuses on same-sex *couples*, Miss. Code § 93-17-3(2) (2003) ("adoption by couples of the same gender is prohibited"). Several other states have legislated on the status of gays or lesbians as prospective adoptive parents. *See* Ala. Code § 26-10A-6 (2003) (amended by a joint resolution in 1998 stating "that we hereby express our intent to prohibit child adoption by homosexual couples"); Okla. St. Ann. § 7007-1.4.A.6.f. (2003) (indicating that among the duties and responsibilities of the child welfare system is "prohibiting homosexuals from adopting children."). In addition, regulations promulgated by the Department of Family Services in Arkansas preclude gays or lesbians from serving as foster parents and restrict foster placements to households in which no gay or lesbian resides. Adopted Emergency Rule, Family Serv. Policy and Procedure Manual, Ark. Dept. Human Serv., 2003 Ark. Reg. 3477.

Utah forbids adoptions by persons who are "cohabiting in a relationship that is not a legally valid and binding marriage under the laws of" Utah. UTAH CODE § 78-30-1(3)(b) (2003). New Jersey was the first state formally to lift a ban against unmarried-couple adoptions in 1997, as part of a consent decree. *Holden v. New Jersey Dept. of Hum. Svcs.,* Sup. Ct. N.J., No. C-203-97. The decree settled litigation brought by the American Civil Liberties Union on behalf of a gay couple. The two men sought to adopt the two-year-old foster child they had cared for since his birth. The resulting policy created parity in the adoption rights all adult couples in New Jersey, whether married or unmarried, opposite-sex or same-sex. *Id.*

Clearly, however, the *Lofton* case has garnered the most attention nation-wide. Florida's Section 63.042(3) was passed in 1977, promoted by anti-gay activist Anita Bryant. The plaintiffs' challenge to the statute has received substantial publicity, due in part to the support of television personality Rosie O'Donnell, who reportedly "came out" for the purpose of assisting the plaintiffs. Michael T. Morley, Richard Albert et al., *Developments in Law and Policy: Emerging Issues in Family Law*, 21 YALE L. & POL'Y REV. 169, 198 (2003).

2. ***The Eleventh Circuit Decision in*** **Lofton**. The unanimous panel of judges in *Lofton* held that Florida's prohibition on adoptions by gays and lesbians is rationally related to the state's goal of furthering the best interests of adopted children. The court emphasized the deferential nature of the rational basis test, and asserted that a family headed by a married heterosexual couple provides "an optimal social structure for educating, socializing, and preparing future citizens to become productive participants in civil society. . . ." Although the notion that such families are superior environments for childrearing is, in the court's own words, an "unprovable assumption," the court held that this assumption can "nevertheless . . . provide a legitimate basis for legislative action." The Eleventh Circuit flatly rejected the petitioners' claims that in *Lawrence v. Texas,* reprinted *supra* at page 847, the United States Supreme Court identified a fundamental right of private sexual intimacy which the Florida law now infringes. If the Supreme Court had premised *Lawrence* on such a fundamental right, strict scrutiny of the statute would be required, making it highly unlikely that the statute would withstand review. As the notes on pages 860-866 of this chapter suggest, the standard of review used by the Supreme Court in *Lawrence* was not clearly articulated in Justice Kennedy's majority opinion. Thus, in applying *Lawrence*, reviewing courts must grapple with this lack of clarity.

In contrast to *Lofton,* the court in *Goodridge v. Massachusetts* (reprinted in Chapter 2, beginning on page 104) concluded that it did not need to reach the question of whether *Lawrence* required strict scrutiny of the challenged statute. It held that the Massachusetts statute restricting marriage to opposite-sex couples was unconstitutional even under the rational basis test. Thus, although both courts ultimately applied a rational basis test, the version applied by the Massachusetts court was substantially more searching than that applied in *Lofton*. This more "heightened" form of rational basis review, sometimes referred to as "rational basis with bite," has been used by the Supreme Court in a small number of important equal protection cases, such as *Romer v. Evans*, which is discussed in this chapter at page 846. For further discussion of this standard of review, see, e.g., Gerald Gunther, *Foreword: In Search of Evolving Doctrine on a Changing Court: A Model for a Newer Equal Protection*, 86 HARV. L. REV. 1, 33-34 (1972); Gayle Lynn Pettinga, Note, *Rational Basis with Bite: Intermediate Scrutiny by Any Other Name,* 62 IND. L.J. 779 (1987). The Massachusetts Supreme Judicial Court in *Goodridge* stated quite clearly that "[n]ot every asserted rational relationship is a 'conceivable' one, and rationality review is not 'toothless.'" 798 N.E.2d 941, 960, n.20 (2003) (noting also that "[s]tatutes have failed rational basis review even in circumstances where no fundamental right . . . is implicated"). Thus, in effect, the two courts applied different standards of review, despite the "rational basis" label.

The *Lofton* and *Goodridge* courts also differed markedly in their interpretations of the body of social science research that examines the effects on children of parenting by gays or lesbians as contrasted with heterosexuals. As discussed earlier in this chapter, see note 4, page 1054 *supra*, all of the major scientific organizations concerned with children's health and psychological development (*i.e.*, American Academy of Pediatrics, American Psychological Association, American Psychiatric Association, American Psychoanalytic Society) have endorsed gay and lesbian adoptions. Each of these organizations has concluded that the relevant empirical research reveals no significant or relevant differences between children raised by gay or lesbian parents and those raised by heterosexual parents on a host of measures of psychological and social adjustment. Despite these appraisals of the literature, the *Lofton* court deferred to the possibility that the legislature "might find it premature to rely on a very recent and still developing body of research. . . ." One might observe, however, that this body of research, like most others, will always be "developing." Professor Michael Wald has noted, "as a practical matter, there may never be sufficient research to convince the skeptics." *Same-Sex Couple Marriage: A Family Policy Perspective*, 9 VA. J. SOC. POL'Y & L. 291, 328 (2001). Thus, at one level, the debate between those who would and those who would not extend to gays and lesbians the same opportunities to become parents as are enjoyed by heterosexuals is a debate over who bears the burden of proof as to whether being parented by gays or lesbians is deleterious to children, and importantly, how heavy is that burden. The highly deferential rational basis test applied by the *Lofton* court placed the burden squarely and heavily on the shoulders of those who assert that the law should not disadvantage gays or lesbians who seek to adopt. Arguably, the burden is so heavy that the scientific method will always be an inadequate tool with which to challenge a court's or legislature's unsubstantiated assumptions about human functioning and development. Yet, there is another interpretation of the *Lofton* court's rejection of the scientific findings in favor of "unprovable assumptions" and "the accumulated wisdom of several millennia of human experience." It is that these assumptions and that "wisdom" are merely euphemisms and serve to reveal the court's underlying reliance traditional notions of "morality." Given the *Lawrence* Court's explicit rejection of traditional notions of morality without more as a basis for constitutional decision-making, one can argue that the *Lofton* opinion is inconsistent with *Lawrence*.

[b] Parenting Disputes Between Former Same-Sex Partners

In the past several decades, increasing numbers of lesbian couples have jointly planned the conception and parenting of children, effecting those plans through the artificial insemination of one of the women. If no second-parent adoption follows the conception and birth of the child, the legal status of the biological mother's partner is uncertain. In several jurisdictions, after the same-sex partnership dissolves, the nonbiological "de facto" parent has sued to obtain legal recognition of her relationship with her former partner's biological child, as in *V.C. v. M.J.B.,* below.

V.C. v. M.J.B.

748 A.2d 539 (N.J. 2000)

(*V.C. v. M.J.B.* is reprinted on page 655, Chapter 6).

NOTES

1. *Custody and Visitation Claims by De Facto Parents.* (See note 3, pp. 664, Chapter 6).

2. *Reconciling Second-Parent Adoption with De Facto Parent Cases.* California, New York, and Vermont all permit second-parent adoptions, and all have rejected de facto parent claims by same-sex partners. Can these positions be reconciled? In *Titchenal v. Dexter,* 693 A.2d 682 (Vt. 1997), the Vermont Supreme Court cited to *B.L.V.B. And E.L.V.B.,* 628 A.2d 1271 (Vt. 1993), in noting that Vermont affords lesbian couples a method to establish the partner's legal relationship with the child via second-parent adoption. New York considered the questions in the reverse chronological sequence. In *in re Jacob,* Chief Judge Kaye argued that allowing second-parent adoption "avoids the sort of disruptive visitation battle we faced in *Alison D.* in which the petitioner had to concede "that she is not the child's 'parent.'" The most emphatic statement of this sort was made by a California court in *Nancy S. v. Michele G.,* 228 Cal. App. 3d 831, 279 Cal. Rptr. 212 (App. 1991). In *Nancy S.,* the court underscored that the mother's partner had *not* adopted the children, which she could have done under state law. It expressed concern that endorsement of the partner's theories of functional, de facto, or equitable parenthood could force the courts to "face years of unraveling the complex practical, social, and constitutional ramifications of this expansion of the definition of a parent." 228 Cal. App. 3d at 841, 279 Cal. Rptr. At 219. Acknowledging that the children are the ones who suffer in situations such as this, the court placed the blame on the mother's partner who did not avail herself of the opportunity to adopt the children. 228 Cal. App. 3d at 84, n.8, 279 Cal. Rptr. at 219, n.8. Thus, it appears that California, New York, and Vermont, in providing same-sex partners with the option to adopt their partner's biological children, hold out this option as the *exclusive* mechanism whereby these partners can establish their legal relationship with the child.

On the other hand, as noted above, second-parent adoption is not available in all jurisdictions. In Wisconsin, one year after interpreting the state's adoption statute to bar a second-parent adoption in *Angel Lace M.*, 516 N.W.2d 678 (Wis. 1994), the Wisconsin Supreme Court held that a former same-sex partner's visitation claims may be heard under the court's general equitable authority. *Custody of H.S.H-K,* 533 N.W.2d 419 (Wis. 1995) (see discussion of *H.S.H.-K* by the New Jersey Supreme Court in *V.C. v. M.J.B.,* page 657 *supra*).

3. *Incorporating the Child's Perspective?* For arguments that the law should incorporate the child's perspective when determining the legal status of parent-like figures under certain circumstances, see, *e.g.*, Katharine T. Bartlett, *Rethinking Parenthood as an Exclusive Status: The Need for Legal Alternatives When the Premise of the Nuclear Family Has Failed,* 70 VA. L. REV. 879 (1984). Professor Barbara Bennett Woodhouse urges that "[a] child who has formed a parent-child relationship with a nonbiological co-parent or de facto parent has a right to legal recognition and protection of this relationships . . ." *Children's Rights in Gay and Lesbian Families: A Child-Centered Perspective,* in CHILD, FAMILY, AND STATE 273, 285 (S. Macedo & I.M. Young eds. 2003).

The drafters of Section 2.03 of the ALI *Principles of the Law of Family Dissolution* included within the definition of "parent," for purposes of custody and visitation decisions, categories referred to as *parents-by-estoppel* and *de facto parents*. In so doing, they sought to create predictability, to protect expectations, and to recognize functional parent-child relationships in order to protect the interests of children. *See ALI Principles,* Chapter 2. *See also* Katharine T. Bartlett, *U.S. Custody Law and Trends in the Context of the ALI Principles of the Law of Family Dissolution,* 10 VA. J. Soc. POL'Y & L. 5, 44-47 (2002) and discussion of the *ALI Principles* § 2.03 in Chapter 6, note 3, pages 664-666. The *Principles* have engendered much scholarly commentary, and some writers argue that the Principles extend the notion of parent too broadly, *see, e.g.,* Gregory A. Loken, *The New "Extended Family" — "De Facto" Parenthood and Standing Under Chapter 2,* 2001 B.Y.U.L. REV. 1045 (criticizing the proposals for potentially authorizing parental rights in multiple parties and promoting increased indeterminacy in and interference with parent-child relationships), while others question whether the outlook is sufficiently child-centered, Barbara Bennett Woodhouse, *Horton Looks at the ALI Principles,* 4 J.L. & FAM. STUD. 151 (2002) (arguing that the *ALI Principles* still retain vestiges of legal emphasis on adults' rights over children's needs).

4. *Constitutional Claims of Mother or Partner.* To what extent is recent constitutional precedent likely to affect current law defining the rights of biological mothers and their same-sex partners in such contests? Does *Troxel v. Granville,* 530 U.S. 57 (2000) (reprinted at page 667), limit the claims of persons who do not have traditional legal parental relationships with children? Presently, the impact of *Troxel's* deference to parental objections in claims for non-parent visitation on cases like *V.C.* is unknown. State courts have issued a range of interpretations of *Troxel,* giving parental preferences more or less weight, and revealing that inquiries are necessarily fact-specific.

For further discussion of *Troxel*, as well as its implications for de facto parent claims by same-sex partners, see Chapter 6.

Does the biological mother's same-sex partner have a constitutional claim to her relationship with the child she has coparented? The answer is likely "no." The U.S. Supreme Court in *Smith v. O.F.F.E.R.*, 431 U.S. 816, 843 (1977), acknowledged that "biological relationships are not [the] exclusive determination of the existence of a family," asserting that family relationships can stem from "emotional attachments that derive from the intimacy of daily association." *Id.* at 844. Yet, in *O.F.F.E.R.*, where the rights of foster parents were pitted against those of the children's legal parents, the Court stated, in no uncertain terms, that whatever liberty interests exist in foster parent-child relationships, that "interest must be substantially attenuated" as against the interests of a child's natural parents. *Id.* at 846–47. The analogy between foster parenting and de facto parent cases like *V.C.* is imperfect, in that foster parents necessarily agree, by contract with the state, to a *temporary* relationship with the child. Yet, in *O.F.F.E.R.*, the Court reinforces the primacy of "natural parents" in the constitutional schema, much as it did in *Troxel*. Thus, whereas courts, if not restrained by *Troxel,* can rely on equitable doctrines and state visitation statutes to authorize continued contact between de facto parents and children over parental objections, it is unlikely that these decisions will be grounded in constitutional doctrine.

5. *Adjudicating Claims by Former Same-Sex Partners Under the Uniform Parentage Act.* In note 7, on page 1055, we indicate that the California Supreme Court has held that a woman can be determined to be a child's legal mother based on her performance of either of two biological functions: contributing the ovum used to conceive the child, or gestating the pregnancy and giving birth. In reaching this result, the court relied on provisions of the UPA (1973), as adopted by California, and provisions of California's Evidence Code. The case in which this holding was announced, *Johnson v. Calvert*, 19 Cal. Rptr. 494, 851 P.2d 776 (1993), involved a dispute between a gestational surrogate and the married couple who had hired her, where the husband and wife had contributed the genetic material from which the child was conceived. The court held that in cases such as this one, in which each of two women has a legally-valid claim to maternity, "intent" to be the child's parent could to break the tie between the two claimants. While the court did not elaborate substantially on the concept of "intent," it is clear from the court's application of this test to the facts of the case that it is the pre-conception intent that is relevant. The test goes beyond the mere "intent" to conceive a child, however, and extends to the *purpose* of conceiving a child. The "intentional parent" is the parent who set in motion the reproductive process *in order to* conceive a child that *she would raise as her own*. Thus, the court held, "under our analysis, in a true 'egg donation' situation, where a woman gestates and gives birth to a child formed from the egg of another woman with the intent to raise the child as her own, the birth mother is the natural mother under California law." 19 Cal. Rptr. at 500, 851 P.2d at 782, n.10. In *Johnson v. Calvert*, the woman from whose ovum the child was conceived, and who had employed the surrogate with the intent of becoming the legal parent to the child, prevailed over the gestational surrogate. The court did not address additional fact scenarios, other than to state: "In what we must hope will be the extremely rare situation in which neither the gestator nor the woman who provided the ovum for fertilization is willing to assume custody of the child after birth, a rule recognizing the intending parents as the child's legal, natural parents should best promote certainty and stability for the child." 19 Cal. Rptr. at 501, 851 P.2d 783.

In 1998, a California court of appeal adjudicated the parentage of a child conceived through an assisted reproductive process initiated by the Buzzancas, a married couple. *Buzzanca v. Buzzanca*, 72 Cal. Rptr. 280. The evidence was clear that, at the time the reproductive process was initiated, Mr. and Mrs. Buzzanca were the intended parents. For reasons not discussed in the published opinion, neither of the intended parents contributed genetic material. An embryo created from a donated egg and donated sperm was implanted in a gestational surrogate (who was not the donor of the egg). Analogizing the circumstances of both parents to that of the husband of a woman who is artificially inseminated with donor sperm with the consent of her husband, which is addressed in the 1973 Uniform Parentage Act as adopted by California, Cal. Fam. Code § 7613 (2004), the court held that the intended parents are the legal parents. Thus, in this case, the court held that the intended father, who had since divorced the intended mother, could not disclaim child support obligations on the grounds he was not the child's legal father.

Extension of the reach of Cal. Fam. Code § 7613 to circumstances beyond that in which a man is consenting to his wife's insemination with donor sperm opened the door to other contexts in which an individual sets in motion a reproductive process with the intent of becoming the legal parent of the resulting child. It was only a matter of time before this and related legal theories grounded in the UPA were employed by a same-sex partner of a child's biological parent who seeks to establish legal parentage in circumstances where that partner jointly planned and initiated the conception of a child with the biological parent, and who, with the biological parent's consent, intended to serve as that child's other legal parent. Recently, two cases were decided by courts of appeal in California, relying on particular sections of those California's statutes derived from the UPA (1973). In May 2004, in *Elisa Maria B. v. Superior Court*, 13 Cal. Rptr. 3d 494, the Third District Court of Appeal in California rejected the claim of one woman that her former lesbian partner was a parent under Sections 7611 and 7613 of California's Family Code. These sections were derived from Sections 4 of the UPA (1973), reprinted on page 957 *supra*. Furthermore, the court distinguished *Buzzanca* on the basis that the intended parents in that case were legally married at the time the husband provided consent for the assisted reproductive technology which resulted in the conception of their daughter Jaycee. The court relied, instead, on the well-established jurisprudence in California rejecting the claims of de facto, psychological, or equitable parenthood. See discussion in note 2 *supra*.

In June 2004, the Second Circuit Court of Appeal in California reached a different result in *Kristine Renee H. v. Lisa Ann R.*, ___ Cal. Rptr. ___, 2004 WL 1465100. In this case, as in *Elisa Maria B.*, two lesbian partners had jointly planned for one of them to conceive a child through artificial insemination, and for both of them to raise the child as co-parents. Strengthening the non-biological intended parent's claims in this case was the existence of a "prebirth judgment" issued by a family court, based on the partners' stipulation that they were "joint intended legal parents" of the unborn child. *Id.* at ___. Acknowledging the interpretation of the Third District Court of Appeal in *Elisa Maria B.*, the Second Circuit court concluded that neither the gender or marital status of the intended parents should affect the outcome of parentage determinations under the UPA. It held that the former same-sex partner of the biological mother was indeed a legal parent, and that the family court had jurisdiction to adjudicate matters of custody and visitation with the child.

Clearly, this area of law is developing at a rapid pace, and these two cases are likely to reflect only the beginning of litigants' attempts to apply the UPA and case law developed in assisted reproduction contexts to maternity and paternity claims by former same-sex partners. In one particularly interesting case, two lesbian partners shared the biological functions of maternity, with one contributing the ovum and the other gestating the offspring. *See K.M. v. E.G.*, 118 Cal. App. 4th 477, 13 Cal. Rptr. 3d (2004). While application of *Johnson v. Calvert* to such a situation would appear to vest maternity in both women if both women were determined to be intended parents, the First District Court of Appeal in California concluded in May 2004 that only one woman was an intended parent. It relied on an egg donor consent form signed by the partner who contributed the ovum, and a corroborative oral agreement between the women. This evidence persuaded the court that both women had, at the time they planned and executed the assisted reproductive process, intended for only one of them, the woman who gestated the pregnancy, to have the legal status of mother. According to the court, subsequent changes of heart by the partner donating the eggs did not alter the determination of maternity, nor did the post-birth development of a parent-like relationship between the egg donor and the child. As such, this case reinforced the notion that intentionality in this line of cases is limited to certain pre-conception points in time, such as when the parties plan and execute the reproductive process. Furthermore, the case reinforced California's rejection of doctrines that recognize *acquisition* of parental status based upon post-birth conduct creating what other state courts characterize as de facto, psychological, or equitable parental status.

PROBLEMS

Problem 9-26. Two women, Beth and Amy, lived together as intimate partners for seven years. They planned that Beth would become pregnant by artificial insemination so that the two of them could raise a child together. During these seven years, the women shared all of those aspects of their lives as a married couple would typically share. The two participated together in selecting a physician and an anonymous donor of the sperm (based on nonidentifying information provided by the fertility clinic). They also discussed names for the not-yet-conceived child, and agreed that the child's last name would be a hyphenated version of Beth and Amy's last names.

It took two years of artificial insemination attempts before Beth became pregnant. The two women shared the financial cost of the procedures. Beth and Amy learned that Beth was pregnant, and jointly made preparations for the birth of twin boys. They shared the financial costs of the prenatal care, participated jointly in prenatal classes, and set up a nursery in their home. Amy was Beth's "coach" during labor and delivery. They named one boy after Amy's father and the other after Beth's grandfather, giving both boys the hyphenated last name. They shared typical parenting functions during the first six months of the boys' lives, both providing for the boys' care and support relatively equally during that period. Yet, when the boys were six months old, the women decided to end their partnership. At Beth's request, Amy moved out and took an apartment a few blocks away from the home where they had lived together. For the next three months, the women cooperated amicably in the care of the twins. Although the boys' primary residence was with Beth, the boys would spent about 30% of their time with Amy. Amy voluntarily paid Beth $1,000 a month to help with the boys' support. Beth, however, curtailed Amy's contact with the boys gradually thereafter. By the time the boys were one year old, Beth refused Amy any further contact with the boys. At that point in time, Amy stopped making support payments.

Address each of the following questions, and indicate whether you think the result would differ depending upon the jurisdiction in which the women lived. Also note whether there are any particular facts not provided above that would assist the claims of either party.

    (A)   Is Amy likely to succeed in a claim for joint custody of the twins?

    (B)   Is Amy likely to succeed in a claim for visitation with the twins?

    (C)   Is Beth likely to succeed in a claim for child support from Amy?

    (D)   Is Amy likely to succeed in an attempt to adopt the twins?

Problem 9-27. Assume the same facts as Problem 9-27 except here the women separated just before learning that Beth was pregnant. They attended counseling to see if they could resolve their differences and reconcile, but the counseling was not successful in achieving this goal. Amy offered to assist Beth with support for the twins, and made voluntary payments of approximately $1,000 per month for the first eight months after the twins' birth. Although Beth initially permitted Amy to take the boys for an overnight visit every other week, Beth curtailed the overnight visits after two months, allowing Amy to take the twins for a few hours on alternate Saturday afternoons only. When the twins became one year old, Beth refused to allow Amy further visitation. Amy then stopped making support payments. Address the same four questions set forth in Problem 9-27 above and indicate whether you think the result would differ depending upon the jurisdiction in which the women lived. Also note whether there are any particular facts not provided above that would assist the claims of either party.

Problem 9-28. Assume the same facts as Problem 9-27 except the women separated before Beth learned she was pregnant, but Beth never informed Amy of the pregnancy. Amy learned Beth was pregnant from a mutual friend a few weeks before the twins were born. Amy contacted Beth, and offered to provide whatever assistance Beth needed, including financial support for the boys. She also requested the opportunity to have a relationship with the twins. Beth rebuffed all of Amy's overtures, and refused to allow Amy to see the twins. Address the same four questions set forth in Problem 9-27 above and indicate whether you think the result would differ depending upon the jurisdiction in which the women lived. Also note whether there are any particular facts not provided above that would assist the claims of either party.

Part IV

Parent and Child

Chapter 10

STATE REGULATION OF THE PARENT-CHILD RELATIONSHIP

§ A. THE NATURE OF THE RELATIONSHIP

The parent-child relationship is generally regarded as fundamental to society and entitled to substantial legal protection. But a rule protecting parental decisionmaking from state interference may sometimes conflict with other important values. The state has a *parens patriae* interest in protecting the welfare of children as vulnerable members of society and an instrumental interest in producing healthy, well-educated and productive future citizens. Parental choices may undermine these interests. Parental authority may also conflict with claims of autonomy by the child, or with claims of non-parents who have an interest in the child. This chapter explores a variety of dilemmas the law confronts in defining the relationships among parent, child, and state.

[1] PARENTAL AUTONOMY AND STATE AUTHORITY: THE CONSTITUTIONAL BOUNDARIES

Parental autonomy refers to control over the many aspects of a child's upbringing — aspects that influence personality, opportunities, and values. The traditional explanation for parental autonomy is that parental *rights* are the natural and logical quid pro quo of parental *obligations*. Another justification is that by reason of biology, societal norms, and the bonds of affection, parents are the most motivated and well-situated persons to act in their children's best interests. Recognizing a strong form of parental autonomy enhances their motivation and ability to do so and protects parental investment in the rearing of their children. *See* Scott & Scott, *Parents as Fiduciaries*, 81 VA. L. REV. 2401(1995); Scott, *Parental Autonomy and Children's Welfare*, 11 WM. & MARY BILL OF RTS. J. 1071(2003). In addition, extending broad autonomy to parents in individual family units promotes society's interests in diversity and cultural pluralism.

As the cases in this section demonstrate, parental authority over children has been elevated to the status of a constitutionally protected interest during the last century. This relatively recent development can be understood not as an enhancement of parental autonomy but as a response to state policies challenging parental authority. Until the late nineteenth century, parental authority was almost absolute and state involvement in the family was minimal. Parental decisions about education, discipline, and the employment of their children received little state supervision. The Juvenile Court, established as a Progressive reform at the turn of the twentieth century, was based on the notion that the state has a responsibility for the welfare of children and an interest in the rearing decisions made by their parents. Thus, the long term trend has been toward expanded state involvement in the family. In response to this trend, the Supreme Court has clarified that parents have an interest in their relationship with their children that is protected under the Due Process Clause of the Fourteenth Amendment. In the cases that follow, the Court has attempted to define the boundary between parental and state authority.

MEYER v. NEBRASKA

262 U.S. 390 (1923)

[Nebraska made it a crime "to teach any subject to any person in any language other than the English language," except that foreign languages could be taught "as languages" to a pupil who has "successfully passed the eighth grade." The state supreme court rejected a constitutional challenge. Review was granted by the United States Supreme Court.]

MR. JUSTICE SUTHERLAND delivered the opinion of the Court.

[The Nebraska Supreme Court] held that the statute . . . did not conflict with the Fourteenth Amendment, but was a valid exercise of the police power. The following excerpts from the opinion sufficiently indicate the reasons advanced to support the conclusion.

> The salutary purpose of the statute is clear. The legislature had seen the baneful effects of permitting foreigners, who had taken residence in this country, to rear and educate their children in the language of their native land. The result of that condition was found to be inimical to our own safety. To allow the children of foreigners, who had emigrated here, to be taught from early childhood the language of the country of their parents was to rear them with that language as their mother tongue. It was to educate them so that they must always think in that language, and, as a consequence, naturally inculcate in them the ideas and sentiments foreign to the best interests of this country. The statute, therefore, was intended not only to require that the education of all children be conducted in the English language, but that, until they had grown into that language and until it had become a part of them, they should not in the schools be taught any other language. The obvious purpose of this statute was that the English language should be and become the mother tongue of all children reared in this state. The enactment of such a statute comes reasonably within the police power of the state. . . .

That the State may do much, go very far, indeed, in order to improve the quality of its citizens, physically, mentally and morally, is clear; but the individual has certain fundamental rights which must be respected. The protection of the Constitution extends to all, to those who speak other languages as well as to those born with English on the tongue. Perhaps it would be highly advantageous if all had ready understanding of our ordinary speech, but this cannot be coerced by methods which conflict with the Constitution — a desirable end cannot be promoted by prohibited means.

For the welfare of his Ideal Commonwealth, Plato suggested a law which should provide: "That the wives of our guardians are to be common, and their children are to be common, and no parent is to know his own child, nor any child his parent. . . . The proper officers will take the offspring of the good parents to the pen or fold, and there they will deposit them with certain nurses who dwell in a separate quarter. . . ." In order to submerge the individual and develop ideal citizens, Sparta assembled the males at seven into barracks and entrusted their subsequent education and training to official guardians. Although such measures have been deliberately approved by men of great genius, their ideas touching the relation between individual and State were wholly different from those upon which our institutions rest; and it hardly will be affirmed that any legislature could impose such restrictions upon the people of a State without doing violence to both letter and spirit of the Constitution.

The desire of the legislature to foster a homogenous people with American ideals prepared readily to understand current discussions of civic matters is easy to appreciate. Unfortunate experiences during the late war and aversion toward every characteristic of truculent adversaries were certainly enough to quicken that aspiration. But the means adopted, we think, exceed the limitations upon the power of the State and conflict with rights assured to plaintiff in error. The interference is plain enough and no adequate reason therefor in time of peace and domestic tranquility has been shown.

The power of the State to compel attendance at some school and to make reasonable regulations for all schools, including a requirement that they shall give instructions in English, is not questioned. Nor has challenge been made of the State's power to prescribe a curriculum for institutions which it supports. Those matters are not within the present controversy. Our concern is with the prohibition approved by the Supreme Court. . . . No emergency has arisen which renders knowledge by a child of some language other than English so clearly harmful as to justify its inhibition with the consequent infringement of rights long freely enjoyed. We are constrained to conclude that the statute as applied is arbitrary and without reasonable relation to any end within the competency of the State.

As the statute undertakes to interfere only with teaching which involves a modern language, leaving complete freedom as to other matters, there seems no adequate foundation for the suggestion that the purpose was to protect the child's health by limiting his mental activities. It is well known that proficiency in a foreign language seldom comes to one not instructed at an early age, and experience shows that this is not injurious to the health, morals or understanding of the ordinary child.

Reversed.

PIERCE v. SOCIETY OF SISTERS

268 U.S. 510 (1925)

[Oregon law required every child between 8 and 16 to attend public schools, with certain limited exceptions. Plaintiff. . . . private schools obtained an injunction against enforcement of the statute, which would have diverted most of their students. The Supreme Court affirmed, holding that the statute violated the Due Process clause of the Fourteenth Amendment. While emphasizing the effect of the statute upon the plaintiffs' property interests, the Court also observed:]

Under the doctrine of *Meyer v. Nebraska,.* . . . the Act of 1922 unreasonably interferes with the liberty of parents and guardians to direct the upbringing and education of children under their control. . . . [R]ights guaranteed by the Constitution may not be abridged by legislation which has no reasonable relation to some purpose within the competency of the State. The fundamental theory of liberty upon which all governments in this Union repose excludes any general power of the State to standardize its children by forcing them to accept instruction from public teachers only. The child is not the mere creature of the State; those who nurture him and direct his destiny have the right, coupled with the high duty, to recognize and prepare him for additional obligations.

NOTE

In *Meyer* and *Pierce,* the Supreme Court announced a right of parents to rear their children as they see fit without undue interference from the government. Although the Court used these opinions as the basis of constitutionally protected privacy rights in the 1960s and 1970s, *Griswold v. Connecticut,* 381 U.S. 479 (1965), *Eisenstadt v. Baird,* 405 U.S. 438 (1972), *Roe v. Wade,* 410 U.S. 959 (1973), their standing as liberal landmarks has been challenged. Professor Barbara Woodhouse argues that *Meyer* and *Pierce* are grounded in traditional views that parents have property-like rights in their children, and that the opinions effectively "constitutionaliz[e] a patriarchal notion of parental rights. Woodhouse, *"Who Owns the Child?"* Meyer *and* Pierce *and the Child as Property,"* 33 WM. & MARY L. REV. 995 (1992).

It important not to exaggerate the extent of parental authority in making rearing decisions. In the area of education, as Justice Sutherland explains in *Meyer,* parental authority is preempted by state compulsory education requirements, under which children must continue their education until a statutorily-prescribed age, and by state curriculum requirements. *See infra.*

PRINCE v. MASSACHUSETTS

321 U.S. 158 (1944)

[Sarah Prince, a Jehovah's Witness, appealed her conviction of an offense involving her 9 year old niece and ward, Betty Simmons, under a Massachusetts statute regulating child labor. Ms. Prince had allowed Betty to accompany her when she went out in the evening to preach in the streets. Betty, who testified that she was also an ordained minister of the Jehovah's Witness sect, offered Watchtower and Consolation magazines to passers-by for 5 cents a copy. Betty later testified that "it was her religious duty to perform this work" and that failure would bring condemnation "to everlasting destruction at Armageddon."

Ms. Prince was charged and convicted under a Massachusetts statute that provided in part:.

"No boy under twelve and no girl under eighteen shall sell, expose or offer for sale any newspapers, magazines in any street or public place."

Any parent [or] guardian . . .who compels or permits such minor to work in violation" of the statute was also guilty of an offense.]

MR. JUSTICE RUTLEDGE delivered the opinion of the Court.

The case brings for review another episode in the conflict between Jehovah's Witnesses and state authority.

. . .

Appellant . . . rests squarely on freedom of religion under the First Amendment, applied by the Fourteenth to the states. She buttresses this foundation, however, with a claim of parental right as secured by the due process clause of the latter Amendment. *Cf. Meyer v. Nebraska* . . . These guaranties, she thinks, guard alike herself and the child in what they have done. Thus, two claimed liberties are at stake. One is the parent's, to bring up the child in the way he should go, which for appellant means to teach him the tenets and the practices of their faith. The other freedom is the child's, to observe these; and among them is "to preach the gospel . . . by public distribution" of "Watchtower" and "Consolation," in conformity with the scripture: "A little child shall lead them."

. . .

. . . Against these sacred private interests, basic in a democracy, stand the interests of society to protect the welfare of children, and the state's assertion of authority to that end, made here in a manner conceded valid if only secular things were involved.

The rights of children to exercise their religion, and of parents to give them religious training and to encourage them in the practice of religious belief, as against preponderant sentiment and assertion of state power voicing it, have had recognition here . . . [Here, the Court cites *Pierce* and *Meyer*.] It is cardinal with us that the custody, care and nurture of the child reside first in the parents, whose primary function and freedom include preparation for obligations the state can neither supply nor hinder. And it is in recognition of this that these decisions have respected the private realm of family life which the state cannot enter.

But the family itself is not beyond regulation in the public interest, as against a claim of religious liberty. . . . And neither rights of religion nor rights of parenthood are beyond limitation. Acting to guard the general interest in youth's well being, the state as parens patriae may restrict the parent's control by requiring school attendance, regulating or prohibiting the child's labor, and in many other ways. Its authority is not nullified merely because the parent grounds his claim to control the child's course of conduct on religion or conscience. Thus, he cannot claim freedom from compulsory vaccination for the child more than for himself on religious grounds. The right to practice religion freely does not include liberty to expose the community or the child to communicable disease or the latter to ill health or death. . . . [T]he state has a wide range of power for limiting parental freedom and authority in things affecting the child's welfare; and that this includes, to some extent, matters of conscience and religious conviction.

But it is said the state cannot do so here. This, first, because when state action impinges upon a claimed religious freedom, it must fall unless shown to be necessary for or conducive to the child's protection against some clear and present danger, . . . and, it is added, there was no such showing here. The child's presence on the street, with her guardian, distributing or offering to distribute the magazines, it is urged, was in no way harmful to her, nor in any event more so than the presence of many other children at the same time and place, engaged in shopping and other activities not prohibited. Accordingly, in view of the preferred position the freedoms of the First Article occupy, the statute in its present application must fall. . . . [F]inally, it is said, the statute is, as to children, an absolute prohibition, not merely a reasonable regulation, of the denounced activity.

Concededly a statute or ordinance identical in terms with Section 69, except that it is applicable to adults or all persons generally, would be invalid. But the mere fact a state could not wholly prohibit this form of adult activity, whether characterized locally as a "sale" or otherwise, does not mean it cannot do so for children. Such a conclusion granted would mean that a state could impose no greater limitation upon child labor than upon adult labor. . . .

The state's authority over children's activities is broader than over like actions of adults. This is peculiarly true of public activities and in matters of employment. A democratic society rests, for its continuance, upon the healthy, well-rounded growth of young people into full maturity as citizens, with all that implies. It may secure this against impeding restraints and dangers, within a broad range of selection. Among evils most appropriate for such action are the crippling effects of child employment, more especially in public places, and the possible harms arising from other activities subject to all the diverse influences of the street. It is too late now to doubt that legislation appropriately designed to reach such evils is within the state's police power, whether against the parent's claim to control of the child or one that religious scruples dictate contrary action.

It is true children have rights, in common with older people, in the primary use of highways. But even in such use streets afford dangers for them not affecting adults. . . . What may be wholly permissible for adults therefore may not be so for children, either with or without their parents' presence.

Street preaching, whether oral or by handing out literature, is not the primary use of the highway, even for adults. While for them it cannot be wholly prohibited, it can be regulated within reasonable limits in accommodation to the primary and other incidental uses. But, for obvious reasons,. . . .the validity of such a prohibition applied to children not accompanied by an older person hardly would seem open to question. The case reduces itself therefore to the question whether the presence of the child's guardian puts a limit to the state's power. That fact may lessen the likelihood that some evils the legislation seeks to avert will occur. But it cannot forestall all of them. The zealous though lawful exercise of the right to engage in propagandizing the community, whether in religious, political or other matters, may and at times does create situations difficult enough for adults to cope with and wholly inappropriate for children, especially of tender years, to face. Other harmful possibilities could be stated, of emotional excitement and psychological or physical injury. Parents may be free to become martyrs themselves. But it does not follow they are free, in identical circumstances, to make martyrs of their children before they have reached the age of full and legal discretion when they can make that choice for themselves. Massachusetts has determined that an absolute prohibition, though one limited to streets and public places and to the incidental uses proscribed, is necessary to accomplish its legitimate objectives. Its power to attain them is broad enough to reach these peripheral instances in which the parent's supervision may reduce but cannot eliminate entirely the ill effects of the prohibited conduct. We think that with reference to the public proclaiming of religion, upon the streets and in other similar public places, the power of the state to control the conduct of children reaches beyond the scope of its authority over adults, as is true in the case of other freedoms, and the rightful boundary of its power has not been crossed in this case.

. . .

The judgment is affirmed.

Mr. Justice Murphy, dissenting.

. . . The great interest of the state in shielding minors from the evil vicissitudes of early life does not warrant every limitation on their religious training and activities. The reasonableness that justifies the prohibition of the ordinary distribution of literature in the public streets by children is not necessarily the reasonableness that justifies such a drastic restriction when the distribution is part of their religious faith. *Murdock v. Pennsylvania, supra*, 319 U.S. 111. If the right of a child to practice its religion in that manner is to be forbidden by constitutional means, there must be convincing proof that such a practice constitutes a grave and immediate danger to the state or to the health, morals or welfare of the child. *West Virginia State Board of Education v. Barnette*, 319 U.S. 624, 639. The vital freedom of religion. . . . cannot be erased by slender references to the state's power to restrict the more secular activities of children.

The state, in my opinion, has completely failed to sustain its burden of proving the existence of any grave or immediate danger to any interest which it may lawfully protect. . . .

WISCONSIN v. YODER

406 U.S. 205 (1971)

MR. CHIEF JUSTICE BURGER delivered the opinion of the Court.

On petition of the State of Wisconsin, we . . . review a decision of the Wisconsin Supreme Court holding that respondents' convictions of violating the State's compulsory school-attendance law were invalid under the Free Exercise Clause of the First Amendment to the United States Constitution . . . [W]e affirm. . .

[The Wisconsin statute required attendance at school for all children until the age of 16. Respondents were three Amish parents who refused to send their children (aged 14 and 15) to school beyond the eighth grade.]

On complaint of the school district administrator for the public schools, respondents were. . . .convicted of violating the compulsory-attendance law in Green County Court and were fined the sum of $5 each.[3] Respondents defended on the ground that the application of the compulsory-attendance law violated their rights under the First and Fourteenth Amendments.

. . . . As a result of their common heritage, Old Order Amish communities today are characterized by a fundamental belief that salvation requires life in a church community separate and apart from the world and worldly influence.

. . . . Amish beliefs [also] require members of the community to make their living by farming or closely related activities. Broadly speaking, the Old Order Amish religion pervades and determines the entire mode of life of its adherents. . . .

Amish objection to formal education beyond the eighth grade is firmly grounded in these central religious concepts. They object to the high school, and higher education generally, because the values they teach are in marked variance with Amish values and the Amish way of life; they view secondary school education as an impermissible exposure of their children to a "worldly" influence in conflict with their beliefs. The high school tends to emphasize intellectual and scientific accomplishments, self-distinction, competitiveness, worldly success, and social life with other students. Amish society emphasizes informal learning-through-doing; a life of "goodness," rather than a life of intellect; wisdom, rather than technical knowledge; community welfare, rather than competition; and separation from, rather than integration with, contemporary worldly society.

---

[3] Prior to trial, the attorney for respondents wrote the State Superintendent of Public Instruction in an effort to explore the possibilities for a compromise settlement. [H]e suggested that perhaps. . . . the Amish could satisfy the compulsory-attendance law by establishing their own vocational training plan similar to one that has been established in Pennsylvania. . . . Under the Pennsylvania plan, Amish children of high school age are required to attend an Amish vocational school for three hours a week, [to study] English, mathematics, health, and social studies by an Amish teacher. For the balance of the week, the children perform farm and household duties under parental supervision, and keep a journal of their daily activities. The Superintendent rejected this proposal on the ground that it would not afford Amish children "substantially equivalent education" to that offered in the schools of the area. . . .

Formal high school education beyond the eighth grade is contrary to Amish beliefs, not only because it places Amish children in an environment hostile to Amish beliefs with increasing emphasis on competition in class work and sports and with pressure to conform to the styles, manners, and ways of the peer group, but also because it takes them away from their community, physically and emotionally, during the crucial and formative adolescent period of life. During this period, the children must acquire Amish attitudes favoring manual work and self-reliance and the specific skills needed to perform the adult role of an Amish farmer or housewife. They must learn to enjoy physical labor. Once a child has learned basic reading, writing, and elementary mathematics, these traits, skills, and attitudes admittedly fall within the category of those best learned through example and "doing" rather than in a classroom. And, at this time in life, the Amish child must also grow in his faith and his relationship to the Amish community if he is to be prepared to accept the heavy obligations imposed by adult baptism. In short, high school attendance with teachers who are not of the Amish faith — and may even be hostile to it — interposes a serious barrier to the integration of the Amish child into the Amish religious community. . . .

The Amish do not object to elementary education through the first eight grades as a general proposition because they agree that their children must have basic skills in the "three R's" in order to read the Bible, to be good farmers and citizens, and to be able to deal with non-Amish people when necessary in the course of daily affairs. They view such a basic education as acceptable because it does not significantly expose their children to worldly values or interfere with their development in the Amish community during the crucial adolescent period. In the Amish belief higher learning tends to develop values they reject as influences that alienate man from God.

On the basis of such considerations, Dr. Hostetler [an expert on Amish society] testified that compulsory high school attendance could not only result in great psychological harm to Amish children, because of the conflicts it would produce, but would also, in his opinion, ultimately result in the destruction of the Old Order Amish church community as it exists in the United States today. The testimony of Dr. Donald A. Erickson, an expert witness on education, also showed that the Amish succeed in preparing their high school age children to be productive members of the Amish community. He described their system of learning through doing the skills directly relevant to their adult roles in the Amish community as "ideal" and perhaps superior to ordinary high school education. The evidence also showed that the Amish have an excellent record as law-abiding and generally self-sufficient members of society.

Although the trial court in its careful findings determined that the Wisconsin compulsory school-attendance law "does interfere with the freedom of the Defendants to act in accordance with their sincere religious belief" it also concluded that the requirement of high school attendance until age 16 was a "reasonable and constitutional" exercise of governmental power, and therefore denied the motion to dismiss the charges. The Wisconsin Circuit Court affirmed the convictions. The Wisconsin Supreme Court, however, sustained respondents' claim under the Free Exercise Clause of the First Amendment and reversed. . . .

I

There is no doubt as to the power of a State, having a high responsibility for education of its citizens, to impose reasonable regulations for the control and duration of basic education. Providing public schools ranks at the very apex of the function of a State. Yet even this paramount responsibility was, in *Pierce,* made to yield to the right of parents to provide an equivalent education in a privately operated system. . . . As that case suggests, the values of parental direction of the religious upbringing and education of their children in their early and formative years have a high place in our society. Thus, a State's interest in universal education, however highly we rank it, is not totally free from a balancing process when it impinges on fundamental rights and interests, such as those specifically protected by the Free Exercise Clause of the First Amendment, and the traditional interest of parents with respect to the religious upbringing of their children so long as they, in the words of *Pierce,* "prepare [them] for additional obligations." 268 U.S. at 535. . . .

II

. . . A way of life, however virtuous and admirable, may not be interposed as a barrier to reasonable state regulation of education if it is based on purely secular considerations; to have the protection of the Religion Clauses, the claims must be rooted in religious belief. Thus, if the Amish asserted their claims because of their subjective evaluation and rejection of the contemporary secular values accepted by the majority, much as Thoreau rejected the social values of his time and isolated himself at Walden Pond, their claims would not rest on a religious basis.

III

Neither the findings of the trial court nor the Amish claims as to the nature of their faith are challenged in this Court by the State. . . . Its position is that the State's interest in universal compulsory formal secondary education to age 16 is so great that it is paramount to the undisputed claims of respondents. . . .

The State advances two primary arguments [in support of its contention that its interest in its system of compulsory education outweighs the established religious practices of the Amish]. . . It notes, as Thomas Jefferson pointed out early in our history, that some degree of education is necessary to prepare citizens to participate effectively and intelligently in our open political system if we are to preserve freedom and independence. Further, education prepares individuals to be self-reliant and self-sufficient participants in society. We accept these propositions.

However, the evidence adduced . . . is persuasively to the effect that an additional one or two years of formal high school for Amish children in place of their long-established program of informal vocational education would do little to serve those interests. Respondents' experts testified at trial, without challenge, that the value of all education must be assessed in terms of its capacity to prepare the child for life. It is one thing to say that compulsory education for a year or two beyond the eighth grade may be necessary when its goal is the preparation of the child for life in modern society as the majority live, but it is quite another if the goal of education be viewed as the preparation of the child for life in the separated agrarian community that is the keystone of the Amish faith.

The State attacks respondents' position as one fostering "ignorance" from which the child must be protected by the State. No one can question the State's duty to protect children from ignorance but this argument does not square with the facts disclosed in the record. Whatever their idiosyncrasies as seen by the majority, this record strongly shows that the Amish community has been a highly successful social unit within our society, even if apart from the conventional "mainstream." Its members are productive and very law-abiding members of society; they reject public welfare in any of its usual modern forms. The Congress itself recognized their self-sufficiency by authorizing exemption of such groups as the Amish from the obligation to pay social security taxes. . . .

. . . .There can be no assumption that today's majority is "right" and the Amish and others like them are "wrong." A way of life that is odd or even erratic but interferes with no rights or interests of others is not to be condemned because it is different.

The State, however, supports its interest in providing an additional one or two years of compulsory high school education to Amish children because of the possibility that some such children will choose to leave the Amish community, and that if this occurs they will be ill-equipped for life. . . . However, on this record, that argument is highly speculative. There is no specific evidence of the loss of Amish adherents by attrition, nor is there any showing that upon leaving the Amish community Amish children, with their practical agricultural training and habits of industry and self-reliance, would become burdens on society because of educational short-comings. Indeed, this argument of the State appears to rest primarily on the State's mistaken assumption, already noted, that the Amish do not provide any education for their children beyond the eighth grade, but allow them to grow in "ignorance.". . .

There is nothing in this record to suggest that the Amish qualities of reliability, self-reliance, and dedication to work would fail to find ready markets in today's society. Absent some contrary evidence supporting the State's position, we are unwilling to assume that persons possessing such valuable vocational skills and habits are doomed to become burdens on society should they determine to leave the Amish faith, nor is there any basis in the record to warrant a finding that an additional one or two years of formal school education beyond the eighth grade would serve to eliminate any such problem that might exist. . . .

IV

Finally, the State, on authority of *Prince v. Massachusetts*, argues that a decision exempting Amish children from the State's requirement fails to recognize the substantive right of the Amish child to a secondary education, and fails to give due regard to the power of the State as *parens patriae* to extend the benefit of secondary education to children regardless of the wishes of their parents. Taken at its broadest sweep, the Court's language in *Prince*, might be read to give support to the State's position. However, the Court was not confronted in *Prince* with a situation comparable to that of the Amish. . . .; this is shown by the Court's severe characterization of the evils that it thought the legislature could legitimately associate with child labor, even when performed in the company of an adult. . . .

This case, of course, is not one in which any harm to the physical or mental health of the child or to the public safety, peace, order, or welfare has been demonstrated or may be properly inferred. The record is to the contrary. . . .

Contrary to the suggestion of the dissenting opinion of Mr. Justice Douglas, our holding today in no degree depends on the assertion of the religious interest of the child as contrasted with that of the parents. It is the parents who are subject to prosecution here for failing to cause their children to attend school, and it is their right of free exercise, not that of their children, that must determine Wisconsin's power to impose criminal penalties on the parent. . . . The children are not parties to this litigation. The State has at no point tried this case on the theory that respondents were preventing their children from attending school against their expressed desires, and indeed the record is to the contrary. The State's position from the outset has been that it is empowered to apply its compulsory-attendance law to Amish parents in the same manner as to other parents — that is, without regard to the wishes of the child. That is the claim we reject today.

Our holding in no way determines the proper resolution of possible competing interests of parents, children, and the State in an appropriate state court proceeding in which the power of the State is asserted on the theory that Amish parents are preventing their minor children from attending high school despite their expressed desires to the contrary. Recognition of the claim of the State in such a proceeding would, of course, call into question traditional concepts of parental control over the religious upbringing and education of their minor children recognized in this Court's past decisions. It is clear that such an intrusion by a State into family decisions in the area of religious training would give rise to grave questions of religious freedom comparable to those raised here and those presented in *Pierce*. On this record we neither reach nor decide those issues.

The State's argument proceeds without reliance on any actual conflict between the wishes of parents and children. It appears to rest on the potential that exemption of Amish parents from the requirements of the compulsory-education law might allow some parents to act contrary to the best interests of their children by foreclosing their opportunity to make an intelligent choice between the Amish way of life and that of the outside world. The same argument could, of course, be made with respect to all church schools short of college. There is nothing in the record or in the ordinary course of human experience to suggest that non-Amish parents generally consult with children of ages 14–16 if they are placed in a church school of the parents' faith.

Indeed it seems clear that if the State is empowered, as parens patriae, to "save" a child from himself or his Amish parents by requiring an additional two years of compulsory formal high school education, the State will in large measure influence, if not determine, the religious future of the child. Even more markedly than in *Prince,* therefore, this case involves the fundamental interest of parents, as contrasted with that of the State, to guide the religious future and education of their children. The history and culture of Western civilization reflect a strong tradition of parental concern for the nurture and upbringing of their children. This primary role of the parents in the upbringing of their children is now established beyond debate as an enduring American tradition. . . .

. . . *Pierce* stands as a charter of the rights of parents to direct the religious upbringing of their children. And, when the interests of parenthood are combined with a free exercise claim of the nature revealed by this record, more than merely a "reasonable relation to some purpose within the competency of the State" is required to sustain the validity of the State's requirement under the First Amendment. To be sure, the power of the parent, even when linked to a free exercise claim, may be subject to limitation under *Prince* if it appears that parental decisions will jeopardize the health or safety of the child, or have a potential for significant social burdens. But in this case, the Amish have introduced persuasive evidence undermining the arguments the State has advanced to support its claims in terms of the welfare of the child and society as a whole. . . .

In the face of our consistent emphasis on the central values underlying the Religion Clauses in our constitutional scheme of government, we cannot accept a parens patriae claim of such all-encompassing scope and with such sweeping potential for broad and unforeseeable application as that urged by the State.

V

. . . .[W]e hold . . . that the First and Fourteenth Amendments prevent the State from compelling respondents to cause their children to attend formal high school to age 16. . . . It cannot be overemphasized that we are not dealing with a way of life and mode of education by a group claiming to have recently discovered some "progressive" or more enlightened process for rearing children for modern life.

Aided by a history of three centuries as an identifiable religious sect and a long history as a successful and self-sufficient segment of American society, the Amish in this case have convincingly demonstrated the sincerity of their religious beliefs, the interrelationship of belief with their mode of life, the vital role that belief and daily conduct play in the continued survival of Old Order Amish communities and their religious organization, and the hazards presented by the State's enforcement of a statute generally valid as to others. Beyond this, they have carried the even more difficult burden of demonstrating the adequacy of their alternative mode of continuing informal vocational education in terms of precisely those overall interests that the State advances in support of its program of compulsory high school education. In light of this convincing showing, one that probably few other religious groups or sects could make, and weighing the minimal difference between what the State would require and what the Amish already accept, it was incumbent on the State to show with more particularity how its admittedly strong interest in compulsory education would be adversely affected by granting an exemption to the Amish. . . .

Affirmed.

MR. JUSTICE POWELL and MR. JUSTICE REHNQUIST took no part in the consideration or decision of this case.

MR. JUSTICE STEWART, with whom MR. JUSTICE BRENNAN joins, concurring. . . .

. . . .[T]here is no suggestion whatever in the record that the religious beliefs of the children here concerned differ in any way from those of their parents. Only one of the children testified. The last two questions and answers on her cross-examination accurately sum up her testimony:

Q. So I take it then, Frieda, the only reason you are not going to school, and did not go to school since last September, is because of *your* religion?

A. Yes.

Q. That is the only reason?

A. Yes. (Emphasis supplied.)

MR. JUSTICE WHITE, with whom MR. JUSTICE BRENNAN and MR. JUSTICE STEWART join, concurring.

. . . It is possible that most Amish children will wish to continue living the rural life of their parents, in which case their training at home will adequately equip them for their future role. Others, however, may wish to become nuclear physicists, ballet dancers, computer programmers, or historians, and for these occupations, formal training will be necessary. . . . [A]lthough the question is close, I am unable to say that the State has demonstrated that Amish children who leave school in the eighth grade will be intellectually stultified or unable to acquire new academic skills later. . . .

. . . I join the Court because the sincerity of the Amish religious policy here is uncontested, because the potentially adverse impact of the state requirement is great, and because the State's valid interest in education has already been largely satisfied by the eight years the children have already spent in school.

MR. JUSTICE DOUGLAS, dissenting in part.

. . . The Court's analysis assumes that the only interests at stake in the case are those of the Amish parents . . . and those of the State. . . . The difficulty with this approach is that, despite the Court's claim, the parents are seeking to vindicate not only their own free exercise claims, but also those of their high-school-age children.

It is argued that the right of the Amish children to religious freedom is not presented by the facts of the case, as the issue before the Court involves only the Amish parents' religious freedom to defy a state criminal statute imposing upon them an affirmative duty to cause their children to attend high school.

. . . .

. . . .[I]t is essential to reach the question to decide the case. . . . If the parents in this case are allowed a religious exemption, the inevitable effect is to impose the parents' notions of religious duty upon their children. Where the child is mature enough to express potentially conflicting desires, it would be an invasion of the child's rights to permit such an imposition without canvassing his views. . . . And, if an Amish child desires to attend high school, and is mature enough to have that desire respected, the State may well be able to override the parents' religiously motivated objections.

Religion is an individual experience. It is not necessary, nor even appropriate, for every Amish child to express his views on the subject in a prosecution of a single adult. Crucial, however, are the views of the child whose parent is the subject of the suit. Frieda Yoder has in fact testified that her own religious views are opposed to high-school education. I therefore join the judgment of the Court as to respondent Jonas Yoder. But Frieda Yoder's views may not be those of Vernon Yutzy or Barbara Miller. I must dissent, therefore, as to respondents Adin Yutzy and Wallace Miller as their motion to dismiss also raised the question of their children's religious liberty. . . .

This issue has never been squarely presented before today. . . . [W]e have in the past analyzed similar conflicts between parent and State with little regard for the views of the child. Recent cases, however, have clearly held that the children themselves have constitutionally protectible interests.

These children are "persons" within the meaning of the Bill of Rights. We have so held over and over again. . . .

On this important and vital matter of education, I think the children should be entitled to be heard. While the parents, absent dissent, normally speak for the entire family, the education of the child is a matter on which the child will often have decided views. He may want to be a pianist or an astronaut or an oceanographer. To do so he will have to break from the Amish tradition.

It is the future of the student, not the future of the parents, that is imperiled by today's decision. If a parent keeps his child out of school beyond the grade school, then the child will be forever barred from entry into the new and amazing world of diversity that we have today. The child may decide that that is the preferred course, or he may rebel. It is the student's judgment, not his parents', that is essential if we are to give full meaning to what we have said about the Bill of Rights and of the right of students to be masters of their own destiny.[3]

If he is harnessed to the Amish way of life by those in authority over him and if his education is truncated, his entire life may be stunted and deformed.

---

[3] The court below brushed aside the students' interests with the offhand comment that "[w]hen a child reaches the age of judgment, he can choose for himself his religion." *Wisconsin v. Yoder*, 182 N.W.2d 539, 543 (Wis. 1971). But there is nothing in this record to indicate that the moral and intellectual judgment demanded of the student by the question in this case is beyond his capacity. Children far younger than the 14-and 15-year-olds involved here are regularly permitted to testify in custody and other proceedings. . . . Moreover, there is substantial agreement among child psychologists and sociologists that the moral and intellectual maturity of the 14-year-old approaches that of the adult. See, *e.g.*, J. Piaget, THE MORAL JUDGMENT OF THE CHILD (1948); D. Elkind, CHILDREN AND ADOLESCENTS 75–80 (1970); Kohlberg, *Moral Education in the Schools: A Development View*, in R. Muuss, ADOLESCENT BEHAVIOR AND SOCIETY 193, 199–200 (1971); W. Kay, MORAL DEVELOPMENT 172–183 (1968); A. Gesell & F. Ilg, YOUTH: THE YEARS FROM TEN TO SIXTEEN 175–182 (1956). . . .

The child, therefore, should be given an opportunity to be heard before the State gives the exemption which we honor today.

The views of the two children in question were not canvassed by the Wisconsin courts. The matter should be explicitly reserved so that new hearings can be held on remand of the case. . . .

NOTES

1. *Religious Free Exercise or Parental Autonomy?* Is *Yoder* a First Amendment free exercise case or a Fourteenth Amendment parental auton-omy case? It would seem that the *Yoder* parents prevailed only because the "way of life" they sought to protect was "rooted in religious belief." On the other hand, the core claim by the Amish parents was that they had a right as parents to inculcate their children in their values, beliefs, and adult roles without undue interference from the state. Put another way, the Amish would certainly *not* have a right to insist that anyone *other* than their children be subject to this inculcation. Thus, it is clear that the Court is recognizing a parental right as well as a right to free expression of religion.

What if the claim arises out of parents' adherence to philosophical or cultural views instead of religious belief? In *In re McMillan*, 226 S.E.2d 693 (N.C. App. 1976), a North Carolina appeals court upheld a decision that Native American children were neglected because their parents had failed to send them to the public schools. The court rejected the parents' argument that their decision was based on the failure of the public schools to present adequate instruction in American Indian heritage and culture, and that their deeply rooted cultural convictions, like religious beliefs, were entitled to constitu-tional protection. In rejecting this argument, the court distinguished *Yoder*: "There is no showing that Shelby and Abe McMillan receive any mode of educational programs alternative to those in the public school. There is also no showing that the Indian heritage or culture of these children will be endangered or threatened in any way by their attending school."

The *Yoder* Court seems to recognize that the Amish community (and not just the Amish parents) has an interest that is affected by the state regulation. The case for an exemption from the compulsory attendance regulation rests in part on the importance to the survival of the community of integrating the younger members through training for their life roles. Should the court be concerned with the community's interest? Do communities have rights? In Chapter 11 we will return to this theme in discussing arguments for racial matching of minority children (particularly African American and Native American children) in adoption placement. *See* pp. 1259-78.

2. *Reconciling* Yoder *and* Prince. The Supreme Court struggles to distin-guish *Yoder* from *Prince* on the ground that *Prince* dealt with the "evil" of child labor, while *Yoder* involves no threat of harm to the child or to public welfare. Are you persuaded? The Amish parents in *Yoder* would not seem to have a more compelling interest than Ms. Prince, who claimed that the activity of street preaching with her child was critically important to their salvation. The different outcomes in the two cases may also be due to the Court's view that the *state's* interest in *Yoder* was less substantial than that asserted in

Prince. In fact, the *Yoder* Court did not seem to take very seriously the claim that the state's interest in a productive educated citizenry was negatively affected by the exemption sought by the Amish parents. The Amish community, after all, was very productive and self-sustaining, imposing no burden on the rest of society. On the other hand, does *Prince* really implicate the state's interest in prohibiting child labor?

An element of the state's interest in education that the *Yoder* Court ignores is in educating citizens to become participants in democratic government. This interest is surely undermined by deferring to the Amish parents. The case suggests a tension (as do *Meyer* and *Pierce)* between important political values. On the one hand, democracy requires political participation by citizens. A society could not function well if the Old Order Amish traditions of withdrawal and isolation were widespread. The "melting pot" metaphor suggests a process of assimilation through which diverse ethnic and religious groups come to share a common culture and values. On the other hand, we also endorse a competing "quilt" metaphor. An important political norm in our country is respect for cultural, religious and ethnic diversity, and a belief that groups in our society should maintain their identity and not be submerged in the mainstream. Commentators have criticized parental authority to inculcate their children by educating them in a segregated environment.

See note 6, *infra* for a discussion of home schooling.

3. *Should the Child's Views be Heard?* Justice Douglas' dissent in *Yoder* is well known, perhaps because it was the first suggestion in a Supreme Court opinion (albeit a dissent) that children might have a legally protected interest separate from (and possibly in opposition to) that of their parents in participating in important decisions affecting their welfare. This dissent has provided authority (and inspiration) for advocates seeking expanded rights of self-determination for minors, and influenced the arguments supporting reproductive rights of minors.

Justice Douglas would require confirmation from the child before honoring the parents' claim, but the majority leaves unresolved the question of what would happen if the child's views differ from that of the parents. Clearly, *Yoder* at least contemplates the possibility that even in that case, the parents' desire will prevail. The decision, then, is one which protects a parent's right to make decisions deemed beneficial to the child, not the child's right to make choices for herself.

4. *Special Accommodations and Vouchers — the Establishment Clause.* Any state accommodation to parental requests for special treatment in recognition of their religious beliefs is vulnerable to Establishment Clause objections. The Supreme Court dealt with this tension in a case that involved a separate school district created for Hasidic Jews in New York to provide a religiously acceptable setting for Hasidic students who needed special education services. The Hasidic village of Kiryas Joel is located entirely within the Monroe-Woodbury Central School District. Most children in the village attended private Hasidic schools, but these schools could not provide special education services. The school district took the position (in response to several Supreme Court opinions dealing with the provision of services to the parochial schools) that it could only provide services to the Hasidic students in the public schools, while the Hasidim sought services to be provided by the district in its religious schools. The legislature, in an effort to resolve the conflict, created a separate school district in the village. In *Board of Educ. of Kiryas Joel Village School District v. Grumet*, 512 U.S. 687 (1994), the Supreme Court decided that the legislative action violated the Establishment Clause of the First Amendment. Although the Court suggested that the state could accommodate religious groups by alleviating particular burdens, the New York legislature had gone too far, because it conferred a special benefit on the Hasidic community of Kiryas Joel that it was unlikely to make available generally to other religious groups. The legislature's response — to make the benefit potentially available to other groups who wanted to establish a separate school district — was struck down by a New York appellate court because, although the criteria were formally neutral, in fact only the village of Kiryas Joel would qualify. *Grumet v. Cuomo*, 647 N.Y.S.2d 565 (N.Y. App. Div. 1996); *aff'd* 681 N.E. 2d 340, (N.Y. 1997). *See* Greene, *Kiryas Joel and Two Mistakes about Equality*, 96 COLUM. L. REV. 1 (1996) (criticizing the Court and defending special school district as an example of "group exit" and the village's incorporation as an exercise of "appropriate public power"); Eisgruber, *The Constitutional Value of Assimilation*, 96 COLUM. L. REV. 87 (1996) (criticizing the districts as "government-sponsored segregation"); Lupu, *Uncovering the Village of Kiryas Joel*, 96 COLUM. L. REV. 104 (1996) (criticizing Greene's accommodation argument).

In recent years, legislatures have initiated voucher programs aimed at offering low income parents a choice of educational alternatives for their children attending inferior inner city schools. The Supreme Court has upheld a Cleveland, Ohio program that provided tuition aid to children attending participating public or private schools against an Establishment Clause challenge. *Zelman v. Simmons-Harris*, 536 U.S. 639 (2002). In an opinion by Justice Rehnquist, a divided Court rejected the argument that the program effectively was a tax benefit to religious schools because 96% of the children receiving aid attended such schools. The Court emphasized that the program was enacted for a secular purpose, to provide educational aid to poor children in a failing school system, and the assistance was provided directly to parents who then directed the aid to religious schools. The Court held the program was neutral toward religion and could not be interpreted as endorsement of a religious message. Parents were making a "true private choice" and the constitutionality of the program did not, in the Court's view, depend on the fact that most private schools in Cleveland (and in most cities) happened to be religious schools. Justice Souter in dissent argued that the parents receiving aid did not have a "genuine choice" because few non-religious schools were available and were too expensive for voucher recipients. Thus, the program had the impermissible effect of advancing religious education. For an opinion finding an Establishment Clause violation in a curricular program, *see Doe v. Rhea Co. Bd. Of Education*, 188 F. Supp. 2d 904 (E.D. Tenn. 2002) (enjoining program of Bible instruction taught by students from a local religious college and rejecting school board's claim the program was voluntary; students were not told this and no student ever opted out).

School voucher programs and other policies to improve the quality of education for poor urban children have attracted considerable academic interest. *See* JAMES DWYER, RELIGIOUS SCHOOLS VERSES CHILDREN' RIGHTS (1998); Ryan, *Schools, Race, and Money,* 109 YALE L.J. 249 (1999)(arguing that only policies which promote integration (including vouchers) will lead to enhanced academic achievement of poor urban children); For an analysis of *Zelman,* see Fried, *Five to Four: Reflections on the School Voucher Case,* 116 HARV. L. REV. 163 (2002).

5. ***School Curriculum and Parents' Constitutional Rights.*** How far should the parents' authority to direct their child's education extend? An important issue that courts have addressed since *Yoder* is whether parents should be able to protect their children who are students in public school from exposure to material in the curriculum that seriously offends their religious beliefs.

Parental challenges of sex education or family life education programs were common in the 1970's and 1980's. Since the 1960's, school districts have offered these programs, largely in response to concerns about increased teenage sexual activity, which in turn has resulted in increases in teen pregnancy and venereal disease. Parents' objections to these programs have been based on a claim that, by educating children about sexuality, the state interferes with parents' authority to instruct their children on moral issues according to their religious beliefs. Most commonly, parents have claimed that sex education programs (and regulations authorizing such programs) violate the Free Exercise and Establishment Clauses and interfere with parental rights under the Due Process Clause of the Fourteenth Amendment. Many programs have excusal policies, allowing parents to opt out of the program. These have been routinely upheld. *See e.g. Smith v. Ricci,* 445 A.2d 501 (N.J. 1982). But what about a compulsory program? In *Brown v. Hot, Sexy, and Safer Productions,* 68 F.3d 525 (1996), the court rejected a challenge by parents and their children to a compulsory AIDS awareness program presented in a school assembly that involved sexually suggestive skits and lewd language. The court rejected the parents' claim that their constitutionally protected privacy and substantive due process rights to rear their children under *Meyer* and *Pierce* "encompasses a. . . . right to dictate the curriculum at the public school to which they have chosen to send their children." *Id.* at 533. Such a right, in the court's view, would require the school to customize the curriculum of any child whose parents raised moral objections. The court also rejected the parties' free exercise claim, finding the burden to religious expression to be far less substantial than that experienced by the parents in *Yoder.*

Parents have also challenged textbooks used in public schools on religious grounds. In *Mozert v. Hawkins Cty. Bd. of Education,* several fundamentalist families challenged the textbook series used in an integrated reading curriculum in the Hawkins County public schools. 647 F. Supp. 1194 (E.D. Tenn. 1986). The parents sought an exemption for their children from classes in which the offensive textbooks were used, asserting that the textbooks violated their Free Exercise rights by requiring them to choose between a free public education and the exposure of their children to ideas that offended their religious beliefs. They objected, in particular, to descriptions in the textbooks of magic, witchcraft, situational ethics, humanistic values, and the theory of evolution and to material reinforcing views that might influence a child to become "a feminist, a humanist, a pacifist, an anti-Christian, a vegetarian or an advocate of a 'one-world government.' " Reversing the district court, the circuit court held that the offending textbooks did not burden the parents' Free Exercise rights. *Mozert v. Hawkins Cty. Bd. of Educ.*, 827 F.2d 1058 (6th Cir. 1987), *cert. denied*, 484 U.S. 1066 (1988). The opinion stressed the importance of the state's secular purposes in teaching independent thinking, critical judgment, logical decisionmaking and tolerance. The Court also emphasized that the students were not required to affirm or deny any belief or engage in any practice that contradicted their religious belief.

Why did the *Mozert* plaintiffs lose? One reason may be that vindication of their claims would require too drastic a remedy. While the *Yoder* plaintiffs could be accommodated by excusing their own children from two years of secondary education, accommodating these plaintiffs would seem to require a revision of major aspects of the educational curriculum for all children in the affected grades (in *Mozert*, all elementary and secondary grades; in *Smith*, grades 1–8).

Some states have acted to enhance parental authority to influence their children's education. A recent Texas statute, the Parents' Rights and Responsibilities Act, TEX. EDUC. CODE ANN. §§ 26.003–26.010 (Vernon 2000), gives rights to parents in dealing with their children's school, including the right to petition ("with the expectation that the request will not be unreasonably denied") on behalf of their children to add or change a course, graduate early, and to withdraw from a class or other school activity that conflicts with their religious beliefs. The statute does not authorize parents to remove a child from a course for an entire semester; nor does it "exempt a child from satisfying grade level requirements. . . . in a manner acceptable to the school district. . . ." *Id.* at § 26.010.

The issues raised by *Mozert, Smith,* and other cases discussed in this note have generated scholarly commentary. *See* Stolzenberg, *"He Drew a Circle that Shut Me Out": Assimilation, Indoctrination and the Paradox of a Liberal Education*, 106 HARV. L. REV. 581 (1993); Lupu, *Where Rights Begin: The Problem of Burdens on the Free Exercise of Religion*, 102 HARV. L. REV. 933 (1989); Mykkeltvedt, *Tension Between the Religion Clauses of the First Amendment:* Mozert v. Hawkins County Public Schools, 56 TENN. L. REV. 693 (1989).

6. *Home Schooling*. Almost all states provide a generally applicable exception from compulsory school attendance requirements for children receiving adequate instruction at home — although most courts that have considered the issue have found no constitutional parental right to withhold children from school for non-religious reasons. Recent years have seen an upsurge in home schooling by parents, many of whom are fundamentalist Christians who believe that public school education undermines their efforts to convey their religious and moral values to their children. Regulations vary among states as to whether home schooling is tolerated or discouraged. Under some statutes, home schooling is subject to the same regulation and standards as non-public schools and parents who provide instruction may be required to meet teacher certification requirements. *See* FLA. STAT. ANN. § 232.02 (West 1998) (requiring either teacher certification or maintenance of academic portfolio and annual evaluation). At the other end of the continuum, some states give a blanket exemption from compulsory school attendance laws to parents who remove their children from school because of religious conviction. *See* VA. CODE ANN. § 22.1-254.1 (2002). Most states subject children who are educated at home to standardized evaluation of their educational progress. How should performance of home-schooled children be measured to evaluate the adequacy of their educational progress? Against the mean performance of public school students? Against their own prior performance? Should the adequacy of performance be based on each student's aptitude?

For other home schooling laws, see, *e.g.*, COLO. REV. STAT. § 22-33-104 (2002); OHIO REV. CODE ANN. § 3321.04 (Anderson 2002); OR. REV. STAT. § 339.030 (2003). *See also Care and Protection of Charles,* 504 N.E.2d 592 (Mass. 1987); *Appeal of Peirce,* 451 A.2d 363 (N.H. 1982) (applying regulations enacted by state board of education). Some courts have allowed home schooling through liberal interpretation of compulsory education laws. *See, e.g., Delconte v. North Carolina,* 329 S.E.2d 636 (N.C. 1985). *See generally* Mawdsley, *Parent's Rights to Direct Their Children's Education: Changing Perspectives,* 162 EDUC. L. REP. 659 (2002).

The extent to which parents should have authority to control children's education has been the focus of academic interest. Stephen Gilles has argued for strong parental authority to make educational choices for their children. Gilles, *On Educating Children: A Parentalist Manifesto,* 63 U. CHI. L. REV. 937 (1996). He challenges liberal theorists such as Amy Gutman and Bruce Ackerman, who assert that children must receive a liberal education to enable them to choose among competing conceptions of the good. Gilles' argument rests in part on the liberal commitment to pluralism and toleration. He also argues that parents have better incentives to take into account their children's best interest than does the state, and that the interest of individuals in nurturing and being nurtured in a parent-child relationship is more foundational than the state's interest in educating future citizens. In contrast, James Dwyer argues that parents have no right to inculcate their children generally or to school them at home. Dwyer, *Parents' Religion and Children's Welfare: Debunking the Doctrine of Children's Rights,* 82 CAL. L. REV.1371 (1994). Emily Buss argues that exposure to different peers is critically important to adolescent development in a heterogenous society, and that home schooling is undesirable in ways that have not been acknowledged. *See* Buss, *The Adolescents' Stake in the Allocation of Educational Control Between Parent and State,* 67 U. CHI. L. REV. 1233 (2000). For further consideration of the issues raised by home schooling, see Lerner, *Protecting Home Schooling through the* Casey *Undue Burden Standards,* 62 U. CHI. L. REV. 363 (1995) (applying undue burden standard from abortion rights context to state regulation of home schooling); Lupu, *Home Education, Religious Liberty, and the Separation of Powers,* 67 B.U.L. REV. 971 (1987) (arguing against home education statutes).

PROBLEM

Problem 10-1. The Johnsons are members of a religious sect that teaches, among other things, that the body is fundamentally sinful, with urges and pleasures that must be fought and overcome through an allegiance to God.

They object strongly to the instruction which their daughter, Mary, is scheduled to receive in her high school physical education class, which teaches that certain bodily urges are "healthy," and stresses the importance of having a positive self-image. The Johnsons consider these teachings heretical and likely to lead Mary to question her religious training. When they object to the high school principal, he seeks your advice on how to respond. The principal has no doubt about the sincerity of the Johnsons' objections. What do you advise him to do?

[2]   THE CHILD'S CLAIM OF AUTONOMY AGAINST PARENTAL AND STATE AUTHORITY

The legal regulation of children, for the most part, defines the boundary between parental and state authority. In Section B, we examine state intervention of abuse and neglect grounds, an important context in which the boundary is defined. Sometimes, however, parental authority over their child is contested by the child herself. In this section, we explore conflicts that arise when the child seeks autonomy against parents or the state. In these parent-child disputes, the parent or the child seeks either enforcement or invalidation of various statutory, constitutional or common law rights. In these disputes, constitutional claims by both parents and children are frequent. The legal tension common in these cases is between the child's liberty claims, the parents' interests in privacy and autonomy, and the state's interests in the child's welfare.

[a]   Claims of Independence by the Child from Parental Authority

In re WELFARE OF SNYDER

532 P.2d 278 (Wash. 1975)

HUNTER, Associate Justice. [Paul and Nell Snyder], petitioners, seek review of the . . . Juvenile Court's finding that their daughter, Cynthia Nell Snyder, respondent, was an incorrigible child. . . . The issue . . . is whether the juvenile court's determination is supported by substantial evidence.

Cynthia is 16 years old, attends high school, and has consistently received above average grades. . . . [A]s Cynthia entered her teen years, a hostility began to develop between herself and her parents. . . . Cynthia's parents, being strict disciplinarians, placed numerous limitations on their daughter's activities, such as restricting her choice of friends, and refusing to let her smoke, date, or participate in certain extra-curricular activities within the school, all of which caused Cynthia to rebel against their authority. These hostilities culminated in a total collapse of the parent-child relationship. . . .

On [June 18], Mr. Snyder . . . removed Cynthia from the family home and delivered her to the Youth Service Center. As a result, Cynthia was placed in a receiving home. On [July 19], . . . Cynthia filed a petition in the Juvenile

Department of the Superior Court . . . alleging that she was a dependent child as defined by RCW 13.04.010(2) and (3), which provide:

> "[D]ependent child" shall mean any child under the age of eighteen years: . . .
>
> (2) Who has no parent, guardian or other responsible person; or who has no parent or guardian willing to exercise, or capable of exercising, proper parental control; or
>
> (3) Whose home by reason of neglect, cruelty or depravity of his parents or either of them. . . . is an unfit place for such child; . . .

 . . . . On [October 12], the juvenile court held that the allegations attacking the fitness of Cynthia's parents were incorrect, at least to the extent that they alleged dependency, and that Cynthia should be returned to the custody of her parents. Cynthia did return to the family residence, where she remained until [November 16]. At that time, following additional confrontations in her home, Cynthia went to Youth Advocates, a group which assists troubled juveniles, who in turn directed her to the Youth Service Center. On November 21, 1973, Margaret Rozmyn, who was in charge of the intake program at the center, filed a petition alleging that Cynthia was incorrigible as defined under RCW 13.04.010(7), which provides:

> For the purpose of this chapter the words "dependent child" shall mean any child under the age of eighteen years: . . .
>
> (7) Who is incorrigible; that is, who is beyond the control and power of his parents, guardian, or custodian by reason of the conduct or nature of said child;. . . .

 . . . .

[O]n December 18,. . . . Commissioner Quinn, upon hearing the comments and conclusions of the counseling psychiatrists chosen by the parents, decided that Cynthia was to be placed in a foster home, under the supervision of the probation department of the juvenile court, and that she and her parents were to continue counseling, subject to subsequent review by the court. The parents immediately filed a motion for revision of the commissioner's decision, which was denied by the Superior Court . . . in August of 1974. . . .

The sole issue . . . is whether there is substantial evidence in the record . . . to support the juvenile court's determination. . . . Her parents contend that Cynthia is not incorrigible, as a matter of law, since the only evidence to support such a finding is their daughter's own statements. We disagree.

A child is incorrigible when she is beyond the power and control of her parents by reason of her own conduct. . . . [T]he issue of who is actually responsible for the breakdown in the parent-child relationship is irrelevant. . . . The issue is whether there is substantial evidence to support a finding that the parent-child relationship has dissipated to the point where parental control is lost and, therefore, Cynthia is incorrigible. It is for this reason that Cynthia's conduct, her state of mind, and the opinion of Doctor Gallagher, the psychiatrist chosen by Mr. and Mrs. Snyder, are of such paramount importance. This child has established a pattern of refusing to obey her parents and, on two occasions, has, in effect, fled her home by filing petitions in the juvenile court in order that she might be made a ward of the court. Cynthia's adamant state of mind can be best understood by considering her clear and unambiguous testimony in response to her attorney's direct examination. . . .

[In addition to the testimony of the parents and a sister, the court considered the testimony] of Dr. Gallagher, who met with Cynthia and her parents, and reported that counseling would not be beneficial until all of the individuals backed away from [their] hard and fast positions. . . .

It is implicit that the. . . .parents believe the juvenile court has given sympathy and support to Cynthia's problems in disregard of their rights . . ., and that the juvenile court has failed to assume its responsibility to assist in the resolution of the parents' problems with their minor child. We find this presumption . . . unsupported.

. . . [N]umerous attempts were made by the juvenile court commissioner to reconcile the family differences, as evidenced by its unsuccessful attempt at sending Cynthia home subsequent to the disposition of the first petition, the attempt to gain assistance through professional counseling, and the numerous and extensive exchanges between Commissioner Quinn and the Snyder family during the proceeding. The avenues for counseling were to remain open and counseling of both parties was to continue, which was interrupted by the interposition of the application by the parents for our review.

The decision . . . is affirmed.

NOTES

1. Court Intervention in the "Intact" Family. The threshold decision for the state to make when presented with a parent-child conflict is whether to intervene at all. If courts were generally available as a forum of appeal from parental authority, considerable time would be consumed deciding such issues as how late teenagers can stay out, whether they should be required to eat their vegetables and whether they can use the car. In addition to the judicial resources this would involve, such intervention would constitute a level of intrusion into family life that most would consider unacceptable. For this reason, the basic premise of the law is that within broad boundaries arranged to protect children from abusive or neglectful parents, courts deny relief to children challenging parental authority. However, this may not be true where parents can not exercise control or discipline over their children. In most states, the juvenile court has authority to intervene where children are "incorrigible," "beyond parental control" or "in need of supervision," even where there is no abuse or neglect. The cases usually involve children who run away from home, are truant, violate parental or legal curfews or other rules, or engage in drug or alcohol use. VA. CODE ANN. §§ 16.1-278.4–16.1-278.5(2003)(stating criteria for court intervention in situations where the child is either in need of supervision or services). As in *Snyder*, state intervention is often initiated by parents, frustrated at the child's resistance to their authority. What is unusual about *Snyder* is that ultimately, the parents changed their minds and the state supported the child in overriding parental authority.

Although Cynthia agreed with the state intervention in her case, courts generally have considerable authority to impose coercive restrictions on children who are beyond parental control. A Washington court upheld, against a constitutional challenge, a court order imposing geographic restrictions on the movement of an adolescent, after she was found to be an "at-risk youth" under Washington's Family Reconciliation Act. *In re M.G.*, 11 P.3d 335 (Wash. Ct. App. 2000). The order, requested by the girl's parents because she had repeatedly run away, shoplifted, drunk alcohol, violated their rules, and engaged in other self-destructive behavior, prohibited her from going into two districts of the city where she shoplifted and drank alcohol. The court concluded that her status as an at-risk youth justified applying a rational basis test to restrictions on her constitutional right to travel. The court then evaluated the curtailment of the girl's rights under the three-part test in *Bellotti v. Baird. See* Section A2c, *infra.* The court found that her past behavior demonstrated her vulnerability and inability to make good decisions and, thus, the first two *Bellotti* factors were satisfied. As to the third factor, the importance of the parental role, the court emphasized the importance of supporting parents who were struggling to protect their children's welfare.

2. *Consequences of Independence and the Legal Status of Emancipation.* Cynthia sought freedom from her parent's authority, and yet her goal was not to be independent. Under the juvenile court order, she received state support and supervision in foster care. A variant on this theme involves minors who want to be free of their parents' authority and yet seek to enlist the courts to enforce parents' obligation to provide financial support. Some courts have not been sympathetic to this kind of claim. In *Roe v. Doe*, for example, the New York Court of Appeals reversed a trial court decision ordering the father, a wealthy attorney, to pay support to his daughter who refused "to conform to his reasonable demands." 324 N.Y.S. 2d 71 (1971). The daughter, a college student in Kentucky who had moved into her own apartment, rejected her father's directive to either return to the dormitory or return home. In rejecting her petition for support, the court emphasized the right of parents to impose reasonable regulations on the child. For where the child abandons the home "to avoid parental discipline or restraint, [she] forfeits the claim to support." Where parents' regulations are not reasonable, however, they cannot escape their support obligation.

A more typical kind of case arises where either the child or the parent provides evidence that the child is self-supporting and capable of living on her own without adult care or supervision. In this situation, most states provide a mechanism by which a minor child can become "emancipated" from her parents. The legal consequence of emancipation is that the child acquires some rights and privileges of adulthood and that the parents no longer have custody of or the obligation to support the child. In fact, although a child seeking to escape parental authority can bring an emancipation action, it is far more typical for the issue to be litigated because a parent seeks to avoid a child support obligation where a claim is brought by a third party who provided services (such as medical treatment) to the child. *See* Chapter 5 for a discussion of emancipation in connection with child support at pp 453-54.

Traditionally, the common law found emancipation triggered by the minor's marriage, *e.g.*, *Meyer v. Meyer,* 493 S.W.2d 42 (Mo. App. 1973), military service, *e.g.*, *LaVoice v. LaVoice,* 214 A.2d 53 (Vt. 1965), or living apart from her parents, *e.g.*, *Town v. Anonymous,* 467 A.2d 687 (Conn. Super. Ct. 1983) (16-year-old daughter who had voluntarily left parents' home to live with putative father of her baby was emancipated); *see Holt v. Holt,* 633 S.W.2d 171 (Mo. App. 1982) (19-year-old son who had left home to live with others, retaining his monthly earnings of $900 emancipated); *but see In re Marriage of Robinson,* 601 P.2d 358 (Colo. App. 1979) (parents' financial obligations continue during child's temporary employment away from home) for a discussion of cases decided under common law emancipation principles.

Many states have now enacted statutes that prescribe the requirements and procedures for attaining emancipation. *See, e.g.*, CAL. FAM. CODE §§ 7001–7003 (West 1994); CONN. GEN. STAT. ANN. § 46(b)-150 (West Supp. 2003), §§ 46b-150b-e (West 1995); OR. REV. STAT. ANN. § 419B.558 (2003). Such statutes provide for a judicial declaration of emancipation on the traditional grounds, such as marriage and military service, and also where the minor "willingly lives separate and apart from his parents" and "is managing his own financial affairs." CONN. GEN. STAT. ANN. § 46b-150b (West Supp. 2003). In one Connecticut case, the court rejected the parents' claim that their 16-year-old son was emancipated despite the fact that he had lived away from home for many months and had dropped out of school. *In re Thomas C.,* 691 A.2d 1140 (Conn. Super. Ct. 1996). The boy lived at home at the time of the petition and was supported by the parents, who wanted to use the emancipation order as a "legal wake up call," to encourage more cooperative behavior. Each statute includes a list of the consequences of emancipation, making clear, for example, that the emancipated minor can consent to his own medical treatment, transfer interests in real property or enter into other binding contracts. *See, e.g., id.* at § 46b-150d. Nowhere are emancipated minors treated as adults for purposes such as voting or drinking.

Professors Carol Sanger and Eleanor Willemsen studied the emancipation process under the California statute. *See* Sanger and Willemsen, *Minor Changes: Emancipating Children in Modern Times,* 25 U. MICH. J. L. REFORM 239 (1992). The authors' findings suggest that the statute, enacted as a reform measure to remove legal disabilities from mature minors who were living independently, may fail to serve their interests. Although the process is technically initiated by the minor, emancipation was often urged upon the minor by parents in situations of family conflict. The process itself was simple and quick, requiring no waiting period, counseling, or investigation. The authors found that, in cases involving parental consent, judges take the parents' signature as a proxy for a best interest determination and rubber stamp the petition. They also found that many emancipated minors were not employed or in school. The authors concluded that emancipation under the California statute operates as an unsupervised out-of-home placement for children in dysfunctional families and that it may serve parents' interest rather than the interests of the affected children.

What legal responses could ameliorate the problems that Sanger and Willemsen identify? Is emancipation simply a bad idea for most adolescents, who need the legal protection that minority status confers? On this question, consider the materials in the following section.

3. _Can Children "Divorce" Their Parents?_ Cynthia Snyder clearly was
not emancipated under either traditional rules or those of the recent statutes.
Nor did her parents' behavior constitute abuse or neglect under ordinary
standards, even though they may have been unusually strict in their demands.
Why then did the court intervene, in effect liberating the girl from parental
authority? _Snyder_ concludes that the daughter's attitude toward her parents
had become so negative that she was "incorrigible" and that the statute did
not require either parental assent or a finding of parental fault. As thus
applied, the statute seems to offer the child an option of "divorce" from the
parents, a result probably not intended by the legislature. Should the state
intervene in family to allow adolescents to "divorce" their parents simply
because they object to their discipline? Perhaps only adolescents who can be
self-sufficient should be allowed to challenge parental authority in this way
— by bringing an emancipation petition. Remember that after the decision,
Cynthia's support was assumed by society. For a criticism of _Snyder_ as being
out of step with the law's traditional deference to the authority of fit parents,
see Hafen, _Children's Liberation and the New Egalitarianism: Some Reservations About Abandoning Youth to Their Rights,_ 1976 B.Y.U. L. REV. 605.

In a more recent Florida case that received a great deal of media attention,
11-year-old Gregory Kingsley brought an action to terminate the parental
rights of his biological mother. Gregory's foster parents were eager to adopt
him and, initially, the state Department of Health and Rehabilitative Services
(HRS) was reluctant to proceed. With the encouragement of his foster father,
who later became the boy's attorney of record, Gregory petitioned to terminate
his mother's parental rights, and also filed an adoption petition. Other
petitions to terminate his mother's parental rights were later filed by his
guardian ad litem, HRS, and his foster parents. Gregory claimed a fundamental liberty interest in freedom from abuse and neglect. The trial court ruled
that Gregory had standing to bring an action to terminate parental rights on
his own behalf. The appellate court, _Kingsley v. Kingsley,_ 623 So. 2d 780 (Fla.
App. 1993), held that unemancipated minors lack the capacity to initiate legal
proceedings in their own names, but upheld the termination of parental rights
on the basis of abandonment. The trial court's error regarding Gregory's
standing to sue was found to be harmless, in light of the petitions filed on
his behalf. Chief Judge Harris, dissenting in part, strongly argued against
the suggestion in an amicus brief that the child's right to be free of abuse or
neglect gave the child a right to participate in the decision about who will
raise him. _Id._ at 790 n.2. He emphasized, "Florida recognizes no cause of action
that permits a child to divorce his parents . . . [T]here is no right to change
parents simply because the child finds substitutes he . . .likes better or who
can provide a better standard of living." _Id._ at 790. The dissenting judge
described the filing of the petition by Gregory as an "artful maneuver" by his
attorneys. _Id._ at 791.

PROBLEMS

Problem 10-2. Ozzie and Harriet seek your advice on controlling their 14-
year-old son, Bruno. Although he has never gotten into legal trouble, they
consider him somewhat unruly and undisciplined, and therefore decided to

send him to a private military academy instead of the public school. For the second time now, however, Bruno has stayed away from home in order to avoid going to the school. On the last occasion, he stayed with his Aunt Happy for five days and attempted to attend public school again, but the Aunt sent him home when the parents insisted. This time, he has been with Aunt Happy for two days, and she seems reluctant to force him out. She keeps urging Ozzie and Harriet to come talk to him and work out some compromise. They are confident that they have made the correct decision about schooling, however, and have no interest in negotiating with their son. They want to know whether the law might be of any assistance to them. You've known Ozzie and Harriet for some time now, and they seem to you like concerned, caring people, although strict and somewhat rigid. What do you advise?

Problem 10-3. Bob and Anna Manson have come to you for advice about their options for responding what they view as a crisis involving their 22-year-old daughter, Elizabeth. Elizabeth, who has always had emotional problems, graduated from college and was at loose ends about what to do with her life when she became involved with what the Mansons feel is a religious cult. The leader, who calls himself "the Holy One," demands extraordinary discipline and absolute obedience to his commands by his followers. The group lives together in an ashram and follow a rigid schedule of programmed communal mediation, lectures, rituals, meals and work from early morning until late night. Elizabeth has hardly seen her parents since she moved into the ashram. They saw her last week and were shocked by the transformation. Their daughter told them that she had renounced all her former relationships and that they were no longer her parents. She had dedicated her life to achieving purity by following the Holy One. The Mansons believe that Elizabeth has been brainwashed. They have consulted a de-programmer who has promised them that he can assist them to "bring back" their daughter, through an intervention that requires that she be confined for a week in a treatment center. What do you advise the Mansons?

[b]   Minors' Objection to Parental Medical Decisions — The Case of Psychiatric Hospitalization

NOTES

1. *The Constitutional Framework* — Parham v. J.R., 442 U.S. 584 (1978). Parents can make most medical decisions for their child over the child's objection. Does a child ever have the right to resist medical treatment which the parents wish him or her to have? The Supreme Court addressed this question in *Parham v. J.R.*, a class action suit challenging Georgia's procedures for commitment of minors to state psychiatric hospitals. Under Georgia law, parents could "voluntarily" admit their minor child to a state psychiatric hospital over the child's objection, if the hospital administrator found "evidence of mental illness" and that the child was "suitable for treatment." The Court in *Parham* acknowledged that this parental decision differs from more routine health care decisions because the child has a liberty interest in the decision that is protected under the Due Process clause of the Fourteenth Amendment. The Court upheld the Georgia statute against a due process challenge, however, finding the statutory procedures adequate to protect against an erroneous decision to commit. (The requirements included a "neutral factfinder" to determine that the statutory requirements for commitment were met and periodic review of the decision). The Court concluded that the factfinder could be a "neutral physician," not connected with the child's treatment, and that no adversary hearing was needed.

In determining the required level of due process, the Court balanced the interest of the parent seeking hospital admission, that of the child desiring to avoid erroneous admission, and the state's interests in promoting the mental health of children and in appropriate use of mental health facilities. The opinion emphasized the long historical tradition in Western civilization favoring parental authority over their children and the sound presumption that parents usually act in their child's interest. The Court discounted the plaintiffs' objection that parents might have a conflict of interest in this situation, and that their decision might be an effort to rid the family of a difficult child. It also downplayed the stigma attached to psychiatric hospitalization, suggesting that the child was more likely to be stigmatized by untreated mental illness. Finally, the Court concluded that state facilities would have no reason to treat children who were not in need of hospitalization. In balancing these interests, the Court analyzed the risks of full adversary pre-commitment hearings:

> [A] problem with requiring a formalized factfinding hearing lies in the danger it poses for significant intrusion into the parent-child relationship. Pitting the parents and child as adversaries often will be at odds with the presumption that parents act in the best interests of their child. It is one thing to require a neutral physician to make a careful review of the parents' decision; it is a wholly different matter to employ an adversary contest to ascertain whether the parents' motivation is consistent with the child's interests.
>
> Moreover, it is appropriate to inquire into how such a hearing would contribute to the successful long-range treatment of the patient. Surely, there is a risk that it would exacerbate whatever tensions already exist between the child and the parents. Since the parents can and usually do play a significant role in the treatment while the child is hospitalized and even more so after release, there is a serious risk that an adversary confrontation will adversely affect the ability of the parents to assist the child while in the hospital. . . .

442 U.S. at 610.

2. *Criticism of* Parham. *Parham* has been criticized on several grounds. The most important challenge has been directed at the Court's assumption that parents who seek to admit their children to psychiatric facilities seldom have a conflict of interest. A description of the *Parham* plaintiffs suggests why critics are skeptical. J.L. was admitted to the hospital at age 6 by his mother and stepfather (his parents were divorced) after being expelled from school because he was aggressive and uncontrollable. Because of his erratic disruptive behavior, efforts to return him to his family were unsuccessful and stressful for the family; ultimately his parents relinquished parental rights. J.R. was in state custody at the time he was admitted to the hospital (and had not lived with his parents for many years). Thus no parent was available to look out for his interest, even if the Court's assumptions about parents as decisionmakers in this context were accurate.

Researchers have indicated that children and adolescents in psychiatric hospitals generally do not suffer from the severe mental disorders of institutionalized adults. Lois Weithorn points out that most juveniles admitted to psychiatric facilities manifest conduct or personality disorders or have psychological adjustment problems associated with normal development. Many, like J.L., are troublemakers whose conduct is disruptive to family harmony. Weithorn points out that the youthful behavior that leads parents to admit their children to psychiatric hospitals is often indistinguishable from that dealt with by the juvenile justice system. Weithorn, *Mental Hospitalization of Troublesome Youth: An Analysis of Skyrocketing Admission Rates*, 40 STANFORD L. REV. 773, 788–91 (1988).

Critics of *Parham* and of policies that permit parents to admit their children to psychiatric facilities without an adversary proceeding do not argue that children who are admitted by their parents are not in need of any treatment, but rather that hospitalization is often an inappropriate intervention, because it severely disrupts the child's life, is stigmatic, restrictive, and often ineffective. Weithorn, among others, argues that community-based interventions, particularly those that allow the child to remain in the family, are less disruptive and more effective than hospitalization. *Id.* at 792–98. Parents may choose psychiatric hospitalization because community programs are not available, or because reimbursement is inadequate or unavailable. Medical insurance policies tend to provide a strong incentive to choose inpatient psychiatric treatment over other options, because outpatient treatment usually receives minimal coverage. *Id.* at 814–15.

3. *Statutory and Judicial Regulation of Psychiatric Hospitalization.* Some statutes provide greater procedural protection of minors whose parents seek psychiatric hospitalization than the *Parham* Court found to be constitutionally required. For example, in Virginia, parents can voluntarily admit their child who is under the age of 14 to a psychiatric facility, but if a minor who is 14 or older objects to commitment, she is entitled to a hearing, at which she is appointed a guardian *ad litem* and the court evaluates whether the commitment is in her best interest. VA. CODE ANN. §§ 16.1-335 *et. seq.* (2003). The standard for the involuntary commitment of minors under the statute is somewhat broader than the involuntary commitment standard applied to adults. *See id.* at § 16.1-345(1). The Virginia statute extends the procedural requirements to private hospitals, which many critics believe are highly motivated to fill beds, and may admit minors where hospitalization is inappropriate. *See* Weithorn, *supra* at 818–20. In other states, parental admission to private hospitals is subject to little regulation.

The Florida Supreme Court recently addressed the issue of what procedural requirements apply to admission to residential treatment facilities of children who have been adjudicated dependent and are in state custody. *M.W. v. Davis*, 756 So. 2d 90 (Fla. 2000). The case involved a 15-year-old with a history of psychiatric illness; the involved mental health experts disagreed about his placement, with some advocating therapeutic foster care. The court concluded that the statutory procedures for involuntary commitment were not required in this situation, and that the decision of the judge for a temporary placement with no evidentiary hearing, based on knowledge of the case and experts' reports, met the constitutional due process requirements of *Parham*.

For commentary on *Parham*, compare Watson, *Children, Families and Courts: Before the Best Interests of the Child and* Parham v. J.R., 66 Va. L. Rev. 653 (1980) (arguing that parents should be able to commit their children without fear that their judgments will be countermanded), with Note, *The Supreme Court, 1978 Term,* 93 Harv. L. Rev. 60, 93–94, 97–98 (1979) (arguing that given the curtailment of liberty at issue, *Parham* provides too few procedural safeguards).

PROBLEM

Problem 10-4. Jessica and Harrison are the parents of 14-year-old Laura, who lately has been causing them a great deal of concern. She no longer sees her old friends, her grades have plummeted, and she spends a lot of time lying on her bed listening to music. When she emerges from her room, Laura, who was a very cheerful pleasant child until recently, snarls at her parents and starts fights with Sam, her brother. The few friends who come by to see Laura seem to be fringe types who she would not have associated with a year ago. Lately, Laura has stayed out all night a couple of times, and refused to tell her parents where she was. The household has been in a continuous uproar for months, and Jessica and Harrison are desperate. Jessica took Laura to a psychiatrist, who after talking to Laura for an hour, told Jessica that her daughter was very depressed, and needed to be hospitalized. Laura is vehemently opposed and refuses to consent to hospitalization. Jessica and Harrison consult you seeking legal advice.

[c]　The Child's Claim of Reproductive Privacy and Regulation of Sexuality

[i]　Minor's Independent Access to Abortion

BELLOTTI v. BAIRD (II)

443 U.S. 622 (1979)

[Massachusetts enacted the following statute:]

If the mother is less than eighteen years of age and has not married, the consent of both the mother and her parents [to an abortion to be performed on the mother] is required. If one or both of the mother's parents refuse such consent, consent may be obtained by order of a judge of the superior court for good cause shown, after such hearing as he deems necessary. . . .

[After a federal court found the statute to be unconstitutional, the Supreme Court ordered the district court to abstain and to certify questions to the Massachusetts Supreme Judicial Court to ascertain the statute's precise meaning [*Bellotti v. Baird I*, 428 U.S. 132 (1976)]. The Massachusetts court's response was paraphrased by the United States Supreme Court as follows:]

1. In deciding whether to grant consent to their daughter's abortion, parents are required . . . to consider exclusively what will serve her best interests.

2. The provision . . . that judicial consent for an abortion shall be granted, parental objections notwithstanding, "for good cause shown" means that such consent shall be granted if found to be in the minor's best interests. . . .

3. Even if the judge . . . finds "that the minor is capable of making, and has made, an informed and reasonable decision to have an abortion," he is entitled to withhold consent "in circumstances where he determines that the best interests of the minor will not be served by an abortion."

4. As a general rule, a minor who desires an abortion may not obtain judicial consent without first seeking both parents' consent. Exceptions to the rule exist when a parent is not available or when the need for the abortion constitutes "an emergency requiring immediate action." Unless a parent is not available, he must be notified of any judicial proceedings brought [under the statute].

5. The resolution of . . . cases and any appeals that follow can be expected to be prompt. The name of the minor and her parents may be held in confidence. . . .

6. [The state statute which provides] that certain classes of minors may consent to most kinds of medical care without parental approval, does not apply to abortions, except as to minors who are married, widowed, or divorced. Nor does the State's common-law "mature minor rule" create an exception to [the abortion statute].

[After the federal district court declared the statute to be unconstitutional in light of the state court interpretation, the state appealed to the Supreme Court.]

MR. JUSTICE POWELL announced the judgment of the Court and delivered an opinion, in which THE CHIEF JUSTICE, MR. JUSTICE STEWART, and MR. JUSTICE REHNQUIST joined. . . .

. . . .

II

A child, merely on account of his minority, is not beyond the protection of the Constitution. . . . This observation, of course, is but the beginning of the analysis. . . . We have recognized three reasons justifying the conclusion that the constitutional rights of children cannot be equated with those of adults: the peculiar vulnerability of children; their inability to make critical decisions in an informed, mature manner; and the importance of the parental role in child rearing. . . .

A

The Court's concern for the vulnerability of children is demonstrated in its decisions dealing with minors' claims to constitutional protection against deprivations of liberty or property interests by the State. With respect to many of these claims, we have concluded that the child's right is virtually coextensive with that of an adult. For example, the Court has held that the Fourteenth Amendment's guarantee against the deprivation of liberty without due process of law is applicable to children in juvenile delinquency proceedings. . . .

These rulings have not been made on the uncritical assumption that the constitutional rights of children are indistinguishable from those of adults. . . . Viewed together, our cases show that although children generally are protected by the same constitutional guarantees against governmental deprivations as are adults, the State is entitled to adjust its legal system to account for children's vulnerability and their needs for "concern, . . . sympathy, and . . . paternal attention."

B

Second, the Court has held that the States validly may limit the freedom of children to choose for themselves in the making of important, affirmative choices with potentially serious consequences. These rulings have been grounded in the recognition that, during the formative years of childhood and adolescence, minors often lack the experience, perspective, and judgment to recognize and avoid choices that could be detrimental to them. . . .

C

Third, the guiding role of parents in the upbringing of their children justifies limitations on the freedoms of minors. The State commonly protects its youth from adverse governmental action and from their own immaturity by requiring parental consent to or involvement in important decisions by minors. But an additional and more important justification for state deference to parental control over children is that "[t]he child is not the mere creature of the State; those who nurture him and direct his destiny have the right, coupled with the high duty, to recognize and prepare him for additional obligations." *Pierce v. Society of Sisters*, 268 U.S. 510 (1925). . . . Thus, "[i]t is cardinal with us that the custody, care and nurture of the child reside first in the parents, whose primary function and freedom include *preparation for obligations the state can neither supply nor hinder.*" *Prince v. Massachusetts, supra*, 321 U.S. at 166, (emphasis added). . . .

Properly understood, then, the tradition of parental authority is not inconsistent with our tradition of individual liberty; rather, the former is one of the basic presuppositions of the latter. Legal restrictions on minors, especially those supportive of the parental role, may be important to the child's chances for the full growth and maturity that make eventual participation in a free society meaningful and rewarding. Under the Constitution, the State can "properly conclude that parents and others, teachers for example, who have [the] primary responsibility for children's well-being are entitled to the support of laws designed to aid discharge of that responsibility." *Ginsberg v. New York*, 390 U.S. at 639.

III

The question before us . . . is whether [the statute], as authoritatively interpreted by the Supreme Judicial Court, provides for parental notice and consent in a manner that does not unduly burden the right to seek an abortion. . . . [P]arental notice and consent are qualifications that typically may be imposed by the State on a minor's right to make important decisions. As immature minors often lack the ability to make fully informed choices that take account of both immediate and long-range consequences, a State reasonably may determine that parental consultation often is desirable and in the best interest of the minor. It may further determine, as a general proposition, that such consultation is particularly desirable with respect to the abortion decision — one that for some people raises profound moral and religious concerns. . . .

But we are concerned here with a constitutional right to seek an abortion. The abortion decision differs in important ways from other decisions that may be made during minority. The need to preserve the constitutional right and the unique nature of the abortion decision, especially when made by a minor, require a State to act with particular sensitivity when it legislates to foster parental involvement in this matter.

A

The pregnant minor's options are much different from those facing a minor in other situations, such as deciding whether to marry. A minor not permitted to marry before the age of majority is required simply to postpone her decision. She and her intended spouse may preserve the opportunity for later marriage should they continue to desire it. A pregnant adolescent, however, cannot preserve for long the possibility of aborting, which effectively expires in a matter of weeks from the onset of pregnancy.

Moreover, the potentially severe detriment facing a pregnant woman . . . is not mitigated by her minority. Indeed, considering her probable education, employment skills, financial resources, and emotional maturity, unwanted motherhood may be exceptionally burdensome for a minor. In addition, the fact of having a child brings with it adult legal responsibility, for parenthood, like attainment of the age of majority, is one of the traditional criteria for the termination of the legal disabilities of minority. In sum, there are few situations in which denying a minor the right to make an important decision will have consequences so grave and indelible. . . .

For these reasons, as we held in *Danforth*, "the State may not impose a blanket provision . . . requiring the consent of a parent or person *in loco parentis* as a condition for abortion of an unmarried minor during the first 12 weeks of her pregnancy." [*Planned Parenthood of Central Missouri v. Danforth,* 428 U.S. 52,] at 74 (1976). Although such deference to parents may be permissible with respect to other choices facing a minor, the unique nature and consequences of the abortion decision make it inappropriate "to give a third party an absolute, and possibly arbitrary, veto over the decision of the physician and his patient to terminate the patient's pregnancy, regardless of the reason for withholding the consent." 428 U.S. at 74. We therefore conclude that if the State decides to require a pregnant minor to obtain one or both parents' consent to an abortion, it also must provide an alternative procedure[22] whereby authorization for the abortion can be obtained.

A pregnant minor is entitled in such a proceeding to show either: (1) that she is mature enough and well enough informed to make her abortion decision, in consultation with her physician, independently of her parents' wishes; or (2) that even if she is not able to make this decision independently, the desired abortion would be in her best interests. The proceeding in which this showing is made must assure that a resolution of the issue, and any appeals that may follow, will be completed with anonymity and sufficient expedition to provide an effective opportunity for an abortion to be obtained. In sum, the procedure must ensure that the provision requiring parental consent does not in fact amount to the "absolute; and possibly arbitrary, veto" that was found impermissible in *Danforth*.

B

. . . [A]s authoritatively construed by the highest court of the State, the statute satisfies some of the concerns that require special treatment of a minor's abortion decision. It provides that if parental consent is refused, authorization may be "obtained by order of a judge of the superior court for good cause shown, after such hearing as he deems necessary." A superior court judge "must disregard all parental objections, and other considerations, which are not based exclusively on what would serve the minor's best interests." The Supreme Judicial Court also stated: "Prompt resolution of a proceeding may be expected. . . . The proceeding need not be brought in the minor's name and steps may be taken, by impoundment or otherwise, to preserve confidentiality as to the minor and her parents. . . . [W]e believe that an early hearing and decision on appeal from a judgment of a Superior Court judge may also be achieved." The court added that if these expectations were not met, either the superior court in the exercise of its rulemaking power, or the Supreme Judicial Court would be willing to eliminate any undue burdens by rule or order.

Despite these safeguards,. . . . [the statute] falls short of constitutional standards in certain respects. We now consider these.

(1)

Among the questions certified . . . was whether [the statute] permits any minors — mature or immature — to obtain judicial consent to an abortion

---

[22] As [the statute] provides for involvement of the state superior court in minors' abortion decisions, we discuss the alternative procedure described in the text in terms of judicial proceedings. We do not suggest, however, that a State choosing to require parental consent could not delegate the alternative procedure to a juvenile court or an administrative agency or officer. Indeed, much can be said for employing procedures and a forum less formal than those associated with a court of general jurisdiction.

without any parental consultation whatsoever. The state court answered that in general, it does not. . . .

We think that, construed in this manner, [the statute] would impose an undue burden upon the exercise by minors of the right to seek an abortion. As the District Court recognized, "there are parents who would obstruct, and perhaps altogether prevent, the minor's right to go to court." There is no reason to believe that this would be so in the majority of cases where consent is withheld. But many parents hold strong views on the subject of abortion, and young pregnant minors, especially those living at home, are particularly vulnerable to their parents' efforts to obstruct both an abortion and their access to court. It would be unrealistic, therefore, to assume that the mere existence of a legal right to seek relief in superior court provides an effective avenue of relief for some of those who need it the most.

We conclude, therefore, that under state regulation such as that undertaken by Massachusetts, every minor must have the opportunity — if she so desires — to go directly to a court without first consulting or notifying her parents. If she satisfies the court that she is mature and well enough informed to make intelligently the abortion decision on her own, the court must authorize her to act without parental consultation or consent. If she fails to satisfy the court that she is competent to make this decision independently, she must be permitted to show that an abortion nevertheless would be in her best interests. If the court is persuaded that it is, the court must authorize the abortion. If, however, the court is not persuaded by the minor that she is mature or that the abortion would be in her best interests, it may decline to sanction the operation.

There is, however, an important state interest in encouraging a family rather than a judicial resolution of a minor's abortion decision. Also, as we have observed above, parents naturally take an interest in the welfare of their children — an interest that is particularly strong where a normal family relationship exists and where the child is living with one or both parents. These factors properly may be taken into account by a court called upon to determine whether an abortion in fact is in a minor's best interests. If, all things considered, the court determines that an abortion is in the minor's best interests, she is entitled to court authorization without any parental involvement. On the other hand, the court may deny the abortion request of an immature minor in the absence of parental consultation if it concludes that her best interests would be served thereby, or the court may in such a case defer decision until there is parental consultation in which the court may participate. But this is the full extent to which parental involvement may be required. For the reasons stated above, the constitutional right to seek an abortion may not be unduly burdened by state-imposed conditions upon initial access to court. . . .

IV

Although it satisfies constitutional standards in large part, [the statute] falls short of them in two respects: First, it permits judicial authorization for an abortion to be withheld from a minor who is found by the superior court to be mature and fully competent to make this decision independently. Second, it requires parental consultation or notification in every instance, without affording the pregnant minor an opportunity to receive an independent judicial determination that she is mature enough to consent or that an abortion would be in her best interests. Accordingly, we affirm the judgment of the District Court insofar as it invalidates this statute and enjoins its enforcement.

. . . .

[Justice Stevens, joined by Justices Brennan, Marshall, and Blackmun, concurred in the judgment, on the ground that the Massachusetts statute was unconstitutional under the Court's earlier holding in *Planned Parenthood of Central Missouri v. Danforth* (428 U.S. 52 (1976)). Justice Stevens emphasized that, in striking down the Missouri statute, the Court had stated:

> "[T]he State does not have the constitutional authority to give a third party an absolute, and possibly arbitrary, veto over the decision of the physician and his patient to terminate the patient's pregnancy, regardless of the reason for withholding the consent." *Id.* at 74, 96 S. Ct. at 2843.

In Justice Stevens' view, the Massachusetts statute, as interpreted by the state Supreme Court, gave an absolute veto over the minor's abortion decision to either her parents or a judge. Thus, it imposed at least as great a burden as did the Missouri law, and was unconstitutional under *Danforth*.]

NOTES

1. *Massachusetts Law after* Bellotti. After *Bellotti*, Massachusetts, following Justice Powell's suggestions, enacted a statute requiring the judge to make a threshold decision about the maturity of the minor seeking abortion, and then address the abortion question only for those minors found to lack the maturity to make the decision herself. *See Planned Parenthood v. Bellotti*, 641 F.2d 1006 (1st Cir. 1981)(denying preliminary injunction against the new statute based on a finding that it satisfied the Supreme Court's directions in *Bellotti*). Professor Robert Mnookin studied the implementation of the statute and reported the following:

> Every pregnant minor who has sought judicial authorization for an abortion has secured an abortion. Between April 1981, when the statute first went into effect and February 1983, approximately 1,300 pregnant minors sought judicial authorization. In about 90 percent of these cases, the Superior Court simply found the minor was "mature" and therefore allowed her to decide for herself. Where the judge concluded the girl was not mature, the court found the abortion to be in her best interest in all but five cases. But even in these five, the girl secured an abortion. In three. . . .instances, when the Superior Court judge initially refused to authorize the abortion, the minor simply went to a neighboring state for the abortion rather than appeal the decision.
>
> What is the explanation for this rather surprising result? Justice Powell's opinion presumed there would be individualized determina-

tions about whether a young woman should have an abortion. Moreover, most of the Superior Court judges were white middle class males, many of whom were morally opposed to abortion. . . .

The basic explanation . . . is that the superior court judges realize that it would be impossible as a legal proposition to justify a finding that a pregnant minor was too immature to decide whether to have an abortion for herself, but that it was in her best interests to bear the child. "There is no way you could substantiate such a decision," John J. Irwin, Jr., a judge who strongly opposes abortion, told the Boston Globe. "I can't see any abortion that wouldn't be ordered or sanctioned by the courts under this law." In the words of another Superior Court judge who indicated that he once gave permission for an abortion to an eleven-year-old, "[t]he law puts judges in the ridiculous position of being rubber stamps."

Mnookin, *Bellotti v. Baird: A Hard Case,* in IN THE INTEREST OF CHILDREN 239–40 (R. Mnookin ed. 1985).

2. *Parental Consent Provisions.* Since *Bellotti,* the adequacy of by-pass procedures under various parental consent statutes has been reviewed by courts with mixed results. A federal appeals court approved the district court's rejection of parents' battery claim against an abortion clinic for performing an abortion on their daughter without their consent, as required under Tennessee's Parental Consent Act. *Blackard v. Memphis Area Medical Center for Women, Inc.,* 262 F. 3d 568 (6th Cir. 2001), *cert. denied,* 535 U.S. 1053 (2002). Because the statute had been enjoined, at the time of the minor's abortion, no adequate by-pass procedure existed to consider her petition for waiver of consent. Under *Bellotti,* the court concluded, the state can require parental consent, but only if it provides a judicial by-pass procedure, under which the minor can get judicial consent. *See also City of Akron v. Akron Center for Reproductive Health, Inc.,* 462 U.S. 416 (1983)(no alternative judicial procedure explicitly provided and Court refused to construe the ordinance as providing one); *American College of Obstetricians v. Thornburgh,* 737 F.2d 283 (3d Cir. 1984) (enjoining parental consent statutes pending clarifying state regulations concerning the judicial consent procedure). *But see Planned Parenthood v. Ashcroft,* 462 U.S. 476 (1983) (upholding statute that requires consent of one parent, interpreting it to require by-pass hearing with *Bellotti* maturity and best interest evaluation). *See Planned Parenthood of Southern Arizona v. Lawall,* 307 F.3d 783 (9th Cir. 2002) (upholding Arizona consent statute as requiring reasonable efforts to protect minor's anonymity (a *Bellotti II* requirement), despite disclosure of minor's identity by court employee). An earlier Arizona statute had been found unconstitutional by the same federal appellate court on vagueness grounds. *Planned Parenthood of Southern Arizona v. Lawall,* 193 F.3d 1042 (9th Cir. 1999).

3. *Parental Notification Statutes.* Some states have not required parental consent when minors seek abortion, but rather have established parental notification requirements. The first Supreme Court opinion confronting the issue was *H.L. v. Matheson,* 450 U.S. 398 (1981). At issue in *Matheson* was a Utah statute (UTAH CODE ANN. § 76-7-304 (1974)), requiring a physician to "notify, if possible" the parents of a "dependent, unmarried, minor girl" prior to performing an abortion on the girl. In an opinion by Chief Justice Burger, the Supreme Court upheld the statute against constitutional attack. The Court emphasized that it was not deciding the constitutionality of the statute as applied to mature minors:

> The Utah statute gives neither parents nor judges a veto power over the minor's abortion decision. . . . As applied to immature and dependent minors, the statute plainly serves the important considerations of family integrity and protecting adolescents which we identified in *Bellotti II*. In addition, as applied to that class, the statute serves a significant state interest by providing an opportunity for parents to supply essential medical and other information to a physician. . . .

> . . . The Utah statute is reasonably calculated to protect minors in appellant's class by enhancing the potential for parental consultation concerning a decision that has potentially traumatic and permanent consequences.

> Appellant . . . contends that the constitutionality of the statute is undermined because Utah allows a pregnant minor to consent to other medical procedures without formal notice to her parents if she carries the child to term. But a State's interests in full-term pregnancies are sufficiently different to justify the line drawn by the statutes. If the pregnant girl elects to carry her child to term, the *medical* decisions to be made entail few — perhaps none — of the potentially grave emotional and psychological consequences of the decision to abort.

> That the requirement of notice to parents may inhibit some minors from seeking abortions is not a valid basis to void the statute as applied to appellant. . . . The Constitution does not compel a State to fine-tune its statutes so as to encourage or facilitate abortions. To the contrary, state action "encouraging child-birth except in the most urgent circumstances" is "rationally related to the legitimate governmental objective of protecting potential life." *Harris v. McRae*, (448 U.S. 297 (1980)). . . .

Justice Marshall, in a dissent joined by Justices Brennan and Blackmun found that the notice requirement burdened the young woman's abortion decision. Although, in the ideal family, a pregnant minor may seek the advice and support of her parents, the dissenting Justices asserted that "many families do not conform to this ideal." . . .

> Many minor women will encounter interference from their parents after the state-imposed notification. In addition to parental disappointment and disapproval, the minor may confront physical or emotional abuse, withdrawal of financial support, or actual obstruction of the abortion decision. Furthermore, the threat of parental notice may cause some minor women to delay past the first trimester of pregnancy, after which the health risks increase significantly. Other pregnant minors may attempt to self-abort or to obtain an illegal abortion rather than risk parental notification. Still others may forsake an abortion and bear an unwanted child, which, given the

minor's "probable education, employment skills, financial resources and emotional resources, . . . may be exceptionally burdensome." *Bellotti II*, 443 U.S. at 642 (Powell, J.). The possibility that such problems may not occur in particular cases does not alter the hardship created by the notice requirement on its face. And that hardship is not a mere disincentive created by the State, but is instead an actual state-imposed obstacle to the exercise of the minor woman's free choice. For the class of pregnant minors represented by appellant, this obstacle is so onerous as to bar the desired abortions. Significantly, the interference sanctioned by the statute does not operate in a neutral fashion. No notice is required for any pregnancy-related medical care. . . .

The dissenting Justices also rejected the state's claim that the notice requirement furthered a "significant state interest," and thus should survive constitutional challenge. The state claimed that the notice requirement permits the parents to provide the physician with medical information, encourages consultation between the parents and the minor woman, and preserves parental rights. Justice Marshall pointed out that since the statutory requirement could be satisfied by a letter or a brief phone call by the physician moments before the operation, it did not promote the transfer of information by the parents. Further, the claim that parental consultation is an important state interest is undermined by the fact that the statute allows minors to consent to other pregnancy-related treatment, including the surgical procedure of caesarian delivery, without notice to their parents. The dissent also challenged the state's claim that the notice requirement protects parental authority and family privacy, recalling the Court's words three years before in *Danforth* (above).

One unresolved issue is whether notification statutes, like consent statutes, must include a judicial by-pass procedure to evaluate maturity and best interest. The statutes that have been reviewed since *H.L. v. Matheson* include such procedures, and legislatures and courts assume that they are required. In *Hodgson v. Minnesota*, 497 U.S. 417 (1990), a splintered (and confusing) five-four decision delivered in part by Justice Stevens, the Supreme Court upheld a Minnesota statute requiring that a minor wait forty-eight hours after both parents have been notified before obtaining an abortion. MINN. STAT. § 144.343(2)–(7) (1988). Other than in emergency situations, the statutory notice and waiting period are mandatory unless the young woman declares herself to be the victim of parental abuse, in which case notice to the proper authorities is required. The Court concluded that the waiting period "would reasonably further the legitimate state interest in ensuring that the minor's decision is knowing and intelligent." A majority of the Justices found the requirement that *both* parents be notified to be an unconstitutional burden on the minor's right to obtain an abortion, which could inflict harm on the pregnant minor when the parents are divorced or the family is otherwise dysfunctional. However, even this requirement was upheld, because Justice O'Connor, who agreed that the two-parent consent requirement was unconstitutional, sided with the four other Justices who found the statute to be constitutional, because she determined that her constitutional objection to the two parent notice requirement was removed by the judicial by-pass procedure which allowed the minor to avoid notifying one or both parents. *See also Lambert v. Wicklund*, 520 U.S. 292 (1997) (upholding provision that parental notice requirement could be waived if notice was not in the petitioner's best interest, as not impermissively narrow).

Since *Hodgson*, lower federal appellate courts have evaluated parental notification procedures. The Tenth Circuit Court of Appeals recently struck down a Colorado notification statute that provided very narrow exceptions to the requirements that parents be notified and required the abortion only be performed after a 48 hour delay. *Planned Parenthood of the Rocky Mountains Services Corp. v. Owens,* 287 F.3d 910 (10th Cir. 2002). The Court found that the statutory exception — that an abortion could be performed without notice or delay if it was necessary to prevent the minor's imminent death and there was insufficient time to provide notification — was too narrow, because it did not allow a physician to perform an abortion when necessary to protect the health of the minor. The court found that such an exception was constitutionally required under earlier Supreme Court precedent requiring an emergency health exception to restrictive state regulation of abortion. Another federal court upheld a Virginia notification statute that included a by pass proceeding and several exceptions, but appeared to give judges discretion to require parental notice even if the minor was found to be mature. *Planned Parenthood of the Blue Ridge v. Camblos* 116 F.3d. 707 (4th Cir. 1997)(3). In 2003, Virginia amended the statute to require notice to parents of mature minors, unless the court determined that notice would not be in the minor's interest. 2003 VA. ACTS CH. 0960.

Research supports the concerns of those who think a notification requirement may impose a substantial burden on some pregnant minors. In fact, most minors consult with their parents voluntarily. In one study, about 60% of minors reported that they told their parents about the abortion. Henshaw & Kost, *Parental Involvement in Minors' Abortion Decisions,* 21 FAM. PLANNING PERSPECTIVES 85 (1992). Of those who did not, 30% said that they feared that they would be kicked out of the house or subject to domestic violence if their parents learned of the abortion. Some observers have suggested that adolescents have unduly pessimistic beliefs about their parents' responses to their pregnancy, but the accuracy of the belief is probably less relevant than the impact on the adolescent's behavior.

According to one author, 43 states have statutes requiring either parental consent or notice before minors can obtain an abortion. Several of those statutes have been struck down under state constitutional provisions. Collett, *Protecting Our Daughters: The Need for the Vermont Parental Notification Law,* 26 VT. L. REV. 101, 106–108 (2001). Vermont, to date, has not adopted a parental involvement statute.

4. *Determination of the Minor's Maturity.* Justice Powell's opinion in *Bellotti v. Baird* emphasized that a minor who establishes that she is "mature enough and well enough informed" has the right to decide whether to terminate her pregnancy independently of her parents. In *H.L. v. Matheson*, the Court emphasized that the issue of notice to parents of a mature minor was not raised by the plaintiff. Although nothing is certain in abortion jurisprudence, the "mature" minor apparently has a right of reproductive privacy that is analogous to that of an adult, and a state seeking to regulate minors' access to abortion must provide a bypass procedure so that minors can demonstrate their maturity. But, what is maturity? What must a minor show to demonstrate that she is sufficiently mature to make her own decision?

Courts apply no consistent standard to evaluating the maturity of minors seeking abortion. Many courts, like those in the Mnookin study (*supra* note 1), find maturity in virtually every case. Others set a very high standard, under which few minors are likely to qualify. In *H.B. v. Wilkinson*, 639 F. Supp. 952 (D. Utah, 1986), a Utah Federal District court analyzed the meaning of maturity under *Bellotti:*

> . . . . [A]s related to a minor's abortion decision, maturity is not solely a matter of social skills, level of intelligence or verbal skills. More importantly, it calls for experience, perspective and judgment. As to experience, the minor's prior work experience, experience in living away from home, and handling personal finances are some of the pertinent inquiries. Perspective calls for appreciation and understanding of the relative gravity and possible detrimental impact of each available option, as well as realistic perception and assessment of possible short term and long term consequences of each of those options, particularly the abortion option. Judgment is of very great importance in determining maturity. The exercise of good judgment requires being fully informed so as to be able to weigh alternatives independently and realistically. Among other things, the minor's conduct is a measure of good judgment. Factors such as stress and ignorance of alternatives have been recognized as impediments to the exercise of proper judgment by minors, who because of those factors "may not be able intelligently to decide whether to have an abortion." [quoting] *American College of Obstetricians & Gynecologists v. Thornburgh*, 737 F.2d 283, 296 (3d Cir. 1984).

The court concluded that the pregnant minor (who was 17 years old and a "very good" student) was "immature," and thus subject to a statutory requirement of parental notification. It described several factors central to this conclusion: the young woman lived at home, was not regularly employed and was financially dependent on her parents (and expected this to continue through college); she engaged in sexual activity several times without using contraceptives, believing that if she became pregnant she could obtain an abortion and deal with any complications without her parents' knowledge; she sought counsel from friends, rather than from family members or church or school officials; she did not consider marriage to be an option as a response to the pregnancy; her demeanor as a witness was initially characterized by nervousness and stress; and she failed to give due consideration to the possibility of post-abortion depression. Based on these facts, the court found the young woman to be "immature, lacking the experience, perspective and judgment to recognize and avoid choice that could be detrimental to herself." 639 F. Supp. at 958. *See also In re Jane Doe*, 566 N.E.2d 1181 (Ohio 1990)(trial court decision that a 17-year-old failed to establish maturity upheld despite minor's superior academic performance and physician's testimony that she understood the risks of the procedure; the court noted the minor's previous abortion and discontinuance of birth control as evidence of immaturity).

Some critics of the maturity requirement have argued that judges' values and attitudes toward abortion affect their decisions about the maturity of young women seeking abortion. *See* Scott, *The Legal Construction of Adolescence*, 29 HOFSTRA U. L. REV. 547 (2000). Do you see evidence of this in *Wilkinson* and *Jane Doe*? One might conclude that some courts would find almost all minors to be immature (perhaps for being foolish enough to become pregnant).

Appellate courts tend to be very deferential to trial court decisions that minors have not demonstrated that they are mature enough to make abortion decisions on their own, emphasizing that the trial judge is in the best position to evaluate maturity. Only when the decision is clearly erroneous, manifestly unjust, or represents an abuse of discretion will it be reversed. The Alabama Supreme Court, for example, has routinely upheld trial court decisions of immaturity. In one case, the appellate court agreed that the minor did not fully consider the emotional consequences of abortion, although she was 17 years old and a student who worked part time to save for college. She had considered alternatives to abortion and acquired information about the procedure from many sources. *Ex Parte Anonymous,* 803 So. 2d 542 (Ala. 2001). *See also In the Matter of A.W.,* 826 So. 2d 1280 (Miss. 2002)(finding no abuse of discretion in denial of abortion, despite 17-year-old minor's reporting suicidal ideation and feelings that having a baby would interfere with college; the child's guardian agreed to the abortion decision, but refused to give consent for religious reasons). Courts will reverse decisions based on illegitimate factors. In *Appeal of L.D.F.,* 280 A.2d 714 (Pa. Super. 2003), for example, the trial court denied the minor's petition because she was 20 weeks pregnant. The appellate court reversed, holding that, in the first 24 weeks, the stage of pregnancy could not be considered, and the minor, who was already a parent and was almost 18 years old, was mature.

Another approach to evaluating the maturity of minors to make abortion decisions is to apply the legal standard for competence to make medical decisions developed under informed consent doctrine. Although legal tests for competence in this context vary, the focus is on capacity for understanding relevant information and for reasoning about the choice. Thus, a judge applying an informed consent standard would examine the minor's understanding of disclosed information about the procedure, its risks and benefits, and available alternatives. She would also inquire into the minor's ability to use this information rationally in making a decision. How does this approach to evaluating maturity to make the abortion decision differ from that of *Wilkinson?* What information considered by these courts would be irrelevant under an informed consent approach?

Are teenagers likely to be competent to make informed treatment decisions using tests developed under the informed consent doctrine — and thus to be "mature" using this approach? One study suggests that adolescents choosing abortion are similar to adults in their decisionmaking process. Ambuel & Rappaport, *Developmental Trends in Adolescents' Psychological and Legal Competence to Consent to Abortion*, 16 LAW & HUMAN BEHAVIOR 129 (1991). A policy statement by the American Psychological Association (APA) Committee on Adolescent Abortion challenges the empirical basis of legal restrictions on adolescent abortion. The statement asserts that psychological theory and empirical research indicate that by mid-adolescence minors are as capable as are adults of conceptualizing and reasoning about medical decisions. Interdivisional Committee on Adolescent Abortion, *Adolescent Abortion: Psychological and Legal Issues,* 42 AMER. PSYCHOLOGIST 73 (Jan. 1987). The APA submitted amicus curiae briefs arguing this position before the United States Supreme Court in *Hartigan v. Zbaraz,* 484 U.S. 1082 (1988)(challenge of Illinois Parental Notice of Abortion Act by physicians on behalf of themselves and their minor patients), and *Hodgson v. Minnesota* (above).

5. *Minors' Abortion Rights under State Constitutions.* Some courts have interpreted their state constitutions to provide more protection of minors' abortion rights than has been recognized under the federal Constitution. For example, the New Jersey Supreme Court struck down that state's parental notification statute under the equal protection provision in that state's constitution, although it recognized that the statute satisfied the federal Constitution. *Planned Parenthood of Central N.J. v. Farmer,* 762 A.2d 620 (N.J. 2000). Under the statute, a minor's right to obtain an abortion was conditioned on notification of her parents, unless she obtained a judicial waiver. Applying a balancing test developed earlier, the court found substantial and unjustifiable burdens on one class of young women without an adequate government interest to justify the unequal burden. The court described in detail the costs to young women of being required to notify their parents and the inadequacy of a waiver hearing as a way of avoiding notification (due to delay, threat to anonymity, awkward procedures). It rejected the state's three justifications: that notification protects minors from their own immaturity, promotes family structure, and protects parental rights. As to the first, the court pointed out that state law recognized minors' maturity in matters relating to sexuality, substance abuse, etc., and that the collective opinion of health care professionals presented to the court supported the view that minors were mature enough to make a decision about abortion. As to the second justification, the court indicated that young women who sought abortion without telling their parents were often in dysfunctional or abusive families. The minor's pre-existing relationship with her parents determined whether she told them about abortion, whether the law required notification or not. Finally, the court dismissed the parental rights argument on the ground that the minor seeking abortion is exercising her independent constitutionally protected rights.

In contrast, the California Supreme Court decided that a statute requiring parental consent for abortion or judicial authorization did not violate the minors' right to privacy under that state's constitution, CAL. CONST. ART. I, § 7. *American Academy of Pediatrics v. Lundgren,* 940 P.2d 797 (Cal. 1997). Upholding the lower courts' rulings, the Supreme Court concluded that, although the privacy right under the California constitution was independent of and broader than the Federal right, the statute did not violate the minor's state constitutional right, because minors have a more limited privacy interest than do adults and a reduced expectation of privacy. Further, the intrusion of the procedure was minimal and was justified because of the state's compelling countervailing interest in the minor's health.

Martin Guggenheim, in a thoughtful analysis of *Bellotti* and other Supreme Court opinions on adolescent abortion, has concluded that *Bellotti* effectively eviscerated the privacy rights of pregnant adolescents provided earlier by the Court in *Danforth* (discussed in the *Bellotti* opinion). Guggenheim challenges the coherence of adolescent abortion doctrine, with its emphasis on an intrusive by-pass procedure. Guggenheim, *Minor Rights: Adolescent Abortion Cases*, 30 HOFSTRA L. REV. 589 (2002).

PROBLEM

Problem 10-5 Sarah Johnson, age 15, has petitioned your court for permission to abort without notifying her parents. Sarah is a 10th grade honor student who has become pregnant by her boyfriend. She testifies that she does not want to tell her parents about her decision because they will be upset with her; they do not know that she is sexually active and they do not like her boy friend. She also thinks they will be angry because her mother talked to her last year about using contraceptives if she became sexually active. Sarah wants the abortion because everyone at school will laugh at her when her pregnancy starts to show and she will not be able to be a cheerleader. She hates the way she would look if she were pregnant — "like a blimp." She also thinks that, if she has the baby, she will have to drop out of school for a while and will lose a grade, which she really does not want to do. The psychologist who evaluated Sarah testifies that she understands the medical procedure, including its risks and benefits. She also understands the alternatives available to her, and is firm about choosing abortion. What is your response to Sarah's petition?

[ii] Regulation of Access to Contraceptive Treatment

CAREY v. POPULATION SERVICES INTERNATIONAL

431 U.S. 678 (1977)

MR. JUSTICE BRENNAN delivered the opinion of the Court (Parts I, II, III, and V), together with an opinion (Part IV), in which MR. JUSTICE STEWART, MR. JUSTICE MARSHALL, and MR. JUSTICE BLACKMUN joined.

Under New York Educ. Law § 6811 (8) (McKinney 1972) it is a crime (1) for any person to sell or distribute any contraceptive of any kind to a minor under the age of 16 years. . . A three-judge District Court for the Southern District of New York declared § 6811 (8) unconstitutional in its entirety under the First and Fourteenth Amendments of the Federal Constitution insofar as it applies to nonprescription contraceptives, and enjoined its enforcement as so applied. We affirm.

. . . .

The District Court . . . held unconstitutional, as applied to nonprescription contraceptives, the provision prohibiting the distribution of contraceptives to those under 16 years of age. Appellants contend that this supervision of the statute is constitutionally permissible as a regulation of the morality of minors, in furtherance of the State's policy against promiscuous sexual intercourse among the young.

[T]he extent of state power to regulate conduct of minors not constitutionally regulable when committed by adults is a vexing one, perhaps not susceptible of precise answer. . . . "Minors, as well as adults, are protected by the Constitution and possess constitutional rights." *Planned Parenthood of Central Missouri v. Danforth,* 428 U.S. 52 (1976). . . . On the other hand, we have held in a variety of contexts that "the power of the state to control the conduct of children reaches beyond the scope of its authority over adults." *Prince v. Massachusetts,* 321 U.S. 158, 170 (1944).

Of particular significance to the decision of this case, the right to privacy in connection with decisions affecting procreation, extends to minors as well as to adults. [*Danforth*] held that a State may not impose a blanket provision . . . requiring the consent of a parent or person *in loco parentis* as a condition for abortion of an unmarried minor during the first 12 weeks of her pregnancy. . . . State restrictions inhibiting privacy rights of minors are valid only if they serve "any significant state . . . that is not present in the case of an adult." . . .

Since the State may not impose a blanket prohibition, or even a blanket requirement of parental consent, on the choice of a minor to terminate her pregnancy, the constitutionality of a blanket prohibition of the distribution of contraceptives to minors is *a fortiori* foreclosed. The State's interests in protection of the mental and physical health of the pregnant minor, and in protection of potential life are clearly more implicated by the abortion decision than by the decision to use a nonhazardous contraceptive.

Appellants argue, however, that significant state interests are served by restricting minors' access to contraceptives, because free availability to minors of contraceptives would lead to increased sexual activity among the young, in violation of the policy of New York to discourage such behavior. The argument is that minors' sexual activity may be deterred by increasing the hazards attendant on it. The same argument, however, would support a ban on abortions for minors, or indeed support a prohibition on abortions, or access to contraceptives, for the unmarried, whose sexual activity is also against the public policy of many States. Yet, in each of these areas, the Court has rejected the argument, noting in *Roe* that "no court or commentator has taken the argument seriously." The reason for this unanimous rejection was stated in *Eisenstadt:* "It would be plainly unreasonable to assume that [the State] has prescribed pregnancy and the birth of an unwanted child [or the physical and psychological dangers of an abortion] as punishment for fornication." We remain reluctant to attribute any such "scheme of values" to the State.

Moreover, there is substantial reason for doubt whether limiting access to contraceptives will in fact substantially discourage early sexual behavior. Appellants themselves conceded in the District Court that "there is no evidence that teenage extramarital sexual activity increases in proportion to the availability of contraceptives," . . . and accordingly offered none. . . . Appellees, on the other hand, cite a considerable body of evidence and opinion indicating that there is no such deterrent effect. Although we take judicial notice, as did the District Court, . . . that with or without access to contraceptives, the incidence of sexual activity among minors is high, and the consequences of such activity are frequently devastating, the studies cited by appellees play no part in our decision. It is enough that we again confirm the principle that when a State, as here, burdens the exercise of a fundamental right, its attempt to justify that burden as a rational means for the accomplishment of some significant state policy requires more than a bare assertion, based on a conceded complete absence of supporting evidence, that the burden is connected to such a policy. . . .

[MR. JUSTICE POWELL concurred in finding the New York's prohibition to be unconstitutional, but strongly rejected the rationale that the statute in restricting minors' access to contraceptives violated a fundamental right of minors to make reproductive decisions. He stated:]

 . . . [T]his provision prohibits parents from distributing contraceptives to their children, a restriction that unjustifiably interferes with parental interests in rearing their children. *Cf. Ginsberg v. New York*, 390 U.S. at 639 and n. 7. "[C]onstitutional interpretation has consistently recognized that the parents' claim to authority in their own household to direct the rearing of their children is basic in the structure of our society. 'It is cardinal with us that the custody, care and nurture of the child reside first in the parents, whose primary function and freedom include preparation for obligations the state can neither supply nor hinder.' " *Ibid.*, quoting *Prince v. Massachusetts, supra*, at 166. Moreover, this statute would allow the State "to enquire into, prove, and punish," *Poe v. Ullman*, 367 U.S. 497, 548 (1961) (Harlan, J., dissenting), the exercise of this parental responsibility. The State points to no interest of sufficient magnitude to justify this direct interference with the parental guidance that is especially appropriate in this sensitive area of child development.

But in my view there is considerably more room for state regulation in this area than would be permissible under the plurality's opinion. It seems clear to me, for example, that the State would further a constitutionally permissible end if it encouraged adolescents to seek the advice and guidance of their parents before deciding whether to engage in sexual intercourse. *Planned Parenthood*, 428 U.S. at 91 (STEWART, J., concurring). The State justifiably may take note of the psychological pressures that might influence children at a time in their lives when they generally do not possess the maturity necessary to understand and control their responses. Participation in sexual intercourse at an early age may have both physical and psychological consequences. These include the risk of venereal disease and pregnancy, and the less obvious mental and emotional problems that may result from sexual activity by children. Moreover, society has long adhered to the view that sexual intercourse should not be engaged in promiscuously, a judgment that an adolescent may be less likely to heed than an adult.

MR. JUSTICE STEVENS, concurring in part and concurring in the judgment. . . .

There are two reasons why I do not join Part IV. First, the holding in [*Danforth*] that a minor's decision to abort her pregnancy may not be conditioned on parental consent, is not dispositive here. The options available to the already pregnant minor are fundamentally different from those available to nonpregnant minors. The former must bear a child unless she aborts; but persons in the latter category can and generally will avoid childbearing by abstention. Consequently, even if I had joined that part of [*Danforth*], I could not agree the Constitution provides the same measure of protection to the minor's right to use contraceptives as to the pregnant female's right to abort.

Second, I would not leave open the question whether there is a significant state interest in discouraging sexual activity among unmarried persons under 16 years of age. Indeed, I would describe as "frivolous" appellees' argument that a minor has the constitutional right to put contraceptives to their intended use, notwithstanding the combined objection of both parents and the State. . . .

The State's important interest in the welfare of its young citizens justifies a number of protective measures. Such special legislation is premised on the fact that young persons frequently make unwise choices with harmful consequences; the State may properly ameliorate those consequences by providing, for example, that a minor may not be required to honor his bargain. It is almost unprecedented, however, for a State to require that an ill-advised act by a minor give rise to greater risk of irreparable harm than a similar act by an adult.

Common sense indicates that many young people will engage in sexual activity regardless of what the New York Legislature does; and further, that the incidence of venereal disease and premarital pregnancy is affected by the availability or unavailability of contraceptives. Although young persons theoretically may avoid those harms by practicing total abstention, inevitably many will not. The statutory prohibition denies them and their parents a choice which, if available, would reduce their exposure to disease or unwanted pregnancy.

The State's asserted justification is a desire to inhibit sexual conduct by minors under 16. Appellants do not seriously contend that if contraceptives are available, significant numbers of minors who now abstain from sex will cease abstaining because they will no longer fear pregnancy or disease. Rather appellants' central argument is that the statute has the important *symbolic* effect of communicating disapproval of sexual activity by minors. In essence, therefore, the statute is defended as a form of propaganda, rather than a regulation of behavior.

Although the State may properly perform a teaching function, it seems to me that an attempt to persuade by inflicting harm on the listener is an unacceptable means of conveying a message that is otherwise legitimate. The propaganda technique used in this case significantly increases the risk of unwanted pregnancy and venereal disease. It is as though a State decided to dramatize its disapproval of motorcycles by forbidding the use of safety helmets. One need not posit a constitutional right to ride a motorcycle to characterize such a restriction as irrational and perverse.

Even as a regulation of behavior, such a statute would be defective. Assuming that the State could impose a uniform sanction upon young persons who risk self-inflicted harm by operating motorcycles, or by engaging in sexual activity, surely that sanction could not take the form of deliberately injuring the cyclist or infecting the promiscuous child. If such punishment may not be administered deliberately, after trial and a finding of guilt, it manifestly cannot be imposed by a legislature, indiscriminately and at random. This kind of government-mandated harm, is, in my judgment, appropriately characterized as a deprivation of liberty without due process of law.

NOTES

1. *Contraception, Abortion, and Reproductive Privacy.* Justices Brennan, Powell, and Stevens each seem to focus on a different constitutional flaw in the New York statute. Justice Brennan suggests that what is at stake is minors' constitutionally protected interest in reproductive privacy. Justices Stevens and Powell join in the result, although they disagree with Justice Brennan's characterization of the problem, with Justice Stevens observing that it would be "frivolous" to suggest that minors have a constitutional right to put contraceptives to their intended use. He reasons instead that it would be "irrational and perverse" for the state to prescribe pregnancy or venereal disease as punishment for fornication. In the opinion of Justice Powell, the statutory restrictions violate the interests of parents. In what way? Does Justice Powell think that minors themselves have any interest independent of their parents?

Do you agree with Justice Brennan that contraception and abortion decisions are similar? Is the argument that minors should have the authority to make independent decisions about contraceptive use without involving their parents stronger (or weaker) than the case for legal autonomy for adolescents to make decisions about abortion? Both decisions, of course, allow the minor to avoid the burden of an unwanted pregnancy. However, the decisions have some distinguishing features. The urgency of the abortion decision is absent in the decision about contraceptive use, which, ideally, is "future oriented." Arguably (although perhaps unrealistically), parental consultation would be beneficial for some minors making the latter decision. On the other hand, contraceptive use is not complicated by the interest in fetal life. Franklin Zimring provides a thoughtful analysis of these issues in THE CHANGING LEGAL WORLD OF ADOLESCENCE 65–69 (1982).

Some support for Justice Brennan's view comes from a recent Georgia Supreme Court decision finding, under the Georgia constitution, that minors can have a right of privacy that protects private acts of sexual intimacy between persons legally able to consent. *In re J.M.*, 575 S.E.2d 441 (Ga. 2003). The court overturned the statutory rape conviction of a 16-year-old who had consensual sex with his 16-year-old girlfriend.

2. *Minor Consent Statutes.* In many states, minors can obtain contraceptive treatment without parental consultation. National Research Council, RISKING THE FUTURE: ADOLESCENT SEXUALITY, PREGNANCY, AND CHILDBEARING (1986). Minors' consent statutes designate specific medical treatments that minors can obtain on their own, including treatment for venereal disease and substance abuse, psychotherapy, and contraceptive treatment.

The Maryland statute provides, for example, that "A minor has the same capacity as an adult to consent to treatment for. . . .contraception. . ." MD. CODE ANN., HEALTH GEN. SECT 20-102(c)(5)(2000 & Supp. 2003). *See also* VA. CODE § 54.1-2969 (Michie 2002); COLO. REV. STAT. SECT. 13-22-105 (2002) (minor can obtain birth control information and supplies when referred. . . .by another physician, a clergyman, a family planning clinic, a school. . . ."). In general, these statutes treat minors as adults in obtaining particular treatments that promote their welfare, in situations in which they would hesitate to involve their parents. Thus, the policy objective may have little to do with promoting adolescent autonomy.

Statutes facilitating free access to contraceptive treatment for minors without parental consent can be justified under a paternalistic rationale. Teenage pregnancy has become a serious social and public health problem in this country, because many teenagers are sexually active and fail to use contraceptives. Among developed countries, the United States is surpassed only by Russia in its teen pregnancy rate. Singh & Daroch, *Adolescent Pregnancy and Childbearing: Levels and Trends in Developed Countries*, 32 FAM. PLANNING PERSPECTIVES 14 (2000). The U.S. rate is far higher than Canada and European countries. Alan Guttmacher Institute, CAN MORE PROGRESS BE MADE? TEENAGE SEXUAL AND REPRODUCTIVE BEHAVIOR IN DEVELOPED COUNTRIES (2001). Birth rates among unmarried teens increased by over 60% in the 1980s, resulting in a rate of almost 50 births per 1000 women in the 15–19 year age group. Ventura, *Recent Trends in Teenage Childbearing in the United States*, 74 (4) STAT. BULL. (Metro. Life Ins. Co.) (1994). There is some evidence that the rate of teen pregnancies has peaked and may be declining. Center for Disease Control, TEENAGE BIRTHS IN THE UNITED STATES: STATE TRENDS, 1991–2000, (2002). Nonetheless the problem is serious; teenage pregnancy carries substantial social costs. Each year, one million teenage girls become pregnant, and almost 500,000 babies are born to teenage mothers. Pregnancy carries greater health risks for adolescents than for adult women. Teenage mothers are less likely than their peers to complete high school, even though pregnant students and teenage mothers can no longer be excluded from public high school. Teenage mothers (and fathers) have fewer employment opportunities than their peers as adults, and are overrepresented in lower-paying unskilled jobs. While some of the discrepancy is linked to pre-pregnancy academic aptitude, socioeconomic status and educational expectations, pregnancy and parenthood are important disabilities. Children of teenage parents have more health problems and are more likely to require public assistance than children of older mothers. A somewhat dated but still useful description of studies of teenage pregnancy are reported in Scott, *Adolescent's Reproductive Rights*, in CHILDREN, MENTAL HEALTH AND THE LAW (N.D. Repucci et al. eds, 1984); National Research Council, RISKING THE FUTURE, *supra*.

School systems in many cities have initiated efforts to provide teenagers with direct access to contraceptives in public high schools, as part of an effort to reduce teenage pregnancy and venereal disease (particularly AIDS). These initiatives have often been met with resistance from community and religious groups. Courts generally have rejected challenges to condom distribution programs in schools. A Federal appellate court concluded that a Philadelphia program did not interfere with fundamental parental rights where the program was voluntary and parents could refuse to allow their children to participate. *Parents United for Better Schools Inc. v. Philadelphia Bd. of Educ.* 148 F.3d 260 (3rd Cir. 1998). *See also Curtis v. School Committee of Falmouth,* 652 N.E.2d 580 (Mass. 1995)(rejecting claim by students and parents that school sponsored condom program violated their right to familial privacy, parental liberty, and free exercise of religion), Sanders, *Kids and Condoms: Constitutional Challenges to the Distribution of Condoms in Public Schools,* 61 U. CIN. L. REV. 1479 (1993). A study comparing Massachusetts schools with and without condom programs found no higher rates of sexual intercourse in the schools in which condoms were available. Blake, et al., *Condom Availability Use in Massachusetts High Schools: Relationships with Condom Use and Sexual Behavior,* 93 AM. J. PUBLIC HEALTH 955 (2003). The researchers found, however, that twice as many teens in these schools who were sexually active used condoms as compared to teens in the schools without programs. The authors suggested that the adoption of a condom program not only provided easy access to condoms, but also signaled approval of condom use by those in authority.

Some authors have challenged regulations that require parental consent to contraceptive treatment for minors. Arons, *Misconceived Laws: The Irrationality of Parental Involvement Requirements for Contraception,* 41 WM. & MARY L. REV. 1093 (2000). For an opposing view, see Wardle, *Parents' Rights vs. Minors' Rights Regarding the Provision of Contraceptives to Teenagers,* 68 NEB. L. REV. 216 (1989).

Teenage pregnancy has been the subject of book-length studies. The problem of desired pregnancy and childbirth among poor teens is the subject of Musnick, YOUNG, POOR, AND PREGNANT (1993). (Note however that studies have found that over 80% of pregnancies among 15–19 year old women are unintended). *See also* LUKER, DUBIOUS CONCEPTIONS: THE POLITICS OF TEENAGE PREGNANCY (1997).

§ B. OVERRIDING PARENTAL AUTHORITY IN ORDER TO PROTECT ENDANGERED CHILDREN

Issues of child abuse and neglect arise in numerous types of legal actions. The most common, and the type focused on in this section are civil actions brought by the state for the purpose of intervening in a parent-child relationship to protect a child. Subsections 1 through 3 explore questions relating to what conditions or parental behavior constitute abuse and neglect. When the state establishes grounds for intervention, a variety of dispositions are possible, such as monitoring the child in the home or temporarily removing the child from the home. Many children found to be neglected or abused are placed in foster care; special issues relating to possible tort liability arising from state intervention in families, and the legal structure of foster care are covered in subsection 4. Subsection 5 addresses questions raised when the state seeks to terminate parental rights.

The state may also bring a criminal action against a parent, guardian or other party for child abuse or neglect. While the issues are similar, criminal defendants are constitutionally entitled to certain protections not required in civil proceedings. The constitutional problems which arise, particularly with respect to special rules intended to deal with the difficulties of proving child abuse and statutes or rules relating to child witnesses, are the focus of subsection 6, *infra*.

Child abuse and neglect are regulated by the state through mandatory reporting statutes. These statutes typically require certain professionals to report to an appropriate state official when they have "reason to believe" that a child has been abused or neglected. While reporting laws initially focused on physicians, today most jurisdictions require reports from any health care personnel as well as social service workers, teachers and other school personnel. Law enforcement officers and child care workers are also often covered. *See* Meriwether, *Child Abuse Reporting Laws: Time for a Change*, 20 FAM. L.Q. 141, 145–46 (1986). A few states, such as North Carolina, impose a duty upon "any person" who has reason to suspect that abuse or neglect has occurred. *See* N.C. GEN. STAT. § 7B-301 (2000). Typically, reporting statutes confer immunity upon persons who make reports, even when the reports are based on questionable information. For example, in *L.A.R. v. Ludwig*, 821 P.2d 291 (Ariz. App. 1991), a counselor who was aware of the couple's marital problems was found to be immune from tort liability for a report to child protective services alleging the father's sexual abuse of his daughter that was based entirely upon the mother's report. *See also, e.g., Storch v. Silverman*, 186 Cal. App. 3d 671 (1986) (interpreting reporting statute to confer absolute immunity upon those required to report child abuse and qualified immunity for those reporting voluntarily). For mandated reporters who do not report, however, criminal sanctions may follow. *See, e.g., Kimberley S.M. v. Bradford Central School*, 649 N.Y.S.2d 588 (1996) (teacher who failed to report that she was told by student that her uncle sexually abused her could be held liable, even though report was not substantiated). *But see Wilson v. Darr,* 553 N.W.2d 579 (Iowa 1996) (priest counselor exempt from reporting duty); *Childers v. A.S.,* 909 S.W.2d 282 (Tx. App. 1995) (parents not required to report child's inappropriate sexual conduct with friend). The problem of false reporting (and statutes designed to deal with the problem) is another issue covered in subsection 6.

Do attorneys have an obligation to report child abuse? This issue presents a conflict between the attorney-client privilege and the policy of protecting children. Rosencrantz, *Rejecting "Hear No Evil, Speak No Evil:" Expanding the Attorney's Role in Child Abuse Reporting*, 8 GEO. J. LEGAL ETHICS 327 (1994); Mosteller, *Child Abuse Reporting Laws and Attorney-Client Confidences: The Reality and the Spector of the Lawyer as Informant*, 42 DUKE L.J. 203 (1992).

[1]   STANDARDS FOR STATE INTERVENTION IN CHILD ABUSE AND NEGLECT CASES

Minnesota Statutes §§260.012, 260C.007 (2003)

§260.012. Duty to ensure placement prevention and family reunification; reasonable efforts

(a) Once a child alleged to be in need of protection or services is under the court's jurisdiction, the court shall ensure that reasonable efforts including culturally appropriate services by the social service agency are made to prevent placement or to eliminate the need for removal and to reunite the child with the child's family at the earliest possible time, consistent with the best interests, safety, and protection of the child. . . .

(b) "Reasonable efforts" means the exercise of due diligence by the responsible social service agency to use appropriate and available services to meet the needs of the child and the child's family in order to prevent removal of the child from the child's family; or upon removal, services to eliminate the need for removal and reunite the family. . . . The social service agency has the burden of demonstrating that it has made reasonable efforts.

§260C.007. Definitions

Subdivision 6. "Child in need of protection or services" means a child who is in need of protection or services because the child:

(1) is abandoned or without parent, guardian, or custodian;

(2) (I) has been a victim of physical or sexual abuse, (ii) resides with or has resided with a victim of domestic child abuse as defined in subdivision 5, (iii) resides with or would reside with a perpetrator of domestic child abuse or child abuse as defined in subdivision 5, or (iv) is a victim of emotional maltreatment as defined in subdivision 13,

(3) is without necessary food, clothing, shelter, education, or other required care for the child's physical or mental health or morals because the child's parent, guardian, or custodian is unable or unwilling to provide that care;

(4) is without the special care made necessary by a physical, mental, or emotional condition because the child's parent, guardian, or custodian is unable or unwilling to provide that care including a child in voluntary placement due solely to the child's developmental disability or emotional disturbance;

(5) is medically neglected, which includes, but is not limited to, the withholding of medically indicated treatment from a disabled infant with a life-threatening condition. . . . [Ed. Note: The remainder of this paragraph is set forth in section B2, *infra*.]

(6) is one whose parent, guardian, or other custodian for good cause desires to be relieved of the child's care and custody. . .;

(7) has been placed for adoption or care in violation of law;

(8) is without proper parental care because of the emotional, mental, or physical disability, or state of immaturity of the child's parent, guardian, or other custodian. . . .

. . . .

Subdivision 13. "Domestic child abuse" means:

(1) any physical injury to a minor family or household member inflicted by an adult family or household member other than by accidental means. . . .

Subdivision 15. "Emotional maltreatment" means the consistent, deliberate infliction of mental harm on a child by a person responsible for the child's care, that has an observable, sustained, and adverse effect on the child's physical, mental, or emotional development. "Emotional maltreatment" does not include reasonable training or discipline administered by the person responsible for the child's care or the reasonable exercise of authority by that person.

. . . .

In re JUVENILE APPEAL (83-CD)

455 A.2d 1313 (Conn. 1983)

SPEZIALE, CHIEF JUSTICE. This is an appeal by the defendant . . . from the order . . . granting temporary custody of her children to the commissioner of the department of children and youth services.

The defendant and her six children lived in a small apartment in New Haven. They had been receiving services from the department of children and youth services (hereinafter DCYS) as a protective service family since 1976, and were supported by the Aid to Families with Dependent Children program. Michelle Spicknall, a DCYS caseworker, was assigned to the defendant's case in January 1979. In the next nine months she visited the defendant's home twenty-seven times. She considered the family situation "marginal," but noted that the children were "not abused [or] neglected." It was Spicknall's opinion that the children were very happy and active, and that they had a "very warm" relationship with their mother.

During the night of September 4–5, 1979, the defendant's youngest child, nine month old Christopher, died. The child was brought by ambulance to Yale-New Haven Medical Center where resuscitation was unsuccessfully attempted by his pediatrician, Dr. Robert Murphy. No cause of death could be determined at that time, but the pediatrician noticed some unexplained superficial marks on Christopher's body.

Because of Christopher's unexplained death, the plaintiff commissioner of children and youth services seized custody of the defendant's five remaining children on September 5, 1979, under authority of the "96-hour hold" provision of General Statutes §17-38a(e), which permits summary seizure if the commissioner has probable cause to believe that a child is "suffering from serious physical illness or serious physical injury or is in immediate physical danger from his surroundings, and that immediate removal from such surroundings is *necessary to insure the child's safety. . . .*" (Emphasis added.)

On September 7, 1979,. . . . DCYS filed petitions of neglect under General Statutes §46b-129(a) for each of the defendant's children. Accompanying each petition was an affidavit for orders of temporary custody asking that the court issue temporary ex parte orders to keep the five children in DCYS custody under authority of §46b-129(b)(2). The petitions alleged, in addition to Christopher's unexplained death, that the defendant's apartment was dirty, that numerous roaches could be found there, that beer cans were to be found in the apartment, that the defendant had been observed drinking beer, that on one occasion the defendant may have been drunk, that a neighbor reported that the children once had been left alone all night, and that the two older children had occasionally come to school without having eaten breakfast. On the basis of these allegations, on September 7, 1979, the court granted, ex parte, temporary custody to the commissioner pending a notice hearing on temporary custody set for September 14, 1979, within ten days of the ex parte order as required by §46b-129(b)(2). The court also set October 1, 1979, for a hearing on the neglect petitions. [The hearing was continued, and never rescheduled.]

At the September 14 temporary custody hearing, DCYS presented testimony of Spicknall confirming and elaborating on the conditions of the defendant's home and on the defendant's beer drinking. Christopher's pediatrician testified concerning Christopher's treatment and physical appearance when the child was brought to the hospital on September 5. The doctor also testified that. . . the external marks on Christopher's body were not a cause of death, that no internal injuries were found, and that the child had had a viral lung infection. He also explained, on cross-examination, the term "sudden infant death syndrome" and its pathology. At the conclusion of the state's case, the court found "probable cause" and ordered temporary custody of the children to remain with the plaintiff commissioner of children and youth services.

The defendant appealed to this court claiming that General Statutes §46b-129(b) violates the due process clause of the Fourteenth Amendment both because it is an impermissible infringement on her right to family integrity, and because the statute is unconstitutionally vague. The defendant also claims error in the trial court's determination that "probable cause" is the standard of proof in a temporary custody proceeding. We conclude that §46b-129(b) is constitutional; however, we do find that the trial court erred when it decided that "probable cause" is the standard of proof in a temporary custody proceeding.

I

Constitutionality of General Statutes §46b-129(b)

A. *Family Integrity*

In administering [Connecticut's policy of protecting children], courts and state agencies must keep in mind the constitutional limitations imposed on a state which undertakes any form of coercive intervention in family affairs. The United States Supreme Court has frequently emphasized the constitutional importance of family integrity. . . .

B. *Criteria for Coercive Intervention by the State*

Where fundamental rights are concerned we have a two-part test: "[1] regulations limiting these rights may be justified only by a 'compelling state interest,' and . . . [2] legislative enactments must be narrowly drawn to express only the legitimate state interests at stake." *Roe v. Wade,* 410 U.S. 113, 155 (1973). The state has a substantial interest in protecting minor children.

Studies indicate that the best interests of the child are usually served by keeping the child in the home with his or her parents. . . . Even where the parent-child relationship is "marginal," it is usually in the best interests of the child to remain at home and still benefit from a family environment.

The language of §17-38a(e) clearly limits the scope of intervention to cases where the state interest is compelling, as required by the first part of the test from *Roe v. Wade, supra.* Intervention is permitted only where "serious physical illness or serious physical injury" is found or where "immediate physical danger" is present. It is at this point that the child's interest no longer coincides with that of the parent, thereby diminishing the magnitude of the parent's right to family integrity; and therefore the state's intervention as *parens patriae* to protect the child becomes so necessary that it can be considered paramount. A determination that the state interest is compelling does not alone affirm the constitutionality of the statute. . . . The second part of the due process analysis . . . requires that statutes affecting fundamental rights be "narrowly drawn to express only the legitimate state interests at stake." General Statutes §17-38a(e) meets this part of the test by requiring, in addition to the compelling need to protect the child, that the assumption of temporary custody by the commissioner be immediately "necessary to insure the child's safety." This phrase requires that various steps short of removal from the home be used when possible in preference to disturbing the integrity of the family. The statute itself mentions supervised in-home custody, but a wide range of other programs short of removal are a part of existing DCYS procedure.

. . . Because we hold that General Statutes §46b-129(b) may be applied only on the basis of the criteria enunciated in §17-38a, we reject the defendant's claim that §46b-129(b) is unconstitutional.

In the instant case, no substantial showing was made at the temporary custody hearing that the defendant's five children were suffering from either serious physical illness or serious physical injury, or that they would be in immediate physical danger if they were returned to the defendant's home. The DCYS caseworker admitted at trial, as did the state's counsel at argument before this court, that without the unexplained death of Christopher there was no reason for DCYS to have custody of the other children. The medical evidence at the hearing indicated no connection between Christopher's death and either the defendant or the conditions in her home. While the final autopsy report was not available at the hearing, the pediatrician testified that the marks on Christopher's body were not related to the child's death. There was, therefore, no evidence before the court to indicate whether his death was from natural causes or was the result of abuse. Yet with nothing before it but subjective suspicion, the court granted the commissioner custody of the defendant's other children. It was error for the court to grant to the commissioner temporary custody when no immediate risk of danger to the children was shown.

. . . [S]hortly after the orders of temporary custody were granted, the state received the final autopsy report which effectively exonerated the defendant from any wrongdoing in Christopher's death. The reason for the custody order then no longer existed. It was then incumbent on DCYS to reunite the family. "In this situation, the state cannot constitutionally 'sit back and wait' for the parent to institute judicial proceedings. It 'cannot . . . [adopt] for itself an attitude of "if you don't like it, sue,"'" *Duchesne v. Sugarman,* 566 F.2d 817, 828 (2d Cir. 1977).

This court notes, however, that the defendant mother took no steps either to revoke custody under General Statutes §46b-129(f) or to pursue a judicial resolution of the neglect petitions. We are even more concerned that the attorney for the children took no steps to protect their interests in family integrity by insisting on a resolution of the neglect petitions, and failed to represent their interests before this court. . . .

Petitions for neglect and for temporary custody orders, like the petitions to terminate parental rights in *Duchesne v. Sugarman,* "are particularly vulnerable to the risk that judges or social workers will be tempted, consciously or unconsciously, to compare unfavorably the material advantages of the child's natural parents with those of prospective adoptive parents [or foster parents]." *In re Juvenile Appeal (Anonymous),* 420 A.2d 875.

This case clearly shows that these dangers do exist; it is shocking that the defendant's children have been in "temporary" custody for more than three years. This is a tragic and deplorable situation, and DCYS must bear full responsibility for this unwarranted and inexcusable delay. . . .

II

Burden of Proof; Standard of Proof

. . . .

In this case, the unexplained death of Christopher, combined with the marks on his body, was sufficient to support a finding under §17-38a(e) that there was probable cause to believe that the defendant's other children might be "in immediate physical danger," as required for removal from the home under the standards enunciated earlier in this opinion. Therefore, both the initial seizure by DCYS under the ninety-six hour hold provision of §17-38a(e), and the court's decision to issue an ex parte temporary custody order under the first step of § 46b-129(b)(2) on September 7, 1979, were entirely proper.

The court below erred, however, at the second step of § 46b-129(b)(2) when it confirmed its order of temporary custody after taking evidence at the temporary custody hearing on September 14, 1979, and October 1, 1979. . . . The defendant claims that the court erred by presuming neglect and by requiring "probable cause" as the burden of proof, thereby effectively shifting the burden of proof to the defendant. We agree. We hold that the burden of proof is always on the state when it seeks to remove children from the home. We hold further that the standard of proof to be used in temporary custody hearings under General Statutes §46b-129(b)(2) is the normal civil standard of a fair preponderance of the evidence. . . .

NOTES

1. *Incidence of Neglect and Abuse Cases.* It is virtually impossible to estimate accurately the frequency of child abuse and neglect in this country today. The findings of studies intended to demonstrate the incidence of abuse and neglect, one expert writes, "are a direct consequence of the definition used. Thus, estimates of the number of children abused and neglected each year range from 60,000 to 4.5 million. . . . Comparing these findings is indeed like comparing apples and oranges." Besharov, *Improved Research on Child Abuse and Neglect through Better Definitions,* in FAMILY VIOLENCE 42, 43 (D. Besharov ed., 1990). There were 2.7 million reports of child abuse and neglect in 2001, of which 903,000 were found substantiated. U.S. Department of Health and Human Services, Admin. on Children, Youth and Families, *Child Maltreatment—2001,* reprinted in STATISTICAL ABSTRACT OF THE UNITED STATES 217–218 (2003). The number of reported cases was 500,000 in 1977. U.S. Department of Health, Education and Welfare, Children's Bureau, *National Analysis of Official Child Abuse and Neglect Reporting 1977,* 3, 5–6 (1979). How much of this increase is due to mandatory abuse reporting laws, discussed above and in subsection 6, is impossible to say. Some variation may also be due to the different sources of data.

2. *Stages of a Legal Action for Child Abuse or Neglect.* An abuse and neglect case may proceed through several stages. The emergency proceedings at issue in *In re Juvenile Appeal* allow state intervention (usually taking temporary custody of the child) in emergency circumstances, without notice and a hearing. In most states, emergency custody without a hearing (ex parte) may continue for only a few days; in Connecticut, the period is 96 hours; in Minnesota, 24 hours (MINN. STAT. ANN. §260C.181, subd. 1 (West 2003); and in North Carolina, only 12 hours (N.C. GEN. STAT. §7B-501 (West 2003). In most jurisdictions, this emergency custody period may be extended after a hearing on temporary custody.

For the state to justify intervention beyond the short periods of time allowed under the emergency hearing procedures, regular child protection hearings must be held. These hearings are often divided into two stages: the jurisdictional or adjudicatory stage, and the dispositional stage. In the first stage, the state must show that one of the grounds for state intervention exists *See* MINN. STAT. § 260C.007, subd. 6, *supra* (defining child in need of protection services). If grounds for intervention are established, the court then proceeds to determine the appropriate disposition of the case, such as supervision in the home or removal of the child from the home. In most states, the termination of parental rights occurs under still another set of procedures, and as a matter of constitutional law, termination must satisfy stricter due process standards than are required in ordinary abuse and neglect proceedings. These special standards are discussed in subsection 5.

3. ***Standards for State Intervention to Protect Children.*** The dilemma facing child protection policy is to create standards that permit intervention only when parental conduct threatens the child's welfare, and then to actually help the child, without causing unnecessary harm and disruption. On one hand, there is a natural tendency to intervene when a child is thought to be mistreated. On the other hand, intervention will often turn out to be mistaken or based on bias, as in *In re Juvenile Appeal,* or it may be unhelpful, because of disruption to the child and limitations in agency resources or skills. Commentators and practitioners divide roughly into two camps – the interventionists and the non-interventionists. Interventionists have faith in the skills of courts and social workers to recognize and repair the damage caused by inadequate homes. Non-interventionists place more emphasis on the harm caused children, even neglected children, by interventions that undermine parental authority and disrupt the parent-child bond, even if the parents are less than optimal. The non-interventionists also focus on the quality of the placements available for children removed from their homes, which is often far from ideal; the interventionists insist that such problems would be alleviated if society would devote more resources to the critical problem of helping children in need.

In BEFORE THE BEST INTERESTS OF THE CHILD (1979), J. Goldstein, A. Freud & A. Solnit ("GFS") argue for a strong non-interventionist position. GFS advocate coercive intervention only in cases in which the parents have violated immunization, education or labor laws; a parent has been convicted of a sexual offense against the child; the parent has inflicted, or attempted to inflict serious bodily injury to the child; or the parent has refused to authorize non-experimental medical care, the denial of which will result in the child's death. *Id.* at 193–94. Under these standards, no intervention is allowed for sexual abuse not established in a criminal conviction, emotional abuse and neglect, failure to provide medical care where a child's health, but not life, is endangered, and severe neglect based upon "inadequate parenting," where no serious injury to the child has yet occurred. For a critical analysis of GFS, see Wald, *Thinking About Public Policy Toward Abuse and Neglect of Children: A Review of "Before the Best Interests of the Child,"* 78 MICH. L. REV. 645 (1980).

A more moderate approach is represented by the *Model Standards Relating to Abuse and Neglect* (Tentative Draft 1981), drafted as part of the

Juvenile Justice Standards Project, a major juvenile law reform project of the Institute of Judicial Administration (IJA) and the American Bar Association (ABA) in the 1970's. These standards are broader than GFS, allowing intervention when "the child is suffering serious emotional damage" for which parents are unwilling to get treatment; the child has been sexually abused or allowed to be sexually abused by the parent; the parent's failure to supervise the child creates a substantial risk of imminent serious bodily injury; or the parent does not provide medical treatment which may "cure, alleviate, or prevent him/her from suffering serious physical harm which may result in death, disfigurement, or substantial impairment of bodily functions." Because they restricted state intervention to a greater extent than was (and is) allowed under the statutes of most states, however, these proposed standards were never adopted by the sponsoring organizations, although 20 volumes of Juvenile Justice Standards were adopted by the ABA and IJA. For analysis of these matters by Michael Wald, see *State Intervention on Behalf of Neglected Children: A Search for Realistic Standards*, 27 STAN. L. REV. 985 (1975) (Wald I); Wald, *State Intervention on Behalf of "Neglected" Children: Standards for Removal of Children From Their Homes, Monitoring the Status of Children in Foster Care, and Termination of Parental Rights*, 28 STAN. L. REV. 623 (1976) (Wald II). *See also* Mnookin, *Foster Care — In Whose Best Interest?*, 43 HARV. EDUC. REV. 599 (1973).

Professor Marsha Garrison, more sympathetic to the interventionist camp, has charged that minimum intervention advocates have (1) not adequately supported the claim that state intervention poses serious risks to children; (2) overlooked the importance of state intervention in cases where assistance is voluntarily sought (about one-half of child welfare caseloads); (3) proposed standards which are vague and obscure; and (4) been overly optimistic about the consequences of non-interventionist reforms. *See* Garrison, *Child Welfare Decisionmaking: In Search of the Least Drastic Alternative*, 75 GEO. L.J. 1745 (1987).

4. *Corporal Punishment and Physical Abuse.* State statutes define physical abuse in terms of either actual physical injury or risk of injury. *See, e.g.*, IND. STAT. ANN. § 34-1-1(1)(1997) (including as a child in need of services one whose ". . . physical . . . health is seriously endangered due to injury by the act or omission of the child's parent. . ."). There is wide societal disagreement about where the boundary between physical abuse and permissible corporal punishment by parents should be drawn. Some statutes describe "excessive corporal punishment" as abuse. On the other hand, "reasonable" corporal punishment used for disciplinary purposes is generally treated as a parental privilege. *See, e.g.* COLO. REV. STAT. ANN. § 18-1-703 (2002); *State v. Jones* 747 N.E.2d. 891 (Ohio App. 2000) (criminal child abuse statute not meant to punish "reasonable. . .discipline," but only corporeal punishment that causes substantial injury). Courts in civil abuse proceedings also are called upon to determine whether corporeal punishment constitutes abuse.

Do switch marks and bruises qualify as excessive punishment? In *In re Ethan H.*, 609 A.2d 1222 (N.H. 1992), a trial court finding of abuse was reversed on appeal in a case involving a physician mother, who struck her seven-year-old with a belt six times when he ignored her admonition at dinner not to throw food. The court noted that the child, who had bruises still visible after five days, suffered no lasting harm, and the physician asked to evaluate the injuries by the children's services reported that he did not believe that the injury constituted child abuse. The mother testified that she believed in corporal punishment "done judiciously" and that she believed that the circumstances warranted it. She introduced testimony that the child bruised easily and that he was playing happily outside shortly after being punished. The trial court decided that Ethan was an abused child, because "a bruise . . . by its plain meaning is an injury," and the mother expressed her intent to discipline him through "strappings" in the future. The supreme court rejected this reasoning, finding no evidence that the bruises constituted "harm or threatened harm to his health or welfare," the statutory requirement for a finding of abuse. *See also In the Interest of J.P.,* 692 N.E.2d 338 (Ill. App. 1998) (reversing trial court decision that mother's use of wooden spoon to paddle child for disciplinary purposes was abuse).

Acceptance of corporal punishment has declined generally over the past generation. In recent years, critics have argued that corporal punishment by parents should be banned in this country as it has been in many European countries. There is a strong trend toward prohibiting physical punishment in schools and day care centers. Many critics point to research findings that indicate that physical punishment is ineffective and has detrimental effects on children's welfare. *See* Pollard, *Banning Child Corporal Punishment,* 77 Tul. L. Rev. 575 (2003); Johnson, *The Parental Corporal Punishment Defense — Reasonable and Necessary or Excused Abuse?* 1998 U. Ill. L. Rev. 413. The Pennsylvania Supreme Court recently acknowledged that social attitudes about child abuse have changed, but concluded that this was irrelevant to the question of whether a father's moderate corporeal punishment, administered for purposes of discipline, could be treated as child abuse. *Chronister v. Brenneman,* 742 A.2d 190 (Pa. 1999). Declining to express either approval or disapproval of physical punishment, the court determined that the father's conduct did not come within the statutory definition of child abuse.

5. *Sexual Abuse.* Child sexual abuse is generally defined in terms of the commission of certain criminal, sexual acts with a child. *See, e.g.,* N.C. Gen. Stat. §§ 14-27.2, 14-27.3 (2000) (all degrees of rape and crimes against nature with a juvenile); § 14.202.1, 14.202.2 (taking indecent liberties with a juvenile); § 14-90.16 (preparation of obscene photographs involving a juvenile, promoting prostitution of a juvenile, and sexual exploitation). In recent years, this issue has received a great deal of attention in the media and public awareness has increased. This perhaps has led to more aggressive state intervention practices and to some uncertainty (and controversy) about what constitutes sexual abuse that warrants intervention. Is it sexual abuse when parents shower with their children? Sleep with them? Only for older children? A federal appeals court concluded that a social worker engaged in an arbitrary abuse of power when she ordered a father (like the mother in *Ethan H.,* a physician) to leave his home or have his 3-year-old taken into social service custody, based on an anonymous tip that he sexually abused the child. *Croft v. Westmoreland Children and Youth Services*, 103 F.3d 1123 (3rd Cir. 1997). The tip described and (based on the evidence) grossly distorted an incident in which the child was found walking outside naked at night. Although the parents provided witnesses who fully corroborated their innocent explanation of the incident, the social worker remained concerned about what she viewed as inconsistencies in the parents' stories and about the father's report that he put vaginal cream on the child when she had a rash. The social worker admitted in testimony that she had no opinion about whether abuse occurred when she ordered the father to leave the home but the agency policy was that a parent accused of sexual abuse must "prove beyond any certainty that there was no sexual abuse before she was permitted to leave the child with [that] parent." The appeals court reversed summary judgment for the county, finding that the county violated the parents' constitutionally protected liberty interest in family privacy, because there was no reasonable ground to believe that the child had been sexually abused, and thus no authority to remove her from her parents.

Croft and *Ethan H.* are unusual cases because the parents are physicians. Poor families are far more likely to be subject to state intervention generally than middle and upper class families, in part, probably for legitimate reasons, and in part, perhaps, because social service agencies and courts may be reluctant to challenge parents who have means and social status.

Many legal issues relating to physical and sexual abuse involve how to prove rather than how to define it. These issues are considered in Section B6 *infra*.

6. *Emotional Abuse and Neglect.* One of the most controversial areas in child abuse and neglect law is that of emotional abuse and neglect. While in the past, open-ended abuse and neglect statutes typically allowed state intervention where the family circumstances presented the risk of emotional damage to a child, see Wald II, *supra,* at 628–29, the trend has been in favor of limiting intervention for emotional neglect. Subdivision 15 of Minn. Stat. § 260.015, set forth above, like many statutes today, provides that emotional neglect or "maltreatment" cannot be found absent "consistent, deliberate, infliction of mental harm" that has some "observable, sustained, and adverse" effects on the child's development. State intervention would not be warranted under this statute merely on the grounds that a parent is engaged in conduct *likely* to cause emotional damage to the child; some actual symptoms of neglect or maltreatment must be shown to already exist.

The assumptions supporting limiting intervention on grounds of emotional neglect are familiar ones: that professionals are unable to accurately predict whether emotional damage will result from parental conduct, and that emotional neglect is a vague category, inviting the insertion of personal values in decisions to intervene, and failing to give parents fair warning of societal criteria for intervention. GFS, *supra,* at 75; see also Wald I, *supra,* at 1000–04 (detailing harmful nature of intervention based upon vague standards more generally). Another difficulty is that a child's emotional problems may be due to environmental or hereditary factors, rather than parental conduct. GFS, *supra,* at 75–77. Finally, even if the parents' treatment of the child is reprehensible, it is often unclear whether intervention will make things better or worse. Some authors, nonetheless, advocate more aggressive proactive intervention in cases of emotional maltreatment. *See, e.g.*, McMullen, *The Inherent Limitations of After-the-Fact Statutes Dealing with Emotional and Sexual Maltreatment of Children*, 41 DRAKE L. REV. 483 (1992).

7. Inability to Parent. Many emotional neglect cases arise in circumstances in which the parent is mentally disabled or has emotional, psychiatric or substance abuse problems which impair his or her ability to provide adequate parental care for the child. State intervention in these cases may be sought under grounds that a parent is "unable or unwilling to provide" appropriate care to the child. *See* MINN. STAT. §260.015 subdiv. 6, *supra*. Again, drawing the line between cases in which a parent is truly unable to care adequately for the child and those in which the parent can provide adequate, if only marginal, care is a difficult task, made more difficult by the fact that the inadequate parent may have no culpability. *See In re Jeannette S.,* 156 Cal. Rptr. 262 (Cal. App. 1979). If the child is in danger because of the parent's conduct, however, even though there has been no demonstrable harm, courts will intervene and remove the child. *See, e.g., In re B.K.,* 429 A.2d 1331 (D.C. App. 1981) (schizophrenic parents subjected infant to risk from roughhousing, dangerous conditions of home, etc.)

8. Failure to Supervise. A parent's failure to supervise their child is a common basis for an abuse or neglect report. *See In re JA*, 962 P.2d 173 (Alaska. 1998), *In re Esmerelda B.*, 14 Cal. Rptr. 2d 179 (Cal. App. 1992). In many of these cases, there is no demonstrable harm to the child. Should harm be required before state intervention is authorized on grounds of failure to supervise? A "harm" requirement limits potentially undesirable intervention and also reduces the chance of intervention based upon personal or cultural differences between the parent and the judge or social worker. On the other hand, if actual harm is required, more children may be left in dangerous circumstances without assistance or protection.

Courts vary in response to deaths of children due to their parents' failure to supervise, and surrounding circumstances play an important role in the outcomes. In a recent Virginia case, a 21-month old child died of hyperthermia when her father left her in the family van for seven hours on a sweltering day. Kevin Kelly, father of 12 children, who was responsible for the children while his wife was in Ireland, received a token jail sentence despite the jury's recommendation that he serve a year in jail. *See* White, *Father Gets Scant Jail Time in Death*, Wash. Post, Feb. 22, 2003, at A01. Kelly told the police that he thought that the child had been removed from the van by an older child. Although members of the Kellys' church testified that the family was close knit and the children were hard-working and well-behaved, neighbors reported that other children had been left in the van before. White, *Inquiry Expands in Death of Girl*, Wash. Post, Jun. 1, 2003, at B1. In contrast, consider *State v. Goff,* 686 P.2d 1023 (Ore. 1984), in which a mother left her two children, ages eight and 22 months, at home alone at 9:30 p.m. while she attended a Halloween party at a local tavern. She left the older child watching television, with the telephone numbers of the tavern and a friend's residence directly across the street. Both children died in a fire that started before the mother returned (for the second time) at 2 a.m. An appellate court reversed the mother's conviction of child neglect, on the grounds that there was "no evidence of a substantial and unjustifiable risk that defendant should have recognized would be likely to endanger her children." The Oregon Supreme Court reversed, reinstating the criminal conviction.

9. *Federal Child Protection Legislation.* Since 1980, state child protection statutes have incorporated provisions dictated by Federal legislation. The Adoption Assistance and Child Welfare Act of 1980 (AACWA) made federal matching funds for foster care and adoption assistance available if states adopted prescribed standards for intervention in abuse and neglect cases. 42 U.S.C.A. §§670–676 (West 1996 & Supp. 2003). The most important requirements are that the state must make reasonable efforts to prevent removal of children from their homes and to reunify the family once removal occurs (42 U.S.C. §671(15)); a case plan must be developed that is designed to achieve placement in the least restrictive setting available (42 U.S.C. §§671(16), 675(1), 675(5)(B)); and the child's status must be periodically reviewed (42 U.S.C. §675(5)(B)). If the child cannot be returned home, a plan must be made for the child's adoption, legal guardianship or other permanent placement. *Id.*

In 1997, Congress enacted the Adoption and Safe Families Act P.L. 105-89 to facilitate adoption of children in foster care. The new statute amended the requirements of the AACWA to provide that the state may place the child in foster care without making reasonable efforts to retain her in the home in the following cases: i) cases involving "aggravated circumstances" (abandonment, chronic abuse, sexual abuse); ii) cases in which the parent has committed murder or voluntary manslaughter of another child, or iii) cases involving felony assault resulting in serious bodily injury to any child. The new statute also directs states to initiate termination of parental rights for children who have been in foster care for 15 of the preceding 22 months.

The Supreme Court has held that the AACWA requirement that the state make "reasonable efforts" to preserve and reunify families was not intended by Congress to create a private right of action in child beneficiaries of the Act under §1983 of the Civil Rights Act. *Suter v. Artist M.*, 503 U.S. 347 (1992). *Suter* was a class action suit against the Illinois Department of Children and Family Services for injunctive and declaratory relief claiming that the Department violated the reasonable efforts requirement because it failed to promptly assign caseworkers to children in state custody. After *Suter*, parents and children who seek to challenge a state's failure to make reasonable efforts to avoid removal of a child or to reunify the family must rely on state statutory or regulatory requirements (often based on the Federal statutory requirements), as no direct remedy is available for a state's failure to enforce the requirements of the Federal statute. Before *Suter*, some courts had provided this relief, relying directly on the obligation created under AACWA. *See, e.g. In re S.A.D.*, 555 A.2d. 123 (Pa. Super. Ct. 1989) (no finding of neglect by parents where state agency failed to make reasonable efforts to assist homeless mother to find suitable housing for herself and her child).

10. *Abuse of Other Children and by Other Adults.* Should a parent's abuse of a child constitute grounds for state intervention as to other children in the same family? Many courts have held that abuse or neglect of one child may not be established based upon facts constituting abuse or neglect of another. *See, e.g., In re Appeal in Cochise County Juvenile Action No. 5666-J,* 650 P.2d 459 (Ariz. 1982). Some courts have concluded that abuse of another child in the household is relevant, but that the judge has discretion to weigh the evidence. *See, e.g. Matter of Nicholson,* 440 S.E.2d. 852 (N.C. App. 1994) (no mandate to remove child whose half-brother died at hands of mother and stepfather, victim of shaken baby syndrome.) Other courts go further, and in severe enough circumstances, find that abuse of one child establishes that other children are in "imminent danger." *See, e.g., In re S.G.,* 581 A.2d 771 (D.C. App. 1990) (sexual abuse of 12-year-old girl by stepfather since she was seven years old warranted finding of neglect as to stepfather's younger three children); *In re Christina Maria C.,* 453 N.Y.S.2d 33 (App. Div. 1982) (physical brutalizing of seven-year-old boy warranted finding that one-year-old half-sister was in imminent danger of excessive physical punishment).

In some circumstances, potential child abuse may consist of allowing another person to abuse the child. Typically, where a parent ignores or condones abusive conduct by another (often the mother's boyfriend or husband), most statutes allow a finding of abuse against that parent for failure to protect the child. The Illinois Supreme Court sustained the murder convictions of two mothers whose young children died from physical abuse administered by the mothers' boyfriends. *People v. Stanciel,* 606 N.E.2d 1201 (Ill. 1992). For more on this general topic from a feminist perspective, see Roberts, *Motherhood and Crime,* 79 Iowa L. Rev. 95 (1993).

If the primary abuser is removed from the home, removal of the child may not be necessary. Minnesota statutes specifically authorize the court to remove an abusing party from the dwelling. *See* Minn. Stat. § 260C.148 (2003).

[2] FAILURE TO PROVIDE MEDICAL TREATMENT FOR THE CHILD

[a] The Minor Child

NEWMARK v. WILLIAMS

588 A.2d 1108 (Del. 1991)

Moore, Justice.

Colin Newmark, a three year old child, faced death from a deadly aggressive and advanced form of pediatric cancer known as Burkitt's Lymphoma. . . . The Delaware Division of Child Protective Services ("DCPS") petitioned the Family Court for temporary custody of Colin to authorize the Alfred I. duPont Institute ("duPont Institute"), a nationally recognized children's hospital, to treat Colin's condition with chemotherapy. His parents, Morris and Kara Newmark, are well educated and economically prosperous. As members of the First Church of Christ, Scientist ("Christian Science") they rejected medical treatment proposed for Colin, preferring instead a course of spiritual aid and prayer. The parents rely upon provisions of Delaware law, which exempt those who treat their children's illnesses "*solely* by spiritual means" from the abuse and neglect statutes. Thus, they opposed the State's petition. *See* 10 *Del.C.* § 901(11) & 16 *Del.C.* § 907 (emphasis added). The Newmarks also claimed that removing Colin from their custody would violate their First Amendment right. . . to freely exercise their religion. . . .

The Family Court rejected both of these arguments and awarded custody of Colin to DCPS. . . .

We heard this appeal on an emergency basis. . . .

. . . . In late August, 1990, the Newmarks noticed that [Colin] had lost most of his appetite and was experiencing frequent vomiting. The symptoms at first appeared occasionally but soon worsened.

The Newmarks reluctantly took Colin to the duPont Institute for examination. The parties stipulated that this violated the Newmarks' Christian Science beliefs in the effectiveness of spiritual healing. The parties further stipulated that the Newmarks acted out of concern for their potential criminal liability. . .

Dr. Meek [a pediatric oncologist]. . . diagnosed Colin's condition as Burkitt's Lymphoma,[and] recommended . . . a heavy regimen of chemotherapy.

Dr. Meek opined that the chemotherapy offered a 40% chance of "curing" Colin's illness. She concluded that he would die within six to eight months without treatment. The Newmarks, learning of Colin's condition only after the surgery, advised Dr. Meek that they would place him under the care of a Christian Science practitioner and reject all medical treatment for their son. . . . There was no doubt that the Newmarks sincerely believed. . . that the tenets of their faith provided an effective treatment. . . .

. . . . [W]e turn to the novel legal question whether, under any circumstances, Colin was a neglected child when his parents refused to accede to medical demands that he receive a radical form of chemotherapy having only a forty percent chance of success. . . Other jurisdictions differ in their approaches to this important and intensely personal issue. Some courts resolved the question on an *ad hoc* basis, without a formal test. . . . [Others, such as t]he California Court of Appeals in *In re Ted B.,* 189 Cal. App. 3d 996, 235 Cal. Rptr. 22 (1987), employed the best interests test to determine if a child was neglected when his parents refused to permit treatment of his cancer with "mild" chemotherapy following more intense treatment. *Ted B.* weighed the gravity, or potential gravity of the child's illness, the treating physician's medical evaluation of the course of care, the riskiness of the treatment and the child's "expressed preferences" to ultimately judge whether his parents' decision to withhold chemotherapy served his "best interests." Finally, the Supreme Judicial Court of Massachusetts, in *Custody Of A Minor,* 375 Mass. 733, 379 N.E.2d 1053 (1978), utilized a tripartite balancing test which weighed the interests of the parents, their child and the State to determine whether a child was neglected when his parents refused to treat his leukemia with non-invasive chemotherapy. . . .

While we do not recognize the primacy of any one of the tests employed in other jurisdictions, we find that the trial court erred in not explicitly considering the competing interests at stake. The Family Court failed to consider the special importance and primacy of the familial relationship, including the autonomy of parental decision making authority over minor children. The trial court also did not consider the gravity of Colin's illness in conjunction with the invasiveness of the proposed chemotherapy and the considerable likelihood of failure. . . .

Any balancing test must begin with the parental interest. . . . The primacy of the familial unit is a bedrock principle of law. . . . We have repeatedly emphasized that the parental right is sacred which can be invaded for only the most compelling reasons. . . .

[T]he essential element of preserving the integrity of the family is maintaining the autonomy of the parent-child relationship. . . .

Parental autonomy to care for children free from government interference therefore satisfies a child's need for continuity and thus ensures his or her psychological and physical well-being. . . .

Parental authority to make fundamental decisions for minor children is also a recognized common law principle. . . . [T]he common law recognizes that the only party capable of authorizing medical treatment for a minor in "normal" circumstances is usually his parent or guardian.

Courts, therefore, give great deference to parental decisions involving minor children. . . .

We also recognize that parental autonomy over minor children is not an absolute right. Clearly, the State can intervene . . . where the health and safety of the child and the public at large are in jeopardy. *See Prince[v. Mass.]*, 321 U.S. at 166–67.

. . . . [C]ourts have accepted the doctrine of *parens patriae* to justify State intervention in cases of parental religious objections to medical treatment of minor children's life threatening conditions. . . . [I]n *Prince*, 321 U.S. at 170,. . . [t]he Court found that parental autonomy, under the guise of the parents' religious freedom, was not unlimited. . . .

Parents may be free to become martyrs themselves. But it does not follow they are free, in identical circumstances, to make martyrs of their children before they have reached the age of full and legal discretion when they can make that choice for themselves. *Id.*

The basic principle underlying the *parens patriae* doctrine is the State's interest in preserving human life. . . . In its recent *Cruzan* opinion, the Supreme Court announced that the state's interest in preserving life must "be weighed against the constitutionally protected interests of the individual." 497 U.S. 261 (1990). . . .

The individual interests at stake here include both the Newmarks' right to decide what is best for Colin and Colin's own right to life. . . .

. . . .

All children indisputably have the right to enjoy a full and healthy life. Colin, a three year old boy, unfortunately lacked the ability to reach a detached, informed decision regarding his own medical care. This Court must therefore substitute its own objective judgment to determine what is in Colin's [best interests]. There are two basic inquiries when a dispute involves chemotherapy treatment over parents' religious objections. The court must first consider the effectiveness of the treatment and determine the child's chances of survival with and without medical care. . . . The court must then consider the nature of the treatments and their effect on the child. . . .

The "best interests" analysis is hardly unique or novel. Federal and State courts have unhesitatingly authorized medical treatment over a parent's religious objection when the treatment is relatively innocuous in comparison to the dangers of withholding medical care. . . . [C]ourts are reluctant to authorize medical care over parental objection when the child is not suffering a life threatening or potential life threatening illness. *See In re Green*, 292 A.2d 387, 392 (1972) (court refused to authorize corrective spine surgery on minor). . . .

The linchpin in all cases discussing the "best interests of a child". . . is an evaluation of the risk of the procedure compared to its potential success. This analysis is consistent with the principle that State intervention in the parent-child relationship is only justifiable under compelling conditions. The State's interest in forcing a minor to undergo medical care diminishes as the risks of treatment increase and its benefits decrease. . . .

[M]ost courts which have authorized medical treatment on a minor over parental objection have . . . noted that a different situation exists when the treatment is inherently dangerous and invasive. . . . *Muhlenberg Hospital*, 128 N.J. Super. at 503, 320 A.2d at 521 ("if the disputed procedure involved a significant danger to the infant, the parents' wishes would be respected.")

Applying the foregoing considerations to the "best interests standard" here, the State's petition must be denied. . . . Colin's proposed medical treatment was highly invasive, painful, involved terrible temporary and potentially permanent side effects, posed an unacceptably low chance of success, and a high risk that the treatment itself would cause his death. The State's authority to intervene in this case, therefore, cannot outweigh the Newmarks' parental prerogative and Colin's inherent right to enjoy at least a modicum of human dignity in the short time that was left to him. . . .

Dr. Meek. . . testified that the cancer was "a very bad tumor" in an advanced disseminated state. . . . She accordingly recommended that the hospital begin an "extremely intensive" chemotherapy program scheduled to extend for at least six months. . . .

Dr. Meek prescribed "maximum" doses of at least six different types of cancer-fighting drugs during Colin's chemotherapy. This proposed "maximum" treatment represented the most aggressive form of cancer therapy short of a bone marrow transplant. The side effects would include hair loss, reduced immunological function creating a high risk of infection in the patient, and certain neurological problems. The drugs also are toxic to bone marrow.

[T]his form of chemotherapy also would adversely affect other parts of Colin's body. . . . The chemotherapy would reduce Colin's white blood count, and it would be extremely likely that he would suffer numerous infections. Colin would require multiple blood transfusions with a resultant additional risk of infection. . . .

The physicians planned to administer the chemotherapy in cycles, each of which would bring Colin near death. Then they would wait until Colin's body recovered sufficiently before introducing more drugs. . . . The doctor noted that it would then be necessary to radiate Colin's testicles if drugs alone were unsuccessful. Presumably, this would have rendered him sterile.

Dr. Meek also wanted the State to place Colin in a foster home after the initial phases of hospital treatment. Children require intensive home monitoring during chemotherapy. . . . She believed that the Newmarks, although well educated and financially responsible, were incapable of providing this intensive care because of their firm religious objections to medical treatment.

Dr. Meek ultimately admitted that there was a real possibility that the chemotherapy could kill Colin. In fact, assuming the treatment did not itself prove fatal, she offered Colin at "best" a 40% chance that he would "survive."[12] Dr. Meek additionally could not accurately predict whether, if Colin completed the therapy, he would subsequently suffer additional tumors. . . .

No American court, even in the most egregious case, has ever authorized the State to remove a child from the loving, nurturing care of his parents and subject him, over parental objection, to an invasive regimen of treatment which offered, as Dr. Meek defined the term, only a forty percent chance of "survival". . . .

> [The court cites several cases in which the disputed treatment was ordered, but was less invasive or the prospect of success greater than in the case before it, including a New York case in which the prospect for a "cure" with treatment was 25–30%. *In re Application of L.I. Jewish Med. Ctr.,* 147 Misc. 2d at 725, 557 N.Y.S.2d at 241. The court distinguished this case on the ground that the Jehovah's Witness parents were not per se opposed to the prescribed chemotherapy, but to the blood transfusion that accompanied it. The court also cites an Ohio case in which the child was placed in state custody because the parents refused to consent to the amputation of the child's shoulder and arm. *In re Willmann,* 493 N.E.2d at 1383 (Ohio App.) The court acknowledges that the mandated treatment was invasive, but notes that the child had a 60% chance of survival with the surgery.]

The aggressive form of chemotherapy that Dr. Meek prescribed for Colin was more likely to fail than succeed. [I]t was also highly invasive and could have independently caused Colin's death. Dr. Meek also wanted to take Colin away from his parents and family during the treatment phase and place the boy in a foster home. This certainly would have caused Colin severe emotional

---

[12] Dr. Meek . . . stated that the term "survival", as applied to victims of leukemia or lymphoma, refers only to the probability that the patient will live two years after chemotherapy without a recurrence of cancer.

difficulties given his medical condition, tender age, and the unquestioned close bond between Colin and his family.

In sum, Colin's best interests were served by permitting the Newmarks to retain custody. . . . Parents must have the right at some point to reject medical treatment for their child. Under all of the circumstances here, this clearly is such a case. The State's important and legitimate role in safeguarding the interests of minor children diminishes in the face of this egregious record.

Parents undertake an awesome responsibility in raising and caring for their children. No doubt a parent's decision to withhold medical care is both deeply personal and soul wrenching. It need not be made worse by the invasions which both the State and medical profession sought on this record. Colin's ultimate fate therefore rested with his parents and their faith.[13]

NOTES

1. Overriding Parents' Refusal of Medical Treatment. As *Newmark* suggests, courts are generally inclined to be deferential toward parents' decisions not to seek conventional medical treatment for their children, especially when their decisions are based on religious convictions. Many courts will not override parents' refusal of treatment unless the decision poses a serious threat of the child's death or permanent impairment. At one level, this stance is puzzling in the context of general policies that guide state intervention. Courts seem far more ready to intervene and even remove children from their parents in situations of neglect where the harmful consequences for the child are far more uncertain. *See* Section B1, *supra*. Indeed, where the parents' failure to obtain medical treatment is part of a general pattern of neglect and inadequate care (*e.g.*, the parents repeatedly fail to bring the child to medical appointments that are part of a regimen to treat a chronic condition), medical neglect may justify intervention. Judicial deference is reserved for affirmative parental decisions not to seek treatment — usually (but not always) based on parents' religious beliefs. Intelligent thoughtful parents like the Newmarks, who decline treatment on the basis of their Christian Science beliefs, are representative of parents whose decisions are respected by courts. Moreover, almost all states have statutes that protect parents' decisions to seek spiritual treatment for their children rather than conventional medical treatment for their children. *See* note 2, *infra*.

What makes *Newmark* somewhat unusual is that Colin faced almost certain death without treatment. Did the court give this adequate consideration? The opinion focuses primarily on the harm of the treatment and the prognosis *with* treatment, emphasizing the invasive nature of the chemotherapy regimen and the prediction that, at best, the likelihood of survival was 40%. The court is surely correct that ordering invasive and painful treatment that offers no real hope would be hard to justify. But is that the case here? Putting aside the parents' religious beliefs, would most people accept those odds and get treatment for themselves or their children, given the alternative? If so, should the Newmarks' wishes be respected, when the outcome almost certainly is the

---

[13] Tragically, Colin died shortly after we announced our oral decision.

child's death? Professor James Dwyer has sharply criticized deference to parental authority on the basis of religious belief in this context. Dwyer, *Parents' Religion and Children's Welfare: Debunking the Doctrine of Parents' Rights*, 82 CAL. L. REV. 1371 (1994).

The American Academy of Pediatrics asserts that children should receive effective treatment despite parents religiously-based objections "when such treatment is likely to prevent substantial harm or suffering or death." Committee on Bioethics, American Academy of Pediatrics, *Religious Objections to Medical Care*, 99 PEDIATRICS 279 (1997). Would the Academy support a treatment order in *Newmark*?

Parents who insistently reject treatment, based on obviously irrational beliefs, do not fare as well. In *A.D.H. v. State Dept. of Human Resources*, 640 So. 2d. 969 (Ala. Civ. App. 1994), the court ordered AZT treatment over the mother's objection for an HIV-infected child. The court justified the intervention for this (presumably) fatal condition, despite the side effects of the treatment, because it would likely slow the progress of the disease, and also because the mother denied that the child was HIV-infected.

Most courts will order treatment over parents' objections when the child's life is at stake. *See, e.g., Custody of a Minor*, 379 N.E.2d 1053 (Mass. 1978); *Custody of a Minor*, 393 N.E.2d 836 (Mass. 1979). Chad Green had lymphocytic leukemia which had responded to chemotherapy. With the leukemia in remission, Chad's parents discontinued treatment and refused to resume treatment until ordered by the court. The court declined to allow them to supplement chemotherapy with "metabolic therapy" that included laetrile and vitamins, persuaded by the state's physicians that the laetrile would actually harm the child by causing cyanide poisoning. The parents then fled with the child to Mexico, where he received laetrile treatment and died at age three. When his parents later returned to Massachusetts, they were held in contempt for having violated the court order, but were not fined or imprisoned because, in the judge's view, they had already been punished enough. *Judge Declines to Punish Parents in Laetrile Case; Father Apologizes to Judge over Couple's Actions*, N.Y. TIMES, Dec. 9, 1980, at B21.

Sometimes, courts order treatment over parents' religious objections, even though the child does not face death without treatment. In *In re Sampson*, the New York Court of Appeals upheld the trial court's order that 15-year-old Kevin Sampson should be treated surgically to remediate extensive disfiguring neurofibromatosis on his face and neck. 323 N.Y.S.2d 253 (App. Div. 1971). Because of his condition, Kevin had been exempted from school attendance requirements and was virtually illiterate. His mother, a Jehovah's Witness, did not oppose the surgery, but objected to the required blood transfusions. Describing Kevin's appearance as "grotesque and repulsive," the court concluded his condition severely interfered with his development and that his chance for a normal useful life without surgery was "virtually nil." Although a surgeon described the surgery as involving a high level of risk, which would decline as Kevin got older, the court declined to delay the procedure until Kevin was an adult because of what it viewed as overriding "developmental and psychological factors." Sampson may seem like a case in which the parents' decision not to treat should receive deference. The parental choice posed no risk to the child's life, while the court-ordered surgery did pose serious risk, which would likely decrease as Kevin matured. Also, the parental decision was based on religious conviction clearly protected under the First Amendment. Did the *Sampson* court believe (based on its own values) that Kevin's life was not worth living without the surgery? Would intervention be permitted in *Sampson* under the American Academy of Pediatrics standard described above?

2. *Religious Objections and the Faith-Healing Exceptions to Child Neglect Statutes.* Almost every state provides an exemption from (or defense to prosecution under) child abuse laws for parents who rely on their belief in faith healing rather than conventional medical treatment. *See, e.g.*, ARIZ. REV. STAT. ANN. §8-201.01 (West 1999)(no child who in good faith is being furnished Christian Science treatment by a duly accredited practitioner shall, for that reason alone, be considered to be an abused, neglected, or dependent child"); IND. CODE ANN. §35-46-1-4 (Michie 1988)) ("It is a defense [in a criminal child abuse action] that the accused person, in the legitimate practice of his religious belief, provided treatment by spiritual means through prayer, in lieu of medical care, to his dependent child.")

When a child dies as a result of the parents' rejection of conventional forms of medical treatment that could have saved the child in favor of faith healing, a split of authority has developed over whether parents can be prosecuted for homicide. Some courts have rejected parents' defenses based on religious accommodation provisions of child abuse statutes. *See, e.g.*, *Hall v. State*, 493 N.E.2d 433 (Ind. 1986) (upholding parents' conviction for reckless homicide, on grounds that spiritual healing exemption is not a defense to homicide); *Walker v. Superior Court*, 763 P.2d 852 (Cal. 1988), *cert. denied*, 491 U.S. 905 (1989) (upholding conviction for involuntary manslaughter of mother whose four-year-old daughter died of meningitis after having been treated exclusively by accredited Christian Science practitioners, because the faith healing exemption applies only to misdemeanor section in which it appears and not to manslaughter and child endangerment prosecutions). In *Commonwealth v. Twitchell*, 617 N.E.2d 609 (Mass. 1993), the Court concluded that the Christian Science parents, who failed to obtain medical treatment for their child's obstructive bowel, could be convicted of involuntary manslaughter when he died, if they recklessly or wantonly violated their parental duty. The statutory spiritual treatment exemption did not bar prosecution, or result in a lack of fair notice to the parents that they might face criminal prosecution. However, the appellate court concluded that the trial court erred in refusing to allow the parents to offer as an affirmative defense an Attorney General's opinion that could be interpreted to bar prosecution.

Other courts have found that criminal conviction under these circumstances is unconstitutional. In *Hermanson v. State*, 604 So. 2d 775 (Fla. 1992), the Supreme Court of Florida held that, because the state child abuse statute includes a religious accommodation provision, the subsequent prosecution for manslaughter of parents was a denial of Due Process. The Court reasoned that the statute gave no notice that parents, acting pursuant to the religious accommodation provision, might be subject to criminal liability. The lower court, relying on *Walker v. Superior Court*, upheld the parents' conviction on the ground that the religious accommodation provision in the child abuse statute provided no protection from criminal liability. The Supreme Court, however, concluded the statute failed to clearly "indicate the point at which a parent's reliance on his or her religious beliefs in the treatment of his or her children becomes criminal conduct." The Court suggested that the issue is purely one of fair notice (and not one of parents' Free Exercise rights under the First Amendment.) Thus, presumably, clear statutory delineation of protected and criminal conduct could support prosecution of parents under similar facts. *See also State v. McKown,* 461 N.W.2d 720 (Minn. Ct. App. 1990), *aff'd* 475 N.W.2d. 63 (Minn. 1991), *cert. denied,* 502 U.S. 1036 (1992) (same result on similar facts).

Is it possible to give parents "fair notice" that their conduct of consulting a faith healer is privileged under the child abuse statute, but may lead to liability for homicide if the child dies? Some courts seem to believe that the child's deteriorating condition in itself should lead parents to take affirmative steps when prayer has failed to heal. For example, consider the following:

> . . . From what started as a common . . . bacterial infection which responds to the most basic of modern antibiotics . . . Seth Miskemens died. First came illness, then more serious illness, then suffering, and then as valiant a struggle as his tiny heart and his weakened lungs would permit. And then after enduring for as long as he could the tremendous pain inherent in the multiple diseases that were attacking him, and then with a raging infection in his tiny chest, he weakened, he faltered, and he died. There is no more gentle way to describe it.

State v. Miskimens, 490 N.E.2d 931, 938 (Ohio Misc. 1984).

Statutory religious accommodation exemptions have generated considerable controversy. Some observers argue that they harm children's welfare. *See, e.g.* Dwyer, *The Children We Abandon: Religious Exemptions to Child Welfare and Education Laws as Denials of Equal Protection to Children of Religious Objectors,* 74 N.C.L. REV. 1321 (1996). The exemptions have also been criticized as provisions designed to benefit a particular religious group. Most of these statutes were enacted in response to lobbying efforts by Christian Scientists and, partly on this ground, have been subject to constitutional challenges. Consider the Delaware statute, for example, which exempts from the definition of "neglected child" children who receive treatment by spiritual means "in accordance with the tenets and practices of a recognized church. . . by a duly accredited practitioner thereof." 10 DEL. CODE § 901(11) (1999). In a part of the *Newmark* opinion not included above, the court suggests that this provision may violate the Establishment Clause. The court concluded that the statute was designed to benefit Christian Scientists, noting that the language (typical of many statutes) reflects the belief that only approved Christian Science practitioners can conduct spiritual healing. Moreover, the statute invited judicial inquiry into the validity of parents' religious beliefs and practices. The court declined to resolve the constitutional question, which had not been raised by the parties, but it invited a future challenge. [Although the Newmarks argued that their refusal was protected by the statute, the court did not rely on the exemption in reversing the court-ordered treatment.]

See also State v. Miskimens, supra (finding exemption to violate the Establishment Clause and Equal Protection Clause). Should the state be permitted to challenge its own duly enacted statute on which parents have relied?

Does the fact that Christian Scientist parents generally are educated professionals affect the societal response to their decision not to seek treatment, which results in the death of a child? Is it possible to approach the dilemma without making some assumptions about both the welfare of children and the validity of a particular set of religious (or nonreligious) beliefs? The approach of states that allow the religious exemption, but hold parents liable if the child dies, may be a reasonable compromise, allowing parents considerable latitude to act according to their religious beliefs, but signaling that there are clear limits to the freedom. On this topic generally, see Treene, *Prayer-Treatment Exemptions to Child Abuse and Neglect Statutes, Manslaughter Prosecutions, and Due Process of Law*, 30 Harv. J. Legis. 135 (1993).

3. *Treatment Refusals for Mature Minors.* Is parental refusal to consent to life-saving treatment for a child more readily justified if the child is an adolescent who agrees with the parents' decision on the basis of her own religious belief? In this situation, the minor may be competent to make the decision herself, and, indeed, a few courts have held that mature minors can refuse life saving treatment. In *In re E.G.*, 549 N.E.2d. 322 (Ill. 1989), the Illinois Supreme Court reversed a trial court decision ordering blood transfusions for a 17-year-old suffering from leukemia over the objection of the minor and her mother, both Jehovah's Witnesses. Applying the state's mature minor doctrine, the court concluded that a minor who is mature enough to "exercise the judgment of an adult" has a right to refuse treatment, unless her interest is overridden by other interests. In this case, the parental interest aligned with that of the child, leading the court to conclude that treatment should not be ordered. Was the case correctly decided? One concern might be that a dependent minor is not well situated to make an autonomous medical decision, and that intervention is appropriate where her life is at stake.

Should the fact that a mature child concurred with her parents' decision to refuse treatment be available as a defense to a manslaughter charge after the child's death? One court has rejected this claim brought by parents of a 16-year-old who died of untreated diabetes. *Commonwealth v. Nixon*, 761 A.2d 1151 (Pa. 2000), *cert. denied* 532 U.S. 1008 (2001). Both the parents and the child belonged to the Faith Tabernacle Church, a sect which rejected medical treatment in favor of spiritual treatment. The court rejected the parents' argument that the mature minor doctrine provided them with an affirmative defense to the manslaughter charge, if they could demonstrate that their daughter had the requisite maturity to refuse treatment. Distinguishing *E.G.*, above, the court concluded that the Pennsylvania statute created specific exceptions to the general rule that minors lack the capacity to consent to medical treatment and did not recognize a general mature minor exception.

PROBLEMS

Problem 10-6. As hospital legal counsel, you are told that physicians have concluded that the only real prospect for saving the life of an eight-year-old girl is a kidney transplant, and that the only potentially successful donor of likely success is her healthy twin sister. The attending physicians are confident that the children's parents will consent to such an operation if so advised by the physicians. Although it is a major operation with some risk, the healthy sister should be able to recover and live a normal life, apart from any speculative problems she might encounter if her remaining kidney were to become diseased. Should the hospital go forward with the operation on the basis of the parents' consent? If judicial authority is sought, is it likely to be granted?

Problem 10-7. Assume the same facts as Problem 10-6 except that the parents refuse to consent. The ill sister will die shortly if the operation is not performed. Should the hospital seek judicial authority for the operation? If it does, should the court grant it?

[b] The Infant

MINNESOTA STATUTES §260C.007 (2003)

Subd. 2a (5) . . . The term "withholding of medically indicated treatment" means the failure to respond to the infant's life-threatening conditions by providing treatment, including appropriate nutrition, hydration, and medication which, in the treating physician's . . . reasonable medical judgment, will be most likely to be effective in ameliorating or correcting all conditions, except that the term does not include the failure to provide treatment other than appropriate nutrition, hydration, or medication to an infant when, in the treating physician's . . . reasonable medical judgment:

(i) the infant is chronically and irreversibly comatose;

(ii) the provision of the treatment would merely prolong dying, not be effective in ameliorating or correcting all of the infant's life-threatening conditions, or otherwise be futile in terms of the survival of the infant; or

(iii) the provision of the treatment would be virtually futile in terms of the survival of the infant and the treatment itself under the circumstances would be inhumane. . . .

NOTES

1. *The "Baby Doe" Regulations.* Both federal and state law regulate decisions to withhold medical treatment from critically ill infants. The Minnesota statute set forth above is patterned after the Child Abuse Amendments of 1984, (amending The Child Abuse Prevention and Treatment Act of 1974, (CAPTA) 42 U.S.C. §§5101–5107 (2002). This law conditions federal financial assistance to states for programs relating to child abuse and neglect on the incorporation of many child protection standards into state law. The federal rules relating to withholding of medically-indicated treatment apply only to infants.

Federal intervention in this area began in 1982 in the wake of public controversy over the death of a Downs Syndrome baby ("Baby Doe") whose Bloomington, Indiana parents refused to consent to necessary but routine, lifesaving surgery. *In re Guardianship of Infant Doe,* No. 1-782 A157 (Ind. 1982). The Reagan administration enacted regulations under Section 504 of the Rehabilitation Act of 1973, 29 U.S.C. §794 (1982), which prohibits recipients of federal funds from discriminating against an "otherwise qualified" individual "on the basis of his handicap." The theory was that by denying a handicapped newborn medical treatment that other children would receive, the hospital violated the statutory nondiscrimination provision. The problems with the theory were (a) the parents, not the hospital, are the source of consent for medical treatment, but only the hospital was covered by the Act, as a recipient of funds, and (b) it was far from clear how to apply, in the medical context, the Act's criterion of "otherwise qualified." The Supreme Court eventually held that Congress had not intended the Rehabilitation Act to apply to such cases, thus voiding the regulations. *Bowen v. American Hosp. Ass'n,* 476 U.S. 610 (1986). By then enacting the Child Abuse Amendments, Congress subsequently established the authorization found lacking in *Bowen.* The Minnesota statute represents typical state legislation based on the federal requirements.

To evaluate the difficult conceptual issues in this area, it is helpful first to understand the wide variation in the medical circumstances in which nontreatment issues arise. In one group of cases that include children with Downs syndrome and spina bifida, non-treatment is no longer an issue. Downs Syndrome yields a very wide range of mental disabilities and it is difficult to tell at birth how severe a particular child's mental handicap will be. The condition itself presents no special medical requirements, but, as newborns, Downs Syndrome babies suffer disproportionately from intestinal blockages (experienced by the Bloomington Baby Doe). An infant with an intestinal blockage will shortly die of starvation without corrective surgery, since he cannot ingest food — which was what happened to the Bloomington baby. Surgery to repair the intestinal blockage is relatively minor, involves little risk, and would be performed without question on an otherwise healthy baby. For children with spina bifida, surgery early in life to close the lesion to prevent infection is often indicated. Today, few would argue against performing surgeries over the parents' objections for children with these conditions.

Other conditions where the outcome is very unpredictable present more difficulty. For example, some infants are born so prematurely that their prognosis and prospects for survival are highly uncertain. Because of advances in neonatal technology, infants whose birth weight is very low and whose respiratory and other bodily systems are not developed at birth can receive sophisticated treatment that greatly improves their chances for survival compared to those that such infants faced a generation ago. Often, however, both the likelihood of survival and the extent of physical or mental impairment if the child survives are very uncertain. Moreover, in some cases, the treatment itself will cause great pain and discomfort for the child. In evaluating the burdens of the treatment and its uncertain outcome, people will vary in the decisions that they reach for their children. Should the law impose a particular choice?

Finally there are cases in which the prognosis is grim and the child's prospects for a minimally satisfying life are slim. The child may face a life which predictably will be very brief; or which, whatever its duration, will be filled with pain and discomfort; or the child's impairment may be so profound that she will have little ability to function mentally or physically — she may be unable to see, hear, sit, walk, understand language or relate to other people. Where the child does not face imminent death, many observers believe that the decision about treatment is not straightforward or simple. If the child cannot look forward to "a life worth living," the question becomes whether medical efforts should be made to sustain the child's life. The federal regulations reflect the view that society, or parents, should not be making judgments about whether a child should receive medical treatment based upon the quality of life that the child can expect. On the other hand, adults, at least in practice, are able to (and do) make this decision for themselves. How much pain should a child have to endure?

The fears of those favoring regulation of medical decisionmaking in this area are (1) that doctors may overestimate the severity of the handicap and underestimate its treatability; and (2) that parents may have a conflict of interest. A severely handicapped child may be seen as an onerous burden to avoid, as well as a threat to the welfare of other siblings whose access to parental time and resources will be sharply curtailed as a result of the handicapped child's demands. We may not be able to tell whether a parent's decision is based entirely on considerations of the disabled child's interests. Should we care? Perhaps, if the parental decision is one which could rationally be made by someone considering only the child's interests, it should not matter what the parents' actual motivations are.

Should newborn cases be treated differently from those involving treatment of older children? One argument is that because the parents of older children will normally have formed a relational bond with the child, they will be more likely to make decisions with that child's best interests in mind, and we thus should more readily defer to their judgment. Another concern is that the parents of a newborn may be peculiarly handicapped in their ability to make a reasoned dispassionate decision in the child's interest. They may be in a state of shock, having anticipated the joyous occasion of the birth of a child, only to be confronted with the unhappy news of the child's condition. Further, the mother's own medical condition may undermine her ability to deal with the crisis and confront the tragic, circumstances.

2. *The Debate About Non-Treatment.* Recent years have seen considerable efforts to ensure, through devices such as living wills, that adult patients can decline additional medical care in appropriate circumstances. Indeed, the Supreme Court has suggested that it is their right, at least where they express their wishes clearly enough. *Cruzan v. Harmon,* 497 U.S. 261 (1990). Does respect for newborns as human beings compel the conclusion that they also have this right? Some so argue. *See, e.g.,* Parness & Stevenson, *Let Live and Let Die: Disabled Newborns and Contemporary Law,* 37 U. MIAMI L. REV. 43 (1982). Newborns are not like adults, however, for they cannot speak for themselves. This difference is critical, for the right to die is based upon the principle of autonomy and a commitment to the right of an individual to choose whether he or she wishes to receive further medical treatment. When one person makes a decision that *someone else* should not receive treatment, an autonomy-based right to die would not seem to apply. *See* Ellman, *Can Others Exercise an Incapacitated Patient's Right to Die?,* 20 HASTINGS CENTER REPORT, Jan./Feb. 1990, at 47. It was essentially on this reasoning that *Cruzan* held that a state is not constitutionally compelled to permit surrogate decisionmakers to terminate life-sustaining treatment for a patient who had not made his or her own wishes in the matter clear. However, unless someone can make this decision for the severely-ill newborn, an option for release from pain and illness that adults value is unavailable.

The exclusion of "quality of life" considerations under federal law does not reflect the norms of the medical profession. A study in a neonatal intensive care unit over a 3-year period in the 1990s suggested that medical care is withdrawn or withheld resulting in death only in the most extreme cases, but that quality -of-life concerns affect the decisions in many cases. Wall & Partridge, *Death in the Intensive Care Nursery: Physician Practice of Withdrawing or Withholding Life Support,* 99 PEDIATRICS 64 (1997). A large percentage of the decisions were based on a conclusion that treatment was "futile" based on imminent death — which is a basis of withholding treatment under the regulations. The American Medical Association Code of Medical Ethics, § 217 (1994), also provides that the quality of life of the severely disabled newborn is a factor to be considered in treatment decisions. Scholarly commentary has also been critical of the federal law, in large part because of its failure to allow adequate consideration of quality of life factors. *See, e.g.,* Rhoden, *Treatment Dilemmas for Imperiled Newborns: Why Quality of Life Counts,* 58 S. CAL. L. REV. 1283 (1985). *See also,* Minow, *Beyond State Intervention in the Family: For Baby Jane Doe,* 18 U. MICH. J.L. REF. 933 (1985) (criticizing adversarial structure promoted by state intervention mechanisms and suggesting strategies for building more trust in medical decisionmaking).

The issue of non-treatment of newborns has always had a political\ideological dimension and religious groups have argued that non-treatment violates the infant's right to life. In a highly publicized case in Virginia, a mother, based on her religious convictions and supported by right-to-live advocates, challenged the hospital for providing routine care but no respiratory support to her anencephalic infant. *Matter of Baby "K" (Three Cases),* 16 F.3d 590 (4th Cir. 1994), *cert. denied* 513 U.S. 825 (1994). This child had a sufficiently developed brainstem that her basic respiratory functions could continue unassisted for some time. The court held that the hospital was obliged to place the child on a ventilator when needed, under the federal Emergency Medical Treatment and Active Labor Act. The decision is puzzling, at a minimum, because, as the dissenting judge pointed out, the statute was intended to deal with a very specific problem: hospital "dumping" of patients with no medical insurance. It requires covered hospitals to provide stabilizing treatment in emergency medical situations, to ensure that they do not turn away uninsured patients. The language of the act can nonetheless be read as requiring the hospital to provide any person with an "emergency" medical condition with either stabilizing treatment or appropriate transfer to another institution. By considering the child's episodic bouts with respiratory distress, rather than the anencephaly, as the relevant medical condition, the court concluded that the Act required repeated treatment by the hospital. *See* Flannery, *One Advocate's Viewpoint: Conflicts and Tensions in the Baby K*

Case, 23 J.L. MED. & ETHICS 7 (1995) (discussion by attorney for Baby K's mother).

What happens if parents choose to treat a child who meets the criteria for withdrawal? Ordinarily the parent's decision controls, but under some circumstances courts will override a parental decision to treat. In *In re K.I.*, 735 A.2d 448 (D.C. 1999), a District of Columbia appellate court upheld an order not to aggressively resuscitate a neglected two-year-old over the mother's objection. The child was in a comatose state from conditions that ultimately were caused by her premature birth (and her mother's neglect); she was able to feel pain, but had no cognitive awareness. The putative father agreed with the DNR order. The court rejected the mother's argument that she be allowed to make the decision under a substituted judgment standard, holding that the best interest standard was appropriately applied in the case of a neglected child in state custody whose parents were not in agreement about his care.

The article which initially focused attention on the Baby Doe issue is Duff & Campbell, *Moral and Ethical Dilemmas in the Special-Care Nursery*, 289 NEW ENG. J. MED. 890 (1973). Among the most influential, subsequent works on the moral and ethical issues are President's Commission for the Study of Ethical Problems in Medicine and Biomedical and Behavioral Research, Pub. No. 83-17978, *Deciding to Forego Life Sustaining Treatment* (1983) (containing section specifically on newborns); P. RAMSEY, ETHICS AT THE EDGES OF LIFE (1978) (rejecting assessments of the baby's probable quality of life as a basis for treatment decisions); Robertson, *Involuntary Euthanasia of Defective Newborns: A Legal Analysis,* 27 STAN. L. REV. 213 (1975); For more recent treatment of the issues, *see* CAPLAN, BLANK & MERRICK, COMPELLED COMPASSION: GOVERNMENT INTERVENTION IN THE TREATMENT OF CRITICALLY ILL NEWBORNS (1992); Fine, *Government as God: An Update on Federal Intervention in the Treatment of Critically Ill Newborns*, 34 NEW ENG. L. REV. 343 (2000).

PROBLEM

Problem 10-8. Baby Jane is born on Nov. 1, and her parents come to consult you shortly thereafter. The child has a number of severe congenital defects. The parents and their doctors have agreed not to perform surgery on her, but the doctors are nervous because of a recent call to the hospital from county welfare department officials who are aware of the baby as a result of a complaint filed with them by a nurse on the hospital staff. The parents anticipate a neglect proceeding may be brought.

Consultations with the attending physicians reveal that the child was born with a lesion high on her back, exposing the spinal cord (spina bifida). There is also an abnormality on the spine above the lesion. She has massive hydrocephalus (fluid on the brain) and very little brain tissue as a result of the damage caused by the hydrocephalus. Regardless of what care is provided, the physicians believe the child will be so severely retarded she will never talk or understand speech. They are not certain that she will ultimately be able to recognize people and be able to smile. As a result of spinal cord damage, she will never be able to walk, sit up or become continent. Another physician with experience treating such children, however, gives a more optimistic prognosis regarding her intellectual development, saying that some similar babies he had cared for ultimately developed I.Q.s of 60 or 70. He is not confident that this child will be so fortunate, however.

Aggressive treatment would ultimately involve 30 to 45 surgeries to deal with problems such as curvature of the spine and urinary problems, as well as shunts to drain the fluid from the brain. The immediate question is whether to perform surgery to close the opening on the back, to prevent infection which could be fatal, and to drain the fluid on the brain, to make the baby easier to handle and prevent further damage. The attending physicians estimate that with aggressive treatment, the child would still probably not survive more than a year, although survival up to 20 years is conceivable. Without aggressive treatment, her life span will probably be between six weeks and six months.

As a result of their discussions with physicians, the parents have concluded that the child would be better off without treatment. On the other hand, if they will be compelled ultimately to authorize surgery, they would prefer to begin immediately, so as to give their daughter the best chance of success. They want to know their prospects for resisting legal challenges to their right to decide upon their daughter's treatment. What do you advise under the federal standards adopted by Minnesota?

[3]   ABUSE OR NEGLECT OF THE FETUS

[a]   Court-Ordered Caesareans and Other Mandated Treatment of Mothers

As we have seen, courts sometimes order necessary medical treatment of children over the objections of parents. Can medical treatment of a parent be ordered to save the life of her child? The issue sometimes arises when a pregnant woman refuses medical treatment — most commonly a Caesarian section, — contrary to medical opinion that the procedure is necessary for the child to survive. Although trial courts have occasionally ordered caesareans against the wishes of the mother, almost uniformly, appellate courts have rejected efforts to override the decisions of competent women refusing this invasive medical procedure.

An Illinois court addressed this issue in *In re Baby Boy Doe* 632 N.E.2d 326 (Ill. App. 1994), a case involving a married woman pregnant with her first child, who refused to consent to a caesarian section because of her religious beliefs. The state's attorney petitioned the circuit court to give the hospital custody of the fetus for the purpose of ordering the operation, without which, according to consultants who examined Doe, the child would likely be born dead or severely retarded. The juvenile court denied the state's petition, concluding that the state had failed to establish a legal basis for ordering an intrusive procedure over the objection of a competent person. [A few weeks later Doe gave birth to an apparently healthy baby.]

The appellate court affirmed the trial court's decision, holding that "a woman's competent choice in refusing medical treatment as invasive as a caesarean section during her pregnancy must be honored, even in circumstances where the choice may be harmful to her fetus." The court recognized that the right to refuse unwanted treatment was a protected liberty interest under the Due Process clause; it noted that the Supreme Court had often found "state incursions into the body repugnant to the interests protected by the Due Process Clause." *Cruzan v. Director, Missouri Department of Health* 497 U.S. 261, 287 (1990) (O'Connor, J. concurring). Moreover, both the federal and Illinois constitutions require that a competent adult may refuse medical treatment on religious grounds. The court then turned to Doe's pregnant condition.

[A] woman's right to refuse invasive medical treatment, derived from her rights to privacy, bodily integrity, and religious liberty, is not diminished during pregnancy. The woman retains the same right to refuse invasive treatment, even if lifesaving or of other beneficial nature, that she can exercise when she is not pregnant. The potential impact upon the fetus is not legally relevant. . . .

In Illinois a fetus. . . has the legal right to begin life with a sound mind and body, assertable against third parties after it has been born alive. . . . This right is not assertable against its mother, however, for the unintentional infliction of prenatal injuries. . . . A woman. . . cannot be compelled to do or not do anything merely for the benefit of her unborn child.

The *Doe* court emphasized that courts in general have consistently refused to force one person to undergo medical procedures for the purpose of benefitting another person "even where the two persons share a blood relationship, and even where the risk to the first person is perceived to be minimal and the benefit to the second person may be great." It also rejected the argument that the viable fetus had rights under *Roe v. Wade* 410 U.S. 113 (1973), that supported mandatory treatment.

> The fact that the state may prohibit post-viability pregnancy terminations does not [mean] that the state may intrude upon the woman's right to remain free from unwanted physical invasion of her person when she chooses to carry her pregnancy to term. *Roe* and its progeny. . . make it clear that, even in the context of abortion, the state's compelling interest in the potential life of the fetus is insufficient to override the woman's interest in preserving her health.

Jefferson v. Griffin-Spalding Cty. Hosp. Auth., 274 S.E.2d 457 (Ga. 1981), is a rare reported appellate judicial decision compelling a caesarian procedure. In *Jefferson*, the evidence indicated that due to a condition known as placenta previa, not only was the child almost certain to die unless delivered by caesarean, but the mother's life was also at risk without surgery. Thus, the caesarian ordered in *Jefferson* was to save the life of the mother as well as the fetus. Is that distinction from *Doe* important, given that adults typically have a right to refuse life-saving treatment?

Courts occasionally order surgery where the pregnant woman is incompetent to make the decision. In *In re A.C.,* the mother was dying of cancer, and had a life expectancy of a few weeks in her 26th week of pregnancy when a hearing was convened to determine whether a caesarian delivery should be ordered. 573 A.2d 1235 (D.C. 1990). The physicians testified that the fetus had a 50% chance of survival if delivered immediately, but that its condition was worsening. A.C. was heavily sedated, and the evidence concerning whether she would have agreed to the procedure was ambiguous and conflicting. The trial court ordered the surgery; both A.C. and the baby died shortly thereafter. The Court of Appeals rejected the trial court's decision, emphasizing that the law does not "compel one person to permit a significant intrusion upon his or her bodily integrity for the benefit of another's health." Do you agree with the appellate court? Is this case different from *Baby Boy Doe*, since A.C.'s wishes were unclear? The court's analysis indicates that the surgery could be authorized if clear evidence of the mother's intentions supported this outcome. Does it matter that her mother, apparently the closest family member present, objected to the surgery?

In fact, there is almost no legal precedent, outside *Jefferson,* for compelling one person to undergo surgery for the benefit of another. Consider, for example, a child whose survival depends upon a bone marrow transplant, and for whom the only compatible donor that can be located in time is his father. Most people would find it reprehensible for the father to refuse to donate marrow in this case, but would a court compel him to do so if he refused? There is no authority precisely on point, but such authority as exists suggests that it would not. In *Curran v. Bosze,* 566 N.E.2d 1319 (Ill. 1990), a case discussed in *Baby Boy Doe,* the Illinois Supreme Court declined to order the mother of the healthy half-brothers of a 13-year-old boy with leukemia to consent to have her sons tested for compatibility for a bone marrow donation. Certainly a parent has a greater duty to their child than does a sibling, but is the duty great enough to compel surgery?

The Committee on Ethics of the American College of Obstetricians and Gynecologists has issued an opinion on Maternal-Fetal Conflict, which concludes in part:

> The use of courts to resolve . . . conflict [between maternal and fetal interests] is almost never warranted. Obstetricians should refrain from performing procedures that are unwanted by pregnant women. The use of judicial authority to implement treatment regimens in order to protect the fetus violates the pregnant woman's autonomy. Furthermore, inappropriate reliance on judicial authority may lead to undesirable societal consequences, such as the criminalization of noncompliance with medical recommendations.

ACOG Committee Op. No. 55, Patient Choice: Maternal-Fetal Conflict (Oct. 1987). The American Medical Association's Board of Trustees has adopted a somewhat weaker resolution that allows physicians to seek judicial intervention where the invasion of bodily integrity and health risk to the mother is minimal and the harm to the fetus without surgery is great. Cole, American Medical Association Board of Trustees Report, *Legal Interventions During Pregnancy: Court-Ordered Medical Treatments and Legal Penalties for Potentially Harmful Behavior by Pregnant Women,* 264 J. Am. Med. Ass'n 2663 (1990).

This issue has generated considerable controversy. Nancy Rhoden's treatment of this issue provides comprehensive and insightful analysis. *The Judge in the Delivery Room: The Emergence of Court-Ordered Caesarians,* 74 CAL. L. REV. 1951 (1986). In addition, see Field, *Controlling the Woman to Protect the Fetus,* 17 LAW, MED. & HEALTH CARE 114 (1989); Robertson, *Procreative Liberty and the Control of Conception, Pregnancy, and Childbirth,* 69 VA. L. REV. 405 (1983).

The issue of court-ordered treatment for pregnant women has come up in a few other contexts with varying results. For example, some courts have ordered blood transfusions over the mother's objections. *See, e.g., Raleigh Fitkin-Paul Moran Mem. Hosp. v. Anderson,* 201 A.2d 537 (N.J.), *cert. denied,* 377 U.S. 985 (1964); *In re Jamaica Hosp.,* 491 N.Y.S.2d 898 (Sup. Ct. 1985); *Crouse Irving Mem. Hosp. v. Paddock,* 485 N.Y.S.2d 443 (Sup. Ct. 1985). How is this different from forced caesarians? Many courts see no difference and decline to override the mother's refusal of blood transfusion, which is usually based on religious beliefs. *See In re Fetus Brown,* 689 N.E.2d 397 (Ill. App. 1997) (reversing trial court order of blood transfusion, refused by pregnant Jehovah's Witness woman after surgery caused extreme blood loss; court found transfusion to be invasive procedure and held that competent woman had virtually absolute right to refuse.) Should HIV-positive pregnant women be ordered to submit to perinatal administration of AZT, which can substantially reduce the risk of HIV infection in the child? Most commentators argue against mandatory treatment, in part because of the risks of AZT treatment to the mother. *See, e.g.,* Grizzi, *Compelled Antiviral Treatment of HIV positive Pregnant Women,* 5 U.C.L.A WOMEN'S. L. J. 473 (1995). Grizzi also suggests that the fact that children born to AIDS-infected women are likely to become "AIDS orphans" also argues against intervention. *Id* at 499. For a recent article arguing that pregnant women have a constitutional right to refuse treatment which trumps any state interest in the viable fetus, see Cherry, *The Free Exercise Rights of Pregnant Women Who Refuse Medical Treatment,* 69 TENN. L. REV. 563 (2002).

[b]   Drug Abuse by Pregnant Women

ANGELA M.W. v KRUZICKI

561 N.W. 2d. 729 (Wisc. 1997)

BRADLEY, Justice.

. . . . The petitioner was an adult carrying a viable fetus with a projected delivery date of October 4, 1995. . . . Blood tests performed on May 31, June 26, and July 21, 1995, confirmed [her] obstetrician's suspicion that the petitioner was using cocaine or other drugs. . . . [He] reported his concerns to Waukesha County authorities.

. . . .

In an order filed on September 6, 1995, the juvenile court directed that: the [petitioner's] unborn child . . . be detained under Section 48.207(1)(g), Wis.Stats., by the Waukesha County Sheriff's Department and transported to Waukesha Memorial Hospital for inpatient treatment and protection. Such detention will by necessity result in the detention of the unborn child's mother. . . .

Later that same day, before the protective custody order was executed, the petitioner presented herself voluntarily at an inpatient drug treatment facility. As a result, the juvenile court amended its order to provide that detention would be at the inpatient facility. The court further ordered that if the petitioner attempted to leave the inpatient facility or did not participate in the facility's drug treatment program, then both she and the fetus were to be detained and transported to Waukesha Memorial Hospital.

[T]he County filed a . . . petition in the juvenile court, alleging that the petitioner's viable fetus was in need of protection or services because the petitioner "neglect[ed], refuse[d] or [was] unable for reasons other than poverty to provide necessary care, food, clothing, medical or dental care or shelter so as to seriously endanger the physical health of the child, pursuant to Section 48.13(10) of the Wisconsin Statutes". . . .

> [The juvenile court rejected the mother's claims that it lacked juris-
> diction over her and her viable fetus and her claim that such authority
> would violate the constitutional guarantees of procedural and substan-
> tive due process, as well as equal protection.]

The court of appeals determined that the juvenile court did not exceed its jurisdiction in this case. The court reasoned that the United States Supreme Court, the Wisconsin legislature, and this court have each articulated public policy considerations supporting the conclusion that a viable fetus is a "person" within the meaning of the CHIPS [Children in Need of Protection or Services] statute's definition of "child." The court also held that application of the CHIPS statute to the petitioner did not deprive her of equal protection or due process, since the statute was a properly tailored means of vindicating the State's compelling interest in the health, safety, and welfare of a viable fetus. . . .

We stress at the outset of our analysis that this case is not about the propriety or morality of the petitioner's conduct. It is also not about her consti-tutional right to reproductive choice. . . . Rather, this case is one of statutory construction. The issue presented is whether a viable fetus is included in the definition of "child" provided in Wis.Stat. § 48.02(2). . . .

The [statute] confers on the juvenile court "exclusive original jurisdiction over a child alleged to be in need of protection or services which can be ordered by the court. . . ." § 48.13. A "child" is defined . . . as "a person who is less than 18 years of age." § 48.02(2). The petitioner contends that the Chapter 48 definition of "child" is clear on its face, and mandates the conclusion that Chapter 48 uses the term "child" to mean a person born alive. In support, she asserts that by having no "age," a fetus cannot be a person who is less than 18 years of age. . . . In contrast, the County asserts that courts in this State and other jurisdictions have determined that "child" and "person" are ambigu-ous terms. As such, the County contends that we are required to look beyond the language of the statute for the meaning of "child.". . .

Case law reveals that different courts have given different meanings to the terms "person" and "child." This court has previously held that a viable fetus is a "person" for purposes of Wisconsin's wrongful death statute. On the other hand, the United States Supreme Court has concluded that a fetus is not a "person" under the Fourteenth Amendment to the United States Constitution. *Roe v. Wade*. Perhaps most compelling, courts in other states have arrived at different interpretations of statutory language nearly identical to that in § 48.02(2). *Compare State v. Gray,* 584 N.E.2d 710, 713 (Ohio 1992) (holding that a third trimester fetus is not "a child under eighteen years of age," as provided in Ohio's child endangerment statute), *with Whitner v. State,* No. 24468, 1996 WL 393164, at 3(S.C. July 15, 1996) (concluding that a viable fetus is a "person under the age of eighteen," pursuant to South Carolina's child abuse and endangerment statute). Against this backdrop of conflicting authority, we conclude that the term "child" is ambiguous.

In construing the statute, we turn first to the legislative history. . . .

. . . . The issue of whether the Chapter 48 definition of "child" includes a fetus is one of a controversial and complex nature. One would expect heated dialogue and intense debate if the legislature intended to include fetus within the definition of "child." Yet, we are met with legislative silence.

> [The Court rejected the claim that legislative silence in response to the intermediate appellate court decision signified acquiescence with that court's conclusion that a fetus is a child under the child abuse statute, finding that assertion applicable only to unappealable decisions.]

We turn next to a consideration of context, examining the § 48.02(2) definition of "child" in conjunction with other relevant sections of the Code. . . .

By reading the definition of "child" in context with other relevant sections of Chapter 48, we find a compelling basis for concluding that the legislature intended a "child" to mean a human being born alive. Code provisions dealing with taking a child into custody, providing parental notification, and releasing a child from custody would require absurd results if the § 48.02(2) definition of "child" included a fetus. Each of the provisions addresses a critical juncture in a CHIPS proceeding. Yet, each also anticipates that the "child" can at some point be removed from the presence of the parent. It is manifest that the separation envisioned by the statute cannot be achieved in the context of a pregnant woman and her fetus.

The court of appeals determined, and the County asserts, that some prior decisions of this court support the proposition that a fetus is a child under the Children's Code. For example, the court of appeals analogized the present case to those in which this court has recognized a degree of fetal personhood under tort law. . . .

We find the tort law analogy unpersuasive. . . . Instead, we agree with the United States Supreme Court that declaring a fetus a person for purposes of the wrongful death statute does no more than vindicate the interest of parents in the potential life that a fetus represents. *See Roe.* Indeed, we have recognized that until born, a fetus has no cause of action for fetal injury. . . .

Similarly, we reject the County's argument that the protections accorded fetuses by property law have a bearing on the Children's Code definition of "child." As the dissent below noted, "[P]roperty law does not confer the full rights of personhood upon the fetus. Instead, it creates a means of fulfilling the intentions of testators by protecting the right of a fetus to inherit property upon live birth". . . .

We also find unpersuasive the court of appeals' citation to *State v. Black*, [in which] we held that the defendant was properly charged with feticide, "intentionally destroy[ing] the life of an unborn quick child." Wis. Stat. § 940.04(2)(a). As we noted in that case, "the words of the statute could hardly be clearer." . . .

Black demonstrates the ease and clarity with which the legislature may, if it so chooses, apply a statute to the unborn. In its several amendments to the Children's Code, the legislature has had ample opportunity to state in similarly clear and unambiguous terms that a fetus is a child. Yet, [it] has failed to take such action. . . .

    . . . .

The court of appeals' reliance on *Roe, Black,* and [other precedent]. . . evidences the fundamental error in its analysis. While positing the correct question — whether the legislature intended to include a fetus within the § 48.02(2) definition of "child"—the court of appeals answered a distinctly different one — whether the legislature could, consistent with the United States and Wisconsin Constitutions, have included a fetus within the term "child." Because we conclude that the legislature did not intend to equate a fetus with a child, we do not reach the question answered by the court of appeals.

Finally, the confinement of a pregnant woman for the benefit of her fetus is a decision bristling with important social policy issues. [T]he legislature is in a better position than the courts to gather, weigh, and reconcile the competing policy proposals addressed to this sensitive area of the law. . . .

NOTES

1. *Prenatal Substance Abuse.* The problem of substance abuse by pregnant women has become acute in the past generation, generating a great deal of legal and policy interest. The risks to the child of maternal drug use are serious; Cocaine and heroin use have been associated with seizures after birth, premature birth, retarded fetal growth, low birth weight, various structural abnormalities in the genitals and urinary organs and prenatal strokes and other neurological effects that may result in lasting brain damage. *See* Zuckerman, et al., *Effects of Maternal Marijuana and Cocaine Use on Fetal Growth,* 320 NEW ENG. J. MED. 762 (1989).

Should civil or criminal child abuse laws extend to prenatal drug abuse? Often, as in *Angela M.W.,* the issue is framed as a jurisdictional question of whether harm done to a fetus is injury to a "child" under the statute. Courts are divided in interpreting statutes that are silent about prenatal abuse, with most agreeing with the Wisconsin court. In a recent Oklahoma case somewhat similar to Angela M.W., the trial court took temporary emergency custody of a seven month fetus as a "deprived child," after the mother was arrested for the manufacture and possession of methamphetamine. The court ordered the mother to submit to random drug tests, inspections of her living quarters, and weekly pre-natal medical visits and removed the child from her custody shortly after birth, based on the arrest evidence. The Oklahoma Supreme Court reversed the order, concluding that neither the language of the statute nor legislative intent supported defining a viable fetus as a "child" under the Children's Code. *Starks v. Oklahoma*, 18 P.3d 342 (Okla. 2001). *See also Reinesto v. Superior Court*, 894 P.2d 733 (Ariz. App. 1995) (fetus is not a "child" under criminal child abuse statute); *Comm. V. Welsh*, 864 S.W.2d. 280 (Ky. 1993) (same). A few courts have held otherwise. *See Whitner v. State*, 492 S.E.2d 777 (S.C. 1996) (viable fetus is a "person under the age of eighteen," under child abuse statute).

Some courts decline to frame the issue in this way, focusing instead on whether a positive drug toxicology test on the mother and newborn can be the basis of an abuse finding. In *In re Baby Boy Blackshear*, 736 N.E.2d 462 (Ohio 2000), the Ohio Supreme Court concluded that the plain language of the statute applied to the case of a mother and infant who tested positive for cocaine. Under Ohio's abuse statute, an abused child was a child who "because of the acts of his parents . . . suffers physical or mental injury." The court determined that this provision justified finding the drug-exposed infant to be abused on the basis of the mother's conduct before his birth. New York's highest court concluded that a post-birth positive toxicology test alone was not sufficient to support a finding of abuse. *In re Matter of Dante M.*, 661 N.E. 2d. 138 (N.Y. 1995). However, toxicology results could be considered along with other evidence (in the case, the child's low birth weight, the mother's history of drug use, and testimonial evidence from relatives) to support an abuse finding.

Some state legislatures have enacted special laws addressing the subject. Under the Florida statute, FLA. STAT. ANN. §39.01(30)(g)(1) (2003), "use by the mother of a controlled substance or alcohol during pregnancy, when the child, at birth, is demonstrably adversely affected by such usage" constitutes "harm" to child. MASS. GEN. LAWS ANN. ch. 119, §51A (West Supp. 2003) includes within the definition of abused child one "who is determined to be physically dependent upon an addictive drug at birth." In some states, standards for the termination of parental rights have been expanded to specifically include drug dependency which the parent has failed to have treated successfully. *See* MINN. STAT. §260C.301 (2003), set forth on pp. 1181-2, *infra*.

Efforts by prosecutors to use existing criminal child abuse statutes in prenatal drug use cases have generally not been successful. Some prosecutors have charged mothers under criminal statutes prohibiting the delivery of a controlled substance to a minor. The Supreme Court of Florida reversed the conviction of Jennifer Johnson, whose child was born with traces of cocaine in its blood. *Johnson v. State*, 602 So. 2d 1288 (Fla. 1992). The Court held that such a statute does not apply to the "delivery" of cocaine through the umbilical cord after birth but before the severing of the cord. This conclusion was supported by the provisions of the Florida child abuse statute, quoted above, in which the purpose to treat maternal drug use as a public health issue and not as a crime is clear. *See also State v. Hardy,* 469 N.W.2d 50 (Mich.

1991) (same theory, same result). However, the South Carolina Supreme Court (which earlier found a fetus to be a child under the state's child abuse statute) upheld the homicide conviction of a mother whose child was stillborn where the prosecution demonstrated that the death was caused by the effect of the mother's ingestion of cocaine during pregnancy. *State v. McKnight*, 576 S.E.2d 168 (2003). The Court concluded that the mother's use of cocaine knowing she was pregnant was sufficient to constitute extreme indifference to human life.

A principle that would reach prenatal injuries resulting from cocaine use could apply as well to pregnant women who drink excessively, causing fetal alcohol syndrome. Medical experts have estimated that drinking by pregnant women harms about 2 in 1,000 fetuses and is a leading cause of mental retardation. Lewin, *Drug Use During Pregnancy: New Issue Before the Courts,* N.Y. TIMES, Feb. 5, 1990, at A1. According to a report in the late 1980s, on the Pine Ridge Indian Reservation in South Dakota, approximately 25 percent of the children are born with fetal alcohol syndrome, which can have devastating and permanent effects on a child's development. Kolata, *Alcohol Abuse by Pregnant Indians Crippling a Generation of Children,* N.Y. TIMES, July 19, 1989, at D24. Pregnant women who smoke are also potential targets of regulations. What about pregnant women who maintain poor nutrition? Should a line be drawn between intervention to deter pregnant women from behavior that threatens harm to the fetus and is itself illegal (drug use) and behavior which may harm the fetus but is generally allowed (smoking and drinking)?

A few academic commentators have argued for increased regulation of pregnancy. Janet Stepherson details the debilitating effects of prenatal drug use and urges criminal prosecution of offenders who, if convicted, should be offered the option of prison or probation, the latter conditioned on treatment and avoiding pregnancy. Stepherson, *Stopping Fetal Abuse with No-Pregnancy and Drug Treatment Conditions*, 34 SANTA CLARA L. REV. 295 (1994). Among the commentators who have argued against punitive measures and in favor of better treatment programs are: LAURA GOMEZ, MISCONCEIVING MOTHERS: LEGISLATORS, PROSECUTORS, AND THE POLITICS OF PRENATAL DRUG EXPOSURE (1997); Paltrow, *Pregnant Drug Users, Fetal Persons and the Threat to* Roe v. Wade, 62 ALA. L. REV. 999 (1999); Moss, *Substance Abuse During Pregnancy,* 13 HARV. WOMEN'S L.J. 278 (1990); and Johnsen, *From Driving to Drugs: Governmental Regulation of Pregnant Women's Lives After Webster,* 138 U. PA. L. REV. 179 (1989).

2. *Detection of Maternal Drug Use and the Fourth Amendment.* Does the state's role as protector of children justify policies of detecting prenatal drug use by mothers through involuntary testing? The United States Supreme Court recently struck down, on Fourth Amendment grounds, a public hospital policy of testing pregnant patients suspected of using drugs. *Ferguson v. City of Charleston*, 532 U.S. 67 (2001). Under the policy, created by the hospital in cooperation with the police and public officials, women were tested without their knowledge or consent; positive results were reported to the police. Several women who were arrested after testing positive for cocaine challenged the policy, arguing that the warrantless and nonconsensual drug tests were unconstitutional searches. The federal appeals court held the searches to be reasonable under the "special needs" doctrine, which permits searches that would otherwise be unconstitutional when special needs for law enforcement provide sufficient justification (186 F.3d 469 (4th Cir. 1999)). The Supreme Court reversed, holding that the state's interest in using the threat of criminal sanctions to deter pregnant women from using cocaine and to force them into treatment did not constitute "special needs." Thus, the Court held that searches pursuant to the policy were unreasonable searches in violation of the Fourth Amendment. If the results of the testing were only used in civil child abuse proceedings, would the policy have been justified?

3. *Remedies for Fetal Abuse.* The extension of child abuse laws to protect fetuses clearly established that intervention at birth can be justified on the basis of prenatal conduct. But what remedies are available *during* pregnancy? If the substance abuse is the result of an addiction, only very coercive remedies may be effective. The trial court in *Angela M.W.* took "custody" of the fetus, ordering the pregnant woman into "voluntary" residential drug treatment, with the threat of involuntary commitment in a state hospital if she left. The interference with the mother's personal freedom that would be involved in trying to protect fetuses raises both constitutional and policy concerns. One concern is that the woman who fears prosecution will be unlikely to seek medical assistance during pregnancy or even in delivering the child. Can a court order a pregnant woman to cease smoking, or to maintain a proper diet? Responding to the crisis in alcoholism affecting newborns among some Native American tribes, a Canadian court locked up a woman during her pregnancy to keep her from drinking. *Kolata, supra.* What about ordering long-term contraceptive implants for women addicted to drugs and alcohol? Many experts have argued that the appropriate approach to the crisis in substance abuse among pregnant women is more and better drug treatment programs. These experts believe that the availability of voluntary programs would offer much better protection to fetuses than the punitive use of civil or criminal child abuse laws. Jennifer Johnson (*supra*) and many other women facing prosecutions for endangering their fetuses sought help for their drug problems during pregnancy, but found either long waiting lists, or that the programs would not accept pregnant women.

PROBLEM

Problem 10-9. Jennifer has been found guilty of child abuse for taking heroin while pregnant. The maximum sentence possible is a 30-year jail term. The judge, however, sentences her to 15 years' probation. One of the terms of her probation is that she submit to random drug testing, for one year, and that if she becomes pregnant again, she will submit to a supervised prenatal program. Is the sentence constitutional? Is it wise?

[4] STATE DUTIES ARISING FROM ITS CHILD PROTECTION SYSTEM

DESHANEY v. WINNEBAGO COUNTY DEPARTMENT OF SOCIAL SERVICES

489 U.S. 189 (1989)

CHIEF JUSTICE REHNQUIST delivered the opinion of the Court.

Petitioner is a boy who was beaten and permanently injured by his father, with whom he lived. The respondents are social workers and other local officials who received complaints that petitioner was being abused by his father and had reason to believe that this was the case, but nonetheless did not act to remove petitioner from his father's custody. Petitioner sued respondents claiming that their failure to act deprived him of his liberty in violation of the Due Process Clause of the Fourteenth Amendment to the United States Constitution. We hold that it did not.

I

The facts of this case are undeniably tragic. Petitioner Joshua DeShaney was born in 1979. In 1980, a Wyoming court granted his parents a divorce and awarded custody of Joshua to his father, Randy DeShaney. The father shortly thereafter moved to . . . Winnebago County, Wisconsin, taking the infant Joshua with him. There he entered into a second marriage, which also ended in divorce.

The Winnebago County authorities first learned that [Joshua] might be a victim of child abuse in January 1982, when his father's second wife complained to the police, at the time of their divorce, that he had previously "hit the boy causing marks and [was] a prime case for child abuse.". . . The Winnebago County Department of Social Services (DSS) interviewed the father, but he denied the accusations, and DSS did not pursue them further. In January 1983, Joshua was admitted to a local hospital with multiple bruises and abrasions. The examining physician suspected child abuse and notified DSS, which immediately obtained an order from a Wisconsin juvenile court placing Joshua in temporary custody of the hospital. Three days later, the county convened an ad hoc "Child Protection Team" — consisting of a pediatrician, a psychologist, a police detective, the county's lawyer, several DSS caseworkers, and various hospital personnel — to consider Joshua's situation. At this meeting, the Team decided that there was insufficient evidence of child abuse to retain Joshua in the custody of the court. The Team did, however, decide to recommend several measures to protect Joshua, including enrolling him in a preschool program, providing his father with certain counseling services, and encouraging his father's girlfriend to move out of the home. Randy DeShaney entered into a voluntary agreement with DSS in which he promised to cooperate with them in accomplishing these goals.

Based on the recommendation of the Child Protection Team, the juvenile court dismissed the child protection case and returned Joshua to the custody of his father. A month later, emergency room personnel called the DSS caseworker handling Joshua's case to report that he had once again been treated for suspicious injuries. The caseworker concluded that there was no basis for action. For the next six months, the caseworker made monthly visits to the DeShaney home, during which she observed a number of suspicious injuries on Joshua's head; she also noticed that he had not been enrolled in school and that the girlfriend had not moved out. The caseworker dutifully recorded these incidents in her files, along with her continuing suspicions that someone in the DeShaney household was physically abusing Joshua, but she did nothing more. In November 1983, the emergency room notified DSS that Joshua had been treated once again for injuries that they believed to be caused by child abuse. On the caseworker's next two visits to the DeShaney home, she was told that Joshua was too ill to see her. Still DSS took no action.

In March 1984, Randy DeShaney beat 4-year-old Joshua so severely that he fell into a life-threatening coma. Emergency brain surgery revealed a series of hemorrhages caused by traumatic injuries to the head inflicted over a long period of time. Joshua did not die, but he suffered brain damage so severe that he is expected to spend the rest of his life confined to an institution for the profoundly retarded. Randy DeShaney was subsequently tried and convicted of child abuse.

Joshua and his mother brought this action under [§1983] in the United States District Court for the Eastern District of Wisconsin against respondents Winnebago County, its Department of Social Services, and various individual employees of the Department. The complaint alleged that respondents had deprived Joshua of his liberty without due process of law, in violation of his rights under the Fourteenth Amendment, by failing to intervene to protect him against a risk of violence at his father's hands of which they knew or should have known. The District Court granted summary judgment for respondents.

The Court of Appeals for the Seventh Circuit affirmed . . . holding that petitioners had not made out an actionable §1983 claim. . . .

. . . We now affirm.

II

. . . Petitioners contend that the State deprived Joshua of his liberty interest in "free[dom] from . . . unjustified intrusions on personal security," . . . by failing to provide him with adequate protection against his father's violence. The claim is one invoking the substantive rather than procedural component of the Due Process Clause. . . .

But nothing in the language of the Due Process Clause itself requires the State to protect the life, liberty, and property of its citizens against invasion by private actors. The Clause is phrased as a limitation on the State's power to act, not as a guarantee of certain minimal levels of safety and security. It forbids the State itself to deprive individuals of life, liberty, or property without "due process of law," but its language cannot fairly be extended to impose an affirmative obligation on the State to ensure that those interests do not come to harm through other means. Nor does history support such an expansive reading of the constitutional text. . . . Its purpose was to protect the people from the State, not to ensure that the State protected them from each other. The Framers were content to leave the extent of governmental obligation in the latter area to the democratic political processes.

Consistent with these principles, our cases have recognized that the Due Process Clauses generally confer no affirmative right to governmental aid, even where such aid may be necessary to secure life, liberty, or property interests of which the government itself may not deprive the individual. *See, e.g., Harris v. McRae,* 448 U. S. 297, 317–318 (1980) (no obligation to fund abortions or other medical services) . . . If the Due Process Clause does not require the State to provide its citizens with particular protective services, it follows that the State cannot be held liable under the Clause for injuries that could have been averted had it chosen to provide them. . . .

Petitioners contend, however, that even if the Due Process Clause imposes no affirmative obligation on the State to provide the general public with adequate protective services, such a duty may arise out of certain "special relationships" created or assumed by the State with respect to particular individuals. . . . Petitioners argue that such a "special relationship" existed here because the State knew that Joshua faced a special danger of abuse at his father's hands, and specifically proclaimed, by word and by deed, its intention to protect him against that danger. . . . Having actually undertaken to protect Joshua from this danger — which petitioners concede the State played no part in creating — the State acquired an affirmative "duty," enforceable through the Due Process Clause, to do so in a reasonably competent fashion. Its failure to discharge that duty, so the argument goes, was an abuse of governmental power that so "shocks the conscience" . . . as to constitute a substantive due process violation. . . .

We reject this argument. It is true that in certain limited circumstances the Constitution imposes upon the State affirmative duties of care and protection with respect to particular individuals. . . . [But our prior cases stand only] for the proposition that when the State takes a person into its custody and holds him there against his will, the Constitution imposes upon it a corresponding duty to assume some responsibility for his safety and general well-being. *See Youngberg v. Romeo,* [457 U.S. 307, 317 (1982)] ("When a person is institutionalized and wholly dependent on the State[,] . . . a duty to provide certain services and care does exist"). . . . The affirmative duty to protect arises not from the State's knowledge of the individual's predicament or from its expressions of intent to help him, but from the limitation which it has imposed on his freedom to act on his own behalf. . . .

. . . Petitioners concede that the harms Joshua suffered did not occur while he was in the State's custody, but while he was in the custody of his natural father, who was in no sense a state actor. While the State may have been aware of the dangers that Joshua faced in the free world, it played no part in their creation, nor did it do anything to render him any more vulnerable to them. That the State once took temporary custody of Joshua does not alter the analysis, for when it returned him to his father's custody, it placed him in no worse position than that in which he would have been had it not acted at all; the State does not become the permanent guarantor of an individual's safety by having once offered him shelter. . . .

It may well be that, by voluntarily undertaking to protect Joshua against a danger it concededly played no part in creating, the State acquired a duty under state tort law to provide him with adequate protection against that danger. *See* Restatement (Second) of Torts §323 (1965). . . . But the claim here is based on the Due Process Clause of the Fourteenth Amendment, which, as we have said many times, does not transform every tort committed by a state actor into a constitutional violation. . . .

Judges and lawyers, like other humans, are moved by natural sympathy in a case like this to find a way for Joshua and his mother to receive adequate compensation for the grievous harm inflicted upon them. But before yielding to that impulse, it is well to remember once again that the harm was inflicted not by the State of Wisconsin, but by Joshua's father. The most that can be said of the state functionaries in this case is that they stood by and did nothing when suspicious circumstances dictated a more active role for them. In defense of them it must also be said that had they moved too soon to take custody of the son away from the father, they would likely have been met with charges of improperly intruding into the parent-child relationship, charges based on the same Due Process Clause that forms the basis for the present charge of failure to provide adequate protection.

The people of Wisconsin may well prefer a system of liability which would place upon the State and its officials the responsibility for failure to act in situations as the present one. They may create such a system, if they do not have it already, by changing the tort law of the State in accordance with the regular law-making process. But they should not have it thrust upon them by this Court's expansion of the Due Process Clause of the Fourteenth Amendment.

Affirmed.

Justice Brennan, with whom Justice Marshall and Justice Blackmun join, dissenting.

The Court's baseline is the absence of positive rights in the Constitution and a concomitant suspicion of any claim that seems to depend on such rights. From this perspective, the DeShaneys' claim is first and foremost about inaction (the failure, here, of respondents to take steps to protect Joshua), and only tangentially about action (the establishment of a state program specifically designed to help children like Joshua). And from this perspective, holding these Wisconsin officials liable — where the only difference between this case and one involving a general claim to protective services is Wisconsin's establishment and operation of a program to protect children — would seem to punish an effort that we should seek to promote.

I would begin from the opposite direction. I would focus first on the action that Wisconsin has taken with respect to Joshua and children like him, rather than on the actions that the State failed to take. Such a method is not new to this Court. . . .

[T]o the Court, the only fact that seems to count as an "affirmative act of restraining the individual's freedom to act on his own behalf" is direct physical control. . . . I would recognize, as the Court apparently cannot, that "the State's knowledge of [an] individual's predicament [and] its expressions of intent to help him" can amount to a "limitation of his freedom to act on his own behalf" or to obtain help from others. . . .

Wisconsin has established a child-welfare system specifically designed to help children like Joshua. Wisconsin law places upon the local departments of social services such as respondent (DSS or Department) a duty to investigate reported instances of child abuse. . . . While other governmental bodies and private persons are largely responsible for the reporting of possible cases of child abuse . . . Wisconsin law channels all such reports to the local departments of social services for evaluation and, if necessary, further action. . . . Wisconsin law invites — indeed, directs — citizens and other governmental entities to depend on local departments of social services such as respondent to protect children from abuse.

The specific facts before us bear out this view of Wisconsin's system of protecting children. Each time someone voiced a suspicion that Joshua was being abused, that information was relayed to the Department for investigation and possible action. When Randy DeShaney's second wife told the police that he had "hit the boy causing marks and [was] a prime case for child abuse," the police referred her complaint to DSS. . . . When, on three separate occasions, emergency room personnel noticed suspicious injuries on Joshua's body, they went to DSS with this information. . . . When neighbors informed the police that they had seen or heard Joshua's father or his father's lover beating or otherwise abusing Joshua, the police brought these reports to the attention of DSS. . . . And when respondent Kemmeter, through these reports and through her own observations in the course of nearly 20 visits to the DeShaney home . . . compiled growing evidence that Joshua was being abused, that information stayed within the Department — chronicled by the social worker in detail that seems almost eerie in light of her failure to act upon it. (As to the extent of the social worker's involvement in and knowledge of Joshua's predicament, her reaction to the news of Joshua's last and most devastating injuries is illuminating: "I just knew the phone would ring some day and Joshua would be dead." 812 F.2d 298, 300 [(7th Cir. 1987)].)

Even more telling than these examples is the Department's control over the decision whether to take steps to protect a particular child from suspected abuse. While many different people contributed information and advice to this decision, it was up to the people at DSS to make the ultimate decision . . . whether to disturb the family's current arrangements. . . . Unfortunately for Joshua DeShaney, the buck effectively stopped with the Department.

In these circumstances, a private citizen, or even a person working in a government agency other than DSS, would doubtless feel that her job was done as soon as she had reported her suspicions of child abuse to DSS. Through its child-welfare program, in other words, the State of Wisconsin has relieved ordinary citizens and governmental bodies other than the Department of any sense of obligation to do anything more than report their suspicions of child abuse to DSS. If DSS ignores or dismisses these suspicions, no one will step in to fill the gap. Wisconsin's child-protection program thus effectively confined Joshua DeShaney within the walls of Randy DeShaney's violent home until such time as DSS took action to remove him. Conceivably, then, children like Joshua are made worse off by the existence of this program when the persons and entities charged with carrying it out fail to do their jobs.

It . . . simply belies reality, therefore, to contend that the State "stood by and did nothing" with respect to Joshua. . . . Through its child-protection program, the State actively intervened in Joshua's life and, by virtue of this intervention, acquired ever more certain knowledge that Joshua was in grave danger. . . .

. . . My disagreement with the Court arises from its failure to see that inaction can be every bit as abusive of power as action, that oppression can result when a State undertakes a vital duty and then ignores it. Today's opinion construes the Due Process Clause to permit a State to displace private sources of protection and then, at the critical moment, to shrug its shoulders and turn away from the harm that it has promised to try to prevent. Because I cannot agree that our Constitution is indifferent to such indifference, I respectfully dissent.

[JUSTICE BLACKMUN wrote a separate dissent.]

NOTES

1. *Section 1983 Liability for Failure to Protect After Social Agency Intervention.* A question left open by *DeShaney* was whether the state has a duty to protect children in state custody, such that a child who is wrongfully injured can recover in a §1983 action against the government. *De Shaney* emphasized the difference between government custodial and non-custodial contexts in establishing §1983 liability. Remember that Justice Rehnquist distinguished the situation in *DeShaney*, in which the child was in his father's custody, from the institutional contexts of *Youngberg v. Romeo*. He also stated that the outcome in *DeShaney* might be different if Joshua was mistreated while in the state's custody. Why is this situation different? Is foster care sufficiently analogous to institutionalization to support state liability for failure to protect the child? Most post-*DeShaney* courts concur that the child who is placed in foster care by the state is in custody and has a substantive due process right to reasonable safety, although the liability standard has varied.

Many lower Federal courts have applied a deliberate indifference standard of liability to the government's conduct, a standard applied to violations of the duty owed by the government to prisoners. One court, for example, found that the state could be liable for harm to children in foster care under § 1983 only if it had knowledge or suspicion that the foster parents were child abusers. *Lewis v. Anderson*, 308 F.3d 768 (7th Cir. 2002), *cert. denied* 123 S. Ct. 1500 (2003). *See also Lintz v. Skipski*, 25 F.3d 304 (6th Cir. 1994) (no state liability because worker's response did not amount to deliberate indifference; although some evidence known to the worker suggested children might be sexually abused, she made some effort to protect the children's safety); *Norfleet v. Arkansas Department of Human Services*, 796 F. Supp. 1194 (E.D. Ark. 1992), *aff'd*, 989 F.2d 289 (8th Cir. 1993) (department owes child a "duty of safekeeping" and deliberate indifference to the serious medical needs of the child who died in foster care violated due process).

A few courts have applied a professional judgment standard to liability in the foster care context, expanding the potential for state liability. A federal district court held that a supervising social service worker can be liable to a child who is abused in her foster home if the agent's conduct was "a substantial departure from accepted professional judgment, practice, or standards." *Tyler v. Gray* 1996 WL 355335 (E.D. Pa. 1996.) (quoting *Romeo*). Under the professional judgment standard, the agent can be liable for failure to prevent a "pattern of attacks, injuries, or violent behavior."

Some courts reject any state duty to protect children in foster care. The Fourth Circuit Court of Appeals in *Milburn v. Anne Arundel Cty. Dept. of Social Serv.*, 871 F.2d 474 (4th Cir. 1989), *cert. denied,* 110 S. Ct. 148 (1989), for example, found *DeShaney* applicable even to agency negligence in supervising a child who had been placed in voluntary foster care. Emphasizing that the placement of the child was voluntary, the court concluded that the agency had no duty to protect the child and was not liable for gross negligence in failing to remove the child when he was physically abused in foster care. The court also found that the foster parents were private rather than state actors, in part because they were not paid by the state, and that the foster parents, rather than the state, retained custody. Can foster parents be liable as state actors? The Eleventh Circuit also rejected a claim by siblings in state custody against their foster parents, that they were molested by other foster children in the home. *Rayburn v. Hogue*, 241 F.3d 1341 (11th Cir. 2001). The court concluded that the foster parents were not subject to §1983 actions, because they were private individuals contracting with the state, and not state actors. The appellate court rejected the district court's conclusion that the foster parents became state actors, under a test that looked to whether "the state had so far insinuated itself into a position of interdependence with private parties that it was a joint participant in the enterprise." 241 F.3d at 1347.

Where a child in state custody is placed with a *parent* and then injured, courts have varied in their responses to §1983 claims. The Eighth Circuit Court of Appeals upheld the dismissal of a §1983 complaint in a case in which Family Services returned the child to her father, from whose custody she had earlier been taken, despite the fact that the agency had notice that the father allowed her to have contact with a known pedophile (who later abused her). *S.S. v. McMullen,* 225 F.3d 960 (8th Cir. 2000). The court rejected the child's claim that the state had placed her in a dangerous environment, reasoning that the case was similar to *DeShaney* in that the state did nothing to make her more vulnerable to a risk of harm than she would have been had the state not intervened. The court concluded that the two-year interval of state custody did not increase the risk that she faced. A federal district court reached a different result where a child, placed by the state in his father's custody, was killed when his father poured boiling water on him. *Currier v. Doran*, 23 F. Supp. 2d 1277 (D.N.M. 1998), *aff'd in part and rev'd in part*, 242 F.3d 905, (10th Cir.), *cert. denied*, 534 U.S. 1019 (2001). *DeShaney* was distinguished, because the state, having removed the child from his mother's custody, assumed control over the child. At that point, the court concluded, it had a duty not to create a dangerous condition for the child by knowingly or recklessly relinquishing control to an abusive person, even if it was a family member. Thus, the defendants, social worker and supervisor, were not entitled to qualified immunity and could be held liable for the acts of the third party father if the officials created the danger that caused the harm.

See Kearse, *Competing Constitutional Standards for the State's Duty to Protect Foster Children,* 29 COLUM. J. OF L. AND SOC. PROBS. 385 (1996); Mushlin, *Unsafe Havens: The Case for Constitutional Protection of Foster Children from Abuse and Neglect,* 23 HARV. C.R.-C.L.L. REV. 199 (1988).

2. *Section 1983 Liability for Intervention.* Can social workers be liable under §1983 for their actions in intervening to protect children? Some courts conclude that social workers must be immune from §1983 actions for wrongfully bringing dependency actions that result in removal of the child from the home. A Federal appellate court concluded that absolute immunity was as important here as in the prosecutorial context. "Like a prosecutor, a child welfare worker must exercise independent judgment in deciding whether or not to bring a child dependency proceeding, and such judgment would likely be compromised if that worker faced the threat of personal liability for every mistake in judgment." *Ernst v. Child and Youth Services,* 108 F.3d 486, 496 (3rd Cir.), *cert. denied,* 533 U.S. 850 (1997). *See also Rippy v. Hathaway,* 270 F.3d 416 (6th Cir. 2001), *cert. denied,* 537 U.S. 812 (2002) (social workers' investigation and recommendation regarding return of child in state custody is entitled to absolute immunity; their role is comparable to probation officer making sentencing recommendation).

Some courts have permitted §1983 actions against social workers and against city governments for policies that violate constitutional rights of parents and children. Many of the cases involve aggressive investigations of child sexual abuse that include medical examinations without court orders. In a bizarre California case, city police officers seized two young children from their home on the basis of a "tip" from the children's mentally ill and institutionalized aunt, who claimed that the father and grandparents were involved in Satanic ritual abuse and planned to sacrifice the child. *Wallis v. Spencer,* 202 F.3d 1126 (9th Cir. 1999). The officers took the children at 1 a.m. and subjected them to intrusive genital examinations. The children were not returned to their parents until two months later. The parents and children brought a §1983 claim against the officers and the city on the basis of the unreasonable seizure without a court order and the medical evaluations without parents' consent or presence. The appellate court, reversing a summary judgment order, concluded that the city could be liable if the officers acted pursuant to a city custom or operating procedure of removing children on the basis of a telephone report from Child Protective Services and of subjecting children in protective custody to medical exams without court orders. Similarly, New York parents and their daughter were allowed to bring a § 1983 claim against the city and social workers who removed the child from school and had her examined for sexual abuse in a nearby hospital without a court order. *Tenenbaum v. Williams,* 193 F.3d 581 (2nd Cir. 1999), *cert. denied,* 529 U.S. 1098 (2000). The court concluded that the medical examination without parental consent or court order violated the parents' and child's procedural due process rights and protection against unreasonable seizure, and that removal of the child from school on an emergency basis without a court order was an unreasonable seizure and a violation of the parents' procedural due process rights, if a jury determined that there was sufficient time to safely secure judicial authorization. Here, the removal occurred more than a day after the decision by state officials was made. Since the emergency removal was undertaken pursuant to city policy, the city was liable, although the individual caseworkers were entitled to qualified immunity if it was reasonable for them to believe that they did not violate clearly established rights. *See also Jordan v. Jackson,* 15 F.3d 333 (4th Cir. 1994) (holding the county's failure to train its employees regarding appropriate circumstances for emergency removal under state statute could support a § 1983 action if it demonstrated deliberate indifference).

What incentives will be created for social workers if they face the possibility of liability if they act wrongfully in intervening to protect a child, but no liability if they fail to act? This asymmetry may discourage excessive intervention, but it might also result in under-intervention, reinforcing caution and rewarding shirking.

3. State Tort Actions and Social Worker Immunity. In many states, state tort law may provide a remedy for harms caused by social worker or agency actions or omissions. *See, e.g., Newton v. County of Napa,* 266 Cal. Rptr. 682 (Cal. App. 1990) (immunity recognized for decision to investigate and for actions necessary to conduct meaningful investigation in emergency situations, but not for tortious conduct in connection with certain aspects of investigation (such as strip search)); *Department of Rehab. Servs. v. Yamuni,* 529 So. 2d 258 (Fla. 1988) (upholding finding of liability against caseworker, although reducing $3.1 million jury verdict for failure of agency to protect child from abuse).

In many states, however, social worker actions and omissions are protected by qualified or even absolute immunity. *See, e.g., Marshall v. Montgomery Co. Children's Service Bd.,* 750 N.E.2d 549 (Ohio 2001)(sovereign immunity bars wrongful death claim even if agency failed to investigate reported abuse); *Williams v. State,* 376 N.W.2d 117 (Mich. App. 1985) (upholding immunity for failure to act upon reports of abuse to protect child, who died at age two from starvation).

State law varies, as well, on whether foster parents have immunity for harm caused while they have custody of a child. One issue is whether foster parents are state actors. If not, of course, they can not be sued under Section 1983, *See* note 1 *supra,* although they could still be liable under state tort law. *Compare Nichol v. Stass,* 735 N.E. 2d 582 (Ill. 2000) (foster parents protected by qualified parental immunity (but not sovereign immunity) against negligence claim) *and* TENN. CODE ANN. § 8-42-101(3)(A), (2002) (foster parents covered by rule giving immunity to state officials) *with Mayberry v. Pryor,* 374 N.W.2d 683 (Mich. 1985) (foster parents not protected by defense of parental immunity).

4. Evaluating DeShaney and Liability Policy. Much of the scholarly commentary on *DeShaney* has been extremely critical, especially of the Court's formalistic distinctions used to justify what seems to be an outrageous failure of public agency responsibility. *See, e.g.,* Amar, *Remember the Thirteenth,* 10 CONST. COMMENTARY 403 (1993); Seidman, *The State Action Paradox,* 10 CONST. COMMENTARY 379 (1993); Oren, *The State's Failure to Protect Children and Substantive Due Process: DeShaney in Context,* 68 N.C. L. REV. 659 (1990); Wald, *Government Benefits: A New Look at an Old Gifthorse,* 65 N.Y.U. L. REV. 247 (1990); Strauss, *Due Process, Government Inaction, and Private*

Wrongs, 1989 SUP. CT. REV. 53; Soifer, *Moral Ambition, Formalism, and the "Free World" of DeShaney,* 57 GEO. WASH. L. REV. 1513 (1989). For a rare, but interesting, defense of *De Shaney, see* Armacost, *Affirmative Duties, Systemic Harms, and the Due Process Clause,* 94 MICH. L. REV. 982 (1996). Armacost argues that the Court's refusal to find an affirmative state duty to protect children can be understood as judicial reluctance to second-guess legislative decisions about allocating resources for public services.

Putting aside the constitutional issue, would expansive social worker liability necessarily be good policy? When it appears that a child's injury or death could have been avoided through state intervention, public outrage is very understandable. On the other hand, social workers perform stressful jobs with inadequate resources for low salaries. Burnout is common; in most large city departments, turnover rates are high. Douglas Besharov, former director of the National Center on Child Abuse and Neglect, expressed concern about expansion of social worker liability, and pointed out what easy targets they are:

> They can be blamed if they report suspected child abuse, and they can be blamed if they don't. They can be blamed if they remove a child from parental custody, and they can be blamed if they don't. They can be blamed if they return a child to the home, and they can be blamed if they don't.

D. Besharov, THE VULNERABLE SOCIAL WORKER: LIABILITY FOR SERVING CHILDREN AND FAMILIES (1985). While preferring agency liability to liability for agency individuals, Besharov opposes liability for either agencies or individuals, because it deflects public attention away from the real issues of inadequate financial and political support for child protection. *Id.* at 157–59.

NOTE ON FOSTER CARE

Most children who are removed from their parents' custody due to abuse or neglect enter the foster care system. What is this system and what special legal rights and responsibilities does it create? Children are most often placed in foster homes rather than institutions. Of 545,000 children in foster care in 2000, about 25% were placed with relatives in "kinship" care, almost 50% in non-relative foster homes and less than 18% in group homes or institutions. *See* Children's Bureau, Admin. on Children, Youth and Families, U.S. Dep't. of Health and Human Services, ACFRARS Report at www.acf.dhhs.gov/programs/cb/dis/tables/ index.htm (updated Sept. 3, 2002). Foster parents are typically paid and supervised by a state agency, though the supervision may be fairly loose. Under the typical court order, parents lose custody to the state agency, which chooses a foster parent but retains authority to change the child's placement as it deems necessary to serve the child's interest. At the same time, the rights of the child's natural parents have only been suspended and not permanently severed. The agency thus itself lacks power to make any permanent adoptive placement for the child, although if it believes there are grounds it may seek termination of the biological parents' rights, thus freeing the child for adoption. Children also come into the foster care system through voluntary placements by parents seeking state help in dealing with family crises. Voluntary placement usually requires an entrustment agreement which defines the rights and duties of each party, including when the child is to be returned to the parent.

State-run foster care has been heavily criticized. Ideally, a foster care system works to provide a short term home for children whose parents will soon be able to reclaim them, or a temporary way station for children who will soon be placed for adoption when the rights of their biological parents are severed. In practice, however, children remain in foster care for extended periods, often moving among foster homes for much of their childhood. Foster care "drift" occurs, in part, because agencies and courts are reluctant both to terminate the rights of biological parents and to return the children home. The children affected are most often from poor minority families who cannot afford the private care alternatives available to other families. In response to this problem, law reform efforts in the past generation at the federal and state level have focused on permanency planning for children. Permanency planning has multiple dimensions: a) avoiding unnecessary removal of children from their families; b) promoting speedy and safe reunification with their families of children in foster care; and c) finding a new permanent home in a reasonable time when children can not be reunified with their families. The emphasis has varied at different times; federal legislation, for example, has shifted its focus from reunification to facilitating adoption. The Adoption Assistance and Child Welfare Act of 1980 sought to deter unnecessary removal of children from their families and to encourage remediation and return to parental custody. *See generally* THE ADOPTION ASSISTANCE AND CHILD WELFARE ACT OF 1980: TEN YEARS LATER (North American Council on Adoptable Children 1990). In contrast, the more recent Adoption and Safe Families Act of 1997, Pub. Law No. 105-89, deemphasizes the goal of reunification with parents and focuses on facilitating permanent placement with a new family. *See infra.* The problem of children remaining in foster care for long periods is a difficult one however, and it is unclear, as yet, whether the recent efforts will reduce the number of children in foster care. According to a report in the mid-1990s, about one third of children placed in foster care remain between two and five years, and about 10% spend more than five years in foster care. Testimony of Carol Bevan, representing National Council for Adoption, before the Subcommittee on Human Resources of the Committee on Ways and Means, House of Representatives, 104th Cong., 1st sess., May 10, 1995, at 131–132. *See also* Roger J.R. Levesque, *The Failure of Foster Care Reform: Revolutionizing the Most Radical Blueprint*, 6 MD. J. CONTEMP. LEGAL ISSUES 1, 8 (1995). One thing that has changed as a result of federal legislation promoting permanency planning is that courts play a far larger role than was once true in monitoring and supervising foster care. Hardin, *Child Protection Cases in a Unified Family Court*, 32 FAM. L.Q. 147 (Spring 1998). For a critical analysis of foster care, see Guggenheim, *The Foster Care Dilemma and What to Do About it: Is the Problem That Too Many Children are Not Being Adopted out of Foster Care or that Too Many Children are Entering Foster Care?* 2 U. PA. J. CONST. LAW 150 (1999).

Periodically, a high profile incident brings the problems with a foster care system to public attention. In 2003, New Jersey officials were ordered to release 1300 confidential files of children in state custody, following the death of a 7-year-old Newark boy who was imprisoned with his 4-year-old twin brothers in the basement of his aunt's home, while his mother (who had been subject to abuse petitions) served a prison term. Jones & Kaufman, *New Jersey Opens Files Showing Failures of Child Welfare System*, N. Y. TIMES, Apr. 15, 2003 at A1. The files revealed some cases of horrendous abuse and neglect in foster care and ineptitude and indifference of agency personnel. One child died of AIDS after receiving no medical care for a year. A drug exposed-infant died in foster care, after agency workers placed the child without explaining his medical condition to the foster mother. Numerous children were found to have been beaten and sexually abused, although agency review found the allegations to have been unsubstantiated. Evidence that children in foster care often do not get the protection that justifies removal from their parents fuels criticism of broad intervention policies.

Of course, many children receive nurturing care while in state custody, and some children in long term placements develop deep emotional ties with their foster parents. In a sense, these ties are incompatible with the premise of foster care as a temporary arrangement. Should foster parents have any rights when the agency seeks to remove a foster child from his "psychological family"? In *Smith v. Organization of Foster Families for Equality & Reform (O.F.F.E.R.)*, 431 U.S. 816 (1977), an organization of foster parents claimed that removing children whom they had had in their care for a substantial period of time without a hearing violated their liberty interests under the Due Process Clause. The Supreme Court avoided the constitutional issue, holding that even if such a liberty interest existed, New York's hearing procedures satisfied any due process rights the foster parents might have. The Court's opinion by Justice Brennan, however, provided *dicta* both supportive and disparaging of foster parent claims:

> [T]he usual understanding of "family" implies biological relationships, and most decisions treating the relation between parent and child have stressed this element. . . .
>
> . . . But biological relationships are not [the] exclusive determination of the existence of a family. . . .
>
> [T]he importance of the familial relationship, to the individuals involved and [to society], stems from the emotional attachments that derive from the intimacy of daily association. . . as well as from the fact of blood relationship. No one would seriously dispute that a deeply loving and interdependent relationship between an adult and a child in his or her care may exist even in the absence of blood relationship. At least where a child has been placed in foster care as an infant, has never known his natural parents, and has remained continuously for several years in the care of the same foster parents, it is natural that the foster family should hold the same place in the emotional life of the foster child, and fulfill the same socializing functions, as a natural family. For this reason, we cannot dismiss the foster family as a mere collection of unrelated individuals.
>
> But there are also important distinctions between the foster family and the natural family. First, unlike the earlier cases recognizing a right to family privacy, the State here seeks to interfere, not with a

relationship having its origins entirely apart from the power of the State, but rather with a foster family which has its source in state law and contractual arrangements. The individual's freedom to marry and reproduce is "older than the Bill of Rights," *Griswold v. Connecticut, supra,* 381 U.S., at 486. Accordingly, . . . the liberty interest in family privacy has its source, and its contours are ordinarily to be sought, not in state law, but in intrinsic human rights, as they have been understood in "this Nation's history and tradition." *Moore v. City of East Cleveland,* 431 U.S., at 503. Here, however, whatever emotional ties may develop between foster parent and foster child have their origins in an arrangement in which the State has been a partner from the outset. While the Court has recognized that liberty interests may in some cases arise from positive-law sources, where, as here, the claimed interest derives from a knowingly assumed contractual relation with the State, it is appropriate to ascertain from state law the expectations and entitlements of the parties. In this case, the limited recognition accorded to the foster family by the New York statutes and the contracts executed by the foster parents argue against any but the most limited constitutional "liberty" in the foster family.

A second consideration . . . is that ordinarily procedural protection may be afforded to a liberty interest of one person without derogating from the substantive liberty of another. Here, however, such a tension is virtually unavoidable. Under New York law, the natural parent of a foster child in voluntary placement has an absolute right to the return of his child in the absence of a court order obtainable only upon compliance with rigorous substantive and procedural standards, which reflect the constitutional protection accorded the natural family. Moreover, the natural parent initially gave up his child to the State only on the express understanding that the child would be returned in those circumstances. These rights are difficult to reconcile with the liberty interest in the foster family relationship claimed by appellees. It is one thing to say that individuals may acquire a liberty interest against arbitrary governmental interference in the family-like associations into which they have freely entered, even in the absence of biological connection or state-law recognition of the relationship. It is quite another to say that one may acquire such an interest in the face of another's constitutionally recognized liberty interest that derives from blood relationship, state-law sanction, and basic human right — an interest the foster parent has recognized by contract from the outset. Whatever liberty interest might otherwise exist in the foster family as an institution, that interest must be substantially attenuated where the proposed removal from the foster family is to return the child to his natural parents.

Smith v. O.F.F.E.R., supra, 431 U.S. at 843–47. Claims that foster parents have a Fourteenth Amendment "liberty" interest in the relationship with their foster children have generally been unsuccessful. *See Procopio v. Johnson,* 785 F. Supp. 1317 (N.D. Ill. 1992); *In re Dependency of J.H.* 815 P.2d 1380 (Wash. 1991) (foster parents have no standing to challenge removal). Some courts have reached results more supportive of the claim. Delaware's highest court found that foster parents have standing to petition for guardianship without the consent of the Department of Family Services. *Div. of Family Serv. v. Harrison*, 741 A.2d 1016 (Del. 1999). The court held that the foster parents had a legally protected interest because they had cared for the child for most of his life. *See also In re Jonathan G.*, 482 S.E.2d 893 (W. Va. 1996) (foster parents who had care and custody of abused child for more than two years were entitled to hearing in termination of parental rights proceedings, to determine whether it was in the child's best interests to have a continuing association with them); *Rivera v. Marcus,* 696 F.2d 1016 (2nd Cir. 1982) (foster mother who was half-sister of children has protected "liberty" interest in their custody).

In *Smith v. O.F.F.E.R.*, the Court emphasized that recognizing a protectable interest in foster parents was in tension with natural parents' rights. However, courts sometimes dismiss foster parents' claims where no biological parent is in the picture. In a case that pitted foster parents against the child's grandfather, the Supreme Court of Pennsylvania recently decided that foster parents lack standing to seek custody of a child who had lived with them since he was an infant. *In re G.C.,* 735 A.2d 1226 (Pa. 1999). After Children and Youth Services opposed their petition to adopt the child, the grandfather sought and won physical custody (with legal custody to remain in CYS). The court rejected the foster parents' claim that they were *in loco parentis*, observing that they were paid to care for the child on behalf of the state, that their relationship could be terminated at any time, and that their status was always subordinate to that of the state and the parents. A dissenting justice argued that the foster parents were de facto parents, and questioned what their subordinated status had to do with their standing to contest the grandfather's custody claim

What of the *children's* liberty interests in remaining with foster parents who have provided them with the only stable home they know? Such a claim was not considered by *Smith,* which framed the inquiry solely in terms of the foster parents' rights. A few courts have denied children's claims. *See, e.g., Del A. v. Roemer*, 777 F. Supp. 1297 (E.D. La. 1991) (Adoption Assistance and Child Welfare Act of 1980 did not create a private right of action enforceable by foster children under § 1983). Some critics have argued for legal recognition of the child's interest in a relationship with psychological parents (including foster parents). *See* Holmes, *The Tie That Binds: The Constitutional Right of Children to Maintain Relationship with Parent-like Individuals*, 53 Md. L. Rev. 358 (1994).

Finally, what happens when a foster parent's claim to custody directly conflicts with the claim of a natural parent seeking the child's return? Traditionally, such disputes almost invariably were resolved in favor of the parents through application of the parental rights doctrine. *See, e.g., In re Matter of Michael B.*, 604 N.E.2d 122 (N.Y. 1992) (award of custody to foster parents who had cared for the child for five years reversed because pure best interest test measuring foster parents against biological parents is not appropriate in a parent-third party custody dispute). In recent years, some courts have favored the child's psychological parents in custody disputes between parents and nonparents. *See* Chapter 6, section F. There is a greater reluctance to decide custody disputes in favor of foster parents, however, because of the institutional concerns that are at stake in this context. It is one thing when a psychological parent relationship arises within the voluntary, step-family relationship, or when relatives or neighbors are asked privately to care for the children of others. It is another thing when the state itself either encourages, or coerces, families into substitute parent arrangements which then develop into long-term psychological relationships.

A battleground between foster parents and the agencies with legal custody of their children arises when the biological parents' rights have been severed and the child becomes available for adoption. Traditionally, foster parents have not fared well in claiming the right to adopt or retain custody. *See, e.g., Nye v. Marcus,* 502 A.2d 869 (Conn. 1985). Agencies often have policies excluding foster parents from adoption, for several reasons, including the agency's own need to maintain its foster home "supply." One long-prevailing philosophy was that foster parents, by definition temporary custodians, must maintain an emotional distance from the children to facilitate the children's reunification with their natural parents, and such a distance would not be possible if they saw themselves as potential adoptive parents. In addition, foster parents may not qualify for adoption under age and race criteria sometimes employed by the agencies. *See, e.g., In re Adoption of K.M.,* 668 So. 2d 862 (Ala. App. 1995) (age); *Bledsoe v. Department of Human Resources,* 241 S.E.2d 304 (Ga. App. 1977) (age); *In re Adoption/Guardianship No. 2633,* 646 A.2d 1036 (Md. App. 1994) (race). *See* Chapter 12.

This response has come under fire with increased concern about permanent placement of children who have been removed from their parents' custody. *See, e.g.,* Lazo-Miller, *Foster Parents, Children and Youth Services, and the Court: Can Foster Children Escape the Bermuda Triangle?,* 6 WIDENER J. PUB. L. 181 (1996) (criticizing the rationale employed by Pennsylvania courts in denying foster parents standing to petition for adoption). Recent legislation at the state and federal level facilitates adoption by foster parents. Many state codes today clarify that foster parents are eligible to adopt children in their care and they may be preferred. *See, e.g.,* N.Y. SOC. SERVICES LAW §383 (McKinney's 2003) (giving preference in adoption proceedings to foster parents who have had continuous custody of child for more than 12 months); *Cf.* CAL. WELF. & INST. CODE §366.25(d)(1)(C)(2)(West 1998) (child shall not be removed from stable and permanent foster care environment if to do so would be detrimental to child), applied in *In re Baby Girl D.,* 257 Cal. Rptr. 1 (Cal. App. 1989) (in "post-permanency planning order," foster parents favored over child's aunt). There also is some evidence that courts are becoming more receptive to adoption petitions by foster parents. *See In the Interest of C.F.,* 796 So.2d 922 (La.App. 3 Cir. 2001) (foster parents can petition for termination of parental rights to adopt child where state does not act); *Adoption of Gwendolyn,* 558 N.E.2d 10 (Mass. App. 1990) (clear and convincing evidence of biological parents' unfitness supported finding that child would benefit from adoption by foster parents in whose care she had been for four years)

In general, pressure has been building in recent years to promote the adoption of children in foster care. A study conducted by the National Center for Policy Analysis and the Institute for Children revealed that states vary widely in the per cent of children in foster care who are ultimately adopted, from 10 % in Hawaii to 96 % in North Dakota. Some observers argue that the current system of Federal payments to the states for foster care services encourage states to keep children in foster care. *See* Molotsky, *Adoption Rate in Foster Care Varies Widely among States*, N.Y. TIMES, Aug. 8, 1997, A12. The Adoption and Safe Families Act of 1997, *supra*, encourages states to increase and expedite adoption of abused and neglected children. The statute offers financial incentives to states to move children from foster care to permanent adoptive homes by awarding substantial payments for each adoption. The new law also directs states to initiate termination of parental rights of children who have been in foster care for 15 of the preceding 22 months. It also provides that reasonable efforts at family reunification required under the 1980 Assistance and Child Welfare Act do not apply to severely abused children. *See* Section B5, *infra*.

Some commentators criticize this approach to permanency planning which focuses on efficient termination of parental rights. Children may have meaningful relationships with parents who are unable to provide care by taking custody. *See* Scott & Scott, *Parents as Fiduciaries*, 81 VA. L. REV. 585 (1995). Moreover, many children are not, in fact, adopted after their parents' rights are terminated. Garrison, *Parents' Rights vs. Children's Interests: The Case of the Foster Child,* 22 N.Y.U. REV. L. & SOC. CHANGE 371 (1996). A federal report indicated that in 2000, 75,000 children whose parents' rights had been terminated were in foster care. *See* Children's Bureau AFCARS Report, *supra*.

[5] TERMINATION OF PARENTAL RIGHTS

MINNESOTA STATUTE § 260C.301 (2003)

§ 260C.301. Grounds for Termination of Parental Rights

Subd. 1. Voluntary and Involuntary. The juvenile court may, upon petition, terminate all rights of a parent to a child in the following cases:

(a) With the written consent of a parent who for good cause desires to terminate his parental rights; or

(b) If it finds that one or more of the following conditions exist:

(1) That the parent has abandoned the child. . .

(2) That the parent had substantially, continuously, or repeatedly refused or neglected to comply with the duties imposed upon that parent by the parent and child relationship, including but not limited to providing the child with necessary food, clothing, shelter, education, and other care and control necessary for the child's physical, mental or emotional health and development, if the parent is physically and financially able, and reasonable efforts by the social service agency have failed to correct the conditions that formed the basis of the petition; or

(3) That a parent has been ordered to contribute to the support of the child or financially aid in the child's birth and has continuously failed to do so without good cause . . .; or

(4) That a parent is palpably unfit to be a party to the parent and child relationship because of a consistent pattern of specific conduct before the child or of specific conditions directly relating to the parent and child relationship either of which are determined by the court to be of a duration or nature that renders the parent unable, for the reasonably foreseeable future, to care appropriately for the ongoing physical, mental, or emotional needs of the child; . . . or

(5) That following upon the child's placement out of the home, reasonable efforts, under the direction of the court, have failed to correct the conditions leading to the determination. It is presumed that reasonable efforts under this clause have failed upon a showing that:

(i) a child has resided out of the parental home under court order for cumulative period of 12 months within the preceding 22 months;

(ii) the court has approved the out of home placement plan required [by statute] and filed with the court. . .

(iii) conditions leading to the out of home placement have not been corrected. . .upon a showing that the parents have not substantially complied with the court's orders and reasonable care plan; and

(iv) reasonable efforts have been made by the social service agency to rehabilitate the parent and reunite the family.

This clause does not prohibit the termination of parental rights prior to one year. . .[after a child has been placed out of the home]

It is also presumed that reasonable efforts have failed under this clause upon a showing that:

(A) the parent has been diagnosed as chemically dependent by a professional certified to make the diagnosis;

(B) the parent has been required by a case plan to participate in a chemical dependency treatment program;

. . . .

(D) the parent has either failed two or more times to successfully complete a treatment program or has refused at two or more separate meetings with a caseworker to participate in a treatment program; and

(E) the parent continues to abuse chemicals.

(6) that a child has experienced egregious harm in the parent's care . . . such that a reasonable person would believe it contrary to the best interest of the child or of any child to be in the parent's care; or

. . . .

(8) That the child is neglected and in foster care.

IN RE ADOPTION/GUARDIANSHIP NO. J9610436

796 A.2d 778 (Md. 2002)

CATHELL, Judge.

. . . . The oldest of the two sons, Tristynn, was born on June 18, 1995 to petitioner and Ms. H. who were never married. . . . Petitioner testified that he has permanently terminated his relationship with Ms. H. . . . Ms. H. ultimately abandoned the children and consented to termination of her parental rights.

. . . . Tristynn. . . came into the care of CCDSS on December 28, 1995, at the age of six months, when petitioner went to CCDSS and asked for help in caring for his child. Petitioner testified that there was no electricity in the apartment where the family had been living at the time he brought Tristynn to CCDSS and that he had no food to feed Tristynn. There was no other evidence bearing on the issue of neglect and no evidence of abuse. Petitioner stated that "[I] thought [I] was going to get [my] kids back once [I] got [my] electricity turned back on". . . .

[Petitioner's second son, Edward, tested positive at birth for drugs, and entered the care of CCDSS on June 18, 1996 when he was three weeks old. He was immediately placed in foster care with Mr. and Mrs. M. (with whom he continues to reside)].

The initial permanency plan for both children was to return them to the home of either parent. On May 13, 1997, petitioner was informed that CCDSS's permanency plan had changed from a plan of reunification to guardianship with the right to consent to adoption. That plan was adopted by the court on June 10, 1997.

The adequacy of the reunification services provided to petitioner by CCDSS are disputed. CCDSS claims that the services provided to petitioner were adequate and ultimately unsuccessful. . . . Specifically, CCDSS states that shortly after Tristynn entered foster care, CCDSS began arranging for him to have supervised visits with petitioner. . . . CCDSS claims that they had scheduling problems with petitioner from the beginning of the visitation [and] the initial visitation schedule had to be changed frequently to accommodate petitioner's work schedule. . . . Further, CCDSS claims that during his early visits with the children, petitioner demonstrated trouble in caring for the children, was unable to remember child care techniques repeatedly shown to him by the social worker, had difficulty in choosing age-appropriate toys for the children, and was not able to help Tristynn with his beginning verbal skills. Moreover, CCDSS states that in later supervised visits when petitioner started seeing Tristynn and Edward together, petitioner needed supervision and direction to understand how to properly care for the two children, how to give them both proper attention when the children are together, and to understand the special medical and dietary needs of Edward.

. . . . CCDSS states that other than visitation, petitioner did not request additional services from CCDSS, and [denied] his need for services. The social worker assigned to assist petitioner claimed petitioner was not cooperative, was not truthful, and provided inadequate information.

Finally, unlike CCDSS's usual practice of entering into a new service agreement every six months with those seeking assistance, CCDSS entered into only one Social Services Agreement with petitioner (on July 3, 1996) that had the goal of reunification. The agreement required petitioner to obtain electricity in his apartment, attend parenting classes, complete a domestic violence program, complete an alcohol and drug evaluation, submit to random urine analysis, confirm in advance his intent to keep scheduled visits, be completely truthful with the CCDSS, and remain drug and alcohol free.

Petitioner attended parenting classes, as well as a parents anonymous group, but the social worker believed that petitioner made very little progress. Petitioner finished the first phase of a domestic violence program, but allegedly could not complete the second phase due to his alleged cognitive limitations. Also petitioner completed a drug and alcohol evaluation. . . the evaluator concluding that he did not need treatment.

A social worker also noted that petitioner never prepared a household budget, presumably for when reunification occurred, or came up with a plan for child care. . . . According to CCDSS, petitioner has a reduced mental capacity that renders him incapable of parenting the children on his own.

Insofar as we have been able to discern from the record, CCDSS never offered any specialized services designed to be particularly helpful to a parent with the intellectual and cognitive skill levels CCDSS alleges are possessed by petitioner. We are informed by the amicus brief that such services are available. . . . [F]inancial advising services, family support services, and other programs were available from . . .various Association Retarded Citizens (ARC) entities, and numerous other entities, private and public. None of these services were utilized by CCDSS. . . .

Petitioner. . . . [claims] that the services offered by CCDSS to him were minimal, inadequate, and inappropriate for his particular situation. Moreover, petitioner proffers that he has completed his education, obtained a driver's license, has secured employment, and maintains his own residence, indicating that he can, in fact, parent his own children.

. . . . Petitioner asserts that CCDSS did not fulfill its role as a social service department by seeking out programs specific to petitioner's parenting deficiencies, programs that would aid in the primary and ultimate goal of reunification. The failure, it is argued, of CCDSS to address its services to his specific need has a discriminatory impact.

. . . . CCDSS apparently did not even offer petitioner services to assist him with literacy. . . .

. . . . [A]t CCDSS's request, Neil Blumberg, M.D., conducted a psychiatric evaluation of petitioner. Dr. Blumberg reported that petitioner suffered from a serious intellectual impairment and categorized petitioner as disabled and unfit to parent. Dr. Blumberg noted that standard testing was not and could not be completed because of petitioner's inability to read well. . . .

. . . . Dr. Blumberg testified: "Well I would *probably* categorize his intellectual impairment as—a disability. I mean, it really does hamper him; he's — he — he cannot read. . . ." (Emphasis added). . . .

. . . . The extent to which Dr. Blumberg relies on a person's inability to read in order to find mental "impairment" or "retardation" is troubling, especially when it is used in proceedings to determine whether to terminate parental rights. . . .

. . . . C. Michael Hardesty, an expert in developmental disabilities, who was petitioner's employment supervisor. . . testified to petitioner's strong work ethic, and to petitioner's duties as a house counselor for United Cerebral Palsy. . .including providing assistance like toileting, dressing, and feeding to persons with profound disabilities, such as quadriplegia.

Some CCDSS caseworkers. . .testified that . . . in their view, unsupervised visitation would endanger the safety of the children. The caseworkers, however, did recognize that petitioner. . . demonstrated an ability to learn and improve his parenting skills through his progress in paying attention to and caring for the children. . . . Also, the caseworkers testified that Tristynn called petitioner "Dada" and was happy to see petitioner, and while the visits with Edward were more difficult for petitioner, Edward would at times seek petitioner for comfort. Finally, a social worker observing some of the visits testified that when petitioner needed assistance with the children during the visits he knew to ask for help, and that . . . given the opportunity, petitioner could learn the necessary skills. In essence, even CCDSS testified to a certain degree that reunification in the future was reasonably possible, if not probable.

Petitioner is a thirty-eight-year-old African-American male. He graduated from high school in 1982 and has maintained steady employment as a maintenance/cleaning person, a cook, and for six years as a house counselor. . . . Petitioner. . . has enrolled, voluntarily and without prompting from CCDSS, in remedial reading classes to improve his reading ability. He has attended parenting classes two times per week for approximately three and a half years and he has attended Parents Anonymous. Petitioner has little history of drug or alcohol abuse, and no history of child abuse or willful neglect. He now lives in a two bedroom townhouse, which includes a bedroom for himself and one which would be shared by the boys were they to be allowed to live with him. He testified that his parents live close to his home and that if he were to encounter problems with the children while in his care, he would know to call his parents or CCDSS for help. Finally, petitioner contends that the short visits under supervised conditions, which is all that CCDSS now permits, render it nearly impossible to establish any regularity with the children. . . .

[T]he children are both adjusting well to, and doing well in, their foster homes. . . . Tristynn is happy and is comfortable with his foster parents, but shows affection for petitioner and displays no negative reactions after visits. Mr. and Mrs. F. wish to adopt Tristynn, but expect Tristynn to continue his relationship with petitioner.

. . . . Mr. and Mrs. M. want Edward to know his father, but stated that Edward has had difficulty in visiting with petitioner. . . . Mr. and Mrs. M. wish to adopt Edward at the end of this litigation.

. . . .

[The Court then reviewed the relevant provisions of the Maryland statute regulating adoption/guardianship without parental consent. (Maryland Code (1984, 1999 Repl.Vol.), section 5-313 of the Family Law Article (FL)).]

. . .

(c) In determining whether it is in the best interest of the child to terminate a natural parent's rights as to the child. . ., the court shall give:

(1) primary consideration to the safety and health of the child; and

(2) consideration to:

(i) the timeliness, nature, and extent of the services offered by the child placement agency to facilitate reunion of the child with the natural parent;

(ii) any social service agreement between the natural parent and the child placement agency, and the extent to which all parties have fulfilled their obligations under the agreement;

(iii) the child's feelings toward and emotional ties with the child's natural parents, the child's siblings, and any other individuals who may significantly affect the child's best interest; . . .

(v) the result of the effort the natural parent has made to adjust the natural parent's circumstances, conduct, or conditions to make it in the best interest of the child to be returned to the natural parent's home, including:

1. the extent to which the natural parent has maintained regular contact with the child under a plan to reunite the child with the natural parent. . . .

4. whether additional services would be likely to bring about a lasting parental adjustment so that the child could be returned to the natural parent within an ascertainable time, not exceeding 18 months from the time of placement. . . .

(d) *Considerations following juvenile adjudication.*—(1) In determining whether it is in the best interest of the child to terminate a natural parent's rights as to the child in a case involving a child who has been adjudicated to be a child in need of assistance, a neglected child, an abused child, or a dependent child, the court shall consider the factors in subsection (c) of this section and whether any of the following continuing or serious conditions or acts exist:

(i) the natural parent has a disability that renders the natural parent consistently unable to care for the immediate and ongoing physical or psychological needs of the child for long periods of time;

(ii) the natural parent has committed acts of abuse or neglect toward any child in the family;

. . . .

In cases where the termination of parental rights is involved, there is. . . a strong presumption that the child's best interests are served by maintaining parental rights. It is only when clear and convincing evidence exists that the child's best interests are served by termination, may a parent's constitutional right to parent his child be permanently foreclosed. In our view, in the instant case, considering the allegations made by CCDSS as to petitioner's mental capacity, the parenting and reunification services offered to petitioner were not sufficient and not sufficiently tailored to his alleged specific situation to support a finding that, with sufficient and properly tailored services, he could not maintain a parental relationship with his children. . . . There was evidence of only one reunification agreement between the natural parent and CCDSS. . . . While there may be no easily ascertainable levels of assistance that must be offered when the termination of parental rights of a "disabled" parent is involved, that level is far above the minimal services CCDSS offered [here]. . . .

There was uncontradicted evidence that petitioner had made extensive and extraordinary efforts to further reunification with his children. He had, to the best of his ability, attempted to do almost everything asked of him, and more, in order to become a capable parent. . . . In so far as the record reflects, he maintained as regular a contact with his children as CCDSS would permit. . . . . . . [T]here is little evidence, as opposed to conjecture, that petitioner was inherently disabled to such an extent that he would be unable to care for the needs of the children for considerable periods of time. . . . He had, in fact, cared for the needs of other disabled persons as a part of his steady employment. He could not adequately read, but was taking classes to address that deficiency. He was a high school graduate. He had adequate living facilities. There was no scientific evidence that he was mentally impaired — that was an assumption that was made by CCDSS and Dr. Blumberg, who apparently presumed that he was, but undertook no tests to establish the extent, if any, of such impairment. . . . There was no evidence that petitioner had ever committed acts of abuse or willful neglect in respect to the children. In fact, when he was unable to care for Tristynn for a temporary period he approached CCDSS seeking assistance. . . .

. . . . Upon our review of the record . . . it is evident that there was not clear and convincing evidence. . . sufficient to overcome the presumption that the "best interests" of the children rest in the retention, generally, of petitioner's parental rights, *although at the present time actual custody may not be appropriate.* . . .

[The Court rejected the claim that the children's long relationship with the foster parents was relevant.]. . . . In cases such as this, parents who. . . love their children. . . and seek assistance [from CCDSS]. . . are placed at great risk of losing their children altogether. If. . . the Department places their children. . . with foster parents with whom they bond (and that is the type of foster parents one hopes are found), the natural parent runs the very real risk of later having that bonding in the foster home, created, in part, by CCDSS and court forced inaccessibility to his own children, be a major factor used to later terminate his parental rights. . .

. . . . Our holding today reflects the idea that fundamental constitutional rights, *i.e.,* the child rearing rights at issue here, can only be completely terminated upon the clearest and most convincing evidence that the parent, however poor, uneducated, or disabled, cannot and will not, even with proper assistance, be able to sufficiently parent his children in the reasonable future. . . .

The judgment of the Court of Special Appeals is reversed, and the case shall be remanded to that court for it to reverse the judgment of the Circuit Court. . . .

Dissenting Opinion by WILNER, J.

. . . . This case does *not* involve discrimination against disabled parents or poor parents. It does *not* involve any trampling upon the legitimate parental rights of Mr. F. . . . It is simply a case in which (1) nearly six years ago, two children were found to be in need of assistance by the juvenile court, (2) no appeal from or attack on those decisions has ever been made, (3) efforts were made to reunify the children with their father, but (4) the conclusion was drawn, based on evidence that the trial court found persuasive, that Mr. F. was not in a position, and was not likely to be in a position in the foreseeable future, to be able to care properly for the children, who have special needs, and (5) there *are* prospective adoptive parents willing and able to care for the children on a permanent basis. Everyone seemed to agree that if an adoption proceeds, it should be an open one, in which Mr. F. may maintain contact with the children.

Although parents do have a Constitutional right to raise their children, if they are able to do so, the law allows a court to terminate parental rights, under specified circumstances, when the welfare of the children would best be served by that course of action. . . . It is for the trial judge, not for us, to weigh and consider the evidence. . . . The Court has thrown appellate restraint to the wind, and, in doing so, has not only subordinated the welfare of these two children to its incorrect view of how far the parent's rights extend but has also injected considerable uncertainty into termination proceedings generally.

NOTES

1. *Relationship Between Termination and Neglect Proceedings.* Parents' rights are involuntarily terminated in two large categories of cases. First are cases in which a non-custodial parent has failed to fulfill parental responsibilities. These cases, which often arise when a stepparent seeks to adopt the child, are dealt with in Chapter 11. The other category involves children who have been removed from parents' custody due to abuse or neglect. While all states have separate statutes which set forth grounds and procedures for termination of parental rights, typically the grounds overlap with the substantive standards for abuse and neglect. When termination grounds relate to a prior finding of child abuse or neglect, usually the conditions resulting in removal of the child must have continued for a minimum period without sufficient improvement, despite reunification efforts by the state in the form of remedial services. If abuse is severe, however, or if the parent is found to be unfit and unlikely to be capable of caring for the child in a reasonable time, parental rights can be terminated without providing an opportunity to remediate. Under recent federal legislation that reflects a policy of promoting permanency planning for children in foster care, termination is facilitated in cases of severe abuse; in other cases, the time period for remediation is limited. This legislation is discussed in Note 4 below.

2. *Legal Standards for Termination — Is Parental Unfitness Required?* The Maryland statute applied in *Adoption No. J9610436* provides that parental rights can only be terminated in abuse or neglect cases when termination is in the best interests of the child. As the court's analysis indicates, however, this is a necessary but not sufficient condition. Many statutes are interpreted to require that a parent's rights cannot be terminated without some showing of unfitness, even if the child's interests might be furthered by termination. *See, e.g., In re Kristina L,* 520 A.2d 574 (R.I. 1987). If a state could override parental rights merely because it believes a child could be made better off as a result, it could remove children from their parents' custody to place them in better homes. That is not the law.

Does the Constitution prohibit the termination of a parent's rights without a showing of unfitness? As the Supreme Court opinions that begin this chapter make clear, parents have a fundamental right to rear their children under the Due Process Clause of the Fourteenth Amendment. Although the issue of whether parental unfitness is required for termination has never been directly addressed, a number of Supreme Court decisions have suggested that the termination of parental rights on grounds of the child's interests alone, without any showing of unfitness, is unconstitutional. *See, e.g., Smith v. Organization of Foster Families,* 431 U.S. 816, 862–63 (1977) (Stewart, J. concurring) ("If a State were to attempt to force the breakup of a natural family, over the objections of the parents and their children, without some showing of unfitness and for the sole reason that to do so was thought to be in the children's best interest, I should have little doubt that the State would have intruded impermissibly on the 'private realm of family life which the state cannot enter.' "). The Court has also held, in *Santosky v. Kramer,* that due process requires that termination on statutory unfitness grounds must be proved by clear and convincing evidence. *See* Note 2c, *infra.* Recently, the Court reiterated that parents' right to control the upbringing of their children is a fundamental right, in rejecting the application of the best interest of the child standard to grandparent visitation decisions and requiring courts to give substantial weight to the objection of a fit parent. *Troxel v. Granville,* 530 U.S. 57 (2000). *See* Chapter 6, page 667. Most lower courts assume that unfitness is a constitutional requirement. In *In the Interest of Jane Doe,* 20 P.3d 616 (Haw. 2001), the Hawaii Supreme Court reversed a lower court decision finding the termination statute unconstitutional, because the lower court erroneously concluded that the statute allowed termination on best interests grounds, without a finding of unfitness. The supreme court interpreted the statute to require a finding of parental unfitness and thus to have no constitutional infirmity.

Because a showing of parental unfitness is often required, termination cases can present a tension between protecting the child's interests and respecting parental rights. For example, as the principal case illustrates, the protection of parents' rights may undermine children's relationships with psychological parents. Would the interest of Tristynn and Edward be promoted if their foster parents were allowed to adopt, especially since an open adoption (and a continued relationship with their father) was contemplated? The lower appellate court suggested that an important consideration in the decision was protection of the children's long-term relationships with their foster parents, a consideration that the Court of Appeals rejected out of hand as unfair to the father in this case, and perhaps in general. Some courts allow consideration of the bonds between children and foster parents in the termination decision if separation from foster parents would cause "serious psychological and emotional harm." *See Matter of the Guardianship of J.C.*, 608 A.2d 1312 (N.J. 1992) (announcing this standard).

3. *Is Parental "Fault" Required for Termination?* Should parental rights be terminated even if the parent has done all that he or she can to remediate the conditions that led to removal of the child, but has been unable to assume parental responsibilities because of conditions beyond her control. This question is at the center of *Adoption No. J9610436*; the father's sincere efforts to become a competent parent and the agency's failure to tailor its remedial efforts to his needs are the basis of the court's determination that termination was wrongly ordered. But was the case correctly decided? From the child's perspective, parental "innocence" may not be relevant to the decision of whether termination promotes her welfare. Or is it? Perhaps children receive benefits from ongoing relationships with inadequate parents who are sincerely trying to fulfill their duties, benefits that do not exist where the parent has culpably harmed the child or has not tried to remediate. *See* Scott & Scott, *Parents as Fiduciaries*, 81 VA. L. REV. 2401 (1995).

a. *Mental disability* Perhaps the best example of a "no-fault" ground for termination is the one at issue in *Adoption No. J9610436*, the parent's inability to care adequately for the child because of limited mental capacity. Mental disability does not necessarily mean that a parent is unable to care for a child, see Budd & Greenspan, *Mentally Retarded Mothers,* in BEHAVIOR MODIFICATION WITH WOMEN 479 (Belchman ed. 1984), but it may seriously affect the degree of supervision and guidance the parent can offer. Courts have consistently upheld this ground of termination if its effect is to severely impair parenting ability. *See Tennessee v. Smith*, 785 S.W.2d 336 (Tenn. 1990) ("mental disability" can form the basis for termination of parental rights, even though the acts of mentally disabled parent are not willful). However, modern courts emphasize that mental disability alone is not a sufficient basis for termination of parental rights. In *In re R.C., a Minor,* 745 N.E.2d 1233 (Ill. 2001), the Illinois Supreme Court reversed a lower court ruling holding unconstitutional a statute permitting termination on grounds of mental incapacity. However, the court emphasized that, under the statute, mental condition could be the basis for a finding of unfitness *only* where it renders the parent unable to fulfill parental responsibilities.

A question that frequently arises in cases involving mentally handicapped parents is whether the agency, to fulfill its obligation to undertake "reasonable efforts" to reunify the family, has a heightened obligation to provide appropriate services and support. *See* note 4, *infra.* Although the court in *Adoption No. J9610436* faulted the state for not tailoring its efforts through programs that were directed toward Mr. F's needs, many courts would find standard programs adequate to satisfy "reasonable efforts." *See, e.g., In Interest of D.L.S.*, 432 N.W.2d 31 (Neb. 1988) (where mother's "mental deficiency" was not improved, although she was trying to comply with rehabilitation plan, agency is not required to wait for some indeterminate period, "on the speculative hope that [her] deficiency would be remedied"); *Interest of J.A.L.*, 432 N.W.2d 876 (N.D. 1988) (agency is not required to provide constant, round-the-clock supervision in order to keep the family together).

Where emotional bonds between the mentally handicapped parent and child are significant, the "reasonable efforts" requirement may be more strictly interpreted. *See, e.g. In re E.M.*, 620 A.2d 481 (Pa. 1993) (termination order set aside where trial court failed to sufficiently consider the emotional bond between the children and their mentally impaired mother). In *P.A.B.*, 570 A.2d 522 (Pa. Super. 1990), a termination order was reversed even though reunification was deemed totally unrealistic, because of the positive emotional relationship enjoyed by the parties. Was the father's relationship with the children an important consideration in *Adoption No. J9610436*? Although he had contact with the children, he had never had custody of Edward and only briefly had custody of Tristynn.

Response to mentally disabled parents potentially has become more complicated with the enactment by Congress of the Americans with Disabilities Act (ADA) in 1990. This statute embodies a policy of protection of disabled individuals from discrimination, and it has been invoked in support of mentally disabled individuals facing termination of parental rights. The ADA provides that "no qualified individual with a disability shall, by reason of such disability, be excluded from participation, or denied the benefits of, the services, programs, or activities of a public entity, or be subject to discrimination by any such entity." 42 U.S.C. § 12132. The court in *Adoption No. J9610436* is clearly concerned to avoid discrimination against mentally disabled parents. In a part of the opinion not reprinted here, the court suggested that the ADA constitutes part of the interpretive framework for applying Maryland's statutory termination provisions (although the court declined to decide whether the ADA directly applied to termination decisions). 796 A.2d at 783. A few courts have concluded that the ADA applies to termination proceedings. *See In re C.M.*, 996 S.W.2d 269 (Tex. App. 1999) (ADA creates defense in termination proceeding, but parent waived defense in this case). Other courts have found ADA inapplicable to termination proceedings. For example, Massachusetts' highest court rejected an appeal by a father who argued that the trial court in terminating his parental rights had failed to reasonably accommodate his cognitive disorder and attention deficit disorder, as required under the ADA. *Adoption of Gregory*, 747 N.E.2d 120 (Mass. 2001). The court concluded that proceedings to terminate parental rights do not constitute "services, programs, or activities" under the ADA. [Even without the ADA, the court noted, Massachusetts law directed that the parents' special needs be accommodated, and that parents with children in state custody be offered services that were responsive to handicapping conditions.] Most other courts have reached the same conclusion. *See In re Antony B.*, 735 A.2d 893 (Conn. App. Ct. 1999) (termination proceedings not subject to ADA, and thus federal statute neither provides a defense nor creates special obligations). For a discussion of this topic, see Watkins, *Beyond Status: The Americans with*

Disabilities Act and the Parental Rights of People Labeled Developmentally Disabled or Mentally Retarded, 83 CAL. L. REV. 1415, 1469 (1995); Hayman, *Presumptions of Justice: Law, Politics, and the Mentally Retarded Parent,* 103 HARV. L.REV. 1202, 1269 (1990).

b. *Mental illness.* Similar issues are raised with respect to parents who are mentally ill, although, in general, mental illnesses tend to be more changeable than mental retardation. When the social services agency attempts to terminate a parent's rights based upon mental illness, ordinarily it must show that the illness is permanent, or that there is no reasonable likelihood that the parent will be able to take care of the child in the future. *See, e.g.,* COLO. REV. STAT. §19-5-105(3.1)(a)(I) (disability of such duration or nature as to render the parent unlikely within a reasonable time to care for the needs of the child); N.Y. SOC. SERV. LAW §384-b(4)(c) (2003) (disability will continue for the foreseeable future).

As with cases involving mentally retarded parents, outcomes in termination actions involving mentally ill parents vary. Some courts require special efforts on the part of the state. In *In Matter of Star A.,* 435 N.E.2d 1080 (N.Y. 1982), the mother who suffered from mental illness was receiving treatment from independent sources, and the social workers monitored her treatment, but "apparently did little to channel her toward appropriate psychiatric care when she strayed from her treatments." In the termination proceedings, the court rejected the agency claim that further services would have been duplicative of the services the mother was receiving, holding that the agency's duty to provide services could not be excused by its predetermination that further efforts would be "futile." In *In re Interest of Brown,* 736 P.2d 1355 (Idaho App. 1987), on the other hand, the court concluded that "any course of psychotherapeutic treatment would have been unproductive." because the mother had declined to take advantage of other services offered by the agency, such as help with family budgeting and home maintenance. *Id.* at 1358.

c. *Imprisonment and termination.* Parents who can not fulfill their parental obligations because they are incarcerated are hardly sympathetic, at one level, and yet their absence from their children is not voluntary and they are unable to take steps toward reunification. Can imprisonment per se be a ground for termination? Illinois recently added statutory unfitness ground for termination on the basis of "repeated incarceration" which prevented the discharge of parental duties. Illinois Adoption Act, 750 ILL. COMP. STAT 50/1(D)(s)(2003). Illinois' highest court determined that the termination decision under this ground could include evidence of imprisonment before the child's birth. *In re D.D.,* 752 N.E.2d 1112 (Ill. 2001). Thus, the criminal record of the father, who began serving a 10 year term for aggravated assault shortly after the child's birth, was appropriately considered in the termination decision. Having been imprisoned almost all of his adult life, he had no parenting abilities or interest in meeting the child's needs. The Arizona Supreme Court examined the meaning of unfitness based on abandonment, as applied to an imprisoned father. *Michael J. v. Ariz. Dep't of Econ. Sec.,* 995 P.2d 682 (Ariz. 2000). The court concluded that, although the father's incarceration alone did not constitute abandonment, it also did not justify the father's failure to make more than minimal efforts to support and communicate with the child. Where the father had failed to take steps to protect his legal status, despite advice from the agency with custody of the child to consult counsel, and had not communicated with him through calls or letters, the finding of abandonment was justified.

Some courts have been sympathetic toward prisoner parents. A Florida court held that a four-and-a-half year sentence did not support termination of the father's rights, under a statute that allowed termination in response to an expected sentence that would constitute a substantial portion of the child's minority. *W.W. v. Dep't of Children and Families*, 811 So. 2d 791 (Fla. Dist. Ct. App. 2002). As no other ground existed, termination was not warranted. A termination decision based on the imprisoned father's failure to visit or support the children was reversed by one court, where the Department of Social Services would not permit visits requested by the father and he was not permitted to earn money in prison. *Dep't of Soc. Serv. v. Wilson*, 543 S.E.2d 580 (S.C. App. 2000). The evidence indicated that prior to his imprisonment, the father had fulfilled his parental responsibilities.

4. The Limits of the State's "Reasonable Efforts" Obligation. In most cases, the state is obliged to use "reasonable efforts" to rehabilitate the parents or the conditions that lead to the child's removal before it can initiate termination proceedings. Thus, where the agency has failed to offer appropriate services that would assist the parent to resume his parental responsibilities, the court may decline to terminate parental rights on that ground. However, although successful remedial efforts can lead to reunification, extensive efforts to reunite the family can mean long periods of foster care for the child. Thus, the trend is to puts limits on state's obligation to undertake reunification efforts and the parent's opportunity to remediate. Some courts attach far less importance to the state's remedial obligation than did the Maryland court in *Adoption No. J9610436*. The Connecticut Supreme Court interpreted that state's statute to provide that termination of parental rights could be ordered without proof by the state that reasonable efforts at reunification had been made. *In re Eden F.*, 741 A.2d 873 (Conn. 1999). The case involved a mother suffering from chronic schizophrenia, which had seriously hampered her ability to care for her child. The court upheld termination on the statutory ground that, in response to an earlier neglect finding, she had failed to achieve rehabilitation sufficient to encourage the belief that she would, in a reasonable period of time, be able to resume a "responsible position in the child's life." The statute (which is quite similar to the Maryland statute) directed that, once the termination ground was established by clear and convincing evidence, the court should consider the state's reunification efforts and the services provided to the parent to determine if termination was in the child's best interest. The court concluded that the statute did not require an explicit demonstration by the state that it had made reasonable reunification efforts, and that such a finding was not constitutionally required. If a parent is simply incapable of parenting, regardless of the services provided or if the necessary services would virtually amount to full-time substitute care (see, *In Interest of J.A.L., supra*), the agency may be excused from providing them. Other circumstances in which courts may excuse the agency's failure to provide further services include parental failure to make use of previously offered services, see *In re Kathaleen*, 460 A.2d 12 (R.I. 1983), or parental failure to keep in touch with the agency. *See In re Katina Valencia H.,* 119 A.D.2d 821,(N.Y. App. 1986).

With the increased emphasis on permanency planning for children in state custody in recent years (see Note on the Foster Care System, *supra*), Congress has sought to limit the state's obligation and parents' opportunities for remediation. The Adoption and Safe Families Act of 1997 (ASFA) provides that the state should initiate the termination of parental rights of children who have been in foster care for 15 of the preceding 22 months. 42 U.S.C. § 675 (5)(D). The statute further provides that reasonable efforts are not required where the parent has subjected the child to "aggravated circumstances," as defined by state law, including abandonment, torture, chronic abuse, sexual abuse or has committed a felony assault on the child resulting in serious bodily injury. 42 U.S.C. § 671(a)(15).

It is not yet clear whether the ASFA achieve its goal of expediting termination of parental rights in the interest of permanency planning for children. Although some states amended their termination statutes to conform to this requirement, there is evidence of judicial resistance. The court in *Adoption No. J9610436* does not seem to feel constrained by the Federal statute — and, indeed, criticizes it in a part of the opinion not reprinted here. The Illinois Supreme Court recently reviewed a new statutory provision (enacted in response to ASFA) creating a presumption of parental unfitness when a child has been in foster care for the congressionally-prescribed time period. *In re H.G.,* 757 N.E.2d 864 (Ill. 2001). The court concluded that the statute represented an unconstitutional violation of parents' liberty interest in their relationship with their children. Although the state has a compelling state interest in protecting children, in the court's view, the statutory provision failed strict scrutiny review. It was not narrowly tailored to achieve the state's goal because it defines unfitness solely on the basis of passage of time, and not on parents' inability to care for their children. The court noted that the length of a child's stay in foster care sometimes is due to circumstances beyond the parents' control. [For example, delays resulted because treatment programs could not accommodate parents.] In the case under review, delays of many months were caused by continuances and other problems in bringing the case to trial. The use of time periods was appropriate, in the court's view, only when it was linked to the parent's conduct (*i.e.* addiction or habitual drunkenness for at least a year.) The fact that under the statute the parent could rebut the presumption by showing that termination was not in the child's best interest did not correct the constitutional defect, because a parent able to care for her child (but who satisfied the presumption) should not have her rights determined by a best interest inquiry.

ASFA has been subject to much academic commentary, often quite critical. *See* Herring, *The Adoption and Safe Families Act: Hope and its Subversion,* 34 FAM. L. Q. 329 (2000). Herring argues that ASFA's goal of permanency will be undermined because judges view the statute as unfair, especially where participation in programs is delayed due to lack of resources. *See also* Adler, *The Meaning of Permanence: A critical Analysis of the Adoption and Safe Families Act of 1997,* 38 HARV. J. LEGIS. 1 (2001). Adler criticizes the ASFA goal of permanence as embodying "the ideology of the ideal family." A more neutral analysis is offered by Gendall, *In Search of Permanency: A Reflection on the First Three Years of the Adoption and Safe Families Act*, 39 Fam. & Concil Cts. Rev. 25 (2001).

5. *Burden of Proof in Termination Proceedings.* Both the burden and standard of proof are procedural devices that reflect particular policy choices as to how to weigh the interests at stake in termination proceedings. The state has the burden of proof, and under *Santosky v. Kramer,* 455 U.S. 745 (1982), it must meet its burden by "clear and convincing evidence." In imposing this standard as a matter of constitutional law, the Court focused on the need to protect parental rights by avoiding mistaken terminations — a risk aggravated in termination cases by such factors as (1) the imprecision of the substantive termination standards, (2) the "vast array" of resources which the state could command to prove its case, (3) the trial court's "unusual" discretion, and (4) the vulnerability of poor, uneducated or minority parents to cultural or class bias.

While the *Santosky* rule reflects the Court's emphasis on parental interests, it shows little recognition of the other interests at stake, such as the child's. A normal preponderance of the evidence standard is appropriate if one gives equal priority to avoiding errors on either side; this standard also yields the fewest errors in total. *See* Kaye, *The Limits of the Preponderance of the Evidence Standard: Justifiably Naked Statistical Evidence and Multiple Causation,* 1982 Am. B. Found. J. 487. By adopting the more demanding standard of proof, the *Santosky* court reduces the frequency of mistaken terminations, but at the same time increases the frequency of mistaken *failures* to terminate. This distortion is appropriate if the interests favored by it are sufficiently strong, and is reflected by the criminal law's "beyond a reasonable doubt" standard, which is explained by the assertion that it is better that ten guilty defendants go free than that one innocent person be convicted. *Santosky* concludes that the parents' interests are particularly strong, and assumes that until grounds for termination are established, there is no equally weighty interest on the part of the child.

In his *Santosky* dissent, Justice Rehnquist, joined by Chief Justice Burger and Justices White and O'Connor, emphasized the numerous protections already afforded by the New York statutory schemes relating to abuse, neglect and termination proceedings; parental rights had been terminated in *Santosky* only "after four and one-half years of involvement . . . more than seven complete hearings, and additional periodic supervision of the State's rehabilitative efforts. . . ." *Id.* at 783. Should the prior findings of neglect and abuse made at these hearings establish that the interests of the parent and the child may be in conflict?

The *Santosky* result has been criticized for encouraging "a disproportionately large number" of parental appeals in termination cases, on technical procedural grounds. One judge commented that, "Every right accorded to the parents, every reunification service ordered, every continuance, and especially every appeal taken is purchased at the expense of the person who is in law and morality their primary object of judicial solicitude, namely the child." *In re Micah,* 198 Cal. App. 3d 557, 243 Cal. Rptr. 756 (1988) (Brauer, J., concurring).

Do indigent parents have a constitutional right to court-appointed counsel at termination proceedings? This claim was rejected by the Supreme Court in *Lassiter v. Department of Social Servs. of Durham Cty.,* 452 U.S. 18 (1981). In *Lassiter,* the Court by a 5-4 vote held that the Due Process Clause does not require appointment of counsel for indigent parents in every termination case, but that the issue should be considered on a case-by-case basis, taking into account the complexity of the case and the parent's capacity to proceed without counsel. The Court affirmed termination of the mother's parental rights without benefit of counsel, because the issues were not sufficiently complicated to require counsel.

The Supreme Court found that a parent whose parental rights have been terminated cannot be denied a right to an appeal of the decision because she lacks the means to pay for the record preparation fees. *M.L.B. v. S.L.J.,* 519 U.S. 102 (1996). The Court concluded that a Mississippi statute conditioning the parent's right to appeal on advance payment of the fees violated the parent's equal protection and due process rights. In the case, the mother's parental rights were terminated in an action brought by the custodial father and his wife, who sought to adopt the children. The mother filed a timely appeal, but was unable to pay the $2350 filing fee to reproduce the transcript and other court records. The Court emphasized the importance to the parent of a decision to sever the parent-child relationship in aligning appeals in this category of cases with other types of cases in which indigent parties have a right to appeal — criminal appeals and appeals in cases involving the right to participate in the political process.

Several courts have held that in a termination action, a claim of ineffectiveness of counsel — a claim generally available only in criminal appeals — can provide a basis for appeal. *See, e.g., State ex rel. Juvenile Dep't v. Geist,* 799 P.2d 674 (Or. App. 1990); *Johnson v. J.K.C.,* 781 S.W.2d 226 (Mo. App. 1989) (citing cases from other jurisdictions, including Arizona, California, Colorado, Illinois, Iowa, Kansas, Massachusetts, Michigan, New York, North Carolina and Washington).

In *Guardianship of S.A.W v. Torres,* 856 P.2d. 286 (Okla. 1993), the Supreme Court of Oklahoma held that a minor child who was the subject of an action to terminate the parental rights is entitled to independent representation. In Oklahoma, parents have a right to counsel in a termination proceeding, and, the Court reasoned, the child has an equally important interest at stake.

PROBLEMS

Problem 10-10. Shortly after the birth of their child, Edward M. killed his wife, Julie M., in a violent domestic dispute. Edward received a 10-year jail sentence. Can Edward M.'s parental rights be terminated under the Minnesota statute set forth above? What are the best statutory and policy arguments that can be made on each side of this question?

Problem 10-11. Six-year-old Darla J. was removed from the home on an emergency petition after several suspicious bruises were reported by her teacher to the welfare department. Physical abuse was never confirmed, but upon investigation of the family situation, the welfare department found that the living conditions at the J's home were unacceptable; Mr. & Mrs. J were living with their two other children in a small and somewhat run-down one-bedroom apartment. Neither parent was regularly employed. Because of the home situation, the Juvenile Court found Darla neglected, although her siblings were not removed. For the next four years, the parents visited with Darla only on five occasions. The reason for the lack of visits is unclear, although during this period, the parents have moved frequently without leaving a forwarding address; they themselves seldom initiated contact with Darla. The welfare department has not really attempted to assist the parents in locating better housing and employment, claiming they have been very hard to track down because of the frequent moves.

Darla is now 10 and has emotionally bonded with her foster parents, the S's. Under the Minnesota statute set forth above, are there grounds for termination of parental rights? If so, what about the other two children?

Problem 10-12. Gershon and Golda Jonisz were Polish Jews. Shortly after their daughter Shifra was born in April, 1941, the Germans confined all Jews in the most miserable section of their town surrounded by a wall. In October 1942, Gershon and Golda escaped with 18-month-old Shifra. They soon became persuaded that they ensured Shifra's death as well as their own if they kept her with them. In desperation, they left her on the edge of the forest, near a Polish town, where she was found and taken in by Leokadia, a 34 year old Polish Catholic woman whose husband had been arrested by the Gestapo two years earlier. She named the child Bogusia and cared for her for the remaining three years of the war. Leokadia worked in a German factory to support them, and was without family to care for the child while she was at work. She could not obtain a food ration for the child because that would have raised suspicions among the Germans. Despite a number of close calls, somehow she and the child survived the war.

Golda died in the extermination camp near Maidanek, but Gershon survived and searched for Shifra. In September, 1945, he succeeded. When he appeared at Leokadia's apartment to claim the child, she said "I am not giving up this child to anyone. God sent her to me and means for her to have me." She asked Bogusia if she wanted to go with the stranger who said he was her father. The child held tightly to Leokadia and said "You are my mother. I love only you and we will always be together."

Who should have custody of Shifra-Bogusia? If you believe Leokadia should have custody, should Gershon's parental rights be terminated? If you believe Gershon should have custody, should Leokadia retain any rights? (The facts are borrowed from a true story told in P. HELLMAN, AVENUE OF THE RIGHTEOUS 167–264 (1980)).

[6] PROVING CHILD ABUSE AND NEGLECT

STEWARD v. STATE

652 N.E.2d 490 (Ind. 1995)

DICKSON, Justice.

In prosecutions for child molesting, is child sexual abuse syndrome, profile, or pattern evidence admissible to prove that child abuse occurred?. . .

The defendant, a 52-year-old police officer and family friend of the alleged victims, was convicted of one count of child molesting, a class C felony, for performing sexual intercourse with S.M. when she was 15 years of age;. . . .

As noted by the Court of Appeals, the State presented evidence at trial that S.M.'s behavior was consistent with that of other victims of child sexual abuse in order to prove that sexual contact occurred. The State called Betty Watson, a licensed clinical psychologist with considerable professional experience who had provided treatment for S.M. After stating that common traits or behavioral symptoms are found in teenagers who have experienced sexual abuse,. . . . Dr. Watson testified that S.M. exhibited such symptoms, identifying poor self-esteem, "family problems," association with an older peer group, depression, leaving home without permission, and problems with school behavior and performance. . . .

The State also presented testimony from Michael S. Girton, a minister and executive director of a licensed group residential treatment facility, and his wife, Katherine R. Girton, a caseworker at the facility. After establishing that Rev. Girton had taken courses in "sexual abuse work," including "being able to identify sexual abuse," the State asked him whether, based upon his personal experience, "kids who have known incidents of sexual abuse exhibit certain traits or characteristics or behavior patterns." Rev. Girton answered, "Yes," and described the following types of behavior that he looks for in determining whether there had been sexual abuse:

> "[The girls can be anything from promiscuous, they can be very timid, they can come in with extremely low esteem. Almost exclusively, that is going to be a major characteristic. Some of the different cues can range in areas from being really over timid to different kind of touches and approaches, where you would approach them in different directions or from different manners or methods. You might even put your hand on their shoulder and that might freak them out or something. . . ."

Both Rev. and Mrs. Girton testified that there was a marked change in S.M.'s behavior immediately after S.M. disclosed to them and to Dr. Watson that she had had a sexual relationship with the defendant.

The defendant argues that testimony concerning similarities between S.M.'s behaviors and those of known child abuse victims is not scientifically reliable evidence to prove S.M. was sexually abused and is therefore inadmissible.

1. The Problem

The admissibility of expert testimony regarding child sexual abuse syndrome evidence is controversial and has received substantial criticism. Recognition of the prevalence of child sexual abuse and intensive study of the problem by behavioral scientists did not begin until the mid-1970s. The Child Sexual Abuse Accommodation Syndrome (CSAAS) was first identified by Dr. Roland Summit in a 1983 article in which he described five experiences typically occurring in sexually abused children: (1) secrecy about the sexual abuse, often ensured by threats of negative consequences of disclosure; (2) emotional helplessness to resist or complain; (3) entrapment and accommodation, where the child sees no way to escape ongoing abuse and thus learns to adapt; (4) delayed, conflicted, and unconvincing disclosure of the abuse; and (5) retraction of the child's allegations in an attempt to restore order to the family structure when the disclosure threatens to destroy it. Roland C. Summit, *The Child Sexual Abuse Accommodation Syndrome,* 7 CHILD ABUSE & NEGLECT 177, 181–88 (1983). [hereinafter Summit, The CSAAS]. . . . The syndrome was not intended as a diagnostic device and does not detect sexual abuse. . . Rather, the syndrome was designed for purposes of treating child victims and offering them more effective assistance "within the family and within the systems of child protection and criminal justice," Summit, The CSAAS, *supra*, at 179–80. [I]t helps to explain reactions — such as recanting or delayed reporting — of children assumed to have experienced abuse.

Because children's responses to sexual abuse vary widely, and because many of the characteristics identified by CSAAS, or by similar victim behavior groupings, may result from causes unrelated to abuse, diagnostic use of syndrome evidence in courtrooms poses serious accuracy problems. . . . Summit explains that: some criticism has been a legitimate defense against improper use by prosecutors and expert witnesses called by prosecution. There has been some tendency to use the CSAAS as an offer of proof that a child has been abused. A child may be said to be suffering from or displaying the CSAAS, as if it is a malady that proves the alleged abuse. Or a child's conspicuous helplessness or silence might be said to be consistent with the CSAAS, as if not complaining proves the complaint. Some have contended that a child who retracts is a more believable victim than one who has maintained a consistent complaint. Our discussion today encompasses not only CSAAS but also similar descriptions of "typical" behavior profiles or patterns, whether or not termed "syndromes," all of which we shall refer to generally as "child sexual abuse syndrome," or "syndrome evidence."

[C]hild sexual abuse syndrome evidence [has been offered] for three major purposes: (1) to prove directly — through either implication or explicit testimony of the expert's conclusion — the fact that abuse actually occurred; (2) to counter claims that the testimony or behavior of alleged victims is inconsistent with abuse or otherwise not credible; and (3) to opine that, because the behavioral characteristics of the child comport with the syndrome profile, the child is likely to be telling the truth. In this opinion we explore the first and second of these applications and summarily affirm the Court of Appeals decision [rejecting evidence [offered] for the [third] purpose]. . .

[C]ourts face the challenge of determining under what circumstances, if any, such evidence is admissible, acutely aware of the potentially severe consequences of error in either direction. This challenge is heightened by the distinctive evidentiary problems posed by prosecutions for child sexual abuse: Often these cases pit the word of a traumatized child against that of an adult. Child sexual abuse typically occurs in private, when the abuser is confident that there will be no witnesses. Therefore, the child victim is usually the only eyewitness. The prosecution's case is severely hampered if the court finds the child to be too young to be a witness or incompetent to testify. Even if the child does testify, several factors often limit the effectiveness of this testimony. The child's cognitive and verbal abilities may not enable her to give consistent, spontaneous, and detailed reports of her sexual abuse. A child who must testify against a trusted adult, such as a parent or relative, may experience feelings of fear and ambivalence, and may retract her story because of family pressures or insensitivities in the legal process. Prosecutors face another dilemma when offering the child victim as a witness if the child has delayed reporting the abuse. Jurors may interpret delayed disclosure as evidence of fabrication, especially if defense counsel suggests this conclusion during cross-examination of the child. Further, jurors may hold misconceptions that the child has memory deficits, is suggestible, cannot distinguish between fact or fantasy, or is likely to fabricate sexual experiences with adults. These problems are compounded by the lack of corroborative physical or mental evidence in many child sexual abuse cases.

The utilization of innovative methodologies to address these problems must be balanced with "the preservation of the constitutional right to presumption of innocence in a criminal case." [citation omitted.]. . . . The particular dilemma expert testimony poses in these emotionally charged cases has been aptly described by the Supreme Court of Michigan: Given the nature of the offense and the terrible consequences of a miscalculation — the consequences when an individual, on many occasions a family member, is falsely accused of one of society's most heinous offenses, or, conversely, when one who commits such a crime would go unpunished and a possible reoccurrence of the act would go unprevented — appropriate safeguards are necessary. To a jury recognizing the awesome dilemma of whom to believe, an expert will often represent the only seemingly objective source, offering it a much sought-after hook on which to hang its hat. *People v. Beckley* (1990), 456 N.W.2d 391, 404.

. . . .

A few decisions from other states have held child sexual abuse syndrome evidence inadmissible for any purpose, and some cases have permitted expert testimony opining that, because of the correlation between a child's behavior and the syndrome, the child has been sexually abused. Most jurisdictions, however, have settled somewhere between these two extremes. . . .

It is important to recognize that syndrome evidence is not similarly problematic in all situations. The reliability of syndrome evidence, although highly questionable for purposes of affirmatively proving sexual abuse, is generally accepted for purposes of helping the jury to understand that a complainant's reactions are not atypical of a young sexual assault victim. . . . The syndrome helps explain why many sexually abused children delay reporting their abuse, and why many children recant allegations of abuse and deny that anything occurred. If use of the syndrome is confined to these rehabilitative functions, the confusion clears, and the accommodation syndrome serves a useful forensic purpose. . . .

The use of syndrome evidence for rehabilitative purposes has not met with universal approval. [T]he Pennsylvania Supreme Court prohibited from admission in child sexual abuse cases essentially all expert testimony concerning behavior patterns. *Dunkle*, 602 A.2d 830. The evidence [in *Dunkle*] sought to explain in general terms, without reference to the alleged victim, "why a victim would delay reporting an offense, why a victim might be unable to recall exact dates and times of an alleged offense, and why victims of sexual abuse omitted details of the incident when they first told their stor[ies]." *Dunkle*, 602 A.2d at 831. Permitting such evidence, the *Dunkle* court believed, "would infringe upon the jury's right to determine credibility," because the reasons for delay, inconsistencies, and omissions in victims' allegations "are easily understood by lay people and do not require expert analysis." *Id.* at 836–37. Such a complete exclusion of child sexual abuse syndrome evidence for any purpose is generally not favored. . . .

A contrasting approach has been taken by the Michigan Supreme Court. . . . *Beckley*, 456 N.W.2d at 406. The court cautioned that:

> to assist the jury in understanding the unique reactions of victims of sexual assault, the testimony should be limited to whether the behavior of this particular victim is common to the class of reported child abuse victims.

Id. at 406. The Michigan Supreme Court concluded that it was unwilling to have "the so-called child sexual abuse syndrome . . . introduced as a scientific tool, standing on its own merits as a doctrine or benchmark for determining causality in child sexual abuse cases." *Id.* at 409. However, it also held that:

> persons otherwise properly qualified as experts in dealing with sexually abused children should be permitted to rebut an inference that specific behavioral patterns attributed to the victim are not [sic] uncharacteristic of the class of child sexual abuse victims. Such witnesses should be permitted to testify regarding characteristics of sexually abused children so long as it is without reference to a fixed set of behaviors constituting a "syndrome." *Id.*

. . . . Federal Rule of Evidence 702 was adopted as subsection (a) of the Indiana rule. Subsection (b) of the Indiana rule is unique in its express requirement that expert testimony must be based upon reliable scientific principles. . . .

The United States Supreme Court's *Daubert* decision . . . interpreted Federal Rule of Evidence 702 as requiring that expert testimony "be supported by appropriate validation – *i.e.*, 'good grounds,' based on what is known," and as "establish[ing] a standard of evidentiary reliability." *Daubert*, _____ U.S. at _____, 113 S. Ct. at 2795. The concerns driving *Daubert* coincide with the express requirement of Indiana Rule of Evidence 702(b) that the trial court be satisfied of the reliability of the scientific principles involved. . . . Of particular relevance to our inquiry here are *Daubert's* statements that "scientific validity for one purpose is not necessarily scientific validity for other, unrelated purposes,". . . . 113 S. Ct. at 2796. . . .

> [The Court rejected both direct and indirect use of syndrome evidence to establish that sexual abuse occurred.]

However, we recognize that, once a child's credibility is called into question, proper expert testimony may be appropriate. *Daubert* notes the importance of "a valid scientific connection *to the pertinent inquiry* as a precondition to admissibility." *Daubert*, 113 S. Ct. at 2796 (emphasis added). Because research generally accepted as scientifically reliable recognizes that child victims of sexual abuse may exhibit unexpected behavior patterns seemingly inconsistent with the claim of abuse, such evidence may be permissible under Indiana Evidence Rule 702(a)'s authorization of "specialized knowledge [which] will assist the trier of fact to understand the evidence." Therefore, if the defense discusses or presents evidence of such unexpected behavior by the child, or if during trial testimony the child recants a prior allegation of abuse, a trial court may consider permitting expert testimony, if based upon reliable scientific principles, regarding the prevalence of the specific unexpected behavior within the general class of reported child abuse victims. To be admissible, such scientific evidence must assist the finder of fact in understanding a child's responses to abuse and satisfy the requirements of both Rule 702(b) and the Rule 403 balancing test.

. . . . [W]hen the relevant inquiry is the syndrome's reliability and probative value for rehabilitative and related purposes, "[s]uch evidence may harm defendant's interests, but we cannot say it is unfairly prejudicial; it merely informs jurors that commonly held assumptions are not necessarily accurate and allows them to fairly judge credibility." *Moran v. State*, 728 P.2d at 251–52. . . .

NOTES

1. *Psychological Testimony About Sexually Abused Children.* Child Sexual Abuse Accommodation Syndrome (CSAAS), as *Steward* suggests, became widely known through the work of Roland Summit, discussed in the case. The court reports the five stages described by Summit through which sexually abused children frequently pass. Prosecutors often seek to introduce expert testimony about the syndrome and more generally, about the characteristics and responses of sexually abused children.

As the discussion in *Steward* indicates, the judicial response to this kind of expert testimony has varied, and many courts have limited or rejected it altogether. The receptiveness of courts to this evidence often depends on the purpose for which the prosecution is seeking to introduce it. Expert testimony on CSAAS generally can not be introduced by the prosecution to establish that sexual abuse occurred. *See, e.g., Mindombe v. United States*, 795 A.2d 39 (D.C. App. 2002), *cert. denied*, 537 U.S. 1234 (2003) (expert can not give opinion on whether sexual abuse occurred); *Louisiana v. Chauvin,* 846 So. 2d 697 (La. 2003) (same); *People v. Duell*, 163 A.2d 866 (N.Y. App. 1990). Courts have split on the question of whether evidence that certain behavior is consistent with CSAAS can be introduced to prove abuse if the expert does not explicitly draw the inference that because the child exhibits the behavior, sexual abuse occurred. Many courts have held this evidence to be inadmissible. *See State v. Moran,* 728 P.2d 248, 255 (Ariz. 1986); *People v. Jeff,* 204 Cal. App. 3d 309 (1988). Other courts have allowed such evidence to be admitted as long as the expert does not give an explicit opinion on whether abuse occurred. *See United States v. St. Pierre,* 812 F.2d 417 (8th Cir. 1987); *State v. Reser,* 767 P.2d 1277 (Kan. 1989); *State v. Bachman,* 446 N.W.2d 271(S.D. 1989).

Courts have been more flexible about admitting evidence for purposes of explaining to the jury that the child's conduct is not unusual for victims of sexual abuse. For example, in *Mindombe, supra,* the appellate court upheld the admissibility of expert testimony on the behavioral characteristics of child victims, including the inability to remember events in sequential order, a tendency not to report abuse and to recant, and other reactions to abuse. *See also Kansas, v. McIntosh,* 58 P.3d 716 (Kan. 2002) (allowing testimony that victim's behavior was consistent with behavioral patterns exhibited by sexual abuse victims). Experts have been allowed to testify that delayed reporting by the child is not unusual. *See, e.g., People v. Hampton,* 746 P.2d 947 (Colo. 1987); *State v. Sandberg,* 406 N.W.2d 506 (Minn. 1987). Testimony that recantation by the child is not atypical behavior has also been admitted by many courts. *See, e.g., State v. Moran, supra,* 728 P.2d at 251–52, 254; *Griego v. State,* 761 P.2d 973 (Wyo. 1988). Courts will restrict CSAAS evidence to that which is relevant to the particular child's behavior, which the evidence may explain. Thus, for example, in *People v. Beckley,* 456 N.W.2d 391 (Mich. 1990), evidence of the stages of secrecy and retraction was admissible, while testimony about other stages of CSAAS was not. As *Steward* indicates, most courts using this approach allow the evidence to be introduced for rehabilitative purposes only when the credibility of the claim of abuse is challenged by the defendant.

Some courts have admitted evidence about other traits of sexually abused children that are less directly linked to the reporting of the sexual abuse, such as low self esteem, timidity, or promiscuity. *See e.g. People v. Reinhardt,* 423 N.W.2d 275 (Mich. App. 1988) (testimony that common characteristics of sexually abused girls are guilt and rage); *State v. Myers,* 359 N.W.2d 604 (Minn. 1984) (testimony that fear of men, confusion, nightmares and unusual knowledge of sex for one's age are characteristics of sexually abused children). Other courts have rejected this kind of evidence that involves traits that could be found in many children who are not sexually abused. *See, e.g., State v. Rimmasch,* 775 P.2d 388 (Utah 1989); *Hester v. Commonwealth,* 734 S.W.2d 457 (Ky. 1987).

2. Allegations of Child Sexual Abuse by Adults. Recently, there has been a flood of cases brought by adults claiming that they were subject to sexual abuse as children. Adult children can only sue parents where inter-familial tort immunity has been abolished for intentional acts. *See Doe v. Holt,* 418 S.E.2d 511 (N.C. 1992) (parental immunity doctrine does not reach parents' "willful and malicious acts" and therefore does not bar daughter's tort action against father for sexual abuse); *Barnes v. Barnes,* 603 N.E.2d 1337 (Ind. 1992) (parental immunity doctrine does not protect "intentional felonious conduct" and thus does not bar daughter's tort action against father for assault and rape).

A procedural hurdle for such claims may be the statute of limitations. Even though the statute is typically tolled during childhood, adult plaintiffs alleging childhood sexual abuse could find their actions time-barred. In most states, the action will accrue from the time the plaintiff knew or should have known of the tort. A number of recent cases have allowed such actions to go forward under a "delayed discovery" theory, on the basis of the plaintiff's claim that the psychological stress associated with childhood sexual abuse caused them to repress their memory of it until recently. *See, e.g., Hearndon v. Graham*, 767 So. 2d 1179 (Fla. 2000) (delayed discovery doctrine applies to accrual of action based on claim of childhood abuse and traumatic amnesia); *Clay v. Kuhl*, 696 N.E.2d 1245 (Ill. 1998) (applying statutory delayed discovery rule); *J.L. v. J.F.*, 722 A.2d 558 (N.J. Super. Ct. App. Div. 1999) (court must hold plenary hearing to "determine plaintiffs' state of mind regarding the date they reasonably discovered the injury and causal connection"). In response to such claims, some states have extended the ordinary statute of limitations for a specified period in childhood sexual abuse claims. *See Johnson v. Johnson*, 766 F. Supp. 662 (N.D. Ill. 1991) (12 years). *See also D.M.S. v. Barber*, 645 N.W.2d 383 (Minn. 2002) (6 year statute of limitation period under the delayed discovery statute began to run when the victim reached the age of majority).

Other courts have declined to extend the statute of limitations in these cases. *See Moriarty v. Garden Sanctuary Church of* God, 534 S.E.2d 672 (S.C. 2000) (statute of limitations extended only where there is independent evidence corroborating repressed memory). *M.D.H. v. Westminster Schools*, 172 F.3d 797 (11th Cir. 1999) (delayed discovery rule does not apply to personal injury claims); *Dalrymple v. Brown*, 701 A.2d 164 (Pa. 1997) (discovery rule does not toll statute of limitations in repressed memory cases due to the inability to determine time of memory as objective fact); *Lemmerman v. Fealk*, 534 N.W.2d 695 (Mich. 1995) (discovery rule does not apply to extend statute of limitations). Some states require plaintiffs relying on memory repression to toll the statute to produce corroborating evidence of the alleged abuse, such as contemporaneous physical manifestations or evidence that there were other victims.

In 2003, the Supreme Court held that a California statute enacted after the expiration of a previously applicable limitations period violated the ex post facto clause of Article I of the Constitution when applied to revive a previously time-barred prosecution. *Stogner v. California*, 123 S.Ct. 2446 (2003). The statute, which permitted the prosecution of child sexual abuse charges when the prior limitations had expired if the prosecution began within one year of the victim's report to the police, included a provision that allowed prosecution that would have been barred by prior limitations statutes. The petitioner was indicted in 1998 for child sexual abuse committed between 1955 and 1973. At the time of the abuse, the statute of limitations was three years.

Psychological researchers and therapists are sharply divided on the issue of the validity of claims of recovered memory. At one end of the continuum are therapists who specialize in memory "recovery" and assume that most people who seek therapy were likely sexually abused as children. Their techniques and theories are not generally well-regarded among mainstream psychologists, and their former patients have at times later recanted their accusations. *See* McDowell, *Lies of the Mind*, TIME, Nov. 29, 1993, at 52 (describing therapists who routinely inform patients that problems for which they seek help arise from sexual abuse they have repressed). Much of the recovered memory "industry" has been inspired by a best seller, THE COURAGE TO HEAL (1988) whose authors, Ellen Bass and Laura Davis, have no formal training in psychology or psychiatry. Other therapists accept the validity of repressed memories of sexual abuse, but are concerned about the possibility of contamination through aggressive therapy interventions.

Many research psychologists who study memory are skeptical about whether memories of traumatic events occurring over time (like sexual abuse) can be repressed and then recovered intact, as the repressed memory therapists argue. A group of researchers who were part of a Working Group created by the American Psychological Association to evaluate the scientific evidence on repressed memory asserted that "there is no compelling . . . evidence that once viable memories of traumatic experiences can be submerged and then recovered. . .after many years." Final Report: Working Group of the Investigation of Memories of Childhood Abuse, *Questions and Answers about Memories of Child Abuse,* p. 150, Am. Psychological Association (1995). [The therapist members of the Working Group filed a separate report. *See* Alpert et. al., *Final Report of the American Psychological Association Working Group on Investigation of Memories of Child Abuse.* 4 PSYCHOLOGY, PUBLIC POLICY, AND LAW 931 (1998).] Even if repression is possible, researchers are concerned about the accounts of recovered memories, because of the extensive evidence that memories can be manipulated and "created" rather easily. *Id.* Recovered memory therapists often use methods like suggestion, hypnosis, visualization, and truth serum. Elizabeth Loftus, the foremost authority on memory, observes that "decades of memory research has shown these are sure-fire ways to implant false memories." Loftus, *The Reality of Repressed Memories*, 48 AMER. PSYCHOLOGIST 518 (1993). She describes a study in which their parents' cooperation was elicited to produce a list of four childhood events for each of the adult volunteers. One of the events, having gotten lost on a shopping trip, was false. When asked about the incident, ten percent of the adults responded with a specific elaborated memory of it, and another 15 percent responded to repeated questioning with a vague sense of certainty that it occurred. *See* Goleman, *Miscoding Seen as Root of False Memories*, NEW YORK TIMES, May 31, 1994, at B5, B7 (reporting on paper presented by Loftus at Harvard Medical School). *See also* Loftus & Ketham, THE MYTH OF REPRESSED MEMORY: FALSE MEMORIES AND ALLEGATIONS OF SEXUAL ABUSE (1996). For a review of several books about repressed memory syndrome by both clinicians and researchers (including the Loftus & Ketham book), see Crews, *The Revenge of the Repressed*, N.Y. REV. BOOKS, Nov. 17, 1994 at 54; Dec. 1, 1994 at 49.

If adult children can recover in tort from their parents for childhood sexual abuse that *has* occurred, can the parents recover damages from therapists who implant on their children memories of abuse that *did not* occur? The conventional view is that therapists have no duty to third parties that is breached by their misdiagnosis of their patient's condition. *Bird v. W.C.W.*, 868 S.W.2d 767 (Tex. 1994) (therapist owed no duty to father of child he diagnosed as being the victim of father's sexual abuse). A classic leading case to the contrary is *Tarasoff v. Regents*, 551 P.2d 334 (Cal. 1976) (therapist has duty to warn his patient's likely victim of patient's propensity for violence). Some courts have entertained actions by parents against therapists in "false memory" cases. The Wisconsin Supreme Court recognized an action by parents against therapists who negligently "implant" false memories of abuse in their adult children. *Anneatra v. Midelfort*, 595 N.W.2d 423 (Wisc. 1999). For an analysis of this case and of therapist liability for "false memory syndrome" generally, see Biesterfield, *False Memories and the Public Policy Debate: Toward a Heightened Standard of Care for Psychotherapy,* 2002 WISC. L. REV. 169. Earlier, a California jury awarded $500,000 to Gary Ramona against a therapist who he claimed used hypnotic drugs to con his bulimic daughter into "remembering" false incidents of incest. The daughter herself had testified in the defendant therapists' behalf. Ayres, *Jury Awards Father Who Challenged Memory Therapy*, NEW YORK TIMES, May 14, 1994, at A1. This litigation seems to have dampened some of the enthusiasm for this diagnosis among therapists. *See also Joyce-Couch v. DeSilva*, 602 N.E.2d 286 (Ohio App. 1991) (patient can sue former therapist for false memories).

   3. Sexual Abuse in the Catholic Church. In the past few years much media attention and litigation have centered on sexual abuse allegations against Roman Catholic priests. In a scandal that has shaken the Church and threatens to result in substantial direct and indirect economic loss, allegations have been brought against hundreds of priests in Catholic dioceses across the country. The most publicized crisis involved priests in the Boston Archdiocese, and led to numerous criminal prosecutions of priests and civil suits against the Archdiocese. The angry response directed at the Church in Boston and elsewhere was intensified when it was revealed that Church officials in many areas engaged in a cover-up, relocating abusive priests to unsuspecting churches where the abuse often continued. Cardinal Bernard Law of Boston and many other high officials resigned in the wake of the scandal. In 2003, the Archdiocese settled 542 claims for $85 million. *Boston Archdiocese Settles Sex Abuse Cases for $85 million.* American Catholic.org, Sept. 11, 2003, at www.americancatholic.org/News/ClergySexAbuse. In response to the scandal, Massachusetts legislators have initiated law reforms by imposing a statutory duty on clergy to report suspected abuse cases. *See generally.,* Reilly, *The Sexual Abuse of Children in the Roman Catholic Archdiocese of Boston*, July 23, 2003 (report by Mass. Attorney General); Shields, *Liability of Church or Religious Organization for Negligent Hiring, Retention, or Supervision of Priest, Minister, or Other Clergy Based on Sexual Misconduct,* 101 ALR 5th 530 (2003) (summarizing the state and federal cases involving liability of religious organization for negligent hiring, retention, or supervision of a clergy member based on sexual conduct).

   4. Medical Evidence About Physical Abuse. Courts are much more open to the use of expert testimony in proving physical abuse than sexual abuse. An important issue in these cases is whether the child's injury was intentionally inflicted or accidental. Most courts allow expert testimony by physicians that the child's injuries conform to a pattern that is consistent with "battered child syndrome" or "child maltreatment syndrome." *See, e.g., State v. Wilkerson,* 247 S.E.2d 905 (1978) (citing numerous opinions upholding admissibility of expert testimony on battered child syndrome.) Battered child syndrome was first described by Dr. Harry Kempe and associates, in Kempe et. al. *The*

Battered Child Syndrome, 181 J. AM. MED. ASSOC. 17 (1962), and denotes both the general health and condition of the child and a pattern of injuries that are consistent with abuse and inconsistent with natural and accidental causes. Bruising over the body is common and radiological evidence often indicates multiple fractures inflicted over an extended period of time. Abdominal injuries and spiral fractures of limbs (caused by twisting) are common. *See also* THE BATTERED CHILD (R. Helfer & C. Kempe eds. 1968). Medically this syndrome has become so well recognized that in 1976, a California court held that a physician who failed to report under the child abuse reporting laws a case which presented the symptoms characteristic of this syndrome could be held civilly liable to the child for medical malpractice. *See Landeros v. Flood,* 551 P.2d 389 (Cal. 1976). The diagnosis is admissible only to show there was a non-accidental injury; it cannot identify the perpetrator of the violence. *See State v. Loss,* 204 N.W.2d 404 (Minn. 1973); *People v. Henson,* 304 N.E.2d 358 (N.Y. 1973).

What explains the more stringent limits on expert testimony about CSAAS as compared to battered child's syndrome? The most plausible explanation lies in the nature of the evidence. In the case of battered child syndrome, the expert has examined the particular child's injuries, and is prepared to testify that they are highly unlikely to have arisen from accidental causes. The defendant often has a particular story of how the injury came about, which the expert can address as implausible. The testimony is similar to that offered by medical experts generally, as when, for example, in homicide cases they testify as to the cause of death or the nature of the instrument that caused the injury. In CSAAS, by contrast, the expert has no independent knowledge about the injury, but can testify only as to the common post-attack behavior patterns of sexual abuse victims. Many of these behaviors are common enough that they serve little diagnostic purpose. Others, such as delayed reporting or recantation, would also be exhibited by children who fabricated the account of sexual assault. That is precisely why the prosecution seeks to introduce such testimony: to show the factfinder that the usual inferences about credibility that might be drawn from such behavior do not necessarily apply in sexual abuse cases. The problem, however, even assuming the validity of the expert's general observations, is the prejudicial impact of these observations, given that in a particular case, the child *may be* fantasizing, or even lying, about the incident. Note also that while the battered child syndrome is a medical diagnosis identifying the cause of an injury, CSAAS is a "diagnosis" attached to a particular pattern of behavior that is employed as a therapeutic aid, and one which is not relied upon even by the experts themselves to show that abuse in fact occurred.

5. The "Battering Parent Syndrome." Child abuse research has also established a profile of the psychological, environmental and economic traits of parents who physically abuse their children. For example, parents who batter their children are described as likely to be more impulsive, self-centered, distrustful of others, and immature than other parents; they have lower self-esteem and were often abused as children; and they are often unemployed. With respect to their relationships with their children, abusive parents tend to make premature and unrealistic demands upon their children, and engage in role reversal behavior, looking to their child for comfort and love rather than providing for the child's own needs. *See* Steel & Pollock, *A Psychiatric Study of Parents Who Abuse Infants and Small Children,* in THE BATTERED CHILD (R. Helfer & C. Kempe, eds., 1968). As evidence that a particular parent has abused a child, such psychiatric data is generally considered inadmissible, like other evidence of past acts and character traits. *See, e.g., United States v. Gillespie,* 852 F.2d 475 (9th Cir. 1988) (expert testimony about the general characteristics of child molester inadmissible where defendant did not put his general character at issue); *Haakanson v. State,* 760 P.2d 1030 (Ala. App. 1988) (reversing conviction due to trial court's admission of evidence of sex offender profile); *See also Sanders v. State,* 303 S.E.2d 13 (Ga. 1983); *State v. Loebach,* 310 N.W.2d 58 (Minn. 1981).

This issue may also arise when the defendant seeks to introduce expert testimony about the battering parent's syndrome as part of his defense. In this context, as well, it generally is not admissible. *See, e.g., State v. Friedrich,* 398 N.W.2d 763 (Wisc. 1987); *State v. Miller,* 709 P.2d 350 (Utah 1985); *Pendleton v. Commonwealth,* 685 S.W.2d 549 (Ky. 1985). For a summary of cases dealing with each of these syndromes, see Boresi, *Syndrome Testimony in Child Abuse Prosecutions: The Wave of the Future?,* 8 ST. LOUIS U. PUB. L. REV. 207 (1989).

6. *Other Methods of Proving Child Abuse.* One method used by social workers and other professionals to determine if a child has been abused is interviewing the child with the help of anatomically correct dolls and drawings by the child. Should the results of these interviews be admissible at trial to establish abuse? Some courts have found this evidence lacking in the necessary level of acceptance within the scientific community to qualify as expert testimony. *See, e.g., United States v. Gillespie,* 852 F.2d 475 (9th Cir. 1988) (rejecting expert opinion testimony based upon play therapy with anatomically correct dolls); *In re Amber B.,* 236 Cal. Rptr. 623 (App. 1987) (same). Cases allowing expert testimony about the meaning of a child's doll play or drawings include *Nelson v. Farrey,* 874 F.2d 1222 (7th Cir. 1989); *State v. Keil,* 794 S.W.2d 289 (Mo. App. 1990); *see also United States v. St. John,* 851 F.2d 1096 (8th Cir. 1988) (hearsay statements by ten-year-old child to social worker and clinical psychologist during play therapy with anatomically correct dolls admissible where child unwilling or unable to testify fully about sexual assaults).

MARYLAND v. CRAIG

497 U.S. 261 (1990)

O'CONNOR, J.

I

[Defendant was charged with various sexual offenses against a child who had attended defendant's child care center.]

[B]efore. . . trial, the State sought to invoke a Maryland statutory procedure that permits a judge to receive, by one-way closed circuit television, the testimony of a child witness who is alleged to be a victim of child abuse. To invoke the procedure, the trial judge must first "determin[e] that testimony by the child victim in the courtroom will result in the child suffering serious emotional distress such that the child cannot reasonably communicate." MD. CTS. & JUD. PROC. CODE ANN. §9-102(a)(1)(ii) (1989). Once the procedure is invoked, the child witness, prosecutor, and defense counsel withdraw to a separate room; the judge, jury, and defendant remain in the courtroom. The [child] is then examined and cross-examined in the separate room, while a video monitor records and displays the witness' testimony to those in the courtroom. During this time the witness cannot see the defendant. The defendant remains in electronic communication with defense counsel, and objections may be made and ruled on as if the witness were testifying in the courtroom.

In support of its motion invoking the one-way closed circuit television procedure, the State presented expert testimony that Brooke, as well as a number of other children who were alleged to have been sexually abused by Craig, would suffer "serious emotional distress such that [they could not] reasonably communicate," §9-102(a)(1)(ii), if required to testify in the courtroom. . . .

II

The Confrontation Clause of the Sixth Amendment . . . provides: "In all criminal prosecutions, the accused shall enjoy the right . . . to be confronted with the witnesses against him."

. . . .

We have never held . . . that the Confrontation Clause guarantees criminal defendants the absolute right to a face-to-face meeting with witnesses against them at trial. . . . *Coy* [*v. Iowa*, 487 U.S., at 1012 (1988)] involved the placement of a screen that prevented two child witnesses in a child abuse case from seeing the defendant as they testified against him at trial. . . . In holding that the use of this procedure violated the defendant's right to confront witnesses against him, we suggested that any exception to the right "would surely be allowed only when necessary to further an important public policy" — *i.e.*, only upon a showing of something more than the generalized, "legislatively imposed presumption of trauma" underlying the statute at issue in that case. . . . We concluded that "[s]ince there ha[d] been no individualized findings that these particular witnesses needed special protection, the judgment [in the case before us] could not be sustained by any conceivable exception.". . . Because the trial court in this case made individualized findings that each of the child witnesses needed special protection, this case requires us to decide the question reserved in *Coy*.

The central concern of the Confrontation Clause is to ensure the reliability of the evidence against a criminal defendant by subjecting it to rigorous testing in the context of an adversary proceeding before the trier of fact. The word "confront," after all, also means a clashing of forces or ideas, thus carrying with it the notion of adversariness. . . .

[T]he right guaranteed . . . includes not only a "personal examination," *id.,* at 242, but also "(1) insures that the witness will give his statements under oath — thus impressing him with the seriousness of the matter and guarding against the lie by the possibility of a penalty for perjury; (2) forces the witness to submit to cross-examination, the 'greatest legal engine ever invented for the discovery of truth'; [and] (3) permits the jury that is to decide the defendant's fate to observe the demeanor of the witness in making his statement, thus aiding the jury in assessing his credibility." [*California v. Green,* 399 U.S. 149, 158]. . . .

The combined effect of these elements of confrontation — physical presence, oath, cross-examination, and observation of demeanor by the trier of fact — serves the purposes of the Confrontation Clause by ensuring that evidence admitted against an accused is reliable and subject to the rigorous adversarial testing that is the norm of Anglo-American criminal proceedings.

. . . .

Although face-to-face confrontation forms "the core of the values furthered by the Confrontation Clause," *Green, supra,* at 157, we have nevertheless recognized that it is not the sine qua non of the confrontation right. . . .

. . . Instead, we have repeatedly held that the Clause permits, where necessary, the admission of certain hearsay statements against a defendant despite the defendant's inability to confront the declarant at trial. . . . We have accordingly stated that a literal reading of the Confrontation Clause would "abrogate virtually every hearsay exception, a result long rejected as unintended and too extreme." [*Ohio v. Roberts,* 448 U.S. 56, 63]. Thus, in certain narrow circumstances, "competing interests, if 'closely examined,' may warrant dispensing with confrontation at trial." *Id.,* at 64. . . . .

That the face-to-face confrontation requirement is not absolute does not, of course, mean that it may easily be dispensed with. . . . [O]ur precedents confirm that a defendant's right to confront accusatory witnesses may be satisfied absent a physical, face-to-face confrontation at trial only where denial of such confrontation is necessary to further an important public policy and only where the reliability of the testimony is otherwise assured. . . .

III

Maryland's statutory procedure, when invoked, prevents a child witness from seeing the defendant as he or she testifies. . . . We find it significant, however, that Maryland's procedure preserves all of the other elements of the confrontation right: the child witness must be competent to testify and must testify under oath; the defendant retains full opportunity for contemporaneous cross-examination; and the judge, jury, and defendant are able to view (albeit by video monitor) the demeanor (and body) of the witness as he or she testifies. Although we are mindful of the many subtle effects face-to-face confrontation may have on an adversary criminal proceeding, the presence of these other elements of confrontation — oath, cross-examination, and observation of the witness' demeanor — adequately ensures that the testimony is both reliable and subject to rigorous adversarial testing in a manner functionally equivalent to that accorded live, in-person testimony. [W]e think these elements . . . not only permit a defendant to "confound and undo the false accuser, or reveal the child coached by a malevolent adult," *Coy,* . . . but may well aid a defendant in eliciting favorable testimony from the child witness. Indeed, to the extent the child witness' testimony may be said to be technically given out-of-court (though we do not so hold), these assurances of reliability and adversariness are far greater than those required for admission of hearsay testimony under the Confrontation Clause. We are therefore confident that use of the one-way closed-circuit television procedure, where necessary to further an important state interest, does not impinge upon the truth-seeking or symbolic purposes of the Confrontation Clause.

The critical inquiry in this case, therefore, is whether use of the procedure is necessary to further an important state interest. The State contends that it has a substantial interest in protecting children who are allegedly victims of child abuse from the trauma of testifying against the alleged perpetrator and that its statutory procedure for receiving testimony from such witnesses is necessary to further that interest.

We . . . conclude today that a State's interest in the physical and psychological well-being of child abuse victims may be sufficiently important to outweigh, at least in some cases, a defendant's right to face his or her accusers in court. That a significant majority of States has enacted statutes to protect child witnesses from the trauma of giving testimony in child abuse cases attests to the widespread belief in the importance of such a public policy.

. . . . [W]e will not second-guess the considered judgment of the Maryland Legislature regarding the importance of its interest in protecting child abuse victims from the emotional trauma of testifying. Accordingly, we hold that, if the State makes an adequate showing of necessity, the state interest in protecting child witnesses from the trauma of testifying in a child abuse case is sufficiently important to justify the use of a special procedure that permits a child witness in such cases to testify at trial against a defendant in the absence of face-to-face confrontation with the defendant.

The requisite finding of necessity must of course be a case-specific one: the trial court must hear evidence and determine whether use of the one-way closed circuit television procedure is necessary to protect the welfare of the particular child witness who seeks to testify. . . . The trial court must also find that the child witness would be traumatized, not by the courtroom generally, but by the presence of the defendant. Denial of face-to-face confrontation is not needed to further the state interest in protecting the child witness from trauma unless it is the presence of the defendant that causes the trauma. . . . Finally, the trial court must find that the emotional distress suffered by the child witness in the presence of the defendant is more than de minimis,. . . . [T]he Maryland statute, which requires a determination that the child witness will suffer "serious emotional distress such that the child cannot reasonably communicate," §9-102(a)(1)(ii), clearly suffices to meet constitutional standards.

To be sure, face-to-face confrontation may be said to cause trauma for the very purpose of eliciting truth, *cf. Coy,* but we think that the use of Maryland's special procedure. . . adequately ensures the accuracy of the testimony and preserves the adversary nature of the trial. . . . Indeed, where face-to-face confrontation causes significant emotional distress in a child witness, there is evidence that such confrontation would in fact [disserve] the Confrontation Clause's truth-seeking goal. . . . Brief for American Psychological Association as Amicus Curiae 18–24. . . .

IV

[The Court vacated the judgment of the Maryland Court of Appeals, because that court had imposed too high a standard in requiring that the determination of necessity be made through questioning of the child in the defendant's presence and requiring that the trial court consider less burdensome alternatives, such as two-way television testimony.]

JUSTICE SCALIA, with whom JUSTICE BRENNAN, JUSTICE MARSHALL, and JUSTICE STEVENS join, dissenting.

Seldom has this Court failed so conspicuously to sustain a categorical guarantee of the Constitution against the tide of prevailing current opinion. The Sixth Amendment provides, with unmistakable clarity, that "[i]n all criminal prosecutions, the accused shall enjoy the right . . . to be confronted with the witnesses against him". . . .

Because of [the] subordination of explicit constitutional text to currently favored public policy, the following scene can be played out in an American courtroom for the first time in two centuries: A father whose young daughter has been given over to the exclusive custody of his estranged wife, or a mother whose young son has been taken into custody by the State's child welfare department, is sentenced to prison for sexual abuse on the basis of testimony by a child the parent has not seen or spoken to for many months; and the guilty verdict is rendered without giving the parent so much as the opportunity to sit in the presence of the child, and to ask, personally or through counsel, "it is really not true, is it, that I — your father (or mother) whom you see before you — did these terrible things?" Perhaps that is a procedure today's society desires; perhaps (though I doubt it) it is even a fair procedure; but it is assuredly not a procedure permitted by the Constitution. . . .

II

Much of the Court's opinion consists of applying to this case the mode of analysis we have used in the admission of hearsay evidence. . . .

Some of the Court's analysis seems to suggest that the children's testimony here was itself hearsay of the sort permissible under our Confrontation Clause cases. . . . That cannot be. Our Confrontation Clause conditions for the admission of hearsay have long included a "general requirement of unavailability" of the declarant. . . . "Live" closed-circuit television testimony, however — if it can be called hearsay at all — is surely an example of hearsay as "a weaker substitute for live testimony,". . . which can be employed only when the genuine article is unavailable. . . .

The Court's test today requires unavailability only in the sense that the child is unable to testify in the presence of the defendant. That cannot possibly be the relevant sense. . . .

III

The Court characterizes the State's interest which "outweigh[s]" the explicit text of the Constitution as an "interest in the physical and psychological well-being of child abuse victims," an "interest in protecting" such victims "from the emotional trauma of testifying." That is not so. A child who meets the Maryland statute's requirement of suffering such "serious emotional distress" from confrontation that he "cannot reasonably communicate" would seem entirely safe. Why would a prosecutor want to call a witness who cannot reasonably communicate?. . . . The State's interest here is . . . what the State's interest always is when it seeks to get a class of evidence admitted in criminal proceedings: more convictions of guilty defendants.

And the interest on the other side is also what it usually is when the State seeks to get a new class of evidence admitted: fewer convictions of innocent defendants — specifically, in the present context, innocent defendants accused of particularly heinous crimes. The "special" reasons that exist for suspending one of the usual guarantees of reliability in the case of children's testimony are perhaps matched by "special" reasons for being particularly insistent upon it in the case of children's testimony. Some studies show that children are substantially more vulnerable to suggestion than adults, and often unable to separate recollected fantasy (or suggestion) from reality. . . .

> [As evidence of the injustice of erroneous testimony by children in sexual abuse cases, Justice Scalia describes the charges of sexual abuse brought against 24 adults in Jordan, Minnesota, on the basis allegations by children obtained through questionable investigational techniques. Most of the charges were later dropped. [This case is discussed in the Note on Child Abuse Reform, below. *Eds.*]]

In the last analysis, however, this debate is not an appropriate one. . . . For good or bad, the Sixth Amendment requires confrontation, and we are not at liberty to ignore it. To quote the document one last time. . .: "In *all* criminal prosecutions, the accused shall enjoy the right . . . to be confronted with the witnesses against him" (emphasis added). . . .

NOTES

1. *The Right of Confrontation and the* Craig *Exception.* No special procedure is available to protect the adult witness who is psychologically unable to testify in a criminal proceeding. Because of the defendant's Confrontation Clause rights, the witness simply does not testify, even though that may mean that the court has a less accurate or less complete record on which to decide the case. What is the basis for the *Craig* exception to this rule? The state's concern for the welfare of child witnesses could be addressed, as Justice Scalia suggests, by having the child not testify. That the exception to defendants' Confrontation rights is limited to child abuse prosecutions is likely because of the perceived importance of successful prosecution in these cases. Should child abuse prosecutions have special constitutional standing? Consider the case, for example, of a child who witnessed the murder of a parent, and who would suffer severe emotional distress from recounting the event in open court. One possible distinction between child abuse prosecutions and other cases in which child witnesses might testify is the central importance of the child's testimony in child abuse cases, particularly in sexual abuse where there may be little physical evidence. Also, the defendant may be the child's parent, making it particularly difficult for the child to confront him in court. But while such a rationale might explain why legislatures would want to make a separate rule for child abuse cases, is it a sufficient reason to limit defendant's Confrontation Clause rights?

The critical difference between what the Court allows in *Craig* and what it did not allow in *Coy v. Iowa*, discussed by the Court in *Craig*, lies in the Maryland requirement of a case-by-case determination of the emotional trauma that face-to-face testimony might cause, as opposed to a general rule for all children based upon a general belief about the need to protect them. Under the Iowa rule, struck down in *Coy*, a screen was placed between the child witness and the defendant in all cases. Consider, however, whether this distinction between *Craig* and *Coy* effectively serves to protect defendant's rights. Might it not be less prejudicial for the jury to be told that children's testimony categorically is taken out-of-court, rather than to allow the inference that this child has particular reason to fear this defendant?

Moreover, it may not be possible to escape reliance on general findings, even under a *Craig* standard because courts will likely rely on psychological evidence based upon the usual reactions of children of the same age and circumstances as the proposed witness. In *Lumholt v. Iowa,* 327 F.3d 748 (8th Cir. 2003), for example, a federal appellate court recently held that a pre-trial hearing which consisted solely of the testimony of the children's sex abuse counselor who testified generally about the trauma to children of testifying with their abuser present, was sufficient to support the finding that the victims would be unduly traumatized if required to testify in the courtroom with the defendant present. The court found that *Craig* did not require that the child demonstrate fear in the courtroom, but instead recognized that trauma could include a broad range of emotions that overwhelmed the child's ability to communicate.

2. The Child Victims' and Witnesses' Rights Act. Congress enacted the Child Victims' and Child Witnesses' Protection Law 18 U.S.C.A. § 3509 (West Supp. 1997), in response to *Maryland v. Craig*. The statute was designed to protect alleged child victims as witnesses in federal courts, while conforming to the requirements that the Supreme Court suggested were necessary to protect criminal defendants' confrontation rights under the Sixth Amendment.

The statute provides that, in a proceeding involving an alleged offense against a child, the court may order that a child's testimony be taken in a room outside the courtroom and televised by two-way closed circuit television, if the child is unable to testify in open court in front of the defendant for any of the following reasons:

1. The child is unable to testify because of fear.

2. There is substantial likelihood, established by expert testimony, the child is likely to suffer emotional trauma from testifying.

3. The child suffers a mental or other infirmity.

    4.   Conduct of the defendant or defense counsel causes the child to be unable to testify.

Under the statute, the prosecutor and the defense attorney must be present in the room with the child, and the child is subject to direct and cross-examination. The testimony is transmitted to the courtroom for viewing by all present, including the defendant. The defendant must be provided with a means of private contemporaneous communication with his attorney. The guardian ad litem and an adult attendant (to offer support to the child, but not to assist in answering questions) may also be present in the room with the child.

The statute further provides for videotaped depositions of alleged child victims, which may be introduced later at trial if the child is altogether unable to testify for one of the above reasons.

Federal circuit courts have upheld the use of out-of courtroom closed circuit television testimony by children under this statute against Sixth Amendment challenges. In *United States v. Garcia,* 7 F.3d 885 (1993), the Ninth Circuit Court of Appeals interpreted provisions of the statute as codification of *Maryland v. Craig.* The fact that the child's counselor who testified that the child would experience emotional trauma was not an expert in child testimony was held to go to the weight and not the admissibility of her expert testimony. In *United States v. Etimani,* 328 F.3d 493 (9th Cir. 2003), the same court held that the statutory requirement that the defendant television image be transmitted into the room where the child is testifying is satisfied if the monitor is called to the child's attention and is visible from where she is seated, but that it does "not have to be in her direct field of vision while she is facing forward." *See* Smith, *Validity, Construction and Application of the Child Victims' and Child Witnesses' Rights Statute,* 121 ALR FED. 631 (2002).

3. *State Law Responses.* Some states have experimented with closed circuit television and other devices to avoid face-to-face confrontation between the child witness and the defendant. In child sexual abuse prosecutions, for example, a California statute allows both one-way and two-way closed-circuit television testimony if the child victim is under the age of ten, and if one of the following is found by clear and convincing evidence: that the child or the child's family was threatened with serious bodily harm if the child testifies; that a firearm or other deadly weapon was used during the commission of the crime; that great bodily harm was inflicted on the child during the crime; or that the defendant or defense counsel acted in a way during the trial to cause the child to be unable to testify. CAL. PENAL CODE Supp. 2003). The judge, jury, defendant and all attorneys are outside the child's presence during the testimony and cross-examination. In the room with the child is a television monitor with the defendant's face. *See also* WIS. STAT. ANN. §972.11 (West 1998 and Supp. 2003), upheld in *State v. Thomas,* 442 N.W.2d 10 (Wisc.1989).

The Illinois Supreme Court found that state's Child Shield Act in violation of its state constitution in *People v. Fitzpatrick,* 633 N.E. 2d. 685 (Ill. 1994), after which Illinois amended its constitution. The statutory procedure was very similar to the one upheld by the U.S. Supreme Court in *Craig,* but the court held that the use of closed circuit television violated the defendant's right to face-to-face confrontation, because the Illinois Constitution stated that criminal defendants have the right to "meet witnesses face to face." ILL. CONST. ART. I § 8. The Illinois legislature amended the relevant provision to track the language of the confrontation clause in the U.S. Constitution, and the amendment quickly was ratified by the voters. These developments are discussed in Gilleran-Johnson & Evans, *The Criminal Courtroom — Is it Childproof?* 26 LOY. U. CHI. L. J. 681 (1995).

Some courts have been rather relaxed in applying the statutory procedures regulating the use of closed circuit television. In *Iowa v. Shearon*, 660 N.W.2d 52 (Iowa 2003), for example, the defendant's conviction was upheld, although the child was not instructed that the defendant would be viewing the televised testimony, as the statute required, and the defendant had no means to consult with his attorney during the testimony. The court emphasized the attorney's vigorous cross-examination. *But see Etimani, supra.* For a comprehensive listing of state statutes authorizing these alternative forms of child abuse testimony, see Hagan, *Maryland's Child Abuse Testimony Statute: Is Protecting the Child Witness Constitutional?* 49 MD. L. REV. 463, 472–73 n.83 (1990).

In competency hearings, during which it is determined whether a child is competent to testify, the Supreme Court has held that the defendant, though not his attorney, may be excluded. *Kentucky v. Stincer,* 482 U.S. 730 (1987).

4. Special Exceptions to the Hearsay Rule in Child Abuse Prosecutions. The Supreme Court has considered whether evidentiary rules that allow easier admissibility of certain forms of hearsay in child abuse cases comply with the Sixth Amendment Confrontation Clause. Until very recently, statements by a child about alleged abuse could be admitted into evidence through the testimony of a third party, if the evidence met the requirements established by the Court in *Ohio v. Roberts,* 448 U.S. 56, 66 (1980), for admissibility of hearsay evidence in compliance with the Confrontation Clause. In *Roberts*, the Court held that hearsay statements could be admitted if the declarant was unavailable and the evidence bore "particular guarantees of trustworthiness." The Court in *Wright* applied this test to testimony by a pediatrician describing statements made to him by a 2½-year-old child about her abuse in *Idaho v. Wright*, 497 U.S. 805 (1990). The Court upheld the decision of the Idaho Supreme Court that the hearsay statements did not have sufficient "indicia of reliability" to satisfy defendant's Confrontation Clause rights under *Roberts,* emphasizing that the required "particularized guarantees of trustworthiness" must be established only from the circumstances surrounding the making of the statement, not from other corroboration of the statement offered at trial.

> . . . [T]he use of corroborating evidence to support a hearsay statement's "particularized guarantees of trustworthiness" would permit admission of a presumptively unreliable statement by bootstrapping on the trustworthiness of other evidence at trial, a result we think at odds with the requirement that hearsay evidence admitted under the Confrontation Clause be so trustworthy that cross-examination of the declarant would be of marginal utility. . . .

Id. at 821–26.

In *Crawford v. Washington*, 124 S.Ct. 1354 (2004), the Court, in an opinion authored by Justice Scalia, overruled *Ohio v. Roberts*; thus, the underlying rationale of *Wright* is no longer valid. The Court in *Crawford* held that testimonial hearsay evidence was barred under the Confrontation Clause unless the witness was unavailable and the defendant had a prior opportunity to cross-examine the witness. Basing its analysis on its interpretation of the history of the Confrontation Clause, the Court acknowledged that the purpose of the Clause was to assure reliability, but emphasized that cross-examination was the means through which the Founders sought to achieve this goal. The Court rejected the notion that a judicial determination of the reliability was adequate protection of defendants' Confrontation Clause rights. In a concurring opinion, Justice Rehnquist argued against overruling *Roberts,* a move that would interject great uncertainty into criminal trials. Justice Rehnquist pointed out that the Court could have reached the same outcome under *Wright,* without disrupting long-standing precedent.

Even after *Crawford*, evidence based on a child's statements may sometimes be admitted through a third party witness, where the evidence is not "testimonial." The Court explicitly left for "another day any effort to spell out a comprehensive definition of 'testimonial.'" Thus, although this matter awaits clarification by the Court, some well-recognized exceptions to the hearsay rule may apply after *Crawford*. Hearsay testimony about a child's report of abuse, for example, may be permitted under the excited utterance exception to the hearsay rule. *See, e.g., State v. Boston,* 545 N.E.2d 1220 (Ohio 1989); *Morgan v. Foretich,* 846 F.2d 941 (4th Cir. 1988). Statements made by a child to a doctor for the purpose of receiving medical treatment are another exception that may be applicable in some child abuse and neglect cases, under proper circumstances. *Id.* For a detailed and well-reasoned analysis of the appropriate applications and limitations of this exception in the context of child abuse cases, see Mosteller, *Child Sexual Abuse and Statements for the Purpose of Medical Diagnosis or Treatment,* 67 N.C. L. REV. 257 (1989).

Courts have evaluated the use of videotaped interviews and testimony of child witnesses under the hearsay rule, focusing on the availability of the child and the reliability of the videotaped evidence. In a case in which the child was present at trial, but did not testify, a federal appellate court rejected a videotaped interview of the child by a psychologist, on the ground that the interview lacked guarantees of trustworthiness. *Schaal v. Gammon,* 233 F.3d 1103 (8th Cir. 2000). The court emphasized that the defendant was not present at the interview; the child was not under oath; the child's mother, who had a hostile relationship with the defendant, was present, and the psychologist had a relationship with the child. Pre-recorded videotaped testimony was allowed by the Vermont Supreme Court where the defendant had an opportunity to cross-examine the victim concerning the prior statements. *Vermont v. Cameron,* 721 A.2d 493 (Vt. 1998). *See also Utah v. Thomas,* 974 P.2d 269 (Utah 1999) (videotaped interview allowed where child is found to be unavailable).

In evaluating prosecution efforts to use hearsay evidence in sex abuse prosecutions, many courts focus on maximizing protection of defendants' rights. For example, the Washington Supreme Court reversed a conviction, concluding that, before the trial court admitted hearsay evidence on the ground that the child was unavailable to testify, it should have considered whether she could testify by closed circuit television. *Washington v. Smith*, 59 P.3d 74 (Wash. 2002). *See also Ex parte R.D.W.*, 773 So. 2d 426 (Ala. 2000) (requiring a corrective jury instruction when hearsay evidence is admitted to remind jury that defendant was unable to cross-examine the child whose out-of-court statements were reported by others).

5. *Comparing Criminal and Civil Abuse Proceedings.* Each of the principal cases involved adjudication of criminal, rather than civil, child abuse, and was therefore subject to the stricter due process requirements associated with criminal proceedings. Some rules applicable in proving child abuse or neglect are the same in both civil and criminal actions. *See, e.g.*, N.C. GEN. STAT. §7B-400 *et. seq.* (2000) (certain privileges do not apply in any judicial proceeding, civil, criminal, or juvenile, in which a juvenile's abuse or neglect is in issue). In other matters, such as standard of proof, the rules for proving child abuse and neglect in civil actions may be different from those in criminal proceedings; civil child protective proceedings usually require that findings be supported by a preponderance of the evidence rather than beyond a reasonable doubt. *See, e.g.*, *In re Nicole V.*, 71 N.Y.2d 112, 518 N.E.2d 914 (1987). The one exception, noted above, is that in civil actions to terminate parental rights, proof by clear and convincing evidence is required. *See Santosky v. Kramer*, 455 U.S. 745 (1982). The Sixth Amendment right of confrontation applies only in criminal proceedings, so that the principles established in *Craig* do not directly apply to civil child abuse proceedings. Some states make use of this flexibility, for example, by allowing the judge to interview children *in camera* in civil abuse and neglect proceedings (*see, e.g. In re Appeal of Maricopa Cty. Juvenile Action*, 786 P.2d 1004 (Ariz. App. 1989)), or allowing admission of videotaped interview as evidence, under circumstances which would not be permitted in a parallel criminal proceeding. *See, e.g., In Interest of L.K.S.*, 451 N.W.2d 819 (Iowa 1990). Again, the rules may be stricter in termination proceedings than in other civil abuse and neglect actions. *See, e.g., Welfare of McGree*, 679 P.2d 933 (Wash. App. 1984) (in chambers interview improper in termination of parental rights proceeding, though held harmless error in case). Similarly, there is not an automatic right to counsel in civil child abuse and neglect proceedings as there is in criminal proceedings. *See Lassiter v. Department of Social Servs. of Durham Cty.*, 452 U.S. 18 (1981) (right to counsel in termination of parental cases determined on a case-by-case basis). In most states, however, counsel for parents is appointed. Evidentiary rules may also be less demanding in civil proceedings. *See, e.g., In re Nicole V., supra* (applying New York statute permitting hearsay in civil child abuse proceedings, if properly corroborated, that would not be admissible in criminal prosecution); *In re E.J.R. and F.J.R.S. Children*, 400 N.W.2d 531 (Iowa 1987) (applying Iowa statute allowing admission of hearsay statements in termination actions).

Because criminal consequences may follow from civil proceedings, the question arises whether parents in civil proceedings are entitled to the usual constitutional prerogatives available in the context of the criminal process. *Baltimore City Dep't of Social Serv. v. Bouknight*, 493 U.S. 549 (1990), concerned the whereabouts of a child, Maurice, who previously had been found to be abused. He was removed from the home and later returned to the mother subject to extensive conditions set forth in a court-approved protective supervision order. When the department of social services later became concerned about the child's welfare and were unable to locate him, the court in the civil case ordered the mother to produce the child in court. She refused, asserting the Fifth Amendment privilege against self-incrimination, and was jailed for civil contempt. By a 7-2 vote, the Supreme Court upheld the finding of contempt, concluding that the mother's Fifth Amendment privilege was reduced both by her acceptance of custody subject to the department's conditions and by the fact that the exercise of this privilege would interfere with "the legitimate object of the government's non-criminal regulatory powers." *Id.* at 558. The Court left open the question whether the state could use the testimonial aspects of the mother's production of the child in any subsequent criminal proceeding. This case indicates, once again, the Court's willingness to frame special exceptions to rights otherwise protected by the Constitution in child abuse cases.

NOTE ON CHILD ABUSE LAW REFORM

In recent years, enormous public attention has focused on the national problem of child abuse. Tragic and highly publicized cases fan the flames of public outrage and increase public pressure to develop more effective responses to child abuse. In 2002, for example, a 7-year-old New Jersey boy, Faheem Williams was found dead in the basement of his aunt's Newark home, where he had been kept with his twin 4-year-old brothers who were severely malnourished. Their aunt was supposed to be caring for the boys while their mother served a prison term, and her teenage son was accused of the killing. (The 4-year-olds were also allegedly sexually abused by a friend of the aunt.) The investigation that followed revealed that the boy's mother had been subject of eleven child abuse allegations, and that the social worker who closed the most recent investigation was working on more than 100 other investigations. *See* Jones & Kaufman, *Worker in Abuse Case in Newark Juggled 107 Child Care Inquiries*, N.Y.TIMES, Jan. 8, 2003, at A1. In general, child welfare experts tend to believe that the problem revealed by cases like these is under-intervention, largely due to inadequate resources. *See, e.g.*, The U.S. Advisory Board on Child Abuse and Neglect, Dept. of Health and Human Services, Administration for Children and Families, *The Continuing Child Protection Emergency; A Challenge to the Nation* (1993).

Many critics argue, however, that public concern about extreme cases has generated an over-zealous response to child abuse that causes harm to many innocent people. These criticisms have targeted many different problems. First, there is the problem of false reports. In 1990, the New York State Department of Social Services estimated that 60% of the 130,000 reports of child abuse in 1989 were unsubstantiated, and 15% were intentionally false. Complaints of child abuse by divorcing parents against one another are said to be a particular problem. *See* United Press International, *"Child Abuse Hotline Law Does Not Prevent False Claims,"* May 14, 1990. The law in New York and other states criminalizes false reporting. *See* N.Y. PENAL LAW §240.55 (McKinney 2000) (Class A misdemeanor); FLA. STAT. ANN. §817.49 (West 2000) (first-degree misdemeanor). Of course, an unsubstantiated claim is not necessarily erroneous.

Besides false reports, mistakes also happen. Cases involving intrusive investigations of allegations of sexual abuse have been the subject of numerous civil suits against government officials. In one particularly egregious case, social workers, removed a developmentally delayed 5-year old from school, on the basis of mistaken information about parental sex abuse, and required her to submit to a pelvic examination. *Tenenbaum v. Williams,* 193 F.3d. 581 (2d Cir. 1999), *cert. denied*, 529 U.S. 1098 (2000). Although social workers are often immune from negligence or even recklessness in performing investigations, courts have waived immunity in egregious cases. Parents who are erroneously accused of abusing their children may experience costs that persist after the case is investigated. Their names may be kept in a child abuse information registry for years, even though the complaint is determined to be unfounded.

Practices used in child abuse investigations have also been the subject of intense criticism for their intrusiveness and potential to produce distorted information. *See* Beeman, *Investigating Child Abuse: The Fourth Amendment and Investigatory Home Visits,* 89 COLUM. L. REV. 1034 (1989). Interview techniques used by investigators have been a particular target of criticism. Child abuse investigations may mean multiple interrogations, which are intimidating, exhausting and emotionally traumatic for children. From the defendant's perspective, the principal complaint is that the techniques used in these interrogations are suggestive and coercive, leading investigators to confirm their own suspicions rather than to determine, impartially, whether abuse has actually occurred. Several highly publicized cases have focused this complaint. One, involving 24 adults who were charged with molesting 37 children in the small town of Jordan, Minnesota, is described in Justice Scalia's *Craig* dissent as evidence of the potential for convictions to be based on erroneous testimony. Some of the children in this case "admitted" to the abuse only after multiple coercive interviews. In a more recent case, a 26-year-old woman, Margaret Kelly Michaels, was sentenced to 47 years in prison after being convicted on 115 of 131 counts of sexual abuse against 20 children in a New Jersey preschool. In this case also, children were repeatedly interviewed until they gave responses which confirmed the investigators' suspicions that abuse had occurred. One article on the investigation reports:

> . . .[T]he children were given knives and forks and then asked to show – on an anatomically correct doll – where Kelly had hurt them. On the tapes that I heard, a child's first response more often than not was to poke the doll in the eye or the neck or a knee. Invariably, the listener then hears the voice of [the interviewer] Fonolleras, urging, "Where else? Uh-huh, where else?" After a succession of "where else?" responses, the child winds up poking at a penis, or a vagina, or an anus. Here, the "where elses" stop. Later, Fonolleras's official report typically would not show how a child "described" the penetration of her vagina or his anus.

> Fonolleras was quick to praise those who confirmed his suspicions: "Boy, you're doing so good." But he was stern with those who responded with firm or frequent noes. Here is Fonolleras with one tiny recalcitrant: "If you don't help me, I'm going to tell your friends that you not only don't want to help *me* but that you won't help *them*."

Rabinowitz, *From the Mouths of Babes to a Jail Cell,* HARPER'S MAGAZINE, May, 1990, at 52, 57, 58. Rabinowitz concludes:

> *Believe the children* is the battle cry of the child-abuse militants, who hold as an article of faith that a pederast lurks behind every door and blackboard. But child after child repeatedly said that Kelly Michaels had done nothing — and they had *not* been believed. The prosecutors had brought experts to court to testify that children denying abuse should not be believed. *Believe the children* apparently means — to those raising the rallying cry — believe the children *only* if they say they have been molested. "To believe a child's *no* is simplistic," [the prosecutor] had told the jury.

Id. at 63.

Michaels' conviction was reversed on appeal. *New Jersey v. Michaels,* 642 A.2d 1372 (N.J. 1994) (holding coercive or highly suggestive interrogation techniques created a significant risk that the interrogation itself would distort the children's recollection of events; a pre-trial hearing is required to determine admissibility. Michael later brought a § 1983 claim against the state, state officials, county and city, as well as state-law claims for malicious prosecution, intentional infliction of emotional distress, and abuse of process. The District Court dismissed the suit, holding that the plaintiff failed to state a claim under § 1983 or for malicious prosecution, and that the other claims were time-barred. *Michaels v. New Jersey,* 955 F. Supp. 315 (N.J. Dist. 1996).

The recent willingness of courts to recognize parents' claims in § 1983 actions and in "false memory syndrome," cases, *supra,* suggests that the tide has turned to some extent on the zealous reaction to child sexual abuse. The basic tension remains however, between the goal of providing adequate protection of children who may be vulnerable to maltreatment by their parents and the goal of protecting family privacy and of limiting the costs of intervention.

Chapter 11
ADOPTION

INTRODUCTION

Adoption is the process by which persons other than the biological parents become a child's legal parents. Because every child is born with biological parents recognized by law, the first step in any adoption is the termination of their parental rights. The involuntary termination of parental rights for abusive or neglectful behavior is treated at length in Chapter 10. Most adoptions begin, however, with the voluntary relinquishment of parental rights by the biological parents that typically takes the form of their consent to the adoption. In some cases, the birth parent (usually the mother) seeks to revoke that consent, or may claim that it was not properly obtained. In other cases, the adoptive parent may argue that special circumstances render a biological parent's (usually the father's) consent unnecessary. These issues are treated in section A of this chapter. Section B examines the role of adoption agencies and agency liability for misrepresentation. Section C examines independent adoptions — those arranged outside of adoption agencies. While adoptions entirely within families (*e.g.,* as where an aunt and uncle adopt an orphaned niece or nephew) would be considered independent adoptions, regulatory attention ordinarily focuses on independent adoptions that arise outside of existing families. Section D deals with the effect of a final adoption decree: when it can be later challenged or reconsidered, the impact of the decree on prior legal relationships, and the secrecy usually demanded by state law concerning the now-displaced biological relationships. Finally, Section E examines adoption alternatives — that is, alternatives to conventional adoption which may provide a baby to childless couples. Some, such as baby-selling, are not new, although they can arise with modern variations. Others, such as the separation of the roles of genetic and gestational mother, emerge from biological advances that test traditional legal doctrines.

§ A. CONSENT TO ADOPTION

[1] WHEN IS THE CONSENT OF THE BIRTH PARENTS UNNECESSARY?

The biological parents' consent is ordinarily required before a child can be adopted. The most important exception to this general rule is found in the procedures for dispensing with the consent of the unmarried father. At one time, the unwed father had no parental claims at all, and could be ignored in the adoption process. (Importantly, he also had no responsibilities toward the child.) Beginning in the 1970s, a line of Supreme Court cases (*see* Chapter 9), recognized both procedural and substantive claims of unmarried fathers before their parental rights were severed by adoption, and the adoption process was altered to take their interests into account. Nonetheless, states may still require the unmarried father to take some step, such as recording his paternity claim in a state registry, even to preserve his right to notice of the pending adoption, and the rights of the father who has never shown an interest in his child are limited at best. Thus, many adoptions still take place without paternal involvement or consent. Consent is also unnecessary, of course, if the birth parents' rights have been severed (or are severed in the adoption proceeding) due to abuse, neglect, or abandonment. This topic is examined in Chapter 10. This section focuses on one common fact pattern that presents special problems: the stepparent adoption. In the typical case, the divorced custodial mother remarries, and her new husband seeks to adopt her children — to be the "real father" and not just the stepfather. Often, he has been the de facto father by virtue of his daily presence, his assumption of paternal responsibilities and his establishment of an emotional bond with the child. If the biological father opposes the adoption petition, the mother and her new husband then ask the court to approve the adoption petition without the father's consent. Many state adoption statutes contain language that appear to authorize adoption on some variant of the best-interest standard over the objection of a fit birth parent. Others have what seem to be quite specific criteria. Precise language, however, is still subject to interpretation. Consider the following case.

IN THE MATTER OF J.J.J.

718 P.2d 948 (Alaska 1986)

MOORE, Justice. This is an expedited appeal from an adoption decree whereby a 7-year-old boy was adopted by his stepfather over the objections of the boy's biological father. Because of the biological father's history of nonsupport, his consent was deemed unnecessary.

The primary issue in this case is whether the master erred in finding that for at least a 12-month period, the biological father failed significantly without justifiable cause to provide support required by judicial decree. This finding was sustained by the superior court. . . .

We conclude that the superior court correctly affirmed the master's finding with respect to support and correctly reversed her best interests determination. . . .

On May 25, 1982 the boy's biological parents were divorced. B.J., the biological mother, was awarded custody of the boy and J.B., the biological father, was ordered to pay $200 per month as child support. J.B. made no payments until August 1982, when he made a single $200 payment after being contacted by the Child Support Enforcement Agency (C.S.E.A.).

Thereafter, from September 1982 through March 1983, J.B. made no payments toward the support of the boy. In April and May of 1983 the C.S.E.A. garnished a total of $1,000 of J.B.'s wages to apply toward his child support arrearages. Thereafter, from May through October 1983, J.B. continued to pay nothing toward the boy's support.[2]

---

[2] J.B.'s earnings in 1982 appear to have been $22,518; his earnings during three quarters of 1983 appear to have been $18,750. . . .

In August 1983 the boy's mother and his stepfather, S.J., decided that S.J. should seek to adopt the boy and so advised J.B. In November 1983, shortly before the filing of the adoption petition, J.B. and his new wife paid $1,800 against part of his child support arrearages, after again being contacted by the C.S.E.A.

From December 1981 until the filing of the adoption petition, on December 19, 1983, J.B. had almost no contact with the boy. Twice during the last six months of this period J.B. reportedly informed the boy's mother, B.J., that he now wanted to visit the boy. However, B.J. resisted J.B.'s request for unsupervised visitation with the boy, stating that she believed that J.B. should slowly develop a relationship with the boy after having had no contact with him for such a long period. It does appear that, beginning well before the divorce, J.B. virtually ignored the boy.

During the period since his marriage to B.J., the boy's stepfather evidently established a close parental relationship with the boy.

In December 1983 the boy's stepfather, S.J., filed the petition to adopt him. The biological father, J.B., refused to consent to the adoption. The stepfather contended that J.B.'s consent was unnecessary pursuant to AS 25.23.050(a)(2)(B), because J.B. had "failed significantly, without justifiable cause . . . to provide for the care and support of the child as required by law or judicial decree."

The probate master found that J.B. had, for at least a year, significantly and unjustifiably failed to provide court-ordered support and had lost his right to withhold consent to the adoption. However, the master also found that the adoption decree would not be in the boy's best interests because he was curious about his biological father and seemed interested in knowing him (notwithstanding the boy's attachment to his stepfather). By law an adoption decree would terminate J.B.'s parental rights regarding the boy. . . .

   . . . .

As commentators have noted, the very problem now before us is an increasingly common occurrence, given the increase in divorce and remarriage in our society. Nevertheless, despite voluntarily assumed obligations and the existence of a strong bond between stepparent and stepchild, such a relationship lacks legal protection in the event of the desertion or death of the stepparent's spouse (the custodial "natural" parent). In such an event the noncustodial "natural" parent, even a parent who has rarely paid child support or merely made an occasional gesture of communication, may automatically assert primary rights to take legal custody of the child, despite the child's need for a stable and continuous family relationship. Stepparent adoption assures that the child may remain with his existing family. However, adoption has seemed a harsh remedy when the biological parent refuses consent. . . .

Alaska has adopted a modified version of the Uniform Adoption Act [which] sets forth the circumstances under which an adoption should be granted without a natural parent's consent. . . . Alaska's version of the Act focuses on a noncustodial parent's failure to meaningfully communicate with a child, significant failure to pay child support, and other acts of abandonment.

In this court's prior decisions in this area we have declined to dispense with a noncustodial parent's right to withhold consent to a stepparent adoption as long as the noncustodial parent had made a few perfunctory communications or an occasional gesture of support. In *Matter of Adoption of K.M.M.*, 611 P.2d 84 (Alaska 1980), we found that the biological father's unwillingness to visit his children for over one year was justified by "the mere fact that it was emotionally traumatic for the natural father to see his children and former wife living with a man who had been the father's closest friend." . . . In *R.N.T. v. J.R.G.*, 666 P.2d 1036 (Alaska 1983) this court reversed a superior court's decision to allow a stepfather to adopt the children of R.N.T. because R.N.T. had not maintained meaningful communication with his young children during the 14-month period that he was in prison. We emphasized that parental conduct that causes the loss of a parent's right to consent must be willful . . . Upon reflection, however, we now find that the *R.N.T.* dissent actually presented the better approach:

> R.N.T. states that the terms of his imprisonment and parole effectively prevented him from having contact with his children. This should not be the end of the analysis, as it is for this court, but only the beginning. Not all parents who are incarcerated or on parole are precluded from communicating with their children; it simply is not an automatic condition of imprisonment or parole. The issue that must be addressed is whether the constraints imposed on R.N.T. were the result of his own conduct, in which case his failure to communicate would not be justifiable, or were instead the result of circumstances over which he had no control. . .

We take this opportunity to clarify that, in order for a noncustodial parent to block a stepparent adoption, he or she must have maintained meaningful contact with a child, and must have provided regular payments of child support, unless prevented from doing so by circumstances beyond the noncustodial parent's control. Circumstances resulting from the noncustodial parent's own conduct cannot excuse such a parent's significant failure to provide support or maintain meaningful communication. Moreover, failure to support or to maintain contact with a child should not be excused by the emotional antagonism or awkwardness that may exist between former spouses. . . . Speaking of the noncustodial parent in *K.M.M.*, Justice Matthews [in dissent] observed that "his duty to his children required him to overcome his personal sensibilities." *Id.* This observation applies as well to J.B.'s prolonged noninvolvement with his son, which cannot be justified by J.B.'s and B.J.'s personality differences. . . .

AS 25.23.050(a) specifies: "Persons as to whom consent and notice not required" in adoption cases. This provision provides that consent is not required of . . .

> (2) a parent of a child in the custody of another, if the parent for a period of at least one year has failed significantly without justifiable cause, including but not limited to indigency,
>
> > (A) to communicate meaningfully with the child, or
>
> > (B) to provide for the care and support of the child as required by law or judicial decree. . . .

J.B. contends that the "period of at least one year" of significant nonsupport must immediately precede the adoption petition. We disagree, as do other courts. J.B. also suggests that his occasional payment should suffice to preserve his right to withhold consent to any adoption of J.J.J.

The statute does not say that the period of "at least one year" must immediately precede the filing of an adoption petition. One year is the minimum period which may be considered. Thus the superior court correctly considered the entire 17-month period during which J.B. made only one voluntary payment of $200 on his court-ordered obligation to contribute to J.J.J.'s support.

Sporadic partial payments do not preclude a finding of significant failure to provide child support. . . . Child support payments should be substantial or "regular" and constitute a "material factor" in the support of a child. . . .

The dissent insists that "no rule of law or principle of logic" requires that child support must be "uncompelled." However, the purpose of the waiver-of-consent statute was to provide an objective measure (at least one year) of when a parent has, in the practical sense, forsaken a child. It would make no sense at all to infer parental concern from payments that a government agency has to garnish from the income of a parent who has refused to provide support. Nevertheless, the dissent suggests that payments garnished from a recalcitrant parent's income should signify the same parental concern that voluntary support payments signify, because all court-ordered child support is "compelled" and "there is no certainty what the terms 'compulsion' or 'voluntary' mean" in this context. Actually, at common law all parents have a duty (not a "voluntary" option) to support their children. Court orders for child support set forth the amount of the parent's obligation. Most parents choose to abide by what the courts determine to be the child's financial needs. Garnishment occurs only as a last resort, when a parent has refused to meet this important obligation. . . .

As for J.B.'s 11th-hour (or 19th-month) payment to partially pay off his arrearages a few weeks before the adoption petition was filed, it would be absurd to believe that the legislature meant for a last-minute balloon payment to cancel out the import of a substantial period of nonsupport and noninvolvement. Other courts have expressed similar views: After the required period of one year has passed, resumption of payment of support for a brief period, particularly after the commencement of the adoption proceeding or just prior thereto, is not sufficient to bar an adoption without the consent of the delinquent father by starting a new one year period of non-support under the statute. . . .

We hold that courts shall consider a parent's entire history of support or nonsupport to determine whether that parent has waived his or her right to block a child's adoption by a stepparent[20] . . . .

---

[20] If, for instance, four years ago a parent significantly failed to support a child for a year, but thereafter (for the next three years) fully supported the child until the filing of an adoption petition, a court should find that that parent had not waived his or her right to withhold consent to the child's adoption. Although the dissent labels our position "harsh," this opinion actually considers the broader picture of the problems posed and recognizes that a child needs regular support (and meaningful communication) in the here-and-now. A young child's needs cannot be put on hold for years until a parent might have a "change of heart."

J.B. also argues that his significant failure to support the boy was the excusable result of his ex-wife's resistance to his belated interest in having the boy visit him, in August 1983, after more than a year of no communication at all with him. This, however, is no justification at all. . . . [A] parent's duty to provide child support is not excused by the conduct of others unless that conduct actually prevents performance of the child-support obligation.[23]

Notably, J.B. admitted at trial that he had not been kept from seeing the boy. Moreover, J.B.'s assertion as to his ex-wife's resistance to his sudden request to take the boy for weekends of unsupervised visitation in August 1983 has no bearing whatsoever on his significant failure to provide support for the period from June 1982 through October 1983. Nor does his contention counter the fact that he made virtually no effort to communicate with the boy from April 1982 to August 1983, despite his ex-wife's requests that he do so.

MATTHEWS, Justice, joined by RABINOWITZ, Chief Justice, dissenting.

. . . [T]he father had paid $3,250 of the total support due of $3,800 and was less than three months behind in child support when the petition for adoption was filed.

Two questions of statutory interpretation . . . are presented.

(1) Does the period of at least one year referred to in the statute mean any period of one year or that period which immediately precedes the filing of the petition for adoption?

(2) Should the amounts obtained by the Child Support Enforcement Agency from the father's employer be taken into account as part of the provision of support by the father?

Only if one concludes that the statute refers to any year rather than the year which precedes the filing of the petition for adoption and that the withheld wages cannot be counted as the provision of support, can the conclusion be drawn that the father in this case has waived his right to withhold consent to the adoption of his son. . .

. . . In interpreting AS 20.15.050(a)(2), we have required that it be strictly construed in favor of a natural parent. *In re Adoption of K.M.M.*, 611 P.2d 84, 87 (Alaska 1980). . . . [P]arents should not be deprived of the fundamental rights and duties inherent in the parent-child relationship except for "grave and weighty reasons." This policy of strict construction means that where two interpretations of the statute are reasonably possible, that interpretation which is most protective of the rights of the natural parent is to be selected. Since interpreting this statute to refer to the one year period immediately preceding the petition is reasonable, and since that interpretation is more protective of the rights of the natural parent than construing the statute to refer to any one year period, the former interpretation should be adopted.

. . . . Under a strict "any year" interpretation, if a parent did not support his children for one year long before the filing of a petition for adoption, but since that year had been faithful in supporting them and had made up all

---

[23] This principle applies with equal force to the noncustodial parent's duty to meaningfully communicate with his or her child. Here, if J.B.'s ex-wife resisted his attempt to visit with the boy, J.B.'s remedy lay in taking legal action against his ex-wife for violating his visitation rights.

arrearages, his consent would nonetheless not be required under the statute. Such a result would be extremely unjust in many cases. This harshness may be tempered to some extent by the majority's declaration that "courts shall consider a parent's entire history of support" in determining waiver. The trouble with this is that it cuts us completely adrift from the statute. The purpose of the statute was to provide a relatively simple means by which waiver could be determined. . . .

B. Provision of Support

The majority concludes that only payments which are made without compulsion should count as provision of support by the parent. There are several reasons why this construction should not be adopted.

First, the requirement of non-compulsion is not expressed in the statute, nor may it reasonably be implied. . . . All that the statute calls for is support. . . .

Second, the rule of construction that the statute be interpreted in the manner most protective of the rights of parents indicates that a requirement of non-compulsion should not be read into the statute.

Third, there is no certainty what the terms "compulsion" or "voluntary" mean in the context of court ordered child support. All payments of support under such an order are compelled. . . .

The majority tells us that "the purpose of the waiver of consent statute was to provide an objective measure of when a parent has, in the practical sense, forsaken a child." I agree. It does not follow, however, that coerced payments necessarily indicate abandonment or lack of parental concern. An aggressive former spouse can garnish wages after only a slight delay in payment, and a non-custodial parent may be passively content to provide support in that way. . . . So long as the non-custodial parent visits with his children it cannot be said that, in a practical sense, he has forsaken them.

NOTES

1. *The Traditional Approach.* Until recently, the rights of noncustodial biological parents were accorded great deference when stepparents sought to adopt over parental objection, and many courts continue to be very reluctant to terminate the rights of parents who have demonstrated minimal interest in their children, to allow adoption by a stepparent. Virginia, for example, has been steadfast in its support of parental rights. In *Ward v. Faw*, 253 S.E.2d 658 (Va. 1979), the father had almost no contact with the child for more than 3 years (in part because of military service in Germany). He had made child support payments and sent greeting cards and occasional gifts. In response to the question of why he refused to consent to the adoption, Ward replied that the boy was his only son and that he wanted his name to be "carried on."

The trial court ordered the adoption without the father's consent, under the Virginia statute providing that if the father's consent is withheld contrary to the best interests of the child, the court may grant the petition without such consent. Code § 63.1-225(4) (1977 Cum. Supp.).

Addressing the child's best interests, the trial judge stated:

> [T]he subject child is now living in a stable home, has love and care, and the child is a happy, healthy, outgoing, and well adjusted six year old boy. The fitness of the adoptive parents is unquestionable. . . . [S]ince the natural father has not established a familial or custodial relationship with his son, they are strangers at this time. . . . To deny the adoption and take the child from a stable and happy environment and expose him to the natural father through his visitation rights would be . . . to experiment with the future welfare of this child.

The Virginia Supreme Court reversed, emphasizing the heavy burden on the party seeking to adopt the child over the objections of a fit biological parent.

> [Where] "there is no question of the fitness of the non-consenting parent and he has not by conduct or previous legal action lost his rights to the child, it must be shown that continuance of the relationship between the two would be detrimental to the child's welfare." 192 S.E.2d at 799.

The court gave lip service to the importance of the welfare of the child, but suggested that "the rights of parents may not be lightly severed, but are to be respected if at all consonant with the best interest of the child." 192 S.E.2d at 799. There was no evidence that Ward was unfit, and the stepfather failed to demonstrate that continuance of the relationship between the father and child would be detrimental to the child's welfare. More recent Virginia cases have followed *Faw*. *See Hickman v. Futty*, 498 S.E.2d 232, 236 (Va. App. 1997) ("even when the parent proved unfit, the unfitness ha[s] to make the continuance of the relationship detrimental to the child's welfare").

Other states continue to be protective of parents' rights in stepparent adoptions. A Kansas father who had virtually no contact with his children and had not voluntarily paid child support was found to have fulfilled his parental duties in the two preceding years, because his children received Social Security disability payments under a benefit received by the father due to his mental illness. *Adoption of K.J.B.*, 959 P.2d 853 (Kan. 1998). Thus, "whether by accident or design," he had provided child support, and the trial court's decision to order adoption without his consent was reversed. *See also Mayberry v. Flowers*, 65 S.W.3d 418 (Ark. 2002) (adoption by a stepfather set aside because father had not been provided with the required statutory notice — even though he had actual knowledge of the adoption within a year after the decree, the limitation period for petitioning to set aside adoption); *Moran v. Weldon*, 57 P.3d 898 (Ore. App. 2002) (statute permitting adoption without consent of parent imprisoned under sentence of 3 or more years requires proof of ground for termination in addition to imprisonment).

Statutory language is often not a very precise predictor of the standard that courts apply. Thus, the Virginia statute does not actually require a finding of parental unfitness before the adoption can be permitted without the parent's consent. Rather, it allows the adoption if the court finds the consent was withheld "contrary to the best interests of the child." The same statutory language has been interpreted by other courts to allow for termination of parental rights under a much more relaxed standard. In *Petition of J.O.L.*, 409 A.2d 1073 (D.C. App. 1979), for example, an appellate court upheld a stepparent adoption, interpreting the statute to create what seemed to a best interest standard.

2. *The Modern Trend.* Although *Ward* may continue to represent a common judicial response to petitions to terminate parental rights, *J.J.J.* reflects the modern trend which requires the objecting biological parent to demonstrate that he has earned the right to continued parental status by fulfilling parental responsibilities and maintaining a relationship with the child. Some states have amended their adoption statutes to be more supportive of stepparent adoption. Recent amendments of the New Jersey adoption statute emphasize that the primary consideration is the best interest of the child and not the rights of biological parents. N.J. STAT. ANN. § 9:3-46 (West Supp. 2002). In *In re Adoption of Children by G.P.B., Jr.*, the New Jersey Supreme Court reversed a lower court's decision that the adoption should not go forward because there was no evidence that continuation of the father's parental rights would result in danger of serious harm to the children. 736 A.2d 1277 (N.J. 1999). The supreme court directed reconsideration in light of the new statute.

Although statutory reform has facilitated stepparent adoption, the law in this area is still largely judge-made, as *J.J.J.* and *Ward* illustrate. In interpreting the statutory language strictly against the father, the *J.J.J.* court seems to be committed to a policy of facilitating stepparent adoption, and does not attach much importance to the continuation of the relationship between the child and his biological father. Do you agree with the court's analysis — and with the policy of promoting stepparent adoption in cases like this? The traditional weight that courts have given to the rights of biological parents has been subject to much legitimate criticism; courts have often seemed to view children as the property of their parents. On the other hand, the child's link to her biological parent may be important to her as she grows up, and perhaps it should not be severed too hastily — particularly in a society in which second marriages end in divorce at an even higher rate than do first marriages. This concern may have influenced the thinking of a Pennsylvania court that vacated the termination of the father's rights where the mother and stepfather had separated, even though they had no plans for divorce and the mother supported the adoption. *In re Adoption of J.D.S.*, 763 A.2d 863 (Pa. Super. 2000).

Even the Alaska Supreme Court has interpreted this statute recently more favorably to the biological parent. For example, the court suggested that a father's subsequent imprisonment (for sexually abusing his niece) might justify his failure to pay support during the period before the adoption petition. *In re Adoption of J.B.K.*, 865 P.2d 737 (Alaska 1993). *See also Adoption of J.M.F.*, 881 P.2d 1116 (Alaska 1994) (mother's failure to pay support during a 3-year period that her child was living with her brother and his wife could not be a basis for waiving her right to withhold consent because couple (who initially planned to adopt) had never asked for or expected support.

Many states, like Alaska, permit stepparent adoptions without the natural parent's consent on what may be understood as a variation of the usual "abandonment" test required for severance of parental rights. This ground focuses on two areas of inquiry: whether the parent has maintained a relationship through communication and contact with the child and whether he has provided financial support. See, *e.g.*, CAL. FAM. CODE § 8604 (West 1994) (noncustodial parent's consent to stepparent adoption not required if he willfully fails to communicate or pay child support for one year). On the first issue, courts vary in responding to excuses for lack of contact that implicate culpable conduct by the parent. An Oklahoma court upheld the stepparent adoption, rejecting the father's claim that his failure to maintain contact with the child for the preceding 12 months was due to a protective order prohibiting contact, and to his incarceration for violating the order, for stalking the mother, and for assault and battery against the mother. *Adoption of C.D.M.*, 39 P.3d 802 (Okla. 2001). The court responded that the father's conduct demonstrated that he did not intend to establish a significant relationship with the child, and the adoption was in the child's best interest.

Perhaps reflecting a "get tough on deadbeat dads" attitude, some courts have responded unsympathetically to excuses for non-support offered by parents. *See, e.g., In re Serre*, 665 N.E.2d 1185 (Ohio Com. Pl. 1996) (under similar statute, father's consent to adoption was unnecessary because payment of $70 child support in the preceding year was inadequate; court tightened previous standard under which any payment in preceding 12 months was sufficient to trigger consent requirement); *Dusseau v. Martyn*, 411 N.W.2d 743 (Mich. App. 1987) (stepfather adoption allowed on basis of father's nonsupport; reasons for nonsupport irrelevant since father could have obtained modification of support order for good reason). But see *In re Adoption of Morelli*, 2002 Ohio App. LEXIS 5063 (Ohio App. 2002)(where child's custodians refused father's offers of support, father's failure to support does not justify waiver of consent to adoption).

The father in *J.J.J.* was divorced from the child's mother. Would it make any difference if the parents had never been married? The law traditionally presumed that marriage created parental rights that were entitled to substantial legal protection (even after divorce), whereas unmarried fathers got no legal protection of their relationship with their child, but also had no parental responsibilities. In recent years, the Supreme Court has clarified that unmarried fathers can have a protected parental interest (see discussion in Chapter 9, *supra*) and, as *J.J.J.* suggests, the traditional protection of the rights of divorced fathers is eroding. States have increasingly treated the two groups in a similar manner, allowing termination of parental rights when the father has seriously defaulted on his responsibilities. However, the Supreme Court suggested in *Lehr v. Robertson* (discussed in Chapter 9) that marriage creates the most effective legal protection of the father's opportunity to develop a relationship with his child. Does this suggest that a divorced father should have a more extensive right to withhold consent than does an unmarried father?

3. Uniform Adoption Act. The 1994 Uniform Adoption Act is a comprehensive reform of adoption law. An express goal of the Act is to facilitate adoption and to promote its benefits, not only for children, but also for the adults involved. Although the Act seeks to accommodate the interests of both birth parents and adoptive parents in a coherent regulatory scheme, it does not seek to preserve the ties between the child and her biological parent as a primary goal. As Professor Joan Hollinger, the principal architect of the Act put it:

> [The Act] rejects the view that adoption is a "last resort," to be invoked only after multiple public efforts to preserve or establish a child's ties to biological parents have failed. Instead the Act is premised on the belief that children's ties to the individuals who actually parent them — or who are committed to parenting them — deserve legal protection – even if those ties are psychologically and socially constructed and not biologically rooted[.]

Hollinger, *Adoption and Aspiration: The Uniform Adoption Act, The DeBoer-Schmidt Case, and the American Quest for the Ideal Family*, 2 DUKE J. GENDER L. & POL.15, 17–18 (1995).

The U.A.A. provision dealing with waiver of consent by biological parents is even tougher than the Alaska statute. U.A.A. § 3-504 (c). It provides that a parent's rights will be terminated if he fails to make reasonable and consistent support payments or communicate or visit regularly with the child for a consecutive six-month period. Section 3-504 (c)(2).

The U.A.A. has comprehensive provisions dealing specifically with adoption by stepparents. (Article 4), recognizing that these adoptions, which constitute over half of all adoptions, differ from the placement of the child with a new family. First, there is no transfer to a strange home; the child remains in a family setting with which he is familiar. Beyond this, evaluation of the adopting stepparent is less important than evaluation of other prospective adoptive parents; the custodial parent, who, of course, will not be evaluated, has "selected" the stepparent, and the custodial arrangement is not likely to change whether the adoption goes forward or not. Under the Uniform Act, evaluation of the stepparent is discretionary; the child's inheritance rights from the biological parent are preserved; and continued post-adoption visitation by the biological parent is facilitated. U.A.A. § 4-113. (*See* discussion of post-adoption visitation in section 2 below).

4. *Constitutional Issues*. Does *J.J.J.* violate the father's constitutional rights by terminating parental rights under an unduly strict standard? Recall *Lehr v. Robertson* and the other Supreme Court cases defining the parameters of paternal rights in Chapter 9. Most of those cases dealt with unmarried fathers seeking to withhold consent to adoption by stepfathers. In general, the Court focused on the same issues as do the waiver of consent statutes, suggesting that fathers' rights are constitutionally protected when they fulfill their parental responsibilities — providing financial support and maintaining a relationship with their child. Fathers who have failed to act as concerned parents may find that their parental status is not protected. In principle, a state could impose such a demanding level of support and involvement on the father who seeks to object to adoption that it would amount to an unconstitutional burden on his parental rights. Is *J.J.J.* close to the line?

PROBLEM

Problem 11-1. Alice and Bob come to you to ask about arranging for him to adopt Alice's son, Tim, from her former marriage. The boy is six. Alice left his father, Ed, five years ago, in part, she says, because he abused the child. The uncontested divorce decree was entered four years ago, awarding Alice custody and modest child support. Since then Ed has paid support and visited the child sporadically. After Bob and Alice married two years ago, the support payments gradually ended, as did the visits. It has now been six months since Alice has heard from Ed or received support, and she is not even certain where he is. She has never attempted to enforce her support rights and is content to leave things as they are, except that she and Bob would like to complete an adoption.

What do you do?

ADOPTION INTO A NEW FAMILY

A very different kind of adoption case is one in which an unmarried mother seeks to place a child for adoption with a couple or individual who will assume exclusive parental responsibilities. These cases often involve infants, and they raise serious questions about when the father's consent can be waived and when his objection can block the adoption. The standards applied to stepparent adoption, or to other adoptions of older children, may not be useful in this context. Most statutes provide that consent to adoption is not required of fathers who have failed to maintain a relationship with their child or to provide financial support. However, in infant adoption cases, the father usually has had no opportunity to fulfill these parental responsibilities.

Historically, little attention was paid to the father when the unmarried mother sought to place a child with an adoptive family. The mother's consent was sufficient and adoptions went forward without notice to or consent by the unmarried father. This approach assumed that most men were not interested in taking responsibility for the children they had fathered by unmarried women, and that a consent requirement would impose a costly administrative burden on the adoption process — assumptions that may have been accurate. *See e.g.* Shanley, *Unwed Fathers' Rights, Adoption, and Sex Equality: Gender Equality and the Perpetuation of Patriarchy,* 95 COLUM. L. REV. 60 (1994). In 1972, in *Stanley v. Illinois,* the Supreme Court implied that unmarried fathers have a constitutional right to a hearing to demonstrate that they are fit parents before adoption can proceed without their consent. 405 U.S. 645. State adoption law changed to provide such an opportunity in ways that would avoid undue cost and delay to adoption.

The first issue is to determine which fathers are entitled to notice of the adoption proceedings. The Supreme Court, in *Lehr v. Robertson,* (discussed in Chapter 9) emphasized the constitutional importance of providing the father with the opportunity to step forward and assert his parental rights when the mother decides to place the child — and concluded that New York's putative father registry satisfied this requirement. Registries, available in many states, provide birth fathers with the means to assure that they will receive notice of any adoption proceeding. *See* 750 ILL. COMP. STAT. ANN. § 50/12-1 (West 1999); MINN STAT. § 559.52 (2000).

Where the father's identity or location is unknown, efforts are made to discover his whereabouts or identity under various statutory provisions. Some states provide that an investigation be undertaken to locate the father. LA CIV. CODE ANN. art. 1136(B)(1995). Many states provide for notice by publication of the adoption proceeding (sometimes called "John Doe" notice) when personal notice is not feasible, a method that is generally sufficient to satisfy due process requirements in terminating parental rights. However, a South Carolina court reversed an adoption order in a case where the father challenged the sufficiency of notice published in a newspaper in a county near his residence. *Brown v. Malloy*, 546 S.E.2d 195 (S.C. Ct. App. 2001). The appellate court directed the court to consider whether the father's consent was required (and an order of publication inadequate), because he had tried to demonstrate his commitment to the child and was thwarted from doing so by the mother.

Requirements of notice by publication vary in the extent to which the birth mother's privacy is compromised. A 2001 Florida law, since repealed, required a birth mother to publish her name and physical description and the name or description of recent sexual partners who might conceivably be the child's father. FLA. STAT. ch. 63.087, 63.088 (amended 2003). According to one report, adoptions dropped and abortion increased under the statute, which generally was subject to scathing criticism. *See* Dahlberg, *Florida Ends Scarlet Letter Adoption Law*, LOS ANGELES TIMES May 31, 2003, Pt. 1, p 14. In 2003, an appellate court found the statutory requirement violated Florida's constitutional right of privacy, interfering with the woman's right to choose adoption and with her right not to disclose intimate personal information. *G.P., C.M., C.H & L.H v. State,* 842 So. 2d 1059 (Fla. App. 4th Dist. 2003). The 2003 repealing statute provides that the unmarried father, by virtue of the fact that he has had a sexual relationship with a woman will be deemed to have notice that a pregnancy and adoption proceeding may occur and he has a duty to protect his interests. § 60.088(1)(2003). The amended statute creates an adoption registry for this purpose. In contrast, in some states the mother's name must not be revealed when notice is published. In *S. C. Dep't of Soc. Serv. v. Doe,* 527 S.E.2d 771 (S.C. App. 2000), the court found that requiring publication of the mother's name would undermine her privacy and compromise the confidentiality of the adoption proceedings, something that should happen only under the most extraordinary circumstances.

The fact that a father must be notified of the adoption proceedings does not mean that he will be able to block the adoption. A separate issue is determining if the father's parental rights can be terminated over his objection. The trend in cases involving adoption placement with a new family has been to put a substantial burden on the father who seeks to block the placement. In contrast to stepparent adoption where the child lives with a custodial parent, the adoption of an infant may offer the child the only possibility of a stable permanent home. If the mother consents to adoption and prospective adoptive parents are ready to undertake responsibility for the child, the father generally must demonstrate that he is ready to step in to assume full parental responsibility. *See, e.g., Matter of T.M.K.*, 617 N.W. 2d 925 (Mich. App. 2000)(To properly object to termination of his rights, a putative father must request custody). Under the U.A.A., where the child is under six months, the father's parental rights can be terminated over his objection if any of the following conditions are proved: 1) he has failed to pay the mother's medical expenses, both before and after birth in accordance with his means; 2) he has failed to provide financial support or visit regularly with the minor; or 3) he is unable or unwilling to assume full custody of the child. U.A.A. § 3-504(c)(1). For a child over six months, termination can occur if one of three grounds is established: 1) failure to provide financial support; 2) failure to communicate or visit regularly with the child; or 3) failure to manifest the ability and willingness to assume custody.

Another important consideration is timing. Fathers have a limited period during which to object to the adoption, probably even if the failure to object was not due to the father's fault. If a father comes forward after the adoption process is well underway — or is completed, recognition of his parental rights would cause considerable disruption to the child and to the adoptive family. Thus, for example, in *Robert O. v. Russell K.*, 604 N.E.2d (N.Y. 1992), the Court rejected the petition of a biological father who sought to set aside the adoption of his 18-month-old son, 10 months after the adoption had been finalized, because he was unaware of the child's existence. (*See* discussion of this case in Chapter 9.) The Court emphasized the importance of "promptness and finality" in adoption proceedings, and stated that "[p]romptness is measured in terms of the baby's life, not by the onset of the father's aware-ness." The demand for prompt action by the father at the child's birth is neither arbitrary nor punitive, but instead a "logical and necessary outgrowth of the child's need for the early permanence and stability."

Courts vary in the extent to which they strictly apply statutory time limits and other requirements. The Nebraska Supreme Court recently upheld a statute permitting adoption without the putative father's consent if he did not file notice of his intent to claim paternity within five days of receiving notice of the child's birth, and then file a petition for adjudication of his paternity claim within thirty days. *Adoption of Baby Girl H.*, 635 N.W.2d 256 (Neb. 2001). In this case, the father, an unemancipated minor, filed the petition in the wrong court. *See also Heidbreder v. Carlton*, 645 N.W.2d 355 (Minn. 2002) (father's registration with adoption registry 31 days after child's birth not timely under statute with 30-day time limit; mother's secrecy about her location and disclosure of child's birth on day 31 was no excuse). On the other hand, in a case that distinguishes *Robert O.*, a New Jersey court reversed an adoption order where the father was unaware of the mother's pregnancy or the child's birth until the child was ten months old and had lived with the family seeking to adopt him for nine months. *In re Adoption of a Child by P.F.R.*, 705 A.2d 1233 (N.J. Super. App. Div. 1998). The court concluded that the father's parenting conduct must be evaluated from the time he learned of the child, because only at that point was he able perform the parental functions of care and support. *See also Petition of Doe*, 638 N.E.2d 181 (Ill. 1994)(30 day post-birth time limit not a bar to father's custody petition at almost 60 days where adoptive parents failed to try to identify father). *See also In the Matter of the Adoption of B.V.*, 33 P.3d 1083 (Utah 2001)(father's consent to adoption is required where he came forward in timely manner, petitioned for custody, and agreed to pay reasonable share of pregnancy and childbirth expenses, although he has not yet paid expenses, as statute requires).

Although the parental rights of unmarried fathers are limited and their opportunity to come forward to object to adoption is not open-ended, nonetheless fathers can block adoption if they object to the termination of their parental rights in a timely manner, and they are ready to assume full parental responsibilities. This can result in disruption of an adoption placement, often after the child has been with the adoptive family for a substantial period of time. The problem is exacerbated (often even created) by the fact that the respective rights of the father and adoptive parents are not clarified until a time-consuming appeals process has run its course.

The highly publicized dispute over "Baby Jessica" Claussen is a case in point. *In the Interest of B.G.C.* 496 N.W.2d 239 (Iowa 1992). In that case, the biological father, Daniel Schmidt, filed an affidavit of paternity and a petition for custody in an Iowa court three weeks after the child's birth. However, the litigation and appeals process dragged on for more than two years — largely prolonged by the prospective adoptive parents, the DeBoers. When Schmidt finally prevailed in his custody claim, a sobbing Jessica was removed from the home of the de Boers, who had raised her almost from birth. The case was finally resolved when the United States Supreme Court denied the De Boers' application for a stay of an order of the Michigan Supreme Court directing them to return the child to her biological parents. *DeBoer v. Schmidt*, 509 U.S. 1301 (1993). Under these circumstances, should the fact that the child and biological parents have been separated for an extended period be relevant to the outcome? If so, the incentive for prospective adoptive parents to prolong litigation and appeals is worrisome. Can you suggest procedural reforms that might mitigate the problem? One critic (the Reporter for the Uniform Adoption Act) argues that many of the problems that arose would have been avoided under the Uniform Act. Hollinger, *Adoption and Aspiration: The Uniform Adoption Act, the DeBoer -Schmidt Case, and the American Quest for the Ideal Family*, 2 DUKE J. GENDER L. & POL'Y 15 (1995).

In a somewhat similar Pennsylvania case, a father opposed adoption and sought custody almost immediately after the birth of his child, who had been placed by an adoption agency in the custody of prospective adoptive parents. *B.A.& A.A. v. E.E.*, 741 A.2d 1227 (Pa. 1999). More than three years later, the state supreme court rejected the claim of the prospective adoptive parents, who had refused to relinquish custody, that they had stood *in loco parentis*, and concluded that they lacked standing to challenge the father's custody.

Cases where the child has lived with the adoptive family for years before the dispute is resolved presents a compelling case for applying the best interest standard to consent waiver. However, consider the following:

> If . . . the best interests of the child is to be the determining factor in child custody cases, . . . persons seeking babies to adopt might profitably frequent grocery stores and snatch babies from carts when the parent is looking the other way. Then, if custody proceedings can be delayed long enough, they can assert that they have a nicer home, a superior education, a better job or whatever, and that the best interests of the child are with the baby snatchers. Children of parents living in public housing. . . and children of single parents might be

considered particularly fair game. The law, thankfully, is otherwise. *Petition of Doe,* 638 N.E. 181, 188 (Ill. 1994).

PROBLEM

Problem 11-2 Oscar lived with Daniella and supported her during her pregnancy. About a month before the baby was born, they became estranged and Oscar moved out. When their son was born, Daniella consented to his adoption shortly after his birth, telling the adoptive parents and their attorney that she knew who the father was but would not reveal his name. When Oscar returned from visiting his ill mother in Europe two weeks after the baby's birth, Daniella told him that the baby had died. Right away, Oscar began to investigate, and learned (57 days after the baby's birth) that he was alive. He immediately contested his son's adoption. Under the applicable statute, the father was required to show "a reasonable degree of interest in the child as to the welfare of a newborn child during the first 30 days of life." Should Oscar have standing to challenge the adoption?

[2] OPEN ADOPTION

MICHAUD v. WAWRUCK

551 A.2d 738 (Conn. 1986)

The sole issue in this case is whether a written visitation agreement between a genetic mother and adoptive parents violates the public policy of this state. The plaintiff, Jacqueline Michaud, filed a complaint seeking specific enforcement of an "Open Adoption and Visitation Agreement" between herself and the defendants, James Wawruck and Cynthia Wawruck. [The trial court granted the defendants' motion to strike and rendered judgment in their favor.] We find error and remand the case for further proceedings.

. . . . The Probate Court, on August 31, 1981, terminated the plaintiff's parental rights with respect to her child born on February 5, 1979. . . . [I]n 1982, the plaintiff filed a Superior Court action against the commissioner of children and youth services to set aside the Probate Court's decree terminating her parental rights, on the ground that her consent to that proceeding had been fraudulently procured by the child's father. . . . The plaintiff agreed to withdraw her lawsuit, and to allow the adoption to go forward, in exchange for the [foster parents'] agreement to permit regular visitation between the plaintiff and the child during the child's minor years.[1]

---

[1] The "Open Adoption and Visitation Agreement" provides in relevant part: "1. Adoption. . . . 2. Termination of Rights. The natural mother will withdraw her legal challenge . . . as soon as the adopting parents have approval of their adoption application by DCYS. 3. Visitation. The adopting parents will cooperate fully with the natural-mother in the natural mother's visits with the child both now and after the adoption takes place until the child's 18th birthday. . . . The tender age of the child and her high sensitivity to her, up to the present, state of uncertainty shall be taken into account by the parties. Each of the parties shall at all times in good faith endeavor to maintain in the child respect and affection for the other parties. The rights of

The agreement between the parties was placed on record in the Superior Court on September 16, 1983. Acquiescence in the agreement was noted, in open court, by counsel for the plaintiff, for the defendants, for the commissioner, and for the minor child. The agreement was not, however, made part of the subsequent decree of the Probate Court permitting the defendants to adopt the child, although the parties to that proceeding, . . . were fully aware of its terms. After the adoption had been finalized, the defendants terminated all visitation between the plaintiff and the child.

The trial court, after reviewing these facts, granted the defendants' motion to strike the plaintiff's complaint because, in its view, enforcement of the "Open Adoption and Visitation Agreement" would violate Connecticut's adoption statutes. According to the trial court, adoption, as a creature of statute, must comply strictly with statutory requirements, and the existing statutes governing adoption preclude private "side agreements" that would serve to perpetuate a relationship, after adoption, between a genetic parent and an adopted child. The court noted that termination of parental rights, under General Statutes § 45-61b(g), operates as a "complete severance by court order of the legal relationship . . . between the child and his parent. . . ." Furthermore, under General Statutes § 45-64a, adoption creates new legal relationships in which the adopting parents are completely substituted for the genetic parents of an adopted person. . . . Relying on these statutory provisions, and a number of out-of-state cases, the court concluded that the contract between the parties could not confer upon the plaintiff a specifically enforceable right to visitation after completion of the adoption process.

[T]here is really only one question that we must resolve: did the trial court err in concluding that this agreement violated the public policy reflected in our adoption statutes? We disagree with the trial court's ruling.

The validity of an "open adoption" agreement is a matter of first impression for this court. Before we address the merits of this question, we should note that the title "open adoption," which has apparently become the standard characterization of such agreements, conveys a misleading impression of what such agreements intend to accomplish. The plaintiff does not seek to "open," to set aside or to diminish in any way the adoptive process that has substituted the defendants as the legal parents of the child. The plaintiff's rights are not premised on an ongoing genetic relationship that somehow survives a termination of parental rights and an adoption. Instead, the plaintiff is asking us to decide whether, as an adult who has had an ongoing personal relationship with the child, she may contract with the adopting parents, prior to adoption, for the continued right to visit with the child, so long as that visitation continues to be in the best interest of the child.

Our statutes recognize that visitation encompasses considerations that differ from those that govern custody, guardianship or parental status. . . . [T]he adoption statutes do not expressly make a visitation agreement void as against public policy.

---

visitation shall not be exercised by the natural mother at any time or in such a manner as to interfere with the education and normal social and school activities of the child. Visitation shall be twice a month for three (3) hours each visit at the Wawrucks' home."

[O]ur visitation statute, General Statutes § 46b-59, permits the Superior Court, upon a proper application, to "grant the right of visitation with respect to any minor child . . . to any person. . . . In making, modifying or terminating such an order, the court shall be guided by the best interest of the child. . . . Visitation rights granted in accordance with this section shall not be deemed to have created parental rights in the person . . . to whom such visitation rights are granted. The grant of visitation rights shall not prevent any court of competent jurisdiction from thereafter acting upon the custody of such child, the parental rights with respect to such child or the adoption of such child and any such court may include in its decree an order terminating such visitation rights". . . . All this plaintiff seeks is a court order consistent with the statutory constraints imposed on visitation by § 46b-59.

[W]e are [therefore] unpersuaded that the agreement between the parties in this case violates the public policy of Connecticut. It would be elevating form over substance to allow the plaintiff to obtain visitation rights by filing an appropriate "application" in the Superior Court, but to deny her the opportunity to seek such rights under a contractual umbrella. . . .

Traditional models of the nuclear family have come, in recent years, to be replaced by various configurations of parents, stepparents, adoptive parents and grandparents. . . . We are not prepared to assume that the welfare of children is best served by a narrow definition of those whom we permit to continue to manifest their deep concern for a child's growth and development. . . . In the present case, the "Open Adoption and Visitation Agreement" was openly and lovingly negotiated, in good faith, in order to promote the best interest of the child. The attorney for the child reported that the child thought the agreement between her mother and her soon-to-be adoptive parents would be "the best world that she could imagine." This agreement did not violate public policy, either ab initio or upon the subsequent entry of a decree of adoption.

We therefore remand this case to the trial court for a hearing on the merits of the plaintiff's claim that visitation would now be in the best interest of the child. . . .

NOTES

1. *Open Adoption — A Response to the Complexity of Modern Families.* Traditionally the law has held firmly to the view that a child can have only two parents. On this view, when an adoptive mother or father assumes the role, the relationship between biological parent and child is severed. In recent years, courts increasingly have been receptive to enforcing agreements, such as the one in *Michaud*, between biological parents and adoptive parents under which the biological parent continues to have visitation rights. This trend, sometimes called open adoption, recognizes that modern family relationships are complex, and that the child's interest may be promoted by maintaining important relationships beyond the two-parent nuclear family. As the court in *Michaud* suggests, open adoption can be regarded as a category of nonparent visitation, discussed in Chapter 6, and reflects many of the same policy objectives. However, many of these arrangements, unlike other nonparent visitation, are created on the basis of the parent's conditional consent to

the adoption and the relinquishment of her parental rights. Nonetheless, enforcement of open adoption agreements is not based on a continuation of parental status, but rather on the child's best interest.

The most important benefit claimed by open adoption advocates is that the bond between the biological parent and child is not severed. Even if the parent has been deficient in fulfilling parental responsibilities, it may be beneficial to both the parent and child to continue an established relationship. *See* Scott & Scott, *Parents as Fiduciaries*, 81 VA. L. REV. 2401 (1995) (arguing continued contact after adoption rewards parents who have invested in relationship with child, to the benefit of child). Moreover, when a family is dissolved because parents can no longer care for their children, open adoption permits siblings to maintain contact. Further, the child will grow up knowing her parents, and may have less concern about why she was placed with another family. By encouraging birth parents to give consent to adoption which they might otherwise withhold, open adoption also promotes permanent placement of the child with responsible adults eager to assume the parental role.

Open adoption may also have some costs. Prospective adoptive parents may feel pressured to agree to an arrangement which they do not believe will be a good basis for creating a family, because they feel that they have no options. Conflicts may develop between the adoptive and biological parents which create stress for the child. Particularly with infants, who have little in the way of an established relationship with the biological parent to maintain, the costs may outweigh the benefits.

Open adoptions are most commonly sought in two kinds of cases: adoptions by foster parents or other adults where a child has been placed in foster care due to abuse or neglect, and stepparent adoptions. Open adoption could facilitate stepparent adoption in a broader range of cases, by encouraging the biological parent to consent to adoption, knowing that he will not lose all contact with his child. Moreover stepparents may be encouraged to invest in the parental role if adoption were easier, because the relationship would acquire legal status and protection. Would *J.J.J.* have been a good case for open adoption, given the child's curiosity about his father? This issue was raised in the case (in a part of the opinion not reprinted here), but the court concluded that it had no statutory authority to order continued visitation rights in the father. The court criticized this "all-or-nothing approach" to adoption as "unrealistic," often producing "an unfair result." 718 P.2d at 951. *See also Weinschel v. Strople,* 466 A.2d 1301 (Md. Spec. App. 1983)(mother may enter enforceable contract with father and his new wife, permitting mother's continued visitation after adoption by the new wife, but court retains the right to decline to enforce the contract where it is not in the child's interest). Some statutes permit open adoption only in foster care cases, probably because the goal of promoting permanent placement is compelling in these cases. N.Y. Soc. SERV. LAW § 383-c(5)(b)(ii) (McKinney 2003).

Although many states continue to prohibit open adoption, in recent years, a number of states have authorized the enforcement of visitation agreements between biological and adoptive parents. *See, e.g.,* MASS. GEN. LAWS ANN. ch. 210, § 6(c) (West Supp. 2001); MINN. STAT. § 259.58 (2001)(authorizing agreement between adoptive parent and biological parent, relative, or foster parent); IND. CODE ANN. § 31-19-16-4 (Burns 1997); MD. CODE ANN. FAM. L. § 5-312 (e) (Michie Supp. 2002); NEB. REV. STAT. § 43-162-165 (1999); N.M. STAT. ANN. § 32A-5-35 (Michie Supp. 2002); WASH. REV. CODE ANN. § 26.33.295(1) (1997); WIS. STAT. ANN. § 48.925 (West Supp. 2002). *See also* Samogye, *Opening Minds to Open Adoption*, 45 KAN. L. REV. 619 (1997). The statutes permit courts to enforce post-adoption visitation agreements, but generally do not allow them to order visitation absent agreement. Some statutes limit adoption agreements to foster care situations. All provide for enforcement only when visitation is in the child's interest, but few provide guidance as to when the child's interest is served. An exception is the Nebraska statute; it directs the court to consider whether the child lived with the birth parent for a substantial period and whether an attachment exists between the child and birth parent.

Many courts continue to adhere to the traditional view that, absent statutory authority, post-adoption visitation agreements can not be enforced because adoption terminates all parental rights. *See Matter of Adoption of Child by D.M.H.*, 641 A.2d 235 (N.J. 1994) (new adoption statute did not authorize the enforcement of visitation agreements). Without a statute or clear precedent, the parent who consents to adoption on condition that the adoptive parents agree to visitation may find courts unwilling either to enforce the visitation agreement or to rescind the adoption. This response encourages strategic behavior on the part of adoptive parents. Prospective adoptive parents may agree to visitation to secure a reluctant parent's consent, with the hope or expectation that it will not continue for long.

2. *Open Adoption by Court Order.* Should courts order post-adoption visitation by birth parents in the absence of agreement? Although open adoption agreements have met with a mixed judicial response, most appellate courts find no authority in trial courts to order post-adoption visitation without agreement. Perhaps courts conclude that without the agreement of the adoptive parents, the visitation will very likely *not* be in the child's interest. The Illinois Supreme Court held that a juvenile court exceeded its authority when, after terminating parental rights of the biological parents, it gave appointed guardians the power to consent to adoption on the condition that the adoptive parents agree to continue contact between the children and their parents. *In re M.M.*, 619 N.E.2d 702 (1993). A few appellate courts have found that trial courts have discretion to mandate open adoption. The Supreme Judicial Court of Massachusetts recently held that a new statute authorizing enforcement of post-adoption visitation agreements between biological and adoptive parents did not affect the previously-recognized equitable powers of the probate court to order post-adoption contact absent agreement. *In re Adoption of Vito*, 728 N.E.2d 292 (Mass. 2000).

Prior to the Supreme Court opinion in *Troxel v. Granville*, see Chapter 6, many courts ordered post-adoption visitation with grandparents and other relatives. This seems curious in light of their reluctance to award visitation to birth parents. Do you see differences in the contexts that might justify the different treatment? After *Troxel*, courts have recognized the constitutional constraints on ordering visitation over the objections of the adoptive parents. *See, e.g., J.S. & E.S. v. D.W. & J.W.*, 835 So. 2d 174 (Ala. 2001) (reversing post-adoption grandparent visitation award as violating parental rights, post-*Troxel)*. [This opinion was later reversed on the highly questionable ground that adoptive parents lack fundamental rights, because adoption is a statutory creation. *Ex Parte D.W. & J.W.*, 835 So. 2d 174 (Ala. 2002)].

3. *Open Adoption of Infants.* Is open adoption appropriate when mothers place infants for adoption? In this context, an important justification of open adoption is absent, because no established relationship exists between the mother and child. Thus, it may be questionable whether the child's interest is promoted. Moreover, the continued involvement of the mother with the child could be an ongoing disruption, undermining the ability of the adoptive parents and child to form a family. Adoptive parents, desperate for a child, might reluctantly agree to the condition of continued visitation as the only way to obtain the mother's consent. Nonetheless, this practice has increased in recent years and some observers advocate open adoption of infants as part of a healthy trend away from secretness in adoption — a trend that is also reflected in greater access to adoption records by adult adoptees and birth parents. *See e.g.* Appell, *Blending Families Through Adoption: Implications for Collaborative Adoption Law and Practice*, 75 B.U. L. REV. 997 (1995); Baron & Pannor, *Open Adoption*, in BRODZINSKY & SCHECTER (EDS.), THE PSYCHOLOGY OF ADOPTION 316 (1990). One study found that contact was more likely to be sustained in infant open adoptions than when older children are involved. Berry, et. al., *The Role of Open Adoption in the Role of Adopted Children,* 20 CHILD & YOUTH SERV. REV. 151 (1998). *See also* Haugaard, *Open Adoptions: Attitudes and Experiences*, 4 ADOPTION Q. 89 (2000) (reviewing open adoption studies showing that most adoptive families found this arrangement to have substantial benefits and did not regret choice). *See generally* Annot., *Postadoption Visitation by Natural Parent*, 78 A.L.R.4th 218 (1990); Bartlett, *Rethinking Parenthood as an Exclusive Status: The Need for Legal Alternatives When the Premise of the Nuclear Family Has Failed*, 70 VA. L. REV. 879 (1984).

The Uniform Adoption Act directs the court in stepparent adoptions to determine whether the visitation with the biological parent is in the best interest of the child, and visitation can be ordered over the objection of the adoptive stepparent and the custodial parent. The decision is based on several factors, including the child's preference; the length and quality of the child's relationship with the parent, the likely effect on the child of allowing the relationship to continue; and the likelihood that the parties will be able cooperate. U.A.A. § 4-113 (c).

[3] DEFECTIVE CONSENT AND THE REVOCATION OF CONSENT

If the birth parents' rights are not involuntarily terminated, adoption can proceed only if they consent or "relinquish" their rights. A relinquishment is a voluntary termination of parental rights, often to an agency, which then assumes parental rights and responsibilities. It may place the child for adoption or in a foster home or an institutional setting.

Rather than relinquish parental rights generally, the birth parents may instead consent only to adoption by particular persons. In private adoptions, the birth parents often know the adoptive parents and limit their consent to an adoption by that particular couple. A "blanket consent" to adoption that does not specify the adoptive home can sometimes be used in a private adoption, but many states permit blanket consents in agency adoptions only. The 1994 Uniform Adoption Act requires consent to adoption by a specific adoptive parent in private adoptions. § 2-406(b). Section 2-401(c) of the UAA also requires that a child of 12 years or more must consent to his/her adoption, although a court may dispense with the requirement. Many states have similar provisions.

The reporters are full of cases in which birth mothers seek to reclaim children after releasing them for adoption, by consent or relinquishment. Mothers sometimes succeed even though the release complied with all the statutory requirements. Consider the following materials.

VELA v. MARYWOOD

17 S.W.3d 750 (Tex. App. 2000)

YEAKEL, Justice. This case presents the question of how forthright a licensed child-placing agency must be with an unmarried, expectant mother who seeks its counsel prior to the birth of her child. . . .

In September 1997, Corina, then nineteen years of age and unmarried, learned she was pregnant. . . . Corina, still living with her parents, [had] completed two years at Austin Community College where she had earned high grades and was planning to attend Southwest Texas State University. [She] is a member of a strong, stable, and supportive family. . . [and] has volunteered at her church, with Big Brothers/Big Sisters. . .and with her eight-year-old sister's Brownie troop. . . . A neighbor who had lived next to the Velas for over twenty-one years said that Corina is the envy of all the mothers in the neighborhood.

In February 1998, this pregnant young woman sought counseling services from Marywood, a licensed child-placing agency. . . . She met with a Marywood counselor, Aundra Moore several times. . . [and] informed Moore that she wanted to place her child for adoption. . . . Moore told Corina that. . . . Corina's "wishes and requests" as to what type of family she would place her child with and what type of relationship she would have with her child after adoption would be "considered.". . .

On March 25, Corina and Moore discussed what Marywood terms an "open adoption," a process by which the birth mother expresses her criteria for adoptive parents. Corina requested a Mexican-American, Catholic couple who had no other children. She also told Moore that "she wanted to visit with the child after the adoption.". . .

Moore first showed Corina an "Affidavit of Voluntary Relinquishment of Parental Rights" (the "relinquishment affidavit") on March 30. Moore did not discuss the relinquishment affidavit with Corina and did not explain the meaning of the term "irrevocable"; rather, Moore simply "showed her the form" but did not give her a copy to take with her to study. . . .

Corina selected an adoptive couple at her next counseling session with Moore and had a face-to-face meeting with them on April 8. . . . The prospective adoptive parents met all of Corina's criteria and indicated their willingness to comply with post-adoption visits. Throughout Corina's counseling sessions, she and Moore discussed a "sharing plan," a standard practice of Marywood. A sharing plan ostensibly allows the birth mother to select the adoptive family, visit her child on a regular basis after the adoption, and exchange letters and pictures. . . . The adoptive parents . . . agree in writing with Marywood to conform to this arrangement. . . . [N]either Marywood nor the adoptive parents enter into any agreement with the birth mother. Marywood admits that aside from advocating that the adoptive parents abide by the plan, Marywood can do nothing if the adoptive parents decide, post-adoption, to disregard it. In fact, the executive director of Marywood admits that the sharing plan is an "empty promise". . . . Marywood never discussed the unenforceability of the sharing plan with Corina. . . .

Corina gave birth to a son on April 24. . . . Moore met with Corina on April 26 [and] told Corina that she "would always be able to visit her baby" and that her baby would always know that Corina was his mother. Corina cried throughout the one-and-one-half-hour visit. . . . The child was placed in foster care on April 27.

On April 28, Corina and her parents visited Marywood. Before the meeting, Corina was not aware that she was to sign the relinquishment affidavit then and was undecided as to whether she wanted to sign it. [After a two hour meeting]. . . . eventually, Corina signed the affidavit. During the meeting, and before Corina signed the relinquishment affidavit, Moore told Corina that she would "always be that child's birth mother and that with her sharing plan that she had with the adoptive family that she would have an opportunity to be in that child's life forever"; . . . that the baby would have "two mothers," "both of whom would have input into his life"; that Corina "would be able to see her son grow up". . . . Corina specifically asked what the agency could do to guarantee that she would have continual, post-adoptive visits with the child. Moore responded by "assur[ing] her that . . . the adoptive family has an adoption worker working with them and that they would encourage them to respect what she wished for in terms . . . of sharing and visits. . . ." According to Corina and her mother, these promises are what convinced Corina to sign the relinquishment affidavit. . . .

Before the April 28 meeting, Corina did not have a copy of the relinquishment affidavit and did not review it with her parents. Corina was crying when she signed the affidavit, but Moore testified that "it's very common to have tears." Moore asked Corina if signing the relinquishment affidavit "was what she wanted to do" and informed Corina that once she signed it, she "couldn't undo or take it back." Moore never told Corina that signing the relinquishment affidavit meant that she would "never have any legal rights to see [her] child." According to Corina, Moore told her that she would only be "giving up [her] guardianship of [the child].". . . Corina was not aware and no one informed her that she could have signed a second foster-care agreement to allow herself more time to make the final decision. Moore . . . never told Corina that she could seek legal counsel or another person's opinion. Marywood never revealed to Corina that the relinquishment affidavit could nullify the sharing plan that she believed would allow her a continuing role in her child's life. It is significant that the relinquishment affidavit was never mentioned to Corina until after she and Marywood had devised a sharing plan satisfactory to her. From that point forward, all of Corina's actions and decisions were founded on her belief in and reliance on the sharing plan.

The following day,. . . . Marywood filed a petition to terminate Corina's parental rights. On May 1, Corina was allowed to visit her son for one hour at Marywood. Later that day, Corina called Marywood. Exactly what was said in that phone call is disputed. Moore claims. . . . Corina never indicated that she wanted to terminate the adoption process. Corina claims that she told Moore that she "wanted [her] baby back" and that she "changed [her] mind." She asked if there was anything she could do, including hiring an attorney. Moore responded that there was nothing that could be done. . . . Moore [also] told Corina's mother that the relinquishment was "irrevocable and that it is signed and that there is no way to undo the document.". . .

On May 12, an associate judge recommended termination of Corina's parental rights. . . . Although Corina had that day retained counsel to contest the termination and adoption, the termination occurred before she could intervene. . . . Corina brings this appeal, arguing that (1) there was not clear and convincing evidence that she knowingly and voluntarily executed the relinquishment affidavit, and in fact the evidence shows that she did *not* execute it voluntarily. . . .

To set aside the affidavit, Corina had the burden to prove by a preponderance of the evidence that the relinquishment affidavit was executed as a result of some nature of wrongdoing, such as coercion, duress, misrepresentation, fraud, deception, undue influence, or overreaching. . . .

. . . . [The] court may order termination of the parent-child relationship if the court finds by clear and convincing evidence: (1) that the parent has: . . . (K) executed before or after the suit is filed an unrevoked or irrevocable affidavit of relinquishment of parental rights as provided in this chapter; . . . *and* (2) that termination is in the best interest of the child. . . . A termination decree is complete, final, irrevocable and divests for all time that natural right as well as all legal rights (except for the child's right to inherit). . . .

. . . . Corina argues that "no rational trier of fact could find . . . that the Affidavit of Relinquishment was executed voluntarily and knowingly, rather than as the result of misrepresentation, fraud, overreaching, and coercion.". . .

Corina argues that Marywood affirmatively misrepresented to her facts that induced her to sign the relinquishment affidavit. Specifically, Corina claims that the only reason she signed the relinquishment affidavit was that Marywood led her to believe that she had the right and would continue to play a significant role in her child's life after the adoption, would continue to have contact with her child, and was only giving up guardianship of her child. At the time they were made, these representations were either false or misleading because Marywood knew that Corina would have no legal right to enforce the sharing plan against the adoptive parents. And, because Marywood was in a close relationship with Corina as her counselor, it had a duty to fully disclose that the open-adoption arrangement had no legal effect. Corina also emphasizes that she was never given a copy of the relinquishment affidavit to bring home with her; Marywood never suggested she seek legal advice; and Moore was the only person who ever explained the relinquishment affidavit to her. Thus, Corina insists that she did not voluntarily and knowingly execute the relinquishment affidavit and that she signed only as the result of coercion, misrepresentation, fraud, and overreaching.

. . . . Silence can constitute a misrepresentation: "When the particular circumstances impose on a person a duty to speak and he deliberately remains silent, his silence is equivalent to a false representation. . . ." At common law, the word "fraud" refers to an act, omission, or concealment in breach of a legal duty, trust, or confidence justly imposed, when the breach causes injury to another or the taking of an undue and unconscientious advantage. . . . [T]his "legal duty" may exist if it is established that one has placed special confidence in another where the latter is bound, in equity and good conscience, to act in good faith and with due regard for the interests of the other; it can arise when special confidence is placed in someone thereby giving that person a position of superiority and influence. . . . In general, once a party undertakes to speak, that party assumes a duty to tell the whole truth. Common-law fraud includes both "actual" and "constructive fraud." . . . [C]onstructive fraud encompasses those breaches that . . . tend to deceive others . . . regardless of the actor's intentions. . . .

Overreaching is "tricking, outwitting, or cheating a person into doing an act which he would not otherwise have done.". . .

Marywood, by its own admission, is more than an adoption agency. It provides extensive parental-counseling services and advertises these services to the public. . . . Corina, in seeking counseling from Marywood, was reasonably entitled to rely fully and unconditionally on Marywood's representations. We hold that Marywood owed Corina a duty of complete disclosure when discussing adoption procedures, including any proposed post-adoption plan. Complete disclosure encompassed the obligation to tell Corina the entire truth about the ramifications of the sharing plan she had chosen with Marywood's help and to make her fully aware that it lacked legally binding effect. Marywood's duty springs from two sources. First, when Marywood made a partial disclosure to Corina about the post-adoption plan, it assumed the duty to tell the whole truth. . . . Second, the evidence conclusively establishes that Corina placed special confidence in Moore, who by virtue of the counseling relationship occupied a position of superiority and influence on behalf of Marywood; thus, Moore and Marywood became bound, in equity and good conscience, to act in good faith and with due regard to Corina's interests. . . . This Court has recognized that a "higher obligation is owed to certain groups because of their vulnerabilities.". . . A young unmarried mother considering placement of her child for adoption is clearly vulnerable and is owed that "higher obligation" when she confides in a maternity counselor.

. . . . To determine whether Corina has met her burden of conclusively proving that she did not sign the relinquishment affidavit voluntarily, we must first ascertain if the record contains any evidence to support the district court's finding to the contrary. Marywood argues that it discharged any duty it owed Corina and that there is ample evidence that Corina fully understood the relinquishment affidavit and wanted to proceed with the adoption. . .

Although the face of the affidavit reflects it was signed knowingly and voluntarily, we must consider the surrounding circumstances to determine if Corina's signature on the document was procured by misrepresentation, fraud, or the like. . . . Corina . . . signed and understood [the agreement] in the context of and in reliance on the post-adoption plan that she and Marywood created, a plan that Marywood now admits is an "empty promise." The evidence conclusively establishes that Corina wanted to proceed with the adoption *only* if she could have post-adoption visits with her child; there is no evidence to the contrary. . . .

There is no evidence . . . that Corina was ever told that the post-adoption plan could not be legally enforced. Marywood's words to Corina were at worst deceptive and at best vague. . . . Marywood was obligated to answer Corina's question directly and tell her that the agency could not guarantee post-adoption visits. Instead, in counseling Corina, Moore carefully selected her words and minced her explanation of the sharing plan with the result that Corina understood one thing while Moore meant another. Whether the incomplete disclosure was deliberate or inadvertent, it does not satisfy the duty of full disclosure that Marywood owed Corina.

. . . . We turn our attention now to [the] second hurdle: Has Corina established as a matter of law that the relinquishment affidavit was procured by fraud, coercion, overreaching, or misrepresentation?. . .

. . . . [W]e find conclusive evidence in the record that the relinquishment affidavit was wrongfully procured. Considering only Marywood's version of events, we conclude as a matter of law that its statements and omissions to Corina constituted misrepresentation, fraud, or overreaching. Marywood admits that it told Corina that "with her sharing plan . . . she would "always have a relationship with [the adoptive] family and with [her] child"; . . . that the baby would have "two mothers," "both of whom would have input into his life. . . ." Marywood never told Corina that she would not have any legal right to see her child after she signed the relinquishment affidavit, and even when Corina directly asked if Marywood could guarantee post-adoption visits, Marywood failed to give her a complete answer. Marywood's statements are misleading and stop short of complete disclosure. They are half-truths that would lead a reasonable person in Corina's circumstance to believe that she had a continuing right to see her child according to the terms of the sharing plan. . . . It is undisputed that Corina sought counseling from Marywood to aid her in the difficult decision of whether to keep her child. She was a young woman faced with a life-changing situation. She found comfort in and placed reliance on Marywood's counseling. We need not and do not determine whether Marywood deliberately misled Corina. At a minimum, Marywood's advice and counsel was incomplete. We hold that Corina conclusively established that the relinquishment affidavit was procured by misrepresentation, fraud, or overreaching and therefore was not voluntarily signed. . . .

NOTES

1. *Revocation Rules and Conflicting Policy Objectives.* Like the issue of waiver of parental consent, rules about revocation of consent by the birth parent raise difficult policy (and political) questions. The traditional approach was to permit revocation of consent until the adoption decree was final. *See* Annot., *Right of Natural Parent to Withdraw Valid Consent to Adoption of Child,* 74 A.L.R.3d 421, 435–37 (1976). In a famous case that led to a change in New York law, an educated, 32-year-old Columbian woman was allowed to revoke her consent to the adoption of her nonmarital child, after discovering that her affluent family would help her raise the child. *Scarpetta v. Spence-Chapin Adoption Serv.,* 269 N.E.2d 787 (N.Y. 1971). The court held that the biological mother must be allowed to revoke her consent "unless it is clearly established that she is unfit to assume the duties and privileges of parenthood." The adoptive parents then fled with the child to Florida, whose courts refused to enforce the New York decree. *Scarpetta v. DeMartino,* 254 So. 2d 813 (Fla. App. 1971), *cert. denied,* 262 So. 2d 442 (Fla.), 409 U.S. 1011 (1972). The traditional rule is rare today, but it is not extinct, and still governs in a few states. *See, e.g.,* TENN. CODE ANN. § 36-1-118(a) (1996); PA. CONS. STAT. ANN. tit. 23 2711 (c) (Purdon 2001).The Indian Child Welfare Act also gives a birth parent the right to revoke consent until the adoption is judicially finalized. 25 U.S.C.A. § 1913(c) (West 1983).

In recent years, the trend has been toward making consent irrevocable in a shorter period of time, and limiting the birth parent's opportunity to change her mind. The justification for this reform is that a short revocation period provides greater security to the adoptive family; constructing family bonds is difficult if the parents must deal with uncertainty about whether the child will be removed from them. New York law has changed to reflect this trend. Under the current statute, consent executed before a judge is immediately irrevocable; other consents become irrevocable 30 days after an adoption proceeding has commenced, unless the birth parent gives written notice of revocation during the 30 day period. N.Y. DOM. REL. LAW § 115 (McKinney Supp. 2003). Even a timely revocation triggers only an inquiry into whether the child's "best interests" lie in allowing the adoption or in returning the child to the birth mother, with no presumption that the birth parent should prevail. The 1994 Uniform Adoption Act is representative of this trend, providing that the birth parent must revoke consent within 8 days of the child's birth. § 2-404. Where consent is given before a judge it is immediately irrevocable. § 2-409. Beyond this point consent can only be set aside for fraud or duress. § 2-408(b); 2-409(b). Professor Joan Hollinger, the principal drafter of the Act defended the short revocation period as follows: "One of the greatest needs of adopted children, and one which this act promotes, is finality in adoption proceedings as expeditiously as possible consistent with due process." Andrews, *Cleanup of US Adoption Laws Irks Many Advocates for Children,* CHRISTIAN SCIENCE MONITOR Sept. 7, 1994 at 2.

The modern approach, although applauded by adoption advocates, has been criticized by some feminists and others concerned about the rights of unmarried mothers and of children. *Id.* These critics raise several concerns. First, it is argued that the modern approach favoring adoptive parents benefits middle class families, represented by powerful lobbying groups, at the expense of poor (often) single mothers, a relatively powerless group. Traditional law was based on the plausible assumption that mothers making decisions about adoption need special protection. They are making a difficult choice under very stressful circumstances, and they may be particularly vulnerable to coercion and overreaching. Further, advocates for birth mothers argue, in light of the evidence that many adopted children seek connection with their biological parents and struggle with issues of personal identity, maximizing the possibility that the birth-parent-child relationship can be maintained may serve the child's best interest. For discussion of the feminist perspective and criticism of the contemporary approach, represented by the Uniform Act, see Dowd, *A Feminist Analysis of Adoption*, 107 HARV. L. REV. 913 (1994) (reviewing Elizabeth Bartholet's FAMILY BONDS: ADOPTION AND THE POLITICS OF PARENTING (1993)).

2. *Revocation Policy and Children's Welfare.* An important, though often submerged, issue in this debate is whether adoption promotes children's welfare or itself contributes to adjustment problems in children. Adoption advocates point to the benefits that children gain from growing up in stable adoptive homes, while advocates for birth mothers claim that children adopted at birth are more likely to experience serious emotional problems than other children. The empirical evidence is incomplete, but it does not support the latter claim — particularly when adopted children are compared to children who grow up in single parent families. Although adopted children are more likely to experience mental health problems than children who grow up in intact families with their birth parents, many of the studies that have reached this conclusion have not separated children adopted as infants from those adopted later. The second group includes children who were removed from abusive parents, which may account for some of their emotional problems. Moreover, there is evidence that parents of adopted children are more likely to seek mental health treatment for their children than are other parents. Warren, *Lower Threshold for Referral for Psychiatric Treatment for Adopted Adolescents*, 31 J. AMER. ACADEMY CHILD & ADOLESCENT PSYCHIATRY 512 (1992). Several longitudinal studies have found that adopted children generally did better than children who were raised in single parent families. For a comprehensive review of the research, see Haugaard, *Is Adoption a Risk Factor for the Development of Adjustment Problems?* 18 CLINICAL PSYCHOL. REV. 47–69 (1998). One measure of welfare is income. According to the 2000 census, adopted children live in households with a higher median income ($56,000) than biological children ($48,000). *Adopted Children and Stepchildren: 2000,* U.S. Census Bureau, www.census.gov/Press-release/www/2003/cb03-130.html.

3. *What Constitutes Fraud, Duress or Coercion?* As the *Vela* court indicates, the birth parent's consent to adoption will only be set aside for fraud, duress or coercion. These defenses are not construed broadly; the birth mother may not be allowed to revoke her consent despite the fact that it was obtained under considerable pressure. For example, coercive influence to place the child that comes from the birth mother's own family generally will not be a basis for revocation. In *In re Baby Boy L.*, 144 A.D.2d 674, 534 N.Y.S.2d 706 (1988), the court rejected the revocation petition by a seventeen year old birth mother, whose mother told her that she could not continue to reside at home if she kept the baby. Moreover, it is not sufficient that the mother was persuaded that the child would be better off with the adoptive family. *See In re Adoption of E.W.C.,* 389 N.Y.S.2d 743 (Surr. 1976) (no revocation on duress ground where the adoptive father persuaded the mother to give the baby up).

Would the agency's conduct in *Vela* be sufficient for recission of a commercial agreement? If the mother was affirmatively misled by the agency as to the legal effect of her consent, then the misstatement, if reasonably relied upon, could amount to misrepresentation. Here non-disclosure was the basis of Miss Vela's misunderstanding about the meaning of the revocation document. In commercial contracts, full disclosure is usually not required, and non-disclosure can be the basis of an actionable misrepresentation claim only in limited circumstances. *See* RESTATEMENT (SECOND) OF CONTRACTS § 161. Under standard doctrine, the mother's unilateral mistake about the legal meaning of her consent embodied in an oral "side agreement" would be sufficient to set aside the contract only if the agency knows about the conditional nature of her consent and the non-disclosure amounts to a failure to act in good faith. § 161(B).

The court in *Vela* emphasized, however, that the adoption counselor had a special disclosure duty in light of her relationship to the birth mother and the young woman's vulnerable position. Under general contract doctrine, a duty to disclose arises where the parties have a relationship of trust. § 161(D). The *Vela* court could well have concluded that Ms. Vela could rescind her consent on the basis of undue influence. This basis for revocation can be invoked where a weaker party in a relationship of trust is subject to unfair persuasion by the dominant party. § 177. Other courts have recognized the vulnerability of pregnant women considering adoption and concluded that the adoption agency counselors may have special duties not usually imposed on contracting parties. *See e.g. Adventist Adoption & Family Servs. v. Perry,* 641 P.2d 178 (Wash. App. 1982) (mother was in unfamiliar environment with no independent counsel, and subject to pressure from adoption agency). For a case somewhat similar to *Vela,* in which revocation was allowed, see *In re Dunn,* 656 N.E.2d 1341 (Ohio App. 1995). There, the mother had relinquished her child to an agency under the mistaken belief that only her cousin could adopt the child, and that she would have visitation rights. The court concluded that the agency was aware of the mother's misconception, which was contrary to language of the relinquishment document.

In *Vela,* should it matter that the mother's desire to revoke consent was unrelated to the undisclosed fact that the "sharing plan" was not enforceable?

For general consideration of this topic, see Ely, *Natural Parents' Right to Withdraw Consent to Adoption: How Far Should the Right Extend?,* 31 J. FAM. L. 685 (1992/93); Note, *Rethinking Revocation: Adoption from A New Perspective,* 23 HOFSTRA L. REV. 733 (1995).

4. *Revocation as a Matter of Right.* In California and a few other states, birth parents have a more extensive right to revoke consent in independent adoptions than in agency adoptions. Under California law, if consent is given to a licensed agency, the relinquishment may only be set aside by mutual agreement. In an independent adoption, however, the period for revocation of consent by the birth parent is 30 days. CAL. FAM. CODE § 8814.5 (West 2002). This approach probably reflects some distrust of nonagency adoptions, and a concern that outside of the context of agency regulation and oversight, prospective parents may induce consent, and that mothers are more likely to regret the decision. However, the statutory revocation period has been reduced from 120 to 90 to 30 days over the past decade, suggesting that this distrust is waning. *See, e.g.* CAL. FAM. CODE § 8814.5 (West 1994). In the usual agency adoption, the adoptive parents must also endure a probationary period, which typically lasts six months. Nonetheless, their status is relatively secure (compared to adoptive parents who pursue independent adoptions under laws like that of California), for they are not subject to the second thoughts of the birth mother, whose relinquishment is final. They can lose the child generally only if their own behavior leads the agency to doubt its selection.

5. *Validity of the Minor Mother's Consent.* In most states, a minor parent can consent to adoption despite the ordinary contract rule allowing minors to avoid their agreements. Thus, for example, in *Baby Boy L, supra* note 3, the mother's youth was not an issue. *See, e.g., Norfolk Div. of Social Servs. v. Unknown Father,* 345 S.E.2d 533 (Va. App. 1986) (sustaining adoption order under statute validating minor mother's consent absent proof of "fraud and duress"). Nonetheless, consent of the minor mother's parents is also often sought, perhaps on the view that their participation may help defend against a later challenge based either on the minor's age, or on a claim that her age, along with other factors, suggests that the consent was not competent or voluntary. *See, e.g., Janet G. v. New York Foundling Hosp.,* 94 Misc. 2d 133, 403 N.Y.S.2d 646, 652 (Sup. Ct. 1978), in which the consent of a 17-year-old girl was upset where she "was alone and uncounseled, faced with a printed surrender form prepared by the state." The parents alone could not consent to adoption, of course, because their daughter's parental rights are constitutionally protected. Just as the mature minor has a constitutional right to choose an abortion, she almost surely has a right to decide whether to keep her child.

6. *Pre-Birth Consent.* The mother's pre-birth consent to adoption is not valid in any state. *See, e.g., Anonymous v. Anonymous,* 530 N.Y.S.2d 613, 139 A.D.2d 189 (1988). Indeed, some states provide that the consent may not be validly executed until some time after the birth. *See, e.g.,* ARIZ. REV. STAT. ANN. § 8-107(B) (West Supp. 2002) (72 hours); ILL. COMP. STAT. ANN. ch. 750, § 50/9 (West Supp. 2003) (72 hours); KY. REV. STAT. ANN. § 199.500 (Michie Supp. 2002) (72 hours); MASS. GEN. LAWS ANN. ch. 210, § 2 (West Supp. 2003) (4 days); OHIO REV. CODE ANN. § 3107.08(A) (Anderson 2003) (72 hours).

What explains this universal rule restricting the pregnant woman's freedom to commit to an adoption contract? The rule seems to presume that pregnant women, like minors under the infancy doctrine, are incapable of making competent self-interested contracting decisions. (Of course, as to pregnant women, the presumption extends only to this one kind of transaction.) Such a rule may be justified when a class of individuals is so vulnerable to overreaching that they need protection. Pregnant women may be particularly susceptible to influence, because the situation itself is coercive, in that *some* decision must be made, and all of the alternatives may seem to carry high personal costs. Consent to adoption may be induced by offers of money and medical treatment. Another concern might be that pregnant women cannot make informed competent decisions about adoption because they cannot predict how they will feel about the baby after it is born. Perhaps there is an underlying assumption that relinquishing a child is a decision that is "unnatural" for women, and every effort must be made to assure that it is voluntary, competent and informed. This view seems to underlie some arguments against gestational contracts. *See* Andrews, *infra* page 1322.

Can a pre-birth consent be ratified after the birth by actions of the consenting mother? In *C.M.S. v. Goforth*, 606 N.E.2d 874 (Ind. App. 1993), approximately two weeks before the birth, the mother signed a written consent to adoption by a particular couple. After the birth, she gave the child over to the couple's attorney, but then filed a writ of habeas corpus, seeking the return of the child and the revocation of her consent. The appellate court found that the statute, which provides that a "consent to adoption may be executed at any time after the birth of the child." requires that consent be given after the birth, but decided that pre-birth consent could be ratified by the mother's post-birth behavior.

PROBLEMS

Problem 11-3. Alice, an 18-year-old unmarried woman, living on her own, gave birth in early February. In August, she decided to give the child up for adoption. The procedure was explained to her, including the fact that the adoption itself is not final until six months after the adoption petition is filed. Alice thought this meant that she could get her baby back within six months, but did not express this belief to the agency's counselor. The counselor gave her the agency consent form, which she read. When asked, she responded that she understood the form, and then proceeded to sign it. The form contained no reference to the six-month period, and stated clearly that she surrendered all parental rights to the agency, "voluntarily and unconditionally," conferring upon the agency "absolute and unrestricted power . . . to consent to the adoption of the child without further notice to me."

The surrender took place on Aug. 15. On Sept. 1, the baby was placed in an adoptive home. On Sept. 4, Alice sought the baby's return. She was told that it was too late, and she then brought a habeas corpus action. What result?

Problem 11-4. Fred consults you about his 16-year-old daughter, Vicki, who recently gave birth to a baby girl. Fred is determined that Vicki give the child up for adoption, but in the six months since the birth, she has resisted. To put pressure on Vicki, he has refused to allow her to bring the child into their home. Vicki's cousin has been keeping the baby, and Vicki has spent time with the child there. Two months ago, Fred went to the cousin's house while Vicki was there and told Vicki that if she did not give the child up for adoption, she would have to leave home. Shortly thereafter, Vicki left home, but after a month of living by herself and caring for the baby, she concluded she could not cope on her own, and moved back in with her family. In the last month, Vicki has finally yielded, and Fred wants to start adoption proceedings now, before she changes her mind again.

The baby's father is an 18-year-old high school student of a different race than Vicki and you believe that Fred's intransigence is related to the child's bi-racial identity. You think it is possible Fred might never become reconciled to bringing this baby into the family. Since Vicki moved back home, the baby has been with the father's family. Fred believes the father will go along with whatever Vicki wants to do. What do you advise?

§ B. THE ROLE OF THE ADOPTION AGENCY

[1] AGENCY DISCRETION AND RELIGIOUS MATCHING

[a] Agency Control of the Adoption Process

Adoption agencies perform many critical discretionary functions in the selection and placement of children with adoptive parents. Agencies not only select the adoptive parents, they also typically certify their suitability in the judicial process that confirms the adoption. While a "social study" of the prospective adoptive family is commonly required before a court enters a final adoption decree, in agency adoptions the court typically relies upon the agency's investigation of the family to satisfy this requirement. Where the birth mother has relinquished her child to an agency, state law may require the agency's consent before the court can approve an adoption, effectively barring adoption by anyone not chosen by the agency. *See Fla. Dept. Of Children and Families v. Adoption of B.G.J.*, 819 So. 2d 984 (2002)(trial court lacks authority to reject appropriate placement by agency). The agency also makes arrangements for the care of the child until placement in the adoptive home.

Because there are many more adults seeking to adopt healthy (usually white) infants than there are available infants (see discussion below), agencies can be very selective in placing children. Thus, the criteria by which placement decisions are made become very important. It is not controversial for agency workers, in exercising discretion, to eliminate families with histories of abuse, alcoholism, or instability, but choosing among the many applicants who are basically qualified is more troublesome. Agencies may deal with the large number of suitable prospective parents by employing professional rules of thumb, such as excluding unmarried or single applicants, or applicants over the age of 40. *See*, Annot., *Age of Prospective Adoptive Parents as Factor in Adoption Proceedings*, 84 A.L.R.3d 665 (1978 & Supp. 2003). Other factors that may be important include health, income, stable employment history, marital stability and neighborhood quality. Sometimes efforts are made to "match" children with applicant families of similar physical stock and educational attainment as the child's birth parents, on the premise that the maturing child will fit in better with the family. And of course, agency workers will also make individual judgments about the prospective applicants. While such judgments are based upon the social workers' professional training and experience, they also are necessarily subjective.

Increasingly, the preferences of the birth parents have come to influence agency choices among prospective adoptive homes. This change in practice flows from the shortage of available infants, which has led to competition among agencies to gain placement authority over available infants. By deferring to the birth-mother's preference, agencies can also better compete with the alternative of an independent adoption, in which the birth mother can also select the adoptive parents.

Although adults who want to adopt a child may be frustrated by their exclusion under agency criteria, successful challenges of the agency's initial placement decision is relatively uncommon. Because the agency is expected to exercise judgment and discretion in its choice of adoptive home, there is usually little basis for judicial modification of the agency decision. In general, decisions are vulnerable to challenge only when agencies follow an announced rule employing constitutionally sensitive criteria, such as religion or race.

An agency's placement of a child in the intended adoptive home ordinarily occurs before the adoption is final. During this probationary period, the agency retains legal custody and may withdraw the child from the adoptive home if it concludes that the child's interests so require. Adoptive parents have had some success in challenging agency decisions to withdraw a placement once the child has been living with them. *See, e.g., In re Adoption/Guardianship No. 3598*, 1997 WL 625109, 437 Md. 295 (1997) (court refuses to remove the child born in Virginia from a "suitable home with caring parents" in Maryland, despite violation of Interstate Compact on Placement of Children, because such decision would penalize the only innocent party involved, the child); *In re Adoption of Michelle T.,* 44 Cal. App. 3rd 699 117 Cal. Rptr. 856 (Cal. App. 1st Dist. 1975) (where petitioners had custody of child, agency can not remove and deny adoption due to their ages — 70 and 54). Yet even here, if the agency offers evidence casting serious doubt on the suitability of the adoptive home, its decision will rarely be upset. *See, e.g., Marten v. Thies,* 99 Cal. App. 3d 161, 160 Cal. Rptr. 57 (1979) (prospective adoptive parents separated and agency social workers found mother to be adjusting poorly). Disappointed pre-adoptive parents have claimed agency liability for failure to complete an adoption, arguing breach of contract, negligence, infliction of emotional distress and violation of federal civil rights laws. *See* Annot., *Liability of Public or Private Agency or Its Employees to Prospective Adoptive Parents in Contract or Tort for Failure to Complete Arrangement for Adoption*, 5 A.L.R.5th 860 (1992).

[b] Religious Practice and Affiliation as Placement Criteria

Some criteria used by agencies in making placement decisions are controversial. One factor that has generated considerable litigation, including constitutional challenges, is the religious practice or affiliation of the applicants. The California Supreme Court considered this factor in a famous case involving orphans brought from Cambodia by an evangelical Christian relief organization. *Scott v. Family Ministries,* 135 Cal. Rptr. 430 (1976). This group, World Vision, transferred the children to a licensed California agency, Family Ministries, with instructions that they be placed in Christian homes. After providing medical and recuperative care to one child, Dr. Scott, together with his wife, sought to adopt him. Their application was turned down, on the ground that, as Episcopalians, they were not members of an evangelical Protestant church and thus were not qualified to adopt. The Scotts challenged this decision. The supreme court upheld the trial court order vacating the agency's adoptive placements. The agency, although private, was licensed under California law, with delegated state authority to take custody of children, investigate prospective parents, make decisions about placement, and report to the court. Thus, its actions are state action in the context of the Establishment Clause. For this reason, the court found that religion can only be a factor in the placement decision where the agency matches the child to adoptive parents who are of the same religious faith as the child's birth parents, or where it follows an expressed religious preference of the birth parent. This policy allows the state to retain neutrality while deferring to the right of parents to control their children's religious upbringing. Neither World Vision nor Family Ministries were the children's parents, despite their custodial role — and indeed, the children's parents likely were Buddhist. Thus, the religious criterion was unconstitutional.

As *Scott* suggests, consideration of the religious affiliation in the adoption decision is not categorically excluded. In the exercise of agency discretion, a well-established practice has been to honor the birth mother's preference as to the religious affiliation of the adoptive parents. In many states, "religious preference" provisions either allow or direct the agency to place children with adoptive parents professing the same religious affiliation as the mother, sometimes without regard to whether the mother has expressed this preference.

New York law includes the most comprehensive religious preference provisions. In the leading case of *Dickens v. Ernesto*, 30 N.Y.2d 61, 281 N.E.2d 153, 330 N.Y.S.2d 346, *appeal dismissed*, 407 U.S. 917 (1972), the Court of Appeals upheld the requirement that the agency place the child with adoptive parents of the same religion as the birth parent, if practicable, unless the birth parent affirmatively authorizes otherwise or expresses no religious preference. The court rejected the Department of Social Services refusal to accept applications of prospective adoptive parents with no religious preference. However, the appellate court found no Establishment Clause violation in the religious preference, because it was a relevant consideration in a placement decision made in the child's best interest, and it was only one of several factors taken into account. The preference also did not violate the petitioners' Free Exercise rights, even though it burdened applicants with no religious affiliation. Those applicants could adopt children whose birth parents expressed no religious preference or indicated that religious preference was not important to them. In another New York case, *Orzechowski v. Perales*, 582 N.Y.S.2d 341 (Sup. Ct. 1992), the child, aged 3, had been institutionalized since birth with spina bifida and other disabilities when the adoption application was filed by a Roman Catholic family who had been approved previously as suitable to adopt a child with a physical disability. The child's Jewish parents had released her for adoption, signing a "Declaration of Religious Preference," requesting that she be placed with a Jewish family. The agency declined to place the child with the petitioners, stating in a letter, "Save the issue of religion, we have no objection to placing Nelli in your home. . . (y)ou had impressed us as caring concerned individuals who are ready to provide a loving home for a child." 582 N.Y.S. at 344. The court held that because the preference was the only factor in the decision not to place the child with the prospective parents, it violated the Establishment Clause.

The rationale for honoring the birth parents' preference is premised upon the acknowledged right of parents to raise their child in the religion of their choice. Should parents who relinquish parental rights receive this protection? Particularly, one might question New York's extension of that premise to cases in which there is no expressed preference. As applied to those cases, another argument must be that the policy serves the child's welfare by giving her a sense of connection with her biological roots. Is this persuasive? Some courts have held that an agency may not employ a rule absolutely barring adoption applicants who practice no established religion, even though it may inquire into the applicants' religious practices as one piece of relevant data in a more general assessment of fitness. *See, e.g., In re Adoption of "E.",* 279 A.2d 785 (N.J. 1971) (otherwise qualified parents cannot be excluded solely because they do not believe in a "Supreme Being").

Religious preference laws have been criticized on constitutional grounds, as violating both the Establishment Clause and the Free Exercise Clause. They also have been challenged on policy grounds as contributing to delay in adoption placement. *Dickens* noted that the New York law imposed the matching requirement only where practical and consistent with the child's interests, and courts can rely upon such statutory language to permit adoptions that do not "match." Of course, agencies have a lot of discretion in deciding how extensively to search for matching parents, and how long to delay placement before they are ready to place children with non-matching parents. Professor Martha Minow observed that religious matching is "legally unacceptable if it produces delays and unequal treatment." *All in the Family and in All Families: Membership, Loving and Owing,* 95 W. Va. L. Rev. 275 (1993). *See also* Schwartz, *Religious Matching for Adoption: Unraveling the Interests Behind the "Best Interests" Standard,* 25 Fam. L.Q. 171 (1991); Horwitz, *Accomodation and Neutrality under the Establishment Clause: The Foster Care Challenge,* 98 Yale L.J. 617 (1989).

PROBLEM

Problem 11-5. Peggy O'Connor relinquishes her one-year-old son, Sean, to a public adoption agency in New York. While seeking an adoptive home, the agency places Sean in foster care with the Goldbergs, who become very fond of him. They apply to adopt, but are told that they will not be considered under an agency policy of placing children with adoptive parents who share the birth mother's religion, unless the birth mother instructs them otherwise. On the basis of this policy, the agency is considering only Catholic homes for Sean, and expects to place him in one shortly. In fact, no one at the agency has ever raised the question of the adoptive parents' religion with Peggy.

The agency tells the Goldbergs that they will be happy to consider them for the next Jewish child who becomes available for adoption, since the

Goldbergs appear to be well qualified. The Goldbergs will also be eligible to adopt a non-Jewish child if the birth parents have expressly indicated indifference as to the religion of the adoptive home. In the past five years, the agency has had one Jewish child available for adoption.

The Goldbergs come to you for help in adopting Sean. What do you advise?

THE BABY SHORTAGE AND INTERNATIONAL ADOPTION

The process of choosing who gets to adopt a child becomes critical if the number of families seeking to adopt greatly exceeds the number of children available. This is clearly true in the case of healthy Caucasian infants. The total number of adoptions in this category has declined significantly since 1970. In part, this is due to the availability of effective contraception and abortion, and in part to the fact that the percentage of unmarried white women who place their children for adoption has dropped (from 19% in 1972 to 3% in 1988). Stolley, *Statistics on Adoptions in the United States* in ADOPTION: THE FUTURE OF CHILDREN (1993). The percentage of African American women who place their children for adoption has always been low; African-Americans tend to be more positive in their attitudes about unmarried mothers, including teenagers, raising their children. *See* Lewin, *U.S. is Divided on Adoption, Survey of Attitudes Asserts*, N.Y. TIMES, Nov. 9, 1997 at 16 (reporting survey by Princeton Survey Research Assoc. indicating that 69% of blacks and 35% of whites approved of teenagers raising children themselves). Agencies have placed about 25,000 domestically-born infants each year. *Id.* at 29. The demand is much higher; according to one estimate, a half million Americans want to adopt children in any given year. For relevant statistics, see the National Adoption Information Clearinghouse website www.calib.com/naic/pubs/s_seek. cfm.

One result of the baby shortage is an increase in the adoption of foreign babies by American couples. Approximately 20, 000 children a year were admitted to the United States for adoption in 2001, up from 7000 in 1990. *See* IMMIGRATION AND NATURALIZATION SERVICE STATISTICAL YEARBOOK FOR 2001, 29 [online at www.immigration.gov/graphics/shared/aboutus/statistics/Yearbook2001.pdf]. Foreign adoptions amount to about 13% of all adoptions. At least 70 percent of these adoptions are handled by agencies; the remainder are transacted privately. Overall, about one half of all foreign-born adopted children are Asian, and Korea is the source of the most adopted children, with about 57,000 adopted Korean children in this country. *Adopted Children and Stepchildren: 2000,* U.S. Census Bureau [www.census.gov/Press-release/www/2003/cb03-130.html]. In recent years, however, the largest number of adopted foreign children have come from China and Russia, according to State Department statistics. *Immigrant Visas Issued to Orphans Coming into the U.S,.* Http://travel.state.gov/orphan_numbers.html. Under a 2001 Federal statute, children adopted from other countries by American citizens automatically become citizens. 8 U.S.C. Sect. 1101(b)(1) & (2).

While fulfilling some of the demand for children to adopt, these adoptions have underscored the potential problems in inter-country adoption. Many children have come with undiagnosed physical and psychological problems.

Talbot, *The Disconnected; Attachment Theory: The Ultimate Experiment*, May 24, 1998 N.Y.Times Magazine at 24 (describing attachment problems of Russian and Romanian adoptees). Moreover, there is some evidence that demand by Americans has created a black market in some countries, in which babies are sold by parents or procured through theft, fraud or force. *See, e.g.,* Marquez, *Transnational Adoption: The Creation and Ill Effects of an International Black Market Baby Trade*, 21 J. Juv. L. 25 (2000). The Hague Conference on Private International Law adopted the Hague Convention on Cooperation in Respect to Intercountry Adoption on May 29, 1993. In addition to providing for international recognition of adoptions, the Convention requires each signatory to designate a Central Authority to provide information to other Central Authorities and "eliminate any obstacles to . . . application [of the Convention]." The Central Authorities in the respective countries make reports about the suitability of the adoptive parents and the adoptive child for the adoption process. The United States has signed but not yet ratified the Convention. Ratification is expected in connection with the Intercountry Adoption Act of 2000. *See* pub.bna.com/fl/hr2909.pdf.

For commentary on intercountry adoption, see Strong, *Children's Rights in Intercountry Adoption: Towards a New Goal*, 13 B.U. Int'l L.J. 163 (1995); Carlson, *The Emerging Law of Intercountry Adoptions: An Analysis of the Hague Conference on Intercountry Adoption*, 30 Tulsa L.J. 243 (1994); Carro, *Regulation of Intercountry Adoption: Can the Abuses Come to an End?*, 18 Hast. Int. & Comp. L. Rev. 121 (1994).

[2] TRANSRACIAL ADOPTION

Should agencies place African-American or biracial children with white adoptive parents? This issue has continued to generate controversy over the years, and changing social attitudes have influenced both policy and agency practice. Consider the following material.

DEWEES v. STEVENSON

779 F. Supp. 25 (E.D. Pa 1991)

Waldman, District Judge. Plaintiffs seek to enjoin defendants from refusing to consider plaintiffs as adoptive parents for their foster child, Dante Kirby, and from taking him from the foster home on November 23, 1991 to participate in a National Adoption Center event to attempt to find prospective adoptive parents. Plaintiffs allege that defendants have refused to consider plaintiffs' request to adopt Dante because of their race and in so doing have violated the equal protection and due process guarantees of the Fourteenth Amendment. Plaintiffs also seek a declaration that defendants alleged refusal to consider plaintiffs as adoptive parents violates these Constitutional guarantees. . . .

I. FINDINGS

Plaintiffs are a white couple who have been married for 27 years and who reside in Royersford, Pennsylvania in an almost exclusively white area. Mrs.

DeWees is a high school graduate and housewife. Mr. DeWees is the maintenance manager for a trucking company. Plaintiffs have three natural children, ages 26, 23 and 21 years, and five grandchildren for whom they have cared.

Defendants are the Chester County, Pennsylvania Children and Youth Services Agency (CCCYS), its director and its adoption supervisor, Kay Thalheimer. In January of 1988, plaintiffs applied to CCCYS to be foster parents. During the ensuing review and evaluation process, Mrs. DeWees stated that she did not want to take any black foster children because "[she] did not want people to think that [she] or her daughter were sleeping with a black man." According to Mrs. DeWees, she gave this reason because she was reluctant to give her real reason which was her concern that she would not know how to take care of a black child. Plaintiffs requested for placement children under three years of age because they felt they "couldn't deal with children after three years old." CCCYS approved plaintiffs as foster parents and entered into a foster parents agreement with them on May 9, 1988. The agreement provides, inter alia, that CCCYS shall have all responsibility for planning for any foster child.

Pursuant to the agreement, CCCYS variously placed seven foster children with plaintiffs. They were from two to twenty months in age. Three were black and two were bi-racial. Plaintiffs never received any complaints from CCCYS about their care of any foster child. Plaintiffs' attitude about black children changed and they came "to accept them as any other child."

On November 10, 1989, CCCYS placed Dante Kirby, then two months old, with plaintiffs. Since August 20, 1991, Dante is plaintiffs' only remaining foster child. Plaintiffs understood that Dante's placement with them was not permanent. On three different occasions Dante was to be returned to his parents, but it did not work out as planned.

Dante's mother is white and his father is black. On November 12, 1991, with their consent, their parental rights were terminated by the Chester County Court of Common Pleas.

Plaintiffs have cared well for Dante. They provide him with his own room and interact frequently with him. He plays and interacts well with plaintiffs' grandchildren. They have supplemented the amounts provided by CCCYS for clothing and toys, and have provided Dante with medical care for his respiratory problems. There clearly is a bond of mutual affection between plaintiffs and Dante.

On June 13, 1991, after being advised by Dante's caseworker that Dante's mother and father intended to relinquish their parental rights, plaintiffs wrote to defendant Thalheimer to express an interest in adopting Dante. On July 18, 1991, defendant Thalheimer met with and interviewed plaintiffs for an hour and a half, and then referred them to Dr. Joseph Crumbley for further evaluation of their request to adopt Dante. On August 22, 1991, Dr. Crumbley interviewed plaintiffs at his office in Philadelphia for approximately two hours. Dante was present. In assessing plaintiffs' ability to raise and socialize a bi-racial child, Dr. Crumbley utilized the Workers' Assessment Guide for Families Adopting Cross-Racially and Cross-Culturally of the U.S. Department of Health and Human Services. Ms. Thalheimer is a social worker with

20 years of experience in the field of adoption. She has experience with transracial adoptions. She has placed bi-racial children with white, black and bi-racial adoptive parents respectively. She is white. Dr. Crumbley is a family therapist and consultant with a Ph.D. in social work. He is a consultant to three adoption agencies and among his areas of specialization are child abuse, foster care and adoption. He has experience with trans-racial adoptions. He is black.

Dr. Crumbley forwarded an evaluation and recommendation to Ms. Thalheimer on September 11, 1991. He concluded that although Dante was emotionally attached to plaintiffs, they would not be appropriate adoptive parents. . . . Dr. Crumbley was concerned about plaintiffs' responses that race had "no impact" on developing a child's identity and self-esteem, that addressing racial issues was not important in raising a minority child; and, that they would not prepare Dante to deal with racial discrimination but rather would address the problem if and when it occurred. He was also concerned about plaintiffs' lack of friends in and contact with the minority community, and Mrs. DeWees' statement that she would "not manufacture black friends." Dr. Crumbley concluded that plaintiffs lacked the ability to: be sufficiently sensitive to the needs of a bi-racial child during the critical period of socialization, self-identification and personality development of age two through six years; educate a minority child about prejudice and provide him with the skills effectively to respond to it; and, provide positive bi-racial and minority role models through interaction with the minority community.

Based on her interview and Dr. Crumbley's report, Ms. Thalheimer concluded that plaintiffs lacked the sensitivity to racial issues and inter-racial network of community resources needed properly to raise Dante. She decided not to grant plaintiffs' request to adopt Dante, and so advised them by letter of September 26, 1991.

Since receiving this letter, plaintiffs have a greater realization of the importance of the issues identified by Dr. Crumbley and are willing to undertake any course of action recommended by defendants to prepare to address the needs of a bi-racial child. They are willing to "grow and learn." They have located and are prepared to participate in a support group of trans-racial adoptive families.

In Dr. Crumbley's opinion, the only evidence adduced on the point, plaintiffs could learn to address Dante's race-related psychological and social needs with appropriate counseling, education and training but this would take a substantial period of time and Dante is now at a "critical" point.

The court has no expertise in the area of cross-racial adoption. Nevertheless, the court cannot accept Dr. Crumbley's view that generally only whites with extensive specialized training or who have experienced discrimination themselves will be able adequately to address the needs of a minority child in his or her formative years. The court does find that particular sensitivity, awareness and skills are necessary for a successful trans-racial adoption of a young child, and that Dr. Crumbley based his recommendation on his conclusion that plaintiffs had not demonstrated those qualities and could acquire them only over a long period.

Ms. Thalheimer did not refuse to consider plaintiffs as adoptive parents because of race or any other reason. Rather, she did consider plaintiffs' request to adopt Dante and decided not to grant it. Ms. Thalheimer is currently prepared to place Dante for adoption with any suitable couple, regardless of race, who appear to her to have the awareness, sensitivity and skills to address adequately the needs of a bi-racial child in his formative years. Her decision was based on the perceived best interests of the child, and not on the color of plaintiffs' skins.

II. CONCLUSIONS OF LAW

To sustain their due process claim, plaintiffs must show that they are being deprived of a federally secured right by persons acting under color of state law. . . . Defendants are clearly acting under color of state law. Foster parents do not have a cognizable liberty interest in maintaining a relationship with a foster child vis-a-vis prospective adoptive parents, particularly where the relationship is based on a contract under which the state retains responsibility for the child and places him in a foster home on a temporary basis. . . .

The essence of the equal protection clause is a requirement that similarly situated people be treated alike. . . . Racial classifications are inherently suspect and can survive an equal protection challenge only if they are necessary to achieve a compelling state interest. The state's responsibility to protect the best interests of a child in its custody is a compelling interest for purposes of the equal protection clause. . . . Because of the potential difficulties inherent in a trans-racial adoption, a state agency may consider race and racial attitudes in assessing prospective adoptive parents.

While the degree of plaintiffs' sensitivity and attitudes about racial issues may be related to their race and experience as whites in a white majority society, defendants refused their request to adopt a minority child because of perceptions about their attitudes and not their race. To the extent that perceived attitudes about race and coping with race-related problems motivated defendants' decision, this was Constitutionally permissible in determining the best interests of a young child eligible for adoption.

Plaintiffs have failed to establish on the record adduced and under applicable legal precedent and principles that their due process or equal protection rights have been violated.

III. CONCLUSION

The court has not found that plaintiffs are in any way unfit or could not acquire the knowledge and skills necessary to provide for Dante's future needs. Foster parents play a vital role in our society. They provide a welcome alternative to institutionalization of children without parents able or willing to care for them while the permanent placement process ensues. State agencies have a moral obligation to be sensitive to the position of foster parents who, particularly with extended placements, are likely to develop emotional bonds to the children placed in their homes. Ultimately, however, the state's responsibility to protect and pursue the best interests of children in its custody must take precedence.

This court is not empowered to sit as a super adoption agency review board. The court thus is not passing upon the wisdom of defendants' actions but only on whether they were motivated by Constitutionally impermissible considerations of race. The court has found that defendants made a considered judgment based on professional input and Constitutionally permissible factors.

This finding turns on the importance of awareness of and sensitivity to issues of race in the context of a trans-racial adoption. These factors, in turn, are important largely because of the realities of the larger society in which we live. As the court stated at the hearing on November 20, 1991, it is concerned that the very problems which give rise to race-related concerns may unintentionally be exacerbated by overemphasizing them. It is difficult to make race irrelevant, as it should be, if adoption and other social decisions are driven by racial considerations, however benign. In making adoption decisions, state agencies cannot ignore the realities of the society in which children entrusted to them for placement will be raised, or the affect on children of those realities as documented by professional studies. The court would hope, however, that these agencies also will be mindful of the possibility that an overemphasis on racial issues may retard efforts to achieve a color blind society, and of the need to avoid even the appearance that an adoption decision may have been based on race per se.

NOTES

1. *Race as a Factor in Adoption.* According to a 2000 U.S. Census report, 20% of adopted children live with adoptive parents of a different race from their own. *Adopted Children and Stepchildren: 2000,* U.S. Census Bureau, www.census.gov/Press-release/www/2003/cb03-130. html. Over the past half century, the question of what role race should play in the adoption decision has been the most controversial issue in adoption policy. In the 1950's, transracial adoption was rare; segregation prevailed in adoption placement as in other areas. During the 1960's civil rights movement, transracial placement was viewed by many as an expression of commitment to racial integration and to a "colorblind" society. The growing importance of racial identity to black Americans, however, was reflected in opposition to transracial adoption. In 1972, the National Association of Black Social Workers (NABSW), in a position statement strongly opposed the practice, which it characterized as a form of genocide. This statement and other opposition has had a substantial impact on adoption policy, generating an intense debate (which continues today) about the extent to which race should be a factor in adoption. The number of transracial adoptions has declined dramatically since the early 1970's. This trend may change in the future, however, in response to recent Federal legislation limiting the freedom of agencies to use race matching as a placement factor. *See* note 3 *infra.*

Prior to the recent changes in Federal law, many agencies applied a rule giving a preference to placing a child in a home where the parents will share the child's racial identity. One critic of race matching policies described standard agency practice in the following way: "children should be placed inracially 'if possible' and transracially 'only if necessary.' " Elizabeth Bartholet, *Where Do Black Children Belong? The Politics of Race Matching in Adoption,* 139 PA. L. REV. 1163 (1991). The agency mandate is to make placements which will further the child's interests, and courts have been reluctant to limit consideration of racial factors in making that judgment, so long as the agency did not follow an absolute rule barring parents of another race. In *In re Adoption No. 2633,* 646 A.2d 1036 (Md. Ct. Spec. App. 1994), for example, the court rejected the challenge by white foster parents who had cared for an African American child from birth, of an agency decision granting adoption to an African American couple who had also adopted the child's brothers. Although the court was critical of the agency for trying to create negative evidence about the foster parents, who had given the child excellent care, it concluded that the agency could consider race, particularly given that the child's sibling ties would be maintained through the adoption by the black couple. *See also Tallman v. Tabor,* 859 F. Supp. 1078 (E.D. Mich. 1994) (consideration of race as one of several factors does not violate Equal Protection Clause); *In Petition of R.M.G.,* 454 A.2d 776 (D.C. App. 1982) (consideration of race permitted); *Drummond v. Fulton City Dep't of Family & Children's Servs.,* 563 F.2d 1200 (5th Cir. 1977) (en banc) (same). *See Zitter,* Annot. Race as a Factor in Adoption Proceedings, 34 A.L.R. 4th 167 (2000). Use of race as the *sole* factor in the adoption placement has been found to violate the Equal Protection Clause. *See e.g. In re Moorhead,* 600 N.E. 2d778 (Ohio App. 1991).

Until recently, some states included a same-race preference among statutory adoption criteria. *See* MINN. STAT. ANN. §§ 259.255, 259.28. (West 1996) (preference for adoptive parents of same race; if not possible, to parents who are "knowledgeable and appreciative of the child's racial or ethnic heritage"). *See In re D.L.,* 479 N.W.2d 408 (Minn. App. 1991); *affd* 486 N.W.2d 375 (Minn. 1992)(striking down statute applying racial preference only to children of minority racial heritage); Ark. Code Ann. § 9-9-102 (Michie 1993). However, such statutes now conflict with federal law, and have typically been amended and racial preferences deleted. ARK. CODE ANN. § 9-9-102(b) (Michie 2002); MINN. STAT. ANN. § 260.181 (West 2002). *See* note 3, *infra.*

How can race-matching policies, which explicitly use race as a classification, be reconciled with the constitutional prohibition against racial discrimination, particularly in light of the Supreme Court's opinion in *Palmore v. Sidoti,* 426 U.S. 429 (1984) (reprinted in Chapter 6)? Remember *Palmore* held it unconstitutional for a trial court to take race into account in modifying a custody order when a Caucasian custodial mother married a black man. The Court suggested that even if the child might suffer because of the reactions of others, race could not be considered. "[T]he problems racially mixed households may pose for children . . . can[not] support a denial of constitutional rights." For a provocative argument that adoptive parents' racial preferences for children of the *same* race should be excluded, see Banks, *The Color of Desire: Fulfilling Adoptive Parents' Racial Preferences Through Discriminatory State Action,* 107 YALE L.J. 875 (1998).

Courts have assumed that race-matching policies are permissible as an exception to the general constitutional prohibition of racial classification —

as long as race is not the exclusive factor. One rationale is that the policy is permissible on affirmative action grounds, because it benefits members of victimized groups and is designed to remedy the effects of past discrimination. The Supreme Court's affirmative action decisions offer little guidance on whether race-matching could be justified under this theory. *See Grutter v. Bollinger*, 2003 U.S. LEXIS 4800 (upholding law school policy considering race as admissions factor to promote diversity). *But see Gratz v. Bollinger*, 2003 U.S. LEXIS 4801 (striking down undergraduate admissions policy that using point system and adding points to minority applicants); *Adarand Constructors v. Pena,* 115 S. Ct. 2097 (1995) (holding federal affirmative action program benefitting minority small businesses to strict scrutiny). Professor Elizabeth Bartholet, *supra*, has argued that race-matching, by creating delay in adoption of black children, harms members of a racial minority group, and thus, even a court open to affirmative action claims should reject these policies. *See also* ELIZABETH BARTHELOT, NOBODY'S CHILDREN: ABUSE AND NEGLECT, FOSTER DRIFT, AND THE ADOPTION ALTERNATIVE (1999).

2. *Race-Matching and the Child's Best Interest.* The use of race as a factor in adoption is primarily justified on the ground that the black child's interest will be promoted by placement with parents of the same race. Several benefits could result from such a placement. First, African-American parents may be in a better position to inculcate racial identity and pride. African-American children whose adoptive parents are white may experience unique identity issues. Many believe that white parents will not understand the experience of being black, and that black children will not be able to identify with their adoptive parents or to develop their own identity based on their genetic heritage. They may feel isolated and different from those around them because they lack the security of belonging to a community of people like themselves.

The debate about transracial adoption focuses on whether black children growing up in white families can develop a positive racial identity — and what that concept means. Few would disagree that black children should grow up feeling positive about being black. However, many supporters of race-matching take a stronger normative stance, arguing that it is essential for African American children to grow up identifying with black culture and that this can only happen in a black family. For an analysis of the meaning of racial identity in this context, see Forde-Mazrui, *Black Identity and Child Placement: The Best Interests of the Child and Biracial Children*, 92 MICH. L. REV. 925 (1994). Forde-Mazrui argues that a positive racial identity need not be a strong racial identity, and that white parents can teach their children to value their racial identity. White parents can also inculcate black culture, Forde-Mazrui argues, although probably not as capably as black parents. In a provocative challenge to racial separationism in sex, marriage and adoption, Randall Kennedy advocates that individuals should be allowed to determine their own racial identities and opposes race matching for "assign[ing] children a permanent racial identity." RANDALL KENNEDY, INTERRACIAL INTIMACIES: SEX, MARRIAGE, IDENTITY AND ADOPTION (2003). Kennedy challenges the empirical basis of claims that white parents can not contribute to the development of racial identity in black children.

Placing black children with black adoptive parents is also important, advocates argue, because only black parents can help develop coping skills to deal with the racial discrimination the child will inevitably confront growing up in American society. Although it is not generally argued that parents must themselves have experienced the difficulties that their children will face to help them deal with these difficulties, advocates of race-matching argue that this is the case here. Moreover, removed from the security of the black community, an African American child growing up in a white home and neighborhood may experience even more discrimination than she would in a black family. Perry, *The Transracial Adoption Controversy: An Analysis of Discourse and Subordination*, 21 N.Y.U. REV. OF L. & SOC. CHANGE 33 (1993-94) (describing the importance of "survivor skills" from the "color and community conscious" perspective of opponents of transracial adoption). *See also* Howe, *Redefining the Transracial Adoption Controversy,* 2 DUKE J. GENDER L. & POL'Y 131 (1995) (arguing that policies must be redefined toward facilitating adoption in the black community). How does such an argument apply in a case like *DeWees*, where the child is biracial? *See* Forde-Mazrui, *supra.* There is some evidence that biracial children are not fully accepted in the black community, although there is a tendency, as *DeWees* demonstrates, to assume that these children are indistinguishable from African Americans. *See* Brown, *Biracial Identity and Social Marginality*, 7 CHILD & ADOL. SOC. WORK 333 (1990).

Race matching policies in adoption are also justified under a collective "group rights" theory. If large numbers of African American children are adopted by white families, many will grow up lacking a black racial identity. As a result, the African American community will be diminished and its future will be threatened. This kind of concern underlies the 1972 position statement of the National Association of Black Social Workers, which states, "We . . . have committed ourselves to . . . work to end this particular form of genocide." This theme of minority group rights is powerfully endorsed by the Supreme Court as applied to Native Americans, in its interpretation of the Indian Child Welfare Act in *Mississippi Band of Choctow Indians v. Holyfield,* 490 U.S. 30 (1989) (*see* discussion *infra*). It also received recognition in *Yoder v. Wisconsin* (*see* Chapter 10). *See* Perry, *supra* (describing the stake of the black community in transracial adoption); Howe, *supra*; Townsend, *Reclaiming Self Determination: A Call for Intraracial Adoption*, 2 DUKE J GENDER L. & POL'Y 173 (1995) (describing transracial adoption as the black community's loss of its children).

Proponents of transracial adoption argue that race matching does not promote the interests of children needing adoptive parents. An important concern is that a race matching policy delays permanent placement of African American children and in some cases results in children remaining in foster care limbo for many years. Black children wait on average twice as long as white children for permanent homes, in part because the pool of African American prospective adoptive parents is not large enough to absorb the black children who need adoptive homes (and it is proportionately far smaller than the pool of white prospective parents). Rosettenstein, *Trans-Racial Adoption and the Statutory Preference Scheme: Before the "Best Interests" and After the "Melting Pot,"* 68 ST. JOHN'S L. REV. 137, 142 (1994). Can more black adoptive parents be found for these children? Because of lower income levels and lower proportions of two-parent families, fewer black applicants than whites qualify under traditional agency standards, but agencies now often relax those standards in order to place black children in African American homes. In addition, the use of subsidized adoption can reduce the income problem. The problem is one of a shortage of available black homes rather than a plethora of black children, since unmarried black mothers do not tend to give their children up for adoption. Richie, *The Adoption Story,* AMERICAN DEMOGRAPHICS, March 1986, at 42, 44. A strict race-matching policy can cause additional harm, as suggested by the facts of *DeWees.* Children's lives and family bonds are disrupted when they are taken from white foster parents with whom they have lived for years but who are not permitted to adopt. Remember, the agency in *DeWees* had no other family in mind when it concluded that the DeWees' were not satisfactory adoptive parents for Dante, despite the acknowledged bond between the foster parents and the child. Thus, delay in permanent placement was inevitable as was disruption of the existing family bonds.

Critics of race-matching also argue that the empirical research indicates that transracial adoptions are generally successful, and that, for most African American children in white families, the racial differences do not have harmful effects. In large part, this is true, although the evidence is not completely unambiguous. Several studies have compared black children adopted by white families with other adopted children. A longitudinal study, which followed black children adopted into black and white families for 13 years, reported somewhat more behavioral and academic problems in the transracial group, but the overall adjustment of children in the two groups was comparable. This study found no differences between the two groups in racial identity — in both groups it was strong — and found that the transracial adoptees felt more comfortable with both blacks and whites than did the children in black families. SHIREMAN, GROWING UP ADOPTED: AN EXAMINATION OF MAJOR ISSUES (1988). The largest and most extensive longitudinal study of transracial adoption involved 366 children and compared black and other minority children in white families with white adopted children and white birthchildren over a 12 year period. The researchers found that all three groups of children were similarly integrated into their families. There were no significant differences in self esteem. Of the 18 transracially adopted children who were experiencing serious problems in the final stage of the study, the researchers concluded that only one was race-related. In the remaining 78 families of transracially adopted children, the children in adolescence and young adulthood (many of whom were finishing college and starting families) were fully committed to their adopted families. SIMON & ALSTEIN, ADOPTION, RACE AND IDENTITY (1992); SIMON AND ALSTEIN, TRANSRACIAL ADOPTEES AND THEIR FAMILIES (1987). *See also* VICTOR GROZE, SUCCESSFUL ADOPTIVE FAMILIES: A LONGITUDINAL STUDY OF SPECIAL NEEDS ADOPTION, 6 (1996) (describing research on transracial adoption).

One supporter of transracial adoption argues that the dissimilarity in appearance between the child and adoptive parents is beneficial, contrary to conventional wisdom. Swize, Note: *Transracial Adoption and the Unblinkable Difference: Racial Dissimilarity Serving the Interests of Adopted Children,* 88 VA. L. REV. 1079 (2002). Swize argues that the dissimilarity will help the child to accept both her racial and adoptive identity, and will give her the freedom to develop as an individual.

3. *Congressional Action on Race-Matching.* In the 1990s, Congress intervened to limit the use of race as a factor in adoption. In 1996, Congress prohibited agencies that receive federal funding from delaying or denying adoption on the basis of the race or ethnicity. (Pub. L. No. 104-188, § 1808(a)(3)). This law replaced an earlier more flexible statute, the 1994 Multi-Ethnic Placement Act (MEPA), that discouraged delay, but allowed consideration of race and of the capacity of the adoptive parents to meet the needs of a child of a minority race. 42 U.S.C.A. § 5115a (1994)). The impact of this Federal law is not yet clear. It does not prohibit the use of race as a factor in the adoption decision, so long as it does not result in delay in the placement or serve as the basis for rejecting prospective adoptive parents. It is also not clear whether, under the new law, agencies can consider the adoptive parents' racial and cultural sensitivity and capacity to develop positive racial identity in the child. For example, would *DeWees* be decided differently in light of the Federal statute, given the concerns about the couple's racial attitudes? One court, in a contest between white foster parents and relatives of the African American child, held that race could be considered in evaluating the child's interest in "development, . . .continuity and stability." *In re Shyina B.*, 752 A.2d 1139 (Conn. App 2000). *See also In re Infant Child J.*, 994 P2d 279 (Wash. App. 1999) (upholding consideration of race as factor in adoption choice between two sets of parents; delay in adoption was not caused by race). A Massachusetts court announced that MEPA restricts agencies, but not courts, in considering race as a factor in adoption. *Adoption of Vito*, 712 N.E.2d 1188 (Mass. App. 1999). For a discussion of the statute, see JOAN HOLLINGER, A GUIDE TO THE MULTI-ETHNIC PLACEMENT ACT OF 1994, AS AMENDED BY INTERETHNIC ADOPTION PROVISIONS OF 1996 (1998); Campbell, *Taking Race Out of the Equation: Transracial Adoption in 2000*, 53 S.M.U. L. REV. 1599 (2000) (arguing that the statute has many loopholes that allow consideration of race in adoption); *Recent Legislation — Transracial Adoption — Congress Forbids Use of Race as a Factor in Adoptive Placement Decisions*, 110 HARV. L. REV. 1352 (1997).

4. *Hard-to-Place Children.* Even today, minority children may be hard to place because of agency concerns about transracial adoption. Older children, who often come from families with a history of abuse or neglect, and handicapped children are also hard to place, because most potential adoptive parents want healthy infants. Various programs promote placement of "hard-to-place" children. Agencies may be more flexible in considering single-parent families, older parents or other placements which depart from conventional requirements. Special efforts may be made to recruit adoptive parents, offering adoptive parent financial assistance to provide for their adopted children. This allows the agency to consider families whose income levels might otherwise disqualify them; it also provides resources to help with the unusual expenses which may be incurred in caring for a child with special problems. Policy analysts have long argued that subsidized adoption not only provides a beneficial placement for the child, but it can also save the state money in many cases, because the cost of the subsidy will be less than the cost of maintaining the child in an institution or foster family. *See* Watson, *Subsidized Adoption: A Crucial Investment,* 51 CHILD WELFARE 220 (1972)

Subsidized adoption programs require appropriations, of course. The Adoption Assistance and Child Welfare Act of 1980, 42 U.S.C. § 1305, which amended Title IV of the Social Security Act, established federal involvement in monitoring, delivery and financing of state-subsidized foster care and adoption programs. *See* Bussiere, *Federal Adoption Assistance for Children with Special Needs,* 19 CLEARINGHOUSE REV. 587 (Oct. 1985). The nation-wide adoption assistance program, permanently authorized under Title IV-E of the Social Security Act, 42 U.S.C.A. § 673 (West 1997), is an open-ended entitlement system contributing federal matching funds to states that provide adoption assistance payments to parents who adopt children with special needs. Data gathered by HHS showed that in 2002, 348,700 special needs children were receiving assistance under Title IV-E each month. DEPARTMENT OF HEALTH AND HUMAN SERVICES, ADMINISTRATION FOR CHILDREN AND FAMILIES, FY 2004 BUDGET JUSTIFICATIONS. Courts have held that this assistance is not available for special needs children who are privately adopted. *See, e.g., Glanowski v. N.Y. Dept. of Family Assistance,* 225 F. Supp. 2d 292 (W.D.N.Y. 2002). Parents adopting both special needs and other children receive a $10,0000 federal income tax credit to help them defray the costs of the adoption process. Public Law 107-16 (Sect. 202) (HR 1836)(2001). Another federal law intended to facilitate adoption is the 1997 Adoption and Safe Families Act, Public Law 105-89 (1997), which provides payments to states for special needs adoptions. *See generally* on this subject, McKenzie, *Adoption of Children with Special Needs* in THE FUTURE OF CHILDREN: ADOPTION 62 (Spring 1993).

THE INDIAN CHILD WELFARE ACT OF 1978

In 1978 Congress enacted the Indian Child Welfare Act, which was designed specifically to reduce the incidence of transracial adoption of Native American children. During much of the 1960s, many Indian children were placed in white homes, partly as a result of the Indian Adoption Project. Although one investigator reported that the program was successful for the children (FANSHEL, FAR FROM THE RESERVATION (1972)), opposition from Indian activist groups was intense. The political challenge was a response to both the large number of Native American children who were adopted by whites, losing touch with their Indian heritage, and to the readiness of state courts to terminate the parental rights of Native American parents. Advocates argued that white social workers and judges were contemptuous of Indian culture, or at best evaluated Indian parents without an understanding of Indian traditions as reflected in domestic life and child rearing. The result was "wholesale removal" of Indian children from their homes. These practices threatened the survival of the tribes themselves. As one tribal chief testified at the Senate hearings:

> Culturally the chances of Indian survival are significantly reduced if our children, the only real means for the transmission of the tribal heritage, are to be raised in non-Indian homes and denied exposure to the ways of their People. . . . Probably in no area is it more

important that tribal sovereignty be respected than in an area as socially and culturally determinative as family relationships. (Testimony of Calvin Isaac, *Hearing on S. 1214 before Senate Select Committee on Indian Affairs* (1977)).

The Indian Child Welfare Act of 1978, 92 Stat. 3069, codified in large part at 25 U.S.C. § 1901 et seq. (1983), sought to remedy this problem through both jurisdictional and substantive reforms. The Act overrides conflicting state adoption laws insofar as Indian children are concerned. In pursuit of its express objective of both promoting the welfare of Indian children and preserving the stability of Indian tribes § 1902, the statute gives tribal courts exclusive jurisdiction over the adoption of Indian children living on a reservation, displacing the jurisdiction of state courts. § 1911. For Indian children not domiciled on a reservation, tribal courts have concurrent jurisdiction, but in foster care placement or termination of parental rights cases, either the tribe or the Indian parent can petition and have the case transferred to tribal court. In placing Indian children for adoption, the Act creates a statutory preference for (1) members of the child's extended family, (2) members of the tribe, or (3) other Indian families. § 1915. The Act also creates a statutory rule allowing an Indian parent to revoke consent to adoption at any time prior to the entry of the final adoption decree, thus preserving, for Indian adoptions, a rule that otherwise has been disappearing, see section A3, *supra,* and overriding contrary state law limiting the birth mother's right to revoke, *e.g., Appeal in Pima Cty. Juvenile Action No. 5-903,* 635 P.2d 187 (Ariz. App. 1981); *Adoption of K.L.R.F.,* 515 A.2d 33 (Pa. Super. 1986), *appeal dismissed as moot,* 533 A.2d 708 (Pa. 1987). Parental consent can be set aside for up to two years after entry of the adoption decree where fraud or duress can be shown. § 1913. Finally, the Act contains many provisions applicable to foster care placements and the termination of parental rights, which make such terminations more difficult and which channel removed children to Indian families. For example, termination of parental rights requires a determination, proved beyond a reasonable doubt, and supported by qualified expert witnesses, that the parent's continued custody is likely to result in serious emotional or physical damage. § 1912 (f). There has been some debate over whether the Act's displacement of state law is constitutional, although in general the Act has been sustained. *See, e.g., Guardianship of D.L.L. & C.L.L.,* 291 N.W.2d 278 (S.D. 1980).

For some time, there was also doubt about the extent to which the Act in fact displaced state court jurisdiction in favor of tribal courts, but these doubts were largely resolved in *Mississippi Band of Choctaw Indians v. Holyfield,* 490 U.S. 30 (1989), *rev'g* 511 So. 2d 918 (Miss. 1987). Under the Act, tribal courts have exclusive jurisdiction over Indian children "domiciled" on the reservation. When an Indian mother domiciled on the reservation gives birth to a child off a reservation, does the child assume the mother's reservation domicile, or the off-reservation domicile of the place where she is born? Most courts held that the Act required them to yield jurisdiction to tribal courts, even if the mother had left the reservation for the purpose of relinquishing the child to non-Indian adoptive parents. *See In re Halloway,* 732 P.2d 962 (Utah 1987). Some courts, such as the Mississippi Supreme Court in *Holyfield,* concluded otherwise.

Holyfield involved twin Native American babies who were born to an unmarried Indian mother. Both parents were members of the Mississippi band of Choctaw Indians and were domiciled on a reservation. The children were born 200 miles from the reservation, and both parents signed a consent-to-adoption form within 2 weeks of the birth. The Holyfields, who were not Indian, quickly petitioned for adoption, and the final adoption decree was signed shortly thereafter. Two months later the Tribe petitioned to set the adoption decree aside on the ground that the children were domiciliaries of the reservation, and thus the tribal court had exclusive jurisdiction. The Mississippi Supreme Court concluded that such a child is not domiciled on the reservation and that state courts therefore retain jurisdiction.

In reversing the Mississippi Supreme Court, the United States Supreme Court concluded that Congress intended a uniform national rule of jurisdiction in these cases, rather than making the definition of domicile dependent on state law. This was clear, in the Court's view, because the purpose of the Act was to protect Indian families and tribes from state authority, a purpose that would be undermined if state law could determine the key jurisdictional provision. In defining the meaning of domicile, the Court emphasized that the common law rule was that the child assumed the domicile of its parents (or, in the case of a nonmarital child, its mother), and that application of that common law rule here was particularly appropriate since it is consistent with the Congressional purpose of expanding exclusive tribal court jurisdiction. In what is perhaps the most interesting part of the opinion, the Court was unimpressed by the fact that the parents had voluntarily relinquished their parental rights, and indeed, had gone to great lengths to give birth to the twins off the reservation so that the Holyfields could adopt them. The Court concluded that Congress's purpose was to protect tribal sovereignty over children born to reservation domiciliaries, even where the child's parents seek to avoid tribal authority to facilitate a non-Indian placement of their child. In short, tribal authority trumps the interests of Indian families where the two are in conflict.

> "Tribal jurisdiction under § 1911(a) was not meant to be defeated by the actions of individual members of the tribe, for Congress was concerned not solely about the interests of Indian children and families, but also about the impact on the tribes themselves of the large numbers of Indian children adopted by non-Indians. . . . In addition, it is clear that Congress' concern over the placement of Indian children in non-Indian homes was based in part on evidence of detrimental impact on the children themselves of such placement outside their culture. Congress determined to subject such placements to the ICWA's jurisdictional . . . provisions even in cases where the parents consented to an adoption, because of concerns going beyond the wishes of individual parents. As the 1977 Final Report of the congressionally established American Indian Policy Review Commission stated, in summarizing these two concerns, "[r]emoval of Indian children from their cultural setting seriously impacts long-term tribal survival and has damaging social and psychological impact on many individual Indian children." *Id.* at *1608–09.*

A dissent by Justice Stevens, joined by Justices Rehnquist and Kennedy, would have protected the choice of individual Indian parents by allowing them to choose an off-reservation domicile for their children by intentionally giving birth off the reservation with that purpose. For a criticism of *Holyfield's* emphasis on domicile, see Note, *The Role of Domicile in Adopting Indian Children: Mississippi Band of Choctaw Indians v. Holyfield*, 1990 UTAH L. REV. 899.

One issue that has been the subject of controversy (and litigation) since *Holyfield* is whether the ICWA only applies to children who are part of an "existing Indian family," from which they are being removed. The argument for the "existing Indian family" rule is that Congress' purpose in enacting the ICWA was to preserve American Indian culture by preventing the removal of children from Indian families and tribes. This purpose arguably is only relevant if the child's parents have significant social, cultural or political ties to the tribe. *In re Bridget R.*, 41 Cal. App. 4th 1483 (1996). Thus, if the Indian parent has never lived on the reservation and has no connection with the tribe except membership, or if the child lives with a non-Indian parent before the placement issue arises, tribal jurisdiction under the ICWA may depend on whether the "existing Indian family" rule is applied. In *In re Bridget R.*, the court determined that to apply the ICWA where the father had "no significant relationship with Indian tribal culture" would violate the Due Process and Equal Protection clauses of the Fourteenth Amendment, at least where the children already had been placed with the adoptive parents. For other courts adopting the existing Indian family rule, see *In re Adoption of Baby Girl S.* 690 N.Y.S.2d 907 (Surr. Ct. 1999); *In re Morgan*, 1997 Lexis 818 (Tenn. App.); *Rye v. Weasel*, 934 S.W.2d 257 (Ky. 1996) *In re Adoption of Crews*, 825 P.2d 305 (Wash. 1992); *In re S.C.*, 833 P.2d 1249 (Okla. 1992); *In re Adoption of T.R.M.*, 525 N.E.2d 298 (Ind. 1988).

Some courts have rejected the existing Indian family doctrine as undermining the purpose of the ICWA. For example, *Adoption of Riffle,* 922 P.2d 510 (Mont. 1996), held that the tribe alone has authority to determine whether a child is eligible for tribe membership and thus is an "Indian child," triggering the Act's jurisdiction. *See also A.B. v. K.B.*, 663 N.W.2d 625 (N.D. 2003) (rejecting doctrine); *State v. P.D.C.*, 933 P.2d 993 (Utah App. 1997); *In re Elliott,* 554 N.W.2d 32 (Mich. App. 1996); *In re Adoption of S.S.*, 622 N.E.2d 832 (Ill. App. 1993) ("Congress imposed no express requirement that children be part of an Indian family in order for these provisions to apply"; the ICWA was applicable even though children were not living with Indian family or on reservation); *A.B.M. v. M.H.*, 651 P.2d 1170, 1173 (Alaska 1982).

For a criticism of the existing Indian family doctrine, see Davis, *The Existing Indian Family Exception to the Indian Child Welfare Act,* 7 AM. J. FAM. L. 189 (1993). The author argues that "(f)ashioning levels of 'Indian-ness' thwarts Congress' policy to enhance the Indian community." For an article critical of the ICWA, see Bakeis, *The Indian Child Welfare Act of 1978: Violating Personal Rights for the Sake of the Tribe*, 10 NOTRE DAME J. OF L., ETH. & PUB. POL'Y 543 (1996) (author makes suggestions for amendment of the Act.) For further analysis of the Indian Child Welfare Act, see Hollinger, *Beyond the Best Interests of the Tribe: The Indian Child Welfare Act and the Adoption of Indian Children,* 63 U. Det. L. Rev. 451 (1989); Barsh, *Indian Child Welfare Act of 1978: A Critical Analysis,* 31 Hastings L.J. 1287 (1980). Randall Kennedy challenges the ICWA as part of a broader critique of race matching policies in adoption. Randall Kennedy, Interracial Intimacies: Sex, Marriage, Identity and Adoption (2003).

ADOPTION BY GAYS AND LESBIANS

An important issue in adoption in recent years is whether sexual orientation is a legitimate criterion in the adoption placement. The judicial and legislative response to adoption by gay and lesbian individuals and couples is examined in Chapter 9.

[3] AGENCY LIABILITY FOR MISREPRESENTATION AND FAILURE TO DISCLOSE INFORMATION TO ADOPTIVE PARENTS

JACKSON v. JACKSON
956 P.2d 35 (Mont. 1998)

Reginier, Justice.

[Aaron, the adoptee, was born on November 8, 1983, to Deborah Russell. Based on a psychological evaluation undertaken while she was incarcerated during her pregnancy, Russell was found to have a full Scale I.Q. of 73. The evaluation also strongly suggested that she had an "organic or psychiatric impairment, with 'disorganized, unconventional, diffused, [and] possibly . . . delusional' thinking." In January, 1984, Russell "fed her infant son soda pop, meat, and vegetables, which caused him to aspirate and led to his hospitalization." The State intervened on the basis of this incident, and in a social study prepared in February, Russell was described as retarded and "quite disturbed." A psychological evaluation in June, 1984 described her diagnosis as "paranoid disorder and mild mental retardation."

Aaron's putative father Roger Stevens was diagnosed with "schizophrenic disorder, paranoid type," in a report that the State acquired before the adoption.

Parental rights for both parents were terminated in December, 1984.

The Jacksons applied to become adoptive parents in November, 1983. During the application process, they advised Betty Petek, the state resource worker, that they "could not provide care for a child that had, or might be at risk for, developing a mental disorder." In January 1985, they were contacted by Petek about 15-month old Aaron's availability for adoption. At a meeting with Petek and Dave Wallace, another state worker, they asked whether there was any history of mental illness in Aaron's family. Petek and Wallace did not disclose the contents of the psychological evaluations to the Jacksons in response to their inquiry, although they had copies of the reports in their possession. Instead, they told the Jacksons that the child's parents were not capable of caring for him, and described the feeding incident. They mentioned the possibility of some drug use by the mother, but thought it was minimal. They also suggested that the mother was unable to care for Aaron because she moved around a lot, and lacked sufficient interest to learn the skills she needed to care for her child, but that she was physically healthy. The contents of the evaluations were not disclosed to the Jacksons prior the final adoption in January 1986.

Soon after the adoption, Aaron began to exhibit serious behavioral and emotional problems. He was diagnosed with psychotic disorder, attention deficit hyperactivity disorder, and pervasive developmental disorder, and was periodically hospitalized for psychiatric treatment.

In 1994, the Jacksons sued the State for negligent misrepresentation and negligent disclosure. The Jacksons appealed summary judgment for the State.]

. . . .

The crux of the Jacksons' "wrongful adoption" suit is their allegation that the State negligently misrepresented, and failed to disclose to them, certain material facts regarding the psychological background of their adoptive son's birth mother and putative father. To determine whether Montana law recognizes a cause of action for "wrongful adoption," such as the one initiated in the present case, we must simply determine "whether long-standing common law causes of action should be applied to the adoption context." *Gibbs v. Ernst*, 647 A.2d 882, 886 (Pa. 1994). . . .

Did the District Court err in concluding the State had neither a common law nor a statutory duty to fully and accurately disclose to the Jacksons information in its possession regarding the psychological and medical background of their adoptive son's birth mother and putative father?. . .

A. *Common law duty: negligent misrepresentation*

. . . .

Courts have commonly recognized that a duty on the part of the adoption agency to use due care may arise only when the agency "begin[s] volunteering information to potential adopting parents". . . . Thus, courts will, under certain circumstances, impose upon adoption agencies a duty to use due care and to refrain from making negligent misrepresentations where the agencies undertake to volunteer information to potential adoptive parents.

. . . . [W]e conclude, as has the recent majority of courts addressing this issue, that recognizing a cause of action for negligent misrepresentation in the adoption context will, in fact, promote public policy and ensure that "adoptive parents assume the awesome responsibility of raising a child with their eyes wide open." *Roe v. Catholic Charities*, 588 N.E.2d 354 at 365 (Ill. 1992). . . .

In the instant case, the Jacksons argue the State, in fact, disclosed certain background information regarding Aaron's birth parents, and in doing so, assumed a duty to use due care and to completely and accurately disclose that information. The State, however, argues it made no misleading statements to the Jacksons regarding the psychological background of Aaron's birth mother and putative father, and, therefore, that it assumed no such duty. The State asserts that, although it did provide the Jacksons with a great deal of information about Aaron's background prior to the adoption, it did not provide them with any inaccurate or misleading information regarding the psychological background of his birth parents. Specifically, the State argues its employees knew of no familial predisposition for mental illness, made no attempts to conceal information from the Jacksons, and did not assure them that Aaron would be free from mental illness.

As the State concedes, review of the record indicates that Wallace and Petek did indeed provide the Jacksons with certain information regarding Aaron's background. For example, deposition testimony from the Jacksons indicates that Wallace and Petek informed them of the possibility that Aaron's birth mother had used drugs or alcohol early in her pregnancy, that Aaron had been removed from the custody of his birth mother due to her inability to care for him, and that his birth mother had caused him to aspirate on solid food and soda pop when he was a young infant. . . . We conclude that the State, when it began volunteering such background information to the Jacksons, assumed a duty to do so with due care. Whether the State breached that duty and negligently misrepresented information to the Jacksons is a question of material fact precluding summary judgment in the State's favor.

. . . . [W]e conclude that to require anything less from the State than the exercise of due care in the dissemination of information in its possession to prospective adoptive parents would be simply unacceptable. We recognize that the imposition of such a duty indeed places a slight burden on the State, but conclude that burden is justified in light of the compelling need for adoptive parents to receive all available information regarding a child who may soon become a permanent part of their family. "Full disclosure of a child's medical and familial background" is warranted "not only to enable adoptive parents to obtain timely and appropriate medical care for the child, but also to enable them to make an intelligent and informed decision to adopt." *Mohr v. Comm*, 653 N.E.2d 1104, 1112 (Mass. 1995). Furthermore, we note the imposition of such a duty will increase public trust in our State agencies, and "will give potential parents more confidence in the adoption process and in the accuracy of the information they receive." *Meracle*, 437 N.W.2d at 537. . . . In light of the fact that the State undertook to disclose to the Jacksons certain information regarding Aaron's birth parents, we conclude that public policy considerations justify the imposition of a duty upon the State in the present case.

[The court then concluded that the district court erred in deciding that the risk of injury to the Jacksons was not foreseeable.]

[T]he Jacksons need only demonstrate that the State could reasonably have foreseen that Aaron was at risk for later manifesting an array of psychological and emotional problems, not that the psychological impairments suffered by Aaron's birth mother and putative father have definitively caused Aaron's present difficulties. . . .

B. *Statutory duty: negligent nondisclosure and negligence*

. . . .

[T]he District Court [also] concluded that the State had no statutory duty "to disclose the information which the [Jacksons] claim was withheld in this case" and accordingly rejected the Jacksons' "claim that the [State was] negligent in violating a statutorily imposed duty."

On appeal, the Jacksons argue that the Uniform Adoption Act of Montana, in fact, imposed upon the State a duty to disclose all available non-identifying information regarding Aaron's familial background, sufficient to support their negligence-based claims. . . . In contrast, the State argues it had no statutory duty to disclose to the Jacksons any more medical or psychological information regarding Aaron's birth family than it actually did. More specifically, the State concedes that it had a limited duty of disclosure pursuant to § 40-8-122(1)(c), MCA, but argues it fulfilled that duty by disclosing a variety of background information to the Jacksons. The State next argues it was, in fact, statutorily precluded from releasing the psychological reports at issue in this case.

[T]he State . . . acknowledges that § 40-8-122(1)(c), MCA, required that it file a report with the court stating that, among other things, "medical and social histories [had] been provided to the adoptive parent." The State contends that it complied with this requirement, and that it had no duty, statutory or otherwise, to provide the Jacksons with a more complete medical and social history. . . .

As the State correctly notes, § 40-8-122, MCA, does not specifically identify that information which the State must include in the medical and social histories it prepares, and does not explicitly mandate disclosure of any psychological records regarding a child's birth parents. The State argues that it did disclose other background information to the Jacksons and that it thus complied with the disclosure requirements of § 40-8-122, MCA.

Although § 40-8-122(1), MCA, does not specifically describe that information which the State must include in the medical and social histories it provides to adoptive parents, the State's own policies and procedures manual provides additional detail. The Department of Social and Rehabilitation Services Policies and Procedures Manual (Manual) § CSD-SS 602-1 specifically provides that:

> The child and his adoptive family need to have all available information on the child and his birth family. This information shall include:
>
> 1. Background information on biological parents . . .; . . . .
>
> 3. Child's Social Study with identifying information removed;. . . .
>
> 6. Psychological evaluation; . . .

Although the State's policy and procedures manual does not specifically require that the State disclose psychological evaluations performed on an adoptee's biological parents, it explicitly recognizes that the child and his adoptive family need to have "*all* available information on the child and his birth family." This language, coupled with that portion of § 40-8-122(1)(c), MCA, which mandates that the State provide adoptive parents with "medical and social histories" clearly evidences a statutory duty on the part of the State to fully and accurately disclose all relevant information, including psychological reports, regarding an adoptee and his or her family.

The State next argues, however, that the imposition of such a duty to disclose. . . would conflict with its statutory duties to maintain the confidentiality of the birth parents' medical records. In support of this contention, the State points to that version of § 41-3-205, MCA (1985), in effect at the time of Aaron's adoption by the Jacksons in 1985, which prohibited the State from disclosing information contained in child protection services files to anyone unless authorized by court order.

Although § 41-3-205, MCA, generally prohibited the State from disclosing information contained in child protective services files, it provided an exception permitting such dissemination if authorized by court order. Had it obtained such an order from the court in this case, the State could have complied with the confidentiality requirements of § 41-3-205, MCA, while at the same time complying with its own policy of providing an adoptive family with "*all available information on the child and his birth family*" and with its statutory mandate to provide adoptive parents with meaningful "medical and social histories." Had the State sought, but failed to obtain, such a court order, the State could still have complied with the confidentiality requirements of § 41-3-205, MCA, and its own policy by simply informing the Jacksons that Aaron would not have been an appropriate child for them to adopt in light of their concerns regarding a possible history of mental illness.

Thus, although we recognize the various privacy considerations at issue in this case, we nevertheless conclude that § 40-8-122(1)(c), MCA, construed in conjunction with the State's own policy and procedures manual, gives rise to a statutorily imposed duty on the part of the State to fully and accurately disclose to the Jacksons all relevant background information in its possession, including any reports regarding the psychological health of Aaron's birth parents. Whether the State breached that duty is a genuine issue of material fact precluding summary judgment in the State's favor on the Jacksons' claims for negligent nondisclosure and negligence based upon a lack of informed consent. . . .

　　. . . .

[T]he Jacksons will ultimately need to demonstrate that the State's conduct in allegedly withholding or misrepresenting information regarding Aaron's background led to their decision to adopt Aaron and thereby helped produce the injury in this case. Moreover, we hold the Jacksons will have to demonstrate that, but for the fact that the State withheld and misrepresented certain background information, they would not have adopted Aaron, would not have been injured, and would not have incurred the damages they now claim.

NOTES

1. *Liability for Agency Misrepresentations About Child.* The tort of wrongful adoption is relatively new, first recognized in *Burr v. Stark Cty. Bd. of Comm'rs*, 491 N.E.2d 1101 (Ohio 1986). Yet, according to one court, virtually all states now recognize wrongful adoption claims based on intentional and

negligent misrepresentation. *See Wolford v. Children's Home Soc'y of W. Va.,* 17 F. Supp. 2d 577 (S.D. W. Va. 1998). The early cases found liability on the basis of intentional misrepresentation or concealment by an agency of information about the child's or birth parents' health. In *Burr,* for example, the court upheld a judgment for adoptive parents where agency concealed birth parent's mental illness and history of Huntington's Disease and the child developed serious mental problems. *See also Michael J. v. Los Angeles Cty. Dep't of Adoptions,* 247 Cal. Rptr. 504 (App. 1988)(liability for misrepresentation and concealment).

Most courts, like the Montana Supreme Court in *Jackson,* have also recognized an action for negligent misrepresentation. In *M.H. and J.L.H. v. Caritas Adoption Services,* 488 N.W. 2d 282 (Minn. 1992), the agency suggested to the prospective parents on several occasions that there was a "possibility of incest in the family." As the child grew up he had serious behavior problems. When he was six years old, the adoptive parents learned that his parents were brother and sister, a fact known to the agency at the time of the adoption. The Minnesota Supreme Court held that the agency could be liable on the ground of negligent misrepresentation, even if it had not intended to mislead the parents. The court rejected the argument that making the agency liable for negligent acts would create an onerous burden for adoption agencies that ultimately would discourage adoptions. Liability was not based on failure to investigate the child's background, to undertake tests, or to disclose facts not required by statute. *See also Gibbs v. Ernst,* 647 A.2d 882 (Pa. 1994) (recognizing liability theories of intentional misrepresentation, negligent misrepresentation and failure to disclose, but making clear that there is no duty to investigate). As in *Jackson,* the *Caritas* court emphasized that once the agency undertakes voluntary disclosures, due care must be exercised so as not to mislead the adoptive parents. This point was also emphasized in *Meracle v. Children's Serv. Soc'y of Wis.,* 437 N.W.2d 532 (Wis. 1989), in which the adoptive parents were told, inaccurately, that, although the child's paternal grandmother had died of Huntington's Disease, the child was not at risk. The child did develop Huntington's Disease, and the court held that such affirmative misrepresentations by the agency would support an action for the extraordinary medical expenses and the emotional distress that resulted from the illness. The court stated that "to avoid liability, agencies must simply refrain from making affirmative misrepresentations about a child's health."

Will this lead agencies to disclose as little information as possible? In *Jackson,* remember, the agency found a duty to disclose information as well as a duty to use due care to avoid misrepresentation. Thus, simply not providing information is not an option for the agency seeking to avoid liability. *See* Milks, Annotation, *"Wrongful Adoption" Causes of Action Against Adoption Agencies Where Children Have or Develop Mental or Physical Problems That are Misrepresented or Not Disclosed to Adoptive Parents,* 74 A.L.R.5th 1 (1999).

2. *Liability Based on Failure to Disclose Information.* The question of whether there can be agency liability based on failure to disclose important information has become more salient recently, because many states like

Montana now impose on the agency a statutory duty to disclose information to adoptive parents about the birthparents' and child's medical history. This represents a significant change from the traditional approach. As one author put it,

> The concern that disclosure of medical and family background information might facilitate adoptees' efforts to locate their birth parents and invade the birth parents' privacy has given way to the view that adoptive parents should have access to as complete a medical and social history as possible so as to better prepare for their adopted child's potential medical and social problems.

ADAMEC & PIERCE, THE ENCYCLOPEDIA OF ADOPTION 81–2 (1991). *See also* Blair, *Lifting the Genealogical Veil: A Blueprint for Legislative Reform of the Disclosure of Health Related Information in Adoption*, 70 N.C. L. REV. 681 (1992) (citing statutes). According to one report, 41 states now have statutory disclosure requirements of this type. Lorandos, *Secrecy and Genetics in Adoption Law and Practice,* 27 LOY. CHI. L.J. 277, 295–6 (Winter 1996). Under the 1994 Uniform Adoption Act (§ 2-106), the person placing the child for adoption must supply a report to the prospective adoptive parents that includes a medical and psychological history of the child, including prenatal care and exposure to drugs, history of abuse, and relevant information concerning the medical and psychological history of the parents and relatives, including predisposition to disease, drug or alcohol addiction, and information about the mother's prenatal health. Vermont has adopted the U.A.A., and its supreme court has interpreted its statutory provisions, in light of the intentions of the U.A.A. drafters. In a case in which the adoptive parents were dead and the birth parents supported the adoptee's petition, the appellate court concluded that the trial court had expansive authority to order disclosure, commenting that the legislature was not concerned about the agency's privacy interest. *In re Margaret Susan P.,* 733 A.2d 38 (Vt. 1999).

Should violation of this statutory obligation serve as a basis for civil liability in suits by adoptive parents against agencies for failure to disclose information about the child's background? Many statutes limit or exclude civil liability for violation of the disclosure duty, but where they do not, a number of courts besides *Jackson* have recognized nondisclosure claims. In *McKinney v. State,* 950 P.2d 461 (Wash. 1998), the court dealt former foster parents who adopted a child (after three years) later diagnosed with fetal alcohol syndrome. Only after the adoption did the parents gain access to the child's medical and psychological records, which revealed her mother's alcohol history and her history of abuse. The court determined that the agency could be subject to liability based on its negligent failure to comply with the statutory mandate to disclose medical and social history information to adoptive parents. The Washington statute is more detailed and specific than the Montana statute in *Jackson* in describing the kind of information that must be disclosed, and would seem to more clearly limit the scope of the agency's duty. The court justified the creation of a private cause of action on the basis of statutory duty in this context because the agency is in a relationship of trust and confidence with the prospective adoptive parents. In the case itself, however, the court concluded that the agency's failure was not the proximate cause of the parents' injury, because they were well aware of the child's problems from their years as her foster parents — and the state's disclosure duty does not extend to foster parents.

This is a difficult issue. Clearly, prospective parents have an interest in information about the child's genetic heritage and health background that might affect the child's future development in important ways. However, an onerous burden on agencies to collect information, together with the broad risk of potential liability would impose significant costs on adoption. Consider the burden on Montana agencies after *Jackson*, under which they sometimes might need to acquire a court order to disclose some of the mandated information. [This is no longer required under the statute]. Many courts require a misrepresentation or concealment by the agency and do not base liability on a failure to disclose alone. *See Juman v. Louise Wise Services*, 608 N.Y.S.2d 612 (Sup. Ct. 1994) (parents must establish a false statement of a material fact, reliance by plaintiff, intent to deceive by the defendant and pecuniary loss by the plaintiff); *c.f. Lord v. Living Bridges*, No. Civ. A. 97-6355, 1999 WL 562713 (E.D. Pa. 1999) (Adoption Act, in imposing disclosure duties on adoption agencies, created no private right of action for the negligent breach of those duties).

§ C. REGULATION OF INDEPENDENT ADOPTIONS

Non-agency adoptions of unrelated children have been on the rise for the past two decades. According to one report in the mid-1990s, about 30% of adoptions outside the family are independent. *Report by the Center for the Future for Children Hearings before the Subcommittee on Human Resources of the Committee on Ways and Means*, 104th Cong., 1st Sess. 12–16 (1995). However, some critics have suggested that this form of adoption does not protect the children's interests. Emery, *Agency v. Independent Adoption: The Case for Agency Adoption*, 3 THE FUTURE OF CHILDREN: ADOPTION 139 (1993). Several states bar placement of children outside of the agency process, except where the biological parent places the child with a stepparent or a close relative. CONN. GEN. STAT. ANN. § 45a-727 (West 1997); DEL. CODE ANN. tit. 13, § 904 (1999 & Supp. 2002); MASS. GEN. LAWS ANN. ch. 210, § 11A (West 1998); MICH. COMP. LAWS § 710.55 (2002). A number of states permit non-relative independent adoptions where the parent places the child, but prohibit involvement of an intermediary. The remaining states, while allowing non-agency intermediaries to arrange adoptions, generally still regulate their activities in some way. *See, e.g.*, FLA. STAT. ANN. § 63.097 (West Supp. 2003).

Independent adoption has gained popularity because both adoptive parents and birth mothers see many advantages over agency adoption. Adoptive parents often choose independent adoption as a way to avoid the agency process and long waiting periods. Some prospective adoptive parents may be unable to adopt through an agency because they fail to meet age or marital status criteria, have health problem, or do not practice a religious faith. *See generally* Kleiman, *Caring for Our Own: Why American Adoption Law and Policy Must Change*, 30 COLUM. J.L. & SOC. PROBS. 327 (Winter 1997); Sanger, *Separating From Children*, 96 COLUM. L. REV. 375, 442 (1996); Romano,

Comment, *Intercountry Adoption: An Overview for the Practitioner*, 7 TRANS-NAT'L LAW 545 (1994). The wait for a healthy white infant is far longer through an agency. Romano, *supra,* at 553. Independent adoption would not be possible of course unless birth parents chose to place their children privately. What birth parents like about independent adoption is that they can play a greater role in the selection of the parents, and that the child can go directly into the custody of the parents and not into foster care. *See* Lucas, *Adoption: Distinguishing Between Grey Market and Black Market Activities,* 34 FAM. L. Q. 553 (2000).

Many of the intermediaries arranging non-agency adoptions (that is, matching available babies with adoptive homes) are lawyers. The small group of attorneys who handle many adoptions have received considerable scrutiny. Are they engaged in unethical practices?

[1] WHOM DOES THE ATTORNEY REPRESENT?

Attorneys can face ethical issues in the adoption setting. Usually they represent the adoptive parents, in dealing with birth parents who often do not have legal counsel. The birth mother typically is looking to the adoptive parents to cover many of her expenses, and will rarely have funds to hire her own lawyer. In this situation, can the attorney inform the birth mother about legal matters? In general, attorneys are prohibited from representing two clients whose interests are adverse, although exceptions are sometimes made in situations of full disclosure and consent by both parties. In the adoption context, the potential for conflicts of interest exists between the birth mother and the adoptive parents. Thus, the ABA Standing Committee on Ethics and Professional Responsibility has found that under both the Model Rules of Professional Conduct and the older Code of Professional Responsibility, an attorney may not ethically represent both the adoptive and birth parents in a private adoption, *Informal Opinion 87-1523*, Feb. 14, 1987, reprinted in 13 FAM. L. REP. 1231.

Avoiding violation of the rule against dual representation may be tricky in a somewhat complex legal context in which only one party is represented. It might seem that the adoptive parents' attorney will inevitably meet with the unrepresented birth mother, present her with documents to sign and explain their meaning, and perhaps relay funds to her from the adoptive parents to cover, for example, the medical expenses of pregnancy and childbirth. Do such activities cross the line to joint representation? *See Adoption of Anonymous,* 131 Misc. 2d 666, 501 N.Y.S.2d 240 (Surr. 1986):

> It is not sufficient that counsel advised the natural mother that she represented only the adoptive parents. If counsel for adoptive parents reviews the consent agreement or other legal documents with the natural mother, assists her in locating a place to live and obtains reimbursement of expenses and advises which expenses are reimbursable, a conflict exists. Such conduct is improper and should be avoided. [The] natural mother should be represented by independent counsel of her own selection. . . . The practice of the attorney for the adopting parents acting on behalf of the natural mother . . . is improper.

The New York court's approach would seem to be consistent with the official comment to Rule 4.3 of the Model Rules of Professional Conduct, which cautions that the "lawyer should not give advice to an unrepresented person other than the advice to obtain counsel." Some courts adopt a more relaxed standard, perhaps recognizing the harshness of leaving the birth mother to fend for herself in negotiating the legal hurdles of adoption. *See e.g. In re Petrie*, 742 P.2d 796 (Ariz. 1987).

> . . . . [T]he attorney advised the natural mother that she could obtain her own counsel; however, no lawyer purporting to represent her contacted the attorney in question. The attorney subsequently obtained the natural mother's written consent to adopt, after advising both her and the alleged father of its legal effect. . . . The committee found no unethical activity . . . because the lawyer made clear who he represented and advised the nonrepresented party to seek independent counsel.

Dual representation problems can arise in agency adoptions also. A New York court criticized an attorney who represented both the adoption agency that had legal custody of the child and the petitioning adoptive family, foster parents of the child. In *In re Vincent*, 602 N.Y.S.2d 303 (Fam. Ct. 1993), after the agency had arranged for the termination of the parental rights of the biological parents and submitted its investigative report to the court, the court appointed another agency to provide an independent report. The independent report indicated some problems with the foster parents. The attorney promptly had his client, the agency, remove all children from the foster home of his client, the petitioning adoptive parents. The court concluded that "dual representation should not be permitted because a conflict could arise at any time," and found that the attorney's termination of his relationship with the prospective adoptive parents insufficient.

The 1994 Uniform Adoption Act requires birth parents, adoptive parents and adoption agencies to have separate representation. UAA § 2-405(a)(4). When the birth parent is a minor, she must be expressly advised of her right to independent counsel. UAA § 2-405(d)(5). If a minor parent does not have independent counsel, her consent is presumed to be incompetent. UAA § 2-405(c). UAA § 3-201(a) authorizes court appointment of a lawyer for any indigent, minor or incompetent individual who appears in the adoption proceedings and whose parental rights may be terminated, unless the court finds that the individual possesses adequate means to hire her own lawyer or waives the right to counsel. UAA § 3-201(b) requires the appointment of a guardian ad litem for any minor adoptee in a contested proceeding.

PROBLEM

Problem 11-6. George and August Johnson consulted with Frank Zorro about their interest in adopting a child. The parties agreed that if the Johnsons found a baby for adoption, Zorro would represent them. About eighteen months later, their friend Jessica Ball called them about a child who Jessica had heard was available. Ball called Zorro, telling him she had found a child for the Johnsons, and arranged for the pregnant birth mother, Ann Calley, to meet with him. After the meeting, Zorro wrote the Johnsons, asking them if they were interested in the adoption. In a response that Zorro later described as "equivocal," because it included questions about the adoption and the fees, the Johnsons responded affirmatively. Shortly thereafter, Zorro received a call from another couple, the Buck's, inquiring about adopting another child. When contacted by Zorro, Calley stated that she owed no obligation to the Johnsons. At Zorro's recommendation, she placed the child with the Bucks. [The Bucks were more conveniently located than the Johnsons; had the Johnsons adopted the child, Zorro would have to make appearances in a distant court.] Should Zorro be sanctioned for dual representation? What should the sanction be?

[2] FEE REGULATION AND BABY BROKERAGE

GALISON v. DISTRICT OF COLUMBIA

402 A.2d 1263 (D.C. App. 1979)

NEBEKER, Associate Judge. Appellant Galison was convicted, after trial to the court, of one count of arranging for the placement of a child under sixteen years of age without having been licensed as a "child-placing agency." D.C. Code 1973, §§ 32-785,-788. Appellant Goldstein was convicted of three counts under the same code provisions. Each argued that Congress, in enacting the provisions of . . . the Baby Broker Act. . ., did not intend to reach the conduct proved in these cases. . . .

I. Edward Galison

Appellant Galison is an attorney licensed . . . in. . . New York. Prior to August 31, 1976, his associate, Spiegelman, was contacted in New York by a Florida attorney. The Florida attorney explained that he had been unable to arrange for an adoption in Florida of the expected child of a Florida resident. Upon locating a New York family that would agree to adopt the child, Spiegelman suggested to his Florida contact that the mother come to New York for the child's delivery. The expectant mother, however, indicated that she would be willing to travel only as far as the District of Columbia. The Florida attorney and Spiegelman arranged for the woman and her mother (the grandmother), to stay in the District of Columbia beginning on August 31, 1976.

Upon arrival in the District, the woman had a change of heart and decided that she would keep the child. She so advised Galison, who thereupon came to the District of Columbia and persuaded her that adoption was "the right thing to do." After he informed her that her medical and living expenses in the District would be paid for and that she would receive $2,000 in addition to her medical and living expenses, she executed documents by which she consented to the proposed adoption and authorized the hospital to release her yet-unborn child to appellant.

Later, in September, the expectant mother again desired to abandon the adoption plans and contacted Galison to inform him that she wanted to return to Florida. Galison explained that the prospective parents were waiting for the baby to be delivered and reminded her of the money that they had provided for her. Because of the money involved, the woman decided to remain in the District.

In October, one week before the baby was born, the grandmother telephoned Galison regarding a Washington newspaper article which stated that it was illegal to arrange an adoption without going through an agency. Galison assured the grandmother that his actions were legitimate. Galison then spoke with the woman and played on her sensitivities by telling her that the prospective parents had not contributed any of the money for her expenses, that he had taken the money from his own pocket and that she should consider all the money invested in her thus far. The woman relented.

Subsequent to the October 19th birth of the baby, the mother once again decided that she wanted to keep the baby, but she was "afraid of the money I owed and the money that he had invested in me. I was afraid to back out. I didn't know what to do." The grandmother contacted a social worker, and, as a result, the police were advised of the circumstances of the proposed child placement. Galison, meanwhile, once again attempted to persuade the mother to continue with the planned placement by arguing that it was in everyone's best interest and by reminding her that there was already $6,000 "invested" in her. The grandmother then obtained the release of the baby from the hospital, received approximately $2,200 from Galison, and gave the baby to Galison. Upon leaving the hospital with the baby, Galison was arrested.

> We are asked to decide whether Congress intended the Baby Broker Act to prohibit Galison's activities.

To fulfill the purposes of the Act, i.e., to assure the care and guidance necessary for the welfare of the child and to protect the interests of the District, Congress required registration and licensing of individuals placing children. . . .

> No person other than the parent, guardian, or relative within the third degree, and no firm, corporation, association, or agency, other than a licensed child-placing agency, may place or arrange or assist in placing or arranging for the placement of a child under sixteen years of age in a family home or for adoption . . . [D.C. Code 1973, § 32-785.]

[The court concluded that the adoption had sufficient connection with the District to fall within the Act and affirmed the conviction.]

II. Leonard Goldstein

Appellant Goldstein is . . . licensed to practice law in . . . Maryland and the District of Columbia. His primary business office is in Maryland, and the events recited herein occurred in Maryland except as otherwise noted. The events leading to his three convictions occurred in late 1975 and early 1976, and involved the placement of three infants, referred to at trial as Baby Doe, Baby Roe and Baby Poe, with three married couples, referred to, respectively, as the Norths, the Wests, and the Souths. The natural mothers, as well as the Norths and the Wests, were all residents of Maryland. The Souths resided in Virginia.

Each of the natural mothers was a patient of Dr. Stave or Dr. Rose, associates in the practice of obstetrics and gynecology in Maryland and private attending physicians at the Washington Hospital Center in the District of Columbia. Goldstein and Dr. Stave, although once acquainted, had had no contact for several years when Dr. Stave called Goldstein in late 1975. Dr. Stave advised Goldstein that one of his patients, Miss Doe, was expecting a child and wished to privately place the child for adoption. Goldstein responded . . . that private placements were legal in Maryland and that he . . . would be willing to assist in such a placement. Subsequently, Dr. Stave contacted Mr. and Mrs. North, who had been his patients for infertility [and] they indicated that they would like to adopt Baby Doe. After unsuccessful attempts to obtain . . . an attorney to assist them . . . the Norths obtained Dr. Stave's recommendation of Goldstein. The Norths thereafter retained Goldstein to assist in the proposed adoption.

Upon the recommendation of Dr. Stave, Miss Doe went to the Washington Hospital Center for delivery of her baby. Goldstein arranged with the staff neonatologist to assure confidentiality of the identity of Baby Doe's mother by covering the baby's crib identification with the name "Goldstein." Similarly, all hospital billing accounts were maintained in Goldstein's name and paid out of an escrow fund established through him by the Norths. On the day of Baby Doe's birth, Goldstein secured from a Maryland court a temporary custody decree authorizing the Norths to take custody of the child. (Goldstein had visited Miss Doe and her parents at the hospital for the purpose of obtaining their signatures on various documents related to the Maryland adoption proceedings.) When the child was able to be released from the hospital, the staff. . . released the child to them. Thereafter the Norths adopted the child in accordance with Maryland procedures.

The second placement also was initiated through Dr. Stave, who advised Goldstein that his patient, Miss Roe, wished to place her expected child for adoption. . . . Dr. Stave asked Goldstein whether he knew of anyone interested in adopting the expected child. Goldstein advised a rabbi of the situation and the rabbi, in turn, advised the Wests, who retained Goldstein to assist in the placement.

When Goldstein was advised by Dr. Stave that Baby Roe had been born at Washington Hospital Center, he arranged to meet Miss Roe and her mother at the hospital to obtain their signatures on various legal documents. He then obtained an order of temporary custody for the Wests. . . . The hospital bills were paid from an escrow fund established by Goldstein for the Wests. A hospital nurse released the baby to Miss Roe's mother who, in turn, gave the baby to Mrs. West. Thereafter the Wests adopted the child in accordance with Maryland procedures.

The third placement [followed a similar pattern].

[T]he facts of this case appear, at least in their broadest outlines, to have some similarity to those of Galison's case. Both Goldstein and Galison attempted to place the children of unmarried expectant mothers, domiciled outside the District, who gave birth to their children in the District. In each case, a non-resident attorney participated in dealings between the natural and the adopting families and the hospital. Additionally, both cases present evidence of some child-placement activity being conducted by the defendants within the District.

The dissimilarities distinguishing the two cases, however, are stark. With reference to Goldstein's placements, the mothers' presence in the District was due to medical reasons — to enter the hospital for delivery. In Galison's case, the mother did not come to the District solely for medical reasons nor, in fact, when she changed her mind about giving away her child, did she desire to remain in the District. Far from having made up her mind to give away her child, the mother in Galison's case consistently expressed to Galison her desire not to go through with the adoption plan. Furthermore, there exists no indication that Goldstein, like Galison, negotiated with the mothers in an attempt to persuade them to relinquish their parental rights over the children. On the contrary, Goldstein's contacts with the natural mothers and with the hospital personnel in the District were limited to carrying into effect the unchanged decisions arrived at by the natural mothers previous to entering the District and subsequent to consulting with their physicians in Maryland.

In short, these cases involve lawful Virginia or Maryland adoptions of children born to Maryland residents while in a District of Columbia hospital solely for medical reasons. The decision to place the child was made by each of the natural mothers before entering the District. The mothers evidenced no reluctance to follow their predetermined course after entering the District. Since the mothers were not residing in the District and no coercive activity was employed in an attempt to persuade them to relinquish their children, the District interests which were offended by Galison are not threatened here. Finding no other District interest threatened by Goldstein's conduct, we hold that the Baby Broker Act is inapplicable in his case. . . .

We hold, therefore, that Goldstein's conduct did not violate § 32-785. No District interest sought to be protected by the Act was threatened by Goldstein's placement activities. [The case is remanded with instructions to enter a judgment of acquittal.]

KERN, Associate Justice, concurring in part and dissenting in part:

. . . . I cannot agree that appellant Goldstein's "conduct was not of the type intended to be prohibited by the Act.". . .

. . . . [I]n *Goodman v. District of Columbia*, D.C. MUN. APP., 50 A.2d 812 (1947) . . . the court . . . stated:

> Congress therefore decreed that commercial agents, baby brokers, and even the best-intentioned citizens serving upon a non-commercial basis and from the most humane motives, must none of them be permitted to place children for adoption unless previously investigated, found qualified, and licensed. . . .

> To emphasize that purpose Congress in the plainest language made it unlawful for anyone not licensed to "place or arrange or assist in placing or arranging for the placement" of a child.

What the appellant did is very clear. He "arranged" and "assisted" in placing and personally consummated the placement of the child. He was the intermediary who produced the prospective adopters and arranged contact (indirect though it was) with the mother. . . . It would be difficult to imagine a more clear-cut infraction of the letter as well as the spirit of the law. . . .

NOTES ON INDEPENDENT ADOPTIONS

1. *Regulation of Fees.* The role of attorneys in arranging adoptions has been subject to considerable scrutiny, and some attorneys are accused of coming dangerously close to "baby-selling." *See* Galen, *Baby Brokers: How Far Can a Lawyer Go?* NATL. L.J. 1 (Feb. 9, 1987). Galen describes Seymour Kurtz, who ran four adoption agencies in four states and placed hundreds of mostly white babies each year. He spent $700,000 on national advertising to attract birth mothers, who (according to charges of the Arizona attorney general, who sought to deny his agency a license) were then offered lavish accommodations, vacations and other inducements to agree to adoption. Other attorneys, according to Galen, receive substantial fees for guiding their clients through the process, assisting them in placing ads that will appeal to pregnant women, screening candidates, etc. One way to deter undesirable behavior by intermediaries is through fee regulation, and many states require attorneys to disclose their fees to the court before issuance of the adoption order. If the legal services alone cannot justify the fees, the suspicion arises that they are in fact for brokerage services. Some states regulate the charges that can be made in connection with the adoption, typically by requiring that all expenditures be set out in the adoption petition or some other document filed with a state agency for approval. Others require court approval for fees and direct that only "reasonable and necessary" fees be approved. ARIZ. REV. STAT. § 8-114(D) (West Supp. 2002). Nonetheless, there are reports of brokerage fees as high as $100,000 in states in which regulation is lax. *See* Mansnerus, *Market Puts Price Tag on the Priceless*, N.Y TIMES, Oct. 26, 1998, at A1, which offers an interesting account of the operation of the adoption market.

Internet baby-brokers have recently received attention as a result of a high-publicity case in which an internet broker assisted the mother in placing her twins with a California couple, the Allens, and then with a couple in England the Kilshaws, after the mother became dissatisfied with the Allens. After a highly publicized exchange between the claimants, Mr. Allen was arrested for sexual abuse of another child and it was revealed that Internet adoptions are illegal in England. The mother changed her mind and claimed custody and both couples withdrew. The Internet broker was charged with mail fraud for mishandling at least a dozen adoptions. *See* Dembski, *Adoption and the Internet*, MILWAUKEE SENTINEL J. April 20, 2001, at 18A; McDonald, *Woman Pleads not Guilty to Fraud in Adoption Case,* Copley News Service, March 12, 2003.

2. *Regulation of Payments to the Birth Mother.* Most states bar payments to the birth mother in exchange for her consent to adoption. Beyond a simple statement to that effect, states may try to police all payments to the birth mother in order to ensure that they are proper. Arizona law provides an example. ARIZ. REV. STAT. § 8-114 (West 1997):

A. The court may approve any monies paid to a parent of a child placed for adoption or another person for the benefit of the parent or adopted child for reasonable and necessary expenses incurred in connection with the adoption. These expenses may include costs for medical and hospital care and examinations for the mother and child, counseling fees, legal fees, agency fees and any other costs the court finds reasonable and necessary.

B. A person who wishes to pay the living expenses of a birth parent that exceed one thousand dollars shall petition the court to permit such payment. . . . The court shall approve living expenses that the person has paid, unless found unreasonable. The person who wishes to pay the one thousand dollars in living expenses of a birth mother shall file an affidavit with the court signed by the birth mother verifying that the birth mother has been given written notice and that she understands that the payment of these expenses by any person does not obligate the birth mother to place the child for adoption and that a valid consent to the adoption can only be given after the child's birth without regard to any cost or expense paid by any person in connection with the adoption. A maximum of one thousand dollars may be advanced for birth parent living expenses without a motion. In determining what living expenses are reasonable and necessary, the court shall consider but not be limited to the following factors:

1. The current standard of living of the birth parent.

2. The standard of living necessary to preserve the health and welfare of the birth parent and the unborn child.

3. The existence of alternative financial resources for the birth parent.

C. Except as provided in subsection A, a person shall not be directly or indirectly compensated for giving or obtaining consent to place a child for adoption.

An important difficulty with such statutes lies in distinguishing between permissible reimbursement of the birth mother for her expenses (costs that are "reasonable and necessary") and impermissible "compensation" for her consent to the adoption.

Some courts do not allow reimbursement of the birth mother's living expenses. In *Adoption of Anonymous,* 501 N.Y.S.2d 240 (Surr. 1986), the court rejected as improper reimbursement to the attorney for advances of birth mother's expenses:

Expenses for food, rent utilities, cable TV, travel, flowers and furniture rental in the amount of $7,996.02 were paid on behalf of the natural mother without court review and approval. The law is clear that adoptive parents may reimburse a natural parent only for expenses "on account of or incidental to the birth or care of the adoptive child, the pregnancy or care of the adoptive child's mother or the placement or adoption of the child and on account of or incidental to assistance in arrangements for such placement or adoption." (Domestic Relations Law § 115 [7]). Specifically disallowed . . .

are the following: food and living expense for 13 weeks prior to birth and five weeks after birth ($1,728); rental of apartment in South Carolina [where the birth mother lived] ($1,385); gas, electric and telephone expenses in South Carolina ($639.82); furniture rental in South Carolina ($315.04); cable TV expense ($28.22); travel ($250); and flowers ($28.06). These amounts shall be reimbursed the adoptive parents by their attorney.

But see In re Baby Boy B., 552 N.Y.S.2d 1005 (Fam. 1990) (birth mother may be reimbursed for wages lost in ten weeks' maternity leave from her employment; court decries vagueness in statutory standards for allowable reimbursement).

The 1994 Uniform Adoption Act permits payment by the adoptive parent of medical and counseling expenses of the mother, and living expenses during pregnancy and for up to 6 weeks after birth. The Act provides that the mother is not required to reimburse the birth parents if the adoption does not go through, but that the adoptive parents are not required to make additional payments unless they have agreed to do so regardless of the outcome. (§ 7-103).

Restriction of reimbursement has also been applied to agencies that take an aggressive marketing approach. The Pennsylvania Supreme Court, holding that adoptive parents may pay only for services that "directly benefit" the child, disallowed agency charges not only for the birth mother's room, board and travel expense, but even for prenatal care. It also rejected the agency policy of setting a fee as a percentage of the adoptive parents' income (with a maximum of $7,500). *In re Baby Girl D.,* 517 A.2d 925 (Pa. 1986).

Is there any rationale for the distinction drawn by some courts between medical expenses during the pregnancy (which are generally permitted) and living expenses (which often are not)? It is plausible that the greater the range of expenses that adoptive parents can pay, the greater the inducement to the birthmother to choose adoption over keeping the child (or abortion), and to choose parents who can pay the maximum amount of expenses permitted. Thus, depending on what compensation is permitted, the reimbursement policy may fall along a continuum from "no inducement" to "baby selling." Is there any principled basis on which the line can be drawn?

Is such regulation socially beneficial? Should birthmothers not receive compensation for the costs incurred in going through a pregnancy that will provide valuable benefit to the adoptive parents, and no benefit to the pregnant woman herself? *Galison* offers one argument for the policy against payment of expenses. The woman whose expenses have been paid may feel compelled to consent to adoption after the child is born. That is, the policy against pre-birth consent may be undermined by allowing the mother to accept pre-birth payments that will make her feel obligated to the prospective adoptive parents. A Tennessee couple who were recruited by a Louisiana agency, Beacon House, were given first class plane tickets to Louisiana and provided with an apartment and all living expenses. When they switched agencies after becoming concerned about the tactics of Beacon House, the agency sued them for $24,000. (The suit was later dropped.) *See* Mansnerus, *supra* note 1.

For an analysis of how demand for babies can lead to inadvertent black market adoptions, and argument for greater regulation, see Lucas, *Adoption: Distinguishing Between Grey Market and Black Market Activities,* 34 FAM. L.Q. 553 (2000).

3. *Legal Ban on Unlicensed "Placing Out."* Many "placing out" statutes (like the D.C. statute in *Galison*) are violated even where there has been no payment for brokerage services, because they create a complete bar on the "placement" of children for adoption by anyone not licensed for that purpose. Yet, in the absence of any payment to the intermediary, many courts will decline to find a violation. *See In re Adoption of Baby Girl B.,* 144 Misc. 2d 583, 544 N.Y.2d 963 (Surr. 1989) (court finds no violation where attending physician who found adoptive parents received no fee).

When problems develop after the adoption, however, the broker who violated the "placing out" law may be dealt with harshly, although the absence of a fee may mitigate liability. In *Sarosi v. Commissioner,* 553 N.Y.S.2d 517 (App. Div. 1990), an appellate court considered a sanction ordered by the state Board of Regents against an obstetrician who secretly arranged for the placement of a baby for adoption at the request of the mother's family in violation of the "placing out" provisions of New York Social Services Law. He insisted that the child be placed with Joel Steinberg, his attorney, and Hedda Nussbaum. Steinberg never filed adoption papers. After Steinberg killed another "adopted" child, Lisa, in a highly publicized case, Sarosi was charged and pleaded guilty to a misdemeanor. He was then subject to a disciplinary proceeding that culminated in a Board of Regents decision to revoke Sarosi's medical license.

On Sarosi's appeal, the court concluded that the "penalty of revocation . . . is excessively harsh. . . and an abuse of discretion," and remitted the case for reconsideration of the penalty. The court noted that Sarosi received no fee for delivering or placing the baby and this was the only time he had ever participated in an arrangement for adoption. Many witnesses supported the claim that he was "[a] physician with a heretofore unblemished record, [who] violated a statute which [had] not previously [been] enforced except in cases of black market 'baby selling' [and of which he was unaware]." Commenting on the notoriety of the case, the court questioned whether the Board would have invoked the harsh penalty "if Steinberg and Nussbaum had been the loving parents petitioner had assumed them to be."

The *Gallison* court distinguished the two cases before it on the basis of facts that are not relevant under a strict reading of the statutory language. However, rather than focusing on whether the brokerage was paid, the majority emphasized that Galison, unlike Goldstein, employed questionable tactics to pressure the birth mother into going forward with an adoption she had come to regret. The majority may be correct that the legislature had such conduct in mind when it banned baby brokering, but the dissent is surely right that Goldstein's seemingly blameless conduct also falls within the statutory net. *Galison* thus suggests that the underlying rationale for the prohibition is preventing the coercion of birth mothers. Should the statute focus explicitly on that concern, rather than create a broad ban on all "placing out?"

The 1994 Uniform Adoption Act follows the same approach, allowing placement only directly by the child's parents or through a licensed agency. § 2-101. In direct placement, the parent herself must select the adoptive parents, and is limited to parties with a favorable pre-placement evaluation. Agents may assist in the adoption, but they may not charge brokerage fees or engage in any advertising. § 7-101.

Not surprisingly, courts are reluctant to void adoption orders on the basis of violations of placing out statutes, concluding that such violations are better addressed through penal sanctions.

In exonerating Goldstein, the *Galison* court emphasized that he merely "carried out" the birth mother's "unchanged decisions." This legal response may encourage attorneys to avoid selecting the adoptive parents for the birth mother. Rather, the common practice is to advise adoptive parents to place ads soliciting birth mothers, and deal with the birth mother only after she has spoken with the adoptive parents. *See* Galen, *supra* note 1. Some attorneys may maintain files of interested adoptive parents. Consider whether such practices violate the statutes involved in *Galison*. If not, should brokering statutes be amended to reach them?

4. *Do Independent Adoptions Risk Children's Welfare?* A theme of the criticism of independent adoptions is that unlicensed intermediaries lack the professional skills to make proper placements, even if they operate with the child's interest in mind. Usually, the pregnant women receive no counseling, and inadequate (if any) attention is given to screening prospective adoptive parents. *See* Mansnerus, *supra* at A14-15; Emery, *supra* page 1450. *Sarosi v. Commissioner,* described above, might seem to vindicate this view and thus justify New York's total ban on unlicensed brokerage. One horrendous case, however, does not prove the point, for licensed agencies also do not have perfect placement records. The question is whether, on average, they do better than lawyers and doctors. In fact, the research has found no evidence that independent adoptions yield less favorable placements for children than agency adoptions. The Child Welfare study found that agency social workers, who are often asked to evaluate the adoptive parents for the "home studies" required in independent adoptions, generally view the homes positively and believe they are usually equal or superior to placements made by agencies. Meezan, *supra* at 42, 46–47.

Most states require a "home study" of the prospective adoptive parents before a court issues the final decree in an independent adoption. Thus, independent adoption does not go unscrutinized. In an agency adoption, the agency itself performs the evaluation, and its results are made available to the court. However, agency personnel who also perform home studies in independent adoptions may view their task differently than when evaluating agency applicants. In independent adoptions, they are certifying that the home meets minimal standards, but when the agency makes the placement decision, it is looking for the best possible home for the child. Thus, home studies done in connection with independent adoptions are less thorough, even though they are often conducted by the same people, in part because they are typically done after the child has already been placed in the home, making it less likely that the court would turn down the adoption petition. If a home study had been done on Joel Steinberg and Hedda Nussbaum, is it likely that the subsequent tragedy would have been avoided?

The 1994 Uniform Adoption Act requires a pre-placement evaluation in independent as well as agency adoptions (§ 2-102). In independent adoptions, the pre-placement evaluation "certifies" the prospective adoptive parents. A favorable pre-placement evaluation is a prerequisite for direct placement by the parent.

Underlying the criticism of independent adoption by those who support agency adoption is a belief about the purpose of an adoption "system." Child welfare advocates believe that the placement process is designed to assist children whose parents can not care for them to find good homes; it is truly a social service function. From this perspective, a flourishing independent adoption system may appear to be more focused on satisfaction of the desires of childless adults to acquire children so that they can have a family. In this sense, it is a short step to Landes & Posner's "market for babies," *infra*.

LEGALIZE BABY SELLING?

In a famous 1978 article, Elisabeth Landes and Richard Posner argued that the legal restrictions on fees in private adoption have created a baby shortage with many unfortunate consequences, and that a free market in which adoptive parents and birth mothers could freely negotiate for the transfer of babies offers a solution that should be considered. Landes & Posner, *The Economics of the Baby Shortage*, 7 J. LEGAL STUD. 323 (1978). Under current law, these authors point out, many of the costs of producing and transferring a baby can not be recovered, including the opportunity costs of the birth mother's time when she is unable to work; the pain or other disutility of the pregnancy and delivery; the subjective value of the child to her; and the costs of search by a middleman in locating and bringing buyer and seller together.

These constraints, although they are evaded to an extent in a "gray market," are sufficiently stringent that pregnant women have little incentive to place their children for adoption, rather than keeping or aborting them. At the same time, the authors argue, "constraints on payment discourage the emergence of an effective middleman function," which is a serious problem in a market in which buyers and sellers may have a hard time finding one another. As economists would predict, a clandestine black market in babies has grown up, characterized by high prices and fraud. Moreover, because abusive or neglectful parents have no incentive to choose adoption, they will place their children in foster care instead, even when they do not seriously plan to reacquire the child. This decision may "render the child unadoptable, for by the time the parents relinquish their parental rights the child may be too old to be placed for adoption." *Id.* at 338.

Landes and Posner review the objections to a free market. Many criticisms, they believe, are more aptly directed at a black market than at a legal free market. For example, they challenge the claim that high prices that favor the wealthy would pervade a free market. Prices are high on the black market, they argue, because they include punishment costs. In a free market, prices for children of *equivalent quality* would be much lower. Fraud would also not be a significant problem in a legal market because sellers could give legally enforceable warranties about genealogy, health, etc. The authors describe the effect of a legal market:

> The current illegality of baby selling reduces the benefits of transacting to the buyer by depriving him of the contractual protections that buyers in legal markets normally receive. Prospective adoptive parents would presumably be willing to pay more for a child whose health and genealogy were warranted in a legally enforceable instrument than they are willing to pay under the present system where the entire risk of any deviation from expected quality falls on them. Thus the effect of legalizing the baby market would be not only to shift the marginal cost of baby production and sale downward but to move the demand curve for adoptive children upward. Conceivably these movements could cancel each other out, resulting in no change from the current black-market prices, but even if they did consumer satisfaction would be increased. The same price would buy a higher-quality package of rights. *Id*. at 341.

The authors then address objections to baby selling in a legal market. In response to the criticism that a free market will not promote the best interests of the children, they acknowledge that "free exchange will maximize the satisfaction of the people trading, [and not] . . . the thing traded." *Id*. at 342. However, they question whether adoption agencies do any better "in finding homes for children that would maximize their satisfactions in life." *Id*. at 342–3. Moreover, on their view, criminal prohibitions of child abuse, together with background checks, would effectively screen out prospective parents who plan to abuse their children. Further, they point out that most people do not adopt with such motives, and their willingness to pay is added assurance.

> Few people buy a car or a television set in order to smash it. In general, the more costly a purchase, the more care the purchaser will lavish on it. Recent studies suggest that the more costly it is for parents to obtain a child, the greater will be their investment in the child's quality attributes, such as health and education. *Id*. at 343.

Landes and Posner express skepticism that adoptive and birth parents will be vulnerable to overreaching by middlemen because the decisions involved have such a strong emotional component. They point out that this is true of "other goods and services, such as medical care, that are subject to market exchange." *Id*. at 344.

Finally, the authors address the objection that baby selling will lead to baby breeding, particularly breeding babies with desirable qualities and specified characteristics that could be matched with those desired by prospective adoptive parents. They acknowledge that "any market will generate incentives and improve the product," *(Id*. at 345) but dismiss the concern about eugenically bred babies. As long as it "did not extend beyond infertile couples and those with serious genetic disorders, the impact of a free baby market on the genetic composition and distribution of the human race at large would be small."*Id*.

The greatest long-run effect of legalizing the baby market, according to the authors, is that it would "induc[e] women who have unintentionally become pregnant to put up the child for adoption rather than raise it themselves or have an abortion." *Id*. A legal baby market, they argue, makes sense as a response to contemporary moral standards:

> Now that the stigma [of illegitimacy] has diminished and abortion has become a constitutional right, not only has the flow of babies to the (lawful) adoption market contracted but the practical alternatives to selling an unwanted baby have increasingly become either to retain it and raise it as an illegitimate child, ordinarily with no father present, or to have an abortion. What social purposes are served by encouraging these alternatives to baby sale?

> The symbolic objections to baby sale must also be compared with the substantial costs that the present system imposes on childless couples, aborted fetuses (if they can be said to incur costs), and children who end up in foster care. *Id*. at 346.

The Landes and Posner article has been heavily criticized. *See* Prichard, *A Market for Babies?,* 34 U. TORONTO L.J. 341 (1984) (comprehensively reviewing arguments that the baby market would not in fact work as intended and that, in any event, it would violate important non-economic moral and social values). Additional critiques include Williams, *Spare Parts, Family Values, Old Children, Cheap*, 28 N.E. L. REV. 913 (1994); Cohen, *Posnerism, Pluralism, and Pessimism*, 67 B.U. L. REV. 105 (1987). For a defense of Posner, see Cass, *Coping with Life, Law and Market: A Comment on Posner and the Law and Economics Debate,* 67 B.U. L. REV. 73 (1987). *See also* Posner, *The Regulation of the Market in Adoptions,* 67 B.U. L. REV. 59 (1987), in which Posner responds to some of his critics.

Law imparts a moral as well as an economic message, and one theme of the critics is that an unacceptable message is implicit in the recognition of a baby market — that children are not persons but commodities, the subject of market transactions. Whatever safeguards are provided to protect against maltreatment, the very idea of selling children seems repulsive. See *People v. Daniel,* 241 Cal. Rptr. 3 (1987), in which the court sustained a baby-seller's felony conviction for violation of laws against slavery; Radin, *Market Inalienability,* 100 HARV. L. REV. 1849 (1987). In assessing this concern, would it matter (as Posner suggests it does) if the additional babies sold by moving to a legal market would otherwise have been aborted?

§ D. THE LEGAL EFFECT OF ADOPTION

[1] THE CHILD'S RELATIONSHIP WITH OLD AND NEW RELATIVES

NOTES

1. *Adoptive Parents' Rights and Duties Generally.* The adoptive parents become the child's legal parents, and acquire the parental rights and obligations of birth parents. The transfer of these rights and duties takes place at the time of adoption. Thus, in *Wise v. Gulf States Collection Servs.*, 633 So. 2d 1025 (Miss. 1994), the Mississippi Supreme Court reversed a trial court decision interpreting this principle to impose liability on adoptive parents for a $32,000 hospital bill incurred by their child as a new-born a month before the adoption took place. The Supreme Court ordered summary judgment for the parents. "Just as the adopting parents have no legal right to the child prior to the adoption, nothing in the statute or the case law suggests that they have any legal duties or obligations during that time."

2. *General Inheritance Rights.* What are the inheritance rights of the adopted child in relation to her adoptive family? Can she inherit from her birth parents? Although these questions have different answers in different jurisdictions, some generalizations can be made. The usual modern rule treats the adopted child exactly as if she were the birth child of the adopted parents. This principle is reflected in many modern adoption statutes, which contain language stating, for example, that "issue" includes an adoptive child, or that adoption terminates the right to inherit intestate from a blood relative. *See, e.g., Estate of Carlson,* 457 N.W.2d 789 (Minn. App. 1990) (two brothers adopted after their parents died do not inherit from the intestate estate of a third brother who was not adopted because statute explicitly cuts off inheritance rights from blood relatives).

Many statutes permit the adopted child to take by intestate succession both from and through adoptive parents as well as from and through the biological parents. This is particularly true when the adoption was by a step-parent. A California court held that the decedent's biological children who were adopted by their stepfather were entitled to share his estate with his "adopted in" son, under a California statute that dealt with stepparent adoption. *In re Estate of Dye*, 112 Cal. Rptr. 2d 362 (Ct. App. 2001). The court pointed out that the decedent, who had had no contact with his birth children in the forty years since the adoption, could have avoided the outcome through a will provision. *See also Railey v. Spikes*, 614 So. 2d 1017 (Ala. 1993)(decedent's natural children, who were adopted by the step-fathers who had married their respective mothers, could take decedent's personal property by intestate succession). Some courts have reached a similar result on the ground that the statute does not exclude inheritance from biological parents. A note argues that the intestate succession rights of adoptees should be contingent on a continued family relationship between the natural family and the adoptee. Note, *Intestate Succession Rights of Adopted Children: Should the Stepparent Exception be Extended?*, 77 Corn. L. Rev. 1188 (1992).

For more on the general question of adoption and inheritance, see Reim, *Relatives by Blood, Adoption and Association: Who Should Get What and Why,* 37 Vand. L. Rev. 711 (1984).

3. *Inheritance: Equitable Adoption.* On occasion, courts have accepted claims to an intestate estate under a doctrine called "equitable adoption," which does not require a lawful adoption. Typically, the claimant will have lived with the decedent in what to all appearances was a parent-child relationship. Further, there will be evidence of some agreement by these "adoptive parents" to enter into a formal adoption, which for some reason never took place. Ordinarily, the sole effect of this doctrine is to permit the "adoptee" to inherit intestate as if she were a child of the decedent. In most states, the doctrine does not create an adoption for any other purpose and therefore has no effect outside of the probate context in which it was developed. *But see Atkinson v. Atkinson*, 408 N.W.2d 516 (Mich. App. 1987) (doctrine applied to divorce visitation rights, where mother revealed on divorce that husband of 5-year-old son was not biological father).

Even in the probate context, courts do not apply the doctrine expansively. *See, e.g., Montgomery Board of Ed. v. Browning*, 635 A.2d 373 (Md. 1994) (under equitable adoption doctrine, a child may take by intestate succession *from* a deceased "equitable parent," but not *through* such a party; thus, petitioner whose equitable parent was decedent's sister (who had died before decedent) was not allowed to claim as a niece of the decedent). Further, the clear purpose of the doctrine is to benefit the child. In *Halterman v. Halterman*, 867 S.W.2d 559 (Mo. App. 1993), the court rejected an effort to intervene in a wrongful death action concerning the death of the child of the claimant's former husband, on the ground that she was the child's parent by equitable adoption. The court concluded that the "doctrine is solely for the benefit of a child" and, therefore, appellant, as a non-parent, lacked standing to intervene." For more on equitable adoption, see Jeffries, *Equitable Adoption: They Took Him Into Their Home and Called Him Fred,* 58 VA. L. REV. 727 (1972).

4. *Grandparent Visitation After Adoption.* An adoption may sometimes sever the legal relationship between the child and relatives who are close to him. In one common example, the surviving spouse remarries after the death of one parent, and this new stepparent then adopts the children. Does this end the relationship between the children and the decedent's parents — the children's grandparents until the adoption? The grandparents may be particularly anxious to maintain their relationship with their grandchild when their own child has died, yet the ordinary principle of treating the adopted child the same as a birth child of the adoptive parent would sever their legal relationship. Where the parties maintain cordial relations, no legal issue will arise. But the former grandparents may seek legal relief if denied access to the children. Before the Supreme Court decided *Troxel v. Granville, See* Chapter 6, page 667, courts sometimes ordered visitation in stepparent adoption situations, although seldom in third-party adoption. *See, e.g., In re Adoption/ Guardianship No. 92A41*, 622 A.2d 150 (Md. Sp. App. 1993) (grandparent who had visitation order following death of her daughter could intervene in stepmother's adoption proceeding). One theory behind this distinction is that a child who is adopted by a stepparent remains within his or her "circle of consanguinity," while adoption by strangers terminates the bloodline through which the grandparents' rights were derived. *See Adoption of G.D.L.,* 747 P.2d 282 (Okla. 1987).

Post-adoption grandparent visitation is simply a variation of the larger issue that the Supreme Court dealt with in *Troxel*. In *Troxel* itself, the grandparents' son had died and the children had been adopted by their stepfather (although after the visitation petition was filed). This fact seemed to be unimportant to the Court in its conclusion that the visitation order infringed on the mother's parental rights. Predictably, after *Troxel*, courts will be more restrained in ordering grandparent visitation, although this does not mean that orders will never be issued and upheld. For a discussion of *Troxel* and the judicial and legislative response, see Chapter 6. The Alabama Supreme Court rejected a lower appellate court's judgment that grandparent visitation could not be ordered after *Troxel,* in a case involving grandparent adoptive parents as well as grandparent petitioners seeking visitation. *J.S. & E.S. v. D.W. & J.W.*, 835 So. 2d 186 (Ala. 2002). The maternal grandparents had custody for a while after the parents were found unfit, but they encouraged the paternal grandparents to adopt. Thereafter, the parties' relationship broke down and the adoptive (grand)parents denied the petitioners access to the child. The supreme court concluded that *Troxel* was distinguishable because it involved natural parents. The (questionable) implication is that adoptive parents have more limited fundamental rights, because adoption is a statutory creature.

   5. Grandparent Adoption. Should grandparents be preferred as adoptive parents when their own child's rights have been terminated, against a younger couple who are not related to the child? Here, the importance of maintaining blood relationships may be weighed heavily, but it is not dispositive. An Illinois court upheld a preference favoring foster parents for adoption when they have had custody of a child for more than a year against a challenge by out-of-state grandparents. *In re Adoption of C.D.,* 729 N.E.2d 553 (Ill. App. Ct. 2000). The grandparents were unable to serve as foster parents for their daughter's child when she lost custody because of the state's reunification goals. When her parental rights were terminated, the foster parents, with whom the child had lived for 7 years, intervened in the proceeding to consider the grandparents' adoption petition. The court rejected the grandparents' equal protection and due process claims. It concluded that the grandparents had no "parental" interest, or fundamental rights in the continued relationship with their grandchildren, and that the foster parent preference reflected rational policy goals. Another concern arises when grandparents are viewed as seeking to maintain the tie between the child and a parent who has been determined to be unfit. *See In re J.M.W.*, 492 N.W.2d 686 (Iowa 1992) (upholding court order rejecting grandparents' claims, partly because of age, and also because the grandparents hoped their daughter might develop a relationship with her children). *See* Note, *Permissive Intervention — Grandparents' Key to Entering Adoption Proceedings*, 26 GA. L. REV. 787 (1992).

ABROGATION BY ADOPTIVE PARENTS

   At one time, many states allowed adoptive parents to seek annulment of the adoption decree upon discovery of a previously unknown illness or other physical abnormality in the child, but a 1983 survey concluded that California was the only state retaining such a provision. Note, *Annulment of Adoption Decrees on Petition of Adoptive Parents*, 22 J. FAM. L. 549 (1983). CAL. FAM. CODE § 9100 (West 1994) provides:

   If any child adopted . . . shows evidence of a developmental disability or mental illness as a result of conditions existing before the adoption to an extent that the child cannot be relinquished to an adoption agency on the grounds that the child is considered unadoptable, and of which conditions the adopting parents or parent had no knowledge or notice before the entry of the . . . adoption [decree], a petition setting forth those facts may be filed by the adopting parents or parent with the court which granted the petition for adoption. If these facts are proved to the satisfaction of the court, it may make an order setting aside the order of adoption.

In *Adoption of Kay C.*, 228 Cal. Rptr. 209 (Ct. App. 6th Dist. 1991), an appellate court upheld an order setting aside an adoption of a mentally ill child, aged 9 at the time of adoption. Although the prospective parents expressed concern and inquired about the possibility of emotional problems, the agency did not disclose psychiatric and other mental health evaluation reports diagnosing the child as having a borderline personality disorder and expressing doubts about the success of adoption. The child subsequently was hospitalized and diagnosed with schizophrenia and depression. After efforts at family therapy failed, the adoptive parents petitioned to set aside the adoption. In upholding the order, the appellate court rejected the child's claim that she had a liberty interest in the adoptive family relationship. It also rejected her equal protection claim that the statutory classification based on her developmental disability was suspect. The court held that the classification was rationally calculated to achieve the legitimate state interest of promoting adoption.

Should adoptive parents receive such a "warranty" regarding the child's health? Birth parents do not, although they have more control over the child's pre-natal environment and more confidence about its genetic heritage. The gradual disappearance of provisions like California's suggests that most legislatures have come to believe that the risks as well as the joys of parenthood pass to the adoptive parents, who should be prepared to cope with whatever their newly undertaken responsibilities require.

Perhaps more legitimately, courts occasionally permit revocations in the absence of a specific statute, where a child's serious problems were concealed rather than unknown. *See* Section B2, *supra*; *In re Lisa Diane G.*, 537 A.2d 131 (R.I. 1988) (family court can revoke adoption and allow adoptive parents reimbursement for child-rearing expenses, because of agency's failure to disclose physicians' advice against adoption based on eight-year-old girl's serious behavioral problems).

An adoption decree can sometimes be rescinded on the basis of general rules providing equitable grounds upon which judgments may be set aside. It is usually difficult to make out an equitable claim for setting aside a judgment, and this applies to adoptions as well. Many of these claims involve stepparent adoption, and courts are generally not sympathetic to the stepparent who seeks abrogation of adoption after his marriage to the biological parent ends in divorce. An Ohio court rejected a stepfather's petition to vacate the adoption order, where the mother (his now-former wife) allegedly had coerced him through misrepresentations to adopt her children, for the sole purpose of providing them with financial security. *Joslyn v. Reynolds*, 761 N.E.2d 48 (Ohio 2001). The marriage ended shortly after the end of the one-year time period of the statute of limitations for abrogation applied to stepparent adoptions. The court declined to extend the definition of fraud to allow the stepfather to qualify for an exception to the limitations period. An important consideration that often weighs against abrogation is the impact on the child's financial security. For example, in *In re Baby Boy C*, 596 N.Y.S.2d 56 (App. 1993), where the adoptive parents became estranged after the agency investigation but before the final order of adoption, the appellate court found the husband estopped from withdrawing his consent to adoption. His clear intent to adopt was demonstrated by his actions in paying for the infant children to be brought to this country, joining the adoption petition, and committing to pay for their care. *See also Sell v. Sell,* 714 A.2d 1057 (Pa. Super. Ct. 1998) (no abrogation to avoid child support obligation based on father's claim that Russian adoption decree was not valid because the couple had effectively purchased the child, and his former wife had coerced him into consenting to the adoption).

Courts may be more receptive where the facts are not only compelling but the child's interests are not endangered by rescinding the adoption order. Sometimes abrogation is clearly in the child's interest. In an unusual New Jersey case, the child whose interest was served was not the adopted child, but her child by her adoptive father. *In re Adoption of M*, 722 A.2d 615 (N.J. Super. Ct. Ch. Div. 1998). The court agreed to vacate the daughter's adoption (six years after the final judgment) so that she could marry the child's father, her (soon to be former) adoptive father. (Not surprisingly, the adoptive parents' marriage ended in divorce after the father-daughter relationship came to light.) In a more routine case, a step-father's adoption was abrogated in a case in which the couple, who lived together only a year, separated three weeks after the adoption decree was issued. *Adoption of Children by O.,* 359 A.2d 513 (N.J. Super. Ct. Ch. Div. 1976). The mother had sufficient funds to provide for the children on her own, and neither she, the children nor the adoptive father wanted the adoption to be effective. The court concluded that the children's interest supported vacating this adoption decree. On abrogation generally, see Carroll, *Abrogation of Adoption by Adoptive Parents,* 19 Fam. L.Q. 155 (1985).

PROBLEM

Problem 11-7. Debra was adopted by the Allens at age 3, after having been in state custody for two years. By the time Debra was 5 years old, she had severe behavior problems and was adjudged mentally deficient. Although she was committed to a public institution, two years later she still had not actually gained admission due to overcrowded conditions. The Allens have continued to care for her at home, but they are concerned over the disturbing effect she has on their family life and their other children. They are also anxious to be relieved of the heavy financial burden of caring for Debra, which will continue even after her ultimate institutionalization, since the state charges the parents of children committed to the institution. The Allens have recently learned that the agency had significant information about Debra's child's psychological condition in its possession at the time of the adoption, and did not communicate it to the Allens, although they inquired about potential problems.

The Allens seek your advice about their legal options. They would like to annul the adoption decree, to make the agency responsible for Debra. Advise them on this matter. What other remedies might be available? *See B3, supra.*

[2]   SHOULD ADOPTION RECORDS REMAIN SEALED? THE TREND TOWARD ACCESS TO ADOPTION RECORDS

In the traditional agency adoption, neither the adoptive parents nor the birth parents are given information that will allow them to identify the other. The policy is reinforced by the traditional state laws sealing adoption records once the decree is granted. *See* Annot., *Restricting Access to Judicial Records of Concluded Adoption Proceedings,* 83 A.L.R.3d 800 (1978). A policy of confidentiality has some obvious purposes. It protects the adoptive parents from subsequent inquiries and potential harassment by the birth parents and is consistent with an adoption philosophy that aims to create a parent-child relationship that mimics, insofar as possible, that of the biological family. Confidentiality also reflects the prevailing view that the presence of extra parents can be disorienting and disruptive to a child. Beyond this, it is assumed that many birth parents (particularly unmarried mothers) may want to get on with their lives, secure in the knowledge that they will not be asked to revisit the "mistake" of their youth at some later time.

Many of the concerns supporting confidentiality seem less compelling today. The stigma of illegitimacy is greatly reduced, if it survives at all, and few adoptive parents seek to maintain the fiction of non-adoption. Confidentiality also protected the privacy of a birth mother anxious to conceal her "indiscretion" at a time when non-marital pregnancy had a much greater social significance than it has today. Moreover, concerns about maintaining the integrity of the adoptive family or of not disrupting the birth mother's life become attenuated as time passes, and at least as to the former concern, seem not to be relevant once the adoptee is an adult.

Recently, there has been a great deal of interest in opening adoption records, principally by adopted children but also by birth parents. Psychologists have recognized the importance to many adopted children of having some knowledge of and connection to their biological family. Since the early 1980's state legislatures have responded. More than 20 states have registry laws, under which adoptees, birth parents and adoptive parents can register their willingness to meet one another. *See, e.g.,* CAL. FAM. CODE §§ 9203, 9205 (West 1994 & Supp. 2003); ILL. COMP. STAT. ANN. 750 § 50/18.1 (Smith-Hurd Supp. 2003); ARK. CODE ANN. § 9-9-504 (2002). Other states have "search and consent" provisions: upon petition of the adult adoptee (usually), a search for the biological parent will be undertaken; if found, the parent is asked to consent to a meeting with adoptee. Because they do not rely on both parties taking the initiative, these laws offer a more proactive means of establishing contact than registries. *See* COLO. REV. STAT. ANN. § 19-5-304 (West 2002).

A few states have enacted far-reaching laws providing adopted persons with information about their biological families. The Tennessee statute, for example, gives adoptees, age 21 and older, the right to any information that the state has about their birth parents. TENN. CODE ANN. § 36-1-127-28 (2001). The statute includes a unique mechanism to protect the privacy of birth parents, however. The parent can file a "contact veto," conditioning the release of information on the adoptee's promise not to make contact. Violation results in civil and criminal penalties. In the view of supporters, this approach, borrowed from a law in New South Wales, Australia, satisfies the adoptee's need to know about her birth family without resulting in unwanted intrusion. It has been challenged as a "disastrous invasion of privacy of birth parents" by adoption advocates. Opponents point out that the birth parents must take the initiative to file the contact veto. *See, e.g.*, Lewin, *Tennessee is Focus of Debate on Adoptees Birth Records*, N.Y. TIMES, March 18, 1996, at A1. In 1999, Oregon voters by referendum enacted Measure 58, under which any adopted person over the age of 21 can apply to the state registrar for a copy of his or her original birth certificate. OR. REV. STAT. § 432.240 (1999). Unlike the Tennesee statute, the measure includes no contact veto. *See also* ALA. CODE § 22-9A-12(c) (2001)(access to the original, unaltered birth certificate is available upon written request by the adult adoptee, along with accompanying adoption records). The Alabama statute also permits birth parents to file a "contact preference form" which would be given to the adoptee along with the birth certificate.

The Tennesee and Oregon enactments have withstood quite similar state and federal constitutional challenges brought by classes of adoptive and birth parents. *Does v. Sundquist*, S.W.3d 919 (Tenn. 1999); *Does v. State*, 993 P.2d 822 (Or. Ct. App. 1999). Both courts rejected the claim that the opening of previously confidential records was a government intrusion into decisions about whether to bear children and infringed on birth mothers' constitutional rights of reproductive privacy. The Oregon court noted that the adoption decision, unlike those involving contraception and abortion, is not made unilaterally by the mother; it involves a willing adoptive parent and active oversight by the state. The Tennessee court emphasized that the parents' privacy was protected by the contact veto under that statute. Equally unsuccessful was the argument that the enactments impaired the obligation of contract. Both courts found that the prior adoption statutes offered no guarantee of confidentiality. Nor was there legislative intent to contract with birth mothers to prevent disclosure of their identities to their children. *See also Doe v. Sundquist*, 943 F. Supp. 886 (M.D. Tenn. 1996); upheld in 106 F.3d 702 (6th Cir. 1997) (rejecting federal constitutional challenge of Tennessee statute).

These laws go one large step beyond other reform statutes under which an adoptee, upon reaching adulthood, can obtain much information about her background contained in the adoption records, except for the identity of the birth parents. Thus, for example, the New York statute grants the adoptee access to information about her parents' race, ethnicity, nationality, religion, age, marital status, health, educational level, physical description, occupation, facts and circumstances relating to the cause of adoption, parents' talents, hobbies, special interests, and health history. N.Y. PUB. HEALTH L. § 4138-c(3) (McKinney 2002). New York has resisted efforts to get identifying information, however. In *O'Hearn v. Spence-Chapin Services to Families and Children,* 929 F. Supp. 36 (S.D.N.Y. 1996), for example, a Federal court in New York rejected a breach of contract claim brought by an adoptee, alleging that the agency was obligated to release identifying information to the adoptee under an agreement with the birth mother. The court found the contract to be against public policy, because of the state's strong interest in maintaining the confidentiality of adoption records, and held that the agency had no duty to release identifying information. The Pennsylvania statute provides no list of the kinds of information that can be released, but states that the adoptee can obtain "as much information as will not endanger the anonymity of the natural parent." 23 PA. CONS. STAT. tit. 23 § 2905 (b) (Purdon 2001). In *Appeal of Kasparek*, 653 A.2d 1254 (Pa. 1995), an adult adoptee challenged the court's release of only the age and religion of her parents under the statute. The Pennsylvania Supreme Court, emphasizing the need of adoptees to know about their biological parents, reversed the trial court's decision. The appellate court looked to the kind of information disclosed under the New York statute and others that list specific factors, and concluded that additional information could be disclosed, including information about the relationship between the birth parents and the circumstances of the adoption. The case suggests that a statutory list of factors may be more efficient than the Pennsylvania approach. A list of factors also constrains the discretion of any judge who disapproves of disclosure. *See also* ILL. COMP. STAT. ANN. ch 750 § 50/18.4 & /18.4a (West 1999 & Supp. 2003); MASS. GEN. LAWS ANN. ch. 210 § 5D (West 1998).

To many people, the availability of non-identifying information to the adult adoptee is a sufficient recognition of her interest in knowing about her biological parents, and also preserves the privacy of the birth parents. Some courts point to this access to information as justification for *not* opening identifying records. *Fineberg v. Suffolk Div. of Probate & Fam. Ct. Div.*, 644 N.E.2d 264 (1995). Indeed, the more radical approach of abandoning traditional policies of confidentiality altogether could generate a backlash, perhaps making adoption less attractive to some adoptive and birth parents. The Oregon and Tennessee experiences suggest that birth mothers (and adoptive parents) who made decisions about adoptions relying on confidentiality and nondisclosure may feel that changing the rules about confidentiality of records violates their understanding of the terms of the placement. One solution would be to allow the birth mother, at the time of adoption, to opt out of a policy of future contact or release of identifying information. (This of course does not resolve concerns that the adoptive parents may have.) Many birth mothers might change their minds over time, however, so making that refusal final might limit future contact excessively.

Do many adoptees desire to search for their birth parents? One study concluded that large majorities of both birth mothers and adoptees favor release of identifying information to adult adoptees who seek it; the feelings of adoptive parents were more ambivalent. P. SACHDEV, UNLOCKING THE ADOPTION FILES (1989). For a thoughtful analysis of the arguments for and against open records, see Cahn & Singer, *Adoption, Identity and the Constitution: The Case for Opening Closed Records*, 2 U. PA. J. CONST. L. 150 (1999). Cahn and Singer favor a presumption in favor of open records.

NOTES

1. *Opening Records for Good Cause: Psychological Need.* Traditional adoption laws providing confidentiality usually permit access to adoption records for "good cause," and adoptees have sometimes sought to fit their claim within this test. Although the statutes typically offer little guidance to judges

asked to decide whether sufficient "cause" exists, the cases seem clear that "good cause" is not a pretextual requirement, but requires a substantial reason beyond the interest that adoptees or birth parents may have in learning more about each other. Courts have also rejected constitutional claims. *See In re Adoption of S. J.D.,* 641 N.W. 2d 794 (Iowa 2002)(adult adoptee has no First Amendment free speech right to adoption records); *In re Roger B.,* 418 N.E.2d 751 (Ill.), *appeal dismissed,* 454 U.S. 806 (1981) (same).

What of adoptees who claim that their need to know about their roots is necessary to avoid serious psychological damage? Some courts have distinguished the adoptee's desire to simply know more about her ancestry from "psychological trauma." *See In re Matter of Wilson,* 544 N.Y.S.2d 886 (Sup. Ct. App. Div. 1989). In practice, psychological damage claims are seldom successful. Consider *In re Dixon,* 323 N.W.2d 549 (Mich. App. 1982). Dixon was a 35-year-old married woman with three children, who testified that she suffered from severe depression which had led to suicide attempts due in part to not knowing her biological parents' identities. The court rejected her petition to open her adoption records after undertaking an analysis that balanced the biological parent's privacy rights, the state's interest in fulfilling its statutory agreement with the biological parents that the records would be kept sealed, except for good cause and the adoptee's interest. Although it characterized the adoptee's interest as "the most important," the court declined to find as a matter of law that Dixon had made a showing of good cause. Based on psychiatric testimony, the court concluded that Dixon's illness was due to her treatment in her adoptive home, and suggested that her claim was based on "little more than a 'Psychological need to know' " about her biological parents.

Should the adoptee's interest in knowing about her parents be given greater weight than the biological parent's interest in privacy, given that her need for information about her past was created by the adoption itself, a decision that in essential ways determined her life and about which she had no input. If adoption policy is designed to promote the adopted child's interest, should not her need to know about her biological family receive recognition? Although biological parents views probably are not well represented in the political process, groups representing the interests of adoptive parents also oppose broad access to adoption records, and these groups are quite powerful.

2. *Opening Records for Good Cause: Medical Need.* Sometimes an adoptee or birth parent seeks access to adoption records because genetic information about the birth parents is thought necessary to protect the health of their child. In these situations, it is often possible to provide the relevant information through intermediaries without revealing the birth parents' and adoptee's identity to one another. *See, e.g., In re Rocci,* 96 A.D.2d 743, 465 N.Y.S.2d 330 (App. Div. 1983) (biological mother sought to inform adoptive parents of potential hereditary tendency toward diabetes; trial court instructed to notify adoptive parents but to maintain confidentiality). Similarly, a 56-year-old adopted son sought disclosure of his father's identity to obtain a more complete genetic history that might assist in the treatment of his heart condition and help him regain pilot certification. His adoptive parents were no longer living, and he had already obtained his mother's identity through other sources. Nonetheless, the New York Court of Appeals reversed a trial court order granting him access to records identifying his father, pointing to a statute under which agencies may release medical information with all identifying information redacted. *Golan v. Louise Wise Servs.*, 507 N.E.2d 275 (1987).

3. *Independent Adoptions.* Policies of confidentiality have never been as important with independent adoptions as with agency placements. Even in a period when confidentiality was the norm, studies found that about one-third of the biological parents in independent adoptions knew the identity of the adoptive couple, and most of these reported that they knew how to get in touch with them. The adoptive parents' names were often on the consents signed by the birth mothers. W. MEEZAN, et. al. *supra* at 101–02 (1978). The same study reported that the adoptive parents for the most part were not worried about the biological mother "interfering in the child's life." With the baby shortage creating pressures on adoptive parents to accommodate birth mothers, it seems likely that a new survey would show an even higher proportion of independent adoptions abandoning all pretense of confidentiality.

PROBLEM

Problem 11-8. Michael and Alice adopted John at four weeks. He is now 17, and wants to track down his birth parents. He seeks your assistance because his adoptive parents have told him you were the attorney who handled the adoption. John tells you that he is interested in learning more about his biological heritage, but has no intention of making demands upon his birth parents. His curiosity about his birth parents seems sincere, although he has no special reason, such as medical necessity, to seek them out. He says his relationship with his adoptive parents is good. You call them and they urge you to provide him with any assistance you can, and offer to pay you any appropriate fees. They have full confidence in their son and are happy to support his quest in any way they can.

You have little independent recollection of this particular adoption, but your office records contain enough information about the mother to give someone a pretty good chance at finding her. She was unmarried at the time, but the records also provide some information about the man she identified as the father. As best as you can recall now, you never actually met or dealt with him. Your standard practice at the time in non-family adoptions was to maintain confidentiality. Often, either adoptive parents or birth mothers requested assurances on this point, which you always gave. Your records do not indicate whether such assurances were sought in this particular adoption. John's parents, however, recall the promise of confidentiality which you had made to them 17 years earlier, and say they were now prepared to waive it. Your records do not indicate any separate counsel for the birth mother in this case.

The only relevant state statute provides: "Except upon order of the court for good cause shown in exceptional cases, no person shall disclose from the court records the name or identity of either an adoptive parent or an adoptive child."

What do you do?

§ E. ADOPTION ALTERNATIVES: GESTATIONAL MOTHERS AND THE NEW BIOLOGY

[1] GESTATIONAL MOTHERING CONTRACTS

IN RE BABY M

537 A.2d 1227 (N.J. 1988)

WILENTZ, C.J. In this matter the Court is asked to determine the validity of a contract that purports to provide a new way of bringing children into a family. For a fee of $10,000, a woman agrees to be artificially inseminated with the semen of another woman's husband; she is to conceive a child, carry it to term, and after its birth surrender it to the natural father and his wife. The intent of the contract is that the child's natural mother will thereafter be forever separated from her child. The wife is to adopt the child, and she and the natural father are to be regarded as its parents for all purposes. The contract providing for this is called a "surrogacy contract," the natural mother inappropriately called the "surrogate mother."

We invalidate the surrogacy contract because it conflicts with the law and public policy of this State. While we recognize the depth of the yearning of infertile couples to have their own children, we find the payment of money to a "surrogate" mother illegal, perhaps criminal, and potentially degrading to women. Although in this case we grant custody to the natural father, the evidence having clearly proved such custody to be in the best interests of the infant, we void both the termination of the surrogate mother's parental rights and the adoption of the child by the wife/stepparent. We thus restore the "surrogate" as the mother of the child. We remand the issue of the natural mother's visitation rights to the trial court.

We find no offense to our present laws where a woman voluntarily and without payment agrees to act as a "surrogate" mother, provided that she is not subject to a binding agreement to surrender her child. . . . Under current law, however, the surrogacy agreement before us is illegal and invalid.

I.

In February 1985, William Stern and Mary Beth Whitehead entered into a surrogacy contract. . . .

The contract provided that through artificial insemination using Mr. Stern's sperm, Mrs. Whitehead would become pregnant, carry the child to term, bear it, deliver it to the Sterns, and thereafter do whatever was necessary to terminate her maternal rights so that Mrs. Stern could thereafter adopt the child. Mrs. Whitehead's husband, Richard, was also a party to the contract; Mrs. [Elizabeth] Stern was not. Mr. Whitehead promised to do all acts necessary to rebut the presumption of paternity under the Parentage Act. Although Mrs. Stern was not a party to the surrogacy agreement, the contract gave her sole custody of the child in the event of Mr. Stern's death. Mrs. Stern's status as a nonparty to the surrogate parenting agreement presumably was to avoid the application of the baby-selling statute to this arrangement.

Mr. Stern . . . agreed to attempt the artificial insemination and to pay Mrs. Whitehead $10,000 after the child's birth, on its delivery to him. In a separate contract, Mr. Stern agreed to pay $7,500 to the Infertility Center of New York ("ICNY"). . . .

The history of the parties' involvement in this arrangement suggests their good faith. William and Elizabeth Stern were married in July 1974, having met at the University of Michigan, where both were Ph.D. candidates. . . . [Before they decided to start a family,] Mrs. Stern learned that she might have multiple sclerosis and that the disease in some cases renders pregnancy a serious health risk. Her anxiety appears to have exceeded the actual risk, which current medical authorities assess as minimal. Nonetheless that anxiety was evidently quite real. . . . Based on the perceived risk, the Sterns decided to forego having their own children. The decision had special significance for Mr. Stern. Most of his family had been destroyed in the Holocaust. As the family's only survivor, he very much wanted to continue his bloodline.

Initially the Sterns considered adoption, but were discouraged by the substantial delay apparently involved and by the potential problem they saw arising from their age and their differing religious backgrounds. . . .

The paths of Mrs. Whitehead and the Sterns to surrogacy were similar. Both responded to advertising by ICNY. . . . Mrs. Whitehead's response apparently resulted from her sympathy with family members and others who could have no children; she also wanted the $10,000 to help her family.

. . . . On February 6, 1985, Mr. Stern and Mr. and Mrs. Whitehead executed the surrogate parenting agreement. After several artificial inseminations over a period of months, Mrs. Whitehead became pregnant. The pregnancy was uneventful and on March 27, 1986, Baby M was born. . .

Mrs. Whitehead realized, almost from the moment of birth, that she could not part with this child. She had felt a bond with it even during pregnancy. Some indication of the attachment was conveyed to the Sterns at the hospital when they told Mrs. Whitehead what they were going to name the baby. She apparently broke into tears and indicated that she did not know if she could give up the child. . . .

Nonetheless, Mrs. Whitehead was, for the moment, true to her word. Despite powerful inclinations to the contrary, she turned her child over to the Sterns on March 30 at the Whiteheads' home. . . .

Later in the evening of March 30, Mrs. Whitehead became deeply disturbed, disconsolate, stricken with unbearable sadness. . . . The next day she went to the Sterns' home and told them how much she was suffering.

. . . . She told them that she could not live without her baby, that she must have her, even if only for one week, that thereafter she would surrender her child. The Sterns, concerned that Mrs. Whitehead might indeed commit suicide, not wanting under any circumstances to risk that, and in any event believing that Mrs. Whitehead would keep her word, turned the child over to her. . . .

The struggle over Baby M began when it became apparent that Mrs. Whitehead could not return the child to Mr. Stern. Due to Mrs. Whitehead's refusal to relinquish the baby, Mr. Stern filed a complaint seeking enforcement of the surrogacy contract. . . .

The Whiteheads . . . fled to Florida with Baby M. . . . For the next three months, the Whiteheads and Melissa lived at roughly twenty different hotels, motels, and homes in order to avoid apprehension. From time to time Mrs. Whitehead would call Mr. Stern to discuss the matter; the conversations, recorded by Mr. Stern on advice of counsel, show an escalating dispute about rights, morality, and power, accompanied by threats of Mrs. Whitehead to kill herself, to kill the child, and falsely to accuse Mr. Stern of sexually molesting Mrs. Whitehead's other daughter.

Eventually the Sterns discovered where the Whiteheads were staying, . . . and obtained [a Florida] order requiring the Whiteheads to turn over the child. Police in Florida enforced the order, forcibly removing the child from her grandparents' home. She was soon thereafter brought to New Jersey and turned over to the Sterns. The prior order of the court, issued *ex parte,* awarding custody of the child to the Sterns *pendente lite,* was reaffirmed by the trial court. . . . Pending final judgment, Mrs. Whitehead was awarded limited visitation with Baby M.

The Sterns' complaint, in addition to seeking possession and ultimately custody of the child, sought enforcement of the surrogacy contract. Pursuant to the contract, it asked that the child be permanently placed in their custody, that Mrs. Whitehead's parental rights be terminated, and that Mrs. Stern be allowed to adopt the child, i.e., that, for all purposes, Melissa become the Sterns' child. . . .

. . . . The trial court concluded that the various statutes governing this matter, including those concerning adoption, termination of parental rights, and payment of money in connection with adoptions, do not apply to surrogacy contracts. It reasoned that because the Legislature did not have surrogacy contracts in mind when it passed those laws, those laws were therefore irrelevant. . . . It then held that surrogacy contracts are valid and should be enforced, and furthermore that Mr. Stern's rights under the surrogacy contract were constitutionally protected.

Mrs. Whitehead appealed. . . .

Mrs. Whitehead contends that the surrogacy contract . . . is invalid. . . . With the contract thus void, Mrs. Whitehead claims primary custody (with visitation rights in Mr. Stern) both on a best interests basis (stressing the "tender years" doctrine) as well as on the policy basis of discouraging surrogacy contracts. . . .

. . . .

The Sterns claim that the surrogacy contract is valid and should be enforced. . . As for the child's best interests, their position is factual: given all of the circumstances, the child is better off in their custody with no residual parental rights reserved for Mrs. Whitehead.

II.

Invalidity and Unenforceability of Surrogacy Contract

We have concluded that this surrogacy contract is invalid. Our conclusion has two bases: direct conflict with existing statutes and conflict with the public policies of this State, as expressed in its statutory and decisional law.

One of the surrogacy contract's basic purposes, to achieve the adoption of a child through private placement, though permitted in New Jersey "is very much disfavored." Its use of money for this purpose. . . is illegal and perhaps criminal. In addition to the inducement of money, there is the coercion of contract: the natural mother's irrevocable agreement, prior to birth, even prior to conception, to surrender the child to the adoptive couple. Such an agreement is totally unenforceable in private placement adoption. Even where the adoption is through an approved agency, the formal agreement to surrender occurs only after birth (as we read N.J.S.A. 9:2-16 and -17, and similar statutes), and then, by regulation, only after the birth mother has been offered counseling. Integral to these invalid provisions of the surrogacy contract is the related agreement, equally invalid, on the part of the natural mother to cooperate with, and not to contest, proceedings to terminate her parental rights, as well as her contractual concession, in aid of the adoption, that the child's best interests would be served by awarding custody to the natural father and his wife — all of this before she has even conceived, and, in some cases, before she has the slightest idea of what the natural father and adoptive mother are like. . . .

A. *Conflict with Statutory Provisions*

The surrogacy contract conflicts with: (1) laws prohibiting the use of money in connection with adoptions; (2) laws requiring proof of parental unfitness or abandonment before termination of parental rights is ordered or an adoption is granted; and (3) laws that make surrender of custody and consent to adoption revocable in private placement adoptions.

(1) Our law prohibits paying or accepting money in connection with any placement of a child for adoption.

. . . .

Considerable care was taken in this case to structure the surrogacy arrangement so as not to violate this prohibition. . . . [T]he adopting parent, Mrs. Stern, was not a party to the surrogacy contract; the money paid to Mrs. Whitehead was stated to be for her services — not for the adoption; the sole purpose of the contract was stated as being that "of giving a child to William Stern, its natural and biological father"; the money was purported to be "compensation for services and expenses and in no way . . . a fee for termination of parental rights or a payment in exchange for consent to surrender a child for adoption"; the fee to the Infertility Center ($7,500) was stated to be for legal representation, advice, administrative work, and other "services." Nevertheless, it seems clear that the money was paid and accepted in connection with an adoption.

. . . The payment of the $10,000 [to Mrs. Whitehead] occurs only on surrender of custody of the child and "completion of the duties and obligations" of Mrs. Whitehead, including termination of her parental rights to facilitate adoption by Mrs. Stern. . . .

(2) The termination of Mrs. Whitehead's parental rights, called for by the surrogacy contract and actually ordered by the court, fails to comply with the stringent requirements of New Jersey law. . . .

. . . .

As the trial court recognized, without a valid termination there can be no adoption. . . . [¶] [A] "best interests" determination is never sufficient to terminate parental rights. . . . [¶] In this case a termination . . . was obtained not by proving the statutory prerequisites but by claiming the benefit of contractual provisions. . . The Legislature would not have so carefully, so consistently, and so substantially restricted termination of parental rights if it had intended to allow termination to be achieved by one short sentence in a contract.

Since the termination was invalid, it follows . . . that adoption of Melissa by Mrs. Stern could not properly be granted.

(3) The provision in the surrogacy contract stating that Mary Beth Whitehead agrees to "surrender custody . . . and terminate all parental rights" . . . is intended to be an . . . irrevocable commitment by Mrs. Whitehead to . . . allow termination of her parental rights. . . .

. . . .

[S]trict prerequisites to irrevocability [set in New Jersey statutes] constitute a recognition of the most serious consequences that flow from such consents: termination of parental rights. . . . Because of those consequences, the Legislature severely limited the circumstances under which such consent would be irrevocable. . . .

. . . .

. . . . The provision in the surrogacy contract, agreed to before conception, requiring the natural mother to surrender custody of the child without any right of revocation [creates] a contractual system of termination and adoption designed to circumvent our statutes.

B. *Public Policy Considerations*

The surrogacy contract's invalidity . . . is further underlined [by] New Jersey's public policy. The contract's basic premise, that the natural parents can decide in advance of birth which one is to have custody of the child, bears no relationship to the settled law that the child's best interests shall determine custody. . . .

The surrogacy contract guarantees permanent separation of the child from one of its natural parents. Our policy, however, has long been that to the extent possible, children should remain with and be brought up by both of their natural parents. [As a result of this surrogacy contract] a child, instead of starting off its life with as much peace and security as possible, finds itself immediately in a tug-of-war between contending mother and father.

. . . .

Under the contract, the natural mother is irrevocably committed before she knows the strength of her bond with her child. She never makes a totally voluntary, informed decision, for quite clearly any decision prior to the baby's birth is, in the most important sense, uninformed, and any decision after that, compelled by a pre-existing contractual commitment, the threat of a lawsuit, and the inducement of a $10,000 payment, is less than totally voluntary. Her interests are of little concern to those who controlled this transaction.

Although the interest of the natural father and adoptive mother is certainly the predominant interest, realistically the only interest served, even they are left with less than what public policy requires. They know little about the natural mother, her genetic makeup, and her psychological and medical history. . . .

Worst of all, however, is the contract's total disregard of the best interests of the child. There is not the slightest suggestion that any inquiry will be made at any time to determine the fitness of the Sterns as custodial parents, of Mrs. Stern as an adoptive parent, their superiority to Mrs. Whitehead, or the effect on the child of not living with her natural mother.

This is the sale of a child, or, at the very least, the sale of a mother's right to her child, the only mitigating factor being that one of the purchasers is the father. Almost every evil that prompted the prohibition on the payment of money in connection with adoptions exists here.

The differences between an adoption and a surrogacy contract should be noted. . . . [¶] First, . . . [d]espite the alleged selfless motivation of surrogate mothers, if there is no payment, there will be no surrogates, or very few. That . . . contrasts with adoption; for obvious reasons, there remains a steady supply, albeit insufficient, despite the prohibitions against payment. . . .

Second, the use of money in adoptions does not produce the problem — conception occurs, and usually the birth itself, before illicit funds are offered. With surrogacy, the "problem," if one views it as such, consisting of the purchase of a woman's procreative capacity, at the risk of her life, is caused by and originates with the offer of money.

. . . .

The main difference, that the unwanted pregnancy is unintended while the situation of the surrogate mother is voluntary and intended, is really not significant. . . . On reflection, however, it appears that the essential evil is the same, taking advantage of a woman's circumstances (the unwanted pregnancy or the need for money) in order to take away her child, the difference being one of degree.

. . . .

Intimated, but disputed, is the assertion that surrogacy will be used for the benefit of the rich at the expense of the poor. . . . In response it is noted that the Sterns are not rich and the Whiteheads not poor. Nevertheless, . . . we doubt that infertile couples in the low-income bracket will find upper income surrogates.

In any event, even in this case . . . wealth . . . play[ed] a part. . . [The Whiteheads'] income derived from Mr. Whitehead's labors. Mrs. Whitehead is a homemaker, having previously held part-time jobs. The Sterns are both professionals, she a medical doctor, he a biochemist. Their combined income when both were working was about $89,500 a year and their assets sufficient to pay for the surrogacy contract arrangements.

. . . . There are, in a civilized society, some things that money cannot buy. . .

. . . . In New Jersey the surrogate mother's agreement to sell her child is void. Its irrevocability infects the entire contract, as does the money that purports to buy it.

III.

Termination

[The court found no basis for involuntary termination of Mary Beth Whitehead's parental rights because she was neither unfit nor has she abandoned her child under the applicable statutory standards.]

IV.

Constitutional Issues

[The court first held that constitutional protection of the right to procreate had no bearing on this case because it cannot provide a basis for favoring the claim of either Mr. Stern or Mrs. Whitehead as against the other parent.]

Mr. Stern also contends that he has been denied equal protection of the laws by the . . . statute granting full parental rights to a husband in relation to the child produced, with his consent, by the union of his wife with a sperm donor. N.J.S.A. 9:17-44. The claim really is that of Mrs. Stern [because] she is in precisely the same position as the husband in the statute: she is presumably infertile, as is the husband in the statute; her spouse by agreement with a third party procreates with the understanding that the child will be the couple's child. The alleged unequal protection is that the understanding is honored in the statute when the husband is the infertile party, but no similar understanding is honored when it is the wife who is infertile.

It is quite obvious that the situations are not parallel. A sperm donor simply cannot be equated with a surrogate mother. The State has more than a sufficient basis to distinguish the two situations — even if the only difference is between the time it takes to provide sperm for artificial insemination and the time invested in a nine-month pregnancy — so as to justify automatically divesting the sperm donor of his parental rights without automatically divesting a surrogate mother. Some basis for an equal protection argument might exist if Mary Beth Whitehead had contributed her egg to be implanted, fertilized or otherwise, in Mrs. Stern, resulting in the latter's pregnancy. That is not the case here, however.

[The court declined to rule on Mrs. Whitehead's claim that her constitutional right to companionship of her child was violated.]

V.

Custody

[The Court then resolved the custody dispute between the parents under the best interest of the child standard.]

[T]he trial court's decision awarding custody to the Sterns (technically to Mr. Stern) should be affirmed since "its findings . . . could reasonably have been reached on sufficient credible evidence present in the record." [¶] Our . . . conclusion is based on strongly persuasive testimony contrasting both the family life of the Whiteheads and the Sterns and the personalities and characters of the individuals. The stability of the Whitehead family life was doubtful at the time of trial. Their finances were in serious trouble . . . Mr. Whitehead's employment, though relatively steady, was always at risk because of his alcoholism. . . . The expert testimony contained criticism of Mrs. Whitehead's handling of her son's educational difficulties. [E]xperts noted that Mrs. Whitehead perceived herself as omnipotent and omniscient concerning her children. . . . As to Melissa, Mrs. Whitehead expressed the view that she alone knew what that child's cries and sounds meant. . . . In short, while love and affection there would be, Baby M's life with the Whiteheads promised to be too closely controlled by Mrs. Whitehead. The prospects for wholesome, independent psychological growth and development would be at serious risk.

The Sterns have no other children, but all indications are that their household and their personalities promise a much more likely foundation for Melissa to grow and thrive. There *is* a track record of sorts — during the one-and-a-half years of custody Baby M has done very well, and the relationship between both Mr. and Mrs. Stern and the baby has become very strong. The household is stable, and likely to remain so. Their finances are more than adequate, their circle of friends supportive, and their marriage happy. Most important, they are loving, giving, nurturing, and open-minded people. . . . All in all, Melissa's future appears solid, happy, and promising with them.

Based on all of this we have concluded, independent of the trial court's identical conclusion, that Melissa's best interests call for custody in the Sterns. . . .

[The Court then directed that in the future the mother should be awarded custody *pendente lite* because of "the probable bond between mother and child." Only where the mother is unfit should the natural father in a surrogacy dispute get temporary custody.

The Court remanded the case to determine visitation for Ms. Whitehead.]

NOTES

1. Baby M. *Sequel.* On remand, the trial court granted Mary Beth Whitehead eight hours of unsupervised visitation a week, to increase over the course of the year to two days every two weeks, including an overnight. While observing that "William and Elizabeth Stern are extraordinarily good parents . . . and their daughter is firmly bonded to them," it also concluded that "Melissa is a resilient child who is no less capable than thousands of children of broken marriages who successfully adjust to complex family relationships when their parents remarry." It observed that Melissa had developed a warm and close relationship with her mother.

Mary Beth Whitehead subsequently divorced her husband and remarried. In a 1997 interview, she expressed continuing resentment of the Sterns, although she acknowledged that she worried that her visitation might hurt Melissa. Under the visitation agreement, she saw Melissa on a regular basis, although their time together had been reduced since the child started school. Melissa, according to the interviewer, seemed comfortable with her mother and half-siblings, but expressed some anxiety, "It's weird having two moms." *See* Puzzanghera, *Unhappy Surrogate L.I. Mom Wants to Live Closer to Baby M.* NEWSDAY, Dec. 13, 1997, at 19.

2. *Other Cases.* Courts have varied in their response to gestational agreements. Some have followed *Baby M.*, finding gestational agreements to be unenforceable. In a case in which the mother changed her mind in the sixth month of pregnancy, Massachusetts' highest court rejected a gestational contract on public policy grounds, emphasizing the mother's pre-birth consent and the payment of a fee by the intended parents as the basis for its decision. *R.R. v. M.H.*, 689 N.E.2d 790 (Mass. 1998). The court suggested that these objections would be overcome if no compensation was paid beyond pregnancy-related expenses, and if the mother was not bound by her consent until a suitable period after the child's birth. *See also Weaver v. Guinn*, 31 P.3d 1119 (Or. Ct. App. 2001) (gestational contract and custody agreement not enforceable).

Baby M.'s analysis has not been universally followed, however. In *Surrogate Parenting Assocs. v. Kentucky,* 704 S.W.2d 209 (Ky. 1986), decided before *Baby M.,* the court held that the anti-baby-selling provisions contained in the adoption and custody laws did not apply to gestational agreements. The court reasoned that the legislature's purpose was to prevent the use of financial inducements to pressure a parent to surrender her child, and that this rationale did not extend to gestational contracts in which no child existed at the time of the agreement. It also noted that the intended adoptive mother (the biological father's wife) was not a party to the contract, and suggested that her exclusion avoided application of the state law since baby-selling, the evil at which the law was aimed, cannot arise where the presumed "buyer" is not a party. Elizabeth Stern was not a party to the agreement in *Baby M.,* but New Jersey did not accept this argument. Is the "baby-selling" characterization inapt when the biological father, rather than a stranger, will acquire the child? In *Doe v. Roe,* 717 A.2d 706 (Conn. 1998), the Connecticut Supreme Court rejected the mother's challenge of the trial court's jurisdiction to enter an order terminating her parental rights. The mother argued that the termination was not ordered under either of the exclusive statutory grounds but on the basis of her agreement with the intended parents. The supreme court concluded that the trial court was not ordering termination of her rights per se, but was issuing an order based on the parties' agreement, which it had reviewed for voluntariness.

Although cases like *Baby M.* get much publicity, it is important to remember that most gestational arrangements are carried out successfully, with no change of heart by the mother. Yet legal problems can still arise. The mother will usually have to reexecute a document of surrender after she gives birth, because few courts would accept the surrogate contract itself, executed pre-birth (indeed, pre-conception), as effecting a valid relinquishment of parental rights. The parties will need judicial approval to formalize the adoption, even if they are all in agreement. Will they get it? Many courts have been ready to facilitate the change in the legal status of the parents and child born pursuant to a gestational agreement, where the parties are in agreement about the transfer. Thus, a Massachusetts court ordered the hospital at which a mother would give birth to the genetic child of the intended couple (*see* note 3 *infra*) to designate them as parents on the birth certificate. *Culliton v. Beth Israel Deaconess Medical Center*, 756 N.E.2d 1133 (Mass. 2001). The court emphasized the importance of quickly establishing the identity of the child's legal parents. *See also A.H.W. v. G.H.B.*, 772 A.2d 948 (N.J. Super. Ct. Ch. Div. 2000) (no pre-birth termination of mother's parental rights, as requested by mother, but genetic parents' names can go on birth certificate after 72-hour waiting period).

3. *Egg Donation and "Pure" Gestational Agreements.* Imagine in *Baby M* that Mrs. Stern's medical difficulty was not in carrying the child but in producing healthy eggs. The court's language suggests that if she became pregnant with a donated egg fertilized with her husband's sperm, it might accept an agreement under which Mrs. Stern, and not the egg donor, was considered the legal mother. Such egg donation is now medically available, and has been used to allow even post-menopausal women to bear children. *See* Sauer, Paulson & Lobo, *A Preliminary Report on Oocyte Donation Extending Reproductive Potential to Women over Forty*, 323 NEW ENG. J. MED. 1157 (1990). This situation is directly analogous to artificial insemination by a sperm donor, which is authorized by statute in many states (including New Jersey, as *Baby M.* discusses), and it is hard to argue for different legal treatment of egg donation. In *McDonald v. McDonald,* 608 N.Y.S.2d 477 (App. Div. 1994), a husband in a divorce action claimed custodial rights on the ground that he was the only natural parent available. The court found that the wife was the natural mother of the children; she had arranged with her husband's consent to give birth to the children as the result of the implantation of fertilized eggs produced by her husband's sperm and a donor's eggs.

In fact, Mrs. Stern's actual case appears to be the opposite: she felt pregnancy would put her at medical risk, but nothing in the case suggests she was incapable of producing healthy eggs. Suppose, then, that her egg had been fertilized with her husband's sperm and implanted in Mrs. Whitehead's uterus — in other words, suppose Melissa was Mrs. Stern's genetic child and Mrs. Whitehead's gestational child. Such procedures are also now available and seem likely to be more widely used as women medically incapable of maintaining a successful pregnancy realize that it is still possible for them to have children who are their genetic offspring. Should that affect the outcome of the case? To what extent is Mary Beth Whitehead's legal claim to parental rights based on her gestational role and to what extent does it rest on the fact that she was the child's genetic mother?

This issue has been central in cases of "gestational surrogacy" in which a fertilized embryo is implanted in the woman, and the genetic mother is either the intended mother or a donor, but not the surrogate herself. In these cases, the surrogate is providing only gestational services, a distinction from traditional gestational agreements that courts have found to be critical. A California trial court, in awarding parental rights to the biological mother, described the surrogate's role as analogous to a "foster parent," providing shelter and food to the child. *Science and the Courts Take a New Look at Motherhood*, N.Y. TIMES, Nov. 4, 1990, sec. 4, at 6. The California Supreme Court upheld this decision in *Johnson v. Calvert*, 851 P.2d 776 (Cal. 1993). Where the gestational and genetic mothers were different, the Court concluded, each had a presumptively equal claim to parenthood, having presented "acceptable proof of maternity" under the state's Uniform Parentage Act. In this situation, parental rights should be determined according to the intent of the parties. The gestational agreement demonstrated that the father's wife (the genetic mother) was intended to be the mother. *Johnson* concluded that the surrogate was not exercising procreative choice, but was simply agreeing to provide a service. Is this not true of the mother in the traditional gestational contract? *See Moschetta v. Moschetta*, 30 Cal. Rptr. 2d 893 (App. 1994) (emphasizing that the intent of the parties was relevant only when the gestational mother was not the genetic mother).

Some of the most troubling legal battles can develop when the marriage of the intended parents breaks down before the legal status of the child is clearly established. In a much cited California case, the intended parents contracted with a woman to be the gestational mother of an embryo unrelated to any of the parties. *Buzzanca v. Buzzanca*, 72 Cal. Rptr. 2d 280 (Ct. App. 1998). During the pregnancy the couple separated and later divorced, and the husband disclaimed any responsibility for the child. The appellate court rejected the trial court's conclusion that the child had *no* lawful parents, deciding that the intended parents were the legal parents responsible for the child's care and support. The court compared the father's status to the status of husbands whose parental responsibility is based on consent to their wives' artificial insemination. Here, by consenting to the medical procedure that resulted in the birth of the child, the husband incurred the responsibilities of parenthood. *See also Soos v. Superior Court*, 897 P.2d 1356 (Ariz. App. 1994) (upholding, against challenge by the intended father, the custody rights of his wife, the mother who donated eggs implanted in the surrogate; and finding Arizona statutory provision that the surrogate is the legal mother of the child unconstitutional on equal protection grounds, as applied to the biological mother in this situation).

4. *Fashioning Remedies for Violating Gestational Agreements*. Even if gestational contracts are allowed, should the remedy of specific performance be available to require the gestational mother to surrender the child? Under general contract principles, personal service contracts are not subject to specific performance. This doctrinal rule is grounded in autonomy principles, since forced servitude is akin to slavery. Performance of a gestational contract may seem to raise similar concerns. However, at some point in the pregnancy, performance is completely beyond the mother's control — in the third trimester of pregnancy, the mother is not free to choose *not* to perform; *i.e.,* she can not obtain an abortion, except under unusual circumstances. Nonetheless, many observers have argued against specific performance. Are other remedies more plausibly allowed? Martha Field, for example, argues that the mother should have the right to renounce the contract, keep the child, and return any money received until she transfers the baby to the intended parents. FIELD, SURROGATE MOTHERHOOD: THE LEGAL AND HUMAN ISSUES (1988). Consider whether the couple's motivations should affect the enforceability of their gestational contract. Suppose, for example, that the wife is not infertile, but simply prefers to avoid pregnancy because she does not want to interrupt her career? What if the purpose is to avoid passing on to the child a deleterious gene carried by the mother?

What happens if the child born to the gestational mother is handicapped or abnormal and the contracting couple does not want it? In 1983, Judy Stiver, pregnant under a gestational agreement, gave birth to a severely retarded baby boy. Neither she nor the intended adoptive couple, the Malahoffs, wanted the child, and Mr. Malahoff claimed he was not the father. Blood tests established that Stiver's husband fathered the child, apparently before the insemination. Three lawsuits then resulted. Malahoff sued the Stivers for not producing the child he ordered; the Stivers sued the doctor, lawyer and psychiatrist involved in the gestational mother program for not advising them about the timing of intercourse, and the Stivers sued Malahoff for violating their privacy by making the incident public. The Stivers' also alleged that the child's illness was not genetic but was caused, rather, by a virus transmitted by Malahoff's sperm. Andrews, *The Stork Market,* A.B.A. J. 50, 56, Aug. 1984.

The complications that can arise under gestational arrangements may be the source of much opposition. Many things can go wrong with this form of assisted reproduction, in part because the child is not born into the intended family. This difference from conception by artificial insemination may explain in part why AID (artificial insemination by donor) is relatively uncontroversial, in contrast to gestational agreements. Are most of the problems attributable to uncertainty about parents' rights and responsibilities? Clarifying the legal status of the child and the rights and obligations of the intended parents and the gestational mother could avoid much conflict and uncertainty. Moreover, problems that arise because the intended parents' marriage falters need be no more difficult than in the typical divorce involving children. Disputes between the gestational mother and the intended parents about the gestational mother's conduct during pregnancy can be subject to legal regulation known in advance. (i.e. if the gestational mother refuses abortion under specified conditions of genetic abnormality, the intended parent has no further obligation.) Even clear legal rules may not protect the child, however. For example, any rule releasing the father from liability (and parental responsibility) due to the gestational mother's conduct, may harm the child. Perhaps the only approach that would fully protect the child is to allocate the risk to the father. Is it possible to deal adequately with the risks to children produced by gestational contracts? If not, should they be discouraged?

5. *Statutory and Regulatory Activity.* Although a few states had statutes dealing with gestational contracts before *Baby M,* there has been considerable legislative activity since the New Jersey opinion, and nearly half the states now have statutes regulating gestational agreements. The statutes run the gamut, from criminalizing the agreements to enforcement under prescribed conditions. Only a few states prohibit gestational agreements and subject the parties to criminal penalties. *See, e.g.,* MICH. COMP. LAWS §§ 722.851 to 722.863 (2002); ARIZ. REV. STAT. ANN. § 25-218 (2000); UTAH CODE ANN. § 76-7-204 (1999), and WASH. REV. CODE § 26.26.210-250 (West 1997). In *Doe v. Kelley,* 307 N.W.2d 438 (Mich. App. 1981), the Michigan statute withstood a constitutional challenge that it infringed upon the right of procreative choice. Most of the these statutes also criminalize the brokering of gestational contracts. *See, e.g.,* MICH. COMP. LAWS § 722.859(3) (felony punishable by $50,000 fine or 5 years in prison). Some statutes that do not criminalize the conduct of the parties, impose severe sanctions on brokers. Under the New York statute, for example, the participants in any gestational contract are subjected to a civil penalty of up to $500. Commercial facilitation of gestational contracts is subject to a civil penalty of up to $10,000; a second violation is a felony. *See* N.Y. DOM. REL. LAW §§ 121–124 (McKinney 1999). *See also* FLA. STAT. § 63.212(1) (Supp. 2003).

One group of statutes simply declare the contract void, without imposing criminal penalties on the parties, although pre-existing penalties for baby-selling probably apply in some of these states. Several statutes passed in the aftermath of *Baby M* generally took this approach. The New York statute, for example, declares surrogate parenting contracts void and unenforceable and prohibits payment or receipt of compensation in connection with such contracts. *See also* N.D. CENT. CODE §§ 14-18-01 to 14-18-07 (1997) (contracts void). Some statutes only prohibit those agreements that involve payment of compensation to the gestational mother. NEB. REV. STAT. Ch. 25 § 21, 200 (Michie 1995); WASH. REV. CODE § 26.26.210, .250 (West 1997); LA. REV. STAT. ANN. § 9.2713 (1991). Thus, a gestational mother is free to donate her genetic material and gestational services, and to transfer parental rights. See also 85 Md. Op. Att'y Gen. No. 00-035 (Dec. 19, 2000), *available at* 2000 WL 1922187 (gestational agreements involving the payment of a fee for termination of parental rights are illegal and unenforceable; however, violation of this prohibition need not be enforced in the adoption proceeding and is not dispositive on issues of the voluntariness of the birth mother's relinquishment of her rights or to the adoptive parent's fitness).

Other statutes recognize the contract as enforceable, although payments are restricted and the gestational mother has a right of recission for a limited period after birth. *See, e.g.,* FLA. STAT. ANN. § 63.212 (Supp. 2003) ("pre-planned adoption agreements" permitted but gestational mother allowed only reimbursement for medical, legal and "reasonable living" expenses; may decide to keep baby up to seven days after birth; must acknowledge responsibility for child if intended adoptive parents terminate their agreement; all brokerage fees barred); ARK. STAT. ANN. § 9-10-201 (Michie 2002) (child of gestational mother is child of father and his wife, but contract not exempted from separate child-selling prohibition).

Finally, some enactments appear to allow enforcement of gestational contracts. NEV. REV. STAT. § 127.287 (Michie 1998) excludes from baby-selling prohibitions a "lawful contract to act as a surrogate" while also "not prohibit[-ing] a natural parent from refusing to place a child for adoption after its birth." N.H. REV. STAT. ANN. §§ 168-B:1 to B:32 (2001), recognizes gestational contracts that have been judicially approved in advance of the child's birth. The statute requires the contract to limit payments to the gestational mother to pregnancy-related medical expenses; actual lost wages related to pregnancy, delivery and postpartum recovery; health, disability and life insurance during the pregnancy and recovery; reasonable attorney's fees; counseling fees; and costs associated with nonmedical evaluations of the gestational mother and her husband. New Hampshire also provides explicitly that the gestational mother may rescind her agreement to surrender the child within 72 hours of birth.

The Virginia statute, based on one alternative of the now supplanted (see infra) Uniform Status of Children of Assisted Conception Act (1988)(USCACA), is the most comprehensive effort to authorize enforceable gestational agreements, through regulation that seeks to mitigate the problems that have generated opposition to these contracts. VA. CODE ANN. § 20-156 et. seq. (Michie 2000). The statute sets out a complex set of requirements which, if fulfilled, can result in an enforceable gestational agreement under which the child automatically becomes the child of the intended parents: The intended parents must be married and the wife must be unable to bear a child without unreasonable risk; the child must be the genetic child of one of the intended parents; psychological and physical evaluations and a home study are required of both the intended parents and the gestational mother; the gestational mother must be married and must have had at least one pregnancy and delivery; all parties must receive mental health counseling. If these requirements are met, the parties can get advance judicial approval of the contract; then, the child on birth is the child of the intended adoptive parents and is not the child of the gestational mother and her husband. However, the gestational mother can terminate the contract by giving written notice to the court within 180 days of conception. § 20-161. If she terminates in a timely manner, the gestational mother and her husband (if any) are the parents. If prior judicial approval is not obtained, the Virginia statute permits the gestational mother, for 25 days after the birth of the child, to relinquish her parental rights. § 20-162. Thus, without judicial approval, the parties are subject to the standard prohibition of pre-birth consent to adoption. Is the statute effective at reducing the risks of gestational surrogacy?

In 2000, the new Uniform Parentage Act replaced the 1988 USCACA with a new formulation regulating gestational agreements. UNIFORM PARENTAGE ACT, SECT. 8. Acknowledging that gestational agreements are becoming more widely used, the new UPA rejects one USCACA alternative, under which gestational agreements were prohibited and void, on the ground that this approach leaves the legal status of the child uncertain. Instead, the new UPA offers a simplified version of the Virginia statute above, under which the court has discretionary authority to validate a gestational agreement before conception upon finding that a number of requirements are met. These include findings that the intended parents are married and the wife unable to bear a child; the gestational mother has had a prior pregnancy; a home study has been conducted; and the consideration paid the gestational mother is reasonable. A gestational link to one intended parent is not required. Under the UPA, the gestational agreement may not limit the right of the gestational mother to "make decisions to safeguard her health or that of the embryos or fetus." Any party can terminate the agreement before a pregnancy occurs and the court can terminate for "good cause" thereafter. Otherwise the agreement is enforceable and the intended parents become the child's legal parents on birth. An unvalidated agreement is unenforceable and the birthmother and her husband are the legal parents, but it may give rise to child support obligations for the intended parents.

6. *Commentary.* Gestational motherhood has been a subject of great academic interest. The most enthusiastic defense of the practice comes from those who view public policy issues from an economic perspective. *See* Epstein, *Surrogacy: The Case for Full Contractual Enforcement*, 81 VA. L. REV. 2305 (1995); Posner, *The Ethics and Economics of Enforcing Contracts of Surrogate Motherhood*, 5 J. CONTEMP. HEALTH L. & POL'Y 21 (1989). John Robertson defends the enforce-ability of gestational contracts on constitutional grounds. In his view the right of procreative liberty of both the intended parents and gestational mothers are promoted by enforcement. Moreover, the infertile couple's fundamental right to form a family through non-coital means should include enforcement of gestational agreements. ROBERTSON, CHILDREN OF CHOICE (1994). *See Symposium on John A. Robertson's CHILDREN OF CHOICE*, 52 WASH. & LEE L. REV. 133 (1995). Some authors argue that gestational contracts are harmful to children. Brinig, *A Materialistic Approach to Surrogacy: Comment on Richard Epstein's Surrogacy: The Case for Full Contractual Enforcement*, 81 VA. L. REV. 2377 (1995). *See* M. FIELD, *supra;* Bartlett, *Re-Expressing Parenthood*, 98 YALE L.J. 293, 335–37 (1988). *See also* Shultz, *Reproductive Technology and Intent-Based Parenthood,* 1990 WIS. L. REV. 297. For a discussion of different feminist perspectives on gestational arrangements, see *infra.*

Marsha Garrison has offered a comprehensive legal framework for analyzing technologically assisted conception of all types, including conventional and "pure" gestational arrangements as well as artificial insemination by donor (AID), and in vitro fertilization (*see infra*). Garrison, *Law Making for Baby Making: An Interpretive Approach to the Determination of Legal Parentage,* 113 HARV. L. REV. 835 (2000). Under Garrison's interpretive approach, resolution of these matters is governed, to the extent possible, by legal doctrine determining parentage in conventional contexts. Thus, in a standard gestational arrangement, the gesatational mother has parental rights until she relinquishes them after birth under state adoption procedures. In a "pure" gestational arrangement in which at least one intended parent donates gestational material, but the gestational mother has no biological link to the child, Garrison argues that none of the conventional bases for setting aside claims based on biology would favor her claim over that of the intended parents, and they would acquire parental status.

PROBLEMS

Problem 11-9. Alice signs a surrogate mothering contract with Sally and Tom, under which she will bear a child conceived through artificial insemination and turn it over to Tom and Sally for adoption by Sally. She in fact relinquishes the child after birth, as planned, but Sally and Tom never complete a formal adoption. A year later, they break up. On divorce, Tom and Sally each file custody petitions. Alice, having a change of heart when she hears of the divorce, files her own action seeking custody of the child. What result? Suppose that because early attempts at insemination using Tom's sperm were unsuccessful, Alice was actually impregnated with sperm Tom obtained from a friend, who makes no claim on the child?

Problem 11-10. Your jurisdiction has adopted Section 8 of the UPA. You represent Jack and Jill, who have executed an agreement with Mary to bear Jack's child. The court approved the gestational agreement after a hearing in which an adoption agency home study was presented. What would you do in the following circumstances?

(A) In the week following birth, Mary refuses to consent to adoption in accordance with their agreement. She tells Jack and Jill that if the child is not returned, she will suffer grievous psychological injury.

(B) The child is born with Down's syndrome and Jack and Jill do not want it.

(C) When Mary is five months pregnant, an amniocentesis shows that the child has Down's syndrome. Jack and Jill want Mary to have an abortion. If she declines, they do not want the child.

(D) Jill unexpectedly becomes pregnant after Mary is already two months pregnant, and Jack and Jill no longer want Mary's child.

(E) During the pregnancy, Jack and Jill learn that Mary is drinking and using drugs.

(F) Mary requires an emergency Caesarian section at delivery, and the child spends a week in the intensive care nursery. This drives the medical costs associated with the pregnancy and birth from $3,000 to $20,000. The child is now well. Jack and Jill had not contemplated this possibility when they agreed to pay Mary $8,000 plus her medical costs. The additional expenses will be difficult, if not impossible, for them to bear.

THE FEMINIST RESPONSE TO GESTATIONAL CONTRACTS

ANDERSON, *IS WOMEN'S LABOR A COMMODITY?* 19 Philosophy & Public Affairs 71 (1988)

. . . . Contract pregnancy substitutes market norms for some of the norms of parental love. Most important, it requires us to change our understanding of parental rights from trusts to things more like property rights — rights of use and disposal over the things owned. In this practice the mother deliberately conceives a child with the intention of giving it up for material advantage. Her renunciation of parental responsibilities is done not for the child's sake, but for her own (and if altruism is a motive, for the sake of the intended parents). She and the couple who pays her to give up her parental rights treat her rights as a partial property right. They thereby treat the child as a partial commodity, which may be properly bought and sold.

Contract pregnancy transforms what is specifically women's labor — the work of bringing forth children into the world — into a commodity. . . . The application of commercial norms to women's reproductive labor reduces surrogate mothers from persons worthy of respect and consideration to dominated objects of mere use. . . .

The pregnancy contract denies mothers autonomy over their bodies and their feelings. Their bodies and their health are subordinated to the independent interests of the contracting parents, who, through the threat of lawsuits, exercise potentially unlimited control over the gestating mother's activities. The surrogate mother is contractually required to obey all doctor's orders made in the interests of the child's health. . . .

The surrogate industry dominates the birth mother's feelings in ways that deny her autonomy in interpreting her own perspective on her evolving relationship with her child. . . . In the surrogate contract, she agrees not to form or to attempt to form a parent-child relationship with her offspring.

This clause alienates the mother's autonomy to the surrogate industry. One may argue that the surrogate mother has decided in advance that she is not interested in viewing her relationship to her child as parental. Regardless of her initial state of mind, she is not free, once she enters the contract, to develop an autonomous perspective on her relationship with her child. She is contractually bound to manipulate her emotions to agree with the interest of the adoptive parents. Few things reach deeper into the self than a parent's evolving relationship with her own child. Laying claim to the course of this relationship in virtue of a cash payment constitutes a severe violation of the mother's personhood and a denial of her autonomy. . . .

    . . . .

The manipulation of the surrogate mother's emotions inherent in the pregnancy contract also leaves women open to forms of exploitation that involve or border on fraud. A kind of exploitation occurs when one party to a transaction is oriented toward the exchange of gift values, while the other party operates in accordance with market norms of commodity exchange. . . . Surrogate mothers often follow gift norms, while the surrogate agency follows market norms. . . . This situation enables the surrogate agencies to manipulate the surrogate mothers' emotions to gain favorable terms for themselves. For example, agencies screen prospective surrogate mothers for submissiveness, and they emphasize to them the importance of the motives of generosity and love. . . .

Critics of contract pregnancy argue that it reinforces negative stereotypes of women that prevent them from gaining equality with men. It reinforces the gendered division of labor that keeps women subordinate to men by confining them to domestic work. It also supports the sexist view of women as primarily valuable for providing shelter to the genetic offspring of men. . . .

Supporters of contract pregnancy complain that the case against it expresses paternalistic attitudes toward women that reinforce sexist stereotypes. To prohibit these contracts or refuse to enforce them is to imply that women are incompetent to enter into and discharge the obligations of commercial contracts. . . .

This criticism depends upon the flawed individualist, preference-based view of autonomy. . . . It supposes that the only justification for restricting freedom of contract in the interests of one of the parties must rely on a presumption that party is incompetent. But the case against surrogacy rests not on the claim that women are incompetent, but only on the claim that women are not self-sufficient bearers of autonomy. Like men, women require certain social conditions to exercise their autonomy. Among these conditions are freedom from domination, which is secured by retaining inalienable rights in one's person. Contract pregnancy is objectionable because it undermines the social conditions for women's autonomy. It uses the norms of commerce in a manipulative way and commands surrogate mothers to conform their emotions to the interests of the other parties to the contract. . . . And it reinforces motivations, such as self-effacing "altruism," that women have formed under social conditions inconsistent with autonomy and that reproduce these social conditions. . . .

Few policies concerning women have an unambiguous impact on their welfare. To prohibit pregnancy contracts is to deny some women an opportunity to earn income. [T]he financial interests of surrogate mothers are not sufficient, however, to render a favorable judgment on the impact of contract pregnancy on the status of women. At best, contract pregnancy provides a few women with supplements to their household income. Women do not depend on this income for survival, if only because surrogate agencies do not view women in such precarious circumstances as suitable surrogate mothers. While contract pregnancy brings financial rewards to a few women, it reinforces gendered relations of inequality and stereotypes that undermine the status of women in general. . . . Overall, contract pregnancy reinforces the very gender inequalities its proponents hope to overcome.

ANDREWS, SURROGATE MOTHERHOOD: THE CHALLENGE FOR FEMINISTS, 16 Law Med. & Health Care 72 (1988)

. . . .

. . . . [A] growing feminist contingent . . . is seeking to ban surrogacy altogether. But the rationales for such a ban are often the very rationales that feminists have fought against in the contexts of abortion, contraception, non-traditional families, and employment. The adoption of these rationales as the reasons to regulate surrogacy could severely undercut the gains previously made in these other areas. . . .

For some feminists, the argument against surrogacy is a simple one: it demeans us all as a society to sell babies. And put that way, the argument is persuasive, at least on its face. But as a justification for policy, the argument is reminiscent of the argument that feminists roundly reject in the abortion context: that it demeans us as a society to kill babies.

Both arguments, equally heartfelt, need closer scrutiny if they are to serve as a basis for policy. In the abortion context, pro-choice people criticize the terms, saying we are not talking about "babies" when the abortion is done on an embryo or fetus still within the woman's womb. In the surrogacy context, a similar assault can be made on the term "sale." The baby is not being transferred for money to a stranger who can then treat the child like a commodity, doing anything he or she wants with the child. The money is being paid to enable a man to procreate his biological child; this hardly seems to fit the characterization of a sale. . . .

At most, in the surrogacy context, I am buying not a child but the pre-conception termination of the mother's parental rights. For decades, the pre-conception sale of a father's parental rights has been allowed with artificial insemination by donor. This practice, currently facilitated by statutes in at least thirty states, has received strong feminist support. . . .

A second line of argument opposes surrogacy because of the potential psychological and physical risks that it presents for women. Many aspects of this argument, however, seem ill founded and potentially demeaning to women. They focus on protecting women against their own decisions because those decisions might later cause them regret, be unduly influenced by others, or be forced by financial motivations.

Reproductive choices are tough choices, and any decision about reproduction — such as abortion, sterilization, sperm donation, or surrogacy — might later be regretted. The potential for later regrets, however, is usually not thought to be a valid reason to ban the right to choose the procedure in the first place.

With surrogacy, the potential for regret is thought by some to be enormously high. This is because it is argued (in biology-is-destiny terms) that it is unnatural for a mother to give up a child. It is assumed that because birthmothers in traditional adoption situations often regret relinquishing their children that surrogate mothers will feel the same way. But surrogate mothers are making their choices about relinquishment under much different circumstances. . . .

The biological mother in the surrogacy situation seeks out the opportunity to carry a child that would not exist were it not for the couple's desire to create a child as a part of their relationship. She makes her decision in advance of pregnancy for internal, not externally enforced reasons. While 75 percent of the biological mothers who give a child up for adoption later change their minds, only around 1 percent of the surrogates have similar changes of heart. . . .

Entering a surrogacy agreement does present potential psychological risks to women. But arguing for a ban on surrogacy seems to concede that the *government*, rather than the individual woman, should determine what risks a woman should be allowed to face. . . .

Perhaps recognizing the dangers of giving the government widespread powers to "protect" women, some feminists do acknowledge the validity of a general consent to assume risks. They argue, however, that the consent model is not appropriate to surrogacy since the surrogate's consent is neither informed nor voluntary. . . .

[A] strong element of the feminist argument against surrogacy is that women can not give an informed consent until they have had the experience of giving birth. . . . But such an approach is at odds with the legal doctrine of informed consent. . . [which] presupposes that people will predict in advance . . . whether a particular course will be beneficial to them. . . .

The consent given by surrogates is also challenged as not being voluntary. Feminist Gena Corea, for example, in writing about another reproduction arrangement, in vitro fertilization, asks, "What is the real meaning of a woman's 'consent'. . . in a society in which men as a social group control not just the choices open to women but also women's motivation to choose?"

Such an argument is a dangerous one for feminists to make. It would seem to be a step backward for women to argue that they are incapable of making decisions. That, after all, was the rationale for so many legal principles oppressing women for so long. . . .

Various feminists have made the argument that the financial inducement to a surrogate vitiates the voluntariness of her consent. Many feminists have said that women are exploited by surrogacy. They point out that in our society's social and economic conditions, some women — such as those on welfare or in dire financial need – will turn to surrogacy out of necessity, rather than true choice. . . .

There is a sexist undertone to an argument that Mary Beth Whitehead was exploited by the paid surrogacy agreement into which she entered to get money for her children's education. If Mary Beth's husband, Rick, had taken a second job to pay for the children's education (or even to pay for their mortgage), he would not have been viewed as exploited. He would have been lauded as a responsible parent.

It undercuts the legitimacy of women's role in the workforce to assume that they are being exploited if they plan to use their money for serious purchases. It seems to hearken back to a notion that women work (and should work) only for pin money (a stereotype that is the basis for justifying the firing of women in times of economic crisis). It is also disturbing that in most instances, when society suggests that a certain activity should be done for altruism, rather than money, it is generally a woman's activity. . . .

. . . .

Feminists are taking great pride that they have mobilized public debate against surrogacy. But the precedent they are setting in their alliance with politicians like Henry Hyde and groups like the Catholic church is one whose policy is "protect women, even against their own decisions" and "protect children at all costs" (presumably, in latter applications, even against the needs and desires of women).

Some feminists have criticized surrogacy as turning participating women, albeit with their consent, into reproductive vessels. I see the danger of the anti-surrogacy arguments as potentially turning all women into reproductive vessels, without their consent, by providing government oversight for women's decisions and creating a disparate legal category for gestation. Moreover, by breathing life into arguments that feminists have put to rest in other contexts, the current rationales opposing surrogacy could undermine a larger feminist agenda.

NOTE

As the excerpts from Anderson and Andrews indicate, feminists have been divided in their views on surrogacy arrangements. Andrews presents the liberal feminist case against restriction of women's freedom of choice in making reproductive decisions, drawing on the parallels to reproductive autonomy in the context of abortion decisions. *See also* Andrews, *Beyond Doctrinal Boundaries: A Legal Framework for Surrogate Motherhood*, 81 VA. L. REV. 2343 (1995). Other feminists, like Anderson, worry about the commodification of women's reproductive capacities. Many who hold this view argue that surrogacy should be banned because it exploits women for their childbearing capacity. *See, e.g.,* RADIN, CONTESTED COMMODITIES (1996); Ehrenreich, *The Colonization of the Womb*, 43 DUKE L.J. 492 (1993); Rae, *Parental Rights and the Definition of Motherhood in Surrogate Motherhood*, 3 S. CAL. REV. OF L. & WOMEN'S STUD. 279 (1994); Dolgin, *The Law Debates the Family: Reproductive Transformations*, 7 YALE J.L. & FEMINISM 37 (1995).

[2]   OTHER REPRODUCTIVE TECHNOLOGIES

ARTIFICIAL INSEMINATION: HOW DIFFERENT FROM SURROGACY?

Artificial insemination by donor, or AID, has long been used to assist couples who are childless because the husband is sterile. In a simple procedure, first reported in 1799, the woman is artificially inseminated with sperm obtained from a donor, who is typically anonymous. According to a report in the early 1990s, about 30,000 American babies are born via AID each year. *See generally* Gibson, *Artificial Insemination by Donor: Information, Communication and Regulation*, 30 J. FAM. L. 1, 1 (1991-92); ROBERTSON, CHILDREN OF CHOICE: FREEDOM AND THE NEW REPRODUCTIVE TECHNOLOGIES 119 (1994). AID is facilitated by statutes recognizing the woman's consenting husband, rather than the sperm donor, as the child's father. Many statutes are based on the Uniform Parentage Act, which provides that if the husband has consented to artificial insemination, the resulting child is the legitimate child of the husband and wife, and that the sperm donor has no legally recognized relationship with the child. 9A WEST'S U. LAWS ANN. (1979). The statutes typically require the husband's written consent to trigger the automatic recognition of his paternal status (and termination of any paternal claims by the sperm donor). Some statutes require that the implantation be performed by a physician for the legal effect of severing the sperm donor's relationship to occur. CAL. FAM. CODE § 7613 (1994). *See, e.g., Jhordan C. v. Mary K,* 224 Cal. Rptr. 530 (App. 1986) (father's rights were not severed where child was conceived through informal AID performed at home); Annot., *Rights and*

Oligations Resulting from Human Artificial Insemination, 83 A.L.R.4th 295 (1991) (reviewing cases).

Courts have begun to address the legal effects of AID in nonmarital relationships. In a recent California case, the cohabiting partner of a woman whose child was conceived through AID was held to be the legal father. *Dunkin v. Boskey*, 98 Cal. Rptr. 2d 44 (Ct. App. 2000). The couple had executed a written contract, in which each promised never to allege that the child was not the couple's. Later the mother left and denied her partner custody or visitation. The court held the contract to grant paternity rights was binding between the parties. The partner had achieved parental status by virtue of his consent to insemination and assumption of parental duties. *See also In re Parentage of M.J.*, 759 N.E.2d 121 (Ill. App. Ct. 2001) (no support liability by cohabitation partner, absent written consent to AID). A Washington court declined to impose a child support obligation on the former domestic partner of a lesbian mother. *State ex rel. D.R.M. v. Wood*, 34 P.3d 887 (Wash. Ct. App. 2001). The parties had separated during the pregnancy and the partner had provided financial support for several months under a separation agreement, until the mother withheld access to the child. The court held that the partner had no parental status because she had not adopted the child and declined to enforce the separation agreement because of the mother's breach in not allowing contact.

Aside from statutes automatically conferring parental status on the woman's husband, AID has been relatively unregulated until recently. All states require tissue banks, including sperm banks, to screen donors for the HIV virus. But only a few states legislatively mandate more extensive screening. CAL. HEALTH & SAFETY CODE § 1644.5 (West. Supp. 2003); FLA. STAT. ch. 381.0041 (2002); IND. CODE ANN. § 16-41-14-5 (Burns Supp. 2002). Nonetheless, a study by the Office of Technology Assessment in the 1980s found that all sperm banks surveyed screened for HIV antibodies, and most screened for other sexually transmitted diseases and for genetic disorders. *See* U.S. Congress, Office of Technology Assessment, *Artificial Insemination Practice in the United States: Artificial Insemination Report*, at 68–70 (USGPO, Aug. 1988). However, the same survey found that only 44% of physicians who obtained sperm outside of sperm banks even tested donors for the HIV virus. *Id.* at 34–35. For an analysis of donor screening procedures, see Hodgson, *The Warranty of Sperm: A Modest Proposal to Increase the Accountability of Sperm Banks and Physicians in the Performance of Artificial Insemination Procedures*, 26 IND. L. REV. 357 (1993).

The lack of legal attention to AID, in part, reflects the fact that it has been relatively uncontroversial, at least as compared to surrogacy contracts. However, recently attention has focused on this means of assisted conception. One concern is selective breeding. In the early 1980s, a sperm bank called the Repository for Germinal Choice offered customers the sperm of Nobel Prize winners. Nothing in current law would seem to bar or regulate eugenic selection of this kind. *See* Note, *Eugenic Artificial Insemination: A Cure for Mediocrity?*, 94 HARV. L. REV. 1850 (1981). The lack of records about sperm donors and the very strong tradition of anonymity have been questioned in an era in which the needs of adopted children to know something of their past receives considerable deference. The impersonal involvement of the sperm donor in creating a child may result in these fathers having a particularly strong interest in anonymity. Surveys show however, that a substantial percentage of donors would be willing to have contact with their child. Mahlstedt & Probasco, *Sperm Donors: Their Attitudes Toward Providing Medical and Psychological Information for Recipient Couples and Donor Offspring*, 56 FERTILITY & STERILITY 747, 749–752 (1991). The nature of the father's role also raises questions about the impact on the development of the child's self concept of being the product of AID. BARAN & PANNOR, LETHAL SECRETS: THE SHOCKING CONSEQUENCES AND UNSOLVED PROBLEMS OF ARTIFICIAL INSEMINATION 136 (1989).

Despite some disquiet and controversy, AID is a widely used and routine procedure, which continues to be relatively unregulated, at least compared to surrogacy. Do the two means of assisted reproduction raise similar concerns? Some have suggested that the legal recognition of AID but not gestational contracts is impermissible gender discrimination. Rushevsky, *Legal Recognition of Surrogate Gestation,* 7 WOMEN'S RTS. L. REP. 107, 120 n.98 (1982). The argument is that AID is facilitated to accommodate the desires of infertile fathers, but that infertile mothers have no recourse. (Of course, it could also be argued that women are allowed to have biological children when their husbands are infertile, but that men married to infertile wives have no recourse.) AID raises similar if less pronounced concerns about commodification of children; the sperm donor is paid for his genetic material and for his consent to terminate his parental rights, as is the gestational mother. Because gestational service is more burdensome, the market price for the service, not surprisingly, is correspondingly higher than that paid to sperm donors. Concerns about selective breeding are at least as important with AID as with surrogacy. The child may have similar identity issues, created by the severing of the connection with a biological parent. The concern about exploitation, raised by some feminists in opposition to surrogacy agreements, has not been raised in the context of AID. On the other hand, the possibility of multiple children (hundreds?) provided by the same father poses a potential social harm that is absent in surrogacy arrangements.

A problem with surrogacy arrangements that does not arise in AID is that the gestation takes place outside of the relationship of the couple who will be the social parents. As noted earlier, the possibility of complications in that situation — including the gestational mother developing a bond to the child — is formidable. With AID (and with egg donation), after conception, the donor plays no further role, develops no attachment to the child and is unlikely to have any interest.

IN VITRO FERTILIZATION: THE BRAVE NEW WORLD

Currently, in vitro fertilization is most often utilized by married couples who experience difficulty conceiving a child. In its most common and uncontroversial form, in vitro fertilization involves removal of eggs from a woman, which are then fertilized in vitro with her husband's sperm, after which one or more resulting preembryos are implanted in the woman's uterus. In this situation, no disaggregation of genetic, gestational and social parenting functions is anticipated. However, because the process is quite uncertain in its success, many more eggs are harvested and preembryos created than are needed, for later use if the initial implantation does not succeed. The fate of these preembryos, which under current technology, can be cryogenically frozen and preserved for future use, can raise difficult issues. Consider the following case.

KASS v. KASS

696 N.E.2d 174 (N.Y. 1998)

KAYE, Chief Judge.

Although *in vitro* fertilization (IVF) procedures are now more than two decades old and in wide use, this is the first such dispute to reach our Court. Specifically in issue is the disposition of five frozen, stored pre-embryos, or "pre-zygotes," created five years ago, during the parties' marriage, to assist them in having a child. Now divorced, appellant (Maureen Kass) wants the pre-zygotes implanted, claiming this is her only chance for genetic motherhood; respondent (Steven Kass) objects to the burdens of unwanted fatherhood, claiming that the parties agreed at the time they embarked on the effort that in the present circumstances the pre-zygotes would be donated to the IVF program for approved research purposes. . .

. . . .

[At the time the couple undertook the IVF procedure involving cyropreservation, they signed a separate consent form dealing with disposition of the frozen pre-zygotes. The form included the following provision:]

2. In the event that we no longer wish to initiate a pregnancy or are unable to make a decision regarding the disposition of our stored, frozen pre-zygotes. . .,

(b) Our frozen pre-zygotes may be examined by the IVF Program for biological studies and be disposed of by the IVF Program for approved research investigation as determined by the IVF Program.

. . . .

[Only a few weeks later, the couple signed a separation agreement that stated that the pre-zygotes should be disposed of as provided in the consent form. A month later, Ms. Kass commenced the divorce action requesting sole custody of the pre-zygotes.]

[W]e conclude that disposition of these pre-zygotes does not implicate a woman's right of privacy or bodily integrity in the area of reproductive choice; nor are the pre-zygotes recognized as "persons" for constitutional purposes (*see Roe v. Wade*). The relevant inquiry thus becomes who has dispositional authority over them. Because that question is answered in this case by the parties' agreement, for purposes of resolving the present appeal we have no cause to decide whether the pre-zygotes are entitled to "special respect" (*cf., Davis v. Davis*, 842 S.W.2d 588, 596–597). . .

Agreements between progenitors, or gamete donors, regarding disposition of their pre-zygotes should generally be presumed valid and binding, and enforced in any dispute between them. Indeed, parties should be encouraged in advance, before embarking on IVF and cryopreservation, to think through possible contingencies and carefully specify their wishes in writing. Explicit agreements avoid costly litigation in business transactions. They are all the more necessary and desirable in personal matters of reproductive choice, where the intangible costs of any litigation are simply incalculable. Advance directives, subject to mutual change of mind that must be jointly expressed, both minimize misunderstandings and maximize procreative liberty by reserving to the progenitors the authority to make what is in the first instance a quintessentially personal, private decision. Written agreements also provide the certainty needed for effective operation of IVF programs. . . .

While the value of arriving at explicit agreements is apparent, we also recognize the extraordinary difficulty such an exercise presents. All agreements looking to the future to some extent deal with the unknown. Here, however, the uncertainties inherent in the IVF process itself are vastly complicated by cryopreservation, which extends the viability of pre-zygotes indefinitely and allows time for minds, and circumstances, to change. Divorce, death, disappearance or incapacity of one or both partners; aging; the birth of other children are but a sampling of obvious changes in individual circumstances that might take place over time.

These factors make it particularly important that courts seek to honor the parties' expressions of choice, made before disputes erupt, with the parties' over-all direction always uppermost in the analysis. Knowing that advance agreements will be enforced underscores the seriousness and integrity of the consent process. Advance agreements as to disposition would have little purpose if they were enforceable only in the event the parties continued to agree. To the extent possible, it should be the progenitors — not the State and not the courts — who by their prior directive make this deeply personal life choice.

Here, the parties prior to cryopreservation of the pre-zygotes signed consents indicating their dispositional intent. . . . [N]either party disputes that they are an expression of their own intent regarding disposition of their pre-zygotes. Nor do the parties contest the legality of those agreements, or that they were freely and knowingly made. The central issue is whether the consents clearly express the parties' intent regarding disposition of the pre-zygotes in the present circumstances. . . .

The subject of this dispute may be novel but the common-law principles governing contract interpretation are not. Whether an agreement is ambiguous is a question of law for the courts. . . .

. . . . [W]e agree that the informed consents signed by the parties unequivocally manifest their mutual intention that in the present circumstances the pre-zygotes be donated for research to the IVF program.

[A]ppellant and respondent intended that disposition of the pre-zygotes was to be their joint decision. The consents manifest that what they above all did not want was a stranger taking that decision out of their hands. Even in unforeseen circumstances, even if they were unavailable, even if they were dead, the consents jointly specified the disposition that would be made. That sentiment explicitly appears again and again throughout the lengthy documents. . . . The overriding choice of these parties could not be plainer: *"We have the principal responsibility to decide the disposition of our frozen pre-zygotes. Our frozen pre-zygotes will not be released from storage for any purpose without the written consent of both of us, consistent with the policies of the IVF Program and applicable law"* (emphasis added).

That pervasive sentiment — both parties assuming "principal responsibility to decide the disposition of [their] frozen pre-zygotes" — is carried forward in ADDENDUM NO. 2-1:

> "In the event that we * * * are unable to make a decision regarding disposition of our stored, frozen pre-zygotes, we now indicate our desire for the disposition of our pre-zygotes and direct the IVF Program to * * *

> "Our frozen pre-zygotes may be examined by the IVF Program for biological studies and be disposed of by the IVF Program for approved research investigation as determined by the IVF Program."

Thus, only by joint decision of the parties would the pre-zygotes be used for implantation. And otherwise, by mutual consent they would be donated to the IVF program for research purposes. . . .

These parties having clearly manifested their intention, the law will honor it.

NOTE

Disputes between divorcing parties over frozen pre-embryos have increased in recent years. For the most part, parties seeking "custody" for the purpose of implantation have been unsuccessful, but courts have applied different theories to reach this result. In *Davis v. Davis*, 842 S.W.2d 588 (Tenn. 1992), where no agreement between the parties existed, the trial court ruled the embryos were "children" and granted "custody" to the "mother," effectively allowing her to proceed over her husband's objection. The decision was reversed on appeal. The state supreme court reviewed the scientific evidence in the case, the question of the "personhood" of pre-embryos under the state or federal constitutions, the right of procreational autonomy, and the enforceability of any agreements in such cases, and then engaged in an explicit balancing of the rights of the parties in such a case. The court decided that the preembryos could not be considered "persons" (and thus not "children" subject to a "custody" award). Nor were they "property", although the parties "do have an interest in the nature of ownership, to the extent that they have decisionmaking authority concerning the disposition of the preembryos." The court concluded that:

> disputes involving the disposition of preembryos produced by in vitro fertilization should be resolved, first, by looking to the preferences of the progenitors. If their wishes cannot be ascertained, or if there is dispute, then their prior agreement concerning disposition should be carried out. If no prior agreement exists, then the relative interests of the parties in using or not using the preembryos must be weighed.

> Ordinarily, the party wishing to avoid procreation should prevail, assuming that the other party has a reasonable possibility of achieving parenthood by [other] means. . . . If no other reasonable alternatives exist, then the argument in favor of using the preembryos to achieve pregnancy should be considered. However, if the party seeking control of the preembryos intends merely to donate them to another couple, the objecting party obviously has the greater interest and should prevail.

The court insisted, however, that it was not creating an "automatic veto" and, presumably, left the lower courts to balance the interests of the parties in individual cases.

Unlike the New York court in *Kass*, New Jersey and Massachusetts courts have refused to enforce disposition agreements between the parties. In the New Jersey case, the divorcing husband sought to prove that the parties had an oral agreement that they would donate any unused pre-embryos to be implanted, and that he, as a Catholic, had gone forward on that condition. The mother argued that the pre-embryos should be destroyed. *J.B. v. M.B.*, 783 A.2d 707 (N.J. 2001). The court declined to allow the father to offer proof of the agreement, holding that any such agreement was unenforceable as a matter of public policy. In deciding about the disposition of the pre-embryos, the court adopted the *Davis* balancing test, as well as the informal presumption that ordinarily the parent seeking to avoid procreation should prevail. Here, the decision did little to burden the father's procreative rights, since he was free to procreate through some other means. The Massachusetts court reviewed an agreement between the parents (executed as part of the consent agreement to the *in vitro* procedures) giving control of the pre-embryos to the mother in the event of the parties' separation. *A.Z. v. B.Z.* 725 N.E.2d 1051 (Mass. 2000). After raising questions about whether this agreement truly reflected the parties' intentions, the court held that any agreement that would compel one donor to become a parent against his will would be unenforceable (even though at the time of the agreement, he apparently assented). The court cited a strong policy against enforcement of agreements that bind parties to future family relationships. Such a policy enhances freedom of personal choice in these matters. Would the *Kass* court have responded differently to a contract giving the mother custody of the preembryos?

For commentary on the issue of frozen embryos and their disposition, see Note, *Davis v. Davis: Establishing Guidelines for Resolving Disputes Over Frozen Embryos*, 10 J. CONTEMP. L. & HEALTH POL'Y 493 (1994); Comment, *Frozen Embryos: A Need for Thawing in the Legislation Process*, 47 S.M.U.L. REV. 131 (1993); Note, *In Vitro Fertilization: Eliminating the Current State of Limbo Between Pre-Embryonic Rights and the Fundamental Right to Procreate*, 26 WAKE FOREST L. REV. 1217 (1991).

The technology of *in vitro* fertilization presents far ranging possibilities for separating genetic, gestational and social parenting. Consequently, the risk of loss of control over the reproductive process is significant, even in the typical case where the process is initiated by a couple using their own genetic material with the intention of producing their own child. As occasionally happens in gestational surrogacy cases (*see* note 3 *supra*), it is possible to have an embryo of one couple (the genetic parents) implanted in a gestational mother (the gestational parent), in anticipation of transfer of the child after birth to a different couple (the social parents). In this situation, the importance of having clear legal rules about the rights and responsibilities of all parties to the transaction is evident.

A scandal at a fertility clinic at the University of California at Irvine illustrates the need for regulation in this area. Three doctors were accused of taking embryos that were produced by couples under treatment, and implanting them in other women who had been unsuccessful in producing healthy embryos. About 80 patients were involved and the genetic parentage of at least 7 children was in question. Two of the doctors left the country. The third was indicted on mail fraud for allegedly falsely billing insurance companies through the mail, the only charge available in the absence of any more direct regulation of the process. The California legislature quickly enacted a statute making it a felony to transfer or implant human gametes without the informed written consent of both donor and recipient. CAL. PENAL CODE § 367g (West 1999). More than 80 civil law suits were brought. *See* Miller, *Key Issue Absent on Eve of O.C. Fertility Trial Set to Open*, LOS ANGELES TIMES, Apr. 8, 1997, at A1. In 2002, a California court ruled that the request for paternity tests by a couple who believed that another couple receiving fertility treatments from the clinic were raising their now 14-year-old twins was properly denied. *Prato-Morrison v. Doe*, 126 Cal. Rptr. 2d 509 (Cal. App. 2002). Even if a genetic link could be proved, the court held, the child's best interest trumped any rights of the embryo's progenitors.

TABLE OF CASES

[Principal cases appear in capital letters; references are to pages or page and note number(s).]

[Principal cases appear in capital letters; references are to pages or page and note number(s).]

[Principal cases appear in capital letters; references are to pages or page and note number(s).]

[Principal cases appear in capital letters; references are to pages or page and note number(s).]

[Principal cases appear in capital letters; references are to pages or page and note number(s).]

[Principal cases appear in capital letters; references are to pages or page and note number(s).]

[Principal cases appear in capital letters; references are to pages or page and note number(s).]

[Principal cases appear in capital letters; references are to pages or page and note number(s).]

[Principal cases appear in capital letters; references are to pages or page and note number(s).]

[Principal cases appear in capital letters; references are to pages or page and note number(s).]

[Principal cases appear in capital letters; references are to pages or page and note number(s).]

[Principal cases appear in capital letters; references are to pages or page and note number(s).]

[Principal cases appear in capital letters; references are to pages or page and note number(s).]

N

[Principal cases appear in capital letters; references are to pages or page and note number(s).]

[Principal cases appear in capital letters; references are to pages or page and note number(s).]

[Principal cases appear in capital letters; references are to pages or page and note number(s).]

[Principal cases appear in capital letters; references are to pages or page and note number(s).]

[Principal cases appear in capital letters; references are to pages or page and note number(s).]

[Principal cases appear in capital letters; references are to pages or page and note number(s).]

[Principal cases appear in capital letters; references are to pages or page and note number(s).]

X

Y

Z

INDEX

[References are to page numbers.]

[References are to page numbers.]

[References are to page numbers.]

[References are to page numbers.]